THE CONCISE

ENCYCLOPEDIA OF

AMERICAN RADIO

The average American listens to the radio three hours a day. In light of technological developments such as satellite and Internet audio services, some argue that broadcast radio is facing a crisis, while others claim we may be at the dawn of a new radio revolution. *The Concise Encyclopedia of American Radio* is an essential single-volume reference guide to this old yet still evolving medium. It brings together the best and most important entries from the three-volume *Encyclopedia of Radio*, edited by Christopher H. Sterling.

Comprised of more than 300 entries spanning the invention of radio to the Internet, *The Concise Encyclopedia of American Radio* addresses program and music genres, regulations, technology, networks and stations, Old-Time radio as well as other topics related to radio broadcasting throughout its long history. The material is updated throughout and the volume includes nine new entries on topics ranging from podcasting to the potential decline of radio. *The Concise Encyclopedia of American Radio* includes suggestions for further reading as complements to most articles, production credits for programs, and a comprehensive index.

Christopher H. Sterling has served on the George Washington University media and public affairs faculty since 1982, and has authored or edited more than 25 books on media and telecommunication topics, including the original *Encyclopedia of Radio* (2004), and, with Michael Keith, *Sounds of Change: A History of FM Broadcasting in America* (2008). He edited the six-volume *Encyclopedia of Journalism* (2009). For Routledge, he edited six volumes of

historical articles, *The Rise of American Radio* (2007), and co-authored the standard *Stay Tuned: A History of American Broadcasting* (2003). He edits *Communication Booknotes Quarterly* and was the third editor of the quarterly *Journal of Broadcasting & Electronic Media*. His research centers on the history and policy of American electronic media and telecommunications.

Cary O'Dell is a graduate of Southern Illinois University at Carbondale. He is the boards' assistant for the film and recorded sound division of the Library of Congress facility in Culpeper, VA. He is the former archives director for the Museum of Broadcast Communications in Chicago and a former project archivist for the Library of American Broadcasting at the University of Maryland. O'Dell authored *Women Pioneers in Television: Biographies of Fifteen Industry Leaders* (1997) and *Virginia Marmaduke: A Journey in Print from Carbondale to Chicago* (2001).

Michael C. Keith is a member of the Communication Department at Boston College and the author of over 20 books on electronic media, including *Radio Cultures* (2008), *Voices in the Purple Haze* (1997), and *Sounds in the Dark* (2001), and the classic textbook *The Radio Station* (2009). In addition, he is the author of a critically acclaimed memoir, *The Next Better Place* (2003), and numerous short stories. Keith is the recipient of several awards, among them the International Radio Television Society's Stanton Fellow Award and the Broadcast Education Association's Distinguished Scholar Award.

THE CONCISE ENCYCLOPEDIA OF AMERICAN RADIO

Christopher H. Sterling
Editor

Cary O'Dell
Assistant Editor

Michael C. Keith
Consulting Editor

Routledge
Taylor & Francis Group

NEW YORK AND LONDON

Concise edition published 2010
by Routledge
270 Madison Ave, New York, NY 10016

Simultaneously published in the UK
by Routledge
2 Park Square, Milton Park, Abingdon, Oxon OX14 4RN

Routledge is an imprint of the Taylor & Francis Group, an informa business

© 2010 Taylor & Francis

Typeset in Times New Roman by
Taylor & Francis Books
Printed and bound in the United States of America on acid-free paper by
Sheridan Books, Inc.

Library of Congress Cataloging in Publication Data
A catalog record has been requested for this book

ISBN10: 0-415-43391-6 (hbk)
ISBN10: 0-203-86355-0 (ebk)

ISBN13: 978-0-415-99533-7 (hbk)
ISBN13: 978-0-203-86355-8 (ebk)

Contents

Editors' Introduction

Radio means distinct things to different people. For some, radio primarily means the "golden age" of the 1920s through the 1940s when network radio headlined the only broadcast service and provided a variety of programs for all tastes. For such listeners, radio's importance is in its programs and stars, its role as the on-the-spot recorder of history, and in its carriage of period politics, sports, and talk. (It is this period of old-time radio [OTR] that is hotly collectible—books, program premiums, recordings, magazines and equipment of the era.) For others radio means the omnipresent yet sometimes struggling business of the early 21st century with chains of stations under common ownership dependent on syndicated programs and as much advertising as they can sell in an increasingly competitive marketplace. And for still others "radio" does not mean broadcasting at all, but instead refers to the transmission of voice and data, amateur or "ham" station operators, or even reception of music and talk programs on the internet. Each of these meanings, none mutually exclusive, illustrates part of radio's pervasive overall role in society.

Indeed radio—or at least audio—has become part of our daily background, there but "not there" for many if not most of us. As I write this, for example, classical music is playing from an online audio stream, for I am one of those who work better with such soothing background. For decades the only source for music was records—or radio stations. Today you need not look farther than the nearest teenager (talking on their cellphone, planning the next few days on their BlackBerry or similar device, programming their iPod, monitoring television or a video, and "doing homework" on their computer) to realize how omnipresent yet invisible audio (and often radio) can be. And notice how often you hear audio playing in the workplace, in your car, or through ever-present headphones on public transit—and at all hours. Audio—often but no longer always delivered by a radio station—is there virtually all the time.

While much of the focus of present-day media praise and damnation seems focused on video

sources (including those online), radio "was there first." Many complaints about present-day television and cable were first directed at radio, such as a fear that violent or suspenseful programs would overly excite children's imaginations with untold effects over time. Radio also established many elements of present-day electronic media industry structure. Much of what we both enjoy and bemoan today, in other words, was accomplished (or inflicted) by radio long before television or more recent digital options became a reality.

For example, that American broadcasting would depend on advertising was pretty much decided by the late 1920s, despite several concerted efforts (before and after passage of the benchmark 1934 Communications Act) to open up greater opportunities for other funding options. In turn, advertising support meant that American radio would be primarily a medium of entertainment (to attract the largest possible audience for that advertising) rather than the public or cultural service that developed in nations with other approaches to financial support. That national networks would dominate radio news and entertainment in the years before the coming of television (which would later and very quickly adopt the same pattern) was a fact by the early 1930s, with only minor modifications at the margins over the years. That government would have to selectively license broadcaster access to limited spectrum space was obvious by the early 1920s; such a process only became fully effective in 1927. And that government would have little to do with American radio program content, though this has again varied over time, was made clear in the laws of 1927 and 1934, reinforced by numerous court decisions in the years that followed.

When commercial television began in the U.S. in the 1940s, the video medium was able to develop quickly (despite higher costs for all concerned) because radio had already established the commercial structure of the industry, the relationship between government and broadcasters, and a wealth of program formats to further develop. Granted that television added pictures and new generations of stars—but the heavy lifting of innovating an electronic media system had already been accomplished by radio.

This volume is an updated excerpt from the three-volume *The Museum of Broadcast Communications Encyclopedia of Radio* published in 2003. Here the focus is entirely on American radio broadcasting. A companion volume will pull together all the biographical or "people" entries. Both books feature new entries (better than a dozen in each case), and in the present one, the majority of entries have been brought up to date.

Given radio's long history, how can any one reference work include all of its many roles and meanings? What should be "in" and what must be left out? (Another obvious concern is what may have been left out inadvertently or unwittingly.) How much emphasis should be given to technology, economic factors, programs, and organizations? (The "people" part of the story will be the focus of a parallel volume.) What you hold in your hands represents our cooperative compromise answer to such questions—if you will, something of a "work in progress." Our approach is to describe aspects of American radio from its beginnings to the early 21st century. Put another way, what we have tried to assemble is an ideal "first-stop" reference source for most aspects of radio broadcasting

in the U.S. Some of what is described here has been history for upwards of three-quarters of a century, plenty of time to develop a broad appreciation of what remains important.

Our focus in this volume is entirely on American radio *broadcasting*—with some mention of the increasingly important online applications of the technology. Aside from occasional side references, you will find little here on radio defined more broadly—as the primary means of transmission for such services as telephone, television, data and more recent mobile services.

Even within that realm, we have had to make often difficult choices on what to include and how. The present book, for example, does not update the numerous individual station entries (they appear under either "K" or "W"), as those would entail a numbing stream of often minor ownership and programming changes without really shedding much light on the larger picture. Despite our best efforts, however, we have without a doubt missed some favorites or given insufficient emphasis on others. We welcome comments and will keep track of suggestions of new topics (and authors) for possible revisions.

CHRISTOPHER H. STERLING
CARY O'DELL
Washington, D.C.

Acknowledgments to the 2003 Edition

As was the case with the companion *Encyclopedia of Television* (1997), many people have helped make the three volumes of the *Encyclopedia of Radio* a viable project. I am grateful first of all to **Bruce DuMont**, the founder and president of the Museum of Broadcast Communications, for entrusting the overall editorial task to me. He was most persuasive when I expressed concern about the very scope of what he proposed.

In the actual process of designing and editing this project, Michael Keith and Paul Schellinger were absolutely indispensable. **Michael C. Keith** of Boston College served as our consulting editor and was my comrade in arms on this project, serving as consulting editor throughout, or as he put it, on call 24/7/365—and he was. Mike's knowledge of all things radio is unsurpassed, and he constantly got us out of scrapes and errors and urged us on. When we needed an author or had to have an essay checked, he was there with useful input and suggestions. Mike and I co-authored several entries, and I learned more from him every time. This is a far better product for Michael's devotion to it.

Paul Schellinger, the project's final and most important editor at Fitzroy Dearborn, worked hard during the final two years or more to get the many pieces into final form, following up with authors, keeping the undersigned cool, and seeing the project through to completion. And he did it with grace and diplomacy—which was often required! Just keeping track of who was doing what—or for that matter, *not* doing what they had promised—was a huge undertaking. The project most certainly could not have been completed without Paul. And he never once had to throw himself on those bamboo bean poles under his second-story study window because of "just one more" edit or addition—though he got close.

Paul's predecessor **Steve LaRue** was another steady rock for much of this multi-year process—and had a sense of humor to boot. He handled all the correspondence and record-keeping without which no such reference work can be assembled. Likewise Carol **Burwash**, Steve's predecessor, worked with the undersigned to get the project initially designed and under way. You would not have these books in your hands without the steady efforts of these three Fitzroy Dearborn editors.

Dan Wingate, then an archivist with the MBC staff, played a central role in gathering the many photographs. This involved constant contacts with owners of photographs, obtaining permission to use the selected images and seeking photos we needed and could not find. We also appreciate the help of **Chuck Howell** and others at the Library of American Broadcasting who helped greatly with photographs and wrote several entries as well.

Our board of advisers was most helpful, especially at the opening stages of the project in 1998 as we first began to design what would be included, how long entries should be, and initial potential authors to contact. Taken as a group, the board had radio knowledge in depth and breadth, many having years of experience dating back to the golden age of American network radio. Several members played special roles, helping to round up authors for specific categories of entries and then assisting in editing their work. **Graham Mytton** was invaluable as our man in London, gathering authors for virtually all of the British entries. Likewise, **John D. Jackson** assisted greatly with the English and French authors who contributed material on Canada. **Ed Shane** not only assisted as a board member but contributed several important entries himself—as did his spouse. And Ed came back several times offering to do more and to scare up authors—or lean on those who were late. **Michele Hilmes** was especially helpful in suggesting graduate students and other colleagues as contributors. **Peter Orlik** helped a great deal at the very beginning of the process, authoring the first entries that were used as samples for others. **Horace Newcomb** set a high standard to follow with his editorship of the *Encyclopedia of Television*—and helped to train the undersigned when I served on his editorial board.

Finally, we *all* owe thanks to the more than 240 individual authors who have written the 670 essays that make up this radio reference. They undertook all the original research, did the writing, and were generally a patient lot, accepting editorial sugges-tions and queries and working to tighten up their essays as we neared publication. They have waited a while to see their efforts in print, and I hope they are pleased.

CHRISTOPHER H. STERLING
Washington, D.C.
September 2003

Acknowledgments for this Volume

First and foremost, I want to thank **Matthew Byrnie**, senior communications editor with Routledge in New York City, for first suggesting this update project—and the companion volume on radio biography that is forthcoming. While I readily admit I was taken aback by the idea at first, he was right—we all hope the hard work of hundreds of contributors can see new life in this briefer and more focused format. **Cary O'Dell** joined me as assistant editor for this volume—and was the picture of efficient and diligent work. Most of the updates herein are from his efforts. He made good suggestions and offered a fresh look at all of the material—this is a far better product thanks to his efforts. **Gail Love** did a number of the initial updates which are also appreciated. Once again,

Michael C. Keith was on hand "24/7" as he put it, helping as our chief consultant to answer questions, suggest source people or material, and make useful comments. Of the publisher's personnel, **Liz Jones** handled the initial editing, **Jim Henderson** compiled the index, and **Paola Celli** supervised the book's production—we greatly appreciate their time and efforts. That they are based in Cornwall, Scotland and London, respectively, simply underlines how international publishing (as with so many other activities) has become, thanks to the ubiquitous Internet.

CHRISTOPHER H. STERLING
Washington, D.C.
September 2009

Reading About Radio

This very brief survey of some of the better print and online sources about American radio broadcasting supplements the many more specific "further reading" references that appear with the individual entries in this volume. The quantity and quality of research writing about radio has increased in recent years and some of that is evident here. Yet this is by *no* means a comprehensive listing—that would take a volume in itself. It is intended to highlight some of the more useful American radio reference works, emphasizing recent titles.

Ordered by author last name (or title if no author), this survey lists and briefly describes some of the books, websites, and periodicals which are broad in their coverage and thus could be cited under many different entries. The usual warning about website listings applies here: they change and even disappear all too often, and rarely with any warning.

CHRISTOPHER H. STERLING

1. Reference Works

Broadcasting and Cable Yearbook. New York: Bowker, 1935–date, annual. One of the broadcasting industry's standard sources, this includes a directory of all radio stations plus some statistics, and listings of ancillary parts of the industry (networks, station reps, consultants).

Carothers, Diane Foxhill, *Radio Broadcasting from 1920 to 1990: An Annotated Bibliography*, New York: Garland, 1991. Some 1,700 items covering both American and foreign radio appear in this, the most comprehensive published bibliography on radio.

Greenfield, Thomas Allen, *Radio: A Reference Guide*, Westport Connecticut: Greenwood, 1989. Combines topically-arranged narrative discussion of the serious writing about radio along with chapter bibliographies.

Keith, Michael C., *Broadcast Links* website http://www.michaelckeith.com/links.html
Extensive listing, heavily focused on radio both here and abroad, including domestic and international stations, services, periodicals, and radio personalities and programs.

Kittross, John M., editor, *A Bibliography of Theses and Dissertations in Broadcasting, 1920–1973*, Washington D.C.: Broadcast Education Assn., 1973. Probably a majority of these concern or include radio. Includes both topical and

key-word indexes. More recent studies can be sought out with online searches.

Radio Yearbook. Chantilly, Virginia: BIA Financial Network, annual. Profiles all 261 Arbitron radio markets and some 10,000 stations, with full directory information on each station, combining ratings and technical information. Includes metro, ownership, and key station contact information, listing of vendors and service providers.

R&R Directory: Ratings, Industry Directory and Program Supplier Guide website http://www.radioandrecords.com/RRDirectory/Directory_Main.aspx
Online directory of all types of suppliers to radio stations—syndicated programs, equipment, services. Its title has varied.

Siegel, Susan and David S., *A Resource Guide to the Golden Age of Radio: Special Collections, Bibliography and the Internet*. Yorktown Heights, New York: Book Hunter Press, 2006. Provides a well-annotated guide to library and archive collections across the country, a basic bibliography, and a variety of web-based sources.

Sterling, Christopher H., *Electronic Media: A Guide to Trends in Broadcasting and Newer Technologies, 1920–1983*. New York: Praeger, 1984. More than 100 historical time-series tables and explanatory text covering radio (and other services) into the early 1980s.

Sterling, Christopher H., and George Shiers. *History of Telecommunications Technology: An Annotated Bibliography*. Lanham, Maryland: Scarecrow Press, 2000. Includes radio (in Chapter 9) and related topics–some 2,500 sources (books and articles, primarily) in all.

2. Radio's Technical Development

Aitken, Hugh G. J., *Syntony and Spark: The Origins of Radio*. New York: Wiley, 1976. Classic study of the innovative work of Clerk Maxwell, Hertz and Marconi and what they accomplished. Continued in the following volume.

——*The Continuous Wave: Technology and American Radio, 1900–1932*. Princeton, New Jersey: Princeton University Press, 1985. Continues the story of wireless from previous title, focusing on American developments: Fessenden and the alternator, Elwell and the arc transmitter, de Forest and his Audion, radio and cables and the national interest, development of RCA, and the expansion of radio's tube technology in the 1920s.

Clark "Radioana" Collection (Lemelson Center, Smithsonian Institution) website http://invention.smithsonian.org/resources/fa_clark_index.aspx
This is the very detailed finding aid for one of the premier archives on radio's technical (and other) development.

Coe, Lewis, *Wireless Radio: A Brief History*. Jefferson, North Carolina: McFarland, 1996. Provides useful concise survey of the work of many inventors before and after the innovation of broadcasting.

Douglas, Susan J., *Inventing American Broadcasting, 1899–1922*. Baltimore, Marlyland: Johns Hopkins University Press, 1987. Readable scholarly analysis of the combination of technological innovation, institutional development, and the projected visions and business realities that led to the formation of the radio broadcasting business in the early 1920s.

Dunlap, Orrin E. Jr., *Radio's 100 Men of Science*. New York: Harper, 1944. Useful mini-biographies of major inventors and engineers over more than a century.

Hong, Sungook, *Wireless from Marconi's Black-Box to the Audion*. Cambridge, Massachusetts: MIT Press "Transformations: Studies in the History of Science and Technology," 2001. Modern history making good use of archival sources, relating the rise of wireless in years before World War I.

Inglis, Andrew F., *Behind The Tube: A History of Broadcasting Technology and Business*. Stoneham, Massachusetts: Focal Press, 1990. Includes chapters on both AM and FM broadcasting, placing the technology of both within the larger context of industry development, though with a bias toward RCA.

Leinwoll, Stanley, *From Spark to Satellite: A History of Radio Communication*. New York: Charles Scribner's, 1979. A wide-ranging popular history of radio into the 1970s, emphasizing the role of key inventors and developments in the expanding roles of the medium.

Lewis, Tom, *Empire of the Air: The Men Who Made Radio*. New York: HarperCollins, 1991. Well-written analysis of the lives, work and changing relationships of Armstrong, de Forest and Sarnoff, among others—there is a Ken Burns PBS documentary with the same title that is well worth seeing.

Maclaurin, W. Rupert, *Invention and Innovation in the Radio Industry*. New York: Macmillan, 1949 (reprinted, Arno Press "History of Broadcasting," 1971). Thorough treatment with supporting data and much critical analysis of the process and nature of radio inventions. A study of struggles, litigation, progress and failure of both individual inventors and industrial organizations. Includes chapters on FM and television.

Mott, Robert L., *Radio Sound Effects: Who Did It, and How, In the Era of Live Broadcasting*. Jefferson, North Carolina: McFarland, 1993. Written by a radio sound-effects authority, this unique history reviews the development of sound effects in radio drama and comedy programs.

Shoenherr, Steven. *Recording Technology History* website http://history.sandiego.edu/GEN/recording/notes.html Quite good and extensive 20-part site on analog and digital recording technology development.

Sakar, Tapan K., et al., editors, *History of Wireless*. New York: Wiley-Interscience, 2006. Very detailed studies of radio's development, including some chapters reaching beyond broadcast applications. Perhaps the best current engineering-based survey.

Schiffer, Michael Brian, *The Portable Radio in American Life*. Tucson: University of Arizona Press, 1991. Valuable survey from clunky tube receivers to modern transistor models–one of the very few serious books on the listener side of the story.

Shiers, George, editor, *The Development of Wireless to 1920*. New York: Arno Press "Historical Studies in Telecommunications," 1977. This anthology reprints 20 pioneering technical and historical papers tracing developments from the late 19th century, many by the inventors themselves including Fleming, de Forest, Fessenden, Marconi, Carl Braun, Armstrong, Elwell, and Alfred Goldsmith.

3. Radio History

Archer, Gleason L., *History of Radio to 1926* and *Big Business and Radio*. New York: American Historical Society/Company, 1938–39 (2 vols reprinted by Arno Press "History of Broadcasting," 1971). While largely concerned with business aspects, this detailed set of books includes considerable pre-broadcast technical background and context, especially patent and related corporate rivalries. Important as the first attempt at a scholarly history of the business.

Balk, Alfred, *The Rise of Radio: From Marconi Through the Golden Age*. Jefferson, North Carolina: McFarland, 2006. Recent overall history reflects much of the recent research and writing about radio broadcasting.

Barnouw, Erik, *A History of Broadcasting in the United States*. New York: Oxford University Press, 1966, 1968, 1970 (3 vols). Classic and well-written narrative; the first two volumes take the story to 1953 and focus most on radio. These could have been cited as "further readings" in most of the entries that follow.

Bergreen, Laurence, *Look Now, Pay Later: The Rise of Network Broadcasting*. Garden City, New York: Doubleday, 1980. One of the few historical treatments of networks, covering both radio and television eras.

Cox, Jim, *Say Goodnight, Gracie: The Last Years of Network Radio*. Jefferson, North Carolina: McFarland, 2002. Informal history of the American radio networks after World War II amidst rising television competition.

Douglas, Susan J., *Listening In: Radio And The American Imagination*. New York: Times Books, 1999. Largely focused on programs and listener reactions to explore the medium's impact over more than half a century.

Godfrey, Donald G., and Frederic A. Leigh, editors. *Historical Dictionary of American Radio*. Westport, Connecticut: Greenwood Press, 1998. Very useful reference ranging over programs, people, organizations, and topics with dozens of contributors.

Hilliard, Robert L., and Michael C. Keith, *The Broadcast Century: A Biography of American Broadcasting*. Stoneham, Massachusetts: Focal Press, 2010 (5th edn). An informal and illustrated history told in chronological fashion, with many contributed comments from important pioneering figures, and a useful chronological time-line.

Hilmes, Michele, *Radio Voices: American Broadcasting, 1922–1952*. Minneapolis: University of Minnesota Press, 1997. Concentrating on what people heard rather than on the industry or technology, the author focuses on several key programs to illustrate the medium's appeal and success.

Jackaway, Gwenyth L., *Media at War: Radio's Challenge to the Newspapers, 1924–1939*. Westport, Connecticut: Praeger, 1995. Developing radio journalism threatened a key role of daily papers–this relates how the latter tried to suppress the former, though to no avail.

Keith, Michael C., *Talking Radio: An Oral History of American Radio in The Television Age*. Armonk, New York: M.E. Sharpe, 2000. Impressive editing job makes this readable despite about 100 contributors, and gets the reader close to decision-making in the radio business.

Lenthall, Bruce, *Radio's America: The Great Depression and the Rise of Modern Mass Culture*. Chicago: University of

Chicago Press, 2007. Importance of radio ("free" once you had a receiver) amidst economic chaos—reviews the entertainment and informational role of the medium.

Library of American Broadcasting (University of Maryland) website http://www.lib.umd.edu/LAB/
One of the best academic archives of all types of material on radio and television, based on the original Broadcast Pioneers Library collection.

Miller, Jeff, *History of American Broadcasting* website http://jeff560.tripod.com/broadcasting.html
Useful list of links to histories of AM, FM (and television).

Mishkind, Barry, *The Broadcast Archive* website http://www.oldradio.com/
Includes equipment and programming sections and links, plus information about the FCC, old stations, and links to other archives and organizations.

Newman, Kathy M., *Radio Active: Advertising and Consumer Activism, 1935–1947*. Berkeley: University of California Press, 2004. Growth of advertising and the beginnings of some consumer push-back against the commercial messages and pressure.

Smulyan, Susan, *Selling Radio: The Commercialization of American Broadcasting 1920–1934*. Washington, D.C.: Smithsonian Institution Press, 1994. Scholarly study of the policy battles over commercial support of radio (and later television) argues that what resulted – today's commercial system – was by no means a sure thing in the early days.

Sterling, Christopher H., and John M. Kittross, *Stay Tuned: A History of American Broadcasting*. Mahwah, New Jersey: Lawrence Erlbaum, 2002 (3rd edn). Standard history—the most comprehensive one-volume survey available—arranged by periods and then by topic. Extensive historical tables, technology glossary and bibliography.

Sterling, Christopher H., and Michael C. Keith, *Sounds of Change: A History of FM Broadcasting in America*. Chapel Hill, North Carolina: University of North Carolina Press, 2008. First overall history of the "second" radio medium, tracing the ups and downs–and eventual industry domination–of the system.

White, Llewellyn, *The American Radio*. Chicago: University of Chicago Press, 1947 (reprinted by Arno Press "History of Broadcasting," 1971). Old but still useful critical history that finds much wanting in the commercial radio business on the eve of television's introduction.

White, Thomas H., *United States Early Radio History* website http://earlyradiohistory.us/
A wonderfully useful site which offers full copies of a variety of pre-1920 articles and documents plus the author's valuable own research on early radio station list publications, call-letter policies, and the like.

4. Business of Radio

Albarron, Alan B., and Gregory C. Pitts, *The Radio Broadcasting Industry*. Boston: Allyn & Bacon, 2000. Useful survey of the modern business and how it operates.

Cox, Jim, *Sold on Radio: Advertisers in the Golden Age of Radio*. Jefferson, North Carolina: McFarland, 2008. Reviews 20 or so of the major sponsors and their programming, shedding light on an era when advertisers owned or controlled most popular network fare.

Ditingo, Vincent M., *The Remaking of Radio*. Newton, Massachusetts: Focal, 1994. Reviews the changing status of the radio business amidst growing competition, comparing

and contrasting AM and FM and reviewing likely technology changes of the future.

Fornatale, Peter, and Joshua E. Mills, *Radio in the Television Age*. Woodstock, New York: Overlook Press, 1980. Broad description of the industry after three decades of television competition but before cable and the Internet had much impact.

Hettinger, Herman S., *A Decade of Radio Advertising*. Chicago: University of Chicago Press, 1933 (reprinted by Arno Press "History of Broadcasting," 1971). Standard treatment of the creation and first decade of radio advertising, focusing on network-level developments.

Keith, Michael C., *The Radio Station: Broadcast, Satellite, and Internet*. Stoneham, Massachusetts: Focal Press, 2010 (8th edn). All aspects of operating and programming the modern commercial station sales format, news, research, promotion, traffic and billing, production, engineering and consultants. A standard, this has appeared in several languages.

National Association of Broadcasters. *Radio* website http://www.nab.org/AM/Template.cfm?Section=Radio&Template=/TaggedPage/TaggedPageDisplay.cfm&TPLID=68&ContentID=5341
Main industry trade association–this page includes most of their available information about radio.

Pease, Edward C., and Everette E. Dennis, editors, *Radio: The Forgotten Medium*. New Brunswick, New Jersey: Transaction Publishers, 1995. Twenty-two essays from *Media Studies Journal* provide a broad survey of radio today including both structure and content trends.

Radio Advertising Bureau, *Radio Marketing Guide* website http://www.rab.com/public/marketingGuide/rabRmg.html
Includes data on radio audiences, selling effectiveness and some on programming. Regularly updated.

Shane, Ed, *Selling Electronic Media*. Focal Press, 1999. Focuses on the selling of air time and the marketing of radio and television stations–by a top industry consultant.

5. Entertainment Programs

These cover either old-time radio [generally programs prior to 1960], or programming since. For specific programs or formats, see references under relevant entries; included here are only those titles that range widely.

DeLong, Thomas A., *The Mighty Music Box*. Los Angeles: Amber Crest Books, 1980. A broad history of all types of music on the air from initial classical pioneers through the various d formats of the so-called golden years (into the 1950s).

Dunning, John, *On the Air: The Encyclopedia of Old-Time Radio*. New York: Oxford University Press, 1998. Clearly *the* definitive directory of American network and major syndicated radio programs from the 1920s into the 1960s. Often includes full credits and, for important programs, quite lengthy discussion. This is another of the handful of invaluable books that could have been cited in "further reading" for all of the U.S. program entries.

Eberly, Phillip K., *Music in the Air: America's Changing Tastes in Popular Music, 1920–1980*. New York: Hastings House, 1982. Reviews both popular music trends and the central role of radio in spreading music's popularity.

Fisher, Marc, *Something in the Air: Radio, Rock, and the Revolution that Shaped a Generation*. New York: Random

House, 2007. Well-written survey of radio music from the 1950s to the end of the century, showing changing musical taste, the role of key figures both musicians and DJs, and some sense of their impact.

Genco, Louis V., *Old Time Radio* website http://www.old-time.com/
Includes many logs of program series, links to other sites, information on collecting programs.

Grams, Martin, *Radio Drama: A Comprehensive Chronicle of American Network Programs, 1932–1962.* Jefferson, North Carolina: McFarland, 2000. Listed by title with brief description and full list of episodes–especially useful to collectors of OTR programs.

Hilmes, Michele, and Jason Loviglio, editors, *Radio Reader: Essays in the Cultural History of Radio.* New York: Routledge, 2001. Excellent indicator of growing scholarly interest in radio past and present, offering 24 original essays.

Lackman, Ron, *The Encyclopedia of American Radio.* New York: Checkmark Books/Facts on File, 2000. Primarily people and programs with from one to several paragraphs on each. Updates his *Same Time, Same Station* (1996).

MacDonald, J. Fred, *Don't Touch That Dial! Radio Programming in American Life, 1920–1960.* Chicago: Nelson-Hall, 1979. A broad social history, focusing on network programs.

MacFarland, David T., *Future Radio Programming Strategies: Cultivating Listenership in the Digital Age.* Mahwah, New Jersey: Lawrence Erlbaum, 1997. Integrated analysis of audience needs and desires, and various approaches to both music and talk program formats in the competitive 1990s.

Maltin, Leonard, *The Great American Broadcast: A Celebration of Radio's Golden Age.* New York: Dutton, 1997. An affectionate and informal history of network radio's great years into the early 1950s discussing programs, personalities, and behind-the-scenes developments.

Nachman, Gerald, *Raised on Radio.* New York: Pantheon, 1998. A delightful read combining considerable insight, wonderful nostalgia and a fair bit of background information on key programs.

Reinehr, Robert C., and Jon D. Swartz, *Historical Dictionary of Old-Time Radio.* Lanham, Maryland: Scarecrow Press "Historical Dictionaries of Literature and the Arts," 2008. Brief (a paragraph in most cases) entries about key network programs to about 1960.

Shapiro, Mitchell E., *Radio Network Prime Time Programming, 1926–1967.* Jefferson, North Carolina: McFarland, 2002. Valuable charts showing changes in network program schedules over four decades. Use with Summers (below).

Sies, Luther F., *Encyclopedia of American Radio, 1920–1960.* Jefferson, North Carolina: McFarland, 2008 [2nd edn, 2 vols]. Individuals, programs, and stations in thousands of often very brief (one or two lines) entries, with some longer essays on important topics.

Swartz, Jon D. and Robert C. Reinehr, *Handbook of Old-time Radio: A Comprehensive Guide to Golden Age Radio Listening and Collecting.* Metuchen, New Jersey: Scarecrow Press, 1993. Dated, but still useful, this offers extensive information on what program recordings are available.

Summers, Harrison B., compiler, *A Thirty-year History of Programs Carried on National Radio Networks in the United States, 1926–1956.* Columbus: Ohio State University Department of Speech, 1958 (reprinted by Arno Press "History of Broadcasting," 1971). Standard listing of programs with times aired, ratings, etc. Use with Shapiro (above).

Widner, James F., *Radio Days* website *http://www.otr.com/index.shtml* Information on many old network radio programs (including some complete logs), OTR (old time radio) chat room and FAQs and more.

6. Radio Journalism

Bliss, Edward, Jr., *Now the News: The Story of Broadcast Journalism.* New York: Columbia University Press, 1991. The only overall history, roughly the first third of it deals with radio prior to television.

Brown, Robert J., *Manipulating The Ether: The Power of Broadcast Radio in Thirties America.* Jefferson, North Carolina: McFarland, 1998. Case studies of the impact of Franklin Roosevelt, the 1938 *War of the Worlds* broadcast, and Father Coughlin's speeches over the air.

Cloud, Stanley, and Lynne Olson, *The Murrow Boys: Pioneers on The Front Lines of Broadcast Journalism.* Boston: Houghton-Mifflin, 1996. Well-written assessment of the legendary CBS radio (and then television) news team from its initial formation in the late 1930s into the 1980s.

Culbert, David Holbrook, *News for Everyman: Radio and Foreign Affairs in Thirties America.* Westport, Connecticut: Greenwood, 1976. Commentators and how their role developed—one of the earliest serious histories.

Hosley, David H., *As Good as Any: Foreign Correspondence on American Radio, 1930–1940.* Westport, Connecticut: Greenwood, 1984. Traces the rise of news reporting from Europe on the U.S. networks through the Battle of Britain.

Miller, Edward, *Emergency Broadcasting and 1930s American Radio.* Philadelphia, Pennsylvania: Temple University Press, 2003. Reviews coverage of the *Hindenburg* crash, Roosevelt's "Fireside Chat" broadcasts, and escapist drama on "The War of the Worlds" and *The Shadow,* among other programs, assessing the impact of each.

White, Paul W., *News on the Air.* New York: Harcourt, Brace, 1947. Former head of CBS News reviews radio journalism at its height, including a fine chapter on how radio reported World War II's "D-Day" invasion of Europe.

7. Educational/Public Radio

Bianchi, William, *Schools of the Air: A History of Instructional Programs on Radio in the United States.* Jefferson, North Carolina: McFarland, 2008. Once widespread use of noncommercial radio–to carry classes to the home and to distant and rural schools.

LaFollette, Marcel Chotkowski, *Science on the Air: Popularizers and Personalities on Radio and Early Television.* Chicago: University of Chicago Press, 2008. These programs appeared on commercial and educational radio and helped to spread news of science to new audiences.

Lochte, Bob, *Christian Radio: The Growth of a Mainstream Broadcasting Force.* Jefferson, North Carolina: McFarland, 2006. Explores the growth of Christian radio stations which, with a variety of formats, make up a huge segment of the business.

Looker, Thomas, *The Sound and the Story: NPR and the Art of Radio.* Boston: Houghton Mifflin, 1995. Readable assessment of many of the people and programs on NPR in its first quarter-century.

McCauley, Michael P., *NPR: The Trials and Triumphs of National Public Radio.* New York: Columbia University

Press, 2004. As the title suggests, this is a critical history of the national network, focusing on both its key programs, and behind-the-scene developments.

Mitchell, Jack, *Listener Supported: The Culture and History of Public Radio*. Westport, Connecticut: Praeger, 2005. A one-time program director of the network describes how and why it operates as it does.

Slotten, Hugh Richard, *Radio's Hidden Voice: The Origins of Public Broadcasting in the United States*. Urbana: University of Illinois Press "History of Communication," 2009. Examines origins of alternative broadcasting models based especially on a commitment to providing noncommercial service for the public on stations, operated largely by universities and colleges.

Walker, Jesse, *Rebels of the Air: An Alternative History of Radio in America*. New York: New York University Press, 2001. Focuses on community and other alternative stations, mainly in large markets.

8. Radio and Minority Groups

Barlow, William, *Voice Over: The Making of Black Radio*. Philadelphia, Pennsylvania: Temple University Press, 1999. Overall history of black-oriented radio programming and stations.

Halper, Donna L., *Invisible Stars: A Social History of Women in American Broadcasting*. Armonk, New York: M.E. Sharpe, 2001. First attempt at an overall history of the many and varied roles of women in radio (and television)–they are a "minority" in the radio business–highlighting many forgotten pioneers.

Johnson, Phyllis, and Michael C. Keith, *Queer Airwaves: The Story of Gay and Lesbian Broadcasting*. Armonk, New York: M.E. Sharpe, 2001. Only study of its type–focuses primarily on radio personalities and programs.

Keith, Michael C., *Signals in the Air: Native Broadcasting in America*. Westport, Connecticut: Praeger "Media and Society Series," 1995. Nearly all the "Indian" stations are radio outlets, many on reservations and operated by the tribes themselves. Useful assessment of what is provided and the problems such stations face.

——, editor, *Radio Cultures: The Sound Medium in American Life*. New York: Peter Lang, 2008. Important and insightful anthology of original papers examining how radio has impacted different social groups over the decades.

Newman, Mark, *Entrepreneurs of Profit and Pride: From Black-Appeal to Radio Soul*. New York: Praeger "Media and Society Series," 1988. One of the first historical treatments of black radio.

Sampson, Henry T., *Swingin' on the Ether Waves: A Chronological History of African Americans in Radio and Television Broadcasting, 1925–1955*. Jefferson, North Carolina: McFarland, 2005 (2 vols). Amazingly detailed chronology, drawing heavily on contemporary press reports, many of which are quoted here.

Siegel, Susan, and David S. Siegel, *Radio and the Jews: The Untold Story of How Radio Influenced America's Image of Jews, 1920s–1950s*. Yorktown Heights, New York: Book Hunter Press, 2008. Focuses on programs from the "golden age" of network radio, and the ways Jewish characters and ideas were portrayed.

Ward, Brian, *Radio and the Struggle for Civil Rights in the South*. Gainesville: University Press of Florida "New Perspectives on the History of the South," 2004. Some stations played a central role in helping to rally civil rights protests–and reporting on their aftermath.

9. Radio's Audiences

Markedly few book-length studies have appeared on this topic. Nearly all of them predate television's appearance.

Arbitron, *Radio Today Reports Series* website http://www.arbitron.com/home/radiotoday.htm
The radio ratings firm provides overview information on radio and its audiences.

Beville, Hugh Malcolm, Jr., *Audience Ratings: Radio, Television, and Cable*. Hillsdale, NJ: Erlbaum, 1988 (2nd edn). Best historical study of how research methods and different audience research companies developed.

Chappell, Matthew N., and C.E. Hooper, *Radio Audience Measurement*. New York: Stephen Daye, 1944. Creator of telephone-based "Hooperatings" collaborated in this discussion of how commercial ratings were then generated.

Los Angeles Times, In the News: Radio Audiences http://articles.latimes.com/keyword/radio-audiences
Recent articles from the Los Angeles newspaper.

Project for Excellence in Journalism, *Radio Audience Trends* http://www.journalism.org/node/836
Regularly updated report on overall listening levels, as well as more focused studies of specific audience groups.

Lazarsfeld, Paul F., and Patricia Kendall, *Radio Listening in America: The People Look at Radio–Again*. New York: Prentice-Hall, 1948. National survey (updating one from two years before) of who listened to what and with what impact in the days before television's rise.

10. Radio Regulation

Benjamin, Louise M., *Freedom of the Air and the Public Interest: First Amendment Rights in Broadcasting to 1935*. Carbondale: Southern Illinois University Press, 2001. Careful analysis of case law and legislation and how the basics of government's "hands off" approach to radio programming developed.

Bensman, Marvin R., *The Beginning of Broadcast Regulation in The Twentieth Century*. Jefferson, North Carolina: McFarland, 2000. The story of legislation and administrative decision-making from the 1910 Wireless Act through passage of the landmark 1927 Radio Act.

Braun, Mark, *AM Stereo and the FCC: Case Study of a Marketplace Shibboleth*. Norwood, New Jersey: Ablex, 1994. Best analysis of the FCC-industry conflict over the setting of technical standards and impact of the commission's 1982 decision allowing the "marketplace" to decide.

Brinson, Susan L., *The Red Scare, Politics, and the Federal Communications Commission, 1941–1960*. Westport, Connecticut: Praeger, 2004. The impact of political pressure and social fear and how it impacted a federal agency and the stations it licensed.

Federal Communications Commission, *Audio Division, Mass Media Bureau* website http://www.fcc.gov/mb/audio/
Licensing and other information concerning both commercial and public AM and FM stations.

Flannery, Gerald, editor, *Commissioners of the FCC 1927–1994*. Lanham, Maryland: University Press of America, 1995. Useful short (2–3 page) mini-biographies of commissioners of both the FRC (1927–34) and FCC (since 1934).

Foust, James C., *Big Voices of The Air: The Battle Over Clear Channel Radio*. Ames: Iowa State University Press, 2000. Study of a long-lasting policy issue only finally resolved in the 1960s–one of the few such case studies of a specific controversy.

Hilliard, Robert L., and Michael C. Keith, *Waves of Rancor: Tuning in the Radical Right*. Armonk, New York: M. E. Sharpe, 1999. An often-scary study of far right-wing demagoguery over the air with many examples cited—and the concerns such broadcasts raise.

——, *The Quieted Voice: The Rise and Demise of Localism in American Radio*. Carbondale: University of Southern Illinois Press, 2005. Despite regulatory lip service given to the notion of "localism," such content has largely disappeared from commercial stations–the authors describe why.

——, *Dirty Discourse: Sex and Indecency in American Radio*. Ames: Iowa State Press, 2003; Blackwell, 2007 (2nd edn). How pushing the envelope of what is acceptable has worked–and has brought down regulatory wrath on the perpetrators.

Kahn, Frank, Jr., editor, *Documents of American Broadcasting*. Englewood Cliffs, New Jersey: Prentice-Hall, 1984 (4th edn). Dated but still valuable anthology of key policy materials.

McChesney, Robert W., *Telecommunications, Mass Media & Democracy: The Battle for the Control of U.S. Broadcasting, 1928–1935*. New York: Oxford University Press, 1993. Excellent study of the policy debate about government's role over broadcasting before and following the 1934 Communications Act.

Opel, Andy, *Micro Radio and the FCC: Media Activism and the Struggle over Broadcast Policy*. Westport, Connecticut: Praeger, 2004. The rise and potential of Low-Power FM outlets and why they created such controversy.

Paglin, Max D., editor, *A Legislative History of the Communications Act of 1934*. New York: Oxford University Press, 1989. Includes committee hearings and floor debate.

——, *The Communications Act: A Legislative History of the Major Amendments, 1934–1996*. Washington, D.C.: Pike & Fischer, 1999. Continues the previous title with the important amendments such as Communication Satellite Act of 1962, Public Broadcasting Act of 1967, various cable legislation, and the Telecommunications Act of 1996.

Slotten, Hugh R., *Radio and Television Regulation: Broadcast Technology in the United States, 1920–1960*. Baltimore, Maryland: Johns Hopkins University Press, 2000. Three of the six case studies concern radio, including the FRC creation of radio standards, and the rise of FM.

11. Regional and State Radio Histories

This is but a sampling—for the many individual station histories, see relevant entries.

Blanton, Parke, *Crystal Set to Satellite: The Story of California Broadcasting–the First Eighty Years*. Sacramento: California Broadcasters Assn., 1987.

Brouder, Edward W., Jr., *Granite And Ether: A Chronicle of New Hampshire Broadcasting*. Bedford: New Hampshire Association of Broadcasters, 1993.

Doll, Bob, *Sparks Out of The Plowed Ground: The History of America's Small Town Radio Stations*. West Palm Beach, Forida: Streamline Press, 1996. Useful given that most books on radio focus on networks or major markets–this provides something of a balance.

Dorgan, Howard, *The Airwaves of Zion: Radio And Religion in Appalachia*. Knoxville: University of Tennessee Press, 1993. Historical assessment of the symbiosis between religion and radio in one of the nation's poorest regions.

Jaker, Bill, et al., *The Airways of New York: Illustrated Histories of 156 AM Stations in the Metropolitan Area, 1921–1996*. Jefferson, North Carolina: McFarland, 1998. Illustrated history of all of them, some well-known and still with use and others long gone and forgotten.

Poindexter, Ray, *Arkansas Airwaves*. North Little Rock, Arkansas: the author, 1974.

Schroeder, Richard, *Texas Signs On: The Early Days of Radio And Television*. College Station: Texas A&M University Press, 1998. Illustrated history of the rise of radio and then television in the Lone Star state, relying heavily on interviews and original documents.

12. Periodicals

Included are radio-focused titles that appeared in paper or (increasingly) online as of mid-2009, showing their start dates where known. Some are available by subscription, but a number are free.

Broadcasting & Cable (1931) http://www.broadcastingcable.com/
   The principal industry trade weekly which helps to place radio in context with television, cable, and newer services. Covers advertising, programming, regulation, and people in the business. Not as comprehensive after about 1995.

Inside Radio (daily) http://www.mstreet.net/
   Reports radio industry news – station sales, management changes, and stock quotations – plus commentary (and hyperbole) by publisher Jerry DelColliano.

Journal of Radio and Audio Media (1991, twice a year) Covers both history and current issues in a scholarly peer-reviewed format—the first scholarly journal devoted to radio.

R&R: Radio & Records (1971) http://www.radioandrecords.com/RRWebSite20/
   Radio programmers main trade source includes music charts for specific formats, industry tip sheets and interviews, and parallels for music playlist comparisons.

RAIN: Radio and Internet Newsletter http://www.kurthanson.com/
   News and updates on broadcast and online services, including satellite and digital services.

Radio Business Report (1983) http://www.rbr.com/
   Emphasis is on management and marketing issues in commercial radio business.

Radio Daily News http://radiodailynews.com/
   Pulls together radio-related news from a variety of sources.

Radio Ink (1985) http://www.radioink.com/
   Sales and management oriented publication containing articles by industry people who offer insights, opinions, and analysis about trends in advertising and station.

Radio Magazine (1994) http://radiomagonline.com/
   Covers radio technology and is a spinoff of *Broadcast Engineering* magazine.

Radio World (1977) http://www.radioworld.com/
   Intended for station engineers, technicians, and electronics manufacturers of audio products.

Talkers Magazine (monthly) http://talkers.com/online/
   Focused on the people and issues in talk radio.

Taylor on Radio-Info http://www.radio-info.com/newsletters/3-taylor-on-radio-info
   Insightful daily analysis of program and economic events, issues, and trends in all of commercial radio business by a long-time authority on the field.

Advisers 2003 Edition

Contributors 2003 Edition

Michael H. Adams

Alan B. Albarran

Pierre Albert

Craig Allen

Steven D. Anderson

Larry Appelbaum

Edd Applegate

Sousan Arafeh

John S. Armstrong

Philip J. Auter

Robert K. Avery

Glenda R. Balas

Mary Christine Banwart

Warren Bareiss

Ray Barfield

Kyle S. Barnett

Douglas L. Battema

Mary E. Beadle

Christine Becker

Johnny Beerling

Alan Bell

Louise Benjamin

ElDean Bennett

Marvin Bensman

Jerome S. Berg

Rosemary Bergeron

William L. Bird, Jr.

Howard Blue

A. Joseph Borrell

Douglas A. Boyd

John Bradford

L. Clare Bratten

Mark Braun

Jack Brown

Michael Brown

Robert J. Brown

Donald R. Browne

John H. Bryant

Joseph G. Buchman

Karen S. Buzzard

Paul Brian Campbell

Dom Caristi

Ginger Rudeseal Carter

Dixon H. Chandler II

Frank J. Chorba

Lynn A. Christian

Claudia Clark

Kathleen Collins

Jerry Condra

Harold N. Cones

Bryan Cornell

Elizabeth Cox

Steve Craig

Tim Crook

Marie Cusson

Keri Davies

E. Alvin Davis

J.M. Dempsey

CONTRIBUTORS 2003 EDITION

Corley Dennison

Neil Denslow

Steven Dick

John D.H. Downing

Pamela K. Doyle

Christina S. Drale

Susan Tyler Eastman

Bob Edwards

Kathryn Smoot Egan

Lyombe Eko

Sandra L. Ellis

Ralph Engelman

Erika Engstrom

Stuart L. Esrock

Charles Feldman

Michel Filion

Howard Fink

Seth Finn

Robert G. Finney

Margaret Finucane

James E. Fletcher

Corey Flintoff

Joe S. Foote

Robert C. Fordan

Robert S. Fortner

James C. Foust

Ralph Frasca

James A. Freeman

Elfriede Fürsich

Charles F. Ganzert

Ronald Garay

Philipp Gassert

Judith Gerber

Norman Gilliland

Donald G. Godfrey

Douglas Gomery

Jim Grubbs

Joanne Gula

Paul F. Gullifor

Linwood A. Hagin

Donna L. Halper

Tona J. Hangen

Margot Hardenbergh

Jeffrey D. Harman

Dorinda Hartmann

Gordon H. Hastings

Joy Elizabeth Hayes

John Allen Hendricks

Alexandra Hendriks

Ariana Hernandez-Reguant

Robert L. Hilliard

Jim Hilliker

Michele Hilmes

John Hochheimer

Jack Holgate

Herbert H. Howard

Chuck Howell

Kevin Howley

W.A. Kelly Huff

Peter E. Hunn

John D. Jackson

Randy Jacobs

Glen M. Johnson

Phylis Johnson

Sara Jones

Lynda Lee Kaid

Stephen A. Kallis, Jr.

Steve Kang

Michael C. Keith

Ari Kelman

Colum Kenny

John Michael Kittross

Frederica P. Kushner

Philip J. Lane

Matthew Lasar

Laurie Thomas Lee

Renée Legris

Frederic A. Leigh

Lawrence W. Lichty

Lucy A. Liggett

Val E. Limburg

Robert Henry Lochte

Jason Loviglio

Gregory Ferrell Lowe

Christopher Lucas

Mike Mashon

Marilyn J. Matelski

Peter E. Mayeux

Dennis W. Mazzocco

Thomas A. McCain

Jeffrey M. McCall

David McCartney

Tom McCourt

Brad McCoy

Allison McCracken

Drew O. McDaniel

Michael A. McGregor

Robert McKenzie

Elizabeth McLeod

Mike Meeske

Fritz Messere

Colin Miller

Toby Miller

Bruce Mims

Jack Minkow

Jack Mitchell

Jason Mittell

Barbara Moore

Matthew Murray

Graham Mytton

Gregory D. Newton

Greg Nielsen

D'Arcy John Oaks

William F. O'Connor

Cary O'Dell

Robert M. Ogles

Ryota Ono

Peter B. Orlik

Pierre-C. Page

Brian T. Pauling

Manjunath Pendakur

Douglas K. Penisten

Stephen D. Perry

Patricia Phalen

Steven Phipps

Joseph R. Piasek

Gregory G. Pitts

Mark Poindexter

Tim Pollard

Robert F. Potter

Alf Pratte

Patricia Joyner Priest

Dennis Randolph

Lawrence N. Redd

David E. Reese

Patton B. Reighard Andre Richte

Edward A. Riedinger

Terry A. Robertson

Melinda B. Robins

America Rodríguez

Eric W. Rothenbuhler

Richard Rudin

Joseph A. Russomanno

Anne Sanderlin

Erica Scharrer

Steven R. Scherer

Karl Schmid

Clair Schulz

CONTRIBUTORS 2003 EDITION

Ed Shane
Pam Shane
Mitchell Shapiro
Jason T. Siegel
Ron Simon
B.R. Smith
Ruth Bayard Smith
Lynn Spangler
David R. Spencer
David Spiceland
Laurie R. Squire
Michael Stamm
Christopher H. Sterling
Will Straw
Michael Streissguth
Mary Kay Switzer
Rick Sykes
Marlin R. Taylor
Matt Taylor
Herbert A. Terry
Richard Tiner

Regis Tucci
David E. Tucker
Don Rodney Vaughan
Mary Vipond
Randall Vogt
Ira Wagman
Andrew Walker
Peter Wallace
Jennifer Hyland Wang
Richard Ward
Mary Ann Watson
Brian West
Gilbert A. Williams
Sonja Williams
Wenmouth Williams, Jr.
Roger Wilmut
Stephen M. Winzenburg
Richard Wolff
Roosevelt "Rick" Wright, Jr.
Edgar B. Wycoff
Thimios Zaharopoulos

List of Entries

A.C. NIELSEN COMPANY
Developing Radio Ratings

From 1942 to 1964, the A.C. Nielsen Company was a primary provider of U.S. radio ratings. The company pioneered the commercial use of mechanical and then electronic meter devices to automatically record which stations listeners were tuning their receivers to.

Origins

Arthur C. Nielsen (1897–1980) founded his marketing company in 1923 after serving briefly as a naval officer in World War I and working with two Chicago companies. With six employees and $45,000 in capital from Nielsen's former fraternity brothers, the company specialized in performance surveys of industrial equipment. The company went bankrupt twice in its early years. A decade later, Nielsen expanded his service by launching a continuous market research service, the Nielsen Drug Index, to chart the retail flow of specific products. The Nielsen Food Index soon followed. Both were based on the same premise (which was later applied successfully to broadcast ratings): carefully develop a sample of stores and visit them periodically to measure unit sales through audits of purchase invoices and shelf stock. When projected regionally or nationally, these data provided a measure of sales that could be related directly to marketing efforts.

Nielsen entered the radio audience measurement business at the request of clients who found the food and drug indexes useful guides and desired the same assistance in purchasing radio advertising time. In 1936, Nielsen acquired the rights to a mechanical device developed by two Massachusetts Institute of Technology professors, Robert Elder and Louis Woodruff. The "Audimeter" made a graphic record on a filmstrip, providing a continuous record of radio receiver use—when it was on and to which station(s) it was tuned—over a month-long period. These early meters were both costly and cumbersome, especially as the tape had to be picked up by Nielsen personnel before the tabulation of results could begin. The tapes were then shipped to a Chicago plant where they were "read" by specially designed machines. After modifications to the meter, their use was subject to intense experimentation for four years in several Midwestern states.

Radio Ratings

The Nielsen Radio Index (NRI) ratings service, based on the meter system, was introduced commercially in December 1942, in competition with the then-dominant "Hooperatings," which used telephone surveys of sample homes. A key advantage of the Nielsen meter was that its sample (initially just 800 homes in the east-central portion of the U.S.) was not restricted to telephone-owning homes; this was important at a time when upward of a third of homes in some areas lacked the instrument. By 1946 the NRI had expanded service to some 1,100 homes over most of the country. NRI also introduced an improved meter with a mailable tape (it provided measures over two weeks) to speed delivery of the resultant ratings and to render personal staff visits to Nielsen sample homes unnecessary. The streamlined process—which could measure four separate radio receivers—allowed expansion of meter-based ratings to both FM listening and television watching.

By early 1949, the NRI sample had expanded to cover virtually all of the country except for the Mountain time zone, which was especially expensive to serve. In early 1950, Nielsen purchased the Hooper national radio and fledgling television ratings services (Hooper continued local radio market ratings for several years). By this point, Nielsen's "methodology, financial position, organization and widespread industry acceptance rendered him nearly invincible" (Beville, 1988). A year later, the NRI sample was up to 1,500 homes—and its charges to advertisers and broadcasters had nearly doubled. But these were national (network) ratings, not local-market measurements.

The Nielsen Station Index (NSI) debuted in 1954 to measure household use of both radio and television on a local market basis. This service was not audimeter based, but rather combined the use of traditional diaries (in which audience members recorded their listening time) with a "Recordimeter" device, which signaled with light flashes and a buzzer when listeners should make a diary entry and at the same time kept a rough measure of when the receiver was on. This crude meter helped to validate the diary information provided. And the diary could provide what no meter then could—demographic information on the gender and age of the person listening. In 1959, computers were first applied to Nielsen ratings processing and analysis. By the early 1960s, NSI was measuring radio listening in more than 200 markets. But its seeming market dominance would be short-lived, for, as Hugh Beville writes,

> in 1962 Nielsen discontinued quarter-hour ratings because of declining radio listening levels and the rapidly increasing number of radio stations. This cost many client cancellations, which sparked the NSI decision to abandon radio. Not only was television seriously diminishing prime-time radio audiences, but the advent of automobile and portable receivers, plus many new independent stations, was rapidly changing basic radio listening patterns. In 1963 the local radio service was discontinued.
>
> (Beville, 1988)

Contributing to the end of Nielsen radio ratings was a series of congressional hearings into the ratings for both radio and television. Nielsen became a central target in those hearings, in part because of

methodological questions about some of the company's means of ratings data collection. Nielsen's system measured only home viewing, not portables. The out-of-home audience, as it became known, grew with the movement to the suburbs and the use of the automobile. In response to the changing radio audience, Nielsen created an Audimeter to be installed in automobiles. However, when his clients were unwilling to support the investment costs needed to upgrade, he decided to quit the radio business. The Nielsen Company decided to focus its investment efforts on the greater returns potential from television ratings. The end of Nielsen's radio services was a key factor leading to development of RADAR national radio ratings.

Later Years

After leaving the radio ratings business, Nielsen continued to develop its national television network and local-market ratings services. It introduced overnight ("instant") television meters in major markets in the early 1960s and slowly expanded the process to other cities and network ratings. In 1987, Nielsen introduced its still-controversial "people meter," which could measure TV receiver tuning as well as who was tuning in. With Arbitron's departure from television ratings in the late 1990s, Nielsen became the only source of both national and local-market television ratings.

When the elder Nielsen retired in 1976, A.C. Nielsen, Jr., became the company's leader. In 1984 he sold the firm to Dun and Bradstreet, which in 1998 split the marketing and media research aspects of the company. The latter was sold to Lucent Technology and then spun off to a new corporate owner, Cognizant Corporation, in mid-1998. At the end of 1999, Nielsen Media Research was purchased by a Dutch company, VNU NV.

In the first decade of the 21st century, many commercial radio broadcasters, concerned about audience declines reported by Arbitron's new portable people meter (PPM) methodology, sought alternative audience measures for their advertising clients. Late in 2008, Nielsen agreed with two large owners of multiple radio stations, Cumulus Media and Clear Channel Radio, to provide ratings in place of Arbitron's service. Nielsen initially measured about 50 markets for Clear Channel, and 17 for Cumulus, with plans to expand broadly across the country. As they had before dropping out of radio ratings in the mid-1960s, Nielsen's service relied on written diaries, starting with annual week-long sweep periods April and May each year, starting in early 2009. The new diaries are pre-printed with all possible over-the-air stations already listed, and are similar to those Nielsen has used in Britain and other nations. Directly responding to a chief complaint about the Arbitron PPM service, Nielsen is over-sampling black and Hispanic households in its radio ratings.

See also: Arbitron; Audience Research Methods; Audimeter; Cooperative Analysis of Broadcasting; Hooperatings; Portable People Meter; RADAR

Further Reading

Beville, Hugh Malcolm, Jr., *Audience Ratings: Radio, Television, and Cable*, Hillsdale, New Jersey: Erlbaum, 1985; revised edition, 1988.

Buzzard, Karen S., *Chains of Gold: Marketing the Ratings and Rating the Markets*, Metuchen, New Jersey: Scarecrow, 1990.

Buzzard, Karen S., "Radio Rating Pioneers: The Development of a Standardized Ratings Vocabulary," *Journal of Radio Studies* 6 no. 2 (Autumn 1999).

Nielsen, Arthur Charles, "Trends in Mechanization of Radio Advertising," *Journal of Marketing* (January 1942).

Nielsen, Arthur Charles, "Two Years of Commercial Operation of the Audimeter and NRI," *Journal of Marketing* (January 1944).

Nielsen, Arthur Charles, *How You Can Get the Ideal Radio Research Service Complete, Accurate, Impartial, Rapid, Skilfully Applied*, Chicago: Nielsen, 1946.

Nielsen, Arthur Charles, *New Facts about Radio Research*, Chicago: Nielsen, 1946.

Nielsen, Arthur Charles, "Audience Analysis via Audimeter Method," *Broadcasting Yearbook 1947* (1947).

Nielsen, Arthur Charles, *Greater Prosperity through Marketing Research: The First 40 Years of A.C. Nielsen Company*, New York: Newcomen Society, 1964.

Rusch, H.L., "Debut of the First Nielsen Radio Index Data," *The Nielsen Researcher* (October 1939).

U.S. House of Representatives, *Evaluation of Statistical Methods Used in Obtaining Broadcast Ratings: House Report No. 193*, 87th Congress, 1st Session (23 March 1961).

U.S. House of Representatives, *Broadcast Ratings: House Report No. 1212*, 89th Congress, 2nd Session (13 January 1966).

KAREN S. BUZZARD, AND
CHRISTOPHER H. STERLING
2009 REVISIONS BY CHRISTOPHER H. STERLING

ACTIVE ROCK FORMAT

See: Heavy Metal/Active Rock Format

ADULT CONTEMPORARY FORMAT

Adult Contemporary (AC) music emphasizes a mixture of modern day (contemporary) and older popular hit singles.

The AC format has its origins in the arrival and eventual permanence of rock and roll as a music form in the United States during the late 1950s. According to Hyatt (1999), radio stations in the United States at that time wanted to keep airing current popular hits, a staple format that had already attracted listeners for decades. However, these stations did not want to play rock and roll and tried to find a way to keep the popular hits genre without having to play songs with a rock beat. Thus, they turned to popular songs that lacked the "heavy" sounds of rock and roll. These tunes became known by those in the radio industry as "easy listening" or "middle of the road." Hyatt refers to Adult Contemporary as being synonymous with both terms.

Beginning in the 1960s, *Billboard* magazine created a new chart listing the top records considered easy listening and middle of the road, in addition to its pop, rhythm and blues, and country lists of popular songs. *Billboard* gave several names to this chart throughout the 1960s, which listed the top 20 (and during some years the top 15 to 25) singles. These names included "Easy Listening," "Pop-Standard Singles," and "Middle-Road Singles." By 1965 the magazine had settled on "Easy Listening" to describe the chart. Artists listed on this chart included music industry veterans such as Dean Martin, Frank Sinatra, Nat King Cole, and Andy Williams. By the late 1960s, folk artists such as Peter, Paul, and Mary, and Simon and Garfunkel had hits on the "Easy Listening" list. The chart also included instrumentals by Herb Alpert and the Tijuana Brass, film composer Henry Mancini, and Mason Williams during the late 1960s and early 1970s. Also during this period, Hyatt notes, "fewer people who considered themselves easy listening fans were requesting previous favorites like Frank Sinatra and Ed Ames." More notably, crossover between the "Easy Listening" and "Pop" lists started to occur at this time, with artists such as the Carpenters and Bread releasing mellow, rock-type songs that were listed on both charts.

"Easy Listening" music grew in popularity; *Billboard* expanded the chart, lengthening the list from the top 40 singles to the top 50 in 1973. Keith (1987) points out that this genre appealed to the same type of audience who listened to stations featuring soft and mellow rock music. Additionally, during the late 1970s, the number of soft and mellow rock listeners declined as the disco format grew in popularity and as the number of hit music stations increased: "It was out of this flux that the AC format emerged in earnest" (Keith, 1987). *Billboard* renamed the "Easy Listening" chart in 1979, when it became known as "Adult Contemporary." During the next 14 years, the list's length fluctuated between 40 and 50 hit singles of the genre. In 1996 the chart came to list the top 25 singles (Hyatt, 1999).

During the 1980s, the AC format became the nation's most widespread, with its target audience encompassing the 25 to 49 age group, especially women, which made it appealing to advertisers as well. By the time of AC's maturation, its audience base consisted of adults who had composed the teen listenership of Top 40 radio in the early 1970s. AC, also referred to as lite or soft rock, drew in the thirty-something listener by offering "popular, upbeat music without the harshness that often accompanies rock" (Keith, 1987). Typical artists with top AC hits during the 1980s included Lionel Richie, Billy Joel, Whitney Houston, and Phil Collins. Artists popular during the 1970s also hit the chart, such as Cher, Elton John, Barry Manilow, and Barbra Streisand.

Regarding the programming of the AC format, stations that employ the genre place greater emphasis on the music, thus minimizing disc jockey chatter. AC stations might describe themselves as "soft rockers" or as "hot, soft, lite, bright, mix or variety" the phrase "continuous soft rock favorites of yesterday and today" serves as a common line in promotional spots (MacFarland, 1997). The music mix itself combines contemporary singles with hits from the past, though these generally do not include true "oldies." Called "recurrents," these older songs typically have just left the current chart and are usually between six months and two years old (Howard, Kievman, and Moore, 1994). Halper (1991) contends that AC music directors must keep up with the newest adult pop artists, such as those presented on VH1, the slightly more mature version of MTV, the cable music channel.

AC stations present chart toppers, both current and potential, and recurrents in blocks or sweeps, which can last as long as 28 minutes of uninterrupted music. Announcers usually follow these sweeps with recaps of song titles and artists, and commercials are limited to four or five per cluster (MacFarland, 1997). AC stations also may feature contests, all-request hours, programs that feature hits from a particular decade, and lifestyle-oriented news. As with other music-oriented formats, news takes a secondary position, although it is usually presented during drive time. Some stations feature strong onair personalities, especially in the morning, and an upbeat delivery style similar to the Contemporary Hits Radio and Top 40 formats.

By the mid-1990s, AC came in second to country as the most popular format in the United States, even though the number of stations featuring this format dropped between 1989 and 1994. Artists with hits on the *Billboard* AC chart during the 1990s included Mariah Carey, Michael Bolton, and previous hitmakers such as Elton John and Eric Clapton. AC hits of the late 1990s exemplified the soft/lite rock, "easy listening" sounds of early AC, a key characterization of this adult-oriented radio format, as embodied in the chart-topping singles of Canadian singer Celine Dion, who headed the list of all artists with songs spending the most weeks at number one on *Billboard's* AC chart (65, 19 of which were with one song [Hyatt, 1999]).

In the first decade of the new millennium, AC's audience numbers continued to erode as new variations or permutations of it, like the more niched "Mike," "Jack," and rhythmic AC formats—nibbled at its base of younger listeners.

See also: Contemporary Hit Radio/Top 40 Format; Easy Listening/Beautiful Music Format; Middle of the Road Format; Soft Rock Format

Further Reading

Halper, Donna L., *Radio Music Directing*, Boston: Focal Press, 1991.

Howard, Herbert H., and Michael S. Kievman, *Radio and TV Programming*, Columbus, Ohio: Grid, 1983; 2nd edition, as *Radio, TV, and Cable Programming*, edited by Howard, Kievman, and Barbara A. Moore, Ames: Iowa State University Press, 1994.

Hyatt, Wesley, *The Billboard Book of Number One Adult Contemporary Hits*, New York: Billboard Books, 1999.

Keith, Michael C., *Production in Format Radio Handbook*, Lanham, Maryland: University Press of America, 1984.

Keith, Michael C., and Joseph M. Krause, *The Radio Station*, Boston: Focal Press, 1986; 4th edition, by Michael C. Keith, 1997; 5th edition, Boston and Oxford: Focal Press, 2000.

Keith, Michael C., *Radio Programming: Consultancy and Formatics*, Boston: Focal Press, 1987.

MacFarland, David T., *Contemporary Radio Programming Strategies*, Hillsdale, New Jersey: Erlbaum, 1990; 2nd edition, as *Future Radio Programming Strategies: Cultivating Leadership in the Digital Age*, Mahwah, New Jersey: Erlbaum, 1997.

ERIKA ENGSTROM
2009 REVISIONS BY MICHAEL C. KEITH

ADVENTURES IN GOOD MUSIC
Classical Music Program

Created by Karl Haas in 1959, *Adventures in Good Music* is one of the longest running and most widely acclaimed classical music programs in radio broadcast history.

Adventures is syndicated in more than 200 U.S. cities. The U.S. Armed Forces network beams the program to U.S. bases on all continents, and 37

Australian Broadcasting Corporation stations broadcast the show. The program is translated into Spanish in Mexico City, causing the one-hour program to run an hour and a half. And in Germany, at the request of the South German Broadcasting Corporation (Suddeutscher Rundfunk), *Adventures* is available in German under a specially formatted, select series of presentations. The program is also recorded in French for the Canadian Broadcasting Corporation (CBC).

Since 1970, Cleveland classical radio station WCLV has supervised syndication of *Adventures* through its subsidiary, Seaway Productions. Each new syndicated program—recorded by producer and host Karl Haas in his New York studio—is transmitted via Seaway Productions to a domestic satellite that beams the program to stations across the United States. Elsewhere, stations receive the program on magnetic tape reels that are duplicated at WCLV and mailed in advance of program dates.

Karl Haas began his lifetime involvement with classical music at the age of six in his hometown, Speyer-on-the-Rhine, Germany, where he studied piano under the guidance of his mother. At the age of 12, he was performing in a piano trio with friends. As a young man, Haas studied music at Germany's University of Heidelberg. At the onset of Nazi tyranny in the 1930s, Haas fled to Detroit, Michigan, where he studied at the famed Netzorg School of Music and commuted from Detroit to New York to study with the legendary pianist Artur Schnabel.

Haas' radio career began in 1950 at Detroit station WWJ, where he was under contract to host a weekly preview of concerts performed by the Detroit Symphony. His program caught the attention of the CBC, which offered him the position of conducting a chamber orchestra and performing piano recitals for a weekly program. Based on the phenomenal popularity of his Canadian show, CBC requested that Haas incorporate a commentary about his music into the program. Following audiences' favorable response to his lively narratives, in 1959 Detroit radio station WJR hired Haas to develop his own daily one-hour music-plus-commentary program—and *Adventures in Good Music* was born.

The format of *Adventures* has remained nearly the same since its debut. Each program is fashioned around a central theme, punctuated and illustrated with musical selections and enhanced by knowledgeable and often witty commentary originated by Haas. One program may highlight the best of Bach, and yet another may challenge listeners to "Name the Composer" in a musical mystery teaser. Still

other programs may seek to understand and explain the impact of humor in music or how music is relevant to current events.

In creating his *Adventures* calendar, Haas explores both the traditional and the unconventional. A sequence from a typical month commenced with a program honoring the anniversary of Chopin's birthday. By midweek, "In Every Sense of the Word" offered an exploration of the five senses and their musical equivalents. Haas scheduled a traditional St. Patrick's Day salute on March 17. Then, he finished off the month's menu with an unconventional study of "When in Rome..." featuring works by non-Italian composers based on Italian culture.

As an active performer on the recital concert tour circuit, Haas has held a series of biannual "live" *Adventures in Good Music* programs at New York's Metropolitan Museum of Art since 1977.

Adventures has twice been awarded the coveted George Peabody Award for excellence in broadcasting. Haas has received numerous awards in recognition of his outstanding contributions to radio and for furthering the appreciation of classical music. The French Government presented him with the Officer d'academie and Chevalier de l'ordre des arts et lettres awards. In Germany he received the prestigious First Class Order of Merit. In 1991 Haas was awarded the National Endowment for the Humanities' Charles Frankel Award. Additionally, Haas was honored with the National Telemedia Award and has received eight honorary doctorates. In March 1995 Haas was the first classical broadcaster to be nominated for induction into the Radio Hall of Fame in Chicago.

Continuing his broadcast effort to educate and entertain listeners to the joys of classical music, Haas authored the reference book *Inside Music*. Also, in 1993 and 1994 he released three compact discs, *The Romantic Piano, Story of the Bells,* and *Song and Dance,* which marked a new venue for *Adventures in Good Music.*

Karl Haas died at age 91 in Michigan on February 6, 2005.

See also: Classical Music Format

Producer/Creator

Karl Haas

Programming History

Syndicated by WCLV, Cleveland, Ohio
  1959–

Further Reading

Douglas, Susan J., *Listening In: Radio and the American Imagination: From Amos 'n' Andy and Edward R. Murrow to Wolfman Jack and Howard Stern*, New York: Times Books, 1999.

Haas, Karl, *Inside Music: How to Understand, Listen To, and Enjoy Good Music*, New York: Doubleday, 1984.

ELIZABETH COX,
2009 REVISION BY CHRISTOPHER H. STERLING

ADVERTISING

Advertising specifically refers to paid commercial announcements aired by a radio station. Although commercials may sometimes seem distracting to listeners, radio stations from the earliest days recognized that there had to be a way for a station to pay its operating expenses, and by the late 1920s radio stations in the United States had adopted commercial advertising.

Origins

Advertising on radio began amid controversy, as many public figures and some station operators initially felt the new medium should not depend on advertiser support. Secretary of Commerce Herbert Hoover and others believed radio should not be allowed to let advertising invade listeners' homes (although newspapers and magazines had been doing just that for decades). But as there was no other practical means of supporting operating costs, advertising on the air gradually attracted greater support.

The American Telephone and Telegraph (AT&T)-operated New York City station WEAF is generally credited with selling the first radio advertisement (what the telephone company owner termed "toll broadcasting"), although other outlets may have made similar sales at about the same time. On 28 August 1922, the Queensboro Corporation spent $100 for a 15-minute commercial message on WEAF touting a new real estate venture. The same message was repeated for five days and again a month later, resulting in many apartment sales. But despite early sales to an oil company and American Express, paid advertising on the station caught on slowly, for too little was known about radio's sales potential.

The critical turning point came in 1927–28 when several trends combined to increase acceptance of radio as an advertising medium. Among them were the development of national networks (the National Broadcasting Company [NBC] published its first pamphlet touting radio advertising in early 1927);

the reduction of interference (thanks to the Federal Radio Commission [FRC]); better and less-expensive radio receivers (which led to growing audiences); the first scientific audience research on radio; the recognition by pioneering advertisers of what radio could accomplish as a sales medium; the growing interest of advertising agencies (the first book on radio advertising was published in 1927); and the general acceptance by the public of advertising as the means to pay for entertainment programming.

Radio Advertising Expands

The Depression brought about an important change in radio advertising. Commercials became more direct, intent on getting listeners to commit to a purchase and focusing on prices. Some program-length advertisements were accepted by stations hard-pressed to stay in business, as was barter advertising (exchange of station time for goods the station or its personnel could use). Advertising agencies began to develop expertise in radio, and station representative firms began to appear in the early 1930s. Radio's portion of all advertising grew from about two percent in 1928 to nearly 11 percent in 1932.

By the mid-1930s, advertising agencies were not only selling most of radio network time but also were increasingly producing the programs themselves. This control continued into the early years of television. About 60 percent of all radio advertising was placed with networks (primarily NBC-Red and the Columbia Broadcasting System [CBS]) and their owned stations, with the other 40 percent going to regional and local advertising on several hundred other stations. Daytime advertising focused on soap opera audiences, whereas evening or prime-time advertising helped to support the comedy, drama, and variety programs that attracted the largest audiences. Many advertiser names appeared in program titles to emphasize their support (and control). Most advertising revenue went to the most powerful stations in larger cities.

World War II brought great prosperity to radio as advertisers flocked to buy time when newspaper and magazine advertising was limited by paper rationing. Changes in tax laws served to encourage advertising expenditure of funds that would otherwise be taxed up to 90 percent. Such "ten-cent dollars" filled radio's coffers and led to sharp declines in sustaining (not advertiser-supported) program time. Many companies producing war goods advertised to keep their names before the public, and they often supported highbrow programming with limited (but important) audiences.

Radio's post-war years were marked by a shift away from network advertising (because of television competition) and a growth of "spot" campaigns, in which advertisers would buy time on key stations in selected markets. By 1952 local radio advertising reached half of the medium's total time sales. But far more stations were sharing the advertising pie, thus sharply increasing competition. Radio also became a more direct competitor with local newspapers. Despite these trends, overall radio advertising sales increased each year, and, perhaps ironically, helped to support the expansion of television.

FM radio was a minor player in advertising sales for its first several decades. Only in the 1960s did FM outlets begin to see success in their quest for advertisers, thanks to independent programming, stereo, and a growing audience interested in quality sound. One FM station in Los Angeles experimented with an all classified-ad format but quickly failed. By about 1980, FM became the largest radio medium in terms of listeners, and soon among advertisers as well.

Still, the overall growth in radio station numbers meant that many stations were barely surviving, and a substantial proportion actually lost money in many years. Competition among stations, and between radio and other media, became tighter. Listeners noted the gradual increase in time devoted to advertising messages, and "clutter" (multiple messages played consecutively) became an issue.

Types of Announcements

In addition to entertainment programming, radio stations generally air commercials, station promotional announcements (promos), non-revenue generating announcements intended to encourage further radio listening, and public service announcements (PSAs), which air in support of not-for-profit organizations (ranging from the American Red Cross to a local civic group). All four of these categories are generally referred to as *spots* and range up to 60 seconds in length each.

Commercials are played in blocks or sets sometimes consisting of six or more announcements at a time. Depending on spot lengths, a commercial break might consume five continuous minutes of airtime. More than $19.5 billion was spent on radio advertising in the United States in 2002; about three-fourths of that total was spent on local advertising. When the advertising is sold effectively—based on the station's listening audience and program approach—a listener may benefit by receiving worthwhile consumer information.

For the potential advertiser, a radio station is in the *ear leasing* business. Just as the radio station must build listener awareness of its programming, advertising clients need listener awareness of the goods or services they sell and, most importantly, the clients need customer traffic. The job of radio advertising is to provide the ears of listeners who will hear the ad buyer's message and then visit the store or otherwise obtain the product or service advertised.

Sales Department

A sales manager or general sales manager supervises day-to-day station sales operations and helps make revenue projections for the station. The members of the sales staff are usually called account executives (AEs), although some stations may refer to them as marketing executives or marketing consultants.

It is the job of account executives to prospect for potential clients, develop client presentations, secure advertising buys, and service the account. Servicing includes ensuring that ads run when they should, updating ad copy as needed, and, in some smaller markets, collecting payment. Radio account executives are usually paid according to their sales performance. AEs may be paid a straight commission or a percentage of the sales dollars they generate. The latter compensation plan carries a strong incentive for the salesperson to produce results, but it also means the AE has little financial security.

Another approach is to pay the account executive a "draw" against commission. The draw enables the AE to receive minimum compensation based on anticipated sales. Once this minimum is reached, additional compensation is paid through sales commissions. If the AE is paid a commission based on advertising sold—rather than advertising revenue collected from clients—and later has a client who defaults on a bill, the AE may have a "charge back" to the draw and commission. In other words, the account executive must return any income earned on ads that aired but were not paid for. For this reason, many stations pay account executives based on advertising revenue collected rather than advertising sold.

As with any electronic medium, the biggest problem stations face is inventory management. For any station, "inventory" refers to the number of commercials the station has available for sale. Advertising time is a perishable commodity. Any commercial inventory not sold is lost forever. There is no effective way for the station to store, save, or warehouse the unsold commercial inventory for use at a future time when demand is higher, nor can stations effectively place additional commercials in their broadcast schedule. Airing more spots may create a short-term revenue increase, but commercial clutter is cited by listeners as one of the biggest distractions to radio listening. A decline in audience will consequently lessen the station's effectiveness in selling future advertising time.

The radio industry publication *Duncan's American Radio* estimates that radio listening in 2000 was at its lowest level in 20 years. *The Wall Street Journal* cited reasons for decreased listening: a survey of 1,071 respondents by Edison Media Research found listener perceptions of increased ad clutter on many stations. Another study found commuters who owned a cell-phone reported less listening to the radio than a year earlier.

Benefits and Disadvantages of Radio Advertising

Radio advertising, when compared with television, cable, newspaper, or magazine advertising, offers the advertiser some unique advantages. Over the course of a typical week, nearly everyone listens at least briefly. Radio reaches more than three-fourths of all consumers each day and about 95 percent of all consumers during a typical week. That exceeds the number of newspaper readers and television viewers. The typical person spends about three hours listening to radio on an average weekday, almost always while doing something else (especially driving).

There are, of course, disadvantages to advertising on radio. It is virtually impossible to buy advertising on just one or two radio stations and still meet an advertiser's marketing needs. The multitude of stations in most markets and their specialized formats (and thus relatively narrow audiences) often mean an advertiser must purchase time on multiple stations in the same market. Radio is sometimes considered a "background" medium. Listeners often tune-out commercials or, even worse, tune to another station when commercials air. Where people listen to the radio—in cars for example—often makes it difficult for consumers to benefit from such information as telephone numbers, addresses, or other product attributes. When a station's audience is perceived as being small, the client may think the ad buy will not be effective. When the station's listening audience is large, a client may think an ad campaign involves overspending for uninterested listeners.

The first job of the sales staff is to help clients understand how effective radio is when compared with competing advertising media. The second and

more difficult job is to sell advertising time on a specific station. Proliferation of radio stations and continued fragmentation of audiences has made it vital for stations to market a station brand to both listeners and advertisers. Advertisers are no longer buying based solely on a station's audience. They are aware of the listener demographic profile and the station's on-air presence, which includes announcers, music, and promotional events. Listener demographics refers to listener age range, gender, ethnicity, socioeconomic background, consumer spending patterns, and a host of other qualitative variables.

Any advertiser must be concerned with both the formal and the hidden costs of purchasing radio time. The most obvious expense is the stated cost of the time, expressed either as actual dollars charged or in terms of cost per thousand listeners. Hidden cost refers to the quality or nature of the audience an advertiser is buying. How closely does this audience match the advertiser's customer profile? Significant deviation from those consumers whom the advertiser needs to reach probably indicates an inefficient advertising purchase.

Radio station owners and the Radio Advertising Bureau, an industry trade group, work to maintain radio's position as a valuable ad source. Most radio station managers acknowledge that their biggest competitors are not other radio stations in the market playing the same music and attempting to attract the same listener group. The biggest competitors for radio station time sales are usually local newspapers and, to a lesser degree, television stations, billboards, or direct mail. By the turn of the century, radio advertising was accounting for about eight percent of all advertising expenditure—an increase from the medium's low point from the 1950s into the 1980s, but far below radio's network heyday of the mid-1940s.

Radio Advertising Clients

Radio stations generally sell advertising to three distinct groups of clients: local, regional (or "national spot"), and national. The percentage of clients in each category varies with market size and the station's ratings. Small market stations air primarily local ads. Successful stations in large markets command more regional and national advertising. Nearly 80 percent of all dollars spent purchasing radio time are for local advertising.

National advertisers are often involved in local ad sales through cooperative advertising programs. These allow local retailers to share the cost of radio time with a national firm. The national company provides an advertising allowance to the local retailer, usually determined by the dollar value of the inventory purchased from the national company. This advertising allowance can be used to buy ads to promote both the national brand and the local retailer. National manufacturers may also produce radio commercials that only need the local retailer's name added as a "local tag" at the end of the ad.

Advertising Effectiveness

The effectiveness of radio advertising is gauged by measuring the reach and frequency of ad exposure. Reach refers to the number of different people who are exposed to the ad, whereas frequency refers to the number of times different people hear the ad. Even though virtually all of the population will listen to the radio at some point during the week, it will take multiple ads to ensure that all listener segments hear an ad. Also, radio ads probably won't produce the degree of effectiveness the advertiser wants if consumers are exposed to the ad once only.

The nature of radio use suggests that consumers are often engaged in other activities while they listen to radio. To create an impression in the consumer's mind, repeated exposure to the message (frequency) is typically needed. To increase the likelihood that ads will cause the consumer to take action, frequent exposure to the message is desired. The advertiser might schedule multiple days of advertising with one or more ads per hour during a selected time period to increase frequency.

Radio advertising sales depend on quantitatively and qualitatively identifying the listeners to a particular station. Quantity is measured by radio ratings.

Research helps a radio station further quantify the listening audience—advertisers want to know how many people are listening and just who the listeners are, with respect to age, income, or gender. By collecting such listener demographic information, radio advertising effectiveness can be evaluated for specific audience segments, such as women 25 to 49 years of age.

Two of the most common calculations for comparing advertising effectiveness are "Gross Impressions" and "Cost Per Thousand" comparisons. Gross Impressions (GIs) measure the total number of people reached with a given commercial message. GIs are calculated by multiplying the AQH (average quarter hour) persons estimate for the particular daypart by the number of spots to be run in the daypart. The number of listeners or AQH

persons is the number of persons listening to the station in a 15-minute period.

Cost Per Thousand provides a way to compare the cost of reaching the targeted audience either on a single station or among multiple stations. Cost per Thousand determines the cost of reaching a thousand station listeners (sometimes referred to as "Listeners Per Dollar" in some small markets, the calculation could be cost per hundred). The simplest way to calculate Cost per Thousand is to divide the cost of the ad by the number of listeners (in thousands) who are expected to hear the ad.

It is important also to consider listener demographics. A listener profile that better matches a product or service may justify paying a higher Cost per Thousand. Another method for calculating Cost per Thousand is to divide the total cost of the ad schedule by the total number of Gross Impressions. "Reverse Cost Per Thousand" enables an account executive to determine the maximum rate per spot that a competing station can charge to remain as cost-effective as his or her own station.

It is also helpful for account executives and advertisers to know a station's "exclusive cume listeners." Rather than count listeners multiple times during the day, this calculation allows the advertiser to see how many different people listen to the station during a day. A Contemporary Hits Radio format will usually have greater listener turnover and a higher cume because there are usually several stations in a market with this format or a complementary format, and listeners are prone to change stations frequently. On the other hand, the only station in a market will have a smaller exclusive audience or cume.

Optimum Effective Scheduling is a radio ad scheduling strategy that is based on audience turnover. Optimum Effective Scheduling proposes to improve the effectiveness of a client's ad schedule by calculating the number of spots a client should run. Optimum Effective Scheduling was developed by Steve Marx and Pierre Bouvard to balance the desire for ad frequency and reach while producing an effective commercial schedule. Marx and Bouvard use station turnover or T/O (cume audience divided by AQH) times a constant they created, 3.29, to determine the number of spots an advertiser should schedule each week (see Marx and Bouvard, 1993).

From the standpoint of generating ad revenue for the radio station, stations with low turnover are at a disadvantage when using Optimum Effective Scheduling. Their audience listens longer and thus fewer spots are needed to produce an effective schedule of reach and frequency. Assuming ad rates

ADVERTISING

per thousand listeners are reasonably comparable, these stations must attract more clients to generate the same amount of ad revenue as the station with high listener turnover.

Advertising Rates

Radio station advertising rates were once typically printed out on a rate card. Most rate cards were valid for six months to a year. Cards listed the charges for either programs or spot advertisements at different times of the day (dayparts). The card might also specify a price discount as the client purchased more ads per day or per week. This rate card is sometimes referred to as a quantity card or quantity-discount rate card. The quantity card might be an effective way to reward loyal advertising clients but is a poor technique for managing valuable advertising inventory. The radio station, with a limited inventory of commercial time, is discounting the price of its product. The discount applies, no matter what the available advertising situation is like.

Increasingly, replacing formal rate cards is the grid rate card system. Using an inventory tracking software package, the grid allows a radio station to track inventory available for sale. This might mean keeping track of the number of commercial minutes sold or the total number of commercial units (spots) available for sale. The inventory management system also enables the radio station to increase or decrease its ad rate in response to customer demand. When a radio station has sold nearly all the advertising it can effectively schedule, it should be able to charge more for remaining commercial units. A grid rate card enables the station to adjust advertising rates according to the amount of inventory remaining.

Once the station's sales department has established a record with clients of pricing inventory according to demand, account executives may be more effective in pre-selling advertising time, which should decrease the likelihood of lost ad inventory. When retailers place advertising orders earlier, the station can project revenue more effectively. The longer a client waits to buy commercials, the more likely the available supply of ad time will decrease and the price of the remaining time will increase.

Radio advertising continues to be an important business for station owners. Ownership consolidation has increased sales pressures for account executives, but it has also lessened direct competition by decreasing the number of station owners. As radio's fortunes dipped with the general economy in 2007?9, advertising sales came under pressure, as more and more advertisers shifted dollars to the internet, which showed a 17.3 percent increase in revenues, pulling within one percentage point of radio's share of the $150 billion spent in 2007. In an attempt to draw back listeners, Clear Channel, then still the largest single owner of stations in the country, announced plans to limit the amount of advertising clutter per hour on its stations as part of a package of steps taken to revive radio's sound.

On a brighter note, technology offered new opportunities for radio. In test markets Arbitron's Portable People Meters (PPMs) showed up to twice as many listeners for many stations (and drop for others) than previously reported via listener diaries, which translated to larger audience numbers, hence higher advertising rates. An illustration of radio's effort to demonstrate how radio and the internet complement each other, allowing radio to participate in the internet advertising bonanza, was the launching of services such as MyQuu, which combines social networking and interactivity with broadcast radio, allowing listeners to use a cellphone or other device to easily purchase, listen, share and discuss favorite music and bands.

See also: Advertising Agencies; Arbitron; Commercial Load; Demographics; Market; Promotion on Radio; Radio Advertising Bureau; Station Rep Firms; WEAF

Further Reading

Albarran, Alan B., and Gregory G. Pitts, *The Radio Broadcasting Industry*, Boston: Allyn and Bacon, 2000.
Arbitron Ratings Company, *Arbitron Radio Market Reference Guide: A Guide to Understanding and Using Radio Audience Estimates*, New York: Arbitron, 1987; 4th edition, 1996.
Barnouw, Erik, *The Sponsor: Notes on a Modern Potentate*, New York: Oxford University Press, 1978.
Cox, Jim, *Sold on Radio: Advertising in the Golden Age of Radio*, Jefferson, North Carolina: McFarland, 2008.
Dygert, Warren B., *Radio as an Advertising Medium*, New York: McGraw Hill, 1939.
Felix, Edgar H., *Using Radio in Sales Promotion*, New York: McGraw Hill, 1927.
Hettinger, Herman S., *A Decade of Radio Advertising*, Chicago: University of Chicago Press, 1933; reprint, New York: Arno Press, 1971.
Marx, Steve, and Pierre Bouvard, *Radio Advertising's Missing Ingredient: The Optimum Effective Scheduling System*, Washington, D.C.: National Association of Broadcasters, 1991; 2nd edition, 1993.
Midgley, Ned, *The Advertising and Business Side of Radio*, New York: Prentice-Hall, 1948.
Radio Advertising Bureau, www.rab.com.
Seehafer, E.R, and J.W. Laemmar, *Successful Radio and Television Advertising*, New York: McGraw Hill, 1951; 2nd edition, as *Successful Television and Radio Advertising*, 1959.
Shane, Ed, *Selling Electronic Media*, Oxford and Boston: Focal Press, 1999.

Streeter, Thomas, *Selling the Air: A Critique of the Policy of Commercial Broadcasting in the United States*, Chicago: University of Chicago Press, 1996.

Warner, Charlie, and Joseph Buchman, *Broadcast and Cable Selling*, Belmont, California: Wadsworth, 1986; 3rd edition, 1993.

Wolfe, Charles Hull, *Modern Radio Advertising*, New York: Funk and Wagnalls, 1949.

GREGORY G. PITTS AND CHRISTOPHER H. STERLING,
2009 REVISIONS BY GAIL LOVE

ADVERTISING AGENCIES

When radio broadcasting established itself in the United States and United Kingdom in the 1920s, advertising agencies were full-service organizations—planning complete advertising campaigns, producing advertising messages, and placing these messages in various media. In the United States, advertising agencies were initially reluctant to recommend radio advertising to their clients; in time, however, the agencies became supporters of radio advertising and, until the arrival of television, helped build the radio networks. In the United Kingdom, where until 1972 noncommercial radio broadcasting by the British Broadcasting Corporation (BBC) was the rule, advertising agencies lobbied for commercial radio and worked with foreign and pirate radio stations on behalf of clients; however, once commercial radio arrived, UK agencies were slow to embrace it.

Resisting Radio Advertising

The rise of radio advertising in the United States was tentative and slow. Advertising first appeared in 1922 on station WEAF in the form of sponsored time. Other stations gradually accepted sponsored programs, but many broadcasters viewed advertising agencies as competitors and were hesitant to sell them time or allow sponsorships. Anti-advertising rhetoric from listeners, critics, legislators, and regulators fueled opposition as well.

Surprisingly, advertisers and agencies distrusted the notion of radio advertising. Agencies doubted that radio advertisements would work, a sentiment shared by many advertisers. The advertising industry also believed listeners might resent radio sponsorship and, consequently, reject other forms of advertising by the same advertisers. This was of particular concern to print advertisers and their agencies.

For several years agencies warned their clients against using radio advertising. Advertisers had to produce programs themselves with assistance from station personnel. For example, in 1925 Clicquot, a soda manufacturer, worked directly with WEAF to

create the *Clicquot Club Eskimos* music program because its agency did not believe in radio. There were, however, exceptions.

William H. Rankin of the Rankin advertising agency decided to test radio advertising before recommending it to clients. He bought time on WEAF for a talk about advertising but received only a small number of letters and phone calls in response. One, from a prospective client, Mineralava, led to a contract and more radio advertising. Rankin began recommending radio and another client, the Goodrich Company, sponsored a radio series.

Another early exception was the N.W. Ayer agency, which supervised *The Eveready Hour* in 1923. Ayer ensured that the show was professional and identified the sponsor in the name. The favorable attention it received attracted other sponsors to radio, with shows such as the *Bakelite Hour, The Victor Hour,* and *The Ray-O-Vac Twins*. These shows became models for later network programs.

Although opposition to radio advertising persisted into the mid-1920s, most advertising practitioners were beginning to consider its use. To win them over, the newly formed National Broadcasting Company (NBC) and Columbia Broadcasting System (CBS) radio networks hired promoters to persuade those still skeptical about the effectiveness of radio advertising.

In 1928 NBC initiated a promotional campaign to educate and encourage adoption of radio advertising. The networks targeted leading advertisers and agencies with brochures highlighting radio success stories and emphasizing radio's ability to build brand awareness and stimulate dealer goodwill. The networks also offered financial incentives by paying agencies commissions even if they were not directly involved in a client-sponsored show.

NBC loaned its employees to leading agencies to help develop radio departments. N.W. Ayer started the first fullscale radio department in 1928 and others soon followed, employing personnel who migrated from radio. The promoters urged the networks to allow agencies to sell broadcast time and produce programs. In turn, agencies recognized how lucrative program development and production could be.

Accepting Radio Advertising

The promoters' efforts were successful. By the early 1930s agencies were selling time and handling nearly all sponsored network program development and production. Agencies had gained control of prime-time radio listening and achieved great prosperity, and their radio departments became centers of power.

Sponsored radio shows of the 1920s employed "indirect advertising," simple mentions of the program's underwriter with no product description or sales pitch. The networks supported this practice with policies against direct advertising. George Washington Hill, president of the American Tobacco Company, and Albert Lasker, head of the Lord and Thomas agency, pressured the networks to allow explicit advertising messages.

Although Lasker and Hill largely conformed to the indirect advertising requirements when they launched the *Lucky Strike Dance Orchestra in 1928*, Hill, who believed strongly in intrusive radio advertising with explicit product claims, aggressively pursued this goal by forcing the issue with network executives and supporting Lucky Strike with extravagant budgets. Lord and Thomas controlled a large share of NBC's business, so Lasker had leverage as well. By 1931 women were being sold Lucky Strikes with mildness claims by opera and film stars and "slimming" messages suggesting that listeners smoke a Lucky Strike instead of eating something sweet.

The 1930s saw advertising agencies crafting selling environments for their clients in the form of elaborate comedy, variety, and dramatic series. Vaudeville came to radio as agencies began to use star talent. Young and Rubicam created *The Jack Benny Program* for General Foods' Jell-O. Lord and Thomas produced Bob Hope. J. Walter Thompson produced the *Kraft Music Hall* with Bing Crosby and *The Chase and Sanborn Hour* with Edgar Bergen and Charlie McCarthy.

After commercializing prime-time radio, the networks, with agency help, developed a daytime audience of women listeners. The networks developed 15-minute sponsored talks with recurring characters and continuing stories. Soap operas—melodramatic serials typically sponsored by manufacturers of household detergents and cleaners—were born. Most were produced by advertising agencies.

One agency, Blackett, Sample and Hummert, built a reputation for soap opera programming. Glen Sample adapted a 1920s newspaper serial into a radio show, *Betty and Bob,* sponsored by Gold Medal Flour. Sample also developed the long-running *Ma Perkins* for Procter and Gamble's Oxydol. In 1931 Frank and Anne Hummert created a daily NBC serial, *Just Plain Bill,* for Kolynos toothpaste. The Hummerts became highly prolific soap opera creators, developing nearly half the network soap operas introduced between 1932 and 1937. Soap operas were so successful that daytime radio advertising revenues doubled between 1935 and 1939.

Agencies and radio networks were determined to protect their financial success during the Depression. Indeed, their program decisions uniformly ignored economic and social problems. With the exception of *The March of Time,* produced for *Time* magazine by Batten, Barton, Durstine and Osborn, news was all but missing from sponsored programs. Radio's skilled entertainers kept Americans' minds off their despair.

The radio and advertising industries experienced continued prosperity during World War II. Agencies encouraged clients to maintain brand awareness, even if they had no products to sell, and radio benefited from such prestigious sponsorships as *General Motors' NBC Symphony Orchestra* as well as benefiting from paper shortages that limited newspaper ads. Both industries assisted the Office of War Information with insertions of war effort announcements, earning them favorable government treatment when their wartime revenues came under close scrutiny.

U.S. Postwar Changes

Envious of the power held by advertising agencies, the radio networks decided to regain control of programming. The agencies lost ground to independent producers, but the real threat to radio came from the growing medium of network television. Advertisers and their agencies shifted the system of star-studded, sponsored programs to television. Young and Rubicam found that its programs moved so easily to television that from 1949 to 1950 half of the top 10 TV shows were its productions.

Within a decade, network radio serials and soap operas had all but disappeared, taking with them substantial ad revenue. Whereas in 1931 network advertising constituted 51 percent of total radio advertising revenues, by 1960 that had fallen to just 7 percent. Radio survived by serving local listeners with format programming and attracting local advertising.

U.S. agencies became producers of commercials and buyers of spot radio time. Despite periods of renewed interest in radio and a resurgence of radio networks, for national advertisers and their agencies radio was relegated to the role of support medium.

See also: Advertising; Radio Advertising Bureau; WEAF

Further Reading

Arnold, Frank Atkinson, *Broadcast Advertising: The Fourth Dimension*, New York: Wiley, and London: Chapman and Hall, 1931.

Barnouw, Erik, *The Sponsor: Notes on a Modern Potentate*, New York: Oxford University Press, 1978.

Burt, Frank A., *American Advertising Agencies: An Inquiry into Their Origin, Growth, Functions, and Future*, New York: Harper, 1940.

Hower, Ralph M., *History of an Advertising Agency: N.W. Ayer and Son at Work, 1869–1939*, Cambridge, Massachusetts: Harvard University Press, 1939; revised edition, with subtitle dates *1869–1949*, 1949.

McDonough, John, "Radio: A 75-Year Roller-Coaster Ride," *Advertising Age* (4 September 1995).

O'Malley, Tom, *Closedown? The BBC and Government Broadcasting Policy, 1979–92*, London and Boulder, Colorado: Pluto Press, 1994.

Scannell, Paddy, and David Cardiff, *Social History of British Broadcasting, 1922–1939*, Oxford and Cambridge, Massachusetts: Blackwell, 1991.

Seymour-Ure, Colin, *The British Press and Broadcasting since 1945*, Oxford and Cambridge, Massachusetts: Blackwell, 1991; 2nd edition, 1996.

Smulyan, Susan, *Selling Radio: The Commercialization of American Broadcasting, 1920–1934*, Washington, D.C.: Smithsonian Institution Press, 1994.

Wilson, H. Hubert, *Pressure Group: The Campaign for Commercial Television*, London: Secker and Warburg, 1961; with subtitle *The Campaign for Commercial Television in England*, New Brunswick, New Jersey: Rutgers University Press, 1961.

RANDY JACOBS

AFFIRMATIVE ACTION
Diversity in Employment, Programs, and Ownership

Affirmative action mandates equal treatment for all people regardless of gender, age, religion, sexual orientation, etc. The need for programs to assure this equal treatment depends on the amount and nature of discrimination; they are solutions to identified problems of discrimination, not processes unto themselves (Hooks, 1987). Applied to radio broadcasting, affirmative action programs have been related to discrimination in: (1) employment, (2) program content, and (3) station ownership. The rationale for affirmative action in radio was based on the desire of the Federal Communications Commission (FCC) to achieve diversity of information, defined as having many voices express opinions on many issues. The Supreme Court affirmed this goal in *Red Lion v. FCC* (Honig, 1984).

Employment

Federal concern about employment diversity was initiated in the 1968 *Report of the National Advisory Commission on Civil Disorders*. The FCC, based on the public interest standard, responded with a statement about equal employment opportunity (47

CFR 73.2080, section b). The result was an examination of license renewals to determine whether the racial composition of a station's staff was similar to the demographic makeup of the community in which the station was licensed (zone of reasonableness). Short-term renewals, fines, and the threat of possible revocations could result from noncompliance. The FCC responded with a model Equal Employment Opportunity (EEO) program in 1975 to eliminate race and gender discrimination. The Supreme Court affirmed the legality of such oversight by independent regulatory agencies in *NAACP v. Federal Power Commission* (1976). The FCC was committed to programming fairness and accurate representation of minority group tastes and viewpoints (FCC, 1978).

Congress, in the Cable Television Consumer Protection and Competition Act of 1992, required the FCC to monitor employment statistics for women and minorities in the cable and broadcast industries. The FCC's first report found that from 1986 to 1993 the number of women in the national workforce increased by 1.1 percent, in the broadcast industry 2.8 percent, and 3.6 percent in upper-level positions. The number of minorities increased 2.1 percent in the national workforce, 2.2 percent in the broadcast industry, and 2.4 percent in upper-level positions (FCC, 1994).

The FCC's EEO policies were overturned in *Lutheran Church v. FCC* (1998). Essentially, the court found that increasing staff diversity did not necessarily lead to diversity of viewpoints in the marketplace because only a small number of station employees made programming decisions. The policy was also overbroad, much as the Supreme Court found in *Adarand v. Pena* (1995). The court's response to the FCC's request for a rehearing indicated that its decision did not preclude any policies that encouraged "broad outreach" to a diverse applicant pool. The FCC has responded with a Notice of Proposed Rule Making (NPRM) suggesting that broadcasters, cable operators, and other multi-channel video programming distributors could send job announcements to recruitment organizations or to participate in job fairs, internships, etc. They could also devise their own recruitment process. Annual hiring reports would still be filed with the FCC. These rules were adopted two years later (FCC, 2000).

A portion of these rules were overturned in *DC/MD/DE Broadcasters Association v. FCC* (2001). The commission responded with another NPRM suggesting that all media outlets "widely disseminate information about job openings to all segments of the community to ensure that all qualified applicants have sufficient opportunity to compete for jobs in the broadcast industry" (FCC, 2001). These rules were adopted in November 2002. What was once a requirement that media owners represent the diversity of their audiences with equal numbers of minorities on their staffs is now a program that requires them to widely distribute job opening information, attend job fairs, and offer scholarships. Statements by the commissioners decried their inability to be more forceful in this area, but stated that limitations by the courts have greatly diminished the force of regulation. Industry spokespersons were hesitant to support the new rules, saying that EEO has been over-regulated in the past (Greenberg, 2002).

Generally speaking, little was accomplished on equal employment opportunity in radio during the first decade of the 2000s. The FCC did step up its auditing of broadcaster compliance with existing EEO rules by requiring radio stations with more than 11 full-time employees (thus excluding thousands of stations which employ fewer people) to file a "Broadcast Mid-Term Report" (FCC Form 397) four years after their most recent license renewal. The first stations required to file, in June 2007, were those in the DC–Maryland–Virginia–West Virginia radio renewal group.

Program Content

The public interest resulted in two rules requiring diversity in program content: ascertainment and the fairness doctrine. Ascertainment required stations to determine issues of public importance by surveying listeners and community leaders. The fairness doctrine required that these issues be addressed fairly. These rules, plus a decision by the Supreme Court that gave audiences the right to testify before the FCC, *United Church of Christ v. FCC* (1966), resulted in increased minority participation in the 1970s until the FCC began deregulating radio in 1981 (FCC, 1981). Honig and Williams argued that deregulation was the result of a conservative FCC wishing to reduce the workload for radio stations coupled with the loss of influential groups pressuring the FCC about diversity.

Deregulation was necessary because the number of radio stations had increased from 583 in 1941 to 9,000 by the late 1980s, forcing stations to develop specialized formats to attract audiences; radio could no longer provide general services to all of its audiences. The result was the elimination of policy guidelines concerning non-entertainment programming, the ascertainment process, commercial time guidelines, and rigidly formatted program logs

(FCC, 1981). The fairness doctrine was abolished in 1987. The concern for radio format changes ended in 1976 in response to the court decision in cases such as *Citizens Committee to Save WEFM v. FCC* (FCC, 1976). Although the FCC was concerned with empowering broadcasters to select entertainment formats that offered the greatest commercial viability in their markets, the results of these policy decisions might have had an impact on programming oriented toward minority audiences.

The end of program content regulation for purposes of increasing diversity and the move away from numerical goals for employment after 1976 spelled the end of employment and program affirmative action policies. The FCC argued that none of these policies actually increased the diversity of information and turned to station ownership diversity as a solution.

Station Ownership

Diversity of station ownership was a goal of the FCC that assumed that who owned radio outlets would influence, if not determine, program diversity. The assumption was that increasing minority (women and ethnic minorities) owners would increase programming for such underserved audiences and thus serve the public interest. Further encouraging ownership diversity was a two-day meeting resulting from pressure from the National Black Media Coalition and the National Association of Black-Owned Broadcasters in 1977. The resulting FCC policy statement found that despite the fact that minorities comprised approximately 20 percent of the population, they controlled less than one percent of the over 8,500 radio stations. The FCC proposed two solutions to the lack of ownership diversity. First, tax certificates were offered to broadcasters who sold their stations to ownership teams that had a "significant minority interest." Tax certificates allowed sellers to defer capital gains taxes. Second, "distress sales" were authorized for licensees who were scheduled for revocation hearings before the FCC. The rationale was that broadcasters who would likely lose their licenses in such hearings could sell their properties at a reduced cost to minority ownership teams, producing at least some profit from the sale of the station. The market would benefit by increasing station ownership diversity. The government would also save money because costly hearings would be avoided (FCC, 1978). The result of these two solutions was the sale of 82 radio stations to minority owners between 1978 and 1982. Despite this increase, still only 2 percent of broadcast stations were minority owned (Honig, 1984). Former FCC Chair Kennard decried the lack of stations owned by minorities because only 2.5 percent of all broadcast stations had minority owners in 1997 (McConnell, 1998).

The historical basis for ownership diversity can be found in the *Policy Statement on Comparative Broadcast Hearings* (FCC, 1965). Two criteria stipulated by the FCC as integral to deciding between competing applicants for station licenses were diversification of ownership and integration of ownership/management, defined as station owners living and being active in the communities for which the license was granted. Application of these factors to diversity of station ownership was affirmed in *Citizens Communications Center v. FCC* (1974). Direct application to minority owners of broadcast stations was made in *TV 9 Inc. v. FCC* (1973).

The FCC was in the process of re-examining its ownership diversity procedures in the late 1980s. As more Republican members of Congress took office, along with conservative Democrats appointed during the Reagan administration, the FCC began to question its proper role in this area. Nevertheless, Congress made clear in budget resolutions that the FCC was not to make any changes.

The Supreme Court affirmed both the enhancement credits (tax certificates) and distress sales as methods for increasing minority ownership. The court's decision was twofold. First, increasing broadcast diversity was an important government goal. Second, FCC policies of diversifying ownership were determined to be reasonable means of meeting these goals. A substantial amount of data supporting this conclusion was appended to the decision (*Metro v. FCC*).

Similar reasoning was used to support incentives for women to own broadcast stations, but data analyzed by the Court of Appeals failed to meet the second part of the Supreme Court's decision in Metro: no link could be established between increasing female ownership of broadcast stations and the consequent increase in programming for women. Thus, the ownership preference was held to be unconstitutional (*Lamprecht v. FCC*).

Americans for Radio Diversity reported that minority ownership was up to 3.1 percent before the enactment of the Telecommunications Act of 1996. The removal of many station ownership caps has led to massive radio consolidations, however, and minority ownership has declined to 2.8 percent (2000). The decline was due in part to sharply higher station prices, which was brought about by industry consolidation.

Through the first decade of the 21st century, station prices continued to limit ownership opportunities for people of color and women. A 2007 study of FCC data found that women owned only 6 percent of full-power commercial radio outlets while racial or ethnic minorities controlled about 7.7 percent—despite their incidence in the population of 51 and 33 percent, respectively (Turner).

The National Association of Broadcasters has been active for a number of years in raising funds to encourage station purchases by ethnic minorities and women, though rising station prices have limited the success of that initiative. For most of the first decade of the 21st century, the FCC did not even track minority ownership, nor did the Bush Administration's National Telecommunications and Information Administration, which had done so in the 1990s. The inauguration of President Barack Obama in January 2009, however, suggested there might be policy changes forthcoming for both agencies.

See also: African-Americans in Radio; Black-Oriented Radio; Deregulation of Radio; Gay and Lesbian Radio; Hispanic Radio; Native American Radio; Ownership, Mergers, and Acquisitions; *Red Lion* Case; Stereotypes on Radio

Further Reading

Adarand Constructors, Inc. v. Pena, 515 US 20 (1995).
Citizens Committee to Save WEFM v. Federal Communications Commission, 506 F2d 246 (1974).
Citizens Communications Center v. Federal Communications Commission, 447 F2d 1201 (1971).
Federal Communications Commission, *Policy Statement on Comparative Broadcast Hearings*, 1 FCC 2d 393 (1965).
Federal Communications Commission, *Changes in Entertainment Formats of Broadcast Stations*, 60 FCC 2d 858 (1976).
Federal Communications Commission, *Statement of Policy on Minority Ownership of Broadcasting Facilities*, 68 FCC 2d 979 (1978).
Federal Communications Commission, *In the Matter of Deregulation of Radio*, 84 FCC 2d 968 (1981).
Federal Communications Commission, *In the Matter of Implementation of Commission's Equal Employment Opportunity Rules*, MM Docket 94–34 (1994).
Federal Communications Commission, *FCC Adopts New Equal Employment Opportunity Rules*, MM Dockets 98–204, 96–16, 20 (January 2000).
Federal Communications Commission, *In the Matter 0/1998 Biennial Regulatory Review*, MM Docket No. 98–35 (2000).
Federal Communications Commission, *FCC Proposes New Equal Employment Opportunity (EEO) Rules for Broadcasters and Cable*, MM Docket 98–204 (2001).
Greenberg, B., "FCC's New EEO Rules Leave Most Enforcement to EEOC, Courts," *Communications Daily* (8 November 2002).

Holder, Pamela J., "A Square Peg Trying to Fit into a Round Hole: The Federal Communication Commission's Equal Employment Opportunity Regulations in *Lutheran Church Missouri-Synod v. Federal Communications Commission*," *Akron Law Journal* 32 (1999).

Honig, David, "The FCC and Its Fluctuating Commitment to Minority Ownership of Broadcast Facilities," *Howard Law Journal* 27 (1984).

Hooks, Benjamin, "Affirmative Action: A Needed Remedy," *Georgia Law Review* 12 (1987).

Lutheran Church-Missouri Synod v. Federal Communications Commission, 141 F3d 344 (1998).

Metro Broadcasting v. Federal Communications Commission, 497 US 547 (1990).

Mishkin, Paul, "Symposium: Race-Based Remedies: The Making of a Turning Point in Metro and Adarand," *California Law Review* 84 (1996).

National Association of Colored People v. Federal Power Commission, 425 US 662 (1976).

Powell, M.K., *Separate Statement of Michael K. Powell: Review of the Commission's Broadcast and Cable Equal Employment Opportunity Rules and Policies and Termination of EEO Streamlining Proceeding*, MM Docket Nos. 98–204 and 96–16 (1998).

Rathbun, E.A., "Count 'em: 830," *Broadcasting and Cable* (11 October 1999).

Red Lion v. Federal Communications Commission, 395 US 367 (1969).

Schlosser, J., "Wanted: VP of Diversity," *Broadcasting and Cable* (31 January 2000).

Turner, S. Derek, *Off the Dial: Female and Minority Radio Station Ownership in the United States: How FCC Policy and Media Consolidation Diminished Diversity on the Public Airwaves.* Washington, D.C.: Free Press, 2007.

TV 9 Inc. v. Federal Communications Commission, 495 F2d 929 (1973).

United Church of Christ v. Federal Communications Commission, 359 F2d 996 (1966).

Williams, Wenmouth, Jr., "Impact of Commissioner Background on FCC Decisions, 1975–1990," in *Media and Public Policy*, edited by Robert J. Spitzer, Westport, Connecticut, and London: Praeger, 1993.

www.stopbigmedia.com/files/off_the_dial.pdf.

WENMOUTH WILLIAMS, JR.
2009 REVISIONS BY CHRISTOPHER H. STERLING

AFRICAN-AMERICANS IN RADIO

African-Americans have played an important part in American radio broadcasting from the beginnings of the medium. From early experimenters to pioneer radio performers, blacks contributed to the cultural, economic, and technical development of radio broadcasting. Though shackled by discrimination, blacks enthusiastically used their talents on radio during World War II to help America display a united domestic front. The half-century since has seen African-Americans help to change the face of American culture through radio and other media.

Origins

One of the most notable of the pioneering electricity experts was Lewis H. Latimer (1848–1928), son of an enslaved African escapee, who prepared Alexander Graham Bell's telephone patent drawings that afterwards assisted the Boston speech and hearing therapist to actually invent his device. Telephone parts were later used by others to demonstrate the wireless transmission of human speech. Talladega College, a black institution known for its solid science curriculum, provided the educational foundation that inspired Lee de Forest to become an inventor who contributed much to perfecting modern radio broadcasting.

Before World War I, some African-Americans enrolled in those YMCA radio classes that were then available to them in a number of cities, and they gained even greater access to radio technology during the war as part of the war effort. Howard University in Washington, D.C., for example, offered electrical and radio technology classes under contract with the U.S. military.

A number of African-Americans conducted radio experiments after the war by establishing amateur radio-training organizations. Members could learn how to build and repair radio transmitters and receiver sets, how to send Morse code, and how to obtain an amateur operator's license. Miles Hardy established his Pioneer Radio Society in 1921 in New York City. A year later Roland Carrington founded the Banneker Radio Club in Baltimore. One of the most active areas for black ham operators was the midwest. Operators in Ohio, Michigan, Indiana, and Kentucky can be traced to Everett Renfroe who passed his ham operator's examination in Chicago in the early 1920s. (The operators formally initiated an organization, OMIK, in the early 1950s to protect members against racism when they traveled throughout the nation.)

Early Broadcasting

Many African-American musicians took advantage of opportunities to appear on early radio broadcasts. There is evidence that the "father of the blues," W.C. Handy, performed on the Memphis ham radio station of a white amateur, Victor Laughter, as early as 1914. The "Fisk Jubilee Singers" of Fisk University and the "Hampton Singers" of Hampton College are known to have performed live on radio in the early 1920s to raise funds for their financially strapped schools. Morehouse College was repeatedly featured on radio in Atlanta.

The common bond among African-American performers was a desire to display their abilities in a manner that proved black people were equal to others in society.

As American radio developed in the 1920s, the contribution of African-American musicians also increased across the country. Fletcher Henderson's music was broadcast from New Orleans in 1921. The Plantation Club in Los Angeles broadcast Kid Ory's Sunshine Orchestra in 1922. Further up the West Coast, vaudevillian George Dewey Washington made an appearance on Seattle's KFC. Clarence Jones and His Wonder Orchestra were guests on KYW in Chicago. The Symphonium Serenaders entertained KDKA listeners from Pittsburgh. On New York's WJZ, the Melrose Quartet was featured regularly, and Clarence Williams accompanied a variety of black artists for the station. Eubie Blake and Noble Sissle showcased their cast from "Shuffle Along" on Boston's WNAC during the *Boston Radio Exposition* of 1922; a year later, they were on the air at KYW in Chicago. "Shuffle Along" later became so popular on Broadway that Sissle and Noble were able to book cast appearances on New York's WJZ, WEAF, and WHN. For its opening ceremonies, WBBM in Chicago included Jimmie Wade's Moulin Rouge Orchestra. WSBC in Chicago featured remote broadcasts by Frankie "Half Pint" Jaxon, and Hughie Swift's band was heard nightly in Chicago on the same station.

Duke Ellington first performed on radio over New York's WDT and then WHN in 1923. Bessie Smith, "Empress of the Blues," was heard performing live throughout the southwest in 1923 from Memphis station WMC. In Nashville, Deford Bailey, the legendary harmonica player, was featured on WSM. He appeared regularly on radio from 1926 to 1941 and helped establish the great musical tradition of the *Grand Ole Opry.*

New York City was a beehive of African-American radio experimentation during this period. Fletcher Henderson's band, performing at the Roseland, was broadcast remotely on a regular basis. Shows from the Plantation Club in New York, another jazz center for black bands, were broadcast five nights a week. Club Alabam contracted with several different stations to remotely broadcast 47 of its shows. Remote broadcasts from the Savoy Ballroom increased to eight per week. WHN carried a program featuring the great Florence Mills in celebration of her joining the Greenwich Village Follies. A blues marathon show was programmed on WDT. Other New York stations brought in such top entertainers as Antoinette Gaines, LeRoy Smith, Sam Wooding, Revella Hughes, and Eva "The

Dixie Nightingale" Taylor. From St. George's Episcopal Church, vocalist Harry T. Burleigh was heard on WJZ and proclaimed "the leading creative genius of the Negro race."

Local Radio in the 1930s

What is known of African-Americans in and on local radio is still evolving. The paucity of information may be due to the fact that much historical attention has focused on network radio. Some researchers have found, however, that a few Northern stations had begun to observe what was then called "Negro history week," inviting guest speakers to discuss black achievements. Certain important black newsmakers occasionally spoke on a public affairs show, as labor leader A. Phillip Randolph did in 1931. By the mid-1930s, local stations in Baltimore and Philadelphia had at least one weekly program aimed at a black audience. The Museum of the City of San Francisco has discovered that Henry Starr, an African-American, was the leading pianist on KFRC's *Edna Fischer Show,* a variety program in that city during the late 1920s and early 1930s.

The Depression may have created opportunities for African-Americans in many markets during the early 1930s: African-American music was often cheaper than white music for local stations to broadcast because the licensing agency ASCAP had signed few contracts with African-American publishers and writers. A station could thus play recordings by African-Americans and not incur ASCAP fees. Although as early as 1930 there were efforts by black businessmen to purchase a radio station, such efforts would not succeed until 1949.

Strong and continuous local programs by African-Americans began with those of Jack L. Cooper in Chicago during the 1930s. Many scholars credit Cooper as being the patriarch of black radio. His newsboy experience in Cincinnati and later his professional song and dance work on stage may have helped turn his career toward communication: he became an entertainment writer for the *Chicago Defender.* While on assignment in Washington in 1925, Cooper began writing, producing, and starring in his own black vaudeville show on WCAP. Washington's racial laws, however, soon forced Cooper's return to Chicago. There, station WSBC operated successfully by brokering time to various immigrant groups and was receptive to Cooper's desire to produce and air *The All Negro Hour* in 1929. One of Cooper's live broadcasts was threatened in 1932 when the key performer abruptly quit over a pay dispute. Cooper creatively set up a phonograph, placed a microphone in front of it, and played recorded music to maintain the show's broadcast schedule and continuity thereafter. Inadvertently, he had become the first African-American disc jockey. By 1938 Cooper was brokering up to 20 hours of time on WSBC and programming church services on Sundays. Eventually he bought time on several other Chicago stations, replicated his record show, and produced news and public affairs programs that utilized his journalism skills. He also launched the first black advertising agency and radio production company.

Chicago became a focal point for broadcasting recorded black music—a mix of jazz, blues, spirituals, and hymns—when in the early 1940s Al Benson bought time on WGES and complemented Cooper's "time blocks" with his own set of programs. Cooper and Benson each organized training programs and taught young aspirants about radio. They bought and sold time, conducted market research, and wrote and produced advertisements.

The "time block" purchase method and the recorded music program also appear to have been popular among local African-American entrepreneurs in other parts of the country in the late 1930s and early 1940s. In Seattle, Bass Harris appeared on KING; in Washington, D.C., Hal Jackson was on WOOK; in Detroit, Ed Baker was featured on WJLB, while Van Douglas appeared on WJBK; in Hammond, Indiana, Eddie Honesty was on WJOB; and in New York, Joe Bostic appeared on both WCNN and WMAC. As with Cooper and Benson, most early African-American radio personalities were college educated, trained by veteran professionals, or they were experienced entrepreneurs who understood the radio business.

Network Radio and Minstrelsy

With programs such as the hugely popular *Amos 'n' Andy* featuring white performers playing black roles, one must look at the stereotypic roles played by early black performers to understand the kinds of jobs generally available to African-American actors on network radio during the 1930s. For example, Ernest Whitman was employed as Awful for *The Gibson Family*. The role of Gardenia, a humorous character, was played by Georgia Burke on the *Betty and Bob* soap opera. Even Academy Award winner Hattie McDaniel (*Gone With The Wind*) was hired to portray a mammy on the network radio series *Showboat*. McDaniel also played a more endearing role as the lead on the network series *Beulah*—but only after the role had originally been played by a white man.

Positive portrayals of blacks in network drama were rare but not absent entirely. In 1933 Juano Hernandez starred in the CBS series *John Henry, Black River Boat Giant*. Rose McClendon, Dorothy Caul, and Jack McDowell also were cast members. John Henry was portrayed as a powerful but bad ladies' man. More frequently, African-Americans were cast in stereotypical roles on network vaudeville programs including the *Eddie Cantor Show*, *Saturday Night Sewing Club*, and the *Rudy Vallee Show*. Cantor also hired a black female vocalist, Thelma Carpenter, for a regular spot on his show. "Rochester," on *The Jack Benny Program*, was another black stereotype, but much of the humor came from Rochester's "bettering" his white boss.

Performers such as the Golden Gate Quartet, Southernaires, Wings Over Jordan, CBS Trumpeteers, Ethel Waters, Andy Razaf, and Paul Robeson were able to showcase their professional skills nationally at one time or another. The Mills Brothers were especially popular on radio, Duke Ellington had his own network radio show by 1936, and Marion Anderson is legendary if only for her 1939 appearance at the Lincoln Memorial in Washington, which was broadcast nationally.

World War II

With its entry into the war, however, the United States was forced to begin confronting its "Jim Crow" treatment of black people, including the paucity and negative portrayal of African-Americans on radio: the country badly needed racial tranquility at home and among its military servicemen. To help accomplish its objective, the government produced or supported network radio programs that projected African-Americans in a positive light. *Men o' War* was an all-black patriotic musical program series featuring naval personnel; it was broadcast regularly for two years over the CBS radio network. *Freedom's People*, an eight-part program on NBC, highlighted African-American achievements and featured Count Basie, Cab Callaway, George Washington Carver, W.C. Handy, Joe Louis, Jessie Owens, and other outstanding African-Americans. African-Americans portraying positive characters were also written into such network soap operas as *Our Gal Sunday* and *The Romance of Helen Trent*.

A special radio documentary, "Open Letter On Race Hatred," was broadcast on CBS in response to the 1943 Detroit, Michigan, race riot that left 35 dead. In addition, a series of discussion and public affairs programs that addressed black issues and featured black leaders aired nationally on radio networks. Ann Tanneyhill produced a show for CBS in 1943 about black women, called *Heroines in Bronze.* NBC aired programs such as *America's Town Meeting* (which, although it discussed racial issues, did so with white speakers), *The Army Hour, Too Long America,* and others. CBS broadcast *People's Platform, The Negro in the War,* and *They Call Me, Joe,* among others.

Many programs carried by the Armed Forces Radio Service (AFRS) encouraged good race relations among troops. Many programs featured black announcers, recorded music, and live bands. One AFRS station, located at the Blytheville Army Air Corps Base in Arkansas, programmed black local news, events, and recorded music in both the early morning and mid-afternoon that was listened to faithfully by African-American civilians throughout Mississippi County.

Postwar African-American Radio

After the war, African-American men and women began performing live on radio throughout America. Early Lee Wright became the South's first recognized black announcer in 1947 on WROX in Clarksdale, Mississippi. The Delta Rhythm Boys, a local gospel group from the same town, could be heard on records. The famous *King Biscuit Time,* featuring blues men Sonny Boy Williamson and Robert Lockwood, was broadcast on KFFA in Helena, Arkansas. WLAC in Nashville had begun to play a mix of black-oriented music on a nightly basis, even though they still used white announcers.

Magazine reports about the success of African-American disc jockeys began to persuade some white owners of unsuccessful radio stations to begin full-time programming of rhythm and blues music. WDIA in Memphis, Tennessee, was the first such white station to do so. It was the second new station (after KWAM in 1946), to go on the air in Memphis after the war and found survival in the new competitive market very difficult. John Pepper, one of the WDIA owners, was ready to quit. In 1948 the station's general manager and co-owner, Bert Ferguson, read a magazine article about the economic success of programming to African-Americans. Probably he was reading about Jack L. Cooper or Al Benson in Chicago. Shortly afterwards, Ferguson hired Nat D. Williams to create a block of black-oriented programming in the afternoon. Williams' afternoon program soon brought financial success to WDIA and enabled Ferguson to add another time block that featured Maurice "Hot Rod" Hulbert, then A.C. "Mooha" Williams and others until WDIA's entire schedule was

completely filled with various black blocks of rhythm-and-blues and gospel music programming. Full-time black-oriented radio was born.

By the early 1950s, there were reportedly more than 500 blacks working in radio throughout the nation, playing mostly rhythm-and-blues, and working part-time on stations that otherwise provided programming for white listeners. This sudden expansion in the number of black announcers had been driven by the popularity of rhythm and blues music. The sounds conveyed joy and hope in a language that reflected the postwar vision of freedom. The men and women who played the music on radio shared the same hope for the future and spoke the same rhythmic language. The rhyme-language style popular among blacks was used in a variety of situations such as "signifying" contests or when compliments were paid on clothing styles. Al Benson used it on radio, but Jack L. Cooper did not. It was used for laudatory salutes among MCs on the black entertainment "chittlin' circuit" when introducing performers and working the audience. Some scholars trace the rhyme's origin back to Africa. It certainly found its way into the lyrics of Louis Jordan's "Beware" recorded in the mid-1940s. Nat D. Williams was associated with rhyme on Beale Street and later on WDIA. Maurice "Hot Rod" Hulbert, entertainer turned Memphis disc jockey, moved to Baltimore radio and popularized the style. Doug "Jocko" Henderson, a Hulbert admirer, put his signature on the style in Philadelphia and syndicated his *Rocket Ship Show* to five other East Coast markets. Radio personalities such as Jack Gibson and Daddy-O Daily developed rhyme styles mutually exclusive of the Memphis linkage.

African-Americans solidified their positive presence in radio through perseverance and by promoting rhythm-and-blues music; their audience expanded because of improved education and growing wealth among African-Americans. Most major U.S. cities operated a full-time rhythm-and-blues station by the mid-1950s. As black people traveled or communicated, they spread stories about their favorite local disc jockey, among them "Frantic" Ernie, Jack "The Rapper" Gibson, Joe "Joltin Joe" Howard, "The Magnificent" Montague, "Honey Boy" Thomas, "Lucky" Cordell, Sid "The Real" McCoy, Martha Jean "The Queen," or simply, Georgie Woods.

African-American performers and rhythm-and-blues music were adopted by white people and by broadcast institutions at an increasing rate. Among those who championed the new sound were Alan Freed in Cleveland, Dick Clark in Philadelphia,

George Lorenz in Buffalo, and Robert "Wolfman Jack" Smith near Del Rio, Texas. Collectively, recorded rhythm-and-blues performances and the accolades awarded black disc jockeys had made their impression. Imitation by white broadcasters was a respectful cultural compliment.

Station Ownership and Activism

Andrew "Skip" Carter bought KPRS of Kansas City, Missouri, a defunct operation, in early 1949: he became the first African-American to own a commercial radio license. Later that same year, J.B. Blayton purchased WERD in Atlanta. Dr. Haley Bell in Detroit was the first black person to construct a new radio station—WCHB first aired in 1956.

African-American disc jockeys during the 1950s found it necessary to organize professionally in order to help each other improve salaries, working conditions, equal rights, and employment. They formed the National Jazz, Rhythm-and-Blues Disc Jockey Association and attracted national attention in 1956 when members met to defend rhythm-and-blues music against its critics—those who believed that because rhythm-and-blues had black origins it was dangerous for white people to listen to. The group later changed its name to the National Association of Radio and Television Announcers (NATRA).

In the mid-1960s, managing and owning stations moved to the top of the black broadcasters' agenda. The entire black staff of disc jockeys at WVOL in Nashville went on strike in 1964 and helped head salesman, Noble Blackwell, move into the vacated general manager's job. In Chicago, Lucky Cordell was appointed manager at WVON. These moves were seen as milestone achievements within the larger civil rights movement.

Dr. Martin Luther King addressed the 1967 NATRA convention and publicly thanked its members for their valuable support of the civil rights movement. He praised the contributions of African-American announcers in general for using radio to popularize rhythm-and-blues internationally. Commentators have since praised the role played by African-American broadcasters in calming fears in the midst of the urban rebellions in the 1960s. Yet many emphasized the need for radio to open its doors even wider. African-Americans in the mid-1960s still held perhaps only one percent of the 60,000 jobs in commercial radio, and only five of 5,500 licensed radio stations were black-owned.

Pressure from activist groups and changes in federal policy brought sweeping change in the 1970s. NATRA declined as a result of growing conflict within and outside its own ranks over its

priorities. Yet the organization's agenda, to promote ownership of radio stations by blacks, advanced by Del Shields and others, had won support from FCC Commissioner Nicholas Johnson and was also supported by other organizations such as Black Efforts in Soul Television, led by Bill Wright, and subsequently The National Black Media Coalition under Pluria Marshall. The predominately white National Association of Broadcasters along with the National Congressional Black Caucus also lent their efforts to addressing the ownership problem. The first black FCC Commissioner, Benjamin Hooks, was appointed by President Richard Nixon. Overall, this activism led to a modest increase in station ownership and the establishment of The National Association of Black Owned Broadcasters.

Dr. Haley Bell's acquisition of a second Detroit license in the 1960s (to operate WCHD-FM) made him the first African-American to own more than one station. James Brown's two Augusta, Georgia, stations and Percy Sutton's Inner Broadcasting, Inc., based in New York, soon followed. Dorothy Brunson's acquisition of Brown's stations made her the first African-American woman to become a station owner. Cathy Hughes of Radio, Inc. emerged as a legendary figure in radio-station financing, acquisitions, and operations. Hughes had honed her skills in advertising and sales by serving as a radio volunteer in Omaha. In 1971 she began to teach advertising at Howard University, and was soon managing WHUR-FM, owned by the university. By 1980 she had purchased Washington's WOL and added another station to her list in 1987. Deregulation helped Hughes: in the early 1990s she founded Radio One, Inc., and by 2001 her company held 48 radio station licenses and was the main reason African-Americans now owned more than 200 stations. Radio One celebrated its 25th anniversary in 2006 and was still the largest radio broadcasting company that primarily targets African-Americans. Within two years, however, Cathy Hughes and her son Alfred Liggins, Radio One's CEO, came under fire for voting themselves huge bonuses and compensation increases as the company's stock suffered double-digit losses, plummeting to less than a dollar and the company's stations numbered 54 after selling off outlets in the lucrative markets of Los Angeles and Miami. The 1996 Telecommunications Act allowed unlimited groups of radio stations (as well as multiple stations in any single market) to be owned by a single entity: this relaxation of former rules had the effect of pushing up station prices. Often unable to raise the inflated purchase prices—and with existing black-owned stations bought out by the owners of the growing radio chains—black station owners were unable to compete: the number of black-owned stations stagnated then slowly begin to decline. The only bright note was that at the turn of the century, blacks William Kennard and then Michael Powell were successive chairmen of the FCC.

Networks and Wider Distribution

The first African-American network was the short-lived National Negro Network founded by black entrepreneur W. Leonard Evans in 1954. The network signed up 40 affiliates and promised good programming: among its best were a radio drama *The Story of Ruby Valentine* and variety shows hosted by Cab Callaway and Ethel Waters. But lack of advertiser support caused the network's demise after only a few months. Two decades later two networks, the Mutual Black Network and the National Black Network, began providing news and public affairs programming to black-oriented radio stations. Together these networks reached millions of listeners.

Ronald R. Davenport, a former dean of the Duquesne University School of Law, raised enough money to purchase the struggling white-owned Mutual Black Network and assumed management of the company. In the late 1970s MBN became the Sheridan Broadcasting Company. In 1991 Sheridan Broadcasting Network and National Black Network joined forces to operate as equals in a general partnership under a new name, American Urban Radio Networks. The AURN distributes a variety of news and public affairs programming to 250 African-American-oriented radio stations. Toward the end of the new century's first decade, the AURN remained the only African-American owned network. Through three programming networks it distributed over 200 programs weekly to more than 300 radio stations, reaching more than 20 million listeners.

A number of highly visible existing African-American operations have made use of such newer technologies as communication satellites and the internet. For years radio personality Tom Joyner had worked in both Dallas and Chicago simultaneously. He became known as the "fly jock" for his daily commutes between the two cities. Finally, he converted to uplinking his broadcast signal to satellite from his Dallas location and syndicating his program to all radio stations. Joyner, the first African-American elected to the Radio Hall of Fame, was heard in more than 115 markets, reaching more than eight million listeners each week. Many tune into him on the internet.

In addition to Joyner, syndicated black radio hosts like Bev Smith, Michael Baisden and Warren Ballentine, as well as Joe Madison on Sirius/XM, gained a wider audience as well as becoming more influential, thanks in part to the 2008 high-profile presidential campaign of Barack Obama. Other African-Americans taking advantage of satellite and internet broadcasting included 40-year gospel radio veteran Walt "Baby" Love. Darnell's *Black Radio Guide* maintains a growing list of internet-only black radio stations. The heart of the human resource chain is Black College Radio, whose stated purpose is to provide an annual forum for black college broadcasters, professional broadcasters, and members of the music industry to meet and discuss ways to increase minority participation in the broadcasting industry.

Although the playing field for African-Americans has seldom been level, many have persisted and mastered the skills essential for successful leadership. The number of African-Americans who worked in radio between 1920 and 2000 was comparatively small. The quality of their contribution to achieve equity is more significant to radio when culture is placed into a perspective that stretches from Latimer, Gosden, and Correll, to recorded music used in modern programming. The magnitude of African-American presence in radio through jazz, rhythm and blues (or rock and roll), blues, reggae, gospel, salsa, and rap, regardless of the performer's race, is incalculable. According to folk legend Pete Seeger, American music is Africanized music.

See also: Affirmative Action; *Amos 'n' Andy*; *Beulah Show*; Black-Oriented Radio; Black Radio Networks; KFFA; Stereotypes on Radio; WDIA

Further Reading

Abdul-Jabbar, Kareem, and Alan Steinberg, *Black Profiles in Courage: A Legacy of African American Achievement*, New York: Morrow, 1996.
Barlow, William, *Voice Over: The Making of Black Radio*, Philadelphia, Pennsylvania: Temple University Press, 1999.
MacDonald, J. Fred, *Don't Touch That Dial!: Radio Programming in American Life, 1920–1960*, Chicago: Nelson-Hall, 1979.
Randle, William, Jr., "Black Entertainers on Radio," *Black Perspective in Music* (Spring 1977).
Redd, Lawrence N., *Rock Is Rhythm and Blues: The Impact of Mass Media*, East Lansing: Michigan State University Press, 1974.
Thomas, Chandra R., "How Black Radio Found its Voice," *Time* (5 April 2008).

LAWRENCE N. REDD,
2009 REVISIONS BY GAIL LOVE

AGRICULTURAL RADIO
See: Farm/Agricultural Radio

AIR AMERICA

Air America Radio (AAR) is a network that emphasizes liberal political talk shows in contrast to the conservative tone of most syndicated talk programming. From the beginning, however, AAR struggled with insufficient capital, too few affiliate stations, and too many changes in ownership and management.

Air America began in late 2002 when Chicago venture capitalists and political activists Sheldon and Anita Drobny sought to arrange national syndication of Mike Malloy, a local talk show host they admired. Working with a radio consultant, the Drobnys formed AnShell Media, and began to raise funds for a national network (or at least a means of program syndication) building on Malloy's work. News that they were raising funds for a liberal counterpart to radio's dominant conservative talk programming received considerable attention, initial support, and newspaper reports about the pending venture. But when funding came up short, the original investment team sold out to advertising man Evan Cohen who formed Progress Media. Even at this early stage, a growing tension was evident between backers driven by liberal ideology and those seeking a successful broadcasting venture.

By early 2004, staff were hired and an affiliation agreement was struck with New York AM station WLIB, then a low-rated outlet. Indeed, many of AAR's early station contracts were with outlets that had little to lose giving the new programmers a try. On March 31, 2004, Air America Radio Network began operation. AAR's intent was to offer news, public affairs, interview and entertainment programs emphasizing a liberal point of view. Critics (not all of them conservative, either) argued AAR would have trouble finding listeners amidst the right-wing domination of commercial radio talk shows heard on hundreds of stations. Some suggested that the network seemed focused more on election politics than broadcasting. And thanks to the model right-wing talk pundits had created in the late 1980s (after the FCC dropped its Fairness Doctrine), AAR would have to purchase program time on stations.

With some effort, AAR persuaded comedian and commentator Al Franken (1951–) to become the network's chief talent. Well known for skewering the political right, Franken would become AAR's best-known voice for the next three years (he later left to run for a U.S. Senate seat from

Minnesota, winning in a squeaker in 2008). Soon others came onboard. When AAR first aired, many programs seemed more satirical than journalistic—indeed, many of the on-air figures were already known for their entertainment backgrounds. In April 2005, AAR signed Jerry Springer to host *Springer on the Radio*, arguing his notoriety might boost listeners. The controversial Springer said his new venture would be political in nature.

In late 2005 and early 2006 several program hosts and personalities left AAR. In August, nighttime host Mike Malloy (around whose role the network idea had begun four years earlier) was also let go. Some suggested that his criticism of Israeli policy may have been one reason. Observing all of this confusion, many conservative radio talk shows highlighted AAR's problems with considerable glee. By late 2006, AAR was providing nearly 20 hours of original programming daily over 92 stations reaching about 2.4 million listeners in the course of a week. Many of its programs featured call-ins as well as active web-pages and audio and video streaming.

Behind the scenes, however, insufficient capital was a continuing issue, as were disagreements among AAR funders and managers. For example, affiliate stations in Chicago and Santa Monica claimed they had not been paid for AAR programs they aired. Subsequent litigation and bad press contributed to the picture of confusion, as did the loss of stations in two top markets, Chicago and Los Angeles. Faced with this debacle, AAR stopped trying to buy radio stations, and allowed affiliates to carry programming other than AAR's. Just two years after starting, AAR had to shift its New York affiliation to a smaller station, WWRL, another outlet that had traditionally programmed to African-Americans, and it became the flagship affiliate. In October 2006, the network was forced to file for bankruptcy protection (it had lost more than $40 million in 2.5 years of operation). The Santa Monica affiliate that had complained about nonpayment two years earlier sought to freeze the network's accounts. Recriminations were rife, some arguing the network had been overstaffed, yet another sign of its political expectations, rather than broadcast business reality.

In late January 2007, AAR announced plans for its acquisition by the Green Realty Corporation, of New York. When they took control two months later, AAR was down to only 70 stations reaching 1.7 million listeners a week. In an attempt to shore up its revenues, AAR signed with radio giant Westwood One to oversee all network and affiliate station advertising sales. Franken left the air in

February 2007 and began his campaign for a U.S. Senate seat from Minnesota, a race he came within a hair of winning.

By early 2008, AAR was producing 21 hours of weekday network programming for its 62 remaining stations, though only about 40 of those carried most of the schedule. Indeed, some outlets carried only one or two programs. Although AAR programs did well in traditionally liberal towns, ratings were often anemic elsewhere. Yet these small audiences were often hugely loyal to specific talk show hosts, giving their programs greater impact than small audience numbers would suggest. AAR programs were also heard over XM Satellite Radio, and streamed on its own website.

See also: Fairness Doctrine; Pacifica Foundation

Further Reading

Air America website, www.airamerica.com/
Drobny, Sheldon, *How We Created Air America: The New Radio Revolution.* Chicago: Vox Pop, 2007.
Steinberg, Jacques, "Media: Office Politics Give Liberal Radio a Rocky Start," *New York Times* (31 May 2004).
Story, Louise, "Air America to Be Acquired by New York Investor," *New York Times* (30 January 2007).

CHRISTOPHER H. STERLING

ALBUM-ORIENTED ROCK FORMAT

Album-Oriented Rock (AOR) originally referred to 33 1/3 rpm LP vinyl recordings, which distinguished it from the "single" 45 RPM recordings played on the Top-40 format.

AOR's initial popularity in the 1970s signaled the arrival of 1960s counterculture tastes into the American popular music mainstream. But far from embracing the progressive politics, lifestyle, and artistry that gave counterculture music its relevance, AOR programmers capitalized on the increasing popularity of progressive radio incubating in the antiwar, Woodstock-era FM underground by appropriating its unique characteristics. AOR programming consultants replaced the DJ-programmer with a system of cue cards and playlists, turned thematic sets into music "sweeps" designed for Arbitron's ratings methodology, and handed FM station owners a homogeneous and more manageable format. AOR radio, by stripping rock and roll of its rhythm and blues heritage and rejecting its subversive possibilities, significantly contributed to branding rock as a marketable commodity. It also helped move most radio listeners from AM to FM by the end of the 1970s. Although the AOR format prospered at the expense of the radio radicals who

inspired it, some went on to run AOR stations or form broadcast consultancies, while others remained reactionary by joining in less mainstream forms of radio, typically noncommercial in nature.

The AOR playlist comprises selected tracks from rock albums, chosen to attract a target audience. Radio stations utilizing the AOR format skew their playlists to position the station competitively. For example, AOR stations targeting an older audience may include rock from the late 1960s and early 1970s; lighter rock tracks often attract more women; and emphasis on contemporary albums may appeal to a cosmopolitan audience. Such refinements of the AOR format have led to Classic Rock, Soft Rock, and some Alternative formats. Although more than 80 stations identified themselves early in 2009 as being AOR in format, it is probably a label based more on tradition and habit than it is on their actual playlist. So-called "AOR" sounds like equal parts AC, Contemporary Hits and other rapidly diffusing, bleeding formats. Furthermore, in a digital and iPod world, the music industry (and the radio industry by default) is increasingly becoming about the music single, i.e. the 99-cent download, and not about selling or playing whole albums or alternate album tracks, a trend that's completely counter to the primary philosophy and original purpose of the AOR format.

See also: Alternative Format; Arbitron; Classic Rock Format; Progressive Rock Format; Soft Rock Format; Underground Radio

Further Reading

Fornatale, Peter, and Joshua E. Mills, *Radio in the Television Age*, Woodstock, New York: Overlook Press, 1980.
Keith, Michael C., *Voices in the Purple Haze: Underground Radio and the Sixties*, Westport, Connecticut: Praeger, 1997.
Ladd, Jim, *Radio Waves: Life and Revolution on the FM Dial*, New York: St. Martin's Press, 1991.
Neer, Richard, *FM: The Rise and Fall of Rock Radio*, New York: Villard, 2001.

JOSEPH R. PIASEK,
2009 REVISIONS BY CARY O'DELL

ALDRICH FAMILY
Situation Comedy Program

The 20th century may not have invented teenagers, but it supplied the most memorable examples. From 1939 to 1953, the character Henry Aldrich and his imitators defined the standard crises, all poignant yet laughable. Although Henry's stage origin was unpromising, his radio personality carried on the Tom Sawyer/Penrod Schofield/Andy Hardy tradition of a good-hearted innocent who unintentionally causes mischief. Clifford Goldsmith's 1937 play *What a Life!* confined him to the principal's office, accused of stealing band instruments when he had merely cheated on a test in order to attend the dance. Henry's world grew when Rudy Vallee and Kate Smith commissioned sketches for their shows. By 1939 the vignettes expanded to a 30-minute series on the National Broadcasting Company's (NBC) Blue network. Sponsored by Jell-O and introduced by the rousing tune "This Is It," *The Aldrich Family* mingled humor, nostalgia, and complicated plots.

The opening routinely stressed the universality of Henry's zany experiences. For example, the announcer led in to the episode "The Tuxedo" by saying, "Whatever and whenever the Golden Age was, it is less important to most people than the teen age—a time of life made notable by typical American boys like Henry Aldrich and all their mishaps." Adolescence normally involves a tension between conformity and individuation, but Henry's awkward attempts to be a dutiful son/student/ friend/worker as well as an independent individual seldom seem rooted in common experience. Unlike his listeners, he never matured beyond 16. Certainly he honored his parents: the show began with the memorable call from mother Alice ("Hen-ry! Hen-ry Aldrich!"), which Henry answers with an obedient, "Coming, Mother." Talking to father, lawyer Sam Aldrich, Henry resorts to elaborate but ungrammatical politeness: "Do you wish to speak to I, Father?" He tries to carry out their wishes by not leaving doors open, by cooperating with his sister Mary, and by babysitting a rambunctious tyke. Yet he inevitably upsets family order. Once Sam borrows Henry's bicycle and thoughtfully leaves a note on the rake with which his son had promised to beautify the yard. As usual, Henry forgets the leaves, doesn't see the note, and, assuming someone has stolen the bike, calls the police. By the show's end, friends, neighbors, and strangers share his teenage turmoil.

School situations likewise do little to develop Henry as a character. He once masters the Latin pluperfect subjunctive; most other times, his academic milestones mark unpredictable gaffes: when he spills glue on the shop floor and sees his teacher lose his shoe in the mess, or when he is caught on a fire escape by the principal as he tries in vain to return a teacher's grade book that his pal mistakenly picked up because it resembled a mystery story. Friendship and romance also seemed to change

before Henry could understand them. A note from a girl in the next town flatters him so that he rents a costume, intending to escort her to a dance. After seeing her picture, he fobs her off on a rival who also takes his costume. The urge to make money, too, is thwarted by poor information. He buys a furnace-starting concession. The seller neglects to tell him that the owners are in Florida, a fact Henry learns from a postcard sent by the owners to his family. Unfortunately, he has already wrecked the furnace, restarted mail and milk deliveries, and burned a box of the owner's papers. Although Henry mishandles his duties, his good will eventually moderates any possibilities for serious harm.

The plots often center on Henry's quest to acquire some object: a misplaced watch given by his aunt Harriet, who wants to see it again; a tuxedo so he can attend the prom; a straw hat; an antique toy to replace the one he broke in his girlfriend Kathleen's home; a motor scooter that he will receive if he can pass his history test. His cravings for material goods parallel those of the normative middle-class citizen, but his missteps lighten greed with humor. Popular formulas for success often mislead Henry. He thinks he might get rich raising rabbits; he imitates the generosity he's seen in a film and, like the hero of Thornton Wilder's *Heaven's My Destination,* creates chaos; he writes to a Charles Atlas-type muscle developer but misplaces the letter that details his puny dimensions. Henry's ambitions do not liberate him; rather, they entangle others. His father spends some uncomfortable hours trapped in a phone booth; a friend crouches miserably in a basement cubbyhole; his chum Homer Brown, unwittingly engaged to Agnes, finds that Henry's solution is worse than commitment.

Although *The Aldrich Family* provided lasting memories, the cast changed frequently. At least three mothers, seven sisters, seven directors, and three fathers appeared. House Jameson, barely in charge as would-be patriarch Sam, had more authority as *Renfrew of the Mounted.* Ezra Stone was the bestknown Henry—his reedy voice captured the nearly out-of-control mood that characterized each program. After Stone was called to military service from 1941 to 1944, Norman Tokar, Raymond Ives, Bobby Ellis, and Dickie Jones filled in until his return. Clifford Goldsmith relied on seven other writers, but his benign vision of adolescence still shaped their versions. Only Jackie Kelk remained consistent, playing Homer (a role that was a shift for Kelk, who had played the self-confident Terry on *Terry and the Pirates* and helpful Jimmy Olson on *Superman*).

Several shows copied the Aldrich formula of a well-meaning youngster who inadvertently confounds normalcy: *Archie Andrews* and *That Brewster Boy* echoed the male adolescent's turmoil; *Junior Miss, A Date with Judy, Maudie's Diary,* and *Meet Corliss Archer* presented the female version. A series of 11 Henry Aldrich movies between 1939 and 1944 made visual his arrested adolescence, but the film versions employed other actors (Jackie Cooper in the first, Jimmy Lydon in the rest). Likewise, the 1949–53 television program used five Henrys (most notably Bobby Ellis), though it retained Jameson as father, Kelk as Homer, and Leona Powers as Mrs. Brown.

See also: Comedy; Situation Comedy

Cast

Henry Aldrich	Ezra Stone (1939–42; 1945–52), Norman Tokar (1942–43), Dickie Jones (1943–44), Raymond Ives (mid 1945), Bobby Ellis (1952–53)
Sam Aldrich	House Jameson, Clyde Fillmore, Tom Shirley
Alice Aldrich	Katharine Raht, Lea Penman, Regina Wallace
Mary Aldrich	Betty Field, Patricia Peardon, Charita Bauer, Ann Lincoln, Jone Allison, Mary Mason, Mary Rolfe, Mary Shipp
Homer Brown	Jackie Kelk, Johnny Fiedler (1952–53), Jack Grimes (1952–53), Michael O'Day (1952–53)
Will Brown	Ed Begley, Arthur Vinton, Howard Smith
Homer's Mother	Agnes Moorehead, Leona Powers
Kathleen Anderson	Mary Shipp, Ethel Blume, Jean Gillespie, Ann Lincoln
Dizzy Stevens	Eddie Bracken
George Bigelow	Charles Powers
Toby Smith	Dick Van Patten
Mrs. Anderson	Alice Yourman
Willie Marshall	Norman Tokar
Aunt Harriet	Ethel Wilson
Announcers	Harry Von Zell, Dwight Weist, George Bryan, Dan Seymour, Ralph Paul

Creator/Writer

Clifford Goldsmith

Programming History

NBC	July 1939–July 1944; September 1946–April 1953
CBS	September 1944–August 1946

Further Reading

Beers, Dale, "The Aldrich Family Log Website," www.geocities.com/Hollywood/Set/3688/aldrich.html.

Dunning, John, *Tune in Yesterday: The Ultimate Encyclopedia of Old-Time Radio, 1925–1976*, Englewood Cliffs, New Jersey: Prentice-Hall, 1976; revised edition, as *On the Air: The Encyclopedia of Old-Time Radio*, New York: Oxford University Press, 1998.

Goldsmith, Clifford, "Radio Oddities," *Tune In 4* (August 1946).

Harmon, Jim, "When Teen-Agers Were Kids," Chapter 6 of *The Great Radio Comedians*, by Harmon, Garden City, New York: Doubleday, 1970.

Swartz, Jon David, and Robert C. Reinehr, *Handbook of Old Time Radio: A Comprehensive Guide to Golden Age Radio Listening and Collecting*, Metuchen, New Jersey: Scarecrow Press, 1993.

Witham, W. Tasker, *The Adolescent in the American Novel, 1920–1960*, New York: Ungar, 1964.

JAMES A. FREEMAN

ALL NEWS FORMAT

All news is a programming format that continuously provides listeners with the latest news, sports, weather, time, and, in many cases, reports on driving conditions. This format's appeal is directed to a revolving audience continuously tuning in and out.

Radio news traces its origins to KDKA's broadcast of the 1920 presidential election returns. The station announcer requested that listeners mail postcards to the station confirming that they had heard the broadcast. By 1930 NBC and CBS were simultaneously broadcasting *Lowell Thomas and the News,* sponsored by *Literary Digest.* The unusual simulcast, in which NBC broadcast the program to the eastern half of the country and CBS to the western half, became solely the property of NBC within a year. Americans grew accustomed to turning on their radios for the latest news during the late 1930s. By the end of the decade, as social unrest increased in Europe, the voices of radio correspondents William L. Shirer, George Hicks, and Edward R. Murrow became as familiar as those of friends and neighbors. Radio was establishing itself as the leader in reporting events as they were occurring. In 1940 Americans told pollsters for the first time that they preferred radio to newspapers as their primary news source. Coverage of World War II cemented the relationship between radio and its audience across the United States as listeners followed the progress of American troops in Europe and the Pacific.

With the end of World War II and the development of television, radio's role once again shifted. During the 1950s, radio's entertainment programming, including dramas and soap operas, moved steadily to television. Music gradually became the dominant form of programming on radio; at many stations, news was shifted to five minutes at the top of the hour.

In the 1960s radio management took another look at news programming. The trade magazine *Sponsor* described radio at that time as the "new king of the news beat" and attributed its change in status to improvements in technology, increased numbers of experienced news reporters, and recognition that newsmakers were more important than newscasters. Four radio networks were providing regular newscasts to their affiliates: ABC, NBC, and Mutual Broadcasting System (MBS) produced two newscasts hourly, and CBS, with 20 news bureaus worldwide, had nearly 50 correspondents contributing to their news programs.

The first all-news radio format in the United States was used at KFAX in San Francisco on 16 May 1960. General manager J.G. Paltridge and sales manager Ray Rhodes called the new format "newsradio." As was common at the time, KFAX (owned by Argonaut Broadcasting) sold advertisers announcements but no sponsorships of shows. Compared to today's heavy commercial schedule, spots were few, with one commercial per five minutes of news and also at station breaks. The first 25 minutes of an hour consisted of hard news followed by business news, sports, and special features. "Newsradio" died after four months due to its lack of advertisers.

In 1961 Gordon McLendon started the first commercially successful all-news radio station, X-TRA. Located in Tijuana, Mexico, it beamed its powerful signal across the border to southern California. A station promotional announcement trumpeted, "no waiting for hourly newscasts or skimpy headlines on X-TRA NEWS, the world's first and only all-news radio station. In the air everywhere over Los Angeles."

Los Angeles broadcasters were critical of the Mexican station's identification with their city, as the only address announcers mentioned was that of the sales office in Los Angeles. The station's official on-air identification, required by law, was made in Spanish and followed by Mexican music and a description of Mexican tourist attractions. The Southern California Broadcasters Association called this an unethical attempt to camouflage a Mexican station as one located in Los Angeles.

In the early days, X-TRA used "rip and read" reports (stories torn straight from wire service machines and read live on the air). The station was served by the Los Angeles City Wire Service, the Associated Press (AP), and United Press International (UPI). X-TRA also subscribed to a clipping service that provided stories from newspapers in all major U.S. cities and international capitals around the world. No one rewrote the wire copy, and there were no station reporters gathering news or conducting interviews. Newscasters alternated as anchors every 15 minutes, with a half hour in between to prepare for the next news stint. The content was somewhat repetitive, as programmers assumed that the audience would switch to a music station after hearing the most recent news. All newscasters read their copy with the sound (often recorded) of wire service teletype machines in the background, as a report in *Sponsor* magazine described it, "to suggest a newsroom setting."

McLendon brought the all-news format to WNUS (pronounced "W-news") in Chicago in 1964. He advised radio programmers considering the format not to attempt to enliven it with features and "actualities" (sound bites), suggesting that listeners wanted nothing but news. WINS, New York's first all-news radio station, ignored that advice when it switched to round-the-clock news in 1965. Owned by Westinghouse, WINS expanded the McLendon design, emphasizing on-the-scene reports and actualities. Fourteen newscasters, rotating in 30-minute shifts, anchored the newscasts. Mobile units provided live and taped reports from the five boroughs and the outskirts of the metropolitan area. A staff of more than 40 produced the news summaries, sports reports, financial news, and weather reports, plus time and traffic reports. They relied on wire service from AP and UPI and the resources of Westinghouse stations and news bureaus across the country and overseas. Despite the personnel-intensive expense of the operation, WINS started turning a profit six months into its all-news operation.

In 1966 *Broadcasting* reported that all news was a viable, profitable choice for a programming format. There were then four U.S. stations concentrating on news: WINS (New York), KYW (Philadelphia), WNUS (Chicago), and WAVA (Arlington, Virginia), and the Mexican station X-TRA in Tijuana, which also had an audience in the United States. Despite reaching the profit-making point after nine months, WNUS never gained a dominant share of the market, so management changed its program format back to music in 1968. Westinghouse, however, went on to program all news in its stations in Los Angeles and Philadelphia.

CBS's flagship station in New York, WCBS, shifted to all news in 1967, but with its own innovations and significant financial support. WCBS used helicopters for traffic reports and its own weather forecasters. It had more reporters and produced more features than other all-news stations of the period, and it had access to the resources of the respected CBS network news. Among its reporters were Ed Bradley and Charles Osgood, who would make national names for themselves and eventually shift to television news. CBS brass liked the results, and all-news formats were put into place at other CBS owned-and-operated stations in Boston, Chicago, Los Angeles, Philadelphia, and San Francisco.

NBC broke into all-news radio in 1975, introducing News and Information Service (NIS), the first national all-news service. Subscribers paid as little as $750 or as much as $15,000, depending on their market size. Stations would pay for world and national news plus sports and features, all provided by NBC anchors in New York. They broadcast for 47 minutes out of every hour with the format constructed so that subscribers could take the whole 47 minutes or as little as 23 minutes of the hourly format. Unlike traditional affiliations in which a network paid its affiliates or traded commercial availabilities, NIS had to be purchased from NBC. With the network producing the majority of the programming, the all-news format looked financially feasible for medium and small markets for the first time.

Despite the positive appearances, the all-news concept was not successful for NBC. After 18 months NBC had only 62 subscribers, significantly fewer than the projected 150 stations. Industry insiders suggested that the NBC network's unwillingness to commit its owned-and-operated stations contributed to the demise of NIS (only one adopted the all-news format). Audience numbers never reached expectations, resulting in disappointing advertising sales. All news was expensive to produce and simply was not bringing in the necessary income, so NIS went off the air two years after it began. Although it had cost $20 million, its impact on the future of all-news radio had been significant during its short life. After its demise, a number of other all-news stations continued, affiliating with other networks, including CBS. So NBC contributed to the all-news format's expansion from the top ten markets to the medium-sized markets, despite the failure of NIS.

From NBC, CBS, and Westinghouse, three basic models developed for the all-news format, all based on the "format clock." A circle divided into pie-shaped slices indicates specific times during the hour on an analog clock. News, weather, traffic reports, and features are designated on the pie slices. Today's "weather on the fours" or "traffic on the eights" are segments that appear every four and eight minutes within each hour span, based on the traditional format clock.

The Westinghouse model is based on a 20- to 22-minute cycle with short, crisp stories and repetition. This is generally a hard-news approach with headlines, weather, time checks, and traffic reports. For instance, Philadelphia's KYW is famous for announcing, "Give us 22 minutes and we'll give you the world." The CBS model tends to be more informal, with hard news, features, and commentary, having initially used dual anchors and less repetition to establish its format. NBC created a more impersonal sound with the NIS model because it was producing news for all areas of the country rather than tailored for a specific market.

All news was one of the fastest growing formats in the 1970s, but the number of all-news stations started dropping in the 1980s as the news format was combined with a less expensive format that was growing in popularity: talk. The number of news-talk stations increased as all news declined. By 1990 there were only 28 all-news stations in the United States.

Theoretically, "all news" is an attractive format. It lends a sense of gravitas and prestige to stations. Furthermore, listeners to all-news radio tend to be older (35+), better educated and have more income than the average consumer. According to research, all-news audiences also tend to listen more attentively to news than to other formats like music. News stations are also often able to air more ads per hour than most other non-news stations without the risk of driving away listeners. (However, due to the repetitious nature of all-news formats, people do tend to listen for shorter durations.) Unfortunately, "all news" is also one of radio's most expensive formats, demanding a cadre of trained staff (reporters, writers, editors and producers) that stations with other formats can do without.

The *Broadcasting & Cable Yearbook* for 2008 quite generously listed over 700 AM and FM stations across the country that identify themselves as being "all news." But how stations label their content varies and many so-called "all-news" stations are really more talk than news. Increasingly, so-called "all-news" stations fill their airtime, not with local coverage or original reportage, but with long-form syndicated talk shows, often with politically conservative leanings, such as Rush Limbaugh.

Many stations rely heavily upon national news services that feed generic (non-local) news stories and features, and often more than one. The Associated Press, for example, provides audio and text to almost 4,000 stations. Westwood One distributes CBS Radio News, and NBC Radio Network as well as its Shadow Broadcast Services and Metro Networks, which offer a variety of news options and traffic reports. ABC provides radio service to more than 4,000 outlets. Business news has become a hot commodity with such suppliers as Bloomberg Business News Network and CNBC Business Radio, among others. Sports news is provided by ESPN, which has about 700 radio customers.

According to some estimates, there are fewer than 20 true all-*news* stations currently on the air. They adhere to the strict format clock, though today these clocks are often far shorter than the traditional 22 minutes. For example, WTOP in Washington, D.C., advertises itself as providing weather and traffic updates every 10 minutes.

Among the stations who can legitimately call themselves "all news" as of early 2009 included: WCBS and WINS in New York, KNX and KFWB in Los Angeles, WBBM in Chicago, WWJ in Detroit and KYW in Philadelphia, all of which are owned by CBS. Non CBS-owned stations include KQV in Pittsburgh and KOMO in Seattle. Yet even these stations adopt alternate programming outside of drive time. KLIV in San Jose, for example, becomes an all-talk station in the evenings, while KIKK in Houston, which airs news during the day, switches to music starting in the early evening.

See also: KYW; News; News Agencies; Talk Radio; WCBS; Westwood One; WINS

Further Reading

Barfield, Ray E., *Listening to Radio, 1920–1950*, Westport, Connecticut: Praeger, 1996.
Bliss, Edward, Jr., *Now the News: The Story of Broadcast Journalism*, New York: Columbia University Press, 1991.
Charnley, Mitchell Vaughn, *News by Radio*, New York: Macmillan, 1948.
Fisher, Marc, "Blackout on the Dial," *American Journalism Review* 20, no.5 (June 1998).
Julian, Joseph, *This Was Radio: A Personal Memoir*, New York: Viking Press, 1975.
Keirstead, Phillip O., *All-News Radio*, Blue Ridge Summit, Pennsylvania: Tab Books, 1980.
Kotz, Pete, "The Decline of News Radio," *Des Moines Business Record* (26 October 1998).
MacFarland, David T., *Contemporary Radio Programming Strategies*, Hillsdale, New Jersey: Erlbaum, 1990; 2nd edition, as *Future Radio Programming Strategies: Cultivating Listenership in the Digital Age*, Mahwah, New Jersey: Erlbaum, 1997.
Schatz, Robin D., "All-News Radio Holds Its Own in U.S. Media Markets," *International Herald Tribune* (26 June 1996).

SANDRA L. ELLIS,
2009 REVISIONS BY CARY O'DELL

ALL-NIGHT RADIO

All-night radio programming has been a staple of the industry since the 1920s, when stations such as WDAF in Kansas City remained on the air far into the night to accommodate listeners who wanted to hear distant signals. Late-night programs began appearing more widely in the 1930s as the networks scheduled live big band shows, which typically played dance music into the wee small hours (often 2:00 or 3:00 A.M.). Although it is difficult to say which station first offered a regular schedule of all-night broadcasts, certainly one of the pioneers was WNEW-AM in New York. It premiered *Milkman's Matinee* (first broadcast midnight to 6 A.M. and later from 2 A.M. to 6 A.M.) on 6 August 1935, and the program remained on the air until 1992. During the same period, many major-market radio stations experimented with extended hours, with some confining their late-night programs to specific days of the week.

World War II led to a sharp increase in all-night radio programming. Feeling it their patriotic duty, many stations (among them WNAC and WEEI in Boston, WNEW and WOR in New York, WKBW in Buffalo, KDKA in Pittsburgh, WCAU in Philadelphia, and WRVA in Richmond) offered broadcasts for those legions of Americans working graveyard shifts in defense plants and factories.

After the war, all-night talk shows began to appear. Regarded by many as the father of the overnight call-in show, Barry Gray launched his program in New York City in 1945, and his "graveyard gab-a-thons" would remain among the most popular forms of this radio programming daypart. In the 1970s, all-night talk was given a significant boost with the debut of national call-in shows hosted by personalities such as Larry King and other extremely popular and sometimes controversial talkmasters. The use of toll-free 800 numbers enhanced the attraction of this format.

The primary appeal of overnight radio broadcasting lies in its companionability. A 1968 National Association of Broadcasters survey concluded that 60 percent of the all-night audience tunes in to keep from being lonely. All-night radio is also where the subcultures and countercultures tune to stay connected at an hour when the mainstream world is asleep. Insomniacs and third-shift workers, among them bakers, policemen, cab drivers, and convenience store clerks, constitute a substantial part of the loyal listenership of all-night radio. For aspiring disc jockeys and talk hosts, the overnight shift frequently serves as a training ground. It is where stations often put their most inexperienced on-air people to allow them the chance to build their skills. However, for some seasoned professionals, especially those in larger markets, the overnight shift is a preferred slot, because it is a segment of the program clock when rigid compliance to format strictures may be somewhat relaxed, thus providing them with greater opportunity to experiment and flex their creative muscles.

The program content of all-night radio tends to be eclectic. However, since the 1980s there has been a significant rise in the number of stations airing overnight talk shows, often syndicated programs, and canned programming are widely employed to fill the time slot. This period of the broadcast schedule has become famous for an often bizarre mix of program offerings. Psychics, paranormalists, conspiracy theorists, love therapists—to mention a few—are among the unique array of those who hold court over the night-time airwaves at hundreds of radio stations.

Outlets programming music over nights are frequently equally divergent in their approaches. In fact, music stations that feature a primary or single format during the day may shift gears to another, albeit complementary, form of music for their overnight hours. One quality many all-night music stations share in common is their tendency to soften or mellow their sounds to create a mood and atmosphere consonant with the nocturnal landscape. Jazz, blues, folk, and classical music are frequently given more airplay at night than during the day. Of course, not all stations vary or reconfigure their program clocks or playlists between midnight and 6 A.M. In fact, most actually mirror the programming they offer throughout the day and early evenings.

No programming ingredient has been more responsible for establishing loyal overnight followings than the radio personality; many of these have served their audiences for decades. The list of popular all-night hosts is long, if not endless. A partial list would certainly include Jean Shepherd, Norm Nathan, Franklin Hobbs, Joey Reynolds, Larry King, Henry Morgan, Jerry Williams, Jim Bohannon, Joe Franklin, Barry Farber, Larry Glick, Alison Steele, Ira Fistell, Ray Briem, Herb Jepko, Jean King, Larry Regan, Raechel Donahue, Long John Nebel, Wolfman Jack, Barry Gray, Mary Turner, Eddie Schwartz, John Luther, Mel Lindsay,

Rollye James, Stan Shaw, Art Dineen, Hunter Hancock, Doug Stephan, Yvonne Daniels, Al Collins, Don Sainte John, Tom Snyder, Dave Wiken, and Art Ford. Every late-night listener has his or her favorite personality. Perhaps no all-night figure was more popular than Art Bell at the turn of the millennium. Broadcasting from a remote locale (near the infamous "Area 51") in the Nevada desert, Bell attracted an audience that consistently numbered in the millions from coast to coast.

Since 1988, Arbitron has rated overnight time slots at the behest of outlets in markets with potentially large listenerships during this segment of the broadcast schedule. Although all-night hours are not typically viewed as profit centers (in fact, they are more often thought of as "giveaway" zones), many stations have been successful enough in generating revenues to want audience statistics to help promote increased levels of advertising. In fact, the value of all-night radio as an advertising medium has risen in a world that has become increasingly 24-hour oriented.

With continuing fallout from station consolidation and a stronger bottom-line emphasis, live and local all-night programming will decline in the future. Already, some stations are rebroadcasting their daytime programs during overnight hours as a cost-saving measure. Others have axed their late-night and overnight programs in favor of voice-tracking services or syndicated fare. A case in point: Minneapolis's late-nighter Al Malmberg was unceremoniously dumped in early 2009 after 12 years on the air, replaced by syndicated offerings.

In early 2009, night owl audiences could tune into the enduring, paranormal-inclined *Coast-to-Coast AM*, hosted by George Noory, *Overnight America* with Jon Grayson, *The Joey Reynolds Show* or *Midnight Trucking Radio* (originally aimed at long-haulers), among other syndicated shows. Perhaps not surprisingly many overnight and late-night programs focus on issues of love and romance. Dr. Judy Kuriansky's *Love Phones* aired from 1992 to 1998. Dr. Drew Pinsky's more clinically minded *Loveline* has been syndicated since 1995. And one-named radio host Delilah, on the air since 1996, intersperses her nightly advice to the lovelorn and long-distance dedications with generous helpings of self-proclaimed "sappy love songs."

See also: Talk Radio

Further Reading

Douglas, Susan J., *Listening In: Radio and the American Imagination*, New York: Times Books, 1999.

Harper, Jennifer. "No sleep for the curious: Night listener discusses aliens, Bigfoot, angels and presidential hopes," *Washington Times* (13 July 2008).

Keith, Michael C., *Sounds in the Dark: All Night Radio in American Life*, Ames, Iowa: Iowa State University Press, 2001.

Laufer, Peter, *Inside Talk Radio*, Secaucus, New Jersey: Carol, 1995.

Munson, Wayne, *All Talk: The Talkshow in Media Culture*, Philadelphia, Pennsylvania: Temple University Press, 1993.

Richards, Andrew, and Rob Gutierrez. "Over the air, overnight: Talk radio lights up dials when road grows dark," *Washington Times* (7 November 2007).

Shepherd, Jean, *In God We Trust: All Others Pay Cash*, Garden City, New York: Doubleday, 1966.

MICHAEL C. KEITH,
2009 REVISIONS BY CARY O'DELL

ALL TALK FORMAT
See: Talk Radio

ALL THINGS CONSIDERED
Public-Affairs Program

The seminal program of National Public Radio (NPR) first aired from an improvised studio in a run-down Washington, D.C., office building at 5:00 P.M. EDT on Monday, 3 May 1971. *All Things Considered (ATC)* marked the beginning of public radio as we know it. It also marked the culmination of more than a year of soul-searching about the purposes of this new enterprise. The task of defining public radio fell to the initial board of directors of NPR—a collection of managers from the largely moribund world of educational radio—and in particular to board member William Siemering, who declared NPR's first priority to be the creation of "an identifiable daily product which is consistent and reflects the highest standards of broadcast journalism." His report continued:

> This may contain some hard news, but the primary emphasis would be on interpretation, investigative reporting on public affairs, the world of ideas and the arts. The program would be well paced, flexible, and a service primarily for a general audience. It would not, however, substitute superficial blandness for genuine diversity of regions, values, and cultural and ethnic minorities which comprise American society; it would speak with many voices and many dialects.

The editorial attitude would be that of inquiry, curiosity, concern for the quality of life, critical, problem solving, and life loving. The listener should come to rely upon it as a source of information of consequence; that having listened has made a difference in his attitude toward his environment and himself.

There may be regular features on consumer information, views of the world from poets, men and women of ideas and interpretive comments from scholars. Using inputs from affiliate stations, for the first time the intellectual resources of colleges and universities will be applied to daily affairs on a national scale.

National Public Radio will not regard its audience as a "market" or in terms of its disposable income, but as curious, complex individuals who are looking for some understanding, meaning and joy in the human experience.

In the early 1970s, radio news remained a serious enterprise at commercial radio networks. The aura of Edward R. Murrow still surrounded Columbia Broadcasting System (CBS) News. CBS provided ten-minute newscasts on the top of the hour around the clock. The commercial networks maintained extensive staffs of correspondents around the world. It was against that staid but responsible incarnation of commercial radio news that NPR sought to define an "alternative." It needed to separate itself as well from the equally staid and responsible style of traditional educational radio. Although it was located in Washington, D.C., just blocks from the White House, NPR saw itself in an outsider role and took pride in not attending the news conferences to which members of the mainstream media flocked. Siemering asked, "Why do we always think that what the President did today is so important? Maybe it is more important that some unemployed person found a job today? Maybe that should lead our program?"

Siemering urged NPR to distinguish itself from commercial radio and its own past by "advancing the art of the audio medium." That mandate ultimately translated into a distinctive production style that took listeners to the scene of an event or into the lives of ordinary people instead of just talking about them. Producers would use microphones the way television reporters and documentarians used cameras. This was a new approach to radio journalism, because although listeners might recall the sounds of Murrow on the streets of London in World War II or the burning of the dirigible *Hindenburg*, these were the exceptions in radio news reporting before NPR. For the most part, radio news had meant reporters reading scripts. NPR sought to pioneer the regular use of sound in its reporting, drawing mental images more vivid than the pictures seen on television.

Even the titles of its programs suggested open-ended possibilities rather than a well-defined concept.

Public radio's initial news program would be called not *The NPR Nightly News* but *All Things Considered*, suggesting both the unlimited range of its interests and the careful consideration it would give to all issues it tackled.

Siemering drafted the program's purposes as a member of the initial board. He then took on the task of implementing them as NPR's first director of programming. In the six months between his arrival at NPR's temporary facilities in Washington in November of 1970 and the program's debut the following May, Siemering took great care in hiring individuals who resonated with his vision statement. Concern with shared vision and personal compatibility outweighed more traditional standards, such as experience. In a sense, anyone with deep experience in traditional broadcasting and journalism had the wrong experience for what was to be a totally new departure. Symbolizing the priority of innovation over traditional broadcast standards, Siemering turned down an offer from the Ford Foundation to fund the salary of veteran news analyst Edward P. Morgan to anchor the new program. Siemering did not question Morgan's competence. He simply wanted something fresh.

All Things Considered's first anchor and "managing editor," then, was not Edward P. Morgan but a relatively obscure former reporter for *The New York Times* and National Broadcasting Company (NBC) Television named Robert Conley. Conley brought with him one of his former editors at *The Times*, Cleve Matthews, who would direct the news operations. Josh Darsa, formerly of CBS Television, gave NPR another experienced hand and another staff member over the age of 30. In contrast to Conley, Matthews, and Darsa, however, a motley group of young, idealistic, creative, energetic men and women more comfortable with the counterculture than conventional journalism dominated the initial staff of *ATC* and formed its distinctive personality. Men still dominated broadcasting and journalism in 1971, and affirmative action was not yet the law of the land, but Siemering hired as many women as men for the initial staff and insisted on minority representation. Only a staff representative of the whole population, he felt, could produce a program that really served the needs and interests of the whole population.

True to the spirit of the times, the character of the staff, and Siemering's own instincts, the program operated as something of a commune during its first nine months. No one was in charge. Three different individuals hosted the program during that time. The program's vision was open ended, its implementation unreliable, and the working conditions chaotic. NPR management told Siemering he would lose his job if he did not give someone operating authority over the staff and program. After consulting members of "the commune," Siemering gave the task to one of the "senior" members of the staff, 30-year-old Jack Mitchell, who imposed a structure on the previously free format and sought to develop a more consistent personality for the show. He changed the theme music from a playful little tune composed by Don Voegeli (a veteran musician at WHA in Madison, Wisconsin) to a more forceful "news" version of Voegeli's basic melody. He broke the program into three half-hour segments, fixed newscasts at the top of each hour, and organized each half hour to move from "hard news" to softer features. Commentaries by "real people" from across the country were an attempt to realize Siemering's democratic vision of radio. Commentaries by immortal broadcasters such as Goodman Ace, John Henry Faulk, and Henry Morgan provided a link to radio's golden age. Key to the program's evolving personality, however, would be two program hosts, a man and a woman, who would conduct their own interviews in addition to introducing produced reports. Siemering had described the hosting role as a neutral, unobtrusive "picture frame" that never called attention to itself; Mitchell moved the hosts into the picture.

ATC's first hosting team paired Mike Waters, a man with a warm voice and a natural ability to tell engaging stories, with Susan Stamberg, an enthusiastic interviewer willing to laugh out loud and reveal the emotions of a real human being. Stamberg was the first female co-anchor of a major national nightly news program, as NPR pointed out in newspaper ads when American Broadcasting Company (ABC) Television touted its appointment of Barbara Walters to co-anchor its evening network newscast as a "first." As much as her gender, Stamberg's New York accent and brash personality polarized listeners, stations, and the NPR management. When she talked on the air about her son Josh or gave her famous recipe for cranberry relish each Thanksgiving, Stamberg provided a human identity that told the world that this program was different from anything else on the air. Susan Stamberg came to personify *All Things Considered*, NPR, and public radio as a whole. Neither Waters nor Stamberg considered themselves journalists. Neither was especially interested in "news." Indeed, their ability to identify with the lay listener, posing "uninformed" questions that any reasonably intelligent non-expert might ask about complex issues, may have been part of their appeal.

In 1974 *ATC* expanded into the weekend. Waters took over the weekend assignment and was replaced on weekdays by Bob Edwards, another fine voice and excellent reader who, like Waters, provided a calming counterpoint to Stamberg's exuberance and who, unlike Waters, cared deeply about news. Many believe that Stamberg and Edwards set the standard for NPR hosting during their five years together, a period in which listeners in large numbers discovered the program and bonded with the co-hosts and the institution they represented. This "perfect" combination split in 1979, when Edwards moved to host NPR's second major news effort, *Morning Edition.*

Morning Edition grew out of the example of *All Things Considered,* drawing its values, approach, and even its host from the older program. At the same time, however, *Morning Edition* changed *All Things Considered.* It broke up the team of Stamberg and Edwards, of course, but more important, *Morning Edition* turned NPR into a 24-hour-a-day news operation and forced the network to drastically increase its news-gathering capacity. Future ABC News star Cokie Roberts began her broadcasting career at NPR at about that time, joining the indomitable Nina Totenberg, who had come to NPR four years earlier, to become two of Washington's most prominent and respected news reporters. Although Siemering had written that NPR's daily magazine would include "some hard news," the program instead evolved into a primary vehicle for breaking news coverage. NPR transformed itself into a competitive news organization, eventually filling the void for quality journalism created by the decline of serious news reporting and analysis on commercial radio and the simultaneous reduction of foreign news-gathering capacity by those networks. *All Things Considered* became more serious in its approach to news, constantly raising its journalistic standards and focusing increasingly on international news as commercial radio abandoned these interests. The "alternative" to traditional broadcast journalism became the bastion of journalistic standards. The hard news squeezed, but never eliminated, the softer elements of the program that had distinguished *ATC* in its early years.

Sanford Unger, a print reporter with a journalistic résumé far stronger than that of any previous NPR host, symbolized ATC's evolving role as a serious player in the world of Washington journalism when he took over Edward's seat next to Stamberg. Unfortunately, Unger's on-air persona did not match his journalistic prowess. He moved on, to be replaced in 1983 by Noah Adams, who,

like Mike Waters, was an "unknown" from within the NPR staff who had a soothing voice, a near-magical sense of radio, and only a marginal interest in hard news.

Tiring of the daily grind and not quite comfortable with the hardening of ATC's news values, both Stamberg and Adams left the program four years later in 1987–Stamberg to host the new *Weekend Edition Sunday,* a feature-oriented program that would better suit her interests, and Adams to Minnesota to take over the Saturday night slot vacated by Garrison Keillor when Keillor moved to Denmark to live with his new wife.

Thus, in a sense, *All Things Considered* started over in 1987 with a harder journalistic edge. News Vice President Robert Siegel decided to give up his big office for the chance to anchor *All Things Considered.* Reporter Rene Montaigne joined him as co-host for one year. At the end of that year, Garrison Keillor was back on Saturday night, and Noah Adams was back at NPR. The news-oriented Siegel and the feature-oriented Adams might have made an outstanding complementary team had they not both been men. NPR solved the dilemma by adding political and congressional correspondent Linda Wertheimer to the mix as a third host. Siegel, Adams, and Wertheimer would share the hosting duties, and each would have time to do some reporting as well. That arrangement served the interests of the three hosts and the philosophy of NPR's president, Doug Bennet, who chose to downplay individual personalities in favor of NPR's institutional identity as a news organization. Three interchangeable hosts on *All Things Considered* symbolized the interchangeability of reporters and other staff in an organization whose success and credibility should transcend that of any individual.

NPR's next president, Delano Lewis, expanded *All Things Considered* from 90 minutes to two hours in 1995 and moved the program forward by one hour to 4:00 P.M. EDT, to better fit peak afternoon drive-time listening. At the same time, breaks were added within each half hour, dividing the program into shorter segments similar to its companion program, *Morning Edition.* The extra time allowed *All Things Considered* to do more "soft" material among the "hard news."

Beginning with its first Peabody Award in 1973 for its "distinctive approach to broadcast journalism," *All Things Considered* has won virtually every award for broadcast journalism excellence.

All Things Considered continued winning awards in the new century. It added Michele Norris as a host in late 2002, and Melissa Block joined the program as cohost in 2003. Thanks to the sheer luck of having NPR News hosts Block and Robert Siegel and already reporting from Chengdu, China for a special week of *ATC*, the network was able to feature live reports from the scene of a huge earthquake that killed thousands of people in May 2008. It was one of the very few western journalist "voices" able to do so.

See also: Easy Aces; *Morning Edition*; National Public Radio; Peabody Awards and Archive; Public Radio Since 1967

Hosts

Robert Conley (1971), Jim Russell (1971), Mike Waters (1971–74), Susan Stamberg (1972–86), Bob Edwards (1974–79), Sanford Unger (1980–83), Noah Adams (1983–86), Robert Siegel (1986–87), Rene Montaigne (1986–87), Robert Siegel (1988–), Noah Adams (1988–2002), Linda Wertheimer (1988–2002), Michelle Norris (2002–), Melissa Block (2003–)

Programming History

National Public Radio   1971–present

Further Reading

Collins, Mary, *National Public Radio: The Cast of Characters*, Washington, D.C.: Seven Locks Press, 1993.
Engelman, Ralph, *Public Radio and Television in America: A Political History*, Thousand Oaks, California: Sage, 1996.
Looker, Thomas, *The Sound and the Story: NPR and the Art of Radio*, Boston: Houghton Mifflin, 1995.
Siegel, Robert, editor, *The NPR Interviews, 1994*, Boston: Houghton Mifflin, 1994.
Stamberg, Susan, *Every Night at Five: Susan Stamberg's All Things Considered Book*, New York: Pantheon, 1982.
Wertheimer, Linda, editor, *Listening to America: Twenty-Five Years in the Life of a Nation, As Heard on National Public Radio*, Boston: Houghton Mifflin, 1995.

JACK MITCHELL,
2009 REVISIONS BY CHRISTOPHER H. STERLING

ALTERNATIVE FORMAT

Responding to a perceived lack of inventiveness on rock music stations, some musicians and modern rock fans embraced a more experimental, less packaged, alternative sound in the 1990s. Compared to the mainstream rock primarily played on Album-Oriented Rock (AOR) stations, alternative was unpolished and unabashed; its lyrics spoke of both idealism and disenfranchisement. Radio programmers, recognizing a new trend with counter-programming potential, added alternative tracks to their playlists, developing what became known as the *alternative format*. For advertisers and record labels seeking to expand their reach, commercial alternative formats provide a highly targeted and efficient medium similar to the alternative press.

The alternative format has been implemented in a variety of ways. The hard edged modern rock version may include talkups, sounders, and contesting similar to Contemporary Hit Radio (CHR). Adult Alternative Album (AAA) is essentially an album-oriented rock format, but with an alternative playlist. College alternative radio, where much of the sound found its original support, often takes an eclectic approach. Other variants may include shock jocks, techno music, or music with urban appeal.

Although the alternative radio movement emerged in the 1990s, its lineage extends back through the punk rock/new wave movement of the late 1970s and progressive radio of the late 1960s to rebellious rock and roll radio of the 1950s. Each of these movements emerged from a fervent subculture demonstrating a certain disdain for what was perceived as popular music at the time. Characterized by garage bands, small venue live performances, and low budget recordings distributed by independent labels, alternative's back-to-basics approach, rejection of glitzy production, and youthful self-expression have paradoxically had popular appeal as Music Television (MTV), college radio, and rock promoters began successfully packaging and selling the new musical genre to an increasingly fragmented market. Commercial radio success, initially in the San Francisco and Seattle areas, the popularity of alternative music on college campuses, and digital distribution—including MP3 audio files on the internet—have all contributed to the vibrancy of the alternative format.

Alternative has also been known as the anti-format, associated with independent, community stations focused on political issues and social change, such as those operated in the U.S. by the Pacifica group. It may also refer to those global broadcasters with alternative worldviews and alternative means of distribution, such as the internet.

In the latter part of the new century's first decade, HD2 programming—especially in larger markets—witnessed the rollout of some alternative commercial format offerings.

See also: Album-Oriented Rock Format; Contemporary Hit Radio/Top 40 Format; Pacifica Foundation; Progressive Rock Format

Further Reading

Campbell, Richard, *Media and Culture: An Introduction to Mass Communication*, New York: St. Martin's Press, 1998; 2nd edition, by Campbell, Christopher R. Martin, and Bettina Fabos, Boston: Bedford/St. Martin's Press, 2000.

Free Speech Radio News website, www.fsrn.org.

Lasar, Matthew, *Pacifica Radio: The Rise of an Alternative Network*, Philadelphia, Pennsylvania: Temple University Press, 1999.

Vivian, John, *Media of Mass Communication*, Boston: Allyn and Bacon, 1991; 5th edition, 1998.

Walker, Jesse, *Rebels on the Air: An Alternative History of Radio in America*, New York: New York University Press, 2001.

JOSEPH R. PIASEK,
2009 REVISIONS BY MICHAEL C. KEITH

AMALGAMATED BROADCASTING SYSTEM

U.S. Radio Network

The Amalgamated Broadcasting System, which survived as a corporation for 13 months but operated as an actual radio network for a mere five weeks, is better known for the myths surrounding it than for the facts of its brief existence. Despite the claims of many so-called "old-time radio" scholars, Amalgamated was never associated with station WNEW in New York (which did not exist until after the network fell into bankruptcy) and the EW in that call sign did not derive from the initials of Amalgamated's founder, comedian Ed Wynn.

Origins

Amalgamated was founded in the fall of 1932, as a program production agency. Wynn's partners in the venture were Broadway producers Arthur Hopkins and T.W. Richardson, and Hungarian-born violinist and promoter Ota Gygi. Initial press releases hinted that Irving Berlin and Daniel Frohman were interested in the project and that more than a million dollars had been committed by two nationally known agencies.

Despite these claims, nothing further was heard of the venture until January 1933 when George W. Trendle, president of the newly formed All-Michigan Network, announced his alliance with the Wynn group. The New York flagship of the network would be made up of an amalgamation of three small time-sharing stations controlled by Walter Whetstone's Standard-Cahill Corporation: WBNX, WCDA, and WMSG. This would be the first step, declared Trendle, toward building a nationwide chain of low-powered regional stations. Trendle

claimed, without naming names, that five Detroit millionaires were backing the venture and that Wynn had enlisted the support of practically every theatrical man of note and 13 prominent authors.

The next five months were filled with promises but little substance. Wynn went into detail in the trade press describing the policy of the new network, declaring that it would limit advertising to indirect messages at the beginning and end of each program and that he himself planned to appear occasionally on the network once his National Broadcasting Company-Texaco contract expired. Studio space was prepared in a newly constructed building at 501 Madison Avenue in New York City, arrangements were made with Western Union for network lines, and several dates were announced for the start of broadcasting, only to be postponed at the last minute.

The industry was fast losing patience with Wynn's stalling. In the 1 June 1933 issue of *Broadcasting*, editor Sol Taishoff portrayed Amalgamated as an amateurish, slipshod operation, run entirely by show people who were decidedly naive about the realities of the broadcasting business. There was no longer any mention of Detroit millionaires and, even though the son-in-law of President Roosevelt, Curtis B. Dall, joined the company in August as chairman of the board, it was becoming evident to observers that the network's money was coming primarily out of Ed Wynn's pocket.

Operations

The Amalgamated network finally went on the air on the evening of 25 September 1933. Thirteen small Eastern stations carried the initial program—flagship WBNX; WCNW in Brooklyn, New York; WPEN in Philadelphia, Pennsylvania; WDEL in Wilmington, Delaware; WCBM in Baltimore, Maryland; WOL in Washington, D.C.; WCAP in Asbury Park, New Jersey; WHDH in Boston, Massachusetts; WCAX in Burlington, Vermont; WPRO in Providence, Rhode Island; WNBH in New Bedford, Massachusetts; WSAR in Fall River, Massachusetts; and WFAS in White Plains, New York. Despite claims that the network would soon span the continent, no additional stations were ever added.

Critic Ben Gross described the inaugural broadcast as chaotic, but a surviving recording reveals that it was in reality a dull hodgepodge of mediocre talent, the major exception being an appearance by the dynamic Broadway vocalist Jules Bledsoe.

There were no commercial announcements, but on-air credits were quietly slipped into the program for the firms that provided the bar for the guests and the beer they were served. Although Gross claimed that there were hundreds of complaints from listeners unable to hear the broadcast because the noise from the rowdy studio audience drowned out the performers, the recording makes it clear that this was a fabrication. The only complaints noted in a post-broadcast article in *Broadcasting* were from technicians, who suggested that the Western Union telegraph network lines were somewhat noisier than AT&T telephone circuits. Wynn himself was not present for the inaugural, because he was occupied with motion-picture duties in Hollywood and had left Gygi in full charge of the network in his absence.

Collapse

The story of Amalgamated has a beginning and an end, but no middle. No sponsorships were ever sold. During October, a 15-hour-a-day schedule of music and talk was fed to the small eastern hookup that had taken the opening broadcast, but clearance of these sustaining programs (programs not paid for by advertising) proved difficult when affiliates insisted on carrying their own local, sponsored features.

Curtis Dall resigned as chairman of Amalgamated in early October. Ed Wynn returned to New York in mid-October and soon realized the futility of the venture. He resigned on 23 October, claiming to have spent $250,000 on the project with no hope of any return. Subsequent investigation by receivers revealed that Wynn's out-of-pocket investment was closer to $125,000.

At midnight on 1 November the network halted service to its 12 affiliates. On 3 November creditors foreclosed and Amalgamated passed into the hands of the Irving Trust Company. Liabilities totaled $38,000, with $10,000 owed in salaries to the company's 200 employees.

The assets of the network were sold at auction on 18 December, raising $10,841 toward the settlement of outstanding claims. The studio equipment was purchased for $9,800 by advertising executive Milton Biow for use in his new station in Newark, WNEW. WNEW would subsequently lease the former Amalgamated studio space at 501 Madison Avenue for its New York studio.

Ed Wynn resolved to settle all of the network's remaining debts. The stresses involved in the Amalgamated venture contributed to the failure of his marriage in 1937 and ultimately to a nervous breakdown. Ever the promoter, Ota Gygi spent much of 1934 trying to form yet another "new network" among stations in the Midwest, but he had lost all credibility. Several former Amalgamated stations became part of George Storer's American Broadcasting System.

Further Reading

"ABS Auction Sale Raises Back Pay," *Broadcasting* (1 January 1934).
"ABS Bankrupt As Comedian Is Blamed," *Broadcasting* (15 November 1933).
"ABS Chain Makes Debut," *The Billboard* (30 September 1933).
"ABS Swan Song," *Broadcasting* (15 November 1933).
"Amalgamated Net Gets Started," *Broadcasting* (1 October 1933).
"Creative Radio Program Service Headed by Ed Wynn," *Broadcasting* (1 October 1932).
"Ed Wynn Resigns Amalgamated Post," *Broadcasting* (1 November 1933).
Gross, Ben, *I Looked and I Listened: Informal Recollections of Radio and TV*, New York: Random House, 1954.
"New Third Network Embraces Old Plans," *Broadcasting* (1 February 1933).
Taishoff, Sol, "Lack of Practical Broadcaster Hampers Wynn Network Venture," *Broadcasting* (1 June 1933).
Wynn, Ed, "Why a Third Chain?" *The Billboard* (30 September 1933).
Wynn, Keenan, and James Brough, *Ed Wynn's Son*, Garden City, New York: Doubleday, 1959.

ELIZABETH MCLEOD

AMERICAN BROADCASTING COMPANY

The American Broadcasting Company (ABC) came late to the radio game, appearing as an independent network only in 1945. As such, it was a weak player until the 1960s, when ABC was in the vanguard of an attempt to revive and reshape network radio in the age of television.

Origins

ABC—as a network and an owner of major radio stations—was created in the 1940s, when the Federal Communications Commission and the Department of Justice forced the National Broadcasting Company's (NBC) owner, the Radio Corporation of America (RCA), to spin off one of NBC's two radio networks. In 1943 Edward J. Noble, who had made his fortune creating, manufacturing, and selling Life Savers candy, bought NBC's Blue network and three owned and operated stations for $8 million. In 1945 Noble renamed Blue the American Broadcasting Company and began to build ABC. In 1946, for example, he acquired WXYZ-AM in Detroit from KingTrendle Broadcasting for slightly less than $3 million.

The Blue network carried a number of popular shows—including *Just Plain Bill*, *Easy Aces*, *Inner Sanctum Mystery*, and *Lum 'n' Abner*. But generally ABC shows drew last place in ratings in all of Golden Age radio's categories of programming. In the variety category, for example, ABC's *The Alan Young Show* earned but a seventh of the ratings of NBC's *Bob Hope Program*, which broadcast later the same night. The *Andrews Sisters* program drew a third of the ratings of *Your Hit Parade* on the Columbia Broadcasting System (CBS), and *Ted Mack's Original Amateur Hour* always finished far behind *Arthur Godfrey's Talent Scouts*.

Still, Drew Pearson attracted vast audiences with his reports of the goings-on in the nation's capital, and the dramatic and controversial re-creations of the *March of Time* were popular as well, helped by the movie newsreel of the same name and by the program's connection with *Time* magazine. On the prestige side, ABC's regular Saturday matinee broadcasts of the Metropolitan Opera added some class to ABC's image.

It was not that Edward Noble was not willing to acquire top talent. During the late 1940s, Noble and his managers tried to add new shows, such as *Professor Quiz*, *Break the Bank*, *This Is Your FBI*, *Lone Ranger*, *Gillette Fights*, and *Gang Busters*. For example, when ABC bought WXYZ-AM, it acquired *Lone Ranger* and *Green Hornet*. A far more temporary triumph came with the hiring of Milton Berle, for this comic appeared on the ABC radio network for only one year before, looking for a showcase better suited to his visual style, he moved to NBC television and became a national sensation.

There were two notable exceptions. In 1946 Bing Crosby moved to the ABC radio network for reasons of convenience and technical change. Crosby, who was then at the very height of his popularity as a singer and movie star, agreed to move to ABC because NBC was forcing him to broadcast his show live twice, once for the eastern and central time zones and then a second time for stations based in the mountain and pacific time zones. Crosby wanted to use audiotape to record his show at his convenience. ABC executives were more than willing to permit Crosby to use the then-new audiotape technology to record his show ahead of time and then hit the links when listeners thought he was in the studio broadcasting to them.

During summer 1946, Crosby shocked the industry when he announced he was leaving NBC and long-time sponsor Kraft to sign with Philco,

maker of radio sets, and appear on ABC. His weekly salary was announced at a staggering $7,500. Because Philco and ABC permitted Crosby to prerecord his *Philco Radio Time*, he was nowhere near the studio when his show debuted on Wednesday night, 16 October 1946. The Philco show proved a major ratings triumph. Because of its success, three years later, when CBS chief William S. Paley was in the midst of his celebrated "talent raids," he lured Crosby away from his three-year run on ABC. *Philco Radio Time* last ran on ABC on 1 June 1949.

The other exception to ABC's normal ratings mediocrity started in March 1948 when *Stop the Music!* premiered. Listeners quickly embraced this giant jackpot quiz show. With master of ceremonies Bert Parks as its host, musical selections were played by the Harry Salter Orchestra or sung by vocalists Kay Armen and Dick Brown. While a song was played, a telephone call was placed to a home somewhere in the United States, and when the caller answered, Parks called out "stop the music." If the person at home could name the tune, he or she won up to $20,000.

Listeners flocked to ABC on Sunday nights, and by the summer ABC truly had a hit, doubling the audience reached by Fred Allen at NBC and *Sam Spade* on CBS. With ratings high from the beginning, sponsors lined up, and ABC selected Old Gold cigarettes and Spiedel jewelry as the main advertisers. During summer 1948, demand for tickets was so high that the producers moved the show to the 4,000-seat Capitol Theater in the heart of Times Square. But ABC could not sustain the hit, and by 1952 the radio version was off the air. The fledgling ABC television network kept it on the tube—originally as just a simulcast—until 1956.

As the Golden Age in radio was ending, ABC certainly matched Mutual as a radio network, but it was rarely as successful as NBC and CBS. Building ABC as a radio network was always a struggle, yet from a network with 168 owned or affiliated stations as of the October 1943 purchase date, Noble and his managers doubled affiliations within a decade. Indeed, owning and operating radio stations and a network was lucrative enough that Noble—with the help of a $5 million loan from the Prudential Insurance Company of America—was able to launch the ABC television network. By the beginning of the 1950s, ABC not only owned a radio network and the maximum allowable number of AM and FM radio stations, but had also reached the legal limit on television stations as well—five. So successful was ABC that Noble began to attract bidders for his enterprise.

The United Paramount Takeover

In 1951, in what was up to that point the biggest transaction in broadcasting history, United Paramount (the chain of movie houses formerly owned by Paramount Pictures) paid $25 million to add ABC's five television stations, six FM radio stations, and six AM radio stations to its 644 theaters in nearly 300 cities across the United States. The FCC took two years to finally approve the deal. ABC would never have become a modern radio and television corporate powerhouse had it not been acquired by United Paramount, greatly adding to its financial resources. Leonard H. Goldenson, head of United Paramount, began to sell theaters and real estate to generate the cash necessary to build up ABC television first and ABC radio second.

On the radio side, Goldenson faced a challenge. Most of ABC's radio affiliates were lower-power stations in smaller cities. When forced to divest RCA of the Blue network a decade earlier, RCA had stacked the deck, making sure that what he transferred with Blue represented the least valuable of NBC's stations. To generate income, ABC radio management, headed by Robert Kintner, allowed advertising for products considered inappropriate by the mighty NBC and CBS, such as deodorants and laxatives. But in 1953 Goldenson felt radio would need to change as television became America's top mass medium. With AM radio now standard equipment on most new cars, and with the innovation of the inexpensive portable radio set, Goldenson reasoned that a radio market would always exist, but in a different form than had worked in the past. The question for ABC—and for all of radio in 1953—was how best to exploit the changing radio medium.

Goldenson realized that while United Paramount had gained a network with the ABC purchase, more important were the stations located in some of the nation's largest markets. The flagship station in New York City—WJZ-AM—was his most valuable radio asset, worth more than the then-struggling ABC radio network. Still, whereas WNBC-AM had studios at Radio City, WJZ-AM broadcast from a modest renovated building at 7 West 66th Street, one block west of Central Park. On 1 May 1953—six and a half years after the rival network's stations were named WNBC-AM and WCBSAM in honor of their respective parent companies—Goldenson renamed his New York City outlet WABC-AM and worked to make this 50,000-watt powerhouse a metropolitan fixture at "77" on the AM band.

Programming proved harder to change, so Goldenson stuck with what was working for the time being. In the mid-1950s that meant shows such as American Safety Razor's *Walter Winchell* on Sunday nights; Anheuser Busch's *Bill Stern's Sports Reports* at 6:30 P.M. three times a week; General Mills' *Lone Ranger* at 7:30 P.M. on Mondays, Wednesdays, and Fridays; and Mutual of Omaha's *Breakfast Club* in the mornings. Goldenson's innovation was to hire local personalities to develop followings only within the New York City metropolitan market. For WABC-AM, this meant in time Peter Lind Hayes and Mary Healy, Martin Block, Ernie Kovacs, Howard Cosell (and his sports reports), commentators John Daly and Edward P. Morgan, and rock disc jockey sensation Alan Freed.

The transition of WABC-AM to the highest-rated rock station in the United States began modestly with Martin Block's *Make Believe Ballroom,* which Goldenson bought in 1954. But it was the June 1958 hiring of Alan Freed that would signal the future of WABC-AM as a Top 40 profit-generating powerhouse. Freed would soon burn out in the payola scandals, but WABC disc jockeys "Cousin Brucie," "Big Dan Ingram," and others replaced him, and by the arrival of the Beatles in early 1964, WABC-AM had become one of the nation's most-listened-to radio stations.

Goldenson's management team rebuilt the other owned and operated ABC radio stations: WLS-AM in Chicago, WXYZAM in Detroit, KABC-AM (formerly KECA-AM) in Hollywood, KQV-AM in Pittsburgh, and KGO-AM in San Francisco. Each would soon take its place among the top-rated stations in its metropolitan area. Each also beefed up an FM license that had been underutilized.

For example, Chicago's clear channel WLS-AM was transformed from a major-market network affiliate to a rock and roll pioneer, beaming Top 40 hits across the Midwestern states. As the 1960s commenced, WLS-AM had joined the Top 40 elite and was being built up by a number of local disc jockey stars—none hotter, or more famous, than Larry Lujack. For a generation of listeners in the 1960s and 1970s, Lujack created and defined rock and roll.

Similar histories could be traced for all of ABC's major radio stations. In Detroit, for example, WXYZ-AM was also transformed into a radio powerhouse, and by Goldenson's own calculations it functioned as ABC's most profitable radio outlet during the 1950s and 1960s. If the selling of United Paramount's theaters and valuable real estate is properly credited with underwriting ABC television network deals with Hollywood's Walt Disney and Warner Brothers Companies, one must also credit the revenues generated by profitable radio stations such as WXYZ-AM. Indeed, the rebuilding of AM radio stations was going so well that in 1957 Goldenson separated the television side (which required fashioning alliances with Hollywood) from the radio side (which needed to transform existing properties into local hot spots, station by station) of the business. With this separation, Goldenson emphasized that television and radio management required quite different skills.

Leonard Goldenson's Radio Network Innovations

Although Leonard H. Goldenson has never been labeled as one of radio's top leaders—in the league of NBC's David Sarnoff or CBS's William S. Paley—many consider that he ought to be. Despite all the hiring and firing of radio talent during the 1950s and 1960s, ABC management at the top varied little as Goldenson and his small set of advisers built ABC radio (and television) into highly profitable media institutions. By 1985, when he stepped down, Goldenson had created a modern media conglomerate. This small-town poor boy from Pennsylvania, who managed to graduate from Harvard Law School, learned the mass entertainment business at Paramount Pictures and took over its divested theater division in 1950. He already had some experience in television from Paramount's owned and operated television station in Chicago, WBKB-TV. He had no experience in radio, but he knew of its success as an entertainment medium in cities where Paramount operated theaters.

Although most kudos for Goldenson goes to his development of the ABC television network, media historians also recognize his reinvention of network radio. By refashioning a single all-things-to-all-audiences network into four—and later more—specialized radio networks in the late 1960s, Leonard Goldenson earned his place as a radio pioneer. ABC was transformed from a single radio network into the American Contemporary Network, the American Information Network, the American Entertainment Network, and the American FM Network. This specialization would set the model for network radio for the next three decades.

However, Goldenson's most significant innovation almost did not come to be. By the early 1960s Goldenson thought he had built up and milked his major-market stations for as much as he could, and he considered abandoning network radio altogether.

He seriously entertained bids to sell the ABC radio network—plus all its valuable stations—to Westinghouse for a price reported to be $50 million. But once he got over the shock of the unexpected size of Westinghouse's offer, Goldenson figured that this substantial bid by Westinghouse's experienced executives did not signal the end of the Top 40 radio era; rather, new forms of radio broadcasting did have a future. He turned down Westinghouse and successfully continued to build his own radio empire as part of what was (and is) often incorrectly considered simply a television network business operation.

At the time, breaking with the mold of a single network was considered a risky proposition. The executives directly responsible for the network radio turnabout were Hal Neal and Ralph Beaudin, who had made their reputations by turning ABC-owned and -operated stations into rock and roll powerhouses. The four networks were patterned from formats of the day. The American Contemporary Network stressed middle of the road music and soft-spoken middle-aged disc jockeys. The American Information Network was all news and talk, patterned after the all-news local stations that CBS and Westinghouse were then pioneering. The American Entertainment Network was a piped-in Top 40 feed, and the FM network was a grab bag, because no-one honestly knew the future of FM at that point.

In planning the four networks, Goldenson, who was already paying American Telephone and Telegraph (AT&T) for transmission by land lines, figured that four would cost only a bit more than one transmission for facilities that were being under-utilized. Talent could be drawn from owned and operated stations. By late 1966 the plan for the four networks was in place, and Goldenson gave notice to all advertisers and affiliated stations that the year 1967 would be the final year for ABC as a single radio network. During summer 1967, ABC began heavy promotion of the four-network idea, and quadruple feeds commenced on the first day of 1968 to 500 affiliates.

In the first year of the four-network operation, 1968, Goldensen was criticized because ABC lost $8 million. But just four years later the radio division alone was making more than $4 million annually. But by 1972 the network radio division was making $4 million profit per year. As the 1970s ended, ABC's network radio division had 1,500 affiliates and was making $17 million profit per year. In the late 1970s, ABC Contemporary had about 400 affiliates, and the American Information Network had almost 500 affiliates, as did the

American Entertainment Network; however, the American FM Network never moved past 200 affiliates. The recasting and specializing of network radio worked for AM stations, but FM gradually found musical niches that would make them the leaders in radio ratings in most markets by 1980.

Goldenson continued to tinker with the format profile of both ABC's owned and operated stations and its growing number of networks. The advertising community applauded Goldenson's adaptation of focused demographics. In August 1970 ABC separated management of AM from FM owned and operated radio stations, and with the progressive rock format ABC began to remake FM outlets, which had long merely simulcast AM.

Takeovers

As the 1980s commenced, Goldenson began to slow down. In 1980 his ABC television network ranked number one, and he was able to tout ABC's radio stations as among the most popular in the nation. For example, WABC-AM in New York abandoned Top 40—after 22 years—and soon made even more money with "talk."

Goldenson needed to find a suitable successor. He wanted to pass "his" company to someone who had the skills to consistently and profitably run a mature multibillion-dollar media empire. After much looking and interviewing, Goldenson met Thomas Murphy, head of Capital Cities Broadcasting, a 30-year-old media company that as the 1980s began owned seven television stations, 12 radio stations, an assortment of daily and weekly newspapers, and an additional assortment of magazines. Capital Cities was a Wall Street high flyer, known for its efficient management by Murphy and Dan Burke. Goldenson decided that Capital Cities was the logical successor to takeover the ABC radio and television networks he had created.

At the time the deal was announced, in March 1985, it was the largest non-oil merger ever, at $3.5 billion. But although headlines warned of vast changes and ominous negative implications for news and entertainment, none ever really materialized. Murphy, Burke, and their Capital Cities executives simply merged the two media companies, sold off some duplicative properties, and then continued the process of fashioning an even more profitable, even larger media enterprise than Goldenson had created—one that encompassed forms of mass media from print to television and from film-making to radio network and station operation.

In radio, Murphy, Burke, and company changed almost nothing. They tinkered on the margins as they tried to follow (not set) trends. They smoothly and efficiently managed format makeovers as Top 40 rock and roll gave way to other formats of pop music. In general, Murphy and Burke transformed ABC's large-city AM powerhouse stations, often to middle of the road talk-format operations. Consider the example of Chicago's WLS-AM, symbol of the Top 40 era. When Murphy and Burke took over, its ratings were slipping, and so they worked to reformat WLS-AM again, even as FM was draining away listeners. By the early 1990s, WLS-AM became news-plus-talk radio 890, with no "hot jock," but instead the ramblings of Dr. Laura Schlessinger and Rush Limbaugh. Such transformations took place throughout the matrix of ABC stations, as radio continued to provide core profits to the company now known as Capital Cities/ABC.

In 1996 Murphy and Burke themselves neared retirement age, and, as Goldenson had done, they sought an alliance with a company to continue ABC. In 1996 the biggest merger in media history was announced when the Walt Disney Company acquired Capital Cities/ABC. Overnight, Disney, far more famous for its movie making and theme parks, became one of the top competitors in the world of radio.

When Disney announced its takeover of Capital Cities/ABC at the end of July 1996, the headlines blared about vast potential synergies of a Hollywood studio and a television network. Radio was considered an afterthought. Still, with New York City flagship station WABC-AM leading the list, Disney now had important radio promotional outlets in a half-dozen other top-ten media markets: in media market 2 Los Angeles (three stations), in market 3 Chicago (two stations), in market 4 San Francisco (two stations), in market 6 Detroit (three stations), in market 7 Dallas (two stations), and in market 8 Washington, D.C. (three stations).

Disney concentrated on these big cities, but its radio holdings paled in comparison to rival radio powers of the late 20th century such as CBS and Clear Channel. Yet Disney's station reach always remained vast. Disney head Michael Eisner then looked and applied synergies to these urban radio stations. He sold off Capital Cities/ABC's newspapers and other print operations but kept radio—even expanding Disney into more radio with the September 1997 launch of a new network, the ESPN radio network, with its exclusive rights for Major League Baseball for five years. Eisner also rolled out Radio Disney, a live network for families and children under age 12 with a select playlist of special music, much of it from Disney movies and television programs.

Shortly after Eisner stepped down as Disney CEO in October 2005, the company put its 22 ABC radio stations and its radio network up for sale. After a lengthy bidding war with several players, Disney sold its radio holdings to Citadel Broadcasting in a $2.5 billion sale in mid-2007. Citadel marketed the acquisition as "ABC Radio," and created and distributed programming to more than 4,000 affiliates. ABC's parent company, The Walt Disney Company, however, has maintained a place in radio through its on-air and online Radio Disney service, which it markets as the only 24/7, listener-driven radio network for children and families.

See also: Network Monopoly Probe; Radio Disney; Talent Raids; WABC; WLS; WXYZ

Further Reading

ABC Radio, www.abcradio.com.

Berle, Milton, and Haskel Frankel, *Milton Berle: An Autobiography*, New York: Delacorte Press, 1974.

Buxton, Frank, and William Hugh Owen, *Radio's Golden Age: The Programs and the Personalities*, New York: Easton Valley Press, 1966; revised edition, as *The Big Broadcast, 1920–1950*, New York: Viking Press, 1972.

Compaine, Benjamin M., *Who Owns the Media? Concentration of Ownership in the Mass Communications Industry*, White Plains, New York: Knowledge Industry, 1979; 3rd edition, as *Who Owns the Media? Competition and Concentration in the Mass Media Industry*, by Compaine and Douglas Gomery, Mahwah, New Jersey: Erlbaum, 2000.

Federal Communications Commission, Mass Media Bureau, Policy and Rules Division, *Review of the Radio Industry, 1997*, Docket MM 98–35 (13 March 1998).

Fielding, Raymond, *The March of Time, 1935–1951*, New York: Oxford University Press, 1978.

Goldenson, Leonard H., and Marvin J. Wolf, *Beating the Odds: The Untold Story behind the Rise of ABC: The Stars, Struggles, and Egos That Transformed Network Television, by the Man Who Made Them Happen*, New York: Scribner, and Toronto, Ontario: Collier Macmillan Canada, 1991.

Grover, Ron, *The Disney Touch: How a Daring Management Team Revived an Entertainment Empire*, Homewood, Illinois: Business One Irwin, 1991; revised edition, as *The Disney Touch: Disney, ABC, and the Quest for the World's Greatest Media Empire*, Chicago: Irwin Professional, 1997.

Hickerson, Jay, *The Ultimate History of Network Radio Programming and Guide to All Circulating Shows*, Hamden, Connecticut: Hickerson, 1992; 3rd edition, as *The New, Revised, Ultimate History of Network Radio Programming and Guide to All Circulating Shows*, 1996.

Jaker, Bill, Frank Sulek, and Peter Kanze, *The Airwaves of New York: Illustrated Histories 0/156 AM Stations in the Metropolitan Area, 1921–1996*, Jefferson, North Carolina: McFarland, 1998.

Morgereth, Timothy A., *Bing Crosby: A Discography, Radio Program List, and Filmography*, Jefferson, North Carolina: McFarland, 1987.

Quinlan, Sterling, *Inside ABC: American Broadcasting Company's Rise to Power*, New York: Hastings House, 1979.

Rhoads, B. Eric, *Blast from the Past: A Pictorial History of Radio's First 75 Years*, West Palm Beach, Florida: Streamline, 1996.

"Special Report on ABC's Twenty-Fifth Anniversary," *Broadcasting* (13 February 1978).

Thomas, Bob, *Winchell*, Garden City, New York: Doubleday, 1971.

Whetmore, Edward Jay, *The Magic Medium: An Introduction to Radio in America*, Belmont, California: Wadsworth, 1981.

White, Llewellyn, *The American Radio: A Report on the Broadcasting Industry in the United States from the Commission on Freedom of the Press*, Chicago: University of Chicago Press, 1947.

Williams, Huntington, *Beyond Control: ABC and the Fate of the Networks*, New York: Atheneum, 1989.

DOUGLAS GOMERY AND CHUCK HOWELL,
2009 REVISIONS BY GAIL LOVE

AMERICAN FAMILY ROBINSON
Soap Opera Adventure Program

The National Association of Manufacturers (NAM) raised the character concept to an art with the soap opera adventure *American Family Robinson*. Syndicated by the World Broadcasting System from late 1934 to 1940, the 15-minute transcribed episodic drama was an anomaly among the NAM's nearly exclusive investment in printed public and political relations material. The NAM's politics, like its print-oriented publicity, were underwritten by the nation's largest industrial corporations, who were *Robinson* sponsors.

Provoked by the prolabor clauses of the New Deal's National Industrial Recovery Act (NRA), in 1933 the NAM embarked on a campaign of employer opposition that forestalled the imposition of collective bargaining in the steel, chemical, and auto industries. Announcing an "active campaign of education" in September of that year, Association President Robert L. Lund explained that NRA Section 7(a) posed a special threat to employers, given the "untruthful or misleading statements about the law" made by the American Federation of Labor and "communistic groups promoting union organization." Lund concluded that the American public would become favorably disposed toward business's traditional prerogatives and institutional choices if only business leaders would "tell its story."

Drawing upon the "home service personality" expertise of its packaged goods producers, the

NAM led the way in radio with the episodic adventures of the *American Family Robinson*. The program appears to have been proposed by Harry A. Bullis, General Mills vice president and chairman of NAM's public relations committee. The *American Family Robinson*'s drop-dead attacks on the New Deal reflected the print-oriented focus of the NAM's traditional publicity techniques. The interjection of editorial comment into the *Robinson*'s soap opera plot reduced series protagonist Luke Robinson, "the sanely philosophical editor of the *Centerville Herald*," to a caricature of the factory town newspaper editor that the NAM assiduously cultivated with an open-ended supply of pro-industry preprinted mats, columns, and tracts.

Editor Robinson, the program's repository of sound thinking and common sense, is beset by social schemers and panacea peddlers. Some are threatening and even criminal, but most are simply misguided. Among the latter is Robinson's brother-in-law, William Winkle, also know as "Windy" Bill, the itinerant inventor of the "housecar." Bill's meddlesome and uninformed political ideas are as unexpected as his unannounced visits with the Robinsons. More menacing is Professor Monroe Broadbelt, the "professional organizer of the Arcadians, a group using the Depression as a lever to pry money from converts to radical economic theories" (from *American Family Robinson,* cited in MacDonald, 1979).

The story line of the *American Family Robinson* revolves around the resolution of political conflict in the home and immediate community through the application of "time-tested principles." The Robinsons are shocked when their daughter Betty falls under the oratorical spell of Professor Broadbelt, a common criminal whose turn of phrase suggests a certain Hyde Park, New York, upbringing. Complications attend Betty's engagement to the Arcadians' charismatic leader, whose first consideration is his chosen mission: "The upliftment of mankind." Broadbelt's motives, however, are neither idealistic nor romantic. In the next episode, Luke Robinson helps apprehend Broadbelt, who has skipped town with the Arcadians' treasury. Returning to Centerville, Robinson presides over the liquidation of the Arcadian movement by publicly refunding the contributions of its confused and misguided members, including his daughter's.

In certain households, interest in the *American Family Robinson* undoubtedly did exist. The program attracted an articulate audience that appreciated and responded to the NAM's send-ups of New Deal liberalism. From fan mail the NAM learned that listeners responded enthusiastically to

Luke Robinson's comic foil "Windy" Bill. Written into the script as an incidental character, "Windy" soon returned to Centerville with a role expanded to include yet more meddlesome and annoying business. Other changes occurred as characters changed careers and took on new responsibilities. In 1935 Luke Robinson left the editorship of the *Centerville Herald* to become the assistant manager of the local furniture factory. Although Robinson remained the series' protagonist, a new character, "Gus Olsen," a janitor who had made the best of his lot in life, assumed Robinson's place as the managing editor and owner of the *Herald*. A tabloid "Herald" mailed to listeners from "Centerville" announced the changes and included photographs of the "Robinsons" reading their fan mail along with the paper's articles, editorials, cartoon, and crossword puzzle.

When introduced to New York City listeners in 1935, the *American Family Robinson* appeared five days a week until it changed to its regular twice-a-week schedule. In 1940, the last year of broadcast, the series appeared twice a week on 255 stations. NAM specialists considered mid-afternoon the optimum time for broadcasts. According to NAM Vice President for Public Relations James P. Selvage, tests showed that when scheduled between 2:00 and 3:00 P.M., the program had an excellent chance "to reach not only housewives but other members of the family." The *American Family Robinson*, Selvage wrote, presented "industry's effective answer to the Utopian promises of theorists and demagogues at present reaching such vast audiences via radio."

From the outset, Selvage had hoped to interest the National Broadcasting Company (NBC) or the Columbia Broadcasting System (CBS) in broadcasting the *American Family Robinson* on a sustaining basis. Neither was interested, and the series ended up in transcription, recorded and circulated to individual stations by the World Broadcasting System. A review of scripts submitted to NBC in October 1934 resulted in the program's banishment from the network's owned and operated stations as well. Reviewing the series' first three episodes, NBC script editor L.H. Titterton hardly knew what to make of the Robinsons, or the direction the story might take. An outline for the rest of the series and a script of the last episode received three days later confirmed Titterton's suspicion. After meeting with Selvage and Douglas Silver, the scripts' author, Titterton reported that the *American Family Robinson* proposed "to take on a definitely anti-Rooseveltian tendency." "You would probably not find in the entire series any specific sentence that could be censored," Titterton wrote to his network superiors, "but the definite intention and implication of each episode is to conduct certain propaganda against the New Deal and all its work."

Cast

Luke Robinson
The Baron
Miss Twink Pennybacker/Gloriana Day
Windy Bill
Cousin Monty, the Crooner
Professor Broadbelt
Myra
Aunt Agatha
Emmy Lou
Elsie
Mr. Popplemeyer
Letitia Holsome
Gus (Luke's assistant)
Pudgie

Producer/Creator

Harry A. Bullis

Programming History

National Industrial Council syndication, Orthacoustic transcription 1935–1940

Further Reading

Bird, William L., Jr., *Better Living: Advertising, Media, and the New Vocabulary of Business Leadership, 1935–1955*, Evanston, Illinois: Northwestern University Press, 1999.
Ewen, Stuart, *PR! A Social History of Spin*, New York: Basic Books, 1996.
Fones-Wolf, Elizabeth, "Creating a Favorable Business Climate: Corporations and Radio Broadcasting, 1934–1954," *Business History Review* 73 (Summer 1999).
MacDonald, J. Fred, *Don't Touch That Dial!: Radio Programming in American Life, 1920–1960*, Chicago: Nelson-Hall, 1979.
Marchand, Roland, *Creating the Corporate Soul: The Rise of Public Relations and Corporate Imagery in American Big Business*, Berkeley: University of California Press, 1998.
Tedlow, Richard S., "The National Association of Manufacturers and Public Relations During the New Deal," *Business History Review* 50 (Spring 1976).

WILLIAM L. BIRD JR.

AMERICAN FEDERATION OF MUSICIANS

The American Federation of Musicians (AFM) represents some 150,000 members in nearly 400 local unions throughout the United States and Canada. The AFM became infamous during and after World War II under its fiery leader James Caesar Petrillo, who fought tirelessly to preserve the jobs of professional musicians at stations and networks. Petrillo defied President Roosevelt and Congress until the latter passed legislation limiting his right to pressure broadcast stations.

Origins

After several earlier attempts at organization, the AFM was founded in Indianapolis in 1896 following an invitation from Samuel Gompers, president of the American Federation of Labor (AFL), to organize and charter a musicians' trade union. Delegates from various musician organizations, representing some 3,000 musicians, created a charter stating that "any musician who receives pay for his musical services shall be considered a professional musician." The union added the phrase "of the United States and Canada" to its title in 1900. At the St. Louis World's Fair four years later, the AFM discouraged the hiring of foreign bands. It also achieved the first minimum wage scale for traveling orchestras.

The economic impact of World War I and the growing popularity of recorded music led to epic high unemployment of musicians. Prohibition was closing beer halls where musicians had worked, and by the late 1920s and early 1930s, sound-on-film technology had displaced theater orchestras. The 22,000 musicians providing in-theater musical background for silent movies were replaced with only a few hundred jobs for musicians recording sound tracks. As might be expected, the New York, Chicago, and Los Angeles AFM locals were the largest during this period, with about 25 percent of the total membership in the three cities.

AFM and Radio

AFM members initially looked to radio as a godsend, assuming that it would provide for more employment opportunities for members. And indeed larger stations did create or hire individual musicians or even orchestras. But stations in smaller markets relied on recordings or shared (networked) broadcasts of national orchestras to fill their airtime, so music was getting wider circulation, but musicians usually were not.

Development of electrical transcription around 1930 (and sound quality improvements in records sold to consumers) made the problem worse, as it was now easier for stations to produce recorded programs that sounded nearly as good as live performances. After many years of indecision, in 1937 AFM President James Petrillo originated the "standby" approach, pressuring Chicago stations to employ AFM members if recorded music was played, as backup musicians or even as "platter turners" in place of regular on-air personnel. This "featherbedding" tactic (hiring more employees than needed) was adopted by the union and expanded to other areas of the nation in the years before the U. S. entry into World War II. That the standby process originated in Chicago is central to the AFM story, for Chicago became the base of strong AFM leadership for several decades.

A onetime trumpet player ("If I was a good trumpet player I wouldn't be here. I got desperate. I hadda look for a job. I went in the union business," *New York Times,* 14 June 1956), James Caesar Petrillo joined the AFM in 1917 from a rival group. He became head of the Chicago AFM local in 1922 and kept that post for over four decades, in part due to the lack of secret ballot elections and members' fear of him. In 1928 Petrillo had demanded that radio stations in the Chicago market pay musicians for performing on the air, which ironically forced many to use recorded music. The "standby" approach followed, wherein musicians were retained but often not used by broadcasters.

By 1940 Petrillo had been elected national AFM president, a post he would hold until 1958, all the while retaining his local power base (and title) with the Chicago local. He quickly expanded the union's standby tactic, requiring stations across the country that played records (as most did by that time) to hire AFM members as standby players. With strong AFM pressure, by 1944 the practice had spread across the nation, employing some 2000 musicians.

Petrillo and the union drew negative public attention, however, by demanding that the NBC radio broadcast from the National Music Camp at Interlochen, Michigan, be canceled in 1942. (Some of the camp's final performances each season had traditionally been broadcast.) A year later, the camp's leader, Joseph E. Maddy, lost his AFM membership because he was playing with nonmembers. The camp proved unable to get another broadcast outlet for its concerts, though ironically most could not have joined the union in any case because they were too young.

Petrillo did not seem to be concerned with public opinion. The height of his "public be damned" mode came in August 1942, when he pulled AFM members from all recording sessions with the big record companies until they agreed to his pension and related demands. The resulting 27-month ban

continued until late 1944 despite orders by the War Labor Board, pleas from President Roosevelt, and loud complaints in Congress that the AFM leader was not being supportive of the war effort. He stood his ground, and in November 1944, the last of the major recording companies (RCA Victor and Columbia) gave in to AFM demands. AFM gained the payment of 1.5–2 cents from each record sold; the money went into what became a huge performance trust fund. (The fund still helps to support popular free concerts in what is now the Petrillo Band Shell in Grant Park in Chicago.) Growth of the recording business after the war and the increasing number of jukeboxes prompted the AFM to threaten another recording musicians strike in 1948, but the parties involved settled, agreeing to continue paying AFM fees to the performance fund.

Concerned about the developing new media and what impact they might have on musicians, Petrillo in 1945 banned AFM members from performing on television or on FM dual broadcasts with AM unless standby musicians were hired. These bans were lifted only after stations again agreed to his demands for payments to musicians who were often not used at all. He also banned foreign music broadcasts except those from Canada, whose players were often AFM members. Although some of the membership grumbled, Petrillo and his supporters were all-powerful in the union and held sway. Indeed, his supporters reveled in the poor press their president achieved, publishing a booklet of negative cartoons depicting the feisty leader.

Lea Act

But pressure from broadcasters who felt blackmailed into accepting employees they did not need led Congress to take action limiting the union's power. In 1946 Clarence Lea, a Republican from California, introduced legislation to revise the Communications Act by adding a revised Section 506 concerning "coercive practices affecting broadcasting." Passed by overwhelming margins in the House and Senate and quickly signed by President Harry Truman, the Lea Act banned pressure on licensees to employ or make payments for "any person or persons in excess of the number of employees needed by such licensee to perform actual services," or "to pay or agree to pay more than once for services performed." Pre-existing contracts were allowed to stand, but renewals would have to agree with provisions of the new law.

In his usual pugnacious approach, Petrillo appealed the new legislation, using WAAF in

Chicago as a test case, and promised a nationwide strike against radio if the Lea Act was found unconstitutional. The Supreme Court, however, held the act to be constitutional and thus enforceable, and the AFM lost some of its power. Petrillo remained president of the AFM for another decade, but the union gradually slipped out of news headlines.

Digital Protection

The union spent much of its lobbying efforts after 1980 on strengthening the protection of its members' performance work in an increasingly digital sound milieu. This involved working with manufacturers of digital audio equipment (including digital audio tape), record companies (which in 1984 introduced compact discs), and eventually internet music providers, to secure Congressional support. By the early 21st century, AFM was seeking performance payments from radio broadcasters which had never before paid such fees.

See also: Columbia Broadcasting System; Copyright; Music on Radio; Radio Corporation of America

Further Reading

American Federation of Musicians: A Brief History of the AFM www.afm.org/about/about.htm?history.

Burlingame, Jon, *For the Record: The Struggle and Ultimate Political Rise of American Recording Musicians within Their Labor Movement*, Hollywood, California: Recording Musicians Association, 1997.

Countryman, Vern, "The Organized Musicians," *University of Chicago Law Review* 16 (1948–49).

"Petrillo," *Life* (3 August 1942).

Seltzer, George, *Music Matters: The Performer and the American Federation of Musicians*, Metuchen, New Jersey: Scarecrow Press, 1989.

Smith, B.R., "Is There a Case for Petrillo?" *New Republic* (15 January 1945).

U.S. Congress, House Committee on Education and Labor, *Investigation of James C. Petrillo and the American Federation of Musicians: Hearings*, 80th Congress, 1st Sess., 1947.

U.S. Congress, House Committee on Education and Labor, *Restrictive Practices of the American Federation of Musicians: Hearings*, 80th Congress, 2nd Sess., 1948.

U.S. v. Petrillo, 332 US 1 (1947).

Warner, Harry P., *Radio and Television Rights*, Albany, New York: Bender, 1953.

"What's Petrillo Up To?" *Harpers* 86 (December 1942).

White, Llewellyn, "King Canute," and "Petrillo," in *The American Radio*, by White, Chicago: University of Chicago Press, 1947.

CHRISTOPHER H. STERLING,
2009 REVISIONS BY CHRISTOPHER H. STERLING

AMERICAN FEDERATION OF TELEVISION AND RADIO ARTISTS

The American Federation of Television and Radio Artists (AFTRA) is the national labor union or "guild" for talent in television, radio, and sound recordings. It was originally founded on 30 July 1937 as the American Federation of Radio Artists (AFRA), part of the American Federation of Labor (AFL). By 2000, AFTRA had 36 local offices throughout the United States, with a total of 80,000 members, representing performers at over 300 radio and television stations nationwide, and a workforce collectively earning over $1 billion annually under work contracted by the union. The union is still affiliated with the AFL-CIO and is headquartered in New York City.

AFTRA's membership represents four areas of broadcast employment: news and broadcasting; commercials and nonbroadcast, industrial, or educational media; entertainment programming; and the recording business. Members include announcers, actors, newscasters, sportscasters, disc jockeys, talk show hosts, professional singers (including background singers and "royalty artists"), dancers, and talent working in new technologies such as CD-ROM and interactive programming. The union also franchises talent agents who represent AFTRA performers, stipulating talent agency commission fees as well as other regulations regarding the representation of performers in the union's jurisdiction.

AFTRA is party to about 400 collective bargaining agreements nationwide. These agreements generally regulate salaries and working conditions and include binding arbitration procedures for unresolved labor disputes. Union rules require AFTRA members to work only for "signatories" (employers who have signed AFTRA contracts), and members are asked to verify the signatory status of an employer before accepting a job. AFTRA was also the first industry union to establish employer-paid health insurance benefits and portable retirement plans. Any performer who has worked or plans to work in an area covered by AFTRA contracts is eligible for membership. Member dues are based on a performer's previous year's AFTRA earnings. Currently, dues and initiation fees are set by each local office, but the union has plans to implement a uniform national schedule of dues.

The union is governed by volunteer member representatives on both local and national boards of directors. National delegates are elected on a proportional basis from the locals at the union's biannual national convention. The national office publishes basic rates for the national freelance agreements for entertainment programming, commercials, sound recordings (both singing and speaking, such as for talking books), industrials (video- and audiotapes for corporate, educational, and other off-air use), and new technologies. Local AFTRA offices publish local talent guides and offer special services designed to meet local member needs, including skills development seminars, casting hotlines and bulletin boards, and credit unions and tax clinics. Local offices handle staff employment for broadcasters and newspersons at over 300 radio and television stations nationally. Because each signatory station's collective bargaining agreement is negotiated separately, it is up to the local AFTRA office to monitor and distribute information about specific station agreements. Local offices also track rates and conditions of employment for freelance work in each market, including rates for local or regional commercials and programs.

Presently, membership in AFTRA does not guarantee work or membership in other performer guilds, such as the Screen Actors Guild (SAG) or Actors Equity, although in general, both SAG and Actors Equity credit AFTRA membership and employment when evaluating applications. About 40,000 performers are members of both unions, and consequently, AFTRA and SAG have discussed a merger for several years. In 1995 the boards of directors of the two organizations approved a merger that would have created a larger union, given the combined membership of 123,000. Proponents of the merger cited the value of being able to present a united front when negotiating with an industry that was undergoing vast changes. Opponents were uneasy about the merging of the unions' health insurance and pension plans and about higher proposed dues, and were said to be nervous about increasing employment pressure on the 80 percent of SAG members already earning less than $10,000 annually from acting. In early 1999 the merger got only about 50 percent of SAG voter approval, far less than the 60 percent level of approval required by the SAG constitution, although the merger was approved by two-thirds of AFTRA voters.

Following the defeat of the proposed merger between AFTRA and SAG, AFTRA's leadership continued to work toward a restructuring of the union. Between 1990 and 1993, an outside consulting agency had been commissioned to study changes affecting the industries under AFTRA jurisdiction. The study concluded with recommendations that AFTRA strengthen its national office and foster coordination among its historically strong locals. The consultants also recommended that AFTRA become more sophisticated in its use of both internal and external resources in order to match the resources of the companies with which it negotiated. Finally, it recommended that AFTRA provide more benefits and services for members and that the union find ways to involve its membership more fully in decision-making and other union activity. Although the study maintained that AFTRA had "under financed" itself for many years by charging member dues that were among the lowest of any union in the broadcasting industry, the union decided it could not increase dues before first improving its services. Consequently, AFTRA reallocated its dues revenues in a series of internal changes that enabled AFTRA to add to its national staff by 36 percent to provide for better legal, financial, negotiating, and organizing services. The union also worked to enforce its existing contracts more vigorously, started a new research department, and worked to increase its lobbying presence in Washington. As of December 2002 AFTRA and SAG engaged in joint contract negotiations as an attempt to coordinate efforts in the face of continuing media (employer) consolidation.

AFTRA has a long history of supporting equal employment opportunities for women and minorities, and all AFTRA contracts include provisions for diversity and hiring fairness. AFTRA has a scholarship fund for members and dependents called the AFTRA Heller Memorial Foundation, and the union also set up the AFTRA Foundation, a tax-exempt organization funded by voluntary contributions to support educational and charitable causes.

By the 1990s, AFTRA focused on greater protection for its members in an increasingly digital world. An attempt to merge AFTRA and SAG failed in 2003 when by a thin margin the film union failed to ratify the agreement that most AFTRA members approved. With digital distribution of music by Apple (iTunes and the iPod) starting in 2005, AFTRA joined with other unions calling for an ongoing dialogue with employers to ensure fair compensation for performers' work. For example, AFTRA and SAG members agreed with the advertising business to design performer compensation models for commercials appearing on television, radio, internet, and other media. By 2007, more than 40 productions for the internet and other services had been covered in the AFTRA Electronic Media Agreement that sets union standards for jobs.

See also: Technical Organizations; Trade Associations

Further Reading

AFTRA website, www.aftra.com/aftra/history.htm.

Cox, Dan, "SAG, AFTRA Boards OK Merger," *Variety* (30 January 1995).

Johnson, Ted, "SAG-AFTRA's Merge Urge Hits Hurdles," *Variety* (12 February 1996).

Koenig, Allen E., *Broadcasting and Bargaining: Labor Relations in Radio and Television*, Madison: University of Wisconsin Press, 1970.

Koenig, Allen E., "A History of AFTRA," *The NAEB Journal* (July–August 1965).

Leeds, Jeff, "Company Town: Screen Actors Guild Rejects AFTRA Merger," *Los Angeles Times* (29 January 1999).

Madigan, Nick, "Unions War over Marriage Proposal," *Variety* (30 November 1998).

Madigan, Nick, "SAG: Merging or Diverging?" *Variety* (25 January 1999).

MARK BRAUN,
2009 REVISIONS BY CHRISTOPHER H. STERLING

AMERICAN SCHOOL OF THE AIR
U.S. Educational Radio Program

First aired on 4 February 1930, with an 18-year run that ended on 30 April 1948, this Columbia Broadcasting System (CBS) half-hour educational series drew from top radio and educational talent to bring programs to U.S. and international schools and radio listeners.

The show was sponsored for a brief time by the GrisbyGrunow Company to support radio sales, and then CBS chose to retain *American School of the Air* as a sustaining "Columbia Educational Feature" overseen by the network's department of education. In 1940 the program was adapted and expanded to international educational markets in Canada and Latin America and the Philippines under the names *School of the Air of the Americas, Radio Escuela de las Americas*, and *International School of the Air*. Beginning in 1942, the *School of the Air of the Americas* was officially sponsored by the U.S. Office of War Information (OWI). In 1943 the program was deemed the "official channel for news, information, and instructions" by the OWI (CBS *Program Guide*, Winter 1943). In 1944 programs were also broadcast over the 400 stations of the Armed Forces Radio Service. The program was discontinued in 1948.

A number of educational organizations and individuals lent their names and expertise to the *American School of the Air*. Top-level national educators, such as William C. Bagley of the Teachers' College at Columbia University and U.S. Commissioner of Education John W. Studebaker, served on the national board of consultants, and educational consultants were also involved at the state and local levels. National organizations also offered conceptual and resource support to the program.

Each *American School of the Air* season ran from October through April, taking a break for the summer out-of-school months. Typically, the series offered five subseries—one for each day of the week—with titles such as *Frontiers of Democracy, The Music of America, This Living World, New Horizons, Lives between the Lines, Tales from Far and Near, Americans at Work, Wellsprings of Music, Science at Work, Music on a Holiday, Science Frontiers, Gateways to Music, Story of America, March of Science, World Neighbors, Tales of Adventure, Opinion Please*, and *Liberty Road*. Program topics included U.S. and international history and current events; music and literature; science and geography; vocational guidance and social studies; biographies; and many other topics. In 1940 CBS reported that the *American School of the Air* programs were received by more than 150,000 classrooms throughout all 48 states, reaching more than 200,000 teachers and eight million pupils.

Some radio historians typically argue that the *American School of the Air* was part of a political strategy in early struggles over broadcast regulation. In the 1920s and early 1930s, noncommercial and citizen organizations proposed regulation, including frequency reallocation and nonprofit channel and program "set-asides," to ensure that the United States' burgeoning broadcast system would remain, on some level, competitive and in the public's hands. The outcry against establishing a wholly commercial broadcast system compelled the networks to present a clear public-interest face, replete with educational, religious, and labor programming, in order to stave off binding regulation that might compromise network program time and control. CBS's *American School of the Air* was a premier effort of this type.

Educational scholars offer an alternative account of the *American School of the Air*. They focus on the program's role and function as an example of early educational technology and see the program as one of the first concerted experiments in education by radio, complete with supplemental classroom materials, teachers' manuals, and program guides.

See also: Columbia Broadcasting System; Educational Radio to 1967

Cast

Members of the New York radio pool, including Parker Fennelly, Mitzi Gould, Ray Collins, Chester

Stratton; cast of *The Hamilton Family:* Gene Leonard, Betty Garde, Walter Tetley, Ruth Russell, Albert Aley, John Monks

Program Directors

Lyman Bryson, Sterling Fisher, and Leon Levine

Musical Directors

Alan Lomax, Dorothy Gordon, Channon Collinge

Writers

Hans Christian Adamson, Edward Mabley, Howard Rodman, A. Murray Dyer, Robert Aura Smith, and others

Announcers

Robert Trout, John Reed King, and others

Programming History

CBS   February 1930–April 1948

Further Reading

Atkinson, Carroll, *Radio Network Contributions to Education*, Boston: Meador, 1942.

Bird, Win W., *The Educational Aims and Practices of the National and Columbia Broadcasting Systems*, Seattle: University of Washington Extension Series, no. 10 (August 1939).

Boemer, Marilyn Lawrence, *The Children's Hour: Radio Programs for Children, 1929–1956*, Metuchen, New Jersey: Scarecrow Press, 1989.

Cuban, Larry, *How Teachers Taught: Constancy and Change in American Classrooms, 1890–1980*, New York: Longman, 1984.

Smulyan, Susan, *Selling Radio: The Commercialization of American Broadcasting, 1920–1934*, Washington, D.C.: Smithsonian Institution Press, 1994.

SOUSAN ARAFEH

AMERICAN SOCIETY OF COMPOSERS, AUTHORS, AND PUBLISHERS

Established in 1914, the American Society of Composers, Authors, and Publishers (ASCAP) is the oldest music performance rights organization in the United States and the only U.S. performing rights organization whose board of directors (elected by the membership) consists entirely of member composers, songwriters, and music publishers. For almost two decades, it also was the only national organization providing copyright clearance for the broadcasting of music.

Origins

The legal foundation for ASCAP was established in the 1909 copyright law that required permission from the copyright holder in order to perform music for profit in public. With no rights clearinghouse in place, however, copyright holders faced the impossible job of individually monitoring performances of songs to which each held title. Not many years later, composer Victor Herbert was conducting performances of one of his operettas at a New York theater. At dinner one evening in a nearby restaurant, he heard the establishment's house musicians performing his composition "Sweethearts." Herbert became upset that people were paying to hear his melodies in the theater while restaurant patrons were listening to them without paying anything. He brought suit under the 1909 law. A lower court initially ruled against him because the restaurant had charged no admission fee. But the United States Supreme Court reversed the lower court in its 1917 *Herbert v. Shanley* decision. In upholding the composer's claim, justice Oliver Wendell Holmes and his colleagues stated that it did not matter whether or not the performance actually resulted in a profit. The fact that it was employed as part of a profit-seeking endeavor was enough.

In 1914, before the main legal battle began, Herbert gathered eight composers, publishers' representatives, and lyricists for a meeting that ultimately would result in the establishment of ASCAP as their collection agent. In addition to Herbert, charter member composers included Irving Berlin and Rudolph Friml. Buoyed by Herbert's legal triumph three years later, ASCAP expanded its fee-seeking horizons beyond theaters and dance halls to any place where performance for profit took place. These proceeds then were distributed among ASCAP members via a sliding scale based on the number of compositions to which each held title and the musical prestige (not necessarily popularity) of each work.

ASCAP and Radio

By 1923 some radio stations had become profit-seeking (and a very few actually profit-making) enterprises that made widespread use of popular music. ASCAP therefore turned its attention to broadcasting, selecting WEAF, American Telephone and Telegraph's (AT&T) powerful New York outlet, as its test case. An aggressive protector of its own license and property rights, AT&T was not in a position to oppose ASCAP and settled on a one-year license of $500 in payment for all of the ASCAP-licensed music WEAF chose to air. This blanket license arrangement would become the industry standard. ASCAP followed this breakthrough by winning a lawsuit against station WOR in Newark, New Jersey, for the unlicensed broadcast of Francis A. McNamara's ballad "Mother Machree." Because ASCAP-affiliated composers were then the creators of virtually all popular music, stations faced the prospect of either paying up or ceasing to play the tunes that listeners expected to hear.

Perceiving themselves to be at ASCAP's mercy, major-market station owners formed the National Association of Broadcasters (NAB) in 1923 to do battle with the licensing organization. Station radio concerts were far less appealing without the melodies ASCAP controlled, but the annual license fees, which escalated upward from an initial $2.50, were seen as too high for many stations to pay. (Few of them had much revenue, let alone profits, at this point.) In subsequent years, ASCAP used its near-monopoly position in the music industry to charge broadcasters ever-higher rates. Continuous legal skirmishes, congressional hearings, and even frequent NAB-inspired Justice Department antitrust probes of ASCAP served only to raise the financial stakes and intensify the antagonistic relationship between NAB and ASCAP.

In 1931, for instance, ASCAP boosted its overall fees to stations by 300 percent, charging five percent of each outlet's gross income. It then broke off dealings with the NAB and began negotiations with individual broadcasters, offering three-year contracts at three percent of net income for the first year, four percent for the second, and the full five percent by the third year. By 1936 it was demanding five-year licenses.

Formation of a Competitor

When ASCAP announced yet another large increase in license fees for 1939, broadcasters took action and by the following year had established their own licensing organization, Broadcast Music Incorporated (BMI). On 1 January 1941, as BMI labored to build a catalog, most stations stopped paying their ASCAP fees and restricted their music broadcasts to airing songs with expired copyrights and folk songs that had always been in the public domain. Stephen Foster melodies, such as "Jeanie with the Light Brown Hair," became radio staples.

To ASCAP's chagrin, no groundswell of indignation arose from the radio audience. Further, singers and instrumentalists also replaced much of their repertoire with non-ASCAP material in order to keep their lucrative and visibility-enhancing radio bookings. Many performers switched from playing tunes by George Gershwin, Cole Porter, and Irving Berlin to using non-ASCAP music from South America—a key factor behind the sudden 1940s popularity of the rumba, samba, and tango. Combined with government antitrust pressure, these factors resulted in ASCAP agreeing to offer per-program fees as well as blanket license fees and the rollback of rates to about half of what they had been collecting.

By the mid-1950s, the number of BMI tunes played over U.S. radio stations had come to parity with those licensed by ASCAP. Most of BMI's success was attributable to the explosion of rock and roll—a pulsating blend of rhythm and blues, country, and gospel music penned by songwriters outside of ASCAP's traditional constituency. BMI scooped up these composers and rode the rock and roll wave to dominance on many Top 40 format stations.

ASCAP and the Payola Scandal

In 1959 the payola scandal shook the radio industry to its core. Many disc jockeys were accused of taking unreported gifts from record promoters in exchange for "riding" (heavily playing) certain songs (payola). ASCAP added fuel to the fire when its spokespersons maintained that rock and roll, largely the creative product of BMI-affiliated composers, would never have got off the ground without payola. ASCAP claimed that 75 percent of the Top 50 tunes owed their success to payola—a charge meant as much to indict BMI as the practice of payola. With the subsequent passage of amendments to the 1934 Communications Act making payola a criminal offense, the radio industry moved beyond the crisis—but the resulting ASCAP–BMI animosity took a much longer time to cool.

Negotiating Music Rights

As it has for decades, ASCAP negotiates with radio stations mainly through the Radio Music License Committee (RMLC), a select group of broadcasters appointed by the NAB. Although stations technically could negotiate on their own, virtually all rely on the committee to carve out acceptable blanket and per-program license fee structures. For the period through the year 2002, blanket license fees for commercial radio stations were pegged at 1.615 percent for stations with an annual gross revenue over $150,000 or a minimum of one percent of adjusted gross income. For stations billing less than $150,000 per year, a flat fee schedule ranges from $450 to $1,800 depending on income. Noncommercial stations pay an annual fee determined by the U.S. Copyright Office. In 2003 this was pegged at $245 for educationally owned facilities and $460 for all other noncommercial outlets.

From 2003 through 2009, ASCAP employed a different methodology for determining fees stations had to pay. No longer requiring stations to file annual reports documenting the music they played, ASCAP royalties were based instead upon Arbitron ratings with, theoretically, stations that reach the largest audiences paying higher fees than stations that reach fewer people. A rate of 1.65 percent was established for top-tier music stations, whereas 2.4 percent was determined for top-tier nonmusic, i.e. news/talk, stations.

After 2000, ASCAP sought compensation for music streamed over the internet. In mid-2008, the organization finally obtained a federal court order against AOL, RealNetworks and Yahoo regarding royalty payments for online music over the previous several years. ASCAP stood to collect $70 to $100 million from the three service providers. Appeals were pending as this volume went to press. In 2009, representatives from radio and online carriers resumed bargaining with ASCAP to determine fees for 2010 and beyond.

ASCAP determines the amount of airplay garnered by each ASCAP-member song via three methods: electronic logging information from Broadcast Data Systems (BDS), periodic logging by the radio stations themselves, and ASCAP taping of station broadcasts.

With 200,000 members, a full-time staff of 300 and a $500,000,000 annual budget, ASCAP is a powerful industry and legislative force. Along with its mission of distributing royalties to songwriters, the organization also stages three conventions a year, distributes annual awards to recognize often-performed songwriters and publishes various journals and directories.

ASCAP has often incurred criticism for overzealousness. It has been known to lodge devastating fees against small nightclubs who stage weekly musical open-mic nights; in 2008, a Texas bar was hit with a penalty of over $8,000 for allowing local troubadours to sing in its establishment. A Rhode Island club was fined $120,000 for copyrighted works played by its in-house band. Indeed, ASCAP

generated a promotional nightmare in the 1990s when it sought payment from the Girl Scouts of America, arguing that local campfire sing-a-longs constituted a "public performance" and required licensing. Facing strong denunciation, ASCAP later backed down.

See also: Broadcast Music Incorporated; Copyright; Licensing Authorizing U.S. Stations to Broadcast; National Association of Broadcasters; Payola; United States Supreme Court and Radio; WEAF

Further Reading

ASCAP website, www.ascap.com/about/history/
Bumiller, Elisabeth. "ASCAP Asks Royalties from Girl Scouts, and Regrets It," *New York Times* (17 December 1996), p. 1.
Dachs, David, *Anything Goes: The World of Popular Music*, Indianapolis, Indiana: Bobbs-Merrill, 1964.
Lathrop, Tad, and Jim Pettigrew, Jr., *This Business of Music Marketing and Promotion*, New York: Billboard Books, 1999.
Petrozzello, Donna, "ASCAP Restructuring Rates," *Broadcasting and Cable* (12 August 1996).
Ryan, John, *The Production of Culture in the Music Industry: The ASCAP-BMI Controversy*, Lanham, Maryland: University Press of America, 1985.
Smith, Wes, *The Pied Pipers of Rock 'n' Roll: Radio Deejays of the 50s and 60s*, Marietta, Georgia: Longstreet Press, 1989.

PETER B. ORLIK,
2009 REVISIONS BY CARY O'DELL

AMERICAN TELEPHONE AND TELEGRAPH

American Telephone and Telegraph Company (AT&T) was a major contributor to the development of early broadcasting technology and radio networking. As a result of its refinements in vacuum tube technology and the ensuing patent disputes, AT&T became a founding shareholder in the powerful Radio Corporation of America (RCA), built the first commercial radio station (WEAF), and perfected the technology for network broadcasting. Over the years, AT&T's Bell Laboratories has pioneered many technologies used in radio.

Audion and Patent Concerns

Parent company of the Bell Telephone System, AT&T recognized the potential of de Forest's Audion tube as an amplifier for telephone circuits and secured rights to the device. Although the Audion could not be used in radio circuits due to a suit by the Marconi Company alleging patent infringements, AT&T licensed its use for telephone circuitry, quickly refining the technology and thus making transcontinental telephony a reality. AT&T also used vacuum tubes to pursue development of continuous wave transmitters necessary for voice communication as ancillary devices supporting telephone services. At the outbreak of World War I, the U.S. Navy took control of all radio patents, accelerating the development of wireless and radio receiver technology. At the end of the war, large electronic manufacturers such as AT&T, Westinghouse, and General Electric reclaimed their patents.

After the war, U.S. government officials expressed their desire to settle the patent problem quickly in order to keep key radio technology in the hands of a U.S. company. In 1919 RCA was formed as a way to pool the patents and cross-license the various technologies, making the large-scale manufacture of radio vacuum tubes possible. Under the agreement, AT&T's manufacturing arm, Western Electric, gained exclusive rights to produce long-distance transmitters and other key technology used in conjunction with wired communications. By 1922 Western Electric transmitters were powering 30 of America's pioneering radio stations, including such legendary stations as WOR in Newark, New Jersey, WHAM in Rochester, New York, and WSB in Atlanta, Georgia. AT&T soon came to realize, however, that the sale of transmitters to others conflicted with the company's strategy of beginning a nationwide commercial broadcasting service.

Birth of Radio Networking

Beginning in 1877 AT&T started experimenting with the use of telephone lines for transmission of music and entertainment. These experiments used telephones or public address systems to carry program material such as music or speeches. By 1919 AT&T had refined vacuum tube technology to the point where large, elaborate auditorium demonstrations were possible. With the advent of broadcasting, however, the need for high quality connections to bring live events to radio stations became apparent. Soon AT&T undertook experiments to test public acceptance of broadcasting.

In January 1922 AT&T began construction of its own broadcasting facilities. AT&T vice president Walter S. Gifford outlined the commercial "toll" concept of broadcasting, calling for the creation of a channel through which anyone could send out his or her own programs. AT&T originally contemplated building 38 "radiotelephone" stations linked together by the company's Long Lines division. The first two stations were constructed in New

York: WBAY was erected atop the AT&T Long Lines building on Walker Street and WEAF was constructed at Western Electric's Labs on West Street. WBAY signed on to 360 meters (830 kHz) on 3 August 1922. When signal coverage from WBAY proved unsatisfactory due to the steel construction of the Walker Street building, WEAF became the company's principal transmitting facility. In 1923 WCAP, Washington, D.C., was added to AT&T's station lineup.

Both RCA and AT&T started experimenting with interconnecting stations, but RCA was limited to using Western Union telegraph lines, and these proved to be unsuitable for the transmission of high-quality voice and music. The first AT&T network experiment started on 4 January 1923, when engineers connected WEAF in New York, New York, with WNAC in Boston, Massachusetts. Soon after, Colonial H.R. Green, owner of station WMAF, convinced AT&T to provide a link from WEAF to his station in South Dartmouth, Massachusetts. Green agreed to pay AT&T $60,000 for a permanent connection, and WMAF began retransmitting WEAF programming. This arrangement gave AT&T engineers a full-time connection, which they used to experiment with transmission equipment. Other networking experiments followed. On 7 June 1923, WGY in Schenectady, New York, KDKA in Pittsburgh, Pennsylvania, and KYW in Chicago, Illinois, were connected to WEAF. AT&T used the term *chain* to refer to interconnection of radio stations. Later, *chain broadcasting* became the term commonly applied to radio network broadcasting.

Using Long Lines Division's capabilities, WEAF undertook a series of spectacular remote broadcasts that generated great interest among radio listeners and gave WEAF a programming advantage over other stations. Sporting events such as the Princeton–Chicago and Harvard–Yale football games, the Dempsey–Tunney boxing match, and recitals from the Capitol Theater demonstrated that coverage of live events was of great interest to Americans. At the same time, AT&T held control over the capability to provide remote broadcasts via its telephone lines, and it began to refuse to provide hookups to other rival stations owned by RCA's radio group.

In 1924 AT&T connected radio stations in 12 major cities from Boston to Kansas City, Missouri, for special broadcasts of the Republican and Democratic national conventions. One year later, it used its circuits in the first coast-to-coast demonstration. As these experiments continued into 1925, radio network connections regularly linked WEAF and other stations in cities throughout the East and Midwest. AT&T executives began to rethink the company's involvement in broadcasting, however, as disagreements with RCA over the cross-licensing arrangements increased. Finally, in 1926 AT&T decided to discontinue broadcasting operations and sold WEAF to RCA.

RCA created the National Broadcasting Company (NBC) to operate WEAF, WJZ, and its own radio stations. Under the terms of the WEAF sale, NBC was required to lease AT&T lines for network connections whenever possible. NBC decided to form two separate networks to handle stations where there was duplication in coverage area. AT&T Long Lines engineers used red and blue pencils to trace the connection paths for NBC's new networks and NBC adopted the colors as designations for the two networks. The Red Network, with WEAF as the flagship station, was the larger and more important of the two with 25 stations; the Blue Network began with only five stations.

Growth of the Chains

America's growing interest in high-quality programs spurred further AT&T development of networking capabilities. As public interest in high-quality programming grew, many local stations joined one of the two NBC radio networks, but the NBC monopoly in network broadcasting was not to last for long. A small upstart, United Independent Broadcasters, was formed when Arthur Judson decided to establish a new radio network. In early 1927 Judson tried to secure telephone lines for the newly formed network, but AT&T refused to provide connections because it had signed an exclusivity agreement with RCA. By mid-1927 AT&T, under pressure from the Federal Trade Commission, agreed to provide network connections to the new network. That fall, the newly named Columbia Broadcasting System (CBS) began operations with 12 affiliated stations. Soon, chain broadcasting revolutionized radio in the United States.

AT&T played a pivotal role in making network broadcasting a success. Long Lines Division developed elaborate specialized network capabilities that served both full-time networks such as NBC and CBS and specialized regional networks, such as the Don Lee Network in California and the Liberty Broadcasting System in the Southwest.

By 1928 AT&T maintained four broadcast network interconnection systems (called Red, Blue, Orange, and Purple) linking 69 radio stations together with more than 28,000 miles of wire. New York served as the central distribution point for

stations in the East and South, while Chicago, Illinois, and Cincinnati, Ohio, served Midwest stations. San Francisco, California, became a switching point for the West Coast. Both telegraph and voice circuits were used to provide affiliates with networking information and programming channel feeds.

AT&T used an elaborate series of repeater stations to route high-quality audio transmissions across the nation. Special Long Lines operators provided maintenance for the system and switching for network programs. Stations that normally carried Red network programming needed to be manually switched by AT&T personnel when they wanted to carry Blue network programs. Important switching stations, such as Washington, D.C., could switch as many as 30,000 programs each year. To facilitate network quality testing, broadcasters provided musical programming for the Long Lines operators. NBC maintained a legendary jukebox at Radio City that played music whenever either of the networks was not transmitting a program. The jukebox selections provided AT&T engineers with a constant audio source to verify network quality. This practice continued through the mid-1980s, when satellites finally replaced land lines. Broadcasters worked with Bell Labs to develop equipment to interconnect broadcast stations with the telephone network. The VU meter, a visual gauge for measuring audio, was an outgrowth of that cooperation, and special terminology such as *nonemanating outputs* (NEMO), *terminal block*, and *mults* entered broadcast parlance as a result of this relationship.

The cost of renting AT&T broadcast lines was often too high to allow local radio stations to provide live coverage of sporting events. Announcers such as Red Barber and Ronald "Dutch" Reagan—and later Gordon McLendon—made names for themselves recreating games by using sparse information provided by telegraph operators at ball games.

As broadcasting networks grew in power and size throughout the 1930s, AT&T expanded its special services. By 1939 more than 53,000 miles of special circuit wires were used to provide network services. The number of specialized networks maintained by AT&T expanded to 21 just before World War II. Network designations continued to be based on the original engineering color schemes, with NBC having its Red and Blue networks and CBS using ivory, black, pink, scarlet, and other specialized broadcast facilities. Broadcast network operations represented approximately 15 percent of AT&T's $23 million in gross revenue for Private

Line Services in 1933. By 1935 broadcasters were spending more than $10 million a year for telephone lines to link their networks. Some estimate that in 1950 nearly 40 percent of AT&T's $53 million in private network gross revenues represented broadcast services. Revenues generated from broadcasting and other special private services rose throughout the golden age of radio networks, providing AT&T with substantial profits.

With the introduction of television, the decline in network radio led to a decline in AT&T's involvement in linking up network stations. Special services provided by Long Lines during this time were used to create a nationwide television network system for the growing number of television network affiliates. Long Lines continued to provide network connections for radio until the mid-1980s, when domestic communication satellites replaced land lines. The competition from satellite distribution and FCC deregulation in telecommunication services made general land-line distribution of radio unprofitable.

Technical Developments

Bell Telephone Laboratories, created by AT&T in 1925, pioneered many technologies that have expanded the capability of modern radio broadcasters. In the 1930s AT&T invented stereophonic sound systems and microwave transmission, both essential technologies for today's high-quality radio programming. In the late 1940s Bell Labs invented the transistor, the forerunner of modern solid-state electronics, spawning both the transistor radio and solid-state computer era. Other key developments include the communication satellite, the light emitting diode (LED), and the laser. Today's advanced audio technology is partially an outgrowth of the basic scientific research undertaken by AT&T.

See also: Bell Telephone Laboratories; Columbia Broadcasting System; National Broadcasting Company; Network Monopoly Probe; Radio Corporation of America; Stereo; WEAF

Further Reading

Aitken, Hugh G.J., *The Continuous Wave: Technology and American Radio, 1900–1932*, Princeton, New Jersey: Princeton University Press, 1985.
Archer, Gleason Leonard, *History of Radio to 1926*, New York: American Historical Society, 1938.
Archer, Gleason Leonard, *Big Business and Radio*, New York: American Historical Society, 1939.
Banning, William Peck, *Commercial Broadcasting Pioneer: The WEAF Experiment, 1922–1926*, Cambridge, Massachusetts: Harvard University Press, 1946.
Douglas, Susan J., *Listening In: Radio and the American Imagination*, New York: Times Books, 1999.
Sibley, Ludwell, "Program Transmission and the Early Radio Networks," *AWA Review* 3 (1988).

FRITZ MESSERE

AMERICAN TOP 40
Popular Music Program

American Top 40 (*AT40*) is the longest running national music countdown broadcast on American radio during the rock era. In its 30-year history, the show has undergone a series of personnel and ownership changes. The first *AT40* show aired with veteran disc jockey Casey Kasem during the week of 4 July 1970 and was distributed in only seven U.S. markets. By 1980 the show could be heard in nearly 500 markets across the United States.

The original *AT40* program concept was created by Ron Jacobs, who with Tom Rounds founded Watermark in 1969. The program grew out of collaboration between Jacobs and K-B Productions owners Casey Kasem and Don Bustany, who sold Jacobs on the idea of a national music countdown. Despite the initial downturn in the Top 40 music format as the rapid proliferation of new FM stations popularized album-oriented rock in the early 1970s, *AT40* soon found a loyal audience.

AT40 was the first program to turn the popular local Top 40 countdown into a national syndicated show. The three-hour show was distributed weekly on records to radio stations across the United States, using the *Billboard* Top 100 as the source for the countdown. *AT40* was distributed as a boxed record set each week. Records played 30 minutes of the show per side, and the set contained cue sheets allowing stations to integrate local station breaks into the *AT40* program format. The records had to be played in the right order for the countdown to progress correctly. Program segments opened or ended with jingles identifying the program and the program host. By 1978 the general length of popular songs had increased, causing *AT40* to increase its program length from three to four hours per show. Today the show is distributed on compact discs.

One of the reasons for *AT40*'s success was the charismatic, personal voice style of Casey Kasem, the show's longest-serving host. The format initially called for a fast-paced delivery with minimal talk and a quick turnover from song to song. As the program gained momentum, Kasem's knowledge of popular music and his ability to create a sense of intimacy added interest for listeners. As the show expanded its time and found a loyal audience, special features such as the "Long Distance Dedication" became popular segments. Kasem's classic signoff, "Keep your feet on the ground and keep reaching for the stars" became the show's trademark.

AT40's success was challenged in 1979 with the introduction of *The Weekly Top 30* hosted by Mark Elliot and in 1980 with *Dick Clark's National Music Survey*. Both of these shows were aimed at slightly different demographics than *AT40*. *The Weekly Top 30* ended in 1982, and in 1983, *Rick Dees' Weekly Top 40* aired based on the popular music chart listings in *Cashbox* magazine.

In 1988 American Broadcasting Companies (ABC) Radio Networks, which had acquired Watermark, and Kasem were unable to agree to terms for a renewal contract. By this time *AT40* had grown to become the most successful American radio program and was the sixth largest syndicated broadcasting program with an estimated 2.4 million listeners worldwide. The show boasted nearly 1,000 outlets around the world. In July 1988 ABC introduced Shadoe Stevens as the new host of *AT40*. ABC heavily promoted the transition and introduced various new features to distinguish the new show host and keep the format fresh. Stevens hosted the show until 1995. Several broadcasting companies vied for Kasem's talents, and in 1989 he signed a multimillion-dollar, multiyear contract with Westwood One to start a competing program called "*Casey's Top 40*."

The early 1990s saw a substantial change in popular music. In November 1991 *Billboard* changed the way it tabulated the Hot 100. *Billboard's* new methodology led to a substantial increase in rap and other nontraditional pop music genres in the chart, causing many older loyal listeners to tune out. The traditional Top 40 format splintered into derivative formats. In addition, the continuing success of *Rick Dees' Weekly Top 40* and *Casey's Top 40* splintered the market for the Top 40. By 1992 *AT40* had fewer than 275 stations carrying the program in the United States, although it still held the predominant position among overseas listeners.

In 1994 ABC Radio Networks acquired the Westwood One network and ownership of *AT40*. ABC now owned both the Rick Dees countdown and *AT40*. On 24 June 1994, ABC announced that it would cancel the American version of *AT40,* and the last program aired in January 1995. ABC's rights to the program terminated in 1998, and the show reverted back to Kasem and Bustany, the owners of K-B Productions. *AT40* was revived with Kasem as the host in March 1998 under the

ownership of AMFM Networks. In addition to the Top 40 format, there is also an American Top 20 based on the hot adult contemporary format and another geared toward adult contemporary listeners. Even though the format of the new *AT40* is very similar to the original, the chart list is now based on the Mediabase 24/7 hit music charts.

In 2003, the distribution of the program changed to Premiere Radio Networks. *American Top 40* was at that time heard on 127 U.S. stations and 14 outlets internationally.

Hosts

Casey Kasem (1970–88; 1998–), Shadoe Stevens (1989–95)

Creator

Ron Jacobs

Executive Producer

Tom Rounds

Programming History

Watermark Syndication	1970–88
ABC	1988–95
Radio Express	1998–2002
Premiere Radio Network	2003

Further Reading

Durkee, Rob, *American Top 40: The Countdown of the Century*, New York: Schirmer Books, 1999.

FRITZ MESSERE

AMERICAN WOMEN IN RADIO AND TELEVISION

Women have taken part in the business of radio broadcasting from the earliest days of the industry. Although their advancement was often slower than that of their male counterparts, they were able to contribute greatly to the development of radio. As in many professions, women organized groups to provide mutual support in their efforts for advancement and recognition. American Women in Radio and Television (AWRT) is one such organization.

Origins

On 8 April 1951, AWRT held its organizing convention at the Astor hotel in New York. According to the trade publication *Broadcasting and Tele-casting,* 250 women from the fields of radio and television attended this event. They elected Edyth Meserand, assistant director of news and special features at WOR-AM-TV in New York, as the first AWRT president. Appropriately, the keynote speaker at the conference was Frieda Hennock, the first woman to be appointed a commissioner at the Federal Communications Commission (FCC).

Since 1951 AWRT has pursued its stated mission: "to advance the impact of women in the electronic media and allied fields, by educating, advocating, and acting as a resource to our members and the industry." Logically, the majority of members are women, but many men also choose to participate in this effort. The organization carries out its work through more than 30 chapters nationwide.

Function

AWRT provides professional development activities, mentoring, and job-search assistance for its members. The organization sponsors awards for excellence in the profession and publishes information resources, in print and on-line, for members and nonmembers alike. Through its lobbying efforts, AWRT has been an advocate for many causes, including better opportunities for women who aspire to own media organizations and stricter enforcement of equal employment opportunity requirements at television and radio stations. It has argued in favor of a proposal that would require broadcast organizations to keep statistics on minority and female employees, and it has taken a lead role in educating professionals about sexual harassment. At times, AWRT speaks out on behalf of general policy options that its members consider relevant to its mission. For example, the group argued against using auctions to determine spectrum ownership. The basis for this argument was the belief that auctioning broadcast frequencies would work against preserving a diversity of voices in the media marketplace.

One of the most important services AWRT provides is facilitating networking opportunities for its members. At its annual convention, professionals from all areas of electronic media discuss key issues affecting the field as well as more specific topics that are most likely to concern women. Throughout the year, AWRT serves all types of organizations by providing speakers on such topics as promoting diversity in the workplace and managing a diverse workforce.

In addition to these services, AWRT recognizes excellence in electronic media by presenting awards to individuals and companies. These awards are given for outstanding achievements in electronic media, for commitment to the issues and concerns of women, and for achievements in strengthening the role of women in the industry and contributing to the betterment of the community. Its annual Gracie awards, named in honor of broadcast pioneer Gracie Allen, recognize realistic portrayals of women in radio and television programming. Several awards are given each year to commend media contributions "by women, for women or about women." The Silver Satellite awards recognize the outstanding contributions of an individual to the broadcast industry. Among the former winners of this prestigious award are Bob Hope, who won the first Silver Satellite award in 1968, Vincent Wasilewski, former head of the National Association of Broadcasters, Mary Tyler Moore, Barbara Walters, and Pauline Frederick. Other honors given by the organization include the Star Awards, which honor individuals and companies who have shown a commitment to the concerns of women, and the Achievement Awards, which recognize a member who has both strengthened the role of women and contributed to the betterment of the community.

In 1960 the AWRT Educational Foundation was chartered to promote charitable programs, educational services, scholarships, and projects to benefit the community and the mass media. This support not only provides assistance to community organizations in need of funding, it also provides an opportunity for AWRT members and others to become actively involved in serving their communities.

See also: American Women in Radio and Television

Further Reading

AWRT website, www.awrt.org/who_we_are/index.html
Baehr, Helen, editor, *Women and Media,* Oxford and New York: Pergamon Press, 1980.
Baehr, Helen, and Michele Ryan, *Shut Up and Listen! Women and Local Radio: A View from the Inside,* London: 1984.
Creedon, Pamela, J., editor, *Women in Mass Communication,* Newberry Park, California, and London: Sage 1989; 2nd edition, 1993.
Phalen, Patricia, "Pioneers, Girlfriends, and Wives: An Agenda for Research on Women and the Organizational Culture of Broadcasting," *The Journal of Broadcasting and Electronic Media* 44, no. 2 (Spring 2000).
Stone, Vernon A., *Let's Talk Pay in Television and Radio News,* Chicago: Bonus Books, 1993.

PATRICIA PHALEN

AMERICA'S TOWN MEETING OF THE AIR
Public Affairs Program

For much of its 21-year run, *America's Town Meeting of the Air* (1935–56) was a Thursday evening staple in many radio homes. As part of a trend toward panel discussion shows in the 1930s, this series as well as *American Forum of the Air, People's Platform, University of Chicago Roundtable, Northwestern Reviewing Stand,* and *High School Town Meeting of the Air* were sustaining (commercial-free) programs devoted to in-depth political and social discussion. Although *America's Town Meeting of the Air* was not the first of these panel discussion programs on the air, it was the first radio program to offer debate *and* active audience participation.

The first panel discussion program, *University of Chicago Roundtable* (1931–55), was a more reserved, scholarly program featuring University of Chicago professors debating contemporary issues. *American Forum of the Air* (1934–56) developed an adversary format, with two opponents on either side of a controversial issue, which became a popular feature of later panel discussion programs. *America's Town Meeting of the Air*'s innovation was its inclusion of the live audience by using unscreened audience questions as an essential part of the discussion. Because audience members challenged guest speakers and their views, *America's Town Meeting of the Air* was an often volatile and unpredictable hour of radio programming. This serious-minded and popular program recognized the power of audience participation and influenced the format of later public-affairs programs and talk shows.

America's Town Meeting of the Air was the brainchild of George V. Denny, Jr., a former drama teacher and lecture manager. Denny was associate director of the League of Political Education, a New York-based political group founded in 1894 by suffragists that held town meetings to discuss contemporary issues. Legend has it that Denny, shocked by a neighbor's refusal to listen to President Roosevelt because he disagreed with him, sought to raise the level of political discussion in the country. He believed that a radio program could be produced that would mirror the New England town meetings of early America and promote democratic debate. Denny mentioned his idea to the director of the League of Political Education, Mrs. Richard Patterson, who brought the idea to her husband, National Broadcasting Company (NBC) Vice President Richard Patterson. Richard Patterson helped Denny develop the show and gave the hour-long program a six-week trial run in 1935

on the NBC Blue network. Inexpensive and easy to produce, *America's Town Meeting of the Air* was an efficient and effective sustaining program for NBC. From its initial airing over 18 stations on the NBC Blue network, the show reached more than 20 million listeners through more than 225 stations by 1947. The successful program found its home on the NBC Blue (later American Broadcasting Companies [ABC]) network for its entire run.

For most of its life on radio, the program refused to accept sponsors, fearing that commercial interests would interfere with the show's controversial content. For only one year, *America's Town Meeting of the Air* accepted the sponsorship of *Reader's Digest.* In its later years (1947–55), the program accepted multiple sponsors. ABC tried to simulcast the program (somewhat unsuccessfully) on television and radio in 1948–49 and again in 1952, but the program did not translate well to television. After an internal dispute, Denny, the originator of the series, was removed from the program in 1952. Despite the loss of its creator, the program lasted four more years.

America's Town Meeting of the Air welcomed listeners each week with the sound of a town crier's bell and Denny's voice calling, "Good evening, neighbors." Broadcasting from Town Hall (123 West 43rd Street in New York City), Denny assembled a live studio audience of nearly 1,800 to participate in the broadcast. Before these witnesses, the show featured two or more opponents on a controversial issue. To build suspense, each guest would have the opportunity to state his or her position and would then field unscreened questions from the live studio audience and from listeners who sent questions via telegram before the program's broadcast. The program's format was designed by Denny to present a diversity of political and social views and to bring those views into conflict before a live and often raucous studio audience.

The program's commitment to public affairs and controversial issues was established from its first broadcast on 30 May 1935. The topic for the first program was "Which Way for America—Communism, Fascism, Socialism, or Democracy?" Raymond Moley (an adviser to President Roosevelt) defended democracy, Norman Thomas made the case for socialism, A.J. Muste argued for the importance of communism, and Lawrence Dennis explained the benefits of fascism. The show was remarkable for the breadth and depth of the issues debated publicly. *America's Town Meeting of the Air* frequently addressed foreign policy or international disputes (e.g., "How Can We Advance Democracy in Asia?" or "What Kind of World Order Do We Want?"

featuring a debate between H.G. Wells and Dr. Hu Shih, the Chinese ambassador to the United States) as well as domestic issues (e.g., "Does Our National Debt Imperil America's Future?" "How Essential Is Religion to Democracy?" or "Can We Depend upon Youth to Follow the American Way?"). *America's Town Meeting of the Air* also tackled the racial conflicts of the period, featuring prominent African-American scholars and writers such as Richard Wright. One of its most popular shows was the 1944 broadcast entitled "Let's Face the Race Question," with Langston Hughes, Carey McWilliams, John Temple Graves, and James Shepard. Whether discussing the detention of Japanese-Americans during World War II, debating immigration restrictions, or confronting the racial divide in the 20th century, *America's Town Meeting of the Air* offered listeners the opportunity to debate topics that were suppressed or marginalized elsewhere on radio.

In the 1930s and 1940s, prestigious panel discussion programs such as *America's Town Meeting of the Air* were sterling examples of the networks' devotion to public service. Such shows were used by the networks to fulfill their public-interest obligations to the community and to stave off government regulation in early radio. As discussed by Barbara Savage (1999), *America's Town Meeting of the Air* conducted an extensive public outreach campaign to incorporate the listening audience into the program and to increase its public profile.

According to a 1940 sales brochure, NBC supported the development of debate and discussion groups. NBC viewed the program as "a real force of public enlightenment" and an example of the network's "unexampled public service to the men and women of America." Transcripts of broadcasts were published by Columbia University Press. The program encouraged the use of transcripts in schools and sponsored editorial cartoon and essay contests on subjects such as "What Does American Democracy Mean to Me?" Despite the fact that *America's Town Meeting of the Air* originated from New York City, the program also worked carefully to promote regional interest in the program. For six months out of the year, the program traveled around the country, sponsored by local universities and civic groups.

America's Town Meeting of the Air was one of the most popular national public-affairs programs on radio. Nearly 1,000 debate groups were officially formed, and thousands more listened each week in barber shops and community centers around the country. In the 1938–39 season, nearly 250,000 program transcripts were requested; the show typically received 4,000 letters a week. The program was also critically acclaimed for its public service. *America's Town Meeting of the Air* was a multiple winner of the Peabody Award and was also recognized by the Women's National Radio Committee, the Institute for Education by Radio, and the Women's Press Bloc, among other organizations, for its educational qualities and its discussion of economic, political, and international problems.

See also: Public Affairs Programming

Moderator

George V. Denny, Jr.

Announcers

Howard Claney, Milton Cross, Ben Grauer, George Gunn, Ed Herlihy, Gene Kirby

Producer

Marian Carter

Directors

Wylie Adams, Leonard Blair, Richard Ritter

Programming History

NBC Blue	1935–42.
NBC Blue/ABC	1942–56

Further Reading

DeLong, Thomas A., "George V. Denny," in *Radio Stars: An Illustrated Biographical Dictionary of 953 Performers, 1920 through 1960*, by DeLong, Jefferson, North Carolina: McFarland, 1996.

Gregg, Robert, "America's Town Meeting of the Air, 1935–1950," Ph.D. diss., Columbia University, 1957.

MacDonald, J. Fred, *Don't Touch That Dial! Radio Programming in American Life, 1920–1960*, Chicago: Nelson-Hall, 1979.

Savage, Barbara Dianne, *Broadcasting Freedom: Radio, War, and the Politics of Race, 1938–1948*, Chapel Hill: University of North Carolina Press, 1999.

JENNIFER HYLAND WANG

AMOS 'N' ANDY

U.S. Serial (1928–1943); Situation Comedy (1943–1955); Hosted Recorded Music (1954–1960)

Amos 'n' Andy, which began as a nightly serial telling the story of Amos Jones and Andy Brown, two Georgia-born black men seeking their fortunes in the North, dominated American radio during the Depression. Combining character-driven humor with melodramatic plots, the series established the viability in broadcasting of continuing characters in a continued story and, from both a business and creative perspective, proved the most influential radio program of its era, inspiring the creation of the broadcast syndication industry and serving as the fountainhead of both the situation comedy and the soap opera. At its peak in 1930–31, the program's nightly audience exceeded 40 million people.

After 15 years and more than 4,000 episodes, the serial gave way to a weekly situation comedy and the characterizations grew more exaggerated. Today, the original *Amos 'n' Andy* is almost completely forgotten—its substance overshadowed by the unacceptability of white actors portraying African-American characters and lost to the memory of the broadly played sitcom that replaced it. Nevertheless, *Amos 'n' Andy* remains a landmark in U.S. broadcasting history.

Origins

Amos 'n' Andy grew out of *Sam 'n' Henry,* created by Freeman F. Gosden and Charles J. Correll, two former producers of home-talent revues who had begun their careers as a comic harmony team on Chicago radio in 1925. They had been asked by the management of station WGN to adapt the popular comic strip "The Gumps" for broadcasting, but were intimidated by its middle-class setting. Instead, they suggested a "radio comic strip" about two black men from the South moving to the North, characterizations that would draw on Gosden's familiarity since childhood with African-American dialect, and that would enable the performers to remain anonymous—an important consideration if the program should fail.

Sam 'n' Henry premiered on 12 January 1926 as the first nightly serial program on American radio, combining black dialect with certain character traits and storytelling themes from "The Gumps." The early episodes were often crude, but Gosden and Correll gradually learned how to tell involving stories and to create complex human characterizations.

By the spring of 1926 the performers had begun recording *Sam 'n' Henry* sketches for Victor, and the success of these records suggested to the performers that live broadcasting need not be their only course. Accordingly, the partners suggested to WGN that their programs be recorded and the recordings leased to other stations. WGN rejected the proposal, citing its ownership of the series and its characters. Gosden and Correll left WGN in

December 1927, moving to station WMAQ, owned by the *Chicago Daily News,* and negotiated an agreement that included syndication rights. Arrangements were made for advance recordings of each episode on 12" 78 rpm discs that would be distributed to subscribing stations for airing in synchronization with the live broadcast from WMAQ. Correll and Gosden called this a "chainless chain" and, realizing the value of the concept, attempted to secure a patent, but were unable to do so; however, by the early 1930s their idea had formed the basis for the broadcast syndication industry.

Transition

The WMAQ series introduced Amos Jones and Andy Brown as hired hands on a farm outside Atlanta, looking ahead to their planned move to Chicago. Amos was plagued by self-doubts and worried about finding work in the North, whereas the swaggering Andy was quick to insist that he had the answers to everything.

Amos and Andy struggled until they met Sylvester, a softspoken, intelligent teenager patterned after the black youth who had been Gosden's closest childhood friend. Sylvester helped Amos and Andy start their own business, the Fresh Air Taxicab Company, and introduced them to a cultured, successful, middle-class businessman named William Taylor and his bright, attractive daughter Ruby, who soon became Amos' fiancée. They also met the potentate of a local fraternity, George "Kingfish" Stevens, a smooth-talking hustler who insinuated himself and his constant moneymaking schemes into their lives.

Chainless Chain to Network

Within a few months *Amos 'n' Andy* had attracted a national following and the attention of the Pepsodent Company, which negotiated to bring the serial to the coast-to-coast NBC Blue network in the summer of 1929. Amos, Andy, and the Kingfish relocated from Chicago to Harlem at the start of the network run, but otherwise the storyline continued unchanged.

At first, the program was heard at 11 P.M. Eastern time, but Pepsodent sought an earlier time slot for Eastern listeners and NBC was able to clear time at 7 P.M. As soon as the change was announced, thousands of listeners in the Midwest and West wrote to complain about the move and within a week Correll and Gosden had agreed to broadcast twice nightly. This dual-broadcast plan would be widely adopted by other national sponsors as a solution to the time-zone dilemma.

The outcry over the time change offered just a hint of what was to come. By the spring of 1930 theater owners in many cities were being forced to stop the movie playing in order to present *Amos 'n' Andy* over their sound systems to hold an evening audience—dramatic evidence of an unprecedented craze that would endure for nearly two years.

Impact

As a result of its extraordinary popularity, *Amos 'n' Andy* profoundly influenced the development of dramatic radio. Working alone in a small studio, Correll and Gosden created an intimate, under-stated acting style—a technique requiring careful modulation of the voice, especially in the portrayal of multiple characters—that differed sharply from the broad manner of stage actors. The performers pioneered the technique of varying both the distance and the angle of their approach to the microphone to create the illusion of a group of characters. Listeners could easily imagine that they were in the taxicab office, listening in on the conversation of close friends. The result was a uniquely absorbing experience for listeners who, in radio's short history, had never heard anything quite like *Amos 'n' Andy*.

Although minstrel-style wordplay humor was common in the formative years of the program, it was used less often as the series developed, giving way to a more sophisticated approach to characterization. Correll and Gosden were fascinated by human nature, and their approach to both comedy and drama drew from their observations of the traits and motivations that drive the actions of all people; although they often overlapped popular stereotypes of African-Americans, there was at the same time a universality to their characters that transcended race.

Central to the program was the tension between the lead characters. Amos stood as an "Everyman" figure: a sympathetic, occasionally heroic individual who combined practical intelligence and a gritty determination to succeed with deep compassion—along with a caustic sense of humor and a tendency to repress his anger until it suddenly exploded. Andy, by contrast, was a pretentious braggart, obsessed with the symbols of success but unwilling to put forth the effort required to earn them. Although Andy's overweening vanity proved his greatest weakness, he was at heart a poignant, vulnerable character, his bombast masking deep insecurity and a desperate need for approval and affection. The Kingfish was presented as a shrewd,

resourceful man who might have succeeded in any career, had he applied himself, but who preferred the freedom of living by his wits.

Other characters displayed a broad range of human foibles: the rigid, hard-working Brother Crawford, the social climber Henry Van Porter, the arrogant Frederick Montgomery Gwindell, the slow-moving but honest Lightning, the flamboyant Madam Queen. Still other characters stood as bold repudiations of stereotypes: the graceful, college-educated Ruby Taylor; her quietly dignified father, the self-made millionaire Roland Weber; and the capable and effective lawyers, doctors, and bankers who advised Amos and Andy in times of crisis. Beneath the dialect and racial imagery, the series celebrated the virtues of friendship, persistence, hard work, and common sense and, as the years passed and the characterizations were refined, *Amos 'n' Andy* achieved an emotional depth rivaled by few other radio programs of the 1930s.

Above all, Correll and Gosden were gifted dramatists. Their plots flowed gradually from one into the next, with minor subplots building in importance until they took over the narrative and then receding to give way to the next major sequence; seeds for future storylines were often planted months in advance. It was this complex method of story construction that kept the program fresh and enabled Correll and Gosden to keep their audience in a constant state of suspense. The technique they developed for radio from that of the narrative comic strip endures to the present day as the standard method of storytelling in serial drama.

Storylines in *Amos 'n' Andy* usually revolved around themes of money and romance—Amos' progress toward the goal of marrying his beloved Ruby Taylor stood in contrast to Andy's romantic fumblings—with the daily challenge of making ends meet forming a constant backdrop. The taxi-cab company remained the foundation of Amos and Andy's enterprises, but the partners constantly explored other ventures, including a lunchroom, a hotel, a grocery, a filling station, and a 500 acre housing development. Andy invariably claimed the executive titles, whereas Amos shouldered the majority of the work, until Amos' temper finally blazed and Andy was forced to carry his share of the load.

The moneymaking adventures of the Kingfish moved in and out of these plotlines, and through the Depression era *Amos 'n' Andy* offered a pointed allegory for what had happened to America itself in the 1920s: Amos represented traditional economic values, believing that wealth had to be earned, whereas the Kingfish embodied the Wall Street lure of easy money, and Andy stood in the middle, the investor torn between prudence and greed.

Although *Amos 'n' Andy's* ratings gradually declined from the peak years of the early 1930s, it remained the most popular program in its time slot until 1941. Correll and Gosden and their characters had become a seemingly permanent part of the American scene.

The early 1930s saw criticism of the dialect and lower-class characterizations in the series by some African-Americans, but *Amos 'n' Andy* also had black supporters who saw the series as a humanizing influence on the portrayal of blacks in the popular media. A campaign against the program by the Pittsburgh *Courier* in mid-1931 represented the most visible black opposition the radio series would receive—and, although the paper claimed to have gathered hundreds of thousands of signatures against the series, the campaign was abruptly abandoned after six months of publicity failed to generate a clear consensus. Throughout *Amos 'n' Andy's* run, African-American opinion remained divided on the interpretation of the complex, often contradictory racial images portrayed in the program.

A New Direction

On 19 February 1943 Correll and Gosden broadcast the final episode of the original *Amos 'n' Andy.* In a busy wartime world, the era of the early-evening comedy-drama serial was drawing to an end.

Correll and Gosden returned to the air that fall in a radically different format. The gentle, contemplative mood of the serial was replaced by a brassy Hollywoodized production, complete with studio audience, a full cast of supporting actors (most of them African-American) and a team of writers hired to translate Amos, Andy, the Kingfish, and their friends into full-fledged comedy stars. The new *Amos 'n' Andy Show* endured for the next 12 years as one of the most popular weekly programs on the air.

The sitcom initially stuck close to the flavor of the original series; with Amos having settled down to family life, the storylines in the last years of the serial had focused on Andy's romantic entanglements and on his business dealings with the Kingfish. At first the half-hour series continued in this pattern, emphasizing plots that could be wrapped up with an O Henry-like surprise twist at the end. By 1946, however, the Kingfish had moved to the forefront, driving the plots through his eternal quest for fast money and his endless battles with his no-nonsense wife Sapphire. The subtle blend of self-importance, guilelessness, and vulnerability that

had characterized Andy was gradually replaced by simple gullibility, and for the Kingfish's increasingly outlandish schemes to work, Andy had to become not just gullible but more than a little stupid. Amos receded further into the background, his presence reduced to that of a brief walk-on, in which he would tip Andy off that the Kingfish had again played him for a fool. The relaxed intimacy of the original series had been replaced by an increasing emphasis on verbal slapstick. The subtlety of the original characterizations was lost in a barrage of one-liners. At the same time, however, the new series offered African-American performers a doorway into mainstream radio, in both comedic and nondialect, nonstereotyped supporting roles.

In 1948 Correll and Gosden sold the program to the Columbia Broadcasting System (CBS), initiating a chain of events that led directly to William Paley's "Talent Raid," and the network immediately began plans to bring the series to television with an all African-American cast. The TV version of *The Amos 'n' Andy Show* was dogged by controversy as CBS took the characters even further down the path of broad comedy, culminating in a formal protest against the TV series by the National Association for the Advancement of Colored People (NAACP) in 1951. The TV series was cancelled in 1953, but remained in rerun syndication until 1966.

The radio version of *The Amos 'n' Andy Show* was not mentioned in the NAACP protest. Radio was a dying medium, however, and when the weekly show ended in May 1955 the performers had already begun their next series, *The Amos 'n' Andy Music Hall,* a nightly feature of recorded music sandwiched between prerecorded bits of dialogue. Coasting on the familiarity of the characters, this final series ran for more than six years.

On 25 November 1960 CBS aired the final broadcast of *The Amos 'n' Andy Music Hall.* After a brief comeback—in which they provided voices for the 1961–62 American Broadcast Company-TV animated series *Calvin and the Colonel,* which reworked *Amos 'n' Andy Show* plots into funny-animal stories—Correll and Gosden slipped quietly into retirement.

Although audio recordings of most of the situation comedy episodes exist, most of the serial survives only as archival scripts, stored at the University of Southern California and the Library of Congress. Modern discussions of *Amos 'n' Andy* commonly focus more on deconstruction of its racial subtext than on examination of the original program—often obscuring the seminal role Freeman Gosden and Charles Correll played in the development of American broadcasting.

See also: African-Americans in Radio; Situation Comedy; Stereotypes on Radio; Syndication; Talent Raids

Cast

Amos Jones	Freeman Gosden
Andrew H. Brown	Charles Correll
George "Kingfish" Stevens	Freeman Gosden
John "Brother" Crawford	Freeman Gosden
Willie "Lightning" Jefferson	Freeman Gosden
Frederick Montgomery Gwindell	Freeman Gosden
Prince Ali Bendo	Freeman Gosden
Flukey Harris	Freeman Gosden
Roland Weber	Freeman Gosden
William Lewis Taylor	Freeman Gosden
Sylvester	Freeman Gosden
Madam Queen	Freeman Gosden (1931–32), Lillian Randolph (1944, 1952–53)
Henry Van Porter	Charles Correll
Pat Pending	Charles Correll
The Landlord	Charles Correll
Honest Joe the Pawnbroker	Charles Correll
Lawyer Collins	Charles Correll
Henrietta Johnson	Harriette Widmer (1935)
Ruby Taylor Jones	Elinor Harriot (1935–55)
Sapphire Stevens	Elinor Harriot (1937–38), Ernestine Wade (1939–55)
Mrs. Van Porter	Elinor Harriot (1936–38), Ernestine Wade (1939–44)
Mrs. C.F. Van DeTweezer	Elinor Harriot (1936)
Harriet Lily Crawford	Edith Davis (1935)
Pun'kin	Terry Howard (1936–37), Elinor Harriot (1937)
Arbadella Jones	Elinor Harriot (1936–39), Barbara Jean Wong (1940–54)
Genevieve Blue	Madaline Lee (1937–44)
Dorothy Blue	Madaline Lee (1937–38)
Valada Green	Ernestine Wade (1939)
Sara Fletcher	Ernestine Wade (1940–43)
Widow Armbruster	Ernestine Wade (1941–42)
Shorty Simpson	Lou Lubin (1944–1950)
Gabby Gibson	James Baskett (1944–1947)
Reverend Johnson	Ernest Whitman (1944–45)
LaGuardia Stonewall	Eddie Green (1947–49)
Algonquin J. Calhoun	Johnny Lee (1949–54)
Leroy Smith	Jester Hairston (1944–55)
Sadie Blake	Ruby Dandridge (1944)
Ramona "Mama" Smith	Amanda Randolph (1951–54)

Announcers

Bill Hay (1928–42), Del Sharbutt (1942–43), Harlow Wilcox (1943–45, 1951–55), Carleton KaDell (1945–47), Art Gilmore and John Lake (1947–48), Ken Carpenter (1949–50), Ken Niles (1950)

Writers (serial)

Freeman Gosden and Charles Correll (1928–43)

Writers (sitcom)

Bob Ross, Joe Connolly and Bob Mosher, with contributions from others

Creative Producer

Freeman Gosden

Programming History (various networks)

1928–43	*Amos 'n' Andy*
1943–55	*The Amos 'n' Andy Show*
1954–60	*Amos 'n' Andy Music Hall*

Further Reading

Alexander, H.B., "Negro Opinion and Amos and Andy," *Sociology and Social Research* 16 (March–April 1932).

"Amos 'n' Andy," *Time* (3 March 1930).

"Amos 'n' Andy: The Air's First Comic Strip," *Literary Digest* (19 April 1930).

Biel, Michael Jay, "The First Recorded Program Series— Amos 'n' Andy, 1928–29," in *The Making and Use of Recordings in Broadcasting before 1936*, Ph.D. diss., Northwestern University, 1977.

Brasch, Walter M., *Black English and the Mass Media*, Amherst: University of Massachusetts Press, 1981.

Clarke, A. Wellington, "If Amos and Andy Were Negroes: What Numerous Negroes in Various Walks of Life Think of the Boys," *Radio Digest* 25 (August 1930).

Correll, Charles J., and Freeman F. Gosden, *Sam 'n' Henry*, Chicago: Shrewesbury, 1926.

Correll, Charles J., and Freeman F. Gosden, *All about Amos 'n' Andy and Their Creators, Correll and Gosden*, New York: Rand McNally, 1929; 2nd edition, 1930.

Correll, Charles J., and Freeman F. Gosden, *Here They Are: Amos 'n' Andy*, New York: Long and Smith, 1931.

Cripps, Thomas, "Amos 'n' Andy and the Debate over American Racial Integration," in *American History, American Television: Interpreting the Video Past*, edited by John E. O'Connor, New York: Ungar, 1983.

Crosby, John, "Amos 'n' Andy: Ain't Dat Sumpin'!" *Colliers* (16 October 1948).

Crowell, James, "Amos 'n' Andy Tell Their Own Story in Their Own Way," *American Magazine* 109 (April 1930).

Ely, Melvin Patrick, *The Adventures of Amos 'n' Andy: A Social History of an American Phenomenon*, New York: Free Press, and Toronto: Macmillan Canada, 1991.

McLeod, Elizabeth, "Amos 'n' Andy Examined," *Chuck Schaden's Nostalgia Digest and Radio Guide* 24 (June–July 1999).

McLeod, Elizabeth. *The Original Amos 'n' Andy: Freeman Gosden, Charles Correll and the 1928–1943 Radio Serial*. Jefferson, North Carolina: McFarland, 2005.

"On The Air: Amos 'n' Andy," *The New Yorker* (22 March 1930).

Quest, Mark, "Amos 'n' Andy Backstage at WMAQ," *Radio Digest* 24 (March 1930).

Roberts, Harlow P., "A Key to One Sponsor's Success in Radio," *Broadcasting* (15 April 1932).

Ross, Dale Howard, "The Amos 'n' Andy Radio Program, 1928–1937: Its History, Content, and Social Significance," Ph.D. diss., University of Iowa, 1974.

Wertheim, Arthur Frank, *Radio Comedy*, Oxford and New York: Oxford University Press, 1979.

ELIZABETH MCLEOD

AM RADIO

Amplitude modulated (AM) or "standard" radio broadcasting (as the Federal Communications Commission [FCC] referred to AM until 1978) was the first broadcast service. AM dominated American commercial radio through the 1970s, provided the basis for most electronic media regulatory policies, and was the medium for which programs and the programming process were first developed. After decades of growth, however, the AM business is in decline.

AM Basics

AM transmitters modulate (or vary) a carrier wave (the basic signal used to "carry" the sidebands that contain the program information) by its amplitude (loudness) rather than its frequency, and do so many thousands of times per second. Seen diagrammatically, AM waves vary in height, indicating power changes in accordance with the signal being transmitted, rather than frequency, as in FM radio. Electronic static, most of which is amplitude modulated in its natural state, cannot be separated from the desired signal, though engineers spent years attempting to do so.

In the United States, AM channels are 10 kHz wide, whereas in much of the rest of the world by the 1990s, stations were licensed to use 9 kHz (a move to do the same in the United States was defeated by industry pressure in the early 1980s). With careful monitoring, an AM station can transmit from 5,000 to 7,000 cycles per second, which is sufficient for voice and some music, but misses the overtones of true high-fidelity sound. On the other

hand, AM channels, being narrower, allow far more stations to be accommodated per kHz than is the case with FM.

In most countries, AM operates on the medium wave frequencies (in the United States, 535 to 1705 kHz). Such a spectrum location means that signals are propagated along and sometimes just beneath the ground (day and night), and by sky waves bouncing off the ionosphere (night-time only). This process has its benefits and drawbacks. The former comes from the extreme distances a powerful AM signal may travel on a cold, clear, winter evening—1,000 miles and often more. Unfortunately, such transmissions can never be exactly predicted; this leads to frustration in tuning distant stations, and more importantly, interference with other outlets, even though they may be closer to the listener. Further, ground waves and sky waves arrive at the same tuning (listening) point at different times (the sky waves having traveled much greater distances), which also causes interference.

Because of the sky wave problem, more than half of all U.S. AM stations are licensed for daytime operation only (the FCC stopped issuing new daytime-only licenses in 1987). Virtually all remaining stations reduce power in the evening hours as a condition of their licenses. This greatly reduces, but does not eliminate, the sky wave problem. Because so many AM stations were crowded on the air in the half century after World War II, most now must use directional antennas to "steer" their signals away from other stations.

All of these issues make AM engineering very complex. Because of this situation and the fact that more than 500 stations were on the air when effective regulation was established in 1927, there are no allotted channels in AM, as there are with FM and television services. When applying for a license, a new station must convince the FCC that it will not cause intolerable interference to others in the same or nearby markets—a very difficult and expensive thing to prove.

In an attempt to reduce interference and add stability to licensing, the Federal Radio Commission (FRC) in 1928 established three different types of AM radio channels: clear, regional, and local (in descending order of power and coverage area). There were few clear and regional channels and hundreds of local ones. Powerful (50,000 watts) clear channel stations were designed to serve large rural regions about 750 miles across and were located at great distances from one another (at first there were no other stations on clear channels at night—hence the term "clear"). Regional stations were less powerful and covered smaller areas; these stations naturally increased as channels were reused by stations in different areas. Finally, local stations reached only 10 or 20 miles, were separated by a few hundred miles, and soon became the most common type of AM outlet, often using lower power at night, with many operating on the same channel in different areas. The system was simplified in the 1980s.

Short History

AM radio broadcasting originated from the early 20th-century radio telephony experiments of Frank Conrad, Lee de Forest, Reginald Fessenden, Charles Herrold, and others. Early radio broadcast transmitters in the 1920s were manufactured by hand, were hard to adjust and maintain, and delivered uneven and sometimes unpredictable performance. This led to considerable detail in the regulatory requirements established by the FRC after 1927. Stations required a full-time engineer for all the modifications and monitoring required. By 1941 the quality of AM technical equipment was considerably improved.

Until 1941 all U.S. commercial stations—about 600 to 700 at any one time—operated only with AM transmission and competed only with other AM outlets. The radio industry at this time was small and friendly. While by 1941 the largest cities had a dozen stations, many smaller towns had but one or two and large parts of the country had no local radio service at night. Radio networks dominated programming and advertising with relatively few stations surviving as independent operations. By 1941 there were only a handful of educational stations on the air.

AM faced its first competition when the Federal Communications Commission (FCC) approved the creation of FM stations at the beginning of 1941; television arrived by the middle of the same year. The U.S. involvement in World War II limited growth of the new services so that most people could only tune in to AM for the duration of the war. After the war, AM grew from about 900 stations in 1945 to some 2,500 by the early 1950s—a frenetic rate of growth that illustrated public interest in and demand for more local radio service. By the 1960s, the FCC initiated two different freezes on further AM licenses, steering new applicants to the FM band instead. Any town of any size had a full complement of AM stations with no room for more.

AM stations dominated the industry through these four decades: there were more of them, they earned the vast majority of radio industry income, and they reached most of the audience most of the time. Most program developments were focused on AM stations, especially the arrival in the 1950s of top-40 rock stations and their many spin-offs in the years that followed. AM station owners controlled broadcast trade associations and saw FM as merely an expansion of what they already offered.

By 1980, however, AM's competitive situation had changed dramatically. The year before, more people tuned to FM stations for the first time, and the gap continued to widen for the next two decades as FM's higher fidelity won over listeners. FM was expanding faster as well. By the turn of the century, only a quarter to a third of the radio audience regularly tuned to AM outlets. In many cases, AM stations shifted to news and talk formats, abandoning music to higher fidelity FM. Long dominant, AM had become a minor partner in a still expanding radio business. The number of AM outlets was actually in decline by the 1990s as stations left the air unable to attract sufficient listeners and thus to make a case to advertisers. The AM business was in trouble.

Improving AM

Faced with signs of this decline, the industry manufacturers and the FCC pressed for relief by improving AM's limited technical capabilities. The first debate concerned stereo transmission, which many in the business thought held great potential for competing with FM. From 1977 to 1980 the AM industry sought to develop an agreed-upon standard for such a service that could be recommended to the FCC. Unable to make a decision among a half dozen mutually incompatible systems by as many companies, in March 1982 the FCC announced that AM broadcasters were expected to establish their own technical standard, although antitrust laws made it impossible for the industry to overtly collaborate on such a decision. Given this confused situation, few manufacturers built receivers, few stations installed AM stereo transmission capability (about 10 percent of all AM stations on the air), and listeners were never given a reasonable opportunity to accept or reject the technology. By 1992 the AM stereo "experiment" was clearly a failure, with two systems (Kahn and Motorola) still contending to be the final choice. Under a congressional mandate to finally make a choice, the FCC in late 1993 picked the Motorola system as a de facto standard. By then it was largely too late—too few stations (and fewer listeners) cared.

That AM still needed technical improvement in order to compete remained obvious. The FCC asked the National Radio Systems Committee

(NRSC), an industry group acting in an advisory capacity to the commission, to aid in the effort, admitting it was "dealing with no less an issue than the survival of the AM service." Heavily criticized for the AM stereo debacle, the FCC appeared eager to demonstrate a real commitment to AM. In a series of decisions, it adopted NRSC-1 and NRSC-2 standards, which would help to reduce AM interference and encourage manufacturers to create improved receivers.

One AM problem had always been insufficient spectrum space. Despite post-World War II growth, the AM band had remained unchanged since 1952. After the International Telecommunication Union approved a recommendation for Western Hemisphere nations to add to their AM radio bands in 1979, the FCC began to shift existing services out of the affected frequencies, and in 1990 began to actively plan for AM station use of the new band (1605–1705 kHz). Most of the new band was allocated to the United States, although both Mexico and Canada received use of some frequencies as well. After deciding not to license new stations (which would merely exacerbate existing interference), in a series of decisions the FCC selected existing AM outlets (based largely on how much interference they caused or received) to shift from lower frequencies into the new space. Assignments began in 1997 and the first station, WCMZ in Miami, was operating in the new frequencies by late that year. However, the newly relocated stations often reached far smaller audiences as old receivers could not tune the new frequencies. Only time and new sets would slowly change this problem.

At the same time the United States did not adopt another proposal—to narrow AM channels from 10 kHz to 9 kHz, a decision that would have allowed hundreds of new stations on the air. Touted in the late 1970s to help bring U.S. standards in line with those of the rest of the world, the idea was shot down by industry arguments that such spacing would increase interference and would make most digital receivers obsolete, as they were calibrated for 10 kHz channels. Not as overtly stated was a strong industry belief that the last thing AM radio needed was more competing stations.

Decline or Survival?

For more than a decade, the number of operating AM stations has slowly decreased. In 1997, there were 4,811 AM outlets on the air; a decade later, nearly 30 had left the air. Eulogies for the AM band are only outnumbered by plans to "save" the medium. For example, since 2000, iBiquity has been manufacturing and promoting its "HD Radio," which, among other features, enhances AM sound quality to digital levels. Should HD catch on, this might help stem some of AM's decline.

Others see AM's salvation in program innovation. Talk radio has long been housed on AM. Having begun on AM, Rush Limbaugh's phenomenal success briefly buoyed the service, but his program is now largely carried on FM stations. AM talk is now mostly dominated by second-tier talent, political and otherwise, including Laura Ingraham, Michael Medved, Michael Reagan and Stephanie Miller. AM is also open to such emerging genres as all-sports talk (sometimes augmented with feeds from ESPN Radio) and such highly specialized formats as children's radio, "women's" radio, all-agriculture formats and such ethno-centric programming as all-Greek or Korean. As various "oldies" formats across the country redefine their play lists—increasingly playing the hits of the 1980s and even 1990s as opposed to those of the 1960s and 1970s—AM may become a refuge for Baby Boomers unable to find music of their era on FM. Some believe AM's best chance for resurrection lies in its willingness to embrace a hyper-local approach, perhaps by airing everything from a recitation of the local police blotter to coverage of high school sports, to "trading posts" shows where area listeners phone in with either items they are looking to sell or items they are looking to buy.

Perhaps AM's biggest obstacle is in perception: It is often seen as little more than a poor relation to FM. And though AM can serve as a successful incubator for new formats, it lacks the cutting edge, futuristic cachet of satellite and terrestrial digital services.

See also: Clear Channel Stations; Digital Audio Broadcasting; Federal Communications Commission; FM Radio; Frequency Allocation; History; National Radio Systems Committee; Stereo

Further Reading

Edelman, Murray Jacob, "The Licensing of Standard Broadcast Stations," in *The Licensing of Radio Services in the United States, 1927 to 1947: A Study in Administrative Formulation of Policy*, by Edelman, Urbana: University of Illinois Press, 1950.

Emery, Walter Byron, "Standard Broadcast Stations (AM)," in *Broadcasting and Government: Responsibilities and Regulations*, by Emery, East Lansing: Michigan State University Press, 1961; revised edition, 1971.

Fisher, Marc, "In the Internet Age, AM Radio Needs Fine-Tuning." *Washington Post* (4 May 2008), p. M-3.

Huff, W.A. Kelly, *Regulating the Future: Broadcasting Technology and Government Control*, Westport, Connecticut: Greenwood Press, 2001.

Inglis, Andrew E., "AM Radio Broadcasting," in *Behind the Tube: A History of Broadcasting Technology and Business*, by Inglis, Boston: Focal Press, 1990.

Snider, Mike, "HD Radio Sends Strong Signal, but Audience Weak," *USA Today* (8 July 2008), p. 1D.

Special Reports on American Broadcasting, 1932–1947, New York: Arno Press, 1974 (reprints of four Federal Communications Committee reports).

W.A. KELLY HUFF AND CHRISTOPHER H. STERLING,
2009 REVISIONS BY CARY O'DELL

ANTENNA

An antenna is a device designed to either radiate ("send") or intercept ("receive") radio signals in an efficient fashion. Antenna types differ according to the frequency used, the radio service involved, and the specific task at hand. Antenna size and location are important factors in their efficiency. Transmission towers for antennas that send radio signals are nearly always manufactured of steel and are either in the form of self-supporting towers or are supported with guy wires (the latter structure is less expensive but requires more ground); in the United States, they are built to national standards set in 1959 by what is now called the Electronic Industries Alliance. Tower structures are typically either square or triangular in cross-section.

Origins

Washington D.C. dentist and wireless inventor Mahlan Loomis may have been the first user of an antenna with his experiments in the Blue Ridge Mountains west of the capital city in the late 1860s. Loomis' antenna consisted of a wire suspended beneath a high-flying kite. The real inception of modern radio antennas came decades later with Marconi's understanding of the need for a high aerial or antenna to aid in receiving wireless telegraphy signals over large distances. He and other wireless pioneers experimented with many often highly complex antenna designs before settling on the use of three or four wooden (later steel) transmission towers at a given transmitter site.

The design of antenna structures rapidly improved in the years before and after World War I. The spread of broadcasting after 1920 and the use of higher frequencies for radio services prompted development of transmission antennas with greater efficiency. Radio receivers had improved by the late 1920s to the point that they no longer always required external antennas for effective operation, thus making them easier to use and less expensive. The first transmission antennas that could propagate signals in a given direction or pattern (dubbed directional antennas) were developed in the 1930s, allowing a station to transmit its signal to a more specific area and thus help avoid interference with other stations. World War II saw the development and refinement of microwave transmission and special antennas for that service. Much was learned about how the careful location of an antenna tower could have substantial impact on its efficiency. Postwar antenna improvements included substantial refinements in methods of both transmission and reception.

AM Radio

AM radio station antennas make use of the entire transmission tower as a radiating element. To achieve the most efficient radiation, an AM antenna tower's height should equal about half the length of the radio waves being transmitted. For example, an AM station on 833 kHz, where wavelengths are about 360 meters long, should ideally use an antenna tower that is some 180 meters or about 590 feet tall (nearly the length of two football fields). Additionally, because AM makes use of ground waves to distribute its signal, the tower is usually merely the visible part of a complex system that extends under and through the ground. As good ground contact is essential for an efficient ground wave, AM antennas often feature an extensive web of copper cables radiating out from the tower location and buried just below ground level. AM antennas are sometimes located in damp or moist locales (such as swamps or marshes) to aid in ground wave conduction.

Both to help reduce interference and to focus signals where most listeners are, the vast majority of the country's AM stations transmit a directional signal. Rather than the circular coverage pattern that would result from a standard antenna (assuming flat terrain), most AM stations use two or more antenna towers to transmit signals in a pattern away from another station, or away from a body of water or some other physical feature with few listeners, and toward population centers. Multiple AM towers for different stations are often clustered together in antenna "farms" to keep potential obstructions to airplanes at a minimum. In some locations, FM antenna towers and towers for television stations are located within the same antenna farms.

FM Radio

Unlike AM antennas, where the entire tower can assist in radiating the signal, in FM broadcasting the antenna is a relatively small device mounted on top of the transmission tower. This is because the wavelengths in the VHF spectrum used by FM radio are far shorter than in the medium wave spectrum used by AM stations. An FM outlet licensed to operate at 100 MHz, where the wavelengths are about three meters long, only requires an antenna about 1.5 meters (about five feet) in length. As FM stations rarely need a directional pattern, multiple FM antennas for a single station are uncommon. A taller transmission tower allows the antenna element to be mounted higher above average terrain, thus extending this line-of-sight service's coverage.

FM antennas can be polarized in three different ways, each affecting how the signal will be received. Horizontal polarization was long the FM standard in the United States, but most stations now employ circular polarization for better service to car radio antennas of different types. A third type, vertical polarization, is generally restricted to public FM stations seeking to avoid adjacent channel interference with television channel six (which occupies 82–88 MHz, immediately below the lowest frequencies of the FM band).

Other Types: Shortwave and Microwave

Shortwave radio station antennas are very complex because of the many different shortwave bands that may be in use during a typical broadcast period. Extensive antenna arrays of different sizes, often covering a large ground area, help to sharpen reception.

On many transmission towers across the country one can observe various ancillary dishes or horn-shaped antennas, sometimes mounted on the top of a tower, but often attached to its sides. These are nearly always for microwave transmission links, some used for voice or data links, and some for sending television signals for use by distant cable television systems.

All radio antennas in the United States must be built and operated within strict licensing and tower marking requirements. A tower's location, height, and other characteristics are specifically defined in a station's license from the Federal Communications Commission. Generally speaking, a higher antenna will help to extend a station's coverage area, although this is more true for FM than AM services. All transmission towers must be painted in wide bands of red and white to make them more visible in low light conditions, and must be electrically highlighted at night. Jurisdiction over these requirements (as well as locating towers as far away from airports as possible) is shared with the Federal Aviation Administration.

Reception Antennas

Antennas to *receive* AM or FM signals are rarely seen by consumers as they are increasingly built into radio receivers. Some home stereo systems, for example, come with a plastic-and-wire loop antenna for improved AM reception indoors. Likewise an FM antenna, usually a long wire with a "T"-shaped ending, can be attached for better indoor reception.

With the inception of satellite communication in the 1960s, large dish-shaped antennas dubbed "earth stations" were built in several locations around the world. Often huge dishes up to 200 feet in diameter, they were designed to gather in weak satellite signals and boost them to an audible range. Also used to receive satellite-delivered audio signals are back-yard or building-top dishes typically called "television receive-only" ("TVRO") antennas. Direct-to-home reception of audio and video signals can now take place using small dishes of a foot or 18 inches in diameter.

With the introduction of HD Radio toward the end of the first decade of the 21st century, there was some effort by consumer electronics firms to market special antennas to improve reception. Although technical advice differed, most engineers argued that no special antenna was required—that any existing FM antenna (especially an "external" one, meaning outside the receiver) should work well. The primary difference is that the digital signal will either be received, or not. There is no fading away of such a signal at the end of its range—it simply ceases being heard. And no special antenna will make any difference, though a good FM antenna may well be useful.

See also: Audio Processing; Frequency Allocation; Ground Wave; Shortwave Radio

Further Reading

"Antennas and Propagation," in *Proceedings of the Institute of Radio Engineers* (May 1962).
Carr, Joseph J., *Practical Antenna Handbook*, Blue Ridge Summit, Pennsylvania: TAB Books, 1989; 3rd edition, New York: McGraw Hill, 1998.
Collin, Robert E., *Antennas and Radiowave Propagation*, New York: McGraw Hill, 1985.
Hall, Gerald, editor, *The ARRL Antenna Book*, Hartford, Connecticut: American Radio Relay League, 1939; 19th edition, Newington, Connecticut, 2000.
Orr, William I., *Radio Handbook*, 23rd edition, Boston: Newnes, 1997.
Rudge, Alan W., et al., editors, *The Handbook of Antenna Design*, 2 vols, London: Peregrinus, 1982–83; see especially vol. 1, 1982.
Setian, Leo, *Practical Communication Antennas with Wireless Applications*, Upper Saddle River, New Jersey: Prentice Hall PTR, 1998.

Sterling, Christopher H., editor, *Focal Encyclopedia of Electronic Media*, Stoneham, Massachusetts: Focal Press, 1997 (CD-ROM).

CHRISTOPHER H. STERLING,
2009 REVISIONS BY CHRISTOPHER H. STERLING

ARBITRON
Media Research Firm

The Arbitron Company is a media research firm that provides information used to develop the local marketing strategies of electronic media, their advertisers, and agencies. Arbitron has three core businesses: measuring radio audiences in local markets across the United States; surveying the retail, media, and product patterns of the local market consumers; and providing survey research consulting and methodological services to the cable, telecommunication, direct broadcast satellite, on-line, and new media industries. Although begun as an audience measurement service for television, it is currently diversified into a complete service marketing firm.

As radio evolved into quite a different medium after the introduction of television, Arbitron was best able to provide a relatively inexpensive method, the personal diary, for measuring radio's listening audience. Radio stations strove to provide a continuous, distinctive sound, composed largely of music but also including news, talk, sports, and community bulletin information. As radio became more portable and available in cars, more of its audience was away from home.

Arbitron splits the field of radio measurement with Statistical Research Incorporated, whose RADAR service measures radio networks. Thomas Birch's Radio Marketing Research provided major competition for the radio marketplace before Birch left the field in 1991. Arbitron measures 276 local radio markets today by means of an open-ended mail-in personal diary developed by James Seiler (originally an improvement over C.E. Hooper's multimedia diaries). Each member of a household who is over 12 years of age receives a personal diary with a page for each day of the week without printed time divisions.

Origins

Begun by James W. Seiler in Washington, D.C., in 1949 as both a national and local television ratings service, the American Research Bureau (ARB; now known as Arbitron) succeeded because of the inexpensive method—the viewer diary—that it used to measure radio and television audiences. The diary method pioneered by Seiler met broadcasters', advertisers', and agencies' needs for more comprehensive information about the television audience, especially viewer demographics.

Seiler realized that the Federal Communications Commission freeze (1948–52) had artificially restricted television development to East Coast cities and that when the freeze was lifted, stations and the need for measurement would spread to the West Coast. On a trip to the West Coast, Seiler discovered a local service, Tele-Que, that also used a diary method to measure one-week periods. Rather than duplicating the Tele-Que service, Seiler offered to consolidate, and ARB merged with Tele-Que in 1951, which put ARB in a strong position on both coasts. Known for a time as ARB Tele-Que, by 1954 the company was known simply as the American Research Bureau.

Like all services during that period, ARB originally tailored its methods to the nuclear family, which served as the target for enormous volumes of merchandise from manufacturers and advertisers. At that time, the entire household was used as the unit of measurement. Both the diary and the meter were tailored to a lifestyle in which the family gathered around a single console radio or television and listened or watched en masse. Only one diary (called a household diary or set diary) was sent to each family, and the assumption was that the housewife would record listening for the entire family. In an era before multiple sets, only the family room console required a meter, and it generated what were known as household ratings. Diaries allowed other information desired by advertisers and broadcasters to be included, such as the number of color television sets and whether the sets had ultrahigh-frequency receivers.

ARB's first major success was with national television reports, introduced in October 1950. Without national or network ratings, Seiler would later remark, ARB would have been lost in the crowd. Only ARB, Nielsen, and a much smaller rating service called Videodex represented a national cross-section in its sampling. Although the Nielsen network service, the Nielsen Television Index, was Audimeter-based, Nielsen supplemented his meter method at the local level for his Nielsen Station Index with a diary to provide demographics. The development of a meter-plus-diary service was necessitated when, in 1954, ARB introduced an electronic instantaneous meter service, called Arbitron, to supplement its diary method. Videodex, a diary-only service, was discovered to be making up numbers from a discontinued sample of warehoused diaries; this came to light during a

1963 congressional investigation into rating services and their practices. The diary provided data on both gross (or duplicated) and cumulative (or unduplicated) audiences, and data were projectable to estimates of all U.S. television homes.

The ARB diary keepers were randomly selected from telephone directories of all U.S. cities within a 50-mile radius of the television signal. Diaries, mailed to those who agreed to cooperate, were kept for a one-week period. Field personnel made two subsequent calls to ensure continued cooperation. ARB drew new samples for each one-week period.

The ARB grew rapidly throughout the 1950s. Following Hooper's death in a 1955 boating accident, ARB took over his local market reports.

Arbitron

By 1959 Seiler had added a multicity rating service that used the same method as his archrival Nielsen, an electronic household meter. He called his meter service Arbitron. This meter service offered a distinct advantage over Nielsen's mail-in Audimeter and over its own hand-tabulated diaries in use at the time, because Arbitron's data were collected instantaneously. As part of the service, each station was represented by a row of electronic lights on a display board. As viewers switched from one station to another, the lights blinked off in the row for one station and lit up in another row for a different station. Arbitron did not succeed as a national television service owing to a number of factors: stations and networks balked at the cost, Nielsen entangled Arbitron in a lengthy patent litigation suit that drained it of financial resources, and the better-capitalized Nielsen undercut the cost of ARB's station reports.

Arbitron produces estimates for three areas: the metro area, the Area of Dominant Influence (ADI), and the total survey area (TSA). The metro area is short for metropolitan area, the standard metropolitan statistical area as defined by the U.S. census, although it is occasionally more loosely employed. The ADI is an exclusive geographical area consisting of all counties in which the home-market commercial stations receive a preponderance of total viewing or listening hours. The ADI concept divided the United States into more than 200 markets, assigning each station to only the one market where it captured the largest share of audience. The ADI was the first standardized means of defining a market, because previously, media planners had used their own definitions. The ADI paved the way for demographic targeting, because with a boundary for each market, a market's performance could

be related to demographics. The TSA is a non-exclusive marketing area that indicates a station's viewing or listening audience regardless of where the station is located, including areas where stations overlap. Thus, a station could be assigned to more than one TSA if listening occurred in neighboring counties or markets. Unlike television, most radio buys are based on metro areas, because radio competes primarily in the local market against such media competition as newspapers. In 1982 Arbitron switched from four-week to 12-week measurement periods in order to reduce the influence of promotions, giveaways, and other gimmicks used by radio stations to increase listenership. Advertising rates are based on audience size.

Radio Ratings

Arbitron entered the local radio marketplace in 1963 after the Harris hearings, a congressional investigation into the ratings services that resulted in Nielsen's exit from the radio marketplace that same year. ARB's new emphasis on the field of radio audience measurement over television was also partly motivated by RKO Radio's request that Seiler conduct a study that same year of the best way to measure audiences of all media, especially radio. The outcome was the recommendation that the personal diary—a small booklet designed for each individual in the household to carry with him or her throughout the day—be used to measure radio. This was an improvement over the household or set diary previously in use, because for the first time since the mass exodus to television, radio stations were able to report a measurable audience. Radio had shifted from a mass medium where people listened around a single set to a more portable medium because of such technological innovations as the transistor. Now radio's largest audience was its out-of-home listeners, as people listened in such places as at work, in the car, and on the beach, a phenomenon that had not been recorded by the previous method, the household set diary, which conceptualized viewing as occurring at home and as a family.

Ratings Innovator

Arbitron has typically been more technologically and conceptually innovative than its competitors in responding to the marketplace. Dominant firms such as Nielsen find it more profitable to pursue a "fast second" strategy whereby they allow small pioneers a modest inroad before they respond aggressively. Arbitron's research and development, as a result, have led to a significant number of new features in product design. Seiler developed both the all-radio diary, which measured the radio audience separately rather than as part of the television sample, and the personal diary, which was sent to each member of the household.

Seiler began the practice of using a four-week ratings period (rather than the previously used one-week period). Television still uses this four-week period as the basis of its ratings, although radio now uses a 12-week period. Seiler provided the first county coverage studies, which determined station viewership on a county-by-county basis by actual measurement rather than the previously used projections.

Seiler also began the practice of "sweeps" periods, or the simultaneous measurement of all markets based on actual coverage areas. In 1966 ARB developed new survey markets, or ADI, which, in addition to the metro and total survey areas used by rating services during the period, became the industry standard for exclusively defining the geography of local markets. The ADI geography largely replaced the previously used metro areas in television. In failing to copyright the idea, however, ARB opened the door for Nielsen to introduce a somewhat similar concept, the Designated Market Areas. Much of this additional information was made possible by ARB's switch from hand-tabulated methods to use of an electronic Univac 90 computer in 1959. By 1961 ARB was measuring every U.S. television market and had twice produced national sweeps.

By the 1960s Arbitron led the other ratings services in its inclusion of age and sex demographic information; it was able to do so because of its use of the diary method, which asked specific viewers about their viewing. Arbitron's innovation offered advertisers and agencies finer and more discriminating tools to cherry-pick audiences. These innovations, together with its national sample, resulted in Arbitron's quickly emerging as a leader in local market measurement.

After merging with the Committee for Economic and Industrial Research (CEIR) in 1961, ARB expanded its computer facilities. By 1964 many members of the original ARB management, including Seiler, Roger Cooper, and John Landrith, left, citing basic differences between ARB and CEIR policy. CEIR hired new management who were not well received by major agencies. In 1967, faced with agency and station cancellations, CEIR sold Arbitron to Control Data Corporation.

By the mid-1980s, Arbitron radio audience measurement had grown to 420 markets measured four times a year, and the personal diary had become the standard tool for radio. For studies of the radio audience, Arbitron was testing a portable pocket "people meter," a passive sound-measuring methodology, for radio, television, and cable audiences. Adoption of this device was stalled because of a 1993 patent infringement suit filed by Pretesting Company of Tenafly, New Jersey, which had developed a prototype similar to Arbitron's that it had shown to Arbitron in 1994. The device is the size of a handheld beeper. It is worn by respondents and is able to detect, decode, and store signals encoded in television and radio sound transmissions. A recharging base unit collects daily data and feeds them to a central computer. Audio encoding is located at each participating radio and television station. In 1998 Arbitron moved its Portable People Meter system out of the lab and into testing in Manchester, England. By 2003, the People Meter system was being test-marketed in Philadelphia. Later the company expanded to Houston and other major markets. Almost immediately, major controversy arose over its People Meter findings, most pertaining to Arbitron's PPM sample sizes. Eventually, both the states of New York and New Jersey filed lawsuits—and the FCC initiated an inquiry as well—charging Arbitron with false advertising and deceptive business practices for allegedly undersampling black and Hispanic households. The ongoing disputes over the PPM have inspired other companies to introduce their own PPM-like devices in the hopes of competing with Arbitron. It has also encouraged the A.C. Nielsen Company to announce that it would re-enter the field of radio audience measurement after an absence of 45 years.

See also: A.C. Nielsen Company; Audience Research Methods; Cooperative Analysis of Broadcasting; Diary; Hooperatings; Portable People Meter

Further Reading

Arbitron History, New York: Arbitron (10 February 1993).

Beville, Hugh Malcolm, Jr., *Audience Ratings: Radio, Television, and Cable*, Hillsdale, New Jersey: Erlbaum, 1985; revised edition, 1988.

Buzzard, Karen S., *Chains of Gold: Marketing the Ratings and Rating the Markets*, Metuchen, New Jersey: Scarecrow Press, 1990.

Knopper, Steve. "Arbitron Portable People Meter Eavesdrops on Your Musical Life," *Wired* (21 August 2007).

Layfayette, J., "Ratings Blackout: Arbitron Leave Stations Scrambling," *Electronic Media* (25 October 1993).

"Local Operations Continue: Arbitron Drops Scanamerica Ratings Service," *Communication Daily* (3 September 1992).

"Matter of Concern: Arbitron Throws in the Towel," *Communications Daily* (19 October 1993).

KAREN S. BUZZARD,
2009 REVISIONS BY CARY O'DELL

ARCHIVES

See: Museums and Archives of Radio; Old-Time Radio

AUDIENCE

Over the eight decades of radio broadcasting's existence, knowledge about the medium's audience has developed and become more refined. Whereas other entries explore how radio audiences have been studied and measured, the purpose here is to characterize the audience for American radio through time.

Radio's Audience Before Television

The earliest information about radio listeners was at best anecdotal. Stations received letters from listeners (usually responding to a program), which revealed some sense of a program's geographical spread, but little else. What little research there was focused on who purchased receivers—and thus, presumably, who listened. The 1930 census gathered information on radio set ownership showing that half the urban, but only 21 percent of the farm families, owned a receiver. Whereas 63 percent of homes in New Jersey owned a radio, only five percent of Mississippi homes did.

In the early 1920s, and to some degree for several years after that, radio appealed to an upper-class audience. Manufactured receivers were often quite expensive (upwards of $1,000 in current values for better models), and only upper-income people could afford them. Programs and advertising reflected this audience. The Depression and the appearance of a variety of popular programs made radio more attractive to a wider audience.

The first concerted attempt to study patterns of the radio audience more deeply was the work of psychologist Daniel Starch, whose consulting firm conducted personal interviews with some 18,000 families across the country in 1928 and again in 1929–30 under contract to the National Broadcasting Company (NBC). The Starch researchers found that 80 percent listened daily, that radio was used about 2.5 hours per day, that listening was largely a family affair that took place in the evening, and that nearly 75 percent of the audience tuned to one or two favorite stations most of the time.

By the end of the 1930s, more than 90 percent of urban and 70 percent of rural homes owned at least one radio (half the homes in the country had two), and whereas ownership was universal in higher-income households, radios were also found in 60 percent of the poorest homes. The average receiver was on for five hours a day, and listeners developed a fierce loyalty to the characters in favorite programs (especially daily soap operas, one of the first formats whose audiences were carefully studied). Radio was also trusted, as became clear in the panic caused by the 1938 *War of the Worlds* broadcast. Research was finding, however, that as a listener's income and educational level rose, the time spent listening to radio dropped.

During the 1941–45 war, radio became the prime source of news, and listening levels reached their peak. Radio's variety of programs appealed at some time of the day to virtually everyone. Radio was available in nearly 90 percent of households and in a quarter of all cars by 1945. At the end of the 1940s—and the end of radio's monopoly of listeners—studies found that most people liked most of what they heard. Indeed, radio was ranked as doing a better job than most newspapers, churches, schools, or local government, although its reputation slipped a bit from 1945 to 1947, perhaps reflecting the end of wartime news (newspapers replaced radio as the primary news source over the same period).

Growing from related studies of the movie audience, some concern was raised about how radio affected young listeners. Programs that featured suspense and horror were said to keep children awake. Crime programs might encourage violence on the part of listeners. Considerable research was undertaken, especially at universities, but no clear results were forthcoming.

Radio Since Television

The public's growing fascination with television after 1948 initially cut down on radio listening, especially in cities with the handful of early television stations. Network audiences dropped sharply in just a few years. Radio rebounded in the 1950s, but patterns of listening were changing—radio was now largely a daytime (especially morning) medium, whereas television dominated evening time. Ironically, as radio diminished in the eyes of some of its listeners, it became the focus of more academic research. Studies began to assess the sociological and psychological reasons why people listened, but most of what was known about radio's listeners grew out of ratings and other commercial research.

As popular music formats (e.g., *American Top 40*) appeared and as car radios became more common (half of all cars had radios in 1951, 68 percent by 1960), radio became a medium with considerable appeal to a teenage audience. Stations developed many gimmicks to keep young people listening—chiefly the use of contests and giveaways. Most parents were totally lost in this new format.

Another audience was attracted to radio, especially to the relative handful of FM stations offering classical music. These were the high-fidelity buffs who were interested in the best quality audio they could buy. They listened to AM–FM stereo broadcasts in the late 1950s and flocked to FM after stereo standards were approved in 1961. This was a relatively highbrow audience with considerable appeal to some advertisers.

By the mid-1960s, radio was in use for about 25 hours per week in the average household, with half of that from portable and car radios (in 80 percent of cars by 1965), showing radio's expanding ability to travel with its audience. Listening peaked in morning "drive time" and slowly dropped off for the rest of the day, reaching low levels in the evening. Most people turned to radio for news and weather reports and some type of music—and despite the growing number of outlets, most people still listened to only a handful of favorite stations. Radio in many cases had become background sound for other activities at work and at home. Nearly 80 percent of households listened to radio sometime during a typical week.

Until the 1970s, *radio* still meant AM stations for most people, because FM was a limited service catering primarily to an elite audience interested in fine-arts programming. However, as the number of FM stations grew and began to program independently of AM outlets, that medium's appeal increased. FM stations began to appear in ratings in major cities, and in 1979 national FM listening first exceeded that for AM. By the 1990s FM accounted for three-quarters of all radio listening.

The minority listening to AM were tuned to various talk formats, and they wanted to participate. Call-in talk shows became wildly popular, especially those with controversial hosts. Radio became almost a two-way means of expression for such listeners. Some controversy arose in the 1990s over the likely effect of some youth-appeal music lyrics that seemed to promote violent behavior.

By 2000 radio was reaching a wholly new and largely unmeasured audience—listeners tuning in via the internet. A station could now appeal to listeners well beyond its own market and even in other countries. This new mode helped to promote the splintering of radio formats—and their audiences—into more specialized categories.

Listening to traditional radio stations, however, declined during the first decade of the 21st century, and appeared likely to continue to drop. That is not to say people stopped listening, but increasingly they listened online or by using portable digital audio devices. And what they listened to was often not a radio station, but some other audio service (or downloads) providing different music genre. Or, they (some 20 million of them by 2009) tuned to satellite radio rather than terrestrial services.

Indeed, radio stations faced a "perfect storm" of trouble that contributed to these declining listening levels—too many commercials, bland programming that sounded much alike across many stations, and a lack of local news and other reasons to tune in. Most seriously, young people were turning away from radio which they perceived as being old-fashioned and dull. Once gone, they seldom return to traditional radio later. Radio's one bright spot continued to be drive-time listening, especially in the late afternoon.

See also: A.C. Nielsen Company; Arbitron; Audience Research Methods; Automobile Radio; Cooperative Analysis of Broadcasting; Demographics; Hooperatings; Office of Radio Research; Programming Research; Psychographics; Radio, Decline of; Violence and Radio; *War of the Worlds*

Further Reading

Cantril, Hadley, and Gordon W. Allport, *The Psychology of Radio*, New York and London: Harper, 1935.

Lazarsfeld, Paul Felix, and Patricia Kendall, *Radio Listening in America: The People Look at Radio—Again*, New York: Prentice-Hall, 1948.

Lazarsfeld, Paul Felix, and Harry Hubert Field, *The People Look at Radio*, Chapel Hill: University of North Carolina Press, 1946.

Mendelsohn, Harold, *Radio Today: Its Role in Contemporary Life*, Washington, D.C.: National Association of Broadcasters, 1970.

Nielsen, A.C. Co., *The Radio Audience*, Chicago: Nielsen, 1955–64 (annual).

Starch, Daniel, A *Study of Radio Broadcasting Based Exclusively on Personal Interviews with Families in the United States East of the Rocky Mountains*, Cambridge, Massachusetts: Starch, 1928.

Starch, Daniel, *Revised Study of Radio Broadcasting Covering the Entire United States and Including a Special Survey of the Pacific Coast*, New York: National Broadcasting Company, 1930.

Sterling, Christopher H., *Electronic Media: A Guide to Trends in Broadcasting and Newer Technologies, 1920–1983*, New York: Praeger, 1984.

CHRISTOPHER H. STERLING,
2009 REVISIONS BY CHRISTOPHER H. STERLING

AUDIENCE RESEARCH METHODS

The necessary and sufficient condition for success in radio is an audience loyal to its favorite stations and important enough to advertisers to produce reliable levels of advertising revenue. Non-commercial radio station aims are much the same except that the advertising is called *underwriting,* and listener (audience) donations are an important source of revenue.

Research into radio audiences has been a part of radio broadcasting from its beginning. In the earliest days of radio, stations were concerned with audiences at a distance and the distant places where the signal of the station could be heard. Stations relied on motivated listeners to send postcards and letters reporting which programs and stations they had heard.

Newspapers carried stories about the distances at which local stations had reportedly been heard; they also reported which far-distant stations had been received by readers. Consider this report in the *New York Times* (18 March 1924):

Pope Hears Opera on His Radio and Picks Up a London Station

ROME, March 17 (Associated Press)—The radio receiving set at the Vatican has been installed and Pope Pius already has been "listening in." Last night the Pontiff heard the opera "Boris Godunov" played at the Costanzi Theatre in Rome, and later picked up a London station which was broadcasting.

Pope Pius expressed great pleasure at the clearness with which the sound waves were received, notwithstanding the fact that there was some static interference.

The set at the Vatican is said to be powerful enough to pick up some of the stations in America, and an effort is to be made to hear KDKA (Pittsburgh). Up to the present, however, there has been no attempt made to listen in on other than Continental stations.

This interest in the reach of radio signals continues today among shortwave broadcast audiences. Many stations encourage listeners to write or e-mail them about the shortwave programs and personalities they have heard. When listeners correspond with a station, they are rewarded by receiving colorful photo cards (QSL or "distant listening" cards) featuring favorite performers.

By the late 1920s advertising on radio had grown to the point that advertisers desired to know at a quantitative level the reach of their radio commercials. Broadcasters also needed to learn whether they were charging enough for the advertising opportunities they sold. The result was systematic radio audience research.

The principal questions addressed by audience research were (1) who is likely to be in a given station's or program's audience? (2) what is the popularity of a program or station? (3) what is the success of a program or commercial announcement?, and (4) what is the probable success of a program or commercial announcement that has not yet been broadcast?

The term *ratings* is often used by media professionals to refer to all measures of audience listening and sometimes to describe the commercial companies that conduct syndicated audience research. Of greatest weight in the view of broadcasters is the fact that audience research is the principal tool used to persuade advertisers that significant audiences will be delivered for their advertising. The evidence of the future value of a station or network advertising opportunity is measured by the size and composition of the audience provided by particular programming in the past, and these are reported in audience research.

The first national radio survey conducted on a systematic basis took place in 1927 when Frank Giellerup of Frank Seaman Advertising asked Archibald Crossley to study audiences for the Davis Baking Powder Company. In March and April 1928, NBC commissioned Daniel Starch, a Harvard professor and pioneer market research consultant, to conduct an extensive survey east of the Rockies. By the 1929–30 radio season a regular program rating service, Cooperative Analysis of Broadcasting (CAB) had been established, providing routine reports on the audiences of network programs. Significantly, the CAB governing board assured that the Association of National Advertisers controlled the infant rating service. Later, broadcasters rather than advertisers became the prime force in establishing standards and practices for audience research.

Methods of Data Collection

Audience research must always ask what listeners have heard (which programs, which stations). The methods of collecting this data have evolved over the history of radio ratings. They include techniques known as telephone recall, telephone coincidental, roster interviews, diaries, meters, and recorders.

In a telephone recall survey, a radio listener is called by an interviewer from the research company at some time after a program has been presented. The interviewer asks whether the respondent listened. In March 1930 the CAB interviewed regularly in 50 cities using the telephone recall method. Telephone recall interviewers asked respondents about their radio listening in the previous 24 hours, noting the time of listening, who was listening, and the programs and stations heard.

Telephone interviewers using the telephone coincidental technique asked respondents about radio listening taking place at the time of the call. Their questions revealed whether anyone was currently listening to a radio in the household, which family members were listening, and what programs and stations were being heard. In the early years of radio, this method was associated with the research firm of ClarkHooper formed when Montgomery Clark and C.E. Hooper left the Daniel Starch organization in 1934. Later, this technique became known as the Hooperatings. As only one time of listening was researched per telephone call, this style of research was labor-intensive for the interviewer and somewhat expensive. However, it is thought by audience research authorities to be the best measure of audience activity when conducted correctly.

Roster interviews were those in which the respondents were interviewed face-to-face. At designated points in a roster interview, respondents were shown a list of programs and stations and asked to identify those that they remembered hearing within a specified period of time. This method of data collection for audience research was also known as *aided recall measurement*. The roster method was used by The Pulse during the several decades of its history and is associated with Sydney Roslow, a psychologist who formed the organization in 1941.

The diaries used in audience research are special questionnaires in booklet form in which listeners record their times of listening and the stations or programs heard. This method has the advantage of collecting many times of listening over a given period of time (typically a week). The development of this method is often associated with James Seiler, founder in 1949 of the American Research Bureau. Diaries may be kept by an individual for his/her own listening (individual diary) or by one household member for all of the household (household diary). Contemporary radio audience research in the United States and Canada asks that all individuals in selected households maintain individual diaries, a pattern called *flooding the household*.

Listening meters were devices that automatically record times and tuner settings for radio receivers. The first of these was devised by Robert Elder and Louis Woodruff of the Massachusetts Institute of Technology and first used in 1935 for CBS. As radio meters measure the potential listening in a household by monitoring which receivers are on or off at what times and to which signal each is tuned, they produce household ratings. In 1936 market researcher A.C. Nielsen attended a luncheon at which Elder spoke about the Elder-Woodruff Audimeter. He was impressed and bought out the inventors, later establishing a radio meter rating service known as the Nielsen Radio Index.

Portable People Meters

A variety of unsophisticated devices were experimented with in the years following, each used to measure radio listening, before Arbitron perfected its Portable People Meter (PPM) in the late 1990s. The PPM is a device made to be worn or carried, much like a cell-phone or pager, by sample participants as they go about their day. It records, via electronic inaudible codes, all radio signals that are listened to or overheard and reports these readings back to a central processor. As the PPM, unlike written diaries, requires no activity or involvement by the person being sampled (beyond being carried and occasionally recharged) its findings are considered to be of a higher accuracy than the more standard (and now "old-fashioned") diary method.

Since their implementation in the first decade of the 2000s, PPM findings have caused great controversy. Arbitron has been sued (on grounds of false advertising and deceptive business practices) by the attorney generals of New York and New Jersey. It has also received an inquiry from the FCC over PPM sample sizes and methods. And introduction of the PPM had an unexpected byproduct: the controversy inspired A.C. Nielsen to re-enter the radio measurement business it left in 1963. Nielsen published its first radio ratings—obtained by the old standby diary method—in the middle of 2009. Despite their checkered introduction into the marketplace, however, further application of PPMs and PPM-like devices is the next significant step in radio audience measurement.

Samples of Listeners

In the early years of radio broadcasting, samples were typically drawn from phone listings in cities selected because they were served by radio stations affiliated with the networks sponsoring the study. During the 1940s and 1950s there were considerable efforts to produce samples that would be perceived as excellent by researchers in the broadcast and advertising industries.

Different samples are used for audience research with national and local audiences. Because the motive for much research has been to substantiate the value of advertising opportunities, the areas where surveys are conducted are called *markets*.

Networks, advertisers, and others interested in nationwide entertainment and advertising support national market audience surveys. National surveys must give weight not only to every local market, but also to listening in rural areas where national signals may reach. RADAR (Radio's All Dimension Audience Report) conducts the only regular national surveys of the radio audience.

In local-market surveys the sample is drawn from three survey areas. The smallest of these is the metropolitan (metro) area, usually a core urban area as defined by the U.S. Office of Management and Budget. The largest area surveyed in a local-market survey is called the total survey area (TSA), which typically is an aggregate of units of county size, including the relevant metro area or areas. The TSAs of adjacent markets may include the same counties; for example, the total survey area for City A may include Brown County because an important part of the listening in the county is to City A radio stations. At the same time, the TSA for City B may also include Brown county for the same reason. An "exclusive area" is sometimes included, in which each market consists only of those counties where the plurality of listening is to the market being surveyed. In this system of exclusive areas, any particular county can belong to only one market.

Random Sampling

In sampling for audience research, random sampling is preferred, because theoretically a random sample maximizes the probability that a sample will be very similar to the population from which it is drawn. A random sample is one in which each member of the target population is equally likely to be chosen for the survey (participants are chosen at random); each choice is also entirely independent of the others. The first criterion—equal likelihood for selection—requires that the researcher name the "sample frame" from which the sample is to be drawn (i.e., list all members of the target population). In the early days of radio audience research, telephone directory listings were the sample frames. Listed telephones serve best as sample frames when nearly all residential telephones are listed and when nearly all residences are equipped with telephones. In the early years of audience research the first condition was typically met, but telephone penetration had yet to reach its peak.

In the past several decades residential telephone listings have become progressively poorer telephone sample frames. Although nearly all residences now have telephones, fewer and fewer have listed telephone numbers. One of the methods audience

researchers have adopted to cope with this problem is random digit dialing, a method in which all possible telephone numbers within a target area are listed and the sample frame is drawn from that list. A number of variations on this procedure are used as contemporary sample telephone frames. There are sample frames for households rather than telephones; an example is a city directory. Enumerations of households within census tracts (designated by the U.S. Census Bureau for control of their surveys) also serve as household sampling frames. A quite different approach to sample frames is a frame of clusters, which are sampling units that each consist of two or more interviewing units such as residences. A city block, for example, may become a cluster in a sample frame, as it is a cluster of households or interviewing units.

In most contemporary radio audience research, sampling procedures are mixed. Thus, the initial sampling frame could be a residential telephone listing, later supplemented by a second frame of telephone numbers computer-generated at random.

Producing Ratings Survey Reports

Whenever a radio audience report lists a rating (percentage of potential audience) or a listening estimate (numbers of listeners), a degree of error is also implied. This is called *sampling error*, a scientifically determined estimate of the difference between research results if the entire target population were surveyed and those obtained using a sample. The probability that such an error will occur is given by the *confidence interval* listed for any professional research study. The confidence interval standard in audience research is 95 percent, meaning that if the same study were conducted many times, the same results would be obtained at least 95 percent of the time. Commercially produced audience survey reports include descriptions of the methods used for estimating sampling error and confidence intervals.

Stations, networks, and program suppliers who use audience data in their sales and planning prefer to receive audience data at a modest cost, so the research suppliers must not spend more on audience research than their customers are willing to pay. The statistic used to compare the cost basis of competing radio audience research reports is price per "listening mention."

A listening mention is the smallest unit of reported radio listening. It consists of at least five minutes of continuous listening to a certain station or program. One listening mention, then, means that one member of the sample reported listening to a particular station/program for at least five minutes during a 15-minute interval of the time period being surveyed. The telephone coincidental method for collecting listening mentions from audiences is the most expensive method of producing routine audience reports, as any respondent can provide only one listening mention—the one in which the individual was involved at the time of the interviewer's call. The lowest cost per listening mention is nearly always a research method employing a meter or recorder, as analysis of one instrument's data can provide a train of listening mentions over months or even years.

The number of hours per week over which ratings or audience estimates are provided is another cost factor. If every hour of the week were surveyed for listening, a maximum of 672 listening mentions could be recorded. To reduce costs, audience research firms have typically limited the number of hours reported in their surveys. Thus, over the years, they have reported listening during prime time only, or they have excluded the hours of lowest listening (such as those between midnight and dawn).

The break-even cost of an audience survey is reached when the number of clients who will pay for the survey at a designated price meets the cost of collecting, tabulating, and printing the data they are willing to buy. When the number willing to buy increases above the break-even point, then the research company becomes profitable (at times very profitable). This explains why a number of new companies over time have entered into the radio audience research business, although relatively few have survived.

Special Research Studies

A number of research methods are used to study the desirability of using particular songs or groups of songs within the established format of a radio station or network. Each of the following music audience research methods has its advocates and detractors, but all have persisted in one form or another over the past several decades.

Telephone call-out and call-in is a method that focuses on recent musical releases and older (but still fairly recent) songs that have remained popular and are still frequently played. Each music selection being studied is prepared as a recorded *hook*—that is, a representative excerpt of a recording.

In telephone call-out research, the researcher will have previously identified a pool of qualified study participants (listeners to the station in question or to the categories of music being studied). The interviewer plays over the phone one hook at a time

and asks the study participant to respond with phrases such as (1) "I've never heard of it," (2) "I dislike it strongly," (3) "I dislike it moderately," (4) "I don't care," (5) "I'm tired of it," (6) "I like it," or (7) "That's my favorite record."

Stations and networks that make use of call-out research conduct their studies weekly or semi-weekly. Satellite programming services making music available to stations throughout the country conduct this research on a continuing basis in many markets.

In one form of telephone call-in, study participants receive a letter in the mail asking them to participate in the study. The letter identifies a telephone number for participants that connects them to a recording of the hooks for the study. The participant listens to the hooks when convenient, then returns the questionnaire by mail or telephones a researcher who writes down the responses read by the participant from the completed questionnaire.

Auditorium studies are surveys often used to study audience response to "oldies" (songs that were quite popular during the more distant past and that are still popular with at least part of the radio audience) and "standards" (new versions of oldies). Researchers recruit a sample of radio listeners, who assemble in an auditorium or rented meeting room. Hooks of the music are played over high-quality sound systems. Participants then mark their responses to each hook in questionnaire booklets or on digital responders (keypads that summarize responses into a convenient computer file). Auditorium studies commonly include hooks for large numbers of recordings, greatly reducing the cost per hook for respondent data. Because of the effort required to assemble hooks, arrange for facilities, and recruit respondents, auditorium studies are conducted less frequently than call-out or call-in studies.

The relatively low costs of mail and internet surveys make these surveys appealing. However, mail surveys require that study participants recognize songs from written descriptions that may include the name of a song or performer or some words from a song's lyrics. This limitation often leaves researchers wondering whether the music has been correctly identified by study participants. Internet surveys permit playing hooks over a respondent's computer speakers, reducing the possibility that study participants will not recognize the music being studied. Survey questionnaires are then presented for completion on respondents' computer screens. When all answers have been provided, the data is immediately returned to the researcher's computer. As not every radio listener has access to a computer connected to the internet, study participants must be identified in a pre-survey as (1) listeners accessible by internet, and (2) listeners to the radio music being studied.

Radio Program Format Research

Radio program format research concerns the mixture of music, news, and talk programming that is best for a given station or network. Although a number of methods are used in format research, focus groups have received the greatest attention in the literature about radio.

A *focus group* is a group of research participants who are selected for their relevance to the matter being studied. Their viewpoints and opinions are collected with a guided conversation about the research topic. In the case of format studies, one strategy is to recruit a variety of groups—those who listen only to the station in question, those who listen to the station sometimes, and those who never listen to the station but by their media habits show that under some circumstances they could become listeners.

The results of station format focus group studies identify the "position" (reputation) of the station in its market. In addition, the specific language used by study participants during the focus sessions may suggest useful slogans or themes for station promotional campaigns.

Because many radio stations today are owned by corporations that own large groups of stations, station format studies may be a matter of researching format issues in several markets simultaneously. The results may lead to the choice of a station format that will function competitively in all of the group's markets.

See also: A.C. Nielsen Company; Arbitron; Auditorium Testing; Cooperative Analysis of Broadcasting; Hooperatings; Portable People Meter; Programming Research; Pulse, Inc.; RADAR

Further Reading

Astal Media information on PPN, http:/infoppm.astalmedia radio.ca/

Beville, Hugh Malcolm, Jr., *Audience Ratings: Radio, Television, and Cable*, Hillsdale, New Jersey: Erlbaum, 1985; 2nd edition, 1988.

Chappell, Matthew Napoleon, and Claude Ernest Hooper, *Radio Audience Measurement*, New York: Daye, 1944.

Fletcher, James E., *Music and Program Research*, Washington, D.C.: National Association of Broadcasters, 1987.

Lumley, Frederick Hillis, "Methods of Measuring Audience Reaction," *Broadcast Advertising* 5 (October 1932).

Lumley, Frederick Hillis, *Measurement in Radio*, Columbus: Ohio State University Press, 1934; reprint, New York: Arno Press, 1971.

National Association of Broadcasters, *Standard Definitions of Broadcast Research Terms*, New York: National Association of Broadcasters, 1967; 3rd edition, as *Broadcast Research Definitions*, edited by James E. Fletcher, Washington, D.C.: National Association of Broadcasters, 1988.

Routt, Ed, "Music Programming," in *Broadcast Programming: Strategies for Winning Television and Radio Audiences*, edited by Susan Tyler Eastman, Sydney W. Head, and Lewis Klein, Belmont, California: Wadsworth, 1981.

Webster, James G., and Lawrence W. Lichty, *Ratings Analysis: Theory and Practice*, Mahwah, New Jersey: Erlbaum, 1991; 2nd edition, as *Ratings Analysis: The Theory and Practice of Audience Research*, by Webster, Lichty, and Patricia F. Phalen, Mahwah, New Jersey, and London: Erlbaum, 2000.

JAMES E. FLETCHER,
2009 REVISIONS BY CARY O'DELL

AUDIMETER

The Audimeter—for audience meter—was the name of the A.C. Nielsen Company's mechanical, and later electronic, device for measuring radio and television set tuning as a way of determining a show's share of the audience, better known as its ratings.

Origins

In 1929 Claude Robinson, a student at Columbia University, applied to patent a device to "provide for scientifically measuring the broadcast listener response by making a comparative record of… receiving sets…tuned over a selected period of time." Robinson later sold his device for a few hundred dollars to the Radio Corporation of America, owner of NBC, but nothing more came of it at that time.

Many realized that the least intrusive and most accurate way to keep track of listeners' radio tuning would be to attach some kind of mechanical recorder to the set. In 1935 Frank Stanton, a social psychology student at Ohio State University, as part of his Ph.D. dissertation built and tested 10 devices to "record [radio] set operations for as long as 6 weeks." (Stanton was later research director and eventually president of the Columbia Broadcasting System.)

Others experimented with similar devices. Robert Elder of Massachusetts Institute of Technology and Louis Woodruff field-tested their device in late 1935 by measuring the audiences tuning in to Boston stations. But it was Arthur C. Nielsen, a consumer survey analyst with a degree in electrical engineering, whose wealth and fame would be made by the device. In early 1936, Nielsen heard a speech by Robert Elder, who called his device an "Audimeter." At the time the Nielsen Company, a consumer survey business, was primarily a collector of information on grocery and drug inventories.

After receiving permission to use the Robinson-RCA device and some redesign of it, in 1938 the Nielsen Company began tests in Chicago and North Carolina. In 1942, the company launched the Nielsen Radio Index based on 800 homes equipped with the Audimeter, which recorded on a paper tape the stations a radio was tuned to. In the beginning, Nielsen technicians had to visit each of the 800 homes periodically to change the tape and to gather other information from each household based on an inventory of the family's food supply. The Audimeter was usually hidden from view in a nearby closet or some other out-of-the-way place. Respondents were usually given nominal compensation for their participation, and Nielsen usually shared repair costs on any radio in which the meter had been installed. Beginning in 1949, the receiver's tuning was recorded by a small light tracing on and off on 16 millimeter motion picture film that could be removed and mailed back to the Nielsen office in Chicago for examination and tabulation by workers using microfilm readers.

Audimeter Ratings

The Nielsen Company soon supplanted the older and dominant Hooperatings, and Nielsen acquired the C.E. Hooper company in 1950. That year the Audimeter was used to record TV tuning for the Nielsen Television Index (NTI). The company also launched the Nielsen Station Index (NSI), which provided local ratings for both radio and television stations for specific market areas. In the same homes where Audimeters were in use, Nielsen obtained additional information on audience demographics by the use of diaries in which viewers were asked to record their listening and viewing of radio and television.

Throughout most of the 1950s, as television's audience grew rapidly, the measurement of radio audiences by Audimeters provided the most important information used by sponsors, advertising agencies, media buyers, and programmers. As network radio audiences declined and independent Top 40 stations rose, however, local ratings became more important. In 1941 a competitor called Pulse entered the ratings business and, with its ratings based on interviews, eventually eclipsed Nielsen.

In the late 1950s and 1960s there was much criticism of broadcasting in general, resulting from scandals involving rigged quiz shows and disk jockeys being bribed in the "payola" scheme to play specific records, and there followed lengthy congressional investigations of ratings methodologies. As a response, Arthur Nielsen tried to develop a new radio index that would be above criticism but found it would be prohibitively expensive; advertisers and stations resisted higher costs. In 1963 the Nielsen Company ended local radio measurement and the next year withdrew from national radio ratings as well. The Arbitron rating company, founded in 1949 as the American Research Bureau (ARB), continued using meters for many years to supplement its diary method of radio ratings collection.

Audimeters that merely indicate when a receiver is on, and to what station it is tuned, are now obsolete. Advertisers and station operators alike want to know *who* is listening—the listener's income, buying habits, location, level of education, etc. The Audimeter began to give way in television research (the new method was too costly to apply to radio) to the more expensive but also more useful "people meter," which can indicate who is listening by means of a remote control-type device on which each listener punches his or her key to show they are present. The people meter is connected by dedicated data lines to computers in Florida that provide overnight ratings.

Starting in 1999, Nielsen and Arbitron began testing a passive personal people meter device (about the size of a pager or small remote control) that listeners were to wear to record all their electronic media use. Arbitron introduced the device (redubbed a PPM for portable people meter) in selected markets in 2008 to considerable controversy. Nielsen responded by breaking off the cooperative research effort, re-entering the radio ratings market with its legacy written diary method, providing its first competition to Arbitron in more than four decades.

See also: A.C. Nielsen Company; Arbitron; Portable People Meter

Further Reading

Banks, Mark, "A History of Broadcast Audience Research in the United States, 1920–1980, with an Emphasis on the Rating Service," Ph.D. diss., University of Tennessee, Knoxville, 1981.
Beville, Hugh Malcolm, Jr., *Audience Ratings: Radio, Television, and Cable*, Hillsdale, New Jersey: Erlbaum, 1985; 2nd edition, 1988.

Elder, Robert F., "Measuring Station Coverage Mechanically," *Broadcasting* (1 December 1935).

Nielsen Media Research website, www.nielsenmedia.com.

Stanton, Frank Nicholas, "Critique of Present Methods and a New Plan for Studying Listening Behavior," Ph.D. diss., Ohio State University, 1935.

Webster, James G., and Lawrence W. Lichty, *Ratings Analysis: Theory and Practice*, Hillsdale, New Jersey: Erlbaum, 1991; 2nd edition, as *Ratings Analysis: The Theory and Practice of Audience Research*, by Webster, Lichty, and Patricia F. Phalen, Mahwah, New Jersey: Erlbaum, 2000.

LAWRENCE W. LICHTY,
2009 REVISIONS BY CHRISTOPHER H. STERLING

AUDIO MIXER
See: Control Board/Audio Mixer

AUDIO PROCESSING
Electronic Manipulation of Sound Characteristics

Once a sound has been transduced (transformed into electrical energy for the purpose of recording or transmission), the characteristics of that sound can be electronically manipulated. These characteristics include pitch, loudness, duration, and timbre. Thus, the term *audio processing* refers to the art and science of making changes to an audio signal to improve or enhance the original sound or to create an entirely new sound based on the original. There are many technical and creative reasons for audio processing in radio.

In the early days of radio, if the audio going into the transmitter was too loud, the transmitter could be damaged. Even today, because of the potential for interference to other stations caused by overmodulation, the Federal Communications Commission (FCC) has strict rules about modulation limits. Audio processors continuously maintain a station's compliance with these rules.

There are also many creative reasons to process audio. Consider the following examples: a commercial producer needs to transform the talent's voice into that of a space alien. In another commercial, the voices sound a little muffled; re-recording the spot through an equalizer 'to increase the midrange can make the voices sound louder. A third spot as recorded runs too long; it can be shortened by redubbing it through a digital signal processor using the time compression function. These are examples of problems that can easily be solved with the right audio processing in a production studio. Radio stations want their sound to be clean and crisp, bright, and distinctive.

Rock-formatted stations targeting teens and young adults usually want to sound loud, regardless of the particular song being played. These are examples of the types of needs addressed by the processing equipment in the audio chain before the signal goes to the transmitter. A description of the basic characteristics of sound identifies the component parts that are manipulated during audio processing.

Characteristics of Sound

Sound is created when an object vibrates, setting into motion nearby air molecules. This motion continues as nearby air molecules are set into motion and the sound travels. This vibration can be measured and diagrammed to show the sound's waveform. The characteristics of a sound include its pitch (frequency), loudness (amplitude), tonal qualities (timbre), duration (sound envelope), and phase. A sound is described as high or low in pitch; its frequency is measured in cycles per second or hertz. Humans can hear frequencies between 20 and 20,000 Hz but usually lose the ability to hear higher frequencies as they age.

The subjective measurement of a sound's loudness is measured in decibels (dB), a relative impression. The softest sound possible to hear is measured at 0 dB; 120 dB is at the human threshold of pain. The range of difference between the softest and loudest sounds made by an object is called its dynamic range and is also measured in decibels. A live orchestra playing Tchaikovsky's *1812 Overture* complete with cannon fire will create a dynamic range well over 100 dB. The amplitude, or height, of a sound's waveform provides an electrical measure (and visual representation) of a sound's loudness. Timbre is the tonal quality of sound; each sound is made up of fundamental and harmonic tones producing complex waveforms when measured. A clarinet and flute sound different playing the same note because the timbre of the sound produced by each instrument is different. Timbre is the reason two voices in the same frequency range sound different. The sound envelope refers to the characteristics of the sound relating to its duration. The component parts of the sound envelope are the attack, decay, sustain, and release. Acoustical phase refers to the time relationship between two sounds. To say that two sounds are in phase means that the intervals of their waveforms coincide. These waves reinforce each other, and the amplitude increases. When sound waves are out of phase, the waves cancel each other out, resulting in decreased overall amplitude.

Individually or in combination, the frequency, amplitude, timbre, sound envelope, and phase of the audio used in radio can be manipulated for technical and creative reasons. The characteristics of the audio created for radio typically need adjustment and enhancement for creative reasons or to prepare the audio for more efficient transmission.

Processors Manipulate Audio Characteristics

Equipment used to process audio can generally be classified using the characteristics of sound described above. There are four general categories of audio processing: frequency, amplitude, time, and noise. Some processors work on just one of these characteristics; others combine multiple functions with a combination of factory preset and user-adjustable parameters. Some processors are circuits included in other electronic equipment, such as audio consoles, recorders, or microphones. Processing can also be included in the software written for a computer-based device such as a digital audio workstation.

An equalizer is a frequency processor; the level of specific frequencies can be increased or decreased. A filter is a specific type of equalizer and can be used to eliminate or pass through specific narrow ranges of frequencies. Low-pass, band-pass, and notch filters serve specific needs. Studio microphones often contain a processing circuit in the form of a roll-off filter. When engaged, it eliminates, or "rolls off," the bass frequencies picked up by the microphone.

Amplitude processors manipulate the dynamic range of the input audio. Three examples of amplitude processors are compressors, limiters, and expanders. A compressor evens out extreme variations in audio levels, making the quiet sections louder and the loud sections softer. A limiter is often used in conjunction with a compressor, prohibiting the loudness of an input signal from going over a predetermined level. An expander performs the opposite function of a compressor and is often used to reduce ambient noise from open microphones. Most on-air audio processing uses these types of processors to refine the audio being sent to the transmitter. Recorders often have limiter or automatic gain control circuits installed to process the input audio as it is being recorded.

A time processor manipulates the time relationships of audio signals, manipulating the time interval between a sound and its repetition. Reverberation, delay, and time compression units are examples of processors that manipulate time.

Telephone talk shows depend on delay units to create a time delay to keep offensive material off the air. Commercial producers use time compression and expansion processing to meet exacting timing requirements.

Dolby and dbx noise reduction processing are methods of reducing tape noise present on analog recordings. The Dolby and dbx systems are examples of double-ended systems: a tape encoded with noise reduction must be decoded during playback. These types of processing become less important with the shift to digital audio.

Until the 1990s most processing was done using analog audio. Individual analog processors, each handling one aspect of the overall processing needs, filled the equipment racks in production and transmitter rooms. Equalizers, reverb units, compressors, limiters, and expanders all had their role. Digital processors were introduced during the 1990s. These processors converted analog audio to a digital format, processed it, and then converted the audio back to the analog form. Most processing today has moved to the digital domain. These digital signal processors allow for manipulation of multiple parameters and almost limitless fine adjustments to achieve the perfect effect. Modern on-air processors combine several different processing functions into one unit.

Audio Processing in the Audio Chain

Virtually every radio station on the air today uses some type of processing in the audio chain as the program output is sent to the transmitter. The technical reasons for processing the program audio feed date to the earliest days of radio. Engineers needed a way to keep extremely loud sounds from damaging the transmitter. The first audio processing in radio was simple dynamic range control done manually by an engineer "riding gain." The operator adjusted the level of the microphones, raising the gain for the softest sounds and lowering it during the loudest parts. During live broadcasts of classical music, the engineer was able to anticipate needed adjustments by following along on the musical score. Soon, basic electronic processors replaced manual gain riding.

Early processing in the audio chain consisted of tube automatic gain control amplifiers and peak limiters. The primary purpose of these processors was to prevent overmodulation, a critical technical issue with an amplitude-modulated signal. Operators still needed to skillfully ride gain on the program audio, because uneven audio fed to these early processors would cause artifacts, such as pumping, noise buildup, thumping, and distortion of the sound. Early processor names included the General Electric Unilevel series, the Gates StaLevel and Level Devil, and Langevin ProGar.

Broadcast engineers generally consider the introduction of the Audimax by Columbia Broadcasting System (CBS) Laboratories to be the birth of modern radio audio processing. The Audimax, introduced by CBS in the late 1950s, was a gated wide-band compressor that successfully eliminated the noise problems of earlier compressors. The Audimax was used in tandem with the CBS Volumax, a clipper preceded by a limiter with a moderate attack time. In 1967 CBS introduced a solidstate Audimax and the FM version of the Volumax, which included a wide-band limiter and a high-frequency filter to control overload due to FM's preemphasis curve.

The reign of the Audimax was challenged in the early 1970s with the introduction of the Discriminate Audio Processor by Dorrough Electronics. This broadcast compressor/limiter divided the audio spectrum into three bands with gentle crossover slopes, compressing each band separately. Broadcast engineers began to make their own modifications to some of the internal adjustments, adjusting for specific program content and personal preference.

In 1975 Orban Associates introduced the Optimod-FM 8000, which combined compressor, limiter, high-frequency limiter, clipper, 15-kHz low-pass filters, and stereo multiplex encoder into one processor. This unit allowed for higher average modulation without interference to the 19-kHz stereo pilot signal. The Optimod-FM 8000 was replaced by what soon became the industry standard, the Optimod-FM 8100. A digital version, the Optimod-FM 8200, was introduced in 1992. The Optimod-AM was introduced in 1977.

The development of these processors was driven by the need for a reliable method of maintaining compliance with the FCC transmission and interference rules while allowing for creative use and adjustment of processing for competitive advantage. Along with maintaining compliance with regulatory constraints on modulation, interference, and frequency response, engineers and programmers are always looking for ways to make their stations sound better than and different from the others. Some stations have taken creative processing to extremes. During the 1960s WABC in New York was well known for the reverb used on disc jockey voices during music programs.

A station programming classical music has processing needs different from those of an urban format station. Preserving the dynamic range of an orchestral work is critical, whereas maximizing the bass frequency and loudness enhances the music aired on the urban station. Today's processors allow for this kind of flexibility in adjustment based on format and on specific goals for the sound of the station. Audio processing plays an important role in radio stations' competition for listeners. Stations targeted toward teens and young adults want to sound louder, brighter, and more noticeable than their competitors. This is where audio processing becomes something of an art. Programmers and engineers cooperate to adjust processing to attract and maintain listeners. This is a subjective process that involves trial-and-error adjustments and critical listening by station management. There is a fine line between compressing audio to boost overall loudness and creating listener fatigue. Low time-spent-listening numbers in the ratings may not be the fault of poor programming as much as of overprocessed audio.

Audio Processing in the Studios

Much of the audio sent to the on-air processor has already been processed, perhaps as it was originally recorded, dubbed in production, or mixed with other sources in the air studio to create the program output.

One of the most common forms of audio processing in the studio is equalization (EQ), which is the increase or decrease of the level of specific frequencies within the frequency spectrum of the audio being created. Many audio consoles, especially those used in the production studio, have equalization controls on each channel to allow for adjustment of the EQ of each individual audio source. At a minimum, there are controls for low-, medium-, and high-frequency ranges, but many consoles divide the frequency spectrum into more parts. The EQ controls can be used for various creative and technical purposes. Examples include matching the frequency response of different microphones so they sound the same, creating a telephone effect by decreasing the low and high frequencies of the audio from a studio microphone, adding presence to the voices in a commercial by boosting the midrange, or eliminating hum on a remote line by decreasing the low end. Equalization can also be done through an outboard equalizer; the source or console output can be routed to the equalizer for processing. These units usually divide the frequency spectrum into intervals of one-third or one-half of an octave. Each band has a slider to increase or decrease the amount of EQ on that band. Filters, a specific type of equalizer, can be used to eliminate specific narrow ranges of frequencies. Low-pass, band-pass, and notch filters are usually used to eliminate technical problems with the audio or to keep unwanted audio frequencies from getting to the transmitter.

A well-equipped production studio has a number of processing options available to producers. Until the development of digital signal processors, every effect came from a separate unit. Although many of these single-function processors are still in use and are still manufactured, digital multiple-function processors are the norm today. These are generally less expensive than the on-air multifunction processors, and a number of manufacturers provide many different models and options in their studio processor lines. Most units offer a number of factory preset effects with user-adjustable parameters. These units also allow users to create and store their own combinations of effects. The Eventide Ultra-Harmonizer, for example, provides pitch changing, time compression and expansion, delay, reverb, flanging, and sound effects as part of its inventory. The major advantage of these multifunction units is their ability to combine effects. For example, pitch change can be combined with chorusing and reverb. Flanging can be combined with stereo panning. Given the opportunity for user-created presets and parameter adjustments, the possibilities are almost limitless.

These same types of digital effects are also integrated in the software of digital audio workstations and editors. Audio processing can be added after a recording is made on a multitrack editor. The complex waveform of each track can be processed using the same type of multiple-effects options described above. An announcer can be made to sound like a group of elves through the addition of chorusing, pitch change, and reverb; each track can be processed independently. Because the changes are not made to the original sound files, any of the modifications can be easily undone and the original audio remodified.

Microphones in the production and air studios often receive special, full-time processing. An analog or digital microphone processor typically provides compression, limiting, de-essing, equalization, noise reduction, and processing functions designed specifically to enhance vocal characteristics.

Ongoing technological advances have steadily brought down the price of even the most expensive processors. Hence, now even the smallest stations can afford to sound like the very best. Furthermore, thanks to the now omnipresent ownership of such software as Pro Tools, stations can now finesse productions at every stage, not just on the "back end" as was once tradition.

Twenty-first century stations face different sound engineering demands and requirements brought on by other technological innovations. For example, so-called HD Radio, also known as "in-band on-channel" (IBOC), allows simultaneous transmission of multiple digital or analog signals over one frequency. Stations are also working to tailor their signals for reception on iPods and other handheld devices.

See also: Control Board/Audio Mixer; Dolby Noise Reduction; Portable Digital Listening Devices; Production for Radio; Recording and Studio Equipment; WABC

Further Reading

Alten, Stanley R., *Audio in Media*, Belmont, California: Wadsworth, 1981; 6th edition, 2002.

Grant, August E., and Jennifer Harman Meadows, editors, *Communication Technology Update*, 7th edition, Boston: Focal Press, 2000.

Keith, Michael C., *Radio Production: Art and Science*, Boston: Focal Press, 1990.

O'Donnell, Lewis B., Philip Benoit, and Carl Hausman, *Modern Radio Production*, Belmont, California: Wadsworth, 1986; 5th edition, Belmont, California, and London: Wadsworth, 2000.

Reese, David E., and Lynne S. Gross, *Radio Production Worktext: Studio and Equipment*, Boston: Focal Press, 1990; 3rd edition, 1998.

JEFFREY D. HARMAN,
2009 REVISIONS BY CARY O'DELL

AUDIO STREAMING
Carrying Sound on the Internet

Delivering audio-video (AV) content on the internet has been a long anticipated goal for the media. Audio delivery became practical in 1999 with the introduction of better streaming software and the widespread adoption of MP3 compression techniques. By 2001 major internet companies (including software, hardware, and content providers) were jockeying for positions in the new market. Streaming involves sending data but not asking the computer to record it.

Compared to other internet files, AV files are very large. At first, AV was delivered in the same manner as all other files. The user would download (receive) the entire file from a central computer. This method is still used with high-quality compression (for example, MP3 files). But sending the whole file was unacceptable for two reasons. First, it took too long and required too much space on the user's computer, causing the typical home computer memory to fill up quickly. Second, after transfer, the user could keep the whole copy of the AV file. For radio it was not possible to send anything more than simple air checks or short songs, and in any case copyright holders would not allow most songs to be sent.

In 1995 Rob Glaser and company introduced RealAudio—later called RealPlayer and RealOne. The concept was simple. The software would download enough of a sound file to cover the difference between the transmission and play speed. A buffer was created on the user's computer and the file would begin to play. Only a fraction of the file needed to be transmitted before the user could enjoy it. The idea was that the file transfer would be completed shortly before the file was done playing. Continuous streaming would come later as bandwidth and compression increased.

The music industry is working to adopt both models. First, delivering whole files (download) for people to use at will—a sale model. Second, streaming content without giving it to people—a broadcast model. Even if whole files are sent, streaming is often used for more instantaneous delivery of content.

As both a business and as a technology, providing audio streaming to consumers calls for consideration of three components: distribution, players, and content.

Streaming media is produced much like any other media. The target player determines how the content is stored and served. The player is the most visible element in the process. In addition to RealPlayer, Microsoft developed its own MediaPlayer and Apple added streaming capability to its Quick Time software. Finally, the MP3 compression standard allowed software vendors to create streaming media without aligning themselves with a major corporation. The main differences between these players involve cost, compression, ability, and quality.

Once produced, the digital file is encoded in one or more of the streaming formats and stored for use by the appropriate server. The server delivers files as users request them. The server may also add visual content such as advertising or graphic illustrations (such as an album cover).

Continuous programming may be delivered by a never-ending stream or by a playlist format. The latter method sends a list of files to be played rather than a never-ending stream. Playlists may make the entire file available to users, though this is a distinct disadvantage for copyright holders. On the other hand, playlists allow users to skip songs they do not want or to build playlists of their own design.

The competition in players comes down to a software choice, whereas the competition in distribution mainly concerns hardware. Streaming files are not only very large but are also time-sensitive. If a part of the streaming content does not arrive in time, the music will stop. Distribution systems have been developed to deliver streaming files without delay. Newer server systems allow on-demand conversion from one streaming format to another. This means the producer need only store content in one format.

The first method to assure delivery was to increase the speed of delivery. Standard telephone modem delivery—the most widely used form of hooking up to the internet—has peaked at about 56,000 bits per second. Broadband delivery systems for home use are becoming increasingly available, but they are more expensive. Rollout is slow and not nearing the level required for entertainment media.

Content providers have been working to fill stream media. By the end of 2000, there were nearly 4,000 internet radio sites worldwide (just less than a decade later there were over 10,000) with nearly half that number in the U.S. Music led the way as it could be enjoyed before true broadband capacity became available. Most services sought a successful means of generating revenue. Along with the search for programming came issues of copyright and payment. ASCAP and BMI created their first internet payment models in 1998. At about the same time, the Recording Industry Association of America (RIAA) began separate negotiations for web content payments on behalf of artists and musicians. Their efforts resulted in successful lawsuits against MP3.com and Napster. The continuing threat of lawsuits based on the Digital Millennium Copyright Act (1996) caused most content providers to refocus their market. Pure streams of broadcast content nearly stopped in favor of copyright-free content—usually new artists or promotion of traditional media product. Meanwhile, internet broadcasters who continued to stream copyrighted works have, over the years, had to pay a myriad of temporary, intermediate and, at times, retroactive fines and fees. As of this writing, all parties are still debating and attempting to hammer out a final, fixed agreed-upon rate and payment model. Many internet-based businesses, such as Pandora.com, have made it clear that some proposed payment models (for example a per-song, per-play payment formula as opposed to, say, a flat fee based upon a business's annual revenue) could prove prohibitive and drive them out of business. Ironically, many companies that own streamable content—such as record labels—are still struggling to find a way to fully monetize their music via the web.

Content providers faced a second challenge in the early 2000s as the dot-com bubble burst. Unlike most player and distribution companies, many content providers did not have a second line of income and failed as online companies. Most players were supported by major software or hardware platforms. Although distribution systems often saw corporate reorganization, broadband delivery was still seen as an acceptable investment by cable television and telephone companies. Meanwhile, other companies are streaming, or are working to stream, audio over devices like cellphones, personal digital assistants and smart cable television boxes.

See also: American Society of Composers, Authors, and Publishers; Broadcast Music Incorporated; Internet Radio; Virtual Radio

Further Reading

Cosper, Alex, "The History of Internet Radio," (2007), www.tangentsunset.com/internetradio.htmFrance.
Jasmine, "How to record streaming audio," *CNET Reviews* (3 September 2008).
Grant, August E., and Liching Sung, editors, *Communication Technology Update*, Austin, Texas: Technology Futures, 1992; 7th edition, edited by Grant and Jennifer Harman Meadows, Boston: Focal Press, 2000.
Kaye, Barbara K., and Norman J. Medoff, *The World Wide Web: A Mass Communication Perspective*, Mountain View, California: Mayfield, 1999.
Miles, Peggy, and Dean Sakai, *Internet Age Broadcaster: Broadcasting, Marketing, and Business Models on the Net*, Washington, D.C.: National Association of Broadcasters, 1998.
RealNetworks, "Getting Started: A Primer on Streaming Media," www.realnetworks.com/getstarted/.

STEVEN DICK,
2009 REVISIONS BY CARY O'DELLT

AUDIOTAPE

Introduced commercially only in the late 1940s, audio recording tape would transform radio broadcasting by removing the stigma of recorded broadcasts. Development of the technique dated back decades, to work accomplished in several countries.

Origins

Early audiotape technology drew on Danish radio pioneer Valdemar Poulsen's 1898 invention of a device called the "Telegraphone." The mechanical energy of sound was converted into a flow of electric current in a microphone and was then translated into magnetic fields, or "flux," in a small induction coil. Then, as a magnetizable steel wire or tape was drawn rapidly past the induction coil, the steel would retain a portion of that magnetic flux as a record of the original sound. This process became the basis for all later developments in magnetic recording. The Telegraphone was a grand prize winner at the 1900 International Exposition in Paris. However, it was only in the late 1930s and early 1940s that U.S. firms became interested in this technology, and even then, only two firms were actively engaged in commercializing it: the Brush Development Company of Cleveland, Ohio, and the Armour Research Foundation of the Illinois Institute of Technology in Chicago.

In contrast, the development of magnetic recording technology advanced in Europe. A turning point came in the early 1930s, when the German firm Allgemeine Elektricitäts Gesellschaft developed the Magnetophone, a high-quality broadcast recorder capable of superior sound recording and reproduction. In 1944, after almost a decade of production, the most advanced Magnetophones incorporated scores of technical innovations. The German broadcasting authority, Reichs Rundfunk Gesellschaft (RRG), became the major customer for Magnetophones, installing them in nearly all German radio studios. During World War II, the RRG took over the operations of broadcast stations in occupied countries and installed Magnetophones there as well. Thus, by the end of the war, tape recording was a standard feature in many European radio stations.

One of the chief distinguishing features of the Magnetophone system was its special recording tape. Since the late 1920s, the German chemical firm IG Farben had been developing a plastic tape base coated with a magnetic form of iron oxide that could substitute for the heavy, expensive steel recording tape used in previous designs. The particles of oxide on such a tape act as tiny individual magnets, and it was learned that it was possible to record higher frequencies at slower tape speeds than on a solid steel band or wire. The slower speed and the lower cost of materials made the coated tape much cheaper, contributing to its widespread adoption in Germany.

The structure of U.S. broadcasting militated against the creation of a demand for that technology. U.S. radio networks relied heavily on live programming distributed by telephone line. Recording represented a threat, both because the recording of a network program was piracy of the network's product and because it would then be technically possible to operate a network by distributing recorded rather than live programs. The status quo in program technology was reinforced by the oligopolistic structure of the broadcast equipment manufacturing market, which was dominated by firms such as Western Electric and the Radio Corporation of America (RCA). None of these firms would offer magnetic recording equipment until after World War II.

Postwar Innovation

In 1945 the United States enlisted the aid of its businesspeople, scientists, and engineers to collect German scientific and industrial knowledge. Some of those who became intimately familiar with Magnetophone technology while in Germany returned to the United States to play a role in the establishment of magnetic recording manufacturing there.

In 1945 Col. John T. Mullin was part of an Army Signal Corps team investigating the military applications of German electronic technology. He was told by a British officer about a tape recorder with exceptional musical quality at a Frankfurt, Germany, radio station that was being operated by the Armed Forces Radio Service (AFRS). There Mullin found German technicians working for AFRS using Magnetophone audiotape recorder/players. The technological improvements of a constant speed transport, plastic tape impregnated or coated with iron oxide, and the employment of a high AC-bias frequency mixed with the audio signal made these machines high fidelity. The first two machines acquired were turned over to the Signal Corps, and Col. Mullin disassembled two other machines and shipped them to his home in San Francisco. In 1946 Mullin designed custom record/reproduce electronics that improved the performance, rewired and reassembled the Magnetophone machines, and went into a partnership with Bill Palmer for movie soundtrack work, using those machines and the 50 reels of tape he had acquired.

In October 1946 Mullin and his partner Palmer attended the annual convention of the Society of Motion Picture Engineers, where he demonstrated the machine to the sound heads of Metro Goldwyn Mayer and Twentieth Century Fox and to the chief engineer of Altec Lansing. Mullin was then invited to an Institute of Radio Engineers meeting in May 1947 to demonstrate the German Magnetophone. It was there that employees of Ampex, a small maker of electric motors in Redwood City, California, first saw and heard the tape recorder. The U.S. government had arranged for the suspension of all German legal claims to magnetic recording technology and had sponsored its wholesale transfer to the United States. The Commerce Department released its technical reports, captured documents, and patents related to the Magnetophone, allowing any interested manufacturers access to information relating to tape-recording technology. Shortly thereafter, Ampex began its own developmental project.

In 1947 the technical staff of the *Bing Crosby Show* on American Broadcasting Companiy (ABC) arranged to have Mullin re-record original disk recordings of the *Bing Crosby Show* onto tape and then edit them. Crosby had been with the National Broadcasting Company (NBC) until 1944, doing the *Kraft Music Hall* live, but he did not like the regimen imposed by live shows. Because NBC would not permit recorded programs, Crosby took the fall off and returned on the newly formed ABC network with a new sponsor, Philco, because ABC had agreed to let him record on electrical transcriptions as long as his ratings did not diminish. The process required cutting a record and then re-recording; what with sometimes two or three generations, the quality of sound suffered. In July 1947, after the initial demonstration of editing, Mullin was invited to give a demonstration of his equipment for Crosby's producers by taping live side by side with transcription equipment the first show for the 1947–48 season in August at the ABC-NBC studios in Hollywood. Bing Crosby Enterprises then negotiated financing for Ampex for exclusive distribution rights, and Mullin was employed to record the Crosby show on his original German equipment until the Ampex machines became available. Made with the original German tape recorders and 50 rolls of BASF tape, Mullin's first recorded demonstration show of August 1947 was broadcast over ABC on 1 October 1947.

In 1948 Alexander Poniatov and his team of engineers at Ampex introduced the first commercial audiotape recorder based on the Magnetaphone as Ampex Model 200. The first two, with serial numbers 1 and 2, were presented to John Mullin, and numbers 3–12 went into service at ABC. (To meet the contract requirements, Mullin gave his machines to ABC and later received numbers 13–14 for his contribution.)

The Minnesota Mining and Manufacturing Company (3M) of Saint Paul, Minnesota, already had experience in the manufacture of coated films from its line of adhesive tapes. Home tape machines such as the Brush Soundmirror, which used Scotch 100 paper tape supplied by 3M, had been introduced in the consumer market, but these fell far short of professional requirements. Mullin then asked 3M engineers to reverse-engineer the German product using samples of IG Farben tape and

Department of Commerce technical reports. Although the Minnesota company quickly came to dominate the field, much smaller firms successfully broke into the market, competing with 3M.

The Crosby show remained tape-delayed, setting a precedent in broadcast production that remains the norm to this day. Most other network radio and recording artists quickly adopted tape to produce their shows and discs, including Burl Ives and Les Paul. Live broadcasting was soon limited mostly to local disc jockeys spinning the new long-playing 33–1/3 and 45-rpm music discs.

Mullin remained with Bing Crosby Enterprises, recording his shows and others at ABC, until 1951. As the exclusive distributor for Ampex, Bing Crosby Enterprises sold hundreds of recorders to radio stations and master recording studios. In 1951 Mullin and other engineers were spun off as the Bing Crosby Electronic Division to handle development of audio instrumentation and video recording. In 1956 the Electronic Division became the Minicom Division of 3M, where Mullin served as head of engineering and as professional recorder development manager until his retirement in 1975. He died on 24 June 1999 at age 85.

See also: American Broadcasting Company; Recording and Studio Equipment; Wire Recording

Further Reading

Angus, Robert, "History of Magnetic Recording," *Audio* 68, no. 8 (August/September 1984).
Camras, Marvin, editor, *Magnetic Tape Recording*, New York: Van Nostrand Reinhold, 1985.
Hickman, E.B., "The Development of Magnetic Recording," in *American Broadcasting*, compiled by Lawrence W. Lichty and Malachi C. Topping, New York: Hastings House, 1975.
Millard, Andre J., *America on Record: A History of Recorded Sound*, Cambridge and New York: Cambridge University Press, 1995.
Mullin, John T., "The Birth of the Recording Industry," *Billboard* (18 November 1972).
Mullin, John T., "Creating the Craft of Tape Recording," *High Fidelity* 26, no. 4 (April 1976).
Van Praag, Phil, *The Evolution of the Audio Recorder: The "Vintage" Years, Late 1940s-Early 1970s*, Waukesha, Wisconsin: EC Designs, 1997.

MARVIN BENSMAN

AUDITORIUM TESTING
Radio Market Research

Auditorium testing is a method of market research used widely in the radio industry and elsewhere to determine the effectiveness of programming and audiences' preferences in music, voice quality, commercial messages, and other program elements. Its name comes not from the room where the testing takes place, but from the "auditory" nature of the testing; that is, the subjects hear the samples being tested.

A company called ASI (now Ipsos-ASI) first used auditorium testing in the evaluation of TV programs, commercials, and movies in the 1960s. They used what they called the "Preview House" in Los Angeles as a controlled environment for such tests. Forty years later, versions of auditorium testing are still used by numerous market research firms around the world.

The basic methodology in auditorium testing starts with a careful consideration of the goals to be achieved. The client advertiser, radio station, or TV station needs to identify, in the most precise way possible, the boundaries of the testing and how the results will be used. Once the desired outcomes are known, the researchers design a testing strategy to achieve those outcomes.

With the strategy set, the research company screens and selects a group of between 75 and 200 people reflecting the demographic the client wishes to study. That demographic (a grouping according to age, gender, income, etc.) can be a random sample or one that is consistent with the station's current or desired audience, or even a subset of the audience that the client wishes to cultivate.

The assembled test group is then invited into a small auditorium and given instructions for the test. They are rarely told what is being tested or who the client is for the testing. In fact, tests often include decoy selections to keep the participants from guessing which specific radio station or product is being evaluated. The test subjects are instructed to respond to samples of music, voice, messages, images, or other content, providing some sort of rating on a scale created by the researchers. This can be accomplished with written questionnaires, a joy stick-type device that measures responses electronically, or even with a show of hands. Sometimes anecdotal comments are also solicited. Participants in auditorium testing are usually compensated for their time in order to increase the seriousness with which they approach the evaluating. The results are then tabulated and evaluated, with many variables charted, and correlations are made among the different samples tested. Ultimately, the research firm can provide clients with both a review of the raw data and recommendations on how they may proceed to achieve their goals. Auditorium testing is essentially a hybrid of several market research methods, taking the group dynamic of focus groups, the larger size of diary or phone research, and the immediacy of one-on-one surveying.

Bob Goode developed a form of auditorium testing called Electronic Attitude Response System. This method uses a video readout of averaged responses of the participants correlated directly to the audio content being rated and allows researchers to determine the test audience's preferences along with their "tune-out" of program elements. It also provides researchers with a sense of which program elements are more effective if paired with others. For example, a commercial following a weather report may lead to less tune-out than if that same commercial aired after a musical selection.

Music testing is a particular strength of auditorium testing models. Whole pieces within a musical genre can be tested before they are aired on a station. More commonly, however, "hooks," short segments of songs, are tested. In markets where many stations compete for listeners within each programming genre (country, oldies, urban contemporary, etc.), the subtleties of which songs are most liked within each genre can make a major difference in the ratings successes of each station. One firm, The New Research Group, offers 600 to 1,200 musical hooks along with 100 perceptual questions, allowing the client to know not only which music is preferred, but why, in specific descriptive terms, dealing with emotions, motivations, associations, etc.

Research firms "cluster" music that appeals to test audiences in auditorium groups, because people who enjoy one song from the cluster are likely to enjoy others as well. In addition, firms use complex matrix charts to show compatibility between clusters, showing radio programmers how to broaden appeal by including more musical selections without causing tune-out by core listeners.

Auditorium testing, along with other music testing, is seen by some as limiting, in that the short hooks it tests can oversimplify otherwise interesting music that might gain acceptance upon being heard by audiences. For example, a hook from "Hey Jude" by the Beatles might not have tested well, whereas the song in its entirety was a number one hit.

Public and commercial radio stations use research, including auditorium testing, to make program decisions; for example, the Wisconsin Public Radio network has been involved in the Corporation for Public Broadcasting program research, and Denver-based Paragon Research studied public radio stations in eight markets using focus groups, surveys, and auditorium research.

As audio broadens its reach through new technologies such as satellite, Web-casting, and other distribution channels, it is likely that increasing specialization of program channels will occur, making auditorium testing more important in the precise selection of program content.

That being said, the increasing sophistication of audience behavior measurement technology imbedded in some of these new communications media may eventually render traditional auditorium testing too slow and imprecise by comparison for the emerging information needs of the industry.

See also: Audience Research Methods

Further Reading

Clemente, Mark N., *The Marketing Glossary: Key Terms, Concepts, and Applications in Marketing Management, Advertising, Sales Promotion, Public Relations, Direct Marketing, Market Research, Sales*, New York: American Management Association, 1992.

PETER WALLACE

AUTOMATION

Automation in radio refers to a method of broadcasting in which individually recorded program elements are reproduced in assigned order by equipment designed to operate with little or no human assistance. Automation systems were initially capable of performing two tasks routinely performed by disc jockeys: broadcasting music selections and commercial announcements. Refinements to technology subsequently enabled disc jockeys to record (or *voice-track*) their ad-libs in advance and to instruct systems to broadcast them at the appropriate times within the program schedule. The addition of voice-tracking capabilities assisted stations in suppressing criticism that automated broadcasting sounded "canned" in comparison with live, disc jockey-supervised presentations.

Origins

Paul Schafer is credited with automating the studio operation function. After founding Schafer Electronics in 1953 to manufacture remote-control equipment for broadcast transmitters, Schafer extended the application of this technology in 1956 to program automation. Radio station KGEE used the first Schafer automation system to expand its hours of operation and offer night-time service to its Bakersfield, California, listeners. Capable of unattended operation, Schafer's initial system consisted of two Seeburg jukeboxes for music reproduction, three Concertone open-reel tape decks for broadcasting commercial announcements, and an electromechanical switcher for storing programming instructions to control the playback sequence.

Schafer installed an automation system into a motor coach and traveled to radio stations to demonstrate its capabilities. During his visits with station owners and managers, Schafer explained how automation could reduce operating expenses while enhancing the quality of the on-air presentation. Automation systems, he asserted, not only reduced the number of personnel needed to operate the station but also executed programming instructions more reliably and with fewer mistakes than human operators could.

Schafer's identification of the economic and performance concerns were, in the late 1950s, of relatively equal importance to broadcasters. However, the economic incentive would escalate prominently in 1965 when the Federal Communications Commission (FCC) imposed the AM–FM Program Nonduplication Rule. In its effort to stimulate listener interest in the languishing FM service, the FCC reduced AM station simulcasting by their FM sister stations in the nation's 100 largest markets. A majority of the approximately 200 duopoly stations affected by the rule chose to automate their FM facilities rather than incur the expense of hiring additional announcing and engineering staffs. Contributing to the movement toward automation was management's realization that the pool of available talent had been depleted by rapid expansion in both radio and television broadcasting. Demand for qualified personnel had steadily driven up the price of labor during the 1950s. Duopolies in the smaller markets, unaffected by the nonduplication rule, were nonetheless enticed into automating when desirable local talent departed for more lucrative opportunities in metropolitan areas.

Equipment

The manufacture of automation equipment, previously a cottage industry, blossomed during the 1960s. The Radio Corporation of America (RCA) and Gates Radio Company, two prominent broadcast equipment manufacturers, entered into competition with Schafer Electronics. Unlike Schafer's initial design, which had relied upon jukeboxes for vinyl disc reproduction, next-generation systems reproduced program elements with open-reel and cartridge tape machines. This approach provided greater reliability than did the early disc-dependent systems. More important, it afforded programmers opportunities to execute formatics in a manner that more closely emulated the sound of a live, spontaneous broadcast.

As the sophistication of control switchers grew, tape-dependent systems enabled announcers to develop the technique of voice tracking. In approximately 10–20 minutes, announcers could record all of the comments they would normally make during the course of a four-hour, live program. By instructing the automation system to execute their voice recordings at the appropriate times, announcers were freed to pursue other creative activities during their airshifts.

Adapting a station to automated broadcasting did not, in and of itself, liberate operators from the responsibility of creating a program service; it merely facilitated the execution of programming decisions. Rather than attempting to produce tape-recorded libraries of music internally, numerous automated-station operators elected to subscribe to the services of program syndicators. In most instances, syndicators supplied stations with base libraries of recorded music, which were supplemented periodically with reels of music of current popularity.

Syndication

The syndication firm Drake-Chenault, under the supervision of legendary Top 40 programmer Bill Drake, successfully adapted the middle of the road, Top 40, country, and soul formats to automated presentation. By the mid-1970s, approximately 300 stations subscribed to the company's services. The beautiful music format was also used extensively by automated stations. Because its execution emphasized repeated segues between songs, this format was especially adaptable to automation.

Broadcaster reliance on tape-based automation diminished during the 1980s. Among the explanations for the decline in automation's popularity was programmers' perception that listeners desired more announcer involvement within the presentation than even the most sophisticated systems could reliably provide. Although voice-tracked programming resembled live presentation, it nonetheless was incapable of emulating for listeners the spontaneity and interactivity they associated with hearing a live broadcast. An alternative approach, in which syndicators delivered live, hosted presentations simultaneously to multiple affiliates via satellite, became the preferred method of automated operation during this period.

Following the passage in 1996 of the Telecommunications Act, which sharply relaxed radio station ownership rules and led to significant consolidation of station properties, interest in automated broadcasting renewed. Owners who operated multiple stations within markets began to cluster the facilities into single studio complexes. In such situations, automation has enabled owners to share personalities among stations, thereby reducing the number of announcers required to sustain program operations. Systems now store all program elements, including voice-tracked disc jockey commentary, in hard-disk memory. These "jock-in-a-box" systems offer disc jockeys greater voice-tracking flexibility and have narrowed the gap between listeners' perceptions of live and recorded presentation. Clear Channel Communications was making use of this technique in the early 2000s, noting that a small station (say, in Boise, Idaho) could gain the use of an on-air personality for as little as $4,000–$6,000 a year, far less than paying a real DJ on site. The DJ stays in a major market, yet appears to host local programs in multiple locations. Another trend developing among group-owned stations is to interconnect stations in multiple cities via telephone circuits to a central, or hub, production facility. A single announcing staff is thus able to provide each of the stations within the hub with individualized, market-specific commentary using the voice-tracking technique. Industry representatives estimate that approximately one in five stations now employs systems for either fully automated or announcer-assisted operation.

See also: FM Radio; Recording and Studio Equipment; Syndication; Telecommunications Act of 1996

Further Reading

Abrams, Earl B., "Schafer Offers Stations Device for Automatic Radio Programming," *Broadcasting* (17 March 1958).

Abrams, Earl B., "Automated Radio: It's Alive and Prospering," *Broadcasting* (9 June 1969).

Antilla, Susan, "Canned Radio Means Fresh Profits," *Dun's Review* 117 (March 1981).

Bennett, Jeffrey, "RCS NT Number One for WONE," *Radio World* (25 June 1997).

Gentry, Ric, "Profile: Paul Schafer," *Broadcast Management/ Engineering* 23 (April 1988).

Keith, Michael C., and Joseph M. Krause, *The Radio Station*, Boston: Focal Press, 1986; 5th edition, by Keith, 2000.

Pizzi, Skip, "New Directions in Radio Automation," *Broadcast Management/Engineering* 24 (February 1989).

Routt, Edd, James B. McGrath, and Fredric A. Weiss, *The Radio Format Conundrum*, New York: Hastings House, 1978.

BRUCE MIMS

AUTOMOBILE RADIO

First designed in the 1920s as separate radios to be installed optionally in automobiles, the auto or car radio eventually became a standard feature, flourishing in popularity after World War II. Today the auto radio is considered standard equipment on virtually all makes and models of cars.

Origins

Perhaps it was inevitable that two of the 20th century's most popular products—cars and radios—would unite in some way, but numerous technological barriers initially prevented such a marriage. The earliest known radio-equipped car was demonstrated in St. Louis, Missouri, in 1904. In 1922 Chevrolet offered the United States' first factory unit, the Chevrolet Radio Sedan, featuring a modified Westinghouse radio with an elaborate fence-like antenna mounted on the roof. This early option alone cost one-third the price of the car itself. Few were purchased, so Chevrolet discontinued their manufacture.

Radio experimenters continued to fend for themselves. Some adapted portable, battery-powered units for use as travel radios, but interference from the automobile's engine and ignition system thwarted their widespread development. The do-it-yourselfers discovered other obstacles, including exposure to extreme heat and cold, incompatible power supplies from automobiles, and loudspeakers too weak to overcome the noise caused by driving.

Gradually these problems were resolved on several fronts and, like the technical development of the radio itself, auto radio evolved from a combination of discoveries over a period of time rather than in the immediate aftermath of a single breakthrough. Ignition interference, for example, was reduced substantially in 1927 with the invention of the spark plug suppresser, or damp resistance. Within three years, a second development, voltage conversion, allowed simplified operation of the auto radio. Enabling the auto radio to operate independently of a battery system, relying instead upon the car's electrical system, was key to the device's commercial success. By the mid-1930s widespread manufacturing was underway.

This second development, in 1930, was the result of collaborative work between Paul Galvin, Elmer Wavering, and William Lear, who later gained prominence in aviation design. At the time, Galvin manufactured battery eliminators in Chicago, products that permitted battery-operated radios to be run by the 120-volt system of household current. Galvin applied the same principle to his Studebaker automobile, demonstrating it to passersby at a meeting of the Radio Manufacturer's Association in Atlantic City, New Jersey. His first production model, the 5T71, sold for $120 (installed) and became known as a Motorola, a combination of the words *motor* and *Victrola*. That year Chrysler offered a radio as a regular option and was followed soon by other automakers. The price of an average auto radio dropped to $80 by the mid-1930s, one-eighth the cost of a typical car, as opposed to the one-third cost of 10 years earlier.

In 1933 Ford introduced auto radios compatible with specially designed dashboard panels in some of its models. By 1936 the push-button feature was added, enabling motorists to tune to a desired station safely, without glancing away from the road while driving. The adjustable, telescopic "whip" antenna, which improved reception of distant stations, was introduced in 1938.

After World War II, the popularity of the auto radio soared when automakers began to offer them as a pre-installed option. By the late 1950s, Motorola, by now the name of Galvin's company, manufactured one-third of all U.S. auto radios.

Postwar Growth

The development of the auto radio reflected the increasing mobility of the United States itself, but television's arrival in U.S. homes after World War II was swift and nearly complete by the end of the 1950s.

Many radio executives assumed the worst: their medium was dead or dying. In one sense, this was true. The amount of advertising revenue generated by network radio shows dropped by half in the five-year period ending in 1955. Such long-time popular shows as *Amos 'n' Andy*, *Jack Benny*, and *Ma Perkins* either moved to television or disappeared completely. Yet a paradox was emerging; despite the precipitous decline of network radio, more radio stations than ever were on the air (about 2,300 in the United States by the mid-1950s, nearly triple the number immediately before World War II) and more radios were being manufactured than ever. Surveys suggested that TV set owners were more likely to own more than one radio than were non-TV set owners and that radio listeners were tuning in more frequently, to different stations, for shorter durations of time. Television, it appeared, was threatening network radio, but not the medium of radio itself.

"Radio didn't die. It wasn't even sick," said Matthew J. Culligan, National Broadcasting Company's vice president for radio, in 1958.

It just had to be psychoanalyzed.... The public just started liking [radio] in a different way, and radio went to the beach, to the park, the patio, and the automobile.... Radio has become a companion to the individual instead of remaining a focal point of all family entertainment. An intimacy has developed between radio and the individual.

The "disc jockey" and "drive-time" had arrived. Influenced by the auto radio and its motorist listeners, radio became a predominantly music and news service after about 1955.

The new portability of radio was made possible, too, by the development of the transistor in 1948 and by the phenomenal growth of auto radios. By 1953 the first transistorized pocketsize portable radios were available, and five years later the first solid-state (tubeless) auto radios using transistors appeared on the market. In 1952 auto radios were in just over half of America's cars. By 1980 that figure reached 95 percent. The trend reflected, as J. Fred MacDonald put it, "a mobile, affluent, and commercialized America, solidly committed to television for its creative amusement, but still requiring radio for music and instantaneous information."

The proliferation of auto radios (by 1962 some 47 million cars in the United States were equipped) also coincided with the emergence of a distinct "teen culture" in the United States following World War II. The auto radio helped to promote the growth of this emerging youth culture and, like the drive-in restaurant and drive-in theater, it came to symbolize America's new level of mobility. At the same time, auto radio offered more stations. FM had been available, although not widely purchased, in car radios since the mid-1950s. With the medium's growth in popularity, sales of FM-equipped auto radios soared and prices dropped.

Radio in the years since has continually readjusted its approach to programming to meet changing audience needs, and the pervasiveness of the auto radio has remained high. Its technology has evolved in the same way consumer electronics have changed in the home. Digital audio broadcasting, introduced to the consumer in the 1990s, has spawned a new generation of auto radios. Radio continues to attract its largest audiences during commuting hours, a trend well established by the 1960s and continuing 40 years later, thanks to the near universal availability of the auto radio.

The focus of development for automobile radios in the early 21st century centered on reception of digital services, both satellite and terrestrial. The digital satellite broadcasters, XM Radio and Sirius (which merged in mid-2008), relied heavily on automobile listening and a large portion of their overall audience tuned into automobile receivers. Each company signed agreements with different automakers to install tuners in their cars. New car buyers got a 90-day free trial, beyond which they had to subscribe to continue listening. Dealers reported that conversion to subscriptions was running about half of all cars sold with the tuners installed. When the firms merged in 2008, one pending issue was whether and how to make the radios from one company receive signals from the other. One agreement between them called for new "universal" receivers to pick up their signals as well as those from terrestrial digital broadcasters.

The spread (and potential success) of digital or HD (high definition) radio was heavily dependent on getting the new digital receivers into automobiles where most radio listening takes place. The initial problem was one of cost—as with FM radio decades earlier, the new HD receivers cost considerably more than existing analog receivers and automakers and consumers resisted those higher prices. Penetration rates remained low well through the first decade of the 21st century.

See also: AM Radio; FM Radio; Digital Satellite Radio; Motorola

Further Reading

An Analysis of Radio-Listening in Autos, New York: Columbia Broadcasting System, 1936.
Martin, Norman, "Turn Your Radio On," *Automotive Industries* 178, no. 4 (April 1998).
Master Key to Auto Radio, New York: Radio Advertising Bureau, 1962.
Matteson, Donald W., *The Automobile Radio: A Romantic Genealogy*. Jackson, MI: Thornridge Publishing, 1987.
Petrakis, Harry Mark, *The Founder's Touch: The Life of Paul Galvin of Motorola*, New York: McGraw-Hill, 1965; 3rd edition, Chicago: Motorola University Press/Ferguson, 1991.
"Radio Boom," *Time* (27 April 1936).
Radio Takes to the Road, New York: National Broadcasting Company, 1936.
Schiffer, Michael B., *The Portable Radio in American Life*, Tucson: University of Arizona Press, 1991.

DAVID MCCARTNEY,
2009 REVISIONS BY CHRISTOPHER H. STERLING

AWARDS AND PRIZES

As with other American media, the radio broadcasting industry awards itself (and receives from others) a host of annual prizes as a prime means of recognizing key people, programs, and top performances in the business. This entry briefly describes a selection of the longer running and better known national awards available to radio broadcasters. Most are given annually, and many are open to people in both radio and television (and sometimes other media). The means of choosing winners varies tremendously across both prizes and organizations.

Armstrong Awards

Often called "Majors" in honor of inventor Edwin Howard Armstrong's World War I army rank, these awards, established in 1964, are given in recognition of excellence and originality in radio broadcasting in six content categories: news, music, news documentary, education, community service, and creative use of the medium. Additional awards may be given in the areas of technology, innovation in station programming, and outstanding service by an individual or company. Armstrong Foundation, Columbia University, New York.

Clarion Awards

Given in more than 80 categories, including radio, for people and programs concerning women in society. Association for Women in Communications, Arnold, Maryland.

Clio Awards

Given in honor of the best domestic and international advertising, these awards have been given since 1960. They include radio among other forms of advertising. More than 200 are given annually. Clio Awards, New York.

Crystal Radio Awards

Given to as many as ten radio stations per year for overall excellence in community service. National Association of Broadcasters, Washington, D.C.

Edward R. Murrow Awards

(1) Given for outstanding individual contribution to public radio. Corporation for Public Broadcasting, Washington, D.C.

(2) Given for the best news department, spot news coverage, continuing coverage, investigative reporting, news series and documentary, and for overall excellence. Radio Television News Directors Association, Washington, D.C.

Freedom Foundation National Awards

Given for constructive activities on drug abuse education, ecology, patriotic programs, respect for the law, moral and spiritual values, economic education, human dignity and brotherhood. Freedom Foundation, Valley Forge, Pennsylvania.

Gabriel Awards

Given for radio programs or segments in the following categories: arts/entertainment, news/information, religion, coverage of single news story, community awareness campaigns, public service announcements, and short features. National Catholic Association of Broadcasters and Communicators, Dayton, Ohio.

George Polk Award

These vary from year to year but generally are given to honor discernment in a news story or coverage, resourcefulness in gathering information, or skill in relating the story. These are usually given for foreign, national, and local achievements. Long Island University, New York.

Gold Medal Award

Presented each year to an outstanding individual or corporate entity in radio or other electronic media. International Radio and Television Society, New York.

Golden Mike Award

Awarded to a company or an individual that has made an outstanding contribution to the art of broadcasting and the community at large. Broadcast Foundation, Greenwich, Connecticut.

International Broadcasting Award

Given to "the world's best" radio and television commercials from anywhere in the world. There are nine radio categories, and subject matter for the advertisement is open. Hollywood Radio and Television Society, Hollywood, California.

Jack R. Howard Awards

Given in honor of investigative or in-depth reporting. ScrippsHoward Foundation, Greencastle, Indiana.

Marconi Radio Awards

Given to stations or on-air personalities for excellence in and contributions to radio. National Association of Broadcasters, Washington, D.C.

Missouri Honor Medals

Given since 1930 in honor of lifetime achievement by the School of Journalism, University of Missouri, Columbia, Missouri.

National Headliner Awards

For radio network and individual station news, public service, documentary, and investigative reporting. National Headliners Club, Northfield, New Jersey.

National Radio Award

Given to an individual for significant or ongoing contributions to radio from a leadership position. National Association of Broadcasters, Washington, D.C.

New York Festivals Award

Encompasses radio advertising, programming, promotion, news, entertainment, editorials, service features, and public service announcements, among others. International Radio Program and Promotion Awards of New York, New York.

Overseas Press Club Awards

Given annually for radio spot news from abroad, or radio interpretation of foreign news. Overseas Press Club, New York.

Public Radio Program Award

Recognizes excellence in radio programming at the local or national level. Corporation for Public Broadcasting, Washington, D.C.

Radio-Mercury Awards

Given to honor creative excellence in paid radio advertising, these carry some of the largest cash prizes of any of the awards in this entry—upward of $100,000 for the top winner. RadioMercury, New York.

Radio Program Awards

To recognize outstanding programming for community-oriented radio, commercial or public. National Federation of Community Broadcasters, Washington, D.C.

Radio Wayne Awards

Given annually for the top account executive, sales manager, general manager, director of sales, and broadcaster of the year. They are named in honor of the late Wayne Cornils, a senior vice president of the Radio Advertising Bureau. Radio Ink, Miami, Florida.

Sigma Delta Chi Distinguished Service Award

Given for radio editorials or radio reporting. Society for Professional Journalists, Greencastle, Indiana.

Silver Baton Award

Given for outstanding work in news and public affairs during the previous year, covering both network and local radio. Can be given to an individual, program, series of programs, or a station. Alfred I. DuPont-Columbia University Awards, Graduate School of Journalism, Columbia University, New York.

See also: Peabody Awards and Archive

Further Reading

"Major Broadcasting and Cable Awards," *Broadcasting and Cable Yearbook* (annual listing).

CHRISTOPHER H. STERLING

B

BEAUTIFUL MUSIC FORMAT
See: Easy Listening/Beautiful Music Format

BELL TELEPHONE LABORATORIES
At the forefront of communications research, Bell Laboratories for decades was regarded as the largest and most successful private research organization in the world. Created as the research and development division of American Telephone and Telegraph (AT&T), Bell Labs is now a part of Lucent Technologies. Best known for its development of the transistor, laser technology, and information theory, the organization boasts more than 27,000 patents and 11 Nobel laureates. Headquartered in Murray Hill, New Jersey, Bell Labs consists of a global community of some 16,000 people in 16 countries.

It was nearly 50 years after the invention of the telephone when AT&T formed Bell Telephone Laboratories as a subsidiary in 1925. The unit was created to merge and centralize the research and engineering work of AT&T and its manufacturing and supply arm, Western Electric. Frank B. Jewett was its first president.

Bell Labs can be credited with major roles in the development of computer technology, the microelectronics industry, and a host of modern communications technologies. In its first three years of operation, researchers demonstrated long-distance television transmission, sound/motion pictures, the artificial larynx, and the negative feedback amplifier (used to reduce distortion in radio and telephone transmissions). During the 1930s, researchers developed an electrical digital computer, a radio altimeter (a new means of radio transmission), and radio astronomy. In addition, they conducted research on stereophonic sound. During World War II, the U.S. military profited from research at Bell Labs on radar and wireless communications.

One of the most notable Bell Labs inventions was the transistor, a small electronic component with a semiconductor, which is now found in virtually every electronic device and led to solid-state communications and transformation of the electronics industry. The transistor was invented in 1947 when a team of scientists took initial semiconductor research and improved upon it in order to amplify signals in the same way as the vacuum tube did but with more reliability and much less power and space consumption. Bell Labs developed techniques to make the transistor practical, and it eventually became a fundamental and essential component of radio, television, telephone, and entertainment equipment. The transistor radio, one of the first mass-produced products based on this invention, appeared in 1954, quickly becoming the best seller in consumer product history and significantly influencing popular culture. The transistor paved the way for portability, miniaturization, and better car radios. Later, the invention of the integrated circuit, which organizes numerous transistors and other electronic components on a silicon wafer, took the transistor innovation to a new level and sparked the Information Age.

Other key contributions of Bell Labs include the publication of "information theory" in 1948, the invention of laser technology in 1958, and the development of the solar battery and communications satellite by the early 1960s. Bell Labs introduced software-controlled telephone switches long before personal computers, in addition to the first electric microphone for hands-free telephone conversations. Other developments in which Bell Labs researchers assisted included cellular mobile radio, fiber optics, light-emitting diodes, charge-coupled devices (used in cameras), the UNIX operating system, C and C++ programming languages, and High-Definition Television (HDTV).

For more than 50 years, Bell Telephone Laboratories enjoyed financial support from its parent company AT&T, a regulated monopoly that could pass along research costs to customers. The research approach was primarily academic, with a corporate philosophy of giving topflight researchers freedom and autonomy. Bell Labs focused on being the first or best in such areas as publishing papers, setting transmission records, and building the most powerful laser diode. Eleven of its researchers have been awarded the Nobel Prize, nine have received the National Medal of Science, and seven have received the National Medal of Technology. An Emmy Award was earned for the institution's work on HDTV. Nobel Prize winners include Clinton J. Davisson, who demonstrated the wave nature of matter, a foundation for much of today's solidstate electronics. John Bardeen, Walter H. Brattain, and William Shockley were honored with a Nobel Prize in 1956 for inventing the transistor, and Arno Penzias and Robert Wilson received the Nobel Prize for detecting background radiation supporting the Big Bang theory.

By the 1980s competitive pressures and then divestiture led AT&T to refocus its research efforts. The terms of a 1956 agreement with the U.S. Department of Justice restricted what use AT&T could make of technologies unrelated to its core telephone business. Bell Labs had to license others to utilize many of its patents—especially the valuable transistor. The court-ordered 1984 break-up of AT&T, however, freed Bell labs to engage in direct marketing as well as licensing of its innovations. Research Director Arno Penzias pushed to bring wide-ranging research projects more in line with the company's telecommunications business. Although there was concern that Bell Labs would suffer without the former cross-subsidies, AT&T pledged to continue its tradition of both primary and applied research. Critics noted, however, the slow but steady decline of fundamental scientific research in favor of more applied work to develop products to meet customer needs.

Bell Labs experienced a dramatic change in 1996 when AT&T underwent another major restructuring

(a trivestiture), giving up 75 percent of its Bell Laboratories staff to its new off-spring, Lucent Technologies. The remaining 25 percent, made up of computer scientists, mathematicians, and other information scientists remained to form the new AT&T Laboratories, supporting the telecommunications provider's businesses in long distance and other services. Some physical science positions were terminated due to the corporate reorganization.

Bell Labs initially experienced a resurgence under its new parent company, Lucent Technologies, a high-tech company that develops and manufactures telecommunications technology and equipment for AT&T and others. Lucent also gave Bell Labs a higher profile, featuring the research and development unit in the company slogan: "Lucent Technologies. Bell Labs Innovations." About 80 percent of Bell Labs employees are part of and integrated into Lucent's business units. The other 20 percent work for what is called the Central Labs, which consists of three major technical divisions: Advanced Technologies, Technology Officer Division, and Research.

During the 1990s, Bell Labs led the world with more citations than, for example, IBM and top academic institutions. Even today, despite serious cut-backs and reorientation of research priorities, the Labs average better than three patent applications every business day. A number of technologies for the digital audio broadcasting (DAB) market have been patented, including the perceptual audio coding (PAC) algorithm. The PAC encoder converts AM or FM radio signals into high-quality digital signals and enables the transmission of digital audio over a variety of wireless and wireline channels, including in-band, on-channel (IBOC) systems and the internet.

At the dawn of the 21st century, Lucent, like most of the telecommunications industry, experienced financial troubles. As a result, Bell Labs lost funding and people, particularly in the physical sciences. Restructuring and streamlining shifted the focus to addressing the needs of communications service providers. There are now two primary operating units, focusing on wireline networks and mobile networks. Web-based customer solutions and service intelligence are emphasized. Bell Labs continues to be Lucent's innovation engine.

Like much of the telecommunications industry, Bell Labs' parent company, Lucent Technologies, struggled financially at the start of the new century. Bell Labs lost people and funding, and, though the company continued work in the physical sciences, streamlining forced a new focus on addressing needs of communications service providers. A dramatic change at Bell Labs came in 2006, when, after several years of negotiations, Lucent was acquired by its French rival Alcatel for $11.6 billion, producing Paris-based Alcatel-Lucent, the world's leading supplier of equipment for telecommunications networks. Bell Labs and the former Alcatel Research and Innovation, merged under the better-known Bell Labs name. The Labs' efforts continued to focus more on applied than original research. Bell Labs' importance faded as a result of continued Alcatel-Lucent financial losses and management upheaval.

See also: American Telephone and Telegraph; Transistor Radios

Further Reading

Bell Labs Innovations, www.bell-labs.com.

Bell Telephone Laboratories, *Impact: A Compilation of Bell System Innovations in Science and Engineering*, 2nd edition, Murray Hill, New Jersey: Bell Laboratories, 1981.

Buderi, Robert, "Bell Labs Is Dead: Long Live Bell Labs," *Technology Review* 101, no. 5 (September/October 1998).

Feder, Toni, "Bell Labs Research Regroups as Parent Lucent Shrinks," *Physics Today* 54, no. 10 (October 2001).

Mabon, Prescott C., *Mission Communications: The Story of Bell Laboratories*, Murray Hill, New Jersey: Bell Telephone Laboratories, 1975.

Mueser, Roland, editor, *Bell Laboratories Innovation in Telecommunications, 1925–1977*, Murray Hill, New Jersey: Bell Laboratories, 1979.

O'Neill, E.F., editor, *A History of Engineering and Science in the Bell System: Transmission Technology (1925–1975)*, Indianapolis: AT&T Bell Laboratories, 1985.

Service, Robert S., "Relaunching Bell Labs," *Science* (3 May 1996).

Southworth, George C., *Forty Years of Radio Research*, New York: Gordon and Breach, 1962.

LAURIE THOMAS LEE,
2009 REVISIONS BY GAIL LOVE

BEULAH SHOW
Situation Comedy

Based on a character that first appeared in *Fibber McGee and Molly,* this spin-off program marked an important transition. A black character, Beulah was, for the show's first two seasons, portrayed by white men. Only in later seasons did black women play the black characters—including the title character of *The Beulah Show.* For its era, however, the program helped to break racial barriers by introducing blacks to on-air roles.

The Beulah character, merely the latest black domestic in a radio program (Rochester on the Jack Benny program was probably the best known), had first appeared on *Fibber McGee and Molly* in early 1944 and became an instant hit. Portrayed by Marlin Hurt (who had himself been raised by a black maid and had thus picked up some of the "right sound" in childhood, developing a reputation as a good portrayer of blacks on radio), the character soon was delivering lines that became widely popular catchphrases across the country— "Looove dat man!" and the regular stand-by, "Somebody bawl fo' Beulah?"

Beulah was played as a central part of the white middleclass family that employed her. She was good-natured and respectful, but not subservient. Indeed she was often sarcastic, though rarely directly to her employers. She ran the household and solved problems—the core of program stories. Her radio friends included a shiftless boyfriend and the next door domestic, among others.

The weekly series seemed on its way to a long run when Hurt died at age 40 of a heart attack and, lacking its key actor, the program left the air. In the spring of 1947 it returned, with yet another white man (Bob Corley) playing the black domestic. Only that fall, when the program switched to CBS as a 15-minute program every weekday, did a black woman (Hatie McDaniel) begin to play the title part.

The program moved to television for four seasons beginning in 1950, though lacking some of the comic bite of the radio original. Black characters were played by black actors from the beginning— the first network television series where this was so.

See also: African-Americans in Radio; *Amos 'n' Andy*; *Fibber McGee and Molly*; Stereotypes on Radio

Cast

Beulah	Marlin Hurt (1945–46); Bob Corley (1947); Hatie McDaniel (1947–52); Lillian or Amanda Randolph (1952–53)
Bill Jackson	Marlin Hurt (1945–46), Ernie Whitman (1947–53)
Harry Henderson	Hugh Studebaker
Alice Henderson	Mary Jane Croft
Donnie Henderson	Henry Blair
Announcer	Ken Niles (1947), Marvin Miller (1947–53), Johnny Jacobs (1954)

Programming History

CBS (as *The Marlin Hurt and Beulah Show*)	1945–46

ABC	1947
CBS (15 minutes weekdays)	1947–54
ABC-TV	1950–53

Further Reading

Bogroghkozy, Aniko, "Beulah," in volume 1 of *Encyclopedia of Television*, 3 vols, edited by Horace Newcomb, Chicago and London: Fitzroy Dearborn, 1997.

Nachman, Gerald, "No WASPs Need Apply," in *Raised on Radio*, by Nachman, New York: Pantheon Books, 1998.

CHRISTOPHER H. STERLING

BIG D JAMBOREE
Country Music Radio Show

Although the *Big D Jamboree* never rivaled the influence of the mighty *Grand Ole Opry* or even small *Opry* cousins such as the *Louisiana Hayride* and *Wheeling Jamboree,* it was nonetheless a potent regional force that helped raise a number of country music artists, and later rock and roll artists, to national prominence. The radio barn dance, which broadcast on 50,000-watt KRLD in Dallas, Texas, also acted as an important stage for local talent.

The *Jamboree* had its roots in the *Texas Barn Dance,* a live country music show first staged at Dallas' Sportatorium in 1946. The *Texas Barn Dance* became the *Lone Star Jamboree* when it found its first radio home on WFAA in Dallas a year later. However, WFAA already featured a country music stage show (the *Saturday Night Shindig*), so in 1948 the show put down more permanent stakes on the airwaves of KRLD. Rechristened the *Big D Jamboree,* the barn dance debuted over KRLD on 16 October 1948.

KRLD, named for the Radio Laboratories of Dallas, had begun broadcasting on 31 October 1926 and achieved its 50,000-watt designation in 1938. The station's power allowed it to cover a 100-mile radius during daytime hours, and to reach more than 30 states during the night-time hours. The *Big D Jamboree* indeed had a powerful conduit through which to reach its radio audience. In the early 1950s, the *Jamboree* gained wider distribution when the Columbia Broadcasting System (CBS) radio network agreed to feature the show on its *Saturday Night Country Style,* a program that featured various country music barn dances around the United States.

The show that would become the *Big D Jamboree* was the brainchild of Sportatorium owner Ed McLemore (who also staged wrestling matches in his venue), Dallas nightclub proprietor Slim McDonald, and KLIF radio (Dallas) disc jockey Big Al Turner. By the time the show appeared on KRLD, only McLemore still had a hand in producing the show. Turner, the show's host going back to the *Texas Barn Dance* days, emceed the *Big D Jamboree* at KRLD for a short time, but that role soon went to KRLD personality Johnny Hicks, who would be the on-air voice most associated with the program during its run. KRLD's Johnny Harper was the *Jamboree*'s announcer, and he also shared producing credit with McLemore and Hicks.

Cast members of the *Big D Jamboree* who achieved national success in country music included Billy Walker, Sonny James, Ray Price, Lefty Frizzell, Hank Locklin, and Charline Arthur. Many other country music performers visited the *Big D Jamboree* frequently and found it a career-amplifying stage; among them were Jim Reeves, Hank Snow, Ferlin Husky, Hank Thompson, Johnny Cash, and Hank Williams. Local acts who never enjoyed much national fame but who nonetheless expanded their profile in Texas included the Callahan Brothers, Romana Reeves, Sid King and the Five Strings, Jimmie Heap, Gene O'Quin, Riley Crabtree, and Okie Jones.

The rise of rock and roll in the mid- to late 1950s was one of the factors that ultimately silenced the *Big D Jamboree* and other barn dances featured on radio, but ironically the *Jamboree* had a role in fueling the dissemination of the rock sound during the genre's early days. Elvis Presley, who toured frequently in Texas at the outset of his career, appeared often on the program before he became nationally known, as did other important figures such as Carl Perkins and Gene Vincent (who was managed by Ed McLemore). Other notable purveyors of the new sound who also appeared regularly on the *Jamboree* were the Belew Twins, Wanda Jackson, Johnny Carroll, and Werly Fairburn.

By the late 1950s, the *Big D Jamboree*'s way had become uneven as rock and roll increasingly overshadowed country music, the primary staple of the program. The once-vital show limped along into the mid-1960s before fading. The *Jamboree* was briefly revived in 1970, but it failed to recapture the glory that inspired historian Kevin Coffey (2000) to call it "an enviable presence on the Southwestern music scene."

See also: Country Music Format

Hosts

Big Al Turner, Johnny Hicks

Producers

Big Al Turner, Johnny Hicks, Ed McLemore, Johnny Harper

Programming History

KRLD   16 October 1948–early 1960s

Further Reading

The Big D Jamboree Live, Volumes 1 and 2 (compact disc), Dallas, Texas: Dragon Street Records, 2000 (see especially the liner notes by Kevin Coffey).

Cooper, Daniel, *Lefty Frizzell: The Honky-Tonk Life of Country Music's Greatest Singer*, Boston: Little Brown, 1995.

Gals of the Big D Jamboree (compact disc), Dallas, Texas: Dragon Street Records, 2001 (see especially liner notes by Kevin Coffey).

Guys of Big D Jamboree (compact disc), Dallas, Texas: Dragon Street Records, 2002 (see especially liner notes by Kevin Coffey).

Kingsbury, Paul, editor, *The Encyclopedia of Country Music*, New York: Oxford University Press, 1998.

Malone, Bill C., *Country Music U.S.A.*, Austin: University of Texas Press, 1968; revised edition, 1985.

Wilonsky, Robert, "Big D Jamboree," *Dallas Observer* (20–26 May 1993).

MICHAEL STREISSGUTH

BIRCH SCARBOROUGH RESEARCH

Birch Scarborough Research was a radio research firm in competition with Arbitron throughout the 1980s and early 1990s. The measurement of local radio audiences provided by the Birch reports and the qualitative research provided by the Scarborough service helped to fill the void left in syndicated local radio audience measurement after the Pulse organization closed down its operation in April 1978. Perhaps no competitor challenged Arbitron with as much consistency and industry support as did Birch Scarborough in the 1980s.

Birch Scarborough Research began in 1979 when Thomas Birch first started a radio ratings service called Radio Marketing Research. Birch had tested a system for measuring market shares and surveying music audiences by phone that met with success during test runs. Birch's research was first used to help determine programming, and his monthly service grew to include 18 markets by 1980. By March 1982, Birch was able to compete with Media Statistic, taking many Mediatrend subscribers from the other service. This gave him some major market subscribers and lent further credibility to his service. By 1984 Birch served 93 markets with the standard report format and he had hired two former Arbitron

executives to work for his organization, making the service an even greater challenger in the radio research business. The executives were Richard Weinstein, who served as president and would later go on to become executive director of the Electronic Media Rating Council (now known as the Media Rating Council), and William Livek, who served as vice president.

The Birch system relied on telephone interviews that asked respondents to report ("recall") their listening pattern during the past 24 hours. Only one designated person per household was used in the survey, with the phone interviewer asking to speak to the person with the last or most recent birthday, an approach commonly known as the "last birthday" method. The selected respondent was asked about stations heard on the radio during the previous 24 hours, the location(s) (such as at home, at work, or in the car) where the listening took place, and in which time periods the listening took place. (Time periods or "dayparts" included 6 A.M. to 10 A.M. that day, 10 A.M. to 3 P.M. that day, 3 P.M. to 7 P.M. the previous day, and 7 P.M. to midnight the previous day.) The Birch system used predesignated households in its sample; households were randomly selected from the Total Telephone Frame listing developed by A.C. Nielsen for the Nielsen Station Index. Each household was called during the evening hours, with three attempts made to reach the household and the designated respondent.

Birch served as a major competitor to Arbitron in the radio research market for a number of reasons. Its service was fairly inexpensive; it provided monthly data that was delivered every two weeks; and its research included qualitative components. Data collection was done in interview centers that allowed for oversight of interviewers and presumably ensured the quality of responses. And finally, Birch Scarborough laid claim to a response rate of over 60 percent, higher than that of Arbitron.

The basic Birch radio report was provided both monthly and quarterly. Monthly reports provided a combination of findings from the two most recent months of interviewing. Quarterly reports included average quarter-hour listening habits, daily listening habits, and weekly cumulative measures that were broken down by daypart, demographic group, and location of listening. Measures for ratings, shares, and cumulative audience were reported on an average quarter-hour and/or daypart basis.

Birch made efforts to weight its findings and thus balance the results obtained by compiling data from households of different sizes. Weighting was also used with data recorded for different days of the week, as not all respondents could be reached on the same day and their interviews often reflected listening on different days of the week (with different program schedules). Balancing methods were also used to account for disparities in ethnicity, age, sex, and county location factors.

Birch Scarborough conducted a number of studies on its own methodological research throughout the late 1980s and in 1990; for instance, in 1988 it conducted an analysis of those telephone calls placed via random digit dialing that resulted in no answer and busy signals. The results of this study were utilized by Birch to calculate response rates.

In 1989 the firm analyzed the number of attempts that were being made to reach specific demographic groups with its surveys. This analysis found no significant differences by gender or age group in the number of completed interviews. A separate study in 1989 examined the "seven day methods test." It compared the weekly cumulative numbers obtained via singleday interviews that examined listening on the current day and previous day with cumulative numbers based on successive daily interviews throughout the week, finding no significant differences between the two groups of results.

In 1990 Birch Scarborough completed a case study of the Hispanic market to evaluate how Hispanic respondents viewed the Birch interview. Personal interviews were conducted in San Antonio, Texas, and Miami, Florida, to determine (1) how well the respondents understood the Birch interview; (2) how they recalled their listening habits from the previous day; (3) which language they preferred to use during the interview; and (4) how the language used affected their responses. This case study was also used to gather other comments about the Birch survey.

Despite its status at the time as the nation's second-largest market research company, the Birch Radio Ratings Service was discontinued in 1992. Birch Scarborough attributed the move to financial losses. Scarborough Consumer Media and Retail Services continued, and a marketing arrangement made Arbitron the exclusive provider of Scarborough's qualitative data to radio and television stations. This precluded any further competition between the two companies.

See also: A.C. Nielsen Company; Arbitron; Audience Research Methods

Further Reading

Beville, Hugh Malcolm, Jr., *Audience Ratings: Radio, Television, and Cable*, Hillsdale, New Jersey: Erlbaum, 1985; 2nd edition, 1988.

Webster, James G., and Lawrence W. Lichty, *Ratings Analysis: Theory and Practice*, Hillsdale, New Jersey: Erlbaum, 1991; 2nd edition, as *Ratings Analysis: The Theory and Practice of Audience Research*, by Webster, Lichty, and Patricia F. Phalen, Mahwah, New Jersey: Erlbaum, 2000.

MATT TAYLOR

BLACKLISTING

Blacklisting was a highly organized, institutionalized effort to deny employment to individuals assumed to be members of the Communist Party or to have communist sympathies. Begun shortly after the end of World War II, blacklisting in radio was a by-product of the larger hunt for communists led by Senator Joseph McCarthy and others. The senator was not, however, a major figure in the radio version of this witch-hunt. The entertainment industry had its own inspired group.

Some researchers trace the beginnings of blacklisting in radio to the founding in 1947 of *Counterattack: The Newsletter of Facts on Communism*. Three former Federal Bureau of Investigation agents, Theodore Kirkpatrick, Kenneth Bierly, and John Keenan, founded American Business Consultants and began publishing the aforementioned newsletter. They sent copies to advertising agencies, broadcasting executives, and sponsors along with offers to do special investigations. The newsletter listed entertainers of all types along with their supposed communist activities.

Others date the beginnings of blacklisting a little earlier, just after the end of World War II. Evidently a list of between 80 and 100 "undesirables" was circulated among broadcasting executives and shown to directors. At one network, the list came with a memo advising, "For Your Information: Keep these names in mind when casting."

Context

In order to understand blacklisting and why it worked, it is first necessary to understand the political climate of the post-World War II world. The war ended in 1945 with the Soviet Union in control of Eastern Europe. Within four years, communists came to power in China. The atomic bomb became a shared weapon. Alger Hiss and the Rosenbergs became frontpage news when Senator Joseph McCarthy of Wisconsin first proclaimed that there were spies in the State Department in 1950, the same year the Korean War started. In short, it was a time ripe for demagoguery and exploitation. Into this climate of fear stepped the blacklisters.

Blacklisters needed the help of both the general public and the broadcasting industry to succeed. They needed the general public to be afraid of communism, as of a mortal enemy. This meant that any method used to defeat such an enemy was allowable. If the public could be convinced of the danger, then the firing of the occasional innocent actor, writer, and so on would be understandable and permissible. This was, after all, a life-and-death struggle with an enemy who would use any means at his disposal to succeed. Therefore, one must be willing to use any means available to defeat him— including the sacrificing of some civil rights. This "end justifies the means" argument was a relatively strong one, considering the political state of the world. Finally, one also needed the public to believe that the entertainment industry was a prime target of an international communist conspiracy.

Blacklisters needed the broadcast industry, including advertisers and advertising agencies, to believe something else entirely. They needed the industry to believe that they, the blacklisters, could institute product boycotts and that such boycotts could ruin an advertiser, agency, or product. From the late 1940s through the middle 1950s, broadcasters, advertisers, and agencies all acted as if this were possible. From a distance of half a century, it is possible to wonder why broadcasters failed to truly question such assumptions (although some did, at great personal risk), but it is always necessary to remember time and place when discussing blacklisting. What the acceptance of such assumptions meant, however, was that instead of discussing whether blacklisting itself was morally correct, people argued over whether a particular individual should or should not be included on one of the many lists being circulated. Few asked whether the lists should be published to begin with.

Although the impression is often of a large, corporate force instituting blacklisting throughout the entertainment industry, the opposite is closer to the truth. There were Bierly, Keenen, and Kirkpatrick, who founded American Business Consultants and published the regular newsletter, *Counterattack*. In 1950 they would also be responsible for publishing *Red Channels*. There was Lawrence Johnson, a Syracuse supermarket owner; Vincent Hartnett, a talent agent associated with AWARE; Daniel T. O'Shea at the Columbia Broadcasting System (CBS); Jack Wren at Batton, Barton, Durston, and Osborne; and George Sokolsky of the Hearst papers. In addition to the publications of American Business Consultants, there was the American Legion's *Firing Line*, the *Brooklyn Tablet*, and the *American Mercury*. Although not all-inclusive, this list includes many of the major groups and individuals involved in the process.

The avowed goal of blacklisters was to root out communists in the entertainment industry. The following is from the September 1947 issue of *Counterattack*:

> The most important thing of all is to base your whole policy on a firmly moral foundation. Space should not be rented to the Communist Party or to any Communist front. Supplies should not be sold to them. They should not be allowed to participate in meetings or to have time on the air or to advertise in the press. No concession should ever be made to them for any business reason. Communist actors, announcers, directors, writers, producers, etc., whether in radio, theater, or movies, should be barred to the extent permissible by law and union contracts.

How It Worked

The way blacklisting worked was relatively simple. Entertainers of all types were listed along with their supposed communist affiliations. Networks and advertising agencies then used the lists when deciding whom to hire. The names were gathered from a number of different sources. Old editions of the *Daily Worker* were searched for incriminating references. Office stationery, letters, publicity, and the like from groups labeled communist fronts by the U.S. Attorney General's Office or by the blacklisters themselves were also scoured for names. Names were also supplied by friendly witnesses to governmental agencies that were supposedly searching for communist infiltration of the entertainment industry. Prominent among these groups were the Tenney Committee in California and the House UnAmerican Activities Committee of the United States House of Representatives. Sometimes, as was eventually shown in court, the listings contained half-truths. Sometimes they were outright lies. Always, the blacklisters were after "names."

Once an entertainer was "listed" in one of the blacklisters' publications, it became almost impossible to find work. The problem was in the way radio was supported. In theater or film, there is a direct correlation between success and people attending the event, but that was not true in radio. Advertisers placed commercials, often in programs they themselves produced, with the idea that people would hear the advertisement and buy the product. Any negative publicity surrounding the program was thought to reflect on the product itself. Advertisers feared listener boycotts of their products if the programs they produced used actors listed in blacklisting publications.

Lawrence Johnson, a Syracuse supermarket owner and active supporter of blacklisting, was excellent at instilling the fear of a boycott into an advertiser's mind. When notified that a program was using actors listed in *Counterattack* or by AWARE, Johnson would write a letter to the program's sponsor. Johnson would offer to hold a test in his supermarkets. A sign in front of a competitor's brand would say that it sponsored programs that used only pro-American artists and shunned "Stalin's Little Creatures"—a phrase for which Johnson was famous. The sign in front of the sponsor's product was to explain why its maker chose to use communist fronters on its program. Johnson then said he would hold the letter for a few days awaiting a reply. He threatened that if he received no reply, he would send a copy to the United States Chamber of Commerce, the Sons of the American Revolution, the Catholic War Veterans, the Super Market Institute in Chicago, and others. The goal was to scare the sponsor into believing that blacklisters could really create a meaningful product boycott. No-one at the network level ever called the bluff.

The year 1950 became a high-water mark for blacklisting in the United States when American Business Consultants published what may be the most successful blacklist. Appearing just before the outbreak of the Korean War, *Red Channels* listed 151 artists in the entertainment field and their communist affiliations. Although many broadcast executives claimed to be appalled by the names included on the list, the book nevertheless became known as the "Bible of Madison Avenue." Two examples should prove the book's effectiveness.

Irene Wicker was one of those listed in *Red Channels*. Kellogg's had sponsored her *Singing Lady* program. The sponsor dropped the program after the publication showed she had one listing. Her sole citation was that she had sponsored a petition for the re-election of Benjamin J. Davis to Congress. The citation was based on an item in the *Daily Worker*. Wicker claimed she had never heard of Davis and went to great lengths to prove she had never sponsored a petition for his re-election. Her lawyer even got a court order to examine all 30,000 names on Davis's petitions. Wicker's was not among them. Although this "cleared" her, it still did not make her employable, for now she had become controversial.

Another of those listed by *Red Channels* was Jean Muir. A former movie actress, she had been hired by the National Broadcasting Company (NBC) to play the role of the mother in *The Aldrich Family*—a former radio drama being developed for television. *Red Channels* included nine listings for her. When Kirkpatrick was informed that NBC was going to use an actor listed in *Red Channels*, he organized a protest over her hiring. The end result was that Muir was paid in full for her contract but was never seen on the program. The industry never attempted to determine how widespread the protest was. The concern was that there was a protest at all. General Foods, the program's sponsor, issued a press release stating, "The use of controversial personalities or the discussion of controversial subjects in our advertising may provide unfavorable criticism and even antagonism among sizeable groups of customers." The sponsor did not want its product placed in any negative light at all. The publicity surrounding the Muir case had made the whole issue of blacklisting much more public than either the networks or the advertising agencies wanted it to be. As a result of the Muir case, blacklisting became institutionalized. The networks and agencies developed a system whereby all those involved in programs were screened ahead of time. Those found to have some sort of "communist affiliation" were simply never offered employment, rather than fired later. This cut back on some of the negative publicity.

Like Wicker, Muir also tried to clear herself, but she remained unemployable. The real point of the Muir case is that by the end of 1950, the industry had accepted the blacklisters' standard on employability. If someone was listed, the networks would not employ him or her. NBC had tried with Muir, but when confronted with a token protest, NBC caved in, thus allowing *Red Channels* and publications like it to set the standards by which performers would be judged. Understand that Muir was not a part of a communist plot, nor was she a member of the Communist Party. She had merely participated in liberal political activities in the 1930s. For those actions, her career was destroyed.

To speak out against the blacklisters was to put one's own career in jeopardy. Raymond Swing was chief commentator for Voice of America when he was invited to debate blacklisting with Kirkpatrick before the Radio Executives Club of New York. While vigorously defending the American system of government, he attacked those in charge of the radio industry:

> If, by some bleak and dreadful tragedy, American radio should come under the control of persons intent on producing a single conformity of thinking in America, it will not be the pressure groups or the blacklisters who will be to blame, but those now in charge of radio. They have it in their keeping, and what happens to it will be their doing.

After his appearance, Swing found himself under attack by both the blacklisters at *Counterattack* and by Senator Joseph McCarthy. Although it was reported that industry executives applauded Swing's role, they did nothing to change blacklisting in radio. That would be left to a single radio personality—John Henry Faulk.

Blacklisters, and to some degree sponsors and networks, believed themselves to be immune from prosecution. After all, blacklisters merely transcribed their information from other publications. If there was a mistake, it was the fault of the publication from which the information had been gathered. Those listed should sue those publications. Sponsors and networks felt immune because they certainly had a right to hire those people they felt best suited the job. This was to change.

John Henry Faulk

In 1956 John Henry Faulk was elected second vice president of the New York Chapter of the American Federation of Television and Radio Artists (AFTRA). Charles Collingwood was elected President and Orsen Bean first vice president. All had made their antiblacklisting beliefs known. AWARE was particularly upset and sought to get both Bean and Faulk fired. Bean became unemployed almost immediately but was able to rely on his club work as a stand-up comedian. Faulk, however, was vulnerable. He was an employee of CBS Radio and had been doing some television at the time of his election. Shortly after his election, his name appeared in the publications of AWARE, which accused him of collusion and fellow-traveling. His radio sponsors deserted him, and CBS fired him. Faulk then took the unusual step of suing AWARE and Vincent Hartnett. It took six years before the case came to trial. Hartnett eventually admitted, "I was sold a barrel of false information," when questioned about the listings next to Faulk's name. Many of the citations on Faulk were incorrect, and others were intentionally misleading. In 1962 the jury awarded Faulk $3,500,000. The award was later reduced to approximately half a million dollars, and Faulk saw little of the money. Lawrence Johnson, who had avoided testifying, died of an overdose of barbiturates the day the verdict was announced. Thanks to the publicity from this case, blacklisting was, more or less, officially dead.

It was not just a single lawsuit that ended blacklisting but several things that came together in the late 1950s. First, the Faulk lawsuit placed advertisers and networks alike on notice that to maintain an official blacklist was to court financial disaster. Second, advertisers were moving away from the program production end of broadcasting. This removed them from the day-to-day hiring of entertainment personnel and made them less vulnerable to threats. Third, it became widely known that many blacklisted individuals had continued to work under assumed identities with no negative consequences for networks or advertisers. By the late 1950s blacklisters were no longer able to raise the same level of response from the public over their allegations. Combined, these factors helped end the effective reign of blacklisters.

Looking back, the real goal of the blacklisters seems to have been publicity. They were constantly after names. No plot was ever uncovered to use radio to convert the masses to communism. No evidence was ever found of a left-wing conspiracy to blacklist anticommunist actors. No spies were found in the radio industry. Blacklisting became a self-perpetuating effort at continued publicity. It destroyed careers and, in some cases, lives.

The real issue was whether there should have been a blacklist at all. Unfortunately, that particular issue was rarely raised. Yes, there was some editorializing during and after the Muir case, but the bottom line is that *Red Channels* was both accepted and used by networks and advertising agencies alike. Some, such as Edward R. Murrow, raised the issue, but they had difficulty sustaining it. Although on the one hand, Murrow was allowed to fight Senator Joseph McCarthy on his CBS program *See It Now,* on the other hand, the network was running its own in-house blacklisting organization headed by Daniel T. O'Shea.

It is also true that the relative number affected was really quite small when compared with the number of people employed in radio and television. This was of no consolation, however, to the Muirs, Wickers, and others who were ruined by the process. The real conclusion is that the broadcasting industry lacked the will to fight blacklisting. Although it is possible to find exceptions to this pattern, they are most notable because they are exceptions. The industry as a whole allowed both itself and the First Amendment to be battered at the hands of blacklisters.

See also: Aldrich Family; Red Channels

Further Reading

Buckley, William F., Jr., and L. Brent Bozell, *McCarthy and His Enemies: The Record and Its Meaning*, Chicago: Regnery, 1954.

Cogley, John, *Report on Blacklisting*, 2 vols, New York: Fund for the Republic, 1956; see especially vol. 2, *RadioTelevision*.

Dunne, Philip, *Take Two: A Life in the Movies and Politics*, New York: McGraw-Hill, 1980; updated edition, New York: Limelight Editions, 1992.

Everitt, David, *A Shadow of Red: Communism and the Blacklist in Radio and Television*. Chicago: Ivan Dee, 2007.

Faulk, John Henry, *Fear on Trial*, New York: Simon and Schuster, 1964.

Foley, Karen Sue, *The Political Blacklist in the Broadcast Industry: The Decade of the 1950s*, New York: Arno Press, 1979.

Kanfer, Stefan, *A Journal of the Plague Years*, New York: Atheneum, 1973.

Miller, Merle, *The Judges and the Judged*, Garden City, New York: Doubleday, 1952.

Red Channels: The Report of Communist Influence in Radio and Television, New York: Counterattack, 1950.

DAVID E. TUCKER

BLACK-ORIENTED RADIO

Although African-Americans have participated in radio since its inception in the early 1920s, specific programs directed to blacks did not develop in any appreciable form until the late 1940s and early 1950s. Historically, black-oriented radio first provided music and comedy. Later, public affairs, news, and programming for the entire community made their way to the airwaves.

Early Black Radio

The first African-American to have a commercially sustained radio program was Jack Leroy Cooper, a former vaudevillian and entrepreneur who began announcing on Washington, D.C.'s WCAP radio station in 1925. Later, in Chicago, Cooper worked at WSBC, where he started the *All Negro Hour* in 1929. Among Cooper's many accomplishments were hiring African-Americans to work as announcers and salespeople, playing gospel music, broadcasting sports, and developing a missing persons program to help individuals find loved ones. Moreover, Cooper created the concept of the disc jockey when his studio musician walked out: Cooper began playing records and talking between them when a local musician's union demanded that his pianist go on strike. In 1947 *Ebony Magazine* called Cooper the "Dean of African-American Disc Jockeys." By that time he was responsible for more than 50 programs broadcast on four Chicago radio stations.

Early network radio developed programs that included black characters; however, these were often in stereotypical roles. On some shows, such as *Amos 'n' Andy,* whites portrayed blacks on the air in stereotypical fashion, and in other programs African-Americans portrayed themselves in this manner. Most often, African-Americans were featured as maids, butlers, and gardeners and in other vocational or domestic-helper roles.

Amos 'n' Andy became one of the most popular radio programs of all time. African-Americans listened to the show and probably laughed at the antics of its characters, even though the program often portrayed blacks in an unfavorable light. Nevertheless, the National Association for the Advancement of Colored People and some other organizations believed that the program demeaned African-Americans and urged the Columbia Broadcasting System (CBS) to cancel the show.

In the many comedies broadcast on network radio, African-Americans played key roles in the success of the programs. Eddie Anderson earned fame as "Rochester" on the *Jack Benny Show.* Hattie McDaniel played "mammy" roles on the *Optimistic Doughnut Hour* and in the radio series *Showboat.* Later, McDaniel played the lead role in *Beulah.*

During the early years of radio, black music such as jazz and blues was often heard on network radio. Bessie Smith's live blues performance was broadcast from a Memphis radio station in 1924. In addition, groups such as the Hampton Singers performed on radio in that same year. Jazz, especially, received a great deal of airplay through the 1940s. Bandleaders such as Cab Calloway, Duke Ellington, and Thomas "Fats" Waller were among the many African-American musicians who made regular broadcasts on early radio. Marian Anderson, Roland Hayes, and Paul Robeson were among the African-American vocalists heard on early radio broadcasts.

Early non-entertainment programming such as public-affairs programs reported on the status of the black family, educational activities in the black community, farming techniques, and occasionally racial issues. In 1933 CBS broadcast *John Henry, Black River Boat Giant,* a positive drama featuring African-Americans. By the 1940s the National Broadcasting Company's (NBC) *Freedom's People,* an eight-part series featuring dramatic vignettes by African-Americans such as Paul Robeson, Joe Louis, and A. Philip Randolph, was broadcast. Non-network radio broadcasts included Roy Ottley's *New World a'Comin'* and Richard Durham's *Destination Freedom,* which focused on historical treatments of African-American experiences. These programs provided positive portrayals of African-Americans to radio audiences. In addition, radio stations began gospel music and church-service broadcasts in the 1940s.

NBC's Blue network broadcast *America's Negro Soldiers* in 1941. Sponsored by the U.S. Department of War, *America's Negro Soldiers* included patriotic vignettes that highlighted the historical contributions black soldiers made to the U.S. Army. Other program components included music, singing, and tap dancing, but the program omitted references to racial discrimination in American society. CBS's *Open Letter on Race Hatred,* however, examined the causes and consequences of the Detroit Race Riot of 1943. Other radio programs developed for African-American listeners during World War II were "Judgment Day" (1942), "Beyond the Call of Duty" (1943), "Fighting Men" (1943), "Gallant Black Eagle" (1943), and "The Negro in War" (1945).

Postwar Rise of Black-Oriented Radio

By the late 1940s radio began to broadcast programs targeted directly to predominantly African-American audiences. For example, in 1946 CBS and NBC produced specials that highlighted significant events in the African-American community. The CBS program shed a spotlight on "National Negro Newspaper Week," and the NBC program focused on Nat King Cole, the famous singer. Two major factors had an impact on the networks' attempts to reach African-American listeners. First, national advertisers recognized African-American economic power. Thus, companies that produced products such as canned milk, flour, and lard directed their advertising messages directly to black consumers via radio.

Second, television began to siphon off advertising dollars, audiences, and top-name performers from network radio. Aside from the money involved, radio performers soon realized that they would also receive greater exposure to larger audiences on television than on radio. Station owners responded to these developments by changing their formats and playing jazz, rhythm and blues, blues, rock and roll, and other black musical forms to appeal to African-American listeners. They also hired disc jockeys whose words, personalities, and music dramatically increased the number of black listeners. When first introduced, radio stations broadcast rhythm and blues, blues, and other black music formats in segments. A few hours during the day was set aside for these broadcasts. Eventually, stations began to build their entire formats around "black-appeal" programming.

In 1948, for example, WDIA in Memphis, Tennessee, broadcast its first program to black audiences.

Nat D. Williams, pioneer black disc jockey at WDIA, hosted this show and many others for years to come. Soon after the initial broadcast, WDIA began an all-black programming format. Prior to WDIA's efforts, few black-appeal radio stations or programs existed. Notable exceptions included Cooper's *All Negro Hour* and Chicago disc jockey Al Benson's programs. WDIA's programming included public affairs, news, public service announcements, and other community service announcements and promotions.

Radio stations across the United States quickly imitated WDIA, which also became known as the "Mid-South Giant," because of its broadcast signal. The station reached audiences in Mississippi, Tennessee, and Arkansas. Other black-oriented stations hired flamboyant black disc jockeys such as "Jockey" Jack Gibson, also known as "Jack the Rapper," Maurice "Hot Rod" Hulbert, and Peggy Mitchell Beckwith to play music, advertise and promote products, and especially to communicate with African-American listeners. Their unique personalities and knowledge of black music and recording artists catapulted black-appeal radio stations to unprecedented popularity among listeners.

Black disc jockeys in northern urban areas performed a number of other functions at the radio station. They often provided useful public service advice and served as counselors to many of the newly arrived migrants from the South, informing them about where best to shop and how to avoid the dangers in their new urban environments.

The popularity of their radio presentations, sometimes referred to as "personality" radio, began to decline in the late 1950s, mainly as a consequence of the payola scandal and the movement toward formatting in radio. Payola, or the payment of unreported money to play records, was legal but became rampant in the industry. The U.S. government outlawed the practice in the late 1950s. Thus, disc jockeys lost the opportunity to play records they deemed popular or attractive to listeners. Instead, that role eventually became one for program directors and other managers to take over.

Moreover, black-oriented radio stations began using a more tightly controlled music format, which did not allow disc jockeys to express themselves as they had in the past. Instead, black-oriented radio stations began to promote call letters, dial positions, and themes, such as "The Quiet Storm" and "the Black experience in sound."

In addition to the disc jockeys who worked for black-oriented radio stations during these years, African-American news reporters and public-affairs announcers also found jobs. Eddie Castleberry and Roy Woods, Sr., became well known for their announcing and reporting skills.

Throughout the civil rights movement, black-oriented radio stations assisted in the struggle for African-American human rights. Broadcasts from these stations provided listeners with accounts of newsworthy events, such as marches, boycotts, and voter registration drives. Additionally, black-oriented stations were often at the forefront in bringing attention to societal ills suffered by African-Americans, including police brutality and violence directed at them. The Reverend Martin Luther King, Jr.'s sermons and speeches were widely broadcast on black radio stations. Message music from black recording artists such as Curtis Mayfield and Little Milton found airplay on black-oriented radio stations.

Black Music and Black Ownership

Although hundreds of radio stations played black music, hired African-American announcers, and used promotions that appealed directly to black listeners, few of these stations were actually owned by African-Americans. J.B. Blayton bought WERD in Atlanta, Georgia, in 1948, becoming the first African-American to own a commercial radio station. WERD played black music and employed disc jockeys such as Jack Gibson, "Joltin' Joe Howard," and Helen Lawrence to appeal to African-American listeners.

By 1970 African-Americans owned only 16 stations out of more than 7,000 commercially operated facilities. Throughout the 1970s, the number of black-owned radio stations increased to 140. During the late 1980s and 1990s, the number of black-owned radio stations further increased but then started to decline to levels approximating those of the late 1970s.

Several factors contributed to this decline, among them greater consolidation in the radio industry, broadcast deregulation, and advertising practices that had a negative impact on the overall dollars generated by black-owned stations. The combination of consolidation in the radio industry and group owners' greater control over the advertising dollars in local markets left the often poorly financed black-owned radio stations unable to compete economically in today's marketplace, forcing many owners to sell.

In addition, some studies have cited the lack of access to investment capital and the lack of policies and incentives that promote African-American ownership of radio stations. One change adversely affecting black ownership was a Federal Communications Commission (FCC) decision not to "extend enhancement credits" for African-American ownership. Enhancement credits helped make African-American applications more competitive in comparative hearings. Other deregulatory actions adversely affecting black radio station ownership included the relaxing of ownership caps. In 1992, for instance, the FCC relaxed national ownership limits, allowing a broadcaster to own up to 18 AM and FM stations nationally.

Moreover, in 1995 Congress repealed the FCC's tax certificate program. This industry incentive had provided tax benefits to the seller of a media property that was sold to a minority broadcaster. Finally, the passage of the Telecommunications Act of 1996 further deregulated the industry. The act removed all national caps on radio station ownership. On the local level, ownership restrictions were considerably liberalized, allowing increased ownership of stations, up to 50 percent of stations in a market, up to a maximum of eight, depending on market size.

The combined impact of these changes has made it difficult for African-American owners to generate revenues to compete successfully with group-owned stations. These changes, however, do not necessarily affect advertising revenues for all black-oriented radio stations, because many are owned by conglomerates and use scale economies to achieve efficiencies and revenue generation.

Finally, African-American ownership, or the lack thereof, does not affect the number of black formats available to listeners. Black-oriented radio stations play music that African-Americans expect to hear. Many of these stations developed into outlets that emphasized music programming and used promotional slogans such as "Soul Music" stations, "The Total Black experience in Sound," and "The Quiet Storm" to appeal to listeners. Non-entertainment programming on some of these stations, however, suffers when local ownership disappears.

Black-Oriented Radio Formats Today

Though the term is somewhat subjective, there are nearly 500 black-oriented radio stations operating in the United States today. The most popular format on these radio stations is urban contemporary. This format plays music from several genres, including rhythm and blues, urban adult contemporary, dance, urban gospel, rap music, and jazz. Fifty-seven percent of all African-Americans aged 12 and older listen to urban contemporary formatted radio stations. Moreover, black-oriented radio has popular appeal among other ethnic groups, including Asians, whites, and Hispanics. The majority of its listeners, however, are African-Americans—indeed, 90 percent of the listeners to black-oriented stations are minorities. Eighty percent of listeners to the urban contemporary format are minority group members. Other black-oriented formats include "black talk" and blues. General market radio stations attract a 21 percent minority audience.

Black-oriented does not necessarily imply black-owned. According to the National Association of Black Owned Broadcasters (NABOB), only about 240 stations in 2008 were owned by African-Americans, many as a part of black-owned groups like Radio One, Urban Radio Licenses and Tama Broadcasting, Inc. (though black ownership does not always mean that stations will air black-oriented formats).

For years, black-oriented radio stations were often among the most community-minded and public affairs-centered outlets in their community. As with other stations, however, consolidation, the quest for ratings and other economic priorities have caused many black-oriented outlets to sharply curtail or abandon news or public affairs programming. This has triggered criticism of both black-owned and -programmed stations, as many believe such outlets have an inherent responsibility to serve the black community. These concerns have been partially alleviated by successful syndicated black personalities including Steve Harvey, Tom Joyner, and Michael Baisden who help publicize race-related stories often under-reported by mainstream media. Black radio was also credited with mobilizing black voters in the 2008 Presidential election.

Black-oriented noncommercial stations play an important role in both entertaining and informing the African-American community. Sometimes called "community stations," they schedule programs to help communities build strong identities and many allow the public to air controversial and unpopular opinions.

See also: African-Americans in Radio; *Amos 'n' Andy*; Black Radio Networks; Blues Format; Community Radio; Jazz Format; Payola; Urban Contemporary Format; WDIA

Further Reading

Alexander, Keith, "Riding the Signal: Cathy Hughes Takes Command of Radio Airwaves," *Emerge* (1 September 1999).
"Annual Negro Radio Issue," *Sponsor* (1952–56) Berry, Venise T., and Carmen L. Manning-Miller, editors, *Mediated Messages and African-American Culture*, Thousand Oaks, California: Sage, 1996.
Kernan, Michael, "Around the Mall and Beyond," *Smithsonian* 27 (April 1996).
MacDonald, J. Fred, *Don't Touch That Dial!: Radio Programming in American Life, 1920–1960*, Chicago: Nelson-Hall, 1979.
Newman, Mark, *Entrepreneurs of Profit and Pride: From Black-Appeal to Radio Soul*, New York: Praeger, 1988.
Robinson, Eugene, "Drive Time for the 'Jena 6'," *Washington Post* (21 September 2007), p. A19.
Sampson, Henry T., *Swingin' on the Ether Waves: A Chronological History of African Americans in Radio and Television Broadcasting, 1925–1955*. Jefferson, North Carolina: McFarland, 2005 (two vols).
Spaulding, Norman W., "History of Black Oriented Radio in Chicago, 1929–1963," Ph.D. diss., University of Illinois, 1981.
Williams, Gilbert Anthony, "The Black Disc Jockey As a Cultural Hero," *Popular Music and Society* 10 (Summer 1986).
Williams, Gilbert Anthony, *Legendary Pioneers of Black Radio*, Westport, Connecticut: Praeger, 1998.

GILBERT A. WILLIAMS,
2009 REVISIONS BY CARY O'DELL

BLACK RADIO NETWORKS

Although the major national radio networks got their start in the 1920s, a network dedicated to African-American listeners did not make its debut until 1954, when the National Negro network (NNN) went on the air. It differed from the older networks in that it did not own any radio stations, but it resembled them in providing programs to affiliate stations.

Origins

Two driving forces helped launch the NNN. The first impetus had to do with finding a way of reaching African-American consumers. National advertisers, seeking ways to increase market share, decided that by using "Negro-appeal" radio stations they could better achieve their goals. For many national companies, sales to African-American consumers often represented the difference between breaking even and increased sales, and finding a way to reach them with advertising was thus an important goal.

Another driving force for the creation and development of a national black radio network came from a desire by African-American entertainers to reach a national black audience with their programs. Toward those two ends, Leonard Evans, publisher of a black radio trade magazine, organized the NNN in 1954 in order to distribute programming to affiliates. The NNN, for example, produced and distributed *The Story of Ruby Valentine*, a soap opera starring Ruby Dee and

Juanita Hall. African-American entertainers Cab Calloway and Ethel Waters also produced NNN programs. Moreover, other programming on the network represented a range: there was highbrow fare, such as symphony concerts broadcast from black colleges, for example a concert at North Carolina College in Durham hosted by African-American disc jockey Norfley Whitted. There was also personality radio, featuring the latest rhythm and blues, blues, and jazz music. These music programs were hosted by African-American disc jockeys at the various NNN affiliates around the country.

Ruby Valentine was broadcast on 45 radio stations. Pulse ratings indicated that the show received a 20 rating among African-Americans in 1954. The show and its network lasted three years. National advertisers pulled away from the network, realizing that local black DJs had probably more appeal than national DJs.

After the demise of NNN, other attempts to create a black radio network were led by Chicago disc jockey Sid McCoy, whose syndicated programs were heard in 61 markets in 1957. McCoy's programs featured interviews with well-known personalities from the world of music. In 1958 McCoy's *Showcase,* a talk program aimed at African-American listeners, became a staple on radio stations in 32 markets.

Norman Spaulding organized Feature Broadcasting Company in 1960. Feature produced radio programs that covered sports, domestic issues, and black history; it also produced a program moderated by Ethel Waters called *Advice to the Housewife.* These syndicated efforts laid the foundation for more ambitious developments in black radio networking.

Developments in the 1970s

The Mutual Broadcasting System helped launch the first black all-news radio network in 1972, the Mutual Black Network (MBN). The MBN had two principal bases of operation, New York and Washington, D.C. The network produced five-minute news and sports reports and distributed them to its affiliates daily. The New York office was led by veteran broadcast journalist Sheldon Lewis, and long-time news reporter Ed Castleberry headed up MBN's Washington, D.C., office. MBN distributed programming to approximately 90 affiliates, using telephone lines subleased from the Mutual Broadcasting Service. Later, as the number and types of programs increased and changed, MBN used leased satellite transmission facilities to

distribute its programming. MBN employed approximately 50 people, with about half working in each of its two main offices.

Another black all-news radio network got its start just a few months after the MBN operation began. The Sheridan Broadcasting network (SBN) in Pittsburgh was developed as part of the Sheridan Broadcasting Corporation. Ron Davenport, Philadelphia native and entrepreneur, along with other investors purchased four radio stations—WAMO AM/FM (Pittsburgh), WUFO-AM (Buffalo, New York), and WILD-AM (Boston). These stations formed the initial media investments of the Sheridan Broadcasting Corporation.

In 1976 MBN, which had been struggling financially, merged with Davenport's Sheridan Broadcasting Corporation when the latter purchased 49 percent of MBN. In 1979 Sheridan bought the remaining 51 percent of the shares, and it became part of SBN. Upon gaining control of MBN, Sheridan expanded its programming offerings to affiliates to include *Money Smarts,* a financial report broadcast daily, and *Coming Soon,* a movie review program. In addition, the network produced *Major League Baseball Notebook, NFL Playbook,* and the *NBA Report* to provide listeners with coverage of the nation's professional athletes in those sports. In addition to sports coverage, the SBN also broadcast Lou Rawls's *Parade of Stars* telethon, an annual fund-raiser for the United Negro College Fund. By 1990 SBN boasted more than 150 affiliates and grossed more than $15 million in annual revenues.

A third black-owned radio news network was established in 1973 in New York City. The National Black Network (NBN) employed 50 people. NBN used a combination of telephone lines, satellite interconnection, and microwave relays to distribute its programming nationally. NBN broadcast its news to affiliates in Los Angeles, New York, and five other major U.S. cities. Eugene D. Jackson became NBN's first president. Sidney Small played a significant role in securing financing for the organization, and Del Racee, another founding member, brought radio station operations and know-how to the group of founding members.

NBN's initial offerings included *Black Issues and the Black Press,* a weekly 30-minute news show, and *One Black Man's Opinion,* which featured the commentaries of veteran newsman Roy Wood, Sr., and aired five days a week. Also in its lineup of programs was the *Ossie Davis and Ruby Dee Story Hour,* a one-hour weekly series hosted by this husband-and-wife team, featuring poetry, historical anecdotes, interviews, and music. By 1977 NBN served 80 affiliate stations.

BLACK RADIO NETWORKS

Aside from the information and entertainment NBN provided to affiliates and listeners, the network also increased the available options of national advertisers to reach African-American consumers. NBN's demographic profile indicated that it had a 54 percent audience share among African-American women, a 47 percent share of African-American men, and a 73 percent share of the listening audience of African-American teens aged 12–17.

Modern Black Radio Networks

By the end of the 1980s, NBN served 94 affiliates, reaching nearly 20 million African-American listeners each week with news, sports, and information programming. NBN had gross revenues exceeding $10 million by the late 1980s. Its expanded programming services included such shows as *Energy Insight*, a consumers' program, and *Short Cuts*. In addition, the network added a late-night talk show, *Night Talk*, hosted by Bob Law. Its parent company, Unity Broadcasting, continued to expand and purchased two radio stations, WDAS AM/FM.

In 1991 SBN bought NBN, creating the American Urban Radio network (AURN). By 2008 this network had more than 300 affiliates and reached over 20 million listeners weekly. Headquartered in New York, with bureaus in Chicago, Detroit, Atlanta, Pittsburgh, Los Angeles and Washington, D.C., AURN was the only black radio network in America and had satellite capacity to reach over 94 percent of African-Americans. With programming produced exclusively for African-American listeners, it offered affiliates news; public-affairs programs; and syndicated features on finance and money, health, political news, minority business ventures and the only national African-American nightly talk show. In addition, AURN produced sports features, entertainment and celebrity news shows, gospel music shows, a daily report from the White House, a show on surfing the web, and cultural offerings, including programs that focused on black music, comedy, media and women.

Its four programming networks—Pinnacle, Renaissance, STRZ, and The Light—offered more than 200 weekly programs, most of them tied to promotions for events, direct mail campaigns and sweepstakes from AURN's marketing division. Examples included a gospel music cruise, a black college football All-American feature, and black music festivals.

By the late 1990s, AURN had become the third-largest radio network operating in the United States. Its five divisions—entertainment, marketing and promotion, news, public affairs, and sports—produce programs especially designed for African-American listeners. For example, its STRZ Entertainment network offers programs on black music (*USA Music Magazine*), media, comedy (*STRZ Funline*), and shows for women (*Cameos of Black Women*). The news division, American Urban News (AUN)/SBN News, distributes two separate news reports. AUN news is a three-and-a-half-minute news summary, delivered on the hour from 6 A.M. to 10 P.M. each day. The SBN newscast is broadcast in five-minute segments at half past the hour. These satellite-delivered newscasts reach approximately eight million listeners each week.

The Urban Public Affairs network (UPAN) is responsible for special programs, such as those developed for Black History Month, and for regular features covering consumer issues, health, minority business activities, and financial matters. Special programs on UPAN include, for example, memorials created for the Dr. Martin Luther King Jr. birthday holiday and for the national elections (*Election Day: America*).

The Sports network on SBN offers the same programming that it offered prior to the merger of the two black radio groups. The SBN Urban network programs are new, however. This AURN network distributes to affiliates marketing and promotional materials and services, including direct-mail campaigns and sweepstakes promotions.

See also: African-Americans in Radio; Black-Oriented Radio; Mutual Broadcasting System

Further Reading

Barlow, William, *Voice Over: The Making of Black Radio*, Philadelphia, Pennsylvania: Temple University Press, 1999.
Edmerson, Estelle, "A Descriptive Study of the American Negro in the United States Professional Radio, 1922–1953," Master's thesis, University of California, Los Angeles, 1954.
Newman, Mark, *Entrepreneurs of Profit and Pride: From Black Appeal to Radio Soul*, New York: Praeger, 1988.
"NNN: Negro Radio's Network," SPONSOR (20 September 1954).
Spaulding, Norman, "History of Black-Oriented Radio in Chicago, 1929–1963," Ph.D. diss., University of Illinois, 1981.
Williams, Gilbert Anthony, *Legendary Pioneers of Black Radio*, Westport, Connecticut: Praeger, 1998.

GILBERT A. WILLIAMS,
2009 REVISIONS BY GAIL LOVE

BLUE BOOK
Broadcast Policy Statement

More formally titled *Public Service Responsibility of Broadcast Licensees,* this 1946 Federal Communications Commission (FCC) report on radio's program and advertising shortcomings gave rise to a lasting controversy concerning the agency's supervisory role over broadcasting's practices.

Background

FCC concerns about radio advertising and programming were anything but new—they had been a part of commission discussion and some legal cases since the commission's creation in 1934. With the approaching end of World War II, the FCC was better able to focus on domestic issues, and incoming chairman Paul Porter proposed a study of radio program practices on which the commission might base overall policy guidelines that could assist in its station licensing decisions. What several commissioners felt was needed was a comprehensive analysis of program and advertising promises stations made in applying for licenses versus their actual performance three years later when that license came up for renewal.

In mid-1945 former British Broadcasting Company (BBC) official Charles A. Siepmann was hired to work with attorney Elinor Bonteque and the FCC staff to develop a workable study of "promise versus performance" measures, including such measures as the amount of advertising a station carried per hour or week, the proportion of locally produced programs provided, and the proportion of sustaining (nonsponsored) programs offered. Because it was too costly and time consuming to survey all 900 AM radio stations then on the air, a few sample cases would have to be relied on to provide a picture of current industry practices. Even before the study got under way, the commission began to hold up once-routine license renewals in cases where there was evidence of serious promise-versus-performance problems. By early 1946 more than 300 stations—nearly a third of all those on the air—were in license limbo.

What It Said

On 7 March 1946, the FCC released a 149-page mimeographed report in light blue covers titled *Public Service Responsibilities of Broadcast Licensees.* Demand for copies led to a printed version of 59 pages, and it is these that are usually found in libraries and archives today. The "Blue Book" (as it was quickly dubbed by all parties) was divided into five parts: (1) a discussion of the commission's concern with program service (which presented five case studies of specific stations found wanting); (2) the FCC's legal jurisdiction with respect to program service; (3) four specific aspects of the public interest in program service; (4) a review of relevant economic issues; and (5) a summary and conclusion including proposals for future commission policy.

The five case studies in Part I each pinpointed a different problem. KIEV in Glendale, California, was found to have promised considerable local cultural and public service programming and limited advertising—but instead to have provided a largely sponsored recorded music service, meeting almost none of its original promises. WSNY in Schenectady, New York, had been granted a license in a comparative hearing based on programming promises that, at renewal time some years later, had not been fulfilled. Station WTOL in Toledo, Ohio, had obtained a full-time authorization (it had been a daytime-only operation), again based on certain promises concerning local public service programs, which were found "conspicuous by their absence" four years later. Baltimore station WBAL changed ownership in the mid-1930s, and a decade later it was found to be providing a service largely bereft of promised local sustaining programs. And finally, station KHMO in Hannibal, Missouri, obtained a license in a court action in the mid-1930s, based in part on programming commitments that it was not fulfilling by early 1945.

The second part of the Blue Book, concerning the "commission jurisdiction with respect to program service," focused on legal issues raised at the time of the FCC's creation from the former Federal Radio Commission. Written by Bonteque, this section concluded that the FCC "is under an affirmative duty, in its public interest determinations, to give full consideration to program service."

The specifics of that determination were spelled out in Part 3. The Blue Book defined the public interest to include four specific requirements of all radio stations. The first was to carry sustaining programs—those not paid for by commercial sponsors—because such programs provided a vital balance to advertiser-supported programs, especially for minority audiences and program experimentation. Including several fullpage charts illustrating station practices, this was the longest single part (nearly 24 pages in the printed version) of the Blue Book. The second requirement was to carry local and live programs to reflect local community concerns and interests. Excessive reliance on national commercial programs was held to be an example of poor practice. Carrying discussion of public issues was the third requirement. Another lengthy section of eight pages was devoted to the fourth requirement—not carrying too much advertising.

The fourth portion of the Blue Book focused on economic aspects—essentially the profits made by the industry. Here 14 tables demonstrated the substantial returns stations had made during the war, suggesting that a profitable business like radio broadcasting could easily support a larger public service role.

Finally, the Blue Book turned to the role of the public and government with some specific procedural proposals for future regulation (some of this section was written by Siepmann). Among these proposals were creation of uniform definitions of program types, segments of the broadcast day, selection of a composite week on which program reports would be based, some revisions in license and renewal application forms, and procedures on renewal actions. All of these proposals were designed to allow ready comparison of practice across stations. The same section also called for more radio criticism, self-regulation, radio listener councils, and education about radio in colleges and universities.

Impact

Publication of the Blue Book brought forth an instant negative radio industry response, including rhetoric that the government was trying to take control of radio or censor broadcasters. At the least, industry figures argued, they should have had a chance to comment on the cases and methods used and the findings reached before the report was released. Along with other critics, they also held that the FCC had no authority to regulate as it seemed to intend; at the same time, the report was criticized for emphasizing a few bad actors in an otherwise well-meaning and effective industry. Even some of those sympathetic to the report's intent felt the distinction concerning benefits of sustaining and commercial programming was overstated. And the financial section probably overstated the industry's profits, because the war years, in retrospect, were clearly an unusual period (given wartime limits on newspaper advertising to save paper and tax provisions making it beneficial for companies making war products to keep their names in the public eye with radio advertising).

Did the publication have any lasting effect? In the end, no station lost its license for the kind of transgressions described in the Blue Book. Virtually all the licensees designated for renewal hearings because of Blue Book issues were eventually renewed—and hundreds of new stations took to the air as well. Yet the FCC never withdrew or replaced the document, which remained in place as a statement of policy thinking for years to come. Still, a decade later, radio broadcasters were carrying even fewer sustaining programs in what had become a "local," although heavily commercialized, music service. By 1959 the trade weekly *Broadcasting* noted that the report was long out of print and was "now something of a collector's item."

See also: Federal Communications Commission; Regulation

Further Reading

"FCC's Blue Book," *Freedom of Information Center Publication* 90 (1961) (major portions of the text are excerpted here).
Meyer, Richard J., "The Blue Book," *Journal of Broadcasting* 6 (Summer 1962,).
Miller, Justin, *The Blue Book: An Analysis*, Washington, D.C.: National Association of Broadcasters, 1947.
Siepmann, Charles A., *Radio's Second Chance*, Boston: Little Brown, 1946.
Siepmann, Charles A., "Storm in the Radio World," *The American Mercury* (August 1946).
Siepmann, Charles A., *The Radio Listener's Bill of Rights: Democracy, Radio, and You*, New York: Anti-Defamation League of B'nai B'rith, 1948.
U.S. Federal Communications Commission, *Public Service Responsibilities of Broadcast Licensees*, Washington, D.C.: FCC, 1946; reprint, New York: Arno Press, 1974.
White, Llewellyn, "The Blue Book," in *The American Radio: A Report on the Broadcasting Industry in the United States from the Commission on Freedom of the Press*, by White, Chicago: University of Chicago Press, 1947.

CHRISTOPHER H. STERLING

BLUE NETWORK

The Blue network was one of two radio networks operated by the National Broadcasting Company (NBC) from 1927 until 1943. After its sale in 1943, this network continued using the Blue network name for a year, until it was renamed the American Broadcasting Companies (ABC).

Origins

The Blue network, predecessor of the ABC Radio network, traces its roots to the early 1920s, when two informal networks linked a few radio stations in the U.S. Northeast to carry broadcasts from New York. The American Telephone and Telegraph

(AT&T) network was the stronger of the two, feeding sponsored programs and special events from the ompany's New York station, WEAF (later WNBC, now WFAN). Starting in 1923, the second network fed programs from New York station WJZ (now WABC) to other Northeastern stations of the "Radio Group" operated by the Radio Corporation of America (RCA), General Electric, and Westinghouse Electric.

In 1926 a patent agreement reached between the Radio Group and AT&T heralded the beginning of serious network broadcasting in the United States. The agreement provided that the Radio Group would operate radio stations and networks, and AT&T would provide telephone lines to connect stations for network broadcasting. RCA established the National Broadcasting Company, a new corporation, in 1926 to operate local stations and radio networks. In turn, NBC bought WEAF and the telephone company's network from AT&T for $1 million to complete the settlement. NBC then announced that it would provide the best programs available for broadcasting in the United States and that it would provide these programs to other stations throughout the country. NBC was launched with a gala inaugural broadcast from New York on 15 November 1926.

At the time of its establishment, NBC had two stations in both New York (WEAF and WJZ) and Washington, D.C. (WRC and WMAL) as well as two affiliates in several other cities. Instead of duplicating the same program on both stations in the same community, NBC devised a plan starting in early 1927 for two semi-independent networks that would carry separate programs most of the time. These two networks, known as the NBC Red and NBC Blue networks, were originated by NBC's two New York flagship stations, WEAF, the former AT&T station, and RCA's station WJZ. On 23 December 1928, NBC linked together its eastern and Pacific coastal stations, known as the "Orange" network, establishing the first transcontinental network service.

As 1927 began, a number of lavish sponsored programs were on the air. Concerts, classical or semi-classical, were presented by several orchestras. Live radio drama was attempted as early as 1928 by the *Eveready Hour*. Remote pickups of dance bands from New York's hotel ballrooms continued to be a prominent feature of both the Red and Blue networks during late night.

When NBC began in 1927, there were 10 stations on each network. At the end of six months of operation, NBC's Red network had a chain of 15 stations, including WEAF in the East, and NBC

Blue had 10 stations including WJZ. Eight additional stations were affiliated with both networks. In January 1928, one year after the network began regular daily service, NBC had 48 affiliates. Ten years later, in 1938, there were 154 NBC affiliates, including 23 on the Red network and 24 on the Blue, with the remainder choosing programs from both. However, NBC Red had considerably more of the high-power clear channel stations, making it the stronger competitor.

Mode of Operation

From the start, the Red network outstripped the Blue network in terms of popular programming. The NBC Red network enjoyed the heritage of the AT&T chain, whose pre-merger advertisers paid performing talent well, whereas the Radio Group's WJZ had largely used free talent. With the Red network's lineup of powerful stations and strong popular programming, many sponsors insisted on placing their programs on NBC Red. Furthermore, to placate the government during the rapid growth of commercialism on radio, NBC deliberately programmed NBC Blue as a complementary service to the Red network, providing extensive news, public service, and cultural programming. Although NBC Blue had some popular sponsored shows, its schedules consisted largely of sustaining (nonsponsored) public-affairs talk programs, concert music, classic drama, and late-night dance bands. New programs often made their debut on NBC Blue and were moved to the Red network when they became popular. Because the Red network stations carried about three-fourths of NBC's commercial programs, industry observers commented that NBC, from 1927 until 1943, used the Blue network more as a foil than as an all-out competitor with the Columbia Broadcasting System (CBS).

Despite its secondary role, the NBC Blue network launched what was to become radio's first sensationally popular serial drama. In 1929 NBC Blue began carrying the nightly *Amos 'n' Andy* comedy show, which depicted the activities of a group of affable black characters living in Harlem. *Amos 'n' Andy* soon dominated all radio listening in the early evening hour of 7:00 Eastern time. The Cooperative Analysis of Broadcasting reported that more than half of all radio homes in the nation regularly tuned to this program during the 1930–31 season.

During the 1930s, NBC Blue also carried additional five- and six-day-a-week serialized dramas, including *Little Orphan Annie*, *Lum 'n' Abner*, *Vic and Sade*, *Clara Lu and Em*, and *Betty and Bob*.

Several news commentators, including Lowell Thomas, also were heard five nights a week on the network. Other regular NBC Blue network programs included concerts by the NBC Symphony Orchestra, *Sherlock Holmes* and other mystery dramas, and the popular *Quiz Kids* program featuring gifted youngsters. NBC Blue served rural audiences with its *National Farm and Home Hour*, offered adaptations of classic drama on *Radio Guild,* and provided the *Walter Damrosch Music Appreciation Hour* for students.

NBC's main competitor during the 1930s was CBS, which was founded in 1927. NBC and CBS together controlled almost all of the most powerful clear channel and regional stations—so much so that a third rival, the Mutual Broadcasting System (MBS), found it extremely difficult to obtain competitive station affiliations after its founding in 1934. Mutual's complaints to the Federal Communications Commission (FCC) resulted in an investigation of radio network practices beginning in 1938. The FCC concluded that the extent of control exercised by NBC and CBS over the radio network industry was not in the public interest; in 1941 the Commission issued a new set of "Chain Broadcasting Regulations" that made it illegal for one company to operate more than one national radio network.

Separation from the National Broadcasting Company and Network Sale

In January 1942, NBC officially split the operation of the two networks, making the Blue network a separate subsidiary of RCA. After bitter litigation, the U.S. Supreme Court upheld the FCC's action, forcing NBC to sell one of its networks. In October 1943, the FCC approved the $8 million purchase of the Blue network by Edward J. Noble, whose fortune was derived from Life Savers candy. The new company was named the Blue Network, Incorporated. One year later, the network was renamed the American Broadcasting Company (ABC).

In the 1940s, the Blue Network/ABC became a more aggressive competitor of NBC and CBS but continued the public service traditions of NBC Blue. ABC hired conductor Paul Whiteman as its musical director and substituted the Boston Symphony for the NBC Symphony Orchestra and the *Blue Theatre Players* for the *Radio Guild.* The Blue network began carrying the Saturday matinee performances of the Metropolitan Opera early in the 1940s. It also carried a Sunday night blues/jazz show called the *Chamber Music Society of Lower Basin Street.* Both the Opera and *Basin Street* were

hosted by famous opera announcer Milton J. Cross. The Blue network was also known for its stable of mystery programs, including *Sherlock Holmes, Gang Busters,* and *Counterspy,* as well as for its series of children's adventure shows in the late afternoons, including *Jack Armstrong, the All-American Boy.* During the daytime hours, the Blue network also counter-programmed the NBC and CBS soap operas with variety shows, the most famous of which was *Don McNeal's Breakfast Club,* a long-running morning show originating from Chicago.

During the war years of the 1940s, the Blue network was heavily engaged in news broadcasting. However, lacking the resources to maintain a worldwide news operation, the Blue network instead hired a number of commentators who presented a spectrum of views on current events. In this unique arrangement, the network's newsmen ranged from ultraconservative to ultraliberal. However, none was more controversial, nor more sensationally popular than columnist–commentator Walter Winchell, who attracted a huge audience for his Sunday night news and gossip programs. Serious public-affairs programming included the weekly *America's Town Meeting of the Air,* which featured speakers both for and against issues of the day. In another business innovation, the Blue network (and Mutual) offered some of its news programs to local advertisers in an effort to broaden the network's sponsorship and revenue base.

The separation of the Blue network from NBC in 1943 introduced a new and more competitive era for the radio networks. NBC and CBS continued to be the strongest rivals, but the Blue network, no longer subsidized by NBC, had to struggle (with Mutual) for third place in the network industry. Both had growing strength in programming but limited resources for competing in the radio and the soon-to-come television network field. Eventually, in 1953, ABC merged with Paramount Theatres and became a much stronger organization in preparation for the coming of television.

See also: American Broadcasting Company; American Telephone and Telegraph; Mutual Broadcasting System; National Broadcasting Company; Network Monopoly Probe; Radio Corporation of America; WEAF

Further Reading

Archer, Gleason L., *Big Business and Radio,* New York: American Historical Company, 1939; reprint, New York: Arno Press, 1971.
Kisseloff, Jeff, *The Box: An Oral History of Television, 1920–1961,* New York: Viking, 1995.

Lichty, Lawrence W., and Malachi C. Topping, compilers, *American Broadcasting: A Source Book on the History of Radio and Television*, New York: Hastings House, 1975.

Robinson, Thomas Porter, *Radio Networks and the Federal Government*, New York: Columbia University Press, 1943; reprint, New York: Arno Press, 1979.

Summers, Harrison B., editor, *A Thirty-Year History of Programs Carried on National Radio Networks in the United States, 1926–1956*, Columbus: Ohio State University, 1958.

HERBERT H. HOWARD

BLUES FORMAT

The blues radio format is defined most eloquently by blues music itself. Blues songwriters often explore subjects that deal with real-life situations, and it is not uncommon for listeners to contact a blues host between selections to share their testimony after hearing a certain blues selection. Says renowned *King Biscuit Time* disc jockey Sonny Payne, it is the "history of the African-American people" surviving enslavement, postreconstruction, and legal segregation, songs of human beings just dealing with life. The unsugarcoated "facts of life" themes often found in the lyrics can be beneficial, nonetheless. The music helps people forget their problems, and it imbues the human spirit with strength. Like other musical genres, the blues format can serve as a cathartic experience. "The blues is the truth," according to the late legendary record promoter Dave Clark.

Radio Blues and Disc Jockeys

Bessie Smith sang the blues live on WMC, a Memphis, Tennessee, radio station, as early as 1924. The regular remote broadcasts from The Palace on Beal Street appear to have continued until sometime in the 1930s. The legacy of blues presence on Memphis radio programming eventually influenced the owners of WDIA radio, the shape of black radio, and lives of legendary listeners such as B.B. King, Rufus Thomas, and Elvis Presley, whose first commercial success was the recording of Arthur Crudup's "That's Alright Mama."

In the early 2000s, WMPR-FM in Jackson, Mississippi, devoted 11 hours per day to blues. Most blues programs are limited to certain time blocks during a radio station's weekly air schedule. One exception is WAVN-AM in Memphis, which in 2003 devoted its entire program schedule to blues. Many noncommercial radio stations (public, community, and college) have increasingly programmed blues for the past 30 years. At least one radio station in many major markets and college communities can be found devoting selected block schedules to blues. National Public Radio downlinks via satellite a blues program, *Portraits in Blue,* to its affiliates each week. The Handy Foundation in Memphis circles the globe to record live blues concerts and syndicates the performances in a magazine format called *Beal St. Caravan.* Blues programming can be heard on the internet, and the trend is growing rapidly. Emerging satellite services such as Sirius and XM had begun to provide continuous blues programming by the early 21st century.

Disc jockeys who work in the radio blues format often travel to blues festivals around the country to keep up with current trends and developments. They exchange ideas, conduct interviews with historical and leading artists, and then broadcast them on their local blues programs back home. Such periodicals as *Living Blues* and *Big City Blues* can provide invaluable cultural information for the program producer. It is fair to say that most men and women who join the still loose network of blues programmers take that step seriously. In essence, they become part of a respected culture that was pioneered by men and women who struggled valiantly to regain their human dignity and make life better for everyone. A serious blues disc jockey will know— and play—the music of Sonny Boy Williamson, Robert Lockwood, Muddy Waters, or B.B. King. And the blues enthusiast—whether disc jockey or listener—might consider revisiting or discovering the rich origin of the blues radio format, which began in the Mississippi Delta "On the Arkansas Side."

Chicago: Al Benson

During the early 1940s in Chicago, Al Benson (following the precedent of Jack L. Cooper, another Chicago entrepreneur) began purchasing blocks of time on several different radio stations to program black music, much of which was blues. An important key to Benson's success was the format he designed, which permitted him and his hired announcers to speak the language of many transplanted Southerners and to promote the products of sponsors. His use of recorded blues music and his training of young broadcasters such as Vivian Carter and Sid McCoy appears to have accompanied the rise in popularity of black disc jockeys and blues programming. Carter later cofounded Vee Jay Records and helped develop the legendary Jimmy Reed. She launched the Beatles' first recordings in the United States. Benson's block programs, broadcast on various stations, remain a major contribution to the blues radio format. By 1947 there were at least 17 blues-oriented radio programs being broadcast in the United States. Several programs aired on various stations in Los Angeles, and Leroy White and others were very popular in Detroit.

Helena, Arkansas: King Biscuit Time

Helena, Arkansas, located on the west bank of the Mississippi River, is a small city that became home to the longest-running blues program on radio, *King Biscuit Time*. Shortly after KFFA Radio was established in 1941, bluesmen Sonny Boy Williamson and Robert Lockwood, Jr., met with their white childhood friend, Sonny Payne, who worked at the station and helped get them on the air. Sam Anderson, the station manager and part owner, agreed to sell Williamson and Lockwood a block of airtime, but the blues duo had no money. Anderson referred them to a potential sponsor, Max Moore, a wholesale grocer who needed to sell a huge backlog of flour from his warehouse. A financial deal was struck, and a tight program structure was agreed upon.

Williamson and Lockwood opened their 15-minute show Monday through Friday with a theme song that was followed by an Anderson voice-over announcement: "Pass the biscuits boys, it's King Biscuit Time." Mixing performances of blues songs with casual conversation about where the duo would be performing in the area, Williamson and Lockwood were a success. Listeners in a 100-mile radius of KFFA's transmitter embraced the blues program and quickly purchased all of Moore's existing supply of King Biscuit Flour.

KFFA Radio has continued broadcasting *King Biscuit Time*, uninterrupted, for six decades and had logged nearly 14,000 blues shows by the turn of the century. Robert Lockwood, Jr., and the late Sonny Boy Williamson have grown into legends in both the blues and radio programming history. The show made Max Moore wealthy and the late Sam Anderson's KFFA world famous. Sonny Payne now hosts *King Biscuit Time* in a half-hour disc jockey format. Visitors from around the world frequently stop in at the Delta Cultural Center in Helena to catch the program, 12:00 to 12:30 P.M. Some guests even get a chance to be interviewed live by Payne. Each year up to 90,000 blues lovers from around the world flock to Helena, Arkansas, to attend a blues festival in honor of *King Biscuit Time* and the return of Robert Lockwood, Jr., to center stage.

Nashville: WLAC Radio

Francis Hill, a white woman, sang the blues live on WLAC in the late 1930s. Then, sometime in the mid-1940s two black record promoters were welcomed into the WLAC studios by Gene Nobles. One of the promoters is believed to have been Dave Clark. Nobles, white and handicapped, held down the night shift for WLAC's 50,000-watt clear channel signal, which blanketed the South, Midwest, parts of Canada, and the Caribbean. After Nobles began playing a few of the promoters' black records several nights a week, listeners began writing from as far away as Detroit, Michigan, and the Bahamas for more blues and boogie. Nobles came to the attention of Randy Wood, a white businessman in Gallatin, Tennessee, about 40 miles away. Wood bought some advertising spots to promote the sale of several thousand records by black artists that he discovered after purchasing an appliance store. Again, the audience responded and bought out Wood's phonograph stock.

Gene Nobles was soon hosting a blues-oriented program on a radio station that many African-Americans referred to simply as "Randy's" (WLAC). The disc jockey-run show focused on promoting a C.O.D. mail-order system operated by Randy's Record Shop in Gallatin, Tennessee. The primary pitch involved promoting sets of phonograph records made up of five or six unrelated 78-rpm singles. To promote sales, one or two records were played each night from various sets called "specials" (e.g., "The Treasure of Love Special" or "The Old Time Gospel Special").

Ernie's Record Mart and Buckley's Record Shop, both in Nashville, soon imitated the successful Randy Wood format. Each store bought time blocks, which were spread among WLAC's additional blues-oriented programming with traditional spots and per-inquiry advertisements. By the early 1950s WLAC Radio's entire night-time schedule was bought out. John Richburg, Bill Allen, and Herman Grizzard joined Nobles to formulate a powerful programming block from 9:00 P.M. to early morning, Monday through Sunday. All of the disc jockeys were white, but they addressed the audience fairly, respected the culture, and won acceptance and trust from a largely, though not exclusively, black audience. Don Whitehead, an African-American, joined the news staff in the 1960s.

Memphis: WDIA Radio

John Pepper and Bert Ferguson, two white businessmen, found themselves unable to attract white listeners or money to their newly built WDIA Radio just as Randy Wood was gaining success. While on a trip to New Orleans, Ferguson encountered a copy of *Negro Digest* and read a success story about Al Benson. The magazine caused him to recall the 1930s live radio broadcasts from Beale Street featuring the skillful Nat D. Williams. When he returned to Memphis, he sought the assistance of Williams, a black educator, journalist, and Beal Street impresario. In an afternoon block of time, Monday through Friday, Williams developed and hosted a blues-oriented show, and the radio audience bonded with his style, laughter, and cultural knowledge. Williams' success led to the hiring of other black announcers until WDIA's entire programming schedule consisted of blues, rhythm and blues, and gospel. It was the birth of full-time radio devoted to these genres.

WDIA Radio intermingled its music with several public service announcements, called "Goodwill Announcements" by the station, to help educate and inform African-Americans living in the mid-South's tristate region: Tennessee, Arkansas, and Mississippi. A.C. Williams, another educator turned WDIA radio announcer, maintains that the foundation of black political achievement in Memphis, which is now very organized, began with public-affairs programming on WDIA Radio. The station's 1950s programming model remains at the pinnacle of blues radio formats. WDIA's programming philosophy served as a model for other radio legends who continued to promote or program the blues wherever their career paths led them: Maurice "Hot Rod" Hulbert in Baltimore; Martha Jean Steinberg in Detroit; and Rufus Thomas and B.B. King as performers around the world.

Blues Radio Format Diffused

The blues format was still strong in 1953 when more than 500 black disc jockeys were reported to be working in radio, mostly in block formats or part-time situations. A few years later, black military veterans returning home from service brought reports that Europeans loved the "real blues." They cited John Lee Hooker, Howlin' Wolf, Muddy Waters, Sonny Boy Williamson, and others as being revered. Indeed, the Animals, the Rolling Stones, and Canned Heat advanced blues programming on white commercial radio stations in the 1960s after they included blues songs by the great African-American masters on their early albums. Curious fans who studied the origins of English rock performers became more aware of the blues. In addition, 1960s FM radio, in need of program material and open to experimentation, also began playing blues. Many young white soul radio station listeners who became attracted to rhythm and blues

made additional cultural explorations and discovered the blues. The blues format increasingly made its way onto the programming schedules of noncommercial radio as the number of FM public, college, and community radio stations expanded.

As with many specialized music formats, blues listeners hoped their music of choice would become more widely available with the advent of HD2 radio, and by the early 2000s there was some reason for optimism as stations, especially in larger markets, skirmished to find new niches for their digital signals.

See also: Black-Oriented Radio; Black Radio Networks; KFFA; *King Biscuit Flower Hour*; WDIA; WLAC

Further Reading

Redd, Lawrence N., *Rock Is Rhythm and Blues: The Impact of Mass Media*, East Lansing: Michigan State University Press, 1974.
Routt, Edd, James McGrath, and Frederic Weiss, *The Radio Format Conundrum*, New York: Hastings House, 1978.
Williams, Gilbert A., *Legendary Pioneers of Black Radio*, Westport, Connecticut: Praeger, 1998.

LAWRENCE N. REDD,
2009 REVISIONS BY MICHAEL C. KEITH

BOB AND RAY
Radio Comedy Team

From their base in New York City, Bob and Ray affirmed that radio comedy was alive and well, despite the emergence of television, in the late 20th century. Bob Elliott (1923–) and Ray Goulding (1922–1990) were both born in Massachusetts, where they worked at local radio stations before World War II. Coincidentally, after the war they ended up at WHDH, Boston. Elliott was a morning disc jockey, and Goulding did the news. They developed an instant comedic chemistry. "I began staying in the studio," Goulding said, "and bailing him out with some chatter, what with all the awful records he had to play." Soon, the program director asked them to do a 25-minute comedy show before baseball games called *Matinee with Bob and Ray*. Elliott recalled, "They had to have that rhyme, and it's the only reason we're Bob and Ray and not Ray and Bob."

In 1951 Bob and Ray sat in for Goulding's older brother Phil and Morey Amsterdam on WMGM, New York. That stint led to a successful audition for the National Broadcasting Company (NBC).

The network offered them a 15-minute show each evening, and Bob and Ray moved to New York, where they remained for nearly 40 years. Soon they had a two-and-a-half-hour morning show, a half-hour evening show, and a 15-minute live television program in addition to their original show. Early on, the duo decided to call their program *The Bob and Ray Show*, a simple title that they continued to use throughout their career at NBC, which lasted until 1973, and on other stations and networks. The only exception was a TV game show, *The Name's the Same*, which they hosted for ABC television briefly in 1955.

In 1953 Bob and Ray moved their television show to American Broadcasting Companies (ABC) and jumped to WINS radio for the next three years. They began a regular feature on the NBC Radio network program *Monitor* and developed an afternoon show for the Mutual Radio network. By 1956 they had landed at WOR, where they stayed off and on for more than 20 years. They also had a show on the Columbia Broadcasting System (CBS) Radio network in the late 1950s.

Although radio was their primary medium, Bob and Ray also starred as "Bert and Harry" in a long-running series of television commercials for Piels Beer and became regular guests on both the *Today* and *Tonight* shows on NBC television. In 1970 they opened on Broadway with *Bob and Ray: The Two and Only*, a revue based on characters from the radio skits; they subsequently took the show on tour and released a live album of the performance. They appeared in two movies, *Cold Turkey* (1971) and *Author, Author* (1982), and published three books of scripts from their radio shows. They returned to the stage briefly in 1984 with sold-out performances at Carnegie Hall.

In 1981 Bob and Ray were inducted into the National Association of Broadcasters Hall of Fame and were named "Men of the Year" by the Broadcast Pioneers. The next year, the Museum of Broadcasting in New York presented a retrospective of Bob and Ray's career that set attendance records and was held over for four months. During the 1980s more than 200 National Public Radio (NPR) affiliates carried *The Bob and Ray Public Radio Show*. They continued regular radio broadcasts until Goulding's death in 1990. Elliott still plays occasional bit parts on television, often in productions written by and starring his son Chris. Many classic Bob and Ray performances were recorded and remain in circulation.

Humorists as diverse as Bob Newhart, Phil Proctor, and Roy Blount Jr. have paid homage to Bob and Ray. Their comedy has been described as wry, low-key, elegant, restrained, and seductive. The *New York Times* once called them "a couple of master comedians who live in a large, comfortable, friendly house right next door to reality." *Kirkus Review* applauded their ability "to take the stupid words right out of our mouths and, with sweet innocence, toss them in our faces."

Typical Bob and Ray routines feature normal people who do bizarre things—the lighthouse keeper whose lighthouse is 40 miles inland, the professor of penmanship who teaches executives to write illegibly, a world champion low jumper, or the editor of *Wasting Time* magazine. Often the skit involves an interview in which the comedy hinges on one absurdity—the frustration of waiting for answers from the president of the Slow Talkers of America, or the misprint on a script that causes the oblivious host to ask questions that his guest just answered. Recurring characters include the casts of the soap opera "Mary Backstayge, Noble Wife" and of the adventure serial "Tippy, the Wonder Dog;" pompous sportscaster Biff Burns; and the intrepid reporter on the beat, Wally Ballou, who always upcut his cue and thus began each feature:

Wally Ballou standing here with a gentleman my staff tells me is one of the most unusual and interesting interviews we've ever lined up. I wonder if you'd tell us your name, sir?

MAN: No, I'm afraid I can't do that...
BALLOU: You hiding from the police or something like that?
MAN: No, I can't tell you my name because I am one of the very few people in America with a name that is completely unpronounceable.
BALLOU: Well...could you spell it for us?
MAN: That's all you can do with it. It's spelled: W-W-Q-L-C-W.
BALLOU: W-W-Q-L-C-W. Are you sure that's a name and not the call letters of some radio station?
MAN: No, it's my name all right. But there's no way to pronounce it. I've been trying for years and it's got me beat.
BALLOU: I certainly never heard it before. What nationality is it?
MAN: Well, my grandfather came from Iraq, originally. And I've got a hunch that when he changed the letters from the Arabic alphabet into English, he goofed something awful.
BALLOU: I guess that could be. Do you still have relatives back in the old country?
MAN: Oh yeah. Cousins...and things like that.

BALLOU: And how do they pronounce the name?
MAN: They pronounce it Abernathy.
(Elliott and Goulding, 1985)

See also: Comedy; WOR

Robert B. (Bob) Elliott. Born in Boston, Massachusetts, 26 May 1923. Studied at the Feagin School of Drama and Radio, New York City; served in the U.S. Army in Europe, 1943–1946; worked at WHDH Boston, 1946–1951, where he met longtime partner Ray Goulding and began writing and performing radio comedy routines. Elliott and Goulding moved to New York in 1951, and their daily comedy programs became a staple of network and local radio for nearly 40 years. During the period, *The Bob and Ray Show* and the duo's sketches were heard on the NBC, ABC, Mutual, and CBS radio networks, as well as National Public Radio. Elliott and Goulding won George Foster Peabody Awards for their work in 1952 and 1957, and were nominated for Grammy Awards for recorded comedy in 1987 and 1988.

Raymond Chester (Ray) Goulding. Born in Lowell, Massachusetts, 20 March 1922. Served in the U.S. Army from 1942–1946, rising to the rank of 1st Lieutenant. His career was closely connected to that of Bob Elliott, above. Died 24 March 1990, in Manhasset, New York.

Radio Series

1946–51   *Matinee with Bob and Ray*
1951–77   *The Bob and Ray Show*
1983–90   *The Bob and Ray Public Radio Show*

Television Series

The Bob and Ray Show, 1952–53; *The Name's the Same*, 1955

Selected Recordings

Bob and Ray, the Two and Only, 1970; *Vintage Bob and Ray*, 1974; *A Night of Two Stars Recorded Live at Carnegie Hall*, 1987; *The Best of Bob and Ray, Vol. 1*, 1988

Selected Publications

Write if You Get Work: The Best of Bob and Ray, 1975
From Approximately Coast to Coast...It's the Bob and Ray Show, 1983
The New! Improved! Bob and Ray Book, 1985

Further Reading

Balliett, Whitney, "Profiles: Their Own Gravity," *New Yorker* (24 September 1973).

ROBERT HENRY LOCHTE

BORDER RADIO
Mexican-Based Stations Aimed at the United States

Mexico-based radio stations, located in cities near the United States border and often beaming signals of great wattage, offered programs and advertising not always found on U.S. radio stations licensed by the Federal Communications Commission (FCC). At various times in radio history, these "border blasters" temporarily filled programming gaps and advertiser needs that stations licensed in the United States could not or would not provide. But United States-based stations always adapted, and border radio stations would fade into obscurity until the next time that they could successfully counter-program.

Origins

Border radio stations, located in Mexican cities bordering the United States from California to Texas, came into being in the 1930s, when broadcasting became big business and U.S. network programming defined itself through specific genres of programming and advertising. Border stations could transmit more powerful signals than U.S. law permitted, could and did advertise products considered fraudulent under U.S. law, and could and did offer programming—particularly "hillbilly" music—that U.S. networks failed to offer.

Although the U.S. government officially worked through a dominant U.S. network—the National Broadcasting Company (NBC)—and its powerful owner, the Radio Corporation of America (RCA), to expand global markets, "border blasters" looked to fill unserved market niches. Although actual audience comparisons are impossible to make as border stations did not subscribe to ratings services such as Hooper, the border stations' own records of selling products in the 1930s are indeed impressive. The official authorities on both sides of the border never liked these clever entrepreneurs but often could do little about directly shutting them down. Border stations such as XED-AM—located across the border from Laredo, Texas—successfully sold Mexican lottery tickets by mail to listeners in the United States, who could also listen to XED-AM for the results. Lottery promotion was at that time strictly forbidden under U.S. radio law.

The Mexican authorities accommodated "outlaw" radio entrepreneurs—some of whom, such as Dr. John Brinkley, had been denied broadcasting licenses in the United States—because it seemed to them that the United States and Canada had divided up all the long-range frequencies between themselves, allocating none for Mexico. In 1931 Dr. Brinkley opened XER-AM (called XERA-AM by 1935) in Villa Acuna, Mexico; later in the 1930s, Brinkley also bought XED-AM, changing its name to XEAW-AM. Indeed, these constant changes were one of the key traits of border radio, because entrepreneurs knew that they risked prosecution if and when Mexican and U.S. authorities came to some agreement.

Brinkley used border radio and its hillbilly music to make money by selling "medical miracles" that the American Medical Association (AMA) deemed fraudulent. (The AMA had pressured the Federal Radio Commission to get Brinkley off the air.) He built a transmitter with 300-foot towers. Out of the range of American restriction, station XER-AM started broadcasting with a power of 75,000 watts, with a remote studio linked by phone lines to the Rosewell Hotel in Brinkley's new headquarters in Del Rio, Texas. The station started operating in October 1931, with gala celebrations in both towns. XER-AM offered more than just hours of pseudoscientific lectures from Dr. Brinkley: it also featured the stars of country music of the day—singing cowboys, fiddlers, a Mexican studio orchestra, and many guests.

Thanks to XER-AM's amazing power, Brinkley could be heard as far away as Chicago. His busy Mexican lobbyists succeeded in allowing him to boost power, which made XER-AM for a time the most powerful radio station in the world at a shattering one million watts, a signal that for a short time smashed everything in its path and could be heard in New York and Philadelphia—sometimes to the exclusion of all other channels.

Even broadcasting at *only* 100,000 watts (twice the power of the largest American stations), Brinkley was able to reach his potential customers. Significant in radio history, he pioneered the use of electrical transcription discs, even as NBC and the Columbia Broadcasting System (CBS) were insisting that listeners preferred live broadcasts. Brinkley also deserves a place in the history of country music, because he kept alive the career of the fabled Carter Family. But in time both U.S. and Mexican authorities took away his radio stations under the provisions of the North American Regional

Broadcasting Agreement treaty, which mandated what country got to use which frequencies. Brinkley died in 1942, before the U.S. Internal Revenue Service could finish suing him for failure to pay taxes.

Although Brinkley was surely the most extreme case, border stations' power generally ranged from 50,000 to 500,000 watts. Listeners reported hearing Mexico-based signals in all parts of the United States and even in Canada. Network affiliates located near a border signal on the AM dial were often drowned out, or at least interfered with, as border stations overwhelmed them. And, as border stations were beyond any code of good conduct that network radio or U.S. law required, they could sell and say almost anything they wanted; indeed, border stations hawked items and made claims that would have been disallowed and even prosecuted in the United States, such as pitches for miracle medicines and sexual stimulants and the hawking of donations for phony religious institutions.

Consider the case of Crazy Water Crystals, owned by Carr P. Collins, entrepreneur and political adviser to Texas politician W. Lee "Pappy" O'Daniel (elected governor in 1938 and 1940). Crazy Water Crystals promised to revive a sluggish system; the crystals were produced in Mineral Wells, Texas, by evaporation of the town's fabled "Crazy" water. In 1941, when the United States and Mexico began to cooperate as part of the efforts surrounding World War II, Mexican authorities confiscated Collins' station.

Country Music

Border radio fulfilled the needs of the audience for hillbilly music, needs that the networks only partially met with *The Grand Ole Opry* and *The National Barn Dance*. In the 1930s there were many local hillbilly radio shows, but the supply never matched the demand, so border stations often blanketed the United States with songs by the Carter Family, Cowboy Slim Rinehart, Patsy Montana, and others.

The greatest beneficiaries were the Carter Family. To call the Carter Family—A.P. Carter, Sara Carter, and Maybelle Carter—the first family of country music is a historical truth, because their famed Bristol, Tennessee, recording sessions in 1928 established country music as a recording, and later as a radio, musical genre. But by the mid-1930s, their style had been supplanted by that of singing cowboys such as *The National Barn Dance's* Gene Autry and the rising stars of the *Grand Ole Opry*, such as Roy Acuff and Ernest Tubb. Thus, few were surprised that the Carters were tempted by the lucrative contract offered by XERA-AM from 1938 to 1942, to work for Brinkley. They needed the money, and Brinkley gave them unparalleled exposure. Jimmie Rodgers, a nascent country star, helped inaugurate XED-AM in Reynosa, Mexico, for similar reasons.

More obscure hillbilly stars benefited as well. Nolan "Cowboy Slim" Rinehart, often called the "king of border radio," was border radio's answer to Gene Autry and the other singing cowboys. Rinehart began his singing career just as border radio was beginning, and although he first appeared on KSKYAM from Dallas, he gravitated to XEPN-AM in Piedras Negras, Mexico, across the Rio Grande from Eagle Pass, Texas. After his initial appearances on XEPN-AM, the station was deluged with mail, and soon Rinehart was being electrically transcribed and then played on all border stations from Tijuana east to Reynosa. Rinehart had no contract with a U.S. record label, and so he made his additional monies on tour selling songbooks. This was a marginal existence, with few of the paths to fame and fortune enjoyed by those on the *Grand Ole Opry*.

Listeners were dedicated, and some even became country music stars. The case of Hank Thompson is instructive. Born in 1925, Thompson loved these border stations while he was growing up in Waco, Texas: they alone played and programmed country music nearly all day. Border radio should be remembered not only for creating stars, but also as an inspiration for future stars, who as children had access to inspiration around the clock from border stations. Webb Pierce, Jim Reeves, and other stars of the 1950s appeared live on XERFAM with country disc jockey Paul Kallinger partially as a payback. Border stations helped develop the music that would later become known as "country and western," which would by the year 2000 be simply known as country, the most popular format on radio.

Rock and Roll

Top-40 pioneered rock music on U.S. radio. But since U.S. stations avoided playing rock's raunchier records, border stations in Mexico filled the gaps. This phenomenon is exemplified by the career of disc jockey Wolfman Jack, who, in the late 1950s, after a series of disc jockey jobs in the United States, appeared on XERF-AM, across from Del Rio, Texas, and sold collections of hit records while "spinning rock" in his own unique style. Although Wolfman Jack's broadcasts hardly constituted anything new in format radio, other than their utter outrageousness, they became far more famous after the fact as a result of the hit movie *American Graffiti,* a tribute song by the Guess Who, and a nationally syndicated radio program in the United States.

All-News Format

But border radio should not be remembered solely for fostering interest in country and rock music. The first commercially successful all-news radio operation in North America went on the air in May 1961 from XETRA-AM (pronounced "x-tra") from Tijuana, Mexico, and was aimed at southern California, not at Mexican audiences. This 50,000-watt AM station was operated by radio pioneer Gordon McLendon. Before McLendon took over, it was border station XEAK-AM, which played rock music aimed at southern California teenagers. By 1961 there was a glut of rock format stations in southern California, so McLendon tried an all-news format instead. XETRA-AM was a headline service, with a 15-minute rotation that was later stretched to 30 minutes when McLendon discovered that Los Angeles commuters were trapped in their cars for far more than a quarter hour. McLendon went to great lengths to disguise XETRA-AM's Mexican base and tried to make it seem like just another Los Angeles AM radio station. Jingles repeated over and over: "The world's first and only all-news radio station. In the air everywhere over Los Angeles." The only address announced was that of the Los Angeles sales office. The station was required to give its call letters and location every hour, so McLendon ran a tape spoken in Spanish in a soft, feminine voice that was backed by Hispanic music, followed in English by a description of Mexico's tourist attractions, suggesting to listeners that XETRA-AM was running an advertisement for vacations in Mexico rather than the required call letters and station location.

Los Angeles radio competitors complained to the FCC, contending that such masking was certainly unethical and possibly illegal. At first, because of Gordon McLendon's reputation as a radio pioneer, XETRA-AM was able to draw even national advertisers. By 1962, the station was making a profit, in part because it was strictly a "rip-and-read" station employing no actual reporters, only a dozen announcers who rewrote wire and newspaper copy and who frequently rotated shifts so as to make the broadcasts seem fresh and new. In the background the teletype's tick-tick-ticking was ever–present. XETRA-AM sounded as though its announcers were sitting in a busy, active newspaper office. But in the end, like the rock format, this format proved too easy to copy, and with competition came lower profits. Eventually McLendon turned to other, more profitable ventures.

Later Incarnations

In the 1980s, the United States and Mexico reached an international agreement that allowed shared use of clear channel stations. U.S. radio owners now cared less, however, because FM's limited-distance signals had become audience favorites, and AM's long-range radio was less valuable. The border stations went the way of the clear channel AM stations that had once blanketed much of the United States, and with common U.S. owners and all-recorded sounds, the niche programming of FM radio fulfilled the needs of the marketplace far better than the limited number of AM stations that broadcast from the 1930s through the 1960s. There are still border stations, but now nearly all of them create programs in Spanish for audiences in nearby U.S. communities and compete in the major radio markets with dozens of other stations.

See also: All News Format; Country Music Format; *Grand Ole Opry*; Music on Radio; *National Barn Dance*; North American Regional Broadcast Agreement

Further Reading

Carson, Gerald, *The Roguish World of Doctor Brinkley*, New York: Rinehart, 1960.
Fowler, Gene, and Bill Crawford, *Border Radio: Quacks, Yodelers, Pitchmen, Psychics, and Other Amazing Broadcasters of the American Airwaves*, Austin: Texas Monthly Press, 1987.
Garay, Ronald, *Gordon McLendon: The Maverick of Radio*, New York: Greenwood Press, 1992.
Landry, Robert J., *This Fascinating Radio Business*, Indianapolis, Indiana, and New York: Bobbs-Merrill, 1946.
Malone, Bill C., *Country Music U.S.A.*, Austin: University of Texas Press, 1968; revised edition, 1985.
Porterfield, Nolan, *Jimmie Rodgers: The Life and Times of America's Blue Yodeler*, Urbana: University of Illinois Press, 1979.
Routt, Edd, James B. McGrath, and Fredric A. Weiss, *The Radio Format Conundrum*, New York: Hastings House, 1978.
Schwoch, James, *The American Radio Industry and Its Latin American Activities, 1900–1939*, Urbana: University of Illinois Press, 1990.
Whetmore, Edward Jay, *The Magic Medium: An Introduction to Radio in America*, Belmont, California: Wadsworth, 1981.

DOUGLAS GOMERY

BROADCAST EDUCATION ASSOCIATION
Serving Higher Education about Electronic Media

The Broadcast Education Association (BEA), located in Washington, D.C., is a U.S. organization for professors, students, and electronic media professionals who prepare college students to learn more about, and possibly enter, the broadcasting, electronic media, and emerging technologies industries when they graduate. By 2000, the BEA had more than 1,450 individual members (professors, students, and professionals), 250 institutional members (colleges and universities), and more than 85 associate members (associations and companies), as well as several important corporate contributors. The BEA is a 501 (c) 3 not-for-profit higher education association and is primarily funded through membership dues, corporate contributions, industry grants, and publications.

Origins

The association traces its lineage back to 1948, when the University Association for Professional Radio Education (UAPRE) was established with members representing ten colleges and universities. The organization was dissolved in 1955, and a new organization, the Association for Professional Broadcasting Education (APBE), was created. At the APBE's first annual meeting in Chicago in 1956, the organization established the *Journal of Broadcasting*, the first scholarly research periodical about radio and television, which produced its first quarterly issue the following winter. The APBE was established with close ties to the professional broadcasting community through the National Association of Broadcasters (NAB). Membership consisted of academic institutions and NAB member broadcasting stations. The Association's connection to NAB remained very close in the following years. NAB provided an executive secretary, office space, and a substantial yearly cash grant to maintain APBE's operation. The APBE became the Broadcast Education Association in 1973. In 1985 the *Journal of Broadcasting* was renamed the *Journal of Broadcasting and Electronic Media*. The BEA has grown over the years and today includes members from all around the world; it publishes two scholarly journals (it added the *Journal of Radio Studies* in 1998), a quarterly membership magazine, *Feedback*, and issues a variety of student scholarships and holds a vibrant annual national convention.

In its initial years, UAPRE and APBE focused substantially on radio issues and training, just as college and university academic departments did. Published research was largely descriptive and historical, with little focus on the audience and less on research methodology. The emphasis was on educating students for professional careers. The growing focus on television in the 1950s left radio concerns behind. Early annual conventions—well into the 1960s—attracted about 100 faculty and student participants for a day of educational sessions.

As the field matured, so did its research output. NAB and APBE cooperated in a series of annual research grants beginning in 1966. In 1968 the annual convention expanded to two days, and research paper sessions made their appearance, attracting more attendees. By the mid-1970s, articles in the *Journal of Broadcasting and Electronic Media* increasingly reflected more social science research into audience patterns and uses of both radio and television.

The Broadcast Education Association Today

The BEA publishes two respected journals. The *Journal of Broadcasting and Electronic Media* is a quarterly research journal considered to be one of the leading publications in the communication field, with articles about new developments, trends, and research in electronic media. The *Journal of Radio Studies,* officially adopted by BEA in 1998 1998 and re-titled a decade later as *Journal of Radio and Audio Media*, is published biannually and is the first and only publication exclusively dedicated to industry and academic radio research. Additionally, *Feedback*, a membership publication, appears quarterly with articles on pedagogy and industry analysis and reviews of books and instructional materials.

The Association has a paid staff of two (its first part-time executive secretary, Dr. Harold Niven, began work in 1963; he became a full-time paid president in 1984): an executive director and an assistant to the executive director. BEA is governed by a board of directors comprising mainly electronic media faculty and industry professionals. The BEA holds an annual convention in Las Vegas each spring that spans three days and is attended by more than 1,000 people. The convention is held in the days immediately following the NAB convention; on the first day there are often sessions cosponsored by both organizations.

The Association is made up of divisions representing various areas of interest to members. The BEA administers scholarships, a new faculty research grant, and a dissertation award. The Distinguished Education Service Award recognizes someone who has made a significant and lasting contribution to the American system of electronic media education by virtue of a singular achievement or through continuing service on behalf of electronic media education.

The Association serves as a repository for information about teaching and research through its website. Among the resources available is the "BEA Syllabus Project," in which professors can access sample syllabi, course outlines, and textbook choices for a variety of classes in radio, television, and new media. Another popular feature is the website's listing of academic job openings. In 2005, BEA began recognizing important electronic media academic researchers with a Distinguished Scholar Award, awarding several in each of the first three years, and then one per year thereafter.

In 2005, BEA embarked on its second half-century of service to higher education. Adapting trends of other academic organizations, BEA's annual directory and other features migrated from print formats to its website. Its annual convention regularly attracted more than 1,200 attendees for days filled with research panels, product demonstrations, and a growing BEA Festival showcasing the best student and faculty audio, video and online productions of the previous year. And its overall research and teaching focus increasingly included online media services of all kinds.

See also: College Radio; Education about Radio; Intercollegiate Broadcasting System; National Association of Educational Broadcasters

Further Reading

Broadcast Education Association website, www.beaweb.org.
Journal of Broadcasting and Electronic Media, "35th Anniversary Issue Symposium: Founder and Editor Comments," 35, no. 1 (Winter 1991).
Kittross, John M., "Six Decades of Education for Broadcasting and Counting," *Feedback* 45, no. 3 (Fall 1989).
Kittross, John M., "A History of the BEA," *Feedback* 40, no. 2 (Spring 1999).
Niven, Harold, *Broadcast Education*, Washington, D.C.: APBE.BEA, 1965–86 (7 reports).
Niven, Harold, "Milestones in Broadcast Education," *Feedback* 26 (Summer 1985)

STEVEN D. ANDERSON,
2009 REVISIONS BY CHRISTOPHER H. STERLING

BROADCAST MUSIC INCORPORATED

Broadcast Music Incorporated (BMI) brought competition to the business of music performance rights licensing in the United States. Established in reaction to what was perceived by radio broadcasters as predatory pricing by the American Society of Composers, Authors, and Publishers (ASCAP), BMI gradually rose to parity with ASCAP and its songs now dominate the playlists of most contemporary music formats.

Origins

In the years following the 1923 negotiation of its first broadcast performance rights license, ASCAP demanded higher and higher copyright fees from stations for airing the music the public expected to hear. As ASCAP controlled the performance rights to virtually all songs being played by U.S. radio stations, broadcasters believed that they had no choice but to pay the rates ASCAP demanded. But in 1939, faced with the onset of yet another price increase, the broadcasting industry rebelled. Sidney M. Kaye, a young CBS copyright attorney, designed the blueprint for a new licensing agency to be called Broadcast Music Incorporated. As presented to key radio executives in Chicago in the autumn of 1939, broadcasters would, under Kaye's plan, pledge sums equal to 50 percent of their 1937 ASCAP copyright payments as seed money to launch the new organization. In exchange for these payments, participating broadcasters received non-dividend-paying BMI stock (most of which they or their successor companies still hold). On 14 October 1939, BMI's charter as a nonprofit venture was filed, and the agency's offices opened in New York on 15 February 1940.

ASCAP did not take the new effort seriously and soon announced a 100-percent rate increase for 1941 (which would amount to five to ten percent of a station's advertising revenues). In response, 650 broadcasters signed BMI licenses by the end of the year, with only 200 primarily small stations resigning with ASCAP. Broadcasters who were anxious about what the loss of ASCAP material would do to their programming were encouraged to buy BMI stock by a BMI pamphlet that observed, "The public selects its favorites from the music which it hears and does not miss what it does not hear." On 1 January 1941, the broadcasters' boycott of ASCAP officially began.

Setting up a new rights agency was one thing; acquiring music for it to license was quite another. BMI began life with only eight songs, all of which had been commissioned specifically for its catalog from non-ASCAP composers. Although BMI sought to find and sign nonaffiliated writers, radio stations that had turned in their ASCAP licenses had no music to program except these eight tunes and songs with expired copy rights. American radio thus entered the "Jeanie with the Light Brown Hair" era, so named for an incessantly aired public domain tune by 19th-century composer Stephen Foster.

As Foster and folk songs filled the ether, BMI looked for new sources of material to license. The popular works of George Gershwin, Cole Porter, Irving Berlin, and scores of others were all ASCAP-licensed. Music from Britain and the rest of Europe could not be used because foreign composers were members of rights organizations that had signed reciprocal agreements with ASCAP. ASCAP had not entered the South American market in any significant way, however; consequently, the music of Latin America soon came to dominate radio program schedules. The sudden and widespread popularity of sambas, tangos, and rumbas during the early 1940s was thus the result of legal necessity rather than of intrinsic musical merit. Faced with a growing competitive threat from BMI, ASCAP agreed to roll back its rates late in 1941, but it was too late to repair the damage.

ASCAP v. BMI

BMI was now firmly established as a licensing rival. Over the next 15 years, BMI rose to parity with ASCAP principally by signing songwriters that ASCAP had ignored: young mainstream composers rebelling against ASCAP's royalty payout system, which favored more established writers; country-and-western composers from the hinterlands; and later, rock-and-roll songsters who combined black blues and white country stylings into a new, rhythmically pulsating phenomenon. Soon, a number of major publishers such as E.B. Marks and M.M. Cole affiliated with BMI. The organization also advanced seed money to new publishers who agreed to be represented by it. BMI prospered under Kaye, who rose from vice president and general counsel to chairman of the board. He was assisted by Carl Haverlin, a former vice president of the Mutual Broadcasting System who began his BMI career as director of station relations and became its president in 1947.

ASCAP and its select members counterattacked with charges that BMI and the broadcasters were conspiring to promote musical trash. Broadway legend Oscar Hammerstein charged that "BMI songs have been rammed down the public's ears," and other detractors asserted that BMI stood for "Bad Music, Inc." Nevertheless, buoyed by broadcasters' resentment of past ASCAP arrogance and the growing 1950s appeal of the rock-and-roll songwriters whom BMI discovered and nurtured, the new organization came to dominate the radio pop charts.

In 1959 when the payola scandal (illegal payment for record promotion) was fully disclosed, ASCAP sought to make it a BMI issue by maintaining that BMI-dominated rock-and-roll music would never have become popular without under-the-table bribes. With a few high-profile disk jockey firings and the passage of federal antipayola legislation, the radio industry weathered the storm and so did BMI. The organization further insulated itself against future attacks on the quality of its catalog by broadening its musical base. Within a few years, BMI had signed affiliation agreements with jazz composers such as Thelonius Monk, folk writers such as Pete Seeger, classical icons such as William Schuman, and Broadway mainstays Sheldon Harnick and Jerry Bock.

BMI Today

Nevertheless, as a primarily broadcaster-owned-and-directed enterprise, BMI remains vulnerable to the undocumented charge that it is more sympathetic to broadcaster interests than to those of its affiliated composers and publishers. BMI's 2002 rates, however, were very close to those assessed by ASCAP: 1.605 percent of adjusted net revenue for stations billing more than $150,000 and 1.445 percent for stations billing less than that figure. BMI also offers stations both blanket and per-program license options, as does ASCAP, and negotiates with the radio industry through the Radio Music License Committee (RMLC), whose members are appointed by the National Association of Broadcasters (NAB).

Under their BMI license agreements, radio stations periodically fill out BMI logs listing the music played during a given week. Outlets logging at any particular time are selected as part of a sample designed to reflect all sizes, formats, and geographic locales. This sample is then used to project national usage of individual BMI-licensed tunes, with license fee payments accordingly divided among member composers and publishers.

Applying Technology

By the early 21st century, BMI claimed to be among the top 10 percent of the most effective American users of information systems. And it needed to be in order to keep track of more than 6.5 million musical works; some 375,000 songwriters, composers and music publishers; and tens of thousands of establishments—including radio

stations—that BMI licensed. Computerization became central to the collection of performance data, distribution of royalty payments, management of licensing fees and automation of accounting functions (indeed most of this process now takes place on line).

This process began when in 1972 BMI installed a mainframe computer and began to develop a song registration database. Online song registration came two decades later, and the first music industry website went online in 1994. Just a year later came the first internet performing rights license. By 2000, most radio stations also generated their music-use reports electronically. Five years later, BMI acquired a digital recognition technology for tracking music use on radio, television, and digital media, including the internet.

See also: American Society of Composers, Authors, and Publishers; Copyright

Further Reading

BMI Fiftieth Anniversary History Book, available on the BMI website, http:www.bmi.com/library/brochures/history book/index.asp.
Dachs, David, *Anything Goes: The World of Popular Music*, Indianapolis, Indiana: Bobbs-Merrill, 1964.
"Fifth Estater—Francis Williams Preston," *Broadcasting* (23 March 1987).
Lathrop, Tad, and Jim Pettigrew, Jr., *This Business of Music Marketing and Promotion*, New York: Billboard Books, 1999.
Ryan, John, *The Production of Culture in the Music Industry: The ASCAP-BMI Controversy*, Lanham, Maryland: University Press of America, 1985.

PETER B. ORLIK,
2009 REVISIONS BY CHRISTOPHER H. STERLING

BROADCASTING RATING COUNCIL
See: Media Rating Council

BROKERAGE IN RADIO
Buying and Selling Stations

Radio station brokers specialize in the buying and selling of radio stations, representing one side or the other in such transactions. As more stations change hands each year, especially in recent years, the role of the broker is an increasingly important one. Commercial radio station licenses in the United States are issued for a finite period, but after each license term there is an expectation of license renewal. Because the expiration of a radio station's license does not usually correspond to the timing of a station's sale, the Federal Communications Commission (FCC) will readily grant a license transfer from a current licensee to a prospective owner, provided that the prospective owner is an acceptable licensee under the FCC ownership rules. The licensee and the prospective owner must submit a request to the FCC for a license transfer.

The assets associated with a station are sold or transferred to another entity either through a conventional sale or through an exchange of assets commonly called a "swap." Just as is true with the sale of any other business, a variety of external or internal events can cause an owner to consider the sale of a station. Externally, a radio station's geographic market or audience may change in a manner that is incompatible with a particular owner's goals. Internally, the particular financial structure that supports a given station may require that the station be "refinanced" in a manner so comprehensive as to require a sale. Other factors that commonly trigger the decision by a station owner to sell include death and consequent estate issues for shareholders, as well as disagreement among principal owners.

Role of Brokers

Radio station sales can be handled by the owners themselves, their attorneys, accountants, small business brokers, investment banking firms, or specialists such as radio station brokers. As the name implies, radio station brokers are industry-specific agents, and, as such, these brokers specialize in representing buyers or sellers of radio stations. After years of specializing in these kinds of transactions, radio station brokers are often also able to assist their clients in refining the future economic projections for a station's operation. One of a broker's main tasks is to properly guide and manage the expectations of his or her clients. Because station brokers are especially familiar with the radio industry, they can often spot unrealistic economic assumptions made by their clients. When a radio station broker is working for a seller, it is his or her responsibility to coordinate efforts with the station's owner, lawyers, and/or accountants to help ensure a desired economic or strategic result. In those instances when radio station brokers work for buyers, the broker's responsibility is to assist the buying principals and their financial advisers in locating and purchasing radio stations that fit the buyers' criteria.

After a definitive agreement is reached between station buyers and sellers, all radio station license transfers must be approved by the FCC. Radio station brokers will usually encourage owners to obtain legal advice from attorneys who are familiar with the execution and submission of the proper forms required by the FCC. Following correct FCC procedure is imperative, because failure to do so can result in severe fines or even in license revocation by the FCC.

Professional radio station brokers attempt the marketing and sale of radio stations so as to create minimum disruption to a station's personnel, revenue, and profitability. This challenge can be difficult to meet. In order for a station to benefit from being sold at the highest price, it is in the seller's best interest that the greatest number of potential buyers be approached; however, the larger the number of buyers contacted, the more likely it is that the employees of the station will learn that the station is being offered for sale. This awareness can create unpleasant instability among the station's staff. Similarly, station advertisers may also learn that the station's ownership is expected to change, and, as a result, the advertisers may be inclined to limit or change the plans for their advertising expenditures in a manner adverse to the station's economic well-being. Radio station brokers are paid to navigate this difficult road.

How Sales are Made

The normal procedure followed by a station owner who anticipates selling his or her station first includes the choice of a radio station broker or others experienced in the selling of businesses similar to radio stations. Most radio station brokers are known to station owners and are listed in various radio industry publications. Once a broker is selected, a fee structure is negotiated. Fee structures vary depending on the nature and anticipated price for the property being sold. Most frequently, brokerage fees range from six percent to as low as one percent of the sale price. The resulting percentage is related to the size of the transaction, with the larger transactions paying lower percentages to the brokers. The seller should confer with the broker and with various advisers in setting an asking price for the radio station, because a wide array of factors must be considered in the price-setting process. Pricing considerations should include data from comparable sales, past economic performance of the specific assets being sold, and the anticipated future earnings performance for the assets.

Most sellers instruct their brokers to secure assurances of confidentiality from the prospects being approached during the sales process. Such assurances are often contained within a confidentiality agreement that is signed by potential buyers before they are given specific information with respect to a purchase opportunity. Potential buyers are furnished with certain information by the radio station broker about the station being offered for sale, commonly referred to as a "book." The book usually contains general information about the station, economic facts pertaining to the market being served, the station's competition, its audience, and its historical financial performance. The prospective buyer will review the book and based on its information will prepare various financial projections with respect to what the buyer feels the station may earn for its owners over a future period of time. Such future projections are called "pro forma estimates," and each may contain a different set of assumptions with regard to items such as competition, ratings, and revenue. Each buyer typically has his or her own set of pro forma objectives and will measure the relative attractiveness of each acquisition opportunity against these objectives.

Once a buyer becomes relatively comfortable with the material he or she has reviewed, the buyer may seek to enter into a written agreement with the licensee. This document is typically called a "letter of intent." The letter of intent usually sets forth various terms and conditions under which the buyer will proceed. This agreement also sets forth the intent of the buyer with respect to confidentiality, pricing, and timing of the contemplated transaction. The letter of intent typically also includes agreement on the procedure and responsibility for the preparation and negotiation of a definitive purchase and sale agreement to be used in the sale. The letter of intent will frequently provide the buyer with an *exclusive* period of time during which time only this buyer or his or her agents can conduct a thorough investigation of the various factors influencing the station's operation. This period is commonly referred to as the buyer's opportunity to conduct "due diligence." Either at the conclusion of such investigation or at the same time such investigation is progressing, the buyer and seller frequently agree to move cooperatively toward the formulation of a definitive purchase and sale agreement. Sometimes, for various reasons, the seller and buyer eliminate the step that involves a letter of intent and instead move directly to a definitive purchase and sale agreement.

There are a number of factors influencing a buyer's and a seller's decision on whether or not to include a letter of intent in the purchase process. Among the consideration for sellers is whether or not they wish to "encumber" their flexibility in negotiating the sale of the station with other potential buyers during the time a letter of intent is in force. Sellers are also frequently concerned that, notwithstanding an agreement as to confidentiality, word of the possible transaction might "leak" during the period that the station is under a letter of intent. Included in the decision process regarding letters of intent for buyers is whether or not a buyer wishes to expend the money and effort to perform due diligence and to continue contemplating the purchase of a specific station, without any firm rights to actually compel a sale of the station to this particular buyer.

Once a definitive purchase and sale agreement is executed, it is filed for consideration with the FCC. The FCC review process includes an opportunity for the public, the FCC, and other governmental agencies to register any objections to the license transfer. If there are no objections, the FCC will typically render its "preliminary" approval within a generally predictable number of days. Thereafter, there is an additional period of time before the FCC approval automatically becomes a "Final Order." The closing on a station's sale transaction usually takes place within a reasonably short period of time following issuance of the Final Order.

There are many strategies that drive the desire to purchase or sell a particular radio station. The radio station broker becomes conversant with the client's plans with respect to economic goals. FCC legal limitations on station ownership, as well as Department of Justice considerations with respect to market dominance leading to unfair competition, are among the factors that constrain buying and selling strategies. Informed radio station brokers assist their clients in conceptualizing and implementing their acquisition or exit strategies.

Sales Trends

In the 38 years from 1954 through 1992, FCC files indicate that nearly 20,000 radio stations changed ownership—some of them several times. The volume of radio station sales exploded with passage of the Telecommunications Reform Act of 1996. The sudden heated demand for the ownership of radio station "clusters" occurred simultaneous with an extremely robust public stock market, which provided large amounts of investment capital to those companies that were able to take advantage of an unprecedented opportunity to rapidly amass a large number of radio stations. In the four-year period following passage of the act, ownership of 7,839 radio stations changed hands, with well-capitalized radio companies emerging as highly acquisitive in markets of all sizes. As these clustered acquisitions continued, the single- or two-station owners came under increased competitive pressure.

The great gold rush of the mid-1990s did not prove enduring, however. Overall, the number of stations changing ownership decreased from peaks right after the 1996 telecommunications law was passed. Reviewing even-numbered years makes this clear: 1996 (2,157 stations sold), 1998 (1,740), 2000 (1,794), 2002 (769), 2004 (890), 2006 (952), and 2008 (778). The decline has been the result of several factors, chief among them a general leveling off after the rash of late 1990s mass purchases made by the Clear Channel conglomerate. Just as the number of stations being sold has decreased, so too has the amount of money changing hands (i.e. the asking or purchase price of a station) for these stations. Reflecting an economic turndown but also concerns about radio's viability, between 2007 and 2008, total values dropped by half.

Sales will decline in the future, especially amid concerns that the Federal Communications Commission is through with its rollback of earlier ownership rules and indications that it might start placing greater emphasis on racial diversity in ownership. Considering these factors, plus the economic recession of 2007–9, owners looking to sell their stations will no doubt face a very difficult marketplace—as will the brokerage firms who represent them.

See also: Consultants; Clear Channel Stations; Licensing; Ownership, Mergers, and Acquisition

Further Reading

Krasnow, Erwin G., *The Politics of Broadcast Regulation*, 3rd edition, New York: St. Martin's Press, 1982.

Vogel, Harold L., *Entertainment Industry Economics: A Guide for Financial Analysis*, 5th edition, Cambridge and New York: Cambridge University Press, 2001.

JACK MINKOW,
2009 REVISIONS BY CARY O'DELL

CABLE RADIO

Cable radio is a program service offered by a cable television system. Usually providing many different talk and music program types, the service is typically offered as an extra feature to television cable subscribers.

Technology

Technically, cable radio is relatively easy to offer. At a cable system head-end, one or more FM antennae are aimed toward stations that can be received by the cable operator. In the past, most such systems used an all-band approach. That is, local stations across the entire FM radio spectrum (88 to 108 MHz) are received, amplified, and carried on the cable system.

To receive cable radio, a signal splitter at the subscriber's location provides a second connection for the FM tuner. Although many systems charge an extra fee for the service (most are low—$1 or $2 per month), seldom are security measures taken that would require payment before the cable radio feed could be used.

With the introduction of multiple channels on such premium services as Home Box Office (HBO), cable operators often use cable channel space to carry the stereo audio signal of such services to subscribers' homes. Audio from the satellite is fed to an FM modulator located on a locally unused FM channel. Before the availability of television sets that supported stereo audio, such schemes were popular among television fans.

Economics

Just as television superstations developed with a national cable television audience in mind, so have a few radio superstations. Classical station WFMT in Chicago is a notable pioneer in this area. Some cable systems even allow local FM signal origination. This is usually done in conjunction with a nearby college or university. For example, WDBS, a long-time "closed carrier current" station on the campus of the University of Illinois, (Champaign-Urbana) has a spot on the local cable system. Additionally, such local origination is often carried on the audio carrier of locally originated television channels.

The relative ease of hooking home receivers into cable radio service has discouraged its active promotion by cable systems. Subscribers soon learn that they can hook up their cable through an easily purchased splitter and not have to pay a monthly subscriber fee. A few cable systems attempt to eliminate this theft of services either by trapping the range of frequencies through a filter or by using a cable audio converter to shift the service first to an unused frequency range and then to convert it back once the subscriber pays to rent the necessary equipment.

Policy

As cable delivery grew—from only 70 U.S. communities in 1950 to more than 32,000 communities in 1995—over-the-air broadcasters came to believe that they were being denied potential revenue from cable operators. Provisions of the Communications Act of 1934 require that a station that desires to rebroadcast the signal of another outlet must first obtain permission from the originating station. As amended, the Communications Act now prohibits cable operators (and other multichannel video program distributors) from retransmitting commercial television, low-power television, or radio broadcast signals without first obtaining consent.

In mid-1993, faced with the daunting task under new rules of obtaining permission from every FM station within a 57-mile radius of their receiving antennae, many cable systems curtailed their cable radio offerings. Only the locally originated channels, generally stereo audio for a few premium services, remain on the systems.

In 1982, National Public Radio (NPR) commissioned a study on the future of cable audio as a possible revenue stream to support other NPR operations. The report concluded that the future of cable audio, although bright, would only be profitable if such services generated revenue for both the cable operator and, of course, NPR. Three models were proposed. The first relied on advertiser support, very much like traditional over-the-air radio stations. Another model suggested that cable operators might be willing to pay for audio services as long as they could sell them as premium services with an appropriate profit margin built in. The model used for public television, where services are supported by corporate sponsorships and individual donations, was also suggested. In the NPR report, an important element for the success of cable audio was the restriction of access to services through secure channels. The report also noted the superior quality of the processed FM signals it proposed to deliver, as compared to the signals of the all-band FM approach. At the time of the NPR report, digital audio, although technically feasible, was not in wide use because it was cost-prohibitive. And, of course, audio streaming on the internet was years into the future.

The Future

Although NPR provided the vision, it took commercial interests and a breakthrough in technology to actually capitalize on the concept of cable audio services. Especially with the introduction of digital, multichannel, CD-quality audio streams such as those in the Digital Music Express (DMX) and Music Choice (formerly Digital Cable Radio) services—services not available over the air—a small but eager audience signed up for service. The set-top digital converter box is similar to that used for

pay-per-view video events, and it is addressable. In recent years, American Telephone and Telegraph (AT&T) cable services, among others, have included a variety of such audio services as part of their tier of digitally transmitted services.

Although it appears that some form of cable radio will continue into the future, according to Dwight Brooks, a contributing author to textbooks on broadcast programming, cable operators are skeptical about growth for this medium, citing a figure of only 15 percent penetration among basic cable subscribers for audio services. With proper copyright clearance, such services are being effectively marketed to business locations to provide background music services.

As broadband computer connections became more common in the first decade of the 21st century, web-based music services developed in competition with cable television audio channels. Although copyright restrictions complicated the provision of internet music, many services appeared and prospered, often providing a wide choice of musical types, some of them free to users.

A variation on the pay cable radio approach is satellite radio. XM and Sirius began service in 2001–2 with more than 100 channels each, roughly half different music genre and half talk. The service required purchase of a proprietary receiver (most were in cars), and a subscription. The latter included advertising, whereas the music channels were ad-free. The two merged in 2008 and melded their channels that overlapped (and most did), but SiriusXM still offered 150 channels by 2009.

See also: Copyright; Digital Audio Broadcasting; Digital Satellite Radio; Internet Radio

Further Reading

Bartlett, Eugene R., *Cable Television Handbook*, New York: McGraw Hill, 2000.
Crotts, G. Gail, Joshua Noah Koenig, Richard Moss, and Ann Stookey, *Listening to the Future: Cable Audio in the 80s*, Washington, D.C.: National Public Radio, 1982.
Eastman, Susan Tyler, Sydney W. Head, and Lewis Klein, *Broadcast Programming, Strategies for Winning Television and Radio Audiences*, Belmont, California: Wadsworth, 1981; 5th edition, as *Broadcast/Cable Programming: Strategies and Practices*, by Eastman and Douglas A. Ferguson, 1997.
Hollowell, Mary Louise, editor, *The Cable/Broadband Communications Book, vol. 2, 1980–1981*, White Plains, New York: Knowledge Industry, 1980.
Vane, Edwin T., and Lynne S. Gross, *Programming for TV, Radio, and Cable*, Boston: Focal Press, 1994.

JIM GRUBBS,
2009 REVISIONS BY CHRISTOPHER H. STERLING

CALL LETTERS

WJCU. KCBS. WRR. Unique combinations of alphabetic letters such as these, known as *call letters,* are used to identify individual radio (and television) stations. In addition to when they sign on or off, broadcast stations must give an identification announcement each hour—near the top of the hour and during a natural break in their programming. Radio stations give an aural identification, usually an announcer voicing the information, but sometimes a station jingle or musical identification.

According to FCC regulations, legal station identification consists of the station's call letters followed by the location of the station. Nothing can be placed between the call letters and the city of license, with the exception of the name of the licensee and/or the station's frequency or channel number. Station identification regulations (Section 73.1201) are found in the *Code of Federal Regulations,* Title 47, Part 73, Subpart H—"Rules Applicable to All Broadcast Stations."

Current policy assigns call letters east of the Mississippi River with a beginning *W* and those west of the Mississippi with a *K.* All modern call signs consist of the appropriate beginning letter plus three additional letters, and they can have a suffix, such as *-AM* or *-FM,* to denote the actual type of radio station. At one time, the FCC would not release objectionable call letter combinations; even the "mild" *SEX* combination was withheld. However, during the deregulatory 1980s, the FCC became less concerned about this and deferred to the courts in disputes regarding call signs that might be objectionable or too similar to another station's.

In the late 1990s the procedures regarding the designation of call letters were altered when the FCC replaced the existing manual system with an online system for electronic submission of requests for new or modified call signs. Through the FCC's website (www.fcc.gov), stations can determine the availability of call letters, request specific call letters or modify an existing call sign, and determine and submit the appropriate fees.

Historical Origins

The concept of radio station identification has its roots in the maritime industry, for which an International Code of Signals noted in the 1850s that signal flags, which included letters, were to be used to identify vessels. As radio, or rather wireless, developed in the late 1890s and early 1900s, telegraph operators used informal, one- or two-letter call signs as a condensed way to identify their stations. The 1906 Berlin International Wireless Telegraph Convention attempted to formalize a system of three-letter call signs, but at the time there was little cooperation. Individual wireless operators or wireless companies merely chose their own identification, which often consisted of one or two letters or a combination of letters and numbers with little consideration for duplicate calls.

The 1912 London International Radiotelegraphic Convention continued to formalize a system of station identification that was the beginning of the *K* and *W* series assigned to U.S. ships; other letters were assigned to vessels from other nations. The Radio Act of 1912 gave responsibility for licensing of U.S. ships and shore radio stations to the Bureau of Navigation in the Department of Commerce. Call signs were designated as a three-letter random sequence, with *K* calls for the west and *W* calls for the east. What would become early "radio stations" actually fell under the status of Amateur and Special Land Stations, which had a different call-sign system. Nine Radio Inspection Districts were established, and call letters were assigned with the District Number plus two alphabetic letters, such as 6XE, 9XM, or 8MK.

As more and more stations went on the air, the international agreements of 1912 were employed for all stations, and many pioneer radio stations were assigned three-letter *K* or *W* call letters. The dividing line for *K* and *W* stations was originally the eastern state boundaries of New Mexico, Colorado, Wyoming, and Montana; however, this was moved to the Mississippi River in early 1923. Existing stations were allowed to keep their previously assigned call letters. Because of this change and a few quirky assignments, some pioneer stations do not follow the current *K/W* demarcation, notably KDKA in Pittsburgh, KYW in Philadelphia, and WOW in Omaha. The move to four-letter call signs took place in the early 1920s as the number of radio stations coming on the air escalated rapidly and additional call letters were needed.

Call Letters Used to Promote Station Image

Although early call letter combinations were merely random assignments, many modern call signs have been carefully chosen and have a specific context for the particular station. In fact, many stations trademark their call signs. In addition to being the legal identification for a radio station, call letters have become an important artistic or imaging statement used to help market the station. From WAAA (Winston-Salem, North Carolina) to KZZZ (Bullhead City, Arizona), stations have tried to dream up memorable call signs. Even a casual examination of radio call letters will reveal several categories that these station identifiers fall into.

Many stations use their call letters to recognize a current or past station owner or licensee. KABC (Los Angeles) and WCBS (New York) denote the network organization associated with each station. Chicago's WGN stands for "World's Greatest Newspaper," which in turn refers to *The Chicago Tribune* and the station owner, the Tribune Company. KLBJ (AM) and (FM) licensee, The LBJS Broadcasting Company in Austin, Texas, recognizes owner and former first lady Lady Bird Johnson.

Besides the station licensee, a station's format offers a logical reason to request a certain set of call letters. For example, WINS (New York) stands for the basic programming elements of "information, news, and sports." Just as WJZZ (Roswell, Georgia; Smooth Jazz) and WHTZ (Newark, New Jersey; Top 40/Hits) readily describe music formats, WFAN (New York) is the monogram for an all-sports station. WGOD (Charlotte Amalie, Virgin Islands) makes it pretty clear it's a religious station; however, you need to know that WBFC (Stanton, Kentucky) stands for "We Broadcast For Christ." And if you really just don't want to bother with a format description, you could be like WGR (Buffalo, New York) and be the "World's Greatest Radio" station.

From dogs (WDOG, Allendale, South Carolina) and cats (KCAT, Pine Bluff, Arkansas) to frogs (WFRG, Utica, New York) and pigs (KPIG, Freedom, California), station call letters that denote animals are quite common. Even less ordinary beasts make an appearance with WFOX (Gainsville, Georgia); Chandler, Arizona's camel, KMLE; and KEGL, the Eagle, in Fort Worth, Texas. Animal-based call signs are not only memorable, but they make it easy for the station to add an appropriate mascot to their marketing efforts. Even the lowly WORM (Savannah, Tennessee) is accounted for, and the human species isn't left out either, with KMAN (Manhattan, Kansas); KBOY (Medford, Oregon), and WGRL (Noblesville, Indiana).

A station's location—either its city of license or its frequency—has been a prevalent theme for clever call letters. WARE—found in Ware, Massachusetts—is the only current set of call letters that is exactly the same as the city of license. For a number of years WACO in Waco, Texas, was another, but radio station WACO is now KKTK (although there is still a WACO-FM in Waco). Stations in cities of more than four letters have had to settle for using just the first few letters, so we find WPRO in Providence, Rhode Island; WORC in Worcester, Massachusetts; KSTP in St. Paul,

Minnesota; and KSL in Salt Lake City, Utah. AM stations using frequency-based call signs, especially at the upper end of the band, include WTOP (Washington, D.C.) near the "top" of the dial at 1500 and WXVI in Montgomery, Alabama, at 1600. KIOI (San Francisco) is found at 101.3 FM, and near the end of the FM band at 106.5 is KEND in Roswell, New Mexico.

Many radio stations request call letters that help define a characteristic of the locale where the station is found. Pioneer station WSB in Atlanta stands for "Welcome South, Brother." KABL refers to San Francisco's cable car; KSPD to Boise, Idaho's potato or "spud" and in what better market than Detroit would you find station WCAR? Cow country territory gives us KATL (Miles City, Montana), WCOW (Sparta, Wisconsin), and KMOO (Mineola, Texas). You could also do a weather forecast with call signs—from WSUN (Tampa, Florida) and WSNO (Barre, Vermont) to KICY (Nome, Alaska) and KFOG (San Francisco). There's also WWET (Valdosta, Georgia), KDRY (Alamo Heights, Texas), and WIND (Chicago).

Finally, there is another group of call signs that are colorful because the sound or spelling of the letter combination is memorable. For example, there is a WHAK (Rogers City, Michigan), a WHAM (Rochester, New York), and a WOMP (Bellaire, Ohio), as well as a KRAK (Hesperia, California), a KICK (Palmyra, Missouri), and a KPOW (Powell Wyoming). Broadcast journalists will be pleased to learn there is a WHO (Des Moines, Iowa), a WHAT (Philadelphia), a WHEN (Syracuse, New York), a WHER (Heidelberg, Mississippi), and a WHYY (Philadelphia).

Maybe all this call letter image information is making you think WOW (Omaha) and WWEE (McMinnville, Tennessee), but there are many more creative call signs yet to be devised. With a *K* or *W* combined with three other alphabetic letters, there are over 35,000 unique call letter combinations possible, which is almost three times as many as there are current radio stations.

See also: Frequency Allocation; Licensing; Authorising U.S. Stations to Broadcast

Further Reading

Archer, Gleason Leonard, *History of Radio to 1926*, New York: American Historical Society, 1938; reprint, New York: Arno Press, 1971.
Kahn, Frank J., editor, *Documents of American Broadcasting*, New York: Appleton-Century-Crofts, 1968; 4th edition, Englewood Cliffs, New Jersey: Prentice Hall, 1984.
Mishkind, Barry, "A Pause for Station Identification," *Radio World* (30 September 1998 and 28 October 1998).

Peterson, Alan, "WILD, WAKY, KRZY Call Letter Combos," *Radio World* (27 December 1995).
Stark, Phyllis, "Stations Spell Out Tradition," *Billboard* (13 March 1993).
United States Callsign Policies, www.earlyradiohistory.us/recap.htm.

DAVID E. REESE

CAN YOU TOP THIS?
U.S. Comedy Panel Program

Perhaps not believable in an era of fast-changing television program tastes, this simple half-hour (15 minutes in its final NBC season) panel program of three men telling jokes lasted nearly 15 years on network radio. The title came from the attempts of the joke tellers to "top" the previous joke and get a louder measured laugh from a studio audience.

Known as the "Knights of the Clown Table," the program's three starring personalities all shared great joke-telling memories and abilities. Ed Ford had been given the title of "Senator" at a political gathering some years previous (Ford also produced and owned the program); Harry Hershfield was already a well-known cartoonist and after-dinner speaker; and Joe Laurie, Jr., had knocked around vaudeville and other jobs before eventually migrating to radio. Ford was said to be the hardest man to get to crack a smile. Radio program authority John Dunning reports that between the three of them, they probably knew something like 15,000 jokes. And all three (plus joke teller Peter Donald) could and did employ a variety of funny dialects and odd-ball characters.

And indeed, the program did not thrive on originality; many of the jokes used were old. To tie the program to its listeners, the audience was encouraged to send in their best jokes (for which they received $10 for each one used on the air) to be told on the air by joke teller Peter Donald. These were followed by the panelists telling their own jokes in the same vein. Audience applause was judged on a score of from one to a thousand by a "laugh/applause meter" displayed so the panel and studio audience could see it. The joke getting the loudest response (the most decibels on the meter) won. Listeners could win up to $25 if their joke was not successfully topped by the panel.

The series later transferred to television, for five months on ABC (1950–51) and then as a syndicated series two decades later, hosted by Wink Martindale and later Dennis James. The radio series was inducted into the Radio Hall of Fame in 1989.

See also: Comedy

Cast

Jokesters "Senator"	Ed Ford, Harry Hershfield, Joe Laurie, Jr.
Host	Ward Wilson
Joke teller	Peter Donald
Announcer	Charles Stark

Programming History

WOR, New York	1940–45
NBC	1942–48
Mutual	1948–50
ABC	1950–51
NBC	1953–54

Further Reading

Dunning, John, *Tune in Yesterday: The Ultimate Encyclopedia of Old-Time Radio, 1925–1976*, Englewood Cliffs, New Jersey: Prentice-Hall, 1976; revised edition, as *On the Air: The Encyclopedia of Old-Time Radio*, New York: Oxford University Press, 1998.
Ford, Edward Hastings, Harry Hershfield, and Joe Laurie, Jr., *Can You Top This?*, New York: Grosset and Dunlap, 1945.
Ford, Edward Hastings, Harry Hershfield, and Joe Laurie, Jr., *Cream of the Crop: The New Can You Top This? Laugh Roundup*, New York: Grosset and Dunlap, 1947.

CHRISTOPHER H. STERLING

CAPEHART CORPORATION

The history of the Capehart Corporation in Fort Wayne, Indiana, dates back to the late 1920s, when entrepreneur Homer Earl Capehart (1897–1970) established the foundations for the enterprise. Capehart was known for producing quality high-end phonographs, radios, radio-console combinations, and jukeboxes.

Homer E. Capehart was born 6 June 1897 in Algiers, Indiana, and he grew up on a farm. After high school he enlisted in the U.S. Army from 1917 to 1919 and advanced to the rank of sergeant. He joined the J.I. Case Corporation as a salesman and soon earned a reputation as a man who could sell anything. He moved from sales to entrepreneurship, at first manufacturing and selling popcorn poppers. In 1928 he established the Automatic Phonograph Corporation; by 1929 the company was manufacturing "talking machines" and was known as the Capehart Automatic Phonograph Corporation. Capehart served as founder and president from 1927 to 1932. During the 1930s Depression era, when other companies such as Philco and the Radio Corporation of America (RCA) were developing low-priced consumer radio sets to encourage sales, Capehart stood stubbornly behind the company's high-quality, expensive receivers. This decision led the company to the brink of bankruptcy. In the early 1930s, at the height of the Depression, Capehart joined Wurlitzer, a producer of jukeboxes, and as a result the Capehart Corporation was saved. Capehart himself served as vice president of the Wurlitzer Company from 1933 to 1938. The joining of the two companies was a complementary success: Wurlitzer sold jukeboxes, which in turn sold records, which in turn created a demand for the Capehart phonograph. The investment helped make Capehart a wealthy man. Despite success with Wurlitzer, Homer Capehart was forever the adventurer and entrepreneur, and by the end of the 1930s he was ready to move into real estate.

In 1938 the Capehart Company and all its "real estate, plants, factories...all patents, patent licenses and patent application rights, and trade marks" were sold to the Farnsworth Television and Radio Corporation. Farnsworth kept the name Capehart because of its reputation for quality radio and phonograph manufacturing. The Capehart manufacturing entities were retooled to manufacture both Farnsworth and Capehart brand-name radio and television receivers intended for consumer sale. The Farnsworth Corporation was banking on the Capehart organization's reputation for quality to launch its entrance into the manufacturing business. However, World War II intervened, and the plants were converted a second time, this time for the manufacturing of armed forces communication equipment.

Following the war, the name Capehart surfaced again. By 1949 the International Telephone and Telegraph Corporation (ITT) had purchased the Farnsworth Television and Radio Corporation, and the Capehart-Farnsworth division of the company was returned to consumer manufacturing. However, even with the financial backing of ITT, the Capehart-Farnsworth sets were never able to capture a significant share of the radio and television manufacturing market. They were competing against the giants of radio manufacturing at the time—RCA, General Electric, Philco, and Westinghouse. By 1954 the Capehart-Farnsworth division of ITT was split. The Farnsworth Electronic division continued as a wholly owned subsidiary of ITT, but the Capehart manufacturing was sold in 1956 to the Ben Gross Corporation, a holding company. The manufacturing properties in Fort Wayne were retained by ITT, the remaining assets were sold, and the Capehart name disappeared from the history of radio and television.

See also: High Fidelity; Receivers

Further Reading

Godfrey, Donald G., *Philo T. Farnsworth: The Father of Television*, Salt Lake City: University of Utah Press, 2001.

Pickett, William B., *Homer E. Capehart: A Senator's Life, 1897–1979*, Indianapolis: Indiana Historical Society, 1990.

Sampson, Anthony, *The Sovereign State of ITT*, New York: Stein and Day, 1973.

DONALD G. GODFREY

CAPTAIN MIDNIGHT
Adventure Program

Among the many syndicated and network daily serials aimed at younger listeners was this aviation-related program of adventure that involved code-breaking and worldwide travels. The debut of *Captain Midnight* is generally given as 17 October 1938; however, as the show was originally syndicated under the sponsorship of Skelly Oil, it is possible that different stations first aired *Captain Midnight* on different start dates. The initial sponsor owned Spartan Aircraft, and had previously sponsored *The Air Adventures of Jimmie Allen,* another aviation oriented radio serial. The writers from *Jimmie Allen*, Robert Burtt and Wilfred Moore, both World War I pilots, were assigned to create the new show. With pilots scripting the show, the aviation content was accurate.

The initial adventures of the show involved the title character, Charles J. ("Jim" or "Red") Albright, who was referred to primarily by his alias "Captain Midnight," as an independent pilot who acted altruistically to fight wrongdoing, along with his ward, Chuck Ramsay, a girl sidekick, Patsy Donovan, and various others, including a mechanic, Ichabod Mudd. His chief adversary was a criminal, Ivan Shark, who led a gang with his daughter Fury, and two aides, Fang and Gardo. Stories involved adventures in the western United States, Mexico, and Canada.

In 1940, the program changed sponsors and first aired on a national network, Mutual. Ovaltine had previously sponsored *Little Orphan Annie*, a 15-minute adventure serial based on the newspaper comic strip, since 1930. Ovaltine dropped sponsorship of that show in favor of *Captain Midnight*, possibly because the international tensions of the era required a mature hero in the eyes of the sponsor. The initial program under the new sponsor provided the hero with an "origin" story (he earned the code name Captain Midnight because of an exploit during World War I) and a secret organization to head. For *Orphan Annie*, Ovaltine had developed a club (Radio Orphan Annie's Secret Society) and a "Decoder Pin" and these were concepts carried over to *Captain Midnight*. The hero headed a paramilitary organization, the Secret Squadron, which was supposedly set up by a high U.S. government official. Its identifying badge was a cipher device, the Code-O-Graph, which was used, like its *Orphan Annie* predecessors, to decrypt "secret messages" provided at the close of some episodes, to provide a hint of the next day's broadcast.

Most of the main characters from the Skelly show were retained, including Chuck Ramsay, Ichabod Mudd, Ivan Shark, Fury Shark, Fang, and Gardo. One exception was that Patsy Donovan was dropped, and a new girl sidekick, Joyce Ryan, was added. The nature of the Secret Squadron, which was supposed to fight sabotage and espionage, enabled the program to have adventures around the world, including the Caribbean, Central and South America, and China, as well as in the United States. New villains were introduced: the Barracuda shortly before the U.S. entry into World War II, and Baron von Karp, Admiral Himakito, and Señor Schrecker during the war. (An interesting sidelight: well before the 1941 Japanese attack, Captain Midnight found plans for Pearl Harbor in The Barracuda's headquarters in Japanese-occupied China.) After the war, the program continued to be set in locales across the world, and the major villain, Ivan Shark, became prominent again.

The program retained its 15-minute serial format through June of 1949. In September of that year, it changed format to half-hour, complete-in-one-program stories. These alternated with *Tom Mix Ralston Straight Shooters*, running on Tuesdays and Thursdays, until the middle of December, when it went off the air.

The first sponsor, Skelly Oil, aimed most of its products to adults—gasoline, bottled gas, and motor oil. The program attracted a fairly large minority of adult listeners, despite its scheduled spot in the middle of the hour devoted to juvenile programs. This audience carried over to Ovaltine sponsorship. As a result, the vocabulary, dialog, and concepts were more mature than those normally found in a children's adventure show.

One notable aspect of *Captain Midnight* was that women were not relegated to stereotypical roles of the time. Joyce Ryan, a teenage Secret Squadron member, routinely faced the same dangers as her male counterparts, including going on commando raids and participating in aerial dogfights. Likewise, Fury Shark was as courageous as her father, and as scheming. Neither expected special treatment

because of their gender. This was reflected in the handbooks that came with the Code-O-Graph premiums, where both genders were encouraged to go after exciting careers.

A television version of *Captain Midnight* was aired on CBS (1953–57), sponsored by Ovaltine, but it differed significantly from the radio program. When it was re-released as a syndicated show, the hero's name was changed to Jet Jackson, and the new name was spliced into the sound track.

See also: Premiums

Cast

Captain Midnight	Ed Prentiss (1938–39), Bill Bouchey (1939–40), Ed Prentiss (1940–49), Paul Barnes (1949)
Chuck Ramsay	Billy Rose (1938–41), Jack Bivans (1941–44), Johnny Coons (1944–46), Jack Bivans (1946–49)
Joyce Ryan	Marilou Neumayer (1940–46), Angeline Orr (1946–49)
Ivan Shark	Boris Aplon
Ichabod Mudd	Hugh Studebaker (1940–46), Sherman Marks (1946–48), Art Hern (1948–49)
Fury Shark	Rene Rodier (1938–40), Sharon Grainger (1940–1949)
Patsy Donovan	Alice Sherry Gootkin
Kelly, SS-11	Olan Soulé

Creators/Writers

Robert Burtt and Wilfred Moore

Programming History

Syndicated	October 1938–March 1940
Mutual	September 1940–July 1942
NBC Blue	September 1942–June 1945
Mutual	September 1945–December 1949

Further Reading

Kallis, Stephen A., Jr., "The Code-O-Graph Cipher Disks," *Cryptologia* 5, no. 2 (April 1981).
Kallis, Stephen A., Jr., "Flying with the Secret Squadron," *Yesterday's Magazette* 25, no. 1 (January/February 1997).
Kallis, Stephen A., Jr., *Radio's Captain Midnight: The Wartime Biography*, London and Jefferson, North Carolina: McFarland, 2000.
Tumbusch, Tom, *Tomart's Price Guide to Radio Premium and Cereal Box Collectibles: Including Comic Character, Pulp*

Hero, TV, and Other Premiums, Radnor, Pennsylvania: Wallace-Homestead, 1991.

Widner, James F., "Cast Photos for *Captain Midnight*," www.otr.com/cm_cast.html.

Winterbotham, Russell R., *Joyce of the Secret Squadron: A Captain Midnight Adventure*, Racine, Wisconsin: Whitman, 1942.

STEPHEN A. KALLIS, JR.

CAR RADIO

See: Automobile Radio

CAR TALK

Advice and Humor Call-in Program

Few radio programs can deliver on promotional announcements that promise advice on both car repair and human relationships. But then few programs blend the serious and the sophomoric into an hour-long show that is both funny and helpful. National Public Radio's (NPR) *Car Talk* is one.

The hosts, Tom and Ray Magliozzi, better known to their fans as "Click" and "Clack," are brothers who opened a do-it-yourself counter-culture garage in Cambridge, Massachusetts, in 1973. As hippies evolved into people with real jobs and cars became more complicated, the brothers offered more conventional car repair.

In 1977 the Magliozzis were invited to appear on a talk show on WBUR-FM with other area mechanics. Tom accepted, and when he returned the following week, he brought Ray along. Later they were given their own WBUR talk show in which they gave advice and tried to drum up business for their garage. The show is produced by Dewey, Cheetham, and Howe—a company the Magliozzis named with the same self-deprecation that drives the program—and it still originates at WBUR.

In January 1987 NPR host Susan Stamberg invited the brothers to be weekly contributors to NPR's *Weekend Edition*. On October 31 of that same year, *Car Talk* premiered as a national program. After more than ten years on the air, NPR broadcasts *Car Talk* on more than 550 NPR stations nationwide to over 3.8 million laughing fans. The program received the George Foster Peabody Award in 1992. In 1998 the Museum of Broadcast Communications in Chicago inducted Tom and Ray Magliozzi into the Radio Hall of Fame.

Although cars and human responses to cars are the foundations of the show, *Car Talk* is about laughing. Tom and Ray are ready to laugh out loud at themselves, at cars, and at callers. Often the show begins with a humorous piece about a serious issue such as global warming or politics. Sometimes one of the brothers begins with a tirade against oversized automobile engines or people who drive while talking on cell phones.

Both brothers are graduates of the Massachusetts Institute of Technology; Tom has a doctorate in marketing and has taught at Boston and Suffolk Universities. Ray still runs the garage and is a consultant to the Consumer Affairs Division of the Massachusetts attorney general's office. Their education and work backgrounds provide fertile areas for them to make fun of each other, their schools, and all areas of higher education. They also make fun of each other's expertise or lack thereof. When one takes a caller's question, he will often say that the other doesn't know what he's talking about and can't possibly give a good answer. Callers come in for their share of jibes, too, mostly in the form of gentle teasing.

Literary references, puns, and joking references to NPR news reporters and hosts spark the show: for example, reading the standard NPR underwriter line, the Magliozzis remind listeners that "Support for *Car Talk* comes from bogus parking tickets we put on cars all over the NPR parking lot" or that "Support for *Car Talk* comes from the small but regular deductions we make from Carl Kassell's retirement account." Callers are encouraged to banter and allowed to star as story tellers. In the midst of the fun and zany comments, real questions about spark plugs, used cars, problems with mechanics or dealer service shops, and personal issues with cars do get answered.

On the air, Ray is the one who actually tries to answer the automotive questions. He's the director of the show and keeps it moving. Tom make jokes, insults Ray and callers, and laughs the most. Both men are honest to the point of bluntness when it comes to how to deal with bad mechanics or auto manufacturers. Ray says that they started cracking jokes the first time they were unable to answer a caller's questions. The more they laughed, the better they enjoyed the show. And the bigger the audience became. Producer Doug Berman, who has worked with the Magliozzis for 12 years, said in an interview in *Brill's Content*, "They're like the kids in the back of the class that used to joke and make you laugh, and you didn't want to laugh because you'd get in trouble" (Greenstein).

Car Talk is a tightly structured show: it begins with a thought piece, usually humorous. There are three segments that feature phone calls. Most weeks a puzzle is featured in the "third half" of the program. Music from many genres, as long as the lyrics mention something automotive, is used as audio bumpers to separate the segments.

"Stump the Chumps" is an irregular feature in which callers are brought back to reveal whether Click and Clack gave the correct answer to their automotive questions. This feature gives rise to much self-deprecating humor. It also establishes credibility, because most of the time the answer was correct and saved the caller both time and money.

In 2008, the Magliozzis took *Car Talk* to television with an animated series on PBS stations nationwide. Thanks to a contest involving their radio listeners, the show was titled *As the Wrench Turns*. It chronicled adventures in the Click and Clack garage with a cast of additional characters not heard on the radio show. The responses from *Car Talk* fans were backhanded jokes in the spirit of Tom and Ray's own self-deprecating comments: "Don't quit your day job," said one. "There's nothing like a good joke," said another, "and that was nothing like a good joke!"

During the show's closing credits, puns reign. From research statistician Marge Inoverra to pseudonym consultant Norm Deplume, the end of *Car Talk* is a high point. The names are accompanied by the appropriate accent when required. Although the basic names repeat week after week, there's always a new one to catch the ear of the faithful and keep Tom laughing.

Car Talk closes with an underwriting statement that offers a final opportunity to make a joke about another NPR host: "And even though Scott Simon sends his resume to MTV every time he hears us say it, this is NPR, National Public Radio."

See also: Comedy; National Public Radio

Programming History

WBUR-FM   1977–87
NPR (550 stations) 1987–present

Further Reading

Car Talk website, http://cartalk.com/.
Greenstein, Jennifer, "The Car Talk Guys Just Want to Have Fun," *Brill's Content* (October 1999).
Magliozzi, Tom, and Ray Magliozzi, "The Mechanics of Buying a Great Used Car," *Friendly Exchange* (Summer 1999).
Magliozzi, Tom, and Ray Magliozzi, *In Our Humble Opinion*, New York: Penguin, 2000.

PAM SHANE,
2009 REVISIONS BY PAM SHANE

CAVALCADE OF AMERICA
U.S. Radio Drama

Sponsored by E.I. du Pont de Nemours and Company, *Cavalcade of America* established the dramatic anthology program format among a generation of public relations and advertising specialists, as well as its reluctant sponsor, in a period when continuous institutional promotion by radio was not generally practiced and when the value of radio in prosecuting even short-term public relations campaigns was not fully appreciated. Because the DuPont Company's previous radio use had been limited to the efforts of company officials who personally helped underwrite the anti-New Deal talks of the American Liberty League, the National Association of Manufacturers, and other pro-business groups, the debut of *Cavalcade* was a signal event in the conservative seedtime of modern broadcast entertainment. What became the longest-running radio program of its kind debuted 9 October 1935 and ran until 1953 with only two brief lapses. In 1952, *Cavalcade* moved to television, where it remained until 1955. Although *Cavalcade*'s sponsor never relinquished its editorial prerogative, by 1940 DuPont acceded to their specialists' attempts to bury the program's more troublesome aspects in the dramatic subtext of "Better Things for Better Living."

A positive expression of corporate social leadership supervised by the advertising and public relations specialists of Batten, Barton, Durstine, and Osborn (BBD&O), the *Cavalcade* exemplified the higher concepts of corporate public affairs, far removed from the give and take of American party politics, which by 1935 had become manifest in a daily cycle of reaction and attack. By the early 1950s, company advertising and public relations specialists proudly pointed to increasingly favorable opinion polling data associating DuPont with "Better Things for Better Living." Reflecting on BBD&O's long and successful relationship with DuPont, Bruce Barton attributed the turnaround in part to two factors: women's nylons and the *Cavalcade of America*.

BBD&O's aggressive merchandising of *Cavalcade* involved celebrated authors, dramatists, actors, actresses, educators, and historians. From 1935 to 1938 the *Cavalcade*'s historical advisers included Dixon Ryan Fox—the president of Union College and the New York Historical Association—and Professor Arthur M. Schlesinger of Harvard. The arrangement enabled BBD&O to merchandise the program as a contribution to the "new social history" with which Fox and Schlesinger had become identified as co-editors of the 12-volume *A History of American Life*. Suspended between the liberal sensibilities of the new social history, represented by the collaboration of Fox and Schlesinger, and the sponsor's predilection for rhetorical attacks upon Franklin Roosevelt's New Deal, the *Cavalcade* offered a counter-subversive drama of self-reliance, resourcefulness, and defiance animated by the misfortunes of typically natural phenomena: grasshopper plagues, flash floods, fire, drought, dust storms, blizzards, ice floes, and log jams. Successful resolution demanded heroic acts of voluntarism, community spirit, and the sterner stuff that defined a heritage. As one flinty character explained while he helped extinguish a forest fire threatening his town, "What we struggled to get, we fight to keep."

The dramatization of the personal meaning of business enterprise played a role in the *Cavalcade*'s striking use of female protagonists. In its first season, the *Cavalcade* presented a hierarchical schedule of broadcasts beginning with "Women's Emancipation," the story of Elizabeth Cady Stanton, Lucretia Mott, William Lloyd Garrison, and Susan B. Anthony; "Women in Public Service," the story of Jane Addams and Hull House; "Loyalty to Family," the story of frontier widow Ann Harper; and "Self-Reliance," the story of planter Eliza Lucas' efforts to establish indigo in Carolina. Many *Cavalcade* women turned up as agents of production. For example, "The Search for Iron," broadcast in 1938, dramatized the story of the Merrit family's discovery of a massive iron ore deposit in Minnesota's Mesabi Range. The search, spanning three generations, featured matriarch Hepzabeth Merrit, log-hewn home life, and a frontier quest for resources. The concluding "story of chemistry" explained how miners used DuPont dynamite to excavate iron ore from "mother Earth," an example of the modern world's extraordinary engineering feats and of dynamite's use for constructive projects. Not without lighter moments, the "Search for Iron" began, as did many early *Cavalcade* broadcasts, with a medley of popular show tunes, in this case "Someday My Prince Will Come" and "Heigh Ho" from Walt Disney's *Snow White and the Seven Dwarfs*.

By the early 1940s, the *Cavalcade of America* had become the commitment to well-merchandised institutional entertainment that its specialists had long sought. Specialists attributed the *Cavalcade*'s success to its capacity to assimilate the functions of broadcast education and entertainment, with each adjusted to fit the circumstances of the changing leadership of the DuPont Company; the inroads of middle management using positivist audience

research; and the onset of World War II, which made possible and even desirable the expression of democratic sensibilities.

After 1940 the *Cavalcade* featured a new mixture of amateur and academic historians who assumed greater program responsibilities. Professor Frank Monaghan of Yale delivered on-air story introductions. A memorable broadcast performance by poet and Lincoln biographer Carl Sandburg and the performance of poet Stephen Vincent Benét's *The People, Yes* signaled the relaxation of the program sponsor's editorial outlook. Thereafter, the formulaic dramatization of the American past culminating in "better living" distanced itself from the crisis of Depression-era business leadership that had called the *Cavalcade* into being. Ever so slowly, the *Cavalcade* decamped from the usable past for the intimate terrain of "more," "new," and "better living" merchandised in a build-up of stars and stories.

In concert with program producer BBD&O, the National Broadcasting Company (NBC) took the *Cavalcade* on the road for timely broadcast performances before the network's "pressure groups." The first of three remote broadcasts originated from the Chicago Civic Opera House, starring Raymond Massey in Robert Sherwood's adaptation of Sandburg's *Abraham Lincoln: The War Years*. Another starred Helen Hayes in "Jane Addams of Hull House," broadcast from the Milwaukee convention of the General Federation of Women's Clubs. A third program, attended by DuPont's Richmond, Virginia, employees, featured Philip Merivale in "Robert E. Lee," based on historian Douglas Southall Freeman's biography of the general.

Program specialists acknowledged the advantage of featuring characters already familiar to listeners, many of whom regarded historical figures as voices of authority. The ideal protagonist was heroic yet humble. Of the 750 *Cavalcade* radio programs broadcast from 1935 to 1953, biographical treatments of George Washington and Abraham Lincoln led the list (15 programs each), followed by Benjamin Franklin (nine programs) and Thomas Jefferson (eight). Washington personified a recurring *Cavalcade* metaphor cementing America's revolutionary struggle for freedom with business' modern-day struggle to escape the regulatory tyranny of the New Deal. In a dramatization of the first inauguration entitled "Plain Mr. President," for example, the *Cavalcade*'s Washington invoked the "sacred fire of liberty and the destiny of the republican form of government...staked on the experiment entrusted to the American people." Washington prayed that "the invisible hand of the almighty being guide the people of the United States to wise measures, for our free government must win the affection of its citizens and command the respect of the world." The weekly "story of chemistry," entitled "news of chemistry's work in our world," noted that "Washington, the practical economist, would no doubt have been pleased with modern house paints that actually clean themselves."

Gaining the confidence of their sponsor, who at last warmed to the idea of entertainment, the *Cavalcade*'s producers found themselves able to take advantage of a wider range of story material. This new range of material expanded the program's original basis in the historical past and the world of letters to feature adaptations of Hollywood screenplays and original works for radio that dramatized democratic sensibilities. In fall 1940, the *Cavalcade* presented the story of "Wild Bill Hickok" woven around a ballad composed and performed by Woodie Guthrie; "Town Crier" Alexander Woolcott, on loan from the Columbia Broadcasting System (CBS), who performed his "word picture" of "The Battle Hymn of the Republic;" and a special Christmas night broadcast of Marc Connelly's "The Green Pastures" featuring the Hall Johnson Choir. The adaptation of popular screenplays the following season enlarged upon the plan. In November 1941 the *Cavalcade* presented Henry Fonda in "Drums along the Mohawk" and Errol Flynn in "They Died with Their Boots On." In the weeks following Pearl Harbor, the program featured Orson Welles in "The Great Man Votes" and James Cagney in "Captains of the Clouds." The appearance of stars who volunteered personal feelings about the company at the conclusion of select broadcasts spoke volumes for the program sponsor's growing confidence in a corporate public relations strategy inconceivable in the early years of the program.

The *Cavalcade* signaled an appreciation among specialists and business leaders alike that carefully scripted investments in dramatic anthology programming could, in the long run, re-establish a political climate conducive to the autonomous expansion of corporate enterprise. Business' contest with the administration for social and political leadership would continue, specialists hoped, divorced from rhetorical reaction and counterproductive short-term effects.

After World War II, the dramatic anthology became the preferred vehicle of corporate public relations among the clients of BBD&O, with tremendous significance for the television of the 1950s. BBD&O-produced programs included *Cavalcade of America*, *General Electric Theater*, *U.S. Steel Hour*

(Theater Guild on the Air), and *Armstrong Circle Theater*. As the prototype of well-merchandised institutional entertainment, the *Cavalcade* set the precedent for them all, including the merchandising of programs undertaken by *General Electric Theater* host and program supervisor Ronald Reagan.

Ever responsive to the need of the moment, the free enterprise subtext of radio's *Cavalcade* continued unabated. At times, company public relations and advertising specialists seemed incapable of any other than dramaturgical expression. When the DuPont Company became entangled in an antitrust suit in 1949, for example, the *Cavalcade* dramatized the benefits of large-scale monopoly in "Wire to the West," the story of Western Union's consolidation of rival telegraph companies; in "Beyond Cheyenne," a story about "how the packing industry started as small business and became big business;" and in "The Immortal Blacksmith," "a story of the invention of the electric motor by Tom Davenport, ...which never amounted to anything until big companies took hold of it and converted its power into conveniences for the millions." The *Cavalcade*'s sponsor's reluctance to broadcast a more explicit defense spoke for a certain dramatic success.

Narrator/Host

Walter Huston

Announcers

Frank Singiser, Gabriel Heatter, Basil Ruysdael, Clayton "Bud" Collyer, Gayne Whitman, Ted Pearson

Actors

John McIntire, Jeanette Nolan, Agnes Moorehead, Kenny Delmar, Edwin Jerome, Ray Collins, Orson Welles, Karl Swenson, Ted Jewett, Jack Smart, Paul Stewart, Bill Johnstone, Frank Readick, Raymon Edward Johnson, Ted de Corsia, Everett Sloane, Luis Van Rooten, Mickey Rooney, Cary Grant, Tyrone Power, and Ronald Reagan

Producer/Directors

Homer Fickett, Roger Pryor, Jack Zoller, Paul Stewart, and Bill Sweets

Writers

Arthur Miller, Norman Rosten, Robert Tallman, Peter Lyon, Robert Richards, Stuart Hawkins,

Arthur Arent, Edith Sommer, Halsted Welles, Henry Denker, Priscilla Kent, Virginia Radcliffe, Frank Gabrielson, Margaret Lewerth, Morton Wishengrad, George Faulkner, Irv Tunick

Programming History

CBS	1935–39
NBC Blue	January 1940–June 1940
NBC Red	1940–53

Further Reading

Barnouw, Erik, editor, *Radio Drama in Action: Twenty-Five Plays of a Changing World*, New York: Rinehart, 1945.

Barnouw, Erik, *Media Marathon: A Twentieth-Century Memoir*, Durham, North Carolina: Duke University Press, 1996.

Bird, William L., Jr., *Better Living: Advertising, Media, and the New Vocabulary of Business Leadership, 1935–1955*, Evanston, Illinois: Northwestern University Press, 1999.

Burk, Robert F., *The Corporate State and the Broker State: The Du Ponts and American National Politics, 1925–1940*, Cambridge, Massachusetts: Harvard University Press, 1990.

Fones-Wolf, Elizabeth, "Creating a Favorable Business Climate: Corporations and Radio Broadcasting, 1934–1954," *Business History Review* 73 (Summer 1999).

Fox, Dixon Ryan, and Arthur Meier Schlesinger, editors, *The Cavalcade of America*, Springfield, Massachusetts: Milton Bradley, 1937.

Fox, Dixon Ryan, and Arthur Meier Schlesinger, editors, *The Cavalcade of America, Series 2*, Springfield, Massachusetts: Milton Bradley, 1938.

Golden, L.L.L., *Only by Public Consent: American Corporations Search for Favorable Opinion*, New York: Hawthorn Books, 1968.

Marchand, Roland, *Creating the Corporate Soul: The Rise of Public Relations and Corporate Imagery in American Big Business*, Berkeley: University of California Press, 1998.

Miller, Arthur, *Timebends: A Life*, New York: Grove Press, and London: Methuen, 1987.

Walker, Strother Holland, and Paul Sklar, *Business Finds Its Voice: Management's Effort to Sell the Business Idea to the Public*, New York and London: Harper, 1938.

Wolfskill, George, *The Revolt of the Conservatives: A History of the American Liberty League, 1934–1940*, Boston: Houghton Mifflin, 1962.

Wolfskill, George, and John A. Hudson, *All but the People: Franklin D. Roosevelt and His Critics, 1933–39*, New York: Macmillan, 1969.

WILLIAM L. BIRD, JR.

CENSORSHIP

Censorship means prior restraint—stopping something from being published or broadcast before it can appear. Radio censorship often determines who gets to broadcast and what is broadcast. It can take many forms: state monopoly of radio facilities and political expression; program monitoring by military or civilian bodies; "private" censorship of controversial topics by station authorities; specific stipulations of what constitutes acceptable quality and good taste in radio programming; the denial of the right to broadcast to minority groups, religions, races, and ethnicities; the list goes on and on. If censorship is understood more broadly as the regulation of the transmission and reception of representations and opinions, it could be argued to transpire at all levels of the radio communication process—through the actions of governments, networks, stations, advertisers, producers, performers, parents, and listeners themselves.

The "Absence" of Official Radio Censorship in the United States

Officially, no government censorship of regular radio programming has ever existed in the United States. The First Amendment's prohibition of laws concerning speech and the press are the primary barrier to such activity. Under the Radio Act of 1912, the secretary of commerce and labor was obliged to issue radio licenses to all applicants. Section 29 of the Radio Act of 1927 stipulated that:

> Nothing in this act shall be understood or construed to give the Commission the power of censorship over the radio communications or signals transmitted by any radio station, and no regulation or condition shall be promulgated or fixed by the Commission which shall interfere with the right of free speech by means of radio communication.

This clause was reproduced as Section 326 of the Communications Act of 1934, and it has been applied to the Federal Communications Commission's (FCC) oversight of broadcasting ever since.

The real history of radio censorship in the United States, however, has been far less clear-cut than this official situation would suggest. The "no-censorship" clause was designed to allay fears that a government agency might impose its political will against the First Amendment rights of the press. The assumption that censorship was an act of "prior restraint" by the government on a private citizen, company, or organization was reiterated in this legislation. But if we understand censorship to constitute a more diverse set of limitations and restrictions, patterns of censorship have existed throughout the history of American radio broadcasting.

The no-censorship clause was crucial because it differentiated the "democratic" American system of broadcasting from the state-controlled or state-affiliated systems adopted by most other nations (such as Yugoslavia and Britain). The specter of political control loomed over early discussions about radio regulation and justified the adoption of a system that endorsed private commercial development of the airwaves. In the process, censorship was frequently regarded as a black-and-white issue: the presence or absence of government control. The broadcasting industry was highly successful in soliciting support for its two philosophies on the subject: (1) the argument that government censorship was a slippery slope (i.e., once established in any measure, it would tend toward the kind of political despotism present in authoritarian media systems); and (2) the idea that the government should not be allowed to impose its elitist standards of taste and culture on the American public by determining program content (hence, a paternalist radio model was unacceptable).

In the early 1930s, the federal courts recognized the Federal Radio Commission's (and subsequently the FCC's) right to consider past programming performance when deciding whether to renew or revoke a broadcasting license. Because no radio station can legally broadcast without a license, this "subsequent review" power has long been recognized as an indirect form of censorship, producing the "chilling effect" on broadcasters of avoiding controversial material that might antagonize the commission. In truth, the commission has rarely revoked or failed to renew licenses.

The Emergence of Self-Censorship in the United States

Most censorship in American radio has consisted of self-regulation by networks, stations, advertisers, and performers. Except for certain situations involving political candidates, broadcasters can refuse anybody access to their facilities. This "editorial control" has inspired well-founded criticisms that particular political opinions, news items, and entertainment forms have been routinely excluded from the radio airwaves. *Market censorship,* where the commercial basis of the industry discourages the airing of certain "unpopular" topics or minority perspectives, is often responsible for these restrictions. Allegations have also surfaced that networks and station owners—controlled by wealthier, politically conservative individuals—have prohibited left-wing viewpoints and protests against the broadcasting industry from reaching the microphone. Conversely, throughout the 1930s, Republican congressmen and conservative commentators such as Boake Carter objected that stations and networks, fearing or favoring the Democratic

administration, refused them equitable opportunities to air their perspectives.

Private censorship refers to the various program (or advertising) prohibitions undertaken by radio stations and networks. The most commonly restricted subjects during radio's golden age were labor unrest, socialist politics, pacifism, political "radicalism," birth control advocacy, criticism of advertising, anti-Prohibition speeches, unorthodox medical practices, unorthodox religious opinions, excessive excitement in children's shows, "offensive" words, and suggestive situations. Private censorship often stemmed from stations' unwillingness to offend advertisers or listeners (based upon feedback or the assumed preferences of their audience). Such actions were not always unfounded or irresponsible. Popular radio priest Father Charles Coughlin's anti-Semitic remarks resulted in his program's cancellation by a number of stations in the late 1930s and led to his eventual removal from the air. Significantly, however, most networks and many stations responded to Coughlin by formalizing policies refusing to accept paid programming that addressed "controversial" issues. As a result, the limits of radio discourse were further circumscribed.

Obscenity and Indecency in Radio

In response to an outbreak of "radio vandalism," in 1914 the Department of Commerce stipulated that amateur licensees must refrain from profane or obscene words. This preoccupation with maintaining standards of good taste and upholding the moral order continued into the broadcasting era. The one exception to the no-censorship clause of the Radio Act and the Communications Act is the following addendum: "No person within the jurisdiction of the United States shall utter any obscene, indecent, or profane language by means of radio communication."

In other words, this was the one legislated area in which prior restraint was permissible: broadcasters airing obscene, indecent, or profane material could expect license revocation or nonrenewal. During its tenure, the Federal Radio Commission interpreted this clause broadly, arguing that because radio entered the home and was accessible by children, indiscretions in this area were unacceptable. Several licenses for smaller stations were revoked following "vulgar" and "offensive" broadcasts, encouraging a higher degree of caution among other broadcasters. Any mention of "sex" was avoided, leading to the widespread cancellation of academic lectures on venereal diseases and birth control methods.

Self-Regulation

In fact, the larger stations and the radio networks justified their dominance within the industry based upon their ability to uphold "good taste" in programming. The commission supported the notion that "quality radio service" was best represented by vigilant self-monitoring of programs and performers. The corroboration between official government regulation and industry self-regulation solidified in the 1930s. The National Association of Broadcasters (NAB) emerged as the primary industry lobbying group and developed continuing working relations with the FCC and Congress. Dominated by the larger commercial entities throughout its history, the NAB encouraged its members to more aggressively self-censor.

Without formal government outlines of what was permissible over the airwaves, program producers personally took on the obligations of unofficial censorship. Most stations codified their censorship policies, justifying them in terms of universal community interests. KSD, St. Louis, prided itself on its ability to exercise "an inflexible censorship over all programs offered for broadcasting ... [to protect] listeners and advertisers against association with the unworthy." In the early 1930s, the trade magazine *Variety* described how the current policy, "somewhat along the lines of an honor system, makes a censor of everybody in the studio, from actors to control room engineers. Nobody has been taught what to avoid or bar and the material washing is left to personal discretion" (quoted in Rorty, 1934).

This gatekeeping function was formalized as the decade progressed, especially as the networks asserted their oversight functions. The Columbia Broadcasting System's (CBS) 1935 policies focused on children's programming, listing themes that would not be permitted:

> The exalting, as modern heroes, of gangsters, criminals and racketeers will not be allowed. Disrespect for either parental or other proper authority must not be glorified or encouraged. Recklessness and abandon must not be falsely identified with a healthy spirit of adventure.

The National Broadcasting Company (NBC) likewise institutionalized restrictions, prohibiting such subjects as "offcolor" songs and jokes, astrology and fortune-telling, irreverent references to the deity, and "questionable statements." The NAB followed suit, issuing in 1939 a more stringent code of "accepted standards of good taste" for its members. CBS and NBC established "Standards and Practices" and "Continuity Acceptance" departments to enforce "courtesy and good taste" and to

guarantee programming appropriate for "homes... of all types...and all members of the family."

The self-censorship system was similar to that of the motion picture industry, but it differed in certain respects. The Hollywood movie studios submitted scripts and films to a semi-independent body to preview and approve. Radio censorship was less centralized; most radio programs were created (and self-censored) by sponsors and their advertising agencies. Networks and stations were therefore usually dealing with third parties, not their own productions. The sheer volume of radio programming meant that continuous monitoring of all stations' output was impractical. Radio guidelines were also harder to enforce, because most broadcasts were transmitted live. The radio networks and stations required all programs and speakers to submit scripts in advance and forbade ad-libbing, but this cumbersome "blue-penciling" review process was never comprehensively enforced, and it failed to account for misinterpretations or unscheduled deviations from the script during broadcast. Writers and performers frequently challenged the networks' censorship provisions, slipping in double entendres or tiptoeing on the brink of "tastelessness" with their gags and dramas. Nevertheless, major infractions of the self-regulatory codes were few and far between, and the FCC wholeheartedly supported the application of private censorship as a preferential alternative to official program supervision.

The close cooperation between government and big industry objectives in radio that had developed during the 1930s was indicated by the formal alliances forged during World War II. The administration's faith in the ideological integrity of radio business interests was confirmed when President Roosevelt appointed top radio journalists and executives to posts in the Office of War Information (OWI) and the Office of Censorship. Networks, stations, and sponsors obliged the OWI by providing hours of free airtime to government programs and bond drives. Dramatic scripts were rewritten to encourage patriotism, enlistment, and home front support for the war effort. The Office of Censorship issued guidelines of prohibited topics such as weather reports and troop movements, and it required the downplaying of racial antagonisms—all of which broadcasters followed willingly.

Radio Censorship in the United States after World War II

As the networks shifted their interests to television in the postwar period, the tight mechanisms of self-regulation that had developed in the 1930s and 1940s began to break down. Radio stations shifted away from a mass-appeal broadcasting model to a format-based system that targeted particular localities and audience groups. In the process, minority tastes, unorthodox political opinions, and non-mainstream moralities were serviced. In increasingly competitive urban radio markets, commercial broadcasters began to "push the envelope" and schedule controversial and sensational programming. A rise in noncommercial community radio stations resulted in programming that resonated with more politically and aesthetically progressive audiences. The NAB Code of Program Standards was abolished in the 1980s. Censorship re-emerged around the fringes of the electromagnetic spectrum.

In the 1970s, the FCC reprimanded several "indecent" radio broadcasters. The trend toward "topless radio"—call-in talk shows inviting sexual anecdotes from listeners—resulted in fines and warnings from the Commission. Various stations associated with the Pacifica Foundation (a listener-supported organization serving avant-garde tastes and addressing political subjects) were chastised for their indiscretions. Most significantly, Pacifica member WBAI, New York, broadcast an unexpurgated sketch called "Seven Dirty Words" by comedian George Carlin. This resulted in a U.S. Supreme Court decision declaring that, although the sketch was constitutionally protected speech, the FCC had the right to restrict indecent expression over the airwaves. Despite lingering debate that such restrictions were tantamount to violating First Amendment rights, the FCC has aggressively exerted its authority to restrict on-air use of certain indecent words or situations. In the 1990s and 2000s, "shock jocks" across the country continuously pushed the envelope—and regularly paid the penalty for it. Notably, in 2002, WNEW's morning team of Opie and Anthony were fined $357,000 and saw their show cancelled after one of their broadcasts appeared to encourage a couple to have sex in New York's St. Patrick's Cathedral.

Stations began to undergo even greater scrutiny after Janet Jackson's infamous "wardrobe malfunction" during halftime entertainment from the 2004 Super Bowl telecast. Responding to growing public outcry (much of it encouraged by a conservative group monitoring television), Congress raised the minimum per-offense FCC fine to a staggering $350,000, enough to bankrupt many smaller stations. In order to head off problems, many stations began to employ broadcast (or tape) delays (some as long as five minutes in length, though ten seconds was more typical) in order to enable engineers or on-air personnel to catch and edit out questionable content.

Though the Jackson incident was exclusive to television, the repercussions from it have spanned media. Similarly, the case of *Fox TV v. FCC* (which concerned fleeting use of profanity on the air), was decided by the Supreme Court in mid-2009, remanding the case, but seemingly upholding FCC decisions that even such fleeting use of "bad" words was subject to legal action and fines.

Prohibited use of certain words and phrases is not restricted just to comics and disc jockeys, however. Increasingly, musical acts have had to learn to watch their language if they want their records played over the air. Alanis Morrisette, Liz Phair and others have seen their songs undergo editing, "bleeping" or some other alteration in order to insure possible airplay. For example, the Black Eyed Peas reworded their song "Let's Get Retarded" to "Let's Get It Started" in order to be more radio friendly.

"Political Correctness"

During the early 2000s, new concerns, and debate, about censorship arose over issues of patriotism and political correctness. In 2003, controversial anti-President Bush statements made in concert by Natalie Maines, lead singer for the country music act the Dixie Chicks, led to a backlash against them by some country radio stations and their listeners. Under the auspices of patriotism, numerous stations across the nation (including some owned by Cox and Clear Channel) pulled Dixie Chicks music from the air. Multiple station owner Cumulus Media went so far as to ban them from all 42 of their stations. Some stations even staged or promoted public bonfires of Dixie Chicks CDs.

Four years later, on-air comments about the Rutgers University women's basketball team by radio veteran Don Imus resulted in a similar firestorm of controversy. Though Imus issued an on-air apology one day after his April 2007 remarks, within days, he was suspended, saw several of his show's sponsors drop their support, saw MSNBC (which was airing a video version of the show) cancel his program, and some onetime guests announce they would no longer appear alongside him. Less than a month later, CBS Radio fired him. Despite the controversy, Imus would return to the air less than a year later, this time on the ABC Radio Network.

Though these actions by these stations were not, per se, censorship—as they did not involve prior restraint by any arm of government—many decried them as censorship as they did curtail expression and exposure to that expression.

A burgeoning "microradio" movement, which broadcasts to immediate localities using cheap, portable, low-power transmitters, more recently flustered the FCC. Advocates of microradio argue that it allows greater access to the airwaves for marginalized voices. The FCC long refused to license broadcasters under 100 watts and considered such microbroadcasting illegal. In 2000 the FCC began to license low-power FM transmitters; microradio proponents consider this an attempt by the Commission to commercialize the movement and extend its authority over radio content.

Though low power radio is still under the jurisdiction of the FCC, satellite and internet radio is not. (This is due primarily to the fact that neither makes use of scarce spectrum.) The unprecedented on-air freedom promised by satellite radio has attracted a wide array of previously corseted on-air talents, most significantly radio provocateur Howard Stern, who decamped terrestrial radio for Sirius in 2006.

Even if satellite radio is free of government content restrictions, however, the channels are not beyond the reach of political correctness, public opinion or good taste. In May of 2007, Opie and Anthony, who had resurfaced over XM radio in 2005 after being fired from WNEW three years before, ignited controversy once more after a guest went on a 20-minute on-air rant about having sex with two prominent political figures. Though the comments violated no laws, the on-air pair were denounced by various media outlets and faced another public backlash. XM suspended the duo for one month, an action that incited its own protest among free speech advocates.

As with the Dixie Chicks, whether this Opie and Anthony incident is "censorship" is open to debate. The station and industry actions it inspired were not born out of federal interference or prior restraint but, rather, were a reflection of public opinion and corporate and community standards.

A significant censorship issue for the future concerns internet radio, which many forecast will supersede broadcast radio if issues of listener access and portability can be resolved. The international implications are massive, because the delivery of audio over the internet renders discrepancies in signal strength and frequency allocation irrelevant. Censorship based on geographical factors disappears as a result. Internet radio seemingly offers a solution to national/state censorship, representing a technological means to circumvent authoritarian attempts to prohibit or limit broadcast transmissions.

See also: Communications Act of 1934; Controversial Issues, Broadcasting of; "Equal Time" Rule; Fairness Doctrine; Federal Communications Commission; First Amendment and Radio; Internet Radio; Licensing Authorising U.S. Stations to Broadcast; Low-Power Radio/Microradio; Obscenity and Indecency on Radio; Radio Laws; "Seven Dirty Words" Case; Topless Radio; United States Supreme Court and Radio

Further Reading

Brindze, Ruth, *Not to Be Broadcast: The Truth about the Radio*, New York: Vanguard Press, 1937.

Chase, Francis Seabury, Jr., *Sound and Fury: An Informal History of Broadcasting*, New York and London: Harper, 1942.

Coons, John E., editor, *Freedom and Responsibility in Broadcasting*, Evanston, Illinois: Northwestern University Press, 1961.

Hilmes, Michele, *Radio Voices: American Broadcasting, 1922–1952*, Minneapolis: University of Minnesota Press, 1997.

"Imus came back on the radio, after penance for his racial offenses." *National Review* 31 December 2007, p. 14.

Krattenmaker, Thomas G., and Lucas A. Powe, Jr., *Regulating Broadcast Programming*, Cambridge, Massachusetts: MIT Press, 1994.

Lipschultz, Jeremy Harris, *Broadcast Indecency: F.C.C. Regulation and the First Amendment*, Boston: Focal Press, 1997.

Murray, Matthew, "The Tendency to Deprave and Corrupt Morals: Regulation and Irregular Sexuality in Golden Age Radio Comedy," in *The Radio Reader: Essays in the Cultural History of Radio*, edited by Michele Hilmes and Jason Loviglio, New York and London: Routledge, 2002.

Paulu, Burton, *Radio and Television Broadcasting in Eastern Europe*, Minneapolis: University of Minnesota Press, 1974.

Rivera-Sanchez, Milagros, "Developing an Indecency Standard: The Federal Communications Commission and the Regulation of Offensive Speech, 1927–1964," *Journalism History* 20, no. 1 (Spring 1994).

Rorty, James, *Order on the Air!* New York: Day, 1934.

Schlesinger, Philip, *Putting "Reality" Together: BBC News*, London: Constable, 1978; Beverly Hills, California: Sage, 1979.

Smead, Elmer E., *Freedom of Speech by Radio and Television*, Washington, D.C.: Public Affairs Press, 1959.

Summers, Harrison Boyd, compiler, *Radio Censorship*, New York: Wilson, 1939.

Summers, Robert Edward, compiler, *Wartime Censorship of Press and Radio*, New York: Wilson, 1942.

MATTHEW MURRAY,
2009 REVISIONS BY CARY O'DELL

CHILDREN'S NOVELS AND RADIO

Much of the excitement over the introduction of wireless communication and radio broadcasting is reflected in a host of books aimed at younger readers, several series of which appeared before 1930, most of them during the early days of broadcasting in the 1920s. Mistakenly referred to as "dime novels," a phrase more fitting to 19th-century magazine fiction, at least 160 separate volumes focusing on wireless or radio appeared from 1908 to as late as the 1960s. Written for an audience of young boys and girls, there were single titles and series, all promoting the use of wireless and radio technology to save lives, solve problems, win friends, and punish the lawless. The earliest books concentrated on shipboard wireless themes; the youthful characters employed the new invention to warn of storms, pirates, and smugglers. By the 1920s, stories of broadcasting to an audience appeared in a few titles, but mostly plots centered on the hobby of radio-set construction and sending and receiving messages—often in the service of law enforcement, with the moral of the story demonstrating that young people use radio for the greater good.

The earliest such volume, John Trowbridge's *Story of a Wireless Telegraph Boy* (1908) appears to be the first children's book focusing on radio. This was followed by Harrie Irving Hancock's *The Motor Boat Club and the Wireless; or, The Don, Dash and Dare Cruise* (1909); James Otis' *The Wireless Station at Silver Fox Farm* (1910); and one of the famous Tom Swift series—Victor Appleton's (pseudonym for Howard Garis) *Tom Swift and His Wireless Message; or, The Castaways of Earthquake Island* (1911). After 1912 the pace picked up, with several other wireless and radio-related boys titles, including the first multivolume radio series—the six-title *The Ocean Wireless Boys*, in which high school boy Jack Ready and friends use wireless to find a lost ocean liner, warn ships away from icebergs, and fight in World War 1. Likely influenced by the *Titanic* disaster, many of the later wireless stories show how radio can help ensure the safety of ships at sea.

By far the best-known and most hotly collected titles today are the two *Radio Boys* series that appeared in the 1920s under the names of Gerald Breckenridge and Alan Chapman (the latter a pseudonym) for a number of different syndicate authors. Unlike the earlier wireless tales, most of the Chapman series took place on dry land (though each featured a different short preface by *S.S. Republic* wireless hero Jack Binns). The first volume had the boys building a radio in order to win a cash prize, and in others, the boys share their hobby by taking their radio equipment to homes for the aged, hospitals, and other venues where the less fortunate would not otherwise have access to this wondrous new device. Chapman's radio boys were of working-class background, and many of their adventures took place near their small town in New York. In all 13 books of the Chapman series,

the same two story elements are repeated and resolved: a local group of bullies is thwarted using nonviolent methods, and a criminal is brought to justice using radio, resulting in accolades from the community. During the eight-year run of the Chapman series, his boys remained the same age and in the same year in school.

The Breckenridge radio boys series is quite different. Though written during the same period, these boys are of upper-middle-class background: their fathers are doctors, lawyers, and bankers. The Breckenridge radio boys grow up, age, and progress in school during the series. And whereas the Chapman boys spend some time away from their small town, the Breckenridge youth travel the world, go to Yale, and become embroiled in foreign adventure. In a story very atypical of a juvenile series, *The Radio Boys as Soldiers of Fortune* (1925), radio boy-now-man Jack, having graduated from college, gets married and moves to Mexico to learn an aspect of the family business. Jack befriends local citizens who are trying to oust the current dictator and return a popular democracy to power. In a bizarre twist, Jack invents television, called a "televisor," and uses it to spy on the dictator and thus ensure his removal and replacement by democratic forces. This early portrayal of television is quite realistic.

What unites both series is the hobby of radio and its use in keeping communities safe while promoting law and order. What differentiates them is their focus and the career paths depicted in the stories. Whereas the Chapman boys stay in high school and experiment with radio locally, the Breckenridge boys graduate from college and go into banking, medicine, and the law. Not a career in radio for these savvy lads, but the hobby of radio as entertainment, as a way to spend their newfound wealth. Another difference may have been in the focus of the series publisher: Chapman was a pseudonym used by the Edward Stratemeyer Syndicate, the major owner of juvenile series in the first third of the 20th century. Stratemeyer would develop a story synopsis and then hire writers to do the book under the pseudonym, and so volumes in the same series were often written by different writers. Gerald Breckenridge was not part of the syndicate; he used his own name, and it is possible that he enjoyed writing about his boys' aging and progressing through life. Unlike the syndicate writers, Breckenridge likely had more artistic freedom, as long as he sold books.

At least two other *Radio Boys* series were published, and by 1922 a *Radio Girls* series, though of only four titles, appeared. By the next decade, when broadcasting was more fully formed, Ruthe S. Wheeler's *Janet Hardy in Radio City* (1935) featured a high school performer who gets the lead in a film, writes a radio script, and ends up in Radio City for its premiere. Betty Baxter Anderson's *Four Girls and a Radio* (1944) included broadcast entertainment consisting of accordion and vocal, and Julie Campbell's *Ginny Gordon and the Broadcast Mystery* (1956) featured a young woman who discovers she has talent as a radio interviewer and a solver of mysteries.

Radio broadcasting was commonplace when Franklin W. Dixon's *The Hardy Boys and the Short Wave Mystery* (1944) was introduced, but there was still hobby interest. Tracking down the source of an illegal transmission used in a smuggling operation, the boys aid law enforcement and further post-World War II interest in amateur radio. *The Hardy Boys* was but one of several longer juvenile fiction series that featured at least one story centering on radio; others included *The Bobbsey Twins, The Navy Boys, The Brighton Boys,* and *Bert Wilson.* Series that continued into the 1950s, such as *Tom Swift Jr.* and *Rick Brant Electronic Adventures,* used radio and combined it, actually overwhelmed it, with undersea adventure, microelectronics, space science, and robotics, but radio transmission was always at the basis of their experiments, and saving the day—for local law enforcement, the government, the armed services, and the community—was always the overriding use portrayed for radio.

Nearly all such books followed a basic pattern. Running 250 or more pages in most cases, with a frontispiece drawing or painting featuring the heroes at a key point in the story, the books offered fast-moving adventure stories wrapped in gaudy dust wrappers (few of which survive today). Their titles were often formatted with a main title followed by *or* and a subtitle hinting at the excitement within. The writing was often exaggerated and certainly old-fashioned by today's standards, and stories sometimes ended with a cliff-hanging reference to the next book in the series. The heroes or heroines rarely aged, though a series might appear over nearly a decade. Using cheap paper and inexpensively bound, these books were intended to be enjoyed and discarded, and few survive today in good condition.

More than entertainment, the depiction of radio in early juvenile novels may have influenced and reinforced some of the cultural and social convictions held by young people. More than merely a technical device, radio in these novels was almost always related to the ideals and preservation of community and family, career choice, patriotism, and attitudes about law and crime, and the stories may have encouraged their young readers toward discovery and invention as adults. There is a clear "right and wrong" point of view in these books, and the books champion the radio hero who uses wireless and later broadcasting to do good for communities, to preserve a way of life, to promote a common good, and to save lives.

What was the real significance of radio as depicted in such novels? First, the simple stories mirrored the public fantasy and its knowledge and sometimes misunderstanding of communication and later entertainment using this 20th-century invention. The stories traced the evolution of radio from a spark-gapped, Morse-coded curiosity into a powerful medium to which everyone listened. These stories of young men and women of high school age mostly provided escape, but in the process, both the hobby and the business of radio and broadcasting were portrayed as a force for public service, for the good of community, and a way to reinforce our view of ourselves. Overwritten though they are, these books remain a wonderful window on the excitement created first by wireless and later by radio broadcasting. The "gee-whiz" nature of the stories and the central role of radio in each is a good indicator of the general public fascination with cat's whiskers, DXing, silent nights, and crystal sets.

Further Reading

Adams, Mike, "Will the Real Radio Boys Please Stand Up?" *Antique Wireless Classified* 8–9 (September 1991, December 1991, May 1992, and December 1992).

Dizer, John T., Jr., *Tom Swift and Company: "Boys Books" by Stratemeyer and Others*, Jefferson, North Carolina: McFarland, 1982.

Lisle, Larry, "Reading Radio Fiction," *QST* (April 1994).

McGrath, J.J., "Radio Boys Revisited," *QST* (July 1976).

Prager, Arthur, *Rascals at Large; or, The Clue in the Old Nostalgia*, New York: Doubleday, 1971.

Sterling, Christopher H., "Dime Novel Radio," *Old Timer's Bulletin: Official Journal of the Antique Wireless Association* 13 (September 1973).

Sterling, Christopher H., *Children's Novels Devoted to or Including Telegraph, Telephone, Wireless, Radio or Television, 1879–1995*, 5th edition, Washington, D.C.: George Washington University School of Media and Public Affairs, 1996.

MICHAEL H. ADAMS AND
CHRISTOPHER H. STERLING

CHILDREN'S PROGRAMS

Children and teenagers have always been particular fans of radio (and targets for radio's advertisers).

From children's programs in the "golden age" before television to the advent of rock and roll music programming through today's diet of educational and entertainment options, radio has been a consistent element of youth culture.

Radio Before Television

Programs

The early days of radio offered a host of programs specially designed for young audiences, as well as several family-friendly options that encouraged parents and children alike to gather in front of the centrally located radio receiver. In the 1930s and 1940s, children everywhere rushed home from after-school activities and errands to listen closely to a series of three to five consecutively run quarter-hour serials largely sponsored by breakfast food companies, collectively called the *Children's Hour*. In the ever-popular category of children's adventure programs, young listeners followed the interplanetary exploits of *Buck Rogers in the Twenty-fifth Century*, the aviation adventures of *Captain Midnight*, the high school heroics of *Jack Armstrong, the All-American Boy*, or the daunting detective work of *Little Orphan Annie*. Westerns such as *Tom Mix, Sky King*, and the wildly popular *Lone Ranger* sparked the imaginations of children across the country and made "Kemo Sabe" a household phrase.

Science fiction was also a favorite genre for young radio listeners. Adapted from comic books was *Buck Rogers in the Twenty-fifth Century*, on which the hero Buck and his faithful assistant and love interest Wilma fought the evil powers of Killer Kane on the planet Niagara. Other early sci-fi favorites of children included *Flash Gordon, Tom Corbett, Space Patrol*, and *Space Cadet*.

Themes and Messages

Typical themes and messages in the wartime and immediate postwar programs included defending "good"—freedom, justice, honor, and other "American values"—from "evil." A series of episodes, for instance, had Tom Mix fighting an enemy balloon perched over the plains or had Superman rushing off to rescue a captured Lois Lane. The Lone Ranger and Tonto battled the wilds of the desert, and Dick Tracy solved crimes and foiled villains in a number of contexts. Perils and pitfalls plagued characters but were expertly averted by the stars of the shows. The hero concept was omnipresent, with viewers left hoping that they would be as strong, as brave, and as principled as those largely male characters who saved the day time and time again.

In fact, during the period to 1948, the potential for violent and aggressive messages to influence child listeners was a prominent and controversial concern. Newspapers and magazines of the 1930s and 1940s invited experts to comment on the issue, with most suggesting there was little ground for concern, citing psychoanalytic and cathartic theories. The discourse was very similar to the controversy that would later arise about television violence, yet it occurred well before the scholarly attention of psychologists and other researchers to the influence of the media and prior to the research and theories that were advanced to explain and demonstrate the influence of media violence on aggression.

When the country was at war, enemies on such programs as *Terry and the Pirates* and *Chandu the Magician* were from the Far East; in *Little Orphan Annie* or *Jack Armstrong, the All-American Boy*, villains had German, Russian, or Italian accents. Some were blatantly referred to as Nazis or obliquely called spies. The "damsel in distress" was a frequent theme, and often highly stereotypical gender representations prevailed. One exception was Little Orphan Annie, who solved crimes à la Nancy Drew and was even more adventurous and plucky than her comic strip character.

Program Openings and Sound Effects

Attention-getting introductions perked the ears and piqued the interest of youngsters across the country. "Look! Up in the sky…it's a bird…it's a plane…it's *Superman*!" heralded the beginning of a child favorite, as did the sing-along openings of *Little Orphan Annie* ("Who's that little chatter-box…The one with the pretty auburn locks…Who can it be? …It's Little Orphan Annie") or *Jack Armstrong* ("Raise the flag for Hudson High, boys…Show them how we stand"). *Terry and the Pirates* opened to the waterfront sounds and hearty bellows of a busy harbor.

The artful use of sound characterized much of the radio offerings of the day, encouraging the "theater of the mind" that fed off young imaginations. The radio tower communications of *Hop Harrigan* added to the realism and authentic feel of the program. The sirens and screeching brakes of police squad cars in *Dick Tracy* sent many a pulse racing. And of course, the gun sound effect after "Faster than a speeding bullet" and the train sound effect following "More powerful than a locomotive"

143

reinforced the power and strength of the visual image of Superman aroused in children's minds.

Sponsors, Premiums, Announcers

Almost equally entertaining were the commercial jingles and premium offers intertwined with children's adventure plots by such advertisers as Ralston Purina (sponsor of *Tom Mix*), General Mills' Wheaties (*Jack Armstrong*), Kellogg's Pep cereal (*Superman*), and Ovaltine (*Little Orphan Annie, Captain Midnight*). Children saved numerous box tops and anxiously awaited the arrival of program-associated toys and gadgets. Successful receipt of a nail from the shoe of *Tom Mix* horse Tony, a *Dick Tracy* badge, or a secret decoder ring that made sense of encrypted messages in *Little Orphan Annie* instantly elevated a child to envied status in the neighborhood. Millions of boxes of hot or cold cereal and tons of hot cocoa and peanut butter were consumed with the ulterior motive of a *Captain Midnight* Key-O-Matic Code-A-Graph, a *Little Orphan Annie* Shake-Up Mug, a *Green Hornet* ring, or a *Tom Mix* Straight-Shooter Medal. Premiums also encouraged further listening and careful attention to the program, because secret messages were woven into the fabric of plots and called for premium decoders for deciphering. Many children's radio programs also offered club memberships to avid followers and follow-up premiums that complemented past offers.

The sponsorship of an entire radio program by a single advertiser allowed for a blending of program and ad copy that heightened the ability of the ad to entertain. Episodes of *Tom Mix* both began and ended with a musical message promoting the qualities of Ralston cereals. At the beginning of the show, the "Tom Mix Straight-Shooters" asked kids (in a Texas accent) to "Start the mornin' with Hot Ralston" amid the sounds of horse hooves and cowboy yips and yells. At the end of the show, the singers urged listeners to "Take a tip from Tom… go and tell your mom…Hot Ralston can't be beat." The characters, the music, the sound effects, and the sponsors' messages all contributed to the overall theme, in this case a Western, a strategy successfully pursued by many radio programs.

The announcer/host was often used to create a transition from the message of the sponsor to the program and back, or even to speak the commercial message, as well as to introduce the program or unveil the latest premium offer. *The Lone Ranger* and Tonto were introduced by Fred Foy, Brace Beemer, and others, who occupied the announcer role by inviting audience members to "return with

us now to those thrilling days of yesteryear. From out of the past come the thundering hoofbeats." Before his *60 Minutes* tenure, Mike Wallace was a convincing voice for *Sky King* and sponsor Peter Pan Peanut Butter on National Broadcasting Company (NBC) and Mutual in the mid-1940s. Announcer Pierre André read copy that persuaded young listeners to fully experience the escapades of *Captain Midnight* with membership into the Secret Squadron or the purchase of a decoder badge.

Weekend Programming

The programs for children during weekend hours generally involved storytelling, singing, and playing educational games. The target age group was often lower on the weekends as well, with many shows appealing to pre-kindergarten and early elementary school children.

Saturday mornings were populated by Archie, Jughead, Veronica, and friends on *Archie Andrews,* replete with story lines featuring the harebrained hijinks of Jughead and the budding romances between the more suave characters. There was also *No School Today,* in which characters Big Jon and Sparkie would tell various adventure tales to very young listeners. Boston's WCOP ran the *Children's Song Bag* on Saturday mornings, while Mutual affiliates carried a show in which birds sang the notes of popular songs, called the *Hartz Mountain Canary Hour, Canary Pet Show,* and *American Radio Warblers* at various times during its 15-year history (late 1930s to early 1950s). Beginning on WGN in Chicago in 1932 was the *Singing Story Lady,* hosted by Ireene Wicker who, true to her title, sang songs and told stories.

Sunday afternoon's gem was *Quiz Kids,* which offered brain-teasing knowledge questions asked of panelists under 16 years of age (aired from 1940–54). The series began on NBC Blue and ended on Columbia Broadcasting System (CBS): time slots changed, but it was generally broadcast on Sunday in late afternoon or early evening. Hosted by Joe Kelly, *Quiz Kids* featured very intelligent young panelists who defined difficult words and performed other mentally challenging tasks. Sponsors of the show included Alka Seltzer and One-a-Day vitamins.

In many markets, radio personalities and other prominent people (including New York City Mayor Fiorello LaGuardia during a newspaper strike in 1945) read the comics to children on Sunday mornings. Among the most beloved children's radio programs was *Let's Pretend,* which was hosted by Nila Mack and enjoyed a 20-year stint (1934–54) on CBS. In the program, a group of child actors (the "Pretenders") acted out a half-hour story built around the names of three objects sent in by young audience members. The actors also played roles in other charming fairy tales written by Mack. The precursor to *Let's Pretend*, a show called *Adventures of Helen and Mary*, had run for five years before Mack changed the name and made the concept more popular with children by involving more young actors. The enthusiastic opening included a theme song ("Hello, hello…Come on, let's go…It's time for *Let's Pretend*") and a rousing "Hello, Pretenders!" shouted by recurring host Uncle Bill Adams, to which the chorus of child actors would respond "Hello, Uncle Bill!"

Radio After Television (Since 1948)

Music Programming

After television arrived and radio came to be primarily devoted to music, teenage audiences remained among the most loyal fans to radio's new programming. Music is the primary force drawing young people to radio. The lure increases with age: 85 to 95 percent of those aged 2 to 18 who listen to the radio are listening to music programs. From rock and roll in the 1950s through alternative and rap in the 1990s and into the new millennium, teens and music have gone hand in hand. Teenagers use music for relaxation and entertainment as well as to keep up to date on popular trends. Another gratification teens derive from music is its social utility; it is something to talk about with their friends. But perhaps what is unique about teenagers and music is the relationship of music to self-identity. Young people use musical styles and favorite performing artists as ways of defining and expressing themselves in a manner that has no equivalent at any other time in life. Evidence for the relationship between music and identity is not limited to teenagers' uses of radio. It is also apparent in concert T-shirts and other styles of dress, posters and sometimes even lyrics displayed by teens in their bedrooms and school lockers, and their treasured compact disc collections. Research suggests that as teens move toward adulthood, their preferred means of listening to music will not be radio but their own sets of compact discs, tapes, and records.

Music programs such as *American Top 40* (launched in 1970) and *Rick Dees' Weekly Top 40* (launched in 1983) have long drawn faithful young audiences on weekends. The contemporary hit format (Top 40) is highly favored by children. When they become teens, they also like album-oriented/classic rock, country, rap, and alternative.

In addition to Top 40 favorites, children's radio offers musical options not likely to be found on stations targeting an older audience, with a heavy emphasis on songs from Disney or other kids' movies and novelty tunes. A list of the top 30 songs on Radio Disney affiliate WSDZ in St. Louis for 20 January 2003 featured the songs of pop stars Britney Spears, Jennifer Lopez, and 'N Sync, as well as the child-friendly tunes "Hampsterdance Song" by Hampton and the Hampsters and "Who Let the Dogs Out" by Baha Men.

Talk, News, and Educational Programs

Young people also have a wide variety of nonmusic radio programming options. Statistics show that 11- to 18-year-olds in the United States spend an average of five to seven minutes with talk radio per day, five minutes with radio news, and six minutes with other types of radio programs. Many local markets offer their own version of WXPN Philadelphia's *Kid's Corner*, an entertaining combination of talk, games, and novelty songs for 8- to 14-year-olds. One of the most popular features of *Kid's Corner* is the news segment, in which 10- to 17-year-olds who have participated in reporter training workshops present stories they've gathered on such topics as women's issues and politics. Somewhat similarly, National Public Radio (NPR) features *Teenage Diaries*, a program in which teens act as newscasters reporting on themselves. They conduct interviews with friends and family and for several months chronicle many aspects of their lives on audiotape, providing reflections on what it means to be a teenager in contemporary society. The older children become, the more often they tune into such nonmusic radio programs.

Countless stations provide call-in or talk shows tackling youth-oriented issues and subjects of concern, including such diverse topics as cheating in school, romance and young crushes, and struggles with self-esteem and "fitting in." WXPN host Kathy O'Connell has encountered callers interested in talking about light-hearted issues such as their computers or their pets, as well as those eager to discuss more weighty topics such as animal rights and AIDS. Other youngsters call in not to discuss issues but to sing a song, play an instrument, or tell a joke. The program has boasted some 400 attempted calls per night.

Educational children's radio enjoys a niche-market position. Endeavors such as the *Kinetic City Super Crew*, sponsored by the American Association for the Advancement of Science, have proven successful at stimulating children's interest in scientific concepts as well as provoking them to work on science projects at home. This particular 30-minute program was launched in 1993 on several public radio stations across the nation and targeted third to fifth graders. The program showcased four students' attempts at solving problems of the world using science, with the goal of encouraging interest in science as well as advancing knowledge and honing critical thinking skills. The Super Crew, comprising Annalee, Joaquin, Chantel, and Alvin, aged 12 to 16, solved mysteries by "traveling" to different locations around the world and gathering information. A scientific study of over 250 fourth graders found that there were educational benefits for both boys and girls in listening to *Kinetic City Super Crew.*

Radio can also be a source of information regarding politics. Studies have found that children turn to television and radio much more often than to newspapers or magazines when gathering information about politics and political campaigns. The national civics education program *Kids Voting USA* found that children overwhelmingly turn to broadcast media for current events and civics information gathering to complete their school assignments. Children and teenagers are often exposed to the news media when their parents tune in, and they are present in the broadcast news audience in surprisingly large numbers. They use radio and television to provide them with information about public figures, policies, and events. In turn, this knowledge helps shape their opinions, values, and behaviors.

As with adults, radio and other media can also set the agenda of youngsters by highlighting some occurrences as newsworthy while shunning others. Through news bias, be it intentional or inadvertent, radio can also influence young people's interpretations of events. Because children often lack first-hand information to counter media messages, these influences can be stronger and more dramatic for child than for adult audiences.

Cultural Programming and the Arts

Radio has been an outlet as well as a vehicle for appreciation of the arts, including theater and literature. Many radio plays are written for young performers or written by young playwrights. All encourage expression, imagination, and creativity. *Children's Radio Theater*, for example, began in 1977 at WPFW in Washington, D.C., and was picked up by more than 100 public radio affiliates by the mid-1980s. The series featured 30-minute plays written by children aged 5 to 17 and performed by professional actors of all ages. The scripts were chosen by teachers, librarians, and actors affiliated with the nationwide Henny Penny Playwriting Contest. The troupe broadcast its last performance in December 1997 on WPFW in New York City.

In 1994 *Rabbit Ears Radio* was launched, a radio program founded by Rabbit Ears, the Connecticut-based publishers of video and book-and-tapes. It enjoyed a two-year run distributed by Public Radio International. It featured stories narrated by celebrities and was hosted by Mel Gibson and Meg Ryan, who described the history of the story and the music chosen to accompany it and also introduced the narrator. Examples included *John Henry,* narrated by Denzel Washington with music by B.B. King, and *The Velveteen Rabbit,* narrated by Meryl Streep with music by George Winston. Many local radio stations also offer programs in which stories are read to children over the air, often created through collaborations between stations and local libraries or colleges. Examples include Northeast Indiana Public Radio's "Folk Tales from the Briar Patch" offered on two weekday afternoons and "Magic Hat Storytime" broadcast on Sundays on the campus station at Rowan University in Glassboro, New Jersey.

Children's Radio Networks

In addition to individual children's programs, there have also been attempts—some successful, some not—at establishing children's radio networks. In 1990 an early entry into the all-children's radio scene was launched: Orlando-based Kid's Choice Broadcasting network boasted an advisory board at the time that included Peggy Charren of Action for Children's Television fame as well as Peter Yarrow of the musical group Peter, Paul, and Mary, who wrote original music and the theme song for the network. Among the programming alternatives offered by Kid's Choice were a 6 A.M. to 10 A.M. segment called *New Day Highway* (a family show with news, music, and special features), *Curbside Carnival* from 2 P.M. to 6 P.M. (offering story and exercise segments and music from around the globe), and a 10 A.M. to 2 P.M. slot targeted to preschoolers featuring music and information on numbers, colors, and shapes.

Foremost among obstacles preventing adoption of a kids' radio format cited by executives was the difficulty in providing potential advertisers with viable listenership data, because Arbitron didn't measure the presence of young children in the radio audience. Station owners and managers have noted that many advertisers, both local and national, would have welcomed the opportunity to address child audiences with their advertising messages. The potential of another outlet, in addition to television, for peddling the breakfast cereals, snack foods, clothing, and other products favored by a young audience was appealing to many advertisers. The tradition in the industry to base pricing, placement, and other crucial advertising decisions on ratings data that were lacking for children's radio was, however, a real impediment to the growth of children's radio at that time.

Therefore, the decision of Arbitron in 1993 to gather data on children aged 2 to 11 years had the potential to be groundbreaking. Arbitron contracted with the Children's Satellite network's Radio Aahs, the nation's only 24-hour children's network at the time. At the request of advertisers, then-president of the Children's Satellite network Bill Barnett arrived at an agreement with Arbitron whereby they would target households with children aged 2 to 11 in return for a subscription fee. To address the needs of the young audience, Arbitron adopted new strategies of training and assistance: older children filled out their own diaries, and Arbitron also conducted sessions to inform parents about completing surveys for younger children. For Radio Aahs, a network that had already been successful at reaching 15 percent of the nation just three years after its debut in Minneapolis, the ratings information offered the potential of additional growth and strengthening of advertising base for the future. Yet the Arbitron agreement turned out to be short-lived and Radio Aahs resumed the practice of relying on call-in statistics to woo advertisers.

Modern Networks and Programs

Despite the breaking of new ground by Arbitron and Radio Aahs, measuring the 2- to 11-year-old audience is still exceptionally rare today. Nevertheless, the 1990s spawned a remarkable growth spurt in children's radio. The growth was due in part to the mere possibility of obtaining ratings data for young child audiences. It was also attributed to the many pioneers and trailblazers whose occasional forays into children's radio had been largely successful. There was also a commonly held view that the nation's youngsters had been an underserved radio audience for too long. For all of these reasons, a resurgence of additional programs and networks geared toward children occurred in the mid-1990s. Some of these fledgling networks are presently enjoying growing financial success and increasing patronage by young audiences, whereas others have gone belly up.

One of the clear success stories is American Broadcasting Companies' (ABC) Radio Disney, launched in 1997 and targeting 2- to 11-year-olds, boasting 45 subscribing stations and an audience of 1.6 million nationwide in the year 2000, offering pop, soundtrack, and novelty songs as well as safety and education tips and news. Music programming accounts for the vast majority of Radio Disney's offerings, and the network showcases such kid-friendly acts as Weird Al Yankovic, 'N Sync, Backstreet Boys, and teen heart-throbs Christina Aguilera and Britney Spears. The network uses focus groups with parents to determine whether music is appropriate for its audience and has often aired edited or alternate versions of songs to ensure that the family-friendly principle is met. Reactions of audience members are monitored carefully through email and phone calls to the station. Radio Disney also gives away prizes that range from the somewhat typical—compact discs, Pokémon cards, and concert tickets—to the downright luxurious, such as snowboarding trips, visits to space camp, and even a day with a recording artist. Audience research data is gathered by Statistical Research, Inc. and has helped attract sponsors.

Fox Kids network's weekly *Fox Kids Countdown* program had garnered well over 200 affiliates by 1997 and reached an estimated three million listeners, mostly in the 8- to 14-year-old age group. The host is Los Angeles disc jockey Chris Leary, who helps draw in the Sunday morning audience with movie promotions and spots advertising Fox television shows. Songs requested by kids, call-in shows, and guest celebrities help make the program, now called *Fox All Access Countdown*, appealing to its affiliates, 95 percent of which are FM outlets.

In the mid 1990s, the Children's Broadcasting Corporation delivered 24-hour programming through Radio Aahs via satellite to over 40 percent of the country, allowing children aged 2 to 11 to listen to young disc jockeys, games, contests, news, and educational or self-esteem messages. A glimpse at the Radio Aahs programming schedule revealed such educationally entertaining fare as *All-American Alarm Clock* (6 A.M. to 9 A.M.), *Alphabet Soup* (noon to 1 P.M.), and *Evening Theater* (8 P.M. to 9 P.M.). The network also featured weekly live broadcasts from Universal Studios Hollywood and Universal Studios Florida. Later nightly slots were designed for adults tackling parenting issues.

Yet the Children's Broadcasting Corporation soon faced stiff competition from the growing Radio Disney network. Indeed, the two companies were in litigation from 1996 to 2002 as the Children's Broadcasting Corporation filed suit against Radio Disney for breach of contract and use of trade secrets, claiming that after the Corporation hired ABC as a consultant, ABC used that information to design Radio Disney. The Children's Broadcasting Corporation ultimately received an award of $9.5 million, yet the judgment was too little, too late for the struggling network, which had gone off the air in 1998.

Despite new growth for more fortunate kid-friendly options, the late 1990s also saw the demise of a pioneer force in children's radio, KidStar Radio. The Seattle-based KidStar Interactive Media organization had distributed 24-hour children's programming from its home at KKDZ (AM) to AM stations in such major markets as San Francisco, Boston, Houston, and Detroit. The network made its debut in May 1993 and used 45 different interactive phone lines to record kids' input on songs, elicit their views on social issues, and even allow them to leave a message for their state senators. Sponsored programs included *Virtual Safari*, in which kids encountered adventures with animals (sponsored by GapKids), and *Zack and Zoey's Survival Guide*, in which the title characters were eighth graders who passed on words of wisdom from their experiences at school (sponsored by the Disney Channel). Citing the loss of a crucial investment deal, KidStar folded in 1997, leaving its affiliates scrambling to replace the child-oriented music (from disc jockeys ranging in age from 9 to 14), news, sports, and entertainment programming that KidStar Radio had provided.

Today, 2- to 7-year-olds in the United States listen to the radio an average of 24 minutes per day. Eight to 10-year-olds listen for 26 minutes. From age 11 to 13, average radio use is 44 minutes per day, whereas for 14- to 18-year-olds it's 65 minutes per day. The most common times for radio listening among youngsters are after school on weekdays (3 P.M. to 7 P.M.) and on weekends from late morning through the afternoon (10 A.M. to 3 P.M.).

Radio is still an important and consistent presence in the lives of young people. Many fundamental characteristics of radio remain unchanged. In addition to musical programming, modern radio programs for children are still populated by heroes and villains, main characters and sidekicks, and the occasional presentations of aggression and gender stereotypes. The adventures and trials and tribulations deemed interesting or relevant to children and teens are still the focus of many shows, much like in the days of old-time radio. Radio is still used to inform young people of topics, events, and central figures in public life. It remains an outlet or a vehicle for creative expression and appreciation of the arts.

And radio is still a source of distraction, a means of escape, and a companion. Frequently entertaining and often educational, radio remains a means of exercising the imagination of America's youth.

See also: American Top 40; Captain Midnight; Green Hornet; Jack Armstrong, the All-American Boy; Let's Pretend; Little Orphan Annie; Lone Ranger; Radio Disney; Science Fiction Programs; Westerns

Further Reading

Anderson, Arthur, *Let's Pretend: A History of Radio's Best Loved Children's Show by a Longtime Cast Member*, Jefferson, North Carolina: McFarland, 1994.
Boemer, Marilyn Lawrence, *The Children's Hour: Radio Programs for Children 1929–56*, Metuchen, New Jersey: Scarecrow, 1989.
Clark, W.R., "Radio Listening Habits of Children," *Journal of Social Psychology* 12 (1940).
Cooper, Jim, "Arbitron to Measure Children's Radio," *Broadcasting and Cable* (23 August 1993).
Eisenberg, Azriel L., *Children and Radio Programs*, New York: Columbia University Press, 1936.
Garfinkel, Simson, "Children's Science Radio," *Technology Review* 96, no. 7 (1993).
Gordon, Dorothy Lerner, *All Children Listen*, New York: G.W. Stewart, 1942.
Gruenberg, Sidonie Matsner, "Radio and the Child," *Annals of the American Academy of Political and Social Science* 177 (January 1935).
Lyness, Paul I., "Radio Habits of the Young Audience," *Broadcasting* (25 September 1950).
McCormick, Moira, "Children's Radio Continues to Liven Up Airwaves," *Billboard* (9 November 1996).
Nachman, Gerald, *Raised on Radio: In Quest of the Lone Ranger, Jack Benny...*, New York: Pantheon Books, 1998.
Petrozzello, Donna, "Children's Radio: A Format Whose Time Has Come?" *Broadcasting and Cable* (7 October 1996).
Petrozzello, Donna, "Kid Star Calls It Quits," *Broadcasting and Cable* (24 February 1997).
"Radio in the Life of the Child," in *Educational Broadcasting*, Chicago: University of Chicago Press, 1936 (symposium).
Roberts, Donald F., et al., *Kids and Media at the New Millennium*, 2 vols, Menlo Park, California: Henry J. Kaiser Family Foundation, 1999.
Stark, Phyllis, "Slow Growth for Youth-Oriented Talk Shows: Finding Engaging Topics, Vocal Callers among Challenges," *Billboard* (7 March 1992).
Taylor, Chuck, "Radio Disney Tunes In Young Listeners and Turns Youth Pop Craze on Its Ear," *Billboard* (25 March 2000).

ERICA SCHARRER

CITIZENS BAND RADIO
Private Two-Way Radio Service

The Federal Communications Commission (FCC) defines "The Citizens Band Radio Service" (CB) as "a private, two-way, short-distance voice communications service for personal or business activities. The CB Radio Service may also be used for voice paging." In the United States and several other countries, a license is not required. In other countries, a license must be obtained or a fee paid, but no examination is required. Other countries with similar services include Canada, Australia, New Zealand, Japan, the United Kingdom, France, Germany, Italy, and Russia. Though not broadcasting, CB radio is one of the most widely recognized uses of wireless technology.

Stations in the CB service are limited to a power output of 4 watts, with additional restrictions on antenna height. Most stations use AM, but a single sideband (SSB) is allowed with a peak effective power of 12 watts output. In some countries, FM is used. CB radios are used for both fixed and mobile communication over relatively short distances. In the United States, communication at ranges greater than 250 km is prohibited by law.

Prior to the rapid growth of the CB service in the United States during the early 1970s, a Class D license was required, and a small fee had to be paid. A federal court decision made the fees illegal. Faced with no revenue to support the administration of issuing licenses, the FCC issued a blanket authorization allowing the CB service to operate within the constraints of 28 simple rules.

In the early days of the CB service, the FCC was divided into 18 regions. So, for example, call signs beginning with 18W indicated a station was somewhere in region 18 (region 18's central office was in Chicago, for example). The number of applications for CB licenses soon exhausted that call sign format. New calls signs were issued that followed an alphabetical-numerical mix and were issued sequentially. As the service became even more popular, the FCC stopped issuing official call signs completely, but encourages users of the service to identify using the call sign form of *K* followed by the operator's initials and zip code. This can lead to duplication of call signs, but the FCC doesn't seem to be concerned about that.

The Original UHF Service

Citizens Radio is a family of services, not just the one that rose to great heights of popularity during the 1970s. As originally conceived and defined by the FCC—long before cellular mobile telephony—hobby-type conversations were explicitly forbidden in the service. Small businesses, many of which provided a service of some type—locksmiths, delivery services, and plumbers, for example—used the Citizens Radio Service to expedite and run their businesses efficiently. No-one "owned" or was assigned to a particular channel. All users shared the channels available.

The FCC established the first Citizens Radio service in 1947. A group of frequencies in the 460- to 470-MHz range was assigned. This service still exists and is properly called the General Mobile Radio Service (GMRS). A license is required. Recently, the microwave band of 31.0–31.3 GHz was also opened for GMRS operation.

Although UHF frequencies were widely used in military equipment during World War II, the near-microwave nature of the technology involved made production of commercially manufactured equipment expensive. Hobbyists were capable of building the required equipment but faced stiff certification requirements in order to legally use their creations.

Even so, the new service was appealing to some early pioneers. John M. Mulligan, who was employed as a radio engineer, became the first recorded CB licensee in 1958. Mulligan, who had ties to industry, built his own equipment. By year's end, 40 citizens in the United States held FCC licenses in the new service.

The same year, a single 3-W experimental station heralded what would become Class D service, operating in the 27-MHz range, often referred to by its wavelength of 11 m. A total of 23 discrete channels were originally assigned to the Class D service. In 1977, to help relieve the congestion that had developed, The FCC increased the number of channels to 40. Several additional attempts to add more channels have not been successful.

For a few years in the 1950s, the 11-m band was assigned to the Amateur Radio Service as compensation for other spectrum reassigned from the Amateur Service. Amateurs retained the nearby 10-m frequency range.

By the 1960s, hobby magazines were filled with articles on building radio transceivers for the service as well as advertisements for kits that could be assembled. Heathkit, EICO, and Allied made many of the kits available. The EICO transceiver lives on today in reruns of television's *Andy Griffith Show*—it's one of the units seen in the Mayberry courthouse.

Gas Shortage Fuels Popularity

The 1972 gas shortage in the United States played a major role in making the CB service popular. Originally, truck drivers relied on their CB radios to help each other locate fuel. In a short time, the general public caught on and began to purchase CB radios as well.

Seven million units were sold in one year during the peak years of the 1970s. Even though CB has returned to relative obscurity in recent years, an estimated 3.5 million units are still sold each year. Today, the service's value as a traveler's aid and means of emergency communication has largely been supplanted by cellular telephones. CB sales in the trucking and freight industry, however, have never slowed.

Popular culture embraced CB radio, including the jargon developed by truck drivers. Even the FCC has its own "handle"—Uncle Charlie. The song "Convoy," written and performed by C.W. McCall, a marketing executive, helped to fuel sales of CB units. A movie by the same name; another titled simply *Citizens Band*; and the popular movie series *Smokey and the Bandit*, starring Burt Reynolds, Jackie Gleason, Sally Fields, and Jerry Reed, are further evidence of the impact of CB during the period.

Public Service

Long before the advent of 911 emergency telephone systems and cellular phones, CB radio provided an effective emergency communication system. There are numerous examples of how CB radio has been used for public service.

On 23 January 1962, long before CB's rise to popular icon status, Henry B. "Pete" Kreer, a CB enthusiast, recruited the Hallicrafters Company (a manufacturer of radio equipment) to sponsor the REACT program. Kreer got the idea during a Chicago snowstorm after using his CB radio to help a family stuck on an expressway with a very sick child and a disabled car. The REACT concept was simple. Initially, a team consisting of three members agreed to monitor for CB emergencies. Today, there are thousands of teams, with teams in nearly every community, to monitor for emergencies around the clock.

In 1964, with 800 teams in place, it became apparent that trying to monitor all 23 channels was a difficult if not impossible task. REACT called for the establishment of a voluntary National CB Emergency Channel. Thanks to their efforts, in 1967 the FCC designated channel 9 as the CB emergency channel, restricting communication on the channel to that associated with emergency operations.

Although 9 is the only channel on which use is legally restricted, other channels have become de facto standards. Throughout California and western states, channel 17 is the unofficial "trucker's" channel. Nationwide, channel 19 is used by truckers and other motorists, especially for speed-trap advisories. Channels from 30 to 40 are used for SSB communication. Although most CB activity uses AM modulation, SSB is authorized with the advantage that all radiated power is concentrated on the information being transmitted, rather than having a large portion consumed by a carrier wave.

Over the years, some have attempted to make the CB service into an unlicensed version of the Amateur Radio Service by modifying equipment to operate on frequencies not officially assigned, boosting power beyond what is allowed, and erecting antennae at variance with the law. CB operators and amateur radio enthusiasts or "hams" are often indistinguishable in the public mind. Operators in both services assist in natural disasters and provide communication for public events. Although both serve as valuable communication assets, they remain distinct services with different primary purposes.

See also: Ham Radio

Further Reading

Brown, Robert M., *CB Radio Operator's Guide*, Blue Ridge Summit, Pennsylvania: G/L Tab Books, 1969; 2nd edition, by Brown and Paul Doreweiler, 1975.
Buckwalter, Len, *ABC's of Citizens Band Radio*, Indianapolis, Indiana: Sams, 1962; 4th edition, 1976.
Harwood, Don, *Everything You Always Wanted to Know about Citizens Band Radio*, New York: VTR, 1976.
Herbert, Evan, *The Best Book on CB*, Tucson, Arizona: H.P. Books, 1976.
Lieberman, Jethro Koller, and Neil S. Rhodes, *The Complete CB Handbook*, New York: Avon, 1976; as *The Complete 1980 CB Handbook*, New York: Avon, 1980.
Long, Mark, Jeffrey Keating, and Albert Houston, *The Big Dummy's Guide to British C.B. Radio*, Summertown, Tennessee: Book, 1981; revised edition, as *The World of CB Radio*, edited by Long, Keating, and Bonnie Crystal, 1988.
Perkowski, Robert L., and Lee Philip Stral, *The Joy of CB*, Matteson, Illinois: Greatlakes Living Press, 1976.

JIM GRUBBS

CLASSICAL MUSIC FORMAT

Once a radio program staple, classical music has in recent years been relegated to a relative handful of stations, most of them noncommercial FM outlets. Sometimes called "fine-arts" programming, the format combines the playing of classical music with interviews, cultural programs, and news commentary.

Origins

At the inception of radio, classical music was omnipresent. Even before there were formal programs, stations would broadcast singers or orchestras performing familiar classics. Most early studios had a piano, and a pianist on call, useful for last-minute fill-in performances when a scheduled program for some reason could not be broadcast. Although popular music was also played, the classics were relied upon to fill airtime.

Many stations in larger markets retained full orchestras and featured them regularly. Somewhat ironically in light of the situation decades later—when broadcasts of the classics have become increasingly rare—classical music was the first musical style to achieve large-scale exposure on radio. Many people were exposed to classical music for the first time on the radio, because few people could afford live concert hall performances in the few cities where they were available. The provision of such music over the air was also a way of gaining radio respectability among upper-class listeners.

Although a rather extreme example, when station KYW first broadcast in mid-1921 in Chicago, it offered almost nothing but opera from the Chicago Civic Opera. Unfortunately, KYW soon discovered that the audience that wanted to hear opera all the time was relatively small.

Network Classical Music

Radio's golden age was certainly golden for classical music listeners as the Columbia Broadcasting System (CBS) and the National Broadcasting Company (NBC) vied to present prestigious orchestras in live performances from the late 1920s into the 1950s. A typical offering on a Sunday, such programs were also heard on other evenings, and virtually all of the broadcasts were live. Among the better known and longer-running program series were the following:

Voice of Firestone (1927–54, NBC; 1954–57, American Broadcasting Companies [ABC]) offered a mixture of popular and more serious music, becoming more focused on the classics after 1932. The program's theme music was composed by the sponsor's wife. The radio audience declined after the broadcasts were simulcast on television beginning in 1949.

Cities Service Concerts (1927–56, NBC) offered an hour-long program until 1940, then a half hour. The title varied, but for a seven-year period (1930–37) its top star did not. Young Jessica Dragonette (1910–80) became hugely popular with her renditions of classical solo works and developed a devoted following.

New York Philharmonic (1927–53, CBS) was the major offering of the second network. With the Philharmonic conducted by the noted Arturo

Toscanini until 1936, the broadcasts from Carnegie Hall were useful exposure for the orchestra, helping to sell its growing number of recordings.

Philadelphia Symphony Orchestra (1931–57, largely on CBS) helped to popularize the lush "Philadelphia sound" developed first by Leopold Stokowski and after 1938 by longtime conductor Eugene Ormandy.

Music Appreciation Hour (1928–42, NBC Blue) featured conductor Walter Damrosch (1862–1950) providing and explaining classical music to a youthful audience. Broadcast on Fridays for an hour (the program ended when Damrosch refused to cut it to a half hour), the program was widely used in schools across the country.

Sinfonietta (1935–45, Mutual) was one of the few forays into classical music programming by the cooperative network. The orchestra was conducted by Alfred Wallenstein, and the program filled various half-hour time slots.

NBC Symphony Orchestra (1937–54, NBC) marked the epitome of network classical music presentations. Radio Corporation of America's (RCA) David Sarnoff paid dearly to coax Arturo Toscanini (1867–1957) out of retirement by letting him establish his own orchestra and paying a handsome salary. Also featuring conductors Artur Rodzinski and Leopold Stokowski, some recordings of these broadcasts are still available. Regular broadcasts ceased when Toscanini finally retired in April 1954.

The *Bell Telephone Hour* (1940–58, NBC) was actually a half-hour long and melded light classics and sometimes popular orchestral music selected by conductor Donald Vorhees. Sponsored by American Telephone and Telegraph (AT&T), the program helped promote the dignified view the company had of itself and its role in society.

The Longines Symphonette (1943–49, Mutual; 1949–57, CBS) was unusual among these programs in featuring prerecorded programs.

Classics on Local Stations

For most of radio, however, classical music from the 1930s into the 1950s was at best an occasional offering, usually from a network broadcast. A few university-owned stations (e.g., the University of Wisconsin's WHA in Madison) provided classical music among other educational and cultural programs. But, otherwise, classical music largely disappeared from AM stations.

The development of FM radio from the 1940s into the 1950s, however, offered a new lease on life for classical music. By offering the classics (usually with recordings plus some live performances), FM outlets could differentiate themselves from the more common AM stations. Well into the 1960s, to both broadcasters and listeners, classical music meant FM radio—and vice versa. FM stations often published program guides to help listeners (and to sell advertising, though few made money), and they thrived on audiences developed by the high-fidelity craze that began in the 1950s. Many offered musical performances uninterrupted by announcements or commercials (again distinguishing themselves from AM) for those who wished to tape broadcasts off the air.

Major cities soon enjoyed one or more classical music FM stations, including New York's WQXR (1939); Chicago's WEFM (1940), initially owned by Zenith with call letters featuring the chairman's initials), and WFMT (1951), which by 1958 became the first FM outlet reflected in local market audience ratings; WWDC (1947) and WGMS (1948) in Washington, D.C.; WFLN (1949) in Philadelphia; WCRB (1954) just outside of Boston; and WFMR (1956) in Milwaukee, to name only a few examples.

With the appearance of the first AM–FM non-duplication rules from the Federal Communications Commission in the mid-1960s, however, FM's days as a bastion of classical music were numbered. As FM frequencies became more valuable, thanks to the larger audiences (and thus greater advertising income), they employed a wider variety of more widely popular musical formats. Small-audience classical music stations often either were sold or changed their formats to something more lucrative. Classics once again became relatively elusive.

By the turn of the century, classical music programs appealed to only a small portion of the audience and were predominant on only a few dozen commercial and several hundred public radio stations, all catering to audiences with more education and higher income than the norm (and to the advertisers that want to reach them). A typical classical music station in the early 21st century provided not only music but also a blend of other cultural features designed to appeal to its audience.

For nearly three decades, Robert Lurtsema (1931–2000) hosted *Morning Pro Musica* each morning on Boston's WHDH, carried on public radio stations in New York and New England (and later by satellite to stations across the country). The program was broadcast five hours each day of the week (until 1993, when it shifted to weekends only) with musical selections introduced in Lurtsema's widely recognized slow and easy delivery. Programs often focused on a specific composer or theme, but music predominated. Along with Karl Haas'

Adventures in Good Music, Lurtsema's program made classics readily available to sizeable audiences.

Although it continued to shrink on analog FM channels (to perhaps two dozen outlets), classical music proved viable on a handful of satellite digital radio channels, and looked as though it might find appeal on HD2 channels that were still developing at the end of the first decade of the 21st century.

See also: Adventures in Good Music; FM Radio; Metropolitan Opera Broadcasts; WQXR

Further Reading

Chase, Gilbert, editor, *Music in Radio Broadcasting*, New York: McGraw-Hill, 1946.
DeLong, Thomas A., "The Maestros," in *The Mighty Music Box: The Golden Age of Musical Radio*, by DeLong, Los Angeles: Amber Crest Books, 1980.
Dunning, John, "Concert Broadcasts," in *On the Air: The Encyclopedia of Old-Time Radio*, by Dunning, New York: Oxford University Press, 1998.
LaPrade, Ernest, *Broadcasting Music*, New York: Rinehart, 1947.
Morton, David, "High Culture, High Fidelity, and the Making of Recordings in the American Record Industry," in *Off the Record: The Technology and Culture of Sound Recording in America*, by Morton, New Brunswick, New Jersey: Rutgers University Press, 2000.
Stokowski, Leopold, "New Vistas in Radio," *Atlantic Monthly* (January 1935).
"Toscanini on the Air," *Fortune* (January 1938).

CHRISTOPHER H. STERLING,
2009 REVISIONS BY CHRISTOPHER H. STERLING

CLASSIC ROCK FORMAT

Classic Rock is a music radio format that focuses on harder rock music from the late 1960s through the 1980s. It is a derivation of the Album-Oriented Rock (AOR) format that incorporates rock music from the same period along with current selections.

Classic Rock evolved from several earlier radio programming formulas that were attempts to provide alternatives to tightly formatted Top 40 radio stations of the 1950s and 1960s. One of the first was freeform radio, in which disc jockeys were given total control over the music played. Although music genres varied, freeform stations tended to feature music selections generally not heard on Top 40 stations. Freeform radio was also referred to as underground, progressive, or alternative radio.

The Progressive radio format emerged from freeform radio, but it had some structure designed by a music programmer. The Progressive format incorporated a rotation system for music categories. Disc jockeys followed the category rotation system but still had considerable latitude in the selection of specific songs. Progressive served as a bridge between freeform radio and the more mainstream AOR format that developed in the 1970s.

Like its predecessors, AOR was a rebellion against Top 40 in that it avoided chart hits in favor of longer album cuts by popular artists. It brought with it *music sweeps*—uninterrupted series of songs—and a less-structured, more laid-back announcer delivery style. Initially, AOR appealed to a young adult, primarily male audience. During the 1970s AOR grew in popularity as Top 40 waned.

During the 1980s, however, AOR began to lose younger listeners as Top 40 regained popularity with the emergence of MTV. Younger listeners could no longer relate as well to standard AOR artists such as the Doors, the Grateful Dead, and the Moody Blues. As a result, a splinter of AOR, called classic rock, emerged to appeal to adult listeners. The format features hits of the past but with a harder musical edge than other popular music formats for adults. Typical artists in the Classic Rock format include Bob Seger, ZZ Top, Bruce Springsteen, and the Rolling Stones.

The Classic Rock format first appeared in 1983 in Dallas on WFAA-FM. The format often is classified as part of the vintage rock category that also includes the Oldies format. Classic Rock is different from Oldies in that it features rock hits with a harder edge and generally does not include music from the 1950s and early 1960s. Arbitron, a radio audience research firm, includes Classic Rock as one of the 15 formats it recognizes nationally and defines Classic Rock's content as "the same universe of music as Album Rock, but without much current rock."

Some radio programming analysts have predicted that the Classic Rock format will disappear within a decade. They see adult listeners shifting to modern rock or alternative formats in the future, but as the 1990s drew to a close Classic Rock was gaining in popularity among "baby boomer" listeners. According to Arbitron, the format's share of the national radio audience has continued to increase over the past few years, with a peak of 4.9 percent in 2002. Later in the decade the Classic Rock format was making slight inroads to the developing HD2 domain, though it had experienced some erosion on FM analog channels

See also: Album-Oriented Rock Format; Oldies Format; Progressive Rock Format; Rock and Roll Format

Further Reading

Arbitron, *Radio Today*, New York: Arbitron, 1995.
Keith, Michael C., *Voices in the Purple Haze: Underground Radio and the Sixties*, Westport, Connecticut: Praeger, 1997.
Ladd, Jim, *Radio Waves: Life and Revolution on the FM Dial*, New York: St. Martin's Press, 1991.
Neer, Richard, *FM: The Rise and Fall of Rock Radio*, New York: Villard, 2001.
Stuessy, Joe, *Rock and Roll: Its History and Stylistic Development*, Englewood Cliffs, New Jersey: Prentice Hall, 1990; 3rd edition, by Stuessy and Scott David Lipscomb, Upper Saddle River, New Jersey: Prentice Hall, 1999.

FREDERIC A. LEIGH,
2009 REVISIONS BY MICHAEL C. KEITH

CLEAR CHANNEL COMMUNICATIONS INC.

Texas-based Clear Channel Communications Inc. had by the late 1990s become, through mergers and acquisitions, the largest single owner of radio stations in the world with nearly 1,000.

The company began with the 1972 purchase of a struggling San Antonio, Texas, FM station for $130,000 by L. Lowry Mays and B.J. "Red" McCombs. Station KEEZ (later KAJA) operated for a number of years under San Antonio Broadcasting, the original company name. Three years later, Mays purchased WOAI-AM, a pioneering operation that had first gone on the air in 1922. (McCombs retains a 2.5% ownership in Clear Channel Communications. As of early 2003 he owned a number of car dealerships as well as the NFL Minnesota Vikings.)

Clear Channel Communications was incorporated in 1974 and grew quite slowly at first, becoming a publicly traded firm in 1984 and owning a dozen stations in several markets a year later. Clear Channel used a simple formula: buy low-priced stations, build up their revenues while controlling costs, and operate conservatively. By 1990, the company had expanded into television station ownership as well, but it was still just one of a host of group owners of broadcast stations.

Federal Communications Commission (FCC) deregulation of limits on radio station ownership after 1993 fueled the first burst of Clear Channel station purchases, but the 1996 Telecommunications Act provided the key for the huge expansion of Clear Channel. By June of that year, it became the first company to own more than 100 stations. Many of its takeovers involved one or two radio stations at a time; bigger multistation deals would come late in the decade. By 1997, CEO Mays was about halfway up *Forbes* magazine's list of the 400 richest Americans.

The October 1998 takeover of Jacor Communications (then the second-largest owner of radio stations with 230 outlets) in a $2.8 billion stock deal moved Clear Channel toward the front of the radio owner pack. The transaction made Clear Channel the country's second-largest owner in number of stations and the third in total radio revenues. By 1999, radio provided 53 percent of total company revenue; billboards brought in 47 percent. Clear Channel also held equity interests in about 240 foreign radio stations, including outlets in Australia, Denmark, Mexico, and New Zealand.

In an agreement announced in October 1999, Clear Channel paid $23.5 billion to take over AMFM Inc. which owned 444 stations—320 FM and 124 AM stations. Combined with what Clear Channel already owned, this deal made it the largest group owner of stations in terms of numbers of outlets and revenues. But the deal also required the sale of about 110 stations collectively worth $4.3 billion to meet government limits on station ownership in individual markets. Early in 2000 the first 88 stations were sold to 17 companies, seven of which were minority-controlled. Early in 2000, Clear Channel Communications also purchased SFX Entertainment (a concert and sports producer and owner of a number of arenas) for $3.3 billion. The 19 March 2000 issue of *The New York Times* noted that "the company will have operations in 32 countries, [including]…550,000 billboards and 110 entertainment venues. It will also own all or part of 1,100 radio stations, though some are being sold to satisfy regulators."

Clear Channel's brand of advertising synergy—selling combined advertising packages across radio, television, and billboards, especially in markets where it owns stations and billboards (virtually all of the cities where it also owns theaters and arenas)—has clearly played a major factor in its success. Company business strategy, as stated in its 1999 10-K filing with the Securities and Exchange Commission, makes clear the value of growth through acquisition and ownership of multiple stations in the same market:

> We believe that clustering broadcasting assets together in markets leads to substantial operating advantages. We attempt to cluster radio stations in each of our principal markets because we believe that we can offer advertisers more attractive packages of advertising options if we control a larger share of the total advertising inventory in a particular market. We also believe that by clustering we can operate our stations with more highly skilled local management teams and eliminate duplicative operating and overhead expenses. We believe that owning multiple broadcasting stations in a market allows us to provide a more diverse programming selection for our listeners.

Although the company's very size (1,214 stations, of which 485 are in the 100 largest markets, with a total weekly audience of nearly 105 million as of mid-2002, generating $8.4 billion in annual revenue) attracted criticism and not a little carping from industry competitors, Clear Channel attracted further attention early in 2003 when it co-sponsored more than a dozen political rallies supporting the American incursion into Iraq. Stories criticizing these "Rally for America!" events first appeared on the internet and soon broke into general press reports. They argued that the company was supporting the Bush administration just as the FCC was considering changes in radio ownership rules. They also felt Clear Channel stations were programming in similar fashion—a criticism the company firmly denied.

Clear Channel's stock value began to decline from a high of about $90 in 2000 to less than a third of that five years later, reflecting a general downturn in entertainment and information company values as well as concerns about whether the company was simply too large to be effectively managed as a unit. In 2005 Clear Channel split into three separate companies, one focusing on radio broadcasting, whereas the other two dealt with out-of-home advertising and live entertainment events. The Mays family remained in effective control of all three.

In November 2006, however, Clear Channel announced plans to sell control to two private-equity firms for about $26 billion. As a result of the long negotiations (where because of the declining value of some of its properties, the sale price declined to $18 billion), Clear Channel announced plans to sell its TV stations as well as about 500 of its smaller radio stations (generally those outside of the top 100 markets). The television outlets and 161 of the radio stations were sold to Providence Equity Partners, another private-equity firm, in April 2007. But the economic downturn quashed a number of attempted station sales. FCC and Department of Justice approval of the overall deal required that the firm sell many of its stations. Early in 2009, Clear Channel announced many job lay-offs as the nation's economy worsened.

See also: Ownership, Mergers, and Acquisitions

Further Reading

"The Biggest Li'l Broadcaster in Texas," *Fortune* (19 August 1996).
Bryce, Robert, "What? A Quiet Texas Billionaire?" *New York Times* (19 March 2000).

Clear Channel Communications website, www.clearchannel.com.

Elliott, Stuart, "Clear Channel in $3 Billion Deal to Acquire SFX Entertainment," *New York Times* (1 March 2000).

Foege, Alec. *Right of the Dial: The Rise of Clear Channel and the Fall of Commercial Radio*. New York: Faber & Faber, 2008.

Forest, Stephanie, and Richard Siklos, "The Biggest Media Mogul You Never Heard Of," *Business Week* (18 October 1999).

Hagan, Joe, "Radio's 1,200-Station Gorilla," *Inside* (3 April 2001).

Rathbun, Elizabeth A., "Texas Size: Clear Channel Builds a Broadcast Dynasty," *Broadcasting and Cable* (7 October 1996).

Rathbun, Elizabeth A., "Clear Channel's Under-Fire Sale," *Broadcasting and Cable* (13 March 2000).

Viles, Peter, and Geoffrey Foisie, "Clear Channel: Sunbelt Success Story," *Broadcasting and Cable* (23 July 1993).

ALAN B. ALBARRAN,
2009 REVISIONS BY GAIL LOVE

CLEAR CHANNEL STATIONS
Powerful Major-Market Radio Stations

Clear channels refers to a class of high-powered AM radio stations that from 1928 into the early 1980s operated with no (or only one or two) interfering stations broadcasting on their channels during evening hours. In other words, their operating channel was "cleared" of other outlets. The role and status of such stations was a matter of major radio industry controversy for decades. (Clear channel stations should not be confused with the Clear Channel Communications company, the owner of a large number of radio stations in the early 21st century.)

Origins

With its General Order No. 40 issued in August 1928, the Federal Radio Commission (FRC) reserved 40 of the then-96 AM channels to ensure listening options in rural areas. As the FRC put it: "On these 40 channels only one station will be permitted to operate any time during night hours, thus insuring clear reception of the station's program up to the extreme limit of its service range." First referred to by the FRC as cleared or "clear channels" in a November 1931 order, these outlets came to represent the pinnacle of radio broadcasting.

All clear channels were located between 640 and 1200 kHz, and most were on or near the East and West coasts, with several in major Midwestern cities (four were located in Chicago). They were given the privilege of operating without other stations on the same channel in order to provide night-time service to so-called "white areas"—more than half the U.S. land mass—that could not receive a ground-wave primary local radio signal and thus depended on night-time sky wave transmission to receive distant higher-powered outlets.

From the beginning, these elite stations were the focus of controversy. On the one hand they provided service in rural areas that could often receive no other radio signal at night. On the other, they strongly resisted the formation of new local stations to serve such areas. Yet in an indication of things to come, the first clear station was "broken" just six months after the 1928 order when the FRC allowed stations WGY and KGO (both owned by General Electric) to share the same frequency, partially because they were on nearly opposite coasts. Two other clear channels were assigned for use by Canadian stations. With other decisions, only 32 stations remained truly "clear" by the time of the Federal Communication Commission's (FCC) formation in 1934.

At the same time, clear channel stations became identified with requests for higher or "super" power above the 50 kw limit. Cincinnati clear-channel station WLW (700 kHz) was given an experimental authorization in 1934 to use 500 kw of power—ten times that of any other station. Using its experimental W8XO, at first only in evening hours, then full-time, the outlet quickly became first choice of listeners in 13 states and second in six others. Under pressure from competitors in the U.S. and from Canada (unhappy with the station's reach into that country), WLW's daytime use of super power ended in March 1939, although occasional night-time use continued until late 1942.

Soon other clear channels petitioned the FCC for "super power," arguing that they could thus better serve rural areas. Clear channel station managers formed the Clear Channel Group (CCG) in 1934 to put forth the views of independent (not network-owned) stations. The CCG lobbied hard for the use of super power, as well as to protect existing clear channels.

The CCG testified at extensive FCC allocation hearings from 1936 to 1938. The commission's resulting engineering report generally supported the retention of clear channels for their evening rural service. In the late 1930s negotiations that led to the North American Regional Broadcasting Agreement (NARBA), the U.S. was given priority use of 32 of a total of 59 clear channels, whereas Cuba received one, and Mexico and Canada each got six. By this time clear channels were dubbed class I-A, whereas clears that were duplicated by at least one station at night on the same channel were dubbed I-B outlets.

Needing a still stronger lobbying voice, the CCG was largely converted to the Clear Channel Broadcasting Service (CCBS) beginning in 1941. With a larger budget and full-time staff, it became more focused on lobbying and public relations efforts as well as representation of clear channel station owner views before the FCC and Congress. But it faced a growing split between network-owned I-A stations and independent I-A outlets. The CCBS also focused on building alliances with farmer groups to create a stronger lobbying front in favor of retaining the clear channel classification.

Breaking Down the Clears

With the end of World War II, the FCC was able to turn its attention to pressing domestic matters, among them what to do about the simmering clear channel controversy. In early 1945 the commission initiated Docket 6741 to focus discussion on the policy tradeoffs (a few national v. many local services) raised by the continued operation of clear channel stations. This proceeding became the primary arena for continued debate on the future of the I-A stations, including their service role and how much power they would be allowed to use. Some 40 days of hearings were held from January 1946 to January 1948, allowing a host of witnesses on all sides of the controversy to be heard. Many critiqued the clear channel stations for their relative lack of farm and agricultural programming (located in major cities, the clear channel stations programmed chiefly for urban audiences). The FCC briefly considered plans to combine the use of more and smaller AM and FM stations to meet the "white area" unserved audience problem. The CCBS proposed that 20 stations (not surprisingly all CCBS members) be allowed to use up to 750 kw of power. Throughout the hearings, the radio networks argued for retention of the status quo, which had served their interests well.

When the hearings adjourned, the FCC considered two plans that were variations on that proposed by the CCBS plus a third that would break down the clears to allow many other stations on the same channels. Senate hearings on these questions largely repeated the same arguments but also delayed any definitive FCC decision. At that point the commission turned to television allocations and essentially ignored clear channel issues for a decade. Only at the urging of many affected parties did the FCC reopen the Docket in 1958. At this

point virtually all the clears shared their frequencies in daytime hours; this final debate concerned only their retention of cleared status in evening hours when radio signals traveled much further.

Finally, in mid-1961 came resolution of Docket 6741 with the FCC decision that 11 of the 25 Class I-A stations would now be required to share their frequency with at least one unlimited time regional (class II) station. This "breaking" of the clears brought an attempt by the CCBS stations to roll back the commission action in Congress, and long hearings on several bills to do just that resulted. FCC and other radio station opposition killed those potential laws, and, upheld on court appeal, the FCC moved to break down the clear channels over the next several years. In the meantime, the commission considered what to do with the remaining dozen clear channel outlets, including continuing proposals to allow them to operate with super power up to 750 kw. Faced with a continued lack of progress on the issue and continuation of the status quo, in 1968 CCBS closed down its Washington office.

Two decades later the FCC voted to end the long-lasting controversy by allowing up to 125 unlimited time AM stations to use either the remaining clear channels or adjacent channels during evening hours, while protecting a 750-mile coverage radius for the original clear channel outlets. Attempts to roll back this final assault also came to nothing. Clear channel stations, although often still called that and remaining among the most powerful AM outlets, no longer operate as the sole occupants of their frequencies in evening hours. Service to rural "white" areas is now largely provided by a host of regional and local stations.

See also, in addition to individual stations mentioned: Farm/Agricultural Radio; Federal Communications Commission; Federal Radio Commission; Frequency Allocation; Licensing Authorizing U.S. Stations to Broadcast; North American Regional Broadcasting Agreement

Further Reading

Brown, Eric R., "Nighttime Radio for the Nation: A History of the Clear-Channel Proceeding, 1945–1972," Ph.D. diss., Ohio University, 1975.
Caldwell, Louis G., "The Case for Clear Channels and High Power," Statement on Behalf of Certain Clear Channel Station Licensees before the Federal Communications Commission, 6 September 1938.
"The FCC and the Clears," *Broadcast Engineering* (November 1961).
"FCC Cuts Back the Clears," *Broadcasting* (2 June 1980).

Foust, James C., *Big Voices of the Air: The Battle over Clear Channel Radio*, Ames: Iowa State University Press, 2000.

Rogers, George Harry, "The History of the Clear Channel and Super Power Controversy in the Management of the Standard Broadcast Allocation Plan," Ph.D. diss., University of Utah, 1972.

Smulyan, Jeffrey, "Power to Some People: The FCC's Clear Channel Allocation Policy," *Southern California Law Review* 44 (1971).

U.S. House of Representatives, Committee on Interstate and Foreign Commerce, *Clear Channel Broadcasting Stations: Hearings*, 87th Congress, 2nd Session, 1962.

CHRISTOPHER H. STERLING

CLUTTER
See: Commercial Load

COLLEGE RADIO

College radio has a long history. A significant number of the earliest radio stations in the United States, such as WHA (then 9XM) in Madison, Wisconsin, were college stations. Many evolved into large professional enterprises, exemplified by those that are members of National Public Radio. However, "college radio" today generally conjures up a different picture. It might be an image of committed volunteer student disc jockeys playing obscure but artistically valuable music for a small but loyal audience, or it might be of a ragtag bunch of kids playing songs that nobody outside their small circle of friends wants to hear. Regardless, it is safe to say that college radio stations play a significant role in many communities and within the music industry, while differing in numerous ways from their more visible professional counterparts and also among themselves.

Despite the great variety, there are some generalizations that can be made about the underlying purposes of most college stations. For many, the primary focus is educational. Colleges may see this role as including educational and informational programming for the community, but it nearly always means that these stations serve academic departments whose scope includes broadcasting or journalism. College radio provides a training laboratory for students in those disciplines, as well as those in business, marketing, and other fields. Some college broadcasters see their mission as providing an entertainment or information service to the listening public, but they usually define themselves as an alternative to professional, tightly formatted stations. Still others exist primarily as a student activity alongside the myriad other extra-curricular clubs on campus. These stations generally have a faculty or professional staff adviser, but they are operated as a hobby by and for students. Whatever the station's foremost reason for being, nearly all college stations serve multiple purposes, a fact also reflected in the unique programming and structure of many stations.

College radio is often associated with programs that do not adhere to the rigid niche format structure of professional, commercial radio. Some stations adopt a free-form approach in which almost anything goes, from classical music to poetry to punk rock, at the discretion of the person on the air. Another popular option is block programming, airing shows in many different styles but at specified times. One might hear a three-hour heavy metal show, followed by two hours of blues, which then leads into a two-hour mainstream jazz program, and then a half-hour news magazine, followed by a 90-minute sports talk show, two hours of hip-hop, an hour of contemporary jazz, and so on. Limited only by the number of hours in the day and the availability of qualified and interested students, block programming offers the advantage of allowing a station to serve many different constituencies both within the university and among the listening public. Even at stations that do program a single music format, there are often additional programs on the schedule. For example, college radio is often the outlet for play-by-play coverage of a school's athletic teams, particularly at smaller schools or for minor sports at large institutions. Many stations also make a significant commitment to local public-affairs and news programming.

The most popular single format in college radio is alternative rock. Approximately 70 percent of all college radio stations reportedly program the format; however, the specific execution can vary considerably from one station to another. Some stations concentrate on music far outside the mainstream, deliberately ignoring any release that gets played on MTV or professional radio stations, whereas others sound very much like typical commercial alternative rock stations.

However individual stations define *alternative*, college radio has a reputation for playing an important role in nurturing the careers of many top music stars by providing important early exposure. U2, R.E.M., and the Red Hot Chili Peppers are just a few of the many staples of commercial rock radio that first received attention via college radio. It was probably in the mid-to-late 1970s that the recording industry began to take college radio seriously. Record companies developed college radio marketing strategies and resources, including full-time college radio representatives. Radio and record industry trade press, such as *Gavin*, began to report college radio airplay, and college programming was of sufficient importance to attract its own trade journal. *CMJ New Music Report*, first published in 1979, is devoted exclusively to college programmers and the record promoters who target that market.

College radio has more in common with community radio than with professional, commercial broadcasting. However, finance, staffing, and the means of transmission also differ markedly from station to station. Money is a major concern for college radio, because inconsistent funding creates problems for all areas of the station's operation, from programming to engineering.

Most, but not all, college stations are noncommercial. In some cases, the station is licensed by the Federal Communications Commission (FCC) as noncommercial in the part of the FM band below 92 MHz that is specifically set aside for that purpose. Other stations adopt a noncommercial policy by their own choice. Noncommercial stations rely on various combinations of student activity fees, state or college support, listener contributions, and underwriting donations from local business to finance operation. College stations that sell commercial time may also rely in part on these other funding mechanisms for a portion of their budget.

Depending on the station's purpose(s) and budgetary support, a college radio station staff may be all or mostly volunteer; they may have one or more professionals, sometimes a faculty member, involved in a management or advisory capacity; or there may be paid student or professional staff handling day-to-day operations. Students also staff some stations in part or in whole as a requirement in specific classes.

Acquiring an FCC license and following all the rules that apply to broadcasting are beyond the reach of many schools and student organizations. Therefore, many schools have chosen to take advantage of more affordable, accessible, and flexible unlicensed alternatives. Derisively dubbed "radiator radio," these are not broadcast stations but facilities that use campus electric or power lines to distribute their signal. In most cases, these permit either commercial or noncommercial operation and also free the school from the record-keeping and public-interest programming obligations imposed on all licensed radio stations.

The FCC's rules explicitly allow some kinds of very low power broadcasting without a license. These include AM carrier current using the electrical system of campus buildings as the antenna; micropowered AM transmitters; or "leaky coax," an FM alternative utilizing coaxial cable throughout a building or campus as the transmitting antenna. Acceptable unlicensed signals cover an area measured in yards rather than miles, broadcasting to only a single block or even just a single building. Cable television provides another unlicensed alternative, via cable FM or audio on regular cable television channels (perhaps as the audio background on a college or public access "bulletin board" channel). Some schools provide a signal through a public address system to reach audiences in a building's public spaces, a service dubbed "cafeteria" radio. Finally, the emergence of the internet as a means of transmitting programming presents colleges with an additional unlicensed radio outlet.

By the first decade of the 21st century, college radio operated in a shifting milieu. Listening to radio was down—as it was across the board. But college stations were generally working with rather than against the internet—60 percent of them streamed their signals online. Although the online listeners at any one time number at best a few dozen, they are often around the world, helping to build a once college campus-bound signal to a broader clientele.

Where once commercial music stations were a competitor, prime competition for college stations now is the ever-larger number of blogs that talk about music, individual podcasts that play it, and the ubiquitous (especially on campuses) portable MP3 players such as the iPod. But the old-fashioned, usually under-funded campus radio station still provides its listeners with the sense of community it always has, helping to introduce new groups, songs, and sounds.

See also: Alternative Format; Community Radio; Free Form Format; Low-Power Radio/Microradio; National Association of Educational Broadcasters; National Public Radio; Podcast; Ten-Watt Stations

Further Reading

Bloch, Louis M., Jr., *The Gas Pipe Networks: A History of College Radio, 1936–1946*, Cleveland, Ohio: Bloch, 1980.
Brant, Billy G., *The College Radio Handbook*, Blue Ridge Summit, Pennsylvania: Tab Books, 1981.
CMJ New Music Report, www.cmj.com.
College Broadcaster website, www.rice.edu/cb.
Sauls, Samuel J., "Alternative Programming in College Radio," *Studies in Popular Culture* 21 (October 1998).
Sauls, Samuel J., *The Culture of American College Radio*, Ames: Iowa State University Press, 2000.

Sisario, Ben. "College Radio Maintains its Mojo," *New York Times* (7 December 2008), Arts, pp. 1, 26.

GREGORY D. NEWTON,
2009 REVISIONS BY CHRISTOPHER H. STERLING

COLUMBIA BROADCASTING SYSTEM
U.S. National Radio Network

The Columbia Broadcasting System (CBS), America's second radio network, grew out of the United Independent Broadcasters (UIB) network, which was incorporated on 27 January 1927. It became CBS after it was purchased by William S. Paley in 1928, and in the decades that followed CBS played a leading role in the development of network radio and in the evolution of radio broadcasting following the establishment of television as a primary entertainment medium. Today, CBS Radio is part of the media conglomerate Viacom Inc. and serves nearly 1,500 radio stations nationwide with a variety of news, public affairs, information, and sports programs through Westwood One, a program syndication company. Through its radio subsidiary, Infinity Broadcasting, Viacom owns some 180 radio stations in 40 of the nation's largest markets. Infinity manages and holds an equity position in Westwood One.

Origins

The UIB network went on the air on 18 September 1927 with a string of 16 radio stations in 11 states. The network was not well financed, however, losing more than $200,000 in its first year of operation. In order to survive, UIB arranged for backing by the financially strong Columbia Phonograph Company, a leader in the record-pressing business. Columbia bought into UIB for $163,000. UIB, in turn, changed the name of its broadcast arm to the Columbia Phonograph Broadcasting Company. Later, when the network continued to sustain substantial losses, Columbia Phonograph withdrew from the network and took free broadcast time as payment for what it was owed.

One of the early advertisers on UIB was the Congress Cigar Company, which produced and aired *The La Palina Smoker* on the network. The musical program, put together by William Paley (the son of the company's owner) and named after one of its cigars, proved quite a successful advertising tool for the company, doubling sales of the brand in less than six months. Paley was delighted with the results of the program and became fascinated with the radio medium. He spent a great deal of time on his project and learned all that he could about radio and the UIB network. Although UIB was losing money, Paley felt the network had a future, and eventually he decided to buy it. On 25 September 1928, the 27-year-old Paley made it official, purchasing the UIB network for a reported $500,000 of his own money. His father soon bought into the network for $100,000 as a show of support for his son's undertaking.

Paley saw that expansion was a must for his fledgling network and quickly renegotiated the contracts UIB had with its affiliates to achieve three goals: (1) to lower the amount that the network paid stations for the broadcast time they provided; (2) to ensure a long-term association with the stations; and (3) to make sure that UIB was the only network carried by each affiliate. The stations were happy with the arrangement, because UIB was able to hire talent not available to them and to provide better and more programs than the stations could produce themselves locally.

With his existing affiliates taken care of, Paley invited other stations, mainly in the South, to join his new network with contracts similar to those he had just renegotiated. Twelve new stations joined. He later gained a few more affiliates in the Midwest, bringing the UIB network to 48 stations in 42 cities, but none on the West Coast.

By December 1928 UIB was broadcasting 21 hours a week from leased facilities at WABC in New York City and WOR in Newark, Delaware, and it desperately needed a station of its own from which to produce programs. For that purpose, Paley bought WABC in New York for $390,000, after selling shares in the network and investing another $200,000 of his own. WABC (which became WCBS in 1946) thus became the network's first company-owned station.

When Paley had taken over UIB three months earlier, it consisted of three companies: UIB, which supplied the airtime; the Columbia Broadcasting System (the old phonograph company unit), which sold the time to sponsors; and a unit that supplied programs. When Columbia Phonograph left UIB, it insisted that the word *phonograph* be removed from the name of the broadcast arm of the network but allowed UIB to keep the *Columbia* portion. As the on-air part of UIB, the Columbia Broadcasting System was what listeners were familiar with. To preserve this name recognition with radio audiences, Paley reorganized UIB, doing away with the broadcasting unit as a separate entity and merging all three UIB companies into one, named the Columbia Broadcasting System, Incorporated (CBS).

In the first six months of 1929 advertising sales picked up at CBS, and the movie studios began to take an interest in the new network. Just as the movie industry was to fear the impact television would have on theatergoing decades later, the industry was leery of radio broadcasting and decided that a link with the growing medium would be a good financial move. After lengthy negotiations, Paramount paid $5 million for half of CBS in June 1929. As part of the sales contract, the studio agreed to buy back the stock it transferred to CBS to make its 50 percent purchase if CBS earned $2 million within the next two years. Incredibly, CBS met the goal and bought out Paramount, even though the country was then in the depths of the Great Depression.

In 1929 CBS signed the Don Lee group of stations as network affiliates, giving CBS a West Coast link and making it a truly nationwide network. This was also the year it began its first daily news program and its first regular program of political analysis. Late in the year, the network moved into its newly completed headquarters on Madison Avenue in New York with 60 affiliates under contract and annual advertising sales of $4 million.

Development

During the 1930s and 1940s, CBS radio grew from infancy to maturity through a process of trial and error. Programs, largely music, variety, and comedy at first, increased in variety to include drama, soap opera, audience participation and quiz shows and, by the late 1930s, fledgling news efforts.

Early in the decade, with 400 employees in his employ at CBS, William Paley hired a new assistant, Edward Klauber, a former *New York Times* editor who was to become the number-two man at CBS. Another addition to the CBS staff was Paul White, a wire-service reporter who established strong journalistic standards and ethics for the new CBS news organization.

Paley was quick to recognize that growth and revenue for CBS could only come by obtaining new talent and programs to offer to sponsors, and he became adept at finding and signing performers for radio shows. His first big talent coup was to get Will Rogers, America's most popular philosopher–comedian, to agree to do a 13-week series for CBS in the spring of 1930. With Rogers aboard, Paley was soon able to woo comedians Fred Allen, George Burns, and Jack Benny to CBS radio, as well as Morton Downey, Bing Crosby, Kate Smith, and the Mills Brothers, all of whom went on to great success and fame.

CBS acquired its second station, WBBM in Chicago, in 1931 and began laying claim to being the number-one news network by virtue of the number of news bulletins it was airing. The network also began airing the *March of Time*, a weekly dramatization of the major news events of the previous week that was sponsored by *Time* magazine. Although considered melodramatic by some, the program became very popular and remained on CBS until 1937, when it moved to NBC.

Classical music programs were also quite popular in the early 1930s, and CBS signed the New York Philharmonic for Sunday afternoon broadcasts. In addition, the network formed its own Columbia Symphony Orchestra and presented thousands of programs of classical music in the years that followed.

Another popular type of program, which emerged on CBS and NBC in the early 1930s and would enjoy loyal audiences for nearly three decades, was the daily romance serial. Sponsored by the giant soap firms of the day, such as Procter and Gamble, Colgate-Palmolive, and Lever Brothers, the shows became a part of the daily lives of housewives across the country.

In 1933, just as CBS became the largest network with 91 affiliates, a high-stakes battle broke out between the radio and newspaper industries that threatened the network's news function. The conflict grew out of radio's steady rise in popularity, which caused newspaper publishers to fear that the new medium was siphoning off advertising revenue and news audiences. The American Newspaper Publishers Association voted not to print the radio industry's daily program schedules in their papers except as paid advertising. The publishers next pressured the newswire services to stop serving radio stations and networks.

Left without wire-service news, CBS, with the help of sponsorship from General Mills, formed its own news-gathering organization, the Columbia News Service, and placed bureaus in New York, Washington, Chicago, and Los Angeles. It also lined up correspondents as "stringers" in nearly every major American city and negotiated exchange agreements with a number of overseas news agencies in an effort to keep news flowing to the radio audiences. Paul White and his staff prepared three news programs each day at CBS, many times with stories the papers did not yet have. By the time the press–radio war ended some time later, CBS had established a strong commitment to providing news and information to America, a commitment that remains at the core of its modern-day radio offerings.

CBS's *American School of the Air* was a non-commercial supplement to regular classroom instruction, complete with a teacher's manual. The program featured geography, history, English, music, and drama for young people. It was regularly heard by six million children, but it was not able to make CBS the most popular network. During the 1934–35 broadcast season, radio's top five programs were all on NBC.

With 91 stations, CBS had more affiliates than NBC, but it continued to trail NBC in popularity. New programs were produced, and a number of policy changes were made during 1935 in an effort to move the network into the top spot. CBS established standards for the amount of advertising time it would permit per program and for the type of products that it would and would not advertise. Standards were also set that dealt with "fairness and balance" in all news and public information programs.

The extra effort seemed to pay off when, by 1936–37, radio's top five programs were on CBS. This was due largely, however, to the fact that the network had enticed three of NBC's most popular entertainers to the network: variety show host Major Bowes, singer Al Jolson, and comedian Eddie Cantor. *Major Bowes' Original Amateur Hour* was the most popular program of the day. CBS also soon took the *Lux Radio Theater* from NBC.

In an effort to serve as many audiences as possible, CBS also began to present the *Church of the Air* on Sundays and formed an advisory board to set policy for its educational programs and to choose shows suitable for children. In addition, it formed the Columbia Workshop in 1936 as an experimental theater of the air. CBS kept this program unsponsored to give it freedom and a chance to pioneer new radio techniques, especially in sound, electronic effects, and music, and many of the ideas the Workshop perfected later became broadcast industry standards. With many of its scripts written by the best-known writers of the day, such as Dorothy Parker, Irwin Shaw, and William Saroyan, the program achieved great critical acclaim.

Late in 1936, CBS established a base of operations in Hollywood in order to be able to originate radio shows from the West Coast. The move allowed the network to better serve that region and its time zone and gave CBS more access to Hollywood stars.

As the signs of war grew in Europe in 1937, Edward Klauber decided that CBS needed a European director, and the job went to Edward R. Murrow. Once overseas, Murrow hired journalist William L. Shirer, and the pair set about lining up cultural events, concerts, and other programs for CBS. When German troops entered Austria in 1938, Shirer, then in Vienna, flew to London to get the story out, and Murrow went to Austria. Shirer went on the air for CBS from the British Broadcasting Corporation (BBC) studios in London, and Murrow sent a shortwave broadcast from Vienna reporting the German takeover of Austria. The effort was the beginning of CBS's exemplary war coverage. Continuing to report from Europe, Murrow and Shirer put together the *CBS World News Roundup*, the first round-robin international radio news broadcast, with Murrow reporting from Vienna; Shirer from London; and other newsmen in Paris, Berlin, and Rome.

In the late 1930s CBS bought Columbia Records (the company from which it got its name) and opened its new $1.75 million Columbia Square studio/office complex on Sunset Boulevard in Hollywood, California. The network also continued to give its growing audience exciting entertainment programs while providing increasing amounts of news and information.

The War Years

The CBS foreign news staff grew from three, including Murrow and Shirer, to 14, and then to 60 in 1941 as the United States entered the war. Of the war years, CBS President William Paley, who became the Deputy Chief of the Office of Psychological Warfare under General Dwight Eisenhower, later noted:

> [W]e adopted war themes on many of our programs. In dramatic shows, characters met wartime problems; the *American School of the Air* brought war news, information, and instruction to children; *Country Journal* gave farmers help in solving wartime agricultural problems; the *Garden Gate* promoted Victory gardens; *Church of the Air* broadcast talks by chaplains. There were also many new series exclusively about the war: *They Live Forever, The Man Behind the Gun, Our Secret Weapon.* (Paley, 1979)

Kate Smith also conducted hugely successful war bond drives, and some CBS company-owned stations began a 24-hour-a-day schedule, serving as part of an air raid defense system and providing entertainment for defense workers on the overnight shift. CBS's foreign correspondents were its stars of the air. Edward R. Murrow became a hero, even before the United States entered the war, through a series of "rooftop" broadcasts during the 1940 blitz in London; William L. Shirer covered the surrender of France to Germany at Compiègne; Larry Lesueur provided regular shortwave reports from Moscow; and Howard K. Smith provided coverage from Berlin. Others were stationed throughout Europe and in North Africa and Asia.

Paul White oversaw the international news organization on a daily basis with the help of a news team of some 50 members, including a staff of shortwave listeners who kept him abreast of what was happening around the world. Many of the team's members went on to achieve individual fame as writers and commentators: Eric Sevareid, Robert Trout, Charles Collingwood, John Daly, Howard K. Smith, and of course Edward R. Murrow all became well known and gave CBS News great credibility.

In 1943 CBS acquired WCBS-FM in New York, its first FM radio station, and WBBM-FM in Chicago. It also lost its number-two man when CBS vice president Ed Klauber suffered a heart attack and resigned.

On 6 June 1944, CBS went on the air at 12:30 A.M. to begin special coverage of the D-Day invasion, utilizing several of its commentators in New York, print reports from Washington and overseas, and live transmissions from London. Additional coverage was provided by correspondents in other European capitals, who kept the listeners updated on the progress of the invasion, and CBS's Charles Collingwood, who crossed the English Channel in an LST to report on the invasion from the beach at Normandy.

Between 7 December 1941 and 2 September 1945, the day the Japanese surrendered, CBS broadcast 35,700 wartime news and entertainment programs, including Norman Corwin's commemorative show *On a Note of Triumph*, which aired at the end of hostilities in Europe. A similar program, entitled *14 August*, was aired following the Japanese surrender.

Postwar Transitions

As the war ended, Frank Stanton, who had been hired in the 1930s as a research specialist to determine CBS listenership, became the network's president; William Paley moved up to become chairman of the board; and Edward R. Murrow was promoted to vice president and director of news and public affairs. By this time, CBS had once again fallen behind in the ratings battle, as 12 of the top 15 radio shows were on NBC.

By the end of 1947, CBS had put together 36 radio programs, but few were sponsored. It also established a news documentary unit to look at the subjects that were most affecting Americans at the

time. In addition, Murrow resigned as a CBS vice president and returned to the air with *Hear It Now*, a talking history of World War II that evolved into the later television news-documentary program *See It Now*. As it gained popularity, the documentary became a mainstay of CBS programming. CBS also joined the other networks in providing live broadcasts of hearings of the House Un-American Activities Committee, which looked into the alleged presence of communist sympathizers in the motion picture industry.

The following year, CBS increased sponsorship for its own shows to 29, and two of the programs became among the nation's 10 most popular: *My Friend Irma* and *Arthur Godfrey's Talent Scouts*.

Near the end of the decade, CBS tax attorneys discovered a way for radio stars to save tax money by selling their programs as "properties," and CBS was able to "raid" the most popular NBC programs, including *Amos 'n' Andy* and Jack Benny. In January 1949 CBS signed other NBC stars: Bing Crosby; comedians Red Skelton, Edgar Bergen, George Burns and Gracie Allen, Ed Wynn, and Groucho Marx; singers Al Jolson and Frank Sinatra; and band leader Fred Warning. Soon, CBS had 12 of the Hooperating's "First 15," 16 of Nielsen's "Top 20," and an average audience rating that was 12 percent larger than that of any other network. CBS was definitely number one in American broadcasting. By the late 1940s, CBS and its rivals were able to use money made in radio to fund progress in television, with CBS allocating $60 million to that cause.

Decline of CBS Radio Network

By the end of 1955, television's ability to attract radio's evening audience became clear when the Nielsen ratings listed no night-time programs among radio's top 10. Searching for a way to keep radio audiences, CBS beefed up its news offerings and premiered the *CBS Radio Workshop* as a revival of the earlier Columbia Workshop. It showcased some of the best talent of the day and used exceptional imagination and creativity in providing critically acclaimed but unsponsored radio drama.

Between 1957 and 1960, Jack Benny, Bing Crosby, and *Amos 'n' Andy* left the air; CBS radio shortened its schedule and turned over more time to the affiliates; and radio stations across the country began to offer more music and less network programming.

By 1960 all three radio networks hit bottom financially, losing 75 percent of the sales they had had in 1948. CBS began to offer even more news, sports, and information programming, and in November 1960 it canceled its last surviving soap operas, putting an end to a chapter of radio history and relinquishing the genre to television.

As the 1960s progressed, CBS made new arrangements with its affiliates that allowed them to put "packages" of network programs together to meet their needs rather than having to take all the network offerings. With the move, profitability returned, and CBS radio changed fundamentally. No longer would the network be able to *tell* its affiliates what it would offer them; CBS would instead have to *ask* the stations what they needed and try to provide it. In 1974 CBS decided to hire E.G. Marshall to host the *CBS Radio Mystery Theater* in an attempt to reintroduce radio drama and the feel of programs from the golden age of radio. The hour-long show, which was run seven days a week using new scripts and some old production formulas, received mixed reviews, and many affiliates declined to carry it or aired it outside of prime time. It was clear that news, sports, and information programs were all stations wanted from the networks, and CBS vowed to provide it through its strong network news division. The decision has remained in place for nearly three decades.

Today CBS News serves both radio and television station affiliates. On the radio side, there are two entities, CBS Radio News and CBS Radio Sports, that produce news, information, and sports programming for distribution to more than 1,500 stations through Westwood One, a program syndication company.

CBS Radio News provides stations in nearly every major market with hourly newscasts, instant coverage of breaking stories, special reports, updates, features, customized reports, and newsfeed material that alerts the stations receiving CBS material to what will be available to them in the following hours. Among the CBS Radio News productions is the World News Roundup, first broadcast in 1940 and said to be the longest-running newscast in America. CBS Radio Sports provides the affiliated stations with regular sportscasts, customized reports, features, and sporting events coverage.

Early in 2000, CBS merged with Viacom Inc., a global media company with interests in broadcast and cable television, radio, outdoor advertising, online entities, and other media-related fields. Viacom's holdings include MTV, Nickelodeon, VH1, BET, Paramount Pictures, Viacom Outdoor, UPN, TV Land, The New TNN, CMT: Country Music Television, Showtime, Blockbuster, and Simon & Schuster.

In the early 21st century, CBS Radio aggressively restructured and diversified. In June 2008, the company announced that it would place 50 of its mid-sized stations up for sale in order to concentrate on its large market operations. Later that year, CBS announced that it would swap five stations with Clear Channel in exchange for two of the latter's stations in Houston.

CBS also unveiled plans for a new internet radio network to provide access to its 150 stations (plus the AOL Radio network's 200 stations), through a single media player. They announced a similar content and advertising partnership with Yahoo Music's Launchcast internet service as well as the creation of an advertiser-supported portal called Play.it, which allows users to create their own radio "stations." In early 2009, CBS announced it was partnering with LiveNation, a live concert promoter and venue owner, to develop a series of live music events in many of that company's more than 100 venues nationwide.

See also: American School of the Air; Don Lee Broadcasting System; Infinity Broadcasting Corporation; KCBS/KQW; *March of Time*; Network Monopoly Probe; News; Press–Radio War; Talent Raids; WCBS

Further Reading

Archer, Gleason L., "Travails of a Rival Radio Network," in *Big Business and Radio*, New York: American Historical Company, 1939; reprint, New York: Arno Press, 1971.

Bergreen, Laurence, *Look Now, Pay Later: The Rise of Network Broadcasting*, Garden City, New York: Doubleday, 1980.

Buxton, Frank, and Bill Owen, *Radio's Golden Age: The Programs and the Personalities*, New York: Easton Valley Press, 1966; revised edition, as *The Big Broadcast, 1920–1950*, New York: Viking Press, 1972; 2nd edition, Metuchen, New Jersey: Scarecrow Press, 1997.

"CBS at 60," *Television/Radio Age* (28 September 1987).

"CBS: Documenting 38 Years of Exciting History," *Sponsor* (13 September 1965).

"CBS: The First Five Decades," *Broadcasting* (19 September 1977).

"CBS: The First 60 Years," *Broadcasting* (14 September 1987).

Metz, Robert, *CBS: Reflections in a Bloodshot Eye*, Chicago: Playboy Press, 1975.

Paley, William S., *As It Happened: A Memoir*, Garden City, New York: Doubleday, 1979.

Paper, Lewis J., *Empire: William S. Paley and the Making of CBS*, New York: St. Martin's Press, 1987.

Slater, Robert, *This is CBS: A Chronicle of 60 Years*, Englewood Cliffs, New Jersey: Prentice-Hall, 1988.

Sloan, William David, James Glen Stovall, and James D. Startt, editors, *The Media in America: A History*, Worthington, Ohio: Publishing Horizons, 1989; 2nd edition, Scottsdale, Arizona: Publishing Horizons, 1993.

Smith, Sally Bedell, *In All His Glory: The Life of William S. Paley*, New York: Simon and Schuster, 1990.

JACK HOLGATE,
2009 REVISIONS BY CARY O'DELL

COMBO

Announcer–Engineer Combination

The term *combo* is short for combination. In the radio industry, the term refers to a combo announcer, one who combines announcing with engineering duties such as playing recorded music and announcements.

Like all businesses, the radio industry experienced growing pains brought by technological advances. For radio stations, one of the growing pains was a labor cost growing out of the need to hire several employees for a disc jockey program. In the early days of radio, three employees were often needed to broadcast a program: two engineers (one to operate the audio console and to play transcribed materials and another to operate the station's transmitter) and an announcer to present spoken materials. As the industry grew, and as the control room and transmitter operating equipment became more sophisticated, station managers concluded they could save money by using "combo" announcers who could also perform the functions of engineers.

In the infancy of radio, the control room of a radio station operated as follows: the announcer was positioned by a microphone to read, or possibly to ad-lib, material that went on the air. The written material was called continuity and consisted of a daily file of all commercials and public service announcements, in chronological order, to be broadcast by the station. The station log provided a schedule of the announcements and programs, notifying both the announcer and the engineer of what should be read when.

So that the announcer could read a given announcement on the air, the engineer operating the audio console would turn on the microphone using the proper switch and volume control. The volume control, more commonly known as a "fader," "pot," or "mixer," was used to control the volume of audio current. The console contained a number of these faders, located in parallel series near the bottom of the unit. Each microphone, turntable, tape recorder, and network input had its corresponding fader. Another fader was used to control the input of a network into the console. The control room engineer had the responsibility of turning on the correct microphones or turntables and then using the fader to "ride gain," or maintain the appropriate volume for each microphone, each turntable, and so on.

The engineer at the audio control console was responsible for regulating the volume during a specific program or through a series of them. This was especially complex when radio stations broadcast live orchestras or bands, live vocalists, and live announcers. The engineer's responsibility was to regulate the volume so that the quality of transmission would not vary and so that distortion or inaudibility would not distract listeners.

In a relatively simple program, such as one in which an announcer hosted transcribed music, the engineer would turn on the switch for the correct microphone and then cue the announcer by pointing at him to begin reading or talking. During the message, the engineer would make certain the volume level was correct and would prepare to turn on the next microphone, turntable, and so on. Once the message had been read, the announcer would indicate completion of the message by pointing back at the engineer. This would be the signal for the engineer to turn off the microphone and to activate other switches for the next source of sound.

As broadcast equipment improved, stations adopted combo operations, and by the 1950s most small-market stations were combo. By "going combo," one person could operate the control room console, turntables, and tape recorders while also announcing live copy. A combo announcer had to combine several traits: an adequate voice to perform announcing duties and sufficient manual dexterity to simultaneously operate the equipment. Not all people could fulfill both roles.

Station managers also had the combo announcer read and record meters on the station transmitter and make necessary adjustments. Because many AM stations were required to sign off at night or were required to prevent interference with other stations by using directional transmission patterns to control the station's signal, correct transmitter operation was essential.

To perform transmitter adjustments at stations transmitting a directional pattern, a Federal Communications Commission (FCC) First Class radio-telephone operator's license, known as "First Phone," was needed until 1981. Many announcers enrolled in schools that taught them the basic knowledge needed to obtain a First Phone. A person who acquired a First Phone could announce, operate control room equipment, and make transmitter adjustments. First Phone announcers were often paid more than announcers who did not have the First Class FCC license, but the financial savings were important to smaller stations. Paying one combo announcer somewhat more than an announcer without a First Phone was financially preferable to paying several staff members.

Not all AM (and eventually FM stations) employed combo announcers. Stations with union agreements generally continued to subdivide the announcing, engineering, and control room operations. However, the majority of non-union AM and FM radio stations now use combo announcers.

The introduction of digital technology has further altered combo operations. At many stations, recorded material, including music, commercials, and station promotional items, are placed on the hard drive of a computer. The announcer operates the audio console, but the computer controls the programming of the other items, that is, music, recorded commercials, and so on. The announcer only stops the computer for live inserts and then restarts it once the live insertion is complete. The rest of the time, the computer plays recorded music, recorded commercials, and so forth on the air in the correct order. In other cases, the announcer can also prerecord the verbal inserts he or she will include between commercials or recordings, and the computer can present the entire recorded program.

See also: Automation; Control Board/Audio Mixer; Recording and Studio Equipment

Further Reading

Chester, Giraud, and Garnet R. Garrison, *Radio and Television: An Introduction*, New York: Appleton, 1950; 5th edition, as *Television and Radio*, by Chester, Garrison, and Edgar E. Willis, Englewood Cliffs, New Jersey: Prentice Hall, 1978.
Ditingo, Vincent M., *The Remaking of Radio*, Boston: Focal Press, 1995.
Halper, Donna L., *Full-Service Radio: Programming for the Community*, Boston: Focal Press, 1991.
Keith, Michael C., *The Radio Station*, 5th edition, Boston: Focal Press, 2000.

MIKE MEESKE

COMEDY

Comedy on radio was a slow starter. Until the mid-1920s, music and various forms of talk provided most of the infant medium's programming. It is probably no coincidence that the most fertile period for radio comedy—and movie comedy, for that matter—was when times were hardest: the Great Depression and World War II. Americans needed the healthy release of laughter, and the young electronic medium was eager to oblige.

Vaudeville on the Air

Just as movies had first borrowed from the format of the proscenium stage—and later, television borrowed from radio—radio itself also initially borrowed from a preceding medium, vaudeville. As the Depression deepened in the early 1930s, people had less money for live entertainment, and vaudeville performers found themselves increasingly out of work. Fortunately for them, radio was proving to have a voracious appetite for talent, and although it was a major contributor to vaudeville's demise—again, along with movies—it was also something of a savior for many of its performers. Nearly all of radio's first stars came from vaudeville: Ed Wynn, Eddie Cantor, Burns and Allen, Jack Benny, Fred Allen, and many more.

Probably radio's earliest paid entertainers were Billy Jones and Ernie Hare, a song-and-comedy-patter duo. First appearing in 1921, they were known by various names depending on their sponsors: The Happiness Boys (a candy company), The Interwoven Pair (socks), The Best Food Boys (mayonnaise), or The Taystee Loafers (bread).

Not only did radio comedy get its performers from vaudeville, radio adopted vaudeville's form as well. A missing component was the audience itself. Initially, broadcasting executives thought that the sound of laughter might be a distraction to listeners, so members of the technical crew or other visitors to the studio were under strict orders to remain absolutely silent during the performance. This practice didn't last very long: comedians gauge their timing and modulate their acts based on audience reaction. Eddie Cantor was the first to insist that audience members not only be allowed to laugh, but also *encouraged* to do so. Although there was some criticism thereafter that occasionally comedians played too much to the studio audience at the expense of listeners at home, for the most part the radio audience accepted and even came to expect a live audience's reactions.

Another missing element was, of course, sight. Whereas a comedian on stage could engage in all manner of leers, sight gags, takes and double takes, even dropping his pants if things got really desperate, all this was lost on radio. Ed Wynn, "The Perfect Fool," would dress up in costume for his radio shows, saying he thought if he looked and felt funny, he'd sound funny. Yet much of his appeal depended on the broad, physical comedy of the stage, and his radio career was only moderately successful. But once comedians and comedy writers adjusted to this limitation, they learned to exploit it, frequently using it as a magician uses misdirection.

For example, in a scene from *The Jack Benny Program*, a nervous Jack is riding in his vintage Maxwell auto, nagging Rochester to watch where he's going. "But Boss," protests Rochester, "*you're driving!*"

Because it soon became apparent that lengthy monologs grew tiresome to home listeners, a second voice in the form of a foil or "stooge" came into vogue. Frequently it was the announcer who, after introducing the star, would stick around for a few minutes to engage in comedic dialog, usually as the straight man. Graham McNamee bantered with Ed Wynn, Jimmy Wallington with Eddie Cantor, Harry Von Zell and later Kenny Delmar with Fred Allen, and, for more than 30 years, Don Wilson sparred gently with Jack Benny. Sometimes other characters filled this role, often in dialect. Eddie Cantor played straight man to Bert Gordon's "the Mad Russian" whose frenzied opening line, "How do you doooo," never failed to get a laugh. Several comedians called upon their wives. Fred Allen's wife, Portland Hoffa, always entered off-mike screeching, "Mister Aaaallen! Mister Aaaallen!," before launching into a description of Momma's latest letter from home. Mary Livingston was always around to puncture husband Jack Benny's latest pomposity. And George Burns was the quintessential straight man to wife Gracie Allen's scatterbrained humor.

J. Fred MacDonald (1979) writes that this device allowed the comedian to better delineate his own personality. Without Mary, Jack Benny's foibles were less "real" and therefore less funny. Fred Allen—one of radio's all-time great wits—needed someone to react to, establishing a kind of almost detached bemusement that was the basis for much of his observational humor.

During the 1930s, the big, expensive, star-driven comedy–variety shows were the most popular form of entertainment on the air. All had several elements in common: they usually opened with a musical number, followed by a monolog (or dialog), then more music, one or more comedy skits, usually featuring guest stars from other shows or the movies, still more music, and a short closing bit with the guest star before saying goodnight. This formula, with nominal variations, satisfied listeners for more than 20 years.

Ethnicity and Race

And what did audiences laugh about? Frequently they laughed at ethnicity. To the modern ear, much of the humor of that era can seem insensitive, sometimes even bordering on cruel. But this was an America still in the process of digesting the second great wave of immigration, predominantly from Southern and Eastern Europe. Whereas immigrants themselves often listened to the radio to discover their place in the new culture, native-born Americans were tuning in to hear caricatures and stereotypes of the recent arrivals. The Irish were usually portrayed as a police officers, if not as drunks. Asians—usually Chinese—were either obsequious launderers or mysterious and inscrutable villains. Mexicans were lazy, the French were great lovers, the British insufferable prigs. These and other stereotypes were commonly understood by audiences and formed the basis for numerous jokes and comedic situations.

For example, Minerva Pious portrayed the "typical" urban Jewish housewife, Mrs. Nussbaum, who was constantly "Yiddishizing" recognizable names, such as Emperor Shapiro-Hito (for Hirohito), Cecil B. Schlemiel (DeMille), Weinstein Churchill, and Heimie Wadsworth Longfellow. Other ethnic characters who would pop up on various shows were Jack Pearl's German Baron von Munchausen, Harry Einstein's Greek Parkyakarkas, and Mel Blanc's lazy Mexican known only as Si (pronounced sigh).

But in many ways, the ultimate ethnic stereotype was reserved for African-Americans. Just as movie audiences were accustomed to shiftless, superstitious, and subservient black characters like Stepin Fetchit, so were radio audiences offered a succession of black maids, handymen, and janitors whose foibles and frailties were often played for laughs.

But while movies at least provided employment for black actors, radio usually did not. The popular character Beulah, of *The Beulah Show*, was portrayed by a white man, Marlin Hurt. Part of the studio presentation involved Hurt's standing among other actors with his back to the audience, turning around only to bellow his opening line in falsetto "colored" dialect, "Somebody bawl fo' Beulah?" Radio listeners could only wonder at the studio audience's astonished reaction.

The most popular, and longest running, black-impersonation act was the phenomenally successful *Amos 'n' Andy*. Freeman Gosden and Charles Correll, both white men, had come out of the minstrel tradition and they teamed up to create two black characters whose adventures spanned the entire life of radio's so-called "Golden Era." Their format eventually spawned the soap opera and the situation comedy. Another—and perhaps more revolutionary—innovation of *Amos 'n' Andy* was to create in listeners' minds a rich and varied black subculture filled with bankers, lawyers, doctors, and other professionals, along with the more stereotypical scoundrels, braggarts, and ne'er-do-wells—all played by Gosden and Correll. In fact, take away the dialect, and one would be hard pressed to identify much that was particularly "black" about any of the program's plotlines or characterizations. Indeed, were it merely a minstrel show on radio, *Amos 'n' Andy* could hardly have riveted the nation's attention as it did. Listeners may have tuned in for the laughs, but they returned because of the fully developed characters and stories.

Amos 'n' Andy also influenced the creation of other programs, similar in form, if not in content. *Lum 'n' Abner* was a variation on the ethnic comedy known as the "rube" show. It featured two bumpkins who presided over the Jot 'em Down Store in the then-fictitious town of Pine Ridge, Arkansas. (In 1936, the town of Waters changed its name to Pine Ridge.) Creators Chester Lauck and Norris Goff played the title characters and everyone else who happened to come in to the store, such as Grandpappy Peabody, Snake Hogan, Doc Miller, and Squire Skimp. (Laureen Tuttle added female voices in 1937.) Sometimes the stories were complete in a single episode. Sometimes they could extend for weeks. When a woman asked Lum to watch her baby for a few moments, then disappeared, the story went on for 40 episodes.

The town of Cooper, Illinois, "40 miles from Peoria," was the setting for *Vic and Sade*. The Gooks were a so-called typical American couple who lived with their adopted son Rush "in a little house halfway up the next block." John Dunning calls the program an American original, in a category of its own making. Though it was a daily, daytime show, it was in no way a soap opera. In fact, it was not even a serial, but rather presented 10-minute sketches that individually stood on their own. In one episode, for example, Uncle Fletcher drops by the Gooks' house to make a long distance call to a family relative. But the then-complex process of getting a long distance line, coupled with the rest of the family's disputes on the proper telephone protocol, finally sends Fletcher home without ever making the call. Its creator, Paul Rhymer, populated the series with such goofy characters as Dottie Brainfeeble, Smelly Clark, Ruthie Stembottom, and Vic's cousin Ishigan Fishigan who hailed from Sishigan, Michigan, most of whom were only referred to but never heard. It was an understated show that eschewed big laughs in favor of smiles punctuated by occasional chuckles.

Ethnic humor became considerably toned down once World War II was underway and Hitler's racist policy of Jewish extermination became more widely understood. Suddenly it was no longer quite as funny to single out a person's racial or national origins as the basis for laughs. For example, one notices a distinct difference between the prewar and postwar portrayals of Jack Benny's black valet, Rochester (Eddie Anderson). Before the war, Rochester was a razor-carrying, craps-shooting womanizer. After the war, those attributes had all but disappeared. When, in 1945, *The Abbott and Costello Show* aired a sketch involving a Jewish loan shark who wanted two quarts of Lou's blood for collateral, the public criticism was immediate and emphatic.

Character and Cliché

Early radio comedy had been based—as in vaudeville—on jokes or gags. From *The Joe Penner Show* came this exchange. Penner: "Waiter, I must say, this is not very good goulash." Waiter: "I can't understand it. I used a pair of your best goulashes." But within a very few years, radio writers' extensively cross-indexed joke reference files had been exhausted. In 1934 Eddie Cantor called for an end to gag-style comedy, saying the public was no longer fooled by dressing up the old jokes and calling them new. Eventually the gags were subordinated to comedy based on characterization. And no-one was more adept at that than Jack Benny.

Benny's on-air personality developed slowly over the years. In his radio debut in 1932, he is a suave, somewhat self-deprecating host, serving up jokes and quips between musical numbers. By 1940 his character is fully realized: stingy and vain, he supposedly plays the violin badly and never admits to being older than 39. One of the most celebrated episodes of the series is particularly instructive if one listens to the audience reaction. Jack is being held up, and the pistol-wielding thief growls the immortal line, "Your money or your life." Jack's cheapness is so well understood by this time that the studio audience begins to laugh immediately, even *before* he can deliver the intended laugh line, "I'm thinking it over!"—and that only after a very long pause allowing the laughter to build.

Another comedy program that depended heavily on characterization was *The Edgar Bergen/Charlie McCarthy Show*. But the character in question wasn't even really a person—except in the minds of audiences—but rather a ventriloquist's dummy. Charlie McCarthy was depicted as a mischievous and sometimes lascivious 10–12-year-old boy, with Edgar Bergen playing a sort of ambiguous parent figure. Probably because he *was* a dummy, audiences accepted Charlie's sometimes lecherous come-ons to glamorous female guest stars. Had he actually been a child, this could have been highly objectionable.

Related to comedy based on character were the running gags or comedic clichés. These were situations or routines that became funnier by the very fact of their repetition. Audiences came to welcome each new variation on the familiar theme. Two of the most famous were the Benny–Allen feud and Fibber McGee's closet.

On one episode of his program in 1937, Fred Allen, following a dazzling guest performance by a 10-year-old violinist, ad-libbed, "Jack Benny should be ashamed of himself." Fortunately, Benny was listening and thought it was funny, so on his next program he reacted by defending his own prowess on the violin, making some disparaging remarks about Allen in the process, and the "feud" was on. The two programs played the supposed conflict for laughs until Allen finally left the air in 1949.

Fibber McGee and Molly was one of radio's longest running situation comedies. As played by real-life married couple Marian and Jim Jordan, Fibber was a lovable windbag and Molly his patient wife. This program may have had more running gags than any other, the most famous being a hall closet so stuffed full of junk that every time the door was opened everything would come crashing down in a nearly epic cacophony of sound. Listeners at home could either laugh at the closet of their imaginations or at the sound effects wizardry that went into its creation. At the end of the last clink, Fibber would inevitably say, "I've gotta clean out that closet one of these days."

War and Controversy

During World War II, radio comedy played its part in keeping homefront morale high. Most programs integrated war-related themes into their plotlines or sketches. The 1944 New Year's *Jack Benny Program* contains a sketch in which a metaphorical World Series baseball game is played between the Axis Polecats and the Allied All-Stars. Various military campaigns are transformed into hits, sacrifice flies, and walks. As the program ends, General Eisenhower is about to come to bat. Later in 1944, on *Fibber McGee and Molly*, Fibber thinks he has a brilliant idea that will revolutionize post-war travel, but he must travel from his home in Wistful Vista in order to pitch it to some government official. The trains are filled with servicemen either returning from or going on leave. No matter

how hard he tries, Fibber can't get a ticket and is berated by everyone he meets for trying to take up valuable space that could be used by a soldier to get home. At the end of the program, the Jordans step out of character and appeal directly to the audience not to travel unless absolutely necessary. Comedy shows also addressed other topics like scrap drives, War Bonds, victory gardens, the rubber shortage and anything else that helped out "our boys."

The war had another effect on radio comedy. During the 1930s, comedians and writers had avoided potentially controversial topics such as politics in their plots or sketches. The only notable exception to this rule was humorist Will Rogers, whose rural-flavored, good-natured ribbing made his jibes palatable. ("I don't belong to an organized political party," he would say. "I'm a Democrat.") But when Rogers was killed in a plane crash in 1935, radio comedy became essentially a controversy-free zone. For example, at one point in 1940, Fibber McGee apologized for inadvertently saying "china" on the air when he meant dishes, acknowledging that "we can't say anything controversial."

Once America was in the war in late 1941, however, radio comedy took a turn for the political: references to national and world events, governmental leaders, and current issues were woven into scripts. Among the most bitingly satirical of the newer generation of comedians was Henry Morgan, whose program, *Here's Morgan*, began on a local station in New York before getting a spot on the Mutual Network. He once "interviewed" a businessman in a mythical southern state who said the new governor of Georgia—formerly associated with the KKK—was great for his business, manufacturing bed sheets. On another show, in the postwar era when housing was tight, he presented a dialog between two landlords, one of whom expressed dismay that the eighth floor of his tenement had caved in. When asked if anyone was hurt, the landlord replied, "No, just tenants." He wasn't particularly kind to business institutions, either. "You know," he said, "most people think of banks as cold, heartless, large institutions. And they're wrong. There are small ones, too." This kind of humor on radio would have been almost unthinkable only a few years earlier.

Situation Comedy

The postwar era also saw the rise of the situation comedy. Aside from its pictures, the format of the modern-day TV sitcom is virtually indistinguishable from that of its radio progenitor of the 1940s. The

American family was the central location for many of them—*The Great Gildersleeve*, *The Aldrich Family*, *Father Knows Best*, *Blondie*—but sitcoms also found comedy in high school (*Our Miss Brooks*), in the blue collar workplace (*The Life of Riley*), a restaurant (*Meet Me at Parky's*), and even a bar (*Duffy's Tavern*).

One of the most popular was *The Phil Harris-Alice Faye Show*, in which Jack Benny's band leader and his wife, a popular singer and film actress, played fictionalized versions of themselves. The versatile actor–director Elliot Lewis played Frankie Remley, an actual member of Harris' band. The program grew out of the many wisecracks from the Benny show about the band's supposed incompetence (though it was obviously first rate), Harris' presumed inability to read (words *or* music), and Remley's purported drinking. These characteristics were extended and enlarged in the sitcom, and placed within the context of the zany Harris–Faye home life and Phil and Frankie's misadventures.

MacDonald calls these shows middle-class morality tales with the family portrayed as *the* vital American institution. Plots tended to revolve around insignificant misunderstandings that were resolved by show's end. Such core values as trust, love, honesty, and tolerance always triumphed. Of the top 10 programs in the 1947 season chosen by Protestant churches as those most faithfully portraying American life, five were situation comedies.

Television Takes Charge

But by the end of the 1940s, the end of an era was drawing near. After having been postponed first by war, and then by technical problems, television was now ready to take its place as the center of family home entertainment. Radio fought its upstart competitor with, among other things, a weekly, 90-minute comedy–variety extravaganza on NBC called *The Big Show*, hosted by the Broadway and film star Tallulah Bankhead and featuring numerous guest stars from all points on the entertainment compass. But it was too much and too late. Though lavish and expensive, it only lasted two seasons.

Other comedians and sitcoms were rapidly jumping ship to try out the new medium. Most of the old line vaudevillians were unable to make the transition, except for occasional guest appearances on TV variety shows like *The Colgate Comedy Hour*. A few did well, however. Jack Benny first appeared on the small screen in 1950 but continued to do the radio program concurrently with television until 1955. Bob Hope also ended his radio

series in 1955 and continued to perform on television for more than 30 years. Red Skelton was even more successful on television than on radio because so much of his humor was visual. His weekly television series ran from 1951 to 1971 and was usually among the highest-rated shows on the air. But the most spectacular transition from radio to television was made by Milton Berle. His radio career had been indifferent at best, but his broad, visual form of comedy was perfect for the tube. What *Amos 'n' Andy* had done for radio 20 years earlier, Berle did for television: create excitement about the new medium and sell receiving sets.

On the other hand, Fred Allen had retired from radio in 1949, a victim of falling ratings and his own poor health. He did guest spots on television but never seemed really comfortable there. Allen was a "word" man in a visual medium. His last job on the air was as a panelist on the TV game show, *What's My Line?*

One of radio's lasting legacies was the situation comedy format. Although the sitcom found success on radio, it has flourished on television for even longer. Making their way to television from radio were, among others, *The Life of Riley*, *Father Knows Best*, *Burns and Allen*, *The Goldbergs*, *December Bride*, and a reworked form of Lucille Ball's radio series *My Favorite Husband*, retitled *I Love Lucy*.

Wit, Satire, and Shock

Although radio comedy on a national scale dwindled during the 1950s, replaced by local disc jockeys and personalities, there was still room for innovative young comics with a satirical edge to their humor. Bob Elliot and Ray Goulding, more familiarly known as *Bob and Ray*, had started their radio career in Boston, joining the NBC network for a daily 15-minute slot in 1951. Eventually they were heard on all the commercial networks at various times until 1960 and even did several limited series on National Public Radio in the 1980s. Their straight-faced, understated routines were frequently hilarious. They generally used no script, sometimes improvising absurd mock interviews as conducted by ace reporter Wally Ballou ("winner of seven international diction awards"), other times spoofing soap operas with scenes from *One Feller's Family* (a dig at the long-running *One Man's Family*) or *Mary Backstayge, Noble Wife*. The detective series, *Mr. Keen, Tracer of Lost Persons* became *Mr. Trace, Keener Than Most Persons*. They offered numerous ersatz premiums, such as the Bob and Ray Home Surgery Kit or membership in Heightwatcher's

International ("six ample servings of low vitamins and nutrients in artificial colorings"). With parody, verbal nonsense, non sequitur, and wit they created what has been described as a surrealistic Dickensian repertory company, all of it clean, subtle and gentle.

Jean Shepherd's rambling, discursive, free-form style was a lineal audio descendant of that of Henry Morgan. Shepherd's program, *Night People*, was broadcast on New York's WOR from 1956 to 1977 and heard in 27 states, parts of Canada and as far south as Bermuda. He was a comic anthropologist, offering mock commentary on social and cultural trends and behavior. A radio raconteur, he would launch into a rambling chat with a central story in mind, often digressing wildly, sometimes playing "The Sheik of Araby" on the kazoo while rhythmically thumping his knuckles on his head, usually wandering back to his main point just as time was running out on his show. His extemporaneous storytelling has been compared to making pizza in the window of a restaurant.

When broadcasting was largely deregulated in the 1980s, standards for acceptable content were liberalized. This made way for so-called "shock jocks" like Morton Downey, Jr., Don Imus, and Andrew Dice Clay, radio personalities whose routine references to sex and use of crude language resulted in endless controversy, occasional fines from the FCC, and laments that the end of civilization was at hand. None have generated more notoriety than Howard Stern, self-styled King of All Media (AKA Fartman), who parlayed a local show in New York into one of the highest-rated programs in national syndication. Stern's clownish, flamboyant brand of humor is the lowest of low brow. He frequently describes his own sexual fantasies, engages in personal attacks, and serves up his own bizarre take on current events (he once wondered how necrophiliac Jeffrey Dahmer could get a fair trial unless there were more guys on the jury who wanted to have sex with dead men). He is rude, crude, and, to fans, often very funny.

At the other end of the spectrum, both figuratively and literally (being at the bottom of the FM dial) is humor served up by public radio. *Car Talk* features Click and Clack, the Tappet Brothers (Tom and Ray Magliozzi), dispensing car advice between self-deprecating jokes, funny letters from listeners, puzzlers, and features like "Stump the Chumps," in which callers are asked if advice they got from Click and Clack some time previous was any good (frequently it wasn't, but nobody really seems to mind). Michael Feldman's *Whad'Ya Know?* is a two-hour comedy/quiz on which audience members

and callers compete for whimsical prizes. *Wait Wait...Don't Tell Me* plays the week's news for laughs and offers callers who correctly answer questions the highly coveted prize of veteran newscaster Carl Castle's voice on their answering machine. *Rewind* also lampoons the news through comic skits and extemporaneous commentary from guest comedians.

The one real throwback to an earlier era is Garrison Keillor's *Prairie Home Companion*, which, ironically, has been on the air longer than any of the original comedy–variety shows. Broadcast live before a large theater audience, its form—if not its content—is somewhat reminiscent of *The Fred Allen Show*, circa 1940. Host Keillor banters with guests, introduces musical acts (and often sings himself), and performs with his troupe in various comedy sketches and fake commercials for "sponsors" like Powdermilk Bisquits and the Catsup Advisory Board. The centerpiece is a weekly 20-minute monolog, "News from Lake Wobegon," in which Keillor tells stories and ruminates on life in his mythical Minnesota home town.

Although radio has certainly not abandoned comedy, it has yielded to television its place as America's primary purveyor of laughter. Mostly gone, then, is a form of humor that depends on listeners' active participation through imagination. Susan Douglas calls this "dimensional listening." For example, Jack Benny's money vault was never as funny on television as it had been on radio, when listeners conjured up their own visions of moats, chains, gates, and a bearded guard who had not seen the light of day since the Civil War. This was radio's contribution to comedy and has since passed into aural history.

See also, in addition to programs mentioned in this entry: Situation Comedy; Stereotypes on Radio; Variety Shows; Vaudeville and Radio

Further Reading

Buxton, Frank, and Bill Owen, *Radio's Golden Age: The Programs and the Personalities*, New York: Easton Valley Press, 1966; revised edition, as *The Big Broadcast: 1920–1950*, New York: Viking Press, 1972.

Douglas, Susan J., "Radio Comedy and Linguistic Slapstick," in *Listening In: Radio and the American Imagination*, by Douglas, New York: Times Books, 1999.

Dunning, John, *Tune in Yesterday: The Ultimate Encyclopedia of Old-Time Radio, 1925–1976*, Englewood Cliffs, New Jersey: Prentice-Hall, 1976; revised edition, as *On The Air: The Encyclopedia of Old-Time Radio*, New York: Oxford University Press, 1998.

Firestone, Ross, editor, *The Big Radio Comedy Program*, Chicago: Contemporary Books, 1978.

Flick Lives: "A Salute to Jean Shepherd," www.flicklives.com/index.html.

Gaver, Jack, and Dave Stanley, *There's Laughter in the Air! Radio's Top Comedians and Their Best Shows*, New York: Greenberg, 1945.

Harmon, Jim, *The Great Radio Comedians*, Garden City, New York: Doubleday, 1970.

Havig, Alan R., *Fred Allen's Radio Comedy*, Philadelphia, Pennsylvania: Temple University Press, 1990.

Hilmes, Michele, *Radio Voices: American Broadcasting, 1922–1952*, Minneapolis: University of Minnesota Press, 1997.

Lackmann, Ronald W., *Same Time, Same Station: An A–Z Guide to Radio from Jack Benny to Howard Stern*, New York: Facts on File, 1996; revised edition, as *The Encyclopedia of American Radio: An A–Z Guide to Radio from Jack Benny to Howard Stern*, 2000.

MacDonald, J. Fred, *Don't Touch That Dial!: Radio Programming in American Life, 1920–1960*, Chicago: Nelson-Hall, 1979.

Nachman, Gerald, *Raised on Radio*, New York: Pantheon Books, 1998.

Poole, Gary, *Radio Comedy Diary: A Researcher's Guide to the Actual Jokes and Quotes of the Top Comedy Programs of 1947–1950*, Jefferson, North Carolina: McFarland, 2001.

Radio Days: "Comedy Central," www.otr.com/comedy.html.

Wertheim, Arthur Frank, *Radio Comedy*, New York: Oxford University Press, 1979.

ALAN BELL

COMMERCIAL LOAD
Amount of Advertising Carried on Radio

Commercial load refers to the total amount of time commercials are broadcast on radio during an hour or some other specific time period. Radio stations, unlike the print media, have a limited commercial inventory, a finite amount of time available for advertising "spots." A broadcast hour cannot be longer than 60 minutes, and the broadcast day cannot be longer than 24 hours, whereas newspapers and magazines can add as many pages as necessary. Further, only so many commercials can be packed into each hour's programming without losing a significant part of the audience.

At one time, the National Association of Broadcasters (NAB) code recommended a limit of 18 minutes of commercials per hour on radio. But the NAB discarded the code when in 1984 the U.S. Justice Department alleged that the standards, although voluntary, violated antitrust laws by promoting limits that discouraged competition.

Historically, astute station management has carefully limited commercial load. When the legendary Bill Drake reinvented top 40 radio at KHJ in Los Angeles in the 1960s, he maintained an "iron-clad" hourly limit on commercials. Drake ordered that commercials should not exceed 13 minutes, 40 seconds per hour, nearly one-third less than the U.S. average at the time. When FM finally became successful in the late 1960s and early 1970s, listeners perceived it as the "less-commercials band," and operators wanting to maintain their stations' success instituted firm policies limiting the number of spot announcements per hour.

Since the top 40 hit-music format emerged in the 1950s, radio stations have grouped commercials in clusters called "spot sets" (or "stop sets"). A common approach has been to promote longer "sweeps" of uninterrupted music, a strategy that requires fewer but longer commercial breaks. However, an Arbitron/Edison Media Research study found strong support for more frequent, and shorter, spot sets. Fifty-two percent of those surveyed preferred more frequent stops with shorter blocks of commercials, whereas 39 percent prefer longer programming blocks and longer blocks of commercials. The findings led the report's authors to recommend that radio stations consider changes in their spot-clustering paradigms, but only after conducting research of their own audience's listening habits.

The number of commercial minutes each hour is entirely up to the management of each individual station. Increasingly, writers on the topic are concerned that a trend toward increasing the number of commercials per hour is having a negative effect on radio listenership. The Radio Advertising Bureau reported that radio-advertising revenue exceeded $17 billion in 1999, up 15 percent from the previous year. However, radio listenership had declined 12 percent over the past decade, according to the consulting firm Duncan's American Radio, with only 15.4 percent of the national population age 12 and over listening in any quarter hour, 6 A.M. to midnight, down from 17.5 percent in 1989. One of the reasons for the decline, according to Duncan's, is the trend toward higher spot loads. Some sources report stations airing up to 22 commercial minutes per hour.

A 2000 study by Empower Media Marketing of Cincinnati found that the number of paid advertisements on radio stations grew by about 6 percent in the previous year. The greatest increase was in the San Francisco–Oakland–San Jose, California, market, where the number of 10-, 30-, and 60-second spots increased by 20 percent (see Kranhold, 2000). A 2001 Arbitron study found that advertisers perceived radio as the most "cluttered" mass communications medium. Although clutter (or the absence of clutter) was not considered a key criterion by most advertisers, the report recommended reducing spot loads.

Another Arbitron report suggests that higher commercial loads are turning off audiences. In the report titled "Will Your Audience Be Right Back After These Messages?" Arbitron and Edison found that 42 percent of radio listeners had noticed that stations are airing more commercials, although, interestingly, listeners are not as likely to believe that their own favorite station is playing more spots. Young listeners seem to be the most annoyed by the trend. The report found 31 percent of listeners ages 12–24 said they were listening to radio less, whereas 17 percent of listeners in the 25–54 demographic, and 11 percent of those 55 and older, said they were listening to less radio. The report suggests that the greater number of commercials is a major reason for the decline in time-spent-listening. Advertising agencies, on the other hand, suggest the results show the need for more entertaining commercials.

A Washington, D.C., station, WWVZ, seemingly took to heart Arbitron's advice to reduce commercial spot loads. The station implemented a format with only two three-minute commercial breaks per hour. An advertising executive with Hill, Holliday in Boston, Karen Agresti, hailed the station's decision. "Clutter is one of the biggest problems in radio. For a station to take a lower load is great, and I hope more will do it," she said. WBLI-FM (Long Island, New York), a contemporary hits station, cut its commercial load from 16–17 minutes per hour to 10–11 minutes. The station gained 3.5 ratings points among its core audience, women 18–34.

On a much larger scale, the Clear Channel company attempted a similar reinvention in early 2005. Amid much fanfare, it announced its "Less is More" campaign in order to offer listeners to its 1,200 stations more music and fewer commercials. Clear Channel announced it would achieve this by lowering the number of commercials aired per hour (from as many as 18 minutes per hour to 15 minutes) and by airing only 15- and 30-second spots as opposed to the more typical 60 seconds. Additionally, the company vowed to air no commercial break greater than four minutes in length or air any break that consisted of more than six commercials in a row.

In order to make up for any loss of revenue due to this change, Clear Channel also announced that it would be raising its ad rates. Clear Channel justified its rate increases with something of a chicken-and-egg argument, telling clients that though fewer ads would be aired and so ads would cost more, in theory more people would hear them since the

company's new "low ad" stance would entice more listeners to tune in.

Unfortunately, many of its regular advertisers balked at Clear Channel's logic and their proposed price increases (which, of course, also came coupled with edicts to shorten their spots by at least half) and many departed Clear Channel (at least for the time) for more lucrative deals they found in advertising over cable TV or via the internet. Their departure quickly affected Clear Channel's profits; the business quarter after "Less is More" began, the organization reported a 13 percent decline in earnings. Nevertheless, in time, listener ratings did increase and ad revenues have since returned to earlier levels.

Clear Channel has remained committed to clearing on-air clutter by adopting a variety of new advertising methods including the practice of "integration" (where talent incorporates a mention of a sponsor's product as part of their on-air conversation) and via its pioneering use of micro-ads and "blinks," commercials which last as little as five seconds to even one second in duration.

In an attempt to make room for more commercials, some radio (and television) stations have begun using a device called "Cash," which uses audio delay and "intelligent micro-editing" to create up to six minutes of additional commercial time per hour. The use of Cash drew criticism from the president of the American Association of Advertising Agencies, O. Burtch Drake. Drake said radio will not benefit in the long run from creating more clutter. "You can shoehorn more commercials in, but it hurts both the station and the advertiser," Drake said. "That's why we are taking a very strong stand against this kind of technology."

As a way to cut through the clutter, and as an alternative to hiring high-profile celebrity endorsers, some advertising agencies are advising clients to find popular local radio personalities to endorse their products. Ironically, in order to offset its own expenses, Sirius XM is now accepting more advertising on its talk channels, running the risk of alienating its listeners/subscribers who quite possibly signed up for satellite radio in the first place because they didn't want to listen to all that clutter.

See also: Advertising; Arbitron; National Association of Broadcasters

Further Reading

Bachman, Katy, "Listeners and Advertisers Cheer Spot-less Loads," *Mediaweek* (14 December 1998).
Bachman, Katy, "Listeners Turning Off Radio," *Mediaweek* (21 June 1999).

Eberly, Philip K., *Music in the Air: America's Changing Tastes in Popular Music*, New York: Hastings House, 1982.

"Executioner" (article on Bill Drake), *Time* (23 August 1968).

Kiesewetter, John, "Big Radio Airs the Sound of Sameness," *Cincinnati Enquirer* (19 March 2000).

Kranhold, Kathryn, "Advertising on Radio Increases 6%; San Francisco Area Sees 20% Rise," *Wall Street Journal* (12, April 2000).

McBride, Sarah, "Clear Channel Scales Back Ad Time," *Wall Street Journal* (19 July 2004), p. B-4.

McWhorter, Ben, "Sales Insights! Radio's Biggest Spenders Speak Up!" Arbitron study, 2001, arbitron.com/downloads/radiosbiggestpres.pdf.

Moran, Susan, "Radio Slips...," *American Demographics* (May 1998).

Rathbun, Elizabeth A., "Clutter's in the Air," *Broadcasting & Cable* (17 April 2000).

Steinberg, Howard, "Radio as Volume Builder, Not Commodity," *Brandweek* (18 June 2001).

Stine, Randy J., "'Cash' Stokes Advertiser Concerns," *Radio World Newspaper* (1 March 2002).

Taylor, Tom, "Major Warning Signs for Radio," *M Street Daily* (8 December 1999).

"Top 40 Story: Bill Drake," *Radio and Records* (special supplement; September 1977).

Toroian, Diane, "Are Radio Stations Approaching Commercial Overload?". *St. Louis Post-Dispatch* (4 May 2000).

"Will Your Audience Be Right Back After These Messages? The Edison Media Research/Arbitron Spot Load Study" (sponsored by *Radio and Records*), www.edisonresearch.com/SpotLoadSum.htm.

J.M. DEMPSEY,
2009 REVISIONS BY CARY O'DELL

COMMERCIALS

See: Advertising

COMMERCIAL TESTS

Determining Audience Preferences

Radio advertisers have been interested in documenting the effects of their commercials since the 1930s. And since the 1980s, when TV commercials promoting radio stations became a major advertising category for local television stations, radio broadcasters have been interested in testing the efficacy of their TV ads.

Commercials (on radio or television) may be tested at any stage in the process of developing a campaign. For example, concept testing is conducted during the planning and writing stages. The campaign's appeal or its basic assumptions may be studied in focus group discussions. *Focus groups* are groups of survey participants who are chosen for their relevance to the research topic and guided through group discussions of that topic; for example, an advertiser wishing to test the potential effectiveness of a campaign to promote diapers would probably choose young mothers for participants in its focus group discussion.

Each version of an ad to be studied in commercial testing is referred to as an *execution*. If more than one execution has been created for a campaign, the object of commercial testing is to determine which execution will be more effective in producing the desired results for the advertiser. However, only relatively large advertisers produce more than one execution for a campaign. In terms of the number of commercials submitted to testing, the most common situation is a test of a single execution. In this case, the aim of commercial testing is to determine how well the commercial performs with each of its potential target audiences. In addition, testing may suggest the kind of media purchase justified by the effectiveness of the commercial. A poor commercial may not justify heavy spending on media.

What is measured in commercial testing? The most popular measures are called *scorecard measures*. They include recall, copy point recall, affinity toward brand or toward product and/or service, intent to purchase, and comparative brand preference.

Advertising strategists assume that *recall* (remembering) is produced by attention, so measurement of a subject's recall of advertisements is actually a measure of his/her attention to those ads at the time they were presented. Decades of research into advertising indicates that, by itself, consumer recall of a brand or product name is not a powerful inducement to purchase. Because of the relatively simple process for measuring recall and the straightforward analysis of data collected, however, the measure continues to be popular. A typical study to assess recall involves recruiting (by telephone) a sample of adults who watch television during known hours and who are interested in the kind of radio station portrayed in the TV commercial purchased to promote the radio station. Each recruited respondent is sent a videocassette containing a television program in which the test commercial and others are embedded. The morning after viewing the video, an interviewer calls to ask each study participant which products and services appeared in the video and what companies were represented. If 80 percent of respondents recall station KATT, then the recall score is 80 for KATT.

When using *copy point recall*, interviewers ask specific questions about features of the targeted product or features of the commercial. If 60 percent of all respondents can recall the key points from the commercial, the copy point recall is 60.

Affinity is a measure of what a person likes. It is assumed that when a consumer likes (has an affinity for) a product or sponsor, then he/she is more likely to purchase the product. Advertising research confirms a positive correlation between liking and purchase, but the relationship is not strong. Researchers often suspect that liking comes from previous exposures to the product. If a listener tunes to only one call-in show host, even if that consumer rarely listens to that host, the listener may report liking the host out of proportion to the amount of actual listening that takes place. Affinity can also be measured by scales that reflect several dimensions of liking. There is a growing preference for this kind of measure, as it may explain what considerations affect the magnitude of affinity in general. In the case of a call-in show host, listeners may like the fairness of the host and his/her treatment of callers but dislike the topics chosen for discussion on the show. This dislike for topics is likely to account for a lower-than-expected general affinity. Also, liking a product is often quite different from liking its manufacturer or dealer. The owner of a particular brand of car may dislike the quality of service provided by the dealer, so on the general affinity measure, the consumer reflects dislike although he/she retains a strong affinity for the car brand.

The *intent to purchase* question asked of a respondent may be as simple as, "Are you more likely to listen to station KATT after hearing this promotion?" Or the question may be embedded in a scenario such as "Suppose that you go to the store because you have run out of milk. You are making a special trip just for this product. When you get to the store, your favorite brand is sold out. What are the odds that you will go to another store rather than try the brand in this commercial, which is available in your store?" Advertising research shows that intent to purchase is a complicated mental process for the consumer. If a young man has been wearing the same brand of jeans for a number of years and has been pleased with that brand, a long period of time will be required to effect a change of preference to another brand (assuming the brands are similar). So exposure to a test of a radio commercial for the new brand may produce very little change in the intent measure, but that small change may be significant because the consumer previously had never considered a change in brands. This is an especially important point when the products are radio stations, as a consumer's attachment to a radio station is rarely a rational process subject to logical argument. Transfer of emotional allegiances to radio stations may initially occur very slowly, then accelerate at surprising speed.

The commercial test measure of *comparative brand preference* has considerable face validity (that is, it appears to be quite useful and reliable) for advertisers. But it is sometimes complicated to incorporate into a commercial test, and advertising research firms have risen or fallen in the past based on their handling of this measure. A typical comparative preference item might be, "If the brand you currently use was priced at $1.00 and you considered that price fair, what price would be fair for the product you heard about in the commercial?"

Tests of commercials can be performed by nearly all local market research firms. They can also be contracted for by large national firms known for commercial testing, such as Gallup and Robinson or Mapes and Ross.

See also: Audience Research Methods

Further Reading

Fletcher, James E., and Ernest Martin, Jr., "Message and Program Testing," in *Handbook of Radio and TV Broadcasting: Research Procedures in Audience, Program, and Revenues*, edited by Fletcher, New York: Van Nostrand Reinhold, 1981.
Hartshorn, Gerald Gregory, *Audience Research Sourcebook*, Washington, D.C.: National Association of Broadcasters, 1991.
National Association of Broadcasters, Research Committee, *Standard Definitions of Broadcast Research Terms*, New York: National Association of Broadcasters, 1967; 3rd edition, as *Broadcast Research Definitions*, edited by James E. Fletcher, Washington, D.C.: National Association of Broadcasters, 1988.

JAMES E. FLETCHER

COMMUNICATIONS ACT OF 1934

Since 19 June 1934, the often-amended Communications Act of 1934 has served as the basic federal statute governing most forms of interstate and foreign wireless and wired electronic communications originating in the United States. Currently codified in Title 47 of the *United States Code*, the Act created the Federal Communications Commission (FCC) as the expert administrator of the statute. The act sets basic standards for radio station ownership, licensing, and operation in the public interest in the United States and its possessions. Congress' authority to legislate in this area is based on the Commerce Clause of the U.S. Constitution (Article I, Sec. 8). Congress posits that all uses of the electromagnetic spectrum are inherently interstate in nature.

Statutory History

The Communications Act of 1934 repealed and replaced the earlier Radio Act of 1927, itself the first federal statute dealing with broadcasting. The 1934 Act, a quintessential example of "New Deal" legislation, grew from a 1933 Department of Commerce study aimed at assessing the adequacy of federal regulation of electronic media. Decrying the division of regulatory powers among various agencies, the study recommended that Congress consolidate authority over almost all forms of interstate electronic media in a single regulatory agency. The resulting act abolished the Federal Radio Commission, whose authority had been limited to users of the electromagnetic spectrum (including radio stations) and transferred authority to a reconstructed and enlarged entity, the Federal Communications Commission. It shifted responsibility for interstate wired telephony and telegraphy from the Interstate Commerce Commission to the FCC. Portions of the 1934 Act dealing with broadcasting were, for the most part, unchanged from the earlier Radio Act of 1927. The primary purpose of the new law was to strengthen federal oversight of the telephone and telegraph industries and, by placing authority over radio, telephony, and telegraphy in a single agency, to recognize that the industries overlapped somewhat.

The act has been frequently amended since 1934. Most revisions modify just a few sections of the law. Congress, for example, has repeatedly changed parts of the act regulating how broadcasters treat candidates for public office. But Congress has also found it necessary to sometimes adapt the law to large changes in the field of telecommunications that were unanticipated in 1934. Major electronic media revisions have dealt with communications satellites (1962, 1999), public broadcasting (1968), and cable television (1984, 1992). Substantial revision with the Telecommunications Act of 1996 reflected congressional recognition that previously distinct parts of the electronic media were converging and sought to enhance competition between and within segments of the electronic media and, through reliance on marketplace-induced discipline, chipped away at the New Deal philosophy that the FCC's notion of what was in the public interest was inherently preferable to relying on what industry players would do in response to consumer demand. Although the act was written when television was in its infancy, it proved unnecessary to substantially amend it when television emerged in the 1940s and 1950s. For the most part, the radio provisions of the act were simply applied to television.

The Act, the FCC, and Related Agencies

In some respects, the act functions as a bare-bones framework for federal control of electronic media. The agency it created, the FCC, is frequently relied upon to fill in details through enactment of rules and regulations that must be consistent with the act. Radio broadcasters must comply with these FCC rules and regulations, as well as with the language of the statute. Other federal laws, dealing with matters such as antitrust law, copyright law, and advertising law, also apply to radio, although they are not administered by the FCC. The federal statute pre-empts most state or local regulation of broadcasting, although general business, taxation, zoning, equal employment opportunity, and labor laws at the state level apply as long as they do not conflict with federal law.

Under the act, appeals of FCC decisions and actions are usually brought to the U.S. Court of Appeals for the D.C. Circuit, although appeals may sometimes begin in other circuits. Appeals of most FCC enforcement actions not involving licensing go to the U.S. District Courts. The U.S. Supreme Court has occasionally issued significant interpretations of the act. Only twice, however, has the Court found any part of the act unconstitutional: once, in 1996, when Congress tried to regulate indecent internet content, and earlier, in 1984, after Congress prohibited noncommercial educational broadcasters from supporting or opposing candidates for public office.

Major Provisions

Like the Radio Act of 1927, the 1934 Act mandates that the FCC regulate broadcasting in the "public interest, convenience or necessity" (Sec. 307[a]).

The act re-enacted the parts of the Radio Act of 1927 that made the FCC a "technical traffic cop" of the air, so it authorizes the commission to set technical standards for radio. The FCC allocates spectrum space to all users except the federal government (whose spectrum use is overseen by the National Telecommunications and Information Administration, a part of the Department of Commerce). In times of national emergency, the act authorizes the president to assume control over all spectrum users, although that has never happened.

Under the act, radio station licenses can be granted for up to eight years. As radio in the United States is a mature industry, with most licenses granted years ago, broadcasters rarely enter the industry by starting a new station. Rather, most enter the field by purchasing existing stations, a process that requires FCC approval. The act does not give the FCC power to directly regulate radio networks or program suppliers except insofar as those networks are also licensees of stations.

Prior to amendments in 1996, the act allowed for another party to file a competing application against a renewal applicant, and this often led to hearings in which the FCC compared the incumbent to the challenger. In 1996, however, Congress amended the act and eliminated such comparative hearings. Now, the FCC cannot entertain competing applications unless it first finds the incumbent unqualified for renewal. Under the act, broadcasters must be renewed if the station has "served the public interest, convenience, and necessity," if the station has not committed "serious violations... of [the] Act or the rules and regulations of the Commission; and...there have been no other violations by the licensee of [the] Act or the rules and regulations of the Commission which, taken together, would constitute a pattern of abuse" (Sec. 309 [k][i]). It remains possible for outsiders to intervene in the licensing process, however, because the statute still allows anyone to file a Petition to Deny with the FCC, arguing that the incumbent's application for renewal should not be granted. Absent grievous misbehavior, however, incumbents are nearly automatically renewed.

The licensing standards are a mixture of statutory requirements and regulatory requirements created by the FCC. Licensees must be legally, financially, and technically qualified. Under the statute, the ownership of radio licenses by foreigners remains strictly limited to no more than 20 percent of total stock.

The act has been amended to require that most users of the electromagnetic spectrum (e.g., cellular phone systems and common-carrier satellite services) pay spectrum use fees, usually set through spectrum auctions. Congress, however, generally prohibits the FCC from charging broadcasters for spectrum. The theory is that, in exchange for free use of the spectrum, broadcasters provide free over-the-air broadcast services that promote the public interest. Broadcasters do pay small regulatory fees for such things as the processing of license applications by the FCC. Congress expects the FCC, through such fees, to recover annually an amount equal to its own cost of operation. In an economic sense, the FCC is expected to be minimally self-sustaining and, through spectrum auctions where they do apply, to generate substantial surplus revenue for the U.S. treasury.

In 1996 Congress amended the act and greatly liberalized radio ownership. It prohibited the FCC from setting any national limit on the number of stations owned and directed the commission to study (and presumably relax) within-market radio ownership limits.

Regulating Content

The act has long been schizophrenic about the regulation of radio content. Concerned about how they were treated by radio broadcasters, Congress directed in the Radio Act of 1927 that broadcasters provide equal opportunities for opposing candidates for public office to use stations. These provisions, sometimes erroneously called "equal-time" laws, were re-enacted in the 1934 Act and, with some modifications, continue today. The provisions stipulate that radio (and television) broadcasters must treat legally qualified opposing candidates for all elected political offices alike. If a broadcaster, for example, sells advertising time to one candidate, the radio station must, within certain time limits, be prepared to sell equal amounts of time, with comparable audience potential, to opposing candidates at the same rate charged the first candidate. In 1959, however, Congress amended Sec. 315 of the act to exempt most news-related programming from these requirements. In 1971, Congress mandated in a new Sec. 312 [a][7] that radio stations must provide for "reasonable access" to their stations by legally qualified candidates for federal elective office only—state and local offices such as governor or mayor are excluded—but commercial radio stations can fulfill this requirement exclusively through paid advertising time (Sec. 312 [a][7]). During the 45 days before a primary election and the 60 days before a general election, the act specifies that candidates for any office cannot be charged more than the "lowest unit charge" for advertising on stations, and they can never be charged more than other commercial advertisers are charged for comparable uses. When candidates make use of stations under these sections of the act, broadcasters are powerless to censor what candidates say, even if their uses may be libelous, obscene, or offensive to viewers—and thus cannot be held legally liable for what a candidate says.

Despite this regulation of political content, the act's Sec. 326, in language from the Radio Act of 1927, prohibits the FCC from exercising "censorship over the radio communications or signals transmitted by any radio station" and states that "no regulation or condition shall be promulgated or fixed by the commission which shall interfere with the right of free speech by means of radio communication." But, in possibly contradictory terms, it also requires the FCC to regulate radio in the public interest. Between 1934 and 1984, the FCC—relying on the generic public-interest standard—exercised broad, categorical regulation of radio content. Congress has not interfered in the commission's modern pursuit of marketplace-based deregulation and has agreed with the FCC that relying on the marketplace is consistent with the public-interest standard of the act.

The Radio Act of 1927 and the Communications Act of 1934 as originally enacted by Congress forbade the broadcast of "obscene, indecent or profane utterances" by radio. In 1948, however, these sections were moved by Congress from the Communications Act to the United States Criminal Code (18 U.S.C. Sec. 1464). Acting under the public-interest portions of the act, however, the FCC continues to enforce regulations that prohibit obscene radio broadcasts and that attempt to channel indecent broadcasts to times of day when few children are listening.

The statutory framework created by Congress in 1927 and 1934 has proven to be durable and flexible. Without major modification, it accommodated the displacement of AM radio by FM and the creation of satellite-delivered digital radio services. In the early 21st century, it appears that analog terrestrial radio broadcasting, a technology of the 1920s, can be replaced by DAB without major changes to this long-lived statute.

See also: "Equal Time" Rule; Federal Communications Commission; Federal Radio Commission; Licensing Authorizing U.S. Stations to Broadcast; Obscenity and Indecency on Radio; Public Broadcasting Act of 1967; Radio Laws; Regulation; Telecommunications Act of 1996; United States Congress and Radio

Further Reading

Aufderheide, Patricia, *Communications Policy and the Public Interest: The Telecommunications Act 0/1996*, New York: Guilford Press, 1999.

Carter, T. Barton, Marc A. Franklin, and Jay B. Wright, *The First Amendment and the Fifth Estate: Regulation of Electronic Mass Media*, Mineola, New York: Foundation Press, 1986; 5th edition, 1999.

The Communications Act 0f 1934, 47 USC 609 (1934) (Title 47 of the *United States Code*).

Emery, Walter Byron, *Broadcasting and Government: Responsibilities and Regulations*, East Lansing: Michigan State University Press, 1961; revised edition, 1971.

McChesney, Robert Waterman, *Telecommunications, Mass Media, and Democracy: The Battle for the Control of U.S. Broadcasting, 1928–1935*, New York and Oxford: Oxford University Press, 1993.

Olufs, Dick W., III, *The Making of Telecommunications Policy*, Boulder, Colorado: Rienner, 1999.

Paglin, Max D., editor, *A Legislative History of the Communications Act Of 1934*, New York and Oxford: Oxford University Press, 1989.

Paglin, Max D., Joel Rosenbloom, and James R. Hobson, editors, *The Communications Act: A Legislative History of the Major Amendments, 1934–96*, Silver Spring, Maryland: Pike and Fischer, 1999.

HERBERT A. TERRY

COMMUNITY RADIO
Small FM Noncommercial Stations

More than any other broadcast medium, community radio reflects the cultural diversity of a region. In the United States, for example, KILI in Porcupine, South Dakota, airs a morning drive program in the Native American Lakota language; Monterey, Virginia's WVLS broadcasts volunteer-produced community-affairs programs across the Shenandoah Valley. KRZA in Alamosa, New Mexico, offers bilingual programming to southern Colorado and northern New Mexico, and WWOZ fills the New Orleans airwaves with early and modern jazz, blues, gospel, and funk.

Community radio stations may be found in isolated hamlets and major cities. They may feature highly eclectic programming or be geared to serving one community exclusively. In spite of their differences, community stations have several qualities in common: they are governed by the communities they serve; they provide a sounding board for local politics and culture; and they are committed to reaching groups, particularly women and minorities, overlooked by other broadcasters. Community radio stations follow the Pacifica Foundation's practices of volunteer programming and listener sponsorship. Like the Pacifica stations, community stations often feature eclectic music and politically activist news and public-affairs programming. However, these stations tend to be smaller and less structured than Pacifica's high-profile stations. In addition, community stations are locally governed, whereas the licenses of Pacifica stations are held by a central board of directors.

Community radio's history began in 1962 when a former Pacifica KPFA station volunteer, Lorenzo Milam, founded KRAB-FM in Seattle, Washington. Whereas Pacifica was somewhat staid, with a more or less paternalistic approach to programming at the time, Milam embraced the then-unheard of notion that radio stations should be run by the listeners themselves. Milam was a man of some financial means, and he eagerly committed his resources to his vision of a truly "public" radio system. In 1968 Milam and his partner, Jeremy

COMMUNITY RADIO

Lansman, founded KBOO in Portland, Oregon, and KDNA in St. Louis, Missouri. Following a series of conflicts between the station's primarily white management and the African-American community, Milam and Lansman sold KDNA to a commercial firm in 1973 for more than $1 million. They used the sale's proceeds to fund 14 community stations around the country in the early 1970s.

The whimsy of Milam's and Lansman's intentions is reflected in the call letters for stations in what they termed the "KRAB Nebula": WORT in Madison, Wisconsin; WDNA in Miami; KOTO in Telluride, Colorado; WAIF in Cincinnati, Ohio; and KCHU ("the wettest spot on the dial") in Dallas, Texas. During the mid-1970s, a community station's typical broadcast day might consist of:

> …music from India blended with readings from esoteric magazines, blues and jazz from very old or very new recordings and the '50s rock and roll antics of Screamin' Jay Hawkins' "I Put a Spell On You," followed by a rare classical recording by Enrico Caruso. Later in the week [listeners] may have turned to a feminist talk program, a program for the gay community… a 12-tone music program, poetry, a noon-hour interview with a flamenco guitarist, music of the Caribbean, news from the Reuters wire service and tapes of speeches by political activists of the '60s. Programs wouldn't necessarily appear at the right times, some announcers had difficulty pronouncing the titles of the works they were introducing, microphones wouldn't always be opened in time to allow a speaker to be heard, and much laughter was heard.
>
> (Routt, et al., 1978)

Community conflicts at KCHU in Dallas led to Milam's withdrawal from the community radio movement. KCHU signed off the air on 1 September 1977, the first community station to cease broadcasting since KPFA's temporary sign-off in 1950.

Nevertheless, the community radio movement continued to grow. In 1975 the National Federation of Community Broadcasters (NFCB) was founded in Washington, D.C., as a professional support and advocacy group by 25 community stations. The community radio movement gradually moved beyond its counter-cultural past to embrace an array of minority-controlled stations serving Native American, Hispanic, and African-American communities. By the late 1990s the NFCB counted 140 member stations around the country. Of these stations, 46 percent are minority-operated, and 41 percent serve rural communities. At the same time, many community radio stations in major metropolitan areas face the "mission versus audience" dilemma that plagues the public radio system. Do these stations stay true to their original mission of serving a variety of small audiences, or do they

focus on capturing a single, larger, and more affluent audience? To ensure their financial survival, some large-market community radio stations have followed their Pacifica counterparts in abandoning their traditional, freewheeling eclecticism in favor of more homogeneous programming designed to attract "marketable" audiences.

At these and other community radio stations, debates over policy, programming, and funding are commonplace. Because of the strong ideological commitment of their participants, relations between volunteers (as well as between volunteers and staffers) may be emotionally charged and highly fractious. Democracy has never been noted for its efficiency, and, at times, dominant factions within community radio stations have adopted authoritarian models of leadership that are the antithesis of community broadcasting. Yet, despite a chronic lack of funds and occasional internecine conflicts, community radio stations continue to erase the line between broadcasters and listeners. Their accessibility, as well as the range of their programming, makes community radio in the eyes of many people the closest approximation to the ideal of "public" broadcasting in the United States.

Despite being heavily affected by the same problems currently facing all of radio (decreasing ad revenues, splintering audiences), as community radio has always emphasized commitment over capital, it will likely endure. It has been bolstered by the Prometheus Radio Project (a group devoted to helping small broadcasters and founding small stations) and by the ongoing efforts of Pacifica. Community radio's survival lies in its ability to give listeners something they cannot get from other broadcasters, be it localized information and news, or a willingness to serve groups rarely addressed by larger broadcasters, including rural residents, minorities, the poor (who may not have easy access to internet-based providers), and even local prison populations.

See also: Alternative Format; College Radio; Localism in Radio; Low-Power Radio/Microradio; National Federation of Community Broadcasters; Native American Radio; Pacifica Foundation; Ten-Watt Stations

Further Reading

Armstrong, David, *A Trumpet to Arms: Alternative Media in America*, Los Angeles: Tarcher, 1981.
Engelman, Ralph, *Public Radio and Television in America: A Political History*, Thousand Oaks, California: Sage, 1996.
Fisher, Marc, "Hear the News from Loudoun County" Well, You Won't Anymore, *Washington Post* (27 May 2008).
Lewis, Peter M., and Jerry Booth, *The Invisible Medium: Public, Commercial, and Community Radio*, Washington, D.C.: Howard University Press, 1990.

Milam, Lorenzo W., *Sex and Broadcasting: A Handbook on Starting a Radio Station for the Community*, 2nd edition, Saratoga, California: Dildo Press, 1972; 4th edition, as *The Original Sex and Broadcasting*, San Diego, California: MHO and MHO, 1988.

Milam, Lorenzo W., *The Radio Papers: From KRAB to KCHU: Essays on the Act and Practice of Radio Transmission*, San Diego, California: MHO and MHO, 1986.

Routt, Edd, James B. McGrath, and Fredric Weiss, *The Radio Format Conundrum*, New York: Hastings House, 1978.

Tom McCourt,
2009 Revisions By Cary O'Dell

CONELRAD

Emergency Warning System

Instituted in 1951, CONELRAD served as America's first mandated nationwide emergency broadcast notification program. It was a direct result of official fears that Russian planes might try striking the United States with atomic bombs.

Only a decade earlier, Japanese aircraft had devastated Pearl Harbor, Hawaii, thus pulling the United States into World War II. Later, members of the Japanese attack force admitted that they had easily navigated to their target by simply homing in on the AM radio signal of Honolulu station KGMB. American military leaders and civil defense planners would not soon forget such a modus operandi, and so they sought to develop a way to keep local broadcast communication flowing without providing a beacon for an enemy.

Soviet Russia's 1949 acquisition of nuclear weaponry reminded nervous U.S. officials that bombers poised to deliver nuclear warheads could adroitly locate any of the several thousand American communities that had an AM radio outlet. On any given day or night in the New York metropolitan area, for example, each Russian flyer in the attacking squadron would have his choice of any one of over a dozen strong, standard broadcast stations. And to make matters worse, maps that ordinary folk, as well as spies, could buy from the federal government for a couple of dollars pinpointed the exact whereabouts of every significant AM transmitter tower.

In 1951 President Harry Truman approved a plan to control all domestic radio waves so that navigators in enemy aircraft could not be aided by listening to an American broadcast station. The plan for *control* of electromagnetic *radiation*, which was simplified into the acronym "CONELRAD," was in practice a complex scheme of transmitter sign-offs and sign-ons, power reductions, and frequency shifts designed to confound hostile bomber crews. It had the potential to confuse loyal Americans, too.

A civil defense pamphlet printed shortly after CONELRAD's implementation explained that "at the first indication of enemy bombers approaching the United States, [the Commanding Officer of the Air Division Defense or higher military authority will instruct] all television and FM radio stations to go off the air." In the days before portable, battery-powered TVs or FM personal or automobile radios, no-one considered either service a reliable means of conveying emergency information. Typically, television and FM stations received their cue to sign-off through a silence-sensor device that detected the sudden absence of key AM outlets, which had also been ordered to be quiet. In daisy-chain fashion, all television, FM, and AM stations would go silent. Along with the TV and FM facilities, many of these AM stations were required to stay dark in order to make way for certain designated CONELRAD AM stations that, during the brief shutdown, had quickly switched their transmitter frequency to either 640 or 1,240 kHz (whichever was closest to each particular station's regular Federal Communications Commission [FCC]-assigned dial position) and then returned to the air with less than normal output power. Understandably, antenna systems customized for, say, 1,600 kHz, suffered efficiency loss when coupled to a jury-rigged 1,240-kHz transmitter. Officials admitted that "the changeover to CONELRAD [frequency and power level] takes a few minutes" and suggested that the understandably anxious public "not be alarmed by the radio silence in the meanwhile."

Once the participating CONELRAD stations resumed broadcasting on their new (640-kHz or 1,240-kHz) wavelength, they were all required to air the same emergency programming instructing the citizenry what to do next. During this information transmission, the CONELRAD outlets would sequentially shut down momentarily. The idea was to have, at any given time during the crisis, ample operating CONELRAD stations to reach the public, while making normal radio station frequency, city-of-origin guides, and transmitter tower maps completely useless from an air-navigational standpoint.

In theory, attempting to decipher the true identity of a CONELRAD station would be like trying to identify which person, in an auditorium filled with whisperers, was intermittently whispering. In practice, though, not all of these elaborately cloaked CONELRAD facilities were effective conduits for vital communication. This was especially true at 1,240 kHz, to which many of the participating stations were switched. In CONELRAD test runs, suburbanites near New Brunswick, New Jersey, tuning to the 1,240 spot occupied by local WCTC and not-too-distant WNEW (now WBBR) New York heard little there but unintelligible crosstalk interference. The 640-kHz CONELRAD setup was the better bet. On that less crowded lower dial position, the result included noticeable station overlapping and some heterodyne whistling, but it delivered readable signals to much of the country.

A young broadcast buff, Donald Browne, recalled rushing home in late April of 1961 from his Bridgeport, Connecticut, high school to catch a CONELRAD dress rehearsal. He described this final CONELRAD system-wide test as sounding "real spooky," like something from *The Twilight Zone* television show. Browne noted that "several primary stations could be heard simultaneously on 640, all with the same program, each slightly delayed or out of phase with the others, like one weird echo effect...and probably scaring more listeners than they informed."

Most Cold War-era radio audiences took CONELRAD quite seriously. The government asked broadcasters to tout the warning system by ubiquitously airing public service announcements capped with a tiny jingle that went, "Six-forty, twelve-forty... Con-el-rad." Then people were urged to "mark those numbers on [their] radio set, now!" Starting in 1953, though, every AM radio sold in America was required to have a civil defense logo triangle factory-printed on its dial at 640 and at 1,240 kHz.

In addition, CONELRAD regulations touched the amateur or "ham" radio community. As with commercial broadcast outlets, amateur stations were required to cease transmitting at the first sign of a CONELRAD activation. The consumer electronics maker *Heathkit* offered an inexpensive automatic alarm unit that would ring a bell and immediately cut-off one's ham transmitter if any local broadcast station being monitored suddenly left the air. CONELRAD architects could take no chances with some unwitting 25-W radio hobbyist who might innocently mention his backyard antenna's whereabouts during an atomic enemy sortie. Hams, as well as staff at nonparticipating CONELRAD radio and TV stations, knew to listen closely to the official 640/1,240 facilities for the "Radio All Clear." Initiated by the Air Defense Commander (or higher military official), this relief meant that the CONELRAD emergency test had ended and heralded the resumption of normal transmissions over regular AM, FM, TV, amateur, and other FCC-licensed frequencies.

By the early 1960s, Soviet missiles, including those they briefly positioned in Cuba, made up a nuclear weapon delivery system far more sophisticated than an airplane navigated via some unsuspecting pop music radio station. Therefore, in 1963 CONELRAD was scrapped as obsolete. Its cumbersome 640/1,240 frequency shifting, power reducing, and on/off sequencing went the way of the wind, but positive aspects of CONELRAD's warning scheme (such as employing a series of primary, participating stations to reach the public) were revamped into the Emergency Broadcast System, which stayed in effect through 1996, when it, in turn, was superseded by the Emergency Alert System.

See also: Emergency Alert System

Further Reading

Beeman, Bess, *A Resolution*, Women's Advisory Council for Defense and Disaster Relief, June 30, 1961 [pamphlet].
"CONELRAD," in *Federal Communications Commission Rules, Regulations, and Standards*, Paragraphs 4.51 through 4.57 (1952).
Kobb, Bennett, "The Last Radio Network," *Northern Observer Newsletter* (November 1990).
United States Federal Civil Defense Administration, *Six Steps to Survival: If An Enemy Attacked Today Would You Know What to Do?* Washington, D.C.: GPO, 1956.

PETER E. HUNN

CONSULTANTS

Radio consultants, also known as "radio doctors" or "hired guns," advise stations on how best to increase listenership and thereby strengthen ratings. Consultants focus on improving a station's image or "sound," refining music playlists, and conducting audience research, all with the end goal of bringing success to a given station.

Development of Radio Consultants

Radio consulting as a profession had its beginnings at the end of the 1950s. By that time, commercial radio had evolved to the point of encompassing distinct programming formats. Rock and roll music changed the radio landscape: formats aimed at specific audiences came into being, notably Top 40, middle of the road, country, and beautiful music. According to Michael C. Keith (1987), radio consulting began in the U.S. Midwest. The first radio consultant, Mike Joseph, decided to start his own business after achieving success as a radio station program director. WMAX-AM in Grand Rapids, Michigan, was Joseph's first client; it found ratings success thanks to Joseph's expertise. More clients soon followed, including WROK in Rockford, Illinois; WKZO in Kalamazoo, Michigan; KDAL in Duluth, Minnesota; and WKBW in Buffalo, New York. Joseph's successive clients each achieved larger audiences, and the business of radio consulting took hold.

As a new subpart of the radio business, consultants initially faced a limited market. However, prospects for those who went into the radio consulting business, usually former station program directors, increased dramatically during the 1960s. During that decade, genre programming blossomed as the number and styles of music programming expanded to meet the needs of specific audiences. Consequently, the resulting fragmentation of formats increased the need for consultants.

Consultants worked at both the individual and agency level; one could work freelance as a one-person operation or at a consulting firm. In addition to these "hired guns" stations brought in to improve their ratings and on-air presentation, program syndicators and station rep companies started to enter the consulting side of the business. Indeed, for the next several decades, many program syndicators would provide their client stations with both the advice and the programming to increase ratings in one convenient package.

The 1960s saw station management in larger markets searching for even larger audiences to attract big advertisers and thus big profits. "Numbers became the name of the game," with a station's goal in any given market to increase listenership: "To be number one was to be king of the hill" (Keith, 1987). With the number-one rating status serving as "the holy grail" of radio stations during that period of "fragout" in programming formats, stations experiencing poor numbers for several ratings periods sought the advice of consultants. The importance of consultants in maintaining a modicum of ratings success became apparent. As Keith notes, "'Call a consultant' became a cry commonly heard when a station stood at the edge of the abyss" (1987).

Although the growth in radio as big business had expanded in the 1960s, the industry saw even more expansion with the rise in popularity of FM during the 1970s. FM contributed to the doubling in the number of stations and the tripling of programming formats—and, of course, to the expansion of consulting opportunities. One particular new format served as a notable example of the significance of the need for and power of the radio

consultant: album-oriented rock (AOR). Prominent radio consultant Donna Halper, in *Radio Music Directing* (1991), relates the power given to consultants by station owners trying out the new format. She quotes Kent Burkhart, one of the industry's best-known consultants and the one-time partner of Lee Abrams, an AOR expert:

> Back in the 1970s, AOR was still a fairly new format, so owners wanted us to have total control. They didn't want to leave anything to chance.... In fact, in those early days of Album Rock, many of the stations didn't even have a music director. They just had a PD [program director] who often guessed what music should be played.

With clients nationwide, Burkhart and Abrams' partnership, Burkhart/Abrams and Associates, became the most powerful consulting firm of the decade. Burkhart and Abrams provided their AOR clients with a playlist based on research, adding new albums each week. Their influence became such that record promoters could count on sales of albums they approved because as many as 100 stations could potentially play them.

Whereas the ascent of FM and the proliferation of format and music genres during the 1970s provided increased employment for consultants, another development—audience research—provided consultants with more complicated tasks. Keith (1987) points out that stations began to rely more on results of surveys, notably those conducted by the Arbitron Company. As FM began luring away AM listeners, smaller AM stations trying to increase listener shares posed a major challenge to consultants, a "Herculean" task that "only a few master consultants were up to."

Ironically, whereas stations had called on consultants to help them during FM's "infancy," the AM market was fertile for the consulting industry in the 1980s. With FM's dominance firmly established by then, the field expanded now to AM: "Radio consultants, who found themselves an integral part of FM's bid for prominence in the 1960s and 1970s, worked on the AM side with as much fervor in the 1980s in an attempt to reverse the misfortunes that befell the one-time ratings leader" (Keith, 1987).

By the mid-1980s, some three decades after Mike Joseph's initial foray into the consulting business, about a third of all radio stations used consultants. There were about 50 individual consultants in 1986; though that number held constant, the consulting business involves a degree of turnaround in that consultants must show positive results in order to remain in business. This number remained constant into the 1990s; of the more than 100 broadcasting consultants listed in various media directories in the United States, more than half specialized in radio (Keith, 1987).

Just as stations had become specialists in certain program formats, with fragmentation and "narrowcasting" helping to stimulate the consulting industry in the 1970s, consultants themselves began to cater to stations' particular program needs in the mid-1990s. Perhaps as an indication of the successes some consultants had achieved by that time, some stations brought in "niche consultants" to help boost ratings during specific dayparts as well as in specific formats. Morning shows in particular served as prime targets for consultants' services (Keith, 1997).

Although Keith (1987) had predicted that increased competition resulting from deregulation all but guaranteed the future of radio consulting in the 1980s, *Billboard* reported a trend toward consolidation of consulting agencies beginning in 1995. For instance, Stark (1995) found that radio consultants started teaming up for long-term joint ventures and referred their clients to rival agencies. Consultant alliances became the product of individual agencies' desire to do whatever it took for a client to succeed. As stations downsized, the demand increased for highly specialized people from "the outside"—consultants—that stations could rent rather than hire full-time.

Consolidation among consultants continued into 1999, and increased competition for work resulted in a shakeout in the business, with some individual consultants being forced to join companies or take other jobs in programming. Media groups—broadcast companies owning several stations—increasingly relied on their own in-house programmers, who effectively took the place of consultants. Additionally, those working for large companies specializing in one format have better long-term prospects than do individual consultants, who must cover several formats. Industry experts predict that those consultants who stay independent will have to provide their clients with expanded services.

Consultant Services

Although radio consultants ultimately aim to improve station ratings, they also advise management on ways to implement a change in format, to gain higher visibility, and to achieve a higher quality of on-air presentation. As their nickname "radio doctors" implies, consultants "diagnose the problems that impair a station's growth and then prescribe a plan of action designed to remedy the ills"

(Keith, 1997). Initially, consultants treated ailments in programming, especially those involving playlists. As the industry increased in complexity, so, too, have the services offered by consultants. These range from making specific observations and suggestions regarding the performance of on-air talent to audience research. The array of services offered depends on the type of consultant.

There are two basic kinds of radio consultant: programming and full-service. Programming consultants focus primarily on the on-air aspect of a station's product—such as playlists and execution of format. Traditionally, they come from the programming side of the business; program directors get into consulting when they have achieved a record of ratings success. One can find consultants who specialize in particular formats, such as country and adult contemporary.

Full-service consultants, in addition to providing clients with programming expertise, offer a "package" of services that covers virtually every aspect of radio station operations: staff training and motivation, music, audience and market trend research, drug and alcohol counseling, sales and management consulting, union and syndication, music suppliers, and record company negotiating. The range of full-service offerings also extends to the use of engineering consultants and advice regarding business operations. Some consulting companies provide clients with programming (program syndicators). Clients can use all the programming services, or just part, either as recorded material or via satellite in conjunction with live announcers (Keith, 1987).

In some cases, station managers give consultants total control, such as when a station changes format or ownership. In other cases, consultants simply give objective advice regarding a station's performance. They also examine the competition and determine what other stations with the same format in a market present the best execution. Consultants also determine what call letters best reflect a station's desired image.

With the consulting industry becoming more specialized, some agencies focus solely on research. Research consultants go through survey data, study a station's market and target audience in terms of socio-economic and financial statistics, and may conduct music research to determine what most appeals to an audience.

Consultants also conduct research to discover what factors about a radio station the listening public likes and dislikes. To this end, consultants use three basic approaches: focus groups, callout research, and music testing. In focus group research, small groups of listeners or potential listeners serve as "sounding boards" regarding certain elements of programming. Researchers document the group's attitudes and emotions concerning a station's music, disc jockeys, news, and contests. Callout research refers to telephone surveys that measure respondents' opinions in empirical form. Music testing involves paying participants to listen to and evaluate songs, usually in an auditorium-like setting. A station then creates its playlist based on the results. Based on these types of research, consultants can make recommendations that have the greatest potential for success in a given market.

Consultants' duties include making in-house visits and examining a station's physical plant. This includes technical assessment of the station's signal strength and clarity. If needed, engineering consultants are brought in to make recommendations regarding the station's equipment.

Consultants usually research their client stations' performance and competition by listening to the station, either live or on tape. When a consultant arrives in the client's market city or town, he or she monitors the station, usually from a hotel room. This leaves the consultant free from distractions in order to assess the client's on-air presentation. Typically, a consultant takes notes on all aspects of a station's "sound." As described by Donna Halper, these include the following: music mix, "listenability," announcer effectiveness, the match between proclaimed format and music played, technical quality, station image, times songs are played, front or back sells, and use of call letters. Consultant Jim Smith looks at certain other basics of on-air execution, including production values, stop sets, newscasts, features, and promotions (Keith, 1987).

In addition to assessing competing stations' products, consultants compare what is aired during specific dayparts and even hours to what their client offers at those times. For example, a consultant would compare station A to station B in terms of songs played, times and lengths of commercial breaks, and the like. The consultant then compiles the information and submits a comprehensive report to the station. As with any type of evaluation, consultants' reports not only include constructive criticism of their client, but also should provide some positive feedback as well.

Consultant Characteristics

Consultant companies can range in size from two or three people to 50, with fees ranging from $500 to more than $1,200 a day. Consultants base their fees on the services the client wants and the size of

the station. Most consultants have backgrounds in broadcasting, usually as station program directors. Those who have broadcasting experience hold a considerable advantage over those who do not. Most also have a thorough knowledge and understanding of radio broadcasting at all levels, including programming, sales, marketing, and promotion. Some obtain formal training in college, notably through research methods and broadcast management courses.

The consulting business as a whole does face obstacles in the radio industry—notably, that of gaining acceptance among broadcasters, who consider consultants a "necessary evil." Industry insiders cite negative perceptions held by some station managers and program directors regarding consultants; despite these perceptions, consultants are not all "charlatans intent on cleaning house and selling fad formats" (Keith, 1987). A good consultant's effectiveness requires, first, that station management make clear to staff the reasons why it is bringing in a consultant. Station managers also need to implement the consultant's recommendations effectively. Those who do often benefit from their investment. As Keith contends, "Statistically, those stations that use programming consultants more often than not experience ratings success" (1997).

By the early 21st century, radio consulting was on the decline for many reasons. Industry ownership consolidation reduced the number of potential clients for such service. The reduced number of music formats aired narrowed options for change. Audience declines and related advertising stagnation (or decline) reduced the funds available to pay consultants, while at the same time making clear new ideas were surely needed. Many smaller shops closed up in the face of dwindling business opportunities.

See also: Programming Strategies and Processes; Trade Associations

Further Reading

Halper, Donna L., *Radio Music Directing*, Boston: Focal Press, 1991.
Keith, Michael C., *Radio Programming: Consultancy and Formatics*, Boston and London: Focal Press, 1987.
Keith, Michael C., and Joseph M. Krause, *The Radio Station*, Boston: Focal Press, 1986; 4th edition, by Michael C. Keith, 1997; 5th edition, Boston and Oxford: Focal Press, 2000.
"Radio Consultants Still in Shakeout," *Billboard* (11 September 1999).
Stark, Phyllis, "Consultancy Alliances Prosper," *Billboard* (10 June 1995).

ERIKA ENGSTROM,
2009 REVISIONS BY CHRISTOPHER H. STERLING

CONTEMPORARY CHRISTIAN MUSIC FORMAT

Part of a growing U.S. trend of religious formats on the air, this development of the past few decades combines the basic tenants of Christianity with popular music approaches that appeal to a broader audience.

Origins

Contemporary Christian Music (CCM) has grown over a long period of time. Its foundations are evident in the early hymns of various Protestant faiths. Overtures of intimacy and sentimentality were mixed with Christian music in the 19th century as the feminine ideal of piety combined with the temperance crusade emerged. Even militaristic themes characterized hymns in the early 20th century as the world and the United States fought several major wars.

By the 1960s, however, Evangelicals began to realize that "Bringing in the Sheaves" on Sundays couldn't begin to compete with weekday broadcasts of "Hey Jude" and "I Can't Get No Satisfaction," especially among younger listeners. Composer Ralph Carmichael began the CCM renaissance with pieces such as "Pass It On" and "He's Everything to Me." Musical creativity burst onto the Christian music scene as the younger generation brought its hippie culture, with music largely devoid of theological divisions, into various churches. Musicians such as Larry Norman, Andrae Crouch, Keith Green, Chuck Girard, and Randy Stonehill added the 1960s flavor of rock and roll to Christian music, thus creating the concept of Contemporary Christian Music.

Variations and Controversy

As with most musical formats, however, the genre of contemporary Christian music has splintered into many different kinds and as a result a controversy arose within the evangelical community that continues today. How, some ask, can Christian music be used to evangelize if it sounds just like secular music? One argument holds that there is nothing in music that makes it Christian. A related controversy is the ability of some Christian musicians to cross over to the secular music world. Radio stations with commercial formats and their audiences either accepted Christian music or Christian artists attempted to create music designed for them. Christian recording artist Amy Grant and the group Sixpence None the Richer both had hit singles in the 1990s that prompted the Gospel Music Association (GMA) to redefine Christian music in association with the annual Dove Awards, which honor Christian recording artists. The GMA's criteria for defining music as Christian is that in any style the lyrics of which are:

> Substantially based upon historically orthodox Christian truth contained in or derived from the Holy Bible; and/or—An expression of worship of God or praise for His works; and/or—Testimony of relationship with God through Christ; and/or Obviously prompted and informed by a Christian world view.

GMA president Frank Breeden commented that "this statement is not intended to be the definition of gospel music for all time, nor is it meant to characterize music made by Christians that may not fit the criteria" (Grubbs, 1998).

These definitional controversies didn't prevent CCM from becoming a multimillion dollar industry by the mid-1990s. CCM's share of 1998 recording industry revenue exceeded the shares of jazz, classical, New Age, and soundtracks according to *Billboard* magazine. CCM record labels did not, however, escape the consolidation fever of the 1990s. By early 1997 three companies controlled all labels that produced CCM: Zomba Group (parent company of Benson Music Group), EMI (parent company of Sparrow, Star Song, ForeFront, and GospoCentric), and Gaylord Entertainment (parent company of Word Music).

Trends that have impacted the radio business have also been reflected in Christian radio. As one example, consolidation is evident with The Way–FM Media Group, which originally owned a single station and by 2009 owned 17 religious-themed stations throughout the U.S. Salem Communications owns over 90 AM and FM stations, all religious in format. Christian radio has also become less localized, serving as a platform for nationally syndicated fare, from individual programs to full music formats. CHRSN (Christian Hit Radio Satellite Network) provides programming to 25 stations in addition to the 17 outlets owned by parent company The Way. The USA Radio Network, known for its news and more inspirational content, supplies programming to over 1,500 stations.

Aspiring Christian musicians can even major in CCM at Greenville College, a Christian liberal arts college in south-central Illinois. Music Department Chair Ralph Montgomery began the program in 1987; the most notable alumni are members of the recording group Jars of Clay.

Contemporary Christian outlets have seen fragmenting of format types. Today "CCM" stations can be almost endlessly subdivided into other format styles including: Adult Contemporary Christian, Alternative Christian, Christian Hit Radio, Country Christian, Gospel, Hispanic, Instrumental, MOR, Praise and Worship, Sacred, Southern Gospel, Specialty and Urban Christian. Other stations focus on Christian-oriented news, talk or preaching. By 2009, almost 3,000 stations were airing some type of religious content. Today, Contemporary Christian music is the second-most popular music format on radio, ceding the top spot to mainstream country.

The internet has proved as pervasive in CCM as elsewhere in radio. Numerous sites deal with every aspect of CCM, from controversies to sites developed by fans of various artists. CCM fans can tune in to their favorite artists through internet-only streaming and radio station websites.

See also: Evangelists/Evangelical Radio; Gospel Music Format; Religion on Radio

Further Reading

NRB Directory of Religious Media (annual).

Balmer, Randall, "Hymns on MTV," *Christianity Today* (15 November 1999).

Grubbs, Deanna, "Gospel Music Association Sets New Criteria for Dove Awards Eligibility," *Gospel Music Association News Release* (30 July 1998).

Howard, Jay R., "Contemporary Christian Music: Where Rock Meets Religion," *Journal of Popular Culture* 26, no. 1 (1992.).

Howard, Jay R., and John M. Streck, "The Splintered World of Contemporary Christian Music," *Popular Music* 15, no. 1 (1996).

Martin, Yvi, "An Education with a Backbeat," *Christianity Today* (15 November 1999).

Olsen, Ted, "Will Christian Music Boom for New Owners?" *Christianity Today* (28 April 1997).

Romanowski, William D., "Roll Over Beethoven, Tell Martin Luther the News: American Evangelicals and Rock Music," *Journal of American Culture* 15, no. 3 (1992).

Schultze, Quentin, "The Crossover Music Question," *Moody Magazine* 93, no. 2 (October 1992).

Solomon, Jerry, "Music and the Christian," www.probe.org/docs/music.html.

LINWOOD A. HAGIN,
2009 REVISIONS BY CARY O'DELL

CONTEMPORARY HIT RADIO/TOP 40 FORMAT

Contemporary hit radio (CHR) is a rock music format that plays the current best-selling records. The music is characterized as lively, upbeat rock or soft rock hits. The playlist generally consists of 20 to 40 songs played continuously throughout the day. Disc jockeys are often upbeat "personalities," and the format emphasizes contests and promotions. CHR stations tend to target a young demographic of both men and women, aged 18–34, with listenership extending into the 35–44 demographic cell.

CHR grew out of Top 40, which was developed in the late 1950s by Todd Storz and Gordon McLendon, who found success in playing the 40 most popular records. By the mid-1960s, the rise of rock music and FM led to audience fragmentation and a revitalized, tighter format with less chatter, refined by programmer Bill Drake. The format was successful but was also criticized for being too slick and dehumanized. The move to FM was initially met with resistance, because FM was regarded as an alternative listening medium. As a result, Top 40 underwent another face-lift and became known as contemporary hit radio.

The trade periodical *Radio & Records* (*R&R*) began using the term *contemporary hit radio* in 1980. The retitling of the format was orchestrated by consulting pioneer Mike Joseph. Joseph's CHR format featured a tight playlist of about 30 records with up-tempo sounds, fast rotations, limited recurrence, chart hit countdowns, and no more oldies and declining records. At that time, CHR songs were by such artists as Blondie, Billy Joel, Christopher Cross, Queen, Dan Fogelberg, and Pink Floyd. The format moved to FM and became virtually non-existent on AM as most radio listening shifted to the higher-fidelity broadcast system. Soon many broadcasters abandoned their soft rock and album-oriented rock (AOR) formats in favor of CHR.

By the mid-1980s, CHR became the highest-rated format. There were two or more CHR stations in many medium to large markets. Close to 800 CHR stations were on the air in 1984, and this number increased to nearly 900 in 1985. In 1987 and 1988 CHR was the number-one format in both New York City and Los Angeles, according to Arbitron market reports.

As more stations flocked to the popular format, some turned to format segmentation as a way to broaden their core audience targets and to counter-program against similar formats in their markets. In the mid-1980s CHR split into two directions. The basic CHR format became a mass-appeal, 12-plus format. A variation on that theme became "adult CHR," which went with softer announcing and added some oldies songs to the musical mix, attempting to appeal to the 25–34 demographic and divert audiences from adult contemporary (AC) stations. Some stations also went with hybrid formats, such as a Top 40/AOR format.

CHR has undergone even more fragmentation in recent years. Today the most common variations include CHR/pop, CHR/rhythmic, and adult CHR/hot AC. CHR/pop most closely resembles the original Top 40 format. It is the most current-based format, playing the hottest-selling popular songs of the day. As a result, the music may vary from rock and pop to dance and alternative, depending on what is most popular at the moment. The style is fast-paced, with lots of audience interaction with on-air personalities. Examples of CHR/pop artists include Madonna, Sheryl Crow, Hootie and the Blowfish, and Red Hot Chili Peppers.

CHR/rhythmic is similarly fast-paced and personality-driven, but it is more dance-oriented than CHR/pop. More dance and urban hits are mixed into the format. Artists include Puff Daddy, En Vogue, Toni Braxton, and Baby Face.

Adult CHR/hot AC focuses on a slightly older demographic of 25–34-year-olds and is dominated more by female artists. The format includes a fair amount of pop alternative. The format includes pop-rock artists such as Alanis Morissette and Natalie Merchant, as well as such traditional hot AC artists as Phil Collins and Gloria Estefan.

Over the years, Top 40/CHR disc jockey announcing styles have changed. The early Top 40 jocks were heavy-voiced, shouting and cajoling their audiences. The mid-1960s change saw a reduction in disc jockey presence, with less chatter and more music. The 1970s saw even less aggressive, more mellow announcers. But with the reformation to CHR in the 1980s, the energetic, big-voiced personality reasserted itself. Irreverent morning shows grew in popularity. Still, audience loyalty is generally to the music and not to the disc jockey.

CHR has replaced and generally become synonymous with the term Top 40, although many still refer to hits-oriented music stations as Top 40, and CHR is sometimes distinguished as using a larger playlist than Top 40. CHR stations feature little, if any, news and public-affairs programming. Syndicated features that reflect the all-hit nature of the format, such as *American Top 40*, are typically aired to help attract listeners. Nonmusic features such as sporting events are rarely programmed, however. Contests and promotions are an integral element of programming at CHR stations. CHR audiences are perhaps more receptive than those of any other format to imaginative and entertaining promotions.

Its "more hits, more often" image led CHR stations to cluster commercials in spot sets after music sweeps. Commercials on CHR stations are designed to sound as slick and entertaining as the music they interrupt. As CHR is production-intensive, liners and catch phrases are vital to the format.

Competition to CHR comes primarily from other CHR stations, which fragment the audience. Formats that share the highest percentages of CHR audiences include Spanish, alternative/modern rock, urban, and AC. AC attracts older demographics and women; AOR draws younger listeners and men. The prospects for CHR are good, however, because analysts believe radio listeners will always be interested in the hot new songs and artists of the day.

After being dismissed in the mid-1990s by some critics and advertisers as too teen-oriented, CHR experienced a resurgence. An Interep Research study attributed its success to an increase in the median age of listeners and to a wide range of music available and suitable to the format. A crossover of playlists became a boon to CHR, as CHR stations were able to play many of the same hits that get airtime on other young adult formats, such as alternative, modern AC, and adult album alternative. Today there is a variation on the format called rhythmic or "Churban" (a blend of CHR and urban).

At the turn of the 21st century, CHR reached 14 million adults weekly in the 18–34 demographic. About 20 percent of the overall audience extends into the 35–44 range, and 8 percent are 45–54 years old. Most CHR listeners are female (56 percent). The CHR format audience is characterized as being active consumers of alcoholic beverages; restaurants; and all entertainment categories, especially movies; as well as of computers and electronic equipment. CHR has a fairly low cost per thousand (CPM), because its audience generally does not have much money, although the young demographic does have very active spending habits.

In 1998 CHR was the fourth-most popular format, behind news/talk, country, and AC. Fall 1998 Arbitron ratings showed Top 40 to be rebounding in all dayparts except midday. By 2002 there were 646 CHR/Top 40 stations in the United States. The format was the 11th-most popular for stations to carry. According to the RAB, by 2008, CHR/Top 40 had moved up to become the seventh-most popular format among radio listeners.

See also: Adult Contemporary Format; Urban Contemporary Format

Further Reading

"CHR Format Grows Up with Former Teens," *Broadcasting* (12 October 1998).

Keith, Michael C., *Radio Programming: Consultancy and Formatics*, Boston and London: Focal Press, 1987.

Lynch, Joanna R., and Greg Gillispie, *Process and Practice of Radio Programming*, Lanham, Maryland: University Press of America, 1998.

MacFarland, David T., *Contemporary Radio Programming Strategies*, Hillsdale, New Jersey: Erlbaum, 1990; 2nd edition, as *Future Radio Programming Strategies: Cultivating Listenership in the Digital Age*, Mahwah, New Jersey: Erlbaum, 1997.

O'Donnell, Lewis B., Philip Benoit, and Carl Hausman, *Modern Radio Production*, Belmont, California: Wadsworth, 1986; 5th edition, Belmont, California, and London: Wadsworth, 2000.

"Shakeout after the CHR Goldrush," *Broadcasting* (22 July 1985).

Sklar, Rick, *Rocking America: How the All-Hit Stations Took Over*, New York: St. Martin's Press, 1984.

LAURIE THOMAS LEE,
2009 REVISIONS BY MICHAEL C. KEITH

CONTROL BOARD/AUDIO MIXER

Device to Manipulate Audio Signals

A radio station's control board (or audio mixer or console, or simply a "board") is the primary piece of studio equipment. It allows for the use of multiple audio signals, such as from a microphone or compact disc (CD) player; allows an operator to manipulate those signals, such as controlling the volume or combining two or more together; and allows signals to be recorded or broadcast. During any of these processes, audio signals can be monitored through meters and speakers.

Functions

Any control board or console serves five basic functions: to select, mix, amplify, monitor, and route an audio signal. An operator can select (input) various sounds at the same time. Most typical of the radio work accomplished with a board is to mix voice and music (or sound effects), as in production of a commercial.

A board can also amplify any sound source. This allows an operator to properly balance sound levels, as when an announcer talks over music (where microphone volume must exceed music volume so the voice is clearly heard).

Monitoring an audio signal can be either visual (by watching volume unit [VU] meters) or aural (by listening to speakers or through headphones).

Finally, the control board is used to route (output) signals to a recorder, another studio, or the transmitter.

The easiest way to understand operation of any control board is to look at one of its individual sound channels. Such a channel includes a group of switches, faders, and knobs in vertical alignment; each group controls one or two sound sources. The number of channels (boards typically have between 12 and 36, or even more) defines its capacity to handle multiple signals. Most boards allow more than one input (microphones, etc.) to be assigned to a each channel, though only one can be selected at a time. Regardless of configuration, the first two channels (from the left) of any board are usually designed for microphones, which always need special amplification. CD players, audio recorders, and other equipment can be patched into the remaining channels.

For any channel, signals can be sent ("output") to one of three destinations: program, audition, or auxiliary. When "program" is selected, a signal is directed to a recorder or transmitter. In the "audition" position, a signal can be previewed off-air. For example, a DJ may play a CD through channel 3 in the "program" position (in other words, on the air), while at the same time previewing another disc or tape through channel 4 in the "audition" position. The "auxiliary" (aux) or "utility" (utl) are often used in production, such as to send signals to another studio.

Volume Control and Monitoring

The volume or gain control is called a slider or fader. Such controls are variable resistors—much like water faucets in function. Raising the fader (pushing it away from you) increases the volume. Some older boards have rotary knobs called potentiometers ("pots"), which fill the same function. Faders are easier to work with, as they provide a quick visual check of which channels are in use and at what level.

One way to judge volume is simply to listen, but this is a relative measure, and what one operator deems loud may seem quieter to another. To more objectively indicate volume, control boards include a volume unit indicator (VU meter). Most use a moving needle on a graduated scale, ideally registering between 80 and 100 percent. Above 100 percent the signal is peaking "in the red" (because that portion of the VU meter scale is usually indicated by a red line) and may distort. On the other hand, a signal consistently below 20 percent—and thus too quiet—is said to be "in the mud." Most newer boards offer VU meters with digital lights (LEDs) to indicate volume.

Sound can be monitored in different ways as it passes through a control board. A common mistake is to run studio monitors quite loud and think all is well, when in reality the program signal going through the audio board may be at too low a level. Most boards also have provision for monitoring their output through headphones. When microphones are on ("live"), monitor speakers in the same control or studio space are automatically muted to avoid feedback howls or squeals.

Another way to monitor (and preview) a sound source is to use a board's "cue" function, which allows any input to be previewed. Shifting a volume control into the cue position, usually marked on the face of the console, routes the audio signal to a cue speaker rather than on the air.

Many control boards have additional features that make them more flexible. For example, some boards will automatically turn a channel on when its fader is moved upward. Others include built-in clocks and timers. Many boards have simple equalizer (EQ) controls that increase or decrease certain frequencies, thus altering the sound of the voice or music by changing the tonal quality. These most often affect a range of frequencies—high, midrange, and low.

Digital Future

Like other radio equipment, the control board is rapidly progressing from analog to digital mode. Incoming audio signals, if not already digital, are converted, and they remain in digital form while being manipulated through the mixer and ultimately output. Such digital boards begin to add new features and capabilities, such as hard disk audio storage. The most striking feature of the digital board is often the addition of an LCD display screen that provides status information for each channel.

Although a digital board offers all the traditional functions of an analog board, it is usually more flexible. For example, instead of just two inputs per channel, a digital board may allow any channel to be assigned to any input. Such user-defined functions allow a board to be custom-designed for a particular use. Another form of digital control board is the virtual audio console. Instead of a physical piece of equipment in the studio, an operator manipulates an image of a control board on a computer screen. A virtual fader or other console control can be managed with simple point-and-click or drag-and-drop mouse commands.

Whether digital or analog, any control board is part mechanical contrivance and part creative component. Although learning its technical operation is fairly easily accomplished, effective utilization of a board takes time and experience.

See also: Audio Processing; Production for Radio; Recording and Studio Equipment

Further Reading

Alten, Stanley R., *Audio in Media: The Recording Studio*, Belmont, California: Wadsworth, 1996.

Gross, Lynne S., and David E. Reese, *Radio Production Worktext: Studio and Equipment*, Boston: Focal Press, 1990; 3rd edition, 1998.

Keith, Michael C., *Radio Production: Art and Science*, Boston: Focal Press, 1990.

McNary, James C., *Engineering Handbook of the National Association of Broadcasters*, Washington, D.C.: National Association of Broadcasters, 1935; 9th edition, as *Engineering Handbook*, edited by Jerry Whitaker, 1999.

Nardantonio, Dennis N., *Sound Studio Production Techniques*, Blue Ridge Summit, Pennsylvania: Tab Books, 1990.

Nelson, Mico, *The Cutting Edge of Audio Production and -Audio Post-Production: Theory, Equipment, and Techniques*, White Plains, New York: Knowledge Industry, 1995.

O'Donnell, Lewis B., Philip Benoit, and Carl Hausman, *Modern Radio Production*, Belmont, California: Wadsworth, 1986; 5th edition, Belmont, California, and London: Wadsworth, 2000.

Oringel, Robert S., *Audio Control Handbook: For Radio and Television Broadcasting*, New York: Hastings House, 1956; 6th edition, Boston: Focal Press, 1989.

Siegel, Bruce H., *Creative Radio Production*, Boston: Focal Press, 1992.

Sterling, Christopher H., *Focal Encyclopedia of Electronic Media* (CD Rom), Boston: Focal Press, 1998.

Thom, Randy, *Audio Craft: An Introduction to the Tools and Techniques of Audio Production*, Washington, D.C.: National Federation of Community Broadcasters, 1982; 2nd edition, 1989.

DAVID E. REESE

CONTROVERSIAL ISSUES, BROADCASTING OF

Broadcasting programs concerning controversial issues of public importance has been a subject of continuing U.S. public policy debate for nearly as long as radio broadcasting has existed. The basic conflict has been between broadcasters, who are concerned about not offending their audiences and advertisers, and the Federal Communications Commission (FCC), who argue—and are often upheld in court decisions—that provision of time for such content is a vital part of the public-interest standard by which broadcast stations are licensed. In recent years much of the controversy has evaporated thanks to deregulation.

This entry *excludes* most discussion of commentators, political candidates, the fairness doctrine, or station editorializing—all directly related, but treated separately in the encyclopedia.

Basis for Concern

Consideration of broadcasts about controversial issues begins with an understanding of three related matters: the First Amendment, censorship, and access. The First Amendment (1791) makes clear that "Congress shall make no law" affecting freedom of speech, of the press, or of religion. Countless statements of political theory and policy as well as numberless court decisions (most having nothing to do with broadcasting) have made clear for decades, that in order to be effective citizens and voters, the public needs to be informed about public issues and the various points of view concerning them. A number of Supreme Court decisions have held that robust public debate is a central component of effective freedom of speech and of the democratic system itself.

Strictly defined, censorship in the American context means *prior restraint* of publication, broadcast, or speech by an act of government. It does *not* usually include private actions (such as those by broadcasters or advertisers) that might limit speech or access to a microphone by others. The term is usually applied far more generally and is often applied to corporate actions to restrict access or debate.

Media access divides into two concerns: media access *to* places or people in order to report news or public (sometimes seemingly private) affairs, and access *by* people (other than a broadcaster or his or her staff) or their ideas to broadcast facilities. Discussion of controversial issues on radio almost always involves the latter.

Shaping a Policy

As the potential value of radio as a means of shedding light on public controversies first became clear in the 1920s, policy-makers and broadcasters alike began to focus on just what radio stations should or could do in support of public-affairs communication. Yet neither the Radio Act of 1927 nor the Communications Act of 1934 (until the latter was amended in 1959) said anything about radio coverage of controversial issues or fairness in doing so. Both acts *did* make clear that government had no right of censorship over radio content. The combination of having no clear statutory requirement to deal fairly with controversial issues on the one hand, with a very clear and firm statement of no censorship on the other hand, has made defining government policy-making in this field difficult.

The first important relevant policy statement— one often still referenced in modern decisions—is

found in an early Federal Radio Commission licensing case in which the commission concluded, "In so far as a program consists of discussion of public questions, public interest requires ample play for the free and fair competition of opposing views, and the commission believes that the principle applies...to discussions of issues of importance to the public" (*Great Lakes Broadcasting Co.*, 1928; see Kahn, 1984).

In the late 1920s and early 1930s, a number of legal cases concerned broadcasters who sought either to obtain or to retain stations as personal mouthpieces (e.g., John Brinkley) or whose programs espoused strong political views with little or no chance for rebuttal by others (e.g., Father Charles Coughlin). In a few short years, most had been forced to share time with others of different views or to leave the air entirely.

Later cases and policy statements echoed the need to cover controversial issues, but to do so fairly. In March 1939, in an FCC statement on objectionable programming practices, one item listed was "refusal to give equal opportunity for the discussion of controversial subjects" this statement underlines the twofold nature of the concern. First, stations should provide discussion of controversial subjects, and second, they should provide a fair balance of views on those subjects. Paralleling the government concern was the 1939 version of the National Association of Broadcasters' (NAB) *Standards of Practice*, which held that "as part of their public service, networks and stations shall provide time for the discussion of public questions including those of a controversial nature."

This relatively early version of the NAB radio self-regulatory code also made clear a long-standing industry practice of not *selling* airtime for the discussion of controversial issues. The code claimed that this was because broadcasters did not want a situation in which only those able to afford the time could be heard. But such a policy also avoided offending either audience members or advertisers with too much controversy. The no-sell provision was largely followed until relatively recently. The downside of all this was that such discussions were nearly always provided as sustaining programs— meaning at the broadcaster's expense. The code provisions remained unchanged until 1948, when the restriction on sponsorship was dropped.

In the meantime, other FCC decisions helped to pin down policy still further. At the end of World War II, the commission held that a station could not establish a blanket policy of not providing any time for discussion of controversial issues (*United Broadcasting Company [WHKC]*, 10 FCC 515,

1945). A year later, three radio licenses in California were renewed despite the stations' refusal to allow a noted atheist to offer his views on the air. The commission reiterated that although "the criterion of the public interest in the field of broadcasting clearly precludes a policy of making radio wholly unavailable as a medium for the expression of any view which falls within the scope of the constitutional guarantee of freedom of speech," there was no obligation on the part of a station to grant the request of any specific person for time to state his or her views (*Robert H. Scott*, 11 FCC 372, 1946).

The FCC Blue Book issued in 1946 devoted several pages to the discussion of public issues, going so far as to raise 19 questions about such broadcasts—but answering none of them. The section concluded that in its decisions on whether a licensee had served in the public interest, the FCC "would take into consideration the amount of time which has been or will be devoted to the discussion of public issues" (Blue Book, 1946, 40). Clearly, trying to avoid such programming was not going to please the licensing authority. Thus, the licensee had to make judgments about what issues to cover and which points of view to present.

The seeming hole in the Communications Act of 1934 was finally filled when a 1959 amendment to Section 315 made clear that licensees had an affirmative obligation "to afford a reasonable opportunity for the discussion of conflicting views on issues of public importance." Nearly four decades after radio broadcasting began, the country's basic communications statute finally and specifically included coverage of controversial issues as being a part of the public interest stations were licensed to serve.

Modern Era: Selling Controversy

The dominance of television in American life by the 1950s naturally shifted regulatory attention to that medium. Most cases concerning controversial issues focused on television programs, though the concerns raised paralleled those first evident with radio. And as discussed elsewhere, most controversial issue program questions were now dealt with in the context of the FCC's fairness doctrine, issued in 1949 and rescinded in 1987. The demise of the fairness doctrine, however, was but one of several factors that changed the face of controversial issue programming.

The end of the doctrine in 1987 made possible substantial expansion of political and other controversial talk programs on radio, because they no longer faced private or government fairness doctrine-based requests for response time. Rush Limbaugh, Oliver North, and many others with decided (usually conservative) political views would have had a difficult time maintaining their controversial programming in the face of a constant barrage of requests from audience members to respond to what they had heard.

Nor did the FCC any longer seem concerned that many stations no longer provided time for discussion of controversial issues. Detailed license renewal forms that asked about station policies concerning the amount of time provided for controversial issue programming disappeared in the 1980s, to be replaced by simple postcard forms with no program-relevant queries whatsoever. The growing number of stations in most markets made regulation of individual outlets seem less relevant. Therefore, neither FCC commissioners nor their staff any longer felt that each station in a market had to provide such programs—as long as at least *some* stations did. Any nearby public radio station was often the selected "mark" to pick up the slack.

More important, the economic basis of radio time devoted to discussion of controversial issues has changed radically. Once shunned by broadcasters, as noted above, the selling of time for expression of points of view, whether in short spots ("editorial advertising" or "advertorials") or in programs, had by the 1990s become accepted practice. No longer did broadcasters have to pick and choose among the minefield of potential controversial issues without even the saving grace of selling time to support programs dealing with such topics. By the early 2000s, controversial issue programs almost always meant time *sold* for that purpose, usually to one or more syndicated talkers with an axe (or several) to grind or an audience large enough to attract advertisers.

Some have argued that radio is thus no longer providing a minimum of public-affairs service to its listeners—that points of view have simply become another commodity for sale to the highest bidder. Others hold that radio is but one information conduit to the modern household and that audiences can obtain as much controversy as they desire from a combination of radio, television, periodicals, and the internet, to name only a few key media. In any case, far more people agree that government supervision or regulation of radio content is not the most effective means of creating an informed electorate.

See also: Blue Book; Censorship; Editorializing; "Equal Time" Rule; Fairness Doctrine; First Amendment and Radio; Politics and Radio

Further Reading

Benjamin, Louise M., *Freedom of the Air and the Public Interest: First Amendment Rights in Broadcasting to 1935*, Carbondale: Southern Illinois University Press, 2001.

Bensman, Marvin R., editor, *Broadcast Regulation: Selected Cases and Decisions*, Lanham, Maryland: University Press of America, 1983; 3rd edition, 1990.

Brindze, Ruth, *Not to Be Broadcast: The Truth about the Radio*, New York: Vanguard Press, 1937.

Fones-Wolf, Elizabeth, *Waves of Opposition: Labor and the Struggle for Democratic Radio*. Urbana: University of Illinois Press, 2006.

Kahn, Frank J., editor, *Documents of American Broadcasting*, New York: Appleton-Century-Croft, 1968; 4th edition, Englewood Cliffs, New Jersey: Prentice-Hall, 1984 (contains "The Great Lakes Statement").

Ripley, Joseph Marion, Jr., *The Practices and Policies Regarding Broadcasts of Opinions about Controversial Issues by Radio and Television Stations in the United States*, New York: Arno Press, 1979.

Smead, Elmer E., *Freedom of Speech by Radio and Television*, Washington, D.C.: Public Affairs Press, 1959.

Summers, Harrison Boyd, editor, *Radio Censorship*, New York: Wilson, 1939.

CHRISTOPHER H. STERLING

COOPERATIVE ANALYSIS OF BROADCASTING

First U.S. Radio Ratings Service

The Cooperative Analysis of Broadcasting (CAB), a nonprofit organization, was the first company to provide regular studies of the radio audience on a continuing basis. From 1929 to 1933 the service belonged to Crossley, Inc., headed by Archibald M. Crossley. With the emergence of the American Association of Advertising Agencies (AAAA) in 1934, Crossley turned over his service to a jointly financed cooperative venture consisting of national advertisers and agencies. By 1936 CAB was supported by the National Association of Broadcasters (NAB) and by 1945 the four major networks.

CAB was a marketing research organization. Its interest was not just in radio listening but in what advertisers in general got out of advertising. Radio program ratings were but one means of answering a number of questions and concerns that CAB addressed. Radio program ratings provided an answer to the question of how large an audience was. During this period, radio advertisers were also program producers, purchasing time periods from the radio networks and filling these periods with their own programs. Sponsors used CAB information about radio's listening audience to build programs that attracted the type of listeners most likely to buy their products. Because radio audiences were broadly based and were not already

predetermined as magazines were by editorial policy, most advertisers concentrated merely on attracting large numbers of listeners.

Origins

Because national advertisers were some of the first companies to explore the use of radio as a means of advertising, it was perhaps not surprising that the Association of National Advertisers (ANA), through its radio commission (or committee), made the first attempt to answer basic questions regarding radio's anonymous audience and the national advertisers' possible customers. Because advertisers created programs and purchased time from networks, the first question that served as the focus for the first generation of audience research was that of network programs' relative popularity: what network programs were the most popular; that is, which programs drew the largest audiences relative to other programs? This question of program ratings served as the focus for CAB.

Crossley had started Crossley Inc. in 1918; it was one of three major organizations (the others being Roper and Gallup) that engaged in political polling. Political polling results were ranked by percentage points, much like ratings. When the ANA returned to Crossley to repeat an earlier audit, Crossley suggested that he should instead study radio's listening audience and listeners' program preferences. Although the radio committee of the ANA decided not to finance the study, the ANA did agree to endorse it if Crossley would underwrite it. By 1929 Crossley had gained endorsement from 30 sponsors, and by 1930 he began field work. Crossley's service functioned primarily as a network program rating service. Crossley, in fact, coined the term *rating*, although initially he used only the "identified listening audience," or what is now called the share, as the base for his ratings. Because national advertisers and agencies had developed Crossley's service, it initially served the 33 cities where the radio networks had outlets.

CAB's Method: The Telephone Recall

Although Crossley used a variety of techniques for different clients, including printed roster, mechanical recorder, personal interview, and coincidental, he selected a simple "next-day recall" telephone method to provide the first regular measure of network program audiences. The coincidental method employs an interview method in which the respondent is asked to state his or her listening to radio at the precise time ("coincidental" with the interview).

COOPERATIVE ANALYSIS OF BROADCASTING

By comparison, next-day recall required respondents to recall behavior for the previous 24 hours. The recall method raised questions about respondent memory. Crossley's technique was to dial a telephone-based list and interview respondents about their previous day's listening.

Crossley chose the telephone recall method for four primary reasons. First, radio and telephone ownership had originally exhibited a high degree of congruence when he began his radio work in 1929—though radio homes would soon outstrip those with telephones. Second, telephones covered a wide area quickly. Third, recall meant that a great deal of information about listeners could be collected at little expense. Finally, sponsor identification was an important concern during the period. As Daniel Yankelovich noted in 1938, for many years advertisers held the belief that recall or registration was the most useful index of advertising effectiveness. Because most sponsors or agencies typically developed their own programs during this period or at least sponsored an entire program, advertisers sought to know the degree of registration between the programs and their product. Recall measured conscious impression. The chief drawback, of course, was that not all homes had telephones. By the late 1930s, twice as many homes had radios as owned telephones, meaning a large proportion of the radio audience was not reached by CAB researchers. Still, over the years Crossley's sample size grew fourfold from its starting point of about 100,000 households.

Enter Hooperatings

Crossley's service, under stiff competition after 1934 with the up-and-coming Hooperatings service, gradually lost ground. The foundation of Crossley's survey technique was originally quota sampling. This was a type of nonprobability sampling, meaning that the degree of sampling error could not be calculated (sampling error is the difference between the sample's results and the results that would be obtained if the whole population were surveyed). Quotas were set as to the number of respondents of varying demographics, such as geographical areas, age, gender, economic levels, and so forth that interviewers were to obtain. The goal in setting quotas was to ensure that the sample was distributed with respect to these characteristics in proportion to presumably known population totals. In response to attacks from C.E. Hooper of Hooperatings, Crossley changed to random sampling, a type of probability sample in which sampling error could be calculated. A random sample ensured that

each unit used in the sample had an equal chance or probability of being selected. He also shifted to the coincidental method, or having interviewers call while the program audience was still tuned to their radios. Hooper also questioned CAB's tabulation procedures, the phrasing of questions asked, and distribution methods.

As the authority of CAB was whittled away by the compiler of a more convincing set of statistics, backers of CAB became alarmed. By January 1946 Hooper had substantial subscribers, and industry backers saw CAB's switch from telephone recall to Hooper's method of telephone coincidental as rendering CAB superfluous. The final straw for CAB was the financial withdrawal of ABC, CBS, and NBC, which left MBS as the only radio network member. The four networks had provided 40 percent of CAB revenues. The three advertising association backers, ANA, AAAA, and NAB, were left holding the bag. An attempt was made to cover this large operating cost gap through increasing dues and assessment. However, CAB had gradually lost more and more ground to Hooper, and in June 1946 CAB suspended its 17-year-old service.

Run as a cooperative membership organization, CAB was operated by a board of governors consisting of advertisers, agencies, and broadcasters. This cooperative structure led to a crucial difficulty that impaired CAB. This structure had hindered its efficient operation, making it much less responsive to the marketplace than Hooper. The committee's divergent idea and politics led to a bureaucratic situation that Crossley called "too many chiefs." Its committee structure meant that decisions were long in the making; decisions were typically compromises and were tied to interest rather than economic considerations; furthermore, results were not measured in terms of profits or loss in the marketplace. Hooper's private enterprise, on the other hand, was conscious of cost, was aware of the degree of acceptance from its clients, and was more responsive in general to the marketplace.

Both CAB's and Hooper's rating services were rating indices limited to a handful of urban cities. Neither provided national size estimates of the number of listeners to a given program, but rather were limited to comparative figures. Neither was designed to measure a true national program audience but was instead limited to urban telephone homes.

See also: Advertising Agencies; Audience Research Methods; Consultants; Hooperatings; Programming Strategies and Processes

Further Reading

Beville, Hugh Malcolm, Jr., "Radio Services—Pre TV (1930–1946)," Chapter I of *Audience Ratings: Radio, Television, and Cable*, Hillsdale, New Jersey: Erlbaum, 1985; revised edition, 1988.

Buzzard, Karen S., *Chains of Gold: Marketing the Ratings and Rating the Markets*, Metuchen, New Jersey: Scarecrow Press, 1990.

Buzzard, Karen S., "Radio Ratings Pioneers: The Development of a Standardized Ratings Vocabulary," *Journal of Radio Studies* 6, no. 2 (November 1999).

Hooper, C.E., "CAB Suspends Ratings Service," *Broadcasting* (24 June 1946).

Womer, Stanley, "What They Say of Two Leading Methods of Measuring Radio," *Printer's Ink* (7 February 1941).

KAREN S. BUZZARD

COPYRIGHT

Protecting Intellectual Property

Copyright is the legal principle that protects the intellectual property rights of the author of a work. Any original literary, audio, or video material can be copyrighted by the author. The author has the exclusive right to control the reproduction, distribution, performance, or adaptation of that work. In order for an author to claim copyright, the work must have been produced in a fixed medium (written on paper, tape-recorded, or even typed onto a computer hard drive). Extemporaneous speeches or performances are not copyrighted.

There is a basic philosophy behind protecting copyright. Those who hope to make a profit from their creations are much more likely to be successful if others are prohibited from using the creations without paying for them. Copyright laws are created to encourage authors to write more with an assurance that their material cannot be illegally reproduced or altered. The U.S. Constitution states that Congress has the authority to "promote the progress of science and useful arts, by securing for limited times to authors...the exclusive right to their respective writings."

Most countries have some form of copyright law. In the United States, the 1976 Copyright Act is the law that provides much of the detail. There are a number of international copyright treaties and conventions, but there is not a single worldwide "copyright registration" that will protect an author's work globally. The United States is a member of the Berne Convention and the Universal Copyright Convention, which recognize copyrights of residents of member nations. Some countries (most notably China) have been criticized for their unwillingness to enforce copyright claims in their country, allowing unlimited copying without compensating the author.

Copyright exists the moment an author creates a work in a tangible form, but without providing notice and registering the work, the author stands little chance of enforcing the copyright. Notice requires that the author provide the word *copyright* or the international symbol ©, the name of the copyright holder, and the date of the copyright. For audio recordings (whether CDs, cassettes, or vinyl), the © symbol is replaced with a ℗ for "phonorecord." Without a notice, a copyright infringer may be able to claim an "innocent infringement." The infringer may successfully claim to have been unaware that the work was copyrighted or may claim not to have known whom to approach to request copyright permission.

Registration with the Copyright Office is a relatively simple procedure. Although registration is not required to have copyright, trying to make a claim in court that copyright has been violated is impossible without registration. In order to register copyright, an author submits a form (available online), a $30 registration fee, and two copies of the work. Although registration can be done months or years after a work is created, there are distinct legal advantages to registering the work within three months of its creation. Only those promptly registering copyright are entitled to recover attorney's fees and statutory damages in a lawsuit.

Radio and Copyright

Radio stations use copyrighted material that they do not own every day. Almost all of the music they play was written by someone other than a station employee. Radio stations are required to pay royalties to the authors of the music they play. To simplify the process, performing rights organizations such as the American Society of Composers, Authors, and Publishers (ASCAP) and Broadcast Music Incorporated (BMI) were created to collect royalties from stations and to distribute the royalties equitably among authors. Stations pay annual blanket licensing fees, which cover the cost of playing any songs from those libraries. The fees are based on the benefit each station derives from the copyrighted music. Highly profitable stations that play a lot of music in large markets are charged much more than are all-talk stations in small markets. Those fees are then equitably divided by the rights organizations based on their own determination of which authors' works were most used.

Not everything a radio station does is covered by music licensing fees. The annual fees paid to performing rights organizations only cover *performances* of the music. Those organizations do not collect fees for other uses of copyrighted material, such as reproducing the work or creating some kind of adaptation. If a radio station uses music in producing a commercial, that is not a performance but is instead the creation of a new, derivative work. Using a piece of copyrighted music in this way without permission of the author is a copyright violation. In order to comply with copyright law, stations or advertisers that use copyrighted music in their commercials need to seek the permission of the copyright holder, usually the author. From that point, it is all a matter of contract negotiation. The author can allow the use for a limited time, charge any fee for the use, or prohibit the use altogether.

Just as a radio station has to pay copyright fees for the music it plays, others might be obligated to pay copyright fees for playing music, even if the music comes from a radio station that has already paid copyright fees. Because the premise of copyright is to reward authors when others benefit from their work, retail establishments, restaurants, and other venues must pay for the use of copyrighted music. If a restaurant plays music that enhances the atmosphere, thereby contributing to its profitability, the restaurant might be responsible for paying a fee for the use of the music. In 1998 the U.S. Congress amended the law to exempt smaller establishments. Retail establishments under 2,000 gross square feet and restaurants under 3,750 gross square feet are exempt from having to pay copyright fees. Larger establishments are expected to pay fees much as a radio station would.

Limitations on Copyright

Copyright does not last forever. Under earlier copyright laws, rights were protected for 28 years and could be renewed for an additional 28 years. In 1978 the law was modified to protect copyright for the life of the author plus 50 years. A more recent modification extended the protection. For works created since 1978, copyright lasts for the life of the author plus 70 years. Because the legislation had to account for changes in existing copyright, duration can be somewhat more complicated for pre-1978 works. Works created before 1978 are generally protected for 95 years, with some rare exceptions (e.g., if a work was created in 1940 and not re-registered 28 years later). Because copyright endures beyond the life of the author, it can be willed just like any other piece of real property that the author owns. In fact, authors can sell or give away their copyrights before death, but the duration is still based on the author's life plus 70 years.

There are instances in which copyright is held not by an individual but rather by a corporation. It would be impossible to calculate the life of the author plus 70 years, because the corporation might go on indefinitely. For these *works for hire*, copyright lasts for 95 years from publication or 120 years from creation, whichever is greater.

There are times when copyright owners have no control over the works they've created. The doctrine of *fair use* allows for certain types of uses without permission or payment to the copyright holder. In determining whether a use is fair, four elements need to be considered: (1) the nature of the use, (2) the nature of the copyrighted work, (3) the amount and substantiality of the original that is used, and (4) the impact of the use on the potential market for the original.

Nature of the Use

Section 107 of the Copyright Act of 1976 states that the fair use of copyrighted works "for purposes such as criticism, comment, news reporting, teaching (including multiple copies for classroom use), scholarship, or research, is not an infringement of copyright." A 1994 U.S. Supreme Court decision determined that parody is also an acceptable purpose for a fair use. The nature of the use can be the sole factor distinguishing a fair use from a copyright infringement. For example, a radio station using a piece of music as the sound bed for a commercial would be infringing copyright. The same piece of music used by the same station as a sound bed for a news story would be a fair use, because news reporting is considered a fair use and so the use of the song as a news story element would be protected. Ironically, the same song used by the same station, if used as production music (e.g., as the theme song for the newscast) would be a copyright infringement. The nature of the use is an important consideration.

Nature of the Copyrighted Work

Authors who don't publish their works have a greater interest in keeping their works out of public sight. A poet or composer who creates work but prefers not to share it has greater protection from a claim of fair use than does a poet or composer who constantly tries to reach the largest possible audience. It would be difficult to claim a fair use of an unpublished work, even if the nature of the use were acceptable.

Amount and Substantiality Used

In order for use of copyrighted material to be considered fair, the amount of the original used should not be excessive. Unfortunately, no legally defined line separates the quantity considered fair from the amount that would not be considered fair. What we do know is that the judgment is made based both on qualitative and quantitative information. Although copying an entire work is not likely to be a fair use, use of just a small percentage of an original might be determined unfair if the use contains the essential part of the copyrighted work. The U.S. Supreme Court ruled that the *Nation* magazine infringed the copyright of Gerald Ford's memoirs when it published "only" a few hundred words from the original: the portion published was at the heart of what people most wanted to know (regarding Ford's dealings with Nixon) and was therefore significant.

Impact on the Potential Market

This is probably the most important consideration in determining whether a use is fair. Uses that harm authors by denying them profits are not likely to be considered fair. The issue is not whether the user profits, but rather whether the copyright owner's profit is reduced. Not-for-profit educational radio stations still must pay to use copyrighted music on the air, even though no-one profits from airing the music. Musical parodies are protected in part because they do not harm the market for the original copyrighted work. The U.S. Supreme Court ruled that a 2 Live Crew parody of Roy Orbison's "Pretty Woman" was a fair use, stating in its reasoning that it could not imagine a potential purchaser trying to choose between the two versions.

An area of fair use where there is still some uncertainty is in home recording. A U.S. Supreme Court decision in 1984 held that video recording of television programs for noncommercial, in-home viewing was a fair use. That decision, however, essentially authorized "time shifting" of TV programs, that is, the taping of a program in order to watch it later. The Court never really addressed the issue of whether an individual would be allowed to amass a collection of videotaped programs as a fair use. The issue will undoubtedly be revisited as advancing digital technology makes high-quality reproductions easier to obtain. The recording industry already fears the possible explosion of MP3 digital audio recordings, many of which are made without compensation to the author. Their reproduction and distribution is made more rapid by the expansion of the internet and the increase of more advanced home computers. If in-home recording is a fair use, and individuals can access thousands of audio files, the recording industry could be severely affected.

Enforcement

In terms of enforcement, the government has no agency charged with seeking out copyright infringements. It is the responsibility of individual authors to protect their own copyrights, and for this reason many copyright infringements are never punished. In the case of music, performing rights organizations seek out copyright violators and take legal action through the courts, if necessary. Commercial studios, publishing houses, and other industries with a vested interest in protecting their copyrights are active in seeking out violators. Major violations are easily caught: ASCAP and BMI know which stations pay their fees and can monitor those that don't and charge them with a violation. Disney Studios is likely to find out if someone releases a film that is substantially similar to one of their own. But there are thousands of small venues where music is performed, hundreds of thousands of photocopiers, and millions of tape recorders. It is impossible for copyright owners to be able to enforce their rights in every possible arena. This does not mean, however, that the laws are any less real. Violations, no matter how small, can still be legally prosecuted. An appropriate analogy might be a traffic light in a small town at 3 A.M. If the light is red, it is still illegal to go. Anyone who does go through the red light is not likely to be caught. Nonetheless, the law still exists. The same is true of copyright. A number of copyright violations are unlikely to be discovered, but they are still violations and can be punished if discovered.

Internet Radio

The potential copyright liability of internet radio became very controversial during the first decade of the 21st century. Both Congress and the Library of Congress (home of the Copyright Office) weighed into the issue. Because of provisions in the 1998 Digital Millennium Copyright Act (DMCA), the Librarian had to consider the issues involved, and a decision on who should pay what. In 2005, he formed a Copyright Royalty Board to take on this function. Especially at issue was how to handle radio services provided only on the internet. Service providers argued they had little or no income. Record companies countered that all users of music should pay something. In many ways, the tussle was reminiscent of the 1920s fight between music licensing agencies and pioneering radio stations.

In 2007 the Copyright Royalty Board set rates for radio stations carried on the Web, internet-only audio services, background music providers (such as Muzak), and satellite digital radio carriers. The DMCA required that royalties be paid to the performers for all digital uses of music except those in an over-the-air digital broadcast transmission or as part of a digital television stream. The royalty is paid to SoundExchange, a firm created by the record companies, and covers both the owners of the copyright in the performance of recorded music and the actual performers of that music. Half of the fees go to performers, and half to the copyright owner (usually the record company). This grows out of the DMCA's granting of a "compulsory license," which allows internet webcasters to use music without the explicit permission of the artists and copyright holder, provided that the webcaster pays this royalty fee.

The law is complex in its royalty payment formula, and requires extensive record keeping—and is thus costly. At its core, it requires payment based on the number of users an internet service is reaching every time a piece of music is played (or "performed"). And there are many restrictions on how often a given piece of music can be played. Although the 2007 decision followed Congressional mandates to require such payments retroactively to the passage of the DMCA nearly a decade before, many internet-only music services shut down, unable to pay bills they argued they could not foresee.

See also: American Society of Composers, Authors, and Publishers; Broadcast Music Incorporated

Further Reading

Middleton, Kent, and Bill F. Chamberlin, *The Law of Public Communication*, White Plains, New York: Longman, 1988; 5th edition, by Kent Middleton, Chamberlin, and Robert Trager, 2000.
Stanford University Libraries: Copyright and Fair Use, fairuse.stanford.edu.
Strong, William S., *The Copyright Book: A Practical Guide*, Cambridge, Massachusetts: MIT Press, 1981; 5th edition, 1999.
United States Congress Senate Committee on the Judiciary, *The Copyright Office Report on Compulsory Licensing of Broadcast Signals*, Hearing before the Committee on the Judiciary, One Hundred Fifth Congress, First Session, November 12, 1997, Washington, D.C.: GPO, 1998.
United States Copyright Office, www.lcweb.loc.gov/copyright.

DOM CARISTI,
2009 REVISIONS BY CHRISTOPHER H. STERLING

CORPORATION FOR PUBLIC BROADCASTING

The Corporation for Public Broadcasting (CPB) was created by the passage of the Public Broadcasting Act of 1967. Conceived as a nonpartisan entity established to promote and protect public radio and television, the Corporation has been embroiled in controversies and conflicts with the very public broadcasting organizations it brought into existence. Despite the best intentions of Congress, the CPB has not been able to sustain a nonpartisan posture through most of its existence.

Origins

When Lyndon B. Johnson signed the Public Broadcasting Act into law on 7 November 1967, the Corporation for Public Broadcasting was created. This landmark legislation became Section 396 of the Communication Act of 1934. In his public remarks at the signing ceremony, President Johnson stated that the Corporation "will get part of its support from our Government. But it will be carefully guarded from Government or from party control. It will be free, and it will be independent—and it will belong to all our people."

Contained in the Corporation's charter is a Congressional declaration of policy that provides, in part, that it is in the public interest to encourage the growth and development of educational radio and television broadcasting; that freedom, imagination, and initiative at both the local and national levels are necessary for high-quality, diverse programming for public broadcasting; that federal support for public broadcasting is appropriate; and that a private corporation should facilitate system development and afford maximum protection from extraneous interference and control. The Corporation's board of directors consists of 15 members appointed by the U.S. President, with the advice and consent of the Senate. No more than eight members may be of the same political party, and all members must be United States citizens. Board members are appointed for a six-year term of office. All officers of the Corporation serve at the pleasure of the board of directors. Each year the CPB must submit an annual report to the President for transmittal to Congress that contains a detailed statement regarding its operations, activities, accomplishments, and financial condition.

CPB and Public Radio

The Corporation for Public Broadcasting was incorporated in 1968 and began the task of staff appointments in 1969. Although the Office of Radio Activities was organized in June 1969 with Albert Hulsen as its first director, the top priority for CPB was television and the formation of a TV interconnection system, the Public Broadcasting Service (PBS). Hulsen, and his successor Thomas Warnock, used this early period to gather information about the performance of public radio in the United States and to begin planning for what would become radio's interconnection system, National Public Radio (NPR), launched in 1971.

CPB and PBS began feuding soon after PBS was created. Lyndon Johnson had since left the White House and President Richard M. Nixon did not like much of what he saw on public television. The Nixon White House started applying pressure on CPB, and the board in turn started applying pressure on PBS. The resulting conflicts between CPB and PBS nearly destroyed the very public broadcasting system that the Corporation had been created to protect. Eventually, a reorganization at PBS and a partnership agreement between CPB and PBS stabilized the system and left television much stronger than its radio counterpart. Public radio would need to engage in major reorganization itself if it hoped to get its share of the funding pie during joint negotiations between CPB, PBS, and NPR. That reorganization came as NPR merged with the Association of Public Radio Stations (APRS) to form a new NPR in May of 1977. This created a new political equation in public broadcasting. No longer could CPB and PBS make unilateral decisions about public broadcasting—whether funding allocations or system development—without considering public radio.

The overall prominence of the Corporation for Public Broadcasting that was witnessed during the first decade following the passage of the Public Broadcasting Act had clearly declined by the beginning of the 21st century. Revisions in Congressional appropriation procedures had substituted funding formulas for board room negotiations. Repeated calls for CPB to be a pass-through agent for the distribution of public monies rather than a policy-making organization for public broadcasting had stripped the Corporation of much of its public stature, and with its loss of image came a drain in talent. Partisan politics had inadvertently been built into the fabric of CPB regardless of the safeguards that had been written into the articles of incorporation. When the Republicans rule, the board is more likely to find liberal political bias in the system's public-affairs programming. When the Democrats are in charge, the system's critics decry insufficient minority programming and barriers to access by independent producers.

CPB was created to help put into practice the visions of public service broadcasting that existed only in the form of idealistic rhetoric. Congress was willing to craft lofty language that gave the Corporation its mandate, but lawmakers were never willing to grant the system the kind of fiscal independence that the original system framers envisioned for the fulfillment of the dream for an alternative system of public radio and television stations that were above partisan politics and commercial marketplace imperatives. Given the political, social, and economic environment in which CPB has been forced to function, it is not surprising that its performance record as a catalyst for the development and preservation of public broadcasting has been no more impressive. Indeed, when all of the political and economic handicaps placed on CPB are factored into the performance equation, one might wonder how the Corporation has been able to sustain the level of effectiveness that it has achieved. Whether the Corporation for Public Broadcasting will be able to fulfill its true potential as a positive agent on behalf of public radio and television in the 21st century will largely depend on whether Congress will at long last create the insulated funding mechanism that was envisioned as vital to the Corporation's functioning some 35 years ago.

Charges of political bias on public television and radio programs, from both conservatives and liberals, have become increasingly common and controversial in recent years and have hastened the exit of one CPB head (Kenneth Y. Tomlinson), derailed the nomination of a proposed board member (*According to Jim* show runner Warren Bell), and caused deep political debates about the appointment of another (Cheryl Halpern). In order to address the partisanship issue, in 2005, the CPB appointed its own internal ombudsman whose job it is to periodically review programs, post-air, and report on their journalistic balance and accuracy.

See also: National Public Radio; Public Broadcasting Act of 1967; Public Radio Since 1967

Further Reading

Avery, Robert K., and Robert Pepper, "Balancing the Equation: Public Radio Comes of Age," *Public Telecommunications Review* 7, no. 2 (March/April 1979).
Burke, John Edward, *An Historical-Analytical Study of the Legislative and Political Origins of the Public Broadcasting Act of 1967*, New York: Arno Press, 1979.
Carnegie Commission on Educational Television, *Public Television: A Program for Action*, New York: Bantam Books, 1967.

Carnegie Commission on the Future of Public Broadcasting, *A Public Trust*, New York: Bantam Books, 1979.
Engelman, Ralph, *Public Radio and Television in America: A Political History*, Thousand Oaks, California: Sage, 1996.
Witherspoon, John, Roselle Kovitz, Robert K. Avery, and Alan G. Stavitsky, *A History of Public Broadcasting*, Washington, D.C.: Current, 2000.

ROBERT K. AVERY,
2009 REVISIONS BY CARY O'DELL

COUNTRY MUSIC FORMAT

At the beginning of the 20th century, "country music" was a version of folk music. With field recordings of the late 1920s, it became categorized as "hillbilly" music, and then after World War II, entrepreneurs renamed it "country and western," a designation used throughout the 1950s and into the 1960s. With the rise of Nashville as the recording center, however, the "western" was dropped, and by the time it became an important radio format, the name "country" was widely accepted. Whatever the name, until the 1960s country music tended to be songs of poor white folk that were passed down generation to generation as the South and then the West were settled.

Early Country Radio

In 1927 Ralph Peer of Radio Corporation of America (RCA) Victor record company began to record country music performers, most notably Jimmie Rogers and the Carter family, and a commercial industry was born. The western side of country music was popularized in cowboy films of the 1930s and 1940s by such stars as Roy Rogers and Gene Autry. On the radio, western stars had regular programs: there were country music performances on live barn dances such as the *National Barn Dance* from Chicago; *Town and Country Time* from Washington, D.C.; and the *Grand Ole Opry* from Nashville.

During World War II, soldiers from the South and West took their music all around the world. In the postwar era, Hank Williams made country songs popular, and he was followed by Jim Reeves and Patsy Cline. As Top 40 took over radio airplay, country music—in the 1960s—emerged as an alternative genre centered in Nashville, with stars such as Johnny Cash, Jimmy Dean, Loretta Lynn, and Dolly Parton.

On radio, country music had long been confined to network programs (such as the *National Barn Dance* from Chicago and the *Grand Ole Opry* from Nashville), small-town stations, and the border radio stations in Mexico. With the decline of network programming and the rise of radio formats, non-network-affiliated stations were playing a substantial amount of country music as early as the late 1940s. Top 40 led the way in terms of playing a selected playlist from one genre of music. Country—from Nashville—did the same as it evolved during the 1960s.

The country music business realized the threat of rock and roll, and in the late 1950s the business reorganized what had been the annual country disc jockeys' convention into the Country Music Association to promote more country music on radio. Although the identity of the first country-formatted station will forever be debated, stations converted from the programming techniques of the network era to those of the format era. Stations such as WARL-AM (Arlington, Virginia); KXLA AM (Pasadena, California); and KDAV-TV (Lubbock, Texas) played live and recorded country music almost all day by 1950.

A generation later, more than 300 radio stations broadcast recorded country music on a full-time basis, and over 2,000 more programmed country for part of the day. The Country Music Association deserves much of the credit for promoting country as an alternative format, but it was certainly helped by the fracturing of rock music during the 1960s and the alienation of its older audience. During the 1950s and 1960s, country format radio moved from its small-town base in the South (as well as in cities such as Los Angeles, where thousands of southerners had moved during the Great Depression) to cities all across the United States.

Country as a Format

By the mid-1960s, advertisers no longer thought of country radio stations as only being listened to by country folk. During the 1950s, it looked as though country would not survive the popularity of rock and Top 40 formatting, but the introduction of the "Nashville Sound"—typified by the now-classic recordings of Patsy Cline—proved that crossover hit making was possible. By the mid-1970s, country had its place in radio, with more than 1,000 stations playing country format. Country had become suburban—it had given a voice to adult problems, such as infidelity, boss hating, and the like, whereas pop music seemed stuck in teenaged concerns. Country radio listeners were therefore older, and were nearly always white.

By the 1990s, one survey determined that country stations were number one in 57 of the top 100 radio markets in the United States. Many surveys found country the most popular format on radio, with such megastars as Garth Brooks, Reba McEntire,

Alan Jackson, and Shania Twain. The country music format had surely reached a high point as the most popular radio music in the country.

Even in the mid-1990s, however, some argued that radio was becoming too formulaic. Country radio aimed programming at adults aged 18–34 who listened on their way to and from work, were made up of more women than men, and lived in the suburbs rather than the cities. Artists who did not appeal to these listeners, including Dolly Parton and Willie Nelson, were simply ignored. Pressed by advertisers seeking younger buyers, country radio ironically abandoned listeners over 49, the very fans who had helped build it into the nation's most popular format.

During the 1990s, grown-up baby boomers embraced country, and so advertisers willingly anted up millions of dollars in advertising spending to reach them. Using Donnelley's Cluster Plus system, in 1990 the Arbitron ratings service found that 40 percent of all country fans fit into the system's most affluent groupings, compared with fewer than one-quarter of all Americans aged 12 and older.

The boom in country radio (and television) is well reflected in the career of Garth Brooks, a star who did not sell his first compact disc until 1989, and who by the close of the century was the best-selling popular music artist in history. American music has never seen a phenomenon like Brooks, who in 1996 at age 34 had reached number two—in just seven years. In the process, he eclipsed Elvis Presley, Michael Jackson, and the Beatles. During the early 1990s he sold an average of eight million "units" per year. Radio stations featured Brooks' latest releases and captured millions of new listeners.

New ways of determining hits helped as well. In 1992, Brooks became the year's top-selling artist based on *Ropin' in the Wind*, released late in 1991, because computers were used to determine what was sold in stores rather than relying on telephone surveys. Brooks became, because of SoundScan computer counting, the first country artist to top *Billboard*'s charts. *Ropin' in the Wind* became the first country album ever to top *Billboard*'s year-end pop album chart. Country radio programmers used SoundScan data (a music sales reporting service for subscribers that integrates weekly retail store reports on how many CDs have been sold, providing results for individual markets, regions, or the nation) to determine their playlists.

The 25 May 1991 *Billboard* chart was the first done on SoundScan, and suddenly 15 more country albums showed up in the Top 200 than had been there a week before. In 1984 the country category showed only eight gold (500,000 sales), four platinum

(1,000,000-plus sales), and seven multiplatinum albums. By 1991 the numbers were 24 gold, 21 platinum, and eight multiplatinum.

At the beginning of the 21st century, the future of the country music format looked bright. The number of young people listening to country music had increased almost 70 percent during the 1990s, and although its popularity was leveling off as the decade ended, no-one predicted that country's core popularity would decline anytime soon. According to the *Simmons Study of Media and Markets*, country music was the choice of one-fifth of the 18–24 population, with growth among those aged 25–34, 35–44, and 45–54, most of these being just the listeners most desired by radio advertisers. As the first decade of the new millennium came to a close, the Radio Advertising Bureau ranked the country music format as the most popular among radio listeners.

See also: Border Radio; Contemporary Hit Radio/Top 40 Format; Gospel Music Format; *Grand Ole Opry*; Music on Radio; *National Barn Dance*; Oldies Format

Further Reading

Carney, George O., editor, *The Sounds of People and Places: Readings in the Geography of Music*, Washington, D.C.: University Press of America, 1978; 3rd edition, as *The Sounds of People and Places: A Geography of American Folk and Popular Music*, Lanham, Maryland: Rowman and Littlefield, 1994.

Keith, Michael C., *Radio Programming: Consultancy and Formatics*, Boston: Focal Press, 1987.

Kingsbury, Paul, editor, *The Encyclopedia of Country Music*, New York: Oxford University Press, 1998.

Lewis, George H., editor, *All That Glitters: Country Music in America*, Bowling Green, Ohio: Bowling Green State University Popular Press, 1993.

MacFarland, David T., *Contemporary Radio Programming Strategies*, Hillsdale, New Jersey: Erlbaum; 2nd edition, as *Future Radio Programming Strategies: Cultivating Listenership in The Digital Age*, Mahwah, New Jersey: Erlbaum, 1997.

Malone, Bill C., *Country Music U.S.A.*, Austin: University of Texas Press, 1968; revised edition, 1985.

Routt, Edd, James B. McGrath, and Fredric A. Weiss, *The Radio Format Conundrum*, New York: Hastings House, 1978.

"Symposium: Country Music Radio," *Journal of Radio Studies* 1 (1992).

DOUGLAS GOMERY,
2009 REVISIONS BY CHRISTOPHER H. STERLING

CRYSTAL RECEIVERS
Simple Early Radio Sets

The crystal receiver, popularly known as the "crystal set," was the device used by most people to listen to radio between 1906 and the early 1920s. The heart of the crystal receiver was the crystal itself, a small piece of silicon or galena, natural elements with the ability to detect radio frequency waves and to rectify or convert them into audio frequency signals. The crystal's ability to detect radio signals was discovered in 1906 by General Henry H.C. Dunwoody and G.W. Pickard. The crystal receiver was inexpensive and easy to construct, making it possible for even a young child to build a radio. Even today, the construction of a crystal receiver from a kit is often a young person's first introduction to radio technology.

As early as 1910, the three basic components and the instructions needed to construct a crystal receiver were available from mail-order electrical supply houses. All one needed was a spool of wire, a crystal detector, and earphones. The crystal detector consisted of a small piece of galena mounted in a lead base, approximately 1/4 inch in diameter, and electrically connected to a terminal. A tiny wire, called a "cat's whisker," made contact with the exposed top of the galena, and its small moveable handle allowed the listener to find the spot on the galena where the radio signal was the loudest. The cat's whisker was connected to a second terminal. One of these terminals was connected to the tuning coil.

A tuning coil was made by winding several hundred turns of thin, insulated wire around an empty oatmeal box or similar cylindrical object. A sliding piece of metal was positioned to move across the exposed coil windings for precise tuning. To the other terminal of the tuning coil a long wire, called the antenna, was connected and strung to a tree in the back yard, the goal being to get it as high as possible. The second terminal of the galena crystal/cat's whisker combination was connected to one wire of a headset or single earphone. The other earphone wire was connected to a ground, usually a metal stake driven into the earth. Sometimes a fourth component, a fixed or variable capacitor, was added to the circuit.

To understand what the crystal receiver meant to the early science of radio, it is necessary to look at the available wireless detector technology in the early years of the 20th century. In Marconi's 1900 wireless, the receiving device used to translate the dots and dashes of his spark transmitter was a coherer, a small tube containing iron filings that closed like a switch when receiving the electromagnetic pulses of the Morse code. Each time the filings cohered, or caused the circuit to close, current from an in-series battery flowed; then, either a buzzer sounded, a telephone receiver clicked, or an inking device recorded a coded symbolic component of the message, a dot or dash. Then a small hammer would tap the filings apart, and the entire process began again to detect the next dot or dash. The coherer could only indicate to a radio operator if a spark signal was present. Such a system might receive five or ten words per minute and was unreliable. And although the coherer was a satisfactory receiver as long as the transmitter was of the spark-gap type, it would not work with the continuous-wave and voice-transmitting systems that quickly replaced the spark. The mechanical coherer did not allow a receiver to "hear" audio, obviously a serious technical impediment to the development of wireless telephone and radio broadcasting.

Between the crude mechanical coherer and the discovery of the detecting properties of the crystal, several intermediate systems of detecting were invented and used by two of the leading early radiotelephone inventors. Between 1900 and 1905, Reginald Fessenden's Liquid Barretter and Lee de Forest's similar Electrolytic Detector were able to detect both continuous-wave code transmission and audio. These were less reliable than the crystal detector that followed, but they did allow radio operators to hear the human voice. By 1906, de Forest was advertising a radiotelephone system with his vacuum tube, the Audion, as the detector. Whether liquid, crystal, or vacuum tube, this new generation of nonmechanical detectors that converted or rectified radio frequency into audio frequency really opened the door for the development of the radiotelephone.

When licensed radio for the public was introduced in 1920, it was believed that the financial basis for the new commercial radio service would derive from sales of manufactured radio sets. Large companies such as Westinghouse and General Electric introduced home radios, the most popular of which was a crystal receiver in a wood box with earphones and instructions, called the Radiola I and the Aeriola Jr. The vacuum tube detector, as pioneered and used by de Forest 15 years earlier, was still too expensive for most families, but there were higher priced radios available that used the crystal as a detector but added a vacuum tube as an amplifier to increase the volume. By the mid-1920s, better programming caused a demand for radios that would play loud enough to drive a horn speaker, and manufacturers introduced radios that used vacuum tubes for both detector and amplifier.

The vacuum tube remained the technology of choice for detecting radio signals until the transistor finally replaced it in the 1960s. And what happened to the crystal receiver? It is still the entry-level radio technology of choice. Its components, in the form of kits, are readily available today. It is almost a rite of passage for a young boy or girl to build a crystal set, and technical museums still offer Saturday morning classes where parents and their children can learn to construct a crystal receiver. There is still a thrill from building your own radio, one that seemingly works by magic, using no batteries, no electricity, one that pulls faint programs from a local AM station, experiencing what your great-grandparents did almost a century ago.

Further Reading

Aitken, Hugh G.J., *Syntony and Spark: The Origins of Radio*, New York: Wiley, 1976.

Greenwood, Harold S., *A Pictorial Album of Wireless and Radio, 1905–1928*, Los Angeles: Clymer, 1961.

Kendall, Lewis F, and Robert Philip Koehler, *Radio Simplified: What It Is—How to Build and Operate the Apparatus*, Philadelphia, Pennsylvania: Winston, 1922; revised edition, 1923.

Sanders, Ian L., *Tickling the Crystal: Domestic British Crystal Sets of the 1920s*, Tunbridge Wells, England: Bentomel Publications, 2001.

Sievers, Maurice L., *Crystal Clear: Vintage American Crystal Sets, Crystal Detectors, and Crystals*, Vestal, New York: Vestal Press, 1991.

Verrill, A. Hyatt, *The Home Radio: How to Make and Use It*, New York: Harper, 1922.

MICHAEL H. ADAMS

D

DEMOGRAPHICS
Defining the Radio Audience

Broadcast Research Definitions describes demographics as:

> a system of categories by which a population is subdivided according to characteristics of the people who comprise it. The same term also describes audience reports which present audiences according to this system of categories. In broadcast ratings demographics most often refer to age and sex categories such as "Men 18–34"or "Women 25–49." The terms may also be used to describe categories based on marital status, education, etc.
>
> (Fletcher, 1988)

Demographics are important in the radio industry in two ways. First, advertisers use demographics to describe their customers and to buy audiences for commercials. This practice is the basic revenue transaction supporting commercial radio. Second, radio stations are programmed to produce audiences with the demographics their advertisers seek.

Core consumers of any product or service account for the day-to-day, year-to-year success of a consumer company. The core consumer spends more or purchases more units in the product/service category in question, and is particularly important to the survival of companies providing such goods/services. For instance, Campbell's Soup identifies its bedrock offering as its condensed soups sold in red-and-white cans. The core consumer of this product purchases a case or more of these soups every month. The demographics of Campbell's core consumers are important to the company, and its

advertising must reach them as well as additional consumers who use their condensed soup less often or seasonally.

These additional consumers are an example of special advertising opportunities for radio. For many years Campbell's has observed that more soup is purchased during the cold seasons and in areas most affected by cold weather. They also know that the typical seasonal purchaser of their soups is a mother with children at home who feels that adding soup to a child's diet in cold weather will improve resistance to colds. As a consequence, Campbell's regularly purchases additional advertising time on radio stations in geographical areas most affected by cold weather and on stations high in the demographic group comprising women aged 30 and over, which presumably includes mothers with children at home.

Origins

In the 1930s, the early years of radio audience reports, the principal demographic of interest to advertisers was the number of households in the audience of particular programs. It was assumed that each household would own one radio receiver and that every member of the household would hear the programs broadcast through the household receiver. The result was that information about the programs tuned into by the household set was the prime information sought by researchers, and advertisers based their strategies on appealing to the product-purchasing decision-makers in the household.

Demographics were so unimportant during radio's Golden Age that the Nielsen Radio Index (NRI) became the principal national radio ratings service in 1950 (right at the end of the period) without having the capability of reporting demographics. The NRI used audimeters attached to respondent receivers at home (and eventually in cars). These devices could only report which programs were accessed by which radios; they could not determine who was listening or whether anyone at all was listening.

The rise of television in the late 1940s marked the rise of demographic information's importance in selling radio time. By 1975—the year before its demise—The Pulse included these demographic categories in its reports: (1) Gender: male, female, total; (2) Age: teens, 18–24, 25–34, 35–49, 50–64, 65 and over, total; and (3) Ethnicity: Black, Hispanic, other, total. In the same year, Arbitron Radio reports included these demographics: (1) Gender: male, female, adults (male and female) and (2) Age: teens, 18–24, 25–34, 35–49, 50–64, 65 +. Special weighting and interviewing procedures were in place for African-American and Latino listeners.

In the mid-1980s Tapscan had become an important selling tool for radio. Tapscan of Birmingham, Alabama, was a provider of radio sales software. The service was available only to full-service clients (stations that purchased all of the regularly scheduled Arbitron surveys of the market in question) of a radio rating service. One of the displays produced by Tapscan analysis was a ranking report that showed which stations in a market had the highest numbers of listeners in each of the demographic categories included in the rating report. If an advertiser wished to sell jeans in a given market, in-house research would reveal that the core jeans consumer was a person in the 18–24 age group, that males were more brand loyal, and that females made more purchases and were more sensitive to price. A Tapscan analysis of the stations in each market would reveal which stations could provide the most young male and female listeners and thus should be included in the jeans campaign.

The greater availability of radio listener demographics and increased use of sales analysis software made possible an important media buying strategy—Optimum Effective Scheduling (OES) or "optimizers." The idea behind OES is that advertisers are best advised to purchase a combination of advertising opportunities from whatever stations in the market are necessary to deliver every listener in the demographic category sought by the advertiser. The software's calculations during data analysis

take into account two factors called *recycling* and *sharing*.

Recycling refers to the tendency of some proportion of an audience to listen during more than one daypart or to more than one program on a given station or network. For example, 25 percent of a radio station's morning drive-time audience is recycled to evening drive-time. This means that only one out of four listeners in the morning will be present in the evening; hence, an advertiser determined to reach the optimum number of target listeners should buy commercials in both morning and evening drive-time.

Sharing refers to listeners of more than one station, which may also be referred to as their having a "duplicated audience." Sharing also implies that there will be some members of the advertising target demographic groups who listen to one station only, so those members' favorite stations must be included in the OES calculation for advertisers who wish to reach them. OES software routines determine how many spots on which stations must be purchased to reach a designated percent of all radio listeners in a particular demographic group.

Optimum effective scheduling has become very important in national and regional media buying. It is also important in planning programming for a radio station. If an important audience listens exclusively to a particular radio station, then advertising from that station must be included in the advertising media plans of any business aiming for the demographic audience delivered by that station.

The need for OES presents some dilemmas to radio programmers. Should a station design its programs for homogeneous audiences from a relatively narrow set of demographic groups, increasing the likelihood that exclusive audiences will be included in buys made using the OES rationale? Or should the station attempt to appeal to a wider range of demographic groups, hoping that each group delivered will be useful to the campaigns of different advertisers? Contemporary radio stations programmed under either of these philosophies are usually prosperous.

One of the most important radio program consultants since the 1980s, Ed Shane, wrote the following while discussing station audiences that are not core to the station:

An essential, of course, is to be able to judge whether there are others in the general audience. A jazz or new age station, for example, may have not only a loyal core, but also may have all the jazz or new age devotees in the market. More than one station has been bitterly disappointed to discover that there was no growth beyond their initial impact

(Shane, 1991)

The situation is even more complicated for station clusters, which are now the norm in the major markets of the United States. Large radio groups today may own stations providing every major radio format, perhaps with five or six or more formats in the same market. The issue of which demographic groups a particular station should target with its programming must be answered by program executives and consultants who are responsible for stations with the same format in many cities, even when that format is failing to deliver its assigned demographics in one market served by the group. At the same time, a cluster of stations in any market attempts to use OES strategies to sell combinations of its stations whenever possible. Sales are often the responsibility of an integrated sales management team charged with selling all of the stations in the cluster.

Demographic Factors

Programmers must look at the demographic characteristics of the market as a whole in light of station formats and audiences already present in the market. The economy of the market is another important consideration. For instance, if the market is characterized by rapid home construction and high levels of home buying, the program planner will recognize that sales of products related to home improvement, major appliances, lawn and garden items, furniture, and interior design are likely to be important sources of revenue in the market. If the community hosts a rapidly growing number of small businesses, business-to-business advertising and ads that direct the attention of business managers to office supply websites will be potentially rewarding.

Various radio program materials produce different demographic patterns among listeners. Most music listeners, for example, gain their music listening preferences during the years in which they are becoming aware of popular music, their teens and young adult years. Although their tolerance for other music may increase over the years, they tend to retain favorites acquired in those formative years. As a consequence, oldies (music no longer in current release but popular with demographic groups socialized to it at a young age) are a major component of popular radio programming. The latest hits tend to be preferred by young audiences, other types of music appeal more consistently to

women, and still others are the choice of blue-collar workers.

A programmer's experience will suggest one or more formats that will attract the desired demographic groups in the market. The station will then conduct studies, perhaps by focus group, to determine listener attitudes about these formats and about the lack of certain music or other radio programming in the market. The focus group discussion may explore the preferences of potential demographics for different parts of the day. Listeners to some formats, although enthusiastic about hearing more of their favorite music, may also wish to hear traffic and weather reports at some time of the day. If talk formats are being studied, popular topics for discussion and the behavior of talk show hosts may be explored in focus groups. Increasingly there will also be discussions about the role of commercials in these formats. Should the commercials be concentrated in a small number of breaks in programming? How many commercials in a row are tolerable?

Format Approaches

The radio station program format will consist of a set of principles or rules for assembling programming. Sometimes these rules are relatively simple: (1) three musical selections should be played in uninterrupted succession; (2) a hit should be heard in this musical style four times per hour; (3) an oldie harking back to the birth of this style should be played at least once per hour; (4) titles and performers should be announced both before and after clusters of musical selections; (5) during early morning hours the time should be announced four times per hour; (6) during commuting hours traffic highlights should be presented twice per hour; and so on.

When the programmer has defined the format, a model tape of the format will be produced in which the music to be played is represented by brief excerpts. This makes it possible for potential listeners to hear all elements of a format in a short space of time (perhaps five minutes), while getting a feel for the music to be included. These model tapes are then played to potential listeners in focus group or auditorium settings. The researcher will also play excerpts of programming from competing stations to measure the competitive appeal of the proposed radio format. The same session may also include examples of promotional materials for the station so that those attractive to the station's target demographic groups can be identified.

When a new station format is broadcast, station management will pay close attention to the demographic groups delivered by the station. An important analysis from audience research reports will be the number of minutes an average listener in a target group listens to the station. This statistic is called "time spent listening" (TSL). The programmer hopes that the station's target demographic groups' TSLs are relatively large and that they will grow after a change in format. It is also significant that exclusive audiences (audiences that tune to only one station) will be apparent in the station's target demographic groups. The exclusive audiences will guarantee the station a place in OES advertising plans. Station promotion will be designed to increase the number of listeners in the target groups, and improvements in programming will be intended to increase TSL for these demographics.

Many stations use satellite or other syndicated sources for their programming. There is some cost associated with acquiring programming in this way. For a syndicator or satellite music service to remain profitable, a similar sort of demographic research is essential.

Although demographic research was not important in the early days of radio, the role of demographics in both contemporary radio programming and advertising sales has become crucial. Commercial radio stations must command audiences in the demographic groups important to their advertisers in order to ensure their own survival.

See also: A.C. Nielsen Company; Arbitron; Audience Research Methods; Commercial Tests; Programming Research; Programming Strategies and Processes; Pulse, Inc.

Further Reading

Beville, Hugh Malcolm, *Audience Ratings: Radio, Television, and Cable*, Hillsdale, New Jersey: Erlbaum, 1985; revised edition, 1988.

Fletcher, James E., *Music and Program Research*, Washington, D.C.: National Association of Broadcasters, 1987.

Fletcher, James E., *Broadcast Research Definitions*, Washington, D.C.: National Association of Broadcasters, 1988.

Fletcher, James E., *Profiting from Radio Ratings: A Manual for Radio Managers, Sales Managers, and Programmers*, Washington, D.C.: National Association of Broadcasters, 1989.

Shane, Ed, *Cutting Through: Strategies and Tactics for Radio*, Houston, Texas: Shane Media Services, 1991.

Webster, James G., and Lawrence W. Lichty, *Ratings Analysis: Theory and Practice*, Hillsdale, New Jersey: Erlbaum, 1991; 2nd edition, as *Ratings Analysis: The Theory and Practice of Audience Research*, by Webster, Lichty, and Patricia F. Phalen, Mahwah, New Jersey: Erlbaum, 2000.

JAMES E. FLETCHER

DEREGULATION OF RADIO
Eliminating Old Rules

Radio deregulation refers both to a specific Federal Communications Commission (FCC) proceeding (1978–81) and to a more general—and continuing—trend of dropping or modifying existing laws, rules, and regulations. Briefly, *deregulation* means to remove or significantly modify existing regulation, either through FCC administrative action or by congressional legislation.

Origins

Contrary to popular opinion, deregulation is not new. Indeed, the basic concept that less government is best is an old shibboleth evident in most aspects of American life. There is a deepseated feeling that cuts across political lines (or most of them) that competition, rather than regulation, will lead to lower prices and higher-quality products or services. Nowhere is this truer than in an expanding industry with new players clamoring to enter the marketplace.

Combining this background with the economics of government in the late 20th century created the seedbed for radio deregulation. On all levels, government was operating at a deficit for much of the period after World War II. Federal deficits mounted annually, forcing Congress and the executive branch to consider ways of cutting costs—or at least of carefully assessing the benefits of new, let alone existing, rules and regulations. Paperwork reduction became a byword after the 1970s as government sought to root out rules that were no longer needed but expensive to maintain.

When deregulatory consideration was applied to broadcasting, it involved a basic review of the practical meaning of the Communication Act's concept of "public interest, convenience or necessity," which had guided FCC decisions since 1934. As society changed, so did at least some views of what government could or should accomplish. To varying degrees an ideological battle, there was at least broad agreement that government could no longer do everything.

In 1972 FCC Chairman Richard Wiley initiated a search for "regulatory underbrush" that could safely be eliminated without harm to broadcasters or their audiences—and within six years the commission had dropped or modified some 800 mostly minor rules. Many concerned small technical changes, and others reduced reporting requirements. This exercise set a larger process in motion.

Radio Deregulation Proceeding: 1978–81

In 1978 the National Association of Broadcasters (NAB), always seeking ways of reducing the burden of government on its member stations, petitioned the FCC to consider dropping four requirements that affected radio. These included processing guidelines (used by the commission staff to decide on the granting of new and renewal license applications) that were designed to limit on-air advertising and promote non-entertainment programming. In addition, the NAB wanted the FCC to drop formal program log requirements as well as the complex process known as "ascertainment," which required licensees to learn more about their community of operation (and reflect that knowledge in their programming).

The petition was a good example of perfect timing, for it paralleled the thinking of many staffers in the FCC's Broadcast Bureau. Prompted in part by the NAB petition for rulemaking, the staff undertook its own studies of the radio business, noting especially how many stations had taken to the air since many of the rules had been established. They also developed a somewhat complex economic policy model that served to question the continuation of the rules the NAB targeted.

In September 1979 the commission issued a *Notice of Inquiry and Proposed Rulemaking* concerning the deregulation of radio. Pragmatic in tone, the long notice (80 pages in tiny *Federal Register* type) conceded that with the removal of the processing guidelines on programming there "will be a tendency toward program duplication and imitation" (Paragraph 144). But it also asked whether this would matter, given how many stations were now on the air, including multiple signals in all but the tiniest towns.

Release of the notice brought forth a torrent of public reaction. In the several months allowed for public comments, some 20,000 were filed, filling shelves of notebooks in the Broadcast Bureau's public file room. They were often emotional—arguing that dropping program guidelines would lead to the elimination of religious or some other kind of minority-interest programming or that letting go of the advertising guideline would lead to a flood of commercials on the air. Some claimed that elimination of the logging requirement would remove a useful tool for those who watched closely how well stations performed. In addition, critics held that elimination of the ascertainment rules would lead to even more "plain vanilla" radio, which would sound the same no matter where a facility was located.

The sheer amount of filed comments took the staff nearly a year to process and consider. Early in 1981, after concerted internal debate, the FCC released a *Report and Order* dropping the four radio rules that the NAB had originally proposed be dropped. On the very day of the order's release, the activist office of communications of the United Church of Christ filed a court appeal and requested that the rule change be stayed pending a final decision. Not surprisingly, the broadcasting industry cheered the FCC decision, restating that the rules being dropped had little to do with program quality or service to listeners.

The U.S. Court of Appeals largely upheld the FCC rulemaking. It remanded for further action one piece of the decision—that concerning the dropping of program logs. The FCC had replaced the logging rule with a requirement that stations develop a list of community problems and programs aired that addressed those problems. The original order called for this to be done annually, and with the court's remand, the FCC made this a quarterly process, with station reports going into each station's own public files rather than being sent to Washington. The change passed muster with the appeals court.

Looking back two decades later, it is difficult to understand the emotions this proceeding created at the time. The issues now seem small and marginal, though at the time many critics saw the FCC decision as a watershed. For if the commission no longer concerned itself with the content that radio stations provided, what was the point of regulation, and what would happen to the industry? How could licenses be issued in the public interest if there was no longer any effective measure of what the public interest was? How could people complain about and seek to improve local station practices if the prime tools they had used previously (the station's local market ascertainment study or composite logs showing a typical week's programming and advertising) were eliminated? These critics argued that the new "problems and programs" listing would not be much use, certainly not in the way the old rules had.

Continuing Deregulation: 1980–2000

The 1981 rulemaking applied only to commercial radio. However, in parallel rulemakings commenced in 1981, the FCC eventually dropped the same four rules for noncommercial radio in 1984, and for television stations a year later. As many had predicted and others had feared, the radio deregulation proceeding paved the way for more substantial actions in the years that followed.

At virtually the same time, the FCC dropped its long and often complex license renewal form, replacing it with a mere postcard with a handful of easy-to-answer questions. Where stations had previously often filed a box of material, the simple postcard itself would often suffice now. Congress joined in the process, lengthening radio station licenses from three years to seven in 1981, and to eight in the 1996 Telecommunications Act. And beginning in 1982, licensees could buy and sell stations like any other property when the FCC dropped its "antitrafficking" rule, which had required that licenses be held for at least three years before they could be sold.

Many rules were not as emotionally charged. Beginning in 1981 the FCC steadily reduced its former requirements on how much engineering expertise a station needed to maintain. Reversing its traditional approach, the commission argued that as long as a station was not creating interference to others, how good or how poor its own signal was would be better regulated by marketplace competition than by stiff rules. A station with poor-quality signals would rapidly lose audience and advertisers. A boon especially to smaller stations, the relaxed rules allowed them to share engineers or merely to have one on-call rather than on the premises.

Higher on the emotional scale was the 1987 elimination of the FCC fairness doctrine. The decision made clear that licensees were the absolute authority on what issues and points of view they aired. Another shibboleth collapsed in 1992, when the FCC first allowed an owner to control more than a single station of each type (AM and FM) in a given market. This spelled the end of the long-established "duopoly" rule, created in the 1940s when there were fewer than 1,000 stations on the air.

The 1996 Telecommunications Act included provisions making it very difficult to challenge a broadcast license (such a process had briefly become a sport in the late 1960s and early 1970s, though few stations actually lost their licenses). The FCC would now have to find the incumbent licensee undeserving of a continued license before it could even consider a possible challenger.

The same act greatly expanded the number of stations anyone could own. In the 1940s the FCC had created de facto rules allowing ownership of no more than seven AM and seven FM stations nationally. As the industry expanded, so did pressure to raise those admittedly arbitrary limits. Finally, in 1985, the FCC increased them by five stations each—to 12 and 12. The limits rose again in 1992, to 18 and 18, and to 20 and 20 by 1994.

With the 1996 Telecommunications Act, Congress eliminated any national cap on radio station ownership. By the turn of the century, the largest radio owners controlled nearly 1,200 stations.

Did all of this deregulation change the face of radio broadcasting? Certainly the economic and structural changes concerning ownership have considerably modified what was once a business of many small groups or individual owners. But the evidence remains inconclusive that elimination of the FCC's radio license processing and content rules two decades ago made any difference that competitive pressures would not have brought about anyway.

Deregulation in the New Century

The three decade-old FCC trend to deregulation accelerated under the Bush Administration (2001–9). Discussed in other entries are the continued commission effort to further deregulate station ownership, as well as the attempts to *re*-regulate indecency on the air. So is the congressionally mandated use of auctions to license stations, which turns the process over to the highest bidder rather than a quest for the best licensee in a given area. On two occasions, in 2003 and again in 2008, the commission commissioned and published (on its website) research studies that surveyed the state of radio broadcasting, including its ownership, economic state, and programming. There was some criticism of who had been selected to undertake the research assignments, let alone the published results, which generally seemed to support the commission's hands-off approach to the medium. There was some suggestion that Chairman Kevin Martin had suppressed research findings that disagreed with his own perception of the facts, but little hard evidence was forthcoming. Finally, the commission agreed in mid-2008 with the plans of the two satellite radio carriers to merge.

That the FCC's views on radio might change yet again seemed evident with the incoming Obama administration in 2009. Among other issues being discussed, (according to press reports) was a possible reinstatement of a version of the former Fairness Doctrine, driven in part by the dominance of right-wing views on radio talk shows. But congressional opinion seemed unlikely to support such a move.

See also: Fairness Doctrine; Federal Communications Commission; First Amendment and Radio; Licensing Authorizing U.S. Station to Broadcast; Localism in Radio; Ownership, Mergers, and Acquisition; "Public Interest, Convenience or Necessity"; Regulation; Telecommunications Act of 1996

Further Reading

Broadcast Deregulation, New York: Station Representatives Association, 1979

Federal Communications Commission, "Ascertainment of Community Problems by Broadcast Applicants: Primer," *Federal Register* 41 (7 January 1976)

Federal Communications Commission, *Inquiry and Proposed Rulemaking: Deregulation of Radio*, 73 FCC 2d 457 (6 September 1979)

Federal Communications Commission, *In the Matter of: Deregulation of Radio—Report and Order in BC Docket 79–219*, 84 FCC 2d 968 (14 January 1981)

Office of Communication of the United Church of Christ v. FCC, 707 F2d 1413 (D.C. Circuit, 1983).

CHRISTOPHER H. STERLING,
2009 REVISIONS BY CHRISTOPHER H. STERLING

DIARY
Method of Audience Research

As the name suggests, a diary is a paper booklet in which a person is asked to record his or her listening to radio or television programs, noting when listening started and stopped, which station the set was tuned to, and other comments. A diary is typically used to record one week of listening, then returned for tabulation. Radio audience estimates, usually called ratings, are based on the tabulation of information obtained from these diaries.

Origins

In the medium's early days, many radio set builders and listeners were not interested in hearing specific programs so much as listening to as many different stations as possible. This "channel-surfing" was called DXing—an abbreviation for distance. DXers kept track of the stations they heard in log books that recorded when they heard a station, the frequency and/or call sign, slogans, programs, and the city of origin. Some computed the distance to the stations they heard, and there were contests sponsored by radio clubs and radio magazines with prizes given to those who compiled the most stations and greatest total distance. Although the diary method existed in the early days of radio, until the rise of television diary-keeping was not the mainstay of radio audience measurement.

The first systematic audience research using diaries was done by Professor Garnet Garrison at Wayne (later Wayne State) University in 1937, though he called it a "listening table." Garrison, who later taught for many years at the University of Michigan, was working on an "experiment developing a radio research technique for measurement of listening

habits which would be inexpensive and yet fairly reliable." He noted that other methods most widely used at the time were the telephone survey, either coincidental or unaided recall, personal interviews, mail—sometimes called fan mail—analysis, surveys, and "the youngster automatic recording." He said that he had borrowed something from each method; as the listening table could be sent and retrieved by mail, it included a program roster, and was thought to be objective. The form he used was a grid from 6 A.M. to midnight, divided into 15-minute segments, that asked respondents to list stations, programs, and the number of listeners. Garrison concluded that "With careful attention to correct sampling, distribution of listening tables, and tabulation of the raw data, the technique…should assist materially in obtaining at small cost quite detailed information about radio listening." Although his methodology was not adopted for about a decade, Garrison's "listening table" is essentially the way radio audience estimates are obtained to this day.

The Columbia Broadcasting System experimented with diaries in the 1940s but apparently thought the data was most applicable for programming research, for which it also used the program (or Lazarsfeld-Stanton) analyzer. CBS used information from diaries primarily to track such things as audience composition, listening to lead-in and lead-out programs, and charting audience flow and turnover. In the late 1940s, C.E. Hooper also added diaries to his telephone sample in areas that could not easily be reached by telephone. But this mixture of diary and coincidental data was never completely satisfactory. Indeed, one of the reasons for Nielsen's Audimeter winning out over Hooperatings was that the telephone method was confined to larger metropolitan areas, where TV first began to erode the radio audience. Hence, Hooper (unlike Nielsen) tended to understate the radio audience and therefore quickly lost the support of radio stations.

Arbitron Diaries

It was not until the end of the 1940s that diaries were introduced on a large-scale basis for providing syndicated audience research. James Seiler, director of research for the National Broadcasting Company's station in Washington, D.C., had for several years proposed using diaries to measure radio. NBC finally agreed to try a survey, not for radio, but for its new TV station in the market, agreeing to help pay for several tests. Seiler set up his own ratings service company in Washington and called it the American Research Bureau. He thought the name sounded very official, even patriotic. Later the name was shortened to ARB, and then to Arbitron when instant television ratings in larger cities were gathered electronically.

The American Research Bureau's first report was based on a week-long diary that covered 11–18 May 1949. By that fall, the company was also measuring TV viewing in Baltimore, Philadelphia, and New York. Chicago and Cleveland were added the next year. In spite of covering more markets the company grew slowly as both TV and the new diary method gained acceptance. Diaries were placed with TV viewers identified by random phone calls. From the beginning, Seiler was careful to list the number of diaries placed and those "recovered and usable." Also, "breakdowns of numbers of men, women, and children per set for specific programs [could] be furnished by extra tabulation."

Tele-Que, another research company, began diary-based television ratings in Los Angeles in 1947. In 1951 Tele-Que merged with ARB, thus adding reports for Los Angeles, San Francisco, and San Diego. During the 1950s ARB emerged as the prime rival to Nielsen's local TV audience measurement, especially after 1955 when it took over the local Hooper TV rating business. By 1961, ARB was measuring virtually every TV market twice a year and larger markets more often.

Local radio reports using the diary method were begun by Arbitron in 1965, nearly a quarter of a century after Garnet Garrison had recommended the method for the audio medium. Arbitron quit the TV measurement business in 1993 and now confines itself to radio.

The diary used by Arbitron today is not much different from the one used more than 50 years ago for television stations. Arbitron now measures more than 100 radio markets continuously and provides monthly ratings for about 150 areas for eight or more weeks each year. Diaries are still placed by phone call, then sent and retrieved by mail. A diary is sent to each member in the household who is 12 or older. The diary format asks the respondent to indicate each time she starts and stops listening to the radio, the call letters or station name, and suggests that if she is not sure of the call letters or station name, she should write in program name or dial setting. Respondents must also indicate whether the station is AM or FM and whether they are listening at home, in a car, or some other place. At the back of the diary are questions about age and gender for audience composition tabulations and other questions, typically on product usage.

Whereas most diaries are still placed by telephone calls, special care is taken to place diaries personally in Spanish-speaking homes and residences in high-density ethnic areas. After careful editing of the diaries' listening reports, audience estimates are published for each market in a "ratings book" and are available online to subscribers for other detailed analysis. In transferring diary entries into computer data, the operators have a number of aids and checks in the computer program that allow them to check the accuracy of call letters in each market and other information. Some radio programmers like to go to Arbitron offices near Washington, D.C., to study the diaries. Images of all entries are available and can be sorted to observe them in many different categories. By examining actual diaries, programmers or a consultant hired by a station can determine whether people remember call letters or station slogans correctly. Often diary-keepers write other comments that might be helpful. More detailed statistical analysis is possible by consulting the ratings book online, which allows subscribers to tabulate persons in the sample by any or all demographic categories. Such manipulations of data allow computation showing favorite station, sharing listeners with other stations, audience in zip code areas, the time spent listening to one station, and other categories, to name just a few.

Advantages

As envisioned by Garnet Garrison, diaries offer some significant advantages that account for their popularity. They offer a relatively inexpensive method for gathering a lot of information over the weekly period. But there are problems associated with the method. Responses—the rate is reported in each rating book—are often from only half of the sample. Younger males, for example, have a low return rate. As the listeners who are more likely to keep a diary and provide accurate information are also likely to listen to some formats more than others, there is continuing controversy about rating results. Recently the growing use of telephone answering machines, cellphones used out of the home, and other factors make it harder to obtain diary-keepers. Nonetheless, millions of diaries recording radio listening and TV watching are processed each year, and the broadcasting industry, advertisers, and advertising agencies depend on (and pay a high price for) the information obtained from a very simple little book that has been around for quite a long time.

Revival

Late in 2008 came word that A.C. Nielsen was reentering the measurement of radio audiences—and using diaries to do so. The corporate move resulted from Arbitron's difficulties with the introduction of its Portable People Meter device and growing displeasure among major radio owners with having to rely on that one company for ratings results that often differed sharply with earlier diary methods. Nielsen's diaries were used in several dozen smaller markets starting in early 2009. It seemed probably that, if successful, the effort might expand to more and larger markets.

See also: A.C. Nielsen Company; Arbitron; Audience; Audience Research Methods; DXers/DXing; Hooperatings; Portable People Meter

Further Reading

Beville, Hugh Malcom, Jr., *Audience Ratings: Radio, Television, and Cable*, Hillsdale, New Jersey: Erlbaum, 1985; 2nd edition, 1988.

Chappell, Matthew Napoleon, and Claude Ernest Hooper, *Radio Audience Measurement*, New York: Daye, 1944.

Lumley, Frederick Hillis, *Measurement in Radio*, Columbus: Ohio State University Press, 1934.

Webster, James G., and Lawrence W. Lichty, *Ratings Analysis: Theory and Practice*, Hillsdale, New Jersey: Erlbaum, 1991; 2nd edition, as *Ratings Analysis: The Theory and Practice of Audience Research*, by Webster, Lichty, and Patricia F. Phalen, Mahwah, New Jersey, and London: Erlbaum, 2000.

LAWRENCE W. LICHTY,
2009 REVISIONS BY CHRISTOPHER H. STERLING

DIGITAL AUDIO BROADCASTING
Replacing Analog Radio Stations

Several different digital radio standards or systems are being operated in different parts of the world. The system that has been in development the longest and that is in full-time operation in the most countries is called EUREKA 147. In the United States, which only selected a national digital standard in 2002, the phrase "high-definition radio" was coming into use by 2003 to suggest a parallel with developments in digital television. This entry surveys digital audio broadcasting (DAB) developments in Britain, Scandinavia, and the United States, with reference to other regions of the world as well.

DAB Basics

Digital audio broadcasting may be seen as the third stage in the use of the electromagnetic spectrum to transmit radio broadcasting services after analog AM and FM, both of which are prone to interference. In AM's case this is caused by static and other unwanted signals, by sky waves reflected from the ionosphere, and by other stations on the same or nearby frequencies. FM's main problems stem from unwanted reflections from high-rise buildings and other objects that cause what engineers term multipath distortion.

There are probably about 2.5 billion receivers with AM or medium wave reception capability in the world. Despite the expansion of FM, AM remains the most widely available means of reception. Both national and international radio broadcasters continue to rely on AM for much of their transmission requirements. The capacity of AM's medium waves to reach beyond horizons and thus much further than FM transmitters makes it essential and irreplaceable. For many countries, DAB is too expensive because a complex and extensive transmitter network is required.

DAB represents a major break with this analog technology. Like all digital systems, it converts the original material into streams of "zeroes" and "ones," which are then reconverted to recreate the original information. DAB, and specifically the EUREKA 147 system, differs from earlier digital systems in being capable of transmitting over a number of different "platforms," including both terrestrial (land) and satellite (delivering services either separately or jointly) and over a large section of the electromagnetic spectrum: from 30 MHz to 3 GHz for mobile reception, and higher for fixed reception.

DAB can be accomplished in any of three ways: (1) in-band, on-channel (IBOC) or in-band, adjacent channel (IBAC) using existing AM and FM terrestrial frequencies (actually blank spaces between frequencies); (2) terrestrially over another broadcast band (S-band in the United States and L-band elsewhere); and (3) by satellite digital audio radio services (SDARS), which bypasses terrestrial broadcasters by sending signals directly to consumers. (*See separate entry*, Digital Satellite Radio.)

The main advantages of DAB, compared with analog radio broadcasting, are many. First, DAB produces a much closer (technically accurate) replication of the original sound reproduced by the receiver, together with easier/automatic tuning than analog techniques.

Second, DAB is more efficient in its use of the radio spectrum and has a lower power requirement. Using the "multiplex" system, a number of radio transmitters carrying multiple signals can "overlap" on the same frequency—if broadcasting the same material. A "single frequency network" means that only one frequency needs to be used to cover a wide area—including a whole country. This compares well with the amount of spectrum needed for analog services. The overall digital signal is produced by 1,536 "carrier frequencies" that are distributed over a 1.5-MHz band. The majority of these carriers are noise-free, and this, coupled with error-correction techniques, means there is no interference to any of the services.

Third, there is at least the potential for many more services in the same spectrum, compared with analog transmissions. This is because the total digital "bit rate" available on the single frequency—12 megabits—can be "sliced" in an almost limitless number of configurations, so more services can be "squeezed" into the same part of the spectrum. However, there is a widely accepted minimum bit rate per second (bp/s) thought to be necessary to provide acceptable quality of either mono or stereo transmissions, and a lower rate to be used for text, graphics, and pictures without causing distortion or interference.

Finally, material other than sound can also be transmitted with the "radio" signal, because many other types of media can also be converted and then reconverted in roughly the same way. Thus digital methods can transform sound broadcasting into a multimedia system.

The main *disadvantages* of digital radio broadcasting are the following: first, a variety of different systems are being developed (unlike AM or FM, there is as yet no agreement on a worldwide standard); second, one transmitter serving a number of different radio services on one multiplex means that less well established, independent organizations are likely to be excluded; finally, listeners will have to buy new radio receivers that are at least initially significantly more expensive than those for analog systems. Indeed, the total consumer expense for this technology will be vastly larger than what stations have to pay out.

DAB in the United States: IBOC

On 1 August 1990, the Federal Communications Commission (FCC) initiated a *Notice of Inquiry* into DAB development and implementation. The FCC and broadcasting business became interested in DAB after learning that Europe was developing its EUREKA 147 system. By 1991 the American radio industry responded with USA Digital Radio (USADR), a partnership of CBS, Westinghouse Electric Corporation, and Gannett to develop an in-band, on-channel (IBOC) system of DAB to eventually replace AM and FM. USADR preferred IBOC over other methods because it allowed

stations to continue existing analog AM and FM service as they developed new digital signals that eliminate multipath and noise and reduce interference.

IBOC DAB has been called the "Holy Grail solution" because broadcasters can convert from analog to digital without service disruption and with low start-up costs, while maintaining their heavily promoted dial positions. Initially the National Association of Broadcasters (NAB) supported DAB implementation using the EUREKA 147 system on L-band (500–1500 MHz), which it believed would give AM and FM equal footing. Incensed broadcasters caused NAB to change their position and support IBOC.

On 26 August 1992, USADR successfully delivered IBOC DAB on the expanded AM band at 1660 kHz in Cincinnati. At the September NAB radio show in New Orleans, USADR demonstrated its system using WNOE-AM and NPR affiliate WWNO-FM. In 1993 NAB's DAB task force officially endorsed IBOC because it believed the FCC would never allocate alternative additional spectrum for DAB. The Electronic Industries Association (EIA), which had held that no system should be selected until all types were tested, struck a compromise with the NAB, agreeing that other systems would not be considered unless IBOC systems were shown not to meet terrestrial DAB requirements.

Although much of the world appears convinced L-band is the best DAB spectrum, the FCC supported use of the S-band (2310–2360 MHz), in part because of the difficulty in shifting existing L-band spectrum users in the United States. Most non-FCC experts agreed S-band will be more expensive and less effective than L-band. As a result of the S-band decision, U.S. DAB will be IBOC, causing global incompatibility. At NAB's 1993 Las Vegas convention, USADR introduced broadcasters to its IBOC system, demonstrating that its IBOC system was more fully developed than any system other than EUREKA 147.

USADR and Lucent Digital Radio (LDR) agreed to work together on IBOC in May 1997, making broadcasters more optimistic about DAB's future. USADR and LDR worked jointly for about 10 months but ended their alliance early in 1998. Digital Radio Express (DRE), another IBOC developer, allied with USADR in late 1999. In October 1998 USADR petitioned the FCC to open a rulemaking proceeding to make its system the DAB standard. In 1999 a number of the larger U.S. radio groups invested in USADR. USADR's new corporate status was important because it demonstrated that much of the radio business believed in

IBOC. Other broadcasters and electronics manufacturers, including receiver makers, soon fell into
line. At NAB's 1999 meeting in Las Vegas, some
broadcasters and manufacturers called for a
"Grand Alliance" like the one struck with digital
television (DTV). Robert Struble, USADR president, accurately stated that as a coalition from the
beginning, USADR already was the Grand Alliance.

The FCC issued a DAB *Notice of Proposed
Rulemaking* on 1 November 1999, more than nine
years after its first *Notice of Inquiry*. The commission
believed it was time:

> to determine whether an IBOC model and/or a model
> utilizing new radio spectrum would be the best means
> of promptly introducing DAB service in the United
> States. By initiating this proceeding now, we can foster
> the further development of IBOC systems, as well as
> new-spectrum DAB alternatives, help DAB system pro-
> ponents identify design issues of public interest dimen-
> sion and, where possible, encourage modifications that
> advance these policy objectives.

In October 2002, the FCC provisionally approved
the technical standard offered by iBiquity digital,
the company controlled by the 15 largest radio
broadcasters. The system allows AM and FM
broadcasters to begin transmitting digital signals,
while continuing to offer their analog service. Initial
broadcast equipment began to reach the market in
late 2002, and the first consumer receivers became
available early in 2003.

Fears remained, however, that using more of a
station's frequency assignment (as the digitized signal
does) might threaten some sub-carrier services such as
reading for the blind, carried by many noncommercial
stations. The FCC order allowed temporary
authority for digital operation until such problems
could be resolved. FM stations may offer digital
signals at all hours, but AM stations are at least
temporarily limited to daytime hours only because
of their more complex evening signal propagation.

Rolling Out HD Radio

By 2008–9, DAB service, now increasingly marketed under the rubric "HD Radio" (a term trademarked by iBiquity, the company formed in 2000
by Lucent Digital Radio and USA Digital Radio,
and holding the key patents) was beginning to take
hold, though still very slowly. Some said HD stood
for "hybrid digital" but the letters seemed to tag
along with the far better-known conversion to
digital television going on at the same time.

The digital radio service faced several problems.
One was that radio leaders were inadvertently

repeating the mistake they made with FM in the
1940s and 1950s by trying to sell the technology
rather than the programming the technology made
available. Another drawback (again paralleling
early FM) was the high cost of receivers—often
several hundred dollars. Car radios were as costly,
and didn't begin to appear until 2006. Yet even
after such an expensive purchase, listeners rarely
found new or different programming. And a third
problem was that people had digital audio options
in the form of subscribing to satellite radio, tuning
in online to digital audio streams, or using their
MP3 players. Finally, most Americans had little
awareness of the service as there was no looming
deadline to end analog AM or FM service and
replace it with digital transmission, as occurred
with television in early 2009.

WDMK-FM Detroit became the first radio station in the U.S. to commercially broadcast with
HD Radio technology on 7 January 2004. By the
end of the year, some 200 stations were doing so.
Major broadcasters swung behind a marketing
campaign for HD radio, seeing the technology as
one way to revive radio's sagging fortunes. By early
2005, the number of HD Radio stations was up to
600. And by the fall of 2008, with receiver costs
having dropped to about $100 and the first por-
tables on the market, some 1,800 stations were
providing HD Radio service, still but a tiny fraction
of the nation's more than 13,000 radio outlets.

Nearly all of the "HD" stations simulcast analog
AM or FM station signals as their primary signal,
though some transmitted old (or different) formats
on one of the digital channels the technology made
available. Some broadcasters argued in chicken-
and-egg fashion that when there were more HD
listeners, they would provide more separate programming—another mistaken throwback to the
early years of FM.

See also: AM Radio; Audio Streaming; Digital Recording; Digital Satellite Radio; FM Radio; Internet Radio;
Virtual Radio

Further Reading

Feder, Barnaby J., "F.C.C. Approves a Digital Radio Tech-
nology," *New York Times* (11 October 2002).
Federal Communications Commission, *Amendment of the
Commission's Rules with Regard to the Establishment and
Regulations of New Digital Audio Radio Services*, Docket
MM 90–357, FCC Rcd 5237 (1990).
Federal Communications Commission, *Digital Audio
Broadcasting Systems and Their Impact on the Terrestrial
Radio Broadcast Service Notice of Proposed Rule Making*,
Docket MM 99–325 (1999); available online at www.fcc.
gov/Bureaus/Mass_Media/Notices/1999/fcc99327.txt

"Heavenly Music: Digital Radio Finally Arrives," *The Economist* (16 March 2002).

HD Radio website, www.hdradio.com/

Henry, Shannon, "Clearing a Path for Digital Radio," *Washington Post* (9 October 2002).

Hoeg, Wolfgang, and Thomas Lauterbach, editors, *Digital Audio Broadcasting: Principles and Applications*, New York: Wiley, 2002.

Huff, W.A. Kelly, *Regulating the Future: Broadcasting Technology and Governmental Control*, Westport, Connecticut: Greenwood Press, 2001.

Lax, Stephen, *Beyond the Horizon: Communications Technologies: Past, Present, and Future*, Luton: University of Luton Press, 1997.

Mirabito, Michael M., and Barbara L. Morgenstern, *The New Communications Technologies*, Boston: Focal Press, 1990; 4th edition, 2000.

Radio Advertising Bureau, Radio listening via new technologies, www.rab.co.uk/news/html/NewTechnologiesQ4O2.htm

"USA Digital Radio and Digital Radio Mondiale To Collaborate On a Worldwide Standard for Digital Radio," *Car Sound & Performance* (22 May 2001).

W.A. KELLY HUFF,
2009 REVISIONS BY CHRISTOPHER H. STERLING

DIGITAL RECORDING

Radio's transition from an analog to a digital medium began with the arrival of the compact disc (CD) in the early 1980s. Since then, radio has embraced digital audio technologies ranging from the first CD players, digital tape recorders, digital effects processors, and digital audio workstations to the more recent introduction of hard disk recorders, digital exciters for transmitters, digital audio consoles, and digital audio file transfer and streaming on the internet.

Digital audio provides superior reproduction of sound and additional benefits useful in a radio station's operation. Except for a station's microphones (which may become the sole analog source at a radio station), it is possible for a radio station's audio chain to be completely digital, from production and storage to playback and processing, before being sent to a digital exciter and on to the transmitter. In the many countries where digital audio broadcasting standards are now in place, transmitters and receivers are now also digital, completing the final links to make radio a totally digital medium. Many radio stations also distribute digital transmissions of their programming on the internet, making a digital version of radio's signal available to listeners with a computer, audio card, and internet connection.

Digital audio has dramatically improved the quality of radio's on-air sound and has also brought many operational enhancements to the production process used to create radio programs. The clear benefits of digital audio have motivated nearly universal adoption among radio stations of some type of digital audio recording and playback equipment. A list of digital audio equipment found in radio stations today includes CD players, CD recorders, open-reel stationary-head digital recorders, rotating-head digital audio tape recorders, mini disc recorders, and hard-disk recording systems. Computers with specialized software and audio cards with inputs and outputs to interface with the other audio equipment in the station provide digital audio replacements for tape recorders, the splicing block, and other production and processing equipment. Digital versions of other equipment, such as audio consoles, telephone hybrids, effects processors, compressors, limiters, microphone processors, studio-transmitter links, on-air audio processing equipment, exciters, and transmitters, are rapidly becoming the standards as aging analog audio equipment is replaced.

Digital Audio Basics

A sound itself is not digital. Sound is created when an object vibrates and causes the molecules of the medium surrounding it (usually air) to vibrate. These vibrations or sound waves are transferred through the air until they reach someone's ear or a microphone. At the microphone, sound is transduced (converted) into electrical energy and becomes analog audio. The characteristics of this electrical energy are analogous to the original sound energy. This electrical energy can be amplified, manipulated, stored, or transmitted as analog audio; however, it can also be digitized and then amplified, manipulated, stored, or transmitted as digital audio.

Digital audio is created by converting analog audio into a stream of binary code, a series of ones and zeroes, representing the measurements of the characteristics of the original sound. This binary code represents measurements made of samples of the original audio representing the sound energy. The binary code can be recorded and stored on any device capable of reading and storing digital data. Magnetic tape, computer floppy disks, hard disks, and optical disks can store the digital information. These data can also be transmitted as pulses through copper wire, fiber-optic cable, or as radio frequency energy through the air. An exact, full-fidelity reproduction of the original audio can be created from the stored or transmitted digital code, copied without generation loss, and easily processed for creative and technical purposes. Unlike analog audio, the digital signal is not as subject to the limitations imposed by the storage medium or the electronics of the equipment. In the analog world, the tape itself adds noise, copying adds more noise, the amplifier adds noise, and so on. The dynamic range and frequency response of the original sound are also reduced as analog audio, because the analog system has inherent limitations in reproducing sound faithful to the original. The methods used to record and process digital audio minimize these limitations.

The digitization of analog audio involves four stages: filtering, sampling, quantizing, and coding. First, the audio is sent through a low-pass filter to prevent unwanted higher frequencies from becoming audible. This process is called anti-aliasing. Then the analog signal is divided, which determines the sampling rate. The more often the signal is sampled and measured, the more accurate the recreation of sound will be. Sampling rates are typically 32 kHz, 44.1 kHz, or 48 kHz. This means the signal is sampled either 32,000, 44,100, or 48,000 times every second. A measurement is made during every sampling period using a multidigit binary number. This binary number is called a word. The number of bits in a word is word length. A 1-bit measurement, for example, would only be able to discriminate between presence and absence of voltage. If n is the number of bits in the word length, the number of levels of measurement is 2n. An 8-bit system provides 256 levels of voltage measurement. A 16-bit system has 65,536 possible levels, and a 20-bit system provides 1,048,576 levels. Systems with more quantizing levels have more accuracy and wider signal-to-noise ratios. The last stage of the digitizing process is the coding stage, in which the bits are placed in a precise order for recording or output to another digital device. During this coding stage, each word is identified in the bit stream. Error correction minimizes the impact of storage defects. The binary code is then distributed or recorded as pulses of magnetic energy.

Moving audio to the digital domain for recording and reproduction purposes provides a number of advantages. Compared to analog audio, digital audio has an improved frequency response, wider dynamic range, immeasurable noise and distortion, and no degradation or generation loss in multiple digital recordings. Some audiophiles have been critical of the digital audio recording process, suggesting that when sound is digitized, it loses its warmth and can sound too sterile and even harsh. Radio has generally rejected those concerns and has continued to replace analog audio equipment with digital equivalents.

The Compact Disc

In 1980 the Philips and Sony corporations joined forces to create an optical disc for digital audio. The two companies agreed on a CD standard, a 12-cm optical disc using 16-bit/44.1-kHz sampling. The CD player and disc were introduced in Europe in the fall of 1982, and in the United States in the spring of 1983. As record and production library companies began to release their catalogs on CD, radio began using CD players in their production and air studios. Manufacturers developed CD players with features such as a shuttle control, as well as a model that played CDs inserted in a special protective case, creating a process similar to the use of a broadcast cartridge machine. The CD changer, capable of handling multiple CDs, was also found useful at many radio stations. Many broadcasters used consumer models because the audio quality was the same for both. Not only did the CDs sound better than the vinyl long-playing and 45-rpm records, but the CD format was also much more efficient to use. CDs could be cued and started faster and, with care to protect the disc from scratches, would allow endless replays without degradation of sound quality. Additional data encoded in the compact disc provided precise track timings, indexing, and continuous monitoring of playing time of tracks and programs.

The CD player uses a laser to read the data encoded in the microscopic circular pits on the disc. The binary code is stored in a series of pits and lands in the disc. A pit is an indentation in the groove; a land is a flat area with no indentation. A photoelectric cell reads the amount of light reflected from the pits and lands and emits voltage to recreate the digital code representing the audio waves. As needed, the digital output of the CD can be converted back to analog audio or sent as digital output to a digital recorder or console. The only problem with the CD was that its content was limited to prepackaged material offered by the manufacturer. However, the recordable CD was soon on the way.

The recordable CD (CD-R) was launched in 1988 but initially was not widely adopted as a production tool by radio. The first CD recorders were relatively expensive, and the disc recording was permanent: the disc could not be erased and recorded on again. Recently, with the introduction of the rewritable CD (CD-RW), lower-cost CD-R recorders, and CD-R drives installed in computers, the recordable CD has attracted more attention from broadcasters, for use as an archival and production tool and as a component in digital automation systems.

The digital versatile disc (DVD) is not yet a factor in the radio environment, but it most likely will be. The DVD is the same diameter and thickness as a CD, but a difference in design and manufacturing provides eight times the capacity of a CD by creating a dual layer. There are currently five recordable DVD formats. DVD-R and DVD+R discs can be recorded only once. DVD-RW and DVD+RW can be rewritten. The DVD-RAM is used for recording computer data only.

Digital Audio Tape and Mini Disc Recording

Although the CD was quickly adopted by most radio stations shortly after its introduction, digital audio recording had a more difficult time gaining a foothold in radio. Commercial digital audio recorders have been available since the 1970s and early 1980s. Sony and Denon introduced adapters that made it possible to record digital audio on videotape recorders. Open-reel two-track and multitrack digital recorders (Digital Audio Stationary Head) were employed in recording studios but were not widely used in radio. By the early 1990s, however, the rotary-head digital audio tape recorder (R-DAT) was finding a place in radio production.

R-DAT machines use essentially the same digitizing scheme as the CD, but they use a rotating helical-scan tape head to record and read the large quantity of information representing the audio signal on the small cassette tape. The result is audio recordings with characteristics similar to the CD with the additional flexibility of being able to record and rerecord. R-DAT recorders were adopted as a cost-effective, high-quality production and on-air playback tool, especially in automation systems. The use of R-DAT has been supplanted somewhat in recent years by other digital formats, including the mini disc.

Although originally intended as a consumer product, the mini disc recorder is finding a niche in broadcasting. The mini disc offers a more portable, less expensive alternative to hard disk recording, and the portable mini disc units provide a digital alternative for field recording. The mini disc offers nonlinear access, track identification, and a recording time of 74 minutes. It has low noise, low distortion, and a wide dynamic range, but its use of data compression limits its use in critical recording.

Computer-Based Recording, Editing, and Digital Distribution

Open-reel analog recordings have at least one advantage over open-reel digital tapes: analog recordings are easier to edit than a digital tape. Because a digital tape has to be running at speed in order to decode the data to recreate the digital audio, digital open-reel recorders record and play on an analog head for editing and cueing purposes. The digital tape can then be marked, cut, and spliced like an analog tape. Physical editing is not possible with the DAT cassette tape, and electronic editing on a DAT recorder requires some finesse. Moving the recorded digital information to a computer hard disk opened the way for the rapid deployment of computer-based digital audio recording and editing systems, which have revolutionized audio production for radio.

By the early 1990s, audio could be recorded to media other than tape. Increased hard disk capacity, faster computer processing speeds, and new compression methods combined to make recording directly to a computer's hard disk a viable alternative to recording on analog tape. Software programs and audio input/output cards were developed to be used on inexpensive personal computers to create digital audio recordings that sounded better than the recordings created on professional analog equipment. Even consumer products could create professional-sounding results in radio production studios. Editing software was introduced that would allow nondestructive editing of the audio material. These programs typically provide a visual representation of the audio waveform, which can be marked, highlighted, cut, copied, pasted, and moved within and between sound files. Precise, noise-free edits are performed that can be readjusted and fine-tuned as needed without destruction of the original sound file.

There are numerous multitrack recording and editing programs used by radio stations, which, when combined with compatible high-quality computer audio cards, allow desktop computers to perform the same functions as multichannel recorders, production consoles, and effects processors—which cost thousands of dollars more—all in one computer.

Once the digital audio exists as a file in a networked computer, local area networks, wide area networks, and the internet allow these sound files to be distributed and shared internally or externally. An increasingly common distribution approach is the use of MP-3 files. The MPEG-1 layer 3 recording technology (commonly known as MP-3) is a digital audio file compression method increasingly used by radio stations to send and receive programs and programming elements through the internet. This form of distribution becomes cost-effective and important as advertising agencies and production companies start to distribute commercials, programming, and other information digitally. As radio groups consolidate and combine station operations and look for economies of scale, digital distribution of content will become even more important. After a commercial is created in the production studio of one of the stations in the group, it can be distributed instantly to all the other stations on the computer network.

Digital Audio Processing

After audio has been converted to digital form, it can be manipulated or processed for creative and technical reasons. Modern radio production studios often have at least one digital effects processor, which efficiently creates various combinations of digital effects, such as echo, reverb, pitch changing, phasing, flanging, and many others. Computer software-based recording and editing programs also have digital audio processing and effects as part of the package. Digital audio processing is also used in the station's air chain, running microphones through processors that convert the signal to digital before processing to strengthen and improve the sound quality of the announcer's voice. Digital processing of the audio signal before it is sent to the transmitter provides one last measure of limiting, compression, and other subtle adjustments to give the station's audio a distinctive, full sound.

Radio and the Portable Revolution

By the end of the first decade of the 21st century, several newer media were increasing demand for ready access to easy and inexpensive digital recording. Radio stations were slowly rolling out HD radio service, slowly creating a likely demand for digital means to record such broadcasts. But most digital audio recording equipment continued to be expensive, thus limiting adoption. At the same time, a variety of portable digital devices (chiefly the iPod, but also other MP3 players) were providing another means for widespread public use of digital recording while on the go. These services posed a competitive threat to radio broadcasters as users could download their own music from recordings or online services without resorting to a broadcast station.

See also: Audio Processing; Audio Streaming; Digital Audio Broadcasting; Portable Digital Listening Devices; Recording and Studio Equipment

Further Reading

Alten, Stanley R., *Audio in Media*, Belmont, California: Wadsworth, 1981; 6th edition, 2002.

Daniel, Eric D., C. Denis Mee, and Mark H. Clark, editors, *Magnetic Recording: The First 100 Years*, New York: IEEE Press, 1999.

Gross, Lynne S., and David E. Reese, *Radio Production Worktext: Studio and Equipment*, London and Boston: Focal Press, 1990; 3rd edition, Oxford and Boston: Focal Press, 1998.

Huber, David Miles, and Robert E. Runstein, *Modern Recording Techniques*, 5th edition, Boston: Focal Press, 2001.

Kefauver, Alan P., *Fundamentals of Digital Audio*, Madison, Wisconsin: A-R Editions, 1998.

O'Donnell, Lewis B., Philip Benoit, and Carl Hausman, *Modern Radio Production*, Belmont, California: Wadsworth, 1986; 5th edition, as *Modern Radio Production: Production, Programming, and Performance*, 2000.

Pohlmann, Ken C., *Principles of Digital Audio*, 4th edition, New York: McGraw-Hill, 2000.

Talbot-Smith, Michael, *Broadcast Sound Technology*, London and Boston: Butterworths, 1990; 2nd edition, Oxford and Boston: Focal Press, 1995.

Talbot-Smith, Michael, editor, *Audio Engineer's Reference Book*, Oxford and Boston: Focal Press, 1994; 2nd edition, 1999.

Watkinson, John, *An Introduction to Digital Audio*, Oxford and Boston: Focal Press, 1994.

Watkinson, John, *The Art of Sound Reproduction*, Oxford and Woburn, Massachusetts: Focal Press, 1998; 2nd edition, 2002.

JEFFREY D. HARMAN,
2009 REVISIONS BY CHRISTOPHER H. STERLING

DIGITAL SATELLITE RADIO

For more than 100 years, radio has been transmitted by electronic analog waves modulated by voice or frequency variance. At the beginning of the 21st century, digital signals beamed from communications satellites could change American radio from a medium with thousands of local stations into a national radio service with only a few content providers. In the new system, a listener could drive from coast to coast and remain tuned to the same CD-quality signal all the way. In the United States, two corporations and hundreds of investors are betting billions of dollars that Americans will embrace the new digital system of satellite radio.

Sirius Corporation v. XM Corporation

Two corporations are at the front of the race to bring satellite radio to the American consumer: Sirius, headquartered at the Rockefeller Center in New York City, and XM, which has its offices on New York Avenue in Washington, D.C. Both companies take a similar approach to satellite broadcasting. Each is beaming a digital signal from a satellite to antennas the size of a playing card. The antennas, mounted in the consumers' cars or homes by suction cups, feed the signal into digital radio receivers that produce CD-quality audio with at least 100 different format selections. As of early 2003, XM offered 70 music channels and 31 talk channels, whereas Sirius advertised 60 music channels and 40 talk channels. Both companies have signed well-known stars to provide special programming for subscribers. Both companies—and here is the big gamble—are charging for their audio services: initially $9.95 (XM) and $13.95 (Sirius, which offers more channels without advertising).

Investors at XM and Sirius are gambling that enough listeners are dissatisfied with the current fare on AM and FM radio stations that they will be willing to pay a small monthly fee to receive programming unavailable on analog terrestrial stations. Executives at both corporations note that almost 30 percent of all recordings sold at music stores come from artists receiving little or no radio airplay. The reasoning goes like this: There may not be enough fans for alternative country acts such as Lyle Lovett or Steve Earle or for new-age performers such as Yanni to support a local radio station format. There are, however, enough of them scattered across the country to make a nationwide satellite feed economically feasible.

Given the sheer cost of both projects, niche programming alone will not offer the kind of return on investment stockholders of either company are looking for. Thus, the need for big-name performers. XM gave a channel to Grammy-winning producer and composer Quincy Jones. Former Yes member Jon Anderson is using the same approach, whereas Ted Nugent gets his own talk show.

Lee Abrams, creator of the album-oriented rock (AOR) sound of the 1970s, provides the consulting for all 50 music formats for XM. Abrams claims that XM will not emulate traditional radio. He understands subscribers are paying for the audio services and expect something different for their money. Abrams delivers expanded selections of classic rock artists such as Bob Dylan, The Beatles, or Led Zeppelin to counter complaints from traditional radio listeners that playlists have become repetitive. Abrams also delivers channels for contemporary alternative rockers as well as multiple jazz, country, and blues formats.

Sirius has given a channel to rock superstar Sting, who produces a daily live show with original and recorded music. With the main studios in New York City, Sirius plans to offer a number of live, in-studio concerts from artists who pass through the city while on tour. National Public Radio (NPR) provides two channels of talk and information, including an original morning program for satellite

listeners only. Programmers point out that Sirius, with multiple rock, jazz, country, blues, and talk formats, plans no commercial advertising at this time, whereas some of XM's channels have up to six minutes of commercials per hour.

Sirius Corporation used to be known as CD Satellite Radio Service. Focus groups and marketing studies found consumers were confusing the name with the audio CDs available in music stores. Furthermore, company executives felt the name CD no longer implied cutting edge technology. So, a name change to Sirius was ordered early in 2000.

Making Satellite Technology Pay Off

Several companies have launched commercial communication satellites. XM hired Sea Launch to place its two Hughes Corporation satellites (named *Rock* and *Roll*) into orbit from an ocean platform located 4,600 miles west of South America. Sirius hired Space System/Loral to build and launch three satellites into orbit from the former Soviet republic of Kazakhstan. The enormous cost of the high orbit satellites for both corporations may be partially offset by leasing unused space on the various transponders to other companies with communications needs.

In order to maintain a constant signal, or footprint, over a specific region of the planet, satellites must remain in roughly the same position relative to the earth. Sirius and XM are using two different systems to meet that goal. XM uses two geostationary satellites positioned at 22,300 miles above the Earth. At that height, the speed of the satellite's orbit matches the speed of the rotation of the earth. Therefore, the satellites appear to be stationary in the sky.

Sirius uses three satellites in an inclined elliptical constellation. Elliptical orbit means the satellites are in a lower orbit moving across the sky. Each satellite spends at least 16 hours a day over the United States and at least one satellite is placing a footprint over the continental U.S. at all times. Both companies have a spare satellite on the ground in case of a catastrophic failure.

What kind of return will the two American corporations need to stay afloat? Wall Street analysts predict that each company will have to attract a minimum of four million subscribers within five years to break even. Such numbers are possible, as has been proven by successful satellite radio ventures in other countries.

Satellite Radio Worldwide

A privately owned American corporation with immense international ties, WorldSpace, is the current leader in digital satellite technology. World-Space claims a potential audience of 4.6 billion people on five continents. Launched in October of 1998, the geostationary satellite Afri-Star offers three overlapping signals to the continent of Africa with 50 audio channels and multimedia programming available on each signal beam. Asia-Star was successfully placed into orbit with a similar programming array over the Asian continent in March of 2000.

A third satellite, Ameri-Star, will service South and Central America as well as Mexico. This satellite has no current plans to broadcast to the United States or Canada. However, World star has signed a cooperative agreement with XM to share technological innovations.

Delivering 24 digital radio signals, Orbit Satellite TV and Radio Network serves the Middle East, North Africa, and parts of Asia with "socially responsible" broadcasts in Arabic and other languages. Originally chartered with the Italian Ministry of Post and Telecommunications, Orbit signed with Telespazio to provide space segment services and launched programming in 1994 with 16 TV and four radio channels. Orbit now boasts business offices and uplink centers throughout the Mediterranean, Middle East, and the Indian Subcontinent.

Orbit first used transponder space on Intelsat satellites, the international telecommunications satellite consortium established by the United Nations. In 1999, Orbit expanded its coverage area by 22 million households when it began to also broadcast on Arabsat, a satellite placed into space by a cooperative of Middle Eastern nations. Orbit contracts with numerous international providers for programming content including CNN and ESPN Radio.

Several other satellites carry digital audio and analog radio programming. The Eutelsat array and the Astra satellites provide a radio footprint over Europe. Panamsat and Brasilsat provide programming for Central and South America. Other countries may well adapt to satellite radio faster than America does. Much of Europe and Asia are already used to the concept of a national radio service. Britain's BBC or Germany's Deutsche Welle have for years broadcast a national signal through the use of relay transmitters. A satellite service is simply a logical extension of that system.

Broadcast Opposition

As early as 1982, the Federal Communications Commission (FCC) began to develop regulations for direct broadcast satellites, or DBS. Signals would be provided to consumers via a 3-m dish antenna. Local broadcasters immediately attacked the proposed service with charges that a national TV service would undermine the localism provided by traditional television broadcasting.

In October 1992, the FCC again acted on an industry DBS proposal, this time for radio. The original proposal called for a Satellite Digital Audio Broadcasting System or DAB to be located within 50 MHz of the S-band (2310–2360 MHz) with the intent to create a system that would provide a national service.

Again, local broadcasters rolled out the same arguments used against the DBS system: "The current number of FM and AM stations serving the United States represents the highest level of audio diversity available in the world." In comments submitted to the FCC the association added, "A competing satellite service presents a potential danger to the United States' universal, free, local radio service and, thus, to the public interest it serves."

A consortium of radio group owners also weighed in with the following comments to the FCC: "National radio stations raise a troubling question of undue concentration of control of the media, an issue that has been consistently a concern to the commission." The joint comments added, "erosion of audiences and advertising revenues caused by satellite radio would inevitably destroy the ability of many [existing] stations to offer these services."

Broadcasters opposed only the national delivery of a digital satellite signal and not the use of digital technology. In fact, the National Association of Broadcasters (NAB) began proposing a system referred to as in-band, on-channel (IBOC). This system would replace terrestrial analog transmitters with digital transmitters for better signal quality and reception. Local broadcasters would then repeat satellite feeds of the various program services with inserts for local advertising and announcements.

However, satellite programmers counter that the broadcasters are overemphasizing the continued importance of localism. Listeners, they say, do not tune exclusively to one station. Although local news, weather, and information are important, research shows many listeners will tune to a station specifically for music or entertainment programming. Satellite programmers believe listeners will tune to their service for specific formats and return to local stations when they need local information. As one programmer stated, "Program directors who think localism is fundamental to successful radio should look at the success of *USA Today*."

The Box in the Car or Home

Ultimately, the success of satellite radio in the United States depends upon whether consumers will buy the new digital receiver necessary to pick up the satellite signal. Sirius and XM settled a patent lawsuit in March of 2000 by agreeing that all digital radios will eventually have the capacity to receive both audio feeds. Deals have now been made with Sony, Alpine, Pioneer, Clarion, and other audio manufacturers to produce the receivers. Major retailers have agreed to market and sell the receivers for $200.00 and up, depending on features and installation.

Some of the retailers, including consumer electronic shops, car sound shops, and automobile dealers, are offering installation for car receivers. Distributors are also marketing a portable device designed to translate a digital satellite signal for existing radios. In January of 2003, Delphi introduced the Sky Fi radio, advertised as the first plug and play portable digital satellite radio.

However, the real key to success is cooperation by major automobile manufacturers in offering digital radios as available equipment in new cars. XM has agreements with General Motors (GM) and Honda. Sirius has a deal with Ford and tentative agreements with Chrysler and five other automakers. The deal with Ford is particularly beneficial because the buyer gets a satellite radio and a two-year subscription to Sirius audio services.

The drawback, if the current marketing arrangement stays in place, is that owners of GM cars will have to take XM audio services, whereas Ford owners will receive Sirius. Will listeners continue to pay for audio services when the initial deals run out with the car companies? As one industry observer put it, "Twenty-five years ago, TV viewers would have thought it odd to pay for watching television." Today, a majority of American homes have cable television and pay a monthly fee for expanded video service.

The Impact on Local Radio

If satellite radio succeeds, there will be some impact on local radio stations.

First, three critical audience-rating categories could be affected: time spent listening, or TSL; average quarter hour listening, or AVQ; and cumulative audience numbers, or cume. If enough listeners tune out local stations to listen to satellite radio, the local stations will report reduced numbers in those categories and will have to lower the rates charged for advertising.

Second, the concept of localism in radio in recent years has really come to mean the ability to generate local ad revenue, rather than the desire to program for regional interests of the community of license. Radio stations are no longer compelled by the FCC to provide specific programming to meet the needs of the local community. Music playlists are almost identical by format in every market. A listener can drive across the country today and find virtually the same 30 or 40 songs being rotated in each format by stations across the dial. If the majority of stations are playing similar music and running many of the same syndicated programs, then the broadcasters' "localism" argument is greatly diminished.

Despite their more than 100 channels of specialized programming, both Sirius and XM radio added subscribers more slowly than expected. Toward the end of 2002, Sirius was reaching only about 30,000 paying customers, whereas XM (which had aired earlier) was reaching more than ten times as many. But each needed more than a million subscribers in order to survive, and in 2002, it appeared such levels would take at least a couple more years to achieve. One result of the slow growth was that their stock prices declined to record low levels, as many observers concluded there was room for only one such service, not two. Both continued to seek additional investors and claimed they were in the competition for the long haul. At the same time, both trimmed their expenses, closing down unused studios and cutting back staff. Talk of consolidation lingered in the air.

Nonetheless, the investors for both XM and Sirius believed that the public would eventually buy into the idea of satellite radio. They believed enough of the public had grown tired of traditional radio's repetitive playlists and commercial saturation to give satellite radio a try at $10.00 per month. Even radio giant Clear Channel Communications hedged its bet by becoming a major investor in XM. It was not clear that satellite radio would succeed as numerous challenges remained. However, executives at XM and Sirius were literally betting millions of dollars that the time was right for a new national radio service.

The two satellite carriers continued their hot competition for another six years. Sirius made an important break-through by hiring New York-based shock jock Howard Stern, who was given his own channel and five-year $500 million deal in 2005 and began his Sirius program in January 2006. Using Stern's appeal to younger listeners, Sirius heavily promoted his program and saw its subscriber totals being to grow. A few months later, the hard-charging former head of CBS, Mel Karmazin, was hired at Sirius CEO. By early 2007, the two carriers had substantially increased their subscriber numbers to more than 15 million.

In March 2007, Karmazin announced that the two companies would seek government permission to merge. There had been hints of this for some time, but any attempt had to overcome the specific FCC ban on such a merger issued as part of the original licenses for the companies to provide service. Karmazin began a blitz of publicity showing how the listener would benefit from the unique programs offered by both firms. Over the air broadcasters, led by the National Association of Broadcasters, ramped up their arguments against the proposed "merger to monopoly." Two government agencies were to share the final word on the proposal—the FCC, and the Justice Department's Antitrust Division. Sirius and XM provided reams of documentation to both and extended their merger deadline while awaiting the government's decision.

At the end of March 2008, the Justice Department signed off on the agreement, making no demands for change in what the companies were offering. The FCC took a good deal longer (more than a year) as chairman Kenneth Martin sought broad support for the merger. Finally, after considerable wrangling, assessment of a nearly $20 million fine for some earlier technical transgressions, the granting of a number of consumer protection benefits (such as no price boost in the basic subscription price for three years) —and despite grumbles from citizen action groups and some in Congress—the commission agreed to the merger on a 3–2 party-line vote in July 2008. Karmazin became head of the merged firm, which was renamed SiriusXM Inc. and headquartered in New York, though retaining some former XM production facilities in Washington.

The timing of the merger, however, could not have been worse. By mid-2008, the country's economy was in a shambles with huge government bailouts of failing financial institutions. Loans were all but impossible to get. Karmazin's merged company saw its stock slip below a dollar a share as car sales (always a key factor in building satellite radio audiences) fell off a cliff. Layoffs became more widespread, and some commentators on the radio business argued that the satellite business model made little sense in an era of portable digital listening and recording devices. A charge was instituted for tuning into the service online (it had been free to subscribers), as well as for multiple subscriptions (as to satellite receivers in different cars).

Indeed, bankruptcy seriously threatened the company by early 2009 when its stock dwindled in value to about a dime. Faced with a $175 million debt payment in February (and others falling due later in the year), negotiations with lenders and possible investors went down to the wire amidst the country's declining economy. Finally Liberty Media's John Malone agreed to advance money to Sirius XM (at an interest rate of 15 percent) with more to come (as much as a half billion dollars all told), in turn for two seats on the company board. CEO Mel Karmazin appeared to have saved his company while adding an aggressive media entrepreneur to his board.

See also: Clear Channel Communications Inc.; Digital Audio Broadcasting; Portable Digital Listening Devices; Virtual Radio

Further Reading

Aherns, Frank, "Radio's Race to Space," *Washington Post* (10 September 2001).
Edgerton, John, "FCC Approves XM-Sirius Merger," *Broadcasting & Cable* (25 July 2008).
Irwin, Neal, "XM Puts Satellite into Space," *Washington Post* (19 March 2001).
Malaysia HITZ Satellite Radio Network, www.astro.com. my/radio/hitz.htm
Markels, Alex, "100 Channels, But Where Are the Subscribers?" *New York Times* (3 November 2002).
RUsirius (The Internet Guide to Satellite Radio), www. rusirius.com
SiriusXM Radio, www.siriusxm.com
WorldSpace Satellite Radio, www.worldspace.com

CORLEY DENNISON,
2009 REVISIONS BY CHRISTOPHER H. STERLING

DOCUMENTARY PROGRAMS

Documentary programs did not play a large role in the history of American radio broadcasting. For three decades from the late 1920s, typically only one or two hours of documentary programs were presented on the national networks during the evening hours. In the 1930s and 1940s there were two to three hours of documentaries each week, during the daytime as well, most of them produced and/or presented in association with educational institutions and intended for students listening in schools. By the late 1940s there were also several hours of documentary and other factual dramas on at weekends, especially on Sunday afternoons (a time period that later would become the "intellectual ghetto" for television).

The documentary programs that were presented, although small in number, often were inventive in their use of voices, music, and sound effects: they created great prestige for the networks and helped stations satisfy requirements for public service programming. Some received much critical acclaim and are still remembered as the pinnacle of radio writing and production.

"Drama documentaries" broadcast during World War II were among the most exciting and accomplished examples of the art of radio and are still studied and enjoyed by students of radio history. Many American documentaries were produced at this time, dealing with U.S. history and patriotism. These programs told war stories about America's fighting men and about its allies—especially the British—or encouraged civilians to conserve resources and support the war effort (and reduce inflation), especially by buying savings bonds. The forms and techniques of such documentaries, combined with the traditions of the film documentary, were precursors to the television documentaries that began in the 1950s.

Origins

The earliest American radio dramas included documentary-type programs such as *Biblical Dramas* and *Great Moments in History*, both on NBC during the season of 1927–28. For several seasons following, at least one radio series presented historical stories or biographies in a dramatic form.

In 1931 the Columbia Broadcasting System (CBS) began *American School of the Air*, which was intended for students. Although this was more specifically an "educational program," it did have documentary elements—and an eavesdropping audience of adults listening at home. The landmark program ran for nearly two decades.

On 6 March 1931, *The March of Time* began airing on CBS and was carried by 20 of the approximately 80 CBS affiliates. Each program dramatized several important news stories. Initially sponsored by *Time* magazine, *The March of Time* had been developed by Fred Smith, who earlier had dramatized news at WLW-Cincinnati and for syndication. Although the news stories were "re-created"—actors portrayed the characters of important events—this was the first important documentary program on radio. Under various sponsors, *The March of Time* was broadcast for 13 seasons and was partly responsible for Time, Inc. developing a monthly newsreel. By the late 1930s, *The March of Time* on film had evolved from a collection of several short reports—the format of the typical newsreel at the time—to a documentary on a single topic. At the end of the 1930s the radio

program was off the air for two seasons, but it returned during World War II, and increasingly it made use of the actual persons featured in the news stories.

During the 1930s and World War II, the high cost of using telephone lines for the transmission of remote stories and the lack of portable, high-quality recording equipment that allowed for easy editing made studio re-creation of events easier and less expensive than coverage of the actual event.

In 1936, to create a better image for itself, the DuPont chemical company began sponsorship of *Cavalcade of America*. A broadcast of 2 September 1936 told "the story of rayon," which was said to "rank with the automobile and radio in its speed of development and in the way it has opened a wide new field of employment." The program dramatized events in American history, although it carefully avoided any mention of gunpowder or dynamite, which were also manufactured by the company. Commercials always spoke of the progress and benefits of chemistry. This program introduced many young listeners to American history; it continued for nearly two decades until the end of most network dramatic programs.

Also in 1936, CBS introduced *We The People*. This program dramatized stories of generally well-known people, using music and a narrator, and was said to be based on actual documents.

In the late 1930s some factual programs were produced with or by the U.S. Office of Education, the Smithsonian Institution, the Library of Congress, the Rockefeller Foundation, and a number of universities. Some, such as *The Ballad Hunter*, produced by John Lomax, about folklore and folk songs, used recordings made on location. Alan Lomax, John's son, also produced a 1941 program with the Library of Congress about people displaced by the Tennessee Valley Authority. Alan Lomax would eventually collect thousands of hours of sound and film recordings, and later develop television documentary series, about folklore.

William Lewis, as CBS vice president of programming, had been given carte blanche by the network for experimental dramas; he assembled the group that created Columbia Workshop. From 1936 until 1941, Columbia Workshop produced experimental dramas and labeled some of these programs "documentaries," especially when they dealt with social problems and issues. In February 1939, *Words Without Music* presented "They Fly Through the Air with the Greatest of Ease," written and directed by Norman Corwin: the program described airmen bombing homes and then strafing the people who fled them. Accompanied by narration, dialogue, and sound effects, the story of the pilots involved them completing their missions of destruction but then being themselves shot down. A pilot describes the sight as one of the bombs hits its target: "Gee, that's fascinating! What a spread! Looks just like a budding rose unfolding!" Although it was not noted during the radio program, the speaker was Vittorio Mussolini, a pilot and the son of Il Duce, the Italian dictator. But Corwin did make this clear in his introduction to the published version of the radio play: "One group of horsemen gave the impression of a budding rose unfolding, as the bombs fell in their midst and blew them up. It was exceptionally good fun."—Vittorio Mussolini. (The younger Mussolini had written his impressions of dropping bombs on Ethiopian cavalry and watching the horses and riders as they were blown to bits.)

The program excoriated "all aviators who have bombed civilian populations and machine-gunned refugees." Although the U.S. was still neutral, and public opinion was evenly divided on the coming war in Europe, CBS was brave not to censor this program or other similar dramas that were based on fact. "They Fly Through the Air with the Greatest of Ease" received an Ohio State Institute for Education by Radio award in May 1939, as the program "best demonstrating the cultural, artistic, and social uses of radio." It was a great boost for Corwin's career, and it was the first of his many dramatized documentaries about the events leading up to World War II and the war itself.

Lewis now told Corwin that he wanted a new series that would build pride among Americans and promote self-awareness of the American heritage. The result was the series *Pursuit of Happiness*, which CBS publicity described as "dedicated to the brighter side of the American scene," bringing us "reminders that today, with thankfulness and humility, we Americans still enjoy our constitutional rights to life, liberty, and the pursuit of happiness." Begun in October 1939, the program presented a spectrum of Americana. It was not an immediate success. But the third program, "Ballad for Americans," a musical written by Earl Robinson and John Latouche and sung by Paul Robeson, received much critical praise. By the time the series ended in May 1940—although there had been many arguments along the way—Corwin had successfully explored his idea of presenting "American sound patterns and phenomena." This series would set the pattern for Corwin's and many other CBS programs throughout the coming time of war.

World War II

On 15 December 1941, all four networks presented the Corwin production "We Hold These Truths," honoring the 150th anniversary of the Bill of Rights: it presented short dramatized stories illustrating the importance of, and conflicts inherent in, each of the rights. Although the program had been in preparation for several months, its broadcast just one week after the attack on Pearl Harbor gave it special emotional appeal. In 1942 Corwin produced a series called *An American in England*, which sought to show how our allies lived, worked, and fought. As previous documentaries had been, these programs were mostly studio-produced dramatizations, but this series distilled research on actual people.

During World War II, the major emphasis of the networks was on reporting the news of the war. Most of that reporting was by newscasters in studios, mainly in New York. There was, of course, much news from London, and some from Asia, transmitted via shortwave—especially at the time of very big stories such as the June 1944 D-Day invasion. The vast majority of such reporting was broadcast live. Recordings were used only sparingly because available equipment was heavy, fragile, unreliable, and required too much battery power for use over long periods.

During the seasons of 1942–43 to 1944–45, radio saw a threefold increase in the amount of documentary programming. Virtually all of the new programs were war related, often produced with the Office of War Information, and included salutes of each branch of the armed services. Because of a special wartime excess profits tax, many companies preferred to buy sponsorship of programs with money that would otherwise go for taxes, and some companies were willing to pay for documentary and information programs that in the past would have had to be self-sustaining. This additional funding meant that broadcasters could produce more elaborate and expensive documentaries.

At the end of the war in Europe, all networks again carried a Corwin-produced dramatized documentary called "On A Note of Triumph." The program was well received and was subsequently released as a phonograph album. On that same night of 8 May 1945, however, the real future of documentary was revealed—although there seems to be no evidence that this change was understood at the time. An NBC program, arranged primarily by Prof. Garnet Garrison of Wayne State University in Detroit, presented a history of the war through phonograph recordings of the most important speeches and events of the war. There was a narrator as well as musical bridges, and some speeches had to be re-created because recordings were not available. This was the first use (on such a scale and for such an important occasion) of a substantial compilation of the actual voices and sounds recorded over a period of years.

Postwar Developments

In June 1946, Norman Corwin left New York for a four-month trip around the world "in a search for common ties and yearnings for world unity." He returned with hundreds of hours of interviews recorded on magnetic wire and acetate discs. By this time plastic magnetic audio tape, to which all of the material was transferred, made editing much easier. The twelve programs produced from this material aired on CBS from 14 January to 1 April 1947 under the series title *One World Flight*.

Although the word "documentary" was now regularly used to describe programs (CBS had formed a documentary unit in 1946), studio re-creation was still the preferred means of presenting nonfiction material. Robert Lewis Shayon created *CBS Is There*, which began 7 July 1947: it dramatized historical events as if they had been covered by CBS correspondents at the time that they happened. For example, on 7 December of that first season, the program was "The Exile of Napoleon," with CBS reporters "covering" the events that marked "the end of the Napoleonic era." The next season the title was changed to *You Are There*, and the program continued on radio until 1950. It later had two runs on CBS television narrated by Walter Cronkite.

Many stations began using audiotape as an aid in gathering news and covering actualities. Yet it was another medium, the phonograph record, that helped show the way to documentary based on audio compilation of bits of recorded sound. In 1948 Fred W. Friendly and Edward R. Murrow compiled a history of the 20th century to that time; marketed as "I Can Hear It Now", it was based on fragments from newsreel sound tracks and on radio recordings. But many items were also re-created, or edited drastically for a more dramatic effect. The success of the record (first released on 78 rpm records, and then re-released in the new LP format), and the several that followed, showed that there was a viable market for audio compilation history.

Working again with Friendly as producer, Murrow made the next significant breakthrough in documentary with his reporting of the 1950 election. "A Report to the Nation" was broadcast just 48 hours after election day; it was a compilation of the voices and sounds of the campaign—speeches, commercials, song, rallies, winners' declarations, and losers' laments. Within a few weeks this new format became the basis of a weekly program called *Hear It Now*, which the announcer introduced "as a document for ear." A segment on 9 February 1951 called "Biography of a Pint of Blood" was not only one of the most dramatic of the series but also showed how audiotape recording would be used in future documentaries. With Murrow narrating, the program offered listeners the story (in interviews, reportage, and the sounds of the events) of one pint of blood—its being donated in the U.S., its transportation to the war front in Korea, and its use in saving a wounded soldier. The Murrow commentary is spare, limited mostly to essentials needed for transition. Now the real reporter was the tape recorder gathering reality sound, to which narration as needed could be added. But with the decline of radio network audiences because of television competition, in April 1951 CBS cut radio advertising rates for the first time ever. The future of broadcast documentary programming, combining with the traditions of the film documentary, was now on television. *Hear It Now* lasted only that first season; it returned to television in the fall as *See It Now*.

Documentary After 1950

During the next half century there were many fine radio and audio documentary programs and series. But none would attract the audience, achieve the critical praise, or reach such large audiences as their counterparts on television.

For four seasons beginning in 1956, NBC Radio presented *Biography in Sound*; often it was the story of a performer and was based on radio, phonograph record, and movie sound clips, as well as recorded interviews with colleagues and historians. Also in 1956 NBC produced 33 half-hour summaries of the history of radio called *Recollections at 30*. Often the phonograph records of radio performers had to be substituted for actual recordings of the radio programs because none could be found—an unfortunate result of the networks' earlier ban on using recordings of programs or of their carelessness: many of the recordings that were made were either lost or destroyed.

From the mid-1950s, most radio stations developed new music formats; there was little radio documentary. Sometimes audio-only reporting was used, especially if it was much less expensive and more convenient than bulky and expensive film equipment. In 1965 there were two notable series about poverty in America. *This Little Light* was a 10-program series produced in Mississippi by Chris Koch and Dale Minor for Pacifica Radio. Westinghouse Broadcasting also produced for the stations it owned a series on poverty called *Outskirts of Hope.*

CBS radio sent its own reporters to cover the Vietnam war, but from the beginning news president Fred Friendly insisted that they also provide TV coverage. ABC produced a weekly radio documentary about the Vietnam War for several years. NBC and CBS produced a very few radio documentaries each year, usually including one that was a summary of news for that year. These documentaries, as well as similar collections from Associate Press Radio, were often also made available as phonograph albums.

Since the 1970s, even smaller and more portable audiorecording equipment has made advances in the documentary art possible, but there are now few stations where radio documentaries can still be heard. Currently, National Public Radio in the U.S., the CBC in Canada and the BBC in Britain each typically broadcast several hours of documentaries each week. Producer David Isay has won numerous awards for his sound documentaries, many of which have aired on National Public Radio.

In December 2000 ABC News produced what it called the first "Webumentary," a biography and recollection of John Lennon on the 20th anniversary of his death.

See also: Cavalcade of America; Hear it Now; March of Time; Re-Creations of Events

Further Reading

Arnheim, Rudolf, *Radio*, London: Faber, 1936.
Bannerman, R. LeRoy, *Norman Corwin and Radio: The Golden Years*, University: University of Alabama Press, 1986.
Barnouw, Erik, editor, *Radio Drama in Action: Twenty-Five Plays of a Changing World*, New York and Toronto: Farrar and Rinehart, 1945.
Hesse, Jurgen, *The Radio Documentary Handbook*, New York: Self Counsel Press, 1987.
Lichty, Lawrence W., and Malachi C. Topping, compilers, *American Broadcasting: A Source Book on the History of Radio and Television*, New York: Hastings House, 1975 (see especially the tables on the types and number of quarter-hours of programming on the networks).
Paget, Derek, *True Stories: Documentary Drama on Radio, Stage and Screen*, Manchester, England: Manchester University Press, 1990.
Radio Documentaries site, www.transom.org
Ryan, Milo, editor, *History in Sound*, Seattle: University of Washington Press, 1963.

LAWRENCE W. LICHTY

DOLBY NOISE REDUCTION
Reducing Unwanted Noise in Broadcasts and Recording

Dolby Noise Reduction (NR) makes audio signals clearer by reducing noise in the signal. There are a number of forms of Dolby NR, but in its simplest form, as applied in Dolby B NR, high-frequency hiss is reduced by about 10 dB using a process called *companding:* on low-level signals, the high frequencies are boosted during recording (or transmission) and then cut by a correspondingly appropriate amount during playback (or reception). Other noise reduction techniques have been applied with Dolby A, C, SR, and S.

Origins

Ray Dolby founded Dolby Laboratories in London in 1965. Dolby's career began in high school when he worked for Ampex Corporation in Redwood City, California. While still in college he worked with a team of Ampex engineers to invent the first practical video tape recorder, which was introduced to the broadcast industry in 1956 (Dolby was largely responsible for the machine's electronics). Dolby graduated from Stanford University in 1957 and received his Ph.D. in physics from Cambridge University in 1961. Dolby Laboratories moved its headquarters to San Francisco in 1976.

The first commercial product from the company was Dolby A, a noise reduction system using audio compression and expansion to reduce background hiss without the discernible side effects of conventional wide-band companders. More than any other feature, the system's freedom from side effects is what differentiated Dolby NR from previous attempts at audio noise reduction and ultimately helped earn its reputation. Also incorporated in this new noise reduction system was the ability to treat only soft signals, leaving unprocessed the loud signals that naturally mask noise.

A consumer version of the noise reduction system, called Dolby B, was released in 1968. Instead of dividing the signal into fixed multiple bands (as did Dolby A), Dolby B NR used a single, less-costly sliding band of compression that reduced noise in the higher frequency hiss region where most of the noise of consumer tape recording occurs. But the system needs the reference levels to be precisely set. Dolby NR is perhaps best known for its use with magnetic tape. The first product to use Dolby B was an open-reel tape recorder made by KLH in 1968, but it made its biggest impact in the compact cassette format; with its inherent tape hiss problem and slow speed, cassette tape was a natural for Dolby B noise reduction.

Applications to Radio

The first experimental FM broadcasts using Dolby NR were made by WFMT in Chicago in June 1971 using the model 320 B noise reduction system. In March 1972 WQXR in New York City began full-time FM broadcasting using Dolby B.

In June 1973 it was proposed that Dolby B be joined with 25 microseconds pre-emphasis for FM broadcasting. In February 1974 this became the Dolby FM system demonstrated to the Federal Communications Commission (FCC). In June the FCC approved Dolby FM broadcasts. By August 1975 about 100 U.S. stations were broadcasting in Dolby FM. The use of Dolby FM moved outside the United States in October when the Canadian Department of Communications approved its use for broadcast.

Reducing Noise in Digital Signals

Concurrent with the development of these analog systems, Dolby Labs began research into digital audio in 1982. The primary goal was to find ways to reduce the amount of data required to transmit and store high-quality digital audio. Dolby Labs moved into the world of digital encoding schemes with AC-1, a refined form of Adaptive Delta Modulation (ADM). AC-1 was introduced in 1984, when bit rate reduction was in its infancy, and adopted the next year for use in a number of direct satellite broadcast and cable distribution systems. The Australian Broadcasting Corporation adopted it for direct broadcast satellite in its AUSSAT I in October 1985.

Dolby began its work in digital radio with the Digital Studio to Transmitter Line (DSTL) system, which was demonstrated for the first time in September 1991 in San Francisco at the National Association of Broadcasting's "Radio '91" conference. DSTL is a design featuring low time-delay implementation of Dolby AC-2, its second-generation digital encoding scheme using ADM. It features two high-quality channels and two auxiliary channels in the same spectrum space used for narrowband FM composite signals. Dolby DSTL was first installed in May 1992 at WWKX FM in Providence, Rhode Island.

Dolby Fax, for linking worldwide facilities with digital audio, began U.S. sales in March 1994. Dolby Fax uses Dolby AC-2 digital audio coding over two ISDN lines for high-quality transmission worldwide. In May 1994 DMX for Business began as the first direct broadcast satellite service, with Dolby AC-3 digital audio.

Dolby Surround is a matrix process that enables any stereo (two channel) medium, analog or digital, to carry four-channel audio. Encoded program material is fully compatible with mono and stereo playback, and listeners with playback systems incorporating Dolby Surround Pro Logic decoding receive four-channel surround sound. In February 1995 the BBC broadcast the first radio production in Dolby surround, "Bomber," on BBC Radio 4, and "Batman," "The Adventures of Superman," and "The Amazing Spiderman" on BBC Radio 1. Italy's Radio 101 has used Dolby Surround for all its evening entertainment programming. In March 1995 "West Coast Live" became the first U.S. radio show to be regularly broadcast in Dolby surround. In January 1997 the first Dolby Surround Pro Logic system for in-car use was launched at the Detroit Motor Show.

Dolby moved into the world of personal computer (PC) Surround Sound in April 1996 when Dolby and Microsoft signed a letter of intent to jointly develop PC surround technologies and specifications supporting the use of Dolby Digital AC-3 and Dolby Surround Pro Logic. Dolby Digital (sometimes known as AC-3 for the technology on which it is based) is a perceptual coding for consumer applications that enables storing and transmitting between one and 5.1 audio channels at a low data rate. Dolby Digital makes it possible to store five audio channels using less data than is needed to store just one channel on a compact disc. This was followed by Dolby Net, a low-bitrate version of Dolby Digital introduced for lowbandwidth applications such as real time streaming internet audio, in November 1996.

In January 1997 Virtual Dolby Surround and Virtual Dolby Digital were introduced at the huge Consumer Electronics Show in Las Vegas. They enable surround sound effects from desktop computers with just two speakers. In October 1999 real time multichannel audio was streamed successfully over the internet using 5.1-channel Dolby Digital.

In 1999 Dolby Laboratories introduced Dolby E, a professional multichannel audio coding technology that allows a single AES/EBU (digital audio) pair to carry up to eight channels of audio, as well as digital metadata, through broadcast facilities. It is a convenient, simple, cost-effective conversion of two-channel broadcast facilities to multichannel audio.

In the world of radio, Dolby Lab's impact has been most felt with Dolby NR, as well as several other programs such as Dolby Surround, DSTL, Dolby Digital, Dolby Fax, and Dolby E. Although no-one can predict the future of radio and the interaction with new technologies, given its track record, Dolby Labs will likely play a role in radio's future—on the airwaves, on the internet, or wherever it goes in the new millennium.

See also: Audio Processing; Audiotape; Digital Recording; High Fidelity; Stereo

Further Reading

Dolby Labs, www.dolby.com.

Eargle, John, *Handbook of Recording Engineering*, New York: Van Nostrand Reinhold, 1986.

Elen, Richard, "Noise Reduction Systems" in *Sound Recording Practice*, edited by John Borwick, London and New York: Oxford University Press, 1976; 3rd edition, Oxford and New York: Oxford University Press, 1987.

Honoré, Paul M., *A Handbook of Sound Recording: A Text for Motion Picture and General Sound Recording*, South Brunswick, New Jersey: Barnes, 1980.

Marco, Guy A., and Frank Andrews, editors, *Encyclopedia of Recorded Sound in the United States*, New York: Garland, 1993.

Runstein, Robert E., *Modern Recording Techniques*, Indianapolis, Indiana: Sams, 1974; 5th edition, by David Miles Huber and Runstein, Boston: Focal Press, 2001.

White, Glenn D., *The Audio Dictionary*, Seattle: University of Washington Press, 1987; 2nd edition, 1991.

Woram, John M., *Sound Recording Handbook*, Indianapolis, Indiana: Sams, 1989.

BRAD MCCOY

DON LEE BROADCASTING SYSTEM

The California-based Don Lee network was one of the longer lasting and more influential of the regional radio networks that first appeared in the 1930s. Before its demise in 1950, the network also pioneered local television broadcasting.

Origins

In 1926 Don Lee (a Los Angeles resident whose wealth had been built on his exclusive distribution rights for Cadillac automobiles in California) purchased KFRC in San Francisco. In 1927 he acquired KHJ in Los Angeles to promote auto sales. He then joined the McClatchy radio stations in 1928 and formed a western network that became affiliated with the Columbia Broadcasting System (CBS).

Don Lee died in 1934, and his son Thomas took over what continued to be known as the Don Lee Broadcasting System. Thomas Lee broke with McClatchy, and in 1936 signed with the Mutual network. Through the remainder of the 1930s and during the 1940s, the Don Lee Broadcasting System served as Mutual's West Coast nerve center. Operations were centered at KHJ in Los Angeles, with KFRC in San Francisco and KGB in San Diego. By the late 1940s the Don Lee Broadcasting System also controlled 17 other stations in smaller California towns. KALE in Portland, Oregon, anchored that state's ten owned-and-operated stations located in smaller Oregon towns. KVI in Seattle and KNEW in Spokane led Washington's nine stations. The properties of the Don Lee Broadcasting System also included three stations in Idaho; KATO in Reno, Nevada; KOOL in Phoenix, Arizona; KCNA in Tucson, Arizona; and KHON in Honolulu, Hawaii.

Pioneering TV

For all its regional radio success, the Don Lee Broadcasting System's truly pioneering work was in television broadcasting. Although RCA is usually given most of the credit for pioneering American television, the Don Lee Broadcasting System deserves at least equal billing. Its radio profits funded television experiments that began as a simple television laboratory in 1930. On 14 November 1930, auto-dealer-turned-broadcaster Don Lee hired Philo Farnsworth protégé Harry Lubcke as his director of television. By 10 May 1931 Lubcke and his staff had built television equipment of sufficient quality to convince the Federal Radio Commission to give the Don Lee Broadcasting System permission to go on the air experimentally. On the last day of 1931, its experimental TV station W6XAO went on the air on a UHF frequency for one hour per day, a schedule maintained through the 1930s.

With a transmitter and studios located in the Lee building's second floor in downtown Los Angeles, TV broadcasting experiments commenced on a slow, steady basis through the 1930s. Highlights included 1933 news footage of a Southern California earthquake as well as USC football games. In October 1937 the Don Lee Broadcasting System presented a gala high-profile premiere, broadcasting both on radio and television the opening of the 27th annual Los Angeles Motor Car Dealers' Automobile Show from the Pan Pacific Auditorium. (This event represented for Don Lee Broadcasting System the equivalent of the more fabled

1939 RCA demonstration at the World's Fair.) Every year the Don Lee Broadcasting System television station broadcast the Pasadena Tournament of Roses Parade, and in 1940 moved its transmitter to the top of Mount Lee, above the fabled "Hollywood" sign. The Don Lee company was apparently on the verge of initiating mass market TV broadcasting—in Hollywood's back yard—but the bombing of Pearl Harbor on 7 December 1941 put further experimentation on hold. Throughout World War II, the Don Lee Broadcasting System concentrated on radio.

Decline

After the war, Thomas Lee continued to concentrate on his highly profitable radio business and thus did not push to convert experimental W6XAO into formally licensed KTSL-TV (KTSL stood for "Thomas S. Lee") until May 1948. This came after Lee opened a $2.5 million radio and television complex at Hollywood and Vine with 18 studios covering 112,000 square feet, for television, AM, and FM broadcasting. Within the studio, Lee management sought to link radio with TV programming, not convinced that television would prove to be a stand-alone medium. Thomas Lee reasoned that simulcasting radio and TV programs would be the wave of the future. The Don Lee Broadcasting System's most famous show, *Queen for a Day*, was an example of this thinking.

Although radio broadcasts of *Queen for a Day* began on 29 April 1945, it would be two years before Lee gave the go-ahead to simulcast the program on the still-experimental TV station W6XAO. But when the simulcast finally occurred, its success led Lee to commit to television. Broadcasting live from a Hollywood theater–restaurant called Moulin Rouge, host Jack Bailey interviewed four or five women who poured out tales of woe. The one receiving the most audience applause became "Queen for a Day" and was showered with gifts, her problems momentarily solved, at least in a material sense. James Cagney's sister Jeanne offered fashion shows in breaks between sob stories. *Queen for a Day* became a Los Angeles sensation through the early 1950s, and later ran on the National Broadcasting Company (NBC) and American Broadcasting Company (ABC) networks.

Thomas Lee's death on 13 January 1950 was the beginning of the end of the Don Lee Broadcasting System. (He had been in poor health for years and either fell or jumped from the 12th floor of his broadcasting center.) Operations continued under long-time vice president Lewis Allen Weiss until

May, when, under the terms of Lee's will, the broadcast properties were put up for sale. In November, General Tire and Rubber Company's bid of $12.3 million was accepted. General Tire folded the Don Lee Broadcasting System into its broadcast empire, which then included the Mutual radio network, the Yankee radio network, and TV/radio station WOR of New York. By the end of the 1950s, nothing remained of the previous Don Lee Broadcasting System as a regional network or a group of influential radio stations.

See also: Mutual Broadcasting System

Further Reading

Murray, Michael D., and Donald G. Godfrey, editors, *Television in America: Local Station History from Across the Nation*, Ames: Iowa State University Press, 1997.
Torrence, Bruce T., *Hollywood: The First Hundred Years*, New York: Zoetrope, 1979.
Writers' Program, *Los Angeles: A Guide to the City and Its Environs*, New York: Hastings House, 1941.

DOUGLAS GOMERY AND CHUCK HOWELL

DRAMA

The American radio industry is and has been the largest in the world. Before the rise of television, U.S. radio drama was creative as well as commercially popular. Radio also provided a marketing dimension for the Hollywood film industry. The political need to gain government support for the network monopoly was one factor behind the substantial network investment in quality sustaining (non-advertiser supported) programs.

As radio reinvented itself as a music medium in the 1950s, dramatic productions quickly fell out of favor. The competition from popular dramatic storytelling on television was too intense. Although the counter-culture movement of youth protest in the 1960s generated a demand for radio that offered a space for intelligent speech and alternative music, it did not support storytelling. Unlike the radio situation in Europe, Canada, and Australia, for example, American radio drama funding was not centralized into one service. Radio drama projects relied on entrepreneurial projects to raise funds from sponsors, private foundations, station budgets, and such public resources for cultural projects as the National Endowment for the Arts and the National Endowment for the Humanities. The developing publishing market for spoken-word cassettes and CDs in the 1980s and 1990s provided further commercial collateral for production budgets.

Origins

Early U.S. drama developed in individual stations across the country. Even before World War I, Charles "Doc" Herrold organized schedules for a station in San Jose, California, which in 1914 included transmitting a live play. A drama series was broadcast by station WGY in Schenectady, New York, in 1922. The WGY players began with a full-length production of Eugene Walter's *The Wolf* and soon established a regular Friday night schedule of two-and-a-half-hour performances of anything from *The Garden of Allah* to Ibsen's *The Wild Duck*. For three years not a single playwright asked for payment. An orchestra provided music in the silences between scenes and acts. By 1923 the WGY players had launched a $500 radio drama prize competition to encourage scripts specifically tailored to the medium. The rules stipulated plays that were "clean," avoided "sex dramas," and employed small casts of five to six characters. One hundred scripts were submitted, but the play selected did not result in a successful broadcast.

As WGY productions began to be shared with other stations by early 1924, some of the actors were paid and other stations started radio drama centers of production. WLW in Cincinnati broadcast *A Fan and Two Candlesticks* by Mary MacMillan, which was followed a week later by the balcony scene from *Romeo and Juliet*. Drama became a weekly event. The transmission of *When Love Wakes*, an original play written by program manager Fred Smith, may have been the first play written especially for radio when it aired 3 April 1923, nine months before the transmission of Richard Hughes' *Danger* on the BBC in January 1924.

During these early years, radio stations realized that it was easier to control sound levels within a studio than to depend upon a theater stage as an arena for drama performance. In WGY's case, engineers designed microphones hidden in lampshades in case actors became nervous at the sight of a bare microphone. Chicago's KYW took to the air specializing in broadcasting operas. *Radio Digest* observed in October 1923 that the radio play was increasing rapidly in popularity and that many eastern stations had their own theatrical groups. That same year, as a publicity device, WLW in Cincinnati provided airtime for the Shuster-Martin School to perform drama readings.

One of the first sponsored dramas was probably included in the *Eveready Hour*, which was launched in December 1923 on WEAF, New York City, to sell Eveready batteries. By 1927 the *Eveready House* program was producing a prestigious drama on a monthly basis, with each production auditioned before the sponsor three weeks before airing. Actors were now being paid $75 to $125 per performance. Rosaline Greene was praised for her portrayal of Joan of Arc.

Golden Age of Popular Radio Drama

The golden age of U.S. radio drama really began in the late 1920s when first the National Broadcasting Company (NBC) and later the Columbia Broadcasting System (CBS) began distributing networked programs. Drama was included along with dance and jazz concerts, because drama had "an aura of respectability." The titles included *Great Moments in History*, *Biblical Dramas*, *Real Folks*, *Main Street*, and *True Story*. For the next three decades, virtually all American network drama and comedy programs were in the format of series in that they used a continuing cast of characters and provided programs on a regular (usually weekly) schedule. Individual episodes usually stood alone, each one a complete story, but such fare was built around continuing characters who would be around the following week. The growing number of network series were supplemented with anthology (sometimes dubbed "prestige") drama programs, whose characters and stories both varied (such as the long-running *Lux Radio Theater*), with no continuing elements save perhaps for a host and regular scheduled air time (and probably a sponsor).

One kind of radio series—the daytime soap opera—offered something additional; their continuing plot lines further focused the series to become a serial that combined continuing characters with stories that often lasted for years, with subplots melding into one another in a never-ending fashion. Each episode depended on the episodes that had gone before and led directly to the following episodes, though stories moved very slowly. Serial announcers usually began each episode with a paragraph or two describing what was happening for listeners who had missed any segments. The plots were purposely designed to hook listeners into regular attendance.

African-Americans and Radio Drama

The cultural gulf separating the white majority from the African-American minority (until the civil rights movement of the 1960s) tended to distort and sometimes censor the presentation of the black identity and storytelling culture. African-American performers had negotiated roles in white-interpreted and -mediated arenas for popular story telling.

Although African-Americans performed some parts in *Amos 'n' Andy* (1928–60), "blacked up" whites Freeman Gosden and Charles Correll played the central characters; Madaline Lee played the duo's secretary Miss Blue; and Eddie Green performed the role of Stonewall, the lawyer. To put it mildly, this was an unsatisfactory context for the expression of African-American identity. Eddie Anderson's role as Rochester, Jack Benny's black valet, represented mainstream participation in radio's popular story-telling culture, but was also controversial in the perpetuation of the "Jim Crow" syndrome of racial stereotyping. Another distorting and comic exploitation of African-American women as maids was the character and series *Beulah* (1945–54). The first actor to play *Beulah* was William Hurt, a white man, who coined the character's famous catchphrases "Love dat man!" and "Somebody bawl for Beulah?" The paradoxical ambiguity of radio's representation of stereotypes became evident in 1947 after Hurt died from a heart attack and the Academy Award-winning African-American actress Hatie McDaniel took over the part.

World War II saw the introduction of positively drawn African-American soldier characters in daytime serials as the U.S. government sought to promote the contribution of black servicemen and reduce racial tension within the armed forces.

The problem of negative racial stereotypes and chronic discrimination against African-Americans' participation was challenged by the work of Richard Durham at WMAQ in Chicago between 1948 and 1950. Durham originated, wrote, and directed a series called *Destination Freedom* that dramatized the stories of black achievers such as Benjamin Banneker, Sojourner Truth, Brooker T. Washington, Marian Anderson, and Joe Louis. Durham had been editor of the black newspaper the *Chicago Defender*. The scripting of 91 half-hour episodes and their production remains a significant event in American radio drama history. The most notable and widely praised episode was the dramatization of the accomplishments of heart surgeons Dr. Daniel Hale Williams and Dr. Ulysses Grant Dailey in "The Heart of George Cotton," originally aired in Chicago on 8 August 1948 and restaged in 1957 on the networked CBS Radio Workshop.

In 1944 Langston Hughes collaborated with the British radio drama producer D.G. Bridson to create a ballad-opera exploring the friendship between black Americans going to war with the people of Britain. The cast included Ethel Waters, Canada Lee, Josh White, and Paul Robeson;

The Man Who Went To War was produced and performed in New York but only heard via shortwave by 10 million BBC listeners in Britain. Langston Hughes also wrote *Booker T. Washington In Atlanta*, commissioned by the Tuskegee Institute and CBS. Despite joining The Writers' War Board after Pearl Harbor in December 1941, he faced blacklisting pressures from the House of Un-American Activities from October 1944. Erik Barnouw wrote that even when American networks had commissioned and produced work by black writers, affiliate stations in the Southern states would often block the broadcast by substituting a local program of musical records.

Sustaining and Prestige Drama

Experimental radio drama of exceptional quality was produced in the United States during the golden age as a by-product of the commercial success of the networks. Advertising profits financed such programming in unsold time. A "marquee status" in radio culture sparked by competition between CBS and NBC helped to generate such programs. Even the poor relation of U.S. radio networks, Mutual (MBS), would commission 21-year-old Orson Welles and his Mercury Theatre to produce a six-part dramatization of Victor Hugo's *Les Miserables* in 1937—ambitious storytelling and dramatic performance on a grand scale. Through a series called *Columbia Workshop* (1936–47), CBS was the first network to experiment with using sound effects for creative and cultural storytelling. Starting in July 1936 the programmers advanced radiophonic techniques for sparking the imagination. The discovery of sound filters that evoked ghostly phenomena gave birth to *The Ghost of Benjamin Street*.

The production of the script *The Fall of the City* by poet Archibald MacLeish presented a social and political attack on totalitarianism and ambition in production. The large "crowd" cast, the special location of performance at New York's Seventh Regiment Armory, and the quality of the cast, which included Burgess Meredith and the young Orson Welles, combined to establish a radio drama broadcast on 4 March 1937 that defined the potential of the medium. *The Fall of the City* invested production confidence in the idea of a drama written in verse for radio. Barnouw (1945) described the resulting competition for prestigious drama projects between the networks. CBS contributed a series of Shakespeare productions featuring John Barrymore. NBC recruited Arch Oboler, who started with a production of his own play *Futuristics* and then persuaded the network to support a series of experimental horror stories, *Lights Out*. Oboler founded a tradition of science fiction horror and melodrama that continued in a series bearing his name.

CBS also signed up Orson Welles and the *Mercury Theatre of the Air* (1938). A formidable production, performance, writing, musical composition, sound design, and directing team of Orson Welles, John Houseman, Howard Koch, and Bernard Herrmann fashioned classic and contemporary novels and plays into highly charged hour-long sequences of live radio entertainment. The subtle sound-design creativity of Ora Nichols advanced the interface of sound and imagination for listeners. The adaptation of the H.G. Wells novelette *The War of the Worlds* at the end of October 1938 would write radio drama into social and cultural history and send Orson Welles and his troubadours to Hollywood.

It was also in 1938 that CBS vice president William B. Lewis hired Norman Corwin to make a series of half-hour programs on Sundays to experiment with poetry. Corwin would become a tour de force in writing and radio drama. The series *Words without Music*, *Pursuit of Happiness*, and *Twenty-Six by Corwin* established his reputation. From his verse play for the festive season of that year, *The Plot to Overthrow Christmas*, to constitutional and historical pageants such as *We Hold These Truths*, Corwin contributed a body of literature and direction for radio that resonated in and had considerable influence on the English-speaking world. The poetics of his writing were also embedded with political poignancy; *They Fly through the Air* was an audio equivalent of Picasso's famous painting on the bombing of Guernica, and his *Seems Radio Is Here to Stay* is a verse essay on the beauty and potentialities of the medium.

An analysis of Corwin's verse play *The Undecided Molecule*, aired only weeks before the detonation of the atomic bombs in Japan in 1945, reveals writing, directing, and performance in advance of its time. Groucho Marks played the role of a judge metaphorically trying the idea of the atom bomb and mankind's use of it in a surreal courtroom. It was a culturally and politically subversive weave of irony, spiced with postmodernist and existential wit and a tour de force of production and performance that served to define Corwin's power and achievement in the history of world radio drama. It was also an elegant and powerful demonstration of radio drama's literary credentials.

Detective Drama

The golden age produced a genre of audio-noir detectives both male and female. *The Adventures of Maisie*, featuring a character who globe-trotted the high seas from one exotic port to the next, began with a man being slapped when asking for a light and the catchphrase "Does that answer your question, Buddy?" *The Adventures of Nero Wolfe*, based on the popular novels by Rex Stout, proved that you could be a good private detective and so fat that your assistant Archie would have to do all your legwork for you. *The Fat Man* (1946–51) had the central character Brad Runyon starting each episode as the announcer spoke these words: "There he goes into the drugstore. He steps on the scale. Weight 237 pounds! Fortune: Danger!" *The Adventures of Philip Marlowe* (1947–51), *The Adventures of Sam Spade Detective* (1946–51), and *The Adventures of the Thin Man* (1941–50) arose out of the successful novels and films featuring the characters so named. The character Nora Charles, first played by Claudia Morgan in the radio series, amounted to a curious blend of femme fatale and positive gender representation. Nora, with a voice that purred with sexuality, was a supersleuth. *Martin Kane, Private Eye* (1949–53) was an example of a radio detective series that made the successful transformation to television. The highly successful *Sherlock Holmes* (1930–36; 1939–46) culminated with British actors Basil Rathbone and Nigel Bruce in the roles of Holmes and Watson.

The invisibility of radio extended the boundaries of imaginative devices in storytelling. *The Shadow* (1930–54) worked best on radio because the character had the power to be invisible. *The Shadow* and other series, such as *The Green Hornet* (1936–52) and *Nick Carter—Master Detective* (1943–55), transplanted the myth of the Western into the urban environment. The Western was also present in U.S. popular drama through, among others, the series *The Lone Ranger* (1934–56). *The Adventures of Dick Tracy* (1935–48) was based on the comic-strip detective created by Chester Gould and is another example of the radio detective genre that cross-pollinated newspaper/magazine comic strips and films.

The police radio series was a cultural mechanism for the mythologizing of Edgar Hoover's FBI or "G-men" and the large-city police departments. Notable series included *Dragnet*, *Call the Police*, *Calling All Cars*, *Crime Does Not Pay*, *Gang Busters*, *Famous Jury Trials*, *Official Detective*, *Renfrew of the Mounted Police*, *Silver Eagle Mountie*, *This Is Your FBI*, *The FBI in Peace and War*, *True Detective Mysteries*, and *Under Arrest*.

The detective genres generated controversy because of their stereotypically negative representations of Asian-Americans. *Charlie Chan* (1932–48) was built around an Asian-Hawaiian private eye who was always played by white American actors. The series *Fu Manchu* (1929–33), arising out of the Collier magazine stories, offered another example of the demonizing and typecasting of Chinese or Asians as "untrustworthy, inscrutable" villains.

"Soap Opera" Drama

Conditions for developing a thriving market of radio serials were ripe in 1930s America. National networks were expanding because they provided "free" entertainment once one owned a receiver. Further, and despite the Depression, there was a continuing market for products that could improve the quality of life in the home, including soap products and washing machines. Radio provided an excellent means of reaching out to the growing market of women concerned with such purchases, and seeking entertainment. Radio could meet the demand for entertainment about family and identity, about fantasy and the idea of home, about struggle against adversity and achievement, and about people who could be admired and respected. From these circumstances, the soap opera was born.

In Los Angeles Carlton Morse began writing episodes for the series *One Man's Family* in 1932; it would last for 28 years. The story of the Barbour family depended on its addictive narrative drive for its success. Radio had become the stage for its own popular American version of Galsworthy's *Forsyte Saga*. In 1939 Morse created *I Love a Mystery*, featuring the exotic adventures of three global adventurers from the A-1 Detective Agency. He wrote every word and directed every script; his craft had him up at 4 A.M. and kept him busy seven days a week. Barnouw (1945) wrote that radio was becoming a mecca for acting talent that could no longer find work in the theater. Radio was helping listeners—and more than a few creative people— buck the Depression.

Serials that charted social mobility and advancement secured lucrative sponsorship because the audience could identify with the reality and aspirations such programs embodied. *The Goldbergs* (1929–50) performed the ritual of a social journey from the Lower East Side of New York City into the middle-class suburbs; Pepsodent was a product that helped enhance the smile on their faces. Writer and actor Gertrude Berg created *The Goldbergs* in her quest to dramatize Jewish family life. Susan J. Douglas (1999) has observed the value of the

research by Herta Herzog into the relationship between women listeners and soap operas: "The melodramatic narratives and strong female characters of daytime serials—coupled with the intimacy of the medium—provided powerful points of identification." Herzog's research in the 1930s showed that, to one woman listener, soap opera "teaches me as a parent how to bring up my child." Popular radio drama during the golden age was an opportunity for women's self-empowerment, and as Barnouw observes, "Almost one-third [of listeners] spoke of planning the day around serials." *Little Orphan Annie* (1930–42) could be comfortably associated with the coziness and nourishment of the Ovaltine bedtime drink. *Myrt and Marge* had the attitude that came with chewing gum made by Wrigley. *Buck Rogers 25th Century* (1932–36, 1939–40, 1946–47) was the kind of dream that listeners could think about when crunching on their breakfast cereals produced by Kellogg's.

Many of the key producers and writers who controlled the form were highly educated and independent women. Irna Phillips probably wrote more words and made more money in the field of soap opera than anyone else. Her prodigious industry was founded in Chicago, and once she hit her stride no-one could match her ability to invent story lines or dictate six scripts a day and write three million words a year. She was the creator of *Today's Children*, *Woman in White*, *Right to Happiness*, *The Guiding Light*, *Road of Life*, and *Lonely Women*. Her gift to the history of gender representation is that she invented and sustained women characters who were role models to American women listeners because they had strength and dignity and could hold their social position equally with men.

Another key center for popular series and serial production was founded and developed by advertising executive Frank Hummert and his assistant Anne S. Ashenhurst, who later became his wife. They established a team of writers distinguished by the talented *Chicago Daily News* reporter Robert D. Andrews, who probably generated more than 30 million words of storytelling for radio. Andrews' first serial story was *Three Days Lost*. Within a year of being hired by the Hummerts he was turning out five radio scripts a day. The author of a book on *How to Write for Radio* was convinced that Andrews was really three or four writers and that his name was the brand title of a writing syndicate. The Hummerts generated legends in the tradition of soap opera entertainment, some of which transferred to television.

In some respects the soap opera boom of the golden age could be described as the "Wild West of

Writing." It was a Klondike for authors, advertisers, and networks because 80 percent of the programming of a network station in a big city market in 1939 was made up of wall-to-wall daytime soap episodes, most of them merely 15 minutes long. Elaine Carrington was an example of a short story writer who found that her ability to produce story outlines and scripts for daytime serials could make her a rich author. She conceived and wrote *Red Adams*, which became *Red Davis* and then *Pepper Young's Family* as the sponsors changed.

In the daytime soap by Jane Crusinberry, *The Story of Mary Marlin* (1935–45, 1951–52), Crusinberry dramatized a character who became a female U.S. senator. *Mary Marlin* was one of the highest-rated daytime serials after 1937, and because Crusinberry retained control of all the writing, the series was able to transcend the political and social compromises that arose from sponsor-controlled "factory writing." During World War II Crusinberry originated and wrote a series called *A Woman of America* (1943–46), which starred Anne Seymour and dramatized the history of achieving women in the United States.

The Legacy of World War II

The political struggle between communism and fascism through the 1930s and the years of World War II coincided with the most intense period of the "Golden Age" of radio. Howard Blue (2002) examines the work of 17 radio dramatists and writers who deployed the radio drama arts in their battle against fascism. Between 1941 and 1945 they were allied with commercial radio networks, private agencies, and U.S. government propaganda organizations that wished to rally the listening imagination in the fight against German Nazism and Japanese militarism.

Blue documents how the chill wind of the Cold War made casualties of left of center writers, directors, and actors who had been politically motivated in their creative engagement with radio drama during wartime. The personal memoir by the radio actor Joseph Julian, published in 1975 as *This Was Radio*, provides a compelling and agonizing account of how Senator Joe McCarthy's witch-hunting could snuff out a career virtually overnight.

The compendium of 25 radio plays edited by Erik Barnouw and published in 1945 as *Radio Drama in Action* represents a significant body of literature from this period of broadcasting. Morton Wishengrad's *The Battle of the Warsaw Ghetto*, broadcast by NBC on the eve of the Day of Atonement in 1943, demonstrated how radio dramatization of actuality could succeed where radio journalism had failed. There was no effective contemporary reporting of the extraordinary rebellion by young Jewish fighters in the Warsaw Ghetto in April 1942. Wishengrad's research and literary imagination combined with the direction of Frank Papp, a music score by Morris Mamorsky, and acting performance by Arnold Moss to represent a vital moment in history.

Radio Drama in the Shadow of Television

With the development of U.S. network television beginning in 1948, radio drama's days were numbered. Within just a few years, audiences and advertisers had begun the rapid migration to the video medium, and network schedules grew sparse. The McCarthy witch-hunts and Cold War paranoia also damaged American radio drama at the same time. Opportunities for significant network projects and corporate sponsorship were not coming to anyone who was perceived to be left of center. Orson Welles, Norman Corwin, and Paul Robeson had characteristics and track records that could be regarded as left wing. Along with thousands of talented writers, actors, and directors, they could be perceived as politically subversive. Blacklisting generated self-censorship and drove a community of artists into exile. Others were silenced, their credentials ruined. Perhaps one of the more absurd manifestations of this cultural anomie was the 1952–54 syndicated series *I Was a Communist for the FBI*, in which film actor Dana Andrews infiltrated organizations as a double agent and week by week roamed episodes with titles such as *The Red Among Us*, *The Red Waves*, and *The Red Ladies*.

Money and talent became concentrated in television. There were courageous and worthy projects, such as *CBS Mystery Theater* between 1974 and 1977 produced by Himan Brown, which tried to turn back the clock. Such ambition and concentration of resources, however, was not sustained by audience figures and the interest of sponsors.

Drama on Public Radio

With the end of commercial radio's golden age in the early 1950s, radio drama was for many years an art hidden behind the cornucopia of television programming. Still, the mutually advantageous relationship between the Hollywood film industry and radio networks during the 1940s and 1950s exemplified by *Lux Radio Theatre*, *Hollywood Hotel/Premiere*, and *Hollywood Star Preview/Star*

Playhouse, Star Theater left seeds for future development and opportunity. In the 1970s Himan Brown produced original radio dramas for CBS radio. Still later, George Lucas donated the sound rights of his *Star Wars* stories to his former university radio station. National Public Radio (NPR) invested more than $200,000 in a 13-part dramatization including members of the film's cast, music composer, and sound designer.

Satellite distribution generated a renaissance in interest in audio drama and created a new audience among young people. In some respects interest in the U.S. *Star Wars* project was similar to the interest shown by young audiences in Britain to the radio series *The Hitchhiker's Guide To the Galaxy*. Filmic music and multitrack sound design techniques combined with the cult of science fiction to produce success.

The period 1971 to 1981 witnessed the development of *Earplay*, a National Public Radio Drama Production Unit based in Madison, Wisconsin, under the artistic direction of Karl Schmidt. The project was substantially funded from federal sources and generated radio drama script competitions for new writers. It eventually developed large-scale collaborations with the BBC in England and commissioned well-known established writers such as Edward Albee, David Mamet, and Arthur Kopit.

National Public Radio's rival American Public Radio (APR, which later became Public Radio International) also generated interest in original spoken word storytelling through the work of Garrison Keillor in Minnesota. NPR, in Washington, D.C., continued to courageously distribute *NPR Playhouse*, but, despite the enthusiasm of producer Andy Trudeau, radio drama became a cultural artifact in the tapestry of U.S. radio. Trudeau even commissioned an original series of new Sherlock Holmes dramatizations starring Edward Petherbridge, and NEH and NEA funding supported worthy cultural drama projects such as Samuel Beckett and German *Horspiel* seasons, which were the initiative of Everett Frost. Unfortunately, the poor take-up by NPR affiliate stations of *NPR Playhouse* programs resulted in its demise in September 2002.

Independent Producers and Radio Drama by Artisans

American radio drama has moved from a mass-appeal service based on daily or weekly series to a far narrower format aimed at small but elite audiences. There would appear to be no shortage of ambition and commitment from small independent producers all over the United States who use efficient modern digital technology to produce original plays and dramatizations that are crafted for a connoisseur audience mainly in public radio. New York-based independent producer Charles Potter and Random House have established a niche interest in the radio Western, with audiobooks that sell well in the retail market and are also carried by some radio stations over the air. The internet, the audio drama cassette/CD/mini disc market, and digital radio offer accessible, low-cost networks of distribution. Furthermore, it is a low-risk genre for ideas and counter-culture. Companies such as Ziggurat, ZBS Foundation, Atlanta Radio Theatre, The Radio Repertory Company of America, Hollywood Theater of the Ear, The Radio Play—The Public Media Foundation, Midwest Radio Theatre Workshop, LA Theatre Works, Shoestring Radio Theatre, and many others have established significant output of original productions. Notable directors/dramatists include Yuri Rasovsky, Eric Bauersfeld, Joe Frank, and David Ossman.

During the 1980s and 1990s, WBAI, the Pacifica radio station in New York, was the arena for an interesting development in the art of the live community radio play. The station's arts director Anthony J. Sloan catalyzed much of this work. Sloan observed that "Most people did taped drama because it's safer. BBC does radio drama every day, but it's canned. I like live radio drama because the adrenaline flows for the actors. They know that not only is this live, but, guess what, it's only one-time. You get some incredible performances." Sloan orchestrated a series of media pageants that have occupied the streets of New York, the studios of WBAI, the satellite frequency of Pacifica Network programming, and the worldwide web with orchestras of musical, dramatic, and acoustic artistic expression fused by captivating, bold narratives. The productions were not short half-hour or one-hour sequences. They spanned five-and-a-half hours of airtime. Philosophically challenging, politically controversial, intellectually stimulating, emotionally invigorating dimensions of communication combined with complex sound production techniques and live performances on the sidewalks of the Lower East Side and various landmarks in the urban geography of New York City. The grassroots dimension of this work was an indicator of how radio drama could strengthen its identity and cultural value with its audiences. The *Leaving(s) Project*, transmitted on the night of 26 January 1996, comprised two live storytelling events over five-and-a-half hours. Larry Neal's play *The Glorious Monster in the Bell of the Horn* was presented before a live audience at the New Knitting Factory in the Tribeca section of Manhattan. The play was structured in the style of the epic opera based on the Brothers Grimm's *Peter and the Wolf*, wherein characters are identified by musical instruments. Then the multimedia event blossomed into "a journey piece" from different locations of the New York metropolitan area. There were six different groups of characters leaving New York for various reasons who were forced to deal with personal crises on their way to an Amtrak train at New York's Penn Station. Their interweaving storylines highlighted current social, political, spiritual, and artistic issues. All the disparate journeys were acted out live with moving microphones on location and culminated in a dramatic finale at Penn station. The realism of the event is indicated by the fact that the fictional characters intended to board the 3:45 A.M. Amtrak red-eye service leaving New York, which was actually waiting to leave one of the platforms at the end of the broadcast. The event began at 10 P.M. on Friday night and continued until 3:45 the following morning. It could be heard in stereo on WBAI 99.5 FM, received by satellite on 360 community radio stations, and heard nationally and internationally on the worldwide web.

Early 21st century U.S. radio drama can be described as "the age of the artisan," whereas the period before the 1950s could be described as "the age of the Network." Audio dramatic techniques are also widely used in advertising and public information spots, so narrative creativity in radio is not a totally lost art.

See also, in addition to individual shows mentioned in this entry: Blacklisting; Hollywood and Radio; National Public Radio; Pacifica Foundation; Poetry and Radio; Public Radio International; Science Fiction Programs; Soap Opera; WBAI; Westerns

Further Reading

Augaitis, Daina, and Dan Lander, editors, *Radio Rethink: Art, Sound, and Transmission*, Banff, Alberta: Walter Phillips Gallery, 1994.

Barnouw, Erik, editor, *Radio Drama in Action: Twenty-Five Plays of a Changing World*, New York and Toronto, Ontario: Farrar and Rinehart, 1945.

Blue, Howard, *Words At War: World War II Radio Drama and the Postwar Broadcasting Industry Blacklist*, Lanham, Maryland: Scarecrow Press, 2002.

Brooke, Pamela, *Communicating through Story Characters: Radio Social Drama*, Lanham, Maryland: University of America Press, 1995.

Burnham, Scott G., "Soundscapes: The Rise of Audio Drama in America," *AudioFile* (July 1996).

Crook, Tim, *Radio Drama: Theory and Practice*, London and New York: Routledge, 1999.

Daley, Brian, and George Lucas, *Star Wars: The National Public Radio Dramatization*, New York: Ballantine Books, 1994.

Douglas, Susan J., *Listening In: Radio and the American Imagination: From Amos 'n' Andy and Edward R. Murrow to Wolfman Jack and Howard Stern*, New York: Times Books, 1999.

Fink, Howard, "The Sponsor's vs. the Nation's Choice: North American Radio Drama," in *Radio Drama*, edited by Peter Elfed Lewis, London and New York: Longman, 1981.

Fink, Howard, "On the Trail of Radio Drama: Organizing a Study of North American and European Practices," *Journal of Radio Studies* 6, no. 1 (1999).

Grams, Martin, Jr., *Radio Drama: A Comprehensive Chronicle of American Network Programs, 1932–1963*, Jefferson, North Carolina: McFarland, 2000.

Guralnick, Elissa S., *Sight Unseen: Beckett, Pinter, Stoppard, and Other Contemporary Dramatists on Radio*, Athens: Ohio University Press, 1996.

Hilmes, Michelle, *Radio Voices: American Broadcasting, 1922–1952*, Minneapolis: University of Minnesota Press, 1997.

Julian, Joseph, *This War Radio: A Personal Memoir*, New York: Viking, 1975.

Kahn, Douglas, and Gregory Whitehead, editors, *Wireless Imagination: Sound, Radio, and the Avant-Garde*, Cambridge, Massachusetts: MIT Press, 1992.

Shingler, Martin, and Cindy Wieringa, *On Air: Methods and Meanings of Radio*, London and New York: Arnold, 1998.

Worlds without End: The Art and History of the Soap Opera (exhibition catalogue), New York: Abrams, 1997.

TIM CROOK

DUFFY'S TAVERN
Comedy Program

—*"Duffy's Tavern, where the elite meet to eat, Archie the manager speaking, Duffy ain't here. Oh, hello, Duffy..."*

Every week, a ringing phone and Archie's nasal New York accent invited listeners into *Duffy's Tavern*, a weekly situation comedy set in a dilapidated pub in the heart of Manhattan's east side. Running the place on behalf of the ever-absent Duffy, Archie the manager and his cohorts—Eddie, Finnegan, Clancy the Cop, Miss Duffy (Duffy's daughter), and others—welcomed a new guest star or guest character every week into a defiantly low-class atmosphere of barbed but friendly give and take.

Duffy's was famous for its play with (and mistreatment of) language, especially Archie's constant malapropisms. "Leave me dub you welcome to this distinctured establishment," Archie said to guest star Vincent Price, "and leave me further say, Mr. Price, that seldom have we behooved such an august presentiment to these confines.... And feel assured, Mr. Price, that your visit is a bereavement from' which we will not soon recover." As comedian Georgie Jessel once chided Fred Allen on *The Texaco Star Theatre*: "Fred! Two split infinitives and a dangling metaphor—people will think this is Duffy's Tavern!"

The pilot for *Duffy's Tavern* aired on 29 July 1940 on the Columbia Broadcasting System (CBS) radio program *Forecast*, which aired previews and pilots of proposed CBS shows in order to gauge audience reaction. The reaction in this case was enthusiastic, and CBS picked *Duffy's* up as a weekly half-hour program beginning in March 1941, running on Saturday nights at 8:30. It moved to two more time slots over the next year, until October 1942, when it switched to National Broadcasting Company's (NBC) Blue network, running at 8:30 on Tuesdays. When NBC Blue became the separate network American Broadcasting Companies (ABC), *Duffy's Tavern* moved to the NBC network proper, where it ran for the next seven years.

Duffy's Tavern was largely the brainchild of its star, Ed Gardner (born Ed Poggenburg), who first created the character of Archie for the CBS program *This Is New York* in 1939. Archie's right-hand man was "Eddie the Waiter," played by Eddie Green, an African-American comedian with a dry wit, who often took the wind out of Archie's sails. Green's part was notable at the time for its lack of stereotype or inferiority: the writers for *Duffy's Tavern* received an award during "Negro History Week" in 1946 for providing Green with such positive, racially inoffensive material.

The most faithful patron of the tavern was the monumentally stupid "Clifton Finnegan," played by veteran radio comic Charlie Cantor (no relation to Eddie Cantor). Cantor had originated the slow-talking, even slower-witted stooge character Socrates Mulligan for the "Allen's Alley" segment on the *Fred Allen Show*, and he eventually transplanted a renamed Mulligan into *Duffy's Tavern*. Cantor was an enormously experienced radio talent, "the Great Mr. Anonymous of radio," appearing on programs such as *The Shadow*, *Abie's Irish Rose*, *Dick Tracy*, *The Life of Riley*, and *Baby Snooks*. At one point he was in such demand that he performed in 26 programs in one week, and for several months he appeared in the same time slot on three different networks in two recordings and one live show.

Ed Gardner's wife Shirley Booth originally played "Miss Duffy," a young woman on the look-out for marriageable men, pursuing them almost as energetically as they fled from her. After Gardner and Booth divorced in 1942, at least 12 different actresses essayed the role of Miss Duffy, most

notably Florence Halop and Sandra Gould, whose combined tenure lasted approximately six years.

In 1944 production moved from Manhattan to Hollywood (though of course the tavern remained eternally in New York), and in 1945, Paramount released a *Duffy's Tavern* feature film, starring the central cast of the radio show as their tavern characters (Gardner, Green, and Cantor, with Ann Thomas as the Miss Duffy du jour), surrounded by literally dozens of Paramount contract players appearing as themselves (among them Bing Crosby, Dorothy Lamour, Alan Ladd, and Paulette Goddard). The film received tepid reviews—critics appreciated the star-studded stage show within the movie much more than the framing story featuring the radio characters—but the radio show itself kept going strong.

An NBC report in March 1949 identified *Duffy's Tavern* as one of the network's top four programs, "vital to the maintenance of a strong position in the industry," alongside Fred Allen, Fibber McGee, and Bob Hope. That year there were rumblings within NBC and rumors in the newspapers that Gardner planned to take the show to CBS; in fact, Gardner went so far as to obtain a release from the program's contract with longtime sponsor Bristol-Myers to free up his options to court another network. However, NBC found *Duffy's* important enough to renegotiate. During the 1949 summer hiatus, Gardner and NBC moved the program in its entirety—including equipment, staff, and performers—to Puerto Rico, to take advantage of a 12-year tax holiday intended to attract new industry.

When *Duffy's* returned to the airwaves in the fall of 1949 with recordings sent in from Puerto Rico, the show had a new sponsor, Blatz Brewing Company, which eventually caused some trouble for NBC. Some stations could not or would not allow beer advertising, and some that allowed beer would not accept the accompanying wine trailer ads, causing a number of stations to drop the program entirely. During its last year, *Duffy's Tavern* relied on multiple sponsors, including Radio Corporation of America (RCA) Victor and Anacin.

At the very end of 1951, despite a temporary rise in ratings after the Puerto Rico move, *Duffy's Tavern* was cancelled. In 1954, a syndicated *Duffy's Tavern* television show appeared, starring Gardner as Archie and Alan Reed (the radio show's Clancy the Cop) as Finnegan, but reviews were strongly negative, and the program did not last. By that time, the tavern's style of humor was considered old-fashioned and long past its prime. During the 1940s, however, *Duffy's Tavern* had been one of the mainstays of radio comedy, and long before television's *Cheers* came along, Duffy's embodied "the place where everybody knows your name."

Cast

Archie the manager	Ed Gardner
Eddie the waiter	Eddie Green
Clifton Finnegan	Charlie Cantor
Miss Duffy	Shirley Booth (1940–43), Florence Halop (1943–44, 1948–49), Sandra Gould (1944–48), Sara Berner, Pauline Drake, Helen Eley, Gloria Erlanger, Margie Liszt, Helen Lynd, Connie Manning, Florence Robinson, Hazel Shermet, Doris Singleton
Clancy the cop	Alan Reed
Wilfred, Finnegan's little brother	Dickie Van Patten
Colonel Stoopnagle	F. Chase Taylor
Dolly Snaffle	Lurene Tuttle

Producer/Creator

Ed Gardner

Producers

Mitchell Benson, Rupert Lucas, Jack Roche, and Tony Sanford

Programming History

CBS	29 July 1940 (pilot aired on Forecast)–June 1942
NBC Blue	October 1942–June 1944
NBC	1944–52

Further Reading

Beatty, Jerome, "What's His Name?" *American Magazine* 136 (July 1943).

Hutchens, John K., "A Very Fine Joint," *New York Times* (23 November 1941).

Mooney, George A., "Talk of the Tavern," *New York Times* (6 April 1941).

"Negro History Week Citations Go to 18 for Aid to Race Relations," *New York Times* (11 February 1946).

"New York Hick," *Time* (21 June 1943).

Schumach, Murray, "Regarding Archie," *New York Times* (2 February 1947).

Williams, Richard L., "Duffy's Latin Tavern," *Life* (13 February 1950).

DORINDA HARTMANN

DXers/DXing
Tuning Distant Stations

DX is the telegrapher's abbreviation for "distance." It came into common use among early amateur radio operators to refer to those who concentrated on working with other operators at great distances. DXing continues as a focus of many modern-day amateurs.

The terms "DX" and "DXing" were also used among radio listeners. In broadcasting's earliest days, radio listeners were known as BCLs, for "broadcast listeners," and those BCLs who were interested in listening not for program content but for the thrill of hearing distant stations were called DXers. Their hobby was (and still is) known as DXing, and their goal was to hear as many stations, from the farthest locations, as possible.

For a time in the early 1920s, long-distance broadcast listening was popular with a large portion of the population. Radio—especially radio from distant places—was a new experience, and everyone wanted to see how far they could "get" with their equipment. However, as the novelty of radio wore off and network broadcasting started, DXing became the preserve mainly of the technically inclined and of hard-core distance aficionados.

Shortwave broadcasting would not come to the attention of most listening hobbyists until around 1924, and so in the United States most DXing before then was done on the standard broadcast (medium wave) band, with domestic stations the targets. The relatively small number of stations and the resulting absence of the channel blocking that is common today, coupled with the prevalence of daytime-only operations, made it possible for a conscientious, well-equipped night hound to hear a large number of the stations that were operating.

DXing's attraction was captured by journalist Charlotte Geer in her 1927 poem "Another One":

You may pick out an average young man
Who has nothing especial "agin it,"
And draw up a comfortable chair
And settle him in it.

Then you mention the call of the West
Thus tempting his spirit to roam
That he early may tire of nooks by the fire
The tame little voices of home.

When the chimes of the clock tinkle ten
The rest of the folks go to bed,
You must then take the youngster in hand
And fasten the phones on his head.

You must lead him and prod him by turns
He'll yawn and seem bored and forlorn
Till he hears that first call from the coast—
And behold a DXer is born.

The "call from the coast" refers to the ability of east-coast listeners, late at night and under the right conditions, to hear stations in California as outlets farther east signed off at local sundown.

Although pioneer radio fans built their own sets, as the number of DXers increased a distinct market was recognized by equipment manufacturers, and soon radios with special features for long-distance reception were being produced. The most important elements to good reception were sensitivity (the ability to pick up weak signals), selectivity (the ability to separate adjacent signals), and frequency readout (the ability to know what frequency the equipment is tuned to). To meet these needs and the like needs of the amateur radio operators, the communications receiver was developed. These receivers, which appeared beginning in 1933 and continue on the market today, emphasize technical capabilities rather than appearance or simplicity of operation. Among the principal early manufacturers of such sets were Hallicrafters, Hammarlund, and National. Today the major producers of high-quality, semiprofessional receivers include Drake, Icom, AOL, and Japan Radio Company.

With the discovery that shortwave signals could propagate around the globe, what had been, in the United States, largely a search for U.S., Canadian, and Caribbean stations on the standard broadcast band took on a worldwide flavor as DXers tried their hand at the shortwave frequencies. Many countries began international shortwave services, and domestic shortwave broadcasting became commonplace in many foreign countries as well, particularly those with large geographic areas to cover. These latter stations made particularly good DX targets. Some listeners also went outside the broadcasting frequencies, preferring to tune in to amateur radio operators; transmissions from ships, planes, and police; and other users of the shortwave spectrum.

The need for up-to-date station information led to the publication of magazines such as *Radio Index*, *All Wave Radio*, and *Official Short Wave Listener Magazine*. These publications were devoted either entirely or in part to DXing. Other magazines had special sections for long-distance radio enthusiasts. Clubs such as the Newark News Radio Club and the International DXers Alliance were formed, and periodic bulletins containing members' "loggings" and other DX information issued. Special broadcasts were scheduled over stations at times when they might not ordinarily be heard, and contests were held to compare DXing prowess.

Besides hearing the stations, many DXers collected QSLs. QSL is the telegraph abbreviation for the acknowledgment of receipt of a signal or a message. QSLs are cards or letters that stations issue to DXers, confirming that it was in fact their station that was heard, based on the listener's description of the programming. QSLs usually take the form of distinctive cards and letters containing information about the station and its location. Some DXers also make it a practice to make audio recordings of their DX catches and thus preserve their listening experiences.

Notwithstanding the common availability of local radio signals over even the simplest equipment, long-distance radio listening still has a devoted following. Although the pervasiveness of high-power, all-night broadcasting has made DXing on the broadcast band more difficult, on the shortwave bands the combination of improved receivers and higher-power transmitters has led to easier tuning and more reliable reception.

As a result, whereas DX was the main objective of long-distance radio enthusiasts during most of radio's developmental period, "shortwave listening"—listening for program content rather than distance—is often the purpose today. Some listeners follow particular specialties. On shortwave they may listen to clandestine radio stations; unlicensed pirate stations; or small stations from exotic parts of the world, such as Indonesia or the Andes. On the broadcast band, some listeners concentrate on domestic stations, whereas others focus on foreign broadcasters.

Although the number of DXers has declined over the years, there is still much truth in the observation made by radio pioneer Hugo Gernsback in 1926: "I can not imagine any greater thrill," he wrote, "than that which comes to me when I listen, as I often do, to a station thousands of miles away. It is the greatest triumph yet achieved by mind over matter."

See also: Ham Radio; Shortwave Radio

Further Reading

Berg, Jerome S., *On the Short Waves, 1923–1945: Broadcast Listening in the Pioneer Days of Radio*, Jefferson, North Carolina: McFarland, 1999.

DeSoto, Clinton B., *Two Hundred Meters and Down: The Story of Amateur Radio*, West Hartford, Connecticut: American Radio Relay League, 1936.

Magne, Lawrence, editor, *Passport to World Band Radio*, Penn's Park, Pennsylvania: International Broadcasting Services (annual; 1984–).

JEROME S. BERG

E

EARLY WIRELESS
Induction and Conduction before 1900

Although Marconi, Lodge, Popov, and their contemporaries were the first electricians to make practical use of electromagnetic waves for communication, varied forms of wireless telegraphy had existed for 50 years before their work at the end of the 19th century. Most of the wireless inventors of this early era were Americans.

Henry and Morse

Joseph Henry, at Princeton University, conducted numerous experiments with induction, or the tendency of a primary electric current in a conductor to stimulate a secondary current in another conductor nearby. During one group of experiments in 1842, which Henry called "induction at a distance," he measured secondary current as far as 200 feet away from the primary circuit. Although the effects were more pronounced with the instantaneous discharge of a Leyden jar (electrostatic induction) at the primary circuit, they were also present when a continuous current passed through a coil (electromagnetic induction). Henry also noted that the wireless electricity seemed to oscillate, but he had no instruments sensitive enough to study this phenomenon. Neither Henry nor his students used induction for telegraphy, but his methods and results were well known to scientists on both sides of the Atlantic.

In the same year, Samuel F.B. Morse, using different technology, devised a working wireless telegraph. Having failed at submarine telegraphy when a ship's anchor hooked and cut the cable, Morse came up with a novel solution to the problem. By then, electricians knew how to use a natural conductor, like earth or water, as the return link to complete an electrical circuit. Morse reasoned that the same natural conductor could replace the wire in the link between transmitter and receiver as well. By attaching the ends of the wires leading from the battery and telegraph key to metal plates, doing the same with wires from a galvanometer, and then submerging the sets of plates on opposite banks, Morse successfully sent a message across a canal some 80 feet wide. The next year, 1843, his assistants sent messages a mile across the mouth of the Susquehanna River.

Morse soon became preoccupied with building a wired telegraph system and never applied for a patent on the wireless scheme. About ten years later, however, James Bowman Lindsay, a Scottish schoolteacher, applied the same natural conduction technology to the task. Apparently Lindsay was unaware of Morse's prior work. By using larger metal plates spaced more widely apart, he increased transmission distance to two miles across the River Tay at Dundee. Lindsay received British patent 1,242 for this invention in 1854, but he failed to raise enough capital to build a prospective transatlantic installation.

Loomis and Ward

American dentist Mahlon Loomis, of Washington, D.C., devised a wireless telegraph system using the upper atmosphere as one conductor, the earth as the other, and the difference in electric potential between the two as the power supply. In 1866 he raised two kites, attached to grounded wires, from mountains in northern Virginia and transmitted a signal between them, a distance of 18 miles. Loomis later adapted this apparatus for telegraphy and, he claimed, telephony. The most interesting facet of this invention was that it worked best when the kites were at the same altitude, leading some historians to speculate that Loomis had hit upon the principle of syntony, or tuned resonance. Although he received U.S. patent 129,971 in 1872, Loomis failed to get a requested appropriation from Congress, and several potential groups of investors went broke in the numerous financial panics that followed the U.S. Civil War.

Another U.S. patent for wireless telegraphy, number 126,356, issued to William Henry Ward of Auburn, New York, actually preceded the Loomis patent by three months. Ward was an author of religious tracts and a vigorous promoter of his own inventions, which included naval signal flags, bullet-making machines, bomb shell fuses, and pomade for the hair. Loomis had made Ward's acquaintance in the late 1850s when Ward agreed to take a set of Loomis-patented false teeth under consignment to a trade show in Europe. Because Loomis furnished no illustrations or model with his patent application, it is difficult to tell how much similarity existed between the two inventions. The Ward wireless telegraph, however, seems to be based on the absurd idea that convection currents in the atmosphere would carry the electric signal to the receiver. Neither system found a ready market.

The 1870s were a busy decade for electricians, whether they were scientists, engineers, or tinkering inventors. Laboratories large and small sprang up in the United States and Europe for both educational and commercial purposes. The new professional societies, as well as academic and trade publications, facilitated communication, so electricians knew what other electricians were doing. Although there was scant progress in wireless telegraphy, there were several interesting events.

Various experiments, including those by Elihu Thompson and Thomas Edison in the United States and by David Hughes in Great Britain, suggested the existence of electromagnetic waves, as predicted by James Clerk Maxwell. Edison called them the "etheric force." Hughes unwittingly built a complete radio system, with a sparking coil as a transmitter and a carbon microphone as a coherer, or receiver. He gave up these experiments, however, when directors of the Royal Society visited his lab

to witness a demonstration and assured him that the effects were due to induction alone.

Wireless Telegraphy

In 1878 Alexander Graham Bell attempted to build a Morse-type wireless telephone using water as a natural conductor. He tested this device the next year with only limited success on the Potomac River near Washington, D.C. When he learned that John Trowbridge at Harvard was pursuing similar research, Bell dropped that idea in favor of one more promising—sending a voice signal on a beam of reflected light.

With a thin diaphragm of reflective mica at the mouthpiece, the device captured light waves from the sun, modulated the light as sound waves moved the diaphragm, and reflected the beam toward the receiver. The receiver was a parabolic reflector coated with silver and aimed at a piece of selenium, a natural photoelectric transducer. Once the selenium converted the light to electricity, the signal traveled to a regular telephone receiver. Bell called it the Photophone, received U.S. patent 235,199 in 1880, and exhibited the device widely in both the United States and Europe. Later experiments proved that the device worked with less expensive lamp-black substituting for the selenium and with any form of radiant energy. The Photophone then became known as the Radiophone, the first application of the term *radio* to wireless communication.

Although European electricians were captivated by the device, and Bell himself thought it a greater invention than the telephone, American Telephone and Telegraph (AT&T) saw no commercial possibility and soon ceased its development. The company continued to exhibit the Photophone as a novelty through the St. Louis World's Fair of 1904, but Bell was so disgusted that he gave his original model to the Smithsonian Institution and halted all active involvement with the company that had once borne his name and was based on his patents.

Amos Dolbear, another early telephone pioneer, became interested in wireless telephony by accident. While working in his lab at Tufts College in 1882, he noticed that he was still hearing sounds from a receiver, even though the wire to the transmitter on the other side of the room was disconnected. Upon examination, he determined that the signal was traveling by electrostatic induction. Through experimentation, Dolbear built a wireless telephone system that employed grounded aerials at both transmitter and receiver and worked well at distances of up to a mile. He demonstrated the invention by transmitting both voice and music at scientific conferences in the United States, Canada, and Europe, receiving U.S. patent 350,299 in 1886. Dolbear's transmitter was capable of generating electromagnetic waves and was in many respects similar to Marconi's of a decade later, but the receiver lacked any device to detect radio waves. Dolbear never attempted to sell his wireless telephone.

In Great Britain during the 1880s, both William Preece and Willoughby Smith developed functional wireless telegraphs to transmit across relatively short distances. They used both natural conduction and induction technologies to solve practical problems such as how to communicate with offshore islands and lighthouses and with workers in a coal mine. Preece, an engineer at the British Post Office, had been interested in wireless since he witnessed Lindsay's work in 1854. Later he became Marconi's chief advocate with the British government.

Moving Telegraphy

The possibility of communicating instantly by telegraph with moving trains generated substantial interest in the United States. William Wiley Smith, a telephone office manager, devised an electrostatic wireless telegraph that used existing lines running beside the tracks and received U.S. patent 247,127 in 1881. Although Smith's invention did not work very well, his partner, Ezra Gilliland, was a childhood friend of Thomas Edison. Three years later, Gilliland convinced Edison to buy the patent, improve the technology, and promote it to the rapidly growing railroad industry as a safety and convenience appliance. Gilliland and Edison's interest in railroad telegraphy grew when they learned that another inventor, Lucius Phelps of New York, had just applied for a patent on a similar system. Phelps, moreover, was preparing to demonstrate a working model in New York City during February 1885. Edison quickly filed a new patent application based on improvements to the prior Smith patent. The Patent Office called the two applications into interference hearings. Meanwhile, Granville Woods, a black inventor from Cincinnati, filed still a third application for a railroad telegraph system. Once again, the Patent Office declared the Woods and Phelps applications to be in interference.

In a series of hearings that ended in 1887, Woods was the ultimate victor. He proved that as early as 1881 he had shown sketches and models of his invention to friends in his neighborhood. Shortly thereafter, he had lost his job and contracted smallpox, delaying his progress. After reading about the Phelps demonstration in *Scientific American*, he quickly gathered his old notes and models and went to his lawyer. In the meantime, the patent examiner determined that the Smith patent, controlled by Edison, had no priority because it used electrostatic induction, whereas the Phelps and Woods inventions used electromagnetic. After this ruling, Edison dropped out of the hearings and merged efforts with Phelps.

Woods received several U.S. patents for his invention, beginning with number 371,241, and Phelps did likewise, starting with number 334,186. But all of this activity was in vain, for the railroads had no interest in wireless telegraphy at that time. With no laws compelling safety or emergency communication improvements, they saw the technology as added expense without compensatory revenue. So none of the inventors profited. Eventually, Edison modified his application and received U.S. patent 465,971 in 1891. He sold the patent to Marconi some years later for a nominal sum. After the failure to market the railroad telegraph, interest in wireless waned in the United States until after Marconi brought his system to the America's Cup races of 1899.

In a widely read article of 1891, John Trowbridge concluded that the technologies of Henry and Morse were inefficient for long-distance wireless communication and, with no tuning mechanism, were limited to a single message at a time. The last champion of natural conduction and induction wireless was probably Nathan Stubblefield, a farmer from Kentucky who learned about electricity by reading *Scientific American* and *Electrical World*. Stubblefield demonstrated an induction wireless telephone for neighbors as early as 1892. He generated considerable publicity in 1902 with a natural conduction wireless telephone that he displayed to enthusiastic crowds in Washington, D.C., and Philadelphia. One remarkable feature of this system was its ability to broadcast a signal to multiple receivers simultaneously. Stubblefield intended to use it to disseminate news and weather information, but he was the victim of a stock fraud scheme that left him destitute. By the time he received U.S. patent 887,357 in 1908 for his induction system, superior technology existed. But he became very paranoid that others were seeking to profit from his work, and he eventually died of starvation in 1928.

Landell and Tesla

Two other inventors had the opportunity to develop wireless communication by electromagnetic waves prior to Marconi but failed to do so. Roberto Landell de Moura, a Catholic priest from Brazil, studied physics at the Gregorian University in

Rome while he prepared for the priesthood. When he returned to Brazil in 1886, Landell set up a laboratory and began electrical experiments. His interest turned to wireless. He built acoustic telephones, a model of Bell's Photophone, and, soon after he learned of Hertz's and Branly's work, his own electromagnetic wave transmitter and receiver. Then he combined the three into one multifunction wireless telephone system. By 1893 Landell was sending messages over distances of five miles. Then, two years later, a powerful bishop witnessed a demonstration. He was so unnerved by the voices coming from nowhere that he declared the apparatus the work of the devil and ordered Landell to stop his work.

Shortly thereafter, fanatics broke into Landell's laboratory, destroyed the apparatus, and set fire to the building. It took Landell five years to regroup, but he eventually received Brazilian patent 3,279 in 1900 and traveled to the United States to pursue patents and development. Hampered by poor legal advice, illness, and inadequate knowledge of the U.S. patent system, Landell nevertheless persisted and received three U.S. patents, beginning with number 771,917 in 1904. By then Marconi and others controlled the market for radio.

Like Landell, Nikola Tesla was trained in physics at a European university. He came to the United States in 1884 to work first for Edison and then for Westinghouse. In his work with high-frequency alternating currents, Tesla discovered that the alternators also generated continuous electromagnetic waves that could be used to transmit signals. He demonstrated this phenomenon as early as 1891 but made no practical application of it until he built a radio-controlled toy boat, for which he received U.S. patent 613,809 in 1898. The next year, he established a laboratory in Colorado Springs, Colorado, from which he intended to send wireless messages to an international exposition in Paris in early 1900. But in the midst of his radio experiments, Tesla became fascinated with the possibility for wireless distribution of electric power through the earth itself and devoted most of the rest of his life to devising methods to accomplish that goal.

Further Reading

Appleby, Thomas, *Mahlon Loomis: Inventor of Radio*, Washington, D.C.: s.n., 1967.

Blake, George G., *History of Radio Telegraphy and Telephony*, London: Radio Press, 1926; reprint, New York: Arno Press, 1974.

Dunlap, Orrin Elmer, *Radio's 100 Men of Science: Biographical Narratives of Pathfinders in Electronics and Television*, New York and London: Harper, 1944.

Fahie, J.J., *A History of Wireless Telegraphy*, London and Edinburgh: Blackwood, and New York: Dodd Mead, 1899; 2nd edition, 1901; reprint, New York: Arno Press and The New York Times, 1971.

Hawks, Ellison, *Pioneers of Wireless*, London: Methuen, 1927; reprint, New York: Arno Press, 1974.

Lochte, Robert, "Reducing the Risk: Woods, Phelps, Edison, and the Railway Telegraph," *Timeline* 16, no. 1 (JanuaryFebruary 1999).

Sarkar, Tapan K., Robert Mailloux, Arthur A. Oliner, Magdalena Salazar-Palma and Dipak N. Sengupta, editors, *History of Wireless*. New York: Wiley-Interscience, 2006.

Seifer, Marc J., *Wizard: The Life and Times of Nikola Tesla*, Secaucus, New Jersey: Carol, 1996.

Sivowitch, E.N., "A Technological Survey of Broadcasting's 'Pre-History,' 1876–1920," *Journal of Broadcasting* 14 (Winter 1969–70).

ROBERT HENRY LOCHTE

EARPLAY
Public Radio Drama Series

Earplay was an anthology series created in an effort to produce a variety of U.S. radio dramas in the late 1970s and early 1980s. Centered at radio station WHA in Madison, Wisconsin, it involved numerous prominent playwrights and scores of actors more than two decades after the last major commercial radio dramas had left the air. *Earplay* was a leading source of drama for member stations of the burgeoning National Public Radio (NPR) network.

The series began in 1971 as a grant proposal submitted to the Corporation for Public Broadcasting by project director Karl Schmidt, a University of Wisconsin professor and station manager of WHA. Schmidt had begun his radio career as a juvenile actor in 1941 and was involved as an actor and director in commercial, public, and armed forces radio. In the 1960s he produced a series of stereo dramas under the auspices of the National Center for Audio Experimentation. In many ways, station WHA, with a long history of producing radio drama, was an ideal place for the development of new forms of that genre. For 30 years the station's School of the Air applied the techniques and forms of drama for instructional purposes. In the early 1970s, WHA had particularly strong ties to Canadian actors and writers, BBC writers and directors, and producers from Radio Nederland.

Under the terms of its grant, the primary purpose of *Earplay* was "to develop drama in audio forms which are intelligible, enjoyable, and useful to more, rather than fewer, people." A second purpose was "the establishment of a testing ground for playwrights and plays." (In the project's latter days, its producers would increasingly disagree as to whether intelligibility or experimentation should predominate.) The creators of *Earplay* proposed an emphasis on original dramas—works by new playwrights that did not demand long attention spans and had strong plot lines, a high degree of intelligibility, enjoyable listening potential, and relevance to life in the United States in the 1970s. There was a conscious effort to "compete with substantial ambient noise levels in the listening circumstance" by emphasizing short dramas (usually less than half an hour long) and avoiding reliance upon subtle sound effects.

Between 1975 and 1979, *Earplay* produced more than 150 radio dramas ranging in length from a few minutes to more than an hour. During those years the dramas were distributed to public radio stations on long-playing records. After 1981 the medium was reel-to-reel tape as part of *NPR Playhouse*. Later the plays were repackaged in half-hour installments under the title *Earplay Weekday Theatre*.

Earplay dramas sounded very different from radio plays of the 1930s, 1940s, and 1950s. Most of them were in stereo, and the acting had a closer, more intimate quality. In some cases the language also was very different and prompted advisories to subscribing stations. In the broadcasts of both Archibald MacLeish's *J.B.* and Edward Albee's *Listening*, for example, there were a half-dozen warnings about "sensitive material." Another departure from U.S. radio tradition was the variable length of *Earplay* dramas, although they were often packaged in one- or two-hour blocks.

Like traditional radio dramas, *Earplay* productions typically involved six or fewer actors, and they often emphasized narration. In most cases the story line was straightforward, but occasionally the plays were more in the realm of the "sound collage."

In their preface to the 1979 *Earplay* program information, the producers noted that the 1979 season reflected a commitment to "give the most promising American playwrights an opportunity to speak to a national audience through the unique medium of radio." During that same year, *Earplay* received both the Peabody Award and the Armstrong Award. The dramas were produced in various locations, including New York, Los Angeles, and Chicago. Most of the postproduction work took place at WHA; the technical director was Marv Nonn.

Among the playwrights commissioned to create *Earplay* dramas were some of the most distinguished of the day: John Mortimer, Donald Barthelme, Larry Shue, Vincent Canby, Alan Ayckburn, Gamble

Rogers, John Gardner, Anne Leaton, Athol Fugard, Tim O'Brien, and Archibald MacLeish. Robert Anderson's play I *Never Sang for My Father* was later adapted into a major motion picture. Other plays went on to success on Broadway: *The Water Engine* by David Mamet, *Lightning* by Edward Albee, and *Wings* by Arthur Kopit, which won the Prix Italia. In order to defray the expense of involving major playwrights, *Earplay* initiated the International Commissioning Group with drama producers in England, Ireland, West Germany, Norway, Sweden, and Denmark, who added rights fees for their countries to *Earplay*'s U.S. fees to provide payments attractive to major playwrights.

Although *Earplay* was carried by a significant number of public radio stations, many years after the series ended Karl Schmidt reflected that its demise came in part from its inclination to raise difficult issues without offering answers, so that the working person coming home after a tiring day would be inclined to pass over them in favor of more refreshing fare. During the late 1970s and early 1980s, Schmidt turned *Earplay* into a series, partly because series were more economical to produce than individual dramas, and partly because he found that many writers preferred structural guidelines to the indefinite length of the earlier format. In order to put *Earplay* resources to the most efficient use, Schmidt stipulated that the episodes in the series were to be approximately half narration and half dialogue. They were: *A Canticle for Leibowitz* (16 half-hours), based on the science fiction novel by Walter Miller, Jr.; *Happiness*, Anne Leaton's multipart radio drama based on the musings of a middle-aged Texas woman; and *Something Singing*, Christian Hamilton's play about abolitionist Amos Bronson Alcott—all of which were distributed through National Public Radio. Contracts allowed three years of use in any and all noncommercial stations in the U.S., with a three-year renewal option that was not exercised.

See also: WHA and Wisconsin Public Radio

Actors

Jay Fitts, Pat King, Carol Cowan, Karl Schmidt, and Martha Van Cleef, Meryl Streep, Vincent Gardenia, Laurence Luckinbill, Brock Peters, Lurene Tuttle, Leon Ames, etc.

Producers/Directors

Karl Schmidt, Howard Gelman, Daniel Freudenberger

Programming History

NPR   1972–86

NORMAN GILLILAND

EASY ACES
Comedy Program

The Easy Aces was a comedy written by Goodman Ace that first aired in 1930 and enjoyed a 15-year run on the Columbia Broadcasting System (CBS) and National Broadcasting Company (NBC) networks. The show was known for simple plot lines that allowed Jane Ace to contort the English language inexhaustibly, while her usually bemused but sometimes horrified husband supplied witty commentary. Like *The Burns and Allen Show, The Easy Aces* relied on the device of a scattered, illogical wife flummoxing the logic and control of her husband. Despite the current anachronistic, even sexist ring of the stereotypical scatterbrained wife, the character had thrived in vaudeville and was still common in mainstream comedy programming well past the middle of the 20th century.

Born in Kansas City, Missouri on 15 January 1899, Goodman Ace's writing talents led him to the *Kansas City Journal-Post* after a stint at haberdashery and other odd jobs. Jane Epstein, also from Kansas City, was born to a local clothing merchant on 12 June 1905. By the time they married in 1922, Ace was regularly exercising his wit in his weekly column of drama and movie reviews for the *Journal-Post*. For instance, while reviewing a play billed as a scenic extravaganza, he offered the comment that the "sets were beautiful—both of them." Since 1922 the paper had sent news to local station KMBC via live feed from a cramped studio off the news room. By the late 1920s Ace's growing interest in radio caused him to approach KMBC's station manager Arthur Church with the proposal for a 15-minute program entitled *The Movie Man*. Church granted Ace the show at the rate of $10 a week, money that supplemented his income from the *Journal-Post*. As a critic in the newspaper and on the air, Ace met many of the vaudevillians and celebrities who performed in Kansas City. He counted George Burns, Gracie Allen, Groucho Marx, Fred Allen, and Jack Benny among his friends, and even contributed jokes to some of Benny's early radio shows.

Ultimately, however, it was chance, not personal acquaintance, that led to the birth of *The Easy Aces* and Ace's initial success on radio. One Friday in late 1930 his broadcast ended, but the following program (which was to feature Heywood Broun)

failed to come through on the network feed. A technician signaled Ace to ad-lib. Jane happened to have been watching from the lobby, so Ace motioned her in, introduced her as his roommate, and the couple bantered fluidly for 15 minutes. They spoke of a local man recently murdered while playing a game of bridge, and during a break Ace instructed Jane as follows: "You be dumb; I'll explain the finer points of bridge, and why murder is sometimes justified." Once on the air she fell effortlessly into character, asking "Would you care to shoot a game of bridge, dear?" and later wondering why "Whenever I lose, you're always my partner."

The audience responded favorably to the broadcast, prompting a local drugstore chain to offer the Aces an initial 13-week contract for two weekly shows. After this contract expired, the advertising firm Blackett-Sample-Humert (BSH) shopped the show around, quickly selling it to the advertisers for Lavoris mouthwash. During this period, the program was broadcast on CBS from Chicago, where Ace negotiated a weekly salary of $500. Foreshadowing future clashes with sponsors, Ace made light of a Lavoris executive's contention that the program had aired five minutes late one evening. The sponsor responded by canceling the show. The Aces then moved to New York, where Frank Hummert of BSH secured the sponsorship that allowed the show to continue.

The initial improvised broadcast established many of the enduring characteristics of *The Easy Aces*. Although the bridge game was eventually abandoned, plots remained fairly uncomplicated. Largely character-driven, typical shows featured Jane visiting a psychiatrist, seeing an astrologer, or serving on a jury. She was the central character from the beginning and her relaxed delivery was the key to the program's continuing popularity. From the beginning, too, Ace's asides imbued the show with an air of sophistication and witty urbanity. The Aces' characters were clearly identified as upper-class and urban—he played a highly paid advertising executive. As Ace later phrased it, they lived "in the typical little eastern town, New York City: population eight million…give or take one."

Jane's misspoken words and phrases, referred to as "janeacesims," were responsible for most of the laughs on the program. Among her weekly linguistic slips were statements that she feared "casting asparagus" on a friend's character, had "worked her head to the bone," made "insufferable friends," and had relatives "too humorous to mention." More often than not, the malapropisms seemed to make a satiric point, such as: "Congress is still in season," or "I got up at the crank of dawn." The seeming deliberateness of her linguistic twists was enhanced by her sober, deadpan delivery. Context might also lead listeners to believe that her deranged phrasing was occasionally intentional. For instance, when Ace got her brother a menial job, she asked him if he would receive a "swindle chair" like the one Ace had. Sometimes the mood was darker, as in "We are all cremated equal."

Although the show appealed to radio insiders and sustained a loyal following, it did not receive high ratings. Ace was proud of the show's low ratings and even bragged about them in the print advertisements for the show. He was disturbed, however, by sponsor Anacin's attempt to encroach on the program's autonomy. When the drug's parent company complained about a change in the music on the show, Ace fired off a letter criticizing Anacin's flimsy packaging. As he later put it, "They thought up a clever answer to that, which was 'You're fired.'"

After losing its sponsorship, *The Easy Aces* spent two years in syndicated reruns until it was revived as *Mr. Ace and Jane*, a 30-minute format with a live audience, a full orchestra, and a larger cast. The show also had a brief run on television in the 1949–50 season, but it did not translate well to that medium. By this time Goodman Ace had started writing for Danny Kaye's television program. In later years he would continue working in television, most notably for Perry Como and Milton Berle. Jane Ace's activities in broadcasting tapered off, and after a stint as *Jane Ace, Disc Jockey* in 1952, she became largely inactive in the field. Jane Ace died in New York on 11 November 1974. Goodman died on 18 March 1982.

See also: Comedy; *George Burns and Gracie Allen Show*

Cast

Ace	Goodman Ace
Jane	Jane Ace
Paul Sherwood, Jane's brother	Leon Janey
Marge	Mary Hunter
Mrs. Benton	Peggy Allenby
Betty	Ethel Blume (1939)
Carl	Alfred Ryder (1939)
Neil Williams	Martin Gabel (1939)
Laura the maid	Helene Dumas
Miss Thomas	Ann Thomas
Announcers	Ford Bond (1930–45), Ken Roberts (1948)

Producer/Creator

Goodman Ace

Programming History

KMBC Kansas City	October 1930–1931
WGN Chicago	late 1931–February 1932,
CBS	March 1932–January 1935
NBC	February 1935–October 1942,
CBS	October 1954–January 1945
as *Mr. Ace and Jane*	February 1948–May 1949

Television

December 1949–June 1950

Futher Reading

Ace, Goodman, *Ladies and Gentlemen, Easy Aces*, Garden City, New York: Doubleday, 1970.
Gaver, Jack, and Dave Stanley, *There's Laughter in the Air! Radio's Top Comedians and Their Best Shows*, New York: Greenberg, 1945.
Singer, Mark, "Goody," *The New Yorker* (4 April 1977).
Wertheim, Arthur Frank, *Radio Comedy*, New York: Oxford University Press, 1979.

BRYAN CORNELL

EASY LISTENING/BEAUTIFUL MUSIC FORMAT

The term *easy listening* refers to a program format characterized by the presentation of orchestral and small-combo instrumental music intended to elicit moods of relaxation and tranquility among its target audience of older adult listeners. Vocal music is intermixed and may include solo artist and choral recordings made popular by recognized personalities as well as "cover" renditions of original performances. Easy listening achieved its greatest popularity in the 1970s and was broadcast predominantly by FM stations. It was common for listeners in major markets to have from three to five such stations from which to choose. In the early 1980s, stations began to defect from easy listening in favor of formats with the youthful orientation advertisers were seeking. The format's popularity declined throughout the 1990s, to the point that easy listening stations by 2000 attracted less than one percent of the radio audience.

Origins

The origin of the phrase *easy listening* is undetermined. Its predecessors, "good music" and "beautiful music," were format descriptors popularized in the 1950s and 1960s by FM stations seeking differentiation from the Top 40 and middle of the road formats that dominated AM radio. Stations initially offered instrumental-laden good music programming to retail business operators on a subscription basis as a means of inducing customer relaxation. Good music programming in the 1950s was transmitted via the FM subcarrier frequency, which precluded reception by the general public. Growing listener interest led broadcasters to shift the good music format to their FM main channels in the early 1960s. The good music format subsequently evolved into beautiful music.

Stations that pioneered the good music format in the late 1950s included several noted AM outlets. KIXL in Dallas; WOR in New York City; WPAT in Paterson, New Jersey; and KABL in Oakland-San Francisco, all defined the easy listening presentation and accelerated the format's popularity. KIXL programmer Lee Seagall emphasized the importance of matching music tempo with the hour of the day—upbeat during the morning but downtempo, soft, and romantic in the evening. Gordon McLendon's KABL relied upon interstitial poetry selections to create distinction. Two evening specialty programs—WOR's *Music from Studio X* and the *Gaslight Revue* on WPAT—influenced WDVR Station Manager/Program Director Marlin Taylor in 1963 to extend the format on this stand-alone FM station to around-the-clock presentation for Philadelphia listeners.

Pairing good music with the FM medium was fortuitous for performers, broadcasters, and listeners. When the Federal Communications Commission directed FM broadcasters in the mid-1960s to curtail the practice of simulcasting the programming of their AM sister stations, this format emerged as the de facto FM format standard. FM broadcasting, in contrast with AM, exhibited the sonic advantages of high-fidelity reproduction and stereophonic sound. The subtle nuances of orchestral performances, diminished by the process of low-fidelity, monaural AM transmission, sprang from FM receivers with astonishing clarity and accuracy. After years of languishing in the shadow of AM radio, the FM medium began to assert its identity as a separate and technically superior mode of broadcasting.

What It Is

Industry followers generally regard the easy listening format as a beautiful music derivative. Beautiful music is a program format featuring soft instrumental and vocal recordings directed to a target audience of predominantly middle-aged female listeners. Lush, melodic, and subdued in its presentation, the format is carefully planned and executed to offer listeners a quiet musical refuge for escaping from everyday distractions. Programmers regard announcer chatter as intrusive and tend to limit the spoken word to brief news reports, time checks, and weather forecasts. Commercial interruptions are similarly minimized, and the construction of message content reflects the format's low-key delivery approach. The objective is to provide listeners with a background musical environment that complements their daily activities.

Beautiful music resides in the development of Muzak, a registered trademark denoting the mood-enhancing background music service pioneered in the 1920s by Brigadier General George Owen Squier. Muzak programming was piped via leased telephone circuits into America's factories to stimulate productivity and into retail stores and restaurants to elevate patrons' spirits.

Programmers for beautiful music and easy listening founded their presentations in the lush, layered string arrangements popularized by the Andre Kostelanetz, Percy Faith, and Mantovani orchestras. Trade publications began using the format labels interchangeably during the mid-1970s. But musicologists cite several distinguishing characteristics between the formats. Beautiful music delved more deeply into the repertoire of 20th-century popular music composers than did easy listening. Tunes by Cole Porter, Jerome Kern, and Hoagy Carmichael—pop music's "standards"—were common fixtures on beautiful music playlists. In contrast, easy listening stations adopted a more contemporary music viewpoint, favoring a greater infusion of fresher sounds. Tunes by Burt Bacharach, Henry Mancini, and John Lennon and Paul McCartney were commonly integrated into the presentation.

Greater distinction between the formats was evidenced by programmers' approaches to vocal music, in terms of both style and quantity. Performances by "traditional" vocalists, such as Perry Como, Andy Williams, and Frank Sinatra, as well as the cover arrangements produced by artists including the Ray Conniff and Anita Kerr choral ensembles, were sparingly interspersed into the presentation of beautiful music. Easy listening stations, which tended to blend instrumentals and vocals on a more proportionate basis, gravitated toward the pop sounds of AM Top 40. Some of the "softer"-sounding hits by Elton John, Billy Joel, the Carpenters, and others qualified for airplay. Up-tempo performances, particularly those punctuated by intrusive guitar licks or intensive percussion, were generally passed over by easy listening programmers.

Key Producers

James Schulke, a former advertising executive and FM radio proponent, established SRP in 1968 to syndicate an approach to the good music presentation that he termed *beautiful music*. Capitalizing on the good music format's mood-music heritage, SRP vice president/creative director Phil Stout constructed each quarter-hour of programming on a foundation of lush orchestral and vocal arrangements of popular music standards. One nuance in execution—the segue—differentiated the beautiful music from the good music format. Stout insisted that transitions between recordings flow in such a manner as to preserve the emotions elicited in listeners by the tempo, rhythm, and sound texture of the performances.

Schulke marketed Stout's concept as the "matched flow" approach to format execution. It was not uncommon for Stout to expend up to two days' effort to assemble a single hour of SRP programming. Collectively, the SRP team's insistence on musical cohesiveness and technical integrity proved successful in attracting and holding listeners. SRP's beautiful music format typically surpassed other formats in Arbitron's "time-spent-listening" measurements, a desirable position for stations catering to advertisers who sought message frequency over reach.

Bonneville was founded in 1970 by Marlin R. Taylor, a veteran programmer who pioneered easy listening on Philadelphia's WDVR in 1963. Taylor meshed a keen music sensibility with an adroit understanding of listeners' tastes in transforming the low-rated WRFM into New York City's number-one FM outlet. Success with WRFM inspired Taylor to launch Bonneville as the vehicle for extending his programming expertise to a clientele that grew in the early 1980s to approximately 180 stations.

Beautiful music prospered in the politically conservative 1970s because its musical message resonated with a nation of silent-majority listeners who had outgrown Top 40 and had never connected with progressive rock, country and western, or ethnic formats. By the end of that decade, more than a dozen syndicators, including Peters Productions, Century 21, and KalaMusic, competed with Bonneville and SRP for affiliates and listeners. As a result, it was common for two or three stations in each of the top 25 markets to vie for a share of the audience.

Beautiful music stations were unable to sustain the momentum, however. "Light" and "soft" adult contemporary (AC) stations, which burgeoned in the latter half of the 1970s, steadily siphoned beautiful music's target listener, the middle aged female, during the 1980s. In a sense, both beautiful music and light AC were easy listening formats (see Josephson, 1986). Unlike beautiful music, which cultivated reputations with listeners as a background music companion, light AC was vocal-intensive, personality driven, and foreground focused in its presentation.

Switching from beautiful music to light AC improved the revenues of many stations. Advertising revenue erosion for beautiful music stations was attributed to the fact that its aging audience was spending a disproportionately low percentage of its disposable income on consumer goods. Light AC stations, whose demographic profiles skewed toward younger female adults, delivered the audience that had become most desired by national advertisers.

During a 1980 industry conference, broadcasters reached general agreement about the perceptual distinctions listeners had drawn between stations that positioned themselves as either easy listening or beautiful music outlets. In an effort to shed negative images of beautiful music as passive, background radio, broadcasters confirmed easy listening as a more appropriate positioning descriptor. The phrase *easy listening*, they agreed, evoked positive and active feelings of involvement by listeners with stations.

Decline

It was a calculated decision made by an industry about to confront a period of dramatic change in listener preferences. Easy listening/beautiful music, which Arbitron reported as radio's number-one format in 1979, slipped into second position behind adult contemporary the following year. The remainder of the 1980s proved to be a period of redefinition for easy listening.

Two distinct waves of defection by instrumental mood music stations occurred, and each was precipitated by advertising industry pressures for stations to deliver younger, more upscale listeners. The first wave, in 1982–83, swept through the major markets. Where multiple easy listening outlets had once competed, now the lower-rated easy listening stations moved in other programming directions. Some of these stations subtly shifted toward soft AC, excising the instrumental music in favor of full-time vocals. Others pursued ratings success with entirely different formats. A second wave of abandonment occurred in 1988–89, when most of the remaining stations vacated easy listening. Traditional, "standards" inspired instrumental music virtually disappeared from the airwaves.

The descriptive phrase *easy listening* became more indefinite in the radio lexicon of the 1990s and 2000s, subsuming not only soft AC but the new age and smooth jazz genres as well. An emphasis on announcer personality and other formatics (sports play-by-play, traffic reports, and promotions) aligned easy listening with other mainstream music formats more closely than ever. As format fragmentation increased during this decade, the phrase *easy listening* generally gave way to variations on the soft AC theme.

See also: Adult Contemporary Format; Formats Defining Radio Programming; Middle of the Road Format; Soft Rock Format

Further Reading

"Beautiful Music, Beautiful Numbers," *Broadcasting* (21 July 1975).
"Beautiful Music's Tag May Change," *Billboard* (6 September 1980).
Borzillo, Carrie, "Beautiful Music Gets a Makeover," *Billboard* (27 March 1993).
Eberly, Philip K., *Music in the Air: America's Changing Tastes in Popular Music, 1920–1980*, New York: Hastings House, 1982.
"Hard Times for Easy Listening: List of Stations Dropping Format Grows," *Broadcasting* (28 November 1988).
Harris, Lee, "A Beautiful Opportunity to Resurrect a Format,' *Radio World* (9 July 1997).
Josephson, Sanford, "Easy Listening vs. 'Soft' Contemporary: Shades of Gray," *Television/Radio Age* (17 March 1986).
Knopper, Steve, "Beautiful Music Gone, Not Forgotten," *Billboard* (21 June 1997).
Lanza, Joseph, *Elevator Music: A Surreal History of Muzak, Easy-Listening, and Other Moodsong*, New York: St. Martin's Press, 1994; London: Quartet, 1995.
"Marlin Taylor Gets Beautiful Ratings with 'Beautiful Music,'" *Television/Radio Age* (7 September 1970).
Opsitnik, James, "Monday Memo," *Broadcasting* (5 November 1990).
Patton, John E., "Easy Listening Shake Out," *Television/Radio Age* (14 March 1983).
Ross, Sean, "Radio Takes Hard Look at Easy Format," *Billboard* (3 December 1988).
Routt, Edd, James B. McGrath, and Frederic A. Weiss, *The Radio Format Conundrum*, New York: Hastings House, 1978.
"A Sour Note for Beautiful Music," *Broadcasting* (23 August 1982).
"Tailored Radio from Marlin Taylor," *Broadcasting* (11 June 1979).

BRUCE MIMS

EDGAR BERGEN AND CHARLIE MCCARTHY SHOW
Comedy Variety Program

Although few would have guessed it when the program first appeared on the air, a ventriloquist act became one of radio's longest-running comedy shows. The creation of Edgar Bergen, the smart aleck Charlie McCarthy character soon had the country in stitches.

The hour-long variety broadcast show was a highly popular format in the mid-1930s, and ventriloquist Edgar Bergen knew that his 17 December 1936 guest spot on Rudy Vallee's *The Royal Gelatin Hour* was a chance to break away from the uncertainties of nightclub engagements, party entertainment jobs, and a declining vaudeville circuit. Newspaper radio pages puzzled over Vallee's decision to "waste" airtime on an act that seemed to require being *seen*, and program insiders had even stronger doubts. However, Vallee asked his audience to give the newcomer a fair hearing, and top-hatted Edgar Bergen and his dummy, Charlie McCarthy, were so successful that they stayed for 13 weeks.

On 9 May 1937, the shy ventriloquist and his brash alter ego began hosting the National Broadcasting Company's (NBC) *The Chase and Sanborn Hour* on Sunday evenings at 8:00, one of radio's most desirable time slots. The Bergen–McCarthy program would see changes of title, length, personnel, sponsorship, and emphasis over the next two decades, but it would remain among the highest-rated of all programs until the summer of 1956, when network radio was rapidly yielding audiences to television.

Chase and Sanborn's program budget could afford a parade of Hollywood guest stars and the weekly services of singers Dorothy Lamour and Nelson Eddy, conductor Werner Janssen, and emcee Don Ameche. In the second half of each program, mischief-making Charlie McCarthy mocked W.C. Fields for his drunkenness and crabbiness. Volleys from the McCarthy–Fields feud are among the best-remembered lines in radio comedy—for instance, Fields' threat to whittle Charlie into a set of venetian blinds and the dummy's punning response, "That makes me shutter." On 12 December 1937, Mae West sent a shiver through the sponsor and network ranks when her sultry reading of an Adam and Eve sketch on the show drew widespread protests. More happily, the program pioneered remote broadcasts from military installations, and in 1939 Bergen introduced his second radio dummy, cheerfully slow-witted Mortimer Snerd.

Becoming a briskly paced half-hour show in January 1940, the retitled *Chase and Sanborn Program* lost regulars Ameche and Lamour and placed renewed emphasis on Bergen and his dummies' interplay with guests such as Charles Laughton, Carole Lombard, Clark Gable, and Errol Flynn. Ray Noble led the orchestra, and, in sketches exploiting the differences between British and American English, he often rivaled Mortimer Snerd in comic "dumbness." Bud Abbott and Lou Costello offered variations on their "Who's on first?" routine. In 1944 Bergen added a third dummy, aging and man-hungry Effie Klinker, who, when asked if she had anything to say to the listeners, blurted out her telephone number to any interested male. The lineup of celebrity guests halted in 1948 when Chase and Sanborn prepared to drop its sponsorship. In a transitional phase, Don Ameche returned with Marsha Hunt for a recurring segment as the eternally at-odds couple, the Bickersons.

Moving to the Columbia Broadcasting System (CBS) in 1949 as a result of William S. Paley's "talent raid" on NBC, *The Charlie McCarthy Show* continued to adjust to rapid changes in radio and in the socio-political climate. Called *The Edgar Bergen and Charlie McCarthy Show* in 1954 and *The New Edgar Bergen Hour* in 1955, Bergen's program now emphasized citizenship in a larger world by inviting scientists, professors, as well as military, political, and diplomatic figures to discuss their careers. Bergen and his friends vacated their regular time slot on 1 July 1956, and except for appearances on his first sponsor's 100th and 101st anniversary programs in 1964 and 1965, Edgar Bergen's radio career had ended. He went on to host a television quiz show in 1956 and 1957. Bergen died in his sleep in 1978 after the third Las Vegas performance of a planned farewell nightclub tour. Charlie McCarthy, who once had his own room in Bergen's Beverly Hills home, is now housed in a Smithsonian Institution display case.

In its early years, the Bergen–McCarthy program prompted an avalanche of Charlie McCarthy books, dolls, spoons, radios, and other products. In most radio households, the show was the measure of Sunday evening family listening, yet Charlie McCarthy's leering attentions to female guests challenged propriety, and today the show's stereotypic treatment of W.C. Fields' drinking, Effie Klinker's "old maid" status, and Mortimer Snerd's good-natured rural stupidity would draw protests from many quarters. Still, the Bergen–McCarthy shows remain among the most popular in "old-time radio" circulation.

In retrospect, Bergen's success lay in his decision to build his act on a cluster of ironic impressions. Opposing the hard-times grain of the 1930s, Bergen and Charlie wore elegant evening clothes, and Charlie's monocle and upper-crust English accent gave an initial impression that was startlingly at odds with his earthy brashness. Charlie assumed the calculating speech rhythm of the schoolyard sharpie, and he wasted little respect on his elders, particularly the sometimes preachy Bergen: "I'll clip ya', Bergie, so help me, I'll mo-o-ow ya' down!" was Charlie's signature threat. Bergen sometimes flubbed his lines, but cocky Charlie rarely did. Charlie often ridiculed Bergen's lip movements and complained that his creator had grown wealthy by stinting on the boy's allowance. Thus Charlie seemed to have the upper hand and the last word, but all the while Bergen's hand and mouth animated the creature of wood and cloth. The two were sharp opposites, yet one was entirely the creation of the other.

See also: Comedy; Variety Shows

Cast

Charlie McCarthy	Edgar Bergen
Mortimer Snerd	Edgar Bergen
Effie Klinker	Edgar Bergen
Series regulars (various periods)	Don Ameche, Dorothy Lamour, Nelson Eddy, W.C. Fields, Dale Evans, Bud Abbott and Lou Costello, Pat Patrick, Jack Kirkwood, and others

Producers

Tony Stanford, Sam Pierce

Programming History

NBC 1937–48
CBS 1949–56

Further Reading

Bergen, Candice, *Knock Wood*, New York: Linden Press, and London: Hamilton, 1984.
Grams, Martin, Jr., *The Edgar Bergen and Charlie McCarthy Broadcast Log*, Delta, Pennsylvania: Martin Grams, Jr., n.d.
Wertheim, Arthur Frank, *Radio Comedy*, New York: Oxford University Press, 1979.

RAY BARFIELD

EDITORIALIZING
Expressing a Station's Point of View

The broadcast of editorials by radio stations has enjoyed an uneven history for both legal and economic reasons. Although legally allowed since 1949 and actively encouraged by the FCC in later years, most stations rarely editorialize on any issue.

An editorial is the expression of the point of view of the station (or network) owner or management. News commentary, in which a single newsperson expresses an opinion about one or more news events, is not an "editorial," because that individual is rarely understood to be speaking for management. The parallel to newspapers is apparent—the editorial page matches what is addressed here, whereas the "op ed" page offers other (and sometimes disagreeing) individual expressions of opinion.

Origins

Many stations took to the air in the 1920s and 1930s specifically so that their owners could express their points of view on one or more controversial issues. Indeed, some early stations that became subject to Federal Radio Commission (FRC) sanctions got into trouble because of their one-sided approach to religious or political issues. Early administrative FRC and court decisions made clear that stations—as part of their requirement to operate in "the public interest, convenience or necessity"—should provide a balanced program menu, allowing a variety of points of view to be expressed. Nothing specific was said about whether or not stations could editorialize in the first place.

At the network level, editorializing was frowned upon in the 1930s. Although "comment" was fairly common among newscasters, and some programs of news "commentary" were common by the late 1930s—indeed, the role of news commentator became more widely recognized—such programs did not express the editorial opinion of network or station management and were thus not looked at in the same way by the regulators.

The *Mayflower* Case

Any question about the legality of station editorials was removed by the *Mayflower* case in 1941. The Yankee Network's WAAB in Boston had presented editorials in 1937–38. This became a matter of legal concern in 1939, when the Mayflower Broadcasting Corporation (one of whose owners was a disgruntled former WAAB employee who felt stations should not editorialize) applied for the same frequency,

throwing the stations into a comparative hearing before the FCC as required by provisions of the 1934 Communications Act. When the commission initially dismissed the Mayflower application for unrelated reasons, the company asked the FCC to reconsider based on the editorializing question. Early in 1941 the FCC issued its final decision, which, although upholding the renewal of WAAB's license, made clear that "a truly free radio cannot be used to advocate the causes of the licensee...the broadcaster cannot be an advocate." The commission argued that given the limited number of frequencies available (and thus the number of stations that could broadcast), each licensee had to remain impartial. In using a public resource (its frequency assignment), a station took on the responsibility of being open to expression of all points of view, not merely its own. Because WAAB had ceased editorializing in 1938 when the FCC questioned the practice, its license was renewed.

Perhaps surprisingly, given broadcasters' fierce defense of their First Amendment rights, there was little industry complaint about the decision. Indeed, many broadcasters were secretly relieved that the FCC had eliminated the editorial option, because they knew that no matter what was said, any editorial could make listeners and advertisers unhappy. As stations grew to depend more on commercial support, avoiding controversy became ever more important.

Encouraging Editorials

Only after World War II did the issue arise anew. Early in 1948 the FCC held eight days of hearings on the question of stations' editorializing and dealing with controversial issues. From those hearings came a mid-1949 decision allowing editorials, in effect reversing the *Mayflower* ban. As the commissioners put it, "We cannot see how the open espousal of one point of view by the licensee should necessarily prevent him from affording a fair opportunity for the presentation of contrary positions." Little did anyone see at the time how this decision—which allowed but did not actively encourage editorials—would lay the groundwork for the hugely controversial fairness doctrine in years to come.

Eleven years later, the commission became more positive, including "editorialization by licensees" as the 7th of 14 specific program types held to be in the public interest. More stations began to offer at least occasional editorials, with some larger outlets hiring dedicated staff for the purpose. But the majority of stations never editorialized, and many others did so only infrequently. For a number of years, *Broadcasting Yearbook* kept track of the number of stations providing editorials. Of AM stations reporting (including most but not all of those then on the air), 30 percent editorialized in 1959, and six years later, 61 percent did, though nearly half of those did so only occasionally.

One indicator of the (temporary, as it turned out) growth of station editorializing was the formation of the National Broadcast Editorial Association (NBEA) in the early 1970s. The association grew to more than 200 members (usually the editorial director of a station); issued a quarterly publication, the *NBEA Editorialist*; and held annual conventions. One of the better-known station editorial directors was Don Gale, of the KSL stations in Salt Lake City, who over two decades broadcast some 5,000 editorials before his 1999 retirement. Each was broadcast three times a day on radio and twice on television. Ed Hinshaw at Milwaukee's WTMJ and Phil Johnson at WWL in New Orleans wrote or broadcast editorials for both radio and television for more than a quarter century.

By 1977 fewer stations reported editorializing activity, and most of those were only doing occasional editorials. A 1982 study identified more than 1,200 stations editorializing, many of them AM-FM-TV combinations. But later surveys suggested that the number was both much smaller and in decline. In September 1991 the NBEA was absorbed by the National Conference of Editorial Writers, most of whose members worked for newspapers.

The decline in station editorials after about 1980 was driven largely by economics. Increasing competition for advertising dollars and the need not to make potential clients irate certainly contributed. The demise of the fairness doctrine in 1987 probably contributed as well. So did the general demise of radio news and public-affairs programming on many stations. Because most focus on music, radio stations no longer compare themselves to newspapers in their community role. With that change in identification came the demise of editorializing.

See also: Controversial Issues, Broadcasting of; Fairness Doctrine; *Mayflower* Decision; News; Public Affairs Programming

Further Reading

Federal Communications Commission, *In the Matter of the Mayflower Broadcasting Corp. and the Yankee Network, Inc. (WAAB)*, 8 FCC 333 (16 January 1941).
Federal Communications Commission, *In the Matter of Editorializing by Broadcast Licensees*, 13 FCC 1246 (1 June 1949).
Federal Communications Commission, *Report and Statement of Policy re: Commission En Banc Programming Inquiry*, 44 FCC 2303 (29 July 1960).
Kahn, Frank J., editor, *Documents of American Broadcasting*, New York: Appelton-Century-Croft, 1968; 4th edition, Englewood Cliffs, New Jersey: Prentice-Hall, 1984.
Sterling, Christopher H., "Broadcast Station Editorials, 1959–1975," in *Electronic Media: A Guide to Trends in Broadcasting and Newer Technologies, 1920–1983*, by Sterling, New York: Praeger, 1984.
Summers, Harrison Boyd, compiler, *Radio Censorship*, New York: Wilson, 1939.

CHRISTOPHER H. STERLING

EDUCATION ABOUT RADIO
Developing University Curricula and Degrees

One measure of a topic's social importance or role is whether colleges and universities conduct research and offer courses (or even degrees) concerning that subject matter. Such academic recognition becomes a touchy question when the topic is largely commercial and enjoys a popular following—as did radio broadcasting by the mid-1920s. The study of mass communication was initially shaped with the first academic programs in newspaper journalism in the early 20th century. Radio broadcasting, however, presented something quite different with its emphasis on popular entertainment.

Origins

Perhaps ironically, the first Ph.D. dissertation on radio broadcasting was published as a book long before college or university organized studies of radio existed. Hiram Jome's *Economics of the Radio Industry* (1925) was based on the author's economics doctorate earned at the University of Wisconsin. Two years later, Stephen Davis' *The Law of Radio Communication* (1927) inaugurated yet another field of serious study, again long before most law schools offered courses on the subject. A series of lectures by radio leaders was delivered as part of a business policy course at the Harvard School of Business in 1927–28 (the lectures appeared as a book), and the first regular course about radio was organized in 1929 at the University of Southern California.

Soon additional scholarly apparatus became evident. The first scholarly journal article concerning radio appeared on the pages of the *Quarterly Journal of Speech* in 1930, when Sherman Lawton discussed principles of effective radio speaking. Two years later he expanded that article into the first collegelevel textbook on radio, *Radio Speech*.

Initial courses began to appear elsewhere, usually within English or speech departments. By 1933 an early survey showed that 16 colleges and universities offered at least one radio course. In 1937 the first comprehensive radio textbook appeared, which would run through four editions over the next two decades—Waldo Abbot's *Handbook of Broadcasting*.

The pace of development speeded up in the final years before World War II. By 1938 another survey showed that more than 300 institutions offered at least one course in radio. Furthermore, eight now offered a bachelor's degree and two offered a master's degree; in 1939 the Universities of Iowa and Wisconsin began offering a Ph.D. with an emphasis in the study of radio broadcasting. By 1939–40 some 360 schools offered about 1,000 courses in 14 different subject categories (including electrical engineering, which was the majority), of which the most common nontechnical topics included radio speech, a survey course, scriptwriting, and program planning/production.

Postwar Expansion

Broadcast education entered a period of substantial growth, and there was a concerted movement to develop standards, if not actual accreditation, for degree programs in radio (and soon television). In 1945 one committee published a brief set of suggested standards for radio degree programs. By 1948 a government survey reported that more than 400 schools provided at least a single radio course, with 35 offering non-engineering degrees in radio broadcasting. However, not everything was in place as television began to make its appearance.

It is often said that a true academic field of study needs at least one national (or international) association of like-minded scholars and a research journal. In 1948 a step was taken toward the first of these with the creation of the University Association for Professional Radio Education (UAPRE), founded by about a dozen universities. The title reflected a tension evident in education for radio—were such courses and degrees designed primarily to turn out personnel for the industry, or was this media education to be more in the liberal arts tradition? UAPRE was set up specifically to accredit university and college degree programs, but it was unable to achieve that goal, though for reasons having nothing to do with radio but rather with the complex politics of establishing any national accrediting process.

By 1950 some 420 colleges and universities offered courses, and 54 provided non-engineering degrees: 30 bachelor's, 15 master's, and three Ph.D.

Five years later, there were at least 81 course sequences leading to radio/broadcasting degrees. In 1955 the UAPRE gave way to the Association for Professional Broadcasting Education (APBE), which a year later began publishing *Journal of Broadcasting* as the first dedicated scholarly journal in the developing field. A year later a national survey reported 93 bachelor's degree programs (3,000 majors), 56 master's degree programs (over 400 students), and 15 Ph.D. programs of study (122 candidates). Broadcast educators now met annually with the National Association of Broadcasters, and many academics were becoming active in the more senior speech and journalism academic organizations. More scholarships, internships, and research opportunities were becoming available every year.

At that point, of course, all eyes were quite literally on television, and radio courses and research began to disappear. A handful of announcing courses survived, but most other broadcast programs focused very strongly on television—and given the costs of such education and the lack of student interest in radio, radio studies were fairly quickly abandoned. However, the field was now sufficiently established to move away from a focus on professional education alone. APBE became the Broadcast Education Association (BEA) in 1973, thereby better recognizing the many liberal arts broadcast programs that had developed.

Radio's Revival

In the 1980s radio began to reappear in college and university curricula. This was due to a combination of factors, first in the industry and then in education.

Certainly the growing number of radio stations (with their entry-level positions for college and university graduates) was a factor. So was the revival of educational and public radio beginning in the 1970s and the reappearance of radio drama documentary broadcasts. The growing complexity of radio formats added a degree of depth to the medium that it had not previously possessed: there was more to study and understand than before. As audience and market research became more widespread and important in radio, people had to be educated in these areas. The explosive popularity of talk radio in the 1980s put radio in the political limelight. Radio was increasingly in the news: with controversial disc jockeys and talk show hosts having impact on elections, its appeal to young people as a possible career option increased exponentially. At the other end of the spectrum, growing interest in the "golden age" of radio increased interest in the history and sociology of radio. As in other parts of American life, more women and minorities were being employed by radio, opening further paths to success in the medium. Technology played a growing role as well, as the radio industry became increasingly computerized and automated, made plans to begin digital operations, and became more widely available on the internet.

Just as radio managers seemed to place more emphasis on the educational credentials of those trying to enter the field, colleges and universities seemed to rediscover radio as well. There were several indicators, including the reappearance of radio-only comprehensive and production-oriented textbooks, the new *Journal of Radio Studies* founded as an annual in 1992 and expanded to twice a year by 1998 (as the first academic journal focused on radio), and the (perhaps belated) formation of a broadcast and internet radio division within BEA in 2000. Radio began reappearing in course titles in university programs across the country, coming full circle seven decades after the academic discovery of the medium.

Despite the hard efforts of many academics, and resulting growth in the output of radio-centric research, however, radio studies in the early 21st century began to meld into a broader audio or media studies frame. One indicator of this was the 2008 title change of BEA's *Journal of Radio Studies* to become the *Journal of Radio and Audio Media*. In one sense this was a healthy trend as it incorporated a theoretically stronger sense of radio's place in American culture past and present, continuing the trend away from practical studio training. It also sought to include the growing mobile digital world of sound. That radio (or audio) was more than "television lite" became more evident. Many cultural researchers are recognizing radio as both reflecting and projecting societal interests and biases. On the other hand, industry consolidation, a growing sense of program sameness, heavy commercial loads, and even limited employment options have all helped to somewhat diminish interest among younger listeners in what many perceive as "old" technology—turning instead to their own portable digital options, rather than listening to or studying about radio.

See also: Broadcast Education Association; College Radio; Educational Radio to 1967; Intercollegiate Broadcasting System; Museums and Archives of Radio; National Association of Educational Broadcasters; Office of Radio Research

Further Reading

Abbot, Waldo, *Handbook of Broadcasting: How to Broadcast Effectively*, New York: McGraw-Hill, 1937.

Davis, Stephen Brooks, *The Law of Radio Communication*, New York: McGraw-Hill, 1927; reprint, 1992.
Directory of Colleges Offering Courses in Radio and Television (annual).
Federal Radio Education Committee, *Suggested Standards for College Courses in Radiobroadcasting*, Washington, D.C.: U.S. Office of Education, Federal Security Agency, 1945.
Head, Sydney W., and Leo A. Martin, "Broadcasting and Higher Education: A New Era," *Journal of Broadcasting* I (Winter 1956–57).
Keith, Michael C. "The Long Road to Radio Studies," *Journal of Broadcasting & Electronic Media* 51 (September 2007), pp. 530–536; www.michaelckeith.com/myspin.html
Keith, Michael C., ed. *Radio Cultures: The Sound Medium in American Life*. New York: Peter Lang, 2008.
Kittross, John Michael, "A History of the BEA," *Feedback* 40 (Spring 1999).
Lawton, Sherman Paxton, *Radio Speech*, Boston: Expression, 1932.
Lichty, Lawrence W., "Who's Who on Firsts: A Search for Challengers," *Journal of Broadcasting* 10 (Winter 1965–66).
Niven, Harold, "The Radio-Television Curricula in American Colleges and Universities," *Journal of Broadcasting* 4 (Spring 1960).
Niven, Harold, "The Development of Broadcasting Education in Institutions of Higher Learning," *Journal of Broadcasting* 5 (Summer 1961).
The Radio Industry: The Story of Its Development, As Told by Leaders of the Industry to the Students of the Graduate School of Business Administration, George F. Baker Foundation, Harvard University, Chicago, New York, and London: Shaw, 1928; reprint, as *The Radio Industry: The Story of Its Development, As Told by Leaders of the Industry*, New York: Arno Press, 1974.
Smith, Leslie, "Education for Broadcasting, 1929–1963," *Journal of Broadcasting* 8 (Fall 1964).

CHRISTOPHER H. STERLING
2009 REVISIONS BY CHRISTOPHER H. STERLING

EDUCATIONAL RADIO TO 1967

Well before radio broadcasting became an entertainment and sales medium, it was used for education. When Charles D. Herrold started the first radio broadcasting station in the United States in 1909, it was largely intended as a laboratory for students of the Herrold School of Radio in San Jose, California. When Lee de Forest, also in the first decade of the 20th century, tested his firm's radio apparatus using recordings of opera and other classical music, it was partly to introduce others to the music he loved.

There has been conflict from the early 1920s until the present between those who believe there is a need for nonprofit educational broadcasting and those who do not. For example, many commercial broadcasters believe that the frequencies occupied by noncommercial educational radio might be better employed for advertising. On the other hand, although its potential has never been fully realized, educational radio—like the internet—has such high potential that its use for education attracted many enthusiastic supporters.

This conflict is pervasive. In the late 1920s, the Federal Radio Commission (FRC) encouraged shared-time broadcasters to persuade educational institutions to give up their licenses. In the early 1930s, the Wagner-Hatfield Amendment was proposed to reserve channels for nonprofits. In 1941 channels were first set aside or reserved for education on the new FM band. In 1946, when the Federal Communications Commission (FCC) issued its "Blue Book" (*Public Service Responsibility of Broadcast Licensees*), it called upon commercial stations to cater to the needs of nonprofit organizations. However, the storm of protest from commercial stations about the "Blue Book" buried this idea at the time.

But although the record shows that educational radio has often been impressively effective in schools and adult education, it frequently was underappreciated. Educational broadcasting was cavalierly dismissed for decades, even though it was originally touted as a great advance. For decades, arguments in favor of a separate educational radio service relied on an analogy with the public service philosophy of agricultural extension intrinsic to the land grant colleges.

Origins: 1920–33

Indeed, one land grant institution, the University of Wisconsin, owns WHA, one of the oldest radio broadcasting stations in the United States. Land grant colleges were interested in outreach—the extension of their expertise to isolated regions. As a result, they first used radio both to provide lectures on topics of more or less general interest and to give specific information on topics intended to serve citizens of their state, such as agriculture and home economics. A few tried to use radio for fund raising in the early 1920s, with very limited success.

A number of stations were merely the tangible results of experiments by engineering and physics faculty and students (such as Alfred Goldsmith, who operated 2XN at City College of New York, 1912–14) who wished to explore the phenomenon of wireless telephony. However, once they had tinkered to their heart's content, the daunting need to find content for their transmissions led, in many instances, to these stations' being turned over to departments of speech, English, music, and extension services. Another reason for this transfer was that the cost of programming, once the technical facilities met the FRC's standards, was a major expense.

Even before World War I, radio telegraph and some radio telephone experimentation had taken place at such colleges and universities as Arkansas, Cornell, Dartmouth, Iowa, Loyola, Nebraska, Ohio State, Penn State, Purdue, Tulane, and Villanova, in addition to Wisconsin. After stations were allowed back on the air in 1919 following the war, regular broadcasting service was started by many of these and others either for extension courses or strictly for publicity.

By 1 May 1922, when the number of radio stations was beginning a meteoric rise, the Department of Commerce's *Radio Service Bulletin* reported that more than 10 percent (23 of 218) of the broadcasting stations then on the air were licensed to colleges, universities, a few trade schools, high schools, religious organizations, and municipalities. This proportion soon climbed, with 72 stations (13 percent) licensed to educational institutions among the 556 on the air in 1923, and 128 (22 percent) of a similar total (571) in 1925.

Although early records are imprecise—noncommercial AM stations were issued the same type of license as commercial ones—many of these stations were short-lived. Not only did it appear that there was no pressing need for educational radio, but also other factors pared the number on the air from 98 in 1927 (perhaps 13 percent of all stations) to half that (43, or 7 percent) in 1933. Although nearly 200 standard broadcast (AM) stations were licensed to educational institutions through 1929, almost three-quarters were gone as early as 1930. The 47 stations that remained, however, were tenacious—and roughly half of them continued to serve their audiences at the beginning of the 21st century.

The number of both commercial and noncommercial stations dropped in the late 1920s, largely because of the expensive technical requirements imposed by the FRC under the Radio Act of 1927. Additionally, the FRC's 1927–29 reallocations and elimination of marginal and portable stations often gave desirable channels to commercial operators at the expense of educational institutions. The costs of new interference-reducing transmitters and other facilities were imposed just prior to the economic dislocations of the Great Depression—which dried up funds for colleges and commercial companies alike.

In addition, many university administrators saw no value in radio. At best, running a radio station, except where it also served curricular needs or could be used effectively by agricultural extension services, seemed to be a lot of work and expense for limited reward during tough times. Many institutions appeared glad that the FRC's new rules gave them an excuse to drop this expensive toy. This lack of interest closed many educational stations.

Into the 1930s, some educational stations found themselves pressured by local shared-time broadcasters to give up their frequencies for full-time use by commercial stations. To sweeten the deal, commercial broadcasters often offered to air some educational programming. Because commercial stations had more lobbying clout and deeper pockets and, in many cases, appeared to be more stable, closing down educational stations sounded very attractive to policy-makers. It also sounded good to timid college administrators who didn't recognize the benefits of using radio for teaching, tended to allocate funding in other directions, and found commercial offers a "win–win" choice—until the promised educational programming was crowded out by advertising-supported programs.

A hard core of educational broadcasters successfully claimed that their stations were serving both the public interest and the interests of their parent institutions. But where there were not enough trained and interested personnel to argue for retention and financial support, many college and university stations no longer had an educational mission—nor, usually, a license.

Concern for their dwindling numbers and interest in ways of using radio effectively led radio educators to band together. In mid-1929, the Advisory Committee on Education by Radio was formed with backing from the Payne Fund, the Carnegie Endowment, and J.C. Penney, but it died before 1930 without having had much effect. In 1930 two rival organizations that would represent educational radio for a decade were organized: the National Advisory Council on Radio in Education and the National Committee on Education by Radio. The council worked with grants from the Rockefeller Foundation and the Carnegie Endowment and called on commercial stations to meet education's needs. The committee, with support from the Payne Fund, asked that nonprofit educational entities be given 15 percent of all station assignments—which would double the number of educational stations; the committee also attacked "commercial monopolies" and disagreed with what it called the "halfway" measures of the council.

One result of the proselytizing by both organizations was a Senate-mandated 1932 FRC survey of educational programs on both commercial and noncommercial stations. Having carefully timed their survey for National Education Week, when most stations scheduled some educational programs, the FRC concluded that commercial stations were adequately filling educational needs. Congress was

not completely convinced, and Senators Wagner and Hatfield sponsored an unsuccessful amendment to the 1934 Communications Act allocating 25 percent of broadcast facilities to nonprofit organizations. After this failed, another dozen of the remaining educational stations began to take advertising in 1933 to meet operating costs and to cover American Society of Composers, Authors, and Publishers (ASCAP) music licensing fees.

The campaign for a set-aside of channels for education continued, resulting in Section 307 (c) of the Communications Act of 1934, which told the new Federal Communications Commission to "study the proposal that Congress by statute allocate fixed percentages of radio broadcasting facilities to particular types or kinds of non-profit radio programs or to persons identified with particular types or kinds of non-profit activities." The FCC held extensive hearings—100 witnesses, 13,000 pages of transcript—in the fall of 1934 and (as might have been anticipated) recommended against reservation of frequencies, for educator cooperation with commercial stations and networks, and for the establishment of another committee.

The resulting Federal Radio Education Committee (FREC) was originally composed of 15 broadcasters; 15 educators or members of groups such as the Parent-Teacher Association; and 10 government officials, newspaper publishers, and others, and it was headed by U.S. Commissioner of Education John Studebaker. "Broadcasters" ranged from network heads to the National Broadcasting Company's (NBC) music and education directors. The committee's purposes were to "eliminate controversy and misunderstanding between groups of educators and between the industry and educators" and to "promote actual cooperative arrangements between educators and broadcasters on national, regional, and local bases." A "subcommittee on conflicts and cooperation" was to try to deal with any friction between "the commercial and the social or educational broadcasters."

Holding On: The 1930s

FREC operated a script exchange (used by 108 stations and a large number of local groups in its first full year) and planned 18 major research projects so it could make valid recommendations. Funding—roughly two-thirds from educational foundations and one-third from the broadcasting industry (through the National Association of Broadcasters)—did not live up to expectations, and roughly half of the projects had to be dropped. Although some useful publications, a supply of standardized classroom receivers, and a great deal of script distribution resulted, the FREC actually held only one full meeting. It disbanded after World War II. Nevertheless, for more than three decades, most educational broadcasters looked to the U.S. Office of Education, headed by Franklin Dunham and Gertrude Broderick, for coordination, sympathy, and low-cost practical assistance.

Because there were then no educational networks of any sort, the exchange of scripts was the best way to give educational stations and their audiences access to programming prepared by others. Beginning in early 1929, the Payne Fund supported daily *Ohio School of the Air* broadcasts on powerful commercial station WLW in Cincinnati. These programs, intended for in-school listening, were produced in the studios of WOSU, then and now licensed to the Ohio State University in Columbus. The Ohio state legislature appropriated money to partly cover production costs, teacher guides, and pupil materials. Later, WOSU, in the center of the state, became the primary transmitter of this program. Another early educational series for below-college-level classroom listening was the *Wisconsin School of the Air*, which began on university-owned WHA in the fall of 1931. WHA started a "College of the Air" two years later.

During radio's "golden age" from 1934 until the end of World War II, educational radio survived— but barely. The 43 educational AM stations on the air in 1933 dropped to no more than 35 by mid-1941. Roughly half had been on the air more than 15 years, 12 were commercially supported, and seven of these were affiliated with a commercial network, airing educational programs only a few hours a day. One was operated by a high school, two were operated by church-affiliated educational groups, nine by agricultural schools or state agricultural departments, and 11 by land grant universities, mostly in the Midwest. Only 11 stations were licensed for unlimited broadcast time, about half of them in the 250- to 5,000-W category.

Commercial stations and national networks regularly scheduled some avowedly educational programming. In the 1920s, commercial broadcasters started "radio schools of the air," lectures, and even courses for credit. WJZ (New York) began such broadcasts in 1923, WEAF (New York) followed, and WLS (Chicago) started its *Little Red Schoolhouse* series in 1924. Such programs, often in association with school boards, were long-lived and useful to the stations' images. For example, WFIL (Philadelphia) aired the *WFIL Studio Schoolhouse*, a series of daily radio programs, complete with teachers' manuals, in the mid-1950s. The *Standard School Broadcasts* (Standard Oil Company) were broadcast over a number of California stations into the 1960s.

A 1928 FRC study of 100 stations in the western United States had found that radio was supplying more features and more plays but fewer children's programs and less educational material than three years earlier. The study also found that, of the 54 hours that the average station was on the air each week, five were devoted to education and lectures other than on farm subjects, and three hours were on farm reports and talks. FCC hearings in 1934 contained testimony that networks and larger stations were more cooperative with educators than were small and independent stations. Although the amount of such programming did not rise appreciably over the next two decades, neither did it fall until most commercial radio adopted all-music formats in reaction to the success of television in the 1950s.

Educational programming tended to be of three kinds: classroom instruction in English, history, social studies, and other disciplines, intended for classes from kindergarten to college; extension study, typically in fields that would be useful to the state or region being served, such as detailed agricultural practices and marketing news; and general cultural programs, such as classical music, which were inexpensive to produce.

Few stations of any sort produced dramatic programs, because the need for proven stories, talented performers, and special skills (such as sound effects) tended to require a major investment in time as well as money. College football and baseball games were often carried on college stations— at least until they became popular enough that more-powerful commercial stations offered to carry them. One potential audience given special attention by nonprofit stations was children, with programs of all types from stories and games to health instruction.

But the failure to provide an adequate number of channels on the AM band for education was not forgotten. National organizations continued to agitate for an adequate number of channels or to coordinate the efforts of existing stations. These groups included the FREC, the National Advisory Council on Radio in Education, the Institute for Education by Radio, the National Association of Educational Broadcasters (NAEB), and the National Committee on Education by Radio.

The Institute for Education by Radio was established at the Ohio State University in 1930 by I. Keith Tyler, and it hosted annual practitioner conferences on educational radio until 1960. Its published proceedings are a good source of contemporary thinking about what radio was doing for education—and might still do with sufficient support.

The NAEB was founded in 1934, but it traced its lineage to the Association of College and University Broadcasting Stations, established during the rush to get education on the air in 1925. NAEB was primarily a program idea exchange during the period up until World War II, but some of its 25 members also experimented with off-the-air rebroadcasting.

The National Committee on Education by Radio, mentioned earlier, worked hard for allocation of educational channels and sponsored annual conferences from 1931 to 1938, when its Rockefeller Foundation funding ended. One of the committee's more interesting initiatives was to help establish local listening councils—groups of critical listeners who would work with local broadcasters to improve existing programs and plan new ones.

In an attempt to secure educational channels without stepping on the toes of commercial broadcasters, the National Committee on Education by Radio proposed that new educational stations be assigned to channels in the 1500–1600 kHz range, just above the standard (AM) broadcasting band of the time. These stations, however, typically would have had less range than those on lower frequencies and would have had to purchase new transmitters and antennas in many instances. Furthermore, there was no way of ensuring that receivers would be built that could pick up this band. As a result, most educators had little enthusiasm. (These frequencies eventually had limited use for high-fidelity AM experimental broadcasting, using 20-kHz-wide channels. In March 1941 they were added to the regular AM band.)

Early in 1938, the FCC reversed its earlier position and established the first specific spectrum reservations for noncommercial broadcast use, in the 41- to 42-MHz band. After the FCC set aside 25 channels for in-school broadcasting, the Cleveland Board of Education was licensed (as WBOE) in November 1938. The next year, this allocation was moved to the 42- to 43-MHz band, and the broadcasters using it were required to change from AM to the new frequency modulation (FM) mode of modulation. The first noncommercial educational FM stations were authorized in 1941. Because FM required a much wider bandwidth, this allocation provided only five channels, on which two fully licensed (and possibly five experimental) stations were transmitting to radioequipped classrooms by late 1941. When commercial FM

went into operation, education was assigned channels at the bottom of the overall band, which were fractionally easier for listeners to receive than higher ones. The interference-free reception and high audio fidelity of FM initially were very attractive, and half a million sets were sold before all civilian radio manufacturing was ended by the demands of World War II.

Postwar Rebirth: To 1967

This opportunity to establish new educational stations was welcomed. Although the wartime construction "freeze" of 1942 exempted educational broadcasting stations, scarcity of construction materials and broadcast equipment—together with the slow decision-making processes of educational institutions—meant that educational FM broadcasting at the end of the war in 1945 consisted of about 25 AM stations, plus 12 FM authorizations and six FM stations on the air. Nevertheless, many potential educational broadcasters used the war years for planning, realizing that finally, after more than a decade of talking about educational radio, they had the means to accomplish it.

But there were complications. In 1945 the FCC shifted the educational FM allotment to 88–92 MHz, at the bottom of a new FM band. Because only a handful actually had to replace transmitters, this change was reluctantly accepted. The number of noncommercial educational FM stations grew substantially after World War II. Although these data are not completely reliable, it appears that there were 10 such stations on the air at the start of 1947 and 85 by 1952, 14 percent of all FM stations then on the air. The number kept rising and the proportion remained respectable: 98 in 1953, 141 in 1958, 209 in 1963, and 326 (16 percent) on 1 January 1968.

Perhaps chastened by earlier experiences with educational AM radio, institutions of higher education, school districts, and nonprofit community groups were initially hesitant to apply for FM licenses. Apart from past disappointments, high costs, and the need for colleges and universities to earmark resources to serve the millions of postwar students, potential operators were wary of the continuing paucity of homes with FM receivers and the possible effects of another new medium, television.

Late in 1948 the FCC, recognizing the burdens of high cost and the limited or campus-only uses planned by some colleges, approved a new class of 10-W stations. These low-power FM stations were immediately popular and constituted more than one-third of the 92 educational FM stations on the air in 1952.

Audiotape recording's potential was first realized by Seymour Siegel of WNYC in 1946. Recording also made it possible to reuse programs; for example, one station was still rebroadcasting some 1945 children's programs in the 1990s—and they still were attracting youthful audiences. In 1951 the Kellogg Foundation provided funds to NAEB to establish a tape duplication operation at the University of Illinois, Urbana, to facilitate a non-interconnected "bicycle network" by which tape recordings of one station's programs were mailed to other stations in succession. Soon, more than 40 stations were participating. The NAEB Tape Network was made possible by the postwar introduction of high-fidelity magnetic tape recorders, which replaced clumsy and fragile 15- or 16-inch transcription discs.

However, some postwar regional or statewide FM networks were established, as in Alabama and Wisconsin. In the latter, eight stations provided a full day's programming to schools, colleges, and adults in most of the state. The National Educational and Radio Center, established in Ann Arbor, Michigan, in 1954 and later moved to New York, eventually started providing some taped radio programs through a subsidiary. At least one independent group of noncommercial stations, affiliated with the Pacifica Foundation, still operates stations across the country; another, the KRAB Nebula, organized by Lorenzo Milam, was more ephemeral.

Many educationally licensed stations programmed a great deal of classical or folk music and jazz, which were timeless and inexpensive. Although education, music, and talk programs were generally inexpensive, news coverage was not, and educational radio therefore played a fairly minor role in the listening habits of most members of radio's audience into the 1960s.

During the period up to 1967, educational radio remained an orphan in many ways. Although given general support in regulatory matters by the FCC and Congress, funding was a perennial local problem. Studies of educational radio usually arrived at the obvious conclusions that money and a national rather than strictly local image were needed. On a local level, some educational radio stations served the public interest economically and well. Some acted both as training laboratories—for example, municipally owned WNYC trained interns from colleges across the country, and its sister station, WNYE, used high school students to create programs for schools throughout New York City—and as sources of a wider variety of programming for the many people who were not well served by the commercial radio broadcasting industry.

Although not the first to lobby, the 1966 Wingspread Conference on Educational Radio as a National Resource came at the right time to argue for federal funding for radio, a proposal that succeeded in including radio in the 1967 Public Broadcasting Act. This provision of some facilities and program funding through the Corporation for Public Broadcasting and NPR after 1967 gave educational radio a very different look.

See also: American School of the Air; Blue Book; Community Radio; Corporation for Public Broadcasting; Federal Communications Commission; History; Low-Power Radio/Microradio; National Association of Educational Broadcasters; National Public Radio; Pacifica Foundation; Public Broadcasting Act of 1967; Public Radio Since 1967; WHA and Wisconsin Public Radio

Further Reading

Atkinson, Carroll, *American Universities and Colleges That Have Held Broadcast License*, Boston: Meador, 1941.

Atkinson, Carroll, *Broadcasting to the Classroom by Universities and Colleges*, Boston: Meador, 1942.

Atkinson, Carroll, *Radio Network Contributions to Education*, Boston: Meador, 1942.

Atkinson, Carroll, *Radio Programs Intended for Classroom Use*, Boston: Meador, 1942.

Baudino, Joseph E., and John M. Kittross, "Broadcasting's Oldest Stations: An Examination of Four Claimants," *Journal of Broadcasting* 21 (Winter 1977).

Bianchi, William. *Schools of the Air: A History of Instructional Programs on Radio in the United States*. Jefferson, North Carolina: McFarland, 2008.

Blakely, Robert J., *To Serve the Public Interest: Educational Broadcasting in the United States*, Syracuse, New York: Syracuse University Press, 1979.

Darrow, Benjamin Harrison, *Radio: The Assistant Teacher*, Columbus, Ohio: Adams, 1932.

Edelman, Murray J., *The Licensing of Radio Services in the United States, 1927–1947: A Study in Administrative Formulation of Policy*, Urbana: University of Illinois Press, 1950.

Engelman, Ralph, *Public Radio and Television in America: A Political History*, Thousand Oaks, California: Sage, 1996.

Frost, S.E., *Education's Own Stations*, Chicago: University of Chicago Press, 1937.

Gibson, George H., *Public Broadcasting: The Role of the Federal Government, 1912–1976*, New York: Praeger, 1977.

Herzberg, Max J., editor, *Radio and English Teaching: Experiences, Problems, and Procedures*, New York and London: Appleton-Century, 1941.

Hill, Harold E., and W. Wayne Alford, *NAEB History*, 2 vols, Washington, D.C.: National Association of Educational Broadcasters, 1965–66.

Levenson, William B., *Teaching through Radio*, New York: Farrar and Rinehart, 1945.

Lingel, Robert J.C., *Educational Broadcasting: A Bibliography*, Chicago: University of Chicago Press, 1932.

Maloney, Martin J., "A Philosophy of Educational Television," in *The Farther Vision: Educational Television*

Today, edited by Allen E. Koenig and Ruane B. Hill, Madison: University of Wisconsin Press, 1967.

Marsh, C.S., *Educational Broadcasting: Proceedings of the National Conference on Educational Broadcasting, 1936*, Chicago: University of Chicago Press, 1937.

Marsh, C.S., *Educational Broadcasting: Proceedings of the National Conference on Educational Broadcasting, 1937*, Chicago: University of Chicago Press, 1938.

McGill, William J., *A Public Trust: The Report of the Carnegie Commission on the Future of Public Broadcasting*, New York: Bantam Books, 1979.

Perry, Armstrong, *Radio in Education: The Ohio School of the Air, and Other Experiments*, New York: The Payne Fund, 1929.

Radio and Education (annual; 1931–34); as *Education on the Air* (annual; 1934–) (proceedings of annual conferences on educational broadcasting).

Robertson, Jim, *Tele Visionaries: In Their Own Words, Public Television's Founders Tell How It All Began*, Charlotte Harbor, Florida: Tabby House Books, 1993.

Siepmann, Charles Arthur, *Radio's Second Chance*, Boston: Little Brown, 1946.

Sterling, Christopher H., and John M. Kittross, *Stay Tuned: A History of American Broadcasting*, 3rd edition, Mahwah, New Jersey: Lawrence Erlbaum, 2002.

Stewart, Irvin, editor, *Local Broadcasts to Schools*, Chicago: University of Chicago Press, 1939.

United States Federal Communications Commission, *Public Service Responsibility of Broadcast Licenses*, Washington, D.C.: Government Printing Office, 1946.

JOHN MICHAEL KITTROSS

ELECTION COVERAGE
Radio Reports of National Campaigns

Elections provided some of the earliest content for the new medium of radio. In 1920, as Westinghouse prepared to issue KDKA's first radio broadcast, they chose to debut with reports of national election results. With a small audience, to whom "simple receiving sets" had been distributed, and advertising placed in the local papers to spark the interest of amateur radio enthusiasts, on the evening of 2 November 1920, the national election returns were broadcast to an audience of perhaps 500 to 1,000 listeners.

The early attraction of radio to politics was not immediately returned in kind by politics, as was evidenced in a comment regarding the 1924 election: "The effect of the election on radio was more important than the effect of radio on the election result" (Chester). However, a dependence on the new medium was soon to follow. Through a historical review of the election coverage on radio, this essay traces the role that radio played in the coverage of political campaigns and the early public dependence on the radio for election coverage.

Early Election Coverage

The first political campaign in which radio played a major role was the 1924 presidential contest. Strategists for President Calvin Coolidge's re-election effort saw the immediate advantages of the medium for "silent Cal," who found radio's requirement of short and simple language more compatible with his own style than the traditional round of presidential candidate stump speeches. One campaign advisor noted, "Speeches must be short. Ten minutes is a limit and five minutes is better" (Chester).

Campaign speeches and addresses by the candidates and other political advocates made up radio's major election coverage in these early days. The Republican Party even purchased their own radio station, on which they broadcast campaign addresses at all available hours in the day. This saturation sparked the Radio Corporation of America (RCA) to suggest that a limit of one hour per day be reserved for political address broadcasting and that such addresses be limited to 15 minutes each. The 1924 election coverage also included the first coverage on radio of the national party conventions. Both the Republican and Democratic conventions were carried to listeners across the nation. Although some political observers were sure that this marriage of radio and elections was a fad, those who predicted that political campaigns would never be the same were closer to the mark.

By the 1928 presidential campaign, 40 million people were able to follow the election campaigns via the radio, which had become an integral campaign tool, so much so that a candidate's "radio personality" was a part of the election dialogue. Republican Herbert Hoover was not an exciting radio personality, but he was credited for not offending his audiences. Democratic opponent Alfred Smith, however, had an accent that tended to alienate voters from the Southern states that he desperately needed to carry. The 1928 campaign also saw the rise in coverage of radio campaign addresses by people other than the presidential candidates themselves. Republicans continued to build on the perceived advantages of brevity in the new medium by creating 30 short speeches that covered the main points of Hoover's campaign. Lasting five minutes each, these were delivered by well-known local people over 174 local stations.

By 1932, with radios in more than 12 million homes, voters witnessed new radio strategies in the presidential campaigns. Franklin Roosevelt established a new precedent in radio address, flying to Chicago to accept his party's nomination prior to the adjournment of the national convention and thus broadcasting his acceptance address by radio from the convention. Other changes in radio coverage evolved during this campaign cycle, with the Columbia Broadcasting System (CBS) and the National Broadcasting Company (NBC) each allotting three periods a week for political addresses and refusing to sell airtime to either party before the parties had officially selected their presidential candidates. During the 1936 campaign, both candidates, Roosevelt and Kansas Governor Alfred Landon, toured the country with many of their speeches broadcast over radio. A unique variation of campaign speeches in the 1936 campaign focused on foreign language broadcasts. Both parties produced radio messages in a variety of languages, with the Republicans using as many as 29 languages in numerous messages varying in length from 100-word spots to 30-minute talks. Although Landon enjoyed many powerful newspaper endorsements, many believe that Roosevelt's victory can be at least partially credited to his effective use of radio during the campaign.

In Roosevelt's last campaign, in 1944, the press noted that Republican nominee Thomas Dewey, then-governor of New York, might be the first real competition Roosevelt had faced in radio performance. It was an unfulfilled prediction; a poll conducted by the American Institute of Public Opinion found that the attitude Dewey conveyed while speaking on the radio hindered audience approval, further underscoring the need for candidates to understand and develop successful radio communication strategies.

During the 1948 election, Democratic incumbent Truman successfully developed his own approach to radio address. As opposed to Roosevelt's manuscript style of speech preparation, Truman found both success and effectiveness in extemporaneous speaking. Truman embarked on a successful "whistlestop" tour during the campaign, and by simply and consistently repeating his message throughout the tour, he inadvertently capitalized on the fundamental nature of radio by reaching masses of voters with the same message.

Throughout the 1948 campaign, a larger percentage of President Truman's speeches were covered by local radio stations than were those of Dewey, again the Republican nominee. Whereas about 50 of the incumbent president's addresses were covered by radio, only about 34 of Dewey's were broadcast to voters. Also significant was the fact that most of Truman's speeches carried on radio were broadcast from his whistlestop tour, giving them a background of excitement and timeliness. The coverage of Truman's speeches was particularly important for him, because the Democratic Party had limited funds to pay for broadcasts. In addition, many of the "whistlestops" where the actual speeches were given did not have local radio stations, and national coverage was essential for his message to reach large numbers of voters. Truman's upset victory was due in part to radio.

In the 1952 election, radio found a mass media partner as television made its first significant appearance in a political election. Although Eisenhower is credited for the first use of presidential televised spot advertising, surveys conducted after the election found that he made his greatest gains on radio (Chester). Nonetheless, the years when radio coverage would dominate elections were over.

Election Advertising

Early in radio coverage of elections, the blending of straightforward coverage and party and candidate advertising in election campaigns was established. By the time of the 1928 election, candidates and parties were routinely purchasing time for the airing of their speeches and messages. Advertising expenditures in 1928 reached $650,000 for the Democrats and $435,000 for the Republicans, as radio stations began charging presidential candidates for airtime after they had given their nomination acceptance speeches. However, during the 1936 campaign, Republicans began to run shorter spot advertisements on behalf of Landon, including language-specific spots directed to the minority and immigrant votes.

In the 1944 presidential election, both parties employed short, one-minute radio spots. The Democrats sought to remind voters that they should blame the Republicans for the Depression with quips such as "Hoover depression," and the Republicans sought to tie the Democrats to the war with slogans such as "End the war quicker with Dewey and Bricker." Testimonial five-minute spots were also employed by the Democrats, with speakers such as vice president Henry A. Wallace and vice presidential candidate Truman.

During the 1948 presidential election, Dewey declined the use of five-minute spot announcements, feeling confident that he was ahead in the polls. The Republican national committee instead made use of 30- and 60-second spot ads to urge the people to vote Republican; the Democrats made very little use of spot announcements. Instead, Truman concentrated on reaching the voters through political speeches broadcast from his whistlestop tour.

With Eisenhower's introduction of televised political spot ads in 1952, radio advertising began to take a back seat to the advertising dollars spent on television. However, as radio stations grew in popularity and number, candidates began to use the target marketing of certain radio stations to reach particular types of voters. The increasing numbers of radio advertising dollars in presidential candidate budgets in the seven decades from 1928 to 2000 is noteworthy. Radio advertising expenditures topped $650,000 in 1928, and by 2000 both parties were spending several million dollars each on radio advertising. A major reason for the resurgence of interest in radio advertising in the 1980s and 1990s has been the ability of radio to target increasingly diverse and segmented audiences.

Election Debates

An idea that was ahead of its time, a proposal for the first presidential debate to be broadcast on radio was actually put forth as early as the 1924 election campaign. Two decades later, radio hosted a 1948 Republican primary debate held in Portland, Oregon; the debate was a forerunner to the famous Nixon–Kennedy debates of 1960. The choice of the issue about which both the leading Republican candidates, Thomas Dewey, governor of New York, and Harold Stassen, former governor of Minnesota, were in complete disagreement set the stage for a traditional, nonmoderated debate. The debate topic focused on whether the Communist Party should be outlawed in the United States. Stassen took the affirmative, and Dewey supported the negative. Although Stassen entered the debate with a slim lead in the state of Oregon, shortly thereafter (and strongly linked to his performance during the radio broadcast debate), he ultimately lost both his lead in Oregon and the Republican nomination.

The first Nixon–Kennedy debate in 1960 has been considered an important turning point in the presidential election. The debate aired on both television and radio. Interestingly, although the television appearance both hindered Nixon and fundamentally affected his future campaign strategies, his radio ratings from the debate were notably positive. Not only did Nixon seem to come across far better than Kennedy, but also those who *heard*, rather than viewed, the debate chose him as the winner by a substantial margin. Debates before and for many years after 1960 were scarce because of the FCC's regulatory view that required *all* candidates to be included—or given equal time. This gradually changed in the 1970s and 1980s, leading to almost regular presidential candidate debates.

To this day debates make up a significant amount of the election coverage available to voters, and many debates are covered simultaneously by radio and television stations. However, so much more attention goes to the television medium that radio coverage of debates does not attract much attention in the modern political system.

Assessment of Modern Election Coverage on Radio and Its Impact

From its beginnings as the medium that brought election returns into the homes of Americans in 1920, radio coverage has evolved into a medium the significance of which in American political coverage is quite limited. As television supplanted radio in the second half of the 20th century, radio's role in election coverage maintained some significance only in lower-level elections, in state and local contests where candidates were unable to expend major resources on television coverage.

Exceptions to the general trend of reduced radio coverage of elections can be found at the national level in the aggressive coverage of the National Public Radio (NPR) system and state public radio outlets. The growth in the 1970s of all-news radio stations in some communities also brought a renewed interest in covering election matters in state and local communities. The all-talk radio formats of the 1980s and 1990s also heightened radio coverage of, and concentration on, political and election matters.

The impact of radio election coverage is not easy to measure. However, by 1944 a Roper survey reported that 56 percent of those interviewed felt they received the "most accurate news" about the presidential campaign from the radio. Although Roper surveys from 1959 to 1980 indicate that the American people's reliance on radio as a news source decreased from 34 percent in 1959 to 18 percent in 1980, American radio listeners' use of this medium to acquaint themselves with local candidates ranked even lower from 1971 to 1984. In 1971, 6 percent of the respondents to a Roper survey indicated that they became acquainted with local candidates through the radio. Although the percentage rose to 10 percent in 1976, from 1980 to 1984 the percentage remained stable at 6 percent. During the presidential election years of 1973, 1976, and 1984, 6 percent, 4 percent, and 4 percent, respectively, indicated radio as a source through which listeners became acquainted with candidates for public office. However, in 1987, 46 percent of the respondents to a Roper survey indicated that the radio was a "somewhat important" source of information for learning about presidential candidates, and

19 percent indicated radio as a "very important" source. This increase probably stemmed in part from the rise in popularity of political talk radio.

More recent polls from the 1990s have reflected the increased attention radio election coverage has received from voters. A Roper survey conducted from May to June 1992 suggested that 18 percent of respondents gathered information about the 1992 presidential election campaign from the radio, with a decrease to 12 percent by November 1992. However, a November 1996 Roper survey found that 19 percent of the respondents indicated that they gathered information about the 1996 presidential election campaign from the radio. Most recently, a November 1998 Roper survey reported that 23 percent of the respondents indicated that they gathered information about the 1998 off-year election campaigns in their state and district from the radio. Within another decade, however, radio's role in election coverage had dwindled along with the rest of radio news as more people turned to internet and cable news sources for the latest election news.

Although radio began its political coverage by broadcasting presidential election results, recognition of the potential impact of radio on the election process came quickly. Whether through radio coverage of candidate addresses, the development of political advertising, or the coverage of major campaign events such as conventions and debates, strategists and ultimately candidates recognized that radio could reach millions of voters. That accessibility thus influenced the need to effectively present the candidate and the candidate's message in this medium.

Undoubtedly, radio's election coverage brought the political process much closer to the American people. Not only could those with a radio in their living room suddenly sit in on their party's national convention, but they could also hear campaign addresses delivered by presidential candidates in distant states. Even more important, the American people could listen to a candidate deliver an address on specific issues in real time, and they could judge for themselves the information as well as the candidate's delivery style and personality. In essence, radio, through its election coverage, handed the American people the opportunity to participate in and make decisions about candidates firsthand without relying solely on press interpretations.

Further Reading

"…And As for Radio," *Broadcasting* (5 September 1988).
Archer, Gleason Leonard, *History of Radio to 1926*, New York: The American Historical Society, 1938.
Berkman, D., "Politics and Radio in the 1924 Campaign," *Journalism Quarterly* 64 (Summer–Autumn 1987).
Carcasson, Martin, "Herbert Hoover and the Presidential Campaign of 1932: The Failure of Apologia," *Presidential Studies Quarterly* 28 (Spring 1998).
Carroll, Raymond L., "Harry S. Truman's 1948 Election: The Inadvertent Broadcast Campaign," *Journal of Broadcasting and Electronic Media* 31 (Spring 1987).
Chester, Edward W., *Radio, Television, and American Politics*, New York: Sheed and Ward, 1969.
Cornwell, Elmer E., *Presidential Leadership of Public Opinion*, Bloomington: Indiana University Press, 1965.
Dobrez, Tom, "Radio: The Secret Weapon," *Campaigns and Elections* 17 (August 1996).
Dreyer, Edward C., "Political Party Use of Radio and Television in the 1960 Campaign," *Journal of Broadcasting* 8 (Summer 1964).
Gest, Ted, "Clinton: Tune-in, It's Party Time," *U.S. News and World Report* (16 September 1996).
Roper, Burns W., *Public Attitudes toward Television and Other Media in a Time of Change*, New York: Television Information Office, 1985.
Summers, Harrison B., "Radio in the 1948 Campaign," *The Quarterly Journal of Speech* 34 (1948).
Swafford, Tom, "The Last Real Presidential Debate," *American Heritage* 37 (February–March 1986).
Willis, Edgar E., "Radio and Presidential Campaigning," *Central States Speech Journal* 20 (Fall 1969).
Wolfe, G. Joseph, "Some Reactions to the Advent of Campaigning by Radio," *Journal of Broadcasting* 13 (Summer 1969).

LYNDA LEE KAID AND MARY CHRISTINE BANWART,
2009 REVISIONS BY CHRISTOPHER H. STERLING

EMERGENCIES, RADIO'S ROLE IN

Radio's news and entertainment roles have long been taken for granted. In times of emergency, however, the medium often rises to the occasion to play a unique public service role. In times of natural or man-made disasters, radio becomes a prime means of social surveillance, a link with the outside world, and a source of information. Radio can mitigate problems by promoting disaster preparedness, keeping people out of harm's way, assisting in rescue coordination and relief efforts, and facilitating rehabilitation and reconstruction efforts. Radio often has the first reports of impending natural disasters, be they tornadoes, hurricanes, or volcanic eruptions. Radio's potential was demonstrated even before the inception of broadcasting. Although wireless aided in rescuing people from several maritime disasters early in the 20th century, notably during the loss of the liner *Republic* in 1909 when more than 1,500 people were saved thanks to a distress call, the 1912 *Titanic* disaster focused public attention on what the medium could do. On her maiden voyage in mid-April of 1912, the huge passenger liner struck an iceberg and began to sink. Her two wireless operators stayed at their posts almost to the end, sending both "CDQ" and the newer "SOS" emergency signals to both nearby ships and the distant shore. The sole operator on the Cunard liner *Carpathia* heard the signals and the ship steamed 55 miles to rescue the 700 survivors in boats several hours after *Titanic* went down. For weeks thereafter, the wireless operators (one of whom perished) were newspaper heroes.

Early Emergency Broadcasting

The new role of radio became clear with two events in the spring of 1937. Massive snow melt flooding of the Ohio and Mississippi Rivers inundated towns and countryside alike, and local stations often were the only link with the outside world for days at a time. Stations that were themselves flooded out loaned their personnel to those still on the air. Regular program schedules were replaced with day and night reporting (sometimes around the clock) and radio broadcasters directed rescue teams where they were most needed. Some stations became arms of official state or federal agencies and provided a personal message service that might normally have been an illegal point-to-point use of radio stations. Radio's immediacy and portability were well demonstrated.

The most spectacular disaster covered on radio was the burning of the German passenger airship *Hindenburg* as it attempted to land in Lakehurst, New Jersey, near New York City on 6 May 1937. Although 36 people were killed in the fiery crash, 62 survived the disaster, which was hard to believe as the nation watched the subsequent newsreel coverage. But people first heard about the crash as Chicago station WLS reporter Herb Morrison reported what was presumed to be a routine landing. Morrison's gripping eye-witness account, in which he cried with a broken voice, "This is one of the worst catastrophes in the world," was aired on the networks the next day, all of them suspending their usual rule against use of recorded programs.

In all too many later natural disasters—floods, tornadoes, and hurricanes—radio stations provided the crucial warnings of impending trouble and then the critical links with rescue help and the outside world. People soon learned to turn to radio if concerned about the weather or some unusual event. Radio's growing transistor-driven portability in the 1950s continued the medium's unique role even in an age of television. Most radio stations have emergency generators and portable studio-transmitter links that allow reporters to get close to the scene of disasters or emergencies and provide on-the-spot reporting.

One sure indicator of radio's central role in emergencies was its use in government emergency communications schemes. Beginning with the CONELRAD system (1952–63), which can still be seen in old radios with tuners marked for the two frequencies (640 kHz and 1240 kHz) to be used in national or regional emergencies, and progressing to the Emergency Broadcast System (1963–97), radio was to play a key role in Cold War civil defense planning and emergency warning schemes.

Radio's Role in More Recent Disasters

In the 1960s, radio's emergency role showed in two man-made emergencies. When President John F. Kennedy was shot in Dallas, Texas, on 22 November 1963, radio was often the first medium most people tuned to; television was far less common in schools and in the workplace then. As that Friday afternoon wore on, one could see people clustered around portable or car radios trying to learn the latest from Dallas, including the swearing in of a new president. During the massive overnight electric power failure in most of northeastern U.S. in late 1965, WBZ's Bob Kennedy became famous for his reassuring radio coverage during the many dark hours in the Boston area. New York DJs and news reporters filled much the same role there in the almost total absence of television reporting. Those who owned battery-powered transistor radios could tune in local radio personalities who did their best to communicate what was going on, how widespread it was, and when the lights began to come back on (the next morning). Many argued later that radio's collective voice helped to avert a widespread panic in the darkness.

In early 1989, stations in the San Francisco Bay area were on top of the Loma Prieta earthquake and provided the first reports of downed bridges and collapsed and burning buildings, and thus assisted in crowd control and channeled rescue workers to where they were most needed. Later that same year, stations in the Caribbean and along the U.S. coast warned of the looming hurricane Hugo, one of the most powerful storms in years. Station WSTA in the Virgin Islands assisted the Federal Emergency Management Agency (FEMA) and for several days was the only source of news and information for and about the people on the devastated island. The station served as a government communications center, emergency police dispatcher, and chief contact for emergency medical personnel. Stations in southern Florida played similar roles when hurricane Andrew struck in 1992 and wiped out many communities south of Miami.

In January 1998 a huge ice storm struck Maine and Eastern Canada, cutting electricity for at least hours, often days, and up to two weeks in some isolated communities. Thousands also lost their telephone connections, and the state's emergency broadcast system was knocked out as well. Hundreds had to move to central shelters. Throughout the storm, two radio stations managed to stay on the air and launched call-in shows. WWBX-FM in Bangor began "Storm Watch" around the clock, combining an aural bulletin board with message relay, town meetings, and a sharing and coordination center. The station linked people with other people, announced the location of shelters, and passed on cold-weather survival tips. WVOM-FM, also in Bangor, stayed on the air thanks to propane gas carried up to its transmitter. It, too, provided a makeshift command center, often a voice in the dark for thousands with portable radios.

A year later, flooding from heavy rains ravaged eastern North Carolina. Stations again scrapped entertainment programming and went into a 24-hour emergency mode, reporting what was happening, linking people with safety spots on high ground, and helping to funnel rescue workers and food supplies where they were most needed.

When terrorists struck New York's World Trade Center (WTC) and Washington's Pentagon on 11 September 2001, radio again came to the fore as a primary means of media communication, especially to those in or near the attacked areas. With the loss of the multistation antenna atop the WTC's North Tower, television reception was lost for much of the metropolitan New York region, save for cable subscribers. While across the nation many tuned to cable news services or the internet, thanks to battery-powered portables, radio was again the prime means of initial news reports and guidance for many listeners.

When Hurricane Katrina pounded New Orleans and surrounding areas in 2005, and more than 40 broadcast stations were knocked off the air by the storm, some continued broadcasting and valiantly carried on throughout the storm assisting residents and, in some cases, even rescue crews in vital ways. New Orleans station WWL newsman Garland Robinette, who urged citizens to evacuate the city before even the mayor's office did, broadcast constantly in the hours leading up to the storm's arrival, during it and in the days to follow. WWL managed to stay on the air though their primary studio was gutted by high winds and rising water levels. Many city residents, unable to reach 911 emergency operators, turned to WWL to report needs for aid or rescue, or simply to let someone know that they were still alive in some outer borough. Clear Channel would eventually pick up the station's signal and simulcast it on the internet so that distant friends and relatives of New Orleans residents could keep abreast of developments.

CBS Radio also supplied constant Katrina coverage, which included the broadcasting of the names of missing children. The station helped reunite 165 children with their families. Residents were also invaluably aided by amateur "ham" radio operators. After cell towers fell and other systems failed, over 500 operators of this traditional technology assisted rescue agencies and relayed messages to and from Red Cross shelters. In Katrina's wake, the FCC empaneled an Independent Panel Reviewing the Impact of Hurricane Katrina on Communications Networks to examine communications failures during the crisis, and also announced creation of a Homeland Security and Public Safety Bureau to ensure against future failures of this magnitude. As reconstruction got underway, the FCC also worked aggressively to assist in rebuilding the communications infrastructure of New Orleans by issuing over a hundred temporary licenses and waivers for microwave links and other radio services.

Although television stations play similar roles, not everyone can receive signals if power is lost. Radio's portability and pervasiveness in cars, offices, schools, and homes makes it the medium of first resort in disasters and emergency conditions.

See also: CONELRAD; Emergency Alert System; *Hindenburg* Disaster; News; World War II and U.S. Radio

Further Reading

Benthall, Jonathan, *Disasters, Relief, and the Media*, London and New York: I.B. Tauris, 1993.
Deppa, Joan, *The Media and Disasters: Pan Am 103*, London: Fulton, 1993; New York: New York University Press, 1994.
Disasters and the Mass Media: Proceedings of the Committee on Disasters and the Mass Media Workshop, February 1979, Washington, D.C.: National Academy of Sciences, 1980.
Flint, J., "FCC Wants to Overhall EBS," *Broadcasting* 122 (1992).
Fortner, Robert S., *International Communication: History, Conflict, and Control of the Global Metropolis*, Belmont, California: Wadsworth, 1993.
Garner, Joe, *We Interrupt This Broadcast: Relive the Events That Stopped Our Lives—from the Hindenburg to the Death of Diana*, Naperville, Illinois: Sourcebooks, 1998.
Harrison, Shirley, editor, *Disasters and the Media: Managing Crisis Communications*, New York: Palgrave, 1999.
Heyer, Paul, *Titanic Legacy: Disaster As Media Event and Myth*, Westport, Connecticut: Praeger, 1995.

Hogan, Warren L., editor, *Hurricane Carla: A Tribute to the News Media, Newspaper, Radio, Television*, Houston, Texas: Leaman-Hogan Company, 1961.

Mooney, Michael MacDonald, *The Hindenburg*, New York: Dodd Mead, and London: Hart-Davis, MacGibbon, 1972.

Newman, Diane, and Joseph Pollet, "Lessons of Katrina and Gustav," *Mediaweek* (29 September 2008), p. 10.

Straubhaar, Joseph D., and Robert LaRose, *Communications Media in the Information Society*, Belmont, California: Wadsworth, 1996; 2nd edition, as *Media Now: Communications Media in the Information Age*, 2000.

"Virgin Islands AM Beats Hugo," *Broadcasting* (30 October 1989).

LYOMBE EKO AND JOANNE GULA,
2009 REVISIONS BY CARY O'DELL

EMERGENCY ALERT SYSTEM
Warning Listeners of Disaster

The Federal Communications Commission (FCC) established the Emergency Broadcast System (EBS) in 1963 to provide the government with a means of quickly contacting U.S. citizens in the event of an emergency. Originally conceived for national defense purposes, its mission was expanded to include natural as well as man-made disasters. The Emergency Alert System (EAS) replaced the EBS system in 1997. Although the technology and specific rules differ, the intent of the EAS remains the same as EBS.

Origins

In the 1950s the United States was increasingly concerned about the possibility of Soviet aggression. During the Cold War, the United States instituted a number of actions to protect itself from a Soviet attack. One fear expressed by the military was that the many American radio transmissions could serve as navigational aids for enemy aircraft (as they had for Japan's 1941 attack on Pearl Harbor). In 1951 the United States instituted a program called Control of Electromagnetic Radiation (CONELRAD). Under this plan, all non-military radio transmissions except for those on two frequencies—640 kHz and 1240 kHz—would cease. The military decided that limiting all transmissions to only those two frequencies would provide the best system for informing the public, while limiting the usefulness of U.S. transmitters for locating military targets. Radio receivers sold after 1953 were required to mark the two designated frequencies with triangles to indicate their civil defense role. This requirement remained in effect until the EBS replaced CONELRAD in 1963.

The fear of Soviet aggression continued in the 1960s, but technology had advanced to the point that radio navigation for foreign bombers was no longer the anticipated threat. Instead, the United States feared a long-distance missile attack, which would not rely on radio navigation, so CONELRAD was replaced with the EBS in 1963. Although still serving the purpose of alerting the nation in the event of foreign aggression, there was no longer a need to order all transmitters off the air. Instead, only those lower-powered stations, usually without the staff or financing to keep a 24-hour emergency operation running, would be ordered off the air during an emergency.

EBS Operations

Unfortunately, the original system was susceptible to frequent false alarms. The early EBS warnings occurred when an EBS station stopped transmitting (known as dropping carrier). Other radio stations, required by law to monitor the EBS station, would then be alerted that the EBS had been activated. The problem was that EBS stations might stop transmitting as the result of a loss of power or because an electrical storm had caused a power surge. In 1973 the dual tone alert system was devised, which dramatically reduced the number of false alarms. EBS activation then required a purposeful triggering of the alert signal by a station employee rather than a station's passive dropping carrier. In the 1970s the EBS was seen as a valuable resource that could be used for more than just defense purposes. Added to the system's mission was notification of such natural disasters as earthquakes and tornadoes. Americans quickly became familiar with the EBS from the weekly tests that were required of all broadcast stations.

EBS was always taken seriously by the FCC, which has disciplined stations that failed to comply with the rules. Some stations ignored weekly tests. Others did not maintain the necessary equipment for monitoring and transmitting a signal. Although those transgressions occurred relatively frequently, it was the occasional willful violation of EBS rules that received the most attention and the most severe penalties. In 1991, during the Persian Gulf War, St. Louis disc jockey John Ulett announced that the United States was under nuclear attack and used the EBS tone to validate the hoax. Two hours later the station apologized for the prank, which management claimed it was unaware of until it actually aired. The FCC was not persuaded by either the apology or the station's lack of complicity and fined KSHE-FM $25,000 for the infraction.

Creating EAS

The need to revise the EBS became increasingly apparent. The two-toned signal was considered to be an annoyance by both broadcasters and listeners. The EBS's success depended on a "daisy chain" of alerts, requiring emergency personnel to contact a station, that station to broadcast a tone, and other stations to receive the tone and retransmit the information. Any breaks in the chain resulted in emergency information not being relayed. In 1989 one station did not rebroadcast an alert about the San Francisco earthquake because the operator on duty did not know how to use the equipment and all the station's engineering staff were attending the World Series baseball game. There have been numerous reports of stations that did not retransmit important weather information because of equipment or operator failure. The overall reliability of the system was called into question.

In 1994 the FCC acted to phase in a replacement of the EBS with the newer EAS by 1997. One change particularly appreciated by broadcasters was the shortening of the length of the alert signal. Instead of the two-tone transmission of nearly 30 seconds, the tone was reduced to only eight seconds. Although weekly testing continues, the alert tone is only required as part of monthly tests, thereby making the system much less intrusive. Weekly tests can actually be conducted that are nearly imperceptible to the audience.

For emergency personnel, EAS is an improvement over EBS because the digital signal can be triggered remotely (or via automation) without the involvement of station employees, thus decreasing the likelihood that messages will go unannounced. What's more, because EAS uses a digital signal, it is not limited to broadcast outlets. Rather, emergency communiqué can be sent via cellphone and soon via text messaging and other modern technologies. It is hoped that this wider use of various media platforms will lower the risk of potential "missed messages," as arose during the April 2007 Virginia Tech school shooting.

The new law required cable systems to participate and made alerts available in Spanish and in visual forms for the deaf. If used at the national level, only the president or his representative can activate the EAS. Local activation can come from several sources, including National Weather Service and Federal Emergency Management Agency offices (something which has been done, for example, in California to broadcast news of imminent natural disasters). In all the years of CONELRAD, EBS, and EAS, there has never been a national activation of an emergency alert.

See also: CONELRAD; Emergencies, Radio's Role in

Further Reading

Chartrand, Sabra, "Warning of Disasters, Digitally," *New York Times* (7 November 1993).
FCC Emergency Alert System webpage, www.fcc.gov/eb/eas
Federal Communications Commission, *Emergency Broadcast System: Rules and Regulations*, Washington, D.C.: Government Printing Office, 1977.
Lambrecht, Bill, "KSHE Is Fined $25,000 for Fake Warning of Nuclear Attack," *St. Louis Post-Dispatch* (25 April 1991).
"Shrill Emergency Broadcast Test Soon to Be a Cold War Relic," *New York Times* (17 November 1996).

DOM CARISTI,
2009 REVISIONS BY CARY O'DELL

EMERSON RADIO
Pioneer of Small Radio Receivers

From the early 1930s into the 1950s, Emerson Radio (not to be confused with the older and larger Emerson Electric Co.) was one of the larger manufacturers of radio receivers in the United States. The company's story parallels the decline of American manufacturing in the late 20th century.

Origins

Victor Hugo Emerson, a former Columbia Phonograph company manager, created the Emerson Phonograph Company in 1915–16. He was already well known in audio circles for his 14 patents in sound recording and reproduction granted from 1893 to 1905, and he continued to receive patents until 1922. His firm manufactured both phonographs and records (including a talking books line for children), riding the early mechanical era recording boom of the World War I years. When business fell off sharply after the war, the company found itself overextended and went into receivership in December 1920.

Benjamin Abrams (1893–1967), his younger brothers Max and Lewis, and Rudolph Kamarak purchased the remaining assets of Emerson Phonograph in 1922 and formed the Emerson Radio and Phonograph Corporation. The senior Abrams would run the operation for the next four decades. After selling off the record business, the new firm entered the radio receiver manufacturing business in 1924 as a small player among several giants and created and marketed some of the first radio-phonograph combination devices. With the advent of the Great Depression and the failure of many other radio manufacturing businesses, Emerson took a new direction.

Emerson and Small Radios

The Depression forced radio manufacturers to provide smaller and cheaper sets, a trend first pursued by several smaller California-based companies. But many of the initial "midget" sets were poorly made and unsuccessful. The image of small radios began to change with a 1932 Emerson product.

The "Model 25" was 10 inches wide, 6.5 inches high and 4 inches deep. It was a four-tube receiver with a 6-inch speaker, weighing about 6 pounds. At a then-low cost of $25.00, the Model 25 sold about a quarter of a million units from late 1932 into the first half of 1933 and helped place Emerson on the map. Demand was so strong that for several months the manufacturing line had trouble keeping up.

Building on this breakthrough success, Emerson quickly focused its attention on other small radios. Some were novelty items built around popular movies (*Snow White and the Seven Dwarfs*), movie or radio stars (*Mickey Mouse*), and even people in the news (the Dionne quintuplets). All of them (as well as similar products from other firms) sold well, as did a $9.95 compact radio of 1937. The "Little Miracle" set of 1938 was a five-tube super-heterodyne receiver offered in a variety of styles and colors as combination and plastic cabinetry began to take over more expensive all-wood cabinets. The 1939 two-tube "Emersonette" took things further—a tiny 6×5-inch receiver selling for $6.95.

Emerson was now making more than one million sets a year. Perhaps the peak of Emerson's prewar success came with the 1940 "Patriot" model, with a design by Norman Bel Geddes based on the American flag (it came in red, white, or blue cabinets with the other two colors as trim).

By 1941, about 80 percent of all radio sales in the U.S. were of compact models, though Emerson was among the first to offer FM receivers when that service began commercial operation that year. But it was on the strength of its small radios that Emerson's portion of the total American radio market rose from a mere 1.5 percent to 17.5 percent between 1932 and 1942. Riding this success, in 1943 the company went public, selling 40 percent of its stock.

Expansion

Emerson produced its first television sets in 1947, although it continued to offer many radio models.

In 1951–52 Emerson first offered a new "pocket" portable radio with subminiature tubes designed by Raytheon. This led to the Model 747 in 1953, a tiny and eminently portable table radio that weighed only 22 ounces. One of the last miniature pre-transistor radios, the Model 747 sold for $40 even though it received poor review notices in *Consumer's Research Bulletin*.

But change was in the air. By 1954 radio made up only 15 percent of company revenues. Emerson offered its first audio tape recorders in 1955 and by the late 1950s was producing combination tiny tube and transistor radios and a growing variety of television models. In 1958, Emerson bought the DuMont consumer electronics manufacturing operation and began to use that brand name along with its own.

Later Developments

Emerson's last full year of independent operation was 1964. The company was sold to National Union Electric in 1965 and absorbed Pilot radio the same year. By the end of the year, the combined firm owned 20 subsidiaries that continued the sale of consumer electronics under both the Emerson and DuMont names. After several years in the red, owing in part to rising consumer electronic imports, the company began to shift away from this focus in 1972.

Major Electronics Corporation of Brooklyn bought the Emerson name in 1973 and four years later renamed itself after the earlier company. It dropped the last U.S. manufactured product (fittingly, a phonograph) in 1980. By 1983–84, imported televisions and videocassette recorders made up two-thirds of company sales. Most were manufactured in Korea but sold under the Emerson name. The once-revered H.H. Scott brand was taken over in 1985, and the company moved to New Jersey. The Scott line was discontinued in 1991.

In October the ever-smaller firm declared bankruptcy, and 60 percent of its stock was taken over by Fidenas Investments, a Swiss firm. Emerson began to retail car audio systems in 1995, licensing its name to several important Korean and Chinese consumer electronic products. But at the turn of the 21st century, the company was down to about 100 employees dealing with product import and distribution. Emerson no longer manufactured anything. About half of its output was sold each year to Wal-Mart and a quarter to the Target discount chain.

See also: Receivers; Transistor Radios

Further Reading

"Emerson Phonograph Company," *Victor and 78 Journal* (Winter 1997–98).

Emerson Radio and Phonograph Corporation, *Small Radio: Yesterday and in the World of Tomorrow*, New York: Emerson Radio and Phonograph Corporation, 1943.

Halasz, Robert, "Emerson," in volume 30 of *International Directory of Company Histories*, edited by Jay P. Pederson, Detroit, Michigan: St. James Press, 2000.

Schiffer, Michael Brian, *The Portable Radio in American Life*, Tucson: University of Arizona Press, 1991.

CHRISTOPHER H. STERLING

"EQUAL TIME" RULE
Political Broadcasting Regulations

Sections of the Communications Act of 1934 and related rules and regulations of the Federal Communications Commission (FCC) require that candidates for political office in the United States be treated equitably in their purchase or other use of broadcast time. These so-called equal time provisions are controversial and have been considerably modified over the years.

The Law

At first—in American elections between 1920 and 1926—there was no regulation of political broadcasting, and some stations did not allow candidates on the air with political appeals. As Congress moved to pass the Radio Act of 1927, the initial bill contained no provisions concerning political candidates' use of radio. Only a Senate amendment that grew out of concern that radio might exert too much control over the political process led to the inclusion of Section 18, which required that:

> If any licensee shall permit any person who is a legally qualified candidate for any public office to use a broadcasting station, he shall afford equal opportunities to all other such candidates for that office in the use of such broadcasting station, and the [Federal Radio Commission] shall make rules and regulations to carry this provision into effect.

The provision did not *require* that political candidates be granted access to airtime, for the section continued, "No obligation is imposed upon any licensee to allow the use of its station by any such candidate." Section 18, without change, became Section 315 of the Communications Act of 1934.

A remarkably small number of amendments have only slightly altered the meaning of these words in the intervening years. The first, in 1952, added a provision prohibiting broadcasters from charging political candidates higher rates than those charged other advertisers for "comparable use." A more fundamental amendment added in 1959 exempted from Section 315 requirements any appearance by a candidate in a "bona fide" (meaning controlled by the broadcaster, not the candidate) newscast, news interview, news documentary, or on-the-spot news coverage if the appearance of the candidate was incidental to the program. Finally, in 1971 Congress narrowed the ability of broadcasters to avoid political advertisements or broadcasts when it modified another section of the act (Section 312 [a][7]) to state that not allowing candidates for federal office (candidates for president, vice president, or for seats in the House and Senate) access to the air might be grounds for revocation of a station's license. Stations could still avoid dealing with candidates for state and local offices.

For decades, broadcasters were caught in a legal bind—Section 315 specifically enjoined them from censoring any remarks made by political candidates, yet stations could still be held liable for any defamatory comments candidates might make. The Supreme Court finally removed this danger by holding in the 1959 *WDAY-TV* decision that, given the no-censorship requirement in the law, stations could not be held responsible for whatever candidates might say.

FCC Rules and Regulations

As required by changing circumstances, over the years the FCC has defined and refined what the relatively few words in Section 315 are to mean in practice. Such definition has focused on phrases such as "legally qualified candidate" "equal opportunities" "use" of a station; how to determine rates charged; and, after 1959, which programs were entirely exempt from the provisions. Indeed, the rules vary for primary and general elections as to who is covered and for what period of time (requiring, for example, an even more stringent "lowest unit charge" price requirement for candidates' advertising 45 days before a primary and 60 days before a general election). Stations must maintain detailed and up-to-date records of all requests for political time and of all actual sales and/or uses of airtime for a period of two years.

These many complications grew steadily more involved after 1960 with an accumulation of numerous FCC decisions and court cases; the confusion finally led to publication by both the FCC and the National Association of Broadcasters of regularly revised booklet-length "primers" or "catechisms," usually in question-and-answer format, of the latest rule interpretations. Despite their complexity—or perhaps because of it—broadcasters, candidates, and the public refer to these rules by the shorthand term of *equal time*, even though far more is involved than merely an equitable provision of time.

As but one example—prior to 1960, debates between or among candidates counted as a "use" requiring Section 315 treatment under FCC rules. For the 1960 election, Congress temporarily suspended Section 315 (leading to the so-called Great Debates between Kennedy and Nixon, which were carried on both radio and television). Effective in 1975, the FCC allowed debates to occur without triggering Section 315 requirements if the debates were sponsored by a disinterested third party—initially, the League of Women Voters. Only in 1983 were broadcasters themselves allowed to sponsor debates as one of the "bona fide" news exemptions in Section 315. National and local debates have increasingly become a staple of American elections since then.

The broadcast industry has attempted repeatedly to have the "equal time" requirements dropped—at least for radio (because of the large number of stations) if not for television as well. Indeed, in the 1980s, a deregulation-minded FCC made the same recommendation to Congress. But all such efforts have generally fallen on deaf ears, given that those who must act to make the change—representatives and senators—are the very people who depend on the access the law provides.

See also: Communications Act of 1934; Fairness Doctrine; Federal Communications Commission; Politics and Radio; Radio Laws

Further Reading

Barrow, Roscow L., "The Equal Opportunities and Fairness Doctrines in Broadcasting: Pillars in the Forum of Democracy," *University of Cincinnati Law Review* 37 (Summer 1968).
Farmer's Educational and Cooperative Union v. WDAY Inc., 360 US 525 (1959).
Federal Communications Commission, Media Bureau. "Political Programming," www.fcc.gov/mb/policy/political/
Friedenthal, Jack H., and Richard J. Medalie, "The Impact of Federal Regulation on Political Broadcasting: Section 315 of the Communications Act," *Harvard Law Review* 72 (January 1959).
Ostroff, David H., "Equal Time: Origins of Section 18 of the Radio Act of 1927," *Journal of Broadcasting* 24 (Summer 1980).
A Political Broadcast Catechism, 3rd edition, Washington, D.C., National Association of Broadcasters, 1956; 15th edition 2000.

CHRISTOPHER H. STERLING

EVANGELISTS/EVANGELICAL RADIO
Conservative Protestant Religious Stations and Programs

Evangelical radio forms a distinct subgenre within religious radio, referring primarily to programs with a teaching/preaching format, often incorporating hymns or other kinds of sacred music. The intent of evangelical radio programming is to convert unbelievers or to reconvert lapsed Christians by stressing the Bible's call to repent and accept Christ as a personal savior.

It is difficult to be precise about what comprises "evangelical radio" as distinct from other forms of religious radio, because in some sense every effort at putting religion on the air constitutes an invitation to learn more about the principles being presented—and because radio itself, as an advertising-saturated medium, is built around an evangelistic pattern. Nearly everything on radio, from ubiquitous 60-second car sales spots to public radio fund drives, has something of an evangelical ring to it.

In addition, the term *evangelical religion* means different things to different groups of people, and the meaning has changed over the course of the 20th century. An *evangelist* can mean any person who seeks to convert another to his or her own religious beliefs. In the popular mind, many tend to link the terms *evangelical* and *fundamentalist*, because both offer a Bible-centered worldview with an emphasis on personal conversion. However, the two are not coterminous. The modern evangelical movement had its roots in the fundamentalist movement of the 1910s and 1920s and maintained ties to fundamentalism through Bible colleges, summer camps, publishing, and radio, but a group of so-called neo-evangelicals decisively broke with fundamentalism by the late 1950s under the leadership of Billy Graham. Contemporary evangelicals occupy a middle ground between liberal religion and fundamentalism. Today, *evangelicalism* refers to a loose coalition of conservative Protestant groups in North America, including Baptists, Holiness-Pentecostalists, nondenominational evangelists, and charismatic Protestants.

Although not all of these traditions have been equally involved in media evangelism, the media have been an important tool of American evangelicals in their quest to fulfill the so-called Great Commission, the instruction of Jesus Christ to his followers: "Go ye into all the world, and preach the gospel to every creature" (Mark 16:15). The preaching of the Christian message in or to every country is considered by many evangelists to be a necessary precondition for the second coming of Christ (e.g., Matt. 24:14), and radio was touted as a providential means to accomplish this important end.

Origins

Revivalism—that is, religious meetings that work through music, word, and emotional appeal to encourage conversion in those attending—lent itself naturally to the new medium of radio in the 1920s. Revivalism grew out of the highly successful late 19th- and early 20th-century mass-audience revival campaigns of Dwight Moody and Billy Sunday and traveling revival movements such as Chautauqua. As promoters of radio evangelism were fond of reminding potential donors, a single broadcast could reach more people than even Dwight Moody had been able to reach in a lifetime. Because folk and campmeeting revivalism was centrally an aural experience—the spoken and heard word being experientially more powerful than the written and read word—the format of revival sermons and meetings made it onto radio with little adaptation.

In fact, radio evangelism is one of the medium's oldest program genres. In the largely unregulated early years of radio broadcasting in the United States, municipal and private stations alike were in search of material to fill time. Evangelists, ever on the lookout for ways to speak to larger and larger audiences, stepped in to fill the need and never left the airwaves, though their presence was not always so sought after by station owners and broadcasters. In addition, some evangelistic denominations and religious organizations developed their own stations to promote gospel on the air: WMBI Chicago (owned by the Moody Bible Institute), KFUO St. Louis (Lutheran Church, Missouri Synod), and KFSG Los Angeles (International Church of the Foursquare Gospel) were three of the earliest, all coming on the air within two years of each other in the mid-1920s; in 2009, all three were still broadcasting as Christian radio stations.

However, once network radio was firmly entrenched, evangelicals found it harder to access airtime, even with donations from loyal listeners and supporters. Their often strident "hellfire and damnation" message worked against both networks' desire for mass audiences and advertisers' appeals for consumer spending, making evangelical radio a risk for network broadcasters. Additionally, airtime became more expensive, and evangelical radio was largely dependent on listener donations for the funds to purchase airtime. The National Broadcasting Company (NBC) and the Columbia

Broadcasting System (CBS) early on developed a policy of donating a block of airtime for religious broadcasting to representatives of the major religious groups in America. As a fragmented and largely grassroots movement from the 1920s through the 1940s, American evangelicalism found itself unable to obtain this donated airtime from the networks.

Instead, evangelical radio focused on buying time on individual stations or developing its own small-scale independent networks. Although Christian benevolent organizations (e.g., the Gideons and the Christian Business Men's Association) made regular and sometimes substantial donations to evangelical radio efforts, most broadcasters relied heavily on individual donations to pay for airtime. Listeners sometimes proved creative and resourceful in scraping together small amounts of money to send to support their favorite broadcasts.

Mutual Broadcasting System—the only national network that then sold time for religion—collected over $2.1 million for its religious broadcasts in 1942. In 1944 this amount had jumped to $3.5 million, a full quarter of the network's income. By 1943, reported *Variety* magazine, an estimated $200 million was "rolling into church coffers each year from radio listeners," allowing racketeers and "religious pirates" to get rich quick without adhering to standards of accounting. Broadcasters' appeals for funds proved increasingly controversial; Mutual eventually prohibited on-air appeals for funding. In the late 1940s, for example, the vigilant director of religious activities at Mutual Broadcasting, Elsie Dick, insisted that Walter Maier (speaker of the *Lutheran Hour* on her network) refrain from using even relatively vague statements, such as "if you want these broadcasts to continue, write to us to assure us of your interest." Broadcasters on Mutual could not follow a request to "pray for the work of this broadcast" with the program's mailing address, as this would violate Mutual's policy against the solicitation of funds. Individual stations that accepted religious broadcasts sometimes also established similar policies. Broadcasters sometimes circumvented these restrictions by offering "free" merchandise such as Bibles, tracts, calendars, or commemorative pins. Through the written requests of listeners for promotional items, broadcasters could build a mailing list for direct-mail appeals instead of using airtime for financial appeals.

Examples of Evangelical Radio

Although it is impossible to be exhaustive in listing all evangelists and their programs throughout the years, a few examples illustrate the genre and its approach to missionizing America and the world: the *Back to the Bible Hour*, the *Radio Bible Hour*, the *Lutheran Hour*, and the *Old Fashioned Revival Hour*.

Started in 1939 by Theodore Epp, the *Back to the Bible Hour* was a daily gospel broadcast and Bible-study program originating from Lincoln, Nebraska. By the mid-1950s, Epp could claim that the "sun never set" on *Back to the Bible*, which was heard somewhere in the world at any given minute through AM, FM, or shortwave. The ministry had its own large two-storey building in downtown Lincoln, where half a million letters were received annually and where some 300,000 copies of the *Good News Broadcaster* and the *Young Ambassador* (the latter aimed at teenagers) were printed and mailed each month. A staff of over 150 workers and volunteers provided music and choir direction for the broadcast, sorted and answered mail, taped and shipped out recordings to stations, staffed a round-the-clock prayer room, and coordinated appearances of Epp and his field evangelists at rallies and meetings. Epp authored 70 books, started a Bible correspondence school, and founded a Back to the Bible Missionary Agency (now International Ministries). At his death in 1985, the program was continued with speakers Warren Wiersbe (1985–92) and Woodrow Kroll (1992–present); it is currently syndicated on over 385 stations and online.

More controversial and colorful was the stridently fundamentalist *Radio Bible Hour* of the Reverend J. Harold Smith, which began in 1935 in South Carolina but for some years was forced off American stations after its pugnacious attacks on the Federal Council of Churches. In 1953 Smith moved the *Radio Bible Hour* to a Mexican border station, XERF, in Ciudad Acuna, just south of the Texas border, where he continued to broadcast until Mexico banned English language religious broadcasts from superpower border stations. The program can still be heard over 50 stations and online.

The *Lutheran Hour*, sponsored by the International Lutheran Laymen's League of the conservative Lutheran Church, Missouri Synod, is the most widely syndicated evangelical radio program. Still heard on 1,200 stations worldwide and online, the *Lutheran Hour* was hosted from 1930 to 1950 by Dr. Walter A. Maier, a professor at Concordia Theological Seminary in St. Louis. His successors continued Maier's sermon-and-song format and its nondenominational approach to Christian outreach.

Finally, perhaps the best-known evangelical radio program was the *Old Fashioned Revival Hour*, the creation of southern California evangelist Charles

Fuller in 1934. Recorded for many years in front of a live audience at the Long Beach Auditorium, Fuller's *Revival Hour* combined lively choral and barbershop-style revival hymns with energetic preaching; the program pulled audiences of 20 million listeners weekly by the mid-1940s. Fuller was also active behind the microphone in bringing together evangelical broadcasters in the 1940s and 1950s to advocate for paid-time programming through the Natianal Association of Evangelicals and the National Religious Broadcasters.

One important thrust of radio evangelism—and a strategy employed by each of the media evangelists noted above—has been to extend religious broadcasting worldwide in the various languages of each nation. Clarence Jones, who worked in the late 1920s on broadcasts from the Chicago Gospel Tabernacle, was one of the pioneers of long-range overseas religious radio. He founded radio station HCJB in Quito, Ecuador. Many North American evangelists, while securing time and broadcast airspace on the AM spectrum, also quietly used shortwave or mailed transcription discs to overseas stations in order to be heard by as wide as possible a swath of the globe. The *Lutheran Hour*, for example, broadcasts in over 130 countries in a multitude of languages, from French to Quechua to Zulu.

Although reaching the far corners of the globe was one goal of radio evangelists, reaching the hearts of listening individuals was the other and related goal. In other words, massive broadcast coverage mattered only as far as that coverage would convert people one at a time.

Trends since the 1960s

Billy Graham's evangelistic mass-media campaigns beginning in 1957 helped catapult evangelicalism back to a position of cultural influence. His *Hour of Decision* program was the first religious broadcast to be carried as a paid-time evangelistic broadcast on the American Broadcasting Company (ABC) radio network. And since the 1960s, the Christian media industry has literally exploded in growth, with television, publishing, music, and internet being added to radio. In 1971 there were 400 stations airing religious programming; in 1999 there were over 1,730 such stations, with 1,400 of those considered "full-time" religious stations airing 15 hours or more of religious programming per week.

Despite the dynamic growth, the format of evangelistic programs on radio has changed remarkably little. In stark contrast to the secular end of the contemporary radio industry, most evangelical radio programs are sponsored by a single organization or ministry. Although some are widely syndicated, nearly all evangelical programs are confined to Christian-format radio stations, in keeping with the radio industry's trend toward niche marketing. Gospel-oriented preaching programs continue to thrive within the world of Christian media, but since the 1960s, some religious broadcasters have expressed concern that evangelical radio is a religious ghetto, serving its own rather than reaching new converts.

As early as 1961, liberal Protestant Charles Brackbill, member of the Broadcasting and Film Commission of the National Council of Churches of Christ in America, criticized what he described as radio evangelism's tired format: "the loud and the sad and the intense voices pouring out on the faithful with their 'heartfelt' pleas for 'letters,' pictures, or books or blessed handkerchiefs." Evangelism, Brackbill argued, should seek to reach the unchurched through proven commercial broadcasting techniques: a quick first impression, a catchy "hook," and lots of repetition. In 1964 the Mennonites tried 30- and 60-second ad spots for the gospel message, criticizing traditional radio programming for attracting "an audience which already has some tendency toward spiritual orientation," in the words of Dr. Henry Weaver, the developer of the series. HCJB founder and director Clarence Jones lamented in 1970 that missionary stations tended to drift in the direction of speaking to believers—who, after all, were the source of any station's continuing funds (incidentally, many of these same concerns would surface over televangelism, where the audience numbers, production costs, and cultural stakes were even higher).

By the late 1980s, some observers expressed concern that evangelism programming would be replaced by magazine or talk-format programs or by Christian music formats. Indeed, one study suggested that only 37 percent of programs on religious stations focused on preaching. National Religious Broadcasters maintains, however, that traditional "preaching" accounts for an overwhelming number of religious radio formats. It is quite possible that stations which engage in heavy sermonizing simply choose not to call it "evangelism" or "preaching" because of those words' "fire and brimstone" connotations. Instead, most stations prefer such softer sounding similes as "teaching" or the increasingly popular term "Christian Talk," often augmented with conservative talk radio programming. In recent years, some outlets, seeking ways to less obtrusively get their message out, simply interrupt long musical interludes with short, pre-recorded messages known as "sermonettes."

Evangelical radio has also become increasingly politicized, with stations and their on-air talent taking vocal stands on issues ranging from banning gay marriage to the 2008 Presidential election. Evangelical broadcasters have been among the most outspoken against the possible reinstatement of the FCC's Fairness Doctrine.

Perhaps more surprisingly, evangelical broadcasters have been among the first to embrace newer technologies. Some estimates suggest there are well over 900 religious-oriented internet radio stations operating, whereas other groups have been prolific in producing and disturbing religious-themed radio podcasts (or "godcasts"). Churches and religious groups have also been among the first to apply to the FCC for low-powered radio station licenses.

Although hugely popular with its core audiences, whether evangelical radio is reaching unchurched listeners remains less clear.

See also: Contemporary Christian Music Format; Gospel Music Format; National Religious Broadcasters; Religion on Radio

Further Reading

Carpenter, Joel A., *Revive Us Again: The Reawakening of American Fundamentalism*, New York: Oxford University Press, 1997.

Dick, Donald, "Religious Broadcasting, 1920–1965: A Bibliography," *Journal of Broadcasting* 9 (Summer 1965).

Directory of Religious Media (annual; 1994–).

Dorgan, Howard, *The Airwaves of Zion: Radio and Religion in Appalachia*, Knoxville: University of Tennessee Press, 1993.

Erickson, Hal, *Religious Radio and Television in the United States, 1921–1991: The Programs and Personalities*, Jefferson, North Carolina: McFarland, 1992.

Martin, William, "The God-Hucksters of Radio," *Atlantic Monthly* 225 (June 1970).

Neely, Lois, *Come Up to This Mountain: The Miracle of Clarence W. Jones and HCJB*, Opa Locka, Florida: World Radio Missionary Fellowship, and Wheaton, Illinois: Tyndale House, 1980.

NRB: National Religious Broadcasters, http://nrb.org.

Schultze, Quentin J., editor, *American Evangelicals and the Mass Media*, Grand Rapids, Michigan: Academie Books/ Zondervan, 1990.

Stout, Daniel A., and Judith Mitchell Buddenbaum, editors, *Religion and Mass Media: Audiences and Adaptations*, Thousand Oaks, California: Sage, 1996.

Sweet, Leonard I., editor, *Communication and Change in American Religious History*, Grand Rapids, Michigan: Eerdmans, 1993.

Ward, Mark, *Air of Salvation: The Story of Christian Broadcasting*, Manassas, Virginia: National Religious Broadcasters, and Grand Rapids, Michigan: Baker Books, 1994.

TONA J. HANGEN,
2009 REVISIONS BY CARY O'DELL

FAIRNESS DOCTRINE
Controversial Issue Broadcasting Policy

Until 1987 (with related parts lasting until 2000), the Federal Communications Commission (FCC) adhered to a series of policy guidelines collectively called the *fairness doctrine*. These guidelines encouraged stations to cover issues of public controversy, and to provide a variety of points of view on those issues. Although they lasted, the policies were among the most controversial of all FCC program regulations.

Origin

A station licensee's duty to present diverse views on public issues was first declared by the Federal Radio Commission in 1928. A dozen years later, however, the FCC reversed direction when it strongly criticized a station for its practice of editorializing. In its 1941 *Mayflower* decision, the FCC concluded that with limited frequencies available for broadcasting, the public interest could not be well served by dedication of a broadcast facility to the support of its own partisan ends. In line with the *Mayflower* decision, broadcasters began to prohibit the sale of commercial time to deal with controversial issues—a policy that also helped them financially as such ads would only serve to anger some listeners and other advertisers.

In 1949 the FCC reversed itself, reconfirming that while stations have an obligation to cover controversial issues of public importance they now could (but did not have to) editorialize. When WHKC in Columbus, Ohio, refused to sell airtime to a labor union, the FCC stated that the station must be sensitive to the problems of public concern in the community and make sufficient time available on a nondiscriminatory basis. The commission concluded that radio stations have the "responsibility for determining the specific program material to be broadcast over their stations." Therefore, they were required to devote broadcast time to "issues of interest in the community served by their stations and [ensure] that such programs be designed so that the public has a reasonable opportunity to hear different opposing positions on the public issues of interest and importance in the community."

To nail down the proposed new policy on editorializing, the FCC held hearings on the matter. From the hearings came a 1949 statement, *In the Matter of Editorializing by Broadcast Licensees*, which placed two primary obligations on the broadcasters. What would become known later as the "fairness doctrine" required broadcasters (1) to cover controversial issues of public importance, and (2) to provide a reasonable opportunity for the presentation of contrasting viewpoints on those issues.

Development

A decade later, in 1959, Congress entered the fray. Legislators amended Section 315 (the political "equal opportunity" section of the Communications Act) to limit the applicability of the requirement to four types of news programs. At the same time, they made more concrete the broadcaster's responsibility to afford reasonable opportunity for the discussion of conflicting views on issues of public importance. This added phrase would cause considerable legal confusion in the future.

By 1967 the FCC had extended what was now commonly referred to as "the fairness doctrine" to include broadcast advertising of cigarettes, reasoning that because smoking was a controversial health issue, broadcasters were therefore required to provide contrasting viewpoints. (This provision lasted until cigarette advertising was removed from the air entirely in the early 1970s.)

Complaining about yet another extension of the fairness doctrine, broadcasters asked what other types of program or advertising might trigger fairness doctrine concerns. To clarify the scope of their doctrine, the FCC instituted a wide-ranging inquiry into the fairness doctrine and its efficacy. As one result, the commission created three "contingent rights of access" policies similar to Section 315: the Zapple rule, the political editorializing rules, and the personal attack rules. The Zapple rule (named for a long-time Senate staff member, Nicholas Zapple, who had been involved with the issue) held that supporters of opposing political candidates must be given approximately the same amount of airtime during election campaigns. In its political editorial rule, the FCC required broadcasters to contact a legally qualified candidate within 24 hours of any station editorial opposing the candidate or endorsing an opponent and to provide a script or tape as well as free time to reply. The political editorial rule pertained only when a station editorial represented the views of the station licensee. Political commentators who were independent of management were subject only to the general fairness doctrine. Finally, the FCC's personal attack rules specified that broadcasters must offer reply time if the honesty, character, or integrity of an identified person or group was attacked during the discussion of a controversial issue of public importance. A person attacked had to be notified within a week of the date, time, and identification of the broadcast. The licensee was required to provide a script, tape, or accurate summary of the attack and offer a reasonable opportunity for the attacked person to respond over the same station at no charge.

The Supreme Court firmly supported the fairness doctrine's constitutionality in its 1969 landmark decision in *Red Lion Broadcasting Co. v. FCC*. Broadcasters argued that the number of commercial radio and TV stations in the country was higher than that of newspapers (for which no such

"fairness" policy existed because of the First Amendment)—and growing. Therefore, they argued that the fairness doctrine was unnecessary because the public suffered no shortage of opportunities to hear different stations and diverse viewpoints. Broadcasters also contended that the fairness doctrine actually "chilled" or curtailed First Amendment rights of broadcasters by encouraging self-censorship—in other words, that many controversial issues might not be covered at all. The Court rejected both of these contentions, asserting that as long as demand for stations exceeded supply (the high sales price of stations was one such indicator), scarcity of spectrum remained, and thus allowed such FCC policies. In addition, the Court ruled that the doctrine did not violate a broadcaster's First Amendment rights as the right of the viewers and listeners to hear diverse viewpoints was paramount to the right of broadcasters to express their views.

Another Supreme Court case decided five years later, *Tornillo v. Miami Herald* (1974), however, concluded that a fairness-type of requirement on newspapers in the state of Florida was clearly unconstitutional. Decided by the same court membership as had decided *Red Lion* five years earlier, the decision showed the stark difference in how the law viewed newspaper and broadcast journalists.

About the same time, the FCC adopted another Fairness Report, which reaffirmed the conclusions of its 1949 decision and upheld the application of a general fairness doctrine requirement for broadcast licensees on both statutory and constitutional grounds.

Demise

Despite the FCC's continuing series of reports and codifications of the fairness doctrine requirements through the 1970s, broadcasters still had problems with the doctrine. They continued to argue that it was too difficult to determine what issues were controversial, which viewpoints should be represented, and suggested that the doctrine was having a "chilling" effect on the flow of ideas: broadcasters would be reluctant to cover controversial issues because according to the doctrine they would be required to report "fairly." In *FCC v. League of Women Voters of California* (1984) the Supreme Court concluded that the scarcity rationale underlying the doctrine might be flawed and that the doctrine might be limiting the breadth of public debate. A footnote suggested that the Court awaited some kind of an indication from the FCC as to whether the conditions that had led to the fairness doctrine (and the *Red Lion* decision) had significantly changed. The doctrine was increasingly difficult to enforce and went against the grain of an increasingly deregulatory commission.

Responding to a complaint brought by a group called the Syracuse Peace Council, on 26 October 1984 the FCC concluded that WTVM-TV (a Syracuse, New York, television station owned by Meredith Corporation), had violated the fairness doctrine in its treatment of a controversy surrounding construction of a nuclear power plant, a conclusion that the Meredith Corporation vigorously contested. A few months later the FCC released another in its series of Fairness Reports to publicly re-evaluate the need for the doctrine. The commission concluded that:

> On the basis of voluminous factual record compiled in this proceeding, our experience in administering the doctrine and our general expertise in broadcast regulation, we no longer believe that the Fairness Doctrine, as a matter of policy, serves the public interests. In making this determination, we do not question the interest of the listening and viewing public in obtaining access to diverse and antagonistic sources of information. Rather, we conclude that the Fairness Doctrine is no longer a necessary or appropriate means by which to effectuate this interest. We believe that the interest of the public in viewpoint diversity is fully served by the multiplicity of voices in the marketplace today and that the intrusion by government into the content of programming occasioned by the enforcement of the doctrine unnecessarily restricts the journalistic freedom of broadcasters. Furthermore, we find that the Fairness Doctrine, in operation actually inhibits the presentation of controversial issues of the public importance to the detriment of the public and in degradation of the editorial prerogative of broadcast journalists.
>
> (FCC, *Inquiry into Fairness Doctrine Obligations of Broadcast Licensees*, 102 FCC 2d 145, 1985)

The report argued that (1) the doctrine was contrary to the public interest because it "chilled" expression, and, therefore, (2) the doctrine was probably unconstitutional. Despite these conclusions, the FCC retained the doctrine because it doubted that it had the power to abandon it. The FCC's legal advisors concluded that with its 1959 amendments in the 1934 act, Congress had formally incorporated the doctrine into Section 315, and thus the FCC could not remove it. Therefore, the FCC asked Congress to abolish the doctrine; Congress did nothing. Meanwhile, in the *Meredith* case, the FCC was in the awkward position of enforcing a doctrine that it was fervently denouncing. On 19 September 1986 the U.S. Court of Appeals for the District of Columbia (D.C.) Circuit cleared up a legal ambiguity by ruling that the

fairness doctrine had never been made a part of the 1934 law but was simply a regulation of the FCC. This meant that the FCC could drop its own regulation.

In the meantime the Meredith Corporation appealed the FCC fairness decision on constitutional grounds. In January 1987 the U.S. Court of Appeals for the D.C. Circuit instructed the FCC to address Meredith's constitutional argument against the fairness doctrine. Faced with this opportunity, on 6 August 1987 the FCC formally announced it would abandon the fairness doctrine on the several bases already argued, chiefly that the doctrine was probably unconstitutional and that it certainly had a chilling effect, exactly opposite from what was intended. The FCC concluded that "the Constitution bars us from enforcing the fairness doctrine," and argued that as the fairness doctrine chilled speech, it could not be construed to be sufficiently narrowly tailored to achieve a substantial government interest—the usual Supreme Court standard for content rules. Therefore, the FCC concluded that the fairness doctrine contravened the public interest.

Shortly after the FCC's decision to drop the fairness doctrine, Congress tried several times to resurrect it by making the doctrine part of federal law. One of the proposed bills stated:

> [The fairness doctrine] ha[s] enhanced free speech by securing the paramount right of the broadcast audience to robust debate on issues of public importance; and [it] fairly reflects the statutory obligation of broadcasters under the [Communications] Act to operate in the public interest [The fairness doctrine] strikes a reasonable balance among the first amendment rights of the public, broadcast licensees, and speakers other than owners of broadcast facilities.
>
> (H.R. Bill 1934, 100th Congress, 1st Session, proposing new Section 315(a) to the Communications Act, 3 June 1987)

President Reagan vetoed the bill, calling the fairness doctrine a "content-based" regulation and antagonistic to the freedom of expression. In a veto message drafted at least in part by former FCC Chairman Mark Fowler (who had long sought to end the doctrine), Reagan claimed that:

> S.742, simply cannot be reconciled with the freedom of speech and the press secured by our Constitution. It is, in my judgment, unconstitutional. Well-intentioned as S.742 may be, it would be inconsistent with the First Amendment and with the American tradition of independent journalism. Accordingly, I am compelled to disapprove of this measure.
>
> (23 *Weekly Compilation of Presidential Documents*, 715–16, 1987)

Congress was unable to override the veto. Attempts to revive the bill in 1989, 1991, and 1993 failed of passage. Such attempts largely ended when Republicans took control of congress in 1994.

The Supreme Court effectively supported the FCC's decision not to continue the doctrine when in 1990 it declined to review a lower court decision upholding the FCC action. Three years later, a federal appeals court decision reaffirmed that the fairness doctrine had been merely a commission policy and not a congressionally mandated law.

Aftermath

After the FCC abandoned the fairness doctrine, it announced it would no longer enforce fairness requirements for broadcast discussions of referenda, initiatives, recall efforts, and bond proposals. However, the commission made clear that its related personal attack, political editorializing, and Zapple rules remained in force. Broadcasters had first asked the FCC to abolish these rules in 1981, following up with at least four more formal requests over the next 16 years; all to no avail.

In December 1998, two leading broadcast trade organizations—the Radio-Television News Directors Association and the National Association of Broadcasters—challenged the constitutionality of the FCC's personal attack and political editorial rules in the U.S. Court of Appeals for the D.C. Circuit. In a series of decisions over the next two years, the FCC was unable to sustain its rules against the Court's firm finding that they appeared to be unconstitutional limits on broadcaster freedom. Angry at the slow-moving commission, in October 2000 the court finally ordered that the rules be vacated (dropped) immediately, and the FCC complied. The last vestiges of the long-lasting fairness doctrine were gone.

Periodic complaints emerged in Congress and elsewhere after the turn of the century about the right-wing sound of nearly all commercial radio talk shows. Rush Limbaugh was a frequent target of both complaints and support. Indeed, many conservative talk show hosts constantly raised the threat of a revived fairness doctrine in an attempt to build audience anger (and regular listening) as well as prompting letters and emails to the FCC and Congress urging lawmakers to leave radio alone. The appearance of the liberal Air America service in 2004, albeit often on low-rated stations, provided some balance to the preponderant right-wing sound of radio rants. Yet its very appearance may have further weakened attempts to revive the doctrine. A few attempts were made to introduce bills that would reinstate some version of the FCC's former policy, but none even received serious consideration at the full committee level in either the House or Senate.

See also: Air America; Controversial Issues, Broadcasting of; Editorializing; Federal Communications Commission; *Mayflower* Decision; "Public Interest, Convenience or Necessity"; *Red Lion* Case

Further Reading

47 USCA section 315 (the "Equal Time" law).
Federal Communications Commission, *Mayflower Broadcasting Corp.*, 8 FCC 333 (1940).
Federal Communications Commission, *In the Matter of Editorializing by Broadcast Licenses*, 13 FCC 1246 (1949).
Federal Communications Commission, *WCBS-TV*, 8 FCC 2d 381 (1967).
Federal Communications Commission, *Letter to Nicholas Zapple*, 23 FCC 2d 707 (1970).
Federal Communications Commission, *Fairness Doctrine and Public Interest Standard* (The Fairness Report), 48 FCC 2d 1 (1974).
Federal Communications Commission, *Memorandum Opinion and Order in Complaint of Syracuse Peace Council against Television Station WTVH*, 2 FCC Red 5043 (1987).
President of the United States, Veto Message, 23 Weekly Compilation of Presidential Document 715–16 (1987).
Rowan, Ford, *Broadcast Fairness: Doctrine, Practice, Prospects*, New York: Longman, 1984.
Simmons, Steven J., *The Fairness Doctrine and the Media*, Berkeley: University of California Press, 1978.
U.S. Congress, United States Senate, Committee on Commerce, *Fairness Doctrine: The FCC's Actions and the Broadcasters' Operations in Connection with the Commission's Fairness Doctrine: Staff Report*, 90th Cong., 2nd Sess., 1968.
United States Supreme Court, *Red Lion Broadcasting Co., Inc. v. FCC*, 395 US 367 (1969).
United States Supreme Court, *Miami Herald Publishing Co. v. Tornillo*, 418 US 241 (1974).
United States Supreme Court, *FCC v. League of Women Voters of California*, 468 US 364 (1984).

STEVE KANG,
2009 REVISIONS BY CHRISTOPHER H. STERLING

FAMILY THEATER
Radio Drama

Broadcasters have often been criticized for making program decisions based on monetary profit rather than a desire to provide educational and thought-provoking content. But throughout the history of radio broadcasting, some producers have used their talents to create programs designed to educate, enlighten, and assist listeners in coping with the difficult situations that arise in everyday life. *Family Theater*, which became one of the longest running weekly drama anthologies in radio history, was one such program.

On 13 May 1945, the Mutual Broadcasting System broadcast a Mother's Day special with an unusual premise—to unite the country in praying the Holy Rosary. The program featured the Sullivans, a family that had lost five sons in a single naval battle during World War II, and included a guest appearance by Bing Crosby and a message from President Truman. This event was the initiative of Father Patrick Peyton, C.S.C, a priest of the Congregation of the Holy Cross who had immigrated to the U.S. from Ireland in 1928. Inspired by the success of this Mother's Day program, Father Peyton, relying largely on private donations, founded Family Theater Productions in 1947. He enlisted the help of Hollywood stars and other media professionals to produce a weekly half-hour radio drama. The series, called *Family Theater*, premiered as a sustaining program on 13 February 1947 on Mutual. Programs emphasized moral problems, and each installment ended with an encouragement to prayer, using Tennyson's famous words, "More things are wrought by prayer than this world dreams of." Although Father Peyton was a Catholic priest, the dramas, by agreement with the network, were nonsectarian. They emphasized moral themes, but were designed as entertainment programming to appeal to a mass audience. The weekly dramas were supplemented by occasional holiday specials.

One of Mutual's contract provisions was that the series had to include at least one Hollywood star each week. The network's commitment to this series was in airtime alone—Father Peyton promised to pay all production costs. In an effort to help with these costs, stars frequently donated their payment back to the producer.

The first *Family Theater* drama, entitled "Flight From Home," starred Loretta Young, James Stewart, and Don Ameche, and was written by True Boardman. Subsequent episodes featured Raymond Burr, Bing Crosby, Irene Dunn, Gary Cooper, Gregory Peck, and dozens of other major Hollywood stars. Although the final original production was completed in 1958, *Family Theater* dramas ran for 22 years. When original radio production was halted so that Family Theater Productions could direct its attention to the newer medium of television, the series continued running in repeats on various stations across the country. Many of the programs were rebroadcast as part of a new series called *Marian Theater*. In total, 482 original

programs were produced, and, at the height of its popularity, the series ran on 429 stations nationwide. These radio programs were broadcast widely outside of the United States: in Canada, Latin America, Spain, Mozambique, Australia, and the Philippines. *Family Theater* won numerous awards for excellence, from trade associations and private organizations, and from non-Catholic as well as Catholic groups. Its motto became a well-known saying in popular culture, "the family that prays together stays together."

Father Peyton died in 1992, but his work continues in the United States and throughout the world. Family Theater Productions, which is now part of the Holy Cross Family Ministries (www. hcfm.org), has six international offices that produce television and radio programs. As of 2000, a dramatic radio series produced in the United States, called *La Historia de Quien Soy* (The Story of Who I Am), continues the spirit of *Family Theater*. The Spanish-language drama focuses on the lives of a fictional U.S. Latino family, and explores issues of ethnicity, morality and faith.

See also: Drama; Religion on Radio

Announcer

Tony La Frano

Host

Father Patrick Peyton, C.S.C

Producers/Creators

Father Patrick Peyton, C.S.C; Bob Longenecker

Programming History

Mutual Broadcasting Company
13 May 1945 (special Mother's Day Broadcast);
13 February 1947–4 July 1956

Further Reading

Peyton, Patrick J., *All for Her: The Autobiography of Father Patrick Peyton, C.S.C.*, New York: Doubleday, 1967.

PATRICIA PHALEN

FAN MAGAZINES

Radio fan magazines serve two popular audiences whose memberships share an intense interest in either the programs and personalities or the technology of radio. The first audience consists of fans who listen to broadcasts, become curious, and seek additional information not provided over the radio. The other group is more concerned with radio's technology, such as amateur and ham radio operators, who are interested in developing and using the technology to both transmit and receive signals using short-wave radio. Both audiences continue to support a number of radio magazines.

Fan magazines enjoyed success because of the large and growing radio audience that was interested in the programs and personalities heard. The magazines were most successful from the mid-1920s through the early 1960s. Fan magazines published a variety of content, including program listings and descriptions. A substantial portion of their content was devoted to radio personalities and included picture stories, hobbies, home life, and any relevant scandal or gossip. Most of the magazines included reader correspondence. Fan magazines helped audiences keep track of programming and stay interested, and they provided information for interaction among other fans.

The oldest group of radio fans are the amateur and ham radio operators. The American Radio Relay League's (ARRL) monthly magazine, *QST*, started publishing in 1916. *QST* was named for the international signal "QST," which means "attention all stations." Still published by the ARRL, *QST* has for years published product reviews and technical articles. Members share tips and tricks for operating and constructing radios. The difference between *QST* and popular fan magazines is the focus on radio technology rather than content. Because the magazine is published by an organized group, it reports news, legal and regulatory issues, and technical information and performs many of the functions of a trade journal.

Radio News

Cosmopolitan, *McClure's*, *Munsey's*, and other general interest magazines provided information about radio in the early 1900s, but it was not until the radio boom of the 1920s that exclusive mass-market radio magazines appeared. The need for a popular publication that served radio audiences was recognized immediately by early broadcasters. For example, KDKA distributed *Radio Broadcasting News* to about 2,000 newspapers. The magazine was developed shortly after the first broadcasts in order to provide background information and program listings that could be published in local newspapers. As radio's popularity increased during the first half of the 1920s, the number of radio magazines grew. By the mid-1920s, there were between 35 and 40 radio magazines serving an audience of nearly one million readers. *Radio News* claimed (May 1926) that the top five radio magazines, including *Radio News*, *Popular Radio*, *Radio in the Home*, *Radio Broadcast*, and *Radio Age*, had over half a million readers.

Radio News was one of the first magazines to capitalize on the radio boom and was founded by one of radio's greatest fans, Hugo Gernsback, who was familiar with both publishing and radio. He published a small radio magazine called *Modern Electrics* in New York in the early 1900s as a way to stimulate sales at his radio electronics store. In 1919 Gernsback started *Radio News* as a general interest radio magazine. Like many of the early radio magazines, the content of *Radio News* appealed to a broad audience of radio enthusiasts. Broadcasting was in its developmental stages, but the popular appeal of radio was already evident. *Radio News* was primarily a "booster" for radio, promoting radio to a developing audience of fans. *Radio News* called itself "Radio's Greatest Magazine," and its early content appealed to the amateur operators and listeners who fueled the early 1920s radio craze. Each issue had a Norman Rockwell-like cover with a scene that showed some aspect of radio in modern American life. The magazine was highly illustrated, and the content was diverse. Much of the content targeted amateur operators at a variety of skill levels by providing technical articles on home construction of radios and on the selection of components and equipment. There were regular features offering technical information and articles discussed receiving and transmitting radio signals. *Radio News* also held contests that challenged readers' technical skills with equipment construction and signal reception (DXing). The magazine even offered lessons in Esperanto, promoted as the international language of amateur radio operators.

Radio News promoted radio as a significant social force that served a variety of needs. There were articles about the people who had developed radio and were shaping its future and about the radio celebrities whose voices and sounds were being recognized across the country. The magazine provided station listings and discussed some of the new successful radio stations, including WRNY in New York, where Gernsback delivered a weekly Tuesday night lecture. There were cartoons, poems, and fictional articles in which radio was a central theme. Readers were encouraged to become knowledgeable about radio in a number of ways. Crossword puzzles required readers to know terms and call letters. There were frequent contests, which included submitting drawings of an "ideal" receiving set, composing four-line verses using standard circuit symbols, or identifying errors in the drawings that appeared on the cover of the magazine. *Radio News* sponsored a "radio play" contest and published the works of the winners and finalists.

Radio News also featured a significant amount of advertising. For example, the index of advertisers for the January 1925 issue lists 381 advertisers and includes 180 pages with advertising (out of 240 total). Equipment and services offered by all segments of the emerging radio industry were advertised. There was also a classified advertising section. *Radio News* used product names in some of its construction articles, although it discontinued the practice after Gernsback was accused of selling out to advertisers. In 1926 *Radio News* claimed that it was second only to *Radio Broadcast* (a successful trade magazine) in its volume of advertising.

Radio News enjoyed its greatest success during the chaotic early 1920s. Advertising revenues dropped significantly as the distinction between professionals, amateurs, and listening audiences became more clearly defined. In the early 1930s, *Radio News* narrowed its appeal to the amateur technical audience and continued publishing technical information until in 1959 it became *Electronics World*.

Radio Guide

The successful popular mass-market fan magazines that emerged in the 1930s served the audiences created by broadcasting. There were more than a dozen popular fan magazines published during radio's golden age, including *Movie Radio, Radio Album, Radio Dial, Radio Digest, Radio Guide, Radioland, Radio Mirror*, and *Radio Stars*. These magazines followed the example set by popular movie fan magazines, which focused on personalities, took readers behind the scenes, and always included pictures or portraits of stars on the cover.

Radio Guide is an example of this kind of fan magazine. *Radio Guide* was published weekly by M.L. Annenberg in Chicago beginning in 1932. By 1936 *Radio Guide* was printed in 17 regional editions and was selling 420,000 copies per week, and the content typified the radio fan magazine of the time. Part of the magazine offered stories and pictorials concerning radio personalities. One pictorial feature called the "Radio Guide Album" included a full-page picture of the cast of a selected network program. There was information and gossip about radio stars and often a short story.

Radio Guide regularly provided short reports about current radio news, shortwave information, and upcoming musical events. Regular features that appeared in the magazine included "Coming Events," "Hits of the Week," "Contests on the Air," "X-word Puzzle," and "Radio Boners." Approximately half of the magazine's content featured a programming guide with day-by-day listings of programs and the stations that aired them. The magazine marked high-quality programs with a star symbol placed next to the listing. Religious programs were identified with a bell symbol. The program section included a log of numerous radio stations, including foreign outlets, and a modest listing of shortwave programs for the week. *Radio Guide* remained an important source of fan support through the early 1940s and laid the groundwork for the same publisher's 1953 creation of the hugely successful *TV Guide*.

Radio Mirror, which started publishing in 1933, changed its name to *TV Radio Mirror* in order to serve the popular interest in television. Fan magazines continued to provide information about radio into the 1960s, but their general content shifted substantially from radio to television. As radio became a medium of music that largely served local markets, the need for mass-market radio fan magazines disappeared.

Web Fan Magazines

The shift from national networks to local programming and the use of syndicated programming have resulted in smaller, more specialized groups of fans for radio programs and fewer opportunities for successful national mass-market fan magazines. A few traditional fan magazines are published in large regional markets, such as the *L.A. Radio Guide* in southern California, but generally the current market for radio fan magazines is limited.

The primary means of reaching fans today is with webpages and e-zines (electronic magazines). E-zines are delivered through the internet and presented in formats that resemble traditional fan magazines. Subscriptions are ordered through a webpage. An example is *Krud Radio*, a fan e-zine that offers a humorous look at radio and arrives by e-mail. About.com is accessed through a webpage and offers a "Guide to Radio" that discusses radio news, conducts polls about a variety of radio topics, provides links to internet audio sites, and includes a chat room for discussing radio topics.

Webpages offer fans the same content found in traditional fan magazines but provide a level of interaction not found in traditional magazines. Talk show host Art Bell's webpage logged more than 5.5 million visitors between January 1997 and January 2000, offering program summaries, archives, a chat room, feature articles, links, a studio camera, audio clips, and more.

Fans sometimes establish "unofficial" webpages that target other fans. Howard Stern's show has a number of unofficial webpages. For example, "Heynow's Webpage" offers a collection of Howard Stern RealAudio files. Stern's associate, Fred Norris, known as the King of Mars, has an unofficial fan site that was started because "everyone else on the show has at least one stupid fan page, so why not Fred."

Internet directories of stations and programs are replacing printed directories in fan magazines. Lists of stations and links to internet audio are provided by a number of websites, including RadioLinks.net, Broadcast.com, Macroradio.net, Radio-Stations.net, Netradio.net, Darnell's Black Radio Guide, and the Massachusetts Institute of Technology (MIT) List of Radio Stations.

Amateur and ham radio operators are experiencing a similar change in their fan magazines. There are still a number of specialized periodicals that target amateurs, but the internet is becoming an increasingly important source of information. Most organizations and publishers that produce magazines for this audience also have webpages, including the ARRL. *AntenneX*, a successful magazine that specializes in antennae for amateurs, is now promoting its website, which logged over two million visitors between 1997 and early 2003. *Ham Radio Online*, offered by the Virtual Publishing Company, provides technical information, news, opinions, cartoons, online discussions, feature stories, up-to-the-minute reports on world disasters, and an online newsletter delivered by e-mail.

The internet has revitalized fan interest by providing sites where smaller and more specialized groups of fans can find the content of traditional fan magazines. In addition, the community of fans using the electronic magazines and websites enjoys a level of interaction that traditional magazines could never offer.

See also: DXers/DXing; Ham Radio; Trade Press

Further Reading

Brown, Michael, "Radio Magazines and the Development of Broadcasting: *Radio Broadcast*, and *Radio News*," *Journal of Radio Studies* 5 (Winter 1998).
Dahlgren, Peter, and Colin Sparks, editors, *Journalism and Popular Culture*, Newbury Park, California: Sage, 1992.
Davis, H.P., "American Beginnings," in *Radio and Its Future*, edited by Martin Codel, London: Harper, 1930; reprint, New York: Arno Press, 1971.
Douglas, George H., *The Early Days of Radio Broadcasting*, Jefferson, North Carolina: McFarland, 1987.
Massie, Keith, and Stephen D. Perry, "Hugo Gernsback and Radio Magazines: An Influential Intersection in Broadcast History," *Journal of Radio Studies 9* (December 2002).
Maxim, Hiram, "The Radio Amateur," in *Radio and Its Future*, edited by Martin Codel, London: Harper, 1930; reprint, New York: Arno Press, 1971.
Peterson, Theodore Bernard, *Magazines in the Twentieth Century*, Urbana: University of Illinois Press, 1968.
Rheingold, Howard, *The Virtual Community: Homesteading on the Electronic Frontier*, Reading, Massachusetts: Addison-Wesley 1993.
Sova, Harry W., and Patricia L. Sova, editors, *Communication Serials: An International Guide to Periodicals in Communication, Popular Culture, and the Performing Arts*, Virginia Beach, Virginia: Sovacom, 1992.
Sterling, Christopher, H., and George Shiers, "Serial Publications," in *History of Telecommunications Technology: An Annotated Bibliography*, Lanham, Maryland: Scarecrow Press, 2000.
Wolseley, Roland Edgar, "Digests, Fans, Comics, Sports," in *Understanding Magazines*, by Wolseley, Ames: Iowa State University Press, 1965.

MICHAEL BROWN

FARM/AGRICULTURAL RADIO

Radio has always had a special place in the lives of farmers and their families. Because of the isolation of rural life, the entertainment and information brought by radio are especially welcome, and up-to-the-minute weather forecasts and agricultural market reports are essential to every modern farmer's business. Even in today's age of television and the internet, farmers still consider radio to be their most important source of agricultural information, and surveys indicate that most of them tune in to farm programs every day.

In 2002, about 75 radio stations, mostly in rural communities, provided what they consider to be a full-time agricultural format, and another 1,000 stations broadcast at least one hour per week of special farm-related programming. In addition, a number of regional and national farm radio networks have evolved to provide stations with specialized programs and advertising.

Federal and state agencies, led by the United States Department of Agriculture (USDA), provide radio reports on topics ranging from the latest research on crop diseases to new agricultural marketing strategies. This information is provided to stations by the USDA in the form of scripts and press releases and as prerecorded audio and video reports that broadcasters can integrate into their own locally produced programs.

On commercial stations, farm programming is generally supported through the sale of advertising. Large corporate producers of agricultural products and services have found radio to be an ideal medium for reaching the widely dispersed farm audience, a group that includes the decision makers of U.S. agribusiness. Farmers who tune in for market reports on these stations are likely also to hear commercials for chemicals, fertilizer, seed, and other agricultural necessities.

Farm programming is also provided by many noncommercial radio stations, especially those associated with land grant colleges and universities with large agricultural research and teaching components. Many of these campuses have strong ties to federal and state farm service offices that provide regionalized agricultural information and programming.

Origins

Radio was just one of several technological innovations in the early part of the 20th century that revolutionized farm life. The telephone, phonograph, automobile, and rural mail delivery all served to greatly reduce the isolation of rural families. But the coming of radio in the 1920s meant that for the first time, farms were instantaneously connected to the outside world. Music, sports, politics, and religion were suddenly available with the twist of a dial. Once-isolated farm families were suddenly a part of the growing national radio audience. In most farm homes, a battery-operated radio became a fixture long before the house was wired for electricity. Perhaps most significant, the radio brought farmers information that had an immediate impact on their livelihoods. Accurate weather reports allowed farmers to time harvests and protect crops from storms, and immediate reports of commodity prices from big-city agricultural markets meant farmers could reap bigger profits and manage operations more efficiently.

In fact, government-produced weather forecasts and agricultural market reports were among radio's first regularly scheduled programs. Initially, these broadcasts were aired experimentally by college and university stations, which were among the first on the air with radio transmitters. As early as 1921 (some sources say earlier) the University of Wisconsin's 9XM (later, WHA) began transmitting agricultural information on a regular schedule. Many other stations soon followed suit.

The USDA was especially quick to recognize radio's potential for reaching the far-flung farm audience. By the mid-1920s the agency had begun producing and distributing not only weather and market reports, but also informational programs on crop and livestock problems, agricultural marketing, and home economics. Scripts were distributed free of charge to radio stations through the USDA's vast network of county extension agents. The county agents themselves often worked closely with local radio stations to supplement programming with information on topics of local concern. At least some of the government-produced radio programs also had a distinctly political purpose: as farmers represented an important national voting bloc, the USDA interspersed the more mundane topics with features and talks that explained and promoted the administration's farm policy.

Early on, businesses that catered to rural customers also saw the potential of programming aimed specifically at the farm audience. Although overt radio advertising was still considered inappropriate in the early 1920s, these companies understood the promotional value of having their names on the air. Sears and Roebuck established the Chicago station WLS ("World's Largest Store") in part to promote its booming mail-order business to rural homes. The company was also instrumental in establishing other early stations in the Midwest and South. In Nashville, the National Life and Accident Insurance Company created the station WSM to help promote its products. In this case, "WSM" stood for the company's slogan, "We Shield Millions."

Stations across the country began to realize that the millions of U.S. farm homes constituted a special audience, and many began to produce and carry programs especially tailored for rural listeners, including those aimed at attracting farm women and children. Indeed, the Federal Radio Commission's radio frequency allocation scheme of 1928, with its high-powered clear channel stations designed to serve large rural areas, was very much driven by a concern (some of it admittedly political) for rural audiences. The National Broadcasting Company (NBC)'s *The National Farm and Home Hour*, begun in 1928, became one of the network's longest-running programs.

As radio developed, the government mounted a major campaign to get more farmers to buy receivers. USDA-authored articles in newspapers and farm periodicals told readers that the radio receiver had become an agricultural necessity. Countless anecdotes were reported of how farmers were able to save their crops by radio's advanced warning of bad weather or to increase their income by using radio reports of market price fluctuations.

But despite these efforts, bad economic times meant the adoption rate in rural areas lagged far behind that in cities. In the 1920s and 1930s many farmers barely eked out a subsistence, and hard cash was always in short supply. In addition, farmers generally lived at great distances from stations and needed to buy more expensive receivers to get satisfactory reception. And despite New Deal rural electrification efforts, many regions still lacked electricity, forcing use of battery-powered radios. By the 1940 census, 92 percent of urban U.S. homes reported owning radios, but only 70 percent of rural farm homes did. The situation among rural nonwhites was far worse. The chronic poverty among minority farmers meant that as late as 1940, only 20 percent owned radios.

Farm Radio and Country Music

Early listener response convinced broadcasters that rural and urban audiences differed considerably in their musical tastes. Farmers, it was believed, much preferred what was then called "hillbilly" music. This style was based on the folk songs commonly performed in rural areas, usually by one or two musicians playing simple stringed instruments. As the need grew for more programming to attract and hold the farm audience, several large stations developed live musical variety shows with a distinctly rural flavor. *National Barn Dance*, from Chicago's WLS, and *The Grand Ole Opry*, from WSM in Nashville, were two of the earliest and most successful.

By providing an audience for budding new performers and a ready market for their records, farm radio music shows played an essential role in the development of country music. Record companies began providing free or low-cost performers in exchange for the promotional value of having their stars heard on radio broadcasts. The fact that Nashville was the home of the powerful WSM and its immensely popular *Grand Ole Opry* was a decisive factor in that city's becoming the country music capital of the world.

The National Association of Farm Broadcasters

Radio stations soon recognized the need for specialized broadcast personnel to produce agricultural news and information programming. The position of station "farm director" was generally filled by someone who knew farming well and who could dedicate full attention to researching and reporting on agricultural issues. Often, male farm directors were assisted by women who were delegated the duties of reporting on rural home economics and hosting homemaker-oriented programs of interviews,

recipes, and household hints. Today, farm broadcasters are often graduates of specialized university programs in agricultural journalism, and, although men still dominate the field, the role of female broadcasters has broadened considerably.

In the 1940s farm directors from several stations met and formed what would eventually be known as the National Association of Farm Broadcasters (NAFB). Today, the NAFB is farm broadcasting's major trade organization, offering members a news service, sales and marketing assistance, and farm audience research.

Farm Radio in the Television Age

The coming of television meant changes throughout the radio industry. Many of the powerful big-city radio stations no longer found it profitable to target rural audiences, and farm radio programming increasingly became the province of the growing number of lower-powered regional or local stations serving rural areas. At the same time, agricultural news and information programs began to appear on many local television stations that served farm audiences.

Yet for a number of reasons, farm radio has remained a viable medium. The low cost and portability of modern radio receivers means today's farm families can own several sets and listen wherever they happen to be. Radios installed in trucks, tractors, and other farm vehicles can accompany farmers throughout the workday. Timely weather forecasts and market reports remain just as important to farmers today as they were in the early days of radio. At the same time, the relatively low cost of operating a local radio station means that farm broadcasters can stay profitable even while appealing to a relatively narrow audience. In fact, it is just this characteristic that attracts agricultural advertisers, who can zero in on their target audience at a relatively low cost. These characteristics mean that farm radio will continue to flourish.

See also: Trade Associations; WHA and Wisconsin Public Radio

Further Reading

Baker, John Chester, *Farm Broadcasting: The First Sixty Years*, Ames: Iowa State University Press, 1981.

Evans, James F., *Prairie Farmer and WLS: The Burridge D. Butler Years*, Urbana: University of Illinois Press, 1969.

Frost, S.E., Jr., *Education's Own Stations: The History of Broadcast Licenses Issued to Educational Institutions*, Chicago: University of Chicago Press, 1937.

Malone, Bill C., *Country Music, U.S.A.*, Austin: University of Texas Press, 1968; revised edition, 1985.

National Association of Farm Broadcasters: About NAFB, "History of NAFB," www.nafb.com/news.cfm.

Rural Radio Listening: A Study of Program Preferences in Rural Areas of the U.S., New York: Rural Research Institute, 1951.

Smulyan, Susan, *Selling Radio: The Commercialization of American Broadcasting, 1920–1934*, Washington, D.C.: Smithsonian Institution Press, 1994.

U.S. Department of Agriculture, Bureau of Agricultural Economics, "Attitudes of Rural People Toward Radio Service: A Nation-Wide Service of Farm and Small-Town People," Washington, D.C.: United States Department of Agriculture, January 1946.

Wik, Reynold M., "The USDA and the Development of Radio in Rural America," *Agricultural History* 62, no. 2 (1988).

STEVE CRAIG

FEDERAL COMMUNICATIONS COMMISSION

The Federal Communications Commission (FCC) is the federal agency charged with regulating broadcasting and other electronic communications media in the United States; it licenses stations to operate in the "public interest, convenience, and necessity." The FCC was created by Congress in 1934 to succeed the Federal Radio Commission. It is an independent federal agency established by the Communications Act of 1934 to regulate domestic interstate and international electronic communication, both wired and wireless.

Because the FCC was established as an independent federal agency, the "checks and balances" on it are not the same as they would be for administrative agencies (such as the Food and Drug Administration), which answer directly to the U.S. president. Although the president selects the chair and the commissioners (who must be approved by the Senate), the president does not have the authority to remove commissioners during their terms. The FCC is much more beholden to Congress, which controls not only appropriations but also the commission's very existence. Since 1981, the FCC is no longer a permanent agency but instead must be reauthorized by Congress every two years. Therefore, Congress' influence over the FCC has increased significantly during the 1980s and 1990s.

The FCC has a dual role: on the one hand, it makes rules and regulations to carry out the Communications Act, but it also serves as a judicial body, hearing appeals of its decisions. As a quasi-judicial agency, the FCC has the duty of both making rules and also serving as an adjudicator in cases dealing with rules violations and challenges. Although the FCC has the responsibility for making, policing, and judging the rules, its decisions are subject to court review. For example, the FCC created a rule requiring regular station identification. It also enforces the rule by asking stations whether they have adhered to it. In cases where stations have been found to violate the rule, the FCC must decide what punishment, if any, to apply. If the offending station challenges the decision, it appeals the judgment to the FCC. In this role, the FCC serves as the equivalent of a federal district court. FCC decisions that are upheld in appeal can then be challenged by appealing directly to the Federal Court of Appeals for the Washington, D.C. Circuit.

Commissioners

The FCC has five commissioners (reduced from seven in 1983), one of whom serves as the chair. Members are appointed by the U.S. president and approved by the Senate. The term of office for commissioners is five years, and they may serve multiple terms. No more than three commissioners from one political party may serve simultaneously.

Although the FCC chair has the same one vote as any of the other four commissioners, the chair has a greater ability to influence the direction of the FCC. The chair's role in selecting issues to pursue sets an agenda for the commission. During the 1970s and 1980s, for example, the FCC adopted a more deregulatory approach, eliminating a number of rules and streamlining the radio license renewal process. Under the leadership of chairmen Richard Wiley, Charles Ferris, and Mark Fowler, the FCC revisited its responsibilities under the concept of the public interest, adopting the philosophy that the public interest is best served by allowing marketplace forces to function. In the 1990s Chairman Reed Hunt decided to investigate the possibilities of high-definition television and formed a task force to study it. Chairman William Kennard pursued the possibility of adding low-power FM stations to the radio band to provide increased opportunities for disenfranchised members of society to be heard. Although no chair has been successful in pursuing all of his interests, each has had the opportunity to set the commission's, and thus to a certain extent the nation's, communications policy agenda.

The majority of commissioners over the years have been lawyers (the last engineer commissioner retired in 1963). FCC commissioners are creatures of politics and as such are often more versed in politics than in technology. A number of commissioners have had no technological background prior to joining the commission. They count on their staff advisers and employees to provide them with the necessary background information. Fewer than half the commissioners have served their full five-year terms. When they leave the commission, they frequently join communications companies or legal firms providing consulting services. Commission staff members often find themselves dealing with former commissioners.

The personality of the FCC changes over time, based on the various personalities of the commissioners who serve and the political climate of the period. Space does not permit a listing of all former FCC commissioners and their contributions, but a few should be noted. Frieda B. Hennock, the first woman appointed to the commission in 1948, served during the critical period of the television "freeze" (1948–52). During those four years, the FCC stopped licensing new TV stations while it decided the issues of color TV, UHF versus VHF transmission, and channel allocation policies. Benjamin L. Hooks, the first African-American commissioner, was appointed in 1972 and worked diligently for the enforcement of equal employment opportunities. Henry Rivera was the first Hispanic commissioner, appointed in 1981. Robert E. Lee has the distinction of having served longer than any other commissioner to date, from 1953 until 1981. William Kennard was the first African-American chairman when appointed in 1993.

FCC commissioners have been perceived alternately as pro and antibroadcasting. FCC chairmen James L. Fly (appointed 1939) and Newton N. Minow (appointed 1961) were public interest advocates who raised the ire of many broadcasters during their respective terms. Fly chaired the FCC during the forced sale of the NBC "Blue" Network. Minow is perhaps best remembered for referring to television as a "vast wasteland" in a speech to the National Association of Broadcasters.

On the other hand, James Quello joined the commission in 1974 after retiring from his position as vice president and general manager of station WJR in Detroit. Quello's Senate confirmation hearings lasted longer than any other commissioner's because a number of public interest groups, fearing that he would be too favorable to broadcast interests (Quello replaced public interest advocate Nicholas Johnson), opposed his nomination. In spite of the lengthy process, Quello was overwhelmingly approved by the Senate. While Quello served as interim FCC chair, *Broadcasting* magazine called him "the broadcasters' chairman." In spite of his strong support of broadcast interests, Quello was critical of indecency on radio.

Staff

Although the FCC has only five commissioners, there are nearly 2,000 staff members in dozens of different departments, including a dozen field offices across the U.S. The five FCC commissioners must officially hold a public meeting at least once a month. The business of the commission is largely conducted as items circulate among the commissioners in between meetings, and at the staff level in the operating bureaus. The FCC is divided administratively into a number of offices and bureaus, to which the bulk of the commission's work is delegated. The six major operating FCC bureaus are Consumer and Governmental Affairs, Enforcement, International, Media, Wireless Telecommunications, and Wireline Competition. Most licensing and regulatory activity undertaken in the name of the FCC occurs at this level.

Of greatest concern to broadcasters is the Media Bureau (previously called the Broadcast Bureau), which regulates AM, FM, and television broadcast stations and related facilities. It assigns frequencies and call letters to stations and designates operating power and sign-on and sign-off times. It also assigns stations in each service within the allocated frequency bands with specific locations, frequencies, and powers. It regulates existing stations, ensuring that stations operate in accordance with rules and in accordance with the technical provisions of their authorizations.

The Media Bureau has five divisions: Audio, Video, Policy, Industry Analysis, and Engineering. The Audio Division receives and evaluates approximately 5,500 applications per year for the nation's approximately 14,000 AM, FM commercial, FM noncommercial educational, and FM translator and booster stations. These applications include station modification applications, applications for new stations, assignment or transfer applications, license applications, and renewal applications.

Since the 1996 Telecommunications Act, radio and television stations are licensed for eight years (into the 1980s, the standard term was only three). Licensees are obligated to comply with statutes, rules, and policies relating to program content, such as identifying sponsors of material that is broadcast. The bureau ensures that licensees make available equal opportunities for use of broadcast facilities by political candidates or opposing political candidates, station identification, and identification of recorded programs or program segments. Licensees who have violated FCC rules, and most especially licensees who have "misrepresented" themselves, are subject to such sanctions as forfeitures (fines), short-term renewals, or (rarely) license revocation.

Other FCC offices are established by the commission as organizational tools for handling the tremendous variety of commission tasks. The current FCC offices are Administrative Law Judges, Communication Business Opportunities, Engineering and Technology, General Counsel, Inspector General, Legislative Affairs, Managing Director, Media Relations, Plans and Policy, and Workplace Diversity.

In its attempt to carry out the wishes of Congress as expressed in the Communications Act, the FCC creates or deletes rules. Proposals for new rules come from a variety of sources both within and outside the commission. To begin assessing a new service or proposal on which it has little information, the commission may issue a Notice of Inquiry (NOI) seeking advice and answers to specific questions. If the FCC plans a new rule, it first issues a Notice of Proposed Rule Making (NPRM). The NPRM gives formal notice that the FCC is considering a rule and provides a required length of time during which the commission must allow public comments. After sufficient comment and discussion, new rules are adopted in FCC Reports and Orders and are published in its own official report series, the *FCC Record*, as well as in the government's daily *Federal Register*. The rules are collected annually into Title 47 of the Code of Federal Regulations.

Licensing

Without a doubt, the greatest power of the FCC is its power to license or not license a station. Since its inception, the commission has modified its rules and procedures for determining the manner in which it grants licenses. In keeping with the directive of the Communications Act, the FCC has always licensed stations to operate "in the public interest, convenience, and necessity." The specific manner in which it has made determinations about individual licensees, however, has undergone changes. For decades, the FCC would examine all applicants for a license to determine which would best serve the public interest, considering a range of characteristics, including preferences for local ownership, minority ownership, experienced ownership, and the character of the owners. Even a station that had been in operation for years faced the prospect of losing its license to a superior applicant in a renewal proceeding. The FCC had to conduct time-consuming and expensive comparative hearings whenever two or more applicants sought the same frequency.

The FCC and the broadcast industry have long been critical of the comparative process, which was largely eliminated by the 1996 Telecommunications Act. Now, existing stations have an expectation of license renewal, provided they have not violated important commission rules. The FCC does not allow a new challenger to draw an existing station that has served the public interest into a comparative process. To avoid comparative hearings in the case of new stations, the FCC in 1999 adopted an auction process similar to what it had used earlier for other nonbroadcast frequencies. Rather than spend months (sometimes years) in comparative hearings, the FCC instead determines whether applicants meet minimum eligibility requirements. If they do, the applicants can then bid for new, available stations or purchase existing outlets.

The FCC does not monitor the broadcasts of radio and television stations. It relies on information provided to it by broadcasters, competitors, and audiences. Determinations about whether a station deserves to have its license renewed are based on documents filed by the station, any public comments the commission receives about that station, and challenges to the renewal by interested parties.

The commission is able to enforce regulations primarily through the *threat* of license action. The majority of license renewals are granted with no disciplinary action by the FCC. However, should the commission find rules violations by a licensee, its actions can range from a letter admonishing a station to fines of up to $250,000 and a short-term renewal of the license, and even to the revocation of a license. It is the threat of this action that keeps broadcasters in compliance.

The FCC has the ultimate authority to revoke a station's license or deny its renewal, although that action has rarely been taken. In more than 60 years, the FCC has taken this action only 147 times: an average of fewer than three per year out of thousands of license renewals. More than one-third of those revocations and nonrenewals were due to misrepresentations to the commission. Although such cases have been infrequent, the FCC has acted severely in cases where licensees have intentionally lied.

In 1998, the FCC revoked the license for Bay City, Texas, station KFCC because the owner "engaged in a pattern of outright falsehoods, evasiveness, and deception." Chameleon Radio Corporation had been awarded a license to serve Bay City, but it attempted to move the transmitter closer to Houston, to the extent that Bay City would not even be served by the station. The FCC cited the station for repeated misrepresentations and lack of candor. Chameleon attempted to argue that the merit of its programming should protect it from revocation. The FCC responded that "meritorious programming does not mitigate serious deliberate misconduct such as misrepresentation." Also that year, licenses were revoked for seven stations in Missouri and Indiana that were owned by Michael Rice through three different corporations. Rice was convicted of 12 felonies involving sexual assaults of children. The FCC was prepared to allow the corporations to continue their ownership of the stations after their assertion that Rice would not be involved in station operation. The commission revoked the licenses on finding that Rice was in fact involved in station operation and that "misrepresentations and lack of candor regarding his role at the stations" was cause for revocation.

Despite all the powers given to the FCC, the 1934 Communications Act specifically states that the commission may not censor the content of broadcasts. According to Section 326, "Nothing in this Act shall be understood or construed to give this Commission the power of censorship over the radio communications or signals transmitted by any radio station." Nevertheless, the FCC's reprimands and fines of stations for broadcasting indecent material at inappropriate times have been upheld by the Supreme Court. The FCC acknowledges its obligation to stay out of content decisions in most areas. The commission has declined to base license decisions on the proposed format of a radio station, and it no longer stipulates the amount of time stations should devote to public service announcements.

Spectrum Management

The FCC also has the important responsibility of managing all users (except the federal government) of the electromagnetic spectrum. This involves two processes. First, the FCC must allocate different uses for different parts of the spectrum in an efficient way that does not create interference. This is followed by the allotment of specific frequencies or channels to particular areas. Licensing of the allotments follows. (AM does not have allotments.) There have been two significant spectrum reallocations affecting radio. In 1945 the FCC moved FM's allocation from 42 to 50 MHz up to its current location at 88 to 108 MHz, more than doubling the available channels but rendering the existing FM receivers and transmitters obsolete. In 1979 the upper end of the AM band moved from 1605 kHz to 1705 kHz to accommodate ten additional AM

channels—a change that took years to implement (the first stations shifted to the new higher frequencies only moved in the 1990s).

A second part of maintaining spectrum efficiency is approving equipment that uses the electromagnetic spectrum. The FCC must be certain that all devices emitting electromagnetic signals do so within their prescribed limits. "Type acceptance" is the FCC process of approving equipment that emits electromagnetic radio waves. In most cases, the evidence for type acceptance is provided by the equipment's manufacturer, who provides a written application with a complete technical description of the product and a test report showing compliance with the technical requirements. An FCC identification number can be found on the backs of telephones, walkie-talkies, pagers, and even microwave ovens. The number does not imply that the FCC has inspected that particular unit but rather that the product meets certain FCC minimal standards designed to avoid interference.

Policy is sometimes the result of inaction by the FCC. For years, the commission was faced with what to do about AM stereo. Rather than choosing a standard from among competing applicants, in 1982 the FCC adopted a marketplace philosophy to allow a winner to emerge from marketplace decisions rather than their own. Many broadcasters believe the introduction of AM stereo was negatively affected by the commission's "decision not to decide." Some stations were reluctant to invest in AM stereo equipment, fearing they might select the losing standard and then lose thousands of dollars. Radio receiver manufacturers had the same concern. The FCC's decision "not to decide" virtually killed any chance for AM stereo.

During the first decade of the 21st century, the FCC focused on three radio issues. By far the most controversial was what—if any—indecent material could be carried on the air. The commission fined many stations for marginal programming, even "fleeting expletives," which it had long ignored. Many of these fines were appealed and were working their way to the Supreme Court as this book went to print. The second issue was technological— the approval and encouragement of HD or "high definition" radio. The commission adopted a technological standard, but did not mandate a specific date for transition from analog AM and FM transmission to digital service. And the third was licensing—specifically the use of scheduled auctions of unused AM and FM frequencies several times a year. Under a mandate from Congress, the FCC will now assign new licensees only after auctions, which raise millions for the U.S. Treasury. The incoming Obama administration in 2009 projected a more activist FCC, but whether this will have impact on radio issues was unclear as this volume went to press.

See also: Blue Book; Communications Act of 1934; Deregulation of Radio; Digital Audio Broadcasting; "Equal Time" Rule; Fairness Doctrine; Federal Radio Commission; First Amendment and Radio; Frequency Allocation; Licensing Authorizing U.S. Stations to Broadcast; Obscenity and Indecency on Radio; "Public Interest, Convenience, or Necessity"; Regulation; Stereo; Telecommunications Act of 1996; United States Congress and Radio

Further Reading

Cole, Barry G., and Mal Oettinger, *Reluctant Regulators: The FCC and The Broadcast Audience*, Reading, Massachusetts: Addison-Wesley, 1978.
Federal Communications Commission Website, www.fcc.gov.
Flannery, Gerald V., editor, *Commissioners of the FCC 1927–1994*, Lanham, Maryland: University Press of America, 1994.
Milliard, Robert L., *The Federal Communications Commission: A Primer*, Boston: Focal Press, 1991.
Kahn, Frank J., editor, *Documents of American Broadcasting*, 4th edition, Englewood Cliffs, New Jersey: Prentice-Hall, 1984.
Krasnow, Erwin G., Lawrence D. Longley, and Herbert A. Terry, *The Politics of Broadcast Regulation*, New York: St. Martin's Press, 1973; 3rd edition, 1982.
Ray, William B., *FCC: The Ups and Downs of Radio-TV Regulation*, Ames: Iowa State University Press, 1990.

DOM CARISTI,
2009 REVISIONS BY CHRISTOPHER H. STERLING

FEDERAL RADIO COMMISSION
Predecessor to the Federal Communications Commission

The first agency created in the United States specifically to license and regulate radio, the Federal Radio Commission (FRC) existed from 1927 to 1934. During that time, the FRC was responsible not only for licensing radio stations in the United States, but also for laying the regulatory foundation that to some extent still exists today.

Origins

The United States passed the Radio Act in 1912, which provided authorization for licensing of radio stations. It was not until 1920, however, that the secretary of commerce began to exercise this authority. Congress had decided to empower the secretary of commerce because radio was seen as

interstate commerce: thus, the Department of Commerce was the logical choice to handle the authorization of these new radio stations.

It did not take long to realize that radio licensing and regulation was a much larger task than could be handled by the secretary of commerce in addition to his regular duties. At the First National Radio Conference in Washington, D.C., in 1922, government officials and amateur and commercial radio operators met to discuss problems facing the infant industry. A technical committee's report resulted in the introduction of legislation in 1923, but it never got out of Senate committee.

At the Second National Radio Conference in 1923, many of the same problems were revisited, most notably concerns about interference. Because interference was greatest in places with the most transmitters (population centers) and less of a problem in remote areas, a recommendation emerged from the conference that the nation be divided into zones and that different rules be established for different zones based on their own specific needs. Again, legislation was introduced into Congress, but it never advanced beyond committee. A third national conference in 1924 produced no legislation either. Finally, the Fourth National Radio Conference in 1925 produced the proposals that would lead to the Radio Act of 1927.

During all this time, the secretary of commerce continued to license radio stations. The difficulty came when secretary Herbert Hoover attempted to *not* license a station. In 1923 Intercity Radio applied for a renewal of its license. The request was denied based on a determination that there was no longer spectrum space available. Intercity appealed the case, and the Federal Circuit Court of Appeals ruled in their favor. According to the court, the 1912 Act authorized the secretary of commerce to grant licenses: it did not grant the authority to deny them. In the court's judgment, the secretary of commerce had to accommodate applicants by finding them spectrum space that would cause the least amount of interference.

The secretary's authority was further undermined in a 1926 court decision. Zenith Radio had been operating a station in Denver with a prescribed allocation limiting it to two hours of broadcasts per week. The station challenged the authorization by using other frequencies not specifically allocated to it. When secretary of commerce Herbert Hoover filed suit against Zenith, the court ruled that Zenith was within its rights, citing a section of the Radio Act that allowed stations to use "other sending wave lengths." For all intents and purposes, such a decision authorized any licensed station to operate on virtually any frequency in addition to the one allocated.

The result of the two court cases was devastating to the secretary of commerce's assumed authority to regulate radio stations. Following the decision in the Zenith case, the secretary sent a letter to the U.S. Attorney General requesting an opinion on the authority vested in the secretary of commerce by the Radio Act. The attorney general's response only reinforced what the courts had already decided. The interpretation of the Radio Act of 1912 was that licensed stations could use virtually any frequency they wanted, at whatever times and using whatever transmitting power they wanted. With the secretary's authority eviscerated, President Calvin Coolidge asked Congress to create new legislation. With the president's endorsement, legislation that had been proposed as a result of the 1925 National Radio Conference moved swiftly through Congress, and the Radio Act of 1927 was signed into law by President Coolidge on 23 February 1927.

Initial Tasks

Central to the 1927 Act was the establishment of the FRC. Instead of having one person overseeing licensing and regulation of radio, a commission of five people appointed by the president and approved by the Senate would handle the duties. Perhaps influenced by the thinking that different geographic regions would have different needs, commissioners were to represent those different regions. When it passed the Radio Act of 1927, Congress naively believed that the FRC would need to act for only one year to straighten out all the confusion in radio regulation and licensing. After that, things would be well enough established that the agency could serve only as an appellate board for actions by the secretary of commerce. W. Jefferson Davis wrote in the *Virginia Law Review* that after the first year, "the Secretary of Commerce will handle most of the problems that arise, and the Commission will probably function only occasionally." Clearly, that was not to be the case. The FRC's authority was made permanent in 1930 and was extended until 1934, when it was replaced by the Federal Communications Commission (FCC).

The FRC got off to what was at best a shaky start, as Congress had not financed it. The FRC came into existence without an appropriation from Congress. The original commissioners were required to do their own clerical work, and engineers had to be "borrowed" from other agencies for several years. Furthermore, Congress confirmed only three of the five nominees from President Coolidge in the

first year. Two of the five appointees died during the Commission's first year. Only one of the original FRC members, Judge Eugene O. Sykes, was still serving just two years later. In spite of these difficulties, the FRC was able to dramatically advance the nation's radio regulatory policy in its eight years of existence, at a crucial time for the development of commercial radio. Even the publication *Radio News* recognized the enormity of the FRC's task and the efficiency with which it worked. In November 1929, the publication stated,

> Not in the history of federal bureaus has any commission ever been called upon to perform so great a task in so short a span of time. The already overloaded departments of the federal government could not have treated with radio problems on this scale without a great increase in personnel and what would have been tantamount to the setting up of a radio commission within the department to which it might have been assigned. By its segregation and absolute independence, radio has been regulated and its major problems have been solved without handicapping any other federal bureau.
> ("Public Interest, Convenience and Necessity," in *Radio News* [November 1929])

The Radio Act of 1927 empowered the FRC with the authority and regulatory discretion that the secretary of commerce had lacked under the Radio Act of 1912. The new act specifically granted the FRC authority to license stations for a limited period of time; to designate specific frequencies, power, and times of operation of stations; to conduct hearings and serve as a quasi-judicial body; and to deny a license or to revoke an existing license. All of these powers had been denied the secretary of commerce.

Legal Challenges

It did not take long for the FRC's enforcement authority to be legally challenged. Technical Radio Laboratory sought a license renewal for its station in Midland Park, New Jersey, and was denied by the FRC because there was not adequate spectrum available. Whereas Intercity had successfully challenged denial of its renewal request, Technical Radio Laboratory was not so fortunate, because the courts found that the FRC was within its authority. Dozens of other cases would follow, with similar results. Congress had taken the appropriate steps to provide the FRC with licensing authority.

According to the Radio Act, the FRC's jurisdiction was based on Congress' authority to regulate interstate commerce. Thus, radio stations that did not transmit across a state line might not have to be regulated by them. In theory, at least, radio stations involved only in intrastate commerce rather than interstate commerce were not subject to federal jurisdiction. Just such an assertion was made in the case of *United States v. Gregg.* An unlicensed Houston station challenged the FRC's authority, claiming that its signal was not interstate commerce. The court accepted the FRC's argument that it had to have authority over all transmissions, even those that did not cross state lines, because otherwise it could not control the interference that might affect other, regulated stations. Leery of raising questions of states' rights, Congress had avoided the issue in the Radio Act of 1927. In 1933 the court extended FRC authority to cover all radio transmissions.

For the most part, the FRC fared quite well in challenges to its regulatory authority. To be sure, there were cases that the FRC did not win, but it certainly won many more than it lost. The Commission's ability to exercise regulatory authority over the broadcast spectrum became greater with each legal decision. In two highly visible cases, the FRC was able to deny license renewals for stations that had not acted in the public interest. In 1931 the court upheld the FRC in denying a renewal to Dr. John R. Brinkley's station, KFKB (Brinkley had been using his station to prescribe medications). Brinkley claimed that the FRC had no authority to censor him. The court held that the FRC was not engaging in censorship by examining the record to determine if a licensee had acted in the public interest. The following year, Dr. Robert Schuler of Trinity Methodist Church appealed the denial of his station license, KGEF, claiming that his free speech rights had been violated. The court rejected that argument on the premise that the Commission was not preventing Schuler from making his vitriolic comments. As with Brinkley, the FRC could use his past record as an indication of how he would serve the public interest.

Defining the Public Interest

Included in the Radio Act of 1927 was the stipulation that the FRC would act "as public convenience, interest, or necessity requires." Likewise, stations were to be licensed to serve the same public interest, convenience, and necessity. Congress borrowed the language from other legislation regulating public utilities. This vague directive from Congress served as the guiding philosophy for the FRC. In one action in 1928, the FRC denied 62 license renewals and modified the operations of dozens more. A month later, the FRC issued a statement to explain its interpretation of the public interest standard and how it was to be applied. As the FRC pointed out

in its statement, "no attempt is made anywhere in the act to define the term 'public interest, convenience, or necessity,' nor is any illustration given of its proper application" (FRC annual report, 166 [1928]). While asserting that a specific definition was neither possible nor desirable, the FRC set forth some general principles regarding the public interest. Perhaps most illustrative of all is the concluding sentence from the FRC's statement: "The emphasis must be first and foremost on the interest, the convenience, and the necessity of the listening public, and not on the interest, convenience, or necessity of the individual broadcaster or the advertiser." The language mirrors the sentiment of Rep. Wallace H. White, cosponsor of the bill that became the Radio Act of 1927, who said:

> We have reached the definite conclusion that the right of our people to enjoy this means of communication can be preserved only by the repudiation of the idea underlying the 1912 law that anyone who will may transmit—and by the assertion in its stead of the doctrine that the right of the public to service is superior to the right of any individual to use the ether.
>
> (67th Cong. Rec. 5479 [1926])

The FRC determined that the public interest is served by having a "substantial band of frequencies set aside for the exclusive use of broadcasting stations and the radio listening public." It also adopted the general premise that the greatest good is served by minimizing interference. It follows from this that denying licenses in order to prevent interference, detrimental though it may be to some prospective broadcasters, serves the greatest good. The commission stated its intent to use the past record of a licensee to determine whether that station was deserving of a license. The reliability of a station's transmissions were also to be considered. Stations that could not be relied upon to transmit at regularly scheduled, announced times or whose transmission frequencies wandered around the spectrum did not serve the public interest. More than 70 years later, these interpretations of serving the public interest are still considered valid.

Also included in the 1928 statement on the public interest was the principle that stations should operate at different classes of service in order to ensure that there would be some stations serving larger geographic areas, while other stations served only small communities. This coincided with Congress' view, which had been stated earlier that same year when the Radio Act of 1927 was amended by the Davis Amendment in 1928. In addition to extending the FRC's authorization beyond its original year, the amendment directed the FRC to devise a scheme for providing equitable radio services in all zones of the country. One week following the FRC's statement on the public interest, it issued a plan for providing different classes of radio service. Each of the nation's zones would have an equal number of channels assigned as clear channels, regional channels, and local channels. Clear channels were designated to be high-power stations audible at a distance, whereas regional and local channels had decreasing coverage areas. Eight clear channels, seven regional channels, and six local channels were assigned to each of the five zones. The FRC's basic concept of clear, regional, and local channels remained in force more than six decades later.

One of the public-interest principles established by the FRC that did not continue with the FCC was the concept that licenses should not be provided to stations that offer services which duplicate those already available. The FRC stated that simply playing phonograph records on the air does not provide the listening public with anything that it cannot otherwise obtain. The FRC would have maintained a licensing scheme that would compare the programming intentions of the applicants. It can also be inferred that the FRC did not favor licensing stations whose formats mirrored those of stations already in the community. Based on today's radio business, that policy clearly did not survive

See also: Censorship; Clear Channel Stations; Controversial Issues, Broadcasting of; First Amendment and Radio; Frequency Allocation; Licensing Authorizing U.S. Stations to Broadcast; Localism in Radio; "Public Interest, Convenience, or Necessity"; Radio Laws; Regulation; United States Congress and Radio

Further Reading

Benjamin, Louise M., "In the Public Interest: The Radio Act and Actions of the Federal Radio Commission," Chapter 5 in *Freedom of the Air and the Public Interest*, Carbondale: Southern Illinois University Press, 2001.

Bensman, Marvin R., "Regulation Under the Act of 1927," Chapter 5 in *The Beginning of Broadcast Regulation in the Twentieth Century*, Jefferson, North Carolina: McFarland, 2000.

Davis, Stephen Brooks, *The Law of Radio Communication*, New York: McGraw-Hill, 1927.

Federal Radio Commission, "Annual Report," Washington, D.C.: Government Printing Office, 1927–33; reprint, New York: Arno Press, 1971.

Goodman, Mark, and Mark Gring, "The Ideological Fight Over Creation of the Federal Radio Commission in 1927," *Journalism History* 26 (Autumn 2000).

Schmeckebier, Laurence F., *The Federal Radio Commission: Its History, Activities and Organization*, Washington, D.C.: Brookings Institution, 1932.

Slotten, Hugh R., "Radio Engineers, the Federal Radio Commission, and the Social Shaping of Broadcast Technology," chapter 2 in *Radio and Television Regulation: Broadcast Technology in the United States, 1920–60*, Baltimore, Maryland: Johns Hopkins University Press, 2000.

U.S. House of Representatives, Committee on Merchant Marine and Fisheries, *Federal Radio Commission: Hearings*, 70th Cong., 2nd Sess. (January–February 1929).

DOM CARISTI

FIBBER MCGEE AND MOLLY
Radio Comedy Series

For three decades, the consummate comedians Jim Jordan (1896–1988) and his wife Marian Driscoll (1898–1961) imitated and mocked the habits of middle-class American homeowners. They began as musicians and vaudevillians. These theatrical experiences, plus several radio series, prepared them for the initial broadcast of *Fibber McGee and Molly* on Tuesday, 16 April 1935. (The show lasted in various forms until 1959.) The Jordans and their writers, mainly Don Quinn and later Phil Leslie, wisely preserved what worked. During the 1940s, fans always voted it one of their favorite programs. Expressions like "Fibber McGee's closet" percolated into popular speech. So did tag lines like Molly's (Marian) "T'aint funny, McGee," Throckmorton P. Gildersleeve's (Hal Peary) "You're a haaard man, McGee," and the Old Timer's (Bill Thompson) "That's pretty funny, Johnny, but that ain't the way I heerd it." (Fibber McGee's overstuffed closet became an American icon, probably for two reasons: it symbolized the unpredictable fullness of the McGees' world, and its sound of falling hip boots, mandolin, Aunt Sarah's picture, and moose head—a triumph of sound effects—consoled listeners who had a similar storage problem. A replica may be seen at the Museum of Broadcasting in Chicago.)

Their modest home at 79 Wistful Vista attracted visitors from a wide variety of social, economic, and ethnic backgrounds. Such conviviality required explanation because McGee was often uncivil, arguing with bankers and bus drivers and department store managers, a dynamo of precarious amiability. Luckily, Molly moderated his bumptious unconviviality so that their many callers simultaneously experienced the contradictory ideals of defensive homeowner and welcoming hostess.

The perilous balance of discourtesy and diplomacy allowed McGee to insult guests and still retain their friendship. Doc Gamble (Arthur Q. Bryan) often received the master's barbs. One time the doctor looked forward to a vacation he said would leave him "ship shape." Ever the deflator of other people's fantasies, McGee agreed that the doctor already looked like a great big "stern wheeler." In keeping with the American spirit of fair play and the aesthetic rule that helplessness is not funny, Doc returned these insults with agility. Once he scolded McGee for being too cheap to buy a proper suit, dubbing Fibber a "rhinestone Jim Brady" and "our little Lucius Booby in that pin-stripe awning he uses for a sport coat."

Similarly, other drop-ins to their parlor had positions that would ordinarily merit respect but instead received impertinence. Policemen were called "lugans" and "larrigans," told to take off their hats, and given false information (asked his name, Fibber replied, "Herman Gibbletripe—and this is my wife Clara"). Mayor LaTrivia (Gale Gordon), outside the McGees' home an effective orator, dissolved into babble at the McGees'. He boasted that the City Council had opposed him, but he had "stuck to [his] guns." Both Fibber and Molly confounded him by asking why an elected official needed weapons, suggesting that he might have been more successful if he had not threatened them, and finally warning him that guns should not be tolerated.

Fibber reacted to aristocrats with a peculiar mixture of envy—which prompted get-rich projects to find a substitute for sugar or turn paper back into cloth—and disdain. Despite all the wealth of grand dames like Abigail Uppington (Isabel Randolph) and Millicent Carstairs (Bea Benedaret), Fibber commented that the latter "acts like a coquettish dray horse." He admired clothing store dummies for their "nonchalant, supercilious, haughty" look: "It takes six generations of money in the family to achieve an expression like that." Molly personalized his sociological dictum: "Yes, it's strange how often a vacant face goes with a full pocketbook, which ought to give you a very expressive countenance."

Because he never seemed to work and borrowed tools without returning them, McGee's own income remained ambiguous. He yearned for money so much that he ripped apart their antique sofa to find $20,000 hidden by an ancestor—$20,000 Confederate, that is. The appearance of a maid on some shows, variously called Beulah (played by a man, Marlin Hurt) or Lena (Gene Carroll, also a man), hinted that he was prosperous; the appearance of a renter, Alice Darling (Shirley Mitchell), a gabby factory worker, on other episodes suggested that he needed spare cash. The general impression was of a household relatively secure in the economic parade.

Located in the middle of the middle class, McGee often was bested by those whom snobs would have considered beneath concern. When Ole Swenson (Dick LeGrand), the Swedish janitor at the Elks' Club, said his boy in the submarine service was on a secret mission, McGee paraphrased loftily, "Sub rosa, eh?" Ole calmly torpedoed the hifalutin' Latin with, "No, submarine." Likewise, the recently immigrated Nick DePopoulous (Bill Thompson) steamrolled over "Fizzer," telling his own tales with nonstop, heavily accented malapropisms.

Far from being disturbed by unpredictable standards for social deportment, people in McGee's universe enjoyed the anarchy. Wallace Wimple (Bill Thompson), the hen-pecked victim of "Sweetie Face," his "big, old wife," just wanted to be alone with his bird book. To avoid her abuse, Wallace secretly rented a room under the name "Lancelot Eisenhower Dempsey"—a name, he explained dreamily, that "just appealed to me somehow. It's such a *brave* name."

Two final visitors show how the give-and-take of their peculiar hosting rituals eliminated barriers. After Fibber read a bedtime story to Teeny (Marian), the precocious little neighbor girl, she asked, "What's a 'Dell'?" Fibber: "Oh, it's a kind of shady nook in the woods where green things grow." Teeny: "You mean like dell pickles." Announcer Harlow Wilcox, ever touting the benefits of Johnson's Wax, delivered his pitches despite McGee's interruptions.

Just as the program democratically blurred social distinctions, the language too evaded rules. McGee frequently delivered such tongue-tangling monologues as:

> When I worked in the big mill there, I was quite the dude. 'Mill Dude McGee' I was known as. Mill Dude McGee, a magnificent mass of muscle and manly manners mesmerizing the maidens in the Midwest and mentioned most every month in many of the men's magazines as the mirror and model for male millinery merchants, meticulous material manufacturers, and miscellaneous members of the metropolitan mob, mighty and magnetic from November through May.

Individual words, like manners, evolved into new forms. After getting Mayor LaTrivia's goat, Fibber bragged to Molly, "He sure gets worked up, don't he? He was just liver with rage."

MOLLY: You mean livid, Dearie.
FIBBER: Go on, livid is a girl's name, like Livid De Haviland.
MOLLY: That's Olivia.
FIBBER: Oh, don't kid me, Snookie. Olivia's a country in South America.

During another episode, Fibber skipped from "subtle to subtitle to scuttle to shuttle to chateau." Such celebrations of social and linguistic independence during decades of Depression, war, and tumultuous recovery that required national conformity explain the enduring appeal of *Fibber McGee and Molly*.

See also: Situation Comedy; Sound Effects; Vaudeville and Radio

Cast

Fibber McGee	Jim Jordan
Molly McGee	Marian Jordan
Teeny	Marian Jordan
Mrs. Abigail Uppington (1936–59)	Isabel Randolph
Nick Depopoulous (1936–59)	Bill Thompson
Widdicomb Blotto	Bill Thompson
Horatio K. Boomer (1936–59)	Bill Thompson
Old Timer (1937–59)	Bill Thompson
Wallace Wimple (1941–59)	Bill Thompson
Wallingford Tuttle Gildersleeve	Cliff Arquette
Throckmorton P. Gildersleeve (1939–59)	Harold Peary
Mayor LaTrivia (1941–59)	Gale Gordon
Foggy Williams	Gale Gordon
Alice Darling (1943–59)	Shirley Mitchell
Beulah (1944–59)	Marlin Hurt
Mrs. Millicent Carstairs	Bea Benaderet
Silly Watson	Hugh Studebaker
Uncle Dennis	Ransom Sherman
Lena	Gene Carroll
Announcer (1935–53)	Harlow Wilcox
Announcer (1953–56)	John Wald

Producers/Directors

Cecil Underwood, Frank Pittman, Max Hutto

Programming History

NBC Blue	April 1935–June 1936
NBC Red	June 1936–1938
NBC	March 1938–September 1959

Further Reading

Griswold, J.B., "Up From Peoria," *The American Magazine* 133 (March, 1942).

Price, Tom, *Fibber McGee's Closet: The Ultimate Log of Performances by Fibber McGee and Molly 1917–1987: A Celebration of the 52nd Anniversary of Fibber McGee and Molly and Jim's 70 Years in Show Business*, 2 vols, Monterey, California: Thomas A. Price, 1987.

Price, Tom, *Performance Logs of Marian+Jim Jordan, #s1–10, 1917–1980*, Monterey, California: Thomas A. Price, 1980 (Contains logs of *Air Scouts*, 1927–1929; *The Smith Family*, 1927–1932; *Farmer Rusk's Top O'Morning*, 1931–1932; Several Short Series, 1931–1934; *Smackout*, 1931–1935; Appearances and Specials, 1917–1980; *Marquette, The Little French Girl*, 1931–1932; *Mr. Twister, Mind Trickster*, 1932–1933; *Kaltenmayer's Kindergarten*, 1932–1935; *Fibber McGee and Molly*, 1935–1959).

Stumpf, Charles, and Ben Ohmart, *Fibber McGee's Scrapbook*, Boalsburg, Pennsylvania: BearManor Media, 2002.

Stumpf, Charles, and Tom Price, *Heavenly Days! The Story of Fibber McGee and Molly*, Waynesville, North Carolina: The World of Yesterday, 1987.

Yoder, Robert M, "The McGee's of Wistful Vista," *The Saturday Evening Post* 221 (April 9 and 16, 1949).

JAMES A. FREEMAN

FILM DEPICTIONS OF RADIO

Radio's depiction in motion pictures initially stemmed from the concurrence of their golden ages, as radio stars were featured in movies, often playing their radio characters. Thereafter, films about radio focused more on radio's producers, dealing with the challenges and ethical issues they faced, or on listeners, depicting the impact radio had on their lives—particularly the medium's ability to unite communities. Mentioned here are many but by no means all of the motion pictures featuring radio-related subjects.

Radio Movies in the Golden Age

Major motion pictures focusing on radio first appeared during the height of Hollywood's studio system in the 1930s and gave fans their first chance to see moving pictures of radio celebrities. Virtually all were comedies or musicals, designed to get the audience's mind off Depression-era realities.

Foremost among these was the series of films beginning with *The Big Broadcast* (1932), which included George Burns, Gracie Allen, and Bing Crosby as employees of a struggling radio station whose survival depends on a group of radio celebrities, including Kate Smith, Cab Calloway, the Boswell Sisters, Arthur Tracy, and The Vincent Lopez Orchestra. This box office success led to a sequel, *The Big Broadcast of 1936* (1935), which finds Burns and Allen with a contraption known as a Radio Eye (what we now call television) on which various stars appear, including Ethel Merman. Still another sequel, *The Big Broadcast of 1937* (1936) followed, wherein Jack Benny is now the radio boss and Martha Raye his secretary; Burns and Allen returned, appearing once again with a host of stars, including Benny Goodman, Benny Fields, and Leopold Stokowski and his orchestra. The final installment, *The Big Broadcast of 1938* (1937), finds W.C. Fields playing twins who race ships that are powered by electricity supplied from radio broadcasts; it starred Raye, as well as Dorothy Lamour, Shirley Ross, and Bob Hope, who sang what became his signature "Thanks for the Memories" for the first time.

Another series of films that tried to mimic the success of the *Big Broadcast* began with *The Hit Parade* (1937), in which a talent search for radio stars turns up a series of celebrities, including Duke Ellington. Sequels included *Hit Parade of 1941* (1940), *Hit Parade of 1943* (1943), *Hit Parade of 1947* (1947), and *Hit Parade of 1951* (1950) and continued the trend of story lines designed to pack in as many acts as possible.

In the same genre of movies about radio stars was *The Great American Broadcast* (1941), which centers on a love triangle between a young woman and two World War I veterans who enter the radio business together, later to become rivals. The finale hinges on a scheme by one of the men to reunite the woman and his wartime friend after they have parted ways, deciding to step aside and let the true lovers reconcile. His scheme involves organizing the first nationwide radio broadcast, an idea originally conceived by his war buddy, who he knows will surface to take credit and be reunited with his love. The broadcast itself features many top-name acts, including Kate Smith, Eddie Cantor, Rudy Vallee, and Jack Benny.

During this era a number of movies were also produced based upon radio programs themselves, giving audiences a chance to see their favorite radio characters in action. These include a movie version of *Ed Wynn, The Fire Chief* simply titled *The Chief* (1933) and starring Wynn. Several films featured characters of the radio comedy *Fibber McGee and Molly*, featuring the radio stars Jim and Marian Jordan. These films started with featured roles for the Jordans, playing their radio characters, in *This Way Please* (1937), followed by starring roles in *Look Who's Laughing* (1941), co-starring Edgar Bergen and Lucille Ball, *Here We Go Again* (1942), with Bergen, Gale Gordon and radio's *Great Gildersleeve* star Harold Peary, and *Heavenly Days* (1944). Peary enjoyed a string of films based upon *The Great Gildersleeve*, including *Gildersleeve on Broadway* (1943), *Gildersleeve's Bad Day* (1943), and *Gildersleeve's Ghost* (1944). Finally, there is *My Friend Irma* (1949), based on the radio sitcom of the same name and starring the radio show's lead actress Marie Wilson. The film featured the debut pairing of Dean Martin and Jerry Lewis, as did a sequel, *My Friend Irma Goes West*

(1950). Band leader and radio star Kay Kyser also appeared in several motion pictures.

What *The Big Broadcast* and its progeny were to 1930s and 1940s radio stars, a series of rock-and-roll radio movies starring renowned disc jockey Alan Freed was to 1950s rock acts. These films included *Rock Around the Clock* (1956), *Don't Knock the Rock* (1956), *Rock, Rock, Rock* (1956), *Mister Rock and Roll* (1957), and *Go, Johnny, Go!* (1959). Showcasing the likes of Bill Haley and the Comets, The Platters, Little Richard, Chuck Berry, and The Moonglows, these movies featured plots that were mainly designed to pack in as many rock performances as possible. Freed's disc jockey career was itself the subject of a later film titled *American Hot Wax* (1978).

Radio Drama on Film

Foremost among films examining challenges facing radio's producers was *FM* (1978). The movie focuses on the successful program director of the number one rock-and-roll station in Los Angeles and his efforts to keep the station's sound from being too influenced by the commercial interests of its corporate owners. The overall theme of the movie is addressed in a pivotal scene, when the new sales manager toasts "to profit, and the quality it brings," to which the program director replies "to quality, and the profit it brings." Highlighting the extreme personalities of the station's air staff, the movie also foregrounds the influence radio has on its community, as the disc jockeys strike rather than give in to over-zealous commercial interests—a move that inspires hundreds of loyal fans to join the protest outside the station.

Director Oliver Stone critically examines the shock jock phenomenon in *Talk Radio* (1988), a film about a late-night talk show host based upon a play by Eric Bogosian. An intense, intelligent examination of hatred, violence, and loneliness in America, all of which are exhibited by callers to a radio program called *Night Talk*, the film is also a study of the host himself, who must suffer the consequences of provoking his late-night listeners to anger. The shock jock is ultimately killed by one of his violent listeners. The film critically examines the capacity of provocative radio talk show hosts to empower society's most troubled members, under the guise of providing entertainment and exploiting radio's First Amendment privileges.

Good Morning Vietnam (1987), perhaps the best known of all the films treated here, was directed by Barry Levinson and tells the partially true story of a wise-cracking, quick-witted disc jockey who joins the staff of Armed Forces Radio Saigon and uses his comic personality to entertain and unite the troops. From presidential impersonations to crass humor, the newcomer (played by Robin Williams) delivers a high-powered series of gags and thinly veiled criticisms of the war, in the process receiving bags-full of fan mail and the contempt of his humorless supervisors. The film also shows a more serious side, as the comic announcer confronts the ethics of army censorship of radio news.

Private Parts (1997) was shock jock Howard Stern's homage to his own rise to power. Based upon his book and starring Stern, the film recounts his career in the radio business, from his first problems with management at a local station, to meeting his long-time on-air companion Robin Quivers, to his network radio days and run-ins with the FCC. A somewhat one-sided retelling of the story, the film presents Stern as a working-class hero who does what he must to entertain the masses, much to the chagrin of his uppity and uptight management counterparts.

Foremost among films focusing on radio's listeners is Woody Allen's *Radio Days* (1987). A nostalgic look at World War II era radio, the film depicts Allen's childhood reminiscences of the role radio played in the lives of his Rockaway Beach family. A mock Martian invasion helps an Aunt see the cowardice of her date; the fantasy of a masked avenger allows a boy to imagine a life apart from suburban humdrum, much as exotic South American music allows his cousin to do the same; game shows or a ventriloquist's act provide occasions for family bonding or discussion; news bulletins following rescue efforts to save a young child who fell down a well help the family put their own petty squabbles in perspective; and war reports help a nation define an era. Throughout the film, Allen affords radio a ubiquitous presence, fondly recalling its role in every aspect of his childhood and lamenting that his memories of radio and its era fade more with every passing year.

Radio's influence in uniting communities is depicted even in films not principally focused upon radio. Hence, the cult classic *The Warriors* (1979) depicts a DJ, shown only as a pair of lips speaking into a microphone, as she helps gang members throughout New York City track and hunt members of the Warriors, who are falsely accused of murdering the charismatic leader of the city's most powerful gang; ultimately, she apologizes to the gang for the urbanite community's error. Another inner city set film that highlights radio's role in a community is Spike Lee's *Do the Right Thing* (1989), a drama about the eruption of racial tension on a

city street in Brooklyn. The disc jockey of the street's storefront radio station serves as a source of news, reason, and inspiration for the community, helping to calm tension and keep the community apprised of neighborhood happenings. Finally there is George Lucas' classic *American Graffiti* (1973), wherein the omnipresent rock music and hip chatter of archetypal disc jockey Wolfman Jack set the mood of the time and binds together the community of young adults coming of age.

Even as many sounded the death knell for radio in the new century, a number of films featured radio, beginning in 2003 with *Radio*, based on the true story of a warm relationship between a high school football coach and a mentally challenged young man nicknamed "Radio" by townspeople because of his always–present portable radio.

American Public Media's *Prairie Home Companion* was the setting for a 2006 ensemble film comedy directed by Robert Altman just five months before the director's death. *A Prairie Home Companion*, written by and starring show creator Garrison Keillor, was a fictional, behind-the-scenes story of the final broadcast of a long-running radio show by the same name. Starring four Oscar winners, the movie received generally favorable reviews.

At least four films centered on talk show hosts and crime. *The Brave One*, a 2007 psychological thriller, starred Oscar winner Jodie Foster as a radio show host who is out for revenge after being brutally attacked by three thugs who kill her fiancé. Foster eventually comes back to her radio show even while nightly roaming the streets as a vigilante killer, accompanied by a running narrative from her radio show that audiences hear as she searches for her attackers. Another 2007 film called *Talk to Me* is the true story of ex-con Ralph "Petey" Greene, who became a popular talk show host in Washington, D.C. Starring Don Cheadle as Greene, the film received favorable reviews, though generating criticism by some who charged it was not true to life in many of the details of Greene's life and activism in the community. In *The Brave One* (2007), Jodie Foster stars as radio show host. Finally, one other similar film was "in production" as this book was going to print. Slated for release in 2009, *Morgan's Summit* features superstar Bruce Willis as the host of a late-night radio show that promotes the power of goodwill and kindness. Willis goes from Mr. Nice Guy to vengeful vigilante after his life is turned upside down by the crime.

Other feature films included *I Am Legend* (2007), where Will Smith, as the allegedly last man alive, uses an abandoned station to broadcast appeals to fellow survivors. Several movies featured radio DJs, including: *The Fighting Temptations* (2003) with Steve Harvey as a DJ; *Burning Annie* (2004) with Gary Lundy as a college station DJ; and *Day of the Dead* (2008), which is partly set in radio station, with Ian McNiece as a DJ.

And a number of early 21st century documentaries focused on radio as well. *Making Waves* (2004) traced the role of low-power FM stations in Arizona. *A Note of Triumph: The Golden Age of Norman Corwin* (2005) reviewed the career of the legendary CBS producer and playwright. The *America Undercover* TV series offered a 2005 episode "Left of the Dial" about the Air America network. *Pirate Radio USA* (2006) focused on unlicensed operations. Changes in the industry were documented in two 2008 films: *Disappearing Voices: The Decline of Black Radio* explored why minority-owned stations were declining; and *Airplay: The Rise and Fall of Rock Radio* explored changing music formats on the air.

See also: Fan Magazines; Hollywood and Radio

Further Reading

Beaver, Frank, *Oliver Stone: Wakeup Cinema*, New York: Twayne Publishers, and Toronto, Ontario: Maxwell Macmillan Canada, 1994.
Hirshhorn, Clive, *The Hollywood Musical*, New York: Crown Publishers, and London: Octopus, 1981; 2nd edition, New York: Portland House, and London: Pyramid, 1991.
Kunz, Don, "Oliver Stone's *Talk Radio*," *Literature-Film Quarterly* 25 (January 1997).
Yacowar, Maurice, "The Religion of *Radio Days*," *Journal of Popular Film and Television* 16 (Summer 1998).

RICHARD WOLFF,
2009 REVISIONS BY GAIL LOVE AND
CHRISTOPHER H. STERLING

FIRESIDE CHATS
President Franklin D. Roosevelt's Use of Radio

The election of Franklin D. Roosevelt to the U.S. presidency in 1932, coincided with the development of radio networks and the growing popularity of radio. Radio was an ideal medium for Roosevelt, whose voice and style of delivery were well suited to the microphone.

Throughout his presidency (1933–45), Roosevelt used radio to talk to Americans about the problems they faced during the Depression and World War II. He inspired listeners to summon their confidence, determination, and courage to combat these threats to the nation's survival. Roosevelt's conversational,

informal radio addresses quickly became known as "fireside chats."

As governor of New York, Roosevelt had used radio to appeal directly to the state's voters, and by the time he entered the White House, he was fully aware of the benefits of the medium. Because many newspaper owners were not supporters of his New Deal programs, Roosevelt found an advantage with radio, which allowed him to speak directly and personally with listeners in their own living rooms. Unable to walk without support after 1921 because of polio, Roosevelt found radio to be an ideal way to project an image of active and powerful leadership.

Roosevelt's press secretary, Steve Early, once noted that Roosevelt liked to picture his audience as a small group sitting around a fireside; this image led to a radio introduction that included the phrase "fireside chat." There are varying opinions as to which of Roosevelt's radio addresses should be classified as fireside chats, with the number placed at between 25 and 31 addresses he made during the 12 years of his presidency. Certainly not all of Roosevelt's radio speeches were in this category, as many of his other radio presentations were tied to ceremonial occasions or political events.

The fireside chats tended to be relatively brief, usually less than 30 minutes, and were structured so that the opening generally focused on a recent event. This was followed by a review of government actions and responses, along with an explanation of the likely impact on the country and the lives of listeners, including the roles they could play in helping to solve problems. Roosevelt's informal language included repetitive devices and simple, easily understood terms. He called for forward, progressive action and expressed optimism and faith in the American people and in divine providence.

Most of the fireside chats were scheduled between 9 P.M. and 11 P.M., and originated from the East Room or the Oval Office of the White House. Frequently, friends or members of the family were in attendance.

Although Roosevelt received assistance with research and preparation, including early drafts, his speeches reflect his own phrasing, personality, and style. Listeners noted that his pleasant and distinctive voice inspired hope and confidence. This played an important part in Roosevelt's ability to communicate ideas and emotions. His relatively slow delivery, clear articulation, and even his Eastern accent contributed to his memorable and successful use of radio.

Early fireside chats described New Deal measures to combat the Depression. Topics included the banking crisis, the National Recovery Administration, the Works Progress Administration, the gold standard, and unemployment. Roosevelt's goal was to assure listeners that his administration was doing everything possible to relieve hardships resulting from economic conditions.

By the late 1930s, although the official U.S. position relative to the war in Europe was one of neutrality, Roosevelt exhibited increasing sympathy for the Allies, and by 1940 the United States was providing nonmilitary support to Britain and France. In a fireside chat during May of that year, Roosevelt urged further American commitment to the Allied cause, and by 19 December, in another radio address, he called on the United States to become the "great arsenal of democracy." Following the Japanese attack on Pearl Harbor, Roosevelt used radio to call on the public for increased industrial production and for the acceptance of necessary restrictions at home during the war effort. During the war, Roosevelt used radio to inform the public, but he also realized that it was important to avoid providing information to the enemy, who could also listen to his broadcasts. Some of the comments in his radio addresses during the war were actually intended for Axis listeners and conveyed the message that the United States was determined and able to persevere to the war's end. The themes of Roosevelt's wartime radio speeches emphasized the nobility of the Allied cause, the inevitability of victory, and the necessity for individual sacrifice. He spoke of the need for more manpower, both military and civilian, and he expressed concern about complacency and overconfidence. Roosevelt used radio to encourage the purchase of war bonds and to describe how everyone could contribute to victory.

Toward the war's end, Roosevelt described the demand for unconditional surrender and plans for a postwar America. In his last fireside chat, delivered 6 January 1945, Roosevelt expressed hope for a United Nations organization, which he described as the best hope for a lasting peace. Franklin D. Roosevelt died 12 April 1945. Roosevelt was the first president to make extensive and continuous use of modern electronic means to speak directly to his constituents. This capability has contributed to the increased power of the executive branch of government. Roosevelt's use of radio allowed him to influence the national agenda and to counter opposing newspaper editorials. His radio addresses played a major role in his popular image, in his being elected four times to the presidency of the United States, and in the success of his efforts to lead the nation through the years of economic depression and world war.

See also: Politics and Radio; United States Presidency and Radio

Further Reading

Becker, Samuel I., "Presidential Power: The Influence of Broadcasting," *Quarterly Journal of Speech* (February 1961).

Braden, Waldo W., and Earnest Brandenburg, "Roosevelt's Fireside Chats," *Speech Monographs* 22, no. 5 (November 1955).

Brandenburg, Earnest, "The Preparation of Franklin D. Roosevelt's Speeches," *Quarterly Journal of Speech* 25 (1949).

Brown, Robert J., "The Radio President," in *Manipulating the Ether: The Power of Broadcast Radio in Thirties America,* by Brown, Jefferson, North Carolina: McFarland, 1998.

Buhite, Russel D., and David W. Levy, editors, *FDR's Fireside Chats.* Norman: University of Oklahoma Press, 1992.

Roosevelt, Franklin D., *FDR's Fireside Chats,* edited by Russell D. Buhite and David W. Levy, Norman: University of Oklahoma Press, 1992.

Rosenman, Samuel Irving, *Working with Roosevelt,* New York: Harper, 1952.

Schlesinger, Arthur Meier, *The Imperial Presidency,* Boston: Houghton Mifflin, 1973.

Smith, B.R., "FDR's Use of Radio in the War Years," *Journal of Radio Studies* 4 (1997).

Winfield, Betty, *FDR and the News Media,* Urbana: University of Illinois Press, 1990.

B.R. SMITH

FIRST AMENDMENT AND RADIO

The First Amendment (1791) to the U.S. Constitution provides, in part, that Congress shall make no law abridging the freedom of speech or of the press. Yet in spite of this proscription, there exist a number of regulations that limit free expression on radio. The very fact that stations must be licensed is a restriction that would be considered clearly unconstitutional if it were applied to print media. On the other hand, the courts have stated that radio broadcasting is entitled to First Amendment protection. The amount of protection is less than that enjoyed by print media, but it is still significant.

The fact that the First Amendment protections extend to radio as well as the press was made clear by a 1948 Supreme Court decision, *United States v. Paramount Pictures,* which stated, "We have no doubt that moving pictures, like newspapers and radio, are included in the press whose freedom is guaranteed by the First Amendment." In order to best understand what free expression rights are due to radio, one needs to examine the rationale for regulating radio. Courts and legal scholars have provided a variety of arguments for regulation that fit into four general categories: scarcity of broadcast frequencies, the broadcast spectrum as a public resource, the need to alleviate interference, and the pervasiveness and power of the broadcast media.

Scarcity

In a 1984 decision, the Supreme Court stated, "The fundamental distinguishing characteristic of the new medium of broadcasting that, in our view, has required some adjustment in First Amendment analysis is that broadcast frequencies are a scarce resource that must be portioned out among applicants." This scarcity rationale has undergone a number of attacks in recent years with the proliferation of media, but in fact it is still considered a valid regulatory rationale. Although the number of radio stations (as well as the number of most other media outlets) has increased, courts continue to accept a scarcity rationale. The reason for this is that scarcity does not depend on the number of existing media outlets but rather on the determination of whether a new applicant stands a good chance of entry to the market. A vast number of existing media outlets implies that diversity exists, not that scarcity has been eliminated. If new applicants want to obtain station licenses and are unable to do so, that implies scarcity. Scarcity is a function of the number of people desiring a station to the number of stations available. As long as applicants exceed available frequencies, scarcity exists. As the Supreme Court noted in its *Red Lion* decision in 1969, "When there are substantially more individuals who want to broadcast than there are frequencies to allocate, it is idle to posit an unabridgeable First Amendment right to broadcast comparable to the right of every individual to speak, write, or publish." This is why there will never be scarcity for newspaper publishers, no matter how many newspapers are published in the United States. In theory, at least, any American can start a newspaper (at least there is no legal restriction). The same is not true for starting a radio station.

In 1943 the Supreme Court supported the notion that scarcity entitled the Federal Communications Commission (FCC) to make judgments about who would best serve the public interest. In *National Broadcasting Company v. United States*, the Court rejected the argument that chain broadcasting rules were a violation of the First Amendment:

> If that be so, it would follow that every person whose application for a license to operate a station is denied by the Commission is thereby denied his constitutional right of free speech. Freedom of utterance is abridged to many who wish to use the limited facilities of radio. Unlike other modes of expression, radio is not inherently available to all. That is its unique characteristic, and that is why, unlike other modes of expression, it is subject to governmental regulation. Because it cannot be used by all, some who wish to use it must be denied. But Congress did not authorize the Commission to choose among applicants upon the basis of their political, economic or social views, or upon any other capricious basis. The licensing system established by Congress in the Communications Act of 1934 was a proper exercise of its authority over commerce. The standard it provided for the licensing of stations was the "public interest, convenience, or necessity." Denial of a station license on that ground, if valid under the Act, is not a denial of free speech.

Public Resource

In 1962 President John F. Kennedy referred to the broadcast spectrum as a "critical natural resource." The federal government typically regulates the use of natural resources to ensure that they are not damaged and that their use is in the public interest. Viewing the spectrum as a public resource results in a philosophy that views users of the public resource as public trustees, who as such can be expected to act according to the dictates of those allowing them to use the resource. The government could have adopted other models for rationing spectrum, but it didn't. The assumption is that those who use the public resource have some degree of public service obligation.

A good example of this requirement is the demand, found in Section 312 of the Communications Act, that broadcasters provide reasonable access to candidates for federal office. This affirmative obligation on broadcasters, which would be unconstitutional if applied to print media, can only be justified under a public-resource rationale. In the 1981 Supreme Court Decision *Columbia Broadcasting System v. Federal Communications Commission*, the Court wrote that such a rule "represents an effort by Congress to assure that an important resource—the airwaves—will be used in the public interest. [The rule] properly balances the First Amendment rights of federal candidates, the public, and broadcasters."

Interference

Undoubtedly the oldest of the regulatory rationales is the assertion that the government must regulate the broadcast spectrum in order to prevent interference. This was provided as rationale for the passage of the Radio Acts in 1912 and 1927. Failure to limit interference would result in a "cacophony" in which no-one would be heard. Thus, the government exercises its authority to limit the free speech of some so that others might be heard. Some might contend that interference and scarcity are actually the same rationale, when in fact they are different. Their connection in broadcast contexts is understandable, because the spectrum is subject to both scarcity and interference. It is possible, however, to have interference when there is no physical scarcity. It is interesting to note that the Supreme Court's 1969 *Red Lion* decision quoted a 1945 print media case involving the Associated Press when it stated "the right of free speech does not embrace a right to snuff out the free speech of others." Clearly, there can be interference without scarcity. In *Red Lion*, the Court stated:

> When two people converse face to face, both should not speak at once if either is to be clearly understood. But the range of the human voice is so limited that there could be meaningful communications if half the people in the United States were talking and the other half listening. Just as clearly, half the people might publish and the other half read. But the reach of radio signals is incomparably greater than the range of human voice and the problem of interference is a massive reality. The lack of know-how and equipment may keep many from the air, but only a tiny fraction of those with resources and intelligence can hope to communicate by radio at the same time if intelligible communication is to be had, even if the entire radio spectrum is utilized in the present state of commercially acceptable technology.

The Supreme Court justified broadcast regulation, in part at least, because of broadcasting's unique physical characteristics.

Pervasiveness and Power

Perhaps most controversial of all the rationales, this claim asserts that broadcast media should be regulated because of the media's unique role in the lives of Americans. In the famous *Pacifica* case (dealing with George Carlin's "Seven Dirty Words" monologue), the Supreme Court stated that "the broadcast media have established a uniquely pervasive presence in the lives of all Americans." Yet no-one would attempt to assert that a small-town radio station has more pervasiveness and power than, say, *The New York Times*. Perhaps a more appropriate term for the Court to have used would have been *invasive* rather than *pervasive*. The Court seemed to be influenced by the fact that radio transmissions come into the privacy of one's home and automobile and are instantly available to children, unlike newspapers, which wait outside our homes for us to collect them and are unreadable by children still too young to read. In *Columbia Broadcasting*

System v. Democratic National Committee in 1973, the Court stated a concern dating back to the 1920s that radio's audience is in a sense "captive" because it cannot simply ignore the messages sent by broadcasters.

It is this rationale that supports limits on broadcast indecency. FCC rules that restrict the use of indecent language during certain hours of the broadcast day (6 A.M. to 10 P.M.) are based on the premise that the audience will consist of a number of minors who should not be subjected to indecent language. Allowing the restriction of indecent material on the air is a recognition of broadcasting's pervasive nature.

First Amendment Protections

In spite of the regulations that do exist, radio is not without First Amendment rights. Section 326 of the Communications Act specifically states:

> Nothing in this Act shall be understood or construed to give the Commission the power of censorship over the radio communications or signals transmitted by any radio station, and no regulation or condition shall be promulgated or fixed by the Commission which shall interfere with the right of free speech by means of radio communication.

Although some might contend that the Section 326 provision is rendered either superfluous by the First Amendment or invalid by rules such as those limiting indecency, the courts have continued to support the general principle that the FCC may not censor broadcasts.

Radio stations also have the right to decide who uses their facilities. The Supreme Court has unequivocally stated that the need to serve the public interest does not require that broadcasters provide access for individuals or organizations. Those who would like to present their positions on public issues have ample opportunity to do so without a government requirement that stations afford them airtime.

The Supreme Court has suggested that the balance between the First Amendment rights of broadcasters and the need for government regulation is not static and that changing conditions might warrant a change in the balance between the two. In the 1973 decision *Columbia Broadcasting System v. Democratic National Committee*, the Court stated, "the history of the Communications Act and the activities of the Commission over a period of 40 years reflect a continuing search for means to achieve reasonable regulation compatible with the First Amendment rights of the public

---

and the licensees." Eleven years later, in *Federal Communications Commission v. League of Women Voters*, the Supreme Court made it even more clear that regulatory rationales were open to review and revision. In two rather significant footnotes, the Court signaled its willingness to accept a regulatory scheme that was less demanding of broadcasters. In addressing the scarcity rationale, the Court wrote, "We are not prepared, however, to reconsider our longstanding approach *without some signal from Congress or the FCC* that technological developments have advanced so far that some revision of the system of broadcast regulation may be required" (emphasis added). Although the Court was not prepared to lay the fairness doctrine or the scarcity rationale to rest, it opened the door for others to do so. After a series of legal actions, the FCC did in fact eliminate the fairness doctrine.

The entire concept of treating broadcast differently from print media has been challenged for some time, but the practice continues. Modifications have been made, and radio has significantly fewer regulations today than it had prior to the deregulation movement that began in the 1970s. Nonetheless, some would assert that the changing nature of mass media will make it more difficult to have different regulatory schemes based on modes of transmission. With media converging as they are, will regulatory policies that treat media differently based on modes of transmission be able to survive? In an era in which both newspaper and radio messages can reach their audience via the internet, should one be regulated differently from the other? These are questions that have been posed for decades, yet our regulatory policy remains essentially unchanged. Broadcast media are subject to regulation based on the four regulatory rationales stated above, whereas the print media are largely unregulated. The amount of regulation that will be tolerated is subject to the balancing engaged in by the Supreme Court, but radio (along with television) continues to be subject to regulation.

Two radio-related First Amendment concerns, both treated in detail elsewhere, came before the FCC during the 21st century's first decade. The most controversial was the commission's seemingly inconsistent treatment of issuing fines for indecent programming; the second concerned possible revival of the defunct (since 1987) Fairness Doctrine.

See also: Communications Act of 1934; Fairness Doctrine; Federal Communications Commission; Federal Radio Commission; Frequency Allocation; Network Monopoly Probe; Obscenity and Indecency on Radio; "Public Interest, Convenience, or Necessity"; *Red Lion* Case; "Seven Dirty Words" Case; United States Congress and Radio; United States Supreme Court and Radio

Further Reading

Associated Press v. United States, 326 U.S. 1 (1945).
Bittner, John R., *Broadcast Law and Regulation*, Englewood Cliffs, New Jersey: Prentice Hall, 1982; 2nd edition, as *Law and Regulation of Electronic Media*, 1994.
Caristi, Dom, *Expanding Free Expression in the Marketplace: Broadcasting and the Public Forum*, New York: Quorum Books, 1992.
Carter, T. Barton, Marc A. Franklin, and Jay B. Wright, *The First Amendment and the Fifth Estate: Regulation of Electronic Mass Media*, 5th edition, New York: Foundation Press, 1999.
Columbia Broadcasting System v. Democratic National Committee, 412 U.S. 94 (1973).
Emery, Walter B., *Broadcasting and Government: Responsibilities and Regulations*, East Lansing: Michigan State University Press, 1961; revised edition, 1971.
Federal Communications Commission v. League of Women Voters of California, 468 U.S. 364 (1984).
Federal Communications Commission v. Pacifica Foundation, 438 U.S. 726 (1978).
Ginsburg, Douglas H., *Regulation of Broadcasting: Law and Policy towards Radio, Television, and Cable Communications*, St. Paul, Minnesota: West, 1979; 2nd edition, as *Regulation of the Electronic Mass Media: Law and Policy for Radio, Television, Cable, and the New Video Technologies*, by Ginsburg, Michael Botein, and Mark D. Director, 1991.
National Broadcasting Company v. United States, 319 U.S. 190 (1943).
Powe, Lucas A. Scot, *American Broadcasting and the First Amendment*, Berkeley: University of California Press, 1987.
Red Lion Broadcasting Company v. Federal Communications Commission, 395 U.S. 367 (1969).
United States v. Paramount Pictures, 334 U.S. 131 (1948).

Dom Caristi,
2009 Revisions By Christopher H. Sterling

FLYWHEEL, SHYSTER, AND FLYWHEEL
Radio Comedy Program

Although much of their fame rests on the dozen films they made between 1929 and 1950, the Marx Brothers, working together and as solo performers, enjoyed a measure of success in radio and later television broadcasting. The National Broadcasting Company's (NBC) weekly comedy *Flywheel, Shyster, and Flywheel* was the first network radio program to feature the Marx Brothers. Or, more accurately, it featured two of the four-member comedy team: Groucho and Chico. The remaining brothers—Harpo's silent clown and Zeppo's straight man—were less suitable for radio. Despite the fact that only 26 episodes were produced between November 1932 and May 1933, *Flywheel, Shyster, and Flywheel* opened up new avenues for the Marx Brothers' comic genius.

Flywheel, Shyster, and Flywheel's origins are typical of many programs produced for American radio during the early 1930s. Following on the heels of its rival's success with the *Texaco Fire Chief Program*, the Standard Oil Company sought a vehicle to promote its new product line: Esso gasoline and Essolube motor oil. Working with its advertising agency, McCann-Erickson, Standard Oil agreed to sponsor a weekly variety program called *Five Star Theater*. Every night of the week featured a different program: detective stories, dramas, musicals, and comedies. As Michael Barson notes in the introduction to his edited collection of the program's scripts, "the jewel of the enterprise was Monday night's entry, *Beagle, Shyster, and Beagle, Attorneys at Law*," which featured Groucho as Waldorf T. Beagle, a wisecracking ambulance chaser, and Chico as his incompetent assistant, Emmanuel Ravelli. Indeed, with four successful feature films to their credit— *The Coconuts, Animal Crackers, Monkey Business*, and *Horsefeathers*— landing even half of the Marx Brothers was quite a coup for Standard Oil.

Beagle, Shyster, and Beagle debuted on 28 November 1932 over the NBC Blue network. Although audience reaction is difficult to gauge, at least one listener, a New York attorney named Beagle, was not amused. Anxious to avoid a lawsuit, the network changed the name of Groucho's character to Flywheel and promptly altered the program's title accordingly. Not surprisingly, the scripts for *Flywheel, Shyster, and Flywheel* are characteristic of the Marx Brothers' penchant for rapid-fire one-liners, puns, putdowns, and malapropisms. And as in their movies, on radio the Marx Brothers had little regard for the rule of law or high society: few cherished American values or institutions were spared a "Marxist" skewering. For example, at the end of one episode, Flywheel (Groucho) advises a would-be philanthropist, "Instead of leaving half of your money to your children and the other half to the orphanage, why not leave your children to the orphanage and the million to me?"

What is most significant about these scripts (the original programs were not recorded, but the majority of the show's transcripts survive in the Library of Congress) is their relationship to the Marx Brothers' film work. In some instances, entire routines from earlier films were reworked for *Flywheel, Shyster, and Flywheel*. For example, some episodes featured plotlines and dialogue taken from the

Broadway hit and subsequent film *Animal Crackers*. Even the name of Chico's character, Emmanuel Ravelli, came directly from this film. Several scenes from *Monkey Business* found their way into episodes of the radio program as well. On the other hand, a number of *Flywheel, Shyster, and Flywheel* scripts foreshadowed the Marx Brothers' later film work. Of particular interest are early drafts of now archetypal routines and dialogue from the Marx Brothers' classic *Duck Soup*. The film's infamous trial sequence owes much of its funny business to a *Flywheel, Shyster, and Flywheel* script, as does Chico's hilarious recitation on his difficulties as a spy: "Monday I shadow your wife. Tuesday I go to the ball game—she don't show up. Wednesday she go to the ball game—I don't show up. Thursday was a doubleheader. We both no show up. Friday it rain all day—there'sa no ball game, so I go fishing." The name of Groucho's character, Waldorf T. Flywheel, would be recycled some years later in the 1941 film *The Big Store*.

The need for this recycling of old gags and testing of new material is understandable. Along with their writers, Nat Perrin and Alan Sheekman, Groucho and Chico soon grew tired of traveling cross-country from Hollywood to New York to do a weekly radio program. In fact, in January 1933, *Flywheel, Shyster, and Flywheel* took the then-unprecedented step of relocating its broadcast from WJZ in New York to Hollywood for a time. Still, the time constraints facing both writers and performers undoubtedly contributed to their willingness to borrow from established routines while refining others. By the middle of 1933, however, it was a moot point. *Flywheel, Shyster, and Flywheel* was taken off the air. Although its ratings were quite respectable, considering the less-than-desirable airtime of 7:30 P.M., the sponsors were disappointed with the show's performance.

Throughout the 1930s and 1940s, Groucho and Chico returned to the airwaves in various guises. In 1934 they were hired by the Columbia Broadcasting System (CBS) to spoof the latest news in a short-lived program called *The Marx of Time*. Both Groucho and Chico struck out on their own as well. Chico made a number of radio appearances as a musical accompanist and band leader, and Groucho served as host for programs such as *Pabst Blue Ribbon Town*. During the war years, the Marx Brothers, including Harpo, made guest appearances on the Armed Forces Radio Service. Of special note, however, is Groucho's role as the judge in Norman Corwin's fanciful courtroom drama from 1945, *The Undecided Molecule*. Groucho's true calling on radio came in 1947 as a quiz show host on *You Bet Your Life*. Curiously, this popular program shuffled between the radio networks before finding a permanent home on NBC.

In an odd but telling postscript, the British Broadcasting Corporation (BBC) began airing recreations of *Flywheel, Shyster, and Flywheel* in 1990. The programs proved quite popular with British audiences and have subsequently been picked up for broadcast in the United States through National Public Radio (NPR).

See also: Comedy; *You Bet Your Life*

Cast

Waldorf T. Flywheel	Groucho Marx
Emmanuel Ravelli	Chico Marx

BBC Cast

Waldorf T. Flywheel	Michael Roberts
Emmanuel Ravelli	Frank Lazarus

Writers

Nat Perin, Arthur Sheekman, Tom McKnight, and George Oppenheimer

Programming History

NBC Blue	28 November 1932–22 May 1933
BBC	1990–92 (19 Episodes)

Further Reading

Adamson, Joe, *Groucho, Harpo, Chico, and Sometimes Zeppo: A History of the Marx Brothers and a Satire of the Rest of the World*, New York: Simon and Schuster, 1973.

Barson, Michael, editor, *Flywheel, Shyster, and Flywheel: The Marx Brothers' Lost Radio Show*, New York: Pantheon, 1988.

Marx, Groucho, *Groucho and Me*, New York: Geis, and London: Gollancz, 1959.

Mitchell, Glenn, *The Marx Brothers Encyclopedia*, London: Batsford, 1996.

KEVIN HOWLEY

FM RADIO

Frequency modulation (FM) radio, more usually called VHF radio outside the United States, began with experiments in the 1920s and 1930s, expanded to commercial operation in the 1940s, declined to stagnation in the 1950s in the face of competition from television, resumed growth in the 1960s, and

rose to dominance of American radio listening by the late 1970s. This entry focuses first on the basics of FM broadcasting and then explores the development of the service in the United States, where it was first invented and developed; finally, this essay turns to selective brief coverage of FM outside the U.S.

FM Basics

FM transmitters modulate a carrier wave signal's frequency rather than its amplitude. That is, the power output remains the same at all times, but the carrier wave frequency changes in relation to the information (e.g., music or talk programs) transmitted. Electronic static (most of which is amplitude modulated) may flow with but cannot attach to FM waves, which allows the desired FM signal information to be separated from most interference by special circuits in the receiver.

Because U.S. FM channels are each 200 kHz wide (allowing a wide frequency swing), a high-quality sound image is transmitted (up to 15,000 cycles per second—almost three times the frequency response of AM signals and close to the 20,000-cycle limit of human hearing), usually in multiplexed stereo. The cost for this sound quality is paid for in spectrum—each FM station takes up 20 times the spectrum of a single AM station, although only a portion is used for actual signal transmission, with the remainder serving to protect signals of adjacent stations. FM radio in the United States is allocated to the very high frequencies (VHF), occupying 100 channels of 200 kHz each between 88 and 108 MHz. Each FM channel accommodates hundreds of stations—there are more than 7,000 on the air at the beginning of the 21st century.

VHF transmissions follow line-of-sight paths from antenna to receiver, and thus FM transmitters (or television stations, which use neighboring frequencies) are limited in their coverage to usually not more than 40 to 60 miles, depending on terrain and antenna height. That limitation is balanced by the lack of the medium wave interference that AM radio has, which is caused by signals arriving from ground waves or sky waves at slightly different times because of the distances covered.

Experimental Development (to 1940)

No one person "invented" FM radio—indeed, the man most credited with developing the system, Edwin Howard Armstrong, readily conceded that point. The first patents concerning an FM transmission system were granted to Cornelius Ehret of Philadelphia in 1905, probably the first such patents in the world. Scattered mentions of FM in subsequent years focused on its negative aspects, suggesting that, based on what was then known, FM would not be a useful broadcast medium. Still, technical work continued, and more than two dozen patents had been granted to various inventors and companies by 1928. Much of the impetus behind research into FM work was the search for a solution to the frustrating interference problem with AM radio. By the late 1920s, it was clear that simply using more AM transmitter power would not overcome static, which made AM unlistenable in electrical storms. Something new was needed.

From 1928 to 1933, Edwin Armstrong, a wealthy radio inventor then on Columbia University's physics faculty, focused on trying to utilize FM in a viable broadcast transmission system. Rather than working with narrow bands as had others before him, Armstrong's key breakthrough was to use far wider channels, eventually 20 times wider than those used by AM. The frequency could then modulate over about 150 kHz (though it normally used far less), leaving 25-kHz sidebands to prevent interference with adjacent channels. This allowed for greatly improved frequency response, or sound quality. Armstrong incorporated various circuits to allow precise tuning of the wide channels, while at the same time eliminating most static and interference. Armstrong applied for the first of his four basic FM patents in 1930 and for the last in 1933; all four were granted late in 1933.

From 1934 to 1941, Armstrong further developed and demonstrated FM, working toward Federal Communications Commission (FCC) approval of a commercial system. After a number of long-distance tests (successfully sending signals up to 70 miles with only 2,000 W of power) in cooperation with the Radio Corporation of America (RCA), Armstrong announced his system to the press early in 1935. A more formal demonstration to a meeting of the Institute of Radio Engineers later that year (and the published paper that resulted) marked the beginning of active FM innovation.

Resistance to the FM idea began to develop at about this time, usually growing out of the competing interests of two other broadcast services. Owners of AM stations, including the major networks, were concerned about the new technology that might totally replace their existing system. And companies already investing heavily in television research, especially RCA, thought that the new video service should receive priority in allocations and industry investment. FM was seen by some as

merely a secondary audio service, albeit a far better one technically.

In July 1936 Armstrong obtained permission from the FCC to construct the world's first full-scale FM station in Alpine, New Jersey, across the Hudson River from New York City. After a technical hearing, the FCC provided initial allocations for FM and television (among other services), granting the fledgling FM technology's backers the right to experiment on 13 channels scattered across three widely separated parts of the spectrum—26, 43, and 117 MHz. Early in 1939 the allocation was expanded to 75 channels located more conveniently between 41 and 44 MHz. In the meantime, Armstrong's experimental station—the world's first FM transmitter—had gone on the air as W2XMN with low-power tests in April 1938.

Developing further experimentation but also looking toward commercial FM operations, the New England-based Yankee Network began to build two large transmitters in 1938–39. General Electric built two low-power FM transmitters at the same time, and the National Broadcasting Company's (NBC) experimental station began operating in January 1940. The first FM station west of the Alleghenies began transmission tests in Milwaukee just a few days later. Transmitters for most of these operations came from Radio Engineering Laboratories. Receivers were first manufactured by General Electric in 1939, with other companies joining in the next year; however, most FM sets cost a good deal more than their AM counterparts.

Early Operations (1940–45)

The FCC became the arena for a 1940 battle over whether or not to authorize commercial FM service, and if so, on how many channels and with what relationship to developing television. In March 1940, more than a week of hearings were held to air the industry's conflicting views over the merits of FM and television. On 20 May 1940, the commission released its decision allowing the inception of commercial FM operation as of 1 January 1941; the decision allocated 40 channels on the VHF band (42–50 MHz), reserving the lowest five channels for noncommercial applicants. Final technical rules were issued a month later. The first 15 commercial station construction permits were issued on 31 October 1940.

As the new year dawned, 18 commercial and two educational stations aired (compared to more than 800 AM stations at the time). The first commercial license was granted to W47NV, affiliated with AM station WSM in Nashville. The first West Coast station, a Don Lee network outlet, went on the air in September 1941. FM outlets briefly used unique call signs that combined the letters used with AM stations with numbers indicating the channel used (e.g., W55M in Milwaukee broadcast on 45.5 MHz). This system was replaced with normal four-letter call signs in mid-1943.

By the end of 1941, and after the United States had entered World War II, the FCC reported 67 commercial station authorizations, with another 43 applications pending. About 30 of the former were actually on the air. Wartime priorities forced the end of further license grants and limited construction material availability after March 1942. By the end of October 1942, 37 stations were in operation, plus an additional eight outlets still devoted to experiments. But construction materials and replacement parts were increasingly difficult to find, and some owners turned back their authorizations or withdrew their applications pending the end of the war.

The first attempt at an FM network, the American network, never made it on the air, largely because of difficulties in constructing the needed affiliate stations in sufficient markets. Programs offered on FM were of two types—duplicated AM station signals (the most common type) or recorded music. Because of the duplicated content of existing stations, FM stations had little appeal for advertisers. Another problem was FM audiences. There were some 15,000 FM sets in use at the beginning of 1941 and perhaps 400,000 by the time manufacturing was stopped early in 1942, compared to 30 million AM equipped households. Most observers expected FM to become an important part of the industry after the war.

Frequency Shift and Decline (1945–57)

The next dozen years—from 1945 through 1957—were both exciting and frustrating as the FM service struggled to become established and successful amidst a broadcasting industry increasingly infatuated with television and still investing considerable sums into the expansion of AM. Initial excitement over FM's potential gave way to a slow decline.

Toward the end of the war, potential operators were already concerned that FM's allocation of 40 channels was not sufficient for expected postwar expansion. To further complicate matters, wartime spectrum and related research suggested that the FM allocation of 42–50 MHz might be subject to cycles of severe sun spot interference. Concerns about television expansion led to demands by some members of the industry for FM's spectrum space to be reallocated to television.

Extensive FCC hearings in mid-1944 aired some of the technical concerns about the FM band, though wartime security limited what could be discussed. Armstrong and his backers argued to retain (or, better yet, to expand) the existing allocation, in part because stations could easily network by picking up each other's signals and passing them on—something that would be impossible were FM to be moved higher in the spectrum (moving lower was out of the question because of existing services). In January 1945 the FCC proposed moving FM to the 84–102 MHz band to avoid the expected atmospheric interference and to gain more channels, for a total of 90. Subsequent proceedings continued the industry split over what to do and how. Finally, in June 1945, the FCC made its decision, shifting FM "upstairs" to the 88–108 MHz band with a total of 100 channels that the service occupies today. Continuing the precedent established in 1941, educational users were assigned to channels reserved for them at 88–92 MHz. The former FM band would be turned over to television and other services after a three-year transition period.

At first it seemed the shift would only disadvantage those stations actually on the air (46 at the time) and those people with FM sets that could not also receive AM signals (perhaps 30,000 old-band FM-only sets in consumer hands). Generally FM's outlook was good. The FCC issued the first postwar grants for new stations in October 1945, and more applications were piling up. Through 1946 there were always at least 200 applications pending, and although the number of stations actually on the air grew fairly slowly, the number of authorized FM stations exceeded 1,000 by 1948—more than all the AM and FM stations on the air just three years earlier. Most applications were coming in from AM stations hedging their bets on the future. Several government agencies issued optimistic publications encouraging still more FM applicants. Two specialized FM trade magazines began to publish. A number of potential FM networks were in the planning stages, and the first, called the Continental network, began operations with four stations early in 1947.

But all was not well. FM's frequency shift was more damaging in the short term than it had seemed. When stations began to transmit on FM's new frequencies, there were few receivers available to pick up the signals. Manufacturers were trying to meet pent-up wartime demand for new AM sets and had little capacity to devote to FM's needs. Thus FM suffered from the lack of a good-sized audience that might appeal to advertisers. Only token numbers of receivers were available until

1950, and by then demand for television sets was threatening capacity devoted to radio. FM's lack of separate programming (after considerable industry argument both ways, the FCC had allowed co-owned AM and FM stations to simulcast or carry the same material) offered little incentive for consumers to invest in one of the rare and expensive FM receivers. A cheap AM set could tune popular local and network radio programs just as well. FM's better sound quality was not enough of a draw. What independent programming did exist was largely classical music and arts material of interest to a relatively small elite. Advertisers saw no reason to invest in FM, especially when FM time was usually given away with AM advertising purchases. Indeed, AM was thriving—more than doubling the number of stations on the air from 1945 to 1950. And the growing concentration on television by broadcasters, advertisers, and the public made FM seem unnecessary.

As these factors combined and intensified, the results soon became apparent. The number of new FM station applications began to drop off, and then overall FM authorizations declined. By 1948 FM stations already on the air, among them some pioneering operations, began to shut down, returning their licenses to the FCC. FM outlets could not be given away, much less sold. The number of stations on the air declined each year. Faced with the seeming failure of his primary invention, Armstrong took his own life in 1954; with the loss of his financial backing, the Continental network had to close down as well.

Rebound (1958–70)

Then, and at first very slowly, FM began to turn around. Reports in several trade magazines late in 1957 picked up the fact that the number of FCC authorizations for FM stations had increased for the first time in nine years. Slowly the pace of new station construction picked up, first in major markets and then in suburban areas. Several factors underlay this dramatic shift.

First, AM had grown increasingly crowded—there were virtually no vacant channels available in the country's major markets. The number of AM stations had doubled from 1948 to 1958, and about 150 more were going on the air annually. However, an increasing proportion of the new outlets were limited to daytime operation in an FCC attempt to reduce night-time interference. FM, with no need for daytime-only limitations, was now the only means of entering major markets. In addition, the major spurt of television expansion was over, and this eased up pressure on time, money, and personnel, which could now be applied to FM.

But aside from overcrowding in AM and television, FM itself had more to offer. In 1955 the FCC had approved the use of Subsidiary Communications Authorizations, which allowed stations to multiplex (to send more than one signal from their transmitter) such nonbroadcast content as background music for retail outlets ("storecasting"). This provided a needed revenue boost. So did the growing number of listeners interested in good music. These "hi-fi" addicts doted on FM operations, and this interest was evident in the increasing availability and sale of FM receivers. A developing high-end audience led advertisers to begin to pay serious attention to the medium.

Another technical innovation gave FM a further boost: the inception of stereo broadcasting. Beginning as early as 1952, some stations, such as New York's WQXR, offered AM/FM stereo using two stations—AM for one channel of sound and an FM outlet for the other. Occasional network two-station stereo broadcasts began in 1958—the same year commercial stereophonic records first went on sale. By 1960, more than 100 stations were providing the two-station system of stereo. But such simulcasting wasted spectrum (two stations with the same content), and the uneven quality of AM and FM provided poor stereo signals. What was needed was a system to provide stereo signals from a single station, and FM's wide channel seemed to offer the means.

In 1959 the National Stereophonic Radio Committee began industry experiments with several competing multiplexed single-station systems. By October 1960 the committee had recommended that the FCC establish FM stereo technical standards combining parts of systems developed by General Electric and Zenith. The FCC issued the standards in April 1961, and the first FM stereo stations began providing service in June. By 1965, a quarter of all commercial stations were offering stereo; by 1970, 38 percent of FM stations had the capability. Though few saw the future clearly, stereo would be a key factor in FM's ultimate success over long-dominant AM stations.

FM's continued expansion led the FCC to establish three classes of FM station in mid-1962. Lower-powered Class A (up to 3,000 W of power and a service radius of 15 miles) and B stations (up to 50,000 W of power and a service radius up to 40 miles) would be granted in the crowded northeastern section of the country as well as in southern California. Higher-powered C stations (up to 100,000 W of power providing a service radius of 65 miles) could be granted elsewhere. A five-year

FCC freeze on most new AM station grants beginning in 1968 helped funnel still more industry expansion into FM as the FCC began to see AM and FM as parts of an integrated radio service.

Of even greater importance to FM's continued growth was a series of landmark FCC decisions from 1964 to 1966 requiring separate programming on co-owned AM and FM stations in the largest markets (those with populations over 100,000). Long concerned about the effect of wasting spectrum space by allowing the same programs to run on both AM and FM, the FCC had been persuaded by industry leaders to allow the practice when FM was weak. Indeed, many FM broadcasters expressed great concern about losing their ability to carry popular AM programming. But FM's growth in numbers and economic strength prompted the move—which further accelerated creation of new FM stations. In just a few years the importance of the FCC decisions (which by the late 1960s had been extended to smaller markets) became apparent as FM audiences increased sharply—bringing, in turn, greater advertiser interest and expenditure to make FM economically viable for the first time in its history. By the early 1980s, when the AM–FM nonduplication requirement was eliminated in a deregulatory move, FM stations were dominant in large part because of their unique programming.

That FM had achieved its own identity was exemplified when one of the big-three networks, the American Broadcasting Companies (ABC), initiated a network of FM stations in 1968. Although relatively short-lived, as the industry increasingly began to think of FM as radio rather than something different, the recognition that such a network gave to FM radio was a tremendous boost in the advertising community. Another indicator was Philadelphia's WDVR, which within four months of first airing in 1963 was the number-one FM station in the city, competing for top spot with long-established AM outlets, an inconceivable development just a few years earlier. Five years later, the same station became the first FM outlet to bill more than $1 million in advertising time. The FM business as a whole reported positive operating income in 1968 for the first time (it happened for the second time in 1973, after which the industry as a whole remained profitable).

The key measure of FM's coming of age, of course, is actual audience use of the service. In 1958, for example, FM was available in about one-third of all homes in such major urban markets as Cleveland, Miami, Philadelphia, and Kansas City. By 1961 the receiver penetration figures for major

cities were creeping up to about 40 percent, and national FM penetration was estimated at about 10 percent, showing how few FM listeners lived in smaller markets and rural areas, many of which still lacked FM stations. By the mid-1960s, FM household penetration in major markets was hovering at the two-thirds mark, and national FM penetration stood at about half that level. Although stereo and car FM radios were initially expensive, increasing production dropped prices and helped to further expand FM availability.

Dominance (The 1970s and Since)

After the many FM industry and policy changes of the 1960s, the 1970s saw FM becoming increasingly and rapidly important economically. Where FM attracted 25 percent of the national radio audience in 1972, just two years later survey data showed FM accounted for one-third of all national radio listening—although only 14 percent of all radio revenues. By 1979 FM achieved a long-sought goal when for the first time, total national FM listening surpassed that of AM stations. Every major market had at least four FM stations among the top 10 radio outlets. Indeed, FM would never lose that primacy, slowly expanding its role until by the turn of the century, FM listening accounted for nearly 80 percent of all radio listening.

Getting there had not been easy and had taken far longer than early proponents had expected. In part, FM's own success got in the way. After years of promoting FM's upper-scale (though small) audiences, often prejudicially dubbed eggheads and high-fidelity buffs, it was hard to shift gears and promote FM's large and growing audience as being tuned to simply "radio." (Indeed, the number of commercial FM classical music stations had actually declined by half since 1963, to only 30 by 1973.) At the same time, the number of educational FM stations expanded dramatically after 1965, greatly aided by the creation of National Public Radio and the appeal of its programs as well as by the availability of increased funding for station development and operation.

But with success came pressure to keep up. As news and talk formats increasingly defined AM (where the poorer sound quality did not matter), FM flowered with a full cornucopia of musical formats and styles. By the early 1970s, FM stations in the nation's largest markets were developing formats every bit as tight and narrow as those of their AM forebears. Each station and its advertisers were appealing to a specific segment of the once-mass radio audience in an attempt to build listener loyalty in a marketplace often defined by too many stations in most cities. By the late 1980s, FM's primary target market was that defined by its advertisers: listeners aged 26 to 34, followed by those 35 to 44 years of age. Only a relative handful of stations target teens, and fewer than 30 percent are interested in listeners aged 55 or older. As compared with its earlier days, FM has become positively mainstream.

FM's success is also seen in the usual marketplace measure—the price of FM stations being sold on the open market. Where top-market stations could literally not be given away in the early 1950s, by the late 1960s, the first million-dollar prices were being quoted. Three decades later, FM stand-alone stations in top markets sold for tens of millions of dollars, and some have sold for well over $100 million. On the other hand, many miss the old days of FM programs aimed at a small, elitist, sometimes cranky but usually appreciative audience. A 1999 FCC proposal to create scores of low-power FM outlets was intended to bring back some of that spirit, but was severely curtailed by Congress in 2000.

Competitive Clouds

By the first decade of the 21st century, FM (indeed, all of radio) was suffering from declining audiences and a sameness of programming. Advertising revenues were flat, or even declining in places as the country's overall economy took a turn downwards by 2008. At the same time, the number of stations continued to grow—up 20 percent from 1996 to 2004. By 2007 there were nearly 6,300 commercial and 2,800 non-commercial FM stations operating—plus close to 800 low-power FM outlets. Yet the medium's overall business outlook was stagnating as competition arose from satellite services and the growing number of portable audio devices. This "perfect storm" situation—more stations dividing stagnant audience and advertising revenue pies—spelled trouble for FM after a generation dominating the radio business.

FM programming witnessed several trends. The variety of music formats continued to evolve, but the overall trend was to less variation and a growing sameness in sound. Fringe formats—such as classical (perhaps two dozen commercial stations remained by 2008) or jazz music—continued to decline while most markets saw growing duplication of the most popular music genre. At the same time, talk (and sports talk) became more common on FM as the one-time "talk on AM, music on FM" tradition broke down. *Washington Post* columnist Marc Fisher deplored the sameness in radio and in

early 2008 stopped regularly reporting on the business, arguing there was too little that was new or different to warrant continuing coverage.

Yet change in consumer audio was taking place, though elsewhere. Increasing use of internet-based radio websites providing audio streaming of a wider variety of music formats attracted a growing number of listeners, despite serious problems concerning copyright payments by service providers. In an attempt to regain momentum, many in radio swung behind HD (for high definition) radio, the digital transmission of sound. By 2009, relatively few stations were offering HD service, and receivers were still priced too high (above $200) for widespread adoption. More seriously, however, too many broadcasters were repeating a mistake that had been made a half century before—touting better-quality sound without offering new and different content. Audiences are attracted by content, not sound quality alone, as FM had learned to its sorrow in the early 1950s. Whether HD radio would help the medium survive its online and satellite competitors was an issue in doubt in 2009.

See also: Don Lee Broadcasting System; Educational Radio to 1967; Federal Communications Commission; FM Trade Associations; Low-Power Radio/Microradio; Radio Corporation of America; Receivers; Stereo; Subsidiary Communications Authorization; Yankee Network

Further Reading

Armstrong, Edwin H., "Evolution of Frequency Modulation," *Electrical Engineering* 59 (December 1940).
Besen, Stanley M., "AM versus FM: The Battle of the Bands," *Industrial and Corporate Change* 1 (1992).
Boutwell, William Dow, Ronald Redvers Lowdermilk, and Gertrude G. Broderick, *FM for Education*, Washington, D.C.: United States Government Printing Office, 1944; revised edition, 1948.
Codding, George A., "Frequency Modulation Broadcasting," in *Broadcasting without Barriers*, Paris: UNESCO, 1959.
Cox Looks at FM Radio: Past, Present, and Future, Atlanta, Georgia: Cox Broadcasting, 1976.
Eshelman, David, "The Emergence of Educational FM," *NAEB Journal* 26 (March–April 1967).
"Evolution of FM Radio: Extracts from FCC Annual Reports," *Journal of Broadcasting* 5 (Spring 1961 and Fall 1961), 6 (Summer 1962), 7 (Fall 1963).
Inglis, Andrew F., "FM Broadcasting," in *Behind the Tube: A History of Broadcasting Technology and Business*, Boston: Focal Press, 1990.
Lewis, Peter M., and Jerry Booth, *The Invisible Medium: Public, Commercial, and Community Radio*, Washington, D.C.: Howard University Press, and London: Macmillan, 1989.
Longley, Lawrence D., "The FM Shift in 1945," *Journal of Broadcasting* 12 (Fall 1968).

Sleeper, Milton B., editor, *FM Radio Handbook*, Great Barrington, Massachusetts: FM Company, 1946.

Slotten, Hugh Richard, "Rainbow in the Sky: FM Radio, Technical Superiority, and Regulatory Decision-Making," *Technology and Culture* 37 (October 1996).

"Special Report: FM Sniffs Sweet Smell of Success," *Broadcasting* (31 July 1967).

Sterling, Christopher H., and Michael C. Keith. *Sounds of Change: A History of FM Broadcasting in America.* Chapel Hill: University of North Carolina Press, 2008.

United States Congress, Senate Special Committee to Study Problems of American Small Business, *Small Business Opportunities in FM Broadcasting*, 79th Congress, 2nd Session, April 10, 1946, Washington, D.C.: GPO, 1946.

Wedell, E. George, and Philip Crookes, *Radio 2000: The Opportunities for Public and Private Radio Services in Europe*, Geneva: European Broadcasting Union, 1991.

CHRISTOPHER H. STERLING,
2009 REVISIONS BY CHRISTOPHER H. STERLING

FM TRADE ASSOCIATIONS
Promoting Radio's Second Service

From the inception of commercial FM radio in 1941, a series of five industry trade organizations appeared—and disappeared—in parallel with the medium's struggles and eventual success. Each was different in its outlook and focus.

The Early Struggle

The first FM group, the National Association of FM Broadcasters Incorporated (FMBI), was created in 1940 to promote the technology as much as the industry. Spearheaded by John Shepherd III of the New England-based Yankee Network and by Walter J. Damm of the *Milwaukee Journal* radio stations (one of which was the first FM station west of the Alleghenies), FMBI published thousands of copies of *Broadcasting's Better Mousetrap* to promote FM's better sound and other qualities. Before and during World War II, a mimeographed newsletter edited by Dick Dorrance appeared regularly to record the slow initial development of the business. FMBI had 43 members by 1943—most of those either on the air or building new stations—and 137 by September 1944. Among its campaigns was a successful move to persuade the Federal Communications Commission (FCC) to modify FM station call letters from letter and number combinations denoting the channel of the station (e.g., W55M, which was on 45.5 MHz) to the more familiar all-letter system used with AM stations. The FCC adopted the plan in 1943. Although FMBI fought the shift of FM frequencies that came in 1945, it worked to put the new spectrum into action.

With the end of the war, FMBI voted in 1946 to merge its activities into the FM Department (later Committee) of the National Association of Broadcasters (NAB), a pattern that would be repeated several times. Initially headed by Robert Bartley, later an FCC commissioner, this arm of the main industry trade association sought a place for FM within an industry dominated by rapidly expanding AM stations and developing television.

Believing that the new medium needed the focused attention of a dedicated organization, broadcasters Roy Hofheintz of Houston and Everett Dillard of Washington, D.C., helped form the FM Association (FMA) in 1946. FMA's primary focus was to get AM broadcasters either to build the FM stations they had applied for or to return their construction permits to the FCC. FMA pressure on the FCC led the agency to terminate many "warehoused" but inactive permits, which were an indicator of FM's coming decline. The FMA ended its short existence with a two-year promotional campaign to brighten the medium's future.

All this activity was to no avail, and FM slipped into decline for most of the 1950s as industry attention turned to television.

FM's Revival

Formation of the FM Development Association (FMDA) in 1956 was one early indicator that FM's fortunes were about to take a turn for the better. Larry Gordon of WBUF (FM) in Buffalo, New York, was its president. Made up of about two dozen independent (without a matching AM station) FM station owners, FMDA sought to get broadcasters to place FM stations on the air. It also attempted to combat escalating music licensing fees being charged by the American Society of Composers, Authors, and Publishers (ASCAP).

In January 1959 a group of FMDA members formed the new National Association of FM Broadcasters (NAFMB). The organization decided to hold its first official meeting prior to the forthcoming annual convention of the NAB in Chicago. With the blessing of the NAB, the NAFMB was allowed to hold its first meeting on the Saturday just prior to the NAB FM Day program; at that time Fred Rabell, an independent FM broadcaster and background music franchisee in San Diego, was elected president. This was a nonpaying position, which he volunteered to accept with the help of his wife, and for nearly three years they operated the NAFMB from their FM radio station KITT.

Rabell was followed by another unpaid leader, T. Mitchell Hastings, Jr., owner of the Concert

Network FM stations in New York City, Boston, Hartford, Connecticut, and Providence, Rhode Island, and the developer of the Hastings FM tuner, America's first FM car radio. Hastings led the NAFMB for three years. (Prior to his death in the mid-1990s, Hastings was chairman of the Armstrong Foundation, dedicated to the propagation of Edwin Armstrong's name as the father of FM radio through its Armstrong "Major Awards," first presented at the NAFMB conventions.)

Another person who played an important role in making the NAFMB successful was James Schulke, NAFMB's first full-time paid president, who had offices in New York City. Schulke was hired in 1963 after an annual donation of commercial airtime by all National Radio Broadcasters Association member stations; this donated time was subsequently sold to the Magnavox Corporation for $150,000. Special research, programming, and marketing studies were developed by the NAFMB in the 1960s as membership grew from its first 50 stations to nearly 500 by 1969. During those formative years, FM broadcasters volunteered their time and resources to advance public and advertiser awareness of FM radio. Dozens of these FM radio pioneers played major roles in the NAFMB, including Abe Voron of Philadelphia, Robert Herpe of Orlando, and James Gabbert of San Francisco.

The impact of NAFMB activities in the 1960s is reflected in the increase in the number of FM radio stations that went on the air. From just 578 commercial stations in 1959, with the majority duplicating the programming of a co-owned AM facility in the same city, the number of on-air FM stations had grown to more than 1,000 by 1963. The promotion of FM stereo multiplexing following the FCC's adoption of FM stereo radio standards in April 1961, as well as the one-year "Drive with FM" campaign in 1965 and 1966 to motivate consumers and the auto industry to have FM and FM stereo available on their auto and truck radios, also played a role in the accelerated growth of FM.

During the 17-year existence of the NAFMB as an organization that would accept only FM station members, the association was the driving force in promoting, researching, marketing, and expanding the visibility of both FM and FM stereo radio in the United States and Canada.

The NAFMB was both the longest-lived and the most successful of the five FM trade groups. It actively worked with the FCC to develop technical standards for FM stereo in 1960–61. A 1963 Harvard University Graduate School of Business study of FM's potential was sponsored by NAFMB and attracted widespread industry attention. The study's prediction of FM's eventual dominance of AM, seen as a pipe dream by many at the time, was borne out by events in the late 1970s. FM's eventual success was heavily aided by the separation of its programming from co-located AM stations in the late 1960s, something NAFMB lobbied the FCC heavily for. The association issued annual program surveys of FM stations in the late 1960s, which showed the growing variety of formats used by FM outlets. It conducted or supported a variety of other studies of the FM industry in response to growing advertiser interest in the medium. At the same time, the Radio Advertising Bureau focused more on FM's potential, and the NAB published its monthly *Fmphasis* newsletter throughout the 1960s.

Because of pressure by AM and AM/FM station owners and operators who wanted to join the NAFMB, in September 1975, during its annual convention in Atlanta, the NAFMB name and membership criteria were changed. The association became the National Radio Broadcasters Association (NRBA), and AM stations were to be admitted into membership. The new members pushed for the association's dedication to seeking regulatory relief from the FCC. Many stations active with NRBA were dissatisfied with the NAB's efforts for radio deregulation and believed that the older radio/TV association was devoting too much of its resources to television issues. Nine years later, in 1984, the NRBA merged with the NAB.

The success of FM radio in superseding AM radio as the dominant aural medium in America was consistently positioned by the NAFMB with the rationale that "in the long run, a quality product always succeeds with the American consumer." The NAFMB was the leading advocate of FM radio and played an important role in the medium's eventual success.

See also: FM Radio; National Association of Broadcasters; Radio Advertising Bureau; Stereo; Trade Associations; Trade Press

Further Reading

Advertisers Are Asking Questions about FM, New York: Radio Advertising Bureau, 1961.

"And Now FM Will Have the Numbers: Special FM Report," *Broadcasting* (29 July 1963).

"A Dramatic Spurt in FM Development," *Broadcasting* (20 February 1961).

"Identity of Audience Gets Attention of NAFMB," *Advertising Age* (4 April 1966).

Mayberry, Joshua J., *New Dimensions for FM Radio*, Presented before 8th Annual NAFMB Convention (30 March 1968).

Mohr, Donald, "The Potential of FM Radio As an Advertising Medium," Master's thesis, New York University, 1961.

"NAFMB Studies Medium's Potential," *Broadcasting* (1 April 1968).

National FM Programming Trends, 1967 and 1968, Washington, D.C.: NAFMB, 1967, 1968.

Sterling, Christopher H., "Second Service: A History of Commercial FM Radio to 1969," Ph.D. diss., University of Wisconsin, 1969.

Lynn A. Christian and Christopher H. Sterling

FORMATS DEFINING RADIO PROGRAMMING

A format is the overall programming design of a station or specific program. It is essentially the arrangement of program elements—often musical recordings—into a sequence that will attract and hold the segment of the audience a station is seeking. There are as many as 100 known formats and variations.

Evolution of Formats

Radio formats developed in response to the competitive threat posed by television and the growing number of competing radio stations. For decades, radio stations had been a mass medium, with each outlet trying to be all things to all people. But as television grew in popularity and as more television and radio stations went on the air, audience fragmentation occurred, prompting radio programmers to seek ways to differentiate their programming and attract audiences. By the mid-1950s, radio programmers were willing to try almost anything to preserve the medium.

One lesson was learned from an independent (i.e., non-network-affiliated) radio station in New York, WNEW, which had successfully programmed a music and news format as early as 1935. Whereas other radio network audiences defected to television, WNEW maintained its audience levels, presumably because its music and news format did not demand long-term or high-level attention from listeners, unlike the typical dramatic productions on the networks. The simpler, less demanding programming apparently allowed listeners to tune in for shorter periods of time and while doing other things, such as household chores.

Another lesson was learned from the success of "countdown" programs such as *Your Hit Parade*, a popular radio network program since the 1940s. Countdown programs tended to play the top 40 or so songs, and audience numbers were very strong. Not surprisingly, some programmers working for independent stations tried playing only the top 40

or so most popular records and were successful. In this sense, they were simply attracting an audience by playing what the audience had already proven they wanted to hear. Station owners Todd Storz and Gordon McLendon were among those who turned the concept into a continuous format, creating the hit-oriented playlist.

Many stations quickly adopted the new approach. But as more stations played the same top 40 songs, a further need for differentiation and refinement arose. In 1957 Storz and programmer Bill Stewart are said to have noted the behavior of jukebox users who repeatedly selected their favorite tunes. Taking this observation back to their Omaha station, they refined the playlist to repeat the most popular hits more often than other songs. Other stations followed suit, positioning themselves as stations that guaranteed the top hits.

Eventually various formats evolved as stations sought to differentiate themselves from competing stations with similar formats. Rock, including soft rock and hard rock, was spun off. Adult contemporary (AC) developed as a way to appeal to an older audience demographic by playing current songs, minus the tunes that appealed mostly to teens. As album sales increased, many stations presumed that listeners wanted to hear certain artists, so they switched to playing primarily album cuts, eventually becoming known as album-oriented rock (AOR) stations. Formats were also distinguished simply by the creative names given them, such as "Hot Hits." The names would sometimes be intentionally vague in order to appear distinct to listeners, while still seeming inclusive of all listeners to advertisers. AM stations also responded to the competition from FM and its superior frequency response and stereo capability by creating information formats such as news, talk, sports, agriculture, and education. Listener perceptions about AM sound quality became entrenched by the 1980s, forcing most AM stations to switch to nonmusic formats to survive.

New formats also emerged, partly because of the increasingly sophisticated ratings reports that provided more detailed demographic data. Stations pushed radio ratings companies to provide specific listener demographic data beyond an overall market headcount in order to justify themselves to advertisers. Once sub-audiences could be clearly identified, a symbiotic relationship emerged, with programmers developing formats that appealed to those audiences. Likewise, music trade magazines such as *Billboard* developed specialized charts that coincided with the formats of stations, and vice versa. Some format names, such as rhythm and blues, were in fact coined by *Billboard*.

Format Categories

The increase in artists, particularly crossover artists, has made it difficult for popular music stations to claim a "pure format," that is, one based on agreement by stations nationwide as to what artists are included and excluded. However, today this definition primarily applies only to classical, big band, and similar formats consisting of older music. Many of the originally pure formats, such as AOR, country, and urban, have split into variations of their respective formats. From the standpoint of promotion, advertising, and ratings classification, it is best for a station to identify with a pure format, but the need to be competitive forces stations to adjust to the demands of the audience and industry. In the 1990s the concept of the "microformat" emerged, whereby syndicated and network music and information programming became fine-tuned to a specific audience and market, relying less on a cookie-cutter approach.

Each of the major music categories—country, AC, rock and urban (black)—has several subdivisions. Country format subcategories include traditional, hot (or young) country, Americana (or alt-country), country gold and the recently coined HANK; each is aimed at a specific demographic group. Adult contemporary (AC) can break down into hot or soft AC and a jazzier version called new adult contemporary/smooth jazz, among others. Urban music is subdivided into urban contemporary, urban adult contemporary, and urban gold. Rock formats include adult album alternative (AAA); contemporary hit radio (CHR); churban (a blend of CHR and urban); active rock (hard/heavy metal); classic rock (popular rock music of the 1960s through the 1980s and, now, occasionally, even the 1990s); and oldies, which is further divided into the decades since 1960. There are many distinct formats such as big band, alternative, contemporary Christian, classical, progressive, and beautiful music/easy listening.

If anything, subdividing of formats and developing of new ones has only increased since 2000. Some "new" formats seem like old ones with different names, such as the so-called ARROW format that loosely translates as "All Rock and Roll Oldies." One of the more innovative and quickly spreading formats of recent years is the JACK format. Created in Canada and allegedly named after DJ "Cadillac Jack" Garrett, JACK prides itself on a musical playlist that is an inch deep but a mile wide, encompassing a catalogue of music that is wildly diverse in styles and eras. JACK (and its country counterpart HANK) is also known for de-emphasizing the DJ's role and for striving for greater musical variety so that a hard rock record could be fol-

lowed by a mellow folk number. Many believe that JACK's success is because its loose, unpredictable nature strongly mimics the random shuffling of iPod players.

Format Popularity

Country continues to reign as the most popular radio format, followed by AC. Though their station numbers are fewer, data suggests that all-talk formats regularly attract more listeners per outlet than does country radio.

Formats are cyclical and can be timely. In the 1990s, modern rock or alternative formats gained in popularity based upon the success of bands like Nirvana. News and talk formats also gained popularity and many migrated heavily from AM to FM. Sports, sports-talk and Spanish-language formats have also gained since the mid-1990s. In some cases, old formats can find a new life. Top 40 enjoyed a resurgence thanks to results from Arbitron's Portable People Meter (PPM). The PPM has recorded more youthful listeners (who were less likely to fill out old-fashioned handwritten ratings diaries) to top 40 outlets.

The 2009 *Broadcasting and Cable Yearbook* ranked radio formats in terms of the number of stations identifying with each style. The top 20 formats were: Country (2,112 outlets); AC (1,738); Christian (1,412); News/Talk (1,277); Oldies (1,053); Sports (1,042); Religious (799); Talk (769); Spanish (768); News (736); Classic Rock (644); Gospel (622); Contemporary Hit/Top 40 (573); Rock/AOR (508); Classical (486); Variety/Diverse (344); Jazz (328); Urban Contemporary (366); Diversified (262); and Alternative (248). Lesser formats included the catchall "Other," Educational, MOR, Progressive, AAA (adult album alternative), Inspirational, Nostalgia, Blues, Top 40, Ethnic, AOR, Black, Full Service, Agriculture, Smooth Jazz, Beautiful Music, Big Band, and, finally, Easy Listening. Only a handful of stations claimed Bluegrass, Children, Folk, Golden Oldies, Soul, and Women's formats, or such ethnic formats as Chinese, French, Greek, Korean, Polish, Russian, and Vietnamese.

New HD channels have provided a new, or second, life (as well as a full-time home in some cases) to many of these more obscure formats and musical styles. And less-popular formats have also found a home on online and satellite services.

Choosing and Creating a Format

Stations switch formats frequently to pursue more profitable demographic segments and in response to shifting audience tastes. According to Eastman, et al., the steps taken in choosing a format involve an evaluation of (1) the technical facilities of the station (i.e., AM, FM, range), (2) the character of the local market, (3) the delineation of the target audience, (4) the available budget, and (5) the potential revenue.

Stations assemble their formats in several ways. Some simply program recordings in a sequence throughout the schedule, whereas others carry different formats during different dayparts. Still others rely on "Format Syndicators," which provide ready-made formats for a fee via satellite feed or music tapes. The formula for constructing a format goes beyond just music and includes a focus on production, personality, and programming.

Format Audience Characteristics

Certain audience demographics are predictors of format preference. For example, listeners to news are more likely to be married and to have lived in the area for at least two years, whereas AOR listeners are more likely to be single and on the move. Some studies also suggest that urban contemporary fans are the heaviest listeners, country listeners are the most loyal, and AC listeners are less involved in their station.

Formats can also be profiled on the basis of education, income, and age. For example, higher education levels are associated with beautiful music and news. In 1998 the highest household median income numbers were associated with AAA ($62,954), news ($62,722), alternative ($55,298), classical ($55,248), and modern rock ($54,488). The two formats appealing most to older audiences are full-service (60.3 years) and nostalgia (59.3 years). Most formats, however, are showing an increase in the median age of listeners, with one exception: news/talk listeners are getting younger.

Finally, where a listener resides has some effect on format popularity. Country is more popular in the South and Midwest, and news and talk formats are listened to most in the West. Spanish has been the most popular format in Los Angeles.

See also, in addition to individual formats discussed in this entry: Programming Strategies and Processes

Further Reading

Eastman, Susan Tyler, Sydney W. Head, and Lewis Klein, *Broadcast Programming: Strategies for Winning Television and Radio Audiences*, Belmont, California: Wadsworth, 1981; 6th edition, as *Broadcast/Cable/Web Programming: Strategies and Practices*, by Eastman and Douglas A. Ferguson, 2002.
Hausman, Carl, Philip Benoit, and Lewis B. O'Donnell, *Modern Radio Production*, Belmont, California: Wadsworth, 1986; 4th edition, 1996.
Lynch, Joanna R., and Greg Gillispie, *Process and Practice of Radio Programming*, Lanham, Maryland: University Press of America, 1998.
MacFarland, David T., *Contemporary Radio Programming Strategies*, Hillsdale, New Jersey: Erlbaum, 1990; 2nd edition, as *Future Radio Programming Strategies: Cultivating Listenership in the Digital Age*, Mahwah, New Jersey: Erlbaum, 1997.
Meril, John, "Listening Down in 98," *Broadcasting and Cable* (29 June 1998).
Routt, Edd, James B. McGrath, and Fredric A. Weiss, *The Radio Format Conundrum*, New York: Hastings House, 1978.
Stein, Joel, "You Don't Know Jack," *Time* (7 August 2005).

LAURIE THOMAS LEE,
2009 REVISIONS BY CARY O'DELL

FREE FORM FORMAT

During the 1960s, FM was ripe for a new form of radio—radio that burst through established format boundaries, emphasizing wholeness over separation and communal action over atomistic listening. *Free form*—in which imaginative disc jockeys combined many types of recorded and live music, sound effects, poetry, interviews, and calls from listeners—was the aural representation of the counterculture movement. Eschewing the slick professionalism, high-pressure salesmanship, and tight formats of AM radio, free form was—and sometimes still is—distinctly spontaneous, experimental, and challenging. At its best, free form is an exhilarating art form in its own right—a synergistic combination of disparate musical forms and spoken words. At its worst, free form may be pandering and self-indulgent.

Origins

Free form's roots developed in both commercial and noncommercial settings. During the mid-1960s, noncommercial community stations were developing across the country, following the lead established by Pacifica stations in California, New York, and Texas. These stations depended heavily on low-paid (often volunteer) programmers whose anti-establishment agendas rejected the tight structure of most corporate, commercial media. At the same time, commercial FM was still in its infancy, and disc jockeys were encouraged to experiment with longer segments and album cuts. Free form developed amidst these experimental venues, catching on quickly among community stations and some commercial FM stations—albeit late at night and on weekends.

Free form most likely originated at WBAI in New York City around 1963–64, with three different DJs: Bop Fass (Radio Unnameable), Larry Josephson (In the Beginning), and the following year with Steve Post's the Outside. Soon, it spread to other stations, notably Pacifica stations KPFA in Berkeley and KPFK in Los Angeles, and privately owned KMPX in San Francisco. KMPX's general manager, Tom Donahue, is often credited as being the driving force behind the "underground radio" movement. Although he did not invent free form, Donahue nurtured it and allowed it to grow from a program shift to an entire format (although *anti-format* might be a better term).

Style

Free-form programmers featured everything from cutting-edge musicians such as Bob Dylan and the Grateful Dead to comedy routines from W.C. Fields and Jonathan Winters. Indian ragas and classical music were heard back to back. Shows started late and ran overtime. Guests wandered in and out of control rooms, sometimes speaking on air, at other times just being part of the scene. Disc jockeys pontificated on the day's topics, their delivery styles ranging from chats with listeners and studio guests to rambling, witty monologues—often within the same program. Interviews and announcements regarding the counterculture and antiwar protests peppered broadcasts increasingly as the 1960s wore on.

Free form's deliberately anarchistic and undisciplined sound was, in effect, a form of participatory theater and gained a considerable following within the counterculture. Listeners called in to programs and were often heard on the air, rallies were announced (and broadcast), and listeners met at live remotes and events sponsored by stations (such as WBAI's 1967 "fly in" at Kennedy Airport, organized by WBAI free form host Bob Foss).

Challenges to Free Form

The popularity of free form reached its peak between 1965 and 1970 and ultimately waned for three primary reasons. Ironically, once established through the success of free form, commercial FM became bound by the same tight formats that defined AM. Also, leaders among free-form disc jockeys, notably WBAI's Larry Josephson, grew weary of underground radio and moved on to other pastures. And the counterculture movement that nurtured free form eventually evolved beyond its communal sentiments. As the movement splintered into subgroups focusing on sexuality, gender, race, and ethnicity, free form gave way to specialty shows on community radio and to the newer, more professional "public" stations affiliated with National Public Radio (NPR).

The 1980s were particularly difficult for free form, as community stations and NPR affiliates began programming more syndicated programming and professionalizing their sound, especially following NPR's near bankruptcy in 1983. Severe internal battles over station control were sometimes waged, with the fate of free form hanging in the balance. Proponents argued that free form was a unique means of expression that the new professionals simply failed to understand. The latter charged that free form's time had passed and that free form appealed to only a tiny fraction of the potential market. Despite such challenges, free form continued to survive at some stations, albeit most often during the late-night hours where it had originally developed.

Contemporary Free Form

Among the community stations and a dwindling number of public stations that still program it, free form has taken on an air of sanctity, hearkening back to the good old days when community radio was central to the underground movement. Yet without a symbiotic cultural context to fuel and inform it, contemporary free form lacks the immediacy and connection with the public that it once held. As such, free form has become a much more personal medium among disc jockeys, and a successful program is one that has smoothly combined a wide variation of sounds reflective of the programmer's moods and inclinations at the moment. Whereas 1960s free form was jarring and often disturbing in its quirky juxtapositions, contemporary free form is more often about flow and seamless segues.

Besides community and public radio stations, most college radio stations also program free-form music to some extent, although the preferred term is "alternative radio." College radio programmers, however, typically lack a historical awareness of free form and have little concept of its cultural implications. Also, college radio's alternative programming is rarely as diverse as free form heard on community and public stations.

Free form's most recent manifestation is on the internet. Community, public, and college stations increasingly broadcast via the web, and some internet-only stations—often the efforts of individuals working from home—advertise themselves as free-form radio. The internet is also an important meeting place for free form enthusiasts, whose webpages and chat groups provide means of sharing information and ideas.

Meanwhile, both satellite radio and HD2 dabbled with the free form concept with the former coopting the 1960s version of the "antiformat" format as manifested in the commercial underground sound of that era and the latter emulating the college radio model.

Free form and alternative radio format names are frequently used as synonyms. Free-form college stations sometimes refer to themselves as alternative. Alternative radio focuses on options to traditional commercial formats, whereas free form provides a less formulaic, more insouciant approach. Further, free form usually employs a "block" program schedule, whereas alternative formatted outlets typically have one primary format.

See also: Internet Radio; KPFA; Pacifica Foundation; WBAI

Further Reading

Armstrong, David, *A Trumpet to Arms: Alternative Media in America*, Los Angeles: Tarcher, 1981.
Bareiss, Warren, "Space, Identity, and Public-Access Media: A Case Study of Alternative Radio Station KUNM Albuquerque," Ph.D. diss., Indiana University, 1997.
"Digging FM Rock," *Newsweek* (4 March 1968).
Engelman, Ralph, *Public Radio and Television in America: A Political History*, Thousand Oaks, California: Sage, 1996.
Keith, Michael C., *Voices in the Purple Haze: Underground Radio and the Sixties*, Westport, Connecticut: Praeger, 1997.
Knopper, Steve, "Free-Form Radio Still on the Dial," *Billboard* (14 January 1995).
Krieger, Susan, *Hip Capitalism*, Beverly Hills, California: Sage, 1979.
Land, Jeffrey Richard, *Active Radio: Pacifica's "Brash Experiment,"* Minneapolis: University of Minnesota Press, 1999.
Lasar, Matthew, *Pacifica Radio: The Rise of an Alternative Network*, Philadelphia, Pennsylvania: Temple University Press, 1999.
Mayor, Alfred, "Accent: Radio Free New York," *Atlantic Monthly* (May 1968).

WARREN BAREISS,
2009 REVISIONS BY MICHAEL C. KEITH

FREQUENCY ALLOCATION
Providing Spectrum for Broadcasting

Governments allocate bands of frequencies, including radio frequencies, for specific uses. Frequency allocation meshes technical limits and options with political and economic realities to create the compromise solutions behind today's broadcast services.

Three definitions are useful. *Allocation* is the broadest division of the electromagnetic spectrum into designated bands for given services (such as AM radio in the medium waves or FM in the very-high-frequency [VHF] spectrum). *Allotments* fall within allocations—they are given channels that are designated for specific places (only FM and television broadcasting have allotments). Finally, *assignments* are allotments that have actual users operating on them (such as a given station using 98.1 MHz, for example)—they are virtually the same as a license to operate.

Frequency allocation can be examined under three broad rubrics. First, frequencies are allocated to classes of service. All radio signals that travel through the air use frequencies that are part of the electromagnetic spectrum. By international agreement this natural resource is divided into bands in which certain kinds of broadcasting occur. Medium-wave (or AM) radio occurs in one part of the spectrum, VHF (or FM) radio in another, VHF and ultra-high-frequency (UHF) television in others, cellular telephony in another, satellite communication in another, and so on.

The frequencies used by different services are a function of three circumstances. First is history. Early experimentation with certain kinds of broadcasting resulted in assumptions that final allocations for that service should occur in the bands, or at the frequencies, originally used. This is because radio and television sets are designed to detect and amplify certain frequencies. Therefore, once such devices begin to be sold, changing the frequency of the service they were designed to use would make them obsolete. This can happen—for instance, in the United States the frequencies used to broadcast VHF/FM were changed in 1945—but the presumption is against such changes if they can be avoided.

Second are the technical needs of a particular service compared to the characteristics of certain portions of the spectrum. For instance, lower frequencies, such as those used for medium-wave/AM radio or shortwave radio, travel farther and propagate in ways that make it possible for them to bypass barriers more effectively than higher frequencies, such as those used for VHF/FM. This makes shortwave an effective means to broadcast transcontinentally or across oceans, medium-wave an effective means to provide national radio services (or international services to contiguous countries), and VHF an effective means to provide local radio services. Satellite television signals are at such high frequencies that they are effectively blocked by buildings, trees, or other obstacles. Such frequencies would be relatively useless if they were used by terrestrial (or land-based) transmitters, but because the satellite signals travel essentially vertically (from the sky to the earth), they can be used for this service as long as the dishes for receiving them are clear of obstacles. They can be affected by electrical storms or heavy thunderstorms, however, so some disruptions of service are inevitable.

Third are the political compromises made by the signatory administrations (or countries) that sign the allocation agreements under the auspices of the International Telecommunication Union (ITU). Such agreements, for instance, can result in an altered frequency band assignment for a particular service, despite uses of another portion of the spectrum in some countries. This is usually the result of a recognized need to rationalize frequency allocations so that transmission and reception devices can be designed using a worldwide standard. Otherwise the economies of scale may not achieve maximum impact, and the devices made may not be manufactured or sold as inexpensively as they would be otherwise. International broadcasting would be impossible if there were not an international allocation for such services, because the radio sets used to listen to them could not tune the same frequencies from country to country.

Frequencies are also allocated within classes of service to particular countries. Some frequencies assigned are exclusive, and others are shared. The less powerful a station is, the less distance its signals travel. Consequently, it can share its frequency with other stations located at a sufficient distance to avoid interference. This is easier with VHF/FM than with medium-wave/AM, because FM signals travel only by line of sight, whereas the propagation characteristics of amplitude-modulated (AM) signals change at dusk, traveling farther via night-time sky waves, which bounce off a layer of the ionosphere and return many hundreds of miles from their origination point. Countries contiguous to one another must share the total frequency allocation for a particular type of service within its region.

Frequencies are also assigned within particular allocations to particular users (or broadcasters). Different carrier frequencies (the center point of a channel—the frequency that appears on your receiver when you tune a specific station) are assigned to individual stations. In the United States, frequencies are assigned by the Federal Communications Commission (FCC) by means of broadcasting licenses. These licenses stipulate the channel (or band of frequencies centered on the carrier) that a station is to use to broadcast, the power it can use (according to the class of service it is licensed to provide), and its hours of operation. AM stations, for instance, use the 535–1705-kHz band, and FM stations use the 88.1–107.9-MHz band. There are 117 AM carrier frequencies that can be assigned and 100 FM frequencies. Because of the propagation characteristics of these two services and the differences in bandwidth (10-kHz bandwidths for AM stations and 200-kHz bandwidths for FM), there were in 2000 about 4,900 AM stations and more than 6,700 FM stations in the United States. In January 2000 the FCC also began a new class of FM service, allowing both 100-W and 10-W stations, which will add many new low-power FM stations to the American broadcast landscape.

The principal exception to these general rules for frequency allocation is the frequencies used for international broadcasting in the shortwave portion of the spectrum. Here, individual stations are not assigned particular frequencies or broadcast power to use. Because the amplitude-modulated carrier waves of shortwave stations have the same propagation characteristics as AM waves generally, shortwave stations must change their frequencies as the seasons change (because the sunspot cycle moves from inactive to active every 17 years) and often as the time of day changes. This is why such stations register their "demands" with the international Frequency Registration Board (FRB), part of the ITU. By registering, they can discover whether they are attempting to use the same frequency as another broadcaster in the same part of the world. Often stations will also collaborate to ensure that their broadcasts will not interfere with one another's.

When radio was just beginning to be used in the early part of the 20th century, scientists believed that there were a limited number of frequencies suitable for broadcasting. When the first stations began to go on the air in about 1919, they used the same few frequencies, and there was significant interference between stations. Shortwave was given its name because people believed that any wavelengths shorter than those first used for radio would be unusable. This was because the shorter the wavelength (and thus the greater the frequency per second with which a wave crosses a particular plane), the more power it takes to move a wave a given distance. In other words, the longer the wave, the farther it will travel with a given transmitter. People thought that if wavelengths became shorter than those used by shortwave, the power required to make them usable would be prohibitively high.

FREQUENCY ALLOCATION

Table 1 International Telecommunication Union Band Allocations

Band Number	Frequencies	Designation	Some Designated Uses
4	10–30 kHz	Very low frequency	Long distance point-to-point broadcasting
5	30–300 kHz	Low frequency	Medium distance point-to-point broadcasting, radio navigation, aeronautical mobile, low-frequency broadcasting
6	300–3000 kHz	Medium frequency	AM broadcasting, short-range communication, international distress
7	3–30 MHz	High frequency	International radio broadcasting; air-to-ground, ship-to-shore, and international point-to-point broadcasting
8	30–300 MHz	Very high frequency	Line-of-sight communication, VHF television broadcasting, FM broadcasting, aeronautical distress
9	300–3000 MHz	Ultrahigh frequency	UHF television broadcasting, space communication, radar, citizens band radio
10	3–30 GHz	Superhigh frequency	Microwave communication, space communication
11	30–300 GHz	Extremely high frequency	Microwave communication, space communication, radar, radio astronomy

Transmitters have become more efficient, however, and new forms of broadcasting (such as frequency modulation and digital broadcasting) have developed that continue to open up new frequencies for use. At the 1992 World Administrative Radio Conference (WARC), the participants provided new allocations for broadcast satellite service. For audio (or sound) broadcasting, the frequencies 1452–1492 MHz, 2310–2360 MHz, and 2535–2655 MHz were agreed to, and the FCC subsequently allocated the spectrum 2310–2360 MHz based on the international allocation adopted for the United States by the 1992 WARC for a Digital Audio Radio Service. The 1992 WARC also adopted an even higher set of frequencies for broadcast satellite service for high-definition television, with 17.3–17.8 GHz assigned to region 2 and 21.4–22.0 GHz for regions 1 and 3. All these new allocations became effective on 1 April 2007.

As seen in Table 1, the ITU has allocated the bands in the electromagnetic spectrum for various uses.

The pattern in these allocations is easy to see. It is useful to note that there are only 20,000 Hz in band 4, 299,970 Hz in band 5, and 2,999,700 Hz in band 6. As the frequencies used for broadcasting rise, the total amount of spectrum available increases not arithmetically (as, for instance, the band numbers do), but exponentially. What this means in practical terms is that the amount of spectrum now available for services has enabled enormously more service, more competition, and more exclusive service allocations at ever-higher frequencies. For broadcasting, this has also meant the opportunity to expand bandwidth as the frequency allocations have risen, thus allowing for higher-fidelity transmissions. Whereas in the AM band, bandwidths of 10-kHz only allow stations to broadcast about half of the frequency response that is within human hearing range, with VHF/FM broadcasting two

signals (left and right) can be broadcast using the entire 20-kHz range and still leave room for sideband broadcasting, guard bands to prevent cross-channel interference, and a broadcasting envelope to prevent atmospheric or man-made interference. Use of even higher frequencies allows the broadcasting of multiple CD-quality digital signals in the same channel, which digital radio delivered by satellite will deliver.

All frequency allocations are based on the use of Hz (or cycles per second) generated by a broadcast transmitter (Hz are named for Heinrich Hertz, whose experiments led to recognition of cycles generated by sound). Human hearing, for instance, can decipher the frequencies from about 20 Hz to 20,000 Hz (or 20 kHz). Any vibrating object creates waves at a particular frequency. Large objects (such as kettle drums or tubas) generate mostly low frequencies, whereas smaller ones (such as flutes or piccolos) generate mostly high frequencies. Tuba sounds travel farther than piccolo sounds do. The same principle applies to broadcast transmitters that generate the carrier waves upon or within which sound is carried to radio or television receivers, with some reservations. Low-frequency signals tend to travel along the ground, and much of their power is absorbed by the earth. As the frequencies increase, more of the signal travels through the air than along the ground, and gradually more of it also becomes a sky wave, which travels up and bounces back to earth. These characteristics mean that less power will actually move a wave at a higher frequency farther than a wave at very low frequencies, despite the fact that the wavelengths are lower at the higher frequency (wavelength and frequency are in inverse relationship). Therefore, when shortwave propagation was discovered in 1921, it was possible to reach as far with a 1-kW transmitter as organizations had used 200 kW to do before using the ground wave of low-frequency broadcasting.

Frequency allocations thus have to be made with several interrelated factors in mind: (1) the type of propagation that will occur at a given frequency (ground, direct, or sky); (2) the type of service that is to be accomplished with a particular allocation (local, national, or international, via terrestrial or satellite transmission); (3) the fidelity required for the service to be provided (for instance, voice, music, video, or CD quality) and the bandwidth necessary to provide that service; (4) whether the allocations must be exclusive or can be shared with other services; (5) existing experimental or other uses that a particular set of frequencies have been put to (thus providing what are called "squatter's rights"); and (6) the political realities of allocation among the different administrations that seek to employ the frequencies for particular uses.

See also: AM Radio; Clear Channel Stations; Digital Satellite Radio; Federal Communications Commission; FM Radio; Ground Wave; Licensing Authorizing U.S. Stations to Broadcast; North American Regional Broadcasting Agreement; Portable Radio Stations; Shortwave Radio; Subsidiary Communications Authorization; Ten-Watt Stations

Further Reading

Glatzer, Hal, *Who Owns the Rainbow? Conserving the Radio Spectrum*, Indianapolis, Indiana: Sams, 1984.
Gosling, William, *Radio Spectrum Conservation*, Oxford and Boston: Newnes, 2000.
Jackson, Charles, "The Frequency Spectrum," *Scientific American* (September 1980).
Joint Technical Advisory Committee, *Radio Spectrum Conservation: A Program of Conservation Based on Present Uses and Future Needs*, New York: McGraw-Hill, 1952; revised and expanded edition, as *Radio Spectrum Utilization: A Program for the Administration of the Radio Spectrum*, New York: Institute of Electrical and Electronics Engineers, 1964.
Levin, Harvey Joshua, *The Invisible Resource: Use and Regulation of the Radio Spectrum*, Baltimore, Maryland: Johns Hopkins University Press, 1971.
Withers, David J., *Radio Spectrum Management: Management of the Spectrum and Regulation of Radio Services*, London: Peregrinus, 1991; 2nd edition, London: Institution of Electrical Engineers, 1999.

ROBERT S. FORTNER

FRESH AIR
Public Radio Arts and Issues Program

Fresh Air host Terry Gross refers to herself and her production team as "culture scouts," seeking the latest in arts, ideas, and issues. The program is one of the most popular on public radio, drawing a weekly audience of more than 4.5 million listeners on some 450 stations. *Fresh Air*'s Peabody Award citation in 1994 noted that "unlike the cacophony of voices that sometimes obscure and polarize contemporary debate, Ms. Gross asks thoughtful, unexpected questions, and allows her subjects time to frame their answers." *Fresh Air*'s guests have ranged from former First Lady Nancy Reagan to filmmaker Martin Scorsese, from hostage negotiator Terry Waite to novelist Joyce Carol Oates, singer Tony Bennett, playwright David Mamet, and thousands more.

Over the years, *Fresh Air* has evolved from a live, three-hour local program to a highly produced hour-long program that runs nationally. David Karpoff created the show in 1974 when he was program director at WHYY (then WUHY) in Philadelphia; he modeled it on *This Is Radio*, a program he had worked on at WBFO in Buffalo. Karpoff was the first host, interspersing live interviews with classical music. He was followed as host by Judy Blank, and when she moved on, Karpoff in 1975 hired Terry Gross, who had been co-hosting and producing *This Is Radio* in Buffalo.

Gross drew complaints by changing *Fresh Air*'s music to jazz, blues, and rock and roll, but she won listeners over with an interview style that was thoughtful and direct. Gross, who was 24 at the time, had broken into radio just two years earlier when she helped produce and host a feminist program at WBFO.

By 1978, when Bill Siemering arrived as station manager at WHYY, Gross was carrying on the entire three-hour program by herself, "playing records," Siemering recalls, "that were just long enough to show one guest out and lead another one in." As a former station manager at WBFO, Siemering had created *This Is Radio* out of the turmoil of campus protest and had then gone on to develop *All Things Considered* as a program director at National Public Radio (NPR). When he arrived at WHYY (then WUHY), Siemering says the station was in a rundown building in West Philadelphia, where the ladies' room plumbing leaked onto Gross' desk. Siemering got a Corporation for Public Broadcasting grant to upgrade the station and was able to hire intern Danny Miller as an assistant producer for *Fresh Air*.

Miller, who eventually became the program's co-executive producer, says the fact that *Fresh Air* began as a local show is an important source of its strength: "The show had years to mature before it went national." Part of that maturation involved cutting back the amount of time on the air from three hours to two in 1983, because, as Gross says, "Danny and I often felt that in order to fill the airtime, we were forced to focus more on the quantity than the quality of guests." At the same time, Gross and Miller added a weekend "best of" edition of the show that became the seed for the weekly national edition that was to follow.

Gross sees the development of the show as a step-by-step evolution. The next step came in the spring of 1985, when WHYY premiered a weekly 30-minute version of *Fresh Air*, distributed by NPR. It appeared at a time when public radio stations on the East Coast were pressing for an earlier start time for the popular newsmagazine *All Things Considered*, which would enable them to capture more of the drive-time audience. Robert Siegel, then the news director at NPR, resisted the idea, feeling that the show was already stretched to meet a 5 P.M. deadline. Siegel saw *Fresh Air* as an answer to the demand for a 4 P.M. start, because its sensibility matched that of *All Things Considered* without duplicating its news content. "It was a very good program," he says, "and Terry is the best interviewer in public radio."

Gross says the program was reconceived in 1987 as a daily arts-and-culture companion to *All Things Considered*. To integrate it further into the *All Things Considered* sound, the new format included a drop-in newscast. *Fresh Air*'s shorter interviews, reviews, and other features were put in the second half-hour so that its pace would match that of the newsmagazine as listeners went from one program to the next. The new *Fresh Air* also featured a recorded interchange between Gross and the hosts of *All Things Considered* in which they discussed what was coming up.

The national version of *Fresh Air* was a hit, both with audiences and with program directors, who liked the show's predictable format because it gave them the flexibility to drop in local material during drive time. However, Gross says she and co-producer Danny Miller grew to feel imprisoned by the rigidity of the format. They were glad, therefore, when the 1991 Gulf War brought new demands on everyone. Even though *Fresh Air* had concentrated on arts and culture, Gross says, "we had to address the war. Everybody was rightly obsessed with it." The producers sought interviews that could supplement the news, looking for what Danny Miller calls "the great explainers," experts on the culture and the history of the region. "Emergencies require change," Gross says, "and emergencies justify change. If an interview ran more than a half-hour,

we let it." The war coverage restored some of *Fresh Air*'s flexibility and expanded its portfolio to include a full range of contemporary issues. Regardless of the subject, Gross applies the same demanding preparation for each interview, reading each author's books, viewing the films, and listening to the CDs that she will discuss. Interviews typically last between 20 and 40 minutes, during which Gross gives her guests the opportunity to rethink and rephrase their answers if they feel they can express themselves better. She prides herself on treating guests with respect, but "that doesn't mean I won't challenge you." Gross' critics have complained that she does not ask confrontational questions, but Bill Siemering says her method is much more effective. "If you're on the attack, all you get is their defense. If you're respectful, you get a lot more."

Many of Gross's interviews (usually done remotely with Gross in Philadelphia, her guest in a different city and the result recorded and edited before broadcast) have generated news. Bill O'Reilly famously terminated an interview in 2003 because of what he saw as Gross's political bias. She engaged in a fractious interview with KISS frontman Gene Simmons in 2002 and a tense one with Lynne Cheney (wife of the then-vice president) in 2005. Perhaps most notably, in 2008, Richard Cizik, then president of National Association of Evangelicals, resigned from his position only days after a *Fresh Air* interview was broadcast during which he said he was reconsidering his stance against same-sex marriage.

In 2004, many of Gross's top talks with actors and other artists were transcribed and issued as a book titled *All I Did Was Ask*. Other interviews have been issued as multi-CD packages: *Fresh Air: Laughs* (2003); *Fresh Air: Writers Speak* (2004); *Fresh Air: Stars* (2007); and *Fresh Air: Faith, Reason, & Doubt* (2008), the latter including conversations on issues of faith, God and religion. In 2009, in its 30th year, the Peabody Award-winning *Fresh Air* has emerged as one of NPR's flagship programs. Gross and her longtime producer Danny Miller have labeled their program "a scattershot history of American culture."

See also: National Public Radio; Peabody Awards and Archive; Public Radio Since 1967

Hosts

David Karpoff, 1974
Judy Blank, 1974–75
Terry Gross, 1975–

Producer/Creator

David Karpoff

Co-producers

Terry Gross and Danny Miller

Programming History

WHYY   1974–85
National Public Radio   1985–

(Note: WHYY continued to produce the program after NPR commenced distribution in 1985)

Further Reading

Clark, Kenneth R., "A Talent for Conversation: NPR's Terry Gross Provides Talk Radio with a Breath of *Fresh Air*," *Chicago Tribune* (19 November 1993).

Dart, Bob, "Fresh and Funky: 'Cultural Scout' for Public Radio Homes In on Truth," *Cox News Service* (January 1994).

Scheib, Rebecca, "Media Diet: Terry Gross," *Utne Reader* (March–April 1997).

White, Edmund, "Talk Radio: Terry Gross," *Vogue* (May 1997).

COREY FLINTOFF,
2009 REVISIONS BY CARY O'DELL

G

GANG BUSTERS
Detective Drama Series

During the 1920s, the American public lost confidence in law enforcement officers as news of bribery and scandal involving real-life police officers became routine. The onset of the Great Depression in the early 1930s exacerbated this situation, and criminals such as Bonnie Parker and Clyde Barrow, Al Capone, and George "Baby Face" Nelson were often portrayed as folk heroes. Hollywood produced films (e.g., *Public Enemy* with James Cagney and *Little Caesar* starring Edward G. Robinson) that presented gangsters as tragic heroes. *Gang Busters*, the first successful regularly scheduled detective drama on network radio, played a major role in restoring America's confidence in law enforcement officials.

Gang Busters was created by Phillips H. Lord, an actor and producer best known for his portrayal of the title character in the radio series *Seth Parker*. Whereas the earlier series was known for its folksy warm feeling, Lord went in a different direction for his next project. *Gang Busters* was a blend of fact and fiction—dramatizations of actual crimes taken from the case files of local and federal law enforcement offices. The series premiered on the National Broadcasting Company (NBC) in 1935 under the title *G-Men*. After a brief run, the series moved to the Columbia Broadcasting System (CBS) in January 1936, and the title was changed to *Gang Busters*. The series also eventually appeared on the American Broadcasting Companies (ABC) and Mutual during its 22-year run.

The format of *Gang Busters* was simple. Each episode opened with a loud, identifiable opening of marching feet, sirens, and machine-gun fire. The series opening became so well known that it led to the phrase "coming on like gangbusters." After the opening sound effects, the narrator would introduce the current episode, followed by an interview with a local law enforcement officer (usually from the locale of the current episode). At the end of each episode was a feature called "Gang Buster Clues," which included information regarding a criminal currently at large. The audience was presented with a detailed description of the wanted person, along with information about how to contact law enforcement officials, and was asked to help bring the suspect to justice. These "clues" led to over 100 arrests during the series' first three years. In subsequent years, many more were brought to justice through this forerunner to several successful television series (e.g., *Unsolved Mysteries* and *America's Most Wanted*).

Lord employed actual law enforcement officials to comment throughout each episode. *Gang Busters'* first narrator was Lewis Valentine, police commissioner of New York City. He was replaced after the first year by Col. Norman Schwartzkopf, former superintendent of the New Jersey State Police (Schwartzkopf's son and namesake would later lead the U.S. troops during the 1991 Persian Gulf War). Schwartzkopf continued as narrator for most of the next ten years. In 1945, Valentine, now the retired police commissioner of New York City, replaced him.

The first episode was a dramatization of the Federal Bureau of Investigation's (FBI) capture and shooting of John Dillinger. Lord had obtained the cooperation of FBI Director J. Edgar Hoover on the condition that only "closed" cases would be dramatized in the series. Subsequent episodes featured the stories of "Machine Gun" Kelley, "Baby Face" Nelson, "Pretty Boy" Floyd, and Bonnie and Clyde. When the series moved to CBS in 1936, it began to feature the stories of lesser-known criminals.

Gang Busters portrayed detectives as modern-day heroes who led glamorous lives and risked their lives in the service of others. The plots were very simplistic plays in terms of "good versus evil," with good always winning. Rarely was any mention made of the causes of such criminal behavior.

Gang Busters had many imitators, most notably *Dragnet*, which began in 1949 and was arguably the prototype for all crime and detective dramas to follow. Unlike that show, however, *Gang Busters'* television history was short. The format was the same as its radio counterpart. Phillips H. Lord appeared in each episode as the narrator in addition to serving as series writer and creator. As in the radio version, clues regarding at-large criminals were presented, along with photographs. The television version premiered in 1952, alternating each week with *Dragnet*. *Gang Busters* was designed as a temporary series because Jack Webb had trouble producing weekly episodes of *Dragnet* on time. Both were very successful, with *Dragnet* ranking 20th among all network prime-time series and *Gang Busters* ranking 14th. However, as was the initial plan, *Dragnet* was continued the following season, and *Gang Busters*, the fill-in, was canceled.

Cast

Actors

Art Carney, Larry Haines, Frank Lovejoy, Don MacLaughlin, Alice Reinheart, Grant Richards, Julie Stevens, Richard Widmark

Chief Investigator

Lewis J. Valentine

Announcers

Roger Forster, Art Hannes, Charles Stark, Frank Gallop, Don Gardiner, H. Gilbert Martin

Narrators

Phillips H. Lord, Col. Norman H. Schwartzkopf (1938–45); Lewis Valentine (1945–57); John C. Hilley; Dean Carlton

Producer/Creator

Phillips H. Lord

Programming History

NBC (as *G-Men*)	1935
CBS	1936–40; 1949–55
NBC Blue	1940–45
ABC	1945–48
Mutual	1955–57

MITCHELL SHAPIRO

GAY AND LESBIAN RADIO

A number of attempts, often short-lived, at broadcasting gay and lesbian programs on radio have occurred since the late 1950s. As of 2002 the United States led the way, with more than 100 original gay and lesbian radio shows, which could be heard in large and small cities across the country; however, only a few of these shows are syndicated overseas. Other countries with such radio programs include Australia, Canada, the United Kingdom, Japan, and New Zealand. Gay radio, which targets a multibillion-dollar market, is not represented by a specific format type; rather, its music and talk programming reflects the socioeconomic and cultural diversity within the gay and lesbian community. Personal expression through "queer radio" empowered gays, lesbians, bisexuals, and transgender communities to seek new ways to work collectively toward providing information, resources, and fellowship to others in the United States and internationally.

Origins

Five Pacifica radio stations—in Berkeley, California; Los Angeles; New York; Houston; and Washington, D.C.—located in cities with the largest populations of lesbians and gays in the United States, aired the queer perspective in their news, public affairs, and literary discussions, even before the 1969 Stonewall Rebellion—the birth of the modern-day gay movement. Pacifica station KPFA-FM in Berkeley went on the air in 1949 and became the first listener-sponsored radio station in the world. Pacifica's second station, KPFK-FM, began broadcasting in Los Angeles in 1959. The following year, philanthropist Louis Schweitzer donated WBAI-FM, New York, to Pacifica.

The poet Allen Ginsburg would propel gay radio into mainstream debate by challenging the boundaries of American radio in 1956, when he read his controversial poem "Howl" on KPFA. Ginsburg's life of drugs, jazz, and a liberal attitude toward sexuality and morality epitomized the Beatnik rebellion against the status quo of the 1950s. In the late 1950s, San Francisco's KPFA aired what is believed to be the first comprehensive gay-rights radio documentary in the United States. The two-hour documentary brought together a small group of physicians, lawyers, and criminologists with the mother of a gay man and Harold L. Call, an editor for the *Mattachine Review* and a member of The Mattachine Society, America's first gay-rights organization, to discuss the rights of gay men.

Then, in 1962, WBAI aired "The Homosexual in America," a 60-minute program focused on the opinions of a panel of psychiatrists. Protests by Mattachine New York organizer Randolfe Wicker demanded equal time from WBAI management. On 16 July 1962, WBAI aired a radio forum with Wicker and six other gay men, which prompted some listeners to file a complaint with the Federal Communications Commission (FCC). The rejected complaint paved the way for future discussions on homosexuality in the electronic media. In essence, the FCC upheld Pacifica's contention that broadcasts addressing gay issues served the public interest, as long as the topics were handled in good taste.

Radio After the Stonewall Rebellion

Queer broadcasting may be traced back to the people who fought for free expression and civil rights. No event revolutionized and liberalized the gay and lesbian movement more than the Stonewall Rebellion. The decision on what needed to be done to achieve equality, tolerance, and ultimately acceptance by all Americans was made during one fateful Friday night on 27 June 1969 on the streets of New York City. A routine police raid on a Greenwich Village bar that served transvestites, lesbians, and gays turned violent after patrons decided not to run away from the police. What might be perceived as an isolated incident to most Americans sent shock waves throughout the queer community. The riots continued in New York City for three days, and The Gay Liberation Front was formed within weeks.

In 1971 Pacifica's KPFK debuted *imru* ("I am; Are you?"), the first weekly gay radio show in Los Angeles, and perhaps in the United States. Another program, *Amazon Country*, celebrated its 25th anniversary in 1999. That year the show was also the recipient of the 1999 Lambda Award for Outstanding Overall Performance by an Organization/

Social-Cultural Group. *Amazon Country* airs on Sunday nights on the University of Pennsylvania's public radio station WXPN-FM, featuring a lesbian/feminist perspective in its music and interviews with artists, authors, and leaders throughout the nation. Since 1974 WXPN has also aired *Q'zine*, a radio magazine show that was originally called *Gaydreams*. It was named partly after a Grateful Dead song and first aired in 1974. Several other queer radio shows were heard mainly on non-commercial college and community radio stations. These programs were almost always volunteer produced, represented the efforts of only a handful of radio collectives, and were limited financially and regionally. The longevity of these shows often depended on the whim of the station manager and program director, and gay and lesbian producers on occasion were forced to compete among themselves for limited time slots.

Repression and Restraint

The 1980s saw a sexual revolution on radio and television—one that prompted public calls for censorship, music labeling, and stronger FCC policies and penalties, as well as for boycotts on stores and stations promoting explicit music. The public outcry against naughty lyrics on the radio seemed stronger than its reaction to Howard Stern's racial and ethnic epithets and verbal gay bashing.

As right-wing conservatism swept the nation during the Reagan era, gay-rights activists were under attack in the mainstream media. The previous victories in civil liberties and free expression were to be challenged once again by the FCC and the religious right. As early as the 1980s, the FCC warned Pacifica that any further broadcast of "Howl" could result in heavy fines or the forfeiture of its license. AIDS would provide the justification and rationale for what would become the widespread abuse of human rights and rise in hate propaganda in the years to follow. It was in this environment that queer broadcasting would push forward and feverishly combat the stereotypical attitudes and hate propaganda that continue to target gays and lesbians.

In 1986 the freedom of queer radio was challenged again by the FCC after Reverend Larry Poland accidentally tuned in to *imru* on KPFK and heard "Jerker," a radio drama about the impact of AIDS on two gay men. The FCC threatened to fine the station "for the patently offensive manner in which the sexual activity was described." The Justice Department declined to take action on the case. In 1991, Pacifica was one of several parties to lead a successful appeal to overturn the 24-hour indecency ban initiated by Congress and put into place by the FCC.

By 1987 the AIDS Coalition to Unleash Power (ACT UP) had attracted mainstream media attention to AIDS issues. "Outing" the famous became "in" among young queers who wanted to end hypocrisy in the media. The sexual revolution of the 1960s was being reinvented by George Michael and Madonna in the electronic media, as both challenged and toyed with gender boundaries in their music and videos. A number of radio stations aired promotional announcements that assured their audiences of "safe" lyrics, and the FCC began to wrestle with "safe harbor" policies designed to protect children from undesirable broadcast content.

The Rise of Queer Music

By the end of the 1980s, Melissa Etheridge and k.d. lang had expanded in popularity beyond college radio and were becoming household names on mainstream radio. The nation seemed ready for something different—and with the rise of alternative radio, a new breed of music was arriving on the scene; its new young audiences embraced the often mystical and mesmerizing video clips of life and love projected across their television screen. For some musicians, it was time for the next step—queer music, in which gays and lesbians would share their experiences about lovers and life partners in their music.

The formation of the National Lesbian and Gay Country Music Association in 1998 was just one example of the trend toward acceptance of queer music in the United States. Other signs toward changing times include the acceptance of country musicians such as Mark Weigle, an independent singer/songwriter who has received regular airplay on Americana shows in Europe. He was nominated (along with Ani DiFranco, Rufus Wainwright, and the B-52's) for two 1999 Gay/Lesbian American Music Awards (GLAMA)—for both Debut Artist and Out Song "If It Wasn't Love." Weigle has been praised by music critics in gay and mainstream music publications such as *Genre, Billboard,* and *Performing Songwriter.* GLAMA is the first and only national music awards program to celebrate and honor the music of queer musicians and songwriters. Its first annual ceremony took place in New York's Webster Hall in October 1996, with about 700 people in attendance. The judges comprised music reviewers from the gay and mainstream media; leaders in radio distribution; executives of major and independent record labels; and those working in performing rights, talent management, and retail. GLAMA's final awards ceremony was held in April 2000; increasing administrative costs were cited as the reason for its demise.

Beyond the Gay Ghetto

In April 1988 Los Angeles radio producer Greg Gordon, a former *imru* producer and host (along with his volunteer staff), created the 30-minute newsmagazine program called *This Way Out*, which began with a weekly distribution to 26 public stations in the United States and Canada. It now airs on more than 125 radio stations—public and commercial—in six countries. The program contains news, author interviews, AIDS updates, humor, poetry, and music recordings by openly gay and lesbian performers rarely heard on commercial radio. The Gay and Lesbian Press Association honored *This Way Out* with its Outstanding Achievement Award in 1988, and the National Federation of Community Broadcasters presented the "Silver Reel" award to its producers in 1991 for their ongoing news and public-affairs commitment to cultural diversity. One affiliate station, Kansas City's KKFI-FM, boasts that more than 500 individuals have presented a myriad of gay, lesbian, and transgender issues across its airwaves. In fact, KKFI is the first and thus far the only station in its market to air a local queer radio program. To some gay media activists, however, the failure to move beyond noncommercial radio and into the mainstream has been a form of "gay ghettoization," or what some queer broadcasters have referred to as "preaching to the choir." For years, noncommercial radio has been the primary vehicle for communicating the queer perspective to the gay community, and increasingly to a straight audience. In 1992 WFNX-FM, a commercial Boston station, debuted *One in Ten*, a three-hour show with a mix of news, entertainment, music, and call-in discussions. In the early 1990s, several other commercial stations experimented, although unsuccessfully, with locally produced programs targeting gay and lesbian audiences.

In 1990 Thomas Davis became the president and general manager of two Amherst commercial stations located in a renowned gay and lesbian community in central Massachusetts. His company's mission was to target listeners outside the gay community, in addition to gays and lesbians themselves. In doing so, the stations would attempt to convey the idea that gays and lesbians function much like any other members of society on a daily basis. As institutional members of the Gay and Lesbian Business Coalition, the stations have been supported on the air by many gay- or lesbian-owned businesses. Programming includes news stories relevant to gays and lesbians, as well as fund-raising efforts for a number of queer community concerns, such as AIDS research and hospice funding.

The year of the largest commercial venture for gay radio was 1992. The KGAY Radio network signed on the air on 28 November 1992 in Denver. KGAY, with its motto "All Gay, All Day," was the inspiration of Clay Henderson and Will Gunthrie. Their previous efforts had included a short-lived 30-minute weekly gay commercial radio show and a weekly gay and lesbian news show called the *Lambda Report*, which first aired on public access cable television in 1989. KGAY Radio was the first attempt to market a 24-hour all gay and lesbian format in America. The KGAY founders planned to use a local Denver station as the headquarters for what they hoped would become a national cable FM operation. The decision to broadcast by satellite from Denver seemed easier and less expensive to the owners than purchasing a commercial radio station in a large or medium market. KGAY's programming was uplinked to satellite dishes in North America, Canada, and the Caribbean. The music and news network was promoted as the first daily media vehicle for the gay and lesbian community in North America. Less than a year after it began, however, the KGAY network, with only a few sponsors and a mostly volunteer staff, failed.

In May 1994 another commercial radio venture was born on adult contemporary WCBR-FM in north Chicago. LesBiGay Radio founder Alan Amberg conversed insightfully every weekday afternoon on America's only drive-time gay radio show, as his signal reached into the Chicago neighborhoods where many gays and lesbians resided. By April 2001, his radio enterprise had logged more than 3,000 hours of programming and had a number of prominent national and local sponsors. Indeed, the show was hailed as the most successful commercial queer radio venture of the 1990s in America, but Amberg was forced to end it in April 2001 because of financial difficulties.

Other stations that have presented themselves as either "gay" in format or have not shied away from openly serving a GLBT constituency include: TWIST, an aural offshoot of TV's gay-themed Logo cable channel, was a short-lived syndicated radio "brand" launched in January 2006; WPYM (Miami), which offset its dance music format with gay-oriented features but left the air in 2008; KHKS (Dallas), which became an HD music station; KNGY (San Francisco), which first aired in 2004 with nearly nonstop dance music but also airs what it bills as

the nation's first openly gay morning show; and KFAI (Minneapolis).

Arguably, the genre's two highest-profile ventures are Sirius's OutQ and Clear Channel's Pride Radio. OutQ was begun by Sirius as a 24-hour channel in 2003 with a mixture of music, talk, news, and advice and features such gay male celebrities as Larry Flick, Derek Hartley, Frank DeCaro, and Michelangelo Signorile. Though originally nearly commercial free (as were most Sirius channels), with time the channel has acquired several national sponsors.

Clear Channel's entry into the field was more surprising considering the company's roster of politically conservative talkers. Nevertheless, Pride Radio, a product of the organization's experimental "format lab," launched in 2006. Heard in more than a dozen markets by 2008, Pride Radio airs a variety of programs.

See also: Affirmative Action; Pacifica Foundation; Stereotypes on Radio

Further Reading

Alwood, Edward, *Straight News: Gays, Lesbians, and the News Media*, New York: Columbia University Press, 1996.
Bednarski, P.J., "Sirius Turns on Gay Radio Channel." *Broadcasting & Cable* (21 April 2003), p. 15.
Gross, Larry, and James D. Woods, editors, *The Columbia Reader on Lesbians and Gay Men in Media, Society, and Politics*, New York: Columbia University Press, 1999.
Hendriks, Aart, Rob Tielman, and Evert van der Veen, editors, *The Third Pink Book*, Buffalo, New York: Prometheus Books, 1993.
Hogan, Steve, and Lee Hudson, *Completely Queer: The Gay and Lesbian Encyclopedia*, New York: Holt, 1998.
Johnson, Phylis, Charles Hoy, and Dhyana Ziegler, "A Case Study of KGAY: The Rise and Fall of the First 'Gay and Lesbian' Radio Network," *Journal of Radio Studies* 3 (1995–96).
Johnson, Phylis, and Michael C. Keith, *Queer Airways: The Story of Gay and Lesbian Broadcasting*, Armonk, New York: M.E. Sharpe, 2001.
Lasar, Matthew, *Pacifica Radio: The Rise of an Alternative Network*, Philadelphia, Pennsylvania: Temple University Press, 1999.
Schulman, Sarah, *My American History: Lesbian and Gay Life during the Reagan/Bush Years*, New York: Routledge, 1994.
"Trends in the Making," *Advertising* (11 August 1998).

PHYLIS JOHNSON,
2009 REVISIONS BY CARY O'DELL

GENERAL ELECTRIC
Manufacturer of Consumer Electronics

General Electric (GE) was instrumental in the shaping of early American radio broadcasting through its creation of the Radio Corporation of America (RCA) in 1919 and its subsequent operation of several pioneering radio stations. GE is a diversified company with holdings in consumer services, technology, and manufacturing. GE operates in more than 100 countries and employs nearly 340,000 people worldwide, including 197,000 in the United States.

Origins

General Electric traces its history to the Edison Electric Light Company, established in 1878 by Thomas Edison, and to the Thomson-Houston Electric Company, established by Elihu Thomson and Edwin Houston in the early 1880s. Both companies grew by the 1890s into leaders in their field and battled over adoption of electrical current standards for the United States. Thomson-Houston promoted alternating current, whereas Edison championed use of direct current. Alternating current was adopted in the United States, and in 1892 the two merged to form GE. GE is the only company that has been listed continuously on the Dow Jones Industrial Index since its inception in 1896.

After the merger, the new company could boast of having some of the best minds in the country. Thomson's financial genius Charles Coffin became GE's first president, and Edison became a director. Thomson helped establish a program of scientific research that led to the creation of GE's Research Laboratory in 1900 under the direction of Dr. Willis R. Whitney. In a career spanning five decades, Thomson was awarded 696 U.S. patents for devices as varied as arc lights, generators, X-ray tubes, and electric welding machines. His successful "recording wattmeter" was a practical method of measuring the amount of electricity used by a home or business. In 1893 a young German, Charles Steinmentz, joined GE, and he proposed new methods of designing machinery using alternating current. After the turn of the century, GE expanded its power-generation business by developing the first steam turbine-generator large enough to power cities. In 1903 GE purchased the Stanley Electrical Manufacturing Company of Pittsfield, Massachusetts. William Stanley, the head of that company, joined GE and pioneered electrical line transmission equipment. He is credited with inventing the transformer, which became the heart of the electrical distribution system. In 1910 GE developed ductile tungsten for light bulb filaments; ductile tungsten is still used in virtually every incandescent lamp.

GE and Radio

By the turn of the 20th century, GE began developmental work in wireless radio, and in 1906, E.F.W. Alexanderson developed a practical alternator to produce the high frequencies needed for reliable long-distance transmission. Later, Dr. Irving Langmuir of GE's Research Laboratory designed an amplifier for Alexanderson's alternator, completing the components of a transoceanic radio-transmitting system. This system was the most powerful generator of radio waves then known, and it became the pivotal point for negotiations with American Marconi, the U.S. subsidiary of British Marconi's worldwide wireless enterprise; these negotiations eventually led to the formation of RCA.

During World War I, the navy had operated most radio stations in the United States, including those using GE's Alexanderson alternator. Naval radio experts became convinced that this equipment was vital to U.S. interests, and after the war Admiral W.H.G. Bullard and Captain Stanford Hooper convinced GE executive Owen D. Young not to sell improved vacuum tubes and the exclusive rights to the Alexanderson alternator to the British subsidiary. In a meeting in May 1919, Young told E.J. Nally of American Marconi that GE would not sell the equipment because the U.S. government did not want control of this equipment to pass into foreign hands. Over the summer the two companies' officers negotiated the sale of American Marconi's assets to GE, and the deal they struck resulted in RCA's incorporation on 17 October 1919.

Shortly after its incorporation, RCA and GE entered into patent cross-licensing agreements with American Telephone and Telegraph (AT&T) and Westinghouse. Under these agreements, all signatories shared their patents. With this patent pooling, RCA quickly became one of the leading companies manufacturing and selling wireless radio equipment. By 1922 the company had moved into wireless' newest application—broadcasting. Radio station WGY began broadcasting from Schenectady, New York, with one of the first U.S. radio dramas, *The Wolf.* As this new phenomenon caught on with the American public, GE, with RCA and Westinghouse, became engaged in a series of intercompany battles with AT&T and its manufacturing arm, Western Electric, over who held what rights in broadcasting. To resolve this issue, AT&T sold its radio interests, and RCA created the National Broadcasting Corporation (NBC) in 1926 to oversee network endeavors in broadcasting.

In the early 1930s the Justice Department filed an antitrust suit against General Electric, Westinghouse, and RCA, alleging restraint of trade. In 1932 the companies signed a consent decree, and GE was forced to divest itself of any interest in RCA.

During the Depression years, GE made important improvements and contributions to X rays, electric ship turbines, and the efficiency of electrical light and appliances. In 1940 GE expanded its business by relaying television broadcasts from New York City and by starting FM broadcasts. During World War II, these operations were suspended, as GE turned its efforts to helping win the war. The company supplied much help to the war effort, from aircraft gun turrets and jet engines, to radar and radio equipment, to electrically heated flying suits. GE made propulsion units for nearly 75 percent of the Navy's ships, and from GE laboratories came new systems for the detection of enemy aircraft and ships.

After the war, GE carried out an extensive program of expansion and decentralization. As a result, autonomous product departments developed. Over the years, GE also expanded its research and development divisions as well as its international efforts. Its many manufacturing lines ranged from consumer products such as light bulbs and consumer electronics, to major appliances such as refrigerators and television sets, to industrial and military equipment such as locomotives, aircraft engines, nuclear reactors, and ICBM guidance systems. In addition, GE moved into services such as insurance, consumer credit, and data processing. In 1957 GE opened the world's first licensed nuclear power plant and entered the mainframe computer business, which it sold in 1970 to Honeywell. Two years later GE developed the TIROS 1 weather satellite. During the 1960s and 1970s, the company continued expanding its lighting, aircraft engine, and electrical equipment businesses both domestically and abroad.

Modern GE

In late 1986 GE bought RCA (and NBC) in a $6.28 billion deal that some say ironically came full circle to the 1930s divestiture. The following July, GE sold off the NBC Radio Network to Westwood One for $50 million so that GE/RCA could concentrate on television and newer consumer media. At the same time, the company began selling the NBC-owned-and-operated radio stations. Over the next ten years, GE and RCA combined their consumer electronics businesses and subsequently sold them to Thomson in exchange for its medical equipment business and $800 million in cash. The companies' combined defense business was also sold, to Martin Marietta for $3 billion. GE/RCA retained ownership of the NBC television operations, and during the 1990s these NBC operations became exceedingly profitable for GE.

In 1989, NBC launched the business financial cable television network CNBC, and GE formed a mobile communications joint venture with Ericsson of Sweden. In 1991 NBC acquired the Financial News network (FNN) and sold its interest in the RCA Columbia Home Video joint venture. In 1994 GE created one of the first major industrial websites, www.ge.com, and two years later NBC and Microsoft joined forces to launch MSNBC, a 24-hour television and internet service. In 1999 GE began e-Business as a key growth initiative. NBC launched NBC Internet (NBCi), a publicly traded internet company that merged the network's interactive properties with XOOM.com and the internet portal Snap.com to form the seventh-largest internet site and the first publicly traded internet company integrated with a major broadcaster. NBCi will use Snap.com as an umbrella consumer brand, integrating broadcast, portal, and e-commerce services. NBC also maintains equity interests in cable channels Arts and Entertainment (A&E) and the History Channel. NBC also has an equity stake in Rainbow Programming Holdings, a leading media company with a wide array of entertainment and sports cable channels. It also holds interests in CNET, Talk City, iVillage, Telescan, Hoover's, and 24/7Media. In partnership with National Geographic and Fox/BskyB, NBC owns and operates the National Geographic Channel in Europe and Asia.

See also: National Broadcasting Company; Radio Corporation of America; Westinghouse

Further Reading

Alexander, Charles, "A Reunion of Technological Titans," *Time* (23 December 1985).

Barnum, Frederick O., III, *His Master's Voice In America: Ninety Years of Communications Pioneering and Progress: Victor Talking Machine Company, Radio Corporation of America, General Electric Company*, Camden, New Jersey: General Electric Company, 1991.

Case, Josephine Young, and Everett Needham Case, *Owen D. Young and American Enterprise: A Biography*, Boston: Godine, 1982.

A Century of Progress: The General Electric Story, 1876–1978, Schenectady, New York: GE Hall of History, 1981.

GE website, www.ge.com.

Hammond, John Winthrop, *Men and Volts: The Story of General Electric*, Philadelphia, Pennsylvania: Lippincott, 1941.

Lewis, Tom, *Empire of the Air: The Men Who Made Radio*, New York: Burlingame Books, 1991.

Loomis, Carol J., "Ten Years After," *Fortune* (17 February 1997).

Nye, David E., *Image Worlds: Corporate Identities at General Electric, 1890–1930*, Cambridge, Massachusetts: MIT Press, 1985.

Reich, Leonard S., *The Making of American Industrial Research: Science and Business and GE and Bell, 1876–1926*, New York: Cambridge University Press, 1985.

LOUISE BENJAMIN

THE GEORGE BURNS AND GRACIE ALLEN SHOW
Comedy Series

For 17 years, Burns and Allen provided one of radio's most enduring comedy series based on the vaudeville tradition.

Vaudeville Origins

George Burns, born Nathan Birnbaum in New York City on 20 January 1896, left school after fourth grade to sing professionally with the PeeWee Quartet. That move led to his career in vaudeville as a singer, dancer, and monologuist (1910–31). Grace Ethel Cecile Rosalie Allen was born 26 July 1906 in San Francisco. She met George after a 1922 New Jersey vaudeville performance he had done with his partner, Billy Lorraine. Gracie, who begun in vaudeville at 14 with her three sisters, wanted to work with Lorraine. She teamed with George instead, and they were married 7 January 1926. They performed together in vaudeville, film, radio, and TV from 1922 until her retirement in 1958.

Gracie played "straight man" until George discovered she was funnier being nice yet dim-witted. George never considered changing Gracie, whom he loved because of her befuddlement and inverted logic. Gracie was a nervous performer, but audiences thought it was an act, part of her giddy, scatterbrained persona. She was uninterested in business, but George enjoyed other responsibilities as script supervisor and manager.

In 1929 Burns and Allen were invited to perform their Vaudeville act in London. After 21 weeks there performing to appreciative audiences at various nightclubs, the duo was asked to go on BBC radio—a successful stint that lasted 26 weeks. The team believed they could experience similar success on American radio.

Network Success

In 1930 the National Broadcasting Company (NBC) rejected them because of Gracie's squeaky, high-pitched voice, but she performed on Eddie Cantor's show in 1931 to rave reviews. A week later Burns and Allen played Rudy Vallee's show, which led to their 15 February 1932 debut on the Columbia Broadcasting System's (CBS) *The Robert Burns Panatella Program*. In 1933 their popularity earned them their own show, which lasted 17 years. *The George Burns and Gracie Allen Show* —also known as *Maxwell House Coffee Time*, *Burns and Allen*, and *The Adventures of Gracie* —presented sketches, music, and vaudeville routines. Among the show's characters was Mel Blanc's Happy Postman, who spoke pleasant and cheerful thoughts but always sounded depressed and near crying.

Originally based in New York, the show made road broadcasts from other cities and military installations throughout the United States. By 1934, the couple began work in film and relocated to Beverly Hills with two adopted children, Sandra Jean and Ronald John. In 1942 ratings dropped temporarily and the sponsor in turn dropped the program. The premise of Burns and Allen as boyfriend and girlfriend no longer worked. George explained: "Everybody knew we were married and had growing children…you have to have truth in a joke just the way you do in anything else to make it any good. If it's basically dishonest, it isn't funny." George finally realized the problem was that he and Gracie were too old to do the boyfriend/girlfriend premise. The jokes were stale, so the format was changed to reflect their status as a married couple and the program experienced a renewal of popularity, attracting 45 million listeners per week.

Many promotional strategies featuring Gracie were employed for the program throughout its run. She went on a show-to-show search for her mythical brother. She ran for president in 1940, receiving several hundred votes. In 1942 bandleader Paul Whiteman wrote *Gracie Allen's Concerto for Index Finger*, which Gracie mentioned constantly on the show. Ultimately, she performed the number at Carnegie Hall and with major orchestras, including the Boston Pops.

George and Gracie were not social commentators, prevailing instead with timeless humor and talented performances. In 1950 they successfully moved to TV, and their 239 episodes continue to air in re-runs decades later. George explained: "We talked in vaudeville, we talked in radio, we talked in television. It wasn't hard to go from one medium to another." Gracie retired after the final TV episode on 4 June 1958, to be Mrs. George Burns, a mother and a grandmother. Only after her 27 August 1964 death did the public discover she had retired because of heart problems.

In his book *Gracie: A Love Story*, George's first line read: "For forty years my act consisted of one joke. And then she died." George continued in TV as an actor, developer, and producer of *Wendy and Me, No Time for Sergeants, Mona McCluskey,* and *Mr. Ed.* In 1975 he returned to film, replacing his late friend Jack Benny in *The Sunshine Boys.* He also starred in the *Oh, God!* trilogy and a handful of other films. George continued TV guest appearances before being slowed by a 1994 fall. He performed in Las Vegas until his death on 9 March 1996.

See also: Comedy; Vaudeville and Radio

Cast

George Burns	Himself
Gracie Allen	Herself
The Happy Postman	Mel Blanc
Tootsie Stagwell	Elvia Allman
Mrs. Billingsley	Margaret Brayton
Muriel	Sara Berner
Waldo	Dick Crenna
Herman, the duck	Clarence Nash
Also featured	Gale Gordon, Hans Conried, Henry Blair
Vocalists	Milton Watson, Tony Martin, Jimmy Cash, Dick Foran
Bandleaders	Jacques Renard, Ray Noble, Paul Whiteman, Meredith Willson
Announcers	Ted Husing, Harry Von Zell, Jimmy Wallington, Bill Goodwin, Toby Reed

Directors

Ralph Levy, Al Kaye, Ed Gardner

Writers

Paul Henning, Keith Fowler, Harmon J. Alexander, Henry Garson, Aaron J. Ruben, Helen Gould Harvey, Hal Block, John P. Medbury

Producer/Creator

George Burns

Programming History

CBS and NBC   15 February 1932–17 May 1950

Further Reading

Blythe, Cheryl, and Susan Sackett, *Say Goodnight, Gracie! The Story of Burns and Allen*, New York: Dutton, 1986.

Burns, George, *Gracie: A Love Story*, New York: Putnam, 1988.

Burns, George, *All My Best Friends*, New York: Putnam, 1989.

Campbell, Robert, *The Golden Years of Broadcasting: A Celebration of the First 50 Years of Radio and TV on NBC*, New York: Scribner, 1976.

Finkelstein, Norman H., *Sounds in the Air: The Golden Age of Radio*, New York: Scribner, 1993.

Harmon, Jim, *The Great Radio Comedians*, Garden City, New York: Doubleday, 1970.

O'Connell, Mary C., *Connections: Reflections on Sixty Years of Broadcasting*, n.p.: National Broadcasting Company, 1986.

Wertheim, Arthur Frank, "Scatterbrains," in *Radio Comedy*, New York: Oxford University Press, 1979.

W.A. KELLY HUFF

GOLDBERGS
Comedy Serial Program

As early as 1937, just 8 years into its 16-year run on radio, *The Goldbergs* was selected by the industry magazine *Radio Daily* as one of the "Programs that Have Made History." Indeed, *The Goldbergs* was a groundbreaking show that influenced both the form and content of later radio and television programming. Amid early radio fare, such as music variety shows and public talks, *The Goldbergs* (along with *Real Folks* and *Amos 'n' Andy*) was one of the first dramatic serials on network radio and one of the first serials to concentrate on family life. *The Goldbergs* demonstrated the power of serials to attract a loyal audience. Its immediate success in 1929 prompted interest in radio programs that regularly featured familiar domestic situations, recurring characters, and continuing story lines.

The Goldbergs was a hybrid program, part comedy, part drama, and part serial; with its continuing story line and domestic focus, the program was the prototype for both later situation comedies and daytime soap operas. Yet *The Goldbergs* is most fondly remembered for its ethnic content. Among the first urban, ethnic comedies in broadcasting, the program spoke eloquently about the experience of immigrants during the Depression and their struggles to assimilate in their adopted country. *The Goldbergs* remains one of the relatively few programs in the history of radio and television to offer a sustained ethnic perspective on American life.

The stories of the Goldberg family—at 1038 East Tremont Avenue, Apartment 3B, in the Bronx—emerged solely from the creator and writer of the series, Gertrude Berg. As Michele Hilmes (1997) writes, "no other daily serial drama reflected so explicitly its creator's own ethnic background." Gertrude Edelstein Berg (1899–1966) was born in Harlem to Russian Jewish parents. As a teenager at her father's resort in the Poconos, Berg began writing plays to entertain the guests. This hobby continued even after Berg married and gave birth to two children. She soon developed a popular skit featuring a wife and mother named Maltke Talnitsky—modeled after her grandmother, her mother, and herself—her no-good husband, and her children. These characters were the earliest forms of the Goldberg family—Molly Goldberg, a Jewish immigrant mother; Jake Goldberg, a tailor and her sympathetic husband; and her two children, Sammy and Rosalie. Gertrude Berg sent a sample script through a family acquaintance to a New York radio station. Berg was offered jobs writing continuity and translating commercials and recipes into Yiddish on radio.

Although Berg's first network offering, about two working-class salesgirls, *Effie and Laurie*, was picked up by the Columbia Broadcasting System (CBS) in 1929, it was canceled after just one broadcast. After this failure, Berg began to shop around her idea for a family comedy based on her earlier skits. Berg claimed that initially "radio studio big wigs" believed audiences would reject a program about Yiddish life. However, the National Broadcasting Company (NBC) saw the promise of radio's first Jewish comedy and aired *The Rise of the Goldbergs* as a sustaining weekly evening series starting on 20 November 1929. Paid $75 a week to write the series and produce the program, Berg controlled all aspects of the show's development, from scripting the program in longhand to paying the performers. Berg, who voiced the character of Molly Goldberg, assembled a cast of New York stage actors to bring the rest of the Goldberg family to life: James Waters as Jake Goldberg, Alfred Ryder as Sammy, and Roslyn Silber as Rosalie. Berg's importance to the series was recognized by fans; nearly 37,000 letters poured in when Berg became ill and was off the air for a week. NBC acknowledged Berg's role, as well: Berg soon earned more than $7,500 a week for the program. By fans and the industry, Berg was considered one of the most important personalities in broadcasting and one of the greatest women in radio.

By the 1931–32 season, the series, retitled *The Goldbergs*, aired six times a week and had become one of the highest-rated programs on radio. On 13 July 1931, the show was picked up by Pepsodent, who sponsored it for the next three years. Berg

ended the serial briefly in 1934 to take the cast and the series on a nationwide promotional tour. When the networks cleared serial dramas from the nighttime air in 1936, *The Goldbergs* moved to daytime until 1945. In January 1938 Berg was signed to a five-year, million-dollar contract to write and star on *The Goldbergs*, making her one of the highest-paid writers on radio. Oxydol and Procter and Gamble picked up sponsorship of the show until the end of its run.

The Goldbergs was a serial that spoke about the economic and social tensions of the 1930s and 1940s, an assimilationist drama about an immigrant Jewish family living on New York's Lower East Side. Many programs focused on typical domestic situations—report cards, dinner guests, schoolyard loves, and Molly's worries about her family. In the early years of *The Goldbergs*, Berg described life in an urban tenement and the attempts of this immigrant family to achieve economic security during the Depression. But, most important, the serial vividly depicted the clash between old and new, yesterday's traditions and today's values, Old World parents and American-born children.

At the heart of this serial drama was the struggle of an immigrant family to assimilate culturally, while still retaining their ethnic identity. Early episodes were marked by generational conflict over how much the family should adapt to life in the United States. The parents, Molly and Jake Goldberg, were ethnic immigrants with "Old World" values. Molly's voice revealed her immigrant background: she spoke with a heavy Yiddish accent and was famous for her "Mollyprops," Yiddish malapropisms that twisted common phrases ("If it's nobody, I'll call back" or "I'm putting on my bathrobe and condescending the stairs"). Their American-born children, Sammy and Rosalie, spoke with relatively little accent and often challenged the traditions of their parents. However, by the end of the serial, the Americanization of Molly's family was nearly complete; like so many other immigrants, the upwardly mobile Goldbergs eventually moved from their New York apartment to the suburbs.

The immigrant experience recounted in *The Goldbergs* clearly resonated in an era characterized by both massive immigration and calls for greater national unity. Although Gertrude Berg moved in more assimilated, upper-middle-class circles, she worked diligently to maintain the "realism" of the ethnic immigrant experience detailed in the series. In 1936, for example, Berg took Dan Wheeler, a writer from the *Radio Mirror*, to the Lower East

Side to witness her research. In an article entitled "How the Ghetto Guides *The Goldbergs*, " Wheeler recounted Berg's conversations with street vendors and immigrant women and her anonymous participation in a Lower East Side charitable club. Her efforts to represent the ethnic experience were appreciated by contemporary audiences. The program was cited at the time by groups such as the National Conference of Christians and Jews for promoting religious and ethnic tolerance.

The continued popularity of the radio program spawned the 1948 Broadway play *Molly and Me*, a comic strip, several vaudeville skits, and a 1950 film. After the program's demise, *The Goldbergs* was briefly revived in 1949–50 for CBS as a 30-minute weekly radio series, but it endured in American culture as a television situation comedy from 1949 to 1955. *The Goldbergs* became one of the most popular comedies of early television, earning Berg the first Emmy Award for Best Actress in 1950. In 1961–62, Molly Goldberg inspired yet another television series, *Mrs. Goldberg Goes to College* (or *The Gertrude Berg Show*). Because of its acuity in representing a common immigrant experience, the magazine *TV Show* appropriately labeled *The Goldbergs* an "American institution" (Merritt, 1951).

See also: Comedy; Jewish Radio Programs; Situation Comedy; Stereotypes on Radio

Cast

Molly Goldberg	Gertrude Berg
Jake Goldberg	James Waters, Phillip Loeb (1949–50)
Sammy Goldberg	Alfred Ryder, Everett Sloane (late 1930s), Larry Robinson (1949–50)
Rosalie Goldberg	Roslyn Silber, Arlene McQuade (1949–50)
Uncle David	Menasha Skulnik, Eli Mintz (1949–50)
Joyce	Anne Teeman
Edna	Helene Dumas
Solly	Sidney Slon
Jane	Joan Tetzel
Seymour Fingerhood	Arnold Stang, Eddie Firestone, Jr.
Sylvia	Zina Provendie
Mr. Fowler	Bruno Wick
Mr. Schneider	Artie Auerback
Esther	Joan Vitez
Mickey Bloom	Howard Merrill
Martha Wilberforce	Carrie Weller
Libby	Jeanette Chinley
Uncle Carlo	Tito Vuolo
Mrs. Bloom	Minerva Pious
Announcer	Clayton "Bud" Collyer, Alan Kent, Art Millet

Creator/Writer

Gertrude Berg

Programming History

NBC	1929–34; 1937 (briefly); 1941 (briefly)
CBS	1935–50

Further Reading

Berg, Gertrude, *The Rise of the Goldbergs*, New York: Barse, 1931.

Berg, Gertrude, and Cherney Berg, *Molly and Me*, New York: McGraw Hill, 1961.

Hilmes, Michele, *Radio Voices: American Broadcasting, 1922–1952*, Minneapolis: University of Minnesota Press, 1997.

Kutner, Nanette, "The Nine Greatest Women in Radio," *Radio Stars* (December 1934).

Merritt, Joan, "Calling: Molly Goldberg," *TV Show* 1, no. 1 (May 1951).

O'Dell, Cary, *Women Pioneers in Television: Biographies of Fifteen Industry Leaders*, Jefferson, North Carolina: McFarland, 1996.

"Programs That Have Made History," *Radio Daily* (3 November 1937).

Seldes, Gilbert, "The Great Gertrude," *Saturday Review* (2 June 1956).

Smith, Glenn D., Jr., *"Something on My Own:" Gertrude Berg and American Broadcasting, 1929–1956*. Syracuse, New York: Syracuse University Press, 2007.

Wheeler, Dan, "How the Ghetto Guides the Goldbergs," *Radio Mirror* 6, no. 2 (June 1936).

JENNIFER HYLAND WANG

GOSPEL MUSIC FORMAT

The gospel music format is a popular genre of radio programming that features generally upbeat music with a Christian message.

Gospel music has long been a staple of radio, particularly in the Bible Belt, and it was featured on several early radio stations, including WFOR in Hattiesburg, Mississippi; KWKH in Shreveport, Louisiana; WSM in Nashville, Tennessee; WVOK in Birmingham, Alabama; and WKOZ in Kosciusko, Mississippi.

Today's gospel music format originated with and grew out of special programming. As local radio stations began to dot the landscape of the United States, many of them featured gospel music on

Sundays, or perhaps 30 minutes to an hour each day. Typically, this special programming featured either white Southern quartets, groups, and soloists (including the Statesmen Quartet, the Blackwood Brothers, the Chuck Wagon Gang, and Tennessee Ernie Ford), or black groups and soloists (such as the Jackson Southernaires, Edwin Hawkins Singers, or Mahalia Jackson).

During the 1980s, some radio stations began to program gospel music exclusively, billing themselves as "all gospel all the time." With deregulation of the broadcasting industry in the 1980s, the number of radio stations significantly increased, and program directors created specialized music formats to target specific audiences. The gospel music format began to burgeon; a number of stations chose it as the only type music they featured, complete with the "clock hour," which delineates and specifies every element of programming during each hour. The clock hour, also known as the "format wheel" or "programming wheel," could be compared to a pie cut into approximately 25 parts. For example, the top of the hour on the format wheel might include five minutes of national news from a network (not a few gospel stations are affiliated with the *USA Radio Network* because its content and style of reporting correlate with issues with which some Christians are concerned). At five minutes past the hour, a number-one song from yesteryear might be featured, followed by a top-ten gospel hit, followed by a totally new selection that might prompt the disc jockey to remark, "And you heard it first right here." In this way, the gospel music format is similar to the structure of a Top-40 station, with on-air personalities using their names, throwing in some pleasantries, and striving to create an image appealing to the target audience—in the case of gospel, a bright, happy, encouraging sound.

Top radio groups such as Jacor, Clear Channel, and Infinity see gospel as a viable format. Capitalizing on audience loyalty to the music, a number of stations have improved their ratings after switching to the gospel format, increasing their average quarter-hour listening shares and paving the way for advertising acceptance. The gospel music format is typically appealing to advertisers, although gospel music stations decline to advertise certain products or services, such as alcoholic beverages or nightclubs. If a gospel music station is airing a sporting event, typically the operator at the station has been instructed to block any network advertisements that pertain to alcohol or tobacco products.

Gospel radio stations have increasingly subscribed to gospel music programming via satellite services. For example, CHRSN (a division of The Way-FM) is one popular supplier of music and voice tracking services, whereas K-LOVE out of Rocklin, CA, beams to over 400 FM Christian stations nationwide. Listeners to such services may perceive that the syndicated announcers are present at the local station, even though these air personalities are part of the download.

Some stations have begun to feature specific gospel subgenres, which have proliferated in recent years. The Dove Awards—the pre-eminent award for nonsecular music—now recognizes music in 12 different categories including Rap/Hip-Hop, Rock, Bluegrass, Traditional, Southern Gospel and Christian Country. Two rapidly rising subformats within the gospel universe are Urban Gospel and Spanish Gospel. Black gospel is currently the fourth most popular format among African-American listeners. In 2008, faith-oriented group owner Salem Communications converted six of its stations to their Spanish-language Radio Luz ("Radio Light") format to meet changing demographics.

See also: Contemporary Christian Music Format; Evangelists/Evangelical Radio; National Religious Broadcasters; Religion on Radio

Further Reading

Collins, Lisa, "Urban Radio Sees the Light," *Billboard Magazine* (2 August 1997).
Schwirtz, Mira, "No Longer up in the Air," *Media Week* (11 May 1998).

DON RODNEY VAUGHAN,
2009 REVISIONS BY CARY O'DELL

GRAND OLE OPRY
Country Music Variety Program

As the 20th century ended, the *Grand Ole Opry* was the most famous and longest-running live radio broadcast still on the air. A traditional radio barn dance, originating on WSM radio from Nashville, Tennessee, the *Opry* has reached homes across the eastern half of the United States. Although it started as a local show and later reverted to that status, through the 1940s and most of the 1950s the *Grand Ole Opry* was a staple on Saturday nights on the National Broadcasting Company (NBC). To most Americans, the *Opry* defined what a radio barn dance was and is. Because of its triumph over all major rivals, exemplified by the centralization of the country music industry in Nashville, the *Grand Ole Opry* occupies an important place in both radio and recording industry history.

The *Grand Ole Opry* made its debut on 28 November 1925 on WSM-AM's Studio B to an audience of 200 people. C.A. Craig, one of the founders of the National Accident Insurance Company of Nashville, Tennessee, owned a radio station during the early 1920s (later called WSM for "We Shield Millions"); in 1925 he hired George D. Hay away from WLS-AM in Chicago to develop a barn dance show for WSM, as Hay had done for WLS with the *National Barn Dance.* Hay began in November 1925, and within a month the new show was a two-hour-long Saturday night staple.

By 1927, as an NBC affiliate, this two-hour local country hoedown followed the network broadcast of the National Symphony Orchestra, which aired Saturday nights from 8 to 9 P.M. One night, probably 8 December 1928, Hay reportedly stated, "For the past hour you have heard music largely taken from grand opera; now we will present the *Grand Ole Opry.*" True or not, the title is now world famous.

Regional success can be measured by the show's need within a few years to move to a new studio, Studio C, which held 500 persons; later, after a series of temporary moves, the show made its permanent home in the 2,000-seat Ryman Auditorium at Fourth and Broadway in downtown Nashville in 1943. The show remained at that location throughout its network radio days and then, in 1974, moved to a new auditorium as part of the opening of the Opryland theme park in suburban Nashville.

The show had started informally as what scholar Charles Wolfe calls "a good natured riot." But although the program seems informal, getting on was always a struggle for the new artist, and many argued that it became more and more commercialized. By the 1930s, "hillbilly" stars had been developed, and some dead singers were immortalized. The music was spread thanks to the diffusion and growth of the population, and even greater stars emerged during the post-World War II era. The Opry management, particularly James Denny, took advantage of this interest, and the network (and many clear channel stations) carrying *Grand Ole Opry* enabled the broadcast to become one of the most popular radio programs in the country. Denny and his colleagues also worked with leading record labels to make Nashville the center of the "country and western" universe.

The *National Barn Dance*, from Chicago's WLS, was already an NBC fixture when a half-hour segment of the *Grand Ole Opry* was added to a number of NBC's regional broadcasts, including 26 stations in the Tennessee area. In 1939 NBC began to carry the *Opry* regularly on a regional basis. Two years later the *Opry* went out all across the NBC network.

The coming of TV and format country radio signaled the end of the barn dance radio show. Yet WSM-AM stuck with the *Grand Ole Opry*, and Nashville became not just one center for the making of country music but the leading one. Indeed, many of the early Nashville recordings were done in WSM studios, until Owen Bradley and others began to fashion "Music Row" several miles west of the Ryman Auditorium. And by the time that Bradley at Decca and Chet Atkins at the Radio Corporation of America (RCA) began to remake "hillbilly" music into crossover country music with stars such as Hank Williams and Patsy Cline, the "Athens of the South" had become "Music City."

See also: Country Music Format; *National Barn Dance*; WSM

Cast

Announcers

George Dewey Hay, Grant Turner

Comedienne

Cousin Minnie Pearl

Singers (partial listing)

Roy Acuff, Hank Williams, Bill Monroe, Patsy Cline, Kitty Wells, Red Foley, George Morgan, Ernest Tubb, Grandpa Jones, DeFord Bailey, Uncle Dave Macon, Eddy Arnold, Loretta Lynn, Hank Snow, Little Jimmy Dickens, Lorrie Morgan, Trisha Yearwood, Vince Gill, Garth Brooks, Emmylou Harris, Ricky Skaggs

Programming History

WSM (and other local Tennessee stations at various times)	1925–present
NBC	1939–57

Further Reading

Eiland, William U., *Nashville's Mother Church: The History of the Ryman Auditorium*, Nashville, Tennessee: Opryland USA, 1992.

Hagan, Chet, *Grand Ole Opry*, New York: Holt, 1989.

Hickerson, Jay, *The Ultimate History of Network Radio Programming and Guide to All Circulating Shows*, Hamden, Connecticut: Hickerson, 1992; 3rd edition, as

The New, Revised, Ultimate History of Network Radio Programming and Guide to All Circulating Shows, 1996.

Kingsbury, Paul, *The Grand Ole Opry History of Country Music: 70 Years of the Songs, the Stars, and the Stories*, New York: Villard Books, 1995.

Malone, Bill C., *Country Music U.S.A.*, Austin: University of Texas Press, 1968; revised edition, 1985.

Wolfe, Charles K., *A Good-Natured Riot: The Birth of the Grand Ole Opry*, Nashville, Tennessee: Country Music Foundation Press and Vanderbilt University Press, 1999.

DOUGLAS GOMERY

GREAT GILDERSLEEVE
Situation Comedy

"Great" is the perfect epithet for the character Throckmorton P. Gildersleeve. First a foil on *Fibber McGee and Molly*, then star of his own program, he was a large man in the tradition of Shakespeare's pleasure-loving Falstaff. Loud but never mean, he began sparring with Fibber, the archetypal windbag, in 1937. His character was honed as the bumptious, explosive Gildersleeve, who typically ended a duel with his exasperated phrase, "You're a harrrd man, McGee!" His very name, coined by script writer Don Quinn, combined dignity (Basil Gildersleeve was a famous Victorian classicist) and inside joke (the actor playing Gildersleeve lived on Throckmorton Place). The character left *McGee*, taking the train from the National Broadcasting Company's (NBC) Wistful Vista to Summerfield on 31 August 1941, thus becoming radio's first successful spinoff. The program would last 16 years, until March 1957. Gildersleeve, or "Gildy" to some, was played by actor Hal Peary to 1950 and by Willard Waterman from 1950 to 1957.

In his new town, Gildy's abrasive personality mellowed as he embraced home, work, and social life. Each contact in Summerville deflated his grandiosity and humanized him. Once he planned to attend a costume ball dressed as an ancestor. He daydreamed about possible relatives—a romantic castaway on a tropical island, a dashing pirate, a Gilded Age tycoon—only to learn that he was descended from Goldslob the Pennsylvania butcher (24 March 1948). His appetites kept housekeeper Birdie Lee Coggins busy. More feisty than most of radio's black domestics, Birdie moderated his pomposity by repeating herself ("You know what I said? That's right! That's what I said"). Birdie often mirrored her employer. Both belonged to fraternal groups (she to "The Mysterious and Bewildering Order of the Daughters of Cleopatra," he to "The Jolly Boys"); both sang well. Her talents and industriousness silently rebuked Gildy's natural sloth. Her chocolate cake won a prize, and when she went on vacation, no-one could prepare a suitable dinner. She also provided a mother surrogate for Gildy's wards, niece Marjorie Forrester and nephew Leroy.

In an era when single-parent families usually implied a widow with children, Gildy was unusual. Like other unmarried guardians (Donald Duck, Sky King), he coped with the younger generation by combining bossiness, wheedling, and exasperation. Marjorie usually abided by his rules, but she began dating a series of boys who fell short of Gildy's expectations. After wedding Bronco Thompson on 10 May 1950 and bearing twins (21 February 1951), she set up her own household next door. Although she dutifully catered to Gildy's whims, double dating with him before the marriage and asking him to babysit after the kids arrived, her in-laws tried his patience. Used to dominating her husband, Mrs. Thompson openly defied Gildy until they bonded on a picnic. But everyone else had become accustomed to their bickering, so they obligingly pretended to spat (22 March 1950).

Leroy gave little promise of accepting maturity: he reacted to his "Unk's" apparently foolish directions with an exasperated "Oh, for corn sakes." Gildy tried patience but often resorted to the ultimate threat, a menacingly drawn-out "Leeeroy." Certainly Leroy needed direction. His academic work would have embarrassed anyone, but it particularly discomfited Gildy, who courted the school principal, Eve Goodwin. Leroy's troubles with bullies, jobs, attractive girls, stolen lumber, and toothaches often defied logical advice, yet they somehow solved themselves.

Gildy seemed to be an unlikely source of practical wisdom. He loitered through his job as water commissioner, sometimes aided by his simple secretary Bessie. His campaign for mayor in 1944 floundered when he lost his temper on a political broadcast. When he discovered that no-one in the city knew him or his job, he hatched a publicity stunt: to dive into the reservoir (23 April 1952). The bungled descent temporarily dampened his quest for recognition. Romance, at any rate, interested him more. Various women with descriptive names like Eve Goodwin and Adeline Fairchild prompted him to buy perfumes and candy from the crusty druggist, Peavey. Gildy should have imitated Peavey's famous tag line, "Well, now, I wouldn't say that," because his amorous crusades never led to the altar. His closest approach, with Leila Ransom, a flirtatious Southern widow, ended when her supposedly dead spouse Beauregard turned out to be alive (27 June 1948).

Gildy's male friends provided enough excitement to compensate for these losses. Judge Horace Hooker, the "old goat" who monitored Gildy's care of Marjorie and Leroy, diminished his ego by staying when Gildy wished to court a lady friend or by demanding vegetarian food when he came for dinner. So did Rumson Bullard, Gildy's wealthy and insulting neighbor, who drove a big car and disdained to invite him to a neighborhood party. The "Jolly Boys"—Peavey, Hooker, Floyd Munson the barber, and police chief Gates—met to gossip and sing. The bonding sometimes frayed, inspiring Chief Gates to plead, "Aw, fellows; let's be Jolly Boys!"

Network politics might have caused disaster, because the original Gildy, Hal Peary, launched his own short-lived Columbia Broadcasting System (CBS) show, *Honest Harold*, in 1950. Luckily, Willard Waterman, a friend of Peary's who often teamed with him on other shows, sounded like him and took over the lead until the show ended in 1957. Both men had fine singing voices and incorporated easy listening songs into the plot.

The two prolonged Gildy's life in movies and television. Peary appeared briefly in four amusing films (*Comin' Round the Mountain*, 1940; *Look Who's Laughing*, 1941; *Country Fair*, 1941; *Unusual Occupations*, 1944) and starred in four others (*The Great Gildersleeve*, 1942; *Gildersleeve's Bad Day*, 1943; *Gildersleeve on Broadway*, 1943; *Gildersleeve's Ghost*, 1944). Waterman was featured in 39 TV episodes (September 1955–September 1956). Radio writers Paul West, John Elliotte, and Andy White followed, sometimes recycling story lines (Gildy's aforementioned dive into the reservoir; his attraction to Bullard's sister from 19 September 1951). However, they overemphasized Gildy's womanizing tendencies for the first 26 programs. Other shows toned down Leroy's mischief, substituted new actors (only three originals remained), and lost a major sponsor. Still, both films and TV communicated some of the great man's foibles and successes familiar to radio fans.

See also: Comedy; *Fibber McGee and Molly*

Cast

Throckmorton P. Gildersleeve	Hal Peary (1941–50), Willard Waterman (1950–57)
Leroy Forrester	Walter Tetley
Marjorie Forrester	Lorene Tuttle (1941–44), Louise Erickson (mid-1940s), Mary Lee Robb (mid-1940s–56)
Judge Horace Hooker	Earle Ross
Birdie Lee Coggins	Lillian Randolph
Mr. Peavey	Richard Legrand, Forrest Lewis
Floyd Munson	Arthur Q. Bryan
Police Chief Gates	Ken Christy
Leila Ransom	Shirley Mitchell
Adeline Fairchild	Una Merkel
Eve Goodwin	Bea Benaderet (1944)
Nurse Kathryn Milford	Cathy Lewis (1950s)
Bashful Ben	Ben Alexander (mid-1940s)
Bronco Thompson	Richard Crenna
Rumson Bullard	Gale Gordon, Jim Backus (1952)
Craig Bullard	Tommy Bernard
Bessie	Pauline Drake, Gloria Holliday
Announcer	Jim Bannon (1941–42), Ken Carpenter (1942–45), John Laing (1945–47), John Wald (1947–49), Jay Stewart (1949–50), Jim Doyle, John Hiestand

Producers/Directors

Cecil Underwood, Frank Pittman, Fran Van Hartesveldt, Virgil Reimer, and Karl Gruener

Programming History

NBC   1941–57

Further Reading

Harmon, Jim, *The Great Radio Comedians*, Garden City, New York: Doubleday, 1970.
"Helpful Hints to Husbands," *Tune In* 4 (July 1946).
Salomonson, Terry, *The Great Gildersleeve: A Radio Broadcast Log of the Comedy Program*, Howell, Michigan: Salomonson, 1997.
Stumpf, Charles, and Ben Ohmart, *The Great Gildersleeve*, Boalsburg, Pennsylvania: BearManor Media, 2002.
Thomsen, Elizabeth B., *The Great Gildersleeve*, www.ethomsen.com/gildy
"Throckmorton P.," *Newsweek* (13 December 1943).

JAMES A. FREEMAN

GREEN HORNET
Juvenile Drama Series

Joining a number of American fictional superheroes already entertaining the large radio audience from the late 1930s through the war and into the 1950s,

The Green Hornet debuted over Detroit station WXYZ on 31 January 1936. The series began simply as *The Hornet* (the descriptive color was added later in order to copyright the title, according to radio historian Jim Harmon). Another brainchild of Detroit station operator George W. Trendle, who also created *The Lone Ranger*, the two half-hour action dramas shared more than classical music themes (for which no copyright fees needed to be paid) and the same creator. In this case, the famous sound of a buzzing hornet was made by a musical instrument called the theremin, and the music was Rimsky-Korsakov's "The Flight of the Bumblebee."

Russo (2001) reports that the first 260 episodes of the series lacked individual titles (they were simply numbered), but those broadcast after 9 August 1938 carried episode names as well. Most if not all of the early scripts (perhaps the first five years) were written by Fran Striker (who also authored *The Lone Ranger*), but they increasingly became a WXYZ team effort for the remainder of the 16-year run. At different times the half-hour drama appeared weekly or twice-weekly.

The protagonist was Britt Reid (also the Green Hornet), who served as a wealthy young newspaper publisher of *The Daily Sentinel* during the day and transformed into evil's arch enemy after sunset. The Green Hornet's mission, according to the opening narration, was to protect us (the law-abiding American citizen) from those "who sought to destroy our way of life." If one listened carefully, one of the series' conceits was made clear—the familial connection of the Green Hornet with his great uncle, the Lone Ranger. References to the earlier legendary figure were abundant. Young Reid was seen as carrying on the family tradition of fighting for justice and the American way. Against the backdrop of an uncertain world, the Green Hornet reassured listeners that the forces of good would always triumph over the forces of darkness. Only three characters knew that Reid was also the Hornet—his father (who appeared rarely), his secretary (who never lets on until late in the series), and Kato.

Kato served as the Green Hornet's faithful valet and partner in crime fighting. Kato also drove the Hornet's famous high-speed car, Black Beauty, during countless breathtaking chases in pursuit of the bad guys. A famous radio legend has it that Kato, who had been described for five years as Japanese, became a Filipino overnight after the 1941 Pearl Harbor attack. Harmon and other sources say, however, that Kato had been described as a Filipino of Japanese ancestry well before the

war began. The role partially reflected a continuing American fascination with things oriental.

Unlike most crime fighters, the Green Hornet did not use lethal weaponry; his gun fired a knockout gas instead of bullets. And in contrast with most other radio superheroes, the Green Hornet often assumed a bad guy persona in order to capture criminals, and this frequently confused law enforcement officials, richly adding to the plotline. He and Kato would always escape the crime scene just before law enforcement officers (and reporters from Reid's own paper) arrived. The final scene would usually feature a newspaper boy hawking the latest headlines of the Hornet's ventures as featured in *The Daily Sentinel*, noting that the Hornet was "still at large" and being sought by police. They never did catch him.

Like other superhero programs of the day, *The Green Hornet* adventure series had its genesis in the pulp detective novels of the 1920s, and the characters also appeared in comic books during and well after the radio broadcasts. The series was resurrected for one season on ABC television in the mid-1960s, riding on the coattails of the tremendously popular *Batman* series.

See also: Lone Ranger; WXYZ

Cast

Britt Reid	Al Hodge (to 1943);
(The Green Hornet)	Donovan Faust (1943); Bob Hall (1944–51); Jack McCarthy (1951–52)
Kato	Tokutaro Hayashi, Rollon Parker, Michael Tolan
Lenore Casey Case	Leonore Allman
Michael Axford	Jim Irwin (to 1938), Gil Shea
Ed Lowery	Jack Petruzzi
Dan Reid	John Todd
Newsboy	Rollon Parker

Announcers

Charles Woods, Mike Wallace, Fielden Farrington, Bob Hite, Hal Neal

Director

James Jewell

Writer

Fran Striker and several others

Programming History

WXYZ, Detroit	January 1936–April 1938
Mutual	April 1938–November 1939
Blue Network/ABC	November 1939–December 1952
ABC (Television)	September 1966–July 1967

Further Reading

Bickel, Mary, *George W. Trendle*, New York: Exposition, 1973.
Harmon, Jim, "From the Studios of WXYZ-III *(The Green Hornet)*" in *The Great Radio Heroes*, Garden City, New York: Doubleday, 1967; revised edition, Jefferson, North Carolina: McFarland, 2001.
Osgood, Dick, *WYXIE Wonderland: An Unauthorized 50-Year Diary of WXYZ Detroit*, Bowling Green, Ohio: Bowling Green University Popular Press, 1981.
Russo, Alexander, "A Dark(ened) Figure on the Airwaves: Race, Nation, and *The Green Hornet*" in *Radio Reader: Essays in the Cultural History of Radio*, edited by Michele Hilmes and Jason Loviglio, New York: Routledge, 2001.
Striker, Fran, Jr., *His Typewriter Grew Spurs: A Biography of Fran Striker—Writer*, Lansdale, Pennsylvania: Questco, 1983.
Van Hise, James, *The Green Hornet Book*, Las Vegas, Nevada: Pioneer, 1989.

MICHAEL C. KEITH AND CHRISTOPHER H. STERLING

GROUND WAVE

A ground wave is a radio signal that propagates along the surface of the earth. It is one of two basic types of AM signal propagation, the other being the sky wave, which travels skyward from the transmitting antenna and then may be refracted back toward earth by the atmosphere. The behavioral characteristics of both types of wave are important both to frequency allocation and to the nature of various radio services.

The term *ground wave* includes three different types of waves: surface waves, direct waves, and ground-reflected waves. Surface waves travel directly along the surface of the earth, following terrain features such as hills and valleys. Direct waves follow a "line-of-sight" path directly from the transmitting antenna to the receiving antenna, and ground-reflected waves actually bounce off the surface of the earth.

Both ground-wave and sky-wave signals can be used to provide radio communication. The distance each type of signal can travel is determined by a number of factors, among them frequency, power, atmospheric conditions, time, and—in the case of ground waves—terrain and soil conductivity.

The principal determinant of which type of signal provides the communication is transmitting frequency. At very low frequencies (below 300 kHz), signal propagation takes place mostly by surface ground waves, which at these frequencies may provide a reliable signal for several thousand miles. At medium frequencies (300 kHz to 3 MHz), surface ground waves may propagate hundreds of miles, and sky waves may travel thousands of miles. At high frequencies (3 to 30 MHz), sky waves provide the principal means of signal propagation, and they may provide usable signals for many thousands of miles. At very high frequencies (30 MHz and above), propagation is largely by ground-reflected and direct ground waves, although at these frequencies the waves generally travel less than 100 miles.

The standard broadcast (AM) band (535–1705 kHz) is a medium-frequency band and is thus characterized by both ground-wave and sky-wave signals. During the day, AM propagation takes place mainly by ground-wave signals; sky-wave signals generally travel through the atmosphere and into space. However, during night-time hours, changes in a portion of the ionosphere known as the Kennelly-Heavyside layer cause the sky waves to be reflected back toward the earth's surface. These refracted sky waves can then provide usable service over many hundreds—or even thousands—of miles, although sky waves are generally more susceptible to interference and fading than are ground waves. A certain amount of AM sky-wave propagation also takes place in the hours immediately before sunset and immediately after sunrise. In contrast, propagation in the FM band (88–108 MHz) takes place by line-of-sight or near-line-of-sight direct and ground-reflected ground waves only.

The complexities of signal propagation in the AM band have presented significant challenges for the allocation of frequencies since the inception of broadcasting in the 1920s. Primary among these, of course, is the presence of both ground-wave and sky-wave signals at various times of the day. The Federal Communications Commission (FCC) has established three service area categories for AM stations: (1) primary service area, in which the ground-wave signal is not subject to objectionable interference or fading; (2) intermittent service area, in which the ground-wave signal may be subject to some interference or fading; and (3) secondary service area, in which the sky-wave signal is not subject to objectionable interference.

Another significant factor is that AM signals—both ground-wave and sky-wave—can cause objectionable interference over a much wider area than that for which they can provide usable service. For example, although a given station may not be able to provide a listenable signal more than 50 miles from its transmitter, that station's signal can still create objectionable interference to other stations on the same frequency over a much wider area. Signals in the FM band do not create this type of wide-area interference, and thus FM stations can be placed geographically closer together on the same frequency.

Perhaps the best illustration of the problems of allocation in the AM band is the dispute over clear channel stations, which began in the 1930s and was not completely resolved until 1980. Clear channel stations were originally created to provide wide-area service to rural audiences through their vast secondary service areas; other stations that were assigned to clear channel frequencies had to sign off at sunset in order to avoid interfering with the dominant stations' sky-wave signals. Clear channel stations sought to maintain and enhance their status by seeking power increases and the maintenance of their clear night-time frequencies. Other classes of stations called for the "breakdown" of clear channels by adding more stations to clear frequencies and by allowing daytime-only stations to broadcast full-time. At the heart of this dispute was an engineering argument over the best way to provide radio service to isolated areas: Clear channel stations maintained that the only way to provide effective rural service was by increasing the power of clear channel stations so that their secondary service areas would expand. On the other hand, other classes of stations called for more stations, located in close geographic proximity to the isolated rural areas, to provide ground-wave service to those areas.

Ultimately, the FCC decided to assign additional full-time stations to use clear channel frequencies, but the FCC protected a substantial portion of the clear channel stations' existing secondary service areas (a roughly 700- to 750-mile radius). Only clear channel stations (now called "Class A" stations) receive protection from interference in their secondary service areas.

The characteristics of ground waves and sky waves are in many cases the determining factors in the purposes for which radio services at various frequencies are used. AM broadcast service can provide reliable ground-wave communication at all times of the day and somewhat less reliable sky-wave communication at night. FM broadcast service can provide reliable line-of-sight service over shorter distances, with less blanketing of interference. Broadcasters in high-frequency bands (shortwave) can provide international sky-wave service.

See also: AM Radio; Antenna; Clear Channel Stations; DXers/DXing; Federal Communications Commission; FM Radio; Frequency Allocation; Shortwave Radio

Further Reading

Federal Communications Commission, *Radio Broadcast Services*, part 73, 47 CFR 73 (2001).
Foust, James C., *Big Voices of the Air: The Battle over Clear Channel Radio*, Ames: Iowa State University Press, 2000.
Jordan, Edward C., editor, *Reference Data for Engineers: Radio, Electronics, Computer, and Communications*, Indianapolis, Indiana: Sams, 1985; 7th edition, 1999.
Orr, William Ittner, *Radio Handbook*, Indianapolis, Indiana: Sams, 1972; 23rd edition, 1992.
Smith, Albert A., Jr., *Radio Frequency Principles and Applications: The Generation, Propagation, and Reception of Signals and Noise*, New York: IEEE Press, 1998.

JAMES C. FOUST

GROUP W
Westinghouse Radio Stations

Westinghouse Broadcasting (Group W after 1963) remained active in radio broadcasting longer than any other company—beginning with the initial airing of Pittsburgh's KDKA in November 1920 and lasting into the late 1990s. Thanks to constant retelling of the KDKA story, the earliest years of Westinghouse Broadcasting are well known, but throughout the history of broadcasting the company was an important owner of both radio and later television stations, eventually merging into the once-independent Columbia Broadcasting System (CBS) network.

Getting into Radio (to 1931)

A Westinghouse engineer, Frank Conrad, had been experimenting with wireless for a number of years, and in 1919–20 he operated amateur station 8XK, playing recorded music one or two nights a week. A September 1920 newspaper advertisement by a local department store seeking to sell receivers to people who wanted to hear Conrad's broadcasts caught the eye of Harry Phillips Davis, a Westinghouse vice president in charge of radio work. Davis perceived that making receivers for a possible new radio service could be the answer to Westinghouse's predicament. He urged Conrad to develop his hobby station into something bigger, and the inauguration of station KDKA on 2 November 1920 was the result.

The success of that initial operation led Davis to the development of a second station, WJZ, at the company meter plant in Newark, New Jersey, in September 1921 (the station was sold to the Radio Corporation of America [RCA] a year later). In the same month, station WBZ took to the air in Springfield, Massachusetts, followed by station KYW in Chicago in December and by WBZA in Boston in 1924. These pioneering outlets made Westinghouse an important early station operator that pioneered many types of program service.

Westinghouse stations were initially located at the factories, which meant that early performers had to learn to entertain in a room filled with electronic equipment, with only an engineer as their audience. Ultimately, the studios were moved to more aesthetically pleasing locations, such as hotels or office buildings.

Experimenting with the potential of shortwave technology, Westinghouse placed KFKX on the air in Hastings, Nebraska, in 1923 to make KDKA's signal more widely available. Another experimental shortwave station, W8XK, was established in Pittsburgh and was soon broadcasting 18 hours per day including a "far north" service to the Arctic. It was joined in 1930 by yet a third station, W1XAZ, in East Springfield, Massachusetts. By the late 1920s, Westinghouse was also pioneering in television research.

Evans Years (1931–55)

On Davis' death in 1931, Walter Evans became the next Westinghouse radio chief. He had joined the company as chief of operations in 1929 and would serve for more than two decades. Evans took a different approach to managing the company's stations and in 1933 signed a contract with the National Broadcasting Company (NBC) network to manage them all, including provision of all local and national programs selling advertising time. The agreement lasted until 1940, when it ended as part of the Federal Communications Commission's (FCC) investigation of national networks, and Westinghouse took over day-to-day operations itself.

Westinghouse operations expanded in the prewar years. Station KYW was moved from Chicago to Philadelphia in late 1934 as part of a deal with the FCC to provide service in underserved areas. Two years later, Westinghouse purchased its first station (it had built its previous operations), WOWO in Fort Wayne, Indiana, along with WGL in the same city, both of which were licensed to a new entity, Westinghouse Radio Stations (WRS). In 1940, WRS took control of all Westinghouse stations, separating the broadcast operations from other company functions.

Westinghouse shortwave (international) stations consolidated operations in Pittsburgh (8XS, which became WPIT in 1939 but closed a year later) and Boston (WIXT, which became WBOS). Westinghouse's international broadcasting was a multilingual operation that by late 1941 was providing 12 hours of programming a day: five hours to Europe and seven to Latin America. Government programs expanded that total to 16 hours just a few months later. Early in 1942, the Boston station was taken over by the government's Office of War Information.

Westinghouse was an early player in FM radio: by 1943 the company owned five FM stations in cities where it also operated AM outlets. Original programming was provided on those FM facilities, but they had all reverted to simulcasting by the end of 1948. That same year, Westinghouse placed its first television station, WBZ-TV in Boston, on the air. As the operation continued to grow, the broadcast subsidiary's headquarters moved several times, finally ending up in New York in 1953, when it became known as Westinghouse Broadcasting Company (WBC), in part because of the addition of television.

McGannon Years (1955–81)

The man who served longest as head of the Westinghouse stations was Donald H. McGannon, who ran the operation from 1955 (after a few interim leaders) until 1981. McGannon soon earned a reputation as a man concerned about public service and program quality as well as profit. He brought Westinghouse back to Chicago with the 1956 purchase of WIND for $5.3 million—at that point the highest price paid for a station. He also began a Washington news bureau to serve his stations in 1957. That same year WBC initiated an arts and classical music format from 4 P.M. to midnight on the four FM stations it still owned. But FM was then a weak service, and by 1970 Westinghouse was down to just two FM outlets, one in Boston and the other in Philadelphia, both programming classical music and suffering from a lack of promotion or advertising.

McGannon faced three serious policy crises early in his tenure. The first concerned Philadelphia's KYW AM and TV. Under at least an implied threat of losing NBC network affiliations for its Philadelphia and Boston television stations, Westinghouse agreed to "trade" its Philadelphia radio and television stations (KYW) for NBC outlets in smaller Cleveland in 1955. Over the next decade various business, FCC, and Congressional investigations brought to light the network threats that had created the deal, and it was undone in 1965, with the KYW stations returning to Philadelphia.

Two other problems briefly threatened Westinghouse licenses. Its Cleveland and Boston radio stations were implicated in the national payola scandal of the late 1950s, and several disc jockeys were fired. Their activities figured in widely covered Congressional investigations. In 1961 antitrust price-fixing convictions against Westinghouse threatened the company's ownership of broadcast stations. Because of the independence of WBC from the parent manufacturing company, its licenses were renewed after several months of threatened FCC hearings. In mid-1963, WBC was renamed Group W.

Because the Westinghouse stations were situated in major cities, they produced sufficient revenue to allow for further acquisitions. In 1962, for example, Westinghouse shut down WBZA in Springfield (which had mainly been simulcasting the much more successful WBZ in Boston for years), making it possible to buy another station, KFWB in Los Angeles, and by 1965 was offering an all-news format on WINS in New York. By the early 1960s, Westinghouse had begun using the term "Group W" to make its owned radio and TV stations more memorable.

A contemporary move was the successful implementation of all-news operations at three major-market radio stations. The conversion began with station WINS in New York, purchased in 1962, which suffered from a weak rock music format. Likewise, KYW had returned to Philadelphia to follow a weak decade of NBC station operation in its place. Westinghouse stations became known for a commitment to news and public affairs (Group W had operated its own news bureau in Washington, D.C., since 1957). All-news operations began KYW and WINS in 1965. KFWB in Los Angeles was purchased in 1966, and two years later it was also converted from rock music to an all-news format. Although not first with the format, Group W was the first to make it a lasting success in major markets.

Only toward the end of McGannon's tenure as Group W chief did the company begin to reconsider FM radio, which by 1980 was dominating national radio listening for the first time. That year Group W purchased two major-market Texas FM stations, KOAX (FM) in Dallas, which soon was renamed KQZY (FM), and KODA-FM in Houston. But although there were adjustments in station lineup, Group W's overall size and contribution to the Westinghouse bottom line (roughly 15–20 percent of annual revenues) remained remarkably stable.

Final Decades (1981–2000)

On McGannon's retirement, Daniel L. Ritchie became Group W's leader and served into the late 1980s, to be succeeded in turn by Burton B. Staniar. The expansion into FM continued with the purchase of KJQY (FM) in San Diego and KOSI (FM) in Denver in 1981. A San Antonio FM station, KQXT, was purchased in 1984; KMEO AM and FM in Phoenix were bought a year later; and WNEW-FM in New York was added to the Group W stable in 1989. Although some outlets were spun off, the overall effect was to slowly grow the company—and to increase the proportion of FM to AM stations.

Group W switched AM outlets in Chicago as well. In the aftermath of Martin Luther King, Jr.'s 1968 assassination, WIND suspended popular on-air figure Howard Miller, whose statements about race and the police were becoming more strident. A breach of contract suit was settled out of court, but the station lost audience steadily for years thereafter and was sold in 1985 to a Spanish-language broadcaster. Three years later, Group W purchased WMAQ, the one-time NBC outlet, thus resuming a role in Chicago radio.

In the late 1990s, Group W underwent a series of mergers and acquisitions that changed the face of the company and eventually caused it to disappear into other entities. The process began with the 1995 purchase by Westinghouse Electric of the weakened CBS network from Lawrence Tisch for $5.4 billion dollars. The deal needed and received several cross-ownership waivers from the FCC, as the radio and television stations of Group W and the network were located in many of the same cities. The new entity controlled 39 radio stations, worth $1.4–1.7 billion, and became the largest group owner in terms of revenues. In buying CBS, Westinghouse purchased a radio division that provided two services Westinghouse had been paying other companies to provide—network news and national sales representation.

In late 1996 CBS/Westinghouse merged with Infinity Broadcasting, combining 83 stations under the CBS Radio Group name, for a time the largest single ownership block in the industry. Over the next couple of years, Westinghouse sold off its traditional manufacturing base (power systems, which had been losing money, and electronic and environmental systems) and its original name to concentrate on the development of its radio and television holdings under the CBS name. The Group W trademark was briefly retained to identify technical support for television distribution and sports marketing, and as owner of record of six AM radio stations, the original KDKA (Pittsburgh), WBZ (Boston), and KYW (Philadelphia), as well as the later-acquired outlets WNEW (New York), WMAQ (Chicago), and KTWV (Houston).

By the turn of the 21st century, however, the radio group was operating under the Infinity name and the one-time Westinghouse (or Group W) stations were merely one integrated part of what had become the country's third-largest group owner of radio stations.

See also: Columbia Broadcasting System; FM Radio; KDKA; KYW; National Broadcasting Company; Network Monopoly Probe; Radio Corporation of America; Westinghouse; WBZ; WINS; WMAQ; WNEW

Further Reading

Broadcasting Yearbook (1935).

Davis, H.P., "The Early History of Broadcasting in the United States," in *The Radio Industry: The Story of Its Development*, Chicago and New York: Shaw, and London: Shaw Limited, 1928; reprint, New York: Arno Press, 1974.

Douglas, George H., *The Early Days of Radio Broadcasting*, Jefferson, North Carolina: McFarland, 1987.

Westinghouse Electric Corporation, *The History of Radio Broadcasting and KDKA*, East Pittsburgh, Pennsylvania: Westinghouse Electric Corporation, 1940.

MARY E. BEADLE, DONNA L. HALPER,
AND CHRISTOPHER H. STERLING

GUNSMOKE
Western Series

Gunsmoke, a western on the CBS Radio Network, was introduced at a time when most radio drama was disappearing. It not only lasted nearly a decade but also spawned television's longest-running drama series. *Gunsmoke*'s devoted fans, who have praised its historical accuracy and realism, would likely attribute the program's longevity to its brilliant writing and acting. Others would say, "it's just a good story."

The stories on *Gunsmoke* provided the groundwork for the so-called adult western, a dominant TV genre for nearly 20 years. There were many radio westerns before *Gunsmoke*, particularly as daytime serials or evening programs, but most of them, such as the even longer-running *Lone Ranger*, were aimed primarily at a young audience.

Origins

Gunsmoke was the result of a collaboration between several writers and producers (all "urban oriented,"

according to William N. Robeson), including John Meston and producer Norman Macdonnell, who worked together at CBS from 1947 on *Escape* and other radio dramas. Robeson, who created *Escape*, admitted that that program was "pretty darned close to *Suspense*." Macdonnell was an assistant director with Robeson, and William Conrad was the announcer on *Escape*. With writer John Meston, several experimental western stories were tried between 1947 and 1950. In 1949 the team also produced two pilots of what they conceived as an "adult western" with a hero named Mark Dillon.

The first *Gunsmoke* program came about when another program was abruptly canceled. Norman Macdonnell and writer Walter Brown Newman used elements from several of Macdonnell's earlier western stories to create "Billy the Kid," the first episode, which ran on 26 April 1952. Although unforeseen at the time, after "Billy the Kid" there would be 412 more episodes of *Gunsmoke*; the final show aired 18 June 1961.

Raymond Burr and Robert Stack (both of whom later became famous TV actors) were considered for the lead role, but at the last moment the job went to William Conrad. While he was the announcer on *Escape* and a veteran radio actor (he would also later star in several TV series), Conrad had just finished the movie *The Killers* and was considered a "heavy." In the pilot, the hero had to narrate much of the story in voice-over. Chester, his assistant, appeared in the first episode, but the part quickly grew larger, and the important characters of Doc and Miss Kitty evolved. From the first show to the last, *Gunsmoke* kept its cast of William Conrad as Marshal Matt Dillon, Georgia Ellis as Kitty Russell, Howard McNear as Doctor Charles Adams, and Parley Baer as Chester Wesley Proudfoot. Although the relations between the four characters held the program together, it was the deep, booming voice of Conrad that provided the program's unmistakable signature. In addition to these regulars, veteran radio actors appeared in episode after episode.

Among fans of radio drama, *Gunsmoke* is considered the best western ever made. The series was marked by high-caliber writing and used only a score of authors during its entire run. Meston wrote 183 stories, and there were three years in which he wrote more than 45 episodes per year. His scripts often concerned the difficulties of frontier life, particularly for women.

After a light Christmas-time show in 1952, Meston wrote "The Cabin," broadcast on 27 December, to assure the audience that *Gunsmoke* had not "gone soft." The episode concerned a young woman named Belle who had been raped. By the end of the program the marshal has killed the men who raped her (though this is not acted out explicitly) and is asked by the woman if he is married. "Too chancy," he replies. Matt tells Belle, "Don't let all this make you bitter, there are lot of good men in the world," and she replies, "So they say." As he heads back to Dodge, Matt ends by noting that the blizzard was gone but it was still bitter cold, "like riding through a vast tomb."

Most of the episodes end violently and tragically, usually with Matt being forced to kill someone. Meston said that violence was rampant in the Old West; there was no medicine, no sanitation, no heat, just sand, little water, and not much food. Meston's view may not be entirely accurate as history, but his shows appealed to an audience raised on the myths of the American West. Meston's scripts were also marked by their mostly factual treatment of Native Americans (called Indians in the shows). The stories often noted that Indians intermarried with whites, suffered as the buffalo were wiped out, were forced into virtual concentration camps, and that federal policy toward the Native Americans was to wipe them out. In "Sunday Supplement" (24 June 1956), a citizen of Dodge says to Matt, "Marshal, you're not standing up for a redskin are you?" Of course he was.

The 19 July 1954 episode, "The Queue," by Meston, is about a Chinese man who has come to Dodge. When others ridicule him and make nasty remarks about foreigners, Matt says, "Except for the Indians we're all foreigners here." Matt learns that the man speaks good English but feigns a Chinese accent because he knows it is expected of him. Kitty also talks of "darn few jobs that a woman couldn't do [she pauses] anywhere." Later the Chinese man is murdered (choked to death by his own pig tail, which is cut off) and robbed of a small box he always carries. Matt tracks down and kills the robbers. The box contains a faded paper indicating that the Chinese man had been honored for his service in the Army of the Potomac in the Civil War, and thus was awarded citizenship. Marshal Dillon suggests that the man be buried at a nearby army fort, whereas they only "plant" the two robbers he has just killed in "Boot Hill." The story was also produced as a first-season TV episode on 3 December 1955.

Although Meston was the principal writer, there were also many scripts by Les Crutchfield and Katherine Hite (Hite was one of the first women writers to work regularly on a western). The program

frequently used three technicians creating sound effects. The sound patterns and music were often used to carry a program when the dialogue was sparse. Macdonnell noted that people who are working just don't talk all the time.

Within two years of its start, the program was a big hit for radio, which was losing programs, stars, and especially advertisers to television. *Gunsmoke* was sponsored by a cigarette company, and soon several other radio westerns appeared on the air. By 1957, however, most weeks' shows had no sponsor but only public service announcements and promotions for other CBS programs, and Meston was spending most of his time writing for the television version. A number of the early radio episodes were adapted for the TV program, which began on 10 September 1955. When it finished its run 20 years later, the TV series boasted 233 half-hour and 402 one-hour episodes. Later four made-for-TV movies were also produced. The final radio broadcast—a repeat—aired in June 1961 as the CBS announcer said matter-of-factly, "This concludes the series of *Gunsmoke*."

See also: Westerns

Cast

Marshal Matt Dillon	William Conrad
Miss Kitty	Georgia Ellis
Doctor Charles Adams	Howard McNear
Chester Wesley Proudfoot	Parley Baer

Producer

Norman Macdonnell

Programming History

CBS   1952–61

Further Reading

Barabas, SuzAnne, and Gabor Barabas, *Gunsmoke: A Complete History and Analysis of the Legendary Broadcast Series with a Comprehensive Episode-by-Episode Guide to Both the Radio and Television Programs*, Jefferson, North Carolina: McFarland, 1990.
Hickman, John, producer, "The Story of Gunsmoke," Washington, D.C.: WAMU, 1976 (an audio history with interviews and excerpts of about five hours, which is available for purchase in a number of old radio and cassette catalogs).

LAWRENCE W. LICHTY

H

HAM RADIO
Hobbyist or Amateur Radio Operators

The Federal Communications Commission (FCC) defines amateur radio operators as "qualified persons of any age who are interested in radio technique solely with a personal aim and without pecuniary interest." Amateur operators are an international phenomenon. Since 1925, the International Amateur Radio Union (IARU) has championed their cause with governments around the world. In the United States, an early amateur radio pioneer named Hiram Percy Maxim organized the American Radio Relay League (ARRL) in 1914. The ARRL is a member of the IARU. There are currently more than 700,000 licensed amateur stations in the United States alone.

Since their beginnings in the early 1900s, amateur radio enthusiasts have also been known as "ham" radio operators. Historians are unsure of how the name came into common usage, but there is strong evidence that the term was bestowed by commercial telegraphers, who considered amateurs to be "ham-fisted"—that is, they sent Morse code very poorly. For many years, operators were also known in official circles as "Citizen Operators"—not to be confused with today's Citizens Band (CB) radio operators.

Although he clearly had commercial interests in mind, the first amateur radio operator was arguably Guglielmo Marconi himself. Until about 1908, all radio experimenters hoped to capitalize on wireless communication. When Marconi successfully sent a wireless signal across the Atlantic in 1901, he used equipment of the same type used by radio hobbyists.

Origins

The history of amateur radio is in essence the history of all wireless communication. Amateurs developed many of the processes key to electronic communication and refined others. In 1909, when the first radio clubs were formed, radio frequency energy was generated by allowing a spark to jump across a wide gap. The frequencies used at the time were in the range of today's commercial AM broadcast band and below (300–6,000 m).

With the onset of U.S. participation in World War I in early 1917, amateurs in the United States were ordered to dismantle their facilities for the duration of the conflict. Technical developments during the war included the replacement of spark-gap transmission with continuous-wave (vacuum-tube powered) transmission. The bandwidth of such emissions is much narrower, is not as prone to interference, and allows clear voice operation. The celebrated November 1920 broadcasts of pioneer station KDKA in Pittsburgh, Pennsylvania, began as experimental amateur programs under the call sign 8XK. The radio transmission of the Dempsey-Carpenter boxing match in 1921, another milestone in early radio, was organized by the National Amateur Wireless Association.

During this period, the issue of who controlled the airwaves was very unclear. In 1926 a federal court declared the only existing law, the Radio Act of 1912, to be essentially unenforceable. The

Radio Act of 1927 created the Federal Radio Commission and federal statutes using the word *amateur* for the first time. The Communications Act of 1934 (which later created the Federal Communications Commission) continued many of the FRC's policies and precedents, including licensing of amateurs.

All amateur activity was again suspended when the United States entered World War II in late 1941; amateurs were only allowed back on the air on 15 November 1945. Within those four years, wartime research opened up new communication options. Single sideband (SSB)—a mode of voice transmission in which the carrier and one of the duplicate sidebands are suppressed—was described in *QST* magazine in 1948. (*QST*, defined as a signal meaning "Calling All Radio Amateurs," is the official house organ of the ARRL.) The popularity and advantages of SSB transmissions were well established by 1960. Whereas most amateur equipment was still powered by vacuum tubes, transistor technology was beginning to appear in both commercial and self-built equipment.

Amateur radio has always been attractive not only to the general citizenry, but also to the rich and famous. Howard Hughes was a licensed amateur radio operator. Senator Barry Goldwater (K7UGA/K3UIG) tried to become the first ham in the White House. Heads of state include the late King Hussein of Jordan (JY1), who encouraged amateur radio as a means of providing technical education for the citizens in his country. Noted radio broadcaster Jean Shepherd (K2ORS) was a very active amateur radio operator. The son of President Herbert Hoover was eventually elected as the president of the ARRL. Marlon Brando operated on the amateur bands from his South Sea compound for many years. Owen Garriott (W5LFL) became the first amateur to operate on board a space shuttle in 1983.

Licensing

With the pressure on the U.S. government to cut costs, in 1984 the FCC created the Volunteer Examiner Program. Tests for all classes of amateur licenses (which were once handled by the FCC) are now administered by approved volunteer examiner programs. In 1991 the privileged place of Morse code, long a tradition and requirement for an amateur license, finally yielded to the first code-free amateur radio license. The FCC administers six classes of operator license, each authorizing varying levels of privileges. The higher classes still require knowledge of Morse code.

In the United States, amateur call signs once consisted of the letter "*W*" and a numeral from 1 to 0, followed by two or three alphabetic characters. (The numerals 1 through 9 are used and roughly translate to geographical regions. For example, the ninth call area includes Illinois, Indiana, and Wisconsin. The numeral 0 [zero] is also used-for the tenth call area.) These replaced the earliest call signs, which consisted of only the numeral and the following letters—often the operator's initials. Prior to World War II, the United States agreed to begin all call signs with prefix letters assigned by international agreement. By 1953, all possible W call signs had been issued, and the K prefix came into use. Today, prefixes include combinations of the letters *W* and *K*, followed by other letters in the alphabet as demand requires. The N prefix is also in use, as well as A.

New Directions

In 1961, through the efforts of a group of amateur operators collectively known as Project OSCAR (Orbiting Satellite Carrying Amateur Radio), thousands of amateur operators around the world listened in on the 50-mW Morse code beacon of OSCAR I as it sent its "HI" message. The relative speed of the code transmitted rudimentary telemetry and told of the condition of the satellite.

The OSCAR satellite rode into space in place of "ballast" on a regularly scheduled rocket launch. Current OSCAR satellites rival early commercial communication satellites (such as Telstar and others) in that they have the capability to relay both voice and data transmissions over half the planet simultaneously. OSCAR satellite experiments in the 1970s served as a prototype for the Global Positioning Satellite Service. Amateurs have also pioneered communication by bouncing signals off of the Earth's moon, off the tails of comets, and via reflection from the aurora borealis. Schoolchildren participate in direct communication with the space shuttle via amateur radio stations.

Morse code, the basis of all early wireless communication, is a very rudimentary form of digital communication. With an abundance of surplus equipment available after World War II, amateur operators adapted teleprinter systems to work via their stations. Later, radioteletype transmissions switched from the five-bit Baudot code to standard ASCII code.

By the early 1980s, with the interest in computers and the availability of components at hobbyist prices, a group of both Canadian and U.S. amateur operators began experimenting with advanced forms of digital communication. Their efforts would eventually lead to the creation of the AX.25 packet protocol—a wireless version of the X.25 protocol that underpinned much of the data communication through the end of the 20th century. Some OSCAR satellites (known as PACSATs or Packet Satellites) are even capable of relaying packet transmissions. Amateurs also experiment with spread-spectrum technologies. This system spreads the information in a transmitted signal over a wide frequency range. Although it is not an efficient use of radio spectrum, its attraction is that it can coexist with narrowband signals using the same frequency range. To narrowband users, the spread spectrum signal appears only as a slight increase in noise level.

The Future

In spite of dire predictions during the 1980s that amateur radio was dying, the number of amateurs in the United States alone by the end of the 1990s stood at 710,000, nearly triple the number of amateurs in 1970. The code-free license, in combination with the popularity of low-cost very-high-frequency (VHF) and UHF portable transceivers and repeater stations, fueled much of the expansion. Growth of the internet, low-cost cellular phone communication, and other new technologies serve as a formidable detractor to future growth, but many amateurs have learned unique ways to marry the two forms of communication. Amateurs have developed shortwave radios and scanners that can be controlled remotely over the worldwide web. Another group provides a real-time experimental navigational service that locates participating amateurs and displays the results on a graphical web interface. Messages move freely from the internet to amateur satellites to amateur packet repeaters. Amateur radio will likely continue to adapt and endure for many years to come.

See also: Shortwave Radio

Further Reading

The ARRL Handbook for Radio Amateurs, Newington, Connecticut: American Radio Relay League, 79th edition, 2002 (updated annually).
Berg, Jerome S., *On the Short Wave, 1923–45: Broadcast Listening in the Pioneer Days of Radio*, Jefferson, North Carolina: McFarland, 1999.
Carron, L. Peter, *Morse Code: The Essential Language*, Newington, Connecticut: American Radio Relay League, 1986; 2nd edition, 1991.
Davidoff, Martin R., *The Radio Amateur's Satellite Handbook*, Newington, Connecticut: American Radio Relay League, 1998.
DeSoto, Clinton, *Two Hundred Meters and Down: The Story of Amateur Radio*, West Hartford, Connecticut: American Radio Relay League, 1936.
Douglas, Susan J., *Listening In: Radio and the American Imagination*, New York: Times Books, 1999.
Fifty Years of A.R.R.L., Newington, Connecticut: American Radio Relay League, 1965.
Grubbs, Jim, *The Digital Novice*, Springfield, Illinois: QSky, 1986.
Helms, Harry L., *All about Ham Radio*, San Diego, California: HighText Publications, 1992.
Jahnke, Debra, and Katharine A. Fay, editors, *From Spark to Space: A Pictorial Journey Through 75 Years of Amateur Radio*, Newington, Connecticut: American Radio Relay League, 1989.
Laster, Clay, *The Beginner's Handbook of Amateur Radio*, Indianapolis, Indiana: Sams, 1979; 4th edition, New York and London: McGraw-Hill, 2000.

JIM GRUBBS

HATE RADIO
Extremist Views on the Air

The messages of extremists are no strangers to radio. From the medium's inception there have been those who have exploited the airwaves to promote their agendas of prejudice and hatred. Despite the obligation of broadcasters to operate as public trustees, programs featuring blatant contempt and unvarnished loathing for different racial, ethnic, religious, political, and lifestyle groups have long been aired. Malevolent and inhumane attitudes and beliefs have unfortunately comprised the core of thousands of radio broadcasts.

Early Rancor on the Air

Beginning in the early 1920s, a number of radio programs were promoting ideological, philosophical, and political rancor. The first nationally successful (and what many consider one of the most influential) use of the airwaves to spread political and social invective were the broadcasts of a Catholic priest, Father Charles E. Coughlin. Coughlin began his radio career in Detroit in 1926 and moved to the Columbia Broadcasting System (CBS) in 1930, where he established the format and approach that right-wing media personalities over the decades have emulated.

Similar to some televangelists today, Coughlin's approach was to target certain groups in order to obtain the support of others and to garner, through his radio talks, millions of dollars in donations. He railed against Jews, labor unions, immigrants, and racial minorities, stirring and reinforcing resentment and hate against these competitors for jobs and social status in pre-World War II, Depression-ridden America. He called for a nation of Christians who would rule politics and the economy. This type of language anticipated the rhetoric that would be employed by far-right radio personalities of the 1990s. Indeed, Coughlin was the forerunner of the Holocaust-deniers and neo-Nazis of today.

Many people think of Walter Winchell, arguably the best-known radio commentator of the 1930s–1950s era, as a precursor to modern radio's Rush Limbaughs. His radio show, begun in 1932, was ostensibly a gossip program, but it expanded into right-wing political commentary. His shows had a huge, loyal audience, and he could affect national policy and make or break an individual's career with a few seconds of on-air commentary. He spread rumors, set styles, waged feuds, and excoriated some politicians while promoting the programs of others; he articulated the public's moods, fears, and prejudices.

The differences between the so-called left and right radio commentators became more pronounced in the late 1940s, when Senator Joseph R. McCarthy (R-Wisconsin) began to exploit Cold War fears and exercised great influence on American thought and action, throwing fear and obeisance not only into the media industries—principally film, radio, and television—but also into leaders and opinion makers of the country. Almost all commentators either supported McCarthyism or, out of fear of being blacklisted, were afraid to criticize him or his methods.

Most commentators in the pre- through postwar era were similar to Fulton Lewis, Jr., who is considered by some as the predominant right-wing commentator of that time and to whom Rush Limbaugh is often compared. Lewis supported McCarthy's contention that the U.S. government was infiltrated by communists and that secret plots were being hatched by communist secret agents throughout the country. This view helped fuel the later witch-hunts that often resulted in the professional, if not mental and physical, destruction of those accused—nearly always without foundation—of being communist sympathizers or fellow travelers.

After McCarthyistic suppression and punishment were no longer a concern to the media and the counterculture of the 1960s began to emerge, the media reinstated some elements of free speech, including several news and public-affairs shows that dealt with controversial issues, and more talk shows. It was not until after full-service radio networks disappeared in the early 1950s and specialized limited-time networks consisting mostly of music took their place—along with community-targeted narrowcasting, also mostly music, on local stations—that talk show hosts with set opinions emerged in force.

The far right seemed to understand more fully than the middle or the left the power of talk radio and quickly deluged stations with calls and opinions and stimulated a demand for, as some put it, loud-mouthed right-wing talk show hosts. One such host was Joe Pyne, who became one of the most popular talk personalities in the country with glib, biting, and unabashedly opinionated comments. A number of hosts, such as Bob Grant, later became famous for using Pyne's caustic approach. Grant often referred to African-Americans as "savages" and used expletives about other targets freely. Grant attributed his reputation to showbusiness techniques, not bigotry. Ira Blue, who hosted a talk show in San Francisco in the 1960s, openly admitted during his on-air reign that the radio talker succeeds most when he is brazenly opinionated.

As the 1950s and 1960s progressed, many right-wing talk show programs and hosts became more subtle, using twisted logic rather than blatant vituperation to persuade their audiences. Meanwhile, right-wing rancor on talk shows went in two distinct directions during the decades that followed. As the number of stations increased, more on-air opportunities existed for fringe advocators. Ranters and ravers, some affiliated with organizations dedicated to violence, found microphones available to them. At the same time, soft-spoken intellectuals dispensing the same bottom line also had their access.

Millennium Waves of Rancor

The 1990s saw the greatest rise in the use of radio by far-right extremist groups, among them white supremacists, armed militias, survivalists, conspiracy theorists, and neo-Nazis. Many of these groups had effectively used the shortwave radio medium to promote their dark agendas in the 1980s, and they sought to go more mainstream with their messages by utilizing the AM and FM bands in the 1990s. Dozens of broadcast stations around the country gave airtime to organizations and individuals intent on denigrating people of color as well as those with non-Christian religious orientations. The bulk of these stations were smaller AM outlets, many of which were battling for their economic survival in the face of vastly declining audiences and shrinking revenues. Far-right programs were a source of income.

Today, far-right hate groups still promote their ideologies over radio stations, but not to the degree that they did prior to the Oklahoma City federal building bombing in 1995. This tragic extremist deed prompted the president to issue an anti-terrorism bill making it clear that anyone employing the airwaves to promote violence and hatred would be hunted down and prosecuted. Technology, however, provided right-wing radicals with yet another way to propagate their racist and antigovernment views. The internet soon became the new home and the preferred medium for hate groups, which relished the freedom and lack of censorship that cyberspace afforded them.

In 1996 a white supremacist organization calling itself Stormfront launched what is considered the first extremist website. A former grand dragon of the Ku Klux Klan, Don Black, operates the internet site, which also features a link for children—"Stormfront for Kids"—run by his 11-year-old son. Within four years, a nearly incalculable number of radical-right websites, replete with sophisticated graphics and chat rooms, were in full operation, and many claimed thousands of hits each week. Several watchdog groups, among them the Simon Weisenthal Center, the Anti-Defamation League, Political Research Associates, and the Southern Poverty Law Center, reported that many of the same organizations and individuals, once so dependent on the airwaves to get their messages out to the public, now download their proclamations of hatred to thousands of websites, thus relegating radio to a secondary medium for their egregious purposes. One cannot help but note an ironic analogy in this migration of radio users to another medium. However, one suspects that the impact of this conversion will be far less traumatic for radio than the one brought on by the rise of television.

Despite the mass exodus of hate radio to the internet in the 1990s, there existed remnants of it in the early years of the new millennium as theNational Alliance continued to distribute its 30-minute program, called *American Dissident Voices*. Only a handful of small stations aired the weekly feature, and, by the latter part of the decade, they, too, had abandoned it.

See also: Controversial Issues, Broadcasting of

Further Reading

Berlet, Chip, editor, *Eyes Right! Challenging the Right Wing Backlash*, Boston: South End Press, 1995.
Milliard, Robert L., and Michael C. Keith, *Waves of Rancor: Tuning In the Radical Right*, Armonk, New York: Sharpe, 1999.
Kurtz, Howard, *Hot Air*, New York: Basic Books, 1996.
Laufer, Peter, *Inside Talk Radio: America's Voice or Just Hot Air?* Secaucus, New Jersey: Carol Group, 1995.

MICHAEL C. KEITH AND ROBERT L. HILLIARD,
2009 REVISIONS BY MICHAEL C. KEITH

HD RADIO
See: Digital Audio Broadcasting

HEAR IT NOW
CBS Documentary Program

Hosted by esteemed newsman Edward R. Murrow, *Hear It Now* was more important in broadcasting's history than its mere six-month run on the Columbia Broadcasting System (CBS) radio network would suggest. The program developed from a series of successful documentary record albums and helped to pave the way for the even more important television documentary series *See It Now*, which presented some of Murrow's finest work.

The Recordings

The idea of making record albums featuring the actual sounds of historical events originated with Fred Friendly, a World War II veteran working as a producer for the National Broadcasting Company (NBC). Friendly saw that the relatively new medium of magnetic tape would make editing sounds recorded during historical events far easier. When Friendly realized that he needed a narrator for his recordings, CBS producer Jap Gude introduced him to newsman Edward R. Murrow and a team was born. Sometime around 1947, Friendly and Murrow approached Decca Records, but that firm was not interested in "talking" records, which were usually money losers. On the other hand, Columbia Records (a subsidiary of CBS) had available capacity as well as interest: a "scrapbook for the ear" they called it.

The initial recording, *I Can Hear It Now, 1933–1945*, was released in the winter of 1948 as a boxed set of five 78-rpm records (10 sides, about 45 minutes total). Murrow provided the historical context and narrated the many soundbites. There was no music or sound other than those of the actual events. To the surprise of virtually everyone involved in the project, the set sold 250,000 copies in the first year, highly unusual for talking records. It was said to be the first financially successful non-musical album.

A second album covering the postwar years (1945–48), with soundbites drawn largely from the extensive archives of the British Broadcasting

Corporation (BBC), came out a year later, and a third, *I Can Hear It Now: 1919–32* (which did use actors for some events when recordings were not available), appeared in 1950. Although the reasons are no longer clear, plans for a fourth album were abandoned. All were issued as 78-rpm albums originally, but some were later reissued in long-playing (LP) format. The title was resurrected in the 1990s for *I Can Hear It Now: The Sixties*, a two-compact-disc set narrated by Walter Cronkite.

The Broadcasts

The idea of broadcasting recorded sounds of historical or present-day events was anything but new. It had been done for *The March of Time* series beginning in 1931, and was often used during World War II. But there had been limited use of such material in part due to the networks' long-standing ban on use of recordings on the air. Something of a pilot program existed in CBS files—a 1948 proposed "Sunday with Murrow" documentary that had never aired for lack of advertiser support. Murrow and Gude now proposed a new program, called simply *Hear It Now* to stress its current-events emphasis, for a half-hour time slot. CBS Chairman William S. Paley so liked the idea, however, that he urged them to make it an hour-long program. Part of the difference in acceptance from the 1948 attempt to 1950 was a change in world events: the Korean War had begun and people once again were interested in world events.

When CBS began to look for a producer for the series, Gude suggested Friendly and CBS hired him away from NBC while the second *I Can Hear It Now* record album was being made. It was an easy choice, given Friendly's role as producer for the recordings and with several radio documentaries for the senior network. The series also provided a vehicle for Murrow upon his return from reporting from the Korean War battlefront.

As it aired, *Hear It Now* included "columnists" covering different subjects: CBS correspondent Don Hollenbeck discussed the media, Abe Burrows dealt with entertainment, and sportscaster Red Barber covered professional teams in several sports. The program had an original musical score by U.S. composer Virgil Thomson. Murrow decided which topics would be included and the order in which they were presented, but he and Friendly wrote the program together. Friendly was the key editor of essential soundbites. The result was a "magazine of sorts, covering the news events of the previous six days in the voices of the newsmakers themselves, by

transcription and hot live microphones" in an era before recordings of actual events were common in radio news (quoted in Dunning, 1998). *Show Business Weekly* said the program, which won a Peabody Award, was "almost breath-taking in scope and concept." It was carried on 173 CBS affiliates. Other networks quickly caught on to the idea and imitated it. NBC's *Voices and Events* and ABC's *Week Around the World* provided essentially the same sort of content, but without Murrow and Friendly. In many ways, the program was a radio vehicle for Murrow, who was then little interested in (and indeed, uneasy about) television. But as the realization became clear that pictures would add considerably to the *Hear It Now* idea, the audio version left the air while video preparations began. *See it Now* premiered on 18 November 1951 and ran until 1955.

See also: Columbia Broadcasting System; Documentary Programs; *March of Time*; News

Commentators

Edward R. Murrow, Red Barber, Abe Burrows, Don Hollenbeck

Writer/Producer

Fred Friendly

Programming History

CBS   15 December 1950–15 June 1951

Further Reading

Bliss, Edward, Jr., *Now the News: The Story of Broadcast Journalism*, New York: Columbia University Press, 1991.
Dunning, John, *On the Air: The Encyclopedia of Old-Time Radio*, New York: Oxford University Press, 1998.
Kendrick, Alexander, *Prime Time: The Life of Edward R. Murrow*, Boston: Little Brown, 1969.
Sperber, Ann M., *Murrow: His Life and Times*, New York: Freundlich Books, 1986.

CHRISTOPHER H. STERLING

HEAVY METAL/ACTIVE ROCK FORMAT

The "Heavy Metal/Active Rock" format encompasses a musical genre that has played a marginal role in commercial radio programming, while the medium of radio has at times played crucial roles in the acceptance, rejection, and content of the music itself. The moniker is the radio industry's term for a category that has gone in and out of style, while maintaining a core fan subculture since heavy metal's emergence in the early 1970s. The music in this format is characterized by a distorted guitar sound, a heavy bass-and-drums rhythm section, and a vocal approach that eschews traditional melodic conventions in favor of an aggressive, emotionally raw sound. The name "heavy metal" was at first uncomfortably accepted by first-generation rock bands such as Led Zeppelin, Deep Purple, and Black Sabbath and later happily adopted by second-generation acts such as AC/DC, Kiss, Blue Oyster Cult, Motorhead, and others.

Initially, few heavy metal bands found a place on commercial radio. Commercial rock radio itself was only then taking shape on the FM dial, as progressive/free-form stations (such as WOR in New York and KMPX in San Francisco) gave way to the new album-oriented rock (AOR) format, at stations such as WNEW in New York and WMMS in Cleveland, designed to reach a larger listening and buying public. Thus, heavy metal was not welcome in the earlier progressive rock format that grew out of the late-1960s counterculture, whose ideology did not complement the nihilism of groups like Black Sabbath. A few bands, however, did find their place on the FM dial in the early 1970s. One band, Led Zeppelin, in fact became central to AOR playlists through much of the decade.

If radio largely ignored heavy metal during the 1970s, in the 1980s the format would find new popularity. By the late 1970s, music on the radio was still functioning much as it had earlier in the decade, due to the continuing influence of AOR, which increasingly programmed the most benign rock music to appeal to the largest audience possible. The heavy metal music that did find its way onto the airwaves was limited to a few songs played endlessly in a station's rotation. The effect was that a few songs on AOR radio came to stand in for heavy metal as a musical genre, and in the process became emblematic of the genre's perceived creative bankruptcy by the end of the decade.

In the late 1970s, competition from new genres such as disco and punk had some influence on American radio formats, but both musical styles returned to the level of subculture within a few years. Meanwhile, heavy metal was being reinvigorated, first by British bands such as Def Leppard, Iron Maiden, and Judas Priest, and then by U.S. bands such as Quiet Riot and Guns N' Roses. By the mid-1980s, heavy metal from bands like Scorpions and Motley Crüe could regularly be heard on American radio. Still, some saw a certain sacrifice in the newfound popularity of the genre on the airwaves. The anticommercial heavy metal of the 1970s gave way, slowly but surely, to a new style sometimes derisively called "lite metal," which meant less emphasis on long instrumental breaks featuring virtuosic guitar solos and greater emphasis on radio-friendly melodies and more traditional pop song structures.

In recent years, the heavy metal format has struggled amidst the relative fragmentation of radio into new formats that have eroded a once-loyal listenership. The format has become one choice in a sea of others, and stations carrying the format increasingly find themselves fighting for audiences in an ever-smaller market share. The emergence of the classic rock format in the mid-1980s and the alternative rock format in the 1990s has meant the loss of both older listeners alienated by newer bands and younger listeners with little allegiance to older heavy metal. Interestingly, the classic rock format has largely not designated earlier heavy metal music as classic. Heavy metal radio was slow to incorporate the music of alternative rock formats after the "grunge" explosion of the 1990s, headed by bands such as Nirvana, Pearl Jam, and Soundgarden. Although grunge had stylistic links to the heavy metal bands of the 1970s, it also embraced the punk aesthetic.

The music played on heavy metal radio in the late 1980s and early 1990s, in comparison, largely catered to the mainstream music industry. Alternative rock formats encroached on both heavy metal and classic rock listeners with the success of stations such as KNDD in Seattle and WHTZ in New York, both of which made significant gains in their respective radio markets. Later in the decade, newer bands stylistically associated with heavy metal, such as Limp Bizkit and Rage Against the Machine, developed. These groups owed much to the emergence of hip-hop music as a predominant popular style in the 1990s. The heavy metal/active rock format has embraced these groups in order to garner younger listeners, while the format expands and absorbs influences in a confusing radio market environment.

Despite the continuing artistic and commercial viability of such metal bands as Metallica, AC/DC and (after a long absence) Guns N' Roses, Heavy Metal had by early 2009 largely fallen out of fashion on the air. This may be because it often finds itself simplistically lumped in with some of the infamous "hair bands" of the 1980s and, hence, is treated more as parody than as a legitimate musical genre. Though no metal-formatted commercial stations exist, there are still some outposts for serious "metal heads," on college radio stations (like

WSOU at Seton Hall University in New Jersey), on some syndicated programming fare—most notably the weekly *Full Metal Jackie*—and online, increasingly the refuge of niche musical styles. Metal has also gotten some renewed attention thanks to an unlikely source—it is the background music for many of the programs used in the videogame phenomenon Guitar Hero.

Within the radio business, though the phrase "Active Rock" has often been used interchangeably with the term "Heavy Metal," in recent years—possibly due to Metal still being so strongly associated with the 1980s—the two terms have split and have come to mean two different things. Active Rock—which is also often called Modern Rock, Heavy Rock, Hard Rock, or just Rock—implies a musical style that, though not "Metal," is rebellious, guitar-heavy and not inclined to anything considered "oldies." Under any name, the format has diminished somewhat in recent years, which is probably inevitable as its key demographic—males aged 18–24—can be a fickle audience. Not only are they quick to age out of the style, they are also often quick to be siphoned off by radio alternatives like iPods, satellite radio and the internet.

See also: Album-Oriented Rock Format; Alternative Format; Classic Rock Format; Contemporary Hit Radio/Top 40 Format; Music on Radio; Progressive Rock Format

Further Reading

Keith, Michael C., *Radio Programming: Consultancy and Formatics*, Boston and London: Focal Press, 1987.
O'Donnell, Lewis B., Philip Benoit, and Carl Hausman, *Modern Radio Production*, Belmont, California: Wadsworth, 1986.
Ross, Sean, "Music Radio—The Fickleness of Fragmentation," in *Radio: The Forgotten Medium*, edited by Edward C. Pease and Everette E. Dennis, London and New Brunswick, New Jersey: Transaction, 1995.
Walser, Robert, *Running with the Devil: Power, Gender, and Madness in Heavy Metal Music*, Hanover, New Hampshire: University Press of New England, 1993.
Weinstein, Deena, *Heavy Metal: A Cultural Sociology*, New York: Lexington Books, and Toronto: Macmillan Canada, 1991.

KYLE S. BARNETT,
2009 REVISIONS BY CARY O'DELL

HIGH FIDELITY

High fidelity is a term used to mean the highly accurate reproduction of sounds within the spectrum of human hearing, usually considered to be between 20 Hz and 20,000 Hz. English engineer Harold Hartley first applied the term in 1926. Much of today's understanding of what constitutes high fidelity reproduction stems from pioneering research into the way humans hear and interpret sound done by Harry Olsen for the Radio Corporation of America (RCA) and Harvey Fletcher at the American Telephone and Telegraph Company's (AT&T) Bell Laboratories.

Origins

Early sound reproduction devices such as Edison's cylindrical phonograph (1877) and Emile Berliner's Gramophone disk developed a decade later demonstrated the feasibility of recording, but they produced tinny sound with significant distortion and limited reproduction of voice and music. The near-simultaneous developments of radio broadcasting and sound motion pictures led engineers to search for ways to improve sound quality.

E.C. Wente's invention of the condenser microphone (1916) and improvements in loudspeaker technology by Rice and Kellogg at General Electric, Peter Jensen and others (1925), greatly improved the ability to record and reproduce audio. In the 1920s Edwin Armstrong's development of the heterodyne circuit improved the sensitivity and selectivity of radio receivers, and Harold Black's discovery of negative feedback provided improved audio reproduction, but several obstacles still prevented accurate reproduction of sound. The surface noise associated with records, coupled with their limited audio range and short playing time, sharply curtailed improvements in mechanical sound reproduction. AM radio transmissions were subject to significant noise and static interference. Engineers thought that reducing the audio bandwidth would reduce annoying whistles and associated distortions.

Simultaneous research into improved audio occurred in Britain, Germany, and the United States, but it was AT&T that spearheaded high-quality audio development. AT&T's Bell Laboratories undertook long-term development of sound reproduction in conjunction with high-quality long-distance telephone service. With the 1922 construction of WEAF, AT&T's flagship New York City radio station, the telephone company carried out research to improve broadcasting microphones, consoles, and transmitters. Bell Labs also developed the transcription turntable using a slower speed (33 1/3 revolutions per minute) to increase playing time to 30 minutes to meet the needs of broadcasters and motion picture engineers. By 1929 the introduction of the matched-impedance recorder, coupled with development of gold master records, increased the attainable frequency response to 10,000 Hz and greatly reduced surface noise for records.

By 1930 both RCA and Bell Labs were experimenting with various means of improving audio quality for records. One year later Leopold Stokowski, the famed conductor of the Philadelphia Orchestra, enlisted Bell Labs' help in setting up an audio test room at the Academy of Music. The first disc recordings capable of accurate sonic reproduction were cut with Stokowski's help, and Bell Labs made more than 125 high-quality recordings of the 1931–32 Philadelphia musical season. During this time Stokowski recorded the first binaural recording using AT&T's new two-styli cutter, developed by Arthur C. Keller, and in 1933 the first U.S. stereophonic transmission over telephone lines occurred when Bell Labs demonstrated a three-channel audio system in Constitution Hall in Washington, D.C. In 1938 Keller received a patent for a single-groove stereophonic disc record system.

Improving Radio

Although various advancements in the technology allowed AM radio to improve substantially, the narrow channel bandwidth adopted by the Federal Radio Commission and static interference problems created technical limitations to full high fidelity transmission. By 1935 radio stations that specialized in quality music were eager to adopt improved technology. The Federal Communications Commission (FCC) licensed four stations on three channels at the high end of the AM frequencies (in the 1500–1600 kHz region) to experiment with high fidelity broadcasting using a wider channel bandwidth. WHAM, a clear channel station that originated Rochester Philharmonic Orchestra broadcasts on the National Broadcasting Company's Blue Network, and WQXR in New York were among the early pioneers of high fidelity AM broadcasting. These stations used new Western Electric transmitters boasting better frequency response with a wider dynamic range. Improved radio receivers capable of better fidelity were manufactured by WHAM's parent company, Stromberg-Carlson, E.H. Scott, and others.

Regularly scheduled high fidelity FM broadcasts began on 18 July 1939 as Edwin Armstrong's station retransmitted classical music programs from New York's WQXR via special telephone lines. That same year, the Yankee radio network began high fidelity FM broadcasting, soon followed by General Electric and others. In 1944 Britain's

Decca records introduced full fidelity recordings capable of reproducing most of the audio spectrum.

Hi-Fi Era

After World War II, rapid improvements in recording and playback technology accelerated the development of true high fidelity sound reproduction. Crosby Research and Ampex (1948) introduced high fidelity tape recorders. The broadcasting and recording industries quickly adopted these new machines. Columbia Records (1948) and RCA Victor (1949) revolutionized the record industry with their respective introduction of the 33 1/3 rpm long play album (LP) and the 45 rpm record. The new records used small microgrooves and a vinyl medium to reduce surface noise and improve fidelity. With the introduction of the LP, entire symphonic movements could be played at home without having to change records. Quality three-speed record changers developed by Webster-Chicago (Webcor), Voice of Music, and Garrard could play stacks of records without interruption. These innovations substantially improved the sound quality of recorded music, making affordable record players available to the general listening public. In 1950 Seeburg introduced its soon-legendary 100 series jukebox, boasting high fidelity amplifiers and large speakers and capable of playing 100 different 45 rpm selections. These jukeboxes were immediate hits with teens and helped usher in the era of the 45 hit single.

By the early 1950s all of the components necessary for accurate sound reproduction were available to consumers and the "high fidelity era" industry began. Fairchild and General Electric introduced magnetic phonograph cartridges, whereas Rek-O-Kut, Thorens, and Grado introduced specialized turntables and tone arms for audiophiles. Webcor's famous model 210 high fidelity tape recorder was introduced and specialized radio manufacturers such as Fisher, H.H. Scott, Macintosh, and Sherwood Labs began selling limited production high fidelity amplifiers and FM tuners. Speaker manufacturers improved the quality of home loudspeaker systems. Jensen's development of the SG-300 triaxial speaker (1949) and bass-reflex enclosure made it possible for enthusiasts to build their own high-quality systems, whereas AR introduced the acoustic suspension system (1954), capable of reproducing powerful bass with small bookshelf enclosures. Altec Lansing and JBL speakers became popular with audiophiles. Specialized magazines such as *High Fidelity* and *Audio* catered to the "hi-fi" enthusiast by reviewing the latest in audio equipment.

Commercial development of stereophonic sound continued throughout the 1950s, culminating with RCA Victor's introduction of the stereophonic LP in 1958 and the FCC's approval of FM stereophonic broadcasting in early 1961. Combination AM/FM phonograph consoles gained popularity throughout the early 1960s, but with the introduction of transistorized equipment and new smaller sound formats such as the audio cassette (1963) and the eight-track (1966), compact stereophonic equipment eventually replaced larger console systems. Although four-channel record systems were introduced in the 1970s, they never received wide acceptance. By 1988 audio cassettes and compact discs were outselling LP records more than three to one.

The introduction of the compact disc player by Sony and Phillips ushered in the beginning of the digital audio era in 1982. Various digital recording formats, including digital audio tape systems (1986), recordable compact discs (1990), and minidiscs (1992) currently provide the capability to make high fidelity recordings that are virtually indistinguishable from the original sound sources. Today, new broadcasting technologies such as satellite-based and in-band digital audio broadcasting and computer data compression advances suggest that even higher-quality broadcast distribution of music is on the horizon.

Indeed, the development of regular digital satellite and terrestrial radio services in the early 21st century further changed the definition of "hi fi" for most Americans. Receivers were initially a slow sell, however, due to their high prices. What attracted buyers was different or original programming—such as channels of satellite radio service—more than an emphasis on high-quality sound.

See also: Digital Recording; Digital Satellite Radio; Dolby Noise Reduction; Receivers; Recordings and the Radio Industry; Stereo

Further Reading

Aldred, John, *100 Years of Cinema Loudspeakers*, www.filmsound.org/articles/amps/loudspeakers.htm

Grado, Joseph, "Audio Milestones: 50 Years and More of Record Playing," *Audio* 81, no. 5 (May 1997).

Jordan, Robert Oakes, and James Cunningham, *The Sound of High Fidelity*, Chicago: Windsor Press, 1958.

Long, John J., Jr., "High Fidelity Broadcasting: Details of the Newly Installed System at WHAM, Rochester," *Communication and Broadcast Engineering* (February 1935).

McGinn, Robert E., "Stokowski and the Bell Telephone Laboratories: Collaboration in the Development of High-Fidelity Sound Reproduction," *Technology and Culture* 24, no. 1 (1983).

Schoenherr, Steven E., "Sound Recording Research at Bell Labs," history.acusd.edu/gen/recording/belllabs.html

FRITZ MESSERE,
2009 REVISIONS BY CHRISTOPHER H. STERLING

HINDENBURG DISASTER

The broadcast of a recording of the 1937 explosion, crash, and incineration of the German zeppelin *Hindenburg* marked the first time NBC played a recording of a news event over its networks. Because the original of that recording was slightly off speed, and because in subsequent years only short excerpts have been broadcast, many people have an incomplete understanding of the reporting of the event.

The Original Recording

On 6 May 1937, at about 6:30 P.M., Herbert Morrison, an announcer and program host from WLS, Chicago, began: "How do you do everyone. We're greeting you now from the Naval Air Base at Lakehurst [New Jersey]." His words were preserved on an experimental portable Presto phonograph disc being made by WLS engineer Charles Nehlsen. Announcer Morrison and engineer Nehlsen had flown to New York on American Airlines, which had DC-3 airliners standing by for connecting flights for passengers bound to many American cities. The broadcast was intended to be good publicity for American Airlines.

Morrison told his listeners that the giant airship had been due that morning, but adverse winds over Newfoundland had slowed the trip. The *Hindenburg* had appeared over New York at noon but had to wait till dusk, when there was less wind, to dock. The ship had left Frankfurt, Germany, two-and-a-half days earlier. This was the first crossing of the season, and also the first anniversary of this air service across the Atlantic.

For about eight minutes Morrison described the hovering *Hindenburg*, its crew, the trip, and carefully related the setting and the preparations for what everyone assumed would be a routine landing. He planned to interview several Chicago-bound passengers. Here is part of his description:

> The ship is riding majestically toward us like some great feather, riding as though it was mighty, mighty proud of the place it's playing in the world's aviation. The ship is no doubt bustling with activities, as we can see, orders are shouted to the crew, the passengers probably lining the windows looking down [at] the field ahead of them, [voice in background over a loudspeaker: "mooring now"] getting their glimpse of the mooring mast. And

these giant flagships standing here, the American Air-lines flagships waiting to rush them to all points in the United States when they get the ship moored. There are a number of important persons on board and no doubt new commander Captain Max Pruitt is thrilled too, for this is his great moment. The first time he commanded the *Hindenburg*, for on previous flights he acted as the chief officer under Captain Leyman. It's practically standing still now, they lowered ropes out of the nose of the ship, and uh, it's been taken ahold of down on the field by a number of men. It's starting to rain again, the rain had slacked up a little bit. The back motors of the ship are just holding it uh, just enough to keep it from. [A shout is heard, from some one apparently standing nearby.]

It burst into flame! [There is a click, as the arm with the needle is knocked off the recording machine. It is replaced by the engineer and Morrison is heard again.]

Get out of the way. Get out of the way. Get this Charlie. Get this Charlie. And it's crashing, it's crashing terrible. Oh my, get out of the way please. It's burning, bursting into flame and it's falling on the mooring mast, and all the folks between it. This is terrible. This is one of the worst catastrophes in the world. Oh, it was four or five hundred feet in the sky. It's a terrific crash ladies and gentlemen, the smoke and the flames now. And the frame is crashing to the ground, not quite to the mooring mast. [His voice is cracking, and he almost seems to cry.] Oh, the humanity and all the passengers screaming around here.

Morrison tells Nehlsen to stop the recording so he can catch his breath. (The recording was stopped five or more times.) He reports that he has "raced down to the burning ship" and met a dazed man who was burned but had survived. Morrison says the man told him that a number of passengers had jumped clear of the ship and were safe.

Until approximately 8:30 P.M., over a span of about two hours, Morrison and Nehlsen recorded some 40 minutes on several discs, including Morri-son's accounts of helping with the wounded and his interviews with survivors. Although he first repor-ted that it would not be possible for anyone to sur-vive, he soon corrected himself. Amazingly, 61 people did survive, but 35 passengers, crewmen, and one ground handler were killed in the fire that lasted just over half a minute.

The first news bulletin describing the tragedy was reported on NBC's Red and Blue networks at about 7:45 P.M. EST. There were later bulletins, and a live report from an NBC mobile unit at about 2:50 A.M.

Morrison hid the four 16-inch discs under his coat and said they had to avoid people—maybe American Airline officials and other reporters—in Newark, Buffalo, and Detroit on their trip back, fearing someone might try to confiscate the recordings. In Chicago they came into the WLS studios through a back freight elevator.

Impact of the Recordings

That next day NBC broke a long-standing rule prohibiting recordings on the networks and pre-sented parts of Morrison's recording and inter-viewed him live from a Chicago studio to which he and Nehlsen had returned. An announcer on NBC Blue said, "we present now one of the most unique broadcasts we have ever presented." Morrison set the scene and a recording was played. WLS later made commemorative copies of the recordings. Most radio, television, and phonograph documentaries, however, use only the most sensational first few seconds, beginning with "It burst into flame."

Broadcast historians long suspected that the ori-ginal discs (or later copies) were recorded too slowly, so that when they were played back they pitched Morrison's voice too high, making him sounding rushed and hysterical. Sixty years later another recording of Morrison at a band remote in May 1938 was found that could be used for refer-ence. Chuck Schaden of the Museum of Broadcast Communication in Chicago produced a restored, speed-corrected version of the original *Hindenburg* broadcast and played it on his program on WNIB 3 May 1997.

Repeated presentations of the slightly off-speed version and the selective use of only a small part of the recordings have given an incorrect impression. Although Morrison was naturally horrified by the explosion and erroneously assumed that all on board had died, he quickly corrected himself as new information became available. Listening to the entire set of recordings reveals that he was generally calm. Despite very difficult operating conditions, his reporting was mostly clear and accurate.

John Houseman, speaking of the Mercury Theater and Orson Welles' production of "War of the Worlds," has recalled that the actor portraying a radio news reporter at the Martian ship in a New Jersey field listened repeatedly to the disc of the *Hindenburg* report, and one of his lines is: "This is the most terrifying thing I've ever witnessed." (Morrison at the *Hindenburg* had said: "Listen folks I'm going to have to stop for a few minutes because I've lost my voice, this is the worst thing I've ever witnessed.")

Morrison, a native of Pennsylvania, had begun his radio career at WMMN in Fairmont, West Virginia. His stint at WLS in Chicago was followed by work at stations in New York, and for many years in Pittsburgh. In the 1960s he returned to

West Virginia to help West Virginia University develop a radio–television program. After Morrison retired from the university, he lived in Morgantown until his death in 1989.

The crash of the *Hindenburg* was a tragic beginning for on-the-spot recording of broadcast news. The original recordings were presented by WLS to the National Archives in January 1938.

See also: Documentary Programs; News; Recording and Studio Equipment; WLS

Further Reading

Chuck Shaden's restored, correct-speed recording of the *Hindenburg* broadcast, including a discussion of his research and his method of correcting the speed, is available from the Museum of Broadcast Communications in Chicago.
"Hindenburg Disaster: Herb Morrison Reporting" website, www.otr.com/hindenburg.html
"WLS Scoops the World," *Broadcasting* (15 May 1937).

LAWRENCE W. LICHTY

HISPANIC RADIO
U.S. Spanish-Language Broadcasting

Whether described as *Spanish-language* or *bilingual*, programming that targets people of Latin-American descent, this has been among the fastest-growing segments of the U.S. radio industry. From its inception in the 1920s to the present, its development has been closely tied to the character of Latin-American immigration to the United States.

Early U.S. Spanish-Language Radio

U.S. Spanish-language radio differed significantly from the Spanish-language press on the key question of ownership. Unlike newspapers, which were largely owned by members of the immigrant community, radio stations that broadcast Spanish-language programming were almost never owned by Hispanics. There were no immigrant-oriented radio stations in the 1930s—only immigrant-brokered foreign language radio *programs*. The principal reason for this was cost. Compared to a small newspaper, the initial capital outlay for radio stations was seen as prohibitively high.

In the first decades of the broadcasting industry, radio station owners found that some hours of the day were less viable commercially. Owners sold these "off hours" for nominal fees to Spanish (and, in other parts of the country, to other minority) language radio programmers, who were responsible for acquiring their own sponsors. In this early

period, radio station owners and advertisers did not think of the Spanish-speaking audience as consumers. This can be attributed to the relative isolation of Mexican and Mexican-American communities—the largest Latino immigrant group then and now—from the rest of society. Spanish speakers were occupationally and residentially segregated from the merchant and business classes, including radio station owners. Until Spanish speakers were conceptualized as a product that could be sold profitably to advertisers, the importance of Spanish-language programming to station owners remained negligible.

However, for immigrant radio producers in the late 1920s and early 1930s, the audience was not in any sense an abstract one. Rather, programming was shaped within the immigrant enclave: face-to-face communication was key. For example, in Los Angeles, broker/programmer Rodolfo Hoyos spent much of his time walking through the commercial district of his southern California *barrio* (neighborhood) making personal calls on potential sponsors of his one-hour daily live music and talk program. During these sales calls on bakeries and *bodegas* (shops), that day's musical selections, or a recent community event that might be mentioned on the air, would also be discussed.

Emblematic of these early Spanish-language radio broadcasters was Mexican musician and radio producer Pedro Gonzãlez. His radio program, *Los Madrugadores* (The Early Risers), began broadcasting from KELW, Burbank, California (just north of Los Angeles) in 1927. The program mixed live performances by Mexican musicians with information about jobs and community services and was extremely popular with the city's Mexican immigrant community. Gonzãlez was, by training and predilection, a musician and performing artist. His response to social and political circumstances of the late 1920s and 1930s transformed him into one of the best-known Mexican-American political figures of his generation, a man *The New York Times* described in an obituary as a "folk hero and social advocate."

Following on the heels of World War I and growing isolationist feelings, and again at the onset of the Great Depression in the late 1920s, the U.S. government deported tens of thousands of Mexican immigrants. Gonzãlez was arrested in 1934 and was subsequently convicted on trumped-up rape charges. He was sentenced to 50 years in prison, all the while protesting his innocence. After sustained protests from the Los Angeles Mexican community, he was released from jail and deported in 1940.

Gonzãlez translated and broadcast advertisements from general market advertisers, such as Folger's Coffee, who were discovering the Spanish-speaking consumer market. Nonetheless, under political pressure after Gonzãlez's arrest, the radio station discontinued all Spanish-language programming. During the early 1930s, other broadcasters in Texas and throughout the Southwest also curtailed their foreign-language programming in response to harassment directed at ethnic broadcasters and the imposition of more stringent radio licensing rules. These rules from the Federal Communications Commission closely examined ownership of stations (one had to be a U.S. citizen) and required that station management be fully aware of the English meaning of all material broadcast.

The reaction of American political and commercial sectors to the emerging Spanish-speaking audience was contradictory. On the one hand, advertisers had begun to recognize the potential profitability of this audience, and radio station owners discovered that by selling blocks of formerly "dead" airtime to immigrant brokers, they could generate increased revenue. At the same time businesses were courting this community, however, politicians, labor unions, and other community leaders were characterizing Mexican immigrants as a threat.

As a cultural complement to mass deportations, in the mid-1930s the Los Angeles district attorney and other government authorities campaigned to ban Spanish from the airwaves. Although many stations continued to program Spanish-language blocks, others wishing to reach Mexican-Americans moved their operations to the Mexican side of the border out of the reach of U.S. authorities. The tension created by the contradictory responses of the Anglo establishment to the Mexican community—commercially welcoming, but politically and culturally rejecting—would continue to shape the development of a Hispanic audience.

The Early Transnational Hispanic Audience

Emilio Azcãrraga, patriarch of the Mexican entertainment conglomerate today known as *Televisa*, began his broadcasting empire with radio stations in the 1930s. Shortly thereafter, he began transmitting music from his Mexico City station XEW, *La Voz de America Latina* (The Voice of Latin America), to a radio station in Los Angeles, which then relayed it to other U.S. stations. In addition, Azcãrraga owned five radio stations along the United States–Mexico border that transmitted directly into the United States. For Azcãrraga and his fledgling

broadcasting empire, the border that separates the United States from Mexico was little more than a bureaucratic nuisance. Mexicans who listened to radio lived on both sides of the official separation of the two countries.

By the 1940s U.S. broadcasters were discovering that the emotional impact of an advertising message delivered in a listener's first language and suggestively enfolded in a program of music or drama, evoking the most nostalgic memories of a listener's far-away birthplace, was infinitely greater than the same message in English. These Spanish-language radio programs were broadcast weekly, not daily, in four states: New York, Arizona, Texas, and California, most of them in the off hours.

The early Spanish-language radio audience in the United States was defined by its "otherness," particularly its continuing close ties to Mexico. When the commercial establishment began to imagine Spanish speakers as members of *their* marketplace, they began to mold Spanish-language radio for an imagined audience more commensurate with that of the dominant, majority society. Immigrant program hosts were urged to shorten their commentary and pick up their pace, so as to better match the quick tempo of the new advertisements they were reading. The length of the music selections was also shortened to make room for more advertising breaks.

Changing the Immigrant Paradigm

In the postwar period outside the Southwest, Spanish-language radio shared off-hour time slots with other foreign-language radio. By the 1950s, German, Polish, Scandinavian, and other foreign-language radio broadcasting began a steady decline. This was largely attributable to the assimilation of European immigrants into the dominant culture. As these peoples were recognized as predominantly English monolingual, the commercial appeal of foreign-language radio programs declined; these consumers could be reached with general radio programming and advertising. As such, foreign-language broadcasting was not as attractive to advertisers and thus not as appealing to radio station owners.

During this period, the number of weekly hours of U.S. Spanish-language radio doubled. Two-thirds originated in the Southwest, the region most heavily populated with Spanish speakers. By 1960 Spanish-language radio accounted for more than 60 percent of all U.S. foreign language radio. Spanish was the only foreign language to command entire stations and entire broadcast days. Because of continuing immigration, U.S. Spanish-language radio was growing at a time when other foreign-language broadcasting was dying.

Radio station owners and their advertisers were among the first to notice (in commercial terms) that the European paradigm of immigration to the United States was not identical to that of Latin-American immigration. Most European immigrants, within a generation or two of their arrival, were socially and economically integrated into the majority culture, losing their European "mother tongue" in favor of English monolingualism. In addition, European immigration to the United States was discontinuous, disrupted by two world wars and the vastness of the Atlantic Ocean. Once new German immigrants, for example, stopped arriving, a generation or so later all but a few reduced their use of German or stopped speaking German completely. Consequently, the market for German-language radio dropped off precipitously.

In contrast, immigrants from Latin-American countries, primarily Mexico, have arrived in a steady stream (of varying size) to the United States for most of this century. Monolingual Spanish speakers settling in the United States renew the life of the language and provide a core audience for Spanish-language radio programming. Today, the Spanish-speaking audience is in many ways the ideal specialized audience. Language, race, and continued close association with Latin America made it an easily identifiable audience. Between 1960 and 1974, spurred by immigration from Cuba and Puerto Rico, the number of radio stations carrying Spanish-language programming doubled.

In the next quarter-century, that number doubled again as immigration from Mexico and Central America increased and, in equal measure, the United States-born Latino population grew. At the same time, the Hispanic audience was "discovered" by Madison Avenue and the narrowcasting broadcasting industry to be "targetable," that is, definable in market terms, and therefore a potentially profitable "niche market."

By 2009 there were more than 700 Hispanic radio stations in the U.S. However, the term "Hispanic radio" is no more accurate or descriptive than saying "American" as many varied formats exist. Spanish-language stations may broadcast anything from all-talk to such musical styles such as salsa, merengue or tejano.

At the start of the new century, various Latin-focused stations enjoyed great success by programming a musical style called "raggaeton." Perhaps best embodied by such artists as Daddy Yankee, raggaeton blends Jamaican reggae and dance hall beats with American hip-hop and other Latin musical influences. The youth-focused raggaeton format eventually gave way to yet another dominant style coined "Hurban" for its melding of "urban" and "Hispanic" appeals. In the middle of the 21st century's first decade more than 30 stations either launched or flipped to the Hurban format, usually with great success. Hispanic-focused radio is now the third-most listened-to format in the country, behind only country music and talk/news formats. Along with its musical taste, the Hurban format is also characterized by its bilingual nature and its open use of "Spanglish," making it appeal to many second-generation Hispanics.

As with other radio, Hispanic stations are shaped by ownership chains like the Spanish Broadcasting System, which owns 20 stations, and Clear Channel, which unveiled its Spanish-language "oldies"-centric La Preciosa network in 14 markets in 2006. But amid the slow decline of the radio business, success of Hispanic radio—in all its forms—seems to be a continuing bright spot as the Hispanic population has become one of the largest minorities in the country. It will account for nearly 15 percent of the population by the end of 2010.

See also: Border Radio

Further Reading

Cobo, Leila, "Spanglish Signals," *Billboard* (13 September 2008), p. 14.

Fowler, Gene, and Bill Crawford, *Border Radio: Quacks, Yodelers, Pitchmen, Psychics, and Other Amazing Broadcasters of the American Airwaves*, Austin: Texas Monthly Press, 1987.

Gutiérrez, Felix, and Jorge Reina Schement, *Spanish Language Radio in the Southwestern United States*, Austin: Center for Mexican-American Studies, University of Texas, 1979.

Lazo, Alejandro, "Hispanic Radio Hits Rough Wave," *Washington Post* (14 July 2008), p. D1.

Ordonez, Jennifer, "America's Hurban Sprawl," *Newsweek* (6 March 2006), p. 10.

Rodríguez, América, "Objectivity and Ethnicity in the Production of the *Noticiero Univision*," *Critical Studies in Mass Communication* 13, no. 1 (1996).

Rodríguez, América, *Making Latino News: Race, Language, Class*, Thousand Oaks, California: Sage, 1999.

Rodríguez, América, "Creating an Audience and Remapping a Nation: A Brief History of U.S. Spanish-Language Broadcasting, 1930–1980," *Quarterly Review of Film and Video* 16, nos. 3–4 (2000).

AMÉRICA RODRÍGUEZ,
2009 REVISIONS BY CARY O'DELL

HISTORY

This entry surveys highlights in American radio broadcasting's development, from the experimental era before 1920 to the rapidly changing industry eight decades later. That history is described using a series of specific periods that help to characterize key developments. Many of the topics touched on here are treated more extensively in their own entries; the reader should use the table of contents as well as the index for more in-depth discussions of specific topics.

Before 1920

Prior to the end of World War I, there was little sustained radio broadcasting, except for occasional experimental and amateur transmissions. This era was characterized by rapid wireless technical innovation over a three-decade period that made broadcasting possible.

After the theoretical foundations of wireless transmission of information were established by James Clerk Maxwell in the 1860s, and the theory was proven with Heinrich Hertz's experiments in the late 1880s, the stage was set for the key innovator, Guglielmo Marconi. Beginning in the mid-1890s he developed and improved the key elements for wireless telegraphy (code) transmission—transmitter, antenna, and receiver. By the end of the 19th century, Marconi was the head of a thriving British company introducing wireless transmission to merchant and navy ships and, with high-powered shore stations, long-distance competition to undersea telegraph cables. Other companies developed in France, Germany, Russia, and the United States, and all shared a common goal—perfecting point-to-point wireless telegraphy as the most lucrative future for wireless. Broadcasting was barely a glint in anyone's eye.

A few early wireless experimenters did stumble onto the key elements of radio broadcasting, beginning with Reginald Fessenden. On Christmas Eve of 1906 he transmitted voice and music in what many consider the first broadcast in the world. Another important inventor–innovator, Lee de Forest, offered occasional broadcasts in 1907 and 1908. Beginning the next year, Charles Herrold initiated a regular radio broadcast service in San Jose, California, as an adjunct to his radio school. He remained on the air (typically for a few hours per week) until World War I. Amateur experimenters in other cities also offered sporadic broadcasts for fellow amateurs to tune in, but these were seen largely as exceptions to the point-to-point focus of most people in the fledgling wireless business.

Recognizing the need for some order among the slowly increasing number of transmitters needing frequencies, Congress passed legislation in 1910

and again in 1912 to regulate the use of wireless at sea. These were followed by the more important Radio Act of 1912, which was to stand for 15 years as the basis for any government regulation of wireless transmission. Following industry advice and expectations, the Radio Act was predicated on wireless as a point-to-point means of communication. It made no mention of, nor provision for, radio broadcasting.

What grabbed the public's imagination early in the 20th century was the role of wireless in some spectacular maritime disasters. In 1909 the White Star liner *Republic* was rammed in the fog by an incoming vessel a few hours outside of New York. Wireless operator Jack Binns called for help (the other ship lacked wireless), and virtually everyone—some 1,500 people—was saved. Radio could not save as many in the horrific *Titanic* disaster of April 1912, when another White Star liner, on her glittering maiden voyage, hit an iceberg and sank, this time taking 1,500 lives with her. But Marconi operators Jack Phillips and Harold Bride stayed at their posts (Phillips died after the vessel sank) and, transmitting both the old "CQD" and newer "SOS" emergency signals, brought a rescue vessel to pick up the 700 survivors, who told the tale that fascinates people still.

Radio played a lesser role in World War I. Demands of reliability and secrecy and the relative immobility of trench warfare made telephone and telegraph service more common than wireless. But military and naval needs and orders helped increase the pace of technical development, and wireless manufacturers rapidly improved both transmitters and receivers. The U.S. Navy took over high-powered transmitting stations from private operators (most other transmitters, including those operated by amateurs, were closed down for the duration of the war) and trained thousands of radio operators to run them. Demand for the best equipment saw development of a Navy-sponsored pooling of patents of different companies to allow the latest developments to more rapidly reach battle fronts.

With the end of the war, Congress briefly considered making permanent the wartime system of government operation of both wired and wireless telecommunications (as was then the rule in most other countries). But despite urging by the Navy, Congress ordered that transmitters be returned to civilian control in 1919–20. The radio industry made plans to expand production and operations in peacetime with the thousands of trained radio technicians and amateurs. Some of them expressed interest in broadcast experiments.

1920–26

The initial period of regular radio broadcasting was one characterized by growth and excitement, little effective regulation, program experimentation, a lack of permanent networks, only limited advertiser interest, and almost no knowledge of its audience.

Among the pioneering American stations taking to the air in 1919–20 (others began at about the same time in Canada and in Europe) were WHA in Madison, Wisconsin (which had begun as a University of Wisconsin physics department transmitter 9XM, sending wireless telegraphy market reports to Wisconsin farmers before World War I); Charles Herrold's station, which became KQW in San Francisco; KDKA in Pittsburgh, Pennsylvania (which had begun as amateur 8XK station in 1916); and Detroit's WWJ, which grew out of amateur operation 8MK.

Each began under a different owner with a different purpose in mind. The University of Wisconsin's WHA, the first educational station on the air, was interested in spreading the university's courses and research to the boundaries of the state. KQW at first continued Herrold's interest in operating his radio school, but it soon passed into the hands of a local church and later a national network interested in commercial operations. KDKA was developed by Westinghouse, which in 1920 was interested in keeping its assembly lines of highly trained personnel together despite the loss of huge government contracts with the end of the war. By providing a radio music and talk service, the company figured it might attract people to buy receivers. Over the next two years, Westinghouse added other stations in different cities. General Electric and the Radio Corporation of America (RCA) entered the radio station business at about the same time. WWJ was the first of many stations to be owned by a local newspaper. Initially seen as another community service, operating a radio station would become a common means of hedging bets as to which medium would survive. Other stations went on the air as auxiliaries to the owner's primary business— a retailer or service firm.

The radio station business began slowly in 1920–21, but it exploded in 1922, when more than 600 stations went on the air. Many went off again in a matter of weeks or months, unable to find a means of supporting operations. Early stations were primitive operations, the studios of which were often merely hotel or office building rooms, with walls covered in burlap to deaden sound and equipped with a microphone and the near-ubiquitous piano. Transmitters were largely hand-built, and many

radiated with less power than a reading lamp. A few stations experimented with temporary hookups, using telephone lines to allow two or more stations to carry the same program at the same time (and perhaps share in its costs)—the germ of networking. But multiple station linkups were largely limited to special sports or political events, such as presidential speeches.

Strictly speaking, there was no "programming" at first—merely different times given over to talk, music, or comedy, and this was usually in an unplanned fashion. The paramount idea was to fill airtime, even for the very few hours that most stations were initially on the air. Ironically, in light of more modern experience, few stations made use of phonograph records. Although records would have been an obvious and easy means of filling time, they were then of low acoustical quality, and their use was considered a poor application of radio's potential. As radio had no ready means of making money, stations could offer no payment to singers and performers, which further limited program options. It was a brief but golden age for amateurs of all types and ages, who would gladly come into the studio just for the chance to have an audience— even an unseen and unheard one. It sounded much like the vaudeville circuit, from whence came many early radio stars.

More formal, preplanned schedules of programs, with clear formats, beginnings, and endings, developed only by the mid-1920s, and then first in the largest markets. One vaudeville pattern that carried over to radio was the "song and patter" team— usually two men with comedy and musical experience—who could easily expand or shorten their act as broadcast time permitted. About the only role for women in early radio was as singers. There was little or no drama or situation comedy, little play-by-play sports, and no regular newscasts or weather reports—all these would come later in the decade or in the 1930s.

Radio was a novelty for its audience as well— indeed, it became a huge fad, which many observers figured would not last, especially as multiple-station interference grew in the mid-1920s, raising listener frustration. But the excitement of hearing disembodied voices and music, often from a considerable distance, was enough to persuade more and more people to build or buy the available crude receivers, which required a fair bit of manual dexterity even to tune in to a nearby station. That ready-made receivers cost a lot was indicated in early radio programs, which included a substantial amount of classical music, aimed at discriminating (i.e., wealthy) ears. Countless radio books and magazines appeared to cater to the growing audience. There was no audience research in this initial period—stations determined who was listening merely by audience mail or requests for cards confirming programs (a spin-off on ham radio "QSL" cards).

Despite this audience interest, the biggest problem broadcasters faced in the 1920s was how to pay for their operations. Although advertising may now seem to have been preordained, there were then many strong arguments against allowing radio to sell airtime. Some observers suggested a tax to pay for programming, others called for voluntary contributions, and still others promoted an annual tax on receivers, a method adopted by many other countries. And a few states or cities operated stations as government services.

Interestingly, it was the American Telephone and Telegraph Company (AT&T) that brought advertising to radio, when their New York station WEAF first offered to sell airtime much as the company did for long-distance telephone calls, dubbing radio's version "toll broadcasting." A 15-minute real estate ad in August 1922 was probably the first radio commercial. Others slowly followed suit, encouraged by initial sales results. Yet these early ads almost never mentioned price—instead they promoted a kind of institutional or image advertising common on today's public radio. Another way advertisers made themselves known was to add their name to the program title or stars—thus the *Lucky Strike Hour* or the *A&P Gypsies*. But many in and out of broadcasting still resisted the notion of bringing business into the home (forgetting perhaps that newspapers and magazines had long done just that). The rapid expansion of advertising came only after 1926, when AT&T sold its stations and ended industry debates over whether the telephone company could force stations to pay a fee for the right to sell advertising.

That radio was developing as more of a business became increasingly evident in the industry's call for firm government licensing policies and related regulations. Secretary of Commerce Herbert Hoover called together four national radio conferences from 1922 to 1925, each of them larger and more strident in calling on Congress to reduce the interference resulting from trying to administer a growing broadcasting system under provisions of the 1912 legislation, which had not foreseen broadcasting. Acting largely on his own, Hoover did succeed in expanding the number of frequencies available for broadcasting from one (833 kHz) in 1920 to three in mid-1922 and to the beginnings of a "band" of frequencies in May 1923. More

frequencies allowed more stations without the need to share time—but only if broadcasters cooperated, because the government had no enforcement power. Court decisions in 1926 took away what little authority Hoover had exercised and increased pressure on Congress to act.

1927–33

The 1927–33 period is one of the most important in the history of broadcasting. By the late 1920s American radio began to take on most of the characteristics of the system still recognizable today—definite program patterns, advertising support, reliable audience research, and far more effective regulation. The latter came with Congressional action early in 1927.

The Radio Act of 1927, though in force for only seven years, would set broadcast patterns that persist to the present. Stations were to be licensed for up to three years, on a specific frequency and with specified power that could only be changed on application to the new Federal Radio Commission (FRC), which had the legal power to enforce its decisions. No longer could stations shift frequency, increase power, or literally move their transmitters overnight, as had become common just before the act became law. The driving impetus of the new FRC and its rules and regulations (first codified in 1932) was to reduce interference on the air so that people could hear stations clearly. A key part of that process was to expand on Hoover's beginnings by allocating most of the modern AM radio "band" of frequencies and by classifying stations by power. A few stations were restricted to daytime-only transmission to reduce evening interference even further. The FRC often had to defend its expanding role in court. A series of four landmark cases in 1928–30 concerning program controls helped confirm the agency's authority and the constitutionality of its licensing decisions. Now subject to federal legislation and rules, it seemed clear radio was here to stay.

The other fundamental change in the business took place at nearly the same time—the development of permanent national networks. The National Broadcasting Company (NBC) was the first, built around the informal network of stations that WEAF had initially developed. After purchase of that station from AT&T late in 1926, RCA formed NBC as a subsidiary that in November 1926 began to operate a continuing network of entertainment and cultural programs.

In fact, NBC began—and would operate until 1943—as two networks, the Red and the Blue. The former was based on WEAF and its connected stations, and the latter was built around RCA station WJZ (also in New York) and a parallel chain of affiliated stations. From the start, the Red network had the stronger stations, greater audience reach, and greater advertiser appeal. NBC's chief competitor, the Columbia Broadcasting System (CBS), had a far more complex birth and only became a stable competitor in 1928. Together, the two New York-based networks soon contributed hugely to radio's expanding audience popularity and advertiser appeal.

Advertising became more widely accepted in this period—at least by the industry, if not by all of its listeners. Based on initial success stories, advertisers and ad agencies had begun to recognize the medium's potential, encouraged by the inception of regular audience research, which had been brought about by the new networks. The first books on radio advertising appeared in 1927. After 1929 the Depression pushed more direct or "hard sell" approaches to radio advertising, first at local stations and more slowly at the network level. Indeed, by 1931–32, major ad agencies had taken on the role of programmers for many networks and a few large station programs, providing casts and even finished productions. The first station representative (rep) firm, Edward Petry, was formed in 1932 to ease the buying of radio spot advertisements in markets across the country. That all of this was successful is indicated in radio's proportion of all advertising, which grew from only two percent in 1928 to nearly 11 percent just four years later. By 1932, an FRC survey found that 36 percent of all radio time had commercial sponsorship, meaning that for 64 percent, networks and stations sustained the costs of production.

With half or more of all broadcast time, music remained the most important kind of program on both networks and local stations, with variety (still drawn heavily from vaudeville) a close second.

Virtually all of these programs were broadcast live, because recorded programming was looked down upon by major broadcasters. Drama and comedy developed more slowly as writers and actors overcame the problem of an audience that could not see the action taking place. Though certainly racist by modern standards, *Amos 'n' Andy* became the first network comedy hit in 1929. The first westerns and thriller dramas began in 1929 and 1930, including such long-lasting hits as *The Shadow*.

Evening network news programs began with Lowell Thomas' weeknight 15-minute program on NBC in 1930. That even in its fledgling state, radio represented a threat to the press became increasingly

obvious, and a short-lived press radio "war" began in 1933, with newspapers and major news associations attempting—unsuccessfully as it would soon turn out—to limit the amount of news reports made available to radio. As it had since 1920, radio continued to cover national political conventions and election nights with the latest voter tallies and analysis.

Radio's audience continued to expand, thanks in part to better and easier-to-tune radio receivers. By 1928 plug-in receivers began rapidly replacing cumbersome battery-powered sets. Speakers improved, and users could tune radios using a single control rather than the former two or three. Radios also became fancier, virtually furniture in their own right, made by dozens of manufacturers. That more people were listening became obvious after 1929 and the inception of regular audience research. Archibald Crossley created the Cooperative Analysis of Broadcasting (CAB) to develop program ratings—how many people were tuning to CBS and NBC programs. The CAB relied on random telephone calls to households for its listening information.

1934–41

Viewed in retrospect, the golden age of network radio programming during the later Depression years saw a flowering of radio creativity in the last peacetime era that had no competition from television. More than 200 stations went on the air, including the first stations to serve many smaller communities. The growing number of stations forced many to utilize directional antennae to avoid interference with other outlets—fully a quarter of all stations used such antennae by 1941. Still, about a third of the nation's listeners got their only reliable evening radio service from one of 52 "clear channel" stations, all located in major cities.

The period's beginning is marked by the FRC's replacement in mid-1934 with the Federal Communications Commission (FCC), which had expanded regulatory responsibilities for wired as well as radio communications. Key provisions of the 1927 act, including most of those concerning radio, simply carried over into the new law.

By this time, success in broadcast station operation meant having an affiliation agreement with CBS or NBC Red or Blue—or, after mid-1934, with the Mutual Broadcasting System—and being able to carry their popular programs. A number of outlets also joined such regional chains as the Colonial or Yankee networks in New England, the Texas network, or the Don Lee network on the

West Coast. The networks' efficient provision of programs and advertising truly dominated radio by the late 1930s. Networks also dominated their affiliates with one-sided contracts that bound the station for up to five years, but bound the network for only one year at a time. This led to an FCC investigation of network operations from 1938 to 1941, which concluded that network control was too strong and that many practices needed change, chief among them the ending of NBC's operation of dual networks.

Most urban and some rural stations programmed 12 hours a day, some for as many as 18. An FCC survey of program patterns in 1938 found that 64 percent of programs were broadcast live (roughly half network and half local), with the remainder being some kind of recording. More than half of all programming was music; talks and dialogues accounted for 11 percent (including President Roosevelt's fireside chats); and nine percent each were devoted to drama, variety programs, and news. Three new types of program soon dominated this period. Daytime hours were soon saturated with dozens of "soap operas," 15-minute domestic serial dramas, broadcast one after the other. By 1940 the national networks devoted no less than 75 hours a week to such programs, some of which would last into the late 1950s. Quiz and audience participation programs also became hugely popular. On the more serious side, news and news commentary programs greatly expanded with the rising world political crisis in Europe and the Far East and the beginning of World War II in 1939. From about 850 hours annually in 1937, network news and commentary programs grew to fill nearly 3,500 hours by 1941.

Perhaps the single most famous radio program, Orson Welles' dramatization of *The War of the Worlds*, was broadcast in October 1938. Realistic in its use of reporters breaking into music programs (as listeners had just heard during the Munich crisis a month before), the hour-long drama panicked millions and demonstrated both how radio had grown in importance in American life and how much it was trusted by its listeners to tell the truth. More than 90 percent of urban households owned a radio, as did 70 percent of rural homes, and half the country's homes now had at least two radios.

All the earlier talk about radio's educational potential (some 200 noncommercial stations took to the air in the 1920s) had dwindled to the activities of about 35 stations by 1941. These survivors, many licensed to universities, provided in-school enrichment and adult cultural and educational programs to small but loyal audiences. Several

national organizations promoted conflicting notions of how radio might best serve educational needs, one urging cooperation with the commercial networks and stations, the other insisting on separation to promote purity of mission.

Another, the National Association of Educational Broadcasters, lasted from 1934 into the early 1980s. Frustrations of educators with an increasingly commercial system led to pressure on the FCC to set aside some channels specifically for noncommercial operations, which resulted in the first such set aside when FM was approved for regular operation in 1941.

1941–45

In part because of wartime paper rationing, which limited newspaper reporting, radio journalism came of age in the war years, supported by high advertising income and popular entertainment programs. But the industry itself grew only a little during the war because of construction and material limitations. Full wartime restrictions remained in force until August 1945.

The proportion of stations affiliated with a network rose from 60 to 95 percent of all stations. Some stations in smaller markets held agreements with more than one network. The FCC's *Report on Chain Broadcasting* (1941) caused a huge controversy, in large part because it called for an end to NBC's operation of two networks, but also because it sought many other changes in the relationship between networks and their affiliate stations. Two years later the NBC Blue network was sold, becoming the basis for the American Broadcasting Company (ABC) in 1945. Radio prospered during the war as advertising spending rose sharply (in part so businesses could avoid simply paying profits out in federal taxes). Whereas a third of all stations reported financial losses in 1939, only six percent did by 1945.

Radio reporters became famous during the war, led by longtime newsman H.V. Kaltenborn on NBC and the CBS team that included Edward R. Murrow in London and William L. Shirer in Berlin. Covering cities under attack and forces fighting in Europe and the Pacific, radio brought the war to listeners at home while also providing propaganda broadcasts by enemy and Allied countries alike.

1945–52

Radio both expanded and contracted in this period—the number of stations more than tripled, but radio networks all but disappeared in the face of television competition. Most of radio's growth took place in smaller markets. What had been a largely AM-centered small industry grew in complexity to include FM and television outlets and networks. One measure of radio's declining glory was the release in March 1946 of the FCC *Blue Book*, which traced wartime profits and compared them unfavorably with radio's heavily commercial programming.

This weakening is most evident in the rapid decline of radio networks, which had dominated the business in 1945 but had all but disappeared by 1952. By then networks provided only a memory of their former service, with daytime soaps, some sustaining dramas, newscasts, and special events—including political year broadcasts. At the same time, their share of radio advertising dropped from nearly half in 1945 to just over a quarter by 1952. Large parts of the broadcast day once programmed by networks were now returned to stations to fill as best they could. One new network—the Liberty Broadcasting System—briefly thrived in 1940–52 based largely on Gordon McClendon's skillful recreations of professional baseball games based only on wire service reports and sound effects.

But radio's chief role in this brief but important period of transition was to provide the revenues that supported expansion of television service. Radio revenue increased each year, though it had to be divided among a vastly larger number of stations, which meant that many radio outlets operated in the red. Noncommercial radio expanded as well, thanks to reserved FM channels.

The most popular dramatic and comedy programs either began to "simulcast" on radio and television, or they moved over to television entirely. The networks began to offer cheaper music and quiz shows, of which *Stop the Music* was one example, to attract listeners by offering a chance at big-money prizes. ABC, the newest and smallest network, broke the longlasting national taboo on recorded programs by using prerecorded transcriptions of many of its programs. Local stations paralleled that practice with "musical clock" programs that provided a local disc jockey with records, weather, news, occasional features—and constant time checks. Affiliates were soon providing more local than network programming—a throwback to the 1930s.

1952–80

This was an era of competition—with radio playing a distinct second fiddle to the country's fascination with television—and of creativity, as radio developed

the many music formats that would give the medium a renewed lease of life. At the same time, the coming of stereorecording and then stereoFM gave that medium a huge boost.

The number of stations continued to expand—by about 100 AM outlets each year, and after 1958 by a revived FM business as well. The rising station population led to problems—where a third of AM stations operated only in the day-time in 1952, fully half were required to do so by 1960 in a continuing FCC attempt to reduce night-time interference. More stations used directional antennae to reduce daytime and evening interference. Indeed, for much of the 1962–73 period, the FCC froze AM applications and tried—largely successfully—to steer radio growth to the FM band. The commission's decision to ban simulcasting by co-owned AM and FM stations in the late 1960s speeded the expansion of FM, which for the first time had a separate identity for most listeners.

Radio networks still demonstrated some program originality in the 1950s. NBC's *Monitor* created a weekend magazine program beginning in 1955, and the same network offered science fiction with *X-Minus-One*; CBS created *Gunsmoke* for radio before transferring the show to television. *Amos 'n' Andy* became a variety program. The last bastion of advertiser-supported network radio was the daytime soap opera, which only finally disappeared in 1960. The networks reverted to "news on the hour" for affiliates.

Freed of their network ties, most local stations at first stuck with middle-of-the-road (MOR) formats, trying to offer a bit of everything to everyone, including music, talk, variety, and features. Of more fundamental importance to radio's future was the slow mid-1950s development of formula or "Top 40" formats, which were dependent on the personality of a local disc jockey and on tightly formatted music and advertising. Tod Storz and Gordon McClendon are both credited with creating the program approach first used by about 20 stations in 1955 and by hundreds by 1960. Top 40 aimed primarily at teens with what became known as rock and roll music, which was based closely on African-American rhythm and blues. The arrival of Elvis Presley in 1956 as the first rock superstar helped cement the new radio trend, though Congressional investigations of payola late in the decade cast doubts, certainly in adults' minds, about the wholesomeness of the format.

Educational radio received a huge boost with the establishment of National Public Radio (NPR) in 1968, the first national network for noncommercial stations. Though excluding hundreds of smaller

FM outlets, the 300 to 400 large-market FM outlets that served as NPR "members" brought listeners the highly popular programs *All Things Considered* and *Morning Edition*, among others.

1980–2000

In one sense, the story of radio since 1980 is turned upside down from its history before that date, because beginning in 1979, radio was increasingly dominated by FM listening. By the late 1980s, FM stations attracted three-quarters of the national audience—and by 1995 nearly 60 percent of the stations. All radio outlets specialized in programming in their attempt to gain and hold a tiny sliver of the audience divided by the early 21st century across more than 13,000 stations.

Two technical developments with AM radio were failures. The first was an FCC attempt to narrow AM channels to 9 kHz (parallel to practice in most of the rest of the world) down from the 10-kHz channels standard since the 1920s. But industry opposition (based on fears of an influx of new competitors) stopped the idea cold in the early 1980s. The second attempted development, offering stereo on AM outlets, was seen by some as one means of slowing AM's decline. Competitors developed a half-dozen mutually incompatible means of delivering stereo in AM's narrow band. Though in 1980 the FCC selected one (by Magnavox) as it had done with prior new technologies, industry ridicule of the decision and the very close parameters of the competing systems led the commission to revisit the matter and in 1982 to allow any stereo system. This experiment in marketplace economics failed because nobody could agree on which system to select (or how best to make such a choice), and thus most stations ignored all of them. That most AM programs by then were talk and news formats less susceptible to the benefits of stereo contributed to the stillborn technology. Extension of the AM band up to 1705 kHz by 1990, the first change since 1952, allowed the FCC to reassign a number of stations to the new frequencies to reduce interference lower in the band.

A popular new format appearing by the late 1980s was nostalgia—"golden oldies"—stations, which allow former teens to relive their childhoods with the music of the 1950s through the 1970s. Another was religious stations. Although such outlets had existed from the early days of radio, by the 1980s hundreds of conservative and evangelical religious broadcasters were becoming a force in the business. By 2000 both AM and FM radio were continuing to grow, with both high expectations

and fears being expressed about the inception of digital audio broadcasting (DAB) in the new century. Further, many radio stations had expanded operations to the internet by means of audio streaming, thus greatly expanding their reach beyond their home markets.

Passage of the Telecommunications Act of 1996 along with related FCC rule changes triggered a wave of consolidation in radio station ownership lasting into the early 21st century. More than 40 percent of all stations changed hands and group owners with more than 100 stations became common; the largest owner controlled more than 1,200 outlets. Additionally, it became possible to own up to eight stations in the largest markets. Critics argued that this consolidation contributed strongly to programming that offered broad appeal but little specialization or inventiveness. One response was the launch of two satellite-delivered subscription digital radio services in the early 2000s, both of them providing 100 channels (with about 60 music and 40 talk formats), many without any advertising.

21st Century Radio

Radio entered the 21st century with expectations of continued expansion and technical change. But the latter began to threaten the former.

Although radio touted the coming of digital sound, especially the FCC-approved HD Radio technology, the new service was rolled out very slowly with little special programming to attract listeners and marketing that emphasized its improved sound. As had happened with FM six decades earlier, such promotion did little to sell expensive HD receivers when the programming could be tuned on cheaper analog receivers.

More successful, at least in the first decade of the century, was digital satellite radio, which by 2009 was serving some 20 million subscribers (still only 10 percent of broadcast radio's audience), suggesting that people would pay for a program service that provided something not heard over the air. The Sirius service touted Howard Stern, lured from broadcast radio to his own satellite channel with a $500 million contract over five years. In 2008 XM and Sirius merged, though they struggled in the country's poor economic climate, which depressed the automobile sales that were central to getting more receivers out to potential audiences.

Back on earth, commercial radio entered a deepening malaise. Audiences stopped expanding and young people, especially, began to desert the medium in droves, opting instead for their iPods and other

MP3 devices as well as internet audio sites (some of which were, of course, broadcasting stations). To such listeners, traditional over-the-air broadcasting appeared quaint and not at all cool. Among the complaints heard from them and many others were the number of commercials per hour, the fact that programming seemed all too similar across stations (a factor made worse by the trend to conglomerate ownership), poor audio quality (compared to the digital services people increasingly used), and a sharp decline in local news and other services. Indeed, many stations offered no news or public-affairs programming at all. Perhaps the biggest problem was in radio station front offices, where many station managers perceived and shared the feeling that radio was in trouble, and perhaps in decline.

By 2008–9, as the nation's economy took a serious downturn, layoffs became widespread in radio, starting with some of the largest conglomerates. Clear Channel and Cumulus, for example, sold stations and dropped many employees, opting for increasingly automated operations. But so did many smaller operations, unable to afford the costs of staff. Program innovation declined (it seemed radio was continually renaming old formats and trotting them out as something new), and advertisers steadily deserted what had once been a strong local marketing medium, spending their dollars on internet websites instead.

Yet people were listening to more music and talk all the time—it simply was reaching them by means other than over-the-air radio broadcasts, picked up on a traditional receiver. Increasingly mobile audiences downloaded music and features to their iPods and cellphones, used audio streaming websites, and listened to podcasts. Radio still was heard by more than 200 million people a week, but increasingly the business seemed like something of a backwater amidst growing competition.

Further Reading

Archer, Gleason Leonard, *History of Radio to 1926*, New York: American Historical Society, 1938.

Archer, Gleason Leonard, *Big Business and Radio*, New York: American Historical Society, 1939.

Barfield, Ray E., *Listening to Radio, 1920–1950*, Westport, Connecticut: Praeger, 1996.

Barnouw, Erik, *A History of Broadcasting in the United States*, 3 vols, New York: Oxford University Press, 1966–70.

Carothers, Diane Foxhill, *Radio Broadcasting from 1920 to 1990: An Annotated Bibliography*, New York: Garland, 1991.

Cox, Jim, *This Day in Network Radio: A Daily Calendar of Births, Deaths, Debuts, Cancellations and Other Events in Broadcasting History*. Jefferson, North Carolina: McFarland, 2008.

Douglas, Susan J., *Listening In: Radio and the American Imagination*, New York: Times Books, 1999.

Fornatale, Peter, and Joshua E. Mills, *Radio in the Television Age*, Woodstock, New York: Overlook Press, 1980.

Godfrey, Donald G., and Frederic A. Leigh, editors, *Historical Dictionary of American Radio*, Westport, Connecticut: Greenwood Press, 1998.

Gomery, Douglas, *A History of Broadcasting in the United States*. Malden, Massachusetts: Blackwell, 2008.

Greenfield, Thomas Allen, *Radio: A Reference Guide*, New York: Greenwood Press, 1989.

Hilliard, Robert L., and Michael C. Keith, *The Broadcast Century: A Biography of American Broadcasting*, Boston: Focal Press, 1992; 3rd edition, as *The Broadcast Century and Beyond*, 2001.

Hilmes, Michele, *Radio Voices: American Broadcasting, 1922–1952*, Minneapolis: University of Minnesota Press, 1997.

Hilmes, Michele, *Only Connect: A Cultural History of Broadcasting in the United States*, Belmont, California: Wadsworth, 2002.

Lenthal, Bruce, *Radio's America: The Great Depression and the Rise of Modern Mass Culture*. Chicago: University of Chicago Press, 2007.

MacDonald, J. Fred, *Don't Touch That Dial!: Radio Programming in American Life from 1920 to 1960*, Chicago: Nelson-Hall, 1979.

Maclaurin, William Rupert, *Invention and Innovation in the Radio Industry*, New York: Macmillan, 1949.

Nachman, Gerald, *Raised on Radio: In Quest of the Lone Ranger, Jack Benny*, New Pantheon Books, 1998.

Reinehr, Robert C, and Jon D. Swartz, *Historical Dictionary of Old-Time Radio*, Lanham, Maryland: Scarecrow Press, 2008.

Settel, Irving, *A Pictorial History of Radio*, New York: Citadel Press, 1960.

Smulyan, Susan, *Selling Radio: The Commercialization of American Broadcasting, 1920–1934*, Washington, D.C.: Smithsonian Institution Press, 1994.

Sterling, Christopher H., *Electronic Media: A Guide to Trends in Broadcasting and Newer Technologies, 1920–1983*, New York: Praeger, 1984.

Sterling, Christopher H., editor, *The Rise of American Radio*, London: Routledge, 2007 (six vols).

Sterling, Christopher H., and Michael C. Keith, *Sounds of Change: A History of FM Radio in America*. Chapel Hill: University of North Carolina Press, 2008.

Sterling, Christopher H., and John M. Kittross, *Stay Tuned: A History of American Broadcasting*, 3rd edition, Mahwah, New Jersey: Lawrence Erlbaum, 2002.

CHRISTOPHER H. STERLING,
2009 REVISIONS BY CHRISTOPHER H. STERLING

HOAXES
Pranks, Policies, and FCC Rulings

Until the early 1990s the Federal Communications Commission (FCC) had taken a relatively laissez-faire attitude toward radio hoaxes, admonishing offenders but avoiding several penalties. From 1975 to 1985 the Commission threw out a number of programming content policies initiated a decade earlier. In 1985 the FCC, under Chairman Mark Fowler's leadership, voted to eliminate its policy of restricting "scare" announcements as part of its deregulation initiatives during the Reagan administration. When the public became subject to a number of hoax abuses, however, in May 1992 the FCC issued a ruling prohibiting pranks that cause immediate public harm or divert resources from law enforcement.

War of the Worlds

Orson Welles perpetrated the first hoax in radio history in his 1938 radio play, *War of the Worlds*. The national public panic over a well-crafted imaginary Martian invasion of the east coast of the United States was the ultimate demonstration of radio's impact on an audience. Subsequently, after the Welles broadcast, the FCC warned broadcasters not to use the words *bulletin* or *newsflash* in entertainment programs and to provide adequate cautionary language in the airing of dramatizations.

Beginning in the 1950s legendary DJs such as Dick Biondi and Wolfman Jack attempted to shock their audiences with crazy stunts and wild antics. Radio stations across the nation undertook many pranks and trickery, such as turkeys thrown out of airplanes and a scavenger hunt for a $1,000 bill hidden in a public library, in the name of fun and higher market ratings. In the 1960s the FCC began a new era of regulation, in part because of what it perceived to be the public's vulnerability to deceptive programming and promotions. In 1960 it issued a policy statement that addressed intentional distortion or falsification of programming (i.e., news staging). In 1966 the FCC issued a stronger policy, which warned against airing "scare" announcements. The 1966 policy was a reaction to specific complaints about radio contests that disrupted traffic, caused property damage, diverted law enforcement, alarmed listeners with imaginary dangers, and threatened life. The FCC stand slowed down the occurrence of hoaxes over the next several years.

Then, in 1974, Rhode Island's WPRO-FM recreated *War of the Worlds*. The program had been promoted as a spoof throughout the day. During the actual broadcast, however, 45 minutes elapsed before the station aired a public disclaimer. One-hundred and forty listeners called the radio station. Although station personnel had warned the local police department of its intent to air the program, the FCC admonished WPRO on the basis of its 1966 statement concerning broadcast of scare announcements.

In another instance, that same year a Tucson, Arizona radio personality, with the help of the news director, faked his own kidnapping. The commission failed to renew the license of KIKX-AM, specifically based on its violation of FCC policies related to the "fake kidnapping" (i.e., news staging, false newscasts, and licensee failure to exercise adequate control over station operations) and to a lesser extent on its technical violations on several station program logs and its Equal Employment Opportunity record. The commission affirmed its position in 1980, and two years later the District of Columbia Circuit Court upheld the decision.

Serious Radio Hoaxes

After the FCC eliminated its scare announcement policy, between 1989 and 1991 a number of serious radio hoaxes popped up across the United States; at least five are documented in the commission's ruling "Regarding Broadcast Hoaxes." Four of these incidents resulted in admonishment by the FCC, although only one resulted in a $25,000 fine. On 2 October 1989 the FCC admonished KSLX-FM in Scottsdale, Arizona, for a stunt that faked the station being taken hostage by terrorist activity. In July 1990 the commission admonished WCCC-AM/FM in Hartford, Connecticut, for reporting a nearby volcanic eruption.

In 1991 three other serious hoaxes were perpetrated by St. Louis' KSHE, Los Angeles' KROQ, and Rhode Island's WALE. On 29 January 1991, KSHE morning personality John Ulett staged a mock nuclear alert during the morning drive-time, complete with a simulated Emergency Broadcast System (EBS) tone and an authentic-sounding civil defense warning that announced that the nation was under nuclear attack. There was no disclaimer until two hours after the broadcast. Four-hundred listeners called the station. The FCC fined KSHE $25,000 based on the false use of EBS during the hoax. The KROQ morning team staged a false confession from an anonymous caller who claimed to have brutally murdered his girlfriend. Police spent nearly 150 hours investigating the case and the incident was featured twice on the syndicated TV program *Unsolved Mysteries*. On 9 July 1991, the WALE news director in Rhode Island announced that the overnight on-air personality had been shot in the head. Police and media rushed to investigate the incident. Upon hearing the broadcast, the program director called the station and told the producer to cease the hoax. When the producer failed to do so, the program director shut off the transmitter. The station went back on the air one minute later, with a disclaimer that aired every 30 minutes for the following 30 hours. Although the program director terminated the news director, the talk show host, and the producer, the FCC admonished WALE for broadcasting false and misleading information and stated that the licensee was not excused by subsequent remedial action.

Anti-Hoax Ruling

The Commission's 1992 anti-hoax rule (Section 73.1217) did not discourage the morning crew at WNOR-FM in Norfolk, Virginia, from staging a series of news reports that the city park built over a landfill was about to explode. Local police, overwhelmed with concerned calls from listeners, filed complaints with the FCC. A month after the WNOR-FM incident, the FCC issued its anti-hoax ruling in an effort to target those incidents involving a false report of a crime or catastrophe. The FCC was eager to clear its docket of what appeared to be a stream of hoax violations and to enact a middle range of enforcement. The commission said that its ruling would provide enforcement flexibility by allowing fines that could range up to $25,000 a day. In the ruling the commission states:

> No licensee or permittee of any broadcast station shall broadcast false information concerning a crime or catastrophe if (a) the licensee knows this information is false, (b) it is foreseeable that broadcasting the information will cause substantial public harm. Any programming accompanied by a disclaimer will be presumed not to pose foreseeable harm if the disclaimer clearly characterizes the program as fiction and is presented in a way that is reasonable under the circumstances.
>
> (amendment to Part 73 Regarding Broadcast Hoaxes, Communications Act, Report and Order, 7FCCRcd4106 [1992])

This ruling clearly demonstrated the FCC's desire to manage promotional content abuses on the airwaves by assigning specific monetary punitive actions for serious hoaxes that posed a substantial threat to the public safety and welfare.

On their Boston broadcast, shock jock team Opie and Anthony reported that the city's mayor had died in a car accident. Intended as a hoax and supposed to be funny, the hoax resulted in their being fired. About a week before the 2008 presidential election, two Canadian radio pranksters reached American vice presidential candidate Sarah Palin on the phone pretending to be French President Nicholas Sarkozy, engaging her in a conversation about hunting, which they aired in Montreal. Palin appeared taken in by the hoax and seemed to believe she was really talking to the French official.

See also: War of the Worlds

Further Reading

Brock, Pope, *Charlatan: America's Most Dangerous Huckster, The Man Who Pursued Him, and the Age of Flimflam.* New York: Crown, 2008.

Cantril, Hadley, *The Invasion of Mars: A Study in the Psychology of Panic*, Princeton, New Jersey: Princeton University Press, 1940.

Cobo, Lucia, "False Radio Broadcast Evokes FCC Investigation," *Broadcasting* (4 February 1991).

Doerksen, Clifford J., *American Babel: Rogue Radio Broadcasters of the Jazz Age.* Philadelphia: University of Pennsylvania Press, 2005.

"FCC Admonishes Station for Airing Hoaxes," *The News, Media, and the Law* 16, no. 1 (Winter 1992).

"FCC Moves to Revamp EBS," *Radio and Records* (25 September 1992).

Fedler, Fred, *Media Hoaxes*, Ames: Iowa State University Press, 1989.

Jessell, Harry A., "FCC Picks up Pace on Indecency Enforcement," *Broadcasting* (31 August 1992).

Johnson, Phylis, and Joe S. Foote, "Pranks and Policy: Martians, Nuclear Bombs, and the 1992 Ruling on Broadcast Hoaxes," *Journal of Radio Studies* 2 (1993–94).

"KROQ Team Suspended after Murder Hoaxes," *Radio and Records* (19 April 1991).

"KSHE Radio Jolts Listeners with Fake Nuclear Bomb News," *St. Louis Post-Dispatch* (30 January 1991).

Ray, William B., *FCC: The Ups and Downs of Radio-TV Regulation*, Ames: Iowa State University Press, 1990.

Tunstall, Jeremy, *Communications Deregulation: The Unleashing of America's Communications Industry*, New York and Oxford: Blackwell, 1986.

PHYLIS JOHNSON,
2009 REVISIONS BY CARY O'DELL

HOLLYWOOD AND RADIO

In this era of studio-owned television networks, it is difficult to remember that only a few years ago, accounts of the history of television and broadcasting cast their relationship in terms of a bitter bicoastal rivalry. Hollywood hated and resisted television as it had radio, these historians said: they turned their back on it and refused to let their stars appear on it, and one studio even forbade television sets from appearing in its films.

If we take a closer look at history, however, nothing could be further from the truth. From the earliest years of radio, Hollywood studios regarded the upstart sound-only medium with a great deal of interest—despite the fact that in those days movies had no voice at all. After a period of experimentation with movie/radio cross-promotion, a few studios attempted to enter the network business.

Thwarted by both economics and regulation, the film industry turned to steady and profitable production for radio, to the point that in the mid-1930s both major networks, the National Broadcasting Company (NBC) and the Columbia Broadcasting System (CBS), constructed major studios of their own in the heart of filmland. This productive relationship continued through the early years of television, and although radio lost its importance in the Hollywood scheme of things as television quickly took over the production of dramatic programs, film companies still maintained a presence in radio station ownership and also in the production of recorded music, so vital to radio's new format mode. The merger mania of the 1980s and 1990s consolidated these cross-ownership positions, as radio, television, film, music, and new media became interlocking parts of the same communications conglomerates.

Origins

One of the earliest instances of film/radio cooperation took place not in Hollywood but on the stage of the Capitol Theater in New York City, part of the Loews/Metro Goldwyn Mayer (MGM) chain. In 1923 theater manager Samuel L. Rothafel entered into an agreement with American Telephone and Telegraph (AT&T) to broadcast his prefilm stage show over their new station, WEAR The results were so positive that the show quickly became a regular feature, called *Roxy and His Gang*, one of the earliest hits of radio broadcasting. Soon other theaters jumped on the bandwagon.

Movies might not have been able to talk, but that didn't mean there wasn't a lot of musical entertainment in the theaters. Many big-city theaters featured elaborate stage shows and enormous theater organs, the musical accompaniments of which animated their film showings. Concerts by theater organists were broadcast over WMAC, WGN, and KWY in Chicago and in many other cities starting in 1925. That year, Harry Warner of Warner Brothers Studios proposed that the film industry as a whole should start a radio network to publicize their pictures. He began by opening a Warner Brothers radio station, KFWB in Los Angeles, and in 1926 a second one, WBPI in New York City. Other studios took note. Pathe, producers of newsreels, announced that they would begin distributing a script version of their news films for delivery over local stations. By 1927 Universal chief Carl Laemmle inaugurated the *Carl Laemmle Hour* over WOR-New York, presenting vaudeville and film stars and giving previews of upcoming pictures.

MGM experimented with the world's first "tele-movie": a dramatic, blow-by-blow narration of MGM's new release, *Love*, starring Greta Garbo and John Gilbert, delivered on the air by WPAP's announcer Ted Husing (usually known for his sports coverage) as it unreeled before his eyes in the Embassy Theater in New York.

That same year, MGM announced an ambitious project with the Loews theater chain: a planned network based on movie materials and promotion that would link over 60 stations in more than 40 cities. This proposal followed a more detailed one announced the previous spring by Paramount Pictures Corporation. Paramount, in conjunction with the Postal Telegraph Company, planned to start up the Keystone network "for dramatizing and advertising first-run motion pictures." Because AT&T had a lock on the land-lines vitally needed to link stations together into a network, and because AT&T had an exclusive contract with the existing radio networks, Paramount needed Postal Telegraph to provide its lines. Despite much excitement in the industry, neither the Keystone Chain nor the MGM/Loews network reached fruition. A combination of regulatory discouragement, exhibitor opposition, and competition from other sources diverted studios' radio ideas in other directions. Paramount shortly thereafter purchased a 49 percent interest in the CBS network, still struggling to compete with its deep-pocketed competitor. Meanwhile, NBC's parent company, the Radio Corporation of America (RCA), acquired its own film studio, Radio-Keith-Orpheum (RKO), in 1929. Though this was intended more as a way to capitalize on RCA's new sound-on-film system than as a radio venture, the era of "talking pictures" would facilitate a renewed interest in the potential of film/radio cooperation.

Depression Years

By 1932 America had been hard hit by the Depression. Film industry profits suffered, as theaters went out of business and box office receipts slowed to a trickle. Radio, however, continued to thrive. As advertising agencies began to take the broadcast medium seriously as an outlet for their customers' campaigns, a new and influential partnership was about to emerge. Dissatisfied with CBS's and NBC's staid approach to programming, several aggressive advertising firms turned their attention to Hollywood's untapped potential for radio-based product promotion. One of the most influential in this Hollywood/agency alliance was John U. Reber of the J. Walter Thompson

Company (JWT), whose plan for radio advertising envisioned big-budget, star-studded productions sponsored by JWT clients over the major radio networks. He determined to form a working relationship with the proven entertainment producers in Hollywood, and by the mid-1930s JWT was producing at least five shows out of each year's top ten, most of them featuring Hollywood talent. Other major agencies included Young and Rubicam, Blackett-Sample-Hummert, and Dancer Fitzgerald. When in 1936 AT&T, as a result of an investigation by the Federal Communications Commission, reduced their land-line rates to the West Coast, a "rush to Hollywood" resulted, and most major agencies, along with the two national networks, opened up studios in Los Angeles. Radio had gone Hollywood.

This productive and profitable association would have great impact on both the radio and film industries. A variety of radio programs developed that centered on movie industry stars, properties, and Hollywood celebrities. The most prestigious was the movie adaptation format pioneered by JWT's *Lux Radio Theater*. Hosted by celebrity director Cecil B. DeMille, *Lux* presented hour-long radio adaptations of recent Hollywood film releases, introduced and narrated by DeMille and featuring well-known film stars. It started on NBC in 1934 but jumped in 1935 to CBS, where it ran until 1954. From 1936 on, the program was produced in Hollywood. Others in this format, often referred to at the time as "prestige drama," included: *Screen Guild Theater, Hollywood Premiere, Academy Award Theater, Dreft Star Playhouse, Hollywood Startime,* and *Screen Directors' Playhouse*. A popular feature of these programs was the intimate, casual interviews with famous stars; DeMille, for instance, would chat at the end of each show with that night's leading actors, often casually working in a mention of the sponsor's product.

The second major venue for Hollywood stars and film promotion was radio's leading genre, the big-name variety show. Starting with the *Rudy Vallee Show* in 1929, almost all of the top-rated programs on the major networks in the 1930s belonged to this genre: the *Kate Smith Hour, Maxwell House Showboat, Shell Chateau* (Al Jolson), the *Chase and Sanborn Hour* (Bergen and McCarthy), the *Jack Benny Program, Kraft Music Hall* (Bing Crosby), *Texaco Star Theater,* the *Eddie Cantor Show, Burns and Allen, Town Hall Tonight* (Fred Allen), and many more. All featured regular guest appearances from Hollywood's best and brightest, often promoting their latest pictures or acting out skits related to film properties. Many stars even-

tually began hosting such programs themselves, especially in the late 1930s and early 1940s. Adolph Menjou and John Barrymore served as hosts for *Texaco Star Theater;* Al Jolson appeared on radio almost exclusively after 1935; and William Powell and Herbert Marshall hosted *Hollywood Hotel* at various times. Some directors also got in on the act: Orson Welles was a frequent variety show guest and often guest-hosted for Fred Allen, and Alfred Hitchcock established a reputation on radio before becoming a television personality. Furthermore, a whole set of Hollywood's secondary ladies became more famous via radio performances than their film careers had permitted: Lucille Ball, Dinah Shore, Joan Davis, Hattie McDaniel, Ann Sothern, and many others began as frequent guest stars, then headlined their own continuing programs on radio and later television.

Dramatic series programs also featured Hollywood talent. Most were the anthology-style programs that would also become early television's most prestigious fare. *First Nighter, Cavalcade of America, Hollywood Playhouse, Grand Central Station, Four Star Playhouse, Ford Theater, Everyman's Theater,* and many others brought film stars to radio in a wide range of stand-alone drama and comedy pieces. During the war years, Hollywood generously donated its talent to morale-boosting programs, sometimes on the regular networks and sometimes for the Armed Forces Radio Service only, such as *Command Performance, Free World Theater, Everything for the Boys, The Doctor Fights,* and many more. Hollywood stars moved freely between film and radio, and they would host and perform just as frequently on television's early dramas. Only in the mid- to late 1940s, however, did film stars begin turning up as leading actors in series comedies and dramas. The situation comedy form, pioneered by radio programs such as *Amos 'n' Andy, The Goldbergs, Fibber McGee and Molly,* and *Vic and Sade,* would be given a new gloss and prestige as Hollywood luminaries, particularly the comediennes mentioned above, moved into regular series production in shows such as *Joan Davis Time, My Favorite Husband, My Friend Irma, Maisie, Our Miss Brooks,* and *Beulah*.

Finally, mention should be made of the ever-popular genre of Hollywood gossip and talk. Many leading figures built their reputations on film industry chitchat, including the print divas Louella Parsons and Hedda Hopper. Walter Winchell also started in print but achieved full status on radio, combining gossip with news-related material. Ed Sullivan, Earl Wilson, and Jimmy Fidler all trafficked in celebrity news and views. A late-developing genre, the so-called breakfast program, presaged the television morning show *Today*, with a combination of host chatter, celebrity guest interviews, and light news. Journalist Mary Margaret McBride pioneered the talk show format on radio in her long-running program of the same name. Another writer, Pegeen Fitzgerald, tried out McBride's formula in an early-morning show called *Pegeen Prefers;* she and her husband Ed would develop the first of the big-time breakfast shows, *The Fitzgeralds.* Others in this genre were *Tex and Jinx* (Tex McCrary and Jinx Falkeberg) and *Breakfast with Dorothy and Dick* (Dorothy Kilgallen and Richard Kollmar).

The film industry came increasingly to rely on the star-producing capabilities of radio as well. Radio personalities starred in many popular Hollywood films, from Freeman Gosden and Charles Correll ("Amos" and "Andy") in *Check and Double Check* in 1929, to special "radio" movies such as *The Big Broadcast of 1936* (and *1937* and *1938*), to the Bing Crosby/Bob Hope/Dorothy Lamour "Road" movies in the 1940s (*Road to Morocco, Road to Zanzibar, Road to Rio,* etc.). Rudy Vallee, Eddie Cantor, and Jack Benny all met with box-office success. Orson Welles' flamboyant production of *War of the Worlds* for the CBS *Mercury Theater of the Air* won him the contract to make *Citizen Kane* in Hollywood.

Radio and Television

As television loomed on the horizon after World War II, movie studios stood in a strong position to move into television production. A combination of network economics, the emphasis on "live" programming during television's early days, and royalty disputes within the film industry would delay the Hollywood/television alliance until the late 1950s. Though the nature of radio changed dramatically once television came onto the scene, some studios did maintain a persistent presence in radio ownership and production. Warner Brothers, Paramount, RKO, and MGM all owned radio stations, and they were to get in on television station ownership early on as well. MGM went into syndicated radio program production and distribution in the late 1940s with such programs as *MGM Theater of the Air* and *Maisie,* starring Ann Sothern. As attention and dollars shifted to television in the late 1940s and early 1950s, and as radio became once again primarily a musical medium, Hollywood stars and on-air production would migrate to the newer medium as well. Soon film studios would dominate prime-time television programming, though

this would not translate into network power until passage of the FCC's financial interest and syndication rules broke up the networks' tight vertical integration in the 1970s. However, just as film companies diversified into television, they also began to acquire interests in the music industry, the new backbone of radio, with frequent cross-promotion between music and film.

Merger Mania

As the 1980s wave of mergers and acquisitions continued into the 1990s, the film majors of yore became part of diversified media conglomerates. Warner became part of the Time/Warner/Turner empire, with more than 50 labels under its imprint, including Warner Music International, Atlantic, Elektra, Rhino, Sire, and Warner Brothers. The conglomerate also has interests in music publishing, record clubs, recording technology, and music distribution. Time Warner accounted for 21 percent of U.S. music sales in 1997. Columbia Pictures was acquired by the Sony Corporation, owner of Columbia Records (acquired from CBS) and associated labels, the Columbia House music club, and other manufacturing and distribution arms, all of which accounted for 15 percent of U.S. music revenues. Universal became a part of the Music Corporation of America (MCA), which was later acquired by Seagram. MCA has long been a major presence in the music industry, with 11 percent of the U.S. market. Its labels include A&M, Decca, Def Jam, Deutsche Grammophon, Interscope, Geffen, MCA, MCA Nashville, Motown, Island, Phillips, Polydor, Universal, and Verve.

In 1995 Paramount was acquired by Viacom, owner of MTV and related cable music channels (M2, VH1), a considerable power in the music business. MTV produces radio programming as well, including radio versions of *MTV Unplugged, MTV News,* and *Weekend Revolution.* In 1995 Viacom announced a partnership with radio's largest program syndicator and station groups, Westwood One, to launch a new MTV Radio network featuring music-related material. The Disney Corporation also holds extensive interests in music recording, and with its merger with American Broadcasting Company (ABC) in 1995, it now owns radio stations that reach 24 percent of U.S. households. Twentieth Century Fox was purchased by Rupert Murdoch's News Corporation in the 1980s and is now linked with satellite music channels worldwide. News Corporation also owns the Australian Mushroom and Festival record labels. And in this age of synergy, the tie between movies and music has become tighter than ever before, with movie sound tracks used to promote artists and recordings, and soundtrack releases often achieving billions of dollars in sales.

In the era of new media, where the lines between film, radio, television, music, recordings, and the internet seem to be growing more blurry every day, the integrated entertainment corporations formerly designated by the term *Hollywood* have fingers in nearly every form of media that reaches into the home—or that reaches the viewer anywhere she or he might be. Now internet radio technology gives companies the ability to go online with their own "radio" services. DisneyRadio.com already provides a schedule of music and features from its films and artists, oriented toward children. Television shows on studio-owned networks promote recordings distributed by the company's record arm, which become hits on pop radio. Recording stars launch film careers; even radio personalities such as Howard Stern might receive a moment of celluloid fame. Though in the United States the days of radio drama and comedy faded, transferring their stars and audiences to television, the film industry continues to play a vital behind-the-scenes role linking radio to a host of other media. Without Hollywood, American radio could never have risen to the heights of creativity and popularity it achieved in its heyday. That the older medium bequeathed this tradition to a newer medium might be radio's loss, but it was television's gain.

See also: Film Depictions of Radio; Television Depictions of Radio

Further Reading

Anderson, Christopher, *Hollywood TV: The Studio System in the Fifties*, Austin: University of Texas Press, 1994.

Balio, Tino, editor, *Hollywood in the Age of Television*, Boston: Unwin Hyman, 1990.

Hilmes, Michele, *Hollywood and Broadcasting: From Radio to Cable*, Urbana: University of Illinois Press, 1990.

Jewell, Richard B., "Hollywood and Radio: Competition and Partnership in the 1930s," *Historical Journal of Film, Radio, and Television* 4, no. 2 (1984).

Lucich, Bernard, "The Lux Radio Theatre," in *American Broadcasting: A Source Book on the History of Radio and Television*, compiled by Lawrence Wilson Lichty and Malachi C. Topping, New York: Hastings House, 1975.

Rothafel, Samuel Lionel, *Broadcasting, Its New Day*, New York and London: Century, 1925.

Smoodin, Eric, "Motion Pictures and Television, 1930–1945," *Journal of the University Film and Video Association* 34, no. 3 (Summer 1982).

Watt, Kenneth, "One Minute to Go," *Saturday Evening Post* (2 April 1938 and 9 April 1938).

MICHELE HILMES

HOOPERATINGS
Radio Ratings Service

Hooperatings was radio's best known and most widely quoted rating service in radio broadcasting during its heyday from 1934 to 1950. C.E. Hooper (1898–1955) pioneered a technique, the coincidental telephone call, that became an industry standard. Hooper sold subscriptions to his ratings information, making his service the first commercial venture in the field of radio ratings. C.E. Hooper, known as "Hoop," was imbued with a mission, and through his salesmanship he made his ratings service famous not just to the broadcasting industry but also to the public.

Origins

Hooper began his business career by selling aluminum utensils from door to door. He went on to earn an MBA (1923) from Harvard Graduate School of Business Administration. He took a job in Yakima, Washington, as assistant manager of the Liberty Savings and Loan Company. Between 1924 and 1926, he was advertising manager at the *Harvard Business Review*. He then took a similar job at *Scribner's Magazine*. He switched from selling space to buying space in 1929 as an account executive for Doremus and Company. After two years, at age 33, he entered the market research field as a member of the Daniel Starch organization.

Daniel Starch had taught business psychology at Harvard when Hooper was a student there. Starch conducted pioneering radio audience research for the new NBC network in 1928 and 1930, and in 1931 established the first continuous service for measuring the readerships of magazine and newspaper advertisements.

Since March 1930, Archibald Crossley had been "rating" broadcasts to estimate audience size for advertisers and for agencies that supported the Cooperative Analysis of Broadcasting (CAB). Crossley used a telephone recall method to ask listeners about their previous day's listening. He limited his surveys to areas of equal network opportunity, the 32 cities where all four networks (National Broadcasting Company [NBC] Red and Blue, Columbia Broadcasting System [CBS] and, after 1934, Mutual) could be heard with equal ease.

Hooperatings Begin

In 1934 Hooper left Starch to go into business as president of Clark-Hooper, a service that measured magazine and newspaper effectiveness. He also entered the field of radio audience measurement that same year using telephone *coincidental* calling when the audience was still listening, a method suggested to him by George Gallup. The team of Clark-Hooper, Inc. was encouraged by a group of magazine publishers who wanted to set up a more valid measure of radio's advertising effectiveness. These publishers were convinced that Crossley's ratings overstated the actual number of radio homes. More popular programs under Crossley's rating system would achieve ratings as high as 40 to 60 percent of the radio audience. To make matters worse, despite the fact that Crossley merely provided a rating index, many broadcasters persisted in projecting CAB ratings to total radio homes, resulting in an astronomical number of radio homes. The reason for this rating inflation was that Crossley initially used only the "identified listening audience," or what is now called the "share" (proportion of people tuned to a given channel based on all those using radio receivers at that time), as the base for his ratings. All of these factors hurt magazines and were factors that Clark-Hooper, Inc. undertook to correct.

Hooper's first important publicity came when, in collaboration with CBS, he estimated the number of adult listeners to President Roosevelt's fireside chat of 10 June 1936 in time for the next day's newspapers.

By 1938 the team of Clark-Hooper, Inc. had disbanded, and Hooper continued alone in the field of radio measurement. Although magazine publishers encouraged Hooper's service, they did not underwrite it. Hooper's method allowed him to innovate such features as the available audience base, resulting in ratings half the size of Crossley's. (The available audience included those not listening as well as those listening, whereas Crossley used only those listening.) Hooper also supplied an average audience rating, rather than give the total program listeners as CAB had done. An average audience rating was a program's total audience divided by the time intervals. Crossley's method, by comparison, presented only the total listeners to a given program in a sample or only the program's total audience. Furthermore, the coincidental technique eliminated what Hooper considered another major flaw with the recall method: the memory factor.

Hooper managed to make his name a household word. CAB reports had been primarily available to the buyers of advertising time, and consequently reports were guarded. Hooper, on the other hand, openly courted the press, making himself and his ratings newsworthy. His name began to appear in a vast assortment of trade magazines. In addition, he was written up in daily newspapers and even garnered a feature article in the *Saturday Evening Post* in 1947. Publicity surrounding Hooperatings rode such a crest during this period that Crossley was later to remark wryly that his defeat could be traced to the fact that his name did not rhyme with anything. (A genius at promotion, Hooper had a field day attaching his name to such derivatives as Hooperuppers, Hooperdowners, Hoopermania, and Hooperhappy.)

Whereas Crossley's reports aided the advertising community, Hooper courted the other side of the street, the networks and the stations. In particular, he did this by introducing services specifically designed to aid stations and networks. Hooper's next move, in the early 1940s, was to introduce his "Stations Listening Area Reports" for local radio markets, quickly signing up 205 local markets to CAB's none. Stations were quick to assume 44.5 percent of the cost of Hooper's operation. Hooper was, of course, weakest in advertising clients, the community sponsoring CAB. This move to local-market reports, together with Hooper's open press policy, made a major impact on CAB's clients—the advertising community.

By 1944 the CAB had lost ground to Hooper's coincidental method, and over time, Crossley also switched his service to the telephone coincidental method. With both services using the coincidental method, with growing costs, and with increasing numbers of interviews yet different results, industry executives began to argue that having two services was repetitive and wasteful. CAB was considered superfluous and was forced out of business in 1946.

In 1945 Hooper made his reports available to advertisers, agencies, and networks. This strategy, which included local stations as a vital part of his service, resulted in both economic and methodological advantages. The economic results were to increase the scope of Hooper's service without excessive financial burden to any one subscriber. In this sense, Hooper operated the first radio pool made up of the commercial interests in radio, a precedent that became an industry norm.

As Frank Nye points out in *"Hoop" of Hooperatings*, the odds had been against Hooper, an unknown selling a deflationary method to those who wanted optimal figures; furthermore, his service was based on a technique one-third more costly and was pitted against a service backed by three powerful associations. Whereas CAB had been developed to serve the advertising community, Hooper had worked the other side of the street, serving stations in 60 cities and their rep firms.

Through Hooper's showmanship, the Hooperatings became increasingly important. Although Hooper took great pains to emphasize in his writings that radio program ratings are measures of quantity, not quality, many critics complained that the ratings took on the sinister quality of being an absolute artistic standard for radio programming.

Although the industry had attacked CAB in particular, telephone-based methods were coming under closer scrutiny in general. In 1929 there were 10.25 million radio homes in the U.S. (approximately 35 percent of all homes), compared to 12.4 million telephone homes (42 percent of all homes). However, the situation changed rapidly when the number of radio homes began to grow substantially faster than the number of telephone homes, raising the question of the representativeness of a telephone-based sample to measure radio. As radio went into World War II, radio homes were approaching saturation and were estimated to reach a national average of 85 percent of all homes, growing at twice the rate of telephone homes. The radio industry was beginning to grumble about the exclusion of listeners on farms, in small towns, and in areas remote from transmitters.

Coming Up on the Outside: Competition from A.C. Nielsen

Hooperatings did not survive the challenge of a new competitor, A.C. Nielsen. Its defeat lay, oddly enough, in the method it had championed, the telephone coincidental, as it attempted to measure the rise of a new advertising medium, television. The year was 1948, a year that brought attacks on two key fronts of the established Hooperatings by the up-and-coming A.C. Nielsen. These two fronts were projectable ratings (ratings projectable to a true national cross-section) and TV ratings.

It became increasingly apparent that Hooper's telephone-based service was doomed if it could not develop a national sample. Hooper's Program Hooperatings measured only urban areas and were not projectable to a national audience. Because projectable ratings required a sample representative of national radio homes, Hooper's key challenge was to develop a representative sample. In April 1948 Hooper launched U.S. Hooperatings, his first projectable service of radio's listening audience. U.S. Hooperatings were an attempt to achieve this national cross-section by adding a diary method to the coincidental method, in order to measure nontelephone homes. Hooper's projectable ratings were not an entity of their own but took the coincidental measurements as a base and projected them to a

national total through information collected from diaries. Hooper planned to charge a separate fee to subsidize this new service, and he planned to operate it on a regular basis if enough subscriptions could be found. His primary client for such a service would be the networks.

However, Nielsen had begun integrating projectable ratings as a feature of his service with no extra charge. In addition, by March 1948 Nielsen had expanded his sample to a national basis. The bottom line was that, until ratings could be projected, they were merely indices of arbitrary value: the numbers were comparable one to another within urban areas but not representative of a national population. Nielsen thus offered a significant product innovation through the development of projectable ratings. Nielsen's projectable ratings offered both a pricing advantage and a superior method. Both strategies resulted in an eventual defeat of Hooperatings. U.S. Hooperatings failed to achieve enough subscriptions to launch the projectable rating service as a regular feature.

A second critical factor in Hooper's defeat by Nielsen was the rise of television. The Hooper network service covered only the larger urban areas with telephone homes. This coverage, however, represented only 20 percent of the population. Television had hit these urban areas the hardest and had made the most impact in cities where Hooper had based his radio rating service. In other words, although radio use was falling in the areas measured by Hooper's network service, it was not falling in 80 percent of the nation's homes. Thus, according to Nielsen, it was utterly unrealistic for Hooper to ignore TV's impact in his network radio cities.

Hooper had based his network program ratings wholly on telephone homes in the urban areas where television had made the greatest inroads. Thus, his sample was attacked for over-weighting the influence of TV on radio listenership. To make matters worse, telephone subscribers were found to own a disproportionate number of TVs, when compared to nonsubscribers. Hooper consequently was accused of shortchanging and deflating radio.

In February 1950 Hooper sold his national ratings services (national radio and national TV ratings) to A.C. Nielsen, Inc. Hooper cited three factors in his decision. First, the number of sponsored network radio programs on the air had dropped 40 percent in three years. Thus, his radio network service had declined because of the flight of advertisers to network TV. Second, Hooper noted the increased competition from Nielsen. According to Hooper, without Nielsen competition, he would have continued his network Hooperatings, "riding the radio curve down and the television curve up." With the growing revenue split between Hooper and Nielsen, even the network TV rating business did not bring the total network ratings to a profitable level. Revenue had dropped from $40,000 annually in January 1949 to $25,000 by January 1950. Third, Hooper stated that television had so changed listening habits in cities with TV service that the averaging of listeners in cities with and without TV was no longer plausible.

The 36-city-based network Hooperatings assumed that "conditions" under which measurements were taken remained relatively constant and that consequently the change in the rating index or rank was a valid indication of change in popularity. Because television came first to the big cities, where Hooper had based his samples, his reports indicated that radio audiences were moving in large numbers to TV. However, this was not true in most of the country. In not being representative, National Hooperatings indices had become essentially meaningless.

Although Hooper quit the national rating business, he planned to continue at the local level with city Hooperatings, city teleratings, area coverage indices, and sales impact ratings. These local markets were now where Hooper was getting two-thirds of his profits. In a prophetic statement, Hooper argued that the shift in their packaging was away from one average index to analytic reports of individual markets and of differences between markets. Hooper left the national rating field for TV and radio to A.C. Nielsen, Inc., and his Audimeter. Though he planned to continue his local market services, Hooper's untimely death in a boating accident prevented these plans from reaching fruition. The American Research Bureau (later Arbitron) purchased Hooper's remaining local service in 1955.

See also: A.C. Nielsen Company; Arbitron; Audience Research Methods; Cooperative Analysis of Broadcasting; Diary

Further Reading

Beville, Hugh Malcom, *Audience Ratings: Radio, TV, Cable*, Hillsdale, New Jersey: Erlbaum, 1985; 2nd edition, 1988.

Buzzard, Karen S., *Chains of Gold: Marketing the Ratings and Rating the Markets*, Metuchen, New Jersey: Scarecrow Press, 1990.

Buzzard, Karen S., "Radio Ratings Pioneers: The Development of a Standardized Ratings Vocabulary," *Journal of Radio Studies* 6, no. 2 (Autumn 1999).

Chappell, Matthew Napoleon, and Claude Ernest Hooper, *Radio Audience Measurement*, New York: Daye, 1944.

Nye, Frank Wilson, *"Hoop" of Hooperatings: The Man and His Work*, Norwalk, Connecticut: n.p., 1957.

Small, C.E., "Biggest Man in Radio: C.E. Hooper," *Saturday Evening Post* (22 November 1947).

KAREN S. BUZZARD

HORROR PROGRAMS

Horror programs occasionally featured classic monsters like vampires and werewolves, but more often were home to the walking dead, disembodied spirits, or unique creations. In the 1940s, *Inner Sanctum's* no-holds-barred formula set the standard, and its "creaking door" is one of radio's best-remembered icons. Listeners never knew what would happen on *Inner Sanctum* or who would be the next victim. In many cases, the episode's narrator turned out to be the murderer! As John Dunning observes, "without benefit of the guilty knowledge, the listener was recruited as the killer's sidekick."

Origins

The real origins of radio horror can be found in the 1930s, but like all popular phenomena, the trend did not occur in isolation. Dime novels had been popular since before the turn of the century, and their direct descendants, the pulp magazines, had become increasingly lurid throughout the 1920s and early 1930s.

Pulps like *Weird Tales* displayed fantastic, horrific, and just plain odd cover images. The March 1923 *Weird Tales* cover, illustrating the story "Ooze," depicts a tentacled, shadowy figure. Horned devils (October 1925), fiendish dwarves (March 1926), wolf-women (September 1927), treacherous druids (October 1930), and monstrous gorillas (September 1929) were common. Stories included Carl Jacobi's "Mive" (January 1932), about carnivorous butterflies, and H.P. Lovecraft's stories of unnamable, lurking monstrosities and rats inside walls. Horror was certainly in the air when Universal Studios inaugurated its series of "monster movies" with 1931's *Dracula* and *Frankenstein*.

Radio's *Collier Hour* serialized stories of Fu Manchu in 1929, complete with menacing fungus and poisonous green mist. "The Shadow" first appeared as a nameless narrator on the *Street & Smith Detective Story Magazine Hour* but would reincarnate in his own program, as an adventurer "with the power to cloud men's minds." Research is now uncovering isolated references to early 1930s horror programs, but the first significant horror program was *The Witch's Tale*, which began on New York's WOR on 28 May 1931.

Written by Alonzo Deen Cole, the series derived from the folk tale tradition. "Old Nancy, the witch of Salem," began by gathering listeners around her fire. "A hunnert and fifteen year old" (her age changed frequently), she sat with "Satan, her wise black cat," inviting listeners to "turn out them lights" and "gaze into the embers" as she wove her tales. Old Nancy's dialect and stories are "straight from the Middle Ages," as Dunning notes. The supernatural dominates, as ghosts seek vengeance, tombs are defiled, and curses are cast. Caucasians laugh at "silly native superstitions" in "Spirits of the Lake" and "The Boa Goddess," only to die horribly. Cole adapted legends like "The Flying Dutchman" and even tackled Mary Shelly's *Frankenstein*. In "The Bronze Venus," a man dies in the arms of a living bronze statue, and in "The Troth of Death," a man betrays his lover, only to be doomed to spend eternity chained to a cemetery.

Nationally syndicated in 1934, the program survived at least half a dozen incarnations. (Ironically, one of the best and most popular surviving *Witch's Tale* episodes, "Four Fingers and a Thumb," originated in Australia.) Adelaide Fitz-Allen, Martha Wentworth, and 13-year-old Miriam Wolfe provided Old Nancy's voice.

In 1934, Wyllis Cooper created *Lights Out* for Chicago's WENR, drastically changing the tone of radio horror. Creative sound effects embellished imaginative nightmares, like people turned inside out, or the "Chicken Heart," which grows to monstrous size. In "Murder Castle," a killer suffocates. "Snake Woman" gains revenge with trained serpents. A chemist discovers "Oxychloride X," a chemical that eats through anything. By 1939, writer Arch Oboler turned to more mainstream fare, claiming that he couldn't keep on topping his own horror stories.

The Hermit's Cave originated in 1935 on Detroit's WJR. It was syndicated nationally by the 1940s, with a later West Coast version. The Hermit (played variously by John Kent, Klock Ryder, Toby Gremmer, and Charles Penman, who also directed) was a cackling counterpart to Old Nancy. He spoke over howling winds, promising "Ghost stories! Weirrrrd stories! And murders, too! The hermit knows of them all!" Detroit acting troupe "The Mummers" produced ghost stories like "A Haunted House," witchcraft tales like "The Red Mark," and grisly fare like "The Vampire's Desire."

By the mid-1930s, local stations were anxious to cash in with programs like WKY's *Dark Fantasy*, which broadcast from Oklahoma City. Network "creepy hosts" like Ted Osborne can be heard on two surviving episodes of *The Black Chapel*, and

Charles Penman hosted *The Devil's Scrapbook* in 1938. Others like *The Devil's Roost* and *The Witching Hour* no longer exist.

Inner Sanctum Mysteries began on 7 January 1941. "Raymond" was a new model for the "creepy host," and *Inner Sanctum* incorporated both strands of previous horror programming—Old Nancy's melodramatic supernatural tales and *Lights Out*'s explicit detail—and added its own unique flavor. Shamelessly theatrical, *Inner Sanctum* resorted to any melodramatic device to engage the listener. Background screams and sudden appearances of characters thought dead were common. Best of all, Raymond relished puns. He professed to keep a "happy medium around to keep in the right spirit." Raymond's moral of an axe murderer story was "Knife can be beautiful if you look out for people with an axe to grind. They may be trying to get a HEAD of you."

Many nonhorror series contained occasional genre trappings during their run. Orson Welles had famously adapted *Dracula* in 1938, and his *War of the Worlds* adaptation frightened thousands. The high profile *Suspense* adapted H.P. Lovecraft's *The Dunwich Horror*, and in "The Diary of Sophronia Winters," Agnes Moorehead's character wallops Ray Collins in the head with an axe. A werewolf stalks "The House in Cypress Canyon."

The Shadow fought monsters like "The Gibbering Things" and "The Weird Sisters" (both written by Alonzo Deen Cole), and *The Hound of the Baskervilles* was periodically reincarnated in *The New Adventures of Sherlock Holmes*. Beginning in 1939, the best-remembered serial adventure, *I Love a Mystery*, depicted gruesome murders and (apparently) supernatural menaces. Jack, Doc, and Reggie often encountered weird horrors like "Temple of the Vampires" or the "Monster in the Mansion," which involved an arm amputation and a headless black cat. A slasher roams the halls as a ghostly baby cries in "The Thing That Cries in the Night."

Still, *Inner Sanctum*'s influence dominated, as new narrator/hosts appeared on other programs. *Suspense* was introduced by "The Man in Black," and by 1942 even a crime melodrama like *The Whistler* featured a nameless host. *The Mysterious Traveler* (Maurice Tarplin) rode a ghostly train, inviting listeners to join "another journey into the strange and terrifying." The Traveler told science fiction (insects seek revenge), ghost stories (haunted honeymoon cottage), and originals like "Behind the Locked Door." In this gem, trapped archaeologists discover sightless, horribly mutated descendants of a lost wagon train. *The Strange Dr. Weird*, who lived "on the other side of the cemetery," was a 15-minute version of *The Mysterious Traveler* and was also voiced by Maurice Tarplin.

A 1942 *Lights Out* revival had new narration, droned by Arch Oboler: "It-is-later-than-you-think." (The original *Lights Out* Chicago series began more effectively with "This is the witching hour. An hour when dogs howl, and evil is let loose on a sleeping world.") *The Haunting Hour*'s opening was similar to the *Lights Out* original, with "Stay where you are! Do not break the stillness of this moment!" but the scripts were *Inner Sanctum* rewrites. *The Sealed Book* from 1945 sounded like *The Hermit's Cave*, as Philip Clarke, "The Keeper of the Book," unlocked "the great padlock," revealing "all the secrets and mysteries of mankind through the ages." Astonishingly, Don Douglas provided *all* the voices on *The Black Castle*.

Mystery in the Air, a 1947 summer replacement series with oily voiced Peter Lorre, adapted classics like "The Tell-tale Heart," "The Black Cat," and "The Horla." Lorre's effective performances usually ended with his screaming insanely. Willis Cooper returned with one of the finest horror/fantasy programs in 1947. *Quiet, Please* was surrealistic, lyrical and subdued. In "Let the Lillies Consider," Cooper asked, "What if plant life could think and plot against us?" A resurrected god appears in "Whence Came You?" and something perches atop an oil rig in "The Thing on the Fourble Board." Each week, the *Quiet, Please* host signed off with, "I'm quietly yours, Ernest Chappell."

The Hall of Fantasy, originally broadcast from Salt Lake City's KALL, was revived by producer/director/writer Richard Thorne for Chicago's WGN in 1949. The show began with sounds of footsteps on wet concrete and featured unusually excellent production values, adapting Poe's "The Cask of Amontillado" and J. Sheridan LeFanu's "Green Tea." Thorne also contributed originals like "The Hand of Botar," in which a man develops intelligence in his right hand, and "The Jewels of Kali," in which a bizarre four-armed body searches the world for four mystical rubies.

Himan Brown's *CBS Radio Mystery Theater* adapted Poe and Shelly in the 1970s and 1980s, and similar radio programming continues today. Recreations are popular at conventions, and amateur groups often mix horror programs and science fiction productions. Still, as Hollywood movies feature increasingly realistic digital effects, it remains for new talents to harness the imagination with the aural medium and convincingly recreate the horror genre on radio.

See also: I Love a Mystery; Inner Sanctum Mysteries; Lights Out; Shadow; Suspense; War of the Worlds

Further Reading

Cole, Alonzo Deen, *The Witch's Tale: Stories of Gothic Horror from the Golden Age of Radio*, edited by David S. Siegel, Yorktown Heights, New York: Dunwich Press, 1998.

Dunning, John, *Tune in Yesterday: The Ultimate Encyclopedia of Old-Time Radio, 1925–1976*, Englewood Cliffs, New Jersey: Prentice-Hall, 1976; revised edition, as *On the Air: The Encyclopedia of Old-Time Radio*, New York: Oxford University Press, 1998.

Gibson, Walter Brown, *The Shadow Scrapbook*, edited by Anthony Tollin, New York: Harcourt Brace Jovanovich, 1979.

Goodstone, Tony, editor, *The Pulps: Fifty Years of American Pop Culture*, New York: Bonanza Books, 1970.

Hand, Richard J. *Terror on the Air! Horror Radio in America, 1931–1952.* Jefferson, North Carolina: McFarland, 2006.

Hickerson, Jay, *The Ultimate History of Network Radio Programming and Guide to All Circulating Shows*, Hamden, Connecticut: Hickerson, 1992.

Server, Lee, *Danger Is My Business: An Illustrated History of the Fabulous Pulp Magazines*, San Francisco, California: Chronicle Books, 1993.

Swartz, Jon David, and Robert C. Reinehr, *Handbook of Old-Time Radio: A Comprehensive Guide to Golden Age Radio Listening and Collecting*, Metuchen, New Jersey: Scarecrow Press, 1993.

DIXON H. CHANDLER II

I

I LOVE A MYSTERY
Adventure/Mystery Thriller Series

Though relatively short-lived (five years in its original run with a three-year revival based on the original scripts), *I Love a Mystery* (*ILAM*) continued its hold on radio aficionados for several decades after it aired. This was due in part to its creator and writer—Carleton E. Morse—but also to the wide-ranging nature of the adventures of the three key characters.

The Radio Serial

A serial with dozens of continuing stories that were usually presented in three-week units for a total of 1,784 episodes, the program varied from 15-minute to half-hour segments depending on the network carrying it. The program was more of an adventure/thriller than a classic detective story, despite its detective agency basis. *ILAM* originated in Hollywood for its original five-year run, moving to New York when the Mutual Broadcast System reused all but five of the original scripts (and added one new script) with a new cast. Adding to later collector confusion, the Mutual series often used different story titles. Though audition tapes were made in 1954 for a revival on CBS, that series never materialized.

In the program, Jack Packard, a one-time medical student, is head of the Triple A-1 Detective Agency, located "just off Hollywood Boulevard and one flight up," whose motto is "no job too tough, no mystery too baffling." At 37, he is older than

the other staff members and is clearly the most cool-headed and clear thinking under pressure. His fellow-adventurers include the Texas-born roughneck "Doc" Long, who loves women and adventure in about that order. The third member of the original trio is Britisher Reggie Yorke, who is refined but also serves as the group's muscle. These original protagonists met in China while fighting the Japanese, and they took over an abandoned detective agency on returning to the United States.

Yorke was written out of the series in 1942 when the actor portraying him took his own life. His character was replaced with distaff interest in the form of handsome secretary Jerry Booker. When she joins the WACs during World War II, her secretarial role is taken on by Mary Kay Brown. The programs concerned exotic adventures, and while they sometimes had far-fetched aspects, the resolution of the stories was always rational and realistic. Each segment ended with a cliff-hanger situation designed to bring listeners back regularly. Unlike many serials, a given *ILAM* story ended before another began.

ILAM in Other Media

Three movies (only the first with a script by Morse) were developed from the series, and a 1967 television pilot film, *I Love a Mystery*, was made though not shown until 1973. No series resulted. An earlier (1956) attempt to develop a television series had also failed.

Don Sherwood created a short-lived 1960s comic strip based on the stories and characters of the radio series. *ILAM* creator Carleton E. Morse wrote one related novel and published it before his death; others were planned but did not appear.

See also: One Man's Family

Programming History

NBC West Coast network	January 1939– September 1939
NBC	1939–40
Blue Network	1940–42
CBS	1943–44
Mutual	1949–52

Cast

Jack Packard	Michael Raffetto (1939–44), Russell Thorson (1949–52), Robert Dryden (1952)
Doc Long	Barton Yarborough (1939–44), Jim Bowles (1949–52)
Reggie Yorke	Walter Paterson (to 1942), Tony Randall (1949–52)
Jerry Booker	Gloria Blondell (after 1942), Athena Lord (1949–52)
Mary Kay Brown	Athena Lord (1949–52)

Creator–Writer–Producer–Director

Carleton E. Morse

Films Based on the Series

I Love a Mystery (1945)
The Devil's Mask (1946)
The Unknown (1946)

Further Reading

Grams, Martin, Jr., "Episode Listing of *I Love a Mystery*" in *Radio Drama: A Comprehensive Chronicle of American Network Programs, 1932–1962*, by Grams, Jefferson, North Carolina: McFarland, 2000.

Harmon, Jim, "Jack, Doc, and Reggie," in *The Great Radio Heroes*, by Harmon, Garden City, New York: Doubleday, 1967.

Morse, Carleton E., *Stuff the Lady's Hatbox*, Woodside, California: Seven Stones Press, 1988.

Packard, Jack, Doc Long, and Reggie York, *I Love a Mystery: The Further Adventures of Jack, Doc, and Reggie*, www.lofcom.com/nostalgia/ilam

Unofficial *I Love a Mystery Page*, www.angelfire.com/on/ilam.

CHRISTOPHER H. STERLING

INFINITY BROADCASTING CORPORATION

Infinity Broadcasting Corporation, a subsidiary of media giant Viacom, is one of the largest radio broadcasting companies in the U.S. Infinity is focused on the "out-of-home" media business, which includes operations in radio broadcasting through Infinity Radio and outdoor advertising through Viacom Outdoor. Infinity's self-characterization of being an "out-of-home" media business comes from the fact that the majority of radio listening and practically all viewing of outdoor advertising occurs outside the consumer's home, from places such as automobiles and public transportation systems. The majority of Infinity's revenue, therefore, is generated from the sale of advertising. Infinity Radio consists of more than 180 radio stations serving over 40 markets. Approximately 94 percent of Infinity's radio stations are located in the 50 largest U.S. radio markets. Infinity also manages and holds an equity position in Westwood One, Inc.

The original Infinity Broadcasting Corporation is not the same as the Infinity currently in existence. The original Infinity was formed by two former Metromedia Communications Corporation executives, Gerald Carrus and Michael A. Weiner, in 1972 and acquired its first radio station in May 1973. Carrus and Weiner planned to emulate Metromedia president John W. Kluge's strategy of acquiring unsuccessful radio stations in the country's largest media markets, where the greatest amount of radio advertising dollars are spent, and developing them.

Seeking someone to run the original Infinity, Carrus and Weiner turned to Mel Karmazin in 1981. Karmazin had spent the previous 11 years working for Metromedia, where he managed the company's AM and FM outlets and gained a reputation for paying substantial amounts of money for on-air talent while exercising the tight-fistedness he had learned from Kluge to keep operating costs down. When Karmazin requested the opportunity to manage one of Metromedia's TV properties, Kluge turned him down, and Karmazin began to consider other options. By offering him a lucrative salary and equity in the original Infinity, Carrus and Weiner were able to lure Karmazin to the company.

The original Infinity, under Karmazin's leadership, substantially increased its acquisitions by paying record prices for top radio stations in large cities. The success of the original Infinity was also based on its ability to acquire the radio broadcast rights to a number of professional sports teams and to seek out high-profile radio personalities for its stations.

One of those high-profile personalities was "shock jock" Howard Stern, who signed on with the original Infinity in 1985 after being fired from WNBC. The original Infinity provided Stern with a national platform. As a result of Stern's bold activities on the airwaves, the company received numerous warnings from the Federal Communications Commission (FCC) that the *Howard Stern Show* was dangerously close to violating indecency standards. The warnings brought substantial publicity to the original Infinity, and the show's ratings soared, to the dismay of the many national and community watchdog groups working to have the show taken off the air. In 1995, as the fines from the FCC escalated, the original Infinity agreed to put the controversy to rest by paying $1.7 million in exchange for the FCC's dismissal of all pending complaints against the company's stations.

Despite the controversy, the original Infinity became popular not only with the listening audience, but also with Wall Street. The original Infinity went public in 1986 and was then bought back in a leveraged buyout in 1988. The original Infinity was again taken public in 1992. Shares issued in 1992 for $17.50 each were worth $170 when the company was eventually purchased in 1996.

In November 1995 Westinghouse Electric Corporation acquired the Columbia Broadcasting System (CBS), creating the nation's largest TV and radio station group. After Congress passed the Telecommunications Act in February 1996, which permitted the expansion of TV and radio station holdings, Westinghouse began considering its options for growth and, recognizing the potential of the radio industry, purchased the original Infinity in December 1996 for $4.7 billion. After acquiring the original Infinity, Westinghouse decided to sell its industrial businesses and reinvent itself solely as a media company. In December 1997 the new media company was launched as the CBS Corporation, the largest radio and television entity in history, with Karmazin as its president and chief operating officer.

With Karmazin at the helm, in September 1998, CBS relaunched Infinity Broadcasting Corporation in the largest initial public offering in media history. The "new" Infinity was created as a wholly owned subsidiary to own and operate CBS's radio and outdoor-advertising business. In addition to his duties at CBS, Karmazin was named president and CEO of Infinity. In May 2000, CBS merged with Viacom and Karmazin became Viacom's COO.

For years, Infinity's most famous and profitable personality was broadcasting firebrand Howard Stern. In 2004, however, with one year still left on his contract with Infinity, Stern announced he was leaving Infinity and terrestrial radio for satellite radio provider Sirius. Stern's departure in many ways signaled the end of Infinity. Amid unsuccessful attempts to refill Stern's time slot and in the wake of Karmazin's resignation in 2005, Infinity was "rebranded" as CBS Radio and split from Viacom. Beginning in 2006, shares of Viacom and CBS Radio began trading as separate entities.

During its lifespan, stations under Infinity included sports-formatted WFAN-AM in New York City, which for years was the nation's top-billing station, and news-talk programmed KDKA-AM in Pittsburgh, the nation's oldest radio outlet. Infinity's roster of talent included, besides Stern, Don Imus, Casey Kasem, Larry King, Charles Osgood and the late Tom Snyder.

See also: Columbia Broadcasting System; Westinghouse

Further Reading

Douglas, Susan Jeanne, *Listening In: Radio and the American Imagination: From Amos 'n' Andy and Edward R. Murrow to Wolf man Jack and Howard Stern*, New York: Times Books, 1999.

Elliott, Stuart, "Media Talk: Infinity Broadcasting Trumpets Its Future After Stern, Heartily," *New York Times* (10 October 2005), p. 6.

Lowry, Brian, "Split from CBS causes static, from stem to Stern," *Variety* (11 August 2008), p. 12.

Quaal, Ward L., and Leo A. Martin, *Broadcast Management: Radio, Television*, New York: Hastings House, 1968; revised 2nd edition, by Quaal and James Anthony Brown, 1976; 3rd edition, as *Radio-Television-Cable Management*, by Quaal and Brown, New York: McGraw Hill, 1998.

Smith, F. Leslie, *Perspectives on Radio and Television: An Introduction to Broadcasting in the United States*, New York: Harper and Row, 1979; 4th edition, as *Perspectives on Radio and Television: Telecommunication in the United States*, by Smith, John W. Wright II, and David H. Ostroff, Mahwah, New Jersey: Erlbaum, 1998.

KARL SCHMID,
2009 REVISIONS BY CARY O'DELL

INNER SANCTUM MYSTERIES
Horror Series

Squeeeeeaakkkk!!!!!! "Good Evening, friends of the inner sanctum. This is your host, Raymond, to welcome you through the squeaking door. Been shopping around for a nice case of murder? Of course you have. And you have come to the right place because the characters on this program simply *kill* themselves to keep you amused. Why only the other day we were accused of making murder our business. But we wouldn't do that friends, oh no, because that would be mixing business with pleasure, and we consider it a *pleasure* to give some stiff the *business* "heh heh heh."

So began one of the most famous openings in radio history. The squeaking door and host Raymond's gallows humor marked *Inner Sanctum Mysteries* as a distinctively campy horror series that reveled in its grisly subject matter. It was one of the first and most successful of radio thriller dramas, a genre that peaked in popularity during the 1940s. *Inner Sanctum* was created, produced, and directed throughout its entire run from 1941 to 1952 by Himan Brown, one of radio's most prolific show-men. Brown balanced the program's macabre humor with carefully chosen organ sounds, blood-curdling screams, and other effects, creating some of the most unsettling sound-scapes ever heard on radio. Brown used the organ to heighten the listener's fear, incorporating sharp stings to spark terror and creating suspense by using what John Dunning has called "doom chords" to signal approaching trouble. Murders were conveyed in the most disturbing manner possible through sound effects: Jim Harmon notes that when Brown wanted to produce the sound of a head being bashed in, he "devised a special bludgeon with which he would strike a small melon" (1967).

Inner Sanctum took its name from a line of Simon and Schuster mystery novels, but its scripts were generally original (although Edgar Allen Poe's work was a favorite of Brown's and was frequently adapted). Like other programs of the genre, *Inner Sanctum* relied on realism to heighten the listener's fear that "this could happen to me!" Ghostly behavior was commonly explained by the presence of a mad relative or an actual dead body that refused to stay quiet. As critics and even the show's own writers have noted, however, *Inner Sanctum's* plots were driven by contrivances and coincidences that were highly implausible. The nurse hired by the judge's wife happens to be the girlfriend of the murderer the judge just sent to the gallows (and she's not happy with him!). The wailing of a man's dead wife that haunts him for 40 years is actually caused by a hole in the wall in which he entombed her body (and which he, so terrified, had never thought to investigate earlier). Frequently, the program employed the device of an insane narrator to throw listeners off track and increase their horror at identifying with a murderer. The violence and gore of the program occasionally got Brown into trouble with parents and with the Federal Communications

Commission, who were particularly concerned that youth, especially, might be unduly traumatized and might even pick up a thing or two about how to carry out a murder. Brown himself was proud of the fact that "[s]hrinks said [the program] was scaring people out of their wits."

Like other programs in the genre, *Inner Sanctum* stories were a counterpoint (some might even say an antidote) to the suburban ideal of the postwar period. Husbands and wives did not get along well in *Inner Sanctum* stories, which were replete with film noir-type characters (including a healthy number of femme fatales) who murdered each other at terrific rates. Titles such as "Til Death Do Us Part," "Til the Day I Kill You," "Last Time I Killed Her," and "Honeymoon with Death" give some sense of the program's portrayal of marriage. Host Raymond took great glee in the violent disintegration of the postwar family and the impossibility of happy coupling; his closing puns or rhymes commented approvingly on the evening's grim outcome: "He hid her body in a bell, and that's where he made his mistake because she *tolled* on him." "Never tangle with a girl with red hair," he would chuckle, "A man is safer in the electric chair" (which, of course, is where this particular man ended up). The trademark tongue-in-rotting-cheek humor of the program is perhaps best conveyed by some of its more amusing titles, including "Hell Is Where You Find it," "The Dead Want Company," "Death Has a Vacancy," "The Meek Die Slowly," "The Girl and the Gallows," "Death Is a Double-Grosser," "The Long Wait Is Over," "The Man on the Slab," "Ring Around the Morgue," "Corpse on the Town," "Corpse without a Conscience," "The Corpse Who Came to Dinner," "Blood Relative," "One Coffin Too Many," and "The Corpse Nobody Loved."

Screen horror great Boris Karloff was the program's regular star for much of its first season, appearing in the Poe classics "The Tell-Tale Heart" and "The Fall of the House of Usher." According to radio program historian John Dunning, Karloff wanted more gore than the networks would allow, and he appeared much less frequently thereafter. *Inner Sanctum* developed its own stable of stars, which included Larry Haines, Mason Adams, Alice Rhinehart, Everett Sloane, Santos Ortega, Lawson Zerbe, and Elspeth Eric. In addition, up-and-coming film stars such as Mercedes McCambridge and Richard Widmark made frequent guest appearances. Although the programs emphasized plot over character, the alternately haunted and psychotic characters gave the actors a chance to stretch their range; women especially got the rare opportunity to narrate stories and play some very unladylike people.

Paul McGrath replaced Raymond Edward Johnson as host in 1945; he set a lighter tone than his predecessor, but the substance of the programs remained the same. Himan Brown attempted to revive the program in other forms in 1959 (as the *NBC Radio Theatre*) and 1974 (as the *CBS Radio Mystery Theatre*), but neither version proved as successful as the original. Of the more than 500 *Inner Sanctum Mysteries* programs produced, more than 100 are available on tape, providing a unique and still entertaining radio legacy.

See also: Horror Programs

Hosts

Raymond Edward Johnson (1941–45), Paul McGrath (1945–52)

Producer/Creator/Director

Himan Brown

Programming History

January 1941–October 1952 (528 episodes)

Further Reading

DeLong, Thomas A., *Radio Stars: An Illustrated Biographical Dictionary of 953 Performers, 1920 through 1960*, Jefferson, North Carolina: McFarland, 1996.

Dunning, John, *Tune in Yesterday: The Ultimate Encyclopedia of Old-Time Radio, 1925–1976*, Englewood Cliffs, New Jersey: Prentice-Hall, 1976; revised edition, as *On the Air: The Encyclopedia of Old-Time Radio*, New York: Oxford University Press, 1998.

Harmon, Jim, "And Here Is Your Host," chapter 4 of *The Great Radio Heroes*, New York: Ace, 1967; revised and expanded edition, Jefferson, North Carolina: McFarland, 2000.

ALLISON MCCRACKEN

INTERCOLLEGIATE BROADCASTING SYSTEM

The Intercollegiate Broadcasting System (IBS) was founded in 1940 by the originators of AM carrier-current college campus radio. Initially, college radio's primary interest concerned exchanging technical information among colleges via this new avenue of transmission. As more college stations were established, the interest evolved to include station management, programming, funding, recruiting, and industry training. Today, IBS is a nonprofit association of student-staffed radio stations located at schools and colleges throughout the United States. Approximately 600 IBS stations operate various types of radio facilities, including closed-circuit, AM carrier-current, cable radio, and Federal Communications Commission (FCC)-licensed FM and AM stations.

The majority of the early college radio stations in the United States were operated under the auspices of campus academic departments of electrical engineering; the primary objectives of these stations focused on the technical aspects of radio broadcasting rather than the public service potential. In 1925, 171 such stations were on the air, but by 1937, only 38 remained in operation. The decline in stations is credited to a general loss of campus interest or funding after the novelty of radio wore off. The few stations that sought to continue as AM broadcasters lost their licenses to commercial interests through comparative hearings before the FCC.

Lobbying in favor of college-based stations led to the FCC's 1938 decision to preserve such stations and to its 1941 and 1945 decisions to reserve FM channels designated for educational use. From the 1960s into the 1980s, the FM stations licensed to colleges and universities in the United States continued to provide leadership for the nation's public radio movement. By the mid-1990s, the majority of the 1,800 noncommercial so-called public radio licenses were granted to colleges and universities.

The formation of IBS was crucial to the preservation of college radio. IBS actively campaigned for reserved FM channels for college radio use. The result was the 1945 continuation of a reserved band of FM frequencies (this time at 88.1–91.9 MHz) where most noncommercial stations are now located. IBS was also active in convincing the FCC to establish the category of Class D (10 W) noncommercial FM stations as an entry-level training ground for college radio. The Class D decision permitted hundreds of fledgling stations to get started; most of these gained momentum and graduated to the increased power of a Class A facility, 100 W.

Increasingly throughout the years, IBS has taken on the fight for the protection of college radio. In 1978, when copyright laws changed to allow performing rights associations to collect fees for noncommercial broadcast performances, IBS presented testimony that resulted in lower rates being applied to college radio than to other classes of broadcast stations. IBS also filed objections against FCC on a proposal governing underwriting announcements.

The IBS favored changes, which were adopted, and gave stations unprecedented latitude in the frequency and content of broadcast announcements, thus encouraging new interest from potential underwriters. Additionally, IBS was the first industry organization to file an FCC Petition for Reconsideration, which resulted in the FCC ruling exempting noncommercial operators from the $35 application permit fee.

IBS is a centralized information source by which college radio remains informed about industry politics, problems, and solutions. IBS lobbies for educational radio through an aggressive campaign of printed materials, e-mail, ground mail, telephone and fax communication, and regional and national seminars and workshops. Beyond addressing the needs of individual member stations, IBS acts as college radio's primary representation before the FCC and other governmental and industry agencies. IBS directors comprise a cross-section of professionals representing a broad range of industry-experienced people who contribute their expertise on a voluntary basis.

The volunteer efforts of IBS personnel make sponsorship of new stations possible. IBS assists in launching new stations through a plan of action that includes advisory tips on conducting a frequency search; purchasing an existing station; and implementation of legal alternatives, such as utilizing on-campus carrier-current AM or cable FM piped into existing cable systems. Additionally, IBS offers basic advice regarding the complicated paperwork involved in filing for FCC permits.

IBS also provides helpful tips to member stations on increasing a station's coverage. IBS advises conducting frequency research to see if expansion is possible. They will assist in discussing the pros and cons of increased power versus increased height. For example, maintaining the same power but increasing the antenna height could give the increased coverage desired.

See also: College Radio; Educational Radio to 1967; Low-Power Radio/Microradio; Public Radio Since 1967; Ten-Watt Stations; WHA and Wisconsin Public Radio

Further Reading

Bloch, Louis M., Jr., *The Gas Pipe Networks: A History of College Radio 1936–45*, Cleveland, Ohio: Bloch and Company, 1980.
Engleman, Ralph, *Public Radio and Television in America: A Political History*, Thousand Oaks, California: Sage, 1996.
Frost, S.E., Jr., *Education's Own Stations*, Chicago: University of Chicago Press, 1937.
Intercollegiate Broadcasting System (IBS) www.ibsradio.org.
McCluskey, James, J., *Starting a Student Non-Commercial Radio Station*, Boston: Pearson Custom, 1998.

ELIZABETH COX

INTERNET RADIO
Delivering Radio Programs Online

Internet radio involves the delivery of audio programming via digital means from one computer to other computers over the internet. It involves both simulcasts of existing over-the-air radio stations and content from internet-only stations. Internet radio was made possible by the 1995 arrival of streaming. Previously, users had to download an entire audio file before being able to listen to it. Even audio clips of short duration could take hours to download. Streaming allows the user to listen to the audio programming as it arrives in real time. This means users do not have to wait for a complete audio file to download before listening to it. Internet radio streaming can involve both live material and archived clips of audio content recorded earlier. In either case, the user must have special software that matches the software used by the station to encode and transmit the data.

Internet radio was a booming enterprise into the late 1990s, but legal decisions and a downturn in internet advertising have effectively shut down many stations today. In 2002, a dispute between internet broadcasters and the music industry came to a head when a copyright appeals board required internet radio stations to pay a per-song, per-listener fee that was prohibitively expensive for many stations. The fee was an especially great hardship for small operations, such as religious broadcasters and college radio stations, and amounted to thousands of dollars more than they made. This led to hundreds of internet-based radio stations shutting down.

By late 2002, a compromise was worked out whereby internet broadcasters could pay royalty fees on a percentage of their revenue instead of on a per-song, per-listener basis. The *Small Webcaster Settlement Act of 2002* was seen as a big victory by small webcasters and by early 2003 many small internet broadcasters were beginning to reappear.

The three leading technologies for delivering internet radio are the RealOne Player, Microsoft Windows Media, and MP3 streaming. Internet radio stations will often select one of the technologies for the delivery of their content. In some cases, stations choose to make their audio stream available in more than one of these formats, allowing listeners to choose the way they want to listen.

Streaming generally sacrifices audio quality because of the need to compress the data for delivery via narrowband (56k) telephone line modems still used by most households. Early internet radio quality was very poor, and many listeners became discouraged by the poor audio quality and problems maintaining a continuous stream. The stream would often stop and buffer (download data before it was used), inhibiting continuous delivery of the program.

Technological improvements and new broadband connections allow better streams and near-CD-quality sound. Listeners with cable modems or telephone DSL (digital subscriber line) services are the biggest beneficiaries. The adoption of these faster broadband connections has been swift; according to a 2008 survey, 55 percent of Americans now have a high-speed connection in the home.

Radio Stations on the Internet

Studies show that internet usage is cutting into time people would otherwise spend listening to broadcast radio. For traditional broadcast stations, delivery of programming on the internet may help recapture some of these listeners and may even generate new listeners in distant locations. Even small-market radio stations can reach the same international audiences as stations in larger markets. The concept of signal strength does not apply in the online world, and all stations start out on equal footing. Location is no barrier, either. It costs no more to send an internet radio program 1,000 miles than it does to send it 10 miles. Online radio listeners say they listen more to radio stations outside their local market than they do to stations in their own locale.

A 2008 study by Arbitron and Edison Media found that 13 percent of the population (or about 33 million people) over the age of 12 were listening to online radio at least once a week, up from 11 percent a year earlier. Such growth gives traditional radio broadcasters cause for concern because listeners have more listening choices online than over the air.

Internet radio listeners are sometimes referred to as "streamies." As a group, streamies represent a very desirable demographic for advertisers. Streamies are among the most active group of internet users, spending more time online than the average internet user. Streamies are twice as likely to click on web ads and to make online purchases and are very interested in new devices to enable even more convenient listening. Internet radio listeners tend to be better educated and come from homes with higher incomes than regular internet users.

Capturing the internet audience and persuading listeners to revisit, however, is made more difficult with such a range of choices. Developing content worthy of repeat visits is one of the biggest challenges for internet broadcasters. Merely having a web presence to promote a station's broadcast operation is not enough. Internet broadcasters are using interactive features such as contests and live chat rooms to gain and hold on to the elusive internet audience. Concert information, celebrity interviews, and fashion information are also important content categories for the young internet radio audience.

Broadcast radio stations have traditionally had strong local identities. On the internet, some stations may decide to adopt a more national identity. Far-flung listeners with ties to a community can stay up to date with "local" news, sports, and community events from anywhere in the world.

Stations looking for a national audience may develop niche programming such as specific music genres or sports. Certain music formats may be more popular than others in the online world. A 1999 Arbitron and Edison Media Research study showed that 91 percent of radio listeners who have internet access prefer alternative rock. The next highest categories were Top 40 (68 percent), classical (68 percent), religious (54 percent), adult contemporary (52 percent), and news/talk (50 percent). The top-rated internet radio stations tend to be eclectic and unique-sounding outlets not commonly found on the air.

Some broadcasters remain unconvinced of the value of internet radio. For one thing, there are far fewer internet-connected computers than there are available radio sets. Internet radio also lacks the portability of broadcast radio and is not generally available in cars, at the beach, a picnic, or other gathering places outside the home or workplace. Sound quality of internet radio varies greatly, and listeners with low-speed modem connections or slow computers are often disappointed with the overall quality. Furthermore, studies have shown that many people sample online stations but don't return regularly. Many broadcasters are still waiting to see a return on their investment in internet radio.

Making Money on Internet Radio

Although broadcast radio is an audio-only medium, internet radio stations are free to offer interactive programming and can include images, animation, and even video. Whereas broadcast radio relies on estimating the size of audiences via ratings, internet radio can measure each time a user accesses a particular page or program and in many cases can provide detailed demographic data about the people visiting their sites.

There are three ways for internet radio stations to make money online; advertising, transactions, and subscriptions. Advertising is the model broadcast stations have adopted and used for decades. The ability of internet radio to reach a global audience means not only the potential for a greater number of listeners, but also that stations may be able to attract national, as well as local, advertisers. Internet radio listeners represent a desirable demographic of technology-savvy young people to advertisers as well.

Besides the standard audio-only commercials so familiar on the radio, internet radio allows stations to generate revenue through graphic advertising banners and pop-up ads as well. The "banner ad" is an easy and effective way to display advertising on a station's website. Stations charge different amounts, depending on banner size, placement, and duration on a page. The banner ad may be placed on the same page listeners go to when they want to listen to the station online. A greater amount can be charged for what are called "click-throughs" (money earned when users click the banner ad and go to the advertiser's site).

Other sources of revenue can be generated through classified ads and direct sales or transactions. For example, many internet radio listeners say that they would like to be able to buy music on a station's site. Advertising on internet radio stations can be tied directly to transactions conducted online. Whereas broadcast radio commercials depend on delayed gratification (listeners hear a commercial and will ideally buy something later), internet radio is more interactive and allows the user to go immediately from the desire to buy directly to a page where a purchase can take place. This immediacy in the online world changes the very nature and approach of advertising for the new medium.

By far the biggest obstacle faced by internet broadcasters is over royalties that have to be paid to music licensing agencies ASCAP and BMI for any music played. After years of haggling, a temporary fee schedule was put in place in 2008, but the issue is continually reopened to determine rates for future years.

Further, and unlike terrestrial radio stations, internet-only broadcasters must pay a performance-based royalty for all music they air. The additional cost inherent in these fees has, over the years, threatened to bankrupt many online providers, including the music service Pandora. How these fees are calibrated has been subject to heated debate over the years. In 2009, after innumerable protests, legal proceedings and Congressional hearings, the US Copyright Board announced it would adopt a royalty rate based on a streaming service's individual business revenues.

Internet-Only Radio Stations

In many cases, internet radio stations exist only on the internet. Often referred to as music "channels," these ventures often play lesser-known groups and alternative music formats. In many cases, internet-only sites are providing original content, multiple channels, and fewer commercials. For artists and labels finding it difficult to get playtime on traditional stations, internet radio provides a viable option for exposure of new music.

The cost for starting up an internet radio station is far less than the cost of building or buying a broadcast station. An internet radio station can be established for less than $10,000 and does not require a license from the Federal Communications Commission.

One of the major targets of internet-only stations is the workplace. There tend to be more computers in use around offices than radio and television receivers. Internet-only stations hope to attract workers disenfranchised by traditional radio by offering more finely niched music choices, fewer commercials, and the opportunity to buy online. However, as internet radio uses a tremendous amount of bandwidth, workers listening to it could put a strain on a company's network and the ability to handle e-mail and other work-related applications.

Personal Internet Radio Stations

New technology and software allow anyone to become an internet radio broadcaster. Individuals can start their own stations and operate them from their homes. All it takes is a computer, an internet connection, and some free software. Users can create and customize their own radio stations online without the trouble of acquiring and setting up a server. Some online sites allow users to create their own playlists of genres and artists and to actually specify how often each is heard. The sites have large archives of music available. Once users have built their "stations" based on their music preferences, they can go to a webpage and listen to their own personalized station. The web address can be given to others so they can listen to the station as well.

One of the most successful audio technologies on the internet is the MP3 format. MP3 (MPEG

Audio Layer 3) is a highly compressed audio format that delivers near-CD-quality sound with very small file sizes. Users can download high-quality MP3 music files even on low-bandwidth connections. Online MP3 sites offer a great deal of free downloadable music, and one is often able to listen to new artists who promote and distribute their music on these sites. MP3 player software is available free online.

These online operations, both internet-only and terrestrial stations that simulcast their signal, will continue to expand, especially considering such new devices as internet car radios and table-top radios that can tune internet signals.

See also: American Society of Composers, Authors, and Publishers; Audio Streaming; Broadcast Music Incorporated; Copyright; Digital Audio Broadcasting; Podcast

Websites

SaveInternetRadio, www.saveinternetradio.org
SoundExchange, www.soundexchange.com
BRS Web-Radio, www.web-radio.fm

Further Reading

Bachman, Katy, "Not Streaming Profits," *Mediaweek* (6 September 1999).

Cherry, Steven M., "Web Radio: Time to Sign Off?" *IEEE Spectrum* (August 2002).
Fulton, Scott M., "Copyright Board Begrudgingly Adopts Revenue-based Streaming Royalties," *Betanews* (29 January 2009).
Graven, Matthew, "Web Radio Days," *PC Magazine* (14 December 1999).
"Internet 9: The Media and Entertainment World of Online Consumers," *Arbitron/Edison Media Research* (5 September 2002).
Kerschbaumer, Ken, "Radio Next for RealNetworks," *Broadcasting & Cable* (26 August 2002).
Kuchinskas, Susan, "Tune It to Internet Radio," *Mediaweek* (19 April 1999).
"New Media Eyes Radio's Audience," *Billboard* (23 October 1999).
Rathbun, Elizabeth A., "Clash of the 'Casters," *Broadcasting and Cable* (6 September 1999).
Shiver, Jube, Jr., "Internet Adds Dimension to Radio," *Providence Business News* (30 August 1999).
"Small Webcasters Get Break on License Fees for Transmissions of Music Recordings, as Authorized by Small Webcaster Settlement Act," *Entertainment Law Reporter* (December 2002).
"Small Webcasters, RIAA Formally Unveil Royalty Accord," *Communications Daily* (17 December 2002).
"Streaming Media Sites Expand: Downloadable Tunes Help Build Audience," *Computerworld* (19 July 1999).
Taylor, Chuck, "Webcasters Reshape Radio Landscape," *Billboard* (5 June 1999).

STEVEN D. ANDERSON,
2009 REVISIONS BY CARY O'DELL

J

JACK ARMSTRONG, THE ALL-AMERICAN BOY
Children's Adventure Series

Even before World War II, Jack Armstrong of *Jack Armstrong, the All-American Boy* (a sort of *Johnny Quest* of the radio airwaves) was the image of the patriot, the great white hope, the upstanding citizen. The creation of former journalist Robert Hardy Andres, *Jack Armstrong, the All-American Boy* was a daily adventure series, the core audience of which skewed just slightly older (and, we can assume, more male) than its closest radio rival, *Little Orphan Annie*. It ran on various networks from 1933–51.

Jack, a perpetual teenager despite his nearly 30 years on the air, was a student and star athlete at Hudson High, where the school fight song (which doubled as the series theme) frequently cheered him on to end-of-the-game saves. But young Jack's real role was as globe-trotting adventurer with his Uncle Jim Fairfield and cousins Billy and Betty. Only barely into the first year of the program, the pep rallies and classrooms of Hudson High were abandoned by Jack and his program's writers in favor of death-defying, hair-raising adventures played out at the four corners of the world. From mountain climbing and airplane flying (Uncle Jim owned a hydroplane) to undersea diving and chasing down evildoers and pirates, from the Arctic Circle and the Philippines to other "wild," "exotic," and "untamed" locales, Armstrong's adventures ran daily in late-afternoon, 15-minute episodes. In true serial format, similar to the Saturday afternoon

matinee escapades of *The Crimson Ghost* and its ilk, each story had a cliff-hanger ending that encouraged listeners to tune in the next day. And millions of kids and preteens did so with near-religious devotion.

This being radio, the producers were free to create outrageous situations and transport their audience to any number of "real-life" places—Jack and company traveled from the Amazon jungle to the Far East via only a few carefully chosen sound effects. A foghorn simulated a ship, and conga drums conjured up images of the darkest places of the dark continent. Meanwhile, the actors never had to leave the comfort of a Chicago radio studio.

Though Jack Armstrong was not technically an orphan, he was one at least symbolically, for in his traipsing around the world with his uncle and cousins, little mention was ever made of Mom and Dad back home.

Though Uncle Jim, with his authoritative voice, was along on all the adventures as a parental role model (a catchall character to represent the entire world of adulthood), it was not unusual to find him missing in action or conveniently at a distance when the real events began, thereby leaving the three youngsters on their own. However, the adultless world that Jack, Bill, and Betty inhabited never devolved into a *Lord of the Flies*-like scenario. Instead, the trio, like a modern-day Tom Sawyer, Huck Finn, and Becky Thatcher with Jack acting as ad hoc leader, proved themselves smart, resourceful, and empowered enough to save the world, a message they no doubt imparted to their youthful audience. As the program ran during the entire duration of World War II, Jack and company did their bit for the war effort, encouraging listeners to plant victory gardens and to write letters to overseas servicemen.

As with Jack's streamlined family situation, his growing-up years were equally simplified. For Jack (and Betty and Billy, for that matter), there was no mention of such staples of adolescence as self-doubt, acne, and romantic yearnings—and no youthful rebellion. Such sentiment and realism would serve not only to turn off most of the young listeners, but would surely also get in the way of all the exciting action. There was no time for planning for the prom in the world of Jack Armstrong!

Not to say that Jack's freewheeling lifestyle did not come under scrutiny during the program's long run. Several sources report that enough mothers (and perhaps fathers, too) wrote to criticize the program for Jack's never being in school that, in response, a few references to homework were eventually dropped into scripts, as was a later character who acted as the children's traveling tutor. Although child psychologist Martin Reymert was engaged to scrutinize each script to make sure it contained no torture or excessive violence, such restraint did not extend to protecting children from heavy-handed consumerism. For *Jack*'s entire run, the show was sponsored by Wheaties, and the show's ongoing celebration of athletics, clear good-versus-evil storytelling, and basic American values worked well for the "breakfast of champions." In addition, *Jack Armstrong* was the airwaves' perhaps most aggressive pitchman for product tie-ins. For the right number of Wheaties box tops, youthful listeners could send in for secret decoders or "hike-o-meters." Girls could send away for a bracelet "just like Betty's."

During its run, the broadcast went through many cast changes, including five different Jacks (the longest-playing one was Charles Flynn, whose voice sounded youthful enough that in his 30s, he was still playing the teen). Eventually, in the program's last years, it dropped Uncle Jim (played for the entire run by Jim Goss) and the others altogether. And Jack, who had become too old to be considered a "boy," became an adult agent for justice in the retitled series *Armstrong of the SBI*.

An entertaining, fun, quaint relic now, *Jack Armstrong, the All-American Boy* —the all-American kid from an all-American town—despite its wild, world-traveling adventures, always had a certain air of innocence about it, portraying a world of honesty and virtue, where the good guys always won.

See also: Premiums

Cast

Jack Armstrong	St. John Terrell (1933), Jim Ameche (1933–38), Stanley Harris (1938–39), Frank Behrens (1939), Charles Flynn (1939–43; 1944–51), Michael Rye (Rye Billsbury) (1943)
Billy Fairfield	Murray McLean (during war years), John Gannon (1933–43), Roland Butterfield, Milton Guion, Dick York (postwar years)
Betty Fairfield	Scheindel Kalish (Ann Shephard) (1933), Sarajane Wells (1933–41), Loretta Poynton (1941–43), Naomi May (1943), Patricia Dunlap (postwar years)
Uncle Jim Fairfield	James Goss
Gwendolyn Duval	Sarajane Wells, Naomi May
Coach Hardy	Arthur Van Slyke, Olan Soulé, Ed Davison
Vic Hardy	Ken Griffin (1950–51), Carlton KaDell (19 50–51)
Captain Hughes	Don Ameche, Jack Doty, Frank Dane
Babu	Frank Behrens
Blackbeard Flint	Robert Barron
Sullivan Lodge	Kenneth Christy
Talia-San	Kenneth Christy
Lal Singh	Michael Romano
Pete	Art McConnell
Dickie	Dick York
Michael	Frank Behrens
Weissoul	Herb Butterfield
Lorenzo	Herb Butterfield
Announcers	David Owen (1930s), Tom Shirley (1930s), Truman Bradley (1930s), Paul Douglas (1930s), Franklyn MacCormack (1940s), Bob McKee (postwar years), Ed Prentiss (1950–51), Ken Nordine (1950–51), Norman Kraft (postwar years)

Creator/Writer

Robert Hardy Andrews

Producer

James Jewel

Programming History

CBS   July 1933–April 1936
NBC   August 1936–September 1941
Mutual   September 1941–July 1942
NBC-Blue   August 1942–August 1947
ABC   September 1947–June 1951

Further Reading

Harmon, Jim, *The Great Radio Heroes*, Garden City, New York: Doubleday, 1967; revised edition, Jefferson, North Carolina: McFarland, 2001.
Harmon, Jim, *Radio Mystery and Adventure: And Its Appearances in Film, Television, and Other Media*, Jefferson, North Carolina: McFarland, 1992.
Nachman, Gerald, *Raised on Radio: In Quest of the Lone Ranger*, New York: Pantheon, 1998.

CARY O'DELL

JAZZ FORMAT

The growth of television in the early 1950s gradually replaced commercial radio as the primary family entertainment medium in the home. Radio adapted to a new role by establishing radio formats. Individual stations targeted narrow audience segments by specializing in news, talk, or any of a variety of music genres.

Although jazz music traces its roots to the formative years of the United States, it did not evolve into a bona fide radio music format until the 1950s. During the 1920s and 1930s, mainstream society viewed jazz music in the same way that rock and roll was viewed in the late 1950s: it was considered decadent. Because jazz was closely identified with black culture and affected by the racism that prevailed nationwide during that time, many of the greatest black jazz artists fled to Europe, some permanently, where they and their music were accepted openly. Paris became a cultural center of American jazz music, and the jazz music genre remains very popular there to this day in clubs and on radio. In fact, jazz radio is probably more popular in Europe than it is in the United States.

What is jazz radio? Jazz fans sometimes refer to it as music by musicians, not electricians. It includes blues, swing, bebop, fusion, Latin, and a number of other subcategories within its overall definition. Music that includes flat line piano, boring guitar, and braying saxophone is sometimes associated with jazz, but not legitimately so. New-wave music is not jazz.

Jazz grew out of blues, ragtime, and Dixieland music during the early 20th century. Following the swing era of the 1930s and 1940s, the style evolved into bebop, modern, cool, and other straight-ahead sounds by the 1960s. By this time, jazz had also been accepted as a legitimate popular art form throughout the United States. American audiences embraced the music as much as the Europeans had a decade earlier.

Jazz radio on the East Coast most likely had its roots in "Symphony Sid" Torin's live WJZ-AM radio broadcasts from the Royal Roost in New York City. Trumpeter Rex Stewart and critic and composer Leonard Feather had their own shows on AM in the early 1950s, as did Felix Grant and Ed Beech. These jazz disc jockeys are important, because early jazz formats were very much personality driven and involved a lot of talk in addition to the music.

"Sleepy" Stein, who was doing all-nighters in Chicago, moved his show to KNOB-FM in Los Angeles in 1956, and West Coast jazz radio was established. KJAZ in San Francisco had Pat Henry. KNOB and KJAZ had similar formats: one-and two-hour programs that were oriented totally toward personalities, with disc jockeys involved in lengthy announcements preceding and following each song played, which included mentioning every player or sideman, the composer, and even the record label. There were not that many jazz recordings at the time, and talkative disc jockey personalities could play virtually every current jazz record release over a 24-hour period. Other jazz radio personalities included Dick Buckley, Howard LaCroft, Frank Evans, Bob Young, Al Fox, Al "Jazzbo" Collins, Jim Gosa, Pete Smith, Dick McGarvin, and Chuck Niles. Niles, probably the "dean" of active jocks, was still doing a regular show on KLON-FM, Long Beach, as the new millennium began.

The growth of FM radio's album-oriented rock and underground formats during the 1970s eroded jazz formats. KKGO in Los Angeles, for example, converted to a classical music format, and KZJZ in St. Louis simply left the air. By the mid-1990s, only a few jazz formats remained on commercial stations. Public radio filled the void, however, with jazz being adopted as a format at several large public and many college stations. In 1977 National Public Radio (NPR) initiated *Jazz Alive*, carried by most NPR stations. By 2009, the two jazz stations with the largest international audiences were both non-commercial: WBGO-FM in Newark, New Jersey, and KJAZZ-FM (formerly KLON) in Long Beach, California. Both of these large public radio stations are carried on numerous cable systems and are relayed via satellite globally.

The format itself has changed as well. Research into audience behavior has demonstrated that most listeners want less talk and more music. This "modal music research" calls for serving a greater number of people, replacing talk with 30-second breaks, limiting the number of announcements, and not airing anything squeaky or long. The jazz format of the future will involve less talk, sharpen the focus of the music, and include memorable moments in jazz history. In all likelihood, the music will be based in the jazz styles made popular in the 1950s and 1960s (i.e., bebop, cool, straight-ahead). The big band era is blending with early rock and roll popular music into a successful commercial format.

Of the over 300 stations that by 2009 described themselves as having a "jazz" format, most actually program a derivative known as "smooth jazz." Around since the mid-1980s, smooth jazz has the distinction of being a radio format longer than it has been a recognized musical style. Musically, smooth jazz is characterized by heavy instrumentals and melody but is devoid of such jazz staples as improvisation. In its early days, it was a style best embodied by the work of George Benson, Kenny G, and Chuck Mangione. In recent years, the genre has expanded to include such artists as David Sanborn, Al Jarreau, and Norah Jones, among others. Although many true jazz aficionados originally decried the smooth jazz style as just one step up from "elevator" music, the format caught on for being equal parts hip and soothing. It also had the appeal of successfully crossing audience boundaries—racial, geographic, and economic. Smooth jazz stations across the country early in 2009 included KIFM in San Diego, KWJZ in Seattle, KTWV in Los Angeles, WYJZ in Indianapolis, and WLTM in Atlanta. Since 2006, the firm Broadcast Architecture has distributed (via satellite) its Smooth Jazz Network with daily and weekly programs hosted by such jazz artists and aficionados as Dave Koz, Ramsey Lewis, and Norman Brown.

On the other hand, some smooth jazz stations have left the air. In 2006–8, smooth jazz stations adopted other formats in New York, Boston, Philadelphia, and other top markets. Some have tried to retain their longstanding jazz fans by offering secondary jazz-focused HD channels. Smooth jazz's decline has been attributed to everything from skewed findings by Arbitron's new Portable People Meter, to a lack of sufficient new music coming out of the genre, to advertisers preferring more uptempo music to surround their messages.

Yet HD radio, satellite radio and multiple on-demand streaming services are providing new venues for jazz radio. The merged SiriusXM satellite service offers a handful of channels devoted to jazz formats. Given that jazz will always target a narrow niche, the new multi-channel environment provides an ideal means for delivering it to fans globally.

See also: FM Radio; National Public Radio

Further Reading

Eberly, Philip K., *Music in the Air: America's Changing Tastes in Popular Music, 1920–1980*, New York: Hastings House, 1982.
Fisher, March, "Smooth Jazz: Gentle Into That Good Night?; As the Genre Declines, Stations Switch to New Formats in D.C. and Nationwide," *Washington Post* (9 March 2008), p. M-5.
Gioia, Ted, *The History of Jazz*, New York: Oxford University Press, 1997.
Harris, Rex, *Jazz*, London: Penguin, 1952.
Kenney, William Howland, *Recorded Music in American Life: The Phonograph and Popular Memory, 1890–1945*, New York: Oxford University Press, 1999.

ROBERT G. FINNEY,
2009 REVISIONS BY CARY O'DELL

JEHOVAH'S WITNESSES AND RADIO

The religious group that took the name Jehovah's Witnesses in 1931 (prior to that date the group preferred the name Bible Students) owned and operated several radio stations in the United States and Canada beginning in 1924, and used syndicated recordings on hundreds of commercial stations to supplement its broadcast outreach between 1931 and 1937. The controversial and often confrontational views of the sect involved it in frequent conflicts with other denominations and with broadcasting regulators.

The story of the Bible Students'/Jehovah's Witnesses' involvement in radio is largely the story of their second president, Judge Joseph Franklin Rutherford—a former Missouri lawyer and substitute judge with a commanding personality and a booming orator's voice. Born in 1869, Rutherford took control of the Watch Tower Society and its associated groups in 1916, following the death of the sect's founder, Pastor Charles Taze Russell. In 1917 Rutherford and several associates were convicted of sedition for their public opposition to the World War I draft; their convictions were overturned in 1919. Upon his release from prison, Rutherford took steps to revive the struggling movement, implementing a renewed program of publishing and public speaking.

As part of this effort Judge Rutherford delivered his first radio address over station WGL in Philadelphia on 16 April 1922. Soon afterward, the Bible Students acquired a plot of land on Staten Island, New York, and began construction of their own broadcasting station.

On 24 February 1924 the Bible Students inaugurated station WBBR. The noncommercial station featured classical music and hymns performed by Bible Student musicians, talks on home economics and other practical subjects, and lectures on the group's complex interpretations of Bible prophecy and chronology by Rutherford and others. The success of WBBR led to the operation of additional Bible Student stations over the next several years, including WORD in Batavia, Illinois (later WCHI), KFWM in Oakland, California, CYFC in Vancouver, British Columbia, CHCY in Edmonton, Alberta, CHUC in Saskatoon, Saskatchewan, and CKCX in Toronto, Ontario.

During 1927 and 1928 the broadcasting activities of the Bible Students began to attract the attention of government regulators. In June 1927 Rutherford testified before the Federal Radio Commission (FRC) to protest a decision denying WBBR's application to share the frequency of station WJZ, owned by the Radio Corporation of America and the flagship of the newly formed National Broadcasting Company's (NBC) Blue network, alleging that NBC was part of a religious/commercial conspiracy seeking to deny his group fair access to the radio audience. Although the FRC dismissed Rutherford's complaint, NBC offered the Bible Students free airtime for the broadcast of a talk by Rutherford. The speech, entitled "Freedom for the Peoples," was delivered on 24 July 1927 and in it Rutherford denounced all other religions, the clergy, big business, and all human governments as agents of Satan. A barrage of complaints received in the wake of this address led NBC to deny Rutherford and the Bible Students any further access to its stations.

The following year the Bible Students ran afoul of broadcasting authorities in Canada. Protests from clergymen over the broadcasts of Bible Student stations in Canada were followed by allegations that the group had on two occasions sold time over its Saskatoon outlet to the Ku Klux Klan. On the strength of these complaints the licenses for the Canadian stations were revoked in March 1928.

Unable to secure time on any established network, the Bible Students turned to a network of their own—buying time on over a hundred stations from 1928 through 1930 for "The Watchtower Hour." Anchored by WBBR, and connected by American Telephone and Telegraph (AT&T) circuits, the "Watchtower Network" functioned for an hour each week, presenting talks by Rutherford and hymns performed by Bible Student musicians.

Increased costs led the organization to discontinue the live network at the end of 1930, replacing it with transcribed syndication. The Watch Tower Society purchased time on local stations and the lectures of Judge Rutherford were distributed on 16-inch shellac transcriptions manufactured by the Columbia Phonograph Company. By 1933 over 400 stations around the world were broadcasting these 12-minute talks. This "wax chain" would be supplemented by occasional live hookups from the organization's annual conventions.

As the Depression deepened, the Witnesses (adopting that name in July 1931) became increasingly combative in their attacks on organized religion, politicians, and big business and this, in turn, brought them into further conflict with station owners and the FRC. Catholic authorities, especially, took offense at Rutherford's statements and pressured station owners to discontinue the broadcasts. In 1933 the Witnesses began a nationwide petition drive for "freedom of broadcasting" and presented more than two million signatures to the FRC in early 1934. Allegations were immediately made that many of the signatures were forged, but the petition led Representative Louis McFadden (R-Pennsylvania) to introduce a bill that would require broadcasters to guarantee free and equal use of air time to all nonprofit organizations. Several Watch Tower Society representatives were among those testifying for this bill in March 1934. Buried under an avalanche of opposition from the National Association of Broadcasters, the established networks, and the Federal Council of Churches of Christ, the bill died quietly in committee.

Opposition to the Witnesses' broadcasts mounted steadily during the mid-1930s, culminating in Philadelphia in 1936 when Catholic leaders urged a boycott of Gimbels Department Store, owners of station WIP, which had carried the Rutherford programs for several years. Stations became increasingly reluctant to sell time to the Watch Tower Society and finally, in October 1937, the organization announced its withdrawal from commercial broadcasting, although it used special hookups for convention broadcasts until 1941.

Rutherford died in 1942 and his successors have moved away from his aggressive stances, ignoring the broadcast media in favor of direct house-to-house canvassing. Station WBBR remained in operation until 15 April 1957, when it was quietly sold. The call letters were changed to WPOW and the once-combative voice of the Watch Tower

Society became a commercial station specializing in recorded music.

See also: Religion on Radio

Futher Reading

1975 Year Book of Jehovah's Witnesses.

"Bible Students Protest," *Broadcasting* (1 February 1934).

Duffy, Dennis J., *Imagine Please: Early Radio Broadcasting in British Columbia*, Victoria, British Columbia: Sound and Moving Image Division, Province of British Columbia, Ministry of Provincial Secretary and Government Services, Provincial Archive, 1983.

Jehovah's Witnesses in the Divine Purpose, New York: Watch Tower Bible and Tract Society, 1959.

"McFadden's Religious Time Bill Believed Defeated at Hearings," *Broadcasting* (1 April 1934).

Penton, M. James, *Apocalypse Delayed: The Story of Jehovah's Witnesses*, Toronto and Buffalo, New York: University of Toronto Press, 1985; 2nd edition, 1997.

Rutherford, Joseph Franklin, *Freedom for the Peoples*, New York: Watch Tower Bible and Tract Society, 1927.

Rutherford, Joseph Franklin, *Government: Speech of World-Wide Interest, Broadcast to All Continents: Hiding the Truth, Why?* Brooklyn, New York: Watch Tower Bible and Tract Society, 1935.

Rutherford, Joseph Franklin, *Enemies: The Proof That Definitely Identifies All Enemies, Exposes Their Methods of Operation, and Points Out the Way of Complete Protection for Those Who Love Righteousness*, Brooklyn, New York: Watch Tower Bible and Tract Society, 1937.

"Rutherford Protests to Radio Commission," *New York Times* (15 June 1927).

"Under Constant Duress," *Broadcasting* (1 April 1934).

ELIZABETH MCLEOD

JEWISH RADIO PROGRAMS

Religious broadcasts usually connote church services and evangelists. Although it is true that most radio religious programs have been directed at a Christian audience, a number of Jewish programs have been on the air since radio's earliest years.

Origins

In March 1922 New York station WJZ's radio listing announced a "radio chapel service," featuring a talk by Rabbi Solomon Foster and music by cantor Maurice Cowan. Although it had been customary for radio stations to offer short inspirational messages (usually in the morning), these were usually provided by well-known Christian clergy. In some cities with large Jewish populations, however, a rabbi was occasionally asked to speak. To the listener in 1922–23, this was something of a social revolution. Most Christians had never met or heard a rabbi before.

Rabbi Harry Levi of Temple Israel, a Reform congregation, was invited to take a turn on a daily religious program that was broadcast over Boston's WNAC in mid-1923. He got such a positive response that he was invited back. By January 1924 WNAC made arrangements to broadcast Temple Israel's services twice a month, certainly the first time most non-Jews had encountered what a Jewish worship service was like. (In March 1926 listeners could also hear a Jewish wedding, as New York's WRNY made Winnie Gordon and Julius Goldberg, along with Rabbi Josef Hoffman, radio stars for a day.) Boston's "Radio Rabbi" Harry Levi became so popular during 16 years on the air that two books of his sermons were issued, and numerous non-Jews who heard him on WNAC wrote him fan letters or came to his temple to ask for his autograph.

Radio in the early 1920s provided its audience with the chance to hear some of Judaism's biggest names, including New York's Rabbi Stephen S. Wise, long regarded by the print media as a spokesman for liberal Jews: both the *New York Times* and *Time* magazine often quoted him. As early as March 1922, Rabbi Wise gave a radio talk to encourage donations to help European Jewish refugees. On a fairly regular basis throughout the 1920s, his speaking engagements were broadcast from a number of cities; Rabbi Wise's sermons were often about the dangers of intolerance, such as a 1924 speech to protest the growing popularity of the Ku Klux Klan. A dynamic orator, Rabbi Wise developed such a following that the radio editors at major newspapers often used a bold headline and a photo to let the audience know that he was about to give another radio sermon.

Radio produced a sort of ecumenism; one listing for New York's WEAF in December 1923 featured Christmas songs for children at 6 P.M. followed by Hanukkah songs at 7 P.M. Seeing the possibilities in radio as a vehicle to promote understanding, Dr. Cyrus Adler, a scholar and president of Dropsie College in Philadelphia, helped to create a weekly program that would not be limited to sermons. In cooperation with the United Synagogues of America, an organization of Conservative Jews, the Wednesday night program went on the air in late August 1923 on WEAF, after first offering an experimental broadcast in May to see if the response would be positive. It was. This weekly Jewish program featured Jewish folk and liturgical music (sometimes sung in Yiddish, sometimes in Hebrew), discussions of Jewish holidays, and a number of famous speakers from all over the United States.

Entertainment

Jewish programming in the 1920s was not only religious in nature. Thanks to radio, listeners were able to hear two famous Cantors—the great cantor Josef (Yossele) Rosenblatt, along with the popular Jewish comedian Eddie Cantor; both appeared at a 1924 banquet to honor the Young Men's Hebrew Association's 50th anniversary. There were also programs of popular music to benefit Jewish causes; Jewish bandleaders and performers such as Irving Berlin, Leo Reisman, and Eddie Cantor were among those who participated. And by the late 1920s, most cities from the East Coast to the West Coast had rabbis on the air, usually around the major Jewish holidays. In addition to rabbis and scholars discussing Jewish customs, there was at least one popular radio show with a Jewish immigrant family as the protagonists—Gertrude Berg had created a comedy–drama called *The Goldbergs*, which began a successful run on the National Broadcasting Company (NBC) in November 1929. It was an era when many performers with ethnic names changed them to sound more "American," yet Gertrude Berg did not hide the ethnicity of her characters, nor did she hide her own ethnicity. She wrote a syndicated advice column for the Jewish press and did speaking engagements on behalf of Jewish charities. And unlike some comedy routines such as "Cohen on the Telephone," a hit record that made fun of a Jewish immigrant who was losing his battle with the English language, the Goldbergs were portrayed sympathetically, and anyone of any religion could identify with their problems. (There were also a number of popular singers and comedians on radio who were Jewish, such as Jack Benny, Fanny Brice, and Al Jolson, but at a time when anti-Semitism still flourished, most Jewish entertainers did not make overt mention of their religion.)

By the 1930s, some network programs featured Jewish themes. One of the earliest was *Message of Israel*, first heard on NBC Blue in late 1934 and hosted by Lazar Weiner, the music director of New York's Central Synagogue. Boston's Harry Levi was invited to speak on this program, which featured some of America's best-known Reform rabbis, in 1937 and again in 1938.

There were also a number of charitable and philanthropic organizations that provided radio programs, such as Hadassah, the Federation of Jewish Charities, and the American Jewish Joint Distribution Committee. Also, when a special occasion took place, such as the 50th anniversary of the Jewish Theological Seminary in March 1937, highlights from the event were broadcast. At a time

when Federal Communications Commission (FCC) guidelines called for a certain amount of religion and public service, such programs served a useful purpose for the station, while providing the Jewish organizations far-reaching exposure they would not otherwise have received.

And then there was the rabbi who decided to leave the pulpit to become a radio singer. Rabbi Abraham Feinburg took the air name "Anthony Frome" known as the "Poet Prince of the Airwaves," he could be heard singing love songs on several New York stations from 1932 to 1935, at which time he gave it all up and went back to being a rabbi again. On the other hand, there was a famous opera singer who also became a cantor; his radio concerts were critically acclaimed whether he was doing Hebrew prayers or portraying the lead tenor role in "La Traviata." Jan Peerce was discovered by the famous impresario Samuel Rothafel (better known as Roxy) while singing at a hotel banquet in 1932. Soon, he was singing on NBC Blue's *Radio City Music Hall of the Air*, and by 1941 at the Metropolitan Opera, where he performed for 27 years. But throughout his life, as he had done in his neighborhood synagogue before he became famous, Peerce would chant the Jewish liturgical prayers at the High Holy days. He also made a number of recordings of sacred Jewish music, some of which have been reissued.

During the 1930s a few radio stations were airing mainly ethnic and foreign-language programs, brokering out segments of the day to particular groups. One of the best known ethnic stations was New York's WEVD, where some long-running Yiddish programs made their home; thanks to WEVD, it was possible to hear anything from folk songs to entire Yiddish plays. And because WEVD had a working agreement with a Jewish newspaper called the *Forverts* ("Forward"), there were always commentators and critics who discussed the news from a Jewish perspective. WEVD also had Moses Asch, who would go on to found Folkways Records, but who in the mid-1930s hired and recorded many of the performers whose music was played on WEVD. America in the 1930s still had many immigrants who missed the culture of the old country, and radio helped to provide it. One program, *Yiddish Melodies in Swing*, went on the air on New York's WHN in 1939, and in 1941 fans were still waiting in line to get tickets to be in the studio audience.

Speaking Out

However, the 1930s became a more serious time for Jewish broadcasters as the situation in Europe worsened. As news of Hitler and the Nazis dominated newspapers, some Jewish radio programs began providing news and information that the network newscasts were hesitant to mention. Nazi military conquests were front-page news, but it was not until the 1940s that newspapers such as the *New York Times* finally decided the extermination of Jewish people was a major story. Thus, it was up to the Jewish press, and the news commentators on Jewish programs (along with a few non-Jewish commentators who spoke out, most notably NBC's Dorothy Thompson), to make sure the story was told. Rabbi Stephen Wise took to the airwaves to condemn fascism overseas while also condemning bigotry in America, as personified by Father Charles Coughlin, the anti-Semitic radio priest. The chairmen and women of many Jewish organizations, such as the American Jewish Committee and the Jewish Labor Committee, decried the persecution of Jews in Europe and tried to raise funds to help them. But Jewish public-affairs programs were usually short and were seldom on the air more than once a week. Although they did call attention to the problems Jews faced, they could not compensate for the lack of coverage the rest of the week.

Ethics and Culture

The next major network program with a Jewish theme came from the Jewish Theological Seminary. Developed by seminary president Louis Finkelstein, *The Eternal Light* first aired on NBC in October 1944, featuring radio dramas about biblical personalities and famous Jewish men and women past and present. It often presented thought-provoking stories with ethical dimensions, and it was still on the air (having moved to television) in the 1980s, celebrating its 40th anniversary in 1985. Among the famous performers who were heard on this award-winning program over the years were Ed Asner, Gene Wilder, and E.G. Marshall. At the height of its popularity, this program was heard on more than 100 stations, and it won a Peabody Award for excellence.

Some Jewish celebrities began to offer their own radio shows, making use of Jewish or Yiddish culture. From 1951 through 1955, parodist and comedian Mickey Katz starred in his own radio show on KABC in Los Angeles, and in the 1960s, actor and folksinger Theodore Bikel starred in *Thedore Bikel at Home*, which aired on FM stations in New York, Chicago, and Los Angeles. Some announcers who began their careers doing Jewish-oriented programming in the 1930s or 1940s could still be heard many years later. Zvee Scooler, who had originally

been an actor in Yiddish theater, did commentary on WEVD for four decades. Max Reznick, whose show *The Jewish Hour* included everything from parodies to cantorial records to the popular style of Jewish jazz known as "klezmer," was on the air on several Washington, D.C., stations from the 1940s until he retired in 1986. Ben Gailing's Jewish program *Fraylekher Kabtsen* (The Happy Poor Man) was on the air in Boston for more than 50 years. And in Chicago, Bernie Finkel's *Jewish Community Hour* celebrated its 37th anniversary in the summer of 2000.

Jewish Programs Today

Jewish music or commentary was readily available on radio as the new century began. There were radio talk shows with Jewish themes, such as *Talkline with Zev Brenner,* heard on stations in New York and New Jersey. (Brenner had even started an all-Jewish radio station, WLIR, Long Island, N.Y., in May 1993, and after that venture, he resumed his job as a radio and cable television talk host.) Another popular radio program with a loyal following combined requests and dedications with a wide range of Jewish music, plus commentary from an Orthodox point of view—*JM in the AM* ("Jewish Moments in the Morning") with Nachum Segal had been on the air since 1983 on WFMU in Jersey City, New Jersey. The growth of the internet enabled Jewish programs from foreign countries (including Israel) to be heard in America. The internet was also helpful to those Jewish programs that at one time were heard on small AM stations; they could now broadcast on the world wide web and gain a much larger potential audience. Newspaper owner Phil Blazer was among those who took advantage of the new technology; the *Phil Blazer Show* has been on radio in Los Angeles since 1965, but it began webcasting in 2000. Talk show host Zev Brenner also began doing webcasting, and Boston radio host Mark David, whose show *Yiddish Voice* aired on WUNR in Brookline, MA, also made his program available over the internet. National Public Radio has aired holiday concerts of Jewish music at Hanukkah (including one concert featuring Theodore Bikel), and a number of Jewish recording artists are making their music available to be heard or downloaded.

Unlike the Jewish radio programs of the early days, there are not as many radio sermons or famous radio cantors, although there certainly are Jewish programs that have a moral or ethical dimension and shows that stress Jewish theology. There are even internet programs that teach Torah

(Jewish Bible) online and play sound files to help with singing and pronunciation.

Although much of Jewish radio programming today is oriented toward music, there are also shows about Israel and current events. And even though tolerance is much more a part of American life than it was during radio's early years, myths and stereotypes still exist; when a celebrity utters an anti-Jewish remark, or when there are questions about Jewish beliefs (such as in 2000 when U.S. Senator Joseph Lieberman, an Orthodox Jew, was the Democratic candidate for vice president), agencies such as the Anti-Defamation League or the American Jewish Congress send spokespeople to address the issue on radio and television talk shows.

One continuing controversy is the presence on the air of so-called Messianic Jewish programs, such as Sid Roth's syndicated *Messianic Vision* or *Zola Levitt Presents*, which is now heard over the internet in addition to its long run on television. Messianic programs are broadcast by Christian stations, but their intention is to convert Jews. Hosts claim they are still Jewish even though they have accepted Christianity; they use Hebrew words and Jewish terminology to disguise evangelical Christian concepts, such as referring to Jesus as "Yeshua HaMoshiah," with the hope that Jewish listeners will be less threatened by a show that says one can convert to Christianity without leaving Judaism. These shows have evoked some vehement protest from leaders of the organized Jewish community, who object to what they feel is a distortion of Jewish teachings and accuse the hosts of using deceptive tactics.

Now that there is no longer an FCC guideline encouraging religious programming, few stations are willing to give free time to a religious show. As a result, the majority of religious programs on the air are sponsored by Christian denominations or individual preachers. With the radio networks no longer providing free time, and with production costs so expensive, there are few if any religious shows of the caliber of *The Eternal Light* on radio anymore. In fact, most of the popular music stations air no religious programs at all, and yet there are still Jewish programs on radio, just as there were in the 1920s. The shows offer a wide range of styles: some are traditional, with old-timers who play the great cantorial music of the past and reminisce about the old days, but others are quite modern and exemplify the interests of the younger audience. One such show is heard on WSIA, Staten Island, New York; it features Jewish women's music and is hosted by Michele Garner, who calls herself

the "Rockin' Rebbetzin" (the Yiddish word for a woman who is married to a rabbi is *rebbetzin*, and not only is her husband Eliezer a rabbi, but he too does a show on WSIA, playing Jewish rock music). Thanks to Jewish radio shows and the performers who love European Jewish culture, the Yiddish language is being kept alive; klezmer music has enjoyed a rebirth and newfound popularity with a younger demographic. Jewish radio shows are also proving helpful to Jews-by-choice, people who have converted to Judaism on their own and now want to learn more about Judaism's various customs and musical traditions. Although it is certainly true that most religious programs on radio are done by and for Christians, there continues to be a consistent Jewish presence on the air, with shows that help to create a sense of community and a sense of identity.

Another interesting trend is the resurgence of Yiddish radio programs. Although only a few American Jews speak the language, there has been great interest in reviving it, especially given its impact on Jewish music and theater in the Golden Age of Radio. Leading this effort is the Yiddish Radio Project, which, beginning in March 2002, (some excerpts appearing in late 2001), could be heard on National Public Radio. Much of the work restoring the recordings and doing the historical research was done by a New York author and musician, Henry Sapoznik. A two-volume compact disc has been issued by the Yiddish Radio Project containing the first ten episodes of the NPR program, and the Project has a website with updated information (see below).

See also: Goldbergs; Religion on Radio; Stereotypes on Radio; WEVD

Further Reading

Fine, Joyce, "American Radio Coverage of the Holocaust," www.motlc.wiesenthal.com/resources.books/annual5/chapo8.html.
Goldman, Ari, "For Orthodox Jews, a Gathering Place on the Air," *New York Times* (24 September 2000).
Kun, Josh, "The Yiddish Are Coming: Mickey Katz, Anti-Semitism, and the Sound of Jewish Difference," *American Jewish History* 87, no. 4 (1999).
Leff, Laurel, "A Tragic Fight in the Family: The New York Times, Reform Judaism, and the Holocaust," *American Jewish History* 88, no. 1 (2000).
Shandler, Jeffrey, and Elihu Katz, "Broadcasting American Judaism," in *Tradition Renewed: A History of the Jewish Theological Seminary*, edited by Jack Wertheimer, vol. 2, New York: Jewish Theological Seminary, 1997.
Siegel, David S., and Susan Siegel, *Radio and the Jews: The Untold Story of How Radio Influenced America's Image of Jews, 1920s–1950s*. Yorktown Heights, New York: Book Hunter Press, 2007.

Wishengrad, Morton, *The Eternal Light: Twenty-Six Radio Plays from the Eternal Light Program*, New York: Crown, 1947.

Yiddish Radio Project website, www.yiddishradioproject.org.

DONNA L. HALPER

JINGLES

Station identification jingles—catchy musical motifs often accompanied by vocals—are a basic ingredient of the sound of radio stations in most regions of the world. Although they are most associated with pop and rock music commercial radio services, jingles are also common in speech-based stations and even in publicly funded radio services.

Jingles are principally used by stations to insinuate their names and slogans into the minds of listeners. In so doing, jingles help ensure that, when questioned by audience researchers, listeners will recall particular stations over their rivals. This is especially vital for commercial stations, whose advertising rates are largely dictated by the results of such surveys.

In addition to this near-brainwashing technique of implanting the station names in the minds of listeners, radio jingles can be regarded as having the following attributes:

- They provide a positive, confident, "station sound" and a general "feel-good" factor.
- They promote the most important programming elements, for example, the style and quantity of music, contests, and local information.
- They "announce" different program elements, such as news, weather, sports, and disc jockey names.
- They serve as a way of "changing gears" between different program elements, for example, between news, commercial stop-sets, and travel information.
- They serve as a way of making musical transitions, for example, between slow- and fast-paced music.

Origins

The first known singing radio jingle was done in the mid-1920s, when Ernie Hare and Billy Jones, known as "The Happiness Boys," sang songs for a number of consumer products. By the late 1930s, advertising jingles had developed to a sophisticated level of production, often involving singing choirs and full big band orchestras. The station identification jingle developed naturally from this by the 1940s: WNEW in New York, for example, asked recording artists to sing short ditties incorporating the station's call letters.

By the mid-1950s radio station management saw the jingle as part of the battle for audience ratings success in a marketplace that was becoming ever more competitive—not just with other radio stations but with the new medium of television. In this period, radio stations were rapidly moving away from the "full-service" network model with a variety of programs and toward local operations, with most adopting one of three or four basic formats, and managements had to convince listeners that their stations were in fact better than and different from the opposition. They therefore marketed and promoted in ways similar to those of any consumer product. The fact that the station jingles sounded very similar to the advertising jingles of products and services was no coincidence: they were often written, performed, and produced by the same companies.

The "founding fathers" of station jingles as a distinct entity were Bill Meeks and Gordon McLendon. The latter bought KLIF in Dallas in 1947 and appointed Meeks as his music director with a specific brief to put together live music shows. As with so many innovations, the modern station jingle happened by accident: the jingles were used as a way of bridging the time needed in live broadcasting to set up each new vocal group.

Meeks left KLIF to start his own company, Production Advertising Marketing Service (PAMS), in Dallas in 1951. By the mid-1950s he was compiling individual station jingles into "packages"— whole series of jingles using variations of the same musical structure and slogans—to different stations across the country. By the end of 1964 the primary business of PAMS had become station jingles, and the company became the world leader in a new stratum of services to the radio industry. Meanwhile, McLendon hired another musical director, Tom Merriman, who developed and elaborated on the station identification jingles at KLIF; other stations in different parts of the United States heard these and asked for customized sets of their own. Merriman also left KLIF and in 1955 formed the Commercial Recording Corporation; his company produced some of the first jingles specifically for Top 40 radio, which was rapidly emerging as the number-one radio format.

There was a good deal of creativity and innovation in this period. PAMS is credited with being the first company to use the Moog synthesizer and the Sonovox—a device originally developed to enable people who had lost the use of their vocal chords to make intelligible speech—to create an extraordinary electronic "singing" voice. The "variable station logo" technique meant that many disparate programming elements could be linked and blended using variations on the same musical motif, often with lyrical variations of the same slogan or "positioning statement."

Despite this, the overall style of these jingles—close vocal harmonies and lush orchestrations common in the pre-rock and roll period—was outdated even by the late 1950s, and yet, curiously, the style persisted for at least another 20 years. It appears that for many years, the radio jingle was accepted by the listening public as being a musical genre of its own, with no need to bow to changes in popular music.

Occasionally, though, attempts were made to overcome this anachronism by somewhat cheekily adopting more contemporary styles: one of the PAMS jingle sets adopted the Beatles' sound, even using the group's trademark "yeah yeah." Even here, though, the jingles outlasted the creations of the form on which they were based. Stations playing more contemporary formats belatedly moved away from the traditional close harmonies and lush orchestrations, seeing these techniques as distinctly "uncool" and embarrassingly old-fashioned (U.S. FM rock stations had always taken this view of jingles and had consequently eschewed them from the start).

In 1974 former PAMS employee Jonathan Wolfert and his wife Mary Lyn set up a new company, JAM (Jon and Mary)—also based in Dallas, the world's center for station jingles—which quickly established itself as one of the leading companies in the jingles field. In 1976 they secured the contract for the most famous and imitated Top 40 radio station in the world—WABC in New York—which used PAMS jingles from 1962 to 1974. Probably the most-played jingle in the world was recorded for this station in the spring of 1976—lasting just two-and-a-half seconds. In 1990 Wolfert bought up the rights to the jingles from PAMS (which had suspended operations in 1978 after a series of financial crises). These jingles were still in demand in many radio markets throughout the world—especially on golden oldies stations, which had their own station names and slogans sung over the original music tracks, often using many of the same singers.

Modern Era

The length of station jingles varies greatly, although most average between five and seven seconds. JAM also claims to have recorded the longest known jingle—for WYNY in the fall of 1979—which lasted three-and-a-half minutes. "The New York 97 Song" is a vocal and musical narrative of a day in the life of a listener in New York, with repeated use of the station location, frequency, and call letters—"New York 97, WYNY."

The international ubiquity of the station identification jingle cannot simply be explained as the result of the competitiveness of the U.S. commercial radio system. Jingles are used in radio services in very different types of economic and media systems. For example, the British public service broadcaster, the British Broadcasting Corporation (BBC), which held a monopoly on domestic radio in the United Kingdom until 1973, began using PAMS jingles in 1967 on its new rock and pop network, Radio 1. This service was set up on instructions from the government after it had produced legislation outlawing the "pop pirates" of the mid-1960s—many of which had copied U.S. Top 40 and beautiful music formats and used jingles from PAMS in Dallas. Radio 1 ordered the same series of jingles that had been used by the most commercially successful of the offshore pirates, the Texan-backed Radio London. Even though the BBC carried no commercials and had no authorized competition during the late 1960s and early 1970s, its managers thought that station jingles had become an essential part of pop music programming and youth culture. Many other state broadcasters have also felt the need to invest in the "Dallas Sound" of jingles, as have the publicly funded armed forces radio networks of both the United States and the United Kingdom. The jingles have also been sung in languages other than English: the U.S. radio jingle can be fairly regarded as a form of cultural imperialism, albeit one of a benign nature.

By the mid-1980s, a new vogue for electronically produced "Sweepers," with a spoken rather than sung vocal track, became the vogue on many contemporary hit radio and adult contemporary stations. As with all commercial operations, the jingles business—dominated in the world market by JAM and TM Century—had to adapt to these new demands or face extinction. In the late 1990s, there was some indication that the fashion had moved, if not full circle, then perhaps 180 degrees, when many stations—especially those targeted to the baby boom generation, which had grown up with the Dallas Sound—began investing in the more traditional type of jingle production, albeit with a more contemporary edge.

Although fashions in station jingles will no doubt evolve still further, the one constant need for stations faced with ever more competition for listeners' loyalty is to ensure that they promote themselves on the air in the most attractive and distinctive audio fashion possible.

See also: Promotion on Radio

Further Reading

Chapman, Robert, *Selling the Sixties: The Pirates and Pop Music Radio*, London and New York: Routledge, 1992.
Douglas, Susan J., *Listening In: Radio and the American Imagination*, New York: Times Books, 1999.
Fong-Torres, Ben, *The Hits Just Keep on Coming: The History of Top 40 Radio*, San Francisco, California: Miller Freeman Books, 1998.
Garay, Ronald, *Gordon McLendon: The Maverick of Radio*, New York: Greenwood Press, 1992.
Hilmes, Michele, *Radio Voices: American Broadcasting, 1922–1952*, Minneapolis: University of Minnesota Press, 1997.
Keith, Michael C., *Voices in The Purple Haze: Underground Radio and the Sixties*, Westport, Connecticut: Praeger, 1997.
MacFarland, David, T., *The Development of the Top 40 Radio Format*, New York: Arno Press, 1979.

RICHARD RUDIN

K

KCBS/KQW

San Jose, California (later San Francisco)
Station

KQW, San Jose, was one of the pioneering radio stations in the United States, the eighth to receive a Department of Commerce license, which was granted on 9 December 1921. But the major significance of KQW was that its owner, Charles Herrold, was the first person to operate a broadcast station. And although being one of the earliest stations to go on the air is important, it is the story of how Herrold got there, beginning in 1909, that makes KQW important. Today KQW is the 50,000-W all-news KCBS in San Francisco.

Charles Herrold, after dropping out of Stanford University in 1899 and spending a decade as a freelance inventor and college instructor, decided to go into business for himself. He borrowed money from his father and in 1909 opened the Herrold College of Wireless and Engineering in a downtown San Jose bank building. The purpose of the college was to prepare young men for what was becoming a lucrative profession: wireless operator. Herrold also had a vision of inventing a new technology for a radiotelephone. Wireless was primarily Morse code-based, but several inventors were just beginning to find ways to make the wireless talk. Herrold had invented and patented a system based on an oscillating DC arc, a device with its roots in the bright arc lighting of the day. His patents were for a water-cooled carbon microphone, an array of arcs burning under liquid, and a unique antenna system.

Between 1912 and 1917, Herrold, his wife Sybil, and his assistants and students at the school began a broadcasting station, regular in schedule and announced in the newspapers, with programming consisting of phonograph music and news read from the local papers. It was new, it was popular, it attracted students to the college, and it allowed Herrold to have audio content for his radio-telephone inventing. Prior to 1912, the students on the air identified the station by saying, "This is the Herrold college station broadcasting from the Garden City bank in San Jose." Later, Herrold used the call sign FN, and in 1916 he received an experimental radiotelephone license, 6XE. The evidence indicates that Herrold's small audiences began to look forward to the broadcasts, and he would have continued them were it not for the United States' entry into World War I. In April 1917, all amateurs and experimenters were ordered to cease all radio activities.

When the ban on radio activity was lifted in 1919, the arc technology once used successfully by Herrold was obsolete. So in 1919, Herrold opened a store in San Jose and built radios as a source of income. He wanted to return to the air and broadcast as before, but he lacked money for the equipment. By December 1921, Herrold had applied for and received a license as KQW, and a new transmitter using vacuum tubes was put on the air.

Like many broadcasters in the early 1920s, Herrold did not have a way to support his station. Advertising was in its infancy, and local stations had to share dial space, making it difficult for listeners to separate stations amid the interference.

Many stations were sold or just went off the air, their operators giving up. In 1925 Herrold turned over his KQW license to the First Baptist Church of San Jose. In exchange for the license, the church agreed to retain and pay Herrold as its chief engineer. After a year, his contract apparently up, the church, citing financial problems of its own, fired Herrold. A headline in the San Jose paper read, "Father of Broadcasting Fired!"

In 1926 Fred Hart approached the church and offered to run KQW and make a profit with agricultural programming. In return, Hart promised the Baptists that KQW would air their Sunday morning services. The station made money as an agricultural news outlet, and Hart soon bought the station. By the end of the 1920s, broadcasting was a fully formed business, but Fred Hart still had his eye on the historical significance of his station. Contacting Charles Herrold, then a freelance sales representative for several Bay Area stations, Hart asked Herrold to try to resurrect some of the early 1909 to 1917 history and bring in materials and photos of the early station, and a promotion was developed around this information.

In 1934 Hart sold KQW to Ralph Burton and Charles McCarthy of San Francisco, and its power was soon raised to 5,000 W. In 1942, KQW began its affiliation with the Columbia Broadcasting System (CBS). The main studios were moved to the Palace Hotel in San Francisco, although legally KQW was still licensed to San Jose, so its transmitter had to remain there. KQW was an important station during World War II, acting as a relay for shortwave transmissions for the Pacific Coast, along with airing well-known CBS network personalities. In 1945 KQW attempted one final time to publicize its pioneer history. An engineer was sent with a disc recorder to the local rest home where the aging Charles Herrold was spending his final days. A one-hour historical documentary was written, produced, and aired, with Herrold's recorded voice used at the end of the show. The actor hired to portray Herrold was Jack Webb.

After the end of World War II, KQW and CBS fought a long Federal Communications Commission battle with another station over the rights to relocate to 740 kHz and to increase power to 50,000 W. In 1949 the call letters were changed from KQW to KCBS, and the transmitter was relicensed and legally moved to San Francisco; a 50,000-W transmitter went into operation in 1951. Throughout the 1950s KCBS operated as a "full-service" station, airing a combination of news, personality, music, and CBS network offerings.

It was not until the late 1950s that CBS rediscovered that KCBS might have some status as a pioneer station. Research leading to this celebration began in 1958, when San Jose State University professor Gordon Greb discovered the Herrold history in a private local museum. The curator had pieces of the early Herrold arc transmitter technology and strong evidence that the long-forgotten broadcasts took place. Greb located the still-living witnesses to the events, including Herrold's first wife and son and former students and teachers at the Herrold school. Greb located a collection of Herrold correspondence, patents, and photographs from the important pre-1920 period. In 1959, 50 years after Herrold's 1909 beginning, a "50th Anniversary of Broadcasting" was staged by KCBS and San Jose State University's journalism department. A Herrold arc transmitter was reassembled from parts found in a local museum, and dignitaries and personalities from CBS in New York were brought to San Jose, where dinners and a parade highlighted a week of celebration. Several historical audio documentaries were aired, and a congressional resolution proclaiming KCBS the first radio station was read into the public record in Washington, D.C.

Then the most important event in the Herrold/KQW/KCBS story took place: the publication in 1959 of Greb's article in the *Journal of Broadcasting*. This story of Charles Herrold not only became the scholarly basis for the KCBS claim but also provided the historical community with evidence of Herrold's work, which has found its way into subsequent broadcast history texts.

What about the KCBS claim of "first station?" The most significant study on first broadcaster claims was published in the *Journal of Broadcasting* in 1977. In a study of four claimants by two respected historians, it was determined that KDKA in Pittsburgh could claim the title of "oldest station," because that station began on the air in 1920 and has continued, uninterrupted, to broadcast up until the present. KCBS, because of the lapse between when Herrold left the air during World War I and his return as KQW in 1921, was deemed not to be the oldest, but it could legitimately claim to be the "first station." In an ironic twist, the two large station owners, Westinghouse with KDKA and CBS with KCBS, who battled for years in the court of public opinion for the title of first broadcaster, are today owned by the same company—Viacom.

See also: Columbia Broadcasting System; KDKA

Further Reading

Adams, Mike, producer, writer, and director, *Broadcasting's Forgotten Father: The Charles Herrold Story* (video-recording), www.kteh.org/productions/docs/docherrold.html

Baudino, J.E., and John M. Kittross, "Broadcasting's Oldest Stations: An Examination of Four Claimants," *Journal of Broadcasting* 21 (Winter 1977).

The Broadcast Archive: Radio History on the Web, www.oldradio.com

The Charles Herrold Historical Site, www.charlesherrold.org

Greb, Gordon, "The Golden Anniversary of Broadcasting," *Journal of Broadcasting* 3, no. 1 (Winter 1958–59).

Schneider, John F., "The History of KQW/KCBS," Master's thesis, San Francisco State University, 1990.

MICHAEL H. ADAMS

KCMO

Kansas City, Missouri Station

KCMO-AM is known both regionally and nationally for two reasons: (1) it was once a high-power, 50,000 W station that could be received across a large portion of the Midwest; and (2) because the station once employed Walter Cronkite, who has mentioned it often in discussing his early career. Originally based in Kansas City, Missouri, its studios are now located in a nearby Kansas suburb. It now operates on 10,000 W during the day and 5,000 W at night.

The KCMO call was first used in 1936 for a station formerly known as KWKC (which had been on the air since the 1920s) that was taken over by investors Lester E. Cox and Thomas L. Evans. By the mid-1950s, the station suffered from low power (100 W) and no network affiliation.

Walter Cronkite, who worked for the station at that time, recalled in his biography that KCMO did not subscribe to a news wire. Cronkite, who was assigned the air name "Walter Wilcox" while at KCMO, recalls announcing sports play by play (from Western Union telegraph wire dispatches), covering news, and eventually leaving the station (but not before meeting his wife-to-be Betsy Maxwell, another station employee) when he had a dispute with management over how to react to reports of a fire at City Hall. Cronkite's version of the story is that he wanted to verify the seriousness of the fire—which turned out to be minor—with the fire department, but the station's program manager wanted to go on the air with false reports of people jumping from the building. Cronkite says that he was fired for "daring to question management's authority" and that his KCMO experience "cooled any thought I had that radio might be an interesting medium in which to practice journalism" (*A Reporter's Life*, 1996).

KCMO made major advances in solving its coverage problems by increasing to 1,000 W in 1939 (the same year it received National Broadcasting Company [NBC] network affiliation), to 5,000 W in 1940, and to 50,000 W (daytime, with reduced power at night) in 1947, at which time it was assigned the frequency of 810 AM, which it occupied until the late 1990s.

The station's most stable period (and its longest continuity of ownership) began not in the golden age of radio, but as radio was being surpassed by television in 1953, when the Meredith Corporation purchased KCMO at a cost of $2 million. Under Meredith, the station heavily promoted the range and quality of signal that its 50,000 W gave it, allowing it to reach listeners across western Missouri, much of Kansas, and parts of Iowa and Nebraska. Despite its strong daytime signal, however, its reduced power and especially its directional pattern at night often resulted in poor reception after dark in the Kansas suburbs.

Under Meredith, the station built a strong news department, and from the 1950s through the 1970s KCMO offered popular and country music formats (at one time referring to its air sound as a combination of the two). After serious losses in ratings in the late 1970s, Meredith invested heavily in a news format in 1980, at one point employing well over a dozen people in news-related capacities alone. The hoped-for surge in audience never came, however, and the news format evolved to a less expensive talk format, which also failed to move the station to a dominant position in the market. In 1983 Meredith sold KCMO to Fairbanks Communications, beginning a string of ownership changes with subsequent sales to Summit (1983), Gannett (1986), Bonneville (1993), Entercom (1997), and Susquehanna (2000).

MARK POINDEXTER

KDKA

Pittsburgh, Pennsylvania Station

KDKA in Pittsburgh began operation in 1920 and is often called the oldest regular broadcast station in the United States. The station, still owned by Westinghouse (now merged with Columbia Broadcasting System [CBS]), pioneered in many areas during its initial years on the air. Within months of its debut, the station broadcast the first regularly scheduled church services; the first program broadcast from a theater; the first on-air appearance by a Cabinet member (the Secretary of War); and the first sporting event, a 10-round boxing match, soon followed by regularly broadcast baseball scores. KDKA developed the first orchestra exclusively used on radio, another precedent soon adopted by many other stations. The station had by then hired the first full-time radio announcer, Harold W. Arlin, a Westinghouse engineer. And a regular farm program was begun in mid-1921.

Westinghouse experimented with different means of extending and improving KDKA's signal. A shortwave station, KFKX, was placed on the air in Hastings, Nebraska, in 1923 and another followed in Pittsburgh. These and others lasted into World War II, eventually under government operation. They were one means of providing KDKA's "Far North Service" that sent the sounds of home to explorers and pioneers in northern Canada in the 1920s and early 1930s, often their only connection with the outside world.

Origins

KDKA radio began as experimental radio station 8XK in the Wilkinsburg, Pennsylvania, garage of Frank Conrad, an electrical engineer employed by the Westinghouse Corporation's East Pittsburgh plant. Conrad's experimental station was established as a point-to-point operation to test radio equipment manufactured by Westinghouse for U.S. military use in World War I. In 1919 the U.S. government canceled Westinghouse's remaining military contracts and the corporation was facing idle factories. Conrad was among the first to put his 8XK back on the air as an amateur radio telephone station and in contact with ham (amateur) radio operators. Conrad's main concerns were with the quality of his signal and the distance it would travel. He would read from newspapers and then await reports from listening posts commenting on the quality of the reception.

The people operating the listening posts soon tired of hearing news they had already seen in the newspapers and they grew weary of hearing Conrad's voice. One of them suggested that Conrad play a phonograph record. Conrad did so and soon the Westinghouse headquarters received a flood of mail requesting newer music and specific song titles. Frank Conrad had become the world's first disc jockey.

The news of Conrad's airborne music reached a department manager at Pittsburgh's Joseph Home Department Store, who realized that people who wanted to listen to Conrad might want to purchase assembled radios. An ad was placed in the *Pittsburgh Sun*'s 29 September 1920 issue, featuring

wireless sets for $10.00. That ad was seen by Harry P. Davis, a Westinghouse vice president who realized that a vast potential market could be developed for home wireless sets and that Westinghouse already had the ideal product: the SCR-70, a radio receiver made for the U.S. military in the recently concluded world war.

Decisions were made to move Conrad's station to the roof of the East Pittsburgh plant's administration building, to install a stronger transmitter, and to redesign the station for public entertainment. All was to be ready by early November 1920, a presidential election year. On 2 November, the Harding-Cox election results were broadcast by KDKA, the newly assigned call letters on its Department of Commerce license. The success of KDKA was rapidly assured, and soon many newspapers across the country were publishing the station's program schedule (usually an hour of music and talk in the evening).

According to Baudino and Kittross (1977), KDKA is the oldest U.S. station still in operation, as reckoned by the following standards: KDKA (1) used radio waves (2) to send out noncoded signals (3) in a continuous, scheduled program service (4) intended for the general public and (5) was licensed by the government to provide such a service.

Later Developments

The station's frequency shifted several times in the 1920s, between 950 and 980 kHz, and one final time in March 1941 (due to the North American Regional Broadcasting Agreement) to 1020 kHz, which it still uses. KDKA became a 50,000-W clear channel operation by the late 1920s. In 1933, Westinghouse turned over daily management of KDKA and its other radio stations to the National Broadcasting Company (NBC) network, an arrangement that lasted until 1940.

Beginning in 1927, engineers experimented with FM transmission, using that mode for KDKA signals several hours a day. A Westinghouse commercial FM outlet was on the air in Pittsburgh by April 1942, initially programmed separately but simulcasting the AM outlet by 1948. Likewise, KDKA personnel experimented with a crude system of television in the late 1920s. However, a regular television operation appeared only when Westinghouse purchased DuMont's Channel 2 (then the only television station in Pittsburgh), dubbing it KDKA-TV, in January 1955.

As it did to most other stations, the decline of network programming brought hard times to KDKA for several years as management attempted a host of middle-of-the-road format ideas in the struggle to maintain listener loyalty, a challenge shared by other major-market stations. In 1954 disc jockey Rege Cordic was hired from competing station WWSW and his huge morning drive-time popularity (in part because of his zany characters and fake commercials) helped propel KDKA up the ratings ladder over the next decade, until he left for Los Angeles. A decision in 1955 to resume broadcasts of Pittsburgh Pirates baseball games also contributed to KDKA's renewed popularity. Station newscasts expanded from several years of rip-and-read wire service-based summaries to a full news staff with substantial local presence.

The station celebrated its half-century anniversary in 1970 with considerable promotion and again laying claim to being the oldest radio station in the country. At that time it was the ratings leader in its market, reaching 50 percent more homes than its nearest competitor. In July 1982 KDKA became one of the first AM outlets to provide stereo service. A decade later the station switched from its long-time "full service" or "middle-of-the-road" programming to take on a news/talk format that continued into the new century.

See also: Group W; Westinghouse

Further Reading

Baudino, Joseph E., and John M. Kittross, "Broadcasting's Oldest Stations: An Examination of Four Claimants," *Journal of Broadcasting* 21 (Winter 1977).

Davis, H.P., "The Early History of Broadcasting in the United States," Chapter 7, *The Radio Industry: The Story of Its Development*, Chicago: A.W. Shaw, 1928.

Douglas, George H., "KDKA," *The Early Days of Radio Broadcasting*, Jefferson, North Carolina: McFarland, 1987.

It Started Hear: The History of KDKA Radio and Broadcasting, Pittsburgh, Pennsylvania: Westinghouse, 1970.

KDKA website, www.kdkaradio.com.

Kintner, S.M., "Pittsburgh's Contributions to Radio," *Proceedings of the Institute of Radio Engineers* 20: 1849–1862 (December 1932).

Myer, Dwight A., "Up from a Bread-Board—KDKA's Tale," *Broadcasting*, 24 November 1941.

Saudek, Robert, "Program Coming in Fine. Please Play 'Japanese Sandman'," *American Heritage: The Twenties* (August 1965).

REGIS TUCCI AND CHRISTOPHER H. STERLING

KFFA

Helena, Arkansas Station

Starting in the 1940s, KFFA played an important role in disseminating blues music to black listeners throughout the upper Mississippi Delta region of the mid-South. The primary showcase for the station's blues offerings was the *King Biscuit Time*, a program that gave valuable exposure to blues performers and that inspired various young black listeners to pursue careers in blues music. The station's black-appeal programming also served as an example to other stations in the region that would later target the black audience.

Sam W. Anderson, a former superintendent of schools in Dyess, Arkansas, conceived the idea of establishing KFFA and recruited John Thomas Franklin and J.Q. Floyd to join him in the investment. Operating as the Helena Broadcasting Company, the men put the station on the air on 19 November 1941. Within a few months, KFFA was carrying a regularly scheduled blues music program.

At the time of KFFA's inception, blacks in the Mississippi Delta region had begun enjoying a measure of increased prosperity, in part because wage labor in farming had replaced the sharecropping system. As a result, businesses had begun marketing more frequently to blacks. Max Moore, who distributed flour through his Interstate Grocer Company, was seeking to market a high-quality flour to blacks and approached KFFA about sponsoring a program that would reach his target population. The new station, ready to try anything that might succeed, inaugurated *King Biscuit Time*, which aired blues music from 12:15 to 12:30 P.M. Monday through Friday. Named for Moore's high-grade flour, the show featured bluesman Rice Miller (also known as Sonny Boy Williamson II), a harmonica player who attracted a large number of listeners who, in turn, began to spend their dollars on the sponsor's product. The show became so popular that Moore began marketing to blacks a cornmeal dubbed "Sonny Boy Meal" after *King Biscuit Time*'s star.

Although KFFA and Max Moore paid Rice Miller very little, the musician could advertise his gigs, which helped fill the venues he played. Club owners, therefore, were more likely to book Miller and to pay him more because of his radio-fueled prominence. Shortly after *King Biscuit Time* debuted, Miller, who had initially performed solo, began recruiting a band for the broadcast. First came Robert Lockwood, Jr., on guitar, and then James "Peck" Curtis on drums and Robert "Dudlow" Taylor on piano. Exposure on KFFA helped promote these men's careers. Furthermore, throughout the 1940s and 1950s bluesmen such as Muddy Waters, Little Walter Jacobs, Houston Stackhouse, Robert Nighthawk, Joe Willie "Pintop" Perkins, and Willie Love appeared on KFFA, reaching audiences that otherwise would never have heard their music; each would go on to enjoy influential careers in the world of blues music.

As KFFA became an important amplifier for blues music in the 1940s, it was inevitable that aspiring blues performers would be influenced by the music and musicians they heard on the station. James Cotton, a well-known harmonica player, was so inspired by the sounds he heard as a child on *King Biscuit Time* that he traveled to Helena to learn from Rice Miller. America's foremost blues performer, B.B. King, also paid close attention to the sounds of *King Biscuit Time* during his boyhood in the Mississippi Delta. "We'd come in from the fields for our noon meal and relax by listening to Sonny Boy," wrote King in his 1996 autobiography. "He had him some famous songs like 'Fattening Frogs for Snakes,' but nothing made him as famous as this show, sponsored by King Biscuit Flour. I'd been listening to it so long, I felt like I knew Sonny Boy personally."

In the immediate wake of *King Biscuit Time's* burgeoning success, other blues music shows joined the KFFA schedule as advertisers saw the value of reaching the black audience. By the mid-1950s, more than 30 hours of KFFA's weekly programming was black-oriented. The station's success with the black-appeal programming that began in the early 1940s served as a significant model for other stations. The station helped fuel a small groundswell of black-oriented programming in the mid-South and was a major impetus in the rapidly growing number of black voices that actually appeared behind the microphones on mid-South radio in the 1940s. The growth of black-oriented programming on mid-South stations like KFFA culminated in the all-black format that debuted on Memphis radio station WDIA in 1949. Just as KFFA promoted the dissemination of blues music, it also promoted black-appeal programming.

Except for a few years in the 1980s, KFFA's *King Biscuit Time* has continued to broadcast on weekdays around noontime, but now disc jockey Sonny Payne provides the music. Payne, who was working at KFFA on the day Rice Miller debuted on *King Biscuit Time*, has carried on the blues tradition at the station, featuring plenty of Rice Miller's recordings and helping to coordinate Helena's annual King Biscuit Blues Festival. KFFA is currently owned by Delta Broadcasting, which bought the station from the Helena Broadcasting Company in 1980.

See also: Black-Oriented Radio; Blues Format; *King Biscuit Flower Hour*

Further Reading

Cantor, Louis, *Wheelin' on Beale: How WDIA-Memphis Became the Nation's First All-Black Radio Station and Created the Sound That Changed America*, New York: Pharos Books, 1992.

Dates, Jannette Lake, and William Barlow, editors, *Split Image: African Americans in the Mass Media*, Washington, D.C.: Howard University Press, 1990.

George, Nelson, *The Death of Rhythm and Blues*, New York: Pantheon Books, 1988.

Hoffman, Larry, "Interview with Robert Lockwood, Jr.," *Living Blues* 26, no. 3 (June 1995).

Khatchadourian, Sonia, "A Ray of Sunshine in the Blues," *Living Blues* 22, no. 3 (May/June 1991).

King, B.B., and David Ritz, *Blues All around Me: The Autobiography of B.B. King*, New York: Avon Books, and London: Sceptre, 1996.

Newman, Mark, *Entrepreneurs of Profit and Pride: From Black-Appeal to Radio Soul*, New York: Praeger, 1988; London: Praeger, 1989.

Palmer, Robert, *Deep Blues*, New York: Viking Press, 1981; London: Penguin, 1982.

Poindexter, Ray, *Arkansas Airwaves*, n.p., 1974.

MICHAEL STREISSGUTH

KFI

Los Angeles, California Station

KFI radio was one of three Los Angeles radio stations to emerge from 1922's early broadcasting confusion and survives today as one of the top radio stations in the United States.

Origins

The story of KFI begins with California's leading Packard automobile distributor, Earle C. Anthony. He became one of the most important early radio station owners, not only on the West coast, but also in the entire nation. An article in the *Saturday Evening Post* gave Anthony the idea to use radio to communicate between his Packard auto dealerships. He built a 50-W transmitter on his kitchen table and on 16 April 1922 began broadcasting in Los Angeles as KFI radio.

The KFI studios were on the roof of his Packard dealership at 1000 South Hope Street, at the corner of 10th (now Olympic) and Hope in downtown Los Angeles. The station started out with only two employees, who put the station on for a few hours per day. They would then take KFI off the air for a dinner break and return to the air for the evening program. One man booked talent for programs, announced them on the air, played musical accompaniments, and, when necessary, filled in program gaps with music. The other man's job was to take care of the technical aspects of putting the programs on the air. In 1923 KFI presented the "June Bride Contest of 1923." The winner had her wedding broadcast over KFI. The bride and groom also received $1,000 worth of electrical appliances (a tidy sum in those days).

With radio becoming the new national fad, KFI did its part to help new listeners. People who bought a crystal set or a more complicated radio could call KFI for help. The station would then send out a technician to help them set up their radio and antenna. KFI is also one of four stations that claim to have used musical chimes between programs before the National Broadcasting Company (NBC) began using them. The chimes were also used when KFI signed on the air each evening in the early 1920s. By the time KFI celebrated its fourth anniversary in 1926, the station boasted a staff of 20 people in the program, technical, and office departments.

Anthony soon realized that KFI could attract new customers into his car dealership. Programs were carefully tailored to the tastes of listeners that Anthony believed would buy Packards. High-class musical and educational programs were featured. The Los Angeles *Herald* and *Examiner* newspapers cooperated with KFI to provide news coverage in the early years. To promote both the station and his car business further, Anthony made sure that the station identification announcements always included the words "This is KFI, Los Angeles. The Radio Central Super Station of Earle C. Anthony, Incorporated, California Packard Distributors." The words "KFI-PACKARD" were also placed on the transmitter towers atop the Packard dealership to keep KFI radio in the public's mind as they traveled through that section of Los Angeles. Program listings in magazines and newspapers during the mid-1920s show that Anthony advertised Packard cars on KFI through such programs as the *Packard Six Orchestra*, *Packard Ballad Hour*, and *Packard Radio Club*.

Development

KFI soon initiated a policy of cooperating with schools, government agencies, and civic groups. In 1924 the first broadcast of a symphony orchestra in the West was presented over KFI; it also sponsored the first remote broadcast of a complete opera from the stage. That same year the first West coast network was set up when KFI exchanged programs with KPO in San Francisco. Over 500 miles of telephone lines connected the two stations. Another "first" was a broadcast of the Hollywood Bowl Summer Concert Season. As the station gained a reputation for its good programming and public service, nearly every important person who visited Southern California made it a point to be heard over KFI's microphone. A mid-1920s favorite of KFI listeners was real-life detective Nick Harris, a forerunner of the "who-done-it" shows. Harris would tell stories proving the folly of committing crime. The Nick Harris program remained a KFI feature through the 1930s.

KFI started a steady growth in popularity and began increasing its output power: from 50 to 500 W in early 1923, to 5,000 W by 1927, and finally to 50,000 W in 1931, all on 640 kHz (since May 1923). The station's signal had already been heard coast to coast on cold winter nights, and radio fans in England and Australia sent in letters in 1924 and 1925 reporting reception of KFI—this owing to occasional sky wave reception. In 1927 KFI supplied the remote equipment for NBC to provide the first national radio coverage of the Rose Bowl football game from Pasadena. KFI's slogan, "A National Institution," made sense when readers of *Radio Listeners Guide* magazine voted KFI as the only West coast station among the 10 most-popular radio stations in the United States. KFI's program schedule was listed regularly in the *New York Times* and other Eastern newspapers.

KFI had several talented announcers on its staff over the years, including two of the most popular men heard on network radio throughout the 1930s and 1940s. Don Wilson was KFI's chief announcer from 1929 to 1933. He later gained fame as Jack Benny's longtime announcer on radio and TV. Ken Carpenter also served as chief announcer at KFI, was later heard on many network radio shows, and was chiefly identified with Bing Crosby's *Kraft Music Hall*. Roger Krupp was another network announcer who did local work on KFI. Chet Huntley was a newscaster from 1937–39 at KFI, years before he became a household name on NBC television's *Huntley Brinkley Report* in the 1950s and 1960s.

As an original NBC affiliate, KFI brought music, comedy, and dramatic programs from New York and Hollywood into Southern California homes, along with the daytime soap operas. The long-time NBC favorites included shows such as Jack Benny, Burns and Allen, *Fibber McGee and Molly*, Fred Allen, Abbott and Costello, and many others. KFI continued to carry its share of local programming, such as *Packard Fiesta* and *Great Moments in History*. One long-time KFI feature that started in 1938, *Art Baker's Notebook*, was heard on the station for two decades.

By December 1939 KFI (and co-owned station KECA) had grown so much that it moved to new studios and offices at 141 North Vermont Avenue. The building included the latest broadcasting equipment and a 250-seat theater for audiences to see local KFI shows on the air.

During World War II, KFI was the station Southern Californians tuned to each night at 10 P.M. to hear the latest war news from reporter John Wahl, sponsored by Richfield gasoline. The 15-minute newscast was followed by *Inside the News*, with Jose Rodriguez and Sid Sutherland and later John Burton. Because the area surrounding Los Angeles was mostly agricultural at the time, KFI presented daily farm news reports and had a full-time farm director. Farmers were also served by KFI with nightly fruit frost warnings in the winter, at 8 P.M. each night. These were heard on KFI into the early 1970s.

Postwar Development

In the 1950s KFI's all-night talk show, *Ben Hunter's Nite Owls*, became quite popular. During the 1960s the station changed from block programming to middle-of-the-road music with local disc jockeys, local and NBC news on the hour, and Los Angeles Dodgers baseball. Later, morning personalities Al Lohman and Roger Barkley tickled listeners' funny bones on KFI from 1969 until 1986.

KFI founder Earle C. Anthony died in 1961. His corporation held the KFI license until the station was sold to Cox Broadcasting in 1973 for $15.1 million. The music on KFI gradually changed to a more contemporary Top 40 format, with several air personalities over the years, including Dave Hull, Bob Hudson, Dave Diamond, and Sonny Melendrez. The station also moved from the more than 30-year-old studios on Vermont to a new facility at 610 South Ardmore Avenue in late 1975.

Since the late 1980s KFI has turned from broadcasting music and become one of the most listened to talk radio stations in the United States, using the slogan "More Stimulating Talk Radio." KFI's program director, David G. Hall, is behind much of that success. The station has been the flagship for such talk hosts as Dr. Laura Schlessigner and Phil Hendrie. KFI also has an award-winning local news staff of 16, who have won many Golden Mike and Associated Press awards. As of early 2001, KFI was owned by Clear Channel Communications.

See also: Clear Channel Communications Inc.; National Broadcasting Company

Further Reading

"A Baby Earle Anthony Wouldn't Give Up," *Broadcasting* (18 October 1971).

Blanton, Parke, *Crystal Set to Satellite: The Story of California Broadcasting, the First 80 Years*, Los Angeles: California Broadcasters Association, 1987.

Blond, Stuart R., *Earle C. Anthony*, Oakland, California: Packard Club, 1985.

Carr, Marc, "When 500 Watts Was a Super Station," *Radio Life Weekly* (16 January 1944).

Higby, Mary Jane, *Tune In Tomorrow; or, How I Found the Right to Happiness with Our Gal Sunday, Stella Dallas, John's Other Wife, and Other Sudsy Radio Serials*, New York: Cowles, 1968.

Poindexter, Ray, *Golden Throats and Silver Tongues: The Radio Announcers*, Conway, Arkansas: River Road Press, 1978.

JIM HILLIKER

KGO
San Francisco, California Station

When West Coast residents first tuned to KGO on 8 January 1924, the station was an innovative business experiment. The General Electric Company (GE) wanted to sell radio sets by attracting consumers to the new medium. During the next 75 years, KGO would symbolize the powerful "key stations" of radio's golden age, develop and name a major new radio format, and be recognized as one of the nation's most successful radio stations.

Early Years

KGO's first studios and transmitter were built at a GE factory in Oakland. This mid-coast tower site reached listeners up and down the West Coast. Its power of 1,500 W at 790 kHz made it one of the five most powerful stations in the nation. It switched to 810 kHz in 1941. KGO's first program schedule totaled six hours weekly: 8–10 P.M. on Tuesday, Thursday, and Saturday. Most radio shows of this era were produced live in the station's studios. San Francisco's enormous wealth of musical, dramatic, and educational talent provided the station with an unlimited supply of performers. Adding studios in the St. Francis Hotel in May 1924 encouraged participation by world famous touring artists.

When radio drama was born on the networks in the late 1920s, KGO reacted by producing local plays. The station employed a full-time dramatic director for the *KGO Players*, a weekly drama. These shows broke new ground by fully enhancing the spoken word with music and sound effects. Top orchestras and community events were also broadcast live. But as broadcast hours expanded, all programming could not remain local. In 1927 both KGO and KPO became San Francisco affiliates of the National Broadcasting Company (NBC). KGO was affiliated with NBC's Red Network and KPO was affiliated with NBC's Blue Network. KPO later became KNBC, then KNBR.

A momentous turning point in KGO's history occurred in 1929, when NBC assumed management of the station, named it the key station for the Blue and Gold networks on the West Coast, and moved it into NBC's studios with KPO. This placed KGO in the creative environment where nationally broadcast network programs such as *One Man's Family* were being produced. (It was the first network radio serial to originate in San Francisco, became the longest-running serial drama in U.S. radio history, and paralleled the golden age of radio from 1932 to 1959.)

In 1942 NBC, KGO, and KPO moved to a $1 million state of the art studio then-called the most perfect plant of its kind ever designed. Ten air-conditioned studios were mounted on springs with suspended walls and ceilings for perfect soundproofing and acoustics. One studio seated an audience of 500 people. NBC was ordered by the Federal Communications Commission (FCC) to sell the Blue Network in 1943 for antitrust reasons. The change gave KGO a new owner, the American Broadcasting Company, and a network re-named ABC (in 1945).

When the FCC authorized an increase to 50,000 W in 1947, a new three-tower transmitting facility was built near the Dumbarton Bridge. This facility included the first multitower directional antenna system in San Francisco. Three 300-foot towers were anchored in salt water and guided KGO's signal in a north–south direction. The station was then billed as "The Sunset Station" because of its powerful nighttime coverage of the Pacific Coast region from Alaska to Mexico. The new transmitting facilities also doubled KGO's daytime coverage area. One of the towers partially collapsed during the 17 October 1989 Loma Prieta earthquake, but the station returned to the air in less than five minutes.

The explosive growth of television in the 1950s captured radio listeners and marked an end to the so-called golden age of radio. As KGO's network shows such as *Don McNeill's Breakfast Club* suffered declining ratings, the station turned to personality disc jockeys. Innovative programs such as *Coyle and Sharpe* (a combination of *Bob and Ray* and *Candid Camera*) and broadcasts by *Les Crane Live from the Hungry I* were featured. But by 1962 the ratings placed "The Sunset Station" eighth in the San Francisco market.

Introducing Talk

The most significant transformation in KGO's history came in 1964 when station manager Don Curran engineered a dramatic change in format by introducing an all-day talk format and leading a team that invented the terms *newstalk* and *infotainment*. The success of this experiment proved the viability of talk radio and eventually led to its expansion into a major new radio format; by 1998 talk radio was being offered by more than 1,000 stations and earned a national audience share of 10 percent. By 1978 KGO had become the most popular radio station in the Bay Area among persons 12 and over.

In October 2000 KGO celebrated its 75th anniversary by continuing its dominance of the nation's fourth-largest market for more than 20 consecutive years. The station's 6.3 share among persons 12 and over captured the number one slot for the 90th consecutive San Francisco Arbitron Ratings book. *Radio Ink* wrote, "This is something that has never occurred in a major market in America before." About 850,000 different listeners tuned in to KGO each week at that time.

A long list of "firsts" contributed to these impressive ratings. KGO was the first Bay Area station with helicopter traffic reports. Its 27-member news department was the first to send a local radio reporter to cover national and international news. In 1997 KGO ranked as the 14th highest-billing station in the nation with revenues of more than $30 million. In 1994 Duncan's *Radio Market Guide* called NewsTalk 810 "the most admired station in the nation." KGO's strengths lay in hiring and keeping enormously talented people and in understanding, serving, and relating to the people and issues of the Bay Area to an extraordinary degree.

In 2000 NewsTalk 810 was one of the first stations in the nation to add a "Push to Talk" feature to its website (www.kgo.com). This allowed visitors to the website to participate in talk shows via the internet with one click of the mouse. And the industry trend to ownership of multiple stations in a single market brought KGO's management team a fresh challenge from owner ABC/Disney—to duplicate their success at sister newstalk station KSFO-FM.

Further Reading

Broadcast History Website: Schneider, John, "Voices out of the Fog: A History of Broadcasting in the San Francisco Bay Area," www.adams.net/~jfs

Duncan, James H., Jr., editor, *Duncan's Radio Market Guide*, Kalamazoo, Michigan: Duncan Media Enterprises, 1984.

Fracchia, Charles A., *Fire and Gold: The San Francisco Story*, Encinitas, California: Heritage Media, and San Antonio, Texas: Lammert, 1994.

McKinsey and Company, et al., *Radio in Search of Excellence: Lessons from America's Best-Run Radio Stations*, Washington, D.C.: National Association of Broadcasters, 1985.

Rhoads, Eric, "Mirror, Mirror on the Radio," *Radio Ink* 8 (November 2000).

Talkers Magazine Online, www.talkers.com

JERRY CONDRA

KHJ

Los Angeles, California Station

The second-oldest station in Los Angeles, KHJ was a broadcast pioneer and prominent originator of network programming during radio's golden age. In the late 1960s, KHJ became the most-imitated radio station in North America following a dramatic ratings turnaround by means of a variant of the basic Storz Top 40 formula.

KHJ began broadcasting with 5 W at 760 kHz on 13 April 1922 from a 10- by 12-foot room atop the Los Angeles *Times* building. Although the *Times* operated the station, C.R. Kierulff, an electrical pioneer, founded it. The first program included "The Star Spangled Banner," an address by *Times* publisher Harry Chandler, vocal selections, a comedy routine, news bulletins, and children's bedtime stories. Three days later the station aired Easter services. The *Times* purchased the KHJ call letters (kindness, health, joy) from Kierulff in November 1922 and increased power to 500 W. During its earliest years, KHJ stopped broadcasting for three minutes out of each 15-minute period in order to clear the air for distress calls. On 31 December 1922, KHJ broadcast throughout New Year's Eve, reported to be an unprecedented event.

As radio entered its golden age, KHJ became the principal West Coast affiliate of Mutual and the flagship of the regional Don Lee network, which was named for its owner, an automobile sales tycoon. The station originated numerous network programs, including the Columbia Broadcasting System (CBS) show *Hollywood Hotel*, hosted by Louella Parsons (during the years before CBS acquired station KNX). Other programming included Raymond Paige and a 50-piece staff orchestra, *Chandu the Magician*, Eddie Cantor, Burns and Allen, *Queen for a Day*, and *Hopalong Cassidy*.

Some prominent figures in mass communication passed through KHJ during its early years. Sylvester (Pat) Weaver, later president of the National Broadcasting Company (NBC), was an announcer in 1934. Helen Gurley Brown, later responsible for revamping Hearst's *Cosmopolitan*, answered listeners' letters while she was a student.

In 1950 RKO General (Tire) purchased the Don Lee broadcast properties, which included KHJ, KHJ-FM, and KHJ-TV. As music and news began to dominate local radio programming in the 1950s, KHJ featured disc jockeys and popular records. In the early 1960s, the station featured the talk personality format that had been successful at RKO General's WOR in New York. Nevertheless, by the end of 1964 KHJ had not developed a niche in the competitive Los Angeles market. In the ratings, the regional facility—on 930 kHz with 5 kW of power and a directional antenna at night—was a lusterless 17th from the top.

The management of RKO General's radio division announced that KHJ would undergo a complete change of programming by May 1965. Although initially opposed to rock and roll or country and western, management chose to pursue an around-the-clock contemporary music format that would draw the bulk of young listeners without offending any other segment of the potential audience. That decision set in motion a chain of events that ultimately brought KHJ from virtual obscurity to legendary status.

In early 1965 RKO General retained "two men who had previously taken 'average' stations and transformed them into number one ranking in areas similar to our own." Those specialists were Gene Chenault and Bill Drake. Chenault was licensee of KYNO in Fresno, the original Top 40 station in the central valley of California. Drake had worked for Gerald Bartell's WAKE in Atlanta and KYA in San Francisco prior to joining Chenault as program director of KYNO. Drake's programming had led KYNO to victory in a tough ratings battle with KMAK, Chenault's tough Fresno competitor.

After Drake's success with KYNO, he and Chenault formed a consulting service. Their first client was KGB in San Diego, which rose from lowest to first in ratings on the 63rd day of Drake–Chenault programming. The success of KGB brought Drake–Chenault to the attention of RKO general management.

Drake and Chenault brought in Ron Jacobs, who had been program director of their Fresno opponent, KMAK, to be the new program director at KHJ. Drake and Jacobs crafted a streamlined version of Top 40 for KHJ centered on a very limited playlist of contemporary favorites aired, when possible, in sweeps of two or three songs. Most sound effects associated with Top 40 (e.g., horns, tones, beepers) were eliminated. A cappella jingles by Johnny Mann were short. Commercial loads were cut to 12–13 minutes per hour and clustered in strategically scheduled stop sets. News aired at 20 minutes past the hour or 20 minutes before the hour to counterprogram competitors' newscasts on the hour or at five minutes before the hour. The mix was given an on-air slogan, "Boss Radio."

Jacobs premiered a "sneak preview" of the Boss Radio format in late April 1965. Compared with other Los Angeles Top 40 stations (KFWB, KRLA in Pasadena), KHJ was noticeably uncluttered. KHJ rose to lead Los Angeles ratings during the first six months with Drake–Chenault as consultants. At the height of its popularity in the late 1960s, KHJ attracted one out of four Los Angeles radio listeners. After KHJ's phenomenal success, RKO General signed Drake and Chenault as consultants for KFRC in San Francisco, CKLW in Windsor (Detroit), WOR-FM in New York, WRKO in Boston, and WHBQ in Memphis.

By 1968 stations paid Drake–Chenault up to $100,000 annually for Bill Drake's services. Although Drake–Chenault consulted a total of only nine stations (including KAKC in Tulsa), the influence of their 1965 win in the tough Los Angeles market diffused throughout the radio broadcasting industry as managers across the nation copied the KHJ format and conservative playlist. Drake–Chenault also attracted critics who blamed the widespread imitation of the KHJ playlist for constrained promotional efforts for innovative music during the late 1960s.

The turnaround of KHJ is a classic business success story of personalities, competition, performance, and impact. In 2000, KHJ continued to thrive with a successful Spanish-language format, and the Drake–Chenault sound remained popular in Los Angeles via KRTH's (formerly KHJ-FM) oldies format, which is reminiscent of KHJ during the late 1960s.

See also: Contemporary Hit Radio/ Top 40 Format; Don Lee Broadcasting System; Mutual Broadcasting System

Further Reading

"Adviser Becomes Boss: Drake Signs with RKO," *Broadcasting* (16 October 1972).
Fornatale, Peter, and Joshua E. Mills, *Radio in the Television Age*, Woodstock, New York: Overlook Press, 1980.
"A History of Rockin' Times: A *Radionow!* Interview with Gene Chenault," *Radionow!* 2, no. 2 (1992).
Jacobs, Ron, *KHJ: Inside Boss Radio*, Stafford, Texas: Zapoleon, 2002.
MacFarland, David T., *The Development of the Top 40 Radio Format*, New York: Arno Press, 1979.
Puig, C., "Back When Jocks Were Boss," *Los Angeles Times* (25 April 1993).
"Rock and Roll Muzak," *Newsweek* (9 March 1970).

ROBERT M. OGLES

KING BISCUIT FLOWER HOUR
Syndicated Showcase for Rock Artists

During the 1970s and 1980s, the *King Biscuit Flower Hour* presented recorded concert performances by more than a thousand artists, including the Rolling Stones, the Who, Eric Clapton, Elton John, U2, John Lennon, Elvis Costello, Aerosmith, the Beach Boys, the Fixx, Led Zeppelin, and many current and future members of the Rock and Roll Hall of Fame. It was the first live performance radio show to offer a glimpse into the daily lives of rock bands on tour. At its peak of popularity, more than 300 U.S. radio stations carried the *King Biscuit Flower Hour*, and the syndicators estimated that the weekly audience surpassed five million listeners.

The program's name pays homage to *King Biscuit Time* (later called *King Biscuit Flour Hour*), a famous radio program that originated in 1941 on KFFA, Helena, Arkansas. Sponsored by the makers of King Biscuit Flour and hosted by Sonny Boy Williamson and Robert Lockwood, Jr., *King Biscuit Time* showcased the country blues music of the Mississippi Delta region, one of the important roots of rock and roll. Every important performer who played the honky tonks and juke joints along the "Chittlin' Circuit" from New Orleans to St. Louis appeared on the show until it left the air in 1967. Helena is now the site of the annual King Biscuit Blues Festival, which keeps the musical tradition alive.

Bob Meyrowitz and Peter Kauff were the first producers for the *King Biscuit Flower Hour*. Their company, DIR Broadcasting, began syndicating the program in 1973. The first show featured John McLaughlin's Mahavishnu Orchestra, a popular jazz-fusion band; Blood, Sweat and Tears; and an unknown group named Bruce Springsteen and the E Street band. For the next 17 years, the format remained the same. Live performances were interspersed with backstage interviews and minimal intrusion from the hosts for continuity. Venues ranged from stadiums to large auditoriums to small clubs. Every hour featured 50 minutes of music heard just as it had been performed before the live crowd.

Later, the company began a similar weekly series featuring country music artists. Production of the original *King Biscuit Flower Hour* ceased in 1990, with a library of more than 24,000 master tapes of classic rock and roll live performances. Soon thereafter, King Biscuit Entertainment bought the series and began syndication of reruns in the United States and Great Britain.

In 1996 King Biscuit Entertainment started releasing a limited number of *King Biscuit Flower Hour* performances on tapes and compact discs, using the syndicated program as a promotional vehicle. Although the classic rock radio format suffered from declining audience shares in the mid-1990s, *King Biscuit Flower Hour* retained its syndication base because its library contained material from other genres such as new wave, modern rock, blues, and alternative.

For the 25th anniversary of *King Biscuit Flower Hour* in 1998, the syndicator produced a two-hour special retrospective program, released a commemorative double compact disc, and made an important announcement. Production had begun on a new series of live performances for future *King Biscuit Flower Hour* programs. King Biscuit Entertainment also added a streaming media website (king-biscuit.com) to promote the radio series and sale of recordings and related merchandise. At the turn of the millennium, the *King Biscuit Flower Hour* could be heard weekly on nearly 200 radio stations in the United States as well as on BBC2 in Great Britain.

See also: KFFA; Rock and Roll Format

Programming History

Nationally Syndicated
18 February 1973–present

Further Reading

Cohodas, Nadine, "The King Biscuit Blues Festival: The Sonny Boy Legacy in Helena," *Blues Access* 31 (Fall 1997), www.bluesaccess.com/No_31/kbbf.html
King Biscuit Radio: The Legendary King Biscuit Flower Hour Radio Show, www.king-biscuit.com/right_about3.html#kingbiscuit
Taylor, Chuck, "King Biscuit to Observe Its 25th," *Billboard* (11 July 1998).

ROBERT HENRY LOCHTE

KMOX
St. Louis, Missouri Station

KMOX (112.0 kHz) is a 50,000-W clear channel AM radio station in St. Louis, Missouri. The station is best known for the talk-centered format it introduced in 1960, which for many years gave it the largest market share of listeners of any radio station in the top 50 U.S. markets. KMOX was put on the air on Christmas Eve (the origin of the X in the station's call letters) in 1925 by a group of investors called "the Voice of St. Louis." In 1927 it began carrying programs from United Independent Broadcasters, which later became the Columbia Broadcasting System (CBS), initially receiving $50.00 per hour of broadcast time. CBS has owned and operated the station since 1932.

KMOX was a fairly typical network station until February 1960 when, faced with erosion of audience to television and with competition from new radio stations that had joined the market in the postwar period, KMOX initiated a radical change in format and became one of the first stations in the United States to offer a talk-centered format. Although a number of stations pioneered the talk format in the 1960s (including KABC in Los Angeles), KMOX was unusual both in the success it achieved with the format (moving rapidly to first in the market) and in the amount of influence that was exerted over the station for decades by a single individual—Robert F. Hyland, Jr., who became general manager of KMOX in 1955 and CBS vice president in 1959 and who continued in both those roles until his death at the age of 71 in 1992.

A number of characteristics set KMOX's air sound apart from that of other stations. In an industry where the norm is short stints for on-air talent, under Hyland's direction the station developed a reputation for just the opposite—talent stayed for decades. From the 1960s through the early 1990s, KMOX's style and content were often closer to those of the British Broadcasting Corporation (BBC) or public radio in the United States than to those of other commercial stations. The style was slightly formal, sometimes described as "dignified," and placed emphasis on both breadth and depth of information. Talk often consisted of a brief interview with a public figure or an expert on topics ranging from medicine to plumbing, followed by telephone calls from listeners. Although he eventually allowed some pure "open line" discussion in which the on-air talent simply chatted with callers, Hyland demanded even then that information of substance be a part of the presentation. If callers were kept on the line too long, Hyland would often reprimand hosts for "back fencing" or engaging in "therapy" with a listener, rather than keeping the discussion on topic. Hyland said in 1960 that one of the purposes of the new talk-oriented format was to educate in addition to entertain.

One of the puzzling paradoxes of KMOX was how it could sound so much like noncommercial, public service radio and yet achieve ratings so much higher than such stations usually do. In 1976 KMOX had a 26 share of the audience in its market, with its nearest competitor holding less than a nine share. The best clue to understanding this success may be found in a common saying that had developed among journalists and politicians in Missouri by the 1970s: "KMOX is more like a newspaper than a radio station." It was sometimes called St. Louis' "third newspaper" (when the *Globe-Democrat* and the *Post-Dispatch* were the other two) and then the "second newspaper" after the *Globe-Democrat* ceased publication. It was idiosyncratic (running marches and prayers as part of a morning ritual) and involved in its community, much like some of the famous editor-dominated newspapers of the 19th century, such as Horace Greeley's *New York Tribune* and Joseph Pulitzer's *St. Louis Post-Dispatch*. The approach Hyland used to advance his radio station was indeed similar to what Pulitzer had tried successfully in the same city almost a century earlier: heavy community involvement (Hyland was reputed to have belonged to approximately 100 different organizations), aggressive investigative reporting, and a combination of entertainment (Hyland tied up all the major professional sports teams for KMOX and carried play-by-play broadcasts of important college games as well) and serious reporting, all seasoned with heavy self-promotion and one editorial campaign after another. Shortly after he became general manager, Hyland made KMOX the first CBS-owned station to carry editorials (the first was in advocacy of fluoridation of St. Louis county water and accused the county government of cowardice for refusing to take a stand). Hyland also followed the lead of newspapers and had KMOX endorse specific candidates for office.

The format that gave KMOX dominance and made it one of the most valuable properties owned by CBS (chairman William Paley once called it "the jewel in the CBS crown") was expensive. At its peak, the station employed more than 100 people, more than 70 of them full-time, and kept a number of "retainers" on the payroll, especially in sports, so that the station would have access to them and so that they would not sell their on-air services elsewhere (a practice that was abandoned as too expensive not long after Hyland's death). The station was intensely local, so much so that when President John F. Kennedy was assassinated in 1963, Hyland ordered the staff to break away from the CBS network feed and to focus on reaction to the assassination in the St. Louis area.

KMOX's similarity to a newspaper illustrates its strengths as well as its vulnerability. The station's high costs required continued high ratings in order to remain profitable, and it could not maintain those ratings as younger people turned away from KMOX's type of serious talk, much as they had also turned away from newspapers. In 1989 a headline in the *Post-Dispatch* read "How Long Will KMOX Be No. 1?" and the accompanying article reported that the station (although still strong overall and especially among the older population) held only a 9.2, percent share of the audience aged 18–34. In the 1990s the share in that critical age group would drop even more, to less than 5.0. Even more important, by 2002 the station's overall share had dropped to below 10, which, although still enough to make it number one in the market, was down dramatically from what it had been a decade earlier. The shift from AM to FM listening and the aging of its audience had finally caught up with KMOX.

Robert Hyland maintained until his death in March of 1992 that KMOX should not trivialize or tabloidize its programming, asserting in a 1990 speech to the St. Louis Press Club:

> The fact that we live in a fast-paced, entertainment-oriented age does not relieve us of the responsibility to live up to the sacred trusts inherent in our profession. Virtually everyone reads newspapers, hears radio and views television. It must be our sacred mission that what they read, hear and view shall have meaning and import beyond filling space and killing time.

Hyland argued that as long as the station maintained its stronghold on major-league play-by-play sports, young listeners would learn its dial position and would eventually turn to KMOX as they got older and became more interested in being informed than in the latest music trends.

Following Hyland's death, a number of changes took place at the station and at CBS that would change KMOX's sound. Much of the station's long-standing on-air staff left. Bob Hardy, who had been on the air for more than 30 years, died, and Jim White and Anne Keefe, also on the air for decades, retired. Jim Wilkerson left for a competing station in a 1996 talent raid that also grabbed two other established voices at KMOX (Wendy Wiese and Kevin Horrigan), transplanting the station's morning sound almost intact to the competing station. But the most drastic change to come to KMOX in the wake of Hyland's death took place in 1994, when a key daytime slot once used for local interviews was turned over to Rush Limbaugh's nationally syndicated show. The decision to put Limbaugh on the air appears to have been primarily defensive—Limbaugh had begun running on a competing station, and the choice was either to have him on KMOX or to compete against him. Limbaugh went on the air from 11 A.M. to 2 P.M. in April 1994, and late in 1999 he was still scheduled in that period. The decision to put Limbaugh on the air may or may not have saved KMOX from further ratings erosion, but it definitely changed the station's sound in three significant ways: (1) where KMOX had long been intensely local, Limbaugh's show has no sense of a particular place; (2) Limbaugh uses various news vignettes and excerpts to support discussion centering on a conservative political point of view; and (3) his sometimes frenetic delivery style is quite different from the calm, public service radio tone that even the younger, post-Hyland KMOX hosts employ.

In 1996 major cutbacks, including reductions in staff, were ordered by Westinghouse, the new owner of CBS. When one irate program host, Kevin Horrigan, walked out and took a job with a competing station, he charged that KMOX was in "chaos," that "part-timers and college kids are writing news and producing shows," and that "everything is being done on the cheap." The cause of the problem, according to the *Post-Dispatch*, was that Westinghouse was demanding a 40 percent profit margin, meaning that the station would have to produce a profit of about $9 million on total advertising sales of about $22.5 million per year, or about double what its past profits had been.

In November 2002 another program host, former CNN correspondent Charles Jaco, was fired (for reasons KMOX management never publicly revealed), and as he left Jaco blasted station management for "dumbing down" its program content in an attempt to raise ratings. The controversy over Jaco's firing (which was covered extensively by St. Louis news media) came on the heels of a number of setbacks, including the erosion of the station's dominance in professional sports play by play. By 2001, KMOX no longer had broadcast rights for the games of the St. Louis hockey and football teams, although it did still provide play-by-play for Cardinal baseball games. In the first years of the 21st century, KMOX could be viewed as embattled, owing to its decline in ratings and to increasingly negative coverage by other media, including the *St. Louis Post-Dispatch* (a 2002 headline proclaimed the station was "losing its grip on listeners") and the *St. Louis Journalism Review* (which in its December 2002/January 2003 issue carried an article on what it referred to as the "unsavory underside" of KMOX in which allegations of right-wing

bias and anti-union policies appeared). However, the station could also be viewed as a survivor: in 2002, more than a decade after a newspaper article questioned how long it could remain in the top position, KMOX was still the number one station in St. Louis in total audience.

See also: Columbia Broadcasting System; Talk Radio

Further Reading

Chin, Sandra Hardy, *At Your Service: KMOX and Bob Hardy, Pioneers of Talk Radio*, St Louis, Missouri: Virginia Publishing, 1997.
Gallagher, Jim, "How Long Will KMOX Be No. 1?" *St. Louis Post-Dispatch* (4 December 1989).
Rains, Sally, and Bob Rains, *The Mighty 'Mox: The 75th Anniversary History of the People, Stories, and Events that Made KMOX a Radio Giant*, South Bend, Indiana: Diamond Communications, 2002.

MARK POINDEXTER

KNX
Los Angeles, California Station

From its beginnings in a small bedroom of a Hollywood residence more than 80 years ago, KNX has grown to become one of the nation's most substantial all-news radio stations. KNX is the oldest radio station operating in Los Angeles and one of the oldest stations in the United States.

Origins

What eventually became KNX started as a 5-W amateur radio station, with the call sign of 6ADZ. The station was built and operated in a back bedroom of his Hollywood home by Fred Christian, a former shipboard wireless operator. KNX historical records indicate that on 20 September 1920 Christian began broadcasting records he had borrowed from music stores, in return for plugs on the air. It is not known how often Christian provided such broadcasts at 200 m/1500 kHz, and he had to leave the air quite often so other amateur radio operators could take their turns at their common hobby.

Christian's main occupation was running the Electric Lighting Supply Company on West Third Street in Los Angeles, selling parts for people to build their own receivers and broadcasting music for them to enjoy. By late 1921 the U.S. Department of Commerce decided to license radio stations that could broadcast music and entertainment to the public, thus removing congestion from amateur radio bands. On 8 December 1921 Christian was granted a license for 360 m (833 kHz), with the call letters KGC.

Christian soon grew tired of broadcasting only recorded music. He moved KGC to the top of the California Theatre Building in downtown Los Angeles. His plans were to broadcast "live" music from the theater. KGC took up the new call sign of KNX when it moved on 1 May 1922. Christian built a new 50-W transmitter to send its signal to more listeners. (The station was briefly off the air a year later while a new 100 W transmitter was installed.) The station was also known as the "California Theatre Radiophone" between 1922 and 1924. Because there were so few available frequencies and no viable government regulation, stations during that period had to share airtime. KNX negotiated with about 15 active radio stations in the Los Angeles area to determine each month the hours the stations would go on the air. KNX usually featured Carli Elinor's California Theatre Concert Orchestra of 50–60 musicians during an afternoon or evening broadcast four days a week, along with music from the theater's organ. The orchestra often performed musical scores from movies playing at the theater, to draw KNX listeners to see the films. Several early Hollywood film celebrities were heard over KNX, including Conrad Nagel, Wallace Reid, Harry Langdon, and Lon Chaney.

Radio magazines of the day that printed KNX program schedules also showed ads for the Electric Lighting Supply Company. Christian sold radios and radio parts to help defray the cost of running the station, because advertising on radio was not common yet. He sold KNX to the Los Angeles *Evening Express* newspaper on 14 October 1924, and the station shifted from 833 to 890 kHz and increased power from 100 W to 500 W. Under the leadership of owner–publisher Guy C. Earl, KNX soon promoted itself to radio fans as "The Voice of Hollywood" and used that slogan for many years. Earl had used KNX before to promote his newspaper and soon sold advertising regularly on the station. When KNX showed a profit of $25,000 in 1925, Earl focused more of his time on the radio side, and other Los Angeles stations took notice of what selling advertising could do for them. In the mid- and late 1920s, KNX offered a daily schedule from early morning to late night. One regular feature was music from Ray West's Cocoanut Grove Orchestra from the Hotel Ambassador. KNX also offered listeners sports and a variety of informational talks, plus drama from the KNX players. From its earliest days, news was an important part of KNX's broadcast day.

In late 1928 KNX shifted from 890 to 1050 kHz and moved to the Paramount Pictures lot in Hollywood. The station increased transmitter power to 5,000 W in 1929 and doubled that in 1932. Earl sold the Los Angeles *Evening Express* but stayed in radio, running KNX under the ownership of the Western Broadcasting Company. When KNX moved its offices and studios again in 1933, to the corner of Vine Street and Selma Avenue, station power was boosted to 25,000 W and finally to 50,000 W in 1934. In 1936 KNX moved to Sunset Boulevard.

CBS Ownership

KNX was sold to the Columbia Broadcasting System (CBS) for $1.25 million in 1936, then the highest price ever paid for a radio station. New KNX/CBS studios were constructed and opened on 30 April 1938 at 6121 Sunset Boulevard. The Hollywood landmark station remains there today. Known as Columbia Square, the studios were home to several top-rated radio shows through the 1940s, including *Silver Theater*, *Melody Ranch* with Gene Autry, *Lucky Strike Hit Parade*, Jack Benny, Burns and Allen, Edgar Bergen and Charlie McCarthy, and Red Skelton. The long-running *Lux Radio Theatre* originated from the Vine Street Playhouse nearby. During World War II, *GE Radio News* with Frazier Hunt was heard. Local shows such as *The Housewives Protective League*, *Hollywood Melody Shop*, and *Hollywood Barn Dance* were favorites with southern California listeners. On 29 March 1941 KNX shifted its frequency one last time, to 1070 kHz.

In the late 1940s comedian Steve Allen worked at KNX as a disc jockey, but he soon turned his airtime into a very popular late-night interview and comedy show. The program got Allen noticed by CBS executives and was a springboard to his highly successful subsequent TV career. Bob Crane, who gained fame on TV's *Hogan's Heroes*, was a very funny morning personality on KNX from 1956 to 1965. During this time KNX had become mostly a music station with news and sports features.

In April 1968 KNX initiated an all-news format and soon operated the largest radio news department in the western United States. KNX claims to have won more awards for broadcast journalism than any other radio station in the United States. These honors include Best Newscast Award from the Associated Press and Best Newscast Award from the Radio-TV News Association (RTNA) 27 times in the past 30 years. KNX has also won more than 150 Golden Mikes from the RTNA.

Further Reading

Blanton, Parke, *Crystal Set to Satellite: The Story of California Broadcasting, the First 80 Years*, Los Angeles: California Broadcasters Association, 1987.

JIM HILLIKER

KOA

Denver, Colorado Station

As a 50,000-W clear channel station, KOA is said to stand for "Klear Over America." One of the first radio stations in Denver, KOA later became one of the West's most popular stations. KOA's powerful signal is capable of reaching 38 states in the evening hours, and the station has been heard in Canada, Mexico, and nearly every state in the United States under the right atmospheric conditions.

Changing Hands

KOA went on the air on 15 December 1924 and was authorized for 1,000 W at 930 kHz. Built and operated by the General Electric Company, the station underwent many changes in operating power and dial position before settling at 50,000 W in 1934 and at 850 kHz in 1941.

KOA underwent many ownership changes over the years. The station became affiliated with the National Broadcasting Company (NBC) in 1928. In 1929 NBC took over operation of KOA from General Electric, and the license was officially assigned to NBC in 1930. However, the actual change of ownership did not occur until NBC bought the transmitter from General Electric in 1934. NBC added a sister station, KOA-FM (later KOAQ-FM, now KRFX-FM), in 1948. The stations were sold to the Metropolitan Television Company (MTC) in 1952. One of MTC's principal stockholders was legendary radio, television, and motion picture entertainer Bob Hope. This group added a television station in 1953, channel 4 KOA-TV (now KCNC-TV). Bob Hope sold his interest in 1964, and General Electric repurchased the station in 1968. In 1983 General Electric sold KOA-AM and sister station KOAQ-FM to Belo Broadcasting. In 1987 KOA was sold to Jacor Broadcasting, which merged with Clear Channel Communications in 1999.

Programming

The opening broadcast in 1924 was launched with much fanfare. With colorful prose, the station avowed its purpose "to serve with special intimacy the states that lie in the great plain—from the Dakotas and Minnesota to Texas—to the Mississippi and beyond; to spread knowledge that will be of use to them in their vast business—to further their peoples' cultural ambitions—to give wider play to their imaginations, and make melody in their ears—to bid them lift up their eyes unto these western hills whence comes new strength" (cited in *Colorado Mac News*, 1984)

In the early days, a large number of KOA radio listeners were farmers, and the station had a heavy emphasis on farm, weather, and agriculture market-related programming. *Farm Question Box* and *Mile High Farmer* were two of the longest-running and most popular agriculture-related programs on the station.

KOA claims a number of historical "firsts" in broadcasting. On 18 February 1927 KOA did a remote broadcast of the "hole-ing through" of the Moffatt Tunnel, which was at the time the longest railroad tunnel in the world. Using the railroad's telegraph circuit, which ran to the entrance of the tunnel, KOA engineers ran lines more than 3.5 miles into the tunnel to broadcast the event. On 15 November 1928 KOA engineers lugged a transmitter to the top of Pikes Peak near Colorado Springs to become the first station to originate from atop a 14,000-foot peak in the Rockies. On 6 May 1936 KOA successfully broadcast a concert nationwide from a specially equipped Radio Corporation of America (RCA) Victor train heading into Denver. Leopold Stokowski conducted Stravinsky's *The Firebird* with a portion of the Philadelphia Symphony Orchestra on board. On 27 February 1937, a ski official involved in a ski race at Berthoud Pass in Colorado was set up with one of NBC's first "pack sets" on his back and a catcher's mask with a microphone mounted inside. The idea was for him to describe what he saw and felt as he sped down the mountain. The nation waited to hear how it felt to ski down a challenging mountain course. The technical apparatus worked perfectly, but the skier forgot to talk, and all the nation heard was several minutes of heavy breathing and the rush of air.

For a number of years, the KOA Staff Orchestra, an allstring ensemble, was featured on the NBC network as a sustaining program. Such programs as *Golden Memories, Rhapsody of the Rockies*, and *Sketches in Melody* spread the fame of the KOA Staff Orchestra across the country.

The 1960s and 1970s saw the development of KOA as a news powerhouse. The station built a reputation as a leading source of news and information throughout the Rocky Mountain West.

On 18 June 1984 outspoken KOA talk show host Alan Berg was murdered in front of his condominium in Denver. The slaying, which had political and religious overtones, generated a tremendous amount of national media coverage because of the circumstances. Berg took on many groups on his high-rated talk show, including right-wing Christians, knee-jerk liberals, and the Ku Klux Klan. There were connections between Berg's death and a group called "The Order," a white supremacist group in Colorado and the Pacific Northwest. The murder weapon was later found in the home of Gary Lee Yarbrough of Sandpoint, Idaho, a member of The Order.

Today, KOA concentrates its efforts as a news/talk/sports station. The station has the largest news-gathering staff in the market and carries play-by-play coverage of the Denver Broncos National Football League team, the Colorado Rockies baseball team, and the University of Colorado football games. The station's internet address is www.koaradio.com, which includes the KOA broadcast signal.

Further Reading

"A Brief History of the 50,000 Watt 'Voice of the West,'" *Colorado Mac News* (3 December 1984).
KOA website, www.koaradio.com
Singular, Stephen, *Talked to Death: The Life and Murder of Alan Berg*, New York: Beach Tree Books, 1987.

STEVEN D. ANDERSON

KOB

Las Cruces/Albuquerque, New Mexico Station

KOB was a pioneering noncommercial, educational radio station established in Las Cruces, New Mexico, in the years after World War I. Affiliated with the New Mexico College of Agriculture and Mechanic Arts (NMA&MA)—now New Mexico State University—and supported by the college's engineering department, KOB began as an experimental student project using equipment salvaged from the U.S. Army. Ralph W. Goddard, a professor of engineering at NMA&MA, organized the school's Radio Club on 11 October 1919. The campus organization soon acquired not only a 500-W Marconi standard Navy spark transmitter and 60-foot tower, but also three experimental radio licenses—5CX, 5FY, and 5FZ. License 5XD, which would become KOB, was granted on 3 June 1920.

In 1922, 500 new stations began broadcasting and KOB was one of them, going on the air on 5 April. Programming included market and stock reports,

live performances, recorded music, weather reports, and news accounts provided by two El Paso newspapers, the *Times* and *Herald-Post*. The college's Agricultural Extension Service was an early ally for KOB and provided ongoing support for the radio project's contributions to rural life in southern New Mexico.

Goddard, who was eventually named Dean of Engineering at NMA&MA, was a key figure in the growth and development of KOB. He was responsible for guiding the station from its beginning as a project of the Radio Club—which was largely interested in amateur and relay work—to its status a few years later as a station broadcasting to all of New Mexico. He led efforts to expand the station's programming, facilities, and wattage, negotiating for clear channel status and a power allotment of 5,000 W with the Federal Radio Commission (FRC); both were granted on 11 November 1928. By March of the following year, the station had been approved for an allotment of 10,000 W, making it the most powerful college radio station in the United States and the country's 13th-most powerful station of any type. In the fall of 1929, Goddard applied for FRC permission to double the station's power again, which would increase its power to 20,000 W.

Ironically, even as KOB developed as one of the country's premier radio stations, its support from the university community decreased. In spite of continuing interest in and contributions to the station by the Agricultural Extension Service, local civic groups, and segments of NMA&MA, the college administration began suggesting in late 1928 that Goddard should start looking for a buyer for the station. This diminished administrative support for KOB would ultimately prove fatal. Goddard's dream of building an educational radio station that would broadcast throughout most of the Southwest dissolved with his tragic death on New Year's Eve, 1929. While attempting to shut the station down for the afternoon, Goddard—whose shoes were soaked from a walk in the rain—was electrocuted. Although another NMA&MA professor was named station director and the application for 20,000-W status was approved, KOB never recovered from the loss of its founder and most ardent supporter. Lacking his hands-on leadership and personal drive, station staff could muster neither adequate management expertise nor local support to keep KOB on the air. When the FRC began sending off-frequency reports and complaints that the station was not modulating, the college decided to accept a lease-purchase offer from T.M. Pepperday, owner of the *Albuquerque Journal*.

The station's assets were subsequently leased to the *Journal* in the fall of 1931; all equipment was transferred by truck more than 200 miles to Albuquerque in September 1932; and KOB's first broadcast from Albuquerque aired on 5 October 1932. The station's disposition was completed in August 1936, when NMA&MA sold KOB to the *Journal*'s newly formed subsidiary, the Albuquerque Broadcasting Company. KOB affiliated with the National Broadcasting Company (NBC) the following year.

KOB is one example of the way in which a number of noncommercial, educational radio stations were transferred from public to private ownership in the 1930s. Lacking financial resources, institutional support, and strong leadership, this flagship western station could not endure as a publicly owned, noncommercial entity. Like many college stations, KOB's purchase and network affiliation helped to facilitate the development of a network-dominated broadcasting system in the United States. Many local listeners in Las Cruces were grieved by the station's departure, and the New Mexico State Legislature conducted an extensive debate about the station's sale to a private company. Governor Floyd Tingley, a New Dealer with close ties to Franklin D. Roosevelt, suggested that KOB become a state owned-and-operated public station, an idea that would be echoed in later discussions of state public networks elsewhere.

The North American Regional Broadcasting Agreement (1941) forced KOB (and many other U.S. stations) to change frequencies. In 1941 KOB moved to 1030 kHz, the same channel used by a Boston clear channel outlet. Later that year, just before U.S. entry into World War II, KOB moved again, this time thanks to a Federal Communications Commission (FCC) temporary permit, to 770 kHz, a clear channel frequency then used by what is now WABC in New York. The potential for mutual interference between the stations led to the longest legal battle in FCC history. Attorneys for each station inundated the commission with legal attempts to force the other outlet off the shared frequency. KOB was allowed to raise its power to 50,000 W in the daytime but was required to drop back to 25,000 W at night in an attempt to protect the New York station. In 1956 KOB was also required to install a directional antenna to reduce interference with WABC. By 1962 it had FCC permission to raise its night-time power to 50,000 W. Legal filings from both outlets continued to plague the FCC into the early 1980s, when KOB's final appeal to overcome WABC's primary status on the channel was turned down. Both stations remain on 770 kHz today, with KOB continuing to shield the New York outlet by means of directional antenna patterns.

A KOB television station was added in 1948, and in 1967 an affiliated FM outlet was added in Albuquerque. The station changed hands several times; it was purchased by Hubbard Broadcasting in 1957, which operated KOB for three decades before selling it in 1986. It changed hands again several times in the 1990s, by which time its call letters had been changed to KKOB. On 15 October 1994 the station was purchased by Citadel Communications, and by 2000 it was programmed as news/talk.

In the meantime, the university that had first supported the radio outlet lost its right to free airtime in 1951, although for a number of years that arrangement continued informally. Ralph Goddard's important role in its early years was remembered when the Las Cruces university again became a licensee in 1964 and placed KRWG (Goddard's initials) on the air as the first college/university FM station in the New Mexico. It, too, was joined by a television outlet with the same call letters eight years later.

Further Reading

Velia, Ann M., *KOB, Goddard's Magic Mast: Fifty Years of Pioneer Broadcasting*, Las Cruces: New Mexico State University Press, 1972.

GLENDA R. BALAS

KPFA
Berkeley, California Station

KPFA-FM in Berkeley, California, is the first station of the Pacifica radio network and the first listener-sponsored station in the United States. Poet, philosopher, and conscientious objector Lewis Hill created the station as a means to "help prevent warfare through the free and uncensored interchange of ideas in politics, philosophy and the arts."

KPFA first went on the air 15 April 1949, and controversy dogged the noncommercial station from the start. In a postwar America known for Cold War conformity and rampant consumerism, KPFA brought many nonmainstream voices to its microphones, including African-American actor and activist Paul Robeson, Zen philosopher Alan Watts, leftist commentator William Mandel, Beat poet Lawrence Ferlinghetti, political theorist Herbert Marcuse, film critic Pauline Kael, and voices from the Bay Area's academic, pacifist, and anarchist communities.

Hill created the idea of listener sponsorship in order to fund the station's operation without having to sell commercials. This freed the station of corporate control and gave it the chance to promote political alternatives. The operating funds, Hill theorized, would come if two percent of the potential audience paid $10 a year to support the station.

Listener sponsorship was not the only unusual aspect of the station's operations. In the beginning, despite a bureaucratic hierarchy, everyone on staff at KPFA was paid the same salary, and decisions were made collectively. Also, clocks were removed from on-air studios so that programs could run to their natural conclusions.

Despite such innovations, financial problems and internal tensions among the staff, the volunteers, and the station's advisory board quickly came to the fore. In 1950 the station went off the air for nine months because of lack of funds. The following year, Pacifica received a $150,000 grant from the Ford Foundation, which allowed it to resume broadcasting.

In June 1953 Lewis Hill resigned because of internal political struggles at the station. A new group felt constrained under his leadership. Despite the internecine problems, KPFA continued to make history with its innovative and intellectually challenging programming. Throughout the 1950s, the station's public-affairs programs regularly addressed such hot-button issues as racial segregation, economic disparity, and McCarthyism. In April 1954 a pre-recorded radio program that advocated the decriminalization of marijuana created an uproar and led to the tape's impoundment by California's attorney general.

In August 1954 founder Lewis Hill returned to run the station. But three years later, in late July of 1957, the 38-year-old Hill, suffering from crippling rheumatoid arthritis and depression, committed suicide. He left the following note: "Not for anger or despair/but for peace and a kind of home."

KPFA and Pacifica won numerous broadcast awards for children's programming and for special programs on the First Amendment by legal scholar Alexander Meiklejohn. KPFA's public-affairs director, Elsa Knight Thompson, continued pushing the broadcast envelope despite attempts to censor the station. The Federal Communications Commission (FCC), for example, questioned KPFA's broadcasts of poets Allen Ginsberg and Lawrence Ferlinghetti, broadcasts that the government found to be "vulgar, obscene, and in bad taste."

In 1960 KPFA broadcast a three-hour documentary on the riots following House Committee on Un-American Activities (popularly known as HUAC) hearings in San Francisco. It subsequently broadcast programs on homosexuality, the black-list, and the FBI. HUAC reacted by investigating Pacifica for "subversion," and the FCC investigated "communist affiliations" at the station, but the Commission ultimately renewed KPFA's license after a three-year delay. KPFA later gave extensive coverage to the Berkeley Free Speech Movement, and many University of California, Berkeley, faculty members were heard regularly.

Though the public-affairs programs often stirred controversy, the station's arts programming had a significant impact on the Bay Area's cultural scene. KPFA's first music director, Americo Chiarito, boldly mixed jazz, classical, folk, and other forms of noncommercial music throughout the broadcast day. Over a 25-year period, subsequent music director Charles Amirkanian interviewed and gave exposure to the work of nearly every living composer of importance in the West, including Terry Riley, LaMonte Young, Steve Reich, Lou Harrison, Pauline Oliveros, and John Cage. Philip Elwood, later the jazz critic for the San Francisco *Examiner*, hosted various on-air jazz programs for nearly 40 years. Sandy Miranda's *Music of the World* program featured live music, interviews, and rare recordings that drew a large and devoted following that made significant financial contributions to the station. For nearly a quarter of a century, the station devoted considerable airtime to contemporary poetry and literature under the direction of Erik Bauersfeld.

Through the 1970s and 1980s there was a gradual, if fundamental, shift in how KPFA and the Pacifica network (which by then included stations in New York, Los Angeles, Houston, and Washington, D.C.) defined themselves and their target audience. Unlike the early days in Berkeley, when the audience was presumed to be an elite, educated, intellectual minority, KPFA gradually became known as a "community" radio station. Its audience, and even many on-air programmers, became increasingly defined not by ideas but by gender, ethnicity, race, and class. Third World and women's departments were eventually created at the station. As these and other groups in the community demanded a place on the broadcast schedule, bitter arguments ensued over ideology and over questions about who speaks for whom and which groups deserve access to the microphone.

In 1999 many of these questions came to a head when the Pacifica network attempted to make programming and staff changes at KPFA, removing the station's popular general manager. The network defended the changes as an attempt to increase audience numbers and diversity. Many of the staff and volunteers, as well as activist members of the community, charged that the network was engaging in strong-arm tactics in an attempt to consolidate power and avoid accountability. What started as a personnel matter soon mushroomed into a widely publicized struggle over the station's future, prompting walkouts, strikes, and demonstrations.

Although such controversies have occurred periodically at a number of the Pacifica stations over the years, it was especially ironic that an organization that that has done so much to protect the broadcast of free speech would resort to censorship when its newscasters attempted to cover the story. When KPFA's investigative reporter Dennis Bernstein defied a network gag order by covering the crisis at the station, he was suspended from his job, then arrested along with 51 KPFA staff and activists who refused to leave the building. A live, open microphone caught the entire drama. Pacifica officials then cancelled regular programming and boarded up the station for much of July and September.

But faced with a demonstration of 10,000 angry KPFA supporters, Pacifica relented and permitted KPFA staff to go back to work. This and subsequent controversies at all five Pacifica stations sparked a grassroots campaign to democratize the network. By December of 2001 a new Board of Directors had been assigned the task of revising the foundation's by-laws to give the network's listener-sponsors more say over governance.

See also: Community Radio; Pacifica Foundation; Public Radio Since 1967

Further Reading

Hill, Lewis, *Voluntary Listener-Sponsorship: A Report to Educational Broadcasters on the Experiment at KPFA, Berkeley, California*, Berkeley, California: Pacifica Foundation, 1958.
KPFA website, www.kpfa.org
Land, Jeff, *Active Radio: Pacifica's Brash Experiment*, Minneapolis: University of Minnesota Press, 1999.
Lasar, Matthew, *Pacifica Radio: The Rise of an Alternative Network*, Philadelphia, Pennsylvania: Temple University Press, 2000.
Thompson, Chris, "War and Peace: The Battle for KPFA and the Soul of Pacifica Is Over: Now the Damage Assessment Begins" (*East Bay Express*, 9 January 2002).

LARRY APPELBAUM AND MATTHEW LASAR

KQW
See: KCBS/KQW

KRLA
Los Angeles, California Station

KRLA (1110 kHz) is a 50,000-W AM station serving the Los Angeles market. It was a popular Top 40 station in the 1960s, featuring stand-out radio personalities such as Casey Kasem, Bob Eubanks, Dave Hull, and Bob Hudson. KRLA associated itself strongly with the Beatles at that time, sponsoring several Beatles concerts in Los Angeles. It became the number one station in that market in 1964 and held that distinction for several years. Ironically, it was during KRLA's ratings heyday that its long legal struggle with the Federal Communications Commission (FCC) began. In 1962 the FCC denied a license renewal to station owner Donald Cooke and his company, Eleven Ten Broadcasting, over questionable on-air practices. This set off a 17-year battle, during which KRLA was operated by a nonprofit interim company. The license renewal case for KRLA is a rare instance of FCC license denial based on content and behavior rather than technical considerations.

Origins

The station's history began in 1940 when J.R. Frank Burke and other investors formed the Pacific Coast Broadcasting Company in order to apply for a broadcasting license in Pasadena, California. Burke was a fund-raiser for the Democratic Party and publisher of the *Santa Ana Register*. The FCC issued a construction permit in September 1941, just months before the United States entered World War II and placed a moratorium on all new radio construction. The new station would have the call letters KPAS and operate at 10,000 W on 1110 kHz. By February 1942 an operating license was issued and KPAS went on the air as an unaffiliated station with block programming typical of the time period. Burke's accountant, Loyal King, became the station manager. In addition to music, news, and religious programs, KPAS featured dramatic sketches performed by the Pasadena Playhouse actors. Local programming and public service were hallmarks of the station in the 1940s.

In 1945, Burke sold his interest to religious broadcaster William Dumm, who in turn sold his share in the station to Loyal King two years later. The license was retained by Pacific Coast Broadcasting. The station's call letters were changed to KXLA in 1945 to suggest a more metropolitan target audience. In 1948 King began to run a popular syndicated program called *Country Crystals* and by the early 1950s, KXLA had become a country and western station. Most commercial radio stations in the United States were switching to musical formats at this time, as radio talent and network financing were migrating to television.

In 1958 a major change for the station occurred when New York businessman Donald Cooke signed an agreement to purchase KXLA from Pacific Coast Broadcasting. Cooke's brother, Jack Kent Cooke, was the true interested party, but as a Canadian citizen, he was prohibited by the Communications Act of 1934 from owning a U.S. radio station. In order to help his brother finance the purchase, Jack Kent Cooke would buy the station facilities through his newly formed company, Broadcast Equipment Corporation (BEC). Don Cooke's company, Eleven Ten Broadcasting, would file for the license transfer and lease the facilities from BEC.

In March 1959, the FCC approved the transfer with the understanding that Jack Kent Cooke would have no role in managing the station. In fact, he had already been heavily involved, and in the months to come he would play a significant role in station management by making personnel decisions and planning on-air contests and promotions. The Cookes' intention was to change the format to Top 40 rock and roll and to concentrate on the teenage demographic throughout the Los Angeles market. At midnight on 1 September 1959, the station officially switched over. Nineteen-year-old disk jockey Jimmy O'Neill announced, "You have been listening to KXLA. You are now listening to KRLA-Radio for the young at heart."

Fifteen Years of "Interim" Owner Operation

In August 1959, all southern California stations were required to submit applications for license renewal according to the regular FCC schedule of renewals. KRLA did so, but in July of 1960, the FCC notified Donald Cooke that there would be a hearing for KRLA's license renewal. The FCC was concerned about several problems, including programming promises not being met, falsified logs, fraudulent contests, and the involvement of a noncitizen in station management. Although the hearing examiner recommended a one-year probationary renewal, the FCC denied renewal in 1962. The decision was upheld on appeal and the FCC ordered KRLA off the air. Comparative hearings would be held to determine the new licensee, but the FCC was concerned about leaving the frequency vacant in the meantime, as that meant the Mexican station XERB would be allowed to increase its power under provisions of an international treaty.

Oak Knoll Broadcasting, a nonprofit company, was selected to be the interim owner and licensee of KRLA. Eighty percent of their profits were to go to KCET, an educational TV station, and the other two percent would be distributed to other charities. Oak Knoll took possession of the station in 1964 and continued to operate it until 1979, when a new company, KRLA Incorporated, was finally selected to take over the license, ending the interim period. Oak Knoll's long period in control stemmed from the protracted FCC proceedings required to choose between more than a dozen applicants for the station license.

The early Oak Knoll years were KRLA's strongest in terms of its position in the market. In 1964, KRLA sought to distinguish itself from KFWB, its primary competitor, by focusing on a single band, the Beatles. The station played all of the cuts from Beatles LPs rather than just the hits and provided information about the music and the band members, promoting itself as "Beatle Radio." KRLA also sponsored three Beatles concerts in Los Angeles from 1964 to 1966. This strategy enabled KRLA to become a contender in the competitive and saturated Los Angeles AM market.

During the 1970s KRLA's format changed several times. In 1971 the station switched to album-oriented progressive rock in an attempt to appeal to young people in the counterculture. This move proved unsuccessful, as FM radio was already offering that format with better sound quality. In 1973 KRLA moved to soft rock, which was more successful, but not enough so to make the station profitable. In 1976, under the direction of Art Laboe, KRLA changed to an Oldies format in a successful move to recapture a segment of the dwindling AM audience.

KRLA Incorporated was actually a merger of five of the companies that had applied for the KRLA license in 1964. It operated the station until 1985, when it was purchased by Greater Los Angeles Radio, Inc. Greater Los Angeles Radio moved the studios from the Huntington Hotel in Pasadena, where they had been since 1942, to Wilshire Boulevard in Los Angeles. The transmitter was moved to Irwindale the following year. In 1997 KRLA was acquired by Infinity Broadcasting, a subsidiary of Viacom, and its format was changed to talk radio. Infinity sold KRLA to Disney-owned ABC Radio in 2001. The format was changed to sports programming with an ESPN affiliation and the acquisition of Anaheim Angels baseball games. ABC Radio relaunched the station under the new call letters KSPN and as of January 2003 had swapped frequencies with KDIS-AM (Disney

Radio) on 710 kHz. KDIS, now on the 1110 frequency, is formatted for children with Disney product. The KRLA call letters were acquired by Salem Communications for its talk station KIEV-AM at 870 kHz.

See also: Contemporary Hit Radio/Top 40 Format; Licensing Authorising U.S. Station to Broadcast; Oldies Format

Further Reading

Beem, Donald C., "Standard Broadcast Station KRLA: A Case Study," Masters thesis, California State University at Fullerton, 1980.
Earl, Bill, *Dream-House*, Valencia, California: Delta, 1989; 2nd edition, 1991.

CHRISTINA S. DRALE

KSL

Salt Lake City, Utah Station

In the early days of radio, one of the key groups of licensees was composed of churches. As is the case with many such stations, it is difficult to discuss the vision and role of KSL without considering its church affiliation and the dream to proselytize. The Church of Jesus Christ of Latter-day Saints (LDS; Mormon) acquired a radio station to broadcast general conferences of the LDS Church to people throughout the area without their having to come to the tabernacle on the city's Temple Square. Although the functions and operations of the station's mission have changed dramatically over the years, the religious influence can still be found.

KSL's predecessor, KZN, went on the air on 6 May 1922 and was among the first in the Western United States. It broadcast on 1160 kHz, and was designated a class A (clear channel) station in 1925. The station is still located at 1160 AM. At 8 P.M. on the first day of its broadcast, from atop the building housing the LDS-operated *Deseret News* newspaper, the station broadcast LDS Church President Heber J. Grant, who spoke of the church's mission and doctrine, quoting from the church's scriptures. Some observers felt that President Grant's remarks were the beginning of the fulfillment of a dream voiced earlier that the president of the church could deliver his sermons "and be heard by congregations assembled in every settlement of the Church from Canada to Mexico, and from California to Colorado" (see Anderson, 1922).

During its first years of operation, the station carried the voices of several famous figures. In addition to church authorities, other noted speakers used this new, fascinating, and promising medium. William Jennings Bryan delivered a ten-minute address on 25 October 1922. In 1923 President Warren G. Harding spoke over the station in a broadcast originating from the church's tabernacle. It was the first known instance of a U.S. President speaking over radio in that area.

In June 1924 *The Deseret News* sold KZN to John and F.W. Cope, who planned to overcome some of the station's engineering problems. The call letters were changed to KFPT. Later that year, in October, the station broadcast the general conferences of the LDS Church, an event that was to occur semi-annually through the rest of the century. Listeners could sit at home in their own living rooms next to their radio receivers and attend to the business and spiritual matters of that faith.

In June 1923 the Mormon Tabernacle Choir began its first formal broadcast on KZN (whose call letters were changed to KFPT in 1924, then to KSL in 1925) with the program *Music and the Spoken Word*, a program that continues in the early 21st century. A few years later, when KSL joined the National Broadcasting Company (NBC) as an affiliate, it began a regular Sunday broadcast of the choir. The program continued when, in 1932, KSL moved its affiliation to the Columbia Broadcasting System (CBS). (The radio station is still a CBS affiliate, although KSL-TV is now affiliated with NBC.) It continues as the oldest continuous sustained radio program in America. The program brought fame to the station and the church, as well as a wider audience for the choir and for the tabernacle organ, from their rich acoustical setting in the century-old tabernacle.

As radio developed into a commercial medium, troubles loomed for the Mormon-owned station. Although church leaders saw nothing wrong with the business operation in conjunction with its function as "a factor in the spread of the gospel of Jesus Christ across the world" (see Hinckley, 1947), the church's standards came into conflict with some commercial practices. For example, the church advocated against the use of alcohol and tobacco. Yet network programs carried by KSL contained commercials selling beer and cigarettes, and programs contained themes or characters using these products. Not to carry such programs with their commercials could mean severance from network feeds and a drastic reduction in profits and income. Continuing to carry the programs appeared hypocritical in light of the church's teachings of abstinence from these products. With CBS's position of hard business practices guiding the decision-making process, the church was poised to lose the network affiliation and become a secondary, perhaps insignificant influence in radio in the intermountain area. Policy was established not to accept spot advertising (contracted individually with the station) for beer, wine, or tobacco, but the national network ads would continue to be carried as a necessary evil. KSL would not try to restrict network advertising or interfere with network contracts. KSL-FM was Utah's first FM station, beginning operation on 26 December 1946. Its programming was different and separate from its AM outlet.

Becoming successful as a business, KSL became the flagship station in the church's broadcast ownership, Bonneville International, established in 1964. The group owned radio and television stations in Seattle, Washington, then acquired FM outlets in New York City, Chicago, San Francisco, Los Angeles, Dallas, and Kansas City. As of 2003, Bonneville had 15 stations. From the mid-1960s to 1975, Bonneville operated an international shortwave radio station reaching various countries.

KSL quickly realized that its clear channel signal of 50,000 W AM served more than just Salt Lake City, extending to the entire Western region of the United States. It also tried to reflect a sense of commitment to serve this extended community, as mandated by church president David O. McKay in the mid-1960s. The station moved from broadcasting high school and church basketball tournaments in the 1950s to political broadcasts of substance. Bonneville's production arm created the "Home Front" public-service messages, which sent nondenominational messages about families and values to listeners who might not otherwise tune in to religious programming. These "Home Front" features were distributed to stations throughout the country to air in a variety of programs.

The church influence in KSL's programming has brought occasional criticism of censorship and biased influence. Yet the wide range of political viewpoints, the representations of other religious denominations, and the respect garnished from its news reporting seem to quell such criticism for many observers. One KSL news director disavows any meddling in the news agenda or its coverage of stories, including those local stories critical of church policies. Although some complaints have gone to the Federal Communications Commission, none has been taken seriously enough to limit the church's operation of its stations.

Broadcast management has indicated that today KSL is a station intent to make a profit, "not to evangelize." It is a commercial broadcast enterprise owned by a religious organization "operated strictly as a business and seeking no special treatment" (see

Brady, 1994). Although the station started with a dream to evangelize, the realities of commercial broadcasting make its mission for community good more general in nature.

See also: Mormon Tabernacle Choir

Further Reading

Anderson, Edward H., "The Vacuum Tube Amplifier," *The Improvement Era* 25, no.3 (March 1922).

Avant, Gerry, "Major Events, 1920–1929," *Church News* (13 March 1999).

Brady, Rodney H., *Bonneville at Thirty: A Value-Driven Company of Values-Driven People*, New York: Newcomen Society, 1994.

Donigan, Robert W., "An Outline History of Broadcasting in the Church of Jesus Christ of Latter-Day Saints, 1922–1963," Master's thesis, Brigham Young University, 1963.

Godfrey, Donald G., Val E. Limburg, and Heber G. Wolsey, "KSL, Salt Lake City: 'At the Crossroads of the West'," in *Television in America: Local Station History from across the Nation*, edited by Michael D. Murray and Donald G. Godfrey, Ames: Iowa State University Press, 1997.

Hinckley, Gordon B., "Twenty-Five Years of Radio Ministry," *Deseret News* (26 April 1947).

Lichty, Lawrence, and Malachi Topping, *American Broadcasting: A Source Book on the History of Radio and Television*, New York: Hastings House, 1975.

Limburg, Val E., "An Analysis of Relationships between Religious Programming Objectives and Methods of Presentation Used by Selected Major Religious Program Producers as Compared to the Church of Jesus Christ of Latter-Day Saints," Master's thesis, Brigham Young University, 1964.

Wolsey, Heber Grant, "The History of Radio Station KSL, from 1922 to Television," Ph.D. diss., Michigan State University, 1967.

Zobell, Albert L., Jr., "Twenty Magnificent Years on the Air," *Improvement Era* 52, no. 9 (September 1949).

VAL E. LIMBURG

KTRH
Houston, Texas Station

A longtime news, talk, and information station, KTRH was the starting point for the careers of several national celebrities, including the two best-known anchors on Columbia Broadcasting System (CBS) television.

The history of KTRH meshes with the history of modern Houston. KTRH was a relative latecomer when it signed on the air 5 March 1930. The city had boasted an experimental radio station as early as 1919. Several commercial stations were on the air in the early 1920s, although none lasted longer than a few years. Only rival KPRC, launched by the *Houston Post-Dispatch* during a newspaper convention in the city in 1925, hinted at the promise radio would hold in the city.

The opportunity to build KTRH came as a result of the Great Depression. The economic downturn caused the regents of the University of Texas to decide against supporting their experimental station in Austin, KUT. Houston real estate magnate Jesse H. Jones, builder of Houston's emerging skyline and owner of the *Houston Chronicle*, purchased KUT and had the station's equipment boxed and transported the 165 miles to Houston.

Jones hoped to house his new station at the *Chronicle*, but the paper's editor dismissed the idea. The manager of Jones's Rice Hotel, on the other hand, was enthusiastic about a station's broadcasting from his facility and wanted the station to be "irretrievably tied to the hotel," according to Jesse Jones's nephew, John T. Jones, who would ultimately inherit KTRH from his uncle. The *TRH* in the new station's call letters stood for "The Rice Hotel."

When Ross Sterling, owner of KPRC and the *Houston Post-Dispatch*, suffered financial reverses in 1931, Jesse Jones came to the rescue and briefly controlled the *Post-Dispatch*, the *Chronicle*, and KTRH and KPRC radio stations. Jones gained such power that when he secured the Democratic Party's national convention for Houston in 1928, he also won the hearts of Texas Democrats: all 40 of Texas's electors cast their ballots for Jones's nomination for president, even though New York Governor Al Smith would ultimately win the nomination.

In 1947 the *Chronicle* established the first FM station in Houston and called it KTRH-FM. For its first two years, it simulcast the programming of KTRH-AM, and then it launched a "fine music" program of light classics. After a few years, the station returned to simulcasting. The popularity of album rock music in the late 1960s and early 1970s prompted a change of format and call letters for KTRH-FM. The letters KLOL were chosen because they resembled the 101 dial position.

On the death of Jesse Jones in 1956, the ownership of KTRH, sister station KLOL, and the *Chronicle* passed to Jones's nephew, John T. Jones, who operated the stations under the corporate name "The Rusk Corporation" (named for the downtown street where Jones's offices were located). The *Chronicle* was operated by a private foundation, Houston Endowment, that was established by the elder Jones for charitable purposes.

A graduate of Houston's San Jacinto High School, Walter Cronkite worked part-time at KTRH on his way to a journalism degree at the University of Texas in Austin. During the early 1930s Cronkite worked for the University of Texas newspaper, *The Daily Texan;* at United Press International (UPI); and at several state capital news bureaus at the same time. Dan Rather began working at KTRH in 1950, shortly after his graduation from Sam Houston State University in nearby Huntsville, Texas, where he had been a reporter for both the Associated Press and UPI. Rather's early KTRH broadcasts originated in the newsroom of the *Houston Chronicle* with the clack of wire service teletype machines in the background. "We got (the) bright idea that it would give the news program more authenticity," said John T. Jones. The younger Jones told the story of a *Chronicle* religious editor whose desk was next to Rather's broadcast desk. At the end of each newscast, said Jones, the editor would correct Rather's grammar. In 1956 Rather became the station's news director.

CBS-TV sports anchor Jim Nantz also began his career at KTRH, in 1981. While studying on a golf scholarship at the University of Houston, Nantz was an intern at the station and later host of the *Sportsbeat* call-in program.

KTRH is credited with originating the *Dr. IQ* radio quiz show during the 1930s. Ted Nabors, then KTRH program director, performed as the Doctor, and announcer Babe Fritsch took a roving microphone into the audience to choose contestants who won silver dollars when they answered questions correctly. Fritsch was the first to say, "I have a lady in the balcony, Doctor!" *Dr. IQ* was developed for national broadcast on the National Broadcasting Company (NBC) network beginning in 1939, with Lew Valentine performing as the Doctor and Allan C. Anthony as the announcer.

In the mid-1960s, KTRH began a move to the talk format under general manager Frank Stewart. Although KTRH was not the first station to adopt the new format, it was an early entry into the talk arena. Texas farm and ranch industries prompted KTRH to establish a strong presence in agribusiness reporting, at first with information for area ranchers and later with lawn and garden programs.

In 1981 the station broadcast two live talk shows from the People's Republic of China, a first for U.S. broadcasters. Talk host Ben Baldwin and KTRH vice president and general manger Hal Kemp answered listener questions and described events of their travels, including a rare firepower demonstration by the People's Army Infantry. "They literally blew up a mountain for us," Baldwin reported. The station staged subsequent live broadcasts from China during the early 1980s and aired weekend features prepared by the English language staff of Radio Beijing.

Because KTRH had affiliated with the CBS Radio network in the first year of its operation, one of the stories the Houston radio rumor mill circulated in the 1970s and 1980s was that CBS had a blank check ready if John T. Jones ever decided to sell KTRH. He didn't—and the stories were never confirmed. At Jones's retirement, his son Jesse Jones III, known as "Jay," assumed operation of the stations and acquired properties in San Antonio and Austin, expanding Rusk Corporation holdings.

In 1989 Jacor Communications made a $60 million offer for KTRH and KLOL, but the deal was never consummated. Ultimately, the two stations were sold in 1993 to Evergreen Media for $51 million. Evergreen became Chancellor and later AMFM after mergers made possible by the Telecommunications Act of 1996. KTRH moved to the Clear Channel Communications roster after that company's merger with AMFM.

Further Reading

Boudreaux, Phillip H., "Houston Radio: The First Sixty Years," Senior thesis, University of St. Thomas, 1982.
"KTRH Stages First Live Talk Show from China," *Radio and Records* (6 March 1981).
"KTRH's Zak to Be Honored on and off the Air," *Houston Post* (5 January 1981).
"Radio Peking: The Red Rose of Texas," *Earshot* (25 October 1982).
Writers' Program, *Houston: A History and Guide*, Houston, Texas: Anson Jones Press, 1942.

ED SHANE

KWKH

Shreveport, Louisiana Station

KWKH, a 50,000-W clear channel station, played an important role in the commercialization of country music and rock and roll music during the 1940s and 1950s. In addition, as one of the first radio stations in Louisiana, it helped pioneer radio broadcasting in the state.

The station that KWKH would become first crackled on the air in early 1922. Engineer William E. Antony built the physical operations under the auspices of the Elliott Electric Company; in 1923 a team of investors led by a retailer of radio sets purchased the station, dubbing it WGAQ. One of the investors bought out his partners in 1925 and rechristened the station with his initials. William Kennon Henderson, who owned and operated the Henderson Iron Works and Supply in Shreveport, promptly turned KWKH into his own soapbox. At arbitrary moments during the broadcast day, he

often burst into his studios and grabbed the microphone from his announcer. "Hello world, doggone you! This is KWKH at Shreveport, Lou—ee—siana, and it's W.K. Henderson talkin' to you." He railed against the national debt and chain retail stores and ridiculed over the air anybody who dared to disagree with him. He condemned the Radio Act of 1927 and sparred with both the U.S. Department of Commerce and the Federal Radio Commission, claiming that both favored chain (network) stations over independent outlets.

In the late 1920s, when Henderson applied for a power boost to 10,000 W, federal regulators turned him down, claiming that KWKH was nothing more than a broadcaster of phonograph records. But Henderson argued that his format—which in actuality encompassed more than just record playing—satisfied his listeners' wishes. The rejection only incited the maverick's ranting resolve, and by 1930 Washington conceded to him and granted the increase in power.

As eccentric and egotistical as Henderson was, his desire to see KWKH prosper and expand its signal range helped consolidate radio's presence in Louisiana. His on-air tirades forced people to note the presence of radio, and entrepreneurs looked to the growth of KWKH as an example when they invested their own dollars in radio stations. Furthermore, it was probably Henderson's distaste for the uniformity of chain stations that led KWKH to recruit local talent to perform on its airwaves. The use of local talent, most of whom performed hillbilly music (as country music was known in the 1920s and 1930s), planted the seeds that would grow into KWKH's *Louisiana Hayride*.

In 1932 Henderson sold KWKH to the International Broadcasting Corporation, and the station changed hands again in 1935 when the *Shreveport Times*, owned by oilman John D. Ewing, took control. Under Ewing, KWKH continued the growth that Henderson had initiated, moving to modern facilities in downtown Shreveport's Commercial Building in 1936 and receiving permission to operate at 50,000 W in 1939. (In 1934, probably much to the former owner's ire, KWKH had established a network affiliation with the Columbia Broadcasting System [CBS].) Carrying on Henderson's tradition of hiring local talent, station manager Henry B. Clay, who was Ewing's son-in-law; program director Horace Logan; and commercial manager Dean Upson established the *Louisiana Hayride*, which would become KWKH's most lasting mark on country music history and, indeed, on radio history.

KWKH's *Louisiana Hayride* was a country and western stage show that played weekly on the station from 1948 to 1960. Dubbed "the Cradle of the Stars," the program aired on Saturday nights from Shreveport's Municipal Auditorium and boasted among its cast members musical performers who would be the primary shapers of post-World War II country music. Important country music figures such as Hank Williams, Jim Reeves, and Johnny Cash appeared as regulars on the *Hayride* early in their careers; each used the program as a springboard to broader acceptance. In addition to providing a stage for important country music performers, KWKH and the *Hayride* would leave a lasting mark on the history of rock and roll in the mid-1950s, when singer Elvis Presley became a regular cast member on the show; the exposure he received as a cast member from 1954 to 1956 helped fuel his rise to national prominence.

KWKH's 50,000 W of power gave the *Louisiana Hayride* its muscle. The station's signal stretched like a fan across the southwestern and northwestern regions of the United States and clipped across national borders to reach countries as near as Mexico and as far as Australia. A regular spot on KWKH's Saturday night hoedown, any aspiring country act knew, could attract recording contracts and generate bookings. The *Hayride*'s influence grew mightier in the early 1950s with its insertion into the schedule of a CBS regional network.

However, the *Hayride* would never be as mighty as the *Grand Ole Opry* on WSM in Nashville, Tennessee, and because of that, KWKH failed to hold on to its rising stars. As *Hayride* personalities gained momentum, they inevitably shifted their eyes toward the *Opry* and Nashville, where a colony that included booking agents and music publishers waited to capitalize on the artists' successes. KWKH and Shreveport lacked such ancillary components of the music industry and therefore could not keep name artists on the show very long. The *Louisiana Hayride* became known as an "*Opry* farm club," and, largely because of the constant talent drain, it ceased regular broadcasting in 1960. The program has been reincarnated in various forms over the years, but it has never achieved the influence it enjoyed in the late 1940s and 1950s.

Today, KWKH is owned by Clear Channel Communications, which acquired the station in 1999. Although the *Louisiana Hayride* disappeared long ago from its airwaves, the station still recalls former glories with its "country gold" format, which features vintage country music from as early as the 1940s.

See also: Clear Channel Stations; Country Music Format; *Grand Ole Opry*; WWL

Further Reading

Escott, Colin, George Merritt, and William MacEwen, *Hank Williams: The Biography*, Boston: Little Brown, 1994.

Guralnick, Peter, *Last Train to Memphis: The Rise of Elvis Presley*, Boston: Little Brown, 1994.

Hall, Lillian Jones, "A Historical Study of Programming Techniques and Practices of Radio Station KWKH, Shreveport, Louisiana, 1922–1950," Ph.D. diss., Louisiana State University, 1959.

Logan, Horace, and Bill Sloan, *Elvis, Hank, and Me: Making Musical History on the Louisiana Hayride*, New York: St. Martin's Press, 1998.

Streissguth, Michael, *Like a Moth to a Flame: The Jim Reeves Story*, Nashville, Tennessee: Rutledge Hill Press, 1998.

MICHAEL STREISSGUTH

KYW

Chicago, Cleveland, and Philadelphia Station

One of Westinghouse's original outlets, KYW has been described as "the wandering radio station." Though it has served the Philadelphia area for most of its life, the call letters were also found on stations in Chicago and Cleveland. KYWs wanderlust is a result of the federal government's intermittent efforts to manage how much control large broadcasters had over America's most important cities. In the end, these labors produced voluminous litigation but little in the way of permanent results.

KYW had a Chicago address for only a dozen years, but its early start earned it a place in radio history as a pioneer radio station. In fact, it was Chicago's first radio station. Legend has it that the call letters stood for "Young Warriors."

The station first broadcast from the Commonwealth Edison office in Chicago on 11 November 1921. KYW was originally started as a partnership. Westinghouse provided the transmitter and Commonwealth Edison the broadcast location. For its part, Westinghouse rushed KYW and sister stations WBZ in Massachusetts and WJZ in Newark, New Jersey, to the air as a direct result of the success of KDKA in Pittsburgh. Westinghouse's motivation was to stimulate sales of the crystal radio sets the company manufactured. For five years, KYW was operated as a joint venture, although Westinghouse dominated the partnership. In 1926 the working relationship ended, and Commonwealth Edison eventually became associated with crosstown radio station WENR.

Three notable early programming experiments punctuate KYW's Chicago history. The first broadcast by KYW featured opera, and regular weekly opera broadcasts on the station proved an immediate success. At one point, the opera broadcasts were credited with selling nearly 2,000 radio receivers a week in the Chicago area. Second, KYW featured an early version of children's programming. Early radio personality Uncle Bob (Walter Wilson) broadcast children's stories each night, being sure to finish by 7 P.M. so as not to disturb his listeners' bedtimes. KYW also featured breaking news supplied by the *Chicago Tribune*. Seeing potential in the new medium, the Tribune Company decided to get in on the business itself and launched WGN in 1924.

The Federal Radio Commission soon grew concerned about the large number of stations in Chicago. Westinghouse offered to shift KYW out of Chicago and moved the station on 3 December 1934 to Philadelphia. Then the nation's third-largest media market, Philadelphia would prove less lucrative to Westinghouse than broadcasting from Chicago, then the nation's second most important city.

In its new hometown, KYW continued its tradition of reporting breaking news. For example, KYW covered the June 1937 *Hindenburg* disaster in nearby Lakehurst, New Jersey. From a telephone booth, a KYW reporter described to the radio audience the horrific fire, and the on-the-spot report was broadcast over both National Broadcasting Company (NBC) networks.

The association with NBC would eventually set the stage for KYW's third move—to Cleveland, Ohio. On 22 January 1956, Westinghouse, under great pressure from NBC, which wanted to upgrade its own facilities to a larger market, exchanged its Philadelphia broadcast operations for NBC's Cleveland stations. In consideration for Westinghouse receiving the smaller and less profitable Cleveland outlets, NBC also paid Westinghouse $3 million.

Later, as a result of federal investigation into NBC's actions, it was demonstrated that NBC had forced Westinghouse into the exchange. Had Westinghouse not complied, it would have lost its valuable NBC network affiliation for its budding television operations. The Federal Communications Commission (FCC) ordered the swap undone in 1964 and found NBC culpable of abusing its network power. KYW's call letters were shifted from Cleveland, and the AM, FM, and television stations to which they were attached returned again to Philadelphia in June 1965 (the Cleveland AM station is now known as WTAM, formerly WWWE).

In October 1965, KYW became one of the first radio stations to adopt an all-news format. The format change did not bring immediate ratings success, and, reportedly, the station lost money for several years. The first decade was particularly difficult, given the popularity of crosstown AM contemporary music outlets such as WFIL and WIBG.

Today, KYW's competition comes mostly from FM stations, because KYW has long been the market's leading AM station. Like other historic AM broadcasters, KYW found that information-based spoken-word programming can be effective against music-based FM competitors. In programming its allnews format, the station uses a 30-minute news wheel and features traffic reports every ten minutes. The station does particularly well in the winter season, when the station issues snow-related closing notices for schools in eastern Pennsylvania, southern New Jersey, and northern Delaware. Arbitron reports that KYW, in addition to regularly being one of the top-three radio stations in the market, has a weekly cumulative audience of well over one million listeners.

Though technically the radio station is not on a full clear channel frequency, the 50,000-W signal produced from the station's directional antenna can regularly be heard across the northeastern United States, far outside the station's primary Delaware Valley coverage area. The station has been located at 1060 kHz since 1941. The studios of KYW radio are housed on Independence Mall within sight of the Liberty Bell. It shares the same building as its sister television station, KYW-TV 3, now a Columbia Broadcasting System (CBS) television affiliate. The television station was Philadelphia's first when it began experimental operations just as W3XE in 1932

Despite Westinghouse's historic attempts to keep its network-owning rivals at arm's length, the company, disappointed by its prospects in manufacturing, eventually decided to concentrate on broadcast programming and merged with the CBS network in 1995. Subsequently, the Westinghouse identity disappeared. Today, the license to KYW radio is owned by Infinity Broadcasting, the radio company closely associated with CBS.

See also: Hindenburg Disaster

Further Reading

Samuels, Rich, "It All Began with an Oath and an Opera: Behind the Scenes at Chicago's First Broadcast," *Chicago Tribune* (8 November 1993).
Shanahan, Eileen, "FCC Orders NBC to Return Station," *New York Times* (30 July 1964).

A. Joseph Borrell

L

LESBIAN RADIO
See: Gay and Lesbian Radio

LET'S PRETEND
Children's Program

The theme song sounded each Saturday morning to the delight of children listening to this Columbia Broadcasting System (CBS) program:

Hello, hello,
Come on let's go!
It's time for *Let's Pretend*.
The gang's all here and standing near
Is Uncle Bill, your friend.
The story is so exciting from the start right to the end.
So everyone, come join the fun.
Come on and let's pretend!

Let's Pretend was so popular that it became the prototype of children's programming, and its creator, Nila Mack, became the director of children's programming for the CBS network.

Let's Pretend was a half-hour children's radio program heard on CBS during the late-Saturday-morning time slot. Its forerunner was *The Adventures of Helen and Mary*, which began on 7 September 1929 and ran until 17 March 1934, with writer Yolanda Langworthy and director Nila Mack.

One week after the end of *Helen and Mary*, *Let's Pretend* began. Using her background as a Broadway actress and vaudevillian, Nila Mack wrote and directed this children's program for most of its 20-year run. Drawing on her own childhood memories, Mack based the program on variations of familiar children's tales from the Grimm brothers, *The Arabian Nights*, Andrew Lang, and Hans Christian Andersen. She freely adapted each story to emphasize human virtues. For example, her annual Christmas show, *House of the World*, promoted the themes of brotherhood and tolerance.

Mack felt that children should tell the stories and be the voices of the characters. She established an ensemble of versatile juvenile talent with members who could easily shift from being a young princess one week to an aging witch the next. She chose her cast from auditions open to any child interested in being considered. She tested each one for the ability to be versatile and to ad lib easily—especially to cover up any production mishaps that might occur during the actual broadcast.

Many of these young performers went on to stage and screen careers. For example, Nancy Kelly scored a major hit on Broadway and in film as the mother in *The Bad Seed*, and Dick Van Patten went on to television fame in *I Remember Mama* and *Eight Is Enough*.

Salaries began at $3.50 per show—less than half the going rate for many long-running shows. However, being on the program was considered an honor and a serious undertaking. Arthur Anderson, an 18-year veteran of the show, wrote of this theatrical experience in glowing terms. Anderson's book, *Let's Pretend: A History of Radio's Best Loved Children's Show by a Longtime Cast Member* details the cast members' view that this was an opportunity to learn a craft whilst actually doing a radio program live over the airways. Other actors, such as Arnold Stang and Jimmy Lydon, have recounted the rigors of maintaining Mack's standard of excellence.

Musical conductor Maurice Brown's theme became one of the hallmarks of juvenile radio—especially in 1943, when he used the newly allowed sole program sponsor as the subject for the violin-backed lyrics:

> Cream of Wheat is so good to eat.
> Yes, we have it every day.
> We sing this song; it will make us strong.
> And it makes us shout HOORAY.
> It's good for growing babies.
> And grown-ups too to eat.
> For all the family's breakfast,
> You can't beat Cream of Wheat!

Having a sponsored children's program was a departure from the norm for CBS. The broadcast company felt that it was not prestigious to permit commercials to air on *Let's Pretend*. However, economic considerations must have won out, because Cream of Wheat became the long-time sponsor in the 1940s.

In addition to the musical commercial program introduction, the show also added an "Uncle Bill" played by Bill Adams, who greeted children with his "Hellooo, Pretenders!" The children in the studio audience would respond, "Hellooo, Uncle Bill." Then Bill would call out, "How do we travel to *Let's Pretend*?" Some child would suggest a mode of transportation—such as a magic carpet.

Imaginative sound effects were the mainstay for building effective theater of the mind for all the children tuned in each Saturday. In her article "Writing for Children," published in *Off Mike*, Mack paid tribute to sound department head Walter Pierson:

> Fortunately for me, he is an imaginative person, for when I spoke of needing the effect of "moon beams shimmering," a "flying trunk," a "magic carpet," he didn't blink an eye. I even had a flying trunk (on the second-hand side) that flew and zoomed, when it finally landed and bumped its way to a stop, it made the audience laugh.

After Mack died of a heart attack on 20 January 1953, Jean Hight replaced her as director. Johanna Johnston became the show's writer. The last broadcast of *Let's Pretend* was on 23 October 1954.

Mack was lauded as "the fairy godmother of radio." As a tribute to her genius during the final two years of the show, the Nila Mack Award was bestowed on the actors who gave the best performances.

See also: Children's Programs

Cast

Host	"Uncle" Bill Adams
Helen	Estelle Levy (Gwen Davies)
Mary	Patricia Ryan
Announcers	George Bryan, Jackson Wheeler, Warren Sweeney

Producers/Creators/Directors

Yolanda Langworthy, Nila Mack, Jean Hight

Programming History

CBS   March 1934–October 1954

Further Reading

Anderson, Arthur, *Let's Pretend: A History of Radio's Best Loved Children's Show by a Longtime Cast Member*, Jefferson, North Carolina: McFarland, 1994.

Boemer, Marilyn Lawrence, "Let's Pretend," in *The Children's Hour: Radio Programs for Children, 1929–1956*, Metuchen, New Jersey: Scarecrow Press, 1989.

MARY KAY SWITZER

LIBERTY BROADCASTING SYSTEM

The Liberty Broadcasting System (LBS) was created by broadcaster Gordon McLendon in 1948. Headquartered in Dallas, the network grew quickly from a state, to a regional, and finally to a full-fledged national network within three years. By then, the 458-affiliate LBS was the second-biggest radio network in America.

LBS's popularity among station affiliates and listeners centered on its heavy schedule of sports programming. LBS flagship station KLIF in Dallas had become well known for its broadcasts of major-league baseball games, most of which were expertly re-created in the KLIF studios by Gordon McLendon. Radio station owners in nearby communities reached by KLIF's signal found many of their listeners attracted to McLendon's baseball games. The owners were soon inquiring about carrying the games, and before long enough of them had signed on as KLIF affiliates for McLendon to decide to formally launch LBS.

The McLendon success with baseball game re-creations resulted from a peculiar scarcity of "live" game coverage on the established radio networks. Major-league teams during the 1930s and 1940s held tight reins over broadcast rights to their baseball games. Radio stations that broadcast these games reached fans within a well-defined and limited coverage area. And because most major-league teams of the period were located in the Northeast and Midwest, baseball fans outside these areas had only the World Series broadcasts to satisfy their interest in major-league games. LBS stepped in to fill the void. An audience ranging in size between 60 and 90 million listeners proved that the network fulfilled a need that major-league club owners had either failed to recognize or ignored.

Although Gordon McLendon's re-created baseball games were popular, he decided in 1949 to challenge the major-league baseball establishment's prohibition of LBS live coverage from the ballparks. A complaint filed with the U.S. Justice Department, suggesting that major-league team owners were violating antitrust laws, finally opened the door for LBS to begin live game coverage. During the 1950 season alone, McLendon signed contracts to carry a minimum of 210 major-league baseball games. The games, numbering about eight per week, were split between American League and National League teams. Besides its baseball games, LBS carried a full slate of weekend college and professional football games during the fall. Noted sportscaster Lindsey Nelson was hired to announce many of these games.

McLendon expanded LBS programming beyond baseball in 1950. Expansion came when McLendon saw his network as now fully in competition with the older, more established National Broadcasting Company (NBC), Columbia Broadcasting System (CBS), American Broadcasting Companies (ABC), and Mutual networks. The traditional program fare that had made these networks popular was copied by LBS with varying degrees of success. Thus, the LBS daily broadcast hours were lengthened and filled with variety shows, musical shows, quiz shows, and soap operas. A number of these were produced in LBS studio facilities in Dallas, and a few were produced and aired from remote facilities in New York and Hollywood. An LBS repertory company supplied the talent for the soap operas; an in-house orchestra supplied live music; and a team of reporters located in Washington, D.C., supplied six daily newscasts for the fledgling network.

The early success enjoyed by LBS was described as phenomenal, especially given the network's youth and the inexperience of Gordon McLendon in running a radio network. Equally phenomenal was the network's success in competing with television's popularity at a time when NBC, CBS, and ABC were de-emphasizing their roles in network radio. What set LBS apart for the moment was McLendon's decision to concentrate his network's most popular programming during daytime hours, which had not yet been heavily infiltrated by television.

Any optimism for the network's future, however, disintegrated in 1951 when the major LBS advertiser, Falstaff Brewing Company, moved its advertising from LBS to Mutual. Loss of Falstaff's income revealed how few national advertisers—and the revenue that such advertisers provided—LBS had attracted. Too much effort had been placed in developing and programming the network, and too little effort had gone toward creating an effective and productive commercial sales apparatus.

In need of an immediate source of cash to keep LBS afloat, McLendon turned to Houston oilman and multimillionaire Hugh Roy Cullen. Cullen agreed to invest $400,000 in LBS and to loan the network an additional $600,000. In return, Cullen received 50 percent ownership of the network. Critics later charged that strings attached to the deal meant that Cullen would have a radio network platform by which to broadcast his ultraconservative political views. Little evidence exists to suggest that Cullen took such advantage of his LBS co-ownership.

The political issue became moot in 1952, when major-league baseball owners decided that broadcasters henceforth would have to negotiate coverage rights with individual baseball clubs rather than collectively with the National and American Leagues. The costs of coverage rights had escalated significantly over the previous year; now they were likely to rise to even greater heights. Added to Gordon McLendon's financial predicament at this point was the refusal of several major-league teams to negotiate any LBS coverage rights whatsoever. A much-reduced baseball schedule meant that LBS affiliates began departing the network. McLendon reacted by filing a $12 million antitrust suit against major-league baseball. The suit never went to trial, however. In January 1955 major-league owners offered Gordon McLendon $200,000 to settle the suit. McLendon had little choice but to accept, as LBS was by then in bankruptcy.

The end for LBS came quickly. Gordon McLendon announced to LBS affiliates on 6 May 1952 that LBS programming would be cut immediately from 16 hours to eight hours daily. One week later, on 15 May, McLendon announced to affiliates that LBS was suspending operation at 10:45 P.M. on that date. The network filed for bankruptcy two weeks later.

Gordon McLendon continued in radio with great success, but he never again ventured into network broadcasting. McLendon gained much fame in later years as a radio program innovator, but he always regarded his days as an LBS play-by-play baseball announcer as the most memorable of his career.

See also: Re-Creations of Events; Sports on Radio

Further Reading

Garay, Ronald, *Gordon McLendon: The Maverick of Radio*, New York: Greenwood Press, 1992.
Glick, Edwin, "The Life and Death of the Liberty Broadcasting System," *Journal of Broadcasting* 23 (Spring 1979).
Harper, Jim, "Gordon McLendon: Pioneer Baseball Broadcaster," *Baseball History* (Spring 1986).
Nelson, Lindsey, *Hello Everybody, I'm Lindsey Nelson*, New York: Beech Tree Books, 1985.
Schroeder, Richard, *Texas Signs On: The Early Days of Radio and Television*, College Station: Texas A&M University Press, 1998.

RONALD GARAY

LICENSING AUTHORIZING U.S. STATIONS TO BROADCAST

Because they must use frequencies on the electromagnetic spectrum, and to avoid as much interference as possible, no transmitter (broadcasting or otherwise) may operate without a federal license. In the United States, such licenses have been required since 1912, although many of the details of both procedure and substance have changed since then. Since 1934, the Federal Communications Commission (FCC) has been the source of federal licenses for all who would broadcast.

Origins

The Radio Act of 1912 vested the Secretary of Commerce and Labor with the authority to license radio transmitters in the United States. Administration of this provision before World War I presented no serious problems, as there was far more spectrum available than people wanting to use it. After the war, however, the demand for frequencies increased dramatically, especially after the 1920 inception of broadcasting. By 1925 there were many more would-be broadcasters than available frequencies, and Secretary of Commerce Herbert Hoover attempted to accommodate all applicants by limiting operating power levels and permissible hours of operation. In 1926 the courts ruled that Hoover had no power to place such conditions on operations, and the situation deteriorated into chaos. In response, Congress passed the Radio Act of 1927, giving the newly created Federal Radio Commission the power to license and regulate

radio broadcasting. Those powers were transferred in 1934 to the FCC.

The Communications Act of 1934, as amended, requires the FCC to license radio broadcasters in the public interest, convenience, and necessity. Originally, broadcast licenses lasted no longer than three years, but various changes in the act lengthened the license period, until with the 1996 amendments all broadcast licenses were extended to run for eight years. During the license term, the licensee has exclusive use of a particular frequency in a specific location. However, licensees do not "own" the frequencies they use; they are considered trustees of the spectrum, which is owned by the public. As public trustees, licensees must operate their stations to serve the public's interest.

Qualifications

In order to receive a broadcast license, applicants must be legally, technically, and financially qualified, as specified in the Communications Act and in FCC rules. To be legally qualified, applicants must be citizens of the United States or corporations with no more than 20 per cent foreign ownership. Parent companies of corporate licensees must have no more than 25 per cent foreign ownership. Applicants must not be in violation of FCC media ownership rules (that is, they cannot already own the maximum number of radio stations in a market) and must meet certain "character" guidelines. Character qualifications relate to certain kinds of criminal convictions and antitrust violations. Lying to the commission is considered a serious character defect—one that almost certainly would disqualify an applicant.

Applicants demonstrate financial qualifications in many ways. If the applicant is applying for a new station, financial qualification is shown by certifying that the applicant has enough money to build the station and operate it for three months without significant advertising revenues. To be technically qualified, applicants must demonstrate the technical proficiency to build and operate the station and to comply with the commission's technical regulations. In most situations, applicants hire engineering consultants to meet their technical needs.

Getting on the Air

If an applicant is seeking a license for a new radio station, the applicant must first find an unused frequency that can be used in or near the community to be served. For AM stations, finding a frequency requires a complex engineering study to determine which frequency could be used in the proposed service area without causing harmful interference to other stations. For FM, the process of finding a usable frequency is often easier, because FM channels are allotted (positioned before licensing) across the country based on specified mileage separation requirements rather than signal interference contours.

Once a frequency has been located, the applicant files an application for a construction permit (CP) with the commission. If the applicant meets the basic qualifications for licensing and the application is not otherwise contested, the commission will grant the CP application. Once the CP is granted, a permittee typically has one year to build a station and begin technical and program testing. Assuming the testing is successful and no other problems arise, the permittee applies for the actual broadcast license, which is then routinely granted by the commission.

Complications in licensing typically arise when more than one party applies for the same frequency in the same market. These are known as mutually exclusive applications, because only one license can be granted for use of the frequency. Prior to 1994, when confronted with mutually exclusive radio applications, the FCC decided which applicant would best serve the public interest (and thereby be awarded the license) through an often lengthy and costly "comparative hearing." These trial-like hearings, presided over by a special FCC employee known as an administrative law judge (ALJ), involved the presentation of evidence, witnesses, and cross-examination. After the hearing, the ALJ would consider all the evidence and pick a winner based on the commission's comparative criteria. Several levels of appeal within the commission were then available to the losing applicants.

The commission's comparative criteria were twofold: diversification of media ownership and best practicable service to the public. The diversification of ownership criterion favored applicants with little or no existing media ownership: the commission at that time favored new owners in an attempt to diversify media ownership. The second criterion, best practicable service to the public, considered issues such as broadcast experience, efficient use of the frequency, and the extent to which the owners would also be integrated into the management of the station. In 1994 the District of Columbia Court of Appeals struck down the FCC's comparative licensing criteria, finding no nexus between the criteria and applicant qualifications. The FCC now settles mutually exclusive application situations through lotteries and spectrum auctions.

Most radio station owners today do not receive their licenses by applying for a new frequency but instead purchase the licenses from other licensees. License transfers must also be approved by the commission in order for the FCC to determine whether the transferee meets the basic qualifications of a radio licensee.

Renewals

The most common licensing situation in the United States today involves the renewal of an existing license. Upon the expiration of a radio license, the licensee must apply to the commission for a renewal. At that time, FCC personnel review the application to determine whether the licensee has performed in the public interest during the previous license term. If the licensee has a good record and no-one objects, the renewal application is routinely granted. The vast majority of licenses are renewed in this way—more than a thousand of them each year.

Nonrenewal of a license, though rare, might be based on any number of factors. The commission might not renew a license if it finds that the licensee has engaged in willful or repeated violations of the act or the commission's rules, has changed its ownership without informing the commission, or has in some way lied to the commission. If the violations are not severe enough to warrant nonrenewal, the commission has the power to issue a short-term renewal or to order special reporting requirements during the license term.

Until 1996, any time a station's license came up for renewal other applicants could also apply for the frequency. This led to what the commission referred to as a "comparative renewal," in which the past performance of the incumbent licensee was compared to the paper promises of the challenging applicant. As with other mutually exclusive licensing situations, comparative renewal cases were decided in a trial-like hearing. In 1996 Congress amended the Communications Act to disallow competing applications at renewal time. According to the revised law, existing broadcasters are judged as to their fitness to continue as licensees. If they continue to be qualified, their licenses are renewed. New applications for the frequency are allowed only when the incumbent licensee is judged unfit and the license renewal is denied.

In all licensing situations, interested parties, including members of the public who live in a station's listening area, have the opportunity to challenge the grant of a license by filing a "petition to deny" the application. If the petition alleges a "substantial and material question of fact," that is, an allegation so serious that if true it would call into question the basic qualifications of the applicant, the commission must hold a hearing on the application.

Section 312 of the Communications Act lists the actions that would justify revocation of a license during the license term. Such actions include willful and repeated violations of the Act, falsifying information, violation of relevant provisions in the U.S. criminal code (e.g., broadcasting lottery information or obscene material), and failure to provide reasonable access to airtime to candidates for federal political office.

Auctions

For decades, the basic FCC policy on licensing new stations operated as described above, changing very little. Early in the 21st century, however, the FCC substantially changed how it issued licenses for new stations. Under a 1997 mandate from Congress to seek new ways to generate revenue by auctioning frequency spectrum, the regulatory agency stopped accepting and acting on most individual license applications—a sharp break from its traditional role.

Instead, and usually several times a year, the FCC's Media Bureau announces a "window" during which applications will be accepted for AM, commercial FM, or educational/public FM construction permits. Each such window is followed by an auction for permits for specified AM frequencies or FM allotments (frequencies in specific towns). The once free radio permits (which only cost filing fees) can now cost thousands of dollars, especially if there are competing applications for specific frequencies, as now occurs more often than in past years. As before, FCC issuing of a license typically follows successful fulfillment of construction permit requirements.

This periodic auction process greatly limited the number of new stations going on the air, though spectrum crowding in major cities had for some years limited new outlet licensing in most urban areas. In early 2009, for example, the FCC website noted that until further notice it was not accepting *any* new applications for most radio stations (save for those in the commercial FM channels) despite (or perhaps because of) some 30,000 inquiries about possible new stations received the previous year. Demand for stations remains high, as attested by continually high sales prices when a station license changes hands.

See also: Communications Act of 1934; Federal Communications Commission; Federal Radio Commission;

Frequency Allocation; Localism in Radio; "Public Interest, Convenience, or Necessity"; Radio Laws; Telecommunications Act of 1996

Further Reading

Browne, Donald R., *Electronic Media and Industrialized Nations: A Comparative Study*, Ames: Iowa State University Press, 1999.
Carter, T. Barton, Marc A. Franklin, and Jay B. Wright, "Broadcast Licensing," in *The First Amendment and the Fifth Estate: Regulation of Electronic Mass Media*, 5th edition, New York: Foundation Press, 1999.
Cole, Barry G., and Mal Oettinger, *Reluctant Regulators: The FCC and The Broadcast Audience*, Reading, Massachusetts: Addison Wesley, 1978.
Edelman, Murray, *The Licensing of Radio Services in the United States, 1927–1947*, Urbana: University of Illinois Press, 1950.
Emery, Walter B., *Broadcasting and Government: Responsibilities and Regulations*, East Lansing: Michigan State University Press, 1961; 2nd edition, 1971.
Federal Communications Commission, Media Bureau, "How to Apply for a Broadcast Station," www.fcc.gov/mb/audio/howtoapply.html
Krasnow, Erwin G., Lawrence D. Longley, and Herbert A. Terry, *The Politics of Broadcast Regulation*, New York: St. Martin's Press, 1973; 3rd edition, 1982.
Sterling, Christopher H., "Billions in Licenses, Millions in Fees: Comparative Renewal and the RKO Mess," *Gannett Center Journal* 2 (Winter 1988).

MICHAEL A. MCGREGOR,
2009 REVISIONS BY CHRISTOPHER H. STERLING

LIGHTS OUT
Horror Series

The first radio horror serial to attract a large following was the National Broadcasting Company's (NBC) *Lights Out*, a Chicago-produced serial that began in 1934 and was broadcast nationwide by the spring of 1935. The brainchild of first Wyllis Cooper and then Arch Oboler, *Lights Out* pioneered many of the horror sound effects and stream-of-consciousness storytelling techniques that would be widely imitated by later programs. Its graphic content was new to radio, and the program's success proved to the industry that listeners' imaginations could be effectively tapped through the skillful combination of sound effects and narrative suggestion. As radio program historian John Dunning has commented, "Never before had such sounds been heard on the air. Heads rolled, bones were crushed, people fell from great heights and splattered wetly on the pavement. There were garrotings, chokings, heads split by cleavers, and, to a critic at *Radio Guide*, 'the most monstrous sound of all sounds, human flesh being eaten'" (Dunning,

1998). Audiences were indeed horrified, some even calling the police. But they were also riveted to their radios.

Lights Out aired late at night throughout its 1930s run. The opening of the show dared the audience to tune in: 12 chimes were followed by a voice announcing, "This is the witching hour!…it is the hour when dogs howl and evil is let loose on the sleeping world. Want to hear about it? Then turn out your lights!" The show's original creator/producer was Wyllis Cooper, a staffer for Chicago's NBC studios. Although his work on the show has been largely overshadowed by that of his successor Arch Oboler, Cooper established *Lights Out*'s basic tone and structure. He combined fantasy and the supernatural with stream-of-consciousness narration to help involve the audience in the reality of its horrors. In particular, Cooper pushed the envelope on gruesome special effects, creating a sort of "can you top this" tradition that was continued by Arch Oboler when he took over the show in 1936 (Cooper moved to Hollywood for a screenwriting career). Real bones (spareribs) were broken on the show to simulate limbs snapping, cabbages were cut in half by meat cleavers to convey heads being bashed in, and wet noodles were crushed with a bathroom plunger to create the sound of human flesh being eaten. One of the program's most famous effects was that of a person being turned inside out, which was accomplished by stripping off a wet rubber glove while crushing a berry basket to simulate broken bones.

Oboler became one of the most famous of radio's auteurs, and his years on *Lights Out* helped establish his reputation as one of the most prolific and imaginative radio writers. Between May 1936 and July 1938, he penned more than 100 *Lights Out* scripts. Oboler continued the *Lights Out* tradition of making the supernatural and science fiction believably scary for the listener, and he has often been compared to Rod Serling and Ray Bradbury in this regard. "I didn't write about little green men," he told media critic Leonard Maltin, "monsters with dripping talons from the special effects department I wrote about the terrors and monsters within each of us" (Maltin, 1997). Oboler's first play, "Burial Services," hit too close to home for many listeners. He told the story of a paralyzed girl being buried alive, and NBC received thousands of horrified letters. Although he never again touched so personal a nerve, Oboler's stream-of-consciousness style, sharp dialogue, and apt metaphors helped pull listeners in by giving his stories a psychological reality. In "Cat Wife," one of Oboler's most famous plays for *Lights Out*, Boris Karloff's duplicitous wife is transformed into an actual human-sized feline, reflecting both her monstrousness to him and his inability to cope with her.

Oboler's plays often contained messages or morals that critiqued greed or man's inhumanity to man. "The Ugliest Man in the World," for example, is not ugly to the woman who loves him. "State Executioner" suggests the horrors of capital punishment and the dangers of greed by having a state executioner execute a man he knows is innocent because he wants the payment; the horror multiplies when he finds out the man was his own son. "The Word" tells of a couple who descend from the Empire State Building to discover that everyone else in the world has disappeared; they conclude that God "got tired of the way [people] were doing things and destroyed them." This couple survived, to make Oboler's point that "plain ordinary people" could make the world a new and better place. Although occasionally heavy-handed, Oboler never hesitated to tackle weighty subjects within the framework of a mass horror genre, winning a new respect for the form.

As the 1930s progressed and the threat of war became clearer, Oboler left *Lights Out* and turned his writing skills to patriotic material. He revived the program for the 1942–43 season, broadcasting from New York over NBC. Oboler hosted the program himself, and its famous beginning became the one that has been most associated with the show since. To the chimes of a gong, Oboler spoke the words "It is later than you think." As John Dunning (1998) has noted, the earlier hour of this series (all the broadcasts were at 8:00 P.M.), made it more accessible to people, and this became the best-remembered year of the series. Scripts were largely recycled from Oboler's previous shows, however, because he was busy doing war work. Its successful 1940s run also owes much to the sudden popularity and growth of the thriller/horror/suspense genre during the war period; *Lights Out* was the granddaddy—and model—of many of the more than 40 such programs that took to the airwaves during that time, most famously *Inner Sanctum* and *Suspense.*

The reputation and influence of the program remained strong long after television supplanted radio. This is due in part to Oboler's status as a celebrated auteur (most of Oboler's shows, unlike Cooper's, are available on tape). But *Lights Out* also stands as pivotal to radio history because it demonstrated the way in which radio programs could push listeners' imaginations to horrifying limits beyond those of reasoned vision. Radio, as horror author (and Oboler admirer) Stephen King has noted, has the ability to "unlock the door of evil without letting the monster out" (quoted in Nachman, 1998). *Lights Out* was the first program to demonstrate and exploit this aspect of radio, to the delight of its terror-stricken fans.

See also: Horror Programs; Sound Effects

Host

Arch Oboler

Narrator

Boris Aplon (1946)

Actors

Boris Karloff, Harold Peary, Betty Winkler, Mercedes McCambridge, Willard Waterman, Arthur Peterson, Betty Caine, Ed Carey, Sidney Ellstrom, Murray Forbes, Robert Griffin, Robert Guilbert, Rupert LaBelle, Philip Lord, Raymond Edward Johnson, and others

Writers/Producers/Directors

Wyllis Cooper, Arch Oboler, Albert Crews, and Bill Lawrence

Programming History

WENR, Chicago January 1934–April 1935
NBC April 193 5–August 1946
CBS October 1942–September 1943
ABC July 1947–August 1947

Further Reading

DeLong, Thomas A., *Radio Stars: An Illustrated Biographical Dictionary of 953 Performers, 1920 through 1960*, Jefferson, North Carolina: McFarland, 1996.
Dunning, John, *Tune in Yesterday: The Ultimate Encyclopedia of Old-Time Radio, 1925–1976*, Englewood Cliffs, New Jersey: Prentice-Hall, 1976; revised edition, as *On the Air: The Encyclopedia of Old-Time Radio*, New York: Oxford University Press, 1998.
Harmon, Jim, *The Great Radio Heroes*, New York: Doubleday, 1967; 2nd edition, Jefferson, North Carolina: McFarland, 2001.
Maltin, Leonard, *The Great American Broadcast: A Celebration of Radio's Golden Age*, New York: Dutton, 1997.
Nachman, Gerald, *Raised on Radio: In Quest of the Lone Ranger, Jack Benny*, New York: Pantheon, 1998.
Stedman, Raymond William, *The Serials: Suspense and Drama by Installment*, Norman: University of Oklahoma Press, 1971; 2nd edition, 1977.

ALLISON MCCRACKEN

LITTLE ORPHAN ANNIE
Children's Serial Drama

A pioneer of the children's serial genre, *Little Orphan Annie* first bowed—or curtsied—in 1930 on Chicago station WGN. On 6 April 1931 it premiered nationally on the NBC Blue Network, later moving to Mutual Broadcasting System. Shirley Bell and Janice Gilbert portrayed Annie during the series' 11-year run; Bell from the beginning until 1940, Gilbert from 1940 to 1942.

Based on Harold Gray's popular comic strip, *Annie* featured 15 minutes of action and high adventure every weekday afternoon or early evening, initially based primarily in her adopted hometown of Tompkins Corners, and later in more exotic, faraway places. She fought all forces of evil, including gangsters and criminals, reminding her faithful listeners at the end of the show to "be sure to drink your Ovaltine." Indeed, the premium toys offered by *Little Orphan Annie* and its long-time sponsor seemed at times to compete with the stories themselves, taking up four to six minutes of the 15-minute broadcast. Children who tuned in were urged to get their own "swell Ovaltine shake-up drinking mug" by sending ten cents and the proof of purchase from an Ovaltine can.

In addition to Bell and Gilbert, other cast members included Allan Baruck and Mel Torme (Joe Corntassel, Annie's best friend), Henry Saxe, Boris Aplon, and Stanley Andrews (Oliver "Daddy" Warbucks), Henrietta Tedro and Jerry O'Mera (Ma and Pa Silo, the farm couple who cared for Annie when Daddy Warbucks was away on business), and Pierre Andre (Uncle Andy, the announcer). The voice of Sandy, Annie's dog, was provided by Brad Barker. Among Annie's favorite expressions were "Leapin' lizards" and "Jumpin' grasshoppers."

The program's writers employed a simple but very effective technique to keep listeners, especially young children, returning to hear the next installment of Annie's adventures: the cliffhanger. Episodes seldom ended with finality or resolution. Instead, story lines "flowed" from one episode to the next, occasionally reaching a conclusion but never without the development of a new story line to take its place. Beginning with *Annie*, this open-ended approach—leaving listeners in suspense at the end of each daily broadcast—was particularly evident for decades to come in children's radio and television programming and motion picture serials. In addition, Annie's radio adventures appealed to youngsters because the episodes often articulated childhood dreams of experiencing the glamour of the adult world.

NBC's radio network connections were not completed for regular U.S. coast-to-coast broadcasting until 1933, two years after *Little Orphan Annie*'s network premiere. As a consequence, *Annie* in its infancy was actually two different programs—one originating in Chicago, the other in San Francisco. Listeners in the eastern and central areas of the U.S. heard Shirley Bell in the lead role, whereas listeners in the far west heard Floy Hughes. Identical scripts ensured some consistency between the two productions, but west coast listeners were no doubt startled to suddenly hear different actors after the program's operations were consolidated in Chicago in 1933.

For over five years *Little Orphan Annie* aired six times a week, going to five times weekly beginning in 1936. The series moved from NBC to Mutual in 1940, at which time Ovaltine, the show's original sponsor, decided instead to put its advertising dollars in *Captain Midnight*, a new children's suspense show. Taking the chocolate drink mix's place as *Annie*'s sponsor was the breakfast cereal Puffed Wheat Sparkies, but by this time other adventure shows were outgunning Annie at her own game. Faced with declining ratings, *Little Orphan Annie*'s last broadcast was on 26 January 1942.

Cast

Little Orphan Annie	Shirley Bell, Floy Hughes, Bobbe Deane, Janice Gilbert
Joe Corntassel	Allan Baruck, Mel Torme
Oliver "Daddy" Warbucks	Henry Saxe, Stanley Andrews, Boris Aplon
Mrs. Mary Silo	Henrietta Tedro
Mr. Byron Silo	Jerry O'Mera
Uncle Andy (announcer)	Pierre Andre
Sandy (Annie's dog)	Brad Barker
Aha	Olan Soule
Clay	Hoyt Allen

Producer/Creator

Based on the comic strip by Harold Gray

Programming History

WGN Chicago	1930
NBC Blue	1931–October 1936
NBC	November 1936–January 1940
Mutual	1940–42

Further Reading

Boemer, Marilyn Lawrence, *The Children's Hour: Radio Programs for Children, 1929–1956*, Metuchen, New Jersey: Scarecrow Press, 1989.

Dunning, John, *Tune in Yesterday: The Ultimate Encyclopedia of Old-Time Radio, 1925–1976*, Englewood Cliffs, New Jersey: Prentice-Hall, 1976; revised edition, as *On the Air: The Encyclopedia of Old-Time Radio*, New York: Oxford University Press, 1998.

Swartz, Jon D., and Robert C. Reinehr, *Handbook of Old-Time Radio*, Metuchen, New Jersey: Scarecrow Press, 1993.

Terrace, Vincent, *Radio Programs, 1924–1984: A Catalogue of over 1800 Shows*, Jefferson, North Carolina: McFarland, 1999.

DAVID MCCARTNEY

LOCALISM IN RADIO
Regulatory Approach

The concept of "localism," or serving a specific community, has always been central to the practice of radio programming and to government policies concerning broadcasting in the United States. In contrast to most of the rest of the world, American radio stations were allocated to local communities and licensed to serve audiences defined by the boundaries of those communities. The Federal Communications Commission (FCC) has described its radio allocation priorities as (1) providing a usable signal from at least one station to everyone and diversified service to as many persons as possible, and (2) creating sufficient outlets for local expression addressing each community's needs and interests. That system of license allocation remains the foundation of American broadcasting. As for programming, local service has frequently been a key element in a station's ability to survive and prosper. Research and experience have consistently demonstrated that local content is one of the things listeners value most highly.

However, economic realities have usually impelled broadcasters toward centralized program distribution. Networks began developing in broadcasting's earliest days, and although the traditional radio networks have long been reduced to providing news and sports for radio, a new generation of networks offering full-time formats appeared as the increased availability of satellite service in the 1980s made such a service viable. By 2000, the emergence of distribution technologies that no longer rely exclusively on nearby transmitters to reach individual audience members—such as direct-to-home satellites and the internet—and the ability of large radio groups to program clusters of stations from a central location led some to suggest that localism is an idea destined to be little more than a quaint relic of a bygone age. Larry Irving (then head of the National Telecommunications and Information Administration) told the 1999 National Association of Broadcasters convention in Las Vegas that localism has "gone the way of the buffalo." Yet other industry observers continue to argue forcefully that the most successful radio stations are those that do the best job of connecting with the localized needs and interests of their audiences. This view holds that localism will be even more important in a future of ever-greater competition from sources such as the satellite-based Digital Audio Radio Services (DARS), offered nationwide since November 2001 by XM Satellite Radio and since 2002 by Sirius.

These contradictory assertions may all, in fact, be accurate, depending on one's vantage point. Much like the phrase "The public interest," the meaning of localism has always been in the eye of the beholder—typically either the FCC or a station licensee. The very vagueness of the term has enabled a variety of regulators, industry spokespersons, and public service advocates to laud the importance of localism in different situations.

Localism in U.S. Broadcast Regulation

As a matter of policy, localism is closely tied to a number of regulatory goals. These are generally expressed as the need to limit centralized (program) power or authority in order to create more diverse content—the robust and varied "marketplace of ideas" central to the American understanding of free speech. For several decades, the FCC has pointed to the importance of localism as a means of providing diverse program content for the furtherance of the public interest. Some policy-makers also argue for the need to protect local communities and smaller interests from being overwhelmed by programs developed by (and for) larger national interests. The desire to diffuse political power has been a running theme throughout American history (the federal system of government is perhaps the most obvious result). Added to the widely accepted notion that the media are capable of exerting great influence on society, the decision to dilute the power of a single broadcast entity—station or especially network—seems an obvious choice.

The commission has a specific charge in the Communications Act to "encourage the larger and more effective use of radio in the public interest." The FCC has generally interpreted this to mean that it should try to allocate the maximum technically feasible number of stations around the country. Thus, structural definitions of localism (in a

geographic or spatial sense) have most often guided policy-makers. This understanding of localism assumes that stations licensed to transmit to a geographically restricted area will focus their programming on the specific needs and interests of the citizens residing in that area. In this context, localism as policy has been put into regulations affecting the distribution of licenses to various communities. Localism is also seen in the bedrock obligation of all broadcast licensees to serve the needs and interests of their community of license (which at one time involved an elaborate process to ascertain the needs of that community) and in the preference that was granted to active local ownership when, prior to 1996, the comparative hearing process was used to choose a licensee from among mutually exclusive competing applicants.

In one of the earliest examples of localism, the Radio Act of 1927 divided the country into five "zones" and, in the case of competing license applications, directed the Federal Radio Commission (FRC) to distribute stations among the zones according to frequency, power, and time of operation, with concern for fairness, equity, and efficiency. The Davis Amendment, added one year later, required the FRC to provide *equality* of service, in terms of both transmission and reception, in each of the five zones. These sections, with slight modification, passed into the Communications Act of 1934. Although the zone system was repealed in 1936 and the law was modified to require once again that the FCC simply provide a fair, efficient, and equitable distribution of radio service to each state and community, localism was (and is) undeniably a powerful concern in Congress.

Another significant, and more recent, example of the FCC's structural concern with localism was the decision to drastically restructure the system of FM station allocation in order to increase the number of available stations in the early 1980s. Generally referred to by its FCC docket number (80–90), this order authorized three new classes of stations and modified the interference and operational rules with the goal of allowing first (and sometimes second) FM stations in communities where none had been possible before under the original 1962 Table of Assignments. As a result, the number of FM stations in the United States grew from around 3,000 in 1980 to slightly under 6,000 by the end of 1990 and continued to climb to more than 8,500 by 2003.

Localism and the Business of Radio

However, the growth was not solely good news for the industry or the audience. Many observers lamented the increase in interference in the FM band. The rise in the number of stations combined with the simultaneous deregulation of radio to rapidly escalate station values. Many owners found themselves too far in debt, particularly during the economic downturn in the late 1980s and early 1990s. Sometimes as a result of the significant economic hardships resulting from the combination of increased competition and debt load, sometimes in response to a perceived change in the desires of the audience, stations cut back or eliminated local air staffs and news operations. If the goal of the FCC's restructuring was to create more local content for more communities, the result could best be described as mixed. Although many stations continue to thrive by providing their audience a programming diet heavy with local content and involvement, satellite-provided formats, other syndicated product, and the ever-increasing ease of automating a station combine to create a significant economic incentive for many licensees to reduce localism to commercials and weather forecasts.

This illustrates the inherent conflict between policy rhetoric and the changing economic realities facing licensees. Though frequently lauding localism in policy pronouncements, the FCC has seldom promulgated, and even more infrequently enforced, local program guidelines or requirements. Nearly all of those that ever existed, such as the fairness doctrine, the ascertainment primer, commercial guidelines, and news and public-affairs guidelines, disappeared by the mid-1980s. The reasons behind this deregulatory trend (critics would term it failure) have been hotly debated because they are so complex. The regulatory problem is one of accommodating the various interests—licensees, program producers, audiences, networks, regulators, advertisers—in a rule that comports with common understanding of the First Amendment. Although this task was difficult under the public trustee model of regulation that guided broadcasting's first 50 years, it is practically impossible to set firm local content guidelines under the current regulatory philosophy, which moves much of the control from government policy to marketplace competition.

A further complicating factor is the constant evolution of the media environment. From the system envisioned at the time of the Communications Act in 1934, rigidly structured along relatively narrow geographic lines, radio in the United States moved almost immediately to a distribution system with a wider geographic frame (regional and national sources feeding the majority of programming on "local" stations). From a few hundred local stations linked with relatively new networks at the time the Communications Act of 1934 was written, radio grew decades later to a business of thousands of "local" outlets providing a relatively few national music or talk program formats. Development of internet and satellite distribution has merely enhanced the trend to national program types provided through local outlets. The degree to which any one of those outlets wishes to be truly local (reflecting and projecting its own community) is left to the discretion of the licensee.

The vague nature of localism itself is a final complication. One's understanding of concepts such as "local" or "community" colors any practical application of localism. The term *can* mean full-scale involvement of a station with its community, or (as is more usually the case) it can mean mere mention of local weather (and local commercials) within a syndicated music format heard on hundreds of stations across the country. As traditionally viewed by the FCC, real localism is probably somewhere in the middle, but much closer to the former—and many argue that it's also good business. In his book *Radio Programming: Tactics and Strategy*, programmer and consultant Eric Norberg asserts that localism and human contact are the elements that listeners value most in a station, and that therefore the core of what makes a station successful is the relatable local person on the air. This viewpoint takes on the air of common wisdom in the industry trade press, particularly in advice given to programmers and air talent. Researchers repeatedly find that local information (weather forecasts, traffic information, event news) is one of the top reasons people tune in to radio.

Localism as a Social Construct

Critics, and occasionally even the FCC, have suggested that the goals of localism can be addressed in a different fashion, recognizing that communities frequently form around shared tastes, interests, and ideals without specific reference to a geographic boundary. For example, in the rulemaking that eliminated many of the radio programming guidelines, the commission noted that

> communities of common interests need not have geographic bounds. The economics of radio allowed that medium to be far more sensitive to the diversity within a community and the attendant specialized community needs. Increased competition in large urban markets has forced stations to choose programming strategies very carefully.

(FCC, "Deregulation of Radio," *Notice of Inquiry and Proposed Rulemaking*, 73 F.C.C.2d 457 [1979], at 489)

This alternative view of community can also be seen in the FCC's decision to approve satellite-delivered DARS. Despite the diversity of programming alluded to above, many program interests go unfulfilled by traditional terrestrial radio because the audience for a particular type of music or information is simply too small within the service area of a single station or is otherwise unattractive to advertisers. Beginning in late 2001, however, satellite radio services included program channels that would not be economically viable on a single station in a given market (e.g., five separate jazz channels). The technology can aggregate widely separated audiences in a fashion that does not serve traditional localism but surely adds to content diversity.

Trials of Modern Localism

Sometimes, competing concerns such as spectrum efficiency have prevailed over localism. Prior to 1978, the FCC issued Class D FM licenses to college and community stations, permitting low-power operation (a maximum of 10 W, with a tower height less than 100 feet) in the noncommercial part of the FM band. These stations represented a variety of operational styles, from student-run stations at colleges or high schools to stations licensed to civic groups and generally run by a largely volunteer or all-volunteer staff. By their very nature, these operations were strongly committed to their community and would appear to personify the localism ideal, often featuring material not available through full-power stations.

In 1972 the Corporation for Public Broadcasting (CPB) petitioned the FCC to explore several issues related to more efficient use of the FM channels set aside for noncommercial educational stations. In comments to the commission, they argued (with the support of others, including the National Federation of Community Broadcasters) that the 10-W broadcasters were effectively blocking more efficient use of the spectrum. Essentially, CPB and its supporters were arguing for more stations that met their qualifying guidelines for size and professionalism, at the expense of smaller operations. Supporters of Class D stations, primarily the licensees themselves, countered with various arguments for retaining the service as it was, including the point most relevant here—the truly local nature of the service.

The FCC recognized that the Class D stations were indeed meeting discrete local needs. But in this case, the commission put the emphasis on the efficiency argument put forth by CPB, announcing

new rules that effectively forced existing Class D stations to upgrade their facilities to Class A minimums or else become a secondary service, facing interference or being bumped from their assignments. In the FCC's view at that time, there was not sufficient spectrum available for both full-power, larger coverage area stations and low-power operations (although the commission has long accepted the need for low-powered translator and booster stations that extend the coverage of existing FM and TV stations but are prohibited from originating any programming themselves).

It is somewhat ironic that the FCC issued rules in 2000 that will create a new class of low-powered FM or microradio stations. The rulemaking comes in response to petitions arguing that, in the wake of industry consolidation following the 1996 Telecommunications Act, radio ownership and content are insufficiently diverse, and that current stations often fail to address local needs. Although congressional intervention curtailed the number of LPFM stations that could be licensed, the FCC had issued more than 400 construction permits by the end of 2002, and 73 LPFM stations were on the air in January 2003.

Localism became a contested policy issue again in the early 21st century. The National Association of Broadcasters (NAB) expressed stalwart support of the concept in their legal battle to contain or eliminate digital satellite radio's competitive threat. They argued that national competition from the satellite providers could harm radio's local programming. This seemed hypocritical to many observers given that the radio industry had seemingly abandoned the concept in the continuing consolidation of radio ownership into huge station groups, which largely killed most local programming. Central studios provided news for hundreds of stations located miles apart. Many stations ceased all local public-affairs programming.

Yet when in mid-2004 the FCC initiated an inquiry into the status of localism in both radio and television, broadcasters were quick and sharp with their criticism. The commission formed a senior staff task force to study the issue and hold public hearings. The NAB and other broadcast groups took strong exception to these proceedings, declaring them both unlawful and unnecessary. It appeared that radio industry leaders were in favor of touting localism when it suited their policy concerns, while fighting it if localism requirements might impinge on their prerogatives.

See also: College Radio; Community Radio; Deregulation of Radio; Emergencies, Radio's Role in; Licensing

Authorizing U.S. Stations to Broadcast; Low-Power Radio/Microradio; Pacifica Foundation; Ten-Watt Stations

Further Reading

Barrett, Andrew C., "Public Policy and Radio—A Regulator's View," *Media Studies Journal* 7 (1993).

Collins, Tom A., "The Local Service Concept in Broadcasting: An Evaluation and Recommendation for Change," *Iowa Law Review* 65 (1980).

Federal Communications Commission, *Commission en banc Programming Inquiry, Report and Statement of Policy*, 44 FCC 2303 (1960).

Federal Communications Commission, *Deregulation of Radio, Notice of Inquiry and Proposed Rulemaking*, 73 FCC 2d 457(1979).

Federal Communications Commission, *The Suburban Community Policy, the Berwick Doctrine, and the De Facto Reallocation Policy, Report and Order*, 93 FCC 2d 436 (1983).

Federal Communications Commission Localism Task Force archives, www.fcc.gov/localism/taskforce-archive.html

Hilliard, Robert L., and Michael C. Keith. *The Quieted Voice: The Rise and Demise of Localism in American Radio*. Carbondale: Southern Illinois University Press, 2005.

Jones, Steven G., "Understanding Community in the Information Age," in *CyberSociety: Computer-Mediated Communication and Community*, edited by Steven G. Jones, Thousand Oaks, California: Sage, 1995.

Kelley, E.W., *Policy and Politics in the United States: The Limits of Localism*, Philadelphia, Pennsylvania: Temple University Press, 1987.

Kemmis, Daniel, *Community and the Politics of Place*, Norman: University of Oklahoma Press, 1990.

McCain, Thomas A., and G. Ferrell Lowe, "Localism in Western European Radio Broadcasting: Untangling the Wireless," *Journal of Communication* (Winter 1990).

Milam, Lorenzo W., *Sex and Broadcasting: A Handbook on Starting a Radio Station for the Community*, 2nd edition, Saratoga, California: Dildo Press, 1972; 4th edition, as *The Original Sex and Broadcasting*, San Diego, California: MHO and MHO, 1988.

Norberg, Eric G., *Radio Programming: Tactics and Strategy*, Boston: Focal Press, 1996.

Stavitsky, Alan G., "The Changing Conception of Localism in U.S. Public Radio," *Journal of Broadcasting and Electronic Media* 38 (1994).

GREGORY D. NEWTON,
2009 REVISIONS BY CHRISTOPHER H. STERLING

LOCAL MARKETING AGREEMENTS
Brokered Agreements among Stations

As part of the deregulation of radio ownership initiated by the Federal Communications Commission (FCC) during the late 1970s and early 1980s, radio station owners and operators began to sign program service and/or marketing agreements, known in the industry as local marketing agreements. In 1992 the FCC formally approved this form of ownership and operations agreements, and they became commonplace, particularly in the four years leading to the easing of ownership rules in the 1996 Telecommunications Act.

Alliances for local marketing agreements may be located in the same market, in the same region, or in the same service (AM or FM). The allied owners and operators draw up and sign legal agreements defining financial control over their allied properties, but the owners still maintain their separate licenses and studios. After 1996, it often became simpler to just purchase a station, but local marketing agreements were still used to make transitions to new owners cheaper, easier, and more cost-effective.

A local marketing agreement thus has become a time-brokering agreement between stations that can address either programming or advertising time. Basically, the originating or principal station in the local marketing agreement pays the "affiliate" a monthly fee either to partially simulcast programming or to air original satellite-delivered programming. This type of agreement differs from a satellite format network affiliation arrangement, wherein the affiliate pays for programming. The originating station in a local marketing agreement can strike an arrangement with the leased station for either handling or sharing advertising sales.

The benefits of local marketing agreements to the originating station include expanded coverage area and thus the potential for increased sales of advertising. For example, during the early 1990s, owners of many struggling AM stations signed local marketing agreements to stabilize their flow of profits rather than take on the risks and costs involved in trying to establish a new format.

By 2000, although the number of stations and formats seems endless in major markets, in fact, local marketing agreements allowed two separate radio stations to operate jointly, and so the number of operators (or voices) was actually far fewer than the number of stations (or outlets). Usually the financially strong station reaches a combined operation and sales agreement with, a financially troubled station in the same community to oversee programming and advertising time sales for a percentage of the advertising sales. Although the parties exercising a local marketing agreement are not required to file the agreement with the FCC, the licensee of the weaker partner station is still required to meet the station's maintenance and community standards (although in practice these requirements have become so minimal during the 1990s that this threat of losing a licensee over such a deal offers no risk).

The local marketing agreement policy helped redefine the institutional relationship that had formerly been restricted to affiliation. Indeed, once the FCC in 1992 formally relaxed regulations to allow local radio owners to own and control more than one station in the same service market, a wave of deals took place. One scholar calculated that over 50 percent of the commercial radio stations became involved in some aspect of consolidation between 1992 and 1996, including local marketing agreements. The pace of consolidation has increased tremendously since the Telecommunications Act of 1996 became law, with local marketing agreements used to make the transition to combinations of radio stations.

Local marketing agreements permit the parties to take advantage of cost and organizational structural efficiencies; to dominate a market with variations of one format; to eliminate redundant jobs; to develop broader marketing plans and solutions for advertisers; and, in the end, to increase profits for stockholders and investors. One can simply buy a station, or, to be more flexible in the short run, one can set up a local marketing agreement to test whether a formal alliance might work better. Some owners delay formal merger decisions until they figure out how to consolidate personnel and facilities.

There have been, therefore, numerous examples of different uses of local marketing agreements, as owners have utilized combinations of acquiring stations to form new and, they hope, more profitable alliances. Consider a top 50 market, Charlotte, North Carolina, where in spring 1992 the market was being served by ten radio owners and operators, who owned three AM and 12 FM stations. Two years later, those ten had dwindled to six owners and operators. By fall 1996, Charlotte had consolidated to the point of having only four viable radio owners and operators controlling the same 15 stations. Local marketing agreements created much, though not all, of this consolidation.

In 1994, in reaction to the promiscuous use of LMAs, the FCC began to investigate whether such agreements violated existing duopoly laws. Eventually, the commission determined that an LMA involving brokerage of more than 15 percent of a station's programming can be viewed as "ownership."

Ironically, the rapid rise and widespread use of LMAs foretold their demise. Rampant consolidation frequently led to outright purchases and as a handful of large corporations—Clear Channel, among others—bought up smaller stations, LMAs steadily decreased. They have all but disappeared, becoming relics of the radio business.

See also: Licensing Authorizing U.S. Stations to Broadcast; Ownership, Mergers, and Acquisitions

Further Reading

Albarran, Alan B., *Management of Electronic Media*, Belmont, California: Wadsworth, 1997.
Chan-Olmsted, Sylvia M., "A Chance for Survival or Status Quo? The Economic Implications of the Radio Duopoly Ownership Rules," *The Journal of Radio Studies* 3 (1994).
Compaine, Benjamin M., and Douglas Gomery, *Who Owns the Media?* White Plains, New York: Knowledge Industry, 1979; 3rd edition, Mahwah, New Jersey: Erlbaum, 2000.
Ditingo, Vincent M., *The Remaking of Radio*, Boston: Focal Press, 1995.
Federal Communications Commission, Mass Media Bureau, Policy and Rules Division, *Review of the Radio Industry, 1997*, MM Docket No. 98–35 (13 March 1998, as part of 1998 Biennial Regulatory Review).

DOUGLAS GOMERY,
2009 REVISIONS BY CARY O'DELL

LONE RANGER
Western Adventure Program

The Lone Ranger originated at WXYZ in Detroit, Michigan, in 1933. The program gained in popularity with both child and adult listeners and reached a national audience when it played an instrumental role in the creation of the Mutual Broadcasting System in 1934. In the early 1940s, *The Lone Ranger* moved to the National Broadcasting Company (NBC) Blue Network, which became the American Broadcasting Companies (ABC) in 1945. The Ranger evolved into a variety of media forms, becoming the subject of comic strips, comic books, books for children, novels for adults, films, and television.

In 1932 George W. Trendle, one of the owners of WXYZ, decided that the station could increase its profitability by breaking ties with the Columbia Broadcasting System (CBS) network and locally producing its own programs, including dramatic shows. Trendle called station manager Harold True, dramatic director James Jewell, and other station personnel together to outline the concept for programs to be developed. One concept that emerged from this conference was a show to be aimed at children. Trendle specified several characteristics he felt were essential. The program should be a western and should feature a leading character who would exemplify model behavior for young listeners. This hero should be mature and possess some of the qualities of Zorro and Robin Hood. In subsequent meetings, details were further developed.

The hero was to be a lone operator, perhaps a former Texas Ranger. Finally a name emerged—the Lone Ranger.

With this basic format in mind, Trendle turned to Fran Striker, a script writer in Buffalo, New York, to bring a fully developed Ranger to the radio audience. Striker's scripts for the *Warner Lester, Manhunter* series had gained national attention. Striker had also created his own radio western for WEBR in Buffalo, and elements of this series, *Covered Wagon Days*, may have influenced the content and tone of *The Lone Ranger*. For many years, however, George Trendle countered implications that anyone besides himself could be considered the creator of *The Lone Ranger*, and he insisted that Striker, as well as other WXYZ personnel, sign over legal ownership of the program.

Trial airings of *The Lone Ranger* on WXYZ received limited publicity, and sources disagree as to the exact date of the first actual broadcast of a complete and polished program, with some specifying 30 or 31 January and others 2 February 1933. As the program evolved, the Ranger was given a white horse named Silver and a "faithful Indian companion," Tonto, who addressed the Ranger as "kemo sabe." This gave the Ranger someone to talk to, lessening the need for an announcer's narration of action for the radio audience. Rossini's "William Tell" Overture became the theme music for the show, another example of using classical music in the public domain in order to avoid royalty payments. The music was accompanied by the announcer's enthusiastic and authoritative description of "the daring and resourceful masked rider of the plains who led the fight for law and order in the early western United States." Listeners were invited to "return with us now to those thrilling days of yesteryear. From out of the past came the thundering hoofbeats of the great horse Silver! The Lone Ranger rides again!"

The fame of the Ranger spread beyond Detroit as WXYZ fed the show to the Michigan Radio network. The program was the most important attraction to WLW Cincinnati, WGN Chicago, and WOR New York when they joined WXYZ in creating the Mutual Broadcasting System in 1934. When more distant stations signed up with Mutual, the Ranger's popularity reached a national level.

The show had already gained a huge following before the Ranger's background and the reason why he wore the mask were fully developed. These questions were answered in a 1938 Republic film serial portraying an ambush on a group of five Texas Rangers. They were all believed dead, but one survived. When this lone surviving Ranger recovered, he wore a mask to protect his identity and anonymity. This version of the Ranger's origin was also reflected in the radio program by 1941. The Lone Ranger's secret silver mine provided the means for supporting himself and was the source of his silver bullets.

A basic skeleton plot that was reflected in many scripts featured the development of a complication or problem and a failed attempt at its solution by a character in the story before the Ranger came onto the scene. When the Ranger did appear and successfully resolved the difficulty by the end of the program, someone would ask, "Who was that masked man?" Another would explain, "That was the Lone Ranger!" He was also a master of other disguises, further confounding villainous attempts at revealing his true identity.

Fran Striker, the show's chief writer, involved the Lone Ranger in getting telegraph lines strung across the West, in helping build the Union Pacific Railroad, and in carrying out special assignments for President Lincoln. The Ranger also assisted Buffalo Bill and Wild Bill Hickok. Furthermore, he provided advice to Billy the Kid, General Custer, and Sitting Bull.

One memorable plot concerned the Lone Ranger's discovery of his nephew, Dan Reid, who had been saved from an Indian attack on a wagon train. Reid had been brought up by a pioneer woman who, with her dying breaths, described his family, revealing that the boy's father was the Lone Ranger's brother. Dan Reid's son, Britt, became the Green Hornet, another masked man in a later radio show that was also scripted by Fran Striker.

For much of its radio existence, *The Lone Ranger* was broadcast live on the NBC Blue network (later ABC) on Mondays, Wednesdays, and Fridays. Because of time zone differences, this schedule required three separate live feeds, the first beginning at 7:30 Eastern time. The second feed was produced for the Mountain zone, and the third for the West Coast.

See also: Children's Programs; Westerns; WXYZ

Cast

Lone Ranger	George Stenius (George Seaton) (1933), Jack Deeds, James Jewell, Earle Graser (1933–41), Brace Beemer (1941–54)
Tonto	John Todd
Thunder Martin	Paul Hughes
Dan Reid	Ernie Winstanley, Dick Beals, James Lipton

Butch Cavendish	Jay Michael
Various characters	Paul Hughes, John Hodiak, Rollon Parker, Bob Maxwell, Frank Russell, Ted Johnstone, Jack Petruzzi, Herschel Mayall, Elaine Alpert, Mel Palmer, Fred Rito, Bertha Forman, Ruth Dean Rickaby, Malcolm McCoy, Jack McCarthy, Bill Saunders, Beatrice Leiblee, Harry Goldstein, Lee Allman
Announcer	Harold True, Brace Beemer, Harry Golder, Charles Wood, Bob Hite, Fred Foy

Creator

George W. Trendle

Directors

James Jewell, Charles D. Livingstone

Programming History

Michigan Radio Network	January 1933–34
Mutual	February 1934– May 1942
NBC-Blue	May 1942–44
ABC	1944–54

Further Reading

Bickel, Mary E., *Geo. W. Trendle, Creator and Producer of: The Lone Ranger, The Green Hornet, Sgt. Preston of the Yukon, The American Agent, and Other Successes,* New York: Exposition Press, 1971.

Boemer, Marilyn Lawrence, *The Children's Hour: Radio Programs for Children, 1929–1956,* Metuchen, New Jersey: Scarecrow Press, 1989.

Bryan, J., "Hi-Yo, Silver!" *The Saturday Evening Post* (14 October 1939).

Harmon, Jim, *Radio Mystery and Adventure: And Its Appearances in Film, Television, and Other Media,* Jefferson, North Carolina: McFarland, 1992.

Jones, Reginald M., Jr., *The Mystery of the Masked Man's Music: A Search for the Music on The Lone Ranger Radio Program, 1933–1954,* Metuchen, New Jersey: Scarecrow Press, 1987.

Osgood, Dick, *Wyxie Wonderland: An Unauthorized 50-Year Diary of WXYZ Detroit,* Bowling Green, Ohio: Bowling Green University Popular Press, 1981.

Rothel, David, *Who Was That Masked Man? The Story of the Lone Ranger,* South Brunswick, New Jersey: Barnes, 1976.

B.R. SMITH

LOW-POWER RADIO/MICRORADIO
Small Community Radio Stations

Microradio is a political movement with the goal of putting low-power FM transmitters into the hands of community activists, minority groups, and those with no hope of getting a traditional Federal Communications Commission (FCC) license to broadcast. Under the leadership of Free Radio Berkeley (FRB) founder Stephen Dunifer, instructions are readily available to anyone who wants a low-cost transmitter kit, programming help, and legal representation. Microradio broadcasters are often students and street people without property, and when ordered by the FCC to cease operations, they simply move to another location. FCC enforcement is uneven and has been complicated by recent court rulings. In *United States v. Dunifer* (July 2000), the court ruled against Dunifer's right to broadcast without a license. That decision led activists to pressure the FCC more strongly for a licensed low-power FM service.

Origins

The history of unlicensed radio goes back to the early radio-telephone experimenters who simply went on the air without asking anybody's permission. By the end of the 1920s, the radio spectrum had been divided between commercial, amateur, and experimental users. All were required to have licenses, first from the Federal Radio Commission and after 1934 from the FCC. But there have always been scofflaws, mostly referred to as "pirate broadcasters." From ships anchored offshore with powerful transmitters to radio hobbyists broadcasting entertainment on amateur radio frequencies, there is a long history of unlicensed broadcasting. The most blatant of those illegal operators were usually caught and fined, and their equipment was confiscated. Unlike the modern microradio movement, most such "pirates" were not political activists.

For a time, however, small radio stations were not only allowed, they were actively encouraged. With the inception of FM radio, the FCC encouraged noncommercial operations. When frequencies went begging, the FCC in 1948 initiated a low-power category of stations, the so-called Class D outlets, that might use as little as 10 W of power and cover a very small area with a usable signal. But they were broadcast outlets, often held by nonprofit groups unable to afford anything larger. By the 1970s there were several hundred such stations on the air.

Low-power stations were increasingly resented by the FM radio business, which was rapidly expanding in the 1970s and 1980s. Tiny stations took up valuable frequencies that full-power outlets coveted. In 1978 the FCC began to reverse course, requiring these stations to use at least 100 (and more likely 1,000) W or give way to full-power stations that would provide more services to more listeners. By the mid-1990s, only a handful of the old Class D stations remained, and most of those were preparing to use the required higher amounts of power.

A model for what could develop with radio was borrowed from television. As a result of experiments originating in Canada in the 1970s, the FCC became interested in and eventually approved a class of low-power television stations in the early 1980s. These were to use very low power on VHF channels or up to about 1,000 W on UHF channels that would be "dropped in" among already allotted full-power channels in such a way as to keep interference at a minimum. After years of legal wrangling over how best to handle the mountain of conflicting applications, the FCC was granted the right to hold lotteries among mutually exclusive applications. By 2000 there were hundreds of low-power television outlets on the air, some providing original programs but many connected by satellite and offering typical entertainment programs otherwise not receivable in isolated rural areas.

Ted Coopman (1999) tells of the beginning of the modern microradio movement:

> The modern micro broadcasting movement began on November 25, 1986 in a public housing development in Springfield, IL. Put on the air for about $600, the one-watt station broadcast openly on 107.1 FM as Black Liberation Radio (now Human Rights Radio). The operator, Mbanna Kantako, a legally blind African-American in his mid-thirties, started the station because he felt that the African-American community in Springfield was not being served by the local media. Kantako felt that because the African-American community had a high illiteracy rate, radio would be the best way to reach this community.

According to FRB founder Dunifer, the goal of the microradio movement was to have so many transmitters in use across the country that the FCC would be overwhelmed, finding itself in a situation similar to one it faced in the early 1970s, when the FCC was unable to control the widely popular citizens band radio service. Licensing for that service was eventually dropped. Unlike the "pirates" of the past, who hid from the FCC, microradio proponents act in open defiance of the law, challenging the government to arrest them, to shut

them down. They believe that they are entitled to the airwaves; that they are shut out of the current allocation of FM licenses; and that, because of scarcity and resulting high cost, licenses are available only to the wealthy.

Dunifer was successful in convincing the National Lawyers Guild that the right to broadcast was a civil rights issue, one of giving access to all people, especially those disenfranchised by licensed media. In 1993 Dunifer's ten-watt radio station started operation at 104.1 FM, offering music and political commentary while actively challenging the FCC. In June 1993, the FCC issued a *Notice of Apparent Liability* to Dunifer for unlicensed broadcasting and fined him $20,000. Dunifer was represented by the Lawyers Guild, and in 1995 a U.S. district court in Oakland, California, heard arguments on constitutional issues in Dunifer's case, arguments stating that the FCC had not proved that his broadcasts caused harm to licensed broadcasters. The FCC responded, saying that siding with Dunifer would cause thousands more to go on the air, and the resulting interference would be chaotic.

The attorney arguing the case for Dunifer raised other issues in the hearing that would eventually cause the FCC to study the possibility of a licensed low-power FM service. One such issue was that the 1978 elimination of the Class D ten-watt educational license in favor of licenses for stations over 100 W was overly restrictive and violated Dunifer's First Amendment right to free speech. It was argued that the commission's failure to provide a low-power service did not provide for the public interest, convenience, and necessity required under the Communications Act of 1934. It was further argued that the financial qualifications required for an FM station license violated the equal protection clause of the Constitution. The FCC disagreed on all counts.

In November 1997 Federal District Judge Claudia Wilken ruled in favor of Dunifer, saying the FCC had failed to prove Dunifer had done harm to existing broadcasters. Buoyed by this victory, Dunifer continued to help others get on the air and to promote the creation of a low-power service. But in June 1998 the FCC prevailed in court, and Dunifer was taken off the air, based on the fact that he had applied for neither a license nor a waiver to broadcast and therefore lacked standing to challenge the FCC. In July 1999 Dunifer's attorneys appealed, arguing that the FCC had not acted in good faith when dealing with microradio, citing as evidence a San Francisco applicant's request for such a license, which had been ignored by the FCC.

Development of the microradio movement has been based on a common belief that stations very low in power escape the jurisdiction of the FCC. This misconception is based on Part 15, Subpart D of the FCC rules, which permits unlicensed operation of very low power transmitters. This rule only allows, however, for an effective service range of 35 to 100 feet in the FM band. On AM frequencies, unlicensed transmitters cannot cover a radius larger than about 200 to 250 feet. The FCC argues that if microradio stations are able to reach listeners, they are almost certainly operating illegally.

Low-Power FM

As the number of microradio stations grew and complaints from the National Association of Broadcasters (NAB) increased, the FCC closed a number of unlicensed microradio operations. Both the protests and the microbroadcasting movement continued to grow, however. Media reports suggested that between 500 and 1,000 microradio stations were on the air in 1998, although five years earlier only a handful existed.

In spite of NAB protests, FCC Chair William E. Kennard suggested that proposals to establish a legal microbroadcasting service were worthy of consideration. The FCC issued a *Notice of Proposed Rulemaking* on 28 January 1999 to authorize an LPFM broadcast service. The FCC's *Notice* cited concern about the increasing concentration of ownership of media properties, with concomitant loss of diversity, in addition to suggesting that smaller communities outside metropolitan areas were often deprived of local focus in programming.

In response to its *Notice*, the FCC received thousands of comments representing the views of community groups, labor unions, religious organizations, state and local government, and others. The commission announced that response to the petition had indicated a broad interest throughout the country in the LPFM proposal. Further, the commission's webpage on "Low Power Broadcast Radio Stations" was accessed more than 15,000 times in 1998 alone. The FCC received thousands of additional phone and mail inquiries each year regarding the legality of low-power broadcasting.

The commission's decision was released on 20 January 2000 with the announcement that such a service would, in fact, be established. The FCC's vote created an entirely new type of radio station, one with the intention of enhancing service to underrepresented groups and local communities. The FCC's restrictions were as follows:

These (LPFM) stations are authorized for noncommercial educational broadcasting only (no commercial operation) and operate with an effective radiated power (ERP) of 100 W (0.1 kilowatts) or less, with maximum facilities of 100 W ERP at 30 meters (100 feet) antenna height above average terrain (HAAT). The approximate service range of a 100 W LPFM station is 5.6 kilometers (3.5 miles radius). LPFM stations are not protected from interference that may be received from other classes of FM stations.

(www.fcc.org)

However, late in 2000, under pressure from both the NAB and National Public Radio, Congress passed the Radio Broadcasting Preservation Act which severely restricted the frequencies that LPFM outlets could use. Fearing that a mass introduction of low-powered stations could interfere with existing broadcast signals, especially in urban areas, the Act imposed a rule stating that new stations had to be positioned on the spectrum at least two channels away from already existing (and, presumably, more high-powered) FM stations. What this "third-adjacent channel" clause did essentially was to restrict LPFM almost exclusively to rural areas, as spectrum density in cities meant there was not enough space to allow for the inclusion of additional signals.

As Congress passed this law, it also ordered the FCC to investigate its assumptions. In turn, the FCC hired the Mitre Corporation to study the issue. The resulting Mitre Report (as it has come to be called) was released in 2003 and concluded that the "third adjacent" rule was overly restrictive and that any interference caused by LPFM stations operating in closer proximity to existing signals would be negligible.

Several times during the early 2000s, legislation was introduced to lift the restrictions created by the Broadcasting Perseveration Act. Despite the Mitre Report's conclusions, the NAB has repeatedly vowed to challenge any such legislation, arguing that more than 200 million weekly listeners to local radio should not be inundated with "inevitable" interference that would result from shoehorning more stations onto an already overcrowded radio dial. In November 2007, the FCC issued a report which, among other clarifications, called for Congress to repeal the third adjacent rule.

Several years after the initial announcement of the Low Power (LPFM) service, the FCC had received several thousand applications. Most of the applicants have been from religious organizations, the rest from community foundations and educational entities. Most applications have been in the L1 category, 100 W or less. Only a few have been under the L2 designation, 10 W or less.

While at least some of the original impetus for the LPFM service was to either legitimize or remove from the air the so-called pirates or micro broadcasters, based on the list of applicants, CPs and licenses issued, many observers suggest that the following will likely happen: former big city pirate/micro broadcasters will not receive licenses due to interference concerns in crowded FM markets; most licensees will be religious organizations, schools, and community foundations. And if the experience from the educational FM "boom" of the 1970s is repeated, most of these LPFM broadcasters will eventually lose interest and funding and abandon their licenses, many of which will be taken over by larger NPR broadcasters and well-funded networks and religious organizations.

See also: College Radio; Community Radio; FM Radio; Licensing Authorizing U.S. Stations to Broadcast; Localism in Radio; Ten-Watt Stations

Further Reading

Coopman, Ted M., "FCC Enforcement Difficulties with Unlicensed Micro Radio," *Journal of Broadcasting and Electronic Media* 43, no. 4 (Fall 1999).
The Free Radio Network: Pirate Radio Top 20 Links of All Time www.frn.net/links
New York Free Media Alliance Microradio Documents artcon.rutgers.edu/papertiger/nyfma/str/links.html
Opel, Andy, *Micro Radio and the FCC: Media Activism and the Struggle over Broadcast Policy.* Westport, Connecticut: Praeger, 2004.
Rogue Radio Research: Research and Resources on Micro Radio/Low Power FM www.rougecom.com/rougeradio/
Sakolsky, Ron, "Anarchy on the Airwaves: A Brief History of the Micro Radio Movement in the USA," *Social Anarchism* 17 (July 1992).
Sakolsky, Ron, and Stephen Dunifer, *Seizing the Airwaves: A Free Radio Handbook*, Edinburgh and San Francisco, California: AK Press, 1998.
Soley, Lawrence, *Free Radio*, Denver, Colorado: Westview, 1999.
Yoder, Andrew R., *Pirate Radio Stations: Tuning In to Underground Broadcasts*, New York: McGraw-Hill Professional, 1990.

MICHAEL H. ADAMS AND STEVEN PHIPPS,
2009 REVISIONS BY CARY O'DELL

LUM 'N' ABNER
Comedy Show

A party line rings, two "backwoods" voices respond ("I-grannies, Abner, I believe that's our ring." "I-doggies, Lum, I believe you're right."), and the announcer gently brings us up to date with the latest events here in Pine Ridge, Arkansas, home of the "Jot 'Em Down Store" run by

Columbus "Lum" Edwards and Abner Peabody. On *Lum 'n' Abner*, Chester Lauck (Lum) and Norris "Tuffy" Goff (Abner) performed their homespun country characters for more than 20 years, starting on a local Arkansas station and eventually airing for a time on every major radio network. Lauck and Goff met as boys in a Mena, Arkansas, grade school, and they were performing impressions and blackface comedy together by the early 1920s. In 1931 an Arkansas radio station invited locals to perform for a flood-relief benefit, and Lauck and Goff planned to do their blackface act. Seeing the station overrun with other blackface teams, they instead performed an "Ozarkian humor" routine to great listener response. They were signed to a weekly 15-minute program on KTHS in Hot Springs, Arkansas, and by late summer of that year they had both a sponsor (Quaker Oats) and a foothold on a regional National Broadcasting Company (NBC) station, Chicago's WMAQ. From then on, *Lum 'n' Abner* became an increasingly hot property; whenever Lauck and Goff were not pleased with their time slot, pay, or sponsor, another network gladly wooed them away.

The show's style was wry and folksy, deriving much of its humor from a combination of misfiring schemes and "countrified" misunderstandings of aspects of the everyday lives of their listeners, as when Lum and Abner try to do their taxes or when the town blacksmith, Cedric Weehunt (Lauck), tries to become a ventriloquist without realizing that ventriloquists are supposed to change the dummy's voice and try not to move their lips. The characters were not stooges, though (despite Abner's regular catchphrase—"Huh?"—often uttered after Lum's long and involved explanation of his latest plan): the folks of Pine Ridge always ended up on top. There was a gentle tone to the humor and a relaxed pace to the steadily rolling plot arcs that made the program a long-lived and reliable performer in the ratings.

Some plotlines were self-contained in a single episode, as when Lum and Abner struggle to do their 1942 taxes, first concluding that they owe "the givverment" 8,912 sacks of sugar, then realizing that the government actually owes them (though they decide instead to send along the extra cash in the till to help the war effort). However, more often the plots wove their way onward for weeks, as when the town's richest man, Diogenes Smith, holds a campaign to discover and reward the kindest person in town, which begins a complex train of events in which Lum eventually becomes an unwitting courier of counterfeit money.

Lauck and Goff performed the voices of most of the program's major characters. In fact, for the first six years they performed all of the characters, and those they did not perform (the female characters in particular) were only talked about in the store and never actually appeared on the show. NBC executives were continually pushing to broaden the program's scope; one 1933 memo read, "I have impressed upon the boys the necessity of more action and other characters. Their scripts from now on will have both. They are afraid of women characters, for they feel they can't write the dialogue. However, we will work hard to accomplish this." In the late 1930s female characters did begin to appear occasionally, most often voiced by Lurene Tuttle.

The program was particularly popular in its home setting, rural Arkansas. In 1936, to celebrate *Lum 'n' Abner*'s fifth anniversary on the air, the unincorporated Arkansas town of Waters officially changed its name to Pine Ridge at a ceremony attended most notably by the governor of Arkansas, Lauck, Goff, and town resident Dick Huddleston, a fictionalized version of whom was voiced by Goff on the program. To this day one can visit the "Jot 'Em Down Store" in Pine Ridge, which serves as a *Lum 'n' Abner* museum and which is where the National Lum and Abner Society holds conventions for aficionados. There is also a country store in Kentucky's Fayette County that styles itself the "Jot 'Em Down Store" it dates back to a 1937 visit by Lauck and Goff on their way through the area to buy some horses.

The show's popularity was parlayed over the years into a series of seven feature films starring Lauck and Goff (with appearances by performers such as Zasu Pitts, Grady Sutton, Franklin Pangborn, and Barbara Hale) and produced by RKO, beginning with *Dreaming Out Loud* in 1940 and ending with *Partners in Time* in 1946. One additional film was released by "Howco Productions" much later, in 1956, an odd installment that found Lum and Abner out of the familiar territory of Pine Ridge, traveling to Paris and Monte Carlo. It was actually an edited-together version of three *Lum 'n' Abner* television pilots that the Columbia Broadcasting System (CBS) had originally produced in 1949 to no great acclaim.

In late 1948, during its second stint on CBS, *Lum 'n' Abner* changed from its 15-minute serial-comedy format to a half-hour comedy variety program, including for the first time such trappings as an orchestra and a studio audience. This was how the program seemed to end its days, going off the air in the spring of 1950. But three years later it reappeared once more in its traditional 15-minute format, first for a limited 13-week series and then for a final six-month run.

Lum 'n' Abner is one of the radio programs for which many recordings and scripts still survive. Some tapes are available from commercial sources, but there are also thriving collections circulating in the hands of ordinary fans. *Lum 'n' Abner* may not have the instant modern name recognition of programs such as *Amos 'n' Andy*, but it has made its mark—not only among radio fans, but also on the map of the United States.

Cast

Columbus "Lum" Edwards, Cedric Weehunt, Grandpappy Spears, Snake Hogan	Chester Lauck
Abner Peabody, Squire Skimp, Dick Huddleston, Mousey Gray, Doc Miller	Norris Goff
Ellie Conners, Sgt. V.W. Hartford, Nurse Lunsford	Lurene Tuttle
Diogenes Smith, B.J. Webster, Mr. Sutton	Frank Graham
Detective Wilson, Dr. Roller, Pest Controller, Mr. Talbert, FCC Man	Howard McNear
Duncan Hines, W.J. Chancellor	Francis X. Bushman
Ira Hodgekins, Caleb Weehunt	Horace Murphy
The Baby, J.W. Tiffin	Jerry Hausner
Mr. Talbert's Father	Ken Christy
Dr. Samuel Snide (dentist)	Eddie Holden
Doc Ben Withers (veterinarian)	Clarence Hartzell
Lady Brilton	Edna Best
Rowena	Isabel Randolph
Otis Bagley	Dink Trout

Announcers

Tom Nobles (1931), Charles Lyon (1931), Del Sharbutt (1931–33), Gene Hamilton (1933–34), Carlton Brickert (1934–38), Lou Crosby (1938–44), Gene Baker (1944–45), Forrest Owen (1945–48), Wynden Niles (1948–50), Bill Ewing (1953–54)

Producer

Larry Berns

Directors

Bill Gay, Robert McInnes, Forrest Owen

Writers

Betty Boyle, Norris Goff, Chester Lauck, Roz Rogers, Jay Sommers, Howard Snyder, Hugh Wedlock, Jr.

Programming History

26 April 1931–7 May 1954 (many changes in network and time slots)

Further Reading

"Amid the Native Corn," *Newsweek* (6 October 1947).

Crawford, Byron, "Setting Store by a Name," *Courier-Journal* (Louisville, Kentucky, 24 May 1991).

Hall, Randal L. *Lum & Abner: Rural America and the Golden Age of Radio*. Lexington: University Press of Kentucky, 2007.

Lum 'n' Abner: Frigidaire Announces Sponsorship," *New York Times* (18 August 1948).

"*Lum 'n' Abner* to End," *New York Times* (30 June 1948).

Salomonson, Terry G.G., *The Lum 'n' Abner Program: A Radio Broadcast Log of the Comedy Drama Program*, Howell, Michigan: Salomonson, 1997.

DORINDA HARTMANN

LUX RADIO THEATER
Anthology Drama

One of the most popular and prestigious radio programs for two decades, *Lux Radio Theater* was a dramatic anthology that mainly presented movie adaptations with big-name Hollywood stars.

Lever Brothers had been using celebrities to endorse its Lux Toilet Soap in magazine ads throughout the 1920s, and in 1934 the J. Walter Thompson Advertising Agency proposed to Lever Brothers an extension of this promotional tactic, the sponsorship of a radio drama presenting stars of the stage and screen. The resulting program, *Lux Radio Theater*, aired on the National Broadcasting Company (NBC) and originated from downtown Manhattan, premiering on 14 October 1934. Given its New York locale, the program presented mostly Broadway talent and properties in this early period. During the first season, the show's host was a fictitious character named Douglass Garrick, played by John Anthony and billed as the show's producer. Peggy Winthrop, another fictional character played by Doris Dagmar, supplied commercials. In addition to commercials, the show's framework included a scripted chat session between Garrick and each particular episode's stars.

By the end of its first season, *Lux Radio Theater* was a critical success, but given their sizable investment in the show, Lever Brothers had hoped for higher listener ratings. When the Columbia Broadcasting System (CBS) offered them the advantageous 9 P.M. Monday night slot, *Lux* made the switch to that network and time. The second season brought a few other changes: a new actor, Albert Hayes, played Douglass Garrick; Art Millett was added as announcer; and the Peggy Winthrop character was eliminated.

By the end of the 1935–36 season, ratings still were not where Lever Brothers wanted them. Under the assumption that film stars would draw larger national audiences than Broadway stars, in 1936 *Lux* moved to Hollywood, specifically to the Music Box Theater on Hollywood Boulevard. Producers also hoped to bring in a famous Hollywood name to replace the Douglass Garrick figure as host. They settled on famed movie director Cecil B. DeMille, who, although he was assigned the title of producer, was simply a host figure and often appeared only for dress rehearsals and the actual recordings. It was hoped that DeMille's famed persona as creative tour de force would help lend a prestigious, glamorous image to the show. Additionally, by specifically presenting him as a producer, essentially an authorial voice, *Lux Radio Theater* posed the show as a first-rate cultural experience on par with DeMille's epic film productions. Equally important, framing DeMille as a creative force helped to elide the fact that the show was really created by an ad agency concerned mainly with advertising revenue, rather than solely a culturally beneficial endeavor.

As a result of these changes, the 1936–37 season brought a plethora of stars in movie adaptations, such as Errol Flynn and Olivia de Havilland in "Captain Blood," Irene Dunne and Robert Taylor in "Magnificent Obsession," and Fredric March and Jean Arthur in "The Plainsman." Cooperation between J. Walter Thompson and the Hollywood studios made this possible. The studios would offer the broadcast rights to film properties for a fee (usually no more than $1,000), though sometimes the rights would be offered for free in exchange for publicity on the air. The show's most substantial expense came from talent costs. DeMille made $2,000 per show in this period, and each headlining star received $5,000. (The average yearly salary in the U.S. in 1937 was $1,327.00) Given that a minimum of two headliners per episode was the general rule, talent costs could reach as high as $20,000 per episode.

In 1940 *Lux Radio Theater* changed recording facilities to the Vine Street Playhouse. This venue offered a more spacious stage, and the actors would thus all stand on the stage throughout the whole program, even if their parts were completed in the first act. DeMille sat off to the side at a card table, and an offstage mike provided sound effects and some commercials. The New York version of the show had not been presented in front of an audience, and a change in this policy upon the move to Hollywood resulted in a furious weekly demand for tickets.

The next period of upheaval for *Lux Radio Theater* came in 1944, when DeMille left the show. His departure stemmed from a dispute with the American Federation of Radio Artists (AFRA). A proposition on that year's state election ballot would have allowed a Californian the right to obtain employment without first gaining union affiliation. AFRA strongly opposed this measure and charged all members $1 to fund a battle against its passage. The right-wing DeMille resolutely objected both to AFRA's stance and to their demand that members fund it, and he refused to pay his dollar. This resulted in a suspension of his AFRA membership, meaning he was also barred from any radio work. *Lux* first turned to guest hosts in the interim, including Brian Aherne and Lionel Barrymore, but when it became clear that neither AFRA nor DeMille would relent, the producers settled on a permanent host in William Keighley, a lesser-known Hollywood director. Keighley took on DeMille's role as host and faux-producer; however, he could never match the famed director's prestigious presence and vaunted image.

Keighley retired in 1952 and was replaced by Irving Cummings, a fellow Hollywood director. However, *Lux Radio Theater*'s ratings began a precipitous slide, particularly into 1954, as Lever Brothers and J. Walter Thompson were giving more attention and money to the television version of the program, *Lux Video Theater* (1950–57). In 1954, NBC reclaimed *Lux Radio Theater* and tried to resurrect the show's stately image with a marketing campaign and presentation of "twenty of the greatest Hollywood pictures" during the 1954–55 season. However, this did little to stem the show's decline, and the show aired its final broadcast on 7 June 1955. The television version carried on until 1957, but it never reached the popularity of the radio version, particularly because it could not offer the caliber of stars the radio show had. Only the radio version could tout a history of 926 episodes starring the most famous talent of the era.

Cast

Host "Douglass Garrick"	John Anthony (1934–35)
Other Hosts	Cecil B. DeMille (1936–45), William Keighley (1945–52), Irving Cummings (1952–55), Lionel Barrymore (1945), Walter Huston (1945), Mark Hellinger (1945), Brian Aherne (1945), Irving Pichel (1945)
Announcers	Melville Ruick (1936–40), John Milton Kennedy (1940s), Ken Carpenter (later years)

Directors

Antony Stanford (1934–36), Frank Woodruff (1943), Fred MacKaye (1944–51), Earl Ebi (1951–55)

Programming History

NBC Blue	October 1934–June 1935
CBS	July 1935–June 1954
NBC	September 1954–June 1955

Further Reading

Billips, Connie J., and Arthur Pierce, *Lux Presents Hollywood: A Show-by-Show History of the Lux Radio Theater and the Lux Video Theater, 1934–1957*, Jefferson, North Carolina: McFarland, 1995.

DeMille, Cecil B., *The Autobiography of Cecil B. DeMille*, edited by Donald Hayne, Englewood Cliffs, New Jersey: Prentice-Hall, 1959; London: Allen, 1960.

Hilmes, Michele, *Radio Voices: American Broadcasting, 1922–1952*, Minneapolis: University of Minnesota Press, 1997.

Jewell, Richard B., "Hollywood and Radio: Competition and Partnership in the 1930s," *Historical Journal of Film, Radio, and Television* 4, no. 2 (1984).

CHRISTINE BECKER

M

MAGAZINES
See: Fan Magazines; Trade Press

MA PERKINS
Serial Drama/Soap Opera

A widow whose homespun wisdom guided her family, friends, and neighbors in the fictitious rural community of Rushville Center, *Ma Perkins* was also one of radio's most enduring soap operas, captivating American and, at times, overseas audiences for 27 years, from 1933 to 1960. Throughout its entire run of 7,065 episodes, Virginia Payne portrayed the leading character.

A 15-minute daytime serial drama, *Ma Perkins* premiered on NBC radio on 4 December 1933, three months after its local debut on WLW in Cincinnati, Ohio. Cincinnati-based Procter and Gamble Company, makers of Oxydol soap flakes, initially sponsored the broadcast. The drama was so popular it was picked up by competing networks, CBS and Mutual, at various times, while continuing its broadcasts on NBC as well. CBS acquired exclusive rights to the show in 1949, where it remained until its final broadcast in 1960.

Ma had three children, John, Fay and Evey, whose husband Willie Fitz (portrayed by Murray Forbes, also for all 27 years of the broadcast) managed Ma's lumber yard business. Shuffle Shober, Ma's business partner, was portrayed by Charles Egleston for 25 years, until his death in 1958. Edwin Wolfe succeeded him for the remaining run of the show. Writer Orin Tovrov wrote the scripts for more than 20 years.

Ma Perkins' roots can be traced not only to Cincinnati, but also to Chicago, where advertising executives Frank and Anne Hummert created the program. It was in Chicago that the Hummerts also originated other popular daytime drama serials in the early 1930s, including *The Romance of Helen Trent* and *Just Plain Bill*. Though each of the serials offered different characters with different story lines, they were all products of the Hummerts' desire to present familiar themes that had proven popular with Depression-era listeners seeking some measure of assurance and security in an unstable world. According to Marilyn Matelski, the Hummert approach was a simple formula. "[It] combined fantasies of exotic romance, pathos and suspense with a familiar environment of everyday life in a small-town or rural setting. Combined with an identifiable hero or heroine, this formula produced an overwhelming audience response" (see Matelski, 1988).

The story lines for *Ma Perkins* often reflected the turbulence of the times. In one broadcast during World War II, for example, Ma learns that her son John was killed in combat in Europe. The "news" prompted a flood of letters from devoted listeners expressing their sympathy. Throughout its run, *Ma Perkins* conveyed the vulnerability of life in ways not depicted before on radio. It did so while reaffirming the belief that people could solve their problems so long as they believed in one another. In 1938, Ma offered this observation: "Anyone of this earth who's done wrong, and then goes so far as to right that wrong, I can tell you that they're well on their way to erasing the harm they did in the eyes of anyone decent."

Virginia Payne was only 23 years old when the serial drama premiered, and, remarkably, she never missed a performance in its 27-year run. A Cincinnati native and graduate of the University of Cincinnati, she faithfully dressed the part at countless public appearances and even personally answered many of her listeners' letters. Her down-home language included such expressions as "I ain't sure I understand it" and "Land sakes!"

U.S. audience interest in radio soap operas declined during the 1950s because of the growth of television, and *Ma Perkins* was no exception. By 1960 CBS radio cut three of its ten serials, and NBC dropped its last surviving soap opera; ABC had ended all of its daytime serials the year before. The sponsors that owned the programs abandoned radio in favor of television because of its increasing audience appeal. The transition to television created a vacuum in radio advertising sales, and by 1960 only one-quarter of network radio advertising time was being sold. Local radio, meanwhile, was blossoming: disc jockeys replaced radio network programs in large numbers by the end of the 1950s, and radio station managers discovered that the locally hosted music program proved cheaper for advertisers and more popular to listeners as well. By the 1955–56 season, *Ma Perkins'* radio audience share had fallen to one-quarter of its all-time high in 1944–45. On 25 November 1960, the show's final broadcast featured the family at its traditional Thanksgiving meal:

> "I look around the table at my loved ones and to me the table stretches on and on. Over beyond the other end past Shuffle I see faces somehow familiar and yet unborn, except in the mind of God Someday, Fay will be sitting here where I'm sitting, or Evey, or Paulette They'll move up into my place and I'll be gone, but I find right and peace in that knowledge I give thanks that I've been given this gift of life, this gift of time to play my little part in it," Ma said at the table.

Virginia Payne was only 50 years old when *Ma Perkins* ended. During the 1960s and 1970s she remained active in showbusiness, appearing in radio commercials and touring in such productions as *Life With Father, Becket*, and *Oklahoma!* Shortly before her death in Cincinnati on 10 February 1977, she appeared on radio one last time on *The CBS Radio Mystery Theater*.

See also: Soap Opera

Cast

Ma Perkins	Virginia Payne
Fay Perkins Henderson	Rita Ascot; Marjorie Hannan; Cheer Brentson; Laurette Fillbrandt; Margaret Draper
Evey Perkins Fitz	Dora Johnson; Laurette Fillbrandt; Kay Campbell
John Perkins	Gilbert Faust
Shuffle Shober	Charles Egleston (1933–58); Edwin Wolfe (1958–60)
Willie Fitz	Murray Forbes
Junior Fitz	Cecil Roy; Arthur Young; Bobby Ellis
Paulette Henderson	Nannette Sargent; Judith Lockser
Augustus Pendleton	Maurice Copeland
Mathilda Pendleton	Beverly Younger
Gladys Pendleton	Patricia Dunlap; Helen Lewis
Paul Henderson	Jonathan Holoe
Gregory Ivanoff	McKay Morris
Gary Curtis	Rye Billsbury
Charley Brown	Ray Suber
Tom Wells	John Larkin; Casey Allen

Announcers

Bob Brown, Jack Brinkley, Dick Wells, Marvin Miller, Dan Donaldson

Producers/Creators

Frank and Anne Hummert; Robert Hardy Andrews

Writers

Robert Hardy Andrews, Lee Gebhart, Lester Huntley, Natalie Johnson, and Orin Tovrov

Programming History

WLW, Cincinnati, Ohio	August 1933–December 1933
NBC	1933–49
NBC Blue	February 1937–December 1937; June 1938–November 1938
CBS	January 1938–May 1938; September 1942–November 1960
Mutual	1935–36

Further Reading

Allen, Robert Clyde, *Speaking of Soap Operas*, Chapel Hill: University of North Carolina Press, 1985.

Cox, Jim, *The Great Radio Soap Operas*, Jefferson, North Carolina: McFarland, 1999.

Edmondson, Madeleine, and David Rounds, *The Soaps: Daytime Serials of Radio and TV*, New York: Stein and Day, 1973.

LaGuardia, Robert, *From Ma Perkins to Mary Hartman: The Illustrated History of Soap Operas*, New York: Ballantine Books, 1977.

Matelski, Marilyn J., *The Soap Opera Evolution: America's Enduring Romance with Daytime Drama*, Jefferson, North Carolina: McFarland, 1988.

Stedman, Raymond William, *The Serials: Suspense and Drama by Installment*, Norman: University of Oklahoma Press, 1971; 2nd edition, 1977.

Stumpf, Charles K., *Ma Perkins, Little Orphan Annie, and Heigh-Ho Silver*, New York: Carlton Press, 1971.

DAVID MCCARTNEY

MARCH OF TIME
Docudrama Series

The March of Time, a radio forerunner of today's television "docudramas," was a widely heard and imitated news dramatization program—a "radio newsreel"—that lasted 14 seasons on network radio (1931–45) and led to a famous motion picture documentary series of the same name. *The March of Time* is best remembered by the words of the title spoken by the mellifluous narrator Westbrook Van Voorhis, who also spoke on the newsreel version and ended both by saying "Time marches on."

Origins

The idea for a digest of the news for radio broadcast originated with Fred Smith, the first station director at WLW in Cincinnati. Smith wrote and directed dramas for WLW and introduced many program ideas at the station. In 1925 he hit upon the novel idea of reading various items taken (without permission) from newspapers and magazines. Smith called the program *Musical News;* after each story, a brief musical piece was played by the staff organist.

About the same time, a similar idea was put into print in a new kind of weekly magazine. Henry R. Luce and Briton Hadden, friends since prep school and Yale, quit their jobs at the *Baltimore News* in 1922 to found a magazine that summarized the week's news—an idea they had discussed since their days in boot camp during World War I. The magazine was *Time*, and its first issue appeared 3 March 1923. (Luce ran *Time* alone after the death of Briton Hadden in 1929.)

In 1928, Fred Smith at WLW got permission from *Time* to use an advance, or "makeready," copy of the magazine sent to him by airmail (then just begun) so that he could rewrite items for a weekly news summary on WLW. Soon Smith was hired by Time Incorporated and traveling the Midwest, signing up stations for a daily news summary the magazine would syndicate to radio stations. Beginning on 3 September 1928, 10-minute scripts were delivered by airmail to be read by local announcers on more than 60 stations. In New York, WOR called the program *NewsCasting* and broadcast it from 5:50 P.M. to 6:00 P.M., Monday through Friday. Smith himself was WOR's reader for the first year.

The radio program's title was apparently the first use of the word *newscast*, and it was listed in the *New York Times* radio logs by that title. While at WLW, Smith had coined *radarios*, after *radio* and *scenario*, for original radio plays he wrote and produced. (*Time* was even better known for its neologisms, coining *cinemaddict, newsmagazine,* and *socialite*, among others.) By the spring of 1929, the 10-minute summaries were being carried on as many as 90 stations (up from 60 stations just a half-year earlier)—the first large-scale regular daily news broadcast carried in the United States—but it was never a true network program because each station developed its own script.

Fred Smith next conceived dramatizing the news. In September 1929 he produced a five-minute "news drama" in cooperation with *Time* and submitted his audition program to a number of stations with the title *NewsActing*. Although *newsacting* did not become a household word, the program idea caught on. By December 1929 Smith and a crew of six to eight actors were producing a weekly five-minute drama for distribution by electrical transcription. These programs were not full-scale dramatic productions, but they included sound effects, occasional music, and the portrayal of the voices of actual people involved in the news stories. Within a few months the *NewsActing* records were being broadcast over more than 100 stations nationwide. At the time, other network programs were dramatizing history, but none had tried a weekly presentation of current news.

Henry Luce wanted to advertise *Time* on the radio networks, and on 6 February 1931, an experimental program was sent via telephone wires to the home of a Time Inc. executive where a small group was gathered that included CBS president William S. Paley. Exactly a month later, on Friday, 6 March 1931, *The March of Time* was fed from CBS's New York studios and carried on 20 of the network's affiliates (there were then about 80) at 10:30 P.M. EST. (The program's title was taken

from a Broadway show tune of the same name.)
After a five-second fanfare, the announcer said:

> The March of Time. On a thousand fronts the events of
> the world move swiftly forward. Tonight the editors
> of *Time*, the weekly newsmagazine, attempt a new kind
> of reporting of the news, the re-enacting as clearly and
> dramatically as the medium of radio will permit some
> themes from the news of the week.

Network Years

This first program dramatized the re-election of
William "Big Bill" Thompson as mayor of Chicago, the sudden death of the *New York World* by
merging with the *New York Telegram*, and shorter
segments on French prisoners sent to Devil's Island,
revolution in Spain, prison reform in Romania, a
roundup of news of royalty, an auction of Czarist
possessions in New York, and the closing of the
71st United States Congress.

During the first season the program ran 13
weeks. It returned on 8 September 1932, but as a
sustaining feature because *Time* executives had
decided that they could not afford advertising, which
they said the magazine no longer needed. In the
magazine the editors justified the radio show's cancellation by asking, "should a few (400,000 *Time*
subscribers) pay for the entertainment of many
(9,000,000 radiowners)?" In the 29 February 1932
issue, *Time* also argued, "For all its blatant claims
to being a medium of education, radio contributes
little of its own beyond the considerable service of
bringing good music to millions." In November
1932 the magazine resumed its sponsorship. *The
March of Time* did its part to promote magazine
sales: at the end of each program, listeners were
reminded that they could find more details in the
issue of *Time* magazine soon to be on news-stands.

On 1 February 1935, *The March of Time* newsreel began as a monthly film series in movie theaters.
It began as a typical newsreel with several items in
each issue, but the January 1938 issue focused on a
single topic, "Inside Nazi Germany." After October
1938, single subjects were being treated exclusively
as the series became a documentary rather than
strictly a news series. The documentary series ran
until 1951. Time Inc. also produced historical television documentary series, such as *Crusade in
Europe*, based on the book by General Dwight D.
Eisenhower (1948). The title *The March of Time*
was also used for a syndicated series of television
documentaries produced by David Wolper.

During the 1933–34 season, *The March of Time*
was sponsored by Remington-Rand, and Westbrook

Van Voorhis became the voice of the program. In
1935 there was a variety of sponsors when a daily
15-minute version was tried for one season. In 1938
the program was sponsored by Time Inc.'s *Life*
magazine (purchased by Luce in 1936), and the
announcer worked that title in to the opening of the
program: "Life! The life of the world, its conflicts
and achievements, its news and fun, its leaders and
its common people." The program was not aired
during the 1939–40 and 1940–41 seasons. After
seven years on CBS, it moved to the NBC Blue
network. In July 1942 the format was changed to
only one or two dramatized segments and many
more live, on-the-spot news reports. By the 1944–45
season, *The March of Time*'s last, listeners were
hearing the actual voices of newsmakers on many
network programs.

At the century's end much was being made of
the "synergy" of cross-media ties, the idea being
that the interaction of a media corporation's units
(say, a magazine division feeding story ideas to a
film company) would encourage the making of
products and profits greater than the sum of the
corporation's parts could make by acting alone. *The
March of Time* was one of the first examples of
synergy. Fred Smith's idea of reading a few news
items accompanied by musical selections that became
Musical News, NewsCasting, NewsActing, and *The
March of Time* led to the many "dramatized news"
programs—documentaries and docudramas—on
television today.

See also: Documentary Programs; News

Narrators

Ted Husing, Westbrook Van Voorhis, Harry Von Zell

Programming History

CBS	1931–39
NBC Blue	1941–45

Further Reading

Bohn, Thomas W., and Lawrence W. Lichty, "The March of
  Time: News As Drama," *Journal of Popular Film* 2, no.
  4 (Fall 1973).
Fielding, Raymond, *The American Newsreel, 1911–1967*,
  Norman: University of Oklahoma Press, 1972.
Fielding, Raymond, *The March of Time, 1935–1951*, New
  York: Oxford University Press, 1978.
Lichty, Lawrence W., and Thomas W. Bohn, "Radio's
  March of Time: Dramatized News," *Journalism
  Quarterly* 51, no. 3 (Autumn 1974).

LAWRENCE W. LICHTY

MARKET

Radio markets are defined in geographic, demographic, and psychographic terms. Often, the definition of a radio market involves all three factors.

The primary definition of a market for radio is geographic—the area served by the transmitter's coverage, whether one city, a group of counties, or an entire region. Within that "market," the station establishes its listener base and sells advertising to attract those listeners to area retailers.

The second definition for radio derives from the medium's ability to target individual audience segments. Demographically drawn markets allow stations to focus programming on specific age groups: young adult women, for example, or teenagers. National radio programs define their markets using demographics.

Some markets defy geography and demography and consist of people of similar interests and tastes—psychographics. These similarities are often referred to as "lifestyle characteristics." However, consultant George A. Burns cautions radio marketers to understand the differences: "A group of nude skydivers may have only that in common. Their radio tastes can vary widely. While there may be broad commonalities among listeners to an individual radio station, it seems almost impossible to define them." Burns (1980) suggested that lifestyle characteristics of a particular group *converge at an individual radio station, as far as radio listening is concerned.*

As radio emerged in the 1930s as a viable—and valuable—medium for advertisers, geographic divisions were the most effective and most often used because of network radio's national reach. A 1939 promotional flyer from the National Broadcasting Company (NBC) showed the percentage of radio ownership in each of nine regions of the United States. The same flyer divided radio families by each of the four standard time zones, by size of city, and by whether listeners were in rural or urban locations.

Geography

The specific geographical definition of a market begins with guidelines set by the U.S. government's Office of Management and Budget (OMB). Radio's ratings services base their market areas on OMB's "Metropolitan Statistical Area" (MSA), "Primary Metropolitan Statistical Area" (PMSA), and "Consolidated Metropolitan Statistical Area" (CMSA). The government assigns each county surrounding a major population area to a specific MSA, PMSA, or CMSA.

For the purposes of radio and television ratings, the definitions are modified by the Arbitron Company for radio and Nielsen Media Research for television, based on the needs and desires of their subscribers. Stations subscribing to the ratings service vote on which counties are included in a ratings report and which are excluded or assigned to another market area. Modern media markets are typically defined in three ways: for radio, the Metro Survey Area ("Metro") and the Total Survey Area (TSA); for television, the Designated Market Area (DMA).

As an example, the San Francisco, California, Arbitron ratings report contains data from Sonoma County listeners, and Sonoma County is considered part of the San Francisco Metro in Arbitron ratings reports. Sonoma County radio station operators, however, elected to define their county as a radio market, too. The result was a ratings report for San Francisco and an additional report for Santa Rosa (the largest city in Sonoma County). The ratings for Santa Rosa are duplicated in the San Francisco report, creating what is called an "imbedded market."

In contrast, Philadelphia and Wilmington, Delaware, are similar in that they are geographically side by side. Just as Sonoma County listeners hear San Francisco stations as easily as local outlets, Wilmington listeners can hear Philadelphia stations. However, the two are separate and distinct radio markets, as elected by Arbitron's subscribers in each area. The Philadelphia report and the Wilmington report have no duplication.

The Federal Communications Commission (FCC) generally defines a market area based on the signal contours of individual stations and overlapping signals. The FCC definition thus often differs from the Arbitron definition.

Targeting

Targeting was first found in advertising texts of the early 20th century. There was clear awareness of the use of different periodicals to target various populations: children, farmers, college students, and religious people, for instance. There were "trade" or "class" magazines such as those aimed at plumbers or Masons. Small-town newspapers targeted their audiences specifically, giving local influence to the advertisements. In 1915 Ernest Elmo Calkins suggested "canvassing consumers" in different cities around the country in order to gather information for an ad campaign. Calkins was a pioneer of targeting specific types of people as audiences and creating nongeographic markets.

General Motors advertising was an early example of targeting and segmentation. Trying to work out of a sales slump in the 1920s, the company reorganized its strategy based on price segments. Chevrolet, Pontiac, Buick, and Cadillac automobiles were priced differently and advertised to different markets based on socio-economic criteria.

This led manufacturers to support magazines and radio stations that reached the consumer segments they wanted for their products. Radio at the time was more mass than segmented; however, it became an ideal demographic and segmentation medium, creating communities of like-minded listeners. Writing in *American Demographics* magazine, Joseph Turow recognized the benefit of targeting to specific communities: "Target-minded media help advertisers [target a specific audience] by building primary media communities formed when viewers or readers feel that a magazine, radio station, or other medium resonates with their personal beliefs, and helps them chart their position in the larger world."

Just as media has changed since targeting and segmentation began, so has research. The statistical tools available to the researcher have grown tremendously over the years. The plunging cost of computation makes it both economically and logistically feasible to merge large databases and create new analyses. Researchers are now able to uncover relationships among demographic, attitudinal, behavioral, and geographic elements of the population. Those relationships are called "clusters."

Clusters

The saying "birds of a feather flock together" represents the idea of clustering. By combining demographic data, a market can be grouped into clusters, also known as "geodemographic segmentation systems."

Cluster systems take many demographic variables and create profiles of different individual or household characteristics, purchase behaviors, and media preferences. Most clusters used in media sales and analysis have catchy, descriptive names in an attempt to make them easier to remember. Examples are "Elite Suburbs," "2nd City Society," "Heart Landers," and "Rustic Living"—all from Claritas' PRIZM cluster system.

Marketing Tools magazine claims that cluster systems:

> are especially powerful when used in conjunction with business mapping. Sophisticated mapping software programs easily link demographics to any level of geography (a process called "geocoding"). Some software can pinpoint specific households with neighborhoods from customer data and then create schematic maps of neighborhoods by cluster concentrations.

The geographic element distinguishes clusters from psychographic segments. Another difference is that cluster categories are based on socio-economic and consumer data, not attitudinal data.

When mapping and media mix, Zip codes are often used as a targeting tool. Radio stations tend to use Zip codes to target potential Arbitron diary keepers, but this is not an exact science. In *The Clustering of America* (1988), Michael Weiss introduced the use of Zip codes as a clustering device. His work introduced marketers to age, education, and buying segments originally developed by Claritas Corporation for their PRIZM database. As effective as Weiss was in describing clustering, the net result among media sellers was his Zip code analyses.

With more than 36,000 Zip codes in the United States, precise segmentation is difficult. A Zip code does not constitute a segmented market, even though a single Zip code can contain 35,000 addresses or more. In New York City, because of the density of the population, Zip codes are somewhat cohesive in terms of ethnic and socio-economic mix. In the smallest towns, there may be only one Zip code, thus defying segmentation. That is why the cluster systems were developed.

Lifestyles

Cluster analysis is often confused with psychographics, and the words *psychographics* and *lifestyles* tend to be used interchangeably. There is a difference, though: *psychographics* usually refers to a formal classification system that categorizes people into specific types based largely on psychological characteristics; *lifestyle* is more vague and generally refers to organizing people by attitudes or consumer behavior—"politically conservative," for example, or "avid golfer." Cluster systems are based on purchase behavior (i.e., "owns a cellphone") and demographics (age, sex, income, and education).

According to researcher James Fletcher, qualitative information about lifestyle includes data collected in one or more of the following categories: (1) activities: work, hobbies, social events, vacations, entertainment, club and community activity, shopping, sports; (2) interests: family, home, recreation, fashion, food and wine, media, personal achievement; (3) media behavior: light, medium, or heavy users of electronic media; local newspaper readership; magazine subscriptions; (4) recreation: sports fans, sports participants, travel for recreational purposes, live theater, concerts, movies; (5) social activity: joiners who frequent the social scene or participate in clubs and organizations, house bodies who concentrate on do-it-yourself projects and gardening; (6) purchase patterns: recent purchases, intention to purchase, likely choices when the purchase time arrives; (7) opinion: social issues, politics, business, education, products, culture, the future; (8) demographics: age, sex, education, income, occupation, family size, rent or own housing, geography.

In radio, demographics are often equated with age and sex. In general use, however, the additional elements listed above are all part of demographics. Given radio's ability to create communities of people with similar tastes and attitudes, it can be said that the medium not only serves markets, but also creates them.

See also: Audience Research Methods; Station Rep Firms

Further Reading

Beville, Hugh Malcolm, Jr., *Audience Ratings: Radio, Television, and Cable*, Hillsdale, New Jersey: Erlbaum, 1985; revised edition, 1988.
Burns, George A., *Radio Imagery: Strategies in Station Positioning*, Studio City, California: Burns, 1980.
Burns, George A., *Playing the Positioning Game: Aiming at the Core*, Studio City, California: Burns, 1981.
Dygert, Warren B., *Radio As an Advertising Medium*, New York and London: McGraw-Hill, 1939.
Fletcher, James E., *Handbook of Radio and Television Broadcasting: Research Procedures in Audience, Program, and Revenues*, New York: Van Nostrand Reinhold, 1981.
Fletcher, James E., and Mark E. Dorming, *Profiting from Radio Ratings: A Manual for Radio Managers, Sales Managers, and Programmers*, Washington, D.C.: National Association of Broadcasters, 1989.
Miller, Berna, "A Beginner's Guide to Demographics," *Marketing Tools* (October 1995).
Shane, Ed, *Selling Electronic Media*, Boston and Oxford: Focal Press, 1999.
Turow, Joseph, "Breaking Up America: The Dark Side of Target Marketing," *American Demographics* 19, no. 11 (November 1997).
Weiss, Michael, *The Clustering of America*, New York: Harper and Row, 1988.

Ed Shane

MARKETPLACE
Public Radio Program

Marketplace: The International Magazine of Business and Finance is a daily program on U.S. public radio billed as the "first truly global program using business and economics as its prism to understand the world." The program's trademark is its non-Wall Street approach, designed, in the words of program originator Jim Russell, "for normal human beings, not CEOs." It is known for its hip and sometimes irreverent reporting; it is short on statistical market data and long on feature reporting and analysis. *Marketplace* went on the air on 2 January 1989 and quickly became the fastest-growing national program on public radio, entering 2003 with nearly six million listeners per week. *Marketplace* airs five days per week, with a 30-minute evening program and five nine-minute reports in the morning. It is carried on more than 355 stations throughout the United States and is also heard in Europe on the public radio satellite channel America One and worldwide on the Armed Forces Radio Network. The program is hosted by David Brancaccio and produced by J.J. Yore. *Marketplace* originates in Los Angeles and is distributed by Public Radio International of Minneapolis. In April 2000, Marketplace Productions was acquired by Minnesota Public Radio, which built a new program production center in downtown Los Angeles.

Origins

Marketplace was born at a time when public radio programmers were looking for a business program suitable specifically for public radio. During the summer of 1988, officials at Public Radio International (then the American Public Radio Network [APR]) approached former *All Things Considered* producer Tim Russell with a request that he provide a critique of its daily business program, *Business Update*, which was being produced for public radio by Columbia Broadcasting System (CBS) Radio. Russell's report concluded that, although the program featured solid reporting and was well produced, it had an unquestionably "CBS sound" that did not match the style that listeners had come to expect on public radio. Russell outlined in his report an alternative vision of a public radio business program that was slightly more witty and smart. This type of program, Russell felt, would not necessarily appeal to business professionals, but it could be targeted to a much broader, but still well-educated, audience.

In the fall of 1988, APR officials gathered a group of public radio programmers together at its Minnesota headquarters to discuss Russell's report and his idea for this new kind of business program. The concept won the group's endorsement, though it was agreed that, in order to avoid domination by the media establishment, the program would be produced neither in the Twin Cities nor on the East Coast. Instead, the new show would be produced in California so that it might develop its own voice and foster access to the Pacific Rim business markets. It thus became the first, and only, national daily news program to originate on the West Coast. The name *Marketplace* was selected as the main title specifically because it did not carry the strong Wall Street connotations of the words *business* or *finance*, which were relegated to the subtitle of the program. Russell was hired as the new program's executive producer and general manager, and within three months a staff was hired and the program went on the air, debuting 2 January 1989 from Long Beach, California. The program nearly went off the air after just a few months, but in 1990 USC Radio at the University of Southern California stepped in, offering money, new studios, and help in finding corporate underwriters. The program's original host, Jim Angle, left for a job at ABC in 1993 and was replaced by David Brancaccio, a former KQED public radio reporter (and a San Francisco rock disc jockey before that) who had opened the show's London bureau.

Covering Business

Marketplace draws from international bureaus in Tokyo, London, Beijing, and in South Africa; it has five domestic bureaus. The program features a number of key elements: it defines business as "*anything* having to do with money." It takes an international perspective on the assumption that business shapes world events. The program producers avoid statistics, operating on the maxim of "no data without context." Instead, the show uses an "op ed" approach for background and analysis by featuring a roster of about 75 commentators from a spectrum of cultures, political backgrounds, and ethnicities. It also maintains unique editorial relationships with such traditional sources as the *Economist Magazine*, London's *Financial Times*, and Reuters.

The fact that it is a "business program for the rest of us" is typified by reporting that shows the human side of economics and that attempts to demystify the world of finance (both general manager Russell and morning host Glaser promote their barely passing grades in college economics classes). Host David Brancaccio brags about not having an MBA, and on-air mentions of his home on USC's Fraternity Row and his daily commute to work on a bicycle add to the hip, quirky approach.

The program's trademark irreverence is typified by the background music played when its hosts "Do the Numbers" each day: the song "Stormy Weather" is used when the Dow Jones Industrial Average is down, and "We're in the Money" is played when the Dow is up. It features a variety of non-economic feature stories on the assumption that every topic has some financial or business angle.

Forty-one percent of *Marketplace* listeners are women, and its audience is relatively young: almost 20 percent of its listeners are in the 25–34 age demographic, and nearly 30 percent are 35–44 years old. Its weekly audience, approaching six million listeners, is said to be the second-largest audience in the United States for a TV, cable, or radio business program, behind PBS's *Nightly Business Report*. In 1998 *Marketplace* won a Silver Baton award for broadcast journalism from Columbia University. In 2000, general manager Jim Russell received a Missouri Honor Medal from the University of Missouri's School of Journalism. In 2001 the program won the prestigious Peabody Award.

Cast

Hosts	David Brancaccio
Morning Hosts	Kai Ryssdal, Tess Vigeland

Producer

J.J. Yore

Programming History

Public Radio International   January 1989–present

Further Reading

Ahrens, Frank, "Funny Business: 'Marketplace' Keeps It Light with Humor and Music," *Washington Post* (12 January 1999).

Baxter, Kevin, "Popular 'Marketplace' Brings Business World to Street Level: Radio Program Focuses on Effects of High Finance, Commerce, and Industry on the Average Person," *Los Angeles Times* (1 January 1999).

Marketplace Radio Business News, www.marketplace.org

Puig, Claudia, "They're Putting a Friendly Face on Financial News Radio: For Six Years, 'Marketplace' Has Reached a Literate, Curious Audience, but Not One Necessarily Knowledgeable about Business," *Los Angeles Times* (1 June 1995).

Sarsfield, AnnMarie, "Program Appeals to Novice Investors," *Tampa Tribune* (17 October 1999).

Simon, Clea, "PRI's 'Marketplace' Means Business," *Boston Globe* (7 January 1999).

MARK BRAUN

MAYFLOWER DECISION
FCC Radio License Renewal

The *Mayflower* decision, issued by the Federal Communications Commission (FCC) in 1941, is most noted for its conclusion that, as public trustees, broadcasters could not use their stations to advocate their own causes. In other words, broadcasters should not editorialize.

In 1939 the Yankee Network filed an application to renew the license of its Boston radio station, WAAB. At the same time, the Mayflower Broadcasting Corporation filed an application with the FCC to operate a radio station on the same frequency used by WAAB, thus challenging the renewal of WAAB. In its challenge, Mayflower claimed that WAAB was violating federal law by broadcasting editorials that endorsed certain political candidates for public office.

WAAB did not deny broadcasting the editorials in 1937 and 1938, but the station had discontinued the practice after being questioned by the FCC. As a result of this change in station policy and because Mayflower was found not to be financially qualified, WAAB's license was renewed. But the *Mayflower* decision sent a signal to broadcasters that station editorials were not considered to be in the public interest.

In writing the *Mayflower* decision, the FCC pointed out that the broadcaster has the initial responsibility for the conduct of the station. But because radio frequencies are limited, the interests of the public must be paramount over those of the licensee. Therefore, according to the FCC: "[T]he broadcaster cannot be an advocate. A truly free radio cannot be used to advocate the causes of the licensee. It cannot be used to support the candidacies of his friends. It cannot be devoted to the support of principles he happens to regard most favorably."

In the language of the *Mayflower* decision, the FCC was expressing its interpretation of the Communications Act of 1934 and the phrase "public interest, convenience, or necessity. "Broadcasters are public trustees who have the privilege of using public property—frequency space on the electromagnetic spectrum. Therefore, they are licensed to operate their stations in the "public interest" (as the phrase has been shortened over the years). In *Mayflower*, the FCC stated: "Indeed, as one licensed to operate in a public domain the licensee has assumed the obligation of presenting all sides of important public questions, fairly, objectively and without bias." This was the basis for the FCC policy prohibiting radio editorials.

But that policy was to be challenged when the FCC encountered more station renewal petitions involving coverage of public issues. In the 1945 *WHKC* case, a station license renewal was challenged on the basis of a policy prohibiting the sale of commercial time for programs that discuss controversial subjects. In resolving the case, the FCC accepted an agreement between the station and the labor-union petitioner. The station agreed to change its policy and consider each request for commercial time on an individual basis. The commission noted that "the operation of any station under the extreme principles that no time shall be sold for the discussion of controversial public issues is inconsistent with the concept of public interest established by the Communications Act."

In the 1946 *Scott* decision, the FCC was petitioned to revoke a station's license based on its refusal to make program time available for the discussion of atheism. The licensee of the station defended the refusal based on its "firm belief that it would not be in the public interest to lend our facilities to Mr. Scott for the dissemination and propagation of atheism." The commission stated that the station could not have a policy that denied views "which may have a high degree of unpopularity." Again, balanced coverage of controversial issues became the central point of the petition.

By the late 1940s, the FCC had decided to hold hearings to clear up confusion about its policies in this area. In 1949 the commission issued what came to be known as the "fairness doctrine." The doctrine established the policy that "broadcast licensees have an affirmative duty generally to encourage and implement the broadcast of all sides of controversial public issues over their facilities, over and beyond their obligation to make available on demand opportunities for the expression of opposing views." Ironically, the fairness doctrine also reversed FCC policy banning station editorials.

As a result of broadcaster complaints, the National Association of Broadcasters asked the commission to reconsider its policy on station editorials. After reviewing its policies on coverage of public issues, the FCC concluded that "overt licensee editorialization, within reasonable limits and subject to the general requirements of fairness detailed above, is not contrary to the public interest. Licensee editorialization is but one aspect of freedom of expression by means of radio."

See also: Controversial Issues, Broadcasting of; Editorializing; Fairness Doctrine

Further Reading

Federal Communications Commission, *In the Matter of The Mayflower Broadcasting Corporation and the Yankee Network Inc. (WAAB)* 8 FCC 323 (1941).

Federal Communications Commission, *In Re United Broadcasting Co. (WHKC)*, 10 FCC 515 (1945).

Federal Communications Commission, *In Re Petition of Robert Harold Scott for Revocation of Licenses of Radio Stations KQW, KPO, and KFRC*, 11 FCC 372 (1946).

Federal Communications Commission, *In the Matter of Editorializing by Broadcast Licenses*, 13 FCC 1246 (1949) [later known as the Fairness Doctrine].

Franklin, Marc A., *The First Amendment and the Fourth Estate: Communications Law for Undergraduates.*, Mineola, New York: The Foundation Press, 1977; 7th edition, 1997.

Gillmor, Donald M., and Jerome A. Barron, *Mass Communication Law: Cases and Comment*, St. Paul, Minnesota: West Publishing, 1969; 3rd edition, 1979.

Horwitz, Robert Britt, *The Irony of Regulatory Reform*, New York: Oxford University Press, 1989.

Kahn, Frank J., editor, *Documents of American Broadcasting*, New York: Appleton-Century-Crofts, 1968; 4th edition, Englewood Cliffs, New Jersey: Prentice Hall, 1984.

Nelson, Harold L., and Dwight L. Teeter, Jr., *Law of Mass Communications*, Mineola, New York: The Foundation Press, 1982; 9th edition, 1998.

Pember, Don R., *Mass Media Law*, Dubuque, Iowa: Brown, 1977; 9th edition, Boston, Massachusetts: McGraw Hill, 1998.

FREDERIC A. LEIGH

MEDIA RATING COUNCIL
Industry Self-Regulatory Group

Originally known as the Broadcast Rating Council (BRC) and then as the Electronic Media Rating Council (EMRC), the official sanctioning body for ratings services now goes by the name Media Rating Council (MRC). The MRC works to maintain confidence and credibility in ratings through its self-stated goal of setting standards which ensure that surveys of media audiences are conducted in a manner that encourages quality, integrity, and accurate disclosure of the research process. A nonprofit agency sanctioned by the U.S. Justice Department, the MRC consists of 70 members from broadcast and cable trade associations, media owners, advertising agencies, cable networks, print and internet companies, and national networks.

The MRC is a nonprofit industry organization that is run on its membership fees. Each member organization provides one person to serve on the MRC board of directors, which makes the final decision as to whether reports that have been audited will receive accreditation from the council. Among the members of the New York-based MRC are the National Association of Broadcasters, the Television Bureau of Advertising, the Radio Advertising Bureau, and the Cable Advertising Bureau.

The MRC was established in 1964, when it was known as the BRC. A self-regulatory agency, the BRC was formed in response to an investigation by the House Subcommittee on Communications of the Interstate and Foreign Commerce Committee, under the chairmanship of Oren Harris. The Harris Committee, as it was known, held hearings in 1963 to investigate ratings and audience research. The hearings arose both from an increased focus on television ratings after the quiz show scandals of 1961 and from complaints by advertisers that they couldn't obtain upfront information about research methodology from the Nielsen Company. Essentially, the Harris Committee was concerned that if ratings were defective or deceptive, they would affect programming selections by stations and work in a manner that was not in the public interest.

The credibility and validity of ratings became a growing industry concern as U.S. representatives questioned executives from broadcast-measurement companies about the quality of their research. Faced with the possibility of government interference in the ratings business, broadcast industry leaders obtained permission from the U.S. Justice Department (to avoid any perception of antitrust violations) to set up the BRC, thereby ensuring a means of self-regulation.

The BRC changed its name to the Electronic Media Rating Council in 1982 to include all electronic media, such as radio, television, and cable. The "Electronic" in the council's name was dropped in 1997 when the council started performing audits on print services as well as broadcast services. On 4 September 1996 the *Study of Media and Markets* (a national survey of over 20,000 adults performed by Simmons Market Research Bureau) became the first multimedia research study with a primary focus on print media to receive accreditation from the council. Today the MRC audits organizations such as Mediamark Research (which provides research to all forms of advertising media collected from a single sample) and J.D. Power and Associates (which publishes the annual *Car and Truck Media Studies* to assist with marketing and media strategies).

Audience measurement services voluntarily submit their studies to the MRC for review and possible accreditation. The MRC then commissions audits by an independent accounting firm (currently the Ernst and Young Corporation) to review the data. The ratings services pay the cost of the audit to the

MRC, which in turn pays the auditors. This system allows for some separation between the parties and establishes that the MRC, not the ratings service, is supervising the audit.

Even though the auditing process is voluntary, many organizations still seek accreditation so that they will be considered legitimate in the industry and will therefore be better able to sell their ratings. Organizations seeking accreditation must agree to conduct their service as represented to users and subscribers, undergo MRC audits, and pay for the costs of the audits. The results of the audits are reviewed by the council's board of directors to determine if the ratings service will receive accreditation. Should a report receive accreditation, the organization submitting the report still must re-apply the following year and have the report reviewed on an annual basis. The MRC accredits syndicated services and individual reports, not entire companies. Accredited services and reports carry the MRC double-check logo.

In 1993 the council made an unprecedented move when it voted to suspend its accreditation of the spring Atlanta Arbitron survey, citing an on-air promotional campaign by Atlanta broadcasters that "hyped" (aimed to increase response rates) the survey by urging listeners to cooperate with Arbitron's diary-based system. The council decided that the effort could have an adverse effect on methodology and thus distort the survey results. The move to suspend accreditation met with sharp criticism from the Radio Advertising Bureau (RAB), which was upset with what it believed was an unfair bias toward television. Despite the controversy, the RAB currently holds membership in the MRC.

The MRC has expanded its role over the years but still functions primarily in an effort to maintain rating confidence and credibility. Melvin A. Goldberg, then EMRC executive director, explained in 1989 that obtaining accreditation required adherence to specific minimum standards that outlined basic objectives of reliable and useful electronic media audience measurement research. Acceptance of those standards was voluntary and was one of the conditions of EMRC membership.

According to Goldberg, the minimum standards fell into two groupings: (1) "Ethical and Operations Standards," and (2) "Disclosure Standards." The Ethical and Operations Standards governed the quality and integrity of the overall process of producing ratings. Meanwhile, the Disclosure Standards specified which information a ratings service had to make available to users, to the EMRC, and to its auditing agent. The overall effect of the standards was to assure anyone using EMRC-accredited ratings that the ratings actually measured what they said they did.

Thus, the minimum standards established professional codes of conduct that ratings services had to agree to in order to gain accreditation. For example, a ratings service was required to submit complete information on its survey methodology, including sampling techniques, recruiting procedures, weighting, tabulations, coding and computer software, and the eventual ratings. The standards that Goldberg referred to are still in effect today. However, the MRC has also added electronic delivery requirements that govern the proper way for ratings services to deliver data to a third party electronically. The MRC has also incorporated internet ratings reports into its auditing processes.

The MRC became involved in the early 21st-century controversy over Arbitron's introduction of the Portable People Meter device. In early 2008, the Council voted not to accredit the new PPM service in Philadelphia and New York, the first cities where the new ratings device had been introduced. The chief concern was with how sample audiences were selected for the PPM panels.

MRC's investigation of the new service, as well as the re-introduction by Nielsen of diary research for smaller radio markets, continued as this volume went to press.

See also: A.C. Nielsen Company; Arbitron; Audience Research Methods; Portable People Meter

Further Reading

Beville, Hugh Malcolm, *Audience Ratings: Radio, Television, and Cable*, Hillsdale, New Jersey: Erlbaum, 1985; 2nd edition, 1988.
Goldberg, Melvin A., "Broadcast Ratings and Ethics," *Review of Business* (Summer 1989).
Media Rating Council website, www.mediaratingcouncil.org

MATT TAYLOR,
2009 REVISIONS BY CHRISTOPHER H. STERLING

MERGERS
See: Ownership, Mergers, and Acquisitions

MERCURY THEATER OF THE AIR
Anthology Radio Drama Series

Mercury Theater of the Air was an offshoot of Orson Welles' successful theater company, which had catapulted him to Broadway fame. Using many of the same actors, he put on a series of radio plays in 1938 under the title *First Person Singular*, although the *Mercury Theater* name was better known. At first the show had no sponsor and few listeners, but the success of the legendary "War of the Worlds" episode in 1938 persuaded Campbell's Soup to back it. The radio plays gave Welles national fame and allowed him to branch into films with his seminal *Citizen Kane* in 1941. The originality and technical flair that marked that film applied equally to Welles' radio productions.

By 1938 Welles, an accomplished Shakespearean actor, was becoming a noted radio performer, having worked on *March of Time*; adapted, directed, and starred in the seven-part *Les misérables*; and, most notably, by becoming the voice of *The Shadow*. He was approached by William Lewis, head of programming at Columbia Broadcasting System (CBS), to make nine one-hour adaptations of famous books. Welles' budget of $50,000 for the nine shows was not much, given that he had been earning $1,000 per week, and the shows were slated for an unpromising timeslot against the popular *Edgar Bergen and Charlie McCarthy*. However, the deal did offer Welles creative carte blanche; he did not need to worry about pleasing a sponsor or appealing to any target audience. (CBS made the offer at a time when Congress was threatening legislation aimed at raising radio standards, so owner William S. Paley wanted programs that could turn CBS into a veritable patron of the arts.)

Broadcasts began on 11 July 1938 on the WABC network with "Dracula." Like subsequent performances, it followed Welles' view that "the less a radio drama resembles a play the better it is likely to be." This represented a major departure from many previous programs that had tried to recreate live theater down to the last detail, even including intermissions and chatting patrons. Instead, Welles introduced an omnipresent narrator, himself, who played several roles. This not only allowed Welles to take center stage but also changed the narrator into a storyteller, all the other characters effectively becoming projections of himself. Welles was equally innovative in his use of music. He asked Bernard Herrmann (head of music for CBS) for an unprecedented amount of musical scoring for each drama: up to 40 minutes in 57-minute-long performances. Similar demands were made with regard to sound effects, which overlapped the dialogue instead of occurring at the end of a speech as had been the practice. Welles demanded that even the faintest rustle of leaves be reproduced, despite the fact that very few listeners would have been able to hear these effects on their crackling AM radios. (They can now be appreciated on compact disc recordings, however.)

Nearly all of the dramas performed by the Mercury Players, which included "Treasure Island," "The Thirty-Nine Steps," and "The Count of Monte Cristo," were classics with family appeal. Their tone was not patronizing, but neither were they too advanced for children to appreciate. Welles decided which story to perform each week, but despite opening credits saying that each play was "produced, directed, and performed by Orson Welles," his participation was strictly limited to reviewing the script, making last minute changes, and performing. His long-time collaborator John Houseman and experienced radio man Paul Stewart oversaw the script writing and rehearsals. For the cast, Welles was able to call upon members of the Mercury stage theater such as George Coulouris, as well as other experienced radio actors including Ray Collins, Agnes Moorehead, and Martin Gabel.

Despite this range of talents, the programs rarely attracted more than four percent of the national radio audience until "War of the Worlds" greatly increased Welles' fame. The resulting sponsorship by Campbell's Soup caused the title of the series to be changed to *The Campbell Playhouse Series* in midseason 1939. This new name also reflected the demise of the Mercury Theater, which had fallen apart following a number of unsuccessful theater productions.

Ostensibly, *The Campbell Playhouse Series* was the same program as the *Mercury Theater of the Air*, and the dramas continued to be hour-long adaptations. However, the new and bigger budget allowed Welles to cast star names, including Katharine Hepburn ("A Farewell to Arms"), Laurence Olivier ("Beau Geste"), Gertrude Lawrence ("Private Lives"), and Walter Huston ("Les misérables"), as his co-stars. Former members of the Mercury stage theater continued to work on the show, but they were now reduced to supporting roles. The presence of a star also affected the show's format, as the play would now be sandwiched between segments of talk show style patter as Welles chatted with his guest star. This would invariably include some banal reference to the joys of Campbell's soup. Campbell's also inserted commercial breaks for soup ads into the plays themselves. The *Mercury* broadcasts had been uninterrupted, but now cliff-hangers had to be created to insure that listeners did not tune in a different program during the commercials.

The *Campbell's* plays were also based on noticeably different books. The *Mercury's* eclectic mix of classics was forsaken in favor of more populist and more modern works, primarily bestsellers from the previous decade. There were also reworkings of previous Welles productions, which were an indicator of the extent to which the program lost much of the *Mercury*'s originality and innovation. Welles' contribution also dropped off considerably as he began to concentrate more on theater before relocating to Hollywood. During this period, he would fly to New York on the day of the performance, make the broadcast, and then fly back to Hollywood. The production of the plays was thus left to Houseman and Stewart, with almost no input from Welles at all. However, *Campbell Playhouse* was one of the most popular shows on radio until Welles finally pulled the plug in March 1940 to fully concentrate on cinema. He had considered moving the show to Los Angeles so that his actors could be employed while he worked in films, but Campbell's refused to give up the Broadway panache that the show's New York connection provided. The *Mercury* name did make some sporadic returns to radio whenever Welles needed to raise some quick cash, but these later programs were mainly rehashes of previous performances that added little to the originals.

See also: Drama; Playwrights on Radio; *War of the Worlds*

Cast

The "Mercury Players"	Orson Welles, Ray Collins, Agnes Moorehead, George Coulouris, Frank Readick, Georgia Backus, Bea Benaderet, Everett Sloane, Edgar Barrier

Producers/Creators

Orson Welles and John Houseman

Programming History

WABC (CBS)

| *First Person Singular/* *Mercury Theater of the Air* | July 1938–December 1938 |
| *Campbell's Playhouse* *Series* | December 1938– March 1940; 1946 |

Further Reading

Brady, Frank, *Citizen Welles: A Biography of Orson Welles*, New York: Scribner, 1989; London: Hodder and Stoughton, 1990.
Callow, Simon, *Orson Welles: The Road to Xanadu*, London: Jonathan Cape, 1995; New York: Viking, 1996.
Houseman, John, *Run-through: A Memoir*, New York: Simon and Schuster, 1972; London: Allen Lane, 1973.
Learning, Barbara, *Orson Welles*, New York: Viking, and London: Weidenfeld and Nicholson, 1985.
Naremore, James, *The Magic World of Orson Welles*, New York: Oxford University Press, 1978.
Thomas, François, "Dossier: La radio d'Orson Welles," *Positif* (October 1988).

NEIL DENSLOW

METROMEDIA
Group Owner of Radio Stations

Corporate executive John Kluge made his mark as the founder of Metromedia, a media conglomerate that operated through the 1960s and 1970s both with independent television stations in major U.S. cities and with owned and operated major-market radio stations as well. Although not well known to the general public, Kluge emerged in this period as one of the most powerful media moguls. Kluge proved that independent television stations and big-city radio stations could make millions of dollars in profits by counterprogramming. In 1985, when Australian Rupert Murdoch offered Kluge nearly $2 billion for Metromedia's seven television stations, he sold out and began to reinvent Metromedia. He was out of big-city radio during the late 1980s.

John Werner Kluge surely represents the American success story. Kluge grew up poor in Detroit, but in 1933 he won a scholarship to Columbia University, where he earned a degree in economics. Serving U.S. Army Intelligence during World War II, he returned with little taste for resuming a career in the employ of others. He looked for ways to make money, including buying and selling radio stations.

After World War II, Kluge came to radio (and television) for its advertising power in the growing market of Washington, D.C., where he had served in World War II. Kluge bought and sold radio stations; his first was WGAY-FM in Silver Spring, Maryland, a Washington, D.C., suburb. As radio reinvented itself as a format medium, Kluge bought and sold stations across the United States, with early investments in radio groups including the St. Louis Broadcasting Corporation, Pittsburgh Broadcasting Company, Capitol Broadcasting Company (Nashville), Associated Broadcasters (Fort Worth-Dallas), Western New York Broadcasting Company (Buffalo), and the Mid-Florida Radio Corporation (Orlando).

Kluge became aware of television as an investment possibility when he ran into an acquaintance on a street in Washington, D.C.; the acquaintance casually mentioned that the failed Dumont television network was going up for sale. In January 1959 Kluge acquired Paramount Pictures' share of what remained of DuMont, the television stations of Metropolitan Broadcasting, for $4 million. He then consolidated his radio and television holdings and later bought and sold interests in restaurants, outdoor and direct-mail advertising, and magazines.

Indeed, Kluge never stopped trading radio—if he figured he could make a profit. So in 1982, for example, he sold WMETFM (Chicago) and KSAN-FM (San Francisco) and acquired KHOW-AM and WWBA-FM in Tampa, Florida. Yet with Federal Communications Commission rules permitting Metromedia to own only seven AM and seven FM radio stations, Kluge held on to stations in top markets because they made the most money. Metromedia held WNEW-AM and -FM in New York City, KLAC-AM in Los Angeles (acquired in 1963), and WIPAM in Philadelphia (acquired in 1960) for the longest amount of time. Once a station was acquired, Kluge assigned managers to squeeze maximum profits, not caring what format was used. His stations employed all formats: adult contemporary, beautiful music, all-news—any format that worked in that particular major market.

In his heyday, Kluge grew famous for cutting costs and maximizing revenues; indeed, once he had assembled Metromedia, he moved the operation's headquarters out of expensive Manhattan across the Hudson River to Secaucus, New Jersey, where rents were lower. He secured the cheapest possible programming, and then, even with small audience shares, Metromedia could, with bare-bones costs, make a profit. But not every well struck oil. One disastrous misstep was Kluge's purchase of the niche magazine *Diplomat*. Another was his vision of forming a fourth television network, a venture in which Kluge only lost millions of dollars.

In April 1984 Kluge took Metromedia private, and so he possessed three-quarters of Metromedia stock when he sold the seven television stations to Rupert Murdoch a year later. The eventual sale of the radio stations in the late 1980s would make Kluge more than $100 million, a great deal of money, but little compared to the billions made from the sale of the television stations.

Further Reading

Compaine, Benjamin M., and Douglas Gomery, *Who Owns the Media?* New York: Harmony Books, 1979; 3rd edition, Mahwah, New Jersey: Erlbaum, 2000.

Gelman, Morris J., "John Kluge: The Man with the Midas Touch," *Television Magazine* (July 1964).
Gomery, Douglas, "Vertical Integration, Horizontal Regulation—The Growth of Rupert Murdoch's Media Empire," *Screen* 27, nos. 3–4 (May–August 1986).
Kluge, John W., *The Metromedia Story*, New York: Newcomen Society in North America, 1974.

DOUGLAS GOMERY

METROPOLITAN OPERA BROADCASTS

Performances of New York's Metropolitan Opera have been broadcast regularly on radio since 1931 and occasionally on television since 1977. Milton Cross was the voice of these broadcasts for more than four decades. The continuous support of Texaco (Chevron-Texaco after 2000) from 1940 to 2004 formed what was probably the world's longest-running commercial broadcast sponsorship.

Origins

New York's Metropolitan Opera Association was formed in October 1883, and soon the city was presented with an annual season of fine opera performances by top-drawer orchestras and singers. But for decades the only way to hear and see a "Met" performance was to purchase an expensive ticket and attend a program in New York.

The first hint of an alternative means of delivering opera came on 13 January 1910. With the permission of the Opera's assistant director, wireless inventor (and opera lover) Lee de Forest set up one of his transmitters high in the attic above the stage with a temporary bamboo antenna on the roof. Several microphones were placed on the stage. That first transmission included scenes from *Cavalleria Rusticana* and Enrico Caruso singing in *Pagliacci*, and was heard primarily by other radio operators and some reporters. And what they heard was anything but a clear signal, given the crude equipment of the time. The poor results did not endear the company's management to the rising medium of radio.

Despite radio's later development, opera director Giulio Gatti-Casazza resisted further experimentation with radio microphones for two decades out of a fear of lost ticket sales. He also felt mere *listeners* would lose the visual aspect of opera. Public reasons given for the lack of radio coverage included technical problems with placement of microphones and contracts with lead singers that forbade such transmission. Yet the Met was being bypassed by others.

The Chicago Civic Opera went on the air in 1922 when station KYW debuted with a focus on opera broadcasts. And other performing companies were heard in other cities. So were some performances by the Manhattan Opera Company that then competed with the Metropolitan Opera. The fan magazine *Radio Digest* began an editorial campaign to get the Met to change its mind that same year. Station WEAF wasn't waiting—they formed their own in-studio opera companies, one for grand and one for light opera—and broadcast their performances for several years. The original language of the composer was used, but performances were cut to fit one-hour time slots. And they took place in a studio, not on an opera stage, limiting what could be accomplished. Broadcasts of opera from Europe could occasionally be picked up by U.S. listeners tuning shortwave. The broadcast sound quality left much to be desired, but at least the operas were being heard.

What finally turned the tide was the Met's need for new sources of operating funds during the depression. NBC secured the broadcast rights for the first season, outbidding rival CBS. Broadcasts began with *Hansel and Gretel* on Christmas Day of 1931 with Deems Taylor providing the initial commentary. He received howls of protest when he timed his comments to appear over the music and soon changed his approach. The first broadcasts also featured announcer Milton Cross, who would remain as host until 1975, doing more than 800 broadcasts and missing only two in all those years.

Metropolitan Opera Auditions of the Air was developed as a separate program (1935–58; on NBC until 1937, then Blue/ABC) and also featured commentary by Milton Cross with Edward Johnson, managing director of the Met, as host. Each week aspiring operatic performers would do their best to earn audience support and a contract from the Met.

Despite the interest of a small but vocal audience, sponsorship for the broadcasts was difficult to arrange and harder to perpetuate. Several backers (American Tobacco, RCA, and Lambert drugs) came and went, and by the late 1930s, opera broadcasts from New York were threatened by a lack of continuing advertiser support.

Texaco Sponsorship

Beginning on 7 December 1940, the Texaco oil company took up sponsorship of the weekly broadcasts. Though at first this seemed merely the latest in a changing parade of financial backers, Texaco stuck with the program, pleased with the highbrow audience it attracted. More than six decades later, ChevronTexaco continued to support the Metropolitan Opera broadcasts, forming what was probably the longest continuing relationship of an advertiser and a program in radio history. The broadcasts under Texaco at first continued on NBC, then moved to Blue (which became ABC) until 1958, at which point CBS carried on the series for two years. But Texaco became unhappy with declining network interest and decided to create its own specialized network of stations to carry the Saturday matinees. So in 1960 the Texaco-Metropolitan Opera Radio Network was created, with Texaco arranging for the AT&T connecting lines to link the slowly growing number of stations carrying the broadcasts.

As microphone and other radio technologies improved, so did the sound of the opera on the air. By the late 1940s a more complex multiple microphone technique was being used. The opera company understandably insisted that no microphone be placed where it could be seen, so broadcasts utilized four microphones placed near the stage footlights. These were aimed at the floor to receive a more equal (reflected) sound of the varied singing voices and spoken lines and were supplemented by two more microphones suspended above the orchestra. Stereo transmissions were added in the 1960s. The entire radio operation was upgraded with the move of the Met into its new opera house in New York's Lincoln Center in 1966. The opera network was connected by satellite in the 1980s.

Over the years the opera broadcasts were supplemented with the "Texaco Opera Quiz" and "Opera News on the Air," features that became very popular. On Milton Cross' death in 1975, Peter Allen took over the host role and continued it into the 21st century. In 1977 several operas were televised on the Public Broadcasting Service, which still does three or four such performances each season (with English subtitles). Texaco also supported formation of a Media Center to archive past broadcasts.

Over the years the audience for the programs grew, first in the United States and then beyond. The 20-week (November–April) season of Saturday matinees has long been transmitted throughout the United States and Canada (more than 325 stations across North America), and beginning in 1990, to 27 European countries. Australia and New Zealand joined the network in 1997, and in 2000 the Texaco network welcomed Brazil and Mexico. By the end of the 2000–2001 season, Texaco had sponsored 1,212 Metropolitan Opera broadcasts of 144 different operas.

In May 2003 ChevronTexaco (as the sponsor had become after a 2000 merger) announced that the 2003–04 season of matinee broadcasts would be the last they would sponsor, ending a nearly 65-year run, the longest continuous sponsorship in radio history. The Metropolitan Opera said it would continue the broadcasts and seek new sponsors. ChevronTexaco said the series had been costing about $7 million a year, reaching some 10 million listeners in 42 countries. Their announcement to terminate sponsorship came after the oil company saw a drop in both profits and stock price.

Edward Downs, the opera broadcast quizmaster for many years, died at age 90 on December 26, 2002. ChevronTexaco ceased its support in April 2004. The Annenberg Foundation provided a $3.5 million grant to help keep the broadcasts going for another year, the total cost of which had climbed to twice that amount. The Metropolitan sought further commitments for longer-range financing and by 2008 the annual series was being supported by Toll Brothers (construction) and two foundations.

See also: Classical Music Format; KYW; Music on Radio

Programming History

NBC Red or Blue (sometimes both)	1931–40
NBC Red	1940–43
Blue Network/ABC	1943–58
CBS	1958–60
Texaco-Metropolitan Opera Radio Network	1960–2000
ChevronTexaco-Metropolitan Opera Radio Network	2000–2004

Further Reading

De Forest, Lee, *Father of Radio: The Autobiography of Lee De Forest*, Chicago: Wilcox and Follett, 1950.

DeLong, Thomas A., *The Mighty Music Box: The Golden Age of Musical Radio*, Los Angeles: Amber Crest Books, 1980.

Jackson, Paul J., *Saturday Afternoons at the Old Met: The Metropolitan Opera Broadcasts, 1931–1950*, Portland, Oregon: Amadeus Press, and London: Duckworth, 1992.

Jackson, Paul J., *Sign-Off for the Old Met: The Metropolitan Opera Broadcasts, 1950–1966*, Portland, Oregon: Amadeus Press, and London: Duckworth, 1997.

LaPrade, Ernest, *Broadcasting Music*, New York: Rinehart, 1956.

Metmaniac Opera Archive Online, www.metmaniac.com

Pogrebin, Robin, "Chevron Texaco to Stop Sponsoring Met's Broadcasts," *New York Times* (21 May 2003).

Pogrebin, Robin, "Gift Aims to Keep Met Opera on the Air," *New York Times* (4 December 2003), p. D1.

CHRISTOPHER H. STERLING,
2009 REVISIONS BY CHRISTOPHER H. STERLING

MICRORADIO
See: Low-Power Radio/Microradio

MIDDLE OF THE ROAD FORMAT
Middle of the road (MOR) refers to a form of radio music programming that features popular standards and current hits, mainly adult contemporary in nature. MOR relies on broad-based music that appeals to adults 45 and older, and it serves as a "bridge" between the adult contemporary and easy listening formats. Other industry terms that describe the MOR approach include *full-service, variety, general appeal,* and *diversified* (Keith, 1997).

MOR serves as "one of the oldest and most durable types of programming within format radio" (Howard, Kievman, and Moore, 1994). It finds its origins in the 1940s, when radio offered a variety of program material and before rock and roll as a musical genre spurred the creation of specialized formats. Traditional MOR stations of this radio era appealed to adults by giving them "lots of news, sports, and safe, comfortable music" (Halper, 1991). As more and more stations sought to attract teen audiences, whom they saw as becoming more important as a demographic group, they began to air countdown shows of popular hits during nights and weekends. In this capacity, MOR serves as the predecessor of Top 40 radio.

During the 1950s, television began to displace radio as a source of entertainment programming, as embodied in serialized dramas and the like. Keith (1987) notes that as the networks left radio, stations found themselves having to fill their schedules with recorded music, news, and sports. When rock and roll arrived on the radio scene, marking the start of format specialization, MOR stations modified their playlists to secure the older adult audience. Thus, MOR established itself as a true radio format, characterized by broad-appeal music and a "full-service" function of providing music, news, and sports. By the mid-1950s, "MOR dominated the radio programming scene" (Keith, 1987).

Between the 1950s and 1970s, MOR enjoyed high popularity. But MOR as a programming powerhouse began to lose strength as the radio industry evolved during those decades. As radio became further fragmented, MOR had to contend with competition from new programming styles, such as beautiful music in the late 1950s and soft rock and oldies in the 1960s. Keith (1987) points out that these formats, plus the updating of easy listening station playlists and the rise of adult contemporary, took away some of MOR's audience. Because MOR was a mainstay of AM, its numbers fell further as FM grew in popularity in the 1970s, with mellow rock taking away the younger side of its demographic, 25- to 40-year-olds.

By the 1980s, the MOR audience consisted mainly of the 45 and older crowd, with a number-two Arbitron rating in AM listenership and a number-11 ranking among the 12 formats listed for FM (Keith, 1987). Indeed, some believed that by the mid-1980s, MOR ceased to exist altogether, as other programming formats, especially adult contemporary, took its place.

Music-wise, the traditional MOR format through the years consistently centered on popular standards that emphasized melody more than a beat (Howard, Kievman, and Moore, 1994). Indeed, Hyatt (1999) considers the term *middle of the road* as synonymous to *adult contemporary* and *easy listening*. The term *middle of the road* accurately describes this type of music, which is similar to the more modern adult contemporary genre—neither too soft nor too raucous, music that walks the line musically, "avoiding anything too old, too new, too upbeat, or too solemn," as Keith (1987) describes it. Asserts Gregory (1998), "MOR was coined by broadcasters to describe a style of popular music that is high on melody, but short on substance."

Traditional MOR station playlists might include "traditional" pop vocalists such as Frank Sinatra, Tony Bennett, Rosemary Clooney, Ella Fitzgerald, Perry Como, and Peggy Lee; big band acts such as Benny Goodman and Glenn Miller; and relatively "contemporary" acts such as Helen Reddy, Olivia Newton-John, Barbra Streisand, Roger Whittaker, Ray Conniff, and Sergio Mendez (Howard, Kievman, and Moore, 1994; Keith, 1987, 1984). Crossover artists who found success in the MOR format during the 1970s included the Carpenters, Glen Campbell, and Anne Murray (Keith, 1984).

During the 1980s and 1990s, notes Gregory (1998), further updating of the MOR style came with the crossover success of artists with soul and rhythm and blues backgrounds, such as Whitney Houston, Toni Braxton, and Luther Vandross. The demarcation between MOR and adult contemporary formats eroded even further during this time, if one believes Gregory (1998) when he asserts that "the whole concept of what MOR actually represented was embodied by Canadian Celine Dion, Elton John and the modern musicals of Andrew Lloyd Webber and Tim Rice." In short, when considering the range of artists found on station playlists, MOR and adult contemporary mirror each other in terms of melodic style, but the MOR playlist includes older standards.

In addition to the inclusion of older tunes, MOR differentiates itself from other similar formats in its use of on-air personalities and its added emphasis on news. For example, whereas adult contemporary stresses music, MOR "has always been the home of the radio personality" (Keith, 1984). On-air announcers and disc jockeys enjoy considerably more freedom on MOR than on other music-based formats; they often choose individual selections to play and may have extensive programming experience (Howard, Kievman, and Moore, 1994). Indeed, "MOR personalities often serve as the cornerstone of their station's air product" (Keith, 1997).

Though fewer traditional MOR stations existed in the late 1990s, the format, encompassing heavy news and informational programming, still found success in the larger metropolitan markets. Just as the radio industry as a whole had experienced "frag-out" during the 1970s, the MOR label became delineated at the end of the 20th century with descriptors such as "nostalgia," "golden oldies," and "adult standard." Stations employing the MOR genre in the late 1990s reflected this emphasis on music favored by its older-adult audience through slogans such as "Unforgettable Favorites," "The Original Hits Station," "Station of the Stars," "The Greatest Music of All Time," "The Memory Station," and "Great Songs, Great Memories."

By the early 2000s, as Baby Boomers and Yuppies matured yet remained musically attuned, the term MOR mutated yet again. Although standards by Frank Sinatra and Peggy Lee are still considered MOR fodder, for some stations, so too is music from Sheryl Crow, Diane Krall, U2, Whitney Houston, Harry Connick, Jr., and the group Train, among others. Some more modern-leaning MOR stations are also broadening their playlists by including everything from rock "power ballads" to recent country hits, soft AC selections and smooth jazz numbers. Increasingly, MOR, as a format, is becoming harder to define as it varies from station to station. Though almost 200 stations—mostly AM—still describe themselves as MOR to those in the business, few do so on the air. Instead, they prefer such euphemisms as "Mix," "Classic Hits" and "Ultimate Hits," as the term "Middle of the Road" long ago took on the connotation of something old, bland and only a few degrees removed from background music.

See also: Adult Contemporary Format; Easy Listening/Beautiful Music Format; Formats; Oldies Format

Further Reading

Gregory, Hugh, *A Century of Pop*, Chicago: A Capella, 1998.
Halper, Donna L., *Radio Music Directing*, Boston and London: Focal Press, 1991.

Howard, Herbert H., and Michael S. Kievman, *Radio and TV Programming*, Ames: Iowa State University Press, 1986; 2nd edition, as *Radio, TV, and Cable Programming*, by Howard, Kievman, and Barbara A. Moore, 1994.

Hyatt, Wesley, *The Billboard Book of Number One Adult Contemporary Hits*, New York: Billboard Books, 1999.

Keith, Michael C., *Production in Format Radio Handbook*, Lanham, Maryland: University Press of America, 1984.

Keith, Michael C., and Joseph M. Krause, *The Radio Station*, Boston: Focal Press, 1986; 4th edition, by Michael C. Keith, 1997; 5th edition, Boston and Oxford: Focal Press, 2000.

Keith, Michael C., *Radio Programming: Consultancy and Formatics*, Boston and London: Focal Press, 1987.

ERIKA ENGSTROM,
2009 REVISIONS BY CARY O'DELL

MINNESOTA PUBLIC RADIO

One of the major trends in public radio during the 1990s has been the growth of "superstations," the signals of which, relayed by repeater antennae and satellites, may blanket an entire region or reach halfway across the United States. The first, and leading, public radio superstation is Minnesota Public Radio (MPR), which extended into seven states and Canada by the late 1990s.

MPR originated with KSJR-FM, a classical music station licensed to St. Johns University, which went on the air in Collegeville, Minnesota—approximately 75 miles northwest of Minneapolis—on 22 January 1967. William Kling, a St. Johns graduate, served as the station's program director. In the fall of 1969, a student announcer from the University of Minnesota named Garrison Keillor took over hosting duties of KSJR's *Morning Program* and began telling stories in addition to spinning records. By 1971 Keillor had changed the program's name to *A Prairie Home Morning Show* and enjoyed a wide following, ultimately leading to the wildly successful *A Prairie Home Companion*. Kling had left the station for a job at the Corporation for Public Broadcasting in 1969, but he returned two years later when St. Johns turned control of KSJR over to a nonprofit concern, Minnesota Educational Radio. Kling obtained federal funding and foundation grants to develop a St. Paul-based regional news service, and the group changed its name to Minnesota Public Radio in 1974. In addition to completing a network of its six licensees in 1975, Minnesota Public Radio also pioneered radio reading services for the blind through the use of FM subcarriers.

Under Kling's leadership, Minnesota Public Radio grew at a phenomenal pace in the 1980s. To capitalize on the success of *A Prairie Home Companion*, MPR founded the Rivertown Trading Company in 1981 to sell merchandise connected to the program. In April 1983 MPR launched American Public Radio (APR) as an independent corporation and rival to National Public Radio (NPR); MPR also initially provided the bulk of APR's programming. The statewide MPR network grew to include 12 stations by 1985. Two years later the Rivertown operation was reorganized as the Greenspring Company, a for-profit subsidiary of MPR. Kling's fund-raising and entrepreneurial skills were reflected in the fact that by 1988 MPR received nearly $5 million from listeners, more than $3 million in government funding, and close to $8 million in revenues from broadcasting and other activities, including *Minnesota Monthly* magazine and catalog sales. By the end of the 1980s, MPR was operating 17 licensees, with another station under construction and applications for four more stations on file with the FCC.

MPR President Kling claimed that MPR moved into an area only after a community requested that it do so, and he insisted that the community finance station construction and the first year of operation. In late 1989 residents of Sun Valley, Idaho, applied to the FCC for a permit to install a translator and a 100-W station with MPR's assistance; soon, MPR's signal was bouncing off the mountains of Idaho. Not surprisingly, these expansionist policies led to direct conflicts with local stations. MPR established a transmitter near Grand Forks, North Dakota, in 1990, although the area already was served by AM and FM public stations licensed to the nearby University of North Dakota. Much of MPR's programming was the same as that of the local stations, who could not hope to match MPR's marketing and production resources and who watched helplessly as MPR skimmed off the cream of their subscriber base.

MPR's profits from Greenspring (which Kling termed an "experiment in 'social purpose' capitalism") also began to attract considerable attention from those outside the organization. Although MPR was ostensibly a separate entity, its ties to Greenspring represented a potential conflict of interest and led to an inquiry by the Minnesota attorney general's office. MPR ultimately was cleared of wrongdoing and sold its catalog business to Minneapolis retailer Dayton Hudson for $120 million in March 1998. Kling personally received $2.6 million from the deal. Minnesota Public Radio also began operating the Public Radio Music Source (PRMS) in conjunction with 66 other public radio stations in January 1993. Participating stations advertise a toll-free number for listeners to purchase the CDs on their station's playlist. In return, the station earns up to 10 percent of the gross from sales. However, critics argue that PRMS encourages stations to narrow their programming and aggressively promote particular releases, with the result that public radio increasingly resembles its commercial counterparts.

MPR spent much of the 1990s consolidating its sprawling operations, and it expanded into southern California in 1999 when it took over Pasadena's financially beleaguered KPCC. Its defenders (and many listeners) argue that Minnesota Public Radio is a paragon of professionalism and vision that will serve as a model for public radio in the 21st century, but its detractors claim that MPR is driven by little more than cut-throat competitive imperatives. Both would agree that MPR rejects the traditional model of public radio, in which stations serve small geographic areas with programming that is not considered commercially viable. In its embrace of professionalism, expansion, and entrepreneurship, Minnesota Public Radio has in many ways set the agenda for public radio in the United States.

In early 2004, Minnesota Public Radio split with its offspring, PRI, and announced it would distribute its national programming under the name American Public Media. By the end of the first decade of the 21st century, MPR was providing three different services: News & Information; Classical Music; and The Current (one station and a music events blog), heard over a 38-station regional radio network and serving a regional population of five million people. MPR was supported by nearly 100,000 members (active subscribers) and had more than 750,000 listeners each week, the largest audience of any regional public radio network. It made full use of podcasts and blogs in addition to traditional radio broadcasting.

See also: National Public Radio; *Prairie Home Companion*; Public Radio International; Public Radio Since 1967

Further Reading

Engelman, Ralph, *Public Radio and Television in America: A Political History*, Thousand Oaks, California, and London: Sage, 1996.
Ledbetter, James, *Made Possible by: The Death of Public Broadcasting in the United States*, New York and London: Verso, 1997.
McCourt, Tom, *Conflicting Communication Interests in America: The Case of National Public Radio*, Westport, Connecticut, and London: Praeger, 1999.
Minnesota Public Radio website, http://minnesota.public radio.org/

Witherspoon, John, Roselle Kovitz, Robert K. Avery, and Alan G. Stavitsky, *A History of Public Broadcasting*, Washington, D.C.: Current, 2000.

TOM MCCOURT,
2009 REVISIONS BY CHRISTOPHER H. STERLING

MONITOR
News and Features Program

A breakthrough in radio journalism formats, *Monitor* premiered on the NBC network in 1955. It was the first regular radio broadcast to employ the magazine format, offering a mix of late-breaking news, interviews, features, humor, and music. The weekend broadcasts continued for nearly 20 years.

The arrival of television in the United States after World War II prompted a dramatic shift in the habits of radio listeners. By the mid-1950s Americans owned more radios and chose from more radio stations than ever, but instead of being the center of attention in the living room, radios had been moved into the kitchen, the bedroom, and the automobile. Surveys suggested that listeners were tuning in more frequently and for shorter periods of time, while performing other tasks around the home, at work, or while driving. This high rate of listener turnover made it difficult for soap operas, variety shows, and concert performances to maintain their audiences, and such shows began disappearing from network schedules. Programming began to emphasize news, music, and local personalities, or disc jockeys, reflecting radio's new role inside—and outside—the typical American home.

Symbolizing this trend was *Monitor,* which premiered on NBC radio on 12 June 1955 as a weekend feature for local affiliates to carry at their discretion, either in its full, 40-hour Friday night-through-Sunday package, or as selected portions to complement local schedules. As *Monitor* did not employ actors or use complex production techniques, its budget was relatively modest. Its electronic theme, nicknamed the "*Monitor* beacon," became a familiar sound to millions of listeners over the next 20 years. A multiple series of variably pitched and paced beeps, the theme allowed affiliates to leave or join the network at scheduled times and also identified the program to its audience.

With its novel potpourri of segments entailing sports, news, interviews, comedy, music, and commentary, *Monitor* became a commercial success. In 1956, Patrick D. Hazard described *Monitor*'s unique format:

> First of all, in a magazine-type broadcast, it is possible to mix levels of taste in the material presented—some-

thing for everyone, in the *Life* [magazine] tradition of photojournalism. And just as in one issue of that magazine, one may see "horror" photos as well as a brilliant color essay on a phase of American art history, so a listener dialed to *Monitor* [may] psychologically tune out, by degrees, program material not compelling to him. There is flexibility of appeal.

(See Hazard, 1956)

This same flexibility in programming permitted greater numbers of advertisers to sponsor smaller blocks of time, a reflection of the new economic order of radio in the 1950s.

Broadcasting magazine had given a sense of *Monitor*'s flavor at the time the program was debuting:

NBC said a typical hour on the weekend service might include the following: the first segment of a trip through Paris with *Monitor*'s roving European correspondent (succeeding segments would be positioned throughout the rest of the day); a dramatic highlight from a current hit Broadway play or movie; live or taped appearances by people at the top of the news that weekend; comedy of all types, including live and recorded routines by stars from all fields of show business, both jokes and stories; a *Monitor* exclusive—which might be a dive with the atomic-powered submarine, the *Nautilus*, firing a rocket at White Sands or visiting Birdland, New York's mecca of jazz; a behind-the-scenes visit with a top star of Broadway or Hollywood; plus, of course, *Monitor*'s basic news, time, weather, sports and local features,

(*Broadcasting*, 11 April 1955)

Monitor was the brainchild of Sylvester L.(Pat) Weaver, a former Young and Rubicam advertising executive who had joined NBC in 1949 as its vice president in charge of television. By the end of 1953, in a climate of tension and uncertainty, he was promoted to president of NBC. In its radio and television audience ratings, NBC was trailing rival CBS, and Weaver vowed to radically change his network's fortunes with new directions in programming. The networks, he said, "must gamble on shows, on talent, on projects; and we will lose in doing this all too often. But only a great network can afford the risk, and that is essentially why the great network service is so important to this country." In addition to *Monitor*, Weaver created *Today* and *The Tonight Show* for NBC television, and he also is credited with the programming strategy of offering occasional specials in lieu of regular shows.

Because of its success, *Monitor* was later imitated on CBS and ABC radio and is arguably a model for the style employed by National Public Radio's *All Things Considered*, beginning in 1971, and *Morning Edition* in 1979. The *Monitor* style also inspired the creation of television magazines,

beginning in 1968 with CBS's *Sixty Minutes*, and later with NBC's *Dateline*, ABC's 20/20, and many others.

Scores of well-known radio personalities hosted *Monitor* segments during its 20-year run, including Ben Grauer, Hugh Downs, Gene Rayburn, Bert Parks, Hal March, Jim Backus, Ed McMahon, Henry Morgan, Joe Garagiola, Garry Moore, Bill Cullen, Cindy Adams, Wolfman Jack, Don Imus, and Robert W. Morgan. It began as a 40-hour weekend broadcast, airing almost continuously from Friday night to midnight Sunday, but was later shortened to 16 hours, from 1961 until 1974. In its final months of production, *Monitor* was offered for 12 live hours each weekend, with nine repeat hours. Its final broadcast was Sunday, 26 January 1975, hosted by John Bartholomew Tucker.

See also: National Broadcasting Company

Creator

Pat Weaver

Producer

James Fleming

Programming History

NBC   June 1955–January 1975

Further Reading

Hazard, Patrick D., "Weaver's Magazine Concept: Notes on Auditioning Radio's New Sound," in *The Quarterly of Film, Radio and Television* 10, no. 4, Berkeley: University of California Press, 1956.
"NBC Radio: Pioneer in New Programming," *Tide* (3 December 1955).
"NBC Radio Tells Plans for 'Monitor,' Its 40-Hour Weekend Program Service," *Broadcasting* (11 April 1955).

DAVID MCCARTNEY

MORMON TABERNACLE CHOIR
Choral Group Broadcasts

The Mormon Tabernacle Choir's broadcast program, *Music and the Spoken Word*, began soon after The Church of Jesus Christ of Latter-day Saints began broadcasting in 1922 on KZN (today's KSL) radio in Salt Lake City. Only rehearsals were broadcast occasionally at first, in part because the musicians were skeptical of the fidelity of radio. The first formal broadcast came on 26 June 1923, when President Warren G. Harding also spoke. The choir began its regular live performance schedule when KSL became an NBC affiliate, and on 15 July 1929 the first regular network Tabernacle Choir program was aired nationally. Today, it claims the title, "longest running continuous network radio program in America" with more than 3,600 broadcasts to its credit. The performance is delivered live when every Sunday morning more than 2,000 radio, television, and cable operations broadcast the program worldwide.

Choir History

The Mormon Choir first sang in Utah's Salt Lake Valley more than 150 years ago, coming into existence in 1847. There was no "Tabernacle" or organ at that time so the group sang in an improvised bower of trees where adobe blocks and poles supported the roof of leaves and branches. From this beginning it played a central part in the early church's commitment to celebrate culture—both sacred and secular events. The historic auditorium, the Tabernacle, is a dome-shaped building in Salt Lake's Temple Square, first used in 1867. The Tabernacle organ was installed that same year and it has become the most recognized symbol of the choir.

In 1849 John Perry, a Welshman, became the choir's first regular director. Perry was followed by others who brought formality and discipline to the choir organization. Evan Stephens, also from Wales, conducted the choir for 27 years. Under his leadership, the choir grew from 125 singers to over 300. Stephens directed the choir on its first major concert tour in 1893 and is credited with laying the foundation for the choir's growing international acclaim.

The choir program tradition consists of song, organ recitals, and a short nondenominational sermon dubbed the "Spoken Word." For more than 40 years, Richard L. Evans provided the latter—thought-provoking, inspirational messages usually two to three minutes in length, all eventually published in a series of books. Upon his death, Evans was replaced by J. Spencer Kinard, who worked for 19 years. He was replaced by the current voice, Lloyd Newell.

The Choir on the Air

The choir began its national broadcast history with the NBC network in 1929, when KSL became an affiliate. When KSL switched to the CBS network in 1933, the choir followed. The "Spoken Word" unit of the program was added in 1936.

It is no wonder that the fidelity of these first programs was questioned by the musicians. As the story goes, KZN/KSL apparently owned only one microphone in those early days. Thus, according to a prearranged plan, the station briefly went off the air as a courier dashed across the street from the station to the Tabernacle carrying that one microphone. There, a tall stepladder was installed near the organ console, and the announcer climbed to his precarious perch atop that ladder holding the microphone that was to pick up both the music and the announcer's words.

Coverage of the choir has grown with technology. In 1948, television broadcasts began in Salt Lake and the choir was among the station program lineup. In 1961, it became a part of the church's launch into international shortwave radio. In the 1970s, the choir took part in the first satellite broadcasts. Today, choir presentations use radio, television, cable, satellite, motion picture recording technology, and the internet in its world-wide distribution. The choir has made more than 150 recordings (some of them CDs), five of which have attained gold status with sales of over 500,000, and two have received platinum awards for sales of more than one million. Perhaps best known is their classic recording of "Battle Hymn of the Republic," recorded with the Philadelphia Orchestra, for which the choir was awarded a Grammy in 1959.

See also: KSL

Further Reading

Evans, Richard L., *Unto the Hills*, New York: Harper, 1940.
Evans, Richard L., *This Day and Always*, New York: Harper, 1942.
Godfrey, Donald, Val E. Limburg, and Heber Wolsey, "KSL, Salt Lake City: At the Crossroads of the West," in *Television in America: Local Station History from Across the Nation*, edited by Michael D. Murray and Donald G. Godfrey, Ames: Iowa State University Press, 1997.
Hicks, M., *Mormonism and Music: A History*, Urbana: University of Illinois Press, 1989.
Jeffery, Charles, *The Mormon Tabernacle Choir*, New York: Harper and Row, 1979.
Limburg, Val E., "Mormon Tabernacle Choir," in *Historical Dictionary of American Radio*, edited by Donald G. Godfrey and Frederic A. Leigh, Westport, Connecticut: Greenwood Press, 1998.
Mormon Tabernacle Choir website, www.musicandthespoken word.com

ELDEAN BENNETT

MORNING EDITION
Newsmagazine Program

For millions of Americans, weekday consciousness begins with *Morning Edition:* the clock radio turns itself on to the razzle of B.J. Liederman's theme music or the resonant calm of host Bob Edwards.

The program began on 5 November 1979. After National Public Radio (NPR) scored a success with its afternoon newsmagazine, *All Things Considered*, the network's member stations wanted a morning service. They were not necessarily looking for a program. Most member stations at the time ran classical music in the morning, but they wanted news and feature elements they could drop into those programs. Unlike *All Things Considered*, which had evolved on the air, *Morning Edition* was to be a planned creation, conceived by a committee with input from stations and guidance from audience researchers. The format was to be a two-hour series of segments, with a mix of news, sports, arts, and features. None of the segments was to be longer than nine minutes, with fixed times so that stations could take what they wished and cover the rest with local news, weather, and traffic. But production of the pilot was handed over to two morning newsmen from the immensely popular Washington commercial station WMAL. As former producer Jay Kernis recalls, "they knew how to do *AM* drive-time radio, but they broke the promise of public radio. They ignored the audience we'd been building." The pilot failed. Host Bob Edwards remembers them as sounding "like a bad talk show in a small market."

NPR's news director, Barbara Cohen, fired the producers and the first two hosts. Kernis, the arts producer, was promoted to senior producer and "given ten days to re-invent the show and teach the staff how to produce it." Frank Fitzmaurice came in as executive producer to oversee the program's news content. Bob Edwards, who had spent five years as cohost of *All Things Considered* with Susan Stamberg, was recruited to fill in as host for 30 days, until the network could find someone to take over.

Jay Kernis recalls how he and Edwards thought through the role that began Edwards' more than two decades as the solo host of the program. "A host is not an announcer," Kernis says. "A host is the glue that holds the show together. There should be this vortex of information, and in the calm center, there should be the host, Bob, steady Bob, carrying it all back to you."

Kernis also preached to his staff that the show's strict format should be liberating rather than restricting, a concept he says he got from the late

arts producer Fred Calland, who pointed out that *All Things Considered* had to create a new architecture in its relatively free-form 90 minutes every day. The program could succeed or fail, depending on whether that structure was successful. With *Morning Edition*, the architecture was a given. As Calland put it, "you know the perimeters of the canvas, now you can paint."

One example of working within the structure came when Kernis had to write a short piece of advance copy for Bob's interview with American haiku poet Nick Virgilio, to be read just before newscaster Jean Cochran delivered the top stories. He did it in classic, 17-syllable form:

> Some words hit; some hurt.
> Jersey poet writes *haiku*.
> News from Jean Cochran.

Resources were stretched thin in the early days of the program. *All Things Considered* was not anxious to share its small pool of reporters, and some reporters preferred being heard on the established afternoon flagship. This meant that Edwards had to get at the news through live interviews, often a dozen or more in a day. Kernis credits three of NPR's most successful female reporters, Cokie Roberts, Nina Totenberg, and Linda Wertheimer, with seeing the audience potential in *Morning Edition* and doing extra work to make sure their reports got on its air.

Morning Edition's voracious format made more room for commentators, too, such as retired sportscaster Red Barber, whose weekly chats with Edwards were one of the program's most popular features for a dozen years.

Morning Edition's producers say the feel of the program is governed by two factors: it is the first thing many people hear each day, and the format is designed to be shared with local stations.

Executive producer Ellen McDonnell says that listeners need to be nudged into their day: "I tell our substitute hosts 'you're up; we're not. People don't want to be blown out of bed.'" Though the show has aired vivid personalities, including Susan Stamberg, Alex Chadwick, and Renee Montaigne as substitute hosts, senior producer Greg Allen says that focus groups consistently favor Bob Edwards' reassuring, understated style. "When Bob's on vacation, we get letters from listeners urging us to bring him back."

The fact that *Morning Edition* begins the day means that its news content is more anticipatory than that of *All Things Considered*. Producers look for items about what's coming up in the day, and what those events are likely to mean for the listener.

Producer Jay Kernis says he decided early on that if he could not know which 20 minutes of the show listeners were going to hear, he would try to make sure that any 20 minutes contained some news, some arts, and some feature. Although the program no longer has specific times dedicated to arts or sports, producers still try to maintain a mix that balances hard news with human emotion. Ellen McDonnell says, "you need a smile, music, a commentary. When the news is grim, we try to be cognizant of the time of day. We don't sugar-coat the news, but we don't have to report every graphic detail." Edwards and McDonnell say that *Morning Edition* aims for a certain civility. McDonnell keeps in mind that "we're a guest who's been invited into your home or your car." Edwards points out that, in the morning at least, "people want that familiar voice, the radio friend."

In March 2004, NPR's programming vice president removed Bob Edwards as *Morning Edition* anchor, provoking a huge listener outcry. Some called their local stations to complain and others withdrew financial support. Edwards was just months shy of celebrating a quarter century in his role (and three decades with the network). Though asked to stay on as a senior correspondent, Edwards chose to leave and in July took up a new role hosting his own channel at XM Satellite Radio.

In December 2004 NPR gave the *Morning Edition* host positions to Renee Montagne (generally based at NPR West, formed two years earlier in Culver City, California) and Steve Inskeep (who broadcast from Washington), both of whom had acted as temporary co-hosts since April. Montagne had hosted *All Things Considered* for two years, and Inskeep had reported for NPR programs since 1996. The changes were more than cosmetic or limited to personnel. The anchor/hosts frequently travel and report from distant locations, most notably during Hurricane Katrina in 2005, and on the several occasions when Montagne sent back reports from Afghanistan. And the program took on a more aggressive breaking news role as well.

See also: All Things Considered; National Public Radio

Host

Bob Edwards (1979–2004)
Renee Montagne and Steve Inskeep (2004–)

Contributors

Baxter Black, Frank Deford, Joe Davidson, John Feinstein, David Frum, Matt Miller, Patt Morrison, Judy Muller, Ruben Navarette, Kevin Phillips,

John Ridley, Cokie Roberts, Amity Shlaes, Kenneth Turan

Programming History

National Public Radio   5 November 1979–present

Further Reading

Collins, Mary, *National Public Radio: The Cast of Characters*, Washington, D.C.: Seven Locks Press, 1993.
Looker, Tom, *The Sound and the Story: NPR and the Art of Radio*, Boston: Houghton Mifflin, 1995.
Siegel, Robert, editor, *The NPR Interviews, 1996*, Boston: Houghton Mifflin, 1996.
Stamberg, Susan, *Every Night at Five: Susan Stamberg's All Things Considered Book*, New York: Pantheon, 1982.
Stamberg, Susan, *Talk: NPR's Susan Stamberg Considers All Things*, New York: Turtle Bay Books, 1993.
Wertheimer, Linda, editor, *Listening to America: Twenty-five Years in the Life of a Nation, As Heard on National Public Radio*, Boston: Houghton Mifflin, 1995.

COREY FLINTOFF,
2009 REVISIONS BY CHRISTOPHER H. STERLING

MORNING PROGRAMS

Morning programming developed slowly in radio, an ironic fact given that morning or "drive-time" would by the 1960s become the most valuable radio broadcast time to advertisers seeking the largest audiences available.

Origins

Radio stations were slow to program morning hours as there was seemingly little audience interest in listening so early. Radio began, as an evening service, only gradually moving into daytime hours. Beginning in larger cities, however, by the mid-1920s many stations had expanded their schedules to program the entire day. Their schedules included early morning hours, sometimes beginning at 7 or 8 A.M., and usually offered some type of uplifting talk and/or music. Among the best known of the pioneers was Charles K. Field, who created the "Cheerio" personality for early morning KGO listeners in San Francisco starting in 1927. At the same time Anthony Snow was broadcasting home-spun philosophy as "Tony Wons" to Chicago listeners over WLS. Both soon moved to the national scene for lengthy network runs into the 1930s. A few other stations offered a variety of music and talk. Baltimore's WCAU began its *Morning Musical Clock* in 1927 or perhaps earlier (station records are unclear), built around a theme of the passing early morning time. It was still on the air two decades later. The program title would in future years come to label a format on many radio stations.

With a growing audience of radio set owners by the late 1920s and slowly awakening advertiser interest in reaching those listeners, the new national networks began to expand their program offerings into earlier daytime hours as well. Programs took many forms, from informal talks and music to those aimed at children. Virtually all were upbeat in tone as befitted the start of the day. Among the first was Field's organ music and talk-filled *Cheerio*, moved from San Francisco and heard for a half-hour daily on NBC at 8:30 A.M. beginning in 1927 and continuing for a decade. *Jolly Bill and Jane*, with music and chatter aimed at children, was also heard daily on NBC at various early morning hours and ran for a decade beginning in 1928. *Gene and Glen* provided early morning comedy (and a multitude of voices) for many years on NBC starting in 1930. *Tony Wons' Scrapbook* moved from Chicago to New York and was heard daily on CBS (and later NBC) during the 1930s. The host would begin each program asking "are yuh listenin'?" and millions of women were. Wons edited nearly a dozen published collections of the poetry and prose he had used on the air.

Golden Years

Network offerings broadened in the 1930s to include drama (*Vic and Sade* began in 1932 on NBC Blue and was first heard at 9:30 A.M.), comedy (*Laugh Club* on NBC-Blue), comedy household hints (*The Wife Saver*, on various morning slots on NBC and NBC-Blue from 1932 until 1943), news commentary (Ann Hard on weekday mornings on NBC), and health (*Health Talk* daily on CBS). In 1940 CBS offered early morning classes from the *American School of the Air*.

As happened with other radio programming, the developing world crisis and eventual outbreak of war in 1941 was reflected in morning programs. Many stations, especially those near military bases, offered morning "Reville" shows, a variation of the "musical clock" format already present in many markets. Early morning network newscasts became a staple on all the networks beginning in 1940. They were heard daily, typically for 15 minutes, and were soon filled with wartime news and information.

As soap operas filled most network daytime hours in the early 1940s, some of the series, such as the CBS drama *Woman of Courage* (1939–42), began as early as 9 A.M. Local stations (and sometimes the networks) took a different tack and offered many homemaking programs at various daytime hours. *Adelaide Hawley Homemaking* was heard most weekday mornings on CBS in 1940.

Networks increasingly focused on talk variety programs for morning hours. Arthur Godfrey's CBS show (so popular he had to give up his local morning program on Washington, D.C.'s WMAL in 1948) and Don McNeill's *Breakfast Club* on ABC had strong audience appeal during the 1940s and 1950s. Such network morning shows became a popular way to start the day along with regular newscasts, a pattern that had developed first during the war.

Postwar "Musical Clocks"

Music-based programming by local stations dramatically expanded daytime program offerings. These "musical clock" or "early bird" or "wake-up" programs had developed in some markets in the 1930s, grew during the war, and expanded greatly in the postwar years. Virtually all of them were based on a combination of music, news, weather, and talk items with constant references to the time and, in larger cities, to traffic conditions. As radio prime time remained the most important listening period (and thus expensive for advertisers), advertising in morning programs could be purchased for one-third to one-half the cost of advertising in the evening hours, and advertisers flocked to the proven ability of early morning radio to sell listeners.

By mid-decade, local station morning broadcast hours were rapidly becoming radio's prime time as network offerings faded away in the face of television competition. Costs to advertisers rose and morning hosts became the new stars of radio. One, Tom Joyner, was in such demand that for many years he hosted a morning show in Dallas and then flew to Chicago for an afternoon drive-time program. He stuck to this grueling schedule for years. The parallel rise of rock and roll music in the 1950s helped fuel a faster-paced morning show still based on a mixture of recorded music and live news, weather, and sports reports. Radio listening became a popular way to make increasingly congested traffic and long commutes more tolerable. In major markets regular traffic reports became an important part of the morning show format.

In the 1970s the morning period spawned the so-called "morning 200" format, a fast-paced, high-energy approach that is known to disregard traditional programming rules. The concept behind this morning programming approach is to create a zany, often irreverent atmosphere designed to keep listeners fully engaged, awake, and on the edge of their car seats during the commute to work and school.

Employing an ensemble cast of characters, its prevailing programming ingredient is comedy and pop-culture chatter usually revolving around hit movies and TV shows, celebrities, and sports. This morning daypart schematic has been refined (toned down in some cases) over the years and has become a mainstay at most larger market contemporary music outlets.

Noncommercial stations also got into the act. Local university and community stations had long provided a mixture of news, features, and, often, classical music. In 1981 National Public Radio developed *Morning Edition* as an expanded long-form news program designed to compete with the more concise commercial radio news programs.

Modern Mornings

Local radio stations seek to provide audiences with personalities who would build a "listener habit" and amass large and loyal followings. In most markets, morning radio hosts became celebrities attracting huge rating numbers that advertisers found compelling and appealing. Among the myriad stars of the sunrise hours was WTIC-AM's Bob Steele, who began entertaining Hartford, Connecticut area listeners in the late 1930s and continued doing so into the 1990s. Steele's tenure on the air, although exceptional, was not atypical, as morning radio hosts around the country often enjoyed greater longevity than other on-air personnel. One indication of the enormous status of certain popular morning hosts is that on occasion radio facilities have actually been named or renamed in their honor. One such example is WPRO's Brine Broadcast Center in Providence, Rhode Island, whose moniker pays tribute to morning radio giant Salty Brine for his nearly half century of service.

Modern morning disc jockeys tend to talk more than they do in other dayparts. They continue to provide a generally upbeat tone just as their forbears did eight decades ago. News and traffic reporters often are part of a "morning team" as a star disc jockey often has a regular sidekick, or co-anchor.

Morning drive time radio—usually defined as being between 6 A.M. and 10 A.M. Monday through Friday—is considered prime real estate in radio broadcasting as it's the time that attracts the most listeners and stations charge their highest rates. Radio does well during these hours as people can't focus on its chief competitors, television or the internet. Often a station's morning show becomes its de facto flagship broadcast. Even if the rest of the broadcast day is filled with syndicated offerings and generic voice-tracking and other automation, morning drive-time will often be preserved as a station's perhaps only live, local programming. Despite the inherent cost of producing rather than carrying a syndicated morning show, stations usually believe that such an expense is offset by what is gained in providing home-grown morning fare: the chance to connect with listeners while generating goodwill within the community.

Nevertheless, as a cost-saving measure, many stations have turned to nationally syndicated morning shows. Programmers have a wide assortment of syndicated offerings from which to choose to create a fit for their audience. They range from sports-themed shows (like ESPN's *Mike and Mike in the Morning*) to shock jock-y (e.g., *Mancow in the Morning*) to African-American-oriented (like Tom Joyner or Steve Harvey) to politics and news (the re-launched Don Imus). Some of the country's other top syndicated morning talkers include *America in the Morning* with Jim Bohannon, Bob and Tom, and Big D and Bubba.

See also: Bob and Ray; Farm/Agricultural Radio; *Morning Edition*; Talk Radio; *Vic and Sade*

Further Reading

Eastman, Susan Tyler, and Douglas A. Ferguson, *Broadcast/Cable Programming: Strategies and Practices*, 5th edition, by Eastman and Ferguson, Belmont, California: Wadsworth, 1996 (see especially chapters 13 and 14).

Field, Charles Kellogg, *The Story of Cheerio*, New York: Garden City, 1936.

Garver, Robert I., "The Musical Clock," in *Successful Radio Advertising with Sponsor Participation Programs*, New York: Prentice-Hall, 1949.

Harden, Frank, Jackson Weaver, and Ed Meyer, *On the Radio with Harden and Weaver*, New York: Morrow, 1983.

Joyner, Tom, Mary Flowers Boyce, and Muriel L. Sims, *"Go with the Bit": The Tom Joyner Morning Show*, Chicago: Johnson, 1999.

Lieberman, Philip A., *Radio's Morning Show Personalities: Early Hour Broadcasters and DJs from the 1920s to the 1990s*, Jefferson, North Carolina: McFarland, 1996.

Wons, Anthony, *'R' You Listening*, Chicago: Reilly and Lee, 1931.

Wons, Anthony, compiler, *Tony's Scrap Book*, Cincinnati, Ohio: Wons, 1929; 1944-45 edition, Chicago: Reilly and Lee, 1944.

MICHAEL C. KEITH AND CHRISTOPHER H. STERLING,
2009 REVISIONS BY CARY O'DELL

MOTOROLA
Radio Manufacturer

Motorola has been a leader in exploring and promoting new uses of radio technology. The Chicago-based company initially focused on radio receivers.

Later, Motorola developed applications of the technology for government, military, and private use, helping radio to realize its potential as a two-way communication tool. In so doing, Motorola became a haven for engineering and high-quality technological innovation.

The Motorola story starts in the 1920s, with a business-savvy young man from north central Illinois. Paul Galvin quickly saw the potential of radio as the medium developed. Galvin and partners formed two companies to produce storage batteries and power converters for radios. Both were closed by 1928, but Galvin continued to believe in the potential of the business. After borrowing $1,000, Paul Galvin and his brother Joseph formed the Galvin Manufacturing Corporation in September 1928.

Galvin Manufacturing quickly moved into the production of private label radios for wholesalers and retailers and experienced some moderate growth. But smaller firms like Galvin's were hit hard by the economic downturn that followed the stock market crash in late 1929. If Galvin Manufacturing was to remain in business, the company needed to develop a landmark product that would mark it as a vital player in radio. Paul Galvin found the cornerstone for his company with the automobile radio.

Although auto radios had been available in the 1920s, they were expensive, difficult to install, and sounded terrible because of static interference from electric devices within the car. Galvin and his associates developed a prototype that solved these problems and installed it in his car in time for the 1930 Radio Manufacturer's Association convention. Galvin drove to Atlantic City for the show and demonstrated his new product to conventioneers who marveled at the innovation.

Galvin Manufacturing's 5T71 was the first commercial radio designed to fit most automobiles and sold for about $120 including installation. In order to create a name that would associate sound with motion, Galvin coined the name Motorola for his radio by combining the word *motor* with *ola* from *Victrola*. Though Galvin Manufacturing retained its original moniker for years, it was the trademarked Motorola name that became famous. By 1936 Motorola was an industry leader and was among the first brands of car radio to include push buttons, fine tuning, and tone controls.

That same year, the Federal Communications Commission (FCC) took action that facilitated Galvin's move into other radio products. After the FCC allocated spectrum space for police communications, Galvin introduced its first AM mobile receiver, called the Police Cruiser, and the following year introduced accompanying transmission equipment. Soon, the need for two-way communications became apparent, so Galvin developed mobile AM transmitters for officers in the field. The cost of a complete system, including one base station and three mobile radios, was about $4,000.

Motorola introduced the first line of improved two-way FM equipment in 1941. This innovation marked the start of a 30-year period in which Motorola engineer Daniel Noble and the company became internationally known for research and development. Motorola later adapted this same FM technology for use in larger commercial and industrial markets as two-way radio communication became commonplace in the 1950s.

During this same era, Motorola became an important supplier to the American military. When World War II broke out in Europe, Galvin assembled an engineering team to develop a lightweight, portable, two-way radio that could be used on the battlefield. Eventually, the U.S. Army awarded Galvin Manufacturing a contract for the Handie-Talkie, a five-pound AM radio with a range of about 1 mile. Galvin manufactured more than 100,000 of the radios before the end of the war. The company also developed a 35-pound FM two-way radio in a backpack with a range of ten miles. This device, the Galvin SCR-300, became better known as the Walkie-Talkie and was hailed by military leaders as a pivotal communication device. Galvin produced 45,000 of the Walkie-Talkies along with jeep and tank radios to aid the war effort.

Galvin Manufacturing became a publicly traded stock in 1943. In 1947 the company formally changed its name to Motorola and prepared to reap the dividends of a booming postwar economy. It did so by continuing to expand on its radio business but also by continued research and development efforts and what company officials call "continuous selfrenewal" into other areas of electronics. In the 1950s, Motorola became an important supplier of automobile radios to Ford, General Motors, and Chrysler. Almost one-third of the car radios on American highways had been made by Motorola as the decade concluded. It was also during this period that Motorola started to manufacture television sets, developed some of the first radio paging systems, and became involved in the semiconductor business. Motorola initially used transistors to miniaturize its own products, leading to a line of pocket-sized radios. Transistors were also crucial in the development of its advanced, two-way Motrac system that ultimately boasted a 50 percent global market share for mobile radios.

Over the years Motorola maintained a partnership with the American government on various projects, including the space program. Motorola systems have played a vital role in tracking and communications between Earth and outer space since the company developed a system for an early satellite mission in 1958.

Despite all this, in the 2000s, the company began to experience serious business problems, partially related to its inability to continue, or duplicate, the success of its once wildly popular cellphone handsets. When the company's earnings dropped 84 percent in the fourth quarter of 2008, Standard and Poor's downgraded Motorola's credit rating to junk status.

To regain its footing, Motorola has undertaken many initiatives from offering the first fully "green" handset (a phone made of recycled plastic water bottles) for its more eco-conscious consumers to the opposite end of the spectrum, a high-end, "prestige" phone with a sapphire crystal display screen for $2,000.

Motorola has also undertaken to encourage schools and universities to go completely wireless. The company has pitched its wireless LAN (WLAN) portfolio as ideal for use by students and faculty, and campuses from Georgia to Texas to India have opted for Motorola wireless solutions in the hopes of saving millions in leased line costs.

See also: Automobile Radio; Receivers

Further Reading

Collins, James C., and Jerry I. Porras, *Built to Last: Successful Habits of Visionary Companies*, New York: HarperBusiness, 1994; London: Century, 1995; 3rd edition, London: Random House Business, 2000.

Crockett, Roger, and Peter Elstrom, "How Motorola Lost Its Way," *Business Week* (4 May 1998).

Motorola website, www.motorola.com/home/.

Motorola, Inc., *Managing Change: Positioning for the Future Summary Annual Report*.

Petrakis, Harry Mark, *The Founder's Touch: The Life of Paul Galvin of Motorola*, New York: McGraw-Hill, 1965; 3rd edition, Chicago: Motorola University Press/Ferguson, 1991.

Tetzeli, Rick, "And Now for Motorola's Next Trick," *Fortune* (28 April 1997).

Weingartner, Fannia, editor, *Motorola: A Journey through Time and Technology*, Schaumburg, Illinois: Motorola, 1994.

STUART L. ESROCK,
2009 REVISIONS BY CARY O'DELL

MOVIES

See: Film Depictions of Radio; Hollywood and Radio

MUSEUMS AND ARCHIVES OF RADIO
Repositories of Radio History

There are many public, private, and academic archives and museums the sole purpose of which is to preserve radio broadcast documents and programs. Most of them have audio and visual recordings, books, periodicals, pamphlets, oral histories, interviews, and other documents that trace the history of radio programming and radio broadcasting. In addition, several archives and museums are devoted to the history of radio technology itself and the development and advancement of this technology. Still others trace the important figures and individuals in radio broadcasting, radio technology, and radio history. There are also dozens of old-time-radio collector's clubs with less extensive collections of radio broadcasts.

Origins of Museums and Archives of Radio

The idea of establishing formal radio museums and archives began in the 1940s, and such institutions were actually developed in the 1970s. The Broadcast Pioneers Library was the first organized library of radio history; it was begun in the 1960s and formally opened in 1972. However, some less formal collections began much earlier. For example, in 1949 the Library of Congress began to collect and preserve some radio programming. At the same time, the National Archives started collecting and preserving programming from governmental sources and began receiving donated new programs and material from radio stations and networks throughout the U.S.

During World War II, the Armed Forces Radio Services began to produce discs in order to bring radio programs to U.S. troops during the war. These discs would later become the basis of privately traded material. During the same period, a few network and syndicated programs were distributed on discs as well.

In the 1950s the Broadcast Pioneers organization unsuccessfully attempted to establish a museum of broadcast history. During the same decade, individuals began seriously recording and collecting radio programs with the introduction of homerecording equipment and the demise of network radio. Reliable and affordable reel-to-reel recorders were first introduced into the consumer market during this time.

However, radio program collecting did not become truly popular until the 1960s, when classic radio programming began to change dramatically and, many felt, to disappear. As a result, many individuals began to realize that preserving such programs was essential for documenting the history of radio. Individuals began to organize for the purpose of exchanging radio programs, information, and resources. As expected, as radio formats rapidly changed, radio stations began to discard their old stored material and programs. These informal groups began collecting such materials, and a collectors movement started to grow. These groups also created newsletters on radio program collecting.

One of the earliest and most influential of the collectors groups was the Radio Historical Society of America, founded by Charles Ingersoll in the 1960s. Ingersoll also started one of the first newsletters for collectors of old-time radio programs, and *Radio Dial* set the standard for those to follow. One of these was *Hello Again*, started in 1970 by Jay Hickerson. It remains the most popular of old-time-radio collector group newsletters. This newsletter was also part of the formation of the Friends of Old Time Radio. *Hello Again* was successful because it brought together more than 100 of the most active program collectors. According to Professor Marvin R. Bensman of the University of Memphis Radio Archives, "Today, approximately 160-plus active collectors comprise the mass of privately collected broadcast material available."

Another factor that helped spawn the radio collector movement was the sale of radio programs to private individuals. J. David Goldin, a former Columbia Broadcasting System (CBS), National Broadcasting Company (NBC), and Mutual engineer, first mass-marketed and sold radio programs. In the late 1960s, Goldin formed Radio Yesteryear, a company that sells audio recordings of classic radio programs. He also started an album subsidiary of the company called Radiola.

A big boost came for the establishment of the first broadcast history library when William S. Hedges, a former NBC executive, began collecting items for the Broadcast Pioneers History Project between 1964 and 1971. This collection, which consists of nearly 13,000 items, including correspondence, articles, and speeches in 540 different subject categories, formed the core collection of the Broadcast Pioneers Library, which opened in 1972 and led to the establishment of the Library of American Broadcasting.

Public and Academic Museum and Archive Collections

Library of American Broadcasting (University of Maryland)

The first formally established institutional radio archive was the Broadcast Pioneers Library, begun in the 1960s and formally opened in 1972. It was housed in the headquarters of the National Association of Broadcasters (NAB) in Washington, D.C., until 1994. It then became part of the library system at the University of Maryland, College Park, and became known as the Library of American Broadcasting, one of the most extensive collections of the history of broadcasting. The collection consists of audio and video recordings, books, periodicals, pamphlets, oral histories, photographs, personal collections, and scripts that pertain to the history of broadcasting. The library features more than 8,000 volumes ranging from engineering manuals to programming histories. It is particularly strong in its book collection from the early part of the 1920s and 1930s, tracing the evolution of broadcasting.

The library's audio holdings include 1,000 interviews, speeches, news broadcasts, special events, and oral histories (with many accompanied by transcripts) of such important radio figures as Edgar Bergen, Norman Corwin, Leonard Goldenson, Lowell Thomas, and William Paley. There are also thousands of recordings in many formats, including more than 8,300 recorded discs, 25,000 photographs, and 10,000 CDs of commercials in its Radio Advertising Bureau Collection. Also housed here are many specialized collections from radio performers, executives, broadcast engineers, writers, producers, and magazine publishers. Highlights include political speeches from Franklin D. Roosevelt, Winston Churchill, and Harry S. Truman in the Donald H. Kirkley collection; more than 160 recordings of congressional hearings, political speeches, and other media events of the 1960s and 1970s in the Daniel Brechner Collection; and The Center for Media and Public Affairs Collection, which contains talk radio programs.

Some of its other holdings include some 7,000 pamphlets, ranging from 1920s Bell Laboratories radio engineering bulletins to promotional materials from broadcast networks; the Westinghouse News Collection (1958–82), which consists mainly of raw feeds from the Washington bureau; the Associated Press Radio Competition Collection (1967–68), which contains samples of radio journalism, almost exclusively from California.

There is also a collection of government documents that includes the Navigation Bureau List of Radio Stations (1913–27), Federal Radio Commission (FRC) and Federal Communications Commission (FCC) decisions, and congressional reports and hearings.

The museum acquired the Chester Coleman Collection of the NAB Library and Historical

Archive in June 1998. This collection includes more than 4,000 books and periodicals. The NAB collection also includes historical meeting and convention minutes, newsletters, promotional materials, and scrapbooks.

National Public Broadcasting Archives (University of Maryland)

An additional archive housed at the University of Maryland is the National Public Broadcasting Archives (NPBA). The archives originated as a cooperative effort between both educational institutions and broadcasting organizations, including the Corporation for Public Broadcasting (CPB), Public Broadcasting Service (PBS), National Public Radio (NPR), the Academy for Educational Development, and the University of Maryland. The idea was spearheaded by Donald R. McNeil, a former PBS board member who was concerned that the history of public broadcasting was at risk.

The archives, which opened 1 June 1990, form part of the Archives and Manuscripts Department of the University of Maryland Libraries. They consist of historical materials from the major organizations of U.S. noncommercial broadcasting. These include PBS, Children's Television Workshop, CPB, NPR, Agency for Instructional Technology, America's Public Television Stations, Association for Educational Telecommunications and Technology, Public Service Satellite Consortium, and the Joint Council for Educational Telecommunications.

The NPBA also has personal papers from many influential public broadcasting figures and a reference library containing basic studies of the broadcasting industry, rare pamphlets, and journals on relevant topics. The archives also house a collection of audio and video programs from public broadcasting's national production and support centers and from local stations. There is also a collection of oral history tapes and transcripts from the NPR Oral History Project.

Museum of Broadcast Communications (Chicago, Illinois)

The Museum of Broadcast Communications is devoted solely to radio and television broadcasting and is housed on two floors of the Chicago Cultural Center. (The Museum was scheduled to relocate to new premises in Chicago's River North area as of Spring 2004.) The museum's purpose is to educate the "public, teachers, and students about the profound influence of radio, television, and advertising in our world." It does this via hands-on

exhibits, broadcasting memorabilia, a public archives collection, and educational outreach programs.

The Museum was founded in 1987 by Bruce DuMont, the nephew of television pioneer Allen B. DuMont, using private contributions. It consists of changing exhibits, radio and television archives, a Radio Hall of Fame, an Advertising Hall of Fame, the Lynne Harvey Radio Center, and a gift shop. The museum's public archive, the Arthur C. Nielsen Jr. Research Center, contains over 85,000 hours of television and radio broadcasts, commercials, and newscasts, with 13,000 television programs, 4,000 radio broadcasts, and 11,000 television commercials, all of which can be screened on site in one of 26 study suites. All programs in the archive's collection are cross-referenced and cataloged in a fully computerized retrieval system. The collection focuses on Chicago television news, talk/interview programs, documentaries, political broadcasts, programs of its Radio Hall of Fame inductees, sports programming, and "Golden Era" television dramas.

Included in its archives is an extensive historic radio program collection, the Chuck Schaden Radio Collection, which contains more than 50,000 programs and is considered to be the largest of its kind in the United States. The Lynne Harvey Radio Center features a live, weekly broadcast of *Those Were the Days*, by radio historian Chuck Schaden, complete with a live studio audience, as well as other live broadcasts. The museum also hosts many special events, including an annual induction ceremony into its Radio Hall of Fame, which pays tribute to the legends of radio. The Hall of Fame was founded by the Emerson Radio Corporation in 1988 and was taken over by the Museum of Broadcast Communication in 1991. There is also a collection of vintage radio and television sets from local donors. Due to financial difficulties, the MBC and its archives were closed to the public by the end of the 21st century's first decade. As it sought to complete its new home, the museum staged small-scale events as well as its annual Radio Hall of Fame induction ceremonies.

The Paley Center for Media (New York City and Beverly Hills, California)

Formerly, the Museum of Television and Radio, the Paley Center adopted its most recent name change in 2007 in order to better reflect its attention to all types of media in the internet age. The bicoastal Center is devoted to radio and television broadcast history, particularly focusing on the individuals and programs that make up that history. The museum was founded in New York in 1975 by William S.

Paley, chairman of CBS, as the Museum of Broadcasting. The museum changed its name and moved to a larger headquarters in September 1991. The New York museum's holdings include some 100,000 radio and television programs, as well as 10,000 commercials. It also includes two screening rooms, two theaters, a group listening room, 96 individual booths equipped with television and radio consoles, a research library, and a gift shop. In addition, there are three public galleries that display broadcast industry artifacts.

In March 1996 the Los Angeles branch of the museum opened in Beverly Hills. It has the same features as its East Coast predecessor. Because Los Angeles is the number-one radio market in the United States, the Los Angeles museum offers more of an emphasis on radio than the New York branch (which focuses more on television). In addition, when radio was in its heyday during the 1930s and 1940s, many shows were made in Los Angeles. According to Norm Pattiz, a trustee of the museum and chairman of Westwood One, "We're now in the No. 1 and No. 2 radio markets, with exactly the same material available at both museums."

Both locations offer seminars by critics, directors, producers, performers, journalists, and writers, including University Satellite Seminars, and both offer a wide variety of programs from the collection in two screening rooms and two main theaters, as well as constantly changing special exhibits. Programming from current series and exhibitions is shown throughout the day.

American Radio Archives and Museum (Thousand Oaks, California)

The American Library of Radio and Television is part of the Special Collections Department of the Thousand Oaks Library System. Its holdings focus specifically on the history of radio rather than on the individuals in the profession. The library was founded in 1984 after the Thousand Oaks Library System broke away from the Ventura County System. The newly formed Library Foundation and the Friends of the Library decided that they wanted the library to focus on larger programs and a research collection. Specifically, they were anxious to fill a niche in the Los Angeles area by focusing on a special historical collection. They chose broadcasting because several of the library organizers had extensive contacts in the radio broadcasting industry.

Along with Maryland's Library of Broadcasting, the American Library of Radio and Television offers one of the largest collections of broadcasting documents in the United States, and it has an extensive reference collection of radio materials including 23,000 radio and television scripts, 10,000 photographs, 10,000 books on the history of radio and television broadcasting, pamphlets, sound recordings, periodicals, 200 maps and charts, manuscripts and personal papers, 5,000 audio recordings, and 50 oral history tapes.

In addition, the library contains archives of such notable individuals and stations as Norman Corwin, Bob Crosby, Monty Masters, Carlton E. Morse, Rudy Vallee, and KNX AM. Their Radio Series Scripts Collection contains scripts from 1930 through 1990, and their Radio Sound Recordings Collection contains recordings from 1932 to 1994.

The museum was adding to its existing space in 2009. The $30 million expansion will provide the museum and archive with 44,000 square feet of display and storage space as well as a student radio theatre, engineering and disc jockey booths, and a specially designed listening room named after radio writer and producer Norman Corwin.

The George Clark Radioana Collection at the Smithsonian Institution

The George H. Clark Radioana Collection is a part of the National Museum of American History of the Smithsonian Institution. The collection was assembled by George Clark of the Radio Corporation of America (RCA) and is one of the most extensive collections of documents and publications on the history of wireless and radio in the United States. It was transferred from the Massachusetts Institute of Technology to the National Museum of American History in 1959. The collection occupies more than 276 linear feet of shelf space, but it has not been fully indexed.

The collection is particularly strong from 1900 through 1935. There is extensive biographical information on the men who developed the technical aspects of radio and the industry; information on the inception, growth, and activities of radio companies, most notably the National Electric Signaling Company and RCA; and photographs of all aspects of radio.

The United States Library of Congress and the National Archives

Both the United States Library of Congress and the National Archives in Washington, D.C., have collections of voice recordings and radio programs. The Library of Congress has received donations of transcriptions of old radio shows. There are over

500,000 programs in their collection, including a large number of British Broadcasting Corporation (BBC) and Armed Forces Radio and Television Service (AFRTS) recordings. The library also has a large collection of radio-related items, such as early folk and regional programs, as well as a large selection of NBC Radio's broadcast discs from 1935 to 1970, which cover the Depression, World War II, postwar recovery, and radio comedy and drama programs. Other radio collections include the WOR-AM collection, United Nations recordings, Library of Congress concerts and literary recordings, and the Armed Forces Radio Collection. There is also an extensive collection from the U.S. Office of War Information (OWI), which, between 1944 and 1947, transferred thousands of items used to support the war effort to the Library of Congress. These items include OWI sound recordings, photographs, and a small number of research papers. In addition, the Motion Picture, Broadcasting, and Recorded Sound Division holds nearly 50,000 acetate disc recordings of foreign and domestic radio broadcasts.

Though maintaining a presence at the Library's main location in downtown Washington, D.C., much of the Library of Congress's film and audio collection has been moved to the Library's new National AudioVisual Conservation Center located in Culpeper, Virginia. Formerly a storage area for the Federal Reserve, the Culpeper facility was turned over the Library of Congress in 1998 and its buildings and storage units substantially rebuilt with a $120 million grant from the Packard Foundation. It opened in mid-2005. Due to its location and construction (which include state-of-the-art environmental controls), the Culpeper center is the optimal storage space for film, audio and other electronic media.

The National Archives of the United States also features a broad collection of radio-related material. Most of these are housed at the Special Media Archives Services Division's Motion Picture, Sound, and Video unit at Archives II in College Park, Maryland. The holdings include 150,000 reels of film, 160,000 sound recordings, and 20,000 videotapes. These materials were obtained from both public and private sources. The sound recordings catalog includes radio broadcasts, speeches, interviews, documentaries, oral histories, and public information programs. The library indicates that the earliest recording they have dates from 1896, with the bulk of their recordings coming from between 1935 and the present.

Some of the specialized catalogs in the holdings include the NPR catalog, which contains NPR news and public-affairs broadcasts from 1971 to 1978, and the Milo Ryan Photoarchive Collection, which includes 5,000 recordings, primarily of CBS-KIRO radio broadcasts from 1931 to 1977. These materials were originally kept at the University of Washington and contain news and public-affairs programs, speeches, interviews, wartime dramas, and daily World War II news programs. The library also features the American Broadcasting Companies (ABC) radio collection, which consists of 27,000 radio broadcasts of news and public-affairs programs from 1943 to 1971.

Duke University Library Advertising History Archive

Duke University Library has a special Advertising History Archive that is part of the John W. Hartman Center for Sales, Advertising, and Marketing History. The advertising history collection located in the Hartman Center is the J. Walter Thompson Company Archives. The J. Walter Thompson Company is one of the world's oldest, largest, and most innovative advertising firms. The collection documents the history of the company and, as part of this, its role in radio broadcasting. The J. Walter Thompson Company's Radio Department produced some of the most popular radio shows on the air during the 1930s and 1940s. These include *Kraft Music Hall*, *Lux Radio Theater*, and *The Chase and Sanborn Hour*. These and other Thompson programs are housed in the collection.

In 1979 the J. Walter Thompson Company Archives were formally established in the company's New York Office. In 1987 Chief Executive Officer Burt Manning authorized the gift of the entire collection to Duke University. The archives contain over 2,000 linear feet of printed and manuscript materials, nearly two million items in all, half of which are advertisements. The archives house the Radio-Television Department files, which include microfilm of scripts of most of the agency-produced radio and television shows from 1930 to 1960, including *Kraft Music Hall*, *Lux Radio Theatre*, and *Lux Video Theatre*. Most of the holdings in the archives are open to researchers except for recent and unprocessed materials.

University of Memphis Radio Archive

The University of Memphis Radio Archive is a collection of broadcast programs that was started over 30 years ago by Dr. Marvin R. Bensman of the Department of Communication. Bensman began his radio collection from original transcriptions, private collectors, and other institutional collections. The collection is intended to be a representative sampling of most series and shows.

The collection is housed in the Microforms Department of the McWherter Library at the University of Memphis. Individuals may request audiocassettes of these radio programs. Programs have been selected because they give a sense of the history and development of broadcasting. They feature the key events that influenced the regulation of broadcasting and of broadcasting programming. Some highlights of the archive include Westinghouse's 50th Anniversary program; the history of broadcasting from the 1920s to the 1970s; 50th anniversary shows about the development of the BBC, NBC, and CBS; early pioneer broadcasters and/or inventors; Aimee Semple McPherson's broadcasts; the American Society of Composers, Authors, and Publishers' (ASCAP) Cavalcade of Music concert in 1940 consisting of live performances by musical stars including Berlin, Handy, and others; *Year-end Reviews*; CBS Radio Workshops; World War II broadcasts; numerous movie dramatizations; and classic comedies.

National Jewish Archive of Broadcasting (New York City)

A subsidiary of The Jewish Museum, the National Jewish Archive of Broadcasting was established in 1979 with the purpose "of collecting and preserving television and radio programs pertaining to the Jewish experience." The broadcasting archives contain in excess of 3,000 television and 600 radio programs.

Freedom Forum's Newseum (Washington, D.C.)

Underwritten by the nonprofit Freedom Forum, the Newseum is devoted to issues of the First Amendment and to stimulating greater understanding between the press and the public. Founded in 1997 and originally located in the Rosslyn area of Arlington, Virginia, the Newseum reopened in its new 250,000 square foot facility (three times its original size) on Pennsylvania Avenue in 2007. The new seven-story building contains 12 exhibit areas, 14 major galleries, and 15 theaters. Although the Newseum contains a detailed "history gallery" which contains over 6,000 items, documenting the history of news gathering and news dissemination from ancient times to the satellite age, the facility is also known for its interactive exhibits (130 in all) that allow visitors to "participate" in the journalistic process. Working radio and television studios are also part of the building's design.

Motorola Innovation Center (Schaumberg, Illinois)

Formerly the Motorola Museum of Electronics, the Innovation Center occupies 25,000 square feet on the company's 325-acre headquarters in the northern Chicago suburbs. Using an array of exhibits and artifacts, the museum traces the history of electronics, including radio and wireless communications, through vintage Motorola products and the company's own historic advertising.

The David Sarnoff Library (Princeton, New Jersey)

Built in 1967 by RCA, the Sarnoff Library celebrates the life and achievements of communications visionary David Sarnoff and the history of the Radio Corporation of America (RCA) from 1919 to 1985. The Library, which also maintains a small museum, houses Sarnoff's papers and memorabilia as well as notebooks, reports, publications, artifacts and over 20,000 photographs, all related to RCA and its research laboratories.

Private/Personal Museum and Archive Collections

American Museum of Radio and Electricity (Wallingham, Washington)

The Bellingham Antique Radio Museum is a nonprofit museum located in Bellingham, Washington. It is a private collection gathered over the past 25 years by Jonathan Winter, who started collecting radios when he was a child. The collection spans the history of radio from the time it began through the early 1940s and features over 1,000 antique radios on display. The Bellingham Antique Radio Museum, as it was originally called, opened in 1988 in a small room and moved to larger quarters in downtown Bellingham in 1990. In 2001 the museum moved to a new, larger facility.

In addition to its collection of antique radios, there is other material on display highlighting the history of radio technology, including historical photographs; books and magazines from radio's early days; microphones, coils, tubes, speakers, and other parts; biographies of people involved in radio history; audio clips of some of the more historic broadcasts; and clips of radio entertainment shows from the early days of broadcasting.

In 2004, the Museum signed on its low-power, community radio station, KMRE 102.3 FM, which re-airs historic radio broadcasts as well as original, locally produced programming. The station is also streamed over the internet.

Auman Museum of Radio and Television (Dover, Ohio)

Built around the private collection of Larry Auman, the Auman Museum contains over 300 vintage television sets dating from the 1920s through the 1950s. Its vintage radio collection dates from the 1900s and includes early wireless sets, "breadboards" and crystal apparatus as well as later floor and tabletop models. The museum also holds extensive radio and television memorabilia including related props, games, toys and comic books. The museum, along with maintaining a web presence, is open by appointment.

The Pavek Museum of Broadcasting (St. Louis Park, Minnesota)

The Pavek Museum of Broadcasting, located in St. Louis Park, Minnesota, a suburb of Minneapolis, houses a large collection of antique radios, televisions, and other broadcasting memorabilia and equipment, including an actual old-time radio studio. The mission of the museum is to provide a broader knowledge of how pioneers in electronic communications affected the evolution of society, to stimulate a new recognition of the practical and real contributions that exploring science and the communication arts can bring, and to provide a permanent and living repository for the preservation of these historic items.

The museum opened in 1988, and most of its collection comes from the original Joseph R. Pavek Collection. Pavek, an electronics instructor for Dunwoody Institute, started his collection in 1946. He also had his own electronics business, and he began storing his collection at his business. By the 1970s he began to look for someone to take over the collection, house it, staff it, and make it available to the public. In 1984, unable to find such a person, he was set to sell the collection, but Earl Bakken, the inventor of the pacemaker, stepped in and, with Paul Hedberg of the Minnesota Broadcasters Association, formed the nonprofit organization that became the umbrella for the museum.

The Pavek collection consists of over 1,000 radio receivers, transmitters, and televisions from the first half of the 20th century. Highlights of the collection include a working 1912 rotary spark-gap transmitter, crystal radios of the early 1920s, a collection of vacuum tubes (including several original de Forest Audions), and a large collection of radio literature. Additional donations from radio and television stations and from other collectors have greatly increased the size of the original collection.

Included at the museum is the Charles Bradley Collection, which has examples from over 60 Minnesota radio and television manufacturers from the 1920s and 1930s. There are also many examples of historic broadcast equipment on display, such as cameras, consoles, and microphones. The museum also houses the Jack Mullin Collection, which documents the history of recorded sound, with over 125 years of audio recording technology, starting with the earliest days of the phonograph. Mullin is credited as being the person who brought back two tape recorders from a German radio station while serving in the Signal Corps at the end of World War II. At the time, tape recording was an unknown technology in the United States, and Mullin was immediately hired by Bing Crosby to tape record his popular radio program for broadcast, the first use of tape recording in American broadcasting.

Also featured in the archives is the Pioneer Broadcaster Series, which preserves videotaped interviews with radio pioneers. The museum also has an educational program with classes, workshops, and exhibits for both children and adults. There is also a library of technical and service information on electronics and electronic communication. Besides the permanent collection, the Pavek also displays items on loan from other private collections. Since 2001, the Pavek has developed its own Hall of Fame which honors Minnesota area broadcasters for their lifetime achievement.

U.S. National Marconi Museum (Bedford, New Hampshire)

The U.S. National Marconi Museum was created by the Guglielmo Marconi Foundation in 1995 to help publicize the name of Marconi, the "Father of Wireless." The museum is located in Bedford, New Hampshire, and the collection features equipment, historical literature, and audiovisual presentations on the development of radio communications. It features displays of early Marconi wireless equipment, along with the progression of radios up to a current cellular telephone exhibit. The museum also features a restoration room for repairing vintage radios, a machine shop, and a facility room for educational lectures to school groups and for meetings of electronic-oriented organizations.

The John Frey Technical Library contains thousands of radio communication periodicals, some in a series dating from 1920. All the publications are indexed and cataloged on CDROM and can be accessed by internet on the library computer. The library also features hundreds of engineering, text, and reference books.

Museum of Radio and Technology (Huntington, West Virginia)

The Museum of Radio and Technology is a small, private collection consisting of old radio and television sets, and it is staffed exclusively by volunteer museum members. It features several displays, including a radio shop of the 1920s and 1930s that has a variety of radios from that era, including battery radios; horn speakers; a wind-powered generator; a radiotelevision sale room featuring radios, television sets, and wire recorders; a Gilbert toy display; a vintage hi-fi room with tubetype audio equipment and related components such as amplifiers, tuners, tape recorders, receivers, microphones, and turntables. The highlight of the display is the Western Electric transmitter, a 1930s 5,000-W AM transmitter complete with power supply components and studio equipment. The Museum also administers the West Virginia Broadcasting Hall of Fame.

The Radio History Society's Radio & Television Museum (Bowie, Maryland)

The Radio History Society is a nonprofit organization dedicated to the preservation of radio and television history. In June 1999 the society opened its new Radio-Television Museum in Bowie, Maryland, housed in a fully restored turn-of-the-century building.

The Radio Historical Society owns a large collection of old literature and radio artifacts relating to the history of radio and television broadcasting. Some of their collection includes radio sets from the 1920s through the 1960s plus local broadcast memorabilia. Their permanent and changing exhibits include home receivers, novelty radios, broadcast microphones, and communication and ham radio equipment. They also maintain a display area at George Washington University's Media and Public Affairs Building in downtown Washington, D.C., with changing displays.

Society to Preserve and Encourage Radio Drama, Variety, and Comedy

The Society to Preserve and Encourage Radio Drama, Variety, and Comedy (SPERDVAC) is an organization of old-time radio enthusiasts that has assembled one of the most important and well-maintained radio program archives in the world. There are over 20,000 original transcription discs, as well as a large library of printed materials and scripts. In addition, there are over 2,000 reels of old-time radio available only to its members. SPERDVAC also produces a monthly newsletter and a catalog listing the thousands of shows in its collection, and it hosts monthly meetings and annual conventions in the Los Angeles area.

Western Historic Radio Museum (Virginia City, Nevada)

Devoted to vintage radio equipment and memorabilia from 1910 to 1950, the Western Historic is located in Virginia City, near Reno, Nevada. Built largely around the personal collection of Henry Rogers, the collection contains vintage amateur radio equipment and transmitters as well as radios from Zenith, Radiola and other manufacturers. The museum concentrates its collecting on sets and equipment from the Reno and Carson area.

The National Museum of Communications (Irving, Texas)

Founded in 1983 by broadcast enthusiast Bill Bragg, its multitude of artifacts vary from a 1611 King James Bible to the microphone used by Walter Cronkite on his final *CBS Evening News* broadcast, and Charlie Chaplin's movie camera.

"Virtual" Museums

The advent of the internet has also allowed various private collectors of radio hardware (receivers, tubes, related equipment) to create their own online exhibits devoted to radio's past. Three examples are the Virtual Collins Radio Museum (at Collinsmuseum.com); Jim's Antique Radio Museum (at Antiqueradiomuseum.org); and Mike Simpson's Midwest Radio Museum (at Midwestradiomuseum.com), and there are doubtless others.

See also: Old-Time Radio; Peabody Awards and Archive

Further Reading

Godfrey, Donald G., editor, *Methods of Historical Analysis in Electronic Media*. Mahwah, New Jersey: Lawrence Erlbaum Associates, 2006.
Godfrey, Donald G., compiler, *Reruns on File: A Guide to Electronic Media Archives*, Hillside, New Jersey: Erlbaum, 1992.
Hedges, William, and Edwin L. Dunham, compilers, *Broadcast Pioneers History Project; Third Progress Report and Historical Inventory*, New York: Broadcast Pioneers, 1967.
Hickerson, Jay, *What You Always Wanted to Know about Circulating Old-Time Radio Shows (But Could Never Find Out)*, n.p.: 1986.

Lichty, Lawrence W, Douglas Gomery, and Shirley L. Green, *Scholars' Guide to Washington, D.C., Media Collections*, Baltimore, Maryland: Johns Hopkins University Press, and Washington, D.C.: Woodrow Wilson Center Press, 1994.

Pitts, Michael R., *Radio Soundtracks: A Reference Guide*, Metuchen, New Jersey: Scarecrow Press, 1976; 2nd edition, Metuchen, New Jersey, and London: Scarecrow Press, 1986.

Sherman, Barry, et al., "The Peabody Archive and Other Resources," *Journal of Radio Studies* 1 (1992).

Siegel, Susan, and David S. Siegel, *A Resource Guide to the Golden Age of Radio: Special Collections, Bibliography and the Internet*. Yorktown Heights, New York: Book Hunter Press, 2006.

Smart, James Robert, compiler, *Radio Broadcasts in the Library of Congress, 1924–1941: A Catalog of Recordings*, Washington, D.C.: Library of Congress, 1982.

Swartz, Jon David, and Robert C. Reinehr, *Handbook of Old-Time Radio: A Comprehensive Guide to Golden Age Radio Listening and Collecting*, Metuchen, New Jersey, and London: Scarecrow Press, 1993.

JUDITH GERBER,
2009 REVISIONS BY CARY O'DELL

MUSIC ON RADIO

Music has been a staple of radio programming since the medium's creation in the early 1920s. Indeed, David Sarnoff's historically fabled memo—real or not—foresaw radio's potential future as a "music box." Before radio, to be able listen to music one had to play an instrument (most often a piano), purchase a poorly recorded disc, or pay to attend a live performance. Radio broadcasting changed that by offering frequent free musical performances for the simple purchase of a radio receiver.

Radio music history can be divided into two eras, divided by a short but confusing transition period. During the first (to 1950), most music was broadcast live as a part of a variety of radio formats, both network and local. The second era (since 1955) followed a brief and difficult transition but soon saw station programmers regularly playing music using specific short lists of recordings. This focus on specific formats has defined radio music, with only the conversion from various disc formats to audiotape and then back to digital discs and tapes changing the means of recording and playback. Indeed, technical change underlies any historical analysis of music on radio. The phonograph record as a means of listening to music preceded radio, but it was radio broadcasting that vastly expanded the musical recording industry—first on 78-rpm records, then, after the war, on 33 1/3-rpm long-playing records and 45-rpm records into the 1960s. Thereafter came a decade or so of analog audiocassettes, and finally, at the end of the 20th century, compact discs and other digital formats.

Network Tin Pan Alley Era (to 1950)

Music as a popular radio program genre started when many advocated the new medium as a means to bring high-art music such as opera and orchestral recitals to the mass public. But although European classical music never disappeared from radio's schedule as radio entered the network era during the late 1920s, its presence quickly gave way to popular music and in particular to variety shows starring musical talents such as Rudy Vallee and Al Jolson. New York City's Tin Pan Alley created the music that big bands and their singers offered radio listeners.

By the early 1930s, both the National Broadcasting Company (NBC) and the Columbia Broadcasting System (CBS) had discovered genres of musical programs that the public preferred. The networks tried classical music; varieties of popular music; and what might be called light or background music, which was designed for listeners involved in activities other than dedicated listening. But although broadcasting classical concert music suggested that radio was providing a "good" to the masses, comedy and variety shows created the mass audiences advertisers sought. Broadcasts of the Chicago Civic Opera on NBC Blue (Saturday), the Cities Service Orchestra on NBC Red (Friday), the Edison Electric Orchestra on NBC Blue (Monday), and the Paramount Symphony Orchestra on CBS (Saturday) maximized prestige but drew small audiences.

Variety shows proved to be the most successful means of creating a profit with music programming. These shows varied depending on how pop music was emphasized—from a comic host with a musical guest to a musical host with a comic as guest. The latter—the musical variety program—became the most popular network radio genre during the 1930s. Top attractions centered more and more on name bands, including Guy Lombardo's Orchestra on CBS or the Paul Whiteman Orchestra on NBC, both broadcast on Monday nights.

Through the 1930s, so-called light music offered the second-largest musical category of radio shows; for example, Jesse Crawford played the pipe organ on CBS on Sunday nights, Lanny Ross (later of *Your Hit Parade* fame) soothed his audiences on NBC on Saturday nights, and—in a rare case of sponsor naming—The Wheaties Quartet performed as intended background music on CBS on Wednesday nights.

By the mid-1930s, NBC and CBS were offering some of the most popular free musical entertainment during those hard times. Indeed, sales of phonograph records plunged during the Great Depression as fans substituted listening to music on the radio for the relatively expensive purchasing of individual phonograph records. Radio became the place where new popular tunes were introduced, and their creators and players became musical stars.

Although during the day local stations still offered non-network live music from the community, prime time had become big time for radio listeners and programmers. Yet stations in large cities did maintain orchestras to play for the local programming. In reality the music that most fans sought came primarily from New York City and then in small doses from Los Angeles-based studios that used musical talent associated with movie making.

By 1940 classical concert music still offered prestige, but on fewer and fewer programs. A star system developed as NBC put together its own classical orchestra, led by Arturo Toscanini. At CBS, William S. Paley signaled that his star was Andre Kostelanetz, who by 1940 was on the air not one night, but two. NBC continued to hire a classical orchestra in order to identify itself as the higher-class network, and by the early 1940s they had scheduled the Boston Symphony, the Firestone Concert, the Minneapolis Symphony, and the Rochester Philharmonic Orchestra.

Judging by the number of shows offered in 1935, radio listeners seemed to prefer a named band with an identifiable sound to a group with the name of its sponsor—even if that was a full classical orchestra. Yet some names in the light music category could and did become pop music stars, such as Kate Smith, who had high ratings in 1935 despite being on the air for only 15 minutes on CBS on Saturday nights.

By 1935 variety shows—which had always had a popular music component—reigned as the most popular of radio's genres. No list can be complete, but the big bands of the day could be found throughout the schedules of NBC and CBS—including the Bob Crosby orchestra, Fred Waring, Horace Heidt, Paul Whiteman, and the "waltz king" Wayne King. Guy Lombardo's orchestra remained a fixture on CBS on Monday nights, symbolizing more and more that the name was in the band and its singers, not in some amalgamation fashioned directly by the sponsor.

In short, the popular mainstream music of the 1930s and 1940s was found primarily on network radio. Orchestras were hired to perform live to generate a studio-made "high-fidelity" sound before

the innovation in the late 1940s of 33 1/3-rpm and 45-rpm records. In-house studio orchestras were formed to provide background music for dramatic shows as well.

Big bands played remotes for dances in such ballrooms as the Aragon in Chicago and the Pacific Square in San Diego, at beach or other waterside attractions (the Steel Pier in Atlantic City and the Glen Island Casino in New Rochelle, New York), at restaurants (the Blackhawk in Chicago, the Copacabana in New York City), and at major hotels in most big cities. Such remotes offered popular venues for radio broadcasting through the 1940s and symbolized the hot new sounds for dancers of the era.

The rise of "name" singers was another emerging trend. Through the 1930s singers, led by Bing Crosby, learned to use the microphone for effect, not simply as a means of broadcasting. Ratings spiked when Crosby and Frank Sinatra—as well as Rosemary Clooney, Ruth Etting, Helen Kane, Peggy Lee, and Doris Day—were scheduled. Soloists hardly represented the lone form of popular radio singing. There were duos, trios, and quartets—from the Ink Spots to the Mills Brothers, from the Andrews Sisters to the Boswell Sisters. Singing intimately and in a number of styles, all based on Tin Pan Alley arrangements, became a true art form through radio broadcasting.

The war years proved to be the final hurrah for the musical variety show. National defense bond rallies often functioned as all-star radio variety shows, meant to outdo all other radio extravaganzas. Programs such as *Music for Millions, Treasury Star Parade*, and *Millions for Defense* not only drew needed bond sales but also were beamed overseas or recorded for later playback for the troops fighting in Europe and the Pacific. The top stars of network radio toured for the United Service Organizations (USO) and went abroad to entertain soldiers near the fronts. Indeed, radio star and big band leader Glenn Miller was killed while traveling from one such show to another. The war years also proved the crest for big band singers on network radio. Kate Smith and Dinah Shore, for example, starred in some of the most popular shows on radio.

This system of making live music came apart, however, because of the demands of its most famous star, Bing Crosby. Crosby hated the necessities of live broadcasting, which demanded a rigid schedule that included doing shows twice (once for the Eastern and Central time zones and then a second time for Mountain and Pacific time zones). In 1946 Cosby moved his top-rated show from

NBC to ABC to obtain relief. ABC, desperate for ratings, allowed Crosby to prerecord his *Philco Radio Time* using newly developed audiotape technology. He did not have to be in the studio when his show debuted (on 16 October 1946), nor weekly as it ran on ABC until June 1949. At that point William S. Paley, head of CBS, also gave in to recorded music programs and as a part of his famous "talent raids," offered Crosby more money than ABC could afford.

Even though Tin Pan Alley and its allies in Hollywood largely dominated music played on the radio through the 1940s, there were alternatives. In particular, hillbilly music shows were becoming hits on the networks and on many local stations, particularly on small-town outlets in the South and West.

NBC led the way on the network level with *The National Barn Dance* and *The Grand Ole Opry*, both on Saturday nights. Numerous Southern stations offered live music, particularly during early morning hours. The demand for hillbilly music exceeded the supply, and so border stations based in Mexico blasted at 1 million W music by hillbilly favorites such as the Carter Family, Jimmie Rodgers, Cowboy Slim Rinehart, and Patsy Montana.

The Carter Family—a trio composed of A.P. Carter, Sara Carter, and Maybelle Carter—was the first family of country music, and their famed 1928 Bristol, Tennessee, recording sessions kicked off a new genre of popular music. Jimmie Rodgers was also at those Bristol sessions and should be counted among the creators of hillbilly music. Nolan "Cowboy Slim" Rinehart, "the king of border radio," was a singing cowboy who, because of border stations' power, was heard across the nation as much as his more popular rival, singing cowboy Gene Autry. Cowgirl Patsy Montana teamed up with Rinehart for a series of transcribed duets during the 1930s and became so popular that her 1935 recording "I Wanna Be a Cowboy's Sweetheart" became the first million-selling record by a female hillbilly artist.

Ethnic artists found it more difficult to gain access to even local radio. In particular, although African-Americans were developing rhythm and blues music, the genre could rarely be heard on the radio during the 1930s and 1940s. Race records and juke joints offered the sole outlets, but the music was there and rich in form and style for the great change that was about to happen to radio music broadcasting.

Transition (1948–55)

Beginning in the late 1940s, NBC and CBS committed themselves to network television. They transferred their big bands and pop singers—plus some symphonic music—to TV and used profits from network radio to fund their new, and in the future far more profitable, medium. This worked well for the networks, and Bing Crosby, Kate Smith, Tommy Dorsey, and particularly Dinah Shore became mainstays of network television programming of the 1950s.

Their departure—and that of most other network programming—left radio stations looking for something new. Stations would find their salvation and reinvention in rock, an amalgamation of country and race forms. As rock was developing through the early and middle 1950s, Todd Stortz and Gordon McLendon pioneered Top 40 radio. They developed a short list of top tunes and played them over and over again. Teenagers of the 1950s—not interested in the big band, Tin Pan Alley music of their parents—embraced Top 40 radio. AM radio stations—looking for something to fill their time as network programs migrated to television—looked to Top 40 as their salvation.

There were sizable vested interests in keeping the live musical variety show going. These included the performing music societies, the American Society of Composers, Authors, and Publishers (ASCAP) and Broadcast Music Incorporated (BMI). Even more concerned was the American Federation of Musicians, the performer's union which tried to slow adoption of the innovative recording techniques—tape and discs—which union leaders and members feared (correctly) would lessen the demand for their live services. These parties, in addition to many parents and religious leaders, found rock music subversive and threatening. Even NBC tried to keep the variety musical show alive on radio with *The Big Show* on Sunday nights in 1951, but with no success.

Format Radio (Since 1955)

The symbol of the Top 40 revolution in radio was singer Elvis Presley. Gone were the big bands, dominated by brass and woodwinds, with dozens of players; these had been replaced by combos of a drummer and a couple of guitars. The electric guitar gave the necessary amplified sound and beat. The singer, who had been just one part of the big band, was now moved to the forefront, and with Chuck Berry, the singer sang his or her own compositions (so the songwriters of Tin Pan Alley were no longer needed). And, most important, the music of the margins—hillbilly and race—moved to the forefront as the amalgam labeled rock and roll. Elvis was the "hillbilly cat." Chuck Berry grew up in St. Louis listening to both *The National Barn Dance* and *The Grand Ole Opry*. After more of a struggle, blues music, later dubbed rhythm and blues in its urban form, came to mainstream rock in the form of Detroit's "Motown Sound."

Rock, country, and rhythm and blues formats spawned a myriad of newer sub-formats for radio stations that wanted to be more than just "the other" Top 40 station in town. Taking but a single example, the history of country symbolizes how one marginal form became mainstream in the last half of the 20th century—indeed the top format in all radio by the century's turn.

As rock splintered into many subtypes, each with devoted audiences, country rose to become the music that many white Americans listened to, in part because during an era of civil rights unrest, country recognized and appreciated that its roots were not tinged by music with more direct African-American roots. Country had its origins in the folk and hill-billy music that was so marginal during the network radio era—save for the popular "barn dance" programs. For advertisers, country attracted white, middle-class, suburban America—the audience they most wanted to reach.

Entrepreneurs provided a new name, and "country and western" was used into the 1960s. With the rise of Nashville (Tennessee) as an important recording center, however, the "western" was dropped, and by the time country format radio took off, the name was simply "country." What would become known as the "Nashville sound" worked as Hank Williams made country songs popular as pop music—an approach also heralded by Jim Reeves and Patsy Cline. By the 1960s, country emerged as an alternative genre, with stars such as Johnny Cash, Jimmy Dean, Loretta Lynn, and Dolly Parton. As rock seemed to lose its roots in the 1970s, country became an even more popular radio format. By the 1980s many surveys found country to be the most popular format on radio. A once marginal music style had become a dominant form of pop music, all made from a central location in Nashville.

With the innovation of portable and automobile radios, radio listening moved out of the home and became ubiquitous, particularly with the advent of the Walkman. The average person listened more than three hours per week. Advertisers targeted ethnic groups (principally African-Americans and Latinos), different age groups, income classes, and genders with different types of music. Adult contemporary music worked best for those 25–34 years old, whereas album-oriented rock was aimed at teenagers; their college-aged cousins seemed to prefer classic rock and contemporary hits radio. Country generally appealed to an older audience.

Creating a complete inventory of these format formulas is pointless as formats are constantly being created, imitated, refined or subdivided. By 2009, the annual *Broadcasting and Cable Yearbook* listed 68 active formats. Arbitron was tracking 57 formats, nine of them exclusively Spanish language. Format types range from adult album alternative (or "AAA") to urban contemporary, variety (at least four or more different formats employed by a station), Vietnamese and those appealing to women.

In the 1990s, country music was among the most popular formats on U.S. radio. Country spun off the gospel music format and, later, the Contemporary Christian format. Country composers and stars were heavily influenced by the rock stylings they grew up with; superstar Garth Brooks, for example, claimed the group KISS as his key influence. Indeed, during the 1990s, one could more easily find a Willie Nelson or Loretta Lynn "classic" tune covered and then played on an adult contemporary, beautiful music, or easy listening station than on a country outlet. Other formats that enjoyed popularity at the turn of the century included hybrids like Contemporary Rock and Rhythmic Oldies as well as Urban and Hot AC. Perhaps the most tuned by young listeners was Hip-Hop. It inspired the newest incarnation of the Top 40/CHR format because the Hip-Hop sound dominated music charts nationally.

By the early 2000s, although the country format retained the most stations nationwide, talk programming (including such derivatives as sports talk) came increasingly to dominate, threatening to drive music to radio's periphery. It seemed ironic that just as music on radio took a hit, the music industry launched a campaign to charge stations performance-related fees, as is already required of satellite and online services. Proposed legislation would require a similar charge (some call it a tax) be paid to singers and musicians for airing their works.

Despite this, music will remain a vital mainstay of radio. It is, after all, why many people tune in to radio in the first place. It is also a necessary and economical airtime filler. And it is certainly central to HD outlets, nearly all of which are built around niche musical tastes. WAMU in Washington, D.C., for example, launched an all-Bluegrass HD channel after the primary signal adopted all talk. WBCN in Boston began a commercial-free "indie" and "ultra-new" rock HD channel to supplement its main signal.

See also, in addition to individual formats discussed above: American Federation of Musicians; American

Society of Composers, Authors, and Publishers; Broadcast Music Incorporated; Classical Music Format; Formats Defining Radio Programming; *Grand Ole Opry*; Metropolitan Opera Broadcasts; *National Barn Dance*; Recordings and the Radio Industry; Talent Raids; Walkman

Further Reading

DeLong, Thomas A., *The Mighty Music Box: The Golden Age of Musical Radio*, Los Angeles: Amber Crest Books, 1980.

Eberly, Philip K., *Music in the Air: America's Changing Tastes in Popular Music, 1920–1980*, New York: Hastings House, 1982.

Fornatale, Peter, and Joshua E. Mills, *Radio in the Television Age*, Woodstock, New York: Overlook Press, 1980.

Fowler, Gene, and Bill Crawford, *Border Radio*, Austin: Texas Monthly Press, 1987.

Hickerson, Jay, *The Ultimate History of Network Radio Programming and Guide to All Circulating Shows*, Hamden, Connecticut: Hickerson, 1992; 3rd edition, as *The New, Revised, Ultimate History of Network Radio Programming and Guide to All Circulating Shows*, 1996.

Joyner, David Lee, *American Popular Music*, Madison, Wisconsin: Brown and Benchmark, 1993.

Landry, Robert John, *This Fascinating Radio Business*, Indianapolis, Indiana: Bobbs-Merrill, 1946.

MacDonald, J. Fred, *Don't Touch That Dial!: Radio Programming in American Life, 1920–1960*, Chicago: Nelson-Hall, 1979.

Malone, Bill C., *Country Music U.S.A.*, Austin: University of Texas Press, 1968; revised edition, 1985.

Routt, Edd, James B. McGrath, and Frederic A. Weiss, *The Radio Format Conundrum*, New York: Hastings House, 1978.

Sanjek, Russell, and David Sanjek, *American Popular Music Business in the 20th Century*, New York: Oxford University Press, 1991.

Whetmore, Edward Jay, *The Magic Medium: An Introduction to Radio in America*, Belmont, California: Wadsworth, 1981.

DOUGLAS GOMERY,
2009 REVISIONS BY CARY O'DELL

MUSIC TESTING

Determining Radio Audience Preferences

There has never been as great a need for accurate music research data in the radio industry as there is today. Not only are many more entertainment options available to potential listeners, but also the expectations for ratings and profit performance continue to increase. As a result, programmers of music-oriented stations have adopted a variety of research methods to better understand their listeners' attitudes toward particular songs.

Requests

Perhaps the most easily overlooked source of music data is a station's request line. Many programmers recognize requests as an inexpensive and simple way to collect music information. Instructing disc jockeys to tally songs that people care enough about to request is an easy and cheap way to obtain a daily glimpse of titles that excite listeners. However, programmers should be careful not to place too much confidence in request data. Listeners with enough spare time to place requests may not best represent a station's audience. To better ensure that a station's entire audience range is represented, programmers rely on more scientific methods.

Callout

The primary method of music testing is callout research. Callout consists of trained interviewers telephoning randomly selected listeners of a particular station and having them use a pre-established scale to rate 15 or 20 "hooks" from songs the station plays. A hook is a brief lyrical segment, often the title or chorus, that captures the essential quality of the song.

According to Tony Novia of *Radio and Records* magazine, callout began in the 1970s when broadcasters believed they could predict which new songs would become popular by having listeners rate hooks from the very latest releases. Unfortunately, because the songs were so new and had not received any airplay, respondent unfamiliarity resulted in unreliable data. Beginning in the 1980s, programmers realized that callout was an effective tool for obtaining data about familiar music. The hook, in effect, was just long enough to "jog the memory about a song in question" (Novia, 2000). Today, most users of callout recommend that songs not be included in research until they reach a high level of familiarity through airplay. For example, radio consultant Guy Zapoleon reports that a general rule is to have a song play at least 100 times on a station before placing it into callout.

During callout, respondents provide data after each hook is heard over the phone line. First, they are asked if they recognize the song. If they do, a favorability-scale question is generally asked next. For example, listeners may rate the song on a scale of 1 to 10, where 1 means they dislike the song very much and 10 means they like the song very much. Another type of data often obtained during callout is a fatigue or burnout measurement. Listeners are asked, "Are you tired of hearing this song on the radio?" Especially in contemporary music formats, fatigue data is important for determining when to decrease airplay of a popular song title.

Perhaps the biggest benefit of callout research is the ability to gather music data quickly, easily, and inexpensively. These benefits result in the ability to generate weekly reports on current music. Drawbacks to callout include the reliance on hooks, the brevity of which sometimes fail to capture the essence of a song; the comparative low fidelity of telephone lines, which may negatively bias results; and the high refusal rates of respondents, which can be expected any time researchers make unscheduled telephone calls. Two newer and less prevalent music testing techniques, the personal music test and call-in research, have been developed to address these shortcomings.

Call-in and Personal Music Tests

As is implied by its name, call-in research consists of listeners telephoning a station's research department to complete music tests. This method allows listeners to provide information at their convenience. A similar method involves invitations to visit the station's website, where listeners can participate in a music test in which audio of hooks (or even of entire songs) is streamed. There are several drawbacks to these two methods that must be kept in mind. First, just as with those who request songs, listeners who have the time or interest to phone a station or visit its website to participate in a music survey may not be representative of listeners in general. Second, there is no way to adequately prevent one listener from providing opinions more than once, thereby biasing the results.

A personal music test attempts to combine the scheduling convenience of call-in with the representativeness and quality control of callout. Using this music testing method, telephone interviewers call a random selection of station listeners and schedule an appointment for them to visit a research facility at a convenient time. Upon their arrival, listeners are given a hook tape of current music and a personal cassette player with headphones. Listeners work through the hooks, providing ratings for each hook at their own pace. The personal music test ensures that respondents devote the undistracted time required to provide valid data. Furthermore, because telephone lines are not involved, the fidelity of the music being tested is much closer to what is actually heard over the air. A major drawback to the personal music test, however, is cost, because most stations employing the method have found that a financial incentive is necessary to increase participation.

Auditorium Music Tests

Although the methods mentioned above tend to be used to collect opinions of fewer than 30 current songs, auditorium music tests (AMTs) are generally employed to test between 350 and 700 older songs. Familiarity with the titles is assumed; the goal here is to determine the best-liked "gold" music among the station's target audience. For oldies formats, the method is often used to determine the entire playlist; therefore, oldies programmers conduct AMTs each quarter, whereas more contemporary music stations can afford to do them only once or twice a year. AMTs consist of inviting between 75 and 150 randomly selected listeners to an auditorium and playing a hook tape for them. The shared sense of purpose and controlled environment are key benefits to this method. One drawback is the cost of auditorium rental and respondent incentives. Another is the possibility of respondent fatigue, which can be lessened by scheduling breaks periodically during hook presentation.

In recent years, to offset these issues and allay high costs, use of auditorium groups is declining as they become more like traditional focus groups. New methods and technologies have also been adopted within the industry. Some stations and research firms utilize CDs, which are mailed to participants' homes for their opinions. Much music testing is also being done online with users listening to snippets of songs over the internet. However, because of cutbacks and budget constraints, many stations have had to cease music polling and testing altogether, causing program directors to rely on nothing more scientific than their own gut instincts.

See also: Audience Research Methods; Auditorium Testing

Further Reading

Eastman, Susan T., Douglas A. Ferguson, and Timothy P. Meyer, "Program and Audience Research," in *Broadcast/Cable Programming*, 5th edition, edited by Eastman and Ferguson, Belmont, California, and London: Wadsworth, 1997.
Kelly, Tom, *Music Research: The Silver Bullet to Eternal Success*, Washington, D.C.: National Association of Broadcasters, 2000.
Lynch, Joanna R., and Gillispie, Greg, "Creating an Image," in *Process and Practice of Radio Programming*, by Lynch and Gillispie, Lanham, Maryland: University Press of America, 1998.
MacFarland, David T., *Contemporary Radio Programming Strategies*, Mahwah, New Jersey: Erlbaum, 1990; 2nd edition, as *Future Radio Programming Strategies: Cultivating Leadership in the Digital Age*, 1997.
Norberg, Eric, G., "Promoting Your Station," in *Radio Programming: Tactics and Strategy*, by Norberg, Boston and Oxford: Focal Press, 1996.

Novia, Tony, "Reach Out and Touch Some Listeners," *Radio and Records* (11 February 2000).

Porter, Chris, "Music Testing: Pros and Cons," *Radio and Records* (28 August 1998).

Zapoleon, Guy, "When to Put a Song into Callout," *Radio@ Large* (15 July 1999).

ROBERT F. POTTER,
2009 REVISIONS BY CARY O'DELL

MUTUAL BROADCASTING SYSTEM
National Radio Network

The Mutual Broadcasting System was unique among the four national radio networks. Whereas the other networks originated most of their programming from studios in New York City and Hollywood, Mutual was a cooperative program-sharing venture the member stations of which around the country provided most of the programming. As the last major network to be established, Mutual's stations tended to be the ones the other networks did not want: low-powered rural stations with limited listening areas. Thus, although Mutual was eventually to proclaim itself the nation's largest radio network based on the number of affiliates it served, it was continually mired in last place in a four-way race.

Mutual and its affiliates created many memorable programs, such as *The Adventures of Bulldog Drummond, Buck Rogers, Double or Nothing, 20 Questions, The Falcon, The Green Hornet, The Shadow, Sherlock Holmes, The Lone Ranger, Dick Tracy, Queen for a Day,* and *Captain Midnight,* and featured personalities such as the controversial Father Charles E. Coughlin, Dick Clark, Merv Griffin, Mike Wallace, and, in later days, Larry King. But the network's fourth-place status and chronically weak financial position often resulted in its best programs being lured away to the deeper-pocketed competing networks.

Creating a Fourth Network

Because local radio listening areas, or markets, varied widely in both population and number of stations locally available, the three-network system (National Broadcasting Company [NBC] Red, NBC Blue, and the Columbia Broadcasting System [CBS]) worked well in some places and not as well in others. Markets with three local stations willing to affiliate with a network (despite the advantages, not all stations desired affiliation) were ideally suited to the status quo. Markets with fewer than three stations frequently saw a station affiliated

with more than one network, with one network considered the station's primary affiliation and another network constituting a "secondary" affiliation. In markets with four or more stations desiring network affiliation, somebody, obviously, was going to be disappointed. In a competitive environment with four or more stations, the affiliation contracts usually went to the more powerful stations.

The early 1930s saw several attempts to start a fourth radio network, from the Amalgamated Broadcasting System (headed by popular radio comedian Ed Wynn, often billed as "the perfect fool": the network folded in five weeks) to an American Broadcasting Company (no relation to today's ABC) that lasted a few months. Among the many reasons for the high failure rate, two deserve special consideration, because they were to resurface continually as formidable challenges to anyone trying to compete with NBC or CBS. The first was the fact that the three major networks already had solid relationships with the best advertisers, and they still had much airtime to sell. In many ways, a sustaining program represented an unsold commercial slot. Ideally (for the network), the entire schedule would be commercial. Thus, the sales representatives at NBC and CBS aggressively went after advertisers to buy more time, often offering discounted rates to large advertising accounts. Any start-up radio network was going to have a tough time convincing advertisers to stray from the majors. A second problem was the ragtag nature of most of the stations not already signed with NBC or CBS. As much as these stations wanted network affiliation, this accumulation of largely low-powered and/or rural stations would not be very attractive to national advertisers.

Ironically, the company that was finally to establish a fourth network started life with no national network intentions. In 1934 four powerful independent (non-network) stations banded together to form the Quality Group. The purpose of the group, which consisted of WOR (New York), WGN (Chicago), WLW (Cincinnati), and WXYZ (Detroit), was twofold. First, they would share their better sustaining programs among themselves. Second, they would offer an alternative to the producers of commercial programs who wanted access to four major metropolitan markets without going through one of the established networks. As a Quality Group spokesman stated, "We will endeavor to make suitable time arrangements for advertisers seeking to broadcast in important markets through the use of a few stations having high power and a vast listening audience. Each station will remain independent and make its own decision in accepting programs. Several programs are now broadcast over this group of stations by mutual agreement." The "mutual" nature of the cooperative venture apparently struck a chord, because the organization was almost immediately renamed the Mutual Broadcasting System (MBS). By the time it celebrated its first anniversary in 1935, Mutual carried 2.0 hours of commercial broadcasts and 40 hours of sustaining broadcasts per week. The anniversary was bittersweet, however. The one non-stockholding partner in the venture, WXYZ, had just jumped ship to NBC Blue. Mutual was able to replace WXYZ in the Detroit market by signing CKLW, an across-the-border Canadian station that had served as the area's CBS affiliate. CBS had dumped CKLW in favor of yet another Detroit station, WJR, when it increased its power to 50,000 W.

More significantly, a major schism regarding the future of the company was developing among the three owner stations. Desiring to increase the operation's revenue, WGN and WOR wanted to open Mutual up into a broader network serving more stations. WLW was opposed to this plan. Whereas the metropolitan locations of WGN and WOR (Chicago and New York City) gave them local access to millions of listeners, WLW got most of its audience through the far-flung reach of its night-time 500,000-W signal. If Mutual began to sign affiliates in the cities reached by WLW's signal, the station reasoned, WLW would lose much of its audience to these local stations. WLW wanted MBS programming to remain exclusively available to the original four markets to preserve its own unique appeal to its geographically widespread audience.

WLW was outvoted. By early 1936 some individual Mutual programs (but not the complete network schedule) were being carried on a network of nine stations. By the fall of 1936, Mutual announced expansion to the West, signing affiliation agreements with the Don Lee regional network in California and with several Midwest stations along the American Telephone and Telegraph (AT&T) line, which was leased to carry the network's signal to the West Coast. At the same time, WLW announced that it was turning in its MBS stock. It remained an MBS affiliate for many years, even continuing to supply Mutual with some original programming. Its own schedule, however, became increasingly a mix of MBS and NBC. The Federal Communications Commission (FCC) eventually decided that the "superstation" experiment was a failure, placing WLW at too much of a competitive advantage over other stations, and

WLW became a regular 50,000-W clear channel station. The Don Lee network picked up WLW's stock, as well as one-third of the cost of the expanded network operations. Before the network hookup to California was in operation, Mutual signed a Washington, D.C., station and another regional network, Colonial, as a New England affiliate. Thus by the end of 1936, Mutual was a true transcontinental network, albeit one with huge gaps (most significantly, the southern half of the United States). Despite this expansion, MBS executives remained committed to the network's unique vision. Company President W.E. Macfarlane emphasized the independent nature of Mutual's affiliates by noting, "The Mutual Broadcasting System was organized with the purpose of presenting better programs, allowing stations to maintain their independence, and creating a network of stations which would serve the country's listening audience and still allow stations to fulfill obligations to their various local communities."

By 1937 Mutual was serving 51 affiliates. The complete network schedule consisted of 30 3/4 hours of commercial programs and 93 1/4 hours of sustaining programs per week. Within a year, the total number of affiliates was up to 51. Yet increasingly, Mutual was finding itself frustrated by the major networks. Many of its new affiliates were only secondary Mutual stations. These stations owed their primary allegiance (and best broadcasting hours) to one of the major networks. On these stations, Mutual only got the broadcast times the major networks did not want: the hours with the fewest listeners that were the most difficult to sell to national advertisers. Because of its weak position relative to the other networks, Mutual became an early practitioner of "counter-programming." If the most popular program on radio in a given time slot was a drama, Mutual would schedule a musical show opposite it.

The FCC Network Probe

Early in 1938, in part responding to growing complaints from Mutual about its difficulty in competing with the entrenched New York-based networks, the FCC initiated a probe of possible network monopolistic practices. Data soon confirmed some of Mutual's complaints—CBS and NBC, with three networks between them, dominated the strongest stations across the country. Mutual was having trouble getting a competitive foothold in the business.

Mutual's winning of the rights to provide the baseball World Series broadcasts in 1938 and 1939 brought other network practices into sharp contrast. CBS and NBC ordered their affiliates to stick with their own network programs, even when those stations wanted to carry the highly popular games (and Mutual was willing to provide them). The closed-door approach of the New York networks certainly helped to underline Mutual's anti-competitive arguments.

Based in part on information provided by Mutual, the FCC issued its final report on chain broadcasting in May 1941, calling for a host of changes in the relationship between networks and their affiliates. After a fierce legal battle, and several long congressional hearings, the rules were upheld in a landmark Supreme Court decision in 1943. NBC and CBS were forced to modify many of their affiliation contracts, somewhat evening the playing field for Mutual.

The Decline of Mutual and Network Radio

The MBS continued to expand through the 1940s, reaching 400 affiliates in 1947. It became the first network to include FM stations in its lineup, although these affiliations were plagued in the beginning by a dispute with the American Federation of Musicians that prohibited any musical programs from being carried over FM stations without an additional fee. The expanded Mutual network now reached 84 percent of the nation's radio homes, although only 60 percent of the network's programming was actually carried over the entire system.

Although the post-World War II structure of Mutual was basically the same as it had always been—a program-sharing cooperative owned by three major stockholders (WGN, WOR, Don Lee) and a few minor stockholders (including the New England-based Colonial regional network)—major changes in the broadcasting landscape and in Mutual's corporate structure loomed on the horizon.

After decades of development, television was finally ready for its commercial launch immediately following World War II. Although CBS, NBC, ABC, and an electronics firm named DuMont all announced plans for television networks, Mutual's stand on the matter was ambivalent. Although WGN, WOR, Don Lee, and some Mutual affiliates were getting into television, MBS announced in 1948 that it would "leave actual video operations to its stockholder stations." The decision was made that these stockholder stations might provide programming to MBS affiliates, but that such programming, for the time being, would be outside of Mutual. Although he assumed that MBS would eventually become the fourth television network, MBS president Edgar Kobak stated, "I have a hunch that a few years from now survival may be difficult and one way to survive is to be careful now. That's what we at Mutual are doing." Survival for Mutual would indeed soon become difficult, and the decision not to actively develop a television arm would be one of the major contributing factors.

In 1943 General Tire and Rubber bought the Colonial network, giving it a small stake in MBS. In 1950 it expanded its broadcast holdings with the acquisition of the Don Lee network (giving the company 38 percent ownership of MBS), and its purchase of WOR the following year made it the controlling partner in Mutual, with 58 percent of the stock. Under the new corporate name of General Teleradio, the company acquired the remainder of Mutual's outstanding stock to become the sole owner of MBS. General Teleradio bought RKO-Radio Pictures in the mid-1950s. General's interest in the studio was solely to obtain its backlog of old theatrical movies as programming for General's growing roster of independent television stations. General had no intention of getting into the theatrical film business or of using RKO's studios as a production center for a possible MBS television network. Content to run its television outlets as independent stations, the newly renamed RKO-General immediately liquidated the film studio and, in 1957, sold MBS to oil tycoon Armand Hammer. The company would pass through the hands of five more owners in the next three years.

In the fall of 1958, Mutual was sold again, this time to Hal Roach Studios. A venerable producer of theatrical short comedies in the 1920s and 1930s, Roach had become a major television producer in the 1950s. By the late 1950s, however, the company was in the throes of serious financial reversals, compelling it to accept a buyout offer from a businessman named Alexander Guterma. Guterma immediately announced plans to combine the Roach operation and MBS into a broadcasting power-house of both radio and television networks, the latter of which would be supplied with programming from the Roach Studios. Within months, however, the Guterma empire collapsed under allegations of stock fraud.

In February 1959, MBS was sold by the Hal Roach Studios to recording executive Malcolm Smith. Smith sold MBS within months to a new set of owners, the McCarthy-Ferguson Group, who entered the network into bankruptcy reorganization.

During the transition from Smith to McCarthy-Ferguson, a final peculiar twist to the Roach-Guterma era emerged. In an effort to save his flagging business empire, Alexander Guterma had accepted $750,000 in January 1959 from the dictator of the

Dominican Republic, Generalissimo Rafael Trujillo, in exchange for up to 425 minutes per month of favorable coverage of the Dominican Republic on Mutual radio news broadcasts. Negative reports on the Dominican Republic would not appear on MBS. The arrangement was reported to federal authorities by the new MBS management, who had found themselves accosted by agents of the Dominican Republic demanding performance on the deal or return of the money. In addition to his problems with the Securities and Exchange Commission, Guterma found himself tried and convicted of failing to register himself as an agent of a foreign principal.

In April 1960, McCarthy-Ferguson sold the network to the giant manufacturing company 3M, which was seeking to diversify into new fields. By the 1960s, however, network radio had become little more than a news-delivery service. As a corollary enterprise to the news division of a television network, a radio news service could return a profit. Despite the fact that it could boast the largest number of affiliates of any radio network, over 500 in 1967, with no television operation to share the costs of news gathering Mutual was locked in a terminal slide toward oblivion.

Despite the inevitability of its demise, MBS lasted considerably longer than most industry analysts expected (and longer than the pioneering NBC Radio Network). The end for Mutual came on 18 April 1999. Its final owner was the Westwood One radio group, which had bought Mutual from Amway in 1985. Shortly before Mutual's demise, Westwood One had turned most management decisions over to CBS Radio, which saw Mutual as redundant to other services offered by both Westwood One and CBS. The last Mutual stations were offered affiliation with Westwood One's CNN Radio operation to replace the departed 65-year-old Mutual network.

Shortly after its final signoff, Mutual's vault of over 40,000 audiotapes, dating between 1955 and 1999, were donated by Westwood One to the archives of George Washington University. Included in the collection were full broadcasts of *The Larry King Show* and *The Jim Bohannan Show* as well as live broadcasts covering major news events.

See also: American Broadcasting Company; Columbia Broadcasting System; National Broadcasting Company; Network Monopoly Probe; Westwood One; WGN; WLW; WOR

Further Reading

"After 50 Years the Feeling's Still Mutual," *Broadcasting* (10 September 1984).
Crater, Rufus, "What Happens to MBS?" *Broadcasting-Telecasting* (15 October 1951).
Federal Communications Commission, *Report on Chain Broadcasting*, Washington, D.C.: Government Printing Office, 1941; reprint, New York: Arno Press, 1974.
"First 12 Years of Mutual Network: A Study in 'Operations Grass Roots'" *Variety* (23 October 1946).
"Grand Jury Indicts Guterma Trio: Charged with Selling MBS as Dominican Propaganda Vehicle," *Broadcasting* (7 September 1959).
The Money Faces of Mutual, New York: Mutual Radio Networks, 1974.
"New Giant Growing in Radio-TV?" *Broadcasting* (15 September 1958).
Robertson, Bruce, "Mutual Reaches Its 20th Birthday," *Broadcasting-Telecasting* (27 September 1954).
Robinson, Thomas Porter, *Radio Networks and the Federal Government*, New York: Columbia University Press, 1943.

RICHARD WARD,
2009 REVISIONS BY CARY O'DELL

N

NARROWCASTING

Narrowcasting is the process of identifying or selecting a specific portion of the overall radio audience and designing a station's programming to attract and retain that audience. Other related terms include *audience fragmentation, target audience, listener segmentation, niche audience,* and *format-specific, cultural-specific,* or *audience-specific programming.*

Narrowcasting stands in contrast to the older word *broadcasting*, which was borrowed from the agricultural industry. To a farmer, broadcasting means to sow seeds as widely as possible throughout a field; in radio, stations transmit their signal widely throughout their coverage area. In the early decades of radio, stations designed their programming to meet the needs of the largest, widest possible audience. However, stations could not always meet everyone's needs adequately, and portions of the population were left underserved or neglected by programming intended for an aggregate audience.

During the 1930s and 1940s, some independent, non-network stations in larger U.S. markets sold air time to African-American or non English-language programmers. In addition, some country and folk listeners could find programs to meet their needs in the various barn dance and jamboree shows around the country, although few stations featured around-the-clock music for rural listeners.

After World War II, the number of radio stations on the air increased dramatically, increasing the pressure on each outlet to find programs that would appeal to at least some listeners. Managers of newer stations who were willing to forgo the "golden age" approach to programming focused their programs to attract specific audiences; as a result, African-American and country stations first appeared in the late 1940s and early 1950s. During the same period, Top 40 programmers reached out to teens, and middle-of-the-road stations attracted older audiences: thus the first true formats were born.

The practice of narrowcasting is of particular interest to advertisers, because even though audiences are typically divided by listening characteristics, listener segmentation also results in buyer segmentation. When special audiences are targeted for specific products, the result is a more efficient use of advertising dollars. Teens are more likely to buy acne medicine and soft drinks. Mature audiences are more prone to invest in luxury cars, health care products, or mutual funds. This improved efficiency can be illustrated by the question, "Would you rather stand on the street and try to sell hot dogs to all the people passing by or would you rather talk to ten hungry people?" On the street, a salesperson will meet many people, but not all will be prepared to purchase. On the other hand, ten hungry people may find themselves quite interested in the prospect of a hot dog, if the salesperson can only locate them.

Over time, the practice of narrowcasting has enhanced the partnership between stations and advertisers. Various narrowcast formats divide the total audience into listener groups according to the demographic characteristics of age, gender, culture, or income. The station programmer's job is to design a total package of program elements, including music, news, IDs, liners, and public service announcements, to attract and retain their specific audience. The advertiser's task is to match audiences with products. A successful link of programs, audiences, and advertisers results in a more efficient and, in the long run, more economical effort enabling stations to deliver audiences to advertisers.

The 2009 *Broadcasting and Cable Yearbook* recognizes 70 different radio formats in use. But even these categories can be further subdivided. For example, country stations might program just country's current top 40 or a mix of contemporary hits with vintage classics, or they might air an alternative country playlist, also known as "alt country" or "Americana." Similarly, Contemporary Christian has various subsets such as Christian Hit Radio, Southern Gospel, Praise and Worship, and even "alternative" Christian music. Many stations are experimenting with hybrid formats such as country-flavored "Hank FM" or the more rock-oriented "Jack" format. Hank, supposedly named after Hank Williams, loosely translates as "(He) Plays Anything Country" and airs a highly varied playlist, whereas "Jack" formats pride themselves on their diversity, programming AC and rock hits from several decades.

In seeking niche audience, stations have even gone so far as to adopt—though usually only briefly—such highly topical formats as all-Beatles, all-Elvis or all-comedy. These formats quickly wear out their novelty and appeal to both listeners and advertisers. Other specialized formats can be popular but problematic. For example, in the early 2000s, many Spanish-language stations began programming a musical style known as *reggaeton*. But although it garnered many listeners, they tended to skew very young and advertisers—from breweries to auto makers—did not find it fruitful to air their ads over *reggaeton* stations.

Narrowcasting can also be used in a technical, rather than programming, sense. Again, the opposite of *broad*casting—which strives to send out a free signal to the largest number of recipients—narrowcasting makes its signal receivable to only those who specifically request or pay for it, or own the hardware necessary to receive it. Cable radio, subscription-based services and satellite radio are all examples of such narrowcasting.

See also: Formats Defining Radio Programming; Programming Strategies and Processes

Further Reading

Fornatale, Peter, and Joshua E. Mills, *Radio in the Television Age*, Woodstock, New York: Overlook Press, 1980.
Ganzert, Charles, "Platter Chatter and the Pancake Impresarios: The Re-Invention of Radio in the Age of Television, 1946–1959," Ph.D. diss., Ohio University, 1992.
Hall, Claude, and Barbara Hall, *This Business of Radio Programming: A Comprehensive Look at Modern Programming Techniques Used throughout the Radio World*, New York: Billboard, 1977.
MacFarland, David, *The Development of the Top 40 Radio Format*, New York: Arno Press, 1979.
Routt, Edd, James McGrath, and Frederick Weiss, *The Radio Format Conundrum*, New York: Hastings House, 1978.

CHARLES F. GANZERT,
2009 REVISIONS BY CARY O'DELL

NATIONAL ASSOCIATION OF BROADCASTERS
Broadcast Trade Organization

The National Association of Broadcasters (NAB) is the primary trade association of the American broadcasting industry. The NAB represents the industry before the Federal Communications Commission (FCC), Congress, and other government entities and takes a proactive role in acquainting the public with the importance of radio and television communications.

Members of the association set policies and make decisions on industry-wide matters through a board of directors composed of radio and television broadcasters elected by fellow members. This joint board is subdivided into a radio and a television board, each with its own chair. The joint board also has a chairman. NAB is overseen by a full-time president.

NAB has an extensive committee structure that enables it to draw on the specialized knowledge of its members in dealing with industry causes and in making recommendations to the board of directors. These committees are composed of representatives of individual stations, broadcast groups, and the networks. Active member support and participation are the basis for NAB decisions and activities.

According to its charter, NAB operates "to foster and promote the development of the arts of aural and visual broadcasting in all forms; to protect its members in every lawful and proper manner from injustices and unjust exactions; to do all things necessary and proper to encourage and promote customs and practices which will strengthen and maintain the broadcasting industry to the end that it may best serve the people."

Origins

The early history of NAB is closely tied to the issue of using recorded music in early radio broadcasts of the 1920s. At that time, broadcasters freely used phonograph records without compensating the artists involved, in spite of a 1917 court decision that upheld the right of creative artists to license their products under provisions of the 1909 copyright act. By early 1922 the declining sale of phonograph records in the face of radio broadcasting caused the American Society of Composers, Authors, and Publishers (ASCAP) to look for ways to recover lost royalties directly from broadcasters. ASCAP, founded in 1914, provided the means for artists to license and copyright their creative efforts.

In April 1922 ASCAP determined that the radio reproduction of copyrighted songs fell under the "public performance for profit" portion of the copyright law and that the copyright owners were entitled to compensation from the broadcasters. ASCAP notified all broadcast stations of their intention to collect royalties for their members, but the announcement was largely ignored by the fledgling industry.

After finding little success pursuing its aims within the broadcast industry as a whole, ASCAP decided specifically to move against Westinghouse, General Electric (GE), the Radio Corporation of America (RCA), and a few other giants of the new industry. ASCAP called for a conference to discuss the issue, but it was once again ignored. The broadcasters agreed to a meeting only after ASCAP threatened to sue them for copyright infringements if they did not meet.

At the meeting on 20 September 1922, ASCAP presented as its major concern artists' rights to royalty payments, whereas broadcasters expressed their desire not to pay royalties. Of major importance to the broadcasters was the payment of performers; at that time, many musicians performed on radio free for the exposure, and broadcasters felt that if they paid some, they would have to pay them all. The broadcasters told ASCAP that they would go on the air with "The Old Gray Mare, She Ain't What She Used to Be" rather then pay ASCAP for the privilege of broadcasting the latest ASCAP licensed hit, "My Bromo-Seltzer Bride." The meeting ended without resolution.

Organization by Zenith's McDonald

The second ASCAP-broadcaster conference occurred one month later, on 25 October 1922. At this meeting, broadcasters expressed sympathy for the artists' position but stated that they could not afford to pay for the music if it would lead to paying all composers, individual performers, and orchestras. ASCAP responded by filing a suit and notifying all broadcasters that it was revoking all temporary licenses for broadcast of ASCAP members' music. Additionally, ASCAP established a rate schedule that fixed fees for the use of music at $250 to $5,000 per year per station depending on the size of the station's audience (determined by location, wattage, and profits). The arbitrary nature of the ASCAP action caused a small group of broadcasters, organized by "Commander" Eugene F. McDonald, Jr., founder-president of Zenith Radio Corporation (and station WJAZ), to meet in Chicago in early 1923 to form an organization to oppose ASCAP; this organization would become the National Association of Broadcasters.

The group, all pioneer broadcasters, moved quickly from a discussion of ASCAP to the need for a regulatory body for radio similar to the Interstate Commerce Commission. At this initial meeting of concerned broadcasters, McDonald first used the name "Federal Communications Commission" for such a group. They also considered rules and regulations that they felt should apply to a free enterprise system for radio.

Shortly after this meeting, McDonald, who knew little of the music business, called on his friend and business colleague Thomas Pletcher, president of the QRS Music Company, for advice. He told Pletcher that his group of broadcasters believed that authors and composers should be paid directly for their contributions, rather then through ASCAP, but that they did not know how to proceed with the organization. Pletcher suggested that the group hire Paul B. Klugh (a knowledgeable, recently retired music roll manufacturer) as secretary of the new organization. McDonald successfully recruited Klugh, who assumed the position of executive chairman. McDonald embarked on a campaign to persuade RCA, GE, Westinghouse, and American Telephone and Telegraph (ATT) to join the fledgling group, but he was initially unsuccessful.

The actual organizational meeting for the NAB was held in the studios of WDAP (Chicago) on 25 and 26 April 1923, with 54 representatives of various radio constituencies. Representatives of ASCAP presented their positions and, after discussion, left the meeting. A committee was then formed to propose the structure for an organization that would carry out the aims of the broadcasters. The committee consisted of McDonald (WJAZ), T. Donnelley (WDAP), J.E. Jenkins (WDAP), W.S. Hedges (WMAQ), P.B. Klugh, R.M. Johnson (Alabama Power and Light Company), and George Lewis (Crosley Manufacturing Company). The group, known as "the Committee of Seven," reported on 26 April 1923, and their recommendations were accepted: the association was to be known as The National Association of Broadcasters, NAB's offices would be established in New York City, and they would employ a managing director. Paul Klugh was selected as the managing director by a unanimous vote. Two other meetings were held in 1923 with the main subject of discussion being the development of an NAB "music bureau" of copyright-free music.

The first annual meeting of the National Association of Broadcasters was held in conjunction with the annual National Radio Show held in New York on 11 October 1923. This meeting, called to order by Chairman Klugh in the Commodore Hotel in New York City, resulted in the election of the first real officers of the NAB. McDonald was elected president. A number of addresses were presented, and the group received a list of holdings in the NAB Music Bureau. A discussion of legislation plans was also undertaken. The group wanted to accomplish two goals with their legislation: (1) music copyright revision and (2) modernization of the 1912 Radio Act. During the meeting, McDonald conducted a test of the size of the audience at WJAZ by asking listeners to send in paid telegrams acknowledging their reception. The audience was estimated to be 400,000, based on receiving 4,284 telegrams in four hours. The public relations coup resulted in considerable publicity for the young broadcasters' group.

In conjunction with the 1923 Chicago Radio Show in November, McDonald and his good friend Thorne Donnelley of WDAP, both officers of the NAB, along with Chicago station KYW, conducted an audience census to determine music preference in the Chicago listening area. For 12 days the stations requested listeners to write in telling what they most desired to hear. The three stations received a total of 263,410 pieces of mail, with WJAZ receiving 170,699; WDAP, 54,811; and KYW, 37,900. It was estimated that not more than 1 in 50 listeners would respond, which suggested that the three stations were being heard by an audience of more than 13 million.

In 1924 ASCAP attempted to flex its muscle and thus created a situation that brought the music copyright problem before Congress. The Edgewater Beach Hotel (home of WJAZ) had always paid a fee to ASCAP for the music used in its dining room. Because at times this music had also been broadcast live over WJAZ, ASCAP refused to renew the performance license for the music unless a broadcast license was also secured, even though the hotel no longer allowed WJAZ to broadcast the music. The broadcasters determined that this situation was a good legal test case. The fact that McDonald's WJAZ was involved and that he was also president of the NAB undoubtedly was an important factor in choosing this incident for the test case.

On 22 February 1924, Senator C.C. Dill, at the urging of the NAB, introduced a bill to the Senate that amended the Copyright Act of 1909 to make radio performances of copyrighted material essentially legal and royalty-free. A nasty battle ensued, with ASCAP waging a publicity campaign encouraging all musicians to join the fight. NAB, small and new, had little money to fight back, and a plea to broadcasters for financial help brought nothing.

The NAB cause was represented by NAB President McDonald, Executive Secretary Klugh, and Counsel Charles Tuttle. In January 1925, the ASCAP-supported Perkins Bill (H.R. 11258) was introduced in the House. This bill called for massive changes in the copyright law in general and particularly in those portions concerned with radio broadcasting.

Years of debate followed. The NAB endorsed its stand at each succeeding annual conference. McDonald's involvement also continued. As NAB president, he was appointed one of ten members of the Copyright Committee of the Fourth National Radio Conference called by then Commerce Secretary Herbert Hoover in Washington on 9 November 1925. The fight to avoid paying royalties, however, was rapidly being lost, and the NAB and ASCAP entered secret negotiations. McDonald stepped down as president of the NAB in 1926 as he began a battle with Secretary Hoover over frequency allocations, but he continued his strong involvement with NAB for many years, holding a variety of offices.

NAB Radio and Television Codes

The NAB has been involved in voluntary compliance broadcast codes since 1929, when it produced its first "Code of Ethics" in an attempt to pre-empt the Federal Radio Commission from imposing such a code. In 1939, attempting to avoid FCC action regarding children's programs, the NAB issued a "Radio Code" dealing with profanity and limits on commercial time in children's programming. NAB issued a guide for broadcasters in 1942 covering security in wartime broadcasting. Although compliance with these codes was voluntary, many NAB members subscribed to them, and the various NAB radio and television codes existed until they were dropped in 1982 after a court case found a portion of the code unconstitutional. Today the NAB operates under a "Statement of Principles" dealing with program content.

The NAB expanded greatly in 1938 and has grown with the broadcasting industry, incorporating other groups in the industry. The FM Broadcaster Association became a department of NAB in 1945, and in 1951 the Television Broadcasters Association also merged with NAB. Springing from NAB membership in 1959, a new and independent National Association of FM Broadcasters met for the first time; by 1984, the 2000-member group, then named the National Radio Broadcasters Association, merged with NAB. NAB also accepts associate members in fields allied to broadcasting.

The Modern NAB

Although much of the association's focus since the 1950s has been on television, cable, and newer media, radio continues to occupy NAB lobbying and developmental efforts. NAB championed FM in the 1960s and 1970s, publishing a monthly newsletter tracing industry developments. In the early 1980s, NAB fought strenuously and eventually successfully to beat back an FCC proposal to reduce AM channels from 10 kHz to 9 kHz, parallel to much of the rest of the world. The association argued that such a move would increase interference and make many push-button radios obsolete. At the same time, NAB supported efforts to create AM stereo and to select a technical standard for the service.

In the late 1990s, NAB radio interests focused on digital radio and on developing a successful technical standard to allow digital audio broadcasting (DAB) service to begin. At the same time, NAB fought hard against allowing satellite digital services to develop, because they would threaten the local stations represented by the association. And NAB fought against the highly popular introduction of low-power FM stations (LPFM) in 2000, arguing that the potential for hundreds of new stations would greatly increase interference problems. NAB maintains an ongoing educational program on its agenda.

The huge annual four-day NAB conventions, which now attract more than 115,000 attendees, are held every spring (in Las Vegas since the early 1970s) and devote considerable conference time and exhibition space to radio and audio topics. A fall conference focused entirely on radio programming and operations is also held, and radio-related publications are issued regularly. With more than 100 full-time employees housed in its own modern building in Washington, D.C., the NAB has gained a reputation as one of the strongest and most effective lobbies in the nation's capital. Part of this strength comes from the clout inherent in member stations, which provide airtime for political candidates and which will readily call congresspersons to express their views. Although the association had a well-deserved reputation for political clout in the nation's capital, it did not always win its lobbying battles. The fight over the merger of the Sirius and XM satellite radio companies in 2007–8 was bitter, coming as it did after decades of debate over whether to even allow such services at all. The NAB argued before Congress and the FCC that approval of the deal was simply a "merger to monopoly" and would make nonsense of any future government moves to control media ownership. Though it seemed likely the association might sue to overturn the FCC decision to approve the merger, no such suit was forthcoming. Observers suggested the NAB had bigger concerns on other radio issues (such as the music industry's renewed campaign to seek payment for recordings played) and wanted to preserve its political and legal strength.

See also: American Society of Composers, Authors, and Publishers; Broadcast Music Incorporated; FM Trade Associations; Trade Associations

Further Reading

Barnouw, Erik, *A History of Broadcasting in the United States*, 3 vols, New York: Oxford University Press, 1966–70; see especially vol. 1, *A Tower in Babel: To 1933, 1966*, and vol. 2, *The Golden Web, 1933 to 1953*, 1968.

Cones, Harold, and John Bryant, *Eugene F. McDonald: Communications Pioneer Lost to History*, Record of Proceedings, 3rd International Symposium on Telecommunications History, Washington, D.C.: Independent Telephone Historical Foundation, 1995.

Hilliard, Robert L., and Michael C. Keith, *The Broadcast Century: A Biography of American Broadcasting*, Boston: Focal Press, 1992; 2nd edition, Boston and Oxford, 1997.

Mackey, David, "The Development of the National Association of Broadcasters," *Journal of Broadcasting* 1 (Fall 1957).

National Association of Broadcasters website, www.nab.org

Smith, Frederick, "Fees for Composers—None for Broadcasters," *Radio Age* (February 1923).

Smulyan, Susan, *Selling Radio: The Commercialization of American Broadcasting, 1920–1934*, Washington, D.C.: Smithsonian Institution Press, 1994.

HAROLD N. CONES AND JOHN H. BRYANT,
2009 REVISIONS BY CHRISTOPHER H. STERLING

NATIONAL ASSOCIATION OF EDUCATIONAL BROADCASTERS

The National Association of Educational Broadcasters (NAEB) was the oldest professional educational broadcasting organization in the United States, founded as the Association of College and University Stations in 1925. Until its demise in 1981, the NAEB served as the nation's most influential force in the establishment and preservation of an alternative system of noncommercial educational (public) radio stations.

Origins

The historical roots of American public radio extend back at least as far as those of commercial radio broadcasters. Early in the 1900s experimental stations began appearing in electrical engineering departments of universities and colleges across the country, the first being station 9XM (now WHA) at the University of Wisconsin in Madison. Unfortunately, the primary motivation for building many of these stations was limited to the study of technical considerations, without much concern about the programming and service potential of this new electronic medium. By 1926, roughly half of these early stations had gone off the air, but among those remaining, there was a growing interest in exploring educational uses for radio.

Secretary of Commerce Herbert Hoover had already begun a series of annual National Radio Conferences in Washington, D.C., and it was at the fourth of these gatherings, on 12 November 1925, that a group of educational broadcasters created a new organization, the Association of College and University Broadcasting Stations. At first, this fledgling collective of broadcast pioneers was loosely knit and had no specific purpose other than to support and promote radio for educational use. Membership was open to all educational institutions that operated radio stations, but even with annual dues set at only $3.00, less than half of the qualified institutions joined the association during its first few years of existence. Documentation for this period is extremely limited, but it is clear that the members struggled against enormous odds to hold the organization together, as the Great Depression began to bring financial hardships to institutions of higher learning.

The first formal convention of the 25-member association was held on the Ohio State University campus in Columbus in July of 1930, convened in conjunction with the Institute for Education by Radio. Recent licensing actions by the Federal Radio Commission were seen as clearly favoring the commercial use of radio at the expense of educational development. Hence, there was a growing sense of urgency that something needed to be done to stem the tide of lost licenses for educational institutions. Association president Robert Higgy, Director of Ohio State's WOSU, launched a campaign to seek legislation that would reserve a portion of the radio spectrum exclusively for noncommercial educational use. Association members joined with other educational radio advocates, including the National Advisory Council on Radio in Education and the National Committee on Education by Radio, in that pursuit over the next several years. However, when the Communications Act was signed into law on 19 June 1934, the provision for which they had fought so hard had been deleted. Instead, Congress specified that the newly created Federal Communications Commission would study the matter of nonprofit allocations to educational institutions and report back on their findings.

Reorganization and Name Change

When the association members gathered on 10 September 1934, in Kansas City, Missouri, for their annual meeting, there was a renewed determination to influence the work of the FCC. A new constitution was adopted and the organization's name was changed to the National Association of Educational Broadcasters. This new label better reflected the interests of existing members, particularly those that were producing educational programs which were being broadcast over commercial radio stations. The NAEB members rededicated themselves to three goals: reserving channels for educational use, establishing a national headquarters, and creating a mechanism for program exchange. Toward this third goal, three committees were established, each to study a specific means of program exchange: shortwave transmission between stations, the establishment of a chain network, and the recording of programs.

The FCC hearings that stemmed from the congressional statute to study the matter failed to result in the desired educational reservations, though the NAEB continued to lobby both the FCC and members of Congress in the years to follow. When the NAEB assembled in Iowa City on 9 September 1935, each of the program exchange committees made their reports. The use of shortwave interconnection was judged impractical, but there was some optimism expressed that federal and state appropriations might enable the creation of a chain network at some future date. However, the only short-term means of program exchange seemed to be to record programs and exchange them among stations through the U.S. mail service. The goal of establishing a national office was still well beyond the members' reach.

The NAEB continued to meet annually through 1938 but suspended its regular meeting schedule during the years 1939–41. Throughout this period the association achieved modest accomplishments, including purchasing of sound transcription equipment, beginning the publication of a regular newsletter, creation of a radio script exchange, and successfully lobbying the FCC to reserve designated "curricular channels" in 1938, though the authorization of FM broadcasting would render this initial lobbying victory moot. The continued efforts by the NAEB culminated in the FCC's acceptance of the reservation principle when the Commission first authorized FM service in 1941, reserving the five lowest channels for noncommercial educational use. Four years later, the FCC shifted the placement of FM broadcasting to its present location, and set aside the lowest 20 channels (88–92 MHz) for educational use.

Although membership in the association during the early 1940s did not increase significantly, the organization gained greater cohesion and confidence as representatives from member stations worked cooperatively on a variety of association initiatives, including FM channel reservations. Efforts were stepped up to get educational institutions to apply for construction permits for FM stations, and discussions about establishing a national headquarters with paid personnel continued to gain momentum. In an attempt to encourage more stations into operation, the NAEB convinced the FCC to liberalize its FM rules by creating a new Class D license in 1948 that allowed stations to broadcast with as little power as 10 W, thus greatly reducing the costs of transmitter equipment and ongoing operations for the many colleges and universities that wanted to mount student-operated radio stations.

In 1949, the long-envisioned program exchange was formally begun when station WNYC in New York City made five sets of recordings of the *Herald Tribune Forum* series that were mailed among 22 NAEB member stations in a distribution system that came to be known as the bicycle network. Prompted by the success of this bicycle tape network, University of Illinois Dean Wilbur Schramm offered a plan at the 1950 NAEB convention in Lexington, Kentucky, to house the network headquarters on his Urbana, Illinois, campus, with funding generated by a series of grants. The following year the NAEB received a major grant from the W.K. Kellogg Foundation to fund a

permanent national headquarters and distribution center at the University of Illinois. A series of other major grants were soon forthcoming, and both the financial posture and the services provided by the NAEB improved significantly. Increases in NAEB membership quickly followed, and by January of 1954 there were 218 members and 78 stations participating in the tape network. The national headquarters staff had expanded to seven full-time employees. After nearly 30 years of struggling for its own survival, the NAEB had become the dominant force in U.S. educational broadcasting.

Organizational Transitions

During the 1950s, the NAEB greatly improved its stature within the educational community, both nationally and internationally. Increased human and financial resources enabled the association to exhibit expanded leadership and professional development for the educational broadcasting establishment. Workshops, seminars, and regional conferences soon complemented the annual convention. In 1956, a sister organization of individual members from a wide range of educational professions—the Association for Education by Radio-Television (AERT)—merged with the NAEB and brought with it a scholarly publication, the *AERT Journal*. The following year, the association began publication of the *NAEB Journal*, in addition to the monthly *NAEB Newsletter* and other occasional reports and monographs. By the 1959 convention in Detroit, Michigan, it was evident that the NAEB's ever-widening vision had outgrown its home in Urbana, Illinois.

From the inception of the national headquarters at the University of Illinois, the NAEB had operated with an elected president from one of the member stations and a full-time executive director located at the national office. It was time to move the national headquarters to Washington, D.C., and to hire a full-time president. On 1 September 1960, the NAEB's new offices opened in the DuPont Circle Office Building at 1346 Connecticut Avenue, NW. The new president who would lead the organization into a new era of educational broadcasting was William G. Harley, a former elected NAEB president and chairman of the board of directors who had gained national prominence as manager for the highly successful WHA-AM-FM-TV stations at the University of Wisconsin.

Harley moved quickly to establish the NAEB as a lobbying force on Capitol Hill, while expanding the number of grants that enabled the NAEB to enhance its intellectual position. A new publication, the *Washington Report*, was created to help keep members posted on important developments in the capital city. The NAEB Radio Network took full advantage of the Washington connection by producing a new public affairs show, *Report from Washington*, that was sent by air mail to the Center in Urbana for distribution to member stations. Harley also secured letters pledging support from both presidential hopefuls, Richard M. Nixon and John F. Kennedy, as a way of building bridges with the new administration. And among the first academic projects to come out of this period was the commissioning of Marshall McLuhan to prepare a report on the new media's role in the future of education. The book resulting from that project, *Understanding Media*, remains one of the most influential mass communication publications of the 20th century.

NAEB leaders had long advocated that the association should be more of a professional organization than a trade association in the traditional sense. The influx of individual members brought about by the merger with AERT in 1956 and the growing ranks of members from closed-circuit instructional television facilities were causing growing dissatisfaction with the existing governance structure, which was controlled by radio and television station representatives. At the 1963 NAEB convention in Milwaukee, Wisconsin, the members voted unanimously to reorganize the association into four divisions: Radio Station Division, Television Station Division, Instruction Division, and Individual Member Division. Each was to elect its own board, with the four boards comprising the NAEB Board of Directors. Offices and support staff for each of the units would be established within the national headquarters.

For radio interests, the reorganization was a major step forward. Television representatives had been exercising more and more control over the NAEB since the mid-1950s. Growing numbers of radio representatives wanted a separate organization of their own but knew full well that they did not have the resources to go it alone. The reorganization gave radio the independence it needed to chart a new course, while allowing it to benefit from the largesse of the higher television station dues. The new configuration also afforded the opportunity for a new name—National Educational Radio (NER)—while remaining under the NAEB umbrella. In the spring of 1964, the radio board appointed WUOM (University of Michigan) production manager Jerrold Sandler to be NER's first executive director. The tape exchange network—now officially named the National Educational Radio Network—remained in Urbana.

Under Sandler's guidance, NER acquired the kind of representational and leadership presence in Washington, D.C., that the radio representatives had envisioned. In addition to continuing the program exchange system, the new division became far more active on Capitol Hill, raised major grants for program and research projects, built relationships in the international community, provided a unified voice in professional circles, offered consulting advice to member stations, and distributed grants-in-aid to support special projects. During 1966–67, Sandler contracted with Herbert W. Land Associates to conduct a national study of the status of educational radio in the United States. The resulting report, *The Hidden Medium: Educational Radio*, offered the documentation needed for Sandler to lobby Congress on behalf of radio during the drafting of what had been the Public Television Act of 1967. As a direct result of Sandler's efforts, radio was written into the language during the eleventh hour, and the final legislation was called the Public Broadcasting Act of 1967.

A Forecast of Demise

Although passage of this historic legislation dramatically changed educational radio and television for the better, it signaled the beginning of a transformation that would eventually mean an end to the NAEB. The Act created the Corporation for Public Broadcasting (CPB), which was charged with strengthening the newly relabeled *public* radio and television stations in the United States. This mandate led to the creation of the Public Broadcasting Service (PBS) and National Public Radio (NPR). In 1971, NPR began live national network interconnection of member stations, and the National Educational Radio Network soon merged with NPR. For a number of months, NAEB continued to represent radio stations before Congress, but by 1973, the stations had created a new lobbying and public relations organization—the Association of Public Radio Stations (APRS)—and so NAEB ceased its radio representation function. (APTS would later merge with NPR in 1977.)

Just as NPR and APRS took over the functions of NAEB's Radio Division, PBS soon acquired the functions of the Television Division. By the mid-1970s, the NAEB was again forced to undergo a major reorganization and a redirection of its mission solely as a professional organization. When Harley retired in 1975, James A. Fellows became NAEB's last president. Fellows worked tirelessly to revitalize the association and to generate a solid funding base through individual member services.

A variety of public telecommunication institutes on such topics as management skills, graphic arts, instructional design, and audience research methods were scheduled throughout the country. The publications program was expanded with the creation of *Public Telecommunications Review*, a research index and reprint series, and later with the *Current* newspaper. Members were served by various professional councils, ranging from broadcast education and research to engineering and management. The annual convention afforded additional professional training opportunities and a career placement center. In short, the NAEB attempted to become the professional standard bearer for the public broadcasting industry.

Despite a herculean effort by Fellows and his ever-shrinking staff, the NAEB could not sustain itself as an organization supported solely by individual members. At its final convention at the Hyatt Regency Hotel in New Orleans on 3 November 1981, NAEB board chairman Robert K. Avery recalled the association's important accomplishments over the preceding 56 years. With the vote taken to declare bankruptcy, he brought down the final gavel and dissolved the organization.

See also: Educational Radio to 1967; National Public Radio; Public Broadcasting Act of 1967; Public Radio Since 1967

Further Reading

Avery, Robert K., Paul E. Burrows, and Clara J. Pincus, *Research Index for NAEB Journals: NAEB Journal, Educational Broadcasting Review, Public Telecommunications Review, 1957–1979*, Washington, D.C.: National Association of Educational Broadcasters, 1980.

Blakely, Robert J., *To Serve the Public Interest: Educational Broadcasting in the United States*, Syracuse, New York: Syracuse University Press, 1979.

Hill, Harold E., and W. Wayne Alford, *NAEB History*, 2 vols, Urbana, Illinois: National Association of Educational Broadcasters, 1966.

Witherspoon, John, Roselle Kovitz, Robert K. Avery, and Alan G. Stavitsky, *A History of Public Broadcasting*, Washington, D.C.: Current, 2000.

ROBERT K. AVERY

NATIONAL ASSOCIATION OF EDUCATIONAL BROADCASTERS TAPE NETWORK
Early Program Exchange

The National Association of Educational Broadcasters (NAEB) Tape Network was the first formal agreement among educational broadcasters to allow for the exchange of programs for rebroadcast. This system was important because it provided for the sharing of much-needed program materials between financially strapped broadcast stations across the United States.

Origins

In the 1930s a growing concept of educational broadcasting was developing at a few scattered stations, most of which were loosely affiliated with colleges and universities. Representatives held annual conventions, which led to formation of the Association of College and University Broadcasting Stations, predecessor to what became the NAEB. The group's primary purpose was to persuade the government to set aside radio channels for state-, college-, and university-operated stations. Another goal was to develop a mechanism for program exchange.

These broadcasters watched the successful sharing of programming taking place in commercial radio through the National Broadcasting Company (NBC) Red and Blue networks and the Columbia Broadcasting System (CBS). A network for educational radio was discussed but was dismissed as too costly; an idea for a script exchange met with little enthusiasm. A few stations did exchange scripts, but few of these exchanges resulted in produced programs.

In 1932 NAEB secured a $500 grant from the National Advisory Council on Radio Education and purchased a wire recorder. The device was to be circulated among stations for recording programs for air. In 1949 the director of New York's municipal station WNYC, Seymour Siegel, made five sets of recordings of the *Herald Tribune Forum* and distributed them to 22 NAEB member stations throughout the year. This event marks the start of what was labeled a "bicycle" (mailed tape exchange) network.

Postwar Developments

In 1950 NAEB was able to secure more funding, this time from the Kellogg Foundation. The purpose of the grant was to support a systemized national noncommercial education and culture tape network to serve the growing demand for educational radio programming. The exchange system delivered programming from the British Broadcasting Corporation (BBC), the Canadian Broadcasting Corporation (CBC), and domestic stations and production centers. In its first year, what became the National Educational Radio (NER) network mailed over 500 hours of programming to 52 NAEB member stations coast to coast.

A network headquarters was established in Urbana, Illinois. Programs were duplicated on high-speed equipment. A fee was established for member stations, and within five years the organization was modestly financed but self-sustaining. By 1967 it was estimated that the network distributed some 35,400 hours (more than 80 million feet of tape) of educational radio programming in the United States on a budget of less than $60,000.

Sample bulletins from the early years of the tape exchange demonstrate diverse program offerings. Program topics included physical sciences ("The Impact of Atomic Energy"), social sciences ("Woman's Role in Society"), mental and physical health ("The Effects of Smoking"), and arts and literature ("The Alabama String Quartet"). Children's programming was a category listed in early bulletins, but specific examples are difficult to find. Networks supplied their affiliates with tapes to be used in local schools as well. Subject matter for kindergarten through 12th grade included science, foreign languages, guidance, language arts, music and art, safety and health, and social studies.

Most of the programs distributed by the tape network in return for the regular affiliation fee consisted of offerings from individual affiliates. Production costs for these programs were generally covered by the local stations. Some stations enhanced programs with modest grants from organizations such as the National Home Library Foundation and the Johnson Foundation.

The network also delivered some special programming to affiliates at no additional cost. For instance, a 30-minute *Special of the Week* produced out of the University of Michigan featured addresses by national and world leaders on public affairs. In addition, an 11-program series by WGBH Boston (*A Chance to Grow*) examined how families dealt with critical changes in their lives. The series featured interviews with families and was produced with the aid of grants and contributions. The government also provided some "no-charge" programs, such as a panel discussion from a conference held by the Selective Service System at the University of Chicago. And finally, the Library of Congress had a special arrangement with the tape network to allow the network to distribute certain readings and lectures given by the library.

Programs were also provided to affiliates from a wide variety of international sources. Regular contributors to the network included the BBC (*Translantic Forum*, *The World Report*, and *Science Magazine*), Radio Netherlands, Berne, Italian Radio, UNESCO, and the CBC, among others.

While the tape exchange network was still in a growth mode, educational broadcasters were still pushing for a more permanent way to exchange programming—a real network. In September 1965 some 70 NER stations linked together for a historic live interconnection to broadcast three hours of German national election results coverage.

In 1966 at a NER conference (The Wingspread Conference), 70 leaders from the industry, government, the academic community, philanthropy, and the arts came up with a seven-point plan for developing educational radio that included a national production center and the use of communications satellites for transmitting noncommercial programming. A concrete step toward centralized programming was made in March 1967 when NER set up a Public Affairs Bureau in Washington. However, a centralized network was yet to come. During the Carnegie Commission's study of 1965–67, the need for an interconnected educational radio system was again stressed. The Public Broadcasting Act (1967) that followed set the stage for the development of that network. In the years following the passage of the act, educational broadcasters met to plan the network. Finally, on 3 May 1971, the goal of national programming distribution sources for noncommercial radio broadcasters was realized, when National Public Radio premiered its first live show—*All Things Considered*. Other programs and a satellite interconnect to allow members to share programming would follow. Educational broadcasters no longer had to duplicate and mail tapes to deliver shared programs to the public.

See also: Educational Radio to 1967; National Association of Educational Broadcasters; National Public Radio; Public Radio Since 1967

Further Reading

Blakely, Robert J., *To Serve the Public Interest: Educational Broadcasting in the United States*, Syracuse, New York: Syracuse University Press, 1979.

Herman W. Land Associates, *The Hidden Medium: A Status Report on Educational Radio in the United States*, New York: Herman W. Land Associates, 1967.

Saettler, L. Paul, *A History of Instructional Technology*, New York: McGraw Hill, 1968.

Siegel, Seymour N., "Educational Broadcasting Comes of Age," in *Education on the Air: Twenty-First Yearbook of the Institute for Education by Radio*, Columbus: Ohio State University, 1951.

Witherspoon, John, Roselle Kovitz, Robert K. Avery, and Alan G. Stavitsky, *A History of Public Broadcasting*, Washington, D.C.: Current, 2000.

PAMELA K. DOYLE

NATIONAL BARN DANCE
Country Music Variety Program

Although the *Grand Ole Opry* is best remembered because it survived far longer, the WLS *National Barn Dance* before World War II ranked as America's most popular country music program. After being picked up by the National Broadcasting Company (NBC) network in 1933, and sponsored and supported by Miles Laboratories' Alka-Selzer, the WLS *National Barn Dance* became a Saturday night radio network fixture.

The show's longtime home was WLS-AM, a pioneering and important station in Chicago, named by owner Sears-Roebuck to herald itself as the "World's Largest Store." First under Sears, and then after 1928 with new owner *Prairie Farmer* magazine, the focus of this clear channel station was always the rural American. Clear channel status made WLS-AM a fixture in homes throughout the Midwestern farm belt.

Originally called the *WLS Barn Dance*, by 1930 the program had expanded to fill WLS's Saturday nights. When the NBC Blue network began on 30 September 1933 to run a portion, sponsored by Miles Laboratories' Alka-Seltzer, the program was renamed the *National Barn Dance*. Though NBC varied the program's length (from 30 to 60 minutes and back, again and again), from 1936 to 1946, the network always penciled the *National Barn Dance* on the schedule starting at 9 P.M. on Saturday nights. Indeed, in 1940 when NBC picked up the *Grand Ole Opry*, the *National Barn Dance* was already a network fixture, signaling to all who paid attention to radio industry trends a growing interest in the "hillbilly" musical form.

The statistics were impressive. For example, on 25 October 1930 nearly 20,000 fans poured into Chicago's massive International Amphitheater for a special performance, and an estimated 10,000 had to be turned away. The popularity peak of the *National Barn Dance* came during World War II, but after the war the *Opry* surpassed its predecessor in ratings, and the shift to Nashville was underway. NBC dropped the *National Barn Dance* in 1946.

But in its heyday, beginning with a move in 1932 to the Loop's Eighth Street Theater, the success of the *National Barn Dance* could literally be seen as crowds lined up for precious Saturday night tickets and regularly filled the theater's 1,200 seats for two shows. Stars included those remembered by country music historians (Bradley Kincaid, Arkie the Arkansas Woodchopper, and Lulu Belle and Scotty) and those who would help define popular culture of the 20th century (Gene Autry).

Bradley Kincaid was one of country music's first popular sellers. He was a student in Chicago in 1926, having moved there from his native Kentucky, when a friend suggested he try out for the hillbilly show on the radio. Kincaid borrowed a guitar, practiced a few ballads he had learned from his family, and soon was a star. His name is usually lost in country music history, but Kincaid helped define the genre as it emerged during the 1920s and 1930s.

Missourian Luther Ossenbrink renamed himself "Arkie, the Arkansas Woodchopper" when he arrived at WLS in the middle of 1929 after some experience on the radio in Kansas City. While playing the fiddle, guitar, or banjo, he sang and told cornball jokes. Sears executives must have loved his favorite song, "A Dollar Down and a Dollar a Week."

Although the husband-and-wife singing duo, Lulu Belle and Scotty (Wiseman), who appeared from 1935 through 1958, may have been the *Barn Dance*'s most enduring act, to the world Gene Autry symbolized the star-making power of the *National Barn Dance*. Autry appeared during the early 1930s as the "Oklahoma Yodeling Cowboy," but when his "Silver Haired Daddy of Mine" became a hit, he was off to Hollywood and became part of radio legend.

Following NBC's dropping of the *National Barn Dance*, the program reverted to again being a local show until 1949, when the American Broadcasting Companies (ABC) radio network, sponsored by the Phillips Petroleum Company, picked up the show. The ratings on ABC were anemic, and so by the mid-1950s the *National Barn Dance* was a faded memory for everyone except the aging Chicagoans who continued to embrace its radio and television versions. The Eighth Street Theater closed on 31 August 1957, and WLS abandoned it.

In 1960, many of the former *National Barn Dance* regulars appeared on Chicago's WGN-AM under the name *WGN Barn Dance*. But after the Tribune Company, the owner of WGN, syndicated the show for television in the 1960s with limited success, Tribune executives closed the show for good in 1971.

See also: Country Music Format; *Grand Ole Opry*; WGN; WLS

Cast

Hosts	Hal O'Halloran (pre-network), Joe Kelly (1933–50)
Announcer	Jack Holden

Performers (partial listing)	Bradley Kincaid, Gene Autry, George Gobel, Red Foley, Homer and Jethro, Lulu Belle and Scotty, Louise Massey Mabie and the Westerners, Arkie, the Arkansas Woodchopper, Wilson Sisters, Dolph Hewitt, Hoosier Hotshots, Pat Butrum

Producers

Walter Wade, Peter Lund, Jack Frost

Director

Bill Jones

Programming History

WLS	April 1924–September 1933
NBC-Blue	September 1933–June 1940
NBC-Red	June 1940–September 1946
ABC	March 1949–March 1950

Further Reading

Baker, John Chester, *Farm Broadcasting: The First Sixty Years*, Ames: Iowa State University Press, 1981.
Evans, James F., *Prairie Farmer and WLS: The Burridge D. Butler Years*, Urbana: University of Illinois Press, 1969.
Malone, Bill C., *Country Music U.S.A.*, Austin: University of Texas Press, 1968; revised edition, 1985.
Summers, Harrison Boyd, *A Thirty-Year History of Programs Carried on National Radio Networks in the United States, 1926–1956*, Columbus: Ohio State University, 1958.
WLS Magazine (12 April 1949) (special 25th anniversary issue entitled "Stand By").

Douglas Gomery

NATIONAL BROADCASTING COMPANY

While now focused on television, the National Broadcasting Company (NBC) was the first purpose-built national radio network, although it continues as such today in name only. Begun with an emphasis on public service program orientation, NBC became a very profitable commercial venture that helped to dominate—and define—radio's golden age.

Origins

The origins of NBC lie in the extensive political and legal maneuvering of its parent company, the Radio Corporation of America (RCA), in the 1920s. One member of the RCA group, AT&T, found its phone lines could be used not only for remote broadcasts but could also connect stations together in a "chain" or network. AT&T announced the formation of 38 "radio telephone" stations linked by telephone lines, the purpose of which was not to provide programming but rather to "provide the channels through which anyone with whom it makes a contract can send out their own programs," an arrangement that soon became known as "toll broadcasting."

But RCA was operating its own New York City station as well. WJZ began operations as a Westinghouse outlet in 1921 but was purchased by RCA two years later. Unlike AT&T, RCA's interest in the medium was based on its desire to sell more receivers, the assumption being that entertaining programs would result in the sale of more sets. Thus, by 1923 there were two factions battling for control of radio: the "Telephone Group" led by AT&T and Western Electric, and the "Radio Group" consisting of RCA, General Electric (GE), and Westinghouse. AT&T sold its interest in RCA when conflict became inevitable and refused to allow any station aligned with the Radio Group to use its telephone lines to establish a network.

With the threat of government intervention looming, it was left to RCA General Manager David Sarnoff to broker a compromise. He proposed that "all stations of all parties [be put] into a broadcasting company which can be made self-supporting and probably revenue-producing, the telephone company to furnish the wires as needed." This marked the creation of NBC, which began operation in November 1926 with Merlin H. Aylesworth, former managing director of the National Electric Light Association, as president. Although ownership of NBC was originally divided among RCA, GE, and Westinghouse, AT&T profited the most, as it controlled the wires that would eventually connect thousands of stations nationwide (a franchise that would be extended even further with the introduction of television). In short, AT&T got to keep the toll without having to worry about the broadcasting.

Consolidation and Growth

NBC immediately adopted the practice of toll broadcasting by selling studio space and a time slot—"four walls and air" in trade lingo—to interested advertising agencies and their sponsor-clients. RCA also decided to operate two NBC networks, with WEAF as the flagship station of NBC-Red and WJZ anchoring NBC-Blue (the colors apparently derived from either the company's color-coded program charts or the pencil lines AT&T engineers drew to map the wire paths for the two networks).

NBC grew rapidly in size and profitability. In 1927 the network had 48 affiliates, including both the Red and Blue networks, and lost almost $500,000 in net income; by 1932—when RCA assumed complete ownership of the network—it had 85 affiliates and pretax profits of $1.2 million.

As both networks grew, so did the interest of advertising agencies and sponsors, who saw network radio as an increasingly effective way to reach a national audience of consumers. Fortunately for advertisers, the ability to reach a mass audience with radio intersected with an expansion of the American economy in the 1920s. In 1929 Merlin Aylesworth proclaimed that radio was "an open gateway to national markets, to millions of consumers, and to thousands upon thousands of retailers."

Soon, major advertising agencies were enthusiastically embracing the new medium, a revolution that was not dampened by the Great Depression. The NBC schedule in the 1930s was dominated by shows named for their sponsors, such as *The Chase and Sanborn Hour, Cliquot Club Eskimos,* and *Maxwell House Showboat.* By the early 1930s, the economic structure that would dominate radio for the next 20 years had emerged. The networks learned to be the middleman, selling time to advertising agencies that produced the commercial shows on behalf of paying sponsors, while their affiliates were responsible for developing a rapport with local audiences.

Throughout the decade, NBC continued to flourish. A sharper distinction between the Red and Blue networks came into focus. NBC-Red was home to the most popular programs, including *Fibber McGee and Molly, One Man's Family,* and *Amos 'n' Andy,* as well as such stars as Bob Hope, Jack Benny, and Fred Allen. Not surprisingly, it accounted for most of NBC's profits. NBC-Blue, on the other hand, was somewhat schizophrenic in character, as it was the home of cultural programming of the highest quality—the NBC *Symphony* led by Arturo Toscanini chief among them—but also was the dumping ground of sustained (unsponsored) programming that as often as not placed fourth in the ratings behind NBC-Red, CBS, and the less successful (after 1934) Mutual Broadcasting System. Still, Blue served as something of a loss leader for RCA, as it was frequently touted by the company as a prestigious public service. Blue also allowed NBC to cultivate a reputation superior to that of CBS, which was always a special consideration for David Sarnoff.

NBC's economic strength derived almost wholly from its affiliate relationships. In 1932, the network initiated a plan to pay its affiliates a fee for every network-originated, sponsored program that the affiliate carried on its schedule. In return, the affiliate agreed to purchase NBC's sustained programs at a rate lower than what the station might typically produce in-house. This à la carte system still allowed the affiliates some freedom to pick and choose among the various network offerings, and although many of the larger stations objected to what they considered an inadequate reimbursement for their time costs, the arrangement allowed NBC to provide nationwide coverage to paying advertisers. However, both NBC and CBS continued to extract more concessions from their affiliates throughout the 1930s, knowing there was no shortage of local stations eager to accept whatever demands the networks might place upon them. As a result, government intervention became almost inevitable.

Report on Chain Broadcasting: 1941

Although the economic structure of commercial broadcasting was consolidated in the early 1930s, its regulatory parameters were slightly more fluid. In March 1938 the Federal Communications Commission (FCC) initiated an investigation into all phases of the broadcast industry, primarily at the instigation of the Mutual Broadcasting System. Mutual complained to the FCC that it was unable to expand into a national operation because NBC and CBS had affiliation agreements with more than 80 percent of the largest radio stations in the country.

The result of that inquiry, the 1941 *Report on Chain Broadcasting,* was highly critical of the network–affiliate relationship, and the regulations derived therein signaled the beginning of an ongoing battle between broadcasters and the government over monopoly practices. To NBC and CBS, the rules set by the *Report* threatened to undermine the very structure of the broadcasting industry.

Most crucial among these were the establishment of strict limits on the length of affiliation contracts; the loosening of affiliation ties by allowing stations to broadcast programs from other networks or sources; the power of affiliates to reject network programs if the stations felt the offering was not in the public interest; and, most dramatically, the abolition of the practice of "option time." This provision struck directly at the heart of network operations, and NBC, CBS, and Madison Avenue howled in protest. Option time was a standard feature of every affiliation contract, giving the network the legal right to pre-empt a station's schedule for network programming. CBS affiliates agreed to give up their entire broadcast day if the network demanded it; NBC was slightly less stringent, asking for options on eight-and-a-half hours a day, including the profitable 8 P.M. to 11 P.M. evening block. The stations were compensated for all hours claimed by the networks at a rate adequate to cover the loss of potential sales to local advertisers (these local rates were set by the network as well, a procedure also abolished by the 1941 regulations). It was a profitable arrangement. The affiliates received popular national programming, relieving them of the chore of local production, and were compensated for their airtime—NBC took in three times more money from time sales than it dispensed in compensation and could guarantee advertisers a national audience.

The networks bitterly denounced the new regulations and brought suit in federal court to stop their implementation, but it was pressure from the business and advertising communities that caused the FCC to revise the chain broadcasting rules in an October 1941 supplemental report. The commission reasoned that while it remained unconvinced by the NBC and CBS contention that option time was indispensable to network operations, "it is clear that some optioning of time by networks in order to clear the same period of time over a number of stations for network programs will operate as a business convenience." As a result, the networks were permitted to maintain control over the 8 P.M. to 11 P.M. slot, the most heavily attended and profitable portion of the broadcast day. Thus, the prime-time schedule remained closed to independent and local producers on affiliate schedules.

Of more direct impact to NBC was the regulation that "no license shall be issued to a standard broadcasting station affiliated with a network organization which maintains more than one network." In other words, either Red or Blue had to go. Despite some public grumbling, RCA was not entirely unhappy with this ruling, having long considered the sale of Blue as a possible source of financing for television activities. Still, NBC filed suit in federal court challenging the Chain Broadcasting rules, but in May 1943, the Supreme Court ruled for the FCC in *NBC v. the United States*. Five months later, RCA sold the Blue Network to Life Savers magnate Edward J. Noble for $8 million. The sale provided RCA with a cash infusion with which to prepare NBC-TV for an anticipated boom following World War II and led to the formation of the American Broadcasting Company (ABC) in 1945.

NBC Radio and the Emergence of Television

The immediate postwar era was enormously profitable for radio as pent-up consumer demand, combined with a shift from military to domestic manufacturing, unleashed a spectacular buying binge. However, television loomed on the horizon, and the new medium promised to have a dramatic impact on network radio. In 1945, 95 percent of all radio stations were network affiliates; in 1948—the year NBC, CBS, and ABC began seven-day-a-week television broadcasting—the figure was 68 percent and dropping fast.

Ironically, the end of network radio as a source of major entertainment was hastened by the CBS "talent raids" of 1948–49. In order to attract NBC's biggest radio stars, CBS designed a clever finance mechanism that had the practical effect of placing performers under long-term contract to the network. It was an elegant scheme: radio stars (who were otherwise taxed at personal income rates of up to 75 percent) would incorporate themselves and, in turn, license their company to CBS. The amount paid by CBS would be considered a capital gain and taxed at 25 percent. As a result, NBC performers left the network in droves for CBS, starting with *Amos 'n' Andy* creators Freeman Gosden and Charles Correll in September 1948, soon followed by Jack Benny, George Burns and Gracie Allen, Red Skelton, Bing Crosby, and Edgar Bergen.

The talent raids certainly paid off for CBS in terms of income (a profit increase of almost $7 million), more successful programming (12 of the top 15 radio shows in 1949), and tangential publicity. Most important, radio provided both the financial and programming foundation for the network's television operation. Every star brought over in the talent raids eventually appeared on CBS-TV, draining resources away from NBC.

As television continued to attract an increasingly larger audience, major advertisers rapidly left radio and moved their dollars into the new medium. By the early 1950s, the trend toward television was readily apparent. Fewer and fewer network-originated radio shows were made available to affiliates, whereas the number of programs that were simulcast (broadcast simultaneously on both radio and TV) increased. By the end of the decade, stations across the country began severing their network affiliations to produce their own programming, an action unthinkable during radio's heyday.

In 1960 NBC stopped production on its last remaining daytime radio serial, *True Story*, and thereafter existed almost solely as a news feed to subscribing stations. In 1986 RCA (including NBC) was purchased by GE (in a sense returning to its original owner), and that same year the network formally split its broadcasting divisions. NBC Radio was then sold to radio conglomerate Westwood One, which continues to maintain "NBC Radio Networks" as a separate brand, although in reality the network has no journalistic responsibility for newscasts labeled as "NBC."

See also: American Telephone and Telegraph; Blue Network; Network Monopoly Probe; Radio Corporation of America; Talent Raids

Further Reading

Archer, Gleason Leonard, *History of Radio to 1926*, New York: American Historical Society, 1938; reprint, New York: Arno Press, 1971.

Archer, Gleason Leonard, *Big Business and Radio*, New York: American Historical Company, 1939; reprint, New York: Arno Press, 1971.

Bilby, Kenneth W., *The General: David Sarnoff and the Rise of the Communications Industry*, New York: Harper and Row, 1986.

Campbell, Robert, *The Golden Years of Broadcasting: A Celebration of the First 50 Years of Radio and TV on NBC*, New York: Scribner, 1976.

Cook, David, "The Birth of the Network: How Westinghouse, GE, AT&T, and RCA Invented the Concept of AdvertiserSupported Broadcasting," *Quarterly Review of Film Studies* 8, no. 3 (Summer 1983).

Federal Communications Commission, *Report on Chain Broadcasting*, Washington, D.C.: GPO, 1941.

Federal Communications Commission, *Supplemental Report on Chain Broadcasting*, Washington, D.C.: GPO, 1941.

Fifty Years with the NBC Radio Network, New York: NBC, 1976.

"The First 50 Years of NBC," *Broadcasting* (21 June 1976).

Hilmes, Michele, *Hollywood and Broadcasting: From Radio to Cable*, Urbana: University of Illinois Press, 1990.

Hilmes, Michele, editor, *NBC: America's Network*. Berkeley: University of California Press, 2007.

National Broadcasting Company, *NBC and You: An Account of the Organization, Operation, and Employee-Company Policies of the N.B.C.: Designed As a Handbook to Aid You in Your Daily Work*, New York: NBC, 1944.

National Broadcasting Company, *NBC Program Policies and Working Manual*, New York: NBC, 1944.

"NBC 60th Anniversary Issue," *Television/Radio Age 33* (May 1986).

"NBC: A Documentary," *Sponsor* 20, no. 10 (May 1966).

Sarnoff, David, *Looking Ahead: The Papers of David Sarnoff*, New York: McGraw-Hill, 1968.

Smulyan, Susan, *Selling Radio: The Commercialization of American Broadcasting, 1920–1934*, Washington, D.C.: Smithsonian Institution Press, 1994.

"A Study of the National Broadcasting Company," *The Advertiser* 14, no. 9 (1943).

MIKE MASHON

NATIONAL FEDERATION OF COMMUNITY BROADCASTERS
Trade Association

The National Federation of Community Broadcasters (NFCB) is a membership organization representing more than 200 radio stations in the United States; it provides legal, technical, and logistical support for community-oriented, educational, and non-commercial broadcasters. Under its leadership, the community radio sector of U.S. broadcasting has emerged as a viable service in major urban centers and rural communities across the country.

In 1973 a group of dedicated community broadcasters met in Seattle to consider the possibilities of coordinating their efforts and promoting community radio throughout the United States. Two years later, in the summer of 1975, the National Alternative Radio Konference (NARK) convened in Madison, Wisconsin. The conference participants—an assortment of radio enthusiasts, artists, musicians, and community activists from across the country—resolved to form a national organization that would represent the interests of community broadcasters before the U.S. Congress and federal regulators. Within a matter of months, the newly formed NFCB located its headquarters in the Washington, D.C. apartment of two of the conference organizers, Tom Thomas and Terry Clifford. From these humble beginnings, the NFCB began its lobbying efforts in support of community-oriented radio. From the outset, the NFCB had two goals: to influence national broadcast policymaking and to secure federal grant money to support this new, locally oriented radio service.

Central to the NFCB's mission is enhancing and increasing diversity in radio broadcasting. Throughout its history, the NCFB has placed special emphasis on opening up the airwaves to women, people of color, and other cultural minorities whose voices are largely absent from mainstream media. In this way, the NFCB promotes volunteerism, supports localism, and encourages the development of programs and services specifically designed to address the needs and interests of underserved audiences. For example, community volunteers program music and public-affairs programming on WFHB in Bloomington, Indiana; WVMR is the only broadcast service for people living in the isolated region of Pocahontas County, West Virginia; and member station KBRW provides multilingual programming for native peoples in Alaska's North Slope region.

In addition, the NFCB provides all manner of technical and logistical support for community broadcasters. To that end, the NFCB has developed training materials that outline the procedures for license applications, describe the use of broadcasting equipment, and offer practical suggestions for enlisting local community support. Some of these publications include *The Public Radio Legal Handbook*, a reference guide to broadcast regulations; *Audiocraft*, a textbook on audio production techniques; and the *Volunteer Management Handbook*, which provides useful strategies for securing and maintaining an enthusiastic volunteer base. Crucially, the NFCB also provides the legal and engineering expertise necessary to successfully secure a broadcasting license from the Federal Communications Commission (FCC). Moreover, through its monthly newsletter, *Community Radio News*, and its annual conventions, the NFCB continues to keep its member stations abreast of ongoing policy debates, new funding initiatives, and the latest technological innovations. Finally, the NFCB established the Program Exchange service in recognition of the need for new and existing stations to round out their broadcast schedules. This scheme encouraged community broadcasters across the country to trade tapes produced by member stations as well as programming developed by independent producers. Not only did this service help offset the costs associated with program production, it also had the added benefits of creating an informal network between community stations and helping to define community radio's national identity.

Under the auspices of the NFCB, the community radio movement of the late 1970s challenged the conventions of commercial radio, forever changing the landscape of U.S. broadcasting. The NFCB successfully lobbied the U.S. Congress, regulatory bodies, and government funding agencies to support noncommercial broadcasting in general and community broadcasting in particular. Most important, perhaps, in its commitment to community access, control, and participation, the NFCB popularized listener-supported radio. This model, first championed by Lewis Hill and the Pacifica stations, encourages community residents to become involved in every aspect of the local radio station: management, governance, finance, promotion, and production. Like the Pacifica stations and those associated with Lorenzo Milam's KRAB nebula, NFCB member stations seek to enhance radio's role in the civic, cultural, and social life of the community. Unlike commercial radio, which shies away from innovative and controversial programming, NFCB member stations encourage local cultural expression and support community activism.

Over time, as the organization's influence with industry leaders and policy-makers grew, the NFCB became firmly entrenched in the Washington establishment. As a result, the NFCB's fortunes became linked to those of National Public Radio (NPR) and the Corporation for Public Broadcasting (CPB). For a time, this relationship proved beneficial to both parties. For example, in 1982 the NFCB organized the first Minority Producers Conference, which was instrumental in diversifying the staff at public and community radio stations across the country. However, the NFCB's relationship with the CPB has been a source of controversy among some community radio advocates. For instance, the NFCB and NPR supported the FCC's 1978 termination of 10-W Class D stations, a prohibition that has fundamentally altered the character of community radio in the United States and that has, more recently, prompted the rise of the so-called microradio movement.

Over the past decade, community radio stations have grown increasingly dependent upon CPB funds, such as the Community Service Grant, to support their efforts and improve their services. However, the eligibility requirements for these funds were far beyond the means of small stations with modest resources. As a result, these stations were confronted with the unpleasant choice between shutting down or hiring professional staff to generate income, produce or acquire more "polished" programming, and oversee the station's daily operation. This condition seriously undermines community participation and has led to the "professionalization" of community radio. In recent years, some community stations have become little more than supplemental outlets for the nationally produced programming of NPR, effectively consolidating the public radio sector and eliminating community radio's greatest strength: its localism. Furthermore, until being discontinued in 2003, the NFCB's Healthy Station Project, with its emphasis on attracting upscale demographics to community stations, has been sharply criticized for its chilling effect on community radio's news and public-affairs programming and the attendant homogenization of music and cultural fare.

Following a period of considerable internal unrest and organizational restructuring, the NFCB moved its headquarters to San Francisco in 1995 and began sharing its operation with Western Public Radio, a not-for-profit radio training and production center. In 2002, NFCB relocated again, this time across the bay to Oakland. With new offices, facilities, and staff, NFCB launched exciting new initiatives, including various workshops which train community broadcasters and volunteers in newer technologies, website strategies and the FCC application process (the latter specifically geared towards minorities and rural populations). The NFCB has also operated a National Youth in Radio Training Project, Latino Radio Summits and Native Public Media (NPM, working with Native American outlets), each with the goal of promoting radio among their groups. The NFCB administers various awards each year. Along with recognizing a community radio "Volunteer of the Year" they also bestow a Golden Reel award to radio producers and an annual Bader Award for lifetime achievement. As a politically minded entity, the NFCB has argued against further deregulation of radio and has long been an outspoken voice against payola corruption.

See also: Community Radio; Corporation for Public Broadcasting; Low-Power Radio/Microradio; National Public Radio; Pacifica Foundation; Public Radio Since 1967; Ten-Watt Stations; Trade Associations

Further Reading

Barlow, William, "Community Radio in the U.S.: The Struggle for a Democratic Medium," *Media, Culture, and Society* 10 (1988).

Bekken, Jon, "Community Radio at the Crossroads: Federal Policy and the Professionalization of a Grassroots Medium," in *Seizing the Airwaves: A Free Radio Handbook*, edited by Ronald B. Sakolsky and Steven Dunifer, Edinburgh and San Francisco, California: AK Press, 1998.

Hochheimer, John L., "Organizing Democratic Radio: Issues in Praxis," *Media, Culture, and Society* 15 (1993).

Lewis, Peter M., and Jerry Booth, *The Invisible Medium: Public, Commercial, and Community Radio*, London: Macmillan, 1989; Washington, D.C.: Howard University Press, 1990.

Milam, Lorenzo W., *Sex and Broadcasting: A Handbook on Starting a Radio Station for the Community*, 2nd edition, Saratoga, California: Dildo Press, 1972; 4th edition, as *The Original Sex and Broadcasting*, San Diego, California: MHO and MHO, 1988.

KEVIN HOWLEY,
2009 REVISIONS BY CARY O'DELL

NATIONAL PUBLIC RADIO
Noncommercial Radio Network

National Public Radio (NPR) is the U.S.'s largest public radio producer and distributor, providing more than 100 hours of news and cultural programming each week to more than 600 member stations. The network is probably best known for its drive-time newsmagazines, *Morning Edition* and *All Things Considered*, but it produces a wide range of radio fare, including music and cultural programs, such as *Performance Today* and *Jazz Profiles*, and the nationwide call-in program *Talk of the Nation*. In the course of its 30-year history, the network has won virtually every major broadcast award and has figured prominently in the nation's political and artistic life.

Origins

Public radio in the United States had its origins in the 1920s, when low-budget community and college stations sprang up around the country. Hundreds of such stations took hold in the early, unregulated days of radio, but not many of these "educational stations" survived the Depression, especially as commercial broadcasters saw radio's potential as a vehicle for massmarket entertainment and lucrative advertising.

The National Association of Educational Broadcasters (NAEB) argued that educational stations could not compete for spectrum space with commercial giants such as the National Broadcasting Company (NBC) and the Columbia Broadcasting System (CBS). In 1945 the NAEB convinced the Federal Communications Commission (FCC) to allot the low end of the radio dial to educational broadcasters, winning 20 FM channels, from 88 to 92 MHz. The allotment gave educational radio the stability to build up a small but hardy core of stations.

The Public Broadcasting Act

By the early 1960s, educational broadcasters were exploring the possibility of networking to help fill their program days. Don Quayle, the first president of NPR, recalls "there was a general feeling, both in television and in radio, that no single station had the resources to do the quality of programming we wanted." Quayle helped link up educational radio and television networks in the northeastern United States that were among the precursors of NPR.

Those networks lacked the resources to do much more than instructional broadcasting until the mid-1960s, when President Lyndon Johnson called on the Carnegie Foundation to look into the possibility of a federally funded broadcasting system. After a two-year study, the Carnegie Commission firmly backed the idea of federal funding, but it envisioned a far wider focus, distinguishing between educational and *public* broadcasting.

The commission offered 12 recommendations for the new service, including public-affairs programming that sought insights into controversial issues, diversified programming in which minorities were represented, and coverage of contemporary arts and culture. The commission's recommendations dealt only with television, but President Johnson, a successful radio station owner himself, was sympathetic to radio advocates who fought to be included. Critics argued that adding hundreds of weak and needy radio stations to the measure would dilute the federal funding and drag the whole project down. Supporters pointed out that radio could offer more services than television at a far cheaper cost.

Congress passed the Public Broadcasting Act in October 1967 and included radio, but the funding available to the newly formed Corporation for Public Broadcasting (CPB) quickly dwindled from a proposed $20 million to $5 million. Without financial support from the Carnegie Commission, CBS, the Communications Workers of America, and the Ford Foundation, CPB would not have been able to fund much programming.

In 1969 CPB sponsored a conference in San Diego that laid the foundation for National Public Radio, an entity that, unlike its television counterpart, the Public Broadcasting Service, would produce as well as distribute programs. The corporation invited Bill Siemering, then the station manager of WBFO in Buffalo, New York, to help conduct the discussion. Siemering had already articulated a vision for the service in an essay called "Public Radio: Some Essential Ingredients," in which he argued that public radio should be "on the frontier of the contemporary and help create new tastes," but that it also had to meet the information needs of the public.

Don Quayle was chosen as the organization's first president, not long after he had made a presentation to the Ford Foundation showing that he could interconnect all the qualified public radio stations "for less than [New York public station] WNET spent on television." Quayle hired Bill Siemering as the network's first program director and set him to work on what was to be its first regular program, *All Things Considered.*

National Public Radio Goes On the Air

National Public Radio was incorporated on 26 February 1970 with 90 charter stations. The network set up offices and studios in Washington, D.C., closer to the heart of the nation's politics than the big commercial networks, which had long been based in New York. NPR officially went on the air in April 1971, offering live coverage of the Senate hearings on Vietnam. Less than a month later, on 3 May 1971, the network aired its first edition of *All Things Considered.* Siemering, who directed the first program himself, recalls that it got off to a "rocky and exhilarating" start, with host Robert

Conley unable to hear the cues in his headphones. But as to content, it fulfilled practically all the elements that Siemering had outlined. The program went on the air as thousands of antiwar demonstrators filled the streets of Washington in what was to be the last major protest of the Vietnam War. Reporter Jeff Kamin brought back tape of the chanting and the sirens as police waded into the crowds of demonstrators and made more than 7,000 arrests. The same program featured a young black woman speaking dreamily about her heroin addiction. As Siemering had promised, the program transmitted "the experience of people and institutions from as widely varying backgrounds and areas as are feasible." It spoke "with many voices and dialects." Siemering says that it also illustrated many of the network's goals: "using sound to tell the story; and presentation of multiple perspectives rather than a single truth."

Over the next few months, the program took shape. Siemering found a distinctive voice and sensibility for the program and the network in Susan Stamberg, who became the first woman to host a daily national newsmagazine. Stamberg was paired with Mike Waters and later with Bob Edwards. The network offset its limited resources and relatively inexperienced staff with a creative, conversational approach that began to gather fans. Producers at the network tried to explore the possibilities of the medium, emulating the sound-rich work of the Canadian Broadcasting Corporation (CBC) in Canada and the German producer Peter Leonhard Braun at *Sender Freies Berlin.*

During the first decade, cultural programming was a strong component of the network's output. Bob Malesky, now the executive producer of NPR's weekend programming, puts it this way: "*All Things Considered* was experimental, while concert programs gave stations the solid base to build a day's programming around, for what was still a largely conservative audience. NPR's first arts program was *Voices in the Wind*, and during its five-year life span (1974–1979), it was second only to *All Things Considered* in station usage." NPR also provided stations with *Folk Festival USA* (1974–79) and *Jazz Alive* (1977–83), both the work of producer Steve Rathe. In 1982, the network launched the *Sunday Show*, a five-hour cultural newsmagazine that won a Peabody Award for its first year but, like *Jazz Alive*, fell victim to the NPR financial crisis in 1983.

Expanding Role

For its first five years, NPR functioned primarily as a production and distribution center for its member stations, which had grown over the years to 190. The network took on a bigger role in 1977, after a merger with the stations' lobbying organization, the Association of Public Radio Stations. Don Quayle had left the network in 1973 to become a senior vice president at CPB, and the merger took place under President Lee Frischnecht. NPR offered member services, including training, management assistance, and help with program promotion. The network also began representing the member stations' interests before Congress and the FCC.

The network gained a great deal more national visibility under its third president, Frank Mankiewicz, who was hired in 1977. Mankiewicz came to the job from a background in freelance journalism and politics. He had been Robert Kennedy's press secretary during the presidential campaign that ended with the senator's assassination in Los Angeles, and he had managed the presidential campaign of Senator George McGovern. He had barely heard of NPR. He recalls that he got the job after promising the board that he "would do whatever was necessary so that people like me will know what NPR is."

Mankiewicz's first coup was getting permission for NPR to do live coverage of the Panama Canal debate in the Senate in 1978. It was the first live broadcast ever from the Senate floor. He chose NPR's Senate reporter, Linda Wertheimer, to anchor the coverage, despite complaints from station managers who worried that a woman would sound "too shrill."

Mankiewicz also fostered the network's longtime goal of offering a morning program service. When *All Things Considered* was first conceived, many public radio stations were not even on the air in the mornings. Bill Siemering says he felt that a new staff creating a new kind of program needed to work together on the day's news, without having to contend with the problems of preparing a program overnight, so the network's flagship program was designed for afternoon drive-time. But the network was well aware that radio's biggest audience was in the morning, and NPR was eager to reach it. Mankiewicz also believed that if listeners tuned to an NPR program in the morning, there was a good chance the dial would remain there the rest of the day.

Mankiewicz says he saw his chance to start a morning program when CPB President Henry Loomis offered him a big chunk of money. Loomis pointed out one day that CPB, unlike most federally funded agencies, received its appropriation in a lump sum at the beginning of the fiscal year. That meant that the money accrued a lot of interest in the course of the year, about $4 million. Loomis, a radio fan, asked Mankiewicz what he would do with that money if he got it. "I'd use it to start a morning radio program." Loomis liked the idea and put up the money to start *Morning Edition*, which went on the air in November 1979. After the member stations roundly rejected a pilot version of the program, Bob Edwards was lured from his position as *All Things Considered* co-host with Susan Stamberg to take over *Morning Edition* on a temporary basis. Edwards stayed on, and the program became a hit.

Morning Edition marked an important departure in program style for the network. Whereas *All Things Considered* flowed relatively freely through its 90 minutes, from beginning to middle to end, *Morning Edition* was conceived as a *program service*, structured into rigid segments that member stations could either use or replace with their own local news, weather, and traffic reporting. The success of the *Morning Edition* format led many station managers to lobby for similar changes in the afternoon program, changes that the producers resisted until the mid-1990s.

The demands of providing material for two major programs each day also forced a significant change in the structure of the organization. In the early years, all reporters and producers worked directly for *All Things Considered*, tailoring their work to the eclectic and free-flowing style of that program. The advent of *Morning Edition* meant that the same reporters had to write and produce for the more rigid time constraints of the program service as well. To avoid having reporters pulled by the conflicting demands of the two shows, the news department adopted a "desk" system like those at major newspapers. Editors with specific expertise and experience set up a national desk, a foreign desk, a science desk, and so on. Reporters now worked for NPR news, rather than for a particular show.

In 1980 the network made a striking improvement in its sound quality with the launch of the nation's first satellite-delivered radio distribution system. Overnight, the programs went from the tinny, telephone quality of a 5 kHz phone line to the clarity and intimacy of the studio. Mankiewicz likes to joke that he told the technicians to add a bit of static to the broadcast for the first few days, "to lend an air of verisimilitude" to the otherwise too-perfect sound. The satellite also expanded the network's delivery capacity from a single channel to four, allowing stations to choose alternative programs without having to wait for the tapes to arrive in the mail.

The satellite meant that listeners could hear complex, skillfully layered sound without the degradation of telephone lines, and it cleared the way for the golden period of NPR documentaries. In 1980 the network broadcast a 13-part series by former *Voices in the Wind* producer Robert Montiegal called *A Question of Place*. The series used sound to bring to life the work of writers and thinkers such as James Joyce, Michel Foucault, Simone de Beauvoir, and Bertrand Russell. The following year, writer James Reston, Jr., producer Deborah Amos, and host Noah Adams used tape from the last days of the Jonestown religious cult to show how a leader's egomania led to the mass suicides of more than 900 people in Guyana. The network even branched into radio theater, with the series *Earplay*, *Masterpiece Radio Theater*, and a radio version of the George Lucas hit film *Star Wars*.

Financial Crisis

NPR was riding high and spending freely in 1983. Under Frank Mankiewicz, the network's membership had grown to more than 250 stations, and as he had promised, it was familiar to people like him, people in politics, the arts, and business. When Mankiewicz took over in 1977, the network was dependent on the federal government for 90 percent of its funding. By 1983 corporate underwriting, foundation grants, and other income had brought that figure down to around 50 percent. But the network was not in good financial shape. The network's chief operating officer, Tom Warnock, came to Mankiewicz with the news that NPR might be as much as $2 million in debt. As Warnock delved deeper, the estimate of the debt grew, finally reaching $9 million, a third of the network's budget. Subsequent audits revealed that NPR's accounting was so sloppy that some of the spending could not be tracked. As an example, the network had issued more than 100 American Express cards to its administrators, who ran up hundreds of thousands of dollars in bills for entertainment and travel. Teetering on the edge of bankruptcy, the network slashed department budgets and ultimately had to lay off about 100 people. The staff of the cultural programs department shrank from 33 to eight. Mankiewicz says he could have saved the situation with an ordinary bank loan, but political differences with the CPB's leadership made that impossible. In the end, Mankiewicz resigned.

Ronald Bornstein, the director of telecommunications at the University of Wisconsin, took over as acting president, leading a rescue team of lawyers and accountants from some of the top firms in Washington. For the first and only time in its history, the network went directly to its listeners to help pay off the debt, by including a fund-raising segment in *All Things Considered*. The member stations were wary of allowing the network to raise money from among their contributors, and only about a third of them chose to carry the segments. Even so, the "Drive to Survive" brought in $2.25 million in just three days. The balance of NPR's debt was to be paid off over a three-year period, under the terms of a loan agreement that was hammered out in often-rancorous negotiations with the CPB.

Messy and embarrassing as it was, NPR reported the story of its near-disaster as it happened. That, too, was part of Mankiewicz's legacy. "By that time, NPR had cast itself unambiguously as a news organization, so the standards of news applied to it," recalls Doug Bennet, who took over as president in 1983. Bennet says that what Mankiewicz "really did was to establish NPR in the news niche, and that was genius. Before, there was some news, but nowhere near the scale of investment or the staff." Scott Simon, then the network's Chicago bureau chief, was brought in to report on the financial crisis, interviewing beleaguered staffers and disgusted members of Congress. Bennet found himself taking over at an organization that was tense and distrustful.

Return to Stability

Bennet recalls that during his first one-and-a-half years, he had to cut the budget eight more times, as new deficits were discovered, but he says, "I never believed that NPR would disappear." Bennet's first task was to develop a plan that would reassure the stations and Congress that NPR could be turned around.

The feud with the CPB eventually led the CPB to open up its funding process so that NPR would not be the only recipient. CPB created a Radio Fund, permitting any radio organization to apply for the money. The new funding system was approved without NPR's knowledge, to the fury of station managers. NPR had lost its funding monopoly and faced the prospect of presiding over an ever-diminishing cut of the pie. Doug Bennet recalls sitting in a bar with then-Board Chairman Don Mullally, charting out a radical and risky new funding plan on a bar napkin. The business plan, announced in February 1985, proposed giving all the CPB money to the member stations and letting them use it to acquire programming wherever they wished. "We were saying to the stations, you can take this money and run, if you want to," Bennet says, "and for about five years, it was a much more market-like relationship." NPR's biggest competitor in that market was American Public Radio (APR).

APR was formed by a group of stations led by William Kling, the president of Minnesota Public Radio. The group had long been critical of NPR's cultural offerings and established its own network to acquire and distribute programs. APR's strongest offering was Garrison Keillor's *Prairie Home Companion*, once rejected by NPR's Mankiewicz as elitist and patronizing to middle-American values. *Prairie Home Companion* quickly became the most popular program on public radio.

Bennet says that, despite the funding pinch, he felt NPR had to prove that it could go forward. "We had to show we weren't locked in a zero-sum game, that we could invent and invest." Bennet backed the development of new programs, such as *Weekend Sunday* and *Performance Today*. The new funding scheme meant that new programs "had to be viable from a market standpoint," Bennet says. "The concept behind *Performance Today* was to showcase contemporary American performances— last night's, if possible—and to give stations a show that funders would support." The network also picked up new programs for distribution, including *Car Talk*, *Fresh Air with Terry Gross*, and *Afropop*, a review of African popular music that Bennet says "was always my proof that the NPR audience was willing to consider all kinds of music, and not just Brahms."

The new programs exemplified the deep change in NPR's mission that took place in the aftermath of the funding crisis, a change from offering listeners an alternative to being a force in the marketplace. Bennet says that NPR formally established that building its audience was an important goal, something that had been debatable in the past. Along with the funding control, stations had assumed more power over programming by refusing to buy any program that seemed unlikely to draw a significant audience in their area. The result was a gradual strengthening of the hard-news content of the magazine programs, leaving much of the network's arts and cultural programming struggling.

News took an even stronger hold as NPR's foreign desk reached out to report more and more ambitious stories. In 1986 NPR's coverage of the overthrow of Philippine President Ferdinand Marcos was more comprehensive than any of its previous reports. Cadi Simon, then the foreign editor, described the change in Mary Collins' (1993) book *National Public Radio: The Cast of Characters*, saying NPR "treated the story like an ongoing news event rather than just coming back and gathering tape." The network applied the same technique to later stories, including the Tiananmen Square uprising in China and the fall of the Berlin Wall, preparing the ground for full-scale reporting on the Persian Gulf War. Simon told Collins, "The coverage of the Gulf War did not happen in a void. It came out of a network that was established, a mind-set that we had come into."

The network fielded some of its top reporters during the 1991 war, including Deborah Amos, Deborah Wang, Scott Simon, John Hockenberry, John Ydstie, and Neal Conan. Conan was among a group of correspondents who were captured and held for several days by Iraqi forces. Their reporting on the war and its aftermath—the oil-field environmental disaster in Kuwait and the Kurdish refugee crisis in northern Iraq—showed that NPR could compete with the television networks and with 24-hour cable news. It was a pattern that would be repeated throughout the decade in places such as Ethiopia, Bosnia, and Kosovo. The network's round-the-clock coverage of the war strengthened NPR's weekend programs and led to the creation of a nationwide call-in show, *Talk of the Nation*.

NPR was also establishing itself as a strong source of political news, with coverage of the presidential campaigns and political conventions. The network's top political correspondents included Linda Wertheimer, Cokic Roberts, Mara Liasson, Brian Naylor, Elizabeth Arnold, and Peter Kenyon. NPR's legal affairs correspondent, Nina Totenberg, enhanced the network's reputation with her coverage of the Supreme Court. In 1987 Totenberg broke the story that Supreme Court nominee Douglas Ginsburg had smoked marijuana while he was a professor at Harvard Law School in the 1970s. The story led to Ginsburg's withdrawal. In 1991 Totenberg reported Anita Hill's allegations of sexual harassment against another Supreme Court nominee, Clarence Thomas. Both stories put NPR squarely in the media spotlight.

Expansion

By the time it celebrated its 20th anniversary in 1991, NPR had grown to nearly 400 member stations nationwide. When Doug Bennet stepped down as president in 1993, the network had begun extending its reach around the world, with the establishment of an international service, beamed by satellite to Europe through the World Radio network in London. Over the next five years, that network evolved into NPR Worldwide, reaching more than 50 countries and territories, from Antarctica to Finland.

NPR's new president, Delano Lewis, oversaw the establishment of the NPR Foundation, designed to help insulate the network against financial crises like the one that had nearly destroyed it ten years earlier. Lewis, the first African-American to head the network, was a former telephone company executive with broad connections to the business and political communities in Washington. He expanded the network's fundraising base and strengthened relations with the member stations. In 1994 the network moved into its own building, at 635 Massachusetts Avenue in Washington, D.C. The move allowed NPR to bring all its news, production, and administrative operations under one roof and provided state-of-the-art facilities for production.

The expansion of production facilities came as NPR was returning to the creation of sound-rich, highly textured documentaries. In 1992 the network had begun *Radio Expeditions* as a joint venture with the National Geographic Society. In 1994 it premiered the 26-part series *Wade in the Water: African-American Sacred Music Traditions.*

NPR also began exploring the possibilities of the internet. The network launched its website in 1994, and the following year it teamed with the Progressive network, using RealAudio technology that allows users to hear prerecorded audio files of the programs online.

After a long struggle, *All Things Considered* moved to capture a bigger segment of the national drive-time audience by advancing its East Coast start time to 4 P.M. and expanding from 90 minutes to two hours. Although not as rigidly segmented as *Morning Edition*, the new *All Things Considered* format provided more fixed points at which member stations could insert local programming. Two years later, in 1997, *Morning Edition* also stretched its airtime, moving to a 5 A.M. start.

The network expanded its own programming and its program distribution in the late 1990s. NPR's *Performance Today* grew from five to seven days a week in 1996. The following year, the network introduced *Sounds Like Science* and began distributing more programs produced by member stations, including the talk shows the *Diane Rehm Show* and *Public Interest* and the sports program *Only a Game*. In 1998 NPR premiered its cross-country news quiz *Wait, Wait Don't Tell Me* and a short-lived music and popular culture program, *Anthem.*

The network expanded its presence on the world wide web in 1998, making an agreement with Yahoo!, the internet media company, to provide selected audio content to *Yahoo! News*. When new president Kevin Klose took over in 1999, the company was entering an agreement with Minnesota Public Radio to create an online network supplying interactive news, information, arts, and entertainment.

Klose, a former head of the government's Radio Liberty and Radio Free Europe, says he wants to bring NPR to its fulfillment as a major player in the world of news and information. He is pressing to move the network into new technologies, including satellite radio, which would allow NPR to provide some programming directly to its listeners for the first time ever, without going through its member stations. Klose says a major challenge for NPR's future will be how to become a multimedia enterprise without compromising its values.

Former President Doug Bennet sees other challenges, including the danger of commercialization at NPR, in which underwriting credits come to sound more and more like advertising. "I think it's a terrible mistake," he says, "to give up the niche of a non-advertising entity to compete ineffectively for advertising." Kevin Klose says he wants to make sure that NPR's "content is not penetrated by commerce."

Governance and Funding

Unlike most commercial networks, NPR does not own or operate any of its member stations. The private, nonprofit corporation is a membership organization, a structure that Klose says is "at the heart of its dynamism." It is governed by a 17-member board composed of the NPR president, ten station managers elected by the membership, and six public members chosen by the board and confirmed by the member stations. The member stations are autonomous entities, most often licensed to colleges and universities or community groups. In exchange for their dues and program-licensing fees, NPR stations receive programming, professional training for staff members, help in promoting programs, and representation in Washington on issues affecting public broadcasting.

On average, member stations take about 27 percent of their programming from NPR. Local staff members produce about 48 percent of the station's program content, and another 25 percent comes from other public radio producers and distributors, such as Public Radio International.

More than 92 percent of the U.S. population now lives within reach of an NPR member station. The stations have a combined audience of some 19 million people, of whom more than 13 million listen to programming provided by the network.

The typical member station gets about a quarter of its funding from its listeners, soliciting donations with on-air and direct-mail appeals. Stations that are licensed to educational institutions generally get around 19 percent of their revenues from their colleges or universities. Corporate donors provide around 17 percent of station support, and about 14 percent comes from CPB. The remainder comes from foundations and other sources.

Although it was created with an infusion of federal money, NPR no longer receives any direct federal funding for general support. Slightly more than half of its funding comes from dues and program fees paid by the member stations. Most of the rest of its $80 million budget is contributed by private foundations and corporations.

21st Century Expansion

During the first decade of the 21st century, NPR evolved into a major media company with 750 employees, its programming heard on more than 860 public radio stations. Its overall audience doubled to 26 million weekly listeners. Audiences for NPR programming added nearly eight million listeners, an increase of 40 percent. In the five years following 2003, NPR launched five programs: *CPRN* (Classical Public Radio Network), *Day to Day*, *News & Notes*, *Tell Me More*, and the short-lived *Bryant Park Project* (the two-hour program aired in 2007–8).

In November 2003, Joan Kroc, widow of the founder of the McDonald's fast food chain, bequeathed $225 million to NPR–by far the organization's biggest donation ever. Indeed, Kroc's gift was the largest individual monetary donation ever given to an American cultural institution, and was twice the size of NPR's annual budget. Over the years, Kroc had given the Los Angeles KPBS radio and television stations some $8 million. Starting in 2004, the bequest underwrote expansions of NPR News staff and facilities, including the naming of several Joan B. Kroc Fellows each year to train in public radio journalism. By the end of the decade, NPR News operated more than 35 news bureaus, about half of them outside the U.S.

In March 2008, NPR purchased a former telephone company building at 1111 North Capitol Street, NE, in Washington as its future headquarters—its third in the capital city. Plans for the new 360,000 square foot facility include a 60,000 square foot space for NPR News operations and public space for live programs and events. All of NPR's Washington-based journalism, multimedia, technical distribution, and management activities will be housed in the new facility, to be occupied in 2012 after extensive rebuilding including a ten-storey office tower.

NPR's Application Programming Interface (API) was introduced in July 2008. Web developers and listeners can use the API tool to access, organize and display NPR reporting and programs, including work produced by NPR member stations, on their personal websites and blogs. They can customize based on more than 130 topics, or choose stations and reporters of greatest interest. The API was designed to provide access to some 15 years of NPR and station-produced content, including audio, text, and photography, for developers to easily incorporate into their sites and blogs and share with larger audiences. API marked an expansion of NPT's three-year podcast program which serves over 14 million podcast downloads of news and cultural programming per month.

See also: All Things Considered; *Car Talk*; *Fresh Air*; *Morning Edition*; National Association of Educational Broadcasters; *Prairie Home Companion*; Public Broadcasting Act of 1967; Public Radio International; Public Radio Since 1967; *Star Wars*

Further Reading

Adams, Noah, *Noah Adams on "All Things Considered": A Radio Journal*, New York: Norton, 1992.
Collins, Mary, *National Public Radio: The Cast of Characters*, Washington, D.C.: Seven Locks Press, 1993.
Edwards, Bob, *Fridays with Red: A Radio Friendship*, New York: Simon and Schuster, 1993.
Engelman, Ralph, *Public Radio and Television in America: A Political History*, Thousand Oaks, California: Sage, 1996.
Looker, Thomas, *The Sound and the Story: NPR and the Art of Radio*, Boston: Houghton Mifflin, 1995.
McCourt, Tom, *Conflicting Communications Interests in America: The Case of National Public Radio*, Westport, Connecticut: Praeger, 1999.
NPR News Releases, 2000-Date, www.npr.org/about/press/
Siegel, Robert, editor, *The NPR Interviews, 1996*, Boston: Houghton Mifflin, 1996.
Stamberg, Susan, *Every Night at Five: Susan Stamberg's All Things Considered Book*, New York: Pantheon, 1982.
Stamberg, Susan, *Talk: NPR's Susan Stamberg Considers All Things*, New York: Turtle Bay Books, 1993.
Wertheimer, Linda, editor, *Listening to America: Twenty-five Years in the Life of a Nation, As Heard on National Public Radio*, Boston, Houghton Mifflin, 1995.
Witherspoon, John, Roselle Kovitz, Robert K. Avery, and Alan G. Stavitsky, *A History of Public Broadcasting*, Washington, D.C.: Current, 2000.

COREY FLINTOFF,
2009 REVISIONS BY CHRISTOPHER H. STERLING

NATIONAL RADIO SYSTEMS COMMITTEE
Recommending New Technical Standards

A cooperative entity of the broadcast and consumer electronics industry, the National Radio Systems Committee (NRSC) recommends technical standards relating to radio broadcasting in the United States. It is particularly concerned with development of standards for both digital audio broadcasting and the radio broadcast data system. The NRSC was originally established in 1985 and initially investigated aspects of AM radio transmission. It has since taken on several other projects.

NRSC members are generally engineers, scientists, or technicians with in-depth knowledge of the subject being studied. They may be from companies, nonprofit organizations, or government entities. Anyone who has a business interest in the technology being investigated by the NRSC is welcome to join and participate. Meetings are held on an as-needed basis. Member organizations fund the participation of NRSC committee participants.

The NRSC receives information from a variety of sources—the companies interested in manufacturing new devices, the International Telecommunication Union (ITU) and other bodies that deal with worldwide standards, and the Federal Communications Commission (FCC). In turn, it monitors and assists with technical testing of proposed new systems.

The NRSC accomplishes its work by establishing subcommittees to focus discussion and development efforts. Two were active as the new century began—one concerning digital audio broadcasting (DAB) and the other concerning radio broadcast data systems (RBDS, or simply RDS). In April 1998 the NRSC suspended activities of a third subcommittee (concerned with high-speed FM subcarriers) because the group had reached an impasse in its deliberations to develop a voluntary standard.

As recommendations emerge from the subcommittees, they are considered and voted upon by the full NRSC membership. These final agreements are in the form of recommendations to both industries (electronic media and consumer electronics) and to the FCC, which must issue any formal standards decisions.

The DAB subcommittee worked for several years to agree upon a final technical standard for in-band, on-channel ("IBOC") digital radio for the United States. The subcommittee also established working groups to compare and contrast two potential DAB systems (one developed by USA Digital Radio and the other by Lucent Digital Radio). By late 2002, there were two operating satellite-delivered digital radio services in the U.S., and the FCC had issued an NRSC-recommended standard for terrestrial digital radio service.

The RBDS subcommittee originally approved RBDS standards in 1993 and last revised and updated them in 1998. Largely based on the European system, the RBDS signal is a low bit-rate data stream transmitted on the 57-kHz subcarrier of an FM radio signal. Radio listeners know RBDS mostly through its ability to permit RBDS-equipped radio receivers to display station call letters and search for stations based on their program format. In addition, special traffic announcements can be transmitted to RBDS radios as well as weather or other emergency alerts.

During the first decade of the 21st century, the NRSC committees and working groups continued to meet regularly, issuing occasional technical guidelines for analog radio as well as the developing digital audio (HD Radio) technology. Among reports on the latter was an early 2007 assessment of "surround sound" issues and resources.

See also: Digital Audio Broadcasting; Digital Satellite Radio; Radio Broadcast Data System

Further Reading

National Association of Broadcasters: The National Radio Systems Committee, www.nab.org/SciTech/nrsc.asp
National Radio Systems Committee website, www.nrsc standards.org/.

CHRISTOPHER H. STERLING,
2009 REVISIONS BY CHRISTOPHER H. STERLING

NATIONAL RELIGIOUS BROADCASTERS
Trade Association

The National Religious Broadcasters (NRB) is a trade association of more than 1,200 Christian radio and television stations, most of which broadcast from an evangelical Protestant perspective. Full membership in the NRB is granted to those who meet financial accountability standards and sign a sevenpoint "Statement of Faith." The organization has grown from a small group of separatist broadcasters in the 1940s to a professionally staffed organization with both political and spiritual influence.

Origins

By the 1940s, radio airtime had become so valuable that commercial nonreligious stations began placing preachers in Sunday morning time slots. Networks preferred to offer organized religious groups "sustaining," or free, airtime to meet government requirements for religious or public-affairs programming. Time was offered to organizations representing Roman Catholics, Jews, and mainline Protestants through the Federal Council of Churches (later know as the National Council of Churches). However, evangelical churches, such as the Southern Baptists and the Assemblies of God, were not members of the mainline Protestant organization and were not allowed to share in the free air-time.

Disgruntled evangelical broadcasters joined churches, parachurch ministries, and educators in the 1942 formation of the National Association of Evangelicals (NAE). Two years later the NAE chartered the formation of the National Religious Broadcasters to address more specifically the concerns of evangelical radio stations and programs. The NRB grew to become independent of the NAE, although the two groups remained affiliated until 2001, when the NRB voted to formally end the relationship after the NAE began accepting members who were part of the National Council of Churches. The National Association of Evangelicals today represents over 50 denominations and 250 parachurch ministries.

The National Religious Broadcasters set up headquarters near Washington, D.C., as a major function of the organization was lobbying the Federal Communications Commission. The NRB also created a code of ethics for broadcast ministries and has provided legal advice to members. The group, however, was mostly unsuccessful in securing free broadcast time for evangelical ministries, so in the late 1940s members began to buy airtime and start their own Christian radio stations. The success of Billy Graham, Oral Roberts, Rex Humbard, and others led to an explosion of Christian programming in the 1960s and 1970s.

The NRB began holding its annual convention in Washington, D.C., in 1956, attempting to influence politicians and FCC commissioners. For more than 30 years, the annual D.C. meetings attracted thousands of increasingly vocal Christian communicators, who took credit for helping to elect born again President Jimmy Carter and conservative Ronald Reagan (who addressed the NRB delegates). The NRB was also instrumental in influencing the government to redefine equal employment laws to allow Christian radio stations to use faithbased criteria when hiring new employees.

NRB Executive Director Ben Armstrong led the organization's growth from 1966 to 1989; over that period, the NRB quadrupled in size to include almost 100 syndicated television preachers and three major religious TV networks. The religious broadcasting audience grew from around five million in the mid-1960s to more than 25 million two decades later. The most successful radio member has been *Focus on the Family* with Dr. James Dobson, which started in 1977 and currently airs on more than 3,000 radio stations in 95 countries.

By the early 1980s, the NRB had become the spiritual and political voice for the estimated $2 billion religious radio and television industry, but the end of that decade saw a dramatic decline in the religious broadcasting industry. In 1987 former NRB member Jim Bakker, who hosted the daily *PTL Club*, resigned his radio and television ministry after it was revealed that his organization had been paying a woman to keep quiet about her sexual encounter with him. The following year brought more scandal and controversy: Oral Roberts was chastised by the media for stating that God would "call him home" if he did not raise $8 million; Pat Robertson of the Christian Broadcasting Network briefly ran for president of the United States; and evangelist Jimmy Swaggart was accused of soliciting a prostitute. Nationally, Christian broadcasters experienced a dramatic decline in their audiences, and some lost up to three-fourths of their contributions.

The NRB, accused of not properly monitoring the ethical standards of its members, responded to the crisis by strengthening financial accountability procedures and tightening membership requirements. By the 1990s, leader E. Brandt Gustavson moved the annual convention to other cities, trading the politically-oriented meetings of Washington, D.C., for a more spiritual emphasis outside the beltway. By the end of the decade, religious broadcasters had stopped the decline in audience and contributions and saw a slow growth in the trust of those looking for spiritual programming. In 2002 the group ousted new president Wayne Pederson after only one month in office for his criticisms of members who were better known for their politics than their ministries. New leader Frank Wright attempted to keep NRB's spiritual focus while increasing its political influence, President George W. Bush addressed the group several times during his presidency and, in the run up to the 2008 Presidential election, Republican candidates John McCain and Mitt Romney both either addressed the organization or met with its leaders.

As an often potent lobbying force, the NRB has campaigned on Capitol Hill against proposed gay marriage legislation and publicly come out against reinstatement of the FCC's Fairness Doctrine (fearful that its reinstatement could force religious broadcasters to grant "equal time" to alternative, nonreligious viewpoints after their broadcasts). The NRB has also challenged some hate crime legislation, concerned that under such laws the messages of some sermons (on topics ranging from homosexuality to out-of-wedlock childbirth) might be construed as "hate speech." Today some major evangelical religious broadcasters are not members of the NRB because they wish to avoid the full financial disclosure required by the organization. Ministers who receive more than $500,000 annually in donations must meet the strict standards of the Evangelical Council for Financial Accountability. Smaller ministries must still meet the NRB in-house standards, but denominational and church-sponsored broadcasters are exempt from the financial accountability requirements. Associate, non-voting memberships that do not require signing the NRB's "Statement of Faith" are available to secular organizations or mainline churches. (Ironically, despite the organization's own policy, the NRB has argued grounds of religious freedom to question the government's authority to obtain financial details about over-the-air ministries.)

Religious Radio Today

"Sustaining" or free radio time is no longer given to the three major religious bodies, and mainline churches are generally unwilling to compete with the big dollars spent by evangelicals. But the current environment can be traced to the unwillingness of mainline churches to share their free time in the 1940s, forcing NRB members to buy airtime in order to get their gospel message over the airwaves. Some non-evangelical denominations are gradually budgeting for media time, and a network of Roman Catholic radio stations was started in the United States in 1999. Most Catholic broadcasters are not members of the NRB but are part of the Catholic Academy for Communication Arts Professionals.

With the fourth-largest format among commercial stations and a directory that lists over 1,600 radio stations playing religious programming at some point during the broadcast week, the National Religious Broadcasters has grown to become a significant political, economic, and spiritual organization for the evangelical Christians who use radio to spread their gospel.

See also: Contemporary Christian Music Format; Evangelists/Evangelical Radio; Gospel Music Format; Jewish Radio Programs in the United States; Religion on Radio

Further Reading

Armstrong, Ben, and William F. Fore, *The Electric Church*, Nashville, Tennessee: Nelson, 1979.

Barnhart, Joe E., and Steven Winzenburg, *Jim and Tammy: Charismatic Intrigue Inside PTL*, Buffalo, New York: Prometheus Books, 1988.

Ellens, J. Harold, *Models of Religious Broadcasting*, Grand Rapids, Michigan: Eerdmans, 1974.

Hedges, Chris, "Feeling the Hate with the National Religious Broadcasters," *Harper's* (May 2005), p. 55.

Melton, J. Gordon, Phillip Charles Lucas, and Jon R. Stone, editors, *Prime Time Religion: An Encyclopedia of Religious Broadcasting*, Phoenix, Arizona: Oryx Press, 1997.

Ward, Mark, *Air of Salvation: The Story of Christian Broadcasting*, Grand Rapids, Michigan: Baker Books, 1994.

STEPHEN M. WINZENBURG,
2009 REVISIONS BY CARY O'DELL

NATIONAL TELECOMMUNICATIONS AND INFORMATION ADMINISTRATION
Federal Policy Agency

The National Telecommunications and Information Administration (NTIA) is a Department of Commerce agency responsible for advising the Executive Branch on matters of domestic and international telecommunications and information policy. This includes managing federal government uses of the radio spectrum, which is used for wireless microwave or satellite-based broadcasting and telecommunications.

Background

The NTIA's role today carries the legacy of the Commerce Department's radio activity, which began in the early 1900s. The cabinet-level Department of Commerce and Labor was established on 14 February 1903. Because the earliest uses of radio were both commerce- and navigation-based, the Department of Commerce and Labor was involved with establishing radio standards, procedures, and equipment requirements in conjunction with national navigation, ship outfitting, and lighthouse communications. The April 1912 *Titanic* disaster highlighted the need for greater commercial, government, and amateur radio standardization and regulation procedures. These were included in the Radio Act of 1912, which required radio apparatus on all passenger steamers and established a system of allocating and assigning both frequencies and licenses to commercial, government, and amateur radio operators. These administrative duties fell primarily to the Commerce Department's Bureau of Navigation.

On 4 March 1913, ten years after the creation of the Department of Commerce and Labor, President Taft signed legislation dividing the unit into separate Labor and Commerce Departments. Increasingly, the Commerce Department was called upon for research and development of radio's commercial and defense applications, including "the investigation and standardization of methods and instruments employed in radio communication," which fell primarily to the Bureau of Standards. In 1916 it developed a radio laboratory—the predecessor of the current Institute of Telecommunication Services (ITS). The Commerce Department's early radio development efforts also extended to the general public. For example, the Bureau of Standards determined standards for homemade crystal detector sets and distributed instructions for constructing them in 1922.

The second secretary of commerce, Herbert Hoover, served from 1921 to 1929. Intent on harnessing the commercial power of radio advances, Hoover convened four national radio conferences to discuss how new radio technologies and capabilities should be regulated in light of increasingly diverse and complex demand. In 1927 a new Radio Act created a Radio Division in the Department of Commerce and an independent Federal Radio Commission (FRC). The FRC relieved the Bureau of Navigation's licensing, frequency allocation and assignment, and transmitter power output regulation duties. Enforcement oversight and technical research duties fell to the Department of Commerce's Radio Division. With creation of the Federal Communications Commission (FCC) in 1934, the Department of Commerce retained oversight of government radio spectrum allocation and technical research.

NTIA Origins

It was Executive Branch activity in the late 1960s and early 1970s, however—particularly in the Nixon administration—that resulted in the current configuration of the NTIA. An Office of Telecommunications Policy (OTP) was created within the Executive Office of the President in 1970. Under its first director, Dr. Clay Whitehead, OTP worked to coordinate federal agency concerns

about telecommunication. (In one administrative response, the Federal Communications Commission formed its own Office of Plans and Policies to deal with longer-range studies, so as not to let OTP completely control that role.) OTP became involved in both electronic media questions as well as telephone industry concerns. After Nixon resigned from office in August 1974, OTP was guided by an acting director. When President Jimmy Carter took office in 1977, officials initiated a planning process to decide how to deal with OTP. Henry Geller, former FCC general counsel, headed up a team to assess what was needed and how best to accomplish that need. The result was to shift OTP out of the Executive Office of the President and to the Department of Commerce.

The NTIA was created in 1978 by merging the Executive Branch's Office of Technology Policy and the Department of Commerce's Office of Telecommunications. This merger was effected through Reorganization Plan No. 1 of 1977 and Executive Order 12046 of 27 March 1978.

Responsibilities

The NTIA's radio-related policy, technical, research, and spectrum-management functions are overseen through five offices and three staff groups.

Domestically, the Office of Policy Analysis and Development (OPAD) develops policy recommendations for the Executive Branch regarding common-carrier, broadcast, cable, digital, radio spectrum, wireless, and information technologies. It focuses on promoting universal, affordable radio, television, and telecommunications in the public and commercial sectors and works alongside the FCC. OPAD was instrumental in developing legislation and a computerized system for auctioning excess government radio spectrum for nongovernmental use. It also gathers data and makes recommendations to encourage minority radio and television station ownership through its Minority Telecommunications Development Program. The Office of Telecommunication and Information Applications undertakes funding for new technology demonstration projects, with a specific focus on underserved public sector areas.

The Office of Spectrum Management (OSM) oversees planning and policy strategy and implementation of federal government radio spectrum use in conjunction with its advisory Interdepartmental Radio Advisory Committee. This includes spectrum for federal government radio transmitters such as those used by the Department of Defense, the National Aeronautics and Space Administration

(NASA), the National Park Service, airport communication, and public safety and emergency services. The OSM also offers technical and policy courses to interested international parties on spectrum makeup and management. The OSM deals specifically with federal government radio spectrum use, whereas the FCC deals with nongovernmental uses of spectrum; the two coordinate their activities closely.

Government spectrum applications overseen by the NTIA include defense; Voice of America facilities; radar and voice communications necessary for weather radio and flood warning services, commercial and pleasure aeronautical and maritime traffic, and weather satellite systems; and floodwater management systems and time signals. Government spectrum ranges throughout the 0- to 300-GHz range; at this writing, the government has more than a quarter million assignments: 43 percent for defense, 19 percent for resource management, 18 percent for public safety, 13 percent for transportation, and eight percent for other purposes.

The Office of International Affairs provides policy and technical counsel regarding international radio frequency spectrum allocation, the Global Information Infrastructure initiative, and other issues of legal and technical standards to advance U.S. commercial interests. In this capacity, it works closely with the State Department and with such international bodies as the International Telecommunication Union, the Organization for Economic Cooperation and Development, the World Trade Organization, the International Telecommunications Satellite Organization, the International Mobile Satellite Organization, the Organization of American States InterAmerican Telecommunications Commission, the Asia Pacific Economic Cooperation Telecommunications Working Group, and the Southern African Regional Telecommunications Restructuring Program.

ITS undertakes engineering research for the NTIA. From its laboratory in Boulder, Colorado, ITS generates knowledge about domestic and international infrastructure development and enhancement, more effective use of radio spectrum, and resolving various technical concerns of federal, state, and local governments and of commercial and non-profit industries and organizations. The Federal Technology Transfer Act of 1986 is the legal basis for any of these activities that require sharing government facilities or resources, including radio spectrum.

NTIA is a relatively small agency—about 300 people, compared to the FCC's 2,000 or more. The former concentrates on mid- and long-range policy, whereas the latter focuses on day-to-day licensing and related decisions. They must and do work closely together on spectrum matters. In its near quarter-century of operation, NTIA has waxed and waned in importance, often depending on the political trends and personalities of the times. Although critics have claimed NTIA should stand for "not terribly important agency," the NTIA has performed significant duties related to radio and radio spectrum management.

See also: Federal Communications Commission; Frequency Allocation

Further Reading

Bowers, Helen, editor, *From Lighthouses to Laserbeams: A History of the U.S. Department of Commerce, 1913–1988*, Washington, D.C.: U.S. Department of Commerce, 1988.

Cabinets and Counselors: The President and the Executive Branch, Washington, D.C.: Congressional Quarterly, 1989; 2nd edition, 1997.

National Telecommunications and Information Administration, www.ntia.doc.gov/

National Telecommunications and Information Administration: Office of Spectrum Management, www.ntia.doc.gov/osmhome/osmhome.html

SOUSAN ARAFEH

NATIVE AMERICAN RADIO
Native Owned and Operated Stations

Native American radio is perceived as a way to help retain the languages and traditions of the tribes as well as a method for communicating to Native Americans who speak a Native tongue exclusively. Many older Native Americans use English as a second language, if they use it at all, and are unserved by "Anglo" broadcasting stations. Native-operated stations are also seen as potential tools to help combat the negative images and false impressions of Native Americans often prevalent in mainstream society.

Origins

Hundreds of years of exploitation and oppression by non-Native Americans, mainly whites, served as the primary impetus behind the establishment of Native-controlled broadcast media. In the 1960s Native Americans resoundingly rejected the paternal rule of the "Great White Father" in Washington in favor of playing a greater role in their own affairs and destiny. In the eyes of many, an historic

Native American action at Alcatraz in 1969 was another catalyst for the creation of Native-controlled radio outlets in the United States. Dozens of statements (by those occupying the island in San Francisco Bay) concerning the plight of Natives were broadcast via Pacifica's KPFA-FM. The station loaned the Native Americans on the island a Marti transmitter to relay their messages to its studios in Berkeley, which it then broadcast live. Radio Free Alcatraz, as it was called, focused on the impoverished state of Native American affairs, demanding that attention be paid to Native American health, education, and cultural issues. From the perspective of those who occupied the tiny island, radio was the medium whereby the truth could be conveyed. It could leap barriers and roadblocks and reach the ears and hearts of the public.

The Red Power Movement was born against a backdrop of civil unrest stemming from a call by African-Americans and other minorities for equal rights. Out of this crusade came the American Indian Movement (AIM) in the late 1960s. Driving AIM was the restoration of Native pride and identity through the preservation of Native American culture and language. AIM's primary function was to call attention to the human rights violations against Native Americans and to ensure that the Native American culture would not be exterminated. AIM's seizure of Wounded Knee, South Dakota, in 1973, and its use of the media to dramatize the situation, raised Native awareness of the potency of electronic media, which was an integral part of the organization's strategy to expose to the world what it perceived as gross injustices against its people. This particular incident would be a key factor in the development of Native-controlled and operated broadcast stations.

Ray Cook, executive director of what was formerly the Indigenous Communications Association in the early 1990s, holds that AIM helped plant the seed that led to the creation of Native electronic media. In interviews with the author of this entry, he also cites the 1934 Native American Restoration Act as providing the initial interest among Native Americans in the potential use of radio to achieve a voice of their own. The Economic Opportunity Act of 1965 also helped set the stage for the creation of tribally licensed radio stations, as it permitted Native American organizations and tribes to work independently of the Bureau of Indian Affairs (BIA) while developing social, economic, and educational agendas.

The construction of the first Native-owned radio stations began in 1971 at the height of the Native American rights movement and today number over two dozen. With but one exception (CKON on the border of Canada and New York state), all Native American broadcast facilities operate under the auspices of the Federal Communications Commission. Tribal governments or local school boards typically are the principal licensees. KILI-FM in Porcupine, South Dakota, is, however, licensed to a corporation.

Patterns of Operation

Support for Native-operated stations comes from a variety of sources, chief among them the Corporation for Public Broadcasting and the National Telecommunications and Information Administration (NTIA). Although the former was instrumental in launching the now defunct Indigenous Communications Association, NTIA breathed life into several Native broadcast projects through its Public Telecommunications Program. Of the 33 (figure varies due to frequent start-ups and occasional shut-downs) Native stations in the United States, only four are commercially licensed. As such they have little to do with the funding sources so vital to the existence of their broadcast brethren. The public broadcasting initiatives of the 1970s and 1980s (which made funds widely available for Native radio projects), coupled with the lack of a sufficient economic base for advertiser-supported stations in most Indigenous communities, has resulted in a predominantly noncommercial medium.

The majority of Native stations broadcast west of the Mississippi, whereas Alaska and New Mexico boast the largest number of Indigenous outlets. All but three Native stations have ethnically diverse or mixed staffs, whereas KDLG, KABR, and KCIE limit their hiring to Native Americans exclusively. However, at this writing, only four have staffs that are less than 50 percent Native American. Most Native stations serve rural audiences with a mixture of diverse and often eclectic programming. Music is the primary programming ingredient with a host of genres, among them country, rock, jazz, and rap. Most Native stations air traditional tribal music and language programs and receive additional programming in English and Native American from American Indian Radio on Satellite (AIROS). Many Native American leaders are now looking to Native American radio to play a vital role in the preservation of their indigenous languages.

In 2007, the National Federation of Community Broadcasters announced formation of Native Public Media (NPM), a task force dedicated to assisting Native American broadcasters. With NPM's help, 37 Native nations applied to the FCC for broadcast licenses though only a dozen tribes received them.

Despite webcasting's ubiquitous nature for the rest of radio, Native American radio tends to stress traditional service over internet options. The reasons are both practical and democratic: regardless of wealth, literacy level or level of technical knowledge, tribal members have wide access to radio receivers. Hence traditional broadcasting can reach the widest audiences, enabling inter-community communication, facilitation of information during emergency situations (such as dangerous weather) and even reaching out to non-Native American listeners.

See also: Stereotypes on Radio

Further Reading

Eiselein, Eddie Bill, *Indian Issues*, Browning, Montana: Spirit Talk Press, 1993.

Grame, Theodore, *Ethnic Broadcasting in the United States*, Washington, D.C.: American Folklife Center, 1980.

Keith, Michael C., *Signals in the Air: Native Broadcasting in America*, Westport, Connecticut: Praeger, 1995.

Murphy, James E., "Alaska Native Communications Media: An Over-View," *Gazette* (Fairbanks, Alaska, 1982).

Smith, Bruce L., and M.L. Cornette, *"Eyapaha* for Today: American Indian Radio in the Dakotas," *Journal of Radio Studies* (Summer 1998).

MICHAEL C. KEITH,
2009 REVISIONS BY CARY O'DELL

NETWORK MONOPOLY PROBE

Landmark Policy Decision

Under pressure from many political figures and a fledgling network having trouble competing, the Federal Communications Commission (FCC) launched an investigation of potential radio network monopoly practices early in 1938. The probe lasted until 1941 and became the subject of a landmark Supreme Court case.

Origins

The radio industry had already been the subject of one investigation into possible monopoly practices. On the order of the House of Representatives, in 1923 the Federal Trade Commission (FTC) had examined the radio manufacturing industry's patent sharing and marketing agreements and determined they amounted to an illegal cartel.

The national radio broadcasting networks began operation as the National Broadcasting Company (NBC) in 1926 and the Columbia Broadcasting System (CBS) in 1927; the Mutual Broadcasting System (MBS) had initiated its very different approach in 1934. But very quickly it became apparent the newest network was having a hard time breaking into major radio markets already served by affiliates of the existing networks. Making competition harder, NBC in the 1930s operated "Red" and "Blue" networks that gave it two affiliate stations in larger markets. Between the two of them, sometimes in "competitive cooperation" with a CBS affiliate, these powerful network-affiliated stations could lower prices to the point that a potential newcomer could not break even. By the late 1930s the pattern of network dominance was hard to miss.

Of the 49 most powerful stations (the 50,000-W clear channel outlets) in the United States, 21 were affiliated with NBC Red, 20 were affiliated with CBS, six were affiliated with NBC Blue, and only two had signed with Mutual. On the other hand, of the least desirable (lowest-powered) stations, Mutual led the pack with 111 affiliates, followed by 44 on NBC Blue, 34 connected to NBC Red, and only 18 affiliated with CBS. Of the nearly 200 Mutual stations in 1942, 26 in important cities had contracts with another network that had first call on their best hours. Examined another way, NBC and CBS controlled more than 85 percent of total broadcasting night-time wattage.

To network critics the problem went even deeper. Networks totally dominated their affiliates. Contracts favored the networks at every turn because it was obvious that network affiliation was vital to true financial success in the radio business. Networks were tied to their stations for only a year, whereas stations were often contracted for three to five years. Networks could "option" chunks of affiliate time for network programs. Networks dictated many operational aspects of their supposedly independently owned affiliate stations.

CBS and NBC made a major blunder as the FCC proceedings got under way. The baseball World Series had been carried on all four networks from 1935 to 1938. In 1939 a new sponsor (Gillette) paid the baseball leagues for the rights to broadcast the series exclusively over Mutual. To better distribute the series nationwide, Mutual entered into temporary affiliation agreements with several NBC and CBS affiliates in communities with no regular MBS affiliate in order to permit the stations to broadcast the games. NBC and CBS informed their wayward affiliates that they would not be released from their contractual obligation to run their regular network programming while the games were being played, even though in some cases the requested program pre-emptions amounted to little more than an hour of the daytime schedule. Although a few stations defied their networks and carried the series games anyway, most capitulated. The same drama played out the following year, when Mutual again got exclusive rights to broadcast the series and signed up a large temporary network, only to lose much of it under threats from NBC and CBS.

FCC Decision

After extensive 1938–39 hearings and an initial staff report in 1940, the FCC issued its final chain (network) broadcasting report in May 1941, a 153-page analysis that reviewed past network development and practices. The commission found that NBC and CBS were engaged in a number of anti-competitive practices, and it issued new rules to curtail these practices. The report was one thing; its conclusions and proposed order for rule changes were quite another.

In its most controversial finding, the commission concluded (in the seventh of its eight rule changes) that NBC would have to sell one of its two networks. As the FCC had no direct regulatory role over networks, the wording of the proposed rule was clever: "No license shall be granted to a standard broadcast [AM] station affiliated with a network organization which maintains more than one network." As the FCC licensed all broadcast stations, network structure could be controlled in this indirect fashion. The order made clear that the rule would not be applied if the networks were not operated simultaneously or if there was no overlap in the areas served by the network (such as the many operating regional networks).

Using the same approach, the commission further decreed that stations could not be forced to sign exclusive network contracts that forbade them from pre-empting network programming. Licensees, the commission continued, had the absolute right to accept or reject network programs on a show-by-show basis. Contracts could only bind networks and stations for the same period of time. The effect of the rule changes was to increase the power of the licensee over what it broadcast. Given that the FCC held licensees responsible for what they put over the air, this made eminent sense to the commissioners.

Aftermath

Infuriated and concerned, however, both NBC and CBS mounted a strong attack on the chain broadcasting order. Amidst considerable publicity and press releases, they sued the FCC whilst also persuading sympathetic members of Congress to investigate the agency. In the end both the commission and its new network regulations emerged largely intact.

The networks' lawsuit was eventually (January 1942) dismissed by the Federal District Court for the Southern District of New York, the judge arguing that the court had no jurisdiction. At nearly the same time, however, the U.S. Justice Department brought an antitrust suit against the networks, using the FCC report and data as support. In June 1942, the Supreme Court agreed to review the FCC rules. On 10 May 1943, by a vote of five to two, the court held in favor of the commission, concluding that the rules in no way violated the First Amendment rights of the networks. The court noted the World Series fiasco, commenting that "restraints having this effect are to be condemned as contrary to the public interest irrespective of whether it be assumed that Mutual programs are of equal, superior, or inferior quality." Following the decision, NBC sold its Blue network in 1943, which in 1945 was renamed the American Broadcasting Company (ABC).

The FCC did have to suffer through months of intense congressional scrutiny, in part for the network rules, but also for congressional dislike of activist FCC chairman James Lawrence Fly. The U.S. Senate held hearings on the network rules before which both the CBS and NBC leadership testified. A bit later Representative Eugene E. Cox (Democrat-Georgia) undertook an 18-month investigation of all aspects of the FCC that led to a number of published hearings but little real change. The pressure of all these investigations on the commission, however, clearly took its toll on the personnel and on other regulatory activities.

The chain broadcasting proceeding was only the first of three FCC probes of the networks, although the later investigations (1955–57 and 1978–81) focused almost entirely on television. The 1957 report did include one chapter reviewing radio networks, but noted their decline in the face of television expansion, and thus proposed no further action. Some FCC rules limiting television networks continued for decades, but most were abandoned by the 1990s. The commission had quietly dropped virtually all of its radio chain broadcasting rules decades earlier. The decline of radio networks had made them unnecessary.

See also: Columbia Broadcasting System; Federal Communications Commission; Mutual Broadcasting

System; National Broadcasting Company; United States Congress and Radio; United States Supreme Court and Radio

Further Reading

Bergreen, Laurence, *Look Now, Pay Later: The Rise of Network Broadcasting*, Garden City, New York: Doubleday, 1980.

Columbia Broadcasting System, *What the New Radio Rules Mean*, New York: CBS, 1941.

Federal Communications Commission, *Report on Chain Broadcasting*, Washington, D.C.: Government Printing Office, 1941; reprint, New York: Arno Press, 1974.

Federal Trade Commission, *Report of the Federal Trade Commission on the Radio Industry*, Washington, D.C.: Government Printing Office, 1924.

National Broadcasting Company Inc. v. United States 319 US 190 (10 May 1943).

"Nets Prepare to Operate Under New Rules," *Broadcasting* (17 May 1943).

"The Radio Industry," in *Network Broadcasting: Report of the Network Study Staff*, U.S. House of Representatives, 85th Cong., 2nd Sess., House Report 1297 (27 January 1958).

Robinson, Thomas Porter, *Radio Networks and the Federal Government*, New York: Columbia University Press, 1943; reprint, New York: Arno Press, 1979.

Sarnoff, David, *Principles and Practices of Network Radio Broadcasting*, New York: RCA Institutes Technical Press, 1939.

Statement by Niles Trammell, President, National Broadcasting Company, Before Senate Interstate Commerce Committee, June 17–18, 1941, New York: NBC, 1941.

Sterling, Christopher H., "Breaking Chains: NBC and the FCC Network Inquiry, 1938–43," in Michele Hilmes, editor, *NBC: America's Network*. Berkeley: University of California Press, 2007, pp. 85–97.

U.S. House of Representatives, Select Committee to Investigate the Federal Communications Commission, *Study and Investigation of the Federal Communications Commission: Hearings*, 78th Cong., 1st and 2nd Sess., July 1943–December 1944.

U.S. Senate Committee on Interstate Commerce, *To Authorize a Study of the Radio Rules and Regulations of Federal Communications Commission: Hearings*. 77th Cong., 1st Sess., June 1941.

Why We Need A New Radio Law: Statement by William S. Paley, President of the Columbia Broadcasting System, Delivered Before the United States Senate Committee on Interstate Commerce, June 16, 1941, New York: CBS, 1941.

CHRISTOPHER H. STERLING

NEWS

News did not become a regular feature of radio programming until the early 1930s, although some stations offered occasional news programs as early as the late 1920s. Radio news remains a fundamental, albeit reduced, segment in the program schedule of most radio stations today. For many stations, the genre of "news" has been redefined to include entertainment information as well as hard news. The style of writing and announcing radio news in its early years differs significantly from the writing and announcing style that is now known as broadcast journalism.

Origins (1920–35)

Radio news in the early 1920s was essentially an oral version of national newspaper news. Radio broadcasters took to reading newspaper stories on the air because newspapers were the main source of news and because many radio stations were owned by newspaper companies. In addition, some big-city stations initiated the practice of interrupting regular programming to carry election results or other breaking news events. Radio news reports were a relatively small part of the overall program content for most stations, which followed an "all things to all people" programming strategy by broadcasting a variety of programs, primarily music and variety and various forms of talk, only slowly including regularly-scheduled newscasts.

At first, there were no daily newscasts. Newspaper-owned stations provided sporadic news bulletins as teasers to increase newspaper sales. At other stations, hosts read news as a filler, often without identifying the source of information. A few major-market stations broadcast once-a-week commentaries on current news events, such as those aired in New York by H.V. Kaltenborn, an assistant editor of the *Brooklyn Eagle* newspaper. A few stations carried news of shipwrecks (early operators were required to tune marine emergency bands) or special news events. For example, in 1925 the infamous Scopes "monkey" trial in Tennessee was covered using long-distance telephone lines by WGN radio in Chicago.

With the advent of national network programming, radio newscasts slowly became a feature of the evening schedule. Gathering information primarily from press association newswires, radio networks distributed national news to their affiliate stations through phone lines. However, regular network news did not begin until a 15-minute newscast was inaugurated by NBC's Lowell Thomas in 1930. Two years later, the Lindbergh baby kidnapping became a major network news event, for which networks often pre-empted their regular schedules.

By this time, however, a number of newspapers, fearing radio's growing competition, began to impose limits on radio use of their stories, as well as those supplied by the newspaper-controlled wire services, the Associated Press (AP) United Press (UP), and the International News Service (INS). In response, CBS formed its own news-gathering organization in 1933 by putting together a nation-wide corps of correspondents made up primarily of freelance "stringers." Both NBC and CBS used newly founded independent news services such as Transradio to assist in gathering news during the press embargo.

Eventually realizing that radio stations would continue to find a way to gather and deliver news, newspaper owners proposed a compromise in 1933 called the Biltmore Agreement, after the New York City hotel where it was hammered out. According to the terms of the agreement, CBS was to halt its own news-gathering and both CBS and NBC were to restrict their newscasts to two five-minute news summaries obtained from a newly created Press-Radio bureau. The news summaries were to be aired only after morning or evening newspapers had been published. And radio reporters were limited to providing background information as opposed to detailed news.

However, the Biltmore Agreement was hardly effective. Only a third of radio stations—the network affiliate stations—were bound by it. In addition, the agreement had loopholes that radio stations took advantage of by offering news "commentaries," which the agreement allowed.

Realizing the ineffectiveness of the Biltmore Agreement, two newswire services—UP and INS—broke the news embargo in 1935. Finally, in 1940, AP agreed once again to sell its news services to radio, thus effectively ending the blackout. Re-establishment of radio newswire services coupled with network and local stations' own newsgathering resources provided the necessary preconditions for placing news firmly in the broadcast program schedule.

Golden Age (1935–50)

By the late 1930s, news had become an expected function of radio and it constituted an average of more than ten percent of the radio programming. Individual stations broadcast news that varied in length and depth. Local news gained greater prominence in the average station's program schedule, though it often amounted to just the headlines. By 1938 many radio stations were subscribing to more than one newswire service, and the services were carrying information written especially for radio delivery as opposed to newspaper publication. Several newswire services allowed their news to be sponsored during radio newscasts. Network news reporting was expanded as political crises in Europe and the Pacific deepened. Yet both NBC and CBS also covered many world-wide sporting events and human interest stories in addition to the often grim news of the day.

In 1937 one of the most dramatic news reports ever broadcast was on WLS in Chicago the morning after the German airship *Hindenburg* burned at Lakehurst, New Jersey. Reporter Herb Morrison had intended to record his report on the flight of this airship for archival purposes, but the networks viewed the disaster and Morrison's memorable eyewitness account as so significant that they aired portions of it despite policies allowing only live broadcasts.

Events leading to World War II proved a catalyst for radio news because of a growing public desire for the latest information. To meet the increasing demand for news from abroad, NBC developed a European news operation in 1937, which ushered in a new kind of news reporting that included on-the-spot reports and interviews, commentaries, and actual sounds of people and events being covered "in the field." Both NBC and CBS established foreign news bureaus and developed their first live overseas news reports, which were relayed by shortwave radio to New York City and then by telephone lines to affiliate stations.

CBS expanded news coverage to a half-hour segment for the first time with its *Foreign News Roundup*, which focused on the 1938 German occupation of Austria. *Roundup* originated from key European cities including London, Paris, Rome, Berlin, and Vienna. Reporters in these cities would stand by microphones recounting and assessing events of the day. They could also hear and react to their colleagues' reports. *Roundup* was anchored by Edward R. Murrow in London. Murrow and CBS are largely credited with helping radio to mature into a full-fledged news medium. One notable legacy of Murrow and his team would prove to be the development of "broadcast journalism" as a distinctive syntax of writing and reporting news—conversational and brief writing that incorporates sound from the field, or *actualities*, into the news story. Murrow's actualities often included exploding bombs and screaming sirens.

Some war correspondents were limited to recording their reports before airtime because of government restrictions. But most reporters managed to broadcast their reports live, proving over time that they could do so without breaching military secrets. CBS introduced the term "news analyst" as a replacement for the term "commentator" specifically to avoid the impression that its radio news improperly shaped public opinion.

Although the BBC and other European services widely reported the expanding war after 1939, entry of the United States into the war in late 1941 dramatically increased American radio news reporting. From 1940 to 1944, scheduled network news increased by more than 50 percent. By 1944, NBC-Red was offering 1,726 hours of news annually, and CBS was a close second with 1,497 hours. Despite a postwar decline in overall news hours, news still occupied more than 12 percent of network evening airtime.

Improving technology, such as portable recorders and smaller transmitters, provided the means for such dramatic broadcasts as Edward R. Murrow's recording of a bomber's run over Germany, George Hicks' live coverage of the June 1944 D-Day landings in Normandy, and pick-ups of news from distant Pacific island battlefields. Listeners heard the war begin by radio in 1939 (or in the U.S. on an otherwise quiet Sunday in December 1941)—and heard world leaders announce the end of the war in Europe in May 1945 and in the Pacific just three months later. Millions tuned to the Japanese surrender as it was broadcast from the deck of the battleship *Missouri* in Tokyo Bay in September 1945. And radio carried the resulting celebrations in cities around the world.

Adjustment (1950–70)

Despite the growing diffusion of television into American households in the late 1940s and into the 1950s, radio networks continued providing an extensive schedule of news and commentary for years after World War II. Only after the mid-1950s did network news schedules begin to dip sharply, soon to decline to hourly summaries of top stories. News continued to be an important element of most local station schedules.

Networks attempted to redesign their radio news. Network executives decided that the five-minute news summaries supplied on the hour should now be delivered by experienced reporters with recognizable names, rather than by staff announcers. In addition, the networks tried rolling out "variety news programs" that offered a greater emphasis on feature stories. In 1955, NBC began airing *Monitor*, a mixture of news, music, interviews, dramatic sketches, and sports. *Monitor* was hosted by Frank Blair and Hugh Downs; Gene Shalit did occasional film reviews. ABC began *New Sounds*, a weekday evening series patterned after *Monitor*. In 1960, CBS began *Dimension*, a series consisting of five-minute informational inserts on the half-hour. For all the network's efforts, however, their audience and network radio news continued to decline in the face of television's increasing viewership.

As radio stations increasingly programmed according to some music format by the mid-1950s, news was made a part of the schedule. Only major-market stations provided more than a news headline service.

In the 1960s, news finally became its own radio format. KFAX in San Francisco adopted the first "all-news" format in 1960 with each hour containing 25 minutes of hard news, updated throughout the day. The remaining minutes were filled with sports, business news, and feature stories. But KFAX failed after four months because of a lack of advertising support. The first commercially successful all-news radio station was founded by Gordon McLendon in 1961. McLendon took a rock-and-roll radio station in Tijuana, Mexico, changed its format to hard news, and targeted it at listeners in Los Angeles. News was recycled every half-hour to coincide with the commuting times of drivers going into and out of Los Angeles. No reporters were used—just hard news from the newswires AP, UPI and the Los Angeles City News Service. In 1965, WINS in New York City became an all-news station and began airing the promotional advertisement that has now become standard to Westinghouse (Group W) news stations: "All news, all the time." WINS used its own reporters and focused heavily on local news, as did KYW in Philadelphia, Pennsylvania, and other stations in cities large enough to support the expensive format.

Radio News Formats

Most aspects of modern radio news vary widely among stations, including the number, scheduling, and length of newscasts, the content of stories broadcast, and their order of presentation. Each of these, in turn, may depend on market size, station format, and any news policy of the owners, especially of multiple outlets. Overall, less news is offered on radio today than was the case a decade or two ago.

Although some stations still retain regular newscasts, many music and all-talk outlets focus on feature material. Contemporary Hit Radio (CHR) and Adult Contemporary (AC) stations often still provide brief newscasts, for example; others, such as Country, Easy Listening, and Album-Oriented Rock (AOR), more often run features or have eliminated news, reasoning that not every station in a multistation market has to provide it. If stations affiliate with a network at all, it is most often to carry their brief national newscasts. Some networks are designed to serve up news to fit within specific radio formats.

Through the 1980s the typical pattern for small- and medium-market music stations was to offer five minutes of news on the hour, usually combining world, national, and local stories with a growing emphasis on the latter. World and national news is most often received as an audio feed from a network or syndicated satellite service or as text from the Associated Press, and may be recast to include a local angle.

On stations still offering news, newscasts range from a minute of headlines to three or four minutes long. Most "stories" are now limited to a sentence or two totaling 10–20 seconds—a 60-second story would be very unusual. Stories may contain a soundbite or sound actuality, perhaps bits of an interview. Short newscasts are often devoted to but one or two stories, especially with breaking news. Whereas major-market AM radio stations once offered up to a half-hour of news in morning or afternoon drive-time, that model has all but disappeared as most stations trim or even eliminate news staffs.

The largest markets typically include an all-news AM station. These often utilize a "news wheel" to format their newscasts. This displays the length, order, and content-type of stories to be broadcast over a half-hour or hour cycle, after which the wheel repeats itself. Ideally, each time the news wheel begins again, stories have been refreshed with new information or have been replaced with new stories. The news wheel is especially convenient for listeners who like to know that they can hear a specific type of information (e.g., the weather forecast) by tuning in at exactly :20 and :50 minutes past the hour. As radio news is easier to prepare than reports for TV or newspapers, radio is often quicker at getting breaking news on the air, though internet-based services can be the fastest of all.

Information Sources

Radio stations gather news from a number of sources, including the local newspaper, the telephone, and the field interview. The local newspaper is especially important to smaller stations with a limited budget and news staff. Reporters will rarely admit to using the local newspaper as a primary source of news, instead describing the newspaper as source for obtaining leads to develop news stories. However, reporters at smaller radio stations often do not have the time to gather their own news, so they end up rewriting newspaper stories for their own newscasts.

The telephone is used for conducting interviews with officials and experts—such as politicians, police officers, and coroners—to acquire actualities to be edited later into soundbites. The radio reporter often initiates a phone call from the studio and then records the conversation on tape or computer. FCC regulations specify that reporters must identify themselves as such and name the station they work for and that they must indicate that the station plans to broadcast portions of the interview. All of this has to be done before the reporter begins recording the interview. The telephone is also used to receive live or pre-recorded traffic and weather reports from companies that sell these services to radio stations. *Accuweather* is widely subscribed to for weather information, whereas *Cellular 1* and *Shadow Traffic* are widely subscribed to for traffic information.

Hand-held cassette and minidisc recorders are used by radio reporters to gather actualities from the field. Hand-held recorders are used to record actualities and then to play them back over a telephone line to the studio.

To gather national news, radio stations use newswires, satellite feeds, and the internet. The main newswire subscribed to by both small-market and major-market radio stations is AP; what is left of the UPI agency is used by a small and dwindling number of stations. Typically only the very largest stations in the U.S. subscribe to the other three big international newswire services—Reuters from England, the Agence France Press (AFP) from France, and ITAR-Tass from Russia. Major-market radio stations normally subscribe to regional and city newswire services as well. Newswire services deliver information mainly through satellite downlinks or conventional phone lines connected to a radio station's computer.

Radio stations also use satellite dishes to receive audio news from satellite news feeds. These feeds can be re-broadcast as self-contained newscasts, or they can be used as actualities to be edited into soundbites. Satellite feeds come down at specific times determined by the satellite service. Satellite feeds are provided by the networks CBS, NPR, and CNN, as well as the newswire service AP. They are normally provided free of charge to radio stations in exchange for pre-selected advertising spots in the radio station's program schedule, which will generate revenue for the satellite service. The remaining available spots will be made available for the local stations to fill with news sponsorships. Television is also used to gather information for radio newscasts. The advent of all-news channels and mostly news channels (e.g., CNN, Fox, MSNBC, ESPN, Weather Channel) has allowed radio reporters to monitor nationally developing news stories constantly.

Increasingly, radio stations are relying on the internet to gather national and international news. Many traditional media organizations such as CNN and NBC as well as nontraditional news organizations provide websites with news and information that can be downloaded as text or audio. The internet provides a cheaper alternative to subscribing to a newswire or satellite, but the boundaries for copyright infringement and source credibility are less clear than for newswire or satellite news information.

Regulation and Deregulation of News

For many years, the FCC's licensing renewal guidelines strongly encouraged stations to provide from six to eight percent of total airtime to news and public affairs. Those rules disappeared in the early 1980s, leaving stations to determine their own journalistic role—if any. As a result, in the past two decades many stations have opted out of any news programming at all. However, most small-market Top 40/Contemporary Hit Radio stations have retained news programming because of a traditional listener base that has expectations for local, community-oriented news with a practical quality, such as local events, traffic reports, and high school and college sports.

Industry consolidation in the 1990s has led to further reductions in radio news programming as part of corporate cost-cutting strategies. Multiple stations with common corporate ownership now routinely obtain news by purchasing national news feeds from independent "outsourcing" companies, such as Metro Network's *MetroSource*.

Significantly, the marketplace guideline of deregulation has led many radio stations to air a new kind of news in their program schedules. Today news has come to be defined not strictly as hard news but also as entertainment-oriented information. Medium-market and major-market radio stations have reinforced this redefinition through the news covered in syndicated talk shows they program. National hosts such as Rush Limbaugh, Don Imus, G. Gordon Liddy, Laura Schlessinger, Howard Stern, as well as many local talk-show hosts now feature political, sexual, or celebrity news in their shows. These and other talk-show hosts routinely deliver news stories and then offer their own opinionated comments, after which listeners are invited to engage in the discussion by calling, faxing, or emailing the program.

The continuing decline of radio news has on occasion raised a question of safety. In 2002, a train derailment in Minot, North Dakota, released thousands of gallons of toxic chemicals into the air. After the town's Emergency Alert System failed, authorities attempted to warn citizens over the town's six radio stations. However, all six were operating on an automated basis that Sunday, and no personnel could be contacted quickly. Several hours passed before any of them issued warnings. The Minot incident, widely cited by critics of radio consolidation (Clear Channel owned all six), would kill one person and injure a thousand others. Thankfully, life-threatening incidents like this are rare. Stations explain their lack of news by noting that people now seek their news online and elsewhere. And in most markets, at least one station provides some news service.

See also: All News Format; Documentary Programs; Editorializing; Election Coverage; Fairness Doctrine; Fireside Chats; News Agencies; Politics and Radio; Press-Radio War; Public Affairs Programming; United States Presidency and Radio; World War II and U.S. Radio

Further Reading

Bliss, Edward, Jr., *Now the News: The Story of Broadcast Journalism*, New York: Columbia University Press, 1991.

Charnley, Mitchell V., *News By Radio*, New York: Macmillan, 1948.

Greenfield, Thomas Allen, *Radio: A Reference Guide*, New York: Greenwood Press, 1989.

Hausman, Carl, *Crafting the News for Electronic Media: Writing, Reporting and Producing*, Belmont, California: Wadsworth, 1992.

Lee, Jennifer, "Media: On Minot, N.D., Radio, A Single Corporate Voice," *New York Times* (31 March 2003).

Mayeux, Peter E., *Broadcast News: Writing and Reporting*, Dubuque, Iowa: Wm. C. Brown, 1991; 2nd edition, Prospect Heights, Illinois: Waveland Press, 2000.

McKenzie, Robert, *How Selected Pennsylvania Radio Stations Use Technology to Gather Information for News Programs: A Field Study*, Ph.D. diss., Pennsylvania State University, August 1990.

Sterling, Christopher H., and John M. Kittross, *Stay Tuned: A History of American Broadcasting*, 3rd edition, Mahwah, New Jersey: Lawrence Erlbaum, 2002.

White, Paul W., *News on the Air*, New York: Harcourt Brace, 1947.

ROBERT MCKENZIE,
2009 REVISIONS BY CARY O'DELL

NEWS AGENCIES

For most of their history, radio stations have relied on national sources for much of their news. Other than the radio network news divisions, the prime source for national and international news has usually been one or more of the news agencies (also called news or wire services or press associations), such as the Associated Press (AP), United Press International (UPI), or Reuters. In recent years, the news agencies have provided considerable regional and local news as well. As more radio stations reduce their news staffs (or eliminate them entirely), "rip 'n' read" newscasts based entirely on news agency copy have once again become common.

Cooperative news-gathering began in the United States with the formation of the Associated Press by a number of New York daily newspapers in 1848. Although reorganized several times, the AP has always been a cooperative rather than a profit-seeking venture. The United Press (UP) was begun as a profit-seeking affiliate of the Scripps newspaper chain in 1907, and the International News Service (INS) appeared as another commercial venture in 1909, controlled by the Hearst newspapers. Each of the three was based on service to newspapers, and newspaper-based board members controlled their operation. Radio's arrival and demand for service created big questions for the agencies.

Associated Press

The oldest and largest news agency had the most trouble deciding how to handle the new medium. As early as 1922, when few stations offered news, the AP warned its member newspapers not to allow use of AP news reports on their own radio stations. But in 1924 and 1928, AP did allow election returns to be broadcast. Starting in 1933, AP adopted a policy of allowing radio use of AP news stories only for events of "transcendent importance," and this continued until 1941, long after its competitors were serving broadcasters.

In 1941 AP initiated a radio wire—a news service written for use on the air, as opposed to the traditional service for newspapers designed to be read. Dubbed "Circuit 7760," it operated 24 hours a day under the direction of Oliver Gramling. Within a year AP was serving 200 (of about 750 total) stations in 120 cities, with no stations on its broadcast wire payroll. After the war, some 450 stations were elected to associate membership (an important status within the AP cooperative organization, as radio now had more of a voice in management decisions). By the early 1950s, AP was providing some 75,000 words every 24 hours, written for audio reading, and usually condensed and rephrased from the main newspaper service.

AP news for radio was usually provided in the shape of ready-to-use newscasts of different lengths. This led many smaller stations, lacking their own news staffs, to simply have an announcer assemble a news program from the news agency wire stories

("rip 'n' read"). As more stations developed popular music formats, many relied on this practice for their entire news operation. Now dubbed the AP Radio Network, the agency launched an audio service with actualities (sound recordings from the field) for stations to use in their own newscasts in 1974. Just five years later, the AP Broadcast Wire was said to be the longest leased telecommunication circuit in the world.

In 1980 the AP broadcast service became the first radio network in the world to use a communications satellite. Just four years later, AP owned its own satellite transponder, making it the first news organization to do so. In the meantime, AP had shifted its broadcast operations from New York to Washington, D.C. A decade later, AP was serving just over half the commercial radio stations in the nation with four focused services designed to better serve varied radio formats: AP NewsPower, AP DriveTime, AP NewsTalk, and AP Specialty Wires. To these was added AP All-News Radio in 1994, a 24-hour service of "full packed" radio newscasts that served more than 70 stations by 2000, with another 750 taking news feeds.

United Press and International News Service

The story of UPI and radio is more complex and begins with its two commercial predecessors: the United Press and the International News Service.

The United Press provided a 1924 general election hook-up using WEAF in New York as the base station. UP's president Karl Bickel argued strongly in favor of serving radio in the 1920s and saw the new medium as an exciting development. But his newspaper-dominated board of directors prevented such a service until 1935 when he resigned owing to ill-health at age 53, leaving his successor Hugh Baillie to bring UP service to radio station subscribers. In the meantime, a number of radio stations owned by UP client newspapers had been using UP reports on the air, despite news agency policy banning such practices. In 1943, UP published a *United Press Radio News Style Book*, an indicator of the growing importance of radio to the commercial news agency. By the early 1950s, UP was providing about 70,000 words per day to its radio subscribers.

The smaller and weaker International News Service began a "radio-script" service providing radio material 40 times a week in addition to its regular print service. In the face of AP expansion and success in luring away newspaper clients, however, the weaker INS and UP agreed to merge to form UPI in 1958.

United Press International

With the merger, UPI, under Scripps control, began to provide its client radio stations with audio reports to use in their own news programs. By 1965 clients were receiving about 65 voice stories a day from the UPI radio center in Chicago. Nine years later they were also receiving 20 full newscasts a day with inputs from London and Hong Kong. In 1977 UPI was serving about 900 client stations (almost twice the number reached by the AP). UPI also moved to distribute its radio news service by satellite in the early 1980s.

But UPI was in deep financial trouble. Although intended from the start as a commercial affiliate of a for-profit newspaper company, the agency had fairly consistently lost money. By the 1970s it was rapidly losing newspaper clients to the larger and better-financed AP and began to focus more on its radio station business.

In 1982, after a two-year effort, Scripps sold the company it had founded nearly three-quarters of a century earlier. The sale led to two decades of drastic decline under several successive owners and two separate declarations of bankruptcy. UPI declined from about 1,800 employees at the time of the Scripps sale to less than 200 in mid-2000 when a Unification Church affiliate took control of the remains of the Washington-based news agency.

The UPI radio network was now the central part of the now much smaller news service. It offered 24 hours of fully produced programs for use at the top of each hour plus an actuality service for stations to use in their own newscasts (called "Selectnews," it began in 1992). Although UPI reached some 2,000 stations in 1994 and radio accounted for half of the agency's income three years later, UPI had to end its radio service on 19 August 1999 due to lack of funds, competition from newer news sources, and a drastic drop-off in the number of client stations (to just 400). Its final words:

> This is the final broadcast from UPI Radio. United Press International is getting out of the broadcast news business and has sold its contracts to Associated Press Radio. For those of us suddenly out of work, it's been fun. We feel UPI Radio has done its job well overall, even as we struggled with fewer and fewer resources. So we sign off now with smiles, memories, a few tears but no regrets.

Other Services

Although most stations relied upon their network affiliation (if any), a specialized news service, or AP for world and national news, competing news sources had existed even in the early years of radio. Several entities, for example, had developed to serve radio in the wake of the brief 1930s "war" that limited availability of AP, UP, and INS news feeds. The agencies created the Press-Radio Bureau to combine service from the three in special radio reports, and it lasted until 1938. The Yankee News Service served the New England regional network's affiliates, the Continental Radio News Service based in Washington, and the Radio News Association from Los Angeles also began operation in 1934. Transradio Press Service began at the same time, largely built with former Columbia Broadcasting System (CBS) news people, aimed at serving non-network radio stations. Transradio survived beyond the 1930s (to December 1951, when it closed for lack of sufficient station clients) because stations could again obtain their news from the traditional news agencies.

London-based Reuters made its first radio agreement with the then-commercial BBC in 1922, although with provisions that no news would be broadcast before 7 P.M. in the evening, thus protecting the circulation of evening London dailies. Continuing negotiations in the mid-1920s allowed the BBC to cover current events as they were happening, and by 1929 the now government-chartered BBC received the full Reuters newswire for use in its news programs. Only in 1972 did Reuters begin its first voice news service for local stations in Britain and the United States. By the 1990s the firm had refocused on financial reporting and information and no longer served radio stations.

The expansion (and by the late 1990s, the consolidation) of the radio business contributed to a variety of other radio news services including Unistar (which carried CNN Radio), Capnews, the Business Radio Network, and the USA Radio Network.

The Associated Press discontinued its All News Radio in 2005 because it had not generated a profit. AP Radio News is distributed by satellite to about a thousand radio and satellite affiliates. Its primary elements are live three-minute newscasts at the top of the hour 24/7 and two additional one-minute updates at the half hour and hour weekdays from 6 A.M. to midnight. AP provides news feeds hourly, which are also available on the internet, during which the agency delivers more than 300 audio soundbites (including news, entertainment, format-specific morning material, sports and business).

AP's newer Hosted Custom News is provided to about 1,000 affiliate radio and television websites. The agency supplies video packages to 2,000 newspaper, radio and TV websites. In all, AP Broadcast serves more than 5,500 customers including AOL and other portals. The newest delivery platform is AP Mobile News Network with downloadable applications for iPhones, BlackBerrys (and soon Trios). Subscribers enter their zip code and receive local, national, and world news including photos and video (and soon audio). In a typical 2009 month the service had more than eight million page views on mobile devices.

In 2008, the Canadian-owned Thomson combine took control of Reuters, renaming the latter Thomson Reuters. And CNN announced plans to form a news agency that would serve radio and other media.

This expansion of syndicated news sources paralleled the decline of individual local station news efforts; instead of supporting local station news, these services were increasingly replacing local efforts.

See also: News; Press-Radio War; Yankee Network

Further Reading

Bickel, Karl August, *New Empires: The Newspaper and the Radio*, Philadelphia, Pennsylvania: Lippincott, 1930.

Bliss, Edward, Jr., *Now the News: The Story of Broadcast Journalism*, New York: Columbia University Press, 1991.

Boyd-Barrett, Oliver, *The International News Agencies*, London: Constable, and Beverly Hills, California: Sage, 1980.

Jackaway, Gwenyth L., *Media at War: Radio's Challenge to the Newspapers, 1924–1939*, Westport, Connecticut: Praeger, 1995.

Moore, Herbert, et al., *"More News—After This": The Untold Story of Transradio Press*, Warrenton, Virginia: Sun Dial, 1983.

Morris, Joe Alex, *Deadline Every Minute: The Story of the United Press*, Garden City, New York: Doubleday, 1957.

"News Agencies and Radio Broadcasting," in *News Agencies, Their Structure and Operation*, Paris: Unesco, 1953.

CHRISTOPHER H. STERLING,
2009 REVISIONS BY CHRISTOPHER H. STERLING

NIELSEN
See: A.C. Nielsen Company

NON-ENGLISH-LANGUAGE RADIO

In the United States, the radio boom of 1923 coincided roughly with the legislated end of the largest wave of international immigration in modern history. Some 20 million immigrants arrived on the shores of the United States between 1871 and 1920, some settling permanently, some returning home, and others traveling that route a number of times. The result was a proliferation of people and communities who spoke German, Polish, Spanish, Yiddish, Italian, and other languages. At the end of the 19th century, newspapers were the primary vehicle for the dissemination of information, with countless daily papers from every ethnic and political angle being published every day. As cities grew and the networks of newspaper distribution had not yet expanded, radio became a vital alternative to the printed word.

As early as 1926, foreign-language markets were being identified as potential profit centers. Despite indications by the advertising industry, major networks such as the National Broadcasting Company (NBC) and soon the Columbia Broadcasting System (CBS) were loath to incorporate foreign-language programming into their schedules. (However, for two years beginning in 1928, NBC briefly broadcast *Der Tog*, a Yiddish-language program.) Yet by 1964 more than 340 radio and television stations broadcast non-English-language programs in everything from Italian to Navajo. The majority of these stations were local, low-wattage stations without access to national networks. More recently the number of non-English broadcasts has increased exponentially with the popularization of web-based broadcasting. The development of non-English programming through alternative formats (local versus network and web versus traditional radio) is not coincidental but speaks of a particular power relationship between language and radio.

Throughout radio's history, the number of non-English stations in the United States has been quite significant, which suggests a considerable listening audience despite its traditional exclusion from market studies. As NBC and CBS rapidly grew to dominate the national networked radio dial, numerous local radio stations, generally with a broadcast power between 100 and 500 W, began to spring up in urban areas. Almost always, these stations rented portions of their broadcast day to different community groups who wished to broadcast. Two of the most prominent examples are New York's WEVD and Chicago's WCFL. Founded in 1927, WEVD was owned by the Debs Radio Trust and broadcast programs in at least four languages, whereas WCFL hosted broadcasting in no fewer than 11. In 1924 WOAI in San Antonio, Texas, aired its first Spanish-language broadcast, and Cleveland's WJAY initiated a weekly Polish-language program beginning in 1926.

Following the Federal Radio Commission's reorganization of the radio dial in November 1928, the majority of the stations that carried non-English-language programming found themselves relegated to the low and high frequency margins of the broadcast spectrum. Additionally, the FRC forced many of these stations to share frequencies and therefore also divide up the broadcast day. Broadcasting from the margin and on power that typically ranged from 250 to 1,000 W, these stations cobbled together whatever broadcasting they could, usually comprising a loose coalition of multilingual programs, performers, advertising agents, and sponsors. Few, if any, of these stations could choose to broadcast in only one language. The only significant exception to this rule was organized during the late 1930s, when New York-based station WOV organized 15 east-coast stations into the International Broadcasting Corporation, which served as an Italian-only network, serving an audience of nearly three million listeners.

With the organization of the Federal Radio Commission in 1927 and amid the growing concern about the "decency" of radio programs, Section 29 of the Radio Act of 1927 sought to regulate U.S. airwaves by providing that "whoever utters any obscene, indecent, or profane language by means of radio communication shall be fined not more than $10,000 or imprisoned not more than two years." As it was impossible to listen to every broadcast nationwide, the FRC mandated that broadcasts be recorded if a listener had filed a complaint against that program. In the beginning, these recordings were made on glass plates (78-rpm records could not hold long enough segments, and magnetic recording tape had not yet been invented). This concern about the "decency" of language contributed to a general suspicion about non-English broadcasts and led to additional federal policing and harassment of such programs. Of course, it was also true that non-English broadcasts could elude the surveying ear of the FRC because often FRC monitors could not understand their content.

If non-English-language programs were considered a marginal segment of radio broadcasting in the United States, the incorporation of non-standard English speakers into English-language programs fueled the popular imagination. During the Depression years, the networks established themselves nationally via the appeal of ethno-comedies such as *The Goldbergs* and *Amos 'n' Andy*. These two programs, as some of the first to reach national audiences, drew significantly on cultural, linguistic, and dialectical differences for their humor. In the case of *The Goldbergs*, the common problems of language acquisition (mispronunciation, spoonerisms, malapropisms, etc.) and accent were the source of a great deal of the humor that Molly Berg wrote into the program. *Amos 'n' Andy* drew on a much older tradition of minstrelsy (and

played on its racial stereotypes), but the particular challenge of putting blackface on radio turned the emphasis from appearance to dialect as the primary signifier of difference. Even though the Goldbergs were clearly on the path toward becoming ordinary Americans, whereas Amos and Andy were depicted as unassimilable, in both cases mastery of English was highlighted as the key determinant of mainstream acceptance. These programs clearly appealed to English-speaking audiences as they poked fun at members of non-traditional-English-speaking population groups.

Although culturally and linguistically marginal, non-English-language programs occupied a substantial amount of the radio dial. Statistics for non-English broadcasts during the Depression era are scant, but one source reports that nearly 200 stations out of a total of 850 broadcast non-English-language programs for some part of the day.

In a 1941 anthology entitled *Radio Research* (edited by Paul Lazarsfeld and Frank Stanton), sociologists Arnheim and Bayne published a survey of non-English-language broadcasts. They reported the presence of German, Italian, Yiddish, Polish, Lithuanian, and Spanish broadcasts. However, there were almost certainly Greek, Croatian, Russian, Hungarian, Bulgarian, Romanian, Chinese, Japanese, and Gaelic broadcasts at the time, as well. Although Arnheim and Bayne were primarily interested in the content of a typical broadcast day, their study is the first organized examination of ethnic radio in the United States, representing an early effort to include non-English-speaking audiences in radio market research.

Limitations

As soon as the United States entered World War II, the Federal Communications Commission (FCC) and the Foreign Language Division of the Office of Facts and Figures began investigations of all major East Coast stations (as well as others farther west) that broadcast foreign-language programs. Stations in New York, Philadelphia, Boston, and Chicago were targeted, and Alan Cranston, then-chief of the foreign language division, recommended that certain broadcasters be "barred from the air immediately." Following the removal of a handful of German and Italian broadcasters and a general decline of foreign-language broadcasts, in March 1942, Cranston initiated new programs in German and Italian. The programs, entitled *Uncle Sam Speaks*, were designed to encourage ethnic listeners to join the war effort through volunteering or taking jobs in the defense industry.

Despite this overall reduction in U.S. foreign-language broadcasting, the World War II era also marked the emergence of substantial Spanish-language broadcasting, which has grown exponentially since that time, with about 500 stations including Spanish-language programming by 1980. In the postwar years, broadcasters in Yiddish actively involved themselves in reuniting Jewish refugees with their families by broadcasting names of people who were looking for family members. Despite these brief highlights, the 1940s were devastating to non-English-language broadcasting, with the exception of Spanish broadcasts, which managed steady growth. Not coincidentally, the postwar years also witnessed the near-total domination of radio by the networks.

With the rise of McCarthyism in the 1950s, radio stations that previously housed foreign-language programs began dropping them from their rosters, fearing that broadcasters from Eastern Europe might use their airtime to spread communist propaganda. These station owners were responding to demographic changes, as well; first-generation groups began to give way to their English-speaking children. As language and residence patterns changed, so did cultural tastes, and programming once valued for its cultural specificity began to sound old-fashioned. However, this era should not be seen as the end of foreign-language radio, but rather as a reflection of changing immigration and settlement patterns and changes in the cultural preferences of many European immigrants. Thus, as European-language broadcasts decreased, a sizable immigration from Asia (most significantly from the Philippines, India, and Korea) gave birth to new broadcast options. And Spanish language broadcasting continued its growth.

Since the late 1960s, non-English-language radio in the United States has seen a massive growth in both the overall number of stations, as well as the size and impact of audiences. Stations broadcasting primarily in Spanish, Korean, and Chinese have multiplied in conjunction with the growth of immigrant populations in primarily urban areas. What distinguishes the growth of non-English-language radio programming in the second half of the century from that of the first half is the development of single-language stations that are able to compete in larger metropolitan markets. Whereas network interests choked off the development of single-language radio stations during radio's golden age, the virtual dominance of radio by local interests has opened the door for radio stations that target a particular ethno-linguistic population in a particular area.

Online Radio

Recently, with the popularity of the internet and the increasing availability of web-based broadcasts, non-English "radio" broadcasts are flourishing. For example, www.live-radio.net contains a listing of online broadcasts from radio stations all over the globe in virtually every language imaginable. The two primary interfaces from accessing online media also include simple ways of locating and accessing online broadcasts of all kinds. No longer restricted by the narrow spectrum of radio frequencies, broadcasters can reach audiences of size and scope never before imaginable. At the same time, audiences can tune in to a wider variety of programs originating from more locations, and broadcasting in more languages than has ever before been possible.

With the spread of online broadcast technology and an FCC ruling in 2000 to create a class of low-wattage stations, the future of non-English-language broadcasting is bright, if not in traditional broadcasting. Insofar as non-English-language programs have long been on the margin of mainstream broadcasting, they have also often been in the vanguard of broadcast practices, conventions, and styles. Thus the sheer number of non-English web-based broadcasts should come as no surprise. Their proliferation indicates that the future of radio is wide open, a form of expression that cannot be limited by traditional broadcast practices or geographical location. It also heralds a return to the origins of non-English-language broadcasting in the United States, which were rooted in the needs and preferences of immigrants from other countries.

See also: Hispanic Radio; Internet Radio; Jewish Radio Programs; Native American Radio; Stereotypes on Radio; WCFL; WEVD

Further Reading

Arnheim, R., and M. Bayme, "Foreign Language Broadcasts over Local American Stations," in *Radio Research*, edited by Paul Felix Lazarsfeld and Fred Stanton, New York: Duell, Sloan, and Pearce, 1941; reprint, New York: Arno Press, 1971.

Grame, Theodore C., *Ethnic Broadcasting in the United States*, Washington, D.C.: American Folklife Center, Library of Congress, 1980.

Gutiérrez, Felix F., and Jorge Reina Schement, *Spanish Language Radio in the Southwestern United States*, Austin: Center for Mexican American Studies, University of Texas, 1979.

Hilmes, Michele, *Radio Voices: American Broadcasting, 1922–1952*, Minneapolis: University of Minnesota Press, 1997.

Horton, Gerd, "Unity on the Air? Fifth Columnists and Foreign Language Broadcasting in the United States during World War II," *Ethnic Forum* 13, no. 1 (1993).

Keith, Michael C., *Signals in the Air: Native Broadcasting in America*, Westport, Connecticut: Praeger, 1995.

Klopf, Donald, and John Highlander, "Foreign Language Broadcasting in the Western States," *Western Speech* 29, no. 4 (Fall 1965).

Migala, Jœzef, *Polish Radio Broadcasting in the United States*, Boulder, Colorado: East European Monographs, 1987.

ARI KELMAN

NORTH AMERICAN REGIONAL BROADCASTING AGREEMENT

Sharing Frequencies among the U.S., Canada, Mexico, and the Caribbean

First placed into effect early in 1941, the North American Regional Broadcasting Agreement (NARBA) treaty doled out radio channels to Canada, Cuba, Mexico, and the United States. Renewed after extensive negotiations in 1960, it remained for years the basis for cooperative regulation and interference reduction among these countries until it was replaced by bilateral agreements and treaties affecting all of the Western Hemisphere.

As the number of radio stations in North America grew, countries neighboring the United States felt increasingly squeezed out of valuable medium wave frequencies used for AM radio broadcasting. Naturally the potential for trouble was greatest along the northern and southern borders of the United States, where American stations could—and did—cause interference to outlets in other countries, and vice versa. Given the larger U.S. population and expanding radio industry, American broadcasters sought the lion's share of available frequencies, leaving little to be shared by Canada, Mexico, and Cuba.

In 1937 representatives of the four nations met in Havana and hammered out the gist of a proposed frequency-sharing treaty. The task was not easy: given the great distances covered by AM signals, the work was complex and occasionally contentious. Nevertheless, the treaty was ratified by each nation and entered force on 29 March 1941. At the time, there were about 750 broadcast stations on the air in the United States, most of which had to shift their frequency (some only slightly), primarily to clear some radio channels for expanded use in Mexico. But for the remainder of the decade, the four nations were able to license stations in accordance with NARBA, thus greatly reducing potential interference problems.

The treaty expired in March 1949 after initial attempts to renew it failed. The demise of NARBA occurred despite considerable effort and controversy. The key problem was the dramatic expansion of American broadcasting—to 2,127 stations when NARBA expired—and thus the greater (and steadily expanding) use of spectrum by the U.S. radio industry. At the same time, driven in part by understandable nationalism, governments in the neighboring countries felt they were (again) getting the short end of the frequency stick, because the number of their stations had increased as well.

Cuba was the loudest complainer, even in the late 1940s. It demanded use of more frequencies and threatened to not ratify a NARBA renewal if it did not get them. Likewise, Mexico moved to protect some of the border stations serving American audiences. Complicating matters was the addition of new negotiating players: Haiti, the Dominican Republic, and Britain (on behalf of the Bahamas and Jamaica). Still, after several rounds of engineering work and diplomatic negotiation, a draft of a second NARBA treaty was initialed in 1950. But because of continuing negotiation problems—and rising pressure from big clear channel broadcasters fearful of losing some of their coverage as well as from small daytime-only stations hoping for longer broadcast hours (both groups felt they had given up enough already)—American ratification was delayed.

Between 1953 and 1962, a second NARBA was ratified by Cuba, Canada, the Dominican Republic, and the Bahamas. In 1960 the U.S. Congress ratified it as well, placing the treaty into force despite the lack of agreement from Mexico, Jamaica, and Haiti. Bilateral agreements with Mexico in 1969–70 and again in 1986 (as well as with Canada in 1984), served to keep the lid on potential interference problems and allowed many American daytime-only stations operating on Mexican or Canadian clear channels to begin operations before local sunrise and sometimes to extend operating hours into the evening with greater power. These agreements remain in force as long as the three nations agree.

Politics, always potent in international agreements, became central in dealing with the island nation of Cuba. By the late 1960s, the Castro regime in Cuba was informally ignoring the 1960 NARBA treaty. In 1981 Cuba formally abrogated the agreement and began to build stations that went well beyond the agreement in terms of power and frequencies used. When the United States began propaganda broadcasts into Cuba over Radio Martú, the Castro government retaliated by building high-power transmitters that caused considerable interference, especially with stations in the American South and Midwest. The Federal Communications Commission began to make case-by-case decisions allowing the affected stations to increase their own power—in essence recognizing exactly the kind of "radio war" the original NARBA treaty was designed to prevent.

As for the other nations in the region, the second NARBA treaty was eventually superseded by various Region II (Western Hemisphere) radio broadcasting agreements established under the auspices of the International Telecommunication Union in a series of regional radio conferences.

See also: Border Radio; Frequency Allocation; Licensing Authorizing U.S. Stations to Broadcast

Further Reading

North American Regional Broadcasting Agreement: Final Protocol to the Agreement, Resolutions, and Recommendations, Washington, D.C.: International Telecommunication Union, 1950.

Rankin, Forney Anderson, *Who Gets the Air? The U.S. Broadcaster in World Affairs*, Washington, D.C.: National Association of Broadcasters, 1949.

CHRISTOPHER H. STERLING

NOSTALGIA RADIO
See: Old-Time Radio

O

OBSCENITY AND INDECENCY ON RADIO

Radio has long been considered a guest in the home or car, and so the medium has been constrained in the kinds of language broadcast. The original language of the Radio Act of 1927 (Sec. 29) indicated that "No person within the jurisdiction of the United States shall utter any obscene, indecent, or profane language by means of radio transmission." However, it was not until 1948 that Congress put teeth into this provision by incorporating this prohibition into the criminal code (18 U.S.C.A. 1464). But does such a constraint violate First Amendment rights of free expression? And has the cultural climate of language usage changed since 1948? Do we know what constitutes *obscene* or *indecent* for everyone, or do these meanings differ from one person to another? Is there any good way for the Federal Communications Commission (FCC) or the courts to enforce this measure without violating a provision in the Communication Act (Section 326), let alone the First Amendment, that prohibits the censorship of broadcast communication? These questions complicate any clear answer to or brief discussion of this issue. However, some court decisions and activities of the FCC give us a history upon which we can base an informed discussion.

Developing Concern

Early in the history of broadcasting, those who announced or otherwise spoke on radio did so with a great deal of decorum and civility. Often they would wear formal attire, even though no-one could see them. The language was precise, enunciation was as perfect as possible, and certainly there was neither slang nor profanity. "Radio speakers" were guests in listeners' homes, and they spoke with careful politeness.

The FCC recognized in 1975 that:

> broadcasting requires special treatment because of four important considerations: (1) children have access to radios and in many cases are unsupervised by parents; (2) radio receivers are in the home, a place where people's privacy interest is entitled to extra deference; (3) non-consenting adults may tune in a station without any warning that offensive language is being or will be broadcast; and (4) there is a scarcity of spectrum space, the use of which the government must therefore license in the public interest.
>
> (56 FCC 2nd 97)

However, radio evolved to the point that speakers became less formal and more conversational in their radio dialogues with the listener. American culture was changing. Nudity in over-the-counter magazines such as *Playboy* appeared. Frank discussions about sex were no longer as taboo as they had been previously. It was during this time, in the late 1950s and 1960s, that the U.S. Supreme Court tried yet again to define obscenity issues in the media.

In *Roth v. United States* (1957), the U.S. Supreme Court tried for the first time to establish some definite measure to define obscenity, after noting that it was not protected by the First Amendment. It was a matter of "whether to the average person, applying contemporary community standards, the dominant theme of the material, taken as a whole, appeals to prurient interest."

There was still no certainty as to what *prurient* meant. A definition was left unarticulated in the case of *Jacobellis v. Ohio* (1964): Justice Stewart stated that although he had a hard time defining pornography, "I know it when I see it."

In *Memoirs v. Massachusetts* (1966), the new element added to the definition was that material is patently offensive when it affronts contemporary community standards relating to the description or representation of sexual matters. "Pandering material," that which openly advertises and appeals to erotic interests, was yet another element added to the definition in 1966 *(Ginzburg v. United States)*.

But by 1967, the courts had become flooded with obscenity cases, resulting in confusion. In *Redrup v. New York*, the court articulated a kind of reverse definition: nothing was obscene except when it fell under the specific circumstances of (1) "pandering," (2) failure to uphold specific statutes designed to protect juveniles, or (3) an assault upon individual privacy by publication in a manner so obtrusive as to make it impossible for the unwilling individual to avoid exposure to it. It is perhaps this third provision that prevented obscene language in broadcasting in an era in which such language was becoming common in other media.

By 1973, in one of the last attempts by the U.S. Supreme Court to define obscenity, in *Miller v. California*, the Court fell back to the elements of the "Roth rule" from the 1957 case. It also added the notion of the "SLAPS rule," which takes into consideration whether the work in question lacks "Serious Literary, Artistic, Political or Scientific value." The Court thereby rejected the previous obscenity standard of being "utterly without redeeming social value."

It was during this era that American mass culture continually presented the courts (and, where broadcasting was concerned, the FCC) with dilemmas of staying with the traditional or liberalizing policies to accommodate new language and attitudes about sex.

As American culture changed, how was radio to reflect this shift? Slang expressions, double entendres, dirty jokes, and derogatory terms became popular. Indeed, during that era, some talk radio programs, known as "topless radio," discussed matters of sex in a frank manner. Here, talk show hosts, disc jockeys, and phone-in callers engaged in sexually explicit dialogue, apparently for the express purpose of titillating listeners. Some stations were found to be broadcasting indecent material, however, and were fined by the FCC in 1973.

But the pivotal case as it relates to obscenity or indecency on radio came in the case of comedian George Carlin. In his comedy routine "Seven Dirty Words You Can't Say on Radio or Television," Carlin expressed thoughts about the nature of some taboo words and how nonsensical their expressions were in many colloquialisms. His descriptions poked fun at society's view of such words. His humorous satire examined the "language of ordinary people and our silly attitudes toward those words." Carlin's routine on the subject was recorded and released with the provision "not for broadcast." However, a New York City radio station owned by the Pacifica Foundation aired the dialogue one afternoon. A man heard the broadcast of the dialogue while driving with his young son and wrote a letter of complaint to the FCC. He stated that he could not understand why the recording had been broadcast over the air that the FCC was supposed to control *(FCC v. Pacifica*, 1978).

The challenge worked its way through the courts for nearly five years, from 1973, when it was first aired, until 1978, when the U.S. Supreme Court decided on it. Because of the dilemma between the FCC's need to prohibit indecent broadcasts and the constitutional rights guaranteed by the First Amendment, the U.S. Supreme Court agreed to hear the case. The Court in considering this dilemma had to take into consideration both the changing social climate of increasing latitude and also the fact that the sketch had been broadcast in mid-afternoon, at a time when any child might have been listening. The Court looked at the FCC's enforcement role and its mandate for enforcement from the U.S. Code on indecency and reflected on the cases over the previous decade, which had maintained no First Amendment protection for obscene material. The Court also looked at the careful definitions of *obscenity* and *indecency*.

However, the need for more stringent definitions seemed necessary for broadcasting. One distinction was that *indecency*, unlike *obscenity*, may have First Amendment protection. The concept of *obscenity* uses a more serious standard than does *indecency*, which was defined by the court in the *Pacifica* (1978) case as "intimately connected with the exposure of children to language that describes, in terms patently offensive as measured by contemporary community standards for the broadcast medium, sexual or excretory activities and organs, at times of the day when there is a reasonable risk that children may be in the audience."

The Court went on to suggest that the material might not have been indecent under some circumstances, such as when children would not be present. This notion led to the concept of *safe harbor*, a time, for example late at night, when the number of children listening is minimal and when it might be safe to consider a different standard.

For many succeeding years, the FCC applied this ruling to indecent programming airing before 10 P.M. By 1987 the FCC changed its definition of *safe harbor* and came to consider a more general definition of indecency. Time of day became less of a factor, because children or youth could often be found listening at all hours. Context became the important factor in determining indecency. Later, the Commission returned to the safe harbor idea, changing the start of the harbor to midnight, provided that the questionable materials began with appropriate warnings. It was assumed by the Commission that parents would maintain some control over their children's listening after midnight. Thus, the focus shifted from the FCC's policing to setting up zones in which parents were responsible.

Broadcasters, together with other interested parties, challenged this new post-midnight safe harbor, because there didn't seem to be any data on such a safe zone. However, Congress intervened, and in the 1989 appropriations bill signed by President Reagan, the FCC was required to enforce a ban on indecent and obscene speech 24 hours a day. This was Congressional grandstanding—they knew such a full-time ban would never survive Court review, but they could look virtuous. Courts eventually did overturn the ban.

Further litigation continued well into the next decade with continually varying definitions of *safe harbor*. The FCC decided in 1993 to look at indecency from the other side; rather than addressing the issue of a safe harbor for questionable language, the FCC declared that it would enforce a safe harbor from 6 A.M. to 8 P.M., during which time indecency would not be aired. This left the later evening hours up for grabs, but the Commission still maintained a watch on complaints about indecency.

Elements of indecency evolved from topless radio to " shock jocks," disc jockeys and hosts who used shocking and titillating language to enhance their popularity, language and descriptions to which listeners had become more accustomed. Don Imus and Howard Stern were examples of this type of rawness, and unpredictability became popular. Stern, who proclaimed himself "King of all Media," often asked his guests about their sexual habits. References to women were generally about their sexual attributes. His female co-host was the object of frank discussions about sexual habits, and sometimes he would spank bikini-clad females. Radio leaves everything to the imagination, so it was difficult to determine whether it was the act on radio or the imagination of the listener that made things unacceptable.

Stern, who wrote books about his misadventures, and about whom a movie was made, remained unabashed about his boldness. It was this brash style that took him from one market to the many markets that carried him. As long as there was an audience to listen to his material, it appeared to be socially acceptable, even though most of his audience members were adolescent white males who chuckled at the suggestive material. He spoke of masturbation, incest, and the breast size of famous women, and he included segments on "bestiality dial-a-date." His antics caused him to be fined by the FCC on the basis of violating the federal statute prohibiting the use of obscene, indecent, or profane language on the air. His parent company, Infinity Broadcasting, fought the fines, and they remained in litigation for several years until Infinity moved for a deal to acquire other broadcast stations, a proposal that had to have FCC approval. An agreement was struck, and Infinity paid some of the fines incurred by Stern.

But the shock jock's language and antics continued to trouble some segments of listeners. One church group called for a widespread boycott of products advertised on Stern's shows. The advertisers found that their sales dropped; in turn, they dropped their advertising support of the radio personality. Occasionally, this infuriated Stern, who lashed out against such groups. His infamy was noted in the national press in the spring of 1999, when, while speaking of the shooting tragedy at Columbine High School, he indicated that the shooters were kind of stupid—they should have had sex with those girls before they took them out. This statement put Stern in a questionable light in the minds of many, but his program continued.

Specific challenges regarding the definition of indecency remained problematic. In the early 1990s, an album by the rap group 2 Live Crew, *As Nasty as They Wanna Be*, proved to be troublesome for many. It contained hundreds of sexual references and obscenities. Live performances of material from the album caused arrests of the group members. There was word that some stations tried to air the work, but no complaints ever reached the FCC, and no action was taken against 2 Live Crew by the FCC.

In Santa Barbara, a station licensed to the Regents of the University of California played sexually explicit lyrics in the recorded music "Making Bacon" by the Pork Dudes. A Pacifica station in Los Angeles played excerpts of the play *The Jerker*, about a homosexual dying of AIDS.

Although the story and theme were not found to be objectionable by the FCC, the extensive use of patently offensive language referring to sexual and excretory organs and functions caused the FCC to rule that the broadcast was indecent.

There is an ever-growing list of broadcasts that either have been or could be cited for the use of indecent language. The examples given previously illustrate the problems with definition and enforcement by the FCC.

Profanity can be equally offensive for some listeners, but judgments regarding profanity are highly subjective, and profanity is considered to have different levels of offensiveness as part of the artistic expression. Such complications make it difficult for the FCC to enforce the prohibition of "profane language." *Profanity* is "the use of irreverent or irreligious words, including cursing by invoking deity." In earlier generations, profanity was common but was usually confined to specific groups that would be tolerant of such words—not in "polite, mixed company" and certainly not in broadcasting.

Recently, profanity has become more common, perhaps because of its widespread use in movies. The FCC has viewed profanity as being judged from the perspective of the listener or viewer. Generally, the Commission will not bring action unless a speaker uses profanity so repeatedly in invoking a curse as to cause a public nuisance. So radio announcers and talk show hosts who occasionally invoke deity in a profane manner would not likely incur any action from the FCC. More recently, the use of profanity in everything from the language of some musical artists to prime-time television shows would make any enforcement of the profanity prohibition difficult. Indeed, one letter from a conservative watchdog group in the fall of 1999 about indecent language on network television received the reply from the FCC that as long as language was used "in context," there were no words that could be forbidden. It was a trend that concerned the more conservative observers.

A newer problem is the wide diversity of the media and the invisible nature of those media that are not really "broadcast" and are therefore not punishable under the indecency rule that applies only to "broadcast" language. For example, when one watches premium cable channels and sees R-rated movies with a plethora of obscene, indecent, and profane language, it is easy to get the idea that such language has become acceptable in broadcasting on radio and television. However, cable dissemination is another medium, not a broadcast entity. Although the distinction remains clear in the minds of regulators and enforcers, it may be less clear in the minds of consumers—listeners and viewers. Such popularizing of language once found taboo makes for mixed signals about the implementation of unlawful language in broadcasting.

Was there a legislative cure? In 1996 Congress passed the Communications Decency Act, seeking to protect minors from harmful material, specifically on the internet, but the Act included the term *transmission*, which could be construed to include broadcasting. The American Civil Liberties Union challenged the law on the basis that it violated First Amendment rights. The U.S. Supreme Court in 1997 ruled that the Act's provisions of "indecent transmission" and "patently offensive display" abridged the freedom of speech protected by the First Amendment; the ruling thus struck down the Communications Decency Act.

The convergence of broadcast, cable, and the internet has further confused the picture of exactly what constitutes "indecent, profane or obscene" language and when and under what circumstances such language may be broadcast or prohibited. As social mores change, so too will the laws and policies affecting materials seen in the media or heard on radio.

21st Century Confusion

Creating considerable controversy for much of the first decade of the 21st century was the FCC's seemingly inconsistent treatment of indecent programming on radio stations. Several conservative family values organizations encouraged thousands of people to file complaints about specific broadcasts. The issue was made more pointed for stations accused of violating commission indecency rules when in mid-2006 the fine for such transgressions was increased by Congress to $325,000 per incident (the FCC adopted rules to apply the new fines a year later). Among the criticisms directed toward commission actions was that the agency was not consistently following either legal precedents or its own rules in assessing fines. Several court decisions, some focused on television rather than radio, excoriated the FCC's failure to provide a rational basis for its departure from precedent.

Appeals finally reached the Supreme Court, which issued its conclusions in *Fox Television v. US* in mid-2009. The new decision upheld an FCC decision about a television broadcast, but was narrowly drawn, and did not supersede the *Pacifica v. FCC* (1978) case, which remained the overriding legal precedent for broadcast indecency cases. But further legal action in this controversial area is sure to develop.

See also: Censorship; First Amendment and Radio; Pacifica Foundation; "Seven Dirty Words" Case; Topless Radio; United States Supreme Court and Radio

Further Reading

Action for Children's Television v. FCC, 852 F2d 1332 (1988).
Broadcast Regulation (annual; published by the National Association of Broadcasters Legal Department).
Clark, Anne L., "As Nasty As They Wanna Be: Popular Music on Trial," *New York University Law Review* 65 (1990).
"FCC Takes Strong Stance on Enforcement of Prohibition against Obscene and Indecent Broadcasts," *FCC Fact Sheet* (November 1987).
FCC v. Pacifica Foundation, 438 US 726 (1978).
Federal Communications Commission, Media Bureau. "Fact Sheet: Obscene, Indecent and Profane Broadcasts", www.fcc.gov/cgb/consumerfacts/obscene.html
Federal Communications Commission, "Policy Statement: In the Matter of Industry Guidance on the Commission's Case Law Interpreting Policies Regarding Broadcast Indecency," Washington, D.C.: FCC (Release 01–90), 6 April 2001 (available on www.fcc.gov).
Ginsburg, Douglas H., *Regulation of Broadcasting: Law and Policy towards Radio, Television, and Cable Communications*, St. Paul, Minnesota: West, 1979; 3rd edition, as *Regulation of the Electronic Mass Media: Law and Policy for Radio, Television, Cable, and the New Video Technologies*, by Michael Botein, 1998.
Ginzburg v. U.S., 383 U.S. 463 (1966).
Hilliard, Robert L., and Michael C. Keith, *Dirty Discourse: Sex and Indecency in American Radio*, Ames: Iowa State University Press, 2003.
Infinity Broadcasting Corporation of Pennsylvania, 3 FCC Rcd 930 (1987).
Jacobellis v. Ohio, 378 U.S. 184 (1964).
LaFayette, Jon, "A Stern Challenge," *Electronic Media* (23 August 1993).
Limburg, Val E., "Obscenity: The Struggle for Definition," in *Mass Media and Society*, compiled by Alan Wells, Palo Alto, California: National Press Books, 1972; 4th edition, edited by Wells, Lexington, Massachusetts: Lexington Books, 1987.
Lipschultz, Jeremy Harris, *Broadcast Indecency: FCC Regulation and the First Amendment*, Boston: Focal Press, 1996.
Memoirs v. Massachusetts, 383 U.S. 413 (1966).
Miller v. California, 413 U.S. 1.5 (1973).
Redrup v. New York, 386 U.S. 767 (1967).
The Regents of the University of California, 2 FCC Rcd 2708 (1987).
Reno v. ACLU, 117 S. Ct. 2329 (1997).
Rivera-Sanchez, Milagros, "The Origins of the Ban on 'Obscene, Indecent, or Profane' Language of the Radio Act of 1927," *Journalism and Mass Communication Monographs* 149 (February 1995).
Roth v. U.S., 384 U.S. 476 (1957).
Smith, F. Leslie, Milan D. Meeske, and John W. Wright, II, *Electronic Media and Government: The Regulation of Wireless and Wired Mass Communication in the United States*, White Plains, New York: Longman, 1995.
Zoglin, Richard, "Shock Jock," *Time* (30 November 1992)

VAL E. LIMBURG,
2009 REVISIONS BY CHRISTOPHER H. STERLING

OFFICE OF RADIO RESEARCH
Applied Studies of Audiences

The Office of Radio Research was established in 1937 after the Rockefeller Foundation extended a two-year grant to Hadley Cantril, a psychologist at Princeton University (best remembered for his studies about the effects of Orson Welles' radio broadcast *Invasion from Mars*), and Frank Stanton, a recent psychology Ph.D. from Ohio State University who headed up research for the Columbia Broadcasting System (CBS) and ultimately directed the network as president from 1948 to 1971. The two researchers had proposed a series of studies to broaden the methods for assessing the impact of radio on the public, including the motivations for listening, radio's psychological value to the audience, and the role it played in their lives. Although they had envisioned extensive use of experimental methods, they chose as their research director an Austrian-trained psychologist, Paul Lazarsfeld, who proved to have a deep interest in applied research and methodological innovation. Lazarsfeld had come to the United States on a Rockefeller fellowship in 1933 and remained there after a protofascist government took power in Austria in 1934.

As associate directors, Cantril and Stanton oversaw the work of the office, but Lazarsfeld was in charge of its day-to-day operations, which were initially handled at an office in Newark where Lazarsfeld had already set up an applied social research center in conjunction with the University of Newark. As an intellectual alliance became firmly established between Stanton and Lazarsfeld, Cantril began to withdraw from the project, and the offices, still officially known as the Princeton Office of Radio Research, migrated in 1938 to New York City's Union Square. In 1939, Princeton severed its ties and the project was moved to Columbia University. Given the relatively limited amount of funding available, Lazarsfeld was forced to pursue a wide variety of audience studies, depending often on archival data previously gathered for Gallup polls and radio program audits as well as soliciting applied research projects from commercial organizations. Lazarsfeld was especially adept at secondary analysis of program ratings, with a particular focus on the social differences between the audiences of various programs, an approach that was nurtured by his European concern for social stratification.

In a successful attempt to win additional Rockefeller Foundation support, Lazarsfeld initiated plans to publish the research studies generated by his small staff. Twice, in 1939 and in 1940, he arranged for an entire issue of the *Journal of Applied Psychology* to be wholly devoted to radio research completed by the office; he was also responsible for a thematic compilation of studies in book form, titled *Radio and the Printed Page*, published in 1940. This tradition continued with three volumes of essays titled *Radio Research* that Lazarsfeld and Stanton jointly published in 1941, 1944, and 1949. The major proposal that Lazarsfeld put forth to ensure a three-year renewal of Rockefeller funding to begin in March 1940 was the idea of creating a study involving two large panels of radio listeners to be interviewed at intervals to assess their response to a sequence of radio broadcasts.

Initially, the research was to be centered on a radio program sponsored by the Department of Agriculture, but ultimately the panel design was implemented for a study of the impact of mass media on voting during the 1940 presidential campaign between Democrat Franklin Roosevelt, running for an unprecedented third term, and Wendell Willkie, a Republican utility executive. The unexpected results—only 54 out of 600 panel members shifted from their initial voting preferences between May and November—led Lazarsfeld and his colleagues, Bernard Berelson and Hazel Gaudet, to devise their theory of the two-step flow of communication effects, in which opinion leaders provide a critical interpersonal link between mass media messages and their intended audiences (*The People's Choice*, 1944, 1948).

In the decade of the 1940s, the office supported a number of studies that marked their authors as prominent innovators in communication research, including sociologist Robert Merton's study of Kate Smith's radio war bond campaign; Bernard Berelson's study of the effects of the 1945 New York City newspaper strike; and Herta Herzog's study of the motivations of women soap opera listeners using in-depth interviews, a precursor of focus group methodology. Joseph Klapper, who later headed audience research at CBS, completed his dissertation under Lazarsfeld's direction in 1949. A revised version published in 1960, *The Effects of Mass Communication*, forcefully argued against the notion of powerful mass media. Lazarsfeld also invited fellow European émigrés to the office. Film theorist Rudolf Arnheim analyzed the dramatic content of soap operas, and critical theorist Theodor Adorno studied the role of popular and classical music, although Adorno was uncomfortable with Lazarsfeld's quantitative techniques.

Key to the success of the office may have been the relationship between Lazarsfeld and Stanton.

Lazarsfeld was ever mindful that he needed the confidence of the broadcast industry to acquire access to the data it gathered as well as political support, but he also realized that he had to persuade executives that studies with negative or unorthodox findings might nevertheless help them better understand and run their industry. Stanton not only had financial resources at CBS to fill in funding gaps at the office, but he was an ally who shared Lazarsfeld's commitment to innovative research techniques. Their joint development of what was called the Lazarsfeld-Stanton Program Analyzer reflected their shared zeal. This device, used both at the office and at CBS studios, allowed the simultaneous recording of the individual opinions of a test audience. Ten listeners at a time could indicate when they liked or disliked the program they were hearing. Such an instant audience analysis machine would be replicated 40 years later using networked personal computers.

Curiously, the Office of Radio Research benefited as well from the social and technological disruptions occasioned by the outbreak of World War II in Europe and by the United States' eventual entry into the conflict. The Rockefeller Foundation's support of radio research was motivated in no small part by a concern about the uses of radio programming for propaganda in wartime. And when America found itself at war, social psychologist Samuel Stouffer, who headed research for the U.S. Army, pursued some of his projects using Lazarsfeld's personnel and even the office's program analyzer. Finally, the exigencies of the wartime economy interrupted the development of commercial television in the United States, artificially extending radio's dominant role in American life.

The vitality of broadcast radio and the importance of this wartime research no doubt aided Lazarsfeld in his quest to fully integrate the office into the structure of Columbia University as a research unit in the graduate school. This he achieved in 1945, shortly after renaming his hybrid organization for academic, governmental, and commercial research the Bureau of Applied Social Research. It is unclear whether the name change was an attempt to achieve academic legitimacy, to broaden its research mission, or both, but by the time the bureau celebrated its 20th anniversary in 1957, it had effectively abandoned commercial broadcasting as a focus of study.

See also: Audience Research Methods; Education about Radio

535

Further Reading

Delia, Jesse G., "Communication Research: A History," in *Handbook of Communication Science*, edited by Charles R. Berger and Steven H. Chaffee, Beverly Hills, California, and London: Sage, 1987.

Lazarsfeld, Paul F., editor, "Radio Research and Applied Psychology," *The Journal of Applied Psychology* 23:1 (special issue, February 1939).

Lazarsfeld, Paul F., *Radio and the Printed Page: An Introduction to the Study of Radio and Its Role in the Communication of Ideas*, New York: Duell, Sloan, and Pearce, 1940; reprint, New York: Arno Press, 1971.

Lazarsfeld, Paul F., "An Episode in the History of Social Research: A Memoir," in *The Intellectual Migration: Europe and America, 1930–1960*, edited by Donald Fleming and Bernard Bailyn, Cambridge, Massachusetts: Harvard University Press, 1968; expanded edition, 1969.

Lazarsfeld, Paul F., and Frank N. Stanton, editors, *Radio Research, 1941*, New York: Duell, Sloan, and Pearce, 1941.

Lazarsfeld, Paul F., and Frank N. Stanton, editors, *Radio Research, 1942–43*, New York: Duell, Sloan, and Pearce, 1944.

Lazarsfeld, Paul F., and Frank N. Stanton, editors, *Communication Research, 1948–49*, New York: Harper, 1949.

Merton, Robert K., *Mass Persuasion: The Social Psychology of a War Bond Drive*, New York and London: Harper, 1946.

Schramm, Wilbur, *The Beginnings of Communication Study in America: A Personal Memoir*, edited by Steven H. Chaffee and Everett M. Rogers, Thousand Oaks, California, and London: Sage, 1997.

Sills, David L., "Stanton, Lazarsfeld, and Merton—Pioneers in Communication Research," in *American Communication Research: The Remembered History*, edited by Everette E. Dennis and Ellen Wartella, Mahwah, New Jersey: Erlbaum, 1996

SETH FINN

OFFICE OF WAR INFORMATION
World War II Government Agency

The Office of War Information (OWI) was intended to be the primary voice of the United States government during World War II. It cleared government radio programs and provided background information on the war for use by broadcasters and periodical publishers.

Origins

The Office of War Information began its life as a response by President Franklin D. Roosevelt to the petty sniping and conflicting reports released by rival government information agencies. Established on 13 June 1942 the mission of the Office of War Information was described in Executive Order 9182, as "the facilitation of the development of an informed and intelligent understanding, at home and abroad, of the status and progress of the war effort, and of the war policies, activities, and aims of the Government." The OWI's domestic branch was formed by combining all or parts of three existing entities: the Office of Facts and Figures, the Office of Government Reports, and the Information Division of the Office of Economic Stabilization, whereas its foreign or overseas branch was created from the existing Foreign Information Service of the Office of the Coordinator of Information. The OWI soon expanded its scope beyond the duties of the agencies it replaced, moving into production and policy along with information dissemination.

Although similar to its predecessors in function, the OWI was envisioned initially as having greater authority than the agencies it replaced. But Roosevelt refrained from giving the OWI the necessary teeth to accomplish the task at hand. Many federal departments still had their own information units, and the OWI's authority allowed it only to coordinate their various activities. It could suggest whether a given piece of information should be released or withheld, but it had no recourse if other agencies ignored their advice. Thus, in practice, the OWI had no more real authority than the agencies it replaced had exercised.

Structure of the OWI

Appointed to head the OWI was journalist and former CBS radio commentator Elmer Davis, who as director was to be involved in larger policy issues both at home and abroad. The choice was hailed almost universally in all quarters, for his radio work had given Davis a reputation for honesty and common sense. His associate director was Milton Eisenhower, a former official of the Department of Agriculture. Eisenhower was appointed specifically to handle administrative matters, as Davis had no experience in that area.

Former Office of Facts and Figures head Archibald MacLeish assumed the post of Assistant Director for Policy Development and reported directly to Davis' office. MacLeish's office served as a think tank of sorts for policy questions, which were then referred (with recommendations) to Davis for final action.

The two branch heads for domestic and foreign operations were next in the hierarchy. Robert Sherwood, noted play-wright (*Abe Lincoln in Illinois*) and one-time Republican who became speechwriter and advisor for Franklin Roosevelt, was chosen as Administrative Director for Overseas Operations. Moderate Midwestern publisher and radio station owner Gardner "Mike" Cowles, Jr., was appointed Assistant Director for Domestic Operations.

Foreign Branch Activities: The Voice of America

The difference in the titles of Sherwood and Cowles was no accident. Sherwood, the former head of the Foreign Information Service of the Office of the Coordinator of Information, had centered his burgeoning operation in New York, not Washington, and much of its later work was actually based in England. Davis and Eisenhower had no experience in international affairs, and much of their time would later be spent trying to smooth the ruffled feathers of "a new and often cantankerous staff on the one hand, and dissatisfied executive departments on the other." From the outset Sherwood and the overseas branch maintained a level of autonomy and distance from its superiors (and from congressional criticism) that the domestic branch could not duplicate.

The Voice of America (VOA), the radio service of the overseas branch, was created in the belief that the U.S. was lagging behind both the Germans and the British in the use of radio as a tool of war. Originally part of the Foreign Information Service, its formation predates that of the OWI by several months. John Houseman, a theatrical and radio producer best known for his collaboration with Orson Welles, was appointed by Sherwood to head the Voice of America. Under his leadership, the Voice, as it was known, was a bastion of liberalism. Its sound was unique, making use of agit-prop and experimental radio and theater techniques to communicate its views. Organized on the principal of language desks (much like the shortwave operations of the BBC), the VOA became a haven for expatriates from every nation under Nazi occupation. As a part of the foreign branch, the VOA exercised direct control not only over its programming but eventually over its broadcast facilities, acquiring the use of all 14 of the existing short-wave outlets in the U.S. by early 1943.

Under Houseman, the VOA played an important role in defending America against criticism for the lack of a second front during the dark days before the tide of war had turned. By the summer of 1943, however, as victory began to appear likely for the Allies, the liberal propaganda style of Houseman and his staff gave way to a less dramatic, more journalistic approach, one meant not to rouse people to action but to inform. This trend accelerated after Houseman and many of his adherents

left the VOA. Military news took precedence over the political, and anything smacking overtly of propaganda was dropped (on the principle that those living under Nazi occupation had heard enough of it already). This approach continues to be effective for the VOA to this day.

Domestic Branch Activities

At its peak, the OWI's domestic branch had its finger in nearly every aspect of the war effort, to the dismay of its critics, and scores of federal agencies cleared information through it daily. This broad reach was not to last, however.

In a democracy, a domestic government propaganda operation cannot help but be slightly suspect, even in wartime, so it is surprising that OWI homefront activities went unchallenged as long as they did. Elmer Davis had been on the job a little more than a year before the dam broke. During the spring and summer of 1943 a congressional coalition of Republicans and conservative Democrats attacked the agency, accusing it and its director of using its resources to work for the re-election of Roosevelt in 1944. The fact that its director had been a frequent critic of congressional Republicans before leaving CBS for the OWI made the situation even worse. Davis fought a losing battle with Congress over the organization's domestic activities and budget, even threatening to resign. By the time the situation had eased somewhat in late June, domestic operating expenditures had been trimmed to $2.75 million, a meager amount compared to the $24-million budget approved for the overseas branch. The appropriation was just enough, Davis mused, to avoid "the odium of having put us out of business, and carefully not enough to let us accomplish much." As it was, the cuts forced closings of regional offices around the country. The motion picture production and publishing arms ceased to exist, and much of the responsibility formerly held by the OWI was lost to other government agencies or returned to private-sector entities such as the Advertising Council. As a result, the OWI's domestic operations became precisely those of the "coordinating super-agency" that had been decried.

One of the few domestic activities not drastically reduced in scope was OWI placement of government messages on radio programs and stations, both national and local. As all time was "donated" (participation was mandatory), expenses were minimal. The system put in place to organize this effort was devised and managed by the staff of the OWI Radio Bureau.

The Radio Bureau

According to a preliminary inventory of the files of the OWI, published by the U.S. Government Printing Office in 1952, the Radio Bureau "reviewed, cleared and approved all proposed radio programs sponsored by Government agencies and served as a central point of contact and clearance for other agencies in other relationships with the radio broadcasting and advertising industries." It also "obtained the use of radio programs with a known audience," and "kept the radio industry informed of the relative importance of the many requests for contribution of free time for Government programs."

Within the bureau were various divisions, each with its own specific area of concentration. These included the Government Liaison Division, the Program Services Division, and the Industry Relations Division. The most important, however, was the Allocation Division. Its primary function was the management of the seven "facilities plans," four providing for the orderly inclusion of "action"-oriented messages (those requiring activity on the part of the listening audience, such as "Don't Buy Black Market Meat") and three plans devoted to communicating war-related "background" information (messages which were meant to educate the American people about why they were fighting and what they were fighting for). The seven facilities plans administered by the Allocation Division were developed to "better insure effective, well planned dissemination of all war information (exclusive of war news) via radio."

First and most extensive among the more specific "action" plans was the Network Allocation Plan. The primary goals of this plan included a "determination as to what needs were paramount and deserved priority," an "orderly allocation and distribution of needs over the radio network structure," and a "wise distribution of war messages which would not surfeit audience and harm established listening habits." To accomplish these tasks, an elaborate bureaucracy was developed linking the four national networks, the various national sponsors, and the program-producing advertising agencies to the OWI Radio Bureau's Allocation Division in Washington, D.C. Under this plan every network program classified as entertainment would carry such information as the Allocation Division provided. Shows broadcasting weekly were required to include a message once every month, whereas those airing more frequently, such as the many soap operas of the day, were expected to air two such messages in the same period. Schedules were designed to prevent audience overexposure to any one campaign,

and many radio campaigns could be run simultaneously owing to the large number of programs available for use.

Copies of all OWI allocation directives concerning a specific program were sent to each of the parties involved. The networks appointed OWI liaisons for both sponsored and sustaining programming, whereas sponsors usually delegated the job to someone in their advertising department (often the manager himself). These communications to sponsor and the network-sponsored program liaison were just courtesies, however, as the bulk of radio's creative work at this time was carried on in the radio departments of advertising agencies around the country (though mostly in New York, Chicago, and Hollywood). These agencies were hired by the sponsor to handle every facet of a show, from conception to production. It was through the likes of Kenyon & Eckhardt, Lord & Thomas, BBD&O, and J. Walter Thompson that the government's information truly flowed to the ears of the American people.

OWI information was distributed in the form of a fact sheet that contained the information to be stressed in a program's scheduled allocation. This, along with a cover letter listing the name of the program it was for and the projected date of broadcast, was sent to the ad agency's OWI liaison, usually a staffer in the agency's radio division. Once the information reached the hands of the program's writers, its treatment was completely up to them. Participation was viewed as mandatory, and Radio Bureau staffers monitored broadcasts to verify that assigned allocations had been carried, judging them according to perceived effectiveness at the same time.

The Station Announcement Plan and National Spot Plan were similar in form and function to the Network Allocation Plan but targeted independent stations, syndicated and local sports programming, and other non-network fare.

The final plan in the action group was the Station Live Program Plan, which was under the control of the various OWI Regional Radio Directors who, working with local stations, would try to produce one-shot war programs with more of a hometown flavor. The OWI promoted the importance of a local character coming through over the air so that people would feel more connected to the war effort.

The first of the background information plans was the Feature Series plan. This plan, proposed jointly by the four national networks, called for a "series of network programs embracing background issues of the war which cannot be fully dclineated by radio in any other way." The focus was "not on the progress of the war, and not on the things the citizen must do to help win the war, but on the things the citizen must know and understand about the war effort in order wholeheartedly to play his part during the war and in the establishment of a just and lasting peace."

The next background plan made use of existing network programming in much the same way as the Network Allocation Plan did, but shows on the Special Assignment Plan were those that volunteered their time and talent "over and above" the requirements already set by the Network Allocation Plan. These programs developed a stronger relationship with OWI and were given more personal treatment by the Radio Bureau, along with tremendous access to government facilities and resources.

The final background plan was the Station Transcription Plan, which consisted of "transcribed war programs produced for station use by government agencies." Stations could receive programs upon request. The two main programs offered were *The Treasury Star Parade* (in cooperation with the Treasury Department), which was a three-a-week series, and the OWI's own show, *Uncle Sam*, a five-a-week "strip."

It is not possible to truly gauge the overall importance of radio as a tool of government information dissemination during World War II, even from the vantage point of more than a half-century later. Still, despite the difficulties inherent in its task, the OWI was correct to let radio do the job at home with a minimum of government interference, and in many ways it was a success story of amazing proportions. Some expressed alarm at the use of advertising techniques in the service of the war effort, but a great deal of important government information was communicated effectively to the nation's civilian population using the familiar forms of radio advertising. Though it is hard to isolate radio's impact from other media, its role as a common focal point of American life undeniably helped foster a unity of purpose among those on the home front that may not otherwise have existed. That the work of the former radio arm of the overseas branch, the Voice of America, goes on to this day is an indication of its perceived effectiveness. Though World War II and the Cold War have ended, the VOA continues to serve the foreign policy goals of the United States, broadcasting 900 hours of programming each week in 53 languages.

See also: Politics and Radio; Shortwave Radio; World War II and U.S. Radio

Further Reading

The records of the Office of War Information comprise Record Group 208 of the National Archives.

Burlingame, Roger, *Don't Let Them Scare You: The Life and Times of Elmer Davis*, Philadelphia, Pennsylvania: Lipincott, 1961.

Dryer, Sherman Harvard, *Radio in Wartime*, New York: Greenberg, 1942.

Kirby, Edward Montague, and Jack W. Harris, *Star Spangled Radio*, Chicago: Ziff-Davis, 1948.

Koppes, Clayton R., and Gregory D. Black, *Hollywood Goes to War: How Politics, Profits, and Propaganda Shaped World War II Movies*, New York: Free Press, and London: Collier-Macmillan, 1987.

Shulman, Holly Cowan, *The Voice of America: Propaganda and Democracy, 1941–1945*, Madison: University of Wisconsin Press, 1990.

Steele, Richard, "Preparing the Public for War: Efforts to Establish a National Propaganda Agency, 1940–1941," *American Historical Review* 75 (1970).

Weinberg, Sydney, "What to Tell America: The Writers Quarrel in the OWI," *Journal of American History* 55 (1968).

Winkler, Allan M., *The Politics of Propaganda: The Office of War Information, 1942–1945*, New Haven, Connecticut: Yale University Press, 1978

CHUCK HOWELL

OLDIES FORMAT

The original Oldies radio format featured the greatest pop music hits of the 1950s and 1960s. The format was created in the early 1970s and initially targeted the musical tastes of the 18- to 34-year-old "baby boomers." The format still targets baby boomers today, although they are now predominantly 35–54. This audience was the first generation to grow up with rock and roll. The format's core artists include such 1950s standouts as Elvis Presley, Chuck Berry, Buddy Holly, and the Everly Brothers and 1960s superstars such as the Beatles, Supremes, Beach Boys, and Four Seasons.

The Oldies format was based on a segmentation strategy that targeted older Top 40 listeners. Top 40 was the first radio format to target a young audience, and from its inception in the late 1950s through the late 1960s, it was virtually the only younger-appeal format. When musical styles changed in the late 1960s and early 1970s, a certain portion of the Top 40 audience ceased to relate to the current style of popular music. This disenfranchisement created a format void that was ultimately filled by the creation of the Oldies format.

Top 40 stations play mostly current hits, with a few oldies thrown in each hour. For Oldies stations, the entire focus is on 1950s and 1960s oldies, although some first-generation Oldies stations occasionally played current hits, calling them "Future Gold." This practice was dropped when Oldies stations discovered that their audience didn't want to hear current music, not even one song an hour. Research showed the audience wanted Oldies music exclusively, and this exclusivity became the format's most powerful listener benefit. The success of this appeal was the genesis for the format's most popular positioning statement, "All Oldies. All The Time."

The Oldies format was a natural, evolutionary outgrowth of Top 40 radio. Consequently, it was shaped by the same cultural factors that affected our society at that time. In the 1950s and 1960s America was a "mass market" society. There were few media choices. Most markets had one or two daily newspapers; three network TV stations (American Broadcasting Company [ABC], Columbia Broadcasting System [CBS], and National Broadcasting Company [NBC]); and a handful of AM radio stations. (FM stations didn't gain significant listening levels until the mid-1970s.)

Because of the limited media choices, media (and virtually all other consumer offerings) were targeted to the mass audience. Most radio stations were programmed to appeal to a broad, adult audience. When the Top 40 format was created, it too was programmed to a wide demographic target audience that ranged in age from subteens to people in their 30s and 40s. Therefore, Top 40 music of the day was an amalgam of many tastes and styles and represented a variety of music, including such divergent artists as Fats Domino; Percy Faith; Peter, Paul, and Mary; The Singing Nun; Roger Miller; Herman's Hermits; Dean Martin; James Brown; Cream; and others. This diversity of musical styles is reflected in the playlists of today's Oldies stations.

The first stations involved in the development of the Oldies format included Westinghouse's WIND-AM in Chicago; CBS FM's WCAU-FM in Philadelphia; and the station that became the format's standard bearer, CBS FM's flagship station, WCBS-FM in New York City. Other early Oldies stations included KRTH-FM in Los Angeles, WFYR-FM in Chicago, and KOOL-FM in Phoenix.

The early success of WCBS-FM was notable for two reasons. First, the station operated in the spotlight of the nation's largest market, and anything of consequence that happened in the number-one market made news. Second, it was an FM station that was beginning to get noticeable ratings at a time when the overwhelming majority of all listening still occurred on the AM band.

WCBS-FM's success had a major impact on the format. Radio operators surmised, "If WCBS-FM can pull a three-share in New York City, with all of the stations in that market, imagine what we can pull in ours." What they discovered, in most cases, was that their Oldies station also was able to pull a three-share, which was indicative of the format's appeal at that time.

Oldies was viewed as a niche format. It had a small, loyal audience but was not considered a format that would make a station a market leader. Most Oldies stations were operated on that premise. Generally, they tended to be on the AM dial with inferior signals (at a time when radio listening was increasingly focused on the FM dial). Most ran network or syndicated programming that was not local, they weren't promoted or marketed, and they were low-cost operations with modest profit goals. There were some notable exceptions, but for the most part the radio industry perceived Oldies to be a second-tier format. Like many beliefs, this had the possibility of becoming a self-fulfilling prophecy. As the radio industry did not believe Oldies could deliver big ratings, it did not invest resources in the format, and thus the format did not grow.

This perception lasted until the mid-1980s, when two major broadcasting companies began achieving big ratings with their Oldies properties. Shamrock Broadcasting's WWSW-AM-FM in Pittsburgh, KXKL-FM in Denver, and WFOX-FM in Atlanta and Sconnix Broadcasting's WQSR-FM in Baltimore and WMXJ-FM in Miami served as pivotal success stories that forced the industry to re-evaluate Oldies as a format. These two companies asked the question, "What would happen if you treated an Oldies station like you would any other station? What would happen if you offered local programming, hired programming consultants, did local research, invested heavily in programming and marketing, and—most important—offered the format on FM?" From the late 1980s to the mid-1990s, market after market saw the emergence of a new FM Oldies competitor. Today, Oldies is considered a major radio format, and in virtually every large and medium market, and in most smaller markets, listeners can find at least one station that specializes in it.

See also: Classic Rock Format; Rock and Roll Format

Further Reading

Jack, Wolfman, *Have Mercy: Confessions of the Original Rock 'n' Roll Animal,* New York: Warner Bros., 1995.
Sklar, Rick, *Rocking America: How the All-Hit Radio Stations Took Over,* New York: St. Martin's Press, 1984.

E. Alvin Davis

OLD-TIME RADIO

Broadcast audio programming has been collected by both institutions and interested individuals and most recently has become a battleground of interests. Central to the ability to collect such programs, of course, was the development of a means to make permanent recordings. Broadcasters from the beginning of radio needed some way to record. Initially the only means for recording was cutting a disc. Western Electric had developed the 16-inch, 33 1/3-rpm recording disc for use as the sound tracks for early 1920 "talkies." Sound-on-Film (SOF) optical tracks did not follow until later. The same medium was used in radio to record programs, usually for archiving, but sometimes for program syndication to multiple markets. Those Electrical Transcriptions (ETs) that survived were preserved by sponsors, their advertising agencies, the talent on the shows, and some broadcast engineers.

Beginnings of Programming Collecting

The Library of Congress began to collect and preserve some programming in 1949 in its role as the U.S. copyright depository. The National Archives also collected and preserved programming from governmental sources and increasingly received donated event and news materials from stations and networks. Institutional archives are as variable as the institutions preserving the available material. Funding difficulties led the UCLA Film and Television Archive to concentrate on their film collection and discontinue the development of its radio archive, which consisted of 50,000 ETs and 10,000 tapes of radio dating from 1933 to 1983 (which the Archive still retains). The Milo Ryan Phonoarchive at the University of Washington, obtained from radio station KIRO, consisted of CBS programming from 1938 to 1962. These ETs were subsequently transferred to the National Archives. Material became available as people gained access to more ETs as radio stations began disposing of their stored material and donations were made to institutions. A large source of material was recordings that had been made for Armed Forces Radio to bring radio programs to U.S. troops during World War II. Those ETs that survived and a few network and syndicated discs comprised the basis for collectors in the sixties, when radio as it had been was almost gone. From these and other sources ETs were transferred to audiotape.

Serious collecting of radio programs by individuals was the result of the introduction of home reel-to-reel tape recording decks to the consumer market around 1950. Small groups formed to exchange material, information, and sources on both the East and West coasts. A number of clubs began to trade tapes, the earliest being the Radio Collectors of America. Some of these grew into large organizations of members who gathered and traded from their shared collections, such as the North American Radio Archive (NARA) and the Society to Preserve and Encourage Radio Drama, Variety and Comedy (SPERDVAC). In 1954 Charles Michelson developed a rebroadcast market by obtaining an umbrella agreement to license *The Shadow* to individual radio stations, long-playing record manufacturers, and producers of home-enjoyment tapes. The first aggressively marketed private dealer was J. David Goldin, a former engineer at CBS, NBC, and Mutual, who formed "Radio Yesteryear" and an album subsidiary, "Radiola," in the late 1960s. Michelson began to send "cease and desist" letters to collectors selling any of the series he had licensed.

Newsletters about radio program collecting began to circulate in the late 1960s. The most influential, which set the standard, was "Radio Dial" by the *Radio Historical Society of America* founded by Charles Ingersoll. Carrying on the tradition, the leading newsletter today is "Hello Again" by Jay Hickerson, which began publication in 1970 and tied together more than 100 of the most active collectors at that time. Today, more than 160 active collectors hold the mass of privately collected broadcast material available, but thousands of other collectors maintain some program recordings. No-one knows how many shows survive, but 150,000 or more are documented as existing in Jay Hickerson's *Ultimate History of Network Radio Programming*, which is an attempt to catalog every radio program currently circulating. The publications of *Radio's Golden Age* in 1966 and its updated revision as *The Big Broadcast 1920–1950* in 1973 by Frank Buxton and Gary Owen also increased interest in old radio programs.

Despite the interest of individual private collectors and the growth of institutional archives, the preservation of radio programming faces a crisis stemming from a combination of concerns. The most basic problem is the increasing rate of disposal and destruction of material. The way programs have been recorded—electrical transcription to tape formats—poses problems for preservationists. As transcription turntables disappear and reel-to-reel tape recorders are replaced with cassette recorders (and cassette recorders replaced with CD players), the means for playing the available material is lost or exists only in museums. The need to transfer the older formats into new formats is a time consuming and costly process. Many radio programs have been made available over the world wide web in the downloadable MP3 format, free to anyone with a computer and an internet connection. Some collectors sell home-recorded CDs on their own websites, with as many as 50 or more shows on a single disc. There are numerous sites on the internet dealing with Old-Time Radio (OTR).

Copyrighting and Collecting

Another problem is one of copyright ownership and control. As the nostalgia market for old radio programming has developed, copyright owners became more interested in protecting their copyrights. Ownership of many programs is very complex and depends on contracts with directors, writers, performers, and rights holders of music and other materials used in the broadcasts. Private collectors who charge for duplication or sell programs are more susceptible to copyright problems than are institutions. Under certain conditions specified in the copyright law, libraries and other archives are authorized to photocopy or make other reproductions for research and teaching. However, Congress, through changes in the current copyright law, has placed most old radio programs under copyright even though they aired 75 years ago. Although sound recordings could not be copyrighted until 1972, the underlying script could be copyrighted as an "unpublished work." If producers registered copyrights and then failed to renew them, the script and the show are in the public domain.

Broadcasting Old Radio Programs

Though a multitude of websites now allow OTR to be easily downloaded (often for free) and tapes and CDs of shows are now widely available for over-the-counter purchase (or via eBay), there still exist many outlets that regularly broadcast examples of old-time radio.

The Big Broadcast, hosted by long-time radio man Ed Walker, was by 2009 being broadcast Sunday evenings over WAMU in Washington, D.C., having been on the air since 1964.

Originally hosted by John Hickman, who ran the program until 1990 when Walker took over, it is the longest-running program in that station's history. Broadcaster Lee Michael, drawing on his vast personal collection of OTR, hosts *The Radio Show* every week over KONA in Kennewick, WA. His program, which is also available over the internet via the Olde Tyme Radio Network, has been airing,

in various incarnations, since 2003. And Chuck Schaden has hosted his Chicago-area broadcast *Those Were the Days* since 1970; it is heard over WDCB and streamed on the web.

Finally, the nationally syndicated *When Radio Was* was the creation of radio entrepreneur Carl Armani and his company Radio Spirits. Armani hosted the program's original incarnation; Art Fleming took over in January of 1990, when the show began syndication. The program has changed ownership several times and has frequently changed hosts as well—past hosts have included Stan Freberg and Chuck Schaden. By 2009 its host was Greg Bell, and the program was heard nightly over 200 stations and online. Syndicated on weeknights was the USA Radio Network's *Golden Age of Radio Theatre* hosted by Vic Ives. Via satellite and internet streaming, Bill Bragg's *Yesterday USA* was an OTR-devoted audio offshoot of Bragg's Texas-based National Museum of Communications.

See also: Copyright; Museums and Archives of Radio; Recording and Studio Equipment

Further Reading

Bensman, Marvin, "Radio Broadcast Programming for Research and Teaching," *Journal of Radio Studies* 1, no. 1 (1992).

Cox, Jim, *This Day in Network Radio: A Daily Calendar of Births, Deaths, Debuts, Cancellations and other Events in Broadcasting History.* Jefferson, North Carolina: McFarland, 2008.

Dunning, John, *Tune in Yesterday: The Ultimate Encyclopedia of Old-Time Radio, 1925–1976*, Englewood Cliffs, New Jersey: Prentice-Hall, 1976; revised edition, as *On the Air: The Encyclopedia of Old-Time Radio*, New York: Oxford University Press, 1998.

Godfrey, Donald, editor, *Re-Runs on File: A Directory of Broadcast Archives*, Hillsdale, New Jersey: Erlbaum, 1992.

Hickerson, Jay, *The Ultimate History of Network Radio Programming and Guide to All Circulating Shows*, 2nd edition, Hamden, Connecticut: J. Hickerson, 1992.

Ryan, Milo, *History of Sound: A Descriptive Listing of the KIRO-CBS Collection of Broadcasts of the World War II Years*, Seattle: University of Washington Press, 1963.

Siegel, Susan, and David S. Siegel, *A Resource Guide to the Golden Age of Radio: Special Collections, Bibliography and the Internet.* Yorktown Heights, New York: Book Hunter Press, 2006.

Swartz, Jon D., and Robert Reinehr, *Handbook of Old-Time Radio: A Comprehensive Guide to Golden Age Radio Listening and Collecting*, Metuchen, New Jersey: Scarecrow Press, 1993.

MARVIN BENSMAN,
2009 REVISIONS BY CARY O'DELL

ONE MAN'S FAMILY
Serial Drama

Created by one of broadcasting's neglected auteurs, Carlton E. Morse, *One Man's Family* was radio's most acclaimed and popular primetime serial drama. Relating the multigenerational saga of the Barbours, an upper middle-class family in San Francisco, *One Man's Family* aired 3,256 episodes from 1932 to 1959, making it the longest uninterrupted narrative in the history of American radio. With an opening dedication to "the mothers and fathers of the younger generation and to their bewildering offspring," *One Man's Family* reflected the aspirations and tensions of the American family over three decades.

Morse imbued *One Man's Family* with a novelistic aura. He modeled his series on *The Forsyte Saga*, John Galsworthy's sprawling study of an aristocratic family in late Victorian and Edwardian England. To underscore the literary parallel, Morse divided his series into "books" and "chapters," which were announced at the beginning of each show. The final program closed the run at Chapter 30 of Book 134. The artistic trappings help give *One's Man's Family* a critical legitimacy, making it seem more than soap opera, closer to literature. Much of the critical discourse about the program echoed Gerald Nachman's assessment that the serial "was emblematic of America's ongoing faith in the home as the savior of the nation and the wellspring of its spiritual strength."

A Morse Creation

Louisiana-born Carlton Morse studied drama at the University of California at San Francisco, where he first became intrigued with the city that would take hold of his imagination. After struggling as a journalist, he joined the staff of KGO, the San Francisco radio affiliate of NBC two weeks before the stock market crash of 1929. He began writing scripts for the series *House of Myths* and later wrote for such mystery programs as *Chinatown Tales* and *Split-Second Tales*. He gained a reputation for his "blood and thunder" scripts, including "Dead Man Prowl" and "City of Dead," first heard on NBC *Mystery Serial* and later revived for the syndication series *Adventures by Morse* in the 1940s. Morse also crafted plays based on the files of the San Francisco Police Department for *Barbary Coasts Nights*.

Concerned about increasing juvenile delinquency after World War I, Morse turned his back on the action genre and developed a series that would affirm family bonds. Serving as both producer and director, he chose many young actors with whom he worked at the university and at *Mystery Serial* for a new program that would emphasize relationships over plot. *One Man's Family* debuted on 29 April 1932 as a 13-week trial on NBC's San Francisco, Los Angeles, and Seattle stations. Broadcast weekly from the NBC radio studios at 111 Sutter Street in San Francisco, the program was aired in May to the full West Coast lineup of stations and one year later was carried nationwide, becoming the first program based in the West to be heard regularly in the East.

One Man's Family quickly attained commercial viability. In 1934 Penn Tobacco became a regular sponsor for a year, soon replaced by Standard Brands for the next 14 years. With a half-hour Wednesday evening slot and an increasingly devoted audience, the production moved to Hollywood in 1937. *One Man's Family* achieved its highest rating during the 1939–40 season when it was on on Sunday evenings following the Jack Benny and Edgar Bergen/Charlie McCarthy comedy programs, and ranked among the top five programs in the nation. In September 1949 there was such a public outcry when Standard Brands dropped the series that NBC sustained it until another advertiser could be found. Miles Laboratories became the sponsor in June 1950 and reorganized *One Man's Family* as a daily quarter-hour program. When the series ended on 8 May 1959, Morse mourned its passing with a note to the *Los Angeles Times:* "The signposts for sound family life are now few, and I feel the loss of *One Man's Family* is just another abandoned lighthouse."

The Ensemble

One Man's Family was immediately recognized for its unprecedented realism. Morse's relationship with his cast was partly responsible for the program's authenticity. Morse wrote the scripts with the personal quirks of each actor in mind, and the ensemble responded by sticking with the program for years. When it ended in 1959, many actors were still playing roles that they had originated decades before. J. Anthony Smythe starred as the patriarch Henry Barbour, the crusty, conservative stockbroker, for the entire run of the series. Minetta Lane continued as Fanny Barbour, the patient mother of five children, until 1955, as did Michael Raffetto who held forth as the eldest son Paul, a battle scarred veteran who became the trusted moral center of the family. Page Gilman, the son of NBC vice president Don Gilman, joined the cast as a 15-year-old playing the youngest son Jack and stayed to the cancellation. When Barton Yarborough, who played the mercurial son Clifford, died suddenly in 1951, his character was written out of the script.

The inaugural episode began with a household of seven; by the end of the run the extended family totaled more than 90. The storylines unfolded slowly and realistically, dealing with such traditional serial subjects as romance, marriage, children, and divorce. Morse tried to capture the rhythms of daily life by listening to his actors and the audience. When the actress Bernice Berwin, who played the eldest daughter Hazel, was pregnant, so was her character. Although much of the domestic action centered on the large family home in the wealthy community of Sea Cliff near the Golden State Bridge and their weekend retreat at Sky Ranch, the well-off Barbours were also affected by national events, especially World War II, which threatened the lives of several leading characters. The tragic heroine of the program, Claudia, was lost at sea when Germans torpedoed her ship, a situation constructed by Morse to allow actress Kathleen Wilson to leave the series and raise her own family. Listeners became so upset that their impetuous and star-crossed Claudia was presumably dead, that Morse revived the role with another actress, Barbara Fuller, who stayed until the end of the series.

Impact

One Man's Family became a national ritual as millions of Americans embraced the Barbour family as their own. Many collectibles were marketed to the ardent fans, including cookbooks, diaries, and family albums. Radio satirists Bob and Ray parodied this sentimental side of the series with their look at the "Butcher family" in *One Feller's Family*. Standard Brands and its advertising company J. Walter Thompson were so pleased with the success of *One Man's Family* that they asked Morse to create another radio series. Morse returned to his action roots and conceived *I Love a Mystery*, which employed many of *One Man's Family* regulars. Morse adapted his family serial to television several times. *One Man's Family* was presented first in 1949 as a weekly prime-time series on NBC. Lasting three years, the live, half-hour television version started the Barbour story practically from the beginning, almost where it began decades before on radio. Consequently, none of the radio stars were asked to participate. This first video adaptation is notable because it featured a young Eva Marie Saint as the adventurous Claudia with Tony Randall and Mercedes McCambridge in lesser roles.

Again starting at the beginning, *One's Man Family* was brought to television as an afternoon quarter-hour soap opera in 1954 but lasted only a year. This time Anne Whitfield played Claudia, while she was also playing Claudia's daughter Penelope on radio. Finally in 1958 Morse tried again with a pilot produced for *The Loretta Young Show*, focusing on the relationship between Claudia (Jean Allison) and Johnny Roberts (Keefe Brasselle), an early radio storyline.

Carlton Morse estimated that he wrote more than 10 million words to bring to life his vision of an American dynasty. Like the rest of America, his radio family, although prosperous WASPs, persevered through the Great Depression, World War II, and the beginnings of the atomic age. Morse truly believed that if the integrity and moral strength of the family could stay intact, then no great harm could come to the nation. *One Man's Family* was the embodiment of his patriotic and patriarchal philosophy. If *One Man's Family* is still warmly remembered by radio partisans, Morse's immense talents as a producer/writer/director have largely been forgotten, and references to his creative contribution are missing from several radio histories. *Variety* even misspelled his first name when he died on 24 May 1993 in Sacramento, California. But Morse was diligent to save and copyright his scripts, donating them to Stanford University for serious scholarship.

For those critics who fell under the sway of *One Man's Family*, the collection at Stanford will prove that Morse was not only a pioneer of the serial narrative, but also one of broadcasting's most gifted and compelling storytellers. The program series is one of those honored by the Radio Hall of Fame.

See also: I Love a Mystery

Cast

Henry Barbour	J. Anthony Smythe
Fanny Barbour	Minetta Ellen (1932–55)
	Mary Adams (1955–59)
Paul Barbour	Michael Raffetto (1933–55)
	Russell Thorson (1955–59)
Hazel Barbour	Bernice Berwin (1932–58)
Claudia Barbour	Kathleen Wilson (1932–43)
	Barbara Fuller (1945–59)
lifford Barbour	Barton Yarborough (1932–51)
Jake Barbour	Page Gilman (1932–59)

Creator

Carlton E. Morse

Writers

Carlton E. Morse, Harlen Ware, Michael Raffetto, Clinton Buddy Twiss, Charles Buck

Directors

Carlton E. Morse, George Fogle, Michael Raffetto

Announcers

William Andrews, Ken Carpenter, Frank Barton

Organists

Paul Carson (1932–51), Sybil Chism (1951–54), Martha Green (1954)

Programming History

NBC (NBC Red until 1943) 29 April 1932–8 May 1959

Further Reading

Cox, Jim, "One Man's Family," Chapter 15 of *The Great Radio Soap Operas*, Jefferson, North Carolina: McFarland, 1999.

Herman, James, One Man's Family website, http://www.geocities.com/californiajamesh/OMF/

Morse, Carlton, *One Man's Family Album: An Inside Look at Radio's Longest Running Show*, Woodside, California: Seven Stones Press, 1988.

Nachman, Gerald, "The Royal Family," Chapter 19 of *Raised on Radio*, New York: Pantheon Books, 1998.

One Man's Family Tree website, http://kinnexions.com/reunion/oneman.htm

Steadman, Raymond William, "Family Saga," Chapter 20 of *The Serials: Suspense and Drama by Installment*, 2nd edition, Norman: University of Oklahoma Press, 1977.

RON SIMON

OUR MISS BROOKS
Situation Comedy

One of the most beloved female characters in radio comedy was Eve Arden's Connie Brooks, an English teacher at a Midwestern high school. Miss Brooks was good-humored, witty, and sardonic, a change from the scatterbrained or merely sarcastic female characters who had been plentiful in supporting or co-starring roles in radio comedy up to that time. Miss Brooks was radio's first single woman as lead character in prime time, and Eve Arden brought to the role the character and intelligence that she had become famous for in films such as *Mildred Pierce*. In films, however, Arden had usually played supporting roles, such as the heroine's best friend. *Our Miss Brooks* allowed Arden to shine on her own, and her series became one of the most popular of the postwar period.

Arden was not the first choice for the role of Connie Brooks. Producer Harry Ackerman had originally wanted Lucille Ball, who turned it down, and he had then asked Shirley Booth. Booth refused the series because, Ackerman recalled, "all she could see was the downside of being an underpaid teacher. She couldn't make any fun of it" (quoted in Nachman, 1998). Meanwhile, Columbia Broadcasting System (CBS) President William Paley had become acquainted with Arden and proposed that she do the series. She passed on the original script, but a rewrite by Joe Quillan and Al Lewis proved more to her taste (Lewis would serve throughout the show's run as writer–director). There was still the matter of the broadcast schedule to negotiate, however. The program was scheduled to premiere at the beginning of the summer, which Arden had planned to spend with her children in Connecticut. She asked if the programs could be transcribed, allowing her to do all 15 in a short time and then depart. The network agreed, and *Our Miss Brooks* became one of the first radio programs to be broadcast by transcription. It quickly became the number-one program of the 1948 summer season.

Arden's warm and witty delivery anchored the program, but she was surrounded by an equally talented supporting cast, many of whom went on to fame in film and television. Gale Gordon, famous for his portrayal of Mayor La Trivia on *Fibber McGee and Molly* (and later as Lucille Ball's television nemesis), played Madison High's blustering Principal Conklin. Future film stars Jeff Chandler and Richard Crenna both had prominent roles—Chandler as Miss Brooks' love interest, biology teacher Mr. Boynton, and Crenna as her adoring, mischief-making student Walter Denton. The other women in the cast were Jane Morgan as Brooks' addled landlady Mrs. Davis; Gloria McMillan as the principal's daughter Harriet; and Mary Jane Croft as Miss Enright, a possible competitor for Mr. Boynton's affections.

Stories often revolved around some scheme of Denton's going comically awry (such as his plan to make Miss Brooks teacher of the year); he inevitably involved Miss Brooks in some way, which ended up getting her into hot water with Mr. Conklin. Conklin constantly suspected Brooks of being at the root of whatever problem is at hand (with some justification), but she was adept at mollifying him and helped to protect him from the dreaded school board. As Gerald Nachman (1998) has noted, part of the uniqueness of Brooks' character was that "she treated men with refreshing suspicion—but as undeserving equals." Miss Brooks was always the smartest, most rational, most sophisticated person in any room. In her romance with Mr. Boynton, she was clearly the aggressor in the relationship, trying to figure out ways to manipulate Boynton into asking her out on dates. As she explained to Mrs. Conklin in one episode, "In a moment of weakness, I promised Mr. Boynton the entire weekend." Mrs. Conklin asks, "When did you do that, Miss Brooks?" and she replies, "At lunch in about an hour from now. That is, I'm sure he'll accept—er—invite me." Although Mr. Boynton remained friendly and admiring throughout the series, he was perpetually dim with regard to romance and often seemed more enamored of his frog, McDougall, than of Miss Brooks.

Connie Brooks' spirit, however, remained undaunted by the lack of progress in her romance or the shortcomings of her profession. Although the program addressed some of the problems of being a schoolteacher—especially low wages and lack of appreciation—Brooks' obvious sense of her own worth helped her rise above her circumstances and served as an inspiration to teachers around the country. Eve Arden received thousands of approving letters from teachers, was often asked to address Parent-Teacher Association (PTA) meetings, and was even offered jobs teaching English at various high schools. Most important, perhaps, Brooks suggested that marriage and children were not the only road to fulfillment for young women in the 1950s. The popularity of the program attests to the audience's desire for more alternatives than those that the narrowly defined culture of the postwar period offered them, and Miss Brooks made such an alternative seem not only possible, but thoroughly enjoyable as well.

In 1952 *Our Miss Brooks* moved to television, where it ran successfully until 1956, earning Eve Arden an Emmy as Best Actress. Although she continued to appear on stage and in films, Arden's low, throaty voice was instantly recognizable to fans of the show, and she always remained best known as Miss Brooks. Fortunately, most of the program's eight-year radio run is available in recordings, providing a remarkable testament to one of radio's comedy heroines.

See also: Comedy

Cast

Miss Connie Brooks   Eve Arden

Principal Osgood Conklin	Gale Gordon
Philip Boynton	Jeff Chandler (1948–53), Robert Rockwell (1953–57)
Walter Denton	Richard Crenna
Mrs. Margaret Davis	Jane Morgan
Harriet Conklin	Gloria McMillan
Stretch Snodgrass	Leonard Smith
Miss Enright	Mary Jane Croft
The French Teacher	Maurice Marsac
Jacque Monet	Gerald Moh
Announcer	Verne Smith, Bob Lamond

Producer/Creator

Larry Berns

Director/Writer

Al Lewis

Programming History

CBS   1948–57

Further Reading

Arden, Eve, *Three Phases of Eve: An Autobiography*, New York: St. Martin's Press, 1985.
Nachman, Gerald, *Raised on Radio: In Quest of The Lone Ranger, Jack Benny*, New York: Pantheon, 1998.

ALLISON MCCRACKEN

OWNERSHIP, MERGERS, AND ACQUISITIONS

During radio's first seven decades, through the mid-1990s, ownership of radio stations was limited by Federal Communications Commission (FCC) rules. Since the passage of the 1996 Telecommunications Act, owners have been allowed to own not just a few stations, but hundreds. Through multiple mergers and acquisitions, a handful of new radio owners—led by Clear Channel and Infinity/Columbia Broadcasting System (CBS)—have consolidated hundreds of stations under a single corporate umbrella.

The First 70 Years

During radio's development stage in the 1920s, stations were most often owned and operated as secondary sidelines to other businesses, such as hotels, retail stores, or radio-related businesses such as receiver manufacturing or sales. Newspapers acquired stations out of fear of a new competitor for local advertising dollars. Department stores and hotels bought stations to promote their sales. But with the development of the national networks, the National Broadcasting Company (NBC, owned by radio manufacturer Radio Corporation of America) and then CBS, ownership began to consolidate.

By 1936 about half of all stations were affiliated with a network, but the FCC frowned on networks' directly owning too many outlets. NBC and CBS acquired stations in major cities, reaching most of the population, and these owned and operated units accounted for a quarter of the networks' income. In 1943 the FCC issued a rule limiting owners to no more than one AM and one FM station per market. Thus, groups of stations were developed across multiple markets by both networks and by other firms. Later in the 1940s, the Commission set as seven the number of AM stations that could be owned in common. In 1953 the FCC raised the FM limit to seven and formalized the limit of seven AM and seven FM stations that would define radio ownership for three decades.

The New World of Radio Ownership

The dramatic growth in the number of radio stations led the FCC (under pressure from the broadcast industry) to allow several increases in ownership limits after 1980—to 20 AM and 20 FM stations, for a potential national total of 40 outlets—by the early 1990s. Also gone, as of 1992, was the "duopoly rule" that had limited a single group or individual to no more than a single AM and FM outlet in a single market. On 8 February 1996, President Clinton signed into law the Telecommunications Act of 1996, which, among its many provisions, directed the FCC to eliminate the national multiple radio ownership rule and to relax the local ownership rule. In an Order adopted 7 March 1996, the FCC implemented these provisions, and soon the former ownership limits of seven AM and seven FM stations seemed quaint.

The Telecommunications Act of 1996 loosened but did not eliminate ownership restrictions. For example, in markets with 45 or more commercial stations, a single company may own up to eight stations with no more than five as either AM or FM. If the market has 30–44 commercial radio stations, the total number one owner can acquire drops to seven, with a maximum of four in the same class (AM or FM). For smaller markets, those with 15–29 radio stations, the total "cap" (permitted absolute amount) drops to six, with four of any one modulation. Finally, in markets with fewer than 14 commercial radio stations, the total that any one company can own is five, with no more than three as AM or FM (in each case, up to half the stations in the market).

Passage of the 1996 Act set off the greatest merger wave in radio history. CBS merged with Infinity Broadcasting, and in a telling metaphor Infinity's founder, Mel Karmazin, noted, "it's like combining two ocean front properties." He meant that the new empire would not be some "mom and pop" collection of stations, as had often been the case in the past, but would own seven outlets in New York City, six in Los Angeles, ten in Chicago, eight in San Francisco, and four in Washington, D.C. By 2000, the new CBS/Infinity combination commanded nearly a third of all radio advertising revenues in the top ten markets.

During just the first year after passage of the 1996 law, the FCC calculated that some 2,066 radio stations (about 20 percent of the total) changed owners. As a result of this trading activity, the Commission observed that there were a score of new owners and a significant increase in the number of large group owners—and therefore of concentration of station ownership overall. There were also considerable changes in the composition of the top 50 radio group owners, reflecting mergers between companies on that list as radio groups began to develop into vast empires. And the top media companies continued consolidating: the top ten of 1996 shrank to six by the end of 1997, to a top three by the fall of 1998, and to a Big Two by 2000—Clear Channel and GBS/Infinity after its merger with Viacom. Disney's American Broadcasting Companies (ABC) and Cox's radio division followed as part of major media conglomerates and were the only powers that could offer Clear Channel or Viacom's CBS/Infinity a true challenge.

Clear Channel

Clear Channel Communications, based in San Antonio, Texas, owned more than 900 radio stations by early 2000, the largest radio group in history. It remained the largest in mid-2003, with more than 1,200 stations nationwide. Clear Channel owned stations in the top markets of the United States, yet it was still best thought of as a force in small and medium markets in communities such as Grand Rapids, Michigan (media market 66), and El Paso, Texas (media market 69). Clear Channel had also expanded abroad, acquiring radio stations in Australia, New Zealand, and the Czech Republic.

But Clear Channel's October 1999 purchase of Hicks Muse's collection of radio stations pushed it into an ownership category never fathomed by the creators of the Communications Act of 1934. Hicks Muse, an investment company unknown to the radio business before 1995, owned in excess of 400 stations when it sold to Clear Channel. The deals had come rapidly. In February 1997, in two deals worth more than $1.6 billion, the largest radio group was formed. The combined company, to be called Chancellor Media Corporation, was put together by Hicks Muse; later that month, Hicks Muse took over Evergreen, and the rush was on. Next came the takeover of ten radio properties owned by Viacom for $1.075 billion, bringing Hicks Muse to widespread notice with a then-combined enterprise of 103 radio stations in 21 markets, aggregate net revenues of more than $700 million, and an enterprise value of about $5 billion. With its late 1999 takeover of Hicks Muse, Clear Channel had acquired stations in nearly every radio market in the United States —certainly in every major one. Clear Channel had become the greatest owner of radio in the medium's 80-year history.

CBS/Infinity

CBS/Infinity owned far fewer radio stations than Clear Channel, but its 161 stations by early 2000 placed it in a strong second place. Despite growing to 185 stations by mid-2003, CBS/Infinity had slipped to fourth place in number of stations but remained second in terms of revenue and audience size because the outlets were all located in major markets. With stations in the top ten markets, CBS/Infinity was a media conglomerate, with a very profitable radio division functioning at the heart of the corporation's strategy for the future. Karmazin argued that radio offered an advertising vehicle that even television could not match, because radio could target listeners far more efficiently.

Under Mel Karmazin, founder and head of Infinity Broadcasting (which Westinghouse CBS acquired in July 1996 for $4.9 billion in the costliest merger to that date in radio history), CBS/Infinity radio ownership in the top ten markets had become impressive by 2000. In the next ten markets, CBS/Infinity owned strong radio positions in Atlanta, Minneapolis, St. Louis, Baltimore, and Pittsburgh. All this added up to equal status with Clear Channel, but one that was accomplished in a far different manner.

Disney/ABC

Disney—although far more famous for its other media operations—took sizable revenues from its

radio division, although its radio holdings paled in comparison to CBS, let alone Clear Channel. Yet Disney offered a significant presence because overall it ranked as the largest media conglomerate in the world before the America Online/Time Warner merger early in 2000. Chief Executive Officer Michael Eisner and his management team kept a significant position in radio; Disney did not sell off these assets as it did with the newspapers it acquired from ABC/Capital Cities, but it also chose not to try to match the merger frenzy of its larger radio rivals. Disney surely had the resources to grow into a larger radio power, but as the 1990s ended the company had chosen not to expand. It rested on its ownership of stations in the top media markets and so should best be thought of as a smaller version of CBS/Infinity. Yet radio did not rank high on Michael Eisner's radar, because Disney management looked to expand the television side of ABC with the potential of more sizable synergies. Disney expanded only the AM penetration of ABC radio to provide outlets for its Radio Disney children's network. By mid-2003, Disney/ABC had slipped to ninth place, with 74 stations, though still ranking third in total audience, and fifth in revenue (Table 2).

Cox and Cumulus

Like Disney/ABC, Cox by 2000 represented a diverse media corporation far more famous for other operations. Its radio division was sizable, but the public focused on its newspaper operations, and the company was best known for its newspaper, the *Atlanta Constitution*, and for its move into new media. Although this Sunbelt company had substantial interests in broadcast and cable television, Cox also had a large number of radio stations, with four in Los Angeles, and clusters in Houston, Atlanta, Tampa, and Orlando. Cox merged with New City Communications to add markets such as Tulsa, Oklahoma, and New Haven, Bridgeport, and Norwalk-Stamford, Connecticut. Then the company traded its Los Angeles cluster of outlets to Clear Channel to acquire Houston properties as well as to add stations to their existing clusters. By mid-2003, Cox had more than 75 stations—third in revenue, fourth in audience, but seventh in number of outlets.

Cumulus Media aggregated more than 260 stations by 2003 (second only to Infinity in number of outlets, though ninth or tenth in terms of audience or revenues), buying and consolidating in markets smaller than the top 100. The company's strategy paralleled in the smallest audience-rated markets

Table 2 Radio Station Ownership in Top 10 Markets, by Major Groups: 2000

		Number of Stations Owned by:		
Market		Clear Channel	Infinity/CBS	ABC/Disney
1.	New York	5	6	3
2.	Los Angeles	15*	8	3
3.	Chicago	6	8	5
4.	San Francisco	9	7	3
5.	Philadelphia	6	5	1
6.	Detroit	7	6	4
7.	Dallas/Ft. Worth	8	8	4
8.	Boston	0	5	0
9.	Washington	8	5	3
10.	Houston	16*	4	10
Top-10 Market Stations Owned		80	62	36
Total Stations Owned		959	161	43
Stations Rank		1	4	11
Revenue Rank		1	2	3
Audience Reach Rank		1	2	3

*Some of these will be spun off to meet FCC ownership limits—this process in a number of markets will bring Clear Channel to just under 900 stations.
Source: Who Owns What (10 January 2000)

what Clear Channel had accomplished in markets of all sizes, and what CBS/Infinity achieved in the largest cities.

Minor Mergers and Public Policy

There were holdouts to the radio merger frenzy of the late 1990s. Stubborn single station owners did hang on. WRNR-FM in the metro Washington, D.C., market illustrates the frustrations of operating as a single independent company in a world of radio consolidation. Jack Einstein is a throwback to the days when the FCC restricted ownership of radio. His Annapolis, Maryland-based WRNR-FM sought simply to survive as the bigger consolidated companies took over the Washington, D.C., market. He had no advantages of scale economies to reduce costs, nor could he sell a whole set of stations and formats to big advertisers. The temptation was to cash out, but Einstein—as of early 2000—could not resist the lure of running a radio station programming vintage and progressive rock, and so with a "group" of three stations all in the Washington, D.C., market, the eighth-largest U.S. radio market, he sought narrow formats and held on with his son as featured disc jockey.

The U.S. Department of Justice remains an important player as well. Since the FCC has lifted its ownership limits, it has been up to the antitrust division to determine if a merger violates antitrust laws. During the late 1990s, the Department of Justice negotiated a number of consent decrees, such as one in Cincinnati in which Jacor agreed to reduce its share of the advertising dollars from 53

percent to 46 percent, and another whereby CBS (as a result of its Infinity takeover) had to divest itself of stations in nine separate markets.

Faced with growing complaints about radio's continuing consolidation, however, in mid-2003 the FCC adjusted its radio market rules. The commission replaced its "signal contour" method of defining local radio markets with a geographic market approach used by the Arbitron rating service. The commission concluded that its signal contour method created anomalies in radio ownership that congress could not have intended in the 1996 act. The FCC's 2003 decision closed a seeming loophole by applying Arbitron's definitions of geographic radio markets to better reflect radio industry practice.

Radio Ownership Outlook

The aforementioned top radio groups are among the biggest companies in an ever-consolidating radio industry. There are many others, but they are all far smaller than the dominant companies. Clear Channel, Infinity, Cox, and Cumulus point to a continuing trend toward greater consolidation during the first years of the 21st century as the radio industry continues to adapt to the far looser FCC caps on ownership set in 1996 and modified in 2003.

Although no-one knows how far this consolidation will go—it was considerably slowed by the poor economic conditions of the early 2000s—media conglomerates such as McGraw Hill Companies, the New York Times Company, and the Tribune Company continued to own and operate radio station groups awaiting the radio industry's shakeout from mergers and acquisitions. All had acquired radio years earlier, and by the early 2000s they chose simply to sit on their relatively small holdings as management determined how far a Clear Channel or Cumulus would grow and what effects of that consolidation would spill over to the relatively small holders of radio stations.

Radio's consolidation slowed later in the 21st century's first decade for two fundamental reasons. First and foremost was the slow decline in commercial radio's financial fortunes generally, with audiences and advertising revenues steadily dropping. The dramatic economic turndown in 2008–9 further slowed conglomeration as financial deals became more difficult to arrange. Indeed, the conglomeration trend reversed to a degree as some large groups—Clear Channel and Cumulus among them—began to shed marginal operations and laid off employees. Acquisitions were fairly minor compared to the post-1996 act frenzy.

The single largest deal came late in the decade with the merger of the two satellite radio carriers, XM and Sirius, into a single firm known as Sirius-XM. Sirius CEO Mel Karmazin spearheaded the companies' petition to the FCC and Department of Justice Antitrust Division to change FCC rules and allow what the National Association of Broadcasters complained was a "merger to monopoly." Though government clearance took 18 months to procure, by mid-2008, the merger had taken place, greatly increasing the debt load on SiriusXM just as the economy turned bad and car sales (vital to expanding satellite radio listening) dropped sharply.

See also: Clear Channel Communications Inc.; Deregulation of Radio; Digital Satellite Radio; Federal Communications Commission; Infinity Broadcasting Corporation; Licensing Authorizing U.S. Stations to Broadcast; Localism in Radio; Radio Disney; Regulation; Telecommunications Act of 1996

Further Reading

Albarran, Alan B., *Media Economics: Understanding Markets, Industries, and Concepts*, Ames: Iowa State University Press, 1996; 2nd edition, 2002.

Chan-Olmsted, Sylvia M., "A Chance for Survival or Status Quo? The Economic Implications of Radio Duopoly Ownership Rules," *Journal of Radio Studies* 3 (1995–96).

Compaine, Benjamin M., et al., *Who Owns the Media?* White Plains, New York: Knowledge Industry, 1979; 3rd edition, by Compaine and Douglas Gomery, Mahwah, New Jersey: Erlbaum, 2000.

Ditingo, Vincent M., *The Remaking of Radio*, Boston and Oxford: Focal Press, 1995.

Federal Communications Commission, Mass Media Bureau, Policy and Rules Division, *Review of the Radio Industry*, 1997, MM Docket No. 98–35 (13 March 1998) (issued as part of 1998 Biennial Regulatory Review).

Sterling, Christopher H., "U.S. Communications Industry Ownership and the 1996 Telecommunications Act: Watershed or Unintended Consequences?" in *Media Power, Professionals, and Policies*, edited by Howard Tumber, London and New York: Routledge, 2000.

Who Owns What (M Street Publications, weekly).

Williams, Wenmouth, Jr., "The Impact of Ownership Rules and the Telecommunications Act of 1996 on a Small Radio Market," *Journal of Radio Studies* 5, no. 2 (1998)

DOUGLAS GOMERY,
2009 REVISIONS BY CHRISTOPHER H. STERLING

P

PACIFICA FOUNDATION
Noncommercial Radio Network

The Pacifica Foundation inaugurated the first listener-supported, noncommercial radio network in the United States in the two decades after World War II. By the 1990s it owned five noncommercial FM stations throughout the country: KPFA-FM in Berkeley, California (acquired in 1949); KPFK-FM in Los Angeles (1959); WBAI-FM in New York City (1960); KPFT-FM in Houston (1970); and WPFW-FM in Washington, D.C. (1977). Characterized by unconventional and dissent-oriented programming, Pacifica also provides news and public-affairs material for about 60 affiliated community radio stations.

Pacifist Origins

The Pacifica Foundation was created in 1946 by a small group of World War II-era conscientious objectors (COs) who had participated in the pacifist student club movement of the 1930s. Most of them belonged to the War Resister's League or the American Friends Service Committee. Lewis Hill is generally credited as the guiding force behind the creation of Pacifica. A CO himself, Hill sought the development of institutions that would foster what he called a "pacific world in our time" through the encouragement of public dialogue. In pursuit of nonprofit status, Hill filed Articles of Incorporation with the state of California in the summer of 1946.

The Pacifica Foundation's first project—listener-supported KPFA-FM in Berkeley—received a license in 1948 and went on the air on 15 April 1949. KPFA is recognized as the world's oldest listener-supported noncommercial FM station, but it barely made it through its first five years. Equipped with a 250-W transmitter during a period when hardly anyone owned FM receivers, KPFA was saved by the Ford Foundation from an early death with a $150,000 grant in 1951. This windfall allowed Hill to test his "two percent theory," first articulated in that year. His theory stated that any listener-sponsored radio station could function effectively with the regular monetary support of two percent of a given metropolitan area's radio listeners.

Having obtained a larger transmitter by the mid-1950s, KPFA's early programs reached an audience of approximately 4,000 subscribers, about one-quarter of whom held advanced degrees. The audience regularly tuned in for the commentaries of movie critic Pauline Kael, poet Kenneth Rexroth, and Zen scholar Alan Watts. The station became a mecca for the leading lights of what scholars generally call the San Francisco Literary Renaissance, especially Jack Spicer, Robert Duncan, and Lawrence Ferlinghetti. In 1957 KPFA broadcast the first radio airing of Allen Ginsberg's poem *Howl*, copies of which were subsequently seized at Ferlinghetti's City Lights Books by the San Francisco police department on charges of obscenity.

Transition to Dissent Radio

By 1959 the Pacifica Foundation had inaugurated its second radio station, KPFK-FM in Los Angeles; this acquisition was followed in 1960 by

WBAI-FM in New York City, a gift to Pacifica by a philanthropist.

Although Pacifica came into existence during the early years of the Cold War, it had its ideological roots in 1930s pacifism. In its public-affairs programs Pacifica encouraged town-hall style discussions revolving around pacifist/anarchist questions. A KPFA panel entitled "Does atomic power threaten our civil liberties?" included participants on the political left, center, and right. On its three stations, the organization endeavored to include the commentaries of conservatives such as William Rusher, Russell Kirk, and Caspar Weinberger.

However, the government took far more interest in the handful of communists and communist sympathizers who appeared regularly on Pacifica's three frequencies, such as historian Herbert Aptheker and Sovietologist William Mandel. In 1960 KPFA broadcast Mandel excoriating the House Un-American Activities Committee (HUAC) during his subpoenaed appearance in San Francisco. When, in October 1962, WBAI in New York broadcast the comments of a disgruntled former Federal Bureau of Investigation (FBI) agent, it triggered a complete bureau investigation of the entire Pacifica network, ordered personally by an irritated J. Edgar Hoover. In early 1963 the principals of Pacifica's national board were subpoenaed to appear before the Senate Internal Security Subcommittee, dominated by Senator James Eastland, a personal friend of Hoover.

Seeking public sympathy for the network, Pacifica's leaders gradually revised their ideology, adapting the Federal Communications Commission's (FCC) fairness doctrine to the organization's mission. Rather than attempting to encourage left/right dialog, the network would serve the dissenter and his or her audience. "Just as I feel little obligation to spend time on my broadcasts saying what is wrong with communist governments," declared Pacifica president Hallock Hoffman in 1963, "since everyone hears what is wrong with communist governments from every side, I think Pacifica serves the ideal of balance if it spends little time reinforcing popular beliefs." KPFA public-affairs director Elsa Knight Thompson made a similar appeal in 1970: "Pacifica Foundation was created to implement the 'Fairness' doctrine on the air rather than on paper, but implementing this policy of balanced programming is not achieved by having someone say yes for five minutes and then finding someone to say no for five minutes." "Pacifica is high-risk radio," concluded a 1975 brochure. "When the theater is burning, our microphones are available to shout fire."

Pacifica's tactical response to McCarthyism gave birth to what a later generation would describe as "alternative media." By the early 1960s the growing availability of FM receivers enabled Pacifica to broaden its audience. More than 27,000 people subscribed to a Pacifica station by 1964. By the late 1960s, WBAI staff estimated that approximately 600,000 people tuned in to the station for its melange of music, commentary, and live coverage of the Vietnam antiwar movement, an audience level probably never matched by any Pacifica station since. The network became "free speech, First Amendment" radio, famous for its broadcasts of the remarks of Ernesto "Che" Guevara and for its news dispatches directly from Hanoi.

By 1970 the network's reputation had spread to the point that it caused a backlash. Pacifica station KPFT-FM in Houston went on the air that year, only to have its transmitter bombed twice by the Ku Klux Klan. Ultimately, a Klansman was apprehended while en route to California to continue his sabotage at the Los Angeles and Berkeley stations. In 1971 a WBAI manager spent time in prison for refusing to turn over to the police taped statements of men incarcerated in New York's notorious "Tombs" city jail. Three years later KPFK's manager was incarcerated for refusing to surrender to the FBI taped statements of the Symbionese Liberation Army. So far did Pacifica push the envelope of free speech that the Supreme Court in 1978 ultimately ruled as indecent a 1973 WBAI broadcast of comedian George Carlin's "Seven Words You Can't Say on Television" routine.

Community Radio

As the Pacifica network grew, its public statements became increasingly populist. After the Berkeley Free Speech movement of 1964 and the Columbia student uprising of 1968, the organization's principals spoke in the language of grassroots democracy. "We have been too academic in the past," declared a KPFA news director in 1975, "and now we want to go to the people and get their feelings." Such rhetoric drew to the organization an unprecedented wave of feminists and minority activists who sought the chance to express their feelings without the assistance of white middle-class mediators. These programmers, often adherents of "Third World" ideologies such as Maoism, coexisted uneasily with an earlier generation of Pacifica activists. Ultimately, this generational tension resulted in difficult and lengthy staff strikes at KPFA in 1974 and at WBAI in 1977.

Out of these conflicts came the basic precepts of "community radio": first, that decisions at a Pacifica station ought to be made collectively, and second, that the network should dedicate its efforts to giving the "voiceless" a forum. The principles of Pacifica's fifth acquisition, WPFW-FM in Washington, D.C., most clearly articulated this philosophy. When WPFW was inaugurated in 1977 after seven years of bureaucratic wrangling with the FCC, the station's news director issued a directive to WPFW's news staff that exemplified the idea of community broadcasting: "We are here to tell people what PARTICIPANTS (the perpetrators and those affected) are saying, doing, planning and thinking—NOT what WE THINK they stand for or really mean. Their actions speak louder than your adjectives." Many noncommercial radio stations across the United States adopted this stance and created the National Federation of Community Broadcasters in 1975.

The community radio philosophy allowed the Pacifica network to accommodate an unprecedented new wave of staff who provided distinct programming. At KPFT came a bevy of programs that served the Gulf Coast in no less than 11 different languages. From WPFW in Washington, D.C., a disk jockey broke the news of the 1983 U.S. invasion of Grenada through live telephone interviews with musicians in Jamaica. At all the Pacifica stations, women's and Third World departments sprang up, with refurbished broom closets often functioning as their offices. The organization's self-conscious decision to operate on the ground floor of American life allowed it to billboard the talents of artists such as Whoopi Goldberg, Alice Walker, and Bobby McFerrin long before they became enshrined in American culture. It also enabled Pacifica stations to provide unique coverage of ongoing stories, such as the 1970s campaign to stop the closing of the International Hotel in San Francisco, a refuge for Filipino workers, and the efforts of solidarity groups to challenge U.S. policies in Central America.

Toward a Centralized Network

Although the Pacifica Foundation has crossed swords with the FBI, local police departments, and Senate investigation committees, its most turbulent battles have usually been with itself. After 1980, the most difficult question the organization faced was the extent to which it should centralize its operations and programming schedule. Pacifica began its first experiments with national programming in the late 1970s with the creation of a national news program. These efforts were followed by live "gavel-to-gavel" coverage of the 1986 Senate Iran-Contra hearings and subsequent confirmation hearings on

the candidacy of Robert Bork for the Supreme Court. Emboldened by these successful ventures, the network inaugurated "Democracy Now" in 1996, a one-hour public-affairs program taken by all the Pacifica stations and 65 affiliated community radio stations. By 1997 Pacifica estimated that 700,000 people a week listened to its programming either direct via a Pacifica station or through an affiliate.

But in the 1990s these gains were accompanied by painful purges of volunteers, especially at KPFA and KPFT. Managers who had lost patience with the democratic process initiated these staff reorganizations. They perceived station program schedules as fragmented, broken down into too many individually controlled shows of poor quality. The problem of managing Pacifica frequencies was exacerbated by government policies that, beginning in the late 1970s, limited the amount of local-access, noncommercial airtime available in most metropolitan regions by eliminating most of the educational low-power FM outlets still on the air. Faced with scores of programmers who had hardly anywhere else to go, Pacifica stations found that personnel and programming decisions had become perilous—guaranteed to provoke trouble. In addition, the emergence of the internet in the early 1990s enabled dismissed programmers throughout the network to create effective dissident organizations, complete with discussion lists and websites.

In February 1999, under pressure from the Corporation for Public Broadcasting to increase audience share, the national board of the Pacifica Foundation voted to centralize its operations, removing all station Local Advisory Board (LAB) members from its body. LAB members had sat on the national board since the late 1970s. This reform was followed by the dismissal of KPFA's general manager two weeks before that radio station's 50th anniversary celebration and by the cancellation of programs whose hosts discussed the controversy surrounding that dismissal over the airwaves. These actions exacerbated long-standing frustrations at KPFA and throughout the Pacifica network. On 13 July 1999, after media activists discovered a memorandum from a member of the national board proposing the sale of KPFA or WBAI, the Pacifica Foundation hired a security firm to expel KPFA's staff from the building. More than 50 programmers were arrested. In response, some 10,000 Bay Area residents staged a demonstration demanding the restoration of the station and the resignation of the national board. The crisis became an international cause, receiving press coverage throughout the United States and Europe. KPFA drew expressions of support from as far away as the staff of Serbia's banned Radio B92. KPFA's staff returned to work on 5 August and the board, at a meeting in Houston in late October, pledged not to sell or transfer the license of any Pacifica station.

Unfortunately, the network's leadership continued to try to solve its problems via personnel purges. Later in 1999 Pacifica's executive director removed the news bureau's program director from his position shortly after the Pacifica Network News broadcast a brief story about community radio affiliate dissatisfaction with the service. Then in November of 2000 the general manager of WBAI was removed. Pacifica once again fired staff who protested the dismissal over the station's airwaves. These actions sparked a nationwide listener-subscriber boycott of the network, which, in tandem with three lawsuits filed against the board and a public pressure campaign, forced Pacifica's leadership to sue for peace in the winter of 2001. A settlement resulted in an interim governing board, which set itself the task of creating a more democratic structure for the organization.

A New Start

In late 2003, and after considerable debate, Pacifica affiliate stations agreed to the results of the Pacifica & Affiliates Communications Exchange (PACE) proposals to rebuild the network. The new approach emphasized collaboration and interactivity between Pacifica management, the Pacifica-owned outlets, and the growing number of affiliate stations by establishing shared programming, a review board, an affiliates committee, and administrative and technical liaison services, as well as other venues for dialog.

The Pacifica Foundation owns the Ku-band satellite operating system and (since 2005) internet servers dubbed the Pacifica AudioPort. There are two satellite uplinks (in Berkeley and Washington, D.C.), an MP3 live streaming server, and an MP3 warehouse server. Stations can receive programming via satellite or the internet, or both, depending on which technologies they use locally. A start-up incentive program is offered by Pacifica to encourage prospective affiliate stations that need internet cable access or KU equipment—providing these technologies for the stations during their first year of affiliation.

Since the management unrest at the turn of the century, the number of Pacifica affiliates has grown from 13 in 2002 to 130 by 2008. New stations join every month and include community and college stations, public outlets, low-power operations, and internet radio. Stations in Europe, Africa, and Central America are included in the growing number of international affiliates.

See also: Community Radio; Controversial Issues, Broadcasting of; Educational Radio to 1967; Fairness Doctrine; Free Form Format; KPFA; Public Affairs Programming; Public Radio Since 1967; "Seven Dirty Words" Case; United States Supreme Court and Radio; WBAI

Further Reading

Engelman, Ralph, *Public Radio and Television in America: A Political History*, Thousand Oaks, California: Sage, 1996.
Hill, Lewis, *Voluntary Listener-Sponsorship: A Report to Educational Broadcasters on the Experiment at KPFA*, Berkeley, California: Pacifica Foundation, 1958.
Land, Jeff, *Active Radio: Pacifica's Brash Experiment*, Minneapolis: University of Minnesota Press, 1999.
Lasar, Matthew, *Pacifica Radio: The Rise of an Alternative Network*, Philadelphia, Pennsylvania: Temple University Press, 1999.
Lewis, Peter M., and Jerry Booth, *The Invisible Medium: Public, Commercial, and Community Radio*, London: Macmillan, 1989; Washington, D.C.: Howard University Press, 1990.
McKinney, Eleanor, editor, *The Exacting Ear: The Story of Listener-Sponsored Radio, and an Anthology of Programs from KPFA, KPFK, and WBAI*, New York: Pantheon, 1966.
Pacifica Network website, www.pacificanetwork.org/radio/content/section/4/81/
Post, Steve, *Playing in the FM Band: A Personal Account of Free Radio*, New York: Viking Press, 1974.
Walker, Jesse, *Rebels in the Air: An Alternative History of Radio in America*, New York: New York University Press, 2001.

MATTHEW LASAR

PAYOLA
Illegal Payments to Disc Jockeys

Payola is an undisclosed payment by a music promoter to a broadcaster for the purpose of influencing the airplay of a particular song. This business practice of paying to play has been known to be associated with radio broadcasting since a national scandal rocked the radio industry in the late 1950s, but sheet music publishers were paying popular artists to perform specific songs even before the start of radio broadcasting.

The term *payola* was coined by *Variety* in 1938 in the wake of numerous stories covering music "pluggers" who promoted their songs to big-name orchestra leaders with network radio shows. It was common for as many as a dozen pluggers to attend a remote broadcast begging a popular bandleader to perform their music. In 1935, the National Broadcasting Company (NBC) barred pluggers from entering the Radio Corporation of America (RCA) building in an attempt to insulate directors from the relentless promotion men.

As postwar television viewing grew, many network radio programs disappeared. Local radio stations, forced to develop low-cost local programming, embraced recorded music formats. Local disc jockeys were soon selecting the music of a new generation—rock and roll.

From 1945 until 1959, the number of recording companies grew from about a half dozen to nearly 2000. By the end of the 1950s, large-market radio stations were receiving as many as 250 new record releases each week. With many more records being produced than could be broadcast, record companies followed the industry formula of compensating the most popular platter spinners. Disc jockeys justified payola as "consulting fees" to "audition" new releases. In most cases, payment was legal as long as it was reported on income tax forms.

In addition to cash, disc jockeys were offered gifts, such as liquor, TV sets, clothes, and sometimes prostitutes. In a 1959 *Life* magazine expose, former WXYZ Detroit disc jockey Ed McKenzie remembered that a "record plugger once offered to install a bar in my basement" ("A Deejay's Expose—and Views," 23 November 1959). That same year, covering the Second International Radio Programming Seminar and Pop Music Disc Jockey Convention in Miami Beach, *Time* magazine described the 2,500 attendees as members of "one of the most pampered trades in the U.S." ("Disc Jockeys: The Big Payola," 8 June 1959). Record companies flocked to Florida to backslap the jocks. *Variety* described the convention as a drunken orgy. A headline in the *Miami Herald* exclaimed, "Booze, Broads, and Bribes."

Elected officials noticed the attention payola was receiving in the popular press. It was also a wake-up call for naive station owners and managers who were unaware of payola or who did not mind their popular personalities earning a little extra on the side. When several government investigations were announced, many paranoid station executives conducted their own internal investigations. Fearing eventual action by the Federal Communications Commission (FCC), owners suspended, or in some cases fired, disc jockeys suspected of accepting payola. Many disc jockeys resigned before they were asked questions. Detroit WJBK-TV news director Jack LeGoff was let go after he defended payola on the air as "a part of American business."

His fellow employee, disc jockey Tom Clay, was fired for taking payola, and two other WJBK-AM staffers resigned. The Federal Trade Commission (FTC) began issuing complaints against record labels, and record giant RCA Victor later agreed to a consent judgment to end payola practices. The New York district attorney's office began a payola inquiry and subpoenaed the financial records of a dozen record companies.

The House Legislative Oversight Subcommittee conducted the most highly publicized investigation. In late 1959 it sent investigators to Boston, Chicago, Los Angeles, Milwaukee, New York, and Detroit to examine the payola racket. An aide said the subcommittee "had been receiving complaints from all parts of the country about disc jockeys and music programs." The subcommittee claimed it had received many letters "from irate parents complaining about particular types of music—specifically certain types of rock and roll and the music aimed at the teenage market" ("Hogan Starting Payola Inquiry in Radio and TV," *New York Times*, 20 November 1959). Claiming the moral high ground, the American Society of Composers, Authors, and Publishers (ASCAP) and other publishing interests lobbied Capitol Hill, asserting that payola was the reason rock and roll music existed. The subcommittee began hearings on "Payola and Other Deceptive Practices in the Broadcasting Field" in February 1960. However, the focus was clearly on rock and roll. Critics argued that the hearings were merely a witch-hunt. Broadcasting trade papers believed it was election-year grandstanding by the same politicians who had produced the recent quiz shows scandal. Nevertheless, more than 50 witnesses testified before the committee, including disc jockeys, program managers, radio station owners, record distributors, music surveyors, and FCC officials.

The consequences of the payola hearings and scandal varied. Several popular East Coast disc jockeys who lost their jobs found employment in West Coast markets, including former New York rock and roll pioneer Alan Freed. Freed was later indicted by a Manhattan grand jury on charges of commercial bribery and was penalized by the Internal Revenue Service. In 1960 the Communications Act of 1934 was amended to discourage payola. Stations were required to announce on the air any "promotional considerations" they accepted to broadcast specific programming. This made the licensee responsible for disclosing gifts accepted by its employees. Violators faced fines of up to $10,000 and jail terms of up to one year. As a result of new antipayola regulations and the growing popularity of the Top 40 format, most disc jockeys no longer wielded the power to pick the hits. Managers (program directors) made the final decisions.

Payola did not end with new regulations. After 1960 it simply became more sophisticated. A 1977 FCC investigator explained, "It's not simply a matter of someone handing a disc jockey a $100 bill and a record he is expected to play" ("Say It Again Sam, But You'll Have to Tell the FCC Why," 14 February 1977). Trade lists compiled from the reports of a few select radio stations determined hit songs. Manipulating radio play-lists was more important than frequent airplay. Labels hired independent promoters to do the dirty work of bribery, making it more difficult to trace payola back to record companies. This introduced underground connections to organized crime. Marijuana and cocaine became payoffs in some markets ("drugola").

Detecting and stopping all forms of payola within the radio industry has proved to be nearly impossible. During attempts to crack down on third parties acting as payola bridges between record companies and station personnel, further shocks were sent through the radio and music businesses when, in 2004, then-New York attorney general Eliot Spitzer exposed multiple examples of ongoing "pay for play" practices.

After months of investigation and armed with smoking-gun internal memos and emails detailing outright cash payments and bribes of free trips, laptop computers, Playstations and plasma TVs given to DJs and program directors in exchange for increased airplay of recordings by Jennifer Lopez, Jessica Simpson and other artists, Spitzer's office filed civil charges against Sony Music and its subsidiaries. In mid-2005, Sony agreed to settle with the state. Along with adopting stricter business practices, the company also agreed to "donate" $10 million for use in various New York state-related music education programs and other charities. Eventually, Warner Music was also ensnared in Spitzer's probe and his team expanded its scope beyond record companies by investigating and charging multiple station owner Entercom Communications with payola practices.

Spurred on (or perhaps shamed) by New York's investigation, the FCC launched its own inquiry in April 2006 by issuing formal "letters of inquiry" to such radio giants as Clear Channel, CBS Radio, Entercom, and Citadel. A year later, in a settlement with the Commission, each of these four companies agreed to pay a combined $12.5 million in fines and agreed that their collective 1,653 stations will no longer engage in payola. All four companies were also compelled to air over 8,000 half-hour segments over a period of years, featuring local and unsigned

artists and recording artists from independent labels.

Another industry-coined term for a different behind-the-scenes scheme in broadcasting is *plugola*. Plugola involves a payoff in exchange for hiding a "plug"—in essence, an advertisement within a radio program. These disguised commercials have their roots in the film industry, in which advertisers paid to have brand names strategically placed in film scenes. The practice eventually infested the golden era of radio as promoters provided under-the-table incentives to program producers and writers willing to plant plugs in radio scripts. For the right price, big-name talent would even ad-lib a subtle plug during a coast-to-coast show. By the 1950s a "complimentary" plug for a product or service planted on a top television or radio show cost $250 with neither the network nor program sponsor receiving compensation. Plugola was not examined as closely as payola during the 1959–60 Congressional probe. By that time plug planting was disappearing as network radio eroded and television networks began clamping down on the practice.

Ironically, while the payola scandals dragged on, and as both radio stations and record companies began to face declining fortunes as a result of internet downloads, file sharing and other new technologies, the concept of payola (payment *to* stations) was turned on its ear as record companies began demanding payment *from* stations for the right to air any of their music. In 2007, the recording industry-backed musicFIRST Coalition began lobbying Congress asking for the passage of a law to require radio stations to pay a royalty payment each time a song or piece of music is played (as satellite and internet radio services already do). The coalition held that radio should no longer have free use of recorded music after decades of enjoying that status. Undecided as this volume went to press, the Coalition was facing major opposition from the National Association of Broadcasters, among other entities.

See also: Contemporary Hit Radio/Top 40 Format; Recordings and the Radio Industry; Rock and Roll Format; United States Congress and Radio

Further Reading

Committee on Interstate and Foreign Commerce, *Responsibilities of Broadcasting Licensees and Station Personnel: Hearings* before a Subcommittee of the Committee on Interstate and Foreign Commerce, House of Representatives, 86th Congress, 2nd Session, on Payola and Other Deceptive Practices in the Broadcasting Field, Washington D.C.: GPO, 1960.

Committee on Interstate and Foreign Commerce, Special Subcommittee on Legislative Oversight, *Songplugging and the Airwaves: A Functional Outline of the Popular Music Business: Staff Study* for the Committee on Interstate and Foreign Commerce, House of Representatives, 86th Congress, 2nd Session, Washington D.C.: GPO, 1960.

"A Deejay's Expose—and Views," *Life* (23 November 1959).

"Disc Jockeys: The Big Payola," *Time* (8 June 1959).

"Hogan Starting 'Payola' Inquiry in Radio and TV," *New York Times* (20 November 1959).

"Payola Blues," *Newsweek* (30 November 1959).

"Say It Again Sam, But You'll Have to Tell the FCC Why," *Broadcasting* (14 February 1977).

Segrave, Kerry, *Payola in the Music Industry: A History, 1880–1991*, Jefferson, North Carolina, and London: McFarland, 1994.

Smith, Wes, *The Pied Pipers of Rock 'n' Roll: Radio Deejays of the 50s and 60s*, Marietta, Georgia: Longstreet Press, 1989.

STEVEN R. SCHERER,
2009 REVISIONS BY CARY O'DELL

PAY RADIO

Although at first an odd proposition to American radio listeners, the notion of pay radio—paying to listen to one or more radio program services—is neither new nor rare. And with developing digital services, pay radio is rapidly becoming an accepted part of radio's landscape.

Early Notions

As radio struggled to find a means of financial support in the early 1920s, several suggested options included some means of direct payment by listeners. Station WHB in Kansas City, Missouri, for example, sold tickets in 1924 to an "invisible theater of the air." For a set price, listeners would obtain a literal ticket—but then, of course, those who did not pay could also "attend" the broadcasts, so the idea rapidly died. This was an early example of listener "donations" to help cover the cost of radio broadcasting—an idea still common in public radio and television today.

Outside the U.S., many other nations adopted a system of radio licensing wherein for each radio or household, an annual fee (effectively a service tax) was set by the government to be paid (usually to the postal authorities), with the proceeds being turned over to the national broadcasting service to meet its operational expenses. The British Broadcasting Corporation (BBC) was perhaps the prime example of this type of funding, which continued into the 21st century despite advertising's inroads in commercial systems in most other countries.

Although advertising was adopted widely in the United States by the late 1920s as radio's chief means of support, the beginning of the Depression placed heavy financial pressure on emerging stations and networks. Therefore, additional means of seeking radio revenue were occasionally offered. For example, in 1930, at the tenth anniversary dinner celebration of KDKA's (Pittsburgh, Pennsylvania) first broadcast, one politician suggested developing a radio with a key device, with said key to be sold for a set price (he suggested a dollar) each year.

With the competition of television looming after World War II, the pay radio idea was again briefly touted. Before becoming a U.S. senator, William Benton backed the idea of subscription or pay radio. Listeners would pay $18 for a year (essentially a nickel a day) to receive radio programs without advertising. At about the same time, in 1947–48, several stations expressed interest in a home music service based on patents of the Muzak corporation.

Neither idea came to fruition—in part because of controversy over even introducing the notion of paying for something that was then free to the audience. And with that, any discussion about pay radio disappeared for several decades. Indeed, the heated debate over possible introduction of a pay television service, which raged from 1948 to 1968, made any consideration of pay systems for radio even more remote.

Modern Pay Radio

By the 1990s, however, some radio listeners were paying to receive programs. Many of the nation's cable television systems offered audio channels, usually for an additional monthly subscription fee.

The 1990s also saw development of two new radio technologies, both of which revived notions of pay radio. The first was satellite delivery of many radio channels, some without advertising, in return for an annual subscription fee by listeners— essentially the same idea that Benton had proposed a half-century earlier, updated with a new means of transmission.

Satellite pay radio got a boost when, in early March 1997, the Federal Communications Commission (FCC) approved frequencies for digital satellite radio transmissions to be made available for payment of a monthly subscription fee. Four companies sought to provide the new service— American Mobile Satellite Corporation (Reston, Virginia), CD Radio of Washington, D.C., Digital Satellite Broadcasting (Seattle, Washington), and Primosphere (New York), though in the end only two (operating as XM Radio and Sirius) actually took to the air. The broadcast industry fought satellite radio in a doomed effort to forestall the competition.

Subscription fees for the compact disc (CD) quality digital satellite service ranged from $10 to $13 per month when they were introduced in 2001–02. Available channels—some carrying advertising—included weather, sports, opera, talk, and a variety of musical formats. Service providers focused marketing of the service especially to those spending large amounts of time in their cars, such as urban commuters.

The second technological innovation, finally approved by the FCC in late 2002, was terrestrial CD-quality digital transmission, or digital audio radio (DAR) or broadcasting (DAB). This technology was already available in Japan and parts of Europe, and some American industry figures suggested that listeners might pay a subscription fee for the service, which would mark a vast improvement over AM and FM analog transmissions.

In neither the satellite nor the terrestrial radio systems, however, is the term *pay radio* very widely used, for it carries negative connotations in an advertiser-supported business.

See also: Cable Radio; Digital Audio Broadcasting; Digital Satellite Radio

CHRISTOPHER H. STERLING

PEABODY AWARDS AND ARCHIVE

Now one of the more prestigious prizes granted in broadcasting, the Peabody Awards have since 1941 recognized the best people and programs in both radio and (since 1948) television. From 1,200 entries annually, only about 25–35 programs are selected, making these among the most competitive of broadcast awards.

Origins

In 1938 the National Association of Broadcasters (NAB) formed a committee to establish a prize to recognize distinguished achievement and meritorious service in radio programming. One of the committee members was Lambdin Kay, longtime manager of WSB Radio in Atlanta. Kay became a champion of the awards program and made it his special project. One day, WSB's continuity editor, Mrs. Lessie Smithgall, overheard Kay talking about setting up a fair and impartial system for administering the awards. She suggested that he contact her former professor, John E. Drewry, then dean of the Henry Grady School of Journalism at the University of Georgia, about university sponsorship of the award.

Basing his concept on the Pulitzer program administered at Columbia University, Kay approached Dean Drewry and received his enthusiastic support. Drewry contacted the university's president, Eugene Sanford—who had initiated the first journalism classes at the university in 1913—for his endorsement. Sanford approved the plan to house the broadcasting award at the University of Georgia, and during 1939, the board of regents of the University of Georgia authorized the award to be named in honor of George Foster Peabody, a native Georgian and major benefactor of the university. At the 1939 meeting of the NAB in San Francisco, Kay and Drewry presented the plan to the association and received unanimous support for establishing the Peabody Award.

Peabody, born in 1852 in Columbus, Georgia, moved to New York with his family after the Civil War. Largely self-educated, Peabody became a successful industrialist and financier. He supported humanitarian causes, especially education, and helped finance a library, a forestry school, and a classroom building at the University of Georgia. He was also the university's first nonresident trustee. In appreciation, the university awarded him an honorary degree. After his death in 1938, the university named the broadcasting award for him. Today, the name George Foster Peabody has become synonymous with excellence in electronic media.

The first awards were presented at a banquet at the Commodore Hotel in New York on 31 March 1941 for programs broadcast in 1940 and were jointly sponsored by NAB and the University of Georgia's School of Journalism. The Columbia Broadcasting System (CBS) carried the ceremony live, and the broadcast carried addresses by CBS Chairman William S. Paley and noted reporter Elmer Davis, the recipient of the first personal Peabody Award. After the program, the NAB bowed out of future sponsorship of the awards to avoid any conflict of interest. In 1990, at the 50th anniversary ceremony, the NAB once again sponsored the event.

The Peabody Awards recognized television programs for the first time in 1948. Among early television winners were *Disneyland*, Ed Sullivan, and Edward R. Murrow for his *See It Now* series. Cable television was first recognized in 1981 when Home Box Office (HBO) and *Ms. Magazine* won for "She's Nobody's Baby: A History of American Women in the 20th Century." Over the years, Peabody Award winners for meritorious programming read like a "Who's Who" in broadcasting and cable. A complete list of winners is available on the Peabody website (address listed below).

The Peabody Awards are the most competitive of the many broadcasting honors. The awards are given without regard for program genre, and recipients represent programs in news, documentaries, education, entertainment, public service, and children's shows. Personal and organizational awards are also presented for outstanding achievement in broadcasting and cable. A national advisory board selects the Peabody Award recipients, and its members are practitioners, educators, critics, and other leaders in the broadcast and cable industries.

One by-product of the awards is the formation of one of the country's richest broadcast archives. Housed at the University of Georgia Library, the Peabody Collection dates to 1940 and preserves the best of 20th-century radio and television for today's students and scholars and for future generations. The collection has grown to over 40,000 radio and television programs and related print materials. In breadth and program diversity, the collection contains significant news, documentary, educational, and entertainment programming from radio, broadcast television, and cable.

The collection also reflects the full range of independent, local, and network programming and contains many of the finest, most significant moments in broadcast and cable history. Virtually all major news events, from World War II to today, may be found. In addition to spot news, documentary, and public-affairs programs, the Peabody Award also recognizes excellence in entertainment, educational, children's, and sports programming. One definite advantage of the collection is its accumulation of local programming.

The collection's entry books list submissions and provide information on programs submitted in a given year, with radio and television entries inventoried separately. Entries are listed alphabetically by state and are grouped according to submission categories: news, entertainment, documentary, education, youth/children, public service, and individual/institutional. Each volume has a table of contents, and entries are described in brief paragraphs provided by the submitters.

Because copyright is retained by copyright holders, not the Peabody Collection, no programs are loaned, but researchers may use the collection on site. Generally, shows from 1976 onward may be found in the card catalog of the Media Center of the University of Georgia's Main Library. These programs are listed alphabetically by title within categories. In most cases, screening copies exist for on-site viewing. Many older programs are not readily accessible because screening copies have not been dubbed owing to lack of funding.

In keeping with the times, the scope of the Peabody Awards has been expanded in recent years, making eligible for Peabody consideration not only products created specifically for radio and television broadcast, but also productions produced for any type of electronic distribution including corporate video, educational media, home-video release, the world wide web and CD-ROM. Though in recent years, television product has dominated the winners list, achievement in radio is still regularly recognized. Recent radio recipients of Peabodys include NPR's *Storycorps* and *Mental Anguish and the Military* also from NPR, as well as *Crossing Borders* (a program on illegal immigration) from KUNM; Ira Glass's *This American Life* from WBEZ; and *The Radio Rookies Project* from WNYC.

See also: Museums and Archives of Radio

Further Reading

Peabody Awards, www.peabody.uga.edu/index2.html
Priest, Patricia J., "Mining the Peabody Archive," *Journal of Radio Studies* 1 (1992).
Reid, John Edgar, "A Half Century of Peabody Radio: Tracking Public Service Entries 1940–1989," *Journal of Radio Studies* 1 (1992).
Sherman, Barry L., "The Peabody Collection: A Treasure Trove For Radio Research," *Journal of Radio Studies* 1 (1992).
Ware, Louise, *George Foster Peabody: Banker, Philanthropist, Publicist*, Athens: University of Georgia Press, 1951.

LOUISE BENJAMIN

PHILCO RADIO
Receiver Manufacturer

Philco radios were first introduced by a small Philadelphia electrical manufacturer in 1928. Within two years, they became the top-selling radios in the United States, and they continued to lead the market for more than a decade.

Early Years

In the initial years of radio development, radios operated from electricity provided by batteries. The Philadelphia Battery Storage Company (the Philco trademark was registered in 1919) began producing batteries for radios in the early 1920s, an offshoot of its earlier production of automobile and truck batteries. In 1925 Philco produced an innovation that eliminated the need for batteries and allowed radio owners to operate the set with electricity from a light socket—the "Socket-Power" unit. The company grew quickly with its two radio-related products and soon began sponsoring a national radio broadcast known as the *Philco Hour*, which appeared on National Broadcasting Company (NBC) Blue from 1927 to 1929 and on the Columbia Broadcasting System (CBS) from 1929 to 1931.

The Radio Corporation of America (RCA) introduced a set powered by alternating current (AC) in 1927. Not long after, RCA announced that it would license other manufacturers to use the new AC technology, effectively wiping out the market for radio batteries.

Philco management recognized the challenge to its survival and completely changed the focus of its business. The company chose to design and build its own radios and set mid-1928 as a target date to introduce the new product. Most manufacturers were producing radios that all looked very much alike. Philco chose to change that look. Instead of the sturdy, sensible wooden box that most table-model radios resembled, the company produced a metal case radio in five bright colors. To attract female consumers, Philco offered four of the models decorated with hand-painted floral designs. Each had color-coordinated matching speakers (early radios did not contain internal speakers).

Recognizing the importance of a strong advertising campaign, Philco introduced its radios in expensive double-page color ads exclaiming, "COLOR! VIVID COLOR!" The copy described them as "enhanced with color effects by Mlle. Messaros, one of the foremost colorists in the decorative arts. The colors are applied *by hand* under her personal direction."

In addition to the unusual color sets, Philco also offered three console models, radios that were cabinet-style pieces of furniture based on the Louis XVI period; these were created by an internationally known furniture designer. The striking line of radios would be the first in a long line of innovations from the company. Philco introduced its first eight models at an industry trade show in June 1928.

It was a stunning accomplishment. Many had thought that RCA's new AC-powered radios spelled the end for Philadelphia Battery Storage. Philco's response was an indication of an innovative ability that would stand it in good stead for the next 30 years and help maintain its reputation for superior-quality products.

At the end of 1928, Philco was in 26th place among radio manufacturers. The company's management believed the best way to compete in 1929 was to improve quality and lower prices. At a time

when most manufacturers used the labor-intensive method of assembling each radio individually by hand, Philco borrowed $7 million to convert and expand its facilities for mass production.

Philco advanced to third place in the industry by selling 408,000 radios in 1929. Despite the October 1929 stock market crash, Philco continued to thrive. The $7 million debt was paid off early in 1930. Later that year, Philco increased its employee base from 1,500 in May to 4,000 by September. Orders for radios continued to increase, and the company announced it was hiring 75 men a day. Soon Philco announced the formation of a subsidiary to manufacture Philco-Transitone automobile radios.

The radio manufacturer continued to recognize the value of advertising, and, in an early version of a common promotional technique today, a Philco radio was prominently featured in the hotel room of movie star Bing Crosby in Paramount's 1932 film *The Big Broadcast*. At the same time that the company was proving such a success in radio manufacturing, it was also looking toward the future and diversifying. Noted inventor Philo T. Farnsworth came to Philco in 1931 to join a research team devoted to television development. In 1932 the Federal Radio Commission licensed Philco's experimental television station W3XE. The company also began to produce home appliances. During the 1930s Philco offered a variety of products, including automobile radios, phonographs, radio-phonograph combinations, air conditioners, and refrigerators.

Near the end of the decade, Philco began a shift from the large tabletop "tombstone" and "cathedral" radios (so called because of their shape) and produced smaller and less experience radios. Industry leaders Atwater Kent, Crosley, Majestic, and Zenith initially ignored the shift to undersized table models. Consumers, however, responded quickly to the new, space-saving radios. In 1938 Philco's 10 millionth radio came off the assembly line.

World War II and After

With the United States' entry into World War II, Philco shifted to production of military items, including radios for tanks and planes. The company also trained military personnel in the installation, operation, and maintenance of electronic aircraft equipment. Only after the war's end in 1945 were new radios, phonographs, refrigerators, and air conditioners produced again by Philco.

Philco sponsored two national network programs: *Philco Radio Time*, starring Bing Crosby, and a radio anthology of plays adapted for radio, the *Philco Radio Playhouse*, hosted by actor Joseph Cotten. *Philco Radio Time* was the first pre-recorded program. Prior to its introduction in 1946, all radio programs were broadcast live.

Philco was active in transistor research in the 1950s, producing a number of transistor radio models. The 1960s began a troublesome time for Philco. The company was losing money—more than $4 million in 1961. Ford Motor Company purchased Philco late in 1961. The Philco-Ford division, producing television sets, computers, and satellite communication equipment, once again became profitable.

During the 1970s Americans became more interested in antiques and collectibles, and among the items drawing their interest were cathedral radios from 40 years earlier. Philco-Ford introduced a miniature, transistorized AM–FM replica of its model 90 Baby Grand (originally produced in 1931).

General Telephone and Electronics purchased the Philco division from Ford in 1974 and then sold Philco to North American Philips Corporation, where the division now produces televisions.

See also: Automobile Radio; Receivers; Transistor Radios

Further Reading

"1,250,000 out of 4,200,000 U.S. Radios Sold Last Year Have the Philco Trademark," *Fortune* (February 1935).
Douglas, Alan, *Radio Manufacturers of the 1920s*, 3 vols, Vestal, New York: Vestal Press, 1988–91; see especially vol. 2, 1989.
Johnson, David, and Betty Johnson, *Guide to Old Radios: Pointers, Pictures, and Price*, Radnor, Pennsylvania: Wallace-Homestead Book, 1989; 2nd edition, Iola, Wisconsin: Krause, 1995.
McMahon, Morgan E., *A Flick of the Switch: 1930–1950*, Palos Verdes Peninsula, California: Vintage Radio, 1975.
Ramirez, Ron, and Michael Prosise, *Philco Radio, 1928–1942: A Pictorial History of the World's Most Popular Radio*, Atglen, Pennsylvania: Schiffer, 1993.
Wolkonowicz, John P., "The Philco Corporation: Historical Review and Strategic Analysis, 1892–1961," Master's thesis, MIT, Alfred P. Sloan School of Management, 1981.

SANDRA L. ELLIS

PLAYWRIGHTS ON RADIO

Writing drama for radio was a challenging task, for, unlike on the stage or screen, a radio playwright had to depend solely on sound, dialog, and description to tell a story. The inability to use any visual devices derailed more than a few early would-be radio authors. Those who succeeded, however, created a wonderful art form that flourished for nearly two decades of radio's golden age.

A half century later it is understandable that few people under the age of 60 remember the names of Norman Corwin or any of the other major radio dramatists. Corwin was the dean of America's radio playwrights during the golden age that began in 1935 and lasted until the late 1940s. Poets, novelists, and mystery writers joined Corwin and others who wrote mainly for radio in having their works aired to a vast listening public. A number of writers for the stage also sought out the broadcasting studios. A 1945 anthology of radio plays featured works by a priest, two army sergeants, a Noble prize-winning novelist, a musicologist, and even a blind man. Novelist John Steinbeck, TV personality Steve Allen, and TV newscaster Chet Huntley took brief stabs at radio play writing.

Golden Age Radio Drama

The first golden age radio playwrights were heard on two dramatic anthologies, the *Cavalcade of America* and the *Columbia Workshop*. The former was a showcase for largely patriotic shows; the latter, an experimental dramatic anthology, offered more artistic productions. Soon after the *Columbia Workshop* was launched in 1936, the show received a manuscript for *The Fall of the City*, a play in verse, from Pulitzer prize winner Archibald MacLeish. It dealt allegorically with the growth of fascist dictatorships in Europe. Its broadcast struck a chord and inspired a number of other talented and experienced writers. Because poetry lends itself particularly to aural expression, Stephen Vincent Benét, Edna St. Vincent Millay, and other poets joined MacLeish's ranks on radio. So did William Saroyan, Pare Lorentz, Dorothy Parker, and a number of other prose writers.

Howard Koch and John Houseman

On the eve of Halloween 1938, CBS broadcast what is probably the medum's best-remembered show, an adaptation of H.G. Wells' novel *The War Of the Worlds*. Orson Welles produced and acted in the program. However, despite the popular notion that Orson Welles also wrote the radio script, the primary authors were his two collaborators, John Houseman and Howard Koch.

John Houseman, a Romanian born Jew, was originally a grain dealer until the Depression put him out of business. By 1938, he was a stage producer, director, and writer, working in two undertakings with Welles, the Mercury Theatre (a stage troupe) and the *Mercury Theatre of the Air*. For the latter, a show on CBS, Houseman initially did the writing until he and Welles took on Howard Koch, a tall, shy Columbia Law School graduate, to relieve Houseman. It was Koch who wrote the original script for *War of the Worlds*. Houseman collaborated on two rewrites and Welles applied the finishing touches.

Even after the show created panic nationwide, Koch, its principal author, still remained unknown to the public, for Welles never attempted to set the record straight. After a shift in the Welles–Houseman relationship, Houseman left. Subsequently, Campbell's Soup offered Welles sponsorship of another radio series, and Koch continued as writer. Not long afterwards, Koch became a film writer, most notably co-author of the famed *Casablanca*.

Among the many talented writers who took to radio was Brooklyn-born Lucille Fletcher. After receiving her degree from Vassar College in 1933, Fletcher took a job as a typist in CBS's publicity department. After Norman Corwin produced a play based on a story that she wrote, Fletcher decided to try radio writing herself. One of her first plays was performed on *Mercury Theatre of the Air*. Her most successful one, *Sorry, Wrong Number*, first broadcast in 1943, was translated into 15 languages, made into two films, and served as the basis for two operas. Other radio plays by Fletcher were produced on the *Columbia Workshop* and the *Suspense* series.

In the four or five years before Pearl Harbor, in response to the threat of fascism that had materialized in Europe, a group of writers began to produce a "social consciousness" body of radio drama that displayed a strong concern for human freedom. Thus, Arch Oboler inserted political themes into about a third of the shows he wrote for the horror series *Lights Out*. Like virtually all of these writers in the pre-Pearl Harbor days, however, he did so in an allegorical manner. Also, a year before the Japanese attack, a government official had taken an initiative that led to the creation of *The Free Company*, an allegorical, antifascist series that featured plays by Stephen Vincent Benét, MacLeish, Maxwell Anderson, Robert Sherwood, Marc Connelly, and Sherwood Anderson.

World War II

After Pearl Harbor, both the networks and the government promoted programs intended to boost morale and otherwise assist in the pursuit of victory. Norman Corwin directed two four-network efforts at the request of the government. The first, only a week after Pearl Harbor, celebrated the Bill of Rights. The second, which began two months later, was a 13-part series about the war, for which he

wrote about half of the shows. Its broadcast roughly coincided with production of Arch Oboler's first post-Pearl Harbor series, *Plays for Americans* on NBC. Oboler produced at least 70 "beat the Axis" radio plays in 1942. He played a particularly prominent role in the propaganda campaign against Germany, arguing forcefully that Americans needed to hate the enemy in order to conduct a successful war effort.

Twenty-seven-year-old Ranald MacDougall was one of the writers for the Corwin series. Like many others of his generation, as a boy he had been fascinated by the technology of radio and had wound copper wire around an oatmeal box to make his first set. MacDougall began to write seriously at the age of 12. In his late teens he was working as an usher at New York City's Radio City Music Hall when a conversation with an NBC executive landed him an office job with the network. Eventually MacDougall worked his way onto the script staff. In 1942 he began working for a new war series, *The Man Behind the Gun*, one of the best dramas depicting the war era. Other notable and prolific writers of wartime radio drama included Allan Sloane, Peter Lyon, and poets Stephen Vincent Benét, Langston Hughes, and Norman Rosten. New Jersey-born Millard Lampell and playwright Arthur Miller, both close friends of Rosten, wrote for radio as well.

Allan Sloane, originally a newspaper journalist, broke into radio in 1943 when, temporarily jobless, he walked unannounced into the office of the producer of *The Man Behind the Gun* and handed in a script he had written at home. He was hired within a few days. Peter Lyon, another journalist, got started writing for *The March of Time*, a dramatized news documentary. Later, he also wrote for the *Cavalcade of America*. Like many of his radio colleagues, Lyon was a progressive. Among other interests, he was a strong trade unionist. He and Millard Lampell both wrote for a wartime series entitled *Labor for Victory*. Lyon also served in 1944 as president of the Radio Writers Guild.

In his earlier years Pulitzer prize winner Stephen Vincent Benét was rather indifferent to politics. But during the 1930s, he grew increasingly interested in national and international events and developed wide friendships among European refugees. By the time of Pearl Harbor, he was driven to assist the war effort, attending meetings and giving radio readings of his poetry. His best-known contribution to the war effort was a radio drama in verse, "They Burned the Books."

Langston Hughes had many fewer opportunities with radio than did his white peers. He first wrote for radio in 1940 when CBS asked him to prepare some scripts for a Norman Corwin series. Soon,

Hughes was lending his talent to the war effort even though he found that he was radio's "token" black writer, defending a democracy whose fruits he could not fully share.

Norman Rosten, a protégé of Stephen Vincent Benét, was one of the most prolific writers of radio plays of the 1930s and 1940s. Rosten received part of his preparation for writing radio drama on a playwriting fellowship at the University of Michigan. The broadcast of MacLeish's *The Fall of the City* made him realize radio's potential as a vehicle for poetry. After completing his studies, Rosten returned to New York where, with an introduction from Benét, he began to write patriotic radio plays for the *Cavalcade of America*.

Millard Lampell grew up in the same New Jersey hometown as Allan Sloane. Son of an immigrant garment worker, Lampell, a short, athletic, ebullient, man, worked in his youth as a fruit picker and coal miner. He sold his first piece of writing, an article about fascist groups on campus, while he was in college in West Virginia. After college, Lampell moved to New York City and sang for a while with folk singers Woody Guthrie and Pete Seeger. One Sunday, after they finished a gig, a radio producer who had been in the audience approached Lampell and asked him if he would be interested in writing for radio. Lampell's writing career was off and running.

In 1942 and 1943 Lampell wrote scripts for *It's the Navy* and several other war-related radio programs. In 1943, he was drafted. After training, he was assigned to the Air Force radio section in New Haven, Connecticut. There he wrote, produced, and directed programs. In 1944, Lampell was released from the service to visit veterans hospitals around the U.S. and gather material for radio scripts about returning soldiers. Afterwards, he produced *First in the Air*, a series for the Army Air Forces program. Subsequently he lectured on radio writing at several New York area colleges. In 1946, Lampell went to Hollywood as a contract writer at Warner Brothers.

The fact that Arthur Miller wrote most of his early plays for radio has not been well known. But he wrote perhaps 25 radio plays between 1939 and 1946, most of them war related. New York-born Miller attended the University of Michigan, where he befriended Norman Rosten and began writing plays. After graduation, Miller also moved back East. Within a few months, a film studio offered him $250 a week to work in Hollywood. Miller rejected the offer, opting instead for a job at $22.77 per week with the Federal Theatre, a government work program for writers. At around the same time, the *Columbia Workshop* accepted his first play

for radio. Miller also wrote for a series entitled *The Doctor Fights* and, after Rosten recommended him, for the *Cavalcade of America*.

During the war, Miller was rejected twice for military service because of a knee injury. As a substitute, he took a job in the Brooklyn Navy Yard where he helped recondition ships for service. He also threw himself into writing patriotic shows for radio. He worked quickly, completing a half-hour play in less than a day and spending only three months per year writing for radio. During the other nine he wrote for the stage.

Arthur Laurents graduated from Cornell University in 1940. At the urging of a friend, he enrolled in a radio writing course at New York University. His teacher, a CBS director, was so impressed with a play that Laurents wrote for the course that he sold it to the Columbia Workshop. After that Laurents wrote for numerous commercial shows before moving away from radio in favor of musicals and films.

Morton Wishengrad was born in New York's Lower East Side in 1913 to Russian-Jewish immigrant parents. A tall, thin, and reserved man, he shared many of the concerns of the progressive-minded writers of his generation. Wishengrad's first job was as the educational director, editor, and researcher for the International Ladies Garment Workers Union. During the war he worked for the American Federation of Labor as director of a joint Labor Short Wave Bureau that broadcast to organized labor in Europe. He also wrote scripts for NBC's *Labor for Victory*, the *Cavalcade of America*, and several other shows.

Writing for Minorities

Wishengrad stands out among a number of Jewish radio writers as perhaps the only one to clearly bring his Jewish consciousness to radio. Although he wrote for mainstream shows, Wishengrad is best remembered for his writing for programs that primarily addressed a Jewish audience. In 1943, he produced a script about the battle of the Warsaw Ghetto for the American Jewish Committee. It was one of a very few wartime shows that touched on the Nazis' genocide policy. The following year, Wishengrad began to write for *The Eternal Light*, a new Jewish religious drama series, sponsored by the Jewish Theological Seminary.

Mitchell Grayson and Richard Durham, two African-American radio dramatists, also appealed to special audiences. Grayson, a New York writer, wrote and directed *New World A'Coming*. Durham wrote *Destination Freedom* in Chicago. Both were provocative collections of half-hour black history dramas about prominent African-Americans that helped pave the way for the civil rights movement.

Postwar Era

Despite radio drama's great success from the mid-1930s, by the 1950s the genre was in decline, a consequence of the ascent of television and the postwar increase in commercialization in broadcasting. The latter helped make radio vulnerable to a destructive broadcasting industry blacklist carried out by anticommunist vigilantes. Corwin, Grayson, Hughes, Lampell, Rosten, and virtually all of the other writers discussed here were its targets. By 1957, most radio dramatists also had to write for television and film to make a living.

With the departure of many of the war-era radio dramatists, the American radio audience lost a steady source of progressive ideas. The public also lost some fine entertainment. For a short time, during television's Golden Age, the new medium filled the gap. But then it too faded from its glory days.

See also: Blacklisting; *Cavalcade of America*; Drama; *Lights Out*; *March of Time*; *Mercury Theater of the Air*; *War of the Worlds*

Further Reading

Barnouw, Erik, editor, *Radio Drama in Action: Twenty-Five Plays of a Changing World*, New York: Farrar and Rinehart, 1945.
Benet, Stephen Vincent, *We Stand United and Other Radio Scripts*, New York: Farrar, 1944.
Blue, Howard, *Words at War: World War II Era Radio Drama and the Postwar Broadcasting Industry Blacklist*, Lanham, Maryland: Scarecrow Press, 2002.
Boyd, James, editor, *The Free Company Presents A Collection of Plays about the Meaning of America*, New York: Dodd Mead, 1941.
Brady, Frank, *Citizen Welles: A Biography of Orson Welles*, New York: Scribner, 1989.
Fenton, Charles A., *Stephen Vincent Benét: The Life and Times of an American Man of Letters, 1898–1943*, New Haven, Connecticut: Yale University Press, 1958.
Lampell, Millard, *The Long Way Home*, New York: Messner, 1946.
Laurents, Arthur, *Original Story By: A Memoir of Broadway and Hollywood*, New York: Knopf, 2000.
Liss, Joseph, editor, *Radio's Best Plays*, New York: Greenberg, 1947.
MacDonald, J. Fred, *Don't Touch That Dial!: Radio Programming in American Life, 1920–1960*, Chicago: Nelson Hall, 1979.
Miller, Arthur, *Timebends: A Life*, New York: Grove Press, and London: Methuen, 1987.
Rampersad, Arnold, *The Life of Langston Hughes*, 2 vols, New York: Oxford University Press, 1986–88.

HOWARD BLUE

PODCAST
Melding Radio and Internet

Podcasts are prerecorded audio (or video) broadcasts delivered in digital form to an internet URL with an RSS (really simple syndication) feed allowing segments to be heard automatically as they are made, or on demand by listeners. Looked at another way, a podcast can be seen as an individual broadcast made without recourse to an over-the-air transmitter and antenna, and one that is listened to on a computer rather than a traditional radio receiver. A podcast is an online broadcast. Podcasts allow nearly anyone to become their own mass medium with minimal expense on equipment. And they allow for time-shifted listening at any time convenient to the audience member.

Origins

Podcasting is barely five years old as this book goes to press. Indeed, the term "podcast" first appeared early in 2004 as one of several possible names for the fast-developing means of distributing content to computers—or to iPods (the source of the name) or other MP3 players. The basic technology required for podcasts had largely been in place by 2001, thanks especially to work by programmer Adam Curry and then software designer Dave Winer. One of the final pieces developed was creation of the aggregator podcast receiving software. But the conception of what a podcast might be took a few years to mature. So did an easy means of subscribing to such material.

The first podcasts began appearing in September 2004, with initial podcast networks just two months later, just as mainstream media stories began to talk up the technology and what could be done with it. There were soon some 300 podcasters worldwide. By the middle of the next year, by which time there were ten times as many podcasts available, Apple's iTunes system was modified to allow for podcast downloads and ongoing subscriptions, thus hugely increasing a podcaster's potential audience. As with many other electronic technologies, pioneering users and providers were generally those who enjoyed tinkering with computers and related devices. But podcasts quickly expanded to include those more interested in communicating ideas than with a fascination for the equipment needed to do so.

Early podcast content included politics, movie reviews, technology, and food. Others combined the spreading appeal of blogging with audio. Many regular podcasts appeared and blossomed. One early hit, *The Dawn and Drew Show*, simply aired some of the unscripted conversation of a rural Wisconsin married couple. Even the White House got on board with the weekly presidential radio broadcast being made available in podcast form by 2005. Commercial and educational applications began to appear by 2006. And so did some pornographers, who always seem among the earliest adopters of any new mode of communication.

Broadcasting Podcasts

The first broadcasts to be distributed using podcast technology came in September 2004 from several stations. Talk programs on public radio stations (especially college outlets) were among the first adapters of podcasting as they didn't have to deal with music licensing concerns. NPR and PRI were using podcasts for some of their syndicated programs before the end of the year. Within a year or so—that is, by 2005–6—some radio stations were providing podcasts from their audiences. Some television stations provided audio-only podcasts of their local newscasts.

The lines between cooperation and competition between traditional broadcasters and podcasters were thus blurred almost from the start. A podcast allows for an instant world-wide appeal to very targeted or specialized audiences (much like blogging, which developed at about the same time, though podcasts add audio and thus the appeal of the human voice), thus raising the potential for commercial applications. Podcasts have been used for business and industrial training as well as more general educational support.

See also: Audio Streaming; Digital Audio Broadcasting; Internet Radio; Portable Digital Listening Devices

Further Reading

Acohido, Byron, "Radio to the MP3 degree: Podcasting," *USA Today* (9 February 2005).
Farivar, Cyrus, "New Food for IPods: Audio by Subscription," *New York Times* (28 October 2004).
Mack, Steve, and Mitch Ratcliffe, *Podcasting Bible*, Indianapolis, Indiana: Wiley, 2007.

CHRISTOPHER H. STERLING

POETRY ON RADIO

Poetry has played many roles on radio, from filling dead airtime to giving voice to the grief of mourning, as well as many of the places in between.

Introduction and Themes

Poetry on radio was initially occasional and spontaneous, with an announcer reading a poem before or after a music segment or the farm reports. Ted Malone, who was later to be one of the best-known hosts of poetry on radio, began his career this way. In the late 1920s, quickly substituting for an act that failed to show, the program director thrust an anthology of poetry and a mike at Malone and left him to his fate. His reading was a success, and Malone went on to a radio career of more than 25 years with *Between the Bookends*. Because of the ease of production and minimal expense involved, this tradition expanded in the 1930s and 1940s and continues to this day.

The poetry heard on radio has tended to fall into several categories. Early on and into the golden days of radio it has mostly been of the sentimental or "light" variety, especially on shows that were commercially sponsored. Poetry was often taken from popular magazines, such as *Good Housekeeping* or *Redbook*. Many times it was read over music, sometimes accompanied by philosophizing or "gentle wisdom." When more serious or "highbrow" poetry found its way onto the airwaves, it was usually in a sustaining program, and later in noncommercial radio. Some shows included music underneath, or before or after the poetry, while others were straight readings of poems.

By the late 1930s poetry found a new form with the appearance of radio verse plays. The originators of radio verse plays in the U.S. were Archibald MacLeish and Norman Corwin. It was here that poetry reached its greatest number of listeners, as illustrated by the estimated audience of 60 million for Corwin's "We Hold These Truths" in 1941. The paragraphs that follow, by no means inclusive, highlight selected examples and events throughout the nearly 100 years of radio.

Origins

In the early part of the 20th century, radio was primarily a medium of individuals and amateurs some of whom would occasionally read poems, sometimes just to fill dead air, or sometimes in loosely organized "shows." Unfortunately, because the technology was not easily available to record these "programs," and scripts were rarely kept, few names or titles have survived.

In the early 1920s poetry was often read within other programs, such as variety shows hosted by people such as Major Bowes, Rudy Vallee, and Fred Allen. The earliest poetry appeared on local radio shows, such as a program in Yankton, South Dakota, broadcast in 1921 on WNAX and supported by the Guerney Seed and Nursery Company. One listener won a "poetry" contest with, "the Guerney's are the farmer's friend/ They always will be to the end."

Later, when radio became more structured, stations broadcast identifiable announcers, and programs with titles appeared, such as *Cheerio, Tony's Scrapbook, Between the Bookends*, and *Poet's Gold*. One of the earliest shows featured Edward Godfrey reading poetry on a children's program titled *Stories and Poems Read by Uncle Ed over KDKA* (Pittsburgh, Pennsylvania). Beginning 26 October 1923, it was a variety program, usually lasting 15 minutes, that ranged from imitations of birds and animals to music on the mouth organ and guitar to the reading of poems, some original.

One of the first shows to feature poetry was *Poems*, with Beatrice Meisler reciting poetry each week on WGBS in New York City in 1925. Another was *Poet's Corner*, sponsored by Hewitt's Bookstore, with an unidentified performer reading poetry on KFON in Long Beach, California, in 1926. A third was *Poetry Club*, in which Mrs. David Hugh read and discussed poetry on KHJ, Los Angeles, California, in 1929.

Although most of this early poetry on the radio was of the sentimental type, more serious poetry did appear. As radio became more regulated in the 1920s, one of its roles was to provide a public service, as defined in the Radio Act of 1927. With this in mind, "highbrow" material, including some poetry, also appeared in sustaining programs (programs funded by the station or network without commercial advertising). David Sarnoff, vice president and general manager of RCA, suggested that the masses needed to be uplifted by culture, including poetry. Although these early poetry broadcasts sometimes were on commercial radio, they were not necessarily commercially sponsored and often served as filler between commercially sponsored programs.

Network Radio

Poetry began on the networks in 1929 when CBS asked David Ross, with his fine voice, to read poetry in a half-hour Sunday afternoon sustaining show titled *Poet's Gold*. However, like many radio shows and personalities, Ross began locally, first airing in 1926 on WMAQ, Chicago. *Poet's Gold* continued on CBS into the late 1930s, mostly on Sunday afternoons. Ross read classic and contemporary verse by poets such as Ben Jonson,

Samuel Taylor Coleridge, Percy Shelley, Robert Frost, Edna St. Vincent Millay, and Stephen Vincent Benét, usually over music. *Variety* commented that it was one of the best of the many programs of the 1930s featuring poetry and quiet music. Ross participated in another trend of poetry on radio programs by publishing a related book named after the show, *Poet's Gold*.

Ted Malone (Frank Alden Russell) and Tony Wons (Anthony Snow) were the two major personalities of poetry shows on network radio. On *Tony's Scrapbook* Wons gave down-home wisdom and commentary mixed with sentimental verse from sources such as *Good Housekeeping* and *Redbook*, as well as drawing occasionally from literary giants. Wons' gentle, intimate sounding delivery made him a favorite with female listeners. Popular or "light" poetry was more likely to be commercially sponsored, and Wons was able to find companies to foot the bill, including International Silver and Johnson Wax in the 1930s and Hallmark Cards in the early 1940s. Before that he had supported his program by selling yearly collections of poems read on the air, thus the show's name. CBS participated in the publishing of the scrapbooks and later had a deal whereby the network got a cut of sales from the books in exchange for airtime.

Wons also appeared on other shows. In 1931 he contributed to the *Camel Quarter Hour*, a variety program directed by Erik Barnouw and sponsored by R.J. Reynolds, where he read a poem on each show. In the commercial spirit, he also read two poetically phrased messages about Camel cigarettes, as part of an attempt to market cigarettes to women. From September 1934 to August 1935, Wons appeared on *The House by the Side of the Road*, a half-hour Sunday afternoon dramatic program, sponsored by Johnson's Wax and Allied Products and broadcast on NBC.

Ted Malone hosted *Between the Bookends*, a book review program that also featured conversation and poetry, for more than 25 years. It included Malone's poetry as well as that of others and was usually amusing and almost always uplifting. Malone sat in a studio with the lights dimmed and read poetry to organ accompaniment played by Rosa Rio. To Malone, radio was an intimate medium that fit the simple and sentimental poetry he read. Malone was poetry editor at *Good Housekeeping*, and the poems he read were mostly taken from it and similar magazines. He published several *Between the Bookends* anthologies, which were widely available.

Malone also hosted a 30-minute *Pilgrimage of Poetry* program for one season on NBC Blue that featured 32 of the most famous poets in America. Malone traveled to the homes of writers such as Henry Wadsworth Longfellow, Stephen Crane, Edgar Allan Poe, and Walt Whitman, among others, as a way of sharing their lives with his radio audience. He followed this with a season of *American Pilgrimage*, broadcast from 1940 to 1941, where he visited the homes of such literary stalwarts as Mark Twain and Herman Melville.

Sentimental/Cheerful Poetry

Readings of sentimental/cheerful poetry over a background of organ music or in between announcers' talking and philosophizing had the widest audience for poetry on the radio. *Cheerio*, a program of good cheer that included poetry, was also the broadcast name used by the popular broadcaster and host of the show, Charles K. Field. He read poetry and gave inspirational talks starting in 1925 on local radio in the San Francisco Bay area. He moved to the networks in March of 1927 until he was off the air in April of 1940. Field claimed never to have received a penny from his broadcasting, but he wrote many best-selling books. They contained the poetry and wisdom used on his shows and provided his income. In a program called *Cheerio Exchange*, Field's staff maintained a fund to purchase radios at a discount to be lent to shut-ins.

Moon River was broadcast on WLW (Cincinnati, Ohio) in the 1930s and 1940s. It was one of the best-known and best-loved local shows of the network radio era. It began when WLW's owner, Powel Crosley, Jr., told Ed Bryan to create a poetry show to make use of the organ he had just purchased. Narrated by Bob Brown among others, *Moon River* occasionally found its way to the networks. One reference mentions it being broadcast on NBC Red at 12:30 A.M. on 15 March 1942.

George Work hosted *Melody and Rhyme* from 1927 until his death in 1947. It was broadcast on WNYC on Sunday mornings from 8:00 A.M. to 8:45 A.M. During those 45 minutes, he read four to six sentimental poems over music, or between musical selections.

Edgar Guest's poems were a regular feature of many music-poetry programs. He also had his own radio career as a poet/host. It began in Boston in the 1920s, although Guest was most well known in the Midwest. He hosted his own show in the 1930s on WASH (Grand Rapids, Michigan) and later on a show in which he read poems between selections by the Detroit Symphony on CBS. Guest's career with poetry on radio continued into the 1940s as he

provided poetry for an NBC radio show in 1941 along with Eddie Howard.

Highbrow/Serious Poetry

Although most of the poetry on the radio was of the sentimental variety, there has long been a presence of "highbrow" or serious poetry allied with the more elite poets, poetry establishments, and the academy. One show that included more serious poetry was the previously mentioned *Poet's Gold*. Another was *Poetry Hour* hosted by A.M. (Aloysius Michael) Sullivan, an officer of the Poetry Society of America. Sullivan began broadcasting *Poetry Hour* on WOR/Mutual Network in 1930 and was still on the air into the 1940s. *Poetry Hour* presented the poets reading their own work and discussing techniques and trends in poetry. He presented more than 300 poets on the air including Stephen Vincent Benét, Edgar Lee Masters, Padraic Colum, Sara Teasdale, Mark Van Doren, and Kimball Flaccus. In 1937 this program helped provide an entrée onto the radio airwaves for Norman Corwin, who filled in for Sullivan on several occasions. In 1948 Sullivan created *The Poet Speaks*, which combined the reading of poetry with discussion about it.

Among the highest of the highbrows, Harriet Monroe, the founding editor of *Poetry: A Magazine of Verse*, appeared on *Here, There and Everywhere*, a 15-minute Chicago area program between 1930 and 1936. She also was on CBS's *American School of the Air* in a 10-minute segment on modern poetry.

Radio Verse Plays

The late 1930s brought a new development to the history of poetry on radio with the beginning of radio verse plays. The legendary first broadcast was Archibald MacLeish's verse play for radio *The Fall of the City*, which was broadcast 11 April 1937 from 7:00 P.M. to 7:30 P.M. on CBS. *The Fall of the City*, said critics, represented the American broadcasting industry's discovery of great radio in poetry and at the same time an American poet's discovery of great poetry in radio. In MacLeish's own words, "I realized at the time how much 'The Fall of the City' owed to not being seen, how much it owed to the fact that the imagination conceives it."

The Fall of the City raised the bar for the level of poetry on radio. First, its author was a writer of high repute—MacLeish won the Pulitzer Prize for Poetry in 1933 and later became the Librarian of Congress. Second, the play recognized radio as a literary medium, well suited to verse and poetry. This furthered the view that radio was highbrow and artistic. *Fall of the City* was referred to frequently by critics in later years as an eminent first in literary broadcasting.

It was, however, Norman Corwin who was to become known as "radio's poet laureate." The *New York Times* said that "Corwin writes with a poet's vision, a good reporter's clarity and a technician's precise knowledge of his craft—three attributes that have made him preeminent in radio literature." While Norman Corwin's name eventually overshadowed all others in the world of radio verse plays, he went on to become much more as he made his reputation as a writer, producer, and director.

Corwin began his radio career at WBZA (Springfield, Massachusetts) reading the news and then later hosting a show called *Rhymes and Cadences* in which he read poems aloud. He moved to New York in 1936, where he hosted *Poetic License* beginning in late 1937. It was broadcast from 9:45 P.M. to 10:00 P.M. on WQXR, a New York station then known for its high-quality ("for the discriminating listener") innovative programming. *Poetic License* featured some of the leading poets of the day in conversational poetry, or what was to become known as "talking verse." On one show Corwin presented an adaptation of *Spoon River Anthology* that caught the attention of W.B. Lewis, a CBS vice president, and led to his becoming a major fixture there.

Soon after moving to CBS, Corwin started *Words without Music*, a sustaining show broadcast on Sundays from late 1938 to June 1939. Here Corwin appealed to a variety of listeners by reading poetry from Mother Goose to Walt Whitman, Carl Sandburg, Robert Frost, and occasionally African-American poets such as James Weldon Johnson and Sterling Brown. *Words without Music* used a form called "vitalized" or "orchestrated" poetry that consisted of dramatizing a poem, giving its lines to several voices, and sometimes adding lines and repetition for dramatic effect. By dramatizing poems and/or adding a sense of humor, Corwin opened up the audience for "good" poetry beyond the highbrow, to include those who enjoyed drama and/or comedy.

Words without Music inspired an NBC poetry program *Fables without Music*, featuring Alfred Kreymborg. It was, however, much more serious in tone and subject. Broadcast in the spring of 1939, it consisted of 10 radio verse plays of 15 minutes each.

Among the hundreds of verse plays written for radio in the 1940s are Stephen Vincent Benét's *A Child is Born*, W.H. Auden's *The Dark Valley*, Pearl S. Buck's *Will This Earth Hold?*, Norman Rosten's *Concerning the Red Army*, and Edna St. Vincent Millay's *The Murder of Lidice.*

Postwar Years

After World War II, poetry played a lesser role on network radio. Some earlier shows, such as *Between the Bookends*, survived into the 1950s. Others suffered as the networks became more commercialized and reduced the number of sustaining programs. Norman Corwin left CBS in 1948 because of a contract dispute and moved to Hollywood. In addition, the networks were less interested in promoting these shows. One example was their reduction in support for the publication of books to support and advertise their on-air poetry shows.

Shows containing poetry or of interest to poetry fans did, however, appear, some locally and some on the networks. One was hosted by Mary Margaret McBride, who broadcast from 1935 to 1955, first as Martha Deane, then under her own name. Her guests included Langston Hughes, Mark and Carl Van Doren, Carl Sandburg, and William Carlos Williams.

Like so many artists, poets of the 1950s suffered under the pressures of McCarthyism. Unofficial lists of "communists" included many prominent poets such as W.H. Auden, Archibald MacLeish, Carl and Mark Van Doren, and Stephen Vincent Benét.

New poetry shows that began in the 1950s included *Poetry of Our Time*, featuring author and poet Katherine Anne Porter reading her poetry. Another was *Anthology*, which mixed music, poetry, and other literature in a series presented in cooperation with the Poetry Center of the Young Men's-Young Women's Hebrew Association. It was produced by Steve White, directed by Draper Lewis, and hosted by Harry Fleetwood. Guests included W.H. Auden, Edna St. Vincent Millay, William Carlos Williams, and Wallace Stevens.

David Ross' long career of reading poetry on the air continued in the 1950s with *Words in the Night*, Here Ross read poetry with music provided by guitarist Tony Mattola and vocalist Sally Sweetland. *The Poet Speaks* was heard on WGBH (Boston) featuring Wallace Stevens, E.E. Cummings, and Adrienne Rich, among many others.

Noncommercial and Other Venues

With the decline in network support for poetry, noncommercial and educational radio filled some of the gap. University and other stations serving cultured and academic populations have supported numerous poetry programs that have lasted as long as their mostly unpaid hosts could manage. Broadcasting since the late 1920s, WOSO at Ohio State University did some of the most progressive work in poetry including *Lyric Ohio*, which presented the work of Ohio poets. On the air since 1930, *Invitation to Reading* on WHA at the University of Wisconsin included poetry programs for high school students.

In the late 1950s, music and literature shows made up 70 percent of the schedule for KPFA (Berkeley, California), flagship station of the Pacifica Foundation. In 1959 KPFA broadcast *The Poetry of Lawrence Ferlinghetti* as well as numerous other shows of beat poets from the thriving poetry scene in the San Francisco Bay Area at the time. Chicago's fine arts station, WFMT, has throughout its history featured live and recorded poetry readings. One notable example is Ken Nordine's *Word Jazz*, which was broadcast in the late 1950s and early 1960s.

The Library of Congress' presence on the radio began in the early 1940s with the Radio Research Project headed by Archibald MacLeish. Although poetry was not its main emphasis, the Research Project featured some of it in a series titled *Books and the News*. In 1950, consultant in poetry Conrad Aiken inaugurated the broadcasting of readings over a local radio station, WCFM, under the Library of Congress' sponsorship. These broadcasts continued in the 1950s and included Katherine Garrison Chapin reading the poems of Emily Dickinson as well as the works of other women poets. The programs were broadcast from the Coolidge Auditorium at the Library of Congress and were often aired only locally in Washington, D.C., although some reached a national audience as well.

Since the early 1950s the Library of Congress has continued to have an irregular but important presence on the airwaves. It has often featured the current consultant in poetry (now called Poet Laureate Consultant in Poetry) as well as a long list of distinguished poets of note. The Library of Congress continues to host poetry broadcasts to this day. Recently these have primarily been on WETA-FM in Washington with national distribution via satellite. One example is *The Poet and the Poem from the Library of Congress*, hosted by Grace Cavalieri, which began broadcasting in 1989 and has been annual since 1997. Robert Pinsky provided the first live poetry webcast on the internet from the Library of Congress on 8 October 1998.

The Library of Congress' Archive of Recorded Poetry and Literature contains many broadcasts by known and not-so-known poets. Many recordings were made at local stations and given to the Library for inclusion in the archive. The Archive of Hispanic Literature, also at the Library of Congress, contains the recordings of hundreds of poets, including six or more Nobel Prize winners from Latin America and Spain. It is difficult to know how many of these were broadcast.

The decade of the 1960s opened with a major American poet, Robert Frost, reading a poem he had written at the inauguration of John F. Kennedy. It was broadcast live on radio and began:

A Golden Age of poetry and power,
Of which the noonday's the beginning hour.

At that point he was blinded by the sun and snow and could hardly read his words. Quickly he moved into a poem he knew well, "The Gift Outright," holding his head high as the words reached out. Frost also read on WAMF (Amherst, Massachusetts) many times between 1948 and 1962. Most of those recordings are in the Archive of Recorded Poetry and Literature at the Library of Congress.

In the 1970s, poetry's access to the airwaves increased with the advent of National Public Radio (NPR). Since its beginning in 1971, NPR has broadcast a number of shows that have featured poets and poetry. *Voices in the Wind* broadcast beginning in 1974 with Oscar Brand as host and included Nikki Giovanni, Lucille Clifton, and Allen Ginsberg. *Poet Speaks*, a 30-minute show that originated at WGBH, broadcast with Herbert Kenny as host from April to June 1972. Guests included Richard Eberhart, John Updike, May Sarton, and Allen Tate. Some shows had very limited runs, perhaps one or only a few broadcasts. *Spoon River Anthology* was broadcast in March 1973 in four weekly installments, originating at WGBH. *The Archibald MacLeish Tribute* was broadcast 15 April 1981 with MacLeish and John Ciardi. MacLeish was also interviewed in *Book Beat* on 31 October 1971. *Voice of the Poet* was broadcast 15 January 1975 with Jerome Rothenberg and Marge Piercy among the guests. Some of the other shows that have featured or included poetry are *Talk of the Nation*, *Fresh Air*, and *Children's Radio Theatre*.

Poetry on Radio Today

At the beginning of the 21st century, Garrison Keillor hosted a daily five-minute radio program called *The Writer's Almanac*, in which he notes milestones of the day and closes with a poem or two. It is heard each day on public radio stations throughout the country. Occasionally Keillor also includes poetry in his weekly program *A Prairie Home Companion*. Other short shows similar to *The Writer's Almanac* include *The Osgood File* with Charles Osgood, heard daily on the CBS radio network, and *Bookbeat*, a daily report on new books and authors with Don Swain as host on WCBS in New York.

New Letters on the Air, the radio companion to the printed publication *New Letters*, was first broadcast locally in Kansas City, Missouri, beginning in 1977. *New Letters on the Air* is a half-hour weekly show designed primarily to introduce the author with a short interview and then a number of poems. Typically, the program has about 10 minutes of poetry, 15 minutes of interview, and three minutes of introductions, credits, and musical bridges. *New Letters on the Air* has featured four Nobel Prize Winners, as well as 50 winners of various other literary awards, including the Pulitzer Prize. Approximately one-third of the featured writers are members of ethnic minorities. It has been syndicated over the NPR satellite and broadcast in more than 60 cities. From 1984 to 1995 it was hosted and produced by Rebekah (Presson) Mosby.

The Poet and the Poem is a one-hour show broadcast locally on WPFW in Washington, D.C., nationally by Pacifica Radio, and internationally by the Voice of America. From 1977 to 1997 it was broadcast weekly, first on Thursday, then on Sunday evenings. It has featured more than 2,000 poets ranging from United States Poet Laureates and Pulitzer Prize winners to unpublished and/or fledgling poets of consequence. In *The Poet and the Poem*, host Grace Cavalieri first provides biographical information about the poet who then reads several poems. A poet herself, Cavalieri asks probing and insightful questions that draw the poets out in revealing and informative ways. From 1978 to 1993, the program also hosted an all-day poetry broadcast once a year featuring 35 performers present. Titled *Ribbon of Song*, it featured Sterling Brown among others and the archival works of Paul Laurence Dunbar and Langston Hughes among others. In May (National Poetry Month) of 2000, in celebration of the bicentennial of the Library of Congress, *The Poet and the Poem from the Library of Congress* was a one-hour weekly show with W.S. Merwin, Louise Gluck, Robert Pinsky, and Rita Dove.

Other contemporary shows of note include *Poems to a Listener* with host Henry Lyman on WFCR-FM, Amherst, Massachusetts; *A Moveable Feast* with Tom Vitale and guests such as Allan Ginsberg, Charles Bukowski, and Joyce Carole Oates; *Soundings* with Wayne Pond; *Bookworm* with Michael Silverblatt from KCRW, Santa Monica, California; *Enjoyment of Poetry* with Florence Becker Lennon on WEVD, New York; *Booktalk* with Rus Morgan on WYPL; and *The Book Show* with Douglas Glover.

Poetry continues to be heard on radio in much the way it was in the early parts of the 20th century. It is heard on stations big and small, to inform and entertain, as filler, inspiration, and as something to soothe. As the internet becomes more of a force in radio, more programs will be available live over the web. Recorded poetry as well is becoming available online, being broadcast, or "webcast."

Perhaps the close and continuing association of poetry and radio should come as no surprise. The development of the radio restored the power of the spoken word. Both are reflections of the original oral traditions that gave birth to our literary heritage. In the words of Archibald MacLeish, "The ear is the poet's perfect audience, his only true audience. And it is radio and only radio which can give him public access to this perfect friend."

See also: Drama; Playwrights on Radio

Further Reading

Cifelli, Edward M., *John Ciardi: A Biography*, Fayetteville: University of Arkansas Press, 1997.

Donaldson, Scott, and R.H. Winnick, *Archibald MacLeish: An American Life*, Boston and London: Houghton Mifflin, 1992.

Everett, Michael, editor, *The Radio Book of Verse*, New York: Poetry House, 1939.

Godfrey, Edward, *Stories and Poems Read by Uncle Ed over KDKA*, Pittsburgh, Pennsylvania: Godfrey, 1926.

Kaplan, Milton Allen, *Radio and Poetry*, New York: Columbia University Press, 1949.

MacLeish, Archibald, *The Fall of the City: A Verse Play for Radio*, New York and Toronto: Farrar and Rinehart, and London: Boriswood, 1937.

Malone, Ted, *A Listener's Aid to "Pilgrimage of Poetry": Ted Malone's Album of Poetic Shrines*, New York: Columbia University Press, 1939.

McGuire, William, *Poetry's Catbird Seat: The Consultantship in Poetry in the English Language at the Library of Congress, 1937–1987*, Washington, D.C.: Library of Congress, 1988.

Poetry Broadcast: An Anthology Compiled for Radio Programs, 4 vols, New York: Exposition Press, 1946.

Poetry House, editors, *Poems for Radio*, New York: Poetry House, 1945.

Ross, David, compiler, *Poet's Gold: An Anthology of Poems to Be Read Aloud*, New York: Macaulay, 1933.

Selch, Andrea, "Engineering Democracy: Commercial Radio's Use of Poetry, 1920–1960," Ph.D. diss., Duke University, 1999.

Tate, Allen, compiler, *Sixty American Poets, 1896–1944*, Washington, D.C., 1945; revised edition, edited by Kenton Kilmer, Detroit, Michigan: Gale Research, 1969.

Wons, Anthony, compiler, *Your Dog and My Dog: From Tony Wons' Famous Radio Scrap Book*, Chicago: Reilly and Lee, 1935.

BRAD MCCOY

POLITICS AND RADIO

The late 1920s witnessed the dramatic expansion of radio as it became a powerful new form of mass communication. The 1930 census reported that nearly 70 percent of all homes in the United States had at least one radio. As the 1930s came to a close, more families owned radios than owned telephones and automobiles or subscribed to newspapers. Nowhere was the impact of radio more widespread than in the political arena. Radio had several effects on political discourse and campaigns. It made campaigning more expensive, as the cost of radio airtime added millions to campaign budgets, and it brought the advertising agency into politics. Perhaps even more importantly, radio was the first technological medium that allowed presidents to "go public"—that is, to go over the heads of Congress and directly to the people, thereby changing the method of governance. This entry, detailing radio's impact on the political process, chronicles the major eras of political radio in the U.S., which include: (1) politics and radio in the early years—from Harding to Hoover; (2) Roosevelt and radio; (3) the postwar years and the rise of television; and (4) the rebirth of political radio.

Politics and Radio in the Early Years—From Harding to Hoover

The first president to speak on radio was President Woodrow Wilson in 1919. However, only a few people heard Wilson's address, and those listening could distinguish no more than a few clear words. Historians theorize that if radio had evolved ten years earlier and provided him the opportunity to speak directly to the people, Woodrow Wilson might have been more successful in his appeal for League of Nations membership.

It was not until after the landslide Harding election of 1920 that both the public and politicians realized that radio could be a pragmatic and efficient communication medium. After the election, Harding periodically spoke on the radio concerning national matters. His 1923 State of the Union speech was carried widely, and later that same year, while on a Western tour, Harding energized the populace's acceptance of political radio with a series of commentaries entitled "Stewardship of the Administration." The effects of these radio announcements were swiftly imprinted on the American political landscape. For example, development of radio during the Harding administration was evident in the broadcasting arrangements made for his Western tour. The railroad car in which he traveled was equipped with a radio transmitter in order to broadcast speeches to a large portion of the nation.

There is little doubt that the novelty of these presidential addresses made at least some impression on the populace. Nonetheless, Harding, it seems, was not altogether comfortable with the new medium. A *New York Times* observer reported, "He is dominated by the restraining influence of the radio-telephone amplifiers, into which he has talked while making these addresses. The mechanical contrivance worries him and he is tempted at times to revert to the old style oratory" ("Cordial to Harding, Cold to Speeches," *New York Times*, 25 June 1923).

As troubling as the mechanics of the radio may have been to Harding, his successor, Calvin Coolidge, found the medium to be suitable to him rhetorically, even as he recognized radio's political possibilities. "Silent Cal" was anything but silent when it came to radio broadcasts. In 1924 it is estimated that Coolidge spoke more than 9,000 words per month over radio and that more than 50,000 people heard his voice during the first eight months of 1927, more than had heard any previous president. That radio broadcasts benefited Coolidge is rarely disputed. Both writers and politicians who assessed Coolidge's radio abilities gave him enthusiastic endorsements. Coolidge himself once made the observation, "I am very fortunate that I came with the radio. I can't make an engaging, rousing, or oratorical speech, but I have a good radio voice, and now I can get my message across to them without acquainting them with my lack of oratorical ability" (Chester, 1969). Coolidge tended, however, to refrain from utilizing radio as a tool for practical political or party gain. Even though radio played a large role in establishing Coolidge as president and in getting him re-elected, he did not feel the need to speak habitually to the nation.

Certainly presidential addresses made up the largest number of political programs on radio in these early years, but the public also seemed to pay attention to other political events carried on the airwaves. Starting in 1924, political party conventions were covered by radio and heard by a large audience, and that same election witnessed the beginning of paid broadcast advertising for political parties and candidates. The early years of radio also saw the beginning of radio's use as a medium for advocating political viewpoints. The most famous of these advocates was the "Radio Priest," Father Charles Coughlin, who used radio to promote his views on social and political issues of the day during the 1920s and 1930s.

If Coolidge was the harbinger of radio as beneficial to the democratic ideal, Hoover was the forerunner of radio as an integral part of a campaign. Hoover pushed the Republican party toward spending the major portion of its publicity budget on radio. Indeed, in May 1928 Hoover indicated that he would engineer his campaign largely through radio and films. The use of radio in the 1928 campaign by both Hoover and his Democratic challenger, Alfred Smith, was remarkable on a number of levels. First, despite his interest in drama as a younger man, Smith did not use the radio airwaves well. Problematic was his East Side accent, which may have endeared him to the immigrant population in New York City but which hurt him in the South, where he desperately needed votes. Second, the spending for airtime in this campaign, by both parties, reached nearly $2 million. This represented only about 15 percent of the total publicity budgets of both parties for a medium that was able to reach nearly 40 million voters.

Radio as a political medium was growing rapidly. For example, the League of Women Voters developed a bipartisan series of programs designed to inform voters, claiming to provide background information, differing points of view on issues, and information on the political and voting process. Campaigning notwithstanding, political scientists argue that radio may have had an even more powerful influence upon American presidential politics than simply the obvious effect of helping candidates attract votes. The power of the president rose with the ability to go "over the head of Congress" directly to the American public. The potential power of the presidency was strengthened during the Harding, Coolidge, and Hoover administrations, and radio played an important role in this development.

Roosevelt and Radio

The harshness of the Great Depression, which had shrouded the country since 1929, almost ensured a victory for the Democratic party in the 1932 election. One of the more notable aspects of his nomination was Franklin Delano Roosevelt's outstanding radio speaking ability. He began his campaign with a radio address at Albany, New York, and he accepted the nomination of his party at the convention over radio, breaking the precedent of waiting for a time lapse of one month. Long before his nomination, Roosevelt suspected that the power of radio would be important to his political livelihood. For instance, in an address to the Tammany Speaker's Bureau in 1929, Roosevelt argued that American politics "had passed from an era in which silver tongues had swayed many votes through a period of newspaper domination to the present age in which radio was king" (Chester, 1969).

The election of 1932 witnessed a remarkable juxtaposition of quality versus quantity. Herbert Hoover had, for example, launched his campaign for re-election over the largest political radio hookup in history, nearly 160 stations. The Republican party used 73 hours of network time to boost its candidate, compared to 51 hours for the Democrats, and ultimately Republicans outspent Democrats on the radio. This did little to enhance the possibility of Hoover's being re-elected, however, as he was not a particularly effective performer on the radio.

The 1936 election was one of the more remarkable campaigns in the history of presidential politics. The Republicans chose a notoriously poor public speaker in Kansas governor Alfred Landon. Further, 1936 witnessed the arrival of a third-party candidate, William Lemke of the Union party, whose candidacy was driven by Father Coughlin. Faced with a strong Democratic candidate as well as Father Coughlin's demagoguery, Republican strategists developed and employed several innovative radio strategies to assist their candidate. The innovations included spot radio advertisements for their candidate as well as the radio drama *Liberty at the Crossroads*, which played on WGN in Chicago. One of the more creative techniques was a one-sided "debate" in which Republican linchpin Arthur Vandenburg "debated" a phonographically recorded Franklin Roosevelt. The debate was designed to illustrate Roosevelt's failed campaign promises from 1932. The "debate" caused consternation among the 66 stations scheduled to carry it: 23 broadcast it, 21 cut it off, and the remainder vacillated back and forth. Also during 1936, both parties placed a great deal of emphasis on foreign-language broadcasts, creating about 2,000 political broadcasts altogether. The Democrats had foreign-language transmissions in over a dozen cities, and the Republicans employed 29 languages in everything from 100-word spot advertisements to 30-minute talks.

Roosevelt's overwhelming victories in 1932 and 1936 were due, in part, to his use of radio.

However, these victories were not so much caused by the use of radio in the campaign itself; instead, it was the cultivating of the electorate during his first term in office that ensured Roosevelt's success. Republican innovation aside, the introduction of Roosevelt's "fireside chats" was one of the most effective uses of mediated political communication in the 20th century.

The Postwar Years and the Rise of Television

With the advent of television, Harry Truman as well as other politicians had to adapt to a new broadcast medium. The future of politics in radio also evolved. Significant during the 1948 campaign was a debate that served as the antecedent to the famous televised Kennedy and Nixon debates 12 years later. The leading contender for the Republican nomination in 1948 was Thomas Dewey, but Minnesota Governor Harold Stasson was a strong challenger. The two men faced off at a Portland radio station in May 1948, and Dewey profited from the confrontation. A poll taken by the *Oregonian* showed that Stassen's popularity dropped following the debate, although by the eve of the election his numbers reflected his pre-debate strength.

Harry Truman's most significant innovations in the political use of radio in 1948 were to record press conferences to assist the White House in checking sources and notes. The Truman White House then began to allow radio broadcasters to transmit portions of the recordings to the general public. Truman's administration will probably be best remembered in broadcast history for the ascent of television. Though radio continued to be used, television quickly became the medium that affected the electorate. Truman became the first president to participate in a television broadcast from the White House when on 5 October 1947 he asked people to cooperate in the President's Food Conservation Program.

Although radio would not again dominate the American political scene, radio remained an important medium for political progress in many less developed countries. The Voice of America continues to broadcast political and informational programming around the world, and many nations, divided by political subcultures and a myriad of differing languages, still find radio superior to television as a way of communicating political messages.

Rebirth of Political Radio

Television made a rather subdued entry into politics at the 1948 Democratic convention. Only a handful of cameras provided live coverage for people who owned sets between Boston and Washington. Even so, television was about to create dramatic changes in American politics. Radio had already laid the foundation for these changes. One of the changes that had developed with radio was that it was a more politically neutral medium than the print medium of the press. Barnard (1924) pointed out, "The listener can form his own opinion for the candidate's utterance before the press or the parties can instruct him." Television continued, to a degree, that aura of neutrality.

Although the days of radio *dominance* of presidential politics were over, radio continues to this day to play an important role in political campaigns for state and local elections. Thousands of elections take place in the United States below the presidential level, and in each election cycle radio serves not only to cover candidates and issues in these races, but also to provide the only affordable and viable broadcast medium for campaign advertising. Even in presidential campaigns and many statewide races, radio remains a viable advertising medium because it provides an avenue for targeting much more specific subgroups of the population than television's more generic audience.

The dichotomy between television and radio grew, and by 1956 television had become a more important source of information than radio. However, radio retained an important role in politics. For example, scholars still argue about the controversial finding from the 1960 Kennedy/Nixon debate that Kennedy was judged the winner by those who watched the debate on television, whereas Nixon was thought to be the superior debater by those who heard the debate on the radio. This finding fueled a continuing debate of its own—why some candidates apparently are more successful on television while others excel on radio.

Radio also played a major role in several aspects of the 1968 presidential campaign. The candidacy of Senator Eugene McCarthy of Minnesota was strengthened when he devoted a large portion of his budget for the New Hampshire primary to radio (McCarthy's campaign team created some 7,200 spots for 23 New Hampshire radio stations to run within a three-week period). The impact of McCarthy on the 1968 primaries was due in large part to his use of radio in New Hampshire. Richard Nixon also relied on radio in his 1968 campaign: believing the studies that touted his superiority on radio in the 1960 debates, Nixon delivered radio addresses on 14 straight nights leading up to the general election. Not only did Nixon use radio extensively again in his 1972 re-election campaign, but he regularly devoted time to major radio addresses during his presidency.

Not until Ronald Reagan would a president give such attention to radio as a method of communicating with the American public. Unhappy with press representation of his policies, Ronald Reagan initiated regular Saturday afternoon radio broadcasts in order to talk directly with the people. George Bush occasionally delivered radio addresses as well, though less frequently than Reagan. President Bill Clinton returned to Reagan's routine of Saturday radio conferences. The general consensus has been that the effects of these messages are limited and may be of more importance in creating news for other media to disseminate. For instance, even though barely half of all radio stations broadcast Reagan's radio addresses, coverage of the talks by the television networks was extensive, and thus Reagan may have succeeded in putting many of his ideas on the table by using the media to emphasize his own agenda.

Another political radio phenomenon developed in the 1980s and 1990s. Political talk radio erupted in the 1980s with impressive audience demographics. For example, in 1995 Rush Limbaugh attracted nearly 20 million listeners, 92 percent of whom were registered voters, 39 percent of whom had college degrees, and 30 percent of whom had a family income of over $60,000. Industry officials argue that talk radio affects politics and elections by reaching a small target group of active citizens. The decline in the popularity of political talk radio in the late 1990s, however, suggests that the dramatic impact attributed to political talk radio in the 1992 and 1996 elections may not be repeated in the next millennium.

The next development in radio's marriage with politics will undoubtedly evolve from its melding with yet another new medium, the internet. Increasingly, radio stations are finding outlets for their programming through internet broadcast, and political talk radio as well as campaign advertising and airing of political issue positions are all sure to provide increased venues for political impact.

Finally, radio set the stage for a new type of political communication. Radio and television are more intimate in nature, bringing political leaders and candidates into the home, where families watch and listen to the candidate in informal settings. Roosevelt's fireside chats introduced a new model of communication, that is, one leader or candidate sitting in his or her living room speaking with millions of people also sitting in the privacy of their living rooms (Jamieson, 1988). These intimate settings allow a politician to educate, to remind, and

in large part to garner support for his or her programs. Radio was the building block upon which politically intimate communication developed and the springboard for the success of television in the political arena.

Although radio may not have revolutionized politics, it did help to change the atmosphere in which the political system operated. Radio may have limited the old-style political oratory and led to the new genres of intimate political address represented well by Ronald Reagan and Bill Clinton. Radio also increased the president's ability to "go public" with issues, forever altering the political dynamics of interaction between the executive and legislative branches.

It is significant that only a few years after the advent of radio in the political arena, one of the greatest radio politicians, Roosevelt, came to the forefront. Very early in the Roosevelt years it was clear that he demonstrated in his low-key fireside chats a mastery of intimate personal delivery. But by 1932, this was altogether natural. Radio was, by then, clearly the way a president spoke to the nation's people.

Decline?

With important exceptions, radio's political role and importance declined in the early 21st century. As news and public-affairs programming disappeared from a growing number of stations, so, too, did programming concerning candidates and political races and issues. One exception to that trend was the continued ranting of right-wing talk show hosts who often commented (at great length) on candidates and controversies. Indeed they dominated much of radio's public-affairs programming. The 2008 presidential campaign saw substantial use of radio spot advertising in key swing states, in part because radio is cheap next to television advertising.

The other exception was begun by Ronald Reagan in the 1980s and was continued by most of his successors–the brief weekly radio message from the president. George Bush used the format regularly through the early 2000s. Barack Obama provided such broadcasts even before being sworn into office in January 2009 and continued them as a part of his administration's outreach to the public. In a sign of the times, however, the weekly broadcast, typically released on a Saturday, could also be heard over the internet.

See also: Controversial Issues, Broadcasting of; Editorializing; Election Coverage; "Equal Time" Rule; Fairness Doctrine; Fireside Chats; First Amendment and Radio;

News; Talk Radio; United States Congress and Radio; United States Presidency and Radio

Further Reading

Archer, Gleason Leonard, *History of Radio to 1926*, New York: American Historical Society, 1938; reprint, New York: Arno Press, 1971.

Barber, James David, *The Pulse of Politics: Electing Presidents in the Media Age*, New York: Norton, 1980.

Barnard, Eunice F., "Radio Politics," *New Republic* 38 (19 March 1924).

Becker, Samuel L., "Presidential Power: The Influence of Broadcasting," *Quarterly Journal of Speech* 67 (1961).

Braden, Waldo W., and Earnest Brandenburg, "Roosevelt's Fireside Chats," *Speech Monographs* 22, no. 5 (November 1955).

Casey, Robert D., "Republican Propaganda in the 1936–1937 Campaign," *Public Opinion Quarterly* 1 (1937).

Chester, Edward W., *Radio, Television, and American Politics*, New York: Sheed and Ward, 1969.

"Cordial to Harding, Cold to Speeches," *New York Times* (25 June 1923).

Cornwell, Elmer E., Jr., *Presidential Leadership of Public Opinion*, Bloomington: Indiana University Press, 1965.

Dryer, Sherman H., "Air Power," *Colliers* 106 (14 September 1940).

Freidel, Frank Burt, *Franklin D. Roosevelt: The Triumph*, Boston: Little Brown, 1956.

Hollander, Barry A., "Political Talk Radio in the '90s: A Panel Study," *Journal of Radio Studies* 6, no. 2 (Autumn 1999).

Jamieson, Kathleen Hall, *Eloquence in an Electronic Age: The Transformation of Political Speechmaking*, New York and Oxford: Oxford University Press, 1988.

Kernell, Samuel, *Going Public: New Strategies of Presidential Leadership*, Washington, D.C.: CQ Press, 1986; 3rd edition, 1997.

Martin, Howard H., "President Reagan's Return to Radio," *Journalism Quarterly* 61 (1984).

Tulis, Jeffrey K., *The Rhetorical Presidency*, Princeton, New Jersey: Princeton University Press, 1987.

Willis, Edgar E., "Radio and Presidential Campaigning," *Central States Speech Journal* 20 (1969).

Wolfe, G. Joseph, "Some Reactions to the Advent of Campaigning by Radio," *Journal of Broadcasting* 13, no. 3 (Summer 1969).

LYNDA LEE KAID AND TERRY A. ROBERTSON,
2009 REVISIONS BY CHRISTOPHER H. STERLING

PORTABLE DIGITAL LISTENING DEVICES
All Audio, All the Time

A revolution in "radio" listening took hold in the first decade of the 21st century as digital technology enabled more people to carry small portable devices with which to listen to recorded music, and even broadcasts. Just as the transistor radio of the 1950s and Walkman of the 1980s and 1990s opened a new window of listening and portability, the newer devices were having a substantial impact on audiences–and the radio business–by the end of the new millennium's first decade.

These players shared several features that ensured their success and rapid adoption by millions. While they were pricy at first, retail prices dropped quickly as production picked up. They were small and easy to carry virtually anywhere, featuring tiny "earbud" earphones that are almost invisible. They were easy to use and logical to operate. And they had a large–and rapidly expanding–capacity for recorded music. Indeed, they provided the first truly individualized music service that could travel anywhere.

Developing MP3 Technology

Many minds contributed to digital compression. Some early speech compression techniques were proposed by scientists in the U.S. in the 1970s. What became the MP3 (or Moving Picture Expert Group-1, Audio Layer 3) digital compression technology useful for music was developed in Germany. Karlheinz Brandenburg, then a doctoral student working at Nuremberg, was the chief innovator, beginning his research in the early 1980s. After completing his doctorate, starting in 1993, he and a research team at Germany's Frauenhofer Institute continually experimented with sound technology, determining how much compression could be achieved before listeners noted a deterioration in sound quality. It turned out that a compression factor of ten was achievable with no noticeable drop-off in perceived audio quality. After years of work, the International Standards Organization recognized the MPEG-1, Audio Layer 3 (or MP3) standard in 1992. Workable codes were released over the next several years, opening up many manufacturing and business opportunities. Millions in royalties paid to the Frauenhofer Institute have, in turn, funded many other research projects.

MP3 is a digital file format that compresses any digital file (such as a song) into a smaller size. For example, a 33 MB song recorded on a CD compresses down to about 3 MB. The smaller file can be more easily and quickly moved around the internet. Such files can be downloaded far faster than uncompressed music files. MP3 music files are of CD quality, depending on their bit rate, and that quality depends on the complexity of the signal being recorded and the encoder.

The compressed format makes possible the use of MP3 portable players. One of the first was released in 1998, raising alarm among record manufacturing companies. As with many break-through technologies, there have been many patent conflicts over MP3 technology and its applications. The Frauenhofer Institute, Texas Instruments, and Alcatel-Lucent are among the participants in these legal fights.

iPods

By far the best known of the new generation of listening devices (eventually with about 70 percent of the total market) is Apple's now ubiquitous iPod, first introduced in October 2001. Developed in less than a year by a 30-member team headed by Tony Fadell, the device combined breakthroughs in design, ease of use (thanks to a multipurpose scroll wheel), and battery life. Some of its innovations came from other companies working with Apple.

Just months earlier, on January 9, Apple had introduced iTunes for its Mac computers, a program that converted audio CDs into compressed digital audio files, organized digital music collections, and allowed listening to internet radio. The new iPod device had the capacity to record up to a thousand songs—but was criticized at first for its high price ($400), and the fact that it lacked compatibility with the widely used PC computer (it was made to work with Mac computers). Despite this, the iPod sold 125,000 units by the end of the year.

By March 2002, a new iPod with twice the recording capacity (and ability to work with the Windows operating system) was announced. Even smaller and more capable iPods appeared in succeeding years, and prices dropped as they sold by the thousands—a total of three million by mid-2004. BMW fitted its cars with an iPod interface allowing its use while on the road, using the automobile speakers. Soon other car brands became iPod ready. By 2006, some 50 million had been sold, and an FM tuner was been made available as one option. A year later several airlines announced iPod-friendly ports in their seats, by which time nearly half of Apple's corporate income derived from the iPod. Apple's later introduction of the hugely successful iPhone expanded the technology in new ways. By the fall of 2008, Apple had sold more than 173 million iPod devices, which were then available in a variety of models, colors and prices. It seemed everyone was carrying one—certainly most people below the age of 35.

Impact

MP3 players, and especially the iPod, soon were having widespread impact. Given that a third of all people in the U.S. over the age of 12 used one by 2008, this is no surprise. They were even used in educational situations from grade school through college. Some argued that listening to an iPod served to isolate users from one another.

In any case, they had an almost immediate impact on radio broadcasting—as use of an iPod or other device usually meant one was listening to downloaded music, not a broadcast signal. As iPods appealed strongly to the young, radio was losing what had been an important audience segment.

See also: Digital Recording; Transistor Radios; Walkman

Further Reading

Ewing, Jack. "How MP3 was Born," *Business Week* (5 March 2007).
Hormby, Tom and Dan Knight. *A History of the iPod* (September 2007).
Levy, Stephen. "The Perfect Thing," *Wired* (November 2006).
Schlender, Brent. "Apple's 21st-Century Walkman," *Fortune* (November 2001).

CHRISTOPHER H. STERLING

PORTABLE PEOPLE METER
Refining Radio Research

The Portable People Meter (often erroneously referred to as "personal" people meter) is the latest technological innovation for the measurement of radio listenership. Developed by Arbitron, the PPM, though still relatively new as this volume went to press, had already radically altered the radio business and ignited controversy, legal action and government intervention.

A small device about the size of a cell-phone or iPod, the PPM is intended to be worn around the neck or on the belt of an Arbitron-selected participant who does not mind having his or her daily radio listening constantly and consistently monitored. The PPM functions by picking up and electronically reporting back to Aribitron specially encoded, inaudible ID codes embedded into broadcast signals of participating stations.

Unlike previous audience measurement methods, the PPM requires no active participation by an individual (the survey participant) beyond being worn on their person during the day and periodically recharged in a company-provided recharger, probably overnight. The PPM does all the work by documenting all "exposures" that a person has to a particular broadcast signal whether they are hearing a station in the car, in a grocery store, the back of a cab or simply in ambient fashion while walking down a street.

As thorough and far more reliable as it is considered over standard written diary surveys (which inevitably rely on the memory and often goodwill of the person being surveyed), the PPM's inability to differentiate between "hearing" and "listening" to a particular station is one of its greatest drawbacks.

The device was originally tested by Arbitron in Manchester, England, and the company undertook its first American testing in Philadelphia before rolling PPMs out in Houston in mid-2007. This was followed by deployment in Los Angeles and Chicago and other top markets. Almost immediately, PPM findings called into question many long-held assumptions about radio listenership. First, data suggested that people listened to (or, at least, overheard) almost twice as many different radio stations as thought previously. Although this meant that many stations had much bigger audiences, it also meant that other stations had far fewer—at least according to the PPM—than previously believed. Second, PPM found that people tended to listen to radio more than they have reported previously via diaries and other ratings methods. According to Arbitron findings, 90 percent of adults listened to radio daily, compared to only 50 percent who, on a daily basis, watched primetime TV. PPMs also showed that people tended to listen to radio in shorter increments than believed previously.

Based upon these findings, some stations immediately began to act upon them. As PPMs showed higher ratings for Top 40, modern rock and oldies formats, many lower-rated stations began to reprogram their playlists in the hopes of gaining larger shares of the listening audience.

These findings were not without controversy, however. Both Hispanic and urban radio stations saw steep audience declines based upon PPM reports, causing many groups representing minority owners—including the Association of Hispanic Advertising Agencies and the National Association of Black-Owned Broadcasters (NABOB)—to accuse Arbitron of undersampling minority listeners.

Though Arbitron had not yet launched use of the PPM in New York or New Jersey, complaints about the new method were enough for the attorney generals of both states to file (October 2008) lawsuits against Arbitron, charging the company with false advertising and deceptive business practices, among other charges. The following month, FCC commissioner Jonathan Adelstein called for a formal inquiry into the PPM based upon the actions of New York and New Jersey.

In January 2009, Arbitron agreed to settle the New York and New Jersey lawsuits. Though the company stopped short of admitting fault, they did agree to pay sizable monetary sums in damages to the NABOB and to the Spanish Radio Association. They also agreed to attempt to recruit more sample members, of greater racial diversity, and pledged to sample more cellphone-only homes, as the lack of focus to homes without landlines was another criticism of PPM methodology.

The resolution of these lawsuits did not resolve all of the problems facing Arbitron's PPM. Many stations still refuse to subscribe to the service based upon what they view as the device's ongoing inaccurate and skewed findings. Equally problematic is the fact that radio's Media Ratings Council (the governing body that sets the standards for ratings providers), has yet to give full accreditation to the PPM.

Nevertheless, despite the PPM's difficult entry into the marketplace, many other companies are now hoping to challenge Arbitron's standings in radio ratings by introducing their own PPM-like methods and instruments. Integrated Media Measurement was in early 2009 testing data collection using cellphones in six markets. This system measures station exposures via codes embedded in the audible audio portion of ads and is designed to cover multiple media platforms including TV, DVD, radio, the internet and theatrical films, among others. Another firm, MediaAudit/Ipsos, was also in the early stages of developing and testing a similar system.

Finally, and perhaps most surprisingly, sensing a renewed opportunity, the A.C. Nielsen Company, the pre-eminent voice in television ratings which had left the radio ratings business in 1963, announced in late 2008 that it would re-enter radio listening measurement. Planning to utilize the old-fashioned but accepted diary method, Nielsen initially planned to survey 50 small and midsize markets and report findings by the middle of 2009. They have signed up two former Arbitron clients, multistation owners Cumulus Media and Clear Channel.

Despite the obstacles it has faced, Arbitron continued to forge ahead with plans for wider use of the PPM. Eventually, they hope to have 70,000 units deployed nationwide.

See also: Arbitron; Audience Research Methods

Further Reading

Astral Media PPM Information site, http:/infoppm. astralmediaradio.ca/
Hinkley, David, "Radio Dial: Can the Portable People Meter be Counted On?" *New York Daily News* (22 November 2008).
Knopper, Steve, "Arbitron Portable People Meter Eavesdrops on Your Musical Life," *Wired* (21 August 2007).

CARY O'DELL

PORTABLE RADIO STATIONS

In the early 1920s, hundreds of entrepreneurs were bitten by the radio bug and decided to set up their own stations. In cities all over the United States, local businessmen (and several women) put radio studios in their stores, their houses, their garages, or their factories. However, some station owners had a different plan: to put a radio station in a truck and drive it to cities that had no station of their own. Such mobile stations were called "portables," and from about 1923 to 1928, they were often invited to county fairs, expositions, and amusement parks. The owner would remove the equipment from the truck and set up an actual broadcasting station on the grounds. Most of the portables were not very powerful—between 10 and 50 W—but their purpose was to introduce the new technology to people who lived far from the big cities. Portables also served as a good gimmick to get more people to attend a local sales event: attendees could not only shop but also watch a live radio broadcast. One portable, WTAT (later renamed WATT), was owned by the Edison Electric Illuminating Company, which first put it on the air (and on the road) in the summer of 1923. WTAT was usually driven to the hall in which a home show or electronics exhibition was taking place; Edison personnel would first entertain and then demonstrate the wonders of the company's various products.

Another successful portable operated in Rhode Island and throughout New England. Owner Charles Messter was written up in the *Providence Journal* on 7 January 1925: the reporter discussed some of the cities where the station had been and then explained how the portable worked.

> [Mr. Messter's station, WCBR] consists of a 50-W standard Western Electric transmitter using 600 volts on the plate. He carries storage batteries and a charger so that he will not be caught without power. His three-wire outside antenna is 200 feet long and is usually erected on top of the building in which the outfit is being used The entire outfit can be easily set up and taken down, and this makes practicable its shipment from place to place on short notice.

Perhaps the best-known owner of a portable station operated in the Midwest throughout the mid-1920s. Charles L. Carrell, formerly a theater impresario, operated five portables based in Chicago, and he took them wherever he was hired to broadcast. One of Carrell's portables, WHBM, appeared in East St. Louis in December 1927, having been invited there by the Chamber of Commerce. The station remained for three months of broadcasts, giving many local performers an opportunity to be heard.

Of course, the novelty of portables wore off, but they might have continued their work were it not for the increasing number of stations on the AM band. In November 1925, at the Fourth National Radio Conference, Herbert Hoover, then Secretary of Commerce, stated that the airwaves had become too crowded. He warned that soon, not everyone who wanted to put a new station on the air would be able to do so. This and other problems (such as wave jumping—in which a station operated from a different frequency than the one it had been assigned) would lead to the creation of the Federal Radio Commission (FRC), an agency that had the authority to license and supervise radio broadcasting, in an attempt to bring order to a chaotic situation. The FRC regarded the portable transmitters as part of the chaos. Portables interfered with an already crowded radio spectrum, and the agency decided that eliminating them would be a positive step. It might not solve the problem of crowding—by 1927, there were not that many portables left—but it would at least keep the airwaves free of sudden interference that might be caused when a portable came to town.

The FRC General Order 6 of 26 April 1927 warned that portable broadcasting stations would only be relicensed for a limited period of time—120 days. (Originally, portables tended to operate mainly in the summer, when fairs and outdoor shows were taking place, but some portables had become nearly year-round operations.) It wasn't long before the FRC began to suggest strongly that any portable that wanted to select a specific city of license could become a permanent part of that city, but that licenses to operate portables as portables would not be permitted for much longer. The end came in mid-1928, when the FRC issued General Order 30, officially terminating the portables. Some of the owners, anticipating this, had found homes for themselves and their stations—Charles Messter, for example, joined his friend Harold Dewing in Illinois, where they anchored a portable to the city of Springfield. By 1928 Edison Electric had long since put a full-time station on the air (WEEI) and no longer needed the promotional value of a station in a truck, so WATT was shut down, as were several portables in other cities.

However, the person who owned the most portables was the one who didn't want to see them taken off the air. Charles Carrell demanded a hearing from the FRC, and several months later, he went to Washington to plead his case. Unfortunately for him, the FRC seemed to have its mind made up. After reading Carrell's materials and considering his argument, the Commission decided there was just no room for portables any longer. In fact, the commissioners did not mince words: they called the portables "a menace" and went on to say that permitting the portables would not be in the public interest, because the frequencies they chose were usually already occupied by permanent stations, and the closer together on the dial two stations were, the worse their signals would be received. Thus, the renewal of the portable station licenses could not be allowed.

Carrell took his case to the U.S. District Court on appeal, but the court would not overturn the FRC's ruling. Having lost most of his stations, he moved one of the Chicago portables (WBBZ) to Ponca City, Oklahoma, and made it a permanent station; he moved his family there, too. Only four years after losing his legal battle, he died in 1933 at the age of 58. The station in Ponca City still exists, but its early days as a portable are seldom if ever mentioned. In fact, few people realize how innovative portables were and how, for a brief period of time, they delighted radio fans who had never seen a live radio broadcast before.

See also: Federal Radio Commission; Frequency Allocation; Licensing Authorizing U.S. Stations to Broadcast

Further Reading

"Criticizes Roving Radio: Commission Replies to Appeal from Revocation of License," *New York Times* (27 August 1933).
"Discontinuance of Portable Stations" and "General Order No. 30," in *Second Annual Report of the Federal Radio Commission*, Washington, D.C.: GPO, 1928.
"Licenses for Portable Stations," in *First Annual Report of the Federal Radio Commission*, Washington, D.C.: GPO, 1927.
"Six Appeal Radio Board Orders," *New York Times* (6 January 1929).

DONNA L. HALPER

PRAIRIE HOME COMPANION
Public Radio Comedy Variety Program

Prairie Home Companion (*PHC*) is one of the most successful programs produced on public radio in the United States. The show received the prestigious George Foster Peabody award in 1980 and its creator and host, Garrison Keillor, is considered an American cultural treasure. He was awarded a National Arts and Humanities medal by the Clinton White House in 1999. Nearly four million listeners tune in weekly to more than 500 public

radio stations across the United States for the live two-hour broadcast. The show also airs abroad on America One and the Armed Forces Networks in Europe and the Far East.

Often compared to humorist Mark Twain, Keillor writes the script for each week's show. It includes comedy sketches with recurring characters ("The Lives of the Cowboys," "Guy Noir Private Eye"), mock commercials ("Ketchup Advisory Board," "Bebopareebop Rhubarb Pie," and "Café Boeuf" and the occasional competition ("Talent from Towns under 2,000" contest). Musicians from around the globe provide a diverse mix of live folk, jazz, rock and roll, classical, gospel, and ethnic tunes.

A program host on Minnesota Educational Radio in the early 1970s (it became Minnesota Public Radio in September 1974), Keillor was inspired to try an old-fashioned radio variety show back home in Minnesota after a leave of absence to research the *Grand Ole Opry* for a *New Yorker* magazine article. The show first played in a nearly empty auditorium at Macalester College in St. Paul on 6 July 1974. Twelve people (who paid one dollar for adult admission—50 cents for children) made up the audience. The show's popularity slowly grew, and national broadcasts began in 1980.

By 1987, 13 years after the initial performance, four million listeners were tuning in to hear Keillor open the show with its signature tune, Hank Snow's "Hello Love." In the same year, however, Keillor announced that *PHC* was coming to an end; he was heading off to Denmark to devote himself to writing. There was a farewell broadcast in June 1987 in St. Paul. One year later, there was a second farewell show from Radio City Music Hall in New York. Keillor told the crowd, "It was so much fun leaving that we're coming back to say goodbye again," to enthusiastic applause. The following year, the cast crisscrossed the United States, performing in 13 cities, for the "Third Annual Farewell Tour."

In 1989 Keillor started a new variety show, *The American Radio Company*, broadcast from the Brooklyn Academy of Music. Eventually more than 200 public radio stations carried the program. In 1993 the show moved to Minnesota and its name was changed back to *Prairie Home Companion*. The show was still being broadcast at the dawn of the 21st century.

About half the programs are produced in the Fitzgerald Theater in downtown St. Paul. The remainder are broadcast from a tour of cities scattered across the U.S., as well as Europe. In large civic centers and college auditoriums, fans of all ages gather to see the stage set with its worn Oriental rugs, musical instruments, and microphones. Behind it all there's a clapboard house-front with a light in the upstairs window and several lucky audience members sitting on the front porch.

Dressed in his signature black suit, white shirt, and red tie, Keillor sings tunes he has written during the previous week, accompanied by the house musicians, the Guys' All-Star Shoe Band led by pianist Rich Dworsky. Keillor plugs the fictitious sponsor of the show, Powdermilk Biscuits, "with that whole-wheat goodness that gives shy persons the strength to get up and do what needs to be done."

The audience waits in anticipation as the ensemble cast, actors Tim Russell and Sue Scott, and sound effects wizards Tom Keith and Fred Newman, step up to their microphones. Russell, a master of impersonation, brings roars of laughter as he converses with Keillor in the voices of Presidents Bill Clinton or George W. Bush, Julia Child, Bob Dylan, Ted Koppel, and many other celebrated personalities. Keith is famous for his ability to produce sound effects with his voice (the sounds of animals, automobiles, motorcycles, missiles, helicopters, and explosions) and a variety of props (including a box of gravel, cellophane, and a miniature door).

The musical segments are eclectic and could include a gospel group, a rhythm and blues singer, or a classical pianist. Rockabilly band Jack Knife and the Sharps, guitarist Leo Kottke, mandolin player Peter Ostroushko and singers Suzy Bogguss and Iris DeMent have performed for *PHC* audiences. Special guests may include writers, actors, comedians, or poets (humorists Al Franken and Roy Blount, Jr., authors Studs Terkel and Frank McCourt, U.S. Poet Laureate Billy Collins, comedienne Paula Poundstone, and actress Sarah Jessica Parker have made appearances).

Halfway through the show Keillor reads messages scribbled by members of the audience on small pieces of paper. Birthday wishes, parental advice, and words of affection go out to friends and family across the country. Throughout the show the audience responds with delighted applause to the mix of songs, comedy routines, brief interviews with guests, and commercials for old familiar products and services.

Near the end of PHC, 15–25 minutes are reserved for Keillor's weekly monolog. His opening words, "It's been a quiet week in Lake Wobegon," are greeted with a surge of applause. In Keillor's melodious baritone, the latest tales about the imaginary town's residents (including the Tolleruds, Krebsbachs, and Pastor Ingqvist) lull the audience into a sense of community in the darkened theater. The words flow steadily until finally it all comes to a tidy close, "And that's the news from Lake Wobegon, where all the women are strong, all the men are good-looking, and all the children are above average."

Prairie Home Companion stands at the end of a tradition that stretches back to the earliest days of radio. Its predecessors include such variety programs as *The Eveready Hour, The Rudy Vallee Show* (also called *The Fleischmann Hour*), *The Maxwell House Show Boat* and *The Collier Hour*. With the arrival of television in the 1940s, variety shows disappeared or shifted to the new medium. The old-fashioned variety owes its survival almost completely to the appearance in the 1970s of *Prairie Home Companion*.

By 2009, *Prairie Home Companion* was heard by more than four million listeners each week over nearly 600 public radio stations (many broadcast it more than once), and abroad on America One and the Armed Forces Networks in Europe and the Far East. Daily and weekly podcasts of the "News from Lake Wobegon" monolog segment were also offered.

See also: Comedy; Minnesota Public Radio; Public Radio International

Cast

Host	Garrison Keillor
Actors	Tim Russell, Sue Scott
Sound Effects	Tom Keith, Fred Newman

Producer/Creator

Garrison Keillor

Programming History

Minnesota Public Radio	1974–80
American Public Radio/ Public Radio International	1980–present

Further Reading

Barol, Bill, "A Shy Person Says So Long," *Newsweek* (15 June 1987).

Larson, Charles, and Christine Oravec, "A Prairie Home Companion and the Fabrication of Community," *Critical Studies in Mass Communication* 4 (September 1987).

Lee, Judith Yaross, *Garrison Keillor: A Voice of America*, Jackson: University Press of Mississippi, 1991.

Nelson, Michael, "Church on Saturday Night: Garrison Keillor's *Prairie Home Companion* " Virginia Quarterly Review 77 (Winter 2001).

Prairie Home Companion website, www.prairiehome.org

Scholl, Peter A., "Garrison Keillor and the News from Lake Wobegon," *Studies in American Humor* (Winter 1985–86).

Scholl, Peter A., *Garrison Keillor*, New York: Twayne, and Toronto: Macmillan Canada, 1993.

Selix, Casey, "At Home on the Prairie," *Houston Chronicle* (1 July 1999).

SANDRA L. ELLIS,
2009 REVISIONS BY CHRISTOPHER H. STERLING

PREMIUMS
Toys and Gifts Offered over the Air

The radio premium became a significant device for measuring listeners' product and program loyalties, and it confirmed sponsors' identifications with admired personalities and attractive fictional characters. Rushing strongly through the 1940s, the avalanche of radio premiums—recipe or inspirational booklets, club badges and membership manuals, costume jewelry, character rings and pins, whistles, and other paraphernalia—finally abated with the advent of television.

In radio's early years, premiums were introduced obliquely in unsponsored "talks." Initially forbidden to describe specific products on the air, many companies offered staff representatives to discuss consumer-interest subjects, and afterward the program host might suggest that the speaker's employer had *permitted* him to offer a token of appreciation for the listener's interest—a 1923 recipe booklet from a Chicago meat-packer, for instance. Thus, through the Trojan horse of ostensibly objective information giving, companies could gain listeners' gratitude by dropping logo-marked "gifts" into their mailboxes.

In the 1930s, the postman's premium-bearing burden increased. Premiums were compellingly described in often-lengthy commercials, and they were sometimes integrated into program content. "Missing a commercial proved almost as much a disappointment as missing a moment of the action itself," recalls a veteran children's serial listener; "I enjoyed sending for the advertised products, especially those, like the decoder ring, which became part of the story." To get the required labels or panels, children spooned through boxes of breakfast food, and their mothers baked and fried their way through packages of flour and shortening. Each week thousands of labels, dimes, and postcards reached premium fulfillment addresses in Chicago and St. Louis, and the listener's eager wait began for the mail carrier to bring the Jack Armstrong Hike-o-Meter or the brooch "just like the one our heroine wears in today's episode."

The premium's role in building audience loyalty may be seen in a handwritten note reproduced inside the front cover of Standard Brands' 1938 souvenir script *One Man's Family Looks at Life*, where Paul Barbour, the radio clan's philosopher-son, says, "As you know, this book comes to you not only from *One Man's Family*, but also from the makers of Tender Leaf Tea. When you think of one, think of the other. For Tender Leaf Tea makes it possible for *One Man's Family* to meet *your* family over the radio." Five years earlier, the pioneering serial *Clara, Lu, and Em* had courted such consumer loyalty by offering a 1933 Chicago World's Fair spoon for a Super Suds box top. For a time *David Harum*, the story of a small-town banker and horse trader, gave away a horse each week; later, when the protagonist took up photography, the program promised a working camera for a quarter and a Bab-O cleanser label. Pepsodent toothpaste's sponsorship of *Amos 'n' Andy* produced such premiums as sheet music, scripts of key episodes, and maps of the characters' adopted hometown.

General interest programs of the 1930s also devised apt premiums. *Captain Tim Healy's Stamp Club of the Air* explored the historical or geographical backgrounds of postal designs and would send a starter stamp collection for an Ivory soap wrapper. In an age fascinated by aviation, a shoe store chain's program *Friendly Five Footnotes* encouraged listeners to pick up copies of the booklet *It's Easy to Learn to Fly* at the local outlet. *The Court of Missing Heirs*, dramatizing stories of unclaimed fortunes, published a bulletin listing such cases, and *The University of Chicago Round Table* furnished transcripts of its radio discussions.

Many children's adventure serial premiums were tied to annual memberships in clubs and secret societies, and announcers energetically persuaded the listener to be "the first on your block" to obtain "your very own" message decoder badge, club manual, glow-in-the-dark ring, or other "swell" object for play and display. Don Gordon tutored children to claim their free *Captain Midnight* Flight Patrol membership cards "on the spot" when their parents next filled the gas tank at the Skelly service station, and Ovaltine spokesman Pierre Andre elicited many a "thin dime" for send-away *Orphan Annie* and later *Captain Midnight* premiums. *Jack Armstrong*, Wheaties' serial of a high school athlete turned adventurer, featured devices useful in hiking and camping. In *Tom Mix*, the cowboy hero was able to escape being tied up by nudging a magnifying glass into position so that the sun would burn into the rope, and soon requests for the magnifying glass premium filled Ralston-Purina's redemption offices. Quaker Oats offered each *Sergeant Preston of the Yukon* listener a certificate representing "actual" ownership of a square inch of Klondike land; the property was later forfeited for nonpayment of taxes, but the deed certificate continues to rise in value as an artifact of 1940s childhood.

In the 1950s, radio premiums faded with the single-sponsor programs that had offered them. Some radio shows attempted TV adaptations or simulcasts and continued to feature premiums for a time, but the success of the radio premium, like that of the host program, had depended on the enlarging power of the imagination. The camera would show too clearly that the giveaway periscope was a flimsy thing of plastic or heavy paper and that the soap opera premium jewelry gave off a glassy glare in the black-and-white TV picture. Television would develop its own lures, and the radio premium was put away in closets and memories.

See also: Old-Time Radio; Promotion on Radio

Further Reading

Hake, Theodore L., *Overstreet Presents Hake's Price Guide to Character Toy Premiums: Including Comic, Cereal, TV, Movies, Radio, and Related Store-Bought Items,* Timonium, Maryland: Gemstone, 1996; 2nd edition, York, Pennsylvania: Gemstone, 1998.
Harmon, Jim, *Radio and TV Premiums: A Guide to the History and Value of Radio and TV Premiums,* Iola, Wisconsin: Krause, 1997.
Heide, Robert, and John Gilman, *Dime-Store Dream Parade: Popular Culture, 1925–1955,* New York: Dutton, 1979.
Marchand, Roland, *Advertising the American Dream: Making Way for Modernity, 1920–1940,* Berkeley: University of California Press, 1985.
Stedman, Raymond William, *The Serials: Suspense and Drama by Installment,* Norman: University of Oklahoma Press, 1971; 2nd edition, 1977.
Tumbusch, Tom, *Tomart's Price Guide to Radio Premium and Cereal Box Collectibles, Including Comic Character, Pulp Hero, TV, and Other Premiums,* Dayton, Ohio: Tomart, 1991.

RAY BARFIELD

PRESS–RADIO WAR
Newspapers' Attempt to Stifle Radio News

The Press–Radio War proved to be an early example of the new medium of radio broadcasting competing against established newspapers to define roles and control the flow of information to the public. The radio industry emerged from this so-called war as a formidable medium that could not be restrained by newspaper publishers.

Origins of the "War"

Radio stations broadcast virtually no news in the early days of the medium. Most of what could be considered news broadcasts were actually commentaries delivered perhaps no more than once a week by broadcast pioneers such as H.V. Kaltenborn and Frederic Wile. The Columbia Broadcasting System (CBS) radio network broadcast its first regular daily news summary beginning in early 1929. By that time, the nation's radio listeners had grown to appreciate this broadcast medium's ability to inform them in a timely manner. News broadcasts of election results and the sensational kidnapping of the Lindbergh baby in 1932 had whetted the public appetite for information delivered via radio. An estimated 63 million listeners tuned in to radio broadcasts the day Herbert Hoover was inaugurated in 1929.

The newspaper industry became alarmed at what was clearly becoming a threat to print. Radio threatened to take away the "breaking news" role of newspapers. The newspaper "extra" was becoming a thing of the past by the early 1930s. Perhaps more importantly, newspaper executives feared that the growth of radio news would continue an erosion of advertising revenue from print to broadcast. The newspaper industry was ready to wage "war" against radio.

A committee of the American Newspaper Publishers Association (ANPA) brought two key recommendations to the 1933 ANPA convention. One was for the wire services to stop supplying news material to radio. The other was for newspapers to publish radio program listings only if the radio stations paid for the space as advertising. The wire services (Associated Press [AP], United Press [UP], and International News Service [INS]) were largely controlled by newspaper publishers. Pressure from the publishers led the wire services to stop providing news to radio broadcasters. The newspaper industry mistakenly believed that the removal of wire service access from the radio industry would force broadcasters out of the news business.

The radio industry fought back, largely through the efforts of CBS. CBS president William Paley directed Paul White to establish the Columbia News Service, a news organization that could supply the news needs of CBS network without the help of the wire services. White, a former UP executive, quickly established news bureaus for CBS in major U.S. cities and arranged for part-time stringers (temporary, on-call reporters) in other news centers. The Columbia News Service bought international news reports from foreign news agencies around the world. CBS network continued its broadcasting of news, further angering the newspaper industry. The National Broadcasting Company (NBC) also continued broadcasting the news, largely through the reporting efforts of Abe Schechter, but on a more limited scale than CBS. The newspaper industry retaliated by dropping CBS program listings from many newspapers around the nation.

It was clear that neither broadcasters nor newspaper publishers were happy with how this war was developing. Representatives of Publishers' National Radio Committee, the wire services, and CBS and NBC met in December 1933 in New York City to discuss ways in which they might work out their differences. The two-day meeting, held at the Hotel Biltmore, resulted in a list of understandings that became known as the Biltmore Agreement.

The agreement called for the establishment of a Press–Radio Bureau that would provide news from the wire services twice a day for unsponsored five-minute newscasts on the radio networks. The morning newscasts, however, could only be broadcast after 9:30 A.M. so as to protect sales of morning newspapers, and evening newscasts were to be broadcast after 9:00 P.M. to protect evening newspaper sales. CBS agreed to break up its own news service, and NBC agreed not to begin one. News bulletins of "transcendental" significance would be provided by the Press–Radio Bureau in a timely fashion between newscasts when circumstances dictated.

The terms of the agreement clearly favored the newspaper industry. The radio industry suffered little, however, because the agreement quickly began to unravel. Several factors led to the quick failure of the Biltmore Agreement. First, independent radio stations and even network affiliates not owned by the networks were not included and thus did not feel compelled to adhere to the terms of the agreement. They scheduled newscasts whenever they chose, with whatever information they could put together. Next, news material was provided to radio stations from several new news-gathering services, including the Transradio Press, which had jumped in to provide information to broadcasters at the time when wire services refused to provide news to radio. These new services were referred to in the newspaper industry as "outlaw" press associations, but there was clearly nothing in the Biltmore Agreement that could restrict them. The Press–Radio Bureau then began sending the networks more and more news updates during the day under the agreement's provision that allowed for timely release of "bulletin" information. Finally, in early 1935, UP and INS announced that they would

renew selling news service to radio broadcasters as a way to maintain a competitive position against Transradio and the other "outlaws." AP soon followed. In a little over one year's time, the agreement had fallen apart. The Press–Radio Bureau executive committee would not meet again after May 1935.

The Biltmore Agreement failed owing to both practical and philosophical weaknesses. Practically, the power of radio broadcasting was beyond the point at which arbitrary restrictions imposed by the newspaper industry could be effective. From a philosophic standpoint, the agreement was clearly a narrow-sighted effort to stifle information flow in a democracy. The effort to suppress news in a legitimate, although relatively new, channel of expression was a violation of the principles of press freedom in the United States. Had the effort to restrict news from the radio airwaves been more successful, the clear losers in the matter would have been America's consumers of radio broadcasting.

See also: News; News Agencies

Further Reading

"The Biltmore Agreement," in *Documents of American Broadcasting*, edited by Frank Kahn, New York: Appleton-Century-Crofts, 1968; 4th edition, Englewood Cliffs, New Jersey: Prentice Hall, 1984.
Bliss, Edward, Jr., *Now the News: The Story of Broadcast Journalism*, New York: Columbia University Press, 1991.
Chester, Giraud, "The Press–Radio War: 1933–1935," *Public Opinion Quarterly* 13 (Summer 1949).
Jackaway, Gwenyth L., *Media at War: Radio's Challenge to the Newspapers, 1924–1939*, Westport, Connecticut: Praeger, 1995.
Lott, George E., Jr., "The Press–Radio War of the 1930s," *Journal of Broadcasting* 14 (Summer 1970).
Paley, William S., *As It Happened: A Memoir*, Garden City, New York: Doubleday, 1979.
White, Paul W., *News on the Air*, New York: Harcourt Brace, 1947.

JEFFREY M. MCCALL

PRIZES
See: Awards and Prizes

PRODUCTION FOR RADIO
Creating Radio Programs

Production is an important, if not the most important, function at a radio station. Without production there is no sound from the radio speaker. As used in radio, the term *production* refers to the assembly of various sources of sound to achieve a purpose related to radio programming. Production is the intermediate step that translates ideas into audible content. The preceding steps are planning and writing, and transmission is the last step to deliver the program to the listener.

The production process in radio has changed significantly since radio first became a broadcast medium. All program production was live in the early days: actors, musicians, and announcers gathered around the microphone at the scheduled airtime and created the radio show, commercials and all. However, turntables, records, and recorders soon gave producers the ability to reproduce and enhance production efforts. Today, computers and other digital equipment play major roles in the creation of production for radio.

Early Radio Production

Production for radio during the time of the experimental broadcasts before 1920 was rudimentary: the radio equipment operator spoke into the microphone himself. As the technology of radio improved during the 1920s, interest in radio grew. By the late 1920s, as radio programming had become more complex, the production of those programs required more people and equipment.

At the National Broadcasting Company (NBC) Red network, the person responsible for the complete supervision of a program, including conducting rehearsals, was called the "production director." At NBC Blue, the Columbia Broadcasting System (CBS), and Mutual, he was called the "producer" or "production man." In a 1944 radio production text, Albert R. Crews defined the production director as "a painter who uses a loudspeaker for his canvas; actors, speakers, music, sound effects for his colors; and a mixing panel for his palette. He must consider himself a conductor as well as a partner-creator of a symphony in sound." From the time the completed script was delivered until the program aired, the production director was the final authority on all matters relating to the broadcast. The production director was responsible for devising the best arrangement of musicians, vocalists, speakers, actors, and sound effects technicians in order to create the program.

Radio programming of that era could be grouped into two major categories: spots and programs. Spots varied from ten seconds to five minutes and included commercial announcements, news broadcasts, and weather reports. Programs featuring speech (serials and dramas, speeches, instruction, news commentary, audience participation, sports, and religion), music/song, and novelty/variety ran up to one hour.

Most of these programs were created live in the studio. The typical studio was a large room, usually acoustically isolated in some way from the rest of the building, hung with heavy drapes or acoustical wall treatments. Here the actors, musicians, announcers, and sound effects people were arranged around one or more microphones.

Many programs were broadcast live from remote locations. Stations used what were called "pick-up locations" connected with telephone lines. Theaters, churches, baseball fields, hotels, and dance halls were some of the locations from which radio stations originated live productions of special events or regular programs.

Many of the programs heard on radio throughout these early decades of radio were uncomplicated from a production viewpoint, especially those created at smaller independent stations. One or two people were heard talking or reading, occasionally with musical accompaniment. More elaborate programs were produced by larger stations and the networks. Sponsor messages became elaborate mini-productions within a program. Humor, melodrama, and jingle singers helped create memorable messages. Musicians, singers, actors, and complex live sound effects all contributed to the production of these live commercials.

Drama programs made regular and frequent use of one of the most fascinating aspects of live radio production, the assembly of sound effects to create the illusions that were so important in making radio theater of the mind. Often, a sound effect suggested time and location or created exposition in these dramas. Coconut shells "stomped" in a tray of sand and a few stones created the sound of horses. Crash boxes filled with broken glass were ready to create the sound of glass breaking. The manipulation of uncut broom corn created the sound illusion of walking through brush. Windows and doors mounted in portable frames, a splash tank, and a walking platform were just some of the various mechanical devices used to create realistic, and sometimes unrealistic, sound effects.

From Live to Recorded Production

As productions became more sophisticated, producers also began to use sound effects recorded on discs. These were ten-inch, double-sided discs revolving at 78 rpm and were used to produce effects that could not be created realistically in a studio, such as train and airplane sounds, machinery of various sorts, and sounds of warfare. Often, effects were used in combination, played at variable speeds on multiple turntables that were specifically designed for sound effect reproduction. Changing the speed on an effect often created a realistic sound of something other than the original. For many programs, the sound effects staff and their equipment were the most important part of the production team assembled for a broadcast.

Even before the introduction of the tape recorder, transcription discs were used to record programs for rebroadcast, archiving, or distribution to other stations, but they were also used to create libraries of music, sound effects, and commercials. Thanks to transcription discs, many popular radio programs and commercials from the 1920s through the 1940s have been preserved. A 16-inch transcription disc, revolving at 33 1/3 rpm, could hold 15 minutes of program material. By the late 1940s, CBS had introduced the vinyl long-playing record, the 33 1/3 LP. Although radio also adopted this format as a means of recording and distribution, nothing would match the tape recorder for production purposes.

The Germans developed the magnetic tape recorder during World War II. The "Magnetophon" design was brought back to the United States at the end of the war. In 1946 singer Bing Crosby's program *Philco Radio Time* was the first program to make use of the tape recorder to record and edit the program in advance of airing. The Ampex Corporation produced its first recorder in 1948, and broadcasters quickly began to use the stationary tape recorder in production. Now producers were released from the bonds of time and place. Networks used recorders to delay programs for the different time zones. Advertising agencies were able to put produced commercials on disc and tape, allowing for continuous re-airing by stations and networks. Audiotape also introduced the ability to edit program content, correcting mistakes or making changes by cutting out or inserting additional tape. In 1959 the endless-loop tape cartridge recorder was introduced to radio. This led to a major improvement in the way commercials were aired on radio. A continuous loop of audiotape housed in a cartridge allowed an individual commercial to be selected by the engineer, inserted into the player, and played back immediately without cueing. Broadcast "carts," reel-to-reel recorders, turntables, and microphones were the basic pieces of equipment used in almost every radio station through the early 1990s.

How Production Works: A Hypothetical Case Study

To illustrate the various components of modern radio production and how they interrelate, the first part of a typical broadcast morning at a hypothetical radio station using a digital recording and playback system is described. All of the activities in the following descriptions represent production tasks, either live or recorded.

The morning announcer turns on a computer monitor and loads a playlist containing most of the day's commercials and messages into the computer-based digital audio delivery system, which was installed a year ago to replace the station's aging cart machines and reel-to-reel recorders. The computer used by the announcer in the radio control room, along with those in the production studio, the newsroom, the music director's office, and the traffic director's office, are all connected to a file-server, so that as soon as a recording is created at one location, it is available for playback anywhere on the network.

The announcer begins the broadcast day by playing a sign-on announcement (although increasingly, especially in larger markets, stations remain on the air at all times). This daily message was recorded in the station's production studio a month ago by the production director after the new ownership of the station was approved. After sign-on, the announcer turns on the network feed potentiometer or "pot" in order to air a network newscast, which is coming to the station via satellite. After the newscast, a 60-second commercial for a local furniture store is aired from the digital audio system; this commercial was produced by the afternoon announcer last week. The commercial uses a track from the station's music production library and the announcer's voice, which has been run through a microphone patched through a microphone processor in order to make the voice sound more powerful.

Following this commercial, the announcer turns on the newsroom microphone, and the news director begins the first of several live morning newscasts. The first two stories each require the announcer to insert an actuality or soundbite at the appropriate place in the story, using the minidisc player mounted just above the compact disc (CD) players. These actualities were extracted from an interview the news director recorded over the telephone yesterday afternoon, edited on the newsroom computer, and transferred to minidisc. The newscast concludes with the weather, which the announcer plays from a broadcast cart recorded over the telephone earlier this morning. After the weather, the announcer plays a station jingle, a short recorded musical promotion for the station. This jingle was recorded as part of an image campaign package recorded by a Dallas production company specifically for this station about three months ago. The announcer quickly looks at the computer monitor to make sure that the music playlist for the day is loaded on the other side of the screen and starts the first song of the morning. This selection, along with six other songs, was recorded into the digital audio delivery system yesterday by the music director.

After a second piece of music, the announcer finally opens her own microphone to say good morning. While talking, she adds the sound of a bugle to punctuate her remarks. The bugle, like many other standard sound effects, comes from a library of digitally recorded sounds licensed for broadcast use and is recorded, along with about 20 other sound effects, directly on a stand-alone hard disk recorder. Each sound effect has its own selector button. The first traffic report of the day is scheduled next. The announcer checks the console to make sure that the remote feed is in cue. Right on schedule, the line comes alive. Today the traffic reporter is downtown at the scene of an accident and is using a mobile transmitter. After a short traffic report, the announcer performs the well-practiced routine of reading advertising copy for the sponsor of the traffic report over the traffic music theme played back from the computer. At the end of the theme music, two more recorded commercials are triggered by the computer to start automatically. These came preproduced from the clients' advertising agencies. The first spot was produced at a Los Angeles production house and features four different actor voices and customized music. The second spot was produced for the client through a Chicago advertising agency. The recording itself was made in Chicago, while the voice talent was in New York, connected to the Chicago recording studio by a digital telephone line. The first spot was mailed to the station, and the second was sent as a sound file over the internet. An intern dubbed the first spot using a reel-to-reel recorder in the production studio and placed the second spot in the playlist by using the cut/paste function of the computer.

After several more music cuts, the announcer plays the new morning show contest open. Over the past several days, she has worked in the production studio recording this rather complex opening for the contest using a multitrack digital editor. She used six different segments from previous contest winners, a music bed, sound effects, and several electronic production elements to create the background. Then she voiced her copy through the digital effects processor to completely change the sound of her voice. After the open plays, she reads

the trivia question and asks for the sixth caller. As music plays, she answers the phone until she gets to the sixth caller. After receiving permission to record the call, she feeds the phone input of the console into audition (so that it doesn't go out over the air) and records the contest winner onto the hard disk recorder. With just enough time to electronically edit out the beginning of the phone call, she adjusts the edit markers on the waveform editing screen, presses the cut button, and saves her work. The song ends, and she plays back the contest winner recording on the air, adjusting the output level on the audio console. On to the next commercial break.

This hypothetical excerpt of daily activity in a radio control room effectively illustrates the fact that production is a multilevel activity necessary to create a radio program. Segments of the assembled program might have been produced at different places, different times, and using different equipment. Or the production of a segment might be happening live, concurrent with the program's airing. In some respects, digital recording simplifies the production process. Digital recording into a networked system allows instantaneous delivery of the completed spot, program, or sound element throughout the system. However, there is always the potential for computer or other equipment failure. Radio stations that depend on computer-based audio systems usually implement a redundant backup approach as part of the system or retain some analog equipment for emergency use.

Production Personnel

Most stations have at least one person whose primary function is to record and manage the station's production of commercials, promotional announcements, public service messages, identifiers, and the many other sound elements used hourly and daily on the air. The person primarily responsible for this work is the production director. There are more people involved in a station's production than just the production director, however. As the previous illustration suggests, a large number of people, both outside and inside the station, have responsibilities that are related to production: a reporter editing an interview to create an excerpt to be used in an upcoming newscast; an on-air announcer reading the weather while mixing in a music bed underneath; an account executive dubbing some new spots supplied by a client's advertising agency; a station's disc jockeys on the air live; jingle singers in Dallas recording a new set of jingles for a station in Detroit; an engineer recording or feeding a live airing of an orchestra concert syndicated via satellite; and a sports producer mixing multiple announcer and field microphones with recorded features to create a live baseball broadcast—all are involved in production.

The Recording Process

Since the 1940s recording has become one of the most important parts of the production process. Radio today depends on quality recordings to create the bulk of the program schedule. The recording and production process actually starts outside the radio station for much of the program content. The station modifies most of this material very little. Most music aired by stations today comes to the station already recorded in some format: CD, hard disk, or digitally via the internet. Some commercials come to the station prerecorded; these elements are simply dubbed or rerecorded to an appropriate format for use in the on-air playback equipment.

Much of the material heard on a radio station is, however, recorded in its own production studio. The recording process can be illustrated by following the recording of a typical commercial: (1) a copy writer at an agency or the station writes commercial copy; (2) the producer working for the agency or at the local station reviews the copy and selects appropriate music and sound effects for the spot if not already specified; (3a) the spot can be recorded in real time by mixing all three elements (voice, music bed, sound effects) at the console and routing it to a recorder (reel, cart, or computer); (3b) alternatively, the spot can be mixed as a multitrack production in three successive recordings, recording the music at full volume on track one, voice on track two, and sound effects on track three. The levels can be adjusted during final mixdown and recording to the format to be used for on-air playback. If the copy changes, the producer can go back to the master multitrack recording and either re-record the entire voice track or edit, cutting and pasting the changes from another audio file.

As automation becomes more prevalent and refined in radio, the recording process becomes even more central to the production function. Precision recordings, timed perfectly and recorded digitally, allow customized voice tracking by announcers from remote locations. An announcer working virtually anywhere in the country can function as a shift announcer for multiple stations anywhere, providing individualized current information for each separate station, all during the same shift. Digital distribution, digital recording, and digital automation create the illusion that the announcer is physically present at the station. Radio has truly become a virtual medium.

The Editing Process

A big part of production for radio is the editing of radio program material. Editing of recorded audio material for radio is undertaken for one or more of the following three reasons: (1) to correct mistakes; (2) to shorten or lengthen the running time of an element; or (3) to creatively enhance or change the content. In the days of analog recording, the quickest way to add, delete, or reorder material in a recording was to splice the tape, physically cutting the tape with a razor blade or scissors; then removing, adding, or replacing tape; and finally rejoining the segments with splicing tape. Done well, a splice edit is imperceptible. The editor finds the beginning point of the edit, marking the tape over the playback head on the recorder. The tape is then advanced until the endpoint is found and marked over the playback head. Using a splicing block, an angled cut is made over each mark, followed by the insertion of a similarly marked and cut audiotape segment or the joining of the two ends of tape. Assured that there is no gap or overlap between the two segments of tape, the editor places a piece of specially formulated splicing tape over the splice and then closely trims the excess splicing tape.

The splice block has been all but replaced by the digital editor. There are many brands, types, and approaches to digital editing. Some units are standalone units, a combination of hardware and software. Others are software packages for a computer with sound card. Some are basic two-channel editors; others are multitrack recorder/editors that allow almost unlimited additions of sound layers with no degradation of audio quality. What they all have in common is the ability to allow the editor to visually and audibly determine precise edit points, cut and paste audio from one file to another or to the same file, and perform nondestructive modification of the original audio. Much of the recording and editing work that takes place in radio production studios is focused on commercials.

Producing Creative Commercials

Producing the radio station's commercials is a creative challenge. The production for each spot has to accurately interpret the details of the written copy, capture the mood of the spot as intended by the writer, attract attention, sound different from all the other spots running on the station, and yet be consistent with the overall format and sound of the radio station.

There are many ways to meet the challenges of producing compelling commercials. Turning the process over to an advertising agency is one way. As reviewed earlier, ad agencies were once in almost total control of the radio networks' program and commercial production. Although agencies no longer exercise such a stranglehold on the programming decisions of local stations and networks, much of the advertising content heard on radio today is produced through the efforts of ad agencies representing clients, especially at the network and syndicated program level. These larger clients can afford to pay for the creative writing, production, and celebrity talent used to create memorable advertising. Stations merely schedule and dub or pass through these commercials from the network or syndicator.

Networks are not the only place to find creative spots. There are many techniques and resources available to producers at local stations as well. Radio stations still use music and sound effects production libraries to enhance production. First available on 78-rpm records, then on vinyl LPs, these libraries are now recorded digitally on CD. The production music libraries offer precisely timed versions of instrumental music beds that can be licensed and used as the backgrounds for commercials and other announcements. These music tracks are usually recorded in 10-, 15-, 30-, and 60-second lengths of the same theme. These creatively titled compositions are available in a variety of music styles, tempos, and instrumentation. Most of the music production libraries are buyout libraries: the station pays a flat fee for the right to use the entire library indefinitely. Some libraries use "needle drop" fees (the term goes back to the days of turntables and discs): the station pays a fee for use of a specific music track for a specified length of time for a specific commercial. Some companies specialize in the composition and recording of customized, personalized jingles or music beds for station clients.

Sound effects are usually sold as buyout libraries containing a comprehensive array of digitally recorded sounds of every possible situation, activity, or device. Babies crying, rocket launches, train whistles, wind, rain, and a computer modem are examples of sounds that have been digitally recorded for inclusion in a sound effects library. Continuing a tradition from the early days of radio, the use of sound effects adds realism and interest to radio content.

The Role of Production in Creating a Station's "Sound"

Since the advent of television, radio has gone from being a general interest entertainment medium to

programming using a specialized, formatted approach. Radio stations rely on a "format," or the creation of a consistent mix of programming elements, to attract and maintain a target audience. The station can then maximize its listenership within specific demographic characteristics, carving out a specific niche among all the stations in a competitive market. All the format elements are carefully selected and positioned in order to maximize and maintain listeners. Most formats are music-based, but some formats are based on music alternatives, such as talk, sports, and all-news radio.

The basic components of format are often the same from station to station. Two competing stations could be programming exactly the same music lists. The differences listeners would hear in the stations would stem from the different approaches taken with production and related elements like promotion. Beyond format, production is the key element influencing the sound of a radio station. The music beds used in the commercials, the promotional announcements for the station itself, the station identifiers, the jingles, the voices on the air, and how they deliver content are just some of the many production elements that contribute to the overall sound of the station. Production is what ties the different programming elements together and makes the whole package seamless. Listeners are not necessarily aware of good production, but they certainly notice the lack of it.

During the 21st century's first decade, thanks to radio ownership consolidation and widespread digital production capabilities, the trend of outsourcing radio production intensified. By 2010, everything from voice-over talent (who may not make any attempt to sound local via script or performance), to sound effects libraries and a station's branding or image elements (including promos and station identification announcements) is more likely to be imported from a major market or at least an off-site production facility rather than produced in-house.

See also: Audio Processing; Audiotape; Automation; Control Board/Audio Mixer; Recording and Studio Equipment; Sound Effects

Further Reading

Adams, Michael H., and Kimberly K. Massey, *Introduction to Radio: Production and Programming*, Madison, Wisconsin: Brown and Benchmark, 1995.
Alten, Stanley R., *Audio in Media*, Belmont, California: Wadsworth, 1981; 6th edition, Belmont, California, and London: Wadsworth, 2002.
Carlile, John Snyder, *Production and Direction of Radio Programs*, New York: Prentice-Hall, 1939.

Crews, Albert R., *Radio Production Directing*, Boston: Houghton Mifflin, 1944.

Keith, Michael C., *Radio Production: Art and Science*, Boston and London: Focal Press, 1990.

Keith, Michael C., and Joseph M. Krause, *The Radio Station*, Boston: Focal Press, 1986; 4th edition, by Keith, Boston and London: Focal Press, 1997.

MacDonald, J. Fred, *Don't Touch That Dial!: Radio Programming in American Life, 1920–1960*, Chicago: Nelson-Hall, 1979.

McLeish, Robert, *The Technique of Radio Production: A Manual for Local Broadcasters*, London: Focal Press, and New York: Focal/Hastings House, 1978; 4th edition, as *Radio Production: A Manual for Broadcasters*, Oxford and Boston: Focal Press, 1999.

O'Donnell, Lewis B., Philip Benoit, and Carl Hausman, *Modern Radio Production*, Belmont, California: Wadsworth, 1986; 5th edition, 2000.

Oringel, Robert S., *Audio Control Handbook: For Radio and Television Broadcasting*, New York: Hastings House, 1956; 6th edition, Boston and London: Focal Press, 1989.

Reese, David E., and Lynne S. Gross, *Radio Production Worktext: Studio and Equipment*, Boston and London: Focal Press, 1990; 3rd edition, Boston and Oxford: Focal Press, 1998.

Siegel, Bruce H., *Creative Radio Production*, Boston: Focal Press, 1992.

JEFFREY D. HARMAN,
2009 REVISIONS BY CARY O'DELL

PROGRAMMING RESEARCH

Most programming research conducted today is done to measure motives and habits of a radio station's target audience. The programmer's goal is to deliver audience to advertisers to generate revenue from the sale of advertising time. By 1985 most programming decisions were based on attracting audiences rather than on providing "necessary" information to them. Advertisers tend to trust research conducted by parties outside the station, for example, by ratings companies such as Arbitron. Research data gathered by commercial research organizations and paid for by the radio station owner are considered less reliable, and research conducted in house is the least reliable, according to advertisers. Station programmers use all three types of research to learn listener motivations that will inspire loyalists to listen longer and that will attract new listeners to sample the station.

In-house research is usually more valid to the specific station; it is also much less expensive than vendor research. In-house research begins before the station goes on the air for the first time, with tests of signal strength within the broadcast reach. Dial testing of all signals within the Area of Dominant Influence (ADI) that will be competing for the same audience indicates missing formats that audiences might tune in to if they were available. Once a format is selected and the station is on the air, station telephone call-outs to audience loyalists and potential listeners can help determine which tunes need to be dropped from the playlist because they are too familiar (boring), and which need to be added to make the sound more current. The station programmer uses ethnographic techniques to study lifestyles of the target audience—observing them in everyday settings, reading the magazines and newspapers they read, and noting when they are tuned in to radio.

Psychographic research also provides lifestyle and buying information about the station's audience. The research is survey-based, and the populations are sampled by zip code. The assumption is that people who share a zip code also share values, lifestyles, and consumer motivation. Advertising time is sold based on a match in psychographics between the advertiser's target and the station's audience.

Outside research vendors are contracted to provide a more objective view of audience perceptions of the station's format, programming elements, promotions, and even the call letter colors. Auditorium testing is a quantitative method used to measure music perceptions. As many as 500 subjects, screened for age and other demographics and loyalty to the station or its closest competitor, are gathered in an auditorium (a hotel convention room, for example) to listen to "hooks" of 10–20 seconds of a tune, enough for audiences familiar with the tune to identify it. Between 200 and 500 tunes might be tested for responses of "like" to "dislike," "tired of it," or "unfamiliar." If a tune is familiar and liked, but the audience is tired of it, it is played less frequently on the station despite its national popularity. In addition to music testing, auditorium testing is used to measure response to advertising and marketing campaigns, disc jockeys, talk show hosts, and other talent, including news, contests, and marketing. Focus groups are the most common qualitative method used to understand *why* audience members (about 12 are chosen to participate) respond as they do. The moderator assesses motivation by using psychological projective techniques, brainstorming, laddering, role playing, role reversal, and others. Information from focus groups is usually not generalizable unless a great number of groups are conducted with subjects chosen randomly from a population.

The task for the radio station program director in assessing the value of research data and findings is to ask a number of questions. First, is this a quantitative study? If so, how was the sample drawn? Were there enough subjects to analyze the data statistically? What is the margin of error? Can the findings be generalized to the station's listening population? Second, were the questions asked unbiased? Were they valid (i.e., did they test what the station programmer wanted to know?)? Finally, are the findings reliable? If we did a similar study, with subjects drawn from the same population, would we get similar results?

Responsible researchers address these issues and explain their conclusions in language that is clear to the programmer. The goal is to provide information to enable the programmer to select programming that will "deliver" audiences profitably to advertisers but that will also respond to listeners' "convenience, interest, or necessity." Audience members are to be considered fellow community constituents, not just ears delivered to advertisers.

Although most stations engage in some type of programming research—or hire outside consultants to conduct it for them—economic constriction within the industry in the early 21st century caused most stations to scale back their efforts considerably. For example, instead of conducting studies annually, stations conduct them once every three years. Stations have also turned to larger sample sizes or smaller focus groups (as both are less costly to conduct). Many are now also making greater use of the internet by initiating station-focused online discussions or using the so-called Living Room Music Test. This is done by mailing a CD to a person's home, allowing them to report focus-group-like comments without ever having to leave their house. For some stations, however, music "research" today consists of nothing more than logging onto websites like Mediabase, which tracks other stations' recent plays, and then adopting other stations' playlists as their own. Radio consolidation has centralized many research efforts. Many smaller research firms have been forced out of business as many people feel stations are sounding increasingly alike thanks to program "findings" being applied so widely, regardless of geographic location or other variables.

See also: Audience; Audience Research Methods; Auditorium Testing; Consultants; Demographics; Psychographics

Further Reading

Carroll, Raymond L., and Donald M. Davis, *Electronic Media Programming: Strategies and Decision Making*, New York and London: McGraw Hill, 1993.
Eastman, Susan Tyler, Sydney W. Head, and Lewis Klein, *Broadcast Programming, Strategies for Winning Television and Radio Audiences*, Belmont, California: Wadsworth, 1981.
Eastman, Susan Tyler, and Douglas A. Ferguson, *Broadcast/Cable Programming: Strategies and Practices*, (5th edition), Belmont, California: Wadsworth, 1996.
Vane, Edwin T., and Lynne S. Gross, *Programming for TV, Radio, and Cable*, Boston and London: Focal Press, 1994.

KATHRYN SMOOT EGAN,
2009 REVISIONS BY CARY O'DELL

PROGRAMMING STRATEGIES AND PROCESSES

Programming was born of the combination of scheduling segments and tabulating appearances, yet it has an elusive definition. As Les Brown wrote in the foreword to *Broadcast Programming: Strategies for Winning Television and Radio Audiences* (Eastman), there is "a vast lore of programming wisdom, much of it self-contradictory because what works at one time or place may not work at all at another time or place." In the same textbook, Sydney W. Head worked at a definition:

> Programming is strategy. It deals with the advance planning of the program schedule as a whole. It involves searching out and acquiring program materials and planning a coherent sequence, a program service. Production is tactics. It deals with arranging and maneuvering the people and things needed to put programming plans into action. It selects and deploys the means for achieving program plans on the air.

A program service is much more than the sum of its parts. Decisions about how to combine programs, or program elements, into an effective whole are just as important as decisions about which program items to accept or reject.

Head cautioned that a "seemingly obvious" distinction between programming and production is often overlooked:

> This oversight arises for understandable reasons: in the first place, production is much easier to define, teach, and practice than is programming. The production end product is visible, audible, observable, assessable. Programming, however, is far more elusive. It cannot be practiced unless one has on-air access to an actual station and perhaps a year to await results. Production, on the other hand, can be practiced with modest facilities, and the results can be recorded for instant analysis and evaluation.

Finally, the programming function varies so much in the scope and nature of its operations from one programming situation to another that it is difficult to discern what, if anything, all these situations have in common.

Radio programming changed substantially in the years after the consolidation of major companies.

Stations relied on music formats that could be pre-recorded and voice-tracked; national or regional air talent, especially morning shows that could be fed to other stations in the company; and syndicated talk and sports programming that needed little input from the local station. Programming strategy in post-consolidation radio turned from focused local service to national music lists and talk topics. Listeners perceive a station's music, its personalities, or its talk programming; few listeners perceive "programming" in the way industry personnel do.

Radio's Golden Age

Radio's best-known programming strategies were introduced during the 1930s and early 1940s when network programs emerged featuring former vaudeville stars who, through radio, became a part of everyday life in America. That was a unique period. Radio was the only free entertainment medium (once you owned a receiver) for a nation emerging from a disastrous depression. Radio changed listeners' attitudes about themselves, about their world, and especially about their leisure time. The radio occupied the same central place in U.S. life that television would achieve in the latter half of the century.

The key strategy was to entertain with words and sounds that stimulated listener imagination. The Golden Age of radio has also been called the "theater of the mind" days when listeners turned words and sounds into mental pictures. A man named Raymond opened a squeaking door on *Inner Sanctum* and the stories told behind that door made spines tingle for half an hour. That age also brought *The Shadow*, a Gothic thriller whose main character was a mental projection against a foggy night full of smoke from coal-burning furnaces.

On the lighter side of that period was Fibber McGee's closet, a packed-to-the-gills jumble that fell with a crash to the floor once per episode in an avalanche that usually included samples of the sponsor's product. After the cacophony there was a pause. Finally, a dinner bell crash-tinkled to the floor as punctuation. Each member of the radio audience "saw" each scene exactly as he or she wanted to see it. Each listener "saw" a different show, yet each show was perfect because it was all a product of the mind, stimulated by the spoken word in conjunction with musical interludes and sound effects. (When attempting a television revival of radio's *Fibber McGee and Molly*, the National Broadcasting Company [NBC] left the famous closet out of sight—in the hands of sound-effects experts and the imagination of the viewer.)

Programming strategy evolved quickly. The orchestras, sopranos, and baritones who were radio's first performers were on the air to give receiver manufacturers live demonstrations of the new audio medium. Once radio took hold, the strategy was to amass large audiences for advertisers who longed to have their products associated with those performers who became household names, such as Jack Benny, George Burns and Gracie Allen, Fred Allen, and W.C. Fields.

Surviving the Challenge of Television

The arrival of television abruptly changed radio strategy. As the 1950s began, the radio networks were collapsing under the impact of the new visual medium. Jack Benny's deadpan face could now be seen, not just imagined. Radio performers moved into brightly lit video studios and added scenery, building sets of the houses and neighborhoods that previously had been part of listener imagination.

To owners, radio stations became liabilities, not the assets they had been just a few years before. Many broadcasting companies sold their radio stations to invest in television. Radio entrepreneurs sifted through the wreckage of big-time radio and improvised new ideas to attract audiences. What saved radio during the encroachment of television was what appeared to be a new innovation in programming—the disc jockey.

Programmer Rick Sklar offered this scenario in *Rockin' America: How the All-Hit Radio Stations Took Over* (1984), his story of New York's legendary Top 40 station, WABC:

> Imagine the dilemma of the first person who proposed playing records instead of broadcasting live bands over the radio. Records? Who will listen to records played over the radio? People play records on phonographs. They'll think we're putting one over on them if we play records on the radio. But as early as 1948 the first bands were being laid off.

Playing records wasn't actually new in the mid-1950s. In New York, WNEW's Martin Block had created his *Make Believe Ballroom* program 20 years earlier. Beginning in 1935, Block made music using turntables and "platters," as the 78-rpm records were called, not with a baton or a piano as his contemporaries did.

When radio was disrupted by the introduction of television, broadcasters stretched individual record programs into 24-hour formats. Thus were born Top 40, Middle of the Road, Beautiful Music, and other full-time formats. Each station became something distinct. The days of radio stations' attempts to be "all things to all people" virtually disappeared. Fortunately, however, entrepreneurs who introduced disc jockeys to their radio stations—people such as Todd Storz and Gordon McLendon—did not view the future of radio in terms of its past. The change to format radio stimulated another golden age as teenagers discovered Top 40.

The Top 40 format was an all-new strategy of playing the best-selling 45-rpm records over and over, so the listener was never more than a few minutes away from hearing a favorite song. On Top 40 radio, Elvis Presley was king and so was the disc jockey, who spun the soundtrack to the lives of 1950s teenagers. The Top 40 format began the resurgence of public interest in radio. It also spawned other music-based program services based on the strategy of repetition of songs: the Adult Contemporary, Country, and Urban formats. The all-music strategy was to dominate radio for half a century.

Programming as Science

Michael C. Keith calls programming a radio station during this period "an increasingly complex task." In his book *The Radio Station*, Keith writes "The basic idea, of course, is to air the type of format that will attract a sizeable enough piece of the audience demographic to satisfy the advertiser." The ability to attract and hold an audience requires science as well as art in programming strategy. The science involves studying what motivates the audience to stay with long-form 24-hour music programs.

Examination of the audience was distilled into nine essential questions by Sydney Head in *Broadcast Programming: Strategies for Winning Television and Radio Audiences* (Eastman, Head, and Klein, 1981):

1. How much time does the average person listen to my station?

2. Am I doing a good job of reaching my target audience?

3. How many different groups of people contribute to my station's average audience?

4. What percentage of the listeners in one of my time periods also listen to my station in another time period?

5. During which hours of the day does my station do the best job of reaching listeners?

6. How much of my audience listens only to me and to no other stations?

7. Is my station ahead of or behind the market average of away-from-home listening?

8. Which are the most available audiences during certain times of day?

9. How often do my listeners hear the same record?

The questions are best answered in ratings reports from Arbitron and similar companies. Ratings questions about size and quality of the audience often distract programmers from the issue of usefulness or innovation of the programming itself. Amassing an audience requires constant feedback on how well the audience is satisfied. Yet none of these questions concerns the quality or the content of programming.

Radio is measured not only in terms of cumulative audience (the number of people who tune into a given station in a week) but also by time spent listening (the number of quarter hour segments heard, or "average quarter hours"). The ratings process influences programming strategy, and programmers find themselves aiming their efforts at the ratings methodology rather than the audience by attempting to extend time spent listening in order to increase average quarter-hour shares.

A sure way to effect longer listening is to combine programming elements—hit records, for example—with positions on the clock. If a familiar and popular classic song is played at the top of the hour, then followed in the next music position with a current hit, then by an up-and-coming record, and so on around the hour, the station's programmer sets up a sound that includes a constant change of era or year of origin for each song. The result is a "Hot Clock" or "Music Wheel" that when drawn resembles the face of a clock with lines extending from the center like bicycle spokes separating songs, commercials, and other programming elements. (Hot clocks are not exclusive to music stations. News and news-talk stations use them as well—often calling the visual version a "News Wheel"—to designate places on the hourly clock for certain types of news stories or talk show segments.)

The music programmer further attempts to mix upbeat songs with slow songs, male vocals with female vocals, large production sounds with solo instruments, etc., so that a sense of musical variety is achieved within the hour. This definition of category is from a client memo from the consulting firm Shane Media Services:

What is a category? It's a group of songs organized by a primary characteristic. On the current/recurrent side of the library, categorization is determined by age and amount of play. For example, new songs are put in an "add" or "light" category; these titles receive the least amount of play and are protected by categories made of more familiar songs. This category's function is to introduce new songs in a palatable manner. It's placed on the clock so announcers can sell the songs it includes.

As songs build up play, they begin to be tested in audience research. Songs listeners show interest in are worthy of more play. They move up to medium current—enough rotation for average listeners to develop affection for the songs.

Medium songs that excel in research move to hot current. Hot current is a category determined by value—current songs listeners care about most. Recurrent categories are made of proven hits and age again becomes the primary organizational criterion: hot recurrents are the strongest hits with high play. Medium and bulk recurrents are seven to 14 months old and represent the best of the recent hits.

Gold categories are organized by value: the Power category is made up of the best testing titles, songs listeners want to hear every day. These songs have high "love" scores, high "play more" scores and little "tired of" scores.

The medium or secondary gold category is made of songs listeners like but aren't involved with enough to want to hear daily. Sometimes records are put into secondary gold because high "love" scores are combined with high "tired of" scores. Resting songs by playing them every two to three days instead of daily usually results in higher scores the next time songs are tested.

If a station uses a third level of gold, it's usually made of songs that have sufficient "like" scores but no "love." These are "okay" songs that won't make listeners tune out but also don't cause them to turn up the station or tell their friends to stop working and listen.

Music rotation software such as Selector, Power-Gold, and MusicMaster helps stations achieve balance through elaborate sound codes and type codes. Use of the popular software also allows efficient management and diagnosis of play histories in a music library once criteria are established.

Formats

A brief overview of the major formats will shed some light on programming strategy.

Adult Contemporary (AC)

The most familiar musical selections found on radio are from Adult Contemporary stations. In terms of the number of listeners, AC was the most popular format of the 1980s and 1990s. It has many permutations owing to the broad age range of listeners (25–54) and their diversity of tastes. AC's territory covers the softest jazz instrumental and light rock to modern hits. Collectively, the varieties of AC are radio's most listened-to formats.

Top 40 or Contemporary Hit Radio (CHR)

"Contemporary Hit Radio" was the euphemism used by radio people who thought "Top 40" was a term used by kids. Listening to their public, they discovered that "Top 40" was what people called radio that played the hits. The strategy remains the same as it was during the earliest years of the format: play the best-selling songs and repeat them often.

Rock

Rock music (formerly called "rock and roll") takes many different forms, most of which have resulted in radio formats. For example, Classic Rock is an offshoot of Mainstream Rock. Offering the comfort of familiarity, the Classic Rock format presents a mix of well-known bands, primarily from the 1970s. Then there's the easy-to-identify rift between Mainstream and Modern (or Alternative) rock. Alternative rock music begins as a splinter of some other style. If it grows, it is embraced by the mainstream and is no longer "alternative," thus losing its cachet.

Country

Since the 1970s, Country has been adopted by more stations than any other format. In its earliest days, the Country format was considered to be aimed at a blue-collar audience. As the audience grew and young artists revitalized the music in the early 1990s, the blue-collar image became mainstream. The format scores very well among adults aged 25–54 and is the least prone to audience fragmentation. Its strategy is rooted in the Top 40 tradition: play the most popular songs often. Country stations tend to offer a mix of songs from a broad spectrum of years.

News-Talk

News-talk radio could be called "personality radio," even though the caller interaction and tendency toward political topics often obscures the impact of on-air personalities. Rush Limbaugh and

Dr. Laura Schlessinger were the reigning superstars at the beginning of the 21st century, with hundreds of newcomers trying to establish themselves in second and third place. Programming news-talk requires a talent-driven strategy. Talented program hosts who give the listeners access by telephone to highly interactive, relevant discussions are the big winners.

Marketing as Radio's Product

In the late 1970s and early 1980s, radio station operators changed their focus from product and programming to positioning and perception. The shift was in large part a result of the efforts of consultant George A. Burns, whose books postulated that the way a radio station sounded was secondary to what listeners imagined or perceived about the station. Burns urged his readers to leave "the product dimension" and to enter "the marketing dimension."

Programming had long been radio's primary product concern. However, in the competitive environment after the rise of FM music formats, product alone was not enough to achieve differentiation and success. As Burns wrote in *Radio Imagery: Strategies in Station Positioning* (1980):

> Standard wisdom originally held that fragmentation would provide a wider spectrum of listening opportunities for the public. Indeed, this seemed to be the case at first. Formats such as "classical" and "progressive rock" supplied fuel for the work of spreading FM. AM operators first became aware of FM in a serious way when they noticed "beautiful music" or "progressive rock" beginning to hurt them. Fragmentation began as alternative programming.

As audiences fragmented, more stations became viable listening options even though each station's audience was smaller. For instance, more than 70 stations could be heard in most parts of the Los Angeles metro area in 1999, according to the *M Street Radio Directory*. In smaller cities, too, the number of stations proliferated. Tulsa, Oklahoma, had more than 25 stations serving some segment of its population during that same period. Large numbers of stations usually meant several stations in the same format with little differentiation. To program effectively against direct competition, stations enlisted research companies to test music libraries and to probe audience perceptions. The research allowed stations to play proven, safe songs that received the highest scores and to reduce the risk of unfamiliar or overplayed songs.

Research became part of the marketing loop. With so many stations vying for a diminishing segment of the audience, the paramount concern became keeping a station's name in the forefront of listeners' minds. Naming stations was as much of an art as programming them. Mnemonics like Z-93, Star 104, K-FROG, and FROGGY 98 caught attention because they were memorable. Advertising campaigns urged listeners to remember one station for country music, another for news, and so on.

Station management concerned with marketing did not ignore programming, but they did take programming for granted. Effective programming was accepted as a given, and emphasis shifted to marketing, promotion, and advertising to influence audience recall.

Programming after Consolidation

The Telecommunications Act of 1996 eliminated many radio ownership limits and simultaneously shifted programming strategy. Consolidated ownership now makes it possible for one company to own a cluster of stations in the same market. An operator company that can do so chooses its cluster by format in order to control all or most stations in a format or to minimize competition. Thus, a company may acquire several varieties of rock stations, or both of a city's country stations, or a combination that includes an all-news station, an all-talk station, and an all-sports station, just to cite three possibilities.

Consolidation offers opportunities for cost savings in programming by combining air talents to perform on several stations in a cluster and operating one news department to serve many stations. For instance, Capster Broadcasting Partners assembled a staff of air talents in Austin, Texas, to feed voice tracks to more than 100 stations in the Capstar and AM/FM groups via a wide area network of linked computers. Another approach to cost savings in programming is the "hub and spoke" system employed by Clear Channel Communications, in which a centrally located station in a large or medium market feeds programming to be simulcast in nearby smaller cities.

Radio's consolidation required cost-cutting which gave rise to syndicated programs, both national and regional. Many morning shows lent themselves to syndication, since they provided national, nonlocal content. Among the most successful were Bob and Tom from Indianapolis and John Boy and Billy's *Big Show* from Charlotte, both targeted to rock stations; Steve Harvey from Atlanta, targeted to urban stations; and Los Angeles personality Ryan Seacrest, whose morning show features were repackaged for use in other dayparts on stations across the U.S.

Adding to syndication was the proliferation of voice tracking from remote locations, as stations sought to reduce air talent expenses. The result was a music-intensive "jukebox" sound on many stations, often leading to audience erosion and dissatisfaction.

See also, in addition to individual radio formats (Adult Contemporary, etc.) as discussed above: Arbitron; Audience; Audience Research Methods; Auditorium Testing; Demographics; Music Testing; Office of Radio Research; Programming Research; Promotion on Radio

Further Reading

Burns, George A., *Radio Imagery: Strategies in Station Positioning*, Studio City, California: Burns Media, 1980.

Burns, George A., *Playing the Positioning Game: Aiming at the Core*, Studio City, California: Burns Media, 1981.

Eastman, Susan Tyler, Sydney W. Head, and Lewis Klein, *Broadcast Programming, Strategies for Winning Television and Radio Audiences*, Belmont, California: Wadsworth, 1981.

Eastman, Susan Tyler, and Douglas A. Ferguson, *Broadcast/Cable Programming: Strategies and Practices*, 5th edition, Belmont, California: Wadsworth, 1996.

Fisher, Marc, *Something in the Air: Radio, Rock, and the Revolution that Shaped a Generation*. New York: Random House, 2007

Keith, Michael C., *The Radio Station*, Boston: Focal Press, 1986; 5th edition, 2000.

Ramsey, Mark, *Making Waves: Radio on the Verge*. Bloomington, Indiana: Universe, 2008.

Shane, Ed, *Cutting Through: Strategies and Tactics for Radio*, Houston, Texas: Shane Media, 1991.

Shane, Ed, "The State of the Industry: Radio's Shifting Paradigm," *Journal of Radio Studies* 5, no. 2 (Summer 1998).

Sklar, Rick, *Rocking America: An Insider's Story: How the All-Hit Radio Stations Took Over*, New York: St. Martin's Press, 1984.

ED SHANE,
2009 REVISIONS BY ED SHANE

PROGRESSIVE ROCK FORMAT

Progressive rock is a radio format designed to appeal to rock music fans who were initially represented by the counterculture of the late 1960s. At times referred to as *progressive radio, underground, free form, album-oriented rock* (AOR), *alternative*, and *classic rock*, the progressive rock format has its roots in the underground rock movement in the years leading up to the Woodstock Music Festival in 1969.

As an alternative to the repetitive hit music of Top 40, which was pervasive on AM radio at the time, progressive radio began on undeveloped FM stations as so-called free form programming, an ephemeral concept that encouraged each disc jockey to program his or her own show with a newer and broader brand of rock and roll than merely its pop progeny, interspersing music with commentary that referenced an emerging cultural change in the United States. Progressive radio drew an audience previously unserved by radio, and it is credited with establishing FM as a dominant force in music radio.

By the mid-1970s, FM progressive rock in a variety of permutations spearheaded audience migration to the new frequency band. Although the radio industry paid little attention to FM, FM was handily supported by the recording industry and the electronics industry, both of which had high stakes in high-fidelity products. By the end of the decade "progressive" stations had seized a majority of the mainstream radio audience owing to the widespread popularity of progressive rock music and the ability of FM to broadcast high fidelity in stereo. As progressive music hit the top of the charts, Top 40 stations reacted by retooling their playlists and moving their operations to the FM band, forcing AM to all but abandon music as a viable format in most competitive markets. To distinguish themselves from Top 40's encroachment, many progressive rock stations began adopting the AOR format designation. Though the progressive rock format has all but disappeared, it has been supplanted in many markets by what is called "classic rock," one that programs the music of progressive rock's breakthrough era. Another iteration is the "alternative" format which is based on a musical alternative to mainstream pop music. In either case, progressive rock radio is connected to at least four distinct broadcast formats: rock and roll pioneers such as Alan "Moondog" Freed; shock jocks such as those on satellite radio by the early 21st century; independent broadcasters including LPFM community stations; and online audio services. Indeed, some of progressive rock's young listeners, inspired by the format's original spirit, became webcasters, producing their own progressive streams.

The rock and roll of Elvis Presley, Jackie Wilson, Buddy Holly, The Shirelles, Chuck Berry, and countless others successfully altered radio's musical landscape in the 1950s as disc jockeys developed a relationship with their youthful audiences and an ear for an alternative sound. Similarly, early progressive rock disc jockeys such as Tom "Big Daddy" Donahue brought a new sensibility and attitude to the medium, playing a variety of alternative music styles, including folk music; a more sophisticated brand of rock and roll; and cross-genre hybrids that combined blues, country, soul, funk, or jazz with increasingly amplified guitar rock, creating new subgenres such as folk-rock, progressive country, country rock, jazz fusion, latin rock, acid rock, hard rock, and heavy metal. Progressive stations did not play hit singles. They played albums, sometimes an entire LP at a time. The format was built around artists who broke new ground musically and lyrically. Artists such as The Doors, Jimi Hendrix, Joni Mitchell, Vanilla Fudge, Creedence Clearwater Revival, Crosby, Stills and Nash, Led Zeppelin, Jefferson Airplane, Janis Joplin, Allman Brothers, Santana, Beatles, Rolling Stones, and others certainly had pop hits, but it was their other album tracks that made progressive playlists, songs often distinguished by lyrics that questioned authority, embraced social protest, and celebrated the sexual revolution.

This music did not fit neatly into the under-three-minutes song length common for airplay on Top 40. There were also rare recordings, live performances, and rock star interviews, which added spontaneity and primed the syndication efforts of new radio networks such as Westwood One. And rather than announce the time and temperature, progressive disc jockeys slipped in pithy social commentary and politically charged comedy bits—often in the same breath. The unique combination of music, structure, and editorial point of view conspired to spawn an identity all its own. Not since the seminal rock and roll disc jockeys of the 1950s had radio responded so directly to popular culture. In both eras, too, popularity brought increased scrutiny, claims of amorality, and scandal. And both saw the execution of their respective preformats move from the individual programmer to station owners and consultants who went on to develop successfully marketable formats.

As playlists shrank and advertising increased, purist progressive announcers became disenchanted with an apparent squandering of the airwaves by strictly commercial interests. Some became radio pirates in the spirit of the underground movement, broadcasting without a license from hideout locations. Others joined or started licensed, non-commercial, low-power community radio. Still others abandoned the need to control the music by developing talk show personalities that led to the advent of FM talk and the so-called shock jock.

Early progressive stations were instrumental in introducing and "breaking" new artists and music. They also provided a voice for "lifestyle" news services such as Earth News, the National Broadcasting Company's (NBC) The Source, and the American Broadcasting Companies' ABC FM network, as well as forging opportunities for targeted advertising. Progressive announcers would categorically reject ad copy with hype or that promoted products antithetical to the desires of their perceived audience. Traditionally, progressive stations did not yell at their audiences, sensationalize in the purely promotional sense, or hard sell, except in parody or satire. They adopted a reduced commercial load of 9–15 minutes of advertising per hour as opposed to the 18–30 minutes of Top 40, partly because of the fact that advertisers were not yet sold on the value of the progressive rock audience.

The format's original structural characteristics included commercials scheduled in "spot sets" and music programmed in "song sets," which established the music mix "segue" as an art form, setting a mood that organically led to increased time spent listening. Many progressive rock formatics were so successful in holding audience that they have long been incorporated into other music formats.

Early adapters of commercially successful progressive rock formats include San Francisco's KMPX and KSAN; Boston's WBCN; Los Angeles' KMET and KLOS; Chicago's WXRT; and New York's WOR-FM, WNEW-FM, and WABC-FM/ WPLJ. Perhaps the most consistent preservation of the original progressive rock spirit has been on student-run college radio, as well as on some of the Pacifica stations.

See also: Album-Oriented Rock Format; Alternative Format; Classic Rock Format; Community Radio; Free Form Format; Pacifica Foundation; Underground Radio; WABC; WNEW; WOR

Further Reading

Ditingo, Vincent, *The Remaking of Radio*, Boston and Oxford: Focal Press, 1995.

Fornatale, Peter, and Joshua Mills, *Radio in the Television Age*, Woodstock, New York: Overlook Press, 1980.

Keith, Michael C., *Voices in the Purple Haze: Underground Radio and the Sixties*, Westport, Connecticut: Praeger, 1997.

Routt, Edd, James McGrath, and Frederick Weiss, *The Radio Format Conundrum*, New York: Hastings House, 1978.

JOSEPH R. PIASEK,
2009 REVISIONS BY JOSEPH R. PIASEK

PROMAX
Industry Trade Association

The primary trade organization in electronic media focusing on promotion and marketing, Promax, is a nonprofit, mutual benefit association for promotion and marketing executives in the electronic media. It conducts annual trade conventions, distributes videotapes of award-winning on-air promotions and print materials, and serves as a clearinghouse for ideas and projects related to electronic media promotion via its resource center and weekly fax memos.

Although broadcast and cable television has been its most salient focus, Promax also serves the commercial and noncommercial radio industry. About 10 percent of its 2,000 member companies are in the radio business, mostly from major-market stations and large groups, and from production companies offering creative concepts and marketing services to radio. Among the best known in the radio area have been such companies as Columbia Broadcasting System (CBS) Radio, American Broadcasting Companies (ABC) Radio Networks, and the Westwood One networks. Nearly all large and mid-sized market stations hold membership and send representatives to the annual Promax conventions.

The association's avowed goals are to share promotion and marketing strategies, to share research techniques and information, and to spread the word on new creative concepts and technologies. Like other trade associations, Promax provides the opportunity for the marketing executives of networks and program syndicators to meet with their counterparts at affiliated stations and for production companies and consultants to show off their wares and attract the attention of potential clients.

On a daily basis, a president/chief executive officer (CEO) and a staff of 20 full-time personnel run the association. The president is selected by an executive committee of the 27-person board of directors overseeing Promax. A portion of the board turns over annually, and new directors are elected by the entire association membership. Board members are nominated to represent a mix of networks, studios, stations, cable systems, production companies, distributors, agencies, and consulting companies.

Founded in 1956 as the Broadcasters Promotion Association (BPA) and operating in tandem with the Broadcast Designers Association (BDA) since the late 1970s, the association grew from a few hundred company members to well over 1,000 by the mid-1980s and to nearly 2,000 companies by the year 2000. Administered in the 1970s and 1980s out of Lancaster, Pennsylvania, by Executive Director Lance Webster, the organization's growth in the late 1980s resulted in a move to Los Angeles. Webster is credited with increasing the association's national visibility, stabilizing its procedures and structures, and creating active ties with other trade and educational organizations.

In 1984 the association's name was changed to Broadcast Promotion and Marketing Executives to acknowledge participation by the highest station and network management and to recognize two factors: the rising importance of promotional activities in an increasingly competitive situation and the industry's increased focus on marketing strategies—which involve a broader conception than sales promotion and audience program promotion. But by the early 1990s, the incongruity of a large cable membership had led to still another evolution in the association's name, this time to Promax in 1993. (Although the name is frequently spelled in all capitals, the word is not an acronym; it draws on the association's traditional connection with the field of promotion, adds an x for executives, and hints at "maximum something" to users, an acceptable bit of hyperbole suiting this profession.)

Another major change was the expansion of worldwide promotion conventions, such as the association's first international conference in Leeds, England, in 1990. This became the annual Promax United Kingdom meeting, and it has been followed by Promax Asia, Promax Europe, Promax Latin America, and, in 1999, the first Promax Australia/New Zealand convention. As of 2000, the association had member companies in 35 different countries and was dealing with rapid membership growth outside the United States.

Two individuals clearly stand out as the biggest contributors to the evolution of the association: Lance Webster, publications coordinator in 1979 and executive director for much of the 1980s, and Jim Chabin, president and CEO during most of the 1990s (now president of the Academy of Television Arts and Sciences in Hollywood), who implemented the association's international vision. In 1999 Glynn Brailsford stepped into the joint position of president and CEO of both Promax and BDA and has continued building and consolidating the international partner associations and melding the administration of Promax and BDA.

Association board president in 1980, Tom Dawson, a CBS Radio vice president, was a key individual in building the radio membership in the organization from 1976 to 1988. Elected to the association's Hall of Fame in 1992, Dawson is building an archive and writing a history of the association. Erica Farber, executive vice president at Interep and president of the Board in 1991–92, took on the role of fostering the growth of radio membership. Farber is now publisher and CEO of *Radio and Records.*

The annual North American convention, usually held in the United States, is the centerpiece of

Promax's offerings. Called the Promax Conference and Exposition, by 1999 the association reported that nearly 7,000 industry executives attended. The convention offers about 65 sessions and workshops with some 200 expert speakers and presenters; about one-half of those panels directly or indirectly address radio interests. Topics have included branding and copyright and music, sports, and performance rights, in addition to radio-only panels about contesting and games, image marketing, segmentation research, audience measurement, and audio technologies. By the late 1990s, the internet had become the conference subject of the most riveting interest to radio executives.

At the annual convention, Promax makes the International Gold Medallion Awards for excellence in marketing and promotion, recognizing achievement in 280 categories for local television, networks, cable, radio, and program syndication with gold Muse statuettes or silver certificates. The categories recognize image and program promotion in on-air and print media, as well as multimedia campaigns and contests. Special achievement awards have gone to such celebrities as Casey Kasem, Dick Clark, Stan Freberg, and Chuck Blore.

The BDA was formed in 1978 with the support of what was then BPA, and it has since met annually conjointly with Promax in North America, Europe, and Australia. It spotlights the needs and interests of the creative staffs of stations and advertising agencies and gives its own awards for outstanding artwork at a separate meeting held at the same time and in the same conference site as Promax. It also conducts panel sessions and workshops focusing on cutting-edge design concepts for program guides, magazines and newspapers, outdoor billboards, posters, and transit signs, as well as on-air spots for both television and radio. In recent years, considerable attention has gone to the implementation of creative ideas via digital technology.

In the 1980s, Promax began issuing weekly faxed communications (*PromofaX*), replete with practical ideas for station promotion, many of which are innovative ideas for radio contests or image promotion. Promax also publishes an annual *Image* magazine at the time of the North American convention, which incorporates examples of promotion and marketing in both television and radio from around the world. In addition, Promax conducts periodic surveys that track changes in salaries, status, and backgrounds of commercial promotion managers and changes in the technologies and methods used in daily promotion and image promotional campaigns. It summarizes these results in *PromofaX* and *Image*. Central to member relations,

the Promax Resource Center is a repository for materials about promotion and marketing. It sells audio- and videotapes of panels, workshops, and keynote speakers as well as copies of award-winning print materials.

From 2003 to 2007, Jim Chabin implemented the association's international vision and was responsible for expanding its partner-associations in many countries. On the radio side, first Tom Dawson and then Erica Farber took on the role of fostering growth of radio membership from the late 1970s into the new century. Following peak attendance of about 7,000, after 2007, attendance fell to about half that as ways of responding to the impact of the world economic recession took the front seat. Promax conducts surveys that track changes in salaries, status, and backgrounds of commercial promotion managers and changes in the technologies and methods used in promotion campaigns. It summarizes these results in its publications. Central to member relations, the Promax Resource Center is a repository for materials about promotion and marketing, which sells audio and video tapes of panels, workshops, and keynote speakers as well as copies of print materials. In 2009, Promax expanded beyond its daily faxes and convention magazine with a quarterly intelligence report in the form of a magazine called *Brief*.

See also: Promotion on Radio; Trade Associations

Further Reading

Eastman, Susan Tyler, and Robert A. Klein, editors, *Strategies in Broadcast and Cable Promotion: Commercial Television, Radio, Cable, Pay-Television, Public Television*, Belmont, California: Wadsworth, 1982; 5th edition, as *Promotion and Marketing for Broadcasting and Cable*, edited by Eastman, Klein, and Douglas A. Ferguson, Boston: Focal Press, 2006.

McDowell, Walter, and Alan Batten, *Branding TV: Principles and Practices*, 2nd edition, Boston: Elsevier Science and Technology, 2005.

Promax website, www.PROMAX.org (case sensitive).

PROMAX Image (1993–).

Promax, *Daily Brief* (formerly *PromoFax*), weekly faxed newsletter to members; and *Brief*, quarterly magazine.

SUSAN TYLER EASTMAN,
2009 REVISIONS BY SUSAN TYLER EASTMAN

PROMOTION ON RADIO

During the early years of commercial radio in the United States, most stations had little reason to promote themselves to listeners because of the relative lack of competition in the local marketplace. Moreover, since the homogeneous programming provided by national networks resulted in every station's sounding basically alike, there was little to promote about a station's "distinctive" qualities. By the middle 1950s, however, local radio programmers began experimenting with new entertainment and musical formats in an attempt to regain audiences lost to the upstart medium of television.

Once stations began to differentiate their programming and audiences found a choice of offerings, the need to attract listeners to specific stations intensified. Since then, the variety of station formats and programming has increased, and along with it the value of promotion in the eyes of radio professionals. One reason promotion is vital in today's radio marketplace is the current Arbitron ratings system, which depends on listeners' ability to recall a station's call letters or name when filling out the ratings diary. Arguably, this methodology means that the station with the highest top-of-mind awareness, not the greatest number of actual listeners, may win the ratings battle.

In an effort to increase this station awareness in the local community, stations depend on promotion to help accomplish four major goals: (1) to increase the number of people who sample the station; (2) to give the current audience a reason to listen for a longer time; (3) to provide listeners who must tune out incentives to tune in later; and (4) to create and reinforce the station's image.

Audience acquisition promotions are designed to encourage station sampling by people who don't regularly listen. By necessity, this is accomplished through promotional campaigns designed for and delivered through other media. Television commercials on local stations and cable systems, direct mail pieces, roadside billboards, bumper stickers, T-shirts, key chains, refrigerator magnets, and a variety of other types of promotional merchandise are used to introduce the public to the station's call letters, frequency, format, personalities, and contests. The strategy behind audience acquisition promotions is to inform or remind potential audience members about the programming a station delivers, hoping to match the station's product with listener wants and needs.

Promotions designed to increase the amount of time current listeners spend tuned to the station are called audience maintenance promotions. Often, audience maintenance goals are accomplished through the design and implementation of on-air contests. For example, a music-oriented station might implement a contest in which listeners must hear a specific song, or any song by a specific artist, before phoning the station to try and win a prize. By strategically working with the programming or music departments to determine when the designated song or artist will play, stations can increase the time listeners spend tuned to the station waiting for a chance to win. Other popular variations on this audience maintenance contest include the scavenger hunt (in which listeners wait to hear different items they must collect in order to have a chance to win a prize) and the treasure hunt (in which clues are periodically given for the hidden location of a valuable gift certificate).

Contests may also be designed to provide audience members who must stop listening with incentives to tune back sometime later. These contests are referred to as recyclers, and they take one of two forms. Horizontal recyclers are designed to entice listeners to tune in again at the same time the following day. For example, a common horizontal promotion on music stations is to encourage listeners to fax the midday host a list of their favorite songs. The listener whose list is chosen wins prizes plus gets to hear his or her favorites played during the lunch hour. When stations promote this as a programming element done every weekday at the same time, it recycles listeners to the lunch hour of the following day to see if they have won. Vertical recyclers, on the other hand, are designed to entice listeners to tune in later during the same day. For example, having a morning announcer promote that the next chance to win concert tickets is during the afternoon show recycles those who may have to tune out during the workday to the station for their drive home.

Regardless of the strategic goals of a station contest, promotion directors must keep in mind applicable federal regulations. For example, the FCC prohibits the broadcast of information about most lotteries other than those sponsored by non-profit organizations and state governments. In order for a radio promotional contest to constitute a lottery, it must contain three components: a prize, chance, and consideration. Consideration is something of value paid by the contest participant, such as an entry fee. For example, if a station decided to give away a new car (a prize) to someone chosen at random (chance) from those who bought a ticket to the station's annual concert/birthday party (consideration), that station would violate lottery laws when promoting the contest on air. Stations often alleviate this problem by instructing listeners how to enter without consideration in the official contest rules—which the FCC requires be fully and accurately disclosed. Other laws that may impact radio promotions prohibit the broadcast of obscene content and limit the broadcast of indecent material to certain hours.

Another goal of radio promotion is to establish and reinforce the station's image in the minds of the audience. It is important that every contest, billboard, bumper sticker, and website associated with the station is consistent with the desired image. Often, program directors and promotion departments work together to establish the target image for their station. This way the program director's vision of the station image is known by the promotion department, and they can be sure that all aspects of the promotion mix are developed with the image in mind.

In order to identify a station's target image, a list is sometimes created of words or phrases that would be desirable for listeners to associate with the station. For example, a news station would want to have the image of being dependable, honest, timely, and involved with the community. A rock station, in contrast, would be more interested in being known as the rock concert station, as being knowledgeable about entertainment news, and as the station that gives away music-related prizes. Creating lists such as these can help ensure that the content of radio promotion is consistent with the desired image.

When trying to reinforce station image, however, content may not be the only variable that promotion directors can use. Radio consultant Lee Abrams argues that the sound of on-air promotions can go a long way to improving a station's image. Abrams advises that when creating on-air promotion, stations should "hit the production room and come out with great stuff" (Lynch and Gillispie, 1998). Recent research suggests that Abrams may be correct. Potter and Callison (2000) have experimented with different types of production techniques in on-air promotions and found that promotions containing sound effects, music, and multiple announcers create more positive images in listeners than comparatively simple promotions do.

Promotional activities—from contests and giveaways to billboards and bumper stickers—cost money. Many stations regularly budget for ongoing promotional campaigns, funding them through management's commitment to marketing the station. Sometimes operating capital for promotions at a current-based music station is enhanced by money from an independent music promoter who pays the station for the right to discuss music decisions with the program director on a weekly basis.

In all formats, however, there is increasing pressure to develop more sales promotions than ever before. Sales promotions are campaigns that accomplish marketing and image goals for the station, while simultaneously providing the sales department with tie-ins that can be sold to advertisers. Sales promotions take many forms; for example, co-sponsorship of a contest or event by both the station and the client, remote broadcasts from a client's location where listeners enter to win prizes, coupons for the client's business as the "removable" backs of station bumper stickers, and advertiser logos screen printed on station T-shirts. Anything that the station's promotion can do to help generate advertising revenue can be viewed as a way to offset the cost of the promotion itself.

Despite various off-set possibilities and new "preferred" or "registered" listener opportunities available via the web, the economic downturn of 2008–9 was hard on promotion departments. For many stations, their already small operations have gotten even smaller or been dissolved completely and their duties folded into either a station's sales or programming department. Shrinking promotional departments and budgets have placed many stations in a unique "catch-22" situation: although declining audiences may have caused promotions to be scuttled, the lack of fresh promotions has undermined efforts to gain new or retain existing listeners.

One bright spot for promoters, ironically, has been the consolidation of radio ownership. Though consolidation has negatively affected many aspects of radio broadcasting, consolidation has often allowed for promotion to take on a grander scale. In 2007, for example, Clear Channel orchestrated a multi-city promotion with the cast members of the NBC-TV series *Chuck*, something that would have been impossible before merged ownership.

Though the overwhelming majority of promotions are innocuous affairs that give away T-shirts, concert tickets and the like, sometimes in the pursuit of ratings and "buzz," station promotions can be distasteful or even deadly. Many of the brutal dance marathons of the 1930s were radio-sponsored. A Florida station set off a panic in 2005 when it dressed a handful of listeners as prison inmates and set them loose on a highway. Opie and Anthony angered many when they staged a "Homeless Shopping Spree" in 2006. Perhaps most infamously, in 2007, a 28-year-old mother of three died of water intoxication shortly after taking part in a water-drinking "Hold Your Wee for a Wii" contest for a videogame console, held over KDND in Sacramento, California.

See also: Arbitron; Consultants; Programming Strategies and Processes; Promax

Further Reading

Buchman, J.G., "Commercial Radio Promotion," in *Promotion and Marketing for Broadcasting and Cable*, edited by

Susan Tyler Eastman, Douglas A. Ferguson, and Robert A. Klein, 4th edition, Boston: Focal Press, 2002.

Fisher, Marc, "*Radio Stations and the Promotional Game: A Fatal Attraction*," Washington Post (25 February 2007), p. N-2.

Lynch, Joanna R., and Greg Gillispie, "Creating an Image," in *Process and Practice of Radio Programming*, by Lynch and Gillispie, Lanham, Maryland: University Press of America, 1998.

Newton, G.D., and R.F. Potter, "Promotion of Radio," in *Research in Media Promotion*, edited by Susan Tyler Eastman, Mahwah, New Jersey: Erlbaum, 2000.

Norberg, Eric G., "Promoting Your Station," in *Radio Programming: Tactics and Strategy*, by Norberg, Boston and Oxford: Focal Press, 1996.

Potter, R.F., and C. Callison, "Sounds Exciting! The Effects of Audio Complexity on Listeners' Attitudes and Memory for Radio Promotional Announcements," *Journal of Radio Studies* 7 (2000).

"Too Much Water Hast Thou," *Harper's* (May 2007), p. 28.

ROBERT F. POTTER,
2009 REVISIONS BY CARY O'DELL

PSYCHOGRAPHICS

Grouping Radio Listeners by Psychological Characteristics

Psychographics is the term for a method of market segmentation that groups consumers on the basis of their psychological characteristics. Unlike demographics, which describes consumer or audience attributes such as sex, age, income, or occupation, psychographics is concerned with unobservable personality traits, such as confidence, aggressiveness, extroversion, curiosity, conscientiousness, agreeableness, and so forth. Psychographics draws inspiration from an array of conceptual perspectives, including theories such as trait-factor, motivation, self-concept, psychoanalytic, and social psychology. Lifestyle characteristics—activities, interests, and opinions—are generally considered a conceptual framework distinct from psychographics. In practice, however, blending personalities and lifestyles is key to producing useful marketing information, and lifestyle characteristics are routinely considered part of a psychographic profile.

Development of Psychographics

Although media and market research about consumer psychology was common as early as the 1920s, the term *psychographics* did not appear until the late 1960s and early 1970s, when target marketing emerged as a predominant business and communication strategy. As more and more companies focused product development and communication efforts on narrowly defined consumer groups, advertisers and marketers called for more sophisticated market segmentation techniques. It had become clear that demographic classifications were insufficient because they lacked the detail necessary for crafting the style of persuasive messages advertisers now preferred. Also inadequate were the prevailing methods for collecting psychological data. Researchers often chose in-depth interviews to uncover psychological and lifestyle dimensions about their subjects. Although rich in detail, the qualitative data were unwieldy for marketers. Interviews were time consuming, which realistically limited the total number of conversations, and therefore, the sample sizes of studies. Interviewing also generated a vast amount of material that was slow to code and cumbersome to analyze.

The emergence of psychographic research paralleled the rapid increase of computer accessibility. Psychographics emphasized easily administered survey instruments with objective questions and precoded responses. Computer data analysis helped psychographic studies include large numbers of subjects, which in turn gave them more general results that could be processed in less time.

Psychographics and Radio

Advertisers' increased emphasis on psychographics also coincided with, and contributed to, the resurgence of radio as a marketing medium in the 1960s and 1970s. Radio was moving from a mass-appeal medium, the something-for-everyone sound and style, to a format-driven medium focused on listener niches and format specialization. At the same time, the proliferation of FM was increasing the number of radio stations and, consequently, competition for advertising dollars. Advertisers were looking beyond standard demographic groupings of target audience; they wanted more tightly focused audience profiles. Differentiating station formats and delivering the audiences for which advertisers were asking became an economic necessity. And it also became necessary to back up claims about number and types of listeners with acceptable cumulative (also known as "cume") audience figures and other ratings details. Not only did the fusion of these various factors stimulate format specialization in radio, it also spurred the creation of hyperspecializations—finely tuned variations on the already flourishing number of general format-types.

The division of the daily radio schedule into dayparts also enhanced radio's attractiveness to advertisers intent on applying psychographic research to their media buys. The accent on lifestyle characteristics in psychographics found a perfect complement in the radio programming day. Advertisers could not only narrow the type of listener to whom they were speaking but could also isolate message sending to the time of day most likely to match target consumers' listening habits.

Although some radio stations used psychographic research to profile their own audiences, most commercial stations continued to market their audiences using demographic descriptions. This practice continues today for several reasons, not the least of which is the prohibitive cost of psychographic research. The fact that radio stations do not typically provide psychographic data about their audiences is not, however, a significant barrier to advertiser purchases of radio spots. Advertisers buy airtime based on both demographic and psychographic data and generally have explicit knowledge of what type of listeners they want.

Public radio is an exception. Public stations regularly use audience personality and lifestyle profiles to entice program sponsors and fortify fund-raising efforts. Understanding listeners' motivations for donating to public broadcasting helps stations to construct persuasive messages and, as a result, to boost financial support from listeners.

Psychographic Measures

Many researchers customize their own segmentation studies as they attempt to predict consumer behavior based on psychographic profiles. Instruments designed to measure various constructs, such as learning style, locus of control, sensation seeking, or general personality traits, illustrate potential tools for gathering psychographic data.

A variety of research firms offer proprietary psychographic research models and syndicated research services. Among the best known are the *Yankelovich Monitor* and the Values and Lifestyles Systems (VALS) from SRI International (formerly the Stanford Research Institute). Since 1970 the *Yankelovich Monitor* has published an annual report on the changing attitudes of adults aged 16 and older based on 2,500 two-hour in-home interviews, combined with written questionnaires. The *Monitor* study is designed to identify broad consumer trends and to build in-depth profiles of target segments.

SRI International created the original VALS in 1978. It offered a psychographic typology that categorized American adults into nine mutually exclusive groups based on consumer responses to questions about lifestyles and social values. The VALS segments were revised and renamed in 1989 in an effort to make VALS more useful to SRI's business customers. Rather than classifying consumers by responses to topical, attitude-oriented issues, the new VALS2 system uses eight profile groups that cluster consumers based on fixed psychological qualities.

See also: Audience; Audience Research Methods; Demographics

Further Reading

Gunter, Barrie, and Adrian Furnham, *Consumer Profiles: An Introduction to Psychographics*, London: Routledge, 1992.
Heath, Rebecca Piirto, "The Frontiers of Psychographics," *American Demographics* 18, no. 7 (July 1996).
Keith, Michael C., *The Radio Station*, Boston: Focal Press, 1986; 4th edition, 1997.
Riche, Martha Farnsworth, "Psychographics for the 1990s," *American Demographics* 11, no. 7 (July 1989).
Schulberg, Bob, *Radio Advertising: The Authoritative Handbook*, Lincolnwood, Illinois: NTC Business Books, 1989.

CLAUDIA CLARK

PUBLIC AFFAIRS PROGRAMMING

From the earliest days of broadcasting, public affairs has been a vital part of the program service of most radio stations and networks. Although it has come in various forms through the years, and despite its decline in recent years in commercial radio, this type of programming has been a resilient, integral player in the public's efforts to understand the vital issues of the day.

"Public affairs" is a broadly construed program type in which current issues of public concern are discussed, analyzed, and debated. The issues may be of broad public interest (such as a presidential election) or designed to appeal to a more narrowly based set of interests (such as the building of an overpass by a public school). The "public" may be defined as the general population of listeners or a more narrowly defined segment (gay men, farmers, housewives, etc.). Yet despite the wide variety of approaches to this program type, there have been two basic approaches to its conceptualization: in the more common one, the public affairs program is designed to have an expert or group of experts discuss the matter at hand; in the other, a more widely drawn segment of opinion and analysis is tapped.

Origins

From the inception of regular broadcasting, radio stations (and later the networks) had an interest in maintaining a public affairs presence. Such programs were inexpensive and helped to build radio's public reputation. Among the earliest were speeches given by prominent people—local and national. In 1923 President Warren G. Harding spoke about the World Court in St. Louis. His speech was carried by local station KSD and by AT&T stations in New York and Washington, D.C., producing the largest audience ever to hear a presidential address at one time. Listeners took these programs quite seriously. Later that year, former President Woodrow Wilson's speech on Armistice Day was broadcast by radio stations in New York City and Schenectady, New York; Washington, D.C.; and Providence, Rhode Island, despite his having been in ill health and out of the public eye for some time. (More than 20,000 people showed up at his house the next day to wish him well.) The following summer, 18 stations linked to WEAF, New York, carried coverage and commentary of the 1924 Democratic National Convention. Listeners heard arguments and violent debates between members of the Ku Klux Klan, and also between New York Governor Alfred E. Smith, former Treasury Secretary William Gibbs MacAdoo, and William Jennings Bryan. Heated arguments went on for hours, complete with cheering and booing from the assembled galleries. Fist-fights broke out on the air; they were so tumultuous that the Democratic Party stationed an official censor to stand on the platform in order to shut off the microphone when speeches became too heated.

Despite the popularity of the format, broadcasters found early on that any serious discussion of public affairs was bound to be contentious. Because the espousal of any particular position on a disputed issue was bound to receive favorable comments from those who agreed with it and criticism from those who did not, broadcasters feared alienating any part of their audience, or the current political powers, or (worst of all, from their perspective) existing or potential advertisers. From this concern would come a firm broadcast business stand against allowing purchase of advertising time for expression of views on controversial issues—a ban that lasted well into the 1980s. On 4 April 1922, Hans von (later H.V.) Kaltenborn, then associate editor of the *Brooklyn Eagle*, began a series of half-hour reviews of current world affairs on station WEAF, New York, the radio station of AT&T. These talks were something new for broadcasting, especially his editorial commentary on the affairs of the day. As Kaltenborn notes in his autobiography, *Fifty Fabulous Years* (1950), radio management was reluctant to air such discussions because they feared "the expression of opinion on the air might have dangerous repercussions and might even jeopardize the future of broadcasting." From its beginnings, public affairs programming demonstrated the conflicting pressures on broadcasters of informing the public and protecting the bottom line. Program producers often were caught in a struggle between the public and the commercial interests of station management.

One way to mitigate this "problem" was to air public affairs program series that offered a variety of viewpoints. Among the first public affairs program series were regular broadcasts of *Meetings of the Foreign Policy Association*, which ran on National Broadcasting Company (NBC) Blue from November 1926 to 1940, *Meetings of the Government Club* (NBC, 1926 to 1930), and *Our Government*, a series hosted by journalist David Lawrence discussing the relationships between the federal government, business, and various professions (NBC, 1927 to 1933). In 1929, 227 officials of the U.S. Department of Agriculture gave more than 500 addresses on various issues concerning agricultural issues and policies on NBC stations.

Major Network Series

In the tightening grip of the Depression and the coming of the Roosevelt years, NBC broadcast two public affairs series focusing on economics: *The Economic World Today* (November 1932 to June 1933) and *Economics in a Changing World* (October 1934 to March 1935). During the mid- to late 1930s, NBC broadcast a number of public affairs series explaining the roles of various New Deal programs such as the National Recovery Administration (1933), Federal Housing Administration (three series from 1934 to 1939), and the Social Security Act (1936 to 1940).

By the mid-1930s public affairs programs had become a regular part of network program schedules. Their primary format was either to present debates or discussions between experts on particular issues or to broadcast interviews of prominent individuals by journalists. Although none expected nor achieved large audiences, the relatively small number of listeners were generally those with strong social and political ties, and thus of importance greater than their number. Among the most well known were the *University of Chicago Round Table*, broadcast on WMAQ, Chicago (1931 to 1933), and then on the NBC Red Network (1933 to 1955); *American Forum of the Air*, hosted by Theodore Granik on the Mutual and later NBC networks (1937 to 1956); and *America's Town*

Meeting of the Air, hosted by George V. Denny on the NBC Blue/American Broadcasting Companies (ABC) network (1935 to 1956). All shared the format of a panel presenting various viewpoints on issues of the day to the audience. Based on the notion that somehow "scholarly objectivity" would remove any fear that the program could be controversial, *The University of Chicago Round Table* was aimed at an elite, educated audience (panelists were intellectuals, primarily college professors).

The real breakthrough program was *American Forum of the Air*. Sponsored by Gimbel's Department Store in New York, *American Forum* was initially hosted by store employee and law student Theodore Granik. His idea was to provide legal advice and a weekly discussion of legal issues over the air in a panel discussion format. When the program moved to WOR (Newark, New Jersey), Granik started to move the panel toward more controversial questions in a more adversarial format. Guests included members of Congress, Cabinet secretaries, journalists, and other prominent citizens. The topics discussed included the New Deal, labor unrest, civil rights isolationism, fascism and Communism. (It should be noted that no communists were ever allowed to speak on the program even when the subject was the nature of Communism itself.) The program was considered important enough to be printed verbatim in the Congressional Record, resulting in many floor debates initiated by the program. Fireworks erupted when a heated debate (virtually unknown in radio up to that point) broke out on the subject of prohibition, between New York Congressman Emmanuel Celler and Emma Boole of the Women's Christian Temperance Union. Boole charged members of Congress with being illegal drunkards, arguing that there were "underground passages" running directly from Washington speakeasies to congressional offices. The charges caused a national uproar drawing widespread attention, and a large audience, to the program.

The best-remembered series of public affairs speeches were the Fireside Chats of President Franklin D. Roosevelt. The first of these, on the banking crisis, was broadcast 12 March 1933, just a few days after his inauguration. Speaking to an audience estimated at more than 60 million radio listeners, President Roosevelt explained banking practices, his reasons for instituting a "bank holiday," and a call for people to have confidence in the government's ability to carry out his plans. In 104 radio addresses between 1933 and 1936, Roosevelt drew large audiences and an array of support for his New Deal policies. The series lasted until 1944.

But it was in reaction to a neighbor who refused to listen to anything Roosevelt had to say that George V. Denny, Jr. created the best-known public affairs debate program: *America's Town Meeting of the Air*. For more than two decades, *Town Meeting* was the public affairs program of choice for millions of listeners. The program received more than 4,000 pieces of fan mail per week. More than 1,000 *Town Meeting* debate and discussion clubs were formed in libraries, churches, schools, community organizations, and local homes for people to gather, listen, and then continue the debate long into the night after a program was over. The National Women's Radio Committee named *Town Meeting* the best educational program in the country in 1936. High school students in New York City listened to the programs and then participated in similar classroom discussion the next day. In 1938 and 1939, listeners purchased more than 250,000 copies of program transcripts so that they could have a permanent record of what had been said.

Town Meeting's popularity stemmed largely from the range of program debate and the volatility of its format. From the beginning it hosted debates that easily led to heated argument. The initial broadcast on 30 May 1935 was "Which Way America—Communism, Fascism, Socialism or Democracy?" In other broadcasts, Eleanor Roosevelt debated Mrs. Eugene Meyer on the benefits of the New Deal, and Langston Hughes discussed "Let's Face the Race Question" (at a time when the voices of African-Americans were seldom heard). Other speakers included justices of the Supreme Court, Norman Thomas, William Randolph Hearst, Jr., Cabinet secretaries, members of Congress, leading educators, and noted authors. Whereas other programs eschewed contentious feedback from the audience, *Town Meeting* promoted it; audience condemnation and heckling of speakers was expected. In some programs, speakers came close to physical violence on the air.

An October 1931 talk by British playwright George Bernard Shaw on the Columbia Broadcasting System (CBS) created a major stir. The network had wanted Shaw to come to its London studios to give a talk on the current situation in Europe. Network management's elation at his appearance was deflated when he focused the majority of his remarks on praising the Communist system in the Soviet Union: "Hello, all my friends in America! How are all you dear old boobs who have been telling one another for a month that I have gone dotty about Russia? Russia has a laugh on us. She has us fooled, beaten, shamed, shown up, outpointed, and all but knocked out." A resulting widespread public outcry led CBS executives quickly to broadcast a rebuttal from a clergyman in order to counteract what they feared was Shaw's inference that the communist system was divinely favored.

Among the more notable public affairs programs of the 1940s were *Life Begins at 80* (on Mutual and ABC from 1948 to 1953), a discussion of world affairs by a group of senior citizens that was reportedly so frank in its discussions that programs had to be taped and edited before broadcast; *Juvenile Jury* (carried by Mutual and NBC from 1946 to 1953), a program featuring young people giving their perspectives on current issues of the day; and *Leave It to the Girls* (on Mutual, 1945 to 1949), which started as a discussion program featuring career women talking about problems submitted by their listeners, before becoming more comedic.

By the 1950s much of radio's major programming was migrating to television; public affairs programs either followed this trend or met their demise with the growing popularity of the new medium. In December 1950, CBS began a weekly series, *Hear It Now*, hosted by highly regarded correspondent Edward R. Murrow. The program was short-lived, moving to television in September 1951 as *See It Now*. Another radio program, *Meet the Press*, began in the late 1940s on NBC Radio and also moved to television in the 1950s. (It remains a Sunday morning fixture to this day.) The long-running *America's Town Meeting of the Air* left the air in 1956.

Many local stations continued to produce public affairs programs targeted at specific immigrant groups such as Poles, Basques, Japanese, Haitians, and Mexicans. Typical was the *Hellenic Radio Hour* hosted by Penelope Apostolides at stations around Washington, D.C., between 1950 and 1995. The program was a one-hour broadcast featuring news and discussion by and for the Greek community, as well as aspects of Greek culture.

Noncommercial Programs

While public affairs radio was declining on commercial radio in the 1950s, a newer, more robust format was taking its place: listener-sponsored radio typified by the broadcasts from stations of the Pacifica Foundation, originally of Berkeley, California. Public affairs was one of the four primary areas of station programming. As Eleanor McKinney notes in *The Exacting Ear* (1966), Pacifica Radio's intention was to provide a program service different from that provided by commercial broadcasters, because "(w)e were all convinced that the commercial notion of 'all us bright people in here broadcasting to all you sheep-like masses out there' was completely false."

McKinney cites Lewis Hill, Pacifica's founder, who held that the problem was how to provide listeners with truly provocative programming that addressed significant alternative viewpoints, analyses, and proposals for fixing the major problems of the day. "Radio which aims to do that," Hill argues, "must express what its practitioners believe to be real, good, beautiful and so forth, and what they believe is truly at stake in the assertion of such values." Hill went on to claim that "either some particular person makes up his mind about these things and learns to express them for himself, or we have no values or no significant expression of them."

A cross-section of Pacifica's programs published in 1966 shows that the public affairs commitment of the three stations in Berkeley, Los Angeles, and New York spanned a wide range: a 1953 broadcast of a talk on the "First Amendment: Core of Constitution" delivered before a congressional committee by legal scholar Alexander Meiklejohn; a 1958 hour-long interview with Ammon Hennacy, editor of the *Catholic Worker*, in which he discussed conscientious objection to war and the benefits of a decentralized state; the 1960 broadcast and subsequent documentary productions reporting on House Un-American Activities Committee hearings in San Francisco; a much requested interview by Irish poet and author Ella Young, discussing environmental issues; Supreme Court Justice William O. Douglas discussing racial discrimination, on Independence Day 1962; a documentary, "Freedom Now!" produced from field recordings of blacks and whites during the racial struggles of Birmingham, Alabama, in 1963; and regularly scheduled series of commentaries by William Rusher, editor of the *National Review*, and noted author Ayn Rand. These outlets for a wide range of public affairs remain on the air to this day.

In the 1970s, several former staff and volunteers at the five Pacifica stations (Pacifica had added stations in Houston and Washington, D.C.) were among the first reporters and producers at National Public Radio (NPR). This noncommercial network has been producing two daily news programs (*Morning Edition* and *All Things Considered*) that regularly feature documentaries on a wide range of subjects, such as health care, poverty, environmental concerns, electoral campaign financing, war and peace, famine, and many other subjects.

Although commercial radio largely abandoned its public affairs commitment in the wake of Reagan era deregulation, it remains a vital component of noncommercial and community stations around the country. Public affairs programming is one of the hallmarks of NPR. It provides three daily public affairs talk programs: *Talk of the Nation*, a national call-in program that runs for two hours Monday through Thursday afternoons; *Fresh Air*, a daily hour-long interview program that focuses on the arts and culture, and the ways they are imbedded within current events; and *The Dianne Rehm Show*, a daily two-hour call-in program with many distinguished guests, offering listeners opportunities to hear and participate in lively, thoughtful dialogs on a variety of topics.

NPR also provides stations with three weekly public affairs programs. *Latino USA* and host Maria Hinojosa provide public radio audiences with information about the issues and events affecting the lives of the nation's growing and increasingly diverse Latino communities. News round-ups and acclaimed cultural segments promote cross-cultural understanding and develop a forum for Latino cultural and artistic expression. *Living on Earth*, which has won a number of awards, is hosted by Steve Curwood. The program explores the environment—what people are doing to it and what it's doing to us. In-depth coverage, features, interviews, and commentary examine how the environment affects medicine, politics, technology, economics, transportation, agriculture, and more. The third series, *The Merrow Report*, focuses on education, youth, and learning, hosted by John Merrow.

In 1983 a second public radio programming source, American Public Radio (since renamed Public Radio International or PRI), began operations from the Twin Cities of Minnesota. Its stated mission was "to develop distinctive radio programs and to diversify the public radio offerings available to American listeners. Among APR's first program offerings was a two-hour weekly talk, essay, interview, and listener call-in program, *Modern Times with Larry Josephson*. The program (first aired by local station KCRW in Santa Monica, California) was about the basic moral and philosophical questions posed by current issues such as abortion; Supreme Court decisions; the Joel Steinberg/Hedda Nussbaum tragedy (hosted by Susan Brownmiller); the atomic age (hosted by McGeorge Bundy); and the end of the Cold War (hosted by Arthur Schlesinger, Jr.).

During the Persian Gulf War in 1990, APR carried a half-hour nightly program, *Gulf War: Special Edition*, consisting of reports from more than 20 BBC reporters in the Middle East, combined with CBC coverage. The series, modeled after the *Nightly Vietnam Report* of Pacifica's WBAI (New York), provided international perspectives on the war that were unavailable from any single producer or network.

In 1994 APR changed its name to Public Radio International to focus more of its efforts, in part, on globally relevant programming. *The World*, public radio's first global news program, was begun in 1996.

More recently PRI has provided public radio stations with daily public affairs programming from the British Broadcasting Corporation (BBC) and the Canadian Broadcasting Corporation (CBC). Among the BBC offerings are *Newshour*, a 60-minute thrice-daily program of news reporting, commentary, and analysis; *The World Today*, a 15-minute program that looks into one international issue each day; and *Outlook*, a 25-minute magazine-style program on international issues. The weekly program *Dialogue* is produced by the Woodrow Wilson International Center for Scholars in association with Radio Smithsonian. This program focuses on topics of national, international, historical and cultural affairs.

Alternative Public Affairs Formats

There have also been efforts to broaden the ways in which stations reach out to their audiences to engage them in discussions and actions concerning issues of current interest. A brief experiment in an alternative form of public affairs radio was *America's Hour*, which ran on CBS from July to September 1935. Its aim was to "boost America" while decrying public dissatisfaction at the height of the Depression. The format was an hour-long melodrama on such issues as railroads, hospitals, mining, and aviation; the intent was to praise mutual management/worker relationships, denouncing "radicals who breed discontent." This program was also noteworthy as being the early breeding ground for radio dramatic actors of later prominence: Orson Welles, Joseph Cotten, Ray Collins, Betty Garde, and Agnes Moorehead.

Some of the more interesting public affairs programs were experiments in using the station to initiate dialogue within the community, with the station seen as a forum for the active engagement of various segments of the local community. Two of the earliest such efforts were produced at commercial FM stations. One of these was the work of Danny Schechter at WBCN-FM, Boston, between 1970 and 1977. WBCN was a major pioneer underground or progressive commercial music station in the country. Calling himself "The News Dissector," Schechter created a public affairs format to match the diverse interests of the station's listeners who, he believed, were interested in public affairs not slanted in the traditional way. Writing in *The More You Watch the Less You Know* (1997), Schechter says his approach was to dissect the news; that is, to:

> break it down into elements that explained what was going on, rather than just report the familiar surfaces. [He] wanted to present news that looked at the world from the point of views of people who were trying to change it, rather than those who would keep it the way it was.

Schecter provided in-depth analyses and discussions of such issues as the anti-Vietnam movements, racism and apartheid in South Africa, and the needs and interests of workers in Boston-area manufacturing industries. He sought to bring a more inclusive format to public affairs programs by inviting community activists to participate in discussions of major issues of the day.

Wes "Scoop" Nisker produced public affairs programs in the same vein at KSAN, San Francisco, in the mid-1960s to mid-1970s. Nisker created person-on-the-street packages in which he incorporated a variety of voices, music, and sounds to create programs on subjects such as the annual Gay Pride Day parade, political campaigns, and sex and violence on television. Nisker concluded each broadcast by urging his listeners to become involved directly in the issues of the day, saying, "If you don't like the news you hear on the radio, go out and create some of your own."

Another experiment in engaging the community actively in public affairs was *The Drum* on WBUR, Boston. Begun in 1968 by a consortium composed of staff from WBUR, the Boston mayor's office, Action for Boston Community Development, and local commercial radio and television stations, *The Drum* was an effort to provide both a radio forum for public affairs discussions and a job training site for young adult members of Boston's minority communities. At the time, the only station that had programming targeted at minority communities in Boston signed off at sundown each day. To reach out to these segments of the population, *The Drum* provided a nightly program of news, music, and public affairs features (on issues such as health care, housing, employment, violence, drug abuse, and education) aimed at those communities. Program staff was composed primarily of young men and women recruited from the communities covered. The recruits were contracted to work for the program for a year, during which they were given rigorous training in news and public affairs reporting, writing and program production, announcing,

publicity, and community outreach. At the completion of the training year, commercial radio and television stations provided them with jobs as a means of increasing minority staff presence and, for the stations, as a way to gain larger audiences in inner city communities.

Thus, *The Drum* provided a model, demonstrating ways that local broadcasters could more closely cater to the needs and interests of under-represented communities in their areas while also expanding their audience base. *The Drum* project was terminated in August 1971. However, many former *Drum* trainees are still working in the broadcasting industries as on-air talent and station management.

The 1970s also saw the founding of radio stations produced by and for Native American communities. More than two dozen Native American stations now have their own national satellite network and have garnered a large audience in indigenous communities. On the reservations the stations produce public affairs news and cultural features of interest to the communities. The sole source of Indian news, these stations act as preservers of Native American languages and culture. They have become the new *eyapaha* (a Lakota word for "town crier"). Typical is station KBRW in Barrow, Alaska. The station's management considers its most important product to be programs about Native American issues and interests, local and state news and discussions, broadcasts of local governmental meetings, personal messages, and public service announcements.

Among the longest running of public affairs commentary programs was *Uncommon Sense: The Radio News Essays of Charles Morgan*, which ran on KPFK, Los Angeles, from 1974 to 1991. This was a series of twice-weekly 15-minute essays on current events covering such topics as the power of the multinational oil companies (which Morgan decried as "The Dictatorship of the Petroletariat"), the Rockefeller-sponsored Trilateral Commission, political extremism, and the increasing disconnection between official news and politics and the growing underclass of people of color in south central and east Los Angeles. From the mid-1980s, Morgan added a listener call-in program, *Talk to Me*, that allowed listeners to respond to what he was saying on the air. *Talk to Me's* significance was that Morgan encouraged listeners to debate him and each other in a lively exchange of ideas. This was very different from the "question-the-expert/hang-up-for-the-answer" format that dominated talk radio.

Alternative Radio is a public affairs program service in Boulder, Colorado, that attempts to breach the near-monopoly of corporate control over commercial radio outlets. Founded in 1986 by producer David Barsamian, *Alternative Radio* provides lectures by and interviews with outstanding analysts (and individuals usually shunned by mainstream media sources) on a variety of topics. Barsamian offers the hour-long program free to stations and then sells copies of the programs to listeners. Among recent national program bestsellers are historian Howard Zinn on "The Use and Abuse of History," Vermont independent congressman Bernie Sanders on "Single Payer Health Care," and journalists Molly Ivins on "American Political Culture and Other Jokes" and Barbara Ehrenreich on "Trash Media: The Tabloidization of the News." Other regular speakers are Michael Parenti, Noam Chomsky, Ralph Nader, and Dr. Helen Caldicott.

The Women's International News Gathering Service (WINGS) is an all-woman independent radio production company that produces and distributes news and current affairs programs by and about women around the world. WINGS programs are used by noncommercial radio stations, women's studies, and individuals. Programs can be heard on local radio stations, on shortwave, on the internet, and on cassettes. The WINGS mailing list provides updates on stories and new information about women's media. Headquartered in Austin, Texas, WINGS collects programs and news stories to distribute to public radio stations around the country.

A more recent radio public affairs program with an alternative format is the daily *Democracy Now!* This is a national, listener-sponsored public radio and TV show, pioneering the largest community media collaboration in the country. The program started in 1997 as the only daily election show in public broadcasting, and has since broadened its focus to national and international public issues. In 1998, *Democracy Now!* went to Nigeria, Africa's most populous country, to document the activities of U.S. oil companies in the Niger Delta. The program won the 1998 George Polk Award for the radio documentary "Drilling and Killing: Chevron and Nigeria's Military Dictatorship." In November 1999 *Democracy Now!* produced an eight-day series of special reports on the demonstrations against the World Trade Organization meetings in Seattle, Washington. Following these programs, in 2000 *Democracy Now!* pioneered a unique multi-media collaboration involving nonprofit community radio, the internet, and satellite and cable television through the Free Speech TV satellite channel. This is the first radio public affairs program to utilize, and to engage, voices from around the world via converging communications technologies.

Since 1997, C-SPAN, cable TV's public affairs network, has also aired an aural counterpart. C-SPAN radio simulcasts many of its TV parent's programs, including *Washington Journal*, as well as many programs unique to the radio service including interviews, oral histories, and the proceedings of Congressional committees and press conferences.

For decades, FCC license renewal guidelines held that radio stations should devote a minimum percentage of airtime to discussion of matters of public importance. In support, the commission required stations to regularly survey their communities to ascertain which issues were of greatest importance so that programs on those topics could be provided. They were also compelled to maintain a publicly available written log of what public affairs-oriented programs they had aired throughout the year. Failure to do these things, which the Commission believed belied the station's operation in the "public interest, convenience and necessity," were grounds for revocation of a station's broadcast license. But, in the early 1980s as part of its sweeping deregulation, the FCC removed all of these requirements and, hence, many stations quickly abandoned any commitment to public affairs.

Similarly, though opponents of the Fairness Doctrine argued that its repeal would significantly increase the amount of public affairs programming heard over the airwaves—as broadcasters would no longer be hamstrung by strict "equal time" statutes—once the Doctrine was abolished (in August 1987), that is not what happened. A 2003 study done by the Benton Foundation found that over a quarter of all stations offered no news or public affairs programming at all.

Though the presence of public affairs programming can no longer determine obtaining or losing a license, it can still be factored into regulatory decisions that might affect the station. Hence, many stations still provide at least some public affairs programming, even if they often bury it in low-rated time periods like early Sunday morning. Luckily for many broadcasters, the FCC defines "public affairs" rather broadly: abbreviated newscasts, community calendars, even some types of entertainment can be interpreted as "public affairs."

See also: All Things Considered; Controversial Issues, Broadcasting of; Documentary Programs; Editorializing; Educational Radio to 1967; Fairness Doctrine; Fireside Chats; *Fresh Air*; *Hear It Now*; *Morning Edition*; National Public Radio; Native American Radio; News; Pacifica Foundation; Politics and Radio; Public Radio International; Public Radio Since 1967; *Talk of the Nation*; Talk Radio

Further Reading

Barnouw, Erik, *A History of Broadcasting in the United States*, 3 vols, New York: Oxford University Press, 1966–70; see especially vol. 1, *A Tower in Babel: To 1933*, 1966.

Chase, Francis Seabury, Jr., *Sound and Fury: An Informal History of Broadcasting*, New York and London: Harper, 1942.

Keith, Michael C., *Signals in the Air: Native Broadcasting in America*, Westport, Connecticut.: Praeger, 1995.

McKinney, Eleanor, editor, *The Exacting Ear: The Story of Listener-Sponsored Radio and an Anthology of Programs from KPFA, KPFK, and WBAI*, New York: Pantheon, 1966.

Schechter, Danny, *The More You Watch, the Less You Know: News Wars/(Sub) Merged Hopes/Media Adventures*, New York: Seven Stories Press, 1997.

JOHN HOCHHEIMER,
2009 REVISIONS BY CARY O'DELL

PUBLIC BROADCASTING ACT OF 1967
Creating Public Radio

The Public Broadcasting Act of 1967 was the first federal legislation that enabled Congressional support for a national public radio and television system for the American people. As a direct result of the Act signed into Law on 7 November, the Corporation for Public Broadcasting was created, and subsequently National Public Radio (NPR) and the Public Broadcasting Service (PBS) were established as radio and television distribution networks, respectively.

Origins

Historians are fond of recalling that federal support of public radio in the United States was largely an afterthought. The impetus that led to the creation of the Public Broadcasting Act of 1967 is rooted in efforts to gain public awareness and funding for what was then known as educational television. That the act was rewritten to explicitly include the medium of radio is a testament to the enormous commitment of a handful of radio enthusiasts.

Noncommercial educational radio frequencies were first set aside by the Federal Communications Commission (FCC) in 1938 (for special high-frequency AM stations to broadcast to school classes) and in 1941 for the new FM service. When FM's frequency band shifted in 1945, the educational reservation was shifted as well. In each case, however, the building of stations to use the allocated frequencies was slow in coming. Educational institutions found it difficult to gather funds to put stations on the air and then sustain their ongoing

operation. Many of the educational radio stations that were built during the 1950s and 1960s failed to achieve the professional standards of their commercial counterparts, and hence the audiences for such outlets were relatively small. So little attention was being given to this "hidden medium" that radio representatives had little influence in the power circles of Washington, D.C.

By contrast, the FCC had created noncommercial educational television channels in April of 1952. The medium of television had caught the public's imagination as an educational resource, although except for Ford Foundation grants its early funding picture was comparable to that of educational radio. Concerns about American education during the late 1950s led to the availability of limited monies to support educational television via the National Defense Education Act of 1958, but educational television advocates saw this modest infusion merely as an important first step. A major political offensive was launched by groups such as the National Association of Educational Broadcasters (NAEB) to take advantage of the pro-educational television campaign rhetoric of President John F. Kennedy. This effort reached fruition on 1 May 1962, when President Kennedy signed into law the Educational Television Facilities Act of 1962. The legislation authorized $32 million over a five-year period to construct new stations or improve the coverage of existing stations. During this period the number of educational television stations nearly doubled.

A New Legislative Initiative

The passage of the Educational Television Act of 1962 not only generated new funding for the construction of educational television stations but also created a new awareness and support base in both houses of Congress. Representatives and senators alike who had been actively involved in the passage of the facilities legislation remained openly impressed with the promise of this new educational medium. One of the senators who had helped mount the charge for educational television funding in the 1950s was Lyndon B. Johnson. When Johnson became president of the United States after the Kennedy assassination, educational television appeared to fit well with his Great Society programs.

The Educational Television Stations (ETS) division of the NAEB held a conference on the long-range financing of educational television in December of 1964. That gathering, and the national survey of station needs associated with it, served as the launching pad for creating a blue ribbon commission to study the future of this important educational resource and to make recommendations to the president. Days after the conference concluded, C. Scott Fletcher of ETS had secured funding from the Carnegie Foundation to form the Carnegie Commission on Educational Television, to be chaired by Ralph Lowell. After a year of study, the Commission issued its report— *Public Television: A Program for Action*. President Johnson received and endorsed the recommendations and then called for legislation that would give life to the vision outlined. Educational broadcasters also applauded the report at a second funding conference held in March 1967 that was designed to encourage prompt congressional action. That action came quickly, as Senate hearings on S.1160 began 11 April 1967. But for advocates of educational radio, or public radio as it was now being called, the legislation had a definite weakness: there was no explicit provision for the radio medium. The proposed law circulating in both houses of Congress (S.1160) was for a Public Television Act.

If there is a single individual who deserves credit for changing the course of this legislation it is Jerrold Sandler, executive director of NAEB's National Educational Radio (NER) division. Sandler was well aware of the ETS division's intention to play down the role of educational radio because of its uneven track record. Without fanfare, Sandler began a campaign to have public radio included in the language of the act. Among his initiatives were a conference at the Johnson Foundation's Wingspread Center in Racine, Wisconsin, and the commissioning of a national fact-finding study to demonstrate that public radio was indeed alive and well. The resulting report, *The Hidden Medium: A Status Report on Educational Radio in the United States*, was distributed to Washington policy-makers after the Senate and House bills had already been scheduled for hearings. But even at this late date, the report had a significant impact. Jerrold Sandler's impassioned testimony during the Senate hearings prompted Senator Griffin of Michigan to propose that the bill be broadened to include radio and the name of the forthcoming legislation be retitled the Public Broadcasting Act of 1967. In addition, the name of the oversight agency to be created by the act was changed from the Corporation of Public Television to the Corporation for Public Broadcasting. Public radio had scored a major policy victory.

This landmark legislation became Section 396 of the Communications Act of 1934. Congress mandated the FCC to uphold the law that was designed to "encourage the growth and development of public radio and television broadcasting" in the United States. Yet with all its public-interest language and the creation of a new nonprofit organization to ensure that public radio and television would develop and prosper, the Act failed to provide the insulated long-range funding mechanism recommended in the Carnegie Commission report. That failure would consume the energies of the public broadcasting community for decades to come.

See also: Communications Act of 1934; Corporation for Public Broadcasting; Educational Radio to 1967; National Association of Educational Broadcasters; National Public Radio; Public Radio International; Public Radio Since 1967

Further Reading

Avery, Robert K., "The Public Broadcasting Act of 1967: Looking Ahead by Looking Back," *Critical Studies in Media Communication* 24, no. 4 (October 2007), pp. 358–364

Avery, Robert K., and Robert Pepper, "Balancing the Equation: Public Radio Comes of Age," *Public Telecommunications Review* 7, no. 2 (March/April 1979).

Burke, John Edward, *An Historical-Analytical Study of the Legislative and Political Origins of the Public Broadcasting Act of 1967*, New York: Arno Press, 1979.

Carnegie Commission on Educational Television, *Public Television: A Program for Action*, New York: Harper and Row, 1967.

Herman W. Land Associates, *The Hidden Medium: A Status Report on Educational Radio in the United States*, New York: Herman W. Land Associates, 1967.

Witherspoon, John, Roselle Kovitz, Robert K. Avery, and Alan G. Stavitsky, *A History of Public Broadcasting*, Washington, D.C.: Current, 2000.

ROBERT K. AVERY

"PUBLIC INTEREST, CONVENIENCE, OR NECESSITY"
Regulatory Policy

"Public interest, convenience, or necessity" is perhaps the most significant phrase in the Communications Act of 1934. Through this durable but flexible set of words, first employed in the Radio Act of 1927, Congress guides (but also allows vital discretion to) the Federal Communications Commission (FCC), radio's most important federal regulator. The agency must act in the public interest. In turn, the rules and policies it creates exist, in part, to prod radio licensees to serve the public interest.

Statutory Origins

The earliest federal radio statutes (the Wireless Ship Acts of 1910 and 1912) were short-lived, although the subsequent Radio Act of 1912 lasted for 15 years. Initially written primarily for maritime wireless telephony, these laws proved inadequate when radio expanded to include broadcasting. Courts ruled that the secretary of commerce (the major regulator under the early acts) lacked the discretion or flexibility to adopt new rules or regulations as radio changed. The secretary's actions, courts said, were limited to the specifics of the Act. Broadcasting required new legislation.

After ignoring this problem for several years, Congress finally adopted the Radio Act of 1927. The new statute created a Federal Radio Commission (FRC) and charged it with keeping up with the rapidly changing field of radio. Unlike the secretary of commerce, the FRC could adopt rules and regulations with the force of law. Such discretion, however, required the statutory limitation that Congress provided by mandating that the FRC regulate radio in the "public interest, convenience or necessity." When the Radio Act of 1927 was replaced by the Communications Act of 1934, Congress re-enacted the public interest standard.

The phrase was derived in part from earlier statutes regulating usage of scarce public resources such as public lands and establishing federal agencies to manage natural monopolies such as railways. By creating the FRC and the FCC and giving them this general statutory charge, Congress could step back from the day-to-day details of regulating rapidly changing radio, but it could also always rein in those agencies by saying, formally and informally, that they had not acted in the public interest. In theory, courts could do the same, if it can be argued that an FCC action is not in the public interest. In practice, however, the Communications Act has granted the FCC wide and rarely challenged discretion. For seven decades, the FCC has justified various rules, regulations, and policies under the standard. As radio (and its social and business contexts) has changed, the FCC has repeatedly altered its understanding of what the public interest requires.

Who Determines the Public Interest?

It is not flippant to say that the public interest in radio is whatever a majority of FCC commissioners believe it to be at any given time. There are two limits to this statement, however. First, the FCC runs the risk of being overturned in court if it cannot justify a rule, regulation, or action as being in the public interest. Courts have historically been reluctant to make this finding, however. More often, they either rule that the FCC has not compiled an

adequate record to support its decision—and give the FCC a second chance on remand—or conclude that the commission simply lacked statutory authority to act in the area. FCC actions, of course, must also comply with the Constitution, especially the First Amendment. On rare occasions, courts have ruled that an FCC policy thought to promote the public interest cannot stand because it violates the First Amendment.

Second, the FCC's opinions on the public interest can be undone by Congress, the commission's ultimate source of both budget and policy authority. If FCC rules, policies, or actions substantially distress Congress, legislators can seek to substitute their view of the public interest for the commission's by simply overriding an FCC decision or amending the Communications Act. Such steps are rarely taken, however. It is more common for Congress, through budgetary and oversight hearings, to telegraph warnings to the FCC about its expectations. The FCC usually heeds these warnings and rarely offends Congress even if commissioners believe an offending action to be in the public interest. A mid-2003 package of FCC decisions concerning media ownership sparked considerable congressional concern and disagreement, and an attempt in the Senate to roll back the rules to those existing before the FCC change. But House (and White House) support for the FCC action doomed the Senate initiative.

The FCC is typically a light-handed regulator of broadcasters. In many areas, the FCC leaves them great discretion as to how to fulfill general FCC mandates. Radio broadcasters, for example, must make "reasonable efforts" to provide "reasonable access" to their stations to candidates for federal elective office. In determining what is reasonable, the FCC expects radio broadcasters to consider what would best serve the public interest.

Public Interest Standard and Radio

In the early 1920s, attempts to regulate radio by the secretary of commerce collapsed as courts ruled that the secretary had limited authority to deal with broadcasting. When the Federal Radio Commission was formed in 1927, it had to deal with the consequences of this breakdown. There were more radio stations on the air than the technology of the day could handle, with resulting interference reducing service quality for all. The FRC had to clear the air and reduce the number of licensees.

Some urged that this be done on technical grounds alone, removing from the air stations that caused interference or could not maintain a reliable transmission schedule. Advocates of this approach often pointed to Section 29 of the Radio Act of 1927 prohibiting the FRC from censoring the uses of radio. This limitation, they argued, meant the FRC could not consider the content of the service a broadcaster was providing.

Others concluded, however, that the public interest standard compelled the FRC to consider content, despite the no-censorship clause. The FRC adopted this position and denied licenses and license renewal to radio broadcasters whose content was not at least generally in the public interest. The FRC ruled that the interests of the public, in good service as the commission defined it, were superior to the interests of broadcasters or advertisers. The public interest mandate led the FCC to regard broadcasters as "proxies" or "trustees" for the public. Reasoning that broadcasting was a scarce public resource and that there were more who wanted to broadcast than frequencies to accommodate them, the FCC developed the trusteeship model and assumed the ability to oversee and define the duties of the trustees—radio broadcasters.

The criteria for being a good trustee were not especially burdensome. Licensees were not to run stations solely to serve their own interests or the interests of advertisers. They were not to air programs or hoaxes (such as Orson Welles' 1938 *War of the Worlds* broadcast) that would scare or disrupt the community. They were not to carry programming, such as on-air diagnoses of disease and prescription of remedies, that might cause harm to others. In the very earliest days of the FRC, being a good trustee meant not playing recorded music, on the assumption that people who wanted to hear records could buy them—a public interest perspective the FRC quickly abandoned.

These programming policies eventually evolved into a general FCC expectation that every radio broadcaster would offer a"balanced" or "well-rounded" program service—a something-for-everyone-at-some-time approach that required every radio broadcaster to offer both paid and sustaining (unpaid) programs during the broadcast day that would be of some interest to everyone. These general expectations persisted until the 1960s when radio, as a result of the ascendance of TV, began to develop specialized formats serving narrowly targeted audiences. The FCC acquiesced in this specialization.

Overall, FCC regulation of radio content switched from expecting balanced or well-rounded programming to anticipating that broadcasters would offer minimum amounts of noncommercial, non-entertainment programming and refrain from over-commercialization. Although there were never any specific FCC rules setting quantitative news and public affairs expectations, until the early 1980s radio broadcasters ran the risk of having license renewals designated for review by the full FCC if they failed to offer minimum amounts of news or public affairs shows (eight percent for AM, six percent for FM), or if they ran too many commercials. Under the public interest standard, the FCC also expected that radio broadcasters would regularly and formally, through surveys of community leaders and the general public, ascertain the problems, needs, and interests of their communities and use their findings to formulate noncommercial, non-entertainment programming.

For many years radio broadcasters were also required to comply with the Fairness Doctrine, another policy the FCC promulgated under the public interest standard. This doctrine imposed two obligations on broadcasters: to devote "reasonable" attention to the coverage of controversial issues of public importance in their community, and to provide a "reasonable opportunity" for opposing views on those issues to be heard. The doctrine was never codified in the Communications Act of 1934; rather, it was another example of a policy created by the FCC under the public interest standard.

Public Interest and the Marketplace

During the 1970s, winds of deregulation swept through the regulatory world, including the FCC. Under both Democratic (Carter) and Republican (Reagan) administrations, and in many areas beyond communications (banking, transportation, etc.), the theory was advanced that marketplace forces, rather than regulation, should be relied upon whenever possible. Regulation, including regulation of radio, should be a last resort, used only when the marketplace produced clearly dysfunctional results. Public interest regulation traced its origins to New Deal responses to the Depression, the greatest marketplace collapse in U.S. history. Fifty years later, with a more robust, capitalistic economy in place, economists, industry leaders, and regulators argued that FCC behavioral regulations, such as the Fairness Doctrine and news programming guidelines, were no longer appropriate. The commission, it was argued, should only rarely substitute its assessment of the public interest for what consumers and the radio industry, responding to marketplace forces, wanted and chose to do.

By the 1980s the number of radio stations was also much greater than in the 1930s and 1940s when many FCC public interest regulations began.

The few hundred AM stations of 1934 had grown into thousands of AM and FM stations. With so many more stations on the air, it was argued, members of the public could choose those fitting their own standards or preferences. Radio deregulation orders in 1981 and 1984 eliminated the FCC's expectations about minimal amounts of news and public affairs programs. The commission reasoned that stations should not be compelled to provide specific amounts of such content in the public interest if they did not want to do so and if consumers were uninterested in such content. Other radio stations or perhaps other media would step in and fulfill any need for news if stations decided to cut back. Similarly, the FCC dropped its limits on the amount of time stations could devote to airing commercials. A station running too many commercials would presumably suffer in the marketplace. That marketplace, rather than the FCC, would henceforth protect the public interest from over-commercialization. Finally, the FCC decided that the public interest no longer required broadcasters to formally ascertain the problems, needs, and interests of their communities on a regular basis. Broadcasters out of touch with their communities, it reasoned, would be held in check by marketplace forces, so the rules mandating ascertainment were dropped.

Three years later, again responding to market-place-based theories of deregulation, the FCC dropped the Fairness Doctrine. It concluded that the doctrine might be counter-productive, as it could push broadcasters to play it safe in order to avoid Fairness Doctrine complaints. But more significantly, the commission believed that a multiplicity of voices in the electronic media marketplace of the late 1980s would, if deregulated, better serve the public's interest in receiving diverse and antagonistic information than regulation by the FCC. Some scholars and many radio industry leaders trace the growth of highly opinionated talk radio in the 1990s to the elimination of the Fairness Doctrine, as the FCC no longer believed that it was contrary to the public interest for a broadcaster to be unfair or unbalanced in the treatment of public issues.

Regulation under the Public Interest Standard Today

At the start of the 21st century, little remains of the public interest regulation of radio as practiced during most of the 20th century. All radio broadcasters are expected by the FCC to offer some "issue responsive" programming, but the commission has almost never questioned broadcasters'

interpretations of this vague standard. If licensees prepare and properly place in local public files quarterly "issues/programs" lists identifying at least five issues that have received treatment on the station during the previous quarter, the FCC assumes that the issue-responsive programming obligation has been met. It is considered contrary to the public interest to broadcast false information concerning a crime or catastrophe if it is foreseeable that the broadcast will cause "substantial public harm"—a prohibition aimed mostly at shock-jock hoaxes. The terms and conditions of station contests and promotions must be fully disclosed and, except in extraordinary circumstances, adhered to. Misleading the public about such contests is considered contrary to the public interest.

Since the late 1960s, the FCC has attempted to promote diversity in the broadcast employment marketplace by adopting policies attempting to enhance the employment of minorities and women by broadcasters and the ownership of stations by members of ethnic groups. In the late 1990s, with national standards on equal employment opportunity, affirmative action, and "minority set-asides" shifting, courts questioned and in some instances overturned these FCC policies. Believing that ethnic and gender diversity in employment and station ownership was in the public interest, however, the FCC adopted revised policies that it hoped would survive judicial scrutiny.

In recent years, most debate over serving the "public interest" has arisen over the issue of multiple station ownership. After the Telecommunications Act of 1996 expanded corporate ownership, concern arose that, potentially, a large conglomerate owning a number of stations within a single market would not be in the public interest as it would not allow sufficient diversity of viewpoints.

Later, in mid-2003, the FCC enacted further deregulation of television ownership rules by raising the percentage of homes that could be reached by one company from 35 to 45 percent. This prompted action by the Prometheus Radio Project, a consortium of community radio advocates, who feared a loss of diversity and who foresaw a possible threat to smaller broadcasters and minorities. They filed suit against the FCC in October 2003. *Prometheus v. FCC* was heard by the U.S. Court of Appeals in 2004 with the court voting 2:1 against the Commission's attempt to raise the limits stating that the "diversity index"—the system used by the FCC to weigh cross-ownership—employed "irrational assumptions and inconstancies."

Concerns about monopolies were voiced anew by Prometheus and others just before the proposed merger of satellite radio operators Sirius and XM Radio took place in mid-2008.

Finally, the conversion from analog to digital transmission could engender further public policy debates about whether digital radio should have new and different public interest obligations beyond the minimal obligations imposed currently on analog radio. Public interest advocates are likely to argue for such regulations, whereas the radio industry will surely argue that continued reliance on competition and the marketplace is the course of action most in the public interest.

See also: Blue Book; Communications Act of 1934; Controversial Issues, Broadcasting of; Deregulation of Radio; Editorializing; Fairness Doctrine; Federal Communications Commission; Federal Radio Commission; Hoaxes; Radio Laws; Telecommunications Act of 1996; United States Congress and Radio; United States Supreme Court and Radio

Further Reading

The FCC's broadcasting rules, in part reflecting its implementation of the public interest standard, are codified in Title 47 of the *Code of Federal Regulations, Telecommunication.*

Aufderheide, Patricia, *Communications Policy and the Public Interest: The Telecommunications Act of 1996*, New York: Guilford Press, 1999.

Benjamin, Louise M., *Freedom of the Air and the Public Interest: First Amendment Rights in Broadcasting to 1935*, Carbondale: Southern Illinois University Press, 2001.

Fowler, Marc, and Daniel Brenner, "A Marketplace Approach to Broadcast Regulation," *Texas Law Review* 60 (1982).

Huber, Peter William, *Law and Disorder in Cyberspace: Abolish the FCC and Let Common Law Rule the Telecosm*, Oxford and New York: Oxford University Press, 1997.

Krattenmaker, Thomas G., and Lucas A. Powe, Jr., *Regulating Broadcast Programming*, Cambridge, Massachusetts: MIT Press, and Washington, D.C.: American Enterprise Institute Press, 1994.

Rowland, Willard, "The Meaning of 'The Public Interest' in Communications Policy, Part I: Its Origins in State and Federal Regulation," *Communication Law and Policy* 2, no. 3 (1997).

Rowland, Willard, "The Meaning of 'The Public Interest' in Communications Policy, Part II: Its Implementation in Early Broadcast Law and Regulation," *Communication Law and Policy* 2, no. 4 (1997).

HERBERT A. TERRY,
2009 REVISIONS BY CARY O'DELL

PUBLIC RADIO INTERNATIONAL

Although many people view National Public Radio (NPR) as synonymous with public radio broadcasting in the United States, its rival network, Public Radio International (PRI), actually distributes more programs to public radio stations.

PRI originated as American Public Radio Associates (APR), which grew out of concerns by large-market stations that NPR's control over programming distribution led it to favor its own programs over those produced by member stations. Several of these stations, including Minnesota Public Radio, New York's WNYC, Cincinnati's WGUC, San Francisco's KQED, and KUSC in Los Angeles, founded APR in January 1982. Minnesota Public Radio president William Kling chaired the new organization. From the outset, APR followed an explicitly entrepreneurial model of organization that was frequently at odds with NPR's slow-moving membership model. Whereas NPR was governed by an elected board of station managers, APR operated under an independent board of directors. Whereas NPR developed and produced the majority of its programs, using staff and facilities subsidized by member stations, APR distributed already completed shows from stations and independent producers. Finally, NPR offered an entire program service for a single price to member stations, whereas APR provided individual programs to stations on an exclusive basis.

APR's initial program offering was *A Prairie Home Companion*, which Minnesota Public Radio had syndicated since 1980, after NPR president Frank Mankiewicz had rejected the program as "too parochial." *A Prairie Home Companion* skyrocketed in popularity, ranking second to NPR's *All Things Considered* as an audience (and station fundraising) draw. In 1983 APR incorporated itself as a fully independent organization. The following year, APR began to distribute *Monitorradio*, a news and public-affairs program produced by the *Christian Science Monitor*. In 1985 APR surpassed NPR as the largest supplier of cultural programs in public radio.

APR also benefited from changes in public radio funding in the mid-1980s. Beginning with fiscal year 1987, nearly all federal dollars went directly to stations. Public radio stations could then purchase programs from NPR or from other organizations and stations. By directing federal funds to stations instead of sending money to stations through NPR, local stations gained more control over programming and NPR was buffered from unstable federal funding.

Emboldened by the increase in direct funding, and claiming that NPR's distribution policies (which required member stations to purchase a full schedule rather than individual programs) posed a significant barrier to entry, APR threatened to bring an antitrust suit against NPR. In late 1987 NPR responded by "unbundling" its program service by offering groups of programs, rather than an entire schedule, to stations. However, APR offered producers higher fees, and popular programs such as *Fresh Air, Mountain Stage*, and *Whad'ya Know* began to jump from NPR to APR. NPR responded by further paring back its cultural programming in favor of news and public affairs.

Reflecting its global designs on public broadcasting, American Public Radio changed its name to Public Radio International (PRI) in July 1994. Two years later, PRI made its first venture into program production with *The World*, an ambitious news and public-affairs program designed to compete directly with *All Things Considered*. PRI also distributes the highly popular *Marketplace* financial program, a show that appeals to corporations as well as listeners: by the mid-1990s, *Marketplace* drew four percent of all corporate sponsorship money for public radio and brought in the highest sponsor income of any public radio program.

In 1997 PRI counted 591 affiliates; NPR had 635 member stations. The two networks had long been considered bitter rivals; therefore, many observers were stunned in late 1997 when NPR President Delano Lewis approached PRI president Steven Salyer to discuss the possibilities of merging the organizations, believing that a merger would attract more corporate sponsors to public radio, help position public radio against commercial competitors, and also allow public radio to act quickly on entrepreneurial ventures. The plan died quickly, however. Whereas NPR was controlled by stations, PRI was not interested in station representation. An NPR/PRI merger also would have limited the number of opportunities for program distribution and would have reduced diversity. Yet, given potential economies of scale and declining federal funding for public radio, such a union may someday prove irresistible. In the meantime, many public radio listeners remain understandably confused about the two services, and their relationship. At the time of writing, the two are totally separate program services for noncommercial radio stations, competing for corporate underwriting dollars.

PRI's leaders have stated that their service offers a competitive alternative to NPR, creating more diversity for the public radio system. Indeed, PRI has distributed many of public radio's outstanding programs throughout its history. Yet, much of PRI's success stems from the fact that (unlike NPR) it primarily distributes completed programs, therefore avoiding the costs incurred through production. PRI's attempts at producing programs, such as

The World, have proved to be highly problematic. Competition may lead to more pluralistic programming, yet competition has its pitfalls when applied to public goods and services. Critics have charged that PRI has focused on reaching upscale audiences from the outset, emphasizing classical music and business-oriented news and public affairs programming while relegating the less popular "conscience" items to NPR. More than any other organization, PRI has played an instrumental role in introducing marketplace economics into the public radio system. Although PRI's financial success is incontestable, its overall contribution to public radio remains subject to debate.

By the end of the 21st century's first decade, PRI was providing some 400 hours of programming a week to 800 public radio stations. Many were BBC productions or programs produced elsewhere, but others, including *The Takeaway, PRI's Sound & Spirit with Ellen Kushner, Studio 360* (produced in part by WNYC), and *The World* were produced by PRI itself. According to Arbitron, in 2008 PRI affiliate stations served over 30 million listeners weekly, and its programming was heard by 11 million listeners. Programs are available over the air, on satellite radio, online, and in podcast form.

See also: Fresh Air; *Marketplace*; Minnesota Public Radio; National Public Radio; Public Affairs Programming; Public Radio Since 1967

Further Reading

Engelman, Ralph, *Public Radio and Television in America: A Political History*, Thousand Oaks, California: Sage, 1996.
Ledbetter, James, *Made Possible By: The Death of Public Broadcasting in the United States*, London: Verso, 1997.
Looker, Thomas, *The Sound and the Story: NPR and the Art of Radio*, Boston: Houghton Mifflin, 1995.
McCourt, Tom, *Conflicting Communication Interests in America: The Case of National Public Radio*, Westport, Connecticut: Praeger, 1999.
Witherspoon, John, Roselle Kovitz, Robert K. Avery, and Alan G. Stavitsky, *A History of Public Broadcasting*, Washington, D.C.: Current, 2000.

TOM McCOURT,
2009 REVISIONS BY CHRISTOPHER H. STERLING

PUBLIC RADIO SINCE 1967

Although educational radio had existed for 50 years—longer than commercial radio—a study published in 1967 aptly described it as "the hidden medium." Commercial radio overwhelmed its noncommercial alternative on the AM band through the 1940s. Then, just when the reservation of 20 channels for noncommercial use on the new FM band gave educational radio a new start after World War II, the attention of educational broadcasters switched to television. Radio continued to languish.

The Beginning

A handful of professionally staffed educational stations served mostly rural areas of the country from state universities in 1967. New York City's WNYC and Boston's WGBH were urban exceptions and accounted for much of educational radio's very limited total national listenership. The Pacifica Foundation radio stations in Berkeley, Los Angeles, and New York attracted more notoriety and more listeners than did most educational stations. Voices of political and social dissent, these stations stood somewhat apart from mainstream educational radio stations. They would continue that independent course as leaders of the "community" radio movement separate from, and sometimes in conflict with, the "public" radio discussed in this article.

When educational broadcasters organized to seek federal funding in the mid-1960s, they sought support only for television. Radio, they believed, had no future. Funding educational radio would divert precious resources from television. The clandestine efforts of a small band of maverick educational radio managers, however, quietly slipped the words "and radio" into President Johnson's Public Television Act of 1967. Deputy Undersecretary of Health, Education, and Welfare Dean Costen added those crucial words as he drafted the legislation for the administration. Costen was an old friend and former employee of Ed Burrows, manager of the University of Michigan radio station, WUOM, and a friend of another former WUOM employee, Jerrold Sandler, the Washington lobbyist for educational radio. At the behest of Burrows, Michigan's Senator Robert Griffin sealed radio's victory by amending the name of the 1967 Public Television Act to "Public Broadcasting" and creating a Corporation for Public Broadcasting rather than a Corporation for Public Television. Thus began the modern history of educational—now called public—radio.

Required by law to create a national public radio system out of virtually nothing, the new Corporation for Public Broadcasting (CPB) appointed as director of radio activities Al Hulsen, the manager of the university station at Amherst, Massachusetts, whose soft-spoken style belied a ferocious determination. Hulsen pursued a two-pronged strategy. He offered financial aid to noncommercial stations that reached minimal professional standards: maintaining a staff of at least three full-time members, broadcasting six days per week for 48 weeks a year, and providing a program service of cultural and informational programming aimed at the general public rather than student training, instructional, or religious programming. The minimum requirements were to increase gradually to five full-time staff and 18 hours a day operations for 365 days a year. Though hardly rigorous, these standards excluded all but 72 of the 400 noncommercial radio stations operating in 1969.

The second part of Hulsen's strategy would create a national entity to produce, acquire, and distribute quality programming to those stations. For this part of the strategy, the weakness of the public radio stations proved advantageous. Whereas public television boasted a handful of relatively strong local stations with national programming ambitions that might be thwarted by a single strong national production center, no public radio station felt capable of producing a significant amount of national-quality programming. Moreover, its weakness and obscurity allowed public radio to avoid the scrutiny of the Nixon administration when it put an end to any dreams of a strong "fourth network" for public television. No one objected if the anemic public radio system created a single independent production and distribution entity that could give strong direction and a clear identity.

The argument for a national radio production center went beyond politics, however. Radio programming differed from television programming. Whether commercial or public, television built schedules of unrelated programs from a variety of producers. Contemporary radio stations, commercial or public, built their services around integrated *formats* rather than a series of programs, and such coherence would best be provided by a single production center. An initial planning board incorporated that production center in Washington, D.C. on 3 March 1970 as National Public Radio (NPR).

National Public Radio defined the national identity for public radio. Its initial board of directors, elected by and largely composed of station managers, in turn articulated that identity. Board member William Siemering of WBFO in Buffalo, New York, captured the spirit of the board deliberations and the anti-authoritarian political climate on college campuses in the late 1960s. His "National Public Radio Purposes" set out a series of expectations that significantly modified the formal, elitist quality of traditional educational radio and its model, Britain's British Broadcasting Corporation (BBC). To Siemering and his fellow board members, public radio should be an instrument of direct democracy. It would listen to the nation as much as it would talk to it. Yes, public radio would pursue the highest standards of journalism. Yes, public radio would tap the academic resources of the nation as never before. Yes, public radio would preserve and foster the cultural life of the nation. All of this might have been expected of traditional educational broadcasting. *Public* radio, however, would also reflect the diversity of the nation, giving voice to the unheard, establishing dialog among those who seldom speak with one another, and seeking wisdom in ordinary people as well as those with credentials. In Siemering's memorable phrase, public radio would "celebrate the human experience."

The chief celebrant would be Siemering himself. NPR's first president, Donald Quayle, hired Siemering as his program director and told him to bring into reality the ideals he had so eloquently enunciated. The implementation proved to be more difficult than the promises, all of which were expected to be realized in NPR's first program offering, *All Things Considered*, a 90-minute daily magazine that debuted at 5 P.M., Monday, 3 May 1971. As its title suggested, *All Things Considered was* intended to be something more than a "news" program. It would "contain some news," Siemering said, but *All Things Considered* would also reflect public radio's egalitarian values and a commitment to "quality" in a whole range of topics. Any subject might be considered, as long as it was approached in a considered manner. Quayle and the board intended *All Things Considered* to be public radio's *Sesame Street*, a defining program that would break into the public's consciousness and call attention to this newly defined medium of public radio. The program did indeed come to define public radio, but only slowly and incrementally over the course of the next decade. *All Things Considered* won its first Peabody Award in 1973 and its first Dupont Award in 1976.

All Things Considered contributed to the gradual growth in listenership for and awareness of public radio. The other strand of Hulsen's strategy, building and strengthening local stations, proved to be even more important. The incentive of federal money and the opportunity to bolster their image in their local communities by carrying *All Things Considered* caused universities and other local licensees throughout the country to upgrade their small stations to meet Hulsen's standards or, in many cases, to start new stations from scratch. Hulsen put particular emphasis and resources into upgrading several small college stations with

virtually no listenership in the Los Angeles basin into significant enterprises. He focused on turning the Chicago Board of Education's instructional station into a large, powerful public station covering all of "Chicagoland" from the top of the John Hancock Building. He invested significant federal funds in several production centers, most notably Minnesota Public Radio (MPR), which burgeoned from a student radio station at St. John's College to two statewide networks and the largest locally based operation in public radio.

Listenership doubled in the five years after public radio audiences were first measured in 1973, from roughly two million listeners a week to a little more than four million in 1978. The largest part of that growth came from new and upgraded stations added to the system, and a smaller part came from increased listening to the initial core stations. Federal, state, and local taxes, primarily through state universities, provided more than 80 percent of the funding for these stations. Listeners provided only about 10 percent.

Public radio grew from almost nothing to something real in the 1970s. Nonetheless, it remained in the shadow of public television and found itself responding to the often troubling developments in the visual medium. Although hostile to all media, the administration of Richard Nixon was particularly unhappy about a television system created by Lyndon Johnson's Great Society, supported by tax money, and presumed to be liberal and hostile to Nixon and his policies. The administration was able to express its displeasure through its control of federal appropriations for public media, which the president vetoed in 1972. To strengthen itself politically, public television folded its lobbying activities into its programming organization, the Public Broadcasting Service (PBS), and recruited a politically influential board and board chairman to provide effective leadership.

Public radio might have responded with a parallel structure at NPR. Quayle objected, however, that political activities should be kept separate from an organization like NPR that produced programming, particularly news programming. As a result, public radio established a separate organization in 1973 to handle its lobbying activities, the Association of Public Radio Stations (APRS), with its own board of directors that consisted, as did the NPR board, primarily of elected station managers. The heads of the two largest local public radio organizations, Minnesota Public Radio and Wisconsin Public Radio, assumed the leadership of APRS, and NPR found itself facing a strong rival. William Kling of Minnesota and Ronald Bornstein of

Wisconsin criticized the leadership of NPR. More fundamentally, they rejected the concept of a single national production center. They preferred the television model of program production by the larger stations in the system, the largest of which they happened to manage.

The rivalries within public radio weakened further its already weak position relative to public television, particularly when the two media fought one another over the division of CPB funds between radio and television. Television's victory in formulating CPB's 1975 budget forced the radio system to conclude that the division between NPR and APRS needed to end, and the two organizations merged. In reality, the merger in 1977 constituted a takeover of NPR by the APRS leadership, which vowed to give public radio the dynamism they felt it had heretofore lacked.

The Second Beginning

To provide that dynamism, the board of the "new" National Public Radio chose as president Frank Mankiewicz, son and nephew of Hollywood producers and writers Herman and Joseph. Mankiewicz was a lawyer and a reporter, and he had been press secretary to the late Senator Robert Kennedy and manager of George McGovern's 1972 campaign for president. A showman, a journalist, a politician, and a natural promoter, Mankiewicz had all the qualities that might put public radio on the map. He would provide public radio with a second beginning.

Public radio made important strides in four areas during the Mankiewicz years, 1977–83.

Politics. Mankiewicz resolved the continuing conflict with public television over the division of CPB money by convincing Congress to earmark 25 percent of CPB funding for radio, leaving 75 percent for television, a more favorable division for radio than it had ever had—or even hoped for—in the past.

Visibility. Mankiewicz was everywhere. Suddenly national media paid attention to the hidden medium, in part because of Mankiewicz's perseverance and in part because he gave them programs they could write about. NPR gained particular notoriety with its live broadcast of the Senate debate over the Panama Canal treaty and an exclusive call-in program from the White House with President Jimmy Carter. Public radio gained similar publicity for a radio adaptation of the movie hit *Star Wars*.

Programs. Less important in attracting attention, but ultimately far more important in attracting

listeners, NPR in 1981 added a two-hour *Morning Edition* complement to its showcase afternoon program, *All Things Considered*. Morning, of course, is radio prime time, and Mankiewicz made public radio competitive where it mattered most, lifting listenership not only in the morning but also throughout the day. The birth of *Morning Edition* brought with it a more basic change. With newsmagazines in the morning and the late afternoon, NPR became an around-the-clock news organization and moved firmly into coverage of breaking news. What had been perceived as an "alternative" medium focusing on the offbeat, the whimsical, the arts, ideas, and the lives and opinions of ordinary people in addition to carrying "some news," *All Things Considered* joined *Morning Edition* in focusing more heavily on the news of the day as reported by a greatly expanded system of reporters, most notably the female trio of Nina Totenberg, Linda Wertheimer, and Cokie Roberts. Mankiewicz redefined "alternative" as doing what they other guy does but doing it better. "In depth" replaced "alternative" as public radio's raison d'être.

Satellite Distribution. Congress agreed to fund satellite distribution systems for public radio and television in 1979. The radio satellite dramatically improved the technical quality of public radio's national programming. More importantly, it allowed multiple programs to be distributed at the same time and allowed live program origination from various places in the country other than Washington, D.C. Multiple origination points gave individual public radio stations the ability to send programming to the system without going through NPR in Washington. It made feasible a television model of multiple program producers, long advocated by Minnesota's Kling, the principle architect of the new satellite system.

Though Bornstein and Kling had been largely responsible for his elevation to the NPR presidency, Frank Mankiewicz could not bring himself to accept a diluted role for NPR as leader and sole programmer for public radio nationally. He would not agree to Kling's proposal that NPR fund, distribute, and promote a live weekly variety show that Minnesota Public Radio produced in St. Paul. Perhaps Kling never really expected—or even wanted—Mankiewicz to accept his proposal, for he used the rejection as a rationale to establish a second network in competition with NPR. American Public Radio (APR) would resemble PBS more than NPR. Like PBS, American Public Radio would not produce its own programs. Rather, it would schedule and promote national programs produced by individual stations, particularly those of Minnesota and four other founding stations that Kling brought into his enterprise: WNYC, New York; WGBH, Boston; KUSC, Los Angeles; and WGUC, Cincinnati. Bill Kling served as president of both American Public Radio and Minnesota Public Radio. Headquarters of the new network started in the MPR building before moving to an office building a few blocks away in downtown St. Paul. Ultimately, American Public Radio signaled its independence from its parent by moving out of St. Paul—all the way to Minneapolis. In 1995 APR changed its name to Public Radio International.

APR burst on the public radio scene in 1980 with the St. Paul—based variety show *A Prairie Home Companion*. Veteran MPR announcer and freelance writer Garrison Keillor hosted the show in an intimate style that conveyed listeners to the mythical town of Lake Wobegon, Minnesota, "where all the women are strong, all the men are good looking, and all the children above average." In addition to the News from Lake Wobegon, *A Prairie Home Companion* included a wide range of musical styles, skits, and commercial parodies. When it declined to fund and distribute the program, NPR had claimed that *A Prairie Home Companion* was too regional, but listeners across the country proved otherwise as they turned on their radios Saturday evenings to enjoy the latest from Lake Wobegon.

Beginning national distribution less than a year after the launch of *Morning Edition* by NPR, *A Prairie Home Companion* joined it and *All Things Considered* as the three programs that defined public radio and drew listeners to it. Garrison Keillor became public radio's most recognized personality, his face reaching the cover of *Time* magazine in 1985. *Morning Edition* and *A Prairie Home Companion*, plus continued growth in the number of public radio stations, caused public radio's audience to double again, to over eight million by 1983.

The best of times turned into the worst of times in 1983. The 25 percent budget cuts imposed on public broadcasting by Ronald Reagan launched the crisis, but Frank Mankiewicz's reaction to the cuts almost turned it fatal. In every crisis lies an opportunity, and Bill Kling saw the impending budget cuts at public radio stations as a chance for APR to sell those stations large quantities of low-cost, high-quality programming that would allow stations to reduce staffs and costs. Not willing to let Kling steal this market, Mankiewicz responded with an even better package at an even lower cost—so low, in fact, that it could not support itself. Kling wisely ended his project. Mankiewicz went full speed ahead with his, as part of a burgeoning concept of

entrepreneurial activities that would allow NPR to "get off the federal fix by '86." Whatever federal money Reagan continued to provide should go to support the stations, Mankiewicz said. NPR would support itself by selling programs to stations and selling a wide variety of services to business partners.

Whatever the merits of these projects in the long run, they required substantial cash investments in the short run, and the need for those investments came in the same year that NPR's federal support, which made up most of its budget, dropped by 25 percent. In March 1982 NPR staff realized they would run a $3 million deficit in that fiscal year. Despite drastic cuts imposed by the NPR board, the deficit projection doubled to $6 million a month later, and to $9 million by June: NPR was insolvent. Mankiewicz, other senior officials, and about a quarter of NPR's 500 employees lost their jobs, and the same Ron Bornstein from Wisconsin who had been instrumental in placing Mankiewicz in the NPR presidency took over as interim president. Bornstein arranged a series of loans from the Corporation for Public Broadcasting. NPR's member stations guaranteed repayment of the loans, and NPR continued to operate.

The Third Beginning

The public radio system that emerged from the NPR crisis looked quite different from the system that went into it. Though NPR was still the most important single organization, individual stations asserted their independence and leadership. The stations, after all, had deposed Mankiewicz and guaranteed the loans that saved NPR. Their responsibility for NPR became permanent in 1985, when they and CPB agreed that federal money that had formerly gone directly to NPR would now go to the stations, who would purchase programs from NPR, APR, or other sources. The larger stations in the system banded together as the Station Resources Group (SRG), expressly designed to exert leadership within the system in place of NPR. The SRG contended that the public radio system brought into existence by federal money through the Corporation for Public Broadcasting should no longer look to government as its primary source of funding. Public radio's future rested not with government support, but with the ability of public radio to raise private funds from corporations, foundations, and, above all, directly from listeners. Reagan's 25 percent cut in federal support, and the antigovernment, free-market philosophy it represented, suggested to these stations that government funding was less certain than private money. Moreover, some of them, most particularly Bill Kling of Minnesota, concluded that private funding was preferable to government funding and set out aggressively to seek "underwriting," the euphemism for soft advertising, listener memberships, and major gifts. Again led by Kling, the station managers of the SRG decided that the academic institutions and state and local governments that held the licenses to most public radio stations hampered the new entrepreneurial spirit. Some actually separated from their institutional licensees to become free-standing, not-for-profit corporations; others found ways to operate more independently within their institutional structures.

The results of these efforts were dramatic. By 1998, public radio was a half-billion-dollar-a-year industry, with the private sector providing more than half of its income. Listeners provided 30 percent of public radio's revenue; business 17 percent; and foundations 10 percent. Only 13 percent came from the federal government, and state and local governments generated 30 percent, primarily through the budgets of state universities. By 1998, public radio was reaching more than 20 million listeners each week, ten times its 1973 listenership.

The ability of public radio to raise money through memberships and underwriting depended directly on its ability to attract, hold, and satisfy listeners. Even those most committed to the more traditional mission of public radio recognized that they fulfilled their mission best when their programs reached the most people. Hence, public radio's priorities after 1983 emphasized audience growth through research. The strategy developed by a national Audience Building Task Force in 1986 set the tone for much of the subsequent development of public radio. Recognizing that most public radio listeners listened to commercial radio more than they listened to public radio, the task force determined that the most direct way to increase public radio listening was to get current listeners to spend more time with public radio and to attract more people like the current listeners. Rather than increasing the diversity of programs in order to appeal to more people, the most successful public radio stations focused on programs that appealed most to existing listeners.

Stations set out to eliminate those program elements that they believed caused listeners to tune away to other stations. Out went some of the more esoteric and self-indulgent offerings. A similar fate awaited programs too blatantly academic in tone. The hour or two a week of programs aimed at targeted groups turned off those who were not members of those groups; these programs disappeared

from most stations. Music in general assumed a reduced role, replaced by news and information, the primary appeal of public radio. The music that remained tended to be confined to classical and jazz, and particularly to the more mainstream selections within those genres. Any hopes for a revival of radio drama evaporated in the quest for consistent appeal.

To replace programming that no longer fit, NPR added programs with qualities that echoed the appeal of *Morning Edition* and *All Things Considered* —programs such as *Weekend Edition*, *Fresh Air*, and *Talk of the Nation*. Public Radio International offered *Marketplace*, a daily news program focused on economics that was created by two former producers of *All Things Considered* and that appealed to NPR news listeners. Nonetheless, the biggest public radio "hit" of the 1990s turned out to be a quirky program that followed no known formula. *Car Talk*, a less-than-serious advice program, became the most listened to hour on public radio. It was like no other public radio program, yet it appealed to most of the same people who liked *Morning Edition, All Things Considered*, and *A Prairie Home Companion*. It gave them yet another reason to spend more time with public radio.

Research in the late 1980s demonstrated the wisdom of such a strategy as public radio sought to raise money from listeners. The research found that the propensity to make donations related directly to the loyalty of listeners to the station. Those who spent the most time with public radio were the most likely to give. Those who tuned in only occasionally were less likely to give. Survival and growth, then, depended on each public radio station's becoming extremely important in the lives of some people rather than marginally important to many people. Whereas Siemering's philosophy urged public radio to bring together people of all backgrounds, races, regions, ages, and educational levels, the new imperative suggested focusing on a particular subset of the potential audience.

A subsequent study called *Audience 88* identified the people most attracted to public radio programming. It identified educational attainment as the primary predictor of an interest in public radio programming—not surprising, perhaps, for a medium that began in universities as "educational" radio. The more years of education an individual had, the more likely he or she would be to listen to public radio. A substantial part of the audience had earned advanced graduate and professional degrees. As education correlates directly with income, well-educated public radio listeners tended to be very comfortable financially, but education level, not wealth or social class, predicted loyalty to public radio. Indeed, the most likely of all to love public radio was the individual with a lot of education and a more modest income, the teacher rather than the doctor, the social worker rather than the investment banker. The ultimate public radio listener turned out to be the Ph.D. who drives a cab. In the values and lifestyle terminology of the time, public radio listeners came largely from the psychographic group called "Inner Directed and Societally Conscious."

Public radio had by the end of the 1980s identified its audience and committed itself to serving that audience well, much as commercial media identify target audiences and attempt to give them what they want. Unlike commercial radio, however, public radio formulated its mission and values initially without consideration of an intended audience. It produced programs that reflected the democratic purposes enunciated by Bill Siemering in 1970. It produced programs that sought to be thoughtful, fair, open-minded, and in-depth; programs of substance, not hype; programs that represented the best traditions of the universities that gave birth to public radio, but in an accessible, nonacademic style. It produced programs driven not by commercial values but by the desire to "celebrate the human experience."

New Century Challenges

In the new century, public radio sought to both open its programming and expand its audiences and support. The Public Radio Exchange (PRX), for example, began in mid-2003 as a means of encouraging and enabling independent producers to place their material on public radio stations. After getting started with foundation seed money, its operations were funded by stations paying a subscription fee for a certain number of program hours annually. It encouraged stations to carry programs by cutting through royalty and rights issues. It even encouraged individual listeners to sample programs to encourage stations to carry them.

Public radio's national average audience peaked around 2003 after years of steady growth. By 2005, however, data made apparent that those audiences had not continued to grow, and had, indeed, begun to decline. Where public radio had expanded while commercial stations suffered, it now appeared that the noncommercial outlets had joined the overall radio trend downward. That decline suggested serious ramifications in fund-raising and other measures of public radio viability.

A variety of theories were put forth to explain the stagnation. One was that audiences might be suffering a kind of news fatigue from constant coverage of political and international affairs, and especially the war in Iraq. Although many in public radio argued that local programming was the best way to resist competition, audience data did not support that view. Certainly one issue was music. Classical and jazz (and some folk music) have long been public radio's most popular formats—but their share of all public station listening has declined since 2001. Even eclectic music formats stayed flat.

Competition—from satellite radio (which began in 2001), web-based options, and the growing use of iPods and other MP3 players—have clearly been a factor in these public radio audience declines.

The Corporation for Public Broadcasting initiated a wide-ranging project to "grow" public radio's audiences, but the general economic downturn in 2008–9 added to the medium's concerns.

Listeners who heard this programming, and liked it, self-selected. They chose to listen to programs that resonated with them. This self-selection happened before public radio professionals learned—or cared—who these people were. When public radio decided its life depended on keeping, pleasing, and deepening the loyalty of those listeners, the most effective strategy was clear: public radio needed to commit itself ever more firmly to the original values that attracted those listeners in the first place. Public radio gives its target listeners what they want when it presents programs that reflect the initial academic values of universities, a commitment to depth and quality, and Bill Siemering's faith in the intelligence and openness of ordinary people.

See also: All Things Considered; Car Talk; Community Radio; Corporation for Public Broadcasting; *Earplay*; Educational Radio to 1967; *Fresh Air*; Minnesota Public Radio; *Morning Edition*; National Public Radio; Pacifica Foundation; *Prairie Home Companion*; Public Affairs Programming; Public Broadcasting Act of 1967; Public Radio International; *Soundprint*; *Star Wars*; *This American Life*; WHA and Wisconsin Public Radio

Further Reading

Audience Research Analysis, *AUDIENCE 2010: Reinvigorating Public Radio's Public Service and Public Support.* 2006, www.aranet.com/

Avery, Robert K., "The Public Broadcasting Act of 1967: Looking Ahead by Looking Back," *Critical Studies in Media Communication* 24, no. 4 (October 2007), pp. 358–364.

Collins, Mary, *National Public Radio: The Cast of Characters*, Arlington, Virginia: Seven Locks Press, 1993.

Corporation for Public Broadcasting. *Grow the Audience for Public Radio Project* , www.srg.org/gta.html

Engelman, Ralph, *Public Radio and Television in America: A Political History*, Thousand Oaks, California: Sage, 1996.

Fedo, Michael, *The Man from Lake Wobegon*, New York: St. Martin's Press, 1987.

Harden, Blaine, "Religious and Public Stations Battle for Share of Radio Dial," *New York Times* (15 September 2002).

Herman W. Land Associates, *The Hidden Medium: A Status Report on Educational Radio in the United States*, Washington, D.C.: The National Association of Educational Broadcasters, 1967.

Ledbetter, James, *Made Possible By: The Death of Public Broadcasting in the United States*, London: Verso, 1997.

Looker, Thomas, *The Sound and the Story: NPR and the Art of Radio*, Boston: Houghton Mifflin, 1995.

McDougal, Dennis, "The Public Radio Wars," four part series, *The Los Angeles Times* (8, 9, 10, 11 October 1985).

Porter, Bruce, "Has Success Spoiled NPR?" *Columbia Journalism Review* 29, no. 3 (September–October 1990).

Public Radio Exchange website, www.prx.org/about-us/what-is-prx

Salyer, Stephen, "Monopoly to Marketplace-Competition Comes to Public Radio," *Media Studies Journal* 7, no. 3 (1993).

Savitsky, A.G., "Guys in Suits and Charts, Audience Research in U.S. Public Radio," *Journal of Broadcasting and Electronic Media* 39, no. 2 (1995).

Stamberg, Susan, *Every Night at Five: Susan Stamberg's All Things Considered Book*, New York: Pantheon, 1982.

Wertheimer, Linda, *Listening to America: Twenty-five Years in the Life of a Nation, As Heard on National Public Radio*, Boston: Houghton Mifflin, 1995.

Witherspoon, John, Roselle Kovitz, Robert K. Avery, and Alan G. Stavitsky, *A History of Public Broadcasting*, Washington, D.C.: Current, 2000.

Zuckerman, Lawrence, "Has Success Spoiled NPR?" *Mother Jones* 12, no. 5 (June–July 1987).

JACK MITCHELL,
2009 REVISIONS BY CHRISTOPHER H. STERLING

PULSE, INC.

Audience Research Firm

The Pulse, Inc., provided audience research reports for up to 250 markets from 1941 to 1976. Throughout its history, the company was associated with its founder, Dr. Sydney Roslow.

Origins

In 1940 and 1941 Roslow worked as a psychologist for the Psychological Corporation, a company composed of academic psychologists. In 1939 the corporation had experimented with a roster personal interview technique in an audience study commissioned by station WBEM (Buffalo, New York).

Encouraged by noted social scientist Paul Lazarsfeld, Roslow published the first official *New York Pulse* for October/November 1941. Stations WABC, WEAF, WNEW, and WOR, as well as advertising agency N.W. Ayer, were subscribers to the report, which summarized interviews with 300 respondents per day (2,100 per week). Equal numbers of respondents were assigned to each of the three dayparts included in the report.

World War II slowed the young company. As Roslow went into government service during the war (in the Department of Agriculture in Washington, D.C.), his wife carried on the business. Two large studies were conducted for WCAU (Philadelphia) in 1944 and 1945. Shortly after the war, Pulse added surveys in Boston, Chicago, Cincinnati, Ohio, and Richmond, Virginia. Eventually Pulse became the dominant local radio audience research supplier. By early 1963 Roslow reported that Pulse was publishing reports on 250 markets. Its clients included 150 advertising agencies and 650 radio stations.

At the peak of its popularity, Pulse referred to its research method as "personal house-to-house interviews":

> The emphasis in this survey is that the interview is made at the home. The roster as used in PULSE surveys is a schedule of radio stations and programs by day-part periods. After the introduction the interviewer is instructed to elicit from the respondents an estimate of when they listened to the radio as the first step. To obtain this information, the interviewer tries to proceed hour by hour through the day, beginning with the time the respondent gets up. Then, the respondents are invited to look at the roster and report their listening.

Pulse respondents reported listening at home and away from home, a unique feature of its audience reports during the company's heyday. Listening preferences, demographics, and other measures were also collected.

The sampling procedure for the Pulse surveys was a sample of "sampling points" (geographical locations distributed at random through the survey areas of the market being studied). This process may be clearer by reviewing the particulars from the October–December 1973 Pulse survey of Atlanta, Georgia. According to the report, Metromail (a market research firm under contract to Pulse) selected at random the addresses of telephone households from the counties surveyed. Each of these addresses became the center of an interviewing "cluster" of approximately 15 interviews. In all, the data for Atlanta came from 146 sampling points, with 2,791 persons interviewed (19 persons per sampling point). As the survey period was 7 October through 28 December 1973 (82 days), it can be seen that the survey could have involved as few as two interviewers, each interviewing persons at one sampling point per day.

The counties surveyed were divided into two parts: the central zone, representing the counties where market radio stations delivered stronger signals; and a larger area, the radio station area, where Atlanta stations were not as dominant and listeners lived farther from the business areas of Atlanta.

In most other respects, the Pulse reports present data similar to that in contemporary radio market reports: listening estimates, cumulative estimates, daypart estimates, in-home and out-of-home estimates, etc. Special sampling provisions were instituted for Hispanic and African-American listeners.

Decline

During the 1970s Pulse was gradually supplanted by Arbitron (formerly the American Research Bureau [ARB]) as the dominant radio audience research company. According to Beville (1988), Roslow attributed this trend to several factors. One was the acceptance by advertising agencies of the diary technique for the measurement of television audiences. It was only a small step further to consider personal diary technique (the Arbitron method) acceptable for measuring radio audiences.

A second factor in Roslow's view was that radio advertising was not profitable enough for agencies to buy more than one audience measurement service; that is, they could not afford to buy reports from both Arbitron and Pulse. A third factor was the technology of the Arbitron parent company at the time, Control Data Corporation (CDC). CDC's large computers could produce more elaborate reports in shorter periods of time and sooner after completion of data collection than the computers available to Pulse.

Another factor in Pulse's loss of business may have been the broadcast industry's All-Radio Methodology Study (ARMS) of 1965. This survey compared the various techniques for collecting radio listening data. ARMS gave the Pulse technique good marks but also provided validation of the personal diary method used by ARB (later Arbitron). In addition, the ARB methods included larger survey areas, making it possible for stations to justify advertising sales on the strength of larger areas included within the surveys of their markets.

During this downward trend in Pulse's business, a number of management changes were also taking place. In 1975, Roslow (who had remained the company's sole owner) retired and moved to Florida after appointing his son Richard president. The following year, two other long-time key officers of the company departed: Laurence Roslow, Sydney's nephew, who had directed all research operations; and sales manager George Sternberg (Sydney's brother-in-law). Left to manage the company, Richard Roslow and his younger brother Peter failed to reverse its fortunes, and in April 1978, Pulse, Inc., closed its doors.

There will always be a lingering nostalgia for Pulse reports among radio managers who remember them, as no other radio audience research methods interviewed listeners face to face. Radio and sales managers had come to feel that this feature alone justified their confidence in the service, as they valued face to face contacts very highly. In addition, the disappearance of Pulse meant that future ratings services for radio had much higher overhead expenses, involving not only huge computers but centralized calling centers and large numbers of workers to collect the necessary data. Prices for rating services inevitably edged upward as well.

See also: Arbitron; Audience Research Methods

Further Reading

Beville, Hugh Malcolm, Jr., *Audience Ratings: Radio, Television, and Cable*, Hillsdale, New Jersey: Erlbaum, 1985; revised edition, 1988.

Fletcher, James E., "Commercial Sources of Audience Information—The Rating Report," in *Handbook of Radio and TV Broadcasting: Research Procedures in Audience, Program, and Revenues*, edited by James E. Fletcher, New York: Van Nostrand Reinhold, 1981.

Hartshorn, Gerald Gregory, editor, *Audience Research Sourcebook*, Washington, D.C.: National Association of Broadcasters, 1991.

The Pulse, *Radio Pulse Atlanta, Georgia, October–November, 1973*, New York: The Pulse, 1973.

Webster, James G., and Lawrence W. Lichty, *Ratings Analysis: Theory and Practice*, Hillsdale, New Jersey: Erlbaum, 1991; 2nd edition, as *Ratings Analysis: The Theory and Practice of Audience Research*, by Webster, Lichty, and Patricia F. Phalen, Mahwah, New Jersey: Erlbaum, 2000.

JAMES E. FLETCHER

Q

QUIZ AND AUDIENCE PARTICIPATION PROGRAMS

Few genres used radio's strengths of live broad-casting, spontaneity, and listener involvement more effectively than audience participation programs and their most successful incarnation, the quiz show. Few genres created as much of a sensation as quiz shows at the height of their popularity, or as much of a backlash when condemned by the insti-tutions of broadcasting. And few genres demon-strated the radical transformation of radio in the television era by so quickly abandoning the very medium that gave birth to the quiz show itself. Although quiz shows are best remembered at the center of the infamous TV quiz show scandals of the late 1950s, the genre had a rich history in the early days of radio.

The quiz show is one of the only genres that could truly be called "native" to broadcasting, not stemming from the common sources of vaudeville, theater, film, or literature. Certainly the program format drew upon a number of important ante-cedents, including newspaper puzzles, parlor games, spelling bees, gambling, carnival contests, and movie-house games such as "Screeno." Despite these varied sources, the specific incarnation of the quiz show on radio was unique, combining the informational content of an educational program, the competitive thrill of sports spectatorship, the humorous patter of comedy and variety shows, and the musical performance featured on much radio programming. The quiz show was the most suc-cessful type of audience participation program,

which was a general term for any program that incorporated the audience—whether in the studio or at home—into the program's proceedings. Other forms of audience participation programs included "stunt" programs, amateur hours, and "sob shows."

Origins

The radio quiz show had its roots in the earliest days of the medium's commercialization in the mid-1920s, albeit in a form quite different from the way the genre would thrive in the 1940s. Question-and-answer quizzes were a common feature of local radio broadcasts on shows such as WJZ-New York's *The Pop Question Game.* On this program and on other segments on local stations, announ-cers would ask questions and provide the correct answers after a pause; there were no contestants or prizes, and the audience was expected to try to guess the correct answer at home. These early question-and-answer shows were not terribly popu-lar and were mostly used to fill time and provide an educational diversion within a fairly barren radio schedule. As radio programming became more sophisticated, these early local quizzes were relegated to the sidelines of the radio schedule.

The first major breakthrough of the audience participation genre occurred in the mid-1930s. As national networks came to dominate the airwaves with their high-priced stars, local unaffiliated sta-tions such as New York's WHN needed to devise innovative formats to compete. In 1934 WHN hired theatrical manager Major Edward Bowes to create an inexpensive program to boost their ratings;

Bowes drew upon a vaudeville tradition in airing an amateur talent contest. The program was a huge hit—within a year, the National Broadcasting Company (NBC) had purchased the show, and Major Bowes' *The Original Amateur Hour* was voted the most popular show of 1935. The formula was simple—parade a succession of unpolished performers in front of the microphone and reward talented individuals with prizes. An additional gimmick caught on, allowing audiences at home to vote for their favorite amateur via telephone, making the show a truly participatory endeavor. As with most successful radio innovations, a number of imitations followed, leading to an all-out amateur craze in the mid-1930s. Although the *Amateur Hour* itself faded in popularity by the end of the decade, its effects lasted far longer through its popularization of the audience participation format.

Although amateur hours showcased ordinary people as the "talent" featured on the radio, they presented traditional forms of entertainment, such as music, comedy, and dancing. It took another program to shift the focus of audience participation to everyday people doing everyday activities. *Vox Pop* emerged on NBC in 1935 with an unusual format—the hosts asked ordinary people questions, broadcasting the resulting dialog as representative of everyday life. Additionally, the program pioneered the practice of giving prizes to its participants, offering both cash and merchandise from sponsors to interesting guests. Other programs followed in *Vox Pop's* footsteps, most notably *We, the People* (1936), as the audience participation format developed into a successful alternative to comedies, musical programs, and dramas.

The quiz show itself developed out of these precedents, taking the contest form from amateur hours and the everyday guests from *Vox Pop*. In 1936 the show hailed as the first radio quiz debuted on Washington, D.C., station WJSV; *Professor Quiz* offered ten silver dollars to the contestant who answered the most questions during each program and invited listeners to send in questions for additional cash prizes if their questions were used on the air. The program was pickcd up by the Columbia Broadcasting System (CBS) in 1937 to great success, leading to numerous clones, including *Uncle Jim's Question Bee*, *Dr. IQ*, *True or False*, and *Ask-It-Basket*. By the late 1930s, quiz shows were established as a popular genre for prime-time radio, with many programs among the top network offerings. The genre established its formula quickly—prizes were modest, questions were intellectual but not too difficult for average listeners, and audience members were invited to participate by sending in their own questions for additional prizes.

Golden Age

Though certainly a fad, quiz shows were able to survive far longer than other radio fads, such as the amateur hour. One reason for the genre's continued success was the creativity of quiz producers in devising variations on the basic formula. One of the first and most successful innovations was NBC's *Information Please*. Producer Dan Golenpaul thought that most quiz show listeners might want to turn the tables on the "know-it-alls" who ran quiz shows and try to "stump the experts." His program, debuting in 1938, offered the chance to do just that— *Information Please* featured a panel of experts on a number of topics, including columnist Franklin Pierce Adams, sportswriter John Kiernan, pianist Oscar Levant, and one rotating guest panelist, all presided over by erudite host Clifton Fadiman. Listeners were invited to submit questions designed to stump the panel, and listeners were rewarded with $10 and an encyclopedia set if they offered a question that could not be answered correctly. The program incorporated a great deal of wit and sophisticated patter among the panel, gave audience members a chance to show up the alleged experts, and created the celebrity panel format that has since become a staple of game shows. The program was hailed not only as fine entertainment but as legitimate education as well, receiving awards from literary magazines and becoming a favorite on college campuses. *Information Please* demonstrated that the quiz show was not dependent on featuring everyday people but could also captivate audiences with celebrities participating in the quizzes.

Whereas *Information Please* succeeded on its intellect and wits, another innovation pushed the genre in the opposite direction. Since the emergence of broadcasting, music has been at the center of radio programming. Quiz shows were quick to incorporate this radio staple to appeal to listeners less interested in intellectual and informational questions. Struggling bandleader Kay Kyser teamed with up-and-coming quiz producer Louis Cowan to devise the *College of Musical Knowledge*, a quiz focused on musical questions interspersed with numbers played by Kyser's band. The program was a hit for Chicago's WGN in 1936 and transferred to NBC in 1938, where it would run for ten years. Similar programs followed *College*'s mixing of quizzes and music in the late 1930s and early 1940s, including *Melody Puzzles*, *Beat the Band*, and *So You Think You Know Music*. But a more controversial example of the musical audience participation program debuted in 1939—NBC's *Pot o' Gold*.

It was not until *Pot o' Gold* that a radio program took full advantage of the widespread availability of the telephone to allow listeners to participate more fully in broadcasting. The program was not a quiz show by most definitions—most of each show consisted of typical band numbers from Horace Heidt and His Musical Knights. But *Pot o' Gold* had a gimmick that made it a national sensation for two years—during each episode, the hosts would spin a large wheel to randomly select a phone number from a collection of telephone books spanning the country. Heidt would then call the number and award $1,000—then a vast sum for most families still suffering the effects of the Great Depression—to whomever answered the phone. The gimmick was a huge success, creating a new type of audience participation program termed the *giveaway*. For two years, the show was enormously popular, leading to reported drops in movie attendance and phone calling during its Tuesday night time slot, as all of America awaited Heidt's lucrative call. The show even spawned a 1941 movie musical (also entitled *Pot o' Gold*), starring Heidt and Jimmy Stewart, that fictionalized the show's origins. Despite the program's success, it was off the air after two years, because it generated as much controversy as popularity.

Some of the controversy surrounding *Pot o' Gold* stemmed from accusations that the mechanism for choosing telephone numbers was biased, not representing some locations and discriminating against people who had moved since phone books had been issued. Other people objected to the telephone system's inability to guarantee that calls would be put through effectively, worrying that they would miss out on the jackpot. And in the 1940s, not everyone owned a telephone. But the biggest controversy involved the Federal Communications Commission's (FCC) accusation that the program was a lottery and thus violated a provision of the Communication Act of 1934. Although the FCC could not censor programming, it was empowered to prevent stations from broadcasting illegal material, including programs that were deemed to violate federal lottery laws. In 1940 the FCC decided that *Pot o' Gold*, along with a number of local programs, violated the lottery section of the Communication Act and recommended that the responsible broadcasters be prosecuted by the Department of Justice. NBC and other broadcasters denied that giveaway programs were lotteries, because no listener needed to provide any money or other

"consideration" (except owning a telephone) to be eligible to win. The Department of Justice refused to prosecute, and the FCC dropped its case, yet broadcasters took the action as a warning; rather than risk being denied license renewal by the FCC, broadcasters canceled or retooled most giveaway programs to make sure they did not violate lottery laws. The link between quiz shows, the FCC, and lottery laws did not disappear, however, and the issue would become even more controversial in the late 1940s.

Although *Pot o' Gold* and other giveaways created a brief sensation, other innovations in the quiz show format proved to have more long-lasting success. Just as *College of Musical Knowledge* thrived by mixing quiz shows with music programs, another genre mixture provided a number of hits: blending children's programming with quiz shows. Cowan, again the crucial innovator, decided to combine the format of *Information Please's* panel of experts with the widespread appeal of precocious children. The resulting hybrid was *Quiz Kids*, which debuted on NBC in 1940 and lasted for 13 seasons. The program featured a panel of erudite children who amazed audiences both with the extent of their knowledge and their more typically childlike personalities. The program was a hit among both adult and child audiences, and many teachers praised the show's ability to make learning and education seem fun and entertaining. Again the quiz show was held up as both entertaining and educational, although that balance would start to shift throughout the 1940s.

Funny Stunts

As the quiz show entered the 1940s, most of the programs were viewed as respectable, entertaining, and even educational. But one innovation would drastically change the tone of the audience participation format, pushing the genre away from the intellectual pursuits of *Information Please* and toward more outlandish and comic pleasures. Ralph Edwards, a radio announcer, decided to capitalize on the audience participation boom. He felt that many potential audience members would enjoy the participatory aspect of quiz shows but were put off by the intellectual nature of shows such as *Information Please* and *Professor Quiz*; thus he set out to devise a quiz show that focused more on humor and participation than on knowledge and education. His inspiration came from a parlor game he remembered playing as a youth— one person would ask another a question, and if the answer were wrong, the person who answered incorrectly would have to pay for his or her mistake by being forced to do some humiliating "consequence." Edwards named his show after the game, and in 1940 *Truth or Consequences* debuted on CBS. The prizes were small—$15 for a correct answer, $5 for performing a consequence—but audiences were enthralled by the show for other reasons. The consequences became the centerpiece of the program, leading contestants purposely to answer questions wrong to perform comic stunts.

Initially the consequences were quick and modest—one contestant had to spell words while sucking on a lollipop, another had to be a one-man band with pots and pans, and a construction worker had to imitate a bawling baby. As the show grew in popularity, sponsor Ivory Soap upped the production budget to devise more elaborate stunts. The show added remote broadcasts, putting contestants out on the streets to interview strangers or to lie in bed with a seal on a New York street corner. The program also upped the ante for cash prizes, often offering large rewards for completing a stunt—one contestant was promised $1,000 if he could fall asleep during the course of the program. In one of the more notorious stunts, Edwards told a contestant that a cash prize was buried on a street corner in Holyoke, Massachusetts; the man immediately boarded a train to dig up his loot, but he was beaten to the punch by hundreds of local residents who intercepted his $1,000 bounty. Another famed stunt resulted after Edwards told audience members to send a contestant pennies to buy war bonds in 1943; the woman received over 300,000 coins as a result, requiring Edwards to provide helpers to open her mail. As a result of such excessive and outrageous participatory stunts, *Truth or Consequences* became a radio sensation in the 1940s, leading the way for other "stunt" shows to reach the air (and for a town in New Mexico to rename itself after the show).

The most notable clone was NBC's *People Are Funny*, starring Art Linkletter. The show took the basic format of *Truth or Consequences*, adding different stunts and Linkletter's comic personality to generate a large fanbase beginning in 1942. One of Linkletter's stunts pitted two contestants against each other to see who could hitchhike across the country faster; the winner was given a new car. Another stunt gave a family their own airplane just for answering the question, "What is your name?" The success of these shows proved the importance of humor to the audience participation format—producers saw that quiz shows did not need to rely on the question-and-answer format to entertain an audience and draw high ratings. *Can You Top This?*

was one successful comic quiz (1940–54)—listeners sent in jokes, which were read on the air; then, a panel of comedians tried to "top" each joke with another on the same topic, and the studio audience judged the results. Another program was *It Pays to Be Ignorant* (1942–51), an outright satire of *Information Please* in which panelists humorously failed to answer questions such as "What animal do you get goat's milk from?" The program was fully scripted with no audience participation, but the parody mined the same terrain as quiz shows. By far the most successful comedy quiz was 1947's *You Bet Your Life*, starring the well-known comedian Groucho Marx; the format was that of a typical quiz show, made distinctive only by Marx's comic ad-libs and friendly harassment of contestants. Soon the show became more focused on Groucho's quips, with the quiz providing only a basic structure for the comedy.

Besides leading to comedy quizzes, the stunt programs popularized another variation on the audience participation format—the ongoing telephone contest. Although *Pot o' Gold* had made the random telephone giveaway an important feature of audience participation programs, it took the well-established success of *Truth or Consequences* to bring the giveaway back after the FCC's concerns in the early 1940s. Edwards started a contest called "Mr. Hush" in 1946—each week a mystery voice read a riddle and a series of clues. Edwards would then call a random phone number, asking whomever answered to identify the mysterious Mr. Hush; after weeks of failed attempts by other listeners, eventually the listener who gave the correct answer of Jack Dempsey won an enormous jackpot of sponsor-provided merchandise. Subsequent contests, such as "Walking Man" and "Mrs. Hush," were expanded to allow listeners to submit their phone numbers along with contributions for health-related charities; Edward's contests raised millions of dollars for organizations such as the March of Dimes and the American Heart Association. These telephone contests became a national sensation, with winners making headlines and boosting ratings to record levels and inspiring another Jimmy Stewart film, *The Jackpot* (1950). Edwards' contests reinvigorated the giveaway format, which would reappear to greater controversy in the late 1940s.

Quiz shows saw little innovation beyond the stunt programs during the war years. Shows like *Information Please*, *Quiz Kids*, and *Dr. IQ* all continued their success, with few new programs competing against their formula. The new shows that did emerge followed the basic formulas set up by the genre's forerunners, with a few added twists.

Two long-lasting programs added a gambling element to the quiz format— both *Take It or Leave It* (1940–52) and *Double or Nothing* (1940–54) allowed contestants either to take their winnings or to risk them on another question for double the amount. The prizes were modest—*Take It or Leave It's* grand prize was $64, leading to a new catchphrase, "the $64 question." This basic format would be revisited on television in the late 1950s by the higher-priced quiz show *The $64,000 Question* and in 1999 by *Who Wants to Be a Millionaire?* Although quizzes went mostly unchanged during World War II, there were concerns about the open microphone featured in all audience participation shows—the U.S. government worried about foreign agents using these programs to communicate coded messages. The U.S. Office of Censorship issued guidelines for programs to avoid "man-on-the-street" interviews like those on *Vox Pop* and to be careful in selecting audience members to participate. Quiz shows joined the war effort, donating prizes to war relief and encouraging listeners to participate in war bond drives.

Sob Shows

Another variant in the audience participation show emerged in the mid-1940s. Many daytime programs had established solid audiences, especially among women, by focusing on human-interest stories. The audience participation format was compatible with this type of program, and thus producers created what were often deemed "sob shows." The most famous and long running of these programs was *Queen for a Day*, debuting in 1945. The program featured a panel of women who testified to the hardships of their lives and told listeners their greatest wish. The studio audience would then judge which woman was most "worthy" of rewards, naming her "Queen for a Day." The Queen would be awarded her wish as well as a package of sponsor-provided merchandise. Although the program capitalized on women's poverty and desperation to garner ratings, it also provided both material and emotional uplift for thousands of women over its 20-year run. Other programs succeeded in the daytime schedule, including both more traditional quizzes like *Double or Nothing* and *Give and Take* and other human-interest contests like *Bride and Groom* and *Second Honeymoon*. Audience participation shows had taken root in daytime schedules, a position they continue to inhabit on television to this day.

If *Queen for a Day* established the emotional potential of audience participation programs, it took *Strike It Rich* to fulfill that potential. CBS brought the show to the air in 1947, almost immediately creating controversy. The program featured down-and-out contestants who competed in a short quiz to win up to $800; the real drama followed, as audience members called in on a "heartline" to offer help, in the form of money, jobs, goods, or services, to the needy contestants. People highlighted their hardships to capture the pity of the enthralled home audience, who listened in high numbers, but controversy followed. Critics decried the program as exploiting human misery for profit. One contestant was successful in garnering pity from the audience and was given a good deal of charity, but it was soon discovered that he was an escaped convict from Texas. The New York Department of Welfare complained that people traveled to the city to appear on the program, only to be refused and end up on the welfare rolls; the Department of Welfare demanded that the program be required to get official licensure for providing public welfare aid to contestants. All of this negative publicity merely boosted the show's ratings, and it transferred to television and ran for over a decade. But the quiz show was still in for its most dire round of negative publicity.

Before discussing the last wave of radio quizzes in the late 1940s, it is important to consider not only the programs that composed the genre on radio, but also the cultural values associated with the genre. Although certain formats were celebrated as "quality" radio (such as prime-time drama) and others were derided as inappropriate (such as soap operas), quiz shows and audience participation programs were seen as mostly harmless entertainment with little controversial content. Nevertheless, many critics felt that the genre promoted the "un-American" value of receiving "something for nothing," because people could receive lavish prizes for answering simple questions (or sometimes just for answering the telephone). Fans of the genre, however, felt that the quiz show offered hope during tough times, giving people the promise that their dire straits might be turned around with a simple phone call. Most people thought the genre was "simple entertainment," although some held up the educational possibilities of quizzes to provide knowledge to the masses and to popularize education among listeners. Some audience members became die-hard fans, looking to participate in the programs enough to call themselves "professional contestants" because they frequented the studio broadcasts in New York. Though audience participation shows ran the gamut of cultural legitimacy—from *Information Please*'s highbrow appeals to *Queen for a Day*'s often shameless exploitation of human misery—the quiz show was generally accepted as a valuable part of the radio schedule.

The radio industry saw the genre in more stark economic terms—quiz shows were an inexpensive programming form, simple to produce, with proven popularity. Sponsors liked the programs because they were a highly profitable format—they required little money for "talent" (only hosts and announcers), needed small writing staffs, and could be produced quickly without many rehearsals. Although prizes were often lavish, especially in the late 1940s, producers usually persuaded companies to contribute products to the prize packages in exchange for on-air mentions; this practice was eventually discontinued by the National Association of Broadcasters (NAB) in 1948, because they felt that sponsors were "freeloading" on their programs. Network censors were a bit less enthusiastic about the genre because the ad-libbed format often led to comments that were viewed as inappropriate and hard to control. Despite general industrial support for the audience participation format, the late 1940s would see quiz shows gain a powerful enemy: the FCC.

Stop the Quiz Show!

Following the success of the phone contests on *Truth or Consequences*, a number of programs emerged to capitalize on the giveaway format in the late 1940s. Shows such as *Get Rich Quick* and *Everybody Wins* used the telephone call as a mechanism to draw in listeners by giving away large jackpots, but the most successful and notorious giveaway was ABC's *Stop the Music!* Premiering in early 1948, the show had a simple premise— a band played songs until the announcer yelled, "Stop the Music!" Then host Bert Parks called a random phone number and asked the listener to identify the song. If the listener got the correct title, he or she would win a prize and a chance at the huge jackpot—usually over $20,000 in merchandise—for identifying the "Mystery Melody." The Cowan-produced show became a huge sensation, with high ratings and widespread press coverage. The program's success sparked other giveaways, such as *Sing It Again*, creating the biggest boom in prime-time quiz shows in radio history. Yet the rise of the giveaways prompted numerous protests by various players within the broadcasting industry.

Fred Allen, whose program had been the perennial ratings champion on Sunday nights, found his show sliding when *Stop the Music!* aired in his time slot. He launched a high-profile antigiveaway

campaign in the press, even offering $5,000 to any listener who, if called by *Stop the Music!*, would claim to be listening to Allen instead, an offer Allen never had the opportunity to fulfill. The NAB also felt that the giveaway trend was potentially a detriment to radio; in 1948 the NAB issued a policy statement positioning itself firmly against "buying an audience" instead of offering solid entertainment programs. But the biggest, and most powerful, enemy to the giveaways was the FCC. In the name of the public interest, the commission issued a policy in August 1948 claiming that giveaways violated lottery laws and threatening to revoke licenses of stations that continued to broadcast the programs. Although the order was immediately enjoined by the courts when ABC filed a lawsuit against the FCC's orders, the policy became a lightning rod for the variety of opinions swirling around the genre in the late 1940s and helped put an end to the radio quiz show.

The FCC's ban received overwhelming press coverage, with critics and commentators taking sides on the matter. Thousands of audience letters poured in to the FCC, expressing divergent opinions on the value of both the programs and the FCC's actions. Critics of the genre condemned it as gambling, pandering to base instincts, and not offering wholesome entertainment. Defenders of quiz shows claimed that they were real-life dramas, that they were more entertaining than scripted programs, and that people did not listen simply for a chance to win. The issue dragged on in the courts for years; it was finally resolved in 1954, when the U.S. Supreme Court ruled (*FCC v. ABC*, 347 US 284 [1954]) that the FCC had misinterpreted the lottery laws—giveaways were legitimate because contestants were not required to provide "consideration" to be eligible to win. Although successful programs like *Stop the Music!* continued while the courts deliberated, new programs were careful to avoid the giveaway format so they would not suffer from negative publicity. By the time the format was cleared, the giveaway had mostly disappeared as a brief fad. Yet shows like *Stop the Music!* had upped the ante for quiz shows, leading to the huge jackpots that would become staples of the prime-time television quizzes of the late 1950s— and of early 2000.

Although the radio quiz show had moments of intense popularity and publicized controversy, its decline was quiet and swift. As television began to spread into more homes in the postwar era, quiz shows were quick to make the transition to the visual format. Unlike dramatic programs, quizzes did not have to create elaborate sets or visuals to appear on television—cameras could easily capture the inexpensive live proceedings that studio audiences had been witnessing for years. Thus programs like *Stop the Music!*, *You Bet Your Life*, *Quiz Kids*, and *Truth or Consequences* all made the transition to television in the early 1950s. Although the networks initially aired these shows on both television and radio, they soon realized that the audiences for radio were dwindling; by removing the shows from the radio, they encouraged fans to purchase televisions when the newer medium became the primary entertainment form of the 1950s. When the TV quiz shows of the late 1950s were exposed as being scripted and "fixed," radio quizzes had long been off the air and thus remained immune from the scandals.

The quiz show was an important part of radio's "golden age," captivating audiences with high-minded questions and emotional appeals, precocious youth and outrageous stunts. Although the format did not last beyond this era of radio broadcasting, its impact is still seen today on television game shows—the inflating jackpots, engaging contestant personalities, amusing celebrity panels, and quick-witted hosts all were conventions established by radio quiz shows. Occasionally radio refers back to these traditions—public radio's *Whad'ya Know* and local stations' call-in giveaways are both updates of classic radio audience participation techniques. Yet these programs were once a broadcasting staple, equal in popularity to better-known genres such as suspense dramas, musical performances, news reports, and celebrity comedy shows. The quiz show was an important, though often ignored, component of radio history, one that warrants a greater examination and appreciation by media historians.

See also: Vox Pop; You Bet Your Life

Further Reading

Adams, Franklin P., "Inside 'Information, Please!'," *Harper's* 184 (February 1942.).

Beatty, Jerome, "Have You a $100,000 Idea?" *American Magazine* 143, no. 3 (March 1947).

Beatty, Jerome, "Backstage at the Give-Aways," *American Magazine* 148, no. 1 (July 1949).

Cox, Jim, *The Great Radio Audience Participation Shows: Seventeen Programs from the 1940s and 1950s*, Jefferson, North Carolina: McFarland, 2001.

DeLong, Thomas A., *Quiz Craze: America's Infatuation with Game Shows*, New York: Praeger, 1991.

Eddy, Don, "Daffy Dollars," *American Magazine* 142, no. 6 (December 1946).

Gould, Jack, "Jack Benny or Jackpot?" *New York Times Magazine* (15 August 1948).

James, Ed, "Radio Give-Aways," *American Mercury* 67 (October 1948).

Lear, John, "Magnificent Ignoramus," *Saturday Evening Post* 216, no. 2 (8 July 1944).

Lear, John, "Part-Time Lunatic," *Saturday Evening Post* 218, no. 5 (4 August 1945).

Marks, Leonard H., "Legality of Radio Giveaway Programs," *Georgetown Law Journal* 37 (1949).

Mittell, Jason, "Before the Scandals: The Radio Precedents of the Quiz Show Genre," in *The Radio Reader: Essays in the Cultural History of Radio*, edited by Michele Hilmes and Jason Loviglio, New York: Routledge, 2002.

Pringle, Henry F., "Wise Guys of the Air," *Saturday Evening Post* 218, no. 45 (11 May 1946).

Robinson, Henry Morton, "Information Please," *Reader's Digest* 34 (January 1939).

JASON MITTELL

R

RADAR
National Radio Ratings Service

Because radio is woven into the patterns of consumers' day-to-day lives, reaching them at home, in the office, and on the road, research is needed to understand how radio's role in today's media mix may be changing. As with the more commonly known television ratings conducted by Nielsen Media Research, Statistical Research Inc. (SRI) uses a sample of radio listeners to determine listener patterns and characteristics. Radio's All Dimension Audience Research (RADAR) was first produced in 1967 and has been produced by SRI since 1972. Using nearly 30 measured networks, RADAR can provide data on national and network radio audiences in a variety of formats to SRI clients.

For its RADAR product, SRI uses an eight-day telephone interview methodology, which it claims establishes a rapport with respondents that allows them to create an accurate and complete picture of radio exposure over the course of one week. SRI also has the ability to merge its respondent data with some three million "clearances" (records of carriage), thus allowing RADAR to provide ratings for specific programs and commercials. Since 1972, SRI has increased the RADAR sample size (from 4,000 to 12,000 respondents annually), the number of measurement weeks (from two to 48 annually), and the frequency of reporting (from annually to quarterly).

One component of the RADAR product allows users to process data and conduct analyses, including profiles of national radio audiences, profiles of network radio audiences, custom electronic ratings books, estimates of the reach and frequency for rotation plans, estimates of the reach and frequency for broadcast schedules, and optimal network radio advertising plans. Another component allows users to combine RADAR data with information from other sources and generate overall reach-and-frequency estimates.

Data from RADAR reach-and-frequency applications can be used as a base for combinations with other information—about radio, the internet, print, or any medium—that the user has obtained and entered. Up to 12 different other-media properties or sources can be included and collectively weighed at the user's discretion.

There are also two RADAR software applications that enable users to estimate audiences for local markets and programs not measured directly by RADAR. With these tools, users can approximate how much a plan's reach may be increased by scheduling units on non-RADAR programming. In addition, users with access to local data can distribute RADAR's national audience data for a particular schedule to individual markets.

The founders and principals of SRI are Gale Metzger, president (formerly with A.C. Nielson, and the first research supplier to be elected chair of the Advertising Research Foundation's Board of Directors), and Gerald J. Glasser, a former professor of business statistics at New York University. In 1990 Metzger and Glasser were joint recipients of the Hugh Malcolm Beville, Jr., Award of the National Association of Broadcasters and the

RADAR

Broadcast Education Association. The SRI founders were cited for "integrating audience research into the broadcast managerial process" and for "superior leadership in the development of the audience measurement field," among other contributions. The SRI staff includes more than 70 full-time employees. The company is based in Westfield, New Jersey.

RADAR studies are based on probability sampling, high response rates, in-depth interviewing by trained personnel, and multiple checks to ensure accuracy. The key component is the sampling process.

Representative Samples

If every member of the population has an equally good chance of being in the sample, it is a representative sample. Through statistical theory, we know that fairly drawn (or random) samples usually vary in small ways from the population. Over time, these small differences tend to average out. A representative sample does not have to be very large to represent the population from which it is drawn, but it does need to be selected in a way that gives all members of the population the same chance of being chosen. Although it is impossible to determine the exact number of listeners spread over a particular area, well-conducted samples generally provide a good estimate.

In sampling, it is common to select a small portion of the entire population to test. If a more accurate estimate is desired, a larger sample is taken. For example, suppose we select 10,000 people to question regarding their radio listening habits. It would be very unlikely that we would get exactly 5,000 that listened to a particular radio station. Likewise, it would be very unlikely to get 0 or 10,000. However, the percent of the listeners we did find in our sample group would be close to the percent that existed in the entire population. In fact, according to sampling theory, the larger the sample we used, the more confidence we would have in our estimated answer. With a sample of 10,000 we might reasonably conclude that the actual percentage would be between 48 and 52 percent of the listeners. This would suggest that possibly one out of every 20 times we would estimate an answer outside this range. With a larger sample, this range might decrease to 49–51 percent, and thus decrease this error probability to more than one out of 30 times.

The RADAR product uses a structured respondent recruiting process. This process includes incentives, advance contacts with potential respondents, and flexibility in the week for which the radio listening data are compiled. This process results in a tabulated sample of about 50 percent.

In addition to the RADAR product, SRI has conducted numerous proprietary studies on radio for the major broadcast networks and programming suppliers. Studies resulting from this work include: the ability of radio commercials to evoke images from familiar TV ads; the way people relate to radio, including the role it plays in their daily lives; awareness of and attention to public radio, as well as reactions of public radio audiences to programming and on-air fund-raising; perceptions of local radio stations—reasons for listening and non-listening, station image, and evaluations of station personalities; and the accuracy ascribed to radio news broadcasts by listeners.

Tracking Trends

Because the methodology of RADAR research has remained consistent, there exists a capability to track trends across more than 25 years of data. For example, trend comparisons have shown that as women have moved increasingly into the labor market, their radio usage has become more similar to men's. In addition, listening itself has also moved outside the home. In 1998, 38 percent of radio usage occurred in homes, as opposed to 61 percent in 1980, and car radio listening has nearly doubled over the same time, from 17 percent to 33 percent. Finally, the FM and AM bands have essentially switched places in terms of listenership during the past 25 years; AM's audience share has dropped from 75 percent to 18 percent, and FM's share has risen from 25 percent to 82 percent.

Arbitron Era

In mid-2001, Arbitron purchased the RADAR service from SRI and continued to expand and improve it through that decade. Arbitron changed the method of gathering network audience data from telephone calls to written diaries —by 2007 some 200,000 of them, a fourfold increase in four years. The number of audio networks reported in RADAR increased from 29 to 58, whereas the number of companies participating doubled from four to eight.

See also: Arbitron; Audience Research Methods

Further Reading

Arbitron's RADAR webpage, www.arbitron.com/national_radio/home.htm

Beville, Hugh Malcolm, Jr., "RADAR," in *Audience Ratings: Radio, Television, and Cable*, Hillsdale, New Jersey: Erlbaum, 1985; 2nd edition, 1988.

Webster, James G., and Lawrence W. Lichty, *Ratings Analysis: Theory and Practice*, Mahwah, New Jersey: Erlbaum, 1991; 2nd edition, as *Ratings Analysis: The Theory and Practice of Audience Research*, by Webster, Lichty, and Patricia F. Phalen, Mahwah, New Jersey, and London: Erlbaum, 2000.

DENNIS RANDOLPH,
2009 REVISIONS BY CHRISTOPHER H. STERLING

RADIO ADVERTISING BUREAU
Radio Trade Association

The Radio Advertising Bureau (RAB) is the sales and marketing arm of the U.S. radio industry. The RAB promotes the effectiveness of radio advertising to potential national advertisers, helps its members effectively market radio advertising to station clients, provides sales training for station employees, and serves as an information resource for station members.

Origins

A Broadcast Advertising Bureau (BAB) was established by the National Association of Broadcasters in 1950, but it quickly failed because of lack of support. A second attempt a year later was more successful, and by 1954 the bureau had all four U.S. networks, more than 835 stations, and 11 station representatives as dues-paying members. At the beginning of 1955, BAB became the Radio Advertising Bureau with a continued aim to provide sales information, especially radio advertising success stories, to prospective advertisers and their agencies. RAB had more than 1,000 station members and a million dollar annual budget by 1959.

The RAB had arrived at a crucial time in radio history. Audiences and advertisers were concentrating on television, and radio was in the midst of its transition from traditional or middle-of-the-road programming aimed at a broad audience to increasing specialization based on various popular music formats, especially variations on Top 40. RAB opened branch offices in Chicago, Los Angeles, and Detroit in the early 1960s. In 1964, RAB initiated the All-Radio Methodology Study (ARMS) audience research program to determine the best ways to measure and describe radio's listeners. On a lighter note, RAB retained comic Stan Freberg to develop a series of commercials touting radio's benefits over television. One of them applied sound effects to create the image of turning Lake Michigan into a huge cherry sundae. It was effectively used for many years.

RAB expanded its efforts and output in the 1970s and 1980s, catering to both large and small radio outlets. Monthly publications, sales meetings, and demonstrations spread the word on how best to utilize radio for advertising. RAB also targeted such large advertisers as Sears and Procter and Gamble—neither of which then advertised on radio—and turned both companies into major users of the medium. A 1989 campaign used brief moments of silence to explore what the world would be like without radio. RAB began to service FM outlets and soon moved to a "radio is radio" campaign, arguing that both AM and FM provided valuable services to advertisers. In 1994 much of the RAB moved to Dallas in a cost-cutting move, though headquarters remained in New York.

RAB Objective

The RAB promotes the effectiveness of radio advertising, helps its members effectively market radio advertising to station clients, provides sales training for station employees, and serves as an information resource for station members. The annual *Radio Marketing Guide and Factbook for Advertisers*, published by RAB, compiles the most recent data on radio audiences, provides information on the top radio advertisers, and includes comparative media information and radio listener facts.

As the primary sales association for the industry, the RAB also tracks the performance and financial health of the radio industry. As many large radio group owners have begun to sell stock through initial public offerings, the RAB has become an important spokesperson for the health and prosperity of the radio industry. More than 5,000 stations, networks, and sales organizations in the United States and abroad are members of RAB.

Member Services

The RAB's Member Services Helpline provides members with access to the radio industry's largest database of marketing, media, and consumer behavior information. The database includes more than a half-million individual reports on some 3,000 different marketing, media, and consumer topics. RAB uses the internet to supply station members with information (its website is www.rab.com). Available on the site is information to help radio account executives prospect for clients, prepare client proposals, make client presentations, and become a marketing resource for advertising clients.

RAB members can find RAB Instant Backgrounds on 160 distinct business categories, products, or services. A radio account executive needing information to prepare presentations for clients as diverse as accountants, a women's clothing retailer, an air conditioning repair service, or warehouse shopping service could obtain specific information about the customers who typically use these services, including competitive characteristics of each business category and the times customers prefer to shop. RAB Research also provides seasonal promotional and sales ideas, consumer information, and media information—including not only facts on radio usage but information to help account executives sell against other media such as newspapers, television, yellow pages, and the internet. An audio library of 1,000 MP3 format commercials, a database of commercial scripts, and a co-op advertising directory are also available online. RAB PROposal Wizard can be downloaded to assist account executives in creating attractive, organized, and problem-solving sales proposals.

Sales Training

A continuing theme for the RAB has been to promote the effectiveness of the radio industry as an advertising medium against other competing media. Although radio broadcasts have entertained and informed listeners since the 1920s, the radio industry receives less than ten cents of every dollar spent on advertising. Newspapers and television receive the greatest percentages of revenue. RAB's efforts are intended to assist local stations in getting a larger share of the local advertising revenue and to see that advertisers nationwide are aware of radio's effectiveness. RAB's awareness campaign, entitled "Radio Gets Results," focuses on how local stations have provided marketing solutions for their clients. Gary Fries, president and chief executive officer of the RAB, described the "Radio Gets Results" campaign as a way to provide the radio industry with documented proof of radio's unique ability to deliver outstanding results for its advertisers.

Professional development of station account executives is another role of the RAB. Radio consolidation, one result of the passage of the Telecommunications Act of 1996, has decreased the number of radio station owners. Large radio groups of several hundred radio stations are now possible. The larger radio ownership groups have done two things to the industry. First, they have put increased pressure on station managers and sales managers to increase revenue. Second, stations are increasingly aware of the need to invest in sales training for their employees.

RAB station members receive daily sales and marketing emails to help sales managers conduct successful sales meetings and to highlight new sales opportunities for account executives. The RAB offers sales training and accreditation through the Academy Certified Radio Marketing Professional. RAB began offering sales training courses in 1973; they estimate that only five percent of all radio salespeople have ever qualified for accreditation. Once the Radio Marketing Professional status is reached, persons wishing to receive advanced designations must combine knowledge gained from studying RAB materials with what they know from their day-to-day experience as radio account executives.

Because the Radio Advertising Bureau is a member-supported trade group, much of RAB's information is available only to members. The RAB's website includes free information, including the "Radio Gets Results" station testimonials, media statistics, links to other sites, and the latest press releases from RAB, which often highlight industry trends. Instant Backgrounds, audio files, the co-op database, and other features are available to members only.

See also: Advertising; Advertising Agencies; Consultants; FM Trade Associations; Promax; Promotion on Radio; Station Rep Firms; Trade Associations

Further Reading

Albarran, Alan B., and Gregory G. Pitts, *The Radio Broadcasting Industry*, Boston: Allyn and Bacon, 2000.

Arbitron Radio Market Report Reference Guide: A Guide to Understanding and Using Radio Audience Estimates, New York: Arbitron, 1996.

Marx, Steve, and Pierre Bouvard, *Radio Advertising's Missing Ingredient: The Optimum Effective Scheduling System*, Washington, D.C.: National Association of Broadcasters, 1990; 2nd edition, 1993.

Radio Advertising Bureau website, www.rab.com

Shane, Ed, *Selling Electronic Media*, Boston: Focal Press, 1999.

Streeter, Thomas, *Selling the Air: A Critique of the Policy of Commercial Broadcasting in the United States*, Chicago: University of Chicago Press, 1996.

Warner, Charlie, *Broadcast and Cable Selling*, Belmont, California: Wadsworth, 1986; 2nd edition, by Warner and Joseph Buchman, 1993.

GREGORY G. PITTS

RADIO BROADCAST DATA SYSTEM
Transmitting Alphanumeric Information

Radio Broadcast Data System (RBDS) is a transitional technology for FM radio, important parts of which will be incorporated into the developing digital radio systems. RDS technology allows a station to transmit an eight character digital message (e.g., station call letters, identification of music being played) to suitably equipped receivers. A small digital readout tells a listener what station is tuned, what music or talk is being provided at the time, as well as other types of information.

Development

The line-of-sight limit to analog FM radio transmission means that many transmitters are required to cover a large geographical area. Adjacent transmitters cannot broadcast on the same frequency because they would interfere with each other. In order to stay tuned to the same radio network or program service, a listener driving long distances would have to constantly seek out a new signal as he moved. Unless the listener knew which transmitter served which area, he would not know the optimal frequency for his favorite network or music or talk program service. This was the problem that engineers sought to solve with the development of RDS beginning in the late 1960s.

Swedish engineers began development of what became RDS in 1976. They sought a means of sending data to radio pagers. Soon a group of broadcast engineers working under the auspices of the European Broadcasting Union (EBU) developed the RDS through the 1970s to meet the requirements of European countries, and subsequently it became a European standard under the umbrella of the Comité Européen de Normalisation Electronique. Initial field tests began in 1980. A large-scale operational trial took place in Germany five years later. Regular service began in Ireland, France, and Sweden, in addition to Germany, in 1987, the same year that Volvo made available the first car radio featuring RDS capability. More European countries—and radio manufacturers—followed over the next two years. By the early 2000s, the number of RDS sets in use totaled over 60 million, most of them in Europe.

Radio Data System Features

RDS technology uses a separate and inaudible digital signal that is a subcarrier (an additional signal) of an FM transmission. An RDS receiver can decode this information to enable digital display of station or program information including the following features.

RDS allows automatic retuning to alternative frequencies. When the radio detects that the signal for a particular program service is becoming poor and hard to hear (due to distance from the transmitter), it seeks another one with the same program identification, and if that station provides better quality, the radio switches over so quickly that the listener is not aware of it. More expensive and sophisticated radios have two tuners at the front of the set, and these are constantly searching for a better service, making for even more efficient switching. Not having to look at the radio to retune while driving has obvious implications for safety on congested roads.

Indicating the type of program provided by the station is one popular RDS feature, and providing additional information such as useful telephone numbers, record titles, and so on via the display is another. This information can be up to 64 characters long and is displayed by scrolling through eight successive character screens. This feature is obviously of more use in home tuners than in moving cars.

On an RDS-equipped radio, the listener is offered an eight-character alphanumeric display of the call letters of the station. With the use of abbreviated indicators, this display can also inform the listener whether that station will provide any sort of traffic or travel program. The radio can interrupt listening when these traffic announcements are being broadcast.

A feature that has made the traffic and travel service work efficiently is the enhanced other networks (EON) feature. This is used to update information stored in a receiver about other program services than the one currently tuned. In other words, a listener can be listening to one radio station or even to a cassette or CD, and if a different local news station is about to broadcast travel information, the receiver can switch away from the primary source of entertainment to that travel information and back at the end of it. If manufacturers were convinced of a demand, they could build sets that would be able to vector onto any particular program type. EON availability is demonstrated by the logo "RDS-EON" which is normally displayed on a radio's front panel or on receiver packing.

Another feature available via RBDS technology is the traffic message channel (TMC). Developed originally in Europe, RBDS-TMC makes it possible to broadcast encoded travel announcements. By means of a voice synthesizer, these can be heard or printed out by the listener in his or her own language regardless of the country through which he or she is driving. Because of the complexity of the process, in order to make the best use of the service, receivers should have two tuners at the front, one listening for conventional RDS services and one tuned to the service carrying the TMC information.

RDS can also supply the smart radio with the current date and time, which adjusts automatically for time zone changes. Among the more subtle features especially useful in Europe is the extended country code, which provides supplementary information to tell the radio in which country (and thus language) it is operating. To keep the RDS system flexible and to adapt to new developments, an "open data application" retains unallocated data groups for control of potential new tasks.

The system can also control the relative volumes of speech and music via a music-speech switch. One feature extensively used in some European countries (and indeed, the feature that began RDS development), is radio paging, which enables broadcasters to use existing networks in a cost-effective way to deliver messages to personal receivers. Up to 40,000 subscribers can take advantage of the service on one program service. There is a related emergency warning system so that those broadcasters who wish to do so can transmit confidential warning messages in the event of a national emergency.

Radio Data System in the United States

Initial RDS demonstrations took place in the United States in 1984 in Detroit. Ford began development work on an RDS-equipped automobile radio. Research and further demonstrations continued in various locations for several years. RDS was demonstrated at the 1986 NAB convention. The National Association of Broadcasters and the National Radio Standards Committee (NRSC) formed a subcommittee to develop an American technical standard recommendation for the Federal Communications Commission. The United States adopted a Radio Broadcast Data System (RBDS) standard in 1993 that added functionality to the basic RDS offering. Further developments in the 1990s sought to retain basic RDS and RBDS compatibility.

As stations are all identified by call letters, a unique set of program identification codes was devised for the transmitter RDS encoders in North America, and a new set of program types was needed to meet the specific needs of the American market. The 31 numerical program type (PTY) codes thus vary in the European RDS and American RBDS systems.

Future

In 2005, Clear Channel launched a RBDS-TMC service. By mid-2008, it claimed to have over 500,000 subscribers across the US and Canada. Though now commonplace in other parts of the world, RBDS's proliferation in the US may be forestalled. Designed as it is for analog FM broadcasting, RBDS arrived just as radio became increasingly digital. Nevertheless, new automobiles are regularly coming equipped with RBDS capabilities and many manufacturers, are producing cellphones and radio receivers that are compatible with RBDS signals.

See also: Digital Audio Broadcasting

Further Reading

Kopitz, Dietmar, and Bev Marks, *RDS: The Radio Data System*, Boston: Artech House, 1999.
RDS Forum website, www.rds.org.uk/
Wright, Scott, *The Broadcaster's Guide to RDS*, Boston: Focal Press, 1997.

JOHNNY BEERLING,
2009 REVISIONS BY CARY O'DELL

RADIO CITY
New York City Headquarters of NBC

Few station or network headquarters are well known as tourist spots. However, Radio City, a central part of Rockefeller Center in midtown Manhattan, has been an exception virtually since it opened in 1933 as the operational headquarters of the National Broadcasting Company (NBC). Public tours are offered, and Radio City has even been the subject of at least three novels.

Origins

In 1928, John D. Rockefeller, Jr., leased 12 acres in midtown Manhattan from Columbia University. Called the "Upper Estate" by the landowner, the plot was bounded by Fifth and Sixth Avenues and 49th Street to 52nd Street, and was then occupied by low-rise brownstones, tenements, and theaters. Rockefeller planned to revitalize the area with three large office buildings and a new Metropolitan Opera House, but the stock market crash of 1929 forced him to scrap the original plans. Still wanting to develop a commercial district on the property, however, Rockefeller hired three architectural firms and a consultant to refine his plans.

In 1930, a $250-million, 11-building project for the area was announced. Raymond Hood had overall architectural control of what would become the largest privately owned prewar business and amusement complex in the world. The first art-deco-style building to open was the Radio-Keith-Orpheum (RKO) Theater, which seated about 3,500 moviegoers (it was torn down in 1954 to make room for an office building). Delayed somewhat by the Depression, the last of the original buildings was not completed until 1940.

In the 1950s what had become known as Rockefeller Center was extended west of Sixth Avenue to incorporate several high-rise office buildings; the Center now comprises 18 buildings. Control of the Rockefeller Center was sold by the family in 1985 in a complex deal. By 1989 the Japanese Mitsubishi company had become the majority owner, but after a real estate turndown, ownership went to Tishman Speyer Properties in 1997.

The centerpiece of Rockefeller Center, however, was the 70-storey building at 30 Rockefeller Plaza, soon known for its chief occupant as the "RCA Building" ("GE Building" after 1986), but often referred to simply as "30 Rock." It opened in 1933.

NBC Headquarters

The Radio Corporation of America (RCA) moved its head-quarters into many floors of the skyscraper in late 1933, bringing the NBC network along with it. NBC occupied its new studios early in November and dedicated them on 18 November 1933.

Studios for the network and its New York flagship station, then WEAF (later WNBC), would eventually occupy 11 floors, of which only the second and fifth had windows. This was part of an unprecedented effort to keep outside sounds isolated. Extensive sound filtration and insulation systems made the many studios among the finest anywhere. Their entire space (4.5 million square feet) was air conditioned, a rarity in that early period. The studios ranged in size from 14 feet by 23 feet to the world's largest studio—78 feet by 135 feet with ceilings 30 feet high. This huge room, Studio 8-H, could accommodate an audience of 1,300 persons.

Not all of the NBC space was immediately used; postwar auditorium studios (Studios 6, 7, and 8) were developed on the sixth and seventh floors as needed. Most studio equipment—master control and the like—was on the fifth floor with 50 tons of backup batteries in case of a power loss. No fewer than 275 synchronized clocks appeared throughout the NBC and WEAF floors.

The new NBC space had also been designed for eventual television operations, although that medium was technically very crude in the early 1930s. Later in the decade, however, NBC began studio television experiments with a much improved all-electronic system that soon extended to two large mobile vehicles, often seen parked outside 30 Rockefeller Center. Right from the start, NBC provided studio tours to the general public, which proved to be highly popular and grew even more so when extended to the new television spaces. By the end of World War II, more than half a million people took either the basic or extended studio tour of NBC every year.

The Radio City Music Hall

Perhaps the most famous single part of the Rockefeller Center complex is the Radio City Music Hall on Sixth Avenue. Built at a cost of about $8 million, it was the largest theater in the world with almost 6,000 seats under a huge arching ceiling. Its handsome art deco interiors were designed by Donald Deskey. It opened on 27 December 1932, and the first of its now-famous Christmas stage shows was offered a year later.

For decades the Music Hall offered movie and stage show combinations that were hugely successful. But as television developed and films began to draw smaller audiences, so did the Music Hall. In 1978 some discussions were held with regard to tearing the place down and erecting another office building; however, the building was granted city landmark status and saved. Its presentations after 1979 focused on what people could not see in their home towns or on television—spectacular stage shows.

In the late 1990s, the Hall underwent a massive $77 million renovation paid for by Cablevision, which currently operates the facility. The complete renovation even included changing each of the nearly 6,000 seats by the company that had made the originals. Much of the original lighting was repaired and rejuvenated, as were all wall surfaces. Computers now control lighting and sound effects, yet much of the Music Hall's original stage equipment remains in place and in use.

See also: National Broadcasting Company; Radio Corporation of America; WEAF; WNBC

Further Reading

Balfour, Alan H., *Rockefeller Center: Architecture As Theatre*, New York: McGraw-Hill, 1978.

Barbour, David, "The Showplace of the Nation Reborn," *Entertainment Design* (April 2000).

Brown, Henry Collins, *From Alley Pond to Rockefeller Center*, New York: Dutton, 1936.

Chamberlain, Samuel, editor, *Rockefeller Center: A Photographic Narrative*, New York: Hastings House, 1947; revised edition, 1952.

Francisco, Charles, *The Radio City Music Hall: An Affectionate History of the World's Greatest Theater*, New York: Dutton, 1979.

Karp, Walter, *The Center: A History and Guide to Rockefeller Center*, New York: American Heritage, 1982.

Loth, David Goldsmith, *The City within a City: The Romance of Rockefeller Center*, New York: Morrow, 1966.

NBC's Air Castles, New York: NBC, 1947.

Novels about Radio City.

Morland, Nigel, *Murder at Radio City: A Mrs. Pym Story*, New York and Toronto, Ontario: Farrar and Rinehart, 1939.

Spence, Hartzell, *Radio City*, New York: Dial Press, 1941.

Wheeler, Ruthe S., *Janet Hardy in Radio City*, Chicago: Goldsmith, 1935.

CHRISTOPHER H. STERLING

RADIO CORPORATION OF AMERICA

No single U.S. communications company has had a more fundamental and important association with the worldwide development of radio broadcasting than the Radio Corporation of America (RCA). Although RCA no longer exists as a separate corporate entity today, having been acquired by General Electric (GE) in 1986, its brand-name products continue to be marketed by Thomson S.A. of France.

Origins

In the early 20th century, the American Marconi Company was a wholly owned subsidiary of Marconi Company, a British corporation. Marconi had a virtual monopoly on maritime ship-to-shore wireless communication when England entered World War I against Germany in 1914. Because of the important role of wireless in maritime operations, President Woodrow Wilson directed the U.S. Navy to assume control of the American Marconi stations and all German-owned stations in 1917 when the United States entered the war. The Navy operated these until the end of the war in 1918, when the U.S. government was reluctant to return control of the American Marconi stations to the British parent company.

Franklin D. Roosevelt was then Assistant Secretary of the Navy, and the experience gained from overseeing operation of these wireless stations during the war convinced him that all radio patents and operations in the United States should be kept under U.S. control. After World War I, British

Marconi and General Electric began negotiations for the GE Alexanderson Alternator, which was the state-of-the-art hardware for long-distance wireless transmission. The U.S. Congress expressed concern that Marconi's acquisition of this equipment would result in a foreign company (and, by implication, a foreign country, albeit a friendly one) gaining complete control over maritime communication, which would not be in the national interest. Congress and the Navy pressured General Electric to buy American Marconi, which it did in October 1919. RCA was established to operate all the American Marconi wireless stations that General Electric had acquired. RCA's charter mandated that all board members were to be U.S. citizens and that stock interest by foreign companies or individuals could not exceed 20 percent. The chief of GE's legal department, Owen Young, was appointed RCA board chairman, and two former American Marconi executives, Edward McNally and David Sarnoff, were appointed its president and commercial manager respectively.

GE and RCA developed cross-licensing agreements that permitted each firm to use the other's radio patents. Over the next three years (through 1922), cross-licensing agreements and RCA stock purchases were made by Westinghouse, American Telephone and Telegraph (AT&T), and United Fruit Company, which had patents on crystal radio, as radio was United Fruit's primary means of communication with its Central and South American plantations. The radio business at that time consisted primarily of international, maritime, and amateur radio services, and just a handful of radio broadcasting stations.

Radio broadcasting grew rapidly during the early 1920s and fostered corporate competition, much of it bitter, over whether the Federal Government or private corporations should control radio broadcasting and how. The corporations, for that matter, where engaged in vicious competition for control and experimented with various ways to shoulder the costs of radio broadcasting and the need for its further development. During this fractious period, AT&T and its manufacturing subsidiary Western Electric were referred to as the "telephone group." WEAF in New York was its first AM station and was in the vanguard for many experiments and innovations during the 1920s. An important experiment was known as "toll broadcasting." The telephone group introduced the first commercial announcements on radio (WEAF) in 1922. RCA, GE, and Westinghouse were referred to as the "radio group" and pooled their development efforts, including operation of the GE and

Westinghouse stations. The two groups had very different ideas about how radio and broadcasting should develop.

The Federal Trade Commission, following a congressional mandate, began an investigation into alleged monopolistic practices brought about as a result of the more than 2,000 pooled patents and cross-licensing agreements. The results of this 1923 investigation led to a binding arbitration agreement between the telephone and broadcasting groups to resolve their differences. Eventually, in 1926 they resolved the disputes when AT&T agreed to leave the broadcasting field, selling the popular WEAF station to RCA. RCA then created the National Broadcasting Company (NBC) as a wholly owned subsidiary of RCA. NBC began a regular network service using WEAF as its flagship program source. In time, 25 stations in different markets were affiliated with the NBC network. Shortly thereafter NBC established a second radio network using Westinghouse's WJZ, also in New York, as its anchor for programming. The WEAF operation was to be known as the Red Network and the WJZ operation was known as the Blue Network, ostensibly because an RCA engineer drew connecting lines in red and blue on a map showing the locations of the stations served by each. NBC became the base for RCA's expansion into commercial radio broadcasting on a national scale.

RCA became a giant in the radio set manufacturing business initially by marketing GE and Westinghouse radios. In 1929 the three companies consolidated their research, manufacturing, and marketing operations. RCA then bought the Victor Talking Machine Company and its famous logo and slogan "His Master's Voice"—the Francis Barraud painting of "Nipper" the Fox Terrier looking into the bell of a Victrola. The $154 million paid for Victor enabled RCA Victor to manufacture its own radios and phonographs at a new plant in Camden, New Jersey. The new RCA Victor then established the RCA Radiotron Company to manufacture radio tubes, and by 1930 RCA controlled a substantial portion of the several markets in which it was active. This raised eyebrows in Washington, and investigations soon followed.

The Justice Department instituted antitrust proceedings that lasted almost three years. Finally, in 1932 the companies signed a compromise consent decree that resulted in GE and Westinghouse divesting themselves of RCA stock, relinquishing their positions on the RCA board of directors, and making their license agreements (dating back to the early 1920s) non-exclusive. RCA was now an autonomous and independent corporation. Its new

president, David Sarnoff, introduced the RCA Photophone in 1932, a device that allowed moviegoers to hear Al Jolson on screen in the first "talkie."

Expansion

The newly independent Radio Corporation of America grew rapidly, expanding some operations to Hollywood, and growing both its manufacturing base and NBC networks. A research and development center opened near Princeton, New Jersey. Research on television focused at RCA's plant in Camden, New Jersey. RCA joined with a chain of vaudeville theaters to start Radio-Keith-Orpheum (RKO) Movie Studios and produced many successful feature films. The NBC radio networks flourished in the 1930s. Rockefeller Center was built in New York City during the early 1930s, and the high-rise building in that complex was named the RCA Building as part of the agreement by RCA to occupy multiple floors, including the first eight (which housed both WEAF and the NBC network facilities), and the top floors (which housed RCA's corporate offices).

RCA's involvement in television began in 1930. Sarnoff hired Vladimir Zworykin, the inventor of the "Iconoscope" (forerunner of today's camera tube) and "kinescope" (forerunner of today's picture tube) away from Westinghouse at the end of the 1920s to establish a laboratory in Camden to develop television. Ten years and $50 million later, Sarnoff introduced RCA's electronic television at the 1939 World's Fair in New York City. Commercial television, using largely RCA technology, began operation in mid 1941.

When the United States entered the war in 1941, RCA plants were converted to war production, making tubes, sound equipment, sonar bomb fuses, mine detectors, and ultimately radar, which was introduced later in the war by the British. Commercial radio and television production resumed less than two months following the end of World War II in 1945. Many new television stations sprang up, resulting in a freeze on authorizations (licensing) by the Federal Communications Commission (FCC) for almost four years, in order to assure equitable allocation of stations and non-interference of signals throughout the country.

Following a round of controversial Congressional hearings, RCA's all-electronic color TV system was adopted as the national standard in 1953. RCA held the patents on that technology at the time, so virtually every color television set produced until the mid-1960s contained RCA parts. All color kinescopes were manufactured by RCA.

When a finished tube came off the assembly line it was given one of several different brand labels, packed into a matching brand-labeled box, and forwarded to an RCA competitor such as General Electric, Sylvania, Philco, or Motorola, if not labeled for sale as an RCA set.

Decline

The 1950s and early 1960s marked the peak of RCA's role in the broadcast and electronics industry. Sarnoff had actively supported the research underlying the company's success in black-and-white and later color television. The firm had developed a huge collection of patents, further strengthening its position. RCA was active in virtually all parts of the electronics field, including military and space communications, and it held major market positions in all those industry segments. At the same time RCA had become a major military equipment manufacturer and had entered the computer business, among others, spreading its resources across new fields.

Sarnoff remained in charge until his 1969 retirement, but other firms made the breakthroughs that would dominate the business in years to come. After Sarnoff's retirement, massive investments in technology that rapidly became obsolete (such as a type of video disc recording and mainframe computers) led to huge losses, weakening RCA in the 1970s (then under the leadership of Sarnoff's son Robert). As manufacturing lagged, soon the NBC television network subsidiary was providing RCA's margin of profit. The younger Sarnoff was soon replaced by a quick succession of other presidents and chairmen as RCA sought to regain its former electronics pre-eminence within a far more competitive and deregulated marketplace. Much of its consumer electronics business (as with other U.S. firms), including radio and television manufacturing, faded in the face of new competition from abroad. The company's attempt to break into the computer manufacturing business resulted in a huge loss—more than $500 million when RCA finally pulled out. When a strong hand was most needed, severe management infighting broke out that would prove fatal to the company's survival as an independent entity.

Finally secret negotiations (initially RCA's board and other leaders were not included) were begun between RCA chairman Thornton Bradshaw and General Electric, which was now rich with profits from manufacturing and takeovers of other companies. The situation was ironic, as GE had created RCA so many years before. Bradshaw said later that some kind of takeover was the only way RCA's many parts might be kept together. But this was not to be.

In 1986 GE took over all of RCA for $6 billion (a huge deal at the time) and shortly thereafter began to dismantle the empire David Sarnoff and others had created. Some parts were incorporated into GE's operations. The research labs that had helped to create television and other products were sold because GE had its own research labs. In 1987 the RCA trade name was also sold for use on consumer products that would now be sold by the French company, Thomson S.A. The NBC radio network that had pioneered national radio programming in the 1920s was sold, as were all of the NBC-owned radio stations.

RCA exists today merely as a product trade name, the giant company that once dominated U.S. radio having disappeared less than two decades after the retirement of its longtime leader.

See also: American Telephone and Telegraph; Blue Network; General Electric; National Broadcasting Company; Westinghouse

Further Reading

Archer, Gleason L., *History of Radio to 192.6*, New York: New York Historical Society, 1938; reprint, New York: Arno Press, 1971.

Archer, Gleason L., *Big Business and Radio, New York: American Historical Company*, 1939; reprint, New York: Arno Press, 1971.

Barnum, Frederick O., III, *His Master's Voice: Ninety Years of Communications Pioneering and Progress: Victor Talking Machine Company, Radio Corporation of America, General Electric Company*, Camden, New Jersey: General Electric, 1991.

Bilby, Kenneth W., *The General: David Sarnoff and the Rise of the Communications Industry*, New York: Harper and Row, 1986.

Demaree, Allan T., "RCA After the Bath," *Fortune* (September 1972).

Douglas, Alan, *Radio Manufacturers of the 1920s*, vol. 3: *RCA to Zenith*, Vestal, New York: Vestal Press, 1991.

Douglas, Susan Jeanne, *Inventing American Broadcasting, 1899–1922*, Baltimore, Maryland: Johns Hopkins University Press, 1987.

Federal Trade Commission, *Report of the Federal Trade Commission on the Radio Industry*, Washington, D.C.: Government Printing Office, 1924; reprint, New York: Arno Press 1971.

The First 25 Years of RCA: A Quarter-Century of Radio Progress, New York: RCA, 1944.

Howeth, L.N., *History of Communications-Electronics in the United States Navy*, Washington, D.C.: Government Printing Office, 1963.

Lewis, Tom, *Empire of the Air: The Men Who Made Radio*, New York: Burlingame Books, 1991.

Sobel, Robert, *RCA*, Briarcliff Manor, New York: Stein and Day, 1986.

Warner, J.C., et al., *RCA: An Historical Perspective*, New York: RCA, 1957, 1958, 1963, 1967, 1978.

Wenaas, Eric P. *Radiola: The Golden Age of RCA, 1919–1929*. Chandler, Arizona: Sonoran Press, 2007.

ROBERT G. FINNEY

RADIO, DECLINE OF

By the close of the 21st century's first decade, American commercial radio showed increasing signs of being in trouble. Indeed, there were widespread indicators of how far the ubiquitous medium had fallen from its former place. And there was a good deal of finger pointing as to the reasons for that decline, but also considerable disagreement as to what could be done about it. Some argued the decline was temporary and that radio would rise again, just as it has in the past. Many others were less sure, fearing that a combination of factors had struck radio with a "perfect storm" from which it would be hard to recover.

Though still ongoing as this was written, radio's problems can be assessed in three broad categories —the medium's loss of local identity, the declining appeal of its programming and thus defection of key parts of its audience, and changing technology.

Localism

For decades both Federal Communications Commission regulators and those in the business have touted radio's local appeal and importance of stations in their markets. Indeed, the FCC considered such localism to be a key factor in licensing decisions. Stations were expected to reflect and project their markets, serving specific local concerns as well as providing entertainment. Only owning one AM and FM outlet in a given market, as was the FCC rule into the 1990s, was another requirement that encouraged localism.

Passage of the Telecommunications Act of 1996, however, laid waste to the foundational idea of localism, though Congress probably didn't foresee or intend that outcome. By eliminating any cap on station ownership nationally, and allowing an owner to control as many as eight stations in each of the largest markets, the new law paved the way for dramatic—and soon harmful—change. In just the first five years after its passage, something close to 40 percent of all stations changed hands. Group (multiple station) owners bought up stations left and right, eventually turning on one another as group owners took over one another. The resulting consolidation meant the loss of local radio voices across the country. More specifically, it often meant

the loss of news and public affairs programming, let alone jobs.

The poster event of what these changes could mean took place in isolated Minot, North Dakota, in early January 2002. When a train derailment near town threatened portions of Minot with a debilitating cloud of ammonia gas early on a frigid morning, city emergency offices could not find a single person at any of Minot's several radio stations. All were on automatic operation (or off the air entirely) and thus could not air emergency warnings to listeners until station personnel were located over the next several hours. Critics argued that as all the Minot stations were controlled by distant group owners (chiefly Clear Channel), there was less concern over local events, good or bad.

Across the country, stations that once touted their local identities became mere extensions of nationally programmed chains of group-owned outlets. Their music or talk formats were determined elsewhere, with little or no local presence. Announcers were often only technically "present" as technology allowed them to perform for many stations in different cities.

Content

People seek out radio because of programming they want to hear. Yet over the last few decades, and at an accelerating rate, radio's menu of content choices has been getting ever narrower. The result is a bland sameness in radio's sound across both stations and markets. Multiple outlets provide the same currently popular music—or perhaps "oldies" from a decade or so ago. Once-common regional differences have largely disappeared. So have such minority-appeal formats as jazz, folk, and classical music—and, often, news. And so have other features that made local stations unique —staff who cared about their community and were often active within it, local news and public affairs programs, and a personal interaction with local advertisers.

Consolidation is one important factor behind the widespread decline of radio news and public affairs programming. A once-thriving aspect of the business (it was the rare station that offered no news), by the early 2000s, a growing number of stations provided no public affairs programming at all. If a group owner controls multiple stations in a market, it may limit news to only one of those outlets, news often fed from a distant location. Even weather and traffic reports are increasingly provided by distant syndicators rather than local reporters.

Some critics argue that radio has sold its soul to right-wing talk show rants and religion, both of which are happy to pay for the airtime they use. The 1987 end of the FCC's Fairness Doctrine removed any concern that stations would have to balance the views of their opinionated talk show hosts or religious programs.

Finally, an old complaint (one first heard in the 1920s) is that radio carries too much advertising. Many stations today have a commercial load exceeding a third of their overall airtime. And the radio spots are ubiquitous and continual, more so as most are 20- or 30-second soundbites aired one right after the other. And they often seem louder than surrounding programs (another old complaint on which evidence is divided). It's hard, argue many would-be listeners, to let a radio receiver play in a work environment with all the advertising broadcasters carry.

Audiences and Advertising

Although radio's overall audience size remained roughly equal year-to-year in the early 2000s, some listener demographic segments were in decline, especially among those groups most sought by advertising time buyers. Younger listeners—those under 25—were increasingly using the competing digital media options rather than radio, which is seen as yesterday's service.

Broadcasters were increasingly unhappy with the Arbitron ratings service by 2008, primarily because the company was beginning to convert its market ratings to data based on new portable people meter devices. Initial results seemed to show sharp audience declines in some types of radio service. The FCC and Congress were asked to investigate and the Nielsen television ratings service announced plans to re-enter the radio market they had left 40 years earlier, providing a more traditional diary-based ratings service for several group owners. The tussle underlined radio's concern with its audience size, makeup, and flow, all of which were of concern to its advertisers.

By late 2008, reports on radio's overall revenues showed a drop each quarter for the previous 18 months. Although 2008 election ads helped bump the industry's revenue, the overall trend was clear —advertisers were departing radio for other venues, chiefly the internet. Overall revenues declined about 7 percent in 2008 (to the lowest level in five years) and were projected to drop 10 percent in 2009. The number of stations changing hands also declined, as did many sale prices.

This decline took place against a general economic downturn in the 2007–9 period, which made radio's revenue situation worse. Advertisers often restrict their expenditure in hard times and radio

has felt the brunt of that trend as many of its usual supporters—finance, retail stores, and automobiles—have been especially hard hit.

Technology

Some have argued that none of the problems discussed thus far would matter as much if radio listeners lacked alternatives. They might have been unhappy with broadcast radio, but would have put up with it had there been no other source of continual audio entertainment. Clearly that is not the case and in recent years a growing number of one-time radio listeners have shifted their listening time and attention to satellite services, portable personal listening devices, and internet-based audio sources. Each of these provides a different threat to over-the-air radio broadcasting.

Satellite radio, in the form of XM and Sirius (which merged in mid-2008) began in 2001 to offer listeners two things—for a subscription price. The lack of advertising on its dozens of music channels met one complaint of critics, whereas the much wider menu of choice met another. Once persuaded to pay for something that had always been free, listeners gained a menu of up to 150 different channels, about half of them providing most forms of music, some fairly esoteric. The talk channels included news and public affairs, sports, and a host of talk formats, albeit most carrying advertising. By late 2008, the satellite radio audience approached 20 million subscribers, not even 10 percent of broadcast radio's listenership, but slowly expanding.

Internet listening developed at about the same time, and provides yet another option to over-the-air listening. While most broadcasters now also offer an online presence, the web has created options for thousands of totally new audio listening options offering every conceivable kind of content. No longer is one's listening restricted to a single market as remains the case in broadcasting. Now one can tune signals from around the nation and world, many only available online. Virtually any kind of content can be found—all types of music, talk in multiple languages, and features found nowhere else. And any laptop (and increasingly, cell-phone) can be a listening device.

Most important, however, has been the spectacular rise of the iPod and other MP3-based portable listening and recording devices (again, including multifeature cell-phones), which pose a greater concern for broadcasters. These allow individuals to create their own changing menu of music without recourse to radio—and thus to control all aspects of their listening experience.

Radio station owners have not ignored this growing competition. To blunt it, they tout coming digital or HD radio as a wonderful new quality sound. They promise multiple digital signals as soon as more people own the requisite receivers. At the same time, however, they are repeating an old mistake in promoting HD radio's sound quality as a means of rebuilding audience interest and loyalty. As happened in the mid-20th century when promoting then-new FM service, radio broadcasters have fallen into the trap of touting a *technology* rather than a *service*. Past experience demonstrates that consumers seek (and are willing to pay for) a desired content service rather than a technology, even one providing more sound quality.

That radio's technological future will be digital is clear, though how quickly that conversion will take place remains less so. Even less obvious is how digital technology may allow owners to increase their programming. Stations will be able to transmit multiple signals once they convert to digital operation, and that will help them compete in what is already a multichannel media mix. But additional signals also carry the danger of further dividing up audiences into listening numbers too small to appeal to advertisers. This is a central conundrum radio managers are grappling with.

Outlook

Yet despite all this, broadcast radio is not about to disappear, and continues to change. Over-the-air radio is the only medium universally available in automobiles (though its competitors are working to catch up). As Americans spend more time in their cars, whether in daily commutes or longer journeys, radio will for some time continue to enjoy an advantage over potential competition.

Indeed, many feel radio is far from declining. Rather, they argue, the medium is going through yet another stage in its long development. Radio has survived predictions of its demise before —especially in the early 1950s when television knocked radio listening out of the nation's living rooms. Radio reinvented itself thanks to rock 'n' roll music, Top 40 formats, and transistor portable receivers that allowed listeners to take radio along anywhere. Radio supporters feel sure that it will overcome its own problems and find a lasting place among growing digital competition.

See also: Advertising; Audience; Clear Channel Communications Inc.; Commercial Load; Digital Audio Broadcasting; Digital Satellite Radio; Ownership, Mergers, and Acquisitions; Podcast; Portable People Meter; Telecommunications Act of 1996

Further Reading

Clifford, Stephanie, "Radio's Revenue Falls Even as Audience Grows," *New York Times* (26 November 2008).
Foege, Alec, *Right of the Dial: The Rise of Clear Channel and the Fall of Commercial Radio*, New York: Faber & Faber, 2008.
Hilliard, Robert L., and Michael C. Keith, *The Quieted Voice: The Rise and Demise of Localism in American Radio*, Carbondale: Southern Illinois University Press, 2005.
Sterling, Christopher H., "Slow Fade? Seeking Radio's Future," in Michael C. Keith, editor, *Radio Cultures: The Sound Medium in American Life.* New York: Peter Lang, 2008, pp. 321–329.
Sterling, Christopher H., and Michael C. Keith, "Clouds in the Air," Chapter 7 of *Sounds of Change: A History of FM Broadcasting in America.* Chapel Hill: University of North Carolina Press, 2008, pp. 177–208.

CHRISTOPHER H. STERLING

RADIO DISNEY
Radio Network for Children

Discussions at ABC about a children's network began as early as 1989, but it was not until 1996 that Radio Disney began broadcasting. Although Radio Disney's format was derivative of its predecessors (ABC Radio's marketing relationship with Radio Aahs resulted in a $30 million judgment against Disney in 1998), its originality resided in its use of Disney characters and its internet site.

By 2008, Radio Disney took a different turn. It was not part of the acquisition of ABC Radio Networks by Citadel Broadcasting in 2007, continuing to be distributed nationally through the Disney Media Networks division of the American Broadcasting Company (ABC). Marketed as the number one 24-hour radio network devoted to kids, tweens (ages 6–14) and families, the Radio Disney internet site promoted its interactivity, urging listeners to "call us" to request a song while promoting a blog, scrolling a "shout-out" feature that showed listener-generated email requests, and continuous streaming of top ten music videos. On-air and internet promotions allowed listeners to win prizes every day, with special contests offering personal visits with artists and celebrities.

With a playlist of pop, rock, soundtrack, oldies and evergreen hits, Radio Disney's unique listener-driven, interactive format empowered young listeners to directly participate in programming. The network, which claimed an audience of over three million kids and tweens and over two million moms, was available to 97 percent of the U.S. via 50 terrestrial radio stations, and SiriusXM satellite radio, iTunes Radio Tuner, a digital satellite and cable music provider and mobile phones. The network, which is both on-air and online, is also available internationally in Japan, Britain, Argentina, Paraguay and Uruguay. In 2008 Radio Disney signed an agreement with media and marketing research firm Arbitron to provide measurement and research of kids, tweens and family radio listening patterns on a national scale, the first time this type of ratings information has regularly been gathered.

Radio had scores of shows for children in the pre-television age, but as those comedies, adventure series, and westerns migrated to the tube, so did their audiences. In fact, Disney's *Mickey Mouse Club* was long responsible for television's ability to keep kids entertained. Consequently, radio essentially abandoned children, reacting to the onslaught of TV with increasingly sophisticated strategies to identify and sell its listeners to advertisers, supported by ratings methodologies that were unable to effectively quantify the under-12 demographic. Although pop music radio has attracted kids since the early days of rock and roll, children had not been directly targeted, nor could they be accurately counted.

Nonetheless, experiments in format radio for children began in earnest in the early 1980s on both commercial and public stations, laying the groundwork for an ongoing children's radio network, which led to Disney's entering the field. A number of concepts for children's radio were tested by the *Children's Radio Network*, established in 1982 by William C. Osewalt; these were broadcast on a handful of underutilized commercial AM stations from Florida to Oregon and eventually found a full-time home at WWTC in Minneapolis. The station's owner, Christopher Dahl, designated WWTC the flagship station for the first full-time kids' radio network, adopting the moniker "Radio Aahs." The network was programmed with specific segments for younger and older children; featured music, contests, and stories; and encouraged audience participation. Because its survival depended on increased distribution and advertising revenues, Radio Aahs entered a marketing relationship with ABC Radio.

It seemed that radio for children would flourish in the 1980s, as others, too, explored opportunities, some supported by Peter Yarrow of the singing group Peter, Paul and Mary and by Peggy Charren of Action for Children's Television. KPAL in Little Rock, Arkansas, had a full-time children's format, and WGN in Chicago was among the affiliates of the short-lived weekly music and news series for children, *New Waves*, which was cohosted by Fred Newman of Nickelodeon and funded by the Markle Foundation.

Public radio's significant children's radio venture, *Kids America* (which started locally in 1984 on New York's WNYC as *Small Things Considered*), was a live, 90-minute daily program distributed by American Public Radio that featured music, wordplay, call-ins, jokes, celebrity interviews, and problem-solving advice for a national audience until 1988.

See also: Children's Programs

Further Reading

Radio Disney website, http://radio.disney.go.com/about/

JOSEPH R. PIASEK,
2009 REVISIONS BY GAIL LOVE

RADIO LAWS
Pioneering U.S. Legislation

Four acts of Congress concerning radio preceded the definitive Communications Act of 1934. The first two focused on maritime wireless telegraphy and are mostly important as initial precedents. The Radio Act of 1912 was to stand for 15 years and was thus in force for the first seven years of regular broadcasting. Its many defects led to the more complex Radio Act of 1927, many provisions of which remain in force three-quarters of a century later.

Origins

The history of congressional action in the field of communications reaches well back into the 19th century with the Post Roads Act of 1866, in which Congress sought "to aid in the construction of telegraph lines and to secure to the government the use of the same for postal, military, and other purposes."

As experimental wireless activity increased after 1903, attempts were made to regulate the "wireless telegraph" industry. Between 1902 and 1912, some 28 bills were introduced in the U.S. Congress to deal with the problem of interference. In 1903 Germany called the First International Convention on radio, and the U.S. Navy made its first attempt to regulate wireless transmission. On 12 July 1904, President Theodore Roosevelt formed an interdepartmental radio advisory board consisting of the departments of commerce and labor, navy, war, and agriculture. Its recommendations constitute the first well-defined radio policy of the U.S. government. One of its recommendations was the necessity for legislation to prevent the control of radio telegraphy by monopolies or trusts by placing supervision in the Department of Commerce and Labor.

In 1906 the German government called the Second International Radio-Telegraph Conference, which was attended by 27 nations. The U.S. Senate's failure to ratify the resulting Berlin Convention caused all government departments concerned with radio to intensify their efforts to obtain legislation for federal supervision of radio usage. The navy department led these efforts, because the commercial wireless companies and amateur interests were opposed to any legislation that would affect their interests.

The marine disaster on 23 January 1909—when the liner *Republic*, with 440 passengers, collided with the Italian *SS Florida*, crowded with 830 immigrants, virtually all of whom were saved thanks to wireless distress messages—focused the public's attention on the safety applications of wireless. Within days there was considerable editorial comment on the role wireless had played in limiting the loss of life, creating such a favorable impression that radio, like life preservers, came to be considered a necessity by individual sea voyagers.

Wireless Ship Acts of 1910 and 1912

On 8 February 1909, President Theodore Roosevelt sent a special message to Congress recommending the immediate passage of legislation requiring, within reasonable limits, ocean-going vessels to be fitted with efficient radio equipment. The Wireless Ship Act of 1910 contained in just one page nearly all that was called for in the 1906 Berlin protocol. The first step to carrying out the provisions of the law was the creation of a radio inspection service.

On the night of 14 April 1912, two months before the Third Wireless Conference was to be held in London, the liner *Titanic*, on its maiden voyage, struck an iceberg 800 miles off the coast of Nova Scotia. The *Titanic* disaster, in which some 1,500 people lost their lives, is often cited as the reason for amending the Wireless Ship Act. However, the subcommittee of the Senate commerce committee had completed its work and the bill had been reported out prior to the *Titanic* disaster. It had become apparent that the United States would have to ratify the 1906 Berlin Convention in order to be invited to a forthcoming London Conference. The new bill became the Wireless Act of 1912. The *Titanic* disaster, however, had awakened congressional

concerns for such legislation and ensured its final enactment.

Radio Act of 1912

The Radio Act of 13 August 1912 was a totally new piece of legislation to provide for the licensing of terrestrial (not maritime) radio operators and transmitting stations. For nearly 15 years, radio operators and radio stations were licensed under this law, which was in effect until 1927.

The law was designed to serve two purposes: (1) to promote safety of life and property at sea and to promote commerce by facilitating the dispatch of ships; and (2) to secure the fullest use of radio communication by means of federal regulation, which was made necessary by the fact that in the state of the art at that time, unregulated use and resulting interference would impair or prevent almost all use. To give effect to these two purposes, both based on the Commerce Clause of the Constitution (Article I, Section 8), Congress provided for licensing and entrusted the administration of the system to the Department of Commerce and Labor's Bureau of Navigation, which previously had inspected ships leaving the United States' harbors for proper wireless apparatus.

The term *radio communication* instead of *radio telegraphy* was used throughout the bill so that its provisions would cover the possibility of the commercial development of radio telephony (or the use of radio waves to carry voice and other noncode signals). One feature of the Radio Act of 1912 that had far-reaching consequences was the fact that 19 specific regulations were embodied in the law, and thus no discretion to make further regulations was allowed to the Secretary of Commerce and Labor. It was the judgment of some members of Congress that doing so would be a surrender by Congress of its powers and would, to all intents and purposes, bestow discretionary legislative power on administrative officers.

Secretary of Commerce and Labor Charles Nagel soon attempted to deny a license to a station that was a subsidiary of certain German interests. Germany did not allow American-owned or -controlled stations to operate in that country, and the secretary wished to apply pressure until a reciprocal arrangement could be made with Germany that would allow U.S. capital the right of investing in and controlling corporations organized under German laws. The secretary of commerce asked for an opinion from the U.S. attorney general concerning his licensing power, and on 22 November 1912, he was advised that Congress had not intended to repose any discretion in the secretary. Although the 1912 opinion clearly restricted the secretary of commerce, he used as a lever a clause that directed him to license for the "least possible interference." However, in reality no-one had been given the authority to meet the new problems that were to arise with the rapid development of radio telephony. The fact that a "normal" wavelength might be written on the face of the license did not give the Department of Commerce (as it was after 1913) actual power of wavelength assignment.

Nevertheless, the assumption of controls was a step forward, and no serious problems arose for some eight years, until the era of regular broadcasting began in 1920. The development of radio broadcasting was delayed first by the threat of government ownership and then by renewal of the patent wars of the radio manufacturing industry. Bills on behalf of the Navy Department, which desired to take over wireless, were presented in January 1917 and again late in 1918. On both occasions, Congress, reluctant to establish outright governmental control, tabled the proposals. The cross-licensing agreements of General Electric, Western Electric, and Westinghouse in 1920–21, involving some 1,200 radio patents, ended the long patent war in radio.

Early Broadcast Regulation

After 1920, the biggest problems the Department of Commerce faced were the licensing of broadcast stations and the control of interference. Twenty bills were placed before the 67th Congress (1921–23); 13 proposed laws were submitted to the 68th Congress (1923–25); and 18 bills were introduced to the 69th Congress (1925–27)—all to regulate radio communication. Of these 51 bills, only one was to pass both houses of Congress—the Radio Act of 1927. Of importance is what took place while these various bills were being debated.

The first step to controlling interference was the closing down of amateur radio transmission. Another reason for stopping amateur work was the fact that many amateurs were attempting "broadcasting." To prevent this, the Department of Commerce began stipulating on all licenses the material that particular classes of licenses could transmit, restricting music, weather, market reports, speeches, news, and so forth to the "limited commercial" or broadcasting stations.

Radio conferences were held to obtain industry support. At the First National Radio Telephony Conference, held at Secretary of Commerce Herbert Hoover's invitation in Washington in 1922,

priorities were assigned to stations according to the services they rendered, with toll stations (i.e., those that sold their airtime) being last on the list. The concepts that the wavelengths being used were public property, that broadcasting should be performed by private enterprise, that there should be no monopoly, and that there must be regulation by the government were presented at these meetings.

The numbers of stations continued to increase, and time sharing became increasingly difficult. The Department of Commerce made available another wavelength for a special class of stations, called Class B. These stations were to be the higher-grade stations in terms of both equipment and programming. Congestion still grew on all three available frequencies. Time sharing of Class B stations began to be required before 1923. The new station classification system with the extra frequency did not solve the problems of interference or time sharing.

The Department of Commerce then decided that a complete band of frequencies was necessary, with specific wavelengths assigned to cities for use by broadcasting stations in those localities. Upon consultation with the navy, which agreed to relinquish its control of the 600- to 1600-m wavelengths to obtain new equipment, the band of 500–1500 kHz was made available exclusively for broadcasting on 15 May 1923.

The Second National Radio Conference in Washington then formally recognized and supported the Department of Commerce's classification system. However, with the increasing number of stations, all of which had great difficulty maintaining a constant frequency with accuracy, the interference and time-sharing problems continued.

A third conference was called by Hoover in an effort to deal with interference. Power increases continued, and experimentation was conducted to reduce the kilocycle separation between adjacent stations. The very success and popularity of broadcasting gave rise to its principal difficulty, which came to a head in 1925. The frequencies of broadcasting stations, which were in 10-kHz bands, provided 89 channels or frequencies. As there were about 578 stations operating in 1925, not every station could have an exclusive frequency, and most of the stations had to share time with one or more stations. This duplicate assignment of frequencies required that stations alternate in the use of the frequencies, for instance, by transmitting on alternate evenings. This was generally recognized as undesirable. In spite of this, the building of stations and the applications for broadcasting licenses increased. Because all of the channels for broadcasting were already completely filled, the Department of

Commerce could see no way of complying with more applications.

The discussions at the Fourth (and final) National Radio Conference in 1925 clearly brought out the fact that broadcasting would be harmed unless a severe check were put on the numbers of stations being authorized. The Department of Commerce in 1926 refused to license any further radio stations, leading to increased pressure from those individuals and corporations who wished to enter this growing field. Scarcity inevitably brought about an increase in the practice of renting the airtime of broadcasting stations to parties who wished to reach the public.

The Zenith Radio Corporation, which had obtained a license in 1925 by promising to restrict their schedule to two hours of operation a week, pressed for either increases in broadcast time or another frequency. Without permission, Eugene F. McDonald placed the company's station, WJAZ, in operation on a Canadian frequency. The Department of Commerce initiated court action, and on 16 April 1926, the court found that the Department of Commerce had no right to make regulations other than those prescribed in the Act of 1912 and could not, therefore, limit a license as to frequency.

Secretary of Commerce Herbert Hoover, instead of appealing the court decision, forced the issue by requesting an opinion on his powers from the attorney general of the United States. This opinion supported the WJAZ-Zenith Company decision and restricted the Department of Commerce's powers to the issuance of licenses to any and all applicants. Because of this decision, at least 100 stations changed frequencies, and over 200 were issued licenses when they applied for them. This created chaos. The main difficulty in achieving legislation was resolving the question of which agency should control radio regulation. Secretary Hoover compromised his stand of keeping the control within the Department of Commerce and agreed to leave some control in the radio service and regulatory and licensing control in an independent commission.

Radio Act of 1927

The Department of Commerce's involvement with broadcast regulation diminished but did not cease. The Act of 1927 was an experiment in the field of administrative legislation, as it combined a semi-independent agency with the Department of Commerce's newly formed Radio Division.

First, the act created a Federal Radio Commission of five members, appointed by the president

with the advice and consent of the Senate. The commission was given broad administrative and quasi-judicial powers to classify radio stations, prescribe the nature of their service, assign frequencies and wavelengths, determine locations for classes of stations, regulate the apparatus used, prevent interference through regulation, hold hearings, and summon witnesses.

The Radio Division of the Department of Commerce retained the power to accept applications for station licenses, renewals, or changes, but these were to be referred to the commission for definite actions. The secretary of commerce might refer to the commission any matter upon which he desired its judgment. An appeal could be made to the commission from any decision or regulation that the Radio Division, through the secretary of commerce, made.

Second, certain purely administrative powers were left in the hands of the secretary of commerce. He was to receive all applications, although he could not act on them. He was to license and fix the qualifications of station operators and suspend such licenses for cause. He was to inspect, through the Radio Division, transmitting equipment; designate call letters; and conduct investigations designed to uncover violations of the act or the terms of the licenses.

Third, this division of labor was to continue for one year only. The secretary of commerce was then to take over all the powers and duties of the Federal Radio Commission except its power to revoke licenses and its appellate powers, and the commission itself was to become merely an appellate body. However, at the end of one year it was apparent that only the worst cases of radio interference had been eliminated, and for the next two years Congress continued the year-by-year status of the commission.

In December 1929 the Federal Radio Commission was made a permanent agency of government. The Radio Division of the Department of Commerce became the field staff of the Federal Radio Commission on 20 July 1932.

The Department of Commerce radio actions influenced almost all of the provisions of the law that was passed in 1927. Through trial and error, the essential ingredients of the regulatory scheme embodied in the Radio Act of 1927 had been developed and refined. The Radio Act of 1927 codified that (1) the radio waves or channels belong to the public; (2) broadcasting is a unique service; (3) not everyone is eligible to use a channel; (4) radio broadcasting is a form of expression protected by the First Amendment; (5) the government has discretionary regulatory powers; and (6) the government's powers are not absolute. Perhaps most importantly, the 1927 law created the principal under which radio was to be regulated—"the public interest, convenience, or necessity," a phrase not defined in the act. Carried over into the definitive 1934 Communications Act, and still in force, the words have been varyingly defined over the years by the courts, adding to a considerable degree to the act's flexibility.

See also: Communications Act of 1934; Federal Radio Commission; Public Interest, Convenience, or Necessity

Further Reading

Aitken, Hugh G.J., "Allocating the Spectrum: The Origins of Radio Regulation," *Technology and Culture* 35 (1994).

Benjamin, Louise M., *Freedom of the Air and the Public Interest: First Amendment Rights in Broadcasting to 1935.* Carbondale: Southern Illinois University Press, 2001.

Bensman, Marvin R., *The Beginning of Broadcast Regulation in the Twentieth Century*, Jefferson, North Carolina: McFarland, 2000.

Garvey, Daniel E., "Secretary Hoover and the Quest for Broadcast Regulation," *Journalism History* 3, no. 3 (Autumn 1976).

Godfrey, Donald G., and Val E. Limburg, "The Rogue Elephant of Radio Legislation: Senator William E. Borah," *Journalism Quarterly* 67 (1990).

Hazlett, Thomas W., "The Rationality of U.S. Regulation of the Broadcast Spectrum," *Journal of Law and Economics* 33, no. 1, (April 1990).

Holt, Darrell, "The Origin of 'Public Interest' in Broadcasting," *Educational Broadcasting Review* 1 (October 1967).

Streeter, Thomas, "Selling the Air: Property and the Politics of U.S. Commercial Broadcasting," *Media, Culture, and Society* 16 (1994).

United States Department of Commerce, Bureau of Navigation, *Radio Communication Laws of the United States*, Washington, D.C.: GPO, 1914.

Webster, E.M., "The Interdepartmental Radio Advisory Committee," *Proceedings of the I.R.E.* 33, no. 8 (August 1945).

MARVIN BENSMAN

RATE CARD

Used by radio stations for decades, rate cards were typically small printed pieces of paper or cardboard (designed to be easily carried in a pocket or wallet), which listed the prices a station charged those who wished to purchase airtime. Rate cards first appeared for both networks and stations in the 1930s, became more important around 1950 with the decline of networks and full program sponsorship, and had largely disappeared by the start of the 21st century.

How They Were Used

Rate card prices were determined based largely upon how many individual "spot" advertisements a client purchased during the year (or how often they did so), with volume discounts offered to those that advertised the most. Early rate cards were often quite simple and consisted of little more than a small grid or table of parts of the day ("dayparts"), prices and a discount for the number of airings of a given spot (such as bulk discounts for airing the same message multiple times). Of these factors, usually the most important was when a spot was to run. Cards might also provide other details on the station or its market. Many stations printed a simplified version of their rate cards in trade magazines or yearbooks.

Though specific rate card price codes varied greatly, times of day were usually designated with a letter or series of letters. For example, "Class A" might denote 10 A.M. to 3 P.M. Monday through Friday whereas "AA" might represent 6 A.M. to 10 A.M. Monday through Sunday. Subsequent letters "B" and "C" might apply to hours with fewer listeners. The designation, "AAA" or something similar often identified the most popular dayparts and, hence, the most expensive for an advertiser to purchase. As rate cards often ended up in the hands of potential advertisers, many listed special deals or "combo" offers as incentives to new or returning buyers.

Traditionally, rate cards were updated or revised two to four times a year in response to a station's most recent Arbitron ratings. Larger markets saw more frequent ratings and thus rate cards. They were often numbered ("Rate Card 27") to be sure that station reps, agencies, and advertisers had the most up-to-date information. Though most stations employed sales people to solicit businesses to advertise on their outlet, some also used local or national station rep firms to provide this service. Rates would then reflect the commissions that such firms charged.

Decline of Rate Cards

By the late 20th century, however, the formal radio rate card began to disappear. Stations sought more flexibility in pricing and volume discount offers, and in highly competitive markets felt they could no longer be constrained by even quarterly rate card updates. Most heavy buyers of radio time considered any amount quoted to them—on a rate card or via a sales professional—as little more than a guideline, the radio industry's version of a new car's factory-direct "sticker" price, something perceived as a starting negotiating point.

Indeed, some stations reversed their sales thinking, and began to see their rates as proprietary information, not to be made known to competing outlets. Other stations were far more open and, after the turn of the century, even posted their rates on the internet. Many large broadcasters (including Clear Channel's stations) dispensed with the classic rate card entirely and adopted a "yield management" system or other complex method to determine their prices.

Yield Management

Yield management is a technique that, in the words of one proponent, involves "selling the right resources to the right customer at the right time for the right price." The method has already been heavily employed, and with great success, in the airline business. Thanks to computer tools, it strives to maximize profits by following, often on an hourly basis, a micro-managed supply-and-demand approach to pricing airtime. For example, airlines offer a wide schema of prices for what is, ultimately, the same perishable service—seats on a flight. The plane goes whether the seat is sold or not. What changes is the number of people who want to travel on that flight, the time of day, season, and how far in advance they book their trip. By paying attention to—some might say exploiting—these variables, airlines and other businesses can charge a wide range of prices for their services.

In similar fashion, the radio industry sells its perishable product (airtime) using yield management logic and pricing techniques. According to Jim Tiller, president of Maxagrid, a company that supplies yield management technology to radio stations,

> if a station has tons of inventory [many spots available for purchase], yield management helps stimulate demand by finding the point on the price curve where you can maximize your revenue while you can find that point in the marketplace where advertisers will see a value.

Yield management software allow stations to create many fast-changing "electronic rate cards" that are tailored to that station's needs, format, demographics and, most importantly, clients. The fluidity of a yield management approach can help generate demand in low-demand situations (by pricing spots low), while maximizing the financial return on high-demand areas.

Similar in many ways to yield management is the "megarate" pricing strategy that many stations have also adopted in recent years. Megarate utilizes computer software that cross-analyzes a variety of criteria including the number of spot availabilities a station has open as well as selling patterns before recommending whether a station should raise or lower its prices for particular dayparts, or other time units.

In 2007, Clear Channel further shook up radio sales and the use of rate cards by initiating a new system for purchasing. It announced a deal with internet powerhouse Google to allow for over-the-web purchase of advertising time on 675 of its stations. These purchases would systematically bypass Clear Channel's vast sales force and could, theoretically, bring to clients greater discounts with each of their purchases. (For the sake of comparison, if Clear Channel's human sales force is considered the equivalent of a traditional travel agent, then this new option is akin to that agent being bypassed in favor of such a direct online booking service as Travelocity). Though Clear Channel and Google have discontinued this practice, the internet rep firm Target Spot offers its clients a similar "self-serve" option via its website for anyone looking to purchase ads on internet-based radio services.

See also: Advertising; Advertising Agencies; Promotion on Radio; Station Rep Firms

Further Reading

Bunzel, Reed E., "Electronic Rate Cards following supply and demand," *Broadcasting* (29 October 1990), p. 37.
Keith, Michael C., *The Radio Station*, 7th edition, Boston: Focal Press, 2007.

CARY O'DELL

RECEIVERS

Over the course of some eight decades of radio broadcasting, receivers for tuning into broadcasts have evolved and become generally lighter, more efficient, and less expensive. They have changed radically in both design and internal features. Although radio receivers are now virtually ubiquitous in homes, cars, and offices, such was not always the case. This entry focuses primarily on U.S. commercial development of consumer radios, with some discussion of developments outside the U.S. as well.

Early Receivers

The earliest consumer radio receivers were relatively crude handmade devices created by amateurs. Throughout the 1920s radio enthusiasts built a variety of sets: sometimes simple crystal tuners, often more complex sets featuring several vacuum tubes (these were sometimes sold as ready-to-make kits). Except for the crystal sets, early radios required power provided by bulky wet-cell batteries and later by rechargeable storage batteries. Users listened using earphones or, by mid-decade, separate horn-shaped acoustic speakers. These early sets were limited in sensitivity (ability to pick up weaker signals) and selectivity (ability to distinguish between signals and to tune sharply) and were not very handsome to look at, consisting of a mass of wires, tubes, batteries (often leaking), and controls. They required careful tuning with several dials, and delivered (by present day standards) poor audio quality.

The first commercial receivers became available in 1920–21, but initial store-purchased sets were expensive and thus limited in appeal. Manufactured initially by Westinghouse and General Electric (for sale under the RCA "Radiola" label) and soon thereafter by other manufacturers, they came with key components simply mounted on boards (termed *breadboards* in the trade) or built into wooden cases (sometimes referred to as *breadboxes*), and they required the same complex battery and antenna rigs used by the home-built sets. As the radio craze peaked in 1922, hundreds of other manufacturers—including Atwater Kent, Crosley, Grebe, and many smaller firms—offered receivers from inexpensive single-tube sets (selling for up to $10) to far more sophisticated multitube receivers selling for well over $100. By 1924 more than a million commercial sets a year were being sold to consumers. Most were hand-wired, thanks to relatively cheap labor (this industry was one of the first modern manufacturing businesses to employ women) and the complexity of their designs.

The first receivers able to operate on AC power, thus eliminating the need for messy batteries, appeared from Atwater Kent, Grigsby-Grunow ("Majestic" radios), and then RCA in 1927–28. From 1924 until 1931, only RCA offered the superior superheterodyne circuit, as the company had purchased Edwin Armstrong's patent. The "superhet" provided far better selectivity and sensitivity than did radios made by other firms. As part of the settlement of an antitrust proceeding, RCA had to make the circuit available to other manufacturers. Superheterodyne circuits dominated radio receivers for decades.

By the late 1920s receiver design was becoming more sophisticated, and the first console (freestanding) "hi-boy" floor models became available as radios became an item of furniture for the home.

Indeed, the design of the wooden cabinetry became an important radio selling point, as did annual model changes (sometimes models changed more frequently than annually), somewhat paralleling automobile sales techniques. Radios were widely sold in various historical "period" styles as well as utilitarian furniture—desks and end tables, for example—all intended to fit with varied home decor. Some table models appeared in all-metal cases, which added to their weight but protected the delicate tubes and circuits. Again attesting to inexpensive labor costs, some were even offered with hand-painted floral designs in multiple colors, made to order. Most radios offered circular dials for selecting stations, leading to users referring to a given frequency "on the dial."

On the eve of the Great Depression, some 60 manufacturers of radios were operating, although four of them held two-thirds of the market and two controlled a third. Fancy console models dominated the radio market. Overproduction, however, helped to force prices down (from an average of $136 in 1929 to about $90 in 1930 and down to $47 by 1932). A host of manufacturers were forced out of the market and then out of business. Depression realities forced a return to cheaper small table model radio receivers, and by the mid-1930s Philco was making a third of them. Crosley and Emerson also specialized in small and inexpensive radios (around $15).

Mass Market Receivers

In part as a move toward greater efficiency, radio circuits, vacuum tubes, and designs all became more standardized. Most table radios (by the mid-1930s, these combined the receiver and loudspeaker in a single enclosure and made up 75 percent of the market) were of the "cathedral," "gothic" (with a rounded or pointed top), or later "tombstone" (with a flat top) design. As economic conditions improved, console radios resumed their former popularity, and better models featuring shortwave as well as medium wave (AM) bands, pushbutton station selection, better speakers, and larger lighted radio dials for easier tuning became available. The first car radios appeared around 1930, although only the more expensive models included radios as factory-installed equipment. By 1938 more than half of the world's radio receivers were in the United States. That radio had become central to daily life is clear as more homes owned radios than owned telephones, vacuum cleaners, or electric irons.

Radios came in an increasing variety of shapes and sizes. Smaller shelf or "mantle" radios became popular because they were easy to move from one room to another. Compact or "midget" radios by Emerson and other firms were made possible by smaller vacuum tubes. Some were manufactured in novelty designs tied to popular radio shows (e.g., Charlie McCarthy or Hopalong Cassidy) or reflecting popular culture (e.g., the Dione Sextuplets) themes. Prices dropped below $10 for some models. In the late 1930s and early 1940s, tabletop sets manufactured from special Bakelite and Catalin plastic resins became popular owing to their reasonable prices and huge decorative appeal. Most sets featured two to three colors and fit in well as bright additions to kitchens and family rooms. Some models were purchased because of their value as both colorful and practical accessories in bedrooms and even bathrooms. (Today many of these same sets are expensive collector's items, costing thousands of dollars.)

In April 1942 manufacture of all civilian radios was halted as part of the U.S. war effort. Finding spare parts grew harder, and thus radio repairs became increasingly difficult as the war continued. Pent up demand led to massive numbers of AM radios being made again starting in late 1945. More than 50 million were sold from 1946 to 1948 alone. The availability of more receivers meant more multireceiver households, a phenomenon that had first appeared in the 1930s. Plastic was now the radio cabinet material of choice, available in many different colors and shapes and less expensive to manufacture than the former wooden casings.

Radios in the 1950s continued the trend to smaller and lighter formats. Few consoles were sold (households devoted available console space to television) as sales concentrated on table radios, most of which were AM only despite the appearance of FM stations. Clock radios with "wake-up" features became popular. Radio technology had changed very little over two decades because designs were still based on the use of vacuum tubes. Only in 1954 did the first tiny transistor models become available, their ready portability a trade-off for very poor sound quality. Only in the 1960s did transistor radio prices drop sufficiently to drive tube models off the market.

FM Receivers

The first FM radio receivers became available in 1941 just as the first FM stations took to the air. Perhaps 400,000 were manufactured before wartime consumer product restrictions came into force. All of the prewar sets were designed for the 42–50 MHz FM band, so when the Federal Communications Commission (FCC) shifted the service up to 88–108 MHz in 1945, the older sets were made obsolete. A few receivers were sold with both old and new FM bands in the 1945–48 period, when dual station operation was allowed. Only very slowly did sets on the new band become available, and then only at prices far higher than comparable AM models. Sales were slow—a tiny fraction of AM levels—and declined into the 1950s.

As FM service began slowly to expand in the late 1950s, however, so did the manufacture and sale of FM receivers. The addition of stereo service in 1961 was a major factor in rising FM receiver sales, as was the growing high fidelity movement (which originated in Britain) among audiophiles. FM reception was a core feature of component stereo systems. Companies such as Fisher, Marantz, and Scott built high-quality tuners that required separate amplifiers and speakers but delivered superb sound.

By the mid-1960s FM radios were found in more than half of the nation's households, but FM radios remained rare in automobiles into the 1970s. FM proponents sought to persuade Congress to require that all radios receive both AM and FM bands (parallel to television legislation that mandated UHF as well as VHF reception capability), but slowly rising FM sales made the attempt unnecessary. As prices came down and more FM stations took to the air, more radios featured both AM and FM tuning capability.

Portable Receivers

Initial portable radios were portable in name only. Handmade "portables" were fragile, bulky, and heavy, even without the required horn speaker and batteries. Yet the ability to take a radio with you was a strong lure, as is evident even in radio advertising of the early 1920s. Some homemade models were tiny and featured earphones. Still, the first commercial portables resembled midsize suitcases, and not light ones at that. One knew they were intended to be portables simply because they had handles. All these difficulties drove the portable radio off the market by 1926–27, and consumers focused on the new plug-in home receivers.

Although many small radios were sold with handles, they still had to be plugged in (they did not operate with batteries), making them what Schiffer (1991) terms *pseudo-portables*, They looked the part, but they were not. Almost no true U.S. portable radios were manufactured in the 1930s save by some smaller companies operating on the fringe of the business. The market was simply too small.

The availability of smaller and more efficient tubes that drew battery power more sparingly helped spark a revival in manufacturer interest in portable radios in 1938–39. Led by Philco and other firms, battery-powered portables began to flood the U.S. market: more than 150 models were available by the end of 1939. Many still looked like cloth-covered suitcases, but now they were small, light, and clearly intended to be carried about. Others made use of the then-new plastic cases and weighed only five or six pounds even with their batteries. Some were even touted as being pocket-sized. Most could also double as plug-in table radios. One of the best was Zenith's TransOceanic, which went on sale early in 1942 featuring several shortwave bands with AM reception, a radio log, special antenna, and a large battery pack. Despite its high price ($100), it was hugely popular in the few months it was available, and it resumed production after the war, lasting in improved models well into the 1960s.

Postwar portables were central to the AM radio boom. Although based on prewar technology, they appeared in bright plastic cases that emphasized modern styling, many of them dubbed "lunchbox" radios because of their size. Manufactured by many companies, these were hugely popular in the late 1940s and into the 1950s, selling more than a million units a year. Smaller "miniature" or "shirt-pocket" models appeared in the early 1950s. No portables included FM tuning, in part because of the limited distance FM stations could transmit.

Announcement of the transistor in 1948 and its first appearance in a small radio (the Regency TR-1 in 1954) sparked a new generation of portables in the late 1950s that emphasized their tiny size, light weight (11 ounces in the Regency's case), long-lasting batteries, and portability. Combined with radio's development of Top 40, the transistor portable helped to transform radio's audience from an at-home family image to an on-the-road active youth image. Yet tube-based (or tube-transistor combination) portables lasted into the early 1960s, in part because of the initial high cost of transistors.

The primary change in the U.S. radio market after 1960 (other than the addition of FM stereo) was less in their technology than their source. Japan began producing small tube portable radios for sale in the United States in the 1950s and sold its first transistor radio (a Sony TR-63) in 1957. Soon thousands of radios were being imported, combining solid (and often better) engineering with low prices. Some U.S. manufacturers shifted set-making (or licensed their designs) to companies in the Far East. The revolution happened quickly; by 1963

there was no U.S. small transistor radio, for they all came from Japan. Cheaper foreign labor soon wiped out U.S. radio (and later television) manufacturing of all types; the final Zenith Trans-Oceanic model of 1973 was made in Taiwan.

In the 1990s some sets (called "smart receivers") featured RDS (Radio Data Systems) technology that enabled AM and FM stations to transmit data to receivers, thus allowing them to perform several automatic functions. Users of such sets could interface with stations and access programming information from them via a built-in light-emitting diode (LED) screen. Radio thus became a visual medium.

Digital Era

Radio's focus in the early 21st century was increasingly on digital reception. In a proverbial "chicken and egg" situation, both satellite and over-the-air digital broadcasting initiatives depended on sufficient listeners to make them viable. Yet listeners would rarely purchase initially expensive digital sets without something unique to listen to.

The first move came from satellite radio carriers. XM initiated service in September 2001, and Sirius a few months later. Both depended on the availability of digital receivers in automobiles given the importance of drive-time listening. Each had its own standard (receivers for one could not tune broadcasts of the other). Marketing campaigns, often linked with consumer electronics outlets, pushed the value of dozens of unique talk and music channels, all in crisp digital sound. Some effort went into promoting sales of desk-top and portable receivers, but the car radio market remained central. When the two carriers merged in 2008, they served nearly 20 million satellite receivers, about 10 percent of the analog radio audience. The merger prompted efforts to develop receivers that could pick up signals from either company's satellites, now that their offerings were melded into a single service.

Slower to develop was a cost-efficient receiver design for terrestrial digital radio broadcasting. FCC approval of the HD Radio standard developed by Ubiquity cleared the question about technical standards, but initial receiver offerings in the middle of the 21st century's first decade were far more expensive than analog sets. Some of the problem was a lack of attractive separate programming for digital listeners—most stations simulcast analog and digital signals if they offered digital service at all. The lack of a firm date for conversion of radio from analog AM and FM to digital transmission also proved a drag on receiver sales. By 2009, only a small minority of radio households owned a receiver able to tune terrestrial digital signals, and questions were being raised about when the service might become viable.

See also: Automobile Radio; Capeheart Corporation; CONELRAD; Crystal Receivers; Digital Audio Broadcasting; Digital Satellite Radio; Dolby Noise Reduction; Early Wireless; Emerson Radio; General Electric; Ham Radio; Motorola; Philco Radio; Radio Broadcast Data System; Radio Corporation of America; Shortwave Radio; Stereo; Transistor Radios; Walkman; Westinghouse; Zenith Radio Corporation

Further Reading

Collins, Philip, *Radios: The Golden Age*, San Francisco, California: Chronicle Books, 1987.

Douglas, Alan, *Radio Manufacturers of the 1920s*, 3 vols, Vestal, New York: Vestal Press, 1988–91.

Geddes, Keith, and Gordon Bussey, *The Setmakers: A History of the Radio and Television Industry*, London: British Radio and Electronic Equipment Manufacturers' Association, 1991.

Grinder, Robert E., and George H. Fathauer, *The Radio Collector's Directory and Price Guide*, Scottsdale, Arizona: Ironwood Associates, 1986.

Hill, Jonathan, *The Cat's Whisker: 50 Years of Wireless Design*, London: Oresko Books, 1977.

Hill, Jonathan, *Radio! Radio!* Bampton, England: Sunrise Press, 1986; 3rd edition, 1996.

McMahon, Morgan E., *Vintage Radio: 1887–1929*, Palos Verdes Estates, California: Vintage Radio, 1973.

McMahon, Morgan E., *Flick of the Switch, 1930–1950*, Palos Verdes Estates, California: Vintage Radio, 1975.

The Old Timers' Bulletin, Breesport, New York: Antique Wireless Association, 1960– (quarterly).

"Radio Broadcasting Receivers," in *Statistics on Radio and Telvision, 1950–1960*, Paris: Unesco, 1963.

Schiffer, Michael Brian, *The Portable Radio in American Life*, Tucson: University of Arizona Press, 1991.

Sideli, John, *Classic Plastic Radios of the 1930s and 1940s*, New York: Dutton, 1990.

Stokes, John W., *70 Yeaars of Radio Tubes and Valves: A Guide for Electronic Engineers, Historians and Collectors*, Vestal, New York: Vestal Press, 1982.

Tyne, Gerald F.J., *Saga of the Vacuum Tube*, Indianapolis, Indiana: Howard W. Sams, 1977.

CHRISTOPHER H. STERLING,
2009 REVISIONS BY CHRISTOPHER H. STERLING

RECORDING AND STUDIO EQUIPMENT

From the carbon microphones used by the early radio experimenters to the virtual studio of today, radio equipment has evolved to meet the demands of changing programming strategies. In the earliest days of radio, the equipment used to create programs was very basic. The radio operator spoke into a microphone connected to a transmitter. Soon, radio control rooms were equipped with mixing consoles to mix and route microphones, remote lines, network feeds, and transcription players. In the 1950s, tape recorders were added to the equipment inventory of the best-equipped radio studios. In the 1960s, broadcast cartridge recorders and players were adopted by broadcasters as the industry standard for recording and playback of commercials and other short-form production.

In the 21st century, the basic functions of recording, editing, and playback are still central to the production process at all radio stations, but the choice of type and brand of equipment is extensive. At many radio stations, most of the recording and studio equipment is now digital, and the computer hard disk and other digital alternatives are the storage media of choice. The typical production and on-air studios of today are equipped with a variety of microphones, mixers, and consoles, analog and/or digital recording and playback equipment, audio processing equipment, and monitors. This essay describes the typical recording and audio equipment that either has been used or is being used in radio studios to meet production needs.

Microphones

The microphone is the most fundamental of all the recording and studio equipment in use today. Most radio production usually starts with a microphone. A microphone is a transducer: it changes the sound energy of an announcer's voice, musical instrument, or other sound into an electrical signal that can then be mixed with other microphones and audio sources to create the radio program. Depending on production requirements and budget, a number of different types of microphones have been used in radio broadcasting.

Microphones can be classified by the method of creating the electrical signal, or the means of transducing the sound. Adapted from their applications in telephones, carbon microphones were the first microphones used in radio. As the carbon microphone was prone to distortion and easily damaged, it was soon replaced by more durable and accurate microphones. Dynamic, or moving-coil, microphones use a diaphragm attached to a moving coil in a magnetic field to generate electrical energy. The dynamic microphone is accurate and fairly inexpensive, making it popular for both studio and remote situations. The Electro-Voice RE-20 and Shure SM-7 are two of the most commonly used dynamic microphones in radio studios today.

Condenser (or more accurately, capacitor) microphones use a built-in battery or phantom power supply from a console or mixer to charge a conductive diaphragm and backplate, creating a changing capacitance that generates the electrical signal. Condenser microphones, because of their wide frequency response, are the microphones of choice in many radio studios.

A third type, the velocity (also known as ribbon) microphone, suspends a strip of corrugated aluminum ribbon in a magnetic field. When the ribbon is vibrated by the sound pressure, an electric current is generated. Although this type of microphone may still be found in some radio studios, the dynamic and condenser microphones are the microphones typically used in today's radio operations.

Microphones can also be classified by pickup patterns. A microphone's pickup pattern describes how the microphone responds to sound coming from different directions. There are three major types of pickup patterns: omnidirectional, bidirectional, and unidirectional. All three types have been or are being used extensively in radio production. An omnidirectional microphone picks up sound uniformly from all directions. The bidirectional pattern picks up sound best from the front and rear, rejecting sound from the sides. A unidirectional pattern picks up sound from the front.

A specific type of unidirectional pattern is the cardioid. Its heart-shaped pattern picks up sound best from the front, with more rejection as the sound source moves to the back. Subcategories of the cardioid pattern are the supercardioid, hypercardioid, and ultracardioid. Each of these successively rejects more sound from the sides, focusing more narrowly on the area in front of the microphone pattern. The pickup pattern of a microphone is determined by the type of pickup element it uses together with the number, size, and positioning of ports in the microphone housing used to direct the pickup of sound. Specific production situations dictate the type of pattern to be used. An omnidirectional microphone works well to pick up a group of people gathered around a microphone. Bidirectional microphones were useful in producing radio dramas because the actors could face each other. Cardioid microphones are especially popular in modern radio production because of their ability to reject unwanted studio noises behind the microphone.

Audio Mixers and Consoles

The audio mixer or console is the focal point of operations in a radio or recording studio. A mixer or console is a device that selects, amplifies, routes, mixes, processes, and monitors input signals, sending the resulting output(s) to the transmitter, recorder, or other destination. A mixer is distinguished from a console in that the mixer is smaller and sometimes portable, and is used for basic production such as mixing the three or four audio sources typically used in a newscast or sportscast. An audio console or audio board is larger and more complex, sometimes with 20 or more channels providing space for the numerous audio selection and processing options needed regularly in on-air and production situations. The console used for on-air operations is designed to be easy to use and efficient in selecting, controlling, and mixing the sources typically needed during a live radio program. The production console, because it is used in recording situations, often has a completely different design and layout from an on-air console. Flexibility, in terms of assigning and processing inputs and outputs, is the key to production console design.

On-Air Console

The electronics and design of on-air consoles have changed significantly from the early days when consoles were large, custom-designed, vacuum-tube units with large rotary controls that dominated the studio. Today's solid state, often digital, fader-control consoles meet the same needs as those first audio consoles. The on-air console is used to select, mix, and control the audio signals used to create the on-air programming of the station. This console's main purpose is to facilitate the simultaneous playback of several microphones, compact disc (CD) players, broadcast cartridge players, and other audio playback equipment. The primary output of this console is typically fed to the final audio processing and on to the transmitter.

Most on-air consoles have similar standard features and layouts. Variation comes from the number of channels and sources that can be connected to the console and special features in processing and monitoring the inputs and outputs. The number of channels on the on-air consoles varies greatly. In small or mostly automated stations, a console with six channels may handle all required operations; stations with complex live programming may have an on-air console with 20 or more channels. Each of these channels has a linear fader control that increases the output of the channel as it is pushed up, allowing the operator to visually monitor the settings of the channels. Each channel usually has two, three, or more selectable inputs to allow alternative sources to be selected depending on specific requirements. For example, channel five on a console may have CD player one as the A input, minidisc player one as the B input, and reel one as the C input. Most on-air consoles have two or three outputs, often labeled program, audition, and utility. Each channel can be assigned individually to program, audition, or utility. The program output is often fed directly to the on-air audio processing equipment and then on to the transmitter. The audition output is often fed to recording equipment, to record telephone calls off-air, for example. Some facilities use the audition and utility feeds to send program material to a second radio station or other location. These outputs usually have corresponding VU (Volume Unit) or LED (Light Emitting Diode) meters to allow for visual monitoring of the audio outputs. The console will also have switchable monitoring of these outputs using loudspeakers and/or headphones. On-air consoles also have a completely separate monitoring circuit called "cue" to allow the operator to preview or cue the audio before it is added to the mix. Each channel, where appropriate, has remote start/stop capability to control an audio source such as a tape recorder or CD player. Other standard console features typically include a digital clock/timer, built-in connection circuits for adding telephones as audio sources, and intercom circuits to facilitate communication with announcers in other studios.

Production Console

Until the 1970s, equipment in most radio production studios was not significantly different from equipment in on-air studios. Each studio was equipped with a console, microphone(s), open-reel audiotape recorder, broadcast cartridge (cart) player, and turntables. A broadcast cart recorder and perhaps additional open-reel audio recorders and audio processing distinguished the studio used for production from the on-air studio. As the popularity of stereo FM radio increased after 1961 and affordable multitrack tape recorders were introduced, the motivation and the means existed to create more elaborate commercial and program productions. The contemporary radio production console reflects this more complex approach. The console is designed to facilitate concurrent selection of more audio sources, compound audio processing of the various signals, and provide flexibility in routing inputs and outputs depending on the specific needs of the production project.

Much of contemporary radio production, especially in larger markets, begins as a multitrack recording project. Generally, multitrack recording involves a two-stage process. In the first stage, the different elements of the production are each recorded individually, at full volume, on separate tracks. The second stage involves playing back all of the separate tracks concurrently, adjusting the relative outputs to their appropriate levels, and mixing down to two-track stereo. This procedure provides a more efficient method of changing one or any combination of elements without re-recording all the elements. Experiments with the mix can be conducted without affecting the final recording. The production console needed to support this method provides the ability to route each of the tracks from a multitrack recorder to a separate fader for adjustment and processing during mixdown.

Digital Console

Digital consoles, which came into widespread use in the early 2000s, accept the digital output of CD players, hard disk recorders, and other digital sources without conversion to analog for the purpose of routing and mixing. Maintaining the signal in digital form minimizes the possibility of noise and other artifacts introduced during conversion to analog and reconversion back to digital. The continuity of the digital signal can be maintained throughout the audio chain. A digital console is different from an analog console in that the audio controls on the surface of the digital console are not physically connected to the audio circuitry. The controls are actuators that send digital control signals to the circuitry to carry out the console functions. These digital signals are commands that can be stored, grouped, recalled, and assigned as needed to various channels. This process creates simplicity and flexibility, allowing console size to remain compact and efficient to operate.

The digital console also provides sample-rate standards conversion and synchronization, converting differing standards from different equipment to one station standard. The CD uses a sampling rate of 44.1 kHz, or 44.1 thousand times per second, to measure the height of the analog signal. Hard disk audio systems usually sample at 32 kHz, whereas digital audiotape uses a 48 kHz rate. The console can generate one standard and all devices can be converted to it, along with providing a reference signal for synchronization.

Most digital consoles also accept analog inputs (open-reel audiotape recorder, microphones, etc.) and provide analog to digital conversion for insertion of these sources into the digital air chain. The console has been the last piece of major radio production equipment to complete its evolution to digital. At the same time, digital developments have, in some respects, eliminated the need for the hard-wired console.

Virtual Console

As more production is created in the digital domain, there becomes less need for an audio console to be a separate piece of hardware, manipulated by an operator. Audio sources can be connected directly to a computer and the functions previously controlled by an operator working a console (such as source selection, routing, mixing, and processing) can be programmed on the computer screen as a software function. In essence, the same process described above for digital console operation can take place entirely within the computer. The virtual console is usually a component of many hard disk recording systems. The console may simply be used to select and route audio sources for two track recording and editing or the console may be the starting point for a complex multitrack recording and editing session. Radio has come a long way from the early days of recording programs on transcription discs.

Transcription Disc Recorder

The earliest recording method used in radio was the transcription disc recorder. Modified from the early phonograph technologies, radio stations began using the transcription recorders and players in the 1920s. By the 1930s, most of the larger radio stations had transcription disc recorders. The recording process used a 16-inch flat disc of aluminum or glass covered with cellulose nitrate in which a lateral or vertical groove was cut. The transcription was cut at a speed of 33 1/3-rpm and provided a transcription time of 15 minutes. These discs were used by affiliate stations to record network programs and play them back at a later time, by program producers to distribute non-network programs to stations, and by local stations to record their own programs for rebroadcast or air check purposes. Even after the introduction of the magnetic tape recorder, the use of transcription recordings continued into the late 1950s.

Open-Reel Audiotape Recorder

The analog open-reel audiotape recorder was introduced to radio in the United States after World War II. Both Rangertone and Ampex Corporation manufactured professional open-reel audiotape recorders based on the designs brought back from

Germany. The analog open-reel audiotape recorder has been an integral part of every radio studio since then. At first, recorders were monaural, recording and playing one track. The two track recorder was then introduced and, as FM radio and stereo transmission developed, soon became the recording standard.

The fundamentals of tape recorder technology have changed little since the tape recorder's introduction. The audiotape used today (when it is used at all, that is) is of better quality, resulting in better fidelity and lower noise, but the electronic principles and mechanics of operation are largely unchanged.

The main components of the open-reel audio tape recorder are the magnetic heads, the tape transport mechanics, the recording and playback electronics, and the tape itself. The magnetic heads of the recorder are the focal point in the process of recording audio on a tape and reading audio from a tape in order to recreate it. There are three heads in a professional recorder, mounted left to right in the following order: erase, record, playback. The tape goes past the erase head first, where any previous signal recorded on the tape is removed during the record function. At the record head, if the tape recorder has been placed in the record mode and a signal is being sent to input of the recorder, this signal will be deposited on the tape, magnetizing the metal particles present on the tape to create an analog of the original sound waves. This signal is now stored on the tape, and as the tape passes the playback head, the arranged magnetized particles create an electrical signal representing the original sound, which is then sent to the output section of the tape recorder electronics.

A tape recorder can be described by the number of tracks it can record or play. A recorder with one head each for erase, record, and play is a one (full) track monaural recorder. Its record and playback electronics are configured using one channel. A recorder with two heads is a two channel, two (or half) track stereo recorder. A recorder with four heads is a four channel, four track recorder. Larger radio production facilities will often have four or eight track recorders available for multitrack radio production. Because multitrack recordings are typically mixed down to two track stereo for on-air playback, the most common audiotape recorder used in radio is the two track stereo recorder.

The open-reel tape transport mechanism is designed primarily to move the tape past the heads at a consistent, exact speed. Tape speeds used in radio are seven-and-a-half inches per second (ips) and 15 ips. Tape reels of seven inches, holding 1200 feet of one-and-a-half mil (thousandths of an inch) tape will record and play for 30 minutes at seven and a half ips. Tape reels measuring 10.5 inches will hold 2400 feet of one-and-a-half mil tape for 60 minutes at seven-and-a-half ips. The tape transport system consists of the motors and tensioning systems to move the tape efficiently from supply side to take-up side. The key component in this process is the capstan and pinch roller. The capstan turns at a precise speed while the pinch roller holds the tape against the capstan, pulling the tape past the heads at the selected speed. Any variation in speed or interference in the transport process will result in inaccurate recording or reproduction. Most recorders also have some type of tape counter to display elapsed time or the amount of tape used.

The open-reel audiotape recorder also has electronic circuitry to support the recording and playback processes. Professional recorders typically have both microphone and line level inputs with individual level adjustments for each channel. The line level input accepts outputs from the console or other equipment, including other recorders. The record mode can be engaged separately for each channel as well. This feature, combined with a feature often called Sel Sync (Selective Synchronization) or Sel Rep (Selective Reproduction) allows the user to listen to material recorded on one channel while recording on the other channel in synchronization with the playback channel. Professional recorders also have monitor selector switches, one for each channel, that allow listening to the source audio at the input or the audio coming from the playback head. These monitor select switches also control the signal sent to the VU meter for visual monitoring of the audio. Output level controls for each channel are also part of the electronics of a professional recorder.

The audiotape itself is an important component of the recording process. Better quality tape costs more but provides better reproduction and long-term storage. Inexpensive tapes will deteriorate faster, causing audio dropouts and flaking of the magnetic oxide coating. Tape thickness is either one or one-and-a-half mils (thousandths of an inch). Open-reel audiotape is available in quarter-, half-, one-, or two-inch widths. The quarter-inch tape is used with full track, two track, and some four track recorders. Multitrack recorders of four or more tracks use half-inch or wider tape. The two-inch tape is used on recorders that record and play 16 or 24 tracks used in professional recording applications.

Broadcast Cartridge Recorder/Player

Shortly after the open-reel audiotape recorder became a mainstay of the radio production process,

the development of the broadcast tape cartridge and recorder/player created another major refinement in the ability of radio to efficiently record and reproduce content. The cartridge recorder and player were introduced to radio in the late 1950s. Using a quarter-inch tape traveling at seven-and-a-half ips, the tape is spliced into an endless loop wound on a single hub so that it comes out from the center of the reel, travels past the record/playback heads, and is rewound on the outside of the hub. A cue tone recorded on the tape when the start button is pressed in the record mode is sensed by the player during playback mode, stopping the tape at exactly the start of the message. A standard sized cartridge allows recording times of five seconds to ten minutes. Multiple messages can be recorded on one cart; each has its own cue (stop) tone. At one time, recording and dubbing carts was the primary activity in any radio production facility. Commercials, jingles, music, news actualities, and any program or message shorter than ten minutes was recorded on a cart. Almost every radio station used carts until the late 1990s, when digital media rapidly began to replace them.

Digital Recording, Playback, and Editing Equipment

The development of digital audio recording and playback equipment has introduced major changes in radio recording and production. The changeover from analog to digital started with the compact disc player. The once ubiquitous turntable is now almost non-existent in radio studios. Radio quickly adopted the CD as a playback medium for music and other programs. A read-only medium until recently, CD recorders and re-writeable CDs are now being used in radio for a variety of purposes, including program production and archival storage.

Digital versions of the audiotape recorder are also being used in radio production. The rotary-head digital audiotape recorder (R-DAT) uses a helical scanning process very similar to that used in a video cassette recorder to record the digital information necessary to encode CD-quality two-channel stereo audio on a small cassette tape. The open-reel stationary head digital tape recorder manufactured today is a multitrack recorder with 24 or 48 tracks, and because of its complexity it is generally found in professional recording studios rather than in radio production studios.

Introduced as a consumer application, the digital minidisc combines the laser optical technology of the CD with the magnetic recording process of tape. The minidisc format has been adopted by many radio stations because it provides digital-quality recording, random access, and portability for field recording, all at a more modest cost than many other digital recording and playback systems. In these facilities, the minidisc recorder/player has replaced the cart recorder/player for recording and playing back short-form programs, announcements, and messages.

Digital options for recording, storing, and playing back radio programming have increased dramatically in recent years. Another option is now the hard disk of a computer. When a sound card is added to a computer with sufficient speed and a large enough hard drive, the computer can effectively replace a tape recorder. As the cost of hard drives has decreased and disk storage space has increased, recording audio on hard drives has rapidly become a viable alternative to tape and disk-based audio recording systems in radio stations. The tapeless digital radio studio exists in many different configurations and formats.

Hard disk recording systems used in radio include self-contained units such as the 360 Systems Shortcut, a hard disk two track recorder/editor, and the 360 Systems Instant Replay, a hard disk audio player, capable of playing back up to 1,000 different audio cuts when a button is pushed. Another approach to the hard disk system is the software-based integrated system installed on a personal computer. The Enco Digital Audio Delivery system and Arrakis Digilink are two of the many examples of this approach to digital audio. These systems integrate, in varying combinations, the mixing and routing functions of a console, audio editing and processing, playback, and automation functions into a single unit. Although hard disk recording allows efficiency, quality, and creativity not possible with tape-based systems, broadcasters must contend with a new set of interface and technical support issues as they adopt these technologies. Hard disks can fail without warning. Where these systems completely replace tape and cartridge-based playback systems, some type of drive redundancy or removable tape or disk-based back-up is a necessary component of the system.

Once cost-prohibitive for many radio stations, digital multitrack recording and editing is now a key feature of much of the digital recording software and equipment. Many of the products are software-based so that any computer with a sound card and a large hard drive can become a digital recorder/editor. Many are self-contained units capable of recording eight, sixteen, or more tracks onto a built-in hard disk, Hi-8 videotape, or removable disk or tape system. Many of these devices

are capable of being synchronized together using MIDI (Musical Instrument Digital Interface) or SMPTE (Society for Motion Picture and Television Engineers) time code so that the number of recording tracks can be expanded.

Digital recording has also changed the methods of editing audio. The process of recording over material to be replaced, dubbing to a new tape, or physically marking, cutting, and splicing the audio tape to remove or insert material has largely been replaced by a virtual editing process that takes place on the computer screen. A visual representation of the waveform of the audio to be edited is displayed on the computer screen or LCD (Liquid Crystal Diode) panel of the hard disk editor. Various editing functions can be carried out by marking and highlighting segments of the waveform. Material can be cut from one file and pasted into another. Adjustments can be made to the beginning and ending points of the audio file. The whole file or just a portion can be programmed to loop continuously. Files can be combined in a virtual over-dubbing mode. Increasingly, of course, use of any type of "hard" audio storage media (e.g., a cassette or CD) is decreasing as even the smallest stations increasingly use digital audio files, which can be stored, edited, and shared via computer work stations.

Audio Processing

In addition to the audio sources, console, and recording devices, most radio recording studios have additional equipment to process the audio for creative and technical reasons. There are four general categories of audio processing: frequency, amplitude, time, and noise. An equalizer is a type of frequency processor, increasing or decreasing selected parts of a sound's frequency response. Equalizer controls are included on many production consoles and in digital audio software programs and are used to refine and enhance the sounds during the recording or production. An amplitude processor is used to control the volume of the audio. Compressors and limiters are commonly used to even out the level of audio. Reverberation and echo units are time processing units that give a sound a distinctive characteristic. Noise reduction processors such as Dolby and DBX units help lower noise caused by analog recording and electronics. Audio processing today is often created digitally, allowing multiple functions to be manipulated. Some processing and effects equipment uses MIDI as an interface system to connect to synthesizers, keyboards, samplers, and other electronic equipment for creative control purposes in radio production.

Monitors

Every studio needs at least one pair of monitor speakers in order to hear the production being created. A speaker performs the exact opposite function from a dynamic microphone; electrical energy is transduced into sound energy when the electrical energy representing the sound is sent through two wires into a magnetic field at the back of the speaker. A moving coil and speaker cone suspended in this field are induced to vibrate by this electrical energy, causing surrounding air molecules to vibrate, creating sound analogous to the original sound. In critical production and recording situations, the monitors must be capable of accurately reproducing the sound from the audio that has been mixed and recorded. Most speakers used as radio studio monitors are dynamic speakers. A separate woofer is used to reproduce the lower frequencies and a tweeter reproduces the higher frequencies. A crossover is an electronic circuit that sends lower frequencies to the woofer and higher frequencies to the tweeter. An acoustic suspension design has speakers and crossover mounted in a sealed box enclosure. The bass reflex design uses a tuned port to release some of the lower frequency sound from the rear of the speaker to combine with the main sound of the speakers, resulting in stronger bass sound. Typically, radio studio speakers are hung from the ceiling or mounted on the walls behind the audio console. This placement, with the speakers slightly angled in toward the operating position, enables the operator to accurately hear the stereo imaging in the mixed sound. Since an open microphone near a monitor speaker will cause feedback, in radio studios a mute circuit is usually used so that when a microphone is turned on, the monitor speaker will be muted. Headphones are worn so that the operator or other personnel may continue to hear the mixed audio while the microphone is on.

Studios

At the beginning of radio broadcasting, studios did not exist; the announcer used a microphone connected directly to the transmitter, housed in whatever space was available, often in a garage or shack. As the process of creating live radio programs grew more sophisticated, so did the studios. Soon the engineers and equipment were housed in a control room, separated from the performers (and often studio audiences) in the studio. A variety of materials including burlap, plush velour curtains, and solid surface baffles were used to control the acoustics of the studios. Larger stations and networks constructed very elaborate and large studio complexes, rich in architectural design and isolated from the rest of the building through special suspensions. Some studios were large enough to seat full orchestras and large studio audiences.

As radio began to rely on local programs featuring recorded music, radio stations began to build smaller, more specialized studios. Initially, most stations relied on an engineer to operate the audio console and adjust the transmitter from the control room while the announcer or program host remained in the announcer booth, receiving cues through the glass separating the two rooms. As transmitters became more stable and stations looked for ways to cut costs, it soon became common for the announcer to also engineer his or her own program. This operational change resulted in a smaller radio studio where the announcer stands or sits at a microphone and console, surrounded by other necessary equipment within easy reach. Although proper acoustic design and isolation is still important in these contemporary studios, audio processing helps overcome acoustical problems. Digital remote equipment also minimizes the need for radio studios. A telephone line and a digital encoder/decoder set make it possible for a radio station to be able to have a studio virtually anywhere.

That the relationship of radio broadcasters and the recording industry was changing, however, became increasingly evident by the end of the first decade of the 21st century. Both radio and the recording businesses were under pressure from competition from internet audio services and growing consumer downloading. As a result, CD sales were down sharply (and many record stores, including several large chains, closed their doors). In the face of this decline in sales, the radio business's stagnating audiences seemed to offer a declining promotional value for the record labels—or so they argued.

Despite the growing menu of competing distribution methods, however, radio remains a central element in the marketing of recordings and in launching new musical acts. This is evident in the recording industry's endless concert and CD promotions carried on radio—and even the cyclical reappearance of payola scandals. The experience of The Dixie Chicks also underlines the continuing symbiosis between radio and recordings. The singers ran into a political backlash after one member made some unscripted remarks about President Bush while the Chicks were performing in London in 2003—and many radio groups and individual station owners pulled their music off the air. Their record sales dropped sharply and a national tour was only partially successful. Despite winning some top recording awards four years later, The Dixie Chicks have been unable to rebuild their top-selling careers without radio exposure.

In 2007 the labels formed the musicFIRST Coalition to lobby Congress for a revision to the nation's copyright laws, requiring radio broadcasters to pay for the use of any recorded music they used. Although standard for satellite and internet-based radio services, such payments had never been required for broadcasters. Terrestrial broadcasters' long-expressed argument had been that exposure of recordings over the air was vital to both businesses —it provided radio programming that attracted listeners, but also encouraged those listeners to purchase music they often first heard over the air and found that they liked. The music-FIRST argument was that in the 21st century, such a trade-off no longer makes sense, especially as the satellite and online providers of music *are* paying. Under their phrase, "fair pay for air play," the coalition sought equity from broadcasters. A major battle between the coalition and the National Association of Broadcasters was building on Capitol Hill as this volume went to press.

See also: Audio Processing; Audiotape; Automation; Control Board/Audio Mixer; Digital Recording; Dolby Noise Reduction; High Fidelity; Production for Radio; Stereo

Further Reading

Adams, Michael H., and Kimberly K. Massey, *Introduction to Radio: Production and Programming*, Madison, Wisconsin: Brown and Benchmark, 1995.
Alten, Stanley R., *Audio in Media*, Belmont, California: Wadsworth, 1981; 5th edition, 1999.
Burroughs, Lou, *Microphones: Design and Application*, Plainview, New York: Sagamore, 1974.
Crews, Albert R., *Radio Production Directing*, Boston and New York: Houghton Mifflin, 1944.
Hausman, Carl, Lewis B. O'Donnell, and Philip Benoit, *Modern Radio Production*, Belmont, California: Wadsworth, 1986; 5th edition, Belmont, California, and London: Wadsworth, 2000.
Kefauver, Alan P., *Fundamentals of Digital Audio*, Madison, Wisconsin: A-R Editions, 1998.
Keith, Michael C., *Radio Production: Art and Science*, Boston: Focal Press, 1990.
Keith, Michael C., and Joseph M. Krause, *The Radio Station*, Boston: Focal Press, 1986; 5th edition, by Keith, Boston and Oxford: Focal Press, 2000.
Oringel, Robert S., *Audio Control Handbook*, New York: Hastings House, 1956; 6th edition, Boston: Focal Press, 1989.
Reese, David E., and Lynne S. Gross, *Radio Production Worktext: Studio and Equipment*, Boston: Focal Press, 1990; 3rd edition, 1998.
Rumsey, Francis, and Tim McCormick, *Sound and Recording: An Introduction*, Oxford and Boston: Focal Press, 1992; 3rd edition, 1997.
Siegel, Bruce H., *Creative Radio Production*, Boston: Focal Press, 1992.
Talbot-Smith, Michael, *Broadcast Sound Technology*, London and Boston: Butterworths, 1990; 2nd edition, Oxford and Boston: Focal Press, 1995.
Talbot-Smith, Michael, editor, *Audio Engineer's Reference Book*, Oxford: Focal Press, 1994; 2nd edition, 1999.
Watkinson, John, *An Introduction to Digital Audio*, Boston and Oxford: Focal Press, 1994.
Watkinson, John, *The Art of Sound Reproduction*, Woburn, Massachusetts: Focal Press, 1998.

JEFFREY D. HARMAN,
2009 REVISIONS BY CARY O'DELL

RECORDINGS AND THE RADIO INDUSTRY

The radio business and music recording industry have been symbiotically related from the inception of broadcasting in the 1920s. Although live music performed on radio initially devastated the record business, radio's improved technology later helped to revitalize the manufacture of recordings. As radio shifted in the 1950s from programs to formats, popular recorded rock music became a staple on the air. Music played on radio promoted record sales—indeed, radio and records (the title of one trade periodical) became virtually inseparable.

Origins

However, radio's relationship with recordings was not so close at first; the two were separated by their differing technologies. Although records were played on some early experimental broadcasts, and on smaller market stations in the 1920s, generally radio avoided the use of recorded music. This was due in part to the poor quality of the largely mechanical recordings of the time, and in part to a widely held feeling that radio should not merely play recordings people could easily buy on their own. This tradition of live radio carried over to the networks as they began forming in the late 1920s. Stations and networks provided hours of live music programming of all types, popular to classical, and the best techniques of studio design and microphone placement became issues of scientific analysis.

Live music on radio nearly doomed the record industry. The poor quality of mechanically recorded records could not hold up to the higher quality of live singing and orchestral music on the air. As record sales declined sharply, many firms left the business. Radio's technology came to the rescue in the form of the electrical transcription (ET). Developed in the late 1920s to allow longer recording times (up to 15 minutes on a side), the 33 1/3 rpm discs featured better frequency response through all-electronic means of recording. They were typically used by stations (WOR in New York was one of the first) to record and sometimes to archive programs. ETs encouraged the development of program syndication as well. Initial attempts failed to sell the better quality 33 1/3 format as commercial records, probably because requiring consumers to buy a new record player in the depths of the Depression was doomed from the start.

The big band music of the 1930s and 1940s was programmed widely on radio and helped to revive record sales. Many programs featured top singers and orchestras whose records were often promoted on the shows. Musicians had plenty of live venues at which to play, and radio carried many of them. At the same time, however, worries about recordings concerned the American Federation of Musicians, which instituted two strikes in the 1940s to preserve live radio in the face of some pressure to allow greater use of recordings.

Even as recording methods improved, the standard commercial recording, a 78-rpm disc, could still play only a few minutes on a side. World War II delayed further progress on all consumer products, but wartime research would contribute to a postwar revolution.

Postwar Revolution

When popular singer Bing Crosby heard about audiotape recording, he offered his top-rated program to a new network (ABC) on the condition that they allow him to record the show to avoid having to perform it twice each time for the East and West Coast time zones. Although networks had stoutly resisted the use of recordings on the air save in emergency situations, ABC was desperate for a popular star to build its competitive position. Crosby got his wish, and the ban on use of recordings began to waste away in the face of this new means of making high-quality recordings that sounded almost live.

In 1947–48, engineers at CBS Laboratories, working under Peter C. Goldmark, developed a considerably enhanced 33 1/3 rpm record that squeezed in more grooves on each side of a 12-inch disc. Other parts of the system were also upgraded,

including the vinyl from which the record was made, the stylus, microphones, amplifiers, and record players themselves. The "microgroove" long-playing (LP) records, with 20–25 minutes of music on each side, were a sensation when introduced on the market. Now consumers could hear opera or symphony concerts without annoying record changes every few minutes. Shortly thereafter, RCA introduced its own version of the improved records, a 45-rpm 7-inch disc, called "extended play" (EP) designed particularly for popular songs. Soon "the 45" became the standard form for selling popular music, while "the 33" was the standard album for longer-form music. Record players were designed to switch among the three speeds, although the 78 quickly disappeared. The most expensive console models combined radios (and soon televisions) with the record player.

As new radio stations flooded onto the air in the late 1940s and the 1950s, they sought programs to attract listeners and advertisers. Live programming was expensive, whereas the use of records was cheaper and thus far more profitable. The result was more playing of recordings on the air—unheard of a mere few years earlier. At the same time a quest for high-fidelity (hi-fi) began to spread from Britain, encouraging an interest in better sound. The new FM stations catered to this interest as did a market for often expensive sound systems. But more attention—and far more money—was focused on the mid-1950s rise of rock-and-roll music.

Rock music saved radio as the networks gave way to television competition. As the Top 40 music system developed in the mid-1950s, record sales grew modestly. After the rise of Elvis Presley in 1956, the growth in sales of 45 and 33 rpm records through the end of the decade was more than 125 percent over previous years. The payola scandal late in the decade served to underline what everyone in the business now understood—that radio's on-air "plays" were essential to popular record sales just as the existence of those records was vital to radio's success. Though more closely controlled after 1960, music companies continued to provide free or heavily discounted records to radio stations to encourage their inclusion on program playlists, and thus to promote record sales.

Record sales continued to skyrocket into the 1960s. Capitalizing on the popularity of rock, radio programmed more of it—and record companies produced more recordings. Radio and records were both aimed at a youthful audience with expendable income, listeners of increasing interest to advertisers. By the 1970s the splintering of music formats as well as the increasing separation of programs between AM and FM stations provided more outlets for recorded music of all types.

Radio's continuing popularity clearly affected music types and formats. "Crossover" music became more common: a specialized recording (say, a country song) might begin to sell well more broadly in the pop music market. Or a specialized song might sell well in another niche market. A crossover can be accidental, but most often it is the result of a deliberate attempt by a music company to bring a song or performer to the attention of more buyers to increase sales. Crossovers have become more common since the 1950s. The constant changing of their music formats by many radio stations has encouraged this constant mixing and changing of musical types.

Modern Era

The arrival of television and especially cable TV channels changed radio's role. By the late 1980s, radio was no longer the sole broadcast outlet for recorded music as listeners flocked to music concerts and channels offering video with sound. Radio remained the most mobile means of listening to music.

Development of the relatively short-lived cartridge and then cassette audio recording devices aided not only radio stations, but also consumers who could now more readily travel with their recordings. The appearance of compact disc (CD) recordings in 1984 soon displaced the LP as the standard consumer recording format, and the even higher capacity of DVDs may do the same to CDs in the early 21st century. Through all these recording format changes, however, radio (along with some cable music channels) continued largely to define what music America liked.

In the late 1990s, internet streaming of music added yet another channel of music delivery to consumers. While the internet offered radio stations far greater reach, this development directly threatened music companies as listeners could download digital copies of desired music without buying it. A host of legal cases, especially involving an internet service called Napster, tested what could and could not be offered online, generally having the effect of limiting downloads only to music that customers paid for. Even here, however, the relationship of music delivery and sales was somewhat symbiotic as recordings (CDs or tapes) were increasingly being sold online as well as through retail outlets.

See also: American Federation of Musicians; Contemporary Hit Radio/Top 40 Format; Internet Radio; Payola

Further Reading

Channan, Michael, *Repeated Takes: A Short History of Recording and Its Effects on Music*, London: Verso, 1995.
Compaine, Benjamin M., and Christopher H. Sterling, et al., *Who Owns the Media? Concentration of Ownership in the Mass Communications Industry*, New York: Harmony Books, 1979; 3rd edition, with subtitle *Competition and Concentration in the Mass Media Industry*, by Compaine and Douglas Gomery, Mahwah, New Jersey: Erlbaum, 2000.
Hickerson, Jay, *The Ultimate History of Network Radio Programming and Guide to All Circulating Shows*, Hamden, Connecticut: Hickerson, 1992; 3rd edition, as *The New, Revised, Ultimate History of Network Radio Programming and Guide to All Circulating Shows*, 1996.
Hull, Geoffrey P., *The Recording Industry*, New York: Allyn and Bacon, 1998.
Kenney, William Howland, *Recorded Music in American Life: The Phonograph and Popular Memory 1890–1945*, New York: Oxford University Press, 1999.
Millard, Andre, *America on Record: A History of Recorded Sound*, Cambridge and New York: Cambridge University Press, 1995.
Morton, David, *Off the Record: The Technology and Culture of Sound*, New Brunswick, New Jersey: Rutgers University Press, 2000.
The M Street Journal (1990–).
Radio and Records, www.rronline.com
Reinsch, John Leonard, *Radio Station Management*, New York: Harper, 1948; 2nd edition, by Reinsch and Elmo Israel Ellis, New York: Harper and Row, 1960.
Sanjek, Russell, and David Sanjek, *American Popular Music Business in the 20th Century*, New York: Oxford University Press, 1991.

Christopher H. Sterling

RE-CREATIONS OF EVENTS
Creative Use of Sound Effects

The term *re-creations* refers to the creative use of sound effects and other inputs to provide a program that is not what it appears to be. To an extent, any radio drama that uses sound effects to create in listeners a mental image involves re-creations. But the most famous examples in radio history involved the use of wire service reports (for the facts) and recorded sound effects (for the color, especially crowd noises such as applause and shouts) to encourage listeners to think they were listening to sports play-by-plays from an observer right on the field rather than, in fact, as visualized by an announcer often hundreds of miles from the scene.

In the early days of radio, news played a relatively small role in radio broadcasting. With entertainment programming serving as the main precedent for new programs, some early radio newscasters re-created events in the news. Given the available technology at the time, radio broadcasters found it difficult to easily produce actualities of people in the news, so the dramatizations of events in the news became a well-accepted substitute.

The best-known example of a news re-creation was *The March of Time*, a program produced by *Time* magazine. *Time* general manager Rob Edward Larsen and Fred Smith of WLW in Cincinnati originally produced a program in 1928 called *News-Casting*, a summary of the news syndicated to about 60 stations. (Larsen receives credit in some sources for coining the term "newscasting.") In late 1929, Smith hit upon the idea of dramatizing the news, and the Larsen–Smith team began producing a program called *News Acting*.

On 6 March 1931, *The March of Time* debuted on CBS, produced by Larsen and Smith and using actors, sound effects and music. The program took its name from its theme song *The March of Time*, composed by Ted Koehler and Harold Arlen. The script of the first program began: "Tonight, the editors of *Time*, the weekly newsmagazine, attempt a new kind of reporting of the news, the re-enacting as clearly and dramatically as the medium of radio will permit, some themes from the news of the week."

Many of the "historical" recordings of early radio broadcasting are, in fact, re-creations. Especially in the 1920s, most radio stations generally did not have the capability to record their programs. The legacy of *The March of Time* made such re-creations acceptable in the late 1940s and early 1950s when a number of records celebrating radio-station anniversaries were released. For example, the recording of "the first broadcast" of KDKA in Pittsburgh on election night, 1920, is actually a re-creation made in the mid-1930s.

Sports, especially baseball games, became popular occasions for radio re-creations. Until the late 1950s, major league baseball franchises were concentrated in the Northeast. No team was located farther west than St. Louis or farther south than Cincinnati. As a way of bringing major league games to vast areas of the nation without big-league teams of their own, radio stations began to re-create games that were taking place in ballparks around the country.

"Dutch" Reagan

Certainly the most famous of the re-creators, now if not then, is Ronald Reagan. "Dutch" Reagan, as he was then known, broadcast more than 600 re-creations of Chicago Cubs games on WOC in Davenport, Iowa, and WHO in Des Moines, Iowa, between 1933 and 1936. The future president's

system was typical of the play-by-play re-creators. Reagan sat in a radio studio in Des Moines, 300 miles away from Wrigley Field, and received a pitch-by-pitch description of the game in progress via telegraph. As Reagan described it many years later:

> Looking through the window I could see [the producer] "Curly" (complete with headphones) start typing. This was my cue to start talking. It would go something like this: "The pitcher (whatever his name happened to be) has the sign, he's coming out of the windup, there's the pitch," and at that moment Curly would slip me the blank. It might contain the information "S2C," and without a pause I would translate this into "It's a called strike breaking over the inside corner, making it two strikes on the batter."

Occasionally the telegraph line would fail and the announcer would have to improvise until it was restored. In those situations, the announcer had to use his wits, as Reagan once was forced to do in a game tied in the ninth inning:

> I knew of only one thing that wouldn't get in the score column and betray me—a foul ball. So I had Augie [Galan] foul this pitch down the left field foul line. I looked expectantly at Curly. He just shrugged helplessly, so I had Augie foul another one and still another. I described in detail the red-headed kid who had scrambled and gotten the souvenir ball. He fouled for six minutes and forty-five seconds until I lost count.

Gordon McLendon

Whereas Reagan's colorful exploits as a play-by-play re-creation announcer are well known because of his later fame as an actor and political figure, the person best known as a practitioner of the skill was Gordon McLendon, "the old Scotchman, 83-years-old this very day" (quoted in Garay, 1992). Recreations had been around since the earliest days of radio and were considered an "honorable practice of the time," according to famed sports broadcaster Lindsey Nelson. But McLendon elevated re-creation to an art with his productions of baseball on the Liberty Broadcasting System (LBS) in the late 1940s and early 1950s.

McLendon was the young owner of fledgling radio station KLIF in Dallas, Texas. One of his early programming ideas at KLIF was to re-create sporting events. In fact, his first re-creation was of a professional football game between the Detroit Lions and the Chicago Cardinals on the day that KLIF took the air, 7 November 1947. But baseball was McLendon's true love.

The leisurely pace of baseball has always allowed play-by-play announcers great freedom, and it was said that in re-creating baseball games, there were no limitations—the broadcaster's imagination could run wild. McLendon started recreating major league baseball games on KLIF in 1948. This soon led to the establishment of LBS. By 1951, 458 affiliates had joined LBS, and the network was second in size only to the Mutual Broadcasting System.

An important aspect of re-creations was the use of sound effects. Author Ronald Garay described McLendon's technique:

> Three or four turntables were kept spinning throughout the re-created games with disks containing the various crowd noises always cued on one or more of the turntables. What would be distinguishable above the crowd noise every so often would be a vendor hollering out the name of a sponsor's product. Gordon's passion for realism and accuracy led him to send an engineer to record every ballpark sound that a radio listener might expect to hear. [Engineer] Glenn Callison recorded many of the sounds at Burnett Field in Dallas. Gordon sent [technician] Craig La Taste to every major league baseball stadium in the country to record sounds identified with each particular stadium.

The success of a re-creation also depended, of course, on the skill of the individual announcer. Author Willie Morris, in his autobiography *North Toward Home* (1967), wrote of McLendon:

> His games were rare and remarkable entities; casual pop flies had the flow of history behind them, double plays resembled the stark clashes of old armies, and home runs deserved acknowledgement on earthen urns. Later, when I came across Thomas Wolfe, I felt I had heard him before, from Shibe Park, Crosley Field, or the Yankee Stadium.

McLendon himself described his approach this way:

> No picture that is shown on television could be possibly as vivid as the picture I painted in my own mind of a baseball game. To me those players were far bigger than life, and Ebbetts Field, even though there were 3,000 people there if you actually were broadcasting from the field, was always in my mind's eye crowded with 35,000 people. The walls were a thousand feet tall that those home runs were hit [over]. I could come out with a far more vivid picture than any that I could have ever painted from the baseball park itself.

The end of this creative but somewhat misleading use of the airwaves came in the early 1950s as both major- and minor-league audience attendance began to decline, in part owing to growing television coverage of the majors. A glimmer of the potential profits from controlling television and radio rights to their franchises pushed baseball

owners to forbid unauthorized use of the activities in their ballparks. They sharply increased the fees charged to LBS for game rights (from $1,000 for a whole season in 1949 to $225,000 just two years later) and then turned the matter over to individual baseball clubs for renegotiation and higher fees. Thirteen of the teams refused to grant LBS rights at all. This fee increase, in conjunction with the departure of key advertisers, spelled the end of re-created baseball games.

See also: Liberty Broadcasting System; *March of Time*; Sound Effects

Further Reading

Fielding, Raymond, *The March of Time, 1935–1951*, New York: Oxford University Press, 1978.
Garay, Ronald, *Gordon McLendon: The Maverick of Radio*, New York: Greenwood Press, 1992.
Harper, Jim, "Gordon McLendon: Pioneer Baseball Broadcaster," *Baseball History* 1 (Spring 1986).
Lichty, Lawrence W., and Thomas W. Bohn, "Radio's March of Time: Dramatized News," *Journalism Quarterly* 51, no. 3 (Autumn 1974).
Morris, Edmund, *Dutch: A Memoir of Ronald Reagan*, New York: Random House, and London: HarperCollins, 1999.
Morris, Willie, *North Toward Home*, Boston: Houghton Mifflin, 1967.
Nelson, Lindsey, *Hello Everybody, I'm Lindsay Nelson*, New York: Beech Tree Books, 1985.
Nelson, Lindsey, and Al Hirschberg, *Backstage at the Mets*, New York: Viking Press, 1966.
Smith, Curt, *Voices of the Game*, South Bend, Indiana: Diamond, 1987; updated and revised edition, New York: Simon and Schuster, 1992.
Wills, Garry, *Reagan's America: Innocents at Home*, Garden City, New York: Doubleday, and London: Heinemann, 1987; revised edition, New York: Penguin, 2000.

J.M. DEMPSEY

RED CHANNELS
1950 Blacklist

In 1950, as Julius and Ethel Rosenberg were being arrested for atomic spying and the Korean War was commencing, the American Business Consultants published *Red Channels, The Report of Communist Influence in Radio and Television*, which formalized the practice of blacklisting in the broadcasting industry. The publication listed 151 performers and artists who were deemed to be communist sympathizers ("fellow travelers" in 1950s parlance). Many of the personalities who were charged and others who were whispered about were denied employment in showbusiness.

The publication of *Red Channels* was an outgrowth of the investigation of communist infiltration of the motion pictures by the House on Un-American Activities (HUAC), chaired by Parnell Thomas in 1947. After World War II, as the Cold War developed between the United States and the Soviet Union, someone suspected of being a supporter of communist and, in many instances, liberal causes could be branded a traitor and forced to reveal his or her political ideology. There was a great concern among certain members of Congress and other patriotic organizations that writers, directors, and actors were using popular culture to spread their nefarious beliefs. Many studio and broadcasting executives, under pressure by the HUAC hearings and by advertiser concerns, agreed never to hire a known communist on staff.

Founded in 1947, the American Business Consultants was a private organization headed by three former Federal Bureau of Investigation agents: John G. Keenan, Kenneth Bierly, and Theodore Kirkpatrick. Proclaiming that the government's efforts had failed to combat the communist message, the group published a newsletter, *Counterattack: The Newsletter of Facts on Communism*, to "obtain, file, and index factual information on communists, communists fronts and other subversive organizations." The group canvassed volumes of the *Daily Worker*, pamphlets of leftist rallies, and unpublished findings of the HUAC committee to uncover names of potential traitors. In June 1950 they published their special report, *Red Channels*, a formal list of 151 people whom the Communist Party used as "'belts' to transmit pro-Sovietism to the American public." The report claimed that the Russians were using radio and television as a means of indoctrinating U.S. citizens even more than press or film. Many of radio's most influential and talented artists were cited, including producers/directors Himan Brown, Norman Corwin, and William Robson; personalities Ben Grauer, Henry Morgan, and Irene Wicker; and commentators Robert St. John, William L. Shirer, and Howard K. Smith. Some retribution was immediate: Wicker, the "Singing Lady" who had entertained children for years on radio, was dropped by her sponsor Kellogg, and Robson, who had directed many of *Columbia Workshop*'s innovative dramas, was mysteriously dismissed from his Columbia Broadcasting System (CBS) assignments, receiving payments until his contract expired.

Many of the 151 industry members were listed because they were social activists, from New Deal supporters to civil rights demonstrators. The writers of *Red Channels* (who were not credited by name)

admitted that not all those named were political radicals; in fact, some "dupes" advanced "communist objectives with complete unconsciousness." Nevertheless, everyone was under suspicion, and *Red Channels* became one of several blacklists circulating on Madison Avenue (though one of the only ones formally published), consulted by broadcasting executives, advertising agencies, and sponsors. Some performers were given the opportunity to recant their previous beliefs or risk being barred from the industry. For a fee, the American Business Consultants also advised radio and television producers as they were casting on which performers had problematic backgrounds.

With the publication of the 215-page *Red Channels*, many companies began to institutionalize blacklisting. CBS, considered the most progressive of the networks, demanded loyalty oaths from its employees and hired a vice president in charge of "security." The other networks quickly followed suit. Batten, Barton, Durstine, and Osborn legitimized the hiring of "security officers" to clear names for the advertising agencies. Both networks and agencies, working as quietly as possible behind the scenes, abided by one principle: don't hire controversial personnel, so that you won't have to fire them.

For many, the *Red Channels* list was the culmination of many years' worth of whispered accusations. Radio director William Sweets had been under investigation since the late 1940s. Sweets directed two hit series, *Gang Busters* and *Counterspy*, for the radio production company Phillips H. Lord, Inc. A charge had been made to the series' sponsors that Sweets, also national president of the Radio Directors Guild, had mandated that only communists could work for him. He was forced to resign and, following the distribution of *Red Channels*, had difficulty finding any employment. Sweets' difficulties were later attributed to Vince Harnett, who had worked in the Lord office and who became a specialist in communist infiltration. As a freelancer, he wrote the introduction to *Red Channels* and worked with Lawrence Johnson's supermarket chain in Syracuse, New York, to boycott products of sponsors that allegedly advertised on shows employing subversives.

The institutional pressure also affected radio news departments. William Shirer had been a member of "Murrow's boys" and was one of radio's most respected commentators. In 1947 he resigned from CBS when his news program lost its sponsor. The *New Republic* (13 January 1947, cited in Cloud and Olson, 1996) charged that after World War II, 24 liberal analysts, such as Shirer, were dropped by the radio networks because of objections from sponsors. Shirer did work for other stations, but after his name appeared in *Red Channels*, no major network regularly employed him again. Considering himself a victim of the blacklist paranoia, Shirer contended "that if the major networks had taken a firm stand in the beginning [by] making a fair determination of individual cases, this thing would never have gotten off the ground."

Before the dissemination of *Red Channels*, discrimination based on political reasons was informal and subjective. The publications of the American Business Consultants commenced systematic ideological screenings, although always behind closed doors. Such blacklisting also coincided with corporate pressures in broadcasting to make a profit in postwar America by pleasing the largest audience possible. Any controversy was strictly to be avoided. Even after the 1954 downfall of one of *Red Channels'* most ardent supporters, Senator Joseph McCarthy, the purging of subversive elements in the entertainment industry persisted quietly into the 1960s. In 1962, when a radio raconteur, John Henry Faulk, won a libel suit against *Counterattack* and other accusers, the mechanics of blacklisting finally became part of the public record just as the process died out.

See also: Blacklisting

Further Reading

Cloud, Stanley, and Lynne Olson, *The Murrow Boys: Pioneers on the Front Lines of Broadcast Journalism*, Boston: Houghton Mifflin, 1996.
Cogley, John, *Blacklisting: Radio-Television*, New York: Fund for the Republic, 1956.
Faulk, John Henry, *Fear on Trial*, New York: Simon and Schuster, 1964.
Foley, Karen Sue, *The Political Blacklist in the Broadcast Industry: The Decade of the 1950s*, New York: Arno Press, 1979.
Navasky, Victor S., *Naming Names*, New York: Viking Press, 1980.
Vaughn, Robert, *Only Victims: A Study of Show Business Blacklisting*, New York: Putnam, 1972.

RON SIMON

RED LION CASE
Landmark Supreme Court Decision

In this 1969 decision, the U.S. Supreme Court upheld the constitutionality of the Federal Communications Commission's (FCC) fairness doctrine and of related personal attack rules. These FCC regulations in some instances required broadcasters to air viewpoints with which they disagreed or to provide airtime to persons criticized by or on the stations. The case is important because it reaffirmed the notion that radio stations' use of a scarce public resource—the electromagnetic spectrum—justified a different First Amendment standard for broadcasting than for print media.

Although the case is commonly referred to as simply *Red Lion*, the court's decision involved a second lower court case as well, *United States v. Radio Television News Directors Association*. Because the two cases involved similar issues, the Supreme Court consolidated them and issued one opinion. The cases involved the FCC's fairness doctrine and a specific application of the doctrine known as the personal attack rules. Under the general fairness doctrine, all radio broadcasters had an affirmative duty to cover controversial issues of public importance in their programming and to provide a reasonable opportunity for all sides of the controversy to be aired. The personal attack rule stated that if a person's character, integrity, or honesty was attacked during the discussion of a controversial issue of public importance, the station airing the attack had to notify the person of the attack; provide a tape, transcript, or summary of the program; and afford the attacked person an opportunity to reply to the attack on the air.

The *Red Lion* litigation arose when WGCB, a radio station licensed to the Red Lion Broadcasting Company in southeastern Pennsylvania, aired a 15-minute syndicated program by the Reverend Billy James Hargis. During the program Hargis discussed a book, *Goldwater — Extremist on the Right*, written by Fred J. Cook. Hargis attacked Cook as being a communist sympathizer, a newspaper reporter who was fired for writing false charges against public officials, and a critic of J. Edgar Hoover and the FBI and of the Central Intelligence Agency. When Cook heard of the broadcast he demanded time to reply on the station pursuant to FCC policy. Red Lion refused, and the FCC ordered the company to afford Cook an opportunity to reply. Red Lion appealed the order, and the U.S. Court of Appeals for the District of Columbia Circuit upheld the FCC's decision. (Years later, respected journalist Fred Friendly alleged that Cook may have been working with the Democratic National Committee, using the fairness doctrine and the personal attack rule to harass stations that carried ultraconservative programming. In response, both Cook and the Committee insisted that Cook had acted alone.)

After the *Red Lion* litigation had begun, the FCC adopted specific regulations clarifying its personal attack rules. The Radio Television News Directors Association challenged the FCC's action in court, and the U.S. Court of Appeals for the Seventh Circuit ruled that the FCC's regulations violated the First Amendment free speech and free press rights of broadcast stations.

In its ruling on the consolidated cases, the Supreme Court confronted two primary legal issues: whether the FCC had jurisdiction under the Commimications Act to adopt the fairness doctrine and its related rules, and whether the policies abridged the free speech and free press rights of broadcasters. Justice Byron White wrote for a unanimous court. (Eight justices voted in the case. Because he had not participated in the oral arguments, Justice Douglas took no part in the Court's decision.)

With respect to the jurisdictional issue, the Court noted that the FCC had been given extensive powers to regulate in the public interest, convenience, and necessity. In previous cases, the power to regulate had been described by the Court as "not niggardly but expansive." The Court also cited various congressional actions that seemingly approved of the FCC's actions in adopting and enforcing the fairness doctrine. Given the Court's own precedents and the implied congressional approval of the FCC's actions, the Court determined that the FCC did in fact have the necessary authority under the act to establish the fairness doctrine and personal attack rules.

Regarding the constitutional issue, the Court first stated that broadcasting was clearly a medium protected by the First Amendment, but that differences in the characteristics of various media justified different treatment under the First Amendment. The Court then addressed the issue of spectrum scarcity. Because of the interference that would result, not everyone who wants to broadcast can do so; there is simply not enough spectrum for all would-be broadcasters. For this reason, Congress enacted legislation giving the FCC the authority to license and regulate broadcasting to serve the public interest. Justice White wrote that, given this scarcity of frequencies, "it is idle to posit an unabridgeable First Amendment right to broadcast comparable to the right of every individual to speak, write, or publish."

The Court determined that the public has a right to hear the voices of those who, because of spectrum scarcity, cannot speak through their own broadcast station. According to Justice White,

> Because of the scarcity of radio frequencies, the government is permitted to put restraints on licensees in favor of others whose views should be expressed on this unique medium. But the people as a whole retain their interest in free speech by radio and their collective right to have the medium function consistently with the ends and purposes of the First Amendment. It is the right of the viewers and listeners, not the right of the broadcasters, which is paramount. It is the purpose of the First Amendment to preserve an uninhibited marketplace of ideas in which truth will ultimately prevail, rather than to countenance monopolization of that market, whether it be by the government itself or a private licensee. It is the right of the public to receive suitable access to social, political, esthetic, moral, and other ideas and experiences which is crucial here. That right may not constitutionally be abridged either by Congress or the FCC.

Having found that the First Amendment rights of viewers and listeners to receive diverse viewpoints were paramount over the First Amendment rights of broadcasters to control the speech over their stations, the Court concluded that the fairness doctrine and its related regulations passed constitutional muster.

The *Red Lion* case is important not so much because of the individual disputes it settled but because of its lasting contribution to our understanding of the First Amendment rights of broadcasters. Even though the FCC stopped enforcing the fairness doctrine in 1987 and the personal attack rule in 2001, the case still stands for the proposition that, because of spectrum scarcity, the government can apply different First Amendment standards to broadcasting than it does to other media.

See also: Controversial Issues, Broadcasting of; Fairness Doctrine; Federal Communications Commission; First Amendment and Radio; United States Supreme Court and Radio

Further Reading

Friendly, Fred, *The Good Guys, the Bad Guys, and the First Amendment: Free Speech v. Fairness in Broadcasting*, New York: Random House, 1976.
Red Lion Broadcasting Company v. Federal Communications Commission, 395 US 367 (1969).

MICHAEL A. McGREGOR

REGULATION

Regulation of radio in the United States began in 1910 when Congress passed modest legislation to control the use of wireless at sea, a law updated in 1912. A separate and more substantial Radio Act of 1912 could not foresee broadcasting. Following the beginning and surge of radio broadcasting in the early 1920s, pressure rose for a new law. The Radio Act of 1927 created an independent commission to determine regulatory policy for radio and broadcasting in the United States. The venerable Communications Act of 1934 expanded the powers of what became the Federal Communications Commission (FCC) to determine regulatory policy, subject to congressional oversight.

Over the past eight decades, government regulation of American radio has varied from minimal oversight, to pervasive control, and more recently to substantial deregulation. Beginning in the late 1970s the commission began adopting less stringent regulatory policies for broadcasters, replacing specific requirements with market-based competition. The Telecommunications Act of 1996 introduced significant relaxation in broadcasting ownership requirements. The 1934 Act, though amended many times, still provides the overarching schema for American radio regulatory policy.

Early Radio Regulation

The "commerce" clause of the U.S. Constitution (art. 1, sec. 8) assigns to Congress the option of regulating interstate and foreign commerce. Early radio stations served as basic communication systems, transmitters of messages that were meant to facilitate commerce and to protect the health and well-being of U.S. citizens. The Wireless Ship Act of 1910 (PL 262, 61st Cong.) reflected congressional intent to institute modest regulatory requirements on the nascent wireless communications industry. Ocean-going ships traveling to or from the United States were required to have transmitting equipment if carrying more than 60 passengers. The secretary of the Department of Commerce and Labor was given the authority to make additional regulations to secure the execution of the 1910 Act.

The 1912 sinking of the *Titanic*, with the tragic loss of 1,500 lives, forced congressional action to meet American international treaty obligations in wireless communication. The 1910 law was expanded, and was followed a few months later by the more comprehensive Radio Act of 1912. The law provided for licensing all transmitting apparatus for interstate or foreign commerce by the secretary of commerce and required that each station operator be licensed and that the government prescribe regulations to minimize interference. Other sections of the act provided for the licensing of experimental stations, regulation over the type of modulation, prohibition against divulging the content of private messages, and a requirement to give preference to distress signals.

The Radio Act of 1912 did not foresee and thus did not mention radio broadcasting. Public interest and service obligations were not discussed except as they pertained to point-to-point communication. However, the emergence of broadcasting after 1920, with the rapid proliferation of new stations seeking licenses and vying for airtime on an extremely limited allocation of frequencies, created administrative problems for Secretary of Commerce Herbert Hoover. The 1912 act allowed the secretary no discretion to develop and modify administrative regulation as needed, depending on changes in the radio business.

In 1922 Hoover convened the first of what became four annual National Radio Conferences designed to elicit voluntary self-regulation by broadcasters and other interested parties. Attendees realized the inadequacy of the 1912 act and many called for better government oversight through more comprehensive legislation. But interference among broadcasting channels dramatically increased as the number of stations proliferated and as operations increased power and moved transmitters; early broadcasting entered a period of chaos without any significant government oversight.

Between 1922 and 1923, Hoover expanded the number of frequencies assigned to radio broadcasting in an attempt to relieve interference conditions. The secretary, who strongly endorsed the notion of self-regulation, had some success persuading stations to share frequencies, limit power, and split up the broadcast day. However, despite his attempt to facilitate solutions, a growing dissatisfaction with time allotments and frequency sharing created problems for Hoover's policy of "associationalism." It was becoming apparent to Hoover and the industry that self-regulation could not solve increasing interference and allocation problems. At the fourth and final radio conference in November 1925, all agreed that "public interest" should be the basis for broadcasting policy. Attendees also convinced the secretary to stop issuing new radio licenses. Thus, the licensing provisions of the 1912 Act were suspended under an ad hoc regulatory policy that was agreed to by government and by the large radio manufacturing and broadcasting interests.

On 16 April 1926, however, a federal appeals court dealt the final blow to the 1912 act when it ruled that the secretary had overstepped his authority. As a result, Hoover was powerless to enforce any operating requirements on licensees (*United States v. Zenith Radio Corp. et al.*, 12 F. 2nd 614 [N.D. Ill. 1926]). Immediately after the *Zenith* decision, stations began switching frequencies, increasing power, and ignoring previously agreed-upon time-sharing arrangements. Interference levels grew dramatically, particularly at night, when signals were prone to long-distance skipping.

Under growing pressure that was fueled by dissatisfaction among broadcasters and the listening public, Congress passed the Radio Act of 1927. The legislation specifically regulated broadcasting for the first time by establishing a framework to regulate the industry and investing decision-making powers in an independent agency. Seven years later, with the passage of the Communications Act of 1934, Congress merged oversight of wired and wireless communication under the new FCC.

The Radio Act of 1927—Real Beginning of Broadcast Regulation

The Radio Act of 1927 (PL 632, 69th Cong.) conceived that a newly constituted Federal Radio Commission (FRC) would be able to resolve numerous interference problems that had emerged during radio's development. Drawing on a combination of earlier legislative efforts introduced by Representative Wallace White of Maine and Senator Clarence C. Dill of Montana, the 1927 legislation provided for continued but more effective licensing and for the assigning of station frequencies, power, and fixed terms for all radio licenses. The legislation also provided for the creation of a temporary commission with authority to designate licensees and to regulate stations' operating conditions. The act asserted a public interest in broadcasting and public ownership of the airwaves, extended considerable rulemaking discretion to the commission, and provided commissioners with considerable discretion to decide questions of law and policy.

One of the significant outcomes of the 1927 act, still debated today, was that broadcasters were accorded more limited rights under the First Amendment than was traditional for the press. The legislation clearly designated the electromagnetic spectrum as part of the public domain, allowing the commission the power to grant rights to users of the spectrum but forbidding private ownership over communication channels. In addition, extreme interference problems encountered with the breakdown of the 1912 act suggested that a real scarcity of available channels existed. This complicated the task of the commission to devise a permanent allocation scheme that would suit all political and business constituents. Because the known radio spectrum and limited engineering capabilities could not afford all who wanted to speak an opportunity to do so, the FRC was empowered to impose rules

and regulations limiting the number of entities actually using the airwaves. Legislators provided the commission with broad discretionary powers, subject to adjudication by the federal courts.

Many of today's expectations for regulatory policy emanate from the 1927 legislation. The Radio Act called for a commission comprising five members, each appointed from and responsible for representing a specific geographical zone of the United States. Congress initially conceived that the agency would dispense with the interference problems within the first year, after which the commission would become a consultative, quasi-judicial body meeting only when necessary. Sections 4 and 9 of the act invoked an undefined public-interest standard and gave commissioners the power to license and regulate wireless stations; federal radio stations were exempt from regulatory oversight. Licensing decisions made by the commission were subject to adjudication by the court of appeals, essentially as a *de novo* review. Legal scholars point to the fact that oversight was essentially a limited review of specific issues within a narrow class of petitioners.

Although the act did not contain specific language to regulate broadcasting "chains" or networks, legislators gave commissioners the ability to "make special regulations applicable to radio stations engaged in chain broadcasting" (sec. 4 [h]). Therefore, whatever control the commission could impose over radio networks had to be accomplished at the station level. Similarly, the act dealt with advertising in a minimal fashion. Some historians point to the fact that advertising was not widely accepted in 1926, when the bill was written, as one possible reason to explain the apparent oversight in the legislation.

Scholars are divided over the effectiveness of the FRC, but they generally give the organization little credit for effecting consistent and strong regulatory policy. During its six-year tenure, relations with Congress were stormy, sometimes to the point of hostility. By the end of its first year, congressional members who wrote provisions of the act called FRC commissioners "cowards" for their lack of regulatory action. Other critics pointed to flawed decision making based on poor information collection. The FRC's inability to resolve interference problems and redistribute licenses caused Congress to impose the Davis Amendment, which called for equality of service standards, in the 1928 reauthorization bill.

The broadcasting industry, led by the Radio Corporation of America (RCA), Westinghouse, and General Electric, succeeded in convincing the FRC that the general framework of broadcasting developed under the secretary of commerce should be retained. Robert McChesney (1993) points out that reauthorizing the existing commercial stations without redistributing licenses caused many non-commercial licensees to have their allocations and times of operation reduced. At the end of the FRC's tenure in 1934, commercial broadcasting was well established in the United States.

Passage of radio legislation clearly reflected the congressional view that the electromagnetic spectrum represented a valuable natural resource that was to be carefully cultivated and conserved for the general population. *United States v. Zenith* had opened the floodgates to far too many licenses, creating substantial interference and chaos for listeners and broadcasters alike. It is not surprising, therefore, that resolution of licensing-related controversies became the first priority of the FRC. Regulatory decisions of the early commission were frequently politically motivated. Client politics stifled regulatory efforts by pitting interests that favored policies to support the growth of a nascent broadcasting industry on one hand against the desires of congressional members who wanted a solution that redistributed licenses along geographical regions on the other. Thus, partisan politics made the FRC sensitive to criticism from both large industry players and the regional constituents of various members of Congress. Furthermore, because only two of the FRC commissioners were actually confirmed by the Senate during the FRC's first term, the initial action of the agency was tentative, depriving the commission of an opportunity to regulate boldly. With passage of the Davis Amendment in 1928, Congress specifically directed the FRC to solve interference problems that plagued the AM band and to provide equalization of services to the different geographical regions of the country. With newly confirmed commissioners and a better sense of purpose, the FRC redistributed the broadcast band in the fall of that year. General Order 40 put into place a structure that allocated certain broadcast frequencies for long-distance, regional, and local services. The outcome of this new engineering calculation was the development of clear channel stations, which came to dominate radio during the 1930s, 1940s and 1950s.

The basic regulatory structure embodied in the Radio Act of 1927 became the basis for the permanent body designated under the Communications Act of 1934. By 1934 broadcasting had evolved into a highly profitable business. The structural components of the network radio system, almost wholly outside the purview of the FRC, had developed into a series of highly successful operations. The breakup of the RCA trust had created powerful forces within the communications industry vying for different segments of the industry. Many of the most powerful broadcasting stations, designated as "clear channels," were licensed to the large broadcasting or radio manufacturing companies, and the FRC's adoption of a system of clear (national), regional, and local AM channels (General Order 40) solidified the interest of stations already on the air, but has lasted in large part to the present as the chief means of allocating channels and reducing interference.

The Federal Communications Commission

The passage of the Communications Act of 1934 (PL 416, 73rd Cong.) established a permanent commission to oversee and regulate the broadcasting and telecommunications industries. In creating the FCC, Congress invested the permanent agency with the same broad regulatory powers that had been given to the FRC. These powers were extended to include wired telecommunications services, which had previously been under the jurisdiction of the Interstate Commerce Commission. Most provisions of the 1927 Act were incorporated word for word into Title III of the more comprehensive Communications Act. The language of both the 1927 and 1934 acts allowed the agency to employ a wide variety of sanctions, incentives, and other tools to fulfill regulatory or policy mandates. Over the years, court rulings concerning the act and appealed FCC decisions have helped to delineate the boundaries of permissible government action.

The new agency did not intend to upset the broadcasting systems that had developed under the Secretary of Commerce and the FRC. However, Congress provided the new agency with some regulatory flexibility by repealing the specific requirements of the Davis Amendment. The general themes of the 1934 act exemplified the principles of the New Deal by consolidating federal powers under one agency and centralizing the decision-making power for all communications industries. Both the 1927 and 1934 acts are significant because they invested regulatory powers in an independent "expert" agency. The realization that broadcast regulation should not be limited to supervision of interference and other technical aspects was fully apparent to legislators.

The newly formed FCC was confronted with the need to develop both an immediate and a long-term agenda. Immediate tasks included identifying and defining what constituted service in the "public interest, convenience, and necessity." The FRC had developed some regulatory policies, but clarification would be needed for long-term administrative policy development. As a corollary to this process, the FCC would have to develop reflective criteria to determine whether stations were doing an acceptable job of meeting their public service obligations. Consistent with this goal, the agency would be required to articulate and give meaning to broad phrases such as *public interest*.

Secondly, the FCC was now charged with developing a plan for utilizing the expanding electromagnetic spectrum. The years between creation of the FRC and creation of the FCC yielded important discoveries regarding the extent and usage of the spectrum. The commission, charged with "the larger, more effective use of radio" (sec. 303 [g]), needed to develop a more complex mechanism for determining which users should be allowed to use what radio band and for what purposes. Different uses would require differing amounts of spectrum space, and conflicting requests for spectrum utilization would require the FCC to make determinations for which services and how many users the spectrum could provide for.

FCC *Annual Reports* through 1939 illustrate that the commission undertook much more sophisticated record collection than the FRC. Between 1936 and 1937, the commission required all broadcasters to file comprehensive information regarding income, property investment, number of employees, and nature and types of programs. The FCC reported much of the statistical data to Congress during 1938. In that same year, the Commission began the first full-fledged review of the practices of chain (network) broadcasting. The initial years of the FCC reflected the need to collect and collate sufficient data to implement a long-term broadcast regulatory policy.

Localism and Trusteeship—A Framework for Broadcast Agenda Setting

The broad nature of the language used in the 1927 and 1934 acts did not prescribe specific tests or mandates for users of the radio spectrum. Consequently, it became necessary for the FRC and FCC to articulate policies that it could use as touchstones for measuring the service of the licensee. Over time, these pronouncements, coupled with rules and regulations, allowed the commission to establish a baseline regulatory policy.

Early decisions of the FRC and the FCC generally illustrate the importance placed on local operation and on a "trusteeship" model in broadcasting.

Local outlets were seen as "trustees" of the public interest, despite the growing power and programming of the radio networks throughout the 1930s and 1940s. These two principles became the bedrock of federal radio policy-making for decades.

The commission realized that defining what constituted acceptable service for a licensee required developing a set of standards that a broadcast licensee could aspire to or be measured against. In *Great Lakes Broadcasting Company et al v. FRC* (37 F. 2nd 993 [D.C. Cir.]), the FRC devised an important set of principles to delineate what constituted public service and to inform licensees as to what their obligations would be as trustees using a natural public resource. The principle of trusteeship was based on a rationale of spectrum scarcity and required broadcasters to provide that:

> the tastes, needs, and desires of all substantial groups among the listening public should be met, in some fair proportion, by a well-rounded program, in which entertainment, consisting of music both classical and lighter grades, religion, education, and instruction, important public events, discussion of public questions, weather, market reports, and news, and matters of interest to all members of the family find a place.

In asserting that stations were trustees, the FCC attempted to develop a policy that scrutinized the economic impact that proposed stations would have on current station trustees. Thus, the FCC denied some licenses when it feared that an applicant had inadequate resources. At other times, the FCC refused to issue a license when an applicant was financially secure but would provide harmful competition to an existing licensee. Taken as a whole, FCC decisions published between 1934 and 1940 do not illustrate how the agency evaluated the merits of potential economic injury, nor do they demonstrate a uniform record of policy-making. Robert Horwitz notes that the FCC's decision to protect the broadcast system resulted in de facto protection of existing broadcasting facilities. In apparent ad hoc fashion, the FCC sometimes approved license applications where there were existing stations, and other times it refused to grant construction permits in cities that had no primary radio service at all. Engineering factors were not critical in many decisions.

Encouraging localism (the idea that stations should reflect their own communities) became the second fundamental principle and proved useful for several reasons. Both network and local programs were being provided to listeners via a local licensee assigned to serve a particular community or via a clear channel station meant to serve a wide geographical area. Although the FCC had very limited control over national networks, it discerned that its power to regulate was essentially the power to control local stations, the stations' relationships with network program suppliers, and the stations' relationship with the community of license. Thus, policy evaluation based on serving the interests of the city of license provided the FCC with sufficient leverage over the whole of the broadcast industry through station regulation.

Regulatory Policies in the 1940s

As the 1930s ended, the FCC expressed concern that radio networks held too much power over licensees through affiliation agreements that prevented stations from programming more independently. The commission's actions during this period illustrate a desire to increase the responsiveness of local licensees to their listening public, reduce the anticompetitive behavior of the powerful radio networks, and effectively increase competition in local broadcasting. In addition, the commission wanted to end the competitive advantage the National Broadcasting Company (NBC) held over the Columbia Broadcasting System (CBS) and the smaller Mutual network as a result of its ability to program both the NBC Red and Blue networks. The Chain Broadcasting Regulations issued in early 1941 were challenged by NBC in *National Broadcasting Company et al. v. United States* (319 U.S. 190 [1943]). The Supreme Court decision, written by Justice Frankfurter, upheld the FCC's authority to regulate the business arrangements between networks and licensees. More important, the decision upheld the constitutionality of the Communications Act and reaffirmed the commission's presumption that it had substantive discretionary power to regulate broadcasting.

But hoped-for changes in the relationship between networks and affiliates failed to emerge. Even though the commission faced increased criticism and oversight hearings between 1942 and 1944 (resulting in the resignation or nonreappointment of several commissioners), FCC staff investigated what licensees proposed to program when they filed applications compared to what they actually programmed. The results of the investigation were summarized in the 1946 "Blue Book." The Blue Book restated the commission's interpretation of what constituted public-interest obligations and articulated four primary concerns: the quantity of sustaining programming aired by the licensee, the broadcast of live local programs, the creation of programming devoted to the discussion of public issues, and elimination of advertising abuse.

Although the Blue Book reflected the first attempt by the FCC to articulate a fully developed policy statement regarding what constituted good service, the FCC never fully enforced application of the service statements it advocated. Still, the Blue Book was an attempt to make broadcasters more responsive to their listeners. First, it articulated the commission's view as to what constituted good service. Second, it started a debate within the industry as broadcasters objected to a perceived governmental attack on their ability to program without censorship or government interference. Third, in an attempt to forestall the promulgation of formal content-based rules, the National Association of Broadcasters strengthened its own self-regulatory radio code. Finally, though perhaps unintentionally, the commission increased record-keeping requirements for broadcasters.

Following the end of World War II (a period of unparalleled prosperity in broadcasting), the commission encouraged local competition by allowing a rapid and dramatic increase in the number of licenses in the standard (AM) broadcast band. Some experts note that the pressure to expand broadcasting may be seen less as a regulatory initiative and more as a result of renewed interest in entertainment due to the end of the Depression of the 1930s and the repeal of war priority restrictions. The expansion of radio broadcasting was further enhanced with the FCC's creation of a new expanded FM band after 1945. As the decade drew to a close, the FCC revoked its former prohibition on station editorializing, thus laying the groundwork for what would become known as the fairness doctrine.

Postwar Radio Policy

The shift in revenue from network to local radio and the increased competition in the AM band forced significant changes in radio programming. Morning and afternoon "drive"-times became major sources of revenue. Stations abandoned the block programming structure typical of network affiliation in favor of generic formats that were stripped across the broadcast week. Because concepts developed in the Blue Book held little significance in the context of this new local competition, the FCC issued a *Programming Policy Statement* in 1960 (25 Fed. Reg. 7291; 44 FCC 2303) to restate a licensee's broadcast obligations. Reflecting the changes in radio with the rise of television, requirements for sustaining programs (those without advertising support) were dropped and other program guidelines were updated.

The 1960 *Programming Policy Statement* required broadcasters to discover the "tastes, needs, and desires" of the people through local area surveys known as "community ascertainment." With the 1960 Policy Statement, the commission delineated a 14-point list of major program elements that broadcasters were supposed to provide for the service area. Broadcasters criticized the laundry-list approach to programming requirements and the agency itself for using specific "quotas" of programs enumerated in guidelines as a litmus test for automatic license renewal.

A decade later, the FCC issued a "primer" that placed significance on programs that were responsive to community problems rather than serving the "tastes, needs, and desires" of the community. In 1976 the commission reaffirmed a commitment to the ascertainment process by making it a continuous requirement. Many felt that with this requirement, combined with other filing requirements, the FCC was imposing a significant record-keeping and filing burden on licensees.

Between 1964 and 1980, the fairness doctrine was fairly rigorously enforced by the FCC, and critics of the doctrine claimed that the specter of a fairness complaint, with its potential for legal entanglements, frequently prevented ("chilled") broadcasters from airing more discussion of public controversies. Supporters of the doctrine claimed that broadcasters merely used the threat of a fairness complaint as an excuse for not airing more controversial material. Despite the fact that in later years it was not always firmly enforced, the mere presence of the fairness doctrine on the books remained a source of discomfort for many broadcasters and First Amendment advocates. Eventually, by the 1980s, because of increasing competition among stations and with various types of radio deregulation already underway, the commission began looking for a way to eliminate its own doctrine—something it eventually did in August 1987.

The FCC also sets policy through behavioral rules meant to provide guidelines for broadcasters as to what is or is not considered acceptable. For example, the ban on indecent language is proscriptive, telling stations the boundaries of acceptable speech. However, despite being provided with a list of verboten words and phrases, what constitutes "obscenity" and "indecency" remains largely a gray area, one that will only partially be settled with the *Fox v. FCC* Supreme Court case. Rules that for years banned some types of cross-media ownership and simulcasting of AM and FM programs (both now repealed) are illustrative of agency rulemaking designed to *structurally* organize the industry.

Radio Deregulation

Serious thinking about deregulation began at the FCC in the mid-1970s, and a move to lift some rules on radio had been outlined in 1979. The 1980 election of Ronald Reagan increased the pace of thinking about radio deregulation. Radio had grown from a few hundred stations in the 1920s to thousands of outlets. Under the lead of FCC Chairman Mark Fowler, the agency pushed to deregulate four required station activities, leaving more up to licensees. The eventual report and order (84 FCC2d 968) eliminated minimal advertising and non-entertainment program guidelines, program log requirements, and rigid approaches to ascertaining community needs. Instead, the commission planned to rely more on "marketplace forces" to provide checks against program or advertising abuses. Many filing requirements were abolished. In the deregulatory process, radio license renewal literally became a pro forma postcard process, increasing most licensees' expectations of renewal. Deregulation, combined with an easing of ownership restrictions in the early 1990s, reflected the agency's attempt to make market economies define broadcasters, who now faced increasing operating costs and stagnant advertising revenues.

If since the 1990s it appears that the FCC has lessened its grip and allowed the radio industry to define itself on marketplace terms, the commission is still diligent in policing practices that are either clearly illegal (like payola) or which threaten to adversely affect broadcasters and the public (such as investigating allegedly biased findings of Arbitron's Portable People Meter or making changes in the merger of XM and Sirius satellite radio).

Commission Regulation as Ad Hoc Policy Making and a Diminishing Public Trustee Model

Robert Horwitz notes that FCC deregulatory policies championed under Mark Fowler (1981–87) mirrored the 50-year-old demands of the broadcasting industry to make the commission a neutral technical oversight agency. The liberal interpretation of the First Amendment, characterized by the equal-time requirements of the FCC's political broadcast rules, faded with the commission's deregulatory efforts. With fewer content and structural controls left in place, radio broadcasting illustrated erosion of the public trusteeship model that had characterized radio since 1927. The dismantling of the trustee concept, combined with the reduction in structural requirements in regulation, left radio open to freer market competition. Passage of the Telecommunications Act of 1996 eased radio station ownership limitations, although the maximum number of stations allowed in any specific market is still restricted.

Even though deregulation and ownership consolidation have increased competition among the top radio stations in most radio markets, critics of deregulation note that the FCC has failed to create a diversity of ownership to mirror the demographic characteristics of America itself. Despite agency attempts to encourage diversity, the number of minority-held licenses has actually decreased, whereas the overall number of station licenses has increased. Other critics point to the failure of AM stereo and the delayed introduction of a digital radio broadcasting standard as indications that the FCC has rarely been successful in inducing the industry to embrace technological innovations. Pirate radio broadcasters and growing disenchantment with increasingly stratified radio programming led the FCC to create a new low-powered FM broadcasting service, which faced strongly negative reactions from the industry and Congress. The commission's decision making can be viewed from a number of useful perspectives. Commission policy can usually be traced on a track parallel to congressional initiatives. For example, with the growth of radio into a large, mature industry, constituent pressure on the agency from members of Congress became less significant, and as a result social regulatory or structural policies were relaxed. Congressional intent, as manifested in legislative efforts such as the Telecommunications Act of 1996, illustrates Congress' desire to treat radio broadcasters less like public trustees and more like a price- and entry-controlled industry segment.

Early critics of the FRC and later the FCC complained that forced social regulation created artificially close ties between the regulatory agency and the broadcasting industry. Under "capture theory" analysis, such a regulatory agency becomes overly concerned with maintaining the economic well-being of the public trustees it licenses. The result is the creation of an oligopoly with limited, managed competition. During the 1980s, both conservatives and liberals promoted broadcast deregulation as a way to deconstruct the relationship that had developed between the regulators and the maturing broadcasting industry. Because competition creates long-term economic uncertainty, deregulation undermines the agency-client relationship.

The success of U.S. radio regulation can be measured in a number of ways. Radio is a vibrant industry with several large competitive players

owning hundreds of radio stations each. Competition for listeners within specific demographic segments in most medium and large radio markets is fierce. Large radio markets support many different formats. Critics of the FCC liberalization policies complain that such policies may serve large listening segments but tend to marginalize smaller populations that seek more diversity in programming or increased access to the media to express divergent viewpoints. Whether one believes that the government should be worried about First Amendment issues largely depends on one's view of whether social regulation should mandate public access to the airwaves. However, a consequence of the expansion of the number of radio outlets and deregulation as a governmental policy is that both factors undermine the public trustee argument. In the long term, radio broadcasting will continue to be more concerned with economics and less concerned with the tastes, needs, and desires of the community of license.

See also: Blue Book; Censorship; Clear Channel Stations; Communications Act of 1934; Controversial Issues, Broadcasting of; Copyright; Deregulation of Radio; Editorializing; "Equal Time" Rule; Fairness Doctrine; Federal Communications Commission; Federal Radio Commission; First Amendment and Radio; Frequency Allocation; Licensing Authorizing U.S. Stations to Broadcast; Localism in Radio; *Mayflower* Decision; Network Monopoly Probe; Obscenity and Indecency on Radio; Payola; Public Interest, Convenience or Necessity; Radio Laws; *Red Lion* Case; "Seven Dirty Words" Case; Telecommunications Act of 1996; Topless Radio; United States Congress and Radio; United States Supreme Court and Radio

Further Reading

Benjamin, Louise M., *Freedom of the Air and the Public Interest: First Amendment Rights in Broadcasting to 1935*, Carbondale, Illinois: Southern Illinois University Press, 2001.
Bensman, Marvin R., *The Beginning of Broadcast Regulation in the Twentieth Century*, Jefferson, North Carolina: McFarland, 2000.
Corn-Revere, Robert, *Rationales and Rationalizations: Regulating the Electronic Media*, Washington, D.C.: Media Institute, 1997.
Davis, Stephen, *The Law of Radio Communication*, New York: McGraw-Hill, 1927.
Dill, Clarence C., *Radio Law: Practice, Procedure*, Washington, D.C.: National Law Book Company, 1938.
Dominick, Joseph R., Barry L. Sherman, and Fritz Messere, *Broadcasting, Cable, the Internet, and Beyond: An Introduction to Modern Electronic Media*, Boston: McGraw-Hill, 2000.
Federal Communications Commission, *Annual Report*, Washington, D.C.: Government Printing Office, 1935–97

(issues for 1935–55 reprinted by Arno Press, New York, 1971).

Federal Radio Commission, *Annual Report*, Washington, D. C.: Government Printing Office, 1927–33; reprint, New York: Arno Press, 1971.

Horwitz, Robert Britt, *The Irony of Regulatory Reform: The Deregulation of American Telecommunications*, Oxford: Oxford University Press, 1989.

Lindblom, Charles E., and Edward J. Woodhouse, *The Policy-Making Process*, Upper Saddle River, New Jersey: Prentice-Hall, 1968; 3rd edition, 1993.

McChesney, Robert W., *Telecommunications, Mass Media, and Democracy: The Battle for the Control of U.S. Broadcasting, 1928–1935*, New York and Oxford: Oxford University Press, 1993.

Rose, Cornelia B., *National Policy for Radio Broadcasting*, New York: Harper, 1940; reprint, New York: Arno Press, 1971.

Rosen, Philip, *The Modern Stentors: Radio Broadcasters and the Federal Government, 1920–1934*, Westport, Connecticut: Greenwood Press, 1980.

Warner, Harry P., *Radio and Television Law*, Albany, New York: Matthew Bender, 1948.

FRITZ MESSERE,
2009 REVISIONS BY CARY O'DELL

RELIGION ON RADIO

The message, "What hath God wrought?" sent over Morse's telegraph in 1837 indicated that religious topics might well be prominent in electronic communications. This proved to be the case when, shortly after Marconi succeeded in transmitting messages by wireless telegraphy in 1895, hymns and prayers were included in the earliest test broadcasts. As stations were granted licenses, religious programming instituted itself as a vibrant and often controversial element in radio.

Beginnings

One of the country's first radio broadcast stations, Westinghouse's KDKA in Pittsburgh, aired *Sunday Vespers* from the nearby Calvary Episcopal Church on 2 January 1921. The pastor was not very interested in the event and so asked his junior associate, Rev. Lewis Whittemore, to conduct the service. In order not to distract those attending, the two KDKA engineers (one Jewish, the other Roman Catholic) donned choir robes. This broadcast was so well received by the listening audience that it soon became a recurring feature of KDKA's Sunday schedule and was presided over by the senior pastor.

In November 1921 the first continuous religious program was broadcast as the *Radio Church of the Air*, and in the following month the Church of the Covenant in Washington, D.C., obtained a broadcast license in order to set up WDM, the nation's first religious radio station. In 1922 Chicago mayor William Hale Thompson invited Paul Rader, who had recently founded the Gospel Tabernacle, to broadcast from a radio station set up in City Hall. Rader quickly grasped the potential reach of radio and negotiated the use of WBBM's studios and airtime on Sundays to run his own once-a-week station, WJBT ("Where Jesus Blesses Thousands"). Besides broadcasting services, Rader presented talks and aired performances by his Gospel Tabernacle Musicians.

Rush to Radio

By 1923 religious organizations held 12 broadcasting licenses and other church groups offered programs to nonreligious channels. That year, fundamentalist preacher R.R. Brown launched the first weekly nondenominational program over Omaha's WOW. Later known as the *Radio Chapel Service*, the program continued until Brown's death in 1964. In 1924 Walter Maier, an Old Testament professor at Concordia Seminary, was the force behind the establishment of KFUO, which still broadcasts from St. Louis under the auspices of the Lutheran Church, Missouri Synod. Also in 1924, Aimee Semple McPherson's International Church of the Foursquare Gospel in Los Angeles set up KFSG. By 1925 the number of religious organizations holding broadcasting licenses had increased to 63. Faced with the explosion of interest in all types of radio, the Department of Commerce passed a rule limiting any new religious or public service stations to broadcasting at 83.3 kilocycles, forcing the sharing of this one frequency by several stations.

Controlling the Flow

On the East Coast in 1923, S. Parkes Cadman started broadcasting services from the Brooklyn YMCA over WEAF and, through a telephone hookup, to a few New England stations. WEAF liked his interdenominational and low-key approach, but other religious groups quickly began pressing for access to the airwaves, so WEAF approached the Greater New York Federation of Churches (GNYFC) for help. It agreed to provide the station with three program streams: Protestantism was represented by the *National Radio Pulpit* (which remained on the air until the early 1970s), whereas Roman Catholics and Jews were given their own airtime. When WEAF became part of NBC, its religious programs became available coast-to-coast.

Sustaining Time

Looking at the varieties of religious broadcasting available and conscious of the diversity of their vast audiences, the networks were eager to keep radical and controversial religious broadcasts off their airwaves. The Federal Council of Churches (which, paradoxically, was subservient to the GNYFC) was consulted by NBC's Religious Advisory Council, which subsequently decided that mainline religious groups would receive sustaining (free) time on the network provided the groups paid their own production costs and avoided proselytizing. All programs would be nondenominational in nature and would be presented by a single speaker so that a preaching format could be maintained.

Under the system of sustaining time, not only were minority groups such as Muslims and Buddhists excluded, but so were Christian Fundamentalists, Evangelicals, Pentecostals and, for many years, Southern Baptists, Lutherans, and other sizable denominations. Mormonism was represented (on CBS) by *Music and the Spoken Word*, featuring the Mormon Tabernacle Choir. In effect, religious broadcasting became segregated—mainline Protestantism, Catholicism, and Judaism were welcomed by the networks at both the local and national levels, whereas Fundamentalists, Evangelicals, and other independent groups were forced to rely on paid broadcasting. Furthermore, NBC refused to sell them any network airtime.

The Federal Radio Commission's (FRC) attempt in 1927 to end the chaos caused by too many stations trying to broadcast on too few available frequencies made matters even more difficult for non-mainstream religious groups. In tightening up its regulations, within six years the FRC had forced about half of the religious radio stations to close because they could not provide the required equipment and personnel.

In 1934 the GNYFC ceded responsibility for religious programming on NBC and CBS to a new committee of the Federal Council of Churches. The mainstream groups accepted the idea of sustaining-time religious broadcasting because it guaranteed them access to large audiences through programs such as *National Radio Pulpit*, *Catholic Hour*, and *Message of Israel*. Cooperation with the networks lessened any threat that they would seek to ban all religious broadcasting because of the often provocative views of conservative groups. Protestant conservatives, however, believed that their voice was being silenced by federal intervention and collusion between mainline religions and liberal network bosses.

Paid-Time Programs

Despite their inability to purchase airtime on the networks and the increased technical regulations on their facilities, many Protestant conservative broadcasters prospered. In 1926, for instance, WMBI, a station sponsored (then and now—it is the nation's oldest audience-supported station) by the Moody Bible Institute, went on the air with up-to-date equipment and a professional staff who avoided both direct financial appeals and demagogic attacks on other religious viewpoints.

Charles E. Fuller was perhaps the quintessential fundamentalist preacher of the 1930s and 1940s. He made his first radio broadcast in 1923, but did not begin a full-time career in religious broadcasting until 1933. The Mutual Broadcasting System (MBS) was happy to sell airtime to Fuller and to other nonmainline religious broadcasters in order to get enough revenue to establish itself in the marketplace. The success of Fuller's *Old Fashioned Revival Hour* (*OFRH*) may be tracked by the number of Mutual stations that carried the program: 66 in 1937, 117 in 1938, and 550 by 1942.

As its name indicates, Fuller's *OFRH* largely followed the format of a revival meeting; its message was simple and represented an amalgamation of conservative religious and cultural values, such as a certain anti-intellectualism and concern with apocalyptic themes. Fuller was given to addressing the audience as his "friends in radioland" and would encourage them to take out their Bibles and gather round the radio set. The *OFRH* was in many ways a model for later broadcasts of a similar nature: its charismatic presenter was at the center of the show, the program was positioned within larger church activities, fundraising activities were emphasized, and production values were kept extremely high.

Walter Maier, who had been instrumental in the founding of KFUO, started *The Lutheran Hour* in 1930. It aired on CBS until the network changed its policy on paid time broadcasting in 1935 and so had to move to the Mutual network. Underwritten by General Motors, *The Lutheran Hour* became the most popular religious program of its day, broadcast in 36 languages over 1,200 stations worldwide, and receiving more mail from listeners than *Amos 'n' Andy*. Unlike many other radio preachers, Maier avoided any sort of star status, insisting that the message rather than the messenger was the only thing that mattered.

Other significant programming was supplied by Paul Rader, the founder of WJBT in Chicago, who by 1930 had an hour-long network show on CBS, the *Breakfast Brigade*, which featured his Tabernacle musicians. J. Harold Smith's *Radio Bible Hour* and Theodore Epp's *Back to the Bible Hour* also had many devoted listeners.

Antibias Stance Strengthened

In 1939 issues concerning sustaining time versus paid time once more came into sharp relief with the decision by the National Association of Broadcasters (NAB) to restrict its member stations from editorializing about "controversial" matters, such as anti-Nazi or anticommunist statements. The NAB was responding, at least in part, to the mounting anti-Semitic and anti-Roosevelt rhetoric in broadcasts on CBS by Father Charles Coughlin, a Roman Catholic priest.

One result of the NAB's actions was that the Federal Communications Commission (FCC) began to deny license renewals to stations judged to have neglected warnings against bias and controversial themes. Further, the FCC insisted that religious broadcasters and other such groups could no longer seek new members or beg for financial contributions over the air. In reaction to the latter ruling, religious broadcasters devised the "free will offering" pitch, which is still used today.

Although by 1941 Coughlin had been removed from the airwaves, the FCC took its antibias stance even further with the "*Mayflower* Decision" which, in commenting upon a Boston radio station, held that "the broadcaster cannot be an advocate." This ruling was relaxed somewhat during World War II when paid time religious programming was allowed to return to evangelization activities as long as national politics were not commented upon.

Mutual Changes Its Course

By 1940 about a quarter of the Mutual network's revenues came from Fuller's *OFRH* and other paid time religious broadcasting. Two things, however, caused it to change its position: it was becoming more financially stable and was looking to further diversify its revenue stream, and in 1942 it was attacked by a liberal interest group, the Institute of Education by Radio, which was opposed to all forms of paid religious broadcasting.

Responding to this onslaught, conservative broadcasters met in St. Louis and set up the National Association of Evangelicals in an attempt to prevent further restrictions on paid religious broadcasts. Despite this move, Mutual announced in 1943 that it intended to make deep cuts in the time it made available for such programs in its 1944

season. The NAE reacted with consternation and worried that individual stations might also try to limit the time sold to religious broadcasters. In 1944, therefore, the members of the NAE decided that they needed to organize an effective pressure group and so set up the National Religious Broadcasters (NRB).

Fuller, forced by Mutual to accept only one half-hour program a week, chose to put a shortened version of *Pilgrim's Hour* in that slot and moved the *OFRH* to a hastily assembled group of independent radio stations, which gave him most of the coverage of the Mutual network. Fuller's solution of non-network syndication through independent stations soon became, and remains, a favorite method for distributing paid religious programming. Mainline religious groups, in fact, also decided in 1944 to start their own syndication campaign through the Joint Religious Radio Committee of the Congregational Christian Church, the Presbyterian Church USA, and the United Church of Canada. Today, in the same way that the NRB supports the conservative or independent wing of Protestantism, mainline Protestantism is represented by the Communications Commission of the National Council of Churches.

After World War II

During World War II, the government froze construction of new stations and the FCC granted few new licenses. By the end of 1945, however, the FCC had already issued more than a thousand licenses for stations and, for the first time since the 1920s, new noncommercial stations began to appear. This provided new outlets for religious programming. Choices also expanded in commercial operations. In 1946, for instance, KDRU in Dinuba, California, began as the first ever Christian radio station run as a commercial enterprise.

In the 1940s and 1950s new voices and new programs found their way onto the airwaves. ABC, the new network founded after the split-up of NBC's Red and Blue networks, aired *The Greatest Story Ever Told* between 1947 and 1956. The Southern Baptists finally got sporadic access to sustaining time for *The Southern Baptist Hour*, and the Christian Reformed Church's *Back to God Hour* started in 1947. The Church of the Nazarene was represented by *Showers of Blessings*, the Seventh Day Adventists had the *Voice of Prophecy*, the Free Methodists produced the *Light and Life Hour*, the Mennonites had their *Mennonite Hour*, and the Assemblies of God sponsored *Sermons in Song*.

Under the direction of the National Council of Catholic Men, the Catholic Church produced four programs: a drama, *The Ave Maria Hour*, *The Catholic Hour* with Fulton Sheen (who presented the program from 1930 until he transferred to television in 1952), *Faith in Our Times*, which was broadcast on the Mutual network, and *The Hour of Faith*. Judaism was represented by one new program, *The Eternal Light*, which ran on NBC from 1946 until 1955. Noted for its excellence, it was funded by NBC and produced in conjunction with Moishe Davis, director of the Jewish Theological Seminary.

Just as many secular shows moved from radio to television, so also did several well-known religious programs. Nevertheless, radio continued to host a wide variety of religious shows. In 1950 *The Hour of Decision* carried Billy Graham's Atlanta Crusade over more than 150 ABC affiliates, and the next year Norman Vincent Peale and his wife Ruth became the first husband-and-wife team to host a religious program on radio.

Decline of Radio Networks

The rise of television caused a huge shakeout in the radio industry. At the same time that conservative and independent religious broadcasters seemed to find new confidence and dynamism, some mainline churches (including some that were having major financial upheavals) appeared to be losing interest in maintaining a vital presence on the radio.

The mainline churches had bought into the notion of sustaining time. As network revenues fell, however, and many local stations wished to maximize their profitability, there was a marked decrease in the amount of time given to sustaining programs and a trend to place these programs into fringe timeslots, either very late at night or early in the morning. The NCC, noting that sustaining time had declined from 47 to eight percent of religious broadcasting, charged that this trend moved against the public interest, but it did not get very far with its complaints.

In 1960 the NRB and the NCC reached a compromise between their two positions, declaring that broadcasters' public service obligations could be fulfilled by either sustaining or paid time. Their announcement banned program-length fund-raising, declaring it unconstitutional, and further stated that religious programs were exempt from the FCC's Fairness Doctrine. The FCC's "hands off" stance facilitated this posture, but it was challenged in 1964 when an author claimed that he had been slandered by a conservative preacher and demanded

equal time to reply on WCCB, a Pennsylvania Station of the Red Lion Broadcast Group. This demand was upheld by the FCC and, ultimately, by the U.S. Supreme Court.

Toward the Current Era

In the mid-1970s, word started to spread that Madelyn Murray O'Hair, a leading atheist, was asking the FCC to put an end to all religious broadcasting. Although a total fabrication, it was taken very seriously by conservatives and independents who had already been riled at an unsuccessful attempt by Jeremy Lanzman and Lorenzo Milam to limit the number of licenses given to religious broadcasters. A result of this was a significant increase in donations to conservative and independent religious broadcasters.

In 1977 James Dobson, a lay psychologist whose "traditionalist parenting" ideas pitted him against the likes of Benjamin Spock, began broadcasting *Focus on the Family* on local radio. Within 15 years his show had grown into the most popular Christian program ever, being broadcast on nearly 1,500 radio stations in the United States and abroad. Unlike many others who started in radio, Dobson insists that he remains happy working in radio and has no desire to move into television.

The NRB became explicitly involved in the political process during the late 1970s. Alarmed at what it considered the "liberal drift" of the Carter Administration, the NRB convened a meeting of religious broadcasters to urge them to become more involved in "educating" Christians about the political process. As a result of this gathering, Jerry Falwell formed the Moral Majority and Pat Robertson not only organized the Freedom Council, but also seven years later launched an unsuccessful campaign to win the Republican presidential nomination. Since the early 1980s, Christian fundamentalists have been active and loyal supporters of Republican candidates for political office.

In 1978 WYIS in Philadelphia, the first religious station owned by African-Americans, went on the air. Although it is conservative in nature, there are other preachers of the "Black Gospel" who are not quite as traditional. Frederick J. Eikerenkoetter II, known to his followers as the "Reverend Ike," began to make a name for himself by preaching a "gospel of prosperity," mailing out "miracle prayer cloths" and pamphlets about how to become rich and stay that way. At one point in the late 1970s, the Reverend Ike had a program in 56 radio markets, but he has since faded into obscurity. The American Muslim community has been served by programs featuring the Honorable Elijah, Malcolm X and, more recently, Minister Louis Farrakhan. Mainstream Muslim radio is now available via the internet.

Jewish radio is largely served by syndicated programs such as *Israel Today Radio* and programs made by the Jewish Federation and the Union of American Hebrew Congregations. There are a few Jewish radio stations, notably in Florida and Boston, but as with the Muslim community, the biggest source of Jewish religious programming can be found through streaming audio on the internet.

Catholic radio appears to have fallen on hard times since the days when it was the responsibility of the National Council of Catholic Men. Certain dioceses, mostly in the Northeast, the states bordering Mexico, and on the West coast, have their own radio stations, and some syndicated programs are produced by groups such as Franciscan Communications, the Christophers, and the Paulists. But given the hierarchical structure of the Roman Catholic church, the lack of a consistent radio strategy is puzzling. In 1999 a group of Roman Catholic entrepreneurs funded Catholic Family Radio, a network with an avowedly conservative viewpoint, but it almost immediately fell into financial difficulties and faced bankruptcy within a year. Mother Angelica's EWTN network, although principally a television operation, also broadcasts on shortwave radio, provides syndicated programming to local stations, and can also be heard over the internet.

Entering the 21st Century

In 2003, www.radio-locator.com listed 1,184 religious radio stations in the United States and Canada, about equally divided between AM and FM. Most carry inspirational and spiritual talk and music, and many of them continued to air sermons. Another 411 stations were listed as "Christian Contemporary" and there were 495 "Gospel" stations, most of these in the South.

Clearly, religious broadcasting by radio continues to flourish, although media consolidation and population shifts have meant that some forms of Christian radio (local stations in Appalachia, for example), are in decline. Conversely, the continuing influx of Hispanics into the United States has meant that considerably more resources are being dedicated to the religious needs of Spanish-speaking peoples.

The excitement that greeted the first religious broadcasts 80 or more years ago has, of course, been considerably tempered. Radio was the first medium that could communicate the sense of a speaker's presence to a mass audience in distant locations. Christians especially hoped that radio broadcasting would allow them to obey the command of Jesus to "Go ye therefore and teach all nations." Experience has shown that radio is not a very efficient tool for gaining converts, but that it can be very useful in providing comfort and support to those already committed to the broadcaster's viewpoint.

Future developments in religious broadcasting by radio will depend on at least three major factors: the creedal and liturgical orientations of the people who will want to listen to the programming, the structures of ownership and control of the media, and ongoing technological developments.

Religious radio stations also call their formats Christian, Gospel, Inspirational, or Sacred. The number of stations with these various formats continued to grow in the early 21st century, but not as rapidly. In 2008, there were nearly 3,000 religious radio stations on the air, of which nearly half (1,400) were noncommercial. Many are relatively low-power repeaters for full-power stations or receive all their programming via satellite. The emphasis in programming is now Contemporary Christian and Praise and Inspiration Music with less time devoted to traditional preaching and teaching. Many Contemporary Christian radio services target young married women with children.

Salem Communications, based in Camarillo, California, dominates commercial religious radio with station clusters in 23 of the top 25 radio markets. Salem offers Contemporary Christian music, Conservative News/Talk, and Preaching and Teaching formats which it also syndicates. Noteworthy noncommercial services include the Educational Media Foundation (EMF) of Rocklin, California, and American Family Radio (AFR) of Tupelo, Mississippi. Both distribute all programming from a central location via satellite to a network of full service stations and translators. EMF networks K-Love (400+ stations) and Air-1 (200+ stations) serve the entire United States with Contemporary Christian music. AFR has about 200 stations, mainly in the rural South, Southwest, and Midwest, and has both Conservative News/Talk and Praise and Inspiration formats. Many AFR stations have been built with the assistance of local churches.

See also: Blue Book; Contemporary Christian Music Format; Controversial Issues, Broadcasting of; Evangelists/ Evangelical Radio; Fairness Doctrine; Gospel Music Format; Jehovah's Witnesses and Radio; Jewish Radio

Programs; Mormon Tabernacle Choir; National Religious Broadcasters; *Red Lion* Case

Further Reading

Alexander, Bobby Chris, *Televangelism Reconsidered: Ritual in the Search for Human Community*, Atlanta, Georgia: Scholars Press, 1994.

Apostolidis, Paul, *Stations of the Cross: Adorno and Christian Right Radio*, Durham, North Carolina: Duke University Press, 2000.

Armstrong, Ben, *The Electric Church*, Nashville, Tennessee: Nelson, 1979.

Bachman, John W., *The Church in the World of Radio-Television*, New York: Association Press, 1960.

Dinwiddie, Melville, *Religion by Radio: Its Place in British Broadcasting*, London: Allen and Unwin, 1968.

Dorgan, Howard, *The Airwaves of Zion: Radio and Religion in Appalachia*, Knoxville: University of Tennessee Press, 1993.

Erickson, Hal, *Religious Radio and Television in the United States, 1921–1991: The Programs and Personalities*, Jefferson, North Carolina: McFarland, 1992.

Hangen, Tona J., *Redeeming the Dial: Radio, Religion, & Popular Culture in America*, Chapel Hill: University of North Carolina Press, 2002.

Harden, Blaine, "Religious and Public Stations Battle for Share of Radio Dial," *New York Times* (15 September 2002).

Hill, George H., *Airwaves to the Soul: The Influence and Growth of Religious Broadcasting in America*, Saratoga, California: R and E, 1983.

Hoover, Stewart M., *Mass Media Religion: The Social Sources of the Electronic Church*, Newbury Park, California: Sage, 1988.

Lochte, R.H., *Christian Radio: The Growth of a Mainstream Broadcasting Force*, Jefferson, North Carolina: McFarland, 2005.

Melton, J. Gordon, et al., *Prime-Time Religion: An Encyclopedia of Religious Broadcasting*, Phoenix, Colorado: Oryx Press, 1997.

Morris, James, *The Preachers*, New York: St. Martin's Press, 1973.

Oberdorfer, Donald N., *Electronic Christianity: Myth or Ministry*, Taylors Falls, Minnesota: Brekke, 1982.

Parker, Everett C., Elinor Inman, and Ross Snyder, *Religious Radio: What to Do and How*, New York: Harper, 1948.

Schultze, Quentin James, editor, *American Evangelicals and the Mass Media: Perspectives on the Relationship between American Evangelicals and the Mass Media*, Grand Rapids, Michigan: Academie Books/Zondervan, 1990.

Ward, Mark, Sr., *Air of Salvation: The Story of Christian Broadcasting*, Grand Rapids, Michigan: Baker Books, 1994.

PAUL BRIAN CAMPBELL,
2009 REVISIONS BY ROBERT HENRY LOCHTE

RENFRO VALLEY BARN DANCE
Country Music Program

One of country music's important radio stage shows, the *Renfro Valley Barn Dance* could be heard in the U.S. South and Midwest from the late 1930s until the late 1950s. Along with the *Grand Ole Opry* on WSM (Nashville, Tennessee), the *Jamboree* on WWVA (Wheeling, West Virginia), the *National Barn Dance* on WLS (Chicago, Illinois), and other similar country music shows, the *Renfro Valley Barn Dance* provided a widely heard forum for country music as it grew commercially in the 1940s and 1950s.

The Saturday night showcase for country music talent debuted on 9 October 1937 over the 500,000-W radio station WLW in Cincinnati, Ohio. Initially, *Renfro Valley Barn Dance* broadcast from the Cincinnati Music Hall and then from the Memorial Auditorium in Dayton, Ohio, but in 1939 John Lair, the program's originator, moved operations to Renfro Valley, Kentucky, some 60 miles from Lexington and not far from Lair's birthplace in Rockcastle County. In Renfro Valley, Lair stationed his show in a converted barn and built around it a rustic pioneer village for tourists to visit. This idea of building a tourist destination around the Renfro Valley stage show predated the *Grand Ole Opry*'s Opryland megaplex by some 30 years.

With the show's physical move to Kentucky came also a move to a new radio station home. In 1941 the 50,000-W WHAS in Louisville began airing the *Renfro Valley Barn Dance*, propelling to the South and Midwest the sounds of the show's country singers and comedians. Over the span of the show's run on radio, it would also be carried by the National Broadcasting Company (NBC), the Columbia Broadcasting System (CBS), and the Mutual Broadcasting System.

Many of the early performers on the *Renfro Valley Barn Dance* had come to the show from WLS radio in Chicago, where John Lair had organized the popular Cumberland Ridge Runners—a musical act on the *National Barn Dance*—and had worked as a music librarian in the 1930s. Former *National Barn Dance* acts on WLS who followed Lair when he headed South were the musical acts Red Foley, Lily May Ledford's Coon Creek Girls, and Karl and Harty. Foley, who was an original investor in the Renfro Valley complex, would go on to be the best-known graduate of the *Renfro Valley Barn Dance*, garnering many hit country songs on the Decca recording label and a prominent spot on the nation's most popular barn dance, the *Grand Ole Opry*. Other nationally known talent who appeared regularly on the *Barn Dance* included comedian Whitey "The Duke of Paducah" Ford (another original investor in the Renfro Valley complex), comedians and song parodists Homer and Jethro, and steel guitar legend Jerry Byrd.

Although the *Barn Dance* gave valuable exposure to country musicians and comics and, in general, helped to establish country music as a commercial force, the show was also important in preserving many of the pre-World War II elements of country music. Founder John Lair was an avid collector of folk songs and ensured that those songs continued to be performed by *Renfro Valley Barn Dance* performers, even as other country music radio shows and performers were forgetting such songs. In addition, as electric instruments and drums became increasingly common in country music during the 1940s, Lair maintained an emphasis on traditional acoustic music, such as that performed by Renfro Valley acts Manuel "Old Joe" Clark, the Callaway Sisters, the Mountain Rangers, and the Laurel County Boys.

As the popularity of the *Renfro Valley Barn Dance* grew in the 1940s, it spun off other musical showcases that brought country music to various audiences. Tent shows featuring *Renfro Valley* talent played one-nighters throughout the East, Northeast, and South. In addition, the Renfro Valley troupe performed on daily shows broadcast over WHAS. For fans of gospel music, Lair and his "Renfro Valley folks" produced the *Renfro Valley Gatherin'*, a program that aired on the CBS network in the 1950s and that still airs today in syndication over more than 150 radio stations in the United States and Canada.

In 1958 WHAS and CBS dropped the *Renfro Valley Barn Dance* from their schedules, marking the end of the show's wide distribution. The program was a victim of the rise of rock and roll music and the decline of network radio. Virtually the only broadcast outlet for Renfro Valley talent would be the tiny radio station WRVK, which Lair established in 1957. As a live performance, however, the *Renfro Valley Barn Dance* continues to be staged every Saturday night, drawing tourists to Lair's pioneer village and often featuring major country music artists. Lair died in 1985 at the age of 91, but his mission to bring country music to the people continues to be fulfilled.

See also: Country Music Format; *Grand Ole Opry*; *National Barn Dance*

Programming History

Mutual	1938; 1946–47
NBC	1940–41
NBC Blue	1941
CBS	1941–49; 1951 (as *The Renfro Valley Country Store*)

Further Reading

Daniel, Wayne W., "A Voice Like a Friendly Handshake," *Journal of Country Music* 16, no. 1 (1993).
Hall, Wade, *Hell-Bent for Music: The Life of Pee Wee King*, Lexington: University Press of Kentucky, 1996.
Kingsbury, Paul, editor, *The Encyclopedia of Country Music: The Ultimate Guide to the Music*, New York: Oxford University Press, 1998.
Malone, Bill C., *Country Music U.S.A.: A Fifty-Year History*, Austin: University of Texas Press, 1968; revised edition, 1985.
McCloud, Barry, editor, *Definitive Country: The Ultimate Encyclopedia of Country Music and Its Performers*, New York: Berkley, 1995.
Rice, Harry S., "Renfro Valley on the Radio, 1937–1941," *Journal of Country Music* 19, no. 2 (1997).
Stamper, Pete, *It All Happened in Renfro Valley*, Lexington: University Press of Kentucky, 1999.

MICHAEL STREISSGUTH

RETRO FORMATS
Oldies/Nostalgia/Classic

Although these programming formats are not identical, they all derive the music they air from years gone by. Whereas the nostalgia station, sometimes referred to as *Big Band*, builds its playlist around tunes popular as far back as the 1940s and 1950s, the oldies outlet focuses its attention on the pop tunes of the 1950s and 1960s. A typical oldies quarter-hour might consist of songs by Elvis Presley, the Beatles, Brian Hyland, Three Dog Night, and the Ronettes. In contrast, a nostalgia quarter-hour might consist of tunes from the pre-rock era performed by Duke Ellington, Benny Goodman, Frank Sinatra, the Mills Brothers, Tommy Dorsey, and popular ballad singers of the past few decades.

Nostalgia radio caught on in the late 1970s, the concept of programmer Al Ham. Nostalgia is a highly syndicated format, and most stations go out of house for program material. Because much of the music predates stereoprocessing (1958), AM outlets are frequently the purveyors of this brand of radio, although in recent years more and more nostalgia programming has appeared on FM because recordings have been remixed in stereo. Music is invariably presented in sweeps, and for the most part disc jockeys maintain a low profile. Similar to easy listening, nostalgia emphasizes its music and keeps other program elements at an unobtrusive distance. In the 1980s, easy listening stations lost some listeners to this format, which claimed a viable share of the radio audience.

The oldies format was first introduced in the 1960s by programmers Bill Drake and Chuck Blore. Whereas nostalgia's audience tends to be over the age of 55, most oldies listeners are somewhat younger. Unlike nostalgia, many oldies outlets originate their own programming, and very few employ syndicator services. In contrast with its vintage music cousin, the oldies format allows greater disc jockey presence. At many oldies stations, air personalities play a key role. Music is rarely broadcast in sweeps, and commercials, rather than being clustered, are inserted in a random fashion between songs.

In the 1990s, oldies stations attracted a broader age demographic than they had in previous years because of a continuing resurgence in the popularity of early rock music. At the same time, nostalgia listener numbers remained fairly static but substantial enough to keep the format on the air in several markets. As of 2002, some 700 radio stations featured one or the other retro sound. A more dance/contemporary approach, called "jammin' oldies," has attracted additional listeners in recent years.

Another variety of vintage radio, classic rock/classic hit (also called boomer rock and adult hits), rose to prominence in the late 1980s. Stations employing this music schematic draw their playlists from the chart toppers (primarily in the rock area) of the 1970s through the early 1990s and often appear among the top-ranked stations in their respective markets.

Whereas classic rock concentrates on tunes essentially featured by album-oriented rock stations over the past quarter century, classic hit stations fill the gap between oldies and Contemporary Hit Radio (CHR) outlets with playlists that draw from Top 40 charts of the same period, although there may be an emphasis on more recent tunes at some classic hit stations.

See also: Album-Oriented Rock Format; Classic Rock Format; Formats; Oldies Format; Rock and Roll Format

Further Reading

Hall, Claude, and Barbara Hall, *This Business of Radio Programming: A Comprehensive Look at Modern Programming Techniques Used Throughout the Radio World*, New York: Billboard, 1977.
Keith, Michael C., *Radio Programming: Consultancy and Formatics*, Boston: Focal Press, 1987.

MICHAEL C. KEITH

ROCK AND ROLL FORMAT
Radio's 1950s Transition

Rock and roll was a hybrid musical form that grew out of rhythm and blues and country boogie, adapting the adult themes of the lyrics found there to the concerns of teenagers. Electric guitars and saxophones were predominant. The rhythm was usually marked by a strong backbeat, though shuffle, swing, straight-eight, rumba, and other rhythms were used. Harmonically, rock and roll adopted the blues chord changes and the standard song structures of the music that preceded it.

Background

Rock and roll radio in the United States was part of a massive set of changes in the industry beginning in the late 1940s and leading to modern formatted radio. After World War II and through the 1950s, the radio industry in the United States underwent fundamental changes, including an increase in the number of AM stations from less than 1,000 in 1945 to about 3,600 in 1960. This radically increased the competition for advertising income, on-air talent, programming materials, and audiences. At the same time, broadcasting networks were shifting their advertising finances, talent, and programming to television, leaving many of the older, established stations in need of programming, income, and management ideas. As television began to dominate the prime-time evening audience, radio increasingly depended on daytime audiences and on audience segments outside the urban, middle- and upper-class living rooms where television was adopted early, audiences such as African-Americans, teenagers, rural dwellers, and the less affluent. The displacement of the living room radio by the television, the postwar increase in the prevalence of car radios, and the later transistor revolution led to a dispersion and segmentation of the audience. People listened outside the family group, as individuals in different rooms of the home and outside the home.

Record shows served the need for cheap programming that appealed to audiences who tended to be listening secondary to other activities. The shows were usually built around a disc jockey personality, who often chose the music and might also work with local record stores and other sponsors. The personality and the music became a programming package with special appeal to targeted audience segments—as opposed to the old network model of wholesome entertainment for the whole family. Rock and roll reflected the shift from mainstream homogeneity to diversity and special-appeal programming.

Origins

In the late 1940s, commercial necessity began to overcome racist habits among radio station owners, managers, and advertisers, who began to program and advertise for African-American audiences and to hire African-Americans as on-air talent and program advisers. The first experiments were so successful that they led to a revolution in what was called "Negro appeal radio," featuring rhythm and blues music and disc jockeys who used the argot of working-class black folks. Disc jockeys in this format quickly became local celebrities, with their personal styles growing correspondingly more flamboyant. Attention-getting nicknames, rapping, rhyming, signifying, and characteristics of older verbal insult games and of the later rap and hip-hop were present in the style of African-American personality disc jockeys. As this became the hot new trend in radio, white disc jockeys learned to talk like hep cats too, and sometimes African-American voice coaches and programming consultants were hired at otherwise segregated radio stations. Later, white proponents of the style, such as Dewey Phillips and Alan Freed, dropped the rhyming and much of the stylized wit, replacing them with a kind of wildness that may have reflected the liberty of white release into black style—as well as the booze and pills they were famous for consuming.

Negro appeal radio was not only a boon to the African-American community but also led to the discovery and development of white audiences for what had been conceived of as race music. Two important contingents were white entrepreneurs, often with working-class roots and rebellious attitudes, and white teenagers with spare time and disposable income. Disc jockeys such as John Richbourg (WLAC, Nashville), Dewey Phillips (WHBQ, Memphis), and Alan Freed (WJW, Cleveland); record producers such as Leonard Chess (Chess Records, Chicago), Sam Phillips (Sun Records, Memphis), and Randy Woods (Dot Records, Nashville); and record store owners and mail-order entrepreneurs such as Randy Woods (who turned mail-order business for Randy's Record Shop in Gallatin, Tennessee, into financing for Dot Records) and Leo Mintz in Cleveland were key players. They were white people with more than casual contact with African-American culture and with their own complicated mix of motives. Although some were primarily exploiting business opportunities, others were responding to a genuine affinity for African-American people and culture, and for others rebelliousness appears to have been the primary motive. The disc jockeys became the spoken voice bringing rhythm and blues music to white teenagers, and thus their rebellion—explicit in their loud, rude, on-air style and implicit in

their love for forbidden black culture—became an essential component of rock and roll.

Heyday and Controversy

Beginning in 1955, rock and roll records became an ever-larger presence on music sales charts. These were songs by both white and black artists, mostly produced by independent record companies, bought by both white and black audiences. Eventually these songs dominated both the pop and the rhythm and blues charts, with notable presence on the country chart as well. In 1956 Elvis Presley made his first release after his contract was bought from Sun records by the major Radio Corporation of America (RCA); "Heartbreak Hotel"/"I Was the One" was in the top 10 of all three charts simultaneously. In the following years, the pop charts became completely dominated by rock and roll and soul, and so many songs crossed over from the rhythm and blues chart to the pop chart that *Billboard* actually suspended a separate listing for a short period in the early 1960s.

Across the same years that rock and roll came to dominate the pop charts, Top 40 radio became the new standard model for popular music radio programming. In this model, the popularity charts were used as a guide to radio programming, with the most popular songs played the most often. Complications about the validity of the charts or about the necessity that radio stations chose songs to play before they could appear on the charts, were ignored. The programming logic was hailed as a dispassionate, even scientific advance. Questions of taste were irrelevant, it was said; the new Top 40 programmers gave the public what it wanted. The result was that the charts and the radio were locked into a positive feedback system, so that some popularity led to more popularity—and rock and roll took over.

Rock and roll was controversial, and not only because of its associations with rebellion and forbidden fun. Though it took a while to catch on in the white middle class, by the late 1950s it swept up teenage interest in a manner that disconcerted adults. Reports of conflict between police and crowds at a few concerts were widely publicized. Exploitation movies capitalized on the association of rock and roll and delinquency. Racists objected to the mixing of black and white musicians and audience members. Rock and roll was predominantly produced by small, independent record companies that quickly came to dominate the older major companies in the popular music market. It was pioneered on independent radio stations, and when it crossed to more established stations, the flamboyant, independent character of the personality disc jockeys came with it. More established interests in the music industry, white backlash groups in the South, conservative ministers, parent–teacher associations, and politicians found a convergence of interests in their suspicion that rock and roll was a conspiracy led by the disc jockeys and damaging to (white) youth.

The payola scandals of 1959–60 were the most prominent component of the antirock-and-roll backlash. The practice of record companies' plying radio and other industry personnel with money and favors was decades old and not illegal; as early as the 1890s, song publishers had aided sheet music sales by paying prominent band leaders to perform their songs. What was new was the power of individual disc jockeys and the success of new, small record companies outside the New York music industry establishment. The disc jockeys were the primary target of the scandal, and station owners used the opportunity to wrest control of programming away from them. The model of management-controlled Top 40 programming spread throughout the industry, and by the early 1960s few disc jockeys anywhere selected their own music to play. The free-spirited and entrepreneurial era of rock and roll radio in the United States was over.

See also: African-Americans in Radio; Black-Oriented Radio; Contemporary Hit Radio/Top 40 Format; Music on Radio; Payola; Recordings and the Radio Industry; Social Class and Radio

Further Reading

Barlow, William, *Voice Over: The Making of Black Radio*, Philadelphia, Pennsylvania: Temple University Press, 1999.

Eberly, Phillip K., *Music in the Air: America's Changing Tastes in Popular Music, 1920–1980*, New York: Hastings House, 1982.

Ennis, Philip H., *The Seventh Stream: The Emergence of Rocknroll in American Popular Music*, Hanover, New Hampshire: Wesleyan University Press, 1992.

Fornatale, Peter, and Joshua E. Mills, *Radio in the Television Age*, Woodstock, New York: Overlook Press, 1980.

Gillett, Charlie, *The Sound of the City: The Rise of Rock and Roll*, New York: Pantheon, 1983.

Jackson, John A., *Big Beat Heat: Alan Freed and the Early Years of Rock and Roll*, London: Macmillan, 1991.

Shaw, Arnold, *The Rockin' 50s: The Decade That Transformed the Pop Music Scene*, New York: Hawthorne Books, 1974.

Smith, Wes, *The Pied Pipers of Rock 'n' Roll: Radio Deejays of the 50s and 60s*, Marietta, Georgia: Longstreet Press, 1989.

ERIC W. ROTHENBUHLER

S

SATELLITE RADIO
See: Digital Satellite Radio

SCIENCE FICTION PROGRAMS

Science fiction programming takes full advantage of radio's ability to transport us through time and space—at a fraction of the cost of a bus ticket. With a well-written story, good voice actors, a few inexpensive sound effects devices, and a willingness to suspend disbelief, we can easily find ourselves lost in *Dimension X*, refugees in a *War of the Worlds*, or leaping tall buildings with our pal *Superman*.

The genre, which traces its roots to the pulp magazines and comic strips of the 1920s, has most often been labeled "thriller drama," but it has actually infused almost every type of fiction, from action-adventure to comedy. There have been sci-fi detective programs, sci-fi adventure shows, sci-fi comedies, sci-fi kids' shows, even sci-fi soap operas. Many programs such as *The Shadow* dealt, at least periodically, with science fiction themes. Regardless of the other elements of a program (or episode), to be science fiction, a work should integrate the relationship between humans and "futuristic themes" such as new technology or alien races.

Science fiction radio dates back to the earliest days of commercial radio. *Ultra Violet*, a program few people remember, was first syndicated as early as 1930. More famous, however, were programs such as *Buck Rogers in the 25th Century*, which was first broadcast in 1932 and is commonly credited as being the first science fiction radio program.

Based on a popular comic strip, *Buck Rogers* was a 15-minute serial that aired five times a week at 7:15 P.M. on the Columbia Broadcasting System (CBS). Aimed predominantly at children, the series focused on Buck, a man from the present (the 1930s) who finds himself transported to the 25th century. The cast of characters included a very strong female character, Wilma Dearing, and the amazing scientist Dr. Huer. Interestingly, many of the fanciful technological devices invented by Dr. Huer in the show became commonplace technologies in the late 20th century. Good and evil were very clearly defined in *Buck Rogers*, and good always prevailed, but there were no truly memorable villains such as *Flash Gordon*'s Ming the Merciless. Like all good serials, most episodes of *Buck Rogers* closed with a "cliff-hanger" ending that left many questions unanswered. Listeners had to "tune in tomorrow" for the next exciting installment. The series and sponsor also held the attention of their audience by allowing them to become "Solar Scouts" and to receive items such as "planetary maps" by responding to Kellogg's premiums.

Superman first arrived from Krypton on the Mutual Broadcasting System in 1940 and is a good example of how science fiction merged with other genres. In this show, also aimed predominantly at children, our superhero fought crime both as Superman and as his alter ego, mild-mannered reporter Clark Kent. "Girl reporter" Lois Lane and "kid photographer" Jimmy Olsen, along with gruff editor Perry White, made up the rest of the regular cast. Often categorized as an action-adventure, crime, or thriller-drama program, the show's central character was an alien with superhuman powers.

Although most 1930s sci-fi radio programming was aimed at children, a few shows were designed for adults. Most of these were episodes of anthology programs such as *Mercury Theater of the Air*, which premiered on CBS in the fall of 1938. On 30 October, just a few short weeks after the premiere, this prestigious drama program, hosted by Orson Welles, pulled off the greatest hoax in radio history— the radio adaptation of H.G. Wells' "War of the Worlds." The pre-Halloween dramatization of Martians landing in Grover's Mill, New Jersey, led some listeners to panic—and many to leave their homes.

Orson Welles' program played on the fears of an audience worried about war in Europe. When actual fighting broke out in 1939, more adult science fiction programs were broadcast as episodes of anthology shows. Series such as *Lights Out*, *Radio City Playhouse*, and *Escape* featured science fiction entries concerning time travel, alien invasion, and world conquest. America, including its radio audience, was becoming more technologically savvy, and more world-weary. Consequently, adult science fiction programs were becoming less reliant on horror and fantasy and more focused on actual science and technology.

By the 1950s, television was pulling a significant number of listeners away from radio. In order to hang on to adult audiences, the radio networks experimented with science fiction series aimed at adult audiences. Several adult anthology series devoted exclusively to science fiction premiered in the early 1950s, including *Year 2000 Plus* on Mutual and *Dimension X* on the National Broadcasting Company (NBC). Later known as *X Minus One*, *Dimension X* was one of the first radio drama series to be recorded on tape rather than broadcast live. As a result, programs could be more involved and could be post-produced to clean up mistakes. As an anthology, stories changed from week to week. Some shows were quite serious, but one of the most famous is an ironic comedy titled "A Logic Named Joe." Originally broadcast on 1 July 1950, this humorous tale is about a world where futuristic computers, or "logics," can do "everything for you." The logics are interconnected in a worldwide web of computers that exchange information. "A Logic Named Joe" takes a comic look at a common theme in science fiction: humanity's fear that technology will take over and corrupt society. Unlike the adult-oriented anthology programs, most series science fiction of the era was limited to such children's shows as *Tom Corbett*, *Space Cadet*, and *Space Patrol*.

As U.S. radio comedy and drama moved to television, science fiction on the radio declined but did not disappear. Later series such as *CBS Radio Mystery Theater* often included science fiction, as well as fantasy and horror themes. National Public Radio stations also imported programs from the British Broadcasting Corporation (BBC) and the Canadian Broadcasting Corporation (CBC). One of the more famous imports, originally aired in England in 1978, was *The Hitchhiker's Guide to the Galaxy* series, which later spawned a BBC television series, several novels, and an interactive computer game.

Radio science fiction programs are actually more plentiful today than they have ever been, thanks to cassette sales, the internet, and a variety of interest groups. Not only are episodes of many classic programs such as "A Logic Named Joe" available for audio streaming, but original programming is being produced, such as the Sci-Fi Channel's web "radio" program, *Seeing Ear Theater*. Thanks to continued interest in the form and some very fantastical technological advances, science fiction radio is not only alive and well, but its future is very exciting.

See also: Children's Programs; Hoaxes; *Shadow*; Sound Effects; *Star Wars*; *War of the Worlds*

Further Reading

Buxton, F., and Bill Owen, *The Big Broadcast: 1920–1950*, New York: Viking Press, 1972.
Science Fiction on Radio, www.mtn.org/~jstearns/sfotr.html
Widner, James F., "To Boldly Go," www.otr.com/sf.html
Widner, James F., and Meade Frierson, III, *Science Fiction — On Radio: A Revised Look at 1950–1975*, Birmingham, Alabama: A.F.A.B., 1996.

PHILIP J. AUTER

"SEVEN DIRTY WORDS" CASE
Supreme Court Decision on Broadcast Obscenity

For five years in the 1970s, the case of the "seven dirty words," in which a complaint by one listener brought the issue of electronic free speech all the way to the Supreme Court, was a direct challenge to the whole underpinning of Federal Communications Commission (FCC) regulation of the airwaves. The "seven dirty words" trial originated when a George Carlin record was played on a New York City radio station and became one of the landmark cases concerning indecency on the public airwaves.

Following in the tradition of his mentor Lenny Bruce, stand-up comedian George Carlin revolutionized comedy with a hip, irreverent attitude and an uninhibited social commentary. By the early 1970s Carlin turned his back on an established, middle-class audience and played almost exclusively to the counterculture. In 1972 he was arrested at the Milwaukee Summerfest while performing one of his satirical routines on language, entitled "Filthy Words" (sometimes called the "Seven Dirty Words You Can Never Use on Television" because of the monolog's central joke). A local judge threw out the charges, but the same routine became the linchpin of a Supreme Court case involving the FCC.

In 1973 Carlin recorded "Filthy Words" for his album *Occupation: Foole*, which was distributed by Little David Records. *New York Times* critic Peter Schjeldahl noted that "Carlin's playing with words, through meaning and emotive permutations, is so mild and earnest it's almost wholesome," and that his "subliminal puerilities are often dissipated by lovely flashes of pure sensitivity." In the earthy monolog, Carlin claims that there are 400,000 words and only seven you can't say on television. On 30 October 1973 a recording of "Filthy Words" was played on the Pacifica Foundation's New York FM station, WBAI. An announcer for the early afternoon program, *Lunchpail*, preceded the album cut with a warning that some listeners might deem Carlin's language offensive.

One month later, the FCC received a complaint from a man who was listening to the station while driving into the city with his 15-year-old son. This was the only objection about the Carlin broadcast that was forwarded to either the commission or WBAI, a listener-supported public radio station.

After writing to WBAI to confirm the broadcast, the FCC used the outraged letter to define the nature of indecency. Ruling that Carlin's recording was not obscene, the commissioners argued that the language was indeed indecent, depicting "sexual or excretory activity and organs, at a time of day when there is a reasonable risk that children may be in the audience." The FCC did not want to censor this material, which it cited as "patently offensive as measured by contemporary community standards for media broadcast," but wished to develop a principle of "channeling," or finding a time of day when the fewest children would be in the audience. Several commissioners thought their statement did not go far enough and wanted indecent language prohibited from the airwaves at any time, but the majority felt that Carlin's material would be appropriate sometime after midnight. The Pacifica Foundation appealed the decision, contending that the definition of indecent did not take into account

any serious literary, artistic, political, or scientific value.

In March 1977 the U.S. Court of Appeals of the District of Columbia overturned the FCC ruling in a two-to-one vote because it violated Section 326 of the Communications Act, which forbids the FCC from censoring any work. Calling the FCC's position "overbroad and vague," Judge Edward A. Tamm of the Appeals Court also deemed the attempt to channel offensive material into the late hours a form of censorship. The FCC appealed.

In July 1978 the U.S. Supreme Court, in a five-to-four split decision, reversed the appeals court and affirmed the FCC's right to limit the use of profane language. In the majority opinion Justice John Paul Stevens wrote that "of all forms of communication, it is broadcasting that has received the most limited First Amendment protection" (*Federal Communications Commission v. Pacifica Foundation* [438 US 726]). No distinction was made between radio and television or between AM and FM radio. Stevens concluded that offensive satire is available elsewhere but should not be broadcast in the afternoon when it is accessible to children. The Carlin broadcast was not labeled obscene, but it was considered by Justice Lewis Powell as "a sort of verbal shock treatment." Justice William Brennan dissented, finding that by its definition of indecency the FCC would deem works by Shakespeare, Joyce, Hemingway, and Chaucer to be inappropriate. He concluded that it is "only an acute ethnocentric myopia that enables the Court to approve censorship of communications solely because of the words they contain."

The Supreme Court's decision did not fully settle the question of what is free expression on the public airwaves. Many writers and producers considered the ruling a major setback to the First Amendment rights of broadcasters. Some newspapers, including the *Washington Post* and the *New York Times*, included editorials in favor of the limited ruling but nevertheless did not print the notorious seven words. FCC chairman Charles Ferris worried that broadcasters would not tackle controversial subjects for fear of the ruling and reassured the industry that so-called indecent language would not be barred in news programs.

But by the end of the 1970s, the growth of cable television transformed the entire world of communications. Home Box Office (HBO) presented the entire "Filthy Words" routine in the special *George Carlin Again* in 1978. This time, Carlin was seen on premium cable, airing in the evening; there were no complaints to the FCC. Given that one has to pay a separate fee to receive HBO programs, the FCC or the courts would likely see such a presentation in a different light than the Carlin broadcast over WBAI. Over the next two decades, competition from cable would largely obliterate the definition of indecency for broadcasters and the FCC. But Carlin's seven words would still rarely be heard on over-the-air radio or television. A clear legal distinction remained between cable service, to which one subscribes, and free over-the-air broadcasting. And the FCC maintained a partial ban on such material, channeling it to the 10 P.M. to 6 A.M. period.

In 2001 the FCC announced new decency guidelines for radio and television broadcasters, making it simpler for stations to determine unacceptable material. The guidelines include instructions about intent and context as well as warnings against repeated swearing and explicit language. Under the new ruling, Carlin's routine would still be problematic if played during morning, afternoon, or evening hours.

Comedian George Carlin died 22 June 2008. As this volume was going to press, the Court was considering the *Fox Television v. U.S.* case, which may update this precedent for electronic media measures of indecency and obscenity.

See also: Obscenity and Indecency on Radio; WBAI

Further Reading

Brenner, Daniel L., and William L. Rivers, *Free but Regulated: Conflicting Traditions in Media Law*, Ames: Iowa State University Press, 1982.
Carlin, George, *Brain Droppings*, New York: Hyperion, 1997.
Douglas, Susan J., *Listening In: Radio and the American Imagination: From Amos 'n' Andy and Edward R. Murrow to Wolfman Jack and Howard Stern*, New York: Times Books, 1999.
FCC v. Pacifica Foundation, 438 US 726 (1978).
Kahn, Frank, "Indecency in Broadcasting," in *Documents of American Broadcasting*, by Kahn, Upper Saddle River, New Jersey: Prentice Hall, 1968.
Lipschultz, Jeremy Harris, *Broadcast Indecency: FCC Regulation and the First Amendment*, Boston: Focal Press, 1996.

RON SIMON,
2009 REVISIONS BY CHRISTOPHER H. STERLING

SHADOW
Crime Drama

In radio drama's heyday, from the 1930s to the mid-1950s, few program openings matched—and perhaps none surpassed—the recognizability of *The*

Shadow's aural calling card. The first straining phrases of Camille Saint-Saëns' tone poem *Le Rouet d'Omphale* (Omphale's Spinning Wheel) are established and begin to fade as the filtered voice cuts through in measured intensity: "*Who* knows *what e-*vil *lurks* in the *hearts* of *men? The Shad*-ow *knows.*" A decidedly unfunny laugh follows, and the rushing music swells again. Here the listener can imagine the unblinking stare of the mysterious figure who has gazed into the dark side of human nature. Thus begun, the late Sunday afternoon broadcasts of *The Shadow* prompted many a schoolchild's nightmares and not a few adults' nervous glances into the evening darkness.

Origins

Although *The Shadow* became one of the best-known characters in radio drama, he first held the more modest role of introducer of stories about other protagonists, dramatized from pulp magazines published by Street and Smith, whose fiction factory had been churning out nickel and dime novels well before the end of the 19th century. Street and Smith's *Detective Story Magazine* and *Western Story Magazine*, both begun during World War I, were well established by the end of the 1920s, but competition tightened as rival mystery and Western publications as well as new aviation, sports, college humor, and romance titles crowded the market. Street and Smith decided to seek new readers through the rapidly evolving rival popular medium, radio.

For *The Detective Story Hour*, first heard on CBS at 9:30 P.M. on 31 July 1930, Harry Engman Charlot wrote scripts based on stories soon to be published in *Detective Story Magazine*. Charlot (whose poisoning death in a seedy Bowery hotel five years later was never solved) also suggested that the host–narrator might be a mysterious figure who told the story from the shadows, his identity disguised. James La Curto was the first to impersonate The Shadow, but after several weeks he accepted a Broadway role and was replaced by Frank Readick, Jr., whose sidelit publicity photographs shielded his face behind a visor mask worn under a broad-brimmed fedora. Stimulated as much by the novelty of the program's mysterious host as by interest in the dramatized samples of Street and Smith fictional wares, listeners rushed to newsstands asking for "The Shadow's magazine." In April 1931 the publisher obliged with the first issue of *The Shadow, A Detective Magazine*, announced as a quarterly publication. Increased demand quickly turned it into *The Shadow Monthly* and then into simply *The Shadow*, published twice a month.

The Detective Story Hour was discontinued after a year, but audience interest led to the revival of The Shadow character as a part of *The Blue Coal Review*, a 40-week Sunday variety series that debuted on 6 September 1931 at 5:30 P.M. on CBS. Half of the hour was devoted to Street and Smith story dramatizations introduced by Readick in The Shadow persona. A few weeks later, Street and Smith reclaimed its Thursday evening 9:30 CBS spot with *Love Story Drama* (retitled *Love Story Hour* later in the season), in which The Shadow recounted tales from *Love Story Magazine*. These hosting duties kept *The Shadow* at work for a year.

In January 1932 Frank Readick was also heard in a Tuesday evening CBS series that used *The Shadow* as the program title for the first time. Other runs featuring Readick and the briefly returning James La Curto were aired in various time slots on NBC and CBS until 27 March 1935. During this period Street and Smith wanted the broadcast tales to reflect the magazine Shadow's protagonist role, whereas Blue Coal, by then a well-entrenched sponsor, did not want to alter the successful format that restricted the on-air *Shadow* to host–narrator duties. In 1937 the impasse was broken when Blue Coal agreed to a trial run in which *The Shadow* would serve as the main character, on the understanding that the program would return to its Shadow-as-host-only format if the public did not welcome the change.

Star Series

With Orson Welles newly cast as *The Shadow*, the program had a sensational re-opening on the Mutual network at 5:30 P.M. on Sunday, 26 September 1937, and it would remain a late Sunday afternoon fixture for many years. Ironically, just as Street and Smith had achieved a radio *Shadow* mirroring the print character's function as an active avenger against law-breakers, the freshened broadcast figure pursued a new direction different from that which the magazine hero had taken from the beginning of the decade.

Having seen a market for *The Shadow*'s own magazine in early 1931, Street and Smith offered the writing task to Walter B. Gibson, an experienced hand at turning out detective stories and a magician skilled enough to be the ghost writer of "how to" manuals published under the names of Harry Houdini, Harry Blackstone, Howard Thurston, and others. Gibson's interest in the occult would help in defining *The Shadow*'s extraordinary

powers. Borrowing names from two literary agents, Gibson began producing The Shadow novels under the pseudonym Maxwell Grant, and when the publisher increased and then redoubled the magazine's frequency, he found himself typing 5,000 to 10,000 words a day while his cabin in rural Maine was literally being built around him. The publisher arranged one meeting between Gibson and an early scripter of the radio series, Edward Hale Bierstadt, but otherwise the handling of the broadcast *Shadow* was left to Street and Smith and to the Ruthrauff and Ryan Advertising Agency. Turning out 28 novels of approximately 60,000 words per issue in the first year and 24 novels in each of the next six years, Gibson wrote of an international network of agents, lookouts, and operatives who reported to *The Shadow*, who himself took a number of guises, aviator Kent Allard being the chief of these. The well-heeled and well-traveled Lamont Cranston, employer of a chauffeur named Stanley, was simply one identity that *The Shadow* assumed as needed when the "real" Cranston was abroad. *The Shadow*'s print tales took him to the Caribbean, Asia, the Pacific islands, and other places where strange religions, philosophies, and practices abounded.

When Ruthrauff and Ryan, the program's packager, planned *The Shadow*'s return to the airwaves in 1937, the agency decided that Lamont Cranston would be the sole alter ego of the crime-fighter. Although the pulp *Shadow* had been a loner, Orson Welles' *Shadow* gained the companionship of "the lovely Margo Lane," first played by Agnes Moorehead, who shared Welles' background in the Mercury Theater and in *The March of Time* dramatizations of news events. According to the announcer's weekly spiel, Miss Lane (named after Margot Stevenson, whom producer Clark Andrews had been dating) was "the only person who knows to whom the voice of the invisible *Shadow* belongs." Whereas the pulp *Shadow* had merely concealed himself in the shadows, the radio *Shadow* had learned "the power to cloud men's minds so they cannot see him." In the fifth episode of the revived series ("The Temple Bells of Neban," broadcast 24 October 1937), Cranston explained to Margo Lane how an Indian yogi had tutored him in "the mesmeric trick that the underworld calls invisibility."

The scripts gave Lamont and Margo a breezy sophistication reminiscent of the marital chat of Nick and Nora Charles in Dashiell Hammett's *The Thin Man* (novel, 1934; film, 1934; radio series, 1941–50) and anticipated the "darling" this and "darling" that conversations of amateur sleuths

Pam and Jerry North in CBS's 1942–54 series *Mr. and Mrs. North*. Always on the go, Lamont and Margo might find danger in Haiti, at the opera, on the road to a ski resort, or in a carnival fun house. Although Margo sometimes saved Lamont from danger or stumbled onto a key clue, she gradually became a convenient bait for psychopaths and a vulnerable "lady in distress" on whom to hang ten minutes' worth of plot tension. The pulp novels' supporting network of crimefighting agents was gone, and Lamont and Margo were generally left to their own resources. Crusty, snapping, and demanding Police Commissioner Weston, representing the civic establishment in contrast to *The Shadow*'s benevolent vigilantism, dealt testily with Cranston on many occasions, and the taxi driver Shrevvy provided comic relief with his self-mocking repetitions of phrase. Even these secondary characters gradually disappeared.

When Orson Welles took the radio lead in *The Shadow*, he was promised that he would not have to attend rehearsals; he arrived at the WOR studios by taxi just before airtime, and the on-air performance was his *only* read-through of each script. His Mercury Theater and other commitments became so demanding, however, that he relinquished The Shadow's role after the regular 1937–38 Blue Coal season and a 1938 transcribed summer season (repeated in 1939) for B.F. Goodrich. (*The Shadow* participated in the tiremaker's commercials, delivering a stern warning about worn tires on slick roads.) Ironically, although Welles was the best-known actor to portray *The Shadow* on radio, his sardonic laugh did not match the scariness of Frank Readick's, whose recorded "Crime does not pay" warning continued to be used at the end of each episode during Welles' tenure.

Bill Johnstone undertook the Cranston/Shadow role on 25 September 1938 and held it through five seasons, while Agnes Moorehead later yielded Margo Lane's part to Marjorie Anderson, and Ken Roberts became something of an institution as the announcer. Bret Morrison inherited the lead for the 1943–44 season but left over salary differences. John Archer and Steve Cortleigh had brief runs in playing *The Shadow* in the usual Sunday afternoon time slot as well as in occasional appearances on the mid-1940s quiz program *Quick as a Flash*, where a rotating series of radio detectives dramatized crimes for the panel to solve. Bret Morrison returned to the lead role in 1945, held it until the program ended in 1954, and later recorded a few new episodes for nonbroadcast tape distribution. In those last years Margo Lane was played by Lesley Woods, Grace Matthews, and Gertrude Warner.

During the late 1930s and early 1940s, most episodes of *The Shadow* began *in medias res*, and the typical Sunday found Lamont, Margo, and their antagonists speeding from place to place by car, motorboat, or private airplane. To make an inquiring visit to a crime scene or to deliver a warning to a miscreant ("The Shadow already knows enough to hang you, Joseph Hart!"), Lamont Cranston often assumed *The Shadow*'s identity shortly before the mid-program commercial break, and his second appearance, at the end of the episode, brought the crack of a handgun and the echoing cries of the guilty as they crumbled, sank, burned, or fell to their deaths. In later years the mad-scientist villains (often lisping and spitting in middle European accents) largely gave way to more commonplace thugs and hoodlums (grumbling in accents of Brooklyn and the Bronx). Early 1950s listeners often felt that they could predict, to the minute, the plot turn when a loudly protesting criminal's death would illustrate *The Shadow*'s view that "The *weed* of crime bears *bitter fruit*. Crime does *not pay*."

Neither Walter Gibson's pulp novels nor *The Shadow*'s radio scripts gave much attention to subtleties of characterization or incident, and listeners have concluded that scarcely any story in all those broadcast years fully made sense. Villains, often nursing misconceptions of being wronged by society or stinging from previous encounters with *The Shadow*, were often megalomaniacs with ambitions for dominating large populations through the risky deployment of flimsy devices. One antagonist strove to block the sun's rays and leave the city in darkness, while in another tale a gang of robbers placed exploding light bulbs in fixtures throughout town so that people would become fearful of using any lights, even car headlights or hospital operating room lamps. In "The Ghost of Captain Baylor" (15 January 1939), The Shadow freed 50 innocent sailors from the island dungeon of a group that was attempting to control naval traffic by rising in a submarine, popping open the hatch, and shooting a machine gun at passing vessels. The Shadow locked the thugs in their own dungeon and left them "to suffer, as long as their lives last, the terrible fate they designed for others," and while this typically articulated bit of poetic justice unfolded, Lamont Cranston's yacht proved capacious enough to return the victims to shore.

The Shadow's own powers and degree of vulnerability sometimes differed from one episode to the next. Although he often seemed able to slip into any cell, cave, locked basement, vault, or ship's cabin, he was nearly burned alive in an ordinary room when its sole window was locked from the outside. In "Appointment with Death" (12 March 1939), a vengeful ex-con tricked The Shadow into swimming toward an island hideout so that the villain might shoot at the gap which the invisible Shadow's body would make in the rippling water. Other antagonists noticed the impressions of The Shadow's feet in deep-pile carpets or sought to trap his image in an early television receiver.

The last episode of *The Shadow* was broadcast on 26 December 1954, five years after Blue Coal had dropped its sponsorship and the same year that the Street and Smith *The Shadow* magazine had ceased publication. Communism and McCarthyism were the shadows then looming over the U.S. horizon, and television had begun to push drama programs from radio. In a 1960s reminiscence, Walter Gibson noted that The Shadow had become a creature of "camp," although he felt that those who derided the series also privately enjoyed it. In 1963 transcriptions of classic episodes were syndicated to WGN and other stations.

In the early 1940s *The Shadow* had been the highest-rated dramatic program on radio, and it prompted a 1940 movie serial starring Victor Jory, a short-lived comic strip drawn by Vernon Greene, a comic book series, three "Big Little Books," and a number of Blue Coal premiums, including ink blotters and glow-in-the-dark rings. The Shadow had been showcased in several "B" features in the 1930s and 1940s, and in 1994 Alec Baldwin starred in a large-budget film adaptation in which lavish costuming and set decoration adorned a typically loose-jointed plot.

The Shadow programs are reasonably well represented in the circulating libraries of radio clubs today, and many episodes starring Welles, Johnstone, and Morrison have been released on commercial records, cassettes, and CDs. Several internet sites offer easy access to program episodes, pulp novel texts, and splashy magazine covers. *The Shadow* persists, too, as a shuddering delight in the memories of those who knew radio before they knew television, when Sunday evening meant sharing Lamont Cranston and Margo Lane's adventures among the obsessively evil and the picturesquely insane. With *The Lone Ranger, Amos 'n' Andy*, and a very few others, *The Shadow* remains an essential figure of golden age radio.

See also: Drama; *Mercury Theater of the Air*; Mutual Broadcasting System; Quiz and Audience Participation Programs; Violence and Radio

Cast

The Shadow/ Lamont Cranston	James La Curto (1930; 1934–35), Frank Readick, Jr. (1930–35), Robert Hardy Andrews (1932), Orson Welles (1937–38; 1939 repeats), Bill Johnstone (1938–43), Bret Morrison (1943–44; 1945–54), John Archer (1944–45), Steve Courtleigh (1945)
Margo Lane	Agnes Moorehead (1937–40), Marjorie Anderson (1940–44), Marion Sharkley (1944), Laura Mae Carpenter (1945), Leslie Woods (1945–46), Grace Matthews (1946–49), Gertrude Warner (1949–54)
Announcer	Ken Roberts (1931–32; 1935; 1937–44), Dell Sharbutt (1934), Don Hancock (1945–47), Andre Baruch (1947–49), Carl Caruso (1949–51), Sandy Becker (1951–35), Ted Mallie (1953–54)

Programming History

CBS	1930–32
NBC	1932–33
Mutual	1937–54

Further Reading

Brower, Brock, "A Lament for Old-Time Radio," *Esquire* 53 (April 1960).
Gibson, Walter Brown, and Anthony Tollin, editors, *The Shadow Scrapbook*, New York: Harcourt Brace Jovanovich, 1979.
Harmon, Jim, *The Great Radio Heroes*, Garden City, New York: Doubleday, 1967.
Harmon, Jim, *Radio Mystery and Adventure: And Its Appearances in Film, Television, and Other Mediums*, Jefferson, North Carolina: McFarland, 1992.
Settel, Irving, *A Pictorial History of Radio*, New York: Citadel Press, 1960.
Stedman, Raymond William, *The Serials: Suspense and Drama by Installment*, Norman: University of Oklahoma Press, 1971; 2nd edition, 1977.

RAY BARFIELD

SHORTWAVE RADIO

Most radio broadcasting takes place in the AM and FM bands (and, outside the United States, in the long wave band—148.5–283.5 kHz). However, the shortwave bands are home to domestic, regional, and international broadcasting as well.

Many different types of radio service use the shortwave frequencies, including maritime, aeronautical, data transmissions, and amateur radio. Within the shortwave spectrum of 1.7–30 MHz (often referred to as high frequency or "HF"), 14 bands have been allocated to shortwave broadcasting (ranges vary slightly in different parts of the world):

2.3–2.495 MHz (120-m band)
3.2–3.4 MHz (90-m band)
3.9–4.0 MHz (75-m band)
4.75–5.06 MHz (60-m band)
5.9–6.2 MHz (49-m band)
7.1–7.35 MHz (41-m band)
9.4–9.9 MHz (31-m band)
11.6–12.1 MHz (25-m band)
13.57–13.87 MHz (22-m band)
15.1–15.8 MHz (19-m band)
17.48–17.9 MHz (16-m band)
18.9–19.02 MHz (15-m band)
21.45–21.85 MHz (13-m band)
25.67–26.1 MHz (11-m band).

The first three of these bands are referred to as the tropical bands and are generally reserved for broadcasting from countries in equatorial regions. The remaining "international" bands are open to everyone. A limited amount of shortwave broadcasting also takes place outside the designated bands.

Origins

The development of shortwave broadcasting traces its roots to early radio experimenters. Known as "hams," these amateur radio operators would utilize their radio equipment to communicate with each other, transmitting on any frequencies they chose.

Exploration of the shortwave bands began as a result of the Radio Act of 1912, which limited amateurs to operation above 1.5 MHz, bands then unexplored and thought to be of little value. All radio transmissions to that point (including those by the hams) had taken place *below* 1.5 MHz. What was widely thought to be ham radio's banishment to useless frequencies above 1.5 MHz proved to be its greatest asset, however, for the hams soon discovered that the reflective properties of the ionosphere made reliable radio transmission over great distances possible on the shortwave frequencies. Moreover, such transmissions could be accomplished with less power and smaller transmitting facilities than had theretofore been required for long-distance communication. (Ham radio

operators continue to be an important element of the modern radio scene.)

Although Marconi had experimented with shortwave spark transmitters as early as 1901, the earliest shortwave broadcaster was Westinghouse engineer Frank Conrad, who experimented with the shortwave rebroadcast of Westinghouse station KDKA in 1921–22. These transmissions were heard in other countries, some of which rebroadcast the programs on their local standard broadcast stations. The long-distance capability of shortwave was a result of the reflective properties of a portion of the ionosphere known then as the Kennelly–Heaviside layer, so named after Britain's Sir Oliver Heaviside and Harvard professor Arthur Kennelly, who had independently suggested the existence of such a phenomenon.

By 1925 some large U.S. stations, including General Electric's WGY, Crosley's WLW, and RCA's WJZ, were simulcasting their regular AM programming on shortwave for experimental purposes. In the United States, it was hoped that shortwave could substitute for the long-distance cables needed to connect AM stations for network broadcasting. The cables were owned by the American Telephone and Telegraph Company (AT&T), which, as a competing broadcaster, was reluctant to lease the cables to others. When AT&T settled its disputes with the radio industry in 1926, ceased its own broadcasting, and agreed to lease its long-distance lines, a commercial rationale for reliance on shortwave as an adjunct to domestic broadcasting was lost.

Several objectives supported the use of shortwave for broadcasting purposes in radio's early days. Most important was basic technical experimentation: determining how far and how reliably signals could be transmitted, and at what times and frequencies. Another objective was to cover remote areas not easily reached by limited-range AM ("medium wave") signals, and thus provide news and entertainment to those not otherwise served by radio.

A third objective was to serve as a unifying national force. In the United States, broadcasting was essentially a private function. The government set technical standards and provided regulation on matters such as frequency, power, and hours of operation, but the broadcasters themselves were private enterprises. In most other countries, however, broadcasting was a government monopoly, and the government the principal broadcaster. (A modified American model was in force in Central and South America, where broadcasting was in mainly private hands, but with government broadcasting permitted as well.) Where the government controlled broadcasting, it was hoped that shortwave would be a useful tool for nation building. In some cases, geography dictated even loftier goals: Britain's "Empire Service," as its early international shortwave broadcasts were known, served as a means of communication with subjects in distant colonies.

The relaying of programs from one country to another by shortwave for rebroadcasting on local AM frequencies was another objective of early shortwave broadcasting. Although in theory such relays would provide a means of enriching local programming, the relays were usually small in scale until World War II, when rebroadcasting took on a propaganda objective. Both Germany and the United States entered into a large number of arrangements with South American stations for the rebroadcasting on local AM frequencies of programs delivered by shortwave.

The use of direct shortwave broadcasting—that is, shortwave programs intended for direct reception by listeners in another country, without local rebroadcasting—also proved a valuable propaganda technique for both sides during World War II. Although the reception of shortwave signals still required special equipment and some technical skill, it was not as complex as in the experimental days. In addition, the directional properties of shortwave—the ability to beam transmissions so as to maximize reception in specified geographic areas—lent itself to shortwave broadcasts specially targeted for particular parts of the globe. Thus Germany had its "U.S.A. Zone," and Italy and Britain had their North American services. The broadcasters made their programs more attractive by using the native language of the target audience.

After the war, the growth of shortwave broadcasting was largely a product of the propaganda needs of Cold War antagonists and the desire of many countries to have a place at the international broadcasting table and a voice that served national pride. Shortwave broadcasting maintained its usual shape, however: international services presented by government broadcasters in the listener's own language, at convenient times, and on multiple frequencies so as to provide the best reception in the target zone.

Although never as prevalent on the shortwave bands as the government broadcasters, private stations use shortwave as well. In some cases these are private AM stations simulcasting on shortwave simply to increase their range. Private religious organizations have also used shortwave as a means of transmitting their message worldwide. This has been a growing phenomenon, with many religious organizations boasting modern, high-power transmitting plants. First in this category was HCJB in Quito, Ecuador, which has been broadcasting religious programs worldwide since 1931. Most private shortwave broadcasting in the United States is by religious stations.

Although its roots can be traced as far back as the 1936–39 Spanish Civil War, jamming became a serious problem in international shortwave broadcasting after World War II. The intentional transmission of noise on or near the frequency of an offending station by a transmitter located in the listener's area was routine in communist countries and was effective in preventing the reception of unwanted broadcasts. One response to jamming was to broadcast on multiple frequencies in the hopes that one would get through. This led to more jamming and rendered significant parts of the shortwave broadcasting bands useless. Jamming largely ceased in 1988–89.

Modern Era

A number of modern trends have affected shortwave broadcasting both positively and negatively. The solid-state revolution greatly simplified the reception of shortwave signals. Frequency drift, a problem for many years in vacuum tube receivers, has disappeared; direct dial tuning has eliminated guesswork in finding the desired frequency; and synchronous detection has improved fidelity. In addition, miniaturization has made possible even portable shortwave receivers with sufficient sensitivity to give good reception. Higher transmitter power has meant stronger shortwave signals, the elimination of jamming has reopened previously unusable band space, and increased international coordination has led to better frequency allocation and less interference.

However, shortwave broadcasting is often underfunded by the parent authorities, and this, along with the absence of a marketplace ethic, has often resulted in unexceptional programming. And despite improvements in the quality of shortwave receivers, several factors, including the superior fidelity of local AM and FM reception, the "second nature" operation of regular radios, the absence of shortwave on car radios, and the scarcity of widely available information on station schedules, have frustrated broad acceptance of shortwave. In addition, communication with faraway places is no longer a novelty. The ubiquity of information media such as cable TV and the internet makes shortwave broadcasting look quaint.

The number of shortwave broadcasters is on the decline. In addition to the loss of many local stations, some of the major broadcasters, including Radio Moscow, Radio Canada International, and the British Broadcasting Corporation (BBC), have reduced their output, sometimes drastically, and some countries have left shortwave broadcasting altogether. In some places, shortwave broadcast time has become a commodity, with high-power stations selling transmitter time to unrelated program producers (often in other nations). Although reliance on someone else's broadcasting facility is not without risk, purchase of airtime on a transmitter closer to the target zone can improve reception and eliminate the producer's need to maintain an expensive transmitting plant, while providing the transmitting station with additional revenue. With the demise of the Soviet Bloc and the introduction of market forces, Western stations have been able to purchase airtime in places that were previously off-limits. Thus, a religious station such as Trans World Radio can be heard broadcasting from Albania and the former Soviet Union. "Freedom" programs also rent time on transmitters in countries not directly related to the broadcaster's underlying message; for example, the Democratic Voice of Burma purchases time on transmitters in Norway and Germany, and the Voice of Tibet has broadcast from the Seychelles.

Internet Era

The other factor leading to a decline in shortwave radio is, of course, the internet. For those with access, tuning to shortwave broadcasts online is far easier as well as less expensive than having to buy and operate a special radio receiver. And a growing number of shortwave broadcasters, including virtually all of those originating in the U.S., are represented online.

Notwithstanding the hurdles that shortwave broadcasting has faced, its oft-predicted demise does not appear imminent. Experiments in the use of the single-sideband transmitting mode and digital shortwave broadcasting continue the effort to improve signal quality, lessen interference, and reduce the power necessary to push broadcast signals around the globe on shortwave.

See also: Ham Radio; Religion on Radio; World War II and U.S. Radio

Further Reading

Berg, Jerome S., *On the Short Waves, 1923–1945: Broadcast Listening in the Pioneer Days of Radio*, Jefferson, North Carolina: McFarland, 1999.

Berg, J. *Broadcasting on the Short Waves, 1945 to Today.* Jefferson, North Carolina: McFarland, 2008.
Berg, J. *Listening on the Short Waves, 1945 to Today.* Jefferson, North Carolina: McFarland, 2008.
Browne, Donald R., *International Radio Broadcasting: The Limits of the Limitless Medium*, New York: Praeger, 1982.
Hale, Julian, *Radio Power: Propaganda and International Broadcasting*, Philadelphia, Pennsylvania: Temple University Press, 1975.
Magne, Lawrence, editor, *Passport to World Band Radio*, Penn's Park, Pennsylvania: International Broadcasting Services (annual; 1984–).
Sidel, Michael Kent, "A Historical Analysis of American Short Wave Broadcasting, 1916–1942," Ph.D. diss., Northwestern University, 1976.
Wood, James, *History of International Broadcasting*, vol. 1, London: Peregrinus, 1992; vol. 2, London: Institution of Electrical Engineers, 2000.
World Radio TV Handbook: The Directory of International Broadcasting, Oxford: WRTH Publications (annual; 1947–).

JEROME S. BERG

SILENT NIGHTS
Enabling Distant Listening

The concept of *silent nights* is unique to American radio broadcasting in the early 1920s. Imagine a time when radio stations went off the air for two days because a president had died: it happened in August 1923, when, out of respect for the late President Harding, numerous stations voluntarily left the air until after his funeral. In the early 1920s, radio stations might also take a day off for a major holiday. A station could shut down because normal hours of operation were still very limited. No stations broadcast 24 hours a day—in fact, few were on for more than four hours, usually just in the evening. Even if a local station were broadcasting, static and interference from other stations might keep listeners from enjoying the entertainment.

In 1920, when regular broadcasting began in the United States, there were only a handful of stations on the air, and they shared a common frequency—360 m (about 833 kHz). Sharing time was not yet an issue. By mid-1922, however, there were over 150 stations, and to have them all share one frequency was impossible. Trying to offer a solution, the government opened another frequency—400 m (750 kHz). It was left to government radio inspectors to seek compromise with the stations to determine the times during which each would broadcast. Broadcast historian Erik Barnouw notes that in Los Angeles there were as many as 23 stations sharing one frequency at any given time.

And then came the idea of silent nights. It probably seemed like a good idea at the time. Stations in a city would voluntarily remain silent for several hours or for an entire evening, thus enabling radio fans to listen in to other cities and receive distant stations. Some cities also used the silent night concept to reduce interference, because with so many stations occupying only two frequencies, reception was getting worse and worse. From late 1922 to the mid-1925, stations grappled with the problem and tried various versions of silent nights. Some cities (such as Boston) couldn't seem to agree on it, so stations would suspend operations for each other if one station had a special broadcast planned; individual stations also agreed to stay silent one night a week to allow other stations more time on the air, but gradually this plan was abandoned. In Minneapolis, according to the *Morning Tribune* (6 October 1923), a "quiet hour" was chosen rather than an entire evening, but this idea also ran into trouble when a major event occurred during the time that was supposed to be the quiet hour.

Silent nights seem to have received the most support in Chicago. According to Barnouw, by 1923 Chicago stations voted to have Monday evenings after 7 P.M. as their silent night. In fact, Chicago was quite organized in its efforts. The Chicago Broadcasters Association sent out a very detailed press release to the major newspapers in early October of 1925 explaining why member stations had voted to continue with their silent night even though many other cities had tried it and given up. The Chicago Broadcasters Association believed that local listeners wanted to hear stations in other cities, and they felt they could bring about goodwill by continuing to make this possible. Atlanta, Kansas City, San Francisco, and Dallas were other cities that experimented with a silent night.

Unfortunately, silent nights didn't solve the problem. Although having stations voluntarily go off the air pleased those people listening for distant stations (called "DXers") the overall problems of crowding and interference were not alleviated by one city's stations going silent for several hours once a week. Also, even in cities where one night was agreed upon, it didn't take long for one or more stations to refuse to cooperate, and soon things were back to where they had begun. The Department of Commerce opened more of what became the AM band in 1923 and 1924, but the result was that even more stations came on the air, and radio columnists were once again noting complaints from listeners regarding poor reception.

By 1926–27 network broadcasting and paid advertising were becoming more common, and

stations could no longer afford a night without revenue. The idea of silent nights, as noble as it may have been, became increasingly rare. In late 1927 even Chicago finally abandoned it, with station owners admitting that as much as they wanted to allow fans to hear distant stations, they also wanted to make a living, and they couldn't do that by staying silent. The days of shutting down for a holiday or going off the air to benefit the DXers were over, for radio had become a business and would be run like one.

See also: DXers/DXing

Further Reading

Barnouw, Eric K., *A History of Broadcasting in the United States*, 3 vols, Oxford: Oxford University Press, 1966–70; see especially vol. 1, *A Tower in Babel: To 1933*, 1966.
"Chicago Ends 'Silent Nights'," *New York Times* (16 November 1927).
"New York Studios Not Likely to Adopt Silent Night Plan," *New York Times* (14 June 1925).

DONNA L. HALPER

SIMULCASTING

As television replaced radio in the 1950s, many previously successful network radio programs shifted to television. For a time, some television programs simultaneously aired their audio portion on network radio stations. Although radio listeners were sometimes annoyed by performers' references to images seen by the television viewer but invisible to the radio listener, the simulcast broadcast, with visual references, often provided a program incentive for the radio listener to purchase a television set. Music and variety programs were especially favored for radio simulcast because there was little or no loss of content for the radio listener. As television grew in popularity, simulcasting of television audio on radio declined.

A far more common form of simulcasting that went on for years involved duplication of AM programming on FM stations. As FM stations began going on the air in the 1940s, FM stations often provided 100 percent duplication of all network programs supplied to an AM sister station. Most new FM outlets were owned by and co-located with AM stations. The former nearly always carried the latter's programs. Broadcasters claimed they were trying to assist the new medium with popular programs from the old, but in fact the chief reason was that because of FM's small audiences, extra program expense made little sense. In reality, of course, simulcasting created little incentive for listeners to purchase an FM receiver. The public saw little advantage in buying an FM receiver to pick up programs they were already receiving from an AM station. About 80 percent of the FM stations signing on the air in the late 1940s were co-owned with an AM station—and most simulcast.

Duplication of programming by FM stations began to decline only in July 1964 when the first rules limiting such practice went into effect. The Federal Communications Commission specified that in markets of 100,000 residents or more, at least half the programming aired on an FM station had to be original. Full implementation of the nonduplication rule took place through the late 1960s, and the rule was extended to small-market stations by the 1970s. Although duplication did not always mean simulcasting, simultaneous delivery of programs from an AM station on an FM station was the most common form of duplication. The nonduplication rule also ended the practice of recording AM programs for playback in a non-simulcast manner. Although widely criticized by broadcasters at the time (who would have to provide separate programming at considerable expense), the end of simulcasting soon provided a huge boost to FM popularity and a concomitant increase in demand for FM receivers.

In the late 1990s, simulcasting took on a very different meaning. Passage of the Telecommunications Act of 1996 allowed operation of multiple radio stations by a single owner in individual markets. Some group owners have used simulcasting to extend the reach of successful urban stations to additional stations in outlying suburban areas. This strategy has also been used to introduce news or talk programs found on AM stations to listeners accustomed to FM stations. Rather than hoping to convince listeners to change their car radio programming to the AM band, a simulcast allows the listener to find the same programming on FM.

A closely related use of simulcasting has been to create a local "network" by purchasing two or more stations, usually FM outlets licensed to communities outside a major metropolitan area, and to simulcast programs on both. When the stations simulcasting the signal are not of sufficient power to cover the market, the simulcast enables listeners to change to a sister "network" station as the listener travels from the coverage area of one station into the coverage area of another.

Before television receivers could accommodate stereo signals, simulcasting was often used as a promotional vehicle for both radio stations and music video channels. Radio simulcast the audio of concerts or music videos that appeared on such cable channels as MTV, VH1 and CMT. The simulcast enabled listeners to watch cable while hearing stereo sound via radio. Many sporting events are regularly simulcast over television and radio as are some high-profile concert events such as the 2005 Live Aid sequel, Live 8.

Often a few video cameras in a radio studio allow radio programs to be simulcast over television. Don Imus had such a setup with cable channel MSNBC before being yanked after his controversial Rutgers women's basketball team comments; he is now seen and heard over cable's Fox Business Network. The sports-oriented *Mike and Mike in the Morning* is carried over both ESPN TV and ESPN Radio every morning. And before departing for satellite radio, Howard Stern had a pseudo-simulcast of his radio show videotaped for airing at a later date over the E! cable channel.

In 2006, notorious morning team Opie and Anthony achieved an unusual first in simulcasting when their XM satellite radio show was simultaneously aired for three hours a day on WYSP in Philadelphia, thus essentially turning their satellite provider into a radio syndicator. Following WYSP's lead, other terrestrial stations also simulcast their program. For a time, CBS's *The Late Show with David Letterman* was simulcast on radio until a royalty agreement with the Director's Guild of America could not be resolved.

A different form of simulcasting became increasingly common during the 21st century's first decade as radio stations streamed their audio on the internet. This was usually done parallel to the over-the-air broadcast (true simulcasting), but could also be archived and retrieved at other times. But royalty issues often derail attempts at simulcasting over the internet, as licensing and royalty payments to recording artists and composers are required for their efforts. However, if arrangements can be resolved (and relays of newscasts and weather reports usually incur no additional fees), simulcasting can be a great boon to broadcasters: if they duplicate signals without having to provide new content, costs are cut.

See also: FM Radio; Programming Strategies and Processes

Further Reading

Albarran, Alan, and Gregory G. Pitts, *The Radio Broadcast Industry*, Boston: Allyn and Bacon, 2001.
Eastman, Susan Tyler, Sydney W. Head, and Lewis Klein, *Broadcast Programming, Strategies for Winning Television and Radio Audiences*, Belmont, California: Wadsworth, 1981; 5th edition, as *Broadcast/Cable Programming:*

Strategies and Practices, by Eastman and Douglas A. Ferguson, 1996.

Smulyan, Susan, *Selling Radio: Commercialization of American Broadcasting, 1920–1934*, Washington, D.C.: Smithsonian Institution Press, 1994.

Sterling, Christopher H., and John M. Kittross, *Stay Tuned: A Concise History of American Broadcasting*, Belmont, California: Wadsworth, 1978; 2nd edition, 1990.

Streeter, Thomas, *Selling the Air: A Critique of the Policy of Commercial Broadcasting in the United States*, Chicago: University of Chicago Press, 1996.

GREGORY G. PITTS,
2009 REVISIONS BY CARY O'DELL

SITUATION COMEDY

Fibber McGee trying to get something out of his junk-filled hall closet without starting an avalanche; Amos 'n' Andy caught up in the Kingfish's latest scheme; Jack Benny considering his options when confronted by a mugger with the classic question, "Your money or your life"—these are but a few of the vivid memories from the "golden era" of radio situation comedy. With their offbeat personality flaws, idiosyncratic neighbors, and disrespectful domestic help, these characters were not just friends to their millions of listeners—they were "family."

Defining a Format

"Family" is, in fact, the linchpin of radio situation comedy. Unlike its comedy/variety relative, the "sitcom" retained the recurring cast of the dramatic serial. In fact, historians once labeled programs such as *The Goldbergs*, *Henry Aldrich*, and *The Life of Riley*, which we call situation comedies today, as "comedy dramas," thus emphasizing their dramatic storyline. Each character in the situation comedy is often a two-dimensional parody of one or two human foibles. Listen to any classic radio sitcom and you often find the "drunk," the "tightwad," the "know-it-all," the "dumbbell," and many other stereotypes. These exaggerated personality flaws define each "family member," and determine how that character interacts with the rest of the show's family, and how he or she will deal with this week's adventure. Radio sitcoms are very consistent in basic structure, but they do vary in length. Although many radio sitcoms ran for 15 minutes, most eventually settled into the more popular 30-minute length. A few even stretch to 45 or 60 minutes, but these are rare.

In the simplistic world of the radio sitcom, with its recurring characters, settings, and themes, stories focus on the main character's adventures—be they big or small. Although most stories were about the central personality, episodes occasionally spotlighted secondary characters. Unlike the radio drama, though, the situation comedy played story lines for laughs.

The basic structure of a radio situation comedy is very consistent. The show's regular cast of characters is (re)introduced to the audience. At the same time, the "comfortable" environment of their sitcom world is made clear. Then someone or something upsets the routine, adding instability to this self-contained world. The storyline takes the characters through a series of dramatic yet comic adventures, each one building until the climax of the show. Along the way the audience is exposed to "running gags" and a comedy of character that transcends the week's episode. The audience also hears commercials, sometimes performed by the characters and "subtly" embedded into the story. Although not a variety show, the radio sitcom would sometimes rely on such variety staples as musical numbers and celebrity guests. At the end of the comedy drama, the adventure is resolved, and the characters are back to where they started. Change is rarely permanent in the radio sitcom world.

The term *family* is used broadly when describing the sitcom cast of characters. It identifies traditional family members but also friends and coworkers. Any group of people that the main character spends significant amounts of time with and cares a great deal for make up his or her sitcom family. Because of this liberal definition of *family*, the situation comedy might be primarily centered on the home but might just as often gravitate to a social gathering place (such as a bar) or a work environment. Any time a small group of characters could gather together, interact, and share adventures, a situation comedy was born. Radio sitcoms have often appeared in the form of soap operas, adventure programs, science fiction, even as variety shows. In fact, among the earliest sitcoms were the fictional adventures of performers such as Jack Benny and Fred Allen as they went about the day-to-day tasks of putting on their variety shows!

An important characteristic of radio comedy was that the home audience had to imagine certain elements. Radio's lack of a visual element created "theater of the mind," allowing listeners to imagine Jack Benny's clunky old Maxwell car (played by veteran voice actor Mel Blanc) and to assume that the many characters in *Amos 'n' Andy* were actually African-American (when in fact they were initially all portrayed by two white actors, Freeman Gosden and Charles Correll). But in its early days, this radio format proved to be a challenge for its stars. Coming primarily from the vaudeville circuit, radio's comedians were accustomed to interacting directly with their audience, and they often relied on visual as well as verbal humor. The former problem was solved by adding an in-studio audience.

Origins

Both radio comedy/variety and situation comedy-programs trace their roots to the days of the touring circuses, burlesque shows, medicine shows, musical reviews, and vaudeville companies that thrived from the late 19th century into the early 20th. Troupes of actors, singers, dancers, poets, and comics—plus an almost infinite variety of more esoteric acts (such as sword swallowers, jugglers, and animal acts)—would take their show on the road, playing in various towns and cities on a pre-determined "circuit." The makeup of these troupes may have differed, but their basic components tended to be similar. An introduction by a master of ceremonies, emcee, or troupe manager would be followed by a wide variety of acts strung together with interim commentary by the emcee. This would often build up to a grand finish featuring a more extravagant sketch or a featured humorist or singer of the day. And in most of these forms, the salesman hawking his products—an early example of a program "sponsor"—was one of the more important parts of the show.

The typical nine-act vaudeville bill would usually include as its seventh act a full-stage comedy or drama playlet as a preliminary act to the bill's climactic eighth act—often a famous comedian or vocalist. Not every vaudeville house could afford playlets featuring well-known stars. Consequently, another sort of playlet, one that relied more upon action than upon stars, was developed. Most of these were comedies, and the vaudeville comic playlet became a well-recognized model for stage comedy. These comedies of situation structure are the ancestors of the modern sitcom.

When the radio networks were first looking for talent in the late 1920s, they turned to the vaudeville circuits for acts that might make the transition to an "audio-only" medium. Radio variety was born of this siphoning of vaudeville talent for use on radio. The radio programs usually included one or two hosts, whose presence provided a skeletal structure for the program, which would showcase a variety of acts by both new and established performers. Radio adopted many vaudeville program types. The situation comedy, or "comic playlet of situation," was one of the last formats borrowed from vaudeville, possibly because it did not promote star value as other formats did.

Sitcoms in Radio's Golden Era

Situation comedy premiered nationally during the 1929–30 radio season with *Amos 'n' Andy*. Soon, situation comedies such as *Our Miss Brooks*, *Beulah*, *Leave It to Joan*, *My Favorite Husband*, *The Goldbergs*, and *My Friend Irma* filled the airwaves, and a new genre for a new medium was born.

Many of the earliest radio sitcoms were not much more than a showcase for vaudeville and film comedians who cobbled together bits from their existing bag of tricks. The Marx Brothers' situation comedy *Flywheel, Shyster, and Flywheel*—a Monday night installment in the *Standard Oil Five Star Theater* series on the National Broadcasting Company (NBC) in the early 1930s—is a prime example. Ostensibly a sitcom about the mishaps of three "shyster" lawyers, scripts were mostly a rehash of gags from the brothers' vaudeville and film performances.

Gradually, though, more and more of the comedy in radio sitcoms was based on character, plot, and storyline. A large number of shows in the 1930s straddled the fence between sitcom and variety show. Stars such as Jack Benny "played themselves," and stories were set around their fictional adventures with their equally fictional friends, family, and coworkers. ("Real person" and radio sitcom star Fred Allen maintained a fake feud with Benny for years, although the two admired each other very much in real life.) In the work environment, stories often involved putting on the star's radio variety show; thus the situation comedy was able to sneak in many of the conventions of the variety format. Although Jack Benny's fictional variety show was never actually heard during the sitcom, audiences were treated to performances by guest acts during "rehearsals" that Jack and other characters were involved in "at the studio."

As radio and its audience evolved, so did the quantity and quality of its programs. The situation comedy became one of the staples of 1930s and 1940s radio entertainment. But sitcoms about "real people" were supplanted by the adventures of fictional characters. Stories about *Fibber McGee and Molly*, *Blondie*, and *Our Miss Brooks* soon dominated the airwaves. In another indicator of radio's impact, *Lum 'n' Abner* was set in the fictional town of Pine Ridge, Arkansas, and in 1936 the real Arkansas town of Waters changed its name to Pine Ridge in honor of the show.

Demise of the Radio Situation Comedy

As radio had borrowed from vaudeville, so television borrowed from radio—for both talent and program formats. Television's first situation comedies were "inherited" from radio, beginning with *The Goldbergs* and *The Life of Riley* in 1949. Network television turned to successful formats on radio, partly as a quick fix to find programming and partly to save money. Three-quarters of early television station owners were already radio station owners.

The direct ancestry of radio to television allowed radio to contribute format styles and even entire programs to the new medium. Many programs, such as *The Chesterfield Supper Club* (hosted by Perry Como), were simulcast in an effort to save money and provide programs for the new medium. Popular radio shows were not necessarily picked up by their respective networks' fledgling television franchises. The big-three radio networks soon foresaw that their future was in television, and bidding wars erupted for the most popular radio programs. Columbia Broadcasting System (CBS) TV "stole" many popular radio shows from rival NBC's radio programs. NBC retaliated, and the American Broadcasting Companies (ABC) participated—but on a smaller scale. Radio networks became a less important part of the national media picture. Most of their familiar program formats shifted to television, as did advertiser dollars. Radio eventually evolved into a provider of music, talk, and news.

Many established radio stars, such as Jack Benny, Red Skelton, Bob Hope, and Fred Allen, attempted to make the transition to television. Some were successful, but others were not. There were many advantages for the situation comedy in the new medium. Viewers could now see how characters fit in with their surroundings. More important, thanks to the television camera, gestures and mannerisms assumed a role impossible on radio. However, there were quite a few problems to overcome in the transition. George Burns and Gracie Allen had to throw out their scripts and learn to memorize their complex verbal comedy routines, and cameras had to be placed so they did not block the live audience that Burns and Allen and other performers needed. Ironically, performers who, several decades earlier, had had to learn how to entertain through sound alone now had to relearn how to *appear* before an audience's very eyes and still stay in character.

When *The Jack Benny Show* first aired on television, Benny had several things to overcome. At first he could not decide between an hour format or a half-hour, so he settled on 45 minutes for his debut program. Future programs settled into the increasingly popular half-hour mold. Sets had to be designed and built to portray what had been left to the imagination on radio. One-time scenes and elaborate sets, such as Benny's famous vault, had to be deleted because of cost or the inability to create them effectively. But now viewers could *see*, not just hear, Benny's slow burn and his look of malaise. Visuals added a wealth of information for the viewer, but producers had to spend a lot on props, costumes, and set pieces to show us all how cheap Jack was.

One of the biggest changes to a transitioning sitcom occurred on the new television version of *Amos 'n' Andy*. Because the entire cast of characters was black, but many of the roles had been played on radio by white series creators Freeman Gosden and Charles Correll, CBS decided to do a four-year talent search for experienced black comedy actors to portray the roles. Only African-American actors Ernestine Wade and Amanda Randolph were retained from the original radio cast. Like its radio ancestor, the television version of *Amos 'n' Andy* relied on many stereotypical sitcom personalities, including ignorant, naive, and conniving characters. During its run and afterward, many groups, such as the National Association for the Advancement of Colored People (NAACP), protested against the wildly popular series because of its negative representation of blacks. In spite of these protests, CBS moved the popular radio show to television, and in 1951 *Amos 'n' Andy* became America's first television sitcom with an all-black cast (it ran for two seasons). The radio version continued but evolved into a quasi-variety show called *The Amos 'n' Andy Music Hall*, which ended in 1955.

By the mid-1950s radio sitcoms—like most network radio formats—had migrated almost completely to television. One strange "reverse crossover" was *My Little Margie*, a sitcom about a well-to-do widower and his 21-year-old daughter, who was intent on "protecting him" from various female suitors. The show premiered on CBS television in June 1952 for a three-month run. NBC ran the series for a few months before it resumed broadcast on CBS in January 1953. At about the same time, the series began producing new episodes for CBS network radio. The television series returned to NBC in September 1953 and stayed there until August 1955. The radio version remained on CBS, but it also ended in 1955.

Only three radio sitcoms, *Our Miss Brooks*, *The Great Gildersleeve*, and *Fibber McGee and Molly*, were still broadcast during the 1955–56 season. *Our Miss Brooks* began on CBS radio in 1948, but it began running on television as well in 1952 with almost the same cast. Both versions of the show ended in 1956. *Gildersleeve*, a character on the *Fibber McGee and Molly* show, spun off into his own radio series in 1941. Although it had a 15-year run on radio, Gildersleeve was not popular enough to make the transition to television. *Fibber McGee and Molly*—which aired for 22 years—left NBC radio in 1957, permanently closing the door on network radio's situation comedy closet. The show reappeared on NBC television for a very short 6-month run in 1959. The characters and situations in the McGee household did not transfer well to the new television neighborhood.

Although radio sitcoms ceased to air nationally in the United States in 1957, the format has not entirely disappeared. Occasionally, comedy dramas have been produced for American public radio. Imports from Canada, the British Broadcasting Corporation (BBC), and other international markets have also made their way to American airwaves. One of the more popular of these was a BBC radio sitcom disguised as a science fiction episodic serial, *The Hitchhiker's Guide to the Galaxy*. It premiered in Great Britain in 1978 and traveled to American public radio in the early 1980s.

See also, in addition to programs mentioned in this entry:
Comedy; Variety Shows; Vaudeville and Radio

Further Reading

Barson, Michael, editor, *Flywheel, Shyster, and Flywheel: The Marx Brothers' Lost Radio Show*, New York: Pantheon Books, 1988; London: Chatto and Windus, 1989.
Buxton, Frank, and William Hugh Owen, *The Big Broadcast, 1920–1950: A New, Revised, and Greatly Expanded Edition of Radio's Golden Age*, New York: Viking Press, 1972.
Dunning, John, *On the Air: The Encyclopedia of Old Time Radio*, New York: Oxford University Press, 1998.
Firestone, Ross, *The Big Radio Comedy Program*, Chicago: Contemporary Books, 1978.
Grote, David, *The End of Comedy: The Sit-Com and the Comedic Tradition*, Hamden, Connecticut: Archon Books, 1983.
Harmon, Jim, *The Great Radio Comedians*, Garden City, New York: Doubleday, 1970.
Josefsberg, Milt, *The Jack Benny Show*, New Rochelle, New York: Arlington House, 1977.
Poole, Gary, *Radio Comedy Diary: A Researcher's Guide to the Actual Jokes and Quotes of the Top Comedy Programs of 1947–50*, Jefferson, North Carolina: McFarland, 2001.
Settel, Irving, *A Pictorial History of Radio*, New York: Grossett and Dunlap, 1967; 2nd editon, New York: Ungar, 1983.
Summers, Harrison Boyd, editor, *A Thirty-Yyear History of Programs Carried on National Radio Networks in the United States, 1926–1956*, Columbus: Ohio State University, 1958.
Wertheim, Arthur Frank, *Radio Comedy*, New York: Oxford University Press, 1979.
Widner, James F., "Comedy Central," www.otr.com/comedy.html

PHILIP J. AUTER

SOAP OPERA
Daytime Radio Drama

Although many critics disagree on when the first-soap opera was actually broadcast, most would concede that the earliest prototype for serial drama appeared on Chicago radio in the 1920s: Irna Phillips' *Painted Dreams*, a mosaic of fanciful stories about heroes, villains, and helpless victims. *Painted Dreams* did not fare very well on local radio initially, but Phillips was never discouraged by her perceived failure. She (along with Frank Hummert, an advertising executive, and his wife Anne) was convinced that a successful serial format in newspapers and magazines could translate well into radio. Within a short time, Phillips and both of the Hummerts were proven right; *The Smith Family*, premiering nationally in 1925, became an instant hit. The program was built around two vaudevillians, Jim and Marion Jordan (who later became Fibber McGee and Molly). Later, *The Smith Family* was joined by *Clara*; *Lu 'n' Em*; *Vic and Sade*; *Just Plain Bill*; *The Romance of Helen Trent*; *Ma Perkins*; and *Betty and Bob*.

The meteoric rise of daytime serial drama was a phenomenon that had not been foreseen by most programmers, and certainly not by any advertisers. In fact, the networks' first impulse was to reject the notion of any type of series targeted toward women. They thought it foolhardy and unprofitable because of the seemingly unattractive listening population of unpaid workers (housewives—unattractive because of their perceived lack of impact on revenues generated for sponsors) during the afternoon time block, and also because of the questionable cost efficiency of providing serious drama in continuous segments.

Despite these reservations, however, the networks decided to experiment with several 15-minute "episodes," provided at discounted prices, to interested sponsors in the early 1930s. Most advertising support for these daytime dramas came from corporations such as the Colgate Palmolive Peet Company and Procter and Gamble, who sold household products to interested female listeners. Thus, the term *soap opera* was coined to describe the melodramatic plotlines sold by detergent companies.

In retrospect, those who gambled on the success of radio soap operas need not have worried; the format seemed to be a perfect complement to the medium. Relying completely on sound, radio producers spread news, information, musical entertainment, and folktales. In minstrel tradition, narrators could easily set the stage for radio drama, providing descriptions of characters and settings for the stories. Within minutes, listeners (mostly women) were ushered into an imaginary world (guided by the narrator) with friends and enemies they might never encounter otherwise. In short, they became participants in a place more exciting, dramatic, and compelling than the home from which they listened.

Thus, the introduction of daytime drama met with as immediate a success as the evening serial counterpart had enjoyed. Devoted listeners faithfully followed the lives and loves of their favorite soap opera characters. And, much to the networks' surprise, housewives were not an unattractive listening demographic to possess. In fact, programmers soon discovered that homemakers, though not directly in the labor force, often controlled the purse strings of the household economy. By 1939 advertising revenue for the popular serials had exceeded $26 million. Less than ten years later, Procter and Gamble was spending over $20 million each year on radio serials. Housewives had indeed found an alluring substitute for previous programming fare (such as hygienic information, recipe readings, and household tips) and were demonstrating their consumer power as well. Network programmers and advertisers had inadvertently stumbled onto an undiscovered gold mine. However, creative programming was not the only reason for the immediate popularity of radio soap operas. To better understand the success of daytime drama in the 1930s, it is important to look at two additional factors: the story formula and its relationship to Depression-era America

Serial Drama and the Cultural Landscape of 1930s America

Irna Phillips was a major contributor to early soap opera formula and content. She concentrated on characterization more than plotline fantasy and later became noted for introducing "working professionals" (doctors and lawyers) to daytime serials. To her, the events were far less important than how they were interpreted or acted upon by her characters. Unlike Phillips, Frank and Anne Hummert believed strongly in plot-driven stories, developing an "assembly-line" or formulaic approach to soap

operas that has continued to be successful in today's media. Together, these radio pioneers created a solid genre for future generations.

The Hummerts originated many of the popular early daytime dramas such as *Just Plain Bill, The Romance of Helen Trent*, and *Ma Perkins*. They based most of their stories in the Midwest—an ideal setting for several reasons. First of all, the Hummerts' ad agency was located in Chicago. Practically speaking, they felt their soap operas should be produced there to cut expenses and to enable them to exert more creative control. Further, since most of the Hummerts' life experience came from the Midwest, they were more confident having their ideas and plots set there. Finally, the Hummerts felt that the Midwest carried with it an accurate reflection of American values, attitudes, and lifestyles. It seemed to be an ideal part of the country for audiences to associate with the familiar themes of daytime drama, known as the "Hummert formula."

The Hummerts' story formula was really quite simple: they combined fantasies of exotic romance, pathos, and suspense with a familiar environment of everyday life in a small-town or rural setting. Combined with an identifiable hero or heroine, this formula produced an overwhelming audience response: people everywhere shared common needs, common values, and common problems.

This broadcast unity of beliefs and attitudes was especially important during the Depression era, when poverty, unemployment, and general political pessimism threatened the very fiber of American family life. Women, in particular, felt threatened. Although most were not laid off from jobs themselves, they found themselves demoralized as those around them, one by one, lost work. Household incomes declined markedly, and women were forced to feed, clothe, and shelter their families with far fewer resources than before. Amid their discouragement, listeners relied on soap opera characters such as Ma Perkins and *Just Plain Bill* Davidson— common folks who could survive despite overwhelming odds. Their victories over the trials and tribulations of daily living gave many Americans the feeling that they, too, could and would survive.

By 1936 soap operas began to dominate the daytime radio dials. *The Goldbergs* moved from its prime-time perch to afternoons (followed in 1937 by *Myrt and Marge*); several Hummert dramas premiered (including *David Harum, Rich Man's Darling, Love Song*, and *John's Other Wife*); and a soon-to-be-famous soap writer, Elaine Carrington, debuted her first work, *Pepper Young's Family*. In 1937 more daytime drama appeared, some worthy of note (such as *The Guiding Light*, the longest-running soap opera in radio/television history), and some better forgotten. However, the total impact of radio serials had finally been realized—both negatively and positively—and as such, the serials became open to criticism from women's groups such as the "Auntie Septics," who argued that storylines with suggestive sex, faulty marriages, and subsequent divorces threatened the survival of the American family unit; or followers of New York psychiatrist Louis Berg, who argued through his "hypodermic theory" that messages from soap operas, when "injected" into American listeners' heads, directly precipitated all sorts of psychosomatic traumas, including blood pressure problems, heart arrhythmias, and gastrointestinal disorders. These political action groups were often supported by male doctors who resented the implied superiority of serial female protagonists. The moral proselytizers ultimately faded away, in large part because of network and advertiser resistance as well as public admonishment of people like Berg, who was found to have based his research solely on his *own* blood pressure and pulse. Soap operas had survived not only the effects of the Great Depression, but the potential ruin caused by their detractors as well.

The 1940s: A Golden Age for Radio Soap Operas

As daytime drama entered the 1940s, several characteristics of serial writing emerged. First, characterization was simple, straightforward, and easily recognizable. As most daytime radio listeners were women, listeners could identify with a woman who led a simple life yet was also a solid citizen and model for others in her mythical community.

Second, characters found themselves in predicaments that were easily identifiable by their listeners, with settings easily imaginable to those who had never traveled far beyond their home environment. As Rudolf Arnheim discovered in his study "The World of the Daytime Serial," soap opera characters seemingly preferred commonplace occurrences in their own hometown, as opposed to problems in an unknown environment. And, when circumstances necessitated travel, the new setting invariably was in the United States. Arnheim surmised that soap opera producers refrained from international travel because they felt listeners would not enjoy a foreign setting that would demand that they imagine a place outside their own realm of experience.

Third, most of the action revolved around strong, stable female characters, who were not necessarily professionals, but who were community cornerstones nonetheless. Men were very definitely the weaker sex in soap opera life—a direct reflection on the primary listening audience during the daytime hours.

Finally, daytime drama was often used as a vehicle for moral discussions or a rededication to American beliefs and values. Soap opera heroines often voiced the platitudes of the Golden Rule as well as the rewards that would come to those who could endure the trials and tribulations of living in a troubled society.

After World War II, economic "happy days" returned and soap operas reflected this boom with more career-oriented characters (especially women). But negative postwar elements also emerged, such as postwar mental stress and alcoholism. All these and more were discussed on Ma Perkins' doorstep—with often easy solutions—keeping the "painted dream" of America alive and well.

Career women became more numerous in the 1940s because of writers like Irna Phillips. Phillips also introduced mental problems and amnesia to daytime drama, to reflect America's postwar interest in psychology. Usually a central character suffered some type of emotional malady such as memory loss, a nervous breakdown, alcoholism, or shell shock as a result of wartime stress. Also, psychosomatic paralysis was a common affliction of the long-suffering soap opera heroes and heroines.

Toward the end of the 1940s, crime emerged as an important plotline theme, especially in the area of juvenile delinquency. This direction was also reflective of the times, for Americans were becoming increasingly concerned about youth crime. Criminal storylines continued throughout the early 1950s and continue to be an important theme in daytime drama on television (although the situations have been updated considerably).

The 1950s: The Move from Radio to Television

In the early 1950s, most soap operas moved from radio to television, and the resulting change in technology was felt at all levels, including scriptwriting, acting, and production. The visual medium of television allowed for a wider choice in soap opera settings, because writers were not forced to limit themselves to the experiential world of radio listeners. Rather, they could take their characters anywhere, as long as they visually established the appropriate setting. However, the visual element in television also had distinct limits, for soap writers could no longer rely on "imagination" to set a scene.

Despite many writers' strong preference for radio, most writers, like Irna Phillips, readjusted themselves to the new medium. Phillips' way to explore television's strengths was to use more reality-based themes in established soap operas like *The Guiding Light* (a Phillips creation, moving from radio to television in 1952) as well as to write new soaps, such as *As the World Turns* (with Agnes Nixon), *Another World* (with Bill Bell), *Days of Our Lives*, and *Love Is a Many Splendored Thing*. Phillips' stories, along with those of other serial writers, such as Roy Winsor (*Search for Tomorrow, Love of Life*, and *The Secret Storm*) and Irving Vendig (*Edge of Night*), were lauded by both viewers and critics: ratings skyrocketed and scholars now asserted that daytime TV drama was both entertaining and informative.

In the mid-1950s, some soap operas expanded to 30 minutes, as compared to the 15-minute capsules of the 1930s and 1940s. Because viewers could now see their characters, plotlines became more slowly paced to capitalize on all the advantages of the visual medium such as character reactions and new locales. In fact, a common plotline such as a marriage proposal could last for weeks in a 1950s television soap. After the male character "popped the question" in *Secret Storm*, for example, several days of programming would be spent learning the reactions of both principal and supporting characters for this event: the bride-to-be, her mother, her old boyfriend, his old girlfriend or ex-wife, his secret admirer, her secret admirer, and so on. The possibilities were endless. Thus, one major plotline could sustain itself for weeks longer on television than would be possible on radio despite the added 15 minutes of programming each day. But was it any more effective? Some would argue yes; others would disagree.

The fact remains that many television soap opera plots in the 1980s and 1990s seemed to have changed little since their birth in the late 1920s. Stories still revolve around issues of love, family, health, and security within a cultural context—much like early radio serial drama. And even today, according to author J. Fred MacDonald (in *Don't Touch That Dial*), TV soap opera characters respond to these issues with the same philosophy as their radio predecessors used, which was best expressed by Kay Fairchild, a central character in a 1940s radio serial called *Stepmother*:

> All we can be sure of is that nothing is sure. And that tomorrow won't be like today. Our lives move in cycles—sometimes that's a good thing to remember, sometimes bad. We're in a dark valley that allows us to hope, and to be almost sure that we'll come out after awhile on top of a hill. But, we have to remember, too, that beyond every hill, there's another valley.

One of the greatest frustrations of serial drama is that the storylines are neverending—though the last seven daytime serials left the Columbia Broadcasting System (CBS) altogether in late 1960. Ironically, this is also one of its greatest attractions. As a result, soap operas are one of most recognized genres of broadcasting today, enjoying consistent audience devotion and popularity in a world where most success is as ephemeral as the last ratings period. And it all began on radio.

See also: Goldbergs; Ma Perkins

Further Reading

Allen, Robert Clyde, *Speaking of Soap Operas*, Chapel Hill: University of North Carolina Press, 1985.
Arnheim, Rudolph, "The World of the Daytime Serial," in *Radio Research, 1942–1943*, edited by Paul F. Lazarsfeld and Frank Nicholas Stanton, New York: Essential Books, 1944.
Buckman, Peter, *All for Love: A Study in Soap Opera*, Salem, New Hampshire: Salem House, 1985.
Cantor, Muriel G., and Suzanne Pingree, *The Soap Opera*, Beverly Hills, California: Sage, 1983.
Cox, Jim, *The Great Radio Soap Operas*, Jefferson, North Carolina: McFarland, 1999.
Cox, Jim, *Historical Dictionary of American Radio Soap Operas*. Lanham, Maryland: Scarecrow Press, 2005
"Era Ends as Soaps Leave Radio," *Broadcasting* (22 August 1960).
LaGuardia, Robert, *Soap World*, New York: Arbor House, 1983.
MacDonald, J. Fred, *Don't Touch that Dial!: Radio Programming in American Life, 1920–1960*, Chicago: Nelson-Hall, 1979.
Matelski, Marilyn J., *The Soap Opera Evolution: America's Enduring Romance with Daytime Drama*, Jefferson, North Carolina: McFarland, 1988.
Matelski, Marilyn J., *Soap Operas Worldwide: Cultural and Serial Realities*, Jefferson, North Carolina: McFarland, 1999.
Rouverol, Jean, *Writing for Daytime Drama*, Boston: Focal Press, 1992.
Schemering, Christopher, *The Soap Opera Encyclopedia*, New York: Ballantine, 1985; 2nd updated and expanded edition, 1988.
Stedman, Raymond William, *The Serials: Suspense and Drama by Installment*, 2nd edition, Norman: University of Oklahoma Press, 1977.
Wilder, Frances Farmer, *Radio's Daytime Serial*, New York: Columbia Broadcasting System, 1945.

MARILYN J. MATELSKI

SOCIAL CLASS AND RADIO

Research in social class attempts to explain how and why societies are divided into hierarchies of power, prestige, or wealth. Studies of social class and media examine how mass media reinforce or reproduce this persistent "stratification" of society. Of all the mass media, radio is an especially rich subject area for the study of social class because radio itself has had several definitions over its history. Each of its several incarnations—wireless telegraph, popular hobby, mass medium, and music utility—presents different opportunities for the exploration of social class.

Radio was a conspicuous newcomer in both U.S. and British culture between 1920 and 1950, the subject of constant debate among scholars, journalists, and politicians. During this period, radio's prominence may be likened to the role of television in today's culture. As a result, nearly all in-depth studies of radio take this golden age as their subject. Very few studies focus on social class in their research; however, from the many cultural, social, and oral histories of radio as well as ethnographic accounts that make up our understanding of radio's audience, it is possible to arrive at some generalizations about radio and social class. Foremost of these is radio's image as an essentially middle-class medium and the creation of a new middle-class culture of consumption and home-centered leisure in the advanced industrial world.

What Is Social Class?

Journalists, critics, and academics often use the concept of class rather casually, referring to the lower, middle, and upper classes, without explaining what they mean by these terms. Typically class is used as a synonym for level of income or wealth. Class is considerably more complex, however, than this casual use suggests. Most media researchers adopt one of two approaches to class: either the approach in the United States that emerged from a sociological tradition in the 1940s and 1950s, or the British Cultural Studies (BCS) approach that developed out of a Marxist literary studies tradition in the 1960s.

American media studies rarely use social class as an object of study or a unit of analysis. Social critic Benjamin DeMott has criticized U.S. culture and other cultural critics for accepting a "myth of classlessness," the assumption that nearly everyone in U.S. culture is (or aspires to be) within the bounds of middle-class taste and values. U.S. media, according to DeMott, reinforce this myth (DeMott, *The Imperial Middle: Why Americans Can't Think Straight about Class*, 1990). On the rare occasion that social class is defined in the sociological tradition, it is often considered a product of

four factors: occupation, education, income, and/or self-identity. As an example of this approach, Melvin Kohn's 1969 book *Class and Conformity: A Study in Values* uses the factors listed above, coupled with statistical analysis, to arrive at useful insights into the workings of social class within families and society.

BCS has grappled with the meanings and definition of social class in a much more critical manner than has sociological analysis in the United States. Accordingly, there are many interpretations of class within BCS. However, most cultural critics would agree that the BCS conception of class fuses the thinking of three important figures: Karl Marx, Antonio Gramsci, and Pierre Bourdieu.

In Marx's conception of class, the divisions between the "three great classes" (capitalist, bourgeoisie, and proletariat) are essentially economic. The capitalist class uses its wealth and property ownership to dominate and organize society according to its own interests.

Antonio Gramsci, an Italian intellectual writing in the 1920s and 1930s, highlighted the role of conflict and negotiation in social structures. Gramsci's theory of "hegemony" states that maintaining control in a social order requires the upper class to constantly *reinvent* its social dominance. Because the upper classes cannot simply dominate all classes at all times, Gramsci argues, class power must operate through the power to define the nature of "prestige" in a society as well as control of political and military force. Gramsci's ideas are significant in their recognition that power relations between social classes are inherently unstable. He also acknowledges schools, families, and media as important battlegrounds in the ongoing struggle for class hegemony. These ideas opened the door to thinking about social class as more than a product of economics, but also a cultural process.

Pierre Bourdieu, a French sociologist, coined the term "cultural capital" to describe how cultural products (books, media) and cultural knowledge (languages, rituals) serve as markers to reinforce social class as it passes from generation to generation. Cultural capital not only helps reproduce social class, but can also translate into an economic advantage and thus a better economic class position for individuals. Using Bourdieu's ideas, media researchers are able to link cultural experiences, such as listening to the radio, accessing the internet, or attending "high art" events such as the opera, directly to the formation and reproduction of social stratification.

Social class can be a powerful analytic tool, a way to better understand group or individual behavior and choices within a historical and social context. However, social class is also difficult to define; the stratification it describes is subject to change and multiple interpretations. Social class may be defined as a product of economic position, cultural position, psychology, or values, yet any particular set of class labels—lower class, working class, middle class, upper class, or elite—will always be inadequate, a simplification of a complex reality. Furthermore, the boundaries between classes are often unclear, and individuals may belong to multiple classes.

Radio: The Middle-Class Medium?

The prevailing attitude toward social class and radio in most historical or institutional research can be summed up by a quote from Fred MacDonald's 1979 book *Don't Touch That Dial:* "Seeking to please an audience of millions of relatively free-and-equal, middle-class citizens, radio inevitably reflected the democratic environment which it served." In other words, radio is widely perceived as a medium successfully catering to all people, serving up a stew of politics, news, sports, music, and drama that represents a perfect mix of the tastes and values of the population as a whole. Some see radio as the beginning of "homogenizing" the culture of the United States. National networks standardized the nation's news and entertainment as it pulled together the first mass audience in history. It ironed out sectional differences and gave the nation a common culture. However, more recent studies have begun to question whether radio is truly a "middle-class medium."

Radio's association with the middle class began early in its history. In her 1987 book, Susan Douglas describes radio's most prominent inventors and entrepreneurs, most of whom emerged from middle-class or upper-middle-class backgrounds. After the turn of the century, thousands of hobbyists converged on the new technology, building transmitters and receivers to experiment and socialize in "the ether." This subculture, Douglas says, was "primarily white, middle-class boys and men who built their own stations in their bedrooms, attics, or garages" (see Douglas, 1987). The amateur operator credited with making the first professional broadcasts, Frank Conrad, was a white, middle-class engineer employed by Westinghouse.

The popular press and news media supported the image of resourceful, average, middle-class boys and men mastering this "new frontier." However, there were female and working-class radio buffs as well. Michele Hilmes (1997) has countered Douglas' description of the amateur operator subculture, arguing that the popular press ignored amateurs outside the mainstream of male, middle-class culture. From its beginnings, Hilmes argues, radio was seen as a threat to established social hierarchies such as class, race, and gender—that is, a threat to the hegemony of white, middle-class values. According to Hilmes, the popular press chose to portray white men and boys as icons of wireless because they were less threatening to the social order than women or working-class male operators.

The opposition between "working-class culture" and "middle-class culture" animates many of the inquiries researchers have made into radio's development as a mass medium. Cultural critics, including Raymond Williams, Jacques Donzelet, and Simon Frith, have noted how radio's success shifted entertainment into the domestic sphere, away from collective spaces such as taverns, dance halls, or simply the front porch or street. Such a change was related to class because outdoor amusements were associated with the lower classes, the "unruly masses," whereas home-based entertainment was considered more genteel and middle-class. In an oral history of early radio, "The Box on the Dresser," Shaun Moores writes that the radio could only become a fixture in the home if it could be accommodated within an existing structure of family relations, routines, and patterns. The radio schedule was quickly shaped to fit the patterns of middle-class family life, intertwining with mother's housework, father's job, and the children's schoolwork and bedtimes. Radio's reorganization of leisure time is one example of how radio interacted with large-scale social transformations in the early 20th century, such as industrialization, urbanization, and the rise of consumer culture. If radio seemed to represent the interests of the middle class, it was in part because middle-class interests were beginning to occupy the culture as a whole.

Radio's threat to established hierarchies extended into its golden age. Hilmes locates class awareness in the advertising men who produced radio's most popular programs, most of whom were well-educated, upper-middle-class men. As the group responsible for filling the radio schedule, they reinforced existing class, race, and gender distinctions through their programming choices. For example, the dialects heard on *Amos 'n' Andy* or *The Goldbergs* and the ethnic stereotypes used by Fred Allen in his "Allen's Alley" sketches reinforced long-standing social differences. Meanwhile, the stories on dramatic programs and soap operas and ubiquitous home economics programs presented middle-class family life as the social norm.

Economic reasoning lay behind this appeal to the middle class. In the United States, radio programs were built with a powerful imperative: to appeal to an identified market of listening consumers. As Eileen Meehan has written, ratings systems developed to measure this market were deeply influenced by class. For instance, the first two widely used ratings methods, the Cooperative Analysis of Broadcasting (CAB) and C.E. Hooper's "Hooperatings," relied on telephone interviews to gather data. However, the telephone was still a relative luxury in the early 1930s. Thus, CAB and Hooperatings did not measure the listening habits of all homes with radios but rather only the habits of homes with radios *and* telephones—homes that represented what Meehan calls the "thoroughly modern, consumer-oriented middle-class" (see Meehan, 1990). Subsequent ratings systems for radio and television, including the Arbitron ratings, still rely on this conception of the audience, literally defining *audience* as only those people that most appeal to advertisers.

Unlike the American broadcasting model, which served predominantly commercial interests, the British Broadcasting Corporation (BBC) was formed to serve the principle of public service. Perhaps as a result, social class is more prominent in British studies of mass media. By most historical accounts, assumptions about class differences and tensions deeply influenced the BBC's programming. "Serious" programs, such as classical music and public affairs, targeted the bourgeoisie, whereas popular "light entertainment," such as dance music, was included for the working-class audience. In a 1983 article, Simon Frith challenged this interpretation of the BBC's popular programming. Frith argued that light entertainment on the BBC was a "middlebrow" form that both entertained a mass audience and fulfilled the BBC's public service charge, but at the cost of producing programs that were wholesome, yet bland and repetitive. David Cardiff revisited Frith's argument in a 1988 article to suggest that comedy on the BBC was also a middlebrow creation, but in no way bland or repetitive. Rather, by simultaneously addressing a mass audience and representing the culture of the elite through comedy, the programs resolved class tensions by deflating perceived differences with laughter.

The construction of middle-class audiences does not tell the entire story of social class and radio. The power of radio (or any form of media) to reshape the identity of its audience is an open debate. Lizabeth Cohen (1989) has questioned the ability of institutions of mass culture—chain stores, movies, and radio—to erase the differences between

classes at the grassroots. In her studies of Chicago's working class, Cohen has pointed out that broadcasting was an intensely local enterprise through the 1920s and into the Great Depression. It featured talks by local personages, ethnic/nationality hours, labor news, church services, and vaudeville acts familiar to local communities. Furthermore, working-class audiences were likely to build their own radios (avoiding high-priced, mass-produced "parlour sets") and engaged in communal listening in stores, social clubs, and neighbors' homes. In other words, rather than blanketing communities with a unified mass culture, early radio promoted affiliations within existing groups through their ethnic, religious, or working-class identities. Similarly, radio had an appeal to rural populations distinct from its urban, middle-class image. As late as the 1940s, the differences between rural and urban life in the United States were stark. To label these families as representative of either the middle class or the working class would be inaccurate, for rural America was a culture apart in many ways. Nonetheless, as Richard Butsch (2000) describes, radio broadcasts as early as the 1920s began to address the particular needs and tastes of rural audiences. Although radios spread slowly into rural areas because of the prohibitive cost of owning and operating the radio sets, they were among the most coveted and prized possessions for rural families. Like Cohen's working-class audiences, rural families built and maintained their own radios and practiced communal listening well after most urban audiences had retreated into isolated domesticity.

The emergence of talk radio as a potent political force over the last 20 years has raised questions about the potential for radio to represent social classes traditionally cut off from political discourse. For instance, the populist uprising that derailed President Bill Clinton's nomination of Zoe Baird for attorney general in 1993 has been attributed to a "spontaneous combustion" of working- and lower-class voices. Benjamin Page and Jason Tannenbaum (1996) have described how mainstream media communicators, influenced perhaps by their own class position, initially treated Baird's tax violations as a trivial matter (she failed to pay Social Security taxes for illegal aliens she had employed). However, an intense reaction materialized through the medium of participatory talk radio, influencing members of Congress and the media and leading to the withdrawal of Baird's nomination. The Baird case may be an exception. In other instances, talk radio commentators have been critiqued for the intensity of their political rhetoric and attraction to scandal. Whether talk radio has inspired a kind of "direct democracy" for the working-class, as the Baird example suggests, or simply given voice to the more angry and intolerant voices in society is a matter for debate.

The case of WCFL, the only radio station to be owned and operated by a labor union, presents another example of working-class interest in radio. The Chicago Federation of Labor founded WCFL in 1926 as a platform to broadcast entertainment and information of interest to the labor unions and the working class. WCFL struggled to survive as a listener-supported station, undermined by a hostile business and regulatory environment, high operating costs, and stiff competition from better-financed commercial stations. By the late 1930s, WCFL had adopted the commercial model of broadcasting. However, the station remained a symbol of resistance to corporate-controlled media and continued to provide news from the perspective of organized labor. WCFL's organizers also hoped to preserve working-class culture, including the music, theater, and art of local ethnic groups and pro-union artists, much of which was being replaced by the avalanche of popular culture coming from Hollywood and New York radio studios. WCFL stayed on the air into the 1970s, although it had lost nearly all pretensions of being the "Voice of Labor." The barriers faced by WCFL are a good illustration of the problems faced by all alternative media. Today only community radio, low-power radio, and, to a lesser extent, public radio provide media outlets for social classes whose art and issues are rarely seen or heard, yet all face perennial problems securing adequate funding and political support, and proving their "relevance" in an industry driven by audience ratings.

Although radio technology and programming have changed dramatically since the 1930s, the economic realities of commercial radio have changed very little. Nonetheless, there are few studies of modern radio that address social class in even a peripheral way. There is some irony here, because the modern radio environment may be more class-inflected than ever. Contemporary radio is marketed to narrow, well-defined niches of the population as ratings companies track the age, gender, ethnicity, and education of audiences in fine detail. Formats are built with a particular audience's tastes, politics, and languages in mind. Meanwhile, the ideal listener is still conceived in terms of his or her ability to buy advertised products. Understanding how society is organized economically and culturally is central to the task of understanding social class, and radio remains a powerful expression of both economics and culture in the 21st century.

See also: Educational Radio to 1967; Pacifica Foundation; Playwrights on Radio; Poetry and Radio; Public Radio Since 1967; Stereotypes on Radio; WCFL

Further Reading

Bolce, Louis, Gerald De Maio, and Douglas Muzzio, "Dial-In Democracy: Talk Radio and the 1994 Election," *Political Science Quarterly* 111, no. 3 (1996).
Butsch, Richard, *The Making of American Audiences: From Stage to Television, 1750–1990*, Cambridge and New York: Cambridge University Press, 2000.
Cardiff, David, "Mass Middlebrow Laughter: The Origins of BBC Comedy," *Media, Culture, and Society* 10 (1988).
Cohen, Lizabeth, "Encountering Mass Culture at the Grassroots: The Experience of Chicago Workers in the 1920s," *American Quarterly* 41, no. 1 (1989).
Douglas, Susan Jeanne, *Inventing American Broadcasting, 1899–1922*, Baltimore, Maryland: Johns Hopkins University Press, 1987.
Frith, Simon, "The Pleasures of the Hearth: The Making of BBC Light Entertainment," in *Formations of Pleasure*, edited by Tony Bennett, et al., London and Boston: Routledge and Kegan Paul, 1983.
Garnham, Nicholas, and Raymond Williams, "Pierre Bourdieu and the Sociology of Culture: An Introduction," in *Media, Culture, and Society: A Critical Reader*, edited by Richard Collins, et al., London and Beverly Hills, California: Sage, 1986.
Godfried, Nathan, *WCFL: Chicago's Voice of Labor, 1926–78*, Urbana: University of Illinois Press, 1997.
Hilmes, Michele, *Radio Voices: American Broadcasting, 1922–1952*, Minneapolis: University of Minnesota Press, 1997.
Kohn, Melvin L., *Class and Conformity: A Study in Values*, Homewood, Illinois: Dorsey Press, 1969; 2nd edition, Chicago: University of Chicago Press, 1977.
MacDonald, J. Fred, *Don't Touch that Dial!: Radio Programming in American Life, 1920–1960*, Chicago: Nelson-Hall, 1979.
Meehan, Eileen, "Why We Don't Count: The Commodity Audience," in *Logics of Television: Essays in Cultural Criticism*, edited by Patricia Mellencamp, Bloomington: Indiana University Press, and London: BFI Books, 1990.
Moores, Shaun, "The Box on the Dresser: Memories of Early Radio and Everyday Life," *Media, Culture, and Society* 10 (1988).
Page, Benjamin, and Jason Tannenbaum, "Populistic Deliberation and Talk Radio," *Journal of Communication* 46, no 2 (1996).
Scannell, Paddy, and David Cardiff, *A Social History of British Broadcasting: Serving the Nation, 1922–1939*, Oxford and Cambridge, Massachusetts: Blackwell, 1991.
Thomson, David Cleghorn, *Radio Is Changing Us*: A Survey of Radio Development and Its Problems in Our Changing World, London: Watts, 1937.

CHRISTOPHER LUCAS

SOFT ROCK FORMAT

The soft rock format of radio programming features songs containing elements of both rock and roll and pop music. This musical subgenre originated in the early days of rock and roll, developed into a separate radio format on FM in the early 1970s, and eventually evolved into the adult contemporary format of the 1980s and 1990s.

The term *soft rock* refers to that side of rock and roll music characterized by, naturally, a softer, less raucous style than classic rock and roll. Stuessy and Lipscomb (1999), in *Rock and Roll: Its History and Stylistic Development*, trace the beginnings of soft rock as a musical trend back to the 1950s and the sock hops popular in U.S. high schools. Danceable, upbeat music needed a counterpart musical style, one to which teenagers could "slow dance." Soft rock also filled a need "to balance the harder mainstream rock with a softer, less raucous alternative, while still maintaining some essential elements of the rock style."

In terms of composition and musical style, Stuessy and Lipscomb describe soft rock songs in general as possessing the following characteristics: slow to moderate beat, a soft backbeat, triple division of the rhythmic pattern, strong emphasis on "beautiful" melodies, harmonies that follow a "major tonic—minor subdominant—major subdominant—dominant" chord progression, chords held for two to eight beats, musically conjunct tunes, love-oriented lyrics, and a lead singer with backup vocals. Regarding the singing found in soft rock music, vocalists might use falsetto, blue notes, and variations of rhythm and blues and gospel style. Specific components aside, the label "soft rock" applies to music that includes either a bass line or a rhythmic pattern derived from rock and roll, or both. Pure pop songs lack these basic rock elements.

Popular artists with soft rock hits during the early days of the genre included "white soft rock" singers Elvis Presley and Pat Boone and "black soft rock" acts such as Frankie Lymon and the Teenagers, the Five Satins, and the Monotones. The songs "Crying in the Chapel" by the Orioles and "Sh-Boom" by the Chords epitomize the softer style of rock music during that era. Other artists whose hit songs exemplified the soft rock style included Paul Anka, Bobby Darin, Frankie Avalon, Johnny Mathis, Connie Francis, and Brenda Lee. Soft rock as a trend continued into the 1960s, with Neil Sedaka, Bobby Vee, Bobby Vinton, and Frankie Valli and the Four Seasons among the more successful teen idols whose songs fit the genre (Stuessy and Lipscomb, 1999).

Although soft rock as a popular music style had already coexisted with harder-edged rock and roll since the 1950s, it became a separate and distinct format during the 1960s, when the radio industry began to experience widespread fragmentation resulting from diversification in the music business itself. Keith (1987) notes that the wide array of popular artists' styles, such as those of the Beatles and Glen Campbell, resulted in myriad format variations: "the 1960s saw the advent of the radio formats of Soft Rock and Acid and Psychedelic hard rock." During this decade of change, there emerged the "chicken rock" stations, those that only "flirted" with rock and roll by airing softer tunes of the popular rock music genre: "While a Chicken Rocker would air 'Michelle' and 'Yesterday' by the Beatles, it would avoid 'Strawberry Fields Forever' and 'Yellow Submarine'" (Keith, 1987).

The soft rock format truly came into its own during the 1970s, when, as Keith (1987) outlines, chicken rock, which appealed to the younger end of the 24–39-year-old adult demographic, evolved into mellow rock, which found its core audience among 18–24-year-olds. Mellow rock, an FM specialty, at first featured playlists containing soft rock tunes both popular and somewhat unknown. Eventually the word *mellow*, a throwback to the 1960s drug culture vocabulary, became outdated. With the change in terminology to soft rock came a narrowing of the soft rock playlist, which included more popular hits of the time. By the mid-1970s, soft rock found its target audience—"the young adult who had grown weary of the hard-driving rock sound but who still preferred Elton John over Robert Goulet" (Keith, 1984).

Soft rockers came from a variety of musical backgrounds, including folk, country and western, and soul. Stuessy and Lipscomb (1999) point to the Carpenters, Barry Manilow, Neil Diamond, America, the Osmonds, John Denver, and Roberta Flack as examples of important artists in soft rock music of the 1970s. Gregory (1998) credits the success of the country-rock band The Eagles with the proliferation of "an entire sub-genre of Soft Rock bands," such as Fleetwood Mac.

As the 1970s came to an end, so, too, did soft rock as a distinct format. Keith (1987) attributes its demise to the emergence of disco as a station format, the rise in popularity of hit music stations, and the updating of playlists featuring "easy listening" music. Soft rock the format might have disappeared, but its style lived on in the 1980s through the music of groups such as Air Supply, the Alan Parsons Project, the Police (and their number-one hit single "Every Breath You Take"), and Huey Lewis and the News (Stuessy and Lipscomb, 1999).

By 2009, the term soft rock was often used interchangeably with adult contemporary. And many SR station playlists did heavily mirror AC outlets. However, some stations (examples include WASH in Washington, D.C., and KEZK in St. Louis), try to emphasize the "rock" in their SR choices, in order to differentiate themselves from the older-skewing AC format, and distance themselves as much as possible from middle-of-the-road. To that end, they play an array of artists—from Adele to Amy Winehouse, Matchbox Twenty, Maroon 5, and The Killers—that are hip and a bit edgy but mellow enough not to disturb co-workers in workplace listening.

See also: Adult Contemporary Format; Middle of the Road Format

Further Reading

Gregory, Hugh, *A Century of Pop*, Chicago: A Cappella, and London: Hamlyn, 1998.

Howard, Herbert H., and Michael S. Kievman, *Radio and TV Programming*, Ames: Iowa State University Press, 1986; 2nd edition, as *Radio, TV, and Cable Programming*, by Howard, Kievman, and Barbara A. Moore, 1994.

Keith, Michael C., *Production in Format Radio Handbook*, Lanham, Maryland: University Press of America, 1984.

Keith, Michael C., *Radio Programming: Consultancy and Formatics*, Boston: Focal Press, 1987.

Keith, Michael C., and Joseph M. Krause, *The Radio Station*, Boston: Focal Press, 1986; 5th edition, by Keith, 2000.

Stuessy, Joe, *Rock and Roll: Its History and Stylistic Development*, Englewood Cliffs, New Jersey: Prentice Hall, 1990; 3rd edition, by Stuessy and Scott Lipscomb, Upper Saddle River, New Jersey: Prentice Hall, 1999.

Erika Engstrom,
2009 Revisions By Cary O'Dell

SOUND EFFECTS

As vaudeville faded from popularity and silent films grew, many of the musicians who created music and sound moved to providing accompaniment for silent films. The dexterity required of these musicians, especially the drummers, allowed them to expand their repertoires to include additional sounds that enhanced the movie for viewers. Robert L. Mott, a sound effects artist from the early days of radio, wrote that the earliest actors who moved from live theater and vaudeville to radio brought with them their props, costumes, and gags. These comedians, who relied on the visual gags for laughter, were often lost when they tried to make it in radio. Radio presented a completely new set of opportunities and problems for actors and producers.

The need for people able to produce sound effects to complement radio performances was recognized early. The earliest use of sound effects in a dramatic radio program was, according to Mott (1993), an unknown radio show in the early 1920s in Schenectady, New York. It wasn't until the late 1920s that the CBS network hired sound effects personnel to work with their dramatic programs. Arthur and Ora Nichols, a husband and wife team who were the first sound effects artists in radio, had been musicians for vaudeville acts. The couple perfected their sound effects skills in movie houses, learning additional instruments and ways to perform sounds so the silent films were more realistic to audience members. Arthur Nichols learned to use drums to provide a more diverse range of sounds. Many of the early sound effects artists were drummers, who found the dexterity instilled by their instrument was useful when producing multiple sound effects at one time. These musicians were also experienced in using a variety of contraptions ("traps") to produce different kinds of sounds.

Before the Nicholses introduced the concept of sound effects to network r adio, writers had to script cues that allowed listeners to understand what was happening. The dialog was often confusing but necessary to let listeners know, for example, that someone was supposed to have knocked on the door. The actors found it as awkward, as did the listeners. With the introduction of sound effects, the listening experience was enhanced for the radio audience.

As if by magic, sound effects aided listeners in more fully visualizing the stories they heard on the radio. Mott (1993) writes that sound effects relied on the art of deception. Nisbett (1962) emphasizes that the responsibility of the sound effects artist is not to reproduce sounds exactly as they are but to *suggest* the sound—that to be too realistic may even be detrimental to the desired effect. Most programs had one or two sound effects artists working on any production, though a network record of eight sound effects people were used for CBS Radio's production of *Moby Dick* in 1977.

A sound effects artist needed a variety of skills and talents to be successful. The first requirement, according to Mott, was timing. The second was to be ambidextrous; there were numerous occasions that required independent movement of each hand simultaneously. Additionally, sound effects artists had to be aware of pitch, timbre, harmonics, loudness, attack, sustain, and decay. These nine components, according to Mott, were integral to producing realistic sound effects. Despite the tremendous amount of skill and work involved in producing sound effects, the artists rarely received mention in the credits of a show. Management believed that to acknowledge that the sounds of radio were merely people creating the noises rather than the actual sound would damage the credibility of the programs.

Types of Sound Effects

Sound effects can be categorized into two types: spot (live) effects and those that are pre-recorded. Spot effects are those sounds that are produced live in the studio, whereas recorded effects are produced independently and inserted into the program at the appropriate time. In the earliest days of radio, spot effects were the only type of sound effect used. The technology for recorded effects was developed for sounds that could not be conveniently created within the studio such as cars, airplanes, weather, large crowds, etc.

Sound effects artists frequently needed to create sounds for ordinary sounds and for extraordinary sounds. Ordinary sounds (those we hear all the time) were often the most difficult to create in a realistic fashion. For example, Mott noted that visually oriented producers were the most difficult to work with, as they often believed that if a telephone bell is to ring, there must be a telephone with the bell to "make it sound like a telephone." The artists were skeptical because experience had shown them that producers often thought it was a telephone ringer until they saw it wasn't attached to a telephone, and only then did they insist that the ringing "Just didn't sound like a real telephone."

In the early days of radio, sound effects artists were often called on to produce sounds that no-one had ever heard before. For example, the early science fiction programs often included an invasion from outer space. The sound effects artists needed to produce sounds of a space ship entering Earth's orbit for an invasion. The artists relied on imagination, creativity, and the odds and ends that comprised the sound effects prop room to create sounds that would induce an audience to believe a space ship was fast approaching Earth.

Important Sound Effects People

Ora Nichols was one of the first sound effects artists and the first female in the industry. Ora and her husband, Arthur, spent 23 years as musicians for vaudeville acts and for silent films in movie houses before entering radio. They worked several years as freelance artists and then were hired at CBS along with Henry Gauthiere and George O'Donnell. They were the first staff sound effects personnel in the fledging radio industry. Ora

Nichols directed the CBS Sound Effects Department for several years until Walt Pierson was hired in 1935 as director. This allowed Nichols to return to her preferred spot as a sound effects artist.

Arthur Nichols brought his skills as a craftsman to create props that were necessary to produce realistic sounds. According to Mott, Nichols spent nine months working on a piece of equipment that could produce a wide variety of sounds, from a small bird chirping to 500 gunshots a minute. Together with his wife, he created many of the props and tools that were used to create many of the sound effects for radio.

Orval White was the first African-American sound effects artist. He started out in 1949 as an equipment man and worked his way up to be a talented and respected sound effects artist. White worked for 22 years on one of best-known programs on CBS, *Gang Busters*. He was, according to Mott, the first and only African-American sound effects artist in radio, television, and film.

Jack Amrhein was considered by directors and peers to be one of the best sound effects artists in radio. His creativity and imagination were his strongest assets. Amrhein worked for the CBS radio network in New York as the sound effects artist for many shows, including *Mr. Keene, Tracer of Lost Persons*; *The Mysterious Traveler*; *Mr. Chameleon*; *The Fred Allen Show*; *Inner Sanctum*; *The Phillip Morris Playhouse*; and *The Robert Q. Lewis Show*.

With the rapid growth of radio, there was rapid growth among the cadre of artists who performed sound effects. CBS expanded its sound effects department from eight artists to 40 in the early 1930s, despite the Depression, hiring engineers, music arrangers, film studio personnel, and other people with varied backgrounds who could contribute diverse skills to the growing department.

As the need for more complex sound effects expanded, four unofficial groups emerged: stars, artists, button pushers, and technicians. Though well known among the sound effects artists, this hierarchy was kept unofficial because CBS wanted to be able to randomly assign personnel to shows rather than having to accommodate requests for certain artists. The producers with shows that were rated highly did request certain personnel, but those requests were fulfilled only when the producers threatened to go to the advertisers. Sound effects personnel soon became specialized with different functions.

Lowest in the hierarchy were the technicians. They designed, built, and maintained the props. Occasionally a technician might fill when needed as a button pusher or for some other minimal sound effect production. The button pushers worked on shows with a limited need for sound effects and, according to Mott, literally pushed buttons to produce those sounds. These could be doorbells, buzzers on game shows, phone ringers, or oven timers on the soap operas. Mott noted that many sound effects artists hated the button pusher shows because they found the work boring, even though it was easy, the pay was the same, and the hours were better.

Next in the hierarchy were the sound effects artists, who made up the majority of the sound effects department at any radio network. These artists were used mostly for prime-time shows (both drama and comedy). Producers did not request them, and they were not paid as much as the artists who were considered stars.

The stars were those personnel at the top of the hierarchy. Mott wrote that these people had an uninhibited approach to performing sound effects. They didn't worry how they looked or what others thought of them. These artists were as successful in eliciting laughs from the studio audience as the comedians. Most often the producers allowed them to improvise, and the more freedom they had in their work, the more they performed for the audience. Some actors accused these sound effects artists of upstaging them, but audiences loved them. The stars demanded and received higher fees, overtime compensation, and a variety of other perks not given to most sound effects personnel.

Techniques for Creating Sound Effects

The tools used to produce sounds and noises varied greatly and often had no apparent connection to the sounds they were used to emulate. For example, in one program, Mott used a bowl of spaghetti to convince the audience a hungry worm was devouring people in their sleep. Other sound effects artists employed large open drums with BB shot to replicate the sound of waves at sea, a thunder screen to create claps of thunder, or a scratch box, a small wooden box with one side of tin. The tin was punched with nail holes, that, when swept with a wire brush, sounded like a steam engine train pulling out of the station.

A concept that became important to realism was layering. Layering sounds means using multiple sounds and mixing them to create a more realistic sound effect, an effort that requires the use of additional people (or recorded sounds). For example, to create the sound of a dinosaur for some of the early radio programs, sound effects artists mixed the sounds of real animals (a lion's roar, an elephant's trumpeting, and a tiger snarling), which when played at a slower speed became the industry standard for the sound of a dinosaur.

Sound effects personnel often had to make extraordinary efforts to create everyday sounds that sounded "right" on radio. For example, they used flash bulbs dropping into a glass for ice, a cork dipped in turpentine and then rubbed on a bottle to create the screech of a monkey or rat. They could squeeze a box of cornstarch to sound like footsteps in the snow or use their arms and elbows to hit a table to sound like a body falling. Splash tanks were important for sounds that required water, such as washing dishes on a soap operaor for creating storms at sea on the dramas.

Footsteps were the most commonly requested sound effect for radio. Most artists had special shoes, called "walking shoes," used only for creating the footsteps on air. The artists paid careful attention to the maintenance of the soles and heels of these shoes to be sure they would produce adequate sounds.

A variety of materials and techniques were used to create the illusion of walking on different surfaces. For example, plywood boards were most commonly used for floors and steps inside buildings such as offices or homes. Sound effects artists preferred a piece of plywood to a portable stair because they found the stairs too limiting; instead they perfected a technique of stepping on the board and then rubbing the sole over the end to replicate the sound of someone climbing or descending the stairs. When the script called for someone going up the stairs, they placed the weight of the step on the sole of the shoe, and for descending stairs, the weight was on the heel. To produce the sound of someone walking on a sidewalk, in the street, or indoors on a concrete floor, they used a slab of marble.

A large wooden box that could be filled with gravel, cornstarch (for footsteps in the snow), or other materials was used when needed, as were palm fronds or broom corn to imitate footfalls or movement through a jungle.

Recorded Sound Libraries

As the technology for recording sounds increased, recorded effects of those sounds not easily reproduced in the studio became commonplace. Initially, recording equipment was large and cumbersome, limiting artists' ability to go into the field and record needed sounds. Manufacturers responded by developing portable equipment that allowed artists the freedom to record realistic sounds to 78 rpm records and to alter the speed at which the records were played back, changing the nature of the sound. These recordings were used to provide general, background noises whereas the manually produced sounds were for specific actions such as someone walking down stairs.

Although recorded sound effects provided standardized sounds, the artists still had to be skilled to produce the correct volume, quality, and speed. According to Robert Turnbull (1951), sound effects artists had to be adept with the record to cross-arm, double-arm, segue, slip-speed, or spot-cue. By 1950, sound effects artists had access to over 15,000 recorded sounds. The major networks had extensive libraries of commercially recorded sounds for their sound effects artists. These were often complemented by a collection of specially recorded sounds that the artists recorded locally.

Well before the coming of television, most sound effects had been reduced to recordings, and stations as well as networks could stock hundreds of discs with all types of recorded sound carefully catalogued and indexed. These could be inserted or brought in under actors creating a precise and smoothly integrated sound—at a fraction of the cost of an extensive live sound effects operation. Virtually all modern television sound effects are achieved in this fashion.

See also: Production for Radio

Further Reading

Creamer, Joseph, and William B. Hoffman, *Radio Sound Effects*, New York and Chicago: Ziff-Davis, 1945.
Mott, Robert L., *Radio Sound Effects: Who Did It, and How, in the Era of Live Broadcasting*, Jefferson, North Carolina: McFarland, 1993.
Mott, Robert L., *Radio Live! Television Live! Those Golden Days When Horses Were Coconuts*, Jefferson, North Carolina: McFarland, 2000.
Nisbett, Alec, *The Technique of the Sound Studio*, New York: Hastings House, 1962; London: Focal Press, 1965.
Turnbull, Robert B., *Radio and Television Sound Effects*, New York: Rinehart, 1951.
Whetmore, Edward Jay, *The Magic Medium: An Introduction to Radio in America*, Belmont, California: Wadsworth, 1981.

MARGARET FINUCANE

SOUNDPRINT

Documentary Series and Media Center

Soundprint is one of the few ongoing nationally broadcast, noncommercial radio documentary series in America. The series is produced by the Soundprint Media Center, Incorporated (SMCI), a nonprofit media production and training facility based in Laurel, Maryland, near Washington, D.C.

Since 1988 *Soundprint*'s weekly broadcasts have featured documentaries by independent radio producers who explore a wide range of topics in half-hour segments. Most of the shows provide more context than one finds in deadline-driven, time-specific radio news stories. The series also provides an outlet for international voices through its documentary exchange program with producers in England, Canada, Australia, New Zealand, South Africa, Scotland, Hong Kong, the Netherlands, and Ireland.

In addition, *Soundprint*'s parent company, SMCI, embraces cutting-edge media technologies. The center maintains state-of-the-art digital audio production facilities and offers world wide web hosting and other internet services.

Soundprint was created in 1986 by the meeting of the minds of some innovative public radio managers and producers. At the Johns Hopkins University station then known as WJHU in Baltimore, Maryland, station managers David Creagh and Dennis Kita hired William Siemering to be the executive producer of their proposed new national documentary series. Siemering was a visionary leader, having co-created National Public Radio's (NPR) flagship daily evening news program, *All Things Considered*. Also, at WHYY in Philadelphia, Pennsylvania, Siemering was a major force behind the creation of the station's celebrated daily national interview program *Fresh Air*. And multi-award winning producers Jay Allison and Larry Massett were two of *Soundprint*'s first documentarians.

Although NPR, the largest of America's public radio networks, maintained its own vehicle for documentaries, *Soundprint* enabled producers outside of the NPR system to air programs dealing with extremely personal issues or with broader societal concerns. For example, one award-winning *Soundprint* show, "Mei Mei: A Daughter's Song" by producer Dmae Roberts (1989), provided an intimate view of a woman's difficult relationship with her mother. The Canadian production "Forever Changed" by Kelly Ryan (1999) examined how people from different walks of life in Nova Scotia dealt with the aftermath of the 1998 crash of Swiss Air Flight 111.

From the start, *Soundprint* encouraged producers to engage listeners aurally in such a way as to allow them to "see" a story through creative sound design—often a complex, multilayered mix of ambient sound, music, narration, and soundbites from event participants. Moreover, *Soundprint* attempts to provide unique perspectives on social, political, cultural, or scientific issues. One of *Soundprint*'s science programs, for example, entitled "A Plague of Plastic Soldiers" produced by Stephen Smith (1996), examined the technological impact of land mines in Southeast Asia—instruments of war that continue to maim and kill long after fighting has ceased. Another program, "Heavy Petting" by Gemma Hooley (1998), humorously chronicled America's infatuation with pets.

The series has always been produced in stereo—technically distinguishing itself from the monaural sound of most radio news programs. And as early as its first broadcast year, *Soundprint* employed the multitrack mixing format used by the music recording industry—enabling the series to better achieve its layered soundscape. In recognition of its technical and contextual daring, the series had won more than 50 major national and international awards through 2002.

Yet for all its success, *Soundprint* has had to wage an ongoing financial battle for survival. Documentary production can be expensive—requiring costly research, travel, sound gathering, editing, and mixing expenses. For the first five years of its life, the series was funded by grants from the Corporation for Public Broadcasting (CPB), the National Endowment for the Arts, and WJHU-FM funds. But as CPB funding (then *Soundprint*'s largest funding source) ended in 1993, WJHU support also dwindled. *Soundprint* executive producer Moira Rankin and technical director Anna Maria de Freitas decided to incorporate the series into a nonprofit company called the Soundprint Media Center, Inc.

The newly formed company landed a major grant from the National Science Foundation (NSF) and rented space at American University's station WAMU-FM in Washington, D.C. But it was clear that the center could not survive on grants alone—especially grants exclusively linked to radio documentary production. So in an attempt to expand its support base, the SMCI began exploring the emerging world of the internet. Through this exploration, the company could also continue to satisfy its desire to utilize new media technology.

In 1994 the SMCI took its documentary series to high school students through the internet and developed some basic webpages for students and teachers. This work led to the center's development of a pioneering mini-network of public broadcasting stations on the internet in 1995. Participating stations included Norfolk, Virginia's WHRO; Athens, Ohio's WOUB; Boston, Massachusetts' WGBH; Minnesota Public Radio; and the Louisiana Public Broadcasting system. Participants could share programs and compare programming strategies through SMCI's online network.

The SMCI later expanded its online efforts by providing the technical architecture, securing the funding, and project-managing "ArtsFest '97," one of the first public broadcasting internet arts festivals. Programming from about 15 non-commercial radio and television stations nationwide was featured almost 24 hours a day during a two-week period. Web users could hear arts programs as varied as cowboy poetry from KGNU-FM in Boulder, Colorado; zydeco music from WWOZ-FM in New Orleans, Louisiana; and radio theater from KCRW-FM in Santa Monica, California.

The SMCI is now continuing its internet innovations by offering database management along with website hosting, updating, and content development. In fact, the company's internet projects have brought in substantial funds from the NSF and the United States Department of Education, as well as contractual work with federal agencies and public radio and television research or production organizations.

SMCI's internet operations have financially bolstered the *Soundprint* radio series. Yet *Soundprint* continues to face challenges. During the mid-1990s, some independent producers boycotted the series until program ownership rights and compensation concerns were resolved. And although *Soundprint* can be heard on stations in several of the country's major markets, the series' station carriage numbers have dropped from a previous high of more than 100 stations during the early 1990s to about 50 stations in the year 2002. Since 1995, radio stations have had to pay for the series. It had been free to affiliate stations when *Soundprint* was distributed by the American Public Radio network (now known as Public Radio International) from 1988–93, and by NPR from 1993–95.

Soundprint produces roughly 45 new documentaries along with 53 re-runs a year. Each week, two half-hour programs are fed via satellite to participating stations throughout the country. Current or archived programs can be heard at *Soundprint*'s website, located at www.soundprint.org

See also: Documentary Programs; Public Radio Since 1967

Hosts

Barbara Bogaev (2000–present), Lisa Simeone (1997–2000), Larry Massett (1988–1997), John Hockenberry (1988)

Creators

William Siemering, David Creagh, Dennis Kita, Larry Massett, Jay Allison

Producers

Moira Rankin, Anna Maria de Freitas

Programming History

American Public Radio/	1988–93
Public Radio International	
National Public Radio	1993–95
Soundprint Media Center, Inc.	1995–Present

Further Reading

Coles, Robert, *Doing Documentary Work*, Oxford and New York: Oxford University Press, 1997.

Conciatore, Jacqueline, "Wary of Losing Rights in New Media, Radio Producers Boycott 'Soundprint,'" *Current* (9 October 1995).

Conciatore, Jacqueline, "CPB Aims to Break Impasse in Talks on Indies Rights," *Current* (20 November 1995).

Conciatore, Jacqueline, "Negotiations Falter, Producers Continue 'Soundprint' Boycott," *Current* (29 January 1996).

"Independents End Boycott on 'Soundprint' Contracts," *Current* (20 January 1997).

Josephson, Larry, editor, *Telling the Story: The National Public Radio Guide to Radio Journalism*, Dubuque, Iowa: Kendall/Hunt, 1983; updated edition, as *Sound Reporting: The National Public Radio Guide to Radio Journalism and Production*, edited by Marcus Rosenbaum and John Dinges, Dubuque, Iowa: Kendall/Hunt, 1992.

Latta, Judi Moore, "Wade in the Water—The Public Radio Series: The Effects of the Politics of Production on Sacred Music Representations," Ph.D. diss., University of Maryland, 1999.

Miller, Doug, "Making Waves: 'Soundprint' Leaves Mark on Radio, Web," *The Laurel Leader* (3 September 1999).

SONJA WILLIAMS

SPORTS ON RADIO

Sports have been a constant feature of radio literally since the beginning of the medium. When Guglielmo Marconi visited New York City in 1899 to demonstrate his wireless telegraphy equipment, he relayed the outcome of the America's Cup yacht race through the ether. Radio sports broadcasts provided some of the first mass-audience programming, enticed Americans to buy radio sets, helped national networks and local stations establish themselves as legitimate entities, and spurred technological and cultural innovations in attempts to capitalize on the appeal of sports. Radio broadcasts of sporting events have also been credited with, or occasionally blamed for, helping to create a sense of national identity, particularly during the 1920s and 1930s.

Origins

Sports—especially boxing, college football, and baseball—became common on some stations as early as the 1920s. The first boxing match broadcast, between heavyweight champion Jack Dempsey and challenger Georges Carpentier on 2 July 1921, was orchestrated by the Radio Corporation of America's (RCA) David Sarnoff and Major J. Andrew White. RCA applied for, and received, a one-day license to broadcast the event using a radio tower borrowed from the Lackawanna Railroad and equipment borrowed from the U.S. Navy. The improvised arrangement, fraught with problems, succeeded in its task. White's narration of Dempsey's victory, which traveled on a signal powerful enough to be received across much of the United States and even in Europe, is credited with sparking a surge in the construction of radio towers and the purchase of receivers. Radio broadcasts of other major bouts, particularly the battles between Dempsey and Gene Tunney in 1926 and 1927 and the Joe Louis–Max Schmeling fights in 1937 and 1938, became mass radio spectacles that attracted audiences of unprecedented size and helped make household names out of broadcasters such as Graham McNamee, Ted Husing, and Bill Stern.

The popularity of college football also grew rapidly in the first two decades of radio. During the 1920s, Notre Dame football became a regional and then a national phenomenon, thanks in part to its prominence on radio, and the annual Army–Navy contest, Ivy League games, and holiday bowl games became nationally recognized events. Bowl games in particular benefited from their appearance on radio: the Rose Bowl, begun in 1927, was carried from the beginning by the National Broadcasting Company (NBC) and became the first coast-to-coast broadcast conducted by the fledgling network. The Sugar Bowl, Orange Bowl, and similar contests begun in the mid-1930s were hyped so vigorously by stations carrying them that radio can be credited for their continued existence. Ted Husing, who began announcing the Orange Bowl in 1937 for the Columbia Broadcasting System (CBS) and hyping the game on his weekly regular-season college broadcasts leading up to New Year's Day, almost single-handedly turned the little-known, sparsely attended event into a major spectacle. His success with the Orange Bowl convinced the industry that other bowl games could become similarly profitable.

Baseball, however, is the most remembered and romanticized radio sport. The inaugural baseball broadcast aired on 5 August 1921, when Harold Arlin called the Pittsburgh Pirates' 8:5 victory over the Philadelphia Phillies on KDKA in Pittsburgh; the first World Series broadcast also occurred that year. These early efforts were little publicized, however, and thus were not widely heard. The next year, however, New York station WJZ's broadcast of the 1922 World Series was heavily publicized by Westinghouse, General Electric, and RCA in an attempt to sell receivers, prompting other New York stations to sign off rather than interfere with the signal. The broadcast was a smashing success: it was heard clearly up to 800 miles away, and immense crowds gathered in front of radio stores to hear the game over loudspeakers.

Demand for baseball broadcasts, especially the World Series, also provoked some of the first experiments in networking. Two New York stations, WJZ and WEAF, were granted broadcast rights to the 1923 World Series; WEAF, owned by telephone giant American Telephone and Telegraph (AT&T), fed the broadcast to WMAF in Massachusetts and WCAP in Washington, D.C. Telephone lines linked seven stations in the Northeast, from Boston to Washington, to carry the Washington Senators' seven-game triumph over the New York Giants in 1924. The World Series quickly became one of radio's biggest and most popular events, with the distinctive voices of McNamee, Husing, Red Barber, Mel Allen, Jack Brickhouse, Jack Buck, Ernie Harwell, and Vin Scully becoming synonymous with baseball over the years for their work behind the microphone during both the regular season and the World Series.

When more regular schedules and commercial radio became established in the late 1920s and early 1930s, sports became more difficult for stations and networks to categorize. Sports resembled news programming in being live, unscripted, and spontaneous, but sports were rarely considered as weighty as other news items. Their mass appeal gave them nearly limitless profit potential, making them resemble entertainment programming, but their spontaneity, timeliness, and control by other entities (team owners, sports commissioners, universities, etc.) limited access and made them difficult to control—particularly because overtime or extra innings could disrupt schedules. In addition, the mixed feelings that outside entities had toward radio broadcasts were a particularly strong obstacle the radio industry had to overcome. Some, such as the Chicago Cubs and Chicago White Sox, viewed radio as a way to expand their sport's (or team's) fan base. Others—such as the New York Yankees, Brooklyn Dodgers, and New York Giants, which agreed to ban baseball broadcasts from 1932 through 1938—considered broadcasts that could be received free of charge a detriment to their box-office revenue. Still others, such as minor-league baseball clubs, believed radio undermined their own profitability while benefiting others in their industry (i.e., the major-league baseball clubs).

Developing Patterns in the 1930s

Reluctant to pay for broadcast rights early in the medium's history, stations and networks initially asked for, and often received, the same treatment as print news media in terms of access to sporting events. There was little exclusivity, and stations competed for listeners rather than for broadcast rights: for instance, during the early 1930s as many as five local stations in Chicago were broadcasting Cubs games from Wrigley Field simultaneously. Although most such broadcasts were noncommercial in character, this approach also allowed radio stations and networks to claim that they met federal responsibility/public service requirements by offering programming of substantial community interest. By the early 1930s, however, most stations accepted advertising revenue for sports programming, spending some of the money to obtain exclusive broadcasting rights. Cereal maker General Mills, Mobil Oil, Goodyear tires, and (after the repeal of Prohibition) numerous beer companies quickly became the major sponsors of major- and minor-league baseball, college football, boxing, horse racing, and, to a lesser degree, college basketball and professional football, in an attempt to reach male listeners.

To reduce costs, stations in the 1920s and 1930s rarely sent announcers on road trips with the local team. Instead, they relied on re-creations: broadcasts produced from skeletal Morse code descriptions of the contest relayed by Western Union to announcers in the radio studio. Baseball announcers became especially famous for their evocative accounts—and for their ingenuity when the wires failed, which announcers usually covered by inventing sudden storms, a ruckus in the stands, or innumerable foul balls. Re-creations slowly disappeared as technology became cheaper and the effects of the Depression were alleviated, and virtually none were heard after World War II except on the Armed Forces Radio Network and on Gordon McLendon's Liberty network.

The networks, oddly, eschewed exclusive sponsorship for sports programming longer than local stations did, for reasons best illustrated by examining the World Series. Network World Series broadcasts from 1926 through 1934 were sustaining fare; NBC and CBS argued that the series was so important to the public that granting exclusive commercial rights to one network would prevent listeners from hearing this sacrosanct event. Because neither network could reach the entire United States through its affiliates, but taken together both could, they contended that non-exclusive rights were imperative. Moreover, the networks contended that commercializing the broadcasts would cheapen the great national pastime. This argument also enabled the networks to justify pre-empting commercial radio programming in order to air the sporting event: because the airtime was not given to another sponsor, an advertising agency that originally paid for the time slot had no basis for complaint.

When the Ford Motor Company acquired exclusive broadcast sponsorship rights to the Series from the commissioner of baseball from 1934 to 1937, the networks feared a backlash from the public, sponsors, and the federal government. Over Ford's objections, NBC and CBS persuaded Baseball Commissioner Judge Kenesaw Mountain Landis to make the broadcast available to all networks and unaffiliated stations; this provision was extended to the Mutual radio network in 1935. This allowed the networks to claim that they met the "public interest, convenience, and necessity" clause codified in the Communications Act of 1934, serving the entire nation in a way that no single station could and alleviating Federal Communications Commission (FCC) concerns. The print media and the public responded favorably to Ford's sponsorship. Jilted sponsors were livid about the arrangement, but they grudgingly agreed to accept compensation from the networks when the networks (legitimately) claimed they had not been privy to the deal. And even though Ford was upset at paying $350,000 for production costs on top of the $100,000 it had spent for exclusive rights, its sales for 1934 doubled, and the sponsorship was publicly hailed as a success.

The networks were ambivalent about this arrangement; although it served several of their needs, each network wanted exclusive rights to the event so it could turn a profit. CBS and NBC executives discussed forgoing their gentleman's agreement and competing for exclusive rights, but neither was able to obtain rights without a sponsor already lined up—and few sponsors were willing to advance the money without rights having been secured. Further, fears about FCC intervention

made the networks reluctant to surrender their "public service" claim, and network executives fretted about how much the exclusive rights to all major sporting events would cost.

The commercial sponsorship model, however, developed quickly. In the wake of Ford's World Series deal, CBS acquired exclusive rights to the 1935 Kentucky Derby, and the major networks began to compete for rights to all major sporting events. College football bowl games, boxing matches, and other major events of national importance were all bought up quickly—except the World Series, the rights to which were already owned by Ford. After the automaker reneged on the final year of its contract, the series was broadcast on a sustaining basis by all major networks in 1937 and 1938. In 1939 Gillette began its long run of exclusive World Series advertising—and the upstart Mutual network acquired exclusive broadcast rights. The deal not only established Mutual's status as a competitive network rather than third banana to the older networks, but also led to FCC investigations of NBC and CBS when affiliates complained that they were pressured not to opt out of their affiliate contracts to carry Mutual's World Series broadcast.

Affiliates' local sports contracts also threatened to destabilize the networks. Although stations often wanted the high-quality programming, national appeal, and other benefits that network affiliation offered, they also wanted to appeal to a local audience—and many regularly pre-empted network programming to air local sports, particularly baseball. The NBC Blue network was particularly lax in policing its affiliates; after all, the high Crossley ratings earned by local baseball team broadcasts in cities such as Pittsburgh and San Francisco helped offset the lower ratings produced by its highbrow public-affairs programming. Both NBC and CBS used the "public interest" clause of the 1934 Communications Act to justify their affiliates' actions to national sponsors, but sponsors increasingly chafed at losing the exclusive access they paid for—particularly in the West, where broadcasts in prime time on the East Coast were often deferred in favor of sporting events in the late afternoon on the West Coast.

Since Television

The advent and diffusion of television throughout the United States in the 1940s and 1950s caused a slow but steady decline in national audiences for radio sports. Sports on American radio became an almost exclusively local or regional affair from the late 1940s through the late 1980s as radio networks declined in prominence and programming shifted from serial comedies and dramas to music, talk, and local-affairs formats. The primary innovation during these years came in the late 1940s, when networks began to cover several baseball or college football games simultaneously, airing different contests regionally while having a national anchor provide updates of distant contests—a practice since imitated by television. Though national broadcasts of regular-season baseball and professional football and of major events such as the World Series and the Super Bowl remain on network radio today, they have a much lower profile than in their heyday.

Radio sports broadcasts were marked by little change from the 1940s through the 1980s. The deregulation of radio and the proliferation of FM stations in the 1980s, however, siphoned listeners from AM radio, and the search for new, profitable formats resulted in a renewed emphasis on sports. The transformation of New York station WNBC into WFAN in 1987 marked the beginning of all-sports radio; other than a morning show hosted by Don Imus, the station devotes its entire programming day to sports talk and sports broadcasts. The debut of ESPN Radio in 1992, with 147 affiliates in 43 states carrying up to 16 hours of programming weekly, was another significant event in sports radio. Initially limited to sports news shows, update segments, and occasional features, the network has expanded to include seasonal baseball and football packages as well as talk shows featuring the likes of "The Fabulous Sports Babe" and Tony Kornheiser that can be acquired through affiliation or syndication, facilitating the development of the all-sports format.

Despite typically small audiences, often less than three percent of the market, the all-sports format's lucrative 25–54-year-old, mostly white, mostly affluent, male demographic has enabled WFAN to become the top-billing radio station in history, breaking the $50 million mark in 1997. Moreover, because sports talk shows are inexpensive to produce, because syndicated shows can be accepted in barter deals from networks like ESPN and CBS, and because local team broadcasts gain loyal audiences, the format offers a higher profit margin than other formats. The format proliferated rapidly: though estimates of the number of all-sports stations vary widely, *Broadcasting and Cable* magazine reported more than 600 all-sports stations by 1998 with four dozen more stations turning to an all-sports format in 1997 alone. A decade later there were over 1,000 sports-focus stations.

Many sports teams have also made their teams' radio broadcast available online, greatly extending their potential fan base without radio networks. The National Hockey League added access to live radio calls through its website, and the National Basketball Association has capitalized on basketball's popularity by allowing ESPN's website to carry its teams' radio broadcasts. Meanwhile, the NBA, NFL, and Major League Baseball have all entered multi-year, multi-million dollar agreements with satellite's SiriusXM Radio.

One of the radio industry's most lucrative and popular formats is an off-shoot of the all-sports approach. Sports talk is like news/talk formats but with sports taking precedence over politics. Sports talk is short on game coverage and long on strong-minded hosts and audience call-ins. On-air conversation can run the gamut from this week's starting line-up to game post-mortems to discussion of sports-related scandals such as steroids. Discussion can be local or national in scope and many sports talk stations augment their own local productions with nationally syndicated programs like *Mike and Mike in the Morning* (ESPN Radio) or programs hosted by the likes of Jim Rome, J.T. the Brick or Dan Patrick.

As with all-sports in the 1990s, the sports talk format spread quickly. In 1999, there were about 150 sports talk stations in the country; there were more than 350 a decade later. And though such stations are not always immediate rating winners, they do score well in their demographics. Sports talk tends to attract audiences that, though primarily male, are nevertheless usually well-educated and possess higher income levels.

Further Reading

Barber, Red, *The Broadcasters*, New York: Dial Press, 1970.

Battema, Doug, "Baseball Meets the National Pastime," in *The Cooperstown Symposium on Baseball and American Culture*, edited by Alvin L. Hall and Peter M. Rutkoff, Jefferson, North Carolina, McFarland, 2000.

Eisenstock, Alan, *Sports Talk: A Journey Inside the World of Sports Talk Radio*. New York: Atria, 2007.

Ghosh, Chandrani, "A Guy Thing," *Forbes* (22 February 1999).

Goldberg, David Theo, "Call and Response," *Journal of Sport and Social Issues* 22, no. 2 (May 1998).

Gorman, Jerry, Kirk Calhoun, and Skip Rozin, *The Name of the Game: The Business of Sports*, New York: Wiley, 1994.

Haag, Pamela, "'The 50,000-Watt Sports Bar': Talk Radio and the Ethic of the Fan," *South Atlantic Quarterly* 95 (Spring 1996).

Halberstam, David J., *Sports on New York Radio: A Play-by-Play History*, Lincolnwood, Illinois: Masters Press, 1999.

Hyman, Mark, "Do You Love the Orioles and Live in L.A.?" *Business Week* (12 May 1997).

McChesney, Robert W., "Media Made Sports," in *Media, Sports, and Society*, edited by Lawrence A. Wenner, Newbury Park, California: Sage, 1989.

Nylund, David, *Beers, Babes, and Balls: Masculinity and Sports Talk Radio*. Albany: State University of New York Press, 2007

Smith, Curt, *Voices of the Game: The First Full-Scale Overview of Baseball Broadcasting, 1921 to the Present*, South Bend, Indiana: Diamond Communications, 1987; revised edition, as *Voices of the Game: The Acclaimed Chronicle of Baseball Radio and Television Broadcasting—From 1921 to the Present*, New York: Simon and Schuster, 1992.

Douglas L. Battema,
2009 Revisions By Cary O'Dell

STAR WARS
Public Radio Drama Series

The 1980 radio drama *Star Wars* was an adaptation of the groundbreaking motion picture of the same name. It can be seen as a radio landmark in several ways. Its production brought to bear the very best stereophonic, multitrack audio technology available. It was a collaboration between a major motion picture production company and a public radio network, with Lucasfilm, Limited, supplying elaborate sound effects and music used in the original motion picture plus promotional and marketing practices hitherto thought beyond the scope of public radio. The series used six-and-a-half hours of airtime to tell a story that, in the motion picture, was originally told in less than 30 minutes of dialog, meaning that the characters could be treated in more depth and the story told in more detail. In addition, the series raised National Public Radio's (NPR) audience ratings spectacularly and brought a new awareness of the high quality of programs broadcast by public radio.

When the motion picture *Star Wars*, written and directed by George Lucas, opened in 1977, it was a great success, lauded for its music, special effects, and rip-roaring approach to telling an adventure story. It immediately became an icon of American culture, so embedded in the popular consciousness that, some time after the motion picture was released, a major shift in the defense policy of the Armed Forces of the United States was titled the Star Wars Strategic Defense Initiative.

A short while after the motion picture opened, Richard Toscan of the University of Southern California (USC) approached George Lucas about making a radio version of the film. This project was to be produced by the university's NPR affiliate,

KUSC-FM. A USC alumnus, Lucas was fascinated by the idea of helping out his alma mater in such a novel way. Adaptations of film scripts were not new to radio—such programs as *Lux Radio Theater* were aired on the commercial networks in the 1940s, often with the stars of the motion picture re-creating their roles on radio as a means of advertising major films. But in the late 1970s, it was a given in the entertainment industry that radio drama, except for a few struggling exceptions, such as *Columbia Broadcasting System (CBS) Radio Mystery Theater* and NPR's *Earplay* and *Masterpiece Radio Theater*, was dead in the United States. The idea for a radio drama made in cooperation with a film company was communicated to NPR head Frank Mankiewicz, who was intrigued by it.

In July 1978 George Lucas' production company Lucasfilm, KUSC-FM, and NPR held initial meetings to get the project underway. In March 1979 an agreement was reached in which, for the price of $1, Lucasfilm subsidiary Black Falcon, Limited turned over to KUSC-FM the rights to write, produce, and broadcast a radio version of *Star Wars*. Lucasfilm also expressed interest in supplying technical help and in assisting to advertise the series. In April 1979 the project was publicly announced as an NPR/KUSC-FM coproduction with the British Broadcasting Corporation (BBC), in cooperation with Lucasfilm. The BBC was brought in by NPR in an effort to launch a cooperative venture with a well-respected colleague organization, experienced in the production of radio drama. But the BBC was uncomfortable with Lucasfilm's control over the script, which was being written by Brian Daley. Daley, who was not the first choice for writer, was familiar with the *Star Wars* stories, having written three novels based on *Star Wars* characters; however, for this undertaking, his scripts were subject to the approval of Lucasfilm's Carol Titelman. Eventually the BBC backed out of its agreement with NPR.

In May 1980 John Madden, who had directed for the National Theater in London and the BBC, as well as *American Playhouse*, was set as the director of the series. Tom Voegeli, who had worked on NPR's *Earplay* drama series, joined the production staff as sound mixer and supervisor of the postproduction period, the period when music and sound effects are added to the voice tracks already recorded by the actors.

Mark Hamill agreed to repeat his motion picture role as Luke Skywalker because he could not see anyone else in the part. Anthony Daniels, a veteran of British stage and radio, was eager to get back into a radio studio, so he, too, repeated his motion picture role as the robot C3PO. In late June 1980, the actors gathered at Westlake Audio Studios in Los Angeles for 13 weeks of recording. Many of the actors, more familiar with acting for screen than for radio, found the two media to be quite different in their demands. The actors had to learn to put the physicality of motion and facial expression into their lines because, in the recording studio, the voice had to do all the acting. With John Madden's help, actors and writer Brian Daley fine-tuned the scripts for the spoken word. Tom Voegeli engineered the stereophonic recording, using sensitive omnidirectional microphones; setting up a scene in which an actor moved across the room, which gave a sense of real spatial movement to the sound of the lines; and placing Anthony Daniels (C3PO) in a separate booth so that his voice could be processed to add a hollow, robotic sound.

The finished recordings of the actors were then taken to Minnesota, where Voegeli added John Williams' music, performed by the London Philharmonic, and sound effects, including the major characters R2D2 and Chewbacca, created by Ben Burtt, both from the original *Star Wars* motion picture. A very small amount of dialog had to be cut to accommodate the prerecorded music, but generally the actor tracks were left as they were originally recorded.

NPR distributed the finished series to its member stations via satellite in stereophonic sound for broadcast in 13 half-hour episodes beginning 2 March 1981. Audience response was overwhelming. In March 1981 NPR's special telephone number for the series received 40,000 calls. The network managed to answer more than 12,000 of the calls, some 7,000 of them from children. During the same period NPR received more than 10,000 letters from *Star Wars* listeners. Many of these people had never listened to public radio before. The network later calculated that its listening audience nearly doubled during the *Star Wars* broadcasts. Lucasfilm had insisted that the release of the radio series be scheduled to coincide with the release of its new motion picture, *The Empire Strikes Back*, and the re-release of the original *Star Wars*. Perhaps not totally coincidentally, all this occurred during the annual public radio fund-raising drive, which saw an enormous increase in donations for that year. In May 1981 NPR's Frank Mankiewicz wrote to Lucasfilm expressing the positive impact of *Star Wars* on the network in terms of audience awareness, fund-raising, and public perception of the quality of NPR's programming.

By June 1981 planning was underway for *The Empire Strikes Back*, the ten-episode radio sequel to *Star Wars*. Recording of the actors' tracks took place over ten days in June 1982, at A and R Studios on Seventh Street in New York City. Many of the *Star Wars* radio actors returned to continue the story. Mark Hamill and Anthony Daniels were joined by Billy Dee Williams, also from the original motion picture cast. Several noted theatrical names were added to the cast list in relatively small parts. *The Empire Strikes Back* was broadcast by NPR beginning 14 February 1982. Subsequently, planning began for a second sequel, *Return of the Jedi*. But all plans had to be laid aside when NPR found itself in a severe financial crisis. Over ten years passed before Highbridge Company, an affiliate of Minnesota Public Radio, managed to raise funds for a six-episode radio production of *Return of the Jedi*, with Tom Voegeli as producer, John Madden as director, and Brian Daley as writer. The actors were recorded in 1996 at Westlake Audio Studios in Los Angeles, and postproduction took place in Minnesota. The finished product was given to NPR, which broadcast it beginning 5 November 1996, bringing to a close the *Star Wars* radio trilogy. The satisfaction gained from this third successful production was tempered by the fact that Brian Daley, the writer of all three of the *Star Wars* radio series, who had become ill and was unable to attend the taping of the actor tracks, had died in February 1996, on the final day of recording.

See also: National Public Radio; Science Fiction Programs

Star Wars

Cast

Antilles	David Ackroyd
Fixer	Adam Arkin
Ben Kenobi	Bernard Behrens
Biggs	Kale Brown
Motti	David Clennon
Tion	John Considine
Grand Moff Tarkin	Keene Curtis
C3PO	Anthony Daniels
Prestor	Stephen Elliot
Aunt Beru	Anne Gerety
Luke Skywalker	Mark Hamill
Uncle Owen	Thomas Hill
Han Solo	Perry King
Darth Vader	Brock Peters
Princess Leia Organa	Ann Sachs
Heater	Joel Brooks
Rebel	John Dukakis
Customer #2	Phillip Kellard
Deak	David Paymer

STAR WARS

Cammie	Stephanie Steele
Wedge	Don Scardino
Narrator	Ken Hiller
Various Roles	James Blendick, Clyde Burton, Bruce French, David Alan Grier, Jerry Hardin, John Harkins, Meschach Taylor, Marc Vahanlan, John Welsh, Kent Williams

Writer

Brian Daley

Directors

John Madden, Tom Voegeli

Producers

Carol Titelman, Richard Toscan

Programming History

NPR   2 March 1981–25 May 1981

Empire Strikes Back

Cast

Ben Kenobi	Bernard Behrens
Trooper	Brian Daley
C3PO	Anthony Daniels
Beta/Trooper	James Eckhouse
Deck Officer	Ron Frazier
Ozzel	Peter Michael Goetz
General Rieekan	Merwin Goldsmith
Veers	Gordon Gould
Renegade Four/ Second Rebel/Trooper	David Alan Grier
Luke Skywalker	Mark Hamill
Emperor	Paul Hecht
Narrator	Ken Hiller
Two-Onebee	Russell Horton
Needa	Nicholas Kepros
Han Solo	Perry King
P.A. Announcer	Michael Levett
Yoda	John Lithgow
Darth Vader	Brock Peters
Renegade Three/First Rebel	John Pielmeier
Piett	David Rasche
Boba Fett	Alan Rosenburg
Princess Leia Organa	Ann Sachs
Wedge	Don Scardino

Lando Calrissian	Billy Dee Williams
RenegadeTwo/ CoordinatingDroid/Zev/ Crewman/Second Trooper/ Superintendent/Guard	Jerry Zaks
Dak	Peter Friedman
Controller	James Hurdle
Imperial Pilot	Jay Sanders
Various Roles	Sam McMurray, Steven Markle, Stephen D. Newman, Geoffrey Pierson

Producer

John Bos

Writer

Brian Daley

Directors

John Madden, Mel Sahr, Tom Voegeli

Programming History

NPR   14 February 1982–18 April 1982

Return of the Jedi

Cast

Jabba the Hutt	Edward Asner
Boba Fett	Ed Begley, Jr.
Anakin Skywalker	David Birney
C3PO	Anthony Daniels
Bib Fortuna	David Dukes
Luke Skywalker	Josh Fardon
General Madine	Peter Michael Goetz
Lando Calrissian	Arye Gross
Emperor Palpatine	Paul Hecht
Han Solo	Perry King
Yoda	John Lithgow
Darth Vader	Brock Peters
Princess Leia Organa	Ann Sachs
Arica	Samantha Bennett
Moff JerJerrod	Peter Dennis
Narrator	Ken Hiller
Barada	Martin Jarvis
Wedge Antilles	Jon Matthews
Mon Mothma	Natalia Nogulich
Admiral Ackbar	Mark Adair Rios
NineDeNine	Yeardley Smith
Major Derlin	Tom Virtue

Various Roles   Samantha Bennett, Ian Gomez, Rick Hall, Andrew Hawkes, Sherman Howard, Karl Johnson, John Kapelos, Ron LePaz, Joe Liss, Paul Mercier, Steven Petrarca, Jonathan Penner, Gil Segel, Nia Vardabs, Ron West

Writer

Brian Daley

Producer

John Bos, Julie Hartley, Tom Voegeli

Director

John Madden

Programming History

NPR   5 November 1996–10 December 1996

Further Reading

Brady, Frank, "A Journey from Outer Space to Inner Space on Public Radio: *Star Wars*," *Fantastic Films* (June 1981).
Collins, Glenn, "Metropolitan Diary: Interviews Anthony Daniels," *New York Times* (16 June 1982).
Daley, Brian, *Star Wars: The National Public Radio Dramatization*, New York: Ballantine Books, 1994.
Daley, Brian, *Star Wars: The Empire Strikes Back: The National Public Radio Dramatization*, New York: Ballantine Books, 1995.
Daley, Brian, *Star Wars: Return of the Jedi: The National Public Radio Dramatization*, New York: Ballantine Books, 1996.
Klinger, Judson, "Radio: Interviews Mark Hamill, Perry King, and Anthony Daniels," *Playboy* (March 1981).
Lindsey, Robert, "Will *Star Wars* Lure Younger Listeners to Radio?" *New York Times* (8 March 1981).

FREDERICA P. KUSHNER

STATION REP FIRMS
Representing Radio Stations to Advertisers

Station representative companies help local radio stations obtain national advertising. They have become known by many names—station reps, rep firms, media reps, sales reps, or simply "reps." Whatever the name, they exist to promote a station and its market and sometimes to assist client stations to improve their advertising appeal with changes in programming. For many years, a station rep firm did not represent competing stations in the same market, but that changed with consolidation of the industry in the late 1990s. From an industry once made up of several hundred companies, the radio station rep business has shrunk to a handful of major players.

Origins

As radio advertising became widespread in the late 1920s, a problem arose that had appeared decades earlier in the newspaper business: how could local stations successfully appeal to advertisers outside their immediate market area? The problem was, in part, a matter of communication, time, and efficiency. The station could not afford to have its own sales representatives in major cities, and advertisers and their agencies could not be troubled to contact dozens or even hundreds of individual stations across the country.

The first—and, as it turned out, temporary—solution was the rise of time brokering. A time broker represented no specific station or advertiser but rather sold (brokered) advertising time from many outlets to advertisers. A time broker might sell time on competing outlets in the same market. For example, around 1930 a broker named Scott Bowen began buying radio time for advertising agencies for a fee and then obtained a commission from the stations when he placed a schedule.

The Katz Agency

Emanuel Katz formed the Katz Agency in 1888 to represent newspapers. In 1931 the company sought to represent radio stations as several of the Katz newspaper clients had acquired radio licenses. Emanuel's son, Eugene Katz, the youngest member of the family and relatively new to the firm, was assigned the responsibility of selling time for the Oklahoma Publishing Company's new radio station, WKY in Oklahoma City. Hoping to organize a southwestern group of National Broadcasting Company (NBC) Radio affiliates, Eugene succeeded in gaining representation of KPRC in Houston, WFAA in Dallas, and WOAI in San Antonio.

Upon his return to New York, Eugene was told by his father to go back to Texas and call off the deal, because other Katz newspaper clients, including the *Houston Post* and *Dallas News*, had complained vigorously. Eugene was forced to withdraw the contracts and was unable to resume soliciting radio clients until a separate division was established in 1935. By that time Edward Petry, Paul Raymer, and the firm Free, John and Fields (later Peters Griffin Woodward) had all established themselves as radio reps, and Katz re-entered radio representation as a latecomer. The first non-newspaper-related radio clients at Katz were WGST, Atlanta; KRLA, Los Angeles; KRNT, Des Moines; and WMT, Cedar Rapids.

The Katz sales staffs for different media were separated after World War II. When television emerged in 1947, Eugene did not make the same mistake that his father had made with radio and moved quickly into television representation. He contracted with most of the big city television stations in the country. Ironically, other radio representatives were reluctant to enter the new medium, leaving Katz dominant until the major television groups such as Storer and Westinghouse formed their own in-house sales organizations. The Katz newspaper representation business continued its downward trend throughout the late 1960s, and the company ceased representing newspapers in 1973 to concentrate on electronic media.

In 1972 one of James Greenwald's first major steps as president of Katz Radio was to begin selling FM radio audience. Until then, most FM stations, if they were sold to national advertisers at all, were coupled with sister AM stations. Nearly all FM stations, except those that programmed classical music, simulcast programming with their AM counterparts, and Katz Radio was particularly steeped in the history of selling only large AM stations. Greenwald visited with the owners of the major Katz AM stations that also had FM stations and first convinced them to sell their fledgling FM stations in combination with their AM stations. In many instances the additional audience, which was essentially sold for the same price as the AM-only audience, resulted in higher rates and larger shares of budgets for the AM station. The Katz clients responded favorably.

When the Federal Communications Commission (FCC) in 1965 passed the rule limiting simulcasting to 50 percent of the program day, Greenwald formed an in-house programming consulting unit within the Radio Division that urged the owners of FM stations to program their FM properties independently. Greenwald foresaw a national sales market rapidly developing that was willing to spend large sums to reach the emerging FM audience. By 1976 national sales on Katz-represented FM stations had grown to represent over 20 percent of the company's total volume. By 1980 it had eclipsed 35 percent, and by 1990, 70 percent.

Eugene, the last member of the Katz family to be associated with the firm, helped to organize the company's sale to its employees in 1976 at the time he retired. Two years later, Katz had 450 employees

and 17 sales offices, and the company represented 170 radio (and 108 television) stations with national spot billings of about $250 million. By 1980 the firm had grown to become the largest representative of radio and television stations in the nation. By the company's 100th anniversary in 1988 (two years after Greenwald retired as chairman), Katz had 1,400 employees in 22 offices and represented 1,440 radio (and 193 television) stations with total billings of $1.5 billion, two-thirds of that in television. By then it was the only rep firm still active in both radio and television.

In 1984 Katz took over the Henry Christal Company (which had specialized in high-power clear channel stations) and spun it off as a division along with RKO Radio Sales, which became the Republic Radio division. Katz took over the John Blair radio business in 1987, and it became the Banner Radio division. Katz also purchased the Jack Masla Company, Eastman Radio, and Metro Radio Sales. Katz set up a Hispanic radio division, and all the Katz divisions competed with one another nationally and in specific markets. By 2000 Katz Radio Group—Katz, Christal, and Clear Channel Radio Sales (set up in 2000, dedicated to the 1,200 stations in 48 states owned by Clear Channel Communications)—represented 2,000 stations in all. Emmanuel Katz died that same year.

Edward Petry

In 1932 Edward Petry established his own radio sales representative company—the first company devoted solely to radio. Petry was the first to develop the notion of "exclusivity," the idea that a station rep should handle only one station in any given market. He also developed a system of rates and standards to the spot broadcasting business that allowed it to grow and flourish. He was also the first rep to open a separate television division. Petry (as with several other rep firms) eventually left the radio business to focus on television.

Both Petry and Katz differed from time brokers in that they provided exclusive representation of client stations, never more than one in a given city. In this way the station rep could "sell" a market and the represented station as the best way to serve that market. By 1935 there were 26 such companies, and by 1937 at least 60 different rep firms were vying for radio station business.

The Industry Matures

Station rep firms increasingly competed with the national networks in the 1930s and 1940s, for the national chains usually represented not only their own stations, but also many of their affiliates. The National Association of Radio Station Reps (which became the Station Reps Association in the early 1950s) filed a complaint in 1947 with the FCC about networks representing non-owned-and-operated affiliate stations. After seven days of hearings in 1948–49 concerned with whether this was a violation of the chain broadcasting rules of the FCC, the commission took no action. American Broadcasting Companies (ABC) stopped representing affiliates in 1952. Only in 1959, by then alarmed at the degree to which television networks already dominated the advertising revenues of the relatively new medium, would the FCC ban networks from acting as reps for their affiliate stations.

With the demise of most programming on radio networks in the face of television competition after 1948, however, a new world opened for station reps. Not only did the networks rapidly fade from the competitive picture, but many more stations were going on the air each year, and each needed representation to reach national advertisers.

Following the Katz example, other radio rep firms were entering the television market. Starting in the late 1950s, a few stations (primarily those controlled by group owners) began again to represent themselves, and by the late 1970s these accounted for about a third of national spot billings for radio and television combined. By the 1970s there were some 230 rep firms, most of them regional, and they increasingly focused on radio or television, but not both.

Ralph Guild and Interep

The man who would change the face of the station rep business, Ralph Guild, began his radio career as an advertising salesman at KXOB in Stockton, California, in 1948. He moved to a similar post at a Sacramento station two years later and became manager of KROY in the state capital in 1955. He turned to the station representative business in 1957 when he joined McGavren-Quinn, then a San Francisco-based rep firm operated by Guild's college classmate Daren McGavren. Later that year, Guild moved to New York to open the company's first East Coast office. He became national sales manager in 1963 and moved up to become a partner of what became McGavren Guild in 1967. The firm was sold to employees in 1975 in an employee stock ownership plan.

In a break with station rep tradition, McGavren Guild began to represent more than one station in a given market. In 1981 Guild formed Interep as a

holding company of separately managed and competing station rep firms. Over the next several years, several rep firms came under the Interep umbrella, including Major Market Radio in 1983 and Group W Radio Sales and Torbet Radio in 1987. Interep became the Interep Radio Store in 1988, all the while expanding its research and related services to both ad agencies and stations. By 1990 there were eight separate rep firms within Interep, which had become the largest radio rep organization. Billings rose from $60 million in sales in 1981 to $500 million by 1990 (half of the radio advertising in the largest 150 markets) and more than $1.25 billion a decade later. Through an initial public offering in December 1999, Interep became a publicly traded company.

With the consolidation of radio station ownership in the late 1990s, the rep companies' policy of exclusivity began to break down as stations changed hands. The huge merger between Clear Channel and AMFM in 1999, for example, caught the Katz and Interep firms in the middle. When Clear Channel gobbled up AMFM (which was the corporate parent of Katz), Guild promptly filed a $56 million lawsuit against Clear Channel for damages arising from Clear Channel's diversion of its business to Katz, and thus its alleged breach of the national sales representation agreement with Interep.

Ongoing conflict and intense competition between the two companies eventually spelled the end of one. In 2003, in a bizarre string of events, Interep lured away many of Katz's top executives and nearly a hundred of its lesser staff. Within a year of the exodus, however, almost all of them—supposedly enticed back with promises of pay raises and bonuses—would return to Katz. What role these internal changes played in Interep's demise is open to debate. Certainly an initiative adopted by Katz thereafter—offing revenue guarantees to clients willing to leave Interep—helped seal the latter's fate. Not long after, Interep would lose two of its largest clients, Cumulus and Radio One; both defected to Katz in 2005. This left Interep with only one remaining major client, CBS Radio. In March 2008, Interep filed for bankruptcy protection and in October for liquidation of the company.

Katz Media Group remains the industry's only national rep firm. Some smaller firms that specialize in specific regions around the country also endure. These include Michigan Spot Sales, Midwest Radio, and Western Regional Broadcast Sales. The internet start-up business Target Spot (Targetspot.com) is now doing for internet audio services what traditional rep firms have done for terrestrial radio. By 2009, Target Spot claimed to represent over a thousand internet portals including 181.FM, Live365.com and CBS Radio.

See also: Clear Channel Communications Inc.; Programming Strategies and Processes

Further Reading

"Katz 100th Anniversary," *Television-Radio Age* (November 1988).

Murphy, Jonne, *Handbook of Radio Advertising*, Radnor, Pennsylvania: Chilton, 1980.

"Pulse Radio Executive of the Year: Ralph Guild," *The Pulse of Radio* (14 January 1991).

"Representatives," in 2000 *Radio Business Report: Source Guide and Directory*, Springfield, Virginia: Radio Business Report, 2000.

Schulberg, Bob, *Radio Advertising: The Authoritative Handbook*, Lincolnwood, Illinois: NTC Business Books, 1989; 2nd edition, by Schulberg and Pete Schulberg, 1996.

United States Congress, House Committee on Interstate and Foreign Commerce, "Network Practices: Network Representation of Stations in National Spot Sales," in *Network Broadcasting*, Washington, D.C.: GPO, 1958.

"U.S. Radio, TV Station, and Cable Representatives," *Broadcasting and Cable Yearbook* (1993–).

GORDON H. HASTINGS, CHRISTOPHER H. STERLING, AND ED SHANE, 2009 REVISIONS BY CARY O'DELL

STEREO

Stereophonic sound, or "stereo" for short, is a system of sound reproduction in which separately placed microphones or loudspeakers enhance the realism of the reproduced sound. The effect of using multiple sound inputs and outputs in separated right and left audio channels is the creation of sound reproduction that is "three-dimensional," as aspects of right- and left-channel sound can be heard separately by persons with normal hearing.

Stereophonic sound is important to radio for two principal reasons. The popularity of stereophonic frequency modulation (FM) broadcasting in the second half of the 20th century contributed to public acceptance of that mode of radio transmission and reception. FM stereogradually became the listening public's preferred medium for receiving music, which makes up the majority of entertainment programming for radio stations in industrialized nations. Second, the controversial method by which the Federal Communications Commission (FCC) authorized amplitude modulation (AM) stereobroadcasting in the United States in the early 1980s is thought by many to have contributed to its relative failure.

History of FM Stereo

Stereophonic radio broadcasting was invented in 1925, when WPAY radio in New Haven, Connecticut, experimented with two-station simulcasting. This early attempt featured the station's broadcast of the right channel of sound on one AM carrier frequency, while a second separate AM signal transmitted the left channel of sound. Despite experiments such as this, the real push for stereophonic broadcasting came in the 1950s, when the United States and British recording industries perfected "high-fidelity" sound reproduction, which included stereophonic recording technologies. The Record Industry Association of America (RIAA) adopted recording industry standards for stereo in January 1959. In the years preceding the adoption of the RIAA standards, interest in stereophonic radio broadcasting also increased. A variation of the technique used in the 1920s by WPAY was used experimentally in 1952 by station WQXR, owned by *The New York Times*. Like the WPAY system, this later variation featured a two-station approach, but with an AM signal for the right channel and an FM frequency for the left. In 1954, station WCRB in Boston began using this type of two-station stereobroadcasting for approximately four hours of programming per week, and for up to 40 hours per week by 1959. Nonetheless, there were problems with this type of stereophonic AM-FM broadcasting, mostly related to the wasted spectrum space of such two-station arrangements and to the fact that listeners needed two radios to get the full stereoeffect; listeners using only one radio receiver received just "half" of the intended sound. Further, the AM channel lacked the frequency response of the FM channel.

Such technical and practical limitations prompted both AM and FM broadcasters to push for the use of single-station, multiple-channel stereobroadcast authorization. Single-station stereobroadcast technology had become a reality with the FCC authorization of FM multiplexing in 1955. Multiplexing refers to the simultaneous transmission of two or more signals over the same radio channel. In FM broadcasting, a "carrier" frequency (the channel's center frequency) and its sidebands transmit the main electronic program information. However, additional electronic information can be transmitted using other frequencies within the station's designated channel, as long as the information generated and modulated on the sidebands does not interfere with the main carrier-frequency signal. This sideband frequency signal is called a "subcarrier," and the second-channel (right or left channel) audio information for FM stereo is carried in a subcarrier transmission. The technique was originally developed as a means to allow FM stations, which were financially struggling at that time, to pick up additional revenue by using the sidebands of their allocated frequencies to carry business background music or financial data information. The same technology that enabled this use of multiplexing for subsidiary communication authorization (SCA) broadcasts could be adapted so that the multiple portions of the signal would carry separate right and left audio channel information.

Developments in AM stereobroadcasting also moved forward. In 1959 AM stereo was successfully tested by the Radio Corporation of America (RCA) in conjunction with Belar Electronics Laboratory. That same year, Philco developed an AM stereosystem that was tested on WABC in New York. Television industry engineers also developed their own adaptations of these stereophonic sound transmission techniques for the audio portion of TV transmission and reception systems.

In 1958 the FCC issued a *Notice of Inquiry* on further uses of FM radio, which included not only stereophonic broadcasting, but also other SCA services such as paging and calling services, traffic light-switching control, radio reading services for visually impaired persons, public utility load management, and specialized foreign language programming. A year later, the FCC separated the question of stereo from the more general SCA inquiry by issuing a *Further Notice of Inquiry*. A new industry testing group was set up in cooperation with the Electronic Industries Association (EIA) in order to sort out the features of the 17 proposed (and mutually incompatible) systems of FM stereo. This engineering test group was called the National Stereophonic Radio Committee (NSRC). Because of antitrust concerns, industry heavyweights RCA and the Columbia Broadcasting System (CBS) did not participate in the standardization testing process.

Boosters promoted FM stereo as "the one big thing" needed to ensure consumer acceptance of FM. Although several stations kept using the AM-FM two-station experimental procedure, most in the industry awaited permission to adopt single station stereo. In the end, the FCC authorized *only* FM stereo in April 1961, accepting with modification the recommendations of the NSRC. In October of that year, the FCC denied petitions for AM stereo authorization, claiming that FM was "the ideal medium" for the development of high-quality stereobroadcasting and that the beneficial effects of AM stereo were *de minimis*. The FCC similarly denied two 1962 petitions to reconsider its negative AM stereo decision.

It appears that there were four overlapping reasons for the FCC to allow stereo FM while denying stereo AM radio or stereo television broadcasting. The most often-cited rationale is that the FCC recognized the need to give struggling FM stations a boost in order to allow them to compete economically with then-dominant AM radio stations. Second, the Commission recognized that FM, with its 200-kHz channel (20 times wider than the width of AM carrier frequencies) had the ability to faithfully reproduce a wider range of frequencies without suffering from fading, interference, or static. This made FM a technically superior medium for broadcasting with the use of sideband stereo technologies. Third, the FCC did not feel that it (or the industry) had adequate resources to introduce FM, AM, and TV stereo simultaneously. Finally, regarding stereo television, FCC engineers felt that "stereo sound mated with the small-screen pictures of a typical television set would be distracting and unsatisfying."

Although FM radio, with its full-frequency stereophonic sound, did gain consumer acceptance over the two decades that followed, the innovation diffusion period for FM stereobroadcasting was relatively protracted. Initially, the cost of stereo-transmission equipment (estimated at $2,000 to $4,000—no small sum in the early 1960s) was considered prohibitive by many unprofitable FM broadcasters of the day, especially since there were too few stereo receivers in the consumer marketplace to make the investment pay off. Consequently, only about 25 percent of all FM stations in the United States were using stereophonic transmitters by 1965, and fewer than 50 percent were broadcasting in stereo by 1971. However, with the gradual growth of the FM industry in the 1970s, fueled by a turn from strictly upscale programming to more progressive rock music formats, a large majority of FM radio stations in the United States were broadcasting in stereo by 1975. In 1978, FM surpassed AM in terms of U.S. listenership.

Interest in AM Stereo Rekindled

The success of FM broadcasting, boosted in no small part by FM's ability to broadcast in stereo, was accompanied by a commensurate decline in AM listenership. By the late 1970s, once-dominant AM stations in several major markets expressed hope that AM stereo might be developed as part of a package of AM improvements that would enable them to compete more effectively with FM stereo.

A number of AM stereo proponents had continued to work on AM stereophonic transmission and reception throughout the 1960s and 1970s. In the early 1960s, CBS experimented with a modification of the AM stereosystem developed by Philco and conducted transmission tests on its New York station, WCBS. AM stereo proponent Leonard Kahn, who in the late 1950s had introduced a "single-sideband" method of AM stereo, also refined his system and conducted stereo tests beginning in 1970 just south of San Diego at the 50,000-W Tijuana, Mexico, AM station XETRA. The FCC granted permission for a six-month test of Kahn's system on WFBR, Baltimore, in 1974. In 1975 RCA demonstrated its AM stereobroadcasting system as its "big draw" at the National Association of Broadcasters (NAB) convention, and Motorola collaborated with a firm called Modulation Systems Laboratory to begin work on its C-QUAM system of AM stereo, which would eventually become the industry standard. Perhaps the greatest development was the 1975 united sponsorship of a new National AM Stereophonic Radio Committee (NAMSRC) under the auspices of the EIA, the NAB, the National Radio Broadcasters Association, and the Broadcasting Cable and Consumer Electronics Society of the Institute of Electrical and Electronics Engineers. Stations WGMS and WTOP in Washington, D.C., volunteered their facilities for on-air tests, and Charlotte, North Carolina's WBT was chosen as the site of the skywave tests. Although early proponent Leonard Kahn refused to participate in the joint-testing process, four companies did submit proposals to the NAMSRC in early 1976, and three systems were eventually tested.

The FCC adopted a *Notice of Inquiry* on AM stereo in 1977, but when no standard was announced by 1980, AM broadcasters grew restless. By that time a political and philosophical shift had taken place in Washington, and the consensus among the increasing number of economists at the FCC was to favor a "marketplace" option. Under this untested mechanism, the FCC would not pick one single AM stereo standard but would instead set only minimal technical standards that would enable any compliant system to be put on the air; theoretically, this system would allow the economics of the free marketplace to select its own de facto standard. Meanwhile, the FCC engineers continued to push for the more traditional single-standard outcome.

At first it appeared as if the traditionalists had prevailed when, in April 1980, an AM stereo-standard decision favoring the Magnavox Corporation's proposal was announced. However, for a variety of reasons, this decision was reversed by the FCC

shortly after it was announced, and in 1982 the commission adopted the "marketplace" option. This experiment was subsequently criticized as "technological Darwinism" and was widely blamed for the ultimate failure of the AM stereo technology to gain public acceptance. Although attractive in theory and certainly politically sensitive to the deregulatory impulse to create a less intrusive FCC, the marketplace experiment ultimately failed. However, it is impossible to sort out the exact reasons for the failure. Many felt that the lack of a single standard proved to be too economically unstable for broadcasters, who were in the position of trying to invest large sums of money in a transmission system that might not be adopted either by competing stations within its market or by portions of its listening audience. Likewise, the marketplace battle was also seen as too confusing for consumers trying to purchase home and auto receivers, which featured up to five different means of decoding AM stereo signals.

After a decade of uncertainty, during which time no AM stereo system emerged as the clear winner in the resulting innovation diffusion process, Congress stepped in and required the FCC to set an AM stereo standard. In 1993 the commission selected Motorola's C-QUAM system as the national AM stereo standard because, although it had not yet reached the level of acceptance that would make it the de facto standard, it nonetheless had the largest share of the AM stereobroadcast transmitter and receiver markets.

Television stereo, also approved in the 1980s, avoided this marketplace skirmish because the consumer electronics industry, through the formation of the Broadcast Television Systems Committee (BTSC) was able to agree on a preferred TV stereo transmission and reception system. As a result, in 1984 the FCC ruled unanimously that the Zenith-dbx TV stereo system's pilot subcarrier frequency would be "protected," without excluding the use of other competing systems. If other systems were to be used, a station would have to choose a subcarrier frequency different from that outlined in the Zenith-dbx standard. This was an unlikely outcome both because the Zenith system was the *only* system recommended to the FCC by the BTSC after exhaustive testing, and because Zenith had purposely used a stereo pilot subcarrier preferred by the television broadcast industry because of its compatibility with existing transmission systems.

The Future of Stereo Radio

A high-capacity FM multiplex broadcast system called Data Radio Channel was proposed in 1996.

It allows for text and graphics to be broadcast while maintaining compatibility with existing stereo-broadcasting technology by multiplexing digital signals at a higher frequency than the baseband FM stereo signals. The system was field-tested in NHK's Tokyo FM station. In the US, Radio Broadcast Data System technologies, which are able to transmit text data such as artist information or station promotional graphics or text, are slowly filtering into the marketplace.

Experiments, which began in the late 1990s, are investigating use of lasers as efficient high-speed subcarrier transmitters of stereo multiplexing. Meanwhile, in another technologically forward step, S-band (2.3–2.6 GHz) and L-band (1.452–1.492 GHz) frequencies are now being utilized by satellite radio service SiriusXM. Additionally, five- and six-channel music-recording techniques, which promise a "beyond stereo" listening experience, are being used in some industries (e.g., film production and exhibition) and will probably catch on with consumers.

See also: AM Radio; Dolby Noise Reduction; FM Radio; Radio Broadcast Data System; Receivers; Recordings and the Radio Industry

Further Reading

Braun, Mark J., *AM Stereo and the FCC: Case Study of a Marketplace Shibboleth*, Norwood, New Jersey: Ablex, 1994.
Johnson, Lawrence B., "Beyond Stereo: Sound Enters a Frontier of Many Dimensions," *New York Times* (10 September 1995).
Prentiss, Stan, *AM Stereo and TV Stereo: New Sound Dimensions*, Blue Ridge Summit, Pennsylvania: Tab, 1985.
Smith, F. Leslie, Milan D. Meeske, and John W. Wright II, *Electronic Media and Government: The Regulation of Wireless and Wired Mass Communication in the United States*, White Plains, New York: Longman, 1995.
Sterling, Christopher H., "Second Service: A History of Commercial FM Broadcasting to 1969," Ph.D. diss., University of Wisconsin, Madison, 1969.
Sterling, Christopher H., "The New Technology: The FCC and Changing Technological Standards," *Journal of Communication* 32, no. 1 (Autumn 1982).
Sunier, John, *The Story of Stereo: 1881–*, New York: Gernsback Library, 1960.
Warren, Rich, "RDS: What's the Story?" *Stereo Review* 62, no. 8 (August 1997).

MARK BRAUN,
2009 REVISIONS BY CARY O'DELL

STEREOTYPES ON RADIO

As with any other mass medium, early radio broadcasts made use of (some more recent critics might say "suffered") stereotypes in dramatic and other programming. Often, the use of clichés simplified groups by labeling them as "other" (that is, outside the mainstream of society) and emphasizing differences between outsiders and the core society. Such reductive portraits may not have promoted universal brotherhood, but they aided radio show popularity by relaxing audiences so that they would continue to listen and to buy the sponsor's products.

The focus here will be primarily on American radio's "Golden Age" (to about 1948) with its greater variety of programs and stereotypes, with a few comments about radio in the years since that time. That there is less stereotyping today is clearly owing to the stronger sense of political and social correctness now pervasive in society.

Precedents

The minstrel tradition began in the 1840s and produced two enduring stereotypes of African-Americans: "Zip Coon" and "Jim Crow." The Zip Coon character was depicted as an individual who wore loud-colored clothes, used language inappropriately (malapropisms), and exhibited an air of self-importance. The Jim Crow character, on the other hand, was mentally slow and exhibited features that Caucasians associated with African-American field hands: speaking slowly and moving sluggishly, with thoughts that seemed to match both speech and movement. In addition to these two enduring stereotypes, other representations of African-Americans included the trusted servant and maid. Thus, from the days of minstrelsy there were also such figures as Uncle Tom or Uncle Remus, Aunt Jemima or Mandy the maid, Preacher Brown and Deacon Jones, Rastus and Sambo and the old Mammy." These stereotypes persisted throughout the 19th century, became part of vaudeville, and later were transferred to radio.

Most Americans accepted these stereotypes as a real depiction of African-Americans; they were, for the most part, unquestioned. Their comical nature became a defining feature of all of such stereotypes. They made Americans laugh and could be easily laughed at. Hence, racial stereotypes of African-Americans served the interest of the status quo by articulating how African-Americans would interact with white society, primarily as comedians and servants.

Stereotypes in Early Radio

Early radio often used stereotypes of other ethnic groups in addition to its portrayal of African-

Americans. For example, there were the *Cliquot Club Eskimos* and the *A&P Gypsies*, both programs featuring orchestras. Moreover, *The Goldbergs* also used heavy dialects and distinct accents, which had been part of the vaudeville and minstrel traditions.

Vaudeville programs that made heavy use of African-American stereotypes were also heard during the early years of radio. For example, the Columbia Broadcasting System (CBS) network broadcast a show featuring George Moran and Charlie Mack, cast as "The Two Black Crows," during the network's *Majestic Theater Hour*. New York radio station WEAF broadcast the *Gold Dust Twins* on Tuesday nights, another show that featured stereotypes of African-Americans (played by two white men, Harvey Hindermeyer and Earl Tuckerman) in 1924.

Variety show formats often featured minstrel routines during the 1920s. *Dutch Masters Minstrels*, for example, was first broadcast by the National Broadcasting Company (NBC) in 1929. Moreover, daytime serials also featured caricatured stereotypes of African-Americans. For instance, in 1929, NBC broadcast a serial based upon the Aunt Jemima trademark of the Quaker Oats Company, the show's sponsor. The focus of the program was the Aunt Jemima character and her family. All members of her family spoke with the heavy black dialect often heard in minstrel shows. (Significantly, and as was usual in this period, white actors played the parts of each character in this show.) Not to be outdone, the Cream of Wheat Company sponsored a program based upon its trademark African-American chef, Rastus. It featured musical selections performed by Rastus' imaginary animal friends and minstrel-type introductions to each song.

Sam 'n' Henry, created by Charles Correll and Freeman Gosden, made its radio debut on WGN, Chicago, in 1926. The program was based upon the minstrel tradition. Although this program never made network radio distribution, it served as the basis for *Amos 'n' Andy* which made its debut on 19 March 1928 on Chicago's WMAQ. The program changed stations and name because WGN refused Correll and Gosden a salary increase; as WGN owned the program/character names, a new name had to be chosen. Radio network NBC picked up the *Amos 'n' Andy* program a year later. As a network program, it soon became immensely popular—even among blacks—because it drew upon the minstrel tradition, made use of vaudeville ethnic humor, and offered sympathetic characters with whom the audience could identify.

Stereotypes of Foreigners, Women, and Children

Stereotypes of foreigners, women, and children appeared on dramatic, adventure, and comedy programs throughout radio's Golden Age. Scripts pictured foreigners, women, and children as predictable creatures who would not cause anxiety in listeners.

Foreigners

Historically, the number of immigrants to the United States between 1925 and 1950 barely equaled the number who entered in one important year—1907. Yet on radio, heavy accents and "ethnic" behavior routinely identified a large number of recent arrivals, nearly all of whose characters agreed to play by American rules. Radio boiled down the enormous Russian empire into Bert Gordon, the Mad Russian of *Eddie Cantor*, or Professor Kropotkin of *My Friend Irma;* all of Mexico's richness was diminished into Pedro, *Judy Canova*'s pal. On *Life with Luigi*, Luigi Basco told his "Mama mia" in Naples about America with the terminal vowels that placed him as one fresh from Ellis Island. Typically, he affirmed the values of his native-born listeners by studying English in night school, avoiding an old-world arranged marriage with Pasquale's daughter Rosa, and singing the ditty, "A-may-ree-kah, I love-a you, you like a papa to me." At least two other shows dealt more cautiously with Italian material: *Little Italy* and *The Great Merlini*.

Similarly, Englishmen, supposed masters of snobbishness, were neutered into stuffy blimps (Harry McNaughton, *It Pays to be Ignorant*; Count Benchley Botsford, *Judy Canova*); cool, work-obsessed police officials (*Scotland Yard*'s Inspector Burke; *Hearthstone of the Death Squad*); or valets (*It's Higgins, Sir*). Even titled gentlemen were domesticated: Lord Bilgewater couldn't compete with *Al Pearce*, and Lord Henry Brinthrope catered to *Our Gal Sunday*. Untitled Britons such as Nicholas Lacey gratefully fit into *One Man's Family*.

French characters, too, lost touch with authentic identity. Jack Benny's violin teacher, Professor Le Blanc, suffered every time Jack produced a tortured "Love in Bloom" from his strings yet stayed because he'd still not been paid. He satisfied some comfortable expectation in the audience about starveling bohemians. *Alan Young* once disguised himself as "Pierre Eclair, decorator" in order to escape the rough treatment a real man might have expected at the hands of his girl's irked father. The supposed French connection to romance justified the character of Mademoiselle Fifi, the sultry flirt on *Eddie Cantor*. Similarly, a heavily accented French teacher at Madison High School generated excitement in *Our Miss Brooks*.

The same Americans who slammed their geographic doors to genuine foreigners admitted through radio a surprising number of often vilified groups, especially Asian, Irish, Jewish, and African-American. Some Asians on the air had been part of earlier tales in other media: *Fu Manchu; Charlie Chan*; Ming the Merciless, dread Emperor of Mongo, enemy of *Flash Gordon*; and *Mr. I.A. Moto*. Many "Easterners" were servants or, at best, sidekicks. *Bobby Benson* had a Chinese cook; so did *Little Orphan Annie* and *Tom Mix*. Ling Wee was a waiter in *Gasoline Alley* and, a little higher on the excitement ladder, Lai Choi San helped Terry against the pirates, Chula assisted on *Island Venture*, and Botak backed up *Green Lantern*. Asians often had simple two-syllable names such as Kato on *The Green Hornet* and Toku on *The Green Lama*.

Other linguistic clichés set Orientals apart from Caucasians. Gooey Fooey, laundryman on *Fibber McGee*, gibbered in a manic singsong; *Fred Allen*'s bumbling sleuth One Long Pan threatened crooks with his "lewoloweh." However, radio soothed listeners by implying that the ancient empires were eager to adopt Western ways. From 1938 to 1940, *This Day Is Ours* told how a dead missionary's daughter carried on his noble religious work, meeting small frustrations with grace because she had so much support from her adoring Chinese proselytes. The VJ episode of *The Charlotte Greenwood Show* (26 August 1945) featured the Chinese refugee Mrs. Lee who spoke, as the stage directions say, "definitely Oxford."

Irish characters used more recognizable words but expressed equally simplified personalities. Many real-life Irishmen had become police officers, so Mike Clancy aided *Mr. Keen*; Harrington helped *Mr. District Attorney*; Sergeant Velie supported *Ellery Queen;* Mullins abetted *Mr. and Mrs. North*; Sergeant O'Hara facilitated *The Fat Man*; and Happy McMann backed up *Martin Kane, Private Detective*. These Irish helpers loyally appreciated their more nimble-witted superiors. Such public servants softened a second Irish cliché, that of the bibulous blowhard. Best exemplified by Molly McGee's Uncle Dennis, this stereotype presented the Irish as ever-thirsty and gregarious. *Duffy's Tavern* seemed the logical gathering place for them.

Jewish roles on radio exuded sentimentality. *The Goldbergs* led this saccharine parade, followed by Izzy Finklestein, the helpful foil on *Kaltenmeyer's Kindergarten*. Some characters, such as Papa David Solomon on *Life Can Be Beautiful*, became earth oracles in the pattern of Molly Berg. Others, such as the Levys of *Abie's Irish Rose*, radiated warm humor. Similarly, another Finklestein on *Houseboat Hannah* and *The House of Glass* series projected exuberant geniality. Mr. Kitzel, one of *Al Pearce and His Gang*, and his namesake on *Jack Benny*—the one who offered hotdogs having a "pickle in the middle, with the mustard on top"—glowed with the same lower-East-Side conviviality that made Pansy Nussbaum on *Fred Allen* so endearing.

Black characters best demonstrate how small a cookie cutter radio used to extract innocuous material from a complex culture. No George Washington Carvers or Marcus Garveys pushed their way to the front of radio's bus. The lethargic Lightning could never do more than run errands on *Amos 'n' Andy*; Molasses 'n' January (*Maxwell House Show Boat*) could only be minstrels; Cyclone could only be a ludicrous handyman for the equally silly *Hap Hazard*. The most independent, Birdy Lee Coggins, kept house for *The Great Gildersleeve*, and Geranium the maid chatted with *Judy Canova*. Even versatile African-American actresses such as Amanda and Lillian Randolph could only serve *Pepper Young's Family* and *Kitty Foyle*. Occasionally these characters bossed their bosses: Rochester van Jones twitted Jack Benny, and Beulah revealed a life outside the McGee household. Usually, like other outsiders, the characters portrayed by black actors merely augmented the lives of the characters they served, apparently content to live in the background and never rebel against middle-class expectations.

Women

Female characters on radio were squeezed into some confining aesthetic corsets. On soap operas they endured, suffered, and occasionally triumphed. Some women assisted male heroes on detective programs, either as compliant secretaries such as Effie Perine on *Sam Spade* or tagalong pals such as Margo Lane on *The Shadow*. Ironically, women were perhaps more fully represented on comedy programs. There they could stretch social molds and carry on at least a century's tradition of amusing, ironic, and flamboyant female speakers. Radio controlled the clichés so they would not discomfit audiences or sponsors. Robert J. Landry suggested in 1946 that the comedy programs (usually aired on Sundays and Tuesdays) repeated formulas because

"American radio fans seem to be profoundly amused by the troublesomely imaginative adult and the juvenile equivalent, or brat" (in *This Fascinating Radio Business*). His typology can be expanded to include six major categories of funny females:

1. The brat
2. The teenager
3. The single working girl
4. The household servant (usually black)
5. The girlfriend or wife
6. The erratics: older spinsters, meddlers, society ladies, rebels.

Replicating Max und Moritz/Hans and Fritz models, brats relentlessly demanded attention or treats or information. Pipsqueak kids rose above gender so that the 10-year old boy on *Daddy and Rollo* couldn't claim much difference from the girlish Teeny who pestered *Fibber McGee*. Many of these characters incorporated the mannerisms of *Baby Snooks*.

Radio exploited the pre-World War I discovery of teenagers by unleashing a gaggle of adolescents. The females varied more than their dithery male counterparts. Admittedly there were the nonstop talkers, such as Gildersleeve's neighbor: by the time she pauses for breath, he has forgotten his message. (She had been commenting on what a quiet man Gildy was.) She belongs with chatty flirts such as Veronica on *Archie Andrews*.

A subdivision of teenage girls, the almost-mother, include Marjorie Forester, who managed much of the *Great Gildersleeve*'s household; Maudie, who kept *Maudie's Diary* with wry sensitivity; *Corliss Archer*; *My Best Girls*, who ran their widowed father's home near Chicago; Harriet Conklin, the mature daughter of *Our Miss Brooks*'s school principal; Babs Riley, who assisted her mom in helping father Chester lead *The Life of Riley*, and Judy Foster, who did more than go out with Ooge Pringle on *A Date With Judy*. All of these buyers into adult responsibility helped to rectify the slur upon young women implied by the twit or coquette images.

The Single Working Girl stereotype offered more memorable characters than their accompanied or married sisters. These plucky females toiled in a world they did not create. Alone but not afraid, they confronted a commercial universe that insisted they were more bother than aid. Most radio singles were eager to remove themselves from the workplace to the sacred space of a kitchen. They lived according to Elizabeth Cushman's maxim, "No girl should remain in business more than five years" ("Office Women and Sex Antagonism," *Harper's*

Magazine). *Maisie* pluckily endured low wages and unpromising boyfriends while dreaming of fulfillment.

The U.S. census for 1950 listed more than 1.6 million "stenographers, typists, and secretaries." However, these vital functionaries appeared on radio as airheads. In 1953 Lorelei Schmeerbaum, stalwart member of the club "Girls Who Say No But Mean Yes" and adviser to *My Friend Irma*, announced that Irma had won the money to go to England. Lorelei's group tells Irma to order everything new. She does, and then wastes the money by buying a ticket to *New* England.

Only a few women workers earned some validity as mature individuals. A predecessor of TV's *Moonlighting*, the 1941 *Miss Pinkerton* allowed one woman to enter a man's world. A pretty, bright, principled young woman who inherited a detective agency, she enlisted as her partner a brash, suggestive guy who both attracted and annoyed her. Likewise, *Penny Williamson*, a war widow with two children, coped poignantly with life in 1950 as a single parent by selling real estate in Middletown. Connie Brooks, the unsinkable English teacher at Madison High, and Miss Spaulding, who taught night school for immigrants on *Life with Luigi*, also managed to stay afloat in the workplace.

Household servants were predictable. One need only think of Beulah (*Fibber McGee and Molly*'s maid), or Geranium (*Judy Canova*) or Nightingale (*A Date with Judy*) to realize how automatically linked were the concepts of "house servant" and "woman of color." Here there exist traces of the wise woman archetype and a certain respect for people whom society often suppressed. Repeatedly, Birdy on *The Great Gildersleeve* moderated her portly employer's pomposity by reminding him of his own need to diet or to get closer to his ward Leroy.

The Girlfriend or Wife represented the grown-up female (as a group comprising nearly half of the total number of women in comedy). Whether she tried to teach *Slapsy Maxie Rosenbloom* that there's more to life than boxing, or to soothe neighbors when *Lorenzo Jones*'s inventions made noise, or to moderate *Fibber McGee*'s bumptiousness, this helper civilized her man. Alice Faye took away Phil Harris' booze; Margaret Anderson sounded as wise as her husband on *Father Knows Best*; Mrs. Blandings altered her husband's schemes to build his dream home; Betty, *Alan Young*'s girl, encouraged him; and Judy Garland on *The Hardy Family* preserved Andy from embarrassment.

Erratics include the many censorious Mrs. Uppington/Mrs. Carstairs (*Fibber McGee and Molly*) types who corrected grammar and chastened mischief. Fussbudgets almost drowned out a small group of revolutionaries such as Lucy Arnaz or *Hogan's Daughter* or Jane Ace (*Easy Aces*). *Charlotte Greenwood* managed to be single, moral, and peppy. When Gracie Allen wandered onto other people's programs during 1937, apparently looking for her brother, she flummoxed normally self-possessed performers such as Walter Winchell, Fred Allen, Ben Bernie, and Singing Sam. The transgressions of erratics could be tolerated because everyone understood that it was temporary.

Children

Golden Age radio drew stereotypes of young characters from two deep wells of tradition. In public Americans looked up to the young. Citizens saw them as the lucky receptacles for their elders' accumulated wisdom and wealth; immigrants valued them because they could make a fresh start, learn to speak English well, and ascend socially. With luck and pluck, some admirable youths strove to succeed in adult-approved universes by helping their families like Horatio Alger heroes, or by comforting their elders with fey wisdom like that of *Pollyanna*, or by traveling so they could learn about grown-up activities like the jolly rovers of G.A. Henty and Edward Stratemeyer. Such characters might be called "collaborators."

The reverse of this optimistic view of children involved annoyance, helplessness, and embarrassment. Out of adult reach, past rational understanding, and immune to good advice, children were sometimes thought to have a life quite different from that of adults. This notion recognized that two forces contended in young people: the desire to belong and the bothersome urge to be an individual. Like the Katzenjammer Kids, spunky tykes discomfited adults. This second group of stereotypes may be called "confounders."

Radio judged, no doubt correctly, that abused, hungry, sexual, angry, homeless, or delinquent children would offend listeners. However, a medium that claimed to be immediate and realistic could not remain silent about young people, so it chose to present them nostalgically. Out of 55 programs that gave significant roles to young characters, 33 presented juniors who collaborated with adults. These collaborators worked to keep families intact. *Mrs. Wiggs of the Cabbage Patch* managed her modest household (during the Depression and on the wrong side of town) with the dependable aid of her little son Billy. The two Nolan kids, Francie and Neely, helped their similarly poor-but-proud family in *A Tree Grows in Brooklyn*. In 1936 *Wilderness Road* (an early version of TV's *The Waltons*) appeared, reporting how five Midwestern "young-uns," the Westons, helped their folks homestead in the 1890s.

Even kids such as the orphans in Buffalo, 1942, on *Miss Meade's Children*—who, in some real world, might exhibit anxiety or use unconventional language—merely frisked through one radio day after another. *Little Orphan Annie* defeated kidnappers and despair throughout the 1930s. *Mommie and the Men* had a level-headed mother managing four "children" in 1945: three kids and one infantile husband. They resembled *My Best Girls*, the three daughters of a widower who dealt amusingly with events in 1944 Chicago. Ethyl Barrymore and her daughter and son cooperated to keep the Thompson family intact on *Miss Hattie*.

Perhaps the most palatable form of the sugary category of home-centered helpers was the comedy program. Jack Barry's son and wife compensated for his flakiness on *It's the Barrys*. In *That's My Pop*, Hugh Herbert's son and daughter supported him (in 1945) because his last job had been peddling sunglasses during the eclipse of 1929. Niece Marjorie Forrester helped her aunt manage *The Great Gildersleeve*.

The kids who glued families together blended with a second subset of collaborators acting in non-residential settings. *Dick Cole* took time off from the Farr Military Academy to foil Nazi-type spies; *Jack Armstrong* skipped out of Hudson High to catch gamblers; and *Frank Merriwell*, no nearer shaving in 1946 than he was in the 1890s, found a huge underground reservoir of water that would enable farmers to make a profit.

Other compliant youths moved beyond home and school to work with adult mentors. Sixteen-year-old *Jimmy Allen* scurried about the 1930s-era Kansas City airport in order to teach 1946 listeners that a bright lad can rise if he keeps his eyes open for mechanics who might sabotage planes. Similarly, Jimmy Olsen and Beanie the office boy worked to keep *The Daily Planet* operating while *Superman* was on the road (or in the air). Junior interned with *Dick Tracy* and Pat Patton. Penny and Clipper aided *Sky King* so enthusiastically that audiences knew the maxims he spouted would inspire them to imitate his career as navy pilot, FBI agent, and rancher-detective. Jimmy, the heir of *Tom Mix*, resembled another apprentice, *Howie Wing*, who was learning to fly (as his name suggests) from Captain Harvey in 1938. Even 10-year old Barney Mallory helped his war-hero uncle Spencer Mallory during 1945 on *The Sparrow and the Hawk*.

A final group of collaborators performed noble deeds with little adult supervision, but still in harmony with adult aspirations. At one end of this spectrum of apparently individuated kids are Isabel and Billy, who hunted under the sea for misplaced toys in *Land of the Lost*. True, they were guided by a talking fish, but still they moved with relative autonomy. In 1935, *Billy and Betty* scampered through perils, contacting adults only when they needed a policeman to take away the criminal they had collared. *Chick Carter* learned so much from his adoptive father that he could pursue criminals on his own or with his pal Sue.

In opposition to the goody-goodies, the confounders were an undisciplined parade of scamps who chipped away at adult composure. They were both male and female, with Red Skelton's "mean widdle kid" complementing Fanny Brice's *Baby Snooks*. For each pair of cooperators such as Tank Tinker who supported *Hop Harrigan*, there were opposites such as Archie and Jughead on *Archie Andrews* or Henry Aldrich and Homer Brown on *The Aldrich Family*. For caretaking niece Marjorie on *The Great Gildersleeve*, there was Leroy, the water commissioner's restive nephew; balancing dutiful daughter Babs was Junior, a true son of his fumbling father on *The Life of Riley*. In contrast to the attentive students of adult mentors (such as *Bobby Benson* and Tex Mason or Little Beaver and *Red Ryder*), there was Teeny, the exasperating kid who flummoxed *Fibber McGee*. Dinky added to the problems on *Today at the Duncans*, and teenagers such as those who dithered on *Junior Miss, Corliss Archer, A Date with Judy,* and *That Brewster Boy* did not exactly rebel, but their enthusiasms often torpedoed parental expectations.

Radio left each confounder's future in amiable doubt: would Harriet Conklin, sensible daughter of the high school principal, eventually marry Walter Denton, nemesis of authority but friend to *Our Miss Brooks*? Radio implied that this class of young people, like foreigners and women, might someday conform to the dictates of middle-class normalcy, but only after amusing tribulations. Darker visions of youth seldom surfaced. A few malevolent children appeared on science fiction programs, but such characters were not typical in radio programs of the day.

Radio Stereotypes since the Advent of Television

After 1947 the radio industry was forced to change owing to the new competition for audiences from television and the subsequent loss of national advertisers, as well as the movement of radio stars and personalities to television. Of necessity, the kinds and types of radio programming changed.

Despite these changes in the medium, racial stereotypes of African-Americans and others did not change quickly; as they had existed prior to radio's Golden Age, they persisted after it ended. In 1948 Joe Scribner developed *Sleepy Joe*, a children's show that used black dialect and "Uncle Tom" stereotypes in its broadcast. *Beulah* made its debut on network radio in 1947. This program made use of the "Mammy" stereotype with African-American actress Hattie McDaniel (of *Gone with the Wind* film fame) in the role of Beulah, after protests forced the network to replace a white man who had originally played the part. In addition to this program, several other network radio programs featured African-American women in stereotypical roles, often cast as maids and servants with flower names. (For example, Ruby Dandridge was cast as Geranium on the *Judy Canova Show*.)

Although the majority of stereotypes on network radio, even after the Golden Age, continued the negative portrayal of African-Americans, other groups were also similarly depicted. Native Americans and immigrant ethnic groups were also stereotyped on network radio after radio's Golden Age. For example, *The Lone Ranger* used the Tonto character to denigrate Native Americans. Significantly, this Native American character referred to the *Lone Ranger* only as "Kemosabe," a word supposedly meaning "wise one" in an otherwise unidentified Indian language.

See also, in addition to individual shows mentioned in this entry: Affirmative Action; African-Americans in Radio; Black-Oriented Radio; Black Radio Networks; Gay and Lesbian Radio; Hispanic Radio; Jewish Radio Programs; Native American Radio

Further Reading

Allport, Gordon W., *The Nature of Prejudice*, New York: Addison Wesley, 1954; abridged edition, New York: Anchor Doubleday, 1958.

Bogle, Donald, *Toms, Coons, Mulattoes, Mammies, and Bucks: An Interpretive History of Blacks in American Films*, New York: Viking, 1973; 3rd edition, New York: Continuum, 1994.

Daniels, Roger, *The Politics of Prejudice: The Anti-Japanese Movement in California, and the Struggle for Japanese Exclusion*, Berkeley: University of California Press, 1962.

Dates, Janette L., and William Barlow, editors, *Split Image: African Americans in the Mass Media*, 2nd edition, Washington, D.C.: Howard University Press, 1993.

Ely, Melvin Patrick, *The Adventures of Amos 'n' Andy: A Social History of an American Phenomenon*, New York: Free Press, 1991.

Gossett, Thomas F., *Race: The History of an Idea in America*, New York: Schocken, 1965.

Helmreich, William B., *The Things They Say behind Your Back*, Garden City, New York: Doubleday, 1982.

Hilmes, Michele, *Radio Voices: American Broadcasting, 1922–1952*, Minneapolis: University of Minnesota Press, 1997.

LaGumina, Salvatore J., editor, *"Wop": A Documentary History of Anti-Italian Discrimination in the United States*, San Francisco, California: Straight Arrow, 1973.

Selzer, Michael, editor, *"Kike!": A Documentary History of Anti-Semitism in America*, New York: World, 1972.

Steinberg, Stephen, *The Ethnic Myth: Race, Class, and Ethnicity in America*, New York: Atheneum, 1981; updated and expanded edition, Boston: Beacon Press, 1989.

Wither, W. Tasker, *The Adolescent in the American Novel, 1920–1960*, New York: Ungar, 1964.

Wu, Cheng-Tsu, editor, *"Chink!": A Documentary History of Anti-Chinese Prejudice in America*, New York: World, 1972.

JAMES A. FREEMAN
("STEREOTYPES OF FOREIGNERS,
WOMEN, AND CHILDREN")

GILBERT A. WILLIAMS
(OPENING AND CONCLUDING SECTIONS)

SUBSIDIARY COMMUNICATIONS AUTHORIZATION

Radio stations, both AM and FM, are permitted to generate programming in addition to their main programs. Subsidiary Communications Authorization (SCA) uses multiplexing techniques and transmits audio or data on a separate channel, but still as part of the modulated carrier. SCA services, called "subcarriers," are not receivable with a regular radio. A special receiver or adapter is required.

Origins

The principle of multiplexing (sending separate signals with one transmitter) was first demonstrated by FM system inventor Edwin Howard Armstrong in the mid-1930s. In 1948 the inventor returned to perfect the multiplex technology and announced it in 1953. Armstrong and his associates saw the system as a way to assist then hard-pressed FM outlets with an additional revenue stream by allowing them the ability to transmit—and sell—a secondary transmission different from the main broadcast signal. This derived from the fact that stations rented or sold the separate receivers needed to pick up the secondary (to the main broadcast channel) transmission, be it music (as most were) or some other format. Early in 1955 the FCC adopted rules for such a service, based in part on the experience from 20 experimental subsidiary multiplex operations already underway. The first new subsidiary communications authorizations were issued in October 1955 to WPEN-FM in Philadelphia and WWDC-FM in Washington, D.C.

In the years that followed, FM stations made wide use of SCAs. Some 30 subcarriers existed by 1958, and more than 600 by 1967. Most were used for "musicasting" (transmitting background music for stores and offices provided either by the station or a service leasing station facilities—the most common application), special news and information services, weather warnings, educational programming, and (by the 1970s) reading services for blind listeners. In the days before widespread FM listenership in the 1970s, operation of SCAs often made the difference between profit and loss (or prevented a larger loss) for stations.

Operations

SCA services are not allowed to disrupt or degrade the station's main programming or the programs of other broadcast stations. Permissible SCA uses fall into two categories: the first includes broadcast transmission of programs or data of interest to a limited audience. Examples include paging services, inventory distribution, bus dispatching, background music, traffic control signal switching, point-to-point or multipoint messages, foreign-language programming, radio reading services for the blind, radio broadcast data systems (RBDS), storecasting, detailed weather forecasting, real-time stock market reports, utility load management, bilingual television audio, and special time signals. The second category includes transmission of signals that are directly related to the operation of the radio station. Examples include relaying broadcast material to other FM and AM stations, distribution of audio networks, remote cuing and order circuits, and remote control telemetry.

Many of the programming requirements for broadcast stations do not apply to SCA programming, including station identification, delayed recording, program logging, and sponsor identification announcements. For FM stations only, SCA operation may continue when regular FM programming is off the air. However, regular hourly station identification must continue. Noncommercial FM stations, usually located between 88.1 MHz and 91.9 MHz, may generate SCA programming for profit. But such stations are then required to provide another SCA channel for any radio reading services for the blind that may request such a channel. The station is limited to charging the radio reading service only for actual operating costs.

There are several technical restrictions for SCA services. SCA subcarriers must be frequency modulated (FM) and are restricted to the range of 20–75 kHz, unless the station is also broadcasting stereo, in which case the restriction is 53–75 kHz. This allows a subcarrier to be modulated at audio frequencies and prevents it from interfering with the main program, as listeners cannot hear modulation above 2.0 kHz. SCA use is secondary to the audio on the main channel and must not interfere with the main broadcast audio channel.

SCA programming is retrieved by a detector in a special receiver, in which a tuned circuit filters out all subcarrier signals except the desired one. A second detector retrieves the information that modulates the selected subcarrier. Generally, tunable subcarrier receivers are prohibited by the FCC.

See also: FM Radio; Licensing Authorizing U.S. Stations to Broadcast

Further Reading

Christiansen, Donald, editor, *Electronics Engineers' Handbook*, 4th edition, New York: McGraw Hill, 1997 (see "Subsidiary Communications Authorizations," "Frequency Modulation Broadcasting," and "FM Stereo and SCA Systems").

Federal Communications Commission: Audio Services Division, www.fcc.gov/mmb/asd/subcarriers/sub.html

Gibilisco, Stan, editor, *Encyclopedia of Electronics*, Blue Ridge Summit, Pennsylvania: TAB Professional and Reference Books, 1985; 2nd edition, 1990.

Gibilisco, Stan, editor, *Illustrated Dictionary of Electronics*, 8th edition, New York: McGraw Hill, 2001.

Parker, Lorne A., *SCA: A New Medium*, Madison: University of Wisconsin Extension, 1969.

DAVID SPICELAND

SUSPENSE

Suspense Thriller

In 1941 there were 16 suspense programs on the radio networks; by the end of the war there were more than 40. The suspense-thriller was the fastest growing genre during the wartime period. The most famous and prestigious of these programs was *Suspense*, which debuted as a series in 1942 after a single episode premiered in the summer of 1940 (this first episode was directed by Alfred Hitchcock, his only direct connection to the show). *Suspense* set the artistic and thematic standard for the programs that followed.

Originally a sustaining program, *Suspense* was promoted as a prestige drama because of the talent of its creative team, its first-rate stars, and the high quality of its original scripts. Producer/director William Spier fine-tuned each episode, coordinating music, actors, and sound to maximum effect and earning himself the nickname of the "Hitchcock of the Air." Bernard Herrmann (famous for his musical scores for Hitchcock films) composed and conducted music for the series until 1948; his theme for the show was used throughout its 20-year run. *Suspense*'s popularity and effectiveness, however, were also due to its realism. Unlike previous thriller programs such as *Lights Out*, *Suspense* programs did not incorporate the supernatural but rather focused on the psychological and social horrors that could be visited on the lives of everyday people. Radio critics of the time saw the growth of the genre as a testament to the audience's need for "escape" during the war, but part of the impact of such programs lay in their ability both to capitalize on the audience's wartime fears and to address some of the feelings of trauma the war produced. This is particularly obvious in the many programs that focused on mistrust between husbands and wives, which tapped into both men's wartime traumas and their fear of women's independence.

Suspense's popularity and influence can be traced to one particular episode during its second year, "Sorry, Wrong Number," which was broadcast on 25 May 1943. This half-hour program, written by *Suspense* regular Lucille Fletcher (Herrmann's wife) and starring Agnes Moorehead, was a watershed moment in the history of radio drama and became perhaps the most famous original radio play of all time. In "Sorry, Wrong Number," Moorehead plays an invalid who overhears a conversation on the telephone between two men who are planning to murder a woman in half an hour. Moorehead's character, known only as "Mrs. Elbert Stevenson," tries desperately to prevent the murder by calling on various public institutions for help—the police, the phone company, public hospitals—but they do nothing for her, and her frustration increasingly borders on hysteria. In the last few moments, she realizes that she is the intended victim, that her husband has paid to have her killed. She calls the police but she's too late, and the play ends with her desperate screams as she is stabbed to death.

The play touched a nerve, and the Columbia Broadcasting System (CBS) was flooded with calls commending the program's realism and Moorehead's performance. The program was repeated within a few months, and then seven more times within the next few years. Audiences identified with a character who ultimately has no control over her fate and whose cries for help are ignored by those in power; the insecurity this created in audiences was enhanced by the fact that the character's killers go unpunished (an exception to Spier's usual policy). The success of the play proved the popularity of the suspense genre and encouraged the proliferation of suspense-thriller programs. It also led to more programs with female leads and narrators (Moorehead herself would become *Suspense's* most frequent star). Finally, it encouraged a focus on domestic tensions in the genre as a whole, in particular making the stalked wife and the killer husband staples of the genre for the next several years. Like film noir of the time, suspense programs seemed to mirror the frustration of many Americans faced with postwar social requirements, particularly the social conformity, suburban ideal, and standards of wealth (husbands frequently killed wives for money) expected of them during the Cold War period.

Although *Suspense* programs developed a stable of talented stars (most notably Nancy Kelly, Cathy Lewis, and Elliot Lewis), producers often called on Hollywood stars to fill the title roles. Frequently, the star's persona was tweaked to accommodate his or her role as a killer or psychotic, adding to both the thrill and the discomfort the program could cause. Stars enjoyed doing *Suspense* programs, in part because it gave them the opportunity to play against their Hollywood images. Ozzie and Harriet Nelson schemed to kill their elderly relative in "Too Little to Live On" (1947); Frank Sinatra played a murdering psychotic in "To Find Help" (1945); Robert Taylor shot and killed his crazed werewolf-wife in "The House in Cyprus Canyon" (1946); and Orson Welles dug into his own living son's skull in the gruesome "Donovan's Brain" (1944). Paul Henried, Joseph Cotten, Charles Laughton, and Lloyd Nolan all killed their wives or girlfriends on the show, and Eve Arden and Geraldine Fitzgerald killed their husbands or boyfriends.

Female stars could look forward to a particularly wide range of meaty roles, in which they had to use their smarts to outwit stalkers as well as to climb the corporate ladder. Some of the more memorable of these include Lucille Ball as a gold digger in "A Little Piece of Rope" (1948), Anne Baxter as a struggling career woman in "Always Room at the Top" (1947), and Ida Lupino as a businesswoman coping with her ex-convict husband in "The Bullet" (1949). *Suspense* also helped shape star personas, first casting Vincent Price as a murdering sophisticate in one of Fletcher's best stories,

"Fugue in C Minor" (1944); in addition, Jimmy Stewart's turn as a paralyzed veteran who believes he is being stalked by his Japanese torturer in "Mission Completed" (1949) anticipates the actor's work for Hitchcock in the 1950s in films such as *Rear Window*.

In later years, the direction of the program shifted to Anton M. Leader and then to Elliot Lewis, but the high quality and star power of the programs continued until the mid-1950s. Comedians and musical stars continued doing interesting variations on their star personas, with Jack Benny as a bank thief in "Good and Faithful Servant" (1952), Red Skelton haunted by dreams in "The Search for Isabel" (1949), and Danny Kaye as a scapegoat for murder in "I Never Met a Dead Man" (1950). Past shows were frequently repeated using different stars. In 1949 *Suspense* made its television debut, and the two shows ran simultaneously until 1954, when Autolite dropped sponsorship of both. The television show ceased production, but the radio program continued until 1962 under multiple sponsorship, making it one of the longest-running programs in radio history. Fortunately, recordings of well over 900 of the program's 945 episodes are available commercially. Listening to them today, they not only provide thrills and chills but are also an invaluable historical record of their time.

Hosts

"The Man in Black" (1942–43), Joseph Kearns or Ted Osborne (1943–47), Robert Montgomery (1948)

Announcers

Truman Bradley, Ken Niles, and Frank Martin (1943–47), Bob Stevenson, Harlow Wilcox (1948–54), Larry Thor and Stu Metz

Actors

Cathy Lewis, Agnes Moorehead, Jeanette Nolan, Hans Conreid, Joseph Kearns, Elliott Lewis, Lurene Tuttle, Mary Jane Croft, Bill Johnstone, William Conrad, Lillian Buyeff, Paul Frees, Irene Tedrow

Producers/Directors

Charles Vanda (1942), William Spier (1942–48, 1949–50), William Robson (1948), Anton M. Leader (1948–49), Elliott Lewis (1950–54), Norman Macdonnell (1954), Antony Ellis (1954–56), William N. Robson (1956–59), Bruno Zirato, Jr. (1959–62), Fred Hendrickson (1962)

Programming History

CBS   22 July 1940 (single episode); June 1942–
                  September 1962

Further Reading

Grams, Martin, Jr., *Suspense: Twenty Years of Thrills and Chills*, Kearney, Nebraska: Morris, 1997.
Kear, Lynn, *Agnes Moorehead: A Bio-Bibliography*, Westport, Connecticut: Greenwood Press, 1992.
Krutnik, Frank, *In a Lonely Street: Film Noir, Genre, Masculinity*, New York: Routledge, 1991.

ALLISON MCCRACKEN

SUSTAINING PROGRAMS

Sustaining programs are those not supported by advertising revenue; the cost of airtime is said to be *sustained* by the network or station. Sustaining programs may be of any format but most are usually (especially in recent years) of some public service variety.

Although never formally required by law, sustaining programs have been seen in the past as a key part of radio's responsibilities under the "public interest" portion of federal regulations concerning radio. The original regulatory theory held that only by providing programs on a sustaining basis could networks or stations offer the diverse points of view and coverage of public affairs that advertisers might not support. Deregulation has swept away most such thinking, and sustaining programs today are few and far between.

Origins

At first, virtually all radio time was provided on a sustaining basis; there was no commercial advertising on the air. Station operators sustained the entire cost of their broadcast activities. This began to change in the early 1920s as various means of supporting the cost of radio broadcasting were discussed and tried and all proved unworkable—except for the sale of airtime for advertising.

After AT&T's New York City station WEAF first sold time in mid-1922, other stations slowly began to do the same. As the potential for revenue became clearer, more stations began the practice, so that by the end of the decade, time sold to advertisers was widely accepted as the standard for broadcasting.

Well into the 1930s, advertiser-supported time was typical only of the most popular programs on the air; substantial portions of the broadcast day were still sustaining. More than a third of U.S.

radio network offerings were sustaining, even on the eve of World War II. Only the lack of print alternatives during paper-short World War II helped to fill most network time slots with paid advertising, reducing sustaining programs to a few public service offerings.

As the most popular (and highly rated) entertainment programs siphoned off advertising, such non-entertainment programs as religion, agriculture, children's shows, public affairs, discussion and talk, and news were offered on a sustaining basis to fill out station and network schedules with the broad program diversity sought by regulators. Many of these were broadcast in daytime hours when fewer people listened to radio. By 1940, "55 out of 59–1/2 daytime hours of sponsored programs per week [carried by the four national networks] were devoted to soap-operas. The broadcasting industry has thus permitted advertisers to destroy over-all program balance by concentrating on one type of program" (Warner, 1948). Similarly, stations in larger markets with more advertiser appeal were carrying fewer sustaining hours.

At the same time, many sustaining programs were providing important radio services. Some experimental drama work appeared, for example, on the Columbia Broadcasting System (CBS) sustaining program *The Columbia Workshop*, beginning in 1936. Stations in a number of larger markets provided sustaining time for programs concerning public affairs, agriculture, children's interests, and other important issues that usually appealed only to a minority of listeners. Although such programs rarely aired in the prime evening time of greatest interest to advertisers, the important fact is that they were provided and were also touted by broadcasters as evidence of their public service role.

The Public Interest

Government and industry perceptions of just what radio's "public interest" responsibilities were comprised a major factor in the long survival of sustaining programs. Prior to the Radio Act of 1927, there were no formal government-mandated rules for radio programs or advertising on the air. The 1927 law established the phrase "public interest, convenience, or necessity" as the guiding principle for government licensing of radio stations. Regulators from the Federal Radio Commission (1927 to 1934) and the Federal Communications Commission (FCC) have attached various measures of importance to the provision of sustaining programs as a key part of meeting the public interest rubric.

The clearest statement of how the FCC saw sustaining programs as a key part of radio's fulfillment of its public interest responsibility came in its 1946 policy statement informally dubbed The Blue Book. In that high-water mark of pro-regulatory thinking—authored in part by former British Broadcasting Corporation (BBC) officials who thought only in terms of sustaining time—the commission's staff held that sustaining programs filled five essential functions: (1) to secure for the station or network a means by which, in the overall structure of its program service, it can achieve a balanced interpretation of public needs; (2) to provide programs that, by their very nature, may not be sponsored with propriety; (3) to provide programs for significant minority tastes and interests; (4) to provide programs devoted to the needs and purposes of non-profit organizations; and (5) to provide a field for experimentation in new types of programs, free from the program restrictions dictated by an advertiser's interest in selling goods. Nearly half of the FCC report was devoted to a detailed discussion of these points and of actual industry practice statistics of sustaining programs during the war years (1940 to 1944).

Industry spokespersons responded by strongly arguing that they could fulfill all of their public service requirements without having broadcasters sustain program costs. Advertisers, they said, were more than willing to take up the slack. And industry economic realities—already evident in radio and soon to be so in television—made it impossible for the FCC to sustain its thinking about sustaining programs. As advertiser demand for radio time expanded after the war, stations sought and often found support for formerly sustaining programs.

When the FCC issued a new program policy statement in 1960, it clearly indicated its acceptance of industry arguments that "There is no public interest basis for distinguishing between sustaining and commercially sponsored programs in evaluating station performance. Sponsorship of public affairs, and other similar programs may very well encourage broadcasters to greater efforts in these vital areas." Sustaining time was now merely that which had not been sold, so it no longer held a special interest for regulators.

When in the early 1980s the FCC removed radio license processing guidelines that called for at least minimal amounts of non-entertainment programming and strongly encouraged public service (i.e., sustaining) messages, another support mechanism for sustaining time disappeared. No longer was the commission interested in how much advertising time a station sold—the marketplace would set the standard.

The decline of the FCC Fairness Doctrine in 1987 took away another prop of sustaining program time. The commission no longer required careful station records demonstrating that various sides of public controversies were being aired even when that meant some had to be given sustaining airtime. On the other hand, expression of controversial points of view in paid time—another long-time industry taboo—was quickly accepted when it became clear that there were plenty of people and institutions eager to buy time in order to broadcast their views. The lapse of the Fairness Doctrine made such sales easier for stations, as they were no longer required to use expensive airtime to provide balancing points of view.

Religion

Religious programs offer a useful window of insight into the subsequent decline of sustaining time. As a category, these were once provided free of charge (i.e., on a sustaining basis) to established or mainline religious groups of the Protestant, Catholic, and Jewish faiths. The major networks offered such programs at least weekly, as did many other stations. Some of these programs ran for decades. For many years it was a proud radio industry policy (a boast?) that time was not to be sold for religious programs, as such programs were offered on a sustaining basis as part of radio's public interest responsibility. But some critics—especially those in smaller religious organizations not included in the mainstream programs—argued that the networks and stations were effectively censoring minority religious viewpoints with their refusal to give equal time to programs from other denominations.

Beginning on the fringes, with small stations in local markets in the late 1940s and early 1950s, evangelical and other generally conservative religious figures began to purchase time from financially strapped outlets happy to make the sales and unconcerned with broader industry policies. Soon larger market stations were doing the same, while continuing to carry their traditional sustaining mainline religious programs. And gradually the mainline programs disappeared, religion on the air being effectively redefined to mean those denominations willing to pay for their time. Such paid programs often spent much of their time (or so it seemed) seeking donations to help purchase still more airtime.

At the beginning of the 21st century, some stations still provide sustaining time for community or other nonprofit organizations. And stations often provide time for their own special campaigns or public service benefits. But for the past four decades, sustaining time has been seen merely as time not (yet) sold, rather than as a special category in and of itself.

See also: Advertising; Blue Book; Controversial Issues, Broadcasting of; Fairness Doctrine; Federal Communications Commission; Public Interest, Convenience, or Necessity; Religion on Radio

Further Reading

Federal Communications Commission, "The Carrying of Sustaining Programs," in *Public Interest Responsibilities of Broadcast Licensees*, Washington, D.C.: GPO, 1946.

Kahn, Frank, "The 1960 Programming Policy Statement," in *Documents of American Broadcasting*, edited by Kahn, New York: Appleton-Century-Crofts, 1968; 4th edition, Englewood Cliffs, New Jersey: Prentice Hall, 1984.

Warner, Harry Paul, "Sustaining Programs," in *Radio and Television Law*, by Warner, Albany, New York: Bender, 1948.

CHRISTOPHER H. STERLING

SWEEP

This term has two quite different meanings in radio, the more usual one concerning music scheduling, and another referring to audience ratings.

Music Scheduling

A sweep describes any lengthy and uninterrupted (meaning commercial- and talk-free) period of radio music. Sweeps are used as both a programming strategy (they are considered a good way to retain listener attention), and a means of promotion. Sweeps at least suggest that a station is playing more music than commercials or interrupting talk.

Pioneered by programming syndicators such as Schulke Radio Productions and Bonneville International, sweeps were first employed in the 1950s. Then-struggling FM outlets were especially open to their use as they lacked advertisers. Sweeps were a boon for early "Beautiful Music" formats since excessive commercial clutter was counterproductive to the relaxing mellow mood the format sought to achieve. From Beautiful Music, the sweep concept migrated to soft rock stations and then other formats. Today, most stations that play music do so in sweeps, something easy to do thanks to expanding automation. Sweeps are also useful during ratings periods as stations will commonly program them to run across and over the quarter-hour to retain listeners. On the other hand, few stations schedule music sweeps during morning and afternoon drive dayparts that are most in demand by advertisers.

Stations frequently seem to play constant one-upmanship in the durations of their sweeps. Although the average sweep is three to four songs in a row (or about 12–14 minutes), some outlets build their reputations on longer sweeps. In 2009, for example station K99 in Great Falls, MT, boasts of its 30-minute sweeps; KFMA in Tucson has sweeps that are 40 minutes long; KXL-FM in Portland, OR, programs 45-minute sweep sessions; and KCIN (Big Kickin' Country) in Cedar City, Utah, proudly promotes a musical interlude that is more than 90 minutes. For promotion, stations may base their sweep length on their frequency. For example, KMXB/Mix 94.1 in Las Vegas regularly play 94 minutes of nonstop music.

Despite its widespread use and the ever-growing length of uninterrupted music, "sweep" is but an informal term, and stations are apt to describe any block of time (from a handful of minutes to an hour-and-a-half) and any number of songs played back-to-back as a "music sweep." Some stations interrupt sweeps just to inform their listeners they are in the middle of "six-in-a-row" or some other musical block. Such pronouncements, even if brief, undermine the purpose of a sweep in the first place.

The spate of commercials—some of them numerous and lengthy—that proceeds or follows a sweep is known as a commercial cluster. Indeed, to make up for loss of ad time during sweep periods, and to avoid tune out during long clusters, some stations are experimenting with "sweeps sponsorship" where a block of music is preceded by an announcement like "This half-hour of music is brought to you by ... ." Although long music sweeps are usually considered listener-friendly, they make the inevitable commercials that follow seem all the more intrusive and out of place.

Finally, a "sweep," should not be confused with a "sweeper(s)" which is a brief (20 seconds or less) pre-recorded segue that identifies a station or delivers some other short bit of information. Also known as "bumpers" or "liners," sweepers can be either produced in-house by a station or purchased (with a variety of voice talent) from specialized providers.

Listener Ratings

The other meaning of sweep concerns audience ratings. In order to determine how many people are actually listening, radio stations depend on various companies (predominately Arbitron) to measure their listener levels via written diaries, Portable

738

People Meters (PPMs) or other methods. It is from these statistics that stations determine how much to charge their advertisers. With thousands of stations in hundreds of markets operating all over the country, it would be impossible to survey every station's audience every minute, let alone every day or even every week. Hence, Arbitron and stations have collectively designated specific time periods throughout the year to evaluate listening levels. These periodic times are called "sweeps" (because they are a sweep of the nation's radio audience). Because the ratings determined during these sweeps periods directly determine how much money stations can charge advertisers, it behooves stations to obtain their largest audiences during these specific survey periods.

The country's 80 largest radio markets are almost continually surveyed by Arbitron, essentially turning the year into one big long sweep. These top markets are surveyed four times a year in 12-week durations, which means only a few weeks a year are not tracked. The nation's next 200 largest markets are polled twice a year also for 12-week periods. These sweeps periods take place between April and June ("Spring") and mid-September through December ("Fall"). The smaller markets are surveyed only once a year.

Full implementation of Arbitron's controversial Portable People Meter (PPM) will greatly alter their surveying calendar. Currently, 14 markets are being electronically surveyed 13 times a year. By 2010, the company plans to be reporting on 50 markets that often.

Arbitron's findings for all these markets are published seasonally in what has come to be called "The Arbitron Book" or, more specifically the "Spring Book," "Fall Book," etc. Understandably, only those stations which are monitored four times a year find it necessary to buy all four yearly Arbitron tomes. The ratings firm releases two additional reports between each ratings book. These are called "Arbitrends" and enable stations to keep closer tabs on how they are performing vis-á-vis competing outlets.

Though "sweeps" do take place in the radio ratings business, the term is far more commonly applied to television ratings where, four times a year (February, May, July, and November), A.C. Nielsen ratings help stations (including the four broadcast networks) determine their ad rates. Just as television entices temporary spikes in audience size by planning important promotions or running contests with high-end prizes, so do radio stations during their respective audience surveys. Policies of both Arbitron and Nielsen try to limit networks and stations from the blatant solicitation of audiences during sweeps periods and against the undue influence of people who are being polled. For example, stations cannot go so far as to host a luncheon or party for area diary keepers, though they can air promotions that encourage all their listeners to remember and record what station they are listening to.

See also: Arbitron; Audience Research Methods; Automation; Easy Listening/Beautiful Music Format; Portable People Meter; RADAR

Further Reading

Arbitron website, www.Arbitron.com
Rocha, Sean, "How Does Sweeps Week Work?" *Slate* (16 February 2004), www.slate.com/id/2095577/

CARY O'DELL

SYNDICATION
Supplementing Local and Network Sources

Stations have three sources of programming: they can produce programming themselves, receive it from a network, or get it from an outside supplier, called a syndicator. For three decades, syndication-provided dramatic series to stations; then, when radio formats changed, syndication provided music-oriented programming. Today, many stations rely on syndication for music and talk programming.

Origins

In the early days of radio, station owners relied on live talent and scratchy-sounding records for programming. The advent of the National Broadcasting Company (NBC) in 1926 and the Columbia Broadcasting System (CBS) in 1927 meant that stations could have access to the top talent in New York City for the production, writing, directing, and performing of programs. (Network programs were delivered to a permanent hookup of stations across the country, which were expected to broadcast the shows simultaneously as they were fed and which were compensated for carrying the programs and their network advertising.) But not all stations could be affiliated to the networks, and not all affiliates were satisfied with network programs and the compensation they received for carrying them.

To meet this demand, shows were distributed on records. The first syndicated radio program is credited to Freeman Gosden and Charles Correll, the creators of *Amos 'n' Andy.* When their series moved to WMAQ, which was owned by the *Chicago Daily News*, they acquired the right to record their program and sell it to other stations. In 1928 the newspaper mailed out the show to 30 stations.

Opposition

Although the idea of stations sharing programs on records seemed logical enough, problems arose. Stations, advertisers, and listeners were reluctant to accept an alternative to live programming. A major difficulty was that records were inferior in sound quality, partly because of the method of recording and partly because of the station's playback equipment. Development of electrical transcription in 1928 helped solve the problem, and stations slowly adopted the playback equipment.

Another problem was that some powerful organizations in the industry had a vested interest in live programming. The American Federation of Musicians insisted that major stations continue to employ staff musicians, even if recorded programming was used. If stations had to pay the salaries, they might as well use the employees rather than buying a recorded program. As transcriptions became more popular, the union stepped up its opposition. In 1942 the president of the musicians' union ordered his members to cease making transcriptions for broadcast use. The battle between syndicators and the union continued until television made the issue moot.

The radio networks also felt threatened by transcriptions. If a station could order a good-quality series through the mail, then who needed a network? Transcriptions also cut into the networks' revenue. Advertisers paid networks on the basis of the number of stations that aired or "cleared" their programs. If too many affiliates used transcriptions, then the networks would be hurt financially.

Network Option Time

To minimize the competition, NBC set up compensation rates to its affiliates in such a way that the use of recordings and the acceptance of national spot advertising were discouraged. These practices ended in 1941 after a Federal Communications Commission (FCC) investigation created new rules controlling network practices.

Both CBS and NBC required that their affiliates be willing to carry a certain amount of network programming at set times of the day. This practice of "optioning" portions of a station's schedule made the syndicator's job more difficult. Sponsors usually wanted their programs to run at the times

when viewing levels were highest, but those were the hours the networks had claimed for themselves. If a station scheduled a syndicated program during those hours, the networks could demand that their own program replace it. Advertisers on syndicated programs had to settle for hours with fewer listeners or for non-affiliated stations, which were usually less prestigious and had smaller audiences. The FCC tried to end the networks' optioning of their affiliates' time with its Chain Broadcasting Rules in 1941, but this move raised so much opposition that the Commission settled for reducing the amount of time the networks could stake out.

The failure to end option time was not the only reason syndicators complained about the Commission. The FCC insisted that announcers state after each record that the program had been transcribed. Syndicators claimed that the practice made their properties seem inferior to live programming. The rule had originated when recorded programs had poor quality, but despite improvement in recording techniques, the policy continued in effect until after World War II.

Advantages

Despite all of these problems, the syndication industry survived. By 1931, 20 percent of the stations in the United States could play electrical transcriptions, including many higher-powered stations. Syndicators claimed that their product was superior to network product because the listener received the best possible performance, without the mistakes that could happen in live situations. And stations could profit, because there was no network to keep commercial minutes and revenue for itself.

National, regional, and local advertisers found the use of syndicated transcriptions beneficial at times. The national advertiser could use syndication as a substitute for or a supplement to the networks. With a recorded program, a sponsor could reach and pay for only a certain region of the country, if desired. Or a seasonal product could be sold using different approaches in different parts of the country.

Stations usually charged less than the networks, and so the advertiser could get a bargain. For example, the Beech-Nut Packing Company syndicated *Chandu, the Magician* to 15 stations. Had syndication not been an option, the sponsor would have had to pay the networks for a cross-country lineup of stations that it didn't need. For local and regional advertisers, syndication was even more attractive. They could have bigname talent at local costs.

The Depression

By 1931, 75 commercially sponsored programs were available by syndication, an increase of 175 percent over the previous year. The most common syndicated shows were musical variety shows, dance bands, and programs that re-created news events.

The Lone Ranger was created on WXYZ in Detroit and syndicated to other stations. The program's success led to the founding of the Mutual Broadcasting Company, a cooperative network that began with the idea of stations sharing programs among themselves.

But as the Depression deepened, the industry faltered. (Sometimes syndicators would sign up some advertisers based on an audition disc but then go out of business if not enough sponsors were found.) During this period, smaller stations and regional advertisers were the main users of syndicated programs.

Two other organizations also became prominent in the syndication industry, NBC and CBS. Both networks maintained that live programs were better, but they recognized that recorded shows might be useful in some circumstances. NBC entered the field in 1935 with three services: a collection of musical numbers, series produced for syndication, and recorded series that had run live on the network. CBS followed in 1940.

Frederic Ziv

Perhaps the leading radio syndicator was Frederic Ziv, who began distributing radio programs in 1937 and later went on to syndicate television programs. He had owned an advertising agency in Cincinnati and wanted to create a product his bakery client could use. Once the program was produced, he started selling it to other stations. This first program was a series aimed at children, *The Freshest Thing in Town*.

World War II brought restrictions on the materials used to make electrical transcriptions, but after the war, radio syndication reached its height of popularity, as more stations went on the air and as the networks concentrated their efforts on television. Two of the more popular syndicated programs were produced by Ziv: *Boston Blackie* and *The Cisco Kid*. Stars such as actor Ronald Colman, singer Bing Crosby, and musician Kenny Baker were available on electrical transcriptions. With the advent of audiotape in the United States, syndicators had a new medium for distribution, and they used it mainly for features and short music programs.

By the mid-1950s, syndicators had to deal with the changes in the radio industry wrought by competition from television. Disc jockeys spinning records had replaced network serial programming. At first, stations desperate to maintain their traditional formats turned to the syndicators to provide the old-fashioned programs, but soon half-hour dramas and adventure shows became rare on radio.

Automated Formats

In the late 1950s, syndicators found another niche. They created hours of recorded music with announcements on audiotape and mailed the reels to stations around the country. Music format syndication offered several advantages to the station. It was cheaper and more reliable than the average live disc jockey. For unpopular time periods, late night and weekends, recorded programming could be the difference between profit and loss for a station. The supply of reels meant that even the smallest town could have an announcer with national appeal and a smoothly produced program aimed at a target audience. The main disadvantage was that the automated programming couldn't be localized. Some stations did use a local announcer during some of the programming in a practice called "live assist."

The FCC provided an impetus to the growth of automated radio by declaring in 1964 that FM and AM stations in the larger markets could no longer simulcast (i.e., carry the same programming at the same time). Because AM radio was the dominant medium at that time, stations scrambled to find programming to put on their FM channels. Automation was a cheap and easy solution.

Other Formats

Other types of programming were also syndicated. In 1968, 300 stations carried a special featuring mythical boxing matches between the all-time best heavyweights. By the mid-1970s, weekly programs were back in style. Successful formats included weekly musical specials, such as the *King Biscuit Flower Hour*, and musical countdowns hosted by Casey Kasem and Dick Clark. *The National Lampoon Radio Hour* and *Dr. Demento* were examples of successful comedies. These programs were carried mainly on weekends.

The mainstay of the industry remained automated programs. The most popular format was "beautiful music," standard songs done without lyrics and in lush arrangements, usually replete with strings. Other formats, though, such as rock and roll and country/western, were also syndicated. By 1977 almost 1,500 stations were fully automated, and another 1,000 relied at least some of the time on automation. The major syndicators were also expected to act as consultants, providing advice on technical matters, promotion, and advertising, as well as format.

Modern Syndication

In the 1980s, satellites made the delivery of programming cheaper and allowed the added quality of timeliness. Disc jockeys could comment on the day's events. A satellite could send a signal to a subscribing station's computer, which could be programmed with local news, commercials, and weather. Several channels of programming could be sent and received at the same time with no loss of quality. A station could carry some programming from one supplier and easily switch to another supplier on the satellite.

A new market developed as AM radio started to lose its audience to FM. Talk shows distributed by satellite began to be in demand. Call-in shows, such as those of Larry King and Tom Snyder, were popular late at night. In 1988 Rush Limbaugh's show was put into syndication for the daytime audience and became successful enough to attract imitators such as Howard Stern and Don Imus. Other types of talkers joined in the competition with topics such as sports, psychological advice, and business information.

Syndicators increased their use of satellites as the cost of equipment went down and as compression technology allowed them to squeeze more signals onto one transponder. The difference between them and networks blurred. Syndicators offered simultaneous delivery of signals to affiliates across the country via satellite, just as networks did, and the type of programming was the same. Traditional networks and syndicators became part of the same companies, as mergers and buyouts led to industry consolidation. Networks didn't always provide compensation, and both industries offered similar formats.

By 2000 the two most successful syndicated radio formats remain the talk show and automated programming delivered by satellite, tape, or disc. With the aid of a computer and the satellite, the syndicator can provide announcing, music, and cues for commercials, local news, and weather. This type of service had existed before but was delivered on tape to the station and was therefore not as versatile. For some markets, the national announcer records local announcements, which can be inserted

smoothly into the program. Short features with medical advice, interviews with stars, and David Letterman's top 10 list are also syndicated.

Syndicated programming can be purchased outright, or the sale may involve barter or a combination of the two (cash plus barter). Some form of barter is the most common method: the producer sells some commercial minutes in the program but leaves time for the station to sell others. In other words, the station trades time for a free program or one with a reduced price. If cash is involved, the cost of the program will depend on the size of the market, its competitiveness, and the station's revenues.

Syndication has become such an omnipresent part of radio that, increasingly, stations are no longer seen as a local resource or for playing a role in the community (once the medium's *raison d'être*) but, rather, as a vehicle for delivering nationally known, high-profile personalities such as Rush Limbaugh and Dr. Laura. One of syndication's newest stars is Ryan Seacrest, whose celebrity-focused, Los Angeles-based morning show is distributed nationally by Premiere Radio Networks. Many stations have anxiously signed up to carry Seacrest, hoping they can glean some of his *American Idol* television success (and his younger demographics) in their ratings.

Though radio syndication was once exclusively the purview of large companies like Westwood One, CBS Radio, and Premiere, in recent years smaller stations are increasingly open to sharing with other outlets a program or two that has proved popular locally. Such an arrangement can be a win–win situation for all—stations which buy the program(s) obtain some cost-effective content while the originating station creates a previously untapped revenue source. However, such small-scale syndicating can be a tenuous undertaking. Should their programs become successful as syndicated properties, the more likely the program or talent is to be swallowed by one of radio's syndication firms.

See also: American Federation of Musicians; *Amos 'n' Andy*; Automation; *King Biscuit Flower Hour; Lone Ranger*; Recording and the Radio Industry; Simulcasting

Further Reading

Becker, Christine, "A Syndicated Show in a Network World: Frederic Ziv's *Favorite Story*," *Journal of Radio Studies* 8, no. 1 (Summer 2001).
Eastman, Susan Tyler, Sydney W. Head, and Lewis Klein, *Broadcast Programming: Strategies for Winning Television and Radio Audiences*, Belmont, California: Wadsworth, 1981; 6th edition, as *Broadcast/Cable/Web*

Programming: Strategies and Practices, by Eastman and Douglas A. Ferguson, 2002.

Keith, Michael C., *Radio Programming: Consultancy and Formatics*, Boston and London: Focal Press, 1987.

Keith, Michael C., and Joseph M. Krause, *The Radio Station*, Boston: Focal Press, 1986; 5th edition, by Keith, 2000.

MacFarland, David T., *Contemporary Radio Programming Strategies*, Hillsdale, New Jersey: Erlbaum, 1990; 2nd edition, as *Future Radio Programming Strategies: Cultivating Listenership in the Digital Age*, Mahwah, New Jersey: Erlbaum, 1997.

Rouse, Morleen Getz, "A History of the F.W. Ziv Radio and Television Syndication Companies: 1930–1960," Ph.D. diss., University of Michigan, 1976.

Routt, Edd, James B. McGrath, and Fredric A. Weiss, *The Radio Format Conundrum*, New York: Hastings House, 1978.

Sterling, Christopher H., and John M. Kittross, *Stay Tuned: A History of American Broadcasting*, 3rd edition, Mahwah, New Jersey: Lawrence Erlbaum, 2002.

BARBARA MOORE,
2009 REVISIONS BY CARY O'DELL

T

TALENT RAIDS

In 1948 Columbia Broadcasting System (CBS) Chairman William S. Paley initiated a raid on the National Broadcasting Company's (NBC) top radio talent in order to compete with the better-fortified network. This bold move changed the balance of power in radio and affected key programming strategies in radio and later in television.

Background

Throughout the 1930s and much of the 1940s, NBC reigned as the dominant radio network. NBC had the financial backing of a wealthy corporate parent in the Radio Corporation of America (RCA), boasted a larger number of affiliated stations than CBS, and had a popular roster of vaudeville-trained comedians. CBS initially tried to even the standings in the mid-1930s by capturing some of NBC's key affiliated stations. Paley also went after some of NBC's talent in 1936, luring such stars as Al Jolson and Major Edward Bowes over to the smaller network. NBC was angered by these maneuvers, particularly because the network thought it had an unwritten agreement with CBS not to participate in such raids. But given CBS's inferior position in the industry, Paley insisted it was the only way he could reasonably compete. NBC battled back heartily, winning back some of its stars and stations.

Thus, after World War II, CBS was still a distant number two. Dissatisfied that his previous coup attempts had failed, Paley began outlining a new strategy. Lew Wasserman and Taft Schreiber of MCA, the mammoth talent agency, ultimately

helped lead Paley to a crafty solution in 1948, during a lunch date with CBS President Frank Stanton. MCA represented Freeman Gosden and Charles Correll, the stars of *Amos 'n' Andy*, and Wasserman offered the popular NBC actors to Paley along with a unique financial arrangement. Stars certainly earned a high salary at NBC (Jack Benny reportedly earned $12,000 a week), but this placed them within a very high income-tax bracket, and they were taxed at a rate as high as 77 percent. Wasserman and Paley thus devised a scheme wherein Gosden and Correll would incorporate, with CBS purchasing the resulting company and its assets, namely the characters and scripts for the shows. The money that CBS subsequently paid out to Gosden and Correll could thus be considered a capital gain, taxed at the considerably lower rate of 25 percent. Moreover, because CBS would now own the properties and names themselves, NBC would not be able to lure its talent back as easily as it did after Paley's first talent raids in the late 1930s.

The Raids

With Gosden and Correll signed, Paley next set his sights on Jack Benny, with Wasserman again brokering the deal. But because Benny and other NBC comedians went by their own names, rather than playing characters as did Gosden and Correll, it was initially unclear if they could legally incorporate their names for CBS to purchase. As a result, when Paley cemented a deal with Benny, the Internal Revenue Service challenged it in federal court. Though the Supreme Court did declare the maneuver legal in 1949, a more immediate obstacle came from Benny's sponsor, the American Tobacco Company, and his corresponding advertising agency, Batton, Barton, Durstine, and Osborn (BBD&O). Benny had a long-term contract with these companies, and they initially objected to the move to CBS, expecting a decline in Benny's ratings, if only because CBS had fewer affiliated stations. BBD&O thus vigorously complained to NBC about the decision to let go of Benny. NBC responded with a major counteroffer to Benny, totaling twice the value of CBS's offer. However, Lew Wasserman again intervened, obtained the NBC contract, changed every mention of NBC to CBS, and reoffered the deal to Benny, who then signed it. Reportedly, the personal attention given to Benny by CBS executives was enough to provide the deciding factor—Benny was continually insulted by the impersonal atmosphere of NBC and had reportedly never even met David Sarnoff, the head of the network's parent firm, RCA.

To counteract the sponsor's concerns about NBC's greater number of affiliates, Paley went to the unprecedented length of offering American Tobacco $3,000 for every rating point that Benny fell below his usual NBC total. Such a drastic move proved that CBS was not planning to merely buy out NBC's talent, but hoped to surpass NBC's success with this same talent. The deal was finally cemented in November 1948, despite the legal uncertainties at that point, and CBS bought Benny's company, Amusement Enterprises, for $2.26 million. Benny's CBS ratings were initially stellar, and despite a ratings decline shortly thereafter, Paley was pleased that he finally had a strategy in place to battle NBC. Bing Crosby, Red Skelton, Edgar Bergen, and George Burns and Gracie Allen were the next NBC stars to head to CBS.

Surprisingly, NBC and Sarnoff had little reaction to this continued upheaval. Some historians simply credit Sarnoff's arrogance for ignoring CBS's moves, and others highlight Sarnoff's belief that paying a performer so much money would set a dangerous precedent, resulting in a system that would give performers too much power over their network bosses. Whatever the reason for NBC's lack of a countermove, these events had the potential to devastate the network's industry standing. Indeed, by the end of 1949, CBS would tout 12 of the top 15 radio shows. But the emergence of television altered the playing field once again, and now both networks had to try out new strategies for the developing visual medium.

The success of its new talent did give CBS a profit infusion that helped launch the company into

television. Lacking the benefit of a deep-pocketed corporate parent like RCA, CBS desperately needed such capital for its first steps into television. Additionally, CBS not only captured the radio ratings lead in 1949, but also held onto that lead right into television and for the next 25 years. Finally, the talent raids related to a crucial industry strategy of developing and scheduling network-owned programming. Such direct connections with talent gave the network more control over their program decisions, rather than sponsors and advertising agencies making these decisions. This would prove to be a key difference between television and radio programming structures. In the end, an initial investment of less than $6 million brought huge benefits—the talent raid nearly eradicated NBC's top line-up of stars, brought CBS to equal status with NBC, and foretold of both networks' coming supremacy in television.

See also: Amos 'n' Andy; Columbia Broadcasting System; *Edgar Bergen and Charlie McCarthy Show*

Further Reading

Barnouw, Erik, *A History of Broadcasting in the United States*, 3 vols, New York: Oxford University Press, 1966–70; see especially vol. 2, *The Golden Web, 1933 to 1953*, 1968.
Bergreen, Laurence, *Look Now, Pay Later: The Rise of Network Broadcasting*, Garden City, New York: Doubleday, 1980.
McDougal, Dennis, *The Last Mogul: Lew Wasserman, MCA, and the Hidden History of Hollywood*, New York: Crown, 1998.
Metz, Robert, *CBS: Reflections in a Bloodshot Eye*, Chicago: Playboy Press, 1975.
Smith, Sally Bedell, *In All His Glory: The Life of William S. Paley*, New York: Simon and Schuster, 1990.

CHRISTINE BECKER

TALENT SHOWS

American radio in its earliest days was similar to an amateur hour, in that early performers were all volunteers, many of whom had great enthusiasm but minimal talent. As radio matured during the 1920s, more selective criteria for getting on the air were established, and that usually meant passing an audition. Local radio shows made a contest out of it—so-called *opportunity nights*, when those who envisioned themselves as tomorrow's radio stars could perform, and listeners voted by sending in postcards. Prizes were not very big, but the thrill of winning seemed to suffice.

Popular network talent shows had higher standards as performers would be heard by a national audience. The biggest shows held several rounds of auditions. To appear on *Roxy and His Gang*, would-be talent first auditioned for "Roxy" himself (Samuel Rothafel); he decided which amateurs would compete on the show. Some network programs also involved sponsors or advertising agencies in the decision-making process; because the money was coming from them, it seemed prudent to consider their input.

A successful show could be quite lucrative for its stars: in 1936, for example, Eddie Cantor was paid $10,000 a week by his sponsor, Texaco gasoline. George Burns and Gracie Allen made the same amount from their sponsor, Grape-Nuts Cereal. And topping the list was the $25,000 a week paid by Chrysler Motor Corporation to Major Edward Bowes. It is no wonder, with the media writing about these big salaries, that the average person dreamed of winning a talent show and becoming a network celebrity.

Radio talent shows became a national craze during the 1930s; with so many people out of work because of the Depression, the idea of striking it rich in radio was especially compelling. One network show that capitalized on this hope was *National Amateur Night*, which ran on the Columbia Broadcasting System (CBS) from December 1934 to December 1936. But thanks to its popular master of ceremonies, it was *Major Bowes' Original Amateur Hour* that would capture the largest audience. Major Edward Bowes (he had earned the rank of major in an obscure Reserve unit during World War I) had started out as a master of ceremonies for *Roxy and His Gang* at the Capitol Theatre in the mid-1920s. A few years later, while he was manager of New York radio station WHN, Bowes and two producers developed a new concept for a talent show: broadcast historian John Dunning (1998) explains that, unlike other shows, in which the master of ceremonies made fun of the contestants, "Bowes saw the amateur hour in terms of a prize fight. The amateurs were the combatants. The bell between rounds [would be] utilized to dismiss an amateur who wasn't making it. The gong was like sudden death, like the hook in the rough-and-tumble days of amateur nights in vaudeville its presence add[ed] another element of suspense."

Major Bowes' Original Amateur Hour debuted on the National Broadcasting Company (NBC) radio network in late March of 1935, sponsored by Chase and Sanborn coffee. The show was an immediate sensation, both in its ratings and in the number of would-be participants. At its highest point, it was receiving more than 10,000 applications a week for the 20 available slots on the

program. The show's opening lines—"the wheel of fortune goes round and round, and where she stops, nobody knows"—became an American catchphrase. But *Major Bowes' Original Amateur Hour* also attracted controversy, with critics questioning how honest the voting process was (people called in to vote for their favorite amateur, leading to charges that a sponsor or any amateur with a lot of friends could easily manipulate the totals) and whether Bowes decided on the winners in advance. And although the show did get huge ratings for a while, it resulted in the discovery of very few major stars—opera star Beverly Sills and crooner Frank Sinatra were the best known of the winners. (Some critics have also suggested that the idea for Major Bowes' program really came from comedian Fred Allen, who did a forerunner of the amateur hour in 1934 as a segment of his NBC show *Town Hall Tonight*.)

Another show that gave amateurs a chance at fame and fortune was *Arthur Godfrey's Talent Scouts*, which started in early July 1946 on CBS Radio and went on TV in 1948. Godfrey, who was also the master of ceremonies of a successful variety show, *Arthur Godfrey Time*, had a special reason for creating *Talent Scouts*. Unlike other talent shows, Godfrey did not give winners cash prizes or gong losers off the stage. Rather, he gave contestants the chance to graduate from *Talent Scouts* and become regular performers on *Arthur Godfrey Time*, a top-rated radio show that would be equally successful on television. Several *Talent Scouts* winners not only joined the "Little Godfreys" on *Arthur Godfrey Time*, but later had their own hit records on radio. Two of the best examples were the McGuire Sisters, whose song "Sincerely" went to number one on the U.S. pop charts in 1955, and the Chordettes, who had three top five songs during the mid-1950s. On the other hand, sometimes Godfrey got it wrong; among those who failed his audition was Elvis Presley.

One other network talent show with appeal was bandleader Horace Heidt's *Youth Opportunity Program*, heard on Sunday nights from 1947 to 1951. But by the early 1950s, most radio talent shows had moved to TV (where a few can still be found). And although the odds of becoming the next big celebrity are very small, the thrill of competing and the chance to get on the air still motivate people to come to auditions, hoping that this time the wheel of fortune will stop for them.

Early 21st century network television borrowed the talent show idea from radio (and earlier television) and aired several hugely popular shows including *American Idol* and *Dancing with the*

Stars. Both programs were inexpensive to produce and offered relative unknowns a chance at stardom (or at least a host of adoring fans).

Further Reading

"Bowes Inc.," *Time* (22, June 1936).
Brindze, Ruth, *Not to Be Broadcast: The Truth about Radio*, New York: Vanguard Press, 1937.
Dunning, John, *On The Air: The Encyclopedia of Old-Time Radio*, New York: Oxford University Press, 1998.
Maltin, Leonard, *The Great American Broadcast: A Celebration of Radio's Golden Age*, New York: Dutton, 1997.

DONNA L. HALPER,
2009 REVISIONS BY CHRISTOPHER H. STERLING

TALK OF THE NATION
Public Radio Call-In Program

Talk of the Nation is a two-hour radio show combining the news experience of National Public Radio (NPR) and the participation of call-in listeners from across the country. For the first four days of the week, the *Talk of the Nation* host (Neal Conan beginning late 2001) discusses a variety of national issues, and on Friday Ira Flatow hosts *Talk of the Nation Science Friday.* As stated by former host Ray Suarez, NPR designed the show to be "a news program that would bring in a caller who really wanted to understand better all the hanging questions out there." Although the show premiered in only nine markets, the midday voice of NPR News and NPR Talk, airing 2 P.M. eastern standard time (EST), boasted more than two million listeners from over 150 markets nationwide by 2001. The show has won several honors including the 1993 Corporation for Public Broadcasting Silver Award.

U.S. President Bill Clinton's presidential pardons in early 2001, U.S. international policies, environmental issues, school privatization, the economics of baseball, and international slavery are examples of the topics broached on *Talk of the Nation.* Jesse Jackson, Stephen King, Ralph Nader, Christopher Darden, Walter Mondale, and Yogi Berra all have graced *Talk of the Nation* as guests. As described by Suarez, "It's not a prissy, pointy-headed intellectual show, but we do give the audience a great deal of credit for being intelligent and literate, and they never let us down."

Originally hosted by John Hockenberry, *Talk of the Nation* began as a series of special call-in shows during the 1990–91 Gulf War and the Soviet coup. These shows received enough interest that

they became a permanent addition to NPR on 4 November 1991. After approximately nine months with the show, Hockenberry departed to become an ABC news correspondent, and although Robert Siegel took over as interim host, it was Brooklyn-born Ray Suarez who took the torch from Hockenberry. Suarez remained the host for the next seven years and received two awards for journalistic excellence, while watching the program's audience double. Specifically, during Suarez's tenure the program won the prestigious Alfred I. duPont-Columbia Silver Baton Award in 1994–95 for "The Changing of the Guard: The Republican Revolution" and for NPR's coverage of the first 100 days of the 104th Congress; the program also won the 1993–94 duPont-Columbia Silver Baton Award for part of NPR's coverage of the South African elections. Suarez has been described by the Copley News Service as a highly intelligent navigator with "the compelling magic of intimacy spun from intense conversations while maintaining his professional distance." Suarez won honors from the *Los Angeles Times*, which listed him as one of "100 People to watch 1996."

By 2000 Suarez followed the path of the host he replaced when he too left *Talk of the Nation* for *The Newshour with Jim Lehrer.* At the end of February 2000, Emmy-award winning writer and reporter Juan Williams replaced Suarez. Williams, who has described radio as "the temperature of our times," and executive producer Greg Allen, took *Talk of the Nation* on the road as part of the continuing series "The Changing Face of America." The series, which debuted in February 2000 in Austin, Texas, travels cross-country on the final Thursday of every month and puts forth a nationally broadcast live town hall meeting. As described by the host, the goal is rather straightforward: "to paint a picture of America at the turn of the century." For example, this format took *Talk of the Nation* to Indiana to look at small-town life and to Los Angeles to look at spirituality. The attitude of the show and its host was described quite eloquently by Williams:

> Talk radio has been boiled down to the point where people tune in to have their prejudices confirmed. The host drives the show by being intentionally provocative and taking very strong views intended to polarize the audience. You tune in to try to see what [outrageous thing] this guy is going to say today, or you tune in to hear him say what you believe but have never articulated. I want people to tune in to *Talk of the Nation* because they want to know what's going on and want to have a full understanding of the arguments that people are making around the country and the different

perspectives. Hearing other people talk about the way they see American life today—that's energizing to me. And if I work as the host of the show, it will be energizing to the audience as well.

(*Minneapolis Star Tribune*, 1 March 2000)

Talk of the Nation has been described by one newspaper as " talk radio at its zenith, a rare quasar of civility and intelligence in the usually rabid world of boom box shriek and shout" (South Florida *Sun-Sentinel*), and the San Diego *Union-Tribune* stated, "In the argumentative archipelago of talk radio, *Talk of the Nation* is an island of civility"; however, the executive producer Allen may have said it best: "The main thing is we want a good talk show. That's what we're there for."

By the end of the 21st century's first decade, *Talk of the Nation* was also available on the internet (which also encouraged listener feedback and participation) and in podcast form. Past programs were made readily available, a good demonstration of how digital media could support analog original material.

See also: National Public Radio; Podcast; Talk Radio

Executive Producer

Leith Bishop

Hosts

John Hockenberry, November 1991–July 1992
Robert Siegel (interim host)
Ray Suarez, April 1993–February 2000
Juan Williams, February 2000–August 2001
Neal Conan, September 2001–present

Further Reading

Bauder, D., "Entertainment, Television, and Culture," *Copley News Service* (14 June 1999).
Becker, Dave, "Not Your Usual Call-In Show," *Wisconsin State Journal* (28 February 1997).
Craggs, Tommy, "Watch Out NPR's 'Talk' Is Coming to Town," *Kansas City Star* (28 September 2000).
Feran, Tom, "Cleveland Is Talk of the Nation As Public Radio Show Stops Here," Cleveland *Plain Dealer* (27 October 2000).
Holston, Noel, "Juan on Juan: New 'Talk of the Nation' Host Unloads," Minneapolis *Star Tribune* (1 March 2000).
Holston, Noel, "Mall of America Is Talk of the Nation," Minneapolis *Star Tribune* (17 May 1995).
Laurence, Robert P., "Suarez Is a Different Voice for Talk Radio," *San Diego Union-Tribune* (5 September 1994).
Talk of the Nation website, www.npr.org/templates/rundowns/rundown.php?prgId=5

Walter, Tom, "Let's Talk about Race, Says NPR Host Williams, at Rhodes Tonight," *Commercial Appeal* (18 April 2000).

JASON T. SIEGEL,
2009 REVISIONS BY CHRISTOPHER H. STERLING

TALK RADIO

Talk radio (sometimes referred to as All Talk) is a general term covering many closely related types of radio programs that do not focus on music or narrative comedy or drama. Most common are interview and call-in programs. Nearly all rely on a host, often a highly opinionated one. Some of the earliest talk programs in the 1920s and 1930s got station licensees in trouble for being one-sided. By the 1990s such polemical radio was common and widely popular. Talk programs today range from serious and balanced discussion of public affairs to scandal-studded rhetoric offering far more heat than light.

By the early 21st century, talk radio had become one of the most popular formats. More than 700 of the 12,000-plus radio stations in the United Statesidentified their program format as talk. An additional 525 were in the hybrid category news/talk. Talk radio tends to be found mostly on commercial AM stations, but it is starting to expand to FM outlets as well. The talk format is generally a mix of interviews and call-in programs frequently hosted by one or more personalities. Content ranges from information to politics to "shock" radio characterized by sexual innuendo and the flouting of social conventions. Many talk show hosts are as famous for the audiences they offend as for those they entertain and attract. News-talk became the generic radio industry term for all stations that carry both news and talk programming. The phrase *talk radio* includes the news-talk format as well as formats that rely on all-conversation programming.

Origins

Legendary Boston talk host Jerry Williams claimed he invented talk radio in 1950 when he worked at an obscure station in Camden, New Jersey, hosting a show called *What's on Your Mind?*

Actually, the form was developed—not as a radio format, but as individual programs—two decades before Williams' arrival. His may have been the first radio show to take calls, but he was hardly the first talker. As early as the 1930s, columnist Walter Winchell and Father Charles Coughlin were sowing the seeds of what would become talk radio. During the following decade, Arthur Godfrey mixed interviews and chat with his musical guests on *Arthur Godfrey Time*, and Don McNeill introduced regular talk segments on his *Breakfast Club* broadcasts from Chicago in the early 1950s.

Talk shows (including Williams' show in Camden) became familiar to listeners in the 1950s as music stations devoted time to discussion of local issues. Most were interview programs, although some stations devoted hours during evenings or overnight to call-in shows. Technology did not allow the protection of a delay system to delete objectionable phone calls. Many station operators avoided airing calls live, and often the host would repeat or paraphrase what a caller said. The motivation behind most early talk programming was to satisfy public affairs requirements as specified in licenses granted by the Federal Communications Commission (FCC).

KLIQ in Portland, Oregon, debuted a format described as All Talk in 1959. *Broadcasting* magazine headlined the story with the words "Talk, Talk, Talk" and called it "Top 30" because the station used 30 different announcers. The new format was a mix of news and talk. Twenty-five minutes of every hour were devoted to a "topic of the day" that listeners called in to discuss. Under special agreement, reporter-announcers read items from 15 national magazines from two to ten days prior to their publication. Taped interviews by British Broadcasting Corporation correspondents in England and Europe were sent daily by plane and aired in three-minute segments.

The term *talk station* came into being when KABC in Los Angeles discarded its music format in 1960 and filled its 24-hour day with talk shows. The station was originally promoted as "The Conversation Station." A four-hour news and conversation program was instituted from 5 A.M. until 9 A.M. using the title *News-Talk*. Not long afterward, KABC's sister station, KGO in San Francisco, adopted the phrase News-Talk as a positioning slogan because it carried news blocks in morning and afternoon drive-time periods with talk shows in between.

Listeners searching for something other than music could tune in Jean Shepherd and other hosts on WOR in the New York area. *Sponsor* magazine trumpeted the advertising and audience successes of WOR's talk radio formula early in 1964. With ratings among the highest in the New York metropolitan area, WOR was grossing $7 million annually. *Sponsor* cited WOR's success as reasons for shifts to talk by WNA Boston, KABC Los Angeles, KMOX St. Louis, and WNBC New York to WOR's success.

The success of early talk formats led to increased industry interest. In May 1965 the National Association of Broadcasters (NAB) featured talk radio at a Chicago programming clinic for program and management executives. The 125 slots quickly filled, and 75 broadcasters who wished to attend were turned away.

Pioneering Talk Hosts

One of the first stars of the new talk radio medium was Joe Pyne, who first appeared on another Los Angeles station that abandoned its music format in the early 1960s—KLAC. Pyne's reputation was built on his style of verbal bombast against almost everyone, guest and caller alike, leading pundits to call his brand of talk "insult radio" because his callers risked verbal skewering ("Look lady, every time you open your mouth to speak, nothing but garbage falls out!"). Pyne's listeners were generally delighted. Pyne had no philosophical leaning except to the contrary. He established the habit of hanging up the phone on callers he disagreed with, a habit later adopted by talk hosts seeking to create the reputation of firebrand.

Pyne achieved some national notoriety, primarily through a short-lived television show. His radio work was not syndicated because technology at that time was too expensive to link stations not already affiliated with one of the three major networks. During a stint at KABC, Pyne took controversy to new heights as a rabid and vocal hater of President John Kennedy. When the president was assassinated in 1963, Pyne was pulled off the air. His exile created opportunity for another KABC host, Bob Grant, who was assigned Pyne's slot during the hiatus.

In 1970 Grant moved to New York and created a name for himself by creating his own brand of controversy. Grant said what he felt, and his comments were often explicitly racist. He held forth for many years at WABC, New York, generally defended by station management as "misunderstood." When black activists picketed WABC after race-baiting by Grant, a WABC spokesman said, "He is extremely angry with rioters and criminals, period. If critics want to say that means blacks, that's their problem."

When the Walt Disney Company acquired WABC with the rest of the ABC Network properties, the tone of management changed. Grant's remarks after the death of Commerce Secretary Ron Brown in a plane crash proved too much for Disney, who yielded to public outcry and pulled Grant off the air. His absence was short-lived, as

New York's WOR hastily made a place for Grant on their schedule and on their WOR Network.

Jerry Williams moved to Boston in 1957 where he sought out topics controversial enough to create talk about him and his show. He was one of very few media people to interview Malcolm X, and Williams took pride in announcing that the Boston TV stations and newspapers did not offer coverage to the black leader. For a brief period in the mid-1960s, Williams moved his show to Chicago and WBBM, where he would pit blacks against whites on the air to, in his words, "start a dialog." The result was often more of a fight. He returned to Boston in 1972, where he became a talk radiofixture until his death in 2003.

New York's Barry Gray was the longest running talk host on radio. He began as a celebrity interviewer in the mid-1940s and was still going strong when he died in 1996. For most of his career Gray was at WMCA in the overnight slot.

Evolution of the Host

Early talk radio was compared to broadcast journalism, but with the added pressures of live radio. As talk radio programmer Bruce Marr wrote:

> Management has to acknowledge that the members of the on-the-air team have their own biases and leave them free to express their stands on the issues being discussed. This philosophy has grown slowly from the understanding that it is fruitless to ask on-air personalities to be unbiased. They are often investigators, sometimes advocates, and biases are doubtless part of their stock-in-trade.

There is structure in the talk show, but there is also enough fluidity for a host to change subjects and reflect the mood and interest of the audience. When an issue or news event is significant enough to capture the attention and interest of the listeners, the talk station changes subjects to respond. Thus a school shooting, a political scandal, or other "hot button" topics could prompt a talk station to abandon a pre-set list of guests or topics and take free-wheeling conversation about the topic at hand.

The most memorable talk hosts have been those whose political leanings are hardly the stuff of balanced journalism. By and large, talk radio is politically conservative. Those attempts at presenting liberal or left-leaning programming have been able to attract only a fraction of the audience that more conservative hosts can attract. The most notable experiment with a liberal bias on a talk station was at KFSO in San Francisco. The programming

was dropped after a few months in favor of a lineup that included conservatives Pat Buchanan and Michael Reagan.

Former Texas Agriculture Commissioner Jim Hightower, a talk host syndicated at one time by ABC Radio, explains talk radio's conservatism this way:

> What happened is the progressive side forgot radio. My generation looked to television and mass demonstrations and other ways of communicating, whereas the conservatives—Ronald Reagan, Paul Harvey—hung in there and continued to build an audience. Now it's just follow the leader. People look across the street and say, "If that sucker is doing well with a conservative, that's what I need, too."

The rise of talk radio has been accompanied by an equally dramatic rise in harsh rhetoric under the guise of political opinion. The combination is often a breeding ground for what Peter Laufer called "hate, scapegoating and stereotyping" in his book, *Inside Talk Radio*. "The talk show demagogues are adept at manipulating anger and turning righteous resentment into fearful hatred of the oppressed," Laufer writes.

In *Hot Air*, Howard Kurtz says that the way to get attention in talk radio is "to shout, to polarize, to ridicule, to condemn, to corral the most outrageous or vilified guests." Kurtz points out that when White House chief of staff Leon Panetta wanted to attack House Speaker Newt Gingrich, he accused Gingrich of acting like "an out-of-control radio talk show host."

Scrappy and Intimate

In an era of blow-dried TV anchors, homogenized sitcoms and cookie-cutter Hollywood sequels, talk radio stands out as unpredictable. It is less politically correct than mass television. "It's more scrappy," said John Mainelli, the programmer who built WABC into a 1990s talk powerhouse. "It's also more intimate because it's radio," he said. That intimacy allowed Boston talk host David Brudnoy the permission to let his audience know that he was gay and that he had AIDS. There was a tremendous outpouring of affection from long-time WBZ listeners who heard Brudnoy's late night program in 38 states. A number of listeners told Brudnoy that his confession had moved them to tell their own families that they, too, had the AIDS virus. As Brudnoy explained it, "Talk Radio is the last neighborhood in town. People know their talk hosts better than they know the person who lives next to them."

Technology and New Networks

In its early days, talk radio was expensive to produce. In addition to a skilled host, the station had to pay a producer, programmer, and engineer. A researcher was also a necessity. Much of talk radio consisted of interviews, easy enough to do over telephone lines, but long-distance charges could be substantial. To make talk radio a success, the stations needed the vast audience provided by large, urban areas. In the 1960s and 1970s it was nearly impossible to make talk a successful format in anything but a large market. It took technological innovation to make talk radio financially feasible.

Chief among the technical factors underlying talk radio as a mass format was the growing commercial success and expansion of FM radio in the 1970s. By 1977, a generation had grown up with their radios tuned as much to FM as to AM. Broadcasters who owned AM stations developed a strategy of counterprogramming to retain audience. Some shifted their programming from music to the spoken word, as KABC and KGO had done a decade and a half earlier. The counter to music programming on FM gave rise to information programming.

Satellite technology gave syndicators the type of access to local stations that only networks had enjoyed previously. Initially, syndicated programs were sent via telephone lines at great expense. By the late 1970s geosynchronous satellites made it possible to distribute radio shows nationwide at a relatively reasonable cost, giving the radio program a national audience of simultaneous listeners. That gave rise to ABC Talkradio, featuring hosts from various ABC-owned talk stations. Host Michael Jackson's mellow Australian accent was networked from ABC's KABC in Los Angeles, as was Ira Fistell's daily program. From San Francisco's KGO came Dr. Dean Edell's medical advice and a general interest talk show with Ronn Owens.

The importance of the telephone caller led to improvements in on-air telephone systems. Nationally syndicated talk shows today use phone systems that handle more than 30 incoming lines. Special automatic gain-control devices compensate for the different levels and sound qualities of the callers' telephones. Specially designed computer software allows the producer and the show host to communicate with one another. Sitting in different rooms, the producer and host can both see on screen the caller's name and location and the topic of interest he or she called to discuss. More advanced versions can create a caller database that can include telephone number, address, regular topic of interest,

occupation, birthday, and zip code. The information is available for the host the next time the listener calls. It can also be used for the radio station's marketing purposes.

Technology also fueled NBC's Talknet, where Bruce Williams answered financial and legal questions in an understanding, fatherly manner. If Williams was father, Sally Jessy Raphael was mother, offering personal advice and relationship counseling. New York personality Bernard Meltzer sounded like a loving grandfather presenting general interest topics. The family doctor was Harvey Rubin, who conducted a daily health program.

New York's WOR Radio, long a leader in talk programming in its own city, used satellite technology to deliver its talk shows to a national audience. Former libertarian candidate Gene Burns, money advisers Ken and Daria Dolan, psychologist Dr. Joy Brown, and others talked about issues that transcended New York. When WOR moved conservative host Bob Grant from rival WABC, he was added to the daily syndication schedule. Comedienne Joan Rivers joined the WOR Network in 1997.

Westwood One Radio Networks inherited the original talk programming of Mutual Radio in a series of mergers that ultimately put Westwood in the CBS family. Once the home of Larry King's overnight talk show, Westwood moved King to afternoons in order to increase his audience. Replacing King overnight was Jim Bohannon, who was the usual replacement when King was on vacation. King's move to afternoons proved unsuccessful, but Bohannon's installation in the overnight chair was a long-term proposition.

Westwood also carried the *Tom Leykis Show* from Los Angeles, the *G. Gordon Liddy Show* from Washington, and *Imus in the Morning* with longtime New York funnyman and curmudgeon Don Imus. Westwood's parent company, Infinity Broadcasting, a division of Viacom after its merger with CBS, also syndicated "shock jock" Howard Stern.

Stern is not a talk host per se, but his program abandoned music in favor of free-wheeling conversation often centered on Stern and his private parts. Stern's program was seldom heard on talk stations; his affiliates were primarily rock music outlets. As one station manager described it, "Stern says what The Who used to sing." That statement reinforces the rock context of Stern's unpredictable broadcasts. In Los Angeles, Stern's program appeared on KSLX, one of a few talk stations on the FM band. In presenting Stern's and other hosts' shows to advertisers, however, KSLX account executives compared them to personalities on rock stations, not to traditional talk personalities such as Rush Limbaugh.

Other syndicators found success as consolidated radio companies attempted to cut expenses. A fledgling network called American View presented host Ken Hamblin. Known as "the Black Avenger," Hamblin was one of only two nationally known black conservative talk hosts in the late 1990s (the other was 2000 presidential candidate Alan Keyes). Cox Radio, owner of several news and talk stations, syndicated hosts Neal Boortz and Clark Howard from WSB in Atlanta for their own stations and others outside the Cox fold. Former WABC host Mike Gallagher created his own network and fed *The Mike Gallagher Show* to more than 200 stations. Jones Radio Networks, best known for long-form music programming, entered the talk field with several programs.

Exponential Growth

Talk radio's growth through the 1990s was fueled by Rush Limbaugh and the network built around the host by entrepreneur Edward F. McLaughlin. A former ABC Radio executive who had been vice president and general manager of KGO, McLaughlin rose to the presidency of the ABC Radio Networks in 1972, a position he held through 1986. In 1987, McLaughlin retired from the network and packaged Limbaugh, then a local Sacramento personality, and KGO's Edell into a fledgling syndication company. Officially called EFM Media (for McLaughlin's initials) the network was known publicly as the "EIB Network" because of Limbaugh's boastful catchphrase, "Excellence in Broadcasting." In 1997, EFM's assets, including *The Rush Limbaugh Show, The Dr. Dean Edell Show*, and the monthly publication *The Limbaugh Letter*, were sold to Jacor Communications and its Premiere Radio Networks. Both Jacor and Premiere were ultimately acquired by Clear Channel Communications.

Premiere began as a syndicator of short-form programming for music stations and developed through mergers and acquisitions into the leading provider of talk radio programming based on sheer numbers of shows. Premiere would ultimately be home to Limbaugh, Dr. Laura Schlessinger, UFO-chaser and expert in the paranormal Art Bell, sports personality Jim Rome, Michael Reagan, Edell, internet publisher Matt Drudge, and Los Angeles satirist Phil Hendrie. Because Premiere was acquired in 1999 by Clear Channel, that company was able to leverage key Premiere talents onto Clear Channel-owned news and talk stations.

Deregulation

If technology was one parent of talk radio, deregulation was the other. For 42 years, radio and television were ruled by the Fairness Doctrine, which required stations to broadcast opposing views on public issues. The Fairness Doctrine was born in 1949 in response to a court case involving the owner of powerful radio stations in Los Angeles, Detroit, and Cleveland, and an early organization of professional newspeople. The newspeople charged the licensee with slanting news on his radio stations.

The doctrine ordered stations to work in the public interest and guarantee equal time for disparate viewpoints. The FCC decided that, contrary to its stated purpose, the Fairness Doctrine failed to encourage the discussion of more controversial issues. There were also concerns that it was in violation of the free speech principles of the First Amendment. The FCC abolished the rule in 1987, leaving talk hosts unrestrained.

Congress tried to reinstate the Fairness Doctrine as law that same year, but President Ronald Reagan vetoed it. Later attempts failed even to pass Congress. Those failures have led many to believe that it will take an act of Congress to bring back the doctrine. In fact, however, the FCC has the power as an independent regulatory agency to re-impose the Fairness Doctrine without either congressional or executive action.

Talk radio as it developed through the 1990s could not exist in the Fairness Doctrine era. In 1987, the year the doctrine was discarded, there were 125 news-talk stations nationwide. By early 2003, there were a total of 1,785 news, talk, and information stations. In 1986, news, talk, and information stations captured 8.7 percent of the national listening audience, good enough for fifth place overall among all radio formats. The Fall 2002 Arbitron Format Trend Report showed news, talk, and information radio as the leading radio format, capturing 16.5 percent of the national radio audience.

Power Shift

The power of talk radio had been felt on a local level since the format's inception. Local stations traditionally staged debates and allowed unprecedented access to politicians. Deregulation merged journalism and populism. The public asked questions that had previously been the domain of reporters and gossip columnists.

Boston's Jerry Williams and listeners who heard his show on WRKO were credited with overturning

Massachusetts' seat belt law in 1988. Williams and other show hosts claimed credit for public opposition to a congressional pay raise and for a boycott against Exxon in the wake of the Alaska oil spill.

At an organizational meeting of the National Association of Radio Talk Show Hosts (NARTSH) in 1989, Williams called talk radio "the greatest forum in history, the last bastion of freedom of speech for plain ordinary folks." The organization attempted to set a political agenda: "It's our government and we're going to take it back from those aristocrats," said Mike Siegel of Seattle's KING Radio on a broadcast from the NARTSH meeting. Siegel later had a short run in syndication on the Premiere Radio Network.

Talk radio created a new dynamic during the 1992 Presidential campaign. Most candidates, prompted by exposure given to independent Ross Perot, appeared on both radio and television talk shows to disseminate their views and corral support. The notable exception was incumbent President George H. Bush, who lost to a regular talk show guest, Bill Clinton. The proliferation of appearances by candidates on both television and radio talk shows prompted *Washington Post* television critic Tom Shales to label the 1991 election "the talk show campaign."

Aides in the Clinton campaign believed their candidate reversed his fortunes in New York with an early morning appearance with Don Imus, morning man on Sports station WFAN heard on a national network. As president, Clinton hosted talk personalities at the White House. California's Jerry Brown surprised political pundits by winning Connecticut's Democratic primary in 1992. Some observers felt his key move was an appearance on Michael Harrison's program then heard on WTIC in Hartford. Brown later hosted his own talk show.

Brown was not the only personality to join the talk host ranks from outside radio. G. Gordon Liddy, of Watergate infamy, had the highest profile because of his national network program. Conservative presidential candidate Pat Buchanan tried his hand for a short while at talk radio. On the local level, former Los Angeles police chief Daryl Gates, former New York Mayor Ed Koch, and former San Diego Mayor Roger Hedgecock gained new careers in their hometowns. Hedgecock became Rush Limbaugh's primary substitute host in 2002.

Audiences and Impact

For a while in the 1990s, talk radio and its effect on politics dominated media discussion. An entire issue of CQ *Researcher* in 1994 was focused on the question "Are call-in programs good for the political system?" A *Newsweek* cover story was headlined "The Power of Talk Radio." Other publications also expressed concern in articles entitled "Tower of Babble," "How to Keep Talk Radio from Deepening America's Divide" and "Talk Radio Lacking Real Dialogue." FCC Chairman Reed Hundt, speaking to members of the NAB, asked if talk radio created "such skepticism and disbelief that as a country we just can't get anything done?" The *New York Times* suggested that "modern politicians have become slaves to public opinion" in the "electronic din" of talk radio. Following the Oklahoma City bombing, there were suggestions that the rhetoric of talk radio might have fueled the bombers' discontent. *World Press Review*, in an article titled "A Bitter, Self-Doubting Nation," suggested that talk radio hosts who were cynical about the federal government and public officials more accurately represented the disillusionment of the U.S. voter than the mainstream press. Editorials and commentators pointed to talk radio's influence on the increasing incivility in U.S. society. Howard Stern continued to draw attention for his sexist and racist talk. Over the airwaves he regularly made fun of women, minorities, and disabled people. Toilet jokes and sex jokes continued to be regular fare on the Stern show in the 21st century.

Scholars began to study talk radio and its effects. In 1995 the Times Mirror Center for People and the Press challenged the view that talk radio listeners were ignorant and ill-informed. The research concluded that talk radio listeners paid close attention to the news and knew what was going on in the world. They were more likely to vote than the average American and were better educated, made more money, and were more focused on the issues than those who did not listen to talk radio. As an indication of its power, some supporters pointed to a three-way political race in Minnesota, where former wrestler turned radio talk host Jesse "The Body" Ventura was elected governor.

Randall Bloomquist, former news/talk editor of *Radio and Records* and a regular observer of the talk radio phenomenon, argues that its ability to influence political developments is heavily dependent on support from mainstream media. Talk show fans do not tune in to get their opinions changed. They listen to the hosts who affirm their personal and political beliefs. Bloomquist suggests that talk radio's power is not in its influence on its own listeners, but in its ability to trigger national media coverage of an issue. That national coverage is what truly affects issues.

Radio market research indicates that the average listener tunes in to talk radio for an hour or less at a time. In 1998, according to the Radio Advertising Bureau, 42 percent of listeners were doing so in their automobiles, 37 percent listened at home, and 21 percent tuned in at work. Most listened to radios while doing something else. In large metropolitan areas, more and more people are commuting greater and greater distances. Those commuters are the perfect captive audience for talk radio. In 1999 national research conducted for *Talkers* magazine, an industry trade journal, indicated that 52 percent of the audience was male, 72 percent had some college education, and nearly 60 percent had an annual household income higher than $50,000.

By the middle of the first decade of the 21st century, these figures had increased across the board. By 2006, there were more than 1,400 talk format stations across the country and they were attracting a weekly radio audience of 47 million listeners. Of these, 63 percent were male, 78 percent had at least one college degree, and most had an annual income of over $75,000.

Early years of the 21st century offered a plethora of syndicated talk product covering a wide assortment of topics for audience tastes from so-called "hot talk" (billed as "rock and roll without the music" and best embodied by Howard Stern and his imitators) to sports-oriented discussions, to politics and current affairs.

By far, however, politically-oriented programs dominate the talk genre, and more particularly conservative talk. Of the top 15 syndicated talk shows on the air in 2009, ten were hosted by politically conservative pundits (including Rush Limbaugh, Sean Hannity, Michael Savage, Glenn Beck, et al.). The dominance of conservative talk as not only a radio genre but also a social and political force was driven home in early 2009 when radio's top-rated talker Rush Limbaugh ignited a firestorm of controversy with comments he made about new president, Barack Obama, stating, "I hope he fails" in regard to the administration's policies. The power and popularity of Limbaugh's statements—at least in terms of his loyal radio audience—soon got him anointed by White House Chief of Staff Rahm Emanuel as the new, de facto leader (and main mouthpiece) of the GOP. Though it was not a title that Limbaugh himself objected to (he challenged the president to a live, on-air debate), the level and appropriateness of Limbaugh's influence was debated by liberals and conservatives. The dominance of conservative politics on talk radio and liberals' inability (with few exceptions) to launch a successful

media counter attack, has served as one basis for many attempts to reinstate the defunct Fairness Doctrine.

See also: Air America; All News Format; All-Night Radio; Fairness Doctrine; *Fresh Air*; Internet Radio; Topless Radio; WOR

Further Reading

Bolce, Louis, Gerald DeMaio, and Douglas Muzzio, "Dial-in Democracy: Talk Radio and the 1994 Election," *Political Science Quarterly* (Fall 1996).
Bulkeley, William M., "Talkshow Hosts Agree on One Point: They're the Tops," *Wall Street Journal* (15 June 1989).
Heath, Rebecca Piirto, "Tuning in to Talk," *American Demographics* 20, no. 2 (February 1998).
Henabery, Bob, "Talk Radio: From Caterpillar to Butterfly," *Radio Business Report* (January 1994).
Hontz, Jenny, "Clinton Points Finger at Talk Radio," *Electronic Media* (1 May 1995).
Hoyt, Mike, "Talk Radio: Turning up the Volume," *Columbia Journalism Review* 31, no. 4 (November/December 1992).
Ivins, Molly, "Lyin' Bully," *Mother Jones* 20, no. 3 (May/June 1995).
James, Rollye, "The RUSH to Talk Continues," *Radio Ink* (17–30 January 1994).
Jost, Kenneth, "Talk Show Democracy," *The CQ Researcher* (19 April 1995).
Keith, Michael C., and Robert Hilliard, *Waves of Rancor: Tuning in the Radical Right*, Armonk, New York: M.E. Sharpe, 1999.
Kurtz, Howard, *Hot Air: All Talk, All the Time*, New York: Times Books, 1996.
Laufer, Peter, *Inside Talk Radio: America's Voice or Just Hot Air?*, Secaucus, New Jersey: Carol, 1995.
Levin, Murray, *Talk Radio and the American Dream*, Lexington, Massachusetts: Lexington Books, 1987.
Marr, Bruce, "Talk Radio Programming," in *Broadcast Programming: Strategies for Winning Television and Radio Audiences*, by Susan Tyler Eastman, Sydney W. Head, and Lewis Klein, Belmont, California: Wadsworth, 1981.
"Medium Is Message at Talk Radio Conference," *Broadcasting* (19 July 1989).
Michaels, Bob, *R&R Talk Radio Seminar 2003: Top Arbitron Performers in News/Talk*, Columbia, Maryland: The Arbitron Company, 2003.
Munson, Wayne, *All Talk: The Talkshow in Media Culture*, Philadelphia, Pennsylvania: Temple University Press, 1993.
Nichols, John. "All's Fair?" *Nation* (25 March 2009), p. 5.
"Programming for Profit with Satellite Talk," *Radio Business Report* (17 May 1993).
Rosenstiel, Thomas B., "The Talk-Show Phenomenon," *Houston Chronicle* (31 May 1992).
Seib, Philip M., *Rush Hour: Talk Radio, Politics, and the Rise of Rush Limbaugh*, Fort Worth, Texas: Summit, 1993.
Shane, Ed, "The State of the Industry: Radio's Shifting Paradigm," *Journal of Radio Studies* 5, no. 2 (1998).
Shane, Ed, "Talk Radio," in *The Guide to United States Popular Culture*, edited by Ray Broadus Browne and Pat

Browne, Bowling Green, Ohio: Bowling Green State University Popular Press, 2001.

Shane, Ed, *Disconnected America: The Consequences of Mass Media in a Narcissistic World*, Armonk, New York: M.E. Sharpe, 2001.

Von Drehle, David, "The Moment," *Time* (16 March 2009), p. 15.

SANDRA L. ELLIS AND ED SHANE,
2009 REVISIONS BY CARY O'DELL

TECHNICAL ORGANIZATIONS
Organizing Radio's Engineers

Four types of technical organizations have emerged during radio's development in the U.S. The first were professional organizations for engineers. The second helped to assemble amateur radio operators and were organized in the early years of radio. The third were company-specific employee organizations begun to counter independent unionization by their radio employees. And the fourth were independent labor unions for radio's engineers and related technicians.

Professional Organizations

Perhaps the most important organizations were those started by leading scientists, electrical engineers, and business leaders to advance the scientific study of radio. These have gone through several iterations but have consistently included the key figures and provided the most important publications.

American Institute of Electrical Engineers

On 13 May 1884, a group of scientists, inventors, and electrical engineers, which included Thomas Alva Edison, Alexander Graham Bell, and Norvin Green, president of the Western Union Telegraph Company, organized the American Institute of Electrical Engineers (AIEE). Spurred in part by an International Electrical Exhibition in 1884, the new AIEE included inventors, entrepreneurs, telegraph operators, and company managers. Technical publications (eventually *Electrical Engineering*), an annual meeting, and even a museum were contemplated. The AIEE changed as the industry became dominated by large manufacturing and service companies that employed "electricians." Creation of research laboratories added more members. AIEE also became centrally involved in the development of technical standards, allowing one company's device to work with another's. And it helped to promote professional standards. But the AIEE became increasingly focused on power

engineering, leaving an opening for a new group focused on wireless and radio.

Society of Wireless Telegraph Engineers

The Society of Wireless Telegraph Engineers (SWTE) was started in 1907 by the head of the Stone Wireless Telegraph Company, John Stone Stone [sic]. In the first years, Stone limited membership in the SWTE to only the employees in his small Boston-based company, although he later permitted the rolls to be opened to the employees of Reginald Fessenden's National Electrical Signaling Company (NESCO) and other companies.

The Wireless Institute

The Wireless Institute (WI), a rival organization to the SWTE, began in 1909 when Robert Marriott organized about 100 wireless U.S. devotees in the United States. Three years later, however, WI membership dropped to 27 members and was teetering on collapse.

Institute of Radio Engineers

The SWTE and Marriott's WI merged on 5 April 1912 and agreed to name the new organization the Institute of Radio Engineers (IRE). The new organization became more international in scope, thus excluding the word "American" in its name. The IRE focused on extending the use of radio to protect and save lives at sea. Because of its ubiquitous nature, radio soon became a tool of war and many IRE members joined the effort as military needs meshed with rapid technical development. By 1916 there were 83 members in the IRE from 11 other countries besides the United States.

In addition to its prestigious monthly, *Proceedings of the IRE*, the IRE focused on improving technical standards as the international radio industry grew into a new economic sector. During the 1920s, the IRE synchronized its scientific and electronic research work with the National Electrical Manufacturers Association and the Radio Manufacturers Association. The IRE also assumed a leadership role as a trade representative for its members of U.S. radio manufacturers and broadcasters such as the Radio Corporation of America (RCA), American Telephone & Telegraph (ATT), and General Electric (GE).

Working for scientific progress and technological insight, the IRE lobbied for a major role in deciding how U.S. radio broadcasting would be regulated. The IRE was invited to participate in a series of National Radio Conferences between 1922 and 1925 that were organized by Secretary of Commerce Herbert Hoover to develop policies concerning station licensing and technology. These four meetings eventually led to Congress passing the Radio Act of 1927.

After World War II, the IRE focused on the developing technologies of television, FM radio, audio recording, and developing standards of excellence in engineering practice. The society delineated its membership along two specialties of interest: broadcast engineers and audio. With the rise of electronic technologies being used by the U.S. military during World War II, the IRE broadened its interest groups with radar, computers, television, solid-state electronics, and space exploration. By 1947, there were nearly 18,000 IRE members.

Institute of Electrical and Electronic Engineers

In January 1963, the AIEE and the IRE merged and formed the Institute of Electrical and Electronics Engineers (IEEE). As of the early 2000s, the IEEE remained the largest professional society in the world with more than a quarter of a million members.

The IEEE quickly expanded to include virtually all arms of electronics as shown by its steadily growing number of specialized technical journals, plus the general appeal *IEEE Spectrum*. Building on the IRE model, the IEEE developed dozens of professional divisions—called societies—each of which held their own meetings and issued their own publications. Among those of particular interest are the societies concerning broadcast technology, consumer electronics, and the society on social implications of technology. A history center was created in 1980.

Society of Broadcast Engineers

Not everyone was pleased with the AIEE-IRE merger, and the Society of Broadcast Engineers (SBE) was one dissident spinoff created at the same time to allow a focus on broadcasting. The SBE's international membership soon covered a broad scope of industry employees: studio and transmitter operators and technicians, supervisors, announcer-technicians, chief engineers of commercial and educational stations, engineering vice presidents, consultants, field and sales engineers, broadcast engineers from recording studios, schools, closed-circuit systems, cable TV, production houses, corporate audio-visual departments, and other facilities. The SBE began in 1977 to certify broadcast

engineers in several categories, including the Certified Broadcast Radio Engineer (CBRE) and Certified Senior Radio Engineer (CSRE). These certifications are renewed every five years. More than 100 local chapters meet regularly. As with other technical bodies, the SBE holds an annual meeting, issues publications, and holds training courses and workshops.

Amateur Radio Groups

To further the developing "ham" hobby, amateur radio clubs began to proliferate early in the 20th century.

The Wireless Club of America

The Wireless Club of America was begun in 1910 by Hugo Gernsback, a Luxembourg immigrant to the U.S. Sometimes referred to as the father of science fiction, Gernsback was an early wireless enthusiast who saw the potential in marketing wireless units to the general public while creating a market for the new technology of amateur radio. By 1912, the *New York Times* reported that there were some 12,000 amateur radio operators in the U.S. and some 122 radio clubs. Most of the meetings for these clubs took place over the air. Message handling, where one operator or groups of operators would relay messages and information to others, became a central feature of amateur wireless clubs. Although these exchanges were most often for fun and fraternal reasons, they were sometimes needed to protect or inform others in public emergencies.

American Radio Relay League

In 1914, Hiram Percy Maxim, a Boston radio enthusiast, contacted others through his Hartford Radio Club and offered to set up a network of relay stations comprised of amateur radio operators. Calling the new network the American Radio Relay League (ARRL), Maxim tapped into the unrealized dreams of many in the field at the time. Within some four months, the League boasted 200 relay stations in the U.S. alone. The ARRL asked the Commerce Department to establish a special license for stations in order to make up a national relay network of stations. Maxim, the ARRL's visionary leader and an MIT graduate, set up a sophisticated system that would serve the nation in the event of war. When the U.S. entered World War I in 1917, amateur radio stations were ordered to close down. At the same time, the military began a full-blown recruitment effort to attract some 6,700 radio operators (many of whom began as amateurs) to the U.S. navy. Instead of being outside of the mainstream, amateur wireless operators became part of the system. After the war, the amateurs were intent upon getting back to where they left off when the war started. By 1921, the Commerce Department listed some 11,000 amateur radio operators in the U.S.

Amateurs were forced off the air again during World War II (1941–45), making ARRL an important means of keeping the hobby alive for what became strong postwar growth. Today ARRL thrives with meetings, the monthly QST, the annual amateur operators' handbook, and a host of other publications. In addition to the ARRL, more regional groups developed. Among them was the Radio Club of America (RCA— *not* to be confused with the former manufacturing company), a New York area group that enjoyed the participation of such key radio figures as Edwin Howard Armstrong, among others.

Technical Unions

The first attempts to organize radio technicians and engineers (often called the "below-the-line" employees to distinguish them from the "above-the-line" creative personnel) occurred in the 1920s. By the 1940s two national labor unions, one devoted to broadcasting, had between them organized most of radio's technical workers. They sought to overcome the relatively low pay and sometimes poor working conditions of workers. Broadcast employees often had to work split shifts, with no pay or time off for holidays, and no overtime pay. The typical wage was about $20.00 per week—$40.00 was big money in the 1930s. The same two unions—The International Brotherhood of Electrical Workers and the Association of Technical Employees—dominate the radio scene today.

International Brotherhood of Electrical Workers

The International Brotherhood of Electrical Workers (IBEW) was formed in 1891 out of several earlier attempts to organize those involved with electrical wiring and manufacturing. IBEW was behind what was probably the first labor strike in radio, in late 1925 at KMOX in St. Louis, Missouri. Concerned with wages and working conditions—the universal labor issues—the strike led to the union's recognition as the bargaining agent for KMOX technicians. In 1931, KMOX became a CBS owned-and-operated station that spread the IBEW idea to others at the network. IBEW also

organized stations in Chicago and in Birmingham, Alabama. In 1939, the union hit the bigtime when it successfully organized the technical employees at CBS. As it made plans to create more broadcast-centered locals on a national basis, however, IBEW increasingly came up against the National Association of Broadcast Engineers and Technicians (see below) in jurisdictional disagreements. In 1951 IBEW organized its broadcasting and recording members into a separate department, though they continued to represent but a tiny part of the larger union.

Association of Technical Employees

In 1933 some 300 employees at NBC formed the Association of Technical Employees (ATE) to represent themselves with the network. A year later they signed their first contract with NBC. This contract set a wage scale of $175.00 per month, rising to $260.00 after nine years' service. The work week was determined to be 48 hours. ATE was the first organization created exclusively to represent radio employees. By 1937 the ATE contract spelled out their jurisdiction, and the first independent (non-network) station joined the unit. A union shop clause came two years later.

National Association of Broadcast Engineers and Technicians

ATE became the National Association of Broadcast Engineers and Technicians (NABET) in 1940. Contracts negotiated the next year set the first eight-hour day. Some 23 small stations were also under NABET contracts. When NBC-Blue split off in 1943 (becoming ABC in 1945), NABET contracts carried over, giving the union two of the major radio networks. Seeking some organizational strength and thus organizing clout, NABET affiliated with the Congress of Industrial Organizations (CIO) in 1951, and changed its name to National Association of Broadcast *Employees* and Technicians, thus retaining the same acronym.

Union Trends

The coming of television in the late 1940s, and later cable television, dramatically increased employment in the electronic media industries—and thus organizing opportunities as well as jurisdictional battles among the unions involved. One union, the International Alliance of Theatrical and State Employees (IATSE), never organized radio workers, building from its 1893 theater and later film bases to expand into television. But both the IBEW and NABET also grew into television, thus precipitating a host of jurisdictional disputes in the 1950s and 1960s, some resolved with strikes and others with arbitration.

The degree of unionization in radio varies greatly by market and region of the country. Union agreements are far more likely at the network level, in large markets, and in the Northeast and West Coast, as well as major Midwest cities. Smaller markets and stations tend not to be subject to union agreements. Recent mergers in the radio business, with huge numbers of stations coming under common control (including multiple stations in the same market) have not thus far had union implications. On the other hand, greater use of automation has trimmed employment ranks as has such FCC deregulation as no longer requiring licensed engineers to supervise radio transmitter operations.

In the constant search for new members and bargaining units, each union emphasizes what it has gained for its rank and file. NABET, for example, listed its accomplishments by the 1990s as the wide-spread acceptance of the union shop, a seven-hour day and 35-hour week, paid vacation and statutory holidays, lay-off and rehiring on a seniority basis, differential pay for night work, discharge only for just and sufficient cause, established grievance procedures (including arbitration), contract provisions covering increased automation, and pension plans. IBEW could make similar claims.

In 1993, NABET sought organizational support with the Communication Workers of America (CWA), heretofore a union of telephone workers, although it had also organized many cable television workers. After a one-year test run in 1993, the two merged into what became the NABET-CWA.

See also: American Federation of Musicians; American Federation of Television and Radio Artists; Ham Radio; KMOX; Trade Associations; WCFL

Further Reading

Brittain, James E., "The Evolution of Electrical and Electronics Engineering and the *Proceedings of the IRE*," *Proceedings of the IEEE*, 77 (June 1989; part 1) and 85 (May 1997; part 2).
"Fiftieth Anniversary of the AIEE," *Electrical Engineering* 53 (May 1934).
Finney, Robert, "Unions/Guilds," in *Encyclopedia of Television*, 3 vols, edited by Horace Newcomb, Chicago and London: Fitzroy Dearborn, 1997.
Gardner, John, "The Below-the-Line Unions," *Television Magazine* 24 (December 1967).
Huntoon, John, *Fifty Years of ARRL*, Newington, Connecticut: American Radio Relay League, 1965.
International Brotherhood of Electrical Workers website, www.ibew.org
Koenig, Allen E., "Labor Relations in the Broadcasting Industry: Periodical Literature, 1937–1964," *Journal of Broadcasting* 9, no. 4 (Fall 1965).
Koenig, Allen E., editor, *Broadcasting and Bargaining: Labor Relations in Radio and Television*, Madison: University of Wisconsin Press, 1970.
McMahon, A. Michal, *The Making of a Profession: A Century of Electrical Engineering in America*, New York: Institute of Electrical and Electronics Engineers, 1984.
Mermigas, Diane, "Unions under Fire," *Electronic Media* (4 and 11 September 1989).
National Association of Broadcast Employees and Technicians website, www.nabetcwa.org/nabet
Radio Club of America, *Seventy-Fifth Anniversary Diamond Jubilee Yearbook, 1909–1984*, Highland Park, New Jersey: Radio Club of America, 1984.
Reader, William Joseph, *A History of the Institution of Electrical Engineers, 1871–1971*, London: Peregrinus, 1987.
Whittemore, Laurens, "The Institute of Radio Engineers— Fifty Years of Service," *Proceedings of the IRE* 50 (May 1962).

DENNIS W. MAZZOCCO AND
CHRISTOPHER H. STERLING

TELECOMMUNICATIONS ACT OF 1996

Changing Radio's Licensing and Ownership Rules

In February 1996 President Bill Clinton signed the Telecommunications Act into law, the result of two decades of industry and congressional effort to update government regulation of the industry. Cast as amendments to the benchmark Communications Act of 1934, the complex 1996 law wrought important changes in the radio industry as a fairly small part of a law primarily addressed to substantial policy change in the telephone business. Provisions of the law contributed to substantial consolidation of station ownership, while at the same time furthering the aims of deregulation.

Origins

The 1934 Communications Act has often been amended in the decades since its passage. Important revisions were enacted every few years as regulated industries changed and expanded. Attempts to replace the law (especially a series of draft "rewrite" proposals from 1976 to 1981) failed to pass, however, because they tried to do too much at one time. The more focused public broadcasting act of 1967 and the cable acts of 1984 and 1992, are examples of more industry-specific legislation that did successfully amend the 1934 law.

Development of what became the 1996 amendments took several years. The issues involved were complex as Congress considered substantial deregulation of and other changes in traditional regulatory approaches to the telephone and electronic media industries. Growing digital convergence among all electronic communications services forced a rethinking of long-accepted regulatory assumptions. At the same time, largely defensive industry positions amidst rapid technical change were deeply entrenched, making compromise difficult (it is nearly always easier to stop legislative progress than to maintain its momentum). Moreover, a continuing trend toward less governmental and more marketplace control was changing the way Congress perceived the telecommunications sector.

For broadcast deregulation was not new. The Federal Communications Commission (FCC) had begun cautious moves in this direction in the mid-1970s, and they accelerated during the Reagan administration in the 1980s. To deregulate radio broadcasting, for example, the FCC lifted a number of "behavioral" regulations (such as guidelines encouraging at least minimal non-entertainment programming) in the early 1980s. Over the next decade, the commission also loosened its "structural" regulation by slowly increasing the number of radio stations any single entity could own from seven AM and seven FM stations (the long-time national limit) to 12 of each type in 1985, raised to 18 in 1992, and 20 by 1994. In an even more basic change, in 1992 the FCC removed a long-time restriction by allowing any entity to own more than one AM or FM station in the same market.

The first potential bills were considered by Congress, then under Democratic control, in the early 1990s, although none of them progressed far. Dramatic changes in telephone industry policy were at the core of each bill; electronic media provisions were relatively minor parts of the proposed legislation. Republican takeover of both houses of Congress in the 1994 elections delayed progress briefly as the long-time opposition party learned how to run things and trained a new cadre of staffers and members in the intricacies of the telecommunications field.

Finally, in the fall of 1995, both houses passed substantial telecommunications deregulation bills, albeit with the differences usually found in the legislative process in which each house acts independently of the other. A conference committee worked for many weeks and early in 1996 produced the compromise bill passed by both houses on the first day of February 1996. The president signed the bill a week later.

Radio Licenses

The new legislation had four important effects on the radio business, two concerning station ownership, and two focused on licensing. Reasoning that, with nearly 13,000 radio stations on the air, old restrictions (established when less than 10 percent of that number existed) could now be eliminated, Congress opted to free the marketplace. Provisions in the 1996 law (a) dropped limits on the number of radio stations that could be owned nationally; (b) increased the local market stations that could be owned by a single entity; (c) lengthened station licenses; and (d) eliminated competitive applications at license renewal time.

The license term change was relatively minor: Section 307 (c) of the 1934 law was changed to extend radio licenses from seven to eight years (until 1981 licenses for radio or television had run for only three years). But the end of potential competitive applications may have more far-reaching impact. Acting on a long-existing industry desire for license "renewal expectancy," the 1996 law added a new subsection (k) to Section 309 of the Communications Act to make clear that existing station licenses will be renewed unless the FCC finds important and continuing transgressions of its rules and regulations to have occurred. Even in such a situation, the commission retains the discretion to renew or deny a license. But the law also forbids the FCC from considering a rival application during a license renewal proceeding—until and unless it has first decided that the existing license must be terminated. Given the FCC's track record over seven decades of license renewals, such terminations are very unlikely. Whereas only a tiny fraction of one percent of all stations were denied renewals under the old rules, the new law makes license renewal virtually automatic in the future.

Station Ownership

Statutory changes governing radio station ownership were more dramatic, as the initial years of station trading after passage of the 1996 law have shown. Stations may now be bought and sold or traded much as with any other business, although the FCC retains the right to approve each new licensee. The 1996 law directed the FCC to eliminate its national cap on radio station ownership (then standing at no more than 20 AM and 20 FM). Any company could now own as many stations as money would allow. Within a month of the law's passage, two radio station groups were approaching 50 stations each—by the end of the year the first group exceeded 100 stations. From there the pace of station buying and selling increased and station prices soared. By early in the 21st century, the largest radio group owner controlled more than 1,200 outlets, by which time 40 percent of all radio stations had changed ownership since 1996.

The market-level situation was more complex. The 1996 law allows a single owner to control up to eight stations in any of the largest markets (more than the *national* cap before 1985) as long as no one owner controls more than half the stations in a given market. The table below provides the specific new limits, and the law allows for even these to be exceeded if such an action "will result in an increase in the number of radio broadcast stations in operation," although just how that might work in practice is not yet clear.

To further complicate matters, in August 1996 the U.S. Department of Justice's Antitrust Division announced that no single market radio owner would be allowed to control more than half of that market's radio advertising revenue. A few group owners had to divest themselves of one or more stations to comply.

In a market with this many radio stations:	*A single entity can control up to this many commercial stations:*
45 or more	Up to 8, no more than 5 in the same service (AM or FM)
30–44	Up to 7, no more than 4 in the same service
15–29	Up to 6, no more than 4 in the same service
14 or fewer	Up to 5, no more than 3 in the same service

Impact on Radio

Although many policy-makers have cited its positive effects, such as eliminating outdated rules, encouraging innovation and development of new technology, and encouraging a more competitive environment, the 1996 law has had negative implications as well. For example, in some smaller markets, only two companies may end up owning all the available stations. The overall number of different radio station owners in the country declined by 39 percent in the first dozen years after passage of the Act.

The Telecommunications Act has also allowed owners of multiple stations to operate multiple outlets with the same personnel (often with voice tracking technology), programming, and administration.

Critics argue that such practices can also lead to more music homogenization and fewer different "voices" (points of view) being heard over the air. Major group owners now significantly control multiple local radio markets and can largely dictate the terms of advertising. CBS, for example, quickly expanded to control 40 percent of all radio revenue in Boston, Chicago, New York, and Philadelphia. At the same time, station ownership by ethnic minorities declined as radio station prices rose and groups expanded. Among FM stations, for example, minority-owned stations declined from 127 to 100 in just the first year after the 1996 law was passed.

When Congress passed the 1996 law, many proponents hailed it as an opportunity to create a procompetitive, deregulatory national framework, as well as more industry employment. Then FCC Chairman William Kennard predicted that the 1996 act would hasten "the transition to a competitive communications marketplace." Commissioner Susan Ness concluded that the main goals of the 1996 amendments were to promote competition, reduce regulation, and encourage rapid deployment of new telecommunication technologies.

On the other hand, commissioner Gloria Tristani later pointed out the dramatic and potentially negative impacts on radio station ownership and operations programming since passage of the Telecommunications Act. Tristani noted that group ownership reduces the number of different and competing voices and opinions heard on local radio stations. More recently, commissioner Michael Copps expressed concern that local radio markets had become oligopolies where programming originated outside the local station "far from listeners and their communities." Even FCC Chairman Michael Powell agreed that the consolidation of radio station ownership "concerned" him. The growing number of group-owned radio stations, of course, mirrors a similar trend in chain-ownership of newspapers, television stations, and cable systems. Many of the conglomerates buying radio stations also own other media.

Although many in Congress, the industry or the FCC continue to trumpet the law's success, more than a decade since its passage there is little question that the act has had a negative impact on radio station ownership and program diversity. The law bred not competition but consolidation. Innumerable radio personnel lost their jobs as corporations bought up stations and then "streamlined" their operations. Radio-related businesses, including brokerage and rep firms, have been weakened or failed as consolidation decreased demand for their services. There is some evidence that the industry's payola scandal early in the new century was made easier by the consolidation engendered by the 1996 law.

Finally, mass ownership of stations has greatly weakened localism and created a homogenous radio programming landscape where everything sounds increasingly alike. In turn, this has driven down listening and stalled ad revenue growth, surely results legislators did not intend.

See also: Clear Channel Communications Inc.; Communications Act of 1934; Deregulation of Radio; Federal Communications Commission; Licensing Authorizing U.S. Stations to Broadcast; Ownership, Mergers, and Acquisitions; United States Congress and Radio

Further Reading

Aufderheide, Patricia, *Communications Policy and the Public Interest: The Telecommunications Act of 1996*, New York: Guilford Press, 1999.

Ferris, Charles D., Frank W. Lloyd, and Harold J. Symons, *Guidebook to the Telecommunications Act of 1996*, New York: Bender, 1996.

Huber, Peter W., Michael K. Kellogg, and John Thorne, *The Telecommunications Act of 1996: Special Report*, Boston: Little Brown, 1996.

Knauer, Leon T., Ronald K. Machtley, and Thomas M. Lynch, *Telecommunications Act Handbook: A Complete Reference for Business*, Rockville, Maryland: Government Institutes, 1996.

Sterling, Christopher H., "Changing American Telecommunication Law: Assessing the 1996 Amendments," *Telecommunications and Space Journal* 3 (1996).

Sterling, Christopher H., "Radio and the Telecommunications Act of 1996: An Initial Assessment," *Journal of Radio Studies* 4 (1997).

Telecommunications Act of 1996, Public Law 104–104, 104th Congress, 2nd Session, February 8, 1996.

Christopher H. Sterling,
2009 Revisions By Cary O'Dell

TELEVISION DEPICTIONS OF RADIO
Fictional Portrayals in American Series

Television's eclipse of radio as the dominant mass medium of entertainment in the decade following World War II was propelled in large measure by the transformation of radio shows into video versions. More than 200 radio programs moved to television, including *The Adventures of Ozzie and Harriet, Truth or Consequences, The Lone Ranger, Your Hit Parade, Suspense, Arthur Godfrey's Talent Scouts,* and *Studio One.* Several comedians who had achieved enormous popularity on radio, such as Jack Benny, George Burns and Gracie Allen, Red Skelton, and Bob Hope, found similar success with their television series.

By the late 1950s, both the radio industry and American life had been profoundly altered by the rise of television. Big-budget network radio shows that appealed to the whole family had given way to cheaply produced local disc jockey programs catering to specialized audiences. Teenagers were an especially attractive market segment as the sale of transistor radios boomed and the age of rock and roll arrived.

The nostalgia many older Americans felt for the glory days of network radio in the 1930s and 1940s was inspiration for a March 1961 episode of *The Twilight Zone* entitled "Static." An elderly bachelor living in a boarding house retrieves his elegant radio console, circa 1935, from the basement. When he's alone in his room, he hears programs from the past. Fearing for his sanity, his former fiancée gives the radio to a junk dealer. Infuriated by her meddling, he gets the radio back and is relieved to find that it still works. When he calls the disbelieving woman to his room to hear for herself, she appears as she did in 1940 as his young sweetheart. He too has become a young man. The radio, a magic machine, sent them back in time and gave the couple a second chance.

But there was no return for the radio industry to its earlier splendor. It adapted to the modern era and itself became grist for TV's storytelling mill. Since the late 1960s a number of television series have had main characters who work in radio stations. *Good Morning, World,* for instance, was a 1967 Columbia Broadcasting System (CBS) situation comedy about a team of early-morning drive-time disc jockeys, Lewis and Clarke, who worked for an overbearing boss at a small station in Los Angeles.

WKRP in Cincinnati

A thoroughly realistic depiction of any occupation or workplace on television is limited by the narrative conventions of drama and comedy. But the spirit and flavor of a profession can be vividly conveyed. The series *WKRP in Cincinnati,* which ran on CBS for four seasons beginning in September 1978, was a show that earned high marks among radio industry insiders for its authentic ambience. WKRP creator, executive producer, and head writer Hugh Wilson received many letters complimenting the show's realism.

The show was, in fact, based on a real station—Atlanta's WQXI, a successful AM/FM combination with a rock format. In the early 1970s, Hugh

Wilson, who was working in advertising in Georgia's capital city, met WQXI salesman Clark Brown at Harrison's, a bar that catered to the media crowd. Through Brown, Wilson was introduced to a number of people who worked in Atlanta radio. In 1977 these friendships proved valuable as a source of inspiration when the vice president for comedy development at CBS gave Wilson the go-ahead to write a pilot for a situation comedy about a radio station.

The premise of *WKRP in Cincinnati* was that the station, a ratings loser with an "elevator music" format, would change to rock and roll. A new young program director, Andy Travis, was brought on board to implement the switch, which alienated some long-time sponsors, such as Barry's Fashions for the Short and Portly.

The other employees of Arthur Carlson, the inept station manager whose mother owned WKRP, were Jennifer Marlowe, a brainy bombshell receptionist; Les Nessman, the naive, conspiracy theorist news director; Herb Tarlek, a salesman with a penchant for wearing white shoes and white belts; Bailey Quarters, Andy's shy assistant; and two disc jockeys—the burned-out hip cat, Dr. Johnny Fever, and the jive-talking sartorial sensation, Venus Flytrap.

Although the focus of *WKRP in Cincinnati* was character development, not the illumination of issues in the radio industry, viewers were introduced to the tribulations that came with the competitive territory. The show's theme song alluded to the uncertain lives of on-air talent and radio managers with a reference to "packing and unpacking up and down the dial." Throughout the 90 episodes, the WKRP staff was faced with many legal, ethical, and business matters that reflected the reality of local radio, including the dwindling length of playlists, the anxiety over the arrival of Arbitron ratings books, the use of programming consultants, the emergence of computer-operated radio stations, and the protests of disaffected listeners.

TV's Talk Radio

Another series of the late 1970s having a radio theme was *Hello, Larry*, a major disappointment for the National Broadcasting Company (NBC). It was hoped that the star power of McLean Stevenson, who had played Lt. Col. Henry Blake in *M*A*S*H* for three seasons, would ensure the success of the show. But viewers did not warm to the series about radio talk show host Larry Alder, who moved from Los Angeles to Portland, Oregon, after a divorce in which he gained custody of two teen-aged daughters. Working with him on his phone-in

show at KLOW were a female producer and an obese engineer. Even a crossover stunt with the popular lead-in series *Diff'rent Strokes*, in which Larry's old Army buddy Phillip Drummond buys the radio station, couldn't generate audience interest.

By the late 1980s, talk radio had become a growth format, and the hour-long dramatic series *Midnight Caller*, which debuted on NBC in October 1988, tapped into the trend. The lead character, Jack Killian, was a San Francisco police detective who had quit the force in despair after he accidentally killed his partner in a shoot-out. His new career as "The Nighthawk," host of an all-night call-in show, allowed him not only to offer advice, but also to become involved in the investigation of crimes and corruption.

The title character of the Fox comedy series *Martin*, which began in 1992, was also a talk show host. He worked for Detroit radio station WZUP until the end of the second season, when the station was sold to a large radio group, the format was changed to country, and Martin was fired by the new owner. Whether they realized it or not, viewers were getting a feel for the fruits of radio's deregulation.

Frasier

In September 1993, *Frasier*, an NBC spin-off of *Cheers*, introduced a radio-related character who would become one of the most popular in television history. Dr. Frasier Crane left his psychiatric practice in Boston, divorced his neurotic wife Lilith, and moved back to his hometown of Seattle, where his new job was hosting a radio advice show.

Unlike *WKRP in Cincinnati*, *Frasier* was not set principally in the workplace. Frasier's home—an ultramodern luxury apartment with a breathtaking view of the Seattle skyline—was just as often the scene of the action. But Frasier revels in his radio celebrity, and troubles at the station often overflow into his personal life. The heartless economics of radio in the 1990s created many complications for Frasier and his colleagues. Changes in management and a slavish adherence to the bottom line in station decision making are the only permanent features of their careers.

In a 1997 seminar at the Museum of Television and Radio, the executive producer of *Frasier*, Christopher Lloyd, acknowledged that faithful realism to the world of radio was not a consideration in the show's production: "We have people that we consult with that kind of help keep us in check as far as how legitimate things are that we do—you know, the buttons that they push and the carts they throw in and out are sort of like what would happen at a radio station. But beyond that, we don't hem ourselves in too much."

One memorable episode of *Frasier* that was based on an actual radio personality, however, took a swipe at Dr. Laura Schlessinger, whose syndicated daily talk show had become a phenomenon by the late 1990s. In the story, Dr. Nora joins the staff of KACL and begins to dispense harsh criticism and questionable advice to her troubled callers, such as calling a bisexual woman an equal-opportunity slut. But despite her rigidly moralistic approach, Dr. Nora in fact has a tarnished past—including two divorces, an affair with a married man, and estrangement from her mother—that renders her righteousness hollow.

Another 1999 episode of *Frasier* parodied the proliferation of crude shock jocks. KACL's new morning team, Carlos and the Chicken, sponsor a contest with a $1,000 prize to the listener who sends in "the best picture of Frasier Crane's humongous ass for our website." Though Frasier laments the success of "so-called humorists who rely on cruel pranks and scatological references," he's warned by his friends and family not to confront the duo or he'll continue to be fodder for their gags. As it turns out, Carlos and the Chicken become victims of their own pettiness and thin skins when an argument over who is the funnier of the two breaks up the team.

Alternate Formats

In 1995 two comedy series with a radio backdrop appeared in prime time. *The George Wendt Show* on CBS was based on a popular program on National Public Radio, *Car Talk*, hosted by brothers Tom and Ray Magliozzi. In the short-lived TV series, unmarried brothers George and Dan Coleman cohosted the radio call-in show *Points and Plugs* from the office of their auto repair shop in Madison, Wisconsin. The more successful entry was NBC's *NewsRadio*, which was set at WNYX, an all-news station in New York City. The domineering and abrupt station owner, Jimmy James, hires yet another in a long succession of news directors. The latest news director (played by Dave Foley), young and energetic, leaves Wisconsin for his big break in a big market. In over his head, he also has to contend with the idiosyncratic personalities of his staff, especially the huge ego of on-air anchor Bill McNeal (played by Phil Hartman).

The cable network American Movie Classics presented an original comedy series, *Remember WENN*, beginning in 1996. The show, set in Pittsburgh during the early years of World War II, soon developed a fanatically loyal audience. In each episode the cast and crew of station WENN struggled to create hours of ambitious daily programming on a shoestring budget—and as a result, viewers were well-schooled not only in the vintage art of sound effects and the logistics of microphone performance, but also in the radio genres of the era.

The heroine of *Remember WENN* is Betty Roberts, who came to the station as the winner of a writing contest with the prize of an unpaid internship. When the station's sole writer is overcome by alcoholism, Betty steps into his job and rises gloriously to the task. The show is evocative of the screwball comedies of the 1930s and 1940s but also weaves in elements of engrossing drama. The overarching theme of *Remember WENN's* four seasons is the sheer romance and unbridled excitement of the medium at its zenith.

Other series that revolved around the radio industry include *The Lucie Arnaz Show* (CBS, 1985); *Knight and Daye* (NBC, 1989); *FM* (NBC, 1989); *Rhythm and Blues* (NBC, 1992); *Katie Joplin* (WB, 1999); and *Talk to Me* (ABC, 2000). Several made-for-television movies also depicted historical events and personalities in American radio, such as *The Night That Panicked America*, the story of the 1938 *War of the Worlds* broadcast, and biographies of Edward R. Murrow and Walter Winchell.

Radio in the Lives of Characters

In addition to television's bounty of direct portrayals of the radio industry, a vast amount of fictional TV programming has embedded in it a sense of the importance radio has always held in the daily lives of American listeners. Throughout the nine seasons of *The Waltons*, for instance, the family radio in the living room was part and parcel of their existence and even served as a key plot element in several episodes. In "The Inferno," aspiring journalist John-Boy travels to Lakehurst, New Jersey, in May 1937 to cover the landing of the German zeppelin *Hindenburg*, the world's largest airship. When he returns to Walton's Mountain after the traumatic incident, there's no need to explain why he's mired in depression. "We heard about it on the Blue Network," says his younger brother Jason. The next day, his little sister Elizabeth makes reference to announcer Herbert Morrison's famous eyewitness account. The night of the disaster, NBC had broken its rigid rules against the broadcast of recordings and aired the dramatic on-the-scene transcription. "Sure sounded gruesome on the radio," says Elizabeth. "The announcer was crying."

As the Depression years gave way to the war years, the Walton's tabletop radio continued to connect them with the world. In the episode "Day of Infamy," Christmas-time 1941 is approaching. Oldest daughter Mary Ellen is planning to go to Hawaii to join her husband Curt, a doctor drafted into the U.S. Medical Corps, when, like millions of other stunned Americans, she learns from the radio that the Japanese had bombed Pearl Harbor.

Brooklyn Bridge, a 1991 series set in 1956, presents radio as an essential element in postwar popular culture. The lead character, 14-year-old Alan Silver, and his 9-year-old brother Nate follow the Dodgers baseball games on the radio with religious devotion. In a 1963 episode of *Leave It to Beaver*, Wally explains to his mother June the redeeming social value of the transistor radio. After every ten records they give a news report. "Heck," says Wally, "that's how Lumpy found out about Cuba."

Whatever changes technology will impose on the production and delivery of television programming in the decades ahead, stories of the American experience will continue to include radio as a key player and a rich source of plots and conflicts. In a world seemingly dominated by images, radio remains the most resilient and ubiquitous mass medium. Radio's pervasiveness in modern life cannot be overlooked by storytellers hoping to create characters and situations that, even if impressionistic, ring true.

See also: Film Depictions of Radio; Situation Comedy

Further Reading

Brooks, Tim, and Earle Marsh, *The Complete Directory to Prime Time Network and Cable TV Shows, 1946–Present*, 7th edition, New York: Ballantine Books, 1999.

Graham, Jefferson, *Frasier*, New York: Pocket Books, 1996.

Kassel, Michael B., *America's Favorite Radio Station: WKRP in Cincinnati*, Bowling Green, Ohio: Bowling Green State University Popular Press, 1993.

Mitz, Rick, *The Great Sitcom Book*, New York: Marek, 1980.

Pease, Edward C., and Everette E. Dennis, editors, *Radio: The Forgotten Medium*, New Brunswick, New Jersey: Transaction Press, 1995.

Stempel, Tom, *Storytellers to the Nation: A History of American Television Writing*, New York: Continuum, 1992.

Zicree, Marc, *The Twilight Zone Companion*, New York: Bantam Books, 1982.

MARY ANN WATSON

TEN-WATT STATIONS
Educational FM Outlets

Ten-watt (Class D) FM stations were created in 1948 as an inexpensive way for noncommercial organizations to operate their own outlets and, at the same time, increase listener traffic on the slow-to-develop FM band. Although educational radio efforts had begun as early as 1930 with the formation of the National Committee on Education by Radio, early operations were limited to a few programs broadcast from commercial AM facilities. By 1936, however, more than three dozen stations licensed to educational entities had managed to get on the air and remain there. Even though these outlets were not operating on frequencies especially reserved for their use, they did provide a service to limited areas of the country and kept the dream of educational radio alive. Consequently, when the Federal Communications Commission (FCC) authorized full-scale FM broadcasting to begin in 1941, five of the original 40 channels (42–50 MHz) were reserved for the use of noncommercial educational institutions. Seven school systems and universities were granted FM noncommercial licenses before wartime priorities brought most FM activity to a halt in early 1942.

At the war's end the FCC moved the FM band to a higher (88–108 MHz) and larger band of 100 channels. The first 20 of these (88.1–91.9 MHz) were again specifically reserved for noncommercial broadcasters. Educators moved quickly to take advantage of this greatly expanded allocation. Their sense of urgency was heightened by the realization that the commercial networks were abandoning their sustaining (unsponsored and often educational or cultural) programming in search of postwar profits.

The cost of building an FM station, however, remained an insurmountable barrier to many educational institutions. In 1948, at the urging of the National Association of Educational Broadcasters, the FCC approved a new low-power category of FM station. These Class D outlets could broadcast at an effective radiated power of just ten watts and were under less stringent operational and licensing requirements than were larger stations. The policy aim was to create a participatory broadcasting entity with low construction and operating costs that would make it affordable to educational institutions of all sizes.

Ten-watt stations were all to be allotted to the first and lowest channel (88.1 MHz) on the FM band. Because the audio portion of television channel 6 ends at 88 MHz, this meant that, by using the fine tuner on their new TV sets, consumers could pull in the signal from their neighborhood Class D radio stations without having to invest in FM radio receivers. If 88.1 had already been spoken for in its locale, a ten-watt applicant was free to request any higher available frequency within the educational band. Although Class D signals seldom carried more than four or five miles unless a more expensive high-gain antenna was deployed, school superintendents and college administrators saw these new audio vehicles as valuable community relations tools.

A typical example was WNAS in New Albany, Indiana, which went on the air in 1949. As chronicled in the high-school oriented *Senior Scholastic* magazine two years later, "Superintendent Henry Davidson wanted a 'voice' for his schools. He couldn't see a way to finance the only kind of station then possible—a high-power station costing from $50,000 to $100,000. He waited until the low-power FM station became a possibility for schools. Then he went into action. He found that a 10-W FM station would cost about $3,000 to build and equip. (Actual final cost $3,500.)" Taking the air on 28 May 1949, WNAS was one of the pioneering Class Ds. But honors as the first such facility were claimed by De Pauw University's WGRE, which had fired up its Greencastle, Indiana, transmitter 33 days earlier.

At the time, the FCC required that stations in other classes have full-time first-class licensed engineers on site to perform required technical functions. In contrast, Class D stations were allowed to use nontechnical third-class license holders to turn the transmitter on and off and operate the station. Technical servicing for a ten-watt outlet could be performed by a second-class operator available on call rather than an on-site first-class holder. Class Ds could also go on and off the air at will, a privilege denied higher power stations and one that meshed well with school and university calendars.

In the ensuing years, scores of Class D stations were built. Although the majority were constructed on college and university campuses, some of the most public-spirited were the licensees of independent school districts. The 20 such stations on the air in 1965 programmed a mix of in-school instructional lessons, general enrichment offerings (such as classical music and drama), and community-oriented services (ranging from school basketball games to school board meetings). The formats of college stations, on the other hand, often were more student-programmed and popular-music focused.

By the end of the 1960s, new realities began to threaten the Class D stations' continued existence. FM was now becoming widely popular—especially with younger listeners. As it rose to prominence, the medium's educational channels became increasingly occupied by high-power facilities whose professional staffs viewed ten-watt operations as inefficient

amateurs clogging scarce spectrum space. That many of these now full-power outlets had originated as Class Ds was seldom mentioned. The raucous and undisciplined material aired by some under-supervised college-licensed Class Ds was used to indict all ten-watt outlets and undermine the case for their continued existence. The passage of the 1967 Public Broadcasting Act and its creation of the Corporation for Public Broadcasting (CPB) also worked against low-power stations. Expanded and more centralized government funding favored support for wide-coverage-area and professionally staffed public broadcast facilities, rather than limited-range student stations or volunteer-heavy ten-watt operations that were impractical to network and incapable of contributing quality programs for national or regional distribution. When National Public Radio (NPR) was founded in 1971, it brought further structure and substance to national noncommercial radio service, but it marginalized Class D stations even more.

In the early 1970s, the public radio establishment introduced via NPR a series of gradually increasing facility, schedule, and personnel requirements for stations to remain NPR members. At the same time, CPB and other federal funding sources dovetailed their requirements for fiscal support with the standards for NPR membership. Although these moves made public radio much stronger, they walled off Class D and other small stations from most external funding. This happened despite the fact that by 1978, 426 outlets (almost half of U.S. noncommercial radio stations) were low-power operations. That same year, the FCC decreed that ten-watt facilities must make plans either to increase output to 100 W or to assume secondary and pre-emptable status (meaning that a higher-power station could take their frequency or push them out of business from an adjoining one). Most Class Ds chose to increase power, although spectrum limitations forced some to relocate.

By 1980, the ten-watts noncommercial station had largely disappeared, except for those which endured as translators. Ironically, in 1999, the FCC proposed a new class of "micro radio" low-power FM outlets designed to better serve neighborhood needs and to advance the cause of minority ownership. These outlets, coined "L2" stations, could operate using up to ten W of power. A "window" for L2 applications was opened briefly by the Commission in 2003, but it has not entertained further inquiries.

See also: College Radio; Community Radio; Corporation for Public Broadcasting; Educational Radio to 1967; Licensing Authorizing U.S. Stations to Broadcast;

Low-Power Radio/Microradio; National Public Radio;
Public Radio Since 1967

Further Reading

Martin, Howard, "Low Power Stations," *The Journal of
College Radio* (November 1972).
McKown, Vernon, "Students Run WNAS," *Senior Scholastic*
(4 April 1951).
Mead, James, "A Study of a Low-Power School Radio Station:
WOAK," Ed.D.diss., Wayne State University, 1965.
Orlik, Peter, *A Survey of Public School Radio in the
United States*, Detroit, Michigan: Wayne State Uni-
versity Mass Communications Center, 1966.

PETER B. ORLIK,
2009 REVISIONS BY CARY O'DELL

THEATER GUILD ON THE AIR
Radio Drama Program

After World War II, the executive officers and
board members of the U.S. Steel Corporation
became willing converts to anthology drama showcasing company voice advertising. Their program
Theater Guild on the Air (the *United States Steel
Hour* after 1952) helped promote the corporation's
public and government relations during reconversion, the postwar period that saw the lifting of price
and wage controls and intertwined negotiation of
agreements with the Truman administration and
the United Steel Workers of America. *Theater
Guild on the Air* featured distinct entertainment and
educational components. By arrangement with
New York's Theater Guild, the program presented
adaptations of plays that had little bearing upon
corporation "messages" (intermission talks) and
messages with little connection to the plays. The
separation of the program's dramatic and editorial
control extended to U.S. Steel executives' admirable
defense of their program in an era of rampant
blacklisting, while the show simultaneously provided
one of radio's last examples of corporate voice
advertising read by corporation officers themselves.

Among large radio sponsors using the anthology
format for institutional promotion, U.S. Steel was
unique in contracting for program production and,
effectively, dramatic control outside of its advertising agency, Batten, Barton, Durstine, and Osborn
(BBD&O). Program production responsibility fell
to the Theater Guild. Founded in 1918, the Guild
aspired to the production of plays not then found in
the commercial theater. The Guild championed the
work of Bernard Shaw, Eugene O'Neill, Maxwell
Anderson, Elmer Rice, Sidney Howard, William
Saroyan, George Gershwin, Richard Rogers, and

Lorenz Hart. By 1945 a back catalog of some 200
Guild productions provided a ready source of
adaptable material for the *Theater Guild on the Air*.
Under contract to U.S. Steel, the Guild supplied
plays and casts, retaining artistic control under
managing director Lawrence Langner, whose long
career as a patent attorney representing inventor
Charles F. Kettering and others enabled his easy
circulation in the world of corporate affairs. The
broadcasts were produced by BBD&O's George
Kondolf, the former director of New York's Federal
Theater Project, and directed by Homer Fickett,
formerly the director of radio's *March of Time* and
the *Cavalcade of America*.

The autonomy enjoyed by the Guild in the
selection and casting of plays, and the confinement
of corporation messages to two intermissions, conformed to the broad goals of public relations
education and entertainment desired by the corporation. In addition to the *Theater Guild on the
Air*'s "commercial aspects," explained U.S. Steel
public relations director J. Carlisle MacDonald, the
program's "two main objectives were (1) To create a
better understanding of the affairs of United States
Steel through a series of weekly, informative messages explaining the corporation's policies and
describing its widespread activities; (2) To provide
the nation's vast listening audience with the finest in
dramatic entertainment by bringing into millions of
homes every Sunday evening the greatest plays in
the legitimate theater." Exemplifying the rewards of
such thinking, the first season's plays ("building
bigger and bigger audiences for U.S. Steel") included *I Remember Mama*, *On Borrowed Time*, and
The Front Page and featured Lynne Fontaine and
Alfred Lunt, Walter Huston, Katherine Hepburn,
Ray Milland, Helen Hayes, Frederick March, Pat
O'Brien, and Walter Pidgeon.

The hour-long *Theater Guild on the Air* featured
two intermission talks prepared by BBD&O and
read by announcer George Hicks, the "Voice of
United States Steel." An American Broadcasting
Companies (ABC) radio newsman who had broadcast the 1944 D-Day invasion in Normandy, Hicks
brought his dispassionate reportorial style to the
delivery of each week's talks. The first described the
policies and objectives of the umbrella corporation,
and the second described the activities of a subsidiary of "United States Steel—the industrial
family that serves the nation." At intermission
time, announcer Hicks served up veritable chestnuts
of institutional promotion: paeans to the widespread ownership of United States Steel corporation stock among all classes of individuals and
hospitals, schools, and charitable organizations; to

the re-employment of veterans; and to the upgrading and training of personnel. An anthology of plays, including two intermission talks, published in 1947 suggests the program's aspiration to low-pressure salesmanship. A talk inserted between the acts of Sidney Howard's *They Knew What They Wanted*, for example, described the latent consequences of United States Steel's vast scale of production, namely, the employment of men and the movement of raw materials. Striving to convey the personal meaning of it all, the text concluded, "So, next time you use any product of steel from a can opener to an automobile, remember—you are benefitting from the skills and energies of literally millions of men who have helped to transfer the raw materials from the earth into the steel out of which come many things to make our lives more comfortable."

Again and again, the United States Steel board of directors expressed satisfaction with their radio program, renewing it on an annual basis from 1946 through the 1952 broadcast season. Chairman of the Board Irving S. Olds and President Benjamin F. Fairless remained sold on the bifurcated production arrangement, owing in part to the corporation's prestigious association with the *Theater Guild* and in part to the public platform that the program provided for Fairless, who personally took to the air to explain the corporation's position during the steel strike of 1949. Anticipating United States Steel's move to television, and with it the improved prospect of an agency-produced show, broadcast producer BBD&O successfully lobbied to change the program's title to the *United States Steel Hour* beginning with the fall 1952 broadcast season. The program's final radio season commenced with Joshua Logan's *Wisteria Trees*, starring Helen Hayes and Joseph Cotten, and concluded with Shakespeare's *Julius Caesar*, starring Maurice Evans and Basil Rathbone.

Hosts

Lawrence Langer
Roger Pryor
Elliott Reid

Announcers

Norman Brokenshire; George Hicks

Programming History

CBS   6 December 1943–29 February 1944
ABC   9 September 1945–5 June 1949

NBC   11 September 1949–7 June 1953 (from 1952 as *United States Steel Hour*)

Further Reading

Bird, William L., Jr., *Better Living: Advertising, Media, and the New Vocabulary of Business Leadership, 1935–1955*, Evanston, Illinois: Northwestern University Press, 1999.

Fitelson, H. William, editor, *Theatre Guild on the Air*, New York: Rinehart, 1947.

Fones-Wolf, Elizabeth, *Selling Free Enterprise: The Business Assault on Labor and Liberalism, 1945–60*, Urbana: University of Illinois Press, 1994.

Fones-Wolf, Elizabeth, "Creating a Favorable Business Climate: Corporations and Radio Broadcasting, 1934–1954," *Business History Review* 73 (Summer 1999).

MacDonald, J. Fred, *Don't Touch That Dial!: Radio Programming in American Life*, Chicago: Nelson-Hall, 1979.

Nadel, Norman, *A Pictorial History of the Theatre Guild*, New York: Crown, 1969.

O'Malley, Thomas, "Every Important Work of Art Has a Message," *Television Magazine* (11 October 1954).

"Steel Melts the Public," *Sponsor* (17 March 1950).

Theatre Guild, *The Theatre Guild Anthology*, New York: Random House, 1936.

"Theatre Guild Show," *Tide* (15 October 1945).

WILLIAM L. BIRD, JR.

THIS AMERICAN LIFE
Public Radio Program

This American Life is an hour-long, weekly public radio program that stretches the boundaries of magazine-style entertainment radio with a poignant honesty and flair rivaling, and even exceeding, the journalistic efforts of groundbreaking programs such as *Morning Edition* and *All Things Considered*.

This American Life's website describes the show as follows: "It's a weekly show. It's an hour. Its mission is to document everyday life in this country. We sometimes think of it as a documentary show for people who normally hate documentaries. A public radio show for people who don't necessarily care for public radio."

The brainchild of former National Public Radio (NPR) reporter Ira Glass, *This American Life* is largely a collection of stories that endeavor to examine America from the inside out. Not unlike Charles Kuralt's video essays gathered "on the road," *This American Life* examines America by examining the lives and challenges faced by individual Americans. It does so with a writing style that is highly conversational and uses an "audio vérité" feel, with the frequent use of natural sound (ambient background sounds) and interview segments that are sometimes raw and unpolished.

Although a team of producers, regular contributors, and guests all provide pieces for the show, the soul of *This American Life* comes from host and producer Ira Glass. A Baltimore native who resisted his parents' idea of a medical career to pursue a career in media, Glass originally sold jokes to radio hosts and eventually found a job editing promotional spots for NPR as an intern at age 19.

During his internship at NPR, Glass immersed himself in all areas of news production and reporting, also filling in as a host on NPR programs *Talk of the Nation* and *Weekend All Things Considered*. As a reporter in NPR's Chicago bureau for six years, Glass emerged as an award-winning education reporter, receiving accolades from the National Education Association, Education Writers Association, and the Harvard Graduate School of Education. His best-known work was a longitudinal profile of several Chicago Public Schools students and the successes and failures of the changes imposed on their respective schools by education reforms.

Each hour-long program of *This American Life* is divided into acts—usually three—which communicate a general theme. Each segment is accompanied by a piece of music that supports the theme—either through its title or through the lyrics.

Among the segment titles *This American Life* aired in 2000 were: "Twenty-Four Hours at the Golden Apple" (a Chicago diner, where poignant stories are told by customers who wander in and out), "Election" (dealing with a high school class election, the production of negative presidential campaign ads, and the genealogy of then-candidate George W. Bush, who, the piece claims, may be related to half of Americans), and "Immigration" (which studies the impact of immigration laws on individuals, including a deported legal alien whose country would not take him back). Contributors range from independent producers whose work is heard on other public radio programs to quirky characters such as "Dishwasher Pete," who share their wisdom and stories of real life.

Distributed by Public Radio International, *This American Life* is produced by WBEZ in Chicago, where it is mixed live each Friday evening for distribution to 370 public radio stations around the country. Glass introduces each segment in his matter-of-fact style, never afraid of a lengthy pause or unconventional voice inflections. Although his delivery appears somewhat unpolished, the sound of the program is anything but. He and his producers spend a great deal of time editing pieces and copy to create the "relaxed" style of the program.

Glass is responsible for many of the stories told on *This American Life*. *Chicago Magazine* said this about his work: "Glass does stories that are casual and intimate in feeling, that seem almost to start in the middle of the story and are told in unfolding scenes. Sort of like a hipster version of Garrison Keillor." Marc Fisher, writing in the *American Journalism Review*, says that, "Glass is the boy wonder, a rumpled genius in the minuscule world of radio documentaries, a quizzical character who hides behind trademark oversized black plastic eyeglass frames and takes radio journalism to places it has not traveled before."

This American Life is a program with a clearly humanist slant, which is expressed through compelling stories and amusing send-ups. Its innovative approach and broad appeal helped land a $350,000, three-year production grant from the Corporation for Public Broadcasting's Program Development Fund in 1997.

As one of the most listened-to public radio programs, it also helps generate significant revenue for stations that carry it during pledge drives. Glass is among the most dedicated of public radio program producers in helping stations with their fund-raising, producing a number of highly effective fund-raising spots for station use and creating gimmicks such as a "decoder" ring as an incentive for listeners to contribute.

This American Life joins *All Things Considered, Morning Edition, A Prairie Home Companion, Michael Feldman's Whad'Ya Know?* and *Car Talk* as one of the leaders in public radio's stable of national programs. The show was honored with a Peabody Award in 1996.

See also: National Public Radio

Host/Producer

Ira Glass

Production Staff

Senior Producer	Julie Snyder
Producers	Alex Blumberg, Diane Cook, Wendy Dorr, and Starlee Kine
Contributing Editors	Jack Hitt, Margy Rochlin, Alix Spiegel, Paul Tough, Nancy Updike, and Sarah Vowell
Writers/Contributors	David Sedaris, Joe Richman, Scott Carrier, Gay Talese, Tobias Wolff

Programming History

PRI   17 November 1995– (remained in production
       as of September 2003)

Further Reading

Barton, Julia, "It Takes Vision to Make Good Radio: Tales
     from *This American Life*," *Salon Magazine* (23 July 1997).
Conciatore, Jacqueline, "*This American Life*: If You Love
     This Show, You Really Love It," *Current* (2 June 1997).
Fisher, Marc, "It's a Wonderful Life," *The American
     Journalism Review* (July–August 1999).
Mifflin, Margot, "*This American Life*: American Lives,
     Radio Journeys," *New York Times Sunday Magazine*
     (7 February 1999).
Sella, Marshall, "A Profile of Ira Glass and the Show: The
     Glow at the End of the Dial," *New York Times Sunday
     Magazine* (11 April 1999).
Snyder, Rachel Louise, "Lunch with Ira Glass," www.salon.
     com/people/lunch/1999/07/16/glass/index.html
This American Life website, www.thislife.org
Verhulst, Kari Jo, "Fearless Curiosity: The Irreverent
     Offerings of *This American Life*," *Sojourners Magazine*
     28, no. 5 (September–October 1999).
Wimsatt, William Upski, "Ira Glass: A Cure for the
     Common Radio," *Horizon Magazine* (1 September 1999).

PETER WALLACE

TOP 40
See: Contemporary Hit Radio/Top 40 Format

TOPLESS RADIO

Multiple sexual partners, methods of self-gratification
and the pleasuring of others, odd sexual procliv-
ities: though these may sound like some of the
recurring topics of shock jocks like Howard Stern,
they are actually examples of the hot topics discussed three decades ago on radio. The format of
such programs became known as "topless radio."

Similar to much of today's "adult talk" radio
and TV, topless radio was a format in which audience members called in to discuss graphically sexual
issues with hosts who tried to titillate the audience
by teasing every explicit detail out of a caller. Although
a predecessor, and perhaps an ancestor, of today's
"adult" radio, topless radioinitially began as quite a
different format and was certainly targeting an
entirely different audience.

Origins

Topless radio's humble beginnings in the United
States date back to the late 1960s, when some AM
talk programs began to experiment with light,
humorous discussions about relationships with
female callers—aimed at younger female listeners.

FM radio stations, with their higher-quality stereo-
signal, had begun replacing AM stations as the place
of choice to listen to popular music. As traditional
talk radio began to fill up the AM airwaves, female
listeners tuned out. The new format was an attempt
to bring younger female listeners to a format (talk)
that attracted predominantly older listeners. Program hosts would ask female listeners to call in to
have a candid discussion about "relationship
issues." Up until then, radio had carefully avoided
direct reference to sex—and innuendo was often
dealt with swiftly by the Federal Communications
Commission (FCC) with "cease and desist" orders.
The medium, and the FCC's oversight of it, lagged
behind television, print, and film of the era in terms
of dealing with explicit subject matter.

The first topless radio programs required callers
to phone the station the night before a program
aired. Hosts would discuss topics with callers off
the air and edit together a program for later
broadcast. Compared to books, film, and even television of the time, the resulting programs were
considered to be quite tame. Despite that, the
format was considered somewhat risqué by the
extremely conservative radio standards of the day.
More important, producers felt the shows sounded
"canned" and dry. So in 1971, KCBS in Los
Angeles began experimenting with live discussions
of sex by women callers that were aimed at female
listeners. A male all-night disc jockey for the station, Bill Ballance, hosted the midday show, *Feminine Forum*.

Topless radio was an instant success and quickly
spread across the nation. By 1973 there were 50–60
stations that allowed only women to call in and
talk about the predetermined topic of the day. As
the format became more popular and spread to
other stations, the content became more explicit.
Truly talented hosts were able to draw extremely
detailed and explicit answers from their callers.
Naturally, listenership grew dramatically.

Complaints to the FCC were also on the rise. As
a result, the commission announced that it did not
consider topless radio to be in the public interest,
as prescribed by the Communications Act of 1934,
and the FCC threatened to take action if the
industry did not police itself. FCC Chairman Dean
Burch considered the format "prurient trash" and
did not feel that the format was broadcasting in the
public interest, convenience, or necessity. Further,
he did not feel that the First Amendment protected
broadcasting discussions of this sort in such an
easily accessible medium—a medium particularly
available to children. Despite these warnings, topless
radio programming did not change.

In 1973 the FCC announced its intention to fine WGLD-FM in Oak Park, Illinois, $2,000 based on two individual excerpts from a show called *Femme Forum*. This was the stiffest penalty then available under the Communications Act of 1934. The declaration did not go without dissent. Two organizations, the Illinois Citizens Committee for Broadcasting and the Illinois Division of the American Civil Liberties Union, along with one FCC member, complained that the ruling was outside the purview of the FCC and went against the organization's goal to maintain broadcasting in the public interest. They stated that the ruling would have a chilling effect on the discussion of important public issues and that, taken as a whole, the content of topless radio programming (specifically *Femme Forum*) was *not* patently offensive by community standards.

Hoping that this would be a test case of the FCC's ability to fine stations based on the commission's perceptions of the obscenity or indecency of the programming, the agency invited WGLD's parent company, Sonderling Broadcasting, to take the case to court. However, Sonderling, stating that they could not afford the cost of testing such broad constitutional issues in the legal arena, paid the fine instead, and the FCC was denied a judicial declaration of its ability to police radio decency. Despite the lack of a court ruling, the FCC achieved its goal. Not only did Sonderling pay the fine, they also canceled their sex-talk show. Indeed, such shows nationwide were canceled or drastically restructured after this event.

Topless radio was quickly banished. Thanks to the Sonderling fine and similar cases over the ensuing years—particularly the "Seven Dirty Words" case in 1978–the FCC managed to keep references to sex on radio primarily limited to risqué jokes and somewhat suggestive song lyrics. However, the FCC was not able to keep this format off the air for long. Not only did sex talk on the radio return, it evolved into a variety of forms, showed up in a number of parts of the day, and sought out multiple audiences. Particularly important were shifts in the regulatory focus of the FCC from behavioral regulation to allowing marketplace competition to "police" the actions of stations. In 1980, Dr. Ruth Westheimer began her serious but frank discussion of sex on local New York radio. In the early 21st century, Dr. Laura Schlessinger's nationally syndicated program dealt with moral and ethical discussions of relationships, sometimes resulting in discussions of sexual behavior and choices.

Another offshoot of topless radio is exemplified by Howard Stern—the self-proclaimed "King of

All Media." In the mid-1980s, Stern and several other national and regional hosts stretched the limits of "patently offensive" to the breaking point—dealing with religion, politics, race, and naturally sex in a manner many consider particularly juvenile. Unlike earlier programming, shock radio sought out the lucrative male 18–49 demographic. These programs caught and held the attention of their audiences with guests from the porn industry, celebrity feuds, off-color phone pranks, stripping on the air, outlandish phone-in contests, and alternative dating games. Surprisingly, corporations backing this type of radio have managed to forestall significant FCC censure—in many cases simply paying massive fines after stalling the organization for a number of years. As the format cannot advance much further than it has, it appears to have simply spread into other parts of the day. Not only is this format aired at night, it has actually become most popular in evening and morning drive-times.

Although the antics in this format have escalated since the early 1970s, topless radio may have helped usher in the new era of explicit radio discussions of sex.

See also: Censorship; Controversial Issues, Broadcasting of; Federal Communications Commission; Licensing Authorizing U.S. Stations to Broadcast; Obscenity and Indecency on Radio; "Seven Dirty Words" Case

Further Reading

Carlin, J.C., "The FCC versus 'Topless Radio'," Master's thesis, University of Florida, 1974.
Pierce, J. Kingston, "How Do Local Stations Boost Ratings? Give Seattle What It Wants—Sex in the Morning," *Seattle Weekly* (8–14 April 1999).
Pierce, J. Kingston, "Radio Raunch," www.seattleweekly.com/features/9914/featurespierce.shtml
Stern, Howard, *Private Parts*, New York: Pocket Star, 1994.
"Touchiest Topic on Radio Now: Talk about Sex," *Broadcasting* 118 (19 March 1993).

PHILIP J. AUTER

TRADE ASSOCIATIONS

The American radio business has organized a variety of trade associations to both lobby government and promote radio to the general public. While the largest and longest-lasting such group has been the National Association of Broadcasters (NAB), many others have focused on more specific concerns or groups, some of them lasting only a few years. This entry details a few such groups (many others, such as NAB, have their own entry) to illustrate the variety of their concerns.

Clear Channel Broadcasting Service

Organized in 1941, the Clear Channel Broadcasting Service (CCBS) was an association of a relative handful of large AM radio station owners whose goal was to operate maximum-powered (50,000 W) AM radio stations on "clear channels" without being subject to co-channel skywave interference from other stations, which might reduce their night-time coverage. Although its stated mission was to conduct "an educational and promotional campaign to acquaint Congress and the members of the public with the need for clear channel stations," the CCBS—the first special-interest trade organization in the broadcast industry—sought to use every political and legal means available to protect the frequencies its members occupied.

By 1934 numerous smaller stations were already asking the FCC for permission to operate on one of the 40 clear channel frequencies. To fight for the preservation of clear channels and repel this potential incursion, and to lobby for *superpower* license grants similar to the 1934–39 experimental permit obtained by WLW, Cincinnati, Ohio, Edwin Craig of WSM in Nashville, Tennessee, organized 13 independently owned (non-network) clear channel stations into the Clear Channel Group. (Stations owned by the National Broadcasting Company [NBC] and Columbia Broadcasting System [CBS] networks were not welcome to join, because it was felt that the networks had their own agendas and were not passionate about, or necessarily even in favor of, the clear channel movement.)

The CCBS was established on 4 February 1941 and eventually became a replacement for the predecessor Clear Channel Group, because the membership was essentially the same and Edwin Craig was the singular driving force behind both organizations. The CCBS, however, took a more aggressive stance than the Clear Channel Group had and, with the support of member station contributions, opened a Washington, D.C., office and employed Vic Sholis, a former public information official for the U.S. Department of Commerce, to lead the cause.

Following World War II, the Federal Communications Commission (FCC) launched a plan to break down a number of the clear channels (by letting other stations use them) in a proceeding labeled as Docket 6741. To fight the plan, the CCBS concentrated on building alliances with farm groups and others living in rural America who would support their claims that protecting the clear channel stations was vital to providing satisfactory service to these vast areas.

Although the CCBS was able to delay action, it was not able to stop the FCC from issuing its decision. This occurred on 13 September 1961, concluding that 13 of the clear channels would be duplicated, with the assignment of one full-time Class II (regional) station to each, with the Commission designating in what area each could be located. CCBS spent the balance of the 1960s seeking congressional reversal of the FCC action while allowing superpower status for several stations. Although it received a degree of support, no bills passed into law. By the 1970s, members' interest in the issue was waning and the organization largely abandoned further legislative battles. The climax of the fight to retain major protected status for clear channel stations came on 20 June 1980, when the FCC released its decision in Docket 20642, declaring that the nation's population would be better served by allowing even more stations to operate on clear channel frequencies than had been permitted under the 1961 decision. Thus, all remaining clear channel stations were now subject to multiple Class II stations, which could operate on what had once been "cleared" channels.

The CCBS, which represented only a limited group of radio stations, was unique as it continued to champion that cause for nearly 50 years. Although CCBS became inactive after the 1980 decision, all of the AM frequencies established as "clear channels" in 1928 are still so designated, and stations originally licensed as Class I still receive a measure of interference protection over and above all other stations on the AM band.

National Association of Farm Broadcasting

By the 1930s, as farm-related broadcasters began meeting informally at various agricultural and broadcast industry gatherings, the need for an organization that focused on their specific needs became evident. On 4 May 1944 the National Association of Radio Farm Directors was officially formed to promote more and better programming directed to American farmers. As TV stations began operating (and, with them, farm-oriented TV reports), the group became the National Association of Television and Radio Farm Directors, adding more than 100 new members, for a total membership of approximately 500. The name was later shortened to the National Association of Farm Broadcasters (NAFB).

Members became aware that to survive, farm programming needed to produce revenue for stations. New emphasis was placed on sales and the acceptance of commercials. By the 1960s the

NAFB had made good progress in becoming a business-oriented organization. They set out to tell about producing results for advertisers and proving there was an audience for farm programs.

Early in 1989 the NAFB employed its first full-time executive director, Roger Olson, who served until 1996 and was followed by Steve Pierson. Under these two men, major focus has been placed on research and obtaining both qualitative and quantitative information about the farm market. By 1998 the NAFB had produced a farm broadcasting presentation on CDROM for use by media sales representatives in telling the story of how radio and television continue to provide the vital information needed by farmers as they labor to feed the nation.

The National Farm Broadcast Service was created in 1992 for the delivery of information via satellite, which also made possible the exchange of news stories and interviews by members.

In 2005, the organization subtly changed its name from the National Association of Farm *Broadcasters* to the National Association of Farm *Broadcasting*, in order to better reflect the inclusion of agribusiness companies, agencies, sales departments, and management in its membership.

Radio-Television News Directors Association

The Radio-Television News Directors Association (RTNDA) was founded in March 1946 under the name National Association of Radio News Editors for the purposes of setting standards for news-gathering and reporting, exchanging ideas, and "convinc[ing] news sources that broadcast reporters were legitimate members of the journalistic profession." Later that year the name was changed to the National Association of Radio News Directors. With the onset of TV news programming, the present name (including the word "Television") was put into place in 1952. Over the years, RTNDA focused on developing both ethical and operational standards for both radio and television news departments.

RTNDA is now a worldwide organization devoted to electronic journalism in all its formats. Thus it represents station and network news executives in radio, television, cable television, and other electronic media in more than 30 countries. By the turn of the century, membership in the RTNDA totaled more than 3,000 news directors, news reporters and editors, educators, and students.

RTNDA offers professional development programs as well as programs for students of journalism and young professionals, including scholarships and short-term paid Capitol Hill internships.

RTNDA also produces an extensive lineup of publications and resources to support the work of electronic journalists, including the *Communicator*, a monthly magazine devoted to reporting on new technological advances, developments in reporting and newsroom management techniques, and topics vital to news facility managers.

Many attend the Association's annual international conference and exposition held in a different city each year. An independent affiliate of the RTNDA is the Radio and Television News Directors Foundation, which promotes "excellence in electronic journalism" through research, education, and training for news professionals and students.

National Association of College Broadcasters

The National Association of College Broadcasters (NACB) is a nonprofit trade organization for student-operated radio stations. NACB is fairly young, having been founded in 1988 by students at Brown University. In their efforts to establish a student TV station at the Providence, Rhode Island-based school, the Brown students realized the need for an entity that could assist student-operated radio and TV stations in their startup efforts and provide a conduit for exchanging programming, operational, and legal information with other student outlets.

NACB exists to provide students a ready resource for advice and information and a venue for exchanging ideas and innovative concepts. Through such events as its annual National Conference, the NACB functions as a link between the academic and professional worlds of the radio/TV industry. It presents an annual awards program, where individuals and station members from the United States and other countries honor the best work in student electronic media. In addition, the NACB devotes itself to encouraging and supporting student stations and individuals in reaching for and attaining high standards so as to enhance the communities they serve, to provide opportunities for individuals with an interest in media and communications, and to argue their position on pending laws or regulations that might affect student media.

The NACB was originally made possible by a $250,000 endowment from CBS. However, after that money was exhausted and, unable to generate sustaining membership or other revenue, the organization suspended operations in 2004.

Radio Music License Committee

The Radio Music License Committee has a very specific function. Made up of broadcasters who volunteer to represent their industry's interests, the committee negotiates with the two largest musical performing rights organizations, American Society of Composers, Authors, and Publishers (ASCAP) and Broadcast Music Incorporated (BMI), to establish acceptable fees and terms for the performance of music by commercial radio stations in the United States.

Originally known as the All-Industry Music Committee, the committee took over this function from the NAB in the early 1940s. The NAB itself had been formed (in 1923) by a group of broadcasters who found ASCAP's fee requests to be unacceptable. In 1970 it was agreed that radio and television's performance of music raised different negotiating concerns requiring different approaches. Hence, the organization divided itself into two separate entities, and the Radio Music License Committee was born. It is an independent body, having no affiliation with the NAB.

Officially, the Committee negotiates on behalf of its member stations—those who voluntarily fund it—yet, for all practical purposes, it represents most of the radio industry, because the blanket and per-performance license fee structure agreed upon applies to all stations and producers. When unable to reach agreement with either ASCAP or BMI, the Committee more than once has commenced litigation under the federally imposed consent decrees, which require both music licensing organizations to set reasonable fees and terms for radio station licenses. Generally, agreements are renewed with the two entities for a four- or five-year term.

Originally headquartered in New York City, the committee relocated to Nashville, Tennessee in 2007.

Broadcast Measurement Bureau

The Broadcast Measurement Bureau (BMB) was a brief experiment by the National Association of Broadcasters to provide a service comparable to that to the Audit Bureau of Circulation (ABC).

Beville (1988) describes the ABC as "a non-profit, tripartite, self-regulatory, voluntary organization established in 1914 and supported by the entire print media and advertising industry." The ABC provides independent audits of circulation figures of newspapers, magazines, journals, and internet media. In its own words, "by creating an independent currency for measuring its value, the ABC makes the sale and purchase of print, exhibition, and internet media both easier and efficient." In the audits, individuals whom the various media assert are in the audiences of a publication or exhibition are independently contacted to assure that they are indeed readers, participants, or viewers as claimed. The governing board of ABC includes representatives of national and regional advertisers, newspapers, and other organizations. Advertisers, agencies, and publications pay an annual fee to receive publications reporting the independent audits.

In 1945—in an attempt to parallel ABC methods for radio—the broadcast industry organized the BMB to conduct radio station coverage surveys. Their method involved a survey form mailed to listeners, who would verify the stations they received and listened to. A private research firm that had conducted some methodological work along these lines was engaged to conduct a national survey. Broadcaster subscriptions supported this study.

Following the apparent success of an initial survey, a second was launched three years later. It did not meet its expenses because of a lack of subscriptions by radio stations. It appeared that some stations, pleased with the results of the first study, did not wish to risk less impressive results in a second survey, whereas other stations, dissatisfied with the first survey, saw no reason to support a survey likely to deliver bad news a second time.

Faced with this lack of support, BMB collapsed. The NAB paid $100,000 to the researchers so that the few broadcasters who had subscribed would receive complete reports. Beville theorizes that BMB was doomed to failure, if the objective was to impress advertisers. In his view broadcaster-supported research would always seem tainted to advertisers and their agencies.

International Radio and Television Society Foundation

The International Radio and Television Society (IRTS) Foundation is a New York City-based service organization whose goal is to "bring together the wisdom of yesterday's founders, the power of today's leaders, and the promise of tomorrow's young industry professionals." The emphasis here is more on education than lobbying.

The IRTS evolved from an organization founded in 1939 when a group of radio executives began meeting informally to discuss mutual interests. Because electronic media face continual change at every level, there is a constant need for development of training and information. IRTS seeks to provide education and ongoing dialog about important communication issues. IRTS membership includes professionals across a variety of disciplines encompassing all modes of electronic content distribution, including radio, broadcast television, cable television, computer, direct broadcast satellite, and telephony.

Each year, IRTS presents approximately 45 programs, including monthly luncheons with a newsmaker as the guest speaker, seminars, and dinners, which help fund the organization's electronic media educational programs. These include a faculty/industry seminar, where university professors meet with industry leaders in New York for five days of intense sessions; the preparation of case studies to assist communications and business school professors in their teaching of media-related topics; minority career workshops; and an annual nineweek summer fellowship program.

Many other radio organizations have appeared and faded away over the years, including those representing radio DJs, sales personnel, financial managers, promotional personnel, stations interested in providing on-air editorials, and classical music stations.

See also: American Federation of Musicians; American Federation of Television and Radio Artists; American Society of Composers, Authors, and Publishers; American Women in Radio and Television; Broadcast Music Incorporated; Clear Channel Stations; Farm/Agricultural Radio; FM Trade Associations; Intercollegiate Broadcasting System; National Association of Broadcasters; National Association of Educational Broadcasters; National Federation of Community Broadcasters; National Religious Broadcasters; Promax; RADAR; Radio Advertising Bureau; Technical Organizations

Further Reading

Audit Bureau of Circulation: *About ABC: The History of ABC*, www.accessabc.com/subi/history.htm

Beville, Hugh Malcolm, Jr., *Audience Ratings: Radio, Television, and Cable*, 2nd edition, Hillsdale, New Jersey: Lawrence Erlbaum Associates, 1988.

Fletcher, J.E., editor, *Broadcast Research Definitions*, Washington, D.C.: National Association of Broadcasters, 1988.

Foust, James C., *Big Voices of the Air: The Battle over Clear Channel Radio*, Ames: Iowa State University Press, 2000.

Marlin R. Taylor and James E. Fletcher,
2009 Revisions By Cary O'Dell

TRADE PRESS
Reporting Radio's Business

The radio or broadcast trade press consists primarily of weekly magazines and newsletters (some now available via internet delivery) that serve an audience of people working within the radio industry—including broadcasters, engineers, managers, program personnel, manufacturers, investors, and others. These publications report what is happening in the radio business and related fields, technological developments and trends, regulatory actions and decisions, and information about people in the industry. They often take a strongly probusiness editorial stance. Some trade periodicals are published as a function of professional organizations, others are published by manufacturing companies, but most are advertiser-supported commercial ventures. Most focus on the American scene, but some deal with comparative or international activities as well.

The trade press excludes publications directed at the general public, including fan magazines, hobby publications, scholarly journals, radio program guides, and the like. A selection of radio-specific titles (most of them American) are highlighted here. Some lasted for only a short time and either disappeared or merged with other periodicals, but others have continued on for decades.

Origins (to 1940)

The earliest related trade periodicals served the electrical and telegraph and telephone industries in the late 19th and early 20th centuries. Journals such as *The Electrical Engineer* (1882–99, weekly) and *Journal of the Telegraph* (1867–1914, monthly) included early reports on wireless telegraphy experiments and applications. The venerable show business papers *Billboard* (1894–present, weekly) and *Variety* (1905–present, weekly) created models of the entertainment trade paper genre that would blossom in the decades to come, and both regularly covered broadcasting from its inception. For a few years from the late 1930s into the early 1940s, *Variety* published an annual *Variety Radio Directory*.

Trade publications focusing on radio broadcasting emerged as regular broadcasting began in the 1920s. Some of these early publications included information of interest to amateurs, broadcasters, manufacturers, and even audience members, but they became more focused as the industry itself began to settle into a pattern. *Radio Broadcast* (1922–30, monthly) was the most important of these early titles, combining feature articles that at first appealed to both listeners and broadcasters. Technical information concerned building and operating receivers as well as station equipment, and the magazine carried more advertising than any of the other early radio journals. The monthly provided its readers with a broad cultural understanding of radio at first, but it became more technical and aimed at industry figures later in the decade, when the masthead noted that it was published "for the radio industry."

Focusing on the equipment side, as many early trade papers did, *The Radio Dealer* (1922–28, monthly) was a pioneer aimed at retailers of radio receivers. *Radio Retailing* (1925–39, monthly) took similar aim and was also supported by manufacturer advertising. Its editor, Orestes Caldwell, eventually served as a member of the Federal Radio Commission (most early editors were radio enthusiasts, and several others emerged as key figures in the development of the radio industry).

Perhaps the most influential of radio industry trade magazines is *Broadcasting* (1931–41, biweekly; 1941–present, weekly). The creation of Sol Taishoff and Martin Codel, this was primarily a newsmagazine from the start, and it built close relationships with the Washington industry and policy community. Taishoff and Codel's combination of journalistic experience with a wide network of contacts rapidly built the magazine into an industry staple, which added an annual yearbook directory number in 1935 (which is still published). Its advertising featured major stations, network and syndicated programs, and broadcast equipment.

As the industry grew in size and complexity, weekly publication was insufficient to follow all the developments and issues. This fact gave birth to *Radio Daily* (1936–50), which began to focus more on television and became *Radio Daily-Television Daily* (1950–62), and finally *Radio-Television Daily* (1962–66), "the national daily newspaper of commercial radio and television." The daily grew in size—from four pages in the 1940s to eight pages in tabloid format with photos. (It published a long-running *Radio Annual* beginning in 1938.) No publication devoted to radio has appeared on a daily basis since, though many broader publications (e.g., *Communications Daily*, which began in 1981) include radio issues and trends.

Radio Faces Television (1940–80)

The rise of a more complex broadcast industry during and after World War II gave rise to more specialized periodicals. *FM* (1940–48, monthly) underwent several title changes as it broadened its coverage to deal with shortwave and television in addition to frequency modulation broadcasting. *Frequency Modulation Business* (1946–48, monthly) was even more focused on management issues, perhaps explaining its shorter life, given FM's quick initial postwar peak and slow demise at the end of the 1940s. Because of wartime production shortages, *Radio Retailing Today* (1942–44, monthly) had a short life. *Radio Showmanship* (began monthly publication in 1939) offered stories and features for advertisers and station executives on program ideas and promotions for different types of products.

As radio began to face fierce competition from television, previously radio-only publications expanded their coverage. *Broadcasting*, for example, became *Broadcasting Telecasting* from 1949 to 1957, devoting increasing space to television beyond that point, and *Radio Daily* focused more and more on the visual medium. *Sponsor* (1946–68, monthly) increasingly focused on television, having begun with a devotion to radio advertising. On the other hand, a growing number of specialized radio-only publications began to appear. *Inside Radio* (1976–present, weekly) is a newsletter aimed at radio executives, programmers, and syndicators that is filled with competitive tips in a no-advertising format.

Development of a host of competitive radio management and programming journals demonstrated radio's post-television comeback and the growing competition among both FM and AM stations. *Radio and Records* (1973–present, weekly), touting itself as "the industry's newspaper," built on the symbiotic relationship between recorded music and broadcasting, including widely used music playlists. Claude Hall's *The International Radio Report* (1978–present, weekly) plays a somewhat similar role, claiming "the most accurate [music popularity] charts in the world." *Radio Only* (1978–present, monthly) calls itself "the management tool" and deals with all aspects of radio management, sales, and programming. *Inside Radio* (1976–present, weekly) is "the confidential newsweekly for radio executives, programmers, and syndicators," focusing on hot news, sales tips, and ratings news. With the dramatic post-1996 ownership changes in the radio business, *Inside Radio* began to issue *Who Owns What* (weekly), a newsletter listing the merger and acquisition activity of major radio group owners.

Company Publications

Several manufacturers published their own trade journals, which sometimes rose above being mere advertising vehicles. Perhaps the first was a product of the Marconi Company, which began publishing the monthly *Wireless Age* in 1913, well before broadcasting began, and continued it until 1925. *RCA Review* (1936–85, quarterly) and *Broadcast News* (1941–68, monthly), both published by the Radio Corporation of America (RCA), largely touted company products and applications but also provided useful information on studios and broadcast equipment. The *Review* offered research papers by RCA engineers. Archival copies remain a useful way to trace station technical development and design. Philips, General Electric, and several other firms issued house organs as well, many of which focused on radio technology.

Association Publications

Issued for members of organizations, such as engineers or broadcast journalists, or for broader trade associations, these often focused on radio. Over the years, for example, the National Association of Broadcasters (NAB) issued many (usually monthly) periodicals concerning radio, including *FMphasis* in the 1960s as the FM industry began to grow again, and *Radio Active*, a monthly, which became *Radio Week* (1988–present, weekly). All of these focused on Washington policy concerns, general industry trends, and NAB activities—and took a strongly pro-industry point of view. The monthly *RTNDA Bulletin* (1952–70) and *Communicator* (1971–88) helped to tie the nation's news directors together with reviews of common problems, though from the beginning the focus was on television rather than radio. With a focus on stations devoted to Christian programs and music, *Religious Broadcasting* (1969–present, monthly) is a publication of the National Religious Broadcasters.

Technical Journals

Engineering association publications are technical in nature or focus on radio production techniques. *The Proceedings of the Institute of Radio Engineers* (1913–62, monthly) was the vehicle for many important technical announcements, including Edwin Armstrong's pioneering FM paper in 1936. Aimed at electrical engineers, its contents were wholly technical, with advertising to match. It has been superseded by a host of publications from the Institute of Electrical and Electronic Engineers. *Audio* (1954–present, monthly) has long dealt with "The World of Sound." It began as *Pacific Radio News* (1917–21), then became *Radio* (1921–47), and later became *Audio Engineering* (1947–54). The *Journal of the Audio Engineering Society* (1953–present, quarterly, monthly, then semimonthly) began as the *Broadcast Equipment Exchange*, a tabloid newspaper dealing with both new and used station equipment. It took on its present title in 1980 and broadened its coverage to station engineering management as well as new technology. *Mix* (1977–present, monthly) is one of the recording industry journals that blur the line dividing radio and sound studio work. First a quarterly and then a monthly, *Mix* offers information on both new technology and its applications.

Non-U.S. Publications

Naturally, a thriving broadcast trade press exists in several other nations as well. There is space here to cite only a few English language titles. *Broadcast* (1973–present, weekly) began in 1959 as *Television Mail* and has become the key trade periodical for British broadcasting, covering all aspects of radio and television, including the British Broadcasting Corporation (BBC) and commercial services. *Broadcaster* (1942–present, monthly) does the same thing for all aspects of Canadian radio and television broadcasting. It provides directory issues listing stations and systems plus related firms and associations twice a year. *Asian Broadcasting* is a Hong Kong-based bimonthly reporting on programming and business aspects of radio and television; it also issues a technical overview covering the region from Egypt to Japan. *The Asian Broadcasting Technical Review* (1969–present, bimonthly) reports on technical developments and equipment trends among Asian nations.

Modern Era (Since 1980)

By the 1980s, specialized radio publications broadened their comeback, encouraged by the continued growth of the industry. *Radio Ink: Radio's Premier Management and Marketing Magazine* (1985–present, monthly) deals with all aspects of commercial radio operation, especially programming. *Digital Radio News* (1990–present, bimonthly) is a newsletter that first appeared just as serious thinking about digital radio began. Although regular digital audio broadcasting has been delayed in the United States, this publication has reported on related terrestrial and satellite developments.

Online Publications

The rise of the internet as a means of effective business communication is very evident in the radio trade press. Indeed, in time, the internet will probably totally transform the whole trade press business. Many radio magazines, including *Billboard, Broadcasting & Cable, M Street, Radio Business Report, Radio Ink*, and *Radio & Records*, offer extensive online versions of their print publications, some available only to subscribers, others to all comers. *Streaming: The Business of Internet Media* (formerly *eRadio*, it is published by Eric Rhodes, who also issues *Radio Ink*) first appeared as a monthly in May 2000 and offers (fittingly) online features. *Radio World* offers readers an email updating service. *FMQB* (*Friday Morning Quarterback*) began in 1968 and is now a 50-plus page glossy weekly, covering programming, management, music, promotion, marketing, imaging, and airplay for various rock and rhythm crossover formats—with an extensive internet presence as well. Online versions of these titles often closely parallel the print editions, even to layout. But online editions often provide more stories and greater depth than the print version can.

Among the internet-only publications tracing the radio business, *Taylor on Radio-Info* (*TRI*) sees long-time radio authority Tom Taylor describe daily doings in commercial and educational radio on a free-on-request online newsletter, with an emphasis on programming and economic issues. *Inside Radio* is another daily online service, this one owned by the M Street publishing house. It created the weekly online *Who Owns What* to keep the fast-changing radio ownership scene current.

Others, such as the *Radio and Internet Newsletter* (founded in 1999), are primarily online publications. Such "publication," of course, is vastly less expensive in that printing and distribution costs are non-existent. Further, online publication allows regular updating, even new daily releases. How many of the internet-only publications can survive without a strong advertising or subscriber base, however, remains to be seen.

See also: Fan Magazines

Further Reading

Brown, Michael, "Radio Magazines and the Development of Broadcasting: *Radio Broadcast* and *Radio News*, 1922–1930," *Journal of Radio Studies* 5, no. 1 (1998).
The First 50 Years of "Broadcasting": The Running Story of the Fifth Estate, Washington, D.C.: Broadcasting, 1982.
Lyons, Floyd, "Publication Dates: Early U.S. Radio Magazines," *The Old Timer's Bulletin* 16, no. 2 (1975).
Slide, Anthony, editor, *International Film, Radio, and Television Journals*, Westport, Connecticut: Greenwood Press, 1985.
Sova, Harry, and Patricia Sova, editors, *Communication Serials*, Virginia Beach, Virginia: Sovacom, 1992.
Sterling, Christopher H., "Periodicals on Broadcasting, Cable, and Mass Media: A Selective Annotated Bibliography," *Broadcasting and Cable Yearbook* (1990–98).
Sterling, Christopher H., and George Shiers, "Periodicals," in *History of Telecommunications Technology: An Annotated Bibliography*, by Sterling and Shiers, Lanham, Maryland: Scarecrow Press, 2000.
Topicator: Classified Article Guide to the Advertising/Communications/Marketing Periodical Press (1965–).
Volek, Thomas, "Examining the Emergence of Broadcasting in the 1920s through Magazine Advertising," *Journal of Radio Studies* 3 (1993–94).

CHRISTOPHER H. STERLING,
2009 REVISIONS BY CHRISTOPHER H. STERLING

TRANSISTOR RADIOS

When the first transistor radio was introduced to the American market during the November 1954 holiday season, no-one recognized it as the precursor to a technological revolution. Apart from electronics buffs, consumers appeared to greet the miniature radios with a collective yawn.

The initial development of transistors in the late 1930s was conducted by physicists working for Bell Laboratories, the research division of American Telephone and Telegraph (AT&T). They were trying to create an electronic device that could replace vacuum tubes, something much smaller that would consume significantly less electricity and generate less heat. World War II interrupted those efforts. In 1948 Bell Labs announced the development of the transistor. William Shockley, John Bardeen, and Walter H. Brattain would share the 1956 Nobel Prize for Physics for its invention.

Texas Instruments (TI) was a small seismic-survey company that built its own survey equipment. During World War II, there was little demand for oil exploration, so the company used its electronics capability to build systems for anti-submarine warfare. In 1952 TI was one of 20 companies that paid Western Electric (the manufacturing division of AT&T) $25,000 for the right to produce transistors.

In 1954 TI constructed a transistorized pocket radio. Concerned that it was introducing an unknown in the consumer electronics market, TI took its six-transistor design to radio manufacturers. The reception, according to marketing director S.T. Harris, was unimpressive. His phone calls, letters, and telegrams to every major radio manufacturer in the United States produced no response.

Finally, in June 1954 a small Indiana company, the Industrial Development Engineers Association (IDEA), agreed that its Regency division would produce and market the 12-ounce, 3-inch by 5-inch radio. Production began in October just in time for Christmas sales in November. The TR-1 sold for $49.95, and the accompanying brochure extolled its pleasures: "in pocket or purse anytime, anywhere, you can be sure to hear that favorite program, be sure not to miss that vital installment of soap or horse or space opera, check scores, weather results, news, have music wherever you go at those times when music adds so much, and the Regency Radio can play for you alone without disturbing others around you or the whole group can share" (White, 1994).

Initially, consumers were slow to adopt transistor radios. After World War II, Americans wanted products that left behind the austerity of the war years. Automobiles and appliances were bigger and flashier. A tiny radio with an earphone resembling a hearing aid did not fit the American shopper's self-image as a prosperous trendsetter—and the relatively high price was an obstacle as well.

It was not until the end of the 1950s that the tiny portable radio would find its niche, but it would take the rock and roll revolution to fuel the increased demand for pint-size radios that teenagers could carry with them wherever they went. In 1955 Bill Haley and the Comets were the first to have a rock and roll record reach number one on the Billboard chart. "Rock Around the Clock" stayed in the number-one slot for eight weeks. A number of music historians mark the occasion as the birth of the rock and roll era.

Radio stations quickly realized that teenagers were a large part of the audience—and that they were clamoring to hear more Elvis, Paul Anka, the Everly Brothers, and others. Stations across the country quickly adopted the new Top 40 format. Parents were less than thrilled with rock music. "Turn that thing down," was the common refrain. Earplugs allowed teenagers to listen to transistor radios without antagonizing adults. The small size also permitted surreptitious listening while huddled under the covers at night after lights out. One of the inventors of the transistor is reported to have joked that he might have reconsidered the invention had he known it would allow kids across the United States ready access to rock and roll.

The head of International Business Machines (IBM), Thomas J. Watson, Jr., was another who recognized the importance of transistors. After reluctant engineers made little effort to incorporate transistor technology in computers they were designing, Watson bought several hundred Regency TR-I radios. He ordered that no more computers be built using vacuum tubes after 1 June 1958. To those engineers who complained, he gave a TR-1 to make his point. Soon IBM was building computers using transistors from TI, $200 million worth by 1960.

American radio manufacturers started building transistor radios in the mid-1950s, with nearly five million radios produced by Admiral, Arvin, Emerson, General Electric, Raytheon, Radio Corporation of America (RCA), Westinghouse, and Zenith by 1957. That same year, the first Japanese transistor radio was sold in the United States. It was manufactured by Tokyo Telecommunications Engineering Company, a new corporation created immediately following World War II. Soon its name would be changed to something catchier for the international market: Sony. Other Japanese companies quickly followed Sony's lead. By 1959, six million radios were coming into the United States from Japan, a highly successful launch into the world market of consumer microelectronics.

In 1960 almost 10 million transistor radios were sold in the United States. That number would increase to 27 million radios in 1969. No longer were they owned exclusively by young people. Americans of all ages had discovered the convenience of a tiny radio that could go anywhere. The transistor radio had become ubiquitous in American life. Baseball fans kept up with the World Series; American soldiers in Vietnam listened to Armed Forces Radio broadcasts.

In the 1960s, innovators realized the transistor radio apparatus fit nicely into a variety of small cases. Model cars, soft drink bottles, and wristwatches were among the many novelty radios that needed only a company's name and message to make it a successful advertising tool. Novelty radios continue to be popular today, coming in every shape imaginable from a radio in a stuffed teddy bear to a fish containing a water-resistant shower radio.

See also: Bell Telephone Laboratories; Emerson Radio; General Electric; Radio Corporation of America; Receivers; Rock and Roll Format; Walkman; Westinghouse; Zenith Radio Corporation

Further Reading

Handy, Roger, Maureen Erbe, and Aileen Antonier, *Made in Japan: Transistor Radios of the 1950s and 1960s*, San Francisco, California: Chronicle Books, 1993.
Schiffer, Michael Brian, *The Portable Radio in American Life*, Tucson: University of Arizona Press, 1991.
Smith, Norman R., *Transistor Radios: 1954–1968*, Atglen, Pennsylvania: Schiffer, 1998.
Ward, Jack, "The Transistor's Early History from 1947 to the 1960s," *Antique Radio Classified* 15 (December 1998).
White, David, "With the Collectors: The Regency TR-1," *Antique Radio Classified* 11 (September 1994).

SANDRA L. ELLIS

U

UNDERGROUND RADIO
Alternative and Free-Form Programming

The 1960s gave rise to one of radio's unique programming genres. During its short existence (1966–72), this format became known variously as progressive, alternative, free-form, psychedelic, and acid and was ultimately dubbed underground radio because of its unorthodox and eclectic mix of music and features and disc jockeys who broke from the traditional delivery style embraced by other youth-oriented stations of the day.

Origin

FM provided the fertile soil from which commercial underground radio would grow. It was where experimentation was permitted, because there was so little to lose at the time. Until the mid-1960s, FM moved along in low gear. A nearly negligible listenership provided FM with little status and currency among the general public and industry. It was perceived by many as the province of the so-called eggheads and the terminally unhip—the place to tune for Mahler and fine-arts programming. Tuning to FM for most people was like choosing to attend a foreign film with subtitles when there was a new action-packed Audey Murphy movie just around the corner. Most 20-year-olds had never tuned between 88 and 108 MHz, because the "in" music and "cool" disc jockeys were spinning the hits on AM.

Many social and cultural factors contributed to the rise of commercial underground stations. The repressive behavior and social conformity of the postwar years led to the volcanic eruption of the 1960s, particularly among youth. Political assassinations, racial upheaval, and an undeclared war in Asia, along with the growing use of mind-altering drugs by young people, contributed to the blossoming of what came to be called the counterculture.

Rock music began to more astutely and candidly reflect the troubles in American culture by incorporating thoughtful and challenging themes and more provocative and innovative scores and arrangements. The increasing popularity of rock albums among youth helped encourage FM stations to abandon their conventional fare and launched them on a quest for disenchanted and disenfranchised radio users—those who had rejected the 45 rpm-driven pop chart outlets. Also enhancing the enthusiasm for FM was its ability to broadcast in stereo—a process that recording companies had embraced for their bestselling groups and a feature that AM lacked.

Breaking the Mold

Several young programmers of the early 1960s had grown weary with the conventional sound of youth-oriented radio. Its frantic disc jockeys and two-and-a-half-minute doowop records left them wanting something more. The repetition and banality of Top 40 stations provided a primary impetus for movement in a very different direction. The pioneers of commercial underground radio, among them Tom Donahue, Larry Miller, Scott Muni, Thom O'Hair, Murray the K, Rosco, and Tom Gamache, took their lead from a couple of early

1960s noncommercial broadcasters and from a handful of innovators on the AM band in the 1950s, all of whom offered listeners a sound antithetical to the highly formulaic formats offered by mainstream stations.

Many stations claim to have debuted the new program genre, but two make the top of the list: WOR-FM in New York and KMPX-FM in San Francisco. The former went on the air in 1966 but changed format within a few months, and the latter was launched in 1967 and marked the beginning of a period in which the underground sound was sustained for several years. Within a year, KMPX lost its on-air staff during a strike to KSAN-FM, which grew to considerable prominence and won a special place in the underground firmament.

Although these stations are traditionally accorded landmark status, development of the underground format was foreshadowed by other stations as early as the 1950s. For example, WJR-AM in Detroit featured the "Buck Matthews Show," which mixed all kinds of music together in a fairly unrestricted, free-form way. Matthews employed a conversational, laid-back announcer style as well, which was atypical for disc jockeys of that day.

Other precursors to FM underground radio could be found on the AM band. For instance, Chicago's WCFL-AM offered a free form mix of rock music in the 1960s. Soon Newton, Massachusetts, had progressive rock over WNTN-AM. Other low-power AM stations experimented with the "open" technique to music programming, despite the fact that the format was nearly the exclusive domain of FM.

A number of noncommercial stations also presaged the arrival of commercial underground radio. Perhaps most significant among them were WBAI-FM and WFMU-FM. At the former, young disc jockey Bob Fass worked the overnight slot airing a program called *Radio Unnamable*. Across the river in New Jersey, college station WFMU-FM's Larry Yurdin was doing much the same thing by offering a creative and innovative mix of sounds. Undoubtedly, like those mentioned above, others helped set the stage for the surfacing of commercial underground radio, which got underway at about the same time on both coasts.

Most radio historians point to WOR-FM in New York as the first commercial outlet to break from the "primary" or single-format approach to music programming. However, the station's free form experiment lasted only a few months, and it was on to other things by the time KMPX-FM in San Francisco introduced Tom Donahue's version of the format in spring 1967. A few months after assuming the programming duties at KMPX-FM,

Donahue took on its sister station, KPPC-FM in southern California, simultaneously working his format magic at both.

The underground radioprogramming genre, the "nonformat" format, as it has been described, was soon emulated by stations around the country. By 1968 dozens of stations around the United States were offering listeners their own brand of underground radio. Most large metropolitan areas (including Detroit, Cleveland, Chicago, and St. Louis) boasted what many were calling "flower power" stations. This was no longer an avant-garde form of radio restricted to the enclaves of the East and West Coasts.

By late 1968 there were over 60 commercial underground radio stations in operation around the country. By the summer of 1969, San Francisco alone could claim a half dozen, whereas New York had only three. One company (Metromedia) owned the two stations that *Billboard* magazine ranked the top underground stations in the country—KSAN (San Francisco) and WNEW (New York).

At this early stage in underground radio's evolution, these two stations were frequently held up as models of the genre. Both attracted listeners and advertisers. Though often compared, the stations had forged their own distinct personas, mainly by creating unique and distinctive sounds that reflected not only the times and the areas in which they broadcast but also the philosophies of their programmers.

The "Nonformat" Format

Programmer Tom ("Big Daddy") Donahue considered the underground radio sound the antidote to Top 40, and by declaring this, he wanted to make it amply clear to everyone that things were being done quite differently at his station. In fact, he even rejected the notion of the term *format*, believing it had little to do with his new brand of radio. In his eyes, underground radio, if anything, was the antithesis of standard format programming because it embraced the best of rock, folk, traditional and city blues, electronic music, reggae, jazz, and even classical selections as opposed to any single type of music. This musical ecumenism was evident at underground stations around the country.

Indeed, the way in which songs were presented by undergrounders was unlike that of any other contemporary radio station at the time. Interestingly, if not ironically, these new outlets did reflect an older adult format, which had been responsible for bringing the FM band to a larger audience in the 1960s. Its name was beautiful music or, as many called it, "elevator" music. It was the Muzak format of the radio world. The common ground between the two seemingly disparate forms of radio programming was the way in which they structured music into sweeps—that is, uninterrupted segments or blocks—typically of a quarter-hour's duration. Evolving from the sweep approach was the idea of music sets, wherein a series of album cuts would establish a particular theme or motif.

Just as the approach to music programming in underground was antithetical to conventional AM radio, particularly Top 40, announcing styles were no less contrary to the long-standing norm. Since the medium's inception in the early 1920s, announcing techniques had undergone relatively subtle changes, never wandering too far from the affected "radio-ese" presentation style. The old-line announcing manner, characterized by its air of formality and self-consciousness, remained prevalent well into the second coming of the radio medium after the arrival of television.

The "stilts," as they have been called, found their way into the FM band as well, migrating to the beautiful music format and others. This announcing style was emphatically rejected by underground stations, which militated against its disingenuous affectations and mannerisms—the hype and histrionics. However, sounding "hip" was considered acceptable and even preferable, but not hip like the "screamers" on Top 40. Underground disc jockeys were intent on projecting a natural, friendly, and mild-mannered "grooviness" when they were on the air. In fact, the "stoned" announcer persona was often an integral part of this radio genre's repertoire. The idea was to be at one with the audience in every way possible. Staying "loose" was the underground disc jockey's mantra.

As with all formats, there are other programming ingredients besides the music and announcing that contribute to a station's general appeal, identity, and overall listenability. News and information broadcasts represent one of those elements. Despite the underground radio's dominant emphasis on album music designed for an under-30 crowd, it differed from other youth-oriented music outlets in that news and public-affairs features were frequently regarded as an integral part of what many of these stations sought to convey to their public. That is, they wished to be perceived as members of the caring and socially conscious community and not simply as record machine operators.

The Fate of the Nonformat Format

As the counterculture movement of the 1960s and early 1970s faded, so did commercial underground radio. Many members of the movement were embracing more mainstream and traditional goals and aspirations, if not values, while the anger and altruism inherent in rock music for nearly a decade bowed to the insipid patter and rhythms of disco and new-wave or "corporate" rock. Underground radio became a thing of the past as the baby boomers sought a less uncertain and chaotic future, taking refuge in that once unsavory realm known as the material world. A survey of published perspectives and conventional wisdom on the 1960s and 1970s and on the underground radio phenomenon itself reveals that numerous factors came into play that ultimately contributed to the nonformat's rather swift departure from the airwaves.

In addition to the changing cultural mores and attitudes, which diminished the relevance and appeal of the underground sound, the growing profitability of FM radio inspired a shift away from the nonformat programming approach to something with more advertiser appeal. Station owners sought greater control over program content to maximize bottom-line figures and profits. The role of disc jockeys in shaping the air product returned to the executive suit. FM was corporatized in the 1970s, and by the middle of the decade, commercial underground radio had been reconstituted in the form of album-oriented rock—a highly structured and formulaic offshoot of the former free form sound.

Further Reading

Anderson, Terry H., *The Movement and the Sixties*, New York: Oxford University Press, 1995.
Fornatale, Peter, and Joshua E. Mills, *Radio in the Television Age*, Woodstock, New York: Overlook Press, 1980.
Görg, Alan, *The Sixties: Biographies of the Love Generation*, Marina Del Ray, California: Media Associates, 1995.
Keith, Michael C., *Voices in the Purple Haze: Underground Radio and the Sixties*, Westport, Connecticut: Praeger, 1997.
Krieger, Susan, *Hip Capitalism*, Beverly Hills, California: Sage, 1979.
Ladd, Jim, *Radio Waves: Life and Revolution on the FM Dial*, New York: St. Martin's Press, 1991.

MICHAEL C. KEITH

UNITED FRUIT COMPANY
Early Wireless System Operator

Spurred by its need to communicate with its many banana plantations and with its shipping fleet, the United Fruit Company became a pioneer wireless operator in the early 20th century. Company operators developed many early radio techniques and helped to pioneer networking of stations and the use of crystal detector receivers in high-humidity conditions.

Origins

Through the merger of the Boston Fruit Company and other companies involved with the production of bananas in the Caribbean, the United Fruit Company was formed in 1899. The largest banana company in the world, the United Fruit Company was also the first transnational, corporate giant in the Americas. During the 20th century, the United Fruit Company would have a significant impact, both positive and negative, on many Central American nations, including Guatemala, Honduras, and Costa Rica. The company's influence in these countries was pervasive, extending into the political, transportation, and communication systems.

At its formation, the United Fruit Company owned banana plantations in seven countries throughout the Caribbean area. The need for efficient means to harvest and transport the perishable banana product was of paramount concern, as errors in the timing of banana deliveries to United States markets often resulted in spoiled cargoes. As a result, the United Fruit Company took an aggressive role in developing railroad links to deliver the bananas to coastal ports for shipping. Because timely communications were essential to coordinate the harvesting and delivery of the bananas, the company also built and maintained telegraph and telephone lines between farms, local company headquarters, and Caribbean ports. Difficult terrain made the construction of land-lines impractical in some areas, however, and the tropical weather conditions and political instabilities often rendered them unreliable when they were built. In addition, communication from shore to ship and from ship to ship required the use of radio. Faced with these obstacles, the United Fruit Company became one of the first companies, and the only major American company, to invest major capital and manpower into developing and adopting the new telecommunications mode of radio.

Implementing Wireless

During the summer of 1903, United Fruit Company employee and electrical engineer Mack Musgrave began investigating the possibilities of using radio for company business in Central America. United Fruit bought its first radio equipment from the American De Forest Wireless Company in 1904 and established its first two stations approximately 150 miles apart at Bocas del Toro, Panama, and Puerto Limon, Costa Rica. In 1906 two more stations were built at Bluefields and Rama, Nicaragua. The expenditures for these and future facilities were great, but the costs were deemed a necessity for company development. United Fruit faced many obstacles in its efforts to establish a radio communications network. One important obstacle was the comparative youth of the radio industry and the experimental nature of its equipment. Unlike the case today, transmission distances were relatively short and required the construction of relay stations throughout the Caribbean. Static, common to the tropics, interrupted transmissions and often made the point-to-point radio links unreliable. In addition, hurricanes destroyed island relay stations with alarming frequency.

By 1908 the United Fruit Company had built six more shore stations and had installed radio equipment on all of its ships. Later known as "The Great White Fleet," these ships delivered bananas but also transported passengers between the United States and the Caribbean. In addition to serving the company's needs in transporting its product, the radio network became an essential tool for ensuring the safety and convenience of the fleet's passengers. Recognizing the further commercial value of the network, United Fruit also made its communications system available to paying customers along the Caribbean coast and thus became Latin America's major commercial alternative to the European owned and operated radio systems of Marconi and Telefunken.

Now an independent provider of radio communications services, United Fruit purchased a controlling interest in the Wireless Specialty Apparatus Company in 1912. This acquisition provided United Fruit with ownership to important radio technology patents and thus the means to develop and manufacture advanced equipment. United Fruit would continue to operate the Wireless Specialty Apparatus Company until 1921 when, through a complicated process of corporate patent pooling, the newly formed Radio Corporation of America became owner of the patent rights.

In 1913 the United Fruit Company radio department was formally incorporated as a wholly owned subsidiary named the Tropical Radio Telegraph Company. The Tropical Radio Telegraph Company took over all company ship stations and most of the land stations. By 1920, the United Fruit Company had invested nearly $4 million in radio. The Tropical Radio Telegraph Company had established an extensive radio network including a radio-telephone communication system serving the general public and the banana trade and connecting many of the principal population centers of the Caribbean to the United States.

The United Fruit Company's remarkable adoption of the fledgling radio technology and its development of a large, privately owned radio communications system in Latin America is a success story. Other companies, including the U.S. Rubber Company subsidiary Amazon Wireless Telephone and Telegraph established in 1901, failed where United Fruit had succeeded. Numerous factors supporting the United Fruit Company's ultimate success in developing its radio system include the dominating U.S. influence in Central America, which assured minimal or no opposition to United Fruit's expansions; the demand for radio communication by passengers on the company ships and by shore customers complementing the banana business communication needs; and the fact that the United Fruit Company's product, bananas, was an economically stable product.

See also: Crystal Receivers; Early Wireless

Further Reading

Douglas, Susan J., *Inventing American Broadcasting, 1899–1922*, Baltimore, Maryland: Johns Hopkins University Press, 1987.
Mason, Roy, "The History of the Development of the United Fruit Company's Radio Telegraph System," *Radio Broadcast* (September 1922).
Melville, John H., *The Great White Fleet*, New York: Vantage Press, 1976.
Schubert, Paul, *The Electric Word: The Rise of Radio*, New York: Macmillan, 1928; reprint, New York: Arno Press, 1971.
Schwoch, James, *The American Radio Industry and Its Latin American Activities, 1900–1939*, Urbana: University of Illinois Press, 1990.
Wilson, Charles Morrow, *Empire in Green and Gold: The Story of the American Banana Trade*, New York: Holt, 1947.

DOUGLAS K. PENISTEN

UNITED STATES CONGRESS AND RADIO
Broadcasting of House and Senate Proceedings

Congress and radio broadcasting have been closely linked for more than 90 years. By virtue of the U.S. Constitution's "commerce clause," Congress has created and amended basic legislation to regulate the industry. It has also funded regulatory agencies and approved appointments to them. But only after years of debate was regular broadcast coverage of Congressional committee and floor activity finally allowed, thereby joining the long-time use of broadcasting media by individual members seeking reelection.

Legislative interest in radio began with the 1910 Wireless Ship Act that regulated maritime use of radio. The Radio Act of 1912 was the first comprehensive radio statute, but it was not designed to regulate radio broadcasting, which did not then exist. During and after World War I, Congress heard testimony from the military and from the Post Office urging federal control and operation of radio broadcasting. Turning away from that option, Congress was perplexed over what to do to regulate early radio broadcasting, and it did not pass the first law designed to regulate broadcasting until the Radio Act of 1927. The new law laid the regulatory foundation of U.S. broadcasting, and most of it is still in effect today. In mid-1934, acting on recommendations from President Roosevelt and its own extensive investigation of communication companies, Congress passed the comprehensive Communications Act of 1934, which is still in force in amended form nearly seven decades later. In the years since, Congress has regularly tinkered with the law, considering and sometimes adopting amendments (of which the Telecommunications Act of 1996 was by far the most extensive). When not actually legislating, Congress plays three other regulatory roles with radio: it provides annual budgets for operation of the Federal Communications Commission (FCC) and related agencies; the Senate approves (nearly always) presidential nominations of FCC commissioners; and commerce committees in both houses regularly conduct "oversight" hearings into industry and FCC activities and decisions.

Seeking to Broadcast Congress

From the inception of radio, some members of Congress perceived the new medium as the perfect way to carry the people's business to those unable to travel to Washington to visit the House and Senate in person. And such coverage would provide radio with just the kind of content that would help popularize the medium.

Efforts to initiate some form of congressional radio began with a resolution introduced by Representative Vincent Brennan (R-Michigan) in 1922 that was intended to allow for the "installation and operation of radiotelephone transmitting apparatus for the purpose of transmitting the proceedings and debates of the Senate and the House of Representatives." Though the Brennan resolution failed, its intent remained alive when Senator

Robert Howell (R-Nebraska) introduced a resolution two years later directing that radio experts from the War and Navy Departments be appointed to study the feasibility of "broadcasting by radio of the proceedings of the Senate and the House of Representatives throughout the country, utilizing the radio stations of the War and Navy Departments." As the Senate discussed the Howell resolution, several arguments were made for and against broadcasting from the congressional chambers that would be repeated in years to come. On the one hand, listeners to congressional debate could hear their elected officials engage in the country's business—and in the process, that debate would be improved in order to give listeners a good impression of Congress. On the other hand, listeners' impressions might be detrimental to congressional members whose speaking skills were not up to radio standards or who were absent during chamber debate.

The report prepared by the War and Navy Departments finally materialized in 1927; the report concluded that broadcasting from the House and Senate chambers would be not only too costly, but also technically infeasible. This effectively ended any substantive efforts to implement congressional radio. Nonetheless, the idea remained alive. In fact, it was invigorated by radio's coverage of President Calvin Coolidge's 4 March 1925 inaugural address. Excitement over the president's radio remarks led the editor of *Radio Broadcast* to "hope that soon Congress will be forced to broadcast its activities." The editor's remark ironically draws attention to another argument that would be used in years to come by congressional broadcasting advocates: that of the imbalance in power that the president's effective use of radio caused with regard to clashes between presidential policy initiatives and congressional policy initiatives.

Efforts to persuade their congressional colleagues to allow broadcasting of Senate and House proceedings were continued by members of both bodies, most notably by Senators Clarence Dill (D-Washington) and Gerald Nye (R-North Dakota), into the 1940s. Meanwhile, parliamentary bodies in other countries experimented with broadcasting deliberative activities during the late 1920s. Germany and Japan were two countries where the idea seemed to be catching hold. The British House of Commons considered but rejected the idea of broadcasting its parliamentary sessions in 1926.

Congressional broadcasting of a very limited and decidedly clandestine nature did occur in December 1932, when the U.S. House voted on the repeal of the 18th Amendment. Radio network representatives had requested permission from House Speaker John Nance Garner (D-Texas) to cover debate on the matter from the House chamber. Undeterred by Speaker Garner's refusal to grant permission, the networks positioned microphones in the doorway of a library adjoining the House chamber and boosted the microphones' volume high enough to pick up the proceedings. Radio listeners had the rare privilege of hearing the repeal vote as it occurred. Afterwards, the *New York Times* took note of the event, saying that "broadcasters have taken a new hope that before long radio will invade Congress just as it has almost every other realm where people speak or sing."

Interest in congressional broadcasting emanated from other directions during the 1940s. For instance, a number of organizations, including the Congress of Industrial Organizations, the Writers War Board, and others, advocated allowing radio coverage of congressional proceedings. World War II certainly stimulated interest in the matter, but more important were the shortcomings of newspapers during the period in properly informing the public about congressional consideration and discussion of important wartime issues. A 1946 poll showed that the general public favored the idea of congressional broadcasting, and a poll of radio executives taken at roughly the same time showed that an overwhelming 70 percent of them also favored such broadcasts.

The first serious consideration of congressional broadcasting occurred during hearings conducted by the Joint Committee on the Organization of Congress in 1945. The committee, co-chaired by Senator Robert M. LaFollette, Jr. (Progressive-Wisconsin) and Representative Mike Monroney (D-Oklahoma), was charged with exploring methods to improve the legislative process. Witnesses at hearings addressed many of the issues about congressional broadcasting that had been raised before. The issues dealt with both style (public reaction to poor or verbose speakers, to the Senate filibuster, or to the absent speaker) and substance (equal treatment of important issues during floor debate and the manner by which chamber proceedings from the House as well as the Senate might be broadcast simultaneously). Advocates for congressional broadcasting failed to win a great following, and in the end the Legislative Reorganization Act of 1946 that evolved from the work of the Joint Committee on the Organization of Congress ignored broadcasting.

Initial Efforts

Interest in congressional broadcasting changed direction by the late 1940s after television forced radio into a secondary role. Members of Congress had grown more at ease with broadcasting in general and thus were willing if not eager to allow television cameras to cover congressional hearings. Rules devised by each congressional committee soon emerged to regulate such coverage; these rules placed television and radio on an equal footing. Committee members had final approval as to whether television and radio could cover committee proceedings, but television and radio networks and stations that controlled the cameras and microphones determined how much of the proceedings would be broadcast. Several famous Senate investigations were televised in the 1950s, including the Kefauver crime hearings in 1951 and the Army-McCarthy hearings in 1954. Radio networks and local stations rarely chose to carry more than short excerpts from committee proceedings during newscasts. Only during the 1970s did National Public Radio (NPR) break tradition by airing some of the more notable congressional hearings virtually gavel-to-gavel, such as a hearing on a new Panama Canal treaty.

Efforts to regularly broadcast House and Senate chamber proceedings were reignited in the early 1970s, possibly owing to successful broadcasts of committee proceedings. The matter received special attention by the Joint Committee on Congressional Operations in 1973. The favorable view taken by the committee—that broadcasting from the House and Senate chambers could help Congress better communicate with the public—led directly to a decision by the House of Representatives to open itself to television cameras and radio microphones in March 1979. The Senate was slower to act but finally opened its own chamber to television and radio in June 1986.

Regular Live Coverage

Ironically, the Senate actually preceded the House in allowing live broadcast coverage to originate from the Senate chamber. A resolution introduced by Senator Robert Byrd (D-West Virginia) in 1977 called for the Senate to allow broadcast coverage of debate over ratification of the controversial Panama Canal Treaty, approval of which would return control of the Panama Canal from the United States to Panama. Senator Byrd's resolution would have allowed both television and radio coverage of the debate, which began on 8 February 1978, but unresolved technical questions forced the Senate to drop plans for television and to allow exclusive coverage to radio. The Columbia Broadcasting System (CBS) and the National Broadcasting Company (NBC) aired portions of the debate,

and NPR aired the entire debate, with only brief interruptions to identify speakers.

Not to be outdone by the Senate, House Speaker Thomas "Tip" O'Neill (D-Massachusetts) announced that beginning on 12 June 1978, radio networks, stations, and news organizations would be able to pick up feeds from the House audio system for broadcast. The decision came in response to a request by Associated Press (AP) Radio. As it happened, AP Radio elected to carry only five minutes of live House debate on the day that radio was finally given a green light to cover chamber proceedings. This brief coverage, however, outdid other radio networks, which carried only brief taped excerpts of House debate during regular newscasts.

Just as rules exist for broadcast of congressional committee proceedings, so do similar rules exist for broadcast coverage of House and Senate floor debate. The Speaker of the House has final authority over all broadcast activity from that body, but House rules also stipulate that coverage of chamber proceedings must be unedited and must not be used for political purposes or commercial advertisements. The Senate Rules and Administration Committee has ultimate authority over the Senate broadcasting system, but the Senate sergeant at arms is authorized to act in the committee's behalf. The same rules on editing and on the political and commercial use of chamber broadcasts that exist in the House also govern the Senate.

Anything that emanates from the microphones in the House and Senate chambers may be broadcast by any radio network or station. As is the case with committee proceedings, neither networks nor stations generally choose to air more than brief excerpts of floor debate. A departure from that practice occurred during the House impeachment and Senate trial of President Bill Clinton. Radio coverage of these two events in 1998–9 was extensive, and over NPR coverage was gavel-to-gavel. NPR and other public broadcasting stations would largely repeat this level of coverage in 2004, for hearings on the 9/11 commission report, and again in 2008, for Iraq War hearings.

Radio and Individual Members of Congress

The unsuccessful efforts to ignite interest in broadcasting chamber debates during the 1920s and 1930s might have stemmed from radio network policies that allowed U.S. senators and representatives free airtime. Records show, in fact, that between 1928 and 1940, CBS allowed some 700 U.S. senators and some 500 House members to speak on the network.

Possibly spurred by the interest shown in congressional radio during the 1945 Joint Committee on the Organization of Congress, in 1948 Robert Coor created a commercial operation known as the Joint Radio Information Facility, which provided a recording studio for individual members of Congress to record speeches and interviews for use by radio networks or local radio stations. Congress brought recording under its own control as part of the Legislative Appropriations Act in 1956, creating separate House and Senate recording studios. Studio operating costs were covered by charges to those members of Congress who actually used them. In later years, both the House and the Senate studios were upgraded for television and for live links with news-gathering organizations via satellite. And besides the congressional studios, individual senators and representatives by the 1990s had access to recording facilities operated by the Democratic and Republican parties.

Radio used purely as a campaign tool—a practice nearly as old as broadcasting itself—stands apart from the other uses of radio already noted. The first known use of radio for campaigning occurred in 1922, when Senator Harry S. New (R-Indiana) used the U.S. Navy's radio station in Washington, D.C., to address his constituents at home. The *New York Times* took note of the occasion, saying that "campaigning by radio soon might leave the field of novelty and become a practical everyday proposition during political fights." The small first step into campaign radio became a rush by 1924.

Radio was readily regarded as a valuable campaign tool, but fears arose over the possibility that those who owned radio stations might create unfair advantages by allowing candidates whom they supported easy access to the airwaves, while refusing to allow use of their radio facilities to candidates whom they opposed. The issue was thoroughly discussed during the Washington Radio Conferences, with the resulting recommendation that Congress include some provision in the Radio Act of 1927 that would ensure not only that there would be equal opportunities for use of radio facilities by candidates for public office, but also that the content of any campaign message via radio would not be censored. The recommendation was approved by Congress and fashioned into Section 18 of the Radio Act, which was transferred intact as Section 315 of the Communications Act of 1934. Section 315 required that equal opportunities be extended to political candidates after their opponents had been granted use of a broadcasting facility. Broadcasters were still free to decide whether to extend initial use of their facilities for campaign purposes.

That changed somewhat in 1971, when Congress amended the Communications Act to include language in Section 312 that required broadcasters to provide time for legally qualified candidates for federal elective office.

Radio and the Contemporary Congress

Radio's coverage of Congress is, in one sense, expanding. Members often design messages to match variously formatted stations in their home districts to reach intended audiences (e.g., a right-to-life argument aired on a gospel outlet). Despite the advent of online services (including dedicated webpages and Facebook profiles), texting and Twitter, radio remains a vital tool in political campaigns. Radio is less expensive than television, has the potential to reach far more voters than online or other digital platforms, and allows candidates to "target" messages. Talk radio, one of the most popular formats early in the 21st century, has an insatiable appetite for guests willing and able to discuss a wide range of issues. By and large, talk radio tends to be dominated more by highly opinionated hosts rather than congressional voices. And it is also heavily dominated by conservative ranters like Rush Limbaugh and Sean Hannity. The political right's seemingly solid hold on the air has caused some representatives (mainly Democrats) to call for reviving the defunct FCC Fairness Doctrine. Though unlikely, a reinstated doctrine is a threat Congress can exert to exact influence over radio.

See also: Communications Act of 1934; "Equal Time" Rule; Politics and Radio; Radio Laws; Telecommunications Act of 1996

Further Reading

Archer, Gleason Leonard, *History of Radio to 1926*, New York: American Historical Society, 1938; reprint, New York: Arno Press, 1971.

Chester, Edward W., *Radio, Television, and American Politics*, New York: Sheed and Ward, 1969.

Garay, Ronald, *Congressional Television: A Legislative History*, Westport, Connecticut: Greenwood Press, 1984.

Garay, Ronald, "Broadcasting of Congressional Proceedings," in *The Encyclopedia of the United States Congress*, edited by Donald C. Bacon, Roger H. Davidson, and Morton Keller, New York: Simon and Schuster, 1995.

Jones, David, "Political Talk Radio: The Limbaugh Effect on Primary Voters," *Political Communication* 15 (1998).

Kahn, Frank J., editor, *Documents of American Broadcasting*, New York: Appleton-Century-Crofts, 1968.

Katz, Jeffrey, "Studios Beam Members from Hill to Hometown," *Congressional Quarterly* 29 (November 1997).

Ostroff, David, "Equal Time: Origins of Section 18 of the Radio Act of 1927," *Journal of Broadcasting* 24 (Summer 1980).

Sarno, Edward, "The National Radio Conferences," *Journal of Broadcasting* 13 (Spring 1969).

Smith, F. Leslie, Milan D. Meeske, and John W. Wright II, *Electronic Media and Government: The Regulation of Wireless and Wired Mass Communication in the United States*, White Plains, New York: Longman, 1995.

RONALD GARAY,
2009 REVISIONS BY CARY O'DELL

UNITED STATES NAVY AND RADIO

During the first two decades of the 20th century, the U.S. Navy served as a principal force in the development of radio communications in the United States. From the introduction of practical radio systems at the turn of the century to the beginning of U.S. radio broadcasting in the early 1920s, the Navy's influence on American radio was powerful and multifaceted. These significant influences included the application and expansion of radio for military and diplomatic purposes, the control of radio communications, technological developments, and the fostering of development in the radio industry.

Origins

At the beginning of the 20th century, electrical communication by telegraph and telephone provided Navy officials with rapid communications between most ports and naval stations worldwide. At sea, the situation was radically different. When a ship left port and disappeared over the horizon, it was isolated from shore communications. Free of new directives from Washington, the captain and fleet could act with complete autonomy.

The invention of radio communications and its application to maritime use brought both benefits and difficulties to the Navy. Some naval officials recognized very early the strategic and tactical benefits of being able to communicate between distant ships and from ship to shore, but the adoption and widespread use of radio on shore and ship installations was slow in coming. The early resistance to radio in the Navy can be attributed to several factors, including the traditional bound bureaucracy and the strong desire of many naval officers to preserve the independence a captain traditionally exercised at sea. To many naval officers, radio was viewed as the ultimate centralizing force from Washington. The Japanese Navy's success in using radio during the 1904–05 Russo–Japanese War aided in diminishing this resistance.

The Navy first tested radio apparatus in 1899, but serious attention and further testing did not occur again until 1901. Over the next decade, the navy tested and purchased various types of wireless equipment from both U.S. and foreign countries, often resulting in stations with unfavorable composite equipment. The Navy was an early and important potential client for new radio companies; it exerted a positive force in developing the U.S. radio industry, but it was also a force to be reckoned with. Inventors eager to gain valuable Navy contracts regularly found themselves frustrated by the Navy's hardball business tactics and lack of respect for patent rights. The Navy simply acquired equipment as needed and from whom they wanted, regularly ignoring patent restrictions. Complicating the Navy's relationship with U.S. radio equipment suppliers was the perception that the Navy often gave preference to foreign companies. A clear exception to this was its negative attitude toward the British Marconi Company.

The Navy's strong aversion to the Marconi Company and its equipment can be traced to concerns about British domination of the world cable system. Navy fears that the Marconi Company would grow to dominate radio communications, and therefore establish a British hegemony over worldwide communications, were very strong. As a result, Marconi equipment was rejected and the Navy began a two-decade-long effort to establish U.S. control of its own radio communications. Radio waves do not recognize national borders, and the need to dominate and so control the ether was a compelling security issue for Navy officials.

Beginning with the 1903 international radio conference in Berlin, the Navy took on the leadership role of representing U.S. radio interests worldwide. This leadership role had great influence over two decades of shaping the evolving international radio regulations. The Navy's influence in directing self-serving lobbying efforts was also ever-present on the Washington political scene. Congress recognized the importance of radio for the Navy and the national interest, placing the Navy in an influential and dominant position, especially for federal funding. Despite the Navy's efforts to support legislation that would wrest control of radio from commercial and amateur interests, however, access to the airwaves by nonmilitary operators and interests prevailed.

World War I

U.S. entry into World War I on 6 April 1917 changed the entire radio communications scene. The following day, with the exception of army-operated transmitters, the Navy took control of all radio stations in the United States, acquiring 53 commercial stations and closing another 28 transmitters. In addition, all amateur radio stations were shut down "for the duration" of the war. In one swift move the Navy had taken control of the entire radio communications system in the United States, along with its existing international ship and port radio system.

Because of the sudden increase in radio communication traffic, Navy orders for equipment from private manufacturers increased dramatically. The Navy's centralized control over the equipping of ship and shore stations produced many improvements in equipment quality and, importantly, standardization in equipment design. The Navy also conducted significant wartime research and development in radio technology, greatly improving the consistency and quality of long-distance radio communications.

With the complete takeover of radio communications by the Navy, the question arose as to what would happen at the war's end. After the armistice on 11 November 1918, Secretary of the Navy Josephus Daniels began a strong lobbying effort for legislation that would leave radio permanently under Navy control. His efforts ultimately failed—Congress was in no mood to continue an activist federal establishment—and government control of the wartime-seized radio stations was eventually relinquished. On 11 July 1919 President Wilson ordered that all commercial stations be returned to their original owners by 1 March 1920. In addition, amateur radio stations were allowed to resume operation on 1 October 1919.

Radio Corporation of America

The Navy's postwar loss of the control of radio communications was a blow to its geopolitical aspirations, but its influence and power were still very significant. The drive to assure the U.S. a major role in global radio communications and to prevent the British Marconi Company from obtaining too strong a foothold in the U.S. communications market resulted in the Navy initiating and facilitating the formation of the Radio Corporation of America (RCA).

The specific technological innovation driving the navy's concern was the Alexanderson alternator, then the only effective means of achieving long-range radio communication. Developed from designs of Reginald Fessenden and greatly improved by General Electric (GE) engineer Ernst F.W. Alexanderson,

rights to the device were controlled by GE. But GE was not interested in getting into the service side of radio; the company defined its role as a manufacturer and sought to sell the devices to recoup its extensive investment. Beginning during the war (1915), the most likely purchaser appeared to be Britain's Marconi Company, which, however, sought full and exclusive rights to the alternator. GE was tempted at what would be a lucrative agreement. Navy officials, including assistant secretary Franklin Roosevelt, however, expressed strong concern about such an important device passing into the hands of even a friendly (but still foreign) country. Navy officials pressed GE to seek a domestic means of selling the alternator.

GE's concern paralleled another: the wartime pooling of radio patents so that manufacturers could perfect the best possible radio equipment for army and navy procurement contracts. The end of the war also ended the patent pools, and companies faced the need to develop a peacetime pool if radio was to continue its development. These related needs—GE's for the alternator, and the industry at large to develop a peacetime patent pool—led to the rise of RCA.

Through a series of complex company buyouts and new patent pooling agreements, General Electric established the Radio Corporation of America as a subsidiary in October 1919, and important technological patents (the alternator among them) were eventually pooled under RCA's corporate umbrella, thus preventing any possibility of British radio communications hegemony within the United States. Ownership in RCA was later spun off and it became the single most important firm in early radio broadcasting development.

See also: Early Wireless; General Electric; Radio Corporation of America; United States Congress and Radio

Further Reading

Aitken, Hugh G.J., *The Continuous Wave: Technology and American Radio, 1900–1932*, Princeton, New Jersey: Princeton University Press, 1985.

Douglas, Susan J., *Inventing American Broadcasting, 1899–1922*, Baltimore, Maryland: Johns Hopkins University Press, 1987.

Gebhard, Louis, *Evolution of Naval Radio-Electronics and Contributions of the Naval Research Laboratory*, Washington, D.C.: Naval Research Laboratory, 1976.

Howeth, Linwood S., *History of Communications Electronics in the United States Navy*, Washington, D.C.: Government Printing Office, 1963.

Hugill, Peter J., *Global Communications since 1844: Geopolitics and Technology*, Baltimore, Maryland: Johns Hopkins University Press, 1999.

King, Randolph, and Prescott Palmer, editors, *Naval Engineering and American Seapower*, Baltimore, Maryland: Nautical and Aviation of America, 1989.

DOUGLAS K. PENISTEN

UNITED STATES PRESIDENCY AND RADIO

On 21 June 1923, when President Warren Harding stepped to the microphone to deliver a speech on the World Court from St. Louis as part of his tour of the western United States, he spoke not just to the citizens of St. Louis, but to those in Washington, D.C., and New York as well. This was the first time that a chain or network of radio stations had been assembled to carry a presidential message simultaneously to several parts of the nation. The speech was heard in St. Louis over KSA and in New York and Washington over American Telephone and Telegraph (AT&T) stations WEAF and WCAP, respectively. Perhaps one million Americans heard Harding speak, more than any president had reached before. No longer was a president bound by the flatness of daily newspaper coverage or the geographical limitations of single-station radio coverage; he now had the potential to speak to the entire electorate at once, a power that would enlarge the "bully pulpit" beyond any expectation of the day. With a single flip of the switch, broadcasters could help a president rise above his adversaries in Congress and go directly to the people.

A strong national broadcasting system contributed to a strong presidency. A politician whose voice commanded attention in every corner of the land simultaneously could build a strong national constituency. Conversely, a strong presidency contributed to a strong national broadcasting system. Presidential speeches created a demand and provided one of the few programs that could unite American interests. The American people were eager to hear their national leader over the fascinating new medium of radio, and broadcasters were pleased to be the purveyors.

Early Experiments in Networking

After the success of his first attempt at chain broadcasting in St. Louis, President Harding tried another major speech in Kansas City and had scheduled still another big speech on 31 July 1923. For the occasion, AT&T assembled its first coast-to-coast linkup stretching from San Francisco to New York. Radio had become such an important part of President Harding's western tour that he installed a powerful radio transmitter in his railroad car to give him a mobile broadcasting studio.

Harding died while on his western trip, and within a few days of his death the National Association of Broadcasters (NAB) was proposing to the new president, Calvin Coolidge, that he substitute radio addresses for public appearances to conserve his health and reach a wider audience. By the end of 1923, as the 1924 campaign approached, President Coolidge heeded the advice and took to the airwaves regularly. When Coolidge spoke to Congress at the end of the year, AT&T assembled a chain of seven stations to carry the speech. The president followed that speech with five additional nationally broadcast addresses. The 1924 party conventions reached an estimated 25 million listeners, and the subsequent campaign provided abundant opportunities for chain broadcasting.

A small group of broadcasters questioned whether politicians should be turned loose on radio. At the NAB's first convention in October 1923, John Shepard, III, of WNAC proposed that a political party applying for airtime be required to give comparable time to a speaker from the opposing party. The NAB accepted the measure and followed these "equal time" ground rules during the 1924 campaign. Presidential speeches, however, were not considered "political" except during campaigns and were not subjected to any "right of reply" mechanism until the campaign actually started. Still, voices were raised early to warn of the dangers of a one-sided political dialog in which the party and congressional opposition had no standing.

By 1924 proponents of chain broadcasting had realized that politics was the perfect bait to lure America into a permanent national system of broadcasting. The presidential election campaign that year provided ample opportunities for demonstrating the virtues of chain broadcasting. AT&T was poised to erect a permanent network of stations and believed that political speeches were an excellent way to ensure frequent use of a system that could reach 78 percent of the nation's purchasing power through the top 24 markets.

The closer the fledgling broadcasting industry could bring itself to the presidency, the higher the status it could bring on itself. Thus, initially there was little concern for the newsworthiness of presidential addresses. Broadcasters saw presidential broadcasting as a means of providing a public service and basking in the prestige of the presidency. Given the open-ended invitation extended early on to presidents by broadcasters, it is no wonder that presidents ever since have regarded their access as a right of the office.

The *New York Times* reported in 1924, "It is a source of wonder to many listeners how a speaker can sit in the White House or stand before Congress and have his voice simultaneously enter the ether over Washington, New York and Providence." The inauguration of Calvin Coolidge on 4 March 1925 showed how far chain broadcasting had come in less than two years. On that day, President Coolidge reached at least 15 million Americans over a hookup of 21 stations from coast to coast. The transmission was so clear that people could hear rustling paper as the new president turned the pages of his text. The inaugural coverage was so successful that talk circulated about broadcasting sessions of Congress. Meanwhile, "Silent Cal" began speaking an average of 9,000 words a month over radio. Although his speeches lacked persuasive content, he was credited with being a strong and effective radio performer.

By the time Herbert Hoover took his presidential oath in 1929, two powerful broadcasting companies supporting three national networks were flourishing. President Hoover spoke on radio 10 times during 1929 and 27 times the following year. By the end of 1930, he had equaled the number of talks Coolidge gave during his entire administration. President Hoover's cabinet reinforced the administration's line by giving even more radio talks. In 1929 the National Broadcasting Company (NBC) devoted from five to 25 hours per week to presidential speeches, reports on national events, and addresses by public figures. By 1930 the government was using 450 hours of broadcasting time on NBC alone.

Despite his unmatched experience on the air, President Hoover was a reluctant and not particularly gifted participant in the broadcasting arena. Aides pushed him into making radio speeches. The president also had the unenviable task of selling an economic program that the American public did not want to hear in the depths of the Depression. Hoover's speeches progressively brought diminishing returns. Soon, everyone realized broadcasting was a two-edged sword; it could not only help elevate presidents but help bury them as well. Broadcasting worked its magic best when the potential for persuasion and good feeling were at a peak, a fact not lost on Hoover's successor.

A Radio Star Is Born

Until Franklin Roosevelt (FDR) became president, the networks were more captivated by the presidency than by any particular occupant of the office. The networks clung tightly to FDR's rising star and used his engaging personality on the airwaves to enhance their own status. Columbia Broadcasting System (CBS) commentator Frederic William Wile was one of the first at the networks to realize how high a priority Roosevelt placed on broadcasting. Wile emerged from a talk with the president-elect predicting that the new president would be "highly radio-minded," which would cause Washington to become more "radio conscious" and the American people to become more conscious of Washington.

Following his success in using radio to push a recalcitrant New York Legislature into action, Roosevelt told Wile that he expected to request time frequently. The new president's fascination with radio was surpassed only by the networks' fascination with him. Merlin Aylesworth, president of NBC, not wanting to miss a piece of presidential action, approached Roosevelt before he was inaugurated to offer him airtime on a regular basis. Although FDR was tempted by the alluring network offer, he feared overexposure and preferred to use the airwaves according to his own timing and his own priorities.

Starting with his first inaugural address, in which he told Americans the only thing they had to fear was "fear itself," the new president proved himself to be an exceptional communicator. The networks quickly realized that Roosevelt had different motivations for using radio than had his predecessors. To him, the medium was no longer a novelty for sending ceremonial greetings; it was a vital tool for persuasion. President Roosevelt used all the intimacy and directness radio could offer to rally support for his policies. Just eight days after being sworn in, FDR put radio to the test. Eschewing his fiery and strained campaign oratory, Roosevelt crafted a subdued, conversational style exclusively for radio. He spoke calmly, intimately, and above all, persuasively in what immediately became known as "Fireside Chats."

As more Fireside Chats poured out of the White House, the American people responded favorably. FDR became a friend and a neighbor who could captivate a nation and develop a truly national constituency. When FDR came to office, one employee could handle all the White House mail. By March 1933, a half-million letters sent the White House scrambling to hire additional staff.

Franklin Roosevelt presented only 28 Fireside Chats during his three terms (and a few months of his fourth), but they had an extraordinary impact on a nation seeking desperately to pull itself out of depression and to win a world war. He boosted his radio speeches' appeal by making them during the "primest" of prime-time (between 9 P.M. and 11 P.M. EST) on weekdays when families were home together. Roosevelt's political adviser Jim Farley said that radio could wash away the most harmful effects once "the reassuring voice of the President of the United States started coming through the ether into the living room."

FDR took advantage of his platform to persuade voters to support him and his programs. Later in the century, broadcasting executives would chafe at a president's using the airwaves solely to persuade voters or Congress to support a particular program, but there was no such resentment of Roosevelt. On the contrary, broadcasting executives delighted in the drama and excitement Roosevelt created. Merlin Aylesworth of NBC effusively wrote President Roosevelt that "I can honestly say that I have never known a public official to use the radio with such intelligence."

Behaviors were locked in during World War II that would greatly influence the way politicians communicated in the coming television age. Americans became even more dependent on the president as a national leader—accustomed to hearing the man who led them through the crisis of the Great Depression, they were prepared to hear him lead them confidently through another. More important, they expected direct communication from the commander in chief. Radio was no longer a novelty; it was a necessity. During the war, Roosevelt always had access to all four networks—CBS, Mutual Broadcasting System, and NBC Red and Blue—simultaneously. When Franklin Roosevelt spoke to the nation two days after the bombing of Pearl Harbor, he achieved the highest ratings of all time; 83 percent of American households that owned radios were listening to the president.

By the end of the Roosevelt administration, presidents had gained a de facto right of access to all radio networks simultaneously, creating a captive audience of millions. Perhaps most important, the president could enjoy this radio access without worrying about a direct rebuttal by the opposition party.

President Versus Candidate

President Roosevelt was a master at inching his presidential addresses closer and closer to election periods to avoid purchasing time from broadcasters. This tactic not only increased his exposure when the voters were starting to focus on the elections but also allowed him to speak without fear of opposition reply. Section 315 of the Communications Act of 1934 required broadcasters to offer "equal time" to opposing candidates during "candidate" uses of airtime. Roosevelt insisted that he was speaking as a "president" rather than as a "candidate" and that his speeches were not subject to the reply rule.

When the president held a Fireside Chat on 6 September 1936 about drought and unemployment, the Republicans charged (to no avail) that the speech was political. Roosevelt used the same successful strategy in the 1940 campaign to make as many free "presidential" rather than paid "candidate" speeches as possible. Roosevelt was particularly adamant about securing free network time for "fireside chats" because toward the end of the campaign, the Democrats were almost out of money. Earlier that year, the NAB had boosted the president's case by ruling that rival political candidates had to prove that FDR's speeches were political, something difficult for an opponent to do. The question of whether addresses were "presidential" or "political" continued into the Truman administration. The Republicans were outraged on 5 April 1947 when NBC, the American Broadcasting Company (ABC), and Mutual carried President Truman's Jefferson Day speech at a $100-per-plate Democratic fund-raising dinner. GOP National Chairman Carroll Reece said the networks' giving airtime constituted an illegal corporate campaign contribution. Reece also charged that "free radio time is a royal prerogative, something to be given without question whenever requested and without regard for the purpose to which it may be devoted."

When television ascended to pre-eminence in the early 1950s, radio was forgotten as a tool of presidential communication. During the Eisenhower, Kennedy, and Johnson administrations, radio found no place in the presidential arsenal—this despite the fact that Vice President Nixon had "won" the first "Great Debate" of the 1960 campaign on radio where people could not see his exhaustion. The televised presidential speech, broadcast simultaneously on all three major networks, had become the oratorical weapon of choice. Radio became a low-key form of communication that President Nixon used in 1973 to downplay the strident debate over highly controversial budget initiatives, choosing to deliver his State of the Union addresses as a series of radio speeches rather than making a formal, more visible presentation before Congress and a nationwide television audience.

Reagan on Radio

It wasn't until 1982 that the presidential radio speech made a comeback with the arrival of Ronald

Reagan in the White House. The administration approached the networks about a series of radio speeches that would be broadcast each Saturday morning from the Oval Office. The Reagan administration saw radio as an opportunity to take its case directly to the people on a sustained basis in a way that would allow the White House total control of the broadcasts. At a time when the president's popularity was sagging, the radio addresses also presented an attractive complement to a broad multimedia offensive. Because the addresses would be broadcast on a traditionally "slow news" day, the White House expected abundant residual media exposure on Saturday network radio and television newscasts and Sunday newspapers. Finally, the White House staff realized how effective "the great communicator" could be on a medium with which he felt so confident.

With the radio speeches, the White House could achieve access in an entirely controlled way. There would be no editing of material, no filtering through reporters' minds, no distracting or nagging questions by the press. It would be a perfect opportunity to "let Reagan be Reagan." Even in the residual coverage, when reporters could edit as they wished, White House aides believed the Reagan momentum would still be present.

On Saturday, 4 April 1982, President Reagan began his radio initiative in the Oval Office with the first of ten five-minute speeches. The president said he was making the speeches to overcome "all the confusion and all the conflicting things that come out of Washington" by bringing "the facts to the people as simply as I can in five minutes." Aides said the speeches' brevity was an effort to prevent having Reagan's message "truncated" or "filtered" by the news media.

The White House staff said that Reagan wrote most of the first ten speeches himself, often rejecting drafts and writing the script in longhand shortly before airtime. Reagan set a folksy, conversational tone in the first address by beginning, "I'll be back every Saturday at this same time, same station, live. I hope you'll tune in." The president's personal input sometimes startled aides.

When President Reagan settled into his radio routine, it was obvious his targets were the Democrats in Congress. The president used six of his first ten speeches to defend his economic programs and to attack the Democrat-controlled House for not supporting him. Not surprisingly, these speeches gained the greatest press coverage: the *Washington Post* carried news about all six of them on the front page, and the broadcasting networks gave them prominent placement on the evening news. Although

it is not difficult for the president to make news, it can be difficult for him to make news that he controls. Therefore, extensive regular coverage in Sunday newspapers and on Saturday network news about subjects that he initiated was a positive sign. Not surprisingly, when President Reagan signed off for the last of his ten speeches, he said, "I'll be back before too long."

After an 11-week hiatus, President Reagan continued his radio speeches on a regular basis. By the end of his term, they had become the longest-running regularly scheduled broadcast initiative ever taken by an American president, establishing Ronald Reagan as the person who resurrected radio as a persuasive tool of the presidency. These speeches also reinforced the value of radio as a campaign tool in non-election years. They brought the president a sustained, controlled forum for his views and significant residual media coverage. The fact that the Republican National Committee continued the radio speeches as paid political broadcasts gave clues to both their purpose and their effectiveness.

Opposition Response

Unlike televised speeches, in which the opposition got to reply on a hit-or-miss basis regulated by the networks, with radio speeches the Democrats in Congress were guaranteed automatic access. The automatic replies to President Reagan's radio speeches gave 28 senators, 41 congressmen, and four non-congressional Democrats an opportunity to go head-to-head with the president. Speaker Tip O'Neill and Senate Minority Leader Robert Byrd chose the spokesmen who wrote their own speeches, with guidance being made available from the leadership.

The opportunity to reply to one of President Reagan's radio speeches was sought by several rank-and-file members, especially younger, less visible congressmen. It was considered an honor and sign of approval to be asked by the Speaker to make the reply. Many members were more interested in the local audience in their districts rather than the nationwide audience. Some media-conscious congressmen heavily promoted the speeches in advance, advising their constituents to listen on Saturday.

The lure of a radio reply was not as appealing to senators and senior House members. The Saturday afternoon time posed an obstacle to recruiting the best and brightest of the party. Many senior members had important weekend commitments that they were not willing to change. Some senators resented the double standards the networks imposed on the Congress. The broadcasters followed President Reagan anywhere in the world for his Saturday speeches but made congressmen and senators come to a studio in downtown Washington, D.C. This gave President Reagan great flexibility—he gave less than one-third of his speeches from the White House—but posed a logistical problem for the Democrats in Congress. Furthermore, listening to the president, drafting a relevant reply, rehearsing it, and presenting it all in one hour did not strike some legislators as the most relaxing way to spend a Saturday afternoon. By the time President Reagan announced his bid for re-election in January 1984, the Democratic leadership and its members seemed ready to give up the Saturday replies. Still, the opportunity for "the loyal opposition" to have automatic, direct access to the president of the United States had been unprecedented, and the Democrats took full advantage of the opportunity.

President Reagan's success with getting residual print and broadcast exposure through his radio addresses caused his successors to carry on the tradition. Although few Americans listen to the Saturday radio speeches live, many see the aftermath of the speeches in the Sunday newspapers, on daily news broadcasts, or Sunday talk shows. The radio addresses have become a significant agenda-setting vehicle for television-age presidents.

Recent Presidents: Since 1990

Reagan's vice-president, George H.W. Bush (1989–93) followed his leader's precedent after his own election, continuing the weekly five-minute broadcasts. And so did Bill Clinton (1993–2001). George W. Bush (2001–9) did so as well, though with the growth of the internet, he became the first president to initiate regular use of the web among other means of getting out the administration's stand on issues and events. The White House website (whitehouse.gov) became a source for the broadcast in addition to its traditional broadcast format. Archived past addresses as well as Spanish translations were also provided. So were written transcripts.

Following his election (November 2008), Barack Obama began to provide weekly addresses on the internet YouTube site in an obvious effort to continue communication with the younger demographic of his national supporters. Video and internet streamed versions of the traditional weekly radio address continued after he took office in January 2009. Thus radio lost its once-unique role in providing the weekly broadcast, though the event continued to be carried by many stations. And, oddly enough, it was still often termed the president's weekly "radio" address.

See also: Election Coverage; "Equal Time" Rule; Fireside Chats; Politics and Radio

Further Reading

Balutis, A., "The Presidency and the Press: The Expanding Presidential Image," *Presidential Studies Quarterly* 7 (1977).

Becker, S., "Presidential Power: The Influence of Broadcasting," *Quarterly Journal of Speech* 47 (February 1961).

Braden, W., and Brandenburg, E., "Roosevelt's Fireside Chats," *Speech Monographs* 22 (November 1955).

Brown, Charlene J., Trevor R. Brown, and William L. Rivers, *The Media and the People*, New York: Holt Rinehart and Winston, 1978.

Chester, Edward W., *Radio, Television, and American Politics*, New York: Sheed and Ward, 1969.

Cornwell, E., "Coolidge and Presidential Leadership," *Public Opinion Quarterly* 21 (Summer 1957).

Craig, Douglas B., *Fireside Politics: Radio and Political Culture in the United States, 1920–1940*, Baltimore, Maryland: Johns Hopkins University Press, 2000.

Foote, Joe S., "Reagan on Radio," *Communication Yearbook* 8 (1984).

Foote, Joe S., *Television Access and Political Power: The Networks, the Presidency, and the "Loyal Opposition,"* New York: Praeger, 1990.

Grossman, Michael Baruch, and Martha Joynt Kumar, "The White House and the News Media: The Phases of Their Relationship," *Political Science Quarterly* 94 (1979).

Grossman, Michael Baruch, and Martha Joynt Kumar, *Portraying the President: The White House and the News Media*, Baltimore, Maryland: Johns Hopkins University Press, 1981.

Han, Lori Cox, "New Strategies for and Old Medium: The Weekly Radio Addresses of Reagan and Clinton," *Congress & The Presidency* 33, no. 1 (2006), pp. 25–45.

Horvit, Beverly, Adam J. Schiffer, and Mark Wright, "The Limits of Presidential Agenda Setting: Predicting Newspaper Coverage of the Weekly Radio Address," *The International Journal of Press/Politics* 13 (2008), pp. 8–28

Minow, Newton N., John Bartlow Martin, and Lee M. Mitchell, *Presidential Television*, New York: Basic Books, 1973.

Paletz, David L., and Robert M. Entman, *Media Power Politics*, New York: Free Press, and London: Collier Macmillan, 1981.

Roberts, Brian, "The Framing Effects of Weekly Presidential Radio Addresses," paper presented before APSA 2008 Annual Meeting, Boston, Massachusetts (28 August 2008).

Rubin, R.L., "The Presidency in the Age of Television," in *The Power to Govern: Assessing Reform in the United States*, edited by Richard M. Pious, New York: Academy of Political Science, 1981.

JOE S. FOOTE,
2009 REVISIONS BY CHRISTOPHER H. STERLING

UNITED STATES SUPREME COURT AND RADIO

The United States Supreme Court has played an important role in defining the relationship between government regulation and radio broadcasters, as well as what is permissible behavior by the broadcasters themselves. Numerous cases decided over six decades help to underpin and sometimes explain current regulatory practices.

Operation and Membership

Mandated by Article III of the U.S. Constitution, the Supreme Court stands at the apex of the judicial branch of the federal government. As its name implies, it is the final arbiter of legal issues involving the Constitution and governmental actions. It acts as an appellate court, meaning that it reviews decisions appealed from lower federal courts and from state supreme courts when cases involve questions of federal law—such as the First Amendment, a common ingredient in many media cases. Cases appealed from different states concerning the same federal issue may also end up in the Supreme Court. To be considered, the losing side in the lower court files a petition for *certiori* or review, along with supporting documents in an attempt to persuade the High Court of the importance of the case and of the wrong done to the litigant.

Unlike federal appeals courts, the Supreme Court need not accept all cases appealed to it. Indeed, the court selects a small portion (about 200 achieve the needed four votes for consideration) of the thousands of cases appealed to it annually. Most are denied (*certiori* or *cert.* denied) without any reason being given, leaving the lower court decision in place. Once a case is accepted, attorneys for each side file briefs (formal written arguments) and the court schedules an oral argument to highlight the key issues and give justices a chance to question counsel. A decision often appears months later, usually with an opinion representing the majority, and often with concurring or dissenting opinions as well.

Though its membership and operations have varied over time, for more than 100 years the court has operated with nine members, one of them designated by the president as Chief Justice of the United States. Appointments to the court, made by the president and subject to Senate approval, are for life-long terms. Vacancies, owing to retirement, death, or resignation (the latter is not common), thus occur at irregular times. President Johnson named the court's first minority justice, Thurgood Marshall (served 1967–1991), and President Reagan named the first woman, Sandra Day O'Conner (served 1981–present). The chief justice is usually a newly appointed justice; only three times in history (most recently in 1986 with William Rehnquist) has a sitting associate justice been so elevated.

Radio Rulings

On numerous occasions since the early 1930s, the court has issued decisions involving radio broadcasting. These have ranged from appeals of FCC decisions to specific sections of the Communications Act or other legislation. Most have concerned procedure and jurisdiction, while others have focused on permissible content. The majority of decisions have upheld commission actions.

The first important Supreme Court case to concern broadcasting was *Federal Radio Commission v. Nelson Brothers Bond and Mortgage Company* (289 US 266, 1933), in which the court upheld the public interest statement in the 1934 Communications Act as being constitutional and not too vague for proper enforcement. The court also found that the commission had substantial discretion in applying the public interest standard to specific situations. Seven years later, in *Federal Communications Commission v. Sanders Brothers Radio Station* (309 US 470, 1940), the court tackled the difficult question of how much the FCC had to be concerned with economic pressure on licensees caused by allowing additional stations on the air. In a decision that provided rhetorical meat for proponents of both sides of the question, the court determined that "economic injury to an existing station is not a separate and independent element to be taken into consideration by the Commission in determining whether it shall grant or withhold a license." Taken together, these first two court decisions served to strengthen the authority of the FCC to read the Communications Act with some discretion.

In *National Broadcasting Company v. United States* (319 US 190, 1943), the court issued a landmark decision that further strengthened the FCC's discretionary power. Upholding the commission's network rules that, among other things, forced NBC to sell one of its two national radio networks (it became ABC in 1945), the court determined that the commission could regulate the business relationships between networks and their affiliates. A decision still widely cited in the legal literature, it included the key rationale for government's control of radio: "Freedom of utterance is abridged to many who wish to use the limited facilities of radio. Unlike other modes of expression, it is subject to governmental regulation. Because it cannot be used by all, some who wish to use it must be denied." The *NBC* case remains one of the most important media decisions of the Supreme Court.

On rare occasions, the FCC comes out on the short end of a Supreme Court decision. In *American Broadcasting Co. v. Federal Communications*

Commission (347 US 296, 1953), the court focused on commission procedures. The radio networks broadcast a variety of quiz programs in the late 1940s, and the commission determined that at least some of them violated the Criminal Code provision banning the broadcasting of lottery information. The Code and existing cases only partially defined what a lottery was, and the FCC had therefore issued a rule further defining what was illegal on the air. It was overturned in the lower court, and the Supreme Court agreed, holding that "the Commission has overstepped the boundaries of interpretation and hence has exceeded its rulemaking power."

More directly focused on program content was *Red Lion Broadcasting Co. v. Federal Communications Commission* (395 US 367, 1969). A conservative religious radio station licensee in Red Lion, Pennsylvania had refused to allow free time to a man who had been attacked on the air during a syndicated religious program. After the station refused FCC orders to comply with its personal attack rules, the case went to court. At the same time, the Radio Television News Director's Association (RTNDA) appealed aspects of the FCC's "Fairness Doctrine." Lower courts found for the FCC in the Red Lion case and against the commission in the RTNDA case. Because they dealt with similar aspects of the law, they were combined when appealed to the Supreme Court. The court's ruling upheld the Fairness Doctrine, again justifying its decision because of the limited spectrum available for broadcasting that provided the groundwork for government regulation of the service. In its widely quoted line, the court concluded "It is the right of the viewers and listeners, not the right of the broadcasters, which is paramount."

Another radio content case came nearly a decade later in *Federal Communications Commission v. Pacifica Foundation* (438 US 726, 1978), which effectively defined that which was indecent, and thus could be broadcast within certain conditions, as opposed to something obscene, which lacks First Amendment protection and may not be broadcast at all. Citing the "uniquely pervasive presence" of broadcasting (in this case a New York City noncommercial FM station) in the home as rationale for some limits on what could be broadcast, the court held (by a narrow 5–4 margin) that the FCC had been right to fine the station for broadcasting material (a satire on dirty words) in the early afternoon that might be permissible late at night when, presumably, children were not present in the radio audience.

In most matters dealing with media content, the Court has held in favor of the First Amendment

and thus against government meddling or interference with media decisions. After a decade of legal wrangling, *Federal Communications Commission v. WNCN Listeners Guild* (1981) resolved once and for all who would determine station formats—a government agency or the marketplace. After 1970, the Court of Appeals for the D.C. Circuit, in a series of cases, had held that the FCC did have to determine whether station format changes were in the public interest. In response, the FCC in 1977 issued a policy statement citing the *Sanders* case (that competition should "permit a licensee to survive or succumb according to his ability to make his programs attractive to the public") and determining that the agency did *not* have to make public-interest determinations concerning format changes. An appeals court decision in 1979 once again held against the FCC position, and the agency appealed to the High Court.

In a 7–2 decision, the Supreme Court held that the lower court had made an "unreasonable interpretation of the act's public-interest standard" and reversed it, agreeing with the FCC finding in favor of marketplace determinations of station formats. The court determined that the FCC policy statement was both reasonable and consistent with the legislative history of the Act. Kahn notes of this decision that "[t]his document is a restatement of the notion that reviewing courts are to grant substantial deference to the discretion of the expert administrative agency Congress established to determine what serves the public interest in broadcasting" (Kahn, 1984).

In sum, the Supreme Court has been called on to determine whether FCC decisions meet Constitutional tests as to their substance or procedure, and in most cases (where lower court decisions have been accepted for review) has supported the federal agency. The court's rationale for upholding federal authority over radio has varied over time, but such rationale usually includes spectrum scarcity and thus the need to select among those who would broadcast, and the pervasive presence of the medium in the home. Combined, these considerations have led to a more limited First Amendment right for radio broadcasting compared to print media.

See also: Censorship; Deregulation of Radio; First Amendment and Radio; Network Monopoly Probe; Obscenity and Indecency on Radio; *Red Lion* Case; Regulation; "Seven Dirty Words" Case

Further Reading

Campbell, Douglas S., *The Supreme Court and the Mass Media: Selected Cases, Summaries, and Analyses*, New York: Praeger, 1990.

Carter, T. Barton, Marc A. Franklin, and Jay B. Wright, *The First Amendment and the Fifth Estate: Regulation of Electronic Mass Media*, Mineola, New York: Foundation Press, 1986; 5th edition, 1999.

Creech, Kenneth C., *Electronic Media Law and Regulation*, Boston: Focal Press, 1993; 3rd edition, Oxford: Focal Press, 1999.

Devol, Kenneth S., editor, *Mass Media and the Supreme Court*, New York: Hastings House, 1971; 4th edition: Mamaroneck, New York: Hastings House, 1990.

Federal Communications Commission v. Pacifica Foundation, 438 US 726 (1978).

Federal Communications Commission v. Sanders Brothers Radio Station, 309 US 470 (1940).

Federal Communications Commission v. WNCN Listeners Guild, 450 US 582 (1981).

Federal Radio Commission v. Nelson Brothers Bond and Mortgage Company, 289 US 266 (1933).

Hindman, Elizabeth Blanks, *Rights vs Responsibilities: The Supreme Court and the Media*, Westport, Connecticut: Greenwood Press, 1997.

Kahn, Frank J., editor, *Documents of American Broadcasting*, New York: Appleton-Century-Crofts, 1968; 4th edition, Englewood Cliffs, New Jersey: Prentice-Hall, 1984.

Lipschultz, Jeremy Harris, *Broadcast Indecency: F.C.C. Regulation and the First Amendment*, Boston: Focal Press, 1997.

National Broadcasting Co. v. United States, 319 US 190 (1943).

Red Lion Broadcasting Co. v. Federal Communications Commission, 395 US 367 (1969).

Ulloth, Dana Royal, *The Supreme Court: A Judicial Review of the Federal Communications Commission*, New York: Arno Press, 1979.

United States v. Edge Broadcasting Co., 509 US 418 (1993).

CHRISTOPHER H. STERLING AND
JOSEPH A. RUSSOMANNO

URBAN CONTEMPORARY FORMAT

Following the arrival of television, radio's new program specialization approach (formats for targeted audiences) provided a previously unavailable venue for a number of music genres, among them rhythm and blues, the "mother" of the urban contemporary radio format. Rhythm and blues, jazz, and black gospel music were developed from the lifestyles and experiences of African-American musicians and artists. Rhythm and blues provided the optimum entertainment and storytelling experiences about life, love, and pain in the African-American community. Artists such as Little Richard, LaVerne Baker, Ruth Brown, Jerry Butler, Jackie Wilson, James Brown, The Platters, The Coasters, The Drifters, Fats Domino, Ray Charles, Chuck Berry, The Spaniels, Faye Adams, Little Anthony and the Imperials, The Moonglows, The Flamingos, The Five Satins, Oscar Brown, Buster Brown, Frankie Lymon and the Teenagers, Big Jay McNeely, and a host of others sang, wrote, and performed their music with a unique flair that captivated listeners throughout the world. These artists provided an excellent source of radio programming material for the development of the rhythm and blues radio format.

In 1946 WDIA-AM, Memphis, Tennessee, became the first radio station to air a complete rhythm and blues radio format. Its 50,000-W signal introduced new African-American musicians and disc jockeys to the airwaves, including B.B. King and Rufus Thomas, who would go on to legendary careers in the music industry. The powerful AM signal provided coverage throughout the Southeastern and Midwestern states. The station was so successful with the rhythm and blues format that its owners proclaimed that there was "gold in the cotton fields of the South." WDIA became the "Mother Radio Station" of the rhythm and blues format, thus laying the historic foundation for this broadcast style and its future offspring, urban contemporary.

Rhythm and blues radio stations grew in number during the 1950s to include such stations as WOOK, Washington, D.C.; WERD, WAOK, Atlanta, Georgia; WRAP, Norfolk, Virginia; WEBB, Baltimore, Maryland; WANN, Annapolis, Maryland; WDAS, WHAT, Philadelphia, Pennsylvania; WLIB, WWRL, New York, New York; KNOLL, San Francisco, California; KGFJ, Los Angeles, California; WVON, Chicago, Illinois; WYLD, New Orleans, Louisiana; WCHB, Detroit, Michigan; WSRC, Durham, North Carolina; WANT, Richmond, Virginia; WILD, Boston, Massachusetts; WJMO, Cleveland, Ohio; KATZ, St. Louis, Missouri; and WAAA, Winston-Salem, North Carolina.

Broadcast groups such as Rollins, Rousanville, Sonderling, Speidel, and United Broadcasting established rhythm and blues stations in large and medium markets throughout the country. Rollins was important because it operated stations in major markets, including WNJR, New York, New York/ Newark, New Jersey; WBEE, Chicago, Illinois; KDAY, Los Angeles, California; WGEE, Indianapolis, Indiana; and WRAP, Norfolk, Virginia. The Sonderling group laid the original foundation for the "new" sound of rhythm and blues radio, soon to be called urban contemporary. Jerry Boulding, program director of WWRL, New York, during the 1960s, was the architect of this new sound of rhythm and blues radio. This air sound, which was very smooth, became the sound of soul on WOL, Washington, D.C.; WWRL, New York; WDIA, Memphis; WBMX, Chicago; and KDIA, San Francisco/Oakland.

The major change that transformed rhythm and blues radio into urban contemporary was the shift of the format from AM stations to FM outlets in the early 1970s. Four radio stations, WBLS-FM, New York; WDAS-FM, Philadelphia; and WHUR-FM, WKYS-FM, Washington, D.C., were major players in this transformation. WBLS-FM in New York received programming directions from veteran disc jockey Frankie Crocker. His efforts transformed WBLS-FM into the number one station with an urban contemporary format in New York City. This success also was responsible for the early ratings erosion of the then-number-one-rated Top 40, 50,000-W WABC-AM. The format of WBLS-FM was a mix of rhythm and blues, jazz, Latin, and gospel. WDAS-FM, Philadelphia, with disc jockey personality Hy Lit and Doctor Perri Johnson, also pioneered in urban contemporary radio. This format was a mix of jazz, blues, rhythm and blues, reggae, Latin, and urban rhythms. The format soon moved the station to high ratings.

Howard University's WHUR-FM in Washington, D.C., first aired in December 1971 with an urban contemporary format. The format was quite similar to the WBLS-FM urban sound, but with an added emphasis of news, educational features, and community programs. Just about every urban contemporary radio station in the United States has adopted one of its programs, *The Quiet Storm*. This program, which features love ballads and slow tunes, was originally aired under the *Quiet Storm* title at WHUR-FM and has become an integral part of the urban contemporary format.

WKYS-FM played a major role in giving the urban contemporary format a mainstream audience and the popular nickname "Kiss." In July 1975 the National Broadcasting Company (NBC) station switched from "beautiful music" to a disco format, a variation of urban contemporary. This helped the station move from a number 17 Arbitron rating to number three in Washington, D.C.

WKYS-FM, Washington, D.C., made format adjustments and moved urban contemporary radio to new programming heights. Veteran radio programmers Donnie Simpson, Bill Bailey, Eddie Edwards, Melvin Lindsay, Ed McGee, Rick Wright, and Jack Harris laid the original foundation. In 2000 WKYS-FM was owned by Radio One, the largest African-American-owned radio broadcasting company in the world.

Urban contemporary is a radio format designed to attract an urban but demographically diverse audience. The overall air sound is that of music performed mainly by African-American artists, with the announcers presenting material such as commercials, features, public service announcements, station breaks, announcements, jingles, and news in various styles ranging from smooth and mellow to wild and zany to authoritative and informational.

Urban contemporary radio stations have become major electronic media entertainment, informational, promotional, and marketing tools. In Washington, D.C., four of the top six stations (WHUR-RM, WKYS-FM, WMMJ-FM and WPCG-FM) are urban contemporary or derivatives thereof, but syndication, technological innovations, and station competition have brought major changes to urban contemporary radio. Most stations have decreased the use of local disc jockeys and moved toward the use of nationally syndicated programs.

One major syndicated urban contemporary service is "The Touch," which is delivered by satellite and downlinked to station affiliates. This service allows staff on-air announcer Tim Garrison to air his *Love Zone* show, with its mellow urban sounds, to audiences at night throughout the world.

The highly popular Tom "Flyjock" Joyner and the Doug Banks Show are two other examples of successful syndicated morning drive-time urban radio programs heard on many stations. The American Broadcasting Company (ABC) radio networks both syndicate radio shows and program a mix of music, news, comedy, contests, political information, features, and interviews with celebrities and people in the news. Both originate from studios in Dallas but also broadcast from various locations around the country, thereby attempting to localize the programming content and focus while still reaching a national audience. In the early 2000s, in keeping with radio's trend to spin off and specialize its formats, urban contemporary also splintered into various format derivatives. Along with Churban, there's also now urban AC, urban jazz and rhythmic contemporary; the latter consists of a mix of dance, upbeat rhythmic pop, hip-hop and R&B hits.

The sound characteristics of urban contemporary have changed from its rhythm and blues roots. This change has been caused by competition from other contemporary formats, such as contemporary hit radio and its variation, called Churban. The latter combines trendy popular musical hits from Top 40 and urban charts and presents it in a tight, fast-paced manner.

To maintain its popularity, urban contemporary radio must seek a balance between the hot, hip-hop, contemporary music choices and the basic staples of radio programming. These staples include the use of local disc jockey personalities, ongoing musical experimentation, creative use of technology, news programs, and programming research for discovery of new audience demographics and format designs.

Though urban contemporary stations have a long history of strong community service, this commitment has weakened in recent years as almost all commercial music stations, across all formats, have scaled back on their news and public affairs programming. However, many UC stations were re-energized in this area after being called upon by black leaders to publicize the cause of the Jena Six in 2007 and to mobilize black voters for the 2008 Presidential election.

See also: Black-Oriented Radio; Blues Format; Formats; Jazz Format

Further Reading

Barlow, William, *Voice Over: The Making of Black Radio*, Philadelphia, Pennsylvania: Temple University Press, 1999.

Fisher, Marc, "Segregated Sounds: Ratings Reflect a Great Divide along Racial Lines," *Washington Post* (1 August 2004).

Williams, Gilbert Anthony, *Legendary Pioneers of Black Radio*, Westport, Connecticut: Praeger, 1998.

ROOSEVELT "RICK" WRIGHT, JR.,
2009 REVISIONS BY CARY O'DELL

V

VARIETY SHOWS

Music and Comedy Formats

Inspired by live stage vaudeville, variety programs on network radio through the 1930s and 1940s—whether oriented to music or comedy—offered significant examples of core network radio programming. Variety programs on network radio proved a powerful lure, but except for the popularity of Arthur Godfrey, they declined and disappeared as radio programming changed in the 1950s.

Origins

Vaudeville started in the late 19th century, and by the early years of the 20th century, it was a staple of mass entertainment in U.S. cities. Jugglers, comics, singers, tumblers, and indeed any talent that could operate in 10- to 20-minute units toured the United States, honing their acts in front of live audiences. This infrastructure of well-practiced talent was in place when radio appeared as a mass medium starting in the 1920s.

Just as radio began to make individual vaudeville stars famous, the new medium slowed and then killed the live vaudeville circuit. Along with the Great Depression, the coming of radio and the arrival of movie sound in the late 1920s ended live stage vaudeville, because live shows could not amortize their costs over huge audiences as did radio and the movies. Thus, vaudeville talent either went west to Hollywood or shifted to radio, particularly the comics and singers whose voices represented the core of vaudeville's appeal.

The National Broadcasting Company (NBC) and the Columbia Broadcasting System (CBS) sought what they called "variety talent" to host shows in prime time. Some long-time vaudeville stars such as Eddie Cantor and Ed Wynn had grown up on the boards and made a successful transition to radio. Others, such as Buster Keaton and Harry Lauder, did not. Indeed, most did not, but Jack Benny and the Marx Brothers smoothly moved to radio (and the movies), bringing their considerable talents to listeners across the United States. Even ventriloquists such as Edgar Bergen thrived in radio, where the skill of throwing one's voice was not necessary, but Bergen's comedy overwhelmed any consideration of the radio inappropriateness of his act.

And the radio variety shows with guest stars thrived. Comics such as Eddie Cantor on Sunday night drew audiences measured in the millions and inspired millions more to purchase radio sets. Others from vaudeville adapted to radio. Will Rogers, for example, who talked on stage as he did his rope tricks, gave up the rope to just tell stories on radio. There was a constant need for new talent, and so amateur hour programs began in 1934 with the introduction of *Major Bowes' Original Amateur Hour*. Scouts roamed the United States looking for skilled entertainers who might win the big prize and then make the next step into radio variety show stardom. According to one report, at the height of his popularity in the late 1930s, Major Bowes received more than 10,000 applications per week, and when local Hoboken, New Jersey, singer Frank Sinatra won, the legend of discovery became firmly established as part of radio's myth.

These radio variety shows seemed safe, because they booked stars who appealed to those in what surveys determined was a group and/or family listening demographic. As was the practice of the day, advertising agencies developed most such programs on behalf of their sponsor clients. Rudy Vallee, for example, was an employee of the J. Walter Thompson advertising agency as a client for Standard Brands. He was not employed by NBC, his network, although most fans surely thought so. But this practice would change as the star system—adapted from the movies and live stage vaudeville—developed and soon dominated.

By the early 1940s, radio stopped inheriting stars from other sources, such as the live vaudeville stage or Hollywood. Instead, radio began to make its own stars. Both Kate Smith and Arthur Godfrey started in radio and then moved to other media to exploit their radio fame.

The Variety Show Schedule

From the beginning—as early as January 1927—listings of network schedules included numerous prime-time variety radio programs. Through the late 1920s, dozens of network prime-time radio variety shows aired on NBC Blue and Red, and later also on CBS. Most programs from this early stage were either music- or comedy-oriented. Musical variety shows made up a third of all prime-time radio at that early point. These shows were headlined by bands or groups of musicians whose very names incorporated references to their sponsors' products: A&P Gypsies, Goodrich Zippers, the Cliquot Club Eskimos, and the Hires (Rootbeer) Harvesters. These were mostly 30- minute shows, with few running an hour.

With the rise of CBS in 1928 came a doubling of variety programming, and although sponsorship still dominated, a new trend arose, because CBS chairman William S. Paley immediately embraced the star system. The first such star was probably *Roxy and His Gang* on NBC Blue, hosted by the noted movie theater impresario, and Roxy's name—not the sponsor's—was above the title. But gradually CBS was to lead the way in exploiting the star system. Such stars would come to equal sponsorship, as Hollywood and then radio itself created the larger-than-life figures the public sought out in their daily listening.

In the early 1930s, with dozens of variety shows on the air, most still featured the names of their sponsors—with new attractions including the Atwater Kent (a radio set manufacturer) Dance Orchestra, the Happy Wonder Bakers, and the Palmolive Hour. But as the 1930s progressed, the stars began to headline in a variation of the star system that Hollywood, and vaudeville before that, had used since the late 19th century. There were variety shows with such names as *The Ben Bernie Orchestra, The Guy Lombardo Orchestra*, and *The Paul Whiteman Orchestra*.

Many combinations of variety talent were tried as NBC and CBS tried to win the ratings war and thus be able to charge more for their increasingly precious airtime. The search was intense for new stars. Some still came over from the New York stage, none more successfully as a variety host and talent than Eddie Cantor, who gained initial stardom as a member of the annual Follies of Florence Ziegfeld. Cantor adapted his talents neatly to radio, and from 1931 through 1949 his NBC variety show was a highly rated network fixture. Jimmy Durante was surely Cantor's biggest rival, but radio-made comic talent such as Bob Hope would take over this subgenre of the variety program.

For example, Fred Waring headed a relatively unknown big band in the 1920s. When he started his radio variety show in 1933 on CBS, he quickly rose to stardom. He moved to NBC in 1939 with a show that was titled *Chesterfield Time* until 1945, when he had become such a big star that his name went into the title. The show became *The Fred Waring Show* and lasted until 1950, spanning the whole of the variety show era.

Rudy Vallee was a nightclub and vaudeville star when he came to radio on NBC in 1929, first in *The Fleischmann Hour*, and then under his own name, with Vallee telling jokes and singing but also delivering guest talent. Vallee first introduced Eddie Cantor, Noel Coward, Beatrice Lillie, Alice Faye, Edgar Bergen, and Red Skelton to radio fans—all of whom would go on to host or star on radio through the 1930s and 1940s. But it was Vallee's name that carried this radio variety show.

Ed Sullivan would become a television variety show legend, but he never claimed that he did any more than simply to offer New York-centric entertainment gossip and to bring as guests the top music, comic, and other talent. Supposedly, comic Fred Allen once remarked that Sullivan would last as long as someone else had talent that radio could showcase.

Some radio-made stars came through the ranks of local stations. For example, bandleader Guy Lombardo and his newly minted Royal Canadians made their radio debut on Chicago's WBBM-AM in 1927, and within a couple of years Lombardo was appearing on the CBS network, of which WBBM was a long-time affiliate.

Robert Ripley proved that stardom could be transferred to a radio variety show—even if it seemed improbable. Ripley had first introduced his *Believe It or Not* newspaper cartoons in 1918; then, using vivid descriptions and sounds, he was able to develop a variety act for NBC, CBS, and the Mutual Broadcasting System. He was a good host as well and invited his guests to share in his glory.

By 1940 the movies and radio were inexorably linked. Long-retired silent film star Mary Pickford—with third husband, bandleader Buddy Rogers—hosted her own variety shows, first titled simply *Mary Pickford and Buddy Rogers* and later titled *Parties at Pickfair*, referring to their posh and noted Hollywood estate. Here was a star play pure and simple. And once performers such as Bob Hope or Bing Crosby became big in radio, they could also go to Hollywood and then smoothly back to radio. Indeed, both CBS and NBC set up major studios in Los Angeles in the late 1930s to take advantage of this growing Hollywood-radio connection.

Program Strategies

Variety shows almost always revolved around music and/or comedy, because the dancing, acrobatics, magic tricks, and other staples of the vaudeville stage had no appeal on radio. There were general variety shows, music-oriented variety shows, and comedy-oriented variety shows. Subgenres included the amateur hours, ethnic music comics (such as Jewish comics who had crafted their comedy on the Catskills circuit), and subcategories of music (such as the barn dance programs, which would later evolve into the country music format radio).

The distinction between programs was in how much of a story was told. *The Jack Benny Show* offered a variety of musical acts with Jack and his gang of comics, but the show was more the story of the Benny group. On the other hand, Al Jolson's various radio variety shows featured the singing of Jolson, with only an occasional sketch and comic guest star.

Sometimes the appeal for radio made little sense. Ben Bernie was a vaudeville star as the genre was dying, killed by the movies. He started on a local New York City radio station in 1923, and thanks to a long-running feud with gossip columnist Walter Winchell, he became famous and was a radio fixture from 1931 until his death in 1943. Like many famous variety talents, he had one strength—in his case, music—but could offer enough talent in comedy, simple patter, and an ability to play master of ceremonies that he could become a star in variety.

Stars were often made by first appearing on a variety show and then moving to their own programs. For example, Dinah Shore was discovered in the late 1930s and early 1940s by Ben Bernie and Eddie Cantor, and by 1940 she was voted top new star in a Scripps Howard newspaper chain national radio poll. A year later, NBC had her on its schedule with her own show.

By the late 1930s, variety, whether categorized as comedy-driven, music-driven, or general, offered the most common program type on network radio. Musical comedy always trailed musical variety, but sometimes it was hard to tell the difference. Indeed, Harrison Summers categorized the *Al Jolson Program* on CBS during the 1937–38 season as "comedy variety." Even programs centered on individual stars frequently filled out their 60-minute time slots with guest stars and so should be thought of as variety shows, such as, for example, *The Edgar Bergen and Charlie McCarthy Program*.

Orchestras dominated, because this was the big band era. There were Horace Heidt, Morton Gould, Russ Morgan, Sammy Kaye, Benny Goodman, and Tommy Dorsey, as well as the long-running Paul Whiteman, Wayne King, and Rudy Vallee.

In the 1940s, bands made their singers into individual stars in their own right. Doris Day, Bing Crosby, and Frank Sinatra could be backed by any band. The fans wanted to hear them as singers, not as appendages of notable big bands. Radio indeed sparked the sales of phonograph records, as stars introduced their new tunes and stylings via radio and then fans flocked to purchase copies of the discs of their favorites.

But there were other forms of music than big bands, notably hillbilly, which was later called country music. On Saturday nights, NBC broadcast both the *National Barn Dance* and the *Grand Ole Opry*, complete with singers, dancers, and comics. But these variety shows borrowed from another, alternative musical tradition and aimed exclusively at a rural audience. Variety shows most often were fed by the New York City-based Tin Pan Alley tradition and then later melded this with the music and comedy coming from Hollywood.

When in 1943 NBC spun off what became the American Broadcasting Company (ABC), the new company began with the *Alan Young Show*, the *Mary Small Revue*, the *Paul Whiteman Radio Hall of Fame*, and the *Woody Herman Band Show*. This is a partial listing, but surely ABC embraced all the strategies and scheduling opportunities that NBC and CBS had pioneered. ABC hit an apex in 1946 when Bing Cosby moved to the network for reasons of convenience and technical change. During the summer of 1946, Crosby left NBC after fulfilling his obligation with long-time sponsor Kraft and signed with Philco (maker of radio and later television sets) for a weekly salary of $7,500. Philco and ABC would permit Crosby to prerecord his *Philco Radio Time* on newly developed audiotape. He did not need to be in the studio when his show debuted (on 16 October 1946), nor as it ran on ABC until 1 June 1949. With the transcription ban broken, Bing Crosby then took advantage of the talent raids by CBS and so switched to a new sponsor—Chesterfield cigarettes—and to a new network—CBS—on which *The Bing Crosby Show* debuted 21 September 1949 and ran until the end of the 1951–52 radio season.

CBS and NBC built studios in both New York and Los Angeles to house these variety productions. Sometimes they simply adapted old vaudeville or movie palaces, but more often through the late 1930s and before building restrictions imposed by World War II, they built original, art deco-style studio spaces made for radio. The early 1930s NBC studio at Rockefeller Center—Radio City—best represented these sizable commitments to variety show's popularity.

Demise

The war years were the final hurrah for the radio variety show. National defense bond rallies often functioned as all-star radio variety shows, meant to outdo all other radio extravaganzas. Programs such as *Music for Millions*, *Treasury Star Parade*, and *Millions for Defense* not only drew needed bond sales, but also were beamed across the ocean or recorded for later playback for the troops fighting in Europe and the Pacific. The stars of radio—led by Bob Hope and Bing Crosby—toured for the United Service Organizations (USO) and went abroad to entertain the soldiers near the fronts. Indeed, radio star and big band leader Glenn Miller was killed in a plane crash while traveling from one show to another.

In the 1940s there was no more popular genre of radio program than variety. But late in the decade, both CBS and NBC shifted their variety stars to their television networks. Music for radio started with the combination of one of network radio's subgenres—hillbilly turned into country music—and another that never appeared on network radio—rhythm and blues. This amalgamation became rock and roll, and television maintained the Tin Pan Alley variety format through the 1950s and 1960s until rock proved so powerful that the variety tradition all but disappeared from television, as it had from radio two decades earlier.

But radio did have a last hurrah during the late 1940s, when CBS's William S. Paley—in alliance with Hollywood agent Lew Wasserman—incorporated stars such as Jack Benny, Red Skelton, Bing Crosby, Groucho Marx, and Edgar Bergen and then had their corporations sell their shows to the networks and sponsors. This incorporation meant vast savings in income taxes for the stars, but it led to the creation of a stable of CBS-housed talent that then transferred—by the middle 1950s—to the dominant CBS television network. By 1949 CBS was winning the radio rating wars with all but four of the top 20 radio shows; a decade later, the ratio would be about the same for CBS television in its battle with NBC.

It was not that participants in the radio variety show tradition gave up easily. There were sizable institutions that had a vested interest in keeping the live variety show going. First, there were the performing music societies: the American Society of Composers, Authors, and Publishers (ASCAP) and the new Broadcast Music Incorporated (BMI). Even more concerned was the union of musicians, the American Federation of Musicians, who tried to slow the innovative recording techniques—tape and discs—that union leaders and members correctly felt would lessen the demand for their live services.

NBC tried to keep the radio variety show alive with *The Big Show* on Sunday nights in 1951, but even this splashy revue could not keep the variety format from switching over to TV. A better symbol of the change was Paul Whiteman, who had hosted many golden age radio variety shows but who in 1947 became an early disc jockey on ABC, symbolizing the transformation to a new form of musical presentation on radio.

One man did keep radio variety alive until 1960 by doing variety in both media—Arthur Godfrey. His morning show was in the variety tradition, and his prime-time hit *Talent Scouts* was able to continue the form through the 1950s, with simulcast over radio until 1956. Godfrey's gift for gab was so popular on radio that he could book whomever he wanted, and fans tuned in. But with the cancellation of first *Talent Scouts* and later his morning show, variety on radio reverted to pure and simple nostalgia. These shows—more than any other form—offer in their preserved form a record of the top variety talent of the first two-thirds of the 20th century.

See also: Hollywood and Radio; *National Barn Dance*; Talent Raids; Vaudeville and Radio; *Your Hit Parade*

Further Reading

Bilby, Kenneth W., *The General: David Sarnoff and the Rise of the Communications Industry*, New York: Harper and Row, 1986.

Buxton, Frank, and William Hugh Owen, *The Big Broadcast, 1920–1950*, New York: Viking Press, 1972.

Crosby, Bing, and Pete Martin, *Call Me Lucky*, New York: Simon and Schuster, 1953.

DeLong, Thomas A., *The Mighty Music Box: The Golden Age of Musical Radio*, Los Angeles: Amber Crest Books, 1980.

Hickerson, Jay, *The Ultimate History of Network Radio Programming and Guide to All Circulating Shows*, Hamden, Connecticut: Hickerson, 1992; 3rd edition, as *The New, Revised, Ultimate History of Network Radio Programming and Guide to All Circulating Shows*, 1996.

Hilmes, Michele, *Hollywood and Broadcasting*, Urbana: University of Illinois Press, 1990.

Joyner, David Lee, *American Popular Music*, Madison, Wisconsin: Brown and Benchmark, 1993.

Lombardo, Guy, and Jack Altshul, *Auld Acquaintance*, Garden City, New York: Doubleday, 1975.

MacDonald, J. Fred, *Don't Touch That Dial!: Radio Programming in American Life, 1920–1960*, Chicago: Nelson-Hall, 1979.

Paley, William S., *As It Happened: A Memoir*, Garden City, New York: Doubleday, 1979.

Rhoads, B. Eric, *Blast from the Past: A Pictorial History of Radio's First 75 Years*, West Palm Beach, Florida: Streamline Press, 1996.

Summers, Harrison Boyd, editor, *A Thirty-Year History of Programs Carried on National Radio Networks in the United States, 1926–1956*, Columbus: Ohio State University, 1958.

DOUGLAS GOMERY

VAUDEVILLE AND RADIO

In a world where vaudeville is all but forgotten, it is difficult to imagine what a great impact this art form had on people's lives. For some immigrants who had talent, it was a way out of poverty. It gave others comfort and cheer when they were lonely. It was catharsis. It was amusement. In some ways, it was remarkably egalitarian. To truly understand the development of radio, one has to understand the vaudeville circuit that nurtured most of radio's early stars and provided the model for many early radio programs.

Origins

The origin of the word "vaudeville" is uncertain; some reference books say it comes from the French drinking songs called "chansons du Val de Vire." Others say it comes from the phrase "voix de ville," meaning "voice of the city" (or "voice of the people"). In Europe the term came to mean comic entertainment, comprised of farce and satire, often

in song or skit. In America vaudeville developed gradually, emerging from the burlesque shows performed in frontier towns and mining camps. As America became more urban, a growing middle class wanted entertainment, and that potential audience included women and children. Vaudeville historian Frank Cullen credits Tony Pastor with giving this form of entertainment some much-needed refinement. Pastor, Cullen writes, used a variety format that would become the standard for vaudeville: his first performances featured "a concert singer, a popular balladeer, a lady who played a [number of] instruments, an Irish act and a comedian who did only clean material."

Vaudeville theaters multiplied; by 1910, there were 2000 of them across the United States. In a world where radio broadcasting did not yet exist, movies were silent, and phonograph records were still fairly new, an enjoyable way to pass the time was to take the family to a vaudeville performance, where there was something for everyone. Some of the comedians used old jokes that the audience knew, and the fans would say the punchline along with the performer. People also sang along if they knew a song, and requests were sometimes taken. Song pluggers, with no radio to promote their potential hits, would persuade performers to do a certain song and then hire people to stand up and request it again or to cheer loudly at the end; the plugger would then stand outside the theater to sell the song on record or sheet music. On the other hand, if spectators did not like a performance or found a routine boring, they might express their disapproval in a chorus of boos. The vaudeville stage was no place for a person with a fragile ego.

The lives of vaudeville performers must have seemed exciting and glamorous to the audience, but the reality of being a performer was endless touring, sometimes playing several theaters a night, staying in cheap hotels, and sharing cramped dressing rooms with others on the same bill. Many impresarios—such as E.F. Albee, Samuel Rothafel, the Shuberts, and Florence Ziegfield—booked the major theaters and acts, though they were not always the kindest people with whom to deal. There was also a hierarchy of vaudeville theaters: the unknowns played in smaller houses and rural towns, whereas the biggest and the best got booked for New York City's Palace Theatre.

Until an entertainer developed a following and became a star, there was not much luxury, and sometimes there wasn't much money. But having to pay some dues did not dissuade the hopefuls: for those who dreamed of being famous, vaudeville was their best chance. In that era before talking

803

pictures and broadcasting, there was a constant need for new and interesting live performers at the many vaudeville houses; some theaters had nine or ten acts on the bill, and performers tried their hardest to be memorable, or at least unique in some way. A few performers who were moderately successful hired their own press agents to get them even more visibility, and, they hoped, better bookings. Nellie Revell, one of the few women press agents, not only worked with vaudeville stars and for several theaters, but also wrote about vaudeville for such publications as *Variety*.

Vaudeville helped the sons and daughters of immigrants become successful in America. Al Jolson and Eddie Cantor are two examples of young men from impoverished immigrant backgrounds whose careers took off thanks to their time on the vaudeville stage. In the North talented black performers often performed as well. (In the South, there was a separate circuit for blacks only.) In New York the legendary black comedian Bert Williams offered his amazing routines consisting of song and dance interfused with comedy; Williams became one of the highest paid black performers of his day and earned the respect of his white colleagues. Earning respect was not easy for a minority performer, especially when vaudeville reinforced every stereotypic representation in society—the greedy Jew, the cheap Scotsman, the drunken Irishman, the unintelligent black man. Williams was able to bring dignity to even those skits where he was supposed to play a bewildered Negro. There was no "political correctness" on the stage—immigrants who could not speak proper English, the nouveau riche who did not know how to behave—any foibles of any group could become the butt of jokes. At the same time, numerous foreign language theaters featured performers who poked fun at life in mainstream America.

Vaudeville on Radio

When radio developed, many of the performers who had made a name for themselves on the stage ignored the new medium. *Variety*, the "bible" of showbusiness, said radio was a fad that would not last, and besides, most stations had no money to pay the big name stars from Broadway. But by 1922 it was obvious that radio was winning new friends every day. Some of the vaudevillians decided that making an appearance on radio might be useful after all. At first, most performers and all of the impresarios had been opposed to going on the air; a 3 March 1922 cover story in *Variety* headlined, "Vaudeville and musicians declare against

Radiophone," with several major impresarios expressing the belief that radio would only encourage people to stay home and not come to the theater anymore. But the novelty and the chance for publicity had already attracted a few entertainers, and more would follow.

One of the first big vaudeville names to do so was comedian Ed Wynn. In February of 1922, he performed the first live play, "The Perfect Fool," on WJZ in Newark, New Jersey. The legend is that Wynn, ill at ease about performing in a silent studio with only an engineer to watch him, gathered up whoever was still in the building, including the cleaning crew and even a few people on the street, and invited them to watch his routine, thus creating the first studio audience. Their natural reactions to his humor greatly aided his timing. Radio made most vaudevillians uncomfortable because in the early days, studios were usually located in factories or on top of a roof, and there was no audience with which to interact. But Ed Wynn's innovation soon changed that, and as stations began building nicer studios (or moving into hotels that had ballrooms) it became acceptable to allow the public to watch performances.

Paying the big names was still a problem, but several of the impresarios decided to expand their use of radio and began putting their stars and theater acts on the air. Samuel Rothafel (better known as "Roxy") and Charles Carrell were two who did very well with this initiative. Roxy broadcast from the Capitol Theater over WEAF in New York City as early as 1923; he would be heard on the NBC network starting in 1927. Carrell, who ran numerous theaters in the Midwest in the mid-1920s, had a novel way of attracting attention to his vaudeville shows: he brought a "portable" station into towns where people had few opportunities to see a performance. His traveling companies then put on a show and the entire event was broadcast on his own station, which often encouraged listeners to make a trip to Chicago (where one of his theaters was located) to see a show in person. Of course, once the networks began operations, the problem of paying talent was solved. Early advertisers hired and paid the most famous stars.

Most of radio's best loved early entertainers got their start in vaudeville: Eddie Cantor, Al Jolson, Ed Wynn, comedienne Fanny Brice, singer Ruth Etting, comedians Jack Benny, George Burns and Gracie Allen, singer Sophie Tucker (who billed herself as the "Last of the Red Hot Mamas"), and many more. Nellie Revell (whose clients had included Jolson) ended up offering her showbusiness gossip column over the air on NBC, under the name "Neighbor Nell." She also invited the stars to her show for interviews.

The variety show on radio operated somewhat as the vaudeville show had—a number of acts in which each performer's job was to win over the audience both in the studio and listening at home. The mid-1930s talent show craze (characterized by Major Bowes' program) also harkened back to vaudeville days when managers offered an "opportunity night" for new performers to try out. If the public liked them, they might win a small prize (Eddie Cantor won $5); the real prize was the chance to come back and perform again, and ultimately to be hired.

Some critics later accused radio of killing vaudeville, but the truth is that the genre had begun to decline before the radio craze really took hold. Perhaps radio hastened its demise, but then, vaudeville really didn't die: it became a part of radio, and later a part of television. Thanks to vaudeville, a generation of entertainers perfected their craft and brought it to the air-waves, where a national audience could appreciate it all over again.

See also: Comedy; *George Burns and Gracie Allen Show*; Jewish Radio Programs; Stereotypes on Radio; Talent Shows; Variety Shows

Further Reading

Csida, Joseph, and June Bundy Csida, *American Entertainment: A Unique History of Popular Show Busmess*, New York: Watson-Guptill, 1978.
Green, Abel, and Joe Laurie, Jr., *Show Biz from Vaude to Video*, New York: Holt, 1951.
Nye, Russel B., *The Unembarrassed Muse: The Popular Arts in America*, New York: Dial Press, 1970.
Sobel, Bernard, *A Pictorial History of Vaudeville*, New York: Citadel Press, 1961.

DONNA L. HALPER

VIC AND SADE
Radio Comedy Serial

For 13 years, from 1932 until 1945, devoted radio listeners tuned in daily to "smile again with radio's home folks," Vic and Sade Gook. Over the course of more than 3,500 scripts, writer and creator Paul Rhymer produced an intimate, idyllic, and eccentric portrait of small-town life in Depression-era America.

Neither its serial format (*Vic and Sade* appeared alongside dozens of daytime soap operas) nor its subject matter (*The Aldrich Family* and *One Man's Family* also featured accounts of white, middle-class American life) made *Vic and Sade* unique.

What distinguished Rhymer's radio tales of life in "the small house half-way up on the next block" were its odd placement on the network schedule, the inimitable perspective of its creator, and its creative use of the aural medium. James Thurber (1948) wrote that amidst the tears and tragedy of daytime soap operas, *Vic and Sade* "brought comedy to the humorless daytime air." Indeed, *Vic and Sade* was one of the earliest and most enduring radio comedies about middle-class families in the American Midwest. Because of its unwavering focus on the humor of domestic life and its large fan following, *Vic and Sade* influenced the shape and form of situation comedies on both radio and television. Using only three (and later four) voices, a microphone, and a vivid imagination, Paul Rhymer collected everyday conversations, trivial events, and mundane details and wove them into fantastic vignettes of small-town life. Few other radio programs capitalized so successfully on the intimacy and imaginative potential of radio as did *Vic and Sade*.

Rhymer wrote all the scripts during the serial's run. His experiences as a young boy growing up in Bloomington, Illinois, served as a model for the Midwestern town life chronicled in *Vic and Sade*. After attending Illinois Wesleyan University, he was hired by the National Broadcasting Company (NBC) in Chicago to write continuity for music programs. As a special assignment, Rhymer was asked by NBC's program director, Clarence Menser, to develop a skit for an up-and-coming client, Procter and Gamble. Although Procter and Gamble did not recognize the early promise of this serial, Menser put the program on the air on a sustaining basis on 29 June 1932. (It was briefly sponsored in 1933 by Jelke and Ironized Yeast.) But not until November 1934 did Procter and Gamble realize its mistake; for the remainder of its run, *Vic and Sade* was sponsored by Procter and Gamble's Crisco. Paul Rhymer quit his position at NBC and devoted himself full-time to writing the serial. Although Rhymer was once fired as a journalist for writing stories about people he had not yet interviewed, his talent for creating stories about eccentric townsfolk was rewarded on radio.

Many contemporaries sought to distinguish *Vic and Sade* from the serials surrounding it on the network schedule. In addition to sharing the format of daytime soap operas (running five times a week), *Vic and Sade* also shared the serials' focus on family life and interpersonal relationships. *Vic and Sade* was set in the Gook household on Virginia Street in Crooper, Illinois. The serial focused on Victor Rodney Gook (Art Van Harvey), a bookkeeper for Plant No. 14 of the Consolidated Kitchenware

Company; his wife, Sade (Bernardine Flynn), a not-so-brilliant housewife who talked in mixed metaphors and malapropisms; their adopted son, Rush (Billy Idelson); and absent-minded Uncle Fletcher (Clarence Hartzell). Each episode focused on the conversations of the Gook family about household events and the daily happenings of their small town—Rush's stomachache; Vic's failure to notice that Sade has cut her hair; or Sade's fight with her best friend, Ruthie Stembottom. As Fred E.H. Schroeder (1978) observed, there is never a scene in *Vic and Sade* "that goes farther than the front porch, attic, or cellar." What distinguished *Vic and Sade* from other daytime serials were its noncontinuous story lines and quirky account of life in Crooper, Illinois. Unlike most radio serials, each episode of *Vic and Sade* was self-contained; the conflict introduced in each episode was often resolved by the end of the 15-minute program.

Through references and conversations of the main characters, a whole town came to life on the air. Listeners knew that Sade was a member of the ladies' Thimble Club, loyally attended the washrag sale at Yamilton's Department Store with Ruthie Stembottom, and specialized in making "beef punkle" ice cream for her family. Vic, the Exalted Big Dipper of his lodge, the Sacred Stars of the Milky Way (Drowsy Venus Chapter), was both antagonized by and devoted to his family. Young Rush often went to the Bijou theater with his friends Smelly Clark, Bluetooth Johnson, and Freeman Scuder to catch a feature film such as *You Are My Moonlit Dream of Love* or *Apprentice Able-Bodied Seaman McFish* when he wasn't playing rummy with Vic and Uncle Fletcher. Listeners knew the places in Crooper, Illinois, visited by Vic and Sade—the Butler House; the Bright Kentucky Hotel; and the Tiny Petite Pheasant Feather Tea Shoppe, which served scalded cucumbers and rutabaga shortcake—and the friends and neighbors who inhabited Vic and Sade's world—Reverend Kidney Slide; Chuck and Dottie Brainfeeble; Jake Gumpox; Rishigan Fishigan of Shishigan, Michigan (who married Jane Bayne from Paine, Maine); and Robert and Slobert Hink, who had brothers named Bertie and Dirtie and sisters named Bessie and Messie. When the eccentric Uncle Fletcher became a permanent character in 1940, the absurdity of the serial reached new heights. Uncle Fletcher entertained audiences with his rambling tales about Vetha Joiner, who went daffy after reading dime novels, or Ollie Hasher, whose friend painted his table every day so he wouldn't have to dust it.

Vic and Sade soon became one of the most popular serials on radio. In fact, in early 1935

Radio Stars reported that business in one South Dakota town literally halted each day so people could listen to the program. That same year, the Women's National Radio Committee named *Vic and Sade* one of the few daytime programs worth listening to. Just four short years after the program's introduction, a promotional offer featured on the show prompted an extraordinary 700,000 requests. By 1938 nearly seven million listeners tuned in daily. Over 600 radio editors polled named *Vic and Sade* the best radio serial. *Vic and Sade* was also admired by contemporary writers and humorists, including Jean Shepard, James Thurber, John O'Hara, Sherwood Anderson, Edgar Lee Masters, Ogden Nash, and Ray Bradbury, for its whimsical and humorous look at small-town America.

In its focus on three or four central characters, *Vic and Sade* remained largely unchanged until the last years of the serial. Art Van Harvey (Vic) was temporarily written out of the show while recuperating from a heart attack, as was Billy Idelson's character (Rush) when the actor enlisted in the navy during World War II. In this period, many of the characters previously only described by the Gooks (such as Orville Wheeney and Mayor Geetcham) were given voice as supporting characters in the serial. Although the program ended its continuous run in 1944, it was briefly revived by the Columbia Broadcasting System (CBS) in mid-1945 as a variety show and in 1946 by the Mutual network as a 30-minute sitcom. Two unsuccessful attempts were made to bring the program to television—to NBC's *Colgate Theater* in 1949 and to a local station, Chicago's WNBQ, in 1957. But the aural magic and the serial's peculiarity did not translate easily to a new visual medium (it was not perhaps until the debut of the *Andy Griffith Show* that eccentric small-town life successfully appeared on television). Although lack of storage space led Procter and Gamble to destroy original recordings of more than 3,000 episodes of the show, some remaining scripts were preserved in two edited volumes and in the archives at the State Historical Society of Wisconsin. Fan clubs such as the Vic and Sadists and the Friends of Vic and Sade and websites such as "Stephen M. Lawson's *Vic and Sade* Fan Page" and "Rick's Old-Time Radio *Vic and Sade* Page" have emerged since the serial's demise to share information, scripts, and the few recordings of the program that remain.

Cast

Victor Gook	Art Van Harvey
Sade Gook	Bernardine Flynn

| Rush Meadows | Billy Idelson, Johnny Coons, Sid Koss |
| Uncle Fletcher | Clarence Hartzell (1940–46), Merrill Mael (briefly in 1943) |

Announcers

Mel Allen, Charles Irving, Bob Brown, Roger Krupp, Ralph Edwards, Vincent Pelletier, Jack Fuller, Glenn Riggs, Clarence Hartzell, Ed Roberts, and Ed Herlihy

Creator/Writer

Paul Rhymer

Directors

Caldwell Cline, Clarence Menser, Earl Ebi, Paul Rhymer, Homer Heck, Charles Rinehardt, Ted MacMurray, and Roy Winsor

Programming History

NBC Blue/ NBC Red/NBC	1932–44
CBS	May 1938–November 1938; 1941–43; August 1945–December 1945
Mutual	March 1941–September 1941; June 1946–September 1946

Further Reading

"Meet Vic and Sade," *Radio Stars* (March 1935).
Rhymer, Paul, *The Small House Half-Way Up in the Next Block: Paul Rhymer's Vic and Sade*, New York: McGraw-Hill, 1972.
Rhymer, Paul, *Vic and Sade: The Best Radio Plays of Paul Rhymer*, New York: Seabury, 1976.
Schroeder, Fred, E.H., "Radio's Home Folks, Vic and Sade: A Study in Aural Artistry," *Journal of Popular Culture* 12, no. 2 (Fall 1978).
Thurber, James, *The Beast in Me and Other Animals*, New York: Harcourt Brace, 1948.

JENNIFER HYLAND WANG

VIOLENCE AND RADIO

Among the issues associated with any medium is a concern about violent and antisocial content. Many of the concerns about television and violence in contemporary society have antecedents in the history of radio. Violence, for the purposes of this entry, is defined as physical aggression toward humans by other humans, or the threat of such aggression. Radio has been associated with both "real" and fictional violence since its inception.

War and Radio's Beginnings

Radio has been related to violence since its inception in the late 19th century. Indeed, radio's applications for purposes of war and defense nurtured its early development. Guglielmo Marconi persuaded Great Britain to utilize his invention for military and commercial ships before the turn of the century. Radios were installed in military ships to enable communication between the sea and the shore, radically changing the nature of sea warfare. The ability to communicate with shore and with other ships greatly enhanced the ship as a weapon.

In the years between 1907 and 1912 in the United States, amateur radio grew steadily, to the agitation of the military. The U.S. Navy became concerned when official messages were undeliverable because of East Coast amateur chatter. President Taft signed the first general radio licensing law in 1912 in part as a response to military concerns. A clause of this law stated that "in time of war or public peril or disaster," the President might seize or shut down any radio station (Public Law No. 264, 62nd Congress, Sec. 2). In 1915 the Navy, acting on a tip from an amateur monitor, took control of a Telefunken-owned station on Long Island, New York, that had been transmitting radio messages regarding movements of neutral ships, presumably to German submarines. On 6 April 1917, as the United States declared war on Germany, all amateur radio operations in the United States were ordered to be shut down. On 7 April all commercial wireless stations were taken over by the Navy. Amateur radio enthusiasts protested the new regulatory atmosphere, but to no avail.

Radio coverage of violence and warfare during World War II ensured radio's place at the pinnacle of journalism. Live reports from Europe enabled audiences to learn about the aggression of Hitler's Germany. Radio contributed to the United States' move out of isolation and into World War II. Journalists such as Edward R. Murrow had broadcast vivid reports of the European conflict that helped convince the populace of the United States that it would be in the best interest of the nation to enter the war. After the bombing of Pearl Harbor, radio brought news of war from both Europe and the Pacific. The American public became adjusted to radio's providing details of violence during the worst war of human history.

Contemporary War and Radio

Radio has played important roles in contemporary violent conflicts. Among the unique uses of radio in wartime occurred during the Gulf War in 1990–91. Israelis tuned in to radio stations for warnings of incoming SCUD missile attacks from Iraq. The Israeli Broadcasting Authority and the radio station of the Israel Defense Forces unified to form the Joint Channel in an effort to keep the Israeli populace informed. The Joint Channel became immensely important to Israeli civilians. An interesting variation was the Quiet Channel. Reacting to audience suggestions, the Joint Channel broadcast silence on one frequency with the exception of missile warning alarms. This permitted Israelis unable to sleep with music or other radio programs an innovative alternative that allowed them to receive missile alarms.

Christine L. Kellow and H. Leslie Steeves (1998) documented the role of radio in the Rwandan genocide of 1994. The government-controlled Radio-Television Libre des Mille Collines (RTLM) served as the propaganda mouthpiece of the Hutu government. Messages intended to incite violence by Hutus against Tutsis were broadcast over Radio Rwanda, the official government station, immediately following the mysterious downing of a plane carrying the presidents of Rwanda and Burundi. With radio as the prominent source of information, RTLM was able to have a greater impact on the Rwandan populaces, both Tutsi and Hutu, in terms of both attitude and behavior. The Hutu-controlled RTLM used reversal techniques, emphasizing Tutsi hatred of the Hutus in order to encourage Hutu hatred of the Tutsis. In this fashion, Rwandan radio audiences were manipulated by messages of violence.

Terrorism

Terrorism has a particular and controversial relationship to media, including radio. To be successful, terrorism relies upon the public reporting of violence. A violent act itself gains nothing without public knowledge of the event. Thus, terrorism is inherently linked to the propaganda value of violence enacted. Terrorist acts are often consciously planned to gain media attention, making media's role even more controversial. The ethics of reporting terrorism are complex. Media organizations face the difficult task of determining what are newsworthy events without encouraging terrorism. At times, radio has inadvertently served the needs of terrorists by reporting police and military activity around the event, placing victims in more

danger. Also of concern is violence directed against radio personnel or stations. Dozens of journalists, some working in radio, are killed every year. Government radio stations are often initial targets in military coups.

Violence and Children

Much of the controversy in recent years concerning television's violent content parallels charges raised against radio in the 1930s and 1940s. Concern over violent programming may be seen in the production process undergone in the making of *Jack Armstrong, the All-American Boy*, broadcast on several radio networks from 1933–51. This serial cliffhanger adventure series featured Jack, a high school athlete, who had many adventures, each and every one of which was examined by child psychologist Martin Reymert before production to ensure that the program was not excessively violent. Still, complaints were heard from critics and some listeners, largely because the program targeted younger, more impressionable listeners.

Mrs. George Ernst of Scarsdale, New York, organized a 1933 campaign against the "Ether Bogeyman" of radio, whose characters were said to be causing nightmares among children. Her group analyzed 40 popular children's radio programs and found 35 unacceptable, including *Little Orphan Annie* and *Betty Boop*, both for violent and suspenseful content. In a 1934 symposium held in New York City, members of the Ethical Cultural Society, the Columbia Broadcasting System (CBS), the National Broadcasting Company (NBC), the Child Study Association of America, and other groups recommended the formation of a clearinghouse to offer a mechanism by which advertisers, the public, and broadcasters might make more informed decisions concerning the content of radio programs, especially those aimed largely at children.

Few studies examined psychological effects of radio listening on children during this period; most focused instead on what children wanted to hear. Paul Dennis (1998) characterized the experts who examined the psychological effects of radio listening during this time as falling into two camps. The dominant view held that dramatic and violent programming was cathartic for children, providing an outlet for tendencies of aggression. A smaller number of researchers argued that violent dramatic content promoted violent behavior, delinquency, and negative emotions.

Proponents of the dominant cathartic model relied on the idea that radio's programming functioned as pragmatic fantasy. In 1924, well before the children's programming boom, Mansel Keith claimed that a 41 percent reduction in juvenile court cases was attributable to radio's provision of adventure and romance for youth audiences. Jersild stated in 1938 that the vicarious enjoyment of excitement was a right of children, for "a cold, intellectual diet does not fill all of their needs." Ricciuti's comprehensive 1951 study found there was no scientific evidence that thriller programs contributed to fears or daydreaming in child audiences. Comparative studies frequently found no difference between audiences of violent radio content and nonlisteners.

Those arguing for scrutiny of violent radio content claimed negative impacts of exposure. The early 1940s witnessed a rise in juvenile delinquency, which was frequently attributed to violence in radio programming and comic books. Herzog (1941) found that 72 percent of fourth to sixth graders who dreamed about radio said their dreams were unpleasant. Several other researchers claimed to have found evidence that dramatic radio program content had a significant influence on children's reality expectations.

Dramatic radio programming sometimes had very tangible and obvious effects. An understanding of both the penetration and the potential impact of radio in terms of perception of violence may be gleaned from an examination of audience reactions to CBS's Halloween broadcast of a dramatic adaptation of H.G. Wells' *War of the Worlds*, on 30 October 1938. The program simulated a news program, with announcers interrupting seemingly standard-formatted programming for reports of aliens invading New Jersey. The American Institute of Public Opinion poll estimated that 1.7 million people believed the program was a newscast, and that 1.2 million people were at least excited by the news, approximately one-sixth of the total audience. Hundreds of people left their homes in fear. Such a mass reaction to dramatized violence in a radio program indicated the potential impact of radio and of American reliance upon the medium as a primary source of information at that time.

By the 1960s social learning theory had gained credence and was used as a foil for the cathartic model. Most of the research community turned away from the cathartic theory for lack of any evidence that such a positive impact existed. Many researchers in the 1960s, generally examining television and not radio, used social learning theory to explain how and why violent content leads to aggressive behavior in audience members.

Research findings concerning violent content of radio remain inconclusive. Many studies indicate that violent content is a cause of social violence, whereas many other studies conclude that violent content is not a cause of social violence. Many social scientists agree that violent media content can be a contributing factor to social violence, but there is disagreement concerning the magnitude of this relationship and the role and extent of other factors.

In 1929 the National Association of Broadcasters (NAB) established self-regulatory practices for program content and advertising. These codes of practices were nonbinding. Often revised, by 1967 the NAB Radio Code reflected the nation's concern for violent material and responsibility toward children. Specifically, the 1967 code stated: "They (radio programs) should present such subjects as violence and sex without undue emphasis and only as required by plot development or character delineation. Crime should not be presented as attractive or as a solution to human problems, and the inevitable retribution should be made clear." Although modified slightly from year to year, the Code wording did not have much impact on radio programming at any time. The Code was eliminated in the early 1980s.

Radio Music and Violence

The violent content in the lyrics of some popular songs broadcast over radio has caused controversy for years. There has been concern about lyrics of music since the first broadcasts of rock and roll records, especially with regard to lyrics dealing with sex, drugs, and violence. In the 1980s and 1990s, the wording of heavy metal, rap, and alternative songs was scrutinized by and became targets of advocacy groups and congressional inquiries. The Parents' Music Resource Center was founded in 1985 by Tipper Gore and Susan Baker, wives of powerful political figures in Washington, to advocate labeling music that dealt with violence, drug usage, suicide, sexuality, or the occult. In 1985 the Recording Industry Association of America agreed to use a uniform warning phrase, "Parental Advisory Explicit Lyrics," for such content.

In 1990, 8.5 percent of all music sold in the United States was classified as rap music, with lyrics often thematically linked to urban lifestyles and hip-hop culture. What became known as "gangsta rap" used themes of crime, violence, antipolice sentiments, and gang activities. Some of the notable figures affiliated with gangsta rap as it became popular in the late 1980s and early 1990s were Ice-T, Easy-E, Dr. Dre, Tupac Shakur, Biggie Smalls, and Ice Cube. Radio was a vital link in the distribution of such music, as after hearing songs on the air listeners then sought out their own copies.

Several politicians and public figures, including Senator Joseph Lieberman (D-Connecticut), Senator Sam Nunn (D-Georgia), and former Education Secretary William Bennett, held a series of news conferences in 1995 to protest lyrics in the music industry that were considered pro-drug, degrading to women, or advocating violence against the police. Senator Bob Dole (R-Kansas) praised the effort, calling for an outright ban on gangsta rap during his presidential campaign of 1996. The advocacy group targeted Time Warner because of its 50 percent ownership of Interscope Records, which served as distributor for such artists as Dr. Dre and the band Nine Inch Nails. The group accused Interscope of distributing music of artists who promoted drug use as well as the rape, torture, and murder of women. Time Warner sold its stake in Interscope records later in 1995, insisting the sale was not precipitated by pressure from the senators' advocacy group.

There have been several efforts by the radio industry to self-censor violent lyrical content. In 1993 WBLS (FM) of New York and KACE (FM) of Los Angeles publicly pledged not to give airtime to the most offensive and violent rap songs. In December 1993 Inner City Broadcasting Corporation, one of the largest African-American-owned broadcasting firms in the United States, announced it had banned lyrics it considered derogatory, sexually explicit, or violent. Entercom Communications, owner of many radio stations around the country, announced in July 1999 that it had adopted a policy to reject any music or advertising with violent content or that condoned violence.

The historical controversies concerning radio's violent dramatic programming and potential impacts on its audience reflect current debates 0concerning violent content of television. The controversy of the 1980s and 1990s concerning violent song lyrics; the contemporary concern with hate groups' use of radio; and the penetration of radio in developing nations, greatly exceeding that of other mass media, ensure that the topic of violence and radio will have great importance into the 21st century.

See also: Obscenity and Indecency on Radio

Further Reading

Cantril, Hadley, *The Invasion from Mars: A Study in the Psychology of Panic*, Princeton, New Jersey: Princeton University Press, 1940.

Dennis, P.M., "Chills and Thrills: Does Radio Harm Our Children? The Controversy Over Program Violence during the Age of Radio," *Journal of the History of the Behavioral Sciences* 34, no. 1 (1998).
Herzog, Herta, *Children and Their Leisure Time Listening to the Radio: A Survey of the Literature in the Field*, New York: Office of Radio Research, Columbia University, 1941.
Jersild, A.T., "Children's Radio Programs," *Talks* 3 (1938).
Kellow, C.L., and H.L. Steeves, "The Role of Radio in the Rwandan Genocide," *Journal of Communication* 48 (1998).
Klapper, Joseph T., *The Effects of Mass Communication*, New York: Free Press, 1960.
Skornia, Harry Jay, and Jack William Kitson, editors, *Problems and Controversies in Television and Radio*, Palo Alto, California: Pacific Books, 1968.

D'ARCY JOHN OAKS AND THOMAS A. MCCAIN

VIRTUAL RADIO

Though a trademarked phrase, Virtual Radio has become a generic term in the radio industry for the practice of using voice tracks to produce a radio station's programming, usually at a location other than at the station. At the most basic level, voice tracking is the integration of prerecorded tracks into music programming, with the intention of giving small market stations access to air talent that only larger markets could afford.

Origin

The true origins of Virtual Radio were tape syndication companies that began to provide services to stations in the 1960s. First was International Good Music, or IGM, which prerecorded classical music with announcer tracks and distributed the programming on tape to automated stations.

In the 1970s, the firm Drake Chenault did the same with Top 40 programming based on the "Boss Radio" concept founder Bill Drake had pioneered at KHJ in Los Angeles. TM Productions—later known as TM Century after a merger—became the largest supplier of syndicated programming for automated radio. Satellite radio formats were never classified as Virtual Radio because they were delivered in real time and not in disassembled form to be reassembled by the radio station.

Further Definition

The phrase was given specific definition in 1997 by The Research Group, a Seattle-based consumer research firm serving the radio industry. As the company expanded beyond audience research studies, it added voice tracking as a service for their client radio stations using announcers from the Seattle area. The new service was termed Virtual Radio, and The Research Group sought trademark registration.

The concept was both praised and derided in the industry—praised by station operators who saw voice tracking from distant studios as a way to reduce costs and increase efficiencies, and derided by local disc jockeys displaced by the systems. Internet chat rooms were filled with postings from air talents complaining about "corporate radio" and the lack of localism that resulted from most virtual radio operations. "How does someone in Seattle know what's going on in Fayetteville, Arkansas?" asked a typical posting on broadcast. net. The answer to that question was in the original plan for voice tracking systems: the local station was expected to provide content information to the voice-tracked disc jockeys so their performances could contain references to events, landmarks and personalities in the town.

Writing in the *BP Newsletter*, Klem Daniels of Broadcast Programming, Inc., stressed that voice tracking "is not an exercise in mediocrity, but a chance to achieve perfection." Daniels said, "Many feel that this is a blow to the creativity that has made great jocks and entertaining radio for years. Actually, only the most talented and creative personalities can make voice tracking a success."

Broadcast Programming (later known as Jones Radio Networks) provided a voice tracking service called Total Radio, and its accompanying *Total Radio Users Guide* asked local stations to provide the following information on a long questionnaire:

Call letters, dial position and station name (i.e., "Mix 96").
A list of personalities and disc jockeys on the station.
What sets your city apart from other area cities?
Manufacturers, football teams, universities, landmarks?
Names of dignitaries and famous residents.
The target audience: Married? Kids? Income level? Hobbies?

A Boon to Cash Flow

The efficiencies and cost savings of Virtual Radio were so lucrative that Capstar Broadcasting Partners built its business plan around computer and internet links among its stations. The first of the links was the Austin, Texas-based Star System, which was first used in Capstar's Gulf Star division, made up of Capstar stations in Texas, Louisiana, and the Southwest. In a 1998 analysis of Capstar's business by Credit Suisse/First Boston financial group, technology, including the Star System,

prompted a "buy" rating for shares of Capstar stock:

Using T-1 lines and other Intranet like systems, Capstar is able to have a DJ in Austin doing a live show in Waco or Tyler. Morning shows are primarily kept local, but other dayparts are done remotely. If the need arises, a local manager can tell a remote DJ what is happening in town over a computer screen, and the DJ can then report. So, if there is a large police chase in Tyler, a DJ in Austin can report on it as if he or she is actually there.

By linking all of its stations to a central location in each "Star" region, interviews of large celebrities can be made to sound local. News and weather are localized, yet music playlists are selected for the individual markets. Thus, local listeners get the researched programming they demand, and Capstar is able to save money on talent by getting more productivity out of each member of its on-air staff. Credit Suisse/First Boston pointed to Capstar's Baton Rouge stations as good examples of the results of using the Star System: in 1997 revenues were up 18 percent and broadcast cash flow was up 45 percent because of the savings on talent. The Star System digital voice-tracking network became part of AMFM, Inc., in a merger with Capstar. AMFM added a second voice track studio location in Fort Lauderdale, Florida. At its height, Star System fed 400 shows a day from the two operations, employing about 50 full-time air talents in each city.

After yet another merger that absorbed AMFM, Inc., into Clear Channel Communications, Clear Channel elected to close the Star System operations in 2001 in favor of its "hub and spoke" voice tracking concept. Hub and spoke is also virtual radio with voice-tracks recorded at major market stations (the hub) and fed to nearby smaller markets in the same region (the spokes). Thus, a Clear Channel station in Columbus, Ohio, would feed voice-tracks to sister stations in nearby Ohio towns. At about the same time Clear Channel closed the Star System, Jones Radio ended their marketing efforts for Total Radio because client demand for the service had dwindled to half a dozen stations. The Research Group had folded Virtual Radio in 1999 when Jacor Communications acquired the company before Jacor's merger with Clear Channel.

Local Input

Virtual Radio remained as a local operation, either in the hub-and-spoke style of Clear Channel or with individual station clusters using in-house talent to feed multiple stations in the same market. It would not be unusual to hear the same voice using one name on a Top 40 station and then later that same day using another name on the co-owned Country station. In some situations, voice-tracked disc jockeys even competed with themselves in the same time slot.

The advantage of voice-tracking within the local station or cluster is the effective use of time and talent. Instead of waiting for songs to end before performing, disc jockeys and other air talent can spend time producing commercials, making local appearances, or selling advertising. Also, by keeping the talents local, it is less likely that they will mispronounce an important local celebrity's name or miss a reference to a local event.

Over time, in some cases, the voice-tracking phenomenon has morphed from short pre-recorded introductions and spot announcements into longer radio features and full programs tailored to sound as though they are emanating directly from the host station. Many companies offer stations "local sounding" national radio shows like Lia's (Lia Knight) nightly country music-themed broadcast and Whitney Allen's *The Big Show*. Meanwhile, Ryan Seacrest's daily gabfest out of Los Angeles is also offered for airing in specially "customized" forms made for different markets. Ironically, this move towards providing full programming content moves the issue of virtual radio/voice-tracking away from one of automation to one of traditional syndication while harkening back to the days of national radio networks.

Alternate Definitions

Though virtual radio still means "voice-tracking" and "hub-and-voice"-like operations, thanks to the internet the term has also come to be used as a generic way of describing any number of mobile and internet-based services and applications.

Strictly speaking, virtual radio means the receiving of broadcast signals (or radio-like programming) through any device other than a traditional radio, for example over a cellphone or the internet. Therefore, all podcasting and audio streaming, including such established online music services as Pandora.com, Radio Paradise, and Sky.fm, can be considered virtual radio. One company that actually calls itself Virtual Radio offers subscribers numerous niche-oriented internet "radio stations" specifically for playing over their cellphones.

See also: Audio Streaming; Automation; Clear Channel Communications Inc.; Internet Radio

Further Reading

Daniels, Klem, "Voice Tracking: Doing It Right," *BP Newsletter* 12, no. 10 (October 1998).

ED SHANE,
2009 REVISIONS BY CARY O'DELL

VOICE-TRACKING
See: Virtual Radio

VOX POP
Radio Interview Program

The radio program *Vox Pop* (from the Latin for "voice of the people"), one of the first "man on the street" interview shows, was also one of the earliest quiz programs. Later it became a popular human-interest program and one of the biggest homefront morale boosters of World War II. It was also probably the best-traveled program in broadcasting history.

Origins

The show began in 1932 at station KTRH in Houston, Texas. Someone had the idea of dangling a microphone on a very long cord out the window of the hotel from which KTRH broadcast so that passersby could be interviewed. Station ad man Parks Johnson and station manager Jerry Belcher took on the task of talking to the man or woman on the street. They started out by asking about current events, then segued into lighter topics. The results were alternately fascinating and hilarious.

Once in those early days, after a large storm had swept through Houston, the hosts found themselves facing an empty street. They had no-one to interview. Necessity being the mother of invention, Johnson quickly relieved the program's crew of all their money, emptied his pockets as well, and had it all changed into dollar bills. He collared an usher from a nearby theater and proceeded to ask him questions, giving him a dollar for every correct answer. Soon the street was mobbed, and the "quiz show" was born.

This device worked very well during the depths of the Depression, and it began to alter the focus of the show. The opinions of the people, their voices, were downplayed as the quiz element gained in popularity. Current events questions were used as a warm-up to the *real* questions, the ones worth a dollar. Johnson often asked questions that originated from everyday life and was known for carrying a notebook with him and jotting down new topics for questions. Participants were asked questions that tested their knowledge of the Bible ("What did Pharaoh's daughter find?") or their vocabulary ("Can you ad-lib?") or questions meant to elicit a humorous response ("Why can't a cat be called 'Fido' or 'Rover'?"). Questions regarding the so-called war between the sexes were practically a regular feature. Such queries as "What makes a person fall in love?" and "What is a woman's place?" were sure to trip up the guest.

Network Popularity

Vox Pop was almost totally unrehearsed, and this spontaneity proved to be a hit with listeners. The show was broadcast from the streets of Houston for more than two years, but it also attracted attention outside of Texas. On 7 July 1935, *Vox Pop* began appearing on the National Broadcasting Company (NBC), broadcasting from the sidewalk at New York's Columbus Circle. The following week, the show took its microphones to the waiting room of Grand Central Station, moving the show around New York City for the rest of the summer. Brief interviews with contestants before the quizzing began became part of the proceedings, and soon *Vox Pop* was dropping in on events as varied as a Hollywood movie premiere and the "Days of '76" celebration in Deadwood, South Dakota.

Into early 1940, the program was still giving away dollar bills at a furious pace, but as the nation edged closer to war, the focus of *Vox Pop* began to change once again. Johnson, a World War I veteran, threw the program wholeheartedly into the war effort at least 17 months before the bombing of Pearl Harbor. The quiz show structure was phased out, and the program changed to a focus on human interest, going into a community or attending an event and deciding beforehand which guests to interview.

The show traveled up to 1,000 miles per week throughout the United States, visiting military bases, military schools, and factories and showcasing different communities that were helping on the home front. Themes such as "Lumber at War," "Food at War," and "Dogs for Defense" were typical of this period; later in the war years, the show's visits included military hospitals. The show broadcast from 45 states as well as to Canada, Mexico, Puerto Rico, and Cuba. At this time, Parks Johnson's wife Louise began helping the show by buying gifts for the interviewed guests. "Mrs. Santa Claus," as she became known, eventually had a budget of $1,000 per week and was quite adept at locating hard-to-find items during the war years. These were halcyon days for *Vox Pop*. The show seems to have connected with the country in a very real way, and its ratings climbed steadily during this period, reaching a respectable 15.3 during the last two years of the war.

Parks Johnson was the guiding force throughout the life of the radio program. Jerry Belcher left the show in 1936 and was replaced by Wally Butterworth, a well-known radio announcer. Butterworth hosted the show with Johnson from 1936 until 1941. Neil O'Malley filled in briefly but was replaced by Warren Hull in 1942. Hull, an actor and announcer who had played the Green Hornet in the movies and was later master of ceremonies for the popular TV program *Strike It Rich*, stayed with the program until *Vox Pop* left the air in 1948.

Advertising Squabble

The show had several sponsors through the years. Deals with Kentucky Club Tobacco and Bromo-Seltzer lasted longest, but it was the sponsor *Vox Pop* had for the least amount of time that made the biggest impact. Lipton Tea sponsored the show in a Tuesday night slot starting in 1946, but the relationship between program and sponsor quickly soured. T.J. Lipton, Inc. thought its products did not get enough attention on the program and insisted that each guest (as many as six per show) be presented with a box of Lipton products before receiving his or her personalized gift. These presentations were in fact commercials, commercials that "must do a hard selling job," according to a memo from Lipton.

Johnson, as sole owner of the show, did not like the new requirement, and after negotiations failed, he took the unusual step of firing his sponsor. Many a sponsor had canceled a program for low ratings, but never had a performer canceled a sponsor! Newspapers around the country picked up the story. Johnson was hailed as a "radio knight," a man of high moral principles who refused to compromise. This favorable publicity meant that *Vox Pop* had little trouble finding a new sponsor, and the show continued until 1948 for American Express. By this time, however, radio was changing, and Johnson was weary of traveling. The last show aired on 19 May 1948, and Johnson retired to his ranch in Wimberly, Texas, where after a second career of civic boosterism he died in 1970.

Hosts

Parks Johnson, Jerry Belcher, Wally Butterworth, Neil O'Malley, Warren Hull

Announcers

Graham McNamee, Ford Bond, Milton Cross, Ben Grauer, Ernest Chappell, Dick Joy, Tony Marvin, and Roger Krupp

Producers/Directors

Arthur Struck, John Becker, Rogers Brackett, Thomas Ahrens, Don Archer, and Glenn Wilson

Programming History

KTRH (Houston)	1932–35
NBC	1935–39
CBS	1939–47
ABC	1947–48

Further Reading

DeLong, Thomas A., *Quiz Craze: America's Infatuation with Game Shows*, NewYork: Praeger, 1991.

Manning, Jerald, "Ready Wally? Ready Parks? How the *Vox Pop* Boys Run Their Show, and Some Questions for You," *Radio Stars* (November 1938).

Sammis, Fred, "The Program on Which YOU Are the Star!" *Radio Mirror* (October 1935).

Sullivan, Ed, "Radio Award," *Modern Screen* (November 1946).

CHUCK HOWELL

WABC

New York City Station

One of the most powerful New York City stations (in terms of both transmission and ratings strength), WABC has been successful first as a Top 40 station and more recently as a talk radio outlet. The flagship station of Disney/American Broadcasting Companies (ABC), WABC traces its history back to 1921. (It should not be confused with another WABC, also in New York City, that served as the flagship for the CBS network and became WCBS in 1946.)

Origins

WABC began broadcasting in 1921 in Newark, New Jersey, with the call letters WJZ, a 3,000-W station owned by the Westinghouse Broadcasting Company transmitting at 833 kHz. Two years later it moved into New York City and was purchased by the Radio Corporation of America(RCA), which in 1926 created the National Broadcasting Company (NBC). NBC, in turn, established its Blue network with WJZ as the flagship station. The station increased its power to 50,000 W in 1935 and changed its frequency several times, finally settling on 770 kHz in 1941.

In 1943 the Blue network and WJZ were sold to Edward J. Noble and Associates, which in 1945 changed its licensee name to the American Broadcasting Companies. Station call letters were altered to WABC in 1953 to reflect the transition. The ABC networks and WABC were taken over by United Paramount Theaters in 1953. Decades later the station and network were sold (1996) to the Disney Corporation.

Programs and Promotion

In the late 1950s WABC was lagging behind New York's leading popular music stations, WMCA and WINS, and was struggling to find its own niche in the highly competitive market. By 1964 WABC was not only the top station in New York, it was also the most-listened-to radio station in America. With weekly audiences of between five and six million from the mid-1960s to the mid-1970s, WABC could be heard in 38 states and Canada. Its Saturday night *Dance Party* with Bruce Morrow (universally known as "Cousin Brucie") reached 25 percent of the total radio audience in the New York metropolitan area.

The phenomenal change in WABC's fortunes is largely credited to the vision of Rick Sklar, station program director from 1963 to 1977. Sklar helped WABC stand out from its competition with a number of approaches. He limited the music playlist while at the same time trying to bridge the generation gap of rock and nonrock listeners. Sklar held weekly music meetings with his staff, assiduously choosing appropriate selections for diverse groups and tapping into the rapidly changing music of the era. The repeated airing of music by the Beatles (and on-air interviews with the members of the group) led to the hyping of the station as "W A Beatle C."

WABC's on-air lineup was built to create recognizable personalities, among them radio legends Harry Harrison, Dan Ingram, and Ron Lundy, as well as one of the best-known disc jockeys in the country, "Cousin Brucie" Morrow. These men had mellifluous voices, but more important, they established a rapport with their devoted listeners and hosted programs that were fun to listen to.

To establish loyalty and to garner attention, the station conducted unusual and ultimately enormously effective promotions. One such gimmick allowed people to vote for the School Principal of the Year. Listeners of all ages could vote as often as they wanted; the idea was to get entire families and school faculties tuned to the station. By the second year of the promotion in 1963, the program was so successful that the station received 176 million ballots—many of them from well beyond the tristate (New York, New Jersey, and Connecticut) standard audience area.

In 1964 WABC sponsored a contest honoring the best and the worst copy of the *Mona Lisa*, which was being flown from Paris to New York for exhibition at the Metropolitan Museum of Art. With Nat King Cole singing the promotional jingle and surrealist painter Salvador Dali serving as the judge, WABC received more than 30,000 entries.

Jingles and slogans were a key aspect of the station and were broadcast constantly. There were special jingles promoting the station's place on the dial, its news and sports reports, its disc jockeys and their timeslots, and—above all—its ranking of songs and attention to music. The station's sounds became so distinct that even listeners tuning in during advertisements knew they were hearing WABC.

News and Talk Radio

The demise of all-music WABC came on 10 May 1982—dubbed by some as "the day the music died"—when "MusicRadio 77" gave way to "News-Talk Radio 77." A range of factors contributed to the need for the switch, among them the development of FM radio with its superior sound quality and the transfer of most music formats (and their audiences) to FM. AM stations like WABC needed to develop viable talk-based formats where sound quality was less crucial. By switching to an all-talk format, WABC was following the trend of many AM stations across the country.

By 2000 WABC was a powerhouse in personality-driven talk radio. As in years past, its promotions emphasize the station's approach: "If you're talkin' about it, we're talkin' about it." The station's two daytime hosts, Dr. Laura Schlessinger (9–11:45 A.M.) and Rush Limbaugh (12–3 P.M.) were the two top-rated hosts in the county; Limbaugh's Excellence in Broadcasting production operation shares studio space in the same building as WABC. Others in

WABC's program lineup include the locally based conservative host Sean Hannity, liberal Lynn Samuels, former New York mayor Rudolph Giuliani, and former Guardian Angel Curtis Sliwa.

The station is also the broadcast home of the New York Yankees and New York Jets, and scheduled programs are pre-empted to broadcast the baseball and football games live. The only indication that WABC was once the premier music station in the nation is a three-hour program on Saturday nights devoted to Frank Sinatra.

See also: American Broadcasting Company; Promotion on Radio

Further Reading

Battaglio, Stephen, "When AM Ruled Music and WABC Was King, *New York Times* (10 March 2002).
Freedom Forum Media Studies Center, *Radio, the Forgotten Medium*, New York: The Center, 1993.
Jaker, Bill, Frank Sulek, and Peter Kanze, "WABC-II," "WJZ," in *The Airwaves of New York*, by Jaker, Sulek, and Kanze, Jefferson, North Carolina: McFarland, 1998.
Musicradio 77 WABC, www.musicradio77.com
Passman, Arnold, *The Deejays*, New York: Macmillan, 1971.
Sklar, Rick, *Rocking America: An Insider's Story: How the All-Hit Radio Stations Took Over*, New York: St. Martin's Press, 1984.
WABC website, www.wabcradio.com

RUTH BAYARD SMITH

WALKMAN
Portable Audio

Begun in 1979 as a risky consumer electronics experiment by Sony and soon after almost a generic term (it was added to the Oxford English Dictionary in 1986), the Walkman was the first personal stereo, a tiny portable cassette tape playback device with a lightweight headset. Perhaps the most important consumer audio product since the development of the transistor radio in the mid-1950s and of stereo FM in 1961, the Walkman and its many imitators became one of the biggest worldwide consumer successes of the 1980s and 1990s. Begun as a tape-playing device, the Walkman changed over the years to add recording capability, radio reception, and eventually digital formats including CDs. The trade name became almost synonymous with any portable radio or disc player.

Origins

The Walkman began with an earnest request from engineer (and Sony co-founder) Masaru Ibuka,

(1908–97) in late 1978 for a device on which he could listen to music while on long international flights from Japan. The first prototype was developed in Sony's tape recorder division in just a few days early in 1979, based on the existing "Pressman," a tape recorder designed for reporters. Given the short time for development, the new device made use of a tape transport and stereocircuits from existing Sony products.

As it was not a sophisticated piece of electronics that provided something technically new, many Sony engineers and some managers were not interested in the device. But Sony co-founder Akio Morita (1921–99), with his strong sense of product appeal and marketing, soon became a strong proponent of the innovation he saw as a potential best-seller. At his urging, engineers added dual headphone connections (the "his and hers" option) to make the device less off-putting, and an orange button mute to reduce volume so that the listener could hear outside sounds without having to remove the headphones (the "hotline function").

Perhaps the most important part of the package was the new lightweight headphones. Sony would emphasize the stylish nature of the tiny headphones in comparison to what people then used—large earmuff-size devices. This attempt to create a headphone culture was risky in a society with a phobia about deafness or other physical impairment. Also risky was the potential market value of a machine that could play cassette tapes but could not record. Batteries could operate the tiny machine for up to eight hours (two decades later batteries could last for 60 hours). Finally, the machine offered quality sound reproduction despite its tiny size—a key selling point. Sensing an untapped market, Morita wanted to focus sales efforts on youngsters during the summer of 1979. There was no advance market testing, in part for lack of time. A relatively low sales price (projected to be about $125) would mean thousands would have to be sold to break even. Morita suggested an initial batch of 30,000—easily twice what their most popular tape recorder sold in a year—and again horrified his colleagues. The first product announcement and demonstration took place in June. Reporters were invited to an outdoor park in Tokyo to demonstrate the many ways the "Walkman," as it was now named, could be used while performing other activities.

Phenomenon

The first Walkmans went on the Japanese market 17 July 1979 (for $200), three weeks later than Morita had hoped. The delay made Sony even more concerned when initial sales were very slow, especially given its huge stock of the devices. By mid-August, however, word of mouth began to propel the Walkman to widespread popularity and sales took off. The first 30,000 were sold in a month, largely to the teenage buyers Morita had projected would be most interested. Sony had to constantly increase production to keep up with demand. Indeed, the first foreign sales had to be postponed for months—despite already running advertising campaigns—just to keep up with burgeoning Japanese demand.

The Walkman device was first sold as the "Soundabout" in the U.S. and Europe only in February 1980. Initially the plan was to sell the device under various names, depending on the country's language, but Sony quickly decided to stick with the Walkman label everywhere, which made advertising campaigns easier and helped the product build a global image.

Some later models added radio reception and by the 1990s were increasingly digital, built around CDs (as the "Discman"). Walkman had become a generic (though still trademarked) term for all the many small, portable CD or tape players and recorders as well as small radios. A variety of Sony models were made available—by 1990 more than 80 different models; by 1999, 180 in Japan alone and more than 600 worldwide. More than 250 million had been sold worldwide by late 1998 at prices ranging from as little as $25 up to $500. By the mid-1990s, the "portable audio product" category of consumer electronics devices was selling more than 25 million units a year. The Walkman principal was extended to television, with the eventual development of the Watchman (tiny portable TVs).

Perhaps the major social impact of the Walkman was to create a "personal sound" space for its users. Now one could listen to a recording or broadcast in a crowd—as in public transportation or even an elevator—without invading others' space. The very unobtrusiveness of the light, tiny device allowed users to carry sound with them almost everywhere—even on strenuous workouts or hikes. The Walkman represented ultimate portability even two decades after its introduction.

While cassette-playing Walkman devices were made by Sony early into the first decade of the 21st century (and even longer in Canada), the basic device increasingly was redesigned to became an MP3 player after 2003, one sold under various product names. It sought to compete with the Apple iPod in terms of features, price and battery life, though with limited success. For one thing, it adhered to a proprietary Sony operating system

WAMU

that limited its use with other devices or content. Later versions, including cellphones, continued this but also accepted MP3 content.

See also: Portable Digital Listening Devices; Receivers

Further Reading

Du Gay, Paul, editor, *Doing Cultural Studies: The Story of the Sony Walkman*, Thousand Oaks, California: Sage, 1997.
Hooper, Judith, and Dick Tersi, *Would the Buddha Wear a Walkman? A Catalogue of Revolutionary Tools for Higher Consciousness*, New York: Simon and Schuster, 1990.
Joudry, Patricia, *Sound Therapy for the Walk Man*, St. Denis, Saskatchewan: Steele and Steele, 1984.
Morita, Akio, Edwin M. Reingold, and Mitsuko Shimomura, *Made in Japan: Akio Morita and Sony*, New York: Dutton, 1986.
Nathan, John, *Sony: The Private Life*, Boston: Houghton Mifflin, and London: HarperCollinsBusiness, 1999.
Patton, Phil, "Humming Off Key for Two Decades," *New York Times* (29 July 1999).
Sanger, David, "Stalking the Next Walkman," *New York Times* (23 February 1992).

CHRISTOPHER H. STERLING,
2009 REVISIONS BY CHRISTOPHER H. STERLING

WAMU

Washington, D.C. Station

WAMU-FM is a public broadcasting FM station in Washington, DC, renowned for its news and commitment to bluegrass music, and as the birthplace of many National Public Radio programs and personalities.

Origins

The station was founded as WAMC in 1948 by a group of radio-inclined American University students who utilized homemade transmitters for their initial broadcasts. After a 1950 robbery, which saw all of the station's equipment vanish, it was silent for a year before signing back on as a 25-W campus station, WAMU-AM, in 1951. During its early campus life, the station was under the auspices of the university's Department of Speech Arts and was located in the communications building.

In 1961, the station switched from AM to FM and signed on as the sixth member of the Educational Radio Network (ERN), the precursor of National Public Radio. WAMU's early programming was a mixture of classical music (including the airing of local concerts), public affairs programs and locally produced talk shows as well as programs supplied by the National Association of Educational Broadcasters, ERN, and the Broadcasting Foundation of America.

After originally only being heard weekdays and for a few hours on the weekends, in 1962, WAMU began broadcasting a full seven-day schedule. The following year it hired its first full-time employees (it had been staffed only by students and volunteers). One of the station's first hires was a young journalist named Susan Stamberg.

Other WAMU on-air talents have included Nate Shaw, George Geesey (who also served as the station's general manager), and Fred Friske. Some of the station's original programming during this period included *Kaleidoscope*, an early radio news magazine, and *Recollections*, devoted to old-time radio. Hosted by John Hickman, it was the predecessor to the station's *The Big Broadcast*, hosted by Ed Walker.

In 1967, WAMU began airing *Bluegrass Unlimited* hosted by Dick Spottswood. It was the station's first foray into bluegrass music, a genre that would later come to dominate WAMU. A decade later, over 20 hours of airtime a week was devoted to bluegrass music. The station began to sponsor its own yearly bluegrass festival beginning in 1979.

WAMU was a charter member of National Public Radio in 1970. On May 3, 1971, the station carried the first broadcast of *All Things Considered*, NPR's daily news program, hosted by former WAMU staffer Susan Stamberg. Despite carrying NPR programs, by 1973, 86 percent of the station's content was being produced in-house, including *The Home Show* hosted by Irma Aandahl, *Stained Glass Bluegrass* hosted by Gary Henderson, and even a full reading of Tolstoy's *War and Peace* performed by Bill Cavness.

In 1978, citing financial constraints and space issues, American University cut its ties with the station and the station was incorporated as an independent nonprofit organization and moved off campus, soon to stage its first on-air pledge drive.

The Modern Station

In 2001, WAMU announced that it would adopt a greater news focus to include a daily three-hour block of news and information programming every weekday afternoon. This was in addition to its continuing airing of its popular talk shows and NPR's *Morning Edition* every morning. This changeover raised many complaints among the station's loyal listeners to bluegrass, who saw their beloved on-air hosts and music banished to the weekends. In order to appease its bluegrass contingent, in late 2001, WAMU launched BluegrassCountry.org, a 24-hour music stream, over the internet. Later, the station would create WAMU 88.5-2, an HD station specifically for bluegrass.

WAMU has served as an incubator for many National Public Radio (NPR) programs. Before moving to network television, Derek McGinty hosted a WAMU talk show beginning in 1991. It was aired over NPR from 1996 until its end in 1998. Diane Rehm, who began her broadcasting career as a volunteer at the station in 1973, saw her talk program *The Diane Rehm Show* go over NPR starting in 1996.

See also: National Public Radio

Further Reading

About WAMU website, http://www.wamu.org/about/
Shallcross, Lynne, "WAMU: Radio Station to Some, Family Newsletter to Others." *Washingtonian*, August 2007, p. 10.

CARY O'DELL

WAR OF THE WORLDS
Radio Drama

Broadcast as part of the *Mercury Theater of the Air* in October 1938, the style and format of *War of the Worlds*, an hour-long live drama, coming just a month after radio's news bulletins about Europe's Munich crisis, pushed some of the U.S. listening audience into a panic—and clearly demonstrated the growing trust in and power of radio broadcasting.

The Script

In 1898 English author and social thinker H.G. Wells (1866–1946) published *War of the Worlds*, a novella concerning an attack on Earth by creatures from Mars. Drawing on fears of a re-arming Germany and concerns about the impact of such modern technologies as the telegraph and improved modes of transport, Wells' invasion story took place in England at the end of the 19th century.

Four decades later, in July 1938, the Columbia Broadcasting System (CBS) radio network began to offer weekly radio adaptations of literary works on the *Mercury Theater of the Air* on Monday evenings at 9 P.M. (changing to Sunday in September). The program featured the cast and producers of Broadway's successful and creative Mercury Theater troupe, headed up by the 22-year-old *wunderkind* Orson Welles (1915–85) and his producer John Houseman (1902–88). For each weekly broadcast, the cast would have only a few days to develop, rehearse, and finally broadcast each script. Several

weeks into the radio season, Welles came upon H. G. Wells' story, which he felt would be perfect for the Halloween eve broadcast of his series.

By this point, Howard Koch (1901–95), undertaking his first professional scriptwriting job, had joined Houseman (who had written all program scripts to that point). In what became his third script for the series, Koch modified the original Wells story to take place in the present time and in tiny Grovers Mill, New Jersey (picked at random), not far from Princeton. Most important, in light of what would happen, Koch applied Welles' idea of a radio news bulletin approach (rather than straight narration) for the first portion of the drama. Listeners would hear what appeared to be news bulletins breaking into ongoing network musical programming. But Koch had to create a modern radio script from the 40-year-old story in less than a week.

He wrote the 60-page script over four days, with about 20 pages at a time being turned over to the producers for their comments and changes. With Houseman's aid, the script was finally finished on Wednesday so that the cast (save Welles, who was committed to Broadway activities) could rehearse on Thursday. The recorded results, however, sounded stilted and dull to all involved, and the script was revised again. Houseman and Koch added bits and pieces to enhance the eyewitness sound of the story with real places and some realistic government voices at key moments. When CBS received a copy on Friday, the network censor also asked for numerous script changes to make the story's fictional basis more obvious. This usually involved the changing of place names or organizations. Whereas the network seemed concerned that listeners might think the story too realistic, Mercury people feared listeners would not stay tuned in or would find the story too fantastic.

Busy with Broadway commitments, Orson Welles did not even see the script until Sunday morning, 30 October—mere hours before it would be broadcast live. At that point he took charge, making further script changes at the opening of the drama to increase the reality of the news bulletins breaking into other programs.

The Broadcast

Sunday evening network radio listening was dominated by Edgar Bergen and Charlie McCarthy on National Broadcasting Company (NBC) Red, the only commercial program in the time slot. On NBC Blue, listeners heard *Out of the West*, narrated dance music from San Francisco presented on a sustaining (noncommercial) basis, while Mutual stations were carrying the WOR symphony orchestra, though many carried a speech by Father Charles Coughlin, as it was sponsored (paid) time. Not all CBS stations carried the Mercury broadcasts—the Boston outlet, for example, was carrying a local program.

At 8 P.M. in CBS Studio 1 on the 20th floor of CBS headquarters at 485 Madison Avenue in New York, the cast and sound effects people were in place. Besides Welles playing Professor Richard Pierson, Dan Seymour played the New York studio announcer, Kenneth Delmar played several roles (he became famous several years later on the Fred Allen show), and Ray Collins also performed several different roles. The music background was by Bernard Hermann. Relatively few listeners heard the program opening—a fairly standard announcement of what was to come followed by Welles setting the stage for the actual inception of the story. Some simply tuned in late, but many were listening to Bergen and McCarthy on NBC and would tune over to CBS after the play had begun. These patterns were a critical factor in the panic created by the program, for when listeners tuned in they heard what seemed like a normal weather forecast and then a cut-away to a hotel orchestra in downtown New York. The music was announced and was just getting underway when an announcer cut in with the first bulletin—about "reports observing several explosions of incandescent gas, occurring at regular intervals on the planet Mars." More music, then another bulletin, followed by a brief interview with a Princeton astronomer played by Welles. Then a bit of piano music, and still another news bulletin about those Mars explosions, but this time adding that "a huge, flaming object, believed to be a meteorite" had fallen on a farm "in the neighborhood of Grovers Mill, New Jersey." After about 20 seconds of a hotel swing band, another announcer broke in—and indeed, the next half-hour was a series of increasingly exciting live on-the-scene reports from different reporters at various points in New Jersey. After the hostile nature of the "invasion" became clearer, about 25 minutes into the program, an announcer said,

Ladies and gentlemen, I have a grave announcement to make. Incredible as it may seem, both the observations of science and the evidence of our eyes lead to the inescapable assumption that those strange beings who landed in the Jersey farmlands tonight are the vanguard of an invading army from the planet Mars.

This was followed by several more reports—from an army detachment and then a bombing aircraft—

all of them giving way to the seeming invincibility of the invaders. By 8:40 P.M., clouds of poisonous gas were reported to have covered Manhattan, and a lone radio operator elsewhere was heard calling out with no response.

At about this point, a CBS announcer made a brief station break, noting that the program in progress was a drama, and then the final portion of the program began. Little remembered today, this consisted of Welles playing the Princeton astronomer, Richard Pierson, fearing he may be the last person on earth. He puts down his thoughts in a diary; then he runs across another survivor and, at the end of the hour, the remains of the invading Martians, killed by earthly organisms and bacteria. This segment ran 20 minutes.

At the end, and "out of character" as he put it, Welles spoke briefly to "assure you that the *War of the Worlds* has no further significance than as the holiday offering it was intended to be." A network announcer wrapped up with a hint of next week's broadcast and a Bulova Watch advertisement for the 9 P.M. hour.

The Effect

The first the program's cast knew of the commotion being caused came as the broadcast ended and police entered the studio, confiscating copies of the script and questioning actors on how much they knew about what was going on outside. Network telephone lines were flooded with calls of concern. Three more times during the evening, CBS announcers made clear the broadcast had been merely a drama and not a real news event. More than half of the stations that carried the play also made their own announcements.

But these cautionary announcements came too late for many listeners. Thousands of them, especially those in the seeming New Jersey and New York "target" zone of the Martian attack, had heard more than enough well before the program was over and were trying to flee the scene. If they heard one of the characters note that people were fleeing, they would, as later reported to researchers, look out the window. If streets were busy, they would assume people were fleeing. If streets were empty, the conclusion often reached was that others had already fled. Amazingly, few of those who panicked thought to tune another radio station to check or even to look at newspaper listings of programs to see what CBS was supposed to be broadcasting at that time. Few even telephoned others. If radio said we were being invaded, then it must be true.

Hundreds of calls were placed to newspapers (the *New York Times* alone received more than 800), radio stations, and police. The Associated Press put out a bulletin to its member papers explaining what had happened. Only slowly on the evening of the broadcast was widespread panic reduced. Though there were many accidents on crowded roadways, luckily no-one was killed.

Over the next several days, there were widespread press reports about what had happened. Ironically, the program's impact that night helped it to gain commercial sponsorship, and it became the *Campbell Playhouse* in December and lasted in modified form until mid-1941.

Fascinated by the reaction to the program, the newly formed Office of Radio Research at Princeton University undertook a research study, under sociologist Hadley Cantril, to determine why so many had been driven to panic. The results, published as a book two years later, were largely based on interviews with 135 listeners. Researchers learned that people had grown accustomed to radio breaking in with important news during the Munich crisis of a month before and that such bulletins were assumed to be true. Of the roughly six million who tuned in, 1.7 million reportedly believed what they heard.

The Aftermath

A number of lawsuits were filed against CBS, all of which were eventually settled out of court. The Federal Communications Commission (FCC) launched a brief investigation out of which came an industry ban on program interruptions for fake news bulletins.

Rebroadcasts or sequels appeared on the anniversary of the original broadcast. In one case, a 1949 Spanish-language sequel in Quito, Ecuador, led to enraged listeners' burning down the station, with several lives being lost. The story became a popular 1953 movie, with the setting shifted to Los Angeles. The first commercial recording of the original broadcast was issued in 1955 by Audio Rarities. "The Night America Trembled," presented on CBS's *Studio One* in September 1957, provided television viewers with a dramatic portrayal of the radio program. Buffalo station WKBS offered an updated version on the 30th anniversary of the original broadcast (30 October 1968), with radio in a Top 40 format style using station disc jockeys and newspeople. It was replayed a year later. Scriptwriter Koch provided a brief 1970 book with his own version of what had happened. For the 50th anniversary (30 October 1988), National Public Radio (NPR) offered a program based on a modified

script by Howard Koch. A long documentary of the whole story appeared on the Discovery Channel in October 1998.

No other single radio program has had such a long-lasting impact as *War of the Worlds*. Both as a highlight of creative radio writing, and as an inadvertent measure of radio's growing place in society, the 1938 drama stands alone.

See also: Hoaxes; *Mercury Theater of the Air*

Programming History

CBS *Mercury Theater of the Air*, Sunday, 30 October 1938, 8–9 P.M.

Further Reading

Cantril, Hadley, *The Invasion from Mars: A Study in the Psychology of Panic*, Princeton, New Jersey: Princeton University Press, 1940.
"Grim Fantasy in Ecuador," *New York Herald Tribune* (15 February 1949).
Homsten, Brian, and Alex Lubertozzi, editors, *The Complete War of the Worlds: Mars' Invasion of Earth from H.G. Wells to Orson Welles*, Naperville, Illinois: Sourcebooks MediaFusion, 2001.
Houseman, John, "The Men from Mars," *Harper's* (December 1948).
Klass, Phillip, "Wells, Welles, and the Martians," *New York Times* (30 October 1988).
Koch, Howard, *The Panic Broadcast: Portrait of an Event*, Boston: Little Brown, 1970.
Noble, Peter, "Orson Scares America," in *The Fabulous Orson Welles*, by Noble, London: Hutchinson, 1956.
"Radio Listeners in Panic, Taking War Drama As Fact," *New York Times* (31 October 1938).
Wolff, G. Joseph, "War of the Worlds and the Editors," *Journalism Quarterly* 57, no. 1 (Spring 1980).

CHRISTOPHER H. STERLING

WBAI
New York City Station

From its inception, WBAI (99.5 FM) has broadcast alternative and often controversial programming to the greater New York City metropolitan area. WBAI has become one of the largest stations in the community radio network, with an operating budget of about $3 million per year.

Origins and Free Speech Heritage

The station became the third in the educational and noncommercial Pacifica network when then-owner and philanthropist Louis Schweitzer donated it to the Pacifica Foundation in the midst of a contentious city newspaper strike in 1959 because he believed that media should be used for the public interest.

WBAI has had a rich and sometimes combative broadcast history and is renowned for programs raising issues related to the First Amendment. In 1968 WBAI incited controversy in a widely publicized incident when a guest on writer Julius Lester's program read an anti-Semitic poem written by one of his students. The airing of the poem, "Anti-Semitism," which vividly described the African-American teenager's views toward the largely Jewish population of schoolteachers, again raised issues of what could and could not be broadcast. Although the United Federation of Teachers union filed a complaint with the Federal Communications Commission (FCC), that agency ruled in favor of the station, asserting that it allowed for "reasonable opportunity for the presentation of conflicting viewpoints."

The most prominent case involved the 1973 broadcast of "Seven Words You Can't Say on Television" by comedian George Carlin. The FCC cited WBAI's owner, Pacifica, for indecency for airing the 12-minute monolog in the early afternoon when children might be in the audience. The case eventually reached the Supreme Court, which ruled in 1978 that the government could regulate "indecent" broadcast speech from the airwaves but could not ban it.

In 1987 WBAI addressed free speech concerns again when it sent the FCC a list of questionable words and phrases without acknowledging that they were from James Joyce's *Ulysses*. Though originally the FCC responded that it could not judge the material until it was broadcast, the agency later ruled that context was critical and allowed the text to be aired as part of a program on Bloomsbury writers.

Programs

WBAI is best known for its extensive, thorough, and often subjective reporting. Beginning in the 1960s the station sent reporters into the South to report on the civil rights movement, including coverage of the murders of three young volunteer workers (James Cheney, Mickey Schwerner, and Andrew Goodman) in 1962. In 1965, WBAI participated with the other two Pacifica stations in holding Vietnam Day "teach-ins," providing non-traditional discussion-type broadcasts.

WBAI pushed the limits even further that same year when program director Chris Koch traveled to North Vietnam to report on the war. His reports were attacked by supporters of the Vietnam War and even by many on the Pacifica Board who were

conflicted about the coverage. After attempts were made to have Koch delete parts of his reports, he and five others resigned. Nearly one-third of station member subscribers also canceled their subscriptions in protest.

WBAI's exhaustive foreign coverage has continued through the years, and long after the mainstream media have left the scene, WBAI has reported from battlefronts in countries such as Iraq, Haiti, and East Timor. Over the years the station has applied the same scrutiny to domestic conditions, examining the practices of the Federal Bureau of Investigation (FBI), federal and state prisons, and city homeless shelters, in addition to other problems.

While news is clearly a mainstay of WBAI's orientation, just as significant are its music and innovative programming. The station is known for introducing free form radio, specifically in *Radio Unnameable*, a program developed in 1963 by WBAI's Bob Fass, which still runs today. The broadcasts—precursors of much subsequent radio—feature a blending of sounds from many different sources. Musicians who would later become popular entertainers appeared regularly on *Radio Unnameable*, among them Judy Collins, Bob Dylan, Jose Feliciano, and Arlo Guthrie (who debuted "Alice's Restaurant" on the show).

It continues its hard-hitting news reporting and also broadcasts an eclectic range of programming, including shows on alternative lifestyles, health, labor, technology—and, of course, music. In the noncommercial "free radio" tradition, WBAI continues to inform, provoke, and rankle its listeners. It has also been honored for its coverage: in 1999 Amy Goodman, the morning co-host of *Wake Up Call*, a local call-in show, won a George M. Polk reporting award for a piece about two unarmed environmentalists who were killed in Nigeria as a result of the Chevron Corporation's involvement with the military there. More recently, the station won a Rodger N. Baldwin Award for outstanding contributions to the cause of civil liberty. As the plaque read, "From the armies converging on Iraq to the march for women's lives in Washington, from the killing fields of East Timor to the mean streets of Manhattan's homeless, WBAI covers the local, national and international scene with a depth and integrity not even conceived of by commercial broadcasting."

Staff Protests

WBAI has regularly been subject to various protests within its own staff. As an operation making heavy use of volunteers, and catering to a broad range of political opinion, heated disagreements are not surprising.

In 1977 a bitter strike over issues of race, staff authority, and finances kept the station silent for seven weeks and still remains one of the most contentious episodes in New York radio history. The strike came about because the staff protested management's reorganization of the station, which they perceived as taking away their power and softening the station programming. Very little was resolved as a result of the strike; it ended when the staff voted (by a narrow margin) to obey a court order requiring them to leave the transmitter room they had taken over.

An even longer and fiercer battle broke out in 1999. Pacifica Foundation management moved to make WBAI sound more professional and mainstream in its programming as they sought larger audiences and additional sources of funding. The move immediately ran into opposition from staffers wedded to their own sometimes controversial programs, often with strong listener support. Many staffers saw the move as an attempt to muzzle unpopular points of view. The host of *Democracy Now!* got into a battle with station management over the direction of her program. By late 2000 a 20-year veteran (including a decade as station manager) had been fired and the staff was in an uproar, talking to newspapers and filing various legal grievances. Soon some staffers were being locked out of the station (somewhat ironically housed on Wall Street) by foundation management. The battle—which had even featured street protests by listeners and disaffected staff—was finally settled in December 2001. WBAI retained the right to work with its own board of directors, only loosely controlled by the foundation in California. After a six-month search, a new station manager was appointed late in 2002.

See also: Community Radio; Educational Radio to 1967; Free Form Format; Pacifica Foundation; Public Radio Since 1967; "Seven Dirty Words" Case

Further Reading

Engelman, Ralph, *Public Radio and Television in America: A Political History*, Thousand Oaks, California: Sage, 1996.
Lester, Julius, *Lovesong: Becoming a Jew*, New York: Holt, 1988.
Post, Steve, *Playing in the FM Band: A Personal Account of Free Radio*, New York: Viking Press, 1974.
WBAI website, www.wbai.org

RUTH BAYARD SMITH

WBAP
Fort Worth, Texas Station

Clear channel WBAP in Fort Worth, Texas, has been a dominant force in Texas and Southwest broadcasting since the very dawn of the radio-television era.

Like many infant stations in the early 1920s, WBAP was an extension of a powerful newspaper, the *Fort Worth Star-Telegram*, published by Amon G. Carter Sr. and Carter Publications. *Star-Telegram* circulation manager Harold Hough convinced a skeptical Carter to put WBAP on the air. Carter grudgingly approved the expenditure of $300 to put the 10-W station on the air on 2 May 1922. "But when that $300 is gone, we're out of the radio business," Carter admonished Hough. Of course, it soon became obvious that radio was more than a $300 experiment. Hough became WBAP's most popular on-the-air personality in the early days, going by the moniker "The Hired Hand."

Dual Channels

For more than 40 years, WBAP shared airspace with WFAA, owned by the *Dallas Morning News*, first on a single frequency, and later, uniquely, on two separate frequencies. It is the only known case of stations sharing more than one frequency.

WFAA had been saddled with a frequency-sharing deal not to its liking with KRLD, owned by the *Morning News'* bitter rival, the *Dallas Times Herald*. The stations were assigned to share 1040 kHz, also a clear channel. *Dallas Morning News* publisher George B. Dealey apparently preferred to cooperate with Carter's station, across 30 miles of then-open prairie, rather than with the station of his intra-city rival. WBAP had been paired with KTHS in Hot Springs, Arkansas. The station found the awkwardness of sharing airtime with such a distant station untenable. So WBAP and WFAA petitioned the Federal Radio Commission (FRC) to allow them to share the 800 kHz channel (820 kHz beginning in 1941), and the FRC granted the change effective 1 May 1929. At the same time, the FRC authorized WBAP and WFAA to broadcast at 50,000 W on 800 kHz, an increase of 100-fold from their previous wattage.

In 1935 the resourceful Carter acquired KGKO in Wichita Falls, Texas, broadcasting on 570 kHz, setting the stage for the unique dual-channel time-sharing arrangement. Carter had the station's license transferred to Fort Worth, and WBAP began broadcasting on KGKO's channel in 1938. Soon WFAA bought into KGKO, and in 1940 the

WBBM

Don Harris enjoyed a career of 33 years on the air at WBAP starting in 1965, in the final years of the dual-frequency days. "There was a 10-second changeover [for each station to sign off and the other to sign on]," Harris recalls. "Sometimes, those WFAA guys would cheat us a couple of seconds, and we would have two or three seconds of dead air [as WBAP waited for WFAA to complete its sign-off]." Harris admitted that sometimes it happened the other way around.

Fort Worth is also known as "Cowtown," and WBAP became famous for a cowbell station identification. The cowbell was almost certainly the innovation of the ubiquitous Hough, the station's most identifiable air personality in the 1920s and 1930s. WBAP claimed that its cowbell jangle was U.S. broadcasting's first "memory signal." The cowbell would be heard when WBAP identified itself before and after exchanging frequencies with WFAA.

WBAP prided itself (then and now) on its farm and ranch programming. A brief 1947 history of the station commented, "The station had a definite field to serve—the vast area of Texas (and West Texas in particular), where distance is most unusual, and which was, and is, a ranching and farming area." Until radio came to Texas, farmers and ranchers relied only on their limited powers of observation to prepare for rough weather. "More than once, ranchers were saved millions of dollars in livestock losses by WBAP's warning of approaching blizzards and storms. National recognition has been given the station for that service," a 1949 *Star-Telegram* article reported.

In the 1940s WBAP broadcast a night-time program from the state prison in Huntsville called *Thirty Minutes behind the Walls*, which was written, performed, and produced by prisoners. WBAP claimed in 1943 that the program received nearly 200,000 fan letters in one month from 45 states, Canada, and Mexico.

As television emerged in the 1950s, the WBAP and WFAA formats gradually evolved toward middle-of-the-road music. The decision by WBAP to hire the legendary Bill Mack to play country music on 820 kHz from midnight to 7:30 A.M. in 1969 marked the first clear break between the two stations. Harris credits general manager James A. Byron, who had been the station's news director, for having the foresight to make the change to country music.

In April 1970 the Federal Communications Commission (FCC) approved the sale of the Belo

Corp's share of the 820 channel to Carter Publications for $3.5 million. Belo and WFAA received WBAP's interest in the 570 channel facilities. The end of the partnership came on 1 May 1970, when WFAA went to 570 kHz full-time and WBAP took over 820 kHz. It was the 41st anniversary of the time-sharing agreement. WFAA radio left the air in 1983.

After the split, WBAP initiated a country music format full-time. Other stations were playing country music, but Harris says WBAP immediately shot right past them and everyone else. "Six months after the change, we were number one in the market," he said, "It was an overnight success, just phenomenal."

In 1973 Capital Cities Communications bought WBAP and WBAP-FM (now KSCS) from Carter Publications for $80 million. In 1996 WBAP and KSCS became part of the merger of Capital Cities/ American Broadcasting Companies (ABC) and the Walt Disney Company. In 1993 WBAP switched from country music to news/talk.

Further Reading

Dempsey, John Mark, "WBAP and WFAA: A Unique Partnership in the Era of Channel Sharing: 1929–1970," *Journal of Radio Studies* 7, no. 1 (Spring 2000).

Glick, Edwin, "WBAP/WFAA: Till Money Did Them Part," *Journal of Broadcasting* 21 (Fall 1977).

"Radio History Made by WFAA and WBAP in New Joint Service," *Dallas Morning News* (8 September 1940).

Schroeder, Richard, *Texas Signs On: The Early Days of Radio and Television*, College Station: Texas A&M University Press, 1998.

"Station WFAA Assigned New Air Channel," *Dallas Morning News* (1 May 1929).

WBAP News/Talk 820: A Brief History of WBAP, wbap.com/aboutwbap.asp

"'We'll Spend but $300' and WBAP Was Begun: Hoover Named Station," *Fort Worth Star-Telegram* (30 October 1943).

"WFAA, WBAP to End Dual Frequency Use," *Dallas Morning News* (25 April 1970).

J.M. DEMPSEY

WBBM

Chicago, Illinois Station

This AM radio station, the long-time Columbia Broadcasting System (CBS) affiliate in Chicago, has been linked to the history of CBS as a radio (and later television) network. Chicago has long been famous as a pioneer in radio, but WBBM-AM never set in motion any significant shows. It simply aired what CBS sent along, and for radio in the late 1940s and network television through the 1970s, this usually meant the top-rated shows being broadcast. There is only one sense in which WBBM was a pioneer, and that was as an early FM station, beginning its broadcasts on 7 December 1941.

With WBBM standing for "World's Best Broadcast Medium," WBBM went on the air on 14 November 1923. WBBM has spent three-quarters of a century on Chicago's AM dial, beginning its life in the basement of the Atlass family home, then moving to the Broadmore Hotel, and then to its long-time home in the Wrigley Building on Chicago's north side. Within three years of its debut, the station bragged that it had aired the first dance music and the first church service, carried regular remote broadcasts, and acquired the leading number of local advertisers.

In 1933 CBS purchased WBBM, and station cofounder H. Leslie Atlass was made its general manager on a lifetime basis as part of the sale. By the late 1930s WBBM transmitted with 50,000 W, and in 1936, the station often ranked number one in Chicago with a significant set of locally produced shows, such as *Piano from Warehouse 39*, *Sunday Night Party*, *One Quarter of an Hour of Romance*, *Dugout Dope*, *Women in the Headlines*, *Radio Gossip Club*, *Man on the Street*, and *Sports Huddle*. But none of these—unlike many other Chicago-based programs—ever made a national splash. From its 410 North Michigan Avenue studio, the station could air from the WBBM Air Theater, which seated 300 persons. Through most of the 1930s and 1940s, it was a clear channel powerhouse at 780 kHz, able to be picked up throughout the upper Midwest and beyond. This meant that WBBM broadcast CBS news into Chicago and served as the Midwest base for the Columbia News Service set up in 1933.

WBBM-FM went on the air on 7 December 1941, but the FM station long merely duplicated the AM broadcast. In recent years, as FM has ascended in popularity, it has tried a number of different music formats. In 2000, WBBM-FM (96.3 FM) had the format of "dance hits," but the station had the same studio as WBBM-AM at 630 North McClurg Court. It was not until well into the 1960s that WBBM-FM did more than duplicate WBBM-AM.

With the rise of television, WBBM-AM needed to reinvent itself. The new format grew out of CBS chairman William S. Paley's desire to come up with a format that was on one hand prestigious (and not simply another rock variation), while also making money. WBBM found this with all-news radio in 1968, and the network reinvented itself as the link among the CBS all-news radio stations. WBBM-AM has provided all-news radio broadcasting in the nation's second city for more than a third of a

century, with classic drive-time formatting. WBBM-FM has not been so lucky and has tried a number of formats that might work—with "dance hits" the format by 2000. Both AM and FM remained at studios at 630 North McClurg Court, though there was talk in 1999 of moving to another part of downtown. WBBM's AM antenna is located on the west side of the region, in Elk Grove Village, and the FM antenna is located atop the landmark John Hancock Building.

See also: All News Format; Columbia Broadcasting System

Further Reading

Boyer, Peter J., *Who Killed CBS? The Undoing of America's Number One News Network*, New York: St. Martin's Press, 1989.
Broadcasting in Chicago, 1921–1989, www.richsamuels.com
Paley, William S., *As It Happened: A Memoir*, Garden City, New York: Doubleday, 1979.
WBBM Newsradio 780, www.wbbm780.com

DOUGLAS GOMERY

WBT

Charlotte, North Carolina Station

Dubbed the "Colossus of the Carolinas," WBT was the first commercially licensed station in North Carolina and, with WSB in Atlanta, was one of the first two such licensees in the southeastern region of the United States. From its debut in 1922, the station has also been one of the region's most powerful. In 1929 William S. Paley purchased WBT, establishing it as a key link in the distribution of the Columbia Broadcasting System (CBS) programming.

WBT's roots stretch back to 1920, when Fred M. Laxton (a former General Electric employee), Fred Bunker, and Earle Gluck began transmitting experimental station 4XD from Laxton's home in Charlotte. Laxton and his friends had constructed the transmitter in a chicken coop behind Laxton's house; they broadcast music from phonograph records to the few people who owned receivers at the time. On 10 April 1922, Laxton, Bunker, and Gluck—operating as the Southern Radio Corporation—received a license from the federal government to broadcast with 100 W of power as WBT. Initially, the station aired from 10:00 to 11:45 in the mornings and from 7:30 to 9:45 in the evenings.

Southern Radio Corporation sold WBT in 1926 to C.C. Coddington, a local Buick automobile dealer, and over the following three years, the station grew to be a regional power. During the years following Coddington's purchase of WBT, the station acquired permission to broadcast at 5,000 W and affiliated with the National Broadcasting Company (NBC).

In the late 1920s William S. Paley of CBS, in fierce competition with NBC to garner affiliates, had begun purchasing established stations in key regions to ensure the expansion of the CBS network. In late 1928 the broadcasting titan bought WABC (later WCBS) in New York, and in 1929, he added to his collection WCCO in Minneapolis, Minnesota, and, with an eye toward reaching the southeastern United States, WBT.

Soon after acquiring WBT, CBS persuaded the Federal Radio Commission to allow the station to broadcast with 25,000 W of power. Four years later, in 1933, the station's power rose to 50,000 W. Listeners from Maine to Florida could clearly receive WBT's signal.

WBT would be a CBS-owned-and-operated station until 1945, when the Federal Communications Commission's (FCC) network rulings forced CBS to divest itself of certain high-power stations. Reluctantly, CBS sold its gold mine in the Southeast to Jefferson Standard Life Insurance Company, the enterprise (known today as Jefferson Pilot) that currently owns the station. WBT would maintain its CBS affiliation and continue to be a powerful outlet for the network's programs.

Just as WBT proved to be an important cog in the distribution of CBS network programming, by the late 1920s the station had also become an important source of local news, information, and entertainment for listeners in the Charlotte region. Led by program director (and later station manager) Charles H. Crutchfield and personalities such as Grady Cole and Kurt Webster, the station broadcast tobacco auctions, professional baseball games, old Confederate veterans reeling off their "rebel yells," country music performances, and other events of local flavor. Many of WBT's local productions were picked up by the CBS network for national and regional distribution.

Numerous entertainers would receive valuable exposure via their appearances on WBT productions. Before achieving fame as *Amos 'n' Andy* over the NBC network, Freeman Gosden and Charles Correll performed on the station in the 1920s. In addition, saxophonist Hal Kemp, who would become a well-known big band leader, had performed over WBT in the 1930s, as had bandleader Kay Kyser. Country music performers, such as the Briarhoppers and Arthur Smith and the Crackerjacks, watched their reputations grow on regularly scheduled WBT programs such as the *Carolina*

Hayride, a weekly barn dance program picked up by the CBS network in the 1940s. Perhaps the best-known of the traditional music performers who emerged from WBT were the Johnson Family Singers, a gospel-singing sextet who, as a result of their success on WBT in the 1940s, broadcast regularly over the CBS network and attracted recording contracts from Columbia and, later, Radio Corporation of America (RCA) Victor. WBT also claimed a role in grooming newsmen for CBS: Charles Kuralt and Nelson Benton worked at the station before going on to the network.

WBT helped pioneer radio broadcasting in the Southeast and became a widely disseminated source of regional news, information, and entertainment. The station would also spawn North Carolinian entertainers and news personalities who would go on to national fame in broadcasting. WBT will be most remembered for its role in building the CBS network.

See also: Columbia Broadcasting System

Further Reading

Eberly, Philip K., *Music in the Air: America's Changing Tastes in Popular Music, 1920–1980*, New York: Hastings, 1982.
Johnson, Kenneth M., *The Johnson Family Singers: We Sang for Our Supper*, Jackson: University Press of Mississippi, 1997.
Wallace, Wesley Herndon, "The Development of Broadcasting in North Carolina, 1922–1948," Ph.D. diss., Duke University, 1962.

MICHAEL STREISSGUTH

WBZ
Boston, Massachusetts Station

One of the Westinghouse group of stations, WBZ Radio went on the air on 19 September 1921, with studios at the Westinghouse Electric plant in East Springfield, Massachusetts, approximately 85 miles west of Boston. WBZ's first broadcast was a remote from the Eastern States Exposition, a large New England county fair; among the speakers helping to dedicate the station were the governors of Connecticut and Massachusetts. WBZ operated on a frequency of 800 kHz, with a power of 100 W. Within several years, the station would move to 900 kHz, and by 1928 it was placed at 990 kHz by the Federal Radio Commission.

By early 1922, WBZ had moved its studio to Springfield's Hotel Kimball. Station programming was typical of radio in those pioneering days: an occasional star but mostly eager amateurs willing to perform free. By early 1924, it was already becoming difficult to get good free talent, as more stations competed for performers. WBZ decided to open a Boston studio in conjunction with the *Boston Herald* and *Boston Traveler* newspapers, from which they got their news at that time; the new station was known as WBZA. The studios were first in Boston's Hotel Brunswick; they moved to the Statler Hotel in 1927 and to the Bradford in 1931. Meanwhile, the Boston station grew in importance, and its ability to attract major talent was a big plus for Westinghouse. WBZ was the first Boston station to broadcast Boston Bruins hockey games (featuring *Herald* sportswriter Frank Ryan doing play-by-play reports), and when not doing sports, the station provided a regular schedule of dance bands, well-known singers, political talks, a storyteller for kids, and a staff of announcers who became very popular in their own right. By March of 1931, it was decided that the WBZ call letters should belong to Boston and the WBZA letters should go to the Springfield station.

In 1926 WBZ began broadcasts of the Boston Symphony Orchestra, and in 1927, the station became one of five original affiliates of the National Broadcasting Company (NBC) Blue radio network. (As time went on, many of the WBZ announcers would be hired by the network.) When WBZ had its tenth anniversary celebration in September 1931, the NBC Blue network carried it. But in April 1932 WBZ got a rather dubious bit of publicity, which showed the perils of live radio. A supposedly trained circus lion (he was trained to roar on cue) was brought to the studio, and for some reason, he broke away and went rampaging through the studios, destroying equipment, terrifying spectators, and injuring seven people before the police arrived and had to shoot him.

By the mid-1930s, WBZ was using 50,000 W; in 1941, the station was moved to 1030 kHz, a dial position it still has today. WBZ began doing a morning show featuring country vocalist Bradley Kincaid during the late 1930s. In 1942 Carl DeSuze joined the station; he would go on to a long career as the morning show host. The programming in the 1930s and 1940s included a daily women's show (radio homemakers were very popular, and WBZ had Mildred Carlson and later Marjorie Mills), as well as an increasing emphasis on news. The WBZ news staff included some of the best-known reporters, many of whom would later go on to join WBZ-TV.

Experiments with FM were taking place in the late 1930s and early 1940s; WBZ used its FM station (W1XK) to broadcast the Boston Symphony Orchestra in 1941, which was probably the first time the orchestra had been heard via the new FM technology. In June 1948 WBZ radio was joined by WBZ-TV, channel 4, and the stations moved into their own new facility, which had been specially designed for both radio and TV.

In the mid-1950s, WBZ moved away from its previously "middle-of-the-road" programming, dropping NBC and abandoning big bands for a more popular, hit-oriented sound. The station hired five well-known announcers and called them "The Live Five" to let the audience know that WBZ was now locally programmed. By the 1960s, WBZ had moved to a soft Top 40 format (detractors called it "chicken rock"—rock without any loud songs), but it still offered a nightly talk show and a heavy news commitment. WBZ's disc jockeys were personalities, and the younger audience found them very entertaining. Disc jockeys such as Bruce Bradley, Dick Summer, and Dave Maynard did more than just play the hits—they also interacted with their fans at numerous remote broadcasts and events: it was the era of the "record hop," and WBZ announcers were masters of ceremonies at dances all over Massachusetts.

By the 1970s, WBZ was moving away from Top 40 to a more Adult Contemporary sound and increasing its news. The station had long been known for public service, raising money for worthy charities; this activity was also increased, such that by the 1980s music was gradually being phased out in favor of longer news blocks, more sports, and more talk shows. By December 1985, WBZ had an all-news and information format during afternoon drive time, and by September 1992 the station completed the transition to being an all-news station.

Ironically, the city where it all began for WBZ—Springfield—was no longer a part of the WBZ game plan after 1962. WBZA was shut down by the parent company in order to buy another station in a larger market. But as a tribute to the station's beginnings, when WBZ celebrated its 50th anniversary in 1971, festivities were held both in Boston and at the Eastern States Exposition in Springfield.

WBZ is one of the few stations that still has its original set of call letters, and it has experienced minimal staff turnover on air: for example, several current members of the sports department have worked there since the 1960s, the news staff includes men and women with 10–15 years of service, and announcers such as Carl DeSuze and Dave Maynard retired after more than 40 years on air. This is a tribute to WBZ's stability: although it is no longer called a Westinghouse station (Westinghouse purchased the Columbia Broadcasting System (CBS) in 1995, and by the end of 1996 the parent company became known as CBS rather than Westinghouse), it is still known for news, public service, sports, and night-time talk shows. The annual telethon/radiothon for Children's Hospital consistently brings in large sums of money; in fact, WBZ Radio has won numerous awards for public service and excellence in broadcasting, including the National Association of Broadcasters' Crystal Award and the Marconi Award. WBZ has consistently earned number one ratings in Boston since the station changed over to an all-news format. And with a signal that can reach 38 states at night, WBZ continues to be among the most respected and most listened-to AM radio stations.

See also: Columbia Broadcasting System; Group W; Westinghouse

Further Reading

"WBZ News Radio 1030 Celebrating 75 Years: 1921–1996," Boston: WBZ, 1996.

DONNA L. HALPER

WCBS

New York City Station

The flagship station of the Columbia Broadcasting System (CBS) radio network, WCBS traces its lineage back to WAHG, which first aired in 1924. It was long the radio home of Jack Sterling and other local radio figures before becoming an all news outlet in 1967.

Origins

WCBS got its start as part of a radio manufacturer's business. Alfred H. Grebe began to make radio receivers in 1922, and two years later he placed WAHG ("Wait and Hear Grebe") on the air on 24 October 1924 at 920 kHz with 500 W of power. As was common at the time, WAHG soon shifted frequencies to 950 kHz and had to share time with another New York City station. By 1926 power had been increased tenfold. That same year, Grebe organized the Atlantic Broadcasting Company and changed the call letters to WABC, moving the studios from Queens into Manhattan.

Grebe had plans to develop a network, following the example set by the National Broadcasting Company (NBC) beginning in 1926. His outlet became one of two New York stations for the new CBS network, because as stations commonly shared time, more than one was necessary for the new network to provide a full week's coverage. Instead, late in 1928 Grebe sold his station to William S. Paley, head of CBS.

Network Station

CBS moved the new flagship station and its network headquarters into 485 Madison Avenue, where both would remain for several decades. The station moved to 860 kHz and by late 1929 was up to 50,000 W of power. The final shift, to the present 880 kHz, came in 1941, part of the readjustment of American stations because of the North American Regional Broadcasting Agreement treaty.

WABC carried virtually all of the developing network's programming, plus some New York-only shows. With the creation of the new American Broadcasting Companies (ABC) in 1945, however, CBS was broadcasting from a station with a competitor's initials, and in November 1946, WABC became WCBS (after involved negotiations, as the new call letters had been used by a small station in Illinois since 1927). At the same time, it began to offer *This Is New York*, a combination of interviews and features on the city that would run for 17 years, first in the morning and finally as an evening program. Another long-lasting program was *Music Til Dawn*, which began in 1953 and lasted until 1970 as an inexpensive way of filling the late night and early morning hours, sponsored by American Airlines (then still headquartered in New York).

With the demise of evening network daytime programs in the early 1950s, WCBS tried a variety of programs with a "middle of the road" approach. Among them was *The Jack Sterling Show*, a morning music DJ show beginning in 1948 that ran for years. Not finding success, WCBS converted to an all news format (for most of its schedule) in August 1967. Ironically, the premier of the new service was delayed when an airplane hit the station's transmitter tower. But, as often happens in such disasters, WCBS was able to use other station facilities while getting its own back on the air full-time. In the early 1970s the remaining non-news programming was terminated, making the station all news, all the time.

In recent years advertised as "WCBS880," the station is formally owned and operated by Infinity Broadcasting Corporation, a publicly traded subsidiary of CBS Corporation. Offices and studios are located in the CBS Broadcast Center on West 57th Street in Manhattan.

See also: Columbia Broadcasting System; Infinity Broadcasting Corporation; North American Regional Broadcasting Agreement

Further Reading

Jaker, Bill, Frank Sulek, and Peter Kanze, "WABC," "WAHG," and "WCBS," in *The Airwaves of New York: Illustrated Histories of 156 AM Stations in the Metropolitan Area, 1921–1996*, by Jaker, Sulek, and Kanze, Jefferson, North Carolina: McFarland, 1998.
WCBS, www.newsradio88.com/main/home/index

CHRISTOPHER H. STERLING

WCCO

Minneapolis, Minnesota Station

The Twin Cities' "Good Neighbor to the Northwest," a 50,000-W, clear channel AM station, is said to have dominated local audience ratings like no other station in the country. Legend has it that radio executives from across the United States would travel to Minnesota and sit in their hotel rooms listening to WCCO in order to "research" its format. They could only shake their heads in wonder. What they heard was a homespun blend of often insipid comedy featuring Scandinavian humor; remote-location broadcasts of amateur glee clubs and ethnic musicians; a schedule heavy on local news, farm markets, and weather; and ubiquitous live chats with political figures such as Hubert Humphrey. It was a sound that could not be duplicated elsewhere, called "Just Folks Radio" by *The Wall Street Journal*. At the height of its popularity, surveys showed WCCO to be the favorite among listeners in 128 counties by a 19 to 1 margin. WCCO was as much a part of the fabric of the Northwest as were snow days in January.

The station's predecessor, WLAG, went on the air in 1922 as a marketing tool for a Minneapolis radio manufacturer. In September 1924 the failed station was resurrected when a promoter convinced executives of the Washburn Crosby Company to buy it (hence the call letters "WCCO"). The company, known today as General Mills, used its new "Gold Medal Station" to promote its many brands of flour and cereal products. The first day's log boasts two home service programs performed by "Betty Crocker," and on Christmas Eve 1926, WCCO aired radio's first singing commercial, "Have you tried Wheaties?"

The station was one of 21 original affiliates of the National Broadcasting Company (NBC) Red Network, but within two years it switched to the fledgling Columbia Broadcasting System (CBS). In 1929 CBS chief William Paley bought one-third of WCCO for $150,000, with an option to buy the rest in three years for $300,000. The station's first general manager, Henry Bellows, was a University of Minnesota rhetoric professor who later served on the Federal Radio Commission and is said to have helped WCCO gain its favorable 50,000-W clear channel designation in the early 1930s. Bellows and his successor at WCCO, Earl Gammons, eventually became CBS vice presidents. Although CBS network programming came to fill about three-quarters of WCCO's broadcast day, Gammons built an immensely loyal audience for local programming in the 1930s. Gammons' trademark was hiring air personalities with a warm, neighborly style of delivery that contrasted with the more sophisticated sound of most New York-based network entertainers. The sound was called "personality radio."

In 1934 the resonant voice of Cedric Adams took over the WCCO evening news, and, bolstered by a night-time signal that spanned half the country, WCCO and Adams together became a U.S. radio phenomenon. He was perhaps the most widely known and highest paid local radio personality for over a quarter of a century. At the height of his popularity, he did a daily five-minute program on CBS and occasionally substituted for network star Arthur Godfrey. WCCO took *Cedric Adams' Open House* on the road, annually logging over 15,000 miles with 49 weekend road trips. At one time his weekend traveling troupe consisted of an accordion player, a magician, three singing sisters, a comedy act, two baton twirlers, an eight-year-old girl who yodeled, and the Minneapolis Aquatennial Queen. CBS executives in New York may have snickered at the hokey lineup, but they never failed to notice the bottom line. Cedric Adams' 12:30 P.M. newscast had the largest Hooperating of any non-network radio show in the country.

In 1938 the station moved from its cramped studios in the Nicollet Hotel to a spacious headquarters in the Minneapolis Elks Club building. The new location had the high ceilings favored by CBS architects and was quickly transformed into an art deco landmark with cream-and-Columbia-blue interiors. It was remodeled in the classic CBS design that had been used in other network projects in Boston, Saint Louis, and Chicago, featuring "floating studios"—in which the floors, walls, and ceilings were separated from the main building structure. Best of all, the new location had a fourth-floor auditorium that seated 700 people. Although unpretentious, with its tiny stage and its stage right main-floor engineering booth, the room became the source throughout the 1940s for some of the country's best live radio. At its peak, the WCCO auditorium was home to seven consecutive individually sponsored live-audience programs on Friday evenings.

The growth of television caused a change in WCCO ownership in the 1950s. Because CBS could own only a minority interest in a Twin Cities television station (it already owned five television stations in other markets), CBS merged WCCO with Mid-Continent Radio and Television in 1952. The firm became Midwest Radio-Television. The Ridder and the Murphy newspaper families held a 53 percent majority, and CBS owned the remaining 47 percent. Two years later Federal Communications Commission (FCC) rules (requiring that minority interests be counted) forced CBS to sell its minority share of the company. The *Minneapolis Star and Tribune* bought this minority interest for $4 million. Under the reorganization, WCCO Radio was set up as an independent entity within the company, controlled by neither the parent company's television nor the newspaper's interests, which now included both the *St. Paul Dispatch-Pioneer Press* and the *Minneapolis Star and Tribune*. This independence probably helped WCCO Radio compete and even thrive in the post-television era and to maintain its market dominance well into the decades that followed. The "variety" programming of the 1960s and 1970s gave way to a more uniform "news-talk" format in the 1980s and 1990s. As late as the mid-1980s, Arbitron showed that WCCO-AM was still the number one rated major-market station in the entire country, although this unusual market dominance was later moderated by local FM competition.

In 1992, 40 years after WCCO was sold to local owners, CBS reacquired the stations, purchasing the assets of Midwest Communications in a deal worth over $200 million. In addition to WCCO Radio and WCCO-TV, the acquisition included WLTE-FM, Minneapolis (formerly WCCO-FM); three smaller television stations in Wisconsin and Minnesota; and the MSC regional sports cable TV channel.

See also: Columbia Broadcasting System

Further Reading

Haeg, Lawrence P., *Sixty Years Strong: The Story of One of America's Great Radio Stations, 1924–1984: 50,000 Watts Clear Channel, Minneapolis-St. Paul*, Minneapolis, Minnesota: WCCO Radio, 1984.
Sarjeant, Charles F., editor, *The First Forty: The Story of WCCO Radio*, Minneapolis, Minnesota: Denison, 1964.
WCCO, 1924–1949: For 25 Years Good Neighbor to the Northwest: The CBS Station in Minneapolis and St. Paul, Minneapolis, Minnesota: n.p., 1949.
Williams, Bob, and Chuck Hartley, *Good Neighbor to the Northwest, 1924–1974*, Minneapolis, Minnesota: n.p., 1974.

MARK BRAUN

WCFL
Chicago, Illinois Station

The Chicago Federation of Labor's (CFL) 1926 plan to open its own radio station initiated one of the most notorious controversies in early broadcasting. As planned by the CFL, the proposal would create the only radio station in the country specifically devoted to the interests of organized labor. The CFL planned to call its new station WCFL and decided to use the same frequency as KGW in Portland, Oregon, and WEAF, the popular American Telephone and Telegraph (AT&T) station in New York City. These plans were drawn without first consulting the U.S. Department of Commerce, which was then charged with station licensing.

When the Commerce Department was approached for a license, the CFL was told that none would be forthcoming. Acting Secretary of Commerce Stephen Davis explained that there was no room in the overcrowded broadcast frequency spectrum to accommodate the station. In response, the CFL declared on 17 May 1926 that the organization fully intended to broadcast with or without a license. The CFL intended to transmit primarily educational programming, including labor-related information, public affairs, and discussions of economic issues, in addition to entertainment features.

CFL secretary Edward N. Nockels protested the commerce department's preferential treatment of corporate giant AT&T. Nockels expressed shock that no room could be found on the airwaves for WCFL, while AT&T's WEAF was able to occupy a clear channel frequency. Nockels wrote Davis asking if it might be possible for WCFL's signal to occupy half of the territory reached by WEAF.

The Department of Commerce intimated that if the CFL broadcast illegally, the department would bring the matter before a federal court to test the legality of the Radio Act of 1912. Nockels said in reply that the CFL was willing to allow the courts to settle the matter. He expressed confidence that the courts would support the CFL's plans. The CFL began construction of its new station, WCFL, without official approval.

Ultimately the CFL was able to secure an inspection for the station from the Department of Commerce, and WCFL received its license. After a week of experimental transmissions, the station officially opened on 22 July 1926 with a special two-hour inaugural broadcast from 6 to 8 P.M. on 491.5 meters, "just a shade away" from WEAF. WCFL broadcast from transmitter facilities on Chicago's Municipal (Navy) Pier, which were linked to studios elsewhere in the city. WCFL was supported by the contributions of labor unions and quickly established itself as "the Voice of Labor."

The station quickly became the target of attacks because of its hindrance of long-distance ("DX") reception of AT&T's WEAF in New York. *Radio Broadcast*, for example, suggested that WCFL had chosen its frequency as a direct attack on AT&T, out of indignation that WEAF could control an exclusive frequency. *Radio Broadcast* engaged in something of a crusade against WCFL, at one point putting the CFL in the same class as the Ku Klux Klan, as both were special-interest broadcasters.

By October 1926, the station was on the air from 6 P.M. until midnight six days a week. The 6–7 slot each evening was devoted to labor issues discussed in a program called CFL *Talks and Bulletins*. The program's length was quickly cut in half, however, because of a lack of material. WCFL filled the remainder of the evening with entertainment features, predominantly music. The station later also offered educational lessons, farm market reports, weather reports, and religious services.

Throughout the history of the CFL's involvement in the station, most WCFL programming was not directly union-oriented, a fact that occasionally generated complaints from union officials but that did not stop the Federal Radio Commission (FRC) from labeling WCFL a "propaganda station." To some extent, WCFL became a victim of General Order 40, issued by the commission in 1928. Severe limitations were placed on the station's activities. WCFL was made to share its frequency, and its power was drastically reduced before the commission finally insisted that the station could not operate in the evening, so as not to interfere with other stations.

After the CFL found that the FRC's stance could not be shifted, the organization sought support for the station from Congress. As a result of congressional pressure, the FRC moved WCFL in 1929 to a new frequency, on which the station could again operate on a full-time basis. When Nockels found that reception of the station was poor on that frequency, the commission allowed the station to return to 970 kHz and to broadcast for an additional four hours in the evening. By 1932 WCFL and the National Broadcasting Company (NBC) had entered into an agreement whereby WCFL would broadcast at 970 kHz full-time and at increased power (5,000 W), despite the NBC station KJR in Seattle, which shared the frequency. The proposal quickly found approval with the FRC.

WCFL faced financial woes in its early days, which were to some extent alleviated by the acceptance of advertising, a practice that began in 1927. The station ushered in a lucrative rock and roll format in 1965 and subsequently became known as the home of some of radio's legendary disc jockeys, including Dick Biondi and Larry Lujack. The station's format change, however, prompted controversy among the membership of organized labor, with AFL-CIO president George Meany asking at one point what rock and roll had to do with the labor movement. By the early 1970s, WCFL had become Chicago's leading rock station.

Emphasis on entertainment, coupled with the competitive pressures of the Chicago commercial radio market, resulted in WCFL's abandoning an ever-increasing portion of its remaining public service programming. In spite of criticisms that the station was no longer significantly engaged in public service, WCFL survived challenges to its 1975 license renewal. Because the station eventually lost its ability to compete adequately in the Top 40 market, however, WCFL switched to an easy listening format in 1976. The station increasingly became a burden on the CFL without financial reward, until WCFL was finally sold for $12 million to the Mutual Broadcasting System in 1979.

Unable to make the station financially viable as an all-news operation (which would have cost twice the then $4 million annual operating budget), Mutual attempted by 1980 to turn WCFL into an adult contemporary music station. However, that failed as well, because most music listening by then was to FM, and AM outlets focused more on talk. Three years later, Mutual sold the station to Statewide Broadcasting, which turned WCFL into a religious music operation. Consistently last in city-wide ratings, WCFL was finally merged with Heftel Broadcasting's WLUP-FM, and in April 1987 the long-time voice of labor became WLUP-AM, an adult rock station.

Further Reading

"Chicago Labor Unions Plan to Build or Buy Station," *New York Times* (21 February 1926).

Godfried, Nathan, "The Origins of Labor Radio: WCFL, the 'Voice of Labor,' 1925–1928," *The Historical Journal of Film, Radio, and Television* 7, no. 2 (1987).

Godfried, Nathan, *WCFL, Chicago's Voice of Labor, 1926–78*, Urbana: University of Illinois Press, 1997.

McChesney, Robert W., "Labor and the Marketplace of Ideas: WCFL and the Battle for Labor Radio Broadcasting, 1927–1937," *Journalism Monographs* 134 (August 1992).

STEVEN PHIPPS

WDIA

Memphis, Tennessee Station

Known as the "Mother Station of the Negroes," WDIA in 1949 became the first black-oriented radio station in the United States. Radio had featured black talent and black-appeal programs since the 1920s, but never before had a station directed its entire broadcast schedule to the black audience. This novel and long-overdue development in radio programming that WDIA pioneered spawned dramatic growth in the number of radio stations tailored exclusively for the black market.

The station, the original studios of which were at 2074 Union Avenue in Memphis, had signed on the air in June 1947 with a white-oriented format that featured country and western music; classical music; and a smattering of news, sports, religion, and children's programs. This format garnered pale ratings, so in the fall of 1948 WDIA's founders, John Pepper and Bert Ferguson, began to experiment with black-appeal programming. It proved to be a profitable decision for the white owners and one that would open opportunities in broadcasting to black men and women. Initially, WDIA featured only a handful of black-oriented programs, but by 1949 the station had made a complete conversion.

To spearhead the new format, Pepper and Ferguson hired Nat D. Williams, a leader, educator, and impresario in the black community of Memphis. Williams's established popularity and ebullient on-air style virtually guaranteed the success of the programs he hosted; he and his shows became the core around which WDIA built the remainder of its black-appeal format.

In establishing the first black-appeal radio station in the United States, Pepper and Ferguson capitalized on the large black population in the Memphis area and its growing postwar prosperity. The ratings and revenue improvements for WDIA were startling and almost immediate. Among the tens of thousands of black Memphians, WDIA was number one. Soon the station was reporting that it attracted 33 percent more daytime listeners on weekdays than did any other Memphis station. Naturally, with more listeners came more advertisers, and although many advertisers, fearing racist backlash, avoided WDIA, they soon shed their fears and latched on to the very real earning potential that the station offered. Ford, Kellogg's, Sealtest, Lipton's Tea, and other companies with deep advertising budgets became regular sponsors of WDIA programs. Confirming that their venture into black-oriented programming had succeeded, Pepper and Ferguson reported in 1951 that their local and national advertising sales had increased 75.4 percent and 80 percent, respectively, in 1950 over 1949.

In 1954, over protest from radio station WMPS in Memphis, the Federal Communications Commission (FCC) granted WDIA the authority to operate with 50,000 W daytime and with 5,000 W night-time with different antenna patterns both day and night. As a result, the station expanded its influence well beyond Memphis into parts of Mississippi, Arkansas, Texas, Louisiana, and Illinois. WDIA claimed to have access to 1,466,618 blacks, or ten percent of the black population in the United States. By 1957 WDIA had the highest ratings and advertising income among radio stations in the mid-South.

Fueled by the example WDIA set and by the general decline in radio audiences, other radio stations sought to bolster their bottom line by becoming exclusively black-oriented. In WDIA's wake followed WMRY in New Orleans, WEFC in Miami, WCIN in Cincinnati, WJNR in Newark, and others.

WDIA employed various tactics to build loyalty among the black population it reached. Noting the success in 1948 of Nat D. Williams—first on his afternoon *Tan Town Jamboree* and then on his morning *Tan Town Coffee Club*—management quickly set about hiring more black talent until virtually the entire on-air staff was black. (Despite this groundbreaking opportunity for black on-air talent, it is important to note that Jim Crow still hovered about WDIA in the 1940s and 1950s: blacks were barred from sales, management, and engineering positions.) Joining Nat D. Williams were disc jockeys Martha Jean Steinberg, Maurice "Hot Rod" Hulbert, B.B. King, and Rufus Thomas, all of whom featured blues, rhythm and blues, and other popular music of the day. (B.B. King and Rufus Thomas would achieve fame as blues and rhythm and blues performers.) Ford Nelson, Theo "Bless My Bones" Wade, and Rev. Arnold Dwight "Gatemouth" Moore presented gospel music programs, and the popular Willa Monroe hosted the *Tan Town Homemaker's Show*, which was geared to women in the radio audience. Blacks who listened to WDIA heard their own voices, which nurtured loyalty to the station as well as pride in the status that blacks had achieved on Memphis radio.

WDIA also built and maintained its listenership with comprehensive community relations efforts. The station's public service pervaded the black community: it traced missing persons, pleaded for blood donors, sponsored baseball teams, and collected food and clothing for needy Memphians. The centerpieces of the station's community focus were its roundtable broadcasts, which often dealt with racism, and the *Goodwill Revue* and the *Starlite Revue*, live concerts that raised money for a school for handicapped black children. Throughout the 1960s, WDIA's programs played an important role in the civil rights movement in Memphis, appealing for black equality and for calm when violence threatened to erupt.

A price was put on WDIA's success when, in 1957, John Pepper and Bert Ferguson sold their station to the Sonderling Broadcast Corporation of Chicago for $1 million. Although Bert Ferguson stayed on as executive vice president and general manager until 1970, many complained that absentee ownership resulted in WDIA's losing its local focus. The entertainment conglomerate Viacom took control of the station in 1980.

In 1983 Ragan Henry of Philadelphia added WDIA to his chain of stations and became the station's first black owner. Henry's ownership capped a period of growing black influence on the station's operations and management. Since the 1960s, blacks had been working in all facets of the station, and in 1972, WDIA welcomed its first black general manager, Chuck Scruggs. In 1996 Ragan Henry sold WDIA to Clear Channel Communications, the company that currently owns and operates the station.

See also: Black-Oriented Radio; Blues Format; Gospel Music Format

Further Reading

Cantor, Louis, *Wheelin' on Beale: How WDIA-Memphis Became the Nation's First All-Black Radio Station and Created the Sound That Changed America*, New York: Pharos Books, 1991.

Dates, Jannette Lake, and William Barlow, editors, *Split Image: African Americans in the Mass Media*, Washington, D.C.: Howard University Press, 1990; 2nd edition, 1993.

King, B.B., and David Ritz, *Blues All around Me: The Autobiography of B.B. King*, New York: Avon Books, and London: Sceptre, 1996.

Newman, Mark, *Entrepreneurs of Profit and Pride: From Black-Appeal to Radio Soul*, New York: Praeger, 1988; London: Praeger, 1989.

Streissguth, Michael, "WDIA and the Rise of Blues and Rhythm and Blues Music," Master's thesis, Purdue University, 1990.

MICHAEL STREISSGUTH

WEAF

New York City Station

WEAF is significant in radio history as the first station to broadcast a paid commercial and as the originating point for American Telephone and Telegraph's (AT&T) pioneering network experiments. AT&T owned the station for only four years, after which it became the flagship of the developing National Broadcasting Company (NBC) network, becoming WNBC after World War II.

Origins

During the 1920s, AT&T was actively involved in the development of radio. The corporation was a member of the radio patent pool (along with the Radio Corporation of America [RCA], Westinghouse, and other companies), owned radio stations, and experimented with networking. It also owned the highest-quality intercity connection circuits in the United States and so was crucial to the efforts of other radio broadcasters to interconnect stations. WEAF actually began as short-lived radio station WBAY. Construction of its antenna was begun in March 1922, and it broadcast its first program on 25 July 1922. WBAY was a technological failure, its signal barely audible. After reconfiguration and location elsewhere in the city, WBAY gave way to WEAF on 16 August.

WEAF was the first station in the United States to broadcast a paid commercial, engaging in what AT&T called "toll broadcasting" at the time. AT&T saw the possibilities for treating radio the same way it treated its long-distance telephone service: it would provide the facilities, and others would provide the content. It would lease its facilities to those who had a message to deliver to the public, just as it provided long-distance service to customers who paid for the time they used its lines. At the same time, it saw toll broadcasting as a means of destroying its most significant rival in the provision of long-distance services, RCA. Although RCA did not own long-distance telephone lines, it had been established in 1919 to provide point-to-point wireless communication services, thus making it a potential rival to AT&T. RCA was also involved in radio broadcasting but planned to provide radio services on a public service model, subsidizing program production and broadcasting through the profits from the sale of radio receivers. AT&T, the long-distance services of which provided massive profits, saw the potential of toll broadcasting to accomplish the same thing, which would give it an unassailable financial base from which to battle RCA.

WEAF broadcast its first commercial on 28 August 1922 at 5 P.M. It was a commercial for the Queensboro Corporation that lasted ten minutes and promoted the sale of apartments in Jackson Heights, New York City. The cost was $50. Queensboro

Corporation quickly became a repeat customer, leasing time from WEAF on five additional occasions over the ensuing few weeks. Its initial broadcast was shortly followed by others for Atwater Kent (a radio receiver manufacturer), Tidewater Oil, and the American Express company.

WEAF did not permit these early advertisements to make direct pitches to the public. It was concerned to preserve the dignity of broadcasting—and of advertising—so it did not allow prices to be mentioned, and the advertisements provided little in the way of graphic descriptions of products. Queensboro's initial advertisement, for instance, told the audience that its apartments had been named to honor Nathaniel Hawthorne, "the greatest of the American fictionists," and invited people to visit the development "right at the boundaries of God's great outdoors." The commercial claimed that just this sort of residential environment had influenced Hawthorne, and it "enjoined" the listeners to "get away from the solid masses of brick" with meager access to the sun. But even this indirect sort of appeal was enough to change the philosophy of broadcasting in America.

WEAF's second significant impact on American radio stemmed from its role as the central point for AT&T's network experiments. The first networked broadcast in the United States occurred on 4 January 1923, when WEAF was connected with WNAC in Boston, although the broadcast lasted only five minutes. In June of that year, WEAF was networked with WGY (Schenectady, New York); KDKA (Pittsburgh); and KYW (Chicago) for a single program broadcast, and the following month WEAF and WMAF (Portsmouth, New Hampshire) were permanently networked, allowing WMAF to take a three-to-four-hour-a-day feed from WEAF. By the middle of 1925 WEAF had become the flagship of the AT&T radio network, which connected 20 stations. All of these early experiments consisted of other stations' carrying programming that originated at WEAF.

National Broadcasting Company Flagship

On 15 November 1926, the true era of network radio arrived when a permanent arrangement was concluded whereby programming could originate at multiple points and be carried by multiple stations. On that date, WEAF originated remote programming from the Waldorf Astoria Hotel ballroom in New York City, and stations in both Chicago and Kansas City originated programs as well. These programs were carried on 21 network affiliate stations and four other stations. This broadcast was the result of complicated industry negotiations.

By the mid-1920s the cross-licensing agreement that formed the basis of the radio patent pool was in jeopardy. RCA and AT&T were part of arbitration hearings that began in early 1924, but before the final report was issued, the legal basis for the cross-licensing agreement itself was called into question, and the arbitrator's report, released in November, essentially affirmed RCA's position, which, among other assertions, denied AT&T's claim that it had an exclusive right to toll broadcasting. On 11 May 1926, AT&T announced that it was forming a separate company to conduct its broadcasting business, and on 7 July the final agreement between AT&T and RCA gave RCA an option to purchase AT&T's broadcasting interests, including WEAF—an option that RCA exercised on 21 July. On 1 November RCA paid the telephone company $1 million for WEAF, which became the flagship station of NBC's "Red" network.

A year later, NBC moved the station's transmitter from downtown Manhattan out to Bellmore, Long Island, increasing its power tenfold, to 50,000 W. Studios moved from what had been AT&T space to a new headquarters at 711 Fifth Avenue, expanding from several rooms to five full floors of operating space. In 1933 the station shifted once more, this time to the new Radio City complex of Rockefeller Center in midtown Manhattan. Nearly 30 studios fed signals to the NBC Red and Blue networks, as well as providing resources for WEAF.

The station's programs were effectively those of the NBC Red network. Only relatively late in its history (during and after World War II) did the outlet develop a local sound for part of the day, adding morning and other talk shows appealing specifically to New Yorkers. In late 1946 the WEAF call letters were dropped, as the station became WNBC.

See also: American Telephone and Telegraph; National Broadcasting Company; Radio City; WNBC

Further Reading

Archer, Gleason L., *Big Business and Radio*, New York: American Historical Company, 1939; reprint, 1971.
Banning, William Peck, *Commercial Broadcasting Pioneer: The WEAF Experiment, 1922–1926*, Cambridge, Massachusetts: Harvard University Press, 1946.
Jaker, Bill, Frank Sulek, and Peter Kanze, "WEAF" in *The Airwaves of New York*, Jefferson, North Carolina: McFarland, 1998.

ROBERT S. FORTNER

WESTERNS
Radio Drama Format

"Hi-yo, Silver, away!," "You betchum, Red Ryder!," and "Happy trails to you" are just a few of the expressions that have entered America's lexicon from the majestic Old West as presented on network programming during the golden age of radio. From the 1930s through the 1950s, westerns entertained millions of listeners—and sold lots of sponsors' products. While westerns varied in their narrative styles and tone, they shared the customary motifs that defined the genre: six-guns and horses, heroes and villains, cowboys and Indians, dusty trails and mountain passes. Radio westerns constitute four overlapping sub-genres: anthology series, singing cowboy shows, juvenile adventures, and so-called adult westerns.

Origins

One of the earliest western series was *Death Valley Days*, broadcast on NBC Blue from 1930 to 1941 and on CBS from 1941 to 1945. As an anthology series, *Death Valley Days* featured new characters each week, although all stories were set in 19th-century California. Stories were reportedly based on fact as collected and dramatized by producer Ruth Cornwall Smith, one of the few women radio producers of the era.

Anthology series not specifically dedicated to the western genre sometimes featured western dramas as well. For example, *Lux Radio Theatre*, which presented weekly radio versions of famous movies, occasionally broadcast western stories such as *The Plainsman* (1937). Similarly, anthology programs featuring original radio dramas, such as *Suspense*, broadcast western radio stories from time to time.

Most radio westerns, however, were episodic series or serials with recurring characters, many of which cultivated fanatically loyal audiences—particularly among children. As such, these programs were a boon to advertisers whose products were carefully associated with the values embodied in and verbalized by mythic, straight-shooting, clean-cut cowboys.

Song-filled programs with a western flavor and recurrent characters included *Grapevine Rancho* (CBS, 1943), *The Hollywood Barn Dance* (CBS, 1943–47), *The National Barn Dance* (various networks, 1924–1950), and *The Grand Ole Opry*, which began in 1925 and continues to this day. Although these musical programs lack some of the generic qualities of the classic western—shootouts, for example—their emphasis on country music and

folksy dialog delved heavily into romanticized imagery of the mythic West. In contrast, *Hawk Larabee* (CBS, 1946–47) also featured songs but leaned in the opposite direction; its primary emphasis was on adventures of the series' protagonist, and songs linked narrative segments.

Children's Series

Juvenile adventure westerns were more ubiquitous than their musical counterparts. The most famous was *The Lone Ranger*, which was developed at Detroit station WXYZ in 1933. The story of the famous western hero quickly became a local sensation. Soon, it functioned as the programming glue that connected stations in the fledgling Mutual radio network. In 1942, the series moved to NBC Blue (later ABC) where it remained until 1955. Throughout its production, the series featured voices of a well-honed stock company who also were heard in other WXYZ programs including *The Green Hornet* (various networks, 1938–52) and *Sergeant Preston of the Yukon* (ABC, 1947–50; Mutual, 1950–55)—the former a Lone Ranger spinoff set in contemporary America (the Green Hornet was the Lone Ranger's great-nephew) and the latter a Canadian Mountie, aided by his famous dog, Yukon King.

The Lone Ranger was warmly received, not only by avid young listeners, but also by the national press as a successful and laudable role model. This was particularly true during World War II when *The Lone Ranger* was peppered with patriotic dialog intended to boost the domestic war effort and overseas troop morale. Also, despite its simplistic storylines and two-dimensional characters, *The Lone Ranger* was a highly polished program penned by a one-man script mill, Fran Striker, who reportedly wrote some 60,000 words of radio dialog per week. The program soon was spun off into highly profitable movie series, a comic strip, and numerous toys.

The tremendous success of *The Lone Ranger* led to many copycat series for young listeners, especially boys. The Lone Ranger's major ratings competitor was *Red Ryder*, heard on various networks from 1942 until the 1950s. Other western heroes were featured in series such as *Hopalong Cassidy* (Mutual, 1950; CBS, 1950–52) and *Wild Bill Hickok* (Mutual, 1951–56). *Tom Mix* (various networks, 1933–50), *Bobby Benson* (various networks, 1932–55), and *Sky King* (various networks, 1946–54) were similar programs set in the modern West.

Among these series' most memorable features was their unrelenting push for sponsors' products, often transforming young listeners into a potent sales force. For instance, in 1939, *The Lone Ranger* mixed hero worship with salesmanship by offering a Lone Ranger badge to listeners who convinced three of their neighbors to buy the sponsor's product. A reported two million such badges were distributed within the first year of the campaign.

Like the singing cowboy programs, juvenile adventure westerns were highly formulaic, once a successful pattern had been established. *The Lone Ranger* episodes, for instance, were formed around recurring narrative elements, beginning with a character and his/her seemingly hopeless problem and moving through the Ranger's appearance and involvement, a trap set for the Ranger, the Ranger's overcoming the trap, his solution of the problem, and resolution of the narrative. Fistfights, gunplay, and chases on horseback were predictable narrative devices. Despite the fact that these programs were intended for young audiences, bloodshed and death were dolled out on a regular basis. In one episode of *The Lone Ranger* from 1939, for example, no less than twelve people were killed within the first three minutes of the program.

Western series with a strong emphasis on cowboy songs and campfire chat included *Gene Autry's Melody Ranch*, which ran on CBS from 1940 to 1956, sponsored by Wrigley's Gum. Episodes of this series consisted of jokes and stories told by Autry and his pals, dramatized tales, and plenty of songs, including the classic closing theme "Back in the Saddle Again." Gene Autry's major ratings competitor was *The Roy Rogers Show*, a program with a similar format that ran from 1937 to 1955. Stars of both series were also featured in popular films of the era.

Contrary to their musical counterparts, heroes of juvenile adventure series tended to live outside the bounds of their communities, even while working to preserve and help expand white society throughout the West. They roamed the frontier looking for adventure and people in need of help, but they never tarried long. (An exception was Red Ryder, who lived with his aunt.) Radio cowboy heroes' combination of placelessness and service to strangers is typical of the western mythos prevalent in other forms of popular culture, such as dime novels and western films, with roots reaching back to James Fennimore Cooper's *Leatherstocking Tale*

Indeed, the western outsider/hero motif has a deep cultural resonance, and given their immense popularity, juvenile western adventures are worth considering as important cultural artifacts. For example, although heroes such as the Lone Ranger deliberately exemplified values such as honesty and

fair play, closer reading also suggests that these programs served to affirm white and male forms of cultural dominance and westward expansion. The Lone Ranger, for instance, may be indebted to Tonto for certain "native" skills such as tracking and healing; nevertheless, power in the relationship is clearly skewed toward the Ranger, as Tonto acts as intermediary between settlers and "hostile" Indians, always under the Ranger's guidance. Similarly, Red Ryder was aided by his Indian protege, Little Beaver. Other sidekicks who helped their white friends tame the West included a Latino character named "Pablo" on *Dr. Sixgun* (NBC, 1954–55) and the Asian Heyboy of *Have Gun, Will Travel* (CBS, 1958–60). A variant of this pattern was *Straight Arrow* (Mutual, 1949–51), whose white hero, Steve Adams, had been raised by Comanches. (One exception to the pattern was *The Cisco Kid*, which was broadcast in the 1940s; in this series, Cisco was a vaguely Latino adventurer who had a humorous sidekick named Pancho.)

Similarly, in juvenile western adventures, female characters tend to be victims in need of heroic rescue, rather than strong, independent forces in their own right. The mythic West of juvenile western adventures, in other words, was rhetorically constructed as a domain to be settled and supervised by white men. Although this was never explicitly spelled out as such, recurring rhetorical tropes in thousands of episodes heard on a regular basis (in combination with accompanying costumes, decoder rings, and other accessories) endowed juvenile western adventures with a ritualized aura, reaffirming dominant values of their era.

Adult Westerns

While juvenile westerns ran well into the 1950s, by 1953 a new breed of western drama appeared. These "adult westerns" were grittier, more realistic, and clearly intended for an older audience. Adult westerns were less the descendants of their juvenile predecessors than they were cousins of western films such as *Shane* and *High Noon*, which were produced at about the same time. These postwar western films (as well as detective movies—with their own radio counterparts) reflected national feelings of postwar disillusion as the U.S. plunged into the Cold War and communists were thought to infiltrate all aspects of American society. In both film and radio, good and evil were far more difficult to distinguish than in juvenile fare. Both heroes and villains were finely shaded, unstable mixes of virtue and vice, suggesting a re-working and reinterpretation of dominant ideological assumptions.

The most notable reluctant hero of the adult radio westerns was Matt Dillon in *Gunsmoke*, played on CBS by gravelly voiced radio veteran William Conrad from 1952–61. Matt Dillon was the Marshall of Dodge City, a frontier town that attracted the worst sorts of outlaw scum ever heard on radio. Dillon's sidekick was his dimwitted deputy Chester Proudfoot, played by Parley Baer. Georgia Ellis played Kitty, and Howard McNear played Doc. Although Kitty's job was never spelled out, *Gunsmoke* creator Norman McDonnell described her as "just someone Matt has to visit every once in a while. We never say it, but Kitty is a prostitute, plain and simple."

Kitty, in fact, represents a complete revolution in portrayals of women in radio westerns; a shrewd, outspoken professional, Kitty is a far cry from the innocent school marm and rancher's daughter common among juvenile western programs. Whereas women on other western programs personified dominant values of white America (specifically values regarding family, religion, and education), Kitty simultaneously represents challenges to the moral status quo and the gutsy determination of independent women.

McDonnell's relish in describing Kitty's profession exemplified the realistic presentation of the West that *Gunsmoke* strove to create. Matt Dillon clearly hates his job, and his decisions are never easy or clear-cut. *Gunsmoke* is also notable for its intense emphasis on sound effects, ranging from the clinking of spurs to ever-present background sounds such as twittering birds and far-off barking dogs. Having established himself as a force in adult radio westerns, McDonnell went on to produce *Fort Laramie*, a series about a Wyoming cavalry outpost broadcast on CBS in 1956.

Other adult westerns of note included *Frontier Gentleman* (CBS, 1958), a well-written, highly polished drama concerning an English newspaper reporter who wandered the Old West. And *Luke Slaughter of Tombstone* (CBS, 1958) was set amidst cattle drives in 19th-century Arizona.

The shift to adult fare among radio westerns can partly be explained by the Cold War milieu within which they were produced. The Red Scare hit the radio industry hard, as many top performers and other creative personnel were blacklisted, while many more were silenced by intimidation. Westerns were removed in time and place from the reality of urban America. As such, they could be arenas in which writers expressed dangerous political concepts and dramatized social issues such as racism, albeit couched in the past and far from contemporary society. (Similarly, adult science fiction—

notably *X Minus One* [NBC, 1955–58]—played upon the same themes, but was set in the future instead.)

Beyond sociopolitical conditions of the times, the development of adult westerns can also be explained by analysis of the economic state of radio in the 1950s. The popular and trade presses had long since announced the death knell of radio drama's golden age, correctly emphasizing television's immediate and immense popularity. As audiences moved toward the newer medium, radio broadcasters needed fresh, new products to hold onto their advertising base. Also, network affiliates were going independent, having discovered that local programs were more lucrative than network fare. Networks, in turn, scrambled to cancel most of their longrunning daytime series and develop evening and weekend programming with ambitious new concepts in order to retain their rapidly dwindling number of affiliates. *Gunsmoke* was clearly such a product. Other new series featuring major film stars were created to keep dwindling audiences tuned to radio. These programs included *Tales of the Texas Rangers* (NBC, 1950), a modern-day western starring Joel McCrea, and *The Six Shooter* (NBC, 1953), starring Jimmy Stewart as a well-meaning, though intensely lethal, gunfighter. Both series were high-quality productions, although of the two, *The Six Shooter* was more in the adult-western mold, given its finely nuanced protagonist, compelling stories, and close attention to historical detail.

Third, the development of adult westerns resulted from changes in the producer/network/sponsor relationship in radio. Prior to the popularity of television, most radio programs were produced by advertising agencies on behalf of sponsors. Censorship was strict, because neither agencies nor sponsors wanted their programs or products associated with controversy. As sponsors moved into television, radio dramas were increasingly produced by networks in the hopes of selling commercial time. If left unsponsored, these "sustaining" programs provided a public-service function for networks. Sustaining programs were touted as experimental venues whereby the networks gave something back to the people for the use of public airwaves. Nevertheless, commercial time on series such as *Gunsmoke* would be sold when possible. Norman McDonnell noted the dilemma of sponsorship versus sustaining programming, quipping "I'd feel great if someone did buy it, but there would be problems. We'd have to clean the show up. Kitty would have to be living with her parents on a sweet little ranch." Whether sponsored or sustaining, network-produced radio dramas, including westerns, were less burdened by direct censorship from the advertising industry.

Decline

Despite the effort put into their development, westerns eventually met the same fate as other forms of network radio theater. The final network radio western was *Have Gun, Will Travel*, last heard on CBS in 1960. *Have Gun, Will Travel* was something of an oddity in radio drama. Whereas most radio westerns, such as *The Lone Ranger* and *Gunsmoke*, moved to television after (or even during the time) they were on radio, *Have Gun, Will Travel* began on television and then was developed for a dual radio/TV presence. As such, the series exemplified not only the end of radio westerns, but also the undeniable ascendancy of television.

Re-runs of original western radio dramas, now often termed "old-time" radio, are still heard on some stations, where they have a loyal following. Also, westerns from radio's golden age are readily available on cassette tapes. Radio Spirits of Schiller Park, Illinois, for example, markets *The Lone Ranger*, *Gunsmoke*, *Frontier Gentleman*, and other series. The Smithsonian Institution, in association with Radio Spirits, similarly offers a package of classic western series for sale on cassette and compact disc. These series are marketed not just as nostalgia but also as first-rate forms of entertainment, which, given their fairly high costs, suggests that many radio westerns retain their vitality decades after their original production.

Although new radio westerns are rarely produced apart from a handful of special-event programs, a descendent of the radio western can be found in books on tape, which feature a variety of western novels read by famous actors. Also, a well-produced series of dramas based on the novels of Louis L'Amour is available, often for sale in interstate highway gas stations—strongly appealing, no doubt, to truck drivers and other lonesome travelers eager to pass the time on long hauls under western skies.

See also: Country Music Format; *Grand Ole Opry*; *Gunsmoke*; *Lone Ranger*

Further Reading

Allen, Chadwick, "Hero with Two Faces: The Lone Ranger As Treaty Discourse," *American Literature* 68 (1996).
Barabas, Suzanne, and Gabor Barabas, *Gunsmoke: A Complete History and Analysis of the Legendary Broadcast Series with a Comprehensive Episode-by-Episode Guide to Both the Radio and Television Programs*, Jefferson, North Carolina: McFarland, 1990.
Bryan, J., "Hi-Yo Silver!" *Saturday Evening Post* (14 October 1939).
Harmon, Jim, *The Great Radio Heroes*, Garden City, New York: Doubleday, 1967.
Holland, Dave, *From Out of the Past: A Pictorial History of The Lone Ranger*, Granada Hills, California: Holland House, 1988.
"Is Network Radio Dead?" *Newsweek* (20 August 1956).
Nachman, Gerald, *Raised on Radio: In Quest of the Lone Ranger, Jack Benny*, New York: Pantheon Books, 1998.
"Network Drama," *Time* (12 January 1959).
"Weeks of Prestige," *Time* (23 March 1950).
Wylie, Max, editor, *Best Broadcasts of 1939–40*, New York: Whittlesey House, 1940.

WARREN BAREISS

WESTINGHOUSE
Electrical and Radio Manufacturer

The Westinghouse Electric Company was founded in 1886 and became well known for both industrial and consumer products, such as washing machines and refrigerators, as well as many consumer electronic products. For many years its widely known advertising slogan was "You can be sure if it's Westinghouse."

Origins

American engineer George Westinghouse (1846–1914) would eventually receive more than 360 patents, including the invaluable one in 1869 for the air brake used by railroads. Although he formed nearly 60 companies, the largest and longest lasting, Westinghouse Electric, was created in 1886, with headquarters in Pittsburgh, Pennsylvania. Westinghouse received numerous honors in the U.S. and abroad. Perhaps his finest tribute came from inventor Nikola Tesla, whose patents for one system of alternating current and the induction motor were acquired by Westinghouse in 1888 and gave the company its early leadership in electric power developments. Westinghouse used Tesla's system to light the World's Columbian Exposition at Chicago in 1893.

By the turn of the 20th century, Westinghouse had become one of the two or three largest electrical manufacturers in America, employing more than 50,000 workers. The company was active in electric power generation, electric traction (trolleys) and railway equipment, and various industrial applications of electricity. A research department was formed in 1904, becoming a division two years later.

In the financial panic of 1907, Westinghouse lost control of the several companies he had founded and then still headed. In 1910, he founded his last firm to exploit the invention of a compressed air spring for absorbing the shock of riding in automobiles. By 1911, however, he had severed all ties with his former companies. He had shown signs of a heart ailment by 1913 and was ordered to rest by doctors. Not long after deteriorating health confined him to a wheelchair, Westinghouse died in March 1914. His last patent was granted four years later.

As with some other electrical companies, Westinghouse Electric began to investigate the manufacturing potential of wireless. During World War I, Westinghouse held huge government contracts to manufacture wireless equipment for the army and navy. Those contracts were canceled with the end of the war in November 1918, leaving the company with a trained cadre of workers and a considerable investment in production equipment but not enough work to keep them busy.

Radio Receivers

To better its manufacturing position for a possible civilian radio market, in 1920 Westinghouse purchased the International Radio Telegraph Co. to obtain important Fessenden heterodyne circuit patents. A few months later, seeking to head off developing competition from the new Radio Corporation of America (RCA), Westinghouse also purchased Edwin Armstrong's regeneration and superheterodyne tuning circuit patents.

At about the same time, a chance event helped pull all the pieces together. Westinghouse engineer Frank Conrad had been experimenting with wireless since 1912. In 1919–20 he operated amateur ("ham") station 8XK, playing recorded music one or two nights a week for the amusement of fellow hams. While hobbyists preferred to build their own equipment, others wanted to tune in as well. A September 1920 newspaper advertisement by a Pittsburgh department store seeking to sell receivers to those who wanted to hear Conrad's broadcasts caught the eye of Harry Phillips Davis, a Westinghouse sevice president in charge of radio work. Davis perceived that making receivers for the public to receive a possible new radio broadcasting service could be the answer to Westinghouse's canceled-contract predicament.

Within a year or so, a very basic Westinghouse crystal receiver marketed as the "Aeriola Jr." could be purchased for about $25 in department stores. A more sophisticated tube set, sold as the "Aeriola

Sr.," offered better reception and cost about $60. Westinghouse was soon turning out thousands of radios from its factories, primarily those in Springfield, Massachusetts. Unlike many other set makers, Westinghouse had the advantage of owning several radio stations, which were useful as a means of promoting company products. In addition to radio receivers, Westinghouse also built transmitters for its own and some other stations. The company made increasingly powerful transmitters throughout the 1920s: whereas a typical station of that time transmitted with 100 W, in the mid-1920s Westinghouse station KDKA was broadcasting with 10,000 W.

Westinghouse's control of the Fessenden, and especially the Armstrong patents, gave the company the clout it needed to enter into agreements with its main competitors, General Electric (GE), RCA, and the Western Electric manufacturing arm of American Telephone and Telegraph. The "patent pool" allowed each company to license the patents of the others, and established a division of the equipment market. The pool had a flaw, however, for it concerned only the international or "point-to-point" radio market, not broadcasting which was then still small and seemingly insignificant. According to the company's version of the story, Westinghouse saw this alliance as a way to get into the international market, but media historians have suggested that Westinghouse felt it could not remain independent and still succeed in outselling the others, especially RCA, which was already solidifying its power and could easily have shut out any meaningful competition. As Westinghouse couldn't beat its competitors, it decided to join them.

After 1922—and until an antitrust case was filed against RCA in 1930—Westinghouse radios were sold under the RCA trade label, usually as "Radiola" receivers. The patent pool agreement reserved 40 percent of the business for Westinghouse while the larger General Electric took 60 percent.

Expanding Consumer Electronics

Westinghouse began to expand its consumer electronics business early on. Television pioneer Vladimir Zworykin undertook his early development work for the television camera tube (dubbed the iconoscope) at Westinghouse before transferring to RCA in 1930. Nearly four decades later, a Westinghouse television camera accompanied the first men to land on the moon.

In 1945, and again fattened by large wartime government contracts (including many for radar, which remained a company specialty), what had long been Westinghouse Electric and Manufacturing

Company reverted to an older and simpler name, becoming known simply as the Westinghouse Electric Corporation.

Postwar Westinghouse products included a full range of radios and phonographs, and soon, television sets. In 1954 Westinghouse formed a Westinghouse Credit Corporation subsidiary that assisted consumers in making major appliances over time. The 1950s were a boom period for the company, the public face of which was the ubiquitous spokesperson Betty Furness, who touted refrigerators and other Westinghouse appliances on prime-time television.

But as was true for all American manufacturers of consumer electronics, competition was fierce, and by the late 1950s inexpensive foreign imports began to cut into sales of radios and related products. Soon Westinghouse-labeled models were being manufactured overseas and American plants were closing down.

Demise

Westinghouse's manufacturing divisions began to show some signs of financial trouble and seemed to lose their way. By the 1970s the firm was beginning to sell off some of its units—including the once-lucrative major appliances division in 1974. The electric lighting business was sold in 1983. On the other hand, Westinghouse also got into the cable business, paying $646 million to acquire the Teleprompter Corporation (renamed Group W Cable) in 1981. When it proved extremely expensive to upgrade the cable systems, they were sold at a profit in 1985. Throughout this period, Westinghouse made some bad real estate loans and made a number of risky acquisitions—all in an attempt to diversify the industrial firm more into the services sector. One important part of the company's service continued to be the broadcast station-owning subsidiary, known as Group W. The East Pittsburgh operations, once the birthplace of commercial radio broadcasting, were closed in 1987. The power transmission and distribution unit was sold two years later.

Major change continued into the 1990s for what had once been one of the country's most stable manufacturing concerns. Layoffs were widespread as a series of restructurings took place. The motor manufacturing divisions were spun off in 1995 to become an independent firm. A new chairman and chief executive officer, Michael Jordan (who had formerly been at PepsiCo), was brought in to redirect Westinghouse.

In 1994 Jordan allied the Group W broadcast stations with CBS in a joint venture. Just a year later came a more dramatic move as Westinghouse

agreed to purchase CBS for $5.4 billion. After the Telecommunications Act of 1996 lifted limits on radio station ownership, Westinghouse acquired a much larger group of radio stations, Infinity Broadcasting. Defense electronics manufacturing was sold off in 1996.

But what was supposed to make a hero of Jordan and save Westinghouse had ironic results. Infinity's chairman, Mel Karmazin, became the largest shareholder in Westinghouse, and as financial columnist Steve Massey (1998) observed, he "had no sentimental attachment to the old Westinghouse." He also did not get along with Jordan. The plan had been for Westinghouse Electric to survive and for Jordan to be in charge. In the end, Jordan was forced out (early retirement, the story went), Karmazin took over, and the Westinghouse name officially vanished from the broadcasting division in December 1997 as the huge entity became known as CBS/Infinity. The nuclear power manufacturing parts of the company were sold in 1999, and with them the Westinghouse Electric Company name, and became a part of the Nuclear Utilities Business Group of British Nuclear Fuels.

See also: Columbia Broadcasting System; General Electric; Group W; Infinity Broadcasting Corporation; Radio Corporation of America; Receivers

Further Reading

Douglas, Alan, "Westinghouse," in *Radio Manufacturers of the 1920s, Volume 3.* Vestal, New York: Vestal Press, 1991.
Massey, Steve, "Who Killed Westinghouse," *Pittsburgh Post-Gazette* (1–7 March 1998); also at www.post-gazette.com/westinghouse/default.asp
Passer, Harold C., *The Electrical Manufacturers, 1875–1900*, Cambridge, Massachusetts: Harvard University Press, 1953.
Prout, Henry G., *A Life Of George Westinghouse*, New York: The American Society of Mechanical Engineers, 1921.
Schatz, Ronald W., *The Electrical Workers: A History of Labor at General Electric & Westinghouse, 1923–60*, Champaign: University of Illinois Press, 1983.
Schiffer, Michael Bryan, *The Portable Radio in American Life*, Tucson: University of Arizona Press, 1991.
Westinghouse history and timeline, www.westinghouse.com/A1.asp
Woodbury, David O., *Battlefronts of Industry: Westinghouse in World War Two*, New York: Wiley, 1948.

DONNA L. HALPER AND CHRISTOPHER H. STERLING

WESTWOOD ONE
Radio Program Service

Westwood One is one of the largest radio service companies in the United States, producing and distributing entertainment, news, sports, talk, and traffic programming to more than 7,500 stations. It runs the nation's largest radio network, which includes National Broadcasting Company (NBC), Columbia Broadcasting System (CBS), Cable News Network (CNN) and Fox radio programs, and maintains an international radio programming service called Westwood One International. It owns local programming subsidiaries Shadow Broadcast Services and Metro Networks, which dominate the industry in localized traffic reports; and it has an ownership stake in an internet radio company called WebRadio.com. With its emphasis on music, personalities, and large-scale events, Westwood One has made a significant contribution to the return of entertainment to network radio.

Origins

Westwood One was founded by Norman J. Pattiz in 1974 after he lost his job as a sales manager at KCOP-TV in Los Angeles. Pattiz had heard a weekend-long Motown music program on local rhythm and blues radio station KGFJ and had the idea of producing such programs for national syndication, as was common in the television industry. Although he had no radio production experience, Pattiz convinced the KGFJ station manager to let him put together another Motown show for national distribution. After nine months of production and lining up advertisers, *The Sound of Motown* aired on about 250 stations and grossed several hundred thousand dollars. The program was provided to the stations at no cost. Local stations were allowed to sell local ad time while Pattiz and KGFJ collected the revenue from national advertisers.

From there Pattiz went on to produce more programs and incorporated his own company, Westwood One, late in 1974. Its name is derived from the Westwood neighborhood of Los Angeles where Pattiz started his new company in a one-room office. In the next nine years, Westwood One would continue to produce programs for syndication and to package the programs with national advertisers, eventually offering 52-week vehicles for those advertisers.

In 1984 Westwood One became a public company. The infusion of capital allowed the company to change quickly from a small syndicator wholly dependent on the success of each program to a national radio network with multiple resources. In 1985 Westwood One acquired the struggling and aged Mutual Broadcasting System from Amway for $39 million. Pattiz consolidated operations and reprogrammed the network, turning the debt-ridden

Mutual into a profit source. Mutual, like other traditional radio networks, had become primarily a distributor rather than a producer of radio programming, although it still retained its news division. By acquiring Mutual, Westwood One was able to offer and market sports, news, and talk radio, as well as its original entertainment programming, becoming a more full-service network. Two years later Westwood One bought the NBC Radio Network from General Electric for $50 million, and in 1989 it launched the Westwood One News and Entertainment Network.

Sharpening the Focus

After several years of expansion, Westwood One found that its debt burden was becoming a problem. NBC Radio was losing $11 million a year when it was purchased by Westwood, but unlike Mutual, its employees were heavily unionized, making cost-cutting more difficult. To make matters worse the radio industry went into a recession shortly after the purchase and advertising revenue declined by nearly 15 percent. In 1988 the company made a secondary stock offering, but after posting continued losses, its stock plummeted. By the early 1990s it became clear that cutbacks had to be made. Pattiz sold off his three radio stations and his trade publication *Radio and Records*. He also consolidated news operations, merged four networks into three, and reduced compensation payments to stations.

By 1994 the company had reduced its debt significantly and could concentrate on its programming. That same year, in an effort to secure station contracts and expand its network capacity, Westwood One made another very significant move. It traded 25 percent of its ownership to Infinity Broadcasting, the largest owner of radio stations in the United States, in exchange for Infinity's Unistar networks. Infinity was hired to take over management and Pattiz gave up the position of CEO while retaining his position as chairman and executive producer of all programming. (He also remained a major stockholder.) Mel Karmazin, then CEO of Infinity, became the new CEO of Westwood One. After merging with Unistar, the company formed two new divisions: Westwood One Radio Networks and Westwood One Entertainment. The networks division managed the six networks, news, and 24-hour formats, and the entertainment division produced programming and live concerts.

In order to tap into the local advertising revenue stream, Westwood One purchased Shadow Broadcast Services in 1996. Shadow provided localized traffic reports as well as local news, sports, weather, and entertainment. Three years later, Westwood bought the number one traffic news service, Metro Networks, in a $900 million stock deal and merged it with Shadow Broadcast Services. In 2000 it added SmartRoute Systems to this lineup, providing wireless and internet services as well. By providing localized products in exchange for ad time, these services account for a substantial percentage of Westwood's revenue.

Shortly after Westwood picked up Shadow Broadcast Services, Karmazin attempted to buy CBS's owned-and-operated radio stations. When CBS CEO Michael H. Jordan declined, Karmazin offered to sell Infinity to CBS in return for allowing Karmazin to run the radio group. Jordan accepted the offer and in December 1996, CBS bought Infinity for $4.9 billion in stock. By the following March, management of the CBS Radio Networks division was spun off to Westwood One. The deal provided that Westwood One would represent CBS Radio Networks, managing its sales, marketing, and promotion, and that CBS would continue to produce and control the programming. CBS, by virtue of owning Infinity Broadcasting, now owned a stake in Westwood One.

After becoming president of CBS in 1998, Karmazin decided to move out of the CEO position at Westwood One, making way for a new full-time president and CEO, Joel Hollander, formerly head of New York station WFAN. Hollander led the company through the Metro acquisition and continued to secure deals for college and professional sports programs, new entertainment venues, and web-based radio programming. In 1999 Westwood made the decision to shut down its Mutual News division, ending the network's 65-year broadcasting legacy. The following year, Westwood bought a six percent stake in WebRadio.com, an internet broadcasting company, and secured an equity stake in Fanball.com, a sportsfantasy multimedia company. In May 2000 Viacom merged with CBS, making Viacom the new parent company of Westwood One. Karmazin became president and chief operating officer of Viacom at that time.

Programs and Operations

Westwood One made a name for itself by focusing on entertainment programming for radio and particularly on large-scale entertainment events. Its advertising slogan became " Westwood One, for the biggest events in radio." In the 1970s, when Westwood first started, traditional radio networks provided mostly news, sports, and talk, and very little

(if any) musical or dramatic entertainment. Starting with *The Sound of Motown*, Westwood went on to produce dozens of radio specials. In the early 1980s, it produced a live broadcast of the US Festival, a four-day rock concert in Riverside, California. Although individual stations such as KRLA had sponsored concerts in the 1960s, no radio network or syndicator had ever produced such a large event for live broadcasting. At that time Westwood also decided to hire its own sound crew and build a state-of-the-art mobile recording studio for concert production. It then produced the first live stereo-radio broadcast from Japan with its concert "Asia from Japan."

When Westwood One began to acquire traditional networks, its youth-oriented entertainment emphasis clashed with the staid culture of the older networks. Although these networks were brought in specifically to provide a wider variety of programming, Pattiz set about to restructure and reprogram them to reflect the energetic style of Westwood One. When Karmazin came on board with the purchase by Infinity Broadcasting, he pushed for expansion into new markets such as traffic and satellite formats. However, as executive producer of programming, Pattiz continued to pursue the exclusive superstar concert broadcasts for which Westwood was known, such as the Rolling Stones, the Eagles, and Barbra Streisand.

Westwood One's network division currently provides programming in several categories. In news it carries Fox News Radio, CNN Radio, NBC Radio Network, CBS Radio News and CBSMarketWatch.com. Both CNN Radio and CBS MarketWatch.com air 24-hour services. The Associated Press (AP) is the primary provider of news content to Westwood's syndicated and network programs. In sports Westwood features broadcasts for the National Football League, the National Hockey League, the National Collegiate Athletics Association, the Olympics, championship boxing, and professional golf. Westwood's talk personalities include Jim Bohannon, Larry King, G. Gordon Liddy, and Tom Leykis. Dozens of music formats are available, including a number of full-time and international services.

Shadow Broadcasting Services and Metro Networks provide local traffic reports, localized news, weather, and sports to hundreds of local radio markets across the country. Each program is customized for the individual station and made to sound as though it is being delivered by local talent. Traffic reports make up the bulk of affiliate contracts, but the other areas, particularly news, are growing with increased demand. The Shadow division has added short-form entertainment and health news reports to its lineup of services. SmartRoute Systems provides traffic, news, sports, and weather information to wireless and web services.

Westwood One also provides prep services such as the MTV Morning Facts and The CBS Morning Resource, which supply stations with interviews, celebrity and entertainment industry facts, soundbites, news, and gossip. Program directors integrate this material into their local programming, using local talent.

The myriad problems that radio suffered in the early 2000s, from increased competition to flat ad sales, were especially hard on Westwood One. Despite a strong lineup of talent and services (which has come to include shows hosted by Adam Carolla, erudite comedian Dennis Miller, Phil Valentine, and Mike O'Meara), the company began to report financial losses and in November 2008 was unlisted by the New York Stock Exchange. This lead to a revolving door of company leadership (one CEO was jettisoned after just ten months). A further blow came in late 2008 when political commentator Bill O'Reilly announced that he would discontinue his highly popular Westwood One-produced daily talk show. Shortly thereafter, long-time Westwood personality Tom Leykis also announced his imminent departure.

See also: Columbia Broadcasting System; Infinity Broadcasting Corporation; Mutual Broadcasting System; National Broadcasting Company

Further Reading

Borzillo, Carrie, "New Challenges Afoot for Network 'King' Westwood One," *Billboard* (8 July 1995).
Dunphy, Laura, "The Advantage of Getting Fired," *Los Angeles Business Journal* (27 December 1999).
Grossman, Lawrence K., "The Death of Radio Reporting," *Columbia Journalism Review* 37, no. 3 (September/October 1998).
Petrozzello, Donna, "Traffic Services Dish Out News," *Broadcasting and Cable* (9 June 1997).
Viles, Peter, "'Leaner, Meaner' Westwood Cuts Losses," *Broadcasting and Cable* (19 July 1993).
Westwood One website, www.westwoodone.com

CHRISTINA S. DRALE,
2009 REVISIONS BY CARY O'DELL

WEVD

New York City Station

WEVD-AM was established in 1927 as a memorial to socialist leader Eugene Victor Debs. A famous unionist and five-time presidential candidate on the Socialist ticket, Debs died in 1926, and the Socialist Party was moved to erect a monument in his honor. The Party raised enough money to buy Long Island radio station WSOM in 1927 and subsequently changed the station's call letters to WEVD. The station signed on at a frequency of 1220 kHz on 20 October 1927, the anniversary of Debs' death, and immediately became an electronic voice for the ideas and causes that Debs had championed.

On a typical day, WEVD would broadcast a mixture of poetry, music, and speeches reflecting the ideals of labor and socialism. The station presented shows for New York's minority population, including a *Jewish Hour*, a *Negro Art Group* program, and shows on African-American literature, music, and history. Debates on topics ranging from foreign policy in Nicaragua to general labor conditions were common. It was station policy to provide free access to labor unions, including, among others, the Teacher's Union, the Union of Technical Men, the Office Workers, the Garment Workers, and the Neckwear Workers. WEVD's fiscal health was dependent on donations from these and other unions. Consequently, the station was plagued with financial difficulties from the start, and plans to increase power and form a network were suspended.

The first task confronting the Federal Radio Commission (FRC) in 1927 was to resolve the problem of congestion on the airwaves. The commission concluded that the solution was to eliminate at least 100 radio stations. Toward that end, the FRC issued its famous General Order Number 32, which asked 164 stations, including WEVD, to show cause why their licenses should not be revoked.

The commission held hearings for two weeks in July 1928 in Washington, D.C., and the WEVD case was the first to be heard. The burden was placed on WEVD and 163 other stations to demonstrate why license renewal would be in the public interest. The FRC insisted that WEVD was placed on the list because of complaints of interference and technical violations. Station officials believed WEVD was singled out because of the unpopular and controversial doctrines expressed in its programming. Station officials invoked the First Amendment, arguing for the right of dissident minorities to free speech and arguing that labor, socialist, and other forms of unpopular rhetoric are in the public interest.

Approximately one month after the hearing, WEVD's license was renewed. Of the 164 radio stations called before the commission, only 81 (including WEVD) escaped adverse action by the FRC. In 1929 WEVD moved to 1300 AM, a frequency it would share with three other stations. By

1930 continued financial problems, the Great Depression, and the weakening of the Socialist Party would bring WEVD into a second confrontation with the FRC. The commission accused WEVD of several operational violations, but station officials again suspected they were being singled out for their unpopular programming.

WEVD's license was renewed in early 1931, but in a highly unusual decision, the FRC changed its mind three days later and revoked the license. The revocation was apparently prompted by a competing applicant, the Paramount Broadcasting Corporation of New York, which vowed to provide better public service. WEVD officials pledged to continue operating the station in defiance of the commission's decision. The FRC decided to grant temporary license extensions to WEVD, during which time the commission would conduct hearings on WEVD's renewal application. One hearing before the commission in 1931 lasted an entire week, which was the longest hearing before the FRC to that time.

In a narrow decision, the FRC finally renewed the license of WEVD in October 1931. However, the delays had involved WEVD in a long and costly battle, and the station's financial problems became acute. The *Jewish Daily Forward* rescued WEVD with a commitment of $250,000, but this and later contributions from the daily newspaper gave that organization effective decision-making power. Within a year, the station's staff was reorganized, and the studios moved to the Times Square area. The Debs Memorial Radio Fund later merged with the Forward Association to run WEVD as a commercial outlet. Six years later the station moved again, to occupy its own building on West 46th Street.

Throughout this period, WEVD shared the broadcast day with other New York stations. Gradually those other operations either sold out, moved, or were taken over by WEVD, which was on the air nearly 90 hours a week by 1938. In the 1980s, the station underwent a host of ownership and frequency changes, selling the AM outlet in 1981 and operating only with FM for much of the decade. In a complex exchange, WEVD sold the now-valuable FM station for $30 million in 1988, and as part of the deal it took over the 1050 kHz AM frequency that had been WSKQ. By the mid-1990s, the 50,000-W station specialized in syndicated talk shows and news programming.

Further Reading

Brindze, Ruth, *Not to Be Broadcast: The Truth about Radio*, New York: Vanguard Press, 1937.

Friendly, Fred W., *The Good Guys, the Bad Guys, and the First Amendment: Free Speech vs. Fairness in Broadcasting*, New York: Random House, 1976.

Godfried, N., "Legitimizing the Mass Media Structure: The Socialists and American Broadcasting, 1926–1932," in *Culture, Gender, Race, and U.S. Labor History*, edited by Ronald Kent, et al., Westport, Connecticut: Greenwood Press, 1993.

Jaker, Bill, Frank Sulek, and Peter Kanze, *The Airwaves of New York: Illustrated Histories of 156 AM Stations in the Metropolitan Area, 1921–1996*, Jefferson, North Carolina: McFarland, 1998.

McChesney, Robert Waterman, *Telecommunications, Mass Media, and Democracy: The Battle for the Control of U.S. Broadcasting, 1928–1935*, New York: Oxford University Press, 1993.

PAUL F. GULLIFOR

WGI
Boston, Massachusetts Station

Although WGI never had expensive studios, it did have a woman engineer/announcer, a morning exercise program, on-air college courses, and the best-known children's show in town. Furthermore, it may have been the first station to run paid commercials, and several well-known performers got their start in those not-very-opulent studios. Yet today, few people know that the Boston station ever existed.

Origins

Harold J. Power fell in love with "wireless" when he was nine years old, and by the time he attended Tufts College, at Medford Hillside (about five miles from Boston), he was already an experienced ham radio operator who enjoyed building his own receiving equipment. After graduating in 1914, he and several fellow hams decided to start their own station, along with a company to manufacture receivers. They named this new venture the American Radio and Research Company; most people knew it as AMRAD. As for the new station, because radio broadcasting was still considered experimental by the Department of Commerce, it received the call letters 1XE. But even six years later, when the station was assigned the commercial call letters "WGI," listeners still thought of it as either "the AMRAD station" or "the Medford Hillside station."

Harold Power became the president of AMRAD, and he soon began to air wireless concerts of phonograph records to promote the new company. In early 1916 this was so unusual that the *Boston Globe* wrote an article about the amazing music programs being heard by the ships at sea. At first, AMRAD targeted the ham radio audience (as there was no commercial broadcasting), but at some point in 1920, everything began to change.

We may never know who was really first to broadcast commercially. Scholars have debated endlessly whether KDKA, WWJ, or any of several other stations were the first, but there is evidence that 1XE was in the elite group of stations on the air in the fall of 1920. Unfortunately, most of AMRAD's and 1XE/WGI's files were long ago destroyed in a fire, but based on the radio columns of several Boston newspaper reporters of the early 1920s and an interesting interview from the manager of a competing Boston radio station, the consensus is that 1XE was on the air at around the same time as the much better-known KDKA.

By the spring of 1921, 1XE was on the air every day with a regular schedule. The station's air staff included a popular woman announcer, Eunice Randall. She read the nightly police reports, gave children their bedtime story several nights a week, sang when a guest didn't show up, and worked as one of the station's engineers—all highly unusual for a woman in those days. Randall also had a show that may have been sponsored—although as with many such arrangements in the early days, it may have been a barter arrangement. Randall's bedtime stories were presented by *Little Folks Magazine*, which may have provided free copies as prizes rather than paying for sponsorship.

The need for revenue was a constant problem for small stations of the early 1920s. Stations owned by individuals or small companies like AMRAD ran into financial trouble when lightning struck their towers or when equipment broke and was expensive to repair. At first, entertainers performed free because radio was a novelty, but eventually the bigger names wanted compensation; small stations had to depend on eager volunteers or up-and-coming performers who would still work in exchange for exposure.

AMRAD had originally been backed by financier J.P. Morgan's son Jack, who had known Harold Power ever since Power worked for him while still in high school. Morgan had been persuaded by Power's dreams of success in the radio business and was a silent partner in AMRAD for its first few years. But although Power had big dreams and good intentions, running a company was problematic for him. AMRAD became famous for good concepts but poor implementation: equipment was often delivered to suppliers late, and AMRAD was slow to react to new trends. Morgan gradually phased out his support of AMRAD,

leaving the company to deal with its own financial problems by 1923.

Decline

In spite of financial and technical problems, 1XE gained fans all over the eastern United States (the station's 100-W signal was even heard in England one night). Guest speakers, from politicians to professors, and even the famous economist Roger Babson, gave talks from Medford Hillside. By late 1921, WBZ was on the air (although it did not yet put a good signal into Boston), but musicians and celebrities continued to appear at the AMRAD station, because it was so close to the theaters and clubs of Boston, whereas WBZ was 80 miles away in Springfield. 1XE became WGI in February 1922: Power later said that he never saw a good reason to get a commercial license until then; he believed his experimental license was sufficient. By March of that year, it was airing Boston's first radio newscasts, courtesy of the *Boston Traveler* newspaper. WGI consistently provided good entertainment throughout the early 1920s: musicians such as *Hum and Strum* and Joe Rines went on to successful careers on the networks and on records; the popular children's show the *Big Brother Club* enjoyed a 45-year run on radio and then TV; and the famous poet Amy Lowell and the African-American actor Charles Gilpin were heard first over WGI, as was Harry Levi, the "Radio Rabbi."

Harold Power's attempt to bring in some revenue at WGI got the station in trouble with the Department of Commerce in the spring of 1922. In early April, Power had accepted money from a car dealer and an advertising agency to air some commercial announcements. Evidently, somebody notified the department (direct advertising was frowned upon, and Secretary of Commerce Herbert Hoover wanted to keep it that way). A series of "cease and desist" letters were sent by Radio Inspector Charles Kolster, beginning on 18 April and continuing into May. His correspondence to the station suggests that WGI aired commercials in April (well before WEAF's first commercial in August) and that the department had to warn WGI management several times before these commercials stopped.

By the fall of 1922, a new station, WNAC, was on the air, owned by the Shepard Department Stores. With substantial financial backing, it paid its talent and soon enjoyed handsome studios as well. In the meantime, AMRAD's financial worries increased, and some of WGI's best performers (and several announcers) accepted jobs at WNAC. Over the next two years, WGI continued to win praise from listeners, magazine editors, and radio columnists, but as more Boston stations came on the air—all with more powerful signals, better equipment, and money to pay the performers—it was only a matter of time before WGI could no longer compete. AMRAD went into bankruptcy in late April 1925, and as a result one of America's pioneer stations came to an end. When a buyer was not found, WGI left the air.

See also: WEAF

Further Reading

Halper, Donna L., "The Rise and Fall of WGI," *Popular Communications* (June 1999).

DONNA L. HALPER

WGN

Chicago, Illinois Station

Named for the "World's Greatest Newspaper," this Chicago radio (and later TV) station was not actually started by its long-time owner, the Tribune Company, but was purchased by the newspaper giant soon after it went on the air in June 1924.

Origins

By no means the first Chicago broadcaster (which was KYW), the *Chicago Tribune* entered radio by providing that pioneering outlet with news and market reports. At least four other stations soon followed KYW on the air. The first station located in the handsome Tribune Tower building was WDAP, which aired from May 1922 until a July tornado destroyed its antenna. The station moved and continued operating with a single (very busy) employee, one Ralph Shugart. When station mail piled up, the second employee, Myrtle Stahl (who would stay in radio until 1960) joined him. In 1923, the Chicago Board of Trade purchased WDAP. By March 1924, however, the *Tribune* had purchased enough airtime to take control of the station, and changed its call letters to WGN. Full page ads in the newspaper announced the "new" station on 28 March 1924, and WGN's inaugural broadcast came the next evening from studios in the Edgewater Beach Hotel.

WGN pioneered a significant number of radio firsts. Probably the best-known special news radio broadcast of the middle 1920s was WGN's broadcasts from the Scopes "monkey" trial from Dayton, Tennessee, which cost the station $1,000 a day in

personal expenses and in telephone lines to send the signals back to Chicago. Freeman F. Gosden and Charles J. Correll, who started together in vaudeville, created *Sam 'n' Henry* for WGN, but in 1929 they were tempted by the National Broadcasting Company's (NBC) greater offer; they then moved to WMAQ and came up with a new form of the same act, *Amos 'n' Andy*, national radio's first great hit. Soap opera pioneer Irna Phillips created *Painted Dreams* on WGN as one of the early soap operas.

Tribune executives tried to take early advantage of radio and newspaper common ownership. In the immediate wake of the Saint Valentine's Day Massacre in 1929, at company expense, WGN installed radio receivers in all 40 of the light blue touring cars driven by members of the Chicago Police Detective Squad. Detectives were instructed to listen to WGN—and only WGN—throughout their shifts. When word of a crime, either in progress or recently completed, reached police headquarters, a dispatcher was instructed to telephone WGN and pass along whatever details were available to the announcer on duty, who interrupted programming and broadcast the information in the form of a bulletin. The nearest squad car would hear the bulletin and rush to the crime scene (but so might others who heard the same bulletin). WGN and the *Tribune* boasted that this experiment was a success, but it lasted only a few years, proving how difficult what would be labeled "synergy" two generations later was to accomplish.

Robert McCormick, long-time *Tribune* editor and publisher, saw radio as an ally, not as an adversary. His most important innovation in radio was to assist in forming the Mutual radio network in 1934. From its studios at 435 North Michigan Avenue, WGN aired Mutual with its 50,000 W and poured the network's offerings into homes all across the upper Midwest.

Through the 1930s and 1940s, WGN functioned as Chicago's link to the Mutual radio network. As a founding station of Mutual—along with WOR (New York), WXYZ (Detroit), and WLW (Cincinnati)—through this period WGN and WOR functioned as the only clear channel stations not affiliated with either NBC or the Columbia Broadcasting System (CBS). On 1 March 1941, W59C (later WGNB) aired as the first WGN-owned FM radio outlet. Just a year before WGN had initiated 24-hour operation, a fairly rare service at the time.

Decline of Mutual

In reaction to TV's growing popularity after 1948, WGN-AM had to lessen its dependence on the

Mutual radio network. WGNB, WGN's FM sister, was donated to Chicago Educational TV (WTTW) in the early 1950s and became WFMT. Receiving fewer network programs as Mutual declined, WGN had to resort to developing its own programming. Station manager Ward Quaal developed local talk stars as many of the radio studios were converted for use by WGN television. In October 1956 Quaal hired Wally Phillips away from another powerhouse clear channel station, WLW in Cincinnati. Along with Bob Bell, who later became WGN-TV's Bozo the Clown, the duo did comedy and talk to entertain Chicago's growing mass of daily commuters. Phillips proved so popular that he also appeared on WGN-TV in *Midnight Ticker*, but it was his solo drive-time show, which debuted in 1959, that lasted until 1986.

In 1961 WGN radio and television moved to a new building on Chicago's north side. At the time the radio station adopted a new slogan: first in sound, first in service, first in sports. By the turn of the century, WGN had long operated as a high-class major-market talk station. Its broadcast day started at 5 A.M. with *The Bob Collins Show*, then switched at 9 A.M. to *The Kathy and Judy Show*, followed by 20 minutes of news starting at 11:55 A.M., and then offered talk with John Williams and Spike O'Dell all afternoon. The evening was allocated mostly to sports broadcasting, and the station, at 720 kHz, broadcast the baseball games of the Chicago Cubs, which was owned by the Tribune Company.

See also: Mutual Broadcasting System

Further Reading

Broadcasting in Chicago, 1921–1989, www.mcs.net/~richsam/home.html
Fink, John, and Francis Coughlin, *WGN: A Pictorial History*, Chicago: WGN, 1961.
Linton, Bruce A., "A History of Chicago Radio Station Programming, 1921–1931, with Emphasis on Stations WMAQ and WGN," Ph.D. diss., Northwestern University, 1953.
WGN Continental Broadcasting Company, *The Wonderful World of WGN*, Chicago: Bassett, 1966.
WGN Radio 720 Online: Chicago's News and Talk, www.wgnradio.com
WGN-TV Online: WGN: Welcome to Chicago's Very Own, www.wgntv.com

DOUGLAS GOMERY

WHA AND WISCONSIN PUBLIC RADIO

WHA (originally 9XM) is significant for three reasons: (1) it has a disputed claim to the title "oldest station in the nation"; (2) it has a strong, and less disputed, claim to having provided educational radio in the U.S. with its guiding philosophy and operating model; (3) it undisputedly pioneered the nation's first statewide FM network, which was later complemented by a second statewide network and the concept of dual program services. Today that network, Wisconsin Public Radio, remains the country's largest institutionally based public radio operation and a significant provider of national programming.

"The Oldest Station in the Nation"

A historical marker on the University of Wisconsin campus proclaims 9XM/WHA to be "the oldest station in the nation." Other stations dispute that claim, of course, but if nothing else, the early history of WHA demonstrates the importance of land grant universities in the early development of radio, particularly in the period before anyone recognized the commercial potential of the medium. The University of Wisconsin's story is emblematic of similar, if smaller-scale, efforts at more than 200 colleges and universities in the second and third decades of the 20th century.

Physicists and engineers began the University of Wisconsin's activities in radio. First Professor Edward Bennet (Engineering) and then Professor Earl Terry (Physics) experimented with radio apparatus in the first two decades of the 20th century. The Commerce Department issued a license for experimental wireless telegraphy station 9XM to Professor Bennet in 1912. The license later was transferred to the Regents of the University, who have been licensed to use radio since 1916, perhaps Wisconsin's strongest claim to the title of "oldest."

In December 1916, 9XM joined stations at the University of North Dakota, the University of Nebraska, and Nebraska Wesleyan University in regularly scheduled daily noontime wireless telegraphy broadcasts of weather and agricultural markets in cooperation with the U.S. Department of Agriculture. With these reports, the four institutions began "broadcasting" in the sense that they sought to serve a dispersed audience on a regular basis. Of course, only those familiar with Morse code could understand the broadcasts, severely limiting the effectiveness of the service. For the most part, local offices in scattered communities received the messages and posted the information for farmers and other citizens to read. By early 1917, however, Wisconsin had added voice to the telegraphic broadcasts, making them accessible to the few ordinary listeners who built or owned receivers. Hence, the historical marker cites 1917 as the beginning of "broadcasting" on station 9XM.

Wisconsin's claim to "oldest" status draws on its exemption from the government order closing down all private radio apparatus during World War I. Rather than cease operations, 9XM formed a partnership with the U.S. Navy to help in developing a cadre to radio operators at the Great Lakes Naval Training Station. That wartime activity allowed the proponents of WHA to trace its continuous operation back to 1916–17, even though the "broadcasts" during the war years could not be heard legally by anyone outside the U.S. Navy.

Broadcasting to the public resumed on a regular basis in 1919, the second date cited on the historical marker as the beginning of continuous regularly scheduled broadcasting. That continuity was not unbroken, however, as 9XM stopped broadcasting for six months in late 1920 in order to build a new, larger transmitter. During those six months of silence, KDKA in Pittsburgh, Pennsylvania, broadcast its famous coverage of the November 1920 election results, an event often cited as the beginning of radio broadcasting. When it returned to the air on 3 January 1921, two months after KDKA's "birth of broadcasting" event, 9XM could no longer be dismissed as an engineering experiment. It had a program director, speech professor William Lighty. It published its program listings in the local paper. It broadcast voice and music. The call letters changed from experimental 9XM to WHA a year later in 1922.

The Wisconsin Idea

The debate over who broadcast *first* obscures the true significance of WHA. More than any other educational station, WHA enunciated a clear mission of public service and implemented it on a scale far beyond any other. WHA developed as a unique broadcasting institution at a unique time. The combination of a progressive state government working closely with a service-oriented university became known as "The Wisconsin Idea," and out of that idea came a unique commitment to serve the state with radio from the campus in Madison, combining education with broader public-service goals.

In its educational role, WHA's programming initially emphasized the practical, particularly agricultural information and "home economics." In this, the radio station complemented the work of the university's network of county agents who assisted farmers and their families throughout the state. The station offered, in addition, music-appreciation series and talks and dramatizations written in

conjunction with faculty members on a wide range of historical, literary, and contemporary topics. In 1932 the charismatic director of WHA for almost 40 years, H.B. (Mac) McCarty, and his meticulous and diplomatic deputy, Harold Engel, gave the umbrella title "College of the Air" to these diverse offerings, which they said would make a college experience available to those whose circumstances had denied them the opportunity. When portable tape recorders liberated radio from the studio in the 1940s, the College of the Air literally moved into the lecture halls of the University of Wisconsin. At its height, lectures from university courses filled three hours each day on the WHA schedule. Faculty lecturers became statewide celebrities.

A year earlier, in 1931, McCarty and Engel had begun a separate series of programs called "School of the Air" for rural "one room school houses," of which Wisconsin still had many. *Let's Draw, Let's Sing*, and *Ranger Mac* provided the art, music, and science lessons otherwise unavailable in small schools without specialist teachers. More than anything else, the School of the Air justified continued state investments in educational radio, particularly in the lean Depression years, and introduced hundreds of thousands of children and their families to the state radio service.

Narrowly defined education constituted only part of the programming mix, however. Variety shows, radio drama, folk, and popular music found their way to the airwaves. The station also pioneered in covering public issues. Radio provided a means for people to learn about issues and to consider alternative directions. In 1931, for example, WHA offered advocates of different farm policies the opportunity to present their views. This led, in turn, to offers of free airtime to all candidates for statewide office, including those of the minor parties, in the 1932 elections and in every subsequent election for the next 40 years. The 1932 "Political Education Forum" marked the first time any American radio station had used its facilities as a forum for public debate. The *New York Times* praised this initiative, and Professor Bennet made it his theme when he testified before Congress in an unsuccessful effort to reserve 25 percent of radio frequencies for noncommercial stations in the Communications Act of 1934.

The State Radio Network

The dramatic boom in commercial radio in the late 1920s and early 1930s forced most educational radio stations off the air, their frequencies taken over by commercial stations, either through purchase or reassignment by the Federal Radio Commission. The handful of educational stations that survived found themselves relegated to inferior "regional" channels and usually only during daytime hours. Whereas in its earlier years WHA transmitted broadly outside Wisconsin, it ended up with a daytime regional frequency in Madison that covered only a portion of the state by day and none of the state by night, when most people listened to the radio. The addition of a second regional daytime station (WLBL) in the central part of the state helped, but it still left WHA with inadequate facilities.

To solve its coverage problems, in the early 1940s WHA proposed to take over the frequency of the National Broadcasting Company (NBC)'s Chicago station, WMAQ, arguing that Chicago had five clear channel stations and Wisconsin had none. Not surprisingly, NBC was able to beat the challenge, as did Atlanta's WSB when WHA proposed to share its clear channel. Thwarted in two attempts to improve its AM facility, Wisconsin looked to the new technology of FM, which had been authorized by the FCC in 1941 but had remained mostly undeveloped in the war years. In 1944, the Wisconsin Legislature created a State Radio Council separate from the university to develop a network of FM stations to carry WHA programming throughout the state. Although legally separate from the University of Wisconsin, the State Radio Council effectively operated as an adjunct to the university broadcasting operation. McCarty headed broadcasting for both the university and the State Radio Council, and WHA was the sole source of programming for the network. In March 1947 the State Radio Council activated WHA-FM in Madison, the first of nine FM stations that would go on the air at the rate of one per year until the network achieved statewide coverage in the mid-1950s. Because McCarty and Engel saw the role of these stations as broader than narrowly defined education, they named the system the Wisconsin State Radio Network or the State Stations rather than the university network or the educational network. Already the oldest and largest educational broadcaster in the country, the Wisconsin operation soared past any potential rival with the state's commitment to build and operate those nine FM stations. On the eve of the Public Broadcasting Act of 1967, the budget of the Wisconsin State Stations tripled that of any other educational radio operation.

Wisconsin Public Radio

McCarty and Engel chose 1967 to retire, just as Congress enacted the Public Broadcasting Act,

which gave a new name and a somewhat different concept to "educational" broadcasting. In a sense, the national legislation vindicated Wisconsin's vision of radio as a public service broader than university-level education. Indeed, the principal author of the vision for the new enterprise that would be called National Public Radio (NPR) was Bill Siemering, a former WHA staff member who often acknowledged his debt to McCarty and the Wisconsin Idea.

Without McCarty to hold his creation together, the university and the Educational Communications Board (successor to the State Radio Council) struggled for control of the state stations. At first, the advocates of a narrow view of educational radio seemed to prevail. Indeed, the Educational Communications Board changed the call letters of WHA-FM to WERN, for Wisconsin Educational Radio Network, its new designation for the State Radio Network. That name, however, ran directly counter to what was happening to the stations. School of the Air programming essentially moved over to television, and programming from NPR replaced some of the College of the Air programming. The State Network was becoming less "educational" at precisely the time it added "educational" to its name.

In 1978 the university and the Educational Communications Board accepted this reality and agreed to designate their joint enterprise "Wisconsin Public Radio." They appointed Jack Mitchell, formerly of NPR, as director of radio for both organizations. They put in place a long-range strategy to provide two formatted services in most parts of the state. One of the services—headed by WERN (the former WHA-FM)—would build a format around music and arts. The other service—headed by WHA (AM)—would feature news and information. The music and news division became a common pattern among public radio organizations that controlled two stations in one community. In 1989 WERN's music and arts service evolved into the "NPR News and Classical Music Network," while WHA's information service narrowed its focus to emphasize unique Wisconsin talk programming, particularly statewide call-in shows on a range of informational, educational, and public affairs topics. As residents across the state talked with academics, authors, officials, advocates, and one another, this service echoed the traditional educational and public-service purposes of the Wisconsin Idea, as did the name of the new service, "The Ideas Network of Wisconsin Public Radio."

As the "Ideas Network" focused inward on the state, Wisconsin Public Radio exported several programs nationally. For a decade in the late 1970s and early 1980s, WHA served as home to public radio's national drama project *Earplay*, under the direction of Karl Schmidt. Although *Earplay* won critical acclaim, it fell victim to the budget cuts of the Reagan administration. Since 1985 WHA has been the home of Michael Feldman's *Whad'Ya Know?*—a comedy quiz program carried by more than 200 public radio stations to a weekly audience of more than one million people. The station also distributes two national advice programs and *To the Best of Our Knowledge*, a weekly two-hour interview magazine covering the world of ideas. Often considered the "brainiest" program on public radio, *To the Best of Our Knowledge* is a fitting product of the radio station that gave America the concept of educational radio.

See also: Educational Radio to 1967; Farm/Agricultural Radio; Minnesota Public Radio; National Public Radio; Public Radio Since 1967

Further Reading

Baudino, Joseph, and John M. Kittross, "Broadcasting's Oldest Stations: An Examination of Four Claimants," *Journal of Broadcasting* 21 (Winter 1977).

Davidson, Randall, *9XM Talking: WHA Radio and the Wisconsin Idea*, Madison: University of Wisconsin Press, 2006.

Engel, Harold A., "Wisconsin's Radio Pattern," *The National Association of Educational Broadcasters Journal* 24 (January 1958).

Engel, Harold A., "The Oldest Station in the Nation," *The National Association of Educational Broadcasters Journal* 25 (February 1959).

The First 50 Years of University of Wisconsin Broadcasting: WHA, 1919–1969, and a Look Ahead to the Next 50 Years, Madison: University of Wisconsin, 1969.

Frost, S.E., Jr., *Education's Own Stations: The History of Broadcast Licenses Issued to Educational Institutions*, Chicago: University of Chicago Press, 1937.

McCarty, H.B., "WHA, Wisconsin's Radio Pioneer: Twenty Years of Public Service Broadcasting," *Wisconsin Blue Book* (1937).

McCarty, H.B., "Educational Radio's Role," *The National Association of Educational Broadcasters Journal* 25 (October 1959).

Penn, John Stanley, "The Origin and Development of Radio Broadcasting at the University of Wisconsin to 1940," Ph.D. diss., University of Wisconsin, 1958.

Penn, John Stanley, "Earl Melvin Terry, Father of Educational Radio," *Wisconsin Magazine of History* 50 (Summer 1961).

Smith, R. Franklin, "Oldest Station in the Nation?" *Journal of of Broadcasting* 4 (Winter 1959–60).

Witherspoon, John, Roselle Kovitz, Robert K. Avery, and Alan G. Stavitsky, *A History of Public Broadcasting*, Washington, D.C.: Current, 2000.

JACK MITCHELL

WHER
Memphis, Tennessee Station

When WHER-AM 1430 broadcast for the first time on 29 October 1955, it was staffed almost entirely by women, a phenomenon never before seen in U.S. radio. An experiment in novelty during a period of declining radio audiences and revenues, WHER would demonstrate and confirm women's competencies in the radio industry and inspire women to pursue careers in the industry.

The brainchild of Memphis record producer Sam Phillips (who first recorded Elvis Presley, Johnny Cash, and other important figures in American music on his Sun Records label), WHER came to life with a $25,000 investment from Kemmons Wilson, the founder of the Holiday Inn hotel chain. Together, Phillips and Wilson formed Tri-State Broadcasting Service, Inc. It was a difficult time for radio in 1955 when the station began operations; television was stealing radio listeners and gobbling up advertising dollars. To remain profitable, station owners sought new ways to reach audiences and looked to audiences that radio had traditionally ignored.

After hiring station manager Dotty Abbott, a veteran radio manager from Phoenix, Phillips selected seven other women (Teresa Kilgore, Marion Keisker, Dot Fisher, Pat McGee, Denise Howard, Barbara Gurley, and Laura Yeargain) to run the station. Phillips' wife Becky, a prominent on-air personality in Southern radio, also joined the team. WHER set up its first studios in several rooms provided by Wilson at the Memphis Holiday Inn (only the third Holiday Inn in existence at the time). Painted in pink and purple pastels, the radio studio featured distinctively feminine decor, somewhat resembling a dollhouse.

Despite skepticism and shock when Keisker's first broadcast aired in Memphis with little warning on the morning of 29 October 1955, the station was an immediate success. Audiences enjoyed tuning in to hear female voices and perspectives on radio. The "girls" lived up to their slogan, "A smile on your face puts a smile in your voice." Their broadcasts were energetic and fun, and they were not afraid to laugh at themselves and their mistakes. Initially the station catered primarily to female homemakers and featured love ballads, jazz, and light content. But as the station evolved, the format matured and diversified. The station fielded competent news and sports staffs, and by the 1960s it programmed one of Memphis' early call-in talk shows, *Open Mike*, hosted by Marge Thrasher. *Open Mike* and the station's other news programs addressed issues of importance in Memphis, such as the city's festering racial tensions that led to the 1968 sanitation workers' strike, the backdrop of Martin Luther King, Jr.'s assassination.

Memphis radio had already seen such experimentation in 1949 when radio station WDIA began offering an all-black format, and although WHER's format was never strictly all-female-oriented, the station's all-female staff did represent the lengths radio entrepreneurs were going to in order to distinguish themselves in the ever-tightening radio market.

Although Sam Phillips and Kemmons Wilson's endeavor bordered on outright gimmickry, the station remained viable for almost 20 years and became a landmark in the history of women's broadcasting. During a period when female reporters were still banned from the National Press Club in Washington, D.C. and most radio stations rarely hired more than one female air personality, WHER boasted a staff of forty women who held positions ranging from general manager to program director to disc jockey. (Among the few stations that adopted WHER's all-girl approach was WSDM, Chicago, which employed "Hush Puppy" Linda Smith, later known as Linda Ellerbee.)

The social upheaval that accompanied the late 1960s would ultimately contribute to WHER's demise. The notion of an "all-girl" radio station that traded on stereotypical feminine qualities seemed out of step with the resurging women's rights movement (hosts of music programs were known as "jock-ettes," and one of WHER's taglines was "One thousand beautiful watts"). As a result, the station added more men to its staff and sought to broaden its appeal. In 1971 (after 16 years on the air) WHER was changed to WWEE, a talk radio station that later became a gospel station. In 1988, Phillips and Wilson sold the station first known as WHER. Currently a WHER broadcasts from Hattiesburg, Mississippi, but the outlet has no connection to the original WHER.

In October 1999, to commemorate WHER's inception, Davia Nelson and Nikki Silva produced a documentary highlighting the history of WHER for National Public Radio's "Lost and Found Sound" series on *All Things Considered*. Also featured on local and national news programs, the women were brought together by Sam Phillips in New York for a reunion.

WHER's female orientation represented radio's general effort to find stable ground in the burgeoning television age of the 1950s, but the station will be best remembered as having played an important role in the development of opportunities for female radio professionals in all areas of radio operations. Many women working in radio today owe a tremendous debt to Sam Phillips and the more than 50 women who worked at WHER from 1955 to 1971.

See also: American Women in Radio and Television

Further Reading

Aherns, Frank, "Memphis's Music Revolution," *Washington Post* (29 October 1999).
Blumenthal, Ralph, "Spinning a Little History in a Studio Painted Pink," *New York Times* (30 October 1999).
Burch, Peggy, "When Radio Did It Her Way," *Memphis Commercial Appeal* (29 October 1999).
Chin, Paula, and Barbara Sandler, "A League of Their Own," *People Weekly* (29 November 1999).

MICHAEL STREISSGUTH AND ALEXANDRA HENDRIKS

WINS

New York City Station

WINS, important as an all-news radio pioneer in the nation's largest market, traces its history back to the 1920s.

Origins

WINS-AM emerged from pioneering WGBS-AM, part of the Gimbels Brothers department store empire. In 1922 Gimbels had put WIP-AM in its Philadelphia store, and thus it was logical that in 1924 Gimbels would follow with a New York City broadcasting station from its landmark 33rd Street and 6th Avenue location. On opening night, Eddie Cantor was the master of ceremonies, with guests George Gershwin, Rube Goldberg, and the Vincent Lopez Orchestra. In November 1928 Gimbels reorganized its radio operations as the General Broadcasting System and announced plans for national expansion. But the General Broadcasting System failed, and on 10 October 1931, as the Depression deepened, Gimbels sold out to William Randolph Hearst, which changed the call letters to WINS (the *INS* stood for Hearst's International News Service).

In July 1932 WINS moved its studios to Park Avenue and 58th Street. Through the 1930s Hearst tried unsuccessfully to use its newspapers, the *New York Journal-American* and the *New York Daily Mirror*, to make WINS a success by carrying feature stories on station programs and stars, including full listings of the daily schedule. WINS moved to 1010 on the AM dial and to new news studios at 28 West 44th Street in the heart of Times Square.

But when these changes brought no higher ratings, in 1945 Hearst sold WINS to Crosley Broadcasting for a reported $2 million, at the time a record amount paid for a single radio station.

Postwar Changes

The deal was consummated in July 1946, and WINS began to carry programming from WLW-AM Cincinnati, including news broadcasts by Gilbert Kingsbury, the Cincinnati Symphony Orchestra, and *Top o' the Morning*. Crosley also tried *Going to Town, Morning Matinee*, and the *Three Corner Club*. New York City was not the Midwest, however, and the station's only ratings winner was New York Yankees baseball.

Crosley owned WINS for seven years before selling the station to a consortium headed by J. Elroy McCaw (a radio station owner on the West Coast), Charles F. Skouras (a movietheater exhibitor), and Jack Keating (a Honolulu and Portland, Oregon, radio station owner) in 1953. Operating as Gotham Broadcasting, WINS was reformatted as a disc jockey station centered on the talents of Mel Allen, Johnny Clark, Jack Eigen, and Jack Lacy. A pivotal moment came when WINS's union contract with musicians expired in the summer of 1954, and McCaw said that WINS would no longer air any live music. The American Federation of Musicians protested, but to no avail.

Disc jockeys Murray "the K" Kaufman, Paul Sherman "the Clown Prince of Rock and Roll," Sam Z. Burns, and Herb Sheldin boosted WINS to the top tier of New York radio. Murray Kaufman became so popular that when the Atlantic record label issued Bobby Darin's "Splish, Splash," composer Darin assigned half the publishing rights to Murray Kaufman's mother so that Murray would plug the song on WINS. This transformation had formally begun in the fall of 1954 when McCaw hired Alan Freed from Cleveland. However, Freed proved so controversial that, despite his popularity, he was fired in May 1958. As the "Fifth Beatle," Murray the K would prove a far more lasting figure.

All News

In July 1962 McCaw and his Gotham group cashed in and sold WINS to Westinghouse Broadcasting Company for a reported $10 million. Westinghouse at first continued to seek a musical format to top market leader WABC-AM, but it never succeeded. So on Monday, 19 April 1965, WINS went to an all-news format, becoming one of the first stations

to make what was then considered a radical format transition. Importantly, WINS pioneered the all-news format in the largest media market in the United States. The station donated its massive music library to Fordham University, and a radio era was over.

WINS-AM became the station where New Yorkers tuned to learn about breaking news. In November 1965, when a major blackout darkened northeastern cities, WINS kept millions informed during the crisis as they listened on battery-powered portable radios. That same year WINS-AM became New York City's first all-computerized news operation, but advanced automation sometimes caused problems. For example, in December 1973 the station falsely reported that New York's Governor Nelson Rockefeller had been stabbed during a visit to Atlanta. Better for the station's image was the March 1974 event when Joseph Yacovelli, wanted for nearly two years by New York City police in connection with the shooting death of underworld leader Joseph Gallo, turned himself in at WINS studios. Yacovelli's attorney said that the purpose of broadcasting the surrender was to protect against police "manufacture" of evidence against his client. Credit for arranging the public surrender went to WINS newsman Paul Sherman, long-time friend of Yacovelli's attorney.

By 2000 WINS was still part of Westinghouse, which was in turn part of media conglomerate Viacom. WINS-AM was simply one profitable AM radio station within a vast group of radio stations, allied with Viacom's other interest in television and film. To New Yorkers, WINS-AM was still "all news, all the time."

See also: All News Format; Westinghouse

Further Reading

Jackson, John A., *Big Beat Heat: Alan Freed and the Early Years of Rock and Roll*, New York: Schirmer Books, 1991.
Jaker, Bill, Frank Sulek, and Peter Kanze, *The Airwaves of New York: Illustrated Histories of 156 AM Stations in the Metropolitan Area, 1921–1996*, Jefferson, North Carolina: McFarland, 1998.
Rhodes, B. Eric, *Blast from the Past: A Pictorial History of Radio's First 75 Years*, West Palm Beach, Florida: Streamline, 1996.
Ward, Ed, Geoffrey Stokes, and Ken Tucker, *Rock of Ages*, New York: Rolling Stone Press, 1986; London: Penguin, 1987.
WINS website, www.1010wins.com

DOUGLAS GOMERY AND CHUCK HOWELL

WIRE RECORDING
Early Means of Preserving Programs

Wire recording technology, used briefly in the 1940s, was an interim approach to recording of radio programs. It helped mark the transition from electrical transcriptions in the 1930s to the soon-to-be-developed plastic tape recording process introduced in the late 1940s and widespread by the 1950s.

Origins

The phonograph and later the wire recorder were developed as dictation devices for stenographers, not for entertainment value. After the 1877 invention of the phonograph, Oberlin Smith, an American mechanical engineer, suggested in the September 1888 issue of *Electrical World* that a thread or ribbon of magnetizable material could record and play sound electromagnetically.

Building on Smith's suggestion, Danish inventor Valdemar Poulsen built the first magnetic recorder in 1893 using a steel piano wire. Poulsen's "telegraphone," patented in 1898, was designed as a dictation device for office use and as an alternative to the phonograph. A working model was demonstrated at the 1900 Paris Exposition and was apparently received well, winning the *Grand Prix*. It was capable of recording for 30 minutes with the wire traveling seven feet per second. Following the device's success, Poulsen and others searched for financial backing but were not successful.

Early wire recording had inherent technical problems. The first wire recorders utilized acoustical (mechanical) technology as opposed to electronic recording. This frequency response was limited; the dynamic recording range did not exceed about 20 decibels, and there were high noise levels and low acoustical output in comparison with other mechanical systems then in place. In time some of these technical problems were overcome. Wire recorders recorded crosswise in a perpendicular direction as opposed to longitudinal magnetization. The discovery of AC or high-frequency bias technique and better recording head design aided the process.

Most wire recording improvements occurred in Europe. In 1930 several movies were completed by Ludwig Blattner in England using a soundtrack recorded on synchronized steel tape. The British Marconi Company acquired Blattner's company and improved the recorder (called the "Blattnerphone") to produce the "Marconi-Stille" machine used by the British Broadcasting Corporation (BBC). But this machine weighed almost a ton and thus was not portable.

In Europe the "Dailygraph" was a wire recorder used for dictation and telephone recording by the Echophone Company. One interesting feature was the device's cartridge loading capability. In 1933 the C. Lorenz Company sold the "Texto-phone," an improved version of the Dailygraph that featured wire or steel bands. Both machines were used throughout Europe to provide a central station telephone answering service or for centralized office dictation systems. The machine was eventually used by Nazi party officials in 1933.

About this time various versions of tape recording entered the marketplace. One example was the "magnetophone" exhibited at the 1935 Radio Exposition in Berlin. The medium used was a 6.5-millimeter-wide plastic tape. Another machine, the German "Lorenz Stahltonmachine," used steel tape. Other steel tape machines followed.

Government-operated radio systems were another catalyst for the development of wire recording in Europe, as a method of storing programming and broadcasting programs across various time zones was needed. Military interest in the United States also spurred wire recording. Immediately prior to the U.S. entry into World War II, wire recorders built by Armour Research Foundation were used for research in submarine detection, language classes, and music recording. Wire recorders also were used increasingly by the U.S. military in the war effort. Manufacturers included Peirce Wire Recorder, the Armour Research Foundation, and Minifon.

An early American pioneer in the development of wire recording was Marvin Camras (1916–95). In 1938 he helped develop a consumer wire recorder, "Model 50," from the Armour Research Foundation. The U.S. military used these wire recorders to train pilots. They were also used to record battle sounds and then play them back, amplified, in places where the D-Day invasion would not take place, thus deceiving the German military. Brush Development (a company in Cleveland, Ohio) also designed and built wire recorders for the U.S. military. One model had a magazine that totally enclosed the spools of wire, level winders, heads, and indicators; it also featured bronze wire. (The first use of stainless steel in 1943 was an important development for wire recorders. It was magnetically superior to previously used carbon steel and even to chromium and tungsten alloy magnet steels; it did not rust or corrode.)

Active Use

After World War II, the production of consumer wire recorders increased until it peaked around

1948. Webster-Chicago and Sears, Roebuck and Company began large-scale wire recorder production. Wire recorders were an alternative to high-priced dictation equipment as they featured advanced electronics and were erasable, a feature not feasible with wax or vinyl. A typical wire machine would use a wire gauge from .004 to .0036 inches. At a speed of 24 inches per second, typical recording time would be 15 minutes, 30 minutes, or one hour. Magnecord produced a wire machine with a frequency response from 35 to 15,000 Hz and flutter below 0.1 percent. (School systems had been among the first to buy wire recorders; a typical model would cost about $150, an affordable price for many school systems. However, the wire would easily snarl and the devices were too difficult for young children to use.)

One of the most popular models was the Webster-Chicago (Webcor) Model 80 because of its low cost, portability, and relative reliability. A similar model was built by Crescent Industries of Chicago. A compact automobile recorder was built by WiRecorder Corporation of Detroit. However, it saw only limited production. Utah Radio Products introduced its "Magic Wire" machine in 1945, touting its ability to record up to 66 minutes of talk or music on one spool. Advertisements emphasized the point that the portable recorder-reproducer had been originally developed for the military.

The value of wire recorded audio segments became clear in postwar radio news departments, several of which were using the device by 1946 and 1947. In January 1948 Mutual's Washington bureau reported that the chairs of all congressional committees had agreed to wire recorder use in committee sessions. By this time some reporters were using wire recorders to create "cut-in" recordings that allowed the broadcast of speech or interview highlights within newscasts.

Decline

The rise of a vastly improved competing device—plastic tape for recording—soon spelled the end of wire recordingas a mainline technology. The formation of Ampex in 1946 (and the financial support of its research by singer Bing Crosby) helped to focus work on seeking an effective means of recording popular weekly shows to avoid live rebroadcasts for different time zones. Wire recording continued to be used for many years by military personnel, who appreciated the ruggedness of the equipment and had less need for high-fidelity recordings.

See also: Audiotape; Recording and Studio Equipment

Further Reading

Camras, Marvin, *Magnetic Recording Handbook*, New York: Van Nostrand Reinhold, 1988.
Lowman, Charles E., *Magnetic Recording*, New York: McGraw-Hill, 1972.
"Magnetic Wire Recorder," *Life* (1 November 1943).
Morton, David, *Off the Record: The Technology and Culture of Sound Recording in America*, New Brunswick, New Jersey: Rutgers University Press, 2000.

DAVID SPICELAND

WJR
Detroit, Michigan Station

Perhaps best known in the latter half of the 20th century for its award-winning news, documentaries, and sports coverage, WJR is a 50,000-W clear channel station with a long and colorful broadcast history.

Origins

When newspaper rival *The Detroit News* put its station WWJ on the air in 1920, *Detroit Free Press* owner and publisher E.D. Stair felt compelled to begin his own station. So WCX, WJR's precursor, began broadcasting on 4 May 1922 from a studio located on the ninth floor of the Free Press Building. Operating at 580 kHz, WCX became known as "The Call of the Motor City." One of its popular programs was a variety show called the *Red Apple Club*, named after WCX's first manager, C.D. Tomy, who offered a "nice red apple" to the first person to call in with the name of the next singing guest. Tomy later became "Uncle Neal" to two generations of listeners who grew up with his children's programs on WJR.

On 16 August 1925, the Jewett Radio and Phonographic Company of Pontiac bought into WCX and moved it to the Book-Cadillac Hotel. The station became WCX/WJR (the "JR" stood for Jewett Radio). Power was increased from 517 W to 5,000 W, making it the second "super power" station in the country (Cincinnati's WLW was the first). For more than two years the *Free Press's* WCX broadcast news, sports and *The Red Apple Club* while WJR aired commercial programs on their shared frequency.

On 20 December 1926 WCX's call letters were changed to WJR and it moved from 580 to 680 kHz. Jewett had hired Leo J. Fitzpatrick, a popular personality from Kansas, as program director in hopes of increasing sales of his radios, but Jewett went out of business. It soon became clear to most radio manufacturers who owned radio facilities that stations could not survive on radio set sales alone.

In 1926 WJR offered several religious programs on a commercial basis, and Sundays were especially profitable. Now station manager, Fitzpatrick persuaded Father Charles Coughlin of the Shrine of the Little Flower in Royal Oak to experiment in using radio for fund-raising. The program was a success and the controversial priest soon became known over the Columbia Broadcasting System (CBS) network for his vitriolic political views.

George A. Richards (president of Pontiac automobiles of southern Michigan) and the Richards-Oakland Motor Car Company bought the *Detroit Free Press's* interest in WJR in 1927 and constructed a street-level studio for it in a showroom in the General Motors Building. It was perhaps the only station in the country to operate a ground-floor studio, and entertainers could be seen by passersby. Its new slogan was "The Goodwill Station." In April 1927 WJR/WCX became affiliated with the Blue Network of the National Broadcasting Company (NBC), and in 1928 the WJR orchestra was formed, beginning almost 40 years of music performed live by various WJR staff.

After the Federal Radio Commission revised the entire broadcasting band in 1928, WCX/WJR moved to 750 kHz. In December 1928 WJR physically separated from WCX. The station installed studios in the new Fisher Building for a token rental fee and regular on-air mentions of its location. On 17 April 1929 WJR bought all of WCX's equipment and WCX left the air. In July 1929 WJR, the Good Will Station, was formed.

In 1932 WJR increased its power to 10,000 W and became "In the Golden Tower." Programs during the 1930s included *Detroit Police Drama*, based on actual crimes, and *The Seven-Day Trial of Vivienne Ware*, featuring Judge John Brennan overseeing a trial and then basing his verdict and sentence on listener votes.

WJR switched from the NBC network to CBS in 1935 and constructed a 50,000-W transmitter. On 29 March 1941 WJR moved again from 750 to 760 kHz, where it remains today. In 1942 it began operating 24 hours a day. Future Federal Communications Commissioner (FCC) James H. Quello was hired in 1947 as publicity and promotions director, rising to become vice president and station manager of WJR 22 years later.

In the 1940s WJR created hundreds of special programs devoted to the war effort. In 1944 owner George Richards began *Victory F.O.B.*, a series that featured a businessman supposedly discussing postwar problems. By this time Richards owned

two other 50,000-W stations. It had become clear that he had a strong political agenda and wished to use his stations to further his causes. According to broadcast historian Erik Barnouw, Richards wanted to use *F.O.B.* to influence the 1944 and 1948 elections. He had a history of encouraging both anti-Semitism and comments against President Franklin D. Roosevelt on his stations. A petition in March 1948 to the FCC from the Radio News Club of Southern California accused Richards of instructing his newsmen to slant, distort, and falsify news. It led to a struggle by Richards to keep his station licenses. Richards died in 1951 during the extensive hearings, but the station licenses were renewed by his family.

The Modern Station

By the late 1950s WJR had developed an intensive news schedule, producing eight five-minute daily newscasts as well as five-minute network news summaries throughout the day. A variety of programs aired in the 1950s, including symphony concerts, opera, and sports. Rock and roll was excluded, according to then-executive vice president Worth Kramer, because it was "music to steal hubcaps by." Popular host J.P. McCarthy began at WJR in 1956 as a staff announcer and took over *Music Hall*, a morning music show, in 1958. He went on to dominate the Detroit market for many years with his blend of music and talk on WJR. In 1959 the station left the CBS network to commit itself to more local programming.

CBS and WJR joined forces again on 30 December 1962. CBS agreed to let the popular WJR censor any network advertisements and programs. It was the only CBS station in the country that didn't broadcast Arthur Godfrey's show live, as it aired at the same time as WJR's showcase program, *Adventures in Good Music* (hosted by Karl Haas, the station's director of fine arts). One of the most celebrated educational programs during the 1960s was the award-winning *Kaleidoscope*, a blend of recorded music and dramatic narrative on a particular topic, hosted by Mike Whorf. WJR was sold to Capital Cities Broadcasting Corporation on 9 September 1964. Its on-air slogan became "The Great Voice of the Great Lakes," and it changed to a middle-of-the-road talk and variety format.

On 1 January 1976 WJR dropped its CBS affiliation and joined the NBC radio network. In early 1983 WJR "Radio 76" began C-QUAM stereobroadcasting. When Capital Cities Broadcasting merged with the American Broadcasting Companies

WLAC

(ABC) in the spring of 1985, WJR's NBC affiliation was dropped for the ABC Information Network.

In 1990 WJR changed to an adult contemporary music/news/talk format but dropped the music in 1993. On 9 February 1996 Capital Cities/ABC, including WJR, was purchased by the Walt Disney Company, and its licensee name was shortened to ABC. WJR continued into the 21st century as "The Great Voice of the Great Lakes" with its award-winning news and sports coverage.

See also: Adventures in Good Music; Columbia Broadcasting System; National Broadcasting Company

Further Reading

On the Air: History of Michigan Broadcasting, http://www. sos.state.mi.us/history/museum/explore/museums/hismus/ special/ontheair/index.html
WJR website, www.wjr.net

Lynn Spangler

WLAC
Nashville, Tennessee Station

WLAC is the powerful radio station in Nashville, Tennessee, that played an influential role in the national diffusion of music recorded by African-American artists from the late 1940s through the mid-1960s. The call letters represent the Life and Casualty Insurance Company of Tennessee, which established the station in 1926. In its early years WLAC was known as the "Thrift Station," reflecting the inscription "Thrift—the Cornerstone" chiseled on the Life and Casualty headquarters building in downtown Nashville.

After operating the station for about a decade, in 1935 Life and Casualty sold WLAC to a company executive, J. Truman Ward. During Ward's tenure as licensee, WLAC enjoyed a close relationship with the Columbia Broadcasting System (CBS). Ward's station manager, F.C. Sowell, served as head of the CBS affiliate group, and the network carried a few of WLAC's local programs coast to coast.

WLAC began operation with 1,000 W of power and increased to 5,000 W within a few years, but in 1941 Ward won a class 1-B clear channel assignment. For full-time operation with 50,000 W at 1510 kHz, WLAC engineers designed a new transmitter facility about seven miles north of Nashville. The antenna system accentuated night-time sky-wave radiation, resulting in a reliable signal that carried the CBS prime-time schedule into 28 states and parts of Canada.

Following World War II, WLAC developed a lucrative niche advertising market by promoting the products of the many small, independent record companies of the period that specialized in "race music" or "sepia and swing." Sometime around 1946 or 1947 WLAC announcer Gene Nobles began to generate a large volume of mail by playing African-American artists on a late-night disc jockey program sponsored by a middle-Tennessee record store. WLAC's management soon recognized the revenue potential of selling access to its widespread night-time audience on a per-inquiry (PI) basis. As network programming dwindled, PI programming on WLAC was gradually extended into the earlier evening hours. During the height of WLAC's PI years, the station maintained a large mail room to handle the orders for products advertised nightly such as 45-rpm recordings, pomade, petroleum jelly, and live baby chicks. These orders were delivered daily to the station by the postal service in large canvas bags. WLAC also sold blocks of time at night for paid religious broadcasts.

In addition to Gene Nobles, the night-time announcing staff included Herman Grizzard, John Richbourg ("John R"), Bill Allen ("The Hossman"), Hugh Jarrett ("Huey Baby"), and newscaster Don Whitehead. The music varied according to the products being pitched. On-air descriptions included "the sweet and the beat," "rock and roll," "rhythm and blues," "spirituals," and "gospel." Several African-American artists who became major recording stars after Motown brought rhythm and blues music into the cultural mainstream have attributed their early success to WLAC airplay in general and in particular to Bill Allen and John Richbourg, both of whom maintained close ties to the recording industry.

Truman Ward sold WLAC back to Life and Casualty in 1953 during the early years of the music-and-news era. His son, Jim Ward, later served as the station's general manager during Life and Casualty's second period as licensee. Although well positioned for a television license, Life and Casualty chose to merge interests with two competing local applicants in order to facilitate the construction of Nashville's third television station, WLAC-TV, in 1954. From 1964 to 1967, WLAC-TV aired a local weekend variety program, *Night Train*, which featured many of the African-American artists heard nightly on WLAC "blues" radio.

Life and Casualty also operated a successful separately programmed FM station during the 1960s and 1970s. From studios on the observation deck of the company's Nashville skyscraper—the tallest building in the southeastern United States

856

when built in 1957—WLAC-FM featured an easy listening format that introduced many middle Tennesseans to FM.

It is important to recognize that during the day, when its signal covered a 125-mile radius of Nashville, WLAC sounded like an entirely different radio station from the one listeners in distant places received via night-time skip signals. Daytime listeners in middle Tennessee, southern Kentucky, and northern Alabama heard a full array of mass-appeal adult programming that included CBS news and features, local news and interview programs, editorials by F.C. Sowell ("The South's Foremost Radio Commentator"), helicopter traffic reports, and upbeat middle-of-the-road music.

In 1971 WLAC introduced Nashville's first news-talk format, but the next year the station dropped its CBS affiliation and switched to a Top 40 music format. WLAC enjoyed several years of good audience ratings with Top 40. It was during those years that the station gradually retreated from its legendary night-time schedule. John Richbourg retired in 1973 rather than play Top 40 music. Bill Allen and Gene Nobles continued to host a few late-night PI shows for long-time sponsors, but by 1977 Top 40 music aired until midnight. The PI and paid religious programming that had distinguished WLAC from other clear channel stations was relegated to overnights.

In 1968 the Life and Casualty Insurance Company of Tennessee was acquired by American General, the Houston-based insurance conglomerate. Life and Casualty's 50 percent interest in WLAC-TV was sold in 1975, and in 1977 WLACAM-FM were sold to the publishers of *Billboard* magazine.

By 1980 historians of popular culture had begun to recognize Gene Nobles as the first person in the United States to play "race music" on a "power" station. WLAC's impact as a principal conduit of rhythm and blues music throughout the eastern half of North America during the 1950s and 1960s has made it one of America's most frequently cited radio stations in historical treatments of the early rock and roll era. In 2003 WLAC was again a CBS affiliate and featured an award-winning all-news-talk format.

See also: Black-Oriented Radio; WSM

Further Reading

Cohodas, Nadine, *Spinning Blues into Gold: The Chess Brothers and the Legendary Chess Records*, New York: St. Martin's Press, and Maidenhead, Berkshire: Melia, 2000.

Cooper, Daniel, "Boogie-Woogie White Boy: The Redemption of 'Hossman' Allen," *Nashville Scene* (4 March 1993).

Egerton, John, *Nashville: The Faces of Two Centuries, 1780–1980*, Nashville, Tennessee: PlusMedia, 1979.

Fong-Torres, Ben, *The Hits Just Keep on Coming: The History of Top 40 Radio*, San Francisco, California: Miller Freeman Books, 1998.

Smith, Wes, *The Pied Pipers of Rock 'n' Roll: Radio Deejays of the 50s and 60s*, Marietta, Georgia: Longstreet Press, 1989.

ROBERT M. OGLES

WLS

Chicago, Illinois Station

Chicago's WLS-AM started as WJR, but in April 1924 the Sears-Roebuck company took over the station and renamed it—in one of the most famous of radio's early logos—for the "World's Largest Store." First under Sears, then after 1928 under a new owner—the *Prairie Farmer* magazine—and finally later in the 20th century under the American Broadcasting Companies (ABC), WLS-AM has long helped define radio broadcasting in Chicago and the upper Midwest. Clear channel status, granted in the early 1930s, made WLS-AM a fixture in homes from Minnesota to Ohio, from the Upper Peninsula of Michigan to the cotton fields of Arkansas and Mississippi.

WLS-AM ought to be remembered as the home base for one of radio's most popular programs of its golden age. Although the *Grand Ole Opry* survived longer, the WLS *National Barn Dance* before World War II pulled in a far larger listenership and ranked as America's most popular country music program. After being picked up by the National Broadcasting Company (NBC) network in 1933, the *National Barn Dance* expanded to all Saturday night once *Prairie Farmer* took charge. Renamed simply *The WLS National Barn Dance*, the show became an NBC Saturday night fixture. Indeed, it was only seven years later, in 1940, that NBC paired the *WLS National Barn Dance* with the *Grand Ole Opry* on the network. The two programs battled evenly during World War II, but the postwar years saw the *Opry* surpass its predecessor in ratings. In time, country format radio, playing recorded music, would replace all barn dance live radio shows—except for the *Opry*.

Still, WLS-AM offered more than the *Barn Dance*. *Prairie Farmer* sold not only its magazines, but also membership in the WLS-Prairie Farmer Protective Union, which promised farmers that it would keep thieves away from listeners' farms. Resident announcers, such as Hal O'Halloran,

857

Martha Crane, Al Rice, Jack Holden, Margaret McKay, and Bill Cline became household names. Ralph Waldo Emerson, organist for WLS, offered an alternative to string hillbilly music. Bill Vickland, the voice of the *Book Shop*, produced live drama. The Sunday School Singers Trio was heard each week on the *Cross Roads Sunday School*. The WLS Staff Orchestra, under Herman Felber's direction, played Tin Pan Alley standards and the latest big band hits. The Chicago Gospel Tabernacle offered another alternative. And Jim Poole offered the necessary reports from the Chicago Live Stock Exchange.

WLS-AM became part of the ABC radio network in 1960. By then, in response to the ascendance of television, WLS-AM needed to reinvent itself. In May 1960 it joined the Top 40 ranks and helped bring mainstream rock sound to the Chicago area through the 1980s. New management hired and promoted many local disc jockey stars—none hotter or more famous than Larry Lujack, who, based at WLS-AM, became one of the symbols of the Top 40 era.

In the 1990s, WLS-AM became news plus talk radio890, adapting to the new ownership by the Walt Disney company in 1995. The program lineup by 2000 included Dr. Laura Schlessinger, Rush Limbaugh, and Electronic Town Hall meetings over radio.

See also: Clear Channel Stations; Country Music Format; Farm/Agricultural Radio; *National Barn Dance*

Further Reading

Baker, John Chester, *Farm Broadcasting: The First Sixty Years*, Ames: Iowa State University Press, 1981.
Broadcasting in Chicago, 1921–1989, www.mcs.net/!richsam/home.html
Evans, James F., *Prairie Farmer and WLS: The Burridge D. Butler Years*, Urbana: University of Illinois Press, 1969.
Hickerson, Jay, *The Ultimate History of Network Radio Programming and Guide to All Circulating Shows*, Hamden, Connecticut: Hickerson, 1992; 3rd edition, as *The New, Revised, Ultimate History of Network Radio Programming and Guide to All Circulating Shows*, 1996.
Stand By (12 April 1949) (special 25th anniversary issue of WLS's magazine).
WLS Newstalk 890 AM website, www.wlsam.com

DOUGLAS GOMERY

WLW

Cincinnati, Ohio Station

"The Nation's Station," founded in Cincinnati in 1922 by Powel Crosley, Jr., was for many years the United States' most powerful radio station, not only in wattage but in the wide geographical range of its audience. From 1935 to 1939, it used 10 times the wattage allowed today. WLW produced and broadcast popular local programming over a large area in Ohio, Indiana, and Kentucky, and also had listeners in Michigan, West Virginia, Illinois, and Tennessee—and in many more states at night. Numerous stars began their careers at WLW (the talent roster includes Fats Waller and Rod Serling), and the station developed programs that were later carried on the national networks. After nearly 80 years WLW remains the most popular radio station in Cincinnati and a large surrounding area, aided by its favorable combination of power and frequency—50,000 W at 700 MHz.

Origins

Crosley, a manufacturer in Cincinnati, Ohio, became interested in radio in 1921 when his son asked for a "radio toy" as a birthday present. Crosley's interest in radio grew to fascination as he built a set for his son from an instruction booklet and an assortment of loose parts. That same year he started an amateur radio station in his home, licensed as 8XAA, and within about a year the Crosley Manufacturing Corporation was the world's largest manufacturer of radio sets and parts. In March 1922 Crosley's station was assigned (at random, as was the practice) the letters WLW as a call sign for a "land radio station" of 50 W on 360 meters. Such a station could have had a range of about 100 miles, but it shared that frequency with hundreds of other stations.

Because he was manufacturing small, inexpensive, and therefore less sensitive radio receivers, Crosley had a more compelling interest in higher power than did many other radio broadcasters. The station's power was increased to 500 W in April 1923, then to 1,000 W a year later, and the Commerce Department announced it might use 5 kW on a "strictly experimental" basis.

At first WLW was operated mainly to provide programming for purchasers of Crosley radio sets "as a medium of advertising and publicity." The company's weekly magazine, distributed to radio retailers and purchasers of new sets, asked listeners to fill out a questionnaire to vote for the type of programs they would most like to hear, out of a choice of music, talk, and drama categories.

The station's earliest programs were musical variety shows featuring amateur talent, talks, and soloists. In August 1922 Crosley hired Fred Smith as station director; he was WLW's first employee.

Smith, who later conceived of the news digest program that became *The March of Time*, inaugurated a regular daytime schedule of market reports, financial news, weather, and recorded music. For the evening hours he arranged musical variety shows and live music remotes. Smith also wrote original radio dramas, the first of which aired on 22 December 1922. On 3 April 1923, WLW broadcast *When Love Wakens*, an original play that Smith wrote especially for radio—probably the first in radio history—and for one station in particular (note the title's initials).

Fred Smith tried many other formats at the station, too, to provide entertainment and information, such as programs for children, lectures to teach swimming, and re-creating a boxing match based on telephone reports from a station staff member at the arena. He also read news items interspersed with musical selections played by an organist in the studio; Smith later revised this news digest program as the basis for the news drama program *The March of Time*.

The U.S. Commerce Department designated WLW as a class B station in June 1923, making the Cincinnati station one of only about 39 (of 500 total stations) in the United States that could use higher power. When the Federal Radio Commission (FRC) set about "cleaning up the broadcast situation" and announced frequency assignment for 694 stations beginning 1 June 1927, WLW was assigned 700 kilocycles (kHz). Soon it was the only station in the United States using that frequency, and thus became a "clear channel" station. It was one of only ten stations using 5 kW of power, and it grew more powerful after 25 May 1928, when the FRC authorized WLW to begin construction of facilities for 50 kW. At that time there were probably only four other stations with that output, but WLW's staff kept producing original programming that (in Crosley's view, anyway) warranted further expansion.

By the late 1920s, WLW was affiliated with both the NBC Red and Blue networks, but the station originated more expensive and high-quality local programming than most other stations in the country. Only the network-owned stations in New York, Los Angeles, and Chicago had staffs as large as WLW's. In June 1929, a hookup was arranged connecting WLS Chicago, WOR New York, and WLW. The Quality Radio Group, as the coalition came to be called, carried each other's programs and made available to advertisers a huge audience in most of the northeastern United States. In 1934 WLW got together with WOR New York, WGN Chicago, and WZYZ Detroit (with its prize show *The Lone Ranger*) to establish the Mutual Broadcasting System (MBS).

Superpower Experiment

In June 1932 the FRC authorized WLW to construct a 500-kW (500,000-W) experimental station and to conduct tests from 1 A.M. to 6 A.M. On 2 May 1934, the station began using this "super power" at all hours after a dedication ceremony in which President Franklin Roosevelt activated the new water-cooled transmitter by pushing a gold key on his desk at the White House. This power increase allowed WLW to transmit with ten times more power than any other AM station—then or now—until 1 March 1939, when the Federal Communications Commission (FCC) refused to renew the "experimental" license for higher power. After a Canadian station in Toronto complained of interference with its signal on 690 kHz, WLW was briefly limited to 50 kW after local sunset. Soon a directional signal was arranged so that no more than 50 kW was transmitted northwest of Buffalo, New York.

The decision to end the 500-kW experiment was controversial and complex for political and technical reasons, but it was primarily the result of complaints by other stations resentful of WLW's enormous economic advantage. A "sense of the Senate" resolution had been passed that directed the FCC to limit stations to 50 kW. The resolution stated that an increase of superpower stations in the United States (at least 15 other clear-channel licensees had applied to the FCC for superpower status) would deprive other local and regional stations of valuable network affiliations and national advertising revenues.

Although its 500-kW experiment was discontinued, WLW had proved that higher power was possible, that it did not cause more than normal interference with adjacent stations, and that it did not blanket out other stations for nearby listeners. Many other AM stations around the world soon began using this much and even more power. However, it was because of its superior programming, not its powerful wattage, that WLW achieved much higher ratings than even the hometown station in many cities in its vast coverage area, which extended in a circle around Cincinnati stretching nearly to Chicago, Detroit, Pittsburgh, and Nashville. (As an indication of WLW's reach, one fundraising appeal during floods on the Ohio River brought donations from 48 states.) In 1936, as part of an FCC study of channel allocations and utilization, a survey returned by more than 32,000 rural listeners (of 100,000 surveys mailed) showed that WLW was by far the favorite station and the listeners' first choice in 13 states and second in six more, from Michigan to Florida and Texas. While its powerful signal made WLW available in homes out of the reach of many other stations at night, its popularity derived from its use of the most popular shows from four networks, a large staff of local talent and specific programming—especially in the early-morning hours aimed at farm audiences—and its geographical position near the center of the agricultural Midwest.

WLW also began a shortwave service and relayed the station's programs around the world until the facility was taken over during World War II for government wartime propaganda broadcasts. In 1942, six new transmitters installed at that facility became the largest installation for Voice of America.

During the 1930s WLW's staff numbered about 350, of whom about 200 worked in the programming division. The station carried programs from both NBC networks (Red and Blue), CBS, and MBS. The station called itself "The Cradle of the Stars," in reference to those who worked there early in their careers, including Virginia Payne (who created the serial heroine Ma Perkins), the Mills Brothers, Andy Williams, writer Rod Serling, Betty and Rosemary Clooney (their younger brother Nick was later a news anchor at WLW's television affiliate), the McQuire Sisters, actor Frank Lovejoy, Red Skelton, Durward Kirby, Eddie Albert, Thomas W. "Fats" Waller, Red Barber, the Ink Spots, Norman Corwin (who quit after only a few weeks when the station refused to broadcast news about labor strikes), and Erik Barnouw. Many performers soon moved on to stations in New York, Chicago, and Los Angeles, and some joked that the call letters WLW stood for World's Lowest Wages.

In the 1930s about 50 percent of all WLW programming was local, 40 percent in evening hours. The station's staff originated programming carried on NBC, especially variety and hillbilly (later called country) music, and many Mutual programs. It also produced original drama—some destined for the networks included *Ma Perkins* (soap opera) and *Mr. District Attorney* (crime). In the late 1930s, station executives added a great deal of agriculture programming, and WLW even started its own experimental farm in an attempt to retain the 500-kW superpower transmitter by providing more unique and rural programming.

The station produced popular early morning hillbilly variety programs and, in cooperation with Ohio State University and the state's department of

education, an educational series for in-school listening. WLW was a "regional" service, nearly a network unto itself. The same could be said of other major clear channel stations such as WGN, WCCO, and WSM, but none matched WLW's quantity of original local programming.

Postwar Change

From 1949 to April 1953, as the station sought to duplicate the huge WLWAM coverage in the new medium of FM (frequency modulation), WLW's programming was broadcast simultaneously on FM stations in Cincinnati, Dayton, and Columbus, Ohio, but the growth of the FM audience was slow. The company concentrated on television. Many WLW radio programs were first simulcast on the television outlet, then later were shown only on TV. In 1955 WLW was the first radio station to provide weather forecasts based on radar (which it shared with the TV station), and in 1958 it became one of the first with helicopter traffic reports. In the 1960s WLW often ranked only third or fourth in Cincinnati ratings (losing out to Top 40 formats), but it had the largest total audience of any station in the city because of its larger coverage area. For example, in 1961 Nielsen reported WLW as having listeners in 184 counties in four states.

As network programming declined in the last half of the 1950s and into the 1960s, WLW became what was often called a Middle of the Road (MOR) station, producing "magazine" programs of news, information, talk, and limited amounts of recorded music during the morning and afternoon hours. Other types of music, including classical all night long, filled most of the rest of the hours. The station's format in the 1970s and 1980s was "adult contemporary." In the 1990s and into the new century, by which time there were many competing stations with a variety of popular music formats (most derived from the earlier Top 40 formula), WLW was usually the station with the highest audience share in the Cincinnati market. The station consistently maintains the largest total audience of any Cincinnati station because it reaches audiences over a wide area in Ohio, Indiana, and Kentucky.

Modern WLW

The programming on WLW is now what is generally described as "full service," being a combination of news, talk, and sports with well-known local personalities—a format that is usually found only on a few stations (mostly 50-kW stations) similar to

WLW in the largest markets with very big revenues. More news and information are offered during peak listening times in the mornings and afternoons. Evenings are generally call-in talk, including sports. Typically WLW has slightly higher overall ratings during the summer and spring, when Cincinnati Reds play-by-play baseball is broadcast.

At the turn of the century, WLW was estimated to have revenues of about $21 million, which would place it in the top 20 of all-talk, news/talk and so-called full service radio stations. All the other full service stations earning more money were in markets larger than Cincinnati (ranked 26th in radio), mostly in New York, Los Angeles, and Chicago, the three largest markets. It is regularly rated among the top 20 stations in other markets in a radius of 35–135 miles from its transmitter in Mason, Ohio, such as Dayton, Columbus, Lima, Lexington, and Fort Wayne. After several changes of ownership and mergers, WLW is now owned by Clear Channel Communications, which operates seven other facilities in the market, and owns more radio stations than any other single company.

See also: Clear Channel Communications Inc.; Clear Channel Stations; Middle of the Road Format

Further Reading

Lichty, Lawrence W., "'The Nation's Station': A History of Radio Station WLW," Ph.D. diss., The Ohio State University, 1964.
Lichty, Lawrence W., "Radio Drama: The Early Years," *National Association of Educational Broadcasters Journal* (July–August 1966).
Perry, Dick, *Not Just a Sound: The Story of WLW*, Englewood Cliffs, New Jersey: Prentice-Hall, 1971.
WLW website, www.700WLW.com

LAWRENCE W. LICHTY

WMAQ

Chicago, Illinois Station

The origins of WMAQ-AM go back to the beginnings of radio when, in the spring of 1922, the *Chicago Daily News* put WGU on the air as a 500-W forerunner of what the National Broadcasting Company (NBC) would turn into a mighty 50,000-W broadcast giant. In 1923 the station acquired formal studios in the LaSalle Hotel; in 1929 the station moved to the new *Daily News* building. Two years later, on 1 November 1931, WMAQ-AM was purchased by the Radio Corporation of America's (RCA) NBC, which moved the studios to the Merchandise Mart and made WMAQ a flagship station.

WMAQ-AM remained a key NBC-owned-and-operated station until General Electric (which purchased RCA, NBC's parent, in 1985) sold it to Group W in 1988. (There was also a WMAQ-FM, which was sold in the early 1970s.) The related television operation—also named WMAQ—was also an NBC-owned-and-operated station in Chicago.

NBC's acquisition of WMAQ-AM gave the network primary Chicago outlets for both its Red and Blue network programming, because WENR-AM had been purchased by NBC earlier. WMAQ-AM was a programming pioneer. Freeman Gosden and Charles Correll started *Sam 'n' Henry* for WGN-AM, but they moved to NBC and WMAQ to become *Amos 'n' Andy* in 1929. Another one of WMAQ's biggest achievements was the discovery of a new act by Marian and Jim Jordan, later widely popular on the show *Fibber McGee and Molly*, who made their first appearance on radio in February 1931. Other first-timers were Count Ilya Tolstoy, son of the noted author; Cyrens Van Gordon, opera star; Lorado Taft, the sculptor; Rosa Raisa, the famed soprano; George Arliss; Ben Hecht; Otis Skinner; Ruth Chatterton; and Jane Addams.

Indeed, the station was within a day of being six months old when it presented the first music appreciation program—on 12 October 1922. Mr. and Mrs. Max E. Oberndorfer began a series of broadcasts with an analysis of the opening program of the Chicago Symphony Orchestra that year. On the following day, WMAQ-AM led the radio industry into the field of children's programs with Mrs. Oberndorfer's *Hearing America First* series. This phase of broadcasting was expanded on 16 October of the same year when Georgene Faulkner, the "Story Lady," gave the first of her *Mother Goose* broadcasts. On 28 November 1922, the first educational broadcast was presented by WMAQ when Professor Forest Ray Moulton, head of the astronomy department at the University of Chicago, gave a lecture on "The Evening Sky." It was the first in a series of broadcasts by University of Chicago professors and was the forerunner of the *University of Chicago Round Table*.

WMAQ-AM also led the field in sports and news broadcasting. It presented one of the first daily play-by-play descriptions of major-league baseball on 20 April 1925 and one of the first play-by-play descriptions of a football game on 3 October 1925. For news, WMAQ-AM ran the first transatlantic news broadcast in history, on 4 December 1928, which consisted of a telephone conversation between John Gunther, then *Chicago Daily News* correspondent in London, and Hal

O'Flaherty, then foreign news editor of the *News*, regarding the condition of King George V, who was seriously ill. WMAQ-AM was also the only Chicago station to broadcast the first presidential inaugural ever put on the air, that of Calvin Coolidge, on 4 March 1925.

That the best in radio entertainment was continually on WMAQ-AM is obvious after a glance at a list of stars, both past and present, who made their radio debuts over Chicago's oldest station. Wayne King, for instance, made his first broadcast anywhere over WMAQ-AM on 28 January 1928. Fred Waring and his Pennsylvanians made one of their earliest broadcasts on WMAQ in August 1922; Ed Wynn made his initial radio broadcast in October 1922; Vincent Lopez made his radio debut in September 1924; and so on.

Because of the success of WMAQ-TV, WMAQ-AM, as a NBC network mainstay, had to reinvent itself as TV forced radio's redefinition. It was never very successful, and so few were surprised when WMAQ-AM was acquired by Westinghouse and became a news/talk station, still based in the NBC Tower on North Columbus Drive.

See also: Amos 'n' Andy; Clear Channel Stations; National Broadcasting Company

Further Reading

Caton, Chester, "WMAQ: Her Independent Years," Ph.D. diss., Northwestern University, 1950.
Linton, Bruce A., "A History of Chicago Radio Station Programming, 1921–1931, with Emphasis on Stations WMAQ and WGN," Ph.D. diss., Northwestern University, 1953.

DOUGLAS GOMERY

WNBC

New York City Station

Begun as WEAF by AT&T in 1922 and becoming the flagship of the new National Broadcasting Company (NBC) network in September 1926, this network-owned-and-operated station's call letters changed to WNBC in November 1946 as part of a process of "rationalizing" network station call letters in the city. Operating with 50,000 W on 660 kHz, WNBC was both the network flagship and a local market station.

With the decline in network radio in the early 1950s, WNBC took on a middle-of-the-road format like many other big-city stations, offering a variety of programs aimed at different tastes during the day, trying to provide something for everyone.

Boston radio humorists Bob and Ray joined the station in 1951 with their parade of characters and radio takeoffs. Public service features such as daily pollen counts and traffic reports became important program elements by mid-decade. From 1954 to 1960, WNBC became WRCA to better promote the initials of owner Radio Corporation of America (the NBC call letters went to a network-owned UHF television station in Connecticut, so the network did not lose control of the identity).

WNBC, as with most stations, had for its entire history signed off the air after its late-evening programs concluded. Beginning in 1952 it began to provide 24-hour service with the *Music through the Night* mixture of easy talk and both classics and light classical music. In 1959 daytime programming featured "wall-to-wall" music, a combination of easy listening and pop tunes and talk. For a time the program could be heard in a kind of stereo with one channel broadcast on the network's AM outlet and the other on the co-owned FM station.

But even in New York City, radio was in decline. By 1962 the station's facilities had shrunk from studios on five floors of the RCA building in Rockefeller Center to just two. A long-time transmitter location on Long Island was closed down and NBC radio shared a transmitter with WCBS, also on Long Island. By the 1960s WNBC was trading more on its traditions and history than its current listenership, and ratings were far from market leaders. From 1964 to 1970, WNBC programmed a talk format, including some of New York's first call-in programs.

By 1970 music had once again taken over, although the format concentration on "66 NBC" (emphasizing the station's location on the AM dial) varied. The music was all contemporary, sometimes current hits and sometimes a mixture of new and older top songs. A major change came with the 1972 hiring of a Cleveland disc jockey, Don Imus, for the morning drive-time period, and the beginning of shock jocks in the New York market. A decade later Howard Stern moved into the afternoon drive-time period. WNBC soon added former TV entertainers Soupy Sales and Joey Reynolds. Although their comments were embarrassing at times, the jocks and their music helped the station climb in audience ratings.

But the ratings turnaround could not save the station. In 1986 parent company RCA was sold to General Electric, which soon decided not to continue radio operations. The NBC network was sold to Westwood One and the New York AM and FM outlets were sold to Emmis Broadcasting. WNBC's last broadcast was heard on 7 October 1988. The next day, its frequency was taken over by WFAN, the city's first all-sports station.

See also: Talk Radio; WEAF

Further Reading

Jaker, Bill, Frank Sulek, and Peter Kanze, *The Airwaves of New York: Illustrated Histories of 156 AM Stations in the Metropolitan Area, 1921–1996*, Jefferson, North Carolina: McFarland, 1998.

Lieberman, Philip A., *Radio's Morning Show Personalities: Early Hour Broadcasters and Deejays from the 1920s to the 1990s*, Jefferson, North Carolina: McFarland, 1996.

The 66 WNBC Tribute Pages, www.imonthe.net/66wnbc

Tracy, Kathleen, *Imus: America's Cowboy*, New York: Carroll and Graf, 1999.

CRAIG ALLEN AND CHRISTOPHER H. STERLING

WNEW

New York City Station

A comparative novelty during network radio's pre-World War II heyday, independently programmed WNEW generated respectable ratings and profit without ties to the likes of the National Broadcasting Company (NBC), the Columbia Broadcasting System (CBS), or Mutual. By the late 1940s, television's widening influence cut deeply into revenues of radio network affiliates that continued to embrace soap operas, sitcoms, and drama. Meanwhile, WNEW's pop music format proved relatively impervious to video competition. Curious broadcast insiders were drawn to WNEW. They wanted to see how the locally programmed AM outlet could succeed with just a handful of disc jockeys, some phonograph records, and a bit of news.

The WNEW story begins in New Jersey, where the station was formed primarily from remnants of comedian Ed Wynn's failed network venture. The performer had tried competing against CBS and NBC with his Amalgamated Broadcasting System, but the effort succumbed to fiscal woes. The Wynn connection is mentioned owing to its legendary nature, but was largely a province of studio facilities acquired from the comic's then-defunct broadcast ownership foray. WNEW more accurately originated from the amalgamation of New Jersey stations WAAM at Jersey City and WODA in Paterson, which time-shared 1250 kHz in the metropolitan region. (Another outlet, WHBI of Newark, occupied the 1250 dial position on Sundays and Monday nights.)

Watch manufacturer Arde Bulova, advertising man Milton Biow, and WODA's owner Richard

O'Dea were principals in the station consolidation. Because—at least for a time—their broadcast enterprise would qualify as the New York area's newest, WNEW seemed a perfect call sign choice. President Roosevelt was selected to inaugurate the station, and on 13 February 1934, he pushed a button in the White House that was wired to a light in WNEW's Carlstadt, New Jersey, transmitter building. The button signaled a singer to belt out the "Star Spangled Banner," and the facility's 1250-kHz channel carried it with 1,000 W. In 1939, its frequency got reassigned to 1280 kHz while the wattage was raised to 5,000.

For two decades, the station's real power came from a metropolitan socialite blessed with an intuitive knack for programming. Bernice Judis had no previous radio industry experience when a friend (wife of co-owner Milton Biow) suggested that she become part of the WNEW staff. Consequently, she thought more like a listener than a detached, by-the-book executive. This, as well as a limited budget, caused Judis to fill much of WNEW's schedule with a pleasant output of pop music records and smooth-voiced announcers skilled at describing the music's performers. Audiences soon equated the station with an endearing kind of companionship that gave them a soundtrack for their daily routine. Ratings rose, prompting Bulova and Biow to name Judis general manager of what had evolved from Newark, New Jersey-based studios to an exclusively downtown New York operation. Judis felt that a city that never slept needed a station that stayed on all night. In 1936 with an early-morning broadcast dubbed *Milkman's Matinee*, WNEW became the first to do so.

The thought of their records being freely spun, even at 3 A.M., irritated some musicians, who would rather perform live and be paid. In a resulting lawsuit, the plaintiff artists were disappointed to learn that because WNEW had purchased the recordings, it could use the transcriptions for any desired purpose. This decision prompted independents in other U.S. communities to proudly play records (a practice "big radio" had considered laughably low class in the 1920s and 1930s). Columnist Walter Winchell so enjoyed the way Judis' announcers deftly rode ad-libs around their discs that he coined their professional title—disc jockey.

In a 1941 frequency swap with co-owned WOV, WNEW was moved from 1280 to 1130 kHz, and power was increased to 10,000 W. This shift also rid WNEW of the time-share arrangement with WHBI. Programs included news, public service, celebrity interviews, and even a series about good grooming. Broadcast schedule diversity included actor James Earl Jones' WNEW debut, circa 1945, in an American Negro Theater radio production. The next year, radio's first two-man morning show hit WNEW's air. This wake-up session garnered a following as loyal as that of the station's cornerstone, *Make Believe Ballroom*, a show on which a recording star might just drop in while disc jockey Martin Block happened to be playing his or her latest release.

A group including general manager Judis purchased WNEW in 1950. The station saw revenues jump due in part to a 1949 quintupling of its transmitter power (to 50,000 W). The group sold to Dick Buckley and associates in 1954. Subsequently, Buckley's principals merged with remnants of the DuMont Television Network, before selling in 1957 to what became John Kluge's prominent Metromedia.

As radio "flagship" for this growing media conglomerate, WNEW received what was arguably the largest and most skilled news department of any independent outlet. By 1961 New York Giants (football) play-by-play broadcasts brought listeners to the 1130 dial position. And the list of excellent air personalities (William B. Williams, Ted Brown, Gene Klavan, Jim Lowe, Bob Landers, Gene Rayburn, and others) made for a very secure-sounding product. That's why, whenever they were in Manhattan, America's most sophisticated pop music icons (such as Dean Martin, Jack Jones, Peggy Lee, Steve Lawrence, and Eydie Gorme) eagerly sampled WNEW. Toting their just-released 33 1/3-rpm album, they would often drop by the Fifth Avenue studios for a surprise on-air appearance.

But by the late 1960s, most advertisers had become more interested in baby boomers and focused their advertising budgets on stations playing records kids demanded. Metromedia watched its venerable AM property slip, whereas WNEW-FM (established in 1958 as the remaining supply of vacant 50,000-W New York City-area FM allocations had dwindled to three) achieved high ratings among the young demographic by dumping its "all-girl" announcers and easy listening music format in favor of progressive rock.

The old WNEW tried attracting new audiences by trying various incarnations of adult contemporary records and sports talk shows. A variety of air-personality and other changes never drained WNEW of broadcasters who could make a shampoo commercial entertaining, but such classic announcing talent was a poor fit with disco-era chart toppers. Fortunately for WNEW, advertising priorities had changed by the late 1970s. Advertising agencies were suddenly interested in America's comfortably affluent 40-plus population, giving the original "good" music, personality, and news station an economic reason to return to the most familiar shelves in its (1930s through 1960s non-rock hits) record library. Targeted listeners gratefully responded. For most, the change represented a surprise homecoming, lifting the station into a second heyday circa 1979. Other AM operators in what was by then an FM world studied this round of WNEW success. Arguably, all music stations that transmit disc jockey patter and recorded music can trace some of their roots to WNEW's original programming practices.

Rupert Murdoch's 1986 Fox acquisition of the Metromedia television properties orphaned WNEW radio. The FM station was bought by Westinghouse (in 1989), and WNEW-AM eventually ended up with the Bloomberg organization for a 1992 rechristening as the 24-hour, business-formatted (Bloomberg Business Radio) WBBR. So great was WNEW's personality-delivered big band/standards void that the *New York Times* came to the rescue. The paper's perennially classical WQXR-AM switched call letters to a mnemonic WQEW (Westinghouse didn't wish to relinquish the WNEW name) and accurately reconstructed, in full AM stereo, WNEW's programming spirit there. That legacy ended in late 1998, when Disney contracted with the *Times* to shift WQEW's programming to a juvenile focus.

See also: All Night Radio; Metromedia; Radio Disney; WQXR

Further Reading

Eberly, Philip K., *Music in the Air: America's Changing Tastes in Popular Music, 1920–1980*, New York: Hastings House, 1982.

Gordon, Nightingale, *WNEW: Where the Melody Lingers On*, New York: Nightingale Gordon, 1984.

Jaker, Bill, et al., "WNEW" in *The Airwaves of New York: Illustrated Histories of 156 AM Stations in the Metropolitan Area, 1921–1996*, Jefferson, North Carolina: McFarland, 1998.

Passman, Arnold, *The DeeJays*, New York: Macmillan, 1971.

Rhoads, B. Eric, *Blast from the Past: A Pictorial History of Radio's First 75 Years*, West Palm Beach, Florida: Streamline, 1996.

PETER E. HUNN

WNYC
New York City Station

For more than 75 years, WNYC, the nation's "most listened to" public radio station (93.9 FM and 820 AM), was funded by New York City municipal tax dollars. The station has weathered a long history of stormy relations as a result of its control at the hands of a line of New York City mayors extending from Mayor John F. Hylan in the 1920s to Mayor Rudolph W. Giuliani in 1995. This mayoral prerogative ended when ownership of the AM and FM stations was sold by the Giuliani administration to the WNYC Foundation, a nonprofit entity, in 1995.

Origins

In 1922 city official Grover A. Whalen, then-commissioner of the Department of Plant and Structures, convinced Mayor John F. Hylan to appoint a committee to study the feasibility of operating a city radio station. The committee recommended the establishment of a municipally owned station, despite opposition from city Republicans and various big-business interests. When Western Electric was the sole bidder for the construction of the station and charged "exorbitant prices" for the use of its wires for remote broadcasts, the city searched for another alternative. In March 1924, a solution appeared in the form of a slightly used 1,000-W broadcasting plant, which Westinghouse sold to the city after removing the equipment from its site at a Brazilian Centennial Exposition in Rio de Janeiro. During construction, an experimental license was granted to "station 2XHB." The station premiered on 8 July 1924, broadcasting from the top of the Municipal Building using the new official call letters WNYC. The opening evening featured crooners and instrumentals by the Police Band and the Vincent Lopez Orchestra. Mayor Hylan and city officials provided stirring orations, solemnized by blessings by clergy from three major faiths. The premier broadcast interfered with broadcasts of ships at sea and annoyed WEAF listeners when the transmission interrupted a broadcast from the Democratic National Convention.

Early broadcast schedules were erratic, beginning in the evenings at approximately 6 P.M. and concluding at around 11 P.M. Live performances from musical artists promoting the sale of sheet music and a series of one-hour foreign language lessons were among the staples of the evening broadcasts. Ad hoc longer broadcast hours accommodated visiting dignitaries and events ranging from band concerts to visiting monarchs, record-breaking aviators, and channel swimmers. H.V. Kaltenborn was an early contributor to WNYC and organized a radio quiz, and *WNYC's Air College* offered scholarly discussion on a variety of topics.

The station's service to the city consisted mostly of a nightly broadcast of missing persons. When Mayor Hylan sought to air a report of progress to the board of aldermen over the air in 1925 while running for his third term of office, the Citizen's Union, a watchdog advocacy group, brought legal action to prevent the mayor from using the station as a tool of propaganda. It was the beginning of a long history of contentious relationships between the mayor or board of city aldermen and the station. In the late 1920s, the station was criticized by a "Freethinker" for broadcasting religious services promoting the Catholic and Jewish faiths. To avoid such criticism, management codified a statement of its mission in 1930; the station would feature music, concerts, and entertainment; talks on current affairs; meetings of civic bodies, associations, and societies; lectures and addresses; and the reception of distinguished visitors.

Upon his election, Depression-era Mayor Fiorello H. La Guardia planned to sell the station as a cost-cutting move. A report by La Guardia aide Walter Chambers argued eloquently for the retention of the station as a public relations arm of the mayor's office. La Guardia detested the station at first, reportedly shouting upon spotting the old-fashioned carbon microphones of WNYC at a speech at the Commodore Hotel in 1934, "Get that damn peanut whistle out of here!" WNYC weathered the Great Depression partially through staffing provided by the Works Progress Administration (WPA) from government relief rolls, and the station embarked on a "Radio Project" to increase cultural programs, vary content, and find new sources of information and entertainment. In 1935 WNYC received a $30,000 WPA grant, and its transmitter was moved to the Greenpoint section of Brooklyn.

Controversies

Almost from its inception, the station was embroiled with federal regulators, fighting to protect its frequency assignment or to maintain broadcast hours. Under the Radio Act of 1927, the station was assigned 570 kilocycles and would be forced to share its frequency with radio station WMCA, broadcasting on alternate days at a reduced power of 500 W. The city fought the assignment, and the Federal Radio Commission agreed that WNYC could swap frequencies with another station also owned by the management of WMCA, at 810 kilocycles. The swap allowed WNYC to operate during the daytime on clear channel until sunset at Minneapolis, when the 50,000-W WCCO assigned to the same frequency came on the air.

In 1937 city councilmen seeking to embarrass Mayor La Guardia accused the station of anti-Semitism and racial hatred following a broadcast discussion of the Arab position on Palestine. The city council attempted to engineer another frequency swap that would have given the 810 AM frequency to the Paulist Fathers and forced WNYC to operate on a half-time basis from frequency 1130. La Guardia successfully fought the move. He was then targeted by political opponents as a supporter of communism for appointing the former secretary to the American Labor Party, Morris S. Novik, as director of radio communications for the city. WNYC was again accused of communist sympathies when the producer George Brandt's National Travel Club program on Soviet Russia on 27 February 1938 expressed admiration for Soviet accomplishments, but station management successfully defended itself against the charges. Concurrently, WNYC began broadcasting city council meetings, and the proceedings quickly became a source of public amusement. The *New York Times* commented that whereas the former board of aldermen had taken 135 years to make fools of themselves, the council had accomplished the same in only two years of radio broadcasts. Despite WNYC political broadcasts, the *New York Post* noted in 1938 that the station also provided more live unrecorded music than any other station in the city.

By 1940 La Guardia was a WNYC enthusiast, using the station to promulgate his political agenda. In 1944 the mayor began a weekly radio show, most memorably reading the Sunday comics to New York City children during a newspaper strike in July 1945. Comedian Fred Allen quipped to the *New York Times*:

> The Mayor's program is a happy blend of *Mary Margaret McBride, Information Please,* and *Gang Busters*. One week the Mayor will tell you how to make Frenchfried potatoes with artichoke roots. The next week he gives you the name of the bookmakers and hurdy-gurdy owners he has chased out of the city.
>
> (cited in Scher, 1966)

Mayor William O'Dwyer, a former district attorney and judge, was the last of the line of early New York City mayors to routinely review the merits of WNYC and contemplate its sale immediately following election. O'Dwyer eventually was convinced to maintain the station and its noncommercial status.

During World War II, the station requested additional hours of broadcast for wartime information, and in 1942 the Federal Communications Commission granted a Special Service Authorization to allow WNYC to broadcast from 6 P.M. until 10 P.M., despite the conflict with Minnesota's clear channel frequency. The additional timeslot was extended after retired Mayor La Guardia lobbied the Columbia Broadcasting System (CBS), owner of the Minneapolis clear channel station, to permit the Special Service Authorization to continue, and the hours were made permanent in 1955. In 1943 New York City launched a companion FM station that would allow WNYC to operate around the clock. Initially, the two stations carried the same programming until sign-off at 10 P.M. for the AM band. In 1953 WNYC also received a permit to construct an ultrahigh-frequency (UHF) band television station, which was renamed WNYC-TV in 1962. In 1987 WNYC moved to 820 kHz and boosted power tenfold—to 10,000 W.

WNYC has built its reputation over the years on its ability to craft a mix of local, national, and world politics; culture; education; the arts; and classical music. The station claims it was the first to broadcast the Japanese attack on Pearl Harbor, and it has broadcast more Senate hearings, conferences, and conventions, including the presidential conventions of smaller political parties, than any other station. In the 1960s, the station offered an outlet for foreign programs and the views of various national news such as the *French Press Review* and the *Review of British Weeklies*. Its broadcast of public hearings on the increase of the New York City subway fare was called "one of the greatest mass civic lessons in the history of radio" by *Variety* magazine. Bob Dylan made his radio debut in 1961 on Oscar Brand's *Folk Song Festival*, and experimental and modern music found an outlet on WNYC.

In 1994 Mayor Giuliani announced that the city would sell the station, and a deal was struck whereby the AM and FM stations would be sold at a reduced price of $20 million to the WNYC Foundation, and the television station would be sold to commercial interests. For the first time, WNYC would be a public- and grant-supported station, and its president would no longer be a political appointee of the mayor but rather hired by the board of the WNYC Foundation. The board appointed Laura Walker, a former producer of Children's Television Workshop, as president. Her management team succeeded in doubling public contributions to the station and raising $1.4 million in June 1995 in a four-day campaign while garnering support from corporations and other high-profile supporters. WNYC 93.9 FM is a member station of National Public Radio (NPR) and of Public Radio International (PRI), and it features

NPR and WNYC news and cultural programming along with classical music. WNYC Radio New York at 820 kHz broadcasts news, talk, and public-affairs programs. In 1998 the station launched a website, wnyc.org, which also allows web users to receive radio programming, both live and in archived segments.

In 2001, the station lost its FM transmitter and antenna in the September 11th attacks on the World Trade Center and temporarily used borrowed transmitters and antenna to simulcast the news talk programming of its AM station over both AM and FM outlets. The subsequent soar in ratings and fund raising was instructive. Within a few months of restoring the FM tower, the station announced it was eliminating five hours of classical music programming each day on the FM channel in favor of more news/talk programming, to the consternation of many listeners and performers who saw WNYC as one of the few outlets for both original and recorded classical programming.

See also: Educational Radio to 1967; Public Radio Since 1967

Further Reading

Gladstone, Valerie, "Having Important (and Generous) Friends Helps," *New York Times* (21 November 1999).
Hinckley, David, "WNYC and Public Radio Become More of a Turn-On," *New York Daily News* (26 August 1997).
Jaker, Bill, Frank Sulek, and Peter Kanze, *The Airwaves of New York: Illustrated Histories of 156 AM Stations in the Metropolitan Area, 1921–1996*, Jefferson, North Carolina: McFarland, 1998.
Lewine, Edward, "Making Radio Waves," *New York Times* (12 January 1997).
Scher, Saul Nathaniel, "Voice of the City: The History of WNYC, New York City's Municipal Radio Station, 1924–1962," Ph.D. diss., New York University, 1966.
Van Gelder, Lawrence, "Morris S. Novik, 93, Early Director of WNYC," *New York Times* (12 November 1996).
Van Gelder, Lawrence, "Footlights," *New York Times* (7 April 1999).
"WNYC-FM to Cut Back Classical Music," *New York Times* (8 March 2002).

L. CLARE BRATTEN

WOR

New York City Station

WOR-AM (710), now a leading talk/news format radio station in New York City that is heard in 35 states, began in 1922 as the New York metropolitan area's second radio station. WOR was constructed as a marketing promotion for the L. Bamberger and Company Department Store, and it originally served the New York area from Newark, New Jersey. Although its transmitter remains in New Jersey, its studios have been located in New York City for more than 70 years.

After New York station WJZ (later WABC) was launched in October 1921, Edgar Bamberger decided to start a radio station to promote both the crystal radio sets sold at the L. Bamberger and Company store and the store itself. Jacob R. Poppele, a former wireless operator for the U.S. Army who worked in the store's radio department, strung up antenna wires and launched station WOR on 22 February 1922 as its chief engineer. Initially, WJZ and WOR alternated daylight and evening hours. WOR operated at 833 kHz with 250 W of power and moved to 740 kHz when it increased its power to 500 W. When the American Society of Composers, Authors, and Publishers (ASCAP) sued WOR for copyright fees in 1923, WOR argued that it was providing a cultural service rather than broadcasting for profit. However, the courts decided that repeated emphasis of the station's sponsorship by L. Bamberger and Company as "one of America's Great stores" excluded it from the realm of charitable enterprises.

Early schedules alternated vocal and instrumental numbers with talk and various programs aimed at self-improvement. One of the most enduring of these early shows was a morning exercise program begun in 1925 featuring Bernarr Macfadden, a physical culture enthusiast and publisher of the magazines *Physical Culture* and *True Story*. Macfadden paid WOR for the privilege of hosting the program. When Macfadden came down with laryngitis, John B. Gambling filled in and eventually took over the morning exercise show. That show ended in 1934, but John Gambling stayed on as a morning fixture. Two succeeding generations of Gamblings have held the morning-show host position since—John A. until 1991 and John R. Gambling for the final decade, 1991–2001.

In 1927 WOR moved to the 710-kHz clear channel frequency. That same year, WOR joined with a group of radio stations enlisted by Arthur Judson and George A. Coats to form the United Independent Broadcasters (UIB), which required that participating stations sell ten hours of station time each week to UIB. WOR was the key station for the UIB group, which merged with Columbia Phonograph Broadcasting System and later became the Columbia Broadcasting System (CBS). However, WOR separated from the CBS chain in 1928 when WABC joined and became the key transmitter station for the chain. Competing department store chain R.H. Macy and Company acquired a controlling interest in L. Bamberger and Company in 1929, and the licensee name for WOR was changed to the Bamberger Broadcasting Service. By 1935 a new 50,000-W transmitter and directional antenna sent WOR airwaves over a "bean-shaped area" up and down the eastern seaboard, garnering it a huge audience.

WOR joined three other major-market stations in 1934 to form the Mutual network, and it was the anchor station for Mutual for many years before leaving the network in 1959. Mary Margaret McBride got her start as *Martha Deane* on WOR from 1934 to 1940. *Uncle Don*, played by Donald Carney, a popular figure with young listeners, told stories and provided avuncular advice. In 1940 Ed Fitzgerald and his wife Pegeen created *The Fitzgeralds*, a breakfast show broadcast from the couple's 16th-floor apartment overlooking Central Park that achieved an audience of two million listeners as they discussed the day's upcoming social events and the morning news. The station featured another long-lived radio family—the McCanns. Alfred W. McCann, a muckraking journalist, used *The McCann Pure Food Hour* to expose the practices of the food industry in the late 1920s. After his death in 1931, son Alfred W. McCann, Jr., took over and was later joined by his wife, Dora, to broadcast *The McCanns at Home* from their house in Yonkers. Daughter Patricia McCann continued the family tradition with *The Patricia McCann Magazine* until 1983.

In 1940 J.R. Poppele oversaw the creation of another WOR entity—New York's first commercial FM station, carrying WOR programs. During the 1940s, the *American Forum of the Air* staged debates on various topics. The station also originated dramatic series, such as *Nick Carter, Master Detective*; game shows; and soap operas. It attracted talent such as Henry Morgan, Cab Calloway, Arlene Francis, and theater critic Jack O'Brian. In the mid-1970s, Jean Shepherd joined WOR and stayed for 21 years as a personality and raconteur. In 1948 Bamberger Broadcasting System became a part of General Teleradio, and in 1952 Don Lee Broadcasting System purchased WOR. In 1955 the station was acquired by RKO Pictures (later RKO General).

WOR-FM developed a new format described as "ahead of its time," featuring "alternative" music such as the Beatles and Rolling Stones album cuts in 1966. It switched to an oldies format called the "Big Town Sound" in November 1967. When, in 1972, it dropped its oldies format and lost half its audience, WOR-FM became WXLO and later WRKS.

Attempting to update its programming in the 1970s, WOR-AM moved increasingly toward a talk format. A 1978 New School of Social Research survey reported that independent stations such as WOR produced more public-affairs programming than network radio competitors. From 1973 and for the next 20 years, "folksy foggy-voiced" radio personality Bernard Meltzer hosted the programs *What's Your Problem?* and *Guidance for Living*, which combined advice on finances, real estate, taxes, and personal problems. During the 1980s, both WOR and its archrival WABC adopted the talk radio format and struggled with revamping their programming to attract a younger audience. In 1988 the Federal Communications Commission (FCC) approved the sale of WOR-AM to S/G Communications, which in turn sold it a year later to Buckley Broadcasting Corporation for $25.5 million, after RKO General lost its licenses because of fraudulent billing practices in the mid-1970s.

Along with its mellow programming personalities, WOR also had its share of controversial figures. Irwin H. Sonny Bloch, a financial talk show host, was aired by WOR until Bloch admitted to swindling his listeners and was jailed. Eric Braverman, a doctor with a weekly show on alternative medicine, lost his medical license in 1996. WOR also hired controversial talk show host Bob Grant from rival WABC-AM in 1996 after Grant was fired for racial slurs against deceased Commerce Secretary Ron Brown.

WOR-AM talk format includes *Rambling With Gambling; Dr. Joy Brown*, a radio psychologist; *The Bob Grant Show*; financial advice from Ken and Daria Dolan; *The Joan Rivers Show; Health Talk* with Dr. Ronald Hoffman; and a food program by *Daily News* critic Arthur Schwartz. The station also carries sports coverage of the New Jersey Nets and Rutgers University.

WOR-AM talk format includes journalist Ed Walsh on *The Morning Show, Dr. Joy Brown*, a radio psychologist; *The Bob Grant Show*, financial advice from Ken and Daria Dolan, and Joan Hamburg, a talk show host wildly popular with women over 30 and whose style is reminiscent of WOR's earlier successes such as *The Fitzgeralds*. *Health Talk* with Dr. Ronald Hoffman, a food program by *Daily News* critic Arthur Schwartz, and an evening talk show host Tom Marr, brought in from Baltimore to replace Joan Rivers, were on the 2003 roster. Joey Reynolds, a former shock jock who is billed by the station as the "Mr. Nice Guy of Night Radio," holds down the night-time hours; his show is distributed by satellite to 35 stations nationwide. WOR does use some outside programming—Fox-syndicated commentator Bill O'Reilly's program *The Radio Factor* is featured during late afternoon hours.

See also: Mutual Broadcasting System; WABC

Further Reading

Jaker, Bill, Frank Sulek, and Peter Kanze, *The Airwaves of New York: Illustrated Histories of 156 AM Stations in the Metropolitan Area, 1921–1996*, Jefferson, North Carolina: McFarland, 1998.

Wilson, George, "With Bob Grant at the Mike, WOR Means 'White Only Radio,'" *New York Amsterdam News* (11 May 1996).

L. CLARE BRATTEN

WORLD WAR II AND U.S. RADIO

A brief radio bulletin brought the reality of another world war to American listeners on 7 December 1941. At 2:26 P.M. EST, the Mutual Broadcasting System (MBS) interrupted coverage of a Sunday afternoon football game to announce that Japanese warplanes had bombed U.S. forces at Pearl Harbor, Hawaii. The other networks quickly followed suit, John Daley of CBS mispronouncing the name of Oahu in his excitement, for example. America and its Allies soon were engaged in a monumental struggle, every aspect of which was in one way or another connected with radio. U.S. radio's prominence during World War II proved to be the medium's journalistic highwater mark. In a sense, radio was the perfect medium to undertake the wartime task of informing, entertaining, and boosting the morale of the American public. In doing so, radio adapted itself to serve three program settings—international, domestic, and military.

Nearly 82 percent of U.S. households and 30 percent of U.S. automobiles were equipped with at least one radio receiver as World War II began, and more than 900 U.S. radio stations, 76 percent of which were affiliated with one of the four major networks—NBC Red, NBC Blue, CBS, and MBS—served listeners before war's end. A demonstration of radio's power to reach listeners occurred on 8 December 1941 when President Roosevelt delivered his noontime address asking that Congress declare war on Japan. A daytime record of 66 percent of radio listeners tuned in to the address. The night-time record was broken the next evening when 83 percent of the audience heard another address by the president.

As the United States entered the war, radio, especially radio news, had achieved stature as a major unifying force. Radio network and station executives who had been reluctant to program anything that appeared to breach the nation's declared neutrality now were able to act in concert. As a result, practically all of the radio programs that listeners were accustomed to hearing—from drama to comedy and from variety show to soap opera—incorporated patriotic, morale-boosting themes.

Radio news during World War II was, for all intents and purposes, NBC and CBS News. CBS News became a force in journalism in a sudden burst of improvised reporting activity at the very outset of the war. On 11 March 1938, when the German army occupied Austria, Edward R. Murrow and William L. Shirer were the only two foreign correspondents employed by CBS Radio. Both, however, were resourceful enough to arrange to cover the *Anschluss*, and at 8 P.M. on 13 March 1938, Murrow and Shirer, along with several newspaper reporters scattered in various European cities, went on the air with live reports of reaction to the German occupation. The CBS *World News Roundup*, as it came to be called, was successful enough to be made a permanent wartime fixture. Radio from then until war's end was not only the chief information source for most Americans, but also the information source that Americans held in highest esteem.

Radio performers such as Jack Benny mixed regular program fare with wartime requests to conserve scarce items or to grow "Victory Gardens." Networks also produced special programs built around stars to make particular mobilization appeals. One such program with Kate Smith, airing on CBS in February 1944, was successful in raising some $112 million in war bond sales. Comedian Bob Hope began a tradition that lasted until the Vietnam War era of taking his show on the road, entertaining radio listeners and military personnel alike at various military locations at home and abroad. The music programs (most of which were in the popular or "pop" category) that filled nearly a third of the network schedules also joined the war effort with the likes of Frank Sinatra or Glenn Miller and his Orchestra performing tunes such as "Praise the Lord and Pass the Ammunition" and "This Is the Army, Mr. Jones."

New dramatic programs such as *Counter Spy* and *Alias John Freedom* incorporated wartime themes exclusively, as did documentary series such as *To the Young*, *Report to the Nation*, and *This Is War*. All of these were meant to stimulate morale as well as to inform listeners about U.S. war policy. Youthful radio listeners were introduced to Americanism and patriotism via the heroic deeds of such characters as Jack Armstrong, Superman, Tom

Mix, and Captain Midnight. These and similar characters battled the treacherous deeds of assorted Axis villains. Messages imploring children to collect paper or to buy war stamps were also inserted into programming especially produced for that age group. And many of the nearly 50 morning and afternoon serials or "soap operas" such as *Young Dr. Malone, Backstage Wife,* and *Front Page Farrell* adapted their plots and characters to wartime situations.

Special programs that demonstrated the unified spirit of the American entertainment industry occasionally appeared throughout the war. One of these, "We Hold These Truths," was produced by the U.S. government and had been intended as a commemoration of the 150th anniversary of America's Bill of Rights. It aired live simultaneously in prime-time on all four U.S. radio networks only eight days after the Japanese attack on Pearl Harbor. Created by noted writer Norman Corwin, "We Hold These Truths" reached a radio audience estimated at the time to have been the largest ever to hear a dramatic performance. President Roosevelt, along with a cast of some of America's most famous performers, including Lionel Barrymore, Walter Huston, Marjorie Main, Edward G. Robinson, Orson Welles, and James Stewart, all lent their voices and talent to a program in which the original intentions of celebration gave way to a more somber call to patriotism.

The U.S. government played other prominent roles in radio programming during the war. For example, *The Army Hour,* financed by NBC but produced by the U.S. Army, began its hourly Sunday afternoon broadcasts in April 1942. *The Army Hour* was produced not only for domestic listeners, but also for military personnel around the globe. The show gave listeners a blend of entertainment and information about the army's mission and featured well-known celebrities and army personnel from privates to generals. For instance, it was here that listeners heard General Jimmy Doolittle tell of Army Air Corps bombing runs over Tokyo. *The Army Hour,* originating from military bases around the globe, remained popular throughout the war.

The U.S. War Department found radio of use in other ways. Noted writers such as Norman Corwin and William Robson were commissioned to prepare scripts for programs meant to raise public perception regarding women serving in the armed forces and regarding the fighting abilities of African-American troops. And when morale problems crept into the numerous military training bases around the country, the War Department requested that

networks provide some entertainment relief by originating programs from the bases themselves. The networks complied, but before the originations began, the networks had to promise to abide by another request—to begin each program with a disclaimer for endorsements by either the army or War Department of commercial products represented by the programs' sponsors.

A number of government agencies produced radio programs that were available to networks and local radio stations wishing to air them. All such programs had to be approved by the OWI, and many of the agencies producing them were assisted by such civilian groups as the Writers' War Board, the War Advertising Council, the Council for Democracy, and the War Activities Committee of the Motion Picture Industry. Members of these wartime organizations devoted time, talent, and expertise to the cause. *Treasury Star Parade* was one such product of this civilian/government collaboration. The 15-minute series was produced by the U.S. Treasury Department and was meant to persuade listeners to buy war bonds. Leading performers of the day donated their dramatic and musical talents to *Treasury Star Parade.* The program, reproduced on electrical transcriptions (called "ETs") that resembled the contemporary long-playing record, was distributed free upon request to over 800 radio stations nationwide.

The government played other key roles during World War II that affected the radio industry. For instance, in April 1942 the FCC discontinued issuing permits to construct both AM and FM stations until war's end. The commission's rationale for its decision was the shortage of construction material resulting from wartime needs and the shortage of trained personnel necessary to operate radio stations. Even before the war had begun, in September 1940, Roosevelt had created the Defense Communications Board (later renamed the Board of War Communications), which was made up of government representatives and civilian representatives of the radio industry and was charged with deciding how best to utilize American radio during the war. The Board's most significant contribution was allowing radio networks and stations to operate as usual with only a modicum of extraordinary government oversight.

Practically all of that oversight came via the Office of Censorship (see following) and units of the FCC. The FCC's Radio Intelligence Division had been created prior to the war to search for unlicensed radio stations. That job became more critical during the war with the threat of clandestine stations broadcasting subversive messages. The

FCC's Foreign Broadcast Intelligence Service also existed prior to the war to monitor and transcribe foreign broadcasts and to make their transcriptions available to the appropriate government agencies.

Voluntary censorship was assisted by an Office of Censorship (OC), which was created by the president's executive order only two days after the Pearl Harbor attack. One of the OC's first objectives was to prepare a code for broadcasters that would include advice on what should or should not be said on the air and how certain kinds of information might be handled.

The OC issued the first of five editions of its *Code of Wartime Practices for American Broadcasters* in January 1942. Because of ways in which the enemy might make use of otherwise innocent kinds of programming, radio station licensees were cautioned to abstain from broadcasting, among other things, weather reports, information about military troop locations or deployments, identification and location of naval ships or military aircraft, military base locations, and casualty counts as a result of military action. Licensees were also cautioned to avoid musical request programs or interview programs that relied on extemporaneous comments and to avoid dramatic content that portrayed the horrors of battle. The OC staff spot-checked network programs for any content that might prove problematic. The staff also reviewed program scripts that networks or stations submitted voluntarily. With few reported breaches of security, the radio industry's ability to look after its own house during the war worked exceptionally well.

The one new FCC unit was the War Problems Division, which the commission established in its law department in 1942 to monitor the nation's 169 radio stations that broadcast all or a major portion of their programming in foreign languages. Because German and Italian were the predominant languages of these programs, there were fears that agents of the Axis powers could easily use the programs to plant subversive messages. The stations could have been ordered off the air, of course, but the FCC realized that they served a significant number of listeners (estimated at 14 million foreign-born and first-generation Americans) who might otherwise listen to shortwave stations originating in Axis countries if they were not served by American stations. In order to police themselves, the stations created the Foreign Language Radio Wartime Control, which adopted a code requiring strict oversight of program content and station employee loyalty. This code eventually was incorporated into the *Code of Wartime Practices for American Broadcasters*.

The abundance of programming for World War II radio was matched by the abundance of advertising. In fact, only one year after the war began, the U.S. radio industry billed a record $255 million for commercial time. And things simply got better after that. Two factors contributed to radio's economic well-being. One was the shortage of newsprint, which curtailed the amount of space many newspapers could allow for advertising. Businesses naturally turned to radio, where no such space constraints existed. As a result, radio's total share of the advertising dollar climbed steadily throughout the war years. The second economic factor favoring radio derived from a tax levied by the government on excess profits as a means of curtailing wartime profiteering. The 90 percent tax on profits exceeding what a company would normally be expected to make was exempted when these profits were spent for advertising. Instead of keeping what amounted to only ten cents for every dollar, companies dumped much of their excess profits into radio advertising.

Radio advertising in the form of program sponsorship also benefited from government largesse. Companies under contract to manufacture war-related products were allowed to count advertising along with other manufacturing costs and to pass along to the government all the bills for doing business. This formula allowed a number of companies to dedicate large amounts of money to sponsoring radio programs. Such sponsorship amounted to paying the full production costs of programs, with the results that a number of network programs either remained in production or were created as a result of funding that came indirectly from the government.

Wartime conditions changed radio advertising content in a number of ways. For one, a number of consumer products either were not available or were in short supply and thus rationed. Companies whose products were thus affected often turned to institutional advertising just to keep their name or brand in the listener's mind. This kind of advertising was particularly beneficial to the fine arts when, for example, a corporation such as General Motors that had no cars to sell nonetheless gave its name to sponsor the NBC Symphony Orchestra. Other companies tied their name or product to the war effort by the messages they chose for their radio commercials. A famous western hat company, for example, mixed its product name with a plea to guard against spreading rumors by admonishing Americans to "Keep it under your Stetson."

Finally, domestic radio stations underwent some wartime changes. Many stations located in markets that were also the homes of important war industries adjusted their broadcast day in order to provide industry and plant workers something to listen to as they worked. Radio was also considered an essential industry by the government, and many key radio station personnel were granted deferments for military duty by the Selective Service System. Of course, although some decisions were made to take advantage of these deferments, many broadcasters still joined the military when duty called. Broadcast engineers in particular provided technical expertise that was useful to the military. They contributed considerably in developing America's wartime electronics capability. And their skills advanced in such ways that the radio engineers who entered World War II left it in 1945 to form the advance troops in postwar development of the television industry.

Military Radio

U.S. military personnel were among the most avid listeners of the shortwave international stations that had been transformed by the OWI into the Voice of America. Programming produced especially for the "G.I." began appearing in early 1942 as a result of the U.S. Army's Bureau of Public Relations (BPR). The BPR's first and perhaps best-known program was *Command Performance*. The one-hour program aired weekly on Sundays and carried a blend of comedy, sports summaries, popular music, and celebrity appearances. The *Command Performance* title derived from the program's key element of entertainers responding to military personnel requests such as singing a special song. The program was produced from several takes, allowing deletion of questionable material or material deemed censorable by the military, and then recorded finally onto wax disks for the Sunday airing. *Command Performance* originated in New York but was moved to Los Angeles shortly thereafter because of the Hollywood talent pool. After producing 44 of the programs, the BPR relinquished control of *Command Performance* to the Armed Forces Radio Service (AFRS).

The AFRS was created in 1942 as a unit within the War Department's Information and Education Division and was headed by Col. Thomas H.A. Lewis. The AFRS was headquartered in Los Angeles and run by staff members from the army and navy as well as civilians. The service was closely connected to the entertainment industry and thus attracted top talent for AFRS programs. By the end of 1943 AFRS had 306 outlets and stations in 47 countries. Each outlet received more than 50 hours of recorded programming per week, delivered by plane, as well as special shortwave programming (e.g., news and ball games) and programs that were produced in the field or at the stations themselves. All programs were reproduced on unbreakable 12-inch vinylite disks, some 83,000 of which were shipped every month from Los Angeles to AFRS outlets. Reuse of commercial programs required cooperation of network and transcription companies as well as concession of rights of entertainers, sponsors, advertising agencies, musicians, copyright claimants, and publishers.

AFRS programs either were produced by the AFRS itself or were network series that had been "denatured." Denaturing meant deleting commercials that normally appeared in the network programs from the transcribed versions heard by the G.I. so as not to give unfair advantage to particular advertisers. There also was fear that soldiers far from home and living under less than ideal conditions would be depressed to hear commercials for food and drink products or goods meant to provide comfort and relaxation. But when soldiers complained of missing the familiar sound of commercials, the army began inserting gag commercials that spoofed the real ones. And as many commercial network programs used the name of the program sponsor in the show's title, completely new openings and closings had to be created by the AFRS and substituted for the actual title. Thus, *Camel Caravan* became *Comedy Caravan* and *Chase and Sandborn Hour* became *Charlie McCarthy*. AFRS also combined dramatic episodes of several programs into anthology-like series with titles such as *Front Line Theater*, *Globe Theater*, and *Mystery Theater*.

Besides entertainment programs, educational and documentary programs were carried on the AFRS network. *Heard at Home* was another combination program that pulled segments from such shows as *The Chicago Roundtable*, *America's Town Meeting of the Air*, and *People's Platform*. The AFRS also produced its own educational programs, such as *Know Your Enemy* and *Know Your Ally*. *Mail Call*, a musical variety program that began in August 1942, was the first AFRS-produced program. For commercially produced shows, several different AFRS offices were responsible for examining program content for security violations, technical quality, authenticity, and compliance with current policy, such as race relations policy. AFRS could not supply all programming needs, and besides, troops preferred the familiarity of U.S. commercial network programs.

Most of the AFRS military radio stations operating in the field were called "American expeditionary stations." Their prototype was a station in Kodiak, Alaska. Soldiers stationed there soon after the war began were unhappy with the unreliable shortwave service in that remote area. To improve matters, the soldiers built and operated their own low-powered transmitter and a makeshift station that broadcast to troops stationed nearby. Programs consisted mainly of recorded music supplemented by occasional news reports as items were received via shortwave.

A more significant makeshift radio operation began in Casablanca shortly after U.S. forces invaded North Africa in November 1942. Present with the troops was Major Andre Baruch, who had been a CBS radio announcer prior to the war and who asked permission of General George H. Patton to construct a radio station for his comrades. The general approved, and Baruch set about molding spare parts into what became the U.S. Army's first expeditionary radio station on 15 December 1942. Major Baruch entertained troops with "platter-chatter" and music from his own limited collection of records. Radio receivers were not plentiful and either had to be purchased from French Moroccan radio shops or built from spare parts. A short time later, soldiers at Anzio were creative enough to build a simple receiving device called "Foxhole Radio" that was similar to the crystal sets of the 1920s.

The idea that radio was an important element in keeping troop morale high led to General Dwight D. Eisenhower's ordering the creation of additional stations that either were stationary or traveled with troops. Transmitters for the 50-W mobile stations were carried in five portable cases and accompanied the Fifth Army as it advanced into Italy. At key locations along the route, permanent stations were established by Major Baruch. By March 1943 these stations were joined to form the Mediterranean Army network. A similar network of stations, called the Armed Forces network, was built to serve American troops stationed in England and began broadcasting in July 1943. And in due course, an equivalent South Pacific operation called the "Mosquito" network was created with stations built on islands scattered throughout the area. All of these stations, of course, carried the AFRS programming supplied on disk, but they also provided listeners with localized programming produced at the stations themselves.

Radio at War's End

Reporting about military matters became more sophisticated as the war progressed. Radio reporters who accompanied troops were assisted in their reporting efforts by field recording techniques using portable wire recorders. During the latter part of the war, these reporters were indirectly assisted by German technical advances that had replaced the difficult-to-edit wire recorders with plastic tape recorders. Captured recorders of this new variety allowed reporters to cover a variety of dramatic wartime events and to quickly get their eyewitness accounts back to their respective networks. Thus, ABC's George Hix provided listeners with vivid accounts of the 6 June 1944 D-Day invasion from his observation point aboard a navy ship. And listeners heard the recorded reactions to nearly incomprehensible horrors on 13 August 1944, when a Mutual reporter first entered Maidanek extermination camp, which had been liberated only a few days earlier by the Russian army.

At least three months of fighting remained in the Pacific when Germany surrendered in May 1945. There was much V-E Day celebrating over the triumph of the Allied forces, and radio was in the thick of it. On 8 May 1945, CBS aired *On a Note of Triumph*, written by Norman Corwin to commemorate the event. *On a Note of Triumph* proved so popular that CBS rebroadcast it live on 14 May. The program eventually was released as a commercial record album, and Simon and Schuster put out a book version of the script that quickly made the best-seller list. The program in a symbolic sense brought radio full circle. Radio had made a commitment of so many of its resources to join in the collective experience that World War II became. Radio and its listeners—wherever they might have been and in whatever endeavor they might have been engaged—had formed a community during the war and had effectively woven themselves into the very fabric of that event.

See also: News; Office of War Information

Further Reading

Bannerman, R. LeRoy, *Norman Corwin and Radio: The Golden Years*, Tuscaloosa: University of Alabama Press, 1986.

Barnouw, Erik, *A History of Broadcasting in the United States*, 3 vols, New York: Oxford University Press, 1966–70; see especially vol. 2, *The Golden Web, 1933 to 1953*, 1968.

Browne, Donald R., *International Radio Broadcasting: The Limits of the Limitless Medium*, New York: Praeger, 1982.

Brylawski, Samuel, "Armed Forces Radio Service: The Invisible Highway Abroad," *The Quarterly Journal of the Library of Congress* 37 (Summer–Fall 1980).

Davis, Elmer Holmes, and Byron Price, *War Information and Censorship*, Washington, D.C.: American Council on Public Affairs, 1957.

Dryer, Sherman Herman, *Radio in Wartime*, New York: Greenberg, 1942.

Garay, Ronald, "Guarding the Airwaves: Government Regulation of World War II American Radio," *Journal of Radio Studies* 3 (1995–96).

Kirby, Edward Montague, and Jack W. Harris, *Star-Spangled Radio*, Chicago: Ziff-Davis, 1948.

Landry, Robert John, *This Fascinating Radio Business*, Indianapolis, Indiana: Bobbs-Merrill, 1946.

MacDonald, J. Fred, *Don't Touch That Dial! Radio Programming in American Life, 1920–1960*, Chicago: Nelson-Hall, 1979.

Redding, Jerry, "American Private International Broadcasting: What Went Wrong—and Why," Ph.D. diss., Ohio State University, 1977.

Rolo, Charles James, *Radio Goes to War: The "Fourth Front,"* New York: Putnam, 1942.

Rose, Ernest, "How the U.S. Heard about Pearl Harbor," *Journal of Broadcasting* 5 (Fall 1961).

Siepmann, Charles Arthur, *Radio in Wartime*, London and New York: Oxford University Press, 1942.

Summers, Robert Edward, *Wartime Censorship of Press and Radio*, New York: Wilson, 1942.

Willey, George, "The Soap Operas and the War," *Journal of of Broadcasting* 7 (Fall 1963).

Winkler, Allan M., *The Politics of Propaganda: The Office of War Information, 1942–1945*, New Haven, Connecticut: Yale University Press, 1978.

RONALD GARAY

WQXR

New York City Station

One of the very few radio stations to begin as part of an experimental TV operation, WQXR (as it became in 1936) and its later FM associate station became in 1944 the voice of the *New York Times* in New York City, renowned for classical music and arts programming. Elliott Sanger, both father and son, played key roles in the station's creation and operation for decades.

Origins

This New York classical music station had a unique start—as the sound channel for a very early experimental *TV* transmitter. In 1929 radio inventor J.V.L. Hogan received a Federal Radio Commission (FRC) license for W2XR, based in Long Island City, New York, to develop a mechanically scanned TV and facsimile service. Whereas the pictures were sent out on 2100 kHz, as of 1933 a second, sound, channel at 1550 kHz was added. In accord with FRC rules of the time, this was one of three 20 kHz channels (each twice the width of existing AM radio channels). Using this new channel, Hogan used classical music recordings as his sound background for the crude pictures. Audience

interest in the music (most could not receive the pictures) prompted the idea of a commercial station providing such content. Indeed, the eventual failure of mechanical approaches to television led to an increased focus on the sound channels.

Working with engineer Al Barber, Hogan focused on providing high-fidelity sound by using special broadcast-only electrical transcription recordings and various filters to improve the music transmitted. Equipment was the best available—or was made especially for W2XR operation. By 1934, using 250 W, the station was on the air four hours daily and was providing a program log for listeners.

The big change came two years later when, teamed with advertising and public relations expert Elliott M. Sanger, the experimental W2XR became commercial station WQXR with 1,000 W of power, still on 1550 kHz. But this was a different kind of commercial operation, because the station (with all of six employees) picked and chose its advertisers and their messages carefully to match the high tone of the programming. WQXR would not accept advertising for products that were in poor taste or represented a bad value—and the method of presentation of those that were accepted "must be in keeping with the quality of the broadcast programs." Prophetically, in light of what happened eight years later when the *Times* bought the station, the original license application stated that the new station would seek to emulate the values of the *New York Times*. Many radios could not even tune in to the station, which was just above what were then the uppermost frequencies on the AM band.

A focus on top-quality sound continued and in 1938, WQXR broadcast the opera *Carmen* as its first tape-recorded program, though the method of recording used was short-lived. Power rose to 10,000 W (on 1560 kHz) in 1941. Hogan and Sanger's Interstate Broadcasting Co. became an FM licensee, with New York's first FM station, W2XQR (with a transmitter loaned by FM inventor Edwin Armstrong) on 26 November 1939, which became W59NY (45.9 MHz) when the FCC approved commercial operation in 1941. When FM call letter rules changed in 1943, the station became WQXQ, and with the service's frequency change it shifted operations up to 97.7 MHz after World War II. Both stations provided the same programming and were now operating from a Fifth Avenue address.

Voices of the Times

In mid-1944, the *New York Times* purchased the stations from Sanger and Hogan for $1 million.

The program emphasis on fine music continued, as did the extensive schedule of live studio performances. Six years later, the studios moved to the *Times* building. In October 1952 the stations began a two-station transmission of stereo, with AM providing the right channel and FM the left. These were replaced in 1961 with the inception of FM multiplex transmission. The AM outlet's power received a final power boost, to 50,000 W, in 1956.

In a decade-long experiment, the New York-based classical programming was shared with more than a dozen "affiliate" stations in the WQXR network. Beginning in 1953 stations from Buffalo, New York, to Boston, Massachusetts, to Washington, D.C., formed the "WQXR Network." It closed 10 years later because of insufficient income and the desire of the other stations to have more local say in their program offerings. December 1963 saw the end of the station's monthly program guide, which had first appeared in 1936 (the *Times* carried the program listings in its pages).

The stations won a Peabody Award in 1959, which noted "no station anywhere has devoted more time or more intelligent presentation to *good* music than has WQXR." In 1967, in response to FCC rules not allowing AM-FM outlets to duplicate their programming, WQXR began to focus on lighter classics, show tunes, and jazz. Several other approaches were tried, but all angered listeners and did not please advertisers. The *Times* briefly considered selling the outlets in 1971, but instead obtained a nonduplication exemption from the FCC and went back to both stations providing the standard classical repertoire that had done so well for so long.

In December 1992 the AM outlet (which over the years had lost much of its audience to its higher fidelity FM twin) became WQEW, with much of the popular music programming that had been on now-defunct WNEW. At the end of 1998 WQEW entered a new stage when the *Times* leased the outlet to Disney for an eight-year period and the format was directed toward children (with a back-up of New York Jets game broadcasts), delivered by satellite and carried by about 40 other stations across the country. WQXR (FM) continued to provide classical music and in January 1997 began an internet website.

In 2009, The New York Times Co., short of cash, sold WQXR in a complex deal with WNYC, a non-commercial operator. The new owner shifted the signal to a higher frequency (105.9 MHz) and continued the classical music format and some of the staff, albeit with less talk and no *Times* news

reports. The former WQXR channel (96.3 MHz) was sold to another commercial operator to help fund the deal.

See also: Classical Music Format

Further Reading

New York Radio Guide, www.nyradioguide.com
Sanger, Elliott M., *Rebel in Radio: The Story of WQXR*, New York: Hastings House, 1973; as *Rebel in Radio: The Story of the New York Times "Commercial" Radio Station*, London: Focal Press, 1973.
Watkin, Daniel J., "More but Selective Music for the New WQXR," *New York Times* (1 October 2009).
"WQXR," in *The Airwaves of New York: Illustrated Histories of 156 AM Stations in the Metropolitan Area, 1921–1996*, by Bill Jaker, Frank Sulek, and Peter Kanze, Jefferson, North Carolina: McFarland, 1998.
WQXR website, www.wqxr.com

CHRISTOPHER H. STERLING

WRR
Dallas, Texas Station

WRR-FM has the distinction of being one of the few municipally owned commercial FM stations in the United States. WRR-AM began broadcasting in 1920; the FM station began broadcasting in 1948. Rising station values convinced the Dallas city government to sell the AM station in 1978, but the city retained the FM service. Although rising station values have again prompted the city to consider selling WRR-FM, the city has so far elected to retain the station and the distinct fine-arts and classical programming contribution the station makes to the city of Dallas.

A Radio Emergency Service

WRR-AM is one of the pioneer radio stations in the United States. In March 1920 WRR was issued a limited commercial license by the Department of Commerce to begin a specialized wireless service. Although WRR claims to be the first station west of the Mississippi River, its original specialized function excludes it from being considered for many of the "firsts" in radio history. WRR was conceived as a two-way communication system to send and receive emergency calls from the city's fire and police departments. Thus its services were not intended for reception by the general public, nor did the station provide general-interest programs in its early years. When not in use, the transmitter's carrier frequency would remain on the air. In the event of a fire or rescue emergency, the silence of the carrier frequency was interrupted with an emergency announcement for firefighters. What would today be termed "programming" was added during the interludes between emergency calls to enable listeners to know that their receivers were set on the correct station frequency.

As with radio in other parts of the United States, the presence of a station and at least limited programming service encouraged listeners to tune in to receive the miracle of wireless transmission. As the radio system developed, the central Dallas fire station served as the base of transmission. Fire Department personnel and dispatchers soon developed an eclectic broadcasting schedule, typical of many early radio stations, consisting of weather reports, joke telling, reading the newspaper on the air, announcing birthdays, and playing music. Such general-interest programming served to encourage more citizens to buy receivers, which in turn increased listener demand for more and improved programming. Eventually, the station was airing not only recorded music but broadcasts of local amateur musicians as well.

The success of WRR led its operation to shift from the fire department to being a municipally operated station. The station began accepting advertising in 1927. By 1939 the station's trailblazer operations led to the construction of a radio building and transmitter tower at the Fair Grounds Park near downtown Dallas. In 1940 the station affiliated with the Mutual Broadcasting System and the Texas State network. Much of the station's format consisted of block programming.

By the 1970s WRR-AM was operating with 5,000 W of power on 1310 kHz. Rising station values led the city of Dallas to sell WRR-AM for $1.9 million in 1978 to Bonneville Broadcasting. Later, Bonneville sold the station to Susquehanna Broadcasting. The station is still on the air using the call letters KTCK and is a profitable all-sports station.

WRR-FM Begins Operation

WRR-FM began broadcasting in 1948, a time when few members of the public owned an FM receiver, but when hopes for the new radio service were high. As with many other FM outlets, WRR-FM began by programming classical music.

WRR-FM has survived a series of city government debates regarding its ownership and operation. Some members of the Dallas City Council have characterized ownership of a commercial radio station as socialism and have viewed the station as being in direct competition with commercial station

owners. WRR-FM has consistently maintained a classical music format with a strong emphasis on local news. It is perhaps the classical format that has enabled the station to continue its status as a municipally owned station. Few commercial station operators would be likely to continue the commercial classical music format if the station were sold. The Dallas-Fort Worth market is also served by a classical and news affiliate of National Public Radio (NPR).

WRR-FM Extends Its Coverage

WRR increased its transmitter power and relocated the transmitter and antenna in 1986. The station currently broadcasts in stereo with 98,000 W on 101.1 MHz. The station's primary coverage radius extends more than 65 miles from its transmitter location, enabling the station to reach listeners in Fort Worth and the suburbs in north Dallas.

Though a commercial radio station, WRR has adopted a tactic of many noncommercial classical-formatted stations. The group "Friends of WRR" is a nonprofit organization whose mission is to support the station's classical programming. WRR also generates revenue by selling time for religious broadcasts, and it sells a weekday half-hour segment at 6 P.M. to a local television station to air the station's local newscast.

WRR programming includes symphonic and opera broadcasts, local arts and cultural programming, and children's programming; the station also broadcasts the bimonthly meetings of the Dallas City Council. WRR-FM continues to be a self-sustaining and profitable radio station. The station is typically one of the 20 most-listened-to stations in the Dallas-Fort Worth radio market, one of the ten largest radio markets in the United States.

Further Reading

Schroeder, Richard, *Texas Signs On: The Early Days of Radio and Television*, College Station, Texas: Texas A&M University Press, 1998.
WRR website, www.wrr101.com

GREGORY G. PITTS

WSB

Atlanta, Georgia Station

Atlanta's WSB radio is the oldest radio station in the South, born of a competition between two Atlanta newspapers. A clear channel station, WSB signed on the air 15 March 1922.

Origins

As early as 1921, ham radio operators in Atlanta were asking for a station. Since the sign-on of KDKA in 1920, radio was becoming a big amateur venture, and Atlanta—and surrounding Georgia—jumped on the bandwagon. A former Navy wireless operator named Walter Tison approached Major John S. Cohen, editor and publisher of *The Atlanta Journal*, to discuss the feasibility of a local radio station. Tison persuaded Cohen, and plans went into action for the new station; Tison would become the first federally licensed operator. George A. Iler, an engineer with the Georgia Power Company, was hired to be the first station director.

The Atlanta Journal and *The Atlanta Constitution*, then rival newspapers, were fighting to get the first Atlanta radio station on the air. On 15 March 1922 *The Journal* won when it received this telegram, signed by acting secretary of commerce C.H. Huston:

> *The Atlanta Journal* is authorized to temporarily broadcast weather reports on the wavelength of four hundred eighty five meters pending action on the formal application for a radio license. Station must use radio call letters WSB repeat WSB and employ commercial second class or higher radio operator licensed by this department.

The telegram ended with these words: "If you desire to broadcast news entertainment and such matter this is permitted on wavelength of three hundred sixty meters only."

According to the station's history, by nightfall the station was on the air with these words, "Good evening: This is the Radiophone Broadcasting Station of *The Atlanta Journal*." That first broadcast came from *The Atlanta Journal* office on Forsyth Street; the station broadcast at a mere 100 W of power. *The Journal* wrote the next day, "Atlanta is on the radio map of the world today." Three months later, according to the station history, that map grew as the station increased to 500 W.

WSB Radio remained a noncommercial station located at *The Journal*'s office for its first three years but moved in 1925 to the Biltmore Hotel. On 9 January 1927, according to the station's official history, WSB became a charter affiliate of the National Broadcasting Company and began to sell advertising. These moves paralleled the station's power boost to 1,000 W.

WSB was a station of firsts. In addition to being the first station in the South, it was the first in the country to have a slogan. According to the station's golden anniversary history, a listener coined the phrase "The Voice of the South," writing, "Because of its remarkable powers of transmission, penetrating alike into lonely cottages in isolated sections and palatial residences in distant cities, WSB has truly become 'The Voice of the South'." A listener contest gave meaning to the call letters WSB—"Welcome South, Brother." Lambdin Key, the first full-time general manager, led programming.

According to the station's official history, WSB was also the first station in the nation to present an entire church service—on Easter Sunday in 1922. The station claims many other firsts, including the first radio fan club, the WSB Radiowls.

By 1933, the station's wattage was increased to 50,000, and WSB had become a permanent and national fixture at 750 kHz. The station made its name by offering first-class news coverage as well as entertainment options.

In December 1939, Governor James M. Cox of Ohio bought the station and *The Atlanta Journal*, adding them to his company that would become the Cox Broadcasting Company. He put J. Leonard Reinsch in charge of the station as general manager. In 1944, Governor Cox made Reinsch managing director of all of his broadcasting properties. Reinsch and former vice president and general manager Elmo Ellis moved the radio station through the initial days of television in Atlanta, a time that saw a national decline in radio usage. Both men saw the station through the turbulent 1960s and into the 1970s. Ellis retired from the station in 1982.

According to the station's history, WSB achieved another first on 16 November 1944, when it put Georgia's first ever Frequency Modulation (FM) station on the air. That station, now known as B 98.5, has changed music format over the years, but it remains a leader and soft rock alternative in the vast Atlanta market.

WSB radio made its last big location move on 28 December 1955 joining its sister television station at Cox's new broadcasting facility known as White Columns, and both remain at that location.

WSB-AM at the turn of the century led its market as an all-news radio station, a format it adopted in the 1980s. It remained a clear-channel station at 50,000 W and was the national broadcasting center for the Atlanta Braves.

Further Reading

Welcome South, Brother: Fifty Years of Broadcasting at WSB, Atlanta, Georgia, Atlanta: Cox Broadcasting, 1974.

Ginger Rudeseal Carter

WSM

Nashville, Tennessee Station

WSM, "The Air Castle of the South," is the powerful radio station in Nashville, Tennessee, largely responsible for that city's emergence as a major entertainment and media center. The call letters WSM represent "We Shield Millions," slogan of the National Life and Accident Insurance Company of Nashville, the station's founding licensee.

Other Tennessee radio stations had already begun broadcasting in Memphis, Knoxville, and Nashville by the time WSM signed on the air in 1925. Although most of the inaugural WSM schedule consisted of programs characteristic of the mid-1920s (i.e., light classical and dance music), some of the station's programs were tailored for the farmers and wage earners who constituted National Life's main business, the sale of weekly premium insurance. Very early in WSM's history, a program of rural-flavored music was modeled after the WLS (Chicago) *Barn Dance*. Shortly after its start, WSM's program became known as the *Grand Ole Opry*. The content of the *Grand Ole Opry* engendered some distaste in certain sections of Nashville, but the "*Grand Ole Opry* Insurance Company" prospered from its affiliation with the broadcast.

A "WS *Empire*" emerged from National Life's 1931 authorization to operate WSM as an unduplicated class 1-A clear channel (650 kHz), with 50,000 W of power full-time and a nondirectional radiation contour. When National Life won the clear channel for WSM, it erected North America's tallest radio tower near Brentwood, about 15 miles south of downtown Nashville. At the dawn of radio's golden age, WSM thus became one of about 25 stations in the United States that could be received reliably at night throughout much of North America.

Although barn-dance programs aired on other clear channel stations during the 1930s and 1940s, Nashville's *Grand Ole Opry* emerged as the leader of that genre for three principal reasons. First, the National Broadcasting Company (NBC) Red network carried a portion of the *Grand Ole Opry* coast to coast for several years starting in 1939, thereby extending the reach of WSM entertainers beyond the range of "clear channel six-fifty." Second, WSM's association with a rural style of music diffused by word of mouth during World War II, as people from various parts of the country served together in the armed forces. Third, touring *Grand Ole Opry* musicians and personalities who entertained World War II troops fostered the image of Nashville as a center for "hillbilly" or "country and western" music.

National Life also was an early commercial FM licensee but abandoned FM broadcasting in favor of television in 1950. The present WSM-FM at 95.5 MHz (formerly WLWM) was purchased in 1968. In 1950 National Life established Nashville's first television station, WSM-TV, which operated without competition for three years. This head start in television did much to solidify WSM's position of dominance in the Nashville radio and television market, which continued at least through the 1970s.

WSM remained a basic affiliate of the NBC radio network during radio's music-and-news era. Only after television displaced much of the evening radio audience in the 1950s did WSM begin to devote large amounts of its weeknight schedule to recorded country and western music. During the day, however, WSM remained a full-service, mass-appeal station. Middle-of-the-road and, later, adult contemporary recorded music filled the time between network features, local news, and business and agricultural reports. The station maintained a staff of musicians who performed pop standards during a live studio morning show well into the 1970s.

By 1968 National Life had become Nashville's largest corporation, the nation's sixth-largest stock life insurance company, and the principal subsidiary of NLT Corporation. In 1972 NLT capitalized on WSM's *Grand Ole Opry* as the theme for Opryland USA, a $40 million entertainment complex followed in 1977 by a $26 million hotel.

The decade of the 1970s probably captures the peak of WSM's influence in Nashville and middle Tennessee. As the radio and television industries began to undergo tremendous change during the late 1970s, NLT broadcasting executives led by Tom Griscom envisioned a way to extend the company's advertising base beyond the reach of WSM, WSM-FM, and WSM-TV. They foresaw the inevitable decline in the audience for AM stations in general and in particular the erosion of the clear channels, as federal regulators increasingly viewed the extensive protection of night-time signals such as WSM's as a vestige of the radio age. They also recognized the widespread market potential of cable television. In response to these structural changes in telecommunications, NLT executives advanced a plan that would fully utilize Nashville's extensive talent pool and NLT's large investment in television production while maintaining *Grand Ole Opry's* core audience.

That plan eventually took form as the Nashville Network. Seed money for the Nashville Network was obtained from the 1981 sale of WSM-TV to George N. Gillette. An even more significant change at WSM occurred that same year, when

NLT was acquired by American General, the Houston financial services giant. Executives at American General made it clear that their interest was limited to NLT's insurance business and that the NLT broadcasting and entertainment operations were to be sold. For a time, there was concern that a single buyer would not be found for WSM, WSM-FM, the Opryland complex, and the Nashville Network. Speculation abounded that splitting the NLT broadcasting and entertainment division through sales to multiple buyers would have the effect of ending the historic *Grand Ole Opry*, which by then had been recognized as the world's longest-running live radio program.

Gaylord Broadcasting Company, a family owned firm itself wholly owned by the Oklahoma Publishing Company (publisher of the *Daily Oklahoman*), stepped in and purchased the NLT broadcasting and entertainment properties as a group in 1983, and the *WSM Grand Ole Opry* continued uninterrupted. In 2000 WSM featured a fine local news department and a country music format carried live on Sirius Satellite Radio.

See also: Clear Channel Stations; Country Music Format; *Grand Ole Opry*; WLAC

Further Reading

Crabb, Alfred Leland, *Nashville: Personality of a City*, Indianapolis, Indiana: Bobbs-Merrill, 1960.
Egerton, John, *Nashville: The Faces of Two Centuries, 1780–1980*, Nashville, Tennessee: PlusMedia, 1979.
Emery, Ralph, and Tom Carter, *Memories: The Autobiography of Ralph Emery*, New York: Macmillan, and Toronto, Ontario: Macmillan Canada, 1991.
Havinghurst, Craig, *Air Castle of the South: WSM and the Making of Music City*, Urbana: University of Illinois Press, 2007
Hoobler, James A., *Nashville Memories*, Knoxville: University of Tennessee Press, 1983.
Ogles, Robert M., and Herbert H. Howard, "The Nashville Network," in *The Cable Network Handbook*, edited by Robert G. Picard, Riverside, California: Carpelan, 1993.
Streissguth, Michael, *Eddy Arnold, Pioneer of the Nashville Sound*, New York: Schirmer Books, and London: Prentice-Hall International, 1997.
Zibart, Carl F., *Yesterday's Nashville*, Miami, Florida: Seemann, 1976.

ROBERT M. OGLES

WTOP

Washington, D.C. Station

"The spot at the top of your dial," WTOP-AM, at 1500 kHz, has been a fixture in the Washington, D.C., market (with various owners, frequencies, and call letters) since 1927. Still an affiliate of the Columbia Broadcasting System (CBS), WTOP was owned by the network from 1932 to 1949 and then by the *Washington Post* before undergoing a series of ownership changes in the 1980s and 1990s. The station's Washington location and the reach of its signal made WTOP a key originating station for CBS, and it launched important careers, including Arthur Godfrey's. In 1969 WTOP became a pioneer of the all-news AM format, and in the 1990s it began providing its signal over the world wide web.

Origins

Although long based in the Washington, D.C. area, WTOP began under different call letters more than 200 miles to the north. A Republican Party political club placed station WTRC on the air in Brooklyn in September 1926. It offered music and some talk programs. Just a year later the station's equipment was sold to John S. Vance, a Virginia publisher with Ku Klux Klan affiliations. Vance's station, first as WTFF and then carrying his initials as WJSV, began broadcasting from Mount Vernon Hills, Virginia, as a self-styled "independent voice from the heart of the nation." CBS purchased WJSV in 1932, took it off the air for three months, then returned to broadcasting from a facility beside the Potomac River in Alexandria, Virginia, using a submarine telephone cable to communicate with a second studio in Washington's Shoreham Hotel. An increasing number of live location broadcasts motivated a full move into Washington in 1933, with a new studio in the Earle Theatre Building. Station engineers set up for Franklin Roosevelt's fireside chats, concerts from Constitution Hall, the visit of George VI and Queen Consort Elizabeth in 1938, and other live broadcasts throughout the 1930s and 1940s.

A complete tape exists of WJSV's broadcast day on 21 September 1939, an invaluable snapshot of radio's golden era. Signing on at 5:58 A.M., the station broadcast *Sundial with Arthur Godfrey* at 6:30, CBS serials (including *The Goldbergs* at noon), a live Roosevelt address to Congress (repeated later in the evening), a Washington Senators baseball game, *Major Bowes' Original Amateur Hour*, and Louis Prima's orchestra at midnight, prior to a 1:00 A.M. signoff. During World War II, because its night-time signal reached the entire East Coast, the station was designated by the Federal Communications Commission (FCC) as a conduit for alerts, and its studios were staffed 24 hours a day even when not broadcasting.

After several frequency changes, the station in 1941 settled at 1500 kHz, at that time the highest AM frequency. This move in turn motivated new call letters, WTOP, adopted in 1943 along with the "top of your dial" slogan. A 50,000-W transmitter had been established in a new international-style building in Wheaton, Maryland, in 1940, where it remains today. (In the 1960s, Sam Donaldson hosted *Music Till Dawn* from the Wheaton transmitter.) The Washington Post Company purchased 55 percent of WTOP in 1949 and assumed full ownership in 1954. Under *Post* control, the station adopted an all-news format in 1969. For 25 years, WTOP-AM shared "Broadcast House" studios and some personnel with WTOP television, channel 9, which was also a Post-Newsweek station and CBS affiliate. The connection ended in 1978 with the sale of the AM station to the Outlet Company of Providence, Rhode Island; WTOP radio moved its studio to an office building next door to Broadcast House. WTOP was acquired in 1997 by Bonneville International Corporation, which also owns classical, contemporary, and country music stations in the Washington market.

From 1947 to 1966, WTOP simulcast its programming on FM. At that point, FCC regulations intervened to stipulate that eight hours daily be separately programmed for FM. In the uncertain regulatory environment, the Post-Newsweek Company eventually sold WTOP-FM for one dollar to Howard University, where it became WHUR. In an attempt to improve its signal in Virginia, another attempt at FM began in 1997, with a signal purchased, upgraded, and moved to 107.7 MHz (near the top of the FM frequency band). In 1998 WTOP launched its website, wtopnews.com. Web newscasts quickly became popular in Washington's government offices (where broadcast signals were sometimes weak), and webcasting figures significantly in WTOP's plans for the future.

Like other AM stations, WTOP had lost audience in the 1960s, and in response the station experimented with a variety of formats before adopting an "all-news" format in 1969. (Originally "all news, all the time," the station soon went from 24 hours a day to a 2 A.M. sign-off; WTOP returned to around-the-clock broadcasting, initially with a talk program, after its purchase by the Outlet Company.) News was a smart choice given the station's history, its location in the political capital, and its affiliations with the *Washington Post* and CBS. Through three subsequent decades of ownership changes and technical developments, WTOP has maintained its highly successful version of all news. One or two anchors coordinate a mix

of live reporting and feeds from CBS. There is a strong emphasis on local reporting, not necessarily focused on the federal government. Local leaders are featured on regularly scheduled call-in shows. Well-coordinated local news resources culminated in WTOP's award-winning live coverage of the July 1998 shootings inside the U.S. Capitol.

In its successful news mix, WTOP's sports coverage emphasizes local professional teams, and "traffic and weather together" appear every ten minutes. WTOP has not been immune to trends that are only marginally related to traditional "news." The long-running *Call for Action* consumer feature was joined in the late 1990s by a series of *Place for the Kids* fund-raising activities for boys clubs and girls clubs. Although on-air personnel still emphasized professionalism over personality, a *WTOP's Man about Town* was created through sponsorship by a luxury automobile. Activities stretching the all-news focus at WTOP had a long-standing precedent: the station for many years broadcast the full season of baseball games by the Baltimore Orioles. By 2000, three technologies—AM, FM, and the world wide web—were delivering WTOP's "all-news" content.

Further Reading

"WTRC," in *The Airwaves of New York*, by Bill Jaker, Frank Sulek, and Peter Kanze, Jefferson, North Carolina: McFarland, 1998.

GLEN M. JOHNSON

WWJ
Detroit, Michigan Station

WWJ Radio was the first radio station in the world to be started by a newspaper, the *Detroit News*, in 1920. By 1924 the radio station was to achieve a number of other first-time events in the history of radio.

Origins

At 8:15 P.M. on 20 August 1920, WWJ radio was born when eight automobile batteries powered what was then called 8MK. The equipment for the station came from a local electrical retail store. The station put out a 20-W signal on that first broadcast. Listeners (mainly ham operators) were asked to call in if they could hear the broadcast.

According to newspaper accounts of the historic event, the first words on the station were spoken by a 17-year-old Canadian named Elton Plant: "This is 8MK calling." A Windsor, Ontario, native, Plant had worked his way up to cub reporter at the *Detroit News* when the managing editor approached him with the idea of going on the air. Plant agreed to do it. He noted later, "It didn't mean a thing as far as I was concerned because I didn't know what it all was."

The name of the station was changed from 8MK to WBL when it received its radio license in October 1921. In March 1922 the call letters were changed again to WWJ, reportedly because listeners kept getting the call letters wrong. Over the years, a dispute developed over whether WWJ in Detroit, KDKA in Pittsburgh or WHA in Madison, Wisconsin, was the oldest radio station in the United States. Those who favor WWJ argue that it was the first station to actually get on the air when wireless restrictions were lifted after World War I.

Initial Programs

Between 1920 and 1924, WWJ aired the first news program, the first election returns (a Michigan race in the summer of 1920), the first complete symphony broadcast, the first regularly scheduled religious broadcast, and the first sports broadcast. The early sports broadcasting duties for WWJ were handled by Ty Tyson, later credited with being the world's first radio sports broadcaster. He got his job at WWJ through an orchestra leader whose band was invited to play on WWJ. Tyson was hired to do weather reports but went on to do sports and live interviews with celebrities such as Charles Lindbergh and Will Rogers. In 1924 he broadcast the first college football game and the Gold Cup powerboat races. On 19 April 1927 Tyson became the first radio sports broadcaster to do a regular season major league baseball game. He was also known for his ability to communicate the essence of the game even when he was not physically present. When the Detroit Tigers played out of town before direct radio lines became common, a telegraph operator in the opponent's park would tap out coded play-by-play messages to Tyson back in Detroit. Tyson would decode the taps and broadcast the plays as if he were seeing them himself.

Later Years

By the mid-1970s, WWJ radio was moving to an all-news format. In 1978 the *Washington Post* acquired WWJ-TV from the Evening News Association. In exchange the Evening News Association acquired WTOP, a Washington, D.C. television station owned by the *Washington Post*. The station

trade followed speculation about forthcoming FCC rules banning local market cross-ownership. The Evening News Association kept WWJ radio. In 1985 the Gannett Company announced that it would sell five broadcast properties to satisfy FCC rules affecting its proposed $717 million purchase of the Evening News Association in Detroit. (FCC rules at the time prohibited companies from owning newspapers and broadcast properties in the same city.) The broadcast properties in Detroit that were to be sold included WWJ radio. WWJ was purchased by Federal Broadcasting, but in March of 1989 the Columbia Broadcasting System (CBS) announced that it had acquired WWJ and its sister station WJOI from Federal Broadcasting for $58 million. WWJ and WJOI continue to be a part of the CBS news family, even though the network has been through several ownership changes, and WWJ remains the only commercial all-news radio station in Michigan.

Baudino, Joseph E., and John M. Kittross, "Broadcasting's Oldest Stations: An Examination of Four Claimants," *Journal of Broadcasting* 21 (Winter 1977).
Baulch, Vivian M., "The Stars Who Turned Detroiters into Couch Potatoes," detnews.com/history/tvhist/tvhist.htm
Bradford, Doug, "Elton M. Plant, Pioneer Voice of Fledgling Radio Station WWJ," *Detroit News* (5 January 1992).
Eden, David, "New Owner Takes over WWJ-TV with 'Sign-on'," *Detroit News* (26 June 1978).
McFarlin, Jim, "Radio's First Voice Gets a Hero's Welcome," *Detroit News* (21 August 1980).
Plant, Elton M., *Radio's First Broadcaster: An Autobiography*, n.p.: Plant, 1989.
"Ty Tyson, the World's First Sports Broadcaster," www.detroitnews.com/history/tyson/tyson.htm

RICK SYKES

WWL

New Orleans, Louisiana Station

The first radio station in the lower Mississippi Valley, WWL has long provided a 50,000-W clear channel voice to one of America's most culturally distinctive cities, serving as a window on New Orleans for much of the nation. This powerful commercial radio station was owned and operated through most of its history by a Jesuit university.

Origins

From the opening of Loyola University of New Orleans in 1914, its physics department offered courses in "wireless telegraphy." By 1922, after several years of accumulating radio equipment to support its curriculum and two years after the U.S. debut of regular broadcasting, Loyola established WWL radio. Although the goals outlined for the station included some educational, cultural, and public service programs (the latter in the form of weather and agricultural reports for farmers), WWL was intended first and foremost to serve as a fundraising tool for the private university. The station's first broadcast, on 31 March 1922, was a direct appeal for funds by the university president. Not only were listeners urged to contribute to a $1.5 million campaign for the construction of six new classroom buildings, but also they were urged to spread word of the university's financial needs to those not fortunate enough to own radio receiving sets.

WWL's first two years saw it off the air more than on. Once the initial enthusiasm wore off, live, original programs became burdensome to produce. The fund-raising appeals were not having the desired effect; the station cost more to operate than it was bringing in. The original 100 W of operating power was reduced to 10 W in an effort to cut costs. This only served to diminish further the station's broadcast range and fund-raising potential.

The station seemed doomed in 1924, when a new physics faculty decided to attempt resuscitation. Committing to a reliable if extremely modest broadcast schedule of one hour per week, WWL's power was increased in increments over the next few years to 500 W. In an effort to find a safe haven from the rampant interference problems of the era, the station moved up the radio dial, from 833.3 kc, to 1070 kc, to 1090 kc, and finally up to 1220 kc.

The Federal Radio Commission permitted WWL to increase its power to 5,000 W, but the Commission moved the station back down the dial to 850 kc, a frequency that it was forced to share with KWKH of Shreveport, Louisiana, a city 350 miles northwest of New Orleans—the stations were too close to both be on the air at the same time. KWKH was owned by W.K. Henderson, a social activist who used his station to broadcast his political views. For the next several years, WWL's growing program schedule had to be squeezed into a complicated time-sharing arrangement with Henderson. Depending on the time of day or day of the week, radio listeners tuning in to 850 kc would hear either WWL's classical music and lectures or Henderson's political harangues.

In 1929 the administration at Loyola made a pivotal decision: the university's goals would be best served if WWL operated as a money-making commercial enterprise, thus providing a continuing endowment to the university. Educational and religious programming, with few exceptions (such as the long-running *Mass from Holy Name Church*), gave way to popular entertainment. However, for WWL to realize its full revenue-producing potential, it needed the reliable source of quality programs that only affiliation with one of the major networks could provide. Although WWL was the most powerful radio station in New Orleans (reaching 10,000 W in 1932), the networks were not interested in a part-time affiliate. As long as it was saddled with the KWKH time-sharing arrangement, WWL would have to continue producing most of its own programming. To this end, Loyola moved the station from the university campus to new studios in New Orleans' Roosevelt Hotel in 1932.

In 1934, KWKH moved to 1100 kc, and WWL achieved full-time status. With this hurdle cleared, negotiations regarding network affiliation could begin in earnest. WWL joined the Columbia Broadcasting System (CBS) on 2 November 1935 with a live, one-hour network show entitled *A City of Contrasts*, which dramatized events from New Orleans history.

The year 1937 saw the debut of *Dawnbusters*, a local morning show featuring live music and comedy. The program would be one of the most popular in WWL's history, running until 1959. In 1938 WWL reached the maximum permissible power of 50,000 W, permitting its signal to cover much of eastern North America at night-time. President Franklin Roosevelt sent the station a congratulatory telegram, noting that the station's far-reaching signal "should be a source of great satisfaction to the Jesuit Fathers who have worked so assiduously building up the station from a small beginning. I trust that its future will be one of great usefulness in the service of God, of Home and of Country." In 1941, to comply with a treaty seeking to reduce interference throughout North America, WWL changed frequencies one final time to its current 870 kHz.

Postwar Change

After World War II, WWL, like all of the nation's AM radio broadcasters, faced a new set of options: expand into television and/or FM or stay the course with AM. WWL's initial decision was to move into FM and leave television to others. WWL's FM station, WWLH, went on the air in 1946. A halfhearted effort from the outset, WWLH mainly simulcast WWL programming. The public failed to buy FM receivers in sufficient quantities to make the enterprise viable, and WWLH went off the air in 1951.

Loyola now decided that television was the more valuable path, but between the Federal Communication Commission's (FCC) four-year freeze on new television licenses and a post-freeze battle with competing interests for the few channel allocations available to the New Orleans market, WWL-TV (channel 4) didn't become a reality until 1957.

With the advent of television and the decline of traditional radio network programming in the late 1950s, WWL's schedule became increasingly centered around local talk shows. WWL's present-day programming is dominated by live, local news programs; "topic of the day" phone-in shows; sporting events; and sports talk programs.

In the late 1980s, the Loyola administration decided to abandon broadcasting. WWL-AM and WWL-TV were sold to different companies, and, through a series of sales and mergers, the AM station has since changed owners several times. Its current ownership, Entercom Communications, holds seven other stations in New Orleans, including WSMB, a long-time National Broadcasting Company (NBC) radio network affiliate that, along with WWL and WDSU, once defined broadcasting in "the city that care forgot."

See also: KWKH

Further Reading

Pusateri, C. Joseph, *Enterprise in Radio: WWL and the Business of Broadcasting in America*, Washington, D.C.: University Press of America, 1980.

RICHARD WARD

WWVA

Wheeling, West Virginia Station

WWVA is the oldest station in West Virginia, and from early in its history it proved to be an important factor in the popularization of country music.

WWVA first aired on 13 December 1926. Founder John Stroebel, a physics teacher and for years an experimenter with crystal sets and wireless telephone, transmitted from his basement in Wheeling. The 50-W station was licensed to broadcast on 860 kHz.

Offering a menu of local information and entertainment, the station received permission to broadcast at 500 W in 1927. WWVA evolved quickly over the next five years. Stroebel sold the station to Fidelity Investments Associates in 1928, and the Federal Radio Commission raised the station's power to 5,000 W in 1929. "The Friendly Voice from out of the Hills of West Virginia" affiliated

with the Columbia Broadcasting System (CBS) in 1931, which helped to fill out the station's program schedule. In 1931 Fidelity Investments sold WWVA to George B. Storer, whose Fort Industry Company (later renamed Storer Broadcasting Company) would hold the license for three decades.

At the time, Storer was collecting a wide array of radio stations, which would make him one of the largest chain owners of radio stations. Under Storer's ownership, WWVA would see its most dramatic developments: the introduction in 1933 of the *Jamboree*, a regular Saturday night broadcast of country music, and the increase of the station's power to 50,000 W in 1941, just as the station moved to 1170 kHz.

The station had featured country music almost since its inception, but the debut of the *Jamboree* on 7 January 1933 would secure its prominent role in the popularization of country music. The show became an important stage for regional artists, whose reputations grew with every appearance, and when the station began broadcasting with 50,000 W, the *Jamboree* became a force in the dissemination of country music in the Ohio Valley and far beyond. WWVA sent the *Jamboree* and country music surging into 18 eastern states and six Canadian provinces during the night-time hours on Saturdays. Along with the *Grand Ole Opry* on WSM (Nashville), the *National Barn Dance* on WLS (Chicago), and the *Louisiana Hayride* on KWKH (Shreveport), the *WWVA Jamboree* was one of a number of widely heard barn dance radio shows that carried country music to large audiences around the nation.

Country music scholar Bill C. Malone (1985) has noted that although many of the barn dance radio programs were important in expanding country music's audience, the *Jamboree* did the most to carry country music to Northeast audiences and to help create new audiences in the Northeast and Canada for country music. The program also helped propel to national prominence the careers of a number of country and bluegrass artists. Artists who prospered from their exposure on the *Jamboree* included Grandpa Jones, Hank Snow, Hawkshaw Hawkins, Wilma Lee and Stoney Cooper, and Reno and Smiley. For a period in the mid-1950s, the CBS network carried the *Jamboree*, giving the program an even wider sphere of influence.

The *Jamboree* wasn't the only conduit for country music on WWVA. Starting in the 1950s, the station featured a popular overnight disc jockey program (hosted for many years by performer Lee Allen, "The Coffee Drinking Nighthawk") that covered the station's wide listening area, and in the

1960s, the station was among the first to adopt a "modern country" format, which featured the lush musical stylings popularized by performers such as Eddy Arnold and Jim Reeves.

WWVA, owned today by AM-FM Incorporated, dropped its all-country programming in 1997 in favor of a news/talk format. But the station's Saturday night country show survives; it is the second-longest-running country music stage show on radio, behind only WSM's *Grand Ole Opry*. *Jamboree U.S.A.*, as the barn dance is known today, still airs from Wheeling's Capitol Musical Hall, which first hosted the show in 1933 (although the show changed venues a number of times after its debut before returning to the Capitol in 1969).

See also: Country Music Format

Further Reading

Kingsbury, Paul, editor, *The Encyclopedia of Country Music*, New York: Oxford University Press, 1998.
Malone, Bill C., *Country Music U.S.A.*, Austin: University of Texas Press, 1968; revised edition, 1985.
Snow, Hank, Jack Ownbey, and Bob Burris, *The Hank Snow Story*, Urbana: University of Illinois Press, 1994.
Tribe, Ivan M., *Mountaineer Jamboree: Country Music in West Virginia*, Lexington: University Press of Kentucky, 1984.
"WWVA-Wheeling," *West Virginia Review* 23, no. 2 (Nov. 1945).

MICHAEL STREISSGUTH

WXYZ

Detroit, Michigan Station

Despite its comparatively remote Midwest location, WXYZ pioneered network radio and radio drama. The station and its *Lone Ranger* series were instrumental in the founding of the Mutual Broadcasting System.

Early Years

WXYZ began life on 10 October 1925 as WGHP, a Class B (medium power) station at 1270 kHz. This frequency was far enough removed from other Detroit stations to avoid serious interference. The WGHP call letters signified founding owner George Harrison Phelps, who had directed automobile advertising for Dodge since 1914. The station secured an affiliation with the fledgling Columbia Broadcasting System (CBS) in 1927 and moved its studios from an alley garage to the 15th floor penthouse of the Maccabees Building, near the Detroit Institute of Arts, and the new Detroit Public Library main branch. The station was a money-loser, however, and when Dodge was purchased by Chrysler Corporation in 192.8, Phelps' agency lost the Dodge account. To lessen the cash crunch, Phelps peddled WGHP to J. Harold Ryan and his brother-in-law George Storer, owners of profitable WSPD in Toledo, Ohio. In October 192.8 these two oil and steel magnates purchased WGHP for $40,000.

WGHP's airtime was now aggressively marketed in a variety of commercial lengths. Just 18 months later as the Depression was deepening, the Storer group sold the station for $250,000 to John Kunsky and George Trendle, owner and manager, respectively, of the Kunsky Theatres movie chain. In July 1930 the new owners unleashed a movie-business-like promotional campaign for their outlet, the call sign of which they also changed to WXYZ—call letters Trendle had persuaded the U.S. Army and Navy (separately) to relinquish. Programming now included *Carl Rupp and His Orchestra*, the first network show to originate from Detroit.

Trendle's background as a newsboy and lawyer and his grasp of management, promotion, and show-business would soon propel the station onto the national stage as he stocked WXYZ with exceptional executives, writers, and on-air talent. All of this potential was nearly discarded, however, when station management decided they were being forced to give up too much time—and therefore advertising revenues—to the Columbia Broadcasting System (CBS). At the end of 1931, WXYZ abruptly canceled its network affiliation and suddenly faced vast amounts of empty airtime for which programming quickly had to be found. Two studios now became four, rehearsals for one show cleared the studio only moments before the cast for another arrived to take the air, and announcers, actors, and musicians jostled each other in the narrow corridors.

Creating National Programs

The first network show to emerge from this creative chaos was *The Lone Ranger*, which debuted in January 1933 with scripts developed by Buffalo syndicated writer Fran Striker and a concept refined by George W. Trendle himself. Only days after the program's first broadcast, the Michigan Radio Network began linking stations in the state's major cities with WXYZ as the key outlet and *The Lone Ranger* as a centerpiece offering. By November the show was also airing over Chicago's WGN, and New York's WOR was added in early 1934. A few weeks later, the series was made available via transcription to stations in seven southern states under the sponsorship of American Bakeries. WXYZ's sales manager H. Allen Campbell then persuaded the general managers of WGN and WOR to expand their relationship into a program-sharing network that would feed multiple programs among their stations as well as to new partners in Cincinnati, Pittsburgh, St. Louis, and Washington, D.C. On 19 September 1934, the seven outlets were linked with telephone lines and became the Mutual Broadcasting System.

In the next year, WXYZ's partner stations began adding far more outlets to Mutual than Trendle thought wise. So while WXYZ continued to feed *The Lone Ranger* to Mutual, it joined the National Broadcasting Company (NBC) Blue Network to secure its own source of programming. In a successful attempt to repeat *The Lone Ranger*'s success, Trendle and Striker debuted *The Green Hornet* in early 1936.

WXYZ's success with these and other programs was recognized in 1937 by *Variety*'s award of its Citation for Showmanship in Program Origination, given each year to the station judged best in new show production. Three years later, to ensure continued access to the talent that made such distinctions possible, WXYZ became the first Detroit station to sign a contract with the American Federation of Radio Artists (AFRA). Future television news stars getting early experience on the station at this time included Douglas Edwards, Hugh Downs, and Myron Wallace, whose first name was changed by WXYZ executives to "Mike."

Postwar Transition

To enlarge its production space, the station moved in 1944 to the Mendelssohn mansion in suburban Grosse Pointe. WXYZ's continued success made it a desirable purchase for the former NBC Blue Network, which had become the separately owned American Broadcasting Company (ABC). ABC badly needed to upgrade its owned-and-operated station holdings, and WXYZ was among the most desirable of its affiliates. In April 1946 the sale was consummated. Key programs such as *The Lone Ranger* and *The Green Hornet* remained the property of George Trendle and long-time station sales executive H. Allen Campbell. The other former station owners, John Kunsky and Howard Pierce, cashed out of the business entirely. The sale of WXYZ marked the end for the Michigan Radio Network stations, which now received program feeds directly from ABC.

Despite wooing by rival WJR, WXYZ sales manager Jim Riddell accepted ABC's Trendle-brokered offer to stay on as the new general manager. A separately programmed WXYZ-FM went on the air on 1 January 1948 at 101.1 MHz, but before the end of the year it reverted to simulcasting the AM station signal. Meanwhile, WXYZ-TV had taken to the air from the Maccabees Building, under the direction of the radio operation's former wire recording technician John Pival. Pival lured some of the radio outlet's top personalities to the television side and the shift of dominance began. As happened around the country, the number of network radio shows withered, to be replaced by local disc jockeys. Chief among them on WXYZ were Paul Winter, Jack Surrell, Ed McKenzie, and Fred Wolf. *The Green Hornet* went off the air in 1952. *The Lone Ranger* hung on, but the last live broadcast was in 1954.

The radio station moved to a caretaker's cottage near the transmitter in 1955 while Fred Wolf's converted house trailer, the "Wandering Wigloo," became a vehicle for a hugely successful remote program; radio executives came from around the country to study the show. Unfortunately for Wolf and other program hosts, however, WXYZ embraced the Top 40 concept in 1958 and tight music formatting now overshadowed individual air personalities. In 1959 the WXYZ television and radio properties moved to the newly constructed suburban Broadcast House—in which radio was relegated to an obscure corner. Four years later, Charles Fritz, former manager of Blair Radio's Detroit office (the firm representing the station to national advertisers), became WXYZ's general manager, but the station's prominence continued to wane. Even though disc jockey Lee Alan's record hops were proving tremendously popular, the station subsequently lost its Detroit market dominance to WKNR (programmed by Mike Joseph). In the years that followed, a string of competitors would continue to beat both the AM and FM (which became the harder-rocking and separately owned WRIF in the 1980s) at the music game.

Fritz bought the AM from ABC in 1984, changed its call letters to WXYT, and thereby launched Detroit's first all-talk outlet. The WXYZ designation thus disappeared from radio but survived as the call letters of the formerly co-owned television station that was purchased by the Scripps Howard News Service in 1986. WRIF (the old WXYZ-FM) continued its mainstream rock format and ultimately was purchased by Greater Media. The AM facility that began it all was acquired by Infinity Broadcasting in 1994. Ironically, when Infinity subsequently merged with CBS, the station found itself owned by the same entity its first owners had unceremoniously jettisoned in 1931.

WXYZ

See also: Clear Channel Stations; *Green Hornet*; *Lone Ranger*; Mutual Broadcasting System;

Further Reading

Harmon, Jim, *The Great Radio Heroes*, Garden City, New York: Doubleday, 1967; 2nd edition, Jefferson, North Carolina: McFarland, 2001.

Lackman, Ronald W., *Remember Radio*, New York: Putnam, 1970.
Osgood, Dick, *WYXIE Wonderland: An Unauthorized 50–Year Diary of WXYZ Detroit*, Bowling Green, Ohio: Bowling Green University Popular Press, 1981.
Zier, Julie, "Fritz Selling Its Detroit AM-FM," *Broadcasting and Cable* (3 January 1994).

PETER B. ORLIK

Y

YANKEE NETWORK
New England Regional Network

The Yankee networkwas one of several regional radio networks from the 1930s into the 1950s that linked stations to share programs and advertising.

Although Boston broadcaster John Shepard III knew little about engineering, he knew enough to hire good people who did understand the technical side of the radio business. In early 1923 he encouraged them to experiment with networking (WNAC linked up briefly with New York's WEAF). It was not long before WNAC in Boston and WEAN in Providence, Rhode Island, were frequently sharing programming, connected by a telephone line. But Shepard wanted to expand: he had begun paying salaries to talented musicians so they would appear on his stations (early radio was still mainly volunteer, so being able to pay was a major plus in getting the big names to appear), and he felt confident he could offer good programs. When the National Broadcasting Company (NBC) and the Columbia Broadcasting System (CBS) were formed in 1926–27, Shepard was convinced that a local network which emphasized New England news, sports, and music would be well received. He called it the Yankee network, and by early in 1930 he had begun signing up a number of stations in New England. The first affiliates were WLBZ in Bangor, Maine; WNBH in New Bedford, Massachusetts; and WORC in Worcester, Massachusetts. In August 1932, *Broadcasting* magazine published a tribute to Shepard, noting that he now had eight affiliates, with number nine soon to go on the air. In 1939,

Shepard would put the first experimental FM station in Massachusetts (W1XOJ) on the air, and it too would carry Yankee network programming. By then, the network had its own house orchestra, a music director, staff vocalists, and a large number of talented performers who could offer the affiliates everything from a radio drama to an evening of hit songs. Always innovative, Shepard sometimes ran synagogue services on the Yankee network, as he would also run church services and sermons by well-known priests and ministers.

Perhaps his biggest innovation was with radio news: in March 1934, thanks in large part to the hard work of editor in chief Leland Bickford, the Yankee News network went on the air. In a jab at newspapers, the network used the slogan "News while it IS news; the Yankee Network is on the air!" A former Boston newspaper reporter, Dick Grant, was hired to run the news department at a time when relationships between radio and newspapers were becoming more contentious. Local newspaper reporters were not amused and tried to bar the network's reporters from getting press passes and covering city hall. But Shepard and his team persisted, and gradually radio reporters gained credibility and came to be accepted as journalists. The Yankee News network made "radio news reporter" a career choice: in radio's first decade, what little news radio stations offered came mainly from newspapers, many of which had agreements with a local station that allowed a reporter to go on the air several times a day with headlines and top stories. But for radio journalists to cover news and generate their own stories (the network even established a news bureau in Washington, D.C.) was something new, and it made the Yankee News network unique in New England.

One popular news program the Yankee network offered was *Names in the News* (late 1930s through early 1940s), in which local heroes and newsmakers were invited to talk about their achievements against a backdrop of Yankee network performers dramatizing the important events that made the guests famous. This was similar to the famous CBS program *The March of Time*, but with a New England emphasis. Such radio newsmagazines were very popular and helped make the news more interesting to the average person.

The more benefits the Yankee network offered, the more New England stations wanted to affiliate. By retaining their affiliation with a national network—which provided the major music, drama, and comedy programs—as well as the regional link, smaller stations benefited from the best of both worlds: professional-sounding local news coverage and access to the best-known national radio stars. By the early 1940s, the Yankee network had 19 affiliates. Shepard was becoming more involved with FM and was also active in Mutual Broadcasting. In late 1937 Bostonians had been shocked when he sold the Shepard Store in downtown Boston; the store in Providence still remained under Shepard family control, however. Shepard invested in technological improvements for his Boston stations—in early 1942, six new studios (for Shepard's AM stations, his FM stations, the Yankee network, and the Yankee News bureau) were dedicated; he was also attempting to organize a national FM network (this venture was not successful; his interest in FM was ahead of its time).

In late 1942 Shepard, rumored to have health problems that led him to sell off various assets, agreed to sell the Yankee network to the General Tire and Rubber Company, although he stayed on as a board member and general manager. (Later, in 1958, long after Shepard's death, the corporate ownership's name would change to RKO [Radio-Keith-Orpheum] General.) Shepard's poor health forced him to retire altogether from radio in 1948; he died two years later. The Yankee network acquired more affiliates and remained a major player in New England through the 1950s. But radio was changing: the youth market wanted Top 40, and news was not as important to that demographic. Affiliates began programming for the younger audience, and gradually they dropped the Yankee network to "play the hits." Although a few stations did remain faithful to the older audience,

allowing the Yankee network to survive into the 1960s, in early 1968, without much fanfare, RKO General disbanded the network, ending its 38 years of distinguished service.

See also: Don Lee Broadcasting System; FM Radio; Mutual Broadcasting System

Further Reading

Bickford, Leland, *News While It Is News: The Real Story of the Radio News*, with Walter Fogg, Boston: G.C. Manthorne, 1935.
"News While It Is News: Yankee Network Sets up Own 24 Hour Service," *Broadcasting* (15 March 1934).

DONNA L. HALPER

YOU BET YOUR LIFE
Comedy Quiz Show

Reruns have made Groucho Marx's *You Bet Your Life* familiar to generations of television viewers. Few fans realize that they are also "watching" radio. For six seasons of its 14-year run, the program was recorded simultaneously for both media. The versions were then edited separately and broadcast on successive nights. Its circumstances of production, editing, and broadcast were just one aspect of the show's distinctiveness. A comedy show masquerading as a quiz, *You Bet Your Life* was "postmodern" before the term was invented.

The origin of *You Bet Your Life* was the appearance by Groucho Marx on a radio variety show in April 1947, when an ad-lib by Groucho led to a verbal duel with Bob Hope that made the segment run many minutes over. Producer John Guedel (who had made Art Linkletter a radio success) immediately went backstage and suggested to Marx a quiz show with an emphasis on ad-libs. Groucho replied, "I've flopped four times on radio before. I might as well compete with refrigerators. I'll give it a try." *You Bet Your Life* premiered Monday, 27 October 1947, on the American Broadcasting Companies (ABC), then moved to Wednesday night as lead-in to Bing Crosby's popular variety show.

A success by any measure, *You Bet Your Life* secured for Groucho the career he sought apart from the Marx Brothers. It also made a celebrity of its announcer and Groucho's comic foil, George Fenneman. The first season sold out the entire stock of its sponsor, Elgin Watches. Groucho received a 1949 Peabody Award as best radio entertainer, with cover stories in *Newsweek* and

Time. Guedel and Marx moved *You Bet Your Life* in 1949 to the larger Columbia Broadcasting System (CBS) network for a longer, 45-week season. (The show continued to precede Bing Crosby's.) A year later, the National Broadcasting Company (NBC) won a bidding war to begin a televised version. The radio broadcasts moved to NBC in October 1950, where they remained in the Wednesday 9 P.M. timeslot. The televised version, recorded simultaneously but edited separately, aired a day later, on Thursdays. At the show's peak, in 1955, the broadcasts drew a combined audience of 35 million. The radio version folded late in 1956, with *You Bet Your Life* continuing on television until 1961.

Though its content was decidedly low-tech— Groucho interviewed contestants and asked simple quiz questions— *You Bet Your Life* was innovative in its production and delivery. *You Bet Your Life* pioneered a version of what became the "live on tape" approach adopted by television talk shows in the 1950s. Guedel's original intention to broadcast live was scrapped, apparently at the last minute, because of concerns about Groucho's ad-libs. The producers then procured acetate disks, of the kind used by Armed Forces Radio, which had the advantage of allowing content to be minimally edited. Later, the program was a pioneer in the use of magnetic tape. For a standard program, one hour of tape was edited down to 26 minutes. When the American Federation of Musicians in 1948 changed its policy to allow network radio shows to be prerecorded, *Daily Variety* attributed the "cry and hullabaloo for tape" to the influence of a single program, *You Bet Your Life.* With the debut of the televised version, the producers recognized the need for separate postproduction for different media. The Wednesday radio program and the Thursday television version were often quite different, to the extent of presenting different contestants because of time shifts during editing.

Ironically, neither version was the spontaneous fest of ad-libs originally conceived by Guedel and Marx. On the contrary, preproduction was as crucial to *You Bet Your Life* as its postproduction editing was. Groucho's writers were disguised in the program's credits, but most of his repartee was scripted. Room was left for spontaneity: for example, Marx declined to meet contestants beforehand, but his writers did extensive preinterviews with them. Genuine ad-libs were always a prospect: director Bernie Smith commented, "At his peak you could never write for this man." Nevertheless, the key was Groucho's ability to deliver scripted lines as if they were ad-libbed. Thus, to a tree

surgeon: "Have you ever fallen out of a patient?" To a cartoonist: "If you want to see a comic strip, you should see me in the shower." To a fat woman: "I bet you're a lot of fun at a party. In fact, you *are* a party." The remarks often had a cruel edge, but as writer Howard Harris observed, "If they weren't insulted, they were insulted."

Scripted ad-libs and edited "live" content were aspects of what might now be called the "postmodern" approach of this quiz show. *You Bet Your Life* was almost pure process, inverting the conventions of its ostensible genre. For example, introductory interviews with contestants, ordinarily perfunctory on quiz shows, occupied half the running time of Groucho's program. Contestants usually appeared in male–female couples—carefully paired to create possibilities for comic repartee—yet despite Groucho's standard compliment to "an attractive couple," they rarely knew each other. The quiz portion of the program was played straight: contestants began with $20 (later $100) and bet on four questions in a set category; the couple with the highest total for each program got a chance at a jackpot question for $1,000 (increased by $500 per week if nobody won). Nevertheless, prizes were never very important; in an era of big-money quiz shows (and scandal), *You Bet Your Life* awarded an average of $333 to 2,100 contestants over a decade. Besides, it was impossible *not* to win: if contestants blew the standard quiz, Groucho would ask a variation of the most famous of all quiz show questions: "Who's buried in Grant's Tomb?" Contestants could also win money accidentally, by speaking the previously announced "secret word."

Periodic journalistic exposes, such as *TV Guide's* 1954 "The Truth about Groucho's Ad Libs," had no effect whatever on his program's popularity. The audience knew they were listening to a comedy program in quiz show guise. If Groucho was funny, nobody cared that his quips were scripted and edited. *You Bet Your Life* presented a perfect match of star and vehicle. Later attempts to duplicate its success on television with Buddy Hackett and Bill Cosby failed. The show's opening audience-response formula turned out to be literally accurate: "Here he is—the one, the only— GROUCHO!"

Host

Groucho Marx

Announcer

George Fenneman, Jack Slattery

Producer/Directors

John Guedel, Bernie Smith, Bob Dwan

Writers

Ed Tyler, Hy Freedman, Howard Harris

Programming History

ABC   October 1947–May 1949
CBS   October 1941–June 1950
NBC   October 1950–September 1956

Further Reading

Arce, Hector, *Groucho*, New York: Putnam, 1979.
Marx, Groucho, and Hector Arce, *The Secret Word Is Groucho*, New York: Putnam, 1976.
Tyson, Peter, *Groucho Marx*, New York: Chelsea House, 1995.

GLEN M. JOHNSON

YOUR HIT PARADE
Musical Variety Program

Your Hit Parade reflected popular music trends of its era, especially the big band sound; the program also helped sell millions of Lucky Strike cigarettes. Yet despite its status as a Saturday night radio staple, *Your Hit Parade* underwent many changes over its long history, notably its continual shifting of length, its scheduled timeslot, and even its network.

Your Hit Parade emerged in early 1935 as the National Broadcasting Company (NBC) looked to fill its Saturday night schedule. The Rogers and Hart ballad "Soon" ranked as the number-one hit. This alliance between big band hits and Lucky Strike cigarettes would continue to define the style and shape of *Your Hit Parade*: as a generation of executives for the American Tobacco Company's Lucky Strike division correctly figured, the public would tune in to the cover versions of hit songs by unknowns, and so show costs would be low while retaining a broad-based appeal.

Although its Saturday night venue never changed, its lineup of announcers, orchestras, and singers surely did. For example, in 1937, when *Your Hit Parade* shifted to the Columbia Broadcasting System (CBS), out went the old talent, and in came the Lanny Ross Orchestra, with Barry Wood and Bonnie Baker as the leading vocalists. But in 1939, out went Ross, and in came the Mark Warnow Orchestra. Such shifts were frequent for the program. Its timeslot and length also varied over the

years. Starting times of 8 P.M., 9 P.M., and 10 P.M. were tried and retried, as running time fell from one hour, to 45 minutes, down to 30 minutes.

Generally the names of the *Your Hit Parade* vocalists and orchestras have been forgotten, with a few exceptions such as Dinah Shore, Frank Sinatra, and Doris Day. Sometimes, to boost ratings, American Tobacco brought in guest stars, including most notably W.C. Fields and Fred Astaire. Indeed, *Your Hit Parade* reached its peak during the World War II years when executives—in a rare spending spree—hired Frank Sinatra, and thus the CBS Radio Theater at Broadway and 53rd Street became the focus of young female fan attention. The theater, which held 1,200, filled with teenagers who roared as Sinatra rendered hits such as "Paper Doll," "You'll Never Know," "Long Ago and Far Away," and "I'll Be Seeing You." In January 1945 Sinatra's contract expired, and rather than pay a higher wage to this budding star, American Tobacco reverted to its low-cost approach. Sinatra would return in September 1946, bringing as his co-star former Les Brown Orchestra star Doris Day, but only temporarily.

If there was an omen of the impending end of radio's *Your Hit Parade*, it was surely when Mark Warnow, the show's longest orchestra leader, died in 1949, immediately after completing his 493rd *Your Hit Parade* broadcast. He was replaced by Raymond Scott, and it was Scott who led the show to television by hiring and developing Snooky Lanson, Dorothy Collins, and Russell Arms. Scott did not change the programming formula.

The constant was that both the radio and television versions featured relative unknowns reprising the most popular pop songs of the week as determined by a national "survey" of record and sheet music sales. (The methodology of this survey was never revealed, but it could hardly have been scientific, as it probably never went beyond calls to a few major city record stores and to the leading publishers of sheet music.) Repeated chart toppers were simply played again and again, with slight variations. "Race" music from and for African-Americans and "Hillbilly" music from and for rural and small-town whites was wholly ignored unless a version "crossed over" and was covered by a mainstream crooner or band. So although Texas western swing band Bob Wills and the Texas Playboys composed, created, and initially recorded "The New San Antonio Rose," it would be Bing Crosby's version that would make it onto *Your Hit Parade*. This Tin Pan Alley focus and inability to deal with the synthesis of Race and Hillbilly music that eventually led to rock and roll signaled the end of the formula and of *Your Hit Parade*—on both radio and television.

See also: Recordings and the Radio Industry

Cast

Vocalists (partial list)	Buddy Clark, Frank Sinatra, Joan Edwards, Freda Gibbson (later Georgia Gibbs), Lawrence Tibbett, Barry Wood, Jeff Clark, Eileen Wilson, Doris Day, Bonnie Baker, Andy Russell
Announcers (partial list)	Martin Block, Del Sharbutt, Andre Baruch, Kenny Delmar, Basil Ruysdael

Programming History

NBC	Spring 1935–Fall 1937
CBS	Fall 1937–Fall 1947
NBC	Fall 1947–Winter 1953

Further Reading

Buxton, Frank, and William Hugh Owen, *The Big Broadcast, 1920–1950*, New York: Viking Press, 1972.

DeLong, Thomas A., *The Mighty Music Box: The Golden Age of Musical Radio*, Los Angeles: Amber Crest, 1980.

Williams, John R., *This Was Your Hit Parade*, Camden, Maine: n.p., 1973.

DOUGLAS GOMERY

YOURS TRULY, JOHNNY DOLLAR
Drama Program

Yours Truly, Johnny Dollar was the last surviving network dramatic show after the inception of television. From 1949 to its demise in 1962, Johnny Dollar entertained those detective fans who had not yet been seduced by "the tube." *Yours Truly, Johnny Dollar* and *Suspense* were the last two original radio dramatic series produced for the Columbia Broadcasting System (CBS), and they ended their run on 30 September 1962.

The radio series recounted the detective cases of Johnny Dollar, "America's fabulous freelance insurance investigator." He would often receive his assignments from Pat McCracken of the Universal Adjustment Bureau, a clearinghouse for several insurance firms. Hartford, Connecticut, the headquarters for many major insurance companies, was his home base, but his assignments took him all over the world. His investigations of such matters

as stolen jewels, paintings, or furs; missing persons; and insurance fraud of various types would inevitably lead to a murder investigation and an encounter with the criminal element. However, Johnny Dollar could take care of himself; he could be as hard-boiled as the toughest detective. His wisecracking betrayed a cynical attitude, and his encounters with women certainly resulted in some suggestive language.

Johnny Dollar was a confirmed bachelor, although he did have a girlfriend, Betty Lewis, who appeared occasionally. He was basically a loner, and each story was told from his firstperson point of view. "Dollar" was a metaphor for the detective's interest in money. Described as the detective "with the action-packed expense account," he tallied each and every expenditure, no matter how small. Each show concluded with the revelation of his total expenses, as if dictating a memorandum to his employer, before he signed off with "yours truly, Johnny Dollar."

The series premiered on 11 February 1949 with a 30-minute episode entitled "The Parakoff Policy," in which the insured was being held for the murder of Mr. Parakoff. Johnny Dollar's encounter with Parakoff's widow allowed for some suggestive dialog. Paul Dudley and Gil Doud wrote the pilot script for the series, and actor Dick Powell auditioned for the title role on 8 December 1948, but he went on to star in *Richard Diamond, Private Detective* instead. Charles Russell was the first of six radio actors to play Johnny Dollar on the air. Russell played the role as the stereotypical hard-boiled investigator with his own little quirks, such as flipping silver dollars to hotel bellboys.

Russell played the role of Johnny Dollar for one year, through 34 half-hour episodes. Edmond O'Brien assumed the role in February 1950, starring in 103 episodes until September 1952, and John Lund continued in the role for the next two years, starring in 92 episodes through September 1954, when the show was canceled, probably because of a lack of sponsorship. Most often the shows were broadcast on a sustaining basis. Wrigley's gum had the longest continuous sponsorship, from 10 March 1953 to 10 August 1954.

Yours Truly, Johnny Dollar returned to the air in October 1955 with a new format, star, and producer/writer/director. Instead of the 30-minute series format, the show moved to a serial format, with five 15-minute episodes per week. The listeners seemed to like this format because it allowed more time for story and character development—75 minutes each week, including commercials or other promotional material, of course. They liked the new star as well. Bob Bailey played Johnny Dollar as a more caring and less cynical and hardboiled investigator. Bailey's portrayal made the hero seem more human, but nevertheless a tough and smart detective. Gerald Mohr, who had played the lead in *The Adventures of Philip Marlowe*, made an audition tape on 29 August 1955, but it never aired. Jack Johnstone, who was responsible for the new directions in the program, began producing and directing the show at this time, and he contributed several scripts before the series ended in 1962.

Bailey played in 55 of these weekly serials before November 1956, when CBS reverted back to the original 30-minute, once-a-week format. Continuing until 27 November 1960, Bailey played in 203 episodes, more than any other star of the series. At that time, the show was moved from Hollywood, where it had been produced from its beginning, to New York City. Robert Readick assumed the role on 4 December 1960 and played in 28 episodes until 11 June 1961, when Mandel Kramer took the part. Kramer played Johnny Dollar for 69 episodes until the series ended with the last case, "The Tip-Off Matter," on 30 September 1962.

Cast

Johnny Dollar   Charles Russell (1949–50), Edmond O'Brien (1950–52), John Lund (1952–54), Bob Bailey (1955–60), Robert Readick (1960–61), Mandel Kramer (1961–62)

Directors

Richard Sanville, Norman Macdonnell, Gordon Hughes, Jaime del Valle, Jack Johnstone, Bruno Zirato, Jr., Fred Hendrickson

Writers

Gil Doud, Paul Dudley, David Ellis, John M. Hayes, E. Jack Neuman, Les Crutchfield, Blake Edwards, Morton Fine, David Friedkin, Sidney Marshall, Joel Murcott, John Dawson, Jack Johnstone, Robert Ryf

Programming History

CBS   February 1949–September 1962

Further Reading

Dunning, John, *Tune in Yesterday: The Ultimate Encyclopedia of Old-Time Radio, 1925–1976*, Englewood Cliffs, New Jersey: Prentice-Hall, 1976; revised edition, as *On the Air: The Encyclopedia of Old-Time Radio*, New York: Oxford University Press, 1998.

Maltin, Leonard, *The Great American Broadcast: A Celebration of Radio's Golden Age*, New York: Dutton, 1997.

Widner, James F., "Yours Truly, Johnny Dollar," www.otrsite.com/articles/widner002.html

Wright, Stewart, "Johnny Dollar," www.thrillingdetective.com/dollar_johnny.html

PHILIP J. LANE

Z

ZENITH RADIO CORPORATION
Radio and Electronics Manufacturer

Zenith Radio Corporation, now Zenith Electronics Corporation, was the longest-surviving American-owned consumer electronics corporation. Founded in 1919 as Chicago Radio Laboratory, Zenith manufactured a wide range of electronic products for 80 years and continues to be one of the most respected and widely known American names in consumer electronics. The United States-based company has been a wholly owned subsidiary of Korean electronics giant LG Electronics since late 1999.

Under the guidance of founding genius "Commander" Eugene F. McDonald, Jr., and innovative financial manager Hugh Robertson, Zenith grew from its beginnings on a kitchen table on Chicago's North Side to a leadership position in radio and, along with archrival Radio Corporation of America (RCA), to continued dominance in the postwar television boom. Along the way, Zenith and McDonald made significant contributions to the very form of the consumer electronics and broadcasting industries. Zenith is best known for the high quality and reliability of its products and its innovative concepts in product development and marketing.

Origins

The founders of what was to become Zenith Radio Corporation were two radio amateurs, Ralph H.G. Matthews and Karl Hassel. Matthews built his first amateur station in Chicago in 1912. In 1913 and 1914 he perfected a distinctive aluminum sawtooth

rotary spark gap disk that later became the company's first product. Matthews also became heavily involved in the newly formed Amateur Radio Relay League (ARRL), and in 1917 his radio call sign was changed to 9ZN. While serving as a radioman at the Great Lakes Naval Training Station at the end of World War I, he met a radio code instructor, Karl Hassel. Upon release from the navy, the two entered into a partnership producing first the aluminum spark gap transmitting disk and then other amateur equipment. They were soon producing complete receivers and transmitters of their own design. Operating as the Chicago Radio Laboratory, the two quickly outgrew their manufacturing space at 1316 Carmen Avenue (actually Matthew's house) and moved into half of a garage on Sheridan Road, on the lakeside grounds of the Edgewater Beach Hotel. The other half of the garage served as the home of 9ZN, one of the best-known amateur stations in the United States. Because their equipment was built for the radio amateur, the earliest advertising was placed in *QST*, the magazine of the American Radio Relay League. By late 1921 *QST* advertisements listed the 9ZN call followed by a small "ith," the origin of the trade name Z-Nith.

In 1921 Eugene F. McDonald became involved with the Chicago Radio Laboratory. McDonald was a savvy businessman who was looking for a business investment when he discovered Matthews, Hassel, and radio. McDonald offered to become a financial partner in their undertaking, and a partnership was formed, with McDonald as the general manager. A period of rapid growth followed.

As demand for the product increased in the spring of 1922, McDonald engaged his friend Tom Pletcher, a well-known figure in the music industry and president of the QRS Music Company, to take over the sales and manufacturing of CRL receivers in his large (and partially empty) new factory. By July, production had reached 15 sets per day.

Because the Armstrong receiver circuit patent was licensed to the Chicago Radio Laboratory, which produced Z-Nith products, McDonald formed Zenith Radio Corporation to become the marketing arm for the Z-Nith radios. The corporation was founded on 30 June 1923 with capital of $500,000 derived from common stock sold at $10 per share.

McDonald's Zenith

In 1923 McDonald built one of Chicago's pioneer radio stations, WJAZ, to stay in contact with the 1923–24 MacMillan Arctic Expedition, which was carrying Zenith radio equipment. The experiment was successful, allowing the expedition to be the first to maintain contact with civilization during the long polar night and generating considerable publicity for the small radio company.

McDonald also equipped the 1925 MacMillan Arctic Expedition with Zenith shortwave equipment. That expedition was the first to use shortwave in the Arctic and the first to fly heavier-than-air craft in the Arctic; it was also Richard Byrd's first introduction to the polar regions. McDonald accompanied the expedition as second-in-command, and the Zenith equipment performed flawlessly. Experimental shortwave communications from the expedition in North Greenland to U.S. Navy vessels in New Zealand played a seminal role in the adoption of shortwave radiofor long-distance communications.

McDonald's work with WJAZ highlighted for him emerging problems with the American Society of Composers, Authors, and Publishers (ASCAP) over royalties for performers whose music was played on the radio. Dissatisfied with the arbitrary nature of ASCAP's rate schedules, McDonald organized a meeting of a small group of broadcasters in Chicago in early 1923 to oppose ASCAP; this organization was to become the National Association of Broadcasters, with McDonald serving as its first president.

By the end of 1924, the production rate at the QRS factory could not keep up with increasing demand, and Zenith resumed manufacturing its own products in a new four-storey plant on Iron Street in Chicago.

In 1925, Zenith introduced the grandest Zenith radio models the company had ever manufactured,

the ten-tube Deluxe receivers. There were five cabinet styles, each handmade: the Colonial, the English, the Italian, the Chinese, and the Spanish. The price for these models ranged from $650 to $2,000 ($5,800 to $21,400 in 2000 dollars) and were the most expensive radios being manufactured at that time. They illustrated the company's commitment to building the very best equipment, regardless of cost.

McDonald became embroiled in another broadcasting battle in 1926, when his WJAZ shifted ("jumped") to another frequency, seeking a less-congested channel, but also challenging the authority of the Secretary of Commerce to assign radio frequencies. On 16 April 1926, the case was decided in federal court in McDonald's favor (*United States v. Zenith Radio Corporation*, 1926), proving finally that the existing frequency allocation laws, dating to 1912, were unenforceable and that the secretary lacked authority.

Zenith Radio Corporation was first listed on the Chicago Stock Exchange in March 1928 and on the New York Stock Exchange in July 1929. Stockholders increased from 250 in April 1928 to 2,750 in April 1929. Fiscal year 1929 earnings exceeded $1 million.

When the stock market crashed in 1929, Zenith found itself with a large inventory of materials to build new sets, but not many finished sets, primarily because of an innovative inventory control plan. That, and the selling of 100,000 shares of stock (worth $1 million) just before the market collapsed, enabled Zenith, with proper management, to ride out the rough times without missing loan payments, borrowing money, or releasing large numbers of employees. The company continued to manufacture high-quality, high-priced radios during the Depression but also added a less expensive line, the Zenette series, to appeal to the average buyer.

Recovery for Zenith began in 1933 when deficits, which had been running at about $500,000 a year, were converted into a $50,000 profit for the fiscal year ending 30 April 1934. At the beginning of 1934, Zenith was the lowest-priced radio stock quoted on the New York Stock Exchange; by the end of 1934, it was the highest. The Depression recovery assumed spectacular proportions for Zenith in 1935, when net earnings returned to the pre-Depression high of just over $1 million. Zenith also undertook major efforts to maintain its distributors' profit margins during the rough times, and Zenith emerged from the Depression with a fiercely loyal band of distributors who would serve the corporation admirably for many decades in the boom ahead.

In 1937 Zenith supplemented its factory space with the addition of the 400,000-square-foot West Dickens Avenue facility. In 1937 the radio industry as a whole showed a 15 percent drop, but Zenith's sales rose. New developments prior to World War II included the chairside radio-phonograph; a "Radio Nurse" baby monitor; and a line of portable radios, including the venerable Zenith Trans-Oceanic radio, which would go on to become the longest lasting radio brand in radio history. By 1938 most Zenith radios contained the Zenith-patented "Wavemagnet" antenna.

The ensuing years were marked by steady progress. The Zenith experimental television station, W9XZV, began operating in black and white in February 1939 and began color transmissions in 1941.

Because of the war, all domestic production stopped on 1 April 1942. Zenith's war efforts centered on development and production of sophisticated frequency meters, work on the V-T proximity fuse, and military-grade radio communications devices. It was through Zenith's efforts that most manufacturers, except RCA, granted the government free license under all patents covering war work. Zenith was awarded the Army-Navy "E" in November 1942, the first of five it would receive. Zenith was given special permission to manufacture only one civilian product during the war years, an inexpensive hearing aid that allowed the hard-of-hearing to be gainfully employed in war work.

Postwar Radio

Zenith planned for the resumption of civilian production in the closing years of the war and was among the earliest to attain volume production after the war. In 1945 Zenith began production of many of its own components, such as loudspeakers, record changers, and coils. The company was also an important early manufacturer of FM receivers. In 1947 Zenith introduced the "Cobra" phonograph arm. In 1948 the company introduced turret tuning for television, allowing the expansion of the tuner for future UHF reception. Zenith acquired television tube manufacturer Rauland Corporation in 1948 and in 1949 introduced the first "black tube" television sets, which quickly became the industry standard. In 1950 Zenith stopped manufacturing automobile radios, in spite of excellent sales, to provide space for the rapidly expanding television business. The continuously variable speed (10–85-rpm) Cobra-Matic record changer was introduced in 1950.

Major expansion of manufacturing occurred again in 1950–51, when a large facility in Chicago was acquired for television production and for Korean War military contracts. The removal of the television station "freeze" in 1952 greatly stimulated the company's television business, and the Zenith turret tuner made Zenith the only sets in production that could be easily converted to UHF. In the fall of 1953 Zenith introduced a three-transistor hearing aid, the first of many solidstate models to follow. By 1954 Zenith was selling more hearing aids than all other companies combined, and their dominance of the industry continued through the 1970s. Zenith entered the high-fidelity market in 1953 and was among the first to provide high-fidelity sound for television receivers. The ultrasonic Zenith "Space Command" remote TV control was introduced in 1956. Zenith's founder, Eugene F. McDonald, Jr., died in 1958.

By the mid-1970s, because of increasing competitive pressures from offshore (mostly Asian) manufacturers of radio and television, Zenith established its own manufacturing operations in Mexico and Taiwan, while forging an alliance with LG Electronics to build Zenith-brand clock radios in Korea. While growing its television business and venturing into new areas such as VCRs and cable set-top boxes, Zenith continued to play a role in transistor and portable radios and in component and console stereos until the company phased out its radio and audio products business in 1982 to concentrate on television and other video-related products. That year, the last of the legendary Trans-Oceanic radios was produced, marking the completion of the four-decade reign of that famous series of multiband shortwave radios.

Still facing tough competition from overseas, in the 1990s the company decided to concentrate on the manufacture of HDTVs and other high-end consumer electronics. However, demand for these items at the time was too limited and Zenith struggled for solvency, posting growing losses before closing its last American factory in 1998 and filing for bankruptcy the following year. It emerged in November 1999 as a wholly owned subsidiary of the Korean manufacturer, LG. Today, Zenith outsources most of its manufacturing, much to LG factories. Its former northern Illinois headquarters in Glenview, Illinois—which once employed over 5,000 workers—has also been shuttered and relocated to a far more modest facility in suburban Lincolnshire.

See also: National Association of Broadcasters; Receivers

Further Reading

Bensman, Marvin, "The Zenith-WJAZ Case and the Chaos of 1926–27," *Journal of Broadcasting* 14, no. 4 (Fall 1970).

Bryant, John H., and Harold N. Cones, *The Zenith Trans-Oceanic: The Royalty of Radios*, Atglen, Pennsylvania: Schiffer, 1995.

Bryant, John H., and Harold N. Cones, *Dangerous Crossings: The First Modern Polar Expedition, 1925*, Annapolis, Maryland: Naval Institute Press, 2000.

Cones, Harold N., and John H. Bryant, *Eugene F. McDonald, Jr.: Communications Pioneer Lost to History*, Record of Proceedings, 3rd International Symposium on Telecommunications History, Washington, D.C.: Independent Telephone Historical Foundation, 1995.

Cones, Harold N., and John H. Bryant, *Zenith Radio, The Early Years: 1919–1935*, Atglen, Pennsylvania: Schiffer, 1997.

Cones, Harold N., and John H. Bryant, "The Car Salesman and the Accordion Designer: Contributions of Eugene F. McDonald, Jr., and Robert Davol Budlong to Radio," *Journal of Radio Studies* 8, no. 1 (Spring 2001).

Douglas, Alex, "Zenith," in *Radio Manufacturers of the 1920s*, by Douglas, vol. 3, Vestal, New York: Vestal Press, 1991.

Zenith Radio Corporation, *The Zenith Story: A History from 1919*, Chicago: Zenith Radio Corporation, 1955.

HAROLD N. CONES AND JOHN H. BRYANT,
2009 REVISIONS BY CARY O'DELL

Index

Numbers in bold refer to main entries

Bell Telephone System 49–50; chains, growth of 51; light emiting diode (LED) 52; Long Lines Division 51; Marconi Company 49–50; mults 51; non-emanating outputs (NEMO) 51; Private Line Services 51–52; radio networking, birth of 50; technical developments 52; terminal block 51; WEAF 50–51; Western Union 50; Westinghouse 50

American Top 40 **52–53**, 53; AMFM Networks 53; *Casey's Top 40* 52, 53; hosts 53; K-B Productions 53; popular music 52; *Rick Dees' Weekly Top 40* 52, 53

American Urban Radio Networks (AURN) 21

American Women in Radio and Television (AWRT) **53–54**; *Broadcasting and Telecasting* 54; Educational Foundation 54; function 54; services 54

Americans for Radio Diversity 15

America's Town Meeting of the Air **55–56**; African-Americans in radio 19; announcers 56; contraversial issues 55–56; moderator 56; public affairs 55; Readers Digest 55; "Which Way for America – Communism, Fascism, Socialism, or Democracy?" 55

Ames, Ed 3

Ames, Leon 242

Amirkanian, Charles 412

Amos, Deborah 506, 507

Amos 'n' Andy **56–61**, 357, 359; announcers 60; automobile radio 88; chainless chain to network 57–58; depression era 58–59; directional change 59; drama of plots 58; Hollywood and radio 365; human foibles on display 58; impact 58; minstrel-style 58; *Music Hall* 59; NAACP 59; racial subtext 59; ratings 59; *Sam 'n' Henry* 57; stereotypes 58, 728; storylines 58; tensions between lead characters 58; transition 57; WGN 57; WMAQ 57

Ampex audiotape 83, 84

amplitude 78

Amrhein, Jack 710

Amsterdam, Morey 113

analog processors 78

Andersen, Hans Christian 421

Anderson, Arthur 421

Anderson, Eddie 101, 229

Anderson, Jon 217

Anderson, Marian 101, 229

Anderson, Marion 18

Anderson, Marjorie 690

Anderson, Maxwell 562, 766

Anderson, Robert 242

Anderson, Sam W. 112, 398

Anderson, Sherwood 562, 806

André, Pierre 144, 428, 581

Andrews, Clark 689

Andrews, Dana 232

Andrews, Robert D. 231

Andrews, Robert Hardy 382, 383, 444

Andrews, Stanley 428

Andrews, William 545

Andrews Sisters 478

The Andrews Sisters Program 36

Angle, Jim 450

Anheuser Busch 37

Anka, Paul 708, 778

Annenberg, M.L. 278

antenna **64–66**; AM radio 64; Electronic Industries Alliance 64; Federal Aviation Administration (FAA) 65; FM radio 64–65; HD radio 65; microwave 65; reception antennas 65; shortwave 65; television receive-only (TVRO) 65

Anthony, Allan C. 417

Anthony, Earle C. 399, 401

Anthony, John 441

Anthony, Susan B. 134

Antony, William E. 418

A&P Gypsies 356, 728, 800

Aplon, Boris 131, 428

Apostolides, Penelope 605

Aptheker, Herbert 552

Arbitron Company **66–69**; A.C. Nielsen Company 2, 3, 66, 67, 68; advertising 10; all night radio and PPMs 28; American Research Bureau (ARB) 66–67, 68; Area of Dominant Influence (ADI) 67; Audimeter (A.C. Nielsen) 76; Committee for Economic and Industrial Research (CEIR) 68; media research 66; Nielsen Station Index 66; PPM samples 68; Pretesting Company 68; Radio Marketing Research 66; radio ratings 67; ratings innovation 67–68; RKO Radio 67; Statistical Research Inc. 66; total survey area (TSA) 67; Videodex 66

Archer, Don 814

Archer, John 690

archives *see* museums and archives of radio; old-time radio

Arden, Eve 545, 546, 735

Area of Dominant Influence (ADI) 67

Arent, Arthur 136

Arkie, the Arkansas Woodchopper 497

Arlen, Harold 663

Arlin, Harold W. 397, 715

Arliss, George 861

Armani, Carl 542

Armed Forces Radio Service (AFRS): African-Americans in radio 19; audiotape 83; sports on radio 715; transistor radios 778; *You Bet Your Life* 889

Armen, Kay 36

Armour Research Foundation 82

Arms, Russell 890

Armstrong, Ben 511

Armstrong, Edwin Howard 300, 301, 347, 348, 733

Armstrong, Jack 382

Armstrong Awards 89

The Army Hour 19

Army-McCarthy hearings (1954) 785

Arnheim, Rudolf 526, 535, 702

Arnold, Eddy 884

Arnold, Elizabeth 507

Arthur, Charline 95

Arthur, Jean 441

Arthur Godfrey Time 749

Arthur Godfrey's Talent Scouts 36, 746

Asch, Moses 388

Ashenhurst, Anne S. 231

Asian Broadcasting 776

Asner, Ed 389

Associated Press (AP) 26, 523, 785, 842

Astaire, Fred 890

Atkins, Chet 330

Atlass, H. Leslie 825

Auden, W.H. 568

audience **69–70**; AM-FM 70; declining listening levels 70; depression era 69; listening peaks 70; radio audience before television 69; radio since television 69–70; *War of the Worlds* 69

audience participation *see* quiz and audience participation programs

audience research methods **71–75**; American Research Bureau 72; Audimeter (A.C. Nielsen) 72; Census

demographics **202–5**; audience definition 202; demographic factors 204; format approaches 204–5
DeMott, Benjamin 704
Dempsey, Jack 627, 714
Denker, Henry 136
Dennis, Lawrence 55
Dennis, Paul 808
Denny, James 330
Denny Jr., George V. 55, 56, 604
Denver, John 708
depression era: advertising in 6; *Amos 'n' Andy* 58–59; audience 69; Hollywood and radio 364–66; KTRH, Houston 417; soap opera 701; syndication 741
deregulation of radio **205–8**; continuing deregulation (1980–2000) 206–7; deregulation (21st century) 207; old rules, elimination of 205; Radio Deregulation Proceeding (1978–81) 206
Deskey, Donald 637
DeSuze, Carl 827
Dewey, Cheetham and Howe 132
Dewey, Thomas 259, 260, 573
Dewing, Harold 578
Diamond, Dave 401
Diamond, Neil 708
diary **208–10**; advantages 209; Arbitron diaries 208–9; audience research tool 72, 208; revival 209–10
Dick, Elsie 269
Dickinson, Emily 569
DiFranco, Ani 321
digital audio broadcasting (DAB) **210–13**; analog replacement 210; automobile radio 88; basics 210–11; HD radio, rolling out of 212; IBOC 211–12
Digital Millennium Copyright Act (1996) 81
digital protection: American Federation of Musicians (AFM) 44; American Federation of Television and Radio Artists (AFTRA) 45
digital recording **213–16**; basics 213–14; compact discs 214–15; computer-based recording 215–16; digital audio, superiority of 213; digital audio processing 216; digital audio tape 215; digital distribution, computer-based 215–16; mini disc recording 215; portable revolution 216; radio and portable revolution 216
digital satellite radio **216–20**; box in car or home 219; broadcast opposition 218; local radio, impact on 219–20; profitability 217; Sirius Corporation *versus* XM Corporation 216–17; worldwide satellite radio 217–18; XM Corporation *versus* Sirius Corporation 216–17
Dill, Senator Clarence C. 669, 784
Dillinger, John 318
Dineen, Art 29
Dion, Celine 4, 459
Dione Sextuplets 651
DIR Broadcasting 404
Disney, Walt 38, 39
Dixie Chicks 659
Dixon, Franklin W. 142
Dobson, Dr. James 511, 678
The Doctor Fights 365
documentary programs **220–24**; post-1950 developments 223–24; postwar developments 223
Dolan, Ken and Daria 751, 868
Dolbear, Amos 239, 240
Dolby noise reduction (NR) **224–26**; audio processing 78; companding process 224; digital signals, noise reduction in 225–26; radio applications 225
Dole, Senator Bob 810

Domino, Fats 540, 796
Don Lee Broadcasting System **226–27**; pioneering TV 226–27; postwar decline 227
Donahue, Raechel 29
Donahue, Tom "Big Daddy" 311, 595, 779, 780
Donald, Peter 129
Donaldson, Dan 444
Donaldson, Sam 880
Donnelley, T. 489, 490
Donzelet, Jacques 705
Doolittle, General James H. 870
The Doors 596
Dorr, Wendy 768
Dorrough Electronics 79
Dorsey, Tommy 479, 681, 801
Doud, Gil 891
Doug Banks Show 797
Douglas, Don 372
Douglas, Justice 667
Douglas, Paul 383
Douglas, Susan J. 170, 231, 705
Douglas, Van 18
Dove, Rita 570
Downey Jr., Morton 160, 170
Downs, Edward 458
Downs, Hugh 462, 520, 885
Dr. Dre 809, 810
The Dr. Dean Edell Show 752
Dragonette, Jessica 151
Drake, Bill 171, 172, 185, 403, 404, 681, 810
Drake, Pauline 236
Drake-Chenault Company 86, 403, 404, 810
drama **227–34**; African-Americans and radio drama 228–29; *Amos 'n' Andy*, drama of plots 58; artisans, radio drama by 233–34; *Cavalcade of America* 133; detective drama 230–31; *Earplay* 241; *Family Theater* 275–76; *Gang Busters* 318–19; golden age of popular radio drama 228; *Green Hornet* 332–34; *I Love a Mystery (ILAM)* 373; independent producers 233–34; *Jack Armstrong, the All-American Boy* 382–84; *Ma Perkins* 443–45; *March of Time* (docudrama) 445–46; *Mercury Theater of the Air* (anthology) 453–55; *One Man's Family* 543–45; playwrights, golden age radio drama 561; prestige drama 229–30; on public radio 232–33; radio drama on film 292–94; radio in shadow of television 232; *The Shadow* 688; soap opera, daytime drama 231–32, 700; social drama and cultural landscape (1930s) 701–2; *Star Wars* 718–21; *Suspense* 734–36; sustaining drama 229–30; *Theater Guild of the Air* 766–67; *War of the Worlds* 819–21; westerns 835–38; World War II, legacy in 232, 869–70; *Yours Truly, Johnny Dollar* 891–92
Dreft Star Playhouse 365
Drewry, John E. 558
The Drifters 796
Driscoll, Marian 289
Drobny, Anita 22
Drobny, Sheldon 22
Drudge, Matt 752
Dudes, Pork 532
Dudley, Paul 891
Duffy's Tavern **234–36**
Duke University Library Advertising History Archive 473
Dumas, Helene 244
Dumm, William 413
DuMont, Allen B. 471

O'Flaherty, Hal 861–62
O'Hair, Madelyn Murray 678
O'Hair, Thom 779
O'Halloran, Hal 857
O'Hara, John 806
old-time radio **541–42**; *The Big Broadcast* 542; broadcasting old programs 542; copyrighting and collecting 542; programming collecting, beginnings of 541–42
oldies format **539–40**
Olds, Irving S. 767
Oliveros, Pauline 412
Olivier, Laurence 454
Olsen, Harry 347
Olson, Roger 772
O'Malley, Neil 813
O'Meara, Mike 843
O'Mera, Jerry 428
One Man's Family **543–45**; ensemble 543–44; impact 544; Morse creation 543
O'Neill, Eugene 766
O'Neill, Jimmy 414
O'Neill, Speaker Thomas "Tip" 785, 792
Opie and Anthony 363
Oppenheimer, George 300
Optimum Effective Scheduling 9–10
O'Quin, Gene 95
Orban Associates Optimod-FM 79
Orbison, Roy 195
O'Reilly, Bill 316, 843, 869
origins: A.C. Nielsen Company 1; advertising 6; African-Americans in radio 16; Air America Radio (AAR) 22; all news format 25–26; *All Things Considered* 30; Amalgamated Broadcasting System 34; American Broadcasting Company (ABC) 35–36; American Federation of Musicians (AFM) 42; American Federation of Television and Radio Artists (AFTRA) 44; American Society of Composers, Authors, and Publishers (ASCAP) 47; *American Top 40* 52; American Women in Radio and Television (AWRT) 53–54; *Amos 'n' Andy* 57; antenna 64; Arbitron Company 66–67; Audimeter (A.C. Nielsen) 75–76; audiotape 82–83; automation 85–86; automobile radio 87–88; black-oriented radio 101–2; black radio networks 104–5; blacklisting 97; Blue Network 108–9; Border Radio 115–16; Broadcast Education Association (BEA) 118–19; Broadcast Music Incorporated (BMI) 120; call letters 127; *Captain Midnight* 130; children's novels and radio 141; citizens band radio 149; classical music format 150–51; Clear Channel Stations 155–56; college radio 157; Columbia Broadcasting System (CBS) 159–60; contemporary christian music format 184; Cooperative Analysis of Broadcasting (CAB) 191; Corporation for Public Broadcasting (CPB) 196; country music format 198; demographics 202–4; deregulation of radio 205; diary 208; documentary programs 221–22; Dolby Noise Reduction (NR) 224–25; Don Lee Broadcasting System 226; early wireless 238; easy listening/beautiful music format 244–45; editorializing 249; education about radio 250–51; educational radio (to 1967) 253–54; election coverage 258–59; emergencies, role of radio in 262; Emerson Radio 265–66; evangelists/evangelical radio 269; fairness doctrine 272; farm/agricultural radio 280–81; free form format 310–11; gay and lesbian radio 319–20; *The George Burns and Gracie Allen Show* 325; *Gunsmoke* 338–39; ham radio 340–41; hate radio 342–43; high fidelity (hi-fi) 347–48; Hollywood and radio 364; Hooperatings 367; horror programs 370–71; Jewish radio programs 387; jingles 391–92; KDKA, Pittsburg 397; KFI, Los Angeles 399–400; KGO, San Francisco 401–2; KNX, Los Angeles 407–8; KPFA, Berkeley, California 411–12; KRLA, Los Angeles 413–14; licensing authorizing U.S. stations to broadcast 424; low-power radio/microradio 436–38; *March of Time* 445–46; *Marketplace* 449–50; Metropolitan Opera, New York 456–57; morning programs 465–66; museums and archives of radio 469–70; National Association of Broadcasters (NAB) 488–89; National Association of Educational Broadcasters (NAEB) 492; National Broadcasting Company (NBC) 498; National Public Radio (NPR) 503; National Religious Broadcasters (NRB) 511; National Telecommunications and Information Administration (NTIA) 513; Native American Radio 514–15; Network Monopoly Probe 516–17; news 518–19; Office of War Information (OWI) 536; Pacifica Foundation 551; pay radio 557; Peabody Awards and archive 558–59; Philco Radio 559–60; podcasts 564–65; poetry on radio 565–66; politics on radio 571–72; production for radio 583; programming strategies and processes 590–91; public affairs programming 602–3; Public Broadcasting Act (1967) 609; "public interest, convenience or necessity" 610–11; public radio (since 1967) 616–18; Pulse, Inc. 622–23; quiz and audience participation programs 624–35; Radio Advertising Bureau (RAB) 633; Radio City, New York 636–37; Radio Corporation of America (RCA) 638–39; radio laws 644–45; receivers 649–50; recordings and the radio industry 660–61; religion on radio 675; rock and roll format 682–83; science fiction programs 685; *The Shadow* 688–89; shortwave radio 692–93; *Silent Nights* 695; soap opera 700–701; sports on radio 714–15; station rep firms 721; Subsidiary Communications Authorization (SCA) 733; sustaining programs 736; syndication 739–40; talk radio 748–49; Telecommunications Act (1996) 758–59; topless radio 769–70; trade press 774–75; underground radio 779; United Fruit Company 782; United States Navy and radio 787; variety shows 799–800; vaudeville and radio 803–4; virtual radio 810; *Vox Pop* 812–13; WABC, New York City 815; Walkman portable audio 816–17; WAMU, Washington, DC 818; WBAI, New York City 821–22; WBAP, Fort Worth 823; WBZ, Boston 826–27; WCBS, New York City 828; WEAF, New York City 833–34; westerns 835; Westinghouse 838–39; Westwood One 841; WGI, Boston 844–45; WGN, Chicago 846; WHA and Wisconsin Public Radio 847–48; WINS, New York City 851–52; wire recording 853; WJR, Detroit 854–55; WLAC, Nashville 856; WLW, Cincinnati 858–59; WNYC, New York City 865; WQXR, New York City 874; WSB, Atlanta 877; WTOP, Washington, DC 879–80; WWJ, Detroit 880–81; WWL, New Orleans 881–82; WXYZ, Detroit 884; Zenith Radio Corporation 893–94
The Orioles 708
Ormandy, Eugene 151
Orr, Angeline 131
Orson, Welles 371
Ortega, Santos 376
Osborne, Ted 371, 735
Osewalt, William C. 644
Osgood, Charles 375, 570
O'Shea, Daniel T. 98, 100

INDEX

WGY, Schenectady, New York 155, 228, 323, 834; AT&T and 50; shortwave radio 692

WHA and Wisconsin Public Radio **847–50**; *To the Best of Our Knowledge* 850; *Earplay* 850; Educational Communications Board 849; *Let's Draw* 848; "Oldest Station in the Nation" 847–48; *Ranger Mac* 848; state radio network 848–49; *Whad'Ya Know?* 850; Wisconsin idea 848; Wisconsin Public Radio 849–50

WHAK call letters 128

Whalen, Grover A. 865

WHAM call letters 128

WHAT call letters 128

WHDH, Amalgamated Broadcasting System and 34

Wheeler, Dan 327

Wheeler, Jackson 422

Wheeler, Ruthe S. 142

WHEN call letters 128

WHER, Memphis **850–51**; *All Things Considered* 851; call letters 128; *Open Mike* 850–51; Tri-State Broadcasting Service 850

Whetstone, Walter 34

White, Andy 332

White, Jim 406

White, Josh 229

White, Justice Byron 667

White, Leroy 112

White, Major J. Andrew 714

White, Orval 710

White, Paul 160, 162, 582

White, Steve 568

White, Wallace 669

White, Wallace H. 288

Whitehead, Don 112, 856

Whitehead, Dr.Clay 513

Whiteman, Paul 325, 477, 478, 801, 802

Whitfield, Anne 544

Whitman, Ernest 18, 60, 94

Whitman, Gayne 135

Whitman, Walt 567, 568

Whitney, Willis R. 323

Whittaker, Roger 459

Whitted, Norfley 105

Whittemore, Rev. Lewis 675

WHN, African-Americans on 17

The Who 404

WHO call letters 128

Whorf, Mike 855

WHRO, Norfolk, Virginia 713

WHTZ call letters 128

WHUR-FM, African-Americans on 20

WHYY, Philadelphia 128, 315, 316, 317, 712

Wicker, Irene 99, 100, 144, 665

Wicker, Randolfe 320

Widmark, Richard 376

Widmer, Harriette 60

Wiersbe, Warren 270

Wiese, Wendy 406

Wiken, Dave 29

Wilcox, Harlow 735

Wilcox, Walter *see* Cronkite, Walter

Wilder, Gene 389

Wile, Frederic William 582, 790

Wiley, Richard 205

Wilken, Federal District Judge Claudia 437

Wilkerson, Jim 406

Williams, A.C. 113

Williams, A. "Mooha" 19

Williams, Andy 3, 245, 860

Williams, Bert 804

Williams, Billy Dee 719

Williams, Bruce 751

Williams, Clarence 17

Williams, Dr. Daniel Hale 229

Williams, Hank 95, 198, 330, 419, 480, 488

Williams, Jerry 29, 748–49, 750, 752–53

Williams, John 719, 847

Williams, Juan 747–48, 748

Williams, Mason 3

Williams, Nat D. 19, 102, 113, 832

Williams, Raymond 705

Williams, Robin 293

Williams, Wenmouth, Jr. 14

Williams, William B. 864

Williams, William Carlos 568

Williamson, Sonny Boy 19, 111, 112, 113, 404

Willis, Bruce 293

Willkie, Wendell 535

Wills, Bob and the Texas Playboys 890

Wilson, Don 166, 400

Wilson, Earl 365

Wilson, Glenn 814

Wilson, Hugh 761–62

Wilson, Jackie 592, 595, 796

Wilson, Kathleen 544

Wilson, Kemmons 850–51

Wilson, Marie 292

Wilson, President Woodrow 571, 603, 638

Wilson, Robert 93

Wilson, Walter (Uncle Bob) 420

Wilson, Ward 129

Winchell, Walter 343, 748, 801, 863

WIND call letters 128

Winehouse, Amy 709

Winer, Dave 564

Wings Over Jordan 18

Winkle, William/ "Windy Bill" 41

WINS, New York City **851–52**; all news 852; all news format 26, 28; call letters 128; *Going to Town* 852; *Morning Matinee* 852; postwar changes 852; *Three Corner Club* 852; *Top o' the Morning* 852; Westinghouse 852

Winsor, Roy 703, 807

Winston, George 146

Winter, Jonathan 474

Winter, Paul 885

Winters Jonathan 311

wire recording **853–54**; active use 853–54; Ampex 854; Brush Development Company 853; "Dailygraph" 853; decline 854; *Electrical World* 853; Magnecord 854; Marconi Company 853; Utah Radio Products 854; Webster-Chicago (Webcor) Model 80 854

Wise, Rabbi Stephen S. 387, 389

Wishengrad, Morton 136, 232, 563

The Witch's Tale 370–71

WJCU call letters 127

WJHU, Baltimore 712, 713

WJLB, African-Americans on 18

WJR, Detroit **854–56**; *Adventures in Good Music* 855; Capital Cities Broadcasting Corporation 855; *Detroit Police Drama* 855; *Free Press* 854; "Goodwill Station" 855; *Kaleidoscope* 855; modern station 855–56; *Music*